1927 EDITION OF

The SEARS, ROEBUCK Catalogue

edited by

ALAN MIRKEN

Bounty Books

A Division of Crown Publishers, Inc.

**See Publisher's Note following Introduction
for explanation of missing pages.**

INTRODUCTION

Many books and films have tried to re-create the America of the boisterous "Roaring Twenties" with varying degrees of success. But to view the twenties as they really were, one can do no better than return to the pages of the Sears, Roebuck and Co. Catalogue.

Out of its pages steps the flapper in all her glory replete with the fashion frills of the day, her flat chest and her bobbed hair. And out of Sears' pages steps her male companion with his full-cut trousers and handsome new "clover-leaf" lapels; their children; and all their family's belongings, necessities, and material desires.

To present the 1920s to the 1970s' viewers, the publishers with good reason have chosen to reproduce Sears' 1927 Fall and Winter Catalogue. This was the heyday of that era—America was experiencing a surging prosperity (although many of Sears' farmer customers had not yet recovered from the sharp recession of 1921–22). With prosperity came the demand for more and more consumer goods which Sears was most anxious to satisfy.

Paradoxically, despite the visible prosperity, Sears apparently was beginning to recognize some of the buying resistance that was to reach depression proportions in the thirties. Much identical merchandise was offered in Sears' Spring and Summer and Fall and Winter catalogs and one startling price pattern emerged. Prices were either identical, or, when different, the Fall and Winter Catalogue published later had lower prices. A Ford seat cushion listed at $5.18 in the spring was only $4.60 in the fall, a meerschaum pipe offered at $3.48 in the spring was only $2.95 in the fall, and even Teenamint catalogued at 42¢ in the spring book was down to 39¢ in the fall.

While turn-of-the-century Sears, Roebuck catalogs relegated ready-to-wear clothing to a modest number of pages at the rear of the book, the 1927 Catalogue featured more than 450 pages of these items, most shown right at the front. America's habits were changing, less time was being devoted to home dressmaking and as usual Sears' Catalogue was reflecting the change. New York was the fashion center in 1927 and the copywriters stressed New York styling. One rare exception was bathing suits for which California was given styling credit for most of those shown in the 1927 Sears Spring Catalogue. (These may be seen in the special supplement at the end of this Bounty reproduction.) Other exceptions were the French designs that appear on page 12.

More fashion notes of particular interest are the fake furs on page 17, the Clara Bow hats "Posed by the Famous Paramount Picture Star" on page 101, and the capsule view of fashions of the period found on the pattern pages, 220 and 221. These provide a quick view of more than seventy varied items.

Between 1920 and 1929 the auto industry underwent a period of marked expansion and grew to number one rank in terms of value of product as well as value added by manufacture. Ford still dominated the industry, but Chevrolet was beginning to challenge that dominance. In 1927, Sears, Roebuck devoted twelve pages to accessories for Fords and two pages for Chevrolet. The rest of the industry got little more than passing attention.

Interest in sports soared in 1927 as evidenced by the tremendous array of sporting goods of all types. Equipment for baseball, golf, tennis, skiing, skating, basketball, boxing, and a host of other activities found space in the catalog's pages. And small wonder! Nineteen twenty-seven was the year Babe Ruth set his famous record, hitting sixty home runs in one season. It was also the year of the controversial Dempsey-Tunney heavyweight championship rematch—the fight in which Tunney retained his championship with the benefit of a much disputed "long count."

The phonograph was obviously enjoying great popularity in 1927. One hundred and four million discs were sold that year in the U.S. and Sears featured a good many of them. Among the top hits offered on page 692 were "Baby Face," "Ain't She Sweet," "Bye Bye Blackbird" and many others still in favor today.

Radio was beginning to gain popularity, but Sears still found it necessary to explain in detail that anyone could install one of its radios by following the carefully worded instructions. By 1932 the growth of radio coupled with the depression would reduce phonograph record sales to a mere 6,000,000. Even more striking was the reduction in sales of phonographs themselves from 987,000 in 1927 to only 40,000 in 1932.

Sears, which billed itself as the World's Largest Store, established its own radio station in 1923 using as its call letters WLS. In 1927 the station was being operated as a service to customers with farm reports interspersed among entertainment programs. The aim apparently was to create more radio sales by providing an incentive for purchase. A similar technique was used by RCA in the early 1960s to create a demand for color television by scheduling an extraordinary number of color programs on the RCA-owned NBC stations.

Collectors can find many items of interest in this 1927 Catalogue. Silver patterns, toys, and furnishings provide numerous treasures. The toys, particularly, reflect the period. Nineteen twenty-seven was the year of Lindbergh's flight to France and naturally there are several toy airplanes. Mechanical trains appear in force, but a full page is devoted to electric trains and equipment. And since Sears' customers could be expected to have free spending money in 1927, an exceptional number of pages is devoted to dolls.

But Sears recognized that all Americans were not completely up-to-the-minute in their living habits and a surprising number of old-fashioned items was still offered for sale. Buggies, once the proudest offering of early Sears Catalogues, still found space on page 1044.

The items in the 1927 Sears, Roebuck Catalogue, reflected the wants of almost everyone, and so preserved for us a most vivid portrait of that period. Here we have before us the merchandise, the styles, the prices to reconstruct the twenties for those who arrived too late and to refresh the memories of those who were there.

—ALAN MIRKEN

Publishers' note regarding this Bounty Edition:

We have retained the continuity and flavor of the original, but in order to keep within a useful format of over 700 pages, we have omitted those pages that were mostly repetitions. Where we believed the present-day interest in a particular section was great enough for preservation in its entirety, such as the toy and doll sections, silver and jewelry sections, we did preserve them. The index will guide you to specific items you may wish to find. Owing to our deletions an occasional item may not be found, but those items will almost certainly be few. The 1927 Fall and Winter Catalogue provides the basis for this Bounty Reproduction. A ten page supplement taken from the 1927 Spring and Summer Catalogue, has been added at the end. These items were included here because we believe they will add an additional dimension to the reader's view of America as it was in 1927. Items in this supplement are not included in the index. The cover illustration by Norman Rockwell was taken from the 1927 Spring and Summer Catalogue.

INDEX *begins on page 550.*

Philadelphia

Kansas City

WE GUARANTEE

To save you money
To deliver all merchandise safely
To satisfy you perfectly

We Guarantee that every article in this catalog is honestly described and illustrated.

We Guarantee that any article purchased from us will give you the service you have a right to expect.

If for any reason whatever you are not satisfied with any article purchased from us, we want you to return it to us at our expense.

We will then exchange it for exactly what you want, or will return your money, including any transportation charges you have paid.

SEARS, ROEBUCK AND CO.

24-Hour Service

We give prompt service at all our stores. Tests show that we ship 99 orders out of every 100 within 24 hours after they are received. See Map on page 258.

OUR ORDER BLANKS
which you'll find in the back of the catalog make it easy to order. We enclose additional blanks with each shipment of goods.

IT'S EASY TO ORDER
Please turn to the simple directions on page 546. How easy it is to measure for wearing apparel will be found on page 548.

Atlanta

Los Angeles

SATISFACTION GUARANTEED OR YOUR MONEY BACK

New York's Loveliest Models Have Posed for You in These Newest Coats

To bring you the most favored of the new season's style offerings, to portray them for you, truthfully, accurately; to make them of the best materials that the market affords and then to price them reasonably, price them to insure you the greatest possible savings, is our obligation to you.

Confident that we have performed that duty well, certain in the feeling that you will find pleasure in going over these style pages, and then renewed pleasure in making your selection here, we present our style offerings of the fall and winter season.

Never have we been so well satisfied with our presentations as we are this season, never do we recall of values being greater, styles more charming or materials more desirable.

To make our illustrations true to life, we have actually photographed our coats from life on New York fashion models so that you may see exactly how they look. What we cannot show you, however, is the excellent fabrics and expert workmanship which have made these coats such splendid values.

And what is true of the women's coat department is true of every style department in this Catalog. On the pages to follow you will find illustrated and described the newest and most desirable fall and winter apparel of every description. Here the stout woman, the woman of short stature, younger women, misses and girls will find coats, furs, dresses, outdoor apparel and housewear of approved style and high quality. And all are priced to mean real savings—worthwhile savings—to you.

Truly, you can dress better for less at Sears.

AMERICA'S Again Proves Its

17K2900
All Wool Suede Velour
Satin de Chine Lining
$27.50
Mandel Fur Trimming

17K2905
All Wool Fancy Sport Plaid Coating
Satin de Chine Lining
$27.50
Manchurian Wolf Dog Fur Collar

True Reproduction of French Model

The style is of Parisian inspiration—the adaptation was made in New York—the result is a coat of chic and beauty. Artfully fashioned of fine quality *All Wool Suede Velour*, a handsome, winter weight fabric of assured durability; the coat is expertly tailored and is enriched by a large shawl collar and deep cuffs of selected grade *Mandel Fur*.

Shows trimming of tailored pin cording, used in the smart manner introduced by "Chanel," the famous French designer. Warm interlining and *Satin de Chine* lining. Average length, 45 inches.

Women's and Misses' Sizes—36, 38, 40, 42, 44 and 46 inches bust measure. **State size.** See page 15 for measuring instructions. Shipping weight, 6 pounds.

17K2900—Medium Green.
17K2901—Reindeer Tan. **$27.50**

Sport Style Coat of Decided Smartness

To really appreciate its true value you must feel the fine quality of its fabric—warm, winter weight *All Wool Sport Plaid* with a pleasing, soft brushed surface.

It is made with large patch pockets and trimmed with lustrous *Rayon* stitching and large novelty buttons.

The handsome collar is of selected, first grade *Manchurian Wolf Dog*—a dense, long haired, sturdy fur, in color to harmonize with the coat.

The garment is interlined and lined throughout with guaranteed *Satin de Chine*. Average length, 45 inches.

Women's and Misses' Sizes—34, 36, 38, 40, 42 and 44 inches bust measure. **State size.** See page 15 for measuring instructions. Shipping weight, 6 pounds.

17K2905—Brown.
17K2906—Gray. **$27.50**

GREATEST STORE
Style Leadership

17K2910
All Wool
Suede Velour

Satin de
Chine Lining

$35.00

Mouflon
Fur Collar

17K2915
All Wool
Suede Velour

Satin de
Chine Lining

$29.50

Baltic
Beaver
Fur
Trimming

17K2920
Deep Pile
Velvety
FRANCIA
Bolivia

Satin de
Chine Lining
$25.50

Mandel Fur
Trimming

Paris Inspired Stunning Coat

This beautiful coat is made as Paris makes them this season—elaborately fur trimmed and boasting smart tailored tucking.

Adapted in fine quality warm winterweight *All Wool Suede Velour*, on swagger straight lines, showing a full length shawl collar and deep cuffs of rich silky haired, selected grade gray *Mouflon Fur*.

It is expertly tailored, heavily interlined and lined throughout with guaranteed *Satin de Chine*. Typical of the best New York models. Average length, 44 inches.

Women's and Misses' Sizes—34, 36, 38, 40 and 42 inches bust measure. State size. See "Measuring Instructions" on page 15. Shipping wt., 6 lbs.

17K2910—Grackle Blue. $35.00

Typical Fifth Avenue Style

You will delight in the beauty and luxurious effect of this stunning New York model, with its deep gauntlet cuffs and novel shape collar of rich *Brown Baltic Beaver Fur* (clipped and dyed coney).

Smartly fashioned of fine quality winterweight *All Wool Suede Velour*. The sides of the model show interesting panel treatments, with tailored tucks, novelty *Rayon* embroidery and ornaments of self material.

Heavy interlining; guaranteed *Satin de Chine* lining. Average length, about 44 inches.

Women's and Misses' Sizes—34, 36, 38, 40 and 42 inches bust measure. State size. See "Measuring Instructions" on page 15. Shipping weight, 6 pounds.

17K2915—Cranberry.
17K2916—Brown. $29.50

Luxuriously Warm Handsome Model

Presenting a rich, smart appearance, this model will make its appeal to women of conservative taste.

Fashioned of the celebrated "*Francia*" Bolivia—an extra warm winterweight fabric of lovely soft velvety texture; has neat adornment of tailored strap inserts and rows of *Rayon* stitching. Large collar and deep cuffs of selected grade *Mandel Fur*.

Made with heavy interlining and lined with guaranteed *Satin de Chine*. Average length, about 46 inches.

Women's and Misses' Sizes—36, 38, 40, 42, 44 and 46 inches bust measure. State size. See "Measuring Instructions" on page 15. Shpg. wt., 6 lbs.

17K2920—Reindeer Tan.
17K2921—Sailor Blue. $25.50

PAUL POIRET
Noted French Designer Created This Lovely Coat

Trimmed with MENDOZA FUR
(DYED CONEY)

Each Coat Bears This World Famous Label

REPLICA OF PAUL POIRET MODEL TRIMMED WITH MENDOZA FUR

Belgian Lynx Coney Fur Trimming

Mandel Fur Trimming

17K3041
All Wool VELANA Suede
All Silk Crepe Lining
$39.75

17K3045
All Wool Broadcloth
Satin de Chine Lining
$24.75

17K3050
All Wool Suede Velour
Satin de Chine Lining
$25.50

This Coat is an exact reproduction of the original model designed by PAUL POIRET the famous Parisian coutourier

Never before has such an offer been made in America. Think of it! A coat of lovely *All Wool Velana Suede*—trimmed with fine *Mendoza* fur, lined with lustrous quality *All Silk Crepe* and designed by the world's most famous fashion creator, Monsieur Paul Poiret of Paris.

The model features a wide flower trimmed collar, deep cuffs and wide band around lower back and sides of *Mendoza Beaver* (clipped and dyed imported coney) and has an original treatment of tucking on the back. In every detail it is a replica of the original Paul Poiret model and each coat bears the label shown above.

Women's and Misses' Sizes—34, 36, 38, 40, and 42 inches bust measure. Average length, 45 inches. See page 15 for measuring instructions. State size. Shipping weight, 5 pounds.

17K3041—Brown. **$39.75**

Coat of Fine Quality

It requires the "best" in the matter of fabric, tailoring and every little detail to make a coat of such simple design give such an effect of elegance, as is the case in this handsome model. Developed in silky lustrous fine quality *All Wool Broadcloth*, a warm, winter weight dressy fabric of guaranteed durability.

It is cut on straight, becoming lines; expertly tailored and made with strap inserts at the sides, that are finished on top with hand embroidered, large silk arrowheads. *Imported Black Belgian Lynx Coney* was used for the flattering large collar and deep cuffs. Coat is warmly interlined and lined throughout with guaranteed *Satin de Chine*. Average length, 47 inches. It is offered at a very modest price.

Women's and Misses' Sizes—34, 36, 38, 40, 42, 44 and 46 inches bust measure. For measuring instructions see page 15. State size. Shipping weight, 6 lbs.

17K3045—Black. **$24.75**

Direct From New York
A Splendid Value

Fashioned of warm, winterweight *All Wool Suede Velour*, this coat has the rich adornment of a large flattering collar and deep cuffs, of selected grade, beautiful *Mandel* fur.

It gains a decided note of chic by having rows of corded tucking at the lower back, finished on each side with lustrous *Rayon* stitched arrowheads. The sleeves also depart from the ordinary, by featuring novel cut inserts and button trimming.

This is an exceedingly smart model; styled as only New York can make them and offered at such a low price as you will only find at Sears.

We guarantee that for $25.50 you will not find anywhere else this season a coat of such sterling worth and quality. Like all of our coats, this model has the full cloth undercollar, wide cloth facings, cloth neckband and careful attention to finish and tailoring; features that have made Sears coats famous.

Coat is heavily interlined and lined with guaranteed *Satin de Chine*. Average length, 46 inches.

Women's and Misses' Sizes—36, 38, 40, 42, 44 and 46 inches bust measure. For measuring instructions see page 15. State size. Shipping weight, 6 pounds.

17K3050—Brown. **$25.50**

Here Is
ECONOMY
Without Sacrifice of Style

Scientifically designed, these coats are guaranteed to fit you perfectly. Long experience in the wearing apparel field, a thorough knowledge of what women require and the tailoring of that knowledge into these garments make a perfect fit certain.

In ordering these coats you need make no "allowances." Just give us your exact measurements, and we guarantee to fit you perfectly.

17K3120
Velour Coating
$10⁹⁸
French Coney Fur Trimming

Another of Our Wonderful Coat Values

With the aid of a dressy collar and cuffs of soft, silky imported *French Coney Fur* and a design that features attractive details and trimmings, this coat gives an effect of decided smartness, yet it can be purchased for the incredibly low price of $10.98.

It is fashioned of winter weight, nearly all wool *Velour Coating*, which is pleasing in appearance and of a sturdy wearing quality. The sides are made with tucked and button trimmed insert panels, that are outlined with lustrous *Rayon* stitching. The sleeves also feature harmonious adornment. Coat is neatly tailored and comes with full lining of high luster, guaranteed durable *Venetian*. Average length, 47 inches. *Women's and Misses' Sizes*—34, 36, 38, 40, 42, 44 and 46 inches bust measure. State size. See page 15 for measuring instructions. Shipping weight, 6 pounds.

17K3120—Brown.
17K3121—Black. **$10.98**

Clothing Order Blank Is on Page 1094

17K3110
Siberian Fur Fabric
$14⁹⁸
Belgian Lynx Coney Fur Trimming

It Looks Like Fur but Costs Very Little

Fur fabric coats are more in demand this season than ever, especially favored by women who admire the luxurious appearance of real fur garments but find them to be more expensive than they desire to pay.

In this coat of *Siberian Fur Cloth* beauty goes hand in hand with economy, for while the silky lustrous deep pile of its fabric gives the effect of the high priced genuine caracul fur, this model can be purchased for the very small sum of $14.98.

It is a smart, delightfully warm garment, fashioned on becoming lines and further enriched with a mushroom shape collar and deep cuffs of imported *Black Belgian Lynx Coney Fur*, which has the dressy appearance of the genuine lynx. For additional warmth and service, the coat is heavily interlined and comes with high luster, guaranteed *Venetian* lining. Average length, 47 inches.

Women's and Misses' Sizes—34, 36, 38, 40, 42, 44 and 46 inches bust measure. State size. See page 15 for measuring instructions. Shipping weight, 6 pounds.

17K3110—Black. **$14.98**

17K3115
Velour Coating
$6⁴⁸

Appealingly Low Priced

It is most unusual to find a coat as inexpensive as this one, possessing so many desirable qualities.

The coat is fashioned of good quality nearly all wool *Velour Coating*, cut on swagger straight lines and made with two large patch pockets. It has a convertible collar of self material and features neat adornment of tailored pin cording, novelty buttons and lustrous *Rayon* stitching. We can recommend it as a genuine bargain at the amazingly low price of $6.48. It comes with full lining of durable mercerized *Twill*. Average length, 47 inches.

Women's and Misses' Sizes—34, 36, 38, 40, 42, 44 and 46 inches bust measure. State size. See page 15 for measuring instructions. Shipping weight, 6 pounds.

17K3115—Black.
17K3116—Navy Blue. **$6.48**

FURS of QUALITY

Two Skin
Fox Fur
Collar

Quality Above All

FOR if the furs you wear are not of dependable quality they will never be satisfactory, regardless of how stylish they appear.

That is why we stress the importance of quality in our furs. Only the better grade of selected choice skins are used by us. Every pelt we buy is carefully examined by expert furriers for possible defects. Every imperfectly dyed or cured skin is at once rejected.

And, furthermore, we never offer a garment made of "pieced" skins. Only the whole pelt, perfectly graded and matched, is good enough for our customers.

Buy your furs, then, from these pages and we guarantee that you will be delighted with the handsome appearance, genuine quality and lasting economy of your purchase.

Every fur we sell is described by both its trade name and its actual name so you will know just what you are getting.

27K5305
*Selected
Quality
Diagonal Cut
Natural
Muskrat*
$199.50

27K5300
*Natural Gray
Opossum Fur
Collegiate Style*
Lined With
Skinner's Satin
and
All Wool Plaid
$129.00

For Simple
Measuring
Instructions
See Page 15

27K5310
*Genuine
Caracul
Fur*
All Silk
Crepe Lined
$198.00

Very Stunning

No fur has greater or more deserved popular appeal, than *Genuine Natural Muskrat*, due to its practical, extra sturdy service, handsome appearance and luxurious warmth. The richness which muskrat alone of all furs can impart is here offered you at a great saving. The skins used for this beautiful coat are of selected quality; the model being made entirely of choice pelts, that are rich in color and have durable silky hair.

The coat is fashioned on swagger, straight lines, showing the pelts assembled in an attractive diagonal pattern. Additional beauty is lent to this model by a large, flattering, convertible collar of genuine silky haired *Brown Fox Fur*. It is interlined and lined with good quality *All Silk Crepe*. Average length, about 44 inches. A remarkable value at our special price.

Women's and Misses' Sizes—34, 36, 38, 40, 42 and 44 inches bust measure. State size. Shpg. wt., 9 lbs.

27K5305
Natural
Muskrat...... **$199.50**

All Silk
Crepe
Lined

Brown
Fox Fur
Collar

Swagger "Tomboy" Model

For misses and small women, we offer here a fur coat of luxurious warmth and appealing smartness. Made of genuine, *Natural Gray Opossum Fur*—only large pelts used and those of a selected grade—dense, long haired, and very sturdy; of a pleasing silvery gray color with rich darker gray markings. The pockets show attractive trimming of *Striped Raccoon Tails*.

The coat is called the "Tomboy" model, having been especially made for hard, strenuous service and cut on loose, comfortable lines in mannish double breasted style. Fastens with large, novelty leather buttons. The sleeves and yoke are lined with guaranteed, genuine *Skinner's Satin* and for additional warmth and practical wear the lower part has *All Wool Plaid* lining. Priced far below what you would have to pay elsewhere for a coat of this quality, and a value typical of those offered by our Fur Department. Average length, about 44 inches.

Misses' and Small Women's Sizes—16, 18, 20 and 22 years; 34, 36, 38 and 40 inches bust measure. State size. Shipping weight, 9 lbs.

27K5300—Natural
Gray.   **$129.00**

Rich and Luxuriously Warm

There is no other item of apparel in a woman's winter wardrobe that can rival a fur coat for its practical features, delightful warmth and for imparting that pleasing assurance of being well dressed. In this stunning New York style coat of *Genuine Caracul Fur*, you will find all these appealing qualities and possess a garment that will give constant pleasure with its beauty, comfort and lasting service, and women know that Caracul is one of the most favored of all furs this season.

This model is made of perfectly matched full sized curly skins, that are dense haired, and rich in appearance. Elegance is also lent to the coat by a deep shawl collar of selected grade, silky haired *Genuine Brown Fox*. It is lined with good quality, durable, *All Silk Crepe*.

We believe this to be one of the most attractive values we have ever offered. Average length, about 45 inches.

Women's and Misses' Sizes—34, 36, 38, 40, 42 and 44 inches bust measure. State size. Shipping weight, 9 pounds.

27K5310—Light
Brown.
27K5311—Black.   **$198.00**

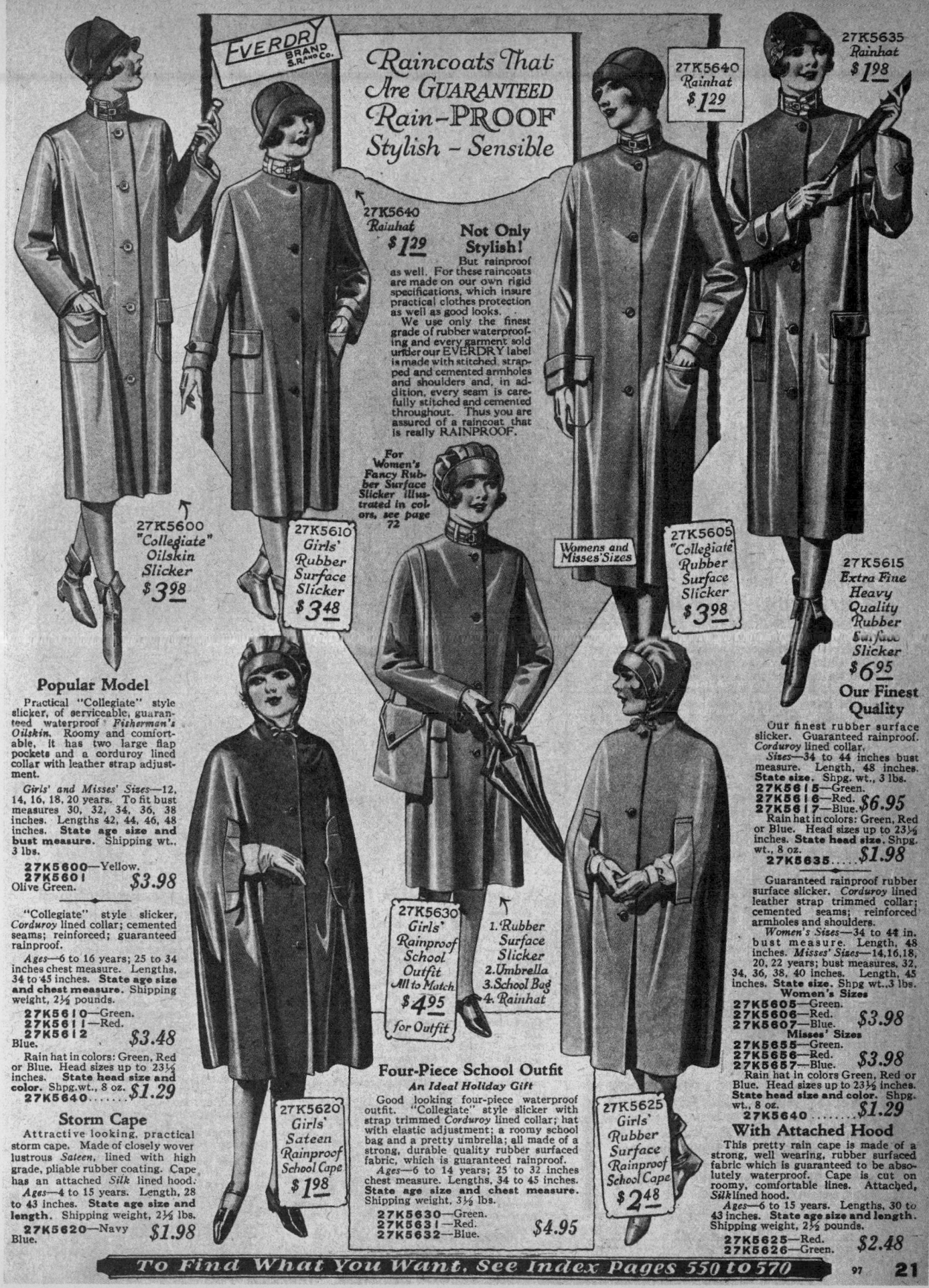

EVERDRY BRAND S. Rand Co.

Raincoats That Are GUARANTEED Rain-PROOF Stylish – Sensible

27K5640 Rainhat $1.29

Not Only Stylish!

But rainproof as well. For these raincoats are made on our own rigid specifications, which insure practical clothes protection as well as good looks.

We use only the finest grade of rubber waterproofing and every garment sold under our EVERDRY label is made with stitched, strapped and cemented armholes and shoulders and, in addition, every seam is carefully stitched and cemented throughout. Thus you are assured of a raincoat that is really RAINPROOF.

27K5640 Rainhat $1.29

For Women's Fancy Rubber Surface Slicker illustrated in colors, see page 72

Womens and Misses' Sizes

27K5635 Rainhat $1.98

27K5600 "Collegiate" Oilskin Slicker $3.98

27K5610 Girls' Rubber Surface Slicker $3.48

27K5605 "Collegiate" Rubber Surface Slicker $3.98

27K5615 Extra Fine Heavy Quality Rubber Surface Slicker $6.95

Popular Model

Practical "Collegiate" style slicker, of serviceable, guaranteed waterproof *Fisherman's Oilskin*. Roomy and comfortable, it has two large flap pockets and a corduroy lined collar with leather strap adjustment.

Girls' and Misses' Sizes—12, 14, 16, 18, 20 years. To fit bust measures 30, 32, 34, 36, 38 inches. Lengths 42, 44, 46, 48 inches. **State age size and bust measure.** Shipping wt., 3 lbs.

27K5600—Yellow.
27K5601 Olive Green. **$3.98**

"Collegiate" style slicker, *Corduroy* lined collar; cemented seams; reinforced; guaranteed rainproof.

Ages—6 to 16 years; 25 to 34 inches chest measure. Lengths, 34 to 45 inches. **State age size and chest measure.** Shipping weight, 2½ pounds.

27K5610—Green.
27K5611—Red.
27K5612 Blue. **$3.48**

Rain hat in colors: Green, Red or Blue. Head sizes up to 23½ inches. **State head size and color.** Shpg.wt., 8 oz.
27K5640......**$1.29**

Storm Cape

Attractive looking, practical storm cape. Made of closely woven lustrous *Sateen*, lined with high grade, pliable rubber coating. Cape has an attached *Silk* lined hood.

Ages—4 to 15 years. Length, 28 to 43 inches. **State age size and length.** Shipping weight, 2½ lbs.

27K5620—Navy Blue. **$1.98**

27K5630 Girls' Rainproof School Outfit All to Match $4.95 for Outfit

27K5620 Girls' Sateen Rainproof School Cape $1.98

27K5625 Girls' Rubber Surface Rainproof School Cape $2.48

Four-Piece School Outfit

An Ideal Holiday Gift

Good looking four-piece waterproof outfit. "Collegiate" style slicker with strap trimmed *Corduroy* lined collar; hat with elastic adjustment; a roomy school bag and a pretty umbrella; all made of a strong, durable quality rubber surfaced fabric, which is guaranteed rainproof.

Ages—6 to 14 years; 25 to 32 inches chest measure. Lengths, 34 to 45 inches. **State age size and chest measure.** Shipping weight, 3½ lbs.

27K5630—Green.
27K5631—Red.
27K5632—Blue.

$4.95

1. Rubber Surface Slicker
2. Umbrella
3. School Bag
4. Rainhat

Our Finest Quality

Our finest rubber surface slicker. Guaranteed rainproof. *Corduroy* lined collar.

Sizes—34 to 44 inches bust measure. Length, 48 inches. **State size.** Shpg. wt., 3 lbs.

27K5615—Green.
27K5616—Red. **$6.95**
27K5617—Blue.

Rain hat in colors: Green, Red or Blue. Head sizes up to 23½ inches. **State head size.** Shpg. wt., 8 oz.
27K5635.....**$1.98**

Guaranteed rainproof rubber surface slicker. *Corduroy* lined leather strap trimmed collar; cemented seams; reinforced armholes and shoulders.

Women's Sizes—34 to 44 in. bust measure. Length, 48 inches. *Misses' Sizes*—14,16,18, 20, 22 years; bust measures, 32, 34, 36, 38, 40 inches. Length, 45 inches. **State size.** Shpg wt..3 lbs.

Women's Sizes
27K5605—Green.
27K5606—Red. **$3.98**
27K5607—Blue.

Misses' Sizes
27K5655—Green.
27K5656—Red. **$3.98**
27K5657—Blue.

Rain hat in colors Green, Red or Blue. Head sizes up to 23½ inches. **State head size and color.** Shpg. wt., 8 oz.
27K5640 ......**$1.29**

With Attached Hood

This pretty rain cape is made of a strong, well wearing, rubber surfaced fabric which is guaranteed to be absolutely waterproof. Cape is cut on roomy, comfortable lines. Attached, *Silk* lined hood.

Ages—6 to 15 years. Lengths, 30 to 43 inches. **State age size and length.** Shipping weight, 2½ pounds.

27K5625—Red.
27K5626—Green. **$2.48**

LITTLE

Especially Designed to Correctly Fit the Woman of Short Figure

17K3205
All Wool
DUVMERE
Suede

Satin de
Chine
Lining

$35.00

Mandel
Fur
Trimming

17K3200
Genuine
VAL-SHORA
All Wool
Bolivia

Fancy Crepe
Lining

$39.95

Manchurian
Wolf Dog
Fur
Trimming

A STYLE IDEA THAT HAS REVOLUTIONIZED WOMEN'S FASHIONS

After years of research our stylists have proved an astonishing fact. Over one-half of the women of America are less than five feet four inches in height. And yet, for years and years, fashion designers have created coats to fit the taller woman only. This has made it difficult for the little woman to find a coat that she could wear without the necessity of expensive alterations which frequently destroy the style lines of the coat.

To meet this problem, we have created a special department for *little women*. On this page and the three pages following you will find the smartest of the new fall styles designed for the petite figure. They are NOT Misses' Coats. They are designed to fit mature women of short stature perfectly.

The coat and sleeve lengths are shorter, the trimmings and other proportions are perfectly balanced, and the result is a garment which we guarantee will fit exactly the woman who is five feet four inches or less in height.

That this special department for *little women* meets a long felt need is proved by the fact that more and more women are turning to it and it is growing larger each season.

You, too, will find the solution of your clothes problem here, and will find a style satisfaction you have never before felt in making your selection from these pages.

Coats on pages 22, 23, 24 and 25 come in special sizes to fit Mature Little Women five feet four inches or less in height. Sizes to Fit Bust Measures: 34, 36, 38, 40 and 42 inches. With Corresponding Coat Lengths: 42, 43, 43, 44, 44, inches. Be sure to state your exact bust measure.

A Coat of Parisian Inspiration

For new fashion ideas we turn to the famous French designers, but for artful adaptations to suit certain types of figures and for such expert tailoring as will assure perfect fit, even they cannot rival the amazing skill of our Fifth Avenue stylists, as for instance the one who reproduced this stunning coat for little women.

This coat has all the chic and beauty of the original Paris model, yet is correctly proportioned and faultlessly tailored to give flattering height and becoming lines to the petite figure. Developed in extra fine quality, delightfully warm, soft finished *All Wool Duvmere Suede*, it is effectively tucked in a distinctive new manner and trimmed with hand embroidered silk arrowheads.

Coat is also enriched with a large shawl collar and deep cuffs of selected grade *Mandel Fur* of brown color with lighter markings.

Comes with warm interlining and guaranteed *Satin de Chine* lining. A truly lovely garment—and a very exceptional value.

Special Sizes for Little Women—34, 36, 38, 40 and 42 inches bust measure. **State size.** See page 15 for measuring instructions. Average length, about 43 inches. Shipping weight, 5½ pounds.

17K3205—Light Brown. **$35.00**

High Grade, Lovely Model

A coat of distinctive style and beauty is offered here for little women; styled in the latest New York manner, made of a choice high grade fabric, trimmed with luxurious fur and—most important of all—cut on correct proportions and artfully tailored, assuring perfect fit.

The model is adapted in finest quality *All Wool "Val-Shora" Bolivia*, a fabric of soft, velvety texture and lustrous dressy finish. It has a handsome large collar and deep cuffs of selected grade *Manchurian Wolf Dog* fur; in the rich coloring of the expensive, genuine Red Fox.

Inverted pleats at the lower sides, centered with *Rayon* stitching, and an appliqued band across the back and at the sides, also enhanced with stitching, are interesting details that lend additional chic to the garment.

It comes with warm interlining and lovely *Brocaded All Silk Crepe* lining.

Special Sizes for Little Women—34, 36, 38, 40 and 42 inches bust measure. **State size.** See page 15 for measuring instructions. Average length, about 43 inches. Shipping weight, 5½ pounds.

17K3200—Black. **17K3201**—Brown. **$39.95**

WOMEN

17K3215
All Wool
Fancy Weave
Sport Cloth
$26⁷⁵
Genuine Red
Fox Fur
Collar

17K3220
Genuine
DUVBLOOM
All Wool Suede
Silk Crepe
Lining
$39⁹⁵
Manchurian
Wolf Fur
Trimming

17K3210
All Wool
DUVMERE
Suede
Satin de Chine
Lining
$29⁹⁵
Mandel
Fur Collar

Exceptionally Smart Sport Coat For Little Women

Of new fashion importance are the coats of fancy fabrics and no longer are they limited to sport wear only, for with rich fur trimmings and clever styling they now look dressy and are considered suitable for almost any occasion.

Their swagger effect is well illustrated in this attractive model which was especially designed for little women. This coat chooses a lovely tapestry weave *All Wool Sport Fabric* of extra fine quality for its development—a fabric of warm winter weight and guaranteed durability.

The model is made with full length tuxedo facings of solid color *All Wool Velour*, which was also used for piping, shown effectively on the cuffs and pockets.

It gains additional smartness with a collar of silky haired, rich looking, genuine *Red Fox*. Also has adornment of novelty buttons and a detachable leather belt.

Comes with warm interlining and good looking, serviceable *Fancy Brocaded* lining. Average length, about 43 inches.

Special Sizes for Little Women—34, 36, 38, 40 and 42 inches bust measure. State size. See page 15 for measuring instructions. Shipping weight, 5½ pounds.
17K3215—Brown Fancy. **$26.75**

Correctly Fashioned by Experts To Fit the Short Figure

This high grade coat, which is identical with the garments sold in the best New York shops, has been artfully fashioned by experts who specialize in apparel for short women. Therefore, it has every assurance of being a correctly proportioned, perfect fitting garment—which after all is one of the most important factors in choosing a coat for any type of figure.

Created on a graceful silhouette of superior quality, soft suede finished *All Wool Duvbloom Suede*—one of the finest of new winter coatings, used only for the most expensive coats. The model shows tiered folds on each side, that were cleverly embodied in an insert panel and topped with lustrous *Rayon* stitching. A luxurious note is lent by rich, fur trimming, using selected first grade *Manchurian Wolf Dog Fur* for the large flattering collar and deep cuffs.

We again assert that if you were to shop in the New York shops, you could hardly find a lovelier or finer garment.

Made with heavy interlining and lined with fine quality *All Silk Crepe de Chine*. Average length, about 43 inches.

Special Sizes for Little Women—34, 36, 38, 40 and 42 inches bust measure. State size. See page 15 for measuring instructions. Shipping weight, 5½ pounds.
17K3220—Sailor Blue.
17K3221—Black. **$39.95**

A Stunning Coat for Little Women

Tiered flounces lend a chic new note to this lovely coat, being featured on the skirt of the garment and topped with soft gathering at either side, effecting a charming, graceful silhouette.

The coat is developed in *All Wool Duvmere Suede*—a high grade, winter weight fabric of dressy appearance. Observe the smartness of the sleeves, with their double cuffs—featuring strap and button trimming. The deep shawl collar is also fashion's latest, made in this case of selected grade *Mandel Fur* in harmonizing color with the coat.

In tailoring and every detail, this coat is all that can be desired, yet its price is incredibly modest—only $29.95. It comes with warm interlining and has guaranteed *Satin de Chine* lining. Average length, about 43 inches.

Special Sizes for Little Women—34, 36, 38, 40 and 42 inches bust measure. State size. See page 15 for measuring instructions. Shipping wt., 5½ lbs. **$29.95**
17K3210—Medium Gray.

It's Easy to Measure for Clothing. See Page 548

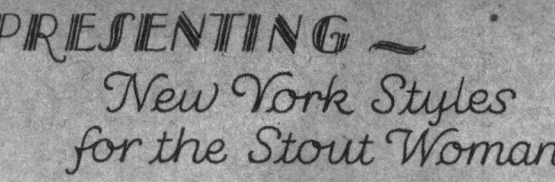

PRESENTING —
New York Styles for the Stout Woman

Trimline BRAND S.R. and Co.

THE foremost style designers of America have spent years in perfecting our TRIMLINE styles for the stout woman.

The smart straight lines and perfect fitting proportions of these coats are expressly designed to give that slenderizing effect which is so desirable, and the perfect tailoring and splendid quality of TRIMLINE coats will prove a revelation to you.

In creating these styles, special attention has been paid to the individual proportions of the stout figure. Every detail of service and comfort is here. These aren't merely large coats cut on ordinary patterns with some width added; they are specially designed to meet the requirements of the larger figure. The back is cut with more fullness, the armholes are cut with greater depths, there is more width and concealed fullness in the skirt.

The result is a coat which will look well and fit well. A coat that will give you greater style satisfaction than any garment which you have heretofore worn, and a coat that will have an almost miraculous effect in slenderizing your figure. The straight, easy lines accent length and break the natural width of the figure by clever cut and trimming. Every attempt has been made to produce a garment in which the larger woman can be comfortably well dressed and confident that she is smartly groomed.

Note particularly the details of workmanship which distinguish our TRIMLINE coats, the wide cloth facing, full cloth under collars, cloth neck bands, high grade linings and warm interlinings.

In ordering your TRIMLINE coats *be sure to state your exact bust and hip measure*, do not allow extra, as our coats are scientifically designed to fit your size correctly. Expert fitters have perfected a chart by which we are able to choose immediately the size that will fit you when we know your measurements.

17K3300
All Wool DUVMERE Suede
Brocaded Silk Warp Lining
$39.50
Vicuna Fox Fur Trimming

17K3305 TEXBLOOM Bolivia
$24.95
Belgian Lynx Coney Fur Trimming

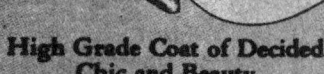

You Can Dress Better for Less at Sears

High Grade Coat of Decided Chic and Beauty

Smart attire has a way of lending poise and assurance to the wearer, but the secret of being smartly attired does not only lie in your choice of a garment that is pleasing in design; it must also have essential features that are best suited to your type of figure—a correct silhouette—clever details—and such expert tailoring as will assure perfect fit.

All these important factors are to be found in this stunning coat, which has been especially designed to fit women of stout figure. It is fashioned on becoming, slenderizing lines of *All Wool Duvmere Suede*, an extra fine quality, soft, suede finish dressy fabric, of warm winter weight.

The high grade tailoring of the coat is especially evidenced by the interesting treatment of insert side panels, that are made with corded tucks, tailored folds and silk embroidered arrowheads. Additional warmth and richness are lent to the garment by a large, flattering shawl collar and deep cuffs, of selected grade, silky furred *Korean Fox (Vicuna Fur)*.

Coat is carefully finished in every detail; heavily interlined and has handsome, durable *Silk Warp Brocaded* lining.

Stout Women's Sizes—41, 43, 45, 47, 49, 51 and 53 inches bust measure. Length, 47 inches. State size. See page 15 for measuring instructions. Shipping weight, 6½ pounds.

17K3300—Light Brown.

$39.50

Smartly Adapted in a Rich, Warm Fabric

A coat of chic New York style is offered here for stout women, becoming in silhouette, slenderizing in effect and desirable in every way—having the pleasing combination of all those little details that mean so much. We can also recommend it to be an exceptional value at $24.95.

The model is fashioned of rich looking "Tex-Bloom" Bolivia, a delightfully warm, durable, winter weight fabric having a soft, velvety texture and a highly lustrous finish. Designed on smart, easy fitting, straight lines, the coat has two convenient pockets at the front, while the back shows clusters of *Rayon* braid adornment and button trimmed pointed tabs.

Beauty is also lent to the garment by a large mushroom shape convertible collar and deep cuffs of selected grade *Belgian Lynx Coney*, a dense, silky haired fur that looks like the expensive, genuine lynx. For added warmth and comfort the coat is heavily interlined and finished throughout with *Patricia* lining (excellent quality, highly lustrous sateen).

Stout Women's Sizes—41, 43, 45, 47, 49, 51 and 53 inches bust measure. Length, 48 inches. State size. See page 15 for measuring instructions. Shipping weight, 6½ pounds.

17K3305—Black.
17K3306—Navy Blue.

$24.95

Slenderizing Styles of the NEW SEASON

Manchurian Wolf Dog Fur Trimming

Belgian Lynx Coney Fur Trimming

Trimline BRAND S.R. and Co.

17K3325 *All Wool VALSHORA Bolivia* $49.95

Brocaded Silk Warp Lining

17K3335 *Fine Quality All Wool Broadcloth* *Satin de Chine Lining* $27.50

This Model Comes in Two Lengths

17K3330 *All Wool Suede Velour* *Satin de Chine Lining* $29.50

Mandel Fur Trimming

Coat of Exceptional Beauty

Our finest coat for stout women. It is a stunning, high grade model, typical of the coats offered in the most exclusive Fifth Avenue shops. In fabric, tailoring and every detail it is all that the most fastidious woman of fashion could desire, yet is very moderate in price.

Artfully fashioned on smart, slenderizing lines of the finest of all Bolivia coatings—richly lustrous *All Wool Val Shora Bolivia*, which is delightfully warm, durable and has a lovely, soft velvety texture. The large, dressy collar and cuffs are of selected, first grade *Manchurian Wolf Dog*—a dense, silky haired fur, famous for its wonderful durability. Made with heavy interlining and lined throughout with *Silk Warp Brocaded* lining.

Stout Women's Sizes—41, 43, 45, 47, 49, 51 and 53 inches bust measure. Length, 47 inches. **State size.** Shipping weight, 6½ pounds.

17K3325—Black. $49.95
17K3326—Brown.

Dressy Smart and Slenderizing

Fashioned by experts who specialize in stout women's apparel, this stunning model combines a style of smartness with a silhouette and clever details, that result in a coat of pleasing, slenderizing effect.

Adapted in silky lustrous, fine quality *All Wool Broadcloth* of a warm, winter weight, the coat is designed on becoming straight lines, showing interesting panel inserts on either side, enhanced with *Rayon* stitching. Richness is lent to the model by a deep shawl collar and cuffs of silky haired, selected grade *Belgian Lynx Coney* fur, which has the appearance of the expensive genuine lynx. Well tailored, modestly priced, desirable garment, warmly interlined and lined with guaranteed *Satin de Chine*. Comes in two lengths, 48 and 45 inches.

Stout Women's Sizes—41, 43, 45, 47, 49, 51 and 53 inches bust measure. **State size.** Shipping weight, 6½ pounds.

17K3335—Black in 48-Inch Length. $27.50
17K3336—Black in 45-Inch Length.

Attractively Fur Trimmed

Warm, winter weight *All Wool Suede Velour* of a soft, fine, durable quality fashions this handsome coat. This model is an excellent choice for stout women, who seek a smart, moderately priced coat with the assurance that it will fit well and lend a becoming, slenderizing effect.

Styled on swagger straight lines, it features height giving, full length panels at either side, outlined with gored seams, finished in pleats and trimmed with *Rayon* stitching. Large mushroom shape collar and deep cuffs of selected grade, fashionable *Mandel* fur.

Coat is carefully tailored, warmly interlined and lined throughout with guaranteed *Satin de Chine* lining.

Stout Women's Sizes—41, 43, 45, 47, 49, 51 and 53 inches bust measure. Length, 47 inches. **State size.** Shipping weight, 6½ pounds.

17K3330—Brown. $29.50
17K3331—Navy Blue.

Youthful, Smart Styles for MISSES

Misses' and Juniors' Sizes—Ages:
14 – 16 – 18 – 20 Years
To Fit Bust Measures
34 – 36 – 38 – 40 Inches

17K3400
All Wool Suede Velour
Satin de Chine Lining
$25.00
Mandel Fur Trimming

Clothing Order Blank on Page 1094.

17K3405
All Wool Plaid Back Sport Coating
All Silk Satin Lined to Hips
$19.98
Mandel Fur Collar

17K3410
Celebrated "FRANCIA" Bolivia
Venesheen Lining
$19.98
Mandel Fur Trimming

17K3415
All Wool Suede Velour
Venesheen Lining
$15.95
Baltic Beaver Fur Collar

A Coat of Youthful Appeal

Style is achieved in this coat by the adaptation of a fine, handsome fabric into a design of decided smartness, producing a garment that is typical of the coats offered in the fashionable New York shops.

The model is developed in warm, winter weight *All Wool Suede Velour*, featuring a silhouette of straight, slender lines made distinctive by novel shape narrow panels that are outlined with tailored tucking. Beauty is also gained by fashionable selected grade *Mandel* fur which was used for the flower trimmed mushroom shape collar and deep cuffs. Lined with guaranteed *Satin de Chine* and interlined for additional warmth.

Average length, 43 inches. Age sizes, 16 to 22 years. Bust measures, 34 to 40 inches. See size scale above; also measuring instructions on page 15. **State age size and bust measure.** Shipping wt., 5½ lbs.

17K3400—Light Brown. **$25.00**
17K3401—Grackle Blue.

Attractive Sport Coat

Fashioned of finest quality firmly woven *All Wool Plaid Back, Sport Coating,* which is of warm winter weight and durable.

Both sides of this fabric were cleverly used; the tweed for the main body of the coat, the plaid for full tuxedo facings and for trimming the large patch pockets. Cut on youthful lines, with raglan cut sleeves, and finished with a dressy collar of *Mandel* fur. *All Silk Satin* lining to the hips; also in the sleeves.

Average length, 42 inches. Age sizes, 14 to 22 years. Bust measures, 32 to 40 inches. See size scale above, also measuring instructions on page 15. **State age size and bust measure.** Shipping wt., 5½ lbs.

17K3405—Dark Tan **$19.98**
with Contrasting Plaid.

A Rich, Warm Fabric

Fashioned of the celebrated *"Francia" Bolivia,* a dressy fine quality coating of soft, velvety texture.

Displays insert tailored strapping and rows of lustrous stitching on either side. It is carefully tailored, neatly finished in every detail, gaining a note of beauty by a large mushroom shape collar and cuffs of selected grade *Mandel* fur. Comes with warm interlining and guaranteed *Venesheen* lining.

Average length, 43 inches. Age sizes, 14 to 22 years. Bust measures, 32 to 40 inches. See size scale above, also measuring instructions on page 15. **State age size and bust measure.** Shipping wt., 5½ lbs.

17K3410—Reindeer Brown. **$19.98**
17K3411—New Sailor Blue.

Exceedingly Smart, Yet Inexpensive

The employment of rows of corded tucking applied in a new and interesting manner, is an attractive feature of this desirable, stylish, moderately priced warm winter coat. Adapted in winter weight, fine quality *All Wool Suede Velour,* it displays the tucking on the sleeves, embodied in panels and centered on the pointed inserts that lend smartness to the sides.

The garment is carefully tailored; cut on becoming youthful lines and finished with a handsome collar of rich brown *Baltic Beaver* (clipped coney) that has the appearance of genuine beaver. It is warmly interlined and lined with guaranteed *Venesheen,* a highly mercerized lining.

Average length, 43 inches. Age sizes, 16 to 22 years. Bust measures, 34 to 40 inches. See size scale above, also measuring instructions on page 15. **State age size and bust measure.** Shipping wt., 5½ lbs.

17K3415—Light Brown. **$15.95**
17K3416—Grackle Blue.

Of Decided Charm Are These
NEW YORK STYLES
for Misses

17 K 3420
All Wool Suede Velour
Venesheen Lining
$16⁹⁸
Mandel Fur Collar

With Smart Fashion Themes

Moderately priced, youthfully styled smart winter coat, fashioned of heavy fine quality *All Wool Suede Velour*, which is a dressy, warm fabric.

Designed on swagger straight lines, the coat shows an interesting treatment of tucking on the sleeves and at the sides, in the latter case finished with hand embroidered arrowheads.

The attractive, becoming, mushroom shaped collar is of selected grade *Mandel* fur.

Coat is warmly interlined and lined with guaranteed *Venesheen*.

Age sizes, 16 to 22 years; bust measure, 34 to 40 inches. See size scale above, also measuring instructions on page 15. **State age size and bust measure.** Average length, 43 inches. Shipping weight, 5½ lbs.

17 K 3420—Light Brown.
17 K 3421
Grackle Blue.   **$16.98**

---

17 K 3425
All Wool Suede Velour
Satin de Chine Lining
$25.00
Belgian Lynx Coney Fur Trimming

Elaborately Fur Trimmed

This coat gains beauty by its full length shawl collar and attractive pointed cuffs, of silky haired, imported *Black Belgian Lynx Coney* fur, which gives the rich effect of genuine *Lynx*. Made of winter weight, fine quality *All Wool Suede Velour*, showing insert pockets at front and a loose tailored fold at the lower sides. Is made with warm interlining and guaranteed *Satin de Chine* lining. Age sizes, 14 to 22 years; bust measure, 32 to 40 inches. See size scale above, also measuring instructions on page 15. **State age size and bust measure.** Average length, 43 inches. Shpg. wt., 5½ lbs.

17 K 3425—Wine.
17 K 3426—Grackle Blue. **$25.00**

Misses' and Juniors' Sizes
14 -16 -18 -20 -22 Years
To fit Bust Measures
32 -34 -36 -38 -40 Inches

---

17 K 3430
All Wool Buxkin Suede Velour
Satin de Chine Lined
$18⁹⁵
Mandel Fur Collar

Distinctively Youthful

The material is *All Wool Buxkin Suede Velour*—warm, dressy and very durable —fashioned into a youthful, smart style with a selected grade *Mandel* fur collar. It has a charming, buckle trimmed bow sash and novel shaped scalloped edge panels on the lower sweep; the latter enhanced with *Rayon* stitching and buttons.

Coat comes with warm interlining and guaranteed *Satin de Chine* lining.

Age sizes, 14 to 22 years; bust measure, 32 to 40 inches. See size scale above, also measuring instructions on page 15. **State age size and bust measure.** Average length, 43 inches. Shpg. wt., 5½ lbs.

17 K 3430—Grackle Blue. **$18.95**

---

17 K 3435
All Wool Velour
$14⁹⁸
Mandel Fur Trimming

Handsome—Warm—and Inexpensive

A charming, dressy effect is lent to this inexpensive coat by a large collar and deep cuffs of selected grade *Mandel* fur and by the smart application of rows of *Rayon* embroidery that are finished with attractive motifs.

It is styled on becoming, youthful lines of sturdy wearing, heavy quality *All Wool Velour*, and for a coat so modestly priced, it shows exceptionally good workmanship and neat tailoring.

Lined throughout with durable, high luster, guaranteed *Striped Venetian*.

Age sizes, 16 to 22 years; bust measure, 34 to 40 inches. See size scale above, also measuring instructions on page 15. **State age, size and bust measure.** Average length, 43 inches. Shipping weight, 5½ pounds.

17 K 3435—Medium Brown.
17 K 3436—Light Navy Blue. **$14.98**

To Insure Correct Fit

To insure correct fit, do not order a size larger than you actually wear. Our size 16 coat, for example, is cut scientifically to fit perfectly a miss of 34 inches bust measure, with ample allowance made for comfortable fullness.

We ask you to note especially the tailoring features which have made these coats famous— the full cloth undercollars, the wide cloth facings, the cloth neckbands, warm interlinings and high grade durable wearing linings.

Baltic
Beaver
Fur
Trimming

All Wool Fabrics Lovely Fur Trimmings and STYLE That Girls Demand

Ages 10 - 12 - 14 - 16 Years
To Fit Chest
Measures 29 - 31 - 33 - 35 Inches

Lengths 36 - 38 - 40 - 42 Inches

To Insure Correct Fit

To insure correct fit, do not order a size larger than your girl actually requires. Our age 10 coat, for example, is cut scientifically to fit perfectly a girl of 29 inches chest measure, with ample allowance made for growth and comfortable fullness. We ask you to note especially the tailoring features which have made our girls' coats famous—the full cloth undercollars, the wide cloth facings, the cloth neckbands, high grade durable wearing linings and warm interlinings. **Clothing Order Blank Is on Page 1094.**

Mandel
Fur
Trimming

17K3600
All Wool
Velour
$10.98

Latest New York Style

This coat has a design of decided smartness, and we guarantee that it will also please with its quality, workmanship and splendid durability. Mothers, too, will be delighted with the extremely low price we have been able to offer—an opportunity to effect economy and still have their daughters stylishly dressed.

Fashioned of warm, winterweight *All Wool Velour*; the garment is enhanced with rich looking *Baltic Beaver (Clipped Coney) Fur* collar and cuffs and it features an attractive treatment of tailored tucking, as well as adornment of *Rayon* stitching and buttons. Comes with strong, serviceable *Striped Venetian* lining. A most unusual value!
Ages—10 to 16 years. **State age size.** Shipping weight, 4½ pounds.

17K3600—Medium Brown.
17K3601—Light
Navy Blue. $10.98

17K3605
All Wool
Suede
Velour
$15.98

17K3610
All Wool
Velour
$12.98

Exceptionally Smart Model

A new and very interesting style treatment is featured in the design of this handsome coat. Adapted in warm, exceedingly fine quality *All Wool Suede Velour*: the model displays attractive pleat finished panels at the lower front, enhanced with buttons and chenille stitching. It also has a novel cut front belt that fastens with an ornamental buckle. The collar and cuffs are of dressy *Mandel Fur*. Coat is warmly interlined and lined with excellent quality, mercerized *Venesheen*. *Ages*—10 to 16 years. **State age size.** Shipping weight, 4½ pounds.

17K3605—Light Brown.
17K3606—Grackle Blue. $15.98

Has Dressy Fur Trimming

Moderately priced, youthfully styled, desirable coat, adapted in winterweight *All Wool Velour*, which is of a quality that insures long, satisfactory service. Coat is cut on swagger, straight lines and features a dressy collar and cuffs of fashionable *Mandel Fur*. It is neatly tailored and has effective trimmings of contrasting color *Velour* and novelty buttons. Comes with strong, mercerized *Twill* lining.
Ages—10 to 16 years. **State age size.** Shipping weight, 4½ pounds.

17K3610—Medium Brown.
17K3611—Light Navy Blue. $12.98

Decidedly Good Value

Fashioned in a pleasing, youthful style of winterweight, serviceable quality *All Wool Velour*; this coat is practical, well made, and desirable in every way. Collar and cuffs of soft gray *French ConeyFur* and attractive novelty *Rayon* braid trimming. Lined with good quality mercerized *Twill*.
Ages—10 to 16 years. **State age size desired.** Shipping weight, 4½ pounds.
17K3615—Light Navy Blue. $12.98

Desirable in Every Way

This handsome coat is practical, warm and a very good value. Fashioned of winterweight, fine quality *All Wool Suede Velour*; it is well tailored, smartly styled, and enhanced with a dressy *Mandel Fur* collar and lustrous *Rayon* embroidery stitching. Has warm interlining and excellent quality mercerized *Venesheen* lining.
Ages—10 to 16 years. **State age size desired.** Shipping weight, 4½ pounds.
17K3620—Reindeer Brown.
17K3621—Wine (Garnet). $14.95

Coat of Rich Appearance

The style is smart; the material is winterweight, fine quality *All Wool Suede Velour*, and the model is richly enhanced with extra fine *Striped Mandel Fur* collar and cuffs as well as lovely *Chenille* hand embroidery—the result, as you see, is a handsome, dressy coat for the young girl. It is warmly interlined and lined with excellent quality mercerized *Venesheen*.
Ages—10 to 16 years. **State age size desired.** Shipping weight, 4½ pounds.
17K3625—Grackle Blue. $19.98

Swagger Sport Model

A serviceable, warm, winterweight *All Wool Fancy Weave Sport Cloth*, fashions this attractive, modestly priced coat. Styled on becoming, youthful lines, it has a handsome *Mandel Fur* collar, and is made with smart, gauntlet shaped cuffs and patch pockets. Has warm interlining and durable *Striped Venetian* lining.
Ages—10 to 16 years. **State age size desired.** Shipping weight, 4½ pounds.
17K3630—Tan. $12.95

Smart and Inexpensive

Note the charming, dressy effect this coat gains, by having a handsome collar and cuffs of fashionable *Mandel Fur* and additional smart adornment of buttons and *Rayon* braid trimmed, contrasting color *Velour* inserts. Coat is made of winterweight, good quality *All Wool Velour* and lined with strong, mercerized *Twill*.
Ages—10 to 16 years. **State age size desired.** Shipping weight, 4½ pounds.
17K3635—Brown and Tan. $13.98

Warm and Sturdy Wearing

Attractive, delightfully warm coat, for the schoolgirl, appropriately styled of sturdy wearing, fine quality *All Wool Sport Plaid*. Made with a handsome *Mandel Fur* collar, it also features *Velour* inserts and metal buttons. Interlined and lined with durable *mercerized Venesheen*.
Ages—10 to 16 years. **State age size desired.** Shipping weight, 4½ pounds.
17K3640—Gray and Red Plaid. $14.75

Attractive New Style

Smartly designed, warm winter coat, fashioned of fine quality, durable *All Wool Suede Velour*. It features graceful pleating and *Rayon* braid trimming at the sides; a smart sash tie bow at the front and has a collar and cuffs of dressy, *Baltic Beaver (Clipped Coney) Fur*. Interlined and lined with excellent quality mercerized *Venesheen*.
Ages—10 to 16 years. **State age size desired.** Shipping weight, 4½ pounds.
17K3645—Green.
17K3646—Light Navy Blue. $16.95

Delightfully Warm and Dressy

For the styling of this handsome coat, we chose fine quality *Francia Bolivia*—a luxuriously warm, deep pile fabric of soft velvety texture. Coat has dressy, *Mandel Fur* collar and cuffs and the sides are trimmed with *Rayon* stitching and self covered buttons. Interlined and lined with excellent quality, mercerized *Venesheen*.
Ages—10 to 16 years. **State age size desired.** Shipping weight, 4½ pounds.
17K3650—Reindeer Brown. $18.48

Our Best Coat for Girls

Paris styled coat of exceptional beauty, adapted in warm finest quality *All Wool "Duvmere" Suede*. In tailoring, design and every detail, it is beyond question a high grade garment. The deep shawl collar and cuffs are of extra fine *Striped Mandel Fur*. Front is made with *Rayon* stitched folds. Coat is warmly interlined and has guaranteed silk satin lining. A super coat value.
Ages—12, 14 and 16 years; also suitable for juniors. **State age size.** Shipping weight, 4½ pounds.
17K3655—Sailor Blue. $25.98

TRULY SMART
Newest Styles
Direct from
New York

Ages 10-12-14-16
Years
To Fit Chest Measures
29-31-33-35
Inches
Lengths
36-38-40-42
Inches

Coney Fur Trimming

Mandel Fur Collar

Mandel Fur Trimming

Mandel Fur Collar

17K3630
All Wool
Fancy Sport
Coating
$12.95

17K3615
All Wool
Velour
$12.98

17K3620
All Wool
Suede
Velour
$14.95

17K3625
All Wool
Suede
Velour
$19.98

Mandel Fur Trimming

Mandel Fur Trimming

Baltic Beaver Fur Trimming

Mandel Fur Trimming

17K3655
All Wool
DUVMERE
Suede
$25.98

17K3635
All Wool
Velour
$13.98

17K3640
All Wool
Sport
Plaid
$14.75

17K3645
All Wool
Suede
Velour
$16.95

17K3650
Genuine
FRANCIA
Bolivia
$18.48

These Coats
Are Fully
Described
on Opposite
Page

Your Orders Shipped Within 24 Hours!

59   41

Styled and Tailored to PERFECTION

for Ages
10-12-14-16 Years
To Fit Chest
Measures
29-31-33-35
Inches

Lengths
36-38-40-42
Inches

Mandel Fur Trimming

Mandel Fur Trimming

17K3665
All Wool
POLAIRE
Mandel
Fur Collar
$10.98

17K3670
All Wool
Fancy
Sport
Coating
Mandel
Fur Collar
$12.98

17K3660
All Wool
Fancy
Sport
Coating
$15.95

17K3675
All Wool
Suede
Velour
$18.95

Mandel
Fur
Trimming

Mandel Fur
Collar

Mandel
Fur
Trimming

Mandel
Fur
Trimming

17K3695
All Wool
Suede
Velour
$16.95

17K3680
All Wool
Duvmere
Suede
$19.98

17K3685
Genuine
FRANCIA
Bolivia
$16.95

17K3690
Genuine
FRANCIA
Bolivia
$19.98

These Coats
Are Fully
Described on
Opposite
Page

Attractive Sport Plaid

Fashioned in a swagger, youthful style of fine quality, winter weight, *All Wool Fancy Sport Plaid*, this coat is attractive, warm, and practical in every way. Enriched with a deep shawl collar and cuffs of dressy *Mandel Fur*, it also gains smartness with a belt at the waistline and by having novel shaped patch pockets. Coat is interlined and lined with excellent quality mercerized *Venesheen*.

Ages—10 to 16 years. **State age size desired.**
Shipping weight, 4½ pounds.
17K3660—Tan. **$15.95**

Low Priced and Stylish

This coat of winter weight *All Wool Polaire* has a collar of fashionable *Mandel Fur* and attractive adornment of *Rayon* embroidery, on the sleeves and pockets. The material is delightfully warm and durable; the style appealingly youthful and the price of the coat is exceptionally low. Made with warm interlining and serviceable striped *Venetian* lining.

Ages—10 to 16 years. **State age size desired.**
Shipping weight, 4½ pounds.
17K3665—Reindeer Brown. **$10.98**

Swagger, Youthful Style

Moderately priced, practical winter coat, for the schoolgirl. Developed in warm, heavy quality *All Wool Fancy Sport Plaid*—an attractive, sturdy wearing fabric. Coat is smart in cut and has a handsome mushroom shaped *Mandel Fur* collar. Trimmed with bandings of *Velour* and small metal buckles. Warmly interlined and lined with strong, mercerized *Twill*.

Ages—10 to 16 years. **State age size desired.**
Shipping weight, 4½ pounds.
17K3670—Green, fancy. **$12.98**

Fine All Wool Fabric

In quality, smartness and tailoring, this coat is all that can be desired. It is also delightfully warm and good wearing. Fashioned in a chic, youthful style of winter weight, fine quality *All Wool Suede Velour*; the coat is richly enhanced with handsome gray *Mandel Fur* and the sides show pin cording and *Rayon* stitching. Has warm interlining and excellent quality, mercerized *Venesheen* lining.

Ages—10 to 16 years. **State age size desired.**
Shipping weight, 4½ pounds.
17K3675—French Blue. **$18.95**

High Grade, Beautiful Model

Latest New York style coat for the young girl, artfully fashioned of lovely, fine quality *All Wool "Duvmere" Suede*—a soft finished, winter weight, durable, dressy fabric. Extra fine striped *Mandel Fur* collar and cuffs and has attractive *Rayon* stitching and a sash tie bow at the front. Warmly interlined and lined with excellent quality, mercerized *Venesheen*.

Ages—10 to 16 years. **State age size desired.**
Shipping weight, 4½ pounds.
17K3680—Reindeer Brown. **$19.98**

Desirable in Every Way

Beautiful deep pile *"Francia" Bolivia*—an extra heavy, luxuriously warm fabric of velvety texture—fashions this youthful, dressy coat. The model is enhanced with a rich looking *Mandel Fur* collar and shows lustrous *Rayon* stitchings on the sleeves and at the sides. Interlined and lined with excellent quality, mercerized *Venesheen*.

Ages—10 to 16 years. **State age size desired.**
Shipping weight, 4½ pounds.
17K3685—Sailor Blue.
17K3686—Gypsy Red. **$16.95**

Luxuriously Warm Coat

This coat is fashioned of extra heavy, deep pile *"Francia" Bolivia*—a delightfully warm, dressy fabric, of soft velvety texture. Coat is expertly tailored, and gains additional beauty by having adornment of striped *Mandel Fur* collar and cuffs and lovely, hand embroidery. Warm interlining and highly mercerized *Venesheen* lining.

Ages—10 to 16 years. **State age size desired.**
Shipping weight, 4½ pounds.
17K3690—Gypsy Red.
17K3691—Sailor Blue. **$19.98**

Has Dressy Fur Trimming

Smartly, youthfully adapted in winter weight, fine quality *All Wool Suede Velour*, and we guarantee it to be delightfully warm and exceptionally well wearing. Has rich, dressy *Mandel Fur* collar and cuffs and further adornment of tailored tucks. Warmly interlined and lined with excellent quality mercerized *Venesheen*.

Ages—10 to 16 years. **State age size desired.**
Shipping weight, 4½ pounds.
17K3695—Brown.
17K3696—Wine (Garnet). **$16.95**

Genuinely GOOD Quality
The Kind That WEARS and WEARS
Beautiful - Becoming Styles

Ages To Fit — 10 -12 -14 -16 Years
Chest Measures — 29 -31 -33 -35 Inches
Lengths — 36 -38 -40 -42 Inches

The Size to Order

All that we require in order to fit your girl perfectly is her actual chest measurement. Our age 10 coat, as an example, has been scientifically designed to fit a girl of 29 inches chest measure, with ample allowance made for growth and comfortable fullness.

We direct your attention also, to features of construction which add materially to the quality of these coats—full cloth undercollars, wide cloth facings, cloth neckbands, high grade, durable linings and warm interlinings.

Mandel Fur Collar

Coney Fur Trimming

17K3700 All Wool Velour $10.98

17K3705 Winter Weight Velour $8.95

17K3710 Winter Weight Velour $9.79

Attractive New Style

A charming treatment of *Rayon* stitched, tiered folds at the sides and a smart fold across the lower back lend a distinctive, new style note to this moderately priced, desirable, winter coat. You will immediately recognize it as a most unusual value, especially when you know of the long, satisfactory wear it will give.

Adapted in warm, heavy quality *All Wool Velour*, a good looking, serviceable fabric; the model has neat workmanship throughout and shows the dressy finish of a *Mandel Fur* collar. Comes with strong, well wearing striped *Venetian* lining.

Ages—10 to 16 years. **State age size.** Shipping weight, 4½ pounds.
17K3700—Light Navy Blue.
17K3701—Wine. **$10.98**

Inexpensive, Pleasing Model

This model makes effective use of tailored tuckings; having them serve as smart adornment at the front and back, as well as on the sleeves and pockets.

The model is fashioned of warm, winter weight, durable quality *Velour*, which is more than two-thirds wool. It is well tailored; has a pleasing, youthful style and is finished with a dressy, convertible collar of handsome *Mandel Fur*. Equally good looking, either buttoned at the neck or unbuttoned, as illustrated. Made with warm interlining and strong, durable, striped *Venetian* lining.

There is genuine economy in the low price we are asking for this beautifully styled, splendidly tailored coat for the young miss.

Ages—10 to 16 years. **State age size.** Shipping weight, 4½ lbs.
17K3710—Light Brown.
17K3711—Wine. **$9.79**

Appealingly Low Priced

For a coat so smart and pleasing in style and practical in every way, this model is a most unusual value at $8.95.

Your daughter will admire the style, so youthfully appealing, and you will be delighted with the economy of your purchase.

Developed in heavy, winter weight *Velour*, which is more than two-thirds wool; the model is designed with pleat finished, attractive insert, side panels, and has adornment of *Rayon* stitching and buttons. It is also enriched with a collar and cuffs of soft *Coney Fur*. Has warm interlining and strong, well wearing, striped *Venetian* lining.

Ages—10 to 16 years. **State age size.** Shipping weight, 4½ pounds.
17K3705—Brown.
17K3706—Light Navy Blue. **$8.95**

Mandel Fur Collar

We Strongly Recommend These Coats
They're Unusual Values!

Smart and Inexpensive

This coat is so dressy in effect that its low price comes as a pleasing surprise. It is warm and sturdy, too, having been fashioned of winter weight *Velour*, about two-thirds wool.

A new side treatment of panels is featured in the design of the coat, trimmed with novelty buttons, knotted straps and *Rayon* stitching. The sleeves are also enhanced with stitching and the collar and cuffs are of soft, silky *Coney Fur*. Coat is warmly interlined and lined with *Mercerized Twill*.

Ages—7, 8 and 9 years. State age size. See size scale. Shipping weight, 4 pounds.

17K3830—Light Navy Blue.
17K3831—Wine.
17K3832—Light Brown. **$8.79**

Swagger Model

From the standpoint of style, service and real economy, this warm, well tailored coat is an excellent choice for the young girl.

Fashioned on swagger lines, of winter weight, sturdy wearing *All Wool Polaire*, it is smartly belted at the waistline; has two attractive patch pockets and a handsome mushroom shape *Mandel Fur* collar. Luxurious warmth is assured by the coat having quilted interlining and *Sateen* lining.

Ages—7, 8 and 9 years. State age size. See size scale. Shpg. wt., 4 lbs.

17K3840 Reindeer Brown. **$8.98**

17K3830 Winter Weight Velour Coney Fur Trimming **$8.79**

17K3840 All Wool POLAIRE Mandel Fur Collar **$8.98**

For Small Children's Coats See Pages 152 and 161.

17K3835 Winter Weight Velour Mandel Fur Collar **$8.98**

17K3845 All Wool Velour Coney Fur Trimming **$8.48**

Guaranteed to Please

Adapted in warm, winter weight *Velour*, about two-thirds wool, this attractive coat has all the features that mothers seek in a serviceable coat for the schoolgirl.

It displays dressy trimming in the form of a *Mandel Fur* collar and pretty *Rayon* embroidery. Coat is interlined and lined with mercerized *Twill*.

Ages—7, 8 and 9 years. State age size. See size scale above. Shipping weight, 4 pounds.

17K3835—Light Navy Blue.
17K3836—Light Brown. **$8.98**

Enhanced With Fur

The style of this coat is appealingly youthful, the material is sturdy and warm.

Made of good quality, winter weight *All Wool Velour*, it shows trimming of tailored pin cording and has a convertible collar and streamer tab endings of soft, silky *Coney Fur*. For extra warmth and service, coat is made with interlining and mercerized *Twill* lining.

Ages—7, 8 and 9 years. State age size. See size scale. Shipping wt., 4 lbs.

17K3845—Wine.
17K3846—Light Navy Blue. **$8.48**

Descriptions of Coats Shown on Opposite Page

Attractive Sport Plaid

A delightfully warm, swagger style coat of heavy, winter weight *All Wool Sport Plaid*. A sturdy wearing, well made garment, smartly trimmed with *Mandel Fur* and harmonizing color velour. Interlined and lined with excellent quality, highly mercerized *Venesheen*.

Ages—7, 8 and 9 years. State age size. Shipping weight, 4 pounds.

17K3850—Gray and Red Plaid. **$12.75**

Distinctive New Design

Adapted in warm, winter weight *All Wool Suede Velour*; this smart new coat has pleated panel inserts and shows adornment of *Mandel Fur* and *Rayon* stitching. Model is interlined and lined with excellent quality mercerized *Venesheen*.

Ages—7, 8 and 9 years. State age size. Shipping weight, 4 pounds.

17K3855—Rust.
17K3856—Grackle Blue. **$12.98**

Lovely, Rich Looking Fabric

This coat is made of a lovely fabric—velvety, deep pile *Francia Bolivia*. A delightfully warm, well made style featuring adornment of a handsome *Mandel Fur* collar and *Rayon* stitching. Has warm interlining and excellent quality, highly mercerized *Venesheen* lining.

Ages—7, 8 and 9 years. State age size. Shipping weight, 4 pounds.

17K3860—Grackle Blue. **$11.50**

Appealing in Every Way

Insert panels, enhanced with pin cording and lustrous *Rayon* stitching are featured on this handsome coat. The sleeves are also adorned with stitching and the model has a dressy collar of *Mandel Fur*. Coat is made of warm *All Wool Suede Velour*. Comes with warm interlining and durable *Sateen* lining.

Ages—7, 8 and 9 years. State age size. Shipping weight, 4 pounds.

17K3865—Light Brown. **$9.98**

Our Finest in Style and Quality

Expertly tailored, handsome model of *All Wool "Duvmere Suede,"* a high grade, winter weight velour. Coat is enriched with a *Mandel Fur* collar and cuffs and has attractive *Rayon* embroidery trimming. Interlined and lined with excellent quality highly mercerized *Venesheen*.

Ages—7, 8 and 9 years. State age size. Shipping weight, 4 pounds.

17K3870—Medium Brown. **$13.48**

An Unusually Good Value

Enhanced with dressy *Mandel Fur*, tailored cording and *Rayon* embroidery, this coat presents a very smart appearance, yet is modest in price. Made of warm winter weight *Velour*, about two-thirds wool. Coat has interlining and *Striped Venetian lining*.

Ages—7, 8 and 9 years. State age size. Shipping weight, 4 pounds.

17K3875—Light Navy Blue.
17K3876—Wine. **$9.48**

Has Dressy Fur Trimming

Winter weight *All Wool Velour* of pleasing quality fashions this coat. Model has dressy, *Mandel Fur* collar and cuffs and pleated panels enhanced with buttons and *Rayon* stitching. Warmly interlined and lined with durable *Striped Venetian*.

Ages—7, 8 and 9 years. State age size. Shipping weight, 4 pounds.

17K3880—Medium Brown.
17K3881—Light Navy Blue. **$9.98**

Latest Style, Dressy Model

Fashioned of beautiful deep pile *Francia Bolivia*, a warm, winter weight fabric with a lustrous, velvety finish. In quality and tailoring it is all that can be desired. Has soft, *Mandel Fur* collar and cuffs; also trimmed with *Rayon* stitching. Interlined and lined with excellent quality, highly mercerized *Venesheen*.

Ages—7, 8 and 9 years. State age size. Shipping weight, 4 pounds.

17K3885—New Gypsy Red. **$12.98**

Very Stylish and Practical

Sturdy wearing, winter weight *All Wool Sport Plaid* fashions this swagger coat. It is practical and delightfully warm. Buckle trimmed strap tabs trim pockets. Coat has collar of handsome *Mandel Fur*. Comes with warm interlining and durable *Striped Venetian* lining.

Ages—7, 8 and 9 years. State age size. Shipping weight, 4 pounds.

17K3890—Dark Plaid. **$10.50**

High Quality
Stylish Coats
for Girls

Mandel Fur Trimming

Ages 7-8-9 Years

Chest Measures 26-27-28 Inches

Lengths 29-31-33 Inches

17K3850 All Wool Sport Plaid $12.75

17K3855 All Wool Suede Velour Mandel Fur Trimming $12.98

Mandel Fur Collar

Mandel Fur Collar

17K3860 "FRANCIA" Bolivia $11.50

17K3865 All Wool Suede Velour $9.98

Mandel Fur Trimming

Mandel Fur Trimming

Mandel Fur Trimming

Mandel Fur Collar

17K3870 All Wool "DUVMERE" Suede Velour $13.48

17K3875 Winter Weight Velour $9.48

17K3880 All Wool Velour Mandel Fur Trimming $9.98

17K3885 "FRANCIA" Bolivia $12.98

17K3890 All Wool Fancy Plaid $10.50

For Descriptions of These Coats See Opposite Page

TRULY BEAUTIFUL FUR TRIMMED COATS

Ages 2-3-4-5-6 Years

Chest Measures
21-22-23-24-25
Inches

Lengths
22-23-24-25-26
Inches

Mandel Fur Trimming

Ages 3 to 6 Years

Mandel Fur Trimming

Ages 3 to 6 Years

Coney Fur Trimming

Ages 2-3-4 Years

Coney Fur Collar

Ages 2-3-4 Years

17K3900
All Wool
Suede Velour
$9.98

17K3905
All Wool
DUVMERE Suede
$11.75

Mandel Fur Collar

17K3940
All Wool
Broadcloth
$8.48

17K3945
Silky Finished
Velvet
Hand Embroidered
$5.95

17K3915
"FRANCIA"
Bolivia
$9.98

Ages 3 to 6 Years

17K3910
All Wool
Broadcloth
$10.50

Ages 2 to 6 Years

Coney Fur Collar

Coney Fur Collar

Mandel Fur Collar

Baltic Beaver Collar and Cuffs

17K3920
All Wool Velour
$5.98

17K3925
Velour Coating
$5.29

Ages 2 to 6 Years

Ages 3 to 6 Years

17K3930
"FRANCIA"
Bolivia
$11.98

17K3935
All Wool Polaire
$7.89

Ages 2 to 6 Years

These Coats Are Fully Described On Opposite Page

Warm Stylish Winter Coats for Little Girls

Handsome, Dressy Model
Enriched with a *Mandel Fur* collar and cuffs and trimmed with attractive *Rayon* braid embroidery, this warm coat of fine quality *All Wool Suede Velour* presents a very smart and dressy effect. It is warmly interlined and lined with excellent quality mercerized *Venesheen*.
Ages—3, 4, 5 and 6 years only. **State age size.** Shipping weight, 2¾ pounds.
17K3900—Light Brown.
17K3901—Grackle Blue. **$9.98**

Our Best Quality Suede Coat
In fabric, style and tailoring this smart little coat is all that can be desired. It is adapted in a high grade, new winter weight cloth—*All Wool Duvmere Suede Velour*—and shows rich adornment of *Mandel Fur*. Additional trimming is lent by novelty buttons and *Rayon* stitching. Warmly interlined and lined with fine quality mercerized *Venesheen*.
Ages—3, 4, 5 and 6 years only. **State age size.** Shipping weight, 2¾ pounds.
17K3905—Sailor Blue. **$11.75**

Smartly Hand Smocked
Lovely model adapted in fine quality silky, lustrous *All Wool Broadcloth*. Styled on fetching lines, it features attractive pockets and hand smocking. Rich *Mandel Fur* collar. Has interlining and durable *Sateen* lining.
Ages—3, 4, 5 and 6 years only. **State age size.** Shipping weight, 2¾ pounds.
17K3910—Reindeer Tan. **$10.50**

Of a Rich, Dressy Fabric
Beautiful, velvety, wool faced *Francia Bolivia* fashions this lovely coat. Smart *Mandel Fur* collar and attractive adornment of *Rayon* embroidery. Warm interlining and durable *Sateen* lining.
Ages—2, 3, 4 and 6 years. **State age size.** Shipping weight, 2¾ pounds.
17K3915—Gypsy Red.
17K3916—Sailor Blue. **$9.98**

Appealing, Low Priced Coat
Warm coat of sturdy wearing, winter weight *All Wool Velour*. Attractive insert panels at lower front. Collar of soft gray *Coney Fur*. Warm interlining and striped *Venetian* lining.
Ages—2, 3, 4, 5 and 6 years. **State age size.** Shipping weight, 2¾ pounds.
17K3920—Light Navy Blue.
17K7001—Wine. **$5.98**

Pleasing in Style and Price
This coat will give comfortable warmth and sturdy wear. Of winter weight, nearly all wool *Velour Coating*. Collar of *Coney Fur* and trimming of buttons and *Rayon* stitching. Striped *Venetian* lining.
Ages—2, 3, 4, 5 and 6 years. **State age size.** Shipping weight, 2¾ pounds.
17K3925—Light Brown.
17K3926—Light Navy Blue.
17K3927—Rust. **$5.29**

Our Finest Coat for Girls
Rich looking, velvety, deep pile *Francia Bolivia*. This lovely coat is dressy and delightfully warm. Well tailored and enhanced with *Mandel Fur* collar and cuffs and *Rayon* stitching. Warm interlining and lustrous *Venesheen* lining.
Ages—3, 4, 5 and 6 years. **State age size.** Shipping weight, 2¾ pounds.
17K3930—Grackle Blue. **$11.98**

Sturdy and Delightfully Warm
Winter weight *All Wool Polaire* of serviceable quality fashions this attractive coat. Collar and cuffs of *Baltic Beaver* (Clipped and Dyed Coney) Fur. *Rayon* embroidery. Warmly interlined. Lined with quilted *Sateen*.
Ages—3, 4, 5 and 6 years. **State age size.** Shipping weight, 2¾ pounds.
17K3935—Rust.
17K3936—Reindeer Brown. **$7.89**

Fetching, Youthful Style
Tailored pin tucking and self covered buttons enhance this little coat of fine quality, silky, lustrous *All Wool Broadcloth*. Neat standing collar and cuffs of soft tan *Coney Fur*. Made with interlining and durable *Sateen* lining.
Ages—2, 3 and 4 years only. Lengths, 21, 22 and 23 inches. **State age size and length.** Shipping weight, 2½ pounds.
17K3940—Reindeer Tan. **$8.48**

Luxuriously Warm and Lovely
Fine quality, rich looking silky finish *Velvet* woven of finest quality mercerized cotton yarn, enhanced with tucking and handmade French knots. Collar of soft *Coney Fur*. Coat is interlined and lined with durable *Sateen*.
Ages—2, 3 and 4 years only. Lengths, 21, 22 and 23 inches. **State age size and length.** Shipping weight, 2½ pounds.
17K3945—Dark Copenhagen Blue. **$5.95**

Ages
2 - 3 - 4 - 5 - 6 Years
Chest Measures
21 - 22 - 23 - 24 - 25 Inches
Lengths
22 - 23 - 24 - 25 - 26 Inches

It's Easy to Order the Right Size
Simply give us the actual chest measure of your daughter, without making any extra allowance, state length you require and we guarantee the coat you receive will be a perfect fit.

Everyone of our girls' coats is cut extra full and large and is designed over scientifically correct patterns to insure easy, comfortable fit with ample allowance made for growth.

All of our girls' coats are carefully tailored with wide cloth facings, full cloth under collar, and cloth neckband. To assure extra warmth—they are nearly all of them fully interlined.

17K3955
All Wool Broadcloth
$6.98
Beaverette Fur Trimmed

17K3950
Wool Faced Chinchilla Cloth
$4.59

Delightfully Warm for Little Ones
Winter weight, wool faced *Chinchilla Cloth* fashions this handsome little coat. Cut on straight lines with two slot pockets at front. Convertible collar of pretty *Gray Persian Lamb Fur Cloth*. *Rayon* stitching and appliqued ornaments. Warmly interlined. Durable *Sateen* lining.
Ages—2, 3 and 4 years only. Lengths, 21, 22 and 23 inches. **State age size.** Shipping weight, 2½ pounds.
17K3950—Light Copenhagen Blue. **$4.59**

Smart and Desirable Style for Little Tots
Prettily fashioned of silky, lustrous *All Wool Broadcloth*, this coat features smart trimming of handmade French knot embroidery and tailored pin tucks. The collar and the balls that finish the streamer tie are of soft *Beaverette* (Clipped Coney) Fur. Comes with warm interlining and durable *Sateen* lining.
Ages—2, 3 and 4 years. Lengths, 21, 22 and 23 inches. **State age size.** Shipping weight, 2½ pounds.
17K3955—French Blue. **$6.98**

Exceptionally Low Priced
This swagger, double breasted style coat of warm, winter weight, nearly all wool *Velour Coating* is a genuine bargain at our special price of $3.98. The material is sturdy and practical; the design is appealingly youthful, and the coat shows nea workmanship throughout. Coat is lined with mercerized twill and has smart trimming of lustrous *Rayon* stitching and novelty buttons.
Ages—2, 3, 4, 5 and 6 years. **State age size.** Shipping weight, 2½ pounds.
17K3960—Brown.
17K3961—Navy Blue. **$3.98**

17K3960
Velour Coating
$3.98

17K3965
Velour Plush
Mandel Fur Collar
Ages 3-4-5-6 Years
$6.48
Ages 7-8-9 Years
$7.48

Appealing, Dressy Model
Fashioned of lustrous, velvety *Velour Plush*, which is dressy, serviceable and delightfully warm, this fetching little coat is all that can be desired, especially with the added appeal of a very low price. The convertible collar is of soft *Mandel Fur*, and the garment is also enhanced with *Rayon* stitching and novelty buttons. For extra warmth and service the coat is interlined and lined with *Sateen*.
Ages—3, 4, 5 and 6 years only. **State age size.** Shipping weight, 2½ pounds.
17K3965—Red. **$6.48**
Same style in ages 7, 8 and 9 years.
17K3897—Red. **7.48**

It's Easy to Measure for Clothing. See Page 548

49

Sturdy Fabrics - Smart Styles
Warm Winter Coats for Girls

Ages	2-3-4-5-6 Years
Chest Measures	21-22-23-24-25 Inches
Lengths	22-23-24-25-26 Inches

We Guarantee Correct Fit

In ordering your girl's coat you do not have to make any extra size allowance. Every one of our girls' coats is cut extra full and large to insure correct, easy fit, and at the same time allow ample room for growth. Just give us the actual chest measure of your daughter, state age size required and we guarantee that you will be delighted with the fit, style and good tailoring of the coat you receive.

Our girls' coats are made with wide cloth facings, full cut under collars, cloth neck bands, and nearly all of them are fully interlined for additional warmth.

Mandel Fur Trimming

Beaverette Fur Trimming

Ages 3-4-5-6 Years

Ages 3-4-5-6 Years

17K3970
Winter Weight Wool Velour

$8.48

Fur Trimmed Dressy Model—Specially Priced

This smartly styled coat is desirable in every way. It is well tailored, good looking and warm, and will stand strenuous hard wear, having been fashioned of winter weight, sturdy quality, *Wool Velour*, which is about two-thirds wool.

The coat is elaborately trimmed with attractive, dressy *Mandel Fur* and the front also shows adornment of novelty *Rayon* embroidery. For extra warmth and service the garment is interlined and lined with good quality *Sateen*.

Ages—3, 4, 5 and 6 years only. **State age size.** Shipping weight, 2¾ pounds.
17K3970—Light Brown.
17K3971 Light Navy Blue. **$8.48**

17K3975
"TRUCURL" Wool Faced Chinchilla Cloth
Scarlet Flannel Lining
Ages 2 to 6 Years
$5.79
Ages 7 to 9 Years
$7.59

17K3990
Velour Coating
$5.95
Coney Fur Trimming

17K3995
Warm Winter Weight "MARTEEN" Cloth

$7.75

Delightfully Warm Sturdy Wearing Attractive Coat

"Marteen" Cloth—a handsome, fleecy napped new fabric, about one-half wool, which has a soft, downy surface, is the pleasing, sturdy coating that fashions this fetching little model. This excellent fabric guarantees unusual warmth, without being at all heavy in weight.

Adapted in a youthful, smart style, it shows pretty adornment of *Rayon* embroidery on the sleeves and below the pockets. The collar and ball trimmings of the streamer tie are of rich looking, soft *Beaverette* (clipped coney) fur.

Coat heavily interlined and lined with good quality *Sateen*.
Ages—2, 3, 4, 5 and 6 years. **State age size.** Shipping weight, 2¾ pounds.
17K3995 Copenhagen Blue. **$7.75**

Swagger, Tailored Model

Warmth and durability—those two essential features that are of foremost importance in a little girl's winter coat—are both guaranteed in this swagger, tailored model. Made of extra heavy, sturdy wearing "Trucurl" *Chinchilla Cloth*, more than three-fourths wool, the coat is trimmed with brass Navy Emblem buttons and has warm, red *Flannel* lining throughout.

Ages—2, 3, 4, 5 and 6 years. State age size. Shipping weight, 2¾ pounds.
17K3975—Navy Blue. **$5.79**
Same style. Ages—7, 8 and 9 years.
17K3895—Navy Blue. **$7.59**

17K3980 **$7.48** *Mandel Fur Trimming*
All Wool Velour

Smart and Practical

Designed in a becoming, youthful style of serviceable, winter weight *All Wool Velour*, this smart little coat is not only pleasing in appearance but delightfully warm and thoroughly practical as well. The collar and ball trimmings on the streamer tie ends, are of dressy *Mandel Fur*, while the lower front of the coat features attractive adornment of buttons and *Rayon* stitching. Coat shows neat workmanship throughout and comes with warm interlining and durable striped *Venetian* lining.

Ages—2, 3, 4, 5 and 6 years. **State age size.** Shipping weight, 2¾ pounds.
17K3980—Light Navy Blue.
17K3981—Medium Brown. **$7.48**

17K3985 **$8.98** *Mandel Fur Collar*
All Wool Suede Velour

Fetching, New Style

Here is an adorable little coat of a smart, new design, cleverly adapted in warm, winter weight *All Wool Suede Velour*—a handsome dressy fabric of fine serviceable quality.

Becomingly fashioned on youthful lines; the coat is well tailored and made with dressy *Mandel Fur* collar. It also features an attractive treatment of pointed tabs at each side of the front as well as adornment of *Rayon* stitching. Comes with warm interlining and durable mercerized *Sateen* lining.

Ages—3, 4, 5 and 6 years. **State age size.** Shipping weight, 2¾ pounds.
17K3985—Wine.
17K3986—Light Brown. **$8.98**

A Very Good Value

From the standpoint of style, service and true economy, this attractive coat is an excellent choice for any little girl. It is becomingly fashioned of winter weight, nearly *All Wool Velour* coating, which is warm and of a sturdy quality. The coat is made dressy by soft, silky *Coney Fur* collar and cuffs and it also shows smart trimming of lustrous *Rayon* stitching. Comes with serviceable *Striped Venetian* lining.

Ages—2, 3, 4, 5 and 6 years. **State age size.** Shipping weight, 2¾ lbs.
17K3990—Navy Blue.
17K3991—Wine (Burgundy). **$5.95**

PRESENTING TO YOU!

The Most Beautiful of the New York Dress Styles

Only 3 Simple Measurements

To Give You a Perfect Fitting Dress

1—Give your ACTUAL bust measure over largest part of bust. Be sure tape measure runs across shoulder blades in back.

2—Give your ACTUAL waist measure.

3—Give your ACTUAL hip measure over largest part of hips.

Draw Tape Close but Not Tight

Give your ACTUAL measurements, do not allow extra inches for fullness as we have already made this allowance. You will find that our dresses are scientifically cut and designed to fit your size correctly.

Be Sure to State Your Height and Weight

31K4000
Light Weight All Wool French Repp
$10.95

31K4005
All Silk Crepe Satin
$13.75

31K4010
All Silk Flat Crepe
$8.98

Tailored Model of Smart Design

This chic frock gives the effect of a swagger suit in front, the illusion being created by the clever treatment of the blouse, which is made with a tailored collar, an insert vestee and a wide hip fold; the latter showing a piped buttonhole trimmed with neat bone buttons.

The model is fashioned of handsome, fine quality, dress weight *All Wool French Repp*, smart in appearance and very serviceable. It was adapted on a becoming silhouette, the skirt having a panel of graceful pleating down front, while the back of the garment is cut on straight, loose lines with a sash belt. Effective trimming is provided by harmonizing *Rayon* chain-stitch embroidery and a self material flower ornament.

Women's and Misses' Sizes—34, 36, 38, and 40 inches bust measure. Dress comes in length 43 inches only, with deep 5-inch basted hem. **State your exact bust measure.** See measuring instructions above. Shpg. wt., 2 lbs.

31K4000—Forest Green. $10.95
31K4001—Navy Blue.

Adapted in a Lovely Fabric

We offer here a gracefully styled frock of extra quality *All Silk Crepe Satin*. This charming model will serve with equal smartness for formal or informal wear.

It features a becoming, collarless neckline, chic draped side panel on the blouse and a deep inverted pleat on the skirt. The insert bands and sash bows at the waistline, as well as the underlay of the pleat on the skirt, are of the dull crepe side of the fabric. Trimming of contrasting color silk *Georgette*, attractive rhinestone studded buttons and rhinestone loop ornaments.

Women's and Misses' Sizes—34, 36, 38, 40, 42, and 44 inches bust measure. Dress comes in length 44 inches with deep 5-inch basted hem. **State your exact bust measure.** See measuring instructions above. Shipping weight, 1½ lbs.

31K4005—Black With Flesh Pink Trimming. $13.75

Featuring Chic New Style Themes

In this frock of good quality *All Silk Flat Crepe* smartness is achieved by a distinctive treatment of pin tucking on the blouse and by the graceful effect lent by groups of pleating on the skirt. It is typical of the latest models shown in the New York shops; slender, yet animated in silhouette and having those clever, pleasing details of design that combine in making it exceedingly chic.

The collar and opening at the neck, as well as the cuffs are trimmed with novelty *Rayon* ribbon, and the double belt straps at the waistline are enhanced with pretty loop ornaments. It is really amazingly low priced for a frock of such attractive style, lovely fabric and good workmanship.

Women's and Misses' Sizes—34, 36, 38, 40, 42 and 44 inches bust measure. Dress comes in length 44 inches only, with deep 5-inch basted hem. **State your exact bust measure.** See measuring instructions above. Shipping wt., 1½ lbs.

31K4010—Navy Blue.
31K4011—Black. $8.98
31K4012—Palmetto Green.

Send Sufficient Money for Postage on Parcel Post Shipments. Any Surplus Will Be Returned

51

As Smart as the Smartest Styles You'll See on FIFTH AVENUE

31K4075
All Wool
Poiret
Sheen
$9.95

31K4085
"Cuddl-Doon"
Worsted and
Rayon Jersey
$9.98

31K4095
All Silk
Flat
Crepe
$10.75

31K4080
All Wool
Repp
$9.98

31K4070
Good
Quality
All Silk
Flat
Crepe
$12.95

These
Delightful Styles
Are Described
on the
Opposite
Page

31K4090
All Silk
Charmeuse
$8.98

31K4100
Fine
Quality
All Silk
Crepe
Satin
$12.95

Latest New York Style Frock

Its beauty is due to its lovely fabric, *All Silk Flat Crepe*, and to the application of diamond shaped chain stitch silk embroidery, on the front, back and sleeves, and its gracefully box pleated skirt. Comes with an overcollar and cuff trimming of contrasting *Silk Crepe*. *Women's and Misses' Sizes*—to fit 34, 36, 38, 40, 42 and 44 inches bust measure. Length, from back of neck to hem, 44 inches only, with deep 5-inch basted hem. **State size.** See measuring instructions on page 15. Shpg. wt., 2 lbs.

31K4070—Green and Tan.
31K4071—Black and Tan. **$12.95**

Tailored Model

Smarter than ever are the tailored frocks of this season, such as you see in this model, of lustrous *All Wool Poiret-Sheen*. It has panels of pleating on the skirt and is adorned with contrasting *Rayon* embroidery. The vestee cuffs and streamer tie are of all *Silk Crepe*. *Women's and Misses' Regular Sizes*—to fit 34, 36, 38, 40, 42 and 44 inches bust measure. Length, from back of neck to hem, 44 inches only, with deep 5-inch basted hem. See measuring instructions on page 15. Shipping weight, 2 pounds.

31K4075—Navy Blue.
31K4076—Brown. **$9.95**

Practical and Very Good Looking

Every woman finds a frock of this type a constant delight. Smart tailored design and fashioned of durable, good quality *All Wool Repp*. The collar, bodice and sleeves show trimming of embroidery. Box pleats lend fullness and a chic effect to the skirt. *Women's and Misses' Regular Sizes*—to fit 34, 36, 38, 40, 42 and 44 inches bust measure. Length, from back of neck to hem, 44 inches only, with deep 5-inch basted hem. **State size.** See measuring instructions on page 15. Shipping weight, 2 pounds.

31K4080—Ashes of Roses.
31K4081—Cocoa Brown. **$9.98**

Smart for Sport or General Wear

A swagger two-piece effect design made of *Rayon and Worsted "Cuddl-doon" Jersey*, appropriate for sport or general wear. It is trimmed with contrasting *All Wool Flasha* Rayon loops and novelty metal discs. The sash belt has metal buckle. *Women's and Misses' Regular Sizes*—to fit 34, 36, 38, 40, and 42 inches bust measure. Length, from back of neck to hem, 44 inches only, with deep 5-inch basted hem. **State size.** See measuring instructions on page 15. Shipping weight, 2 pounds.

31K4085—Medium Blue.
31K4086—Light Brown. **$9.98**

Inexpensive Dressy Type Frock

This charming frock of lustrous *All Silk Charmeuse* is of the latest mode. The skirt is box pleated at front; the pleats restrained by rows of contrasting silk stitching which match the trimming of the belt. A flower ornament and novelty buttons add smartness. *Women's and Misses' Regular Sizes*—to fit 34, 36, 38 and 40 inches bust measure. Length, from back of neck to hem, 43 inches only, with deep 5-inch basted hem. **State size.** See measuring instructions on page 15. Shipping weight, 2 pounds.

31K4090—Black and Red. **$8.98**

Graceful New Style

We offer here a very charming model of good quality *All Silk Flat Crepe*, which makes smart use of *Rayon* embroidery and contrasting *Silk Crepe* trimming. It has softly bloused bodice, made with a jaunty tie and the skirt gains pleasing fullness with rows of shirring. *Women's and Misses' Sizes*—to fit 34, 36, 38, 40, 42 and 44 inches bust measure. Length, from back of neck to hem, 44 inches, with deep 5-inch basted hem. **State size.** See measuring instructions on page 15. Shpg. wt., 2 lbs.

31K4095—Athenia and Tan.
31K4096—Black and Tan. **$10.75**

Style of Appealing Beauty

This lovely frock employs *All Silk Crepe Satin* for its fabric and uses both the lustrous and dull crepe sides in its design. Adornment is lent by contrasting *All Silk Georgette*, fancy buttons, embroidery and buckle ornament. Its price is appealingly modest. *Women's and Misses' Regular Sizes*—to fit 36, 38, 40, 42 and 44 inches bust measure. Length, from back of neck to hem, 44 inches only, with deep 5-inch basted hem. **State size.** See measuring instructions on page 15. Shipping weight, 2 pounds.

31K4100—Brown and Tan.
31K4101—Black and Queen Blue. **$12.95**

Unmistakably NEW YORK

A Splendid Value

Trim looking, inexpensive, tailored style frock of good quality *Half Wool Crepe*, a practical, well wearing garment. Designed on becoming straight lines, with a narrow insert panel of pleating on the skirt; it features neat adornment of lustrous *Rayon* braid, metal buttons and an ornamental buckle. *Women's and Misses' Regular Sizes*—34, 36, 38, 40, 42 and 44 inches bust measure. Length, from back of neck to hem, 44 inches with deep 5-inch hem. **State size.** See page 15 for measuring instructions. Shipping weight, 2 pounds.

31K4115—Brown.
31K4116—Navy Blue. **$5.98**

31K4115
Half Wool Crepe
$5.98

31K4120
All Wool Poiret Sheen with All Silk Flat Crepe Blouse
$16.95

3-Piece Ensemble

31K4110
Good Quality All Silk Flat Crepe
$11.50

31K4105
All Silk Satin Charmeuse
$7.98

Stunning Costume

New York's latest! The swagger box jacket 7nd skirt are of fine quality *All Wool Poiret-Sheen*; the lovely separate blouse of *All Silk Flat Crepe*. Skirt is pleated at front and has a *Seco* bodice lining. *Small Women's and Misses' Sizes*—34, 36, 38 and 40 inches bust measure. Length, from back of neck to hem, 42 inches. Skirt has deep 5-inch basted hem, making length easy to alter. **State size.** See page 15 for measuring instructions. Shpg. wt., 2½ lbs.

31K4120—Navy Blue. **$16.95**

With Attractive New Fashion Themes

Good quality *All Silk Flat Crepe* tucked collar, vestee and cuffs of contrasting-color *Silk Crepe*. Trimmed with pearl buttons and a lovely buckle. A pleasing two-piece effect style. *Women's and Misses' Sizes*—34, 36, 38, 40, 42 and 44 inches bust measure. Length, from back of neck to hem, 44 inches, with 5-inch basted hem. **State size.** Shpg. wt., 2 lbs.

31K4110—Palmetto Green and Tan.
31K4111—Black and Rose Beige. **$11.50**

Lustrous, Dressy, All Silk Satin Charmeuse

The skirt is pleated at front, while the bodice and cuffs show contrasting *All Silk Flat Crepe* trimming. Vestee also shows adornment of embroidery edging and small fancy buttons. The string tie is finished with pretty metal ball pendants and the sash belt has a buckle ornament. *Women's and Misses' Sizes*—to fit 34, 36, 38, 40, 42 and 44 inches bust measure, with 5-inch basted hem. **State size.** Shipping wt., 2 lbs.

31K4105—Black and Beige.
31K4106—Navy Blue and Tan. **$7.98**

BETTERMADE

FOR WOMEN WHO KNOW THE DIFFERENCE

No Other Name So Truly Describes Them

BETTERMADE DRESSES are b-e-t-t-e-r m-a-d-e. Better made than any dresses ever before offered for the price. For we have long felt that there was a definite demand for dresses of such quality—the quality which only the very finest shops in America handle.

In *workmanship* and *tailoring* they leave nothing to be desired. Only the most skilled designers and makers can produce dresses of such quality. And naturally, the *finest* tailors work only with the *best* materials. Every dress in every size is subjected to the most thorough examination for fit and quality. Trimmings are specially selected. Silks and woolens are rigidly tested. We are satisfied with nothing but the best in these dresses.

We present BETTERMADE DRESSES to the women of America who desire to possess the best, confident that they will be fully satisfied—that their purchase will give them unending satisfaction.

31K4125
ALL SILK
FLAT
CREPE
$14.75

31K4135
ALL SILK
CANTON
CREPE
$16.75

31K4130
ALL SILK
GEORGETTE
CREPE
$16.75

We present here a charming "BETTER-MADE" frock that will serve with smartness for almost any occasion. Its charm is due, not only to a style that portrays the latest mode, but to those two additionally important factors—quality and excellent workmanship.

Fashioned of *All Silk Flat Crepe*, it has shirring below the shoulders, a wide band of fine tucking at the waist, tucking on the cuffs and graceful pleating on the skirt. Contrasting color *Silk Crepe* was effectively used for a vestee, overcollar and neat piping. It also shows the adornment of novelty buttons and a handsome buckle.

Women's and Misses' Regular Sizes—to fit 34, 36, 38, 40, 42 and 44 inches bust measure. Length, from back of neck to hem, 44 inches only, with deep 5-inch basted hem. See measuring instructions on page 15. **State size.** Shpg. wt., 2 lbs.

31K4125—Navy Blue with Tan Trimming.
31K4126—Black with Tan Trimming. **$14.75**

A frock such as this lovely and desirable "BETTERMADE" model, can be achieved only by the artful combination of style, plus quality and perfect workmanship.

Adapted in a charming, graceful design of sheer, dainty *Silk Georgette Crepe;* the softly bloused bodice is made over a contrasting Georgette foundation, which is revealed as a yoke at the neck, and serves as a vestee down the front. Contrasting *Georgette* also trims the graceful tie ends and sleeves. The frock also has clusters of narrow folds on front and back, and a group of inverted pleats on the skirt, which is draped over a matching color Georgette drop slip.

Women's and Misses' Regular Sizes—to fit 34, 36, 38, 40, 42 and 44 inches bust measure. Length, from back of neck to hem, 44 inches only, with deep 5-inch basted hem. See measuring instructions on page 15. **State size.** Shpg. wt., 2 lbs.

31K4130—Navy Blue with Beige Trimming. **$16.75**

For the smartly dressed woman, who chooses her frocks for their fine quality and workmanship, we offer this truly lovely "BETTERMADE" model.

Made of *All Silk Canton Crepe*, it shows a long waisted bodice, a bow finished wide girdle and a straight cut skirt with graceful loose pleated panels. Frock has detachable, dainty vestee and cuffs of exquisitely embroidered contrasting *Georgette Crepe*. Other pleasing details include rows of shirring at the shoulders and self covered buttons.

Women's and Misses' Regular Sizes—to fit 34, 36, 38, 40, 42 and 44 inches bust measure. Length, from back of neck to hem, 44 inches only with deep 5-inch basted hem. See measuring instructions on page 15. **State size.** Shpg. wt., 2 lbs.

31K4135—Navy Blue.
31K4136—Black. **$16.75**

DRESSES

THE QUALITY TELLS THE STORY

31K4155
ALL SILK
CANTON
CREPE

REGULAR
SIZES
$14⁷⁵

STOUT
SIZES
$16⁷⁵

31K4140
SILK
STRIPED
ALL WOOL
REPP
$12⁷⁵

31K4145
ALL SILK
CREPE
SATIN
$14⁷⁵

31K4150
ALL SILK
CREPE
ROMAINE
$16⁷⁵

This "BETTERMADE" model of *All Silk Canton Crepe* is fashioned on a chic straightline silhouette. Trimmed smartly with contrasting silk crepe, novelty buttons and a neat buckle, it gives evidence of its excellent workmanship in the expert treatment of folds, inserts and pleated panels.
Women's Regular Sizes—36 to 44 inches bust measure, with length from back of neck to hem, 44 inches. *Stout Women's Sizes*—39 to 53 inches bust measure, with length from back of neck to hem, 48 inches. Dresses have deep 5-inch basted hem, making length easy to alter. **State size.** See measuring instructions on page 15. Shipping weight, 2 pounds.
Regular Sizes
31K4155—Black with Tan Trimming.
31K4156—Navy Blue with
Tan Trimming.   **$14.75**
Stout Sizes
31K4385—Black with Tan Trimming
31K4386—Navy Blue with
Tan Trimming.   **$16.75**

This stunning "BETTERMADE" frock is skillfully fashioned of *All Silk Crepe Satin*, and the designer cleverly used the shimmering lustrous as well as the dull crepe side of the fabric. The frock gains additional chic by having pleat inserts, a graceful jabot frill and trimmings of *Contrasting Color Silk Crepe* and novelty triple loop ornament.
Women's and Misses' Regular Sizes—34, 36, 38, 40, 42 and 44 inches bust measure. Length from back of neck to hem, 44 inches only, with deep 5-inch basted hem, making length easy to alter. **State size.** See measuring instructions on page 15. Shipping weight, 2 pounds.
31K4145—Black with
Rose Beige Trimming.....**$14.75**

This New York model is indicative of the splendid features that make our "BETTERMADE" frocks distinctive and desirable.
Made of *Silk Striped All Wool Repp* in the latest coat effect, with a detachable vestee and cuffs of washable *White Silk Crepe*, it fastens down the front with bone buttons and has flower boutonniere. Of high quality fabric and expert workmanship.
Women's and Misses' Regular Sizes—34, 36, 38, 40, 42 and 44 inches bust measure. Length from back of neck to hem, 44 inches only, with deep 5-inch basted hem. **State size.** See measuring instructions on page 15. Shipping weight, 2 pounds.
31K4140—Navy Blue with White Stripes.
$12.75

Like all of our "BETTERMADE" frocks, it is distinguished by its perfection of make and style.
Adapted of lovely *All Silk Crepe Romaine*, the frock features pin tucking, tiered soft folds, a smart kick pleat and has adornment of two-tone grosgrain ribbon, a handsome novelty buckle and a flower ornament. Made over a matching color silk crepe slip.
Women's and Misses' Regular Sizes—34, 36, 38, 40 and 42 inches bust measure. Length from back of neck to hem, 44 inches only, with deep 5-inch basted hem. **State size.** See measuring instructions on page 15. Shipping weight, 2 pounds.
31K4150—Navy
Blue with Tan Trimming.   **$16.75**

Never Have We Seen Such SPLENDID STYLES for Stout Women

Stout Sizes to Fit Bust Measures 39 to 53 Inches

Trimline BRAND S.R. and Co.

31K4350
Half Wool
Fancy Crepe
$6.98

Very Practical

The style is slenderizing, the material good looking and durable, and the price is very modest, indeed. Adapted in *Novelty Half Wool Crepe* that has a pretty varitone woven *Rayon* plaid pattern, the model shows a wide panel effect down the front, outlined with folds on the bodice and with pleats on the skirt. Has neat trimming of solid color half wool *crepe* and composition buttons.

Special Sizes to Fit Stout Women—39, 41, 43, 45, 47, 49, 51 and 53 inches bust measure. Dress comes in length 48 inches only, with 5-inch basted hem. See page 51 for measuring instructions. **State your exact bust measure.** Shipping weight, 2 pounds.

31K4350—Brown, Fancy
31K4351—Blue, Fancy $6.98

Of Rich Appearance

You will find pleasure in owning this lovely frock of lustrous *All Silk Satin Charmeuse*. It was created on slenderizing lines, that are accentuated by panels of pleating down the front and by the vestee treatment on the bodice, the vestee made of contrasting silk crepe and ecru shade Venise pattern lace. The wide girdle has handsome buckle ornament.

Special Sizes to Fit Stout Women—39, 41, 43, 45, 47, 49, 51 and 53 inches bust measure. Dress comes in length 48 inches only, with 5-inch basted hem. See page 51 for measuring instructions. **State your exact bust measure.** Shipping weight, 2 pounds.

31K4345—Black.
31K4346—Navy Blue. $10.98

31K4345
All Silk
Satin
Charmeuse
$10.98

Attractive — Inexpensive

A graceful effect is lent to this frock by a draped jabot frill collar and by the pleating featured on the front of its skirt; a style treatment that is both smart and slenderizing, making the frock an ideal choice for stout women.

It is fashioned of *Figured Silk Warp Foulard*, that comes in a new, attractive pattern, and the model is prettily trimmed with lustrous satin ribbon. The sash belt has an ornamental metal buckle at front.

Special Sizes to Fit Stout Women—39, 41, 43, 45, 47, 49, 51 and 53 inches bust measure. Dress comes in length 48 inches only, with 5-inch basted hem. See page 51 for measuring instructions. **State your exact bust measure.** Shipping weight, 2 pounds.

31K4340
Navy Blue and Tan. $5.98

31K4340
Figured
Silk Warp
Foulard
$5.98

Descriptions of Styles Illustrated on Opposite Page

Dressy, Attractive Model

This charming frock is fashioned in the latest New York manner, of richly lustrous *All Silk Crepe Satin*, portraying a design that is smart and most flattering to stout women. Trimmed effectively with contrasting color silk *Crepe*; it has a chic, button-trimmed frill on the bodice, and graceful pleating on the skirt, while the waistline is finished with a narrow sash belt showing a rhinestone studded, handsome buckle.

Special Sizes to Fit Stout Women—39, 41, 43, 45, 47, 49, 51 and 53 inches bust measure. Dress comes in length 48 inches only, with 5-inch basted hem. State your exact bust measure. See page 51 for measuring instructions. Shipping weight, 2 lbs.

31K4355—Black and Tan. $14.95

New and Decidedly Smart

A clever treatment of full length narrow panels down the front, and graceful, tiered folds on either side of the skirt give a distinctive and very smart effect to this lovely Trimline frock of fine quality *All Silk Flat Crepe*. The revers and vestee are of contrasting color silk *crepe*, the latter showing adornment of attractive *Rayon* embroidery. Belt is trimmed with a good looking novelty metal buckle.

Special Sizes to Fit Stout Women—39, 41, 43, 45, 47, 49, 51 and 53 inches bust measure. Dress comes in length 48 inches only, with 5-inch basted hem. State your exact bust measure. See page 51 for measuring instructions. Shipping weight, 2 pounds.

31K4360—Navy Blue.
31K4361—Black. $15.98

Of Neat Tailored Style

It is very inexpensive—only $7.98—yet it will give splendid service and please in every way, because the fabric is durable and attractive, while the style of the dress is smart and becoming. Adapted in *Fancy Half Wool Jacquard Crepe*, the garment is cut on slenderizing lines, and has trimming of harmonizing color plain half wool *crepe*, novelty bone buttons and a metal buckle.

Special Sizes to Fit Stout Women—39, 41, 43, 45, 47, 49, 51 and 53 inches bust measure. Dress comes in length 48 inches only, with 5-inch basted hem. State your exact bust measure. See page 51 for measuring instructions. Shipping weight, 2 lbs.

31K4365—Tan. $7.98

So Chic and Practical

The fall and winter wardrobe of the well dressed woman usually includes a good looking cloth dress of this type for general all around service. This one was especially designed for stout women on smart, slenderizing lines and adapted in good quality *All Wool Repp*. It is made with a front panel of harmonizing color Repp and shows trimmings of attractive *Rayon* embroidery, novelty buttons and a metal buckle.

Special Sizes to Fit Stout Women—39, 41, 43, 45, 47, 49, 51 and 53 inches bust measure. Dress comes in length 48 inches only, with 5-inch basted hem. State your exact bust measure. See page 51 for measuring instructions. Shipping weight, 2 lbs.

31K4370—Palmetto Green.
31K4371—Navy Blue.
31K4372—Black. $10.95

Direct From New York

Fashioned in a distinctive new style of fine quality silky lustrous *All Wool Poiret-Sheen*, this handsome dress shows attractive trimming of harmonizing color all wool *French Repp* and is further enhanced with *Rayon* braid and chainstitch embroidery. Created on a slenderizing silhouette, it has a becoming blouse and gracefully pleated skirt, the pleating confined on top with rows of stitching.

Special Sizes to Fit Stout Women—39, 41, 43, 45, 47, 49, 51 and 53 inches bust measure. Dress comes in length 48 inches only, with 5-inch basted hem. State your exact bust measure. See page 51 for measuring instructions. Shipping weight, 2 pounds.

31K4375—Brown.
31K4376—Navy Blue. $14.98

Lovely in Style and Fabric

Designed with unerring good taste by experts who specialize in better grade, stout women's apparel, this charming frock was created on a slenderizing silhouette, of fine quality *All Silk Georgette Crepe*. It is made with graceful, full length front panels; shows a deep inverted fold down the center of the skirt and a narrow sash belt at the waistline. Trimmed with *All Silk Flat Crepe* bands and buttons, as well as with a handsome buckle. Comes with a Seco slip.

Special Sizes to Fit Stout Women—39, 41, 43, 45, 47, 49, 51 and 53 inches bust measure. Dress comes in length 48 inches only, with a 5-inch basted hem. State your exact bust measure. See page 51 for measuring instructions. Shpg. wt., 2 lbs.

31K4380—Navy Blue. $16.75

Designed for *STOUT WOMEN* and Possessing That *SMART* New York *STYLE*

Trimline BRAND S.R. and Co.

Stout Women's Sizes to Fit Bust Measures 39 to 53 Inches

31K4360 All Silk Flat Crepe $15.98

31K4375 All Wool Poiret Sheen $14.98

31K4355 All Silk Crepe Satin $14.95

31K4365 Fancy Half Wool Jacquard Crepe $7.98

31K4370 All Wool Repp $10.95

31K4380 All Silk Georgette Crepe $16.75

These Dresses Are Fully Described on Opposite Page

YOUTHFULLY STYLED
For Misses and Small Women

31K4505
Fancy
All Wool
French Crepe
$9.95

Sizes
14 - 16 - 18 - 20 - 22
Years
To Fit Bust Measures
32 - 34 - 36 - 38 - 40
Inches

31K4515
All Wool
Plaid Velour
$6.95

31K4510
All Silk
Flat Crepe
$8.98

31K4500
Good
Quality
All Silk
Flat Crepe
$10.98

31K4520
All Wool
Ombre
Striped
Jersey with
All Wool
Flannel
$7.98

These Frocks Are Fully Described on Opposite Page

31K4525
Silk Striped
Wool
CHERILAINE
$17.98

31K4530
All Silk
Georgette
Crepe
$15.00

31K4535
All Silk
Crepe
Satin
$9.98

Attractively Styled

The material is lustrous *All Silk Satin Charmeuse*, featuring a tie trimmed convertible collar and pointed yoke on the bodice, a wide insert band at the waist and graceful pleating on the skirt. Novelty metal buttons and contrasting piping.
Misses' Sizes—32, 34, 36, 38 or 40 inches bust measure. Length, 42 inches only with 5-inch basted hem. **State bust measure.** Shpg. wt., 2 lbs.
31K4545—Rustic Brown.
31K4546—Black. **$7.98**

Very Modestly Priced

Silky lustrous, good quality *All Wool Poiret-Sheen.* Pin tucked blouse and sleeves; collar band and tie of contrasting *All Silk Crepe.* Patch pocket of embroidered *Duvetyn.*
Misses' and Small Women's Sizes—32, 34, 36, 38 or 40 inches bust measure. Comes in length 42 inches only, with 5-inch basted hem. **State exact bust measure.** Shipping weight, 2 pounds.
31K4550—Green.
31K4551—Rust.
31K4552—Navy Blue. **$7.89**

Sizes
14-16-18-20-22
Years

To Fit Bust
Measures
32-34-36-38-40
Inches

31K4550
All Wool Poiret Sheen
$7.89

31K4545
All Silk Satin Charmeuse
$7.98

For Simple Measuring Instructions See Page 51

Descriptions of Dresses Shown on Opposite Page

31K4540
Novelty Wool Homespun Velour
$6.98

Smartly fashioned of good quality *All Silk Flat Crepe*, it has a gracefully pleated skirt and attractive box tucking on the sleeves and lower part of the blouse. The over-collar and cuffs are of contrasting silk *Crepe.*
Misses' Sizes—32, 34, 36, 38 or 40 inches bust measure. Length, 42 inches only, with 5-inch basted hem. **State bust measure.** Shipping weight, 2 pounds.
31K4500—Queen Blue.
31K4501—Black and White. **$10.98**

Frock of distinctive style made of fine quality silver maize *All Wool French Crepe.* Shows tucking on the blouse, wide loose folds at the hip and graceful pleating on the skirt. Trimmed with harmonizing all silk *Crepe.*
Misses' Sizes—32, 34, 36, 38 or 40 inches bust measure. Length, 42 inches only, with 5-inch basted hem. **State bust measure.** Shipping weight, 2 pounds.
31K4505—Almond Green.
31K4506—Begonia (Light Rust.) **$9.95**

With box pleating on the skirt and buckle trimmed strap bands as well as exquisite hand embroidery on the blouse, this frock of *All Silk Flat Crepe* achieves a charming effect. Collar and cuffs show contrasting silk edging.
Misses' Sizes—32, 34, 36, 38 or 40 inches bust measure. Length, 41 and 43 inches only, with 5-inch basted hem. **State bust measure and length.** Shipping wt., 2 pounds.
31K4510—French Beige.
31K4511—Palmetto Green.
31K4512—Black. **$8.98**

Tailored frock of attractive *All Wool Plaid Velour.* Styled with graceful pleating on the skirt, it shows effective trimmings of solid color all wool *Flannel*, pretty buttons, a ribbon tie and novelty belt.
Misses' Sizes—32, 34, 36, 38 or 40 inches bust measure. Length, 42 inches only, with 5-inch basted hem. **State bust measure.** Shipping weight, 2 pounds.
31K4515—Blue Plaid. **$6.95**

Two-piece effect sport style frock; blouse made of attractive *Ombre Striped All Wool Jersey*, while the skirt and blouse trimmings are of harmonizing dress weight *All Wool Flannel.* Has novelty metal buckle ornament.
Misses' Sizes—32, 34, 36, 38 or 40 inches bust measure. Length, 42 inches only, with 5-inch basted hem. **State bust measure.** Shipping weight, 2 pounds.
31K4520—Tan.
31K4521—Medium Blue. **$7.98**

Three-piece suit dress. Box jacket and skirt of *Silk Striped All Wool Cherilaine;* separate blouse of *All Silk Flat Crepe.* Tie and kerchief of printed all silk *Crepe.* Skirt is attached to a *Seco* bodice lining.
Misses' Sizes—32, 34, 36, or 38 inches bust measure. Length, 42 inches only, with 5-inch basted hem. **State bust measure.** Shipping weight, 2 pounds.
31K4525—Briar Rose.
31K4526—Light Navy Blue. **$17.98**

Fine quality *All Silk Georgette Crepe.* Harmonizing all silk *Crepe de Chine* slip, a smart kerchief drape at the front and back of the blouse; petal panels on the skirt; a self flower ornament and rhinestone buckle.
Misses' Sizes—32, 34, 36, 38 or 40 inches bust measure. Length, 41 and 43 inches only. **State bust measure and length.** Shipping weight, 2 pounds.
31K4530—Navy Blue.
31K4531—Rose Beige. **$15.00**

Frock of *All Silk Crepe Satin.* The bodice has side drape and is trimmed with a self flower and novelty buttons. Skirt shows panel of pleating at front. Enhanced with contrasting *Satin* and a rhinestone pin.
Misses' Sizes—32, 34, 36, 38 or 40 inches bust measure. Length, 42 inches only, with 5-inch basted hem. **State bust measure.** Shipping weight, 2 pounds.
31K4535—Garnet Red.
31K4536—Black. **$9.98**

31K4555
All Wool Dress Weight Flannel
$7.95

Of Tailored Smartness

Fashioned of *Novelty Wool and Silk Homespun Velour*, this frock is practical and inexpensive. The collar, rever facings as well as the cuffs and piped openings on the pockets are of all wool *Flannel;* also trimmed with pretty bone buttons and a fancy leather belt. Inverted pleats lend pleasing fulness to the skirt.
Misses' and Small Women's Sizes—34, 36, 38 or 40 inches bust measure. Dress comes in length 42 inches only, with 5-inch basted hem. **State bust measure.** Shipping weight, 2 pounds.
31K4540
Medium Blue Fancy. **$6.98**

Handsome and Practical

Chic two-piece effect frock of distinctive design, of soft, good quality *All Wool Dress Weight Flannel.*

New V shape neck, pin tucking at the front and lower fold of the blouse, while the skirt gains smartness with pleating. Trimmed with contrasting color *Flannel*, small metal discs and a novelty metal buckle. This is a well made, durable garment, very modestly priced.
Misses' and Small Women's Sizes—34, 36, 38 or 40 inches bust measure. Dress comes in length 42 inches only with 5-inch basted hem. **State bust measure.** Shipping weight, 2 pounds.
31K4555—Athenia (Medium Old Rose).
31K4556—Blue. **$7.95**

It's Easy to Measure for Clothing. See Page 548

67

GRACEFULLY DESIGNED

for Junior Misses and High School Girls

31K4705
Wool and Rayon Crepe With All Wool Crepe

$6.98

Attractive Model
Smart two-piece effect model, with the blouse made of novelty *Wool Crepe with Rayon Pattern* and the skirt and blouse trimmings of plain, contrasting *All Wool Crepe*. A tie with buckle adornment lends a pleasing style note to the bodice, while the skirt shows graceful pleating.
Junior Sizes—15, 17, and 19 years. *Intermediate Sizes*—14½ and 16½ years. See size scales. **State age size and length.** Shpg. wt., 1½ lbs.
31K4705—Red and Gray.
31K4706—Blue and Gray. **$6.98**

31K4700
All Silk Flat Crepe

$8.59

31K4710
All Wool French Spun Jersey

$7.48

31K4715
All Wool Flasha Velour and Plaid Cashmere

$5.98

Two-Piece Effect
Popular "Tomboy" style dress at a very low price. Blouse is made of *All Wool Flasha Velour*, showing a kerchief and swagger tie of contrasting color *Tub Silk*, while the skirt and wide waistband are of attractive *All Wool Plaid Cashmere*.
Junior Sizes—15, 17 and 19 years. *Intermediate Sizes*—14½ and 16½ years. See size scales. **State age size and length.** Shpg. wt., 1½ lbs.
31K4715—Green.
31K4716—Light brown. **$5.98**

31K4720
Novelty Checked Suiting

$2.95

Youthfully Styled Charming Silk Frock
Good quality *All Silk Flat Crepe*. Trimming of contrasting color silk *Crepe*. Effective shirring trims top of bodice panels and skirt.
Junior Sizes—15, 17 and 19 years. Bust measure, 33, 35 and 37 inches. *Intermediate Sizes*—14½ and 16½ years. Bust measure, 35 and 37 inches. Average length, 42 inches. **State age size and length.** See size scales. Shpg. wt., 1½ lbs.
31K4700—Navy Blue and Red.
31K4701—Rose Beige and Tan. **$8.59**

Junior Sizes			
Ages, Years	15	17	19
Lengths, Inches	41	42	43
To Fit Bust Measure, Inches	33	35	37

Smart, Practical and Inexpensive
This good looking frock so appropriate for school and general wear is youthfully fashioned of soft, well wearing *All Wool French Spun Jersey*. Has wide box pleats at the front and shows effective trimming of harmonizing color *Jersey*.
Junior Sizes—15, 17 and 19 years. *Intermediate Sizes*—14½ and 16½ years. See size scales. **State age size and length.** Shpg. wt., 1½ lbs.
31K4710—Beige and Tan.
31K4711—Gooseberry Green and Palmetto Green. **$7.48**

Wonderful Value at Our Low Price
Attractive *Fancy Checked Cotton Suiting*. Practical for everyday service. Box pleat panels at front, two button trimmed novel pockets. Collar, cuffs and tie of *Sateen*.
Junior Sizes—15, 17 and 19 years. Bust measure, 33, 35 and 37 inches. *Intermediate Sizes*—14½ and 16½ years. Bust measure, 35 and 37 inches. Average length, 42 inches. **State age size and length.** See size scales. Shpg. wt., 1½ lbs.
31K4720—Fancy Check. **$2.95**

Intermediate Sizes		
Ages, Years	14½	16½
Lengths, Inches	40	42
To Fit Bust Measure, Inches	35	37

Descriptions of Dresses Shown on Opposite Page

Richly lustrous *All Silk Satin Charmeuse* is the lovely fabric that fashions this youthful frock. It shows contrasting silk *Crepe, Rayon* hand embroidery and belt with novelty buckle.
Misses' Sizes—32, 34, 36, 38 and 40 inches bust measure. Dress comes in length 42 inches only, with 5-inch basted hem. **State bust measure.** Shpg. wt., 1½ lbs.
31K4610—Rustic Brown. **$8.98**
31K4611—Black.

Charming frock of *All Silk Flat Crepe* with trimming of contrasting silk *Crepe* and lovely silk and chenille hand embroidery. Skirt has panel of shirring; sash belt shows buckle ornament.
Misses' Sizes—32, 34, 36, 38 and 40 inches bust measure. Dress comes in length 42 inches only, with 5-inch basted hem. **State bust measure.** Shpg. wt., 1½ lbs.
31K4615—Mosaic Blue.
31K4616—Athenia.
31K4617—Black. **$8.98**

Made of *All Wool Canton Crepe* into a swagger, youthful design, this frock has a gracefully pleated skirt and shows effective trimmings of contrasting silk *Crepe* and novelty *Rayon* bandings.
Misses' Sizes—32, 34, 36, 38 and 40 inches bust measure. Dress comes in length 42 inches only, with 5-inch basted hem. **State bust measure.** Shpg. wt., 1½ lbs.
31K4620—Rust.
31K4621—French Blue. **$9.95**

New and stunning model, adapted in lovely *All Silk Flat Crepe*. Has chic kerchief collar; box pleated skirt; hand embroidered motif on bodice, and smart contrasting silk *Crepe* trimming.
Misses' Sizes—32, 34, 36, 38 and 40 inches bust measure. Dress comes in length 41 and 43 inches only. **State bust measure and length.** Shpg. wt., 1½ lbs.
31K4625—Dahlia (Dark Orchid).
31K4626—Queen Blue.
31K4627—Black. **$11.75**

Two-piece frock made of plain and checked *All Silk Flat Crepe*. Blouse shows a gracefully draped jabot panel and adornment of novelty metal buttons and piping. The box pleated skirt is attached to a *Tub Silk* bodice lining.
Misses' Sizes—32, 34, 36, 38 and 40 in. bust Dress comes in length 42 in. only, with 5-in. basted hem. **State bust measure.** Shpg. wt., 1½ lbs.
31K4630—Mother Goose (Tan).
31K4631—Black and Black and White Check. **$12.98**

Frock of tailored smartness, adapted in handsome *All Wool Novelty Velour*. It has a new, distinctive design and shows the pleasing adornment of lightweight, solid color all wool *Flannel*, fancy buttons, a swagger belt and a dressy *Mandel Fur* collar.
Misses' Sizes—34, 36, 38 and 40 inches bust measure. Dress comes in length 42 inches only, with 5-inch basted hem. **State bust measure.** Shpg. wt., 2 lbs.
31K4635—Blue Fancy. **$9.95**

Two-piece model blouse of lustrous twill back *Velveteen* and pleated skirt of all wool *Flannel*. The blouse is trimmed with a Roman stripe silk *Crepe* tie and with a suede leather belt. Skirt has attached *Batiste* bodice lining.
Junior and Intermediate Sizes. See size scale above. **State size.** Shpg. wt., 2 lbs.
31K4730—Brown and Tan.
31K4731—Navy Blue and Medium Blue. **$9.98**

Two-piece effect youthful frock, of which the blouse is made of lightweight all wool *Flannel*, while its trimmings, as well as the skirt are of novelty *Plaid Homespun*. Has the latest "Chanel" neckline and the skirt shows graceful pleating at one side.
Junior and Intermediate Sizes. See size scale above. **State size.** Shpg. wt., 1½ lbs.
31K4725—Gooseberry Green. **$5.98**

Sizes
14 - 16 - 18 - 20 - 22 Years
To Fit Bust Measures
32 - 34 - 36 - 38 - 40 Inches

For Misses Who Love NICE FROCKS

31K4615
All Silk
Flat
Crepe
$8.98

31K4620
All Wool
Canton
Crepe
$9.95

31K4630
Good Quality
All Silk
Crepe
$12.98

31K4625
Good
Quality
All Silk
Flat Crepe
$11.75

31K4610
All Silk
Satin
Charmeuse
$8.98

These Two Dresses Come in Juniors and Intermediate Sizes Only

31K4730
Twill Back
Velveteen
and All Wool
Flannel
Two Piece
Frock
$9.98

31K4725
All Wool
Flannel
and Novelty
Homespun
$5.98

31K4635
All Wool
Novelty
Velour
$9.95

These Dresses Are Fully Described on Opposite Page

27K5425
Fancy Knitted
Sport Blouse
$2.98

27K5420
Brushed
All Wool
Sport
Blouse
$2.98

27K5415
Fancy Knitted
Sport Blouse
$3.50

27K5650
Rainhat
$1.98

Junior
Misses
Sizes

Misses
Sizes

27K5430
Fancy Knitted
Sport Blouse
$1.95

27K5645
Alligator
Pattern
Rubber
Surface
Slicker
$5.98

These Styles
Are Fully
Described on
Opposite Page

27K5435
Fancy Knitted
Sport Blouse
$1.98

27K5405
All Wool
Plaid
Lumberjack
Blouse
$4.95

27K5700
All Wool
Tweed
Knickers
$2.98

Hills Khaki
Jean
$1.98

All Wool
Tweed
Stout Sizes
$3.98

27K5440
All Wool
Plaid
Lumberjack
Blouse
$3.98

27K5410
Rainproofed
Leatherette
Sport Jacket
$7.98

Misses
Sizes

27K5400
All Wool Plaid
Lumberjack
Blouse
$3.79

Girls
Sizes

Girl's lumberjack sport blouse of fine quality *All Wool Plaid*, self material convertible collar, hipband and cuffs of knitted all wool worsted. *Ages—7 to 14 years.* **State age size.** Shipping weight, ¾ pound.
27K5400—Tan and Gray Plaid.
27K5401—Blue and Gray Plaid. **$3.79**

All Wool Plaid Flannel, lumberjack style sport blouse, convertible collar, cuffs, hip band and trimmings of *All Wool Worsted Yarn*. *Misses' and Small Women's Sizes*—34, 36, 38 and 40 inches bust measure. **State size.** Shipping weight, 1 pound.
27K5405—Green Combination Plaid.
27K5406—Brown Plaid Combination. **$4.95**

Leatherette sport blouse inner facing of flannel. Corduroy collar; knitted all wool worsted hipband and cuffs. Rainproof and windproof. *Misses' and Small Women's Sizes*—34, 36, 38 and 40 inches bust measure. **State size.** Shipping weight, 1½ pounds.
27K5410—Olive Green.
27K5411—Leather Brown.
27K5412—Black. **$7.98**

Pullover knitted sport blouse of rich Navajo coloring and attractive pattern. Made of soft *All Wool Worsted Yarn* and lustrous *Rayon* (80 per cent worsted; 20 per cent Rayon). *Women's and Misses' Sizes*—34 to 44 inches bust measure. **State size.** Shpg. wt., ¾ lb.
27K5415—Tan, Blue and Red Combination.
27K5416—Powder Blue, Brown and Tan Combination. **$3.50**

Another smart pullover style knitted sport blouse. This one has a colorful striped pattern, and is made of softly brushed, delightfully warm, *All Wool Worsted Yarn*. *Misses' and Small Women's Sizes*—34, 36, 38 and 40 inches bust measure. **State size.** Shipping wt., ¾ lb.
27K5420—Heather Blue and Tan. **$2.98**

Women's fancy pattern pullover style, knitted sport blouse. Made of soft *All Wool Worsted Yarn* with Rayon design (75 per cent worsted; 25 per cent Rayon). *Women's and Misses' Sizes*—34 to 44 inches bust measure. **State size.** Shpg. wt., ¾ lb.
27K5425—Tan Combination.
27K5426—Black and White Combination. **$2.98**

Cricket neck, pullover style knitted sport blouse of smart pattern, *Half Wool Worsted Yarn*, balance cotton and lustrous *Rayon*. *Misses' and Junior Sizes*—12 to 20 years. Bust measure, 30, 32, 34, 36 and 38 inches. **State age size and bust measure.** Shpg. wt., ¾ lb.
27K5430—Tan, Black and Red Combination. **$1.95**

The attractive pattern of this cricket neck style knitted sport blouse, gives it a strikingly smart effect. Made of *Half Wool Worsted Yarn*, balance of cotton and *Rayon*. *Women's and Misses' Sizes*—34 to 44 inches bust measure. Shpg. wt., ¾ lb.
27K5435—Tan and Blue Combination. **$1.98**

Lumberjack blouse of *All Wool Plaid Flannel*. Knitted waistband of *All Wool Worsted*. *Misses' and Small Women's Sizes*—34, 36, 38 and 40 inches bust measure. **State size.** Shipping weight, 1 pound.
27K5440—Blue and Russet Plaid.
27K5441—Red and Tan Plaid. **$3.98**

Latest style raincoat adapted in a fashionable, alligator pattern, rubber surfaced fabric which is guaranteed absolutely waterproof. Model is cut on straight, loose lines; and has a swagger, buckle adjusted belt. All the seams are cemented; the armholes and shoulders reinforced. Length, 48 in. *Women's and Misses' Sizes*—34 to 44 inches bust measure. **State size.** Shpg. wt., 3½ lbs.
27K5645—Green.
27K5646—Red.
27K5647—Blue. **$5.98**
Attractive rain-hat in colors Green, Red or Blue. Will fit head sizes up to 23½ inches. **State head size and color.** Shpg. wt., 8 oz.
27K5650.................. **$1.98**

Tailored knickers in your choice of fine quality *All Wool Tweed* or sturdy *Hill's Khaki Jean Cloth*. *Women's and Misses' Regular Sizes*—24 to 34 inches waist measure. **State exact waist measure.** Shipping weight, 2 pounds.
27K5700—Gray Tweed........$2.98
27K5701—Tan Tweed........ 2.98
27K5702—Tan Khaki Jean.... 1.98
All Wool Tweed Knickers in Stout Women's Sizes—34 to 46 inches waist measure. **State waist measure.** Shipping weight, 2 pounds.
27K5703—Gray Tweed........$3.98
27K5704—Tan Tweed........ 3.98

Your Choice 98¢ each

27K5460 *Mercerized English Broadcloth*

27K5465 *Mercerized English Broadcloth*

Girls' Sizes

27K5455 **$3.79** *Heavy Weight Buckskin Suede Cloth Lumberjack Blouse*

Misses' Sizes

Stylish Blouses and Sports Apparel

You will enjoy this smart lumberjack sport blouse. Made of heavyweight warm *Buckskin Suede Cloth*. Knitted hipband and cuffs of all wool worsted yarn. *Misses' and Small Women's Sizes*—34, 36, 38 and 40 inches bust measure. **State size.** Shpg. wt., 1 lb. **$3.95**
27K5445—Tan.

Lumberjack style sport blouse of good quality *Plaid Cotton Flannel*. Made with large pockets and buttoned cuffs. Has snug fitting knitted waistband. Warm and practical. *Misses' and Small Women's Sizes*—34, 36, 38 and 40 inches bust measure. **State size.** Shipping weight, 1 lb.
27K5450—Russet, Blue and Green Combination Plaid. **$1.98**

Girls' lumberjack sport blouse made of heavyweight *Buckskin Suede Cloth*—a very sturdy, warm fabric. The collar, cuffs and snug fitting hipband are of knitted all wool worsted yarn. *Ages—7, 8, 10, 12 and 14 years.* **State age size.** Shipping weight, 1 lb.
27K5455—Tan. **$3.79**

Tailored blouse of washable *English Broadcloth*. Shows clusters of pin tucking. The "Peter Pan" collar is finished with a ribbon tie. *Women's and Misses' Regular Sizes*—34 to 44 inches bust measure. **State size.** Shipping weight, ¾ lb.
27K5460—White.
27K5461—Tan. **98c**

Smartly styled, well made, tailored blouse of washable *English Broadcloth*. It has a pin tucked front and pointed collar with ribbon tie. *Women's and Misses' Regular Sizes*—34 to 44 inches bust measure. **State size.** Shipping weight, ¾ lb.
27K5465—White.
27K5466—Tan. **98c**

Well tailored knickers of sturdy wearing *Velour Corduroy*. Made with two pockets, buttoned knee cuffs and a buckle adjusted belt. *Sizes*—24 to 34 inches waist measure. **State exact waist measure.** Shpg. wt., 2 lbs. **$2.98**
27K5705—Brown.
Swagger lumberjack blouse, of strong, velvety *Velour Corduroy*. Has knitted hipband and cuffs of all wool worsted yarn. *Misses' and Small Women's Sizes*—34, 36, 38 and 40 inches bust. **State size.** Shipping wt., 1 lb.
27K5470—Brown.
27K5471—Green. **$3.98**

Misses' Sizes

27K5450 *Cotton Flannel Lumberjack Blouse* **$1.98**

Misses' Sizes

27K5445 **$3.95** *Heavy Weight Buckskin Suede Cloth Lumberjack Blouse*

27K5470 *Velour Corduroy Lumberjack Blouse* **$3.98**

27K5705 *Velour Corduroy Knickers* **$2.98**

Imported English Broadcloth Blouses $1.98 each

27K5485 All Silk Pongee $2.98

A Bargain Offer
These smart blouses are of fine quality, washable *Imported English Broadcloth.*
The model on the right is trimmed with pin tucking and has fluted edgings on the collar and cuffs. Ribbon tie.
The one at the left is made in swagger double breasted design, with a tailored collar, pointed revers and pin tucked front.
Women's and Misses' Regular Sizes—34 to 44 inches bust measure. State size. Shpg. wt., ¾ lb.
27K5475—White.
27K5476—Tan.
27K5477 Powder Blue. $1.98
27K5480—White.
27K5481—Tan.
27K5482 Powder Blue. $1.98

27K5480

27K5475

Popular Fabric
Fine quality *All Silk Pongee* is the fabric that fashions this smart, tailored style blouse. It will appear fresh and pleasing after constant laundering. Pin tucking adorns the front on either side of the closing, and the pointed collar is finished with a ribbon tie.
Women's and Misses' Regular Sizes—34 to 44 inches bust measure. State size. Shipping weight, ¾ pound.
27K5485—Tan. $2.98

Sport Blouse
Shown on Figure at Right
Mannish tailored sport shirt of strong, well wearing, washable *English Broadcloth.* Made with buttoned cuffs, breast pocket and swagger fancy figured tie.
Women's and Misses' Regular Sizes—34 to 44 inches bust measure. State size. Shipping weight, ¾ pound.
27K5495 White. 98c

27K5495 Mercerized English Broadcloth 98c

Here you will find the better quality sports apparel priced to show you remarkable savings. This smart attire costs so little yet adds so much to your enjoyment of the out of doors.

27K5490 Part Wool Flannel Sport Shirt $1.79

27K5710 Fancy All Wool Tweed Skirt

Splendid Value
This good looking front pleated skirt of *Fancy All Wool Tweed* is appropriate for sport or general wear. Has attached belt of self material.
Women's and Misses' Sizes—26 to 34 inches waist. Lengths, 24 to 30 inches. State waist measure and length. Shpg. wt., 2 lbs.
27K5710 Tan Mixture. $3.98

Girls' sport shirt of *Half Wool Flannel.* Has buttoned cuffs and two large pockets.
Ages—7, 8, 10, 12 and 14 years. State age size. Shpg. wt., 8 oz.
27K5490 Olive Drab.
27K5491—Gray. $1.79
Trim looking knickers with two pockets, buttoned knee cuffs and a buckle adjusted belt.
Ages—7, 8, 10, 12 and 14 years. State age and exact waist measure. Shipping weight, 2 pounds.
27K5720 Gray All Wool Tweed. $2.79
27K5721 Tan All Wool Tweed. 2.79
27K5722 Tan Khaki Cloth. .98
27K5723 Gray Cotton Tweed. .98

Girls Sizes

27K5720 All Wool Tweed Knickers $2.79
27K5721 Khaki Cloth or Cotton Tweed 98c

27K5725 Good Quality Whipcord Riding Breeches $3.59

Expertly Tailored Riding Breeches
Swagger style, correctly fashioned riding breeches of sturdy *Cotton Whipcord.* Cut on comfortable, easy fitting lines and made with two pockets, lacing at the knee and an adjustable buckled belt. Will give extra long service.
Women's and Misses' Regular Sizes—24 to 34 inches waist measure. State exact waist measure. Shipping weight, 2 lbs.
27K5725—Brown. $3.50

27K5500 Khaki Jean Sport Shirt $1.39
27K5730 Khaki Cloth or Cotton Tweed Knickers 98c

27K5715 All Wool Crepe Knife Pleated Skirt

Graceful Model
Fine durable *All Wool Crepe* skirt, with gracefully knife pleated front, plain back and an attached belt of self material.
Women's and Misses' Sizes—26 to 34 inches waist measure. Lengths, 24 to 30 inches. State waist measure and length. Shipping weight, 2 pounds.
27K5715—Tan.
27K5716 Navy Blue. $3.98

Mannish style sport shirt of good quality *Khaki Jean Cloth.* Has pocket and buttoned cuffs.
Sizes—34 to 44 inches bust measure. State size. Shipping weight, ¾ pound.
27K5500 Khaki Tan. $1.39
Knickers in your choice of strong *Khaki Cloth* or good quality *Cotton Tweed;* adjustable belt and buttoned knee cuffs.
Sizes—24 to 34 inches waist measure. State exact waist measure. Shpg. wt., 2 lbs.
27K5730 Tan Khaki. 98c
27K5731 Gray Cotton Tweed. 98c

27K5505 *Lonsdale Jean Cloth.* $1.39

The Famous Admiral BRAND B.R. AND CO. Middy Blouses

27K5520 *Lonsdale Jean Cloth* 98c

↗ 27K5535 All Wool Flannel $2.98

Girls Sizes

Girls' and Misses' Sizes

↗ 27K5515 Half Wool Flannel $1.98

Excellent value in a smart, regulation style middy, made of strong, well wearing *Lonsdale Jean Cloth.* Has non-rip placket cuffs, braid trimming, deep sailor collar and swagger, long black tie.
Women's and Misses' Regular Sizes—34 to 44 inches bust measure. **State size.** Shipping weight, ¾ pound.
27K5505—White With Blue.
27K5506 All White.
$1.39

High grade *All Wool Flannel* middy. Trimmed with braid and pretty embroidery appliqued ornament.
Girls' Sizes—7, 8, 10, 12 and 14 years. **State age.** Shipping weight, ¾ pound.
27K5535—Scarlet.
27K5536—Navy Blue.
$2.98

Admiral Brand middy of serviceable *Flannel,* about one-half wool. Contrasting color braid and long black tie, deep sailor collar and non-rip placket cuffs.
Misses' and Girls' Sizes—7, 8, 10, 12, 14, 16, 18 and 20 years. **State age size and bust measure.** Shpg. wt., ¾ lb.
27K5515 Navy Blue. $1.98

An exceptionally low price for this good looking, well made middy of strong, sturdy quality *Lonsdale Jean Cloth;* deep sailor collar, swagger long black tie and non-rip placket cuffs. Popular for sport and general wear.
Women's and Misses' Regular Sizes—34 to 44 inches bust measure. **State size.** Shipping weight, ¾ pound.
27K5520—White With Blue.
27K5521—All White. 98c

27K5540 *Mercerized English Broadcloth* 98c

27K5530 *Lonsdale Jean Cloth* $1.29

Girls' and Misses' Sizes

27K5510 $1.29 *Regulation Lonsdale Drill "Gym" Middy*

Girls Sizes

27K5525 *Lonsdale Jean Cloth* 98c

Girls Sizes

Girls' tailored blouse of washable *English Broadcloth.* Neatly pin tucked front and a snug fitting, buttoned waistband. Contrasting color tie, drawn through a buckle ornament.
Girls' Sizes—7, 8, 10, 12, 14 and 16 years. **State age size.** Shipping weight, ¾ pound.
27K5540—White.
27K5541—Tan. 98c

Girls' braid trimmed middy of fine quality *Lonsdale Jean Cloth.* Non-rip placket cuffs; black tie.
Girls' Sizes—7, 8, 10, 12 and 14 years. **State age size.** Shipping weight, ¾ pound.
27K5530—White With Blue.
27K5531—All White. $1.29

Regulation style gym middy, made according to strict specifications, of strong, sturdy wearing, fine quality *Lonsdale Drill Cloth.* Deep sailor collar, breast pocket and lace tie. Service is assured by double stitched seams.
Misses' and Girls' Sizes—7, 8, 10, 12, 14, 16, 18 and 20 years. **State age size and bust measure.** Shipping weight, ¾ lb.
27K5510—White. $1.29

Girls' middy of serviceable *Lonsdale Jean Cloth* or *Hills Khaki Jean Cloth.* Deep sailor collar, tie and non-rip placket cuffs.
Girls' Sizes—7, 8, 10, 12 and 14 yrs. **State age size.** Shpg. wt., ¾ lb.
27K5525—White With Blue.
27K5526—All White.
27K5527—Khaki Tan. 98c

27K5740 *All Wool Plaid* $2.98

27K5735 *All Wool Serge* $2.98

Admiral BRAND Middy Skirts for Wear With Girls' Blouses Above

Two smartly fashioned skirts for the schoolgirl, both made with detachable cambric bodice that fastens with buttons beneath the belt.
One model is in knife pleated style, in your choice of fine quality *All Wool Serge* or *All Wool Crepe.* The other is box pleated of fine *All Wool Plaid Homespun.*
Girls' Sizes—7, 8, 10, 12 and 14 years. **State age size.** Shipping weight, 1½ lbs.
27K5735—Navy Blue Serge. $2.98
27K5736—Navy Blue Crepe. 2.98
27K5740—Tan and Blue Plaid Homespun, 2.98

Smart Two-Piece Outfit

This is a new and very swagger two-piece outfit for the young girl— practical for school, sport and general all around service.
Adapted in warm, sturdy wearing, good quality *All Wool Homespun,* it consists of a pleated skirt with an attached bodice top, and a separate lumberjack style sport blouse that has a stripe pattern knitted collar, cuffs and snug fitting waistband of *All Wool Worsted Yarn.* An exceptional value at $4.98.
Girls' Sizes—7, 8, 10, 12 and 14 years. **State age size.** Shipping weight, 2 lbs.
27K5745—Tan.
27K5746—Blue. $4.98

27K5745 *All Wool Homespun Two-Piece Outfit* $4.98

Girls Sizes

PLAY TIME TRADE MARK REGISTERED

Low Priced Frocks for Girls

Ages 7-8-10-12-14 Years

A Special Offer

Thrifty mothers will appreciate this exceptional bargain. We offer, here, two pretty apron frocks for the schoolgirl at the remarkably low price of $1.00.

One is made of *Blue Checked Gingham* and trimmed with plain *Chambray*; the other of *Rose Color Linene* with checked gingham piping. The materials are fast color and serviceable.

Ages—7, 8, 10, 12 and 14 years. **State age size.** See size scale. Shipping weight, 3 pounds.

31K4820 Two Frocks. **$1.00**

31K4820 Two Apron Frocks for One Price $1.00 for Two

31K4800 Fancy Homespun **$3.98**

Pleasing Model

Trim looking, tailored frock—practical for school and play—adapted in sturdy *Wool and Silk Mixed Homespun* with plaid pattern. It has neat ornament of solid color *All Wool Flannel* bandings, and the front of the bodice shows pretty wool embroidery.

Ages—8, 10, 12 and 14 years. **State age size.** See size scale. Shipping weight, 1½ pounds.

31K4800—Rust Fancy.
31K4801 Green Fancy. **$3.98**

31K4805 All Silk Crepe de Chine or All Silk Changeable Taffeta $4.98

31K4810 Novelty Rayon Crepe $1.98

31K4815 Part Wool Poiret Twill $3.59

Lovely Party Frock

Fashioned of rich looking *All Silk Crepe de Chine or All Silk Changeable Taffeta*, smartly enhanced with shirring and picot edged gathered ruffles. Has flower ornament with two-tone silk satin ribbon streamers.

Ages—8, 10, 12 and 14 years. **State age size.** See size scale. Shipping weight, 1½ pounds.

Crepe de Chine
31K4805—Queen Blue.
31K4806—Navy Blue.
Taffeta
31K4807—Rose.
31K4808—Navy Blue. **$4.98**

Very Low Priced

It is unusual to find a frock so attractive and well made, costing only $1.98. The material is washable *Rayon and Cotton Crepe* of durable quality. Frock is prettily trimmed with contrasting color plain *Rayon Cloth* and novelty buttons.

An ideal dress for school wear, being washable, durable and very good looking.

Ages—7, 8, 10, 12 and 14 years. **State age size.** See size scale. Shipping weight, 1½ lbs.

31K4810—Blue Fancy.
31K4811—Peach Fancy. **$1.98**

Tailored Model

Smart, practical and inexpensive. Fashioned in neat, tailored style of serviceable, good looking *Part Wool Poiret-Twill*. It shows effective trimming of self color, woven check cotton *Poiret-Twill* and pretty composition buttons.

Ages—8, 10, 12 and 14 years. **State age size.** See size scale. Shpg. wt., 1½ lbs.

31K4815—Green. (Medium.)

31K4816—Rust. **$3.59**

Descriptions of Dresses Shown on Opposite Page

The bodice of this smart frock is of fine quality *All Wool Rep-Sheen*, while the skirt and blouse trimmings are of fashionable contrasting *All Wool Flasha Cloth*. Frock also shows adornment of novelty buttons and buckle ornament. Has neat workmanship and will wear well.

Ages—8, 10, 12 and 14 years. **State age size.** See size scale. Shipping weight, 1½ lbs.
31K4825—Red and Tan.
31K4826—Light Blue and Navy. **$4.98**

Good looking, inexpensive, school frock, of *Novelty Woven Cotton Suiting*. This is a well made, practical garment, neatly trimmed with contrasting, two-tone *Cotton Duvetyn*, pretty composition buttons and a novelty embroidered applique ornament.

Ages—7, 8, 10, 12 and 14 years. **State age size.** See size scale. Shipping weight, 1½ lbs.
31K4830—Green Fancy.
31K4831—Raisin Fancy. **$2.48**

This frock is practical, smart, neat in workmanship and unusually low in price. Made of pre-sponged and pre-shrunk, good quality *All Wool Double Warp Serge*, it is effectively trimmed with *Red Cotton Duvetyn*, wool hand embroidery and a handsome buckle.

Ages—7, 8, 10, 12 and 14 years. **State age size.** See size scale. Shipping weight, 1½ pounds.
31K4835—Navy Blue. **$3.79**

Long wearing, *Wool and Silk Velour Homespun* fashions this good looking frock. Collar and cuffs are of all wool Flannel and it has a tub silk tie. Frock is also enhanced with contrasting flannel piping and a pretty appliqued ornament.

Ages—7, 8, 10, 12 and 14 years. **State age size.** See size scale. Shipping weight, 1½ lbs.
31K4840—Tan Fancy.
31K4841—Blue Fancy. **$3.98**

Latest sport style frock designed in clever two-piece effect; the blouse of attractive ombre stripe; the skirt and blouse trimmings of plain cotton *Balbriggan Jersey*. It is a smart, serviceable garment, and a real bargain.

Ages—7, 8, 10, 12 and 14 years. **State age size.** See size scale. Shipping weight, 1½ lbs.
31K4845—Green.
31K4846—Light Brown. **$1.98**

Attractively styled, well made frock, developed in fine quality *All Wool Flannel*. Trimmed with bandings of harmonizing *Silk Crepe*, composition buttons and pretty wool hand embroidery. Will please with its becoming design and attractive material.

Ages—7, 8, 10, 12 and 14 years. **State age size.** See size scale. Shipping weight, 1½ lbs.
31K4850—Rose Beige.
31K4851—French Blue. **$4.98**

Two harmonizing shades of heavy quality *All Silk Flat Crepe* were smartly employed in the styling of this beautiful frock. Pleasing fashion themes and dainty hemstitching are featured in its design, and the skirt is gracefully pleated at the front. Our finest dress for girls.

Ages—8, 10, 12 and 14 years. **State age size.** See size scale. Shipping weight, 1½ lbs.
31K4855—Brown and Tan.
31K4856—Queen Blue. **$7.98**

Adapted on swagger lines of good quality *All Wool and Rayon Cheviot Cloth*, a strong, warm, dressy fabric; this frock is both smart and practical. It shows neat workmanship and has trimming of *Figured Silk Warp Crepe* and composition buttons.

Ages—7, 8, 10, 12 and 14 years. **State age size.** See size scale. Shipping weight, 1½ lbs.
31K4865—Red.
31K4866—Medium Blue. **$4.98**

This frock is exceptionally smart, and its material, *Printed Cordette Velveteen*, is not only very pretty, but warm and serviceable as well. Harmonizing color one-half wool *Poiret-Sheen* and ornamental buttons provide trimming.

Ages—7, 8, 10, 12 and 14 years. **State age size.** See size scale. Shipping weight, 1½ lbs.
31K4870—Green Fancy.
31K4871—Blue Fancy. **$3.98**

Here is a charming frock featuring the pretty combination of fine quality figured and plain *Washable All Silk Radium*. The softly bloused bodice is very stylish and new, while the skirt is made pleasing with box pleating at the front. Belt is trimmed with an ornamental buckle.

Ages—8, 10, 12 and 14 years. **State age size.** See size scale. Shipping weight, 1½ pounds.
31K4875—Queen Blue. **$4.98**

SIZE SCALE

Dresses for ages, years...	7	8	10	12	14
Fit chest measure, inches	26	27	29	31	33
Come in lengths, inches	27	28	32	36	40

See page 548 for Measuring Instructions.

Smart New Frocks for Girls

Ages 7 - 8 - 10 - 12 - 14 Years

PLAY TIME TRADE MARK REGISTERED

31K4825
All Wool
Rep-Sheen
With
All Wool
Flasha
$4⁹⁸

31K4830
Fancy
Novelty
Suiting
$2⁴⁸

31K4835
All Wool
Double
Warp
Serge
$3⁷⁹

31K4840
Wool
Novelty
Homespun
$3⁹⁸

31K4845
Fancy
Balbriggan
Sports
Frock
$1⁹⁸

31K4855
All Silk
Flat
Crepe
$7⁹⁸

31K4865
Wool and
Rayon
Cheviot
$4⁹⁸

31K4870
Checked
Cordette
Velveteen
$3⁹⁸

31K4850
All Wool
Flannel
$4⁹⁸

31K4875
All Silk
Washable
Radium
$4⁹⁸

These Dresses Are Described on Opposite Page

Order Blanks Are in Back of This Catalog

For Practical Service

The young girl will find this two-piece bloomer frock a comfortable, practical garment for school or play. Fashioned in a youthful, becoming style, of good quality, well wearing *Cotton Balbriggan Jersey*, it features pretty trimming of *Ombre* striped jersey, and novelty buttons. Comes with matching balbriggan jersey bloomers.

Ages—7, 8 and 9 years. **State age size.** See size scale. Shpg. wt., 1½ lbs.
31K4960—Queen Blue.
31K4961—Rose.
$1.98

PLAY TIME
TRADE MARK REGISTERED

Bloomer Dresses
for Younger Girls
Ages 7-8-9 Years
To Fill a Long Felt Need

we have added this selection of younger girls' bloomer dresses to our catalog. Appropriately designed for the little girl who is not quite ready for the styles that "big sister" can wear. Mothers have long felt the need of just this particular class of dresses, for girls at this age.

A Genuine Bargain

It is most attractive, and we guarantee that it will launder and wear to your entire satisfaction; yet the price of this two-piece bloomer frock is only 98c. Made of good quality, fast color, washable *Fancy Cotton Print*, it gains added charm by solid color *Cambric* trimmings and touches of hand embroidery stitching. Comes with matching bloomers.

Ages—7, 8 and 9 years. **State age size.** See size scale. Shipping weight, 1½ pounds.
31K4970—Blue Fancy.
31K4971 Rose Fancy. **98c**

31K4970 Washable Fancy Print 98c

31K4960 Novelty Trim Balbriggan Jersey $1.98

31K4965 Good Quality Twill Back Velveteen $4.79

31K4975 All Wool Canton Crepe $5.98

31K4980 Novelty Fancy Suiting $2.59

31K4985 All Wool French Spun Jersey $4.98

31K4990 Woven Novelty Rayon Crepe $1.98

Smart and Dressy

Here is a charming frock of the dressy type, for the young girls of 7 to 9 years, adapted in rich looking good quality *Twill Back Velveteen*. It portrays a design of youthful chic and is attractively trimmed with ecru lace edged, contrasting color *Silk Broadcloth*. Comes with matching color lustrous sateen bloomers.

Ages—7, 8 and 9 years. **State age size.** See size scale. Shipping wt., 1½ lbs.
31K4965—Black. **$4.79**

Ages, years	7	8	9
Fit chest measures, in.	26	27	29
Come in lengths, in.	26	28	30

Fine Quality

Fashioned of lightweight soft pliable *All Wool Canton Crepe*, this charming youthful frock will appeal to mothers who demand our best dress. The latest style, featuring collar, panel and cuffs of contrasting tone fine quality self material. The front displays smart scalloped edge folds, trimmed with fancy *Rayon* braid and novelty buttons. Comes with lustrous sateen bloomers.

Ages—7, 8 and 9 years. **State age size.** See size scale. Shipping weight, 1½ pounds.
31K4975—Palmetto Green.
31K4976 Rust. **$5.98**

Very Good Value

Practical, two-piece bloomer dress of strong, serviceable *Novelty Fancy Cotton Suiting* for young girls. It will delight with its fetching style and mothers will appreciate it for being a well made, low priced durable garment. Has trimming of *Mercerised Broadcloth*, pretty buttons and wool hand embroidery. Comes with separate matching bloomers.

Ages—7, 8 and 9 years. **State age size.** See size scale. Shipping weight, 1½ lbs.
31K4980—Green (Medium).
31K4981—Blue (Medium). **$2.59**

Exceptionally Attractive

Two harmonizing shades of fine quality *All Wool French Spun Jersey*, were prettily combined in the design of this frock for girls of 7 to 9 years. The style is youthful and attractive; the material warm and durable. Wool hand embroidery and pearl buckles provide smart trimmings. Frock comes with separate bloomers of lustrous sateen.

Ages—7, 8 and 9 years. **State age size.** See size scale. Shipping weight, 1½ lbs.
31K4985—Tan and Light Brown.
31K4986 French Blue. **$4.98**

Pleasing Model

This two-piece bloomer frock will please with its youthful appearance and practical qualities. Made of good looking, *Woven Novelty Stripe Rayon Crepe*, a strong, fast color washable fabric. Collar, cuffs and pocket are of solid color mercerized pongette. Frock is trimmed with pretty, *Rayon* hand embroidery and crochet buttons. Comes with matching, separate bloomers.

Ages—7, 8 and 9 years. **State age size.** See size scale. Shipping weight, 1½ pounds.
31K4990—Blue.
31K4991 Lavender. **$1.98**

Homestead Daytime Frocks
The Best Known House Dresses in America
FAMOUS FOR QUALITY AND VALUE

This Garment Also Comes in the famous Snow White Indian Head Cloth

For Women's Aprons See Page 141

Reversible Front Apron

31K5005 Knitted Balbriggan Jersey $1.98

31K5010 Fancy Check Novelty Suiting $3.48

31K5015 Muslin or Chambray 89c Mercerized Broadcloth $1.39 Indian Head Cloth $1.59

31K5020 Mercerized Washable Broadcloth $1.98

31K5025 Cotton Serge $1.98

31K5000 Genuine SIMPSONS Mercerized Pongee $1.98

31K5030 Fancy Figured Rayon $2.98

Most Practical
You will get splendid wear and service from this trim looking frock of good quality Cotton Balbriggan Jersey. The fabric is very durable, and the style of the garment makes it appropriate for the house, street or general everyday wear. It has a buckle adjusted belt and is trimmed with novelty buttons. Women's and Misses' Regular Sizes—34 to 46 inches bust measure. State size. Shipping weight, 1½ pounds.
31K5005—Blue. 31K5006—Tan. $1.98

Decidedly Smart, Yet Inexpensive
This frock is fashioned in an attractive new style of good quality, serviceable Fancy Check Cotton Suiting. In design and pleasing features it is a worthy rival of frocks that are far more expensive. It features effective adornment of solid color flannel. We recommend this dress to be a very satisfactory garment for practical utility. Women's and Misses' Regular Sizes—34 to 46 inches bust measure. State size. Shipping weight, 1½ pounds.
31K5010—Red Check. 31K5011—Blue Check. $3.48

Prettily Hand Embroidered
It is good looking, very inexpensive and decidedly well wearing—a combination that makes this frock desirable for everyday service. Fast color, mercerized Checked Broadcloth of a dependable quality was chosen as its fabric; fashioned into a becoming style and attractively trimmed with colorful hand embroidery. The neck is finished with a ribbon tie. Women's and Misses' Regular Sizes—34 to 46 inches bust measure. State size. Shpg. wt., 1½ lbs.
31K5020—Blue and White. 31K5021—Green and White. $1.98

Double Service Apron
Made with a wide overlapping front, which may be reversed when one side becomes soiled. Can be purchased in serviceable, washable, fast color Muslin, Chambray or Mercerized Broadcloth; also the famous long wearing linen-like snow white Indian Head cloth. Women's and Misses' Regular Sizes—34 to 46 inches bust measure. State size. Shpg. wt., 1½ lbs.
31K5015—White Muslin. 31K5016—Blue Chambray. 31K5017—Pink Chambray. 89c
31K5018—White Broadcloth. $1.39
31K5019—White Indian Head Cloth. $1.59

Attractive Model
Two-piece effect frock of pleasing appearance and practical qualities; adapted in well wearing, lustrous sheen, Fancy Figured Rayon. Has attractive adornment of solid color Rayon cloth. The skirt is smartly pleated at the front and the garment is finished with a buckle adjusted belt. Women's and Misses' Regular Sizes—34 to 46 inches bust measure. State size. Shipping weight, 1½ pounds.
31K5030—Tan and Green. 31K5031—Copenhagen Blue and Tan. $2.98

Pleasing in Style and Fabric
Fashioned in a trim tailored style of serviceable quality Novelty Figured Cotton Serge, this frock is attractive, well made, very practical and an exceptional bargain at $1.98. Cut on becoming, straight lines, it has modish kick pleats on the skirt and is made with two convenient pockets and a jaunty tie. The frock is neatly trimmed with contrasting color broadcloth and small buttons. Women's and Misses' Regular Sizes—34 to 46 inches bust measure. State size. Shipping weight, 1½ pounds.
31K5025—Navy with Tan. $1.98

Will Wear and Wash Well
In addition to its pretty style, this frock is one of those practical garments that looks as fresh and pleasing after constant tubbing as when new, due to its fast color durable fabric, Genuine Simpson's Mercerized Cotton Pongee. It has contrasting pongee collar and cuffs with a silk ribbon tie to match. The front shows cluster tucking and dainty drawnwork effect trimming. Women's and Misses' Regular Sizes—34 to 46 inches bust measure. State size. Shipping weight, 1½ pounds.
31K5000—Tan. $1.98

Send Sufficient Money for Postage on Parcel Post Shipments. Any Surplus Will Be Returned

81

A Page of Comfort and Beauty
Robes ! Negligees !

31K5105
Beacon
Blanket
Cloth
$6.98

31K5110
Warm
Wool Faced
Eiderdown
$6.98

31K5115
Fancy
Blanket
Cloth
$3.98

31K5120
All Silk
Crepe
de Chine
$6.98

31K5125
Genuine
Box Loom
Crepe
$2.98

31K5130
Beacon
Blanket
Cloth
$7.98

31K5135
Velour
Corduroy
$4.98

31K5140
Beacon
Blanket
Cloth
$4.98

31K5145
Beacon
Blanket
Cloth
$5.95

These Robes
Are Described
on Opposite
Page

Homestead REG. U.S. PAT. OFF.

Robes and Negligees Make IDEAL Gifts

Practical Useful! Comfortable

Attractive Robe for Girls

For so modest a price as $2.98 your daughter will have the pleasure and comfort of owning this handsome, delightfully warm robe of soft, fleecy *Imported Striped Cotton Blanket Cloth*. The garment shows lustrous *Satin Ribbon* trimming and has a tassel finished *Rayon* cord girdle. It makes an ideal gift.
Ages—8, 10, 12 and 14 years only. **State age size. Shpg. wt., 2 lbs.**
31K5150—Blue and Tan.
31K5151—Red and Tan. $2.98

Girls Sizes

Trimmed With Quilted Satin

Made of superior quality, soft, fleecy *Beacon Cotton Blanket Cloth*; this attractive robe is luxuriously warm, very durable and practical in every way. It has lustrous, quilted, blue *Satin* trimming, fancy braid piping and a heavy cord girdle.
Women's Regular Sizes—36 to 46 inches bust measure. **State size. Ship. wt., 3 lbs.**
31K5105—Blue Combination. **$6.98**

Luxuriously Warm and Pleasing

This is a high grade, handsome robe, made of soft, fine quality *Eiderdown*, which is about three-fourths wool. Has richly lustrous, two-tone *Satin Ribbon* trimming and a heavy cord girdle.
Women's Regular Sizes—36 to 46 inches bust measure. **State size. Shipping weight, 2½ lbs.**
31K5110—Tan.
31K5111—Lavender.
31K5112—Copenhagen Blue. **$6.98**

Appealing in Every Way

Delightful warmth, splendid service and an appealing low price recommend this robe. Made of soft, fleecy, attractive figured *Cotton Blanket Cloth*, it shows lustrous *Satin Ribbon* adornment and a *Rayon* cord side tie.
Women's Regular Sizes—36 to 46 inches bust measure. **State size. Shipping weight, 3 lbs.**
31K5115—Blue and Tan.
31K5116—Blue and Red. **$3.98**

Lovely Lace Trimmed Model

This charming negligee will lend added pleasure to your leisure hours. Made of fine quality *All Silk Crepe de Chine*, it has exquisite trimmings of gathered *Valenciennes Lace* and *Ribbon Buds*.
Women's Regular Sizes—34 to 46 inches bust measure. **State size. Shipping weight, 1½ lbs.**
31K5120—Rose.
31K5121—Copenhagen Blue.
31K5122—Peach. **$6.98**

Attractively Hand Embroidered

Highly lustrous, two tone *Satin Ribbon* ruffles and beautiful hand embroidery effectively trim this lovely kimono. It is fashioned of *Box Loom Cotton Crepe*, which will wash well and give excellent service.
Women's Regular Sizes—34 to 46 inches bust measure. **Shipping wt., 1½ lbs.**
31K5125—Copenhagen Blue.
31K5126—Rose. **$2.98**

Our Finest Bathrobe

If you are looking for a high grade bathrobe, for your own use or as a gift, choose this luxuriously warm, handsome model of extra fine, ombre tone *Beacon Cotton Blanket Cloth*. Has attractive block checked *Beacon Cloth* trimming; fancy *Rayon* cord edging and a matching cord girdle.
Women's Regular Sizes—36 to 46 inches bust measure. **State size. Shpg. wt., 3 lbs.**
31K5130—Tan. **$7.98**

Charming Lounge Robe

It is fashioned of rich looking, velvety *Velour Corduroy*—a soft, delightfully warm fabric. This robe is gracefully styled and attractively trimmed with *Brocaded Corduroy*.
Women's Regular Sizes—34 to 46 inches bust measure. **State size. Shipping wt., 3 lbs.**
31K5135—Firefly.
31K5136—Copenhagen Blue. **$4.98**

Of Rich Plaid Design

The delightful warmth and practical qualities of this robe will give constant pleasure to its wearer. Made of plaid pattern, fine quality, soft, fleecy *Beacon Cotton Blanket Cloth*, and trimmed with lustrous *Satin Ribbon*. Has heavy cord girdle.
Women's Regular Sizes—36 to 46 inches bust measure. **State size. Shipping wt., 3 lbs.**
31K5140—Blue.
31K5141—Orchid. **$4.98**

Makes an Ideal Gift

For your own use or as a gift, this handsome, luxuriously warm robe of fine quality, soft, fleecy *Beacon Cotton Blanket Cloth* is an excellent selection. Trimmed with rich looking *Satin Ribbon* and a *Rayon* cord girdle.
Women's Regular Sizes—36 to 46 inches bust measure. **State size. Shipping wt., 3 lbs.**
31K5145—Red and Gray.
31K5146—Copenhagen Blue and Tan. **$5.95**

Gracefully Styled

Made of the justly famous, fast color washable, genuine *Serpentine Cotton Crepe*; this charming kimono is assured of being a thoroughly satisfactory garment—one that will wear and wash well. The model is gracefully styled and elaborately trimmed with gathered ruffles of self material. It fastens with a side sash and has a pretty silk bud ornament on the collar. An exceptional value at $1.98.
Women's and Misses' Regular Sizes—34 to 46 inches bust measure. **State size. Shpg. wt., 1½ lbs.**
31K5165—Rose.
31K5166—Copenhagen Blue. **$1.98**

31K5150 Imported Blanket Cloth $2.98

31K5165 Serpentine Crepe $1.98

31K5160 Velour Corduroy $2.98

Handsome Desirable Model

We recommend this charming low priced lounge robe. It is made of rich, velvety *Velour Corduroy*—delightfully warm and handsome. The garment is gracefully fashioned on loose, comfortable lines, with wide kimono sleeves and a tuxedo rever collar. Has pretty silk bud ornament at neck.
Women's and Misses' Regular Sizes—34 to 46 inches bust measure. **State size. Shpg. wt., 3 lbs.**
31K5160—Rose.
31K5161—Copenhagen Blue. **$2.98**

Delightfully Warm Robe

This robe is made of soft, fleecy, *Figured Cotton Blanket Cloth*, which is delightfully warm. Trimmed with *Rayon* cord edging and has a tassel trimmed cord girdle.
Women's and Misses' Sizes—36 to 46 inches bust measure. **State size. Shpg. wt., 3 lbs.**
31K5155—Red and Blue.
31K5156—Tan and Blue. **$2.98**

Beautiful Quilted Robe

This luxuriously warm quilted robe is made of fine quality lustrous, changeable *All Silk Satin* and is lined throughout with *Figured Seco Crepe*. Has a deep tuxedo collar and fastens at one side with tassel trimmed *Rayon* cords.
Women's and Misses' Sizes—34 to 46 inches bust measure. **State size. Shpg. wt., 3 lbs.**
31K5170—Orchid.
31K5171—Copenhagen Blue. **$9.98**

31K5155 Fancy Blanket Cloth $2.98

31K5170 Quilted All Silk Changeable Satin $9.98

Homestead Apron Frocks
Mean Efficiency for Women Who Work
THEY ARE PRACTICAL — DURABLE — ECONOMICAL

31K5240
Sateen
Regular Sizes
98c
Stout Sizes
$1.19

31K5230
Linene or Chambray
$1.00
Mercerized
Broadcloth
$1.48

Reversible Front Apron

31K5255
Gingham
69c

31K5250
Genuine Amoskeag
Gingham
98c

31K5225
Fancy
Figured
Prints
$1.48

31K5245
Percale
Regular Sizes
89c
Stout Sizes
98c

Artist Style Cover-All Smocks for Home or Office Workers

31K5235
Figured
Mercerized
Pongee
$1.98

Genuine Bargain

Here is a neat, well made, practical apron frock, made of good grade, fast color *Check Gingham*; offered at the amazingly low price of 69c. Cut on loose, comfortable lines, it has a collarless square neck; short kimono sleeves and two convenient pockets. Trimmed with *White Piping*. Women's and Misses' Regular Sizes—34 to 46 inches bust measure. State size. Shipping weight, 1½ pounds.
31K5255—Green. 69c
31K5256—Blue.

Pleasing, Practical Apron

Made of strong, serviceable, lustrous *Black Sateen*; this type of apron dress is always favored by women, due to its trim, neat appearance and the fact that it does not soil easily. This garment comes in regular and stout sizes being practical and comfortable for all types of figure. It is cut with generous fullness and prettily trimmed contrasting color *Linene* and *Cretonne*. Women's and Misses' Regular Sizes—34 to 46 inches bust measure. Women's Stout Sizes—48 to 54 inches bust measure. State Size. Shpg. wt., 1½ lbs.

Regular Sizes	Stout Sizes
31K5240 98c Black.	31K5241 $1.19 Black.

Exceptionally Low Priced

Standard grade, fast color, *Fancy Check Amoskeag Gingham* is the strong, serviceable fabric that fashions this good looking, inexpensive apron frock, assuring the garment of being practical and well wearing.

Becomingly styled on comfortable lines; the dress is neatly made and shows pleasing trimming of *White Pique* and pearl buttons. Women's and Misses' Regular Sizes—34 to 46 inches bust measure. State size. Shipping weight, 1½ pounds.
31K5250—Blue.
31K5251—Lavender.
98c

Popular Style Apron Dress

This pretty reversible apron dress is a very useful and sensible garment for general housework. It is fashioned of strong, fast color *Figured Cotton Print*, which will wash well and give splendid service.

The dress is cut on full, comfortable lines and made with wide overlapping front, which may be reversed when one side becomes soiled. The collar, cuffs and pocket trimmings are of solid color *Linene*. A very good value at our low price.

Women's and Misses' Regular Sizes—34 to 46 inches bust measure. State size. Shipping weight, 1½ pounds.
31K5225—Blue.
31K5226—Tan.
$1.48

Pretty Smock

It only costs $1.98 and this small investment will be more than repaid by its practical service and comfort. Made of fast color, *Figured Cotton Pongee* with trimming of solid color *Pongee*. An ideal garment for saving your clothes; used for office work, gardening and as a coverall apron. Women's and Misses' Sizes—34 to 46 in. bust measure. State size. Shpg. wt. 1½ lbs.
31K5235—Green Figured.
31K5236—Rose Figured. **$1.98**

Will Save Your Clothes

The smock has become very popular, due to its practical qualities. It serves as a coverall apron, protecting your clothes from wear and tear, and it is an exceedingly comfortable garment; one that is as easy to put on and take off as a coat. This style may be purchased in fast color *Linene or Chambray* or in fast color *Mercerized Broadcloth* with dotted trimming. Women's and Misses' Regular Sizes—34 to 46 inches bust measure. State size. Shpg. wt., 1½ lbs.
31K5230—Blue Chambray. **$1.00**
31K5231—Blue Broadcloth. **1.48**
31K5232—Blue Linene. **1.00**

Stout and Regular Sizes

Practical, well made apron frock, cut on comfortable lines and neatly fashioned of standard grade *Figured Percale*. Comes in regular and stout sizes at a truly low price. Has two large convenient pockets and is trimmed with pretty *Rickrack Braid*. Women's and Misses' Regular Sizes—34 to 46 inches bust measure. Women's Stout Sizes—48 to 54 inches bust measure. Shpg. wt., 1½ lbs.

Regular Sizes	Stout Sizes
31K5245—Navy Blue Figured.	31K5247—Navy Blue Figured.
31K5246 89c Gray Figured.	31K5248 98c Gray Figured.

Class-mate Hats
TRADE MARK REG.

Perfect Fit Guaranteed
Please Use a Tape Measure

$1.95 — **78K6501** Fits 20½ to 21¼ inches head size. For 10 to 12 years.
Colors: Almond (medium) green, pirate (bright) red, Copenhagen blue or French beige (sand). Measure and state color. Shipping weight, 1¼ pounds.
Delightful felt has charming dress up qualities. In latest ripple brim style. Made of good quality full body felt. Handsome plush applique surrounded with scroll design ribbonzine in attractive color to harmonize. Ribbon has fancy border. Striking value.

78K6504 — Fits 20¼ to 20½ inches head size. For 8 to 10 years. **$1.95**
Colors: Pirate (bright) red, Copenhagen blue, French beige (sand), or rose color. Measure and state color. Shipping weight, 1⅝ lbs.
Unusually 'different' and very smart. Made of good quality full body felt. Odd brim is slashed and makes an attractive visor effect. Novel felt gardenia to match. Narrow ribbon crown band. Snug fitting back.

$1.39 — **78K6508** — Fits 20 to 20¾ inches head size. For 6 to 8 years.
Colors: Almond (medium) green with beaver color plush, sand color with dark Copenhagen blue with sand color. Measure and state color. Shipping weight, 1¼ pounds.
Darling little bonnet has a smart, semi-tam crown. Made of good looking suedelike cloth. Crown tip and brim set off with Rayon (fur-like) plush. Trimmed with cunning little ribbon rosettes and streamers.

Two Sizes: **78K6512** — Fits 6 to 8 years. **78K6513** — Fits 9 to 13 years. **95¢**
Colors: Bright red, bright green or navy blue. State color. Shipping weight, 4 ounces.
Greatest tam of the year! And it's a direct importation. Think of it a genuine French Beret at this remarkably low price. Made of all wool material with a thick suedelike nap. Bias headband fits snugly.

78K6520 — Fits 20 to 20½ inches head size. For 7 to 9 years. **$1.65**
Colors: Oakwood brown with sand color ribbon; Copenhagen blue with sand color bright red with sand color with gooseberry (light) green. Measure and state color. Shipping weight, 1½ pounds.
Smartly tailored felt model. Close fitting shape with novel, inverted tucked crown. New trimming idea of pleated ribbon held under scalloped slashes in crown. Ribbon crown band tied into cunning bow at side. Dainty trimming pin.

78K6524 — Fits 19 to 19¾ inches head size. For 3 to 6 years. **$1.89**
Colors: Copenhagen blue with sand color; bright red with sand color; rose color with sand; or almond (medium) green. Measure and state color. Shipping weight, 1½ pounds.
Gives a smartly dressed up appearance. Shape of good quality full body felt. Brim is cut to point at either side. A flattering line set off with ribbon pleatings. Novel self trimming effects bound with ribbon and joined with perky little bow in front. Dainty ornaments and stitching. Big value.

"Every Girl's Favorite ~ Every Mother's Choice"

$1.65 — **78K6528** — Fits 20½ to 21¼ inches head size. For 10 to 13 years.
Colors: Wild honey (light brown), pirate (bright) red, Copenhagen blue or almond (medium) green. Measure and state color. Shipping weight, 1¾ lbs.
Right smart, and a remarkable value. Flexible, oval brim shape. Made of good quality bengaline. Six-section crown, set off with high grade velveteen. Velveteen brim set off neatly with tucks. Cut away, snug fitting back. Double quills add smart touch.

78K6532 — Fits 20 to 20¾ inches head size. For 7 to 10 years. **$1.65**
Colors: Monkey skin (sand) with Copenhagen blue; almond (medium) green with sand color; black with rose color, or bright red with navy blue. Measure and state color. Shipping weight, 1¾ pounds.
Just like older sister's—and isn't it adorable! Brimless, close fitting felts are quite the smartest. Ribbon bound edge carries clever curve at either side. Evenly pleated ribbon is attractive insert across top. Four brilliant jewels set into felt. High grade design and lovely quality.

78K6536 — Fits 20½ to 21 inches head size. For 8 to 12 years. **$1.89**
Colors: Dark brown with sand color; solid rose color, or solid Copenhagen blue. Measure and state color. Shipping weight, 1½ pounds.
Lovely dressup style and a special "Class-Mate" value. Pretty shirrings of Rayon taffeta set off soft crown between tip and contrasting fold of velveteen. Narrow roll velveteen brim carries attractive border of pleated ribbon. Delicate hand made applique cluster adds cheerful touch.

$1.19 — **78K6540** — Fits 20½ to 21¼ inches head size. For 8 to 10 years.
Colors: Oakwood brown, or French beige (sand color). Measure and state color. Shipping weight ¾ pound.
Present value for fur imitations is unusually attractive in this tam makeup. Top and band carries natural coloring of leopard (sand and brown) spots on a novel furlike cloth foundation. Good quality Paon (high grade velveteen) insert. Perky Paon loops at tip. Bias crown band fits snugly.

Class-mate Always Admired Hats
TRADE MARK REG

For 3 to 6 Years

Cute little set of good millinery felt cloth. Splendid fitting hat has elastic head size adjustment at back. Brim set off with two-tone border. Bag trimmed to match hat with gay colored felt motifs and metallic chain stitch. (Lovely suggestion for holiday gift). *Colors:* **Copenhagen blue with rose color; bright red with sand color, or sand color with oakwood brown. State color.** Shipping wt., set, 1¼ pounds. Hat only, ¾ pound; Bag only 2 oz.

78K6544 Hat and bag set.. **$2.25**
78K6548 Hat alone........ **$1.45**
78K6552 Bag alone............ **88c**

78K6556—Fits 20¼ to 21 inches head size. For 7 to 10 years. **$1.95**
Colors: **Oakwood brown with sand color; solid Copenhagen blue; bright red, or almond (medium) green. State color.** Shipping wt., 1¾ pounds.
Great value dress-up hat. Made of good quality Paon (high grade velveteen). Handsomely shirred crown. Poke brim has under shirring of lustrous **Rayon taffeta.** Dainty ribbon flower appliques set between embroidered stitching. Lovely messaline ribbon side streamers.

78K6560 — Fits 20½ to 21¼ inches. For 10 to 12 years. **$1.89**
Colors: **Oakwood brown with sand color; navy with bright red; sand with gooseberry (light) green, or bright red with sand.** Shipping weight, 1¾ pounds.
Well liked poke of good grade **full body felt.** Creased sectional crown with stitching and clever cut-out design. Showy, good quality ribbon trim.

78K6564—For 3 to 8 years. Head size adjusted with elastic insert. **$1.95**
Colors: **Oakwood brown with crab apple (salmon); Copenhagen blue with rose color; bright red with sand, or rose with sand. State color.** Shipping weight, 1¼ pounds.
Fine grade **velveteen.** Soft pleated brim faced with lustrous **Rayon.** Genuine fur, beaver color. Set off with tiny handmade buds. Ribbon rosettes and streamers.

78K6568—Fits 20¼ to 21 inches head size. For 6 to 8 years. **$1.98**
Colors: **Oakwood brown with touch of tiger lily (salmon color); Copenhagen blue with black; almond green with sand, or sand with rose color. State color.** Shipping weight, 1¼ pounds.
Darling bonnet of fine **Paon velveteen** with lots of shirrings. Tip matches contrasting fullness on brim. Soft edge of gold color lace. Handmade ornament. Ribbon rosettes and streamers.

$1.19
78K6572—For 9 to 12 years. Elastic insert at back adjusts head size.
Colors: **Rose color, bright green, Copenhagen blue, bright red, or sand color. (All with black ribbon.) State color.** Shipping weight, 1 lb.
Good looking, girlish tam of **suedelike cloth.** Neatly tailored. Stitched tucks. Grosgrain ribbon band. Stylish ornament.

78K6600—Fits 20¼ to 21 inches head size. For 8 to 10 years. **$1.89**
Colors: **Oakwood brown with crab apple (salmon color); Copenhagen blue with sand color; bright red with sand color, or black with rose color. Measure and state color.** Shipping wt., 1¾ lbs.
Smart style of good quality **Paon velveteen. Rayon taffeta** shirrings. Corded crown. Neatly tailored with ribbon. Odd ornament.

78K6604 — Fits 20¼ to 21 inches head size. For 7 to 10 years. **89¢**
Colors: **Copenhagen blue, bright red, sand color, or oakwood brown. Measure and state color.** Shipping weight, ¾ pounds.
Great value. Soft, swagger hood style. Made of good quality millinery **felt.** Neatly tailored with self leaflike motifs at side. Joined with fancy metal button. Dandy school and play hat.

78K6596—Fits 20 to 20½ in. For 6 to 8 years. **$1.89**
Colors: **Sand with light green ribbon; bright red with navy blue; Copenhagen blue with sand color, or black with rose color. State color.** Shipping weight, 1¾ pounds.
See the cunning hand painted ribbon band on this stylish tailored **felt.** Fancy cut brim. Trimming pin.

78K6608 — Fits 20½ to 21½ inches. For 9 to 13 years.
Colors: **Rose color, French beige (sand color), bright red, or Copenhagen blue. Measure and state color.** Shipping weight, 1¾ pounds.
Smart, serviceable hat and wonderful value. Made of good quality **full body felt.** Clever ribbon arrangement with tailored loops at side. Novel, celluloid pin. **$1.89**

78K6588—Fits 3 to 7 years. Elastic adjustment. **89¢**
Colors: **Sand color, Copenhagen blue, bright red, or rose color. (All with sand color brim.) State color.** Shipping weight, 1¼ pounds.
Bargain bonnet of **suedelike** material. Shirred **silcot** brim edged with fancy ribbon ruching. Ribbon chin strap.

78K6592—Fits 20¼ to 20¾ inches head size. For 7 to 10 years. **$1.89**
Colors: **Sand color, Copenhagen blue, rose color oakwood brown. Measure and state color.** Shpg. wt., 1¾ lbs.
Fine hat of good quality **full body felt.** Crown has smart creases. Dainty plush blossoms with stem effects of twisted chenille. **Felt** band around back.

89¢ **78K6612**—Fits 10 to 14 years. Elastic adjustment.
Colors: **Bright red, sand color or Copenhagen blue. (All with touch of black.)** State color. Shpg wt., 1 lb.
Greatest tam value. Made of good looking **suedelike cloth.** Trimmed with novelty two-tone braid. Ribbon crown band slipped through smart celluloid ornament. Streamers.

For Style and Quality

See Page 98 for "How to Measure"

$1.98 **78K6616**—Fits 20½ to 21¼ inches head size. For 11 to 13 years.
Colors: Almond (medium) green, oakwood brown, Copenhagen blue or rose color. Measure and state color. Shipping weight, 1¾ pounds.
Draped tam crown is very dressy. Made of good quality Paon velveteen. Smart side roll faced with Rayon taffeta. Full crown shirred into clever oval tip bound with taffeta. Nifty ostrich fancy. Silk lining. Tremendous value.

$1.89 **78K6620**—Fits 20¾ to 21½ inches head size. For 12 to 14 years.
Colors: Sand with oakwood brown; Copenhagen blue with sand color, or rose with claret (dark) red. Measure and state color. Shipping weight, 1¼ pounds.
Stylish shape and serviceable hat. Made in soft, crushable style of novel, velvety-like "Bordoray." Crown set off with bias folds of lustrous satin. Satin brim is pleated and stitched. Cellophone pin. Silk lining.

$1.65 **78K6624**—Fits 3 to 5 years. Elastic insert at back.
Colors: Black with rose color; sand color with Copenhagen blue; oakwood brown with sand color, or solid bright red. State color. Shipping weight, 1¼ pounds.
Cutest bonnet style for little tots. Sectional Paon velveteen crown. Shirred oval brim of bengaline. Matches bias folds through crown. Cunning fur-head ornament. Ribbon streamers.

$2.39 **78K6628**—Fits 4 to 6 years. Elastic insert at back adjusts head size.
Colors: Copenhagen blue, rose color, or wild honey (light brown). State color. Shipping weight, 1¼ pounds.
Our finest bonnet. Adorable shirred brim of lustrous changeable taffeta. Eight section Paon velveteen crown with diagonal rows of soutache braid. Dainty hand made applique. Fine moire ribbon rosettes and streamers. Delightful style and a bargain as well.

Fur Ball Tams, Two Sizes

78K6632—Fits 7 to 9 years. **$1.27**
78K6636—Fits 10 to 13 years. **1.39**
Colors: Bright red, wild honey (light brown), sand color, Copenhagen blue, or black. State color. Shipping weight, 1 pound.
Bargain fur ball tam—such a favorite with youngsters and junior misses. Made of good quality Paon velveteen. Tucked through center. Shirred brim with elastic insert at back to adjust head size. Neat ribbon streamer with genuine fur tassel balls.

$1.89 **78K6640**—Fits 20½ to 21 inches head size. For 7 to 10 years.
Colors: Dark brown with rose color, sand with Copenhagen blue, black with bright red, or beaver color with almond green. State color. Shpg. wt., 1¾ lbs. Rayon plush with bengaline. Ribbon trim. Dainty applique.

$1.65 **78K6644**—Fits 20¼ to 21 inches head size. For 6 to 8 years.
Colors: Sand color, Copenhagen blue, bright red or almond (medium) green. State color. Shipping weight, 1¼ lbs.
Shirred brim (short back) hat of suedelike material. Circle of colorful blossoms. Crown sections edged with braid. Ribbon band and streamers.

$1.65 **78K6648**—Fits 20½ to 21 inches head size. For 8 to 10 years.
Colors: Pirate (bright) red, Copenhagen blue, sand color, almond (medium) green or black. Measure and state color. Shipping weight, 1¾ pounds.
Generally becoming, popular tailored shape. Bargain full body felt hat. Good looking ribbon crown band drawn through novel cellophone buckle.

$1.39 **78K6652**—Fits 21 to 21½ inches head size. For 12 to 14 years.
Colors: Oakwood brown, rose color, Copenhagen blue, sand color or black. (Vari-color stripes). Measure and state color. Shipping weight, 1¼ pounds.
Wonder value! Soft, crushable tam of good quality millinery felt. Stylish brim band, also crown tip set off with bias felt strips. Showy pin ornament.

$1.23 **78K6656**—Fits 20 to 20½ inches head size. For 6 to 8 years.
Colors: Sand color, bright red, Copenhagen blue, or oakwood brown. Measure and state color. Shipping wt., 1¾ lbs.
Remarkable "Classmate" value. Great school hat for early fall and winter wear. Made of full body felt. Grosgrain ribbon crown band and back streamers.

$1.39 **78K6660**—Fits 20¾ to 21½ inches head size. For 11 to 13 years.
Colors: Sand color with oakwood brown, bright red with sand color, Copenhagen blue with sand color, or black. Measure and state color. Shipping weight, 1¾ pounds.
Admired tailored style. Made of good, soft quality full body felt. Novel picot cut brim. Fancy scallops in crown sets off ribbon crown band. Immense value.

$1.29 **78K6664**—Fits 20½ to 21¼ inches head size. For 8 to 12 years.
Colors: Copenhagen blue, sand color, bright red, oakwood brown or black. Measure and state color. Shipping weight, 1¼ lbs.
Smartly designed, self trimmed, soft felt model. Made of good quality felt cloth. Neatly tailored with tucks and stitching. Novel trimming pin.

98¢ **78K6668**—Fits 3 to 6 years. Elastic insert at back.
Colors: Rose color, Copenhagen blue, sand color, or bright red. (All furlike plush to harmonize.) Measure and state color. Shpg. wt., ¾ lb.
Kiddies love this soft, suedelike tam. Lovely band of furlike plush. Self streamer effects with plush balls. Bargain!

Approved Styles

$2.48 **78K8200** — Fits 21½ to 22¼ inches head size. *Colors:* Wild honey (light brown), pearl gray, Copenhagen blue or black. Measure and state color. Shipping weight, 1¾ pounds.
Popular trend for hackle feather trims is smartly expressed on this charming little shape. Striking crown, softly draped in tam fashion of good quality millinery faille. Gay varicolored insertion of narrow ribbon. Becoming brim laid in folds of silk faced velvet. Silk lining. Well made hat and splendid value.

$2.75 **78K8211** — Large size, fits 22½ to 23¼ inches head size. *Colors:* Claret (dark) red, wild honey (light brown), Copenhagen blue, or black. Measure and state color. Shipping weight, 1¾ pounds.
You'll love this flower trimmed felt model. Shape is smart and unusually becoming to a full face. Blocked of very fine, full body felt. Attractive plush poppy appliques over wide grosgrain ribbon crown band having extra narrow border of metallic braid on top. Full silk lining. Compare this hat with $5.00 values elsewhere.

Two-Tone Brim— A Remarkable Value

$1.75 **78K8219** — Fits 21½ to 22 inches head size.
Colors: French beige (sand) and oakwood brown combination; almond green with jungle (dark) green; or briar rose color with claret (dark) red. Measure and state color. Shipping weight, 1¾ pounds.
As smart and attractive as hats of this type offered at much higher prices elsewhere. Made of good quality full body felt. Two-tone effect on this clever wavy brim is the season's new feature. Tall, semi-telescope crown can be folded lower if desired. Novel, tailored ribbon arrangement.

$2.39 **78K8235** — Fits 21½ to 22¼ inches head size.
Colors: Monkey skin (sand), almond green, pirate (bright) red, Copenhagen blue, or black. Measure and state color. Shipping weight, 1¾ pounds.
High grade, genteel designing is displayed in every line of this adorable soft style. Made of extra fine quality full body felt. Brim has stitched border of lovely ribbon. Novel stitched tuck arrangement across back, finished with self loops extending at either side. Pearl-like ornament. Silk lining. Truly exceptional value.

Two Head Sizes

78K8226 — Snug fitting, fits 21 to 21½ inches head size.
$2.85 **78K8227** — Fits 21¾ to 22½ inches head size. *Colors:* Monkey skin (sand), almond green, orchid color, pearl gray, or black. Measure and state color. Shipping weight, 1¾ pounds.
Stylish trimming and smart lines were never more charmingly combined. Clever, snug fitting, hand draped turban of very soft, extra fine quality chiffon finish felt. Smart, machine stitched tucks set through crown. Gracious, ostrich pendant. Silk lining.

$1.95 **78K8230**—Fits 21 to 21¾ inches head size.
Colors: Oakwood brown; claret (dark) red, sand color, or black. Measure and state color. Shipping weight, 1¾ pounds.
With smart hats at this low price who could resist this clever little model? Late, tam style blocked of good quality full body felt. Attractive trimming idea is stitched bands of lustrous ribbon set off with felt ribbon-like band and perky bow on top. Neat buckle ornament. Silk lining.

$2.85 **78K8240** — Fits 21½ to 22 inches head size.
Colors: Wild honey (light brown), almond green, pearl gray, or black. Measure and state color. Shipping weight, 1¾ pounds.
Smart, pleated ribbon brim is an important style factor this season. Here on a crown of softly draped full body felt it is most adorable. Richly trimmed with novelty gold color discs to match metallic ribbon band. Very dressy and distinctly unusual.

$1.95 **Two Head Sizes**
78K8246 — Fits 22 to 22½ inches head size.
78K8247 — Fits 22¾ to 23½ inches. *Colors:* Sand with dark brown ribbon; Copenhagen blue with sand color; almond green with dark green; solid oakwood brown or black. Measure and state color. Shipping weight, 2 lbs.
This new "Vagabond" has a new wide crown, especially becoming to full faces. Soft, wide, pliable brim. Made of good quality full body felt. Handsome tailored ribbon trim. Very special at this low price.

Most Amazing Values

78K8256 — Fits 22 to 23 in. head size. **$2.95** *Colors:* Almond green with jungle (dark) green combination; rose color with claret (dark) red; sand color with oakwood brown, or all black with bright blue appliques. Measure and state color. Shipping weight, 1¾ pounds.
Cheerful cutout appliques enhance the beauty of this stylish, close fitting shape. Features new tam drape crown. Made of lustrous bengaline with high grade silk Lyon's velvet brim and velvet fold in crown. Rows of novelty braid and side ribbon loops complete the trimming. Silk lining.

Two Head Sizes $3.69
78K8260 — Fits 22 to 23 inches.
78K8263 — Fits 23¼ to 24 inches.
Colors: Sand color with oakwood brown; pearl gray with Copenhagen blue, or black. Measure and state color. Shipping weight, 1¾ pounds.
High grade hat of soft make conforms beautifully to your head. Made of fine silk Lyon's velvet with rich quality, millinery satin in soft corded style drape. Satin and velvet sections in tip. Pleated brim is flattering and very dressy. Colorful plush appliques over ribbon loops. Touch of braid. Silk lined.

78K8250 — Fits 21¼ to 22 inches head size. **$2.95** *Colors:* Black with tiger lily (salmon color) facing; oakwood brown with sand color, or Copenhagen blue with rose color. Measure and state color. Shipping weight, 1¾ pounds.
Attractive trimming on a pleasing and well liked shape. Moderate size, short back poke of lustrous millinery satin. Finely pleated **Rayon taffeta** facing. Striking colorful leaf appliques with flat silk covered fruit effect at side. Delightful style for misses and young women. Great value, too.

78K8272 — Fits 22½ to 23¼ inches head size. **$2.75** *Colors:* Gull (light) gray, monkey skin (sand color), Copenhagen blue, jungle (dark) green, or black. Measure and state color. Shipping weight 1¾ pounds.
Perfection of tailored smartness and high grade quality adds to its charm. Made of extra fine, soft full body felt. Stylish, draped crown set off with odd arrangement of narrow felt strips. New, pearl style divided pin. Silk lining. Great "Style Square" value indeed!

Extra fine Soft Velour

78K8264 **$1.95** Snug fitting. Fits 21 to 21¾ inches. *Colors:* French beige (sand color), almond green, pirate (bright) red, Copenhagen blue, or black. Measure and state color. Shipping weight, 1¾ pounds.
Right smart, and a bargain of great merit. Snug fitting, soft turban style of fine quality full body felt. Novel trimming idea is also felt. Silk lined.

Two Head Sizes $2.85
78K8268 — Fits 21½ to 22¼ inches head size.
78K8270 — Fits 22½ to 23¼ inches head size.
Colors: Dark brown with wild honey (light brown); Copenhagen blue with sand color, or solid black. Measure and state color. Shipping weight, 1¾ lbs.
High grade tailoring in this stylish hat. Late sectional tam idea set off with double bias folds of bengaline. Crown band and upper brim of bengaline. Neatly trimmed with novelty braid. Cleverly pleated ribbon ornament. Cellophane pin. Silk lining.

78K9023 **$4.44** Small size. Fits 21 to 22 in head size. *Colors:* Chin Chin (new light Copen) blue, almond green, claret (dark) red, monkey skin (new sand), or black. Measure and state color. Shipping wt., 1¾ lbs.
Last word of ultra smartness! High grade hat of finest quality, genuine clipped fur velour. Close roll brim has novel cut affecting smart one side tab. Also clever shingle cut at back. Slight tam drape. Tuck at right side can be stitched deeper for snugger fit or let out to fit larger. Exquisite divided pin (earring style) ornament with pearl brilliant settings. Fine quality silk lining.

78K8276 — Fits 22½ to 23 inches head size. **$3.95** *Colors:* Autumn brown (taupe-brown), French beige (sand color), Copenhagen blue, or black. Measure and state color. Shipping weight, 2 pounds.
Most stylish shape for well dressed women of the full face type. Stunning new telescope crown. Made of extra fine quality clipped fur velour. Brim has smart, divided feature at side. Handsome, two-tone banded trim with smart pleated arrangement at side. Full silk lining.

Choice of Colors

$1.95 78K8406—Fits 21¼ to 22 inches head size.
Colors: Almond green, wild honey (light brown), Copenhagen blue or black. Measure and state color. Shipping weight, 1¾ lbs.
Delightfully youthful and in good taste for early and late winter wear. Made of lustrous millinery satin. Pleated ribbon brim is unusually becoming. Neat pin tucks give tailored finish to crown. Pleated ribbon rosette at either side. Striking value.

$2.39 78K8398—Fits 21½ to 22¾ inches head size.
Colors: Sand color with Copenhagen blue combination; bright red with sand; solid Copenhagen blue, or black. Measure and state color. Shipping weight, 2 pounds.
Great value and a well liked style. Moderate size, short back poke of **silk faced velvet** combined with lustrous silk millinery **faille.** Shirred velvet bias on upper border. Showy ribbon trim set off with novelty pin.

$2.48 78K8402—Fits 21¼ to 22 inches head size.
Colors: Almond green, rose color, Copenhagen blue or black. Measure and state color. Shpg. wt., 1¾ lbs.
New "halo" turban is quite dressy in this showy makeup. Made of lustrous millinery **faille.** Fancy fold across top has overlay of fancy metallic net. Novelty, gold color flower to match. Silk lining.

$1.95 78K8414—Fits 21¾ to to 22¼ inches head size.
Colors: Oakwood brown with crab apple (salmon) color flowers; black with bright red, or sand with Copenhagen blue. Measure and state color. Shpg. wt., 1¾ lbs.
Great value poke. Slightly wavy brim of lustrous millinery **faille** with bias folds effecting corded like insert. Velvet brim has **faille** facing. Showy flower cluster. Double ribbon band. Silk lining.

$1.95 78K8410—Fits 21½ to 22¼ inches head size.
Colors: French beige (sand), Copenhagen blue, bright red or black. Measure and state color. Shipping weight, 2¼ pounds.
Generally becoming style—besides amazing value at our low price. Wide side, drooping brim that is turned up across back. Made of lustrous millinery **faille.** Deep insert in crown and along upper brim of **silk faced velvet.** Grosgrain ribbon trimming.

$1.95 78K8418—Fits 22¾ to 23½ inches head size.
Colors: Black, navy blue or oakwood brown. Measure and state color. Shipping weight, 1¾ lbs.
Special value hat is one of the most becoming styles for full face types. Attractively draped crown of **silk faced velvet.** Narrow roll brim (short at back) of lustrous **bengaline.** Smart applique of varicolor silk and metallic thread to harmonize.

"Vagabond" Felt Bargain

$1.65 78K8430—Fits 22 to 22¾ inches head size.
Colors: Sand color, oakwood brown, Copenhagen blue or rose color. Measure and state color. Shipping wt., 2 pounds.
Popular utility hat for women and misses. Great value, too, for good quality **full body felt.** Belt style band of felt with buckle finish. Soft and pliable. Brim shapes to suit your fancy. Favorite travel and sport hat for early fall and winter wear.

$1.95 Two Head Sizes
78K8438—Fits 21½ to 22 inches head size.
78K8439—Fits 22¼ to 23 inches head size.
Colors: Almond green with beige (sand); Copenhagen blue with pearl gray; oakwood brown with sand color, or black. Measure and state color. Shipping weight, 1¾ pounds.
Attractive tailoring in this special value hat. Well made and favored shape of good quality silk faced velvet. Millinery **faille** insert made fancy with inverted tucks on bias across front. Neat, ribbon arrangement at side. Novel ornament.

$1.75 78K8422—Fits 21½ to 22¾ inches head size.
Colors: Rose color, Copenhagen blue, French beige (sand) or oakwood brown. Measure and state color. Shpg. wt., 1¾ lbs.
Another **Sears** bargain of unusual merit! Stylish, **full body felt** shape. Brim carries becoming soft ripple across front; narrow roll at back. Good looking small hackle feather pad trims it smartly. Felt ribbon style band.

$1.95 78K8426—Fits 21½ to 22¼ inches head size.
Colors: Copenhagen blue with pearl gray; wild honey (light brown) with sand color; rose color with sand, or black. Measure and state color. Shipping weight, 1¾ pounds.
Inexpensive, yet as attractive as many hats offered elsewhere at double our price. Becoming, close fitting hat of good quality **silk faced velvet.** Folded insert of **Rayon faille** matches underbrim. Gay color plush flower appliques. Metallic stitching.

Note Our Head-Sizes

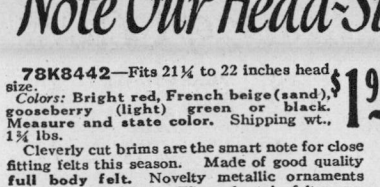

78K8442—Fits 21¼ to 22 inches head size.
Colors: Bright red, French beige (sand), gooseberry (light) green or black. Measure and state color. Shipping wt., 1¾ lbs.

$1.95

Cleverly cut brims are the smart note for close fitting felts this season. Made of good quality **full body felt.** Novelty metallic ornaments punched through brim. These also trim felt crown band. Inverted tuck is telescope suggestion in crown. Splendid style for a low price.

$1.95

78K8446—Fits 21½ to 22¼ inches head size.
Colors: Oakwood brown, Copenhagen blue, sand color, purple or black. Measure and state Color. Shipping weight, 1¾ pounds.
Lovely style and you will marvel at our splendid value. New, tam drape turban. Made of lustrous millinery **faille** that is finely pleated through tip and insert. Contrasting folds are **silk faced velvet.** Novelty pendant style ornament.

78K8450—Fits 21½ to 22¼ inches head size.
Colors: Black with touch of white and gold color, or Copenhagen blue or oakwood brown (with vari-colored trimming to harmonize). Measure and state color. Shipping weight, 1¾ pounds.

$2.39

Delightful dress up hat along with great value. Made of good quality **silk faced velvet.** Corded like treatment of bias bengaline folds. Draped in stylish tam fashion. Novel lacy edge has metallic border. Rayon plush flower applique. Ribbon ends.

SATIN

$1.95

Two Head Sizes
78K8454—Fits 21¼ to 22 inches.
78K8455—Fits 22¼ to 23 inches.
Colors: **Black, sand color, almond green or oakwood brown. Measure and state color.** Shipping weight, 1¾ pounds.
Stylish shape is nicely tailored throughout. Made of good quality millinery **satin.** Inverted tucks add to soft appearance of crown. Stitched brim. Novelty, colorful trimming pin.

Two Head Sizes
78K8458—Fits 21½ to 22 inches.
78K8459—Fits 22¼ to 23 inches.
Colors: **French beige (sand), Copenhagen blue, wild honey (light brown) or black. Measure and state color.** Shipping weight, 1¾ pounds.

FELT

$1.48

Narrow, soft drooping brim is the popular line followed in the smartest tailored hats this season. For our good quality **full body felt** this low price is indeed a bargain. Banded with attractive side trim of good ribbon.

78K8470—Fits 22¼ to 23 inches head size.
Colors: **Black with Copenhagen blue, or oakwood brown with rose color. Measure and state color.** Shipping weight, 2 pounds.

$1.98

Elaborate trimming on a well liked shape and splendid value. Short back poke of good quality **silk faced velvet.** Brim faced with lustrous **Rayon faille.** Becomingly draped crown. Shaded plush applique set off with stitching. Ribbon crown band and loops at side.

Clara Bow Hats

Posed by the Famous Paramount Picture Star

95¢ Each

Ⓐ **78K8462**—Fits 21 to 22 in. head size.
Colors: **French beige (sand color), Copenhagen blue, rose color, pearl gray or black. Measure and state color.** Shipping weight, 4 ounces.
Young women and misses will love the lightweight feeling as it conforms snugly to the head. Soft, crushable make (can be folded into pocket size) of extra fine quality millinery **felt.** Neatly tailored with fine, machine stitched tucks. Trimmed with colorful cutout motifs of felt.

Ⓑ **78K8466**—Has elastic insert at back to insure perfect fit. Fits young women and misses from 21 to 22½ in. head size.
Colors: **Copenhagen blue, sand color, wild honey (light brown) or bright red. Measure and state color.** Shpg. wt., ¾ lb.
Here is a real sport tam. As smart as it can be made of good looking novelty "Bord-o-ray" (ribbed velveteen). Fitted in six sections. Ribbon crown band, trimmed with novel button-like discs. Lined.

Ⓒ **78K8469**—Fits 21 to 22 in. head size.
Colors: **Almond green, wild honey (light brown), bright red, sand color or black. Measure and state color.** Shpg. wt., 4 oz.
Misses and young women delight in this snug fitting mode. So light in weight—conforms perfectly to your head. Made of extra fine quality millinery **felt.** Neatly tailored with machine stitching and tucks. Fancy, contrasting cutout designs of felt trim either side.

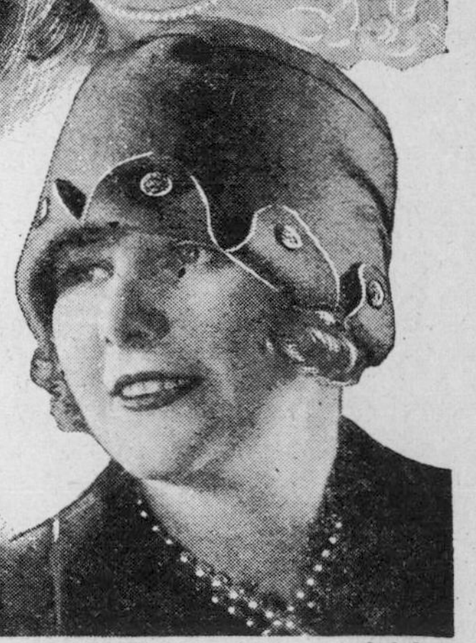

$1.95

78K8474—Large head size, fits 22¾ to 23½ inches.
Colors: **Navy blue, oakwood brown, sand color or black. Measure and state color.** Shipping weight, 1¾ pounds.
Good looking hat and quite a favorite with middle aged and mature women. Bargain too at this low price. Made of good quality **silk faced velvet.** Lower drape in crown of lustrous millinery **faille.** Narrow brim all around (trifle shorter at back). Showy, pleated ribbon ornament. Trimming pin.

78K8478—Fits 21½ to 22½ inches head size.
Colors: **Oakwood brown, bright red, Copenhagen blue, sand color or black. Measure and state color.** Shipping weight, 1¾ pounds.

$1.00

Great value hat indeed for the smart style it represents. Good make as well of fine quality **felt cloth.** Tucked crown. Novel scalloped brim set off with odd metal buttons. Soft, crushable hat. Has no foundation.

Order Blanks Are in Back of This Catalog

$1.98~ **78K8482**—Small size, fits 21 to 21¾ inches headsize. *Colors:* Copenhagen blue with black; sand with dark brown; almond green with dark green; or bright red with black. Measure and state color. Shpg. wt., 1¾ lbs.
Nifty flapper style of full body felt. Tinted felt is clever "halo" trimming, having late style point at either side. Felt strip finishes back. Tiny ornaments also of felt. Silk lining. Dandy value at this low price.

78K9106—Fits 22 to 22½ inches headsize. *Colors:* Dark brown with sand color; navy blue with pearl gray, or black. Measure and state color. Shipping weight, 1¾ pounds. **$2.85~**
Lovely style that is favored for dress up. Becoming side roll shape of silk faced velvet. Several of grosgrain ribbon having slight fullness toward top covers side crown. Cheerful flower spray.

78K8486—Fits 21½ to 22¼ inches headsize. *Colors:* Black with rose color; oakwood brown with sand; sand with Copenhagen blue, or solid black. Measure and state color. Shipping weight, 1¾ pounds. **$1.98~**
Perfect beauty at a very low price. Silk faced velvet prettily tucked to the tip. Narrow **taffeta** silk brim below handsome, wide band of lustrous baronet satin ribbon. Finished with many loops (pompon fashion) at side.

78K8490—Small size, fits 21 to 21¾ inches headsize. *Colors:* Dark brown with wild honey (light brown); jungle (dark) green with almond green, or black with rose color. Measure and state color. Shipping wt., 1¾ lbs. **$2.48~**
New idea. Silk faced velvet has solid ribbon insert in tam drape. Half circles of ribbon complete ensemble with trimming pin to match.

$2.75~ **TWO HEAD SIZES**
78K9112—Fits 21¾ to 22½ inches headsize.
78K9115—Fits 22¾ to 23½ inches headsize. *Colors:* Black or dark brown. Measure and state color. Shpg. wt., 1¾ lbs.
Leading draped turban for the matron, on becoming side roll brim. Splendid value, of good quality silk faced velvet. Fan shaped feather fancy.

$3.48~ **78K9118**—Large size, fits 22½ to 23 inches headsize. *Colors:* Black with Copenhagen blue or oakwood brown with Tiger Lily (salmon color). Measure and state color. Shpg. wt., 1¾ lbs.
Charming style, has delightful dress up qualities. Rayon taffeta crown with piping of velvet joining each bias. Touch of velvet through innerbrim and lower bias around crown. Taffeta facing matches gorgeous, full blown silk and plush rose.

$2.39~ **78K9122**—Fits 21¾ to 22½ inches headsize. *Colors:* Black with choice of pink or Copenhagen blue facing, or oakwood brown with sand color. Measure and state color. Shipping weight, 2½ lbs.
Large brim tailored style is always smart. Made of silk faced velvet. Lustrous baronet satin facing; also satin insert to match velvet on upper brim. Folded satin ribbon band drawn through fancy metal buckle.

$1.95~ **78K8494**—Fits 21¼ to 22 inches headsize. *Colors:* Black with bright red; sand color with almond green, or pearl gray with Napoleon (bright blue). Measure and state color. Shipping weight, 1¾ lbs.
Low price for this good looking hat. Smartly styled turban of moire faille and silk faced velvet drape. Neat trimming pin.

$1.35~ **78K8498**—Fits 21 to 22 inches headsize. *Colors:* French Beige (sand) with touch of Copenhagen blue, rose color with pearl gray, almond green with sand or bright red with navy blue. Measure and state color. Shipping weight, 1¾ pounds.
Wonderful value and style to this good looking tailored hat. Soft utility style for misses and young women. Fine quality, soft millinery felt. Double brim affects becoming ripple. Two-tone twisted felt around crown. Novelty buttons. Lined.

78K8502—Fits 21¼ to 22 inches headsize. *Colors:* Oakwood brown, rose color, Copenhagen blue, or sand color. Measure and state color. Shipping weight, 1¾ pounds. **$1.75~**
Stylish full body felt shape and mighty big value. Showy, sport band is shaded in blending tones to harmonize. Cellophane trimming pin.

78K8506—Fits 21 to 21¾ inches head size. *Colors:* Copenhagen blue, light sand color, Copper leaf (new light copper brown), almond green or black. Measure and state color. Shipping wt., 1¾ pounds. **$1.75~**
Popular shape for misses and young women. Blocked of soft, full body felt. Novel stitched tucks decorate crown. Nice quality grosgrain ribbon in trim tailored arrangement. Bargain!

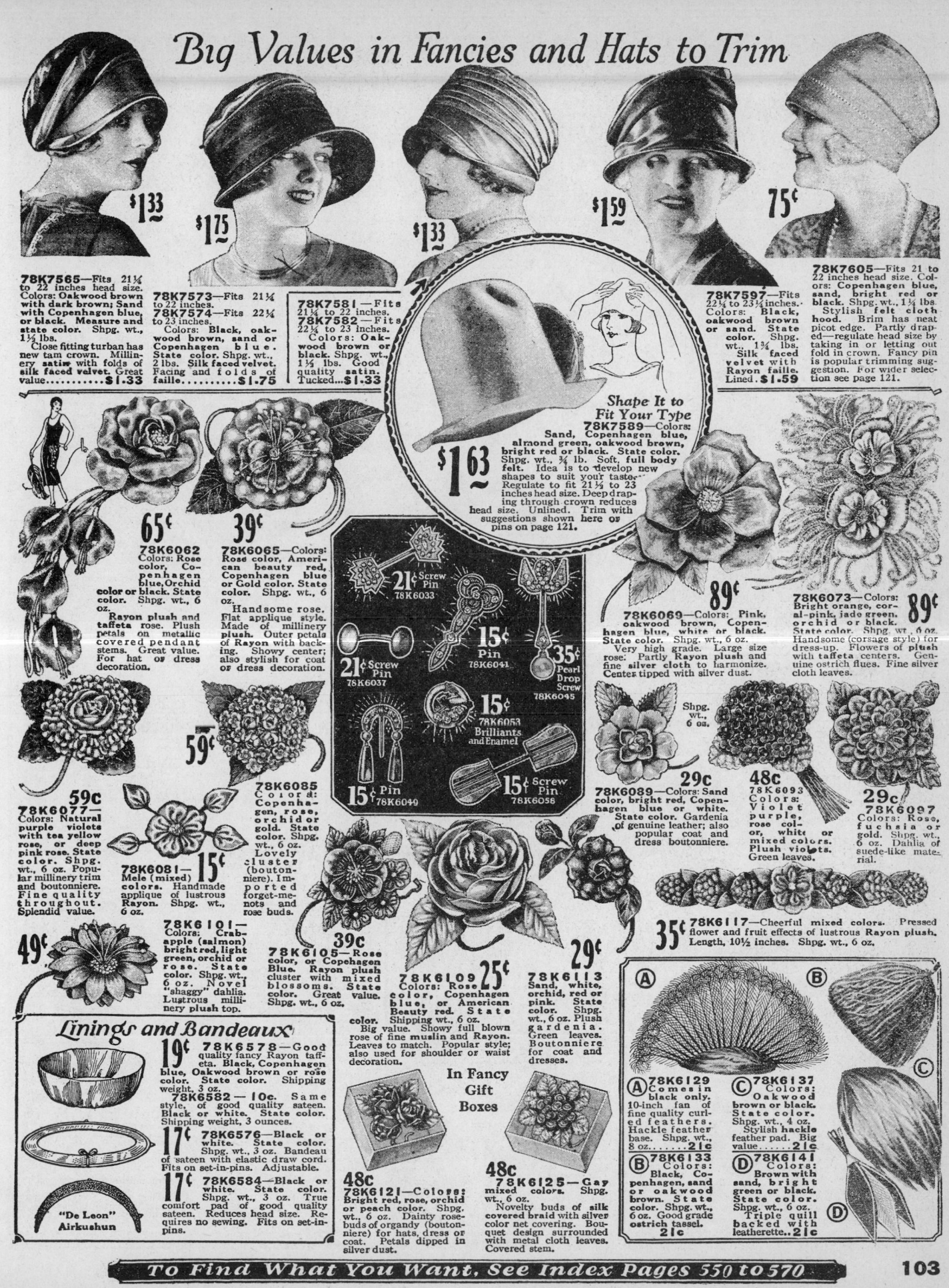

Big Values in Fancies and Hats to Trim

$1.33

78K7565—Fits 21¼ to 22 inches head size. Colors: Oakwood brown with dark brown; Sand with Copenhagen blue, or black. Measure and state color. Shpg. wt., 1½ lbs.
Close fitting turban has new tam crown. Millinery satin with folds of silk faced velvet. Great value..........$1.33

$1.75

78K7573—Fits 21¼ to 22 inches.
78K7574—Fits 22¼ to 23 inches.
Colors: Black, oakwood brown, sand or Copenhagen blue. State color. Shpg. wt., 2 lbs. Silk faced velvet. Facing and folds of faille..........$1.75

$1.33

78K7581—Fits 21¼ to 22 inches.
78K7582—Fits 22¼ to 23 inches.
Colors: Oakwood brown or black. Shpg. wt., 1⅓ lbs. Good quality satin. Tucked...$1.33

$1.59

78K7597—Fits 22¼ to 23¼ inches. Colors: Black, oakwood brown or sand. State color. Shpg. wt., 1¾ lbs. Silk faced velvet with Rayon faille. Lined. $1.59

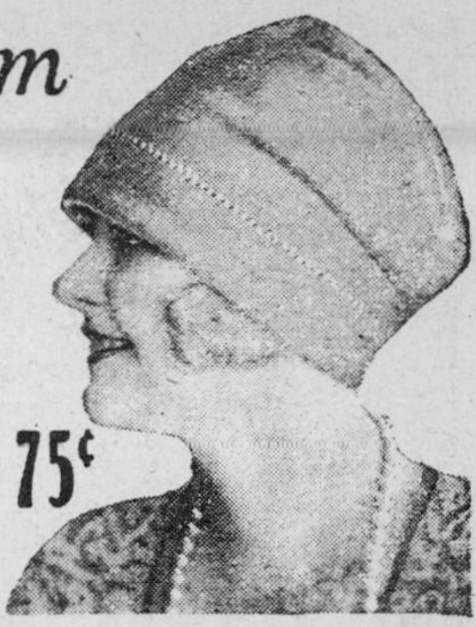

75¢

78K7605—Fits 21 to 22 inches head size. Colors: Copenhagen blue, sand, bright red or black. Shpg. wt., 1¼ lbs.
Stylish felt cloth hood. Brim has neat picot edge. Partly draped—regulate head size by taking in or letting out fold in crown. Fancy pin is popular trimming suggestion. For wider selection see page 121.

Shape It to Fit Your Type

$1.63

78K7589—Colors: Sand, Copenhagen blue, almond green, oakwood brown, bright red or black. State color. Shpg. wt., ¾ lb. Soft, full body felt. Idea is to develop new shapes to suit your taste. Regulate to fit 21½ to 23 inches head size. Deep draping through crown reduces head size. Unlined. Trim with suggestions shown here or pins on page 121.

65¢

78K6062
Colors: Rose color, Copenhagen blue, Orchid color or black. State color. Shpg. wt., 6 oz.
Rayon plush and taffeta rose. Plush petals on metallic covered pendant stems. Great value. For hat or dress decoration.

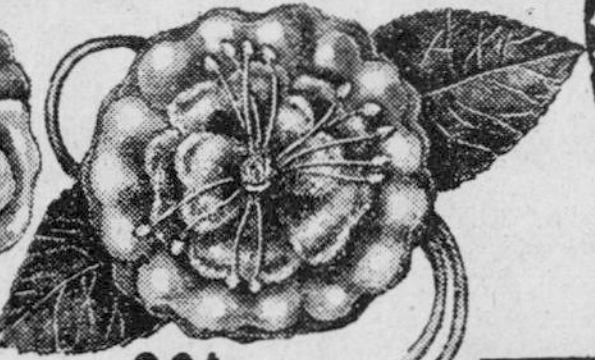

39¢

78K6065—Colors: Rose color, American beauty red, Copenhagen blue or Gold color. State color. Shpg. wt., 6 oz.
Handsome rose. Flat applique style. Made of millinery plush. Outer petals of Rayon with backing. Showy center; also stylish for coat or dress decoration.

21¢ Screw Pin
78K6033
21¢ Screw Pin
78K6037
15¢
Pin
78K6041
35¢
Pearl
Drop
Screw
78K6045
15¢
78K6053
Brilliants
and Enamel
15¢ Pin
78K6049
15¢ Screw Pin
78K6056

89¢

78K6069—Colors: Pink, oakwood brown, Copenhagen blue, white or black. State color. Shpg. wt., 6 oz.
Very high grade. Large size rose. Partly Rayon plush and fine silver cloth to harmonize. Center tipped with silver dust.

89¢

78K6073—Colors: Bright orange, coral-pink, jade green, orchid or black. State color. Shpg. wt., 6 oz. Handsome (corsage style) for dress-up. Flowers of plush with taffeta centers. Genuine ostrich flues. Fine silver cloth leaves.

59c

78K6077—Colors: Natural purple violets with tea yellow rose, or deep pink rose. State color. Shpg. wt., 6 oz. Popular millinery trim and boutonniere. Fine quality throughout. Splendid value.

59¢

78K6085
Colors: Copenhagen, rose, orchid or gold. State color. Shpg. wt., 6 oz.
Lovely cluster (boutonniere). Imported forget-me-nots and rose buds.

15¢

78K6081—Mele (mixed) colors. Handmade applique of lustrous Rayon. Shpg. wt., 6 oz.

49¢

78K6101—Colors: Crab-apple (salmon) bright red, light green, orchid or rose. State color. Shpg. wt., 6 oz. Novel "shaggy" dahlia. Lustrous millinery plush top.

39c

78K6105—Rose color, or Copehagen Blue. Rayon plush cluster with mixed blossoms. State color. Great value. Shpg. wt., 6 oz.

25¢

78K6109
Colors: Rose color, Copenhagen blue, or American Beauty red. State color. Shipping wt., 6 oz.
Big value. Showy full blown rose of fine muslin and Rayon. Leaves to match. Popular style; also used for shoulder or waist decoration.

29¢

78K6113
Sand, white, orchid, red or pink. State color. Shpg. wt., 6 oz. Plush gardenia. Green leaves. Boutonniere for coat and dresses.

Shpg. wt., 6 oz.

29c

78K6089—Colors: Sand color, bright red, Copenhagen blue or white. State color. Gardenia of genuine leather; also popular coat and dress boutonniere.

48c

78K6093
Colors: Violet purple, rose color, white or mixed colors. Plush violets. Green leaves.

29c

78K6097
Colors: Rose, fuchsia or gold. Shpg. wt., 6 oz. Dahlia of suede-like material.

35¢ 78K6117—Cheerful mixed colors. Pressed flower and fruit effects of lustrous Rayon plush. Length, 10½ inches. Shpg. wt., 6 oz.

Linings and Bandeaux

19¢ 78K6578—Good quality fancy Rayon taffeta. Black, Copenhagen blue, Oakwood brown or rose color. State color. Shipping weight, 3 oz.

78K6582—10c. Same style, of good quality sateen. Black or white. State color. Shipping weight, 3 ounces.

17¢ 78K6576—Black or white. State color. Shpg. wt., 3 oz. Bandeau of sateen with elastic draw cord. Fits on set-in-pins. Adjustable.

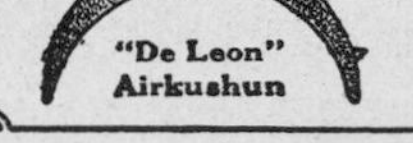

"De Leon" Airkushun

17¢ 78K6584—Black or white. State color. Shpg. wt., 3 oz. True comfort pad of good quality sateen. Reduces head size. Requires no sewing. Fits on set-in-pins.

In Fancy Gift Boxes

48c

78K6121—Colors: Bright red, rose, orchid or peach color. Shpg. wt., 6 oz. Dainty rosebuds of organdy (boutonniere) for hats, dress or coat. Petals dipped in silver dust.

48c

78K6125—Gay mixed colors. Shpg. wt., 6 oz.
Novelty buds of silk covered braid with silver color net covering. Bouquet design surrounded with metal cloth leaves. Covered stem.

Ⓐ

Ⓑ

Ⓒ

Ⓓ

Ⓐ 78K6129—Comes in black only. 10-inch fan of fine quality curled feathers. Hackle feather base. Shpg. wt., 8 oz.......21c

Ⓑ 78K6133—Colors: Black, Copenhagen, sand or oakwood brown. State color. Shpg. wt., 6 oz. Good grade ostrich tassel. 21c

Ⓒ 78K6137—Colors: Oakwood brown or black. State color. Shpg. wt., 4 oz. Stylish hackle feather pad. Big value.......21c

Ⓓ 78K6141—Colors: Brown with sand, bright green or black. State color. Shpg. wt., 6 oz. Triple quill backed with leatherette..21c

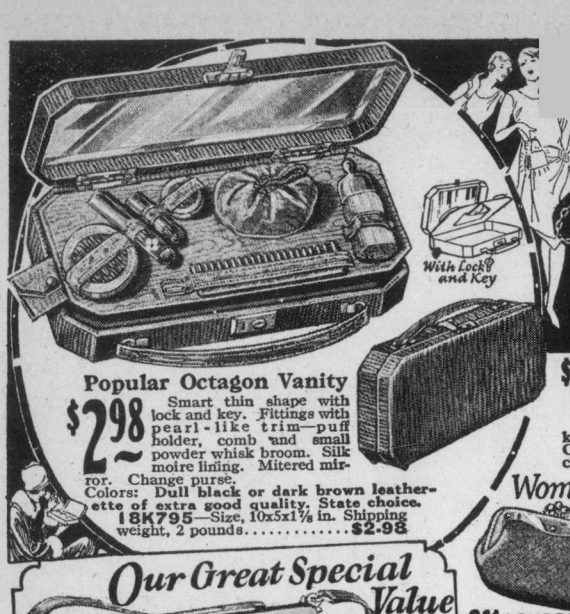

Popular Octagon Vanity

$2.98

Smart thin shape with lock and key. Fittings with pearl-like trim—puff holder, comb and small powder whisk broom. Silk moire lining. Mitered mirror. Change purse. Colors: Dull black or dark brown leatherette of extra good quality. State choice. **18K795**—Size, 10x5x1⅞ in...........$2.98

With Lock and Key

18K810—Colors: White or black silk. State choice. Fine quality silk moire. Entire front covered with very high grade sparkling imitation diamonds (white). Beveled mirror in pocket. Dainty link silver-like chain handle. Correct small size, 4⅜x3¼ inches. Very classy. Shpg. wt., ¾ lb. **$4.98**

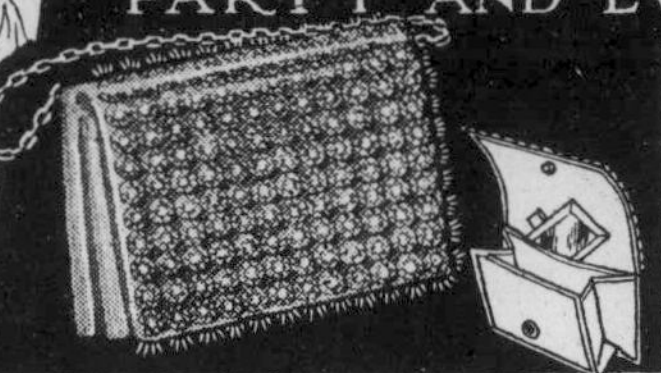

Petitpoint Design

18K824—Black Silk Moire Pouch Bag. Imitation petitpoint floral design. Fancy frame. Change purse. Beveled mirror. Lustrous lining. Size, 7x4½ inches. Shipping weight, ¾ lb. **$2.95**

18K813—Colors: Gold or silver. State choice. Size, 4¼x5 inches. Shipping weight, ¾ pound. Dress Bag of good quality imported tinsel cloth. Jeweled frame. Dainty link chain handle. Beveled mirror. Lustrous lining. Change purse. **$2.95**

Our Great Special Value

$1.98

Without question one of the greatest bag values ever offered, a grade usually sold elsewhere at very much higher prices. Pouch style of good quality boarded cowhide, beautifully embossed in hand tooled effect. Pull tab, real hand laced. Gold color frame with swinging inner change purse. Very roomy. Mirror in long compartment. Moire lining. **18K844**—Colors: Dark brown or black. State color. Size, 9x6⅛ inches. Shipping weight, 1¼ pounds.............$1.98

Womens Coin Purses

21¢ 18K835 Good quality black leather. Two pockets. Nickeled frame. 4 x 2 ½ in. Shpg. wt., 2 oz.

18K837 19¢ Two pockets. Good quality brown leather. Size, 3½x2¼ in. Shipping weight, each 2 oz.

The Ideal **Gift** *for* **Him** *See pages 621 to 623*

Fine Calf
All Leather Lined

$2.98

18K840 Colors: Black and gray, or brown and tan. State choice. Size, 10x6½ inches. Shipping weight, 1¼ pounds. Tailored Bag of genuine top grain calf leather. Very smart with touch of stylish lizard grain leather trim on frame and pull tab. Very roomy. All leather lined. Swinging change pocket. Beveled mirror. Big bargain.

WATERPROOF CRETONNE LINING

$1.00

Please do not confuse this grade with the cheaply made type.

LARGE SHIRRED POCKET

Metal hinges and fastener.

18K847—Size, 11x10x4½ in. Shipping weight, 2 lbs. Improved Hollywood Bags for the woman traveler or for carrying lunches, baby's things or bathing suits. Embossed design in multitone colorings. Fine appearing, sturdily built. Good grade glossy light brown leatherette with tan lizard grain trim. Entirely lined with fancy waterproofed cretonne.

The Paris Special

$2.85

18K852 Colors: Tan and brown, or black and tan. State color. Size, 8⅛x4⅞ in. Shipping weight, 1 lb..........$2.85

Novel Vanity Bag now all the rage. Made of good quality leather in popular alligator grain. Long beveled mirror and shirred pocket for powder puff, etc., concealed under flap. Framed inner change purse. Top strap handle. Moire lining.

RUBBERIZED WATERPROOF LINING

ALL LEATHER

$1.89

18K838—Colors: Black or tan. State color. Shpg. wt., 3 lbs. Boston Bag. Long wearing selected split cowhide. Rubberized lining. Large inner pocket. For business men, women or students, or for babies' things, etc. Strong strap fastener and buckle. Large full 14-inch size. Size, 14x9½x5⅝ in.

New Style Leatherette
Very Popular

$1.00

The Bag of Many Uses

18K839—Full size Boston Bag. Made of a new style cork back leatherette in rich brown color. Looks like real fine leather, is lightweight, waterproof and will give good service. Lock and key. Name plate. Fancy cloth lining. Size, 15x10x5¾ inches. Shpg. wt., 3½ lbs.

Shopping Bag

45¢

18K755 Shpg. wt., ¾ lb. Large and roomy. Strong artificial leather. Cretonne lining. Wide gussets. Double handles. Size, 12x13½ in.

Description of Bags Shown on Opposite Page

(A) **18K862—$3.48** Shipping weight, 1 pound. *Colors:* Light brown, black or gray. State color. Distinctive new style Bag of extra quality goat leather. Has novel pull tab with beveled mirror concealed underneath. Gold colored frame. Swinging change purse. Fine lining. Size, 9½x7 inches.

(B) **18K864—$2.98** Shipping weight, 1 pound. *Colors:* Brown, tan or gray. State color. Chic Back Strap Pouch Bag of pliable goat leather in alligator grain. Center strip of smooth calf, edged in gold color trim. Leather covered frame. Swinging coin purse. Fine lining. Mirror. Attractive enameled ornament. Size, 9¼x5½ inches.

(C) **18K866—$4.95** Shipping weight, 1¼ pounds. *Colors:* Tan, gray or black. State color. Fine Soft Calf Leather Pouch Bag with beautiful embroidered floral design. Carried two ways, either back strap or by top strap handle. Leather covered frame. Swinging gold color change purse. Beveled mirror. Splendid lustrous lining. Size, 9x6¼ inches.

(D) **18K870—$1.95** Shipping weight, 1 pound. *Colors:* Brown, tan, gray or black. State color. Bargain value. Vanity Purse in a new popular style. Good quality leather in wanted alligator effect. Beveled mirror and gold color fittings conveniently placed under flap. Purse in long inside pocket. Good moire lining. Size, 7x4 inches.

(E) **18K874½—$4.95** Shpg. wt., 1¼ lbs. *Colors:* Black, brown or gray. State color and initial wanted. Tailored Pouch of genuine Pin Morocco. Has wide gussets at sides and bottom. Roomy practical bag. Individual enameled initial. Extra high grade plain gold color frame with inner swinging change pocket. Fine lustrous lining. Beveled mirror. Size, 9¼x6½ in.

(F) **18K876—$1.98** Shpg. wt., 1 lb. *Colors:* Brown and tan or black and gray. State choice. Back Strap Bag of boarded grain leather with good quality lizard grain leather in two-tone shade to harmonize. Gold color frame. Swinging change purse. Moire lining. Mirror. An unusual value. Size, 8¼x5¾ inches.

(G) **18K882—$1.98** Shpg. wt., 1¼ lbs. *Colors:* Brown or black. State color. Arm Bag of fine boarded leather in beautiful hand tooled effect. Real hand lacing. Top strap handle. Three roomy pockets. Nicely lined. Change purse and mirror metal frame. Size, 8x4¼ inches.

(H) **18K884½—$2.98** Shipping weight, 1¼ pounds. Print initial wanted. Pouch Bag of genuine calf leather in dark brown with sides and center panel in wanted lizard grain in two-tone tan and brown to harmonize. Individual gold initial stamped on tab pull. Adds that personal touch. Gold color frame. Swinging change pocket. Beveled mirror. Moire lining. Size, 8¼x6 inches.

(I) **18K886—$1.69** Shipping weight, 1¼ pounds. An amazing value. All leather Bag of medium quality in attractive brown alligator grain. Handsome gold color frame with swinging change purse. Fancy lining. Mirror. Size, 8¼x5¾ inches.

(K) **18K888—$1.00** Shipping weight, 1 pound. *Colors:* Brown and tan or Black and gray. State choice. Top Strap Arm Bag of good grade leatherette in reptilian grain with three wide strips of smooth leather. Exceptionally low price. Three roomy pockets. Mirror. Neatly lined. Nickel plated frame. Size, 9x5¼ inches.

(L) **18K890—$1.48** Shipping weight, 1 pound. *Colors:* Brown or Black. State choice. Arm Bag of smooth cowhide leather in tooled design. Top strap. Three pockets. Nickel plated frame. Mirror. Nicely lined. Size, 8¼x4½ inches.

(M) **18K894—79c** Shipping weight, 1 pound. *Colors:* Brown or Black. State choice. Durable leatherette Arm Bag at a special bargain price. Attractive tooled design. Nickel plated frame. Three pockets. Mirror. Neatly lined. Size, 8¼x5 inches.

(N) **18K896—$1.00** Shipping weight, 1 pound. *Colors:* Tan with brown, or black with gray. State choice. Stylish Pouch Bag of good quality lizard grain leatherette with contrasting leather trim on pull tab and outside handkerchief pocket. Gold color frame. Swinging change purse. Neatly lined. Mirror. Big bargain. Size, 8⅝x5⅛ inches.

Newest Shapes and Leathers

(A) $3.48

(B) $2.98 New Back Strap

Long Wear
Fine Leather
Hand Laced

Mirror Under-Tab
(A) $3.48 Special Value

(C) $4.95 Carried Two Ways

Outstanding Value
$4.98 —
Pouch Bag of good quality Spanish style leather in rich dark brown shade beautifully embossed in hand tooled effect. Real hand laced. Gunmetal frame with inner swinging change purse. Large roomy compartment. Gives long wear. Mirror. Suede lining. Exceptional Bargain.
18K868—Size, 7x7 in. Shpg. wt., 1¼ lbs.... $4.98

$1.95
(D)

Fitted Vanity
Smart Alligator Grain

NEW SNAKE TRIM

(E) $4.95
Genuine Morocco

INITIAL ON TAB

(G)

Very Special Value

$2.95 —
Genuine Steerhide Hand Laced
Rich dark brown color with shaded design in hand tooled effect. Flap, suede leather lined. Three deep pockets. Nickel plated frame with swinging change purse. Outside handkerchief pocket. Mirror. Neatly lined. Top strap handle.
18K880—9¼x5¼ in. Shpg. wt.. 1½ lbs. $2.95

$4.98 —
Real Pin Morocco
Many Colors With Enameled Initial
Stunning Pouch Bag of fine morocco leather with leather covered frame and trim in snake effect. Imported gold color fittings on center frame in shirred compartments. Beautifully lined. Coin purse in pocket.
18K872½—Colors: Black, brown, gray, tan, blue, red or green. State color. Print initial carefully. Size, 10x6 inches. Shipping weight, 1¼ lbs... $4.98

(F) $1.98

(G) $1.98 Real Hand Lacing Long Wearing Leather

(H) $2.98 Your Initial in Gold

For Descriptions ~ *See Opposite Page*

(J) $1.69 Alligator Grain Leather

(K) $1.00 Special Leather Trimmed

(L) $1.48 Embossed Cowhide Bargain!

NEW MULTIPLE FRAME

(M) 79¢ "Tooled" Design

(N) $1.00 Outside Handkerchief Pocket

$4.95 —
Newest French Tailored Bag of soft extra quality smooth calf leather, featuring new style gold color frame. Has three large pockets, each pocket really a separate purse. a great convenience. Coin purse. Mirror. Beautifully lined.
18K892—Colors: Black or brown. State color. 9½ x 7½ in. Shipping weight, 1½ lbs.

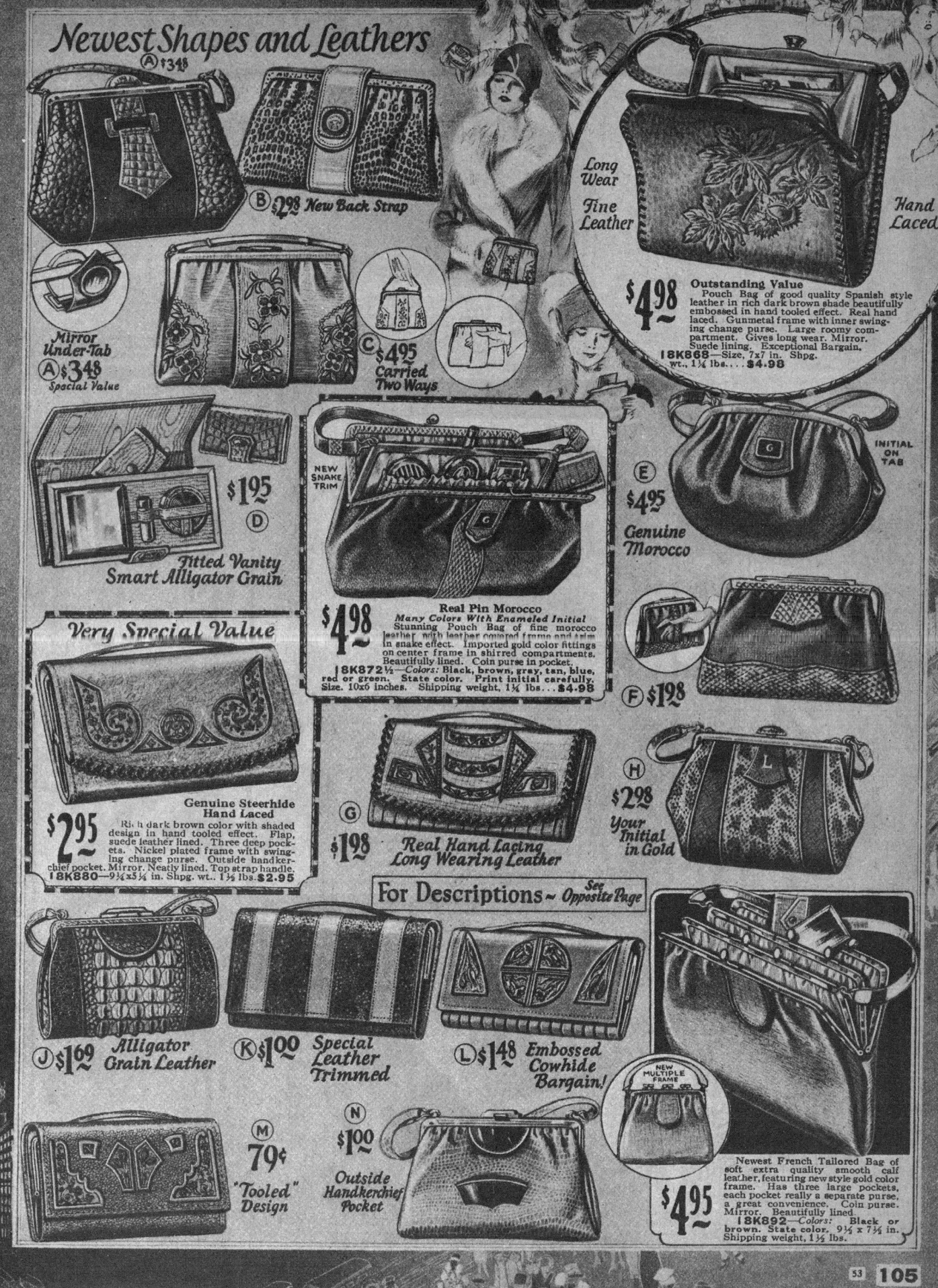

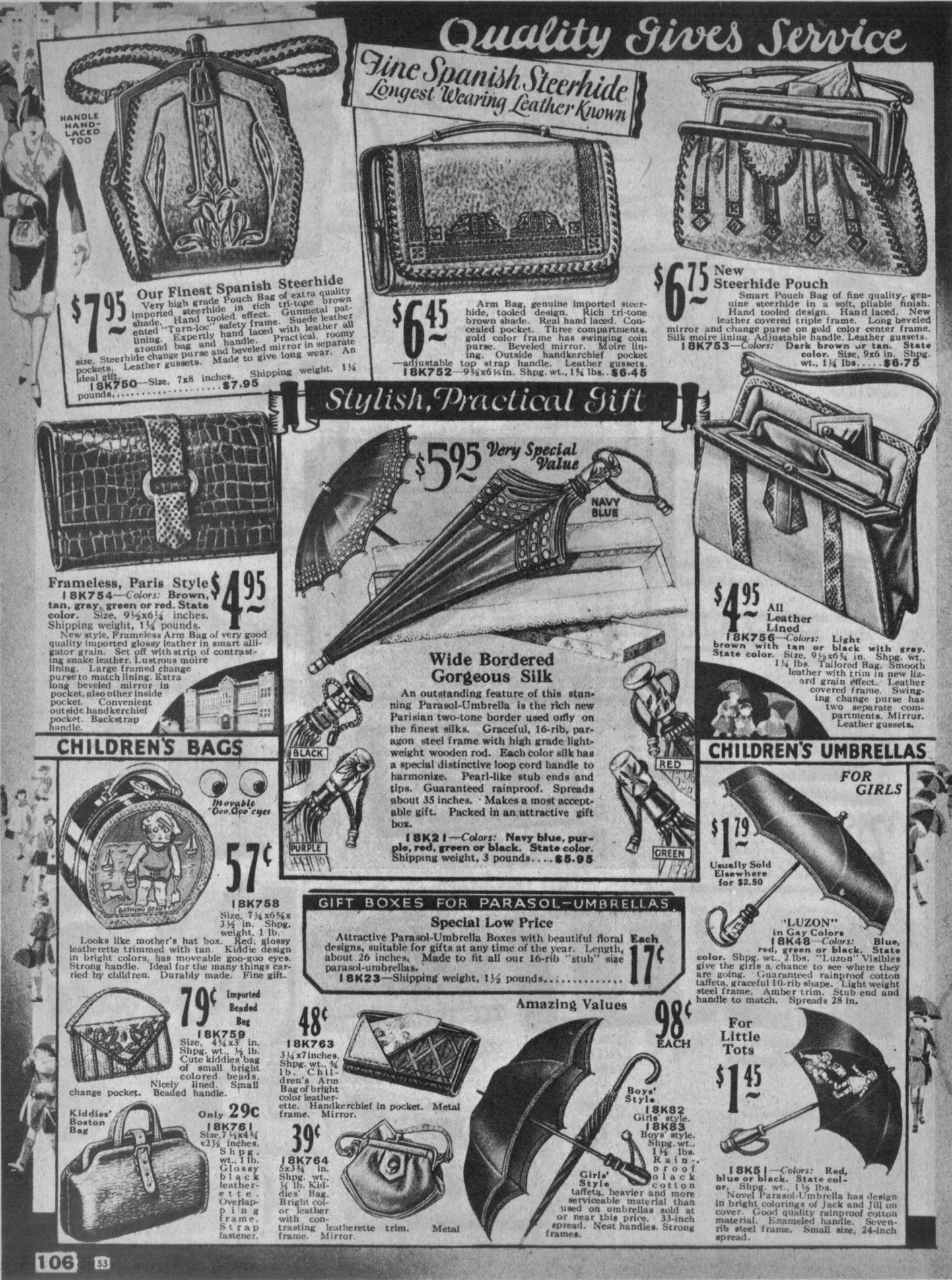

Quality Gives Service

Fine Spanish Steerhide
Longest Wearing Leather Known

HANDLE HAND-LACED TOO

$7.95 **Our Finest Spanish Steerhide**
Very high grade Pouch Bag of extra quality imported steerhide in rich tri-tope brown shade. Hand tooled effect. Gunmetal patented "Turn-loc" safety frame. Suede leather lining. Expertly hand laced with leather all around bag and handle. Practical, roomy size. Steerhide change purse and beveled mirror in separate pockets. Leather gussets. Made to give long wear. An ideal gift.
18K750—Size, 7x8 inches. Shipping weight, 1¾ pounds............**$7.95**

$6.45 Arm Bag, genuine imported steerhide, tooled design. Rich tri-tone brown shade. Real hand laced. Concealed pocket. Three compartments, gold color frame has swinging coin purse. Beveled mirror. Moire lining. Outside handkerchief pocket —adjustable top strap handle. Leather gussets.
18K752—9⅜x6¼ in. Shpg. wt., 1¾ lbs.....**$6.45**

$6.75 **New Steerhide Pouch**
Smart Pouch Bag of fine quality, genuine steerhide in a soft, pliable finish. Hand tooled design. Hand laced. New leather covered triple frame. Long beveled mirror and change purse on gold color center frame. Silk moire lining. Adjustable handle. Leather gussets.
18K753—Colors: Dark brown or tan. State color. Size, 9x6 in. Shpg. wt., 1¼ lbs.....**$6.75**

Stylish, Practical Gift

$5.95 Very Special Value

NAVY BLUE

BLACK

PURPLE

RED

GREEN

Wide Bordered Gorgeous Silk
An outstanding feature of this stunning Parasol-Umbrella is the rich new Parisian two-tone border used only on the finest silks. Graceful, 16-rib, paragon steel frame with high grade lightweight wooden rod. Each color silk has a special distinctive loop cord handle to harmonize. Pearl-like stub ends and tips. Guaranteed rainproof. Spreads about 35 inches. Makes a most acceptable gift. Packed in an attractive gift box.
18K21—Colors: Navy blue, purple, red, green or black. State color. Shipping weight, 3 pounds....**$5.95**

Frameless, Paris Style $4.95
18K754—Colors: Brown, tan, gray, green or red. State color. Size, 9½x6¼ inches. Shipping weight, 1¼ pounds.
New style, Frameless Arm Bag of very good quality imported glossy leather in smart alligator grain. Set off with strip of contrasting snake leather. Lustrous moire lining. Large framed change purse to match lining. Extra long beveled mirror in pocket, also other inside pocket. Convenient outside handkerchief pocket. Backstrap handle.

$4.95 All Leather Lined
18K756—Colors: Light brown with tan or black with gray. State color. Size, 9½x6¾ in. Shpg. wt., 1¼ lbs. Tailored Bag. Smooth leather with trim in new lizard grain effect. Leather covered frame. Swinging change purse has two separate compartments. Mirror. Leather gussets.

CHILDREN'S BAGS

Movable "Goo Goo eyes"

57¢
18K758
Size, 7¼x6⅝x 3¼ in. Shpg. weight, 1 lb.
Looks like mother's hat box. Red, glossy leatherette trimmed with tan. Kiddie design in bright colors, has moveable goo-goo eyes. Strong handle. Ideal for the many things carried by children. Durably made. Fine gift.

79¢ Imported Beaded Bag
18K759
Size, 4¾x3 in. Shpg. wt., ¼ lb.
Cute kiddies' bag of small bright colored beads. Nicely lined. Small change pocket. Beaded handle.

Only 29c Kiddies' Boston Bag
18K761
Size, 7½x4¾ x2¾ inches. Shpg. wt., 1 lb. Glossy black leatherette. Overlapping frame. Strap fastener.

48¢
18K763
3¼x7 inches. Shpg. wt., ¾ lb. Children's Arm Bag of bright color leatherette. Handkerchief in pocket. Metal frame. Mirror.

39¢
18K764
5x3¾ in. Shpg. wt., ¼ lb. Kiddies' Bag. Bright color leather with contrasting leatherette trim. Metal frame. Mirror.

GIFT BOXES FOR PARASOL-UMBRELLAS
Special Low Price
Attractive Parasol-Umbrella Boxes with beautiful floral designs, suitable for gifts at any time of the year. Length, about 26 inches. Made to fit all our 16-rib "stub" size parasol-umbrellas.
18K23—Shipping weight, 1½ pounds.............
Each 17¢

Amazing Values

98¢ EACH
Boys' Style 18K82
Girls' style. 18K83 Boys' style. Shpg. wt., 1½ lbs. Rainproof black cotton taffeta, heavier and more serviceable material than used on umbrellas sold at or near this price. 33-inch spread. Neat handles. Strong frames.

Girls' Style

CHILDREN'S UMBRELLAS

FOR GIRLS

$1.79
Usually Sold Elsewhere for $2.50
"LUZON" in Gay Colors
18K48—Colors: Blue, red, green or black. State color. Shpg. wt., 2 lbs. "Luzon" Visibles give the girls a chance to see where they are going. Guaranteed rainproof cotton taffeta, graceful 10-rib shape. Light weight steel frame. Amber trim. Stub end and handle to match. Spreads 28 in.

For Little Tots
$1.45
18K51—Colors: Red, blue or black. State color. Shpg. wt., 1½ lbs.
Novel Parasol-Umbrella has design in bright colorings of Jack and Jill on cover. Good quality rainproof cotton material. Enameled handle. Seven-rib steel frame. Small size, 24-inch spread.

106
53

The Place to Buy Umbrellas

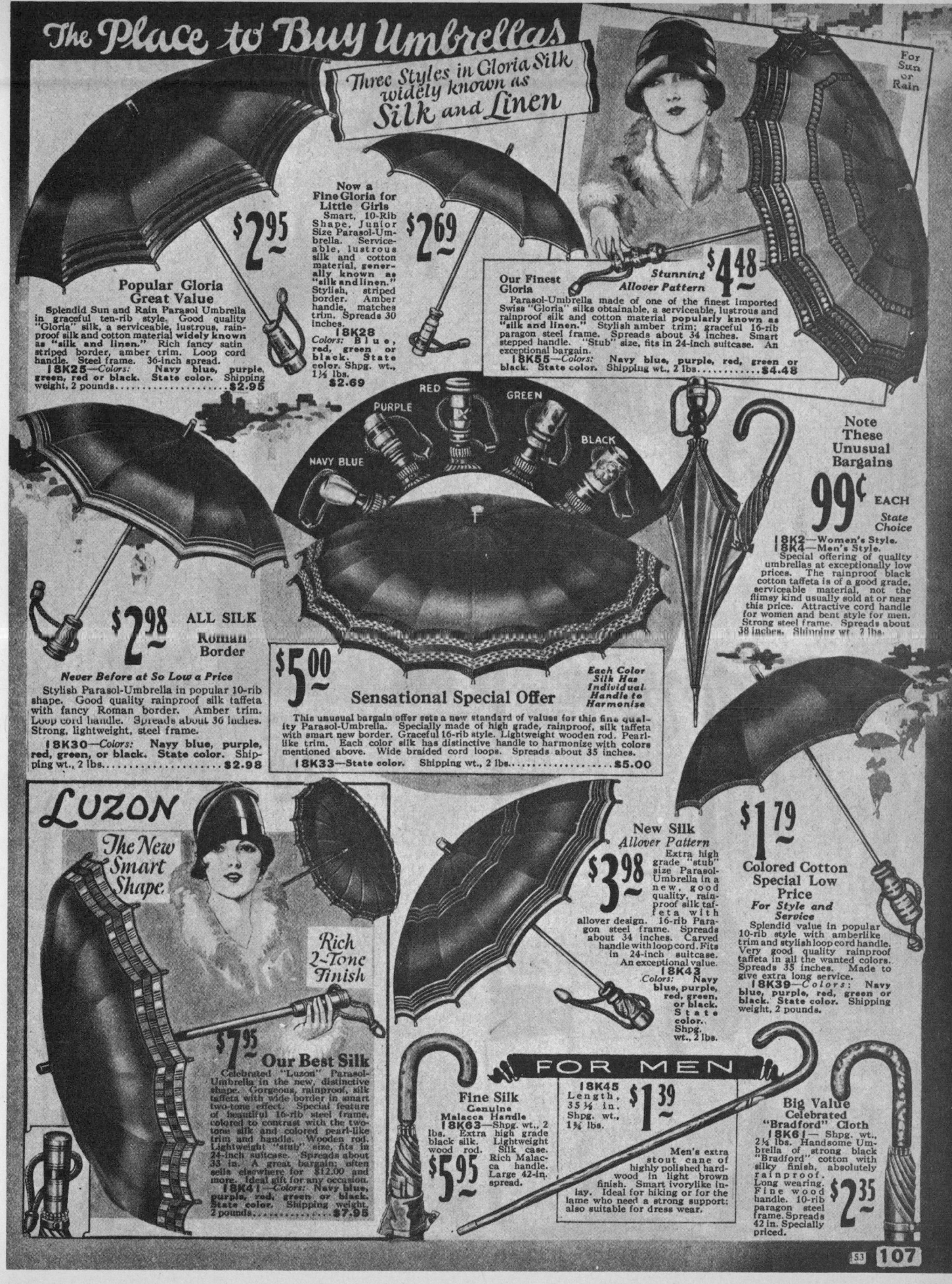

For Sun or Rain

Three Styles in Gloria Silk widely known as Silk and Linen

$2.95
Popular Gloria Great Value

Splendid Sun and Rain Parasol Umbrella in graceful ten-rib style. Good quality "Gloria" silk, a serviceable, lustrous, rainproof silk and cotton material widely known as "silk and linen." Rich fancy satin striped border, amber trim. Loop cord handle. Steel frame. 36-inch spread.
18K25—*Colors:* Navy blue, purple, green, red or black. State color. Shipping weight, 2 pounds.................$2.95

$2.69
Now a Fine Gloria for Little Girls

Smart, 10-Rib Shape, Junior Size Parasol-Umbrella. Serviceable, lustrous silk and cotton material, generally known as "silk and linen." Stylish, striped border. Amber handle, matches trim. Spreads 30 inches.
18K28—*Colors:* Blue, red, green or black. State color. Shpg. wt., 1½ lbs. $2.69

$4.48
Our Finest Gloria Stunning Allover Pattern

Parasol-Umbrella made of one of the finest imported Swiss "Gloria" silks obtainable, a serviceable, lustrous and rainproof silk and cotton material popularly known as "silk and linen." Stylish amber trim; graceful 16-rib paragon steel frame. Spreads about 34 inches. Smart stepped handle. "Stub" size, fits in 24-inch suitcase. An exceptional bargain.
18K55—*Colors:* Navy blue, purple, red, green or black. State color. Shipping wt., 2 lbs..........$4.48

PURPLE **RED** **GREEN**

NAVY BLUE **BLACK**

$2.98
ALL SILK Roman Border

Never Before at So Low a Price

Stylish Parasol-Umbrella in popular 10-rib shape. Good quality rainproof silk taffeta with fancy Roman border. Amber trim. Loop cord handle. Spreads about 36 inches. Strong, lightweight, steel frame.
18K30—*Colors:* Navy blue, purple, red, green, or black. State color. Shipping wt., 2 lbs.................$2.98

$5.00
Sensational Special Offer

Each Color Silk Has Individual Handle to Harmonize

This unusual bargain offer sets a new standard of values for this fine quality Parasol-Umbrella. Specially made of high grade, rainproof, silk taffeta with smart new border. Graceful 16-rib style. Lightweight wooden rod. Pearl-like trim. Each color silk has distinctive handle to harmonize with colors mentioned above. Wide braided cord loops. Spreads about 35 inches.
18K33—State color. Shipping wt., 2 lbs.................$5.00

Note These Unusual Bargains
99¢ EACH
State Choice

18K2—Women's Style.
18K4—Men's Style.
Special offering of quality umbrellas at exceptionally low prices. The rainproof black cotton taffeta is of a good grade, serviceable material, not the flimsy kind usually sold at or near this price. Attractive cord handle for women and bent style for men. Strong steel frame. Spreads about 38 inches. Shipping wt. 2 lbs.

LUZON
The New Smart Shape
Rich 2-Tone Finish

$7.95
Our Best Silk

Celebrated "Luzon" Parasol-Umbrella in the new, distinctive shape. Gorgeous, rainproof, silk taffeta with wide border in smart two-tone effect. Special feature of beautiful 16-rib steel frame, colored to contrast with the two-tone silk and colored pearl-like trim and handle. Wooden rod. Lightweight "stub" size, fits in 24-inch suitcase. Spreads about 33 in. A great bargain; often sells elsewhere for $12.00 and more. Ideal gift for any occasion.
18K41—*Colors:* Navy blue, purple, red, green or black. State color. Shipping weight, 2 pounds.................$7.95

$3.98
New Silk Allover Pattern

Extra high grade "stub" size Parasol-Umbrella in a new, good quality, rainproof silk taffeta with allover design. 16-rib Paragon steel frame. Spreads about 34 inches. Carved handle with loop cord. Fits in 24-inch suitcase. An exceptional value.
18K43—*Colors:* Navy blue, purple, red, green, or black. State color. Shpg. wt., 2 lbs.

$1.79
Colored Cotton Special Low Price
For Style and Service

Splendid value in popular 10-rib style with amberlike trim and stylish loop cord handle. Very good quality rainproof taffeta in all the wanted colors. Spreads 35 inches. Made to give extra long service.
18K39—*Colors:* Navy blue, purple, red, green or black. State color. Shipping weight, 2 pounds.

FOR MEN

Fine Silk
Genuine Malacca Handle
18K63—Shpg. wt., 2 lbs. Extra high grade black silk wood rod.
$5.95
Silk case. Rich Malacca handle. Large 42-in. spread.

$1.39
18K45 Length, 35½ in. Shpg. wt., 1¾ lbs.
Men's extra stout cane of highly polished hardwood in light brown finish. Smart ivorylike inlay. Ideal for hiking or for the lame who need a strong support; also suitable for dress wear.

Big Value
Celebrated "Bradford" Cloth
18K61—Shpg. wt., 2½ lbs. Handsome Umbrella of strong black "Bradford" cotton with silky finish, absolutely rainproof. Long wearing. Fine wood handle. 10-rib paragon steel frame. Spreads 42 in. Specially priced.
$2.35

Women Everywhere Know This Is Corsetry

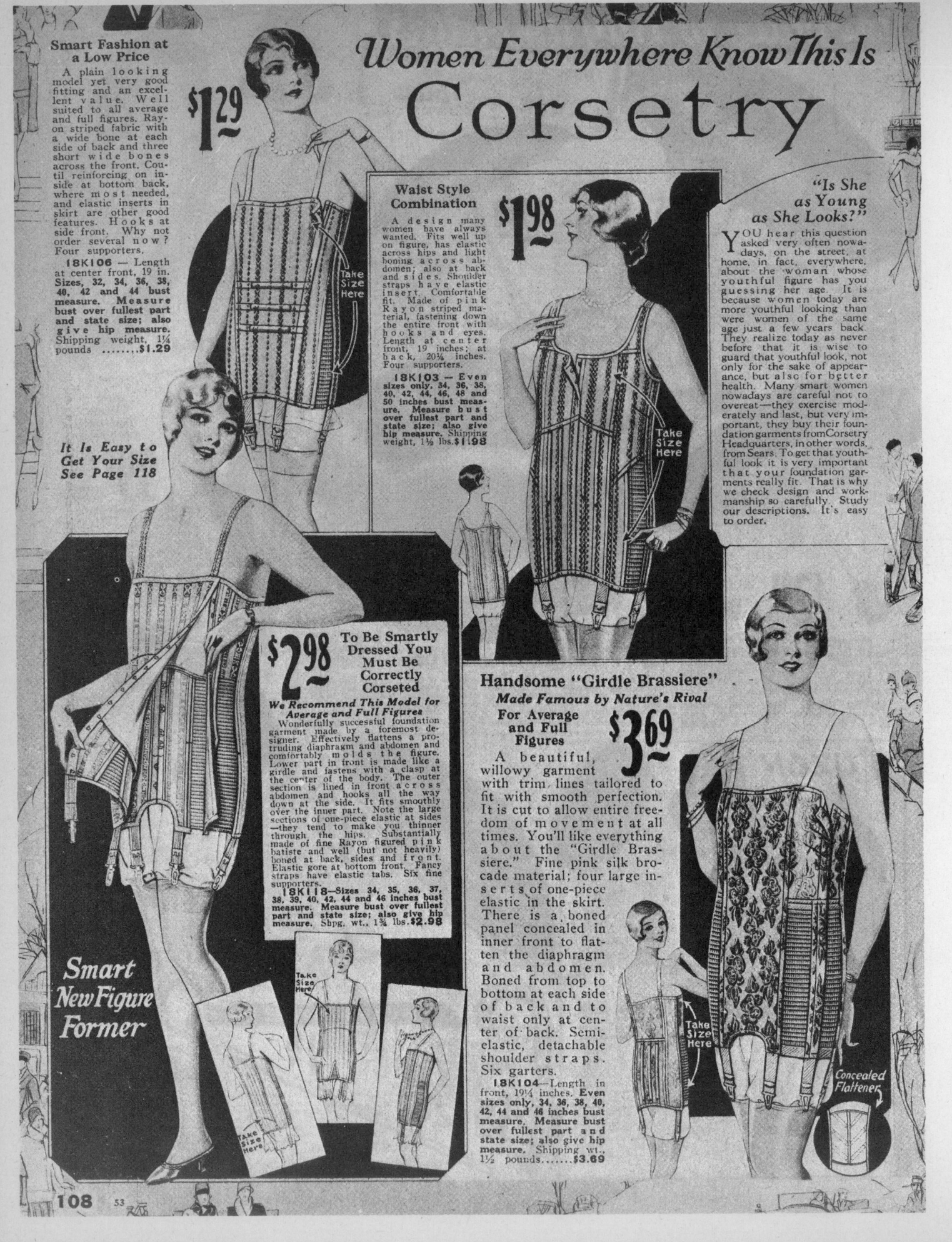

Smart Fashion at a Low Price

$1.29

A plain looking model yet very good fitting and an excellent value. Well suited to all average and full figures. Rayon striped fabric with a wide bone at each side of back and three short wide bones across the front. Coutil reinforcing on inside at bottom back, where most needed, and elastic inserts in skirt are other good features. Hooks at side front. Why not order several now? Four supporters.

18K106 — Length at center front, 19 in. Sizes, 32, 34, 36, 38, 40, 42 and 44 bust measure. Measure bust over fullest part and state size; also give hip measure. Shipping weight, 1¼ pounds $1.29

Take Size Here

It Is Easy to Get Your Size See Page 118

Waist Style Combination

$1.98

A design many women have always wanted. Fits well up on figure, has elastic across hips and light boning across abdomen; also at back and sides. Shoulder straps have elastic inserts. Comfortable fit. Made of pink Rayon striped material, fastening down the entire front with hooks and eyes. Length at center front, 19 inches; at back, 20¾ inches. Four supporters.

18K103 — Even sizes only, 34, 36, 38, 40, 42, 44, 46, 48 and 50 inches bust measure. Measure bust over fullest part and state size; also give hip measure. Shipping weight, 1½ lbs.$1.98

Take Size Here

Take Size Here

"Is She as Young as She Looks?"

YOU hear this question asked very often nowadays, on the street, at home, in fact, everywhere, about the woman whose youthful figure has you guessing her age. It is because women today are more youthful looking than were women of the same age just a few years back. They realize today as never before that it is wise to guard that youthful look, not only for the sake of appearance, but also for better health. Many smart women nowadays are careful not to overeat—they exercise moderately and last, but very important, they buy their foundation garments from Corsetry Headquarters, in other words, from Sears. To get that youthful look it is very important that your foundation garments really fit. That is why we check design and workmanship so carefully. Study our descriptions. It's easy to order.

To Be Smartly Dressed You Must Be Correctly Corseted

$2.98

We Recommend This Model for Average and Full Figures

Wonderfully successful foundation garment made by a foremost designer. Effectively flattens a protruding diaphragm and abdomen and comfortably molds the figure. Lower part in front is made like a girdle and fastens with a clasp at the center of the body. The outer section is lined in front across abdomen and hooks all the way down at the side. It fits smoothly over the inner part. Note the large sections of one-piece elastic at sides —they tend to make you thinner through the hips. Substantially made of fine Rayon figured pink batiste and well (but not heavily) boned at back, sides and front. Elastic gore at bottom front. Fancy straps have elastic tabs. Six fine supporters.

18K118—Sizes 34, 35, 36, 37, 38, 39, 40, 42, 44 and 46 inches bust measure. Measure bust over fullest part and state size; also give hip measure. Shpg. wt., 1¾ lbs.$2.98

Smart New Figure Former

Take Size Here

Take Size Here

Take Size Here

Handsome "Girdle Brassiere"

Made Famous by Nature's Rival

For Average and Full Figures

$3.69

A beautiful, willowy garment with trim lines tailored to fit with smooth perfection. It is cut to allow entire freedom of movement at all times. You'll like everything about the "Girdle Brassiere." Fine pink silk brocade material; four large inserts of one-piece elastic in the skirt. There is a boned panel concealed in inner front to flatten the diaphragm and abdomen. Boned from top to bottom at each side of back and to waist only at center of back. Semi-elastic, detachable shoulder straps. Six garters.

18K104—Length in front, 19¼ inches. Even sizes only, 34, 36, 38, 40, 42, 44 and 46 inches bust measure. Measure bust over fullest part and state size; also give hip measure. Shipping wt., 1½ pounds......$3.69

Take Size Here

Concealed Flattener

the Place to Buy the Modern Garments
Headquarters

Our "Co-Ed"
New Soft Figure Former without Single Bone or Stay

$1.95

We Are the World's Largest Retailers

of Modern Corsetry and buy from the foremost and finest makers in the country. Each new and practical idea is added at once to our line, and among our pages you are sure to find an up to date model just suited to your individuality, giving you correct body control to make your figure lovely.

The tremendous quantities we sell enable us to buy at rock bottom prices, and the savings effected are passed on to our customers, making possible the sensational values we offer. We use only tested fabrics, interlinings, garters, bonings, etc., in our garments. This makes for long wear and satisfaction. Many women have learned of the greater satisfaction of buying Modern Corsetry from our Headquarters and you, too, will be of this vast army if you give us a chance to serve you.

Stunning Model for Average and Stout Figures

Very Special Value

Splendid style with a concealed, flattening and reducing pad with loop supporters attached (note small view indicating concealed features). Of fine lustrous Rayon figured pink batiste with large sections of fine surgical elastic at sides; also at top and bottom of back. Full length boning through back section only. Self material shoulder straps with elastic tabs. 18K173—Even sizes, 34, 36, 38, 40, 42, 44, 46 and 48 inches bust measure. Measure bust over fullest part and state size; also give hip measure. Length, 19½ inches. Shipping weight, 1½ pounds.

$2.79

Its presence—so invisible under your frock. Soft corseting is preferred by many smartly dressed youthful figures and our "Co-Ed" fills the need. Made of Rayon striped pink material with elastic all the way down each side and across the thighs; no boning. The section across abdomen is lined and well stitched to impart just a little support. Hooks at left side and has four supporters. Lgt., center front, 19½ in. 18K125 Even sizes, 30, 32, 34, 36, 38, 40 and 42 inches bust measure. Measure bust over fullest part and state size; also give hip measure. Shpg. wt., 1¼ lbs. $1.95

STYLE HINT:—

Shape Your Figure Into Slim Lines of Beauty by Wearing the Lovely "Pliant-B"

The Justly Famous CorseTrim

Favorite of Thousands
Its Popularity Is Most Certainly Deserved

Corsetrim is a stylish and practical patented garment which gives corset trim to the figure. It confines the bust and hips and diaphragm, is light, yet strong and flexible, and gives all women correct support and the fashionable figure with great ease. Inner girdle attached to each side has elastic at top for comfort and clasps directly at center of body. The front panel, fastening at side, fits over inner girdle, giving slender figure and a graceful, smooth front. Lacing in back from waist down permits perfect hip adjustment. Entire front length, 21 in. 18K172 Corsetrim of fancy weave, durable pink cotton material. Even sizes only, 32, 34, 36, 38, 40, 42, 44, 46 and 48 inches bust measure. Measure bust over fullest part and state size; also give hip measure. See page 118 for "How to Measure." Shipping weight, 1¾ lbs.

$1.69

"Pliant-B"

Our New High Grade Combination Garment

Lower part in front and at sides of back is shaped like a girdle and is cleverly fashioned of various sections of one-piece elastic. It hugs the body ever so comfortably, thereby subtly bringing out the feminine line. Fastens with a broad end clasp at direct body center. The front panel of fine Rayon fabric cares for the bust and fits neatly over the lower part, giving a flat front and longer figure lines. Center of garment at back is of Rayon fabric, with elastic at top for comfort. The elastic along entire bottom edge cups the figure snugly, giving trim hip lines and it expands comfortably when seated. Moderately boned, six garters. 18K110—Color: Pink. Length at front, 19¼ inches. Even sizes, 34, 36, 38, 40, 42, 44, 46 and 48 inches bust measure. Measure bust over fullest part and state size; also give hip measure. Shipping weight, 1¼ lbs.

$4.95

Headquarters for the Celebrated
Dr. Wine's Health Garments

Quickly Adjusted to Your Own Physical Need

Dr. Wine's Improved Health Garments are the result of extensive research work and, in our opinion, are the best garments of their kind ever produced. Scientifically constructed inner belt gently lifts the abdomen and holds it in its natural place most comfortably, thereby assisting nature in bringing permanent relief. Truly wonderful for all women requiring abdominal support or wishing to reduce. Also recommended for women suffering from abdominal troubles and before and after maternity.

Inner belt fastens in center with strong hooks and eyes, each half being fitted with a thin, slightly bent, narrow stay of "Surgic-Alloy" metal which is very easily bent to cup into just the right shape to fit the abdomen. These "Surgic-Alloy" stays can be straightened from time to time as the lines of the figure improve through wearing of this garment. Lower front part of belt has short wire stays for corrective and comfortable abdominal support. Belt is attached to inner sides by lacings and is easily raised, lowered or let out, therefore wonderfully suited to every abdominal need. The outer part fits neatly over the inner belt, giving a smooth and more slender line.

Take Size Here

Dr. Wine's Health Corset

Has the scientifically fitted, health assisting inner belt and all features described above. The corset part of fine pine coutil is boned throughout with strong stays and has elastic insert at top front and at bottom back. Clasps smoothly over inner belt, giving a straight and slimmer figure (see small view at top). It is laced at back and fitted with three pairs of strong supporters. Order size 2 inches smaller than waist measure taken over your corset; give hip measure as outlined on page 118. Shipping weight, 2½ pounds.

$3.98~

Regular Sizes
24, 25, 26, 27, 28, 29, 30, 31, 32, 33, 34, 35 and 36 inches.

$4.95~

Extra Large Sizes
38, 40, 42, 44, 46, 48 and 50 inches.

Order the Model for Your Figure
18K394—Tall Figure Model. Bust, 3 inches; skirt, 15½ inches; clasp, 8½ inches. Note price of sizes.

18K395—Short Average Figure Model. Bust, 2 inches; skirt, 13 inches; clasp, 7½ inches. Note price of sizes.

Dr. Wine's Health Corselet

A single combination garment to take care of the bust, waist, abdomen and hips. Has the scientifically fitted health assisting inner belt and all fine features described above. Outer part of fine Rayon striped fabric has a section of elastic over each hip (see small view) and concealed boning at front; also moderate boning at back and sides. Lacers at back waist down permit perfect hip adjustment.
18K388—Sizes, 34, 36, 38, 40, 42, 44, 46, 48 and 50 inches bust size. Measure bust over fullest part and state size; also give hip measure. See chart on page 118. Shipping weight, 2 pounds.

$3.98~

Take Size Here

Dr. Wine's Slenderizing Health Belt

For General Wear

These belts are today considered one of the highest forms of corsetry. Excellent for home, sport, dress or street wear, not only for the stout but for the average and slender figure, too. They create a stylish contour, support the abdomen in its proper position, reduce the hips and abdominal girth and do away with the pushing of flesh into unsightly bulges and the compression of the diaphragm. Also recommended for obesity, for the tendency of rupture or colon trouble, for pregnancy and after childbirth. Dr. Wine's Health Belt has all the special health assisting features described above and is made of elastic and cloth in front and all cloth back and is correctly boned. The elastic used is special "Armor-Lastic," having a patented regulated stretch. It can be laundered freely without injury. Its life is three times that of ordinary elastic. Fastens in center with strong hooks and eyes. Lacing at sides and bottom front permits wonderful adjustment. Shipping weight, 1½ pounds.

Take Size Here

To Order Your Size

Take waist measure over your corset and deduct 2 inches. (If measure is 36, order size 34.) Note prices of sizes.

$2.98~
18K385—Sizes 24, 25, 26, 27, 28, 29, 30, 31, 32, 33, 34, 35 and 36 inches. Order size as above.

$3.98~
18K386—Extra large sizes, 38, 40, 42, 44, 46, 48, 50 and 52 inches. Order as above.

Prof. Gale Tru-Lift Health Belts

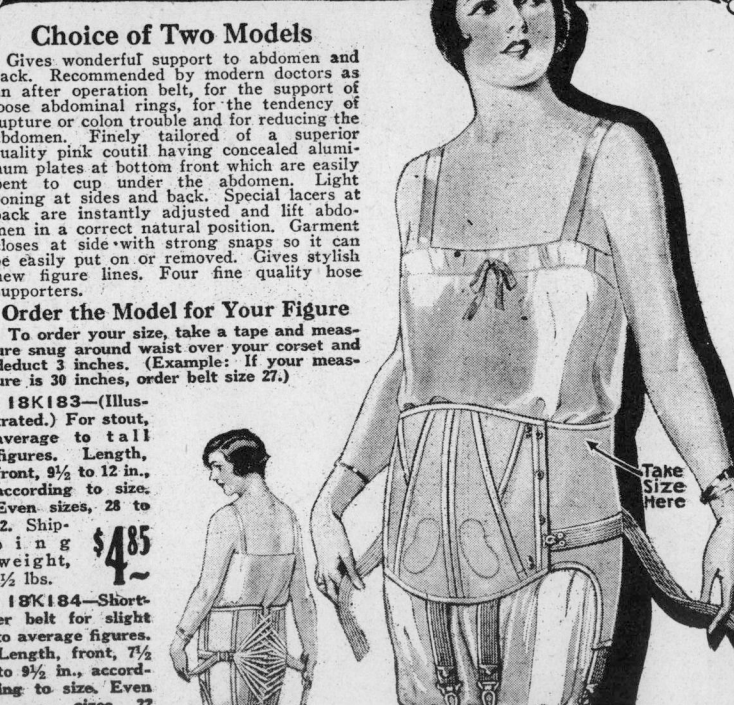

Choice of Two Models

Gives wonderful support to abdomen and back. Recommended by modern doctors as an after operation belt, for the support of loose abdominal rings, for the tendency of rupture or colon trouble and for reducing the abdomen. Finely tailored of a superior quality pink coutil having concealed aluminum plates at bottom front which are easily bent to cup under the abdomen. Light boning at sides and back. Special lacers at back are instantly adjusted and lift abdomen in a correct natural position. Garment closes at side with strong snaps so it can be easily put on or removed. Gives stylish new figure lines. Four fine quality hose supporters.

Order the Model for Your Figure

To order your size, take a tape and measure snug around waist over your corset and deduct 3 inches. (Example: If your measure is 30 inches, order belt size 27.)

18K183—(Illustrated.) For stout, average to tall figures. Length, front, 9½ to 12 in., according to size. Even sizes, 28 to 52. Shipping weight, 1½ lbs.
$4.85~

18K184—Shorter belt for slight to average figures. Length, front, 7½ to 9½ in., according to size. Even sizes, 22 to 44. Shipping wt., 1 lb.
$3.65~

Take Size Here

Our Famous Comfort Corsets

"Bends With the Body"

$3.39 Stylish Stout Figure Model

18K407 Pink. Low bust, 2⅛ inches; long skirt, 14½ inches; broad end clasp, 8½ inches. All odd and even sizes, 23 to 30. Order your corset size 2 inches smaller than waist measure taken over corset. Shipping weight, 2 pounds.

18K409—Extra large sizes, 32, 34, 36, 38 and 40. State size as above. **$3.69**

Well known model that will give slender lines plus the average to tall stout figure. Strong, pink coutil, extra well boned. Large sections of elastic at top and hips. Note reinforced front to flatten figure. Has Coiled Comfort Boning. Extra heavy supporters.

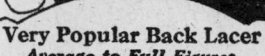

Very Popular Back Lacer
Average to Full Figures

$2.79

18K105—White coutil. Medium bust, 4 in.; skirt length, 14 inches; broad end clasp, 10½ inches. All odd and even sizes, 21 to 30; also 32. Order your corset size 2 inches smaller than waist measure taken over your corset. Shipping wt., 1½ lbs.

Favorite model worn by thousands of satisfied customers. Substantially made of fine white coutil, having roomy skirt and bust. Well boned with our famous unbreakable and non-rustable Coiled Comfort Boning. Stitched belt across abdomen adds strength and gives better abdominal support. Four supporters.

Average and Stout Figures
$3.39

18K344—Pink. Low bust, 2 inches; long skirt, 14¼ inches; clasp, 9 inches. All sizes, 22 to 30; also 32, 34 and 36. Order corset size 2 inches smaller than waist measure taken over corset. Shipping weight, 1¾ pounds.

Laced front corset of strong pink coutil with elastic sections at bust and bottom back. Special sewed down sections of double thickness coutil across hips and front tend to comfortably suppress fleshy thighs and abdomen, giving slimmer hip lines. Boned with our famous Coiled Comfort Boning.

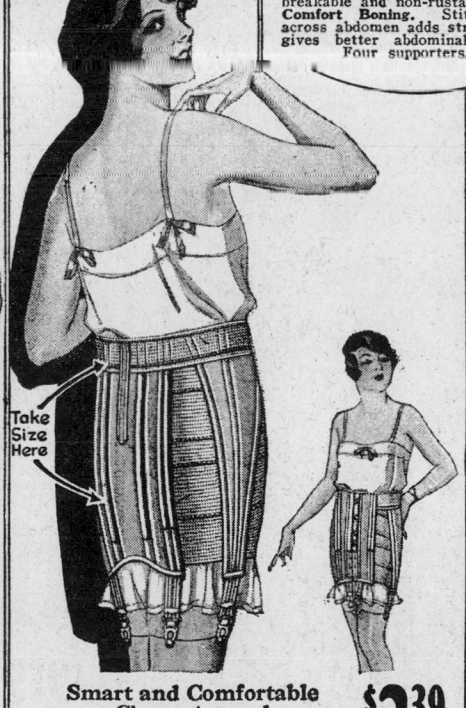

Smart and Comfortable Clasp Around
$2.39

18K140—Low 1½-inch bust. Skirt waist down 13½ inches. Sizes, 25, 26, 27, 28, 29, 30, 31, 32, 33, 34, 35, 36 and 38 inches waist measure. Order your actual waist measure taken over corset and dress; also state hip measure taken about 7½ inches below waist. Shipping weight, 1¾ pounds.

Look youthful and stylish! Flatten your back and take in your abdomen and hips with this new and charming non-lacing model. Well constructed of fine quality pink coutil with four sections of surgical elastic in skirt and elastic across entire top. Has our famous Coiled Comfort Boning which bends with the body. Clasps at center front with a 7½-inch flexible clasp, having three strong hooks below.

Average and Full
$1.98

18K301 — Medium bust, 3 in.; skirt, 14 in.; clasp, 7½ in. All odd and even sizes, 21 to 30; also 32, 34 and 36. Order your corset size like 18K451 at right. Shpg. wt., 1¼ lbs.

Back lacing corset in a free hip full skirt model of Rayon figured pink batiste. Elastic at top, front and sides. Has Coiled Comfort Boning.

For Average and Stout Figures
$2.98

18K451—Pink. Bust, 3¼ inches; skirt, 13½ inches; broad end clasp, 9½ inches. All even and odd sizes, 24 to 30. Order corset size 2 inches smaller than waist measure taken over corset. Shipping weight, 1¾ pounds.

18K453—Extra sizes, 32, 34 and 36. State size as above. **$3.25**

A back lacing model of strong pink coutil well stayed with our famous Coiled Comfort Boning.

Inner belt of elastic and coutil fastens in center and has loop supporters attached, always keeping belt in position and giving real support and smooth lines.

Send Sufficient Money for Postage on Parcel Post Shipments. Any Surplus Will Be Returned

117

IT IS EASY for You to Order Your Size

Fine Back Lacer
For Average to Tall Stout Women

$2.75

For those inclined to be stout, we suggest this high grade back lacing model. Well tailored to give needed support and apparent reduction to the entire figure. Substantially made of fine quality pink coutil with heavy rubber sections at bust and bottom skirt. Double coutil across the front and abdomen makes for longer wear. Well boned at front and more heavily boned at back with double strength rust resisting stays. Fashionable low bust 2 inches; shaped higher at back. Long skirt 14¾. Broad end clasp 9 inches with three hooks below.

18K426—Sizes 24, 25, 26, 27, 28, 29 and 30. Order corset sizes 2 inches less than waist measure taken over corset. Shipping weight, 2 pounds...........$2.75

18K427—Same model as above in extra large sizes, 31, 32, 33, 34, 35, 36, 38 and 40. State corset size as above. Shipping weight, 2¼ lbs....$2.98

Take Size Here

Please do not guess your size—use a tape to measure with as shown here. Follow the measuring directions given for the garment you are ordering and be sure to give us all information requested. If your hips are very much larger than your bust you are better fitted in a back lacing, step-in, or a clasp around model. Please use care in ordering—help us to give you real first class service.

Note Where to Measure

For Bust Size— Measure all around at the fullest part of bust, keeping tape measure well up under arms.

Waist— To get waist size measure all around body at smallest part.

Hips— To get hip size measure all around body, about 7½ inches below waist.

BUST
WAIST
HIPS

Take Size Here

A Favorite with Average and Stout Figures

$1.98

Comfort, Health and Style garments are famous for value, fit and high quality. Anything that goes into the making of them must be of standard and tested quality. Our aim is always to improve rather than cheapen. Models shown on our "Modern Corsetry" pages have real merit. We will not catalog garments made just to sell. The tremendous quantities we use enable us to buy at rock bottom prices so as to make possible the sensational values we offer.

Exceptional value, low bust, back lacing model of good quality pink coutil with elastic at top and bottom back. Made double across abdomen insuring long wear. Well boned with double strength stays. Stylish low bust, 2 inches; skirt, 14 inches; broad end clasp, 9 inches. Four supporters.

18K443—All odd and even sizes, 23 to 30; also 32, 34 and 36 inches. Order corset size 2 inches smaller than waist measure taken over your corset. Shpg. wt., 1½ lbs.

Are You Short?

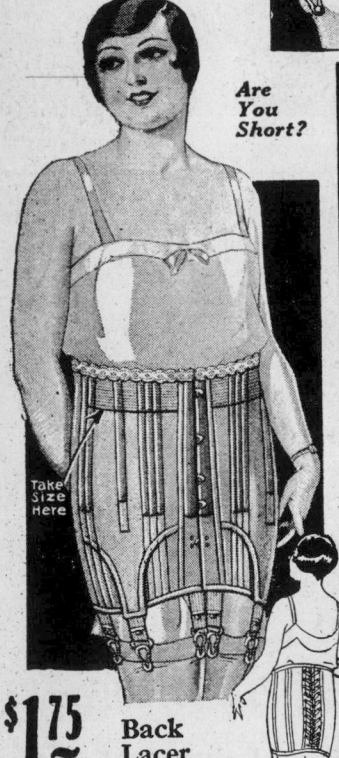

Ever-sta Models

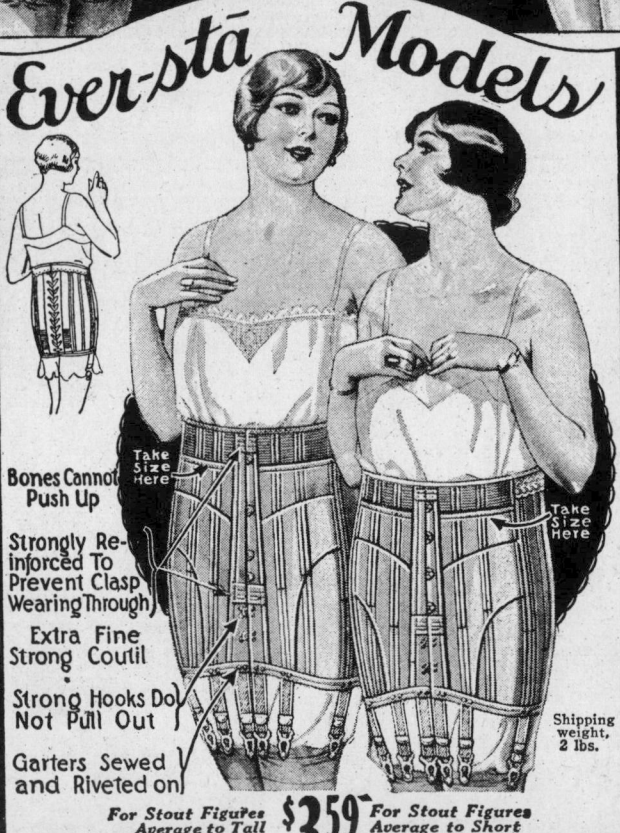

Bones Cannot Push Up

Strongly Reinforced To Prevent Clasp Wearing Through

Extra Fine Strong Coutil

Strong Hooks Do Not Pull Out

Garters Sewed and Riveted on

Take Size Here

$1.75 Back Lacer
For Short Figures Average to Stout

18K142—All even and odd sizes, 24 to 30. Order corset size 2 inches smaller than waist measure taken over corset. Shipping weight, 1½ lbs.

18K144—Extra large sizes, 32, 34 and 36. State size.....................$1.95

Specially designed for short average to stout figures by one of America's leading makers. It is of good quality pink coutil and well boned with non-rustable stays. Double coutil sections across front give wonderful abdominal support and a smooth fitting front; elastic at bust for comfort. Low bust, 2¼ inches; short skirt, 12½ inches. Broad end clasp, 8 inches; six supporters.

For Stout Figures Average to Tall

18K147—Back lacer, bust, 3¼ inches; skirt, 15 inches; broad end clasp, 10 inches. State corset size..............$3.59

Odd and even sizes, 24 to 36 inches; also even sizes, 38 to 44 inches. Order corset size 2 inches smaller than waist measure taken over your corset.

$3.59 EACH

For Stout Figures Average to Short

18K148—Back lacer, bust, 3 inches; skirt, 12½ inches; broad end clasp, 9½ inches. State corset size.....$3.59

Ever-Sta (pronounced ever-stay) means a special patented construction whereby the strong yet resilient boning does not twist or push through the cloth. It also prevents the stripping (stay covering) from wrinkling and causing discomfort. These models have proved immensely popular with our customers. Double sections of coutil across abdomen and sides with heavy elastic at bottom back, molds and reduces flesh through the abdomen and hips. Large inserts of sturdy, comfort giving elastic. Six strong supporters.

Take Size Here

Shipping weight, 2 lbs.

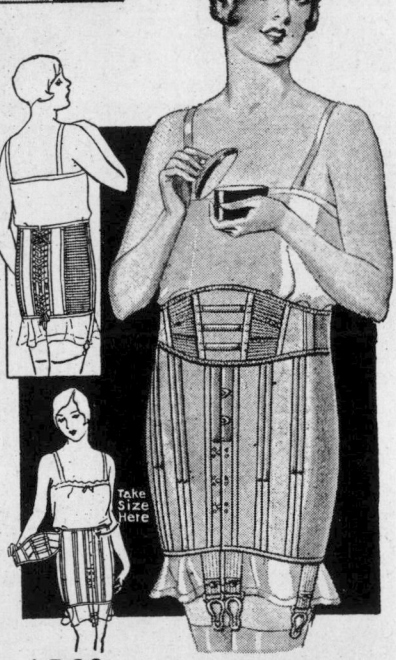

Take Size Here

$2.89 Back Lacer With Diaphragm Reducer

Specially designed for the figure having excess flesh at diaphragm. Reducer of coutil and elastic is lightly boned and extends across the front top of corset hooking at the sides; it can be detached for washing. The corset is made of pink coutil with a wide section of one-piece (14 inch) surgical elastic at each side of back, (see small view above.) It is sent you all laced up at back. Four good supporters.

18K154—Very low bust, 1½ inches; skirt, waistdown, 12½ inches. Short comfortable clasp, 6½ inches with three hooks below. All even and odd sizes, 24 to 32, also 34 and 36 inches waist measure. Order corset size 2 inches smaller than waist measure taken over your corset. Shpg. wt., 1¾ lbs.

Stylish Items *for Your* Special Attention

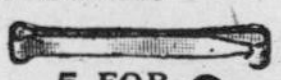

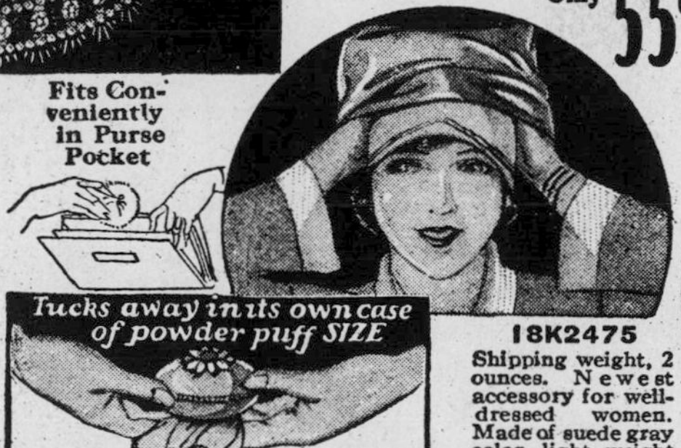

"New Joan Bob Cover"

Rubber Covered Prongs

Stemless Switch Style With Clasp That Holds Securely on Shortest Hair

Change your "bob" style hairdress to the appearance of long hair in an instant with this new hair piece. The patented clasp designed especially to attach securely to even shingled hair. Attached or released with greatest ease. Many becoming dressings can be easily arranged. Also used as a stemless switch if desired. Clasp may be quickly detached for dressings that do not require it. Two qualities. All shades except gray. Shipping weight, ¾ pound.
Send sample for price on gray or white.
18K4303—"Fairy-Touch," Our Strictly First Quality "Stemless," Switches. Shipping weight, ¾ pound.

Length	Weight	
16 inches	¾ ounce	$3.98
18 inches	1¼ ounces	5.75
22 inches	1¾ ounces	8.75

18K4301—Our French Triple Refined Quality Switches. Fine soft grade. Shipping weight, ¾ pound.

Length	Weight	
16 inches	¾ ounce	$1.98
18 inches	1½ ounces	3.25
22 inches	2 ounces	4.65

"Fairy-Touch" Quality Means Highest Grade

Our exclusive brand Strictly Pure First Quality Genuine Human Hair. (No mixtures, no refined hair with misleading names.) That soft, dainty texture like your own, not obtainable in any refined qualities. Perfect workmanship, full weight and length. Beautiful lasting wave. Priced far below what is usually asked for real First Quality Goods. We list below prices for all regular shades and a separate list for gray and white mixtures. Shipping weight, ¾ lb.
18K4477—"Fairy-Touch" First Quality Switches in three separate stems, the most practical style. Be sure to send good sample.

Length	Weight	Regular Ordinary Shade	Gray and White Mixtures
18 inches	1¼ ounces	$3.98	$6.39
20 inches	1½	5.75	7.89
22 in. Note This Great Value	1¾ oz.	$7.95	$9.98
24 inches	2	$9.75	$12.89
26 inches	2½	12.98	14.95
28 inches	3 ounces	14.95	Write for Prices

Our Famous French Triple Refined Switches

Often sold by others as "Finest Quality." Genuine human hair refined by our special process to an exquisitely soft texture. Much superior to cheaply made coarse switches sometimes offered at prices near ours. Permanently wavy. Neat short stems securely woven. Note very low prices. We list below prices for all regular shades and a separate list for gray and white mixtures. Shipping weight, ¾ pound.
18K4458—Three Separate Stem French Refined Switches. Send good size sample of your hair.

Length	Weight	Regular Ordinary Shades	Gray and White Mixtures
18 inches	1¼ ounces	$1.89	$2.39
20 inches	1½ ounces	2.49	2.95
22 in. Special Favorite	1¾ oz.	$3.69	$3.95
24 inches	2¼ ounces	$4.35	$4.95
26 inches	2½ ounces	5.48	Write
28 inches	2¾ ounces	6.45	for
30 inches	3¼ ounces	7.98	Prices

NOTE: If shade varies in front and back send two samples stating preference.

Low Priced Switches Selected Medium Quality
A Very Popular Grade

18K4457—Three Stem Switches, Genuine Human Hair, comes only in black and ordinary brown shades. Send good size sample of your hair. For drabs, blondes, auburns or gray mixtures order 18K4458. Shipping weight, ¾ pound.

Length	Weight	
18 in.	1¼ oz.	$0.98
22 in.	1¾ oz.	1.75
24 in.	2 oz.	2.45

Improved Front Piece at Special Low Price

Popular priced outside piece designed as a covering for thin or faded hair. New improved construction. Quickly adjusted. Held securely with elastic band. Hair finishes about 16 inches. Beautifully marcelled, giving that finished dressy appearance. We match all shades. Send good size sample of your hair. Shipping weight, 1 pound.
"Fairy-Touch," Strictly First Quality
18K4497—Standard Shades only $7.95
Gray and White Mixed 11.98
French Triple Refined Quality
18K4499—Standard Shades only $4.69
Gray and White Mixed 6.48

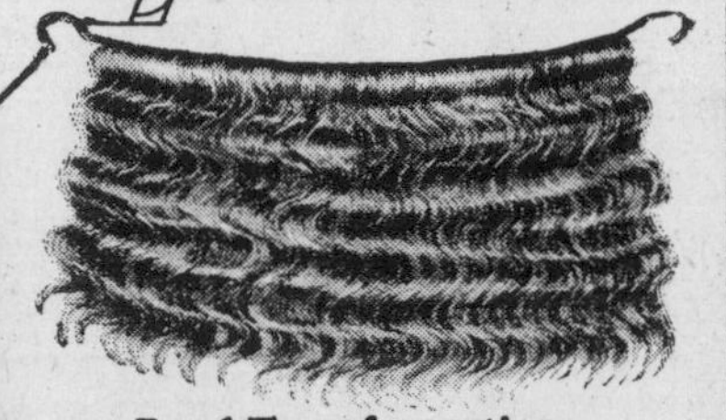

The Patricia Wave

Natural looking Front Piece, hand ventilated center part. Made on silk gauze reinforced by vegetable lace foundations measuring 4½x2 inches. Beautifully marcelled. Hair finishes about 14 inches. Send good size sample to match. "Fairy-Touch" Strictly First Quality. Shipping weight, 1 pound.
18K4447—Standard Shades $10.95
Gray and White Mixed 13.95
French Triple Refined Quality
18K4448—Standard Shades 7.25
Gray and White Mixed 9.45

Band Transformations

Especially desirable for women with thin hair. Usually worn under your own hair. This practical 22-inch band encircles the head. Full length and weight. Three qualities offered. We match all shades. Send good size sample to match. Shipping weight, ¾ pound.
"Fairy Touch"—Strictly Pure First Quality
18K4440—Regular Shades $6.98
Gray and White Mixed 9.95
French Triple Refined Quality
18K4424—Regular Shades $3.19
Gray and White Mixed 4.48
Selected Medium Quality
18K4432—Ordinary Black or Brown Shades. Only.................. $2.29

Women's French Bob Wig

Very fine Imported Wig now at a greatly reduced price. Has natural silk gauze right side drawn parting. Hand ventilated throughout. These beautiful lightweight French wigs are extensively used by women of fashion. Their fine natural appearance makes Milady look her best at all times. Can be had as illustrated above in either curly, wavy or shingled style. State choice. Shipping weight, 1 pound.
18K4401—All ordinary shades. Only....... $26.75

Important Facts About Hair Quality

Few women are well informed on the many grades of human hair. As a result, they are often offered under misleading names. Even experts find it difficult at times to distinguish the difference in quality. Inferior quality soon becomes apparent after wearing the hairpiece. It fades, becomes streaky, straggly or brittle very quickly. Our hair qualities are guaranteed exactly as described, an especially valuable feature in this kind of merchandise.

Latest Hair Style Book

Showing newest fashions in hair dressing arranged by our expert, Madame Annette, who will also cheerfully help you solve any of your hair dressing problems. Ask for hair booklet No. 8556K. Mailed on request, or sent with each hair goods order. Address inquiries to Madame Annette, Hair Goods Department.

How to Order Hair

Send a full length sample, cut from the head close to the roots. (Combings are not good samples.) Pin sample to your order stating whether you wish roots, center or ends matched. We match center unless otherwise specified. We do not make switches or hair pieces from combings.

Made to Order
Perfect Fitting Toupees and Wigs for Men and Women

Expertly made of only finest material. Perfect satisfaction guaranteed. Order from this catalog, if familiar with measurements and instructions required. Otherwise write for illustrated booklet 8287K. Specially made and delivered in about two weeks.
For Men: Our Famous Toupee. A great favorite. Best quality obtainable anywhere, at any price. Now made with durable natural looking silk gauze parting and foundation. Shipping weight, 8 ounces.
18K4423.....................$35.95
18K4423X—For gray shades.......39.75
18K4428—12 Sheets Toupee Plasters, 45c
18K4436.....................$54.75
18K4436X—For gray shades......58.95
Our best men's featherweight full wig. All silk gauze foundation. Natural looking parting. Completely hand ventilated. Finest workmanship and materials. Shipping weight, 8 oz.

We Ship Promptly

We ship most hair goods orders within 24 hours, because we carry a very large stock of average shades. Even special shades usually require only from five to eight days.

Famous *Fairy-Touch* Hair Net IMPORTED

The favorite of American women. Made by hand of selected and thoroughly sterilized genuine human hair that is scientifically handled, giving it better wearing qualities than ordinary nets. Every mesh in every "Fairy-Touch" net is guaranteed perfect. Specially packed in our beautiful "Fairy-Touch" envelopes.
Nets are now much worn at night to protect the marcel or water waves.
Our Famous "Fairy-Touch" Quality Nets are the finest to be had. Handmade of selected human hair, cap shape, easily conform to the hairdress and keep the hair tidy. Choice of two styles. Regular full size for the usual hairdress, or new snug fitting bob size for bobbed hairdress. Every mesh perfect. Our special packing insures receipt in best condition. Colors: Black, blonde, light brown, medium brown, dark brown or auburn (red). State color. Shipping weight, 2 ounces.

Two Styles
Regular Full Size
Snug Fitting "Bob" Size
6 for 43¢
Guaranteed equal to any 10-cent net on the market
DOUBLE MESH *Gives Extra Wear.*
18K2607—Regular Full Size, 6 for 43c
18K2609—New "Bob" Size, Colors, 6 for 43c
18K2610—White or gray. Regular full size .... 4 for 59c

SINGLE MESH
18K2601—Full Size, Cap Shape Single Mesh. All standard colors .... 6 for 43c
18K2602—Cap Shape, White Only .....4 for 52c

Imported Silk Nets

Nets ← 12 for 39¢ →

Elastic Edge Silk Cap Shape
18K2598—Made in France, especially for full cap size, single mesh, to slip over hairdressing fitted with elastic edge to hold in place. Keeps bobbed hair tidy. Durable, good looking perfect nets. Same colors as 18K2600.

Silk Full Size Tied Ends
18K2600—Single Mesh Silk Nets, large size with tied ends, direct from France. Every net perfect. Colors: Black, blonde, light brown, medium brown, dark brown, auburn (red) or gray. Shipping weight, 2 ounces.

Be Your Own Hairdresser

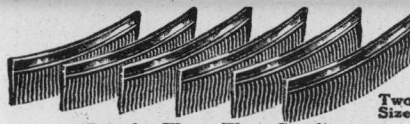

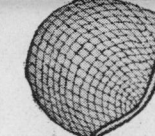

Popular Water Wave Combs
Our well known water wave combs, with extra long crimped teeth. Make deep graceful waves. Usually retail at 10 cents for each comb. Brown shell color. Shipping weight, 7 ounces.
18K2479—5 inches long. Set of 6 .... **35c**
18K2480—6 inches long. Set of 6 .... **39c**

Water Wave Combs Complete Set
6 for 19c
18K2469 — Shipping weight, 5 ounces. Practical 6-inch length with the popular wavy teeth. Usually retail at 5 cents for each comb. Brown shell color.

Popular "O Boy" Curlers and Wavers
Great for Bobbed Hair

6 for 43c
18K2433—Shipping weight, 4 oz. New "O Boy" Snappy Curler now with a heavier rubber covered rod, holds the hair tightly, forming the curls to the very ends. Very practical waver and curler. Constructed so hair is curled without breaking. Can be used for long hair also. Full directions included with each order.

The DupleX Hairpin
"Rules Unruly Bobs"
30 Pins for 11c
Entirely new type hair pin made of flexible steel which holds the hair firmly in place. Each DupleX pin does the work of several ordinary hairpins. Mounted 10 pins to a card.
18K2525—Colors: BLACK or BRONZE. State choice. Shipping weight, 2 ounces.

Large Assortment
15c

18K2522—Shpg. wt., ¾ lb. Cabinet containing about 300 Black Wire Hairpins, assorted sizes, including "invisible" style.

Scolding Locks
Two-Way Hairpins
20c Worth of Pins for **13c**

400 Pins for .... Patented invisible, black enameled wire hairpins. 400 assorted, 1½, 1¾ and 2-inch sizes.
18K2459 — Shipping weight, 4 ounces **13c**

Our Price, **9c**

18K2514
Shpg. wt., 2 oz. "Sta-Rite" Patented Invisible Crimped Wire Hairpins. 100 assorted, 1½ to 1⅝-inch size.

New Imported Water Wave Cap
37c
Large size coiffure Cap especially made for use with water waving combs. Easily fits overcombs, holding them firmly in place; also used for sport wear and as a boudoir cap. Made of a brown mercerized cotton mesh, absorbs moisture and will give long wear. Elastic edge.
18K2470—Shipping weight, 2 ounces.

Save That Wave!
37c
18K2474 Colors: Light blue or light pink. State color. Shipping wt., 2 oz. Smart Imported Coiffure Cap in a lovely new style. Ideal for use as a coiffure cap to hold hairdress in place. Deep full size. Elastic chinband makes cap fit snugly. Made of a fine quality mercerized cotton mesh.

The Green Witch WATER WAVER
$2.45 Set of 6 Wavers
For Marcel Effect Use Green Witch Wavers
Beautiful deep graceful water waves assured with these new patented improved Green Witch Wavers. Dampen hair, insert wavers, lock them in position. Remove wavers when hair is dry and a lovely natural looking wave is there. Makes thin hair appear plentiful; also keeps a permanent wave set. No annoyance of wearing wavers overnight. Made of lightweight silverlike metal. Simple illustrated instructions enclosed are easy to follow. (Extra wavers at 45c each.)
18K2523 — Length, 7¾ inches. Shipping wt., 7 oz. Set of 6.... **$2.45**

Celluloid Hairpins
24 Pins for 23c
18K2508—Brown shell or yellow amber color. State color. 2½ inches long. Shipping weight, each box, 2 oz. Crimped Celluloid Hairpins. Special value.

12 Pins for 25c
18K2503—Brown shell or yellow amber color. State color. Fine Celluloid Crimped Hair pins, 3 inches long.

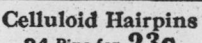

6 Pins for 17c
18K2506—Brown shell or yellow amber color. State color. 3½ inches long, heavy weight. Our best crimped celluloid Hairpins.

12 Pins for 15c
18K2504—Three-inch pins. Crimped Celluloid Hairpins. Brown shell color only.

Challenge Waver

98c
A waver gives the soft effect which is becoming so fashionable. Produces a natural looking style and is easy to operate. To make the prettiest waves use our Challenge Waver. Shipping weight, 1 pound.
57K3720—For 110-volt city current only **98c**

Curling Iron Heater
Heats your iron the safe, clean electric way. Iron is ready for use a short time after the heater is connected. Heavy molded base, guaranteed heating element and strong aluminum tube which keeps the iron warm for some time after the current is turned off. A regular professional heater which may be used with curlers 18K2437, 18K2467 and 18K2471 shown on this page. Shipping weight, each, 2½ pounds.
57K3391—For 110-volt city current only ....
$2.55

Our Most Popular Water Wave Combs

Two Sizes Wavy Pattern With Extra Long Teeth
Improved wavy pattern Water Wave Combs with extra long crimped teeth. They hold fast. Make deep waves more quickly. Dampen hair and leave combs in until dry. Brown shell color. Shipping wt., 7 ounces. Usually sold elsewhere at 60 cents set of 6 combs. Note our prices.
18K2482 5 in. long. Set of 6. **39c**
18K2483 6 in. long. Set of 6. **43c**

New Imported Marcel Iron
83c Easy to Operate
18K2471—Length, 10¾ in. Shpg. wt., ¾ lb. Great bargain. Revolving Handle French Marcel Iron of nickel plated heat retaining steel. Black wood handles. Will not slip—holds ends tightly. Makes large or small waves.

48c

Professional Marcel Iron at Low Price
18K2467—French type Marcel Iron. Compares with irons usually sold at much higher prices. Length, 11 inches. Shipping weight, ¾ pound. **48c**

With Enameled Wooden Handles
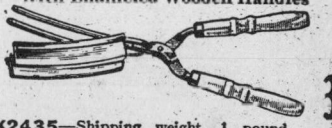
39c
18K2435—Shipping weight, 1 pound. Marcel Waver. Nickel plated and especially made to retain heat. Length, 10½ inches.

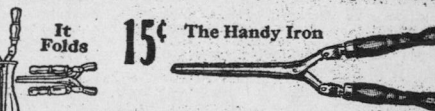
15c
Nickel Plated Marcel Waver
18K2455—Shipping weight, 1 pound. Improved Marcel Waver for making deep graceful hair waves. Nickel plated. Length, 9 inches.

It Folds **15c**
The Handy Iron
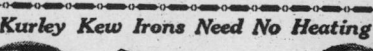
18K2437—Shipping weight, 7 ounces. Folding Curling Iron. Wooden handles. Length, folded, 5¾ inches. Nickel plated. Handy for the woman traveler. Takes up little space.

Kurley Kew Irons Need No Heating
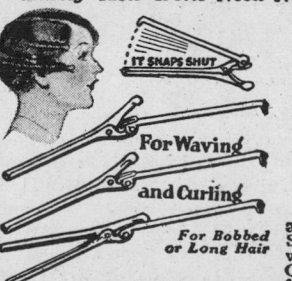
IT SNAPS SHUT
For Waving and Curling
For Bobbed or Long Hair
3 for 25c
Fashioned like a curling iron. Snaps in place with spring lock. Curls the hair from the very ends where most needed and quickly makes deep graceful waves. Simply clasp the ends of the hair with curler as with regular curling iron and roll up (either over or under). For best results use 6 to 9 curlers.
18K2472—Length, closed, 3½ in. Shpg. wt., 4 oz.

Newest Creations

An Exquisite Imported Chamoisuede Glove $1.59 PER PAIR
33K3375 Mode.
33K3376—Silver moon.
33K3377 French blonde.
Sizes, 6 to 8½. Half sizes. State size. Shpg. wt., 3 oz.
Women's Finest Quality Imported Two-Plex (similar to double thickness) Pre-Shrunk Washable Chamoisuede Fabric Gloves. A very chic turnover cuff. Fancy embroidered backs. Kip-knot sewed seams and Bolton thumbs. A high grade glove at a reasonable price.

Mode · Silver Moon · French Blonde · French Blonde · Silver Moon · Almond

How to Measure Your Hand for Size— See Page 1095

Imported Pre-Shrunk Chamoisuede $1.49 PER PAIR
33K3339 French blonde.
33K3340—Silver moon.
33K3341—Mode.
Sizes, 6 to 8½. Half sizes. State size. Shpg. wt., 2 oz.
A style fashioned by Europe's best glove experts. Attractive, smart and stylish Gloves of exquisite design. Made of the finest imported pre-shrunk washable chamoisuede fabric. Latest embroidered turnover cuffs. Beautifully embroidered backs. Kip-knot sewed seams and Bolton thumbs. You cannot buy finer gloves even though you pay considerably more than our price.

Different—The New Tinted Stitching on Cuffs and Backs $1.15 PER PAIR
33K3385—French blonde.
33K3386—Almond.
33K3387—Silver moon.
Sizes, 6 to 8½. Half sizes. State size. Shipping weight, 2 ounces.
The season's smartest and newest novelty Turnover Cuff Gloves. Made of a very fine quality imported pre-shrunk washable chamoisuede fabric. Neatly embroidered backs. Kip-knot sewed seams and Bolton thumbs. A combination of style and quality makes this an outstanding value.

Newest Parisian Creation $1.39 PER PAIR
33K3395—Monkey skin.
33K3396—Silver moon.
33K3397—Mode.
Sizes, 6 to 8½. Half sizes. State size. Shipping weight, 2 ounces.
Individuality of design is emphasized in these smart, strictly tailored Turnover Cuff Gloves for women. Made of the finest imported pre-shrunk chamoisuede fabric, in what is considered the best European factory. Handsomely embroidered backs. Kip-knot sewed seams and Bolton thumbs. Highest quality at lowest possible price.

Silver Moon · Monkey Skin · Mode

Imported French Cuff Style 79c PER PAIR
33K3330—Sand.
33K3331—Gray.
33K3332—Beaver.
33K3334—Sable.
Sizes, 6 to 8½. Half sizes. State size. Shipping weight, 2 ounces.
Smart and Stylish Women's Good Quality Imported Washable Chamoisuede Fabric Gloves. Flare cuffs of French design. Heavily embroidered cuffs and backs. Kip-knot sewed seams and Bolton thumbs. Quality gloves at a low price.

Gray · Beaver · Sable · Sand

A Distinctive Model $1.98 PER PAIR
33K3050—Black.
33K3051—Grain.
33K3052—Gray.
33K3053—Brown.
Sizes, 6 to 8. Quarter sizes. State size. Shpg. wt., 4 oz.
Imported Bandelet Style Gloves which are Fashion's favorite this season. Made of selected lambskin usually called kid. Beautifully embroidered backs. Full pique sewed.

Grain · Black · Gray · Brown

$1.69 PER PAIR
33K3672—Black.
33K3673—Rich tan.
Sizes, 6 to 8½. Half sizes. State size. Shipping weight, 5 ounces.
Women's Fine Quality Mohair Lined Gloves. Made of a good quality imported chrome tanned capeskin. Half outseam sewed. Stitched backs. Popular and stylish gloves that will give warmth and real service.

Rich Tan · Black

33K3662 Black
33K3663 Dark tan **$1.98 PER PAIR**
Sizes, 6 to 8½. Half sizes. State size. Shpg. wt., 5 oz.
Wonderful values are these excellent Quality Capeskin Gloves for women. Made of a fine quality imported chrome tanned capeskin with fleeced lining. Strap wrists. Outseam sewed. Ideal for winter wear.

Dark Tan · Black

Smartly Fashioned Chamoisuede Gloves $1.00 PER PAIR
33K3390—Tortoise.
33K3391—Piping rock.
33K3392—Airedale.
Sizes, 6 to 8½. Half sizes. State size. Shipping weight, 2 ounces.
Fashionable Imported Slip-On Gloves. Made of a fine quality pre-shrunk double-plex (double woven) imported chamoisuede fabric. Newest "saddle stitch" seams and back. The greatest value in fashionable gloves ever offered to our customers.

Piping Rock · Tortoise · Airedale

The Latest All Wool Sport Model 98c PER PAIR
33K3420—Sand.
33K3421—Golden brown.
33K3422—Gray.
Sizes, 6 to 8½. Half sizes. State size. Shpg. wt., 5 oz.
A very new and smart Sport Model Glove for women. Made of a fine quality fully shrunk all wool yarn in the season's newest colors. The newest swagger style button cuff.

Gray · Golden Brown · Sand

A Splendid Value 55c PER PAIR
33K3620—Brown.
Sizes, 6 to 8½. Half sizes. State size. Shpg. wt., 5 oz.
Women's Fur Top Fine Gauge Jersey Cloth Gloves. Durable fleeced lining. Good looking, inexpensive gloves that will give warmth and service.

Brown

$2.75 PER PAIR
33K3695—Black.
33K3696—Rich tan.
Sizes, 6 to 8½. Half sizes. State size. Shipping weight, 5 ounces.
Specially selected, imported capeskin is used in the manufacture of these Gloves. Fine quality fur top. Warm fleeced lining. A style suitable for sport or motor wear. Strap wrist. Outseam sewed. One of our biggest bargains.

Rich Tan · Black

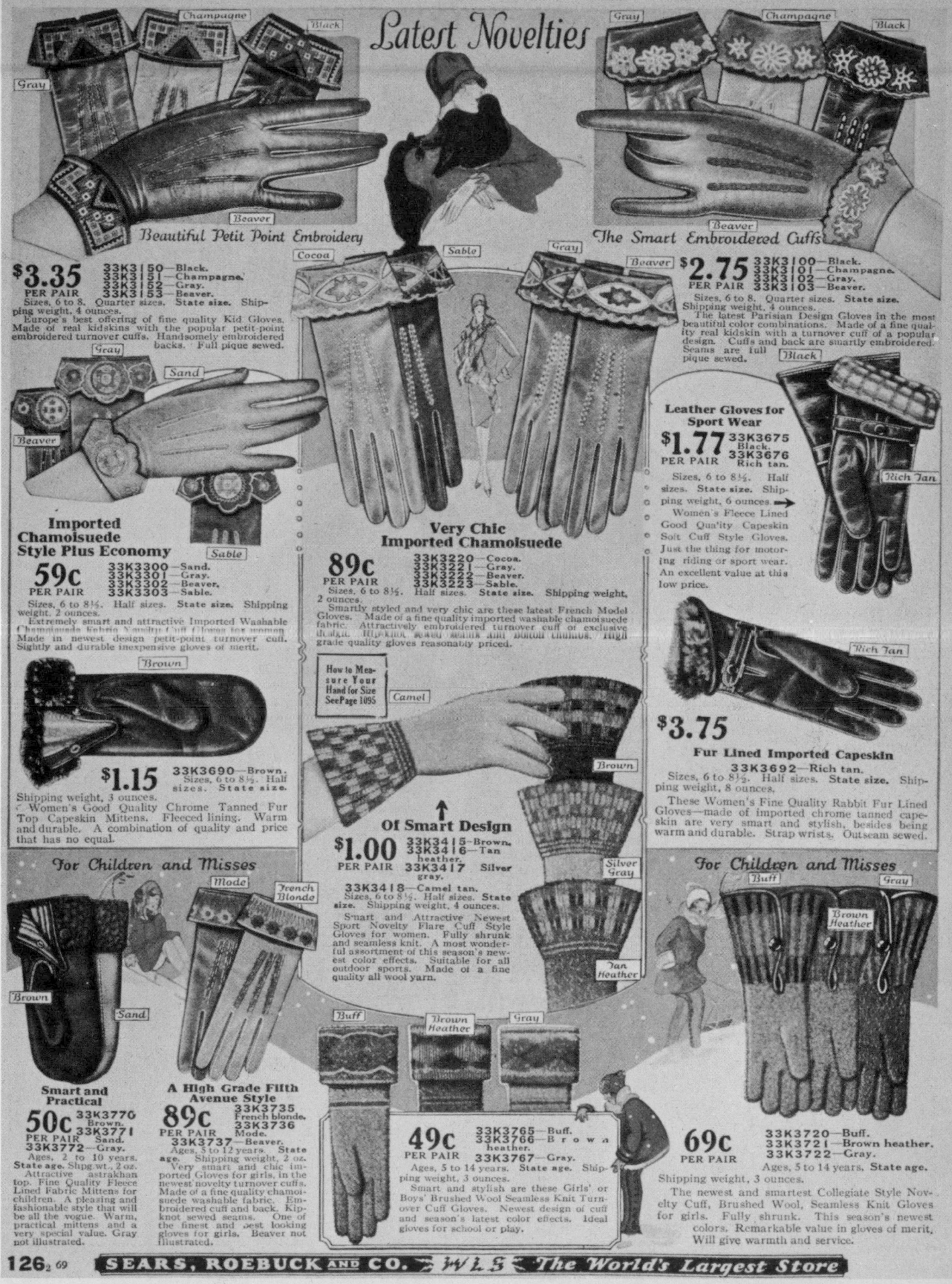

Latest Novelties

Beautiful Petit Point Embroidery

$3.35 PER PAIR
33K3150—Black.
33K3151—Champagne.
33K3152—Gray.
33K3153—Beaver.

Sizes, 6 to 8. Quarter sizes. State size. Shipping weight, 4 ounces.
Europe's best offering of fine quality Kid Gloves. Made of real kidskins with the popular petit-point embroidered turnover cuffs. Handsomely embroidered backs. Full pique sewed.

The Smart Embroidered Cuffs

$2.75 PER PAIR
33K3100—Black.
33K3101—Champagne.
33K3102—Gray.
33K3103—Beaver.

Sizes, 6 to 8. Quarter sizes. State size. Shipping weight, 4 ounces.
The latest Parisian Design Gloves in the most beautiful color combinations. Made of a fine quality real kidskin with a turnover cuff of a popular design. Cuffs and back are smartly embroidered. Seams are full pique sewed.

Imported Chamoisuede Style Plus Economy

59c PER PAIR
33K3300—Sand.
33K3301—Gray.
33K3302—Beaver.
33K3303—Sable.

Sizes, 6 to 8½. Half sizes. State size. Shipping weight, 2 ounces.
Extremely smart and attractive Imported Washable Chamoisuede Fabric Novelty Cuff Gloves for women. Made in newest design petit-point turnover cuff. Sightly and durable inexpensive gloves of merit.

Very Chic Imported Chamoisuede

89c PER PAIR
33K3220—Cocoa.
33K3221—Gray.
33K3222—Beaver.
33K3223—Sable.

Sizes, 6 to 8½. Half sizes. State size. Shipping weight, 2 ounces.
Smartly styled and very chic are these latest French Model Gloves. Made of a fine quality imported washable chamoisuede fabric. Attractively embroidered turnover cuff of exclusive design. Hipstitch sewed seams and button thumbs. High grade quality gloves reasonably priced.

How to Measure Your Hand for Size See Page 1095

Leather Gloves for Sport Wear

$1.77 PER PAIR
33K3675—Black.
33K3676—Rich tan.

Sizes, 6 to 8½. Half sizes. State size. Shipping weight, 6 ounces.
Women's Fleece Lined Good Quality Capeskin Soft Cuff Style Gloves. Just the thing for motoring, riding or sport wear. An excellent value at this low price.

$1.15 33K3690—Brown. Half sizes. State size.
Women's Good Quality Chrome Tanned Fur Top Capeskin Mittens. Fleeced lining. Warm and durable. A combination of quality and price that has no equal.

Of Smart Design

$1.00 PER PAIR
33K3415—Brown.
33K3416—Tan heather.
33K3417—Silver gray.
33K3418—Camel tan. State size. Shipping weight, 4 ounces.

Smart and Attractive Newest Sport Novelty Flare Cuff Style Gloves for women. Fully shrunk and seamless knit. A most wonderful assortment of this season's newest color effects. Suitable for all outdoor sports. Made of a fine quality all wool yarn.

$3.75 Fur Lined Imported Capeskin

33K3692—Rich tan.
Sizes, 6 to 8½. Half sizes. State size. Shipping weight, 8 ounces.
These Women's Fine Quality Rabbit Fur Lined Gloves—made of imported chrome tanned capeskin are very smart and stylish, besides being warm and durable. Strap wrists. Outseam sewed.

For Children and Misses

Smart and Practical

50c PER PAIR
33K3770—Brown.
33K3771—Sand.
33K3772—Gray.

Ages, 2 to 10 years. State age. Shpg.wt., 2 oz.
Attractive astrakhan top. Fine Quality Fleece Lined Fabric Mittens for children. A pleasing and fashionable style that will be all the vogue. Warm, practical mittens and a very special value. Gray not illustrated.

A High Grade Fifth Avenue Style

89c PER PAIR
33K3735—French blonde.
33K3736—Mode.
33K3737—Beaver.

Ages, 5 to 12 years. State age. Shipping weight, 2 oz.
Very smart and chic imported Gloves for girls, in the newest novelty turnover cuffs. Made of a fine quality chamoisuede washable fabric. Embroidered cuff and back. Kipknot sewed seams. One of the finest and best looking gloves for girls. Beaver not illustrated.

49c PER PAIR
33K3765—Buff.
33K3766—Brown heather.
33K3767—Gray.

Ages, 5 to 14 years. State age. Shipping weight, 3 ounces.
Smart and stylish are these Girls' or Boys' Brushed Wool Seamless Knit Turnover Cuff Gloves. Newest design of cuff and season's latest color effects. Ideal gloves for school or play.

For Children and Misses

69c PER PAIR
33K3720—Buff.
33K3721—Brown heather.
33K3722—Gray.

Ages, 5 to 14 years. State age. Shipping weight, 3 ounces.
The newest and smartest Collegiate Style Novelty Cuff, Brushed Wool, Seamless Knit Gloves for girls. Fully shrunk. This season's newest colors. Remarkable value in gloves of merit. Will give warmth and service.

Quality Shaker Knit Sweaters
All Have These Famous Features

① *Hand Finished Throughout*

All Seams have been carefully gone over by experienced hand finishers and looped into a smooth, flat finish. No unsightly or bulky seams on Sears Shaker Sweaters.

② *Knit of Guaranteed All Wool Yarns*

ALL WOOL

Every strand of yarn used in these Shaker sweaters is guaranteed 100 per cent all wool.

③ *Reinforced Non-Sagging Shoulders*

An extra reinforcing strip across the shoulders prevents sagging, assures trim fit and holds the sweater in shape.

Double Body Jersey Lined

Regular Sizes $5.98

38K7040—Red.
38K7041—Buff.
38K7042—Black.
Sizes, 34 to 44 inches bust measure. State size. Shpg. wt., 3½ lbs.

Stout Sizes $6.98

38K7044—Red.
38K7045—Buff.
Sizes, 46 to 54 inches bust measure. State size. Shpg. wt., 4 lbs.

The quality of this All Wool Service Sweater is a guarantee of satisfactory wear. A practical, medium heavyweight garment, knit of good quality all wool yarns in the serviceable shaker stitch. Hand finished throughout. Reinforced shoulders prevent sagging and keep the sweater snug fitting. Large, double fabric, shaped collar and reinforced buttonholes. Extra wool yarn is knit into the sleeves at elbows to provide double wear resistance. Well made and built to give satisfaction. No wardrobe is complete without the ever useful shaker sweater. You will like its warmth and serviceability; you will be proud of its fine, comfortable fit and its rich coloring.

Per Set $6.95 — *Two-Piece Set*

38K7031—White.
38K7032—Jockey red.
38K7033—Camel (light tan).
Sizes, 34 to 44 inches bust measure. State size. Shipping weight, 3¼ lbs.
One of Sears big specials! Every woman who participates in winter sports or who just enjoys walking, will be delighted with this wonderful warm, heavy winter weight Pullover Sweater and Cap Set. Knit of good dependable quality all wool yarn in shaker stitch. Exceptionally well made and hand finished throughout. The sweater has reinforced shoulder seams that prevent stretching or sagging and assure trim fit. Has popular storm collar that may be buttoned high around the neck. Hockey cap to match knit in same close shaker stitch with pompon trim.

38K7013—Camel (light tan). $9.48
38K7007—Maroon.

Sizes, 34 to 44 inches bust measure. State size. Shipping weight, 3½ lbs.
For real warmth, good looks and solid comfort, select this finest quality, sturdy, heavyweight Sweater, knit from excellent quality all wool worsted yarns in the popular shaker stitch. Our best sweater. No bulky machine seams, but hand finished throughout, with reinforced shoulder seams that prevent sagging and insure good fit. Has double fabric, shaped collar that may be worn high around neck. Two knit-in pockets. Will stand lots of hard wear. A remarkable value and a high grade garment which would cost much more elsewhere. We know you will be pleased with the appearance and service this excellent quality sweater will give.

38K7001—Maroon.
38K7003—Navy blue. $7.98
38K7004—White.

Sizes, 34 to 44 inches bust measure. State size. Shipping weight, 3½ lbs.
Women who get out of doors a great deal and need an Extra Heavy Sweater will find this a splendid value. It is knit in a heavy weight of excellent quality worsted and wool yarns in the popular shaker stitch. Beautifully hand finished throughout and made with reinforced shoulder seams, that prevent stretching and give a neat, correct fit. Has large, shaped, double fabric shawl collar and two pockets. A garment that has always been in the lead for popularity. A really big price value.

38K7014—Royal blue.
38K7015—Red. $6.98
38K7016—Buff.

Sizes, 34 to 44 inches bust measure. State size. Shipping weight, 3 pounds.
For downright comfort—warmth without weight and absolute body freedom—slip into this attractive style Sweater! Knit in a medium heavyweight of worsted and wool yarns in the popular baby shaker stitch—that smaller and finer size shaker stitch of fine quality. Beautifully striped in contrasting color. An elastic knitted strip reinforcing the shoulder seam provides both the "give" and extra strength needed for vigorous action; also prevents sagging and stretching. Reinforced buttonholes stitched to hold their shape through the strains and twists of many unbuttonings. Tailored, full fashioned collar. Two pockets. Hand finished throughout. This sweater is a wonder for wear.

38K7037—Buff, blue trim.
38K7038—Red, buff trim. $7.45

Sizes, 34 to 44 inches bust measure. State size. Shipping weight, 3½ pounds.
Women's Double Body All Wool Extra Warm Shaker Sweater. Smartly trimmed with contrasting color. The body is lined with all wool worsted striped jersey to match. A practical sweater from every angle—comfortable, trim, stylish and economical! An elastic reinforcement across the shoulders provides both extra give and sturdy strength. Holds its shape and serves faithfully for years. The tight knit cuffs and double body keep out cold winds. Knit of good quality all wool yarns, and is hand finished throughout. You will be able to get a great deal of comfort from this smart sweater during the winter and will find it a handy coat to have all year round.

Baby Shaker Stitch Sweater (Smaller Stitch)

Fashionable Knitwear for Women

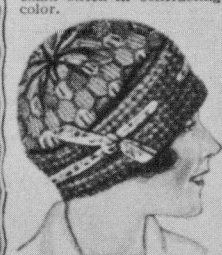

59c
38K8306
Brown and buff.
38K8307
Peacock blue and buff.
Shipping weight, 6 ounces.
Soft, warm Hockey Cap for women or misses. Double thickness all wool yarn, beautifully brushed. Matching color pompon.

98c
38K8365—Silver gray.
38K8364—Buff.
Shipping weight, 7 oz.
Knitted All Wool Brushed Cap. Attractively designed cuff trimmed with wool ornament. The crown has welted seams, with a chain stitch in contrasting color.

Jaunty Astrakhan Knit Sport Set

$2.48 →
38K8302
Brown and buff.
38K8303
Powder blue and pearl gray.
Shipping weight, 1¼ lbs.
For Women and Misses! You will adore the style and comfort of this jaunty Tam and Scarf Set. Fashioned from the popular knit Astrakhan Krimmer Cloth, a closely curled all wool pile, resembling the real fur and is securely knit into a cotton back. The fancy tam is neatly lined with sateen and is most becoming, giving a very dashing appearance to wearer. The set is trimmed with bandings of softly brushed wool. Double fabric scarf is finished with fringe.

38K8313
White and red. **89c**
38K8314
White and powder blue.
38K8315
White and Kelly green.
Shipping weight, 7 oz.
Warm Hockey Cap. Knit in a double thickness of soft all wool yarns trimmed with Rayon stripes. Bushy pompon.

$1.19
38K8316
Wood brown and buff.
38K8317—Copenhagen blue and buff.
Shipping weight, 7 ounces.
Close fitting Turban, for woman or miss. Hand crocheted of all wool yarns. Turned up brim of contrasting color. All wool floral trim. *Hand Crocheted*

38K8304
Peacock blue and buff. **57c**
38K8305— Brown and buff.
Shipping weight, 7 ounces. Women's or misses' Serviceable Hockey Cap of double thickness. Knit from about one-half wool with cotton lining. Trimmed in contrasting color stripes and bushy two-color wool worsted pompon. A fine value.

87c
38K8311—Buff combination.
38K8312—Powder blue combination.
Shipping weight, 8 ounces.
Beautifully blended colorings have made this chic Sport Cap a favorite of fashion for women and misses. The crown, softly draped, is knit in a fancy pattern of wool with Rayon and cotton trimming. The deep cuff of knit Astrakhan Krimmer Cloth continues into inside of hat, affording extra warmth. Knit ribbon of lustrous Rayon is laced through cuff and forms smart bow at one side.

38K8308
Brown and buff.
38K8309
Peacock blue and buff. **79c**
38K8310
Solid maroon.
Shipping weight, 8 ounces.
For all around service, we recommend this warm and heavyweight all wool and seamless, double thickness Knit Hockey Cap for women. Wide roll cuff and bushy pompon.

85c
38K8370—White.
38K8371—Buff.
38K8372—Red.
38K8373
Peacock blue.
Shipping weight, 7 ounces.
Beautiful Sport Hockey Cap for women. Knit in a rope stitch of double thickness from extra good quality soft all wool yarn. Trimmed with large wool pompon. A dandy cap for all around wear. A big value.

Latest Styles for the Schoolgirl

$1.85
38K8206
Powder blue and camel color.
38K8207
Buff and wood brown.
Shipping weight, 1 lb.
A better selection could not be made for the schoolgirl than this stylish set of serviceable knit Astrakhan Krimmer Cloth with brushed stripe trim. The tightly curled all wool pile resembles the real fur and is reinforced in back with cotton. The cap is smartly shaped and is trimmed with two-color pompon. Double fabric scarf with wool fringe. Each set packed in a neat box.

38K8210
Peacock blue and buff. **48c**
38K8211
Brown and buff.
Shipping weight, 6 oz.
Schoolgirls' Good Weight All Wool Brushed and Seamless Knit Hockey Cap of double thickness. Soft and warm. A wonderful value at our price.

French Beret Tam
38K8238—Red.
38K8239
Navy blue.
38K8240
Copenhagen blue. **89c**
Shipping wt., 6 oz.
Seamless Beret Tam for misses and girls. Felted all wool knit cloth.

For Women or Misses

$1.98
38K8300
White and red.
38K8301
Buff and golden brown.
Shipping weight, 1 pound.
Women's and Misses' Attractive Cap and Scarf Set. Knit in the smart popcorn stitch of all wool yarn. The set is of double fabric and is neatly trimmed with the two-color combination. Large, bushy two-color pompon trims cap, and scarf is finished with hand knotted fringe.

$1.35
38K8200
Brown and buff.
38K8201
Peacock blue and buff.
38K8202—Red and buff.
Shipping weight, ¾ lb.
Schoolgirls' Attractive Cap and Scarf Set from all wool yarn with a beautiful brushed Angora finish. The hockey cap is trimmed with pompon. The set is neatly striped in a harmonizing color; scarf finished with fringe. Warm and comfortable.

39c
38K8208
Peacock blue and buff.
38K8209
Red and buff.
Shipping weight, 6 oz.
Schoolgirls' Inexpensive Hockey Cap, knit of one-half wool worsted yarn with cotton knit lining. Neatly striped and set off with daisy pompon. Warmth and style make it a very attractive selection.

67c ↗
38K8218
Brown and buff.
38K8219
Buff and peacock blue.
38K8220
White and red.
Shipping weight, 7 oz.
Close Fitting All Wool Fancy Knit Hockey Cap for schoolgirls. Novelty star design knit in contrasting color in crown. Solid color cuff of double thickness.

69c ↗
38K8212
Buff and peacock blue.
38K8213
Peacock blue and brown.
38K8214
Brown and buff.
Shipping weight, 7 oz.
Schoolgirls' Heavyweight All Wool Seamless Knit Double Fabric Hockey Cap. Prettily striped in contrasting colors. Large wool worsted bushy pompon.

75c
38K8221—Red.
38K8222—Buff.
38K8223—White.
38K8224
Peacock blue.
Shipping weight, 7 oz.
Schoolgirls' Soft, All Wool, Heavy Weight, Seamless Knit Hockey Cap, of double thickness. Trimmed with large, bushy wool pompon. Warm and cozy; dandy for cold weather.

Charming Underthings

Descriptions and Other Colors May Be Found on Opposite Page

Shadowproof Hem

Double Fabric Crotch

Shadowproof Hem

A Tub Silk $2.98 Radium Silk $3.98

B Mercerized Jersey Long 85¢ Short 75¢

C Silk Pongee Pantie $1.69

D Glove Silk $2.95 Rayon $1.95

E Silk Crepe de Chine $2.98

F Better Quality Glove Silk Vest $1.98 Bloomer $2.69 Step-in $2.48

G Searslip Cloth 75¢

H Hand Embroidered Silk Pongee $2.79

Exquisite Rayon Garments

Shadowproof Underlay

Shadowproof Hem

M Fine Quality Rayon $2.95

J Excellent Quality Rayon $2.95

K Fine Quality Rayon Regular $1.95 Stouts $2.48

L Fine Knit Rayon $1.65

R Rayon Jersey Long $1.69 Short $1.49

S Fine Quality Rayon $1.89

T Dainty Rayon 98¢

Descriptions of Underthings Shown on Opposite Page

A $2.98
38K1806—Flesh.
38K1807—Tan.
38K1808—Navy blue.
Sizes, 34 to 44 in. bust measure. State size. Shipping weight, 8 oz. Straight tailored lines prevail in this Costume Slip of soft and firmly woven tub silk, trimmed with hemstitched bodice top and finished with deep shadowproof hem. Pleated over hips for ample fullness.

$3.98
38K1809—Peach.
38K1810—Tan.
Same style and sizes made of heavy quality all silk radium. Will wash beautifully and give excellent service.

Sport Length
B 85¢
38K1936—Tan.
38K1944—Flesh.
38K1934—Navy blue.
38K1938—Green.
Length, 32 in. Shipping weight, 8 ounces. Splendid value in Sport Length. Fine Mercerized Lisle Silk Finish Cotton Jersey Knit Bloomers. Reinforced flat seams and double fabric gusset crotch. Double elastic cuffs are of contrasting color Rayon.

Knee Length
75¢
38K1948—Flesh.
38K1967—Purple.
38K1968—Tan.
Lengths, 25, 27 and 29 inches. State length. Shpg. wt., 7 oz. Same in Knee Length style; single elastic contrasting color Rayon cuff at knees.

C 38K1926—Natural pongee.
$1.69
Lengths, 23 and 25 inches. State length. Shipping wt., 6 oz. French Step-In Panties of soft fine quality all silk pongee, finished at bottom with hemstitching and dainty embroidered organdy medallions. Elastic waistband.

D 38K1236—Flesh.
38K1237—Peach.
$2.95
Sizes, 34 to 44 inches bust measure. State size. Shpg. wt., 8 oz. Delightfully pretty, well made Step-In Chemise of high quality pure glove silk. Trimmed with fine ecru Val lace insertion and edge. Silk ribbon draw. Reinforced crotch.

$1.99
38K1238—Flesh.
38K1239—Peach.
Same style and sizes made of the lustrous Rayon. Can be laundered with the greatest of ease.

E 38K1240—Nile green.
$2.98
38K1241—Flesh.
Sizes, 34 to 44 in. bust measure. State size. Shipping weight, ¾ lb. Excellent value is represented in this Step-In Chemise of silk crepe de chine, topped with dainty and fine quality ecru color Val lace and insertion and finished with lace edging. The embroidered net medallion and Val lace insertion and clusters of pin tucks add an elaborate touch.

F **Vest**
38K1615—Flesh.
38K1625—Peach.
$1.98
Sizes to fit 34 to 44 in. bust measure. State size. Shpg. wt., 7 oz. Pure Thread Glove Silk Vest of better quality, attractively priced so you can own several. Bodice top. Reinforced under arms. Average length, including straps, 31 inches.

Bloomers
$2.69
38K1614—Flesh.
38K1624—Peach.
Medium and large sizes, to fit up to 48 hip measure. State size. Shpg. wt., 8 oz. Women's Pure Thread Glove Silk Bloomers of better quality. Double fabric saddle crotch for longer wear. These bloomers match vest or step-in.

Step-In
$2.48
38K1613—Flesh.
Medium and large sizes to fit up to 44 hip measure. State size. Shipping weight, 7 ounces. Women's Better Quality Pure Thread Glove Silk Step-In Drawers. Cut full and roomy.

G 38K1997—Green.
38K1998—Peach.
38K1999—Pencil blue.
75¢
Lengths, 25, 27 and 29 inches. State length. Shpg. wt., 8 oz. Smart Style Knee Length Bloomers of the well known Searslip Cloth, a high grade, finely woven cotton cloth with the desirable sleek, slippery finish, preventing outer garments creeping up or clinging to the body. Colored elastic garter cuffs. Reinforced crotch.

H 38K1811—Natural pongee.
$2.79
Sizes, 34 to 44 inches bust measure. State size. Shpg. wt., 7 oz. Silk pongee of a good quality that is easily laundered makes this a decidedly practical Slip for any wear. Bodice top is daintily hemstitched. Front is prettily designed with hemstitching and hand embroidered work. Pleated over hips; deep shadowproof hem.

J 38K1803—Coral.
38K1804—Peach.
38K1805—Black.
$2.95
Sizes, 34 to 44 inches bust measure. State size. Shpg. wt., ¾ lb. An appealing style from the standpoints of price and beauty is this lustrous finely knit Rayon Costume Slip, handsomely trimmed with beautiful lace at top and bottom. Beautiful scalloped embroidery also gives the garment an artistic touch. Shadowproof underlay of Rayon is edged with narrow lace. Pleated over hips.

K 38K1724—Flesh.
38K1725—Navy blue.
38K1726—Sand.
$1.95
Sizes, 34 to 44 inches bust measure. State size. Shipping weight, ¾ lb. Costume Slips are the correct foundation of every smart costume. Modeled on slim, straight lines this slip made of better quality knit Rayon is just what you will need. Well tailored with pleats on each side to give the necessary fullness. Deep shadowproof hem.

Stout Sizes
$2.48
38K1727—Flesh.
38K1728—Navy blue.
38K1729—Sand.
Sizes, 46 to 54 inches bust measure. State size. Shipping weight, 1 pound. Same style for stout women.

L 38K1579—Peach.
38K1580 Nile green.
$1.65
38K1581—Orchid.
Lengths, 23 and 25 inches. State length. Shipping weight, 7 ounces. Beautiful Step-In Drawers of fine quality knit Rayon. Lavishly trimmed with ecru color Val lace insertion and embroidered net medallions. Bottom and slashed sides edged with lace. Tiny two-tone satin ribbon bows adorn corners.

M 38K1165—Flesh.
38K1166—Orchid.
38K1167—Green.
$2.95
Sizes, 34 to 44 inches bust measure. State size. Shpg. wt., ¾ lb. Fine enough for the most fastidious woman and lovely enough for the daintiest trousseau. This adorable Gown is fashioned of heavy quality lustrous Rayon. Front of finely embroidered net medallions and clusters of pin tucks; fine ecru Val lace edge around neck and armholes. The bottom is finished with fine double net footing. Can be laundered easily.

R 38K1901—Pansy.
38K1902—Navy blue.
38K1903—Peach.
$1.69
Length, 32 inches. Shpg. wt., ¾ lb. High grade Bloomers of beautiful lustrous Rayon, a fine knitted fabric, soft and clinging. Wears well and launders beautifully without losing its luster. Specially designed non-binding double gusset crotch. Double elastic contrasting color cuffs.

Knee Length
$1.49
38K1904—Nile green.
38K1905—Peach.
38K1912—Pansy.
Lengths, 25, 27 and 29 inches. State length. Shpg. wt., 8 oz. Same, in knee length with single elastic contrasting color cuff.

S 38K1242—Orchid.
38K1243—Flesh.
38K1244—Nile green.
$1.89
Sizes, 34 to 44 inches bust measure. Shpg. wt., 8 oz. You will be pleased with this lovely Step-In Chemise of fine quality knit Rayon. The lace trimming and inserts are of exceptionally fine quality. Tiny tucks lend to its dainty features.

T 38K1229—Peach.
38K1230—Flesh.
38K1231—Orchid.
98¢
Sizes, 34 to 44 inches bust measure. State size. Shpg. wt., ¾ lb. Attractive Step-In Chemise, combining style, beauty and value. Good quality Rayon trimmed with ecru val lace. Lace and ribbon rosette trims front. Retains silky appearance through many washings. A big bargain!

Stylish Slips for Any Frock

Satinette or Sateen

Genuine LINGETTE or Sateen

Fruit of the Loom Mercette or Rayola

Satinette or Cotton Taffeta

98c
38K1716—Peach.
38K1718—White.
38K1719—Black.
38K1730—Purple.
Sizes to fit 34 to 44 inches bust measure. State size. Shipping weight, ¾ pound. A remarkable value is offered in this striped satinette Costume Slip. The material has a beautiful sheen and is very durable. Retains its luster after washing. You have your choice of four popular colors. The bodice top is neatly hemstitched and has same material shoulder straps. Pleated over hips and has deep shadowproof hem.

Stout Sizes $1.19
38K1720—Peach.
38K1721—Black.
Sizes to fit 46 to 54 inches bust measure. State size. Shipping weight, 1 pound. Same as above, for stout women.

Lustrous Sateen 75c
38K1837—Black.
38K1838—Purple.
38K1839—Tan.
38K1802—Flesh.
Sizes to fit 34 to 44 inches bust measure. State size. Shipping weight, ¾ pound. Same style as above, but made in regular sizes of high grade sateen with a lustrous finish. 2-inch hem.

98c
38K1700—Pencil blue.
38K1772—Black.
38K1773—White.
Sizes to fit 34 to 44 inches bust measure. State size. Shipping weight, 8 ounces. Stylish Costume Slip of the famous Fruit of the Loom Mercette Cloth, a firmly woven soft cotton fabric with mercerized finish that will launder beautifully and wear well. The bodice top is finished with neat hemstitching and same material shoulder straps; bottom has two rows of pinked scalloped ruffles.

Rayola Cloth $1.98
38K1714 Blue and gold.
38K1715—Flesh.
38K1705—Navy blue.
Same style and sizes as above, but made of Rayola Cloth, a fine fabric with a closely woven silk and cotton texture, giving a lustrous appearance. Will be a joy as it does not cling or creep up.

$1.48
38K1711—Navy blue.
38K1712—Tan.
38K1713—Purple.
Sizes to fit 34 to 44 inches bust measure. State size. Shipping weight, ¾ pound. Soft, lustrous satinette fashions this Dressy Costume Slip. Bodice is neatly hemstitched and has same material shoulder straps; bottom has deep pleated flounce, gracefully designed with Rayon braid and insert of contrasting color.

Cotton Taffeta
38K1708 Black.
98c
38K1709—Tan.
38K1710—Purple.
Same style and sizes as above, but made of high grade cotton taffeta.

$1.69
38K1827—Tan.
38K1025—Black.
38K1889—Flesh.
Sizes to fit 34 to 44 inches bust measure. State size. Shpg. wt., ¾ lb. A favored material for Costume Slips is this well known genuine striped lingette, which has that rich silk-like soft appearance. It is finely woven of good grade cotton cloth; launders beautifully and gives excellent wear. The round neck and arm openings are finished with neat hemstitching. Draw tape at neck. Pleated over hips and has 2-inch hem.

STOUT SIZES
38K1828 Black. $1.98
Sizes to fit 46 to 54 inches bust measure. State size. Shipping weight, ¾ lb. Same style as above, but for stout women.

Lustrous Sateen—Regular Sizes
38K1795—Black.
38K1796—Flesh. $1.00
38K1799—Tan.
Sizes to fit 34 to 44 inches bust measure. State size. Shipping weight, ¾ lb. Same style as above, but made of good quality, finely woven lustrous sateen.

Send Sufficient Money for Postage on Parcel Post Shipments. Any Surplus Will Be Returned

2 133

Well Made Muslinwear

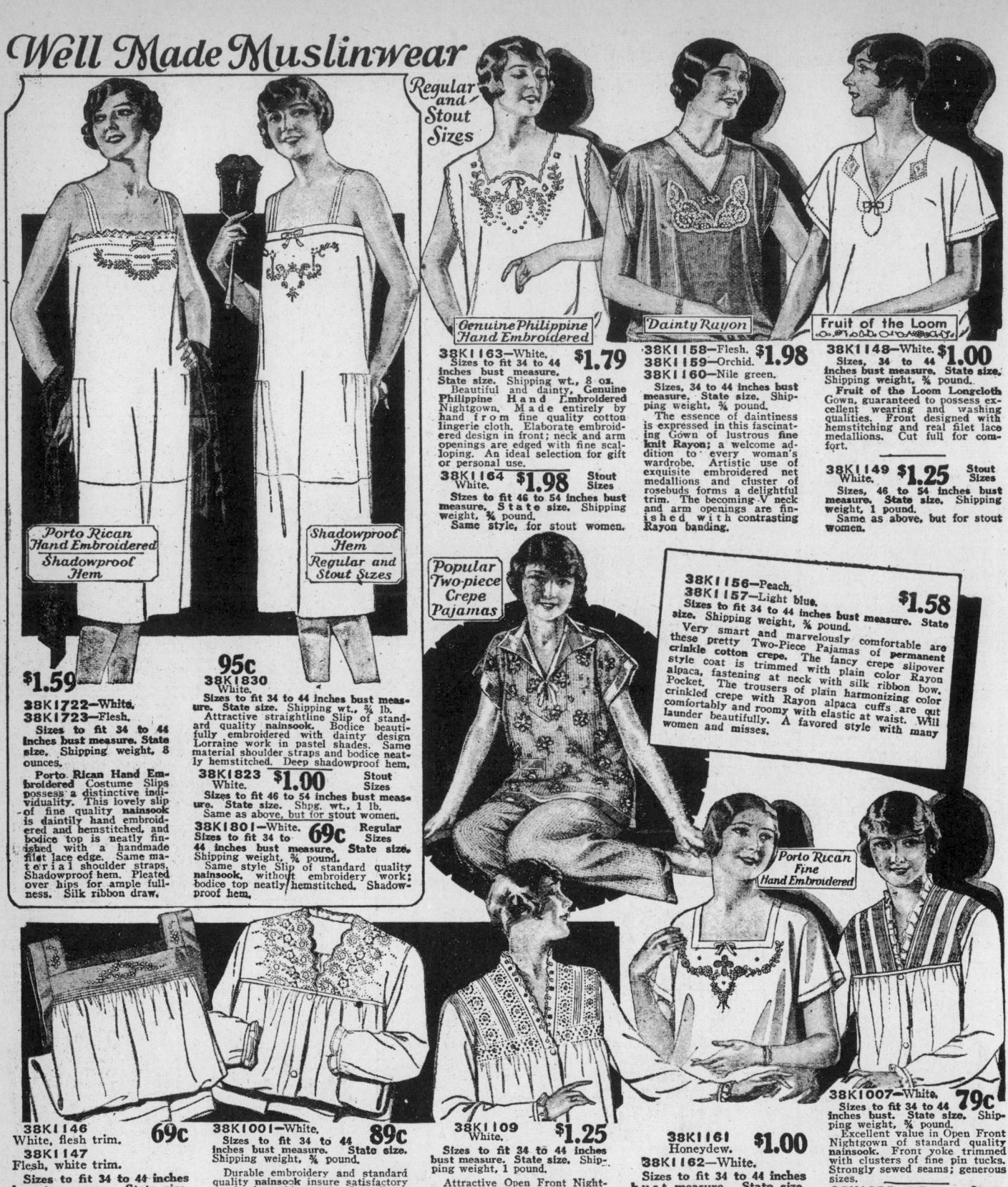

Regular and Stout Sizes

Genuine Philippine Hand Embroidered

38K1163—White. **$1.79**
Sizes to fit 34 to 44 inches bust measure. State size. Shipping wt., 8 oz.
Beautiful and dainty, Genuine Philippine Hand Embroidered Nightgown. Made entirely by hand from fine quality cotton lingerie cloth. Elaborate embroidered design in front; neck and arm openings are edged with fine scalloping. An ideal selection for gift or personal use.

38K1164 **$1.98** Stout Sizes
White.
Sizes to fit 46 to 54 inches bust measure. State size. Shipping weight, ¾ pound.
Same style, for stout women.

Dainty Rayon

38K1158—Flesh. **$1.98**
38K1159—Orchid.
38K1160—Nile green.
Sizes, 34 to 44 inches bust measure. State size. Shipping weight, ¾ pound.
The essence of daintiness is expressed in this fascinating Gown of lustrous fine knit Rayon; a welcome addition to every woman's wardrobe. Artistic use of exquisite embroidered net medallions and cluster of rosebuds forms a delightful trim. The becoming V neck and arm openings are finished with contrasting Rayon banding.

Fruit of the Loom

38K1148—White. **$1.00**
Sizes, 34 to 44 inches bust measure. State size. Shipping weight, ¾ pound.
Fruit of the Loom Longcloth Gown, guaranteed to possess excellent wearing and washing qualities. Front designed with hemstitching and real filet lace medallions. Cut full for comfort.

38K1149 **$1.25** Stout Sizes
White.
Sizes, 46 to 54 inches bust measure. State size. Shipping weight, 1 pound.
Same as above, but for stout women.

Porto Rican Hand Embroidered Shadowproof Hem

Shadowproof Hem *Regular and Stout Sizes*

$1.59
38K1722—White.
38K1723—Flesh.
Sizes to fit 34 to 44 inches bust measure. State size. Shipping weight, 8 ounces.
Porto Rican Hand Embroidered Costume Slips possess a distinctive individuality. This lovely slip of fine quality nainsook is daintily hand embroidered and hemstitched, and bodice top is neatly finished with a handmade filet lace edge. Same material shoulder straps. Shadowproof hem. Pleated over hips for ample fullness. Silk ribbon draw.

95c
38K1830
White.
Sizes to fit 34 to 44 inches bust measure. State size. Shipping wt., ¾ lb.
Attractive straightline Slip of standard quality nainsook. Bodice beautifully embroidered with dainty design Lorraine work in pastel shades. Same material shoulder straps and bodice neatly hemstitched. Deep shadowproof hem.

38K1823 **$1.00** Stout Sizes
White.
Sizes to fit 46 to 54 inches bust measure. State size. Shpg. wt., 1 lb.
Same as above, but for stout women.

38K1801—White. **69c** Regular Sizes
Sizes to fit 34 to 44 inches bust measure. State size. Shipping weight, ¾ pound.
Same style Slip of standard quality nainsook, without embroidery work; bodice top neatly hemstitched. Shadowproof hem.

Popular Two-piece Crepe Pajamas

38K1156—Peach. **$1.58**
38K1157—Light blue.
Sizes to fit 34 to 44 inches bust measure. State size. Shipping weight, ¾ pound.
Very smart and marvelously comfortable are these pretty Two-Piece Pajamas of permanent crinkle cotton crepe. The fancy crepe slipover style coat is trimmed with plain color Rayon alpaca, fastening at neck with silk ribbon bow. Pocket. The trousers of plain harmonizing color crinkled crepe with Rayon alpaca cuffs are cut comfortably and roomy with elastic at waist. Will launder beautifully. A favored style with many women and misses.

Porto Rican Fine Hand Embroidered

38K1146 **69c**
White, flesh trim.
38K1147
Flesh, white trim.
Sizes to fit 34 to 44 inches bust measure. Shipping weight, ¾ pound.
A simple and comfortable Nightgown in the popular Jenny neck slipover style. Made of standard quality nainsook with bands at top and deep armholes of contrasting color; embroidered with neat Lorraine work in pastel shades. Shirred across front. Well made in full sizes. Note the low price!

38K1001—White. **89c**
Sizes to fit 34 to 44 inches bust measure. State size. Shipping weight, ¾ pound.
Durable embroidery and standard quality nainsook insure satisfactory service from this popular Open Front Style Nightgown. Long sleeves. Double yoke in back. Neat and well made over full size pattern. Inexpensive and a popular style with our customers.

38K1002 **98c** Stout Sizes
White.
Sizes to fit 46 to 54 inches bust measure. State size. Shipping weight, 1 pound.
Same style as above, but for stout women.

38K1109 **$1.25**
White.
Sizes to fit 34 to 44 inches bust measure. State size. Shipping weight, 1 pound.
Attractive Open Front Nightgown of standard quality cambric. Yoke trimmed with fine embroidery insertions and clusters of pin tucks. Neck and long sleeves finished with embroidery edge. Double yoke in back.

38K1110 **$1.35** Stout Sizes
White.
Sizes to fit 46 to 54 inches bust measure. State size. Shipping weight, 1 pound.
Same, for stout women.

38K1161 **$1.00**
Honeydew.
38K1162—White.
Sizes to fit 34 to 44 inches bust measure. State size. Shipping weight, 8 ounces.
Porto Rican Hand Embroidered Gowns are a favorite with many women who like fine lingerie. Made entirely by hand from fine cotton lingerie batiste, and daintily trimmed with colored hand embroidered design in front. Ribbon draw. The price, you will note, is very low for such a beautiful gown.

38K1007—White. **79c**
Sizes to fit 34 to 44 inches bust. State size. Shipping weight, ¾ pound.
Excellent value in Open Front Nightgown of standard quality nainsook. Front yoke trimmed with clusters of fine pin tucks. Strongly sewed seams; generous sizes.

38K1008 **89c** Stout Sizes
White.
Sizes to fit 46 to 54 inches bust measure. State size. Shipping weight, 1 pound.
Same, for stout women.

Fruit of the Loom

38K1010 **$1.39** Regular Sizes
White.
Sizes to fit 34 to 44 inches bust measure. Shipping weight, ¾ pound.
Same style as above, made of Fruit of the Loom muslin.

Searstride

Triple Stitched Seams for Extra Strength

Sateen

Perfect Fit in Every Position

Regular Sizes. **69c**	Stout Sizes. **85c**
38K1973—Black.	38K1977—Black.
38K1974—Purple.	38K1978—Flesh.
38K1975—Tan.	38K1979—Purple.
38K1976—Flesh.	Length, 30 in.
Lengths 25, 27 and 29 in.	only. 68-inch
State length.	seat. Shpg. wt.,
Shpg. wt., ¾ lb.	1 lb.

The New Searstride Bloomer. A style that fits every movement of the body perfectly. Made for sturdy wear, because of its extra strength triple stitched seams. Cut full and roomy from better quality lustrous sateen. Has saddle crotch. Elastic at waist and double elastic cuffs at knees.

Blossom Bloomer
Fruit of the Loom

Cannot Rip or Tear

Knit Rayon

Striped Satinette

38K1969—Flesh. **$1.00**	38K1929—White. **85c**	38K1922—Purple. **69c**
38K1970—Peach.	38K1930—Flesh.	38K1923—Green.
38K1971—Pansy purple.	38K1910—Black.	38K1924—Flesh.
38K1972—Nile green.	Sizes, small, medium and	Lengths, 25, 27 and 29 in.

Lengths, 25, 27 and 29 in. State length. Shpg. wt., 8 oz. For the trim figure in Fashion's favor, you will want these lovely **high grade Rayon Jersey Knit Bloomers.** They have the clinging softness of real silk, yet are made full and roomy. Have reinforced double fabric gusset crotch, elastic waist and pretty lace edged ruffle at elastic knees. Launder beautifully in good soap suds.

large. State size. Shipping weight, 8 ounces. Blossom Bloomers made of fine quality Fruit of the Loom Longcloth with seams guaranteed to stand every strain without ripping or tearing at crotch. Will not pull up on the leg nor down at waist. Elastic at waist and knees.

Stout Sizes	
38K1931—White. **95c**	
38K1911—Black.	

Knee length only. Shipping weight, ¾ pound. Same, for stout women; 68-inch seat.

State length. Shpg. wt., 8 oz. High Grade Lustrous Striped Satinette Bloomers in knee length. Made in full sizes for comfort and well finished to insure good service. Reinforced crotch. Double elastic cuffs.

Stout Sizes	
38K1927—Black. **85c**	
38K1928—Flesh.	

Length, 30 inches. Shpg. wt., ¾ lb. Same, for stout women; 68-inch seat.

Double Stitched Seams Throughout

Sateen

Special Seat Construction

Knee Length. **79c**	Length, 31 in. **89c**
38K1989—Flesh.	38K1993—Black.
38K1990—Tan.	38K1994—Green.
38K1991—Purple.	38K1995—Purple.
38K1992—Black.	38K1996—Flesh.

Medium and large hip sizes. State size. Shpg. wt., ¾ lb. Sears Step-Rite Bloomers especially constructed upon different lines from those of the ordinary bloomer. Form fitting in every position, due to special seat construction; fashioned to allow the greatest amount of room where most needed and permit bending or sitting without binding or pulling. Made of superior quality lustrous sateen with elastic at waist and cuffs. All seams are double stitched.

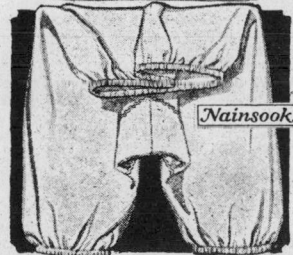

Nainsook

38K1511—White. **35c**
38K1512—Flesh.

Lengths, 25, 27 and 29 inches. State length. Shpg. wt., 7 ounces. Soft finish nainsook Bloomers. Reinforced crotch. Elastic at waist and knees.

Stout Sizes
38K1513—White. **45c**
38K1523—Flesh.

Length, 30 in. only. Shpg. wt., 8 oz. Same, for stout women; 68-inch seat.

Cotton Jersey

Regular Sizes. **29c**	Stout Sizes. **39c**	38K8532—Black. **79c**
38K8510—Black.	38K8525—Black.	38K8533—Navy blue.
38K8511—Flesh.	38K8527—Flesh.	38K8534—Gray.
38K8513—Tan.	Length, 30 inches	Sizes: Medium and large. State

Sizes: Small, medium and large. State size. Shpg. wt., 6 oz. Women's Medium Lightweight Cotton Jersey Bloomers. Knee length. Knit in a close stitch. Double gusset crotch. Warm and serviceable.

only. Extra wide. Shipping weight, 7 oz.

size. Shipping weight, ¾ pound. Women's Medium Heavyweight Knee Length Cotton Jersey Knit Bloomers. Full cut and roomy. Elastic at waist and knees. Improved double fabric gusset crotch. Well made and warm.

Heavy Weight Cotton Jersey

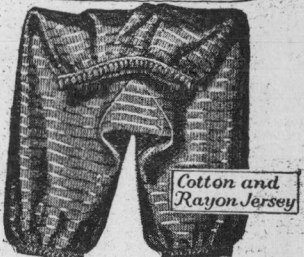

Cotton and Rayon Jersey

38K8507—Black. **49c**
38K8508—White.
38K8509—Flesh.

Sizes: Small, medium and large. State size. Shpg. wt., ¾ lb. Women's Knee Length Medium Weight Bloomers of combed cotton underwear fabric, with neat Rayon stripes. A well made and warm garment that will give good service. Elastic at waist and knees.

Flannelette

38K9576—Gray. **45c**
38K9577—Light stripes.

Lengths, 25, 27 and 29 inches. State length. Shipping weight, ¾ pound. Warm and serviceable Bloomers for women. Well made of good quality flannelette with reinforced crotch; elastic at waist and ruffled knees. Cut over full and roomy pattern.

Genuine LINGETTE

38K1918—Flesh. **98c**
38K1919—Orchid.
38K1920—Navy blue.

Lengths, 25, 27 and 29 inches. State length. Shpg. wt., 8 oz. Smartly dressed women always find Bloomers a neat costume foundation. This splendid value is made of genuine striped Lingette, a silky, soft, striped cotton material of fine quality. Cut over full standard sizes and will wear well. Comfortable saddle crotch. Elastic at waist and double elastic cuffs.

Sateen

38K1501—Black. **59c**
38K1502—White.
38K1503—Purple.

Lengths, 25, 27 and 29 inches. State length. Shpg. wt., ¾ lb. Well made Bloomers of better quality plain sateen. Carefully finished and cut in full, comfortable sizes. Elastic waistband and double elastic cuffs at knees. Saddle crotch.

Stout Sizes
38K1521—Black. **75c**
38K1523—Purple.

Length, 30 inches only. Shipping weight, ¾ pound. Same, for stout women; 68-inch seat.

Wool and Rayon Jersey

38K8529—Navy blue. **$1.98**
38K8530—Gray.
38K8531—Tan.

Sizes: Medium and large. State size. Shpg. wt., ¾ lb. Women's Knee Length, Fine Quality All Wool Worsted Jersey Knit Bloomers with Rayon stripes. Elastic at waist and knees. Medium weight that will keep you warm. Large and roomy.

Fleeced

38K8516—Silver gray. **79c**

Sizes: Medium and large. State size. Shipping weight, 1 pound. Women's Extra Heavyweight Fleece Lined Combed Cotton Knit Bloomers. Elastic at waist and knees. Warm and durable. Gusset crotch. Priced very reasonably.

Excellent Values

Double Thickness Fine Knit Rayon~

Side or Back Closing

Fancy Rayon Brocade Back or Side Closing

Flat-O-Form

Extra Long Waisted

57c

38K671—Peach.
38K672—Flesh.
38K673—White.

Sizes, 28 to 36 inches bust measure. State bust measure. Shipping weight, 2 ounces.

New natural form Bandeau of double thickness lustrous knit fine gauge Rayon. The center is gathered to a fancy silk elastic insert, shaping the bust to the graceful rounded lines now so stylish. Firmly bound. Shoulder straps are of fancy lingerie tape. A very dressy model.

Side Closing	Back Closing
89c	**89c**
38K685	38K684
Flesh.	Flesh.

Sizes to fit 32 to 46 inches bust measure. State bust measure. Shipping weight, 8 ounces.

This long Brassiere is especially designed for stylish trim figure lines. Made of firm and good quality cotton madras with fancy Rayon stripes. Has large inserts of strong elastic at each side and panel in back to hold brassiere trimly to the figure. Special Sta-Flat boning in front effectively controls the diaphragm. Tape shoulder straps wtih inserts of elastic to help prevent slipping from shoulders.

Back Closing	Side Closing
49c	**49c**
38K620	38K621
Flesh.	Flesh.

Sizes to fit 30 to 40 inches bust measure. Shipping weight, 4 ounces.

Daintiness and good quality are combined in this serviceable Bandeau of rich Rayon brocade, finished at top with fancy braid. Particularly popular for slight and average figures. The shoulder straps are of fancy Rayon lingerie tape. Panel of elastic webbing in back for comfort.

38K641—Flesh. 75c

Sizes to fit 32 to 48 inches bust measure. State bust measure. Shipping weight, 5 ounces.

Favored Style Flat-O-Form Brassiere, a garment that rids you of that bulging diaphragm. It is made of durable quality fancy cotton madras. The attached adjustable belt, with elastic diaphragm feature, effectively flattens the diaphragm and holds the brassiere securely in place. Lightly boned. Elastic panel in back with invisible hooking. Tape shoulder straps.

Side Closing

38K648—White.
38K649—Flesh. 55c

Sizes to fit 30 to 44 inches bust measure. State bust measure. Shipping weight, 4 ounces.

This style has been greatly favored by many women. Made of good quality mercerized cotton brocade. Side closing. Has elastic inserts in back over hips. No boning. Top trimmed with braid. Tape shoulder straps.

Lustrous Satinette

Front Closing

49c

38K639—White.

Sizes to fit 30 to 42 inches bust measure. State bust measure. Shipping weight, 4 ounces.

Brassieres made of Indian Head Cloth in this comfortable long stylish model for average figures are very popular. A most convenient feature of this garment is its side fastening, making it extremely easy to hook. Elastic inserts at waistline in back allow the garment to fit snugly without creeping up. No boning. Indian Head is famous for its sturdy wearing qualities. Easy to launder. Tape shoulder straps.

For Women's Knit and Rayon Vests See Page 290

Side Closing

INDIAN HEAD

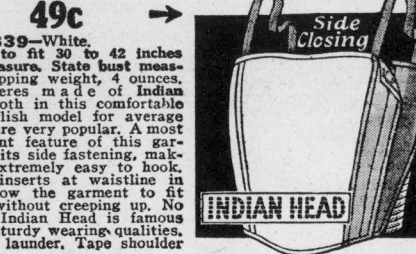

38K637—White.
38K638—Flesh. 23c

Sizes to fit 28 to 40 inches bust measure. State bust measure. Shipping weight, 3 ounces.

A popular and big value is this Bust Confiner for average and slight figures, made of durable quality fancy Rayon striped cotton madras. Elastic web insert in back, fastening with hooks and eyes. Tape shoulder straps. Lightly boned. Purchase several at this low price. Launders beautifully and will give excellent service.

Rayon Striped

Two Special Values for Stout Figures~

Side Closing

98c

38K1245—Flesh.
38K1246—Orchid.

Sizes to fit 34 to 44 inches bust measure. State size. Shpg wt 7 oz.

You will be delighted beyond words with this very low priced Step-In Chemise of nice quality lustrous striped satinette. It has two panels of folds in front caught with ecru color embroidered net medallions and finished across the front of bodice with same trim. The bodice top is trimmed with beautiful pattern ecru color lace and ribbon draw. Satinette shoulder straps. The bottom and deep slashed sides are finished with lace edge.

38K616—White.
38K617—Flesh. 29c

Sizes, to fit 28 to 36 inches bust measure. State bust measure. Shipping weight, 2 ounces.

The ideal Bandeau Confiner designed especially for the miss and slender woman. Made of good quality mercerized cotton brocade. Hooks in back aside of elastic panel. Tape shoulder straps.

Tub Silk

38K610—Flesh. 49c

Same style and sizes as above, but made of fine quality plain tub silk. A very dainty

Brocade Madras or Tub Silk

79c

38K525—Flesh.

Sizes, 36 to 54 inches bust measure. State bust measure. Shipping weight, ¾ pounds.

This Brassiere is especially designed for stout figures. Made of durable quality cotton madras. The important features of this garment are the convenient side opening, the flattening front device of Sta-Flat parallel boning and lacing down the center of the back, which is adjustable for comfortable expansion. Tape shoulder straps. Highly recommended as a favored style.

38K507—Flesh. 75c

Sizes to fit 36 to 54 inches bust measure. Shipping weight, 5 ounces.

This popular style is particularly adaptable to the average and full figure. Made in built-up shoulder style with inserts of covered elastic over shoulders to prevent binding. The elastic webbing at sides of waist and down center of high back offers freedom and extra comfort. It is lightly boned in back. Made of firm quality cotton madras in fancy pattern. Opens in front, a convenient feature.

soft garment, giving firm support. Launders beautifully. Be sure to state bust measure.

Have You Seen the Beautiful Display of Women's Rayon Lingerie? See Page 132.

Styles for All Figures

Side Closing

Front or Back Closing

Fancy Rayon Brocade or Glove Silk

38K614—White.
38K615—Flesh. **55c**
Sizes to fit 28 to 38 inches bust measure. **State bust measure.** Shpg. wt., 2 oz.

For the slight figure, this pretty Uplift Bandeau is very popular. It is made of good quality **cotton madras** with fancy Rayon pattern. Three rows of narrow covered elastic at both sides give comfort and freedom. Fits snugly and raises and supports the busts in an easy natural line without undue pressure. Fastens at side under arm. Neat lace edge and tiny rosebud make a pretty trim. Has fancy lingerie tape shoulder straps.

Front Closing
38K660—White.
38K661—Flesh. **55c**
Sizes, 34 to 48 inches bust measure. Shipping wt., 4 oz.

Back Closing
38K690—White.
38K691—Flesh. **55c**
Sizes, 32 to 44 inches bust measure. Shipping wt., 4 oz.

Women's Comfortable Bandeau Brassiere in waist length for the average figure. Made of durable quality cotton madras. Will not pull up on the figure or above a low bust corset, as the all around elastic waistband is adjustable to all figures and will stay in place. Tape shoulder straps. Lightly boned at sides.

38K603—Flesh. **59c**
Sizes to fit 28 to 38 inches bust measure. State bust measure. Shipping wt., 2 oz.

A dressy Uplift Bandeau, giving a foundation of a smart graceful figure to the slight woman or miss. Made of beautiful **Rayon brocade** of excellent quality with cotton back. Fancy Rayon elastic in narrow back. Shoulder straps of fancy lingerie tape.

Glove Silk
38K674—Flesh. **69c**
Same style and sizes as above, but made of **fine quality pure glove silk.** An ideal material for a costume of this type, a rich piece firm support with elasticity. A soft and dainty bandeau, giving to the bust the graceful lines which are now so stylish.

38K534—Flesh. **55c**
Sizes to fit 30 to 44 inches bust measure. State bust measure. Shpg. wt., 3 oz.

The Boyshform Brassiere is very popular, as it gives your figure that smart boylike flat appearance that so many women desire. Made of fancy batiste of a firm durable quality with Rayon stripes. Cut in one piece; fitted under arms and has elastic waistline. Top neatly trimmed with lace. Hooks down back. No boning. Lingerie tape shoulder straps. If you have not tried this style, place an order for one or more now.

38K626—Flesh. Sizes to fit 30 to 40 inches bust. State bust measure. Shipping wt., 2 oz. **45c**

A neat style Bandeau designed for the young girl or woman with slight or average figure. Beautifully tailored Rayon striped good quality cotton batiste in a fancy pattern. The natural lines of the figure, cut low under the arms and narrow in back. Hemstitched darts trim front. Neatly bound edges. Fancy lingerie tape shoulder straps.

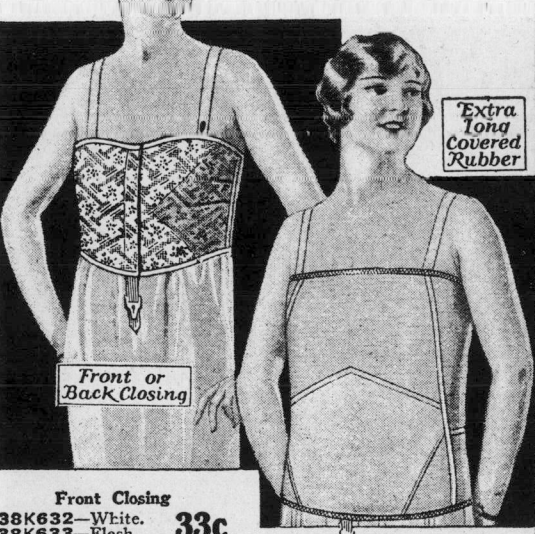

Front or Back Closing

Front Closing
38K632—White.
38K633—Flesh. **33c**
Sizes, 32 to 44 inches bust measure. State bust measure. Shpg. wt., 3 oz.

Back Closing
38K606—White.
38K607—Flesh. **33c**
Sizes, 30 to 40 inches bust measure. State bust measure. Shpg. wt., 3 oz.

Beautiful and durable **Mercerized Cotton Brocade** Bust Confiner; a favored style with many women. A style appropriate for the average and slight figure. Has 4-inch back with elastic insert; lightly boned at sides. Tape shoulder straps. Will launder satisfactorily and give good service.

For Other Bust Supporters See Page 110

Extra long Covered Rubber

38K667—Flesh. **$1.59**
Sizes to fit 32 to 46 inches bust measure. State bust measure. Shipping wt., 1 pound.

Extra Long Style Rubber Brassiere, a successful and very effective garment giving the appearance of slenderness while gently massaging superfluous flesh. Made of scientifically treated rubber, covered on both sides with a soft cotton knit fabric. No rubber can touch the skin. Has front flattening reinforcement over the diaphragm. Can be worn next to the skin or over the undergarments. Hooks down high back. Easily washed.

Linene

38K500—White. Sizes to fit 34 to 48 inches bust measure. State bust measure. Shipping weight, 3 ounces. **35c**

Wonderful value in Women's Durable Brassiere, made of good quality **cambric**, neatly trimmed in front with attractive patterns embroidery in assorted designs. Shield reinforcement under arms. Neat scalloped braid finishes back of neck and armholes. Opens in front.

Front or Back Closing

INDIAN HEAD

38K521—White. Sizes to fit 34 to 48 inches bust measure. State bust measure. Shpg. wt., 4 oz. **59c**

Brassiere of durable quality cotton **linene**, made with front opening, for the average and full figure. Trimmed with neat assorted patterns embroidery, front and back. Made with one-piece back and panels of elastic webbing under arms, permitting extra freedom.

38K520—White. **49c**
Same style as above, without elastic, but with panel of double fabric under arms. State bust measure.

Front Closing
38K630—White. **29c**
Sizes to fit 30 to 48 inches bust measure. State bust measure. Shpg. wt., 3 oz.

Back Closing
38K631—White. **29c**
Sizes to fit 30 to 40 inches bust measure. State bust measure. Shpg. wt., 3 oz.

Keep your figure trim and stylish with this inexpensive and popular Bandeau, made of the reliable Indian Head Cloth, known for its sturdy wearing qualities; launders beautifully. Elastic insert in back. Tape shoulder straps. Lightly boned at sides. Fine for everyday wear.

Round Neck or Bodice Top

Regular and Stout Sizes

38K1606—White. **75c**
Sizes to fit 34 to 44 in. bust measure. State size. Shpg. wt., ¾ lb.
This Built-Up-Style Union Suit is made of better quality crossbar nainsook with round neck neatly hemstitched, and draw tape. A ribbed knit insert across the back provides plenty of stretch and relieves all strain on the garment. Has open crotch with sure lap flap seat. Cut roomy at knees. Buttons down front.

38K1605—White. **85c** Stout Sizes
Sizes to fit 46 to 54 inches bust measure. State size. Shpg. wt., ¾ lb.
Same, but made for stout women.

38K1607—White. **53c** Regular Sizes
38K1608—Flesh. Sizes to fit 34 to 44 inches bust measure. State size. Shpg. wt., 8 oz.
Bodice Top Style Union Suit of standard quality crossbar nainsook. Same material shoulder straps. Top neatly hemstitched. Knitted ribbed insert in back for comfort. Open crotch with sure lap flap seat.

Cozy Flannelette Gowns — Two Leading Values

Stout and Regular Sizes

Regular Stout and Jumbo Sizes

38K9012—Light stripes. **98c**
38K9013—White.
Sizes to fit 34 to 44 inches bust measure. State size. Shipping weight, 1 pound.
Splendid value in **Better Quality Flannelette** Open Front Nightgown. Double front yoke beautifully trimmed with colored Lorraine embroidery work and hemstitching. Double yoke in back. Inexpensive, comfortable and serviceable. A gown sure to please.

STOUT SIZES
38K9060—White. **$1.48**
38K9061—Light stripes.
Sizes to fit 46 to 54 in. bust measure. State size. Shpg. wt., 1½ lbs.
A big value in Extra Size Gown of warm, durable, **better quality flannelette.** The double front yoke is prettily trimmed with hemstitching and colored Lorraine embroidery work. Double yoke in back.

REGULAR SIZES
38K9020—White. **$1.29**
38K9021—Light stripes.
Sizes to fit 34 to 44 in. bust measure. State size. Shpg. wt., 1¼ lbs.
Same as above, but in regular sizes.

38K9048
White, floral pattern. **$1.69**
Sizes to fit 34 to 44 inches bust measure. State size. Shipping weight, 1¼ lbs. Fancy floral design **Windsor Flannelette Nightgown.** High grade flannelette, well known for its soft, firm texture and long wearing qualities. Double yoke, front and back. Double stitched seams.

38K9068
White, floral pattern. **$1.85**
STOUT SIZES
Sizes to fit 46 to 54 inches bust measure. State size. Shipping weight, 1½ pounds.
Same as above, but for stout women.

Windsor Flannelette

Amoskeag Flannelette

38K9024—White. **$1.00**
38K9025—Flesh.
38K9026—Peach.
Sizes to fit 34 to 44 inches bust measure. State size. Shipping weight, 1¼ pounds.
Well made Nightgown of heavy, durable **Amoskeag Flannelette.** The front yoke is attractively trimmed with hemstitching and Rayon scallops. The front and back yokes are made double. An excellent selection.

38K9064
White. **$1.18**
STOUT SIZES
Sizes to fit 46 to 54 inches bust measure. State size. Shipping weight, 1½ pounds.
Same as above, but for stout women.

Resta Flannelette

$1.39
38K9016
White, floral pattern.
Sizes to fit 34 to 44 inches bust measure. State size. Shipping weight, 1¼ pounds.
Dependable quality, soft and long wearing **flannelette** is used in this high grade Gown. Has allover Dresden pattern floral design. Yoke is neatly hemstitched in fancy design and is double, front and back. Cut over full, generous sizes. Our price is very low for this wonderful value.

38K9004—Light stripes. **89c**
38K9005—White.
Sizes to fit 34 to 44 inches bust measure. State size. Shpg. wt., 1 lb.
Well made Nightgown of good quality **flannelette.** Double yoke, front and back, with hemstitching and colored Lorraine embroidery trim on front.

STOUT SIZES
38K9054—Light stripes. **$1.00**
38K9055—White.
Same style. Sizes to fit 46 to 54 inches bust measure. State size. Shpg. wt., 1¼ lbs.

EXTRA EXTRA SIZES
38K9051—Light stripes. **$1.08**
Same style. Sizes to fit 56 and 58 inches bust. State size. Shpg. wt., 1½ lbs.

38K9000
Light stripes. **65c**
Sizes to fit 34 to 44 inches bust measure. State size. Shpg. wt., 1 lb.
A bargain. Women's full cut, well made Nightgown of good quality **flannelette.** Not to be compared with low priced gowns of thin, light weight flannelette sold elsewhere. Yoke trimmed with hemstitching. Double yoke, front and back.

STOUT SIZES
38K9050
Light stripes. **79c**
Sizes to fit 46 to 54 inches bust measure. State size. Shpg. wt., 1¼ lbs.
Same as above, but for stout women.

BLENDOWN
Part Wool Flannelette

38K9043 **$1.48**
Fancy stripes.
Sizes to fit 34 to 44 inches bust measure. State size. Shpg. wt., 1 lb.
For extra warmth and serviceability, we highly recommend this Nightgown made of **Blendown Flannelette.** The texture of a small amount of wool and fine high grade combed cotton yarns assures warmth without bulkiness. You will realize what a splendid value it is for your money. The double front yoke is neatly hemstitched in an attractive design. Well made and cut over full generous sizes. All seams are firmly stitched. Double yoke in back.

38K9007—White. **79c**
38K9006—Light stripes.
Sizes to fit 34 to 44 inches bust measure. State size. Shipping weight, 1 lb.
Women's High Neck, Good Quality Flannelette Nightgown with collar. Double yoke, front and back. Opens in front. It will be economy for you to buy several at this low price.

38K9056
Light stripes. **95c**
STOUT SIZES
Sizes to fit 46 to 54 inches bust measure. State size. Shipping weight, 1¼ pounds.
Same as above, but for stout women.

38K9014—White. **89c**
38K9015—Light stripes.
Sizes to fit 34 to 44 inches bust measure. State size. Shipping weight, 1 pound.
Women who prefer a slipover style Nightgown will find this a remarkable value. Made of good quality flannelette and is cut full and roomy. The front is prettily hemstitched and embroidered with colored Lorraine work. Panels of shirring.

38K9028
Light stripes. **48c**
Sizes to fit 34 to 44 inches bust measure. State size. Shipping weight, 1 lb.
Save money and buy several of these inexpensive Nightgowns. Made of nice quality flannelette in slipover style and cut full and roomy. Round neck and short sleeves neatly hemstitched. Panel of shirring in front. A very low price, indeed!

Full Sizes— Well Made

For the Schoolgirl and Miss

38K9082—Flesh. **98c**
38K9083—Peach.
Sizes to fit 34 to 44 inches bust measure. State size. Shpg. wt., 1 lb. Warm Two-Piece Pajamas for women, made of soft, fleecy and durable flannelette. Cut full and roomy, making them comfortable garments. The slipover style coat is neatly trimmed with hemstitching. The trousers are cut in extra full sizes and have a draw tape at the waist.

$1.39
38K9092 Light stripes.
38K9093 White.
Sizes to fit 34 to 44 in. bust measure. State size. Shpg. wt., 1 lb.
Sleep in warmth and comfort in this One-Piece Sleeping Garment made of good, dependable quality, soft cozy flannelette. Extra full, comfortable cut. The front is neatly hemstitched and has two panels of shirring. Pocket. Opens down front and has drop seat. Ankles have elastic tie with neat ruffles. Well made.

Women's and Misses' Sizes

38K9084 Light **$1.49**
38K9085—White. stripes.
Sizes to fit 34 to 44 inches bust. State size. Shipping wt., 1½ lbs. Two-Piece Pajamas are very popular and this pretty style, made of better quality flannelette, you will find very comfortable and cozy for cold wintry nights. The coat is cut roomy with close fitting round neck and long sleeves. Buttons through smart Rayon frogs. Roomy trousers have draw tape at waist.

MISSES' SIZES
38K9362 Light **$1.29** stripes.
Ages, 12, 14 and 16 years. State age size. Shpg. wt., 1 lb. Same, but for the schoolgirl, miss or small woman.

38K9351 Light stripes, **69c** with feet.
38K9352—Light stripes, without feet. Ages, 7 to 14 years. State age size. Shipping weight, ⅝ pound. Schoolgirls' Warm and Comfortable One-Piece Sleeping Garment of good quality light striped flannelette. Drop seat. High neck and long sleeves.

Resta Flannelette

Misses' and Schoolgirls' Sizes

38K9360 Floral pattern. **$1.29** Ages, 7 to 14 years. State age size. Shipping weight, ¾ lb.
38K9361 Floral pattern. **$1.49** Ages, 16 to 18 years. State size. Shpg. wt., 1 lb. One-Piece Sleeper. Better quality soft and firm flannelette. Hemstitched; panels of shirring. Drop seat; pocket. Elastic at ankles.

Misses' and Schoolgirls' Sizes

38K9554 Light stripes. **73c**
38K9555 Dark gray stripes.
Sizes to fit 34 to 44 inches bust measure. State size. Shpg. wt., ¾ lb.
Women's Princess Slip of warm and good quality flannelette. Well made throughout. Wide flounce finished with neat hem. Neck and arm openings trimmed with shell crocheted edge. Buttons down front. Launders nicely.

Warm Nightgowns for Schoolgirls

38K9201 **59c**
Light stripes.
Ages, 7 to 14 years. State age size. Shipping weight, ¾ lb. Good Quality Flannelette Nightgown for the schoolgirl. Carefully made with a double yoke front and back. The front yoke is neatly hemstitched. Long sleeves. Well made and a wonderful value. At this price you can afford to buy more than one.

38K9204—White. **75c**
38K9205—Flesh.
Ages, 7 to 14 years. State age size. Shipping weight, ¾ lb. A splendid value Flannelette Nightgown for the schoolgirl. Made of plain color good quality flannelette that will give wonderful service. Double yoke front and back; the front yoke is prettily trimmed with colored Lorraine embroidery and hemstitching. Buttons close at neck.

38K9353 **89c**
Light stripes. Ages, 7 to 14 years. State age size. Shpg. wt., ¾ lb.
38K9356 **98c**
Light stripes. Ages, 16 to 18 years. State age size. Shpg. wt., 1 lb. Big value in Schoolgirls' Misses' or Small Women's Sleeping Garment. Made of better quality flannelette. Front closing trimmed with attractive Rayon frogs. Drop seat. Pocket. Full sizes. Cozy and warm.

38K9505—Light stripes. **59c**
38K9507—Gray stripes.
Ages, 7 to 14 years. State age size. Shipping weight, ¾ lb.
Warm Princess Slip for the school girl. Made of good quality flannelette. Buttons in back. Flounce neatly finished with scalloped embroidered edge. Neck and arm openings finished with shell crocheted edge. Warm and comfortable for colder days.

Parcel Post, Express and Freight Rates Are on Pages 42 to 545

Standard Quality Shawls
Guaranteed Values ~ Lower Prices

Fine Quality Honeycomb Shawl for MOTHER OR BABY

38K8037 — Cream-white with black stripes.............. **$5.65**

Average size, including fringe, about 2 yards square. Shipping weight, 1⅛ pounds.

Women's Fine Quality All Wool Shawl with cross hairline stripes. A medium weight wrap, suitable for all occasions. Also finds favor with the aged or infirm person who desires a warm, light color shawl. Will give excellent service.

$1.85

38K8031—White.
38K8032—Black.
38K8033—Gray.
38K8038—Light blue.
38K8039—Pink.

Size, including fringe, about 44x48 inches. Shipping weight, ¾ pound.

Soft All Wool Worsted Shawl of good quality and generous size. Is warm without being heavy. Knit in a fancy honeycomb stitch with beautiful border in assorted designs. A lovely shoulder shawl for women and particularly suitable to wrap baby in.

Larger Size
$2.25

38K8034—White.
38K8036—Gray.

Size, including fringe, about 52x64 inches. Shipping weight, 1 pound.

Larger size Shawl of same quality, warm, all wool worsted yarn; same pattern as above.

Reversible Beaver Shawls (Two Popular Styles)

38K8009—Fancy gray.
38K8010—Fancy brown. **$6.48**

Average size, including fringe, about 2 yards square. Shipping weight, 3 lbs.
Extra Fine Quality Reversible Beaver Shawl. Carefully woven from about ¾ wool and ¼ cotton. Beautiful design in border. Finished with looped fringe. Our best beaver shawl.

38K8087—Fancy gray.
38K8088—Fancy brown.
38K8089—Fancy black. **$4.79**

Average size, including fringe, about 2 yards square. Shpg. wt., 2¼ lbs.
High Grade Reversible Beaver Shawl. Medium heavy weight, closely woven from one-third wool, two-thirds cotton. Very warm. Don't be without one of these cozy warm shawls for winter comfort. Our reasonable price offers you the most for your money.

$1.59

38K8063—Lavender.
38K8064—White.
38K8055—Black.

Size, about 40 inches square. Shpg. wt., ¾ lb.
A Beautiful Shawl or Fascinator to slip around your shoulders when you begin to feel chilly. Knit in a fancy stitch of fine quality all wool worsted yarn and interknit with Rayon of same color. Has fancy designed border. Soft and warm.

87c

38K8026—Gray.
38K8027—Shepherd check.
38K8028—Brown.

Size, including fringe, about 37 inches square. Shpg. wt., 8 oz.
A warm and comfortable Shoulder Shawl for cold weather wear. Knit from one-half wool in a medium weight and finished with attractive striped border. Fringed all around.

38K8029—Gray.
38K8030—Brown. **$1.19**

About 42 inches square. Shipping weight, ¾ pounds.
Same as above, in larger size.

Your Choice of Two Sizes

$1.15

38K8051—White.
38K8050—Black.

Size, about 36 inches square. Shipping weight, 8 ounces.
Women's Fine Quality All Wool Worsted Square Shawl or Fascinator. Knit in a fancy stitch. Has attractively designed border. Warm and comfortable.

Shawl or Auto Wrap

38K8084—Gray.
38K8085—Brown. **$5.25**

Size, including fringe, about 2 yards square. Shipping weight, 3½ pounds.
You will make no mistake in selecting this beautiful, rich looking Shawl of firmly woven all wool yarns in a heavy weight. Hard to duplicate elsewhere at anywhere near this low price. Can also be used for motoring, or wherever you want a good warm robe. Neatly finished with a straight fringe.

$2.85

38K8003—Fancy gray.
38K8004—Fancy brown.

Average size, including fringe, about 64x64 in. Shipping weight, 1¾ lbs.
A warm and comfortable Reversible Beaver Shawl at a low price. Closely woven from cotton with a small amount of wool. Well napped and finished. Has fancy border and fringe. An excellent value at this price.

$4.48

38K8023—Gray.
38K8024—Brown.

Size, including fringe, about 2 yards square. Shipping weight, 1½ pounds.
Fine Quality Cloth Shawl. Woven from all wool. Medium heavy weight. Has fancy border and straight fringe.

$8.95

38K8025—Gray.

Size, including fringe, about 2 yards wide and 4 yards long. Shipping weight, 2¾ pounds.
Same as above, in gray only, double size.

$2.69

38K8011—Gray.
38K8012—Brown.

Size, including fringe, about 64 inches square. Shipping weight, 1¼ pounds.
A Dependable Quality Medium Weight Cloth Shawl. Firmly woven from all wool yarns. Will give good service.

$5.35

38K8013—Gray.

Size, about 64x128 in. Shipping weight, 1¾ pounds.
Same Shawl as above, in gray only, double size.

Healthful and Approved Maternity Wear

For many years we have specialized in the proper selection of Maternity Corsets for expectant mothers. Comfort and proper support are so necessary at this time, and the ordinary corset may be dangerous. A correctly designed Maternity Corset is the only solution. This page has a variety of styles from which you can select the one preferred. Order your corset today. Take present waist measure, without corset, at waistline at hollow of back, less 2 inches for lacing, where special instructions are not given in description.

$2.49
38K226—Pink.

Corset sizes, 22 to 40 inches. State corset size. Shipping weight, 1½ lbs.

A comfortable Maternity Corset of durable quality pink coutil. Has adjustable side lacings with cloth gussets underneath. Inside abdominal support of cotton surgical elastic webbing, hooks at side and is adjustable with elastic lacers. Wide surgical elastic webbing panels at top and panel extending full length down center of back. Flexible boning. Front length, 13 inches; 8-inch clasp, with one hook on skirt. Back length, 14 inches. Height of bust, 8½ inches. Four hose supporters.

$2.48
38K228—Pink.

Sizes, 22 to 38 inches. State corset size. Shpg. wt., 1¼ lbs.

"Berthe May" Maternity Belt or short corset for expectant mothers; also good for invalids or elderly women. Very comfortable. No boning over hips. Four tucks of material are provided inside the corset to allow all the future enlargement that may be needed. Has easy shoe hook front lacing backed with strip of soft plush. Duplex non-rustable steels. Top finished with neat edge. Front length, about 10 inches; back length, 13 inches. Four good hose supporters.

$2.58
38K220—White.
38K222—Pink.

Corset sizes, 22 to 38 inches. State corset size. Shpg. wt., 1¾ lbs.

"Ideal Brand" Maternity Corset of good quality coutil. Adjustable inside abdominal support. Elastic lacings front and sides and cloth gussets underneath. Back lacing. Duplex boning. Front length, 14 inches; 8 inch steel clasp and three strong hooks on skirt. Back length, 15½ inches; height of bust, 3 inches. Embroidery trimming. Four hose supporters.

$1.79
38K207—Pink.

Corset sizes, 22 to 38 in. State corset size. Shipping weight, 1½ pounds.

This wonderful, scientifically made Maternity Corset carries our heartiest recommendation for both comfort and service. Strongly made of coutil, with flexible boning. The smooth fitting, restful back comes well above the waistline. The front pouch, which is strapped and lightly boned to uplift and support the abdomen, is adjustable by lacers at both sides to any type of figure. Closes at side with hooks and eyes. Back lacing. Length of back, 14 in. Four hose supporters.

$2.39
38K221—Pink.
38K218—White.

Corset sizes, 22 to 34 inches. State corset size. Shpg. wt., 1¾ lbs.

"Ideal Brand" Maternity Corset of good quality coutil. Abdominal support with elastic lacers, together with front and side elastic lacers, can be adjusted as needed. Cloth gussets underneath lacers. Embroidery trim. Front length, 13½ in., with an 8-inch steel clasp; three strong hooks. Back length, 16 inches. Height of bust, 3 in. Duplex boning. Back lacing. Four good quality hose supporters.

$2.25
38K216—Pink.

Corset sizes, 24 to 40 inches. State your present waist measure. Do not deduct 2 inches for lacing. Shpg. wt., 1¼ lbs.

Comfortable coutil Maternity Corset with no steels or clasps over sensitive abdomen. Wide front panel is made of soft, pliable elastic webbing. Famous flexible woven wire boning bends comfortably with the body. Corset clasps at side of abdomen with lacings for outlet. Elastic panel at back. Cut low in front and longer in back to give comfortable support. Front length, about 10 inches; back length, 15 in. Four good elastic hose supporters.

For Other Corsets See Pages 106 to 120.

Elastic Laces~

Famous Flexible Woven Wire Boning

$1.59
38K202—Flesh.

Sizes, 24 to 34 inches. State your present waist size. Do not deduct 2 in. for lacing. Shpg. wt., 1¼ lbs.

Many mothers-to-be, who are not accustomed to wearing a corset, will have comfort in this one. The wide elastic section in front prevents any possible pressure and permits greater ease. Lower than the usual corset, but high enough for proper support. Hooks at side, has lacings for necessary expansion. The back section is of strong, serviceable coutil, lightly boned. Four hose supporters. Front length, 10 in.; back length, 12 inches.

$1.39
38K206—White.

Corset sizes, 24 to 38 in. State corset size. Do not deduct 2 inches for lacing. Shipping weight, 1¼ pounds.

Practical and comfortable is this clasp around model Maternity Girdle of coutil at a remarkably low price. Being topless makes it ideal for the woman accustomed to wearing a light girdle. Surgical elastic webbing panels in front and back. Shaped front clasp which cannot dig in at top and flexible boning. Full length lacers at sides for outlet. Front length, 10 in.; back length, 12 in. Four hose supporters.

Comfortable Nursing Brassiere~

85c
38K275—Pink.

Sizes to fit 34 to 48 in. bust measure. State bust measure. Shpg. wt., 7 oz.

A new and improved style Nursing Brassiere. Fastens with hooks and eyes at each side of panel in front without the least inconvenience. The front panel and back are made of durable fancy pattern cotton madras; panels of elastic webbing at waist in front allow comfortable fit. The firm, absorbent, cotton knit, fabric used over busts insures support without pressure.

Waterproof Front

49c
38K276—White.

Sizes, 32 to 46 inches bust measure. State present bust measure taken snugly around body over fullest part of breasts. Shipping weight, 4 ounces.

This Waterproof Brassiere is correctly designed for comfort and protection and should be worn by every careful nursing mother. The front is rubberized nainsook and prevents other clothing becoming wet or soiled; reinforced buttoned nursing flaps. Hooks in front. Back made of strong batiste with elastic panel. Tape shoulder straps.

98c
38K234—White.

Sizes to fit. 34 to 44 inches bust measure. State size. Shipping wt., 1 lb.

Maternity or Hospital Nightgown, opening full length down front. Made of standard quality nainsook with neat front yoke of embroidery insertions, pin tucks and embroidery ruffle at neck. Nursing sections fasten with buttons and are cleverly concealed beneath panels of embroidery. Made in full sizes. Launders well.

$1.69
38K277—Pink.

Sizes 30 to 44 in. bust measure. State present bust measure. Do not make any extra allowance in your measurement. Shpg. wt., 1½ lbs.

Corset Brassiere of durable cotton madras. Shaped inside elastic belt support. Improved high back; elastic panel below waistline. Lacing at sides and inside support can be adjusted. Both hook conveniently at side. Four elastic hose supporters.

$2.75
38K278—Pink.

Same style and sizes as above, but of fine quality fancy mercerized brocade. State size.

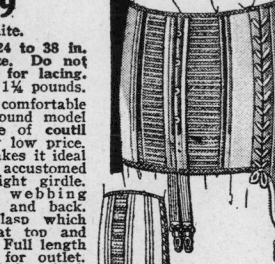

Little Tots' Knitwear
at Money Saving Prices

$2.79
38K7881—White, blue trim.
38K7882—White, pink trim.
One size, for ages up to 12 months. Shpg. wt., 1 lb.
Babies' Attractive Three-Piece Knitted Set—Sweater, drawer leggings with closed feet, and fancy hockey cap. Knit from fine quality all wool worsted yarn in links and links stitch with colored Rayon stripes and hand-made rosebuds. A useful outfit for baby and will make a lovely gift set.

43c
38K8606—White, blue trim.
38K8607—White, pink trim.
One size only, for ages up to 4 months. Shpg. wt., 2 oz. Hand Crocheted All Wool Bootees. Knee length. Embroidered rosebuds. Draw string. A large size better quality bootee.

23c
38K8600—Blue trim.
38K8601—Pink trim.
Infants' size only, for ages up to 3 months. Shipping weight, 2 ounces. Hand Crocheted All Wool White Bootees with contrasting color trim.

Infants' size only, for ages up to 6 months.

Knee Length Legging Bootee
65c
38K8602—Blue trim.
38K8603—Pink trim.
Shipping weight, 4 ounces. This soft and warm all wool knitted white legging Bootee comes well above the knee. Trimmed with contrasting color satin ribbon draw and Rayon rosebuds.

29c
38K8620 Blue trim.
38K8621 Pink trim.
Infants' size only, for ages up to 4 months. Shpg. wt., 2 oz. Hand Crocheted All Wool White Bootees in fancy stitch. Contrasting color trim.

37c
38K8622 Blue trim.
38K8623 Pink trim.
Infants' size only, for ages up to 6 months. Shpg. wt., 2 oz. Hand Crocheted All Wool White Bootees. Contrasting color trim.

$2.98
38K7888 Buff, brown trim.
38K7889—Peacock blue, buff trim.
One size, for ages 1 to 2 years. Shipping weight, 1 pound.
This Cozy and Warm Three-Piece Set consists of sweater, drawer leggings with open feet and close fitting hockey cap. Knit of good quality all wool worsted yarn in fancy links and links stitch. Fancy border trim of contrasting color.

The New Legging With Patented Fastener

$1.65
38K7897—White, blue trim.
38K7898—White, pink trim.
One size only, for babies up to 4 months of age. Shpg. wt., ¾ lb.
This dainty Set, consisting of sweater, cap and bootees is beautifully knit of soft and warm zephyr wool. Trimmed with knitted stripes of contrasting color Rayon and satin ribbon ties. An inexpensive set and a very beautiful gift suggestion.

$1.98
38K7755—White.
38K7756—Red.
38K7757—Buff.
Ages, 1 to 4 years. State age size. Shpg. wt., ¾ lb.
Little Tots' High Grade Belted Style Sweater Coat. Knit in a fancy links and links stitch from extra fine quality soft all wool zephyr yarn.

87c
38K8550—Black.
38K8551—Navy blue.
38K8552—Brown.
Ages, 2 to 6 yrs. State age. Shpg. wt., ¾ lb.
Children's Serviceable Jersey Knit Cotton Drawer Leggings. Fleece lined. Waist fitted with elastic band in back. Cut full and roomy and well made throughout. Priced reasonably.

$1.35
With Feet
38K8554—White.
Without Feet
38K8555—Red.
38K8556—White.
38K8583—Brown.
Ages, 1, 2 and 3 yrs. State age, Shpg. wt., 7 oz.
Children's Fine Quality Heavy Weight All Wool Worsted Knit Drawer Leggings. Fashioned to fit. Draw string at waist.

79c
With Feet
38K8560—White.
Without Feet
38K8561—White.
38K8562—Red.
Ages, 1, 2 and 3 yrs. State age. Shpg. wt., 6 oz.
Warm Drawer Leggings, well knit in a firm stitch from good quality all wool zephyr yarn. Fashioned to fit. Draw string at waist.

$1.98
38K8584—Brown.
38K8585—Navy blue.
38K8586—Buff.
38K8587—Powder blue.
Ages, 2 to 6 yrs. State age. Shpg. wt., ¾ lb.
Introducing the new drawer legging with guaranteed patented fastener. A serviceable Jersey Knit Cotton Drawer Legging, warmly fleeced inside, fastener at legs that can be opened and closed in a jiffy. Draw tape at waist. Cut full and roomy.

For Ages 6 mos. 1 and 2 Years

$1.29
38K8624—White, blue trim.
38K8625—White, pink trim.
Ages, 6 months, 1 and 2 yrs. State age. Shpg. wt., 7 oz.
A soft and warm Sweater Coat for the baby. Knit in a fancy links and links stitch of all wool worsted yarn with contrasting color trim. Very beautiful and will give satisfactory service.

$1.25
38K8608 Blue trim.
38K8609 Pink trim.
One size only, for ages up to 6 months. Shpg. wt., 5 oz.
Infants' beautiful Sacque, knit of best quality all wool white yarn in links and links stitch. Dainty hand crocheted edge. Trimmed with crocheted rosebuds.

89c
38K8626 White, blue trim.
38K8627 White, pink trim.
One size only, for ages up to 5 months. Shpg. wt., 5 oz.
Babies' dainty Sacque. Hand crocheted in a fancy shell stitch; fine quality soft all wool zephyr yarn.

47c
38K8187 White, blue trim.
38K8188 White, pink trim.
For ages up to 2 yrs. State age. Shpg. wt., 3 oz.
Babies' Warm All Wool Worsted Hand Crocheted Cap with ear tabs. Contrasting color trim.

89c
38K8610—White, blue trim.
38K8611—White, pink trim.
One size only, for ages up to 6 months. Shpg. wt., 5 oz.
A dainty Sacque for the wee baby. Knit of soft all wool white yarns in links and links stitch and trimmed with contrasting color Rayon rosebuds and stripes.

69c
38K8634 White, blue trim.
38K8635 White, pink trim.
One size only, for ages up to 4 months. Shpg. wt., 5 oz.
Infants' Pretty Hand Crocheted Sacque of soft and warm all wool zephyr yarn.

33c
38K8636—White, blue trim.
38K8637—White, pink trim.
One size, for ages up to 12 months. Shpg. wt., 2 oz.
Babies' Thumbless Mittens. Knit from soft all wool yarn with lustrous Rayon stripes. Trimmed with Rayon rosebud and has knit cord.

Babies' Outfits at Money Saving Prices

Outfit 38K106 $10.35 46 Pieces

Trimmed in Pink or Blue. State choice. Shipping weight, 7 pounds.

1 White Lawn Dress. Embroidered yoke. Bottom lace and embroidery trimmed.
1 White Nainsook Dress. Embroidered yoke. Bottom finished with embroidery edge.
2 White Nainsook Bishop Style Slips finished with lace edge.
1 White Gertrude Nainsook Underskirt with lace insertion and edged ruffle.
2 White Flannelette Gertrude Underskirts.
2 White Flannelette Sleeping Bags.
1 White Gertrude Nainsook Underskirt with tucks and hemstitched hem.
1 White Flannelette Wrapper. Machine stitched turnback edges and cuffs.
2 White Flannelette Pinning Blankets.
1 Embroidered White Flannelette Sacque.
2 Pairs All Wool Hand Crocheted Bootees. Ankle length.
3 Cream-White Knit Undershirts. About one-fourth wool.
3 Cream-White Flannel Bands. About one-half wool.
3 White Cotton Granite Cloth Bibs.
12 White Cotton Birdseye Diapers, hemmed ready for use. Size, 24x24 in.
1 Pair White Gum Rubber Diaper Pants.
1 White Gum Rubber Crib Sheet. Size, 24x24 inches.
2 Quilted Muslin Pads. Size, 15x17 in.
1 Cake Fine Castile Baby Soap.
2 Books Assorted Size Safety Pins. Nickel plated and rustproof.
1 Can Good Talcum Powder.
1 Book, "How to Take Care of the Baby."

Sears Complete Layettes are a big time and labor saving idea. Each set is complete in itself, and reaches you in a fresh and sanitary condition. A greater saving is made in buying these complete sets than if you were to select each garment separately.

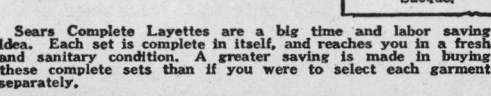

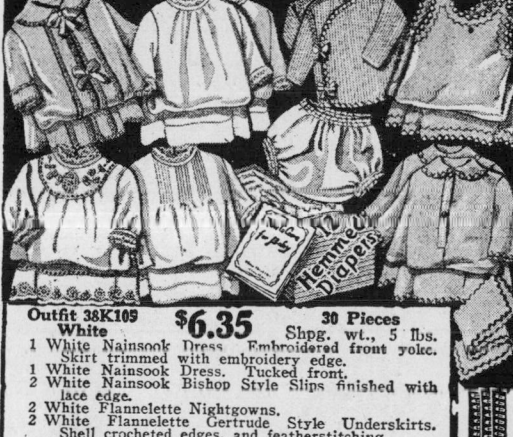

Outfit 38K109 $6.35 30 Pieces
White

Shpg. wt., 5 lbs.

1 White Nainsook Dress. Embroidered front yoke. Skirt trimmed with embroidery edge.
1 White Nainsook Dress. Tucked front.
2 White Nainsook Bishop Style Slips finished with lace edge.
2 White Flannelette Nightgowns.
2 White Flannelette Gertrude Style Underskirts. Shell crocheted edges, and featherstitching.
1 White Flannelette Wrapper. Machine stitched turnback edges and cuffs.
1 Pair White Gum Rubber Diaper Pants. Waterproof and washable.
2 Knitted Cream-White Undershirts, about one-fourth wool.
2 Cream-White Flannel Bands, one-half wool.
2 Pairs All Wool Cream-White Cashmere Stockings.
12 White Cotton Birdseye Diapers. Hemmed ready for use. Size, about 20x20 inches.
1 Book Assorted Size Safety Pins. Nickel plated and rustproof.
1 Book, "How to Take Care of the Baby."

Outfit 38K109 $9.48 44 Pieces

Trimmed in Pink or Blue. State choice. Shipping weight, 6½ pounds.

1 White Lawn Dress, attractive pattern embroidery. Embroidered yoke.
1 White Nainsook Dress. Square embroidery front yoke.
2 White Nainsook Bishop Style Slips finished with lace edge.
1 White Nainsook Gertrude Underskirt, clusters of tucks and embroidery ruffle.
2 White Flannelette Gertrude Underskirts. Featherstitching and shell crocheted edges.
1 White Nainsook Underskirt. Finished with tucks and hemstitched hem.
2 White Flannelette Wrappers. Trimmed with machine stitching.
2 White Flannelette Sleeping Bags.
2 White Flannelette Pinning Blankets.
1 Embroidered White Flannelette Sacque.
2 Pairs All Wool Hand Crocheted Bootees. Ankle length.
3 White Cotton Granite Cloth Bibs.
12 White Cotton Birdseye Diapers. Size, about 20x20 inches. Hemmed.
3 Cream-White Flannel Abdominal Bands, about one-half wool.
3 Fine Ribbed Cream-White Undershirts. Knit from about one-fourth wool.
2 Soft Finish Cotton Turkish Towels. Size about 13x23 inches.
1 Cake Fine Castile Baby Soap.
1 Book, "How to Take Care of the Baby."
1 Can Good Talcum Powder.
1 Book Assorted Size Safety Pins. Nickel plated and rustproof.

Outfit 38K108 $14.98 49 Pieces

Outfit Trimmed in Pink or Blue. State choice. Shipping weight, 9½ lbs.

1 White Lawn Dress. Deep embroidery skirt. Hand embroidered yoke.
1 White Lawn Dress. Embroidered yoke. Skirt has two rows lace insertion and lace edge.
1 White Nainsook Dress. Embroidered yoke.
2 White Nainsook Bishop Style Slips finished with lace edge.
1 Gertrude Style White Nainsook Underskirt. Lace edge ruffle and insertion.
1 White Nainsook Gertrude Underskirt.
2 Gertrude Cream-White Flannel Underskirts. About one-fourth wool. Featherstitched hem.
1 Embroidered Gertrude Underskirt of cream-white flannel. About one-fourth wool.
1 White Flannelette Wrapper. Colored machine stitched turnback border and cuffs.
1 White Flannelette Wrapper. Fancy revers.
3 White Flannelette Sleeping Bags, with draw string.
1 Soft Fleecy Cotton Receiving Blanket.
3 Cream-White Undershirts, knit from about one-fourth wool.
3 Cream-White Flannel Bands, about one-half wool.
12 Absorbent White Cotton Birdseye Diapers, hemmed ready for use. Size, about 24x24 inches.
1 Kleinert's Rubber Coated and Waterproof White Crib Sheet, about ¾ yard square.
2 Pairs Cream-White All Wool Cashmere Stockings.
1 Pair All Wool Hand Crocheted Bootees. Ankle Length.
2 Soft Cotton Turkish Towels. Size, about 13x23 inches.
1 Fancy Embroidered Lawn Bib.
1 Cake Fine Castile Baby Soap.
1 Braided Straw Toilet Basket.
2 White Cotton "Arnold Knit" Wash Cloths.
1 Can Good Talcum Powder.
1 Book, "How to Take Care of the Baby."
2 Books Assorted Size Rustproof Safety Pins.

Send Sufficient Money for Postage on Parcel Post Shipments. Any Surplus Will Be Returned

145

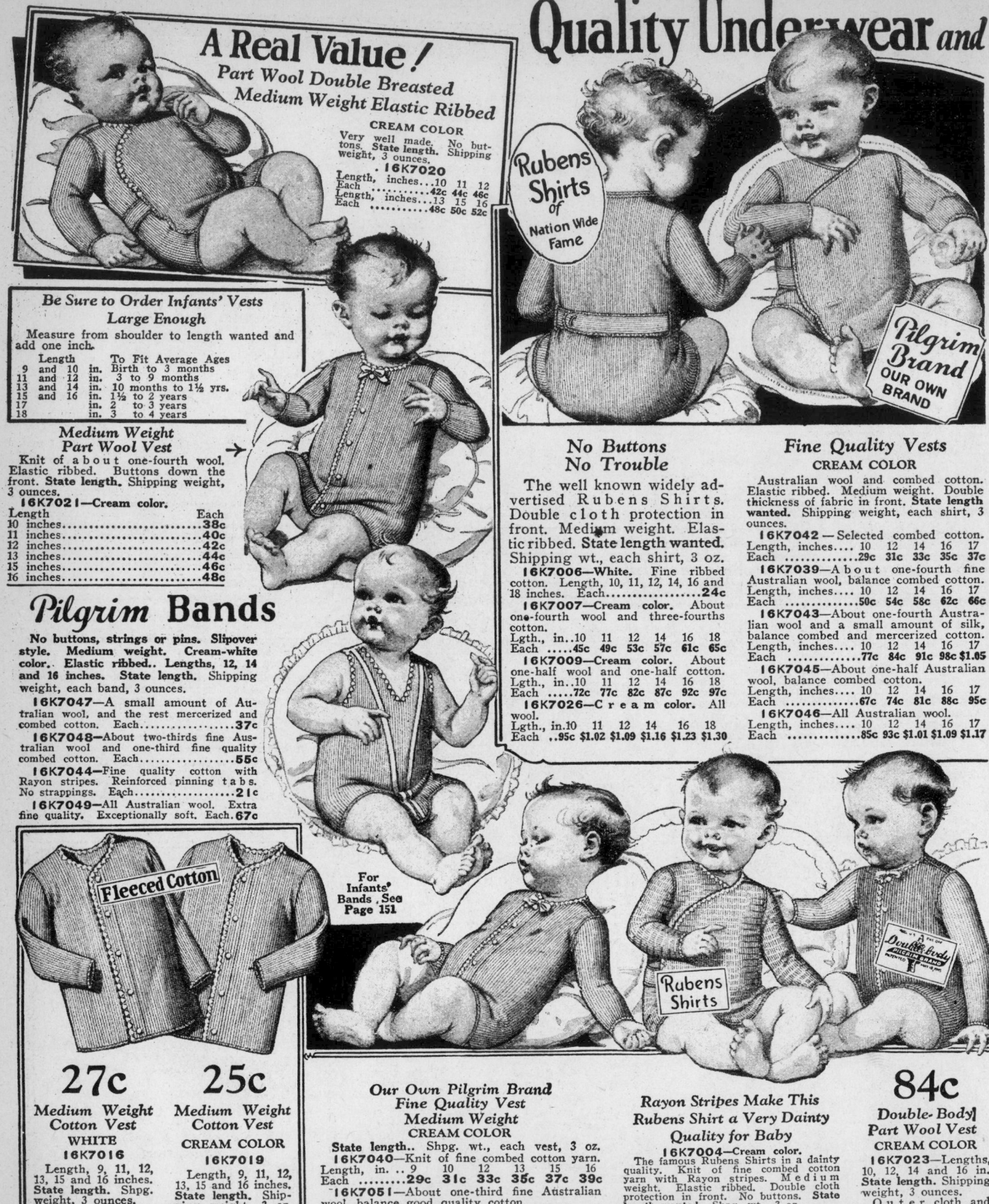

A Real Value!
Part Wool Double Breasted
Medium Weight Elastic Ribbed
CREAM COLOR

Very well made. No buttons. State length. Shipping weight, 3 ounces.

. 16K7020

Length, inches	10	11	12
Each	42c	44c	46c

Length, inches	13	15	16
Each	48c	50c	52c

Quality Underwear and

Rubens Shirts of Nation Wide Fame

Pilgrim Brand OUR OWN BRAND

Be Sure to Order Infants' Vests Large Enough

Measure from shoulder to length wanted and add one inch.

Length	To Fit Average Ages
9 and 10 in.	Birth to 3 months
11 and 12 in.	3 to 9 months
13 and 14 in.	10 months to 1½ yrs.
15 and 16 in.	1½ to 2 years
17 in.	2 to 3 years
18 in.	3 to 4 years

Medium Weight Part Wool Vest

Knit of about one-fourth wool. Elastic ribbed. Buttons down the front. State length. Shipping weight, 3 ounces.

16K7021—Cream color.

Length	Each
10 inches	38c
11 inches	40c
12 inches	42c
13 inches	44c
15 inches	46c
16 inches	48c

Pilgrim Bands

No buttons, strings or pins. Slipover style. Medium weight. Cream-white color. Elastic ribbed. Lengths, 12, 14 and 16 inches. State length. Shipping weight, each band, 3 ounces.

16K7047—A small amount of Australian wool, and the rest mercerized and combed cotton. Each................37c

16K7048—About two-thirds fine Australian wool and one-third fine quality combed cotton. Each................55c

16K7044—Fine quality cotton with Rayon stripes. Reinforced pinning tabs. No strappings. Each................21c

16K7049—All Australian wool. Extra fine quality. Exceptionally soft. Each 67c

Fleeced Cotton

For Infants' Bands, See Page 151

No Buttons No Trouble

The well known widely advertised Rubens Shirts. Double cloth protection in front. Medium weight. Elastic ribbed. State length wanted. Shipping wt., each shirt, 3 oz.

16K7006—White. Fine ribbed cotton. Length, 10, 11, 12, 14, 16 and 18 inches. Each................24c

16K7007—Cream color. About one-fourth wool and three-fourths cotton.

Lgth., in.	10	11	12	14	16	18
Each	45c	49c	53c	57c	61c	65c

16K7009—Cream color. About one-half wool and one-half cotton.

Lgth., in.	10	11	12	14	16	18
Each	72c	77c	82c	87c	92c	97c

16K7026—Cream color. All wool.

Lgth., in.	10	11	12	14	16	18
Each	95c	$1.02	$1.09	$1.16	$1.23	$1.30

Fine Quality Vests
CREAM COLOR

Australian wool and combed cotton. Elastic ribbed. Medium weight. Double thickness of fabric in front. State length wanted. Shipping weight, each shirt, 3 ounces.

16K7042—Selected combed cotton.

Length, inches	10	12	14	16	17
Each	29c	31c	33c	35c	37c

16K7039—About one-fourth fine Australian wool, balance combed cotton.

Length, inches	10	12	14	16	17
Each	50c	54c	58c	62c	66c

16K7043—About one-fourth Australian wool and a small amount of silk, balance combed and mercerized cotton.

Length, inches	10	12	14	16	17
Each	77c	84c	91c	98c	$1.05

16K7045—About one-half Australian wool, balance combed cotton.

Length, inches	10	12	14	16	17
Each	67c	74c	81c	88c	95c

16K7046—All Australian wool.

Length, inches	10	12	14	16	17
Each	85c	93c	$1.01	$1.09	$1.17

Rubens Shirts

Double Body

27c
Medium Weight Cotton Vest
WHITE
16K7016

Length, 9, 11, 12, 13, 15 and 16 inches. State length. Shpg. weight, 3 ounces. Elastic ribbed. Slighly fleeced. Knit of good quality cotton yarn. Well made and finished.

25c
Medium Weight Cotton Vest
CREAM COLOR
16K7019

Length, 9, 11, 12, 13, 15 and 16 inches. State length. Shipping weight, 3 oz. Elastic ribbed. Slightly fleeced. Made of fine quality cotton. Medium weight.

Our Own Pilgrim Brand Fine Quality Vest
Medium Weight
CREAM COLOR

State length.. Shpg. wt., each vest, 3 oz.

16K7040—Knit of fine combed cotton yarn.

Length, in...	9	10	12	13	15	16
Each	29c	31c	33c	35c	37c	39c

16K7051—About one-third fine Australian wool, balance good quality cotton.

Length, in...	9	10	12	13	15	16
Each	65c	69c	73c	77c	81c	85c

16K7059—About one-half fine Australian wool, balance silk.

Length, in...	9	10	12	13	15	16
Each	$1.45	$1.55	$1.65	$1.75	$1.85	$1.95

Rayon Stripes Make This Rubens Shirt a Very Dainty Quality for Baby

16K7004—Cream color. The famous Rubens Shirts in a dainty quality. Knit of fine combed cotton yarn with Rayon stripes. Medium weight. Elastic ribbed. Double cloth protection in front. No buttons. State length wanted. Shpg. wt., 3 oz.

Length	Each
10 inches	35c
11 inches	37c
12 inches	39c
14 inches	41c
16 inches	43c
18 inches	45c

84c
Double-Body Part Wool Vest
CREAM COLOR

16K7023—Lengths, 10, 12, 14 and 16 in. State length. Shipping weight, 3 ounces. Outer cloth and sleeves of fine quality combed cotton. Inside cloth is about one-fourth wool and three-fourths combed cotton.

Hosiery for Infants

A Special Bargain
32c
About One-Half Wool

86K2740—Black.
86K2742—White.
86K2743—Beige.

Sizes, 4, 4½, 5, 5½, 6 and 6½. State size. Shipping weight, 2 ounces.

Warm and exceptionally serviceable stockings. Knit of about one-half fine quality wool and one-half high grade cotton. Medium weight, fine elastic ribbed legs, fully seamless flat knit feet. Silk tipped heels and toes.

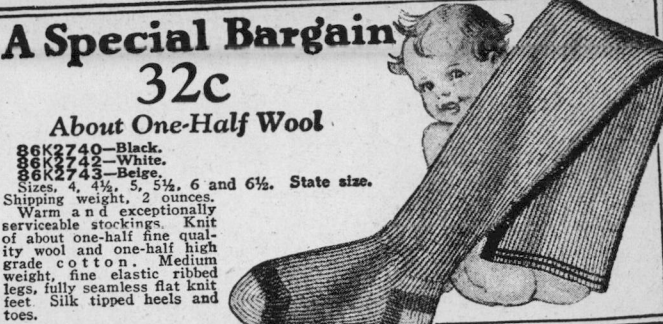

45c
Rayon and Wool

86K2772—Black.
86K2773—White.
86K2774—Pongee.

Sizes, 4½, 5, 5½ and 6. State size. Shipping weight, 3 ounces.

Soft, dainty stockings that will prove very dressy for baby. They are knit of about three-fourths fine quality wool and about one-fourth Rayon yarns. The legs are fine elastic ribbed with flat knit seamless feet.

Pilgrim Babe
All Wool Unshrinkable

43c
Our Own Brand Guaranteed All Wool and Unshrinkable

86K2768—Black.   86K2769—White.

Sizes, 4, 4½, 5, 5½, 6 and 6½. State size. Shipping weight, each pair, 2 ounces.

Our "Pilgrim Babe" Stockings offer mothers the biggest value that can be had anywhere in infants' stockings. They are knit of the finest quality Australian wool, very soft, and comfortable for baby's tender skin. They will not shrink regardless of repeated washings, because they have been put through a special process which makes them non-shrinkable. These stockings are good medium weight. The legs are fine elastic knit and the feet are fully seamless. The toes and heels are daintily tipped with silk.

23c Each Pair
About One-Third Wool

86K2752—Black.
86K2754—Cream-white.
86K2755—Pongee.

Sizes, 4½, 5, 5½ and 6. State size. Shipping weight, 2 ounces.

Knit of about one-third wool and two-thirds cotton and quite able to keep tiny feet warm and comfy. Elastic ribbed legs. Seamless flat knit feet have reinforced heels and toes. Medium weight.

Scale of Sizes for Infants						
Size of Shoe	1 2	3 4-5	6-7	8-8½		
Size of Hosiery	4	4½	5	5½	6	6½

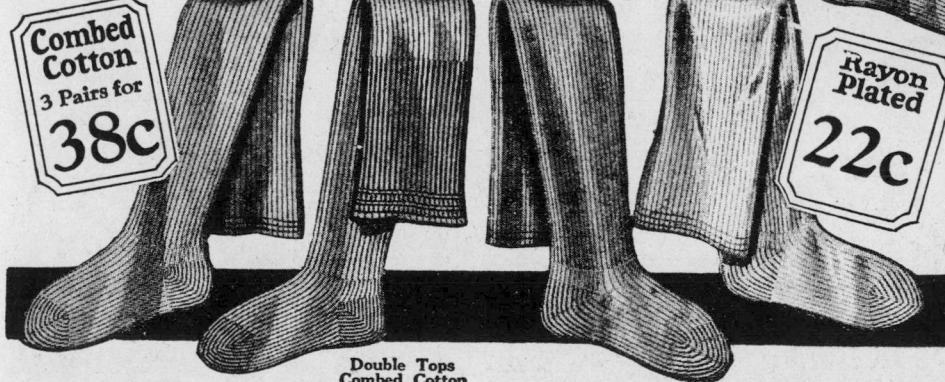

Combed Cotton 3 Pairs for 38c

Rayon Plated 22c

3 Pairs for 38c
Neat and Serviceable Stockings

86K2706—Black.
86K2707—White.
86K2708 — Dark brown.
86K2709—Pink.
86K2710—Light blue.

Sizes, 4½, 5, 5½ and 6. State size. Shipping weight, 3 pairs, 5 oz.

Knit from very good quality combed cotton yarn. Medium weight. Elastic ribbed legs and flat knit seamless feet. Reinforced heels and toes.

Double Tops Combed Cotton
18c Each Pair

86K2727—Black.
86K2728—White.
86K2729—Dark brown.
86K2730—Pongee.

Sizes, 4½, 5, 5½, 6 and 6½. State size. Shpg. wt., 2 oz.

He is a fortunate baby whose mother buys these stockings for him. The good quality combed cotton of which they are made stands for durability and is helped greatly by the double tops. Reinforced heels and toes. Elastic ribbed legs and flat knit seamless feet. Medium weight.

3 Pairs for 30c
Medium Weight Cotton

86K2713—Black.
86K2714—White.
86K2712—Dark brown.
86K2711—Pongee.

Sizes, 4½, 5, 5½ and 6. State size. Shipping weight, 3 pairs, 5 ounces.

Save money buying the three pair lot way. These good quality cotton stockings have flat knit seamless feet and fine elastic ribbed legs. Reinforced heels and toes.

22c Each Pair

86K2700—Black.
86K2701—White.
86K2702—Pongee.
86K2703—Camel color.

Sizes, 4, 4½, 5, 5½, 6, 6½. State size. Shipping wt., each pair, 2 oz.

A fine dressy stocking knit of Rayon reinforced with mercerized cotton to give greater strength. Mercerized cotton heels and toes. Fully seamless.

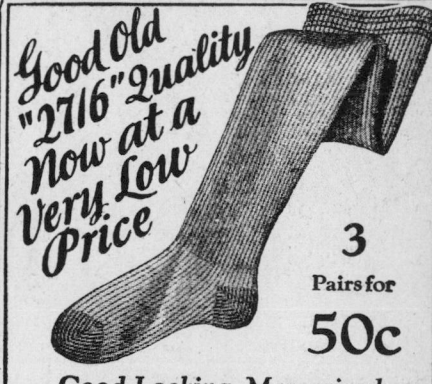

Good Old "27/6" Quality Now at a Very Low Price

3 Pairs for 50c
Good Looking, Mercerized Stockings at a Big Reduction

86K2722—Blush.
86K2716—Black.
86K2717—White.
86K2718—Pongee.
86K2723—Dark brown.

Sizes, 4½, 5, 5½ and 6. State size. Shipping weight, 3 pairs, 5 ounces.

One of our most popular stockings for infants. We buy immense quantities of them, that's why we can sell them so cheap. Medium weight, knit of fine quality mercerized cotton. Fine elastic ribbed legs with flat knit seamless feet. Reinforced heels and toes.

Stylish Coats for Little Tots

For Coats for Larger Girls See Pages 47 to 50.

38K6679—Gray. **38K6680**—Navy blue. **$3.98**
38K6681—Brown. Ages, 1, 2 and 3 years. State age size. Shpg. wt., 2¼ lbs. A Warm and Attractive Double Breasted Overcoat for the baby boy. Made of heavy weight chinchilla cloth of more than three-fourths wool. Snug fitting turnover collar. Belted back. Flap pockets. Lined with good quality sateen.

CAP TO MATCH
38K6846—Gray. **38K6847**—Navy blue. **89c**
38K6848—Brown. Sizes, 19 to 21½ inches headband. State measurement. Shipping weight, 1 pound. Warm and Serviceable Chinchilla Cloth Polo Style Cap with ear tabs. Has woven headband. Chin elastic. Lined with sateen.

38K6673—Rose-wood tan. **$5.98**
38K6674—Copenhagen blue. Ages, 1, 2 and 3 years. age size. Shpg. wt., 1¾ lbs. Pretty Coat of soft and dressy all wool suede velour. Convertible collar of soft coney fur; smart raglan sleeves, fancy tucks and stitching. Sateen lining, warm interlining.

HAT TO MATCH
38K6861—Rose-wood tan. **$1.48**
38K6862—Rose-wood tan. **38K6863**—Copenhagen blue. Hat to match. Hand embroidery and ribbon trim.

38K6661—Peacock blue. **$6.48**
38K6662—Rosewood tan. Ages, 1, 2 and 3 years. State age size. Shipping wt., 2 lbs. All Wool Broadcloth Coat. Coney fur collar; smocked panels. Sateen lining; interlining.

HAT TO MATCH
38K6864—Peacock blue. **$1.59**
38K6865—Rosewood tan. Shipping weight, ¾ pound.

38K6671—Marine blue. **$5.35**
38K6672—Leaf brown. Ages, 1, 2 and 3 yrs. State age size. Shpg. wt., 2 lbs. Girls' Coat of all wool Velour; lined with durable sateen; warmly interlined. Convertible coney fur collar. All around fancy stitching running into panels under pockets.

HAT TO MATCH
38K6860—Marine blue. **$1.58**
38K6861—Leaf brown. Shipping weight, ¾ pound. Coney fur, floral trim.

38K6609—Powder blue. **$3.68**
38K6610—Buff. Ages, 1, 2 and 3 years. State age size. Shipping weight, 2 lbs. A wonderful value! Heavyweight coat of one-third wool chinchilla finish eiderdown cloth. A stylish model, suitable for fall and winter wear. Generously trimmed with Karami cloth, resembling a soft, thick fur. Trimmed with fancy stitching. Quilted sateen lining.

HAT TO MATCH
38K6858—Powder blue. **98c**
38K6859—Buff. Shipping weight, ¾ lb. Hat to match Coat. Elastic across back; Karami cloth shield and Rayon ribbon trim.

$2.50 →
38K6600—Cream-white. Ages, 6 months, 1 and 2 years. State age size. Shipping wt., 1½ lbs. Becoming style in Walking Length Cape Coat of a fine quality two-thirds wool closely woven cashmere. Beautiful embroidered design on cape and finished with embroidered scalloped edge of Rayon. Sateen lining; flannelette interlining.

Hand Embroidered

← **$1.79**
38K6601—Cream-white. Ages, 6 months, 1 and 2 years. State age size. Shipping weight, ¾ pound. This attractive Walking Length Coat is made of finely woven cotton cashmere and is exceptionally low priced. Circular cape on round yoke is beautifully embroidered and finished with scalloped embroidered edge. Embroidered design on skirt to match cape. Lined with cambric and warmly interlined with flannelette.

38K6500 **$2.69**
Cream-white. Infants' size only. Shipping weight, ¾ lb. Our Best Quality Long Coat. Made of finely woven two-thirds wool cashmere. The lined shoulder cape is beautifully hand embroidered with Rayon and finished with scalloped embroidered edge. Sateen lining; flannelette interlining.

38K6501 **$1.98**
Cream-white. Infants' size only. Shipping weight, ¾ lb. Beautiful Long Coat of finely woven cotton cashmere. The cape and skirt are elaborately embroidered in attractive pattern. Cape finished with scalloped edge and braid. Lined with cambric and interlined with flannelette.

Hand Embroidered

$3.89
38K6604—White. **38K6605**—Pink. Ages, 6 months, 1 and 2 years. State age size. Shipping weight, 1½ lbs. Baby's First Walking Length Coat of beautiful quality half wool crepella cloth. Daintily hand smocked below yoke all around and trimmed with silk ribbon rosette. The fancy collar is prettily hand embroidered and finished, like cuffs on sleeves, with hand crocheted edge in Rayon. Sateen lining; flannelette interlining. A beautiful gift for any baby.

Hand Smocked and Embroidered

38K6606—White. **$2.98**
38K6607—Red. **38K6608**—Medium brown. Ages, 1, 2 and 3 years. State age size. Shpg. wt., 2 lbs. A Smart and Serviceable Coat for the little boy or girl. Splendidly made and cut from medium weight chinchilla cloth, one-fourth wool. Lined with quilted sateen.

CAP TO MATCH
38K6752—White. **85c**
38K6753—Red. **38K6754**—Medium brown. Sizes, 19 to 21½ inches headband. State measurement. Shipping wt., ½ lb. Smart Polo Cap of same material as above. Ear tabs.

$1.98
38K6597
Cream-white. Shipping wt., 1½ lbs. A wonder value — only $1.98! An Ideal Outdoor Wrap for baby. Warm bunting made of good quality chinchilla finish eiderdown cloth with an all wool face and cotton back. Neatly trimmed with sateen facing down the front and is warmly lined with soft flannelette. The hood is fitted with elastic to fit snugly over the head and around the face and is lined with mercerized sateen. Wears and launders well.

$2.98
38K6602—White. **38K6603**—Pink. Ages, 6 months, 1 and 2 years. State age size. Shipping weight, 1½ lbs. Beautiful Walking Length Coat for baby to wear on "best" occasions. Made of good quality half wool crepella cloth. Panels of hand smocking make a beautiful trim. Attractive collar is hand embroidered with Rayon; finished, as are cuffs on sleeves, with hand crocheted Rayon edge. Sateen lining; flannelette interlining.

Hand Smocked and Embroidered

$1.79
38K6676—Blue. **38K6677**—Pink. One size only; for babies up to 2 years. Shipping weight, 1 pound. When baby goes visiting, put on this cunning little Cape and just see how adorable it is. Very beautifully knit in the fancy links and links stitch and trimmed with a soft and lovely white Angora brushed collar, cuffs and revers. Daintily hand embroidered and finished with hand crocheted edge of Rayon. Knit cord tie and tassels.

63c
38K8161—White.
For ages up to 3 years. State age. Shipping weight, 3 ounces. Babies' Beautiful Helmet. Prettily hand crocheted from soft all wool zephyr yarn. Crocheted edge and interwoven border of lustrous Rayon. A high grade helmet at a special low price.

98c
38K6824—Powder blue.
38K6825—Buff.
Sizes to fit ages from 2 to 6 years. State age. Shipping weight, ¾ pound. Attractive Winter Weight Semi-Hat of good quality one-fourth wool chinchilla finish eiderdown cloth. Elastic back. Rayon ribbon and fur tail trim. Brim faced with Rayon taffeta. Sateen lining.

$1.35
38K6851—Copenhagen blue.
38K6852—Oak brown.
Sizes to fit ages from 2 to 6 years. State age. Shipping weight, ¾ pound. Smart and Dressy Silky Velveteen Semi-Hat for the little miss. Close fitting crown with elastic back. Sateen lining. The shield is daintily edged with ruffled and shirred Rayon taffeta; colored hand embroidered stitching.

Kozy WRAP

"It Grows"
First a Wrap Then a Coat
$3.69
38K6503—White.
Shipping weight, 2 pounds. Medium weight, double faced cotton Polar Cloth.

38K6504—White, blue trim.
38K6505—White, pink trim.
Shipping weight, 2½ pounds.
Good weight, double faced, soft finish cotton Kozy Down Cloth. **$5.29**
The nationally known "Kozy Wrap." The perfect outdoor garment that will keep out the cold and drafts by means of a patented hood, sleeves and flap. Adjustable to the growth of the baby from birth to the age of 3. Can be made into a coat. A garment of excellent workmanship throughout. Well tailored with double stitched seams. Good quality washable materials. Detachable waterproof pad.

For Children's Hats See Pages 89 to 91

49c
38K6700—White.
Sizes, 12 to 15 inches; to fit ages up to 2 years. State age. Shipping weight, 2 oz. Babies' Pretty Embroidered Jap Silk Bonnet. Trimmed with satin ribbon bow. Val lace edge around face. Lined with good quality sateen; interlined with flannelette.

38K8157—White, blue trim.
38K8158—White, pink trim. **95c**
For ages up to 2 years. State age. Shipping weight, 3 ounces. Daintily Hand Crocheted Cap of lustrous Rayon. Warm, hand crocheted, all wool zephyr lining. Ear tabs and tie strings. Pretty raised design all around.

38K6702—White. **79c**
38K6703—Pink.
Sizes, 12 to 15 inches; to fit ages up to 2 years. State age. Shpg. wt., 7 oz. A Warm and Dressy Bonnet of one-half wool crepella cloth. Shirred and ruffled shield with Rayon braid edge. Trimmed with satin ribbon rosettes and fluting. Sateen lining; flannelette interlining.

$1.59
38K6710—White.
38K6711—Blue.
38K6712—Pink.
Sizes, 12 to 15 inches; to fit ages up to 2 years. State age. Shipping weight, ¾ pound. A Beautiful Bonnet, made of fine quality Radium silk. Ruffled shield neatly shirred. Trimmed with silk ribbon rosettes, criss-cross hand stitching and rosebuds. Lined with Jap Silk; flannelette interlining.

89c
38K6707—White.
38K6708—Blue.
38K6709—Pink.
Sizes, 12 to 15 inches; to fit ages up to 2 years. State age. Shipping wt., 7 ounces. Silk Crepe de Chine Bonnet; shirred and ruffled shield. Trimmed on each side with fancy satin ribbon rosette; tiny rosebud. Val lace edge around face. Sateen lining; flannelette interlining.

85c
38K6706—White.
Sizes, 12 to 15 inches; to fit ages up to 2 years. State age. Shipping weight, 7 ounces. Dressy Little Bonnet made of lustrous silk messaline; lined with sateen; warmly interlined with flannelette. Prettily shirred and trimmed with satin ribbon band, bows and rosebud. Val lace edge around face.

67c
38K6701—Cream-white.
Sizes, 12 to 15 inches; to fit ages up to 2 years. State age. Shipping wt., 3 ounces. Babies' Smart Fall and Winter Bonnet. Made from finely woven two-thirds wool cashmere. Shield daintily embroidered and finished with fancy scalloped edge. Trimmed with satin ribbon rosettes and lace edge around face. Sateen lining; flannelette interlining.

38K8159—White, blue trim. **79c**
38K8160—White, pink trim.
For ages up to 3 years. State age. Shipping weight, 4 ounces. Babies' Warm Helmet. Hand crocheted from soft all wool zephyr yarn. Crown trimmed with pompon and loose chains of Rayon. Cuff crocheted-in fancy stitch, interwoven and edged with Rayon.

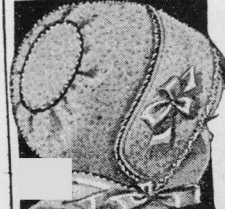

38K6749—White. **59c**
38K6750—Red.
38K6751—Buff.
Sizes, 14 to 16 inches; to fit ages from 1 to 3 years. State age. Shipping weight, 8 ounces. Good, Serviceable Bonnet of one-fourth wool chinchilla finish eiderdown cloth. Wide shield is neatly edged with Rayon cord and trimmed with silk ribbon bow. Lace edge around face. Lined with sateen.

$1.65
38K6853—Sand tan.
38K6854—Copenhagen blue.
Ages, 2 to 6 years. State age. Shipping weight, ¾ lb. Very Becoming Semi-Hat of soft silky velveteen with daintily shirred and ruffled taffeta shield; trimmed with fancy Rayon ribbon and rosettes. Sateen lining. Elastic back.

$1.19
38K6849—Red.
38K6850—Sand tan.
Ages, 2 to 6 years. State age. Shipping weight, ¾ pound. Girls' Stylish and Becoming Semi-Hat of a desirable quality silky velveteen. Crown is gathered onto shirred and ruffled shield and has pretty Rayon taffeta ribbon bows and rosebud trim. Elastic back.

89c
38K8171—Buff.
38K8172—Peacock blue.
For ages up to 8 years. State age. Shpg. wt., 7 oz. Girls' Warm Attractive Cap. Closely hand crocheted from all wool yarn. The crocheted shield is finished with a fancy crocheted edge of wool and Rayon. Trimmed with harmonizing color wool and Rayon pompons. A new and stylish cap.

85c
38K6752—White.
38K6753—Red.
38K6754—Brown.
Sizes, 19 to 21½ inches headband. State measurement. Shipping weight, ¾ pound. A Smart and Serviceable Polo Cap, well made of about one-fourth wool chinchilla finish eiderdown cloth; sateen lining. Neatly trimmed with wool pompon and tassels. Ear tabs.

89c
38K6846—Gray.
38K6847—Navy blue.
38K6848—Brown.
Sizes, 19 to 21½ inches headband. Shipping wt., 1 lb. Little Boys' Warm and Serviceable Chinchilla Cloth Polo Style Cap, about three-fourths wool. Has ear tabs which can be worn inside of cap in mild weather. Trimmed with woven U. S. Marine headband. Chin elastic. Lined with sateen.

85c
38K6757—White.
38K6758—Red.
38K6759—Brown.
Sizes, 14 to 17 inches; to fit ages from 1 to 4 years. State size. Shipping weight, ¾ lb. Child's Warm and Comfortable Winter Weight Poke Bonnet of good quality one-fourth wool chinchilla finish eiderdown cloth. Satin ribbon and fur tail trimming. Sateen lining.

Attractive Baby Clothes

Genuine Philippine Hand Embroidered Dress and Slip

Dress $1.29
Slip 89c

38K5216—White Dress............ $1.29
38K5217—White Underskirt............ .89
Ages, 6 months, 1 and 2 years. State age size. Shipping weight, each, 2 ounces.

This beautiful handmade Dress and Underskirt to match made of very fine quality **nainsook** is an outstanding value. Embroidered and hand finished with a skill in needlework that will delight the mother who loves beautiful baby clothes. The embroidery work, tucks and fancy scalloped edge on dress and Gertrude style skirt are very dainty. A most adorable set and our price is very reasonable.

Hand Embroidered Silk Pongee $1.79
38K5213—Tan. Ages, 1, 2 and 3 years. State age size. Shipping weight, 4 oz. A dainty little frock, made of good quality all silk pongee. Hand running stitching on collar and hem and the hand embroidered designs are of rich colorful Rayon floss. Raglan sleeves. Launders nicely.

Hand Embroidered All Wool Jersey $1.98
38K5214 Powder blue. **38K5215—Tan.** Ages, 1, 2 and 3 yrs. State age. Shipping weight, 7 ounces. One-Piece Dress of soft all wool jersey. Collar of contrasting color broadcloth trimmed with fancy stitching. Pockets, hand embroidered with colorful Rayon floss.

Hand Embroidered Broadcloth 79c
38K5211 Blue. **38K5212—Tan.** Ages, 1, 2 and 3 yrs. State age size. Shipping wt., 7 oz. One-Piece Dress of good quality cotton broadcloth. Delicate hand embroidery forms a panel. Collar prettily hand embroidered, and cuffs on sleeves are of plain white broadcloth.

38K5209 79c
38K5210—Rose. Blue. Ages, 1, 2 and 3 years. State age size. Shipping weight, 7 oz. Pretty Pantie Dress of washable fancy cotton print. White collar, prettily embroidered. Fancy stitching with crocheted buttons forms panels. Panties are made with buttonhole waistband.

98c
38K5208—White. Ages, 6 months, 1 and 2 years. State age size. Shipping weight, 3 oz. Dainty Walking Length Dress for baby. Made of fine quality nainsook, prettily designed with fine Val lace and embroidery medallions and rows of lace insertions at bottom. The lawn ruffle is neatly edged with Val lace. Fancy emboidery yoke is edged with lace insertion. A lovely dress for best occasions.

38K5205 59c
38K5206... 45c White Dress. White Underskirt. Ages, 6 months, 1 and 2 years. State age size. Shipping weight, each, 2 ounces. A pretty Dress and Underskirt to match of fine quality nainsook in walking length style; very reasonably priced. Neat embroidery front yoke, edged with braid. The bottom of dress is trimmed with dainty Val lace insertions and edge, while the Gertrude style underskirt has one row of lace and edge to match.

75c
38K5207—White. Ages, 6 months, 1 and 2 years. State age size. Shipping weight, 3 ounces. Pretty Nainsook Dress for the walking tot. Attractively trimmed with Val lace insertions; bottom neatly finished with embroidery edge. Embroidery and Val lace insertion form pretty front yoke. Silk ribbon rosette. Neck and sleeves finished with lace.

38K5204 39c
White. Ages, 6 months, 1 and 2 years. State age size. Shipping weight, 4 oz. Walking Length Dress of standard quality nainsook with neat embroidery yoke. Item joined to dress with veining.

98c
38K6165—Yellow and white. **38K6166—Blue and white.** Ages, 6 months, 1 and 2 years. State age size. Shipping weight, 8 ounces. Dressy Creeper made of serviceable mercerized cotton poplin. Pretty floral embroidered design on bands in front, forming suspender effect, and on fancy collar. Button across bottom and in back; band at knees. Cord tie at neck. A very pretty creeper that will look adorable on baby boy or girl. Will launder nicely.

85c
38K6153—Blue check. **38K6154—Tan check.** Ages, 6 months, 1 and 2 years. State age size. Shipping weight, 7 ounces. Dandy creeper made in a combination of checked gingham and plain poplin. The waist is embroidered in cute nursery designs. Collar is finished with neat picoted organdy frill. Buttons across bottom and in back. Will launder nicely.

38K6149 59c
Blue. State age size. Shpg. wt., 7 oz. Let baby creep about in these serviceable Creepers, made of sturdy quality chambray that will stand lots of wear. Trimmed with panel of hand smocking. Buttons across bottom and in back. A real big value!

75c
38K6151—Pink check. **38K6152—Blue check.** Ages, 6 months, 1 and 2 years. State age size. Shipping weight, 7 ounces. Dandy Creeper for baby boy or girl. Made of standard quality checked gingham with white poplin collar, cuffs, knee bands and hand embroidered panel down center front. All around belt. Buttons down back and at bottom with envelope flap.

89c
38K6155—Tan. **38K6156—Blue.** **38K6157—Pink.** Ages, 6 months, 1 and 2 years. State age size. Shipping weight, 7 ounces. A pretty and dressy Creeper of mercerized cotton poplin. Daintily hand smocked and embroidered in front. Collar edged with organdy ruffle. All around belt. Buttons in back and at bottom with envelope flap. Elastic at knees.

45c
38K6108—Black. Ages, 6 months, 1 and 2 years. State age size. Shipping weight, 6 oz. These sleeveless Creepers save on laundry and wear of better clothing. Made of lustrous black sateen with red binding. Buttons at shoulders and across bottom. **Band at knees.** Pocket.

Well Selected Styles

Dr. Denton's Sleeping Garments

Our Leader! *Lower Prices*

- Extra Strong Seams
- Unbreakable Rubber Buttons
- Extra Heavy Romper Feet

$1.10 AND UP
Doctor Denton's Sleepers

This well known garment has many splendid features. Made of heavyweight cotton with a small amount of wool; a knit fabric with soft fleecy finish on both sides. Extra full drop seat. Pocket. Feet are especially cut and shaped and made of heavier fabric than body, which means added wear and comfort. Strong seams. Comes in two styles. Age, 2 years, buttons down the back; ages 3 to 10 years button down the front.

38K9324—Natural gray. State age. Shipping weight, each garment, 1 pound.

Ages Years	Each Suit	Ages Years	Each Suit
2..	$1.10	7..	$1.60
3..	1.20	8..	1.70
4..	1.30	9..	1.80
5..	1.40	10..	1.90
6..	1.50		

69c AND UP
Warm Cotton Knit Sleeper

Boys' or Girls' Cozy and Warm Sturdy Cotton Knit Sleeping Garment with soft fleecing inside and outside. Buttons down the front, making it easy for children to dress alone, and has roomy drop seat. Feet have double soles. Pocket. Tie strings at wrists on small sizes. Body, feet and hands are covered, protecting the child even if bed coverings are thrown off. Smooth finish flat lock seams. Strongly made.

38K9322—Natural gray. State age. Shipping weight, each garment, 1 pound.

Ages Years	Each Suit	Ages Years	Each Suit
2..	69c	7..	$0.94
3..	74c	8..	.99
4..	79c	9..	1.04
5..	84c	10..	1.09
6..	89c		

We Have Improved the Quality

Practical Garments

Flannelette

Three-in-One Combination

38K2065—White. Ages, 2 to 8 years.69c Ages, 10 to 14 yrs..85c State age size. Shipping weight, 7 oz.

Cleverly designed Undergarment, three garments in one, combining underwaist and underskirt with bloomer legs sewed to inside of skirt. Made of standard quality nainsook. Buttons in back, has drop seat. Embroidery trim.

49c
38K2004—White. Ages, 2, 3, 4, 5 and 6 years. Shipping weight, 4 oz. Dressy Princess Slip made of standard quality nainsook in slipover style. Ruffle trimmed with tucks and Val lace. Arm openings and neck edged with Val lace. Dainty embroidered medallion. Ribbon draw.

29c
38K9401 Light stripe. **38K9402** Gray stripe. Ages, 2, 4 and 6 yrs. State age. Shipping weight, 7 ounces. Big value in good quality Flannelette Princess Style Underskirt. Cut full and roomy. Neck, armholes and deep ruffle at bottom finished with machine stitching. Slipover style.

55c
38K9508 Gray, **38K9509** Light stripes. Ages, 2, 4 and 6 years. State age size. Shipping weight, 7 oz. Inexpensive, comfortable and warm is this Bloomer Combination made of good quality flannelette. Neck and armholes finished with shell crocheted edge. Elastic at knees. Drop seat. Buttons down back.

"Security" Waist

DOUBLE

35c
38K2305 White. Ages, 2, 3, 4, 5 and 6 years. State age size. Shpg. wt., 3 oz. Good Quality Cambric Underwaist. Adjustable shoulder straps. Taped bone buttons fastened with security triple stitching so buttons will not pull off easily. Eyeleted garter tabs.

29c
38K2303 White. Ages, 2, 3, 4, 5 and 6 years. State age size. Shpg. wt., 3 oz. Cambric Underwaist. Double thickness of cloth over shoulders and under arms for sturdy wear. Taped buttons. Garter tabs. Will launder well.

59c
38K9253 White. **38K9254** Flesh. Ages, 2, 4 and 6 years. State age. Shpg. wt., ¾ lb. Children's Nightgown, well made of warm good quality flannelette. Has double yoke, front and back; front yoke prettily trimmed with colored Lorraine embroidery work and hemstitching.

49c
38K9257 Light stripe. Ages, 2, 4 and 6 years. State age size. Shipping weight, ¾ pound. Warm and comfortable Nightgown for children. Made of good quality flannelette with double yoke in front and back. Front trimmed with neat hemstitching. Will give good service. Full sizes.

Sateen

27c
38K2203 Black. Ages, 2, 4 and 6 years. State age. Shpg. wt., 5 oz. Girls' Better Quality Sateen Bloomers. Full size. Strong seams. Buttonhole waistband; reinforced plackets. Elastic at knees.

35c
38K2231 Gray. Ages, 2, 4 and 6 years. State age size. Shipping weight, 8 ounces. Extra Heavyweight Bloomers. Warmly made of durable gray cotton knit underwear fabric, heavily fleeced on inside. Elastic at waist and knees.

Fleeced

Lower Prices

89c
38K9318. Light gray. Ages, 1, 2, 3, 4, 5, 6 and 7 years. State age size. Shpg. wt., 1 lb. Children's Heavyweight One-Piece Sleeping Garment. Knit from good quality cotton with a small amount of wool. Full cut and extra well made with double stitched seams throughout. Buttons in back. Drop seat with a gusset insert. Made with double sole feet. Handy pocket.

83c
38K9320—White. Ages, 1, 2, 3, 4, 5 and 6 years. State age size. Shipping weight, 1 lb. Children's One-Piece Sleeping Garment. Knit from a good quality pure white cotton yarn. Slightly fleeced both inside and out. Drop seat. Buttons in the front. Draw string at cuffs. Warm feet with double fabric soles. We ask you to compare this sleeping garment, as to finish and workmanship, with any you have seen at a much higher price.

79c / 69c
38K9317 Light gray. Ages, 1, 2, 3 and 4 years......69c Ages, 5, 6 and 7 years......79c State age size. Shipping weight, 1 pound. Special value in Children's One-Piece Cotton Knit Sleeping Garments with feet. Cut full and roomy and well made. Fleece finish. Button in back and have gusset inserted full drop seat. Pocket. Smaller sizes have turnback cuffs with draw string.

"Searstride"
Triple Stitched Seams for Extra Strength

Sateen

39c
38K2239 Black. Ages, 2, 4 and 6 years. State age size. Shpg. wt., 6 oz. Girls' Searstride Bloomers of better quality sateen are specially designed for their comfort and durability. Made with triple stitched seams, bar tacked for extra strength. Inserted strip through crotch for comfort. Elastic waist and knees.

10c
38K3408—White. **38K3410**—Black. Sizes to fit ages 2 to 6 years. State age. Shipping weight, 2 oz. Children's Hose Supporters. Good quality elastic with adjustment for length. Hold stockings securely.

29c
38K2206 Black. **38K2207** White. Ages, 2, 4 and 6 years. State age size. Shipping weight, 5 ounces. Serviceable bloomers of better quality sateen. Full sizes. Strong seams. Elastic at waist and knees. Saddle crotch.

Sateen

for Children

Wool and Cotton

All Worsted Wool

All Worsted Wool

Apple Blossom Flannelette

Taped Buttons

Double Seams BarTacked

38K8411—Gray.
38K8412 Navy blue. **79c**
Ages, 2, 4 and 6 years. State age size. Shpg. wt., ¾ lb.
Every little girl should have some of these Medium Heavyweight Warm Princess Slips. Knit from about one-third wool and two-thirds cotton. Neatly finished with crocheted edges. Launders nicely. Slipover style.

38K8405 $1.48
Cream-white.
38K8406—Gray.
Ages, 2, 4 and 6 years. State age size. Shpg. wt., 8 oz.
Little Girls' Fine Quality All Worsted Wool Princess Slip. Comfortable, soft and warm. Neck, armholes and bottom finished with crocheted edge. A very fine slip.

$1.28
38K8401 White, blue trim.
38K8402 Gray, red trim. Ages, 2, 4 and 6 years. State age size. Shpg. wt., 8 oz.
Soft and Warm All Worsted Wool Princess Slip for the little girl. Skirt is neatly striped. Neck and arm openings finished with hand crocheted edge. Big value!

38K9301 47c
Light stripes.
Ages, 2, 4 and 6 years. State age size. Shpg. wt., 8 oz.
Inexpensive, Warm and Serviceable Sleeping Garment for the children. Made of nice quality flannelette in the popular button down the back style, with feet and drop seat. A splendid value at this low price.

89c
38K9316—Light stripe.
Ages, 2, 4 and 6 years. State age size. Shipping weight, ¾ pound.
These warm and cozy Sleepers for boy or girl are made of the well known Apple Blossom Flannelette, an excellent quality, soft and serviceable material. Well made in comfortably full sizes without feet. Have handy pocket and close in front with Rayon frogs and pearl buttons. Drop seat. A splendid value at this price; order at least two of them.

Back Opening
38K9314.........**85c**
Light stripe.
Front Opening
38K9315.........**85c**
Light stripe.
Ages, 2, 4 and 6 years. State age size. Shipping weight, ¾ lb.
Sears ROLLIC BRAND Sleepers of better quality flannelette for the active boy or girl. Made for longer wear with smooth double stitched seams throughout and taped "Security" buttons which will not pull off. Roomy non-gapping drop seat. Feet are made of double thickness. Can be had in either back or front closing style. Will give extra warmth and wear; made in roomy sizes.

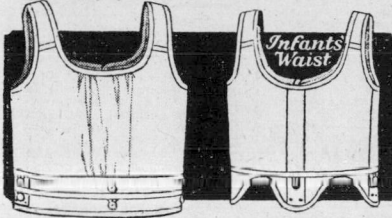

Infants Waist

23c
38K2310—White.
Ages, 2, 3, 4, 5 and 6 years. State age size. Shpg. wt., 3 oz.
Well made Cambric Underwaist for boy or girl. Buttons in back. Reinforced at waistline. Double stitched taped buttons. Eyeleted tabs for garters. Priced very low.

23c
38K2306—White.
Ages, 1, 2 and 3 years. State age size. Shpg. wt., 3 oz.
Infants' Cambric Underwaist with reinforced panels. Metal eyelets on tabs, both front and back, and at hips, for pinning diapers. Back opening Taped bone buttons.

53c
38K9302
Light stripe.
Ages, 2, 4 and 6 years. State age size. Shipping weight, ¾ lb.
Warm and serviceable One-Piece Sleeper for boy or girl of nice quality flannelette. Drop seat. Buttons in front. Trimmed with colored binding and fancy Rayon frogs. Made with feet and has handy pocket.

59c
38K9310
Light stripe.
38K9311 White.
Ages, 2, 4 and 6 years. State age size. Shipping weight, ¾ pound.
Easily laundered, cut comfortably full and made of good quality flannelette, these Sleepers for boy or girl are a fine value. Made without feet. Drop seat. Finished with strongly stitched seams throughout. Handy pocket.

Flannelette

Nainsook

27c
38K2241 Gray stripes.
38K2242 Light stripes.
Ages, 2, 4 and 6 years. Shpg. wt., 6 oz.
Warm and serviceable flannelette Bloomers. Elastic at waist and knees. Double stitched seams. Saddle crotch. Full sizes.

33c
38K2258—White.
Ages, 2, 4 and 6 years. State age size. Shpg. wt., 5 oz.
Standard Quality Nainsook Knickerbocker Bloomers for girls, made on buttonhole waistband. Neatly finished with elastic knee and embroidery ruffle.

59c
38K9304—Light stripe.
38K9305—White.
Ages, 2, 4 and 6 years. State age size. Shpg. wt., ¾ pound.
A sturdy wearing Sleeping Garment of good quality flannelette. Made with strongly stitched throughout. Has drop seat, pocket and feet. Buttons down the back. Big value!

65c
38K9306 Light stripe.
38K9307—White.
Ages, 2, 4 and 6 years. Shpg. wt., ¾ lb.
Warm and comfy Sleeper for children. Made of good weight flannelette that will wash well. Has drop seat, pocket and made with feet. Strongly sewed seams and cut over roomy sizes. Wonderfully nice for cold nights.

79c
38K9312 Blue ground.
38K9303 Pink ground.
Ages, 2, 4 and 6 years. State age size. Shpg. wt., ¾ lb.
One-piece Sleeper. Made of soft and durable flannelette, nicely fleeced on outside and printed with juvenile designs. Seams are strongly stitched. Opens down back and has drop seat. Made with cozy feet. Pocket.

Cotton Jersey

17c
38K2221—Black.
38K2222—White.
Ages, 2, 4 and 6 years. State age size. Shipping weight, 3 ounces.
Little Girls' Warm Cotton Jersey Knit Bloomers. Medium light weight. Elastic at waist and knees. Full sizes.

45c
38K2210—Flesh.
38K2211—Black.
Ages, 2, 4 and 6 years. Shipping wt., 4 oz.
Girls' Bloomers of soft and lustrous fine quality mercerized sateen. Full cut and roomy; made with inserted strip through crotch. Elastic at waist and knees. Strong double stitched seams. Nice for dress wear.

Fine Mercerized Sateen

Khaki Drill or Chambray

ROLLIC PLAY SUITS

Khaki Drill

38K5695—Khaki drill.
38K5694—Blue chambray. **95c**
Ages, 2, 3, 4, 5 and 6 years. State age size. Shpg. wt., ¾ lb. This "Rollic" Brand Play Suit is a splendid garment for play hours, as the active child can romp about without fear of spoiling better clothes. Laundry savers for mothers. Choice of two sturdy materials—both fine values. Buttons at waist, front and back. Trimmed with red piping and red tie. Has drop seat. Elastic knees. Extra well made for rough wear.

38K5693 98c
Ages, 2, 3, 4, 5 and 6 years. State age size. Shipping weight, ¾ lb. Two-Piece "Rollic" Brand Play Suit. The middy or bloomers may be worn separately. Well made of sturdy quality khaki drill. Washes perfectly; wears wonderfully. Middy has regulation sailor collar, red tie and embroidered emblem. Bloomers have elastic at waist and knees.

69c
38K6132—Blue chambray.
38K6133—Khaki cloth.
38K6134—Black sateen.
Ages, 2, 3, 4, 5, 6 and 7 years. State age size. Shipping weight, ¾ pound.
Our popular "Rollic" Brand Play Suit in a choice of three sturdy materials. Save the children's better clothes and lets them romp about; also a laundry labor saver for mother. Neatly trimmed with red in fast color. Pearl buttons. Drop seat. Back closing.

Broadcloth

38K5659 ↑ **$1.69**
38K5666—Tan.
Ages, 2, 3, 4, 5 and 6 years. State age size. Shpg. wt., ¾ lb. A stylish Dress for sister. Made in a combination of plain broadcloth and cotton print. Sturdy, fast color material which will withstand a lot of tubbing. Front is smartly embroidered with hand running stitch, box pleats are held together in front with silk ribbon bow with streamers. Two fancy pockets. Full size bloomers with buttonholes at waistband.

Little Tots' Gum Rubber Apron

← 33c
38K3186
Coral.
38K3187
Blue.
38K3188
Green.
One size only, for ages 2 to 6 years. Shipping weight, 4 oz.
A dainty little Rubber Apron to protect the little tots' dresses. Neatly trimmed with two-color ruffled edge; straps slip over head and cross in back. The apron and ruffled edge pocket are trimmed with bubbles and pipe. Can be easily cleaned with damp cloth. Makes a dandy, inexpensive gift.

For Ages 2 to 6 Years

Sateen

Black.
38K5650 89c
Ages, 2, 3, 4, 5 and 6 years. State age size. Shipping weight, ¾ pound.
A sateen Pantie Dress is always practical and every little girl should have one. This style you will find particularly neat. Made of good grade lustrous sateen, trimmed in medium dark blue with embroidered medallion in front. The new kick pleats afford extra fullness to dress. Roomy bloomers made on buttonhole waistband.

38K4750 45c
Blue and white check gingham.
38K4751—Dark patterns percale.
Ages, 2, 4 and 8 years. State age size. Shipping weight, 8 ounces.
A practical Apron made of good quality checked gingham or attractive dark figured percale. Offers ample protection, as it completely covers the dress. Has handy pocket. Long sleeves. Sash back. Trimmed with white binding.

38K4766 59c
Black.
Ages, 2, 4 and 6 years. State age size. Shipping weight, 8 oz.
A remarkable value in a better quality black sateen. Coverall Apron for the little girl. No girl's wardrobe is quite complete without at least one practical apron. Neck, front, sleeves and pockets are neatly trimmed with rickrack braid in contrasting color. Sash in back. Has excellent wearing qualities and priced low.

Sateen

Our dresses are cut according to a standard scale of sizes to fit the average child. If child is large or small for her age, order in age size (not actual age), according to length from center of shoulder to bottom of hem and chest measure, as given in size scale below. We will be unable to fill your order accurately unless you state age size child wears, not actual age.

SIZE SCALE

Age size	2	3	4	5	6
Average chest measure, in.	21	22	23	24	25
Average length, straight dresses, inches	20	22	23	24	26

DRESSES WITH BLOOMERS MEASURE 3 IN. SHORTER.

Descriptions of Dresses Shown on Opposite Page

A $1.39
38K5669 Navy blue. Ages, 2, 3, 4, 5 and 6 years. State age size. Shipping weight, ¾ pound. Popular One-Piece Regulation Sailor Dress of good quality cotton serge. Trimmed with rows of white braid. Embroidered emblem on sleeve. Poplin tie. Full pleated skirt and all around belt.

38K5670 $2.89
Navy blue. Shipping weight, 1 pound. Same style and sizes, but made of good quality all wool storm serge.

B $1.69
38K5657 Honeydew.
38K5658 Blue. Ages, 2, 3, 4, 5 and 6 years. State age size. Shpg. wt., ¾ lb. Smart, popular two-piece Jumper Dress. Made in a combination of plain and printed washable cotton fabric that will give sturdy wear. Hand embroidered work on collar and fancy pockets. Neatly bound edges. The bloomer combination is well made, buttoning down back to waist, with drop seat. Can be worn separately.

C $2.98
38K5665—Blue.
38K5666—Tan. Ages, 2, 3, 4, 5 and 6 years. State age size. Shipping weight, 1¼ pounds. Popular Pantie Dress for the little girl, charmingly made of soft all wool worsted jersey. Hand embroidery in bright colors of Rayon makes a very artistic trim. Broadcloth collar with hand running stitch. Bloomers on waistband cut full and roomy.

D $3.98
38K5671 Brown and tan.
38K5672 Black and powder blue. Ages, 2, 3, 4, 5 and 6 years. State age size. Shipping weight, 1¼ pounds. Velveteen, rich, silky and warm makes this sweet little Pantie Frock. The raglan sleeves and trim are of all wool plain color challis in contrasting color. Enhanced with hand embroidery and ribbon streamers in pretty colors of Rayon. Panties of lustrous cotton satinette have velveteen cuffs: buttonhole waistband.

E $2.48
38K5663—Blue.
38K5664 Rose tan. Ages, 2, 3, 4, 5 and 6 years. State age size. Shipping weight, 1¼ lbs. Fancy weave homespun of about one-half wool in a splendid, sturdy quality fashions this charming one-piece frock. Smartly finished with velveteen collar and pockets, hand stitched in harmonizing colors. Ribbon streamers.

F $2.98
38K5667 Navy blue.
38K5668 Brown. Ages, 2, 3, 4, 5 and 6 years. State age size. Shipping weight, 1 pound. Practical Pantie Dress, adorable for little girls! Made of all wool soft finish French serge. The front is prettily hand embroidered in colorful Rayon. Fine quality broadcloth collar in contrasting color. Long raglan sleeves. Full size panties are on buttonhole waistband.

G $1.59
38K5655 Navy blue.
38K5656 Red. Ages, 2, 3, 4, 5 and 6 years. State age size. Shipping weight, ¾ pound.
The mother who is seeking an inexpensive dress for little daughter will make a very wise purchase in selecting this Two-Piece Pantie Dress of sturdy quality cotton serge. The collar, top of pockets and cuffs on long sleeves are of contrasting color poplin. Dainty sprays of hand embroidered work above pockets and on collar add a pretty touch to frock. Kick pleats provide extra fullness. Panties are cut full and roomy with buttonhole waistband.

H $1.00
38K5651 Tan.
38K5652 Blue. Ages, 2, 3, 4, 5 and 6 years. State age size. Shpg. wt., 8 oz. A combination of plain and printed cotton pongette makes this a splendid practical Dress for playtime. The hand running stitching is employed to trim the front and to outline the pockets. Full cut bloomers come on buttonhole waistband with the polka dot band at knees. Ribbon bow. A saving value!

J $2.69
38K6171 Blue heather.
38K6172 Brown heather. Ages, 1, 2, 3 and 4 years. State age size. Shipping weight, 1½ pounds. The little fellow will look very appealing in this handsome Two-Piece Suit of warm all wool Jersey cloth in heather mixtures with trimming of contrasting color all wool flannel. The collar and front panel are neatly embroidered with Rayon. Straight leg trousers have buttons and buttonholes at waistline and are neatly lined.

K $2.98
38K6175 Tan plaid.
38K6176 Blue plaid. Ages, 1, 2, 3 and 4 years. State age size. Shipping weight, 1½ pounds. A snappy All Wool Two-Piece Lumberjack Suit for the active little fellow. A warm and serviceable outfit. The jacket blouse of fancy plaid all wool flannel has two pockets. Wrists and hipband of double thickness all wool jersey to match the pants. The straight pants of all wool jersey are neatly lined and have buttons and buttonholes at waistband.

L $1.89
38K6170 Navy blue. Ages, 1, 2, 3 and 4 years. State age size. Shipping weight, 1 pound. This Little fellow's trim Navy Middy Suit is very practical, and we are sure our price is the lowest you will find for a suit of this quality. Made of one-fourth wool flannel with sailor collar, dickey and sleeves trimmed with gold braid; regulation silk emblem on the sleeve, black tie, cord and pocket. Straight pants with buttonholes at waistline.

Just the Dress for Every Occasion

$1.98
38K5661—Chanel red.
38K5662—Navy blue.
Ages, 2, 3, 4, 5 and 6 years. State age size. Shipping weight, 1¼ lbs.
A wealth of smartness is fashioned into this cleverly made Dress of rich looking corduroy velveteen. It is simply made with long raglan sleeves and two pockets; hand embroidered with Rayon in pretty design. The collar is of fine quality broadcloth in contrasting color. Deep hem.

Corduroy

$3.98
38K5673—Green.
38K5674—Powder blue.
Ages, 2, 3, 4, 5 and 6 years. State age size. Shipping weight, 1¼ lbs.
Appropriate for almost any occasion is this Pantie Frock of fine All Wool Crepe. A most effective touch is given to this charming model by the two-color hand embroidered cross stitches, forming a very attractive design in front and finish on collar. Long raglan sleeves. Full size panties with buttonhole waistband.

Fine All Wool Crepe

C *All Wool Jersey* **$2.98**

D *Silky Velveteen* **$3.98**

E *Homespun* **$2.48**

A *Cotton Range* **$1.39** *All Wool Serge* **$2.89**

B *Cotton Print Jumper Dress* **$1.69**

F *All Wool French Serge* **$2.98**

G *Cotton Serge* **$1.59**

H *Hand Embroidered Cotton Pongette* **$1.00**

Descriptions and Other Colors May Be Found on Opposite Page

Cotton Serge

Little Boys' First Suits

J *All Wool Jersey* **$2.69**

K *All Wool Lumberjack Suit* **$2.98**

L *Flannel Middy* **$1.89**

Full Cut Roomy Sizes

Cozy Bathrobe for Boy or Girl
$1.39

38K3653—Brown. **$1.00**
38K5654—Blue.
Ages, 2, 3, 4, 5 and 6 years. State age size. Shpg. wt., 8 oz.
A pleasing style in a One-Piece Dress, made of sturdy quality cotton serge. A splendid choice and inexpensively priced. The collar and trim on fancy pockets are of contrasting color serge. Fancy machine scroll embroidery forms panel down front. Long raglan sleeves. Cord and tassel tie at neck. A style that will give excellent service.

38K3281—Powder blue and buff.
Ages, 2, 4 and 6 years. State age size. Shipping weight, 1 pound.
Every little boy and girl should have one of these warm and cozy Bathrobes. Well made of good quality cotton blanket material in attractive two-color allover pattern. The edges are neatly finished with shell crocheted stitch in harmonizing color. Fastens at neck and around waist with Rayon cord and tassels. Handy pocket. Useful garment and a dandy gift suggestion.

Warm and Cozy Knit Outfits

Warm Togs for Little Tots

35c
38K8104
Red and navy blue.
38K8105
Brown and buff.
One size only, for ages up to 6 years. Shpg. wt., 6 oz.
Warm Hockey Cap, knit in double thickness of one-half wool worsted Contrasting color stripes. Cotton knit lining.

65c
38K8109
White and peacock blue.
38K8110
Brown and buff.
One size only, for ages up to 6 years. Shpg. wt., 6 oz.
Snug Fitting All Wool Hockey Cap. Knit in fancy design through cuff and star on crown. Large wool pompon.

47c
38K8131
White and red.
38K8132
Buff and brown.
38K8133
Navy blue and red.
One size only, for ages up to 6 yrs. Shpg wt., 6 oz.
A soft and warm Hockey Cap for the youngster. Knit in double thickness all wool worsted in fancy pineapple stitch. Neatly striped and seamless.

Hand Crocheted

89c
38K8173
Buff and brown.
38K8174
Peacock blue and buff.
Shpg. wt., 6 oz.
For ages up to 6 years. State age.
Attractive Cap for the little girl; hand crocheted of all wool yarn in fancy allover stitch; hand finished with contrasting color edge.

49c
38K8134—Red.
38K8135—Brown.
38K8136—White.
38K8137
Peacock blue.
One size only, for ages up to 6 years. Shipping wt., 6 oz.
Our Biggest Value! Boys' or girls' warm, double thickness, all wool worsted seamless knit rope stitch Hockey Cap.

Hand Quilted Silk Robe for Crib or Carriage

$1.65
38K3352—Pink. 38K3351—Blue.
Size, about 24x33 inches. Shipping weight, ¾ pound.
A gift that will delight any mother is this exquisite Imported Hand Quilted Japanese Silk Robe. The reverse side and top border are of solid color, while the daintiest little printed floral designs adorn center of cover. This beautiful robe is filled with clean, fluffy white cotton and is hand quilted throughout. Light and soft in weight, beautiful and comfortable; for baby's carriage, crib or bassinet.

38K6692 $4.65
Navy blue.
Ages, 1, 2 and 3 years. State age size. Shipping weight, 2¼ pounds.
Baby Boys' Popular Navy Style Overcoat of heavy weight chinchilla cloth of about three-quarters wool. A nicely tailored coat with heavy red flannelette lining, gilt buttons, convertible collar and emblem on sleeve. Has belted back, trimmed with gilt buttons, and four cozy pockets. A warm overcoat for winter wear, serviceable, well made and, best of all, very moderate in price.

Sailor Hat to Match
38K6760 **95c**
Navy blue.
Sizes, 6¼ to 6¾. State hat size. Shpg. wt., 1 lb.
Little boys' warm and serviceable chinchilla cloth Hat with ear tabs, about three-fourths wool. Ear tabs can be worn inside of cap in mild weather. Trimmed with cotton taffeta U. S. Navy headband. Chin elastic. Lined with sateen.

38K6693 $4.48
Copenhagen blue.
38K6694—Buff.
38K6695
Rosewood brown.
Ages, 1, 2 and 3 years. State age size. Shipping weight, 2 pounds.
Smart little Coat for the little girl. Warm, winter weight one-third wool eiderdown chinchilla cloth. Material is sturdy and practical; neat workmanship and youthful style. Trimmed with fancy stitching and buttons and enriched with all wool astrakhan krimmer cloth. For extra warmth and comfort it has quilted sateen lining. Collar can be worn high or low at neck. Moderate price. Slot pockets.

Hat to Match
38K6855
Copenhagen blue.
38K6856—Buff.
38K6857
Rosewood brown. **$1.15**
One size only, for ages up to 3 years. Shpg. wt., ¾ lb.
Hat to match above coat, trimmed with astrakhan cloth brim and Rayon ribbon bow and streamers. Sateen lining.

$1.98
38K6651
Blue, white trim.
38K6652
Pink, white trim.
One size only, for babies up to 2 years. Shipping wt., 1 lb.
A useful garment for the baby is this pretty Knit Cape of all wool and Rayon. Knit in a fancy stitch with white trim. The long revers and collar have hand embroidered rosebuds in dainty contrasting colors. Knit cord and tassels fasten cape close at neck. A lovely gift for baby.

Cap to match, can be found elsewhere on this page.

Hand Embroidered

$1.19
38K8152
Peacock blue and buff.
38K8153
Brown and buff.
One size, for ages up to 6 years. Shipping weight, ¾ lb.
Little Tots' Serviceable Cap and Scarf Set. Knit in double thickness of all wool yarn with a beautiful brushed Angora finish and striped in contrasting color. Good size seamless scarf. Warm, seamless Hockey Cap, trimmed with wool pompon.

$1.45
38K8169
Powder blue and buff.
38K8170
Red and silver.
One size, for ages up to 6 years. Shipping weight, ¾ lb.
Every girl will long for this wonderful Sport Set of cozy and warm all wool worsted. Knit throughout in a double thickness in a decidedly new popcorn stitch in two-color combination. The becoming Hockey Cap has a solid color wool pompon and the scarf is finished with knotted fringe.

Four Cute Styles Especially for the Baby

Boys Prefer This Style

37c
38K8100—Pink.
38K8101—Light blue.
One size, for ages up to 3 years. Shipping weight, 6 ounces.
Warm, snug fitting Hockey Cap for the baby. Outer surface knit from one-half wool. Rayon trim. Cotton knit lining. Prettily striped and has pompon.

43c
38K8140—Brown and buff.
38K8141—Maroon and gold.
One size only, for ages up to 6 years. Shipping weight, 6 oz.
Boys' Warm Muffler Cap. Knit in a double thickness in an elastic stitch from about one-half wool. This convertible cap can be fastened around the neck to protect the ears and throat from cold and wind or can be worn as the ordinary hockey cap.

48c
38K8119
Light blue.
38K8120—Pink.
38K8121
Solid white.
One size, for ages up to 4 years. Shipping weight, 6 oz.
Dainty Cap for children in warm double thickness. Knit in fancy two-color popcorn stitch of soft all wool worsted yarn with perky pompons at sides. A fine value.

43c
38K8128
White salmon stripes.
38K8129—Peacock blue, white stripes.
38K8130
Red, white stripes.
One size, for ages up to 3 years. Shipping weight, 5 oz.
Babies' Pretty Hockey Cap. Knit in a double thickness of all wool worsted yarns in a fancy stitch with contrasting color Rayon stripes on cuff. A fluffy wool and Rayon pompon perches atop this warm, snug fitting cap.

45c
38K8125—Red.
38K8126
Copenhagen blue.
38K8127—White.
One size, for ages up to 3 years. Shipping weight, 6 ounces.
Beautiful Hockey Cap for the tiny youngster. Double knit in a fancy stitch in a mixture of all wool worsted yarns and lustrous Rayon. Trimmed with bushy Rayon and wool mixed pompon. Warm, serviceable and low priced.

79c
38K8144
Brown and buff.
38K8145—Navy blue and red.
One size, for ages up to 6 years. Shipping weight, 6 oz.
Boys' New Muffler Arcticap. Well made of triple thickness for greater warmth. Outside knit of about one-third worsted wool, interlining of part wool and lining of about one-third brushed wool. Can be pulled down over the ears.

The ARCTICAP Triple Thickness for Extra Warmth

Distinctive Features of These Three Sweaters

HAND FINISHED THROUGHOUT

ALL WOOL

REINFORCED SHOULDER SEAMS

Useful Sweaters Astounding Values
Ages 8 to 14 Years

Knitted OUTERwear deserves the preference

Double Body Jersey Lined

D $2.75

A $4.98

Two-Piece Set

B $4.98 PER SET

C $4.98

E $2.98

Descriptions and Other Colors May Be Found on Opposite Page

J $3.98

L $2.98

F $3.98

G $1.79

H $2.98

Double Body Jersey Lined

K $3.95

M $3.65

IMPORTANT—READ
How to Order Schoolgirls' Sweaters

When ordering a sweater for the schoolgirl, be sure to measure over fullest part ot the bust and order size according to the ages given below:

Age Size Years	Chest Measure of Sweater
7-8	30 inches
9-10	32 inches
11-12	34 inches
13-14	36 inches

Order a roomy and comfortable size.

Descriptions of Sweaters Shown on Opposite Page

A $4.98 — 38K7540 Cardinal red and buff. 38K7542 Peacock blue and gray. Ages, 7 to 14 years. Shipping weight 3 lbs. Girls' Shaker Knit Lumberjack Sport Sweater for winter sport or general outdoor activities. Knit in a real heavyweight shaker stitch of all wool yarns. Beautifully hand finished throughout and made with reinforced shoulder seams, giving a smooth, perfect fitting garment.

B $4.98 PerSet — 38K7533 All white. 38K7534 Jockey red. 38K7535 Camel. Ages, 7 to 14 years. Shipping weight, 2¾ pounds. Schoolgirls' good looking Shaker Knit All Wool Pullover Sweater and Hockey Cap. Knit in the favored shaker stitch of soft all wool yarn in a heavyweight, beautifully hand finished and made with reinforced non-sagging shoulder seams that prevent stretching and give a neat appearance. The cap has double knit turnback cuff with pompon trim.

C $4.98 — 38K7531 Buff. 38K7530 Red. 38K7532 Navy blue. Ages, 7 to 14 years. State age size. Shipping weight, 3 pounds. A practical Shaker Sweater for active girls, in colors they will like. Warmly knit in heavyweight all wool shaker stitch. Beautifully hand finished throughout and made with reinforced non-sagging shoulder seams that prevent stretching and give neat and correct fit. Has shawl collar and two pockets.

D $2.75 — 38K7614 Blue combination. 38K7615 Red combination. Ages, 7 to 14 years. Shipping wt., 1½ lbs. A very handsome Lumberjack Sweater for the schoolgirl. Knit of about one-half fine quality soft wool and balance cotton yarns in fancy Jacquard pattern with a touch of Rayon. The body is nicely lined with knit jersey for extra warmth. The top of pockets, wrists and hipband are finely knit of jersey in harmonizing color.

E $2.98 — 38K7566 Cardinal red. 38K7567 Buff. Ages, 7 to 14 years. State age size. Shipping weight, 2¼ lbs. High grade sweater for the active schoolgirl. Knit of good quality all wool yarn in a medium heavy weight with large collar, turnback cuffs and bottom neatly striped in contrasting colors.

F $3.98 — 38K7624 Royal blue. 38K7625 Red. 38K7626 Buff. Ages, 7 to 14 years. Shipping weight, 2 lbs. Softly knit in a fancy stitch, this youthful model is one of the loveliest sweaters of the season. Finely knit of all wool worsted yarn in a medium weight. Note how well the stripes of contrasting color set off the collar, cuffs, pockets and bottom of sweater.

G $1.79 — 38K7607 Maroon. 38K7606 Navy blue. 38K7608 Brown. Ages, 7 to 14 years. Shipping weight, 2 lbs. This good, sturdy Sweater for schoolgirls will stand the strain of active play. It is knit in a heavy weight from about one-third wool and two-thirds cotton. Has double shawl collar and two pockets. Well made and has long wearing qualities. A splendid value.

H $2.98 — 38K7618 Powder blue combination. 38K7619 Red combination. Ages, 7 to 14 years. State age size. Shipping wt., 1½ lbs. A stunning Pullover Sweater for the schoolgirl for wear indoors or out. Warmly knit from all wool worsted yarns in a fancy pattern; interknit with colorful Rayon. Popular and becoming cricket style. Trimmed in harmonizing color. Very desirable for wear at all times.

J $3.98 — 38K7627 Red plaid. 38K7628 Blue plaid. Ages, 7 to 14 years. Shipping wt., 1¾ lbs. For winter sport and outdoor play schoolgirls will enjoy having this smart Lumberjac' Style Sport Sweater, fashioned of warm, sturdy, fine quality all wool in fancy colors with a convertible collar. Neatly trimmed with jersey knit in plain harmonizing color. Two pockets with buttoned flaps.

K $3.95 — 38K7629 Buff. 30K7630 Peacock blue. Ages, 7 to 14 years. State age size. Shipping weight, 2¼ lbs. A sweater that is ultra new and destined to be very popular is this Smart Astrakhan Knit Krimmer Cloth Sweater for the schoolgirl. The tightly curled all wool pile resembles real fur and is knit into a sturdy cotton back. Body is warmly lined with knitted warm jersey, slightly fleeced for extra warmth. Collar and cuffs are of Rayon in a beautiful combination of pretty colors. The pockets, bottom and cuffs are neatly finished with Rayon braid.

L $2.98 — 38K7616 Powder blue and buff. 38K7617 Leaf brown and buff. Ages, 7 to 14 years. State age size. Shpg. wt., 1¾ lbs. A handsome tailored Sweater Coat for the schoolgirl. Beautifully knit of very soft, fluffy brushed fine wool worsted yarns in a medium weight. The trim is of natural buff. Has close elastic ribbed wrists. A very soft and warm, fine sweater in a smart style. Can be worn nicely under a regular coat for extra warmth.

M $3.65 — 38K7622 Red. 38K7623 Buff. Ages, 7 to 14 years. Shipping weight, 2 lbs. You will feel that $3.65 was well spent for this smart Sweater, it is so warm and comfortable. Knit in a block pattern of all wool worsted yarns and neatly striped in contrasting colors. Has' two pockets. A fine, high grade sweater. A very smart style and an exceptional value at our low price.

$1.75
38K7609—Buff.
38K7610—Powder blue. Ages, 7 to 14 years. State age size. Shipping weight, 1¼ pounds.
The practical usefulness of a knitted Cricket Style Pullover for schoolgirls makes it an ideal garment for sport or general wear. This sweater is smartly fashioned of one-half soft durable wool and one-half cotton yarns, knit in a close elastic stitch. The bottom and cuffs are neatly knit in an array of gay colors to harmonize with the stripes in the body of sweater.

$1.98
38K7611 Buff and brown.
38K7612 Cardinal and navy blue.
38K7613 Peacock blue and gray. Ages, 7 to 14 years. State age size. Shipping weight, 1¾ pounds.
Fashioned of one-half high grade soft wool and one-half cotton yarns, this dandy sweater for the schoolgirl is not only smart and attractive, but durable and warm as well. It is neatly trimmed in contrasting color in a fancy stitch. A good sweater, well worth the price and will give you all the service you expect.

$2.98
38K7537—Maroon.
38K7538—Brown.
38K7539—Buff. Ages, 7 to 14 years. State age size. Shipping weight, 2¼ pounds.
This serviceable Heavyweight All Wool Sweater Coat is very desirable for the schoolgirl at all times. It is well made throughout with double shawl collar that can be buttoned up snug at neck. Has two pockets. A splendid selection at a genuine bargain price. One or two sweaters are always a welcome addition to the schoolgirl's wardrobe, and you will find some very wonderful values on these two pages.

89c
38K7601—Gray. Ages, 7 to 14 years. State age size. Shipping weight, 1¼ pounds.
For all around service, this inexpensive Heavyweight Cotton Sweater for schoolgirls cannot be beat. Fills the demand for any wear and will give satisfactory service. Has roll collar that can be buttoned up around neck and two pockets. A remarkable value at our low price.

$2.98
38K7620—Royal blue.
38K7621—Buff.
Ages, 7 to 14 years. State age size. Shipping weight, 1½ lbs.
The girls will be very enthusiastic about this snappy new sweater. It is a very swagger Lumberjack model, knit in a fancy stitch of soft high grade, all wool worsted yarns with contrasting color stripes. Made with Byron collar, snug fitting hipband and two buttoned pockets. A dandy style for wear with knickers.

$1.59
38K7602—Navy blue.
38K7604—Maroon.
38K7603—Buff. Ages, 7 to 14 years. State age size. Shipping weight, 1½ pounds.
A splendid choice in a practical Sweater for the schoolgirl. Knit in a heavyweight from a small amount of wool, balance cotton. Has two pockets and double roll collar that can be buttoned up close around the neck. Well made and will give excellent service. Offered at a reasonable price.

Underthings for Schoolgirls and Misses

Ages 10 to 18 Years

Rayosheen Rayon

Fruit of the Loom Mercette

Sateen

Shadowproof Hem

Ages 10 to 18 Years

Windsor Washanrede Krinkle Krepe

Knit Rayon

38K2055—Tan.
38K2056—Flesh.
38K2057—Navy blue. **$1.49**
Ages, 10 to 18 years. State age size. Shipping weight, 7 ounces.
An essential item for the schoolgirl and miss is this Dressy Costume Slip of heavy, lustrous Rayosheen Rayon. Made in the tailored straightline style with self material shoulder straps, inverted pleats at sides and 2-inch hem. Lovely for wear under any nice frock.

65c
38K2073—White.
38K2074—Tan.
38K2075—Navy blue.
Ages, 7 to 16 yrs. State age size. Shipping wt., 6 oz.
Simple in style, this neat Costume Slip of Fruit of the Loom Mercette Cloth, a firmly woven mercerized cotton fabric, is an outstanding value. Round neck, armholes and front are neatly hemstitched.

Bodice Top Style
38K2041 65c
Black.
38K2042—Flesh.
38K2058—Tan.
Ages, 10 to 18 years. State age size. Shpg. wt., 8 oz.
Neat Costume Slip for girls; bodice top style. Good quality sateen. 2-inch hem.

Built-Up Shoulder
38K2043 65c
Black.
38K2044—Flesh.
Same, but made in built-up shoulder style. State size.

38K2072 69c
White.
Ages, 10 to 18 yrs. State age size. Shipping wt., ¾ lb.
Costume Slip for schoolgirls and misses of standard quality nainsook. Colored Lorraine embroidery work. Hemstitched top.

38K2066 57c
White.
Same as above, with only one row of hemstitching and without embroidery work. State size.

49c
38K2155
White.
Ages, 7 to 16 years. State age size. Shpg. wt., 8 ounces.
Schoolgirls' Underwaist and Bloomer Combination of better quality crossbar nainsook. Buttons down back to waist. Has drop seat. Elastic knees. Garter tabs.

$1.39
38K2465
Flesh and honeydew.
38K2466
Honeydew and flesh.
Ages, 7 to 16 years. State age size. Shipping weight, ¾ pound.
Pretty Two-Piece Pajamas for girls. Made of good quality Windsor Washanrede Krinkle Krepe that requires no ironing. Daintily trimmed in contrasting color, and slipover style coat has Peter Pan collar with ribbon tie at neck. Pocket. Roomy trousers come with draw string at waistline. A style that will please every girl.

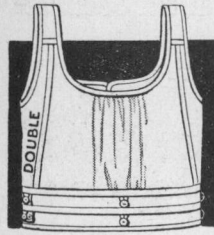

Knit Rayon

38K2163—Flesh. **98c**
Ages, 4 to 10 years. State age size. Shpg. wt., 6 oz.
38K2164—Flesh. **$1.29**
Ages, 12 to 16 years. State age size. Shipping weight, ¾ pound.
Dainty underthings appeal to the little girl and miss, and this beautiful Bloomer Combination, made of fine knit Rayon will surely please her. The popular bodice top has a silk ribbon draw and double knit Rayon shoulder straps with neatly finished edge. Elastic knees and drop seat. A well made garment and a dandy value.

"Searstride" Triple Stitched Seams for Extra Strength

Sateen

Perfect Fit in Every Position

38K2238—Black. **49c**
Ages, 7 to 16 years. State age size. Shipping weight, 7 ounces.
We recommend this wonderful "Searstride" Bloomer for schoolgirls. Splendidly made from good quality lustrous sateen with triple stitched seams for extra strength; well designed saddle crotch for comfort. A bloomer that fits perfectly in every position.

Windsor Washanrede Krinkle Krepe or Fruit of the Loom Longcloth

38K2224—White. **43c**
38K2226—Flesh.
Ages, 7 to 16 years. State age size. Shpg. wt., 7 oz.
Windsor Washanrede Krinkle Krepe Bloomers for schoolgirls. A labor saver for mother, as they require no ironing. Will give excellent wear. Inserted strip of double thickness through crotch. Elastic at waist and knees.

Fruit of the Loom
38K2213 43c Shpg. wt., 7 oz.
White.
Same style and sizes as above, but made of Fruit of the Loom Longcloth. State size.

The Pied Piper Play Bloomers

Sateen

38K2229—Black. **55c**
38K2227—White.
Ages, 4 to 16 years. State age. Shipping weight, 7 oz.
Pied Piper Healthful Play Bloomers of better quality sateen. Permit free movement of the body. Plain band at front waistline and supported by elastic in back. Side openings. Saddle crotch. Double stitched seams. This style is becoming more popular every season.

Sateen or Nainsook

38K2220 39c
Black sateen.
38K2215 29c
White nainsook.
Ages, 7 to 16 years. State age size. Shipping weight, 8 ounces. Schoolgirls' Bloomers made of better quality sateen or standard quality nainsook. Elastic at waist and knees. Well made with strongly sewed seams. Inserted strip through crotch for comfort. Exceptional value.

Double

33c
38K2327—White.
Ages, 7 to 14 years. State size. Shipping weight, 5 oz.
Schoolgirls' Cambric Underwaist. Has double thickness of cloth over shoulders and under arms for longer wear. Double stitched taped buttons. Eyeletted tabs for garters.

Cotton and Rayon Jersey

38K8504—Black. **45c**
38K8502—Tan.
38K8506—Flesh.
Lengths, 20, 22 and 24 in., to fit ages 11 to 16 years. State length. Shpg. wt., 8 oz.
Schoolgirls' and Misses' Medium Weight Bloomers. Knit of cotton underwear fabric with Rayon stripes. Elastic at waist and knees. Gusset crotch.

Knit Rayon

38K2248—Flesh. **85c**
38K2249—Peach.
Ages, 7 to 16 years. State age size. Shipping wt., 7 oz.
Schoolgirls' Fine Knit Rayon Bloomers made with elastic at waist and knees and trimmed with lace edged ruffle. Strong flat seams; double gusset crotch for added wear.

Lustrous Satinette

38K2232—Flesh. **53c**
38K2233—Black.
Ages, 7 to 16 years. State age size. Shipping wt., 7 oz.
Lustrous Striped Satinette Bloomers for Schoolgirls. Made with saddle crotch, giving extra comfort. Elastic waist and knees. Cut full and roomy without bulkiness. Seams double stitched.

Sateen

38K2214—Black. **65c**
Ages, 7 to 14 years. State age size. Shipping wt., 8 oz.
Schoolgirls' Better Quality Sateen Bloomers. Extra full cut. Inserted strip through crotch for comfort. Double seams. Fitted yoke front with elastic at back. Pleats in front provide extra fullness.

A Fine Line of Schoolgirls' Knit Princess Slips Can Be Found on Page 141.

SERVICE FABRICS
GREATEST VALUES

Steadfast Chambray Gingham

Steadfast chambray gingham lives up to its name; no matter how much you order, you'll be glad you bought it. A strong, durable good wearing cloth for women's and children's washable dresses. Popular also for kiddies' rompers and play suits and for men's shirts.

36K4299—Width, 32 inches. Plain colors: Copenhagen blue, Light blue, Light green, Heliotrope, Oxford gray, Pink, Tan or Yellow. Mention color. Shipping weight, per yard, 3 ounces. **13½c A YARD**

Oakman Quality Extra Good All Purpose Khaki

Extra heavy. Khaki, the nation's outdoor clothing fabric. Buy our new Oakman quality; it's extra good grade, a better, stronger, heavier cloth than we have ever sold and it's wonderfully good value. Very heavy weight; well twilled, the kind of cloth that almost never wears out. For tough, long wearing work shirts, sport shirts, overalls, work pants and aprons. Best value we could offer you.

36K1175—Width, 36 inches. Olive tan. **24c A YARD** Shipping weight, per yard, 8 ounces.

Bargain Khaki Cloth

Medium weight; twilled; good grade; liked best for women's and girls' middies, skirts, knickers and blouses for camping; for women's work dresses; also children's overalls and play suits.

36K1172—Width, 36 inches. Olive tan. **17½c A YARD** Shipping weight, per yard, 5 ounces.

Economy Chambray

Seldom have durability and low price been so luckily combined as in Economy Chambray. Attractive designs. Washes well, and wears well. You couldn't get a more satisfactory cloth for everyday dresses and aprons, or for children's wear. Popular also for men's shirts.

36K4604—Width, 29 inches. Plain colors: **8½c A YARD** (1) Pink; (2) Tan; (3) Medium blue; (5) Oxford gray. Stripes: (7) Tan with blue; (8) Light blue with dark blue and white. Order by catalog number and mention pattern number. Shipping weight, per yard, 3 ounces.

Wear Resisting

Oakman Quality Extra Good ALL PURPOSE KHAKI Sears, Roebuck and Co.

Heavy 2:45 Weight **Extra Heavy 2:20 Weight** **Standard Hickory**

Apron Gingham

Leader value. Medium weight, serviceable gingham suitable for aprons and house dresses. A real bargain.

98K4183 Width, 26 inches. Sold only in 10-yard bolts. Checks: Navy blue and white, Black and white, Red and white. Mention color. Shipping weight, 1¾ pounds. **9c A YARD** / **90c 10-YARD BOLT**

White Back Denims

Denim the popular, sensible, economical, work garment fabric. Heavy, strong white back indigo blue denim; will give splendid service for overalls, jumpers, work shirts, pants and factory work aprons.

36K1154—Width, 28 inches. Indigo blue. Shpg. wt., per yd., 8 oz. **16½c A YARD**

Extra heavy weight. A better than ordinary grade; strong, firm, very heavy genuine indigo blue white back denim. Stands the roughest wear and laundering. Gives the most exceptional wear and satisfaction.

36K1157—Width, 28 inches. Indigo blue. Shipping wt., per yd., ¾ lb. **18c A YARD**

Hickory Shirting Guaranteed Value

Especially durable. Strong, heavyweight hickory shirting, priced for real economy. No value anywhere to approach this. Suitable, too, for men's medium weight overalls.

36K1167—Width, 28 in. Indigo blue with white stripes. Shipping wt., per yard, 6 oz. **18c A YARD**

STIFEL

Yard Wide Denim

Stifel Heavy Calico

Stifel quality, the standard work shirt and work dress material for over 75 years. Quality always the same—our price is lowest. Very much heavier in weight than ordinary calico; closely woven and dyed genuine indigo blue. Stands washing and hardest kind of wear.

36K1194—Width, 32 inches. (1) White dot on navy blue; (2) White figure on navy blue; or (3) White stripe on navy blue. Order by catalog number and mention pattern number. Shipping weight, per yard, 5 ounces. **17½c A YARD**

Stifel Twilled Shirting

For sturdy, tough, long wear work shirts. It's the same old reliable Stifel quality and our price is lowest. Extra heavy weight, well twilled; dyed genuine indigo blue. A favorite for men's shirts and overalls and women's work dresses.

36K1196—Width, 28 inches. (1) White dot on navy blue; (2) White figure on navy blue or (4) White stripe on navy blue. Order by catalog number and mention pattern number. Shipping weight, per yard, 5 ounces. **19½c A YARD**

Yard Wide Heavyweight Denim

Yard wide, heavyweight white back, blue faced denim. For overalls, jumpers, coveralls, factory aprons, etc. The extra width of this cloth makes our price unusually low. Make work garments at home, at our especially low prices your savings are doubled.

36K1158—Width, 36 inches. Indigo blue. Shipping weight, per yard, ¾ lb. **23c A YARD**

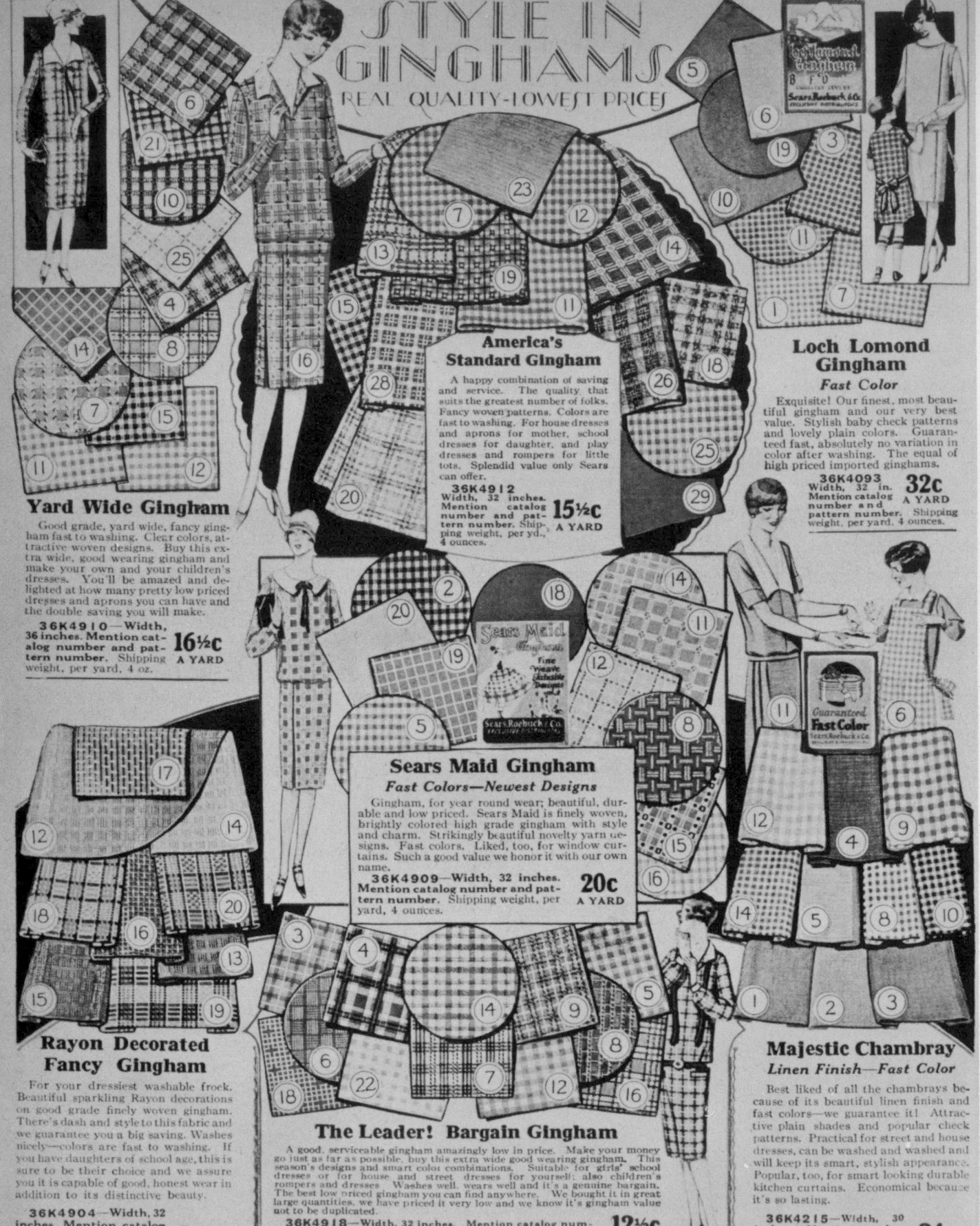

STYLE IN GINGHAMS
REAL QUALITY—LOWEST PRICES

Yard Wide Gingham

Good grade, yard wide, fancy gingham fast to washing. Clear colors, attractive woven designs. Buy this extra wide, good wearing gingham and make your own and your children's dresses. You'll be amazed and delighted at how many pretty low priced dresses and aprons you can have and the double saving you will make.

36K4910—Width, 36 inches. Mention catalog number and pattern number. Shipping weight, per yard, 4 oz. **16½c A YARD**

America's Standard Gingham

A happy combination of saving and service. The quality that suits the greatest number of folks. Fancy woven patterns. Colors are fast to washing. For house dresses and aprons for mother, school dresses for daughter, and play dresses and rompers for little tots. Splendid value only Sears can offer.

36K4912—Width, 32 inches. Mention catalog number and pattern number. Shipping weight, per yd., 4 ounces. **15½c A YARD**

Loch Lomond Gingham
Fast Color

Exquisite! Our finest, most beautiful gingham and our very best value. Stylish baby check patterns and lovely plain colors. Guaranteed fast, absolutely no variation in color after washing. The equal of high priced imported ginghams.

36K4093—Width, 32 in. Mention catalog number and pattern number. Shipping weight, per yard, 4 ounces. **32c A YARD**

Sears Maid Gingham
Fast Colors—Newest Designs

Gingham, for year round wear; beautiful, durable and low priced. Sears Maid is finely woven, brightly colored high grade gingham with style and charm. Strikingly beautiful novelty yarn designs. Fast colors. Liked, too, for window curtains. Such a good value we honor it with our own name.

36K4909—Width, 32 inches. Mention catalog number and pattern number. Shipping weight, per yard, 4 ounces. **20c A YARD**

Rayon Decorated Fancy Gingham

For your dressiest washable frock. Beautiful sparkling Rayon decorations on good grade finely woven gingham. There's dash and style to this fabric and we guarantee you a big saving. Washes nicely—colors are fast to washing. If you have daughters of school age, this is sure to be their choice and we assure you it is capable of good, honest wear in addition to its distinctive beauty.

36K4904—Width, 32 inches. Mention catalog number and pattern number. Shipping weight, per yard, 3 ounces. **22c A YARD**

The Leader! Bargain Gingham

A good, serviceable gingham amazingly low in price. Make your money go just as far as possible, buy this extra wide good wearing gingham. This season's designs and smart color combinations. Suitable for girls' school dresses or for house and street dresses for yourself; also children's rompers and dresses. Washes well, wears well and it's a genuine bargain. The best low priced gingham you can find anywhere. We bought it in great large quantities, we have priced it very low and we know it's gingham value not to be duplicated.

36K4918—Width, 32 inches. Mention catalog number and pattern number. Shipping weight, per yard, 4 ounces. **12½c A YARD**

Majestic Chambray
Linen Finish—Fast Color

Best liked of all the chambrays because of its beautiful linen finish and fast colors—we guarantee it! Attractive plain shades and popular check patterns. Practical for street and house dresses, can be washed and washed and will keep its smart, stylish appearance. Popular, too, for smart looking durable kitchen curtains. Economical because it's so lasting.

36K4215—Width, 30 inches. Mention catalog number and pattern number. Shipping weight, per yard, 3 ounces. **24c A YARD**

Fine Comforter Silkoline

A lightweight, brightly colored, silky looking cotton cloth for covering cotton filled comforters. Especially nice, too, for covering crib comforters and baby carriage robes. Used also for window drapes. Durable, very dainty and low priced.

36K2735—Width, 36 inches. Order by catalog number and mention pattern number. Shipping wt., per yard, 4 oz. **18c A YARD**

Famous Cosy Cottage Cretonne

The cloth of many uses. Exclusive French art designs; we've never had more beautiful styles and colors. You will like the homey, cheery brightness of this standard grade, medium weight, cotton cretonne for comforter coverings, bedspreads, drapes and cushions. Your money never bought better value.

36K2745—Width, 36 inches. Order by catalog number and mention pattern number. Shipping weight, per yard, 4 oz. **15½c A YARD**

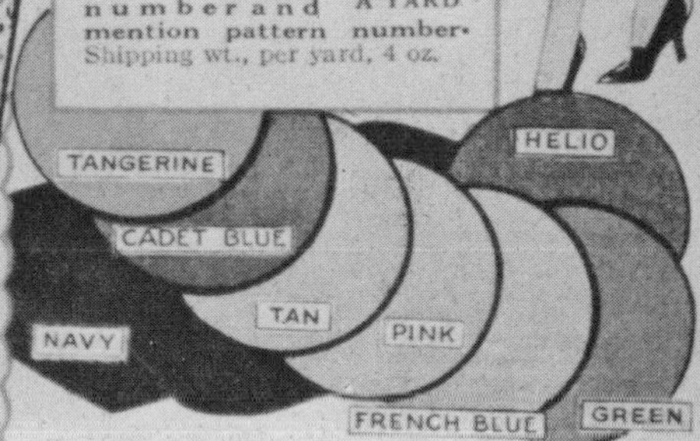

Lovely Sunbeam Challis

Challis is especially suitable for comforter covering; either for new comforters or covering old ones. It is bright and gay with its exclusive French art designs. Good grade, cotton challis, with soft, wool-like finish. Nice, too, for drapes and day bed covers. Lowest price anywhere.

98K2741—Width, 36 inches. Put up at the mill in 10-yard bolts only. Order by catalog number and mention pattern number. weight, 1¾ pounds. **13¾c A YARD** **$1.37 10-YD. BOLT Shipping**

Newest Thing in Colored Crinkled Bed Coverings

Crinkled ground fabric with beautiful flower and leaf design in new two-tone weave, giving the effect of silk. Pattern extends through fabric, making spread reversible, both sides can be used. Colors are fast. Made of strong two-ply cotton yarns. Exceptionally fine value; its beauty and good wear will please you. Four styles, as described below. Durably scalloped all around; neat square corners. Colors: Cream color ground with woven patterns in Blue, Gold or Rose. Order by catalog number and mention color.

See Pages 194 and 195 for other Bed Coverings

98K2470 **$2.78 A SET** Two-piece set. Double bed size. Bedspread—size, 80x90 inches. Bolster cover—size, 27x80 inches. Shipping weight, set, 3¼ lbs.	98K2469 **$2.59 A SET** Two-piece set. Three-quarter or twin bed size. Bedspread — size, 70x90 inches. Bolster cover —size, 27x70 inches. Shpg. wt., set, 2¾ lbs.	**$2.09 EACH** 98K2471—Bedspread only. Double bed size. Bedspread —size, 80x90 inches. Shipping wt., each, 2½ lbs.	98K2472 **$2.50 EACH** Popular "tuck under" style. Forms bedspread and bolster cover over pillows. Double bed size, 80x108 inches. Shipping wt., each, 3 lbs.

Dolly Madison, the Popular Percale

Thousands of housewives look for the Dolly Madison label on percales as they look for the sterling mark on silver. It means to them—Newest Percale Patterns and Colors, High Quality and Lowest Price. Unbeatable percale value.

36K2923—Width, 36 inches. Order by catalog number and mention pattern number. Shipping wt., per yard, 4 oz. **14c A YARD**

TANGERINE • HELIO • CADET BLUE • TAN • PINK • GREEN • NAVY • FRENCH BLUE

Plain Color Percale

The minute you see the attractive colors and feel the smooth, soft finish of this percale, you will know you've made a good purchase. Very popular for street and house dresses, and smocks. Nice also for trimming. High grade cotton cloth, really worth more money.

36K2951 — Width, 36 inches. Order by catalog number and mention color. Shpg. wt., per yard, 4 oz. **13½c A YARD**

Smart Style Prints

A style hit! Latest dress-up patterns in bright gay colors. High grade cotton dress prints ideal for the better grade house dresses and street frocks. Styles for children, too.

36K2921—Width, 36 inches. Order by catalog number and mention pattern number. Shipping weight, per yard, 4 ounces. **15c A YARD**

ATTRACTIVE
WASH FABRICS
PRICED VERY LOW

Lady Cloth New~Smart

Lustrous Charmeuse

Fifi Frocks—Fast Color

HELIO — PEACH — NAVY — TAN — GREEN — ROSE — BROWN — COPE

Strongkloth

Outwears Wear

So strong and durable, we say it "Outwears wear." High grade, smoothly woven mercerized cotton cloth, beautifully designed, in fast colors. For women's and children's stylish frocks; also for window drapes. Strongkloth merits your choice from among our many beautiful cotton fabrics.

36K3306 — Width, 36 inches. Order by catalog number and mention pattern number. Shpg. wt., per yd., 5 oz.

32c A YARD

For a Chic Frock

Lady Cloth has the durability of French flannel, the attractiveness of challis; it's new and very beautiful. Fine in appearance, low in price! High grade cotton cloth with soft wool-like finish; new designs; fast colors.

36K3300—Width, 36 inches. Order by catalog number and mention pattern number. Shpg. wt., per yard, 4 oz.

44c A YARD

The Smartest Fabric

Stylish, dressy, durable fast color charmeuse. Ideal for women's fashionable frocks and children's garments. Made of fine, strong, highly mercerized cotton; looks like silk. Washes well and keeps its satiny luster; colors are fast.

36K3309—Width, 36 inches. Order by catalog number and mention pattern number. Shpg. wt., per yard, 4 oz.

41c A YARD

Seroco Fast Color Linene

High grade guaranteed absolutely fast color mercerized cotton linene; nothing to equal it for children's garments and your own smart frocks, blouses and smocks. Made to stand washing, boiling and sunlight. Great value.

36K5570—Width, 33 inches. Mention color. Shipping weight per yard, 4 ounces.

24c A YARD

36K5026 — White only. Same quality as above. Width, 33 inches.

18c A YARD

Beautiful LYKSILK

It's beautiful and so durable and stylish! Has the distinctive beauty of silk and extreme durability of cotton. High grade, fine weave cotton fabric highly mercerized, you would think it was silk. Choose from a wealth of brightly colored designs; they are this season's latest. Colors are fast; it's wonderful how well it looks after repeated washings. Keeps its luster. Marvelously good value. Quite the thing for your smartest dress up frock and substantial enough for everyday dresses. Patterns are suitable, too, for children's dresses. You'll love the beauty of Lyksilk and the good wear it will give.

36K3307—Width, 36 inches. Order by catalog number and mention pattern number. Shipping weight, per yard, 4 ounces.

55c A YARD

Stylish—Durable

The newness demanded by Fashion is found in this assembly of bright, fast color patterns. For a smart, durable and low priced street or house frock select this appealing fabric; also for fancy aprons, trimmings and children's garments. Good grade medium weight cotton fabric in soft kid-like finish. Colors are fast. Priced low as an introductory offer.

36K3305— Width, 36 inches. Order by catalog number and mention pattern number. Shipping weight, per yard, 4 ounces.

19c A YARD

GOLD — COPE — BLACK — PEACH — BEIGE — ORCHID — SCARLET — SAGE GREEN — STEEL GRAY — CORAL ROSE — NAVY

Guaranteed Fast Color Sateen—Extra Durable

Just what you've always wanted, a guaranteed fast color high grade sateen for your own and your children's bloomers and costume slips. Here it is, a cloth guaranteed by the mill that makes it and further backed by our guarantee. A remarkably good cotton cloth, suitable for a hundred and one purposes. Serviceable and entirely satisfactory for little tots' rompers, children's school dresses, and trimming purposes. Wash and boil the garments, we guarantee the colors will not run or fade. Used, too, for making lamp shades, window drapes, comforter covers and cushion covers. Colors are guaranteed sunproof. Doubly guaranteed, wonderfully good all purpose sateen, priced low.

36K5407—Width, 36 inches. Mention color. Shipping weight, per yard, 4 ounces.

40c A YARD

GREATEST FLANNEL VALUES IN YEARS
LOWEST PRICES

Yard Wide Outing Flannel

The celebrated Jack Frost Outing Flannel at a record breaking low price. Full yard wide, softly napped on both sides. A serviceable, economical cotton outing flannel, always the choice of thousands of women for sleeping garments for the entire family. Extraordinary value.

36K4425—Width, 36 inches. Order by catalog number and mention pattern number. Shipping weight, per yard, 5 ounces.

14c A YARD

Our Best Outing Flannel

Our best yard wide cotton outing flannel affords comfort and the best possible service for your money. Very high grade, heavy weight, strong; heavily napped on both sides. Gives the best satisfaction for day in and day out wear for men's, women's and children's garments. The best value.

36K4958—Width, 36 inches. Order by catalog number and mention pattern number. Shipping weight, per yard, 6 oz.

19c A YARD

Sears Bargain Outing Flannel

Full yard wide, low priced, serviceable cotton outing flannel. Softly napped on both sides. Makes comfortable garments for grownups and children. Good wearing, extra wide and remarkable good value for the money. We name the lowest prices, give you the greatest values.

12c A YARD   **$1.19** 10-YD. BOLT

98K4430—Width, 36 inches. Put up at the mill in 10-yard bolts only. Order by catalog number and mention pattern number. Shpg. wt., 3½ lbs.

Famous Blendown Part Wool Flannel

Though new, it's already a great favorite, because of its beauty and durability. High grade flannel, firmly woven of a small amount of wool, just enough to afford added warmth, balance strong cotton yarns. Napped on both sides. Beautifully styled, really smart looking flannel. The grade that goes into the higher priced ready made garments. Fine for warm, comfy pajamas for the family; children's sleeping suits, underskirts, underwaists, bloomers and petticoats.

36K4444—Width, 36 inches. Order by catalog number and mention pattern number. Shipping weight, per yard, 5 ounces.

23c A YARD

Leader Value Kiddies' Special

Economical 27-inch width, just the thing for kiddies' nightgowns sleeping suits, bloomers and petticoats. Popular for grownups, too. Well napped. A strong, durable cotton outing flannel. It's years since it was sold at such a low price.

10c A YARD   **99c** 10-YD. BOLT

98K4915—Width, 27 inches. Order by catalog number and mention pattern number. Shipping weight, 2 pounds.

Velvedown—Our Best White Shaker Flannel

The world's best white shaker flannel values. Select quality, heavy weight cotton white shaker flannel. Heavily fleeced or napped on both sides. Priced low; quality never varies. Gives splendid wear, remains soft and pliable after washing. Unequaled in value; unequaled in service. For little tots' dresses, kimonos, underskirts and sleeping garments.

36K4168—White only. Width, 27 inches. **13½c** A YARD Shipping weight, per yard, 4 oz.

36K4170—White only. Width, 30 inches. **16c** A YARD Shipping weight, per yard, 5 oz.

36K4171—White only. Width, 36 inches. **18½c** A YARD Shipping weight, per yard, 5 oz.

Slumbersound Baby Flannel

Twilled, napped on both sides. Washes nicely, remains soft. A strong cotton flannel, always in demand for infants' and babies' kimonos, dresses, sacques, underskirts and nightgowns. A Sears famous flannel value; priced low.

36K4800—Width, 27 inches. Plain colors: Blue, Pink or White. Mention color. Shpg. wt., per yd., 4 oz. **13½c** A YARD

Greatest Comforter Values Ever Offered

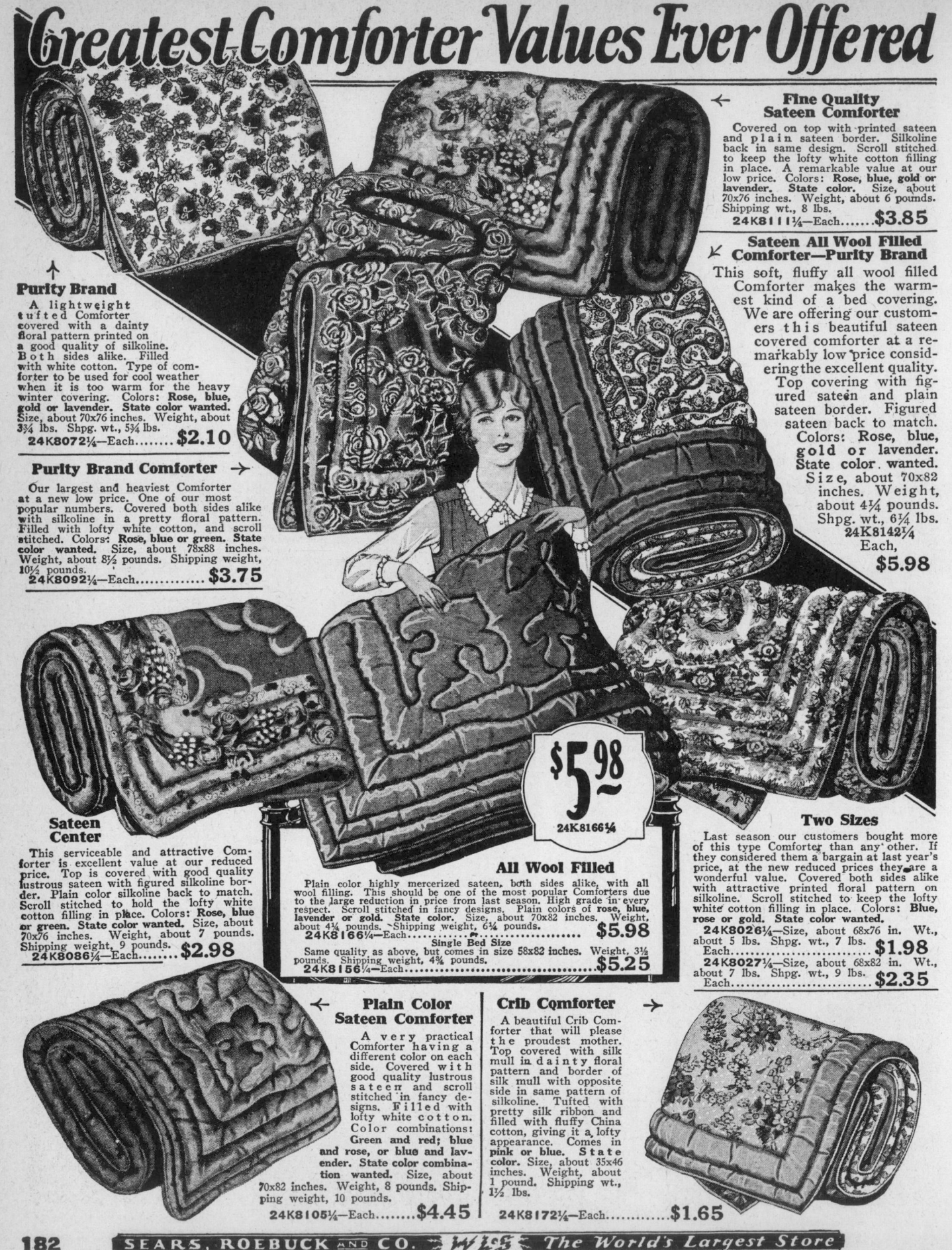

Purity Brand

A lightweight tufted Comforter covered with a dainty floral pattern printed on a good quality of silkoline. Both sides alike. Filled with white cotton. Type of comforter to be used for cool weather when it is too warm for the heavy winter covering. Colors: Rose, blue, gold or lavender. State color wanted. Size, about 70x76 inches. Weight, about 3¾ lbs. Shpg. wt., 5¾ lbs.
24K8072¼—Each........ $2.10

Purity Brand Comforter →

Our largest and heaviest Comforter at a new low price. One of our most popular numbers. Covered both sides alike with silkoline in a pretty floral pattern. Filled with lofty white cotton, and scroll stitched. Colors: Rose, blue or green. State color wanted. Size, about 78x88 inches. Weight, about 8½ pounds. Shipping weight, 10½ pounds.
24K8092¼—Each............. $3.75

Fine Quality Sateen Comforter

Covered on top with printed sateen and plain sateen border. Silkoline back in same design. Scroll stitched to keep the lofty white cotton filling in place. A remarkable value at our low price. Colors: Rose, blue, gold or lavender. State color. Size, about 70x76 inches. Weight, about 6 pounds. Shipping wt., 8 lbs.
24K8111¼—Each...... $3.85

Sateen All Wool Filled Comforter—Purity Brand

This soft, fluffy all wool filled Comforter makes the warmest kind of a bed covering. We are offering our customers this beautiful sateen covered comforter at a remarkably low price considering the excellent quality. Top covering with figured sateen and plain sateen border. Figured sateen back to match. Colors: Rose, blue, gold or lavender. State color wanted. Size, about 70x82 inches. Weight, about 4¼ pounds. Shpg. wt., 6¼ lbs.
24K8142¼ Each, $5.98

$5 98 ~
24K8166¼

Sateen Center

This serviceable and attractive Comforter is excellent value at our reduced price. Top is covered with good quality lustrous sateen with figured silkoline border. Plain color silkoline back to match. Scroll stitched to hold the lofty white cotton filling in place. Colors: Rose, blue or green. State color wanted. Size, about 70x76 inches. Weight, about 7 pounds. Shipping weight, 9 pounds.
24K8086¼—Each........ $2.98

All Wool Filled

Plain color highly mercerized sateen, both sides alike, with all wool filling. This should be one of the most popular Comforters due to the large reduction in price from last season. High grade in every respect. Scroll stitched in fancy designs. Plain colors of rose, blue, lavender or gold. State color. Size, about 70x82 inches. Weight, about 4¼ pounds. Shipping weight, 6¼ pounds.
24K8166¼—Each............... $5.98

Single Bed Size
Same quality as above, but comes in size 58x82 inches. Weight, 3½ pounds. Shipping weight, 4¾ pounds.
24K8156¼—Each............... $5.25

Two Sizes

Last season our customers bought more of this type Comforter than any other. If they considered them a bargain at last year's price, at the new reduced prices they are a wonderful value. Covered both sides alike with attractive printed floral pattern on silkoline. Scroll stitched to keep the lofty white cotton filling in place. Colors: Blue, rose or gold. State color wanted.
24K8026¼—Size, about 68x76 in. Wt., about 5 lbs. Shpg. wt., 7 lbs.
Each........................... **$1.98**
24K8027¼—Size, about 68x82 in. Wt., about 7 lbs. Shpg. wt., 9 lbs.
Each........................... **$2.35**

← Plain Color Sateen Comforter

A very practical Comforter having a different color on each side. Covered with good quality lustrous sateen and scroll stitched in fancy designs. Filled with lofty white cotton. Color combinations: Green and red; blue and rose, or blue and lavender. State color combination wanted. Size, about 70x82 inches. Weight, 8 pounds. Shipping weight, 10 pounds.
24K8105¼—Each....... $4.45

Crib Comforter →

A beautiful Crib Comforter that will please the proudest mother. Top covered with silk mull in dainty floral pattern and border of silk mull with opposite side in same pattern of silkoline. Tufted with pretty silk ribbon and filled with fluffy China cotton, giving it a lofty appearance. Comes in pink or blue. State color. Size, about 35x46 inches. Weight, about 1 pound. Shipping wt., 1½ lbs.
24K8172¼—Each............. $1.65

New Low Prices on Our Most Popular Cotton Blankets

Pennant Brand Cotton Plaid Blankets

24K7093¼	**$1.72**	24K7094¼	**$1.99**
Per pair...............		Per pair...............	
Size, 64x76 inches. Weight, per pair, 2½ lbs. Shipping weight, 3 pounds.		Size, 70x80 inches. Weight, per pair, 3 lbs. Shipping weight, 3½ pounds.	

Amazing Price Reductions

Our prices on these Best Staple Cotton Blankets are one-fifth lower than they were a year ago. This really breaks all records for low price and value. Last year we sold over 100,000 pairs of these blankets. They are so popular with our customers and the growing demand for them every season makes it imperative that we buy tremendous quantities; consequently, we get substantial price reductions and pass the saving on to you. The blankets are made of the finest grade American cotton, and carefully finished so that appearance as well as wearing qualities are yours at these low prices. Neatly overlocked at ends. Attractive plaids of **blue and white, gold and white, pink and white, lavender and white, tan and white or gray and white. State color wanted.**

Extra Fine China Cotton Blankets

24K7164¼	**$2.98**	24K7171¼	**$3.50**
Per pair...............		Per pair...............	
Size, 66x80 inches. Weight, per pair, 3½ lbs. Shipping weight, 4 pounds.		Size, 70x80 inches. Weight, per pair, 4 lbs. Shipping weight, 4½ pounds.	

Lower Prices—Extra Warmth—Sateen Binding

These fine quality China Cotton Blankets are absolutely the finest cotton blankets made, and at our new low prices are wonderful values. A special weaving process makes them much warmer than the ordinary cotton blankets and a great deal more serviceable. The softness of the deep nap gives them the appearance of wool blankets. They are high grade and we know at our low prices they cannot be duplicated elsewhere. Bound at ends with good quality 3-inch sateen. Attractive plaids of **blue and white, gold and white, pink and white, lavender and white, tan and white or gray and white.** State color wanted.

A "Pair" of blankets is one continuous length, twice the size given.
For Pillows See Page 885. For Mattresses See Pages 892 to 895

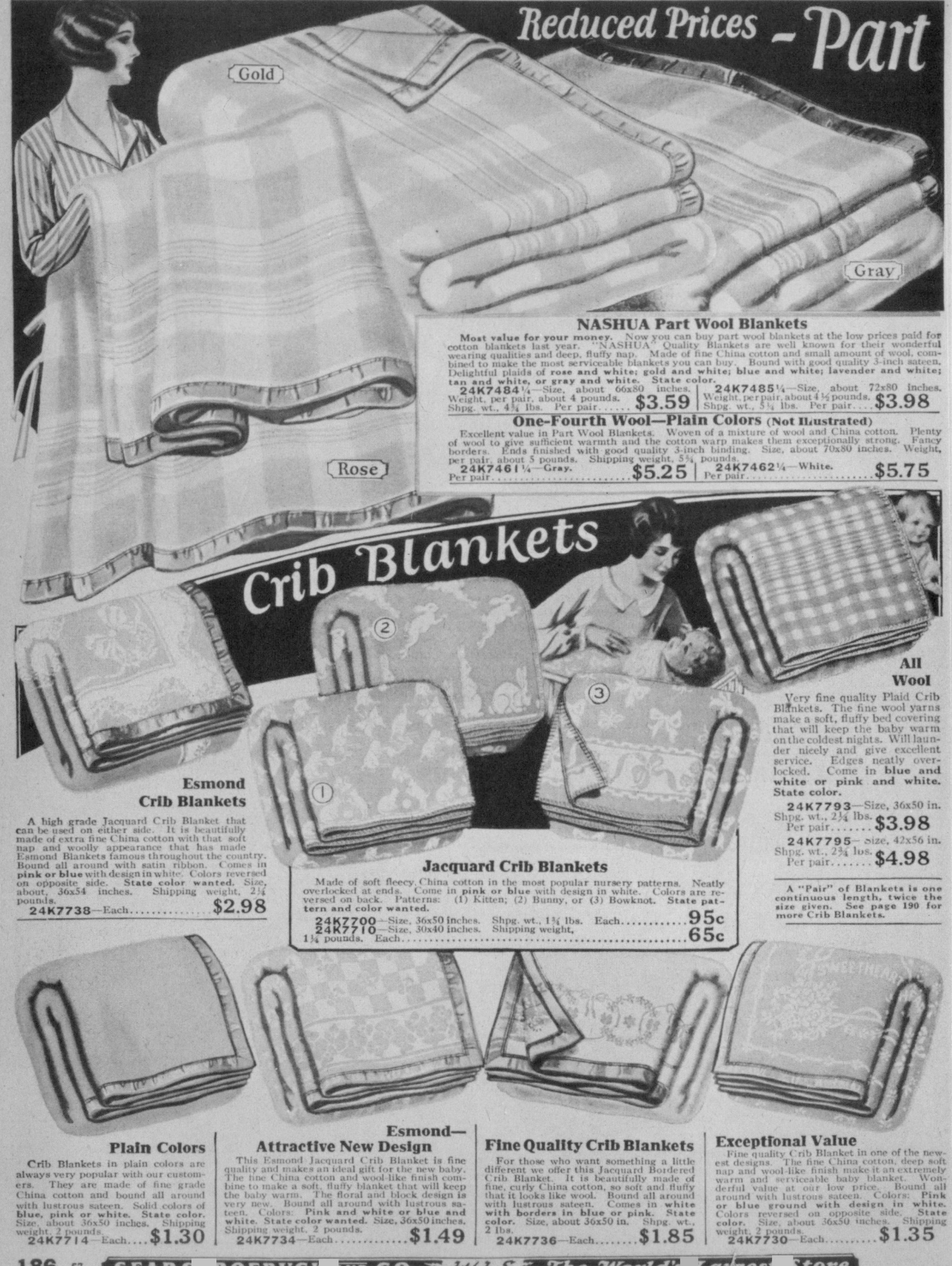

Reduced Prices — Part

Gold

Gray

Rose

NASHUA Part Wool Blankets

Most value for your money. Now you can buy part wool blankets at the low prices paid for cotton blankets last year. "NASHUA" Quality Blankets are well known for their wonderful wearing qualities and deep, fluffy nap. Made of fine China cotton and small amount of wool, combined to make the most serviceable blankets you can buy. Bound with good quality 3-inch sateen. Delightful plaids of rose and white; gold and white; blue and white; lavender and white; tan and white, or gray and white. State color.

24K7484¼—Size, about 66x80 inches. Weight, per pair, about 4 pounds. Shpg. wt., 4¾ lbs. Per pair....... **$3.59** | 24K7485¼—Size, about 72x80 inches. Weight, per pair, about 4½ pounds. Shpg. wt., 5¼ lbs. Per pair... **$3.98**

One-Fourth Wool—Plain Colors (Not Illustrated)

Excellent value in Part Wool Blankets. Woven of a mixture of wool and China cotton. Plenty of wool to give sufficient warmth and the cotton warp makes them exceptionally strong. Fancy borders. Ends finished with good quality 3-inch binding. Size, about 70x80 inches. Weight, per pair, about 5 pounds. Shipping weight, 5¾ pounds.

24K7461¼—Gray. Per pair..... **$5.25** | 24K7462¼—White. Per pair..... **$5.75**

Crib Blankets

Esmond Crib Blankets

A high grade Jacquard Crib Blanket that can be used on either side. It is beautifully made of extra fine China cotton with that soft nap and woolly appearance that has made Esmond Blankets famous throughout the country. Bound all around with satin ribbon. Comes in **pink or blue** with design in white. Colors reversed on opposite side. State color wanted. Size, about 36x54 inches. Shipping weight, 2¼ pounds.

24K7738—Each............. **$2.98**

Jacquard Crib Blankets

Made of soft fleecy China cotton in the most popular nursery patterns. Neatly overlocked at ends. Come in **pink or blue** with design in white. Colors are reversed on back. Patterns: (1) Kitten; (2) Bunny, or (3) Bowknot. State pattern and color wanted.

24K7700—Size, 36x50 inches. Shpg. wt., 1¾ lbs. Each........... **95c**
24K7710—Size, 30x40 inches. Shipping weight, 1¼ pounds. Each................................. **65c**

All Wool

Very fine quality Plaid Crib Blankets. The fine wool yarns make a soft, fluffy bed covering that will keep the baby warm on the coldest nights. Will launder nicely and give excellent service. Edges neatly overlocked. Come in **blue and white or pink and white**. State color.

24K7793— Size, 36x50 in. Shpg. wt., 2¼ lbs. Per pair...... **$3.98**
24K7795— Size, 42x56 in. Shpg. wt., 2¾ lbs. Per pair...... **$4.98**

A "Pair" of Blankets is one continuous length, twice the size given. See page 190 for more Crib Blankets.

Plain Colors

Crib Blankets in plain colors are always very popular with our customers. They are made of fine grade China cotton and bound all around with lustrous sateen. Solid colors of **blue, pink or white**. State color. Size, about 36x50 inches. Shipping weight, 2 pounds.

24K7714—Each............ **$1.30**

Esmond— Attractive New Design

This Esmond Jacquard Crib Blanket is fine quality and makes an ideal gift for the new baby. The fine China cotton and wool-like finish combine to make a soft, fluffy blanket that will keep the baby warm. The floral and block design is very new. Bound all around with lustrous sateen. Colors: **Pink and white or blue and white**. State color wanted. Size, 36x50 inches. Shipping weight, 2 pounds.

24K7734—Each........ **$1.49**

Fine Quality Crib Blankets

For those who want something a little different we offer this Jacquard Bordered Crib Blanket. It is beautifully made of fine, curly China cotton, so soft and fluffy that it looks like wool. Bound all around with lustrous sateen. Comes in white with borders in blue or pink. State color. Size, about 36x50 in. Shpg. wt., 2 lbs.

24K7736—Each........ **$1.85**

Exceptional Value

Fine quality Crib Blanket in one of the newest designs. The fine China cotton, deep soft nap and wool-like finish make it an extremely warm and serviceable baby blanket. Wonderful value at our low price. Bound all around with lustrous sateen. Colors: **Pink or blue** ground with design in white. Colors reversed on opposite side. State color. Size, about 36x50 inches. Shipping weight, 2 pounds.

24K7730—Each........ **$1.35**

Wool Blankets—Better Quality

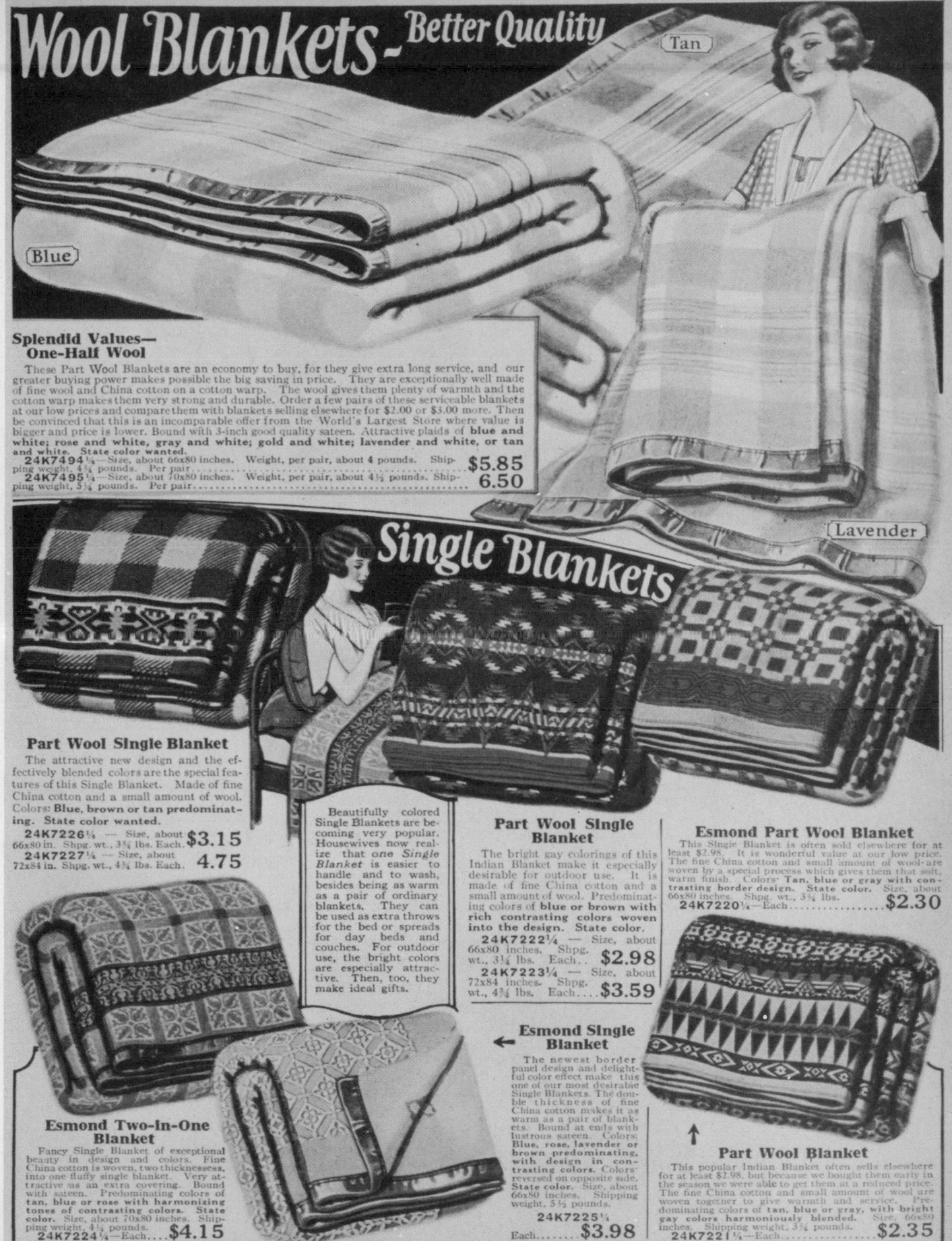

Blue

Tan

Lavender

Splendid Values— One-Half Wool

These Part Wool Blankets are an economy to buy, for they give extra long service, and our greater buying power makes possible the big saving in price. They are exceptionally well made of fine wool and China cotton on a cotton warp. The wool gives them plenty of warmth and the cotton warp makes them very strong and durable. Order a few pairs of these serviceable blankets at our low prices and compare them with blankets selling elsewhere for $2.00 or $3.00 more. Then be convinced that this is an incomparable offer from the World's Largest Store where value is bigger and price is lower. Bound with 3-inch good quality sateen. Attractive plaids of **blue and white; rose and white; gray and white; gold and white; lavender and white, or tan and white.** State color wanted.

24K7494¼—Size, about 66x80 inches. Weight, per pair, about 4 pounds. Shipping weight, 4¾ pounds. Per pair.............**$5.85**
24K7495¼—Size, about 70x80 inches. Weight, per pair, about 4½ pounds. Shipping weight, 5¼ pounds. Per pair....................**6.50**

Single Blankets

Part Wool Single Blanket

The attractive new design and the effectively blended colors are the special features of this Single Blanket. Made of fine China cotton and a small amount of wool. Colors: **Blue, brown or tan** predominating. State color wanted.

24K7226¼ — Size, about 66x80 in. Shpg. wt., 3¾ lbs. Each. **$3.15**
24K7227¼ — Size, about 72x84 in. Shpg. wt., 4¾ lbs. Each. **4.75**

Beautifully colored Single Blankets are becoming very popular. Housewives now realize that one *Single Blanket* is easier to handle and to wash, besides being as warm as a pair of ordinary blankets. They can be used as extra throws for the bed or spreads for day beds and couches. For outdoor use, the bright colors are especially attractive. Then, too, they make ideal gifts.

Part Wool Single Blanket

The bright gay colorings of this Indian Blanket make it especially desirable for outdoor use. It is made of fine China cotton and a small amount of wool. Predominating colors of **blue or brown** with rich contrasting colors woven into the design. State color.

24K7222¼ — Size, about 66x80 inches. Shpg. wt., 3¾ lbs. Each. **$2.98**
24K7223¼ — Size, about 72x84 inches. Shpg. wt., 4¾ lbs. Each. **$3.59**

Esmond Part Wool Blanket

This Single Blanket is often sold elsewhere for at least $2.98. It is wonderful value at our low price. The fine China cotton and small amount of wool are woven by a special process which gives them that soft, warm finish. Colors: **Tan, blue or gray** with contrasting border design. State color. Size, about 66x80 inches. Shpg. wt., 3¾ lbs.
24K7220¼—Each................**$2.30**

Esmond Two-in-One Blanket

Fancy Single Blanket of exceptional beauty in design and colors. Fine China cotton is woven, two thicknesses, into one fluffy single blanket. Very attractive as an extra covering. Bound with sateen. Predominating colors of **tan, blue or rose** with harmonizing tones of contrasting colors. State color. Size, about 70x80 inches. Shipping weight, 5 pounds.
24K7224¼—Each....**$4.15**

Esmond Single Blanket

The newest border panel design and delightful color effect make this one of our most desirable Single Blankets. The double thickness of fine China cotton makes it as warm as a pair of blankets. Bound at ends with lustrous sateen. Colors: **Blue, rose, lavender or brown** predominating, with design in contrasting colors. Colors reversed on opposite side. State color. Size, about 66x80 inches. Shipping weight, 5½ pounds.
24K7225¼
Each.......**$3.98**

Part Wool Blanket

This popular Indian Blanket often sells elsewhere for at least $2.98, but because we bought them early in the season we were able to get them at a reduced price. The fine China cotton and small amount of wool are woven together to give warmth and service. Predominating colors of **tan, blue or gray,** with bright gay colors harmoniously blended. Size, 66x80 inches. Shipping weight, 3¾ pounds.
24K7221¼—Each....**$2.35**

Your Orders Shipped Within 24 Hours!

57 **187**

Our Biggest All Wool Blanket Values

$7.75

$6.98

24K7522¼

Size, 70x80 Inches Weight, 5 Pounds Gray

Usual $10.00 Retail Value

Again Improved Quality on these All Wool Blankets. We had these blankets made for us when the mill was slack and the manufacturing cost was at its lowest; in this way we were able to get much better quality at the same price. These blankets are made of long wool fibers and the splendid construction and firm weaving make them exceptionally serviceable and extremely warm. For real comfort there's nothing like all wool blankets, for they keep out the cold and keep in the heat. We know it isn't possible to buy more in the way of "quality" all wool blankets at $7.75 a pair. That's why we guarantee satisfaction. Come in Gray with blue borders and neatly lock-stitched ends. Shipping weight, 5¾ pounds.

24K7533¼—Per pair... $7.75

Cotton Bathrobe Blankets

Beacon Bathrobe Blanket

Reversible blanket easily made up into a Bathrobe. Beacon Blankets are famous for their delightful colors and novel designs. Made of finest quality China cotton with a smooth, soft finish. Waist cords included. **Colors: Blue, rose, lavender, gray or tan, with design and reverse side in contrasting colors. State color.** Size, about 72x90 in. Shipping weight, 3½ lbs.
24K7242¼—Each..... $4.75

Beacon Bathrobe Blanket

The attractive woven Indian design brings out the beautiful colorings which are a special feature of all Beacon Blankets. Carefully made of fine quality China cotton with a smooth, soft finish. Very easily made into a robe that will give service and satisfaction. Waist cords included. **Colors: Tan, navy blue or gray wtih design and reverse side in contrasting colors. State color.** Size, about 72x90 inches. Shipping weight, 3½ pounds.
24K7232¼—Each........ $4.75

Size, 66x80 Inches Weight, 4 Pounds

All Wool Blanket Offer That Is Incomparable

This is the Best Quality All Wool Blanket it is possible to buy under $7.00 a pair. For the thrifty housewife who wants low priced all wool blankets this is just the number, for it will give wonderful service. Made of long wool fibers, firmly woven so that they will keep you warm on the coldest nights. Bound at ends with lustrous sateen. The softly blended plaids come in blue and white, rose and white, gray and white, gold and white, lavender and white, or black and scarlet. State color combination wanted.

24K7522¼—Size, 66 x 80 inches. Weight, per pair, 4 pounds. Shipping weight, 4¾ pounds.
Per pair................... **$6.98**
24K7523¼—Size, 72 x 84 inches. Weight, per pair, 5 pounds. Shipping wt., 5¾ lbs.
Per pair.................. **$8.95**

Dainty Crib Blankets

All Wool

A pair of extra fine All Wool Blankets for $3.98 is indeed a remarkable value. Made of a selected grade of wool and finished with a deep, soft fluffy nap. Neatly overlocked at ends. White only, with pink or blue borders. State color of border wanted.
24K7780—Size, about 36x50 inches. Shipping weight, about 2¼ pounds.
Per pair..................... **$3.98**
24K7781—Size, about 42x56 inches. Shipping weight, about 2¾ pounds.
Per pair..................... **$4.98**
A "Pair" is one double blanket, twice the size given.

Jacquard Crib Blankets — Fine Cotton

Money saving prices on practical Baby Blankets. They are made of fine cotton and are warm, soft and comfortable for the baby. Neatly overlocked at ends. Come in pink or blue with design in white. Colors are reversed on opposite side. State color wanted.
24K7744—Size, about 30x40 in. Shpg. wt., ¾ lb. Each.......... **55c**
24K7745—Size, about 36x48 in. Shpg. wt., 1 lb. Each......... **85c**

China Cotton — Specially Low Priced

White China Cotton Crib Blankets beautifully made of fine, fleecy China cotton. Will wash easily and give complete satisfaction. A value that would be hard to equal elsewhere. Neatly overlocked at ends. Pink or blue borders. 36x50 inches. Shipping weight, 1¼ pounds.
24K7726—Each..................... **65c**

China Cotton Crib Blankets

Plaid Crib Blankets offered at substantial savings. Made of fine, fleecy China cotton with a soft, wool-like finish. Neatly overlocked at ends. Thrifty housewives will buy these baby blankets for service and economy. Come in plaids of pink and white, or blue and white. State color. Size, about 36x50 inches. Shipping weight, 1¼ pounds.
24K7722—Each..................... **65c**
For Other Baby Carriage Robes, See Page 150

Launderite Sheets and Pillowcases

The Washtub Proves the Quality

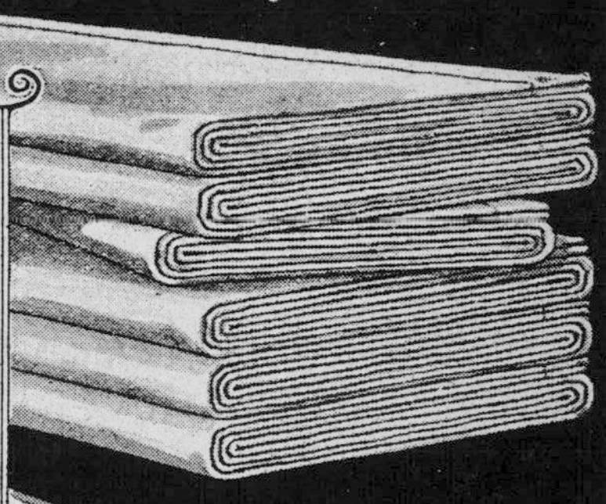

It takes more than just lower cotton prices to make sheet values like this! Only the cash buying power of Sears-Roebuck with their eleven million customers could obtain value like this. Launderite is our own brand. You never bought better value. We take the entire output of a big, busy mill, thus keeping the quality absolutely the same, and the prices at a rock bottom level. Launderite quality is immensely popular because it launders right, wears right and is priced right! Good grade cotton sheets contain no artificial weighting, and lose none of their appearance in washing. The same high quality you've been buying for years. We may cut the price, but we never skimp on quality. Launderite sheets and pillowcases are absolutely guaranteed to please you and save you money.

Hemmed Sheets

Regular Length, 90 Inches
Bleached White

Size, Before Hemming, Inches		EACH
54 by 90	98K1309—For single size bed. Shipping weight, each, 1¼ pounds.	$0.77
63 by 90	98K1310—For extra single or for twin size bed. Shipping weight, each, 1½ pounds.	.84
72 by 90	98K1312—For three-quarter or twin size bed. Shipping weight, each 1½ pounds.	.93
81 by 90	98K1314—For double size bed. Shipping weight, each, 1¾ pounds.	1.00

Extra Length, 99 Inches
Bleached White
Extra Long to Allow for a Generous Tuck-In Under Mattress

Size, Before Hemming, Inches		EACH
63 by 99	98K1320—For extra single or for twin size bed. Shipping weight, each, 1½ pounds.	$0.92
72 by 99	98K1321—For three-quarter size bed. Shipping weight, each, 1¾ pounds.	.98
81 by 99	98K1322—For double size bed. Shipping weight, each, 1¾ pounds.	1.08
90 by 99	98K1307—For extra double size bed. Shipping weight, each, 2 pounds.	1.20

Hemstitched Sheets

Size, Before Hemming, Inches	Regular Length, 90 Inches—Bleached White	EACH
81 by 90	98K1316—For double size bed. Shipping weight, each, 1¾ pounds.	$1.16
	Extra Length, 99 Inches—Bleached White	
81 by 99	98K1324—For double size bed. Shipping weight, each, 1¾ pounds.	1.26

Scalloped Sheets

Size, Before Scalloping, Inches	Extra Length, 99 Inches—Bleached White	EACH
81 by 99	98K1330—For double size bed. Scalloped on double thickness of muslin. Shipping weight, each, 1¾ pounds.	$1.29

Launderite Pillowcases

Hemmed—Bleached White

Size, Before Hemming, Inches		EACH
42 by 36	98K1326—For the ordinary size pillow. Shipping weight, each, 6 ounces.	25c
45 by 36	98K1328—For full size pillow. Shipping weight, each, 7 ounces.	26c

Hemstitched—Bleached White

Size, Before Hemming, Inches		EACH
45 by 36	98K1318—For full size pillow. Shipping weight, each, 7 ounces.	33c

Scalloped—Bleached White

Size Before Scalloping, Inches		EACH
45 by 36	98K1331—For full size pillow. Scalloped on double thickness of muslin. Shipping wt., each, 7 ounces.	34c

Scalloped Sheets and Pillowcases

We recommend these sheets and pillowcases to those who want a dress-up quality. Carefully finished, hand cut scallops on edges, made on double thickness of cloth for extra durability. You'll like the fine appearance and sturdy wearing quality. Not excessively weighted; will wear well and wash well. A set of these sheets and pillowcases will make a lovely and useful wedding or anniversary gift.

98K1345—Sheet. Size, before scalloping, 81x90 inches. Bleached white. Shipping weight, each, 1½ pounds. **$1.10 EACH**

98K1332 — Pillowcase. Size, before scalloping, 42x36 inches. Bleached white. Shipping weight, each, 7 ounces. **29c EACH**

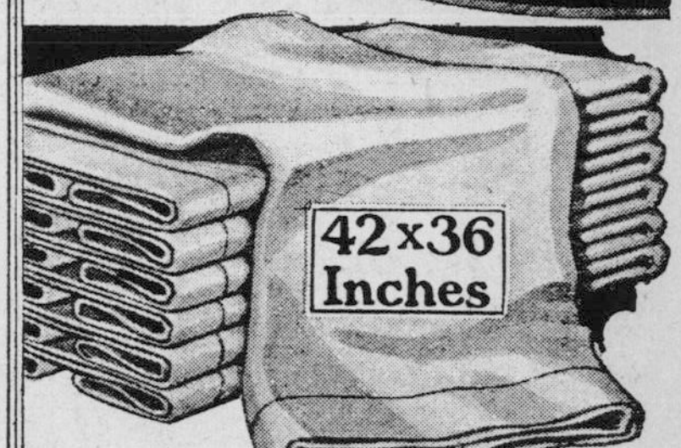

Bleached

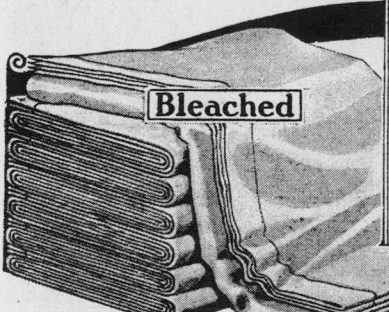

Bargain Pillowcases

Housewives, home makers, bargain hunters, here's a value for all! Standard grade, standard size, bleached muslin pillowcases. You cannot equal this value elsewhere. Not the sleazy pillowcases usually offered elsewhere at this low price, but a good, durable quality that washes well and wears well.

98K1720—Bleached white. Hemmed. Size, before hemming, 42x36 inches. Shipping weight, each, 5 ounces. **17c EACH**

This is a finer and closer weave than the above pillowcase, and a better value for the money. Well made of serviceable bleached muslin. A good wearing pillowcase, nice in appearance and priced very low.

98K1721—Bleached white. Hemmed. Size, before hemming, 42x36 inches. Shipping weight, each, 6 ounces. **19c EACH**

42x36 Inches

Unbleached

Wonder Value Sheets

Wonder Value Bleached Sheets
Great Bargains

Honestly made and honestly valued. Wonder Value, our medium grade sheets, liked for everyday use. Good weight, serviceable sheets priced for big savings. Neatly hemmed at ends. Not excessively weighted and do not become sleazy when washed. Now is the time to lay in a supply of sheets and pillowcases. The favorable cotton market enabled us to save money for eleven million thrifty users of our Wonder Value quality. Prices are the lowest in ten years. It will pay you to order liberally. You will be money ahead.

Size, Before Hemming, Inches		Size, Before Hemming, Inches	
72x90	**76c EACH**	81x90	**83c EACH**

98K1707—Bleached white for three-quarter or twin size bed. Shpg. wt., each, 1½ lbs.

98K1708—Bleached white for double size bed. Shipping weight, each, 1¾ pounds.

For Embroided Pillowcases See Page 244
For Pillows See Page 885

Wonder Value Unbleached Sheets
Wear Longer

The lowest priced ready made sheets in this whole big catalog. They're good, durable, long wearing quality in the natural cream color. In addition to household uses these unbleached sheets are popular for camping and sleeping porches, because they do not readily soil. Unbleached sheets last longer and, in time, washing bleaches them white. This is a great big value you won't want to overlook.

Size, Before Hemming, Inches		Size, Before Hemming, Inches	
72x90	**69c EACH**	81x90	**76c EACH**

98K1702—Unbleached (natural cream color). Hemmed. For three-quarter or twin size bed. Shipping weight, each, 1½ lbs.

98K1703 — Unbleached (natural cream color). Hemmed. For double size bed. Shipping wt., each, 1¾ lbs.

World's Standard Quality
Maysville Carpet Warp and Rug Filler
For Hand Loomed Rugs

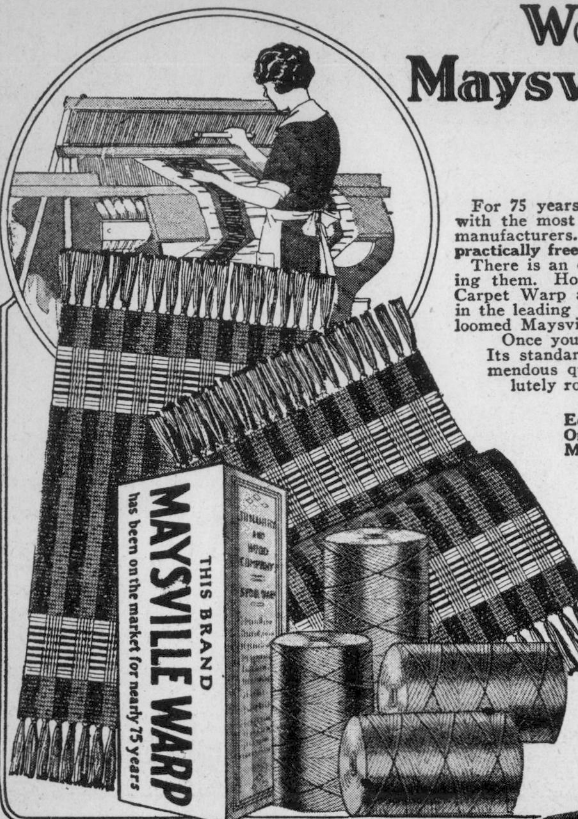

Maysville Carpet Warp

For 75 years rug weavers throughout the country have used Maysville 4-Ply Warp with the most satisfying results. It is guaranteed by both Sears-Roebuck and by the manufacturers. It is standard in yardage, uniform in strength and properly dyed. It is practically free from knots and comes tightly wound on handy half-pound tubes.

There is an ever increasing demand for hand loomed rugs, and a good profit in making them. Housewives everywhere are learning to demand rugs woven of Maysville Carpet Warp and Maysville Rug Filler. Maysville products are nationally advertised in the leading women's magazines, so that weavers find a ready market for their hand loomed Maysville rugs and keep their looms busy the year around.

Once you've tried Maysville Warp and Filler you will never use any other brand. Its standard, uniform quality is backed by long years of experience; and the tremendous quantities we buy enable us to offer our millions of customers an absolutely rock bottom price.

98K6536¼—Carpet Warp only. Colors: Dark brown, Ecru, Light blue, Red, Old rose, Myrtle green, Orange, Reddish brown, Purple, Slate gray, Yellow or Black. Mention color. Shipping weight, per pound, 1¼ pounds. 38c A POUND

98K6538¼—Carpet Warp only. White. Shipping weight, per pound, 1¼ pounds. 34c A POUND

Maysville Rug Filler

Maysville Rug Filler, or Roving, as it is known to the trade, is made of loosely spun cotton in rope form; about the thickness of a lead pencil, it is very soft, lustrous and fluffy. Weavers are enthusiastic about Maysville Rug Filler; it gives that individual, distinctive touch so much to be desired. It is used with Maysville Warp for hand loomed rugs and striking results can be obtained by combining different colors of the Rug Filler in the body of the rug or for beautiful border effects. It makes a firm, strong, good wearing rug. Also used in combination with rags. May we send you an attractive folder and sample card showing actual samples of Rug Filler?

98K6535¼—Rug Filler only. Colors: Dark blue, Dark brown, Garnet, Gold, Golden brown, Light blue, Light gray, Light green, Old rose, Tan; also Black or White. Mention color. Shipping weight, per pound, 1¼ pounds. 36c A POUND

Carpet Looms

If you intend buying a carpet loom, either for professional or home weaving, write us; we will be glad to put you in touch with a manufacturer of the highest grade and best type of loom. These looms are sturdily constructed and will last a lifetime. They are easily within reach as to price.

Latest Patterns
Oilcloths
Newest Colors

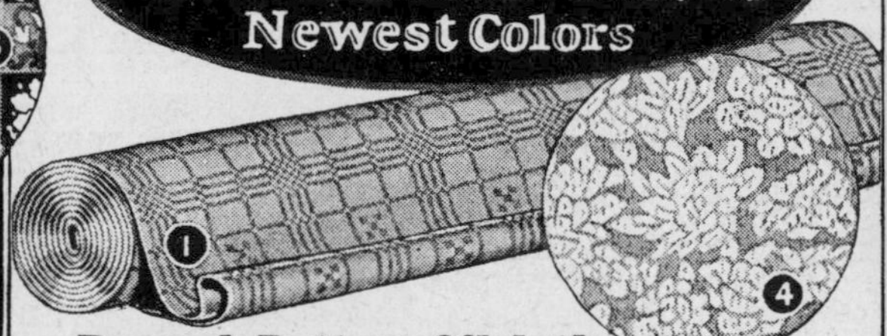

Damask Pattern Oilcloth

Standard weight, high grade table oilcloth. Extra wide. Beautiful patterns, they look like woven damask. Makes a dignified, attractive table covering.

98K6361¼—Width, 56 inches. (1) White checked damask effect; (4) White flowered damask effect. Order by catalog number and mention pattern number. Shpg. wt., per yard, 1½ lbs. Add 1 pound for each additional yard. 36c A YARD

PALMETTO GREEN
ROSE PINK
CANARY YELLOW
MEDIUM BLUE
DARK RED

Latest Thing—Plain Color Oilcloths

High grade oilcloth. Beautiful, bright colors, so popular for covering dining room, kitchen and breakfast nook tables, porch cushions, sunroom drapes, pocketbooks and shopping bags. Bright glazed surface.

98K6350¼—Width, 47 inches. Plain colors as indicated on illustration. Mention color. Shipping weight, per yard, 1¼ lbs. For each additional yard, add ¾ lb. 29c A YARD

For Furniture Upholstery See Pages 813 and 1003

47-Inch Table Oilcloth

High grade, well covered surface oilcloth in standard width for kitchen tables, breakfast tables and smaller size dining room tables. Our low price will save you money. Most attractive patterns you've ever seen. They are high class reproductions of imported oilcloths. Shipped on strong wooden sticks. They reach you in good condition. A mighty big value for the money.

98K6354¼—Width, 47 inches. (1) Plain white; (2) White with blue damask effect; (5) White with red damask pattern; (6) White with gray; (7) White with blue, double border; (10) White with blue. Order by catalog number and mention pattern number. Shipping weight, per yard, 1¼ pounds. Add ¾ pound for each additional yard. 26c A YARD

Extra Wide Table Oilcloth

A firm, heavy quality oilcloth. Comes in a number of bright, colorful designs. Made extra wide for dining room or large kitchen tables. A quality that will wear well and keep its bright, clear colors for a long time. If you are looking for a cheerful, durable and money saving table cover this is the number to order.

98K6356¼—Width, 54 inches. (1) Plain white; (2) White with blue tile; (5) White with blue damask design; (6) White with blue double border pattern. Mention pattern number. Shpg. wt., per yard, 1½ pounds. Add 1 pound for each additional yard. 35c A YARD

Complete Pattern Covers

98 K 6341¼

Women everywhere are learning to appreciate the saving in time and money that our oilcloth luncheon covers offer. They're popular, dainty and durable. They save washing, ironing and mending, and, best of all, they can be had for a fraction of what other materials cost. Two handy sizes in a choice of bright attractive colors. High grade oilcloth; well covered surface; sure to please in every way. Not a section of oilcloth cut from a bolt, but a complete pattern design.

98K6341¼—Size 55 x 55 inches. Blue or Orange on white, damask effect ground. This size comes only in design as shown in this illustration. Mention color wanted. Shipping wt., each, 2 lbs. 62c EACH

98 K 6340¼

98K6340¼—Size, 48x48 inches. Blue or Orange on white, damask effect ground. This size comes only in design as shown in this illustration. Mention color wanted. Shipping weight, each, 1½ lbs. 43c EACH

Sewing Machine Supplies

NEEDLES for Any Make of Family Sewing Machine 18¢ a Doz.

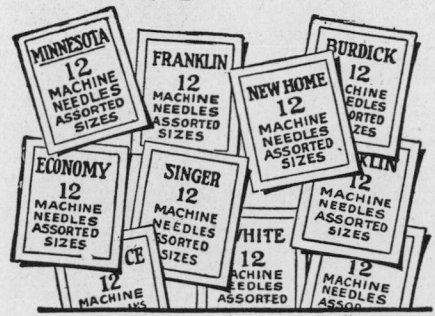

Your sewing machine will do its best work when equipped with the very best needles. We list only the highest grade and they are guaranteed to give satisfaction.

Be Sure to Send a Sample Needle

In ordering needles be sure to send a sample, stuck in a small piece of cloth or heavy cardboard to prevent it from being lost; also mention the name and head number of machine. No order will be filled for less than one dozen needles.

Our needles are put up in packages of twelve, in assorted sizes, and ten of the twelve needles are sizes used for sewing from 40 to 100 thread.

We do not sell needles for special manufacturing machines.

26K306—Sewing Machine Needles.
Shipping weight, 2 ounces. Per dozen........**18c**

For Sewing Cabinets See Page 903

Bias Cutting Gauge

A very useful attachment. The Bias Cutting Gauge is used in making up bias bands for the binder for use in home sewing. The Bias Cutting Gauge is also used for cutting net and chiffon for ruchings, cutting straight bands for pleating and cutting narrow ruffles for baby bonnets and dresses. To use the attachment, place it on the point of the scissors blade as shown in the illustration. By means of the slide "S" you regulate the width of the band. Shipping weight, 1 ounce.
26K4087—Bias Cutting Gauge........... **10c**

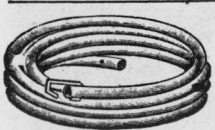

Leather Belt

Sewing Machine Belt. Genuine leather. Long enough for any sewing machine. Complete with hook. Shipping weight, 2 ounces.
26K4046...... **18c**

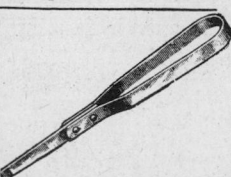

Metal Screwdriver.

4½ inches long, nickel plated. Shipping weight, 1 ounce.
26K4049......... **5c**

The Sewing Light Protects Your Eyes

With Mazda Lamp and New Style Double Plug

This Sewing Lamp is a necessity for the woman who sews. Poor light is one of the worst enemies of eyesight, and nearly all women who sew are common sufferers. Day or night, regardless of where your machine stands, you can depend upon this excellent lamp for your sewing without the slightest trouble.

It reduces your electric light bill inasmuch as it requires only a small part of the electricity needed to light a larger lamp. This Sewing Lamp is handsomely finished in polished nickel and comes complete with special attaching plug, long cord and bulb. Will fit all makes of sewing machines. With mazda light for standard 105 to 115-volt 60-cycle alternating current. Shipping weight, ¾ pound.
26K4009—Sewing Lamp................ **$2.45**
26K4010—Extra bulb for above lamp........**45c**
Shipping weight, 2 ounces.

Miscellaneous Supplies and Stand Parts
For Any of Our Machines

26K910—Greist Ruffler. Shipping wt., 4 oz....**$0.75**
26K1008—Genuine Greist Tucker. Shpg. wt., 4 oz. **.50**
26K6010—Instruction Book. Shpg. wt., 2 oz... **.08**
26K1606—Presser Foot. Shipping wt., 2 oz... **.30**
26K825—Shuttle Carrier. Shipping wt., 2 oz.. **.40**
26K4080—Shuttle Slide, front or back. Shipping weight, 2 ounces.................... **.20**
26K1109—Attachments. Shipping weight, 1 lb. Complete set **1.50**
The complete set of attachments consists of one tucker, one binder, one ruffler, a set of four hemmers, one under braider, one shirring blade and one short presser foot.
When ordering be sure to mention name of sewing machine and give head number.
26K5029—Leg, right or left. State which. Shipping weight, 10 pounds................**$1.75**
26K5020—Brace. Shipping weight, 5 pounds.... **.75**
26K5021—Treadle. Shipping weight, 5 pounds.. **1.00**
26K5022—Band Wheel, not ball bearing. Shipping weight, 4½ pounds **1.00**
26K5028—Band Wheel, complete with ball bearings. Shipping weight, 5 pounds........ **1.75**
26K5023—Dress Guard. Shipping wt., 4½ lbs... **.75**
26K5024—Treadle Rod. Shipping wt., 2 lbs.... **.35**
26K5026—Pitman. Shipping weight, ¾ lb.... **.75**
When ordering stand parts give name and head number of sewing machine and send full size drawing of part wanted.

Shuttle Screwdriver
Nickel Plated Shuttle Screwdriver. Will fit any shuttle. Shipping weight, 1 ounce.
26K4050......... **5c**

Needle Threader
One of the handiest attachments ever manufactured. Threads the needle quickly without straining your eyes. Shipping weight, 2 ounces.
26K4062........ **15c**

SHUTTLES 75¢ Each

The illustrations are exact reproductions. Be sure to compare your old shuttle with the illustrations before ordering. Also mention the name and head number of your machine. If the name of your machine is not shown, send us your old shuttle and we will try to duplicate it.

In some cases it will be found necessary to move the shuttle carrier to the right, so that the new shuttle, which is always a little larger than the worn shuttle, will fit properly. Shipping weight, 3 ounces.

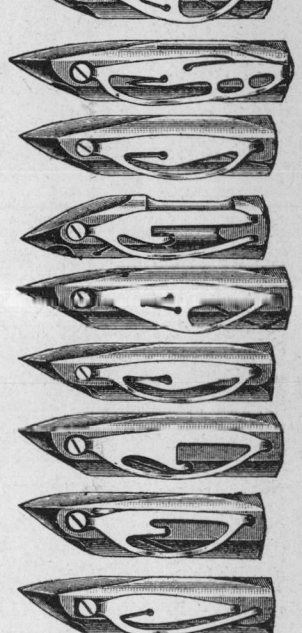

26K429
Burdick
Davis
Elmore
Iowa
Minnesota

26K430
Belmont
C. and C.
Homan
Minnesota

26K436
Old Domestic

26K443
Burdick
Edgemere
Eldredge
Howard
Kenwood
Minnesota

26K447
Franklin
King
Minnesota
Singer

26K490
Champion
Climax
Favorite
New Home
New Ideal

26K501
Amazon
Defiance
Delmar
Home Queen
New Queen

26K532
Dundee
Minnesota
Norwood
Arlington Gem

26K533
Kenmore

26K550
Florence
White

Bobbins
26K620 — Bobbins for Shuttles listed on this page. Shipping weight, 2 ounces.
Per one-half dozen......................**15c**
When ordering bobbins be sure to mention catalog number of the shuttle for which the bobbins are wanted and mention the name and head number of your machine.
26K608—Bobbins for Economy and Franklin Rotary machines. Shpg. wt., 2 oz. 3 for..**25c**

Where to Find Head Number
The head number of machines sold by us will be found on or under the front shuttle slide, on the rear slide or on the stitch regulator plate.

Sewing Machine Oil
To obtain the best results from your sewing machine, to insure and warrant its always running easy and lasting a long time, you must use good oil. For this reason we have had prepared for us a special extra high grade oil. Net contents, 8 oz. Shpg. wt., 1¼ lbs.
30K3394
Per can.......... **16c**

Bobbin Winder Rubbers
Bobbin Winder Rubbers. For all family sewing machines.
When ordering be sure to mention name of sewing machine. Shipping weight, 2 oz. 26K4070......**5c**

$5.00 Down and $5.00 a Month
The FRANKLIN
The Utmost BEAUTY and

HERE is your great opportunity! Equip your home with the most modern, up to the minute sewing machine ever made, at an amazingly low price! We have made many startling improvements, we have developed the sewing machine to the highest efficiency ever achieved. This Franklin Rotary compares with the most expensive models on the market today. Feature for feature, you will find them all on this remarkable Franklin. But look at the difference in price! Figure your savings on this rotary sewing machine which we offer for $59.50 with machines of the same type, which sell for twice as much and more. The Franklin Rotary sews just as smoothly, just as rapidly, with as little effort and brings you the same conveniences as any sewing machine made, bar none.

Every woman wants this newest Franklin just as the owner of an old model automobile wants a new, modern car. The Franklin is far, far ahead of old time sewing machines—you will be most pleasantly surprised at the ease with which you can sew on the Rotary Electric. It brings you, too, many, many new ways to save. In only a short time the Franklin will have paid for itself. It opens the door to a new world, of more and better clothes and of happiness and pleasure in personal achievement.

This efficient, speedy machine is a splendid TIME SAVER; it accomplishes twice the work of any ordinary machine. Attached to any electric socket, it is easy to operate. Starts with a slight pressure on the foot control and is always under your control. Perfect construction, accurate mechanism, scientific design make it a masterpiece. Built to outlive our ironclad 20-year guarantee. We can make this remarkable offer because, by selling direct from factory to you, we have no dealers', jobbers' or salesmen's expenses, and the difference is your gain.

Attachments and Accessories

A full set of the latest improved attachments, made by the famous Greist Company, is furnished with every Franklin. These include tucker, ruffler, shirring blade, under braider, short presser foot, binder and set of four hemmers, different widths.

Accessories furnished without added charge consist of one quilter, three bobbins (and one in the machine), one gauge screw, large nickel plated screwdriver, small nickel plated shuttle screwdriver, oil can filled with oil, foot hemmer and a package of five needles besides one in the machine.

The Sewing Machine Beautiful

THE BEAUTY of this machine attracts your immediate attention. Produced by expert cabinet makers, this lovely piece of furniture in dark walnut finish fits perfectly in any room. Closed, it makes a beautiful table or desk to occupy that vacant corner in your parlor or bedroom, and increases your satisfaction in your tastefully furnished home. Its low price, its extraordinary efficiency, its perfect construction would alone endear it to any housewife, but the added features of beauty and utility make it an unparalleled value. Silent, speedy service for a lifetime of use. The touch of your foot on the foot control sets it whirring, increased pressure speeds it up. All you have to do is guide the material, and both hands are free for that. Double the work in half the time, and twice as well done.

The Truth About Allowances

Allowances on old machines are always misleading. Dealers' prices, of course, are large enough to let them do this and still give them a large profit. The padded price is especially unfair to the purchaser who has no old machine to turn in. When you consider an allowance, compare the net price quoted with ours. You will find that even after the promised allowance is deducted from the dealers' price we can still save you a great deal of money. **The World's Largest Store makes no allowances.** We give you the best materials and workmanship at the lowest prices, and in every case we **Absolutely Guarantee You a Saving.**

Ownership Made Easy

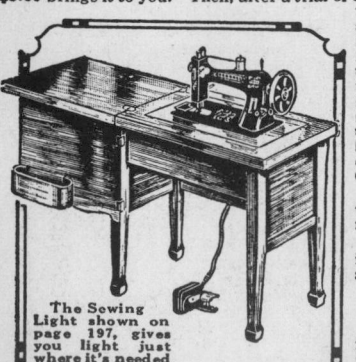

The Sewing Light shown on page 197, gives you light just where it's needed

Open View

The ownership of the Franklin Rotary is now made remarkably easy and simple. Only $5.00 brings it to you. Then, after a trial of 30 days in your own home, using it on your own work under your own conditions and, if you are satisfied, you pay the balance in easy monthly installments. In this manner the Franklin literally pays for itself while you are using it. Should you decide, after the trial, that you do not wish to keep this machine you may send it back and your money, with transportation charges you have paid, will be returned. Remember, we guarantee entire satisfaction with your purchase and we stand back of the Franklin Rotary with this guarantee. Order Your Electric Rotary Today!

Shipped from our store or from the factory in CLEVELAND, OHIO, whichever is nearer you. Shipping weight, 105 pounds.

26K96—Franklin Electric Rotary Sewing Machine, complete with attachments, accessories and instruction book.
Cash Price................. **$59.50**
Easy Payment Price............. **$65.00**
Payable $5.00 with order, balance $5.00 a month. Use Time Payment Order Blank on Page 1092.
Motor supplied is for direct or alternating current, 105 to 115 volts and 25 to 75 cycles. If you need a 32-volt motor allow $2.00 extra.

With This Portable Any
Illustrated on Opposite Page

Another example of the tremendous money saving possibilities of our sewing machines is this Portable Franklin Electric Rotary. For the apartment or small home where the space necessary for a sewing machine cabinet is lacking, this Franklin Rotary Portable Electric is ideal. Constructed with the care and perfection that characterizes every Franklin, it is an invaluable servant. Quiet, inconspicuous and easy to handle, it can be moved anywhere, and quickly put away when not in use. With this practical machine, any room with electrical connections becomes a sewing room. Runs smoothly and silently and is easily controlled by a foot control. The same head, the same motor and the same sewing efficiency of the other Franklin Rotary machines, described on this and the opposite page, are incorporated in the Portable. The motor supplied is for direct or alternating current, 105 to 115 volts, and from 25 to 75 cycles or 32-volt lighting plant. Machine is furnished with wood base and cover of American Walnut. A complete set of attachments and instruction book with each machine.

Shipped from our store or from the factory in CLEVELAND, OHIO, whichever is nearer you. Shipping weight, 60 pounds.

26K94—Franklin Portable Electric Rotary Sewing Machine, complete with attachments, accessories and instruction book.
Cash Price.. **$43.75**
Easy Payment Price **$48.75**
Payable $3.75 with order, balance $5.00 a month. If you need a 32-volt motor allow $2.00 extra. Use Time Payment Order Blank on Page 1092.

ROTARY *Electric* $5.00 Down and $6.00 a Month
in VALUE EFFICIENCY

FOR THE HOME, the hostess, and each member of the household. In this charming table model we have combined beauty and utility to a remarkable degree. Fashionable clothes and fine furniture, what could be more interesting to any woman? Here, in this modern table electric, you find both desires fulfilled. More clothes, more dresses, more underthings, more of the utility and decorative pieces for the home, more frocks and waists for the children and, at the same time, a distinctive table which is both ornamental and useful every day of the year. Where could you buy more for $78.50? What better investment could you make? In only a short time you will have paid for the machine by your savings as a result of your home sewing. Then there is a whole lifetime of additional economy ahead of you!

Remember, that this Franklin Rotary is the finest machine money or modern manufacturing facilities can produce. There is nothing better regardless of the higher prices you are asked to pay elsewhere. Each part is made with watch-like precision and the finished product is a marvel of speed, smoothness, efficiency. Lifetime satisfaction! We guarantee this model for 20 years of perfect operation. We guarantee your complete satisfaction with each smallest detail of construction and operation. If you want the latest improved electric machine on the market today, if you want a sewing machine that will bring you new ease and comfort, that will save you many hours and make of home sewing a delightful pastime, then order this Franklin Rotary now. Its purchase is made so simple because of our **easy payment plan** of only $5.00 down and $6.00 a month, that you can order it at once. Then try it, put it to every test and comparison you wish before you finally decide to keep it.

Special Electric Motor

The powerful motor, attached to the head, is always ready for use. Connect the plug to any convenient socket and the machine is ready for operation. A foot control regulates the speed of the motor, which responds easily and quickly. The motor supplied with machine is for direct or alternating current, 105 to 115 volts, and from 25 to 75 cycles. If you need a 32-volt motor, allow $2.00 extra.

Proof of Satisfaction!

Sears, Roebuck and Co.

It is a great pleasure to tell you that my Franklin Electric sewing machine is everything that can be desired. I have used several other more expensive machines, but prefer the Franklin because it is so easy to manipulate and runs so smoothly. I am more than pleased with it and highly recommend it.

I must congratulate you on the prompt delivery. It was ordered on Saturday, December 18th, and we received it December 23rd. Some service!

Wishing you the best,
Yours truly,
(Mrs.) O. G. Shaw.
Address furnished on request.

Rotary Head

The head is illustrated on the portable shown below. The Rotary type head has a revolving shuttle. The continuous rotary motion insures smooth operation and perfect stitching, as well as increased speed. The working parts, all carefully fitted and beautifully finished, move smoothly, noiseless and free of vibration. All Franklin Electrics are made with Rotary heads. Raising the presser foot releases all tension on the thread, and you can draw the work from under the presser foot without breaking the needles or the thread.

Room Is a Sewing Room

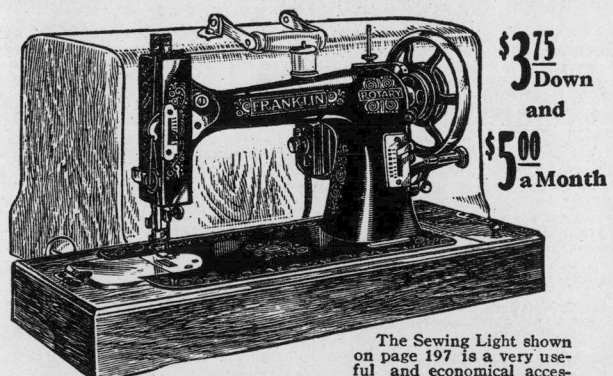

$3.75 Down and $5.00 a Month

The Sewing Light shown on page 197 is a very useful and economical accessory for any sewing machine.

For Prices and Description See Opposite Page

An Investment in Sewing Satisfaction

THE SEWING mechanism of this table electric is entirely hidden when the machine is closed. Yet to open it requires practically no effort at all. Simply take off the removable top, lift up the head, attach the cord to any handy electric socket and there it is, all ready to do your work. With the foot control you have absolute control, you start and stop instantly and can sew fast or slow. The big roomy sewing surface provides ample space without crowding. The motor does all the work, you simply guide the sewing and all your attention may be given to that. You can sew the whole day long without fatigue and you can make the most complicated gowns. The famous rotary principle of construction and operation means vibrationless action, a beautiful, even stitch and marvelous speed. The table is made of genuine American Walnut and exquisitely finished, serves many utility purposes in the home.

Easy Payments—Free Trial

We want to offer our customers every opportunity for demonstrating the usefulness, the economy and the perfection of this Franklin Rotary Electric to their own satisfaction and to help them own it without the slightest financial inconvenience. Order Now, enclosing only the initial payment, try it 30 days. If the Franklin Rotary does not sell itself to you, return it and we will send back every cent you've paid, including any transportation charges you have paid.

Motor supplied is for direct or alternating current, 105 to 115 volts and 25 to 75 cycles. If you need a 32-volt motor allow $2.00 extra.

Shipped from our store or from the factory in CLEVELAND, OHIO, whichever is nearer you. Shipping weight, 110 pounds.

26K97—Franklin Electric Rotary Sewing Machine, complete with attachments, accessories and instruction book. Cash Price.............. **$78.50**
Easy Payment Price.............$88.00
Payable $5.00 with order, balance $6.00 a month. Use Time Payment Order Blank on Page 1092.

See Page 197 for Electric Sewing Light

Open View

Parcel Post, Express and Freight Rates Are on Pages 542 to 545

MINNESOTA
Sewing Efficiency at

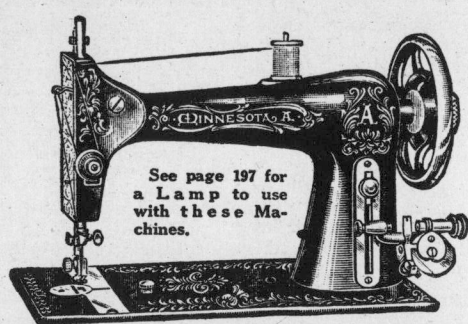

33^{95}

Minnesota Model "A"

In this remarkable six-drawer model we have concentrated our manufacturing facilities and our world wide resources to bring you a reliable sewing machine at a price which has heretofore been unheard of in the whole industry! Try to buy the equal of the Minnesota Model "A" elsewhere, and then compare your saving! Remember, you are buying real quality in this machine, notwithstanding the low price, quality which we back with our 20-year guarantee of satisfaction, quality which, we know will stand the infallible test of service. You can do everything with the Minnesota Model "A" which any other machine will do. You can sew the same clothes, the same garments for your household and you can do the same fine job of it, for this machine makes a beautiful stitch, sews rapidly, is easy to handle and operate. The woodwork is of selected plain oak finish and varnished in a golden oak color. Six enclosed drawers provide room for the many sewing accessories, such as buttons, thread, shears and the like. The head is easy to bring into position, because of the automatic lifting device.

Ninety-Day Trial

There is only one real place to test a sewing machine and that is in your own home. Let us send you this machine, use it on your own work, under your own conditions. If, at the end of ninety days, you have decided that you prefer not to keep the machine, we will return your money, including transportation charges you have paid.

26K226—Six-Drawer Minnesota Model "A" Drop Head Ball Bearing Sewing Machine, fitted with automatic lift, plain oak woodwork, complete with attachments, accessories and instruction book. Shipping weight, 105 pounds. 33^{95}

Sold for Cash Only.....................................

Shipped from our store or from the factory in CLEVELAND, OHIO, whichever is nearer you.

See page 197 for a Lamp to use with these Machines.

Minnesota Model "A" Head

The head is, naturally, the most important part of the sewing machine. The stand, the woodwork, other parts are of minor consideration; the head does the work. In this Minnesota Model "A" Head we have met the demand for a good, serviceable and efficient high arm machine at a medium price. Built of the best materials by skilled mechanics, we have tested and tried every part to make sure that it will give you the years of service you expect. Constant improvement, unfailing supervision, perpetual vigilance have produced a head that we can unhesitatingly guarantee for twenty years of service. Beautifully finished in old gold design decorations upon a black enamel background, the elaborate nickel plated trimmings and graceful outlines lend it a most pleasing appearance.

Special Features

Automatic Bobbin Winder saves time and trouble, and insures a perfectly wound bobbin at all times. Independent Positive Cam Take-Up insures a perfect stitch on any material with steady, regular tension. Automatic Tension Release.

By raising presser foot all tension is released, and work can be drawn from under the foot without bending or breaking the needle or breaking thread. Extra Strong and Large Feed, positive in action, giving even and perfect stitching on all kinds of material.

In a Cabinet of Beauty

38^{45}

Offering you the Minnesota "A" head, with all the quality features of this celebrated machine, in a cabinet of such distinction and at the astonishingly low price of $38.45, is an achievement we are proud of. Don't think that because this cabinet model is so apparently underpriced it can't be a quality machine. You can easily prove its value by trying it on your sewing in your home under our Free Trial and Money Back Guarantee Plan. We are perfectly willing to let this sewing machine be its own demonstrator. Thousands of customers have bought it and know they have made a splendid investment. You, too, will be proud of your purchase for this cabinet type is ideal. No need to provide a hidden nook of your home for storage purposes. You can leave this model right out among the rest of your furnishings where it will add to the attractiveness of your interior arrangement. You will find many purposes for which the cabinet can be used; such as a console, a server or utility table.

Built to Give Lasting Service

The Mechnical construction is identical to the drop head model described at the left. It has the same Minnesota Model "A" Head, the same headlifting device, ball bearing balance wheel, ball bearing metal pitman and automatic bobbin winder. Made of built-up oak stock, the cabinet is large enough to give ample knee room, and a convenient rack on the back of the door holds sewing needs. Finished with gloss varnish in golden oak.

26K244—Minnesota Model "A" Parlor Cabinet Sewing Machine, with automatic lift and ball bearing balance wheel. Complete with attachments, accessories and instruction book.

Shipping weight, 105 pounds. 38^{45}
Sold for Cash only.....................................

Shipped from our store, or from the factory in CLEVELAND, OHIO, whichever is nearer you.

Sewing Machines
Its Lowest PRICE !!!

$31.25

The Minnesota Model "H"

To complete our large assortment of quality sewing machines we have built the Minnesota Model "H" head in a convenient six-drawer cabinet model. Whichever sewing machine you choose from our wide selection you can't buy more downright value than we offer you in this number. The Minnesota "H" dominates the entire sewing machine industry in every way you want to compare it, for quality of workmanship, quality of sewing, ease and efficiency of operation or length of service. Where can you buy so much value for so little money? We specialize in sewing machines. They are our "hobby." We build them as well as they can be built, because we want them to be constant reminders in the homes of our customers, for years and years, of the bargains they can get from the World's Largest Store. For this reason you can have the utmost confidence in the reliability of the Minnesota Model "H." We guarantee it for 20 years and we will gladly send it to you so you can try it in your home for 90 days before you actually decide to keep it. . If at the end of ninety days you have decided you prefer not to keep it, we will return your money, including any transportation charges you have paid.

Special Design

Woodwork of selected, nicely grained plain oak finished in a rich golden oak color. Six drawers are large and roomy and fitted with wooden pulls. An automatic lifting device brings the head into sewing position when the lid is raised, doing away with unnecessary effort. When the machine is open ready for sewing the front apron folds up under the head out of the way, giving more comfort to the operator. A light running, ball bearing stand is well made throughout. In every way it is planned to give you the greatest satisfaction.

26K358—Six-Drawer Minnesota Model "H" Ball Bearing Drop Head Sewing Machine, fitted with automatic lift, plain oak woodwork. Complete with attachments, accessories and instruction book. Shipping weight, 105 pounds. $31.25 Sold for Cash Only..$31.25

Shipped from our store or from the CLEVELAND, OHIO, factory, whichever is nearer you.

A Splendid Cabinet

$36.25

In the low priced field of standard, dependable sewing machines, the Minnesota Model "H" easily takes the lead!

Outstanding in performance, reliable in construction and bigger in value, this machine is a real buy any way you look at it. Surely there is no necessity for you longer to deny yourself the comfort, the economy and the pleasure of owning a sewing machine. Your saving on only a few dresses will more than pay for it. Then you still have all the years ahead of you when the Minnesota "H" will be helping you in countless ways to have more of the luxuries as well as the necessities of life.

We guarantee the Model "H." We guarantee it against all defects of material and workmanship for 20 long years of reliable service. Naturally we couldn't do this unless we were sure of the quality of every small part that goes into it, unless we knew the precision with which each part was made and put together and tested. We would never jeopardize our reputation for handling only quality goods by offering you a sewing machine which didn't deliver the kind of trouble-free service you expect. The Model "H" will solve all your sewing problems. It will do your sewing in a most splendid, efficient manner, with a minimum of effort and exertion on your part. Will sew practically anything from the sheerest silken fabric to the heaviest wool wash garment.

The cabinet is constructed of selected quality oak, thoroughly air seasoned and kiln dried. On the inside of the door is a convenient pocket to hold attachments and accessories. All the everyday service of a splendid, useful piece of furniture is yours when you buy this cabinet model. Moreover, the machine is always handy for immediate use—you don't have to keep it hidden away.

Take Advantage of Our Ninety-Day Offer

26K349—Minnesota Model "H" Hand Lift Parlor Cabinet Ball Bearing Sewing Machine. Complete with attachments, accessories and instruction book. Shipping weight, 100 pounds. $36.25 Sold for Cash Only...$36.25

Shipped from our store, or from the factory at CLEVELAND, OHIO, whichever is nearer you.

The Lamp shown on page 197 can be used with these Machines.

The Head

The Minnesota Model "H" is one of the handsomest, most roomy, high arm sewing machines on the market. Makes the double lockstitch, the same as all high grade machines.

Silent and easy running. All bearings and wearing parts are made of steel, specially selected and properly fitted. The tension on this head is placed on top of the arm and consists of two flexible nickel plated steel plates through which the thread passes. Shuttle is cylindrical and made of fine grade steel. Self threading, being opened at one end for inserting the bobbin, after which the thread is instantly drawn into place by two motions of the hand.

The Minnesota Model "H" is a full size high arm machine. It has the same working space under the arm as the Franklin Minnesota Model "A" or any other up to date sewing machine sold anywhere.

Minnesota Model "H" Four-Drawer

Here is a sewing machine of good quality offered at a startling reduced price. If you have only a small amount of sewing to do, this fine four-drawer model will amply care for your needs. The Minnesota Model "H" Head is light running and well made in every particular, and the ball bearing stand is of our latest type. The attractively designed woodwork is of selected plain oak with gloss varnished finish. The drawer fronts are handsomely embossed and are fitted with wooden knobs. In every way this machine is a remarkable value, the best low priced machine ever offered.

In buying this machine you are absolutely protected by our Twenty-Year Guarantee of your sewing satisfaction.

26K347½—Four-Drawer Minnesota Model "H" Hand Lift Drop Head Ball Bearing Sewing Machine, plain oak woodwork, complete with attachments, accessories and instruction book. Shipping weight, 105 pounds. $27.95 Sold for Cash Only......$27.95

Shipped from factory in CLEVELAND, OHIO.

$27.95

"I Made It Myself! It was no trouble at all. The material arrived from Sears yesterday and I cut it out and finished it all today. The patterns are so easy to follow and Sears have such a splendid assortment of silks and dress goods that I find it very easy to make my own clothes. You say you like the color? That's 'Chin Chin blue', one of the Sears new featured colors. They illustrate a new color on each page, about 12 or 14 colors all told, and you can be sure of just which shade you want. Yes, they show Claret, Jungle green, Pirate red, Rose beige, and all the other new colors. No, I've never found better values anywhere in yard goods, and their service is so prompt."

It is easy to sew with one of our Electric Rotary, Sit-Right Franklin or Minnesota sewing machines. Our easy-payment plan and low prices also make it easy to own one. See pages 198 to 203.

One of Our Big Special Values

89c A YARD

All Wool Flannel

A value we thought so much of that we put it in this prominent place so you wouldn't miss it. You'll be agreeably surprised at the quality you get at this price. Firmly woven twilled flannel. 14K3968—Width, about 36 inches. Colors: Jungle green, Claret wine, Chin Chin blue, Pirate red, Rose beige tan, Napoleon blue, Brown sugar or Athenia. State color. Shipping weight, per yard, 7 ounces.

Half Wool Dress Serge

49c A YARD

A standard, popular, long wearing dress serge priced well below the usual retail price. For children's clothes. 14K3145—Width, about 36 inches. Colors: Navy blue, Tan, Dark French blue, Claret, Brown or Black. State color. Shipping weight, per yard, 6 ounces.

Half Wool French Serge

68c A YARD

A much better quality than our 14K3145. Fine twilled. Firmly woven of good quality wool yarns. A very serviceable, good looking serge. 14K3345—Width, about 36 inches. Colors: Navy blue, Brown, Claret wine, Jungle green, Dark French blue, Tan or Black. State color. Shpg. wt., per yard, 7 ounces.

All Wool French Serge

98c A YARD

Our lowest priced all wool French Serge. A surprisingly nice quality that will give a lot of wear. The new Fall colors are very attractive. 14K3645—Width, about 36 inches. Colors: Navy blue, Brown, Athenia, Napoleon blue, Claret wine, Jungle green, Mother Goose tan, Pirate red, Cream or Black. State color. Shipping weight, per yard, 6 ounces.

All Wool French Serge

$1.19 A YARD

A firm, splendid quality dress weight serge. 14K3055—Width, about 40 inches. Colors. Navy blue, Rose beige tan, Cream, Pirate red, Jungle green, Chin Chin blue, Claret wine or Black. State color: Shipping weight, per yard, 7 ounces.

All Wool French Serge

$1.68 A YARD

Our best French serge. Dress weight. A splendid quality. For dresses or suits. 14K3095—Width, about 54 inches. Colors: Navy Blue, Athenia, Jungle green, French blue, Claret wine, Brown sugar or Black. State color. Shipping weight, per yard, ¾ pound.

All Wool Storm Serge

75c A YARD

A fine quality storm serge for children's clothes. Wonderful wearing quality. 14K3240—Width, about 36 inches. Colors: Navy blue, Brown, black, Claret wine or Pirate red. State color. Shipping weight, per yard, 7 ounces.

Half Wool Batiste

78c A YARD

A nicely finished, firmly woven batiste. This quality especially suited for children's dresses. 14K3149—Width, about 36 inches. Colors: Tan, Cream, Pink, Pirate red, Navy blue, French blue, Claret wine, Palmetto green or Black. State color. Shipping weight, per yard, 6 ounces.

All Wool Batiste

98c A YARD

Batistes or basket weaves are becoming increasingly important as style items. They are light weight, fall softly and dye up beautifully in the newer colors. 14K3039—Width, about 36 inches. Colors: Navy blue, Tan, Jungle green, Cream, Rose, Pirate red, Chin Chin blue, Dark French blue, Claret wine, Athenia or Black. State color. Shipping weight, per yard, 6 ounces.

Part Wool Shepherd Check

58c A YARD

Checks are being prominently styled again for dresses, in combination and as trimming. Always desirable for children's clothes. One-fourth wool. 14K3147—Width, about 36 inches. Medium size Black and white checks only. Shipping weight, per yard, 7 ounces.

All Wool Shepherd Checks

$1.50 A YARD

Our best and only all wool shepherd check. A very nice quality made of the best yarns obtainable. 14K3067—Width, about 40 inches. Medium size Black and white checks only. Shipping weight, per yard, 7 ounces.

For Paper Patterns See Pages 220 and 221.

New Wool Flannels

$1.79 A YARD

Chin Chin Blue (Medium Blue)

All Wool Twilled Broadcloth Flannel

$1.79 A YARD Another smart fabric for the plaid and plain compose feature. This is our standard lightweight broadcloth flannel that we have sold for years and we have the attractive plaids below to match.

14K3081—Width, about 52 inches. For compose with plaids **order the colors illustrated by pattern number.** Additional plain colors without plaids to match are Claret wine, Pirate red, French blue, Brown sugar or Black. State color. Shipping weight, per yard, ¾ lb.

All Wool Plaid Compose Flannel

$1.98 A YARD Most attractive flannel plaids to match our broadcloth flannel shown above. The plaids are the same fine quality. The colors are the new fall shades and the stylish combinations you can fashion are many. You'll like this new idea and this always popular flannel.

14K3083—Width, about 54 inches. Order by catalog number and pattern number. Shipping weight, per yard, ½ pound.

$1.75 A YARD

All Wool Plaid Composé Flannel

$1.75 A YARD Plaids that match the plain colors for the new composé styles. Smart, crisp basket weave flannel. The attractive combinations possible with plaids and plains are many. Sometimes the plaids are used only to trim—also for one tier in the skirt—as the blouse, or skirt, etc. You will like this lightweight material.

14K3604—Width, about 54 inches. Order by catalog number and pattern number. Shipping weight, per yard, 8 ounces.

All Wool Composé Plain Flannel

$1.48 A YARD Composé (the French for combination), is one of the newest style features. Plaids and plain to match are smart. This plain basket weave flannel matches the plaid above. A remarkably bright, stylish color combination. We illustrate one of the many possible combinations. A very nice soft, lightweight quality.

14K3605—Width, about 54 inches. Order by catalog number and pattern number. Shipping weight, per yard, 8 ounces.

$1.59 A YARD AND UP

All Wool Twilled Flannel

$1.59 A YARD Our best selling flannel at a very attractive price. We offer you all the compose color combinations shown above in this popular priced flannel and several other colors. Very serviceable.

14K3948—Width, about 54 inches. Order by catalog number and pattern number the colors above and by name if you want Pirate red, Napoleon blue, Copperleaf or Rose beige tan. Shipping weight, per yard, ¾ pound.

All Wool Flannel

$2.45 A YARD Our best all wool flannel and one of the best flannels obtainable today. We illustrate above some of our two-color composé combinations which are so very smart this season. A beautiful quality. Light weight.

14K3498—Width, about 54 inches. Comes in all the eight colors illustrated above, which please order by pattern number; also Pirate red, illustrated below, which please order by name. State catalog number. Shipping weight, per yard, 8 ounces.

Wash Flannel

88c A YARD Guaranteed fast color, non-shrinkable half wool wash flannel. Light weight. Especially suited for children's clothes.

14K3448—Width, about 36 inches. Colors: Jungle green, Claret wine, Mother Goose tan, Pirate red, Chin Chin blue or Napoleon blue. State color. Shipping weight, per yard, 5 ounces.

$1.98 A YARD

All Wool Cashora

$1.98 A YARD An imitation of Rodier's Kasha. One of the best of the many black shadowed fine yarn fabrics sold as Kasha. A delightful light weight.

14K3201—Width, about 54 inches. Order by catalog number and pattern number the colors illustrated above, and by name Pirate red or Tan. Shpg. wt., per yd., 8 oz.

All Wool Crepe Flannel

$1.98 A YARD One of the new featherweight dress materials. Combines the vogue for crepes with the wanted softness of flannel and in the new fall colorings is exceptionally attractive.

14K3682—Oporto (illustrated on figure at right), Chin Chin blue, Rose beige tan, Jungle green, Pirate red, Brown sugar, Napoleon blue or Copperleaf. State color. Shipping weight, per yard, 8 ounces.

All Wool Striped Flannel

$1.48 A YARD Single line stripes are quite fashionable. They tailor smartly and are a change from plain colors.

14K3087—Width, about 54 inches. Colors: Tan (illustrated), Chin Chin blue, Pirate red, Brown, Cocoa or Copperleaf. State color. Shipping weight, per yard, ¾ pound.

For Paper Patterns See Pages 220 and 221.

Velvets, Velveteens and

Claret
(Medium Wine)

Fur Effects
Resemble Real Fur
$5.48 A YARD The rich pile and natural fur-like markings make these beautiful pile fabrics look more like real fur than any we have ever before offered. Will make handsome, stylish and warm coats and jacquettes. Also an excellent trimming for a cloth coat. 14K7800—Width, about 48 inches. Colors: Leopard (tawny yellow with black spots), Silver Muskrat (gray and brown), or Mink (tan and brown.) State color. Shipping weight, per yard, 1 pound.

Silk Finish Costume Velveteen
Guaranteed Fast Pile
$1.98 A YARD Our fine quality velvety finish costume velveteen with a thick, erect, silky pile on a twill background. The pile is soft and will not rub off. A charming and stylish fabric for your fall and winter dresses, or for a separate jacket for the new ensemble.
14K7340—Width, about 36 inches. Colors: (1) Petunia; (2) Jungle green; (3) Brown sugar; (4) Napoleon blue; (5) Claret wine; (6) Black; also Pirate red, Navy or Dark gray. State color. Shipping weight, per yard, ¾ pound.

Voivelle—A Fancy Corduroy
78c A YARD Voivelle has a rich velvet pile raised in an attractive pattern on a voile-like ground. Few all-cotton fabrics have such a silky feel and drape with such soft graceful beauty. And it is so practical too, because it can be washed. Ideal for sport dresses and coats, for robes, or for children's wear.
14K7600—Width, about 36 inches. Colors: (1) American beauty; (2) Peacock blue; (3) Rose of Sharon; also Pirate red, Brown, Sugar, Pigeon gray, Napoleon blue, Mother Goose, Jade green, Navy or Black. State color. Shpg. wt., per yard, ¾ lb.

For Paper Patterns See Page 220 and 221

Chiffon

All Silk Chiffon Velvet
$5.89 A YARD Our standard fine quality all silk velvet. It has a soft, rich, erect pile. 14K7000—Width, about 39 inches. Black only. Shipping weight, per yard, ¾ lb.

All Silk Transparent Velvet
$7.50 A YARD The finest and most beautiful velvet you have ever seen. All silk, its high erect pile is on a georgette-effect background, making a velvet of unbelievable softness and suppleness. Its graceful drapiness and lovely sheen will fashion most beautifully.
14K7100—Width, about 39 inches. Black only. Shpg. wt., per yard, 8 oz.

Velvets

Chiffon Velvet
Erect, Thick, Silk Pile
$3.48 A YARD Of course you will want at least one velvet dress in your new fall wardrobe, and here is an opportunity to have one at small cost. Our standard, fine quality velvet with a high silk pile on the best woven cotton back. It drapes beautifully, and comes in the season's newest dress shades.
14K7598—Width, about 39 inches. Colors: (1) Claret wine; (2) Jungle green; (3) Chin Chin blue; (4) Cherry bloom; (5) Black; also Brown sugar or Navy blue. State color. Shipping weight, per yard, ¾ pound.

Velvet Finish Corduroy
Narrow Wale. Medium Weight.
58c A YARD This fine quality velvet finish corduroy is soft and lustrous, and is woven of extra fine mercerized cotton yarns. It has made many friends due to its fine wearing qualities and nice appearance. Makes lovely lounging robes and bathrobes, and is also excellent for children's garments, sports wear and men's shirts. Washes well.
14K7300—Width, about 36 inches. Colors: (3) Rose of Sharon; (4) Claret wine; (5) American beauty; (6) Mother Goose; (7) Napoleon blue; also White, Pigeon gray, Palmetto green, Brown sugar, Chin Chin blue, Navy or Black. State color. Shipping weight, per yard, ¾ pound.

Shepherd Check Costume Velveteen
Silk Finish. Twill Back.
$2.48 A YARD Shepherd checks, alone or in compose with a plain velvet like our 14K7340, on this page, are very popular this season. This is a fine quality velveteen with a fast pile. Very attractive.
14K7540—Width, about 36 inches. Colors: (1) Green and black; (2) Blue and black; (3) Red and black; or (4) White and black. State color. Shipping weight, per yard, ¾ pound.

Velvet Finish Corduroy
Wide Wale. Fast Pile.
68c A YARD This is the best quality wide wale corduroy, being woven of the finest cotton yarns. It washes beautifully and wears extremely well. The thick pile is soft and velvety. It makes attractive bathrobes and lounging robes. Also ideal for sports wear and children's clothes.
14K7420—Width, about 36 inches. Colors: (1) Chin Chin blue; (2) Rose of Sharon; (3) Pigeon gray; (4) Palmetto green; (5) Pirate red; also American beauty, Claret wine, or Navy. State color. Shipping weight, per yard, ¾ pound.

Silky

Half Silk Brocaded Lining
88c A YARD This is an attractive lining fabric for your new coat or suit. It is closely woven, soft, and has a lustrous, silky finish. Comes in the newest two-tone effects in a pretty brocaded design.
14K4968—Width, about 36 inches. Colors: (1) Tan and blue; (2) Gray and cerise; (3) Blue and gold; or (4) Rose and gray. State color. Shipping weight, per yard, 4 oz.

New Dress Fabrics

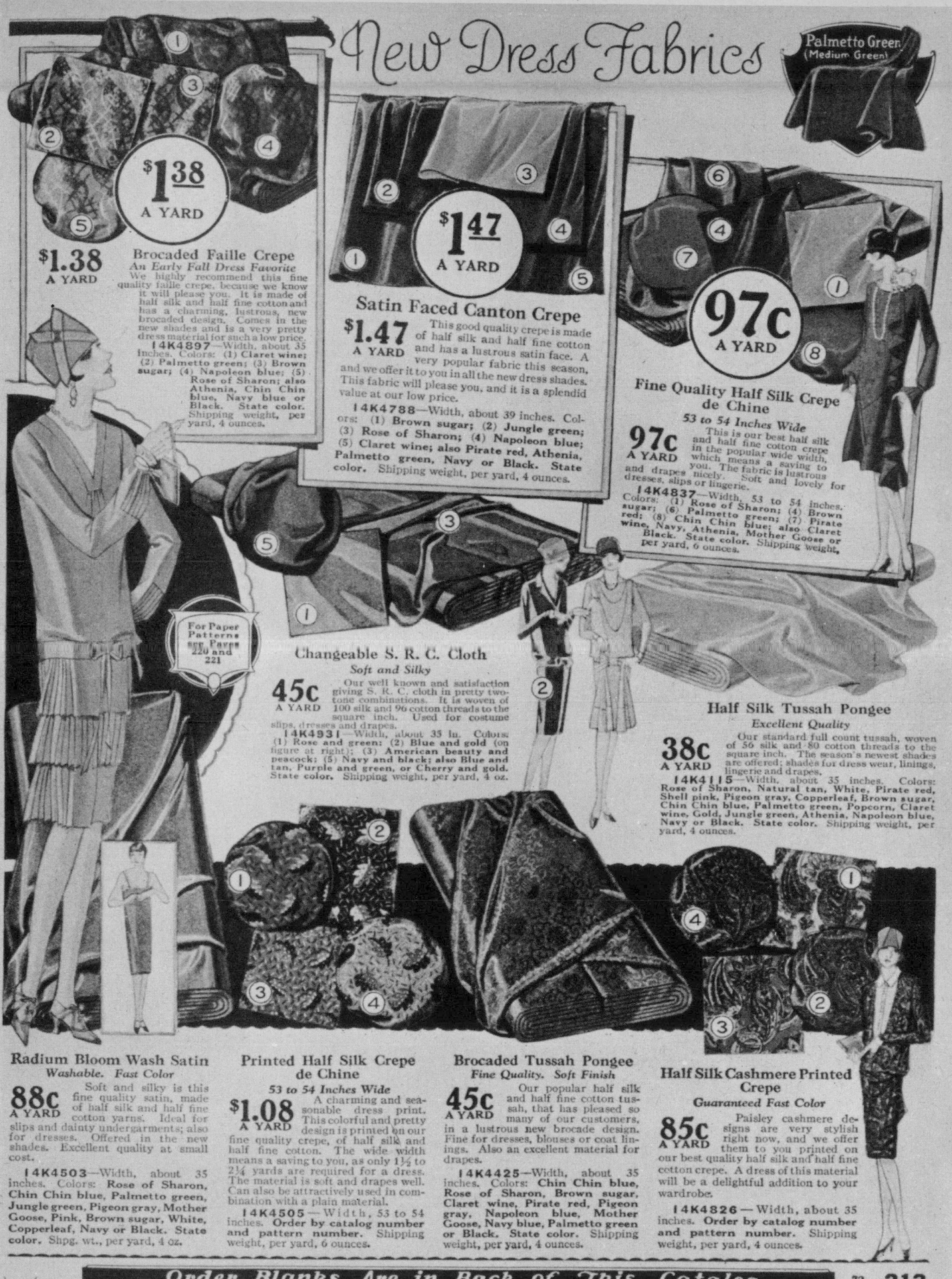

Palmetto Green (Medium Green)

Brocaded Faille Crepe

$1.38 A YARD

An Early Fall Dress Favorite

We highly recommend this fine quality faille crepe, because we know it will please you. It is made of half silk and half fine cotton and has a charming, lustrous, new brocaded design. Comes in the new shades and is a very pretty dress material for such a low price.

14K4897—Width, about 35 inches. Colors: (1) Claret wine; (2) Palmetto green; (3) Brown sugar; (4) Napoleon blue; (5) Rose of Sharon; also Athenia, Chin Chin blue, Navy blue or Black. State color. Shipping weight, per yard, 4 ounces.

Satin Faced Canton Crepe

$1.47 A YARD

This good quality crepe is made of half silk and half fine cotton and has a lustrous satin face. A very popular fabric this season, and we offer it to you in all the new dress shades. This fabric will please you, and it is a splendid value at our low price.

14K4788—Width, about 39 inches. Colors: (1) Brown sugar; (2) Jungle green; (3) Rose of Sharon; (4) Napoleon blue; (5) Claret wine; also Pirate red, Athenia, Palmetto green, Navy or Black. State color. Shipping weight, per yard, 4 ounces.

Fine Quality Half Silk Crepe de Chine

97c A YARD

53 to 54 Inches Wide

This is our best half silk and half fine cotton crepe in the popular wide width, which means a saving to you. The fabric is lustrous. Soft and lovely for dresses, slips or lingerie.

14K4837—Width, 53 to 54 inches. Colors: (1) Rose of Sharon; (4) Brown sugar; (6) Palmetto green; (7) Pirate red; (8) Chin Chin blue; also Claret wine, Navy, Athenia, Mother Goose or Black. State color. Shipping weight, per yard, 6 ounces.

Changeable S. R. C. Cloth

45c A YARD

Soft and Silky

Our well known and satisfaction giving S. R. C. cloth in pretty two-tone combinations. It is woven of 100 silk and 96 cotton threads to the square inch. Used for costume slips, dresses and drapes.

14K4931—Width, about 35 in. Colors: (1) Rose and green; (2) Blue and gold (on figure at right); (3) American beauty and peacock; (5) Navy and black; also Blue and tan, Purple and green, or Cherry and gold. State color. Shipping weight, per yard, 4 oz.

For Paper Patterns see Pages 220 and 221

Half Silk Tussah Pongee

38c A YARD

Excellent Quality

Our standard full count tussah, woven of 56 silk and 80 cotton threads to the square inch. The season's newest shades are offered; shades for dress wear, linings, lingerie and drapes.

14K4115—Width, about 35 inches. Colors: Rose of Sharon, Natural tan, White, Pirate red, Shell pink, Pigeon gray, Copperleaf, Brown sugar, Chin Chin blue, Palmetto green, Popcorn, Claret wine, Gold, Jungle green, Athenia, Napoleon blue, Navy or Black. State color. Shipping weight, per yard, 4 ounces.

Radium Bloom Wash Satin

88c A YARD

Washable. Fast Color

Soft and silky is this fine quality satin, made of half silk and half fine cotton yarns. Ideal for slips and dainty undergarments; also for dresses. Offered in the new shades. Excellent quality at small cost.

14K4503—Width, about 35 inches. Colors: Rose of Sharon, Chin Chin blue, Palmetto green, Jungle green, Pigeon gray, Mother Goose, Pink, Brown sugar, White, Copperleaf, Navy or Black. State color. Shpg. wt., per yard, 4 oz.

Printed Half Silk Crepe de Chine

$1.08 A YARD

53 to 54 Inches Wide

A charming and seasonable dress print. This colorful and pretty design is printed on our fine quality crepe, of half silk and half fine cotton. The wide width means a saving to you, as only 1¾ to 2¼ yards are required for a dress. The material is soft and drapes well. Can also be attractively used in combination with a plain material.

14K4505—Width, 53 to 54 inches. Order by catalog number and pattern number. Shipping weight, per yard, 6 ounces.

Brocaded Tussah Pongee

45c A YARD

Fine Quality. Soft Finish

Our popular half silk and half fine cotton tussah, that has pleased so many of our customers, in a lustrous new brocade design. Fine for dresses, blouses or coat linings. Also an excellent material for drapes.

14K4425—Width, about 35 inches. Colors: Chin Chin blue, Rose of Sharon, Brown sugar, Claret wine, Pirate red, Pigeon gray, Napoleon blue, Mother Goose, Navy blue, Palmetto green or Black. State color. Shipping weight, per yard, 4 ounces.

Half Silk Cashmere Printed Crepe

85c A YARD

Guaranteed Fast Color

Paisley cashmere designs are very stylish right now, and we offer them to you printed on our best quality half silk and half fine cotton crepe. A dress of this material will be a delightful addition to your wardrobe.

14K4826—Width, about 35 inches. Order by catalog number and pattern number. Shipping weight, per yard, 4 ounces.

Coatings and Children's Dress Materials

Brown Sugar (Light Brown)

$1.39 A YARD

$1.98 A YARD

Chinchilla
$1.39 A YARD — Made primarily for children's coats and tams as illustrated, but also fine for school coats. Will wear well. About one-fourth cotton, which is necessary in the making of this popular priced chinchilla to give it wearing quality. A heavy quality. For flannel lining see 14K3948, on page 208.
14K3996 — Width, about 30 inches. Colors: (1) Brown; (2) Dark blue; (3) Tan; (4) Gray; also Claret wine. Shpg. weight, per yard, 1 lb.

For Paper Patterns See Pages 220 and 221

All Wool Suede Velour
$1.98 A YARD — A great value in a velour of good winterweight. Heavy enough without an inner lining. You will get splendid service and have a stylish looking coat at small cost. For children's or women's coats.
14K3818 — Width, about 54 inches. Order by catalog number and pattern number. Shipping weight, per yard, 1¼ pounds.

All Wool Suede
$1.75 A YARD — A remarkable value in a winterweight suede coating. Dull finished as is the vogue, and remarkably clear pretty colors in so low priced a coating. Wonderful wearing quality for either children or grownups.
14K3373 — Width, about 54 inches. Colors: Rose tan (illustrated), Horse chestnut brown (the new reddish brown), Jungle green, Dark claret wine, Sailor blue or Black. State color. Shipping weight, per yard, 1¼ pounds.

All Wool Bolivia Coating
$4.98 A YARD — Bolivia is a very dressy looking cloth coating. The dull soft luster is most charming and this splendid quality is heavy enough for winter coats with just a silk lining. A beautiful Bolivia.
14K3896 — Width, about 54 in. Colors: (1) Tamarack tan; (2) Deep claret wine; (3) Jungle green; (4) Sailor blue; also Sedge (a dark reddish tan), Mole gray, Horse chestnut brown or Black. State color. Shipping weight, per yard, 1¾ lbs.

All Wool "Buxkin" Suede
$2.98 A YARD — This suede is so well known and so popular that we feel our customers already know this quality. One of the best suedes made. Wonderful wearing fabric. With each order of this number we give you a label (as illustrated) to sew in your coat. A guarantee of fine quality.
14K3891 — Width, about 54 inches. Colors: Light claret wine (illustrated), Sailor blue (see figure at left for color), Horse chestnut (the new reddish brown), Sedge (the new brownish tan), Bright Gracklehead blue, Pigeon gray or Navy. State color. Shipping weight, per yard, 1½ pounds.

Dress Fabrics for The Young Miss

Part Wool Dress Checks
59c A YARD — A very handsome, inexpensive check for the children's clothes. Just see how smartly Pattern No. 1 makes up as illustrated on the figure. The other patterns will look as nicely. About one-fourth wool. A crepe weave that will give a lot of wear.
14K3225 — Width, about 36 inches. Order by catalog number and pattern number. Shipping weight, per yd., 6 oz.

Frosted Shadow Dot
78c A YARD — Our frosted check in last fall's catalog was so popular and pleased so many thousands that we are offering you again the same fine cloth in a slightly different pattern. A most attractive frosted dot pattern. Made of about one-fourth wool. A fine wearing fabric.
14K3019 — Width, about 36 inches. Order colors illustrated by number, and Claret wine, Pirate red or French blue by name; also state catalog number. Shpg. wt., per yd., 6 oz.

Half Wool Crepe
59c A YARD — An unusual price for so nice a quality half wool crepe. The colorings are clear and the beautiful finish will stand the hard wear that children give their clothes. One of our very best values.
14K3549 — Width, about 36 inches. Colors: Claret wine, French blue, Brown, Navy blue, Athenia, Black, Mother Goose tan, Pirate red or Jungle green. State color. Shpg. wt., per yd., 7 oz.

Half Wool Plaid
88c A YARD — A firmly woven good looking plaid. A quality which will pleat nicely and holds the pleating. We copied a high priced all wool plaid and we know these attractive colorings will please.
14K3988 — Width, about 36 inches. Order by catalog number and pattern number. Shipping weight, per yard, 7 ounces.

All Wool Crepe
89c A YARD — Our most popular and most serviceable child's dress material. The popular price, the beautiful colors and the crisp, smart look appeal alike to mothers and the children. An extra nice quality.
14K3439 — Width, about 36 inches. Colors: (1) Navy; (2) Tan; (3) Claret; (4) Chin Chin blue; (5) Jungle green; also Brown, Copperleaf, Palmetto, Pigeon gray, Pirate red, Napoleon blue, Athenia or Black. State color. Shipping wt., per yard, 7 oz.

Half Wool Shadow Check Crepe
78c A YARD — An attractive shadow check crepe. Makes very nice looking and exceptionally serviceable clothes for children. Comes in the new colors and can also be used for women's clothes. Medium weight.
14K3137 — Width, about 36 inches. Colors: Pirate red (illustrated), Chin chin blue, Brown sugar, Mother Goose tan, Claret, Athenia, Navy blue, Jungle green or Black. State color. Shipping weight, per yard, 7 ounces.

Shirtings and Lumberjack Fabrics

Pirate Red
(Bright Red)

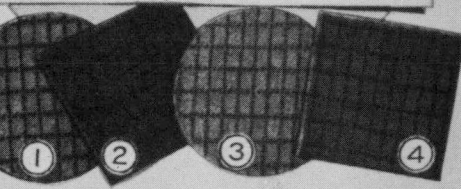

All Wool Plaid Lumberjack

$1.48 A YARD New plaid patterns in the same fine cloth which was so popular and which proved so practical last fall. Wonderful wearing and wonderful looking cloth for the money. Medium weight. About 15 ounces per yard. Knitted bottoms are shown at the right below.

14K3330—Width, about 54 inches. Order by catalog number and pattern number. Shipping weight, per yard, 1 pound.

All Wool Heavyweight Lumberjack

$1.98 A YARD A heavyweight plaid—about 20 ounces per yard. Heavy enough for the boys to wear all winter without an overcoat. Mighty attractive and serviceable colors. Knitted bottoms are shown at left below.

14K3492—Width, about 54 inches. Order by catalog number and pattern number. Shipping weight, per yard, 1½ pounds.

All Wool Small Plaid Shirting

$1.59 A YARD Newest idea in flannel shirts. Small multi-colored plaid. Our illustration doesn't do justice to the colors or the quality. A good wearing, medium weight cloth.

14K3397—Width, about 54 inches. Order by catalog number and pattern number. Shipping weight, per yard, ¾ pound.

Knitted Lumberjack Bottoms

39c EACH Knitted bottoms for the two lumberjacks we list, or can be used on the shirtings if desired. A good, firmly knitted, all wool bottom. This size large enough for men or boys.

14K3924—Size, 9x24 inches. Colors: (1) Pirate red; (2) Tan; (3) Gray; also Black, Navy, or Brown. State color. Shpg. weight, each, 2 oz.

All Wool Flannel Shirting

$1.59 A YARD Small checks, small plaids are the popular fancy shirting patterns this season. Here's a fine quality twilled flannel in a small check. Medium weight. Very low priced for this quality.

14K3097—Width, about 54 inches. Colors: (1) Chevreuse; (2) Palmetto green; (3) Tan; (4) Claret red; also Brown, Pirate red, Navy blue, Cocoa or Rust. State color. Shipping weight, per yard, ¾ lb.

For Paper Patterns See Pages 220 and 221

Eiderdowns

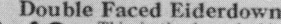

Half Wool Shirting Flannel

39c A YARD You'll be surprised at this quality for so low a price. For women's and children's wear as well as men's shirts. Makes excellent children's play suits because it is washable. Cost is low and wearing quality high.

14K3518—Width, about 27 inches. Colors: Dark gray, Medium gray, Navy blue, Brown, Khaki, Wine or Tan. State color. Shipping weight, per yard, 6 ounces.

Half Wool Shirting Flannel

49c A YARD A cloth of many uses. Play clothes, skirts, blouses, shirts and others. Washes and wears and costs very little. You'll find this material very serviceable.

14K3748—Width, about 36 inches. Colors: Dark gray, Medium gray, Navy blue, Brown, Myrtle green, Wine or Khaki. State color. Shipping weight, per yard, 8 ounces.

Half Wool Shirting Flannel

78c A YARD A remarkable wearing quality at a low price. For either shirts, dresses, or children's clothes. Our customers tell us it is a most satisfactory and serviceable quality.

14K3598—Width, about 54 inches. Colors: Dark gray, Medium gray, Brown, Navy blue, Myrtle green, Khaki, Wine or Tan. State color. Shipping weight, per yard, ¾ pound.

Double Faced Eiderdown

$1.48 A YARD This is the best double faced eiderdown we can buy. There are cheaper ones on the market, but we think it will pay you to buy the best. Half wool.

14K3136—Width, about 36 inches. Comes in Cream only. Shipping wt., per yard, 1 lb.

All Wool Blanket Cloth

$1.98 A YARD Blanket cloth for making receiving blankets, buntings, baby carriage robes. Washes beautifully and is soft and warm. Doesn't stretch.

14K3846—Width, about 36 inches. Comes in Cream only. Shipping wt., per yard, 1 lb.

Single Faced Eiderdown

98c A YARD Deep, downy, woolly faced, knitted on a strong cotton back. For buntings, baby carriage robes and robes.

14K3336—Width, about 36 inches. Colors: Cream, Pink, Light blue, Red, Tan or Light gray. State color. Shipping weight, per yard, 1 pound.

Chinchilla

$1.58 A YARD A nice bathrobe or infant's coating material. Well liked by our customers. Warm, serviceable, and the price is low. A warm wool face on a strong cotton back.

14K3796—Width, 52 to 54 inches. Colors: Navy blue, Brown, Cream, Tan, Pirate red, or American beauty. State color. Shipping weight, per yard, 1 pound.

Wool Muffler Material

98c For 1¼ Yards Finest all wool flannel material for mufflers. Not fringed. You can fringe the ends (make as wide a fringe as you desire), featherstitch the sides, and you have as fine a wool muffler as you could want. About 9 inches wide and 1¼ yards long, which is the popular wool muffler size for men and boys. Will make very desirable presents.

14K3011—Width, about 9 inches. Order by catalog number and pattern number. Shipping weight, each, 2 ounces.

Half Wool Shirting Flannel

95c A YARD Heavier, warmer, more serviceable and a better all around shirting flannel. Well worth the little more it costs. For women's and children's wear as well as shirts.

14K3798—Width, about 54 inches. Colors: Medium gray, Dark gray, Khaki, Navy blue, Brown, Wine, Tan or Dark green. State color. Shipping weight, per yard, ¾ pound.

Extra Fine Flannel Shirting

$1.25 A YARD A wonderful heavy quality. This material goes into shirts retailing as high as $5.00. If you want the best, here it is. Half wool.

14K3998—Width, about 54 inches. Colors: Khaki or Gray mixture. State color. Shipping weight, per yard, ¾ pound.

Rayon Mixed Fabrics

Jungle Green (Dark Green)

Half Rayon Satin
Excellent Quality Rayon Warp
97c A YARD

The demand for this fine quality satin is rapidly increasing. It has a Rayon warp and a fine cotton filling, the Rayon giving it a very lustrous, satiny face. Makes up prettily into dresses, blouses, sport wear or costume slips, and comes in the newest fall shades.

14K4502—Width, about 39 inches. Colors: (1) Chin Chin blue; (2) Claret wine; (3) Palmetto green; (4) Mother Goose; (5) Rose of Sharon; also White, Jungle green, Athenia, Napoleon blue, Pirate red or Black. State color. Shipping weight, per yard, 4 ounces.

Half Rayon Canton Crepe
Lustrous and Durable
48c A YARD

An exceptionally fine quality crepe of half Rayon and half fine cotton. Has the appearance of a higher priced all silk crepe and is just the right weight for fall and winter dress wear.

14K4166—Width, about 35 ins. Colors: Pirate red, Napoleon blue, Rose of Sharon, Pigeon gray, Orange, Brown sugar, Claret wine, Navy, Jungle green, Rose beige, Palmetto green or Black. State color. Shipping wt., per yd., 4 oz.

$1.00 A YARD

Half Rayon Sparkle Satin
Fine Quality—Priced Low
65c A YARD

Our well known Sparkle Satin in the latest colorings. It is made of half Rayon and half fine cotton and will give you lots of wear. Has become very popular for costume slips and dresses.

14K4402—Width, about 35 inches. Colors: (1) Mother Goose; (2) Claret wine; (3) Chin Chin blue; (4) Brown sugar; (5) Pirate red; also Pigeon gray, Rose of Sharon, Palmetto green, Navy or Black. State color. Shipping weight, per yard, 4 ounces.

Half Rayon Canton Crepe
52 to 54 Inches Wide
$1.00 A YARD

One of our biggest sellers in the popular wide width, which means economy in cutting and ease in sewing. Only 1½ to 2¼ yards required to make a dress for a woman of average size. A lustrous and drapey half Rayon and half fine cotton Canton crepe with the appearance of the higher priced all silk Canton crepe. Comes in the very latest dress shades.

14K4266—Width, 52 to 54 inches. Colors: (1) Chin Chin blue; (7) Brown sugar; (8) Claret wine; (9) Rose of Sharon; (10) Napoleon blue; (11) Jungle green; also Palmetto green, Copperleaf, Navy, Black or Pirate red. State color. Shipping weight, per yard, 6 ounces.

For Paper Patterns See Pages 220 and 221

Dot Crepe Faille
98c A YARD

This smart corded effect crepe faille with its attractively neat self color raised dots is woven of silk and Rayon, and has the appearance of a much higher priced fabric. An attractive medium weight material for fall and winter dress wear.

14K4812—Width, about 35 inches. Colors: (1) Jungle green; (2) Claret wine; (3) Brown sugar; (4) Napoleon blue; also Mother Goose, Pirate red, Orange, Chin Chin blue, Jade green, Rose of Sharon, Athenia, Navy or Black. State color. Shpg. wt., per yard, 4 oz.

Brocaded Half Rayon Crepe
58c A YARD

This lovely brocaded crepe with its attractive design and lustrous, silky appearance will make the prettiest dresses and blouses. An exceptionally good quality, made of half Rayon and half fine cotton. Comes in the season's newest colorings.

14K4535—Width, about 35 inches. Colors: (1) Brown sugar; (3) Rose of Sharon; (4) Chin Chin blue; (7) Palmetto green; also Pirate red, Orange, Mother Goose, Napoleon blue, Navy Blue, Pigeon gray or Black. State color. Shipping weight, per yard, 4 ounces.

Printed Half Rayon Crepe
65c A YARD

Our fine quality half Rayon and half fine cotton crepe printed in one of the new fall designs. The colorings are rich and attractive. Makes up into very pretty dresses and blouses.

14K4546—Width, about 35 inches. **Order by catalog number and pattern number.** Shipping weight, per yard, 4 ounces.

Brocaded Half Rayon Alpaca
43c A YARD

The new and popular dress material made of half Rayon and half cotton with a lustrous brocade design on the surface. It's good looking, wears exceptionally well, yet it is inexpensive. Can also be used for linings and drapes. Pretty new colors.

14K4225—Width, about 35 inches. Colors: Palmetto green, Rose of Sharon, Pirate red, Brown sugar, Chin Chin blue, Pigeon gray, Mother Goose, Napoleon blue, Navy or Black. State color. Shipping weight, per yard, 4 ounces.

Half Rayon Plaids and Checks
58c A YARD

Brightly colored plaids and shepherd checks such as these are very smart this season, either used by themselves or combined with plain material in an attractive two-piece costume like that illustrated above. An excellent quality fabric woven of half Rayon and half fine cotton yarns.

14K4780—Width, about 35 inches. **Order by catalog number and pattern number.** Shpg. wt., per yard, 4 oz.

Half Rayon Broadcloth Alpaca
A Splendid Value
58c A YARD

The best quality alpaca obtainable. Woven of half Rayon and half fine cotton yarns it is soft, silky and lustrous. Serviceable and pretty for dresses, linings or drapes. Comes in the season's most wanted shades. For such a good quality as this our price is extremely low.

14K4211—Width, about 35 inches. Colors: Mother Goose, White, Pink, Rose of Sharon, Palmetto green, Brown sugar, Napoleon blue, Shell pink, Pirate red, Chin Chin blue, Pigeon gray, Athenia, Navy or Black. State color. Shipping weight, per yard, 4 ounces.

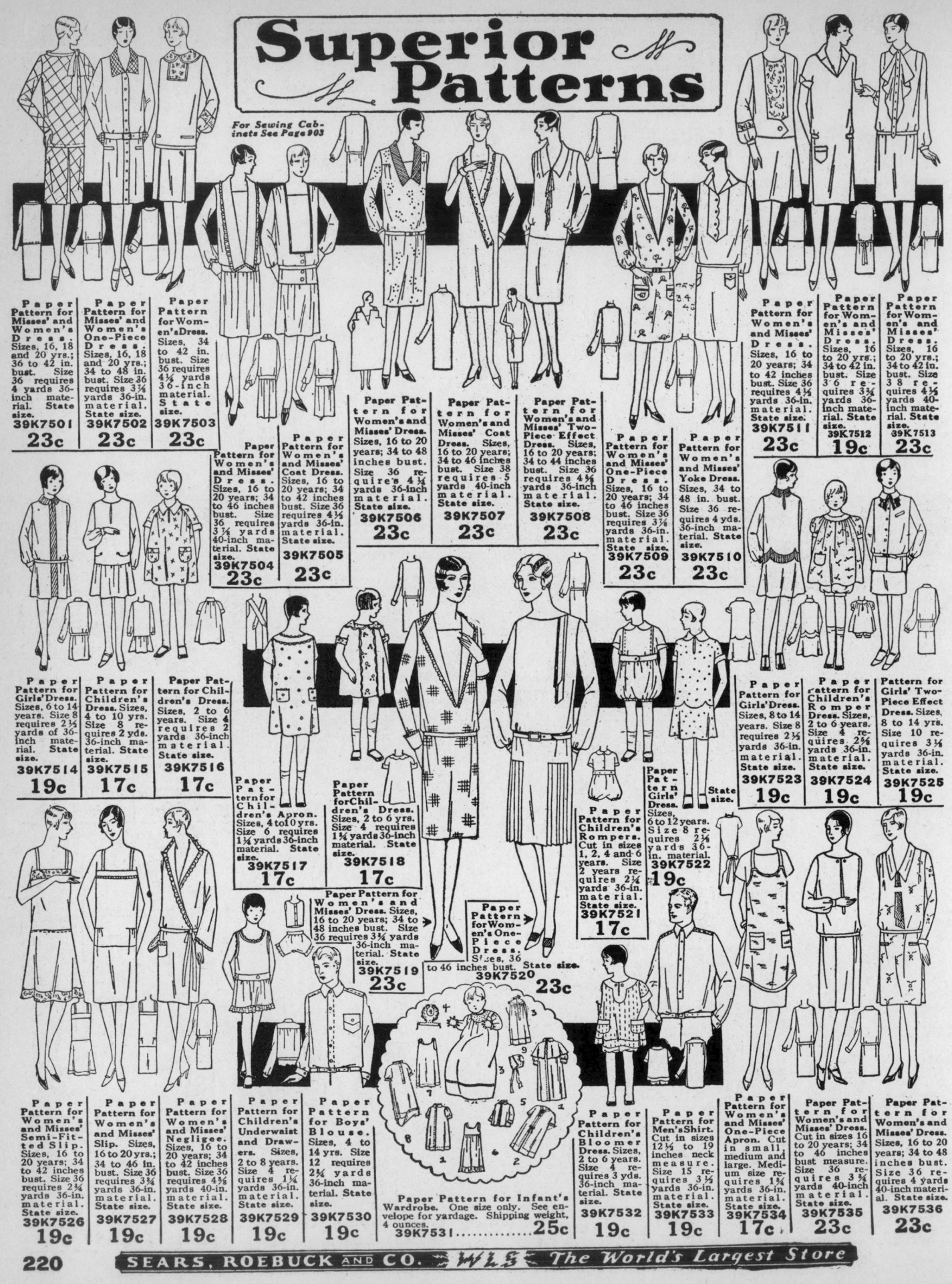

Superior Patterns

For Sewing Cabinets See Page 903

Paper Pattern for Misses' and Women's Dress. Sizes, 16, 18 and 20 yrs.; 36 to 42 in. bust. Size 36 requires 4 yards 36-inch material. State size.
39K7501 **23c**

Paper Pattern for Misses' and Women's One-Piece Dress. Sizes, 16, 18 and 20 yrs.; 34 to 48 in. bust. Size 36 requires 3¼ yards 36-in. material. State size.
39K7502 **23c**

Paper Pattern for Women's Dress. Sizes, 34 to 42 in. bust. Size 36 requires 4¼ yards 36-inch material. State size.
39K7503 **23c**

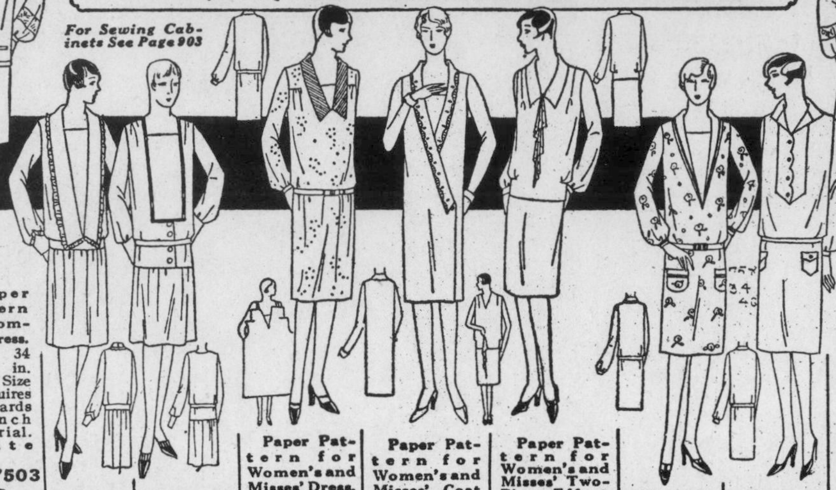

Paper Pattern for Women's and Misses' Dress. Sizes, 16 to 20 years; 34 to 46 inches bust. Size 36 requires 3⅛ yards 40-inch material. State size.
39K7504 **23c**

Paper Pattern for Women's and Misses' Coat Dress. Sizes, 16 to 20 years; 34 to 42 inches bust. Size 36 requires 4⅛ yards 36-in. material. State size.
39K7505 **23c**

Paper Pattern for Women's and Misses' Dress. Sizes, 16 to 20 years; 34 to 48 inches bust. Size 36 requires 4¼ yards 36-inch material. State size.
39K7506 **23c**

Paper Pattern for Women's and Misses' Coat Dress. Sizes, 16 to 20 years; 34 to 46 inches bust. Size 38 requires 5 yards 40-inch material. State size.
39K7507 **23c**

Paper Pattern for Women's and Misses' Two-Piece Effect Dress. Sizes, 16 to 20 years; 34 to 44 inches bust. Size 36 requires 4⅝ yards 36-inch material. State size.
39K7508 **23c**

Paper Pattern for Women's and Misses' One-Piece Dress. Sizes, 16 to 20 years; 34 to 46 inches bust. Size 36 requires 3⅛ yards 36-in. material. State size.
39K7509 **23c**

Paper Pattern for Women's and Misses' Yoke Dress. Sizes, 34 to 48 in. bust. Size 36 requires 4 yds. 36-inch material. State size.
39K7510 **23c**

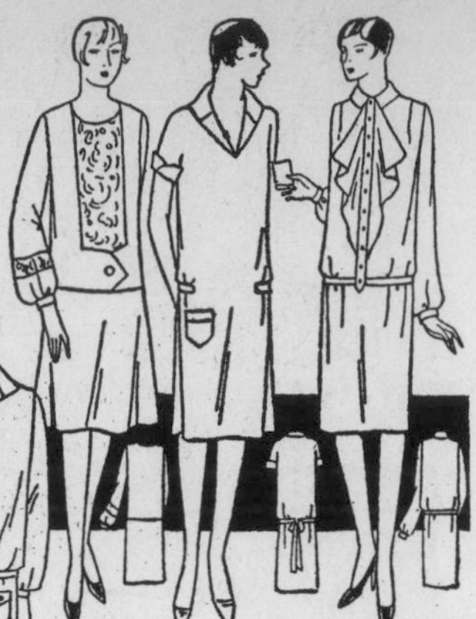

Paper Pattern for Women's and Misses' Dress. Sizes, 16 to 20 years; 34 to 42 inches bust. Size 36 requires 4½ yards 36-in. material. State size.
39K7511 **23c**

Paper Pattern for Women's and Misses' Dress. Sizes, 16 to 20 years; 34 to 42 in. bust. Size 36 requires 3⅜ yards 36-inch material. State size.
39K7512 **19c**

Paper Pattern for Women's and Misses' Dress. Sizes, 16 to 20 yrs.; 34 to 42 in. bust. Size 38 requires 4½ yards 40-inch material. State size.
39K7513 **23c**

Paper Pattern for Girls' Dress. Sizes, 6 to 14 years. Size 8 requires 2½ yards of 36-inch material. State size.
39K7514 **19c**

Paper Pattern for Children's Dress. Sizes, 4 to 10 yrs. Size 8 requires 2 yds. 36-inch material. State size.
39K7515 **17c**

Paper Pattern for Children's Dress. Sizes, 2 to 6 years. Size 4 requires 2 yards 36-inch material. State size.
39K7516 **17c**

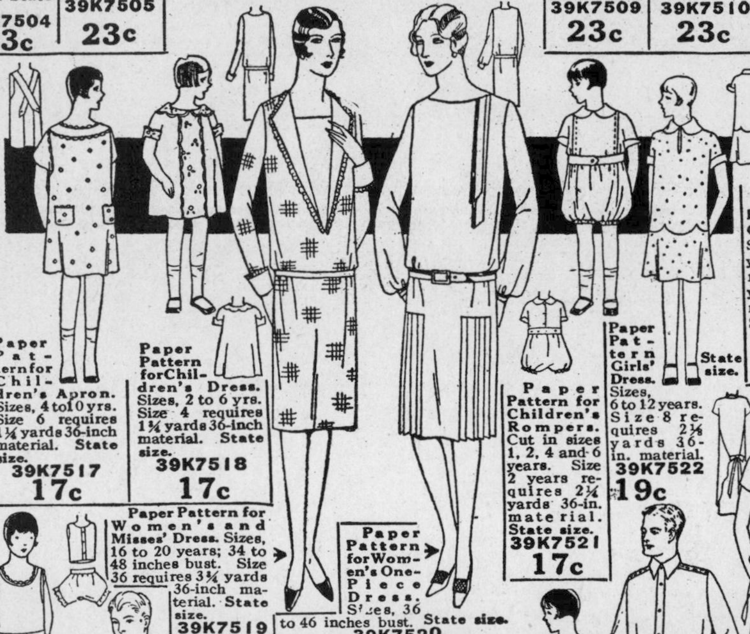

Paper Pattern for Children's Apron. Sizes, 4 to 10 yrs. Size 6 requires 1¼ yards 36-inch material. State size.
39K7517 **17c**

Paper Pattern for Children's Dress. Sizes, 2 to 6 yrs. Size 4 requires 1¾ yards 36-inch material. State size.
39K7518 **17c**

Paper Pattern for Women's and Misses' Dress. Sizes, 16 to 20 years; 34 to 48 inches bust. Size 36 requires 3¾ yards 36-inch material. State size.
39K7519 **23c**

Paper Pattern for Women's One-Piece Dress. Sizes, 36 to 46 inches bust. State size.
39K7520 **23c**

Paper Pattern for Children's Rompers. Cut in sizes 1, 2, 4 and 6 years. Size 2 years requires 2¼ yards 36-in. material. State size.
39K7521 **17c**

Paper Pattern Girls' Dress. Sizes, 6 to 12 years. Size 8 requires 2⅛ yards 36-in. material. State size.
39K7522 **19c**

Paper Pattern for Girls' Dress. Sizes, 8 to 14 years. Size 8 requires 2½ yards 36-in. material. State size.
39K7523 **19c**

Paper Pattern for Children's Romper Dress. Sizes, 2 to 6 years. Size 4 requires 2⅝ yards 36-in. material. State size.
39K7524 **19c**

Pattern for Girls' Two-Piece Effect Dress. Sizes, 8 to 14 yrs. Size 10 requires 3⅛ yards 36-in. material. State size.
39K7525 **19c**

Paper Pattern for Women's and Misses' Semi-Fitted Slip. Sizes, 16 to 20 years; 34 to 42 inches bust. Size 36 requires 2¾ yards 36-in. material. State size.
39K7526 **19c**

Paper Pattern for Women's and Misses' Slip. Sizes, 16 to 20 yrs.; 34 to 46 in. bust. Size 36 requires 3¾ yards 36-in. material. State size.
39K7527 **19c**

Paper Pattern for Women's and Misses' Negligee. Sizes, 16 to 20 years; 34 to 42 inches bust. Size 36 requires 4⅝ yards 40-in. material. State size.
39K7528 **19c**

Paper Pattern for Children's Underwaist and Drawers. Sizes, 2 to 8 years. Size 4 requires 1¼ yards 36-in. material. State size.
39K7529 **19c**

Paper Pattern for Boys' Blouse. Sizes, 4 to 14 yrs. Size 12 requires 2¾ yards 36-inch material. State size.
39K7530 **19c**

Paper Pattern for Infant's Wardrobe. One size only. See envelope for yardage. Shipping weight, 4 ounces.
39K7531............ **25c**

Paper Pattern for Children's Bloomer Dress. Sizes, 2 to 6 years. Size 4 requires 3 yds. 36-inch material. State size.
39K7532 **19c**

Paper Pattern for Men's Shirt. Cut in sizes 12½ to 19 inches neck measure. Size 15 requires 3½ yards 36-in. material. State size.
39K7533 **19c**

Paper Pattern for Women's and Misses' One-Piece Apron. Cut in small, medium and large. Medium size requires 1¾ yards 36-in. material. State size.
39K7534 **17c**

Paper Pattern for Women's and Misses' Dress. Cut in sizes 16 to 20 years; 34 to 46 inches bust measure. Size 36 requires 3¾ yards 40-inch material. State size.
39K7535 **23c**

Paper Pattern for Women's and Misses' Dress. Sizes, 16 to 20 years; 34 to 48 inches bust. Size 36 requires 4 yards 40-inch material. State size.
39K7536 **23c**

OUR PATTERNS ARE ALL CUT TO THESE STANDARD PROPORTIONS

Bust, inches	34	36	38	40	42	44	46	48
Waist, inches	24	26	28	30	32	34	36	38
Hip, inches	37	39	41	43	46	49	52	55

BE SURE TO INCLUDE MONEY FOR POSTAGE ON PATTERNS

Shipping weight, all patterns except baby outfits, 2 ounces; baby outfits, 4 ounces.

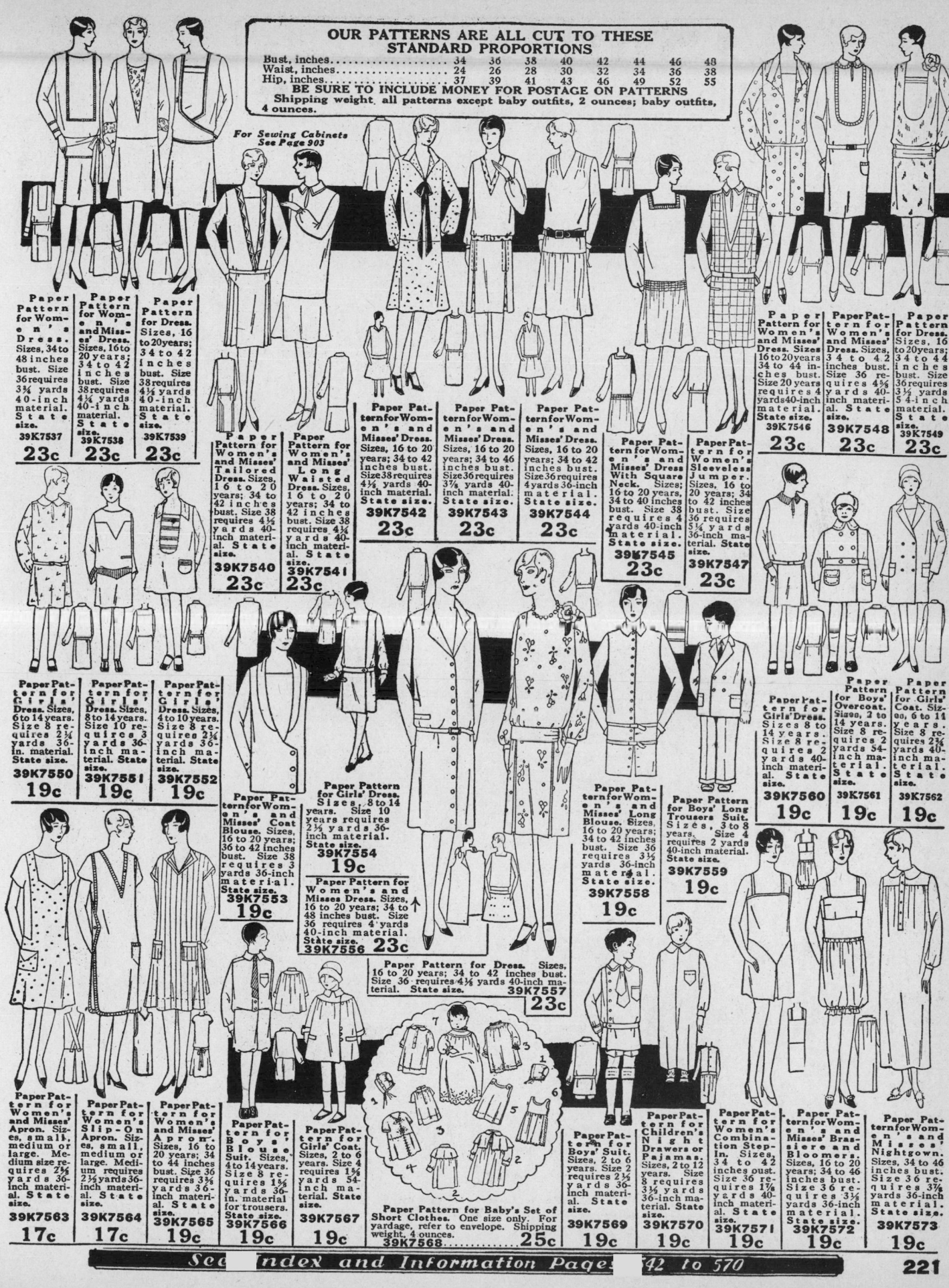

For Sewing Cabinets See Page 903

Paper Pattern for Women's Dress. Sizes, 34 to 48 inches bust. Size 36 requires 3¾ yards 40-inch material. State size. **39K7537 23c**

Paper Pattern for Women's and Misses' Dress. Sizes, 16 to 20 years; 34 to 42 inches bust. Size 38 requires 4¼ yards 40-inch material. State size. **39K7538 23c**

Paper Pattern for Dress. Sizes, 16 to 20 years; 34 to 42 inches bust. Size 38 requires 4½ yards 40-inch material. State size. **39K7539 23c**

Paper Pattern for Women's and Misses' Tailored Dress. Sizes, 16 to 20 years; 34 to 42 inches bust. Size 38 requires 4½ yards 40-inch material. State size. **39K7540 23c**

Paper Pattern for Women's and Misses' Long Waisted Dress. Sizes, 16 to 20 years; 34 to 42 inches bust. Size 38 requires 4¼ yards 40-inch material. State size. **39K7541 23c**

Paper Pattern for Women's and Misses' Dress. Sizes, 16 to 20 years; 34 to 42 inches bust. Size 38 requires 4⅛ yards 40-inch material. State size. **39K7542 23c**

Paper Pattern for Women's and Misses' Dress. Sizes, 16 to 20 years; 34 to 46 inches bust. Size 36 requires 3⅞ yards 40-inch material. State size. **39K7543 23c**

Paper Pattern for Women's and Misses' Dress. Sizes, 16 to 20 years; 34 to 42 inches bust. Size 36 requires 4 yards 36-inch material. State size. **39K7544 23c**

Paper Pattern for Women's and Misses' Dress With Square Neck. Sizes; 16 to 20 years, 34 to 40 inches bust. Size 38 requires 4 yards 40-inch material. State size. **39K7545 23c**

Paper Pattern for Women's Sleeveless Jumper. Sizes, 16 to 20 years; 34 to 42 inches bust. Size 36 requires 5¼ yards 36-inch material. State size. **39K7547 23c**

Paper Pattern for Women's and Misses' Dress. Sizes 16 to 20 years 34 to 44 inches bust. Size 20 years requires 4 yards 40-inch material. State size. **39K7546 23c**

Paper Pattern for Women's and Misses' Dress. Sizes, 34 to 42 inches bust. Size 36 requires 4⅝ yards 40-inch material. State size. **39K7548 23c**

Paper Pattern for Dress. Sizes, 16 to 20 years; 34 to 44 inches bust. Size 36 requires 3½ yards 54-inch material. State size. **39K7549 23c**

Paper Pattern for Girls' Dress. Sizes, 6 to 14 years. Size 8 requires 2¼ yards 36-in. material. State size. **39K7550 19c**

Paper Pattern for Girls' Dress. Sizes, 8 to 14 years. Size 10 requires 3 yards 36-inch material. State size. **39K7551 19c**

Paper Pattern for Girls' Dress. Sizes, 4 to 10 years. Size 8 requires 2⅜ yards 36-inch material. State size. **39K7552 19c**

Paper Pattern for Women's and Misses' Coat Blouse. Sizes, 16 to 20 years; 36 to 42 inches bust. Size 38 requires 3 yards 36-inch material. State size. **39K7553 19c**

Paper Pattern for Girls' Dress. Sizes, 8 to 14 years. Size 10 years requires 2½ yards 36-inch material. State size. **39K7554 19c**

Paper Pattern for Women's and Misses Dress. Sizes, 16 to 20 years; 34 to 48 inches bust. Size 36 requires 4 yards 40-inch material. State size. **39K7556 23c**

Paper Pattern for Dress. Sizes, 16 to 20 years; 34 to 42 inches bust. Size 36 requires 4⅛ yards 40-inch material. State size. **39K7557 23c**

Paper Pattern for Women's and Misses' Long Blouse. Sizes, 16 to 20 years; 34 to 42 inches bust. Size 36 requires 3½ yards 36-inch material. State size. **39K7558 19c**

Paper Pattern for Boys' Long Trousers Suit. Sizes, 3 to 8 years. Size 4 requires 2 yards 40-inch material. State size. **39K7559 19c**

Paper Pattern for Girls' Dress. Sizes 8 to 14 years. Size 8 requires 2 yards 40-inch material. State size. **39K7560 19c**

Paper Pattern for Boys' Overcoat. Sizes, 2 to 14 years. Size 8 requires 2 yards 54-inch material. State size. **39K7561 19c**

Paper Pattern for Girls' Coat. Sizes, 6 to 14 years. Size 8 requires 2⅜ yards 40-inch material. State size. **39K7562 19c**

Paper Pattern for Women's and Misses' Apron. Sizes, small, medium or large. Medium size requires 2⅝ yards 36-inch material. State size. **39K7563 17c**

Paper Pattern for Women's Slip-On Apron. Sizes, small, medium or large. Medium requires 2½ yards 36-inch material. State size. **39K7564 17c**

Paper Pattern for Women's and Misses' Apron. Sizes, 16 to 20 years; 34 to 44 inches bust. Size 36 requires 3⅜ yards 36-inch material. State size. **39K7565 19c**

Paper Pattern for Boys' Blouse Suit. Sizes, 4 to 14 years. Size 8 requires 1⅝ yards 36-in. material for trousers. State size. **39K7566 19c**

Paper Pattern for Girls' Coat. Sizes, 2 to 6 years. Size 4 requires 1⅝ yards 54-inch material. State size. **39K7567 19c**

Paper Pattern for Baby's Set of Short Clothes. One size only. For yardage, refer to envelope. Shipping weight, 4 ounces. **39K7568 .... 25c**

Paper Pattern for Boys' Suit. Sizes, 2 to 6 years. Size 2 requires 2⅛ yards 36-inch material. State size. **39K7569 19c**

Paper Pattern for Children's Night Drawers or Pajamas. Sizes, 2 to 12 years. Size 8 requires 3½ yards 36-inch material. State size. **39K7570 19c**

Paper Pattern for Women's Combination Step-In. Sizes, 34 to 42 inches bust. Size 36 requires 1⅞ yards 40-inch material. State size. **39K7571 19c**

Paper Pattern for Women's and Misses' Brassiere and Bloomers. Sizes, 16 to 20 years; 34 to 46 inches bust. Size 36 requires 3⅛ yards 36-inch material. State size. **39K7572 19c**

Paper Pattern for Women's and Misses' Nightgown. Sizes, 34 to 46 inches bust. Size 36 requires 3⅞ yards 36-inch material. State size. **39K7573 19c**

Dress in Style and Save Half

98¢ EACH

A little of your own time and you can make these beautiful dresses and save half. We furnish all material and trimmings, nothing additional to buy. Just follow our simple directions enclosed with each dress. Our semi-made dresses save you a lot of money and keep you correctly dressed.

The newest styles in women's and children's wash dresses. Priced 98c to $2.19. You save at least a half! Here's the secret of these extraordinary low prices: The dresses are semi-finished and everything you need to complete any of the attractive styles here illustrated is included at the prices we quote. You not alone can make a big saving—one-half or more—but you will have individuality of style both in fabric and design and the satisfaction that comes to those alone who help in the making of their clothes. Each garment comes completely designed and cut out, and in the same envelope we include all necessary trimmings, embroidery floss, buttons and diagram with full instructions—absolutely nothing else to buy. Your dress will look exactly like the illustration on this page.

Shipping weight, any dress on this page, ¾ pound.

A charming afternoon dress made of cotton ENDURAE printed in bright colors in a very original pattern. The novelty collar is designed with attached tie. Four rows of shirring at pleasing front effect. The collar, cuffs and pocket tabs are of plain chambray; two colors of embroidery thread included. Misses' sizes, 16 and 18; women's, 36 to 44. State catalog number and size.
25K6024—Tan with blue..$1.59
25K6025—White with Copenhagen.............$1.59
25K6026—White with rose 1.59

A smart shawl collar and cuffs of white barred dimity adds a charming touch to this model of rich cotton EMBROYDERAE, a novelty weave of varicolored embroidered effects. Misses' sizes, 16 and 18; women's, 36 to 44. State size.
25K6018
Tan 98c
25K6019
Blue 98c
25K6020
Orchid 98c

Afternoon or Street Dress of cotton ENDURAE, a novelty printed fabric. Long roll collar cuffs and pocket tabs are of barred white dimity, edged with fine lace. Vestee effect is made of the same material, biased. Misses' sizes, 16 and 18; women's, 36 to 44. State size.
25K6027—Gold and black....$2.19
25K6028—Red and navy....$2.19
25K6029—Copenhagen and black, $2.19

Here Is What You Get:
1. All the material and findings needed, cut out and ready to sew. 2. All the trimmings. 3. All the buttons. 4. All the embroidery floss. 5. All the neckpieces. 6. All the hooks and eyes. 7. Complete instructions! All you need is a little of your own time.

Attractive model cotton ENDURAE fabric, which lends slenderizing lines, set off by collar, cuffs and pocket tabs of plain color embroidered ENDURETTE. Misses' sizes, 16 and 18; women's, 36 to 44. State catalog number and size.
25K6021—Tan on navy..$1.29
25K6022—Copenhagen on tan 1.29
25K6023—Tan on Copenhagen 1.29

98¢ EACH

Clever Little School Dress Made of Endurette
A beautiful printed cotton fabric. Novelty two-piece effect with three inverted kick pleats and chambray collar, cuffs and front trimmings with two-color embroidery. Finished with narrow ribbon tie. Easy to make. Sizes, 6, 8, 10, 12 and 14. State catalog number and size.
25K6000—Blue on tan........98c
25K6001—Copenhagen on white.98c
25K6002—Rose on white........98c

You'll Like This Pretty Dress
Newest of woven fabrics, cotton EMBROYDERAE, checked dimity for collar and pocket tabs. Vestee effect front, edged with white and self piping—already made up. Embroidered woven stripe effect. Sizes, 6, 8, 10, 12 and 14. State catalog number and size.
25K6003—Medium blue.98c
25K6004—Orchid 98c
25K6005—Peach 98c

A Stylish Dress Easy to Make
This overblouse model is made of cotton SUPER-EMBROY-DERAE, a soft, durable fabric with woven embroidered set-in effects. Sizes, 6, 8, 10, 12 and 14. State catalog number and size.
25K6009—Light tan...$1.59
25K6010—Rose 1.59
25K6011—Medium blue 1.59

Made of genuine 72-100 cotton pongee with pattern printed in INDENTREEN dye, the fastest color known. White broadcloth collar, cuffs and pocket tabs with two-color embroidery. Set-in sleeves. Sizes, 6, 8, 10, 12, 14. State size.
Rose with white............$2.19
25K6013
Copenhagen with white...... 2.19
25K6014
Peach with white............ 2.19

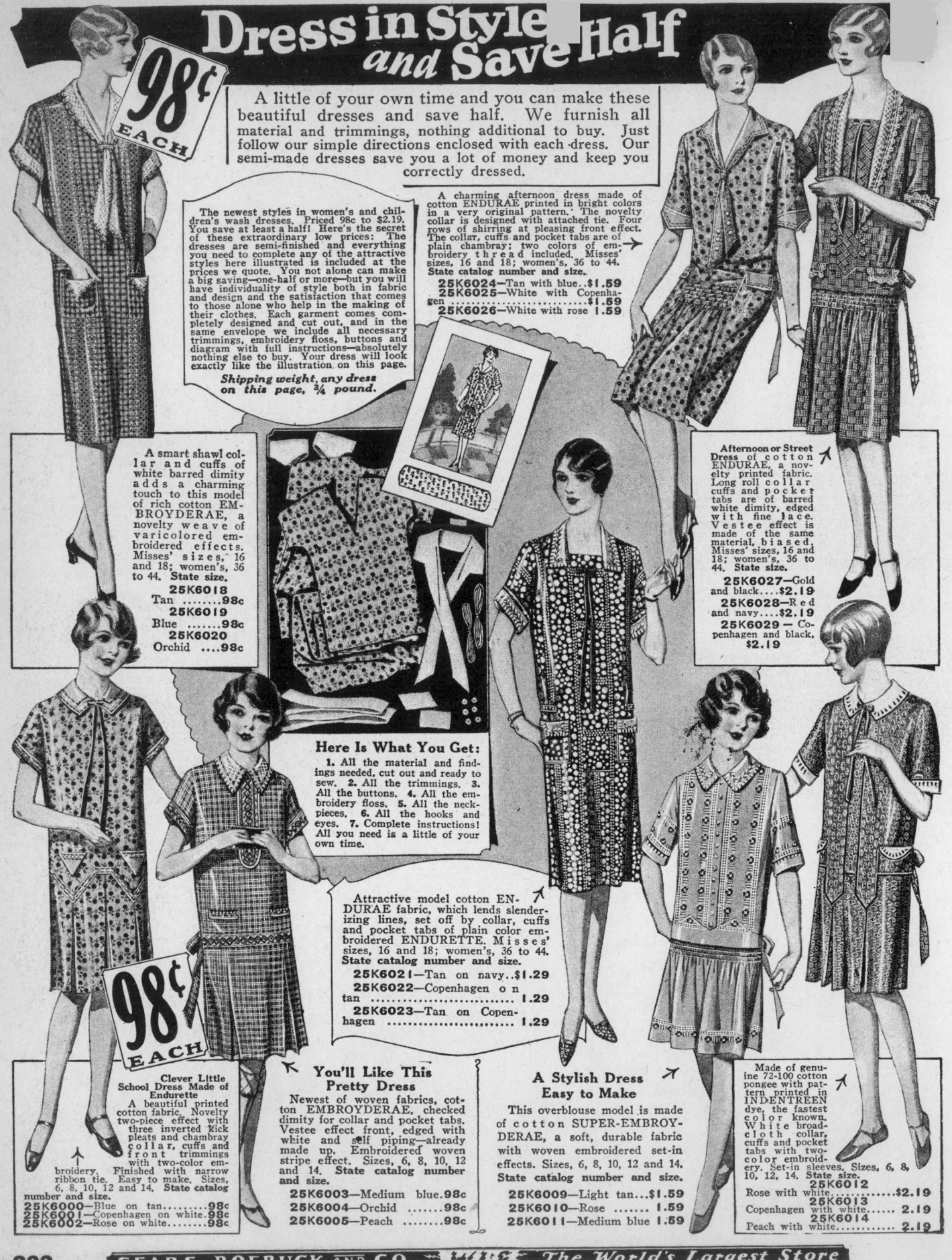

The FAMOUS LOCKERBIE LINENS
Manufactured in Scotland Exclusively for
SEARS, ROEBUCK AND CO.

LINENS
of Quality and Distinction

Ideal Home Set

Our Family Quality

TULIP AND MORESQUE

ARABESQUE AND PEARL

Ideal Home Set

Why? Because It Gives Everyday Service at an Everyday Price and Has a Splendid Appearance. This All Linen Table Set, With Cloth and Napkins Neatly Hemmed, Ready for Use. Put Up in Beautiful Individual Boxes. We Do Not Break the Sets.

Two sizes, to fit either square or oblong tables. Crystal white, in the beautiful Tulip and Moresque design.

19K7900—Size of tablecloth, about 54x54 inches, with six 18x18-inch napkins to match. Shipping weight, per set, 2 pounds. **$3.75 A SET**

19K7902—Size of tablecloth, about 54x72 inches, with six 18x18-inch napkins to match. Shipping weight, per set, 2¼ pounds. **$4.75 A SET**

"Our Family Quality"
The Cloth That Will Stand Everyday Use

The workmanship on these linen cloths is by the same skilled weavers who make the finest linen goods, insuring unusual quality at the price.

Hemmed, ready for use. Soft laundered finish. Two sizes, to fit either square or oblong tables. Pure white in the distinctive Arabesque and Pearl design, as illustrated.

19K7914—Tablecloth. Size, about 54x54 inches. Shipping weight, each, 1¼ pounds. **$2.00 EACH**

19K7916—Tablecloth. Size, about 54x72 inches. Shipping weight, each, 2 pounds. **$2.80 EACH**

Napkins to Match
Sold in Dozens or Half Dozens Only

19K7918—Size, about 18x18 inches. Hemmed. Shipping weight of six, 1 pound. **$1.85 FOR SIX**

A BEAUTIFUL DOUBLE DAMASK QUALITY
With Napkins to Match

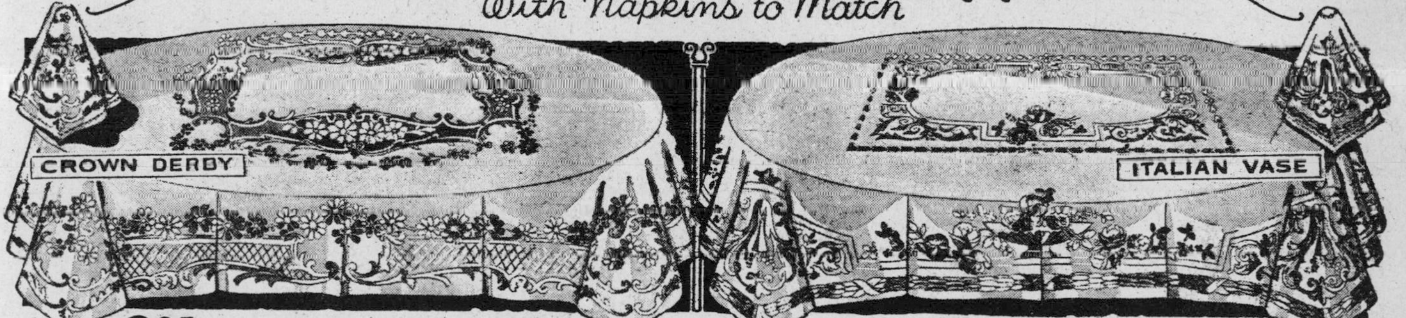

CROWN DERBY

ITALIAN VASE

$6.85 AND UP

$6.85 AND UP

Exquisitely Patterned Pure Linen Double Damask Tablecloths
Finished With the Justly Famous "Meadow" Bleach

A fine weave, with evident refinement and beauty as a result of unusual care in their making, is found in these wonderful Scotch Tablecloths. You will be proud of your selection, both of the pattern and of the quality, which is unexcelled for wearing. Three practical sizes. Put up in attractive individual envelopes, direct from the manufacturer. Bleached snow white. Hemmed, ready for use. Two exquisite patterns, among the most famous of European designs—The Italian Vase or Crown Derby. State pattern wanted.

		Size, About	Shipping Wt.	Each
19K7920	Tablecloth	72x 72 inches	2 pounds	$6.85
19K7922	Tablecloth	72x 90 inches	2¼ pounds	8.00
19K7924	Tablecloth	72x108 inches	2½ pounds	9.65

Napkins to Match in Quality and Pattern
Sold in Dozens or Half Dozens Only
Each half dozen in a separate envelope.

19K7926—Full dinner size, 22x22 inches. Hemmed. Ready for use. State pattern. Shipping wt., of six, 1¼ lbs. **$3.75 FOR SIX**

A REAL SERVICE QUALITY

All Linen Scotch Table Damask Excel All Others for Service

There is no better instance of the extraordinary values received in all of our linens than the low price we quote on this Damask. Long service is guaranteed. Two beautiful designs, especially created for this number—the attractive Rose Brier or stately Chrysanthemum and Maiden Hair. State pattern.

19K7930—Crystal white pure linen. Width, 70 inches. Shipping weight, per yard, ¾ pound. **$1.50 A YARD**

Napkins to Match the Above Damask in Quality and Pattern State Pattern. Sold in Dozens or Half Dozens Only

19K7932—Size, about 21x21 inches. Hemmed, ready for use. Shipping weight of six, 1 pound. **$2.25 FOR SIX**

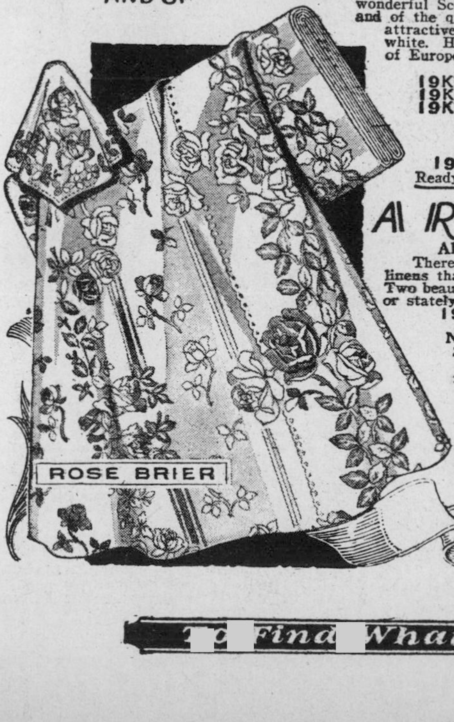

THE FAMOUS LOCKERBIE LINENS
MADE IN SCOTLAND

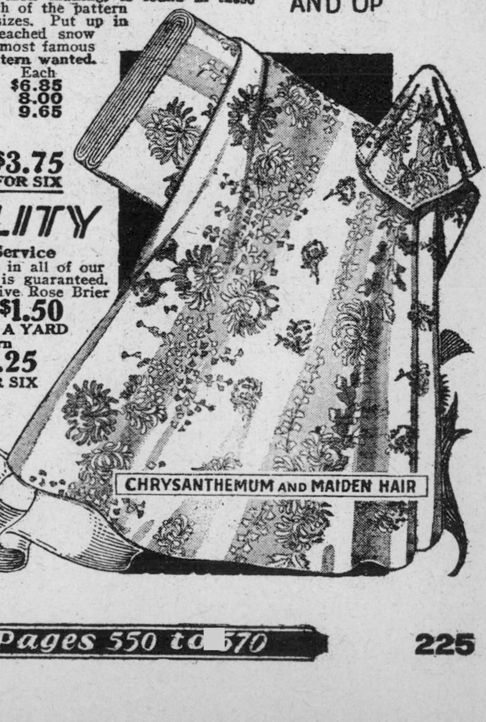

ROSE BRIER

CHRYSANTHEMUM AND MAIDEN HAIR

Distinctive Table Linens

$2³⁵ A YARD   **$1⁰⁰ A YARD**   **90c A YARD**   **$1⁷⁵ A YARD**

The Grade We Recommend
Heavy Weight—"Square Weave"—Full Width Satin Finish Table Damask

This Damask is a specially constructed "Square Weave" Double Damask that will withstand a lot of tear and wear and still retain the beautiful rich satin luster that has made linen so desirable. We do not hesitate to recommend this quality as we know it to be the greatest value that it is possible to offer at this low price. Two beautiful designs: The always popular Rose or attractive Pansy and Basket. State pattern. Width, 72 Inches.

19K6536—Crystal white. Once used, always desired. Shpg. wt., per yd., ¾ lb. Yd. **$2.35**
Napkins to Match the Above Damask in Quality and Pattern. State Pattern.
Sold in Dozens or Half Dozens Only
19K6538—Dinner size, 22 x 22 inches. Hemmed ready for use. Shipping weight of six, 1¼ pounds. **$3.00 FOR SIX**

68 Inches Wide Only $1.00 a Yard
Here Is Where You Get Quality and Low Cost

It is needless to emphasize the fact that this is a wonderful bargain—the price tells the story. All Linen Bleached Table Damask, imported direct from Ireland's best weavers. Will wear well and always look attractive. We save you at least 25 cents on every yard over prices others frequently ask. Floral patterns.
Width, 68 Inches

19K6516—Pure white bleach all linen table damask. Shipping weight, per yard, ¾ pound. **$1.00 A YARD**

A Real Value All Linen Silver Bleach or Cream Table Damask
Width, 64 Inches
90c A YARD

19K6600—Natural cream or silver bleach in pretty floral patterns, similar to illustration. Shipping weight, per yard, ¾ lb.

A strong, durable, table damask, easily laundered, soon bleaches white. Built for daily household wear and tear.

High Quality Imported All Linen Table Damask

Brimful of quality, rich in appearance and will give you abundant service. A "Flower of the Flax" All Linen Lustrous Satin Finish Table Damask, with Napkins to match. Crystal white bleach, in beautiful patterns similar to illustration.
Width, 70 Inches
19K6521—Pure white. Shipping weight, per yard, ¾ pound. A yard.......... **$1.75**
Napkins to Match
Sold in Dozens or Half Dozens Only
19K6523—Size, 22x22 inches. Bookfolded. Unhemmed. Shipping weight of six, 1 pound.
For six................. **$2.35**

What Every Woman Wants

Lily of the Valley   **Chrysanthemum and Circle**

Ben Lomond Linens

$3⁵⁰ Ea. AND UP   **$1³⁹ A YARD**   **$1³⁹ A YARD**

Lily of the Valley Design
Table Damask or Tablecloths Hemmed With Hemmed Napkins to Match

Great economy, durable quality and a mighty low price for such good all linen goods.
Table Damask—Width, 70 Inches
19K7761—Crystal white. Shipping weight, per yard, ¾ lb. **$1.39 A YARD**
Tablecloths—Hemmed, Ready for Use
19K7763—Size, about 70x69 inches. Shipping weight, each, 2 pounds. **$3.50 EACH**
19K7765—Size, about 70x87 inches. Shipping weight, each, 2 pounds. **$4.50 EACH**
19K7767—Size, about 70x104 inches. Shipping weight, each, 2½ pounds. **$5.75 EACH**
Hemmed Napkins Matching Table Damask and Tablecloths
Sold in Dozens or Half Dozens Only
19K7769—Size, about 21x21 inches. Shipping weight of six, 1 pound. **$2.25 FOR SIX**

Chrysanthemum and Circle Design

The biggest value and the best offering of good household linens, presented in a way you have always wanted to buy. All linen.
Table Damask—Width, 70 Inches
19K7781—Pure white. Shipping weight, per yard, ¾ pound. **$1.39 A YARD**
Tablecloths—Hemmed, Ready for Use
19K7783—Size, about 70x69 inches. Shipping weight, each, 2 pounds. **$3.50 EACH**
19K7785—Size, about 70x87 inches. Shipping weight, each, 2¼ pounds. **$4.50 EACH**
19K7787—Size, about 70x104 inches. Shipping weight, each, 2½ pounds. **$5.75 EACH**
Hemmed Napkins Matching Table Damask and Tablecloths
Sold in Dozens or Half Dozens Only
19K7789—Size, about 21x21 inches. Shipping weight of six, 1 pound. **$2.25 FOR SIX**

Hemstitched, Snow White, All Linen Tea Napkins or Doilies
A Superior Quality for the Price
Size, 15x15 Inches

19K1590—Sold in dozens or half dozens only. Shipping weight of six, 8 ounces. **$1.90 FOR SIX**
Beautiful monogram patterns (similar to illustration), in our own "Flower of the Flax" quality. Neatly hemmed and hemstitched all around.

Plain Woven All Linen Table Damask

Superior "Flower of the Flax" quality all linen table damask and napkins suitable for embroidery purposes as well as for tablecloths. Offered in all plain or with a wide satin damask border.
Width, 70 Inches
19K6550—All plain woven, crystal white. Shipping wt., per yard, ¾ lb. **$2.10 A YARD**
Napkins to Match
Sold in Dozens or Half Dozens Only
19K6552—Dinner size, 22x22 inches. Bookfolded and unhemmed. Shipping weight of six, ¾ pound. **$2.75 FOR SIX**

Width, 70 Inches
19K6556—Plain woven beautiful wide satin border. Pure white, per yard, ¾ pound. **$2.25 A YARD**
Napkins to Match
Sold in Dozens or Half Dozens Only
19K6558—Dinner size, 22x22 inches. Bookfolded and unhemmed. Shipping weight of six, ¾ pound. **$3.00 FOR SIX**

All Linen Table Napkins at Rock Bottom Prices

We save you the additional cost in time and money you spend preparing the napkins for use, at no added cost on our goods. These napkins are beautifully hemmed, ready for use. All pure linen, full white bleach.
Three Practical Sizes—Neat Damask Patterns
19K1592—Finished hemmed size, about 18x18 inches. Shipping weight of six, ¾ pound. **$1.35 FOR SIX**
19K1594—Finished hemmed size, about 20x20 inches. Shipping weight of six, 1 pound. **$1.75 FOR SIX**
19K1595—Finished hemmed size, about 22x21 inches. Shipping weight of six, 1¼ pounds. **$2.25 FOR SIX**

All Linen Tablecloths

Napkins to Match

PEACOCK   CASTLE ROCK LINENS   ENGLISH RENAISSANCE

Newest in Patterns

Regular Sizes

19K7860—Tablecloth. Size, about 72x71 inches. Shipping weight, 2 pounds. **$7.95 EACH**

19K7862—Tablecloth. Size, about 72x89 inches. Shipping weight, 2¼ pounds. **$10.00 EACH**

Napkins to Match in Quality and Pattern

Sold Only in Dozens or Half Dozens **$4.50 FOR SIX**

19K7868—Full dinner size, 22x21 inches. Hemmed, ready for use. State pattern. Shipping weight of six, 1¼ pounds.

Our Best Quality Tablecloth
Castle Rock Linen—The Pride of Scotland

All pure linen exclusively patterned full double damask satin finish tablecloths and napkins. Anyone would be proud to own one or more of these superior Castle Rock tablecloths. They are rich in appearance, with a wonderful satin luster only obtainable in Castle Rock quality.

Snow white bleach, one quality in four practical sizes, neatly hemmed with fine, needlework stitching. Each cloth carefully packeted in a separate envelope. Two beautiful artistic patterns, each a high art creation. The stately Peacock or the new English Renaissance. State pattern wanted in ordering.

Best of Quality

Extra Sizes

19K7864—Tablecloth. Size, about 72x107 inches. Shipping wt., 2½ lbs. **$12.75 EACH**

19K7866—Tablecloth. Extra large size, 72x125 inches. Shipping weight, 3 pounds. **$14.75 EACH**

Napkins to Match in Quality and Pattern

Sold in Dozens or Half Dozens Only

19K7868—Full dinner size, 22x21 inches. Hemmed, ready for use. State pattern. Shpg. wt., of six, 1¼ lbs. **$4.50 FOR SIX**

TABLECLOTHS AND NAPKINS *impressively correct*

ST. MARGARET ROSE   **CASTLE ROCK HEMSTITCHED ALL LINEN SETS**   CHRYSANTHEMUM

CHRYSANTHEMUM   LILY AND ADAMS | TULIP AND SCROLL   ROSE AND BAND

Double Service
Extra Value—Specially Priced
All Linen Scotch Damask Tablecloths

The same durable pleasing quality at low cost. Ready to put right on your table. Tablecloths and napkins are durably hemmed. Soft laundered lustrous finish. Crystal white in two wonderful patterns; Chrysanthemum and Basket, or St. Margaret Rose. State pattern.

19K7840—Tablecloth. Size, about 72x70 inches. Hemmed. Shipping weight, 1¾ pounds...... **EACH $4.50**

19K7842—Tablecloth. Size, about 72x88 inches. Hemmed. Shipping weight, 2¼ pounds...... **EACH 5.75**

19K7844—Tablecloth. Size, about 72x105 inches. Hemmed. Shipping weight, 2½ pounds. Each...... **$7.00**

Napkins to Match—State Pattern

Sold in Dozens or Half Dozens Only

19K7846—Dinner size, 22x22 inches. Hemmed ready for use. Shipping weight of six, 1 pound. **$2.90 FOR SIX**

Castle Rock—Hemstitched Sets
All Linen Hemstitched Table Sets in the Soft Laundered Satin Finish —Ready for Use

A famous Castle Rock quality, Scotch full bleached lustrous finish hemstitched pure linen table sets. Nothing like them at the price. Durable and easily laundered. Manufactured for us in our own designs. You cannot secure them elsewhere. Each set boxed. We do not break sets. Can be had in three popular sizes. Patterns: Tulip and Scroll or Lily and Adams. State pattern wanted.

19K1001—For Square or Round Tables. Size, 66x66 inches, with six 20x20-inch Napkins to match. Shipping weight, per set, 3 pounds. **A SET $7.50**

19K1003—For Oblong Tables. Size, 66x84 inches, with six 20x20-inch Napkins to match. Shipping weight, per set, 3½ lbs. **A SET $9.00**

19K1685—Full Dinner Size. Size, 66x101 inches, with twelve 20x20-inch Napkins to match. Shipping weight, per set, 4 pounds. **A SET $12.50**

Full Double Damask Weave
Grass Bleached

High grade exclusively patterned All Linen Tablecloths. "Flower of the Flax" heavy quality, snow white all linen imported satin damask tablecloths of Scotch manufacture. Two distinctive patterns: Chrysanthemum and Ribbon or Rose and Band. State pattern. Hemmed, ready for use.

19K7851—Size, about 72x70 inches. Shipping wt., 2 lbs. **$6.00 EACH**

19K7853—Size, about 72x87 inches. Shipping wt., 2¼ lbs. **$7.00 EACH**

19K7855—Size, about 72x105 inches. Shipping weight, 2½ pounds. Each... **$8.50**

Napkins to Match

Sold in Dozens or Half Dozens Only

19K7857—"Flower of the Flax" quality. Size, about 22x22 inches. Hemmed, matching the above cloths in quality and pattern. State pattern. Shipping weight of six, 1¼ pounds. **$3.25 FOR SIX**

Abundance of Quality in Linen ~ Correctly Priced

Colored Border
A Smashing Value!
Unequaled for Quality and Price

All Linen "Birdseye Weave" Tablecloth Set. One Cloth and Six Napkins

19K1668—One cloth, size, 50x50 inches, with six napkins, size, 14x14 inches. Hemmed, ready for use. Bleached white with fast color borders in Blue, Gold or Rose. State color of border. Shipping weight, per set, 1¼ pounds. **$2.69 A SET**

Each set neatly boxed. We do not break sets.

The Best All Flax Linen Cloth in America for Anywhere Near Our Price
Imported All Linen Satin Damask Tablecloths

Made of all pure flax with no inferior or short end yarns used. We believe the only cloth of this quality offered at our low prices. Comes in three sizes, bleached, hemmed ready for use in patterns similar to illustration.

19K7809—Size, 66x66 in. Hemmed. Shpg. wt., 1¾ lbs... **$2.75 EACH**

19K7811—Tablecloth. Size, 66x84 in. Hemmed. Shpg. wt., 2 lbs... **3.59**

19K7813—Tablecloth. Size, 66x104 in. Hemmed. Shpg. wt., 2¼ lbs.. **4.59**

Napkins to Match—Sold in Dozens or Half Dozens Only

19K7815—Size, 20x20 inches. Hemmed. Ready for use. Shipping weight of six, 1 pound... **1.85 FOR SIX**

Beautifully Patterned
"Household" Tablecloths
A Big Value for Little Money

Full bleached damask tablecloths and napkins to match. Hemmed and laundered, ready for use; expressly for the new bungalow and kitchenette tables. Good quality satin finish all linen damask tablecloths and napkins to match. Pure white, beautifully patterned, similar to illustration.

19K7871—Tablecloth. Size, about 54x54 inches. Shipping weight, each, 1¾ pounds. **$2.00 EACH**

19K7873—Tablecloth. Size, about 54x72 inches. Shipping weight, each, 2 pounds. **$2.69 EACH**

Napkins to Match

Sold in Dozens or Half Dozens Only

19K7875—Size, 18x18 in. Hemmed. Shipping weight of six, 1 pound. **$1.50 FOR SIX**

Send Sufficient Money for Postage on Parcel Post Shipments. Any Surplus Will Be Returned

227

Better Quality Housekeeping Linens

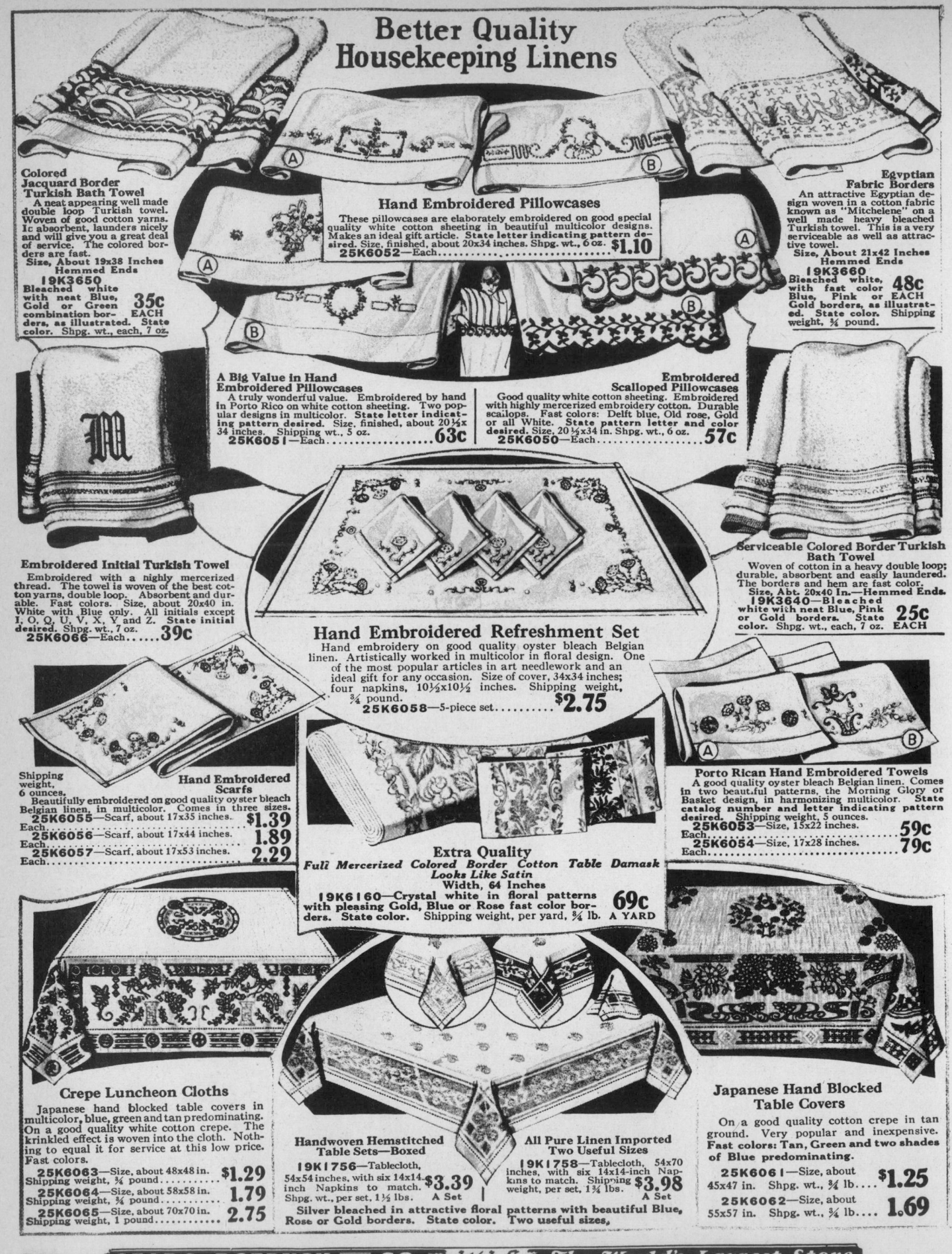

Colored Jacquard Border Turkish Bath Towel
A neat appearing well made double loop Turkish towel. Woven of good cotton yarns. Is absorbent, launders nicely and will give you a great deal of service. The colored borders are fast.
Size, About 19x38 Inches Hemmed Ends
19K3650 Bleached white with neat Blue, Gold or Green combination borders, as illustrated. State color. Shpg. wt., each, 7 oz. **35c EACH**

Hand Embroidered Pillowcases
These pillowcases are elaborately embroidered on good special quality white cotton sheeting in beautiful multicolor designs. Makes an ideal gift article. State letter indicating pattern desired. Size, finished, about 20x34 inches. Shpg. wt., 6 oz.
25K6052—Each........................ **$1.10**

Egyptian Fabric Borders
An attractive Egyptian design woven in a cotton fabric known as "Mitchelene" on a well made heavy bleached Turkish towel. This is a very serviceable as well as attractive towel.
Size, About 21x42 Inches Hemmed Ends
19K3660 Bleached white, with fast color Blue, Pink or Gold borders, as illustrated. State color. Shipping weight, ¾ pound. **48c EACH**

A Big Value in Hand Embroidered Pillowcases
A truly wonderful value. Embroidered by hand in Porto Rico on white cotton sheeting. Two popular designs in multicolor. State letter indicating pattern desired. Size, finished, about 20½x34 inches. Shipping wt., 5 oz.
25K6051—Each.................... **63c**

Embroidered Scalloped Pillowcases
Good quality white cotton sheeting. Embroidered with highly mercerized embroidery cotton. Durable scallops. Fast colors: Delft blue, Old rose, Gold or all White. State pattern letter and color desired. Size, 20½x34 in. Shpg. wt., 6 oz.
25K6050—Each.................... **57c**

Embroidered Initial Turkish Towel
Embroidered with a highly mercerized thread. The towel is woven of the best cotton yarns, double loop. Absorbent and durable. Fast colors. Size, about 20x40 in. White with Blue only. All initials except I, O, Q, U, V, X, Y and Z. State initial desired. Shpg. wt., 7 oz.
25K6066—Each......**39c**

Hand Embroidered Refreshment Set
Hand embroidery on good quality oyster bleach Belgian linen. Artistically worked in multicolor in floral design. One of the most popular articles in art needlework and an ideal gift for any occasion. Size of cover, 34x34 inches; four napkins, 10½x10½ inches. Shipping weight, ¾ pound.
25K6058—5-piece set.......... **$2.75**

Serviceable Colored Border Turkish Bath Towel
Woven of cotton in a heavy double loop; durable, absorbent and easily laundered. The borders and hem are fast color.
Size, Abt. 20x40 In.—Hemmed Ends.
19K3640—Bleached white with neat Blue, Pink or Gold borders. State color. Shpg. wt., each, 7 oz. **25c EACH**

Hand Embroidered Scarfs
Shipping weight, 6 ounces. Beautifully embroidered on good quality oyster bleach Belgian linen, in multicolor. Comes in three sizes.
25K6055—Scarf, about 17x35 inches. Each........................ **$1.39**
25K6056—Scarf, about 17x44 inches. Each........................ **1.89**
25K6057—Scarf, about 17x53 inches. Each........................ **2.29**

Porto Rican Hand Embroidered Towels
A good quality oyster bleach Belgian linen. Comes in two beautiful patterns, the Morning Glory or Basket design, in harmonizing multicolor. State catalog number and letter indicating pattern desired. Shipping weight, 5 ounces.
25K6053—Size, 15x22 inches. Each........................ **59c**
25K6054—Size, 17x28 inches. Each........................ **79c**

Extra Quality
Full Mercerized Colored Border Cotton Table Damask
Looks Like Satin
Width, 64 Inches
19K6160—Crystal white in floral patterns with pleasing Gold, Blue or Rose fast color borders. State color. Shipping weight, per yard, ¾ lb. **69c A YARD**

Crepe Luncheon Cloths
Japanese hand blocked table covers in multicolor, blue, green and tan predominating. On a good quality white cotton crepe. The krinkled effect is woven into the cloth. Nothing to equal it for service at this low price. Fast colors.
25K6063—Size, about 48x48 in. Shipping weight, ¾ pound............ **$1.29**
25K6064—Size, about 58x58 in. Shipping weight, ¾ pound............ **1.79**
25K6065—Size, about 70x70 in. Shipping weight, 1 pound............ **2.75**

Handwoven Hemstitched Table Sets—Boxed
19K1756—Tablecloth, 54x54 inches, with six 14x14-inch Napkins to match. Shpg. wt., per set, 1½ lbs. **$3.39 A Set**
19K1758—Tablecloth, 54x70 inches, with six 14x14-inch Napkins to match. Shipping weight, per set, 1¾ lbs. **$3.98 A Set**
Silver bleached in attractive floral patterns with beautiful Blue, Rose or Gold borders. State color. Two useful sizes.

All Pure Linen Imported Two Useful Sizes

Japanese Hand Blocked Table Covers
On a good quality cotton crepe in tan ground. Very popular and inexpensive. Fast colors: Tan, Green and two shades of Blue predominating.
25K6061—Size, about 45x47 in. Shpg. wt., ¾ lb.... **$1.25**
25K6062—Size, about 55x57 in. Shpg. wt., ¾ lb.... **1.69**

Gifts That Please

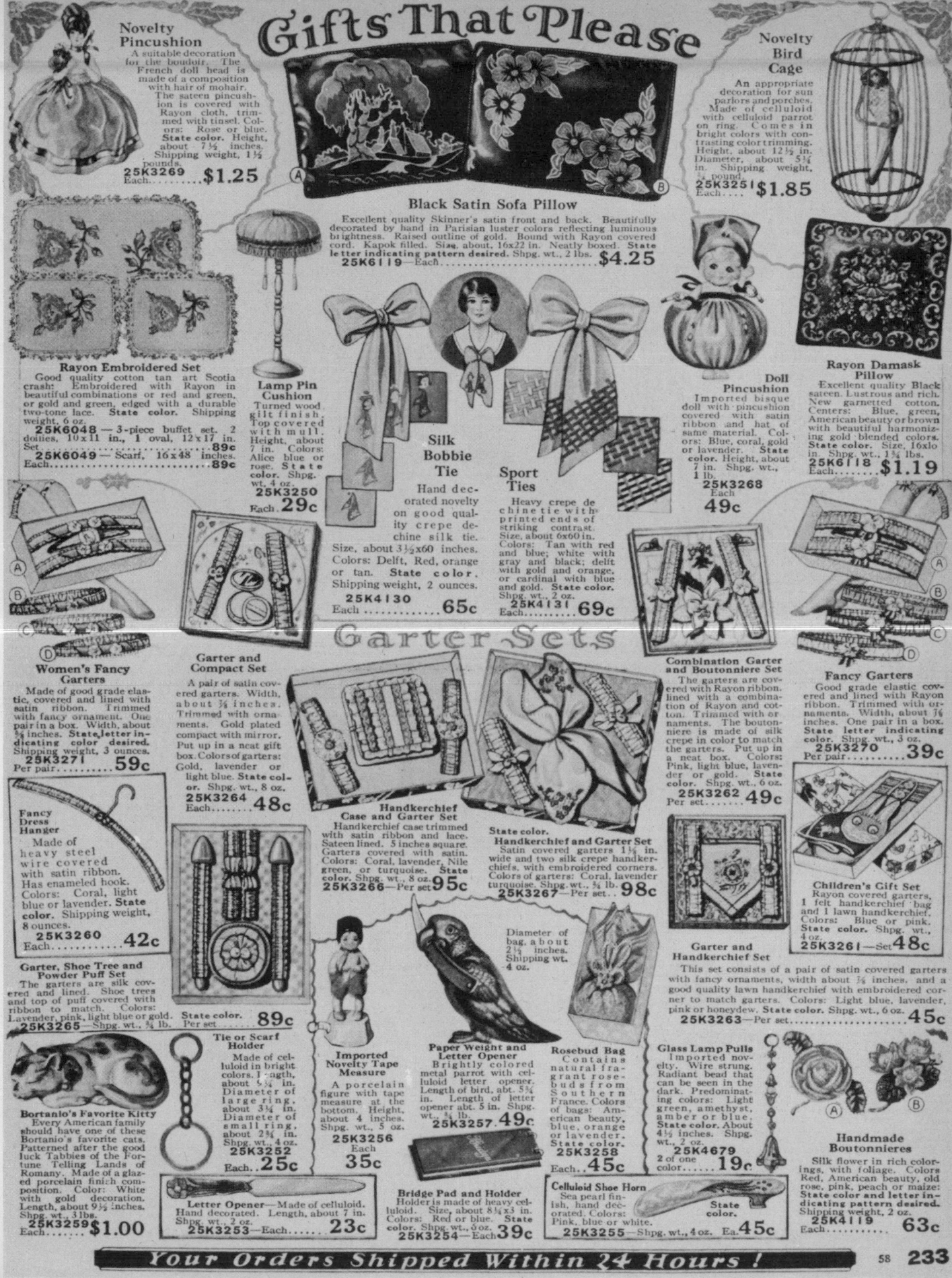

Novelty Pincushion
A suitable decoration for the boudoir. The French doll head is made of a composition with hair of mohair. The sateen pincushion is covered with Rayon cloth, trimmed with tinsel. Colors: Rose or blue. **State color.** Height, about 7½ inches. Shipping weight, 1½ pounds.
25K3269 Each.......... **$1.25**

Black Satin Sofa Pillow
Excellent quality Skinner's satin front and back. Beautifully decorated by hand in Parisian luster colors reflecting luminous brightness. Raised outline of gold. Bound with Rayon covered cord. Kapok filled. Size, about, 16x22 in. Neatly boxed. **State letter indicating pattern desired.** Shpg. wt., 2 lbs.
25K6119—Each.......... **$4.25**

Novelty Bird Cage
An appropriate decoration for sun parlors and porches. Made of celluloid with celluloid parrot on ring. Comes in bright colors with contrasting color trimming. Height, about 12½ in. Diameter, about 5¾ in. Shipping weight, ¾ pound.
25K3251 Each.... **$1.85**

Rayon Embroidered Set
Good quality cotton tan art Scotia crash: Embroidered with Rayon in beautiful combinations or red and green, or gold and green, edged with a durable two-tone lace. **State color.** Shipping weight, 6 oz.
25K6048 — 3-piece buffet set. 2 doilies, 10x11 in., 1 oval, 12x17 in. Set.......... **89c**
25K6049 — Scarf, 16x48 inches. Each.......... **89c**

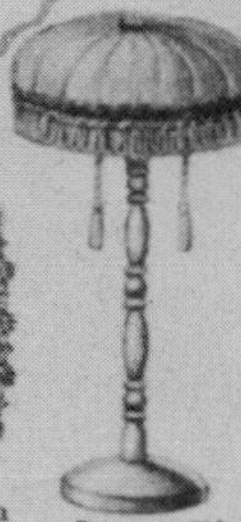

Lamp Pin Cushion
Turned wood gilt finish. Top covered with mull. Height, about 7 in. Colors: Alice blue or rose. **State color.** Shpg. wt., 4 oz.
25K3250 Each. **29c**

Silk Bobbie Tie
Hand decorated novelty on good quality crepe de-chine silk tie. Size, about 3½x60 inches. Colors: Delft, Red, orange or tan. **State color.** Shipping weight, 2 ounces.
25K4130 Each.......... **65c**

Sport Ties
Heavy crepe de chine tie with printed ends of striking contrast. Size, about 6x60 in. Colors: Tan with red and blue; white with gray and black; delft with gold and orange, or cardinal with blue and gold. **State color.** Shpg. wt., 2 oz.
25K4131 Each.......... **69c**

Doll Pincushion
Imported bisque doll with pincushion covered with satin ribbon and hat of same material. Colors: Blue, coral, gold or lavender. **State color.** Height, about 7 in. Shpg. wt., 1 lb.
25K3268 Each **49c**

Rayon Damask Pillow
Excellent quality Black sateen. Lustrous and rich. New garnetted cotton. Centers: Blue, green, American beauty or brown with beautiful harmonizing gold blended colors. **State color.** Size, 16x16 in. Shpg. wt., 1¾ lbs.
25K6118 Each.......... **$1.19**

Garter Sets

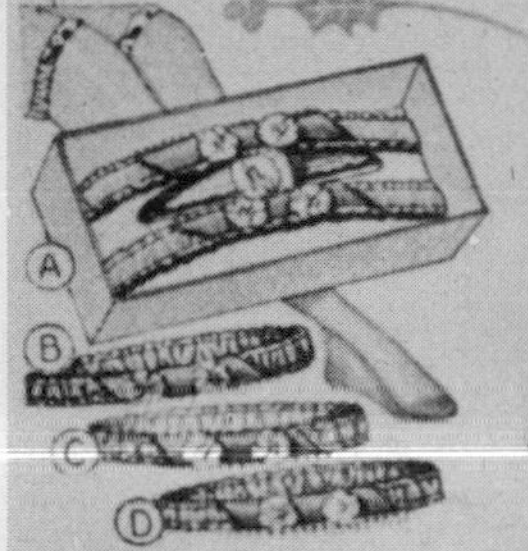

Women's Fancy Garters
Made of good grade elastic, covered and lined with satin ribbon. Trimmed with fancy ornament. One pair in a box. Width, about ⅝ inches. **State letter indicating color desired.** Shipping weight, 3 ounces.
25K3271 Per pair.......... **59c**

Garter and Compact Set
A pair of satin covered garters. Width, about ⅜ inches. Trimmed with ornaments. Gold plated compact with mirror. Put up in a neat gift box. Colors of garters: Gold, lavender or light blue. **State color.** Shpg. wt., 8 oz.
25K3264 Each.......... **48c**

Combination Garter and Boutonniere Set
The garters are covered with Rayon ribbon, lined with a combination of Rayon and cotton. Trimmed with ornaments. The boutonniere is made of silk crepe in color to match the garters. Put up in a neat box. Colors: Pink, light blue, lavender or gold. **State color.** Shpg. wt., 6 oz.
25K3262 Per set.......... **49c**

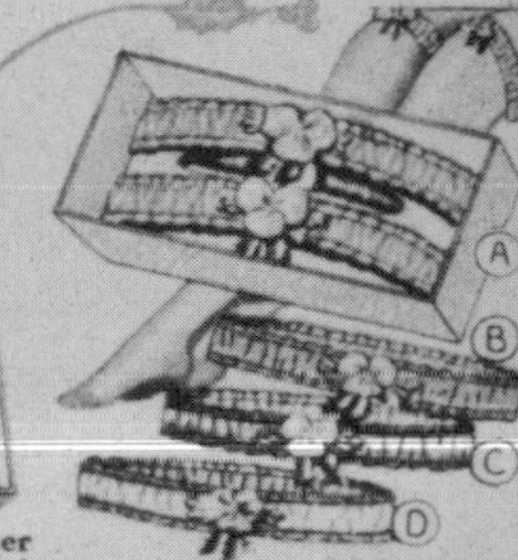

Fancy Garters
Good grade elastic covered and lined with Rayon ribbon. Trimmed with ornaments. Width, about ⅞ inches. One pair in a box. **State letter indicating color.** Shpg. wt., 3 oz.
25K3270 Per pair.......... **39c**

Handkerchief Case and Garter Set
Handkerchief case trimmed with satin ribbon and lace. Sateen lined. 5 inches square. Garters covered with satin. Colors: Coral, lavender, Nile green, or turquoise. **State color.** Shpg. wt., 8 oz.
25K3266—Per set **95c**

State color.
Handkerchief and Garter Set
Satin covered garters 1½ in. wide and two silk crepe handkerchiefs, with embroidered corners. Colors of garters: Coral, lavender turquoise. Shpg. wt., ¾ lb.
25K3267—Per set.. **98c**

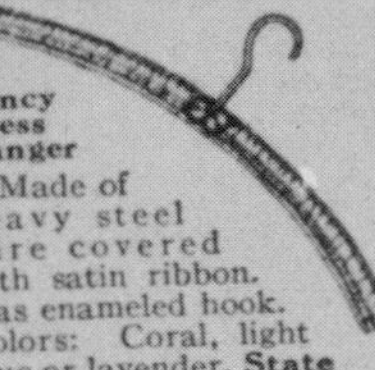

Fancy Dress Hanger
Made of heavy steel wire covered with satin ribbon. Has enameled hook. Colors: Coral, light blue or lavender. **State color.** Shipping weight, 8 ounces.
25K3260 Each.......... **42c**

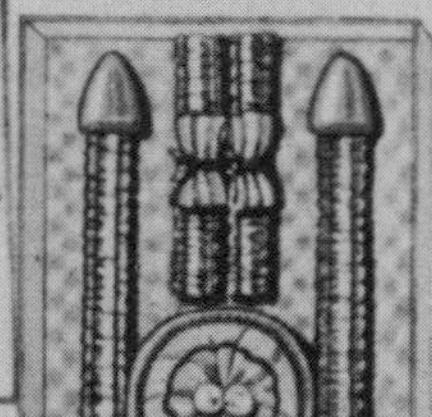

Garter, Shoe Tree and Powder Puff Set
The garters are silk covered and lined. Shoe trees and top of puff covered with ribbon to match. Colors: Lavender, pink, light blue or gold. **State color.**
25K3265—Shpg. wt., ¾ lb. Per set.......... **89c**

Children's Gift Set
Rayon covered garters, 1 felt handkerchief bag and 1 lawn handkerchief. Colors: Blue or pink. **State color.** Shpg. wt., 4 oz.
25K3261—Set **48c**

Garter and Handkerchief Set
This set consists of a pair of satin covered garters with fancy ornaments, width about ⅜ inches, and a good quality lawn handkerchief with embroidered corner to match garters. Colors: Light blue, lavender, pink or honeydew. **State color.** Shpg. wt., 6 oz.
25K3263—Per set.......... **45c**

Bortanio's Favorite Kitty
Every American family should have one of these Bortanio's favorite cats. Patterned after the good luck Tabbies of the Fortune Telling Lands of Romany. Made of a glazed porcelain finish composition. Color: White with gold decoration. Length, about 9½ inches. Shpg. wt., 3 lbs.
25K3259 Each.......... **$1.00**

Tie or Scarf Holder
Made of celluloid in bright colors. Length, about 5¾ in. Diameter of large ring, about 3¼ in. Diameter of small ring, about 2¾ in. Shpg. wt., 4 oz.
25K3252 Each.. **25c**

Imported Novelty Tape Measure
A porcelain figure with tape measure at the bottom. Height, about 4 inches. Shpg. wt., 5 oz.
25K3256 Each **35c**

Paper Weight and Letter Opener
Brightly colored metal parrot with celluloid letter opener. Length of bird, abt. 5¾ in. Length of letter opener abt. 5 in. Shpg. wt., ¾ lb.
25K3257 **49c**

Rosebud Bag
Contains natural fragrant rosebuds from Southern France. Colors of bags: American beauty, blue, orange or lavender. **State color.** Diameter of bag, about 2½ inches. Shipping wt., 4 oz.
25K3258 Each.. **45c**

Glass Lamp Pulls
Imported novelty. Wire strung. Radiant bead that can be seen in the dark. Predominating colors: Light green, amethyst, amber or blue. **State color.** About 4½ inches. Shpg. wt., 2 oz.
25K4679 2 of one color...... **19c**

Handmade Boutonnieres
Silk flower in rich colorings, with foliage. Colors Red, American beauty, old rose, pink, peach or maize: **State color and letter indicating pattern desired.** Shipping weight, 2 oz.
25K4119 Each.......... **63c**

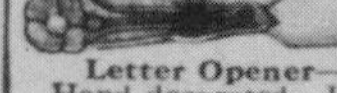

Letter Opener—Made of celluloid. Hand decorated. Length, about 7 in. Shpg. wt., 2 oz.
25K3253—Each...... **23c**

Bridge Pad and Holder
Holder is made of heavy celluloid. Size, about 8¼x3 in. Colors: Red or blue. **State color.** Shpg. wt., 6 oz.
25K3254—Each **39c**

Celluloid Shoe Horn
Sea pearl finish, hand decorated. Colors: Pink, blue or white. **State color.**
25K3255—Shpg. wt., 4 oz. Ea. **45c**

GIFTS From

Antimony

Antimony is a metal with the appearance of silver and is commonly known as "Dutch silver." To clean it, just use a dry, soft cloth. Do not apply any metal polish as it will spoil the surface.

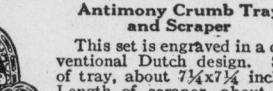

Combination Ash Tray Set

Made of antimony engraved in ship design. The set consists of one container with cover and four ash trays. Size of trays, 3⅛ inches in diameter. Shpg. wt., 1 lb.
25K5403 **$1.39**
Set.....

Ash Tray Set

Made of antimony in engraved Chinese design. The set consists of one cigar tray, about 6x4¼ inches, and four ash trays, about 3½x2½ inches. A practical combination for card parties. Shipping weight, ¾ lb.
25K5400 **$1.10**
Set.....

Antimony Crumb Tray and Scraper

This set is engraved in a conventional Dutch design. Size of tray, about 7¼x7¼ inches. Length of scraper, about 7¼ inches. Shipping weight, 1 pound.
25K5401—Set.. **98c**

Antimony Cigarette Box

An elaborate cigarette box with heavily engraved top in dragon design with Japanese good luck characters. Lined with Sugi wood. Cover is gold plated on the inside. Size, about 6x3½x2½ inches. Shipping weight, 1¾ pounds.
25K5406 **$3.75**
Each.....

Cigarette Box

Made of antimony engraved in a Chinese design showing cranes and bamboo trees. A very acceptable gift. The box is lined with Sugi wood. The cover is gold plated on the inside. Size, about 4⅛x3¼x1¾ inches. Shipping weight, 1 pound.
25K5402 **$1.19**
Each.....

Jewel Box

Made of antimony in octagon shape. The cover is engraved in a Dutch design, satin lined. Length, about 4½ inches. Width, about 3¼ inches. Height, about 1¾ inches. Shipping weight, 1 lb.
25K5407—Ea. **$1.98**

Antimony Powder Box

A beautiful ornament as well as a practical article for the boudoir. Made of antimony. Engraved in a conventional floral design. Has removable glass jar. About 3⅛ inches in diameter. Height, about 2⅝ in. Shipping weight, 1¼ pounds.
25K5409 **$1.39**
Each.....

Miyajima Nut Cracker

This nut cracker is made in the province of Miyajima, Japan, noted for its high class woodenware. Consists of wooden bowl with carved design and hammer. Diameter of bowl, about 7 inches. Length of hammer, about 8 inches. In natural dark brown finish only. Shipping weight, 1 lb.
25K5428 **$1.10**
Set.....

Lacquered Salad Set

Bowl, fork and spoon of oriental wood. Outside finished in black and gold lacquer; inside in Chinese red lacquer. Lacquered fork and spoon to match. Diameter of bowl, about 7¾ in. Length of fork and spoon, about 9½ inches. Shipping wt., 1 lb.
25K5425—Set. **$3.98**

Crumb Tray and Scraper

Made of beautiful lacquered Chinese wood. Finished in Chinese red, black and gold color. Size of tray, about 6⅝x7¼ inches. Length of scraper, about 9¾ inches. Shipping wt., ¾ lb.
25K5424
Set..... **98c**

Carved Crumb Tray and Scraper

Imported Japanese crumb tray and scraper. Hand carved. Made of natural finish cherry wood. Size of tray, about 7x7½ inches. Length of scraper, about 8½ in. Shipping weight, 8 ounces.
25K5430—Set...... **49c**

Miyajima Coaster Set

This coaster set consists of one container and six coasters made of hardwood. The cover of the container and coasters are hand carved with Japanese design. A well polished and neat looking set. Diameter of coasters, about 3 inches. Shipping weight, ¾ pound.
25K5429—Set...... **79c**

"Hakone" Cigarette Box

Has four wooden inlaid doors with space for 20 cigarettes, and one drawer for matches. Natural finish wood with decorative Japanese scenes. Size, about 6 inches high, 3½ inches square. Shipping weight, ¾ lb.
25K5431
Each......... **$1.35**

Lacquered Candlestick Holders

A very desirable and ornamental decoration for the home. Made of Chinese wood. Finished in either Chinese red or black lacquer with oriental decorations finished in gold. State color. Height, about 6 inches. Shipping weight, ¾ pound.
25K5427
Per pair...... **$1.25**

Salad Set

Spoon and fork made of Chinese wood. Chinese red and black lacquered finish. Have inlaid iridescent mother of pearl on the handles. Length, about 11 inches. Shpg. wt., 3 oz.
25K5423—Set. **98c**

Salad Set

Spoon and fork made of natural polished hardwood. Hand carved design on handles. Length, 9½ inches. Shipping weight, 3 ounces.
25K5422—Set.. **35c**

Damascene Cigarette Case

A very appropriate gift. Has gold filled Chinese design inlaid with black enamel. Size, 3½x3¼ inches. Holds 10 cigarettes. Shpg. wt., 6 oz.
25K5439—Each **$1.98**

Damascene Bracelet

A combination of black enamel and gold filled inlaid metal. Bracelet is composed of ten charms, each bearing a different design. Has catch with safety chain. Shipping weight, 4 ounces.
25K5438
Each..... **$1.35**

Lacquered Cigarette Set

Made of Chinese wood. Finished in Chinese red lacquer with gold crest. Set consists of one tray, about 9x5¼ inches, one cigarette box, about 2⅝x3⅝ inches and one match box, about 2x3 inches. Shpg. wt., 1 lb.
25K5426—Set.. **$2.69**

Lemon or Pickle Forks

Made of ivory-bone with flat handle. The handle is carved and painted in Japanese design. Length, about 4¾ inches. Shipping weight, 2 ounces.
25K5437—4 for.. **25c**

Lemon or Pickle Forks

Hand decorated and carved ivory-bone pickle or lemon forks with round handle. Can also be used for candy or glace fruit. Length, 4¾ inches. Shipping weight, 2 ounces.
25K5434—2 for..... **19c**

Penholder

A new Japanese novelty made of ivory-bone with hand carving. Appropriate for favors and prizes. Length, about 6 inches. Shipping weight, 2 ounces.
25K5436—Each...... **23c**

Orange Peeler

A very handy article for peeling oranges. Made of ivory-bone, hand decorated. Length, about 5½ inches. Shipping weight, 2 ounces.
25K5432—2 for..... **17c**

Bookmark

Hand painted and hand carved ivory-bone bookmark decorated with a small tassel. Length, 4¼ inches. Shipping weight, 2 ounces.
25K5435—Each...... **19c**

Letter Opener

Made of ivory-bone with Japanese Maid painted on the handle. Has "Lucky Dog" charm attached. Length, about 5¼ inches. Shipping weight, 2 ounces.
25K5433—Each...... **15c**

Candlestick Holders

Made of antimony in engraved floral design in dull finish. One of the newest shapes in candlestick holders. A very popular table decoration. Diameter at base, 3½ inches. Height, about 1½ inches. Shipping wt., 1 lb.
25K5405
Per pair..... **$1.25**

Candlestick Holders

Made of antimony, engraved in a Dutch design. Height, about 6¼ inches. Diameter at base, about 2¾ inches. Shipping weight, 1 pound.
25K5408
Per pair... **$1.98**

Bud Vase

Artistically designed Bud Vase made of antimony. Engraved in a beautiful ship design. Height, about 6 inches. An ornamental decoration for any home. An appropriate and welcome gift. Shipping weight, ¾ lb.
25K5404
Each..... **98c**

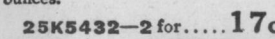
SEARS, ROEBUCK AND CO. *The World's Largest Store*

the ORIENT

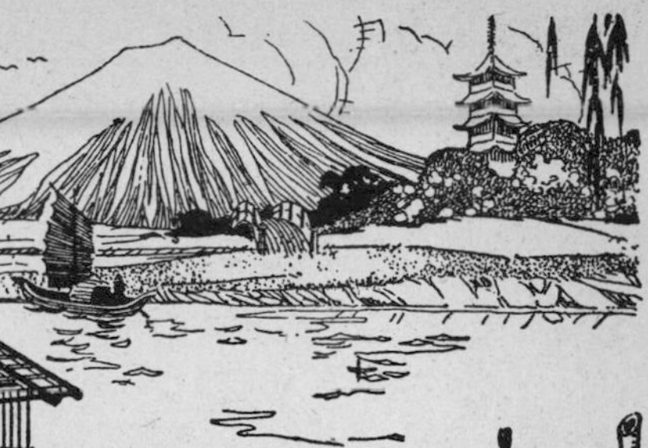

The first five articles listed below are made of heavy Chinese brass. They are handmade and elaborately chased, and make ideal home decorations. Note our exceptionally low prices.

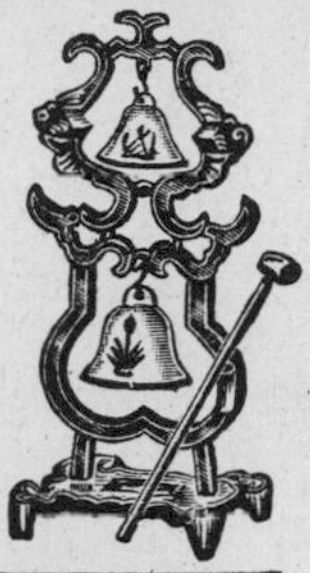

Chinese Dinner Gong

Made of heavy Chinese brass in a typical temple gate design. Has two bells with different chimes. Both stand and bells are hand chased. An appropriate decoration for your dining room. Height of stand, about 9¼ inches; widest width, about 4⅛ inches. Has brass hammer about 5¾ inches long. Shipping weight, 1¾ pounds.
25K5413—Set........... **$2.49**

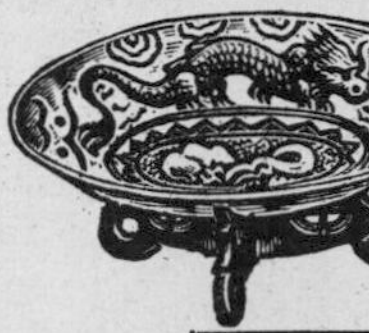

Chinese Brass Bowl

Beautifully chased brass bowl with Chinese dragon design. Each bowl has black Chinese wooden stand. Makes a wonderful fruit or candy bowl. Comes in three sizes as listed below. **State catalog number indicating size wanted.**

25K5414
Diam., 6 in. Shpg. wt., 1 lb. Each....... **98c**

25K5415
Diameter, 8 inches. Shipping weight, 1¾ lbs. Each... **$1.49**

25K5416
Diameter, 10 inches. Shipping weight, 2½ lbs. Each... **$1.98**

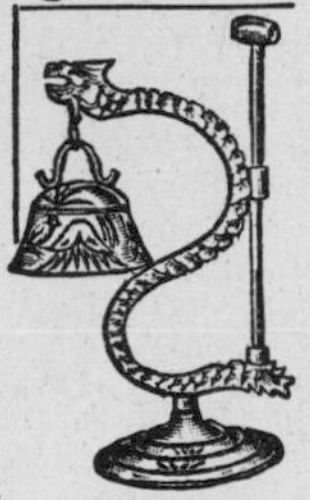

Chinese Brass Dinner Gong

The dragon design stand, as well as the gong, are neatly chased. A very novel and acceptable gift. The set consists of a stand, gong and hammer. Height, about 6½ inches. Shipping wt., 1 lb.
25K5412—Set................... **75c**

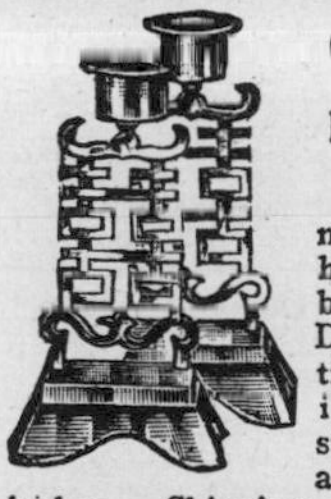

Candle stick Holders

Handmade of heavy brass. Decorative and inexpensive. Ht., about 6¼ inches. Shipping weight, 1½ pounds.
25K5411
Per pair............. **89c**

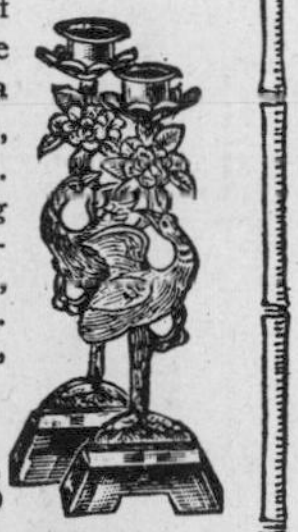

Candlestick Holders

Handmade of heavy Chinese brass in a crane design, hand chased. A rich looking home decoration. Height, about 9 inches. Shipping wt., 2 pounds.
25K5410
Per pair. **$1.85**

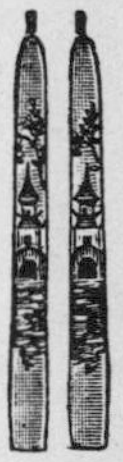

Fancy Candles

Decorated by Japanese artists with crystal beads in multi-color. Length, about 10 inches. Colors: Red, blue, green or orange. **State color.** Shipping weight, ¾ lb.
25K5418
Per pair...... **79c**

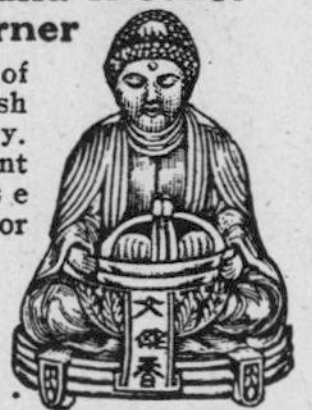

Buddha Incense Burner

Made of brass finish antimony. An excellent incense burner or can be used as an ornament. Height, about 4½ inches. One box of incense included. Shpg. wt., 1¾ lbs.
25K5417—Set. **$1.00**

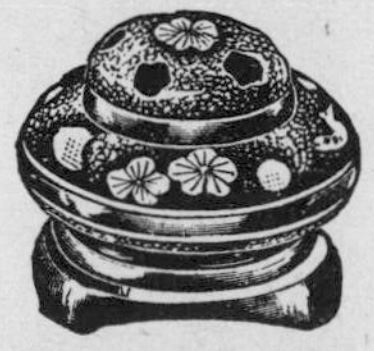

Incense Burner

Made of Japanese pottery known as Tokanabe. The basic color is black, decorated in red and green designs. Diameter, 3¼ in. Height, including pedestal, about 3 inches. Shipping weight, ¾ pound.
25K5419—Each.. **19c**

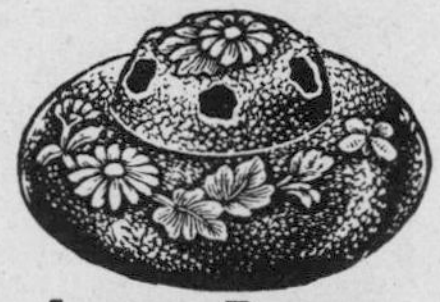

Incense Burner

Made of Japanese pottery known as Tokanabe. The basic color is black, decorated in red and green floral design. Diameter, about 4½ inches. Height, about 3 inches. Shipping weight, 1 pound.
25K5420
Each................. **35c**

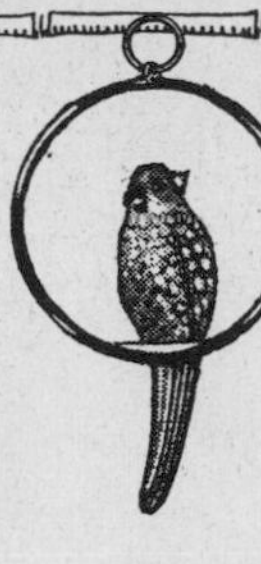

Celluloid Parrot on Ring

An appropriate decoration for sun parlors and porches. Made of celluloid decorated in gay colors. Size of ring, about 8 inches in diameter; length of parrot, about 8¾ in. Shipping wt., 5 oz.
25K5448
Each........ **39c**

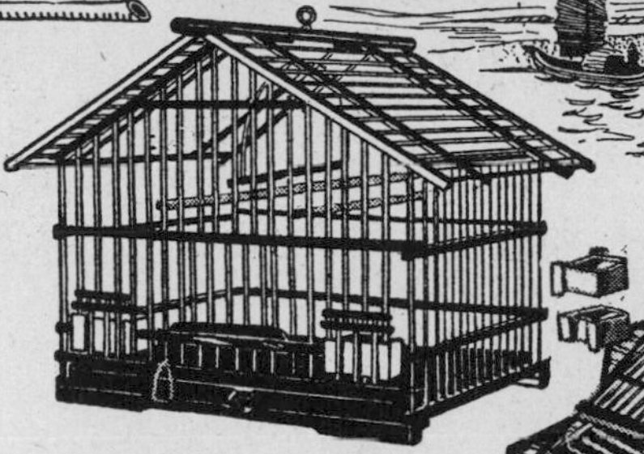

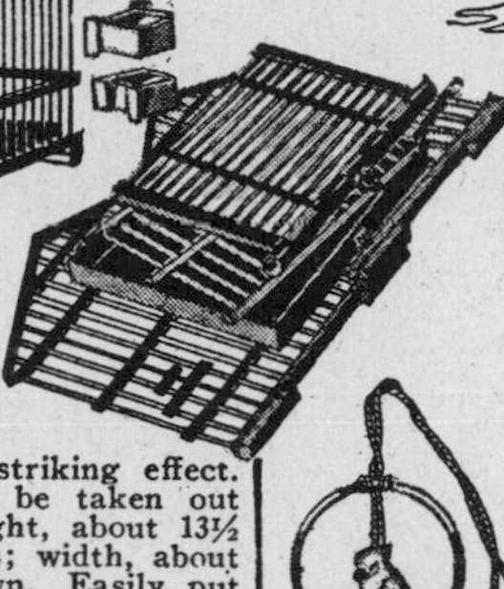

Yamato Bird Cage

Genuine Yamato bird cage entirely made of bamboo with the exception of the floor, which is of black enamel metal. The crosspieces are black lacquered, which gives this cage a very striking effect. The water and seed cups can be taken out without opening the cage. Height, about 13½ inches; length, about 11½ inches; width, about 9¼ inches. Comes knocked down. Easily put together. Shipping weight, 2½ lbs.
25K5453—Each.................... **$2.98**

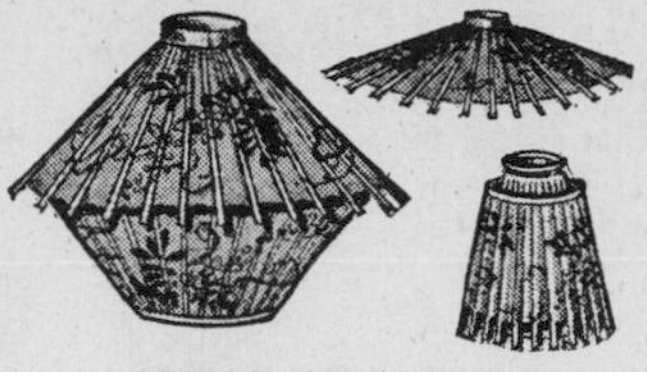

Silk Lamp Shade

Hand painted three-way silk lamp shade with adjustment ring. Can be used in three different styles, as illustrated. In assorted color patterns. Total width of shade, over all, 12 in. Shipping weight, 2 ounces.
25K5444—Each........... **59c**

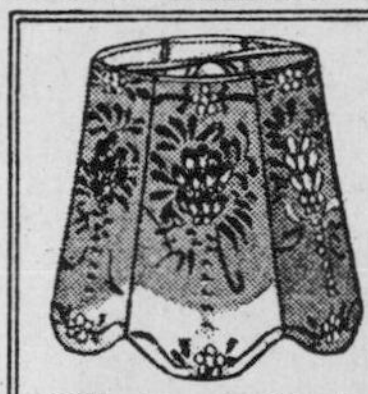

Silk Lamp Shade

Has steel frame covered with Japanese silk. Hand painted. Diam. at the top, 3 in.; at the bottom, 4½ inches; height, 4½ in. Colors: Old rose or Copenhagen blue. **State color.** Shpg. wt., 2 oz.
25K5445
Each........ **49c**

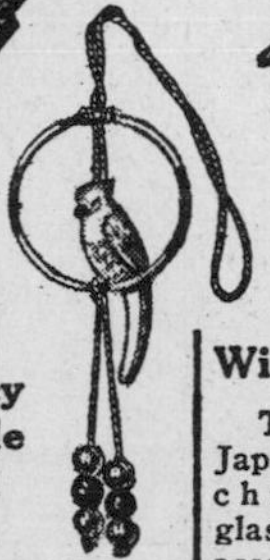

Fancy Shade Pull

Made of Rayon cord with spun glass ring and celluloid parrot. Trimmed with glass beads. Colors: Tangerine, gold, old rose or Alice blue. **State color.** Shipping weight, 4 ounces.
25K5450
19c

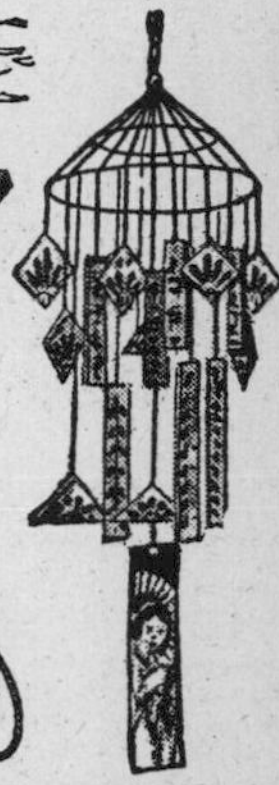

Wind Chime

This pretty Japanese wind chime has 20 glass chimes in assorted colors and sizes. To be hung on the porch or around the house where the breeze may strike it. Total length, about 13 inches. Shipping weight, ¾ lb.
25K5446
Each
23c

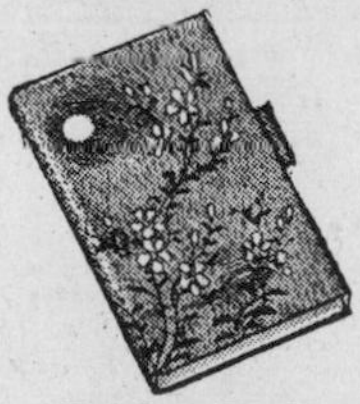

Bridge Pad

Silk covered bridge pad with hand painting in assorted designs and colors. Size, 6½x3¾ inches. Shipping weight, 5 ounces.
25K5442—Each.... **59c**

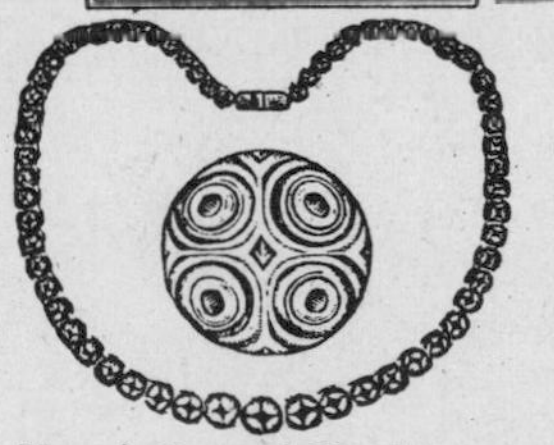

Hand Carved Necklace

A very neat necklace made of hand carved ivory-bone beads. Fastens and unfastens by screw attachment. Length, of string, about 30 inches. Shipping weight, 6 ounces.
25K5440—Each....... **$1.98**

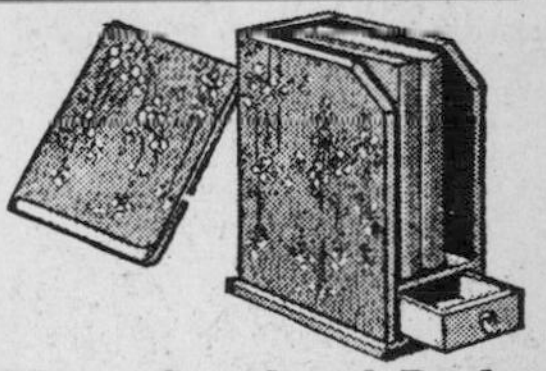

Memo Stand and Books

A unique novelty consisting of three 64-page memorandum books with cabinet. Silk covered and hand decorated in assorted designs and colors. Has small drawer for stamps. Size of books, 2½x3⅝ inches. Size of stand, 4½x2⅝ inches. Shpg. wt., 8 oz.
25K5441......... **$1.00**

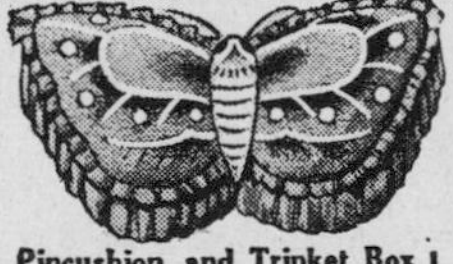

Pincushion and Trinket Box

Has cardboard base covered with silk and hand painted in assorted colors. An attractive and inexpensive gift. Length, about 5 inches; width, about 2½ inches; height, about 1½ inches. Shipping weight, 2 ounces.
25K5443—Each **29c**

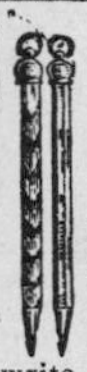

Bridge Pencils

A popular sized pencil for bridge games and gifts. The pencils are automatic and always ready to write. Made of metal, nickel plated. Length, 4¼ inches. Have ring at the top for cord. Shipping wt., 2 oz.
25K5447
2 for......... **25c**

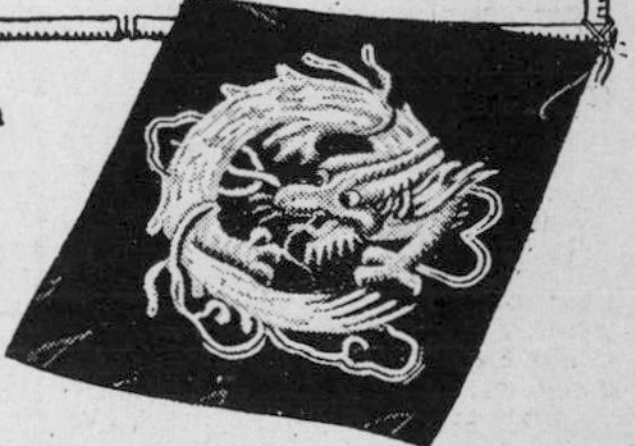

Gold Dragon Pillow Top

Oriental dragon design embroidered in gold tinsel on good grade black satin. The dragon is worked in a raised design and the combination of gold and black makes a most attractive pillow top. Size, over all, 20x20 inches. Shipping weight, 6 ounces.
25K5451—Each........................ **$2.48**

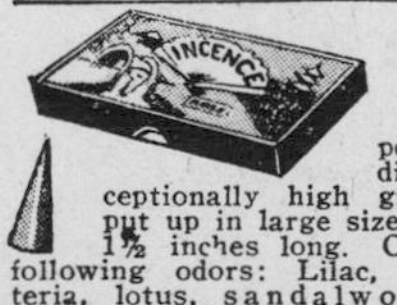

Incense

Made of imported ingredients. An exceptionally high grade incense put up in large size cones, about 1½ inches long. Comes in the following odors: Lilac, violet, wisteria, lotus, sandalwood or rose. **State choice.** Put up a dozen cones to a box. Shipping wt., 1 oz.
25K5421—Per box....... **19c**

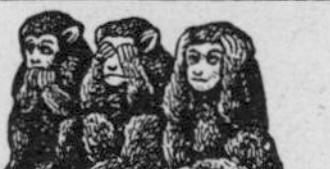

Three Wise Monkeys

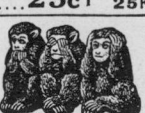

A very popular novelty, symbolic of the oriental race. Representing "Speak no evil, see no evil, hear no evil." Made of brown Tokanabe or Japanese pottery. Height, about 2 inches. Length, about 3 inches. Shpg. wt., 4 oz.
25K5452—Each.......... **13c**

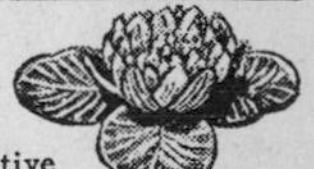

Artificial Water Lily

An effective decoration for acquariums and fish bowls. Will float on the water. Made of wax paper. Assorted colors. Has a striking resemblance to the natural flower. Shpg. wt., 2 oz.
25K5449—Each. **19c**

Decorative Oriental Pottery

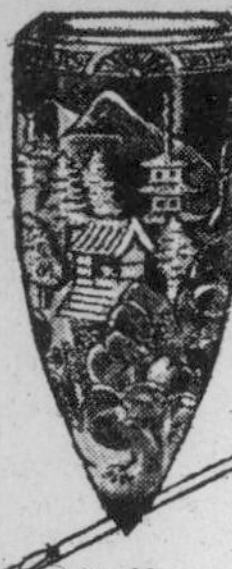

Wall Pocket

Made of Tokanabe pottery. This wall pocket has a slot in back to hang on wall. The color is black, decorated in gay colors in a typical Japanese design. Length, about 9¼ inches. Width at top, about 4 inches. Shipping weight, 2¼ lbs.

25K5470
Each, **79c**

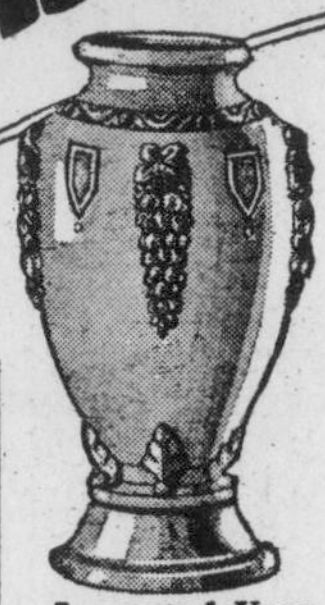

Imported Vase
Made of Japanese Tokanabe pottery in antique design. The color is yellowish tan ornamented with multicolor flowers. Height, about 10 inches. Diameter at base, 4½ inches. Shipping weight, 4¼ pounds.
25K5457
Each, **$1.25**

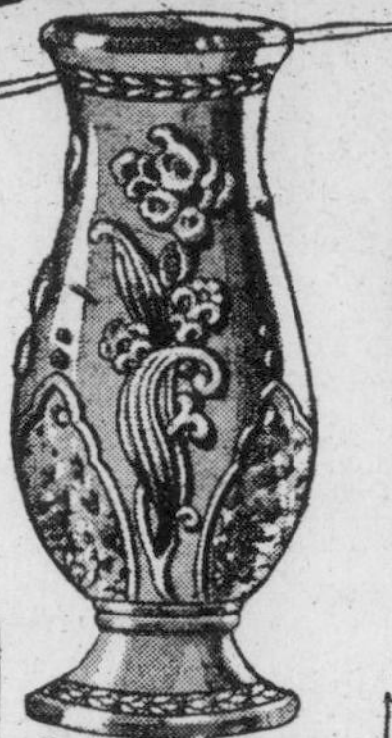

Imported Flower Vase
Made of Japanese Tokanabe pottery in a green color decorated with contrasting colors in a floral design. A very attractive vase. Height, about 12 inches. Diameter at base, 5 in. Diameter at top, 4½ in. Shipping weight, 6 lbs.
25K5456¼
Each, **$1.98**

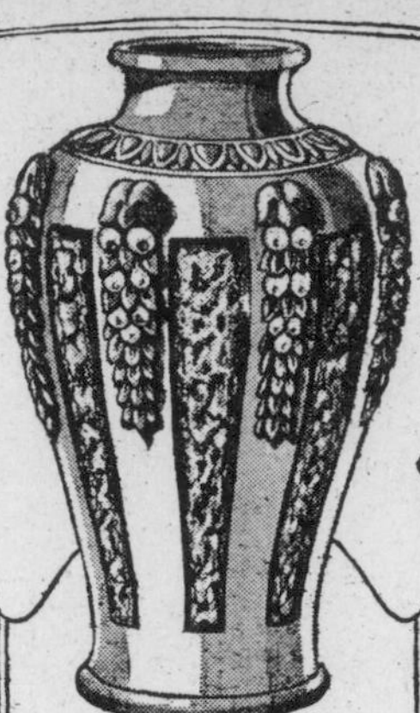

Imported Flower Vase
This decorative and artistically designed flower vase is made of what is known as Tokanabe pottery. A strictly Japanese product. An inexpensive vase appropriate for any home. The color is light brown with harmonizing multicolor ornamentation. Height, about 13 inches. Diameter at widest part, about 8 inches. Diameter at base, 5 inches. Shipping weight, 11 pounds.
25K5455¼
Each **$1.59**

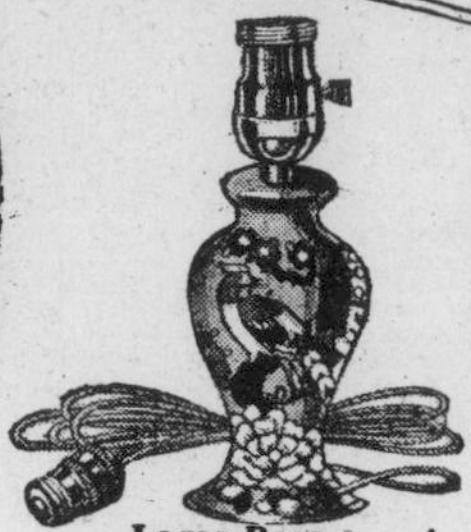

Lamp Base
Made of Imari China, one of the finest porcelain products in Japan. Hand painted in gorgeous oriental design on the following colored grounds: Black, dark blue or tan. **State color.** Fitted with socket for one electric bulb and six yards of Rayon covered cord with plug. Height of base, about 9 inches. Diameter at the foot, about 3 inches. Shipping weight, 2½ pounds.
25K5473
Each, **$1.85**

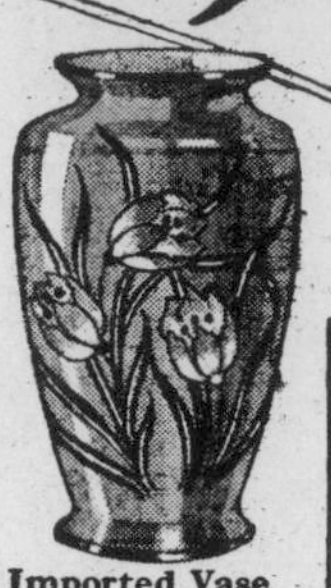

Imported Vase
A graceful and ornamental vase made of "lusterware china." The color of the vase is light Nile green decorated in a floral design of black and orange. Height, about 8¾ inches. Diameter at base, 3¼ in. Diameter at widest part of the top, 5 inches. Shpg. wt., 4 lbs.
25K5458
Each, **$1.39**

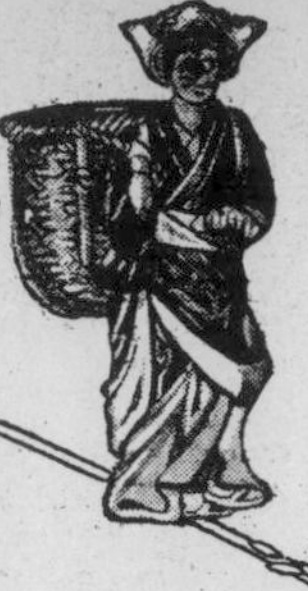

Wall Pocket

One of the most popular designs in wall pockets, "The Japanese Maid." This is made of what is known as "Banko China." Decorated in bright colors. Length, about 9 inches. Shipping weight, 2 pounds.

25K5471
Each, **89c**

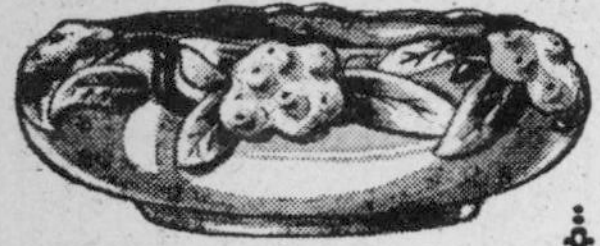

Flower Bowl
Made of imported "lusterware china," with removable block. Can also be used as bulb bowl. Color, outside, tan with contrasting color edge. The inside is a deep blue. The flower block will hold eight stems. Diameter, about 7½ inches. Height, about 2¾ inches. Shipping weight, 3 pounds.
25K5474—Each.... **$1.25**

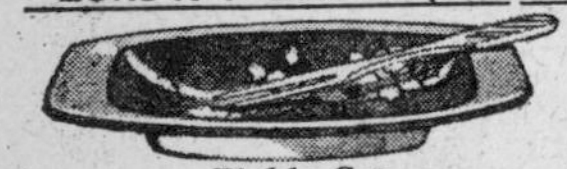

Pickle Set
Consisting of pickle dish and fork. The dish is made of Japanese lusterware with blue body and tan edge. Decorated in floral design. Length of dish, about 6¼ inches; width, about 3 inches. Pickle fork is made of white ivorybone, about 5¼ inches long. Shipping weight, ⅜ pound.
25K5468—Set.......... **49c**

Condiment Set
Consisting of antimony or "Dutch silver" tray with salt and pepper shakers made of Japanese lusterware in a blue and tan combination. An original and unique design. Height of stand, including handle, about 4 inches. Height of shakers, about 2¾ inches. Shipping weight, 1 pound.
25K5465—Per set....... **98c**

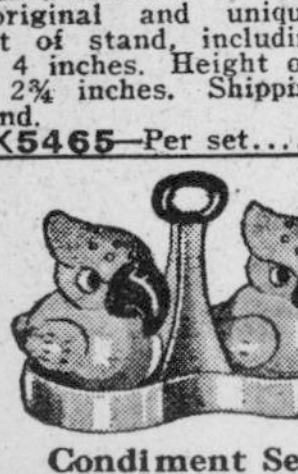

Condiment Set
Made of imported Japanese lusterware. The set consists of one stand, one salt shaker and one pepper shaker. Height of stand, about 3¼ inches; height of shakers, about 2¾ inches. Tan color only. Shipping weight, 1 pound.
25K5472—Per set...... **59c**

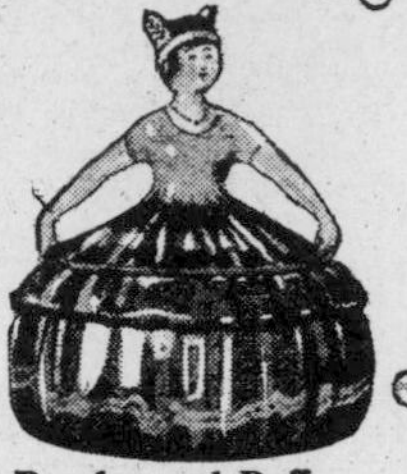

Powder and Puff Container

Made of Japanese lusterware. Color is iridescent turquoise blue with white figure. Diameter, about 4¾ inches; height, about 6 inches. Shipping weight, 1½ pounds.
25K5463
Each............... **$1.75**

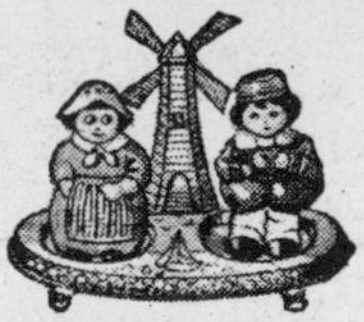

Condiment Set
A typical Dutch design. Consists of a tray made of antimony, commonly known as "Dutch silver," with Japanese lusterware salt and pepper shakers in a Dutch children design. Height of tray, including handle, about 3¼ inches; height of shakers, about 3 inches. Shipping weight, 1 pound.
25K5466
Per set.............. **$1.15**

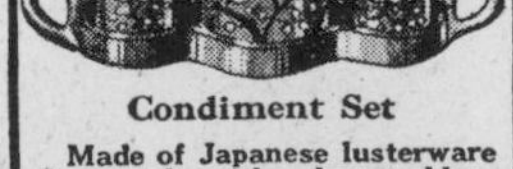

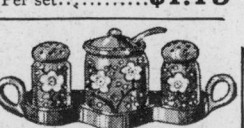

Condiment Set
Made of Japanese lusterware decorated with cherry blossoms. The set consists of one tray, about 6¾ inches long, one mustard jar, about 2¼ inches high and one salt shaker and one pepper shaker, each about 2⅛ inches high. Comes in blue or tan. **State color.** Shipping wt., 1 lb.
25K5467—Per set **85c**

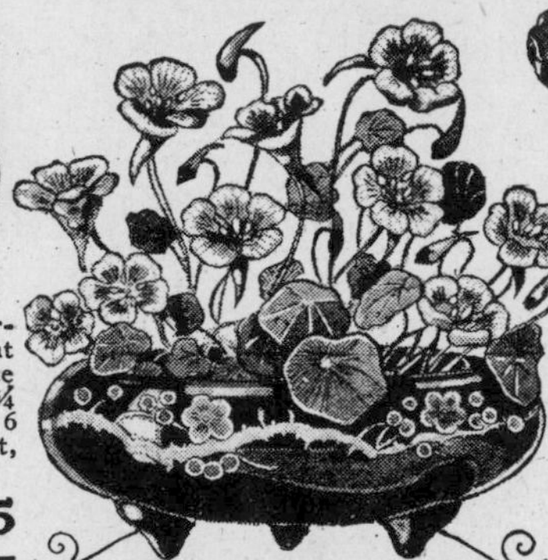

Combination Flower Bowl and Artificial Nasturtiums
A beautiful table decoration. The flower bowl is made of black lacquered Tokanabe pottery with dainty hand painting in gold and red on the rim. Diameter, about 8½ inches; height, about 3 inches. The removable block has holes for ten flowers. The artificial nasturtiums are very natural looking. Made of processed cotton with silk finish. Assorted colors. Average length of flowers, about 12 inches. Shpg. wt., 4½ lbs.
25K5480—Bowl and ten nasturtiums.......... **$1.98**
25K5476—Bowl only. Shipping wt., 4½ lbs..... **1.25**
25K5477—Artificial nasturtiums, made of cotton with silk finish. Assorted colors. Shpg. wt., 8 oz.
6 for.............................. **55c**
25K5478 — Artificial California poppies, made of processed cotton cloth in bright colors. Shipping weight, 8 ounces.
6 for.............................. **69c**
25K5479 — Artificial geraniums, made of a combination silk and waxed paper. Assorted colors. Shipping weight, 8 ounces.
6 for.............................. **69c**

Mayonnaise Set

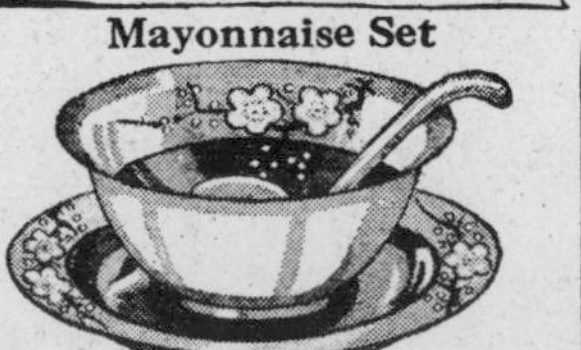

A beautiful set made of Japanese lusterware in a combination color of blue and tan decorated with cherry blossoms. Set consists of plate, bowl and spoon. Diameter of plate, about 6 inches. Diameter of bowl, about 5 inches. Shpg. wt., 2 lbs.
25K5462—Per set....... **$1.29**

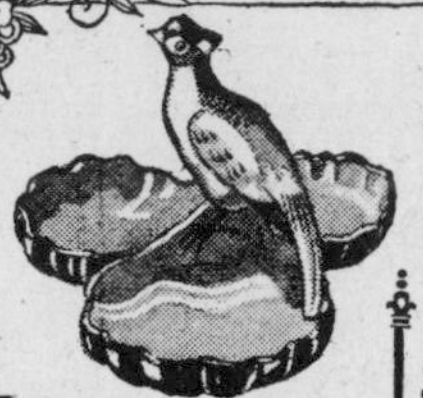

Compartment Nut Tray
Made of "China" in the province of Shofu, Japan, especially noted for its products of high grade porcelain. Finished in bright colors. Triangle shape. Width from point to point, about 5½ inches. Height, about 4 inches. Shipping weight, 1 lb.
25K5464
Each, **55c**

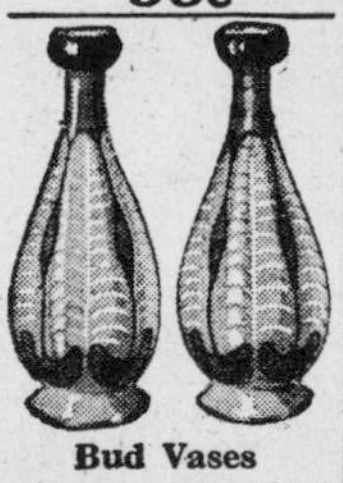

Bud Vases
A graceful and unique design made of Japanese lusterware in a combination of tan and blue, tan predominating. Height, about 6 inches. Diameter at base, about 2 inches. Shpg. wt., 1 pound.
25K5461
Per pair....... **$1.39**

Sleeping Cat
An appropriate home decoration; can also be used for door stop. Made of real china known as "Kutani." Color is white with gold and black decoration.
25K5485—Length, 7 inches. Shipping weight, 3 pounds. Each....... **$2.85**
25K5486 — Length, 8½ inches. Shipping weight, 3½ pounds.
Each **$3.85**

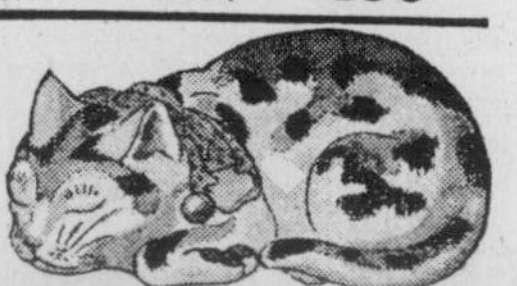

Flower or Bulb Bowl
An inexpensive but attractive bowl. Made of Tokanabe pottery in a dark gray color decorated in multicolor floral design. **Has removable flower block with six holes. Diameter, about 9½ inches. Height, about 3¼ inches.** Shpg. wt., 4½ lbs.
25K5475—Each............ **98c**

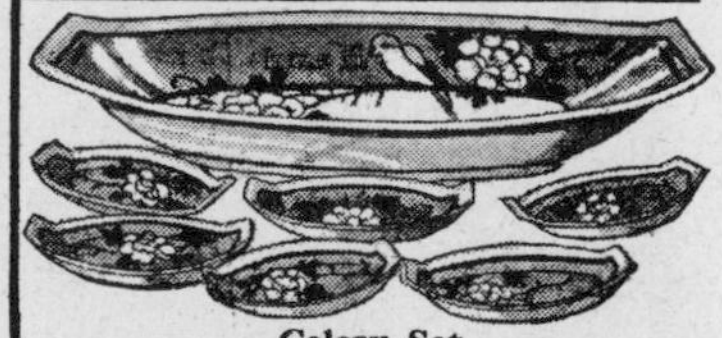

Celery Set
Made of Japanese lusterware consisting of one large dish, about 11½ inches long, 5¼ inches wide, for celery, and six salt dishes, about 3½ inches long and about 2¼ inches wide. The color is a combination of blue and tan. Decorated in flowered design. Shipping weight, 3 pounds.
25K5469—Set.......... **$1.75**

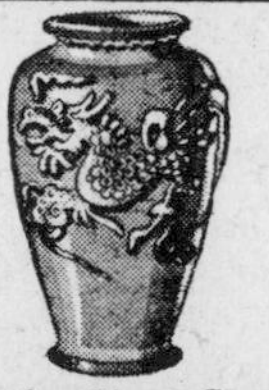

Vase for Short Stem Flowers
Made of Japanese lusterware, ornamented with raised Chinese dragon design in contrasting colors. Height, about 5¼ inches. Diameter at base, about 2 inches. Diameter at widest part at the top, 3 inches. Comes in orange with gray color dragon, or black with gray color dragon. **State choice.** Shipping weight, 1 pound.
25K5459
Each............. **49c**

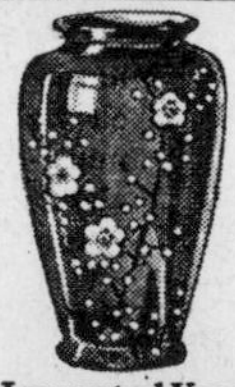

Imported Vase
Made of Japanese lusterware, decorated with cherry blossoms. Height, about 5 inches. Diameter at base, 1¾ inches. Diameter at the widest part at the top, 3 inches. **Colors: Blue or tan. State color.** Shipping wt., 1 pound.
25K5460
Each, **49c**

Latest Fashions in Neckwear

Corsage Flower
A beautiful combination of filmy organdy and plush. Very attractive. Neatly boxed. Diameter, about 5½ inches. Colors: Old rose, orchid, American beauty, peach, pink or red. State color. Shipping wt., 2 ounces.
25K4115
Each............55c

Marvel Set
Very fashionable for high neck dresses. A pleasing combination of cotton net, Valenciennes and Venise lace, with black ribbon. Colors: Cream-white or dark ecru. State color.
25K4140—Per set......65c

Circular Set
Collar is splendid for dresses of round neck. Good quality Venise lace. Light ecru. Shipping weight, 2 ounces.
25K4121
Per set............95c

Miracle Set
Made of imported cotton net and lace. One of the most fashionable collars of the season, with large gauntlet cuffs. Beading for drawing ribbon. Color: Light ecru. Shipping weight, 2 ounces.
25K4143
Per set............$1.10

Linen Set
This collar and cuff set is made of imported linen and daintily trimmed with real handmade crochet lace. Cream-white. Shipping weight, 2 ounces.
25K4139
Per set......39c

Plush Rose
Lustrous plush with muslin backing. For coats, suits, furs, etc. Neatly boxed. Colors: Old rose, orchid, American beauty, peach, pink or red. State color. Diameter, about 4½ inches. Shipping weight, 2 oz.
25K4116
Each............70c

Oriental Set 80¢

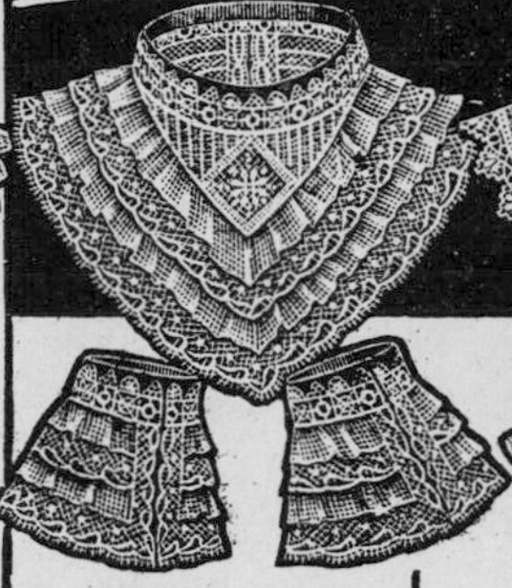

Buster Brown Set
A very dressy set. Made of good quality Valenciennes lace and imported cotton net. Light ecru or dark ecru. State color. Shipping weight, 2 oz.
25K4144
Per set............85c

Silk Georgette Sleeves
Give you a new dress for a little expense. All you have to do is stitch them in. Shirred cuffs. 23 inches long. Colors: Black, tan, navy, red, Copenhagen, white or flesh. State color. Shpg. weight, 2 ounces.
25K4134
Per pair....$1.00

Oriental Lace Set
Embroidered Van Dyke point design on good quality imported cotton net in combination with Venise lace. Light ecru only. Shipping weight, 2 ounces.
25K4149
Per set............80c

Hollywood Set
Very attractive. A beautiful combination of imported cotton net, Valenciennes and Venise lace, with hand crocheted medallion. Collar and cuffs edged with black silk ribbon. Light ecru. Shipping wt., 2 oz.
25K4146 $1.59
Per set............

Oriental Set
Embroidered on good quality imported cotton net. Trimmed with dainty Venise lace. Ecru only. Shipping wt., 2 oz.
25K4141
Per set............45c

Silk Georgette Set
Good quality silk georgette enriched with multicolor petit point medallions and trimmed with the better quality dainty Venise lace. Light ecru. Shipping weight, 2 oz.
25K4148 $1.65
Per set......

Vestee With Real Lace
A beautiful combination of imitation Point D'Alencon and fancy Valenciennes lace. Collar trimmed with real handmade filet. Light ecru. Shpg. wt., 3 oz.
25K4130
Each............$1.95

Novelty Georgette Set
Daintily embroidered on good quality silk Georgette and trimmed with a dainty Venise lace. Colors: White, or light ecru. State color. Shpg. wt., 2 oz.
25K4145
Per set............82c

MARI-LU SET
Fashion's latest creation! Fancy cotton lace. Trimmed with dainty filet lace. Silk ribbon. Color: Ecru. Shipping wt., 2 ounces.
25K4142
Per set............$1.90

Lace Vestee
Good quality Valenciennes and oriental lace. Trimmed with oriental lace. Can be worn with V neck or Buster Brown style. Light ecru. Shipping weight, 2 ounces.
25K4136
Each............95c

Imported Venise

Bromley Collar and Cuff Set
Neatly embroidered on cotton batiste. Trimmed with Venise lace. Light ecru only. Shipping weight, 2 ounces.
25K4123—Per set......59c

Venise Coat Collar and Cuff Set
Better quality. For suit or dress. Light ecru. Shpg. wt., 2 oz.
25K4124
Per set............75c

Chic Venise Bromley Set
Multicolor inserting. Embroidered medallions on sheer batiste. Ecru only. Shipping wt., 2 ounces.
25K4122 80c
Per set......

Crepe De Chine Vestee
A very attractive and fashionable vestee with cuffs. Made of double rich crepe de chine. Has pearl buttons. Colors: White, flesh, champagne, Lanvin green, old rose or powder blue. State color. Shipping weight, 2 ounces.
25K4137
Each............$1.50

Tailored Linen Set
Good quality imported linen with pearl button cuff links. One of the nobbiest sets we have ever shown. Colors: White, ecru, delft, jade, russet (tan) or orange. State color. Tie not included. Shipping weight, 3 ounces.
25K4132
Per set............95c

Sport Windsor Tie
Of silk messaline. Same colors as 25K4132; also black or cardinal. Size, about, 6½x45 in. Shpg. wt., 2 oz.
25K4133—Each......48c

SILK TIE
Good quality crepe de chine. Can be worn as bow or scarf. Colors: Black, tan, red, delft, navy blue, white, jade, brown or orange. State color. Size, about, 3½ x60 in. Shpg. wt., 2 oz.
25K4128 42c
Each............
Same colors as above. Size, 5½x60 in.
25K4129
Each............69c

Silk Windsor Tie
Popular for Buster Brown Collar. Colors: Red, black or navy blue. State color. Size, about, 4¾x35 in. Shipping wt., 2 oz.
25K4126—Each......24c
Better quality. Same colors. State color. Size, 6½x45 in. Shpg. wt., 2 oz.
25K4127—Each......45c

Buster Brown Collar
Neat, dainty collar in a beautiful combination of cotton net and Venise lace. Light ecru only. Shipping weight, 2 oz.
25K4120
Each............49c

Tuxedo Collar
Good quality Venise lace. Suitable for coat or dress. Light ecru only. Shpg. wt., 2 oz.
25K4125
Each............35c

Boudoir Cap
Dainty boudoir cap of Jap silk and Rayon marquisette. Trimmed with ribbon and Valenciennes lace. Colors: Pink, blue, orchid or honeydew. State color. Shpg. wt., 2 oz.
25K4135
Each............48c

Hand Embroidered MADEIRA Decorated Linens

Madeira Buffet Set
Hand embroidered on excellent quality white Irish linen in eyelet and butterfly design. Two round doilies, diameter about 10 inches; 1 oval, 11½x17 inches. Shpg. wt., 6 oz.
25K6113—Set of 3 pieces............$1.98

Printed Sateen Pillows
Filling cotton napper. Multicolor. Size, 21 in. Square or round. State choice. Shpg. wt., each, 1½ lbs.
25K6121—Each...$1.15

Large Sheen-Rayon Pillow
Center of gold color cloth. Cotton and kapok filled. Colors: Rose, blue, gold or green. State color. Shpg. wt., each, 1½ lbs.
25K6126—Oblong. Size, including flounce. 14x32 in. Each $3.29
25K6127—Oval. 22x27 in. Each..$3.29

Rayon Pillows
Excellent quality Rayon faille sofa pillows. Filled with kapok and silk floss. Handmade flower. Colors: Rose, blue or gold. State color. Shipping weight, each, 1 pound.
25K6124
Round. 18 in. Each....$2.00
25K6125—Oval. 15x20 in. Each............$2.00

Madeira Oval Doilies
Hand embroidered on white Irish linen. Rose scallops. Shpg. wt., 2 oz.
25K6114
6x12 in. Each............70c
25K6115—10x14 in. Each.$1.40
25K6116—12x18 in. Each. 1.90

Madeira Tea Napkins
Hand embroidered on excellent quality white Irish linen in bow-knot and eyelet design. Size, about 12x12 inches. Shipping weight, six, 8 ounces.
25K6117—Box of 6. $3.50

Hand Painted Bedroom Set

All Fast Colors

Save Money Here

Novelty bedspread set. Hand painted. Made of good quality unbleached (cream color) cotton sheeting. This is the best low cost set ever put on the market and our low price has never been equaled. Hand painted in multicolors that are fast. The dainty and popular bluebird is the design and it comes with blue or rose predominating. Durable overlocked edges to match. Set consists of 5 pieces, which can be bought separately. Colors: Rose or blue. State color.
25K6096—Scarf. Size, about 12x49 inches. Shpg. wt., 5 oz. Each.....29c.
25K6097—Valance and pair of curtains. Valance, 11x35 inches. Curtains, 17½x77 inches each. Headed ready to hang. Shipping weight, 1¾ lbs...98c
25K6098—Bedspread. Size, about 85x100 in. Shpg. wt., ¾ lb. Each.$1.98
For other Bedspread sets, See page 193

Our Best Pillow
A beautiful house decoration of radiant sheen Rayon, ornamented with five rows of Rayon covered soutache braid with smocking, and antique gold net. Colors: Rose, blue, gold or lovebird green. State color. Size, 18x26 inches. Shipping weight, 1½ pounds.
25K6128—Each....$4.95

Stamped Scalloped Pillowcases
Stamped on good quality linen finish white cotton sheeting. With hand cut scallops and stamped with very attractive designs. Easy to embroider. Size, finished, 20½x34 inches. Order by catalog number and state pattern desired. Shipping weight, 6 oz.
25K6076—Each......57c

Linen Set

Excellent quality imported ivory-white linen, enriched with heavy Venise lace medallions and trimmed with Venise lace of excellent quality. Shpg. wt., 5 oz.
25K6107—Vanity set. 1 oblong, 6½x14 in.; 2 doilies, 10x14 in. Set of 3 pieces......$1.15
25K6108—Buffet set. 2 doilies, 9 in. round; 1 oval, 12x17 in. Set of 3 pieces..$1.15
25K6109—Scarf, 17x50 in. Each...............$1.15

Krinkled Dresser Scarf
A very striking scarf of cotton krinkled krepe interwoven with Rayon. Trimmed with ecru cotton lace in Cluny design. Size, 16x49 inches. Color of center: Rose, blue or gold. State color. Shipping weight, 5 ounces.
25K6103—Each. 60c

Stamped Tubing Pillowcases
Stamped on excellent quality white cotton pillowcase tubing. With hemstitched edges for crocheting. Comes without lace. Order by catalog number and state number indicating pattern desired. Size, finished, 21x35 inches. Shipping weight, 6 ounces.
25K6075—Each....................................55c

Embroidered Hemstitched Pillowcases
Good quality white cotton sheeting. Embroidered with mercerized thread in rose, blue, gold or white. State color. Size, 20½ x33 inches. Shipping wt., 5 oz.
25K6099—Each...............39c
For Pillowcases, See Page 192

Lace Trimmed Linen Scarf
Center of scarf is made of imported linen with hemstitching. Oyster white. Trimmed with durable cotton lace in Cluny design. A wonderful value. Size, about 15½x49 inches. Shipping weight, 5 ounces.
25K6102—Each..... 70c

Hand Crocheted Doilies
Imported from Japan. White cotton centers with drawnwork.
25K6110—Doily. Diameter, 8½ in. Shpg. wt., 2 oz. Each....17c
25K6111—Doily. Diameter, 10½ in. Shipping weight, 2 oz. Each....26c
25K6112—Centerpiece. Diameter, 18 in. Shipping weight, 3 oz. Each....59c

Lace Trimmed Pillowcases
Of good quality white cotton sheeting. Enriched with 4 imitation Irish crochet medallions and trimmed with dainty durable cotton lace in hand crocheted effect. Size, about 21x35 inches. Comes packed 1 pair in a neat box. Shpg. wt., 1 lb.
25K6100—Box of 2....$1.25

Japanese Hand Blocked Table Covers
Standard quality white cotton cloth printed in two shades of blue. Fast color. Seamed. Don't confuse this number with those of inferior quality.

	Size, About	Shpg. Wt.	Each
25K6104	45x45 in.	¾ lb.	$0.75
25K6105	60x60 in.	1 lb.	1.15
25K6106	70x70 in.	1 lb.	1.60

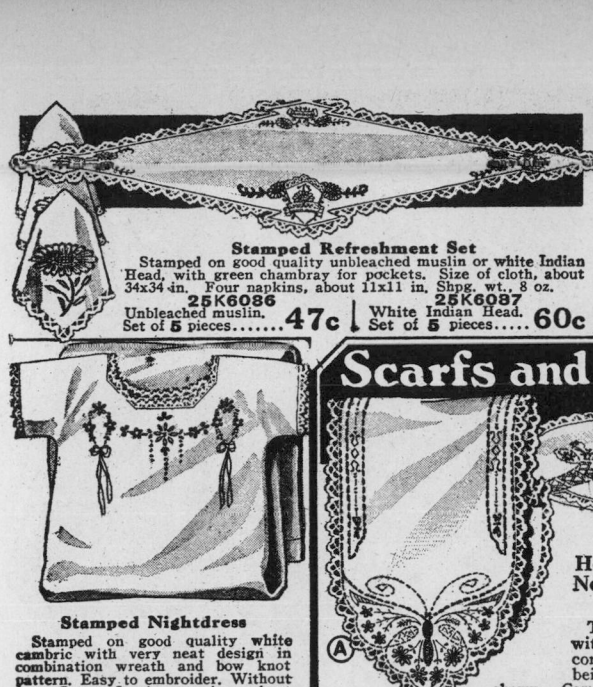

Stamped Refreshment Set
Stamped on good quality unbleached muslin or white Indian Head, with green chambray for pockets. Size of cloth, about 34x34 in. Four napkins, about 11x11 in. Shpg. wt., 8 oz.
25K6086
Unbleached muslin.
Set of 5 pieces...... **47c**
25K6087
White Indian Head.
Set of 5 pieces...... **60c**

Stamped Hot Pot Holder
Tinted in multicolors, on good quality unbleached muslin. Durably bound edges in fancy gingham with three gingham pads matching edging. Shipping wt., 3 oz.
25K6101
Holder and 3 pads.. **48c**

Stamped Goods

Stamped Vanity and Buffet Sets
Stamped on white linen finish cotton cloth. Hemstitched edges for crochet. Comes without lace.
25K6067—Vanity set. Consists of two doilies, 9x9 inches; 1 oblong, 6¼x15½ inches. Shipping weight, 3 ounces. Per set.. **28c**
25K6068—Buffet set. Two doilies, 10x10 inches; 1 oblong, 10½x13 inches. Shipping weight, 3 ounces. Per set.. **29c**

Scarfs and Centerpieces to Match

Here Are Two of the Best Novelty Stamped Sets We Have Ever Offered!
Two unique patterns of scarfs with centerpieces to match. They combine the special features of being easy to embroider and very showy. Come stamped on white cotton linen finish embroidery cloth, or on natural brown embroidery art linen of good quality. Order by catalog number and state letter indicating pattern desired. Without lace, but with hemstitched edges.

25K6070—White scarf, 17x45 inches. Shipping weight, 5 ounces. Each.. **45c**
25K6071—White centerpiece, 34-in. diameter. Shipping wt., 5 oz. Each.. **59c**
25K6072—Brown linen Scarf. Size, about 17x45 in. Shpg. wt., 5 oz. Each.. **63c**
25K6073—Brown linen, Centerpiece, 34 in. diameter. Shpg. wt., 5 oz. Each.. **85c**

For Other Table and Dresser Scarfs, See Page 818

Stamped Baby Dress
Ready made sheer white nainsook. Yoke inserted with hemstitching. Shpg. wt., 3 oz.
25K6091 Infants' dress. **75c**
25K6092 One year old child's dress. **75c**

Stamped Nightdress
Stamped on good quality white cambric with very neat design in combination wreath and bow knot pattern. Easy to embroider. Without lace. Comes flat in one piece, about 36x100 in. Shpg. wt., 8 oz.
25K6077—Each........ **59c**

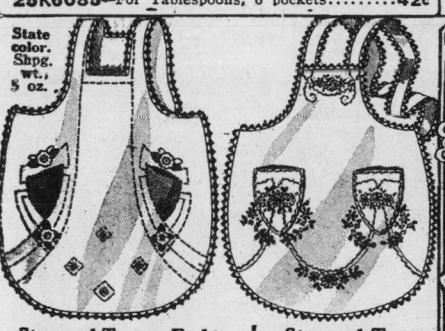

Stamped Silverware Holders
A popular article in art needlework. Keep your silverware in order. Good quality cream color cotton art crash lined throughout with Canton flannel. Durably bound edges. Shipping weight, 5 ounces.
25K6082—For Knives, ... **12c**
25K6083—For Forks, 12 pockets............ **42c**
25K6084—For Teaspoons, 12 pockets........ **42c**
25K6085—For Tablespoons, 6 pockets........ **42c**

Stamped Buffet or Dresser Set
Stamped on good quality white linen finish cotton cloth. With hemstitched edges for crocheting, and novel design easy to embroider. Size, two doilies, 11x17 inches; 1 oval, 17x23 inches. Shipping weight, 5 ounces.
25K6069—Per set.......... **47c**

Stamped Gertrude
Ready made sheer white nainsook with frill and dainty white lace. Size, 1 year. Shpg. wt., 3 oz.
25K6090
Each, **59c**

Eleven-Piece Stamped Set

State color. Shpg. wt., 5 oz.

Stamped Tea or Fudge Apron
On good quality unbleached (cream color) muslin. Stamped in a very effective design, easy to embroider, with blue or old rose linene pockets sewed on. Without trimming. Length, 36 inches. All sewed up.
25K6089—Each.,.... **47c**

Stamped Tea Apron
Stamped on good quality unbleached muslin. Easy to embroider. Without lace. Length, 31 inches. Shipping weight, 5 oz.
25K6088 Each.......... **28c**

A Practical and Attractively Designed 11 Piece Set
Stamped on good quality white cotton embroidery cloth with linen finish. Stamped on one piece, size, 36x106 inches. Set consists of 1 cloth, size 34x34 inches.; 6 napkins, size 12x12 inches; 1 scarf, size 17x43 inches. Three-piece buffet set consists of two doilies, 10x16 inches, and 1 oval, 16x22 inches. Comes without lace. Shipping weight, 1 pound.
25K6074—Set of 11 pieces... **$1.10**

Stamped Luncheon Sets
Stamped on excellent quality white linen finish cotton cloth with four napkins to match, size, 12x12 inches. Without lace.
25K6078—Size, 36x36 inches. Four napkins. Shipping wt., 8 oz. Per set.. **79c**
25K6079—Size, 45x45 inches. Four napkins. Shpg. wt., ¾ lb. Per set... **$1.19**
25K6081—Size, 54x54 inches. Four napkins. Shpg. wt., 1 lb. Per set...... **1.39**

Dainty Dimity Stamped Curtains
Stamped on good quality striped cotton dimity in a very pleasing design in outline embroidery. White only. Size, about 18x34 inches. Shipping weight, 3 ounces.
25K6090—Per pair......... **42c**

Stamped Bedspreads

Stamped Krinkled Krepe Bedspread
Material good quality unbleached cotton (cream color) Krinkled Krepe. Stamped in the ever popular basket design which is easy to embroider, in the long and short stitch. Comes without fringe. For fringe see page 256. Size, about 81x94 in. Shipping weight, 2 pounds.
25K6094—Each.......... **$2.19**
Same pattern as above, on good quality unbleached (cream color) cotton sheeting. Size, about 81x94 inches. Shpg. wt., 2 lbs. **$1.30**
25K6095—Each.......... **$1.30**

Easy to Embroider

Quality Laces — Imported Valenciennes Lace Edges and Insertions to Match — Low Prices

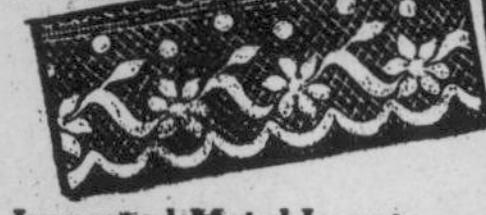

Imported Metal Lace Edges
With neat design. Colors: Gold or silver. **State color.** Shipping weight, per yard, 1 oz.

	Width, About	Per Yard
25K353..	¾ in.	12c
25K354..	1⅛ in.	17c
25K355..	1½ in.	23c

Imported Metal Lace Edges
In floral design. This style of lace is very much in use at the present time. Colors: Gold or silver. **State color.** Shipping weight, per yard, 1 ounce.

	Width, About	Per Yard
25K350—Edge..	3⅛ in.	55c
25K351—Edge..	4½ in.	69c
25K352—Edge..	5½ in.	85c

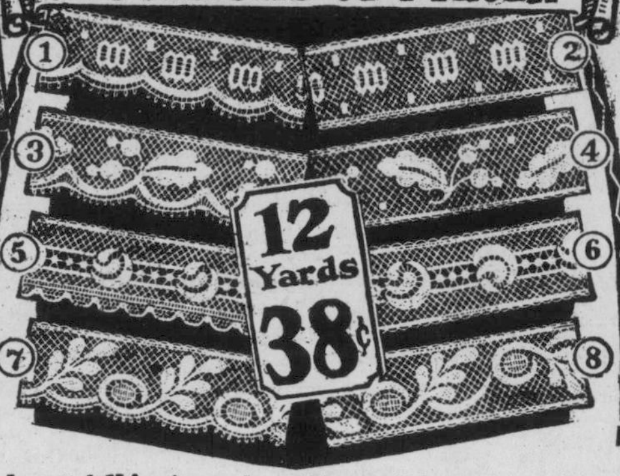

Imported Valenciennes Lace Edges and Insertion to Match
Lace of this character is used very extensively for all kinds of trimming purposes. The designs are very neat. Made of good quality cotton thread. Color: White only. **Order by catalog number and state number indicating pattern desired.** Sold only in 12-yard pieces. Width, about ⅝ inch. Shipping weight, 2 oz.
25K299—12-yard piece........................38c

Imported Silk Chantilly Lace Edges
In floral design. Colors: Black or white. **State color.** Shipping weight, per yard, 1 oz.

	Width, About	Per Yard
25K414..	3 in.	19c
25K415..	3⅞ in.	23c
25K416..	4¾ in.	29c

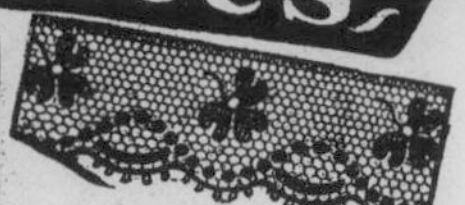

Imported Silk Chantilly Lace Edges. In neat design. Colors: Black or white. **State color.** Shipping wt., per yard, 1 oz.

	Width, Abt. In.	Per Yard
25K385—Edge...	¾	7c
25K386—Edge...	⅞	8c
25K387—Edge...	1¼	10c
25K388—Edge...	1⅝	14c

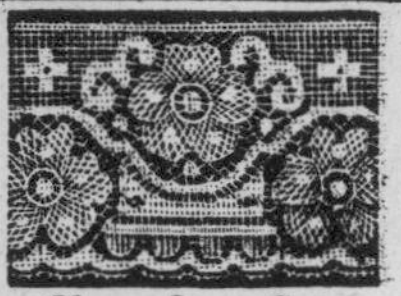

Cluny Lace Set
Attractive set at a popular price. Colors: Ivory white or ecru. **State color.** Shipping weight, per yard, 1 oz.

	Width, About	Per Yard
25K782—Edge..	2¼ in.	6c
25K783—Edge..	4½ in.	11c
25K784—Ins....	2¼ in.	6c

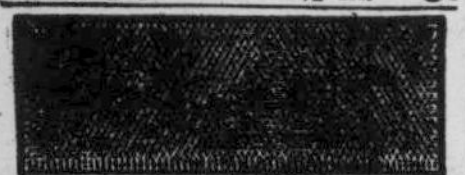

Imported Cotton Net Footings. Colors: Black, white, ecru, pink, orange, sky blue, heliotrope, gold, flame, Copenhagen blue, nile or peach. **State color.** Shipping weight, per yard, 1 oz.

	Width, About	Per Yard
25K420........	1 in.	5c
25K421........	1⅜ in.	7c

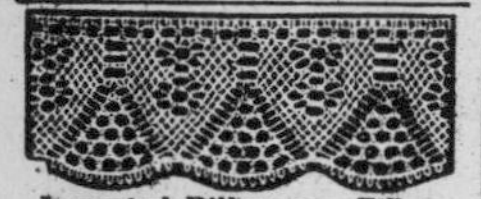

Imported Pillowcase Edges
Shipping weight, per yard, 1 ounce.

	Width, About	Per Yard
25K110—Edge..	2 in.	4c
25K111—Edge..	2⅜ in.	5c
25K112—Edge..	3½ in.	6c
25K113—Edge..	4⅛ in.	8c

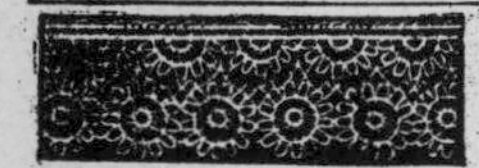

Imported Teneriffe Lace Set
Colors: White or ecru. **State color.** Shipping weight, per yard, 1 oz.

	Width, About	Per Yard
25K274—Edge..	½ in.	5c
25K275—Edge..	⅝ in.	6c
25K276—Edge..	1 in.	8c
25K277—Ins....	½ in.	6c

Imported Valenciennes Lace Set
Color: White only. Shipping weight, per yard, 1 ounce.

	Width, About	Per Yard
25K245—Edge..	½ in.	4c
25K246—Edge..	¾ in.	5c
25K247—Edge..	⅞ in.	6c
25K248—Edge..	1⅛ in.	7c
25K249—Ins....	¾ in.	5c

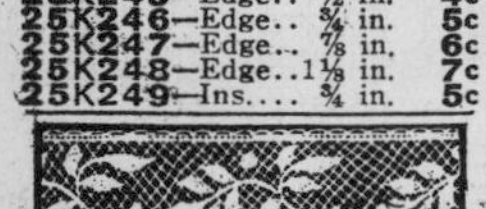

Imported Valenciennes Lace Set
Color: White only. Shipping weight, per yard, 1 oz.

	Width, About	Per Yard
25K270—Edge..	⅝ in.	6c
25K271—Edge..	¾ in.	7c
25K272—Edge..	1 in.	8c
25K273—Ins....	⅝ in.	6c

Imported Baby Valenciennes Lace Set
Shipping weight, 2 ounces.

	Width, About	12-Yd. Piece
25K324—Edge..	¼ in.	36c
25K325—Ins....	¼ in.	36c

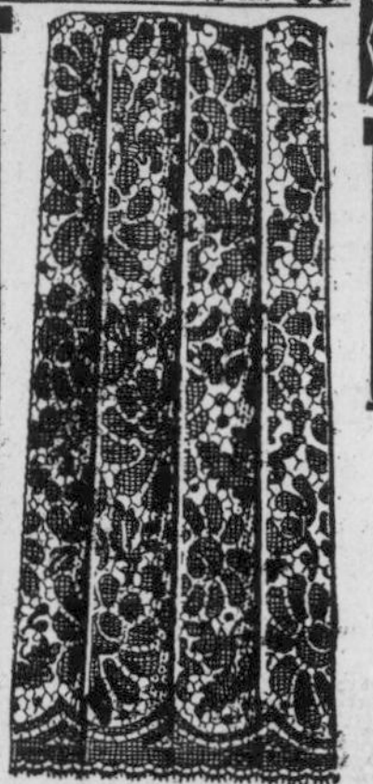

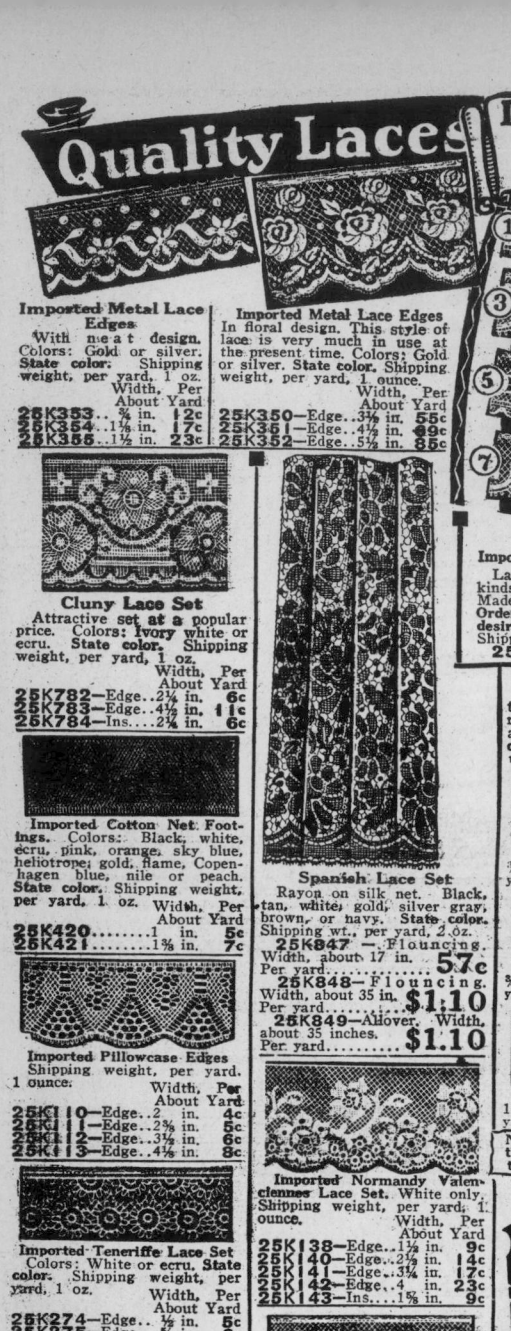

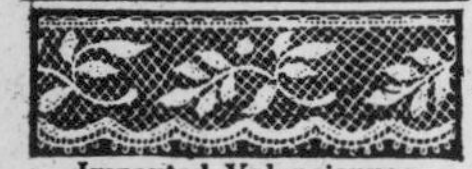

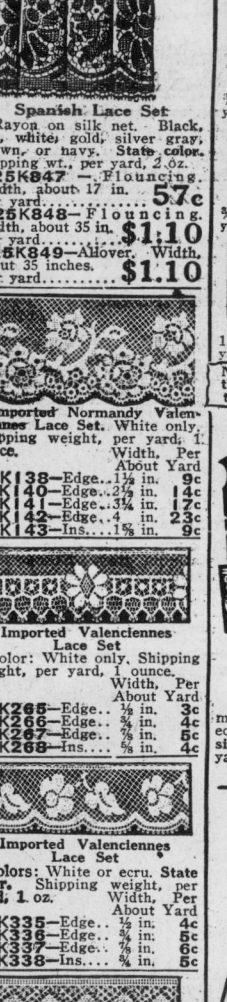

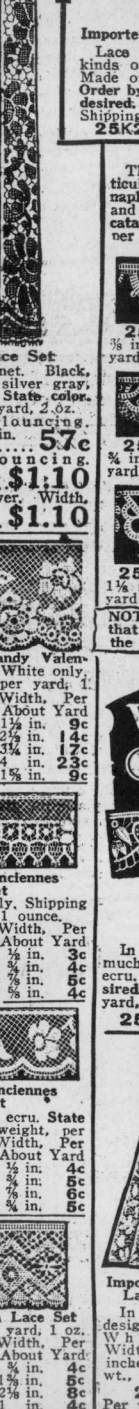

Spanish Lace Set
Rayon on silk net. Black, tan, white, gold, silver gray, brown, or navy. **State color.** Shipping wt., per yard, 2 oz.
25K847 — Flouncing. Width, about 17 in. Per yard.............. 57c
25K848—Flouncing. Width, about 35 in. Per yard.......... $1.10
25K849—Allover. Width, about 35 inches. Per yard......... $1.10

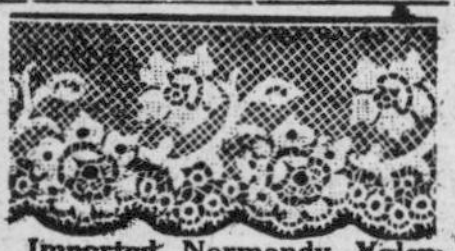

Imported Normandy Valenciennes Lace Set. White only. Shipping weight, per yard, 1 ounce.

	Width, About	Per Yard
25K138—Edge..	1½ in.	9c
25K140—Edge..	2⅓ in.	14c
25K141—Edge..	3¼ in.	17c
25K142—Edge..	4 in.	23c
25K143—Ins....	1⅝ in.	9c

Imported Valenciennes Lace Set
Color: White only. Shipping weight, per yard, 1 ounce.

	Width, About	Per Yard
25K265—Edge..	½ in.	3c
25K266—Edge..	¾ in.	4c
25K267—Edge..	⅞ in.	5c
25K268—Ins....	⅝ in.	4c

Imported Valenciennes Lace Set
Colors: White or ecru. **State color.** Shipping weight, per yard, 1 oz.

	Width, About	Per Yard
25K335—Edge..	½ in.	4c
25K336—Edge..	¾ in.	5c
25K337—Edge..	⅞ in.	6c
25K338—Ins....	¾ in.	5c

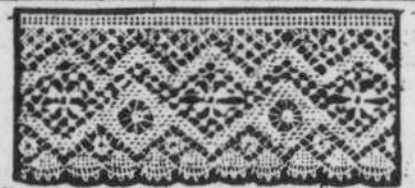

Imported Torchon Lace Set
Shipping weight, yard, 1 oz.

	Width, About	Per Yard
25K105—Edge..	¾ in.	4c
25K106—Edge..	1⅜ in.	5c
25K107—Edge..	2⅛ in.	8c
25K108—Ins....	1 in.	4c

Crochet Art Laces
The popular trimming for embroidered pieces. Particularly adapted for buffet sets, scarfs, centerpieces, napkins, vanities, towels, aprons, curtains, pillowcases and bedspreads. Made in white, cream or ecru. **State catalog number and color when ordering.** **Shpg.** wt., per yard, 1 oz.

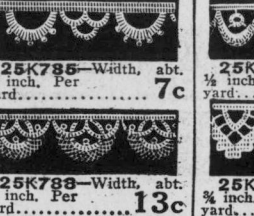

25K785—Width, abt. ⅜ inch. Per yard................ 7c

25K786—Width, abt ½ inch. Per yard........... 8c

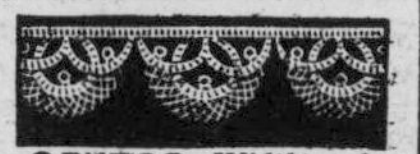

25K788—Width, abt. ¾ inch. Per yard............... 13c

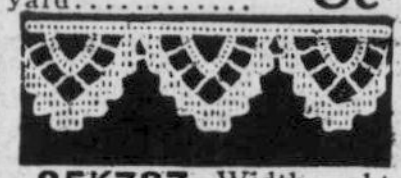

25K787—Width, abt. ¾ inch. Per yard............ 11c

25K789—Width, about 1⅛ inch. Per yard............... 14c

25K791—Width, abt. 1 inch. Per yard............ 16c

NOTE—Unless otherwise specified it will be understood that the laces on this page are made of cotton, that the color is white and that they are machine made.

Imported Venise Lace Edges

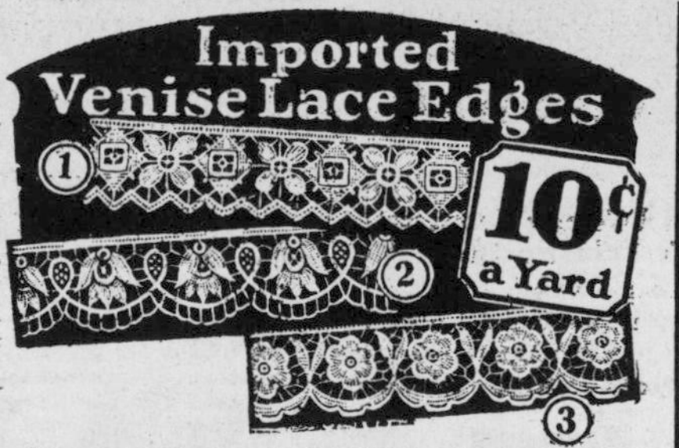

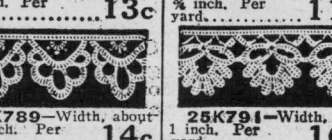

In neat patterns. Lace of this character is very much used for trimming purposes. Colors: White or ecru. **State color and number, indicating pattern desired.** Width, about ¾-inch. Shipping weight, per yard, 1 ounce.
25K659—Per yard.............................10c

Imported Lace Allovers

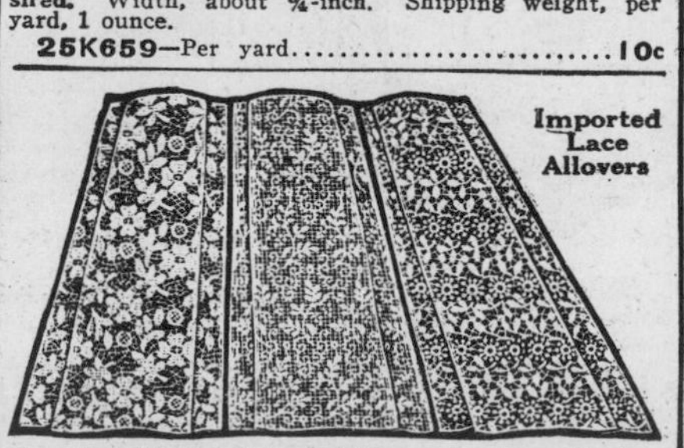

Imported Shadow Lace Allover
In neat floral design. Color: White only. Width, about 34 inches. Shipping wt., per yd., 2 oz.
25K316
Per yard......69c

Imported Oriental Lace Allover
Colors: White or ecru. **State color.** Width, about 18 inches. Shpg. wt., per yard, 2 oz.
25K755
Per yard...89c

Imported Venise Lace Allover
Colors: White or ecru. **State color.** Width, about 18 inches. Shpg. wt., per yard, 2 oz.
25K756
Per yard.$1.45

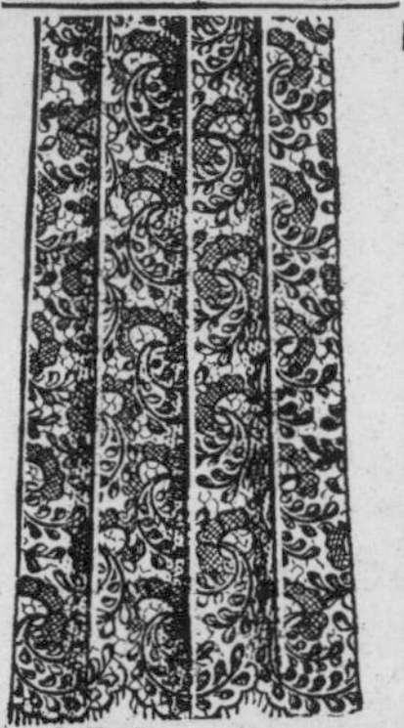

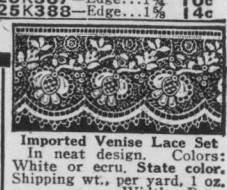

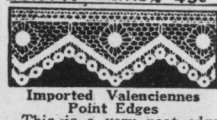

Silk Lace Set
Black, tan, white, gray or ecru. **State color.** Shipping weight, yard, 2 ounces.
25K833 — Edge. Width, about 6 inches. Per yard.35c
25K834 — Edge. Width, about 12 inches. Per yard.65c
25K835 — Flouncing. Width, about 17 in. Yard.95c
25K836 — Flouncing. Width, abt. 35 in. Yd..$1.65
25K837—Allover. Width, about 35 in. Per yard..$1.65

Imported Fancy Lace Set
Used for all kinds of fancy-work purposes. Shipping wt., per yard, 1 oz.

	Width, About	Per Yard
25K114—Edge..	2 in.	12c
25K115—Edge..	2¾ in.	15c
25K116—Edge..	4½ in.	21c
25K117—Ins....	2¾ in.	15c

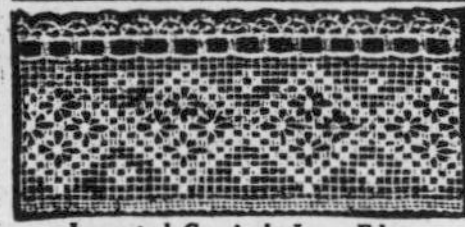

Imported Camisole Lace Edge
Width, about 3½ inches. Takes about ¼-inch ribbon. Shipping wt., per yard, 1 oz.
25K307—Per yard...19c

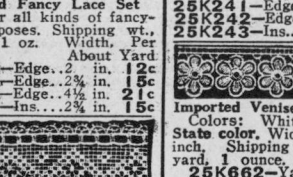

Imported Valenciennes Lace Beading Edge
Takes ⅛-inch ribbon. Width, about 1 inch. Shipping wt., per yard, 1 ounce.
25K333—Per yard... 7c

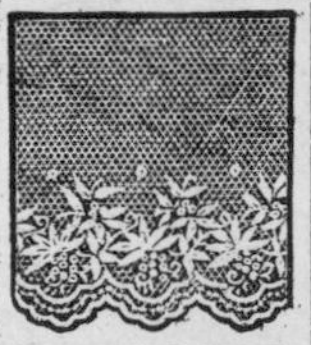

Imported Oriental Lace Edges
Colors: White or ecru. **State color.** Shipping weight, per yard, 1 oz.

	Width, Abt., In.	Per Yard
25K440 Edge....	3	16c
25K441 Edge....	4¾	25c
25K442 Edge....	6¼	33c

Imported Venise Lace Set
In neat design. Colors: White or ecru. **State color.** Shipping wt., per yard, 1 oz.

	Width, Abt. In.	Per Yard
25K444—Edge.	2	32c
25K445—Edge.	2¾	49c
25K446—Edge.	3½	57c
25K447—Ins...	2¾	49c

Imported Valenciennes Point Edges
This is a very neat edge and makes a dainty trimming. Color: White only. Shipping weight, per yard, 1 ounce.

	Width, Abt. In.	Per Yard
25K300—Edge..	¾	4c
25K301—Edge..	1	5c
25K302—Edge..	1⅛	6c
25K303—Edge..	1⅜	7c

Imported Calais Valenciennes Set
Colors: White or ecru. **State color.** Shipping wt., per yd., 1 oz.

	Width, Abt. In.	Per Yard
25K239—Edge..	⅝	4c
25K240—Edge..	1	5c
25K241—Edge..	1½	7c
25K242—Edge..	1¾	11c
25K243—Ins....	1⅛	5c

Imported Venise Lace Edge
Colors: White or ecru. **State color.** Width, about ⅝ inch. Shipping weight, per yard, 1 ounce.
25K662—Yard 16c

Imported Venise Lace Edge
Colors: White or ecru. **State color.** Width, about ¾ inch. Shipping weight, per yard, 1 ounce.
25K661—Yard 14c

Imported Tatting Lace Set
Color: White only. Shipping wt., per yard, 1 oz.

	Width, Abt. In.	Per Yard
25K310—Edge..	½	4c
25K311—Edge..	¾	5c
25K312—Edge..	1	6c
25K313—Ins....	⅝	4c

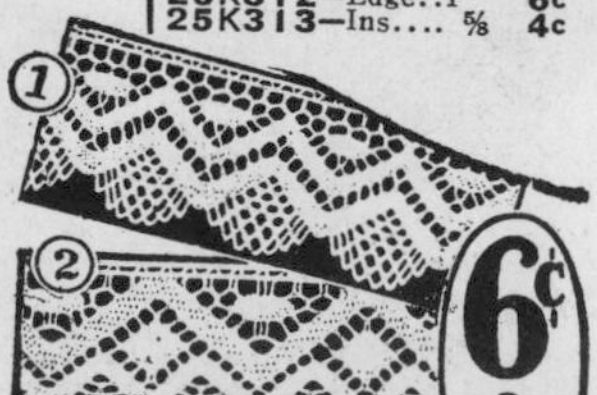

Imported Heavy Torchon Lace Edges
This style of lace is used extensively as a trimming for all kinds of fancy work. Color: White only. Width, about 2½ inches. **Order by catalog number and state number indicating pattern desired.** Shipping weight, per yard, 1 ounce.
25K205—Per yard.........6c

BUTTONS

We do not accept orders for smaller quantities than those listed in our catalog.

SCALE OF SIZES AND SHIPPING WEIGHTS

Lines	12	14	16	18	20	22	24
Size, inches	1/4	5/16	3/8	7/16	1/2	9/16	5/8
Shpg. wt., dozen, ounce	1	1	2	2	2	2	2
Lines	27	30	36	45	60	80	
Size, inches	11/16	3/4	7/8	1 1/8	1 1/2	2	
Shpg. wt., dozen, ounce	2	2	2	3	4	4	

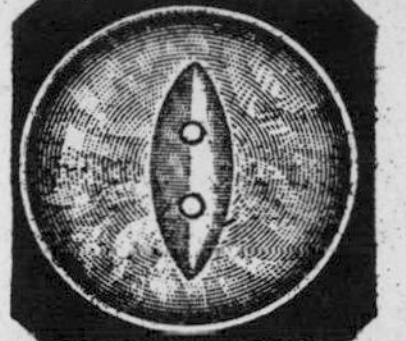

White Fisheye Pearl Buttons

25K5082 — First quality pearl buttons, made from fresh water white pearl. **State size.**

Size, Line	Per Doz.
12	6c
14	6c
16	7c
18	8c
20	9c
24	10c
30	14c
36	16c

Iridescent White Ocean Pearl Buttons

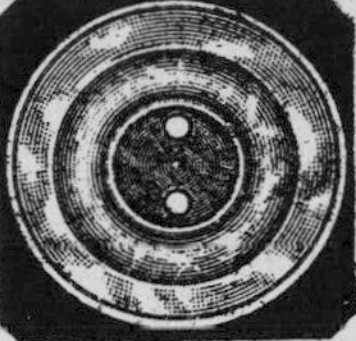

25K5095 These buttons are made of ocean pearl, which has a beautiful iridescent luster like the colors of the rainbow, and will make a striking trimming for any garment. They are made in ring design which further tends to bring out the exceptional luster. **State size.**

Size, Line	Per Doz.
14	9c
16	10c
18	12c
20	14c
22	16c
24	19c
30	25c
36	40c

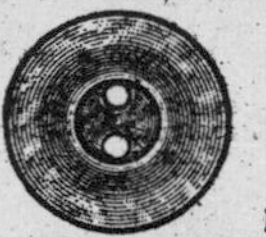

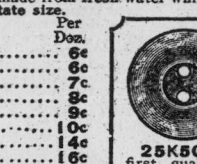

Cup Shape Fresh Water Pearl Buttons

25K5078—Made of first quality clear white pearl in two-hole cup shape. Just the button for shirtwaists and undergarments. **State size.**

Size, line	14	16	18
Per doz.	6c	6c	7c
Size, line	20	22	24
Per doz.	8c	9c	10c

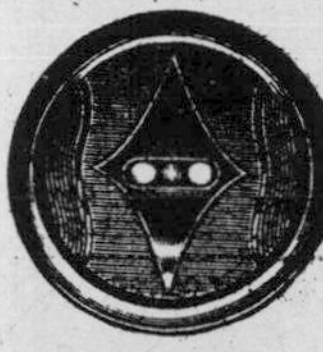

Colored Vegetable Ivory Buttons

A new and neat design; will make a very attractive trimming. Colors: Black, tan, brown, light green, red, Copenhagen, navy blue or orange. **State size and color.**

25K5120

Size, line	24	30
Dozen	20c	24c
Size, line	34	42
1/2 doz.	18c	33c

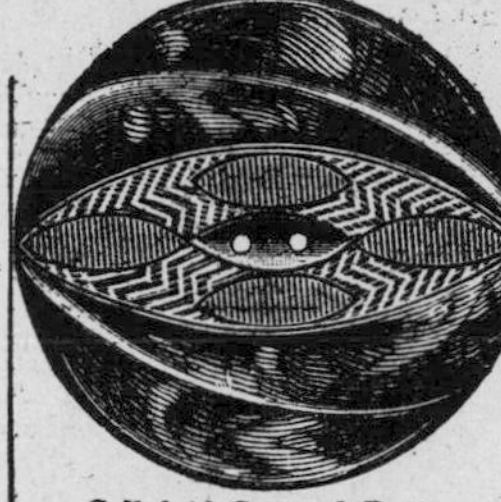

Celluloid Covered Buttons

Sutiable for women's and children's coats. Come in the following variegated colors: Black, tan, gray, Copenhagen blue, dark red or brown. **State color and size.** **25K5083**

30 line. Per dozen........25c
45 line. Per 1/2 dozen........24c
60 line. Per 1/2 dozen........36c
80 line. Per 1/4 dozen........33c

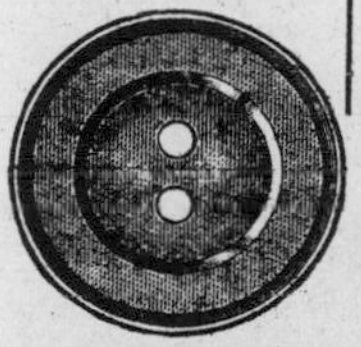

Colored Vegetable Ivory Trimming Buttons

25K5104—A popular design in a vegetable ivory button. Colors: Black, brown, navy blue, dark red, tan or gray. **State color and size.**

24 line. Per dozen........17c
30 line. Per dozen........22c
36 line. Per 1/2 dozen........19c
45 line. Per 1/2 dozen........33c

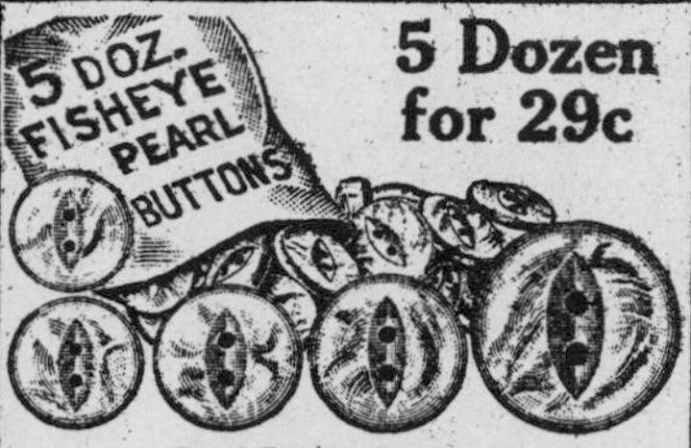

5 Dozen for 29c

Pearl Button Assortment

Contains the most popular sizes of good quality fisheye white pearl buttons. One dozen each size, 16, 18, 20, 22 and 24-line two-hole buttons. Shpg. wt., 6 oz.
25K5130—Assortment of 5 doz.. **29c**

BUCKLES

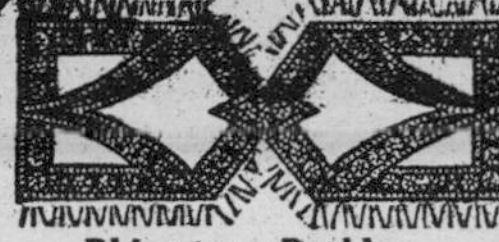

Rhinestone Buckles

Rich looking and stylish. Made of white metal set with rhinestones. Length, about 3 1/2 in. Width, about 1 1/4 in. Silver finish only. Shipping weight, 2 ounces.
25K5106
Per set........ **$1.50**

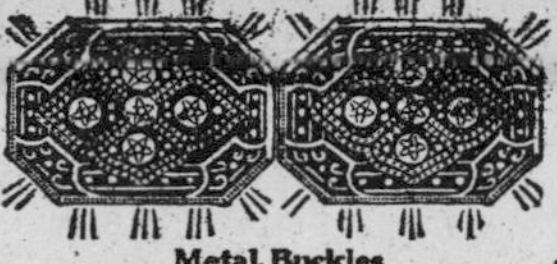

Metal Buckles

Imported metal buckles set with rhinestones. A most popular design. Size, about 1 1/8x2 7/8 inches. Gold or silver finish. **State color.** Shipping weight, 2 ounces.
25K5093—Per set.... **59c**

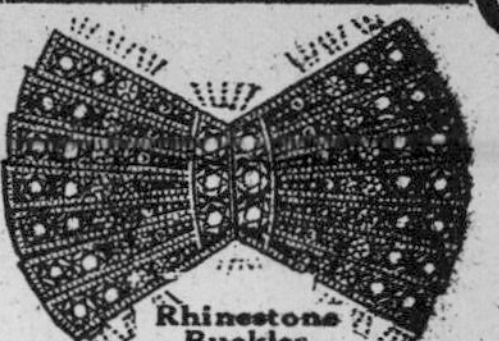

Rhinestone Buckles

One of the most popular shaped and effective buckles. Made of white metal, set with rhinestones in fan shape. Length, about 2 1/8 inches. Silver finish only. Shpg wt., 2 oz.
25K5105—Set.. **$1.00**

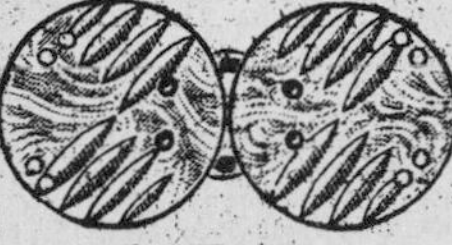

Pearl Buckles

A very popular trimming for dresses. Made of iridescent ocean pearl. Diameter of each buckle, about 1 1/8 inches. Colors: Iridescent white or natural black. **State color.** Shipping wt., 2 oz.
25K5089
Per set........ **29c**

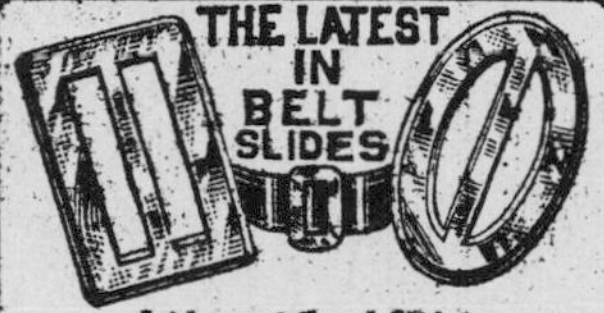

Iridescent Pearl Slides

Made of iridescent ocean pearl. Used for trimming dresses and millinery. Come in iridescent white or natural black. **State catalog number, size and color.** Shipping weight, 2 ounces.

25K5096—Oblong.
1 x1 1/4-inch. Each........17c
1 1/4x2 -inch. Each........29c

25K5097—Oval.
1 1/4-in. Each. 17c 2-in. Each. 29c

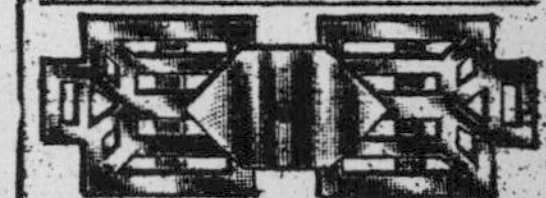

Latest in Fancy Metal Buckles

May be used for all purposes where buckles are used. Colors: Gold with steel center or steel with gold center. **State color.** Size, 1 1/8x2 1/8 in. Shipping weight, 2 ounces.
25K3785—Per set.. **21c**

Koh-I-Noor Shoe Fastener and Ornament

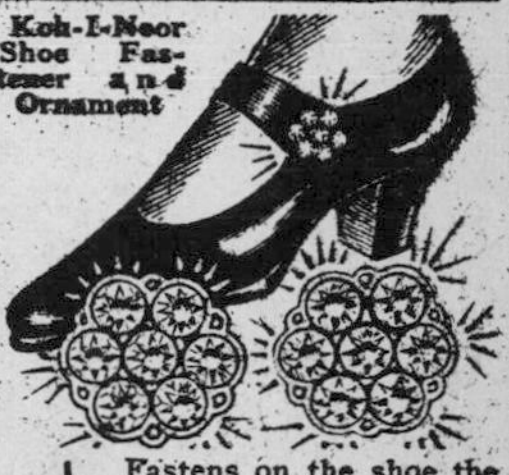

Fastens on the shoe the same as bachelor button; interchangeable. Button part is made of white metal set with rhinestones. Easy to put on. Set consists of one pair rhinestone fasteners with complete attachments. Size, about 1/2 inch. Shipping wt., 2 oz.
25K5107—Set. **59c**

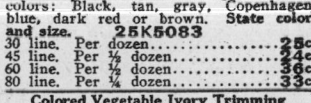

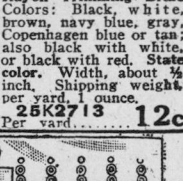

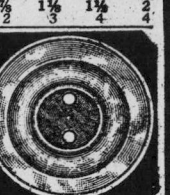

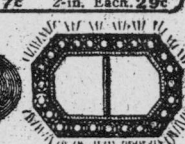

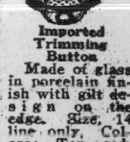

Metal Slide

A popular trimming for dresses, made of metal with filigree work and set with rhinestones. Size, abt. 1 3/4x1 inch. Silver or gold finish. **State color.** Shipping weight, 2 oz.
25K5092
Each........ **33c**

Rhinestone Slide

A stylish trimming for dresses. Made of white metal set with rhinestones. Size, abt. 1 7/8x1 1/4 inches. Silver finish only. Shipping weight, 2 ounces.
25K5101
Each........ **50c**

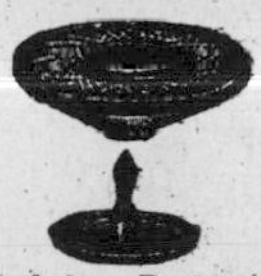

Bachelor Buttons

Lock or unlock by raising top. Black or khaki. Size, 27 line. **State color.** Shpg. wt., 2 oz.
25K5094
Pkg. of 6... **8c**

22

Bone Buttons

Colors: Black or white. **State color and size.** Shpg. wt., of 6 doz., 5 oz.
25K5091
22 line. 6 doz. 17c
27 line. 6 doz. 21c

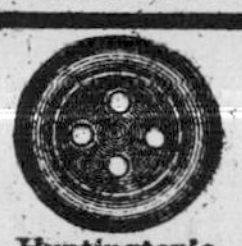

Huntington's "Ever On" Rubber Button

Will not break going through the wringer. Made of vulcanized rubber. White or black. **State size and color.** **25K5087**
22 line. Doz.... 8c
27 line. Doz.... 9c

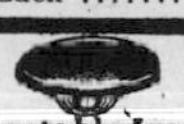

Vegetable Ivory Buttons

A popular design for trimming dresses, shirt waists and children's garments. Colors: Black, white, gray, lavender, green, red, tan, navy, Copenhagen blue, light blue or tangerine. **State color.**
25K5071—Size, 16 line only.
Per dozen.. **10c**

Rhinestone Buttons

Set in dull glass background. Size, 10 line. Colors: White with black back, or white with white back; also in red, jade, royal blue, amethyst with white back. **State color.**
25K5099 Per dozen. **9c**

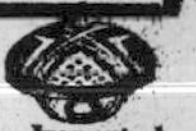

Imported Trimming Button

Made of glass in porcelain finish with gilt design on the edge. Size, 14 line only. Colors: Tan, red, royal blue, gray, green or black. **State color.**
25K5108
Per dozen.... **9c**

Rayon and Tinsel Braid

Comes in the following colors combined with gold tinsel: Black, Copenhagen, gold, orange, rose, red, brown, tan or jade. **State color.** Width, about 3/8 inch. Shpg. wt., per yd., 1 oz.
25K2717
Per yard........ **8c**

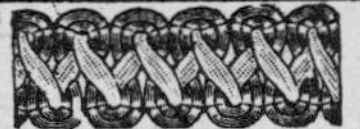

Rayon Trimming Braid

Colors: Black, white, brown, navy blue, gray, Copenhagen blue or tan; also black with white, or black with red. **State color.** Width, about 1/2 inch. Shipping weight, per yard, 1 ounce.
25K2713
Per yard........ **12c**

Embroideries

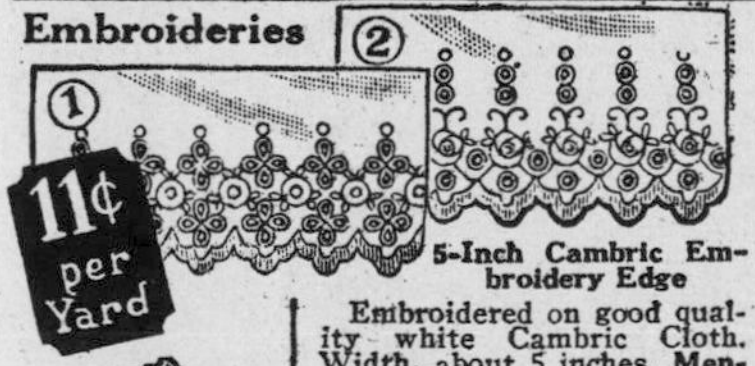

5-Inch Cambric Embroidery Edge

Embroidered on good quality white Cambric Cloth. Width, about 5 inches. **Mention pattern number.**
25K2014
Per yard........ **11c**

Shpg. wt., all embroideries, per yard, 1 oz.

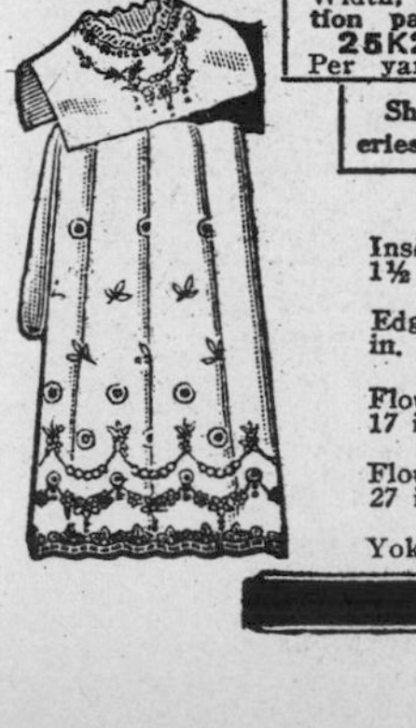

Swiss Baby Set

25K2020
Insertion. Width, about 1 1/2 in. Per yard... 13c
25K2021
Edge. Width, about 4 in. Per yard...... 23c
25K2022
Flouncing. Width, about 17 in. Per yard.... 57c
25K2023
Flouncing. Width, about 27 in. Per yard.... 79c
25K2024
Yoke to match. Ea. 29c

DRESS TRIMMINGS

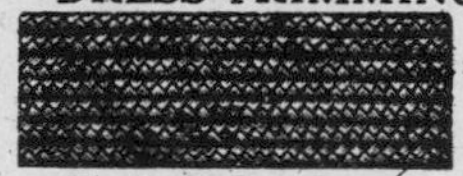

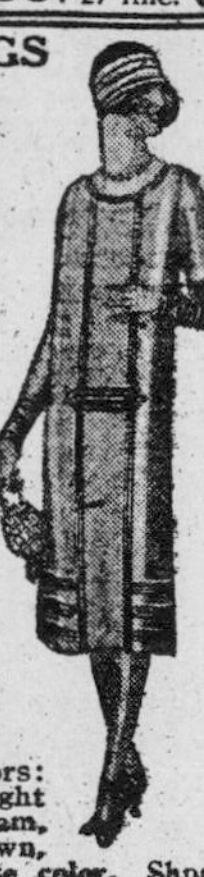

F. A. Quality Rayon Trimming Braid

Colors: Black, white, tan, navy blue, brown, cardinal, jade, gold, Copenhagen, orchid, rose or gray. **State width and color.** Shipping weight, per yard, 1 ounce.

25K2730

Width, Abt.	Per Yd.
3/8 inch	5c
5/8 inch	7c
3/4 inch	9c
15/16 inch	10c
1 1/8 inches	12c

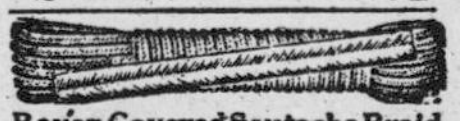

Rayon Covered Soutache Braid.

Width, about 1/8 in. Colors: Black, white, navy blue, light blue, pink, Alice blue, tan, cream, dark green, scarlet, wine, brown, gray, gold or cardinal. **State color.** Shpg. wt., 2 oz. Sold only in 6-yard pieces.
25K3774—6-yard piece........ **9c**
25K3776—Gold or silver colored tinsel covered soutache braid. **State color.** 6-yard piece........20c

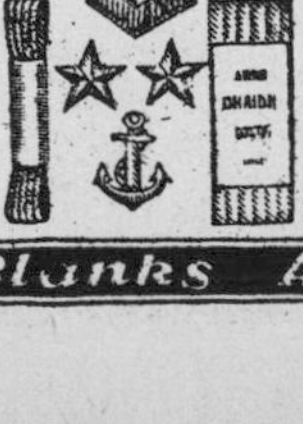

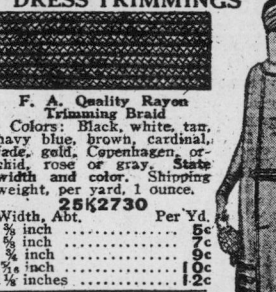

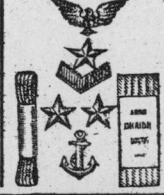

Rayon Embroidered Combination Middy Set

This comprises the eagle, three stars, anchor, chevron, middy lacer and a 3-yard piece of Peter Thompson braid. Colors: Black, white, red, navy blue or gold. **State color.** Shipping weight, 2 ounces.
25K3763
Per set........ **23c**

Rayon Trimming Braid

Color combinations: Black and Persian; navy blue and Persian; brown and Persian; tan and Persian, or gray and Persian. **State color.** Width, about 1 3/4 in. Shipping weight, per yard, 1 ounce.
25K2710
Per yard........ **33c**

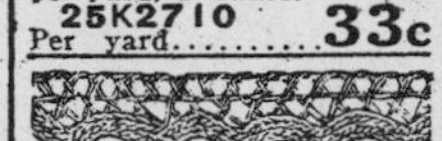

Very Neat Tinsel Edge

May be used for trimming lamp shades, dresses, etc. Colors: Antique gold, bright gold, steel or silver. **State color.** Width, about 3/8 inch. Shipping weight, per yard, 1 ounce.
25K2704
Per yard........ **10c**

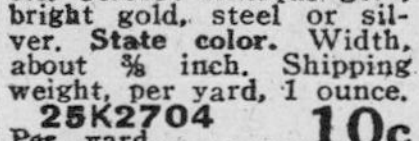

Fancy Metal Braid

Can be used for lamp shades; also for dress trimming. Colors: Antique gold or steel. **State color.** Width, about 1/2 inch. Shpg. wt., per yd., 1 oz.
25K2720
Per yard........ **10c**

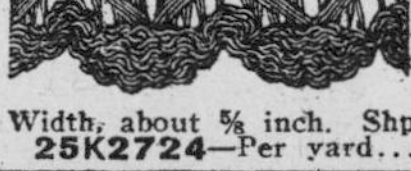

Fancy Metal Edge

Very desirable for trimming lamp shades and fancy work; also for dress trimming. Colors: Antique gold or steel. **State color.** Width, about 5/8 inch. Shpg. wt., yard, 1 oz.
25K2724—Per yard........ **15c**

Rayon Rosebud Trimming

Combination colors: Rose and light blue; pink and light blue; pink and green; pink and white, or light blue and white. **State color.** Width, about 3/8 in. Shpg. wt., yd., 1 oz.
25K2716—Yd. **21c**

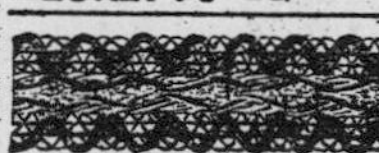

Rayon Fancy Novelty Trimming

Combinations with tinsel: Rose, green, Copenhagen, cardinal, lavender or black. **State color.** Width, about 1/2 in. Shpg. wt., per yard, 1 oz.
25K2700—Per yd.. 7c

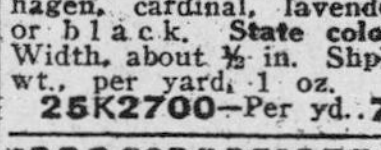

Rayon Buttonhole and Trimming Braid

Saves making buttonholes. Colors: Black, navy blue, dark brown, Copenhagen, gray, tan or white. **State color.** Size of braid, 1/8 in.; 1/2-in. loop. Shpg. wt., per yard, 1 oz.
25K2703—Per yd. 9c

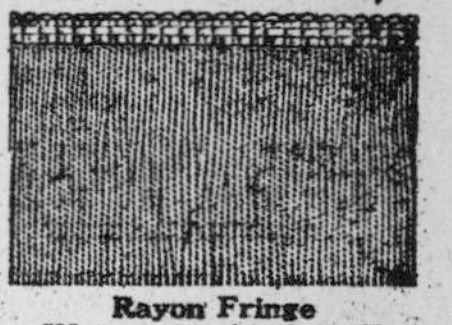

Rayon Fringe

Woven top border. For dress trimming; also for lamp shades, etc. Colors: Black, navy blue, brown, white, Copenhagen blue, tan, gold or old rose. **State color and width.** Shpg. wt., per yd., 1 oz.

25K2722

Width, Abt.	Per Yd.
2 inches	19c
4 inches	39c
6 inches	59c
12 inches	97c

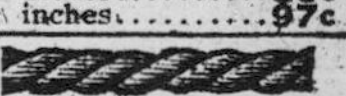

Rayon Covered Cord

Colors: Black, white, pink, navy blue, medium brown, tan, cardinal, gold, gray or Alice blue. **State color.** Width, about 1/8 in. Shpg. wt., per yd., 1 oz.
25K2796—Per yd. 5c

Rayon Tassels

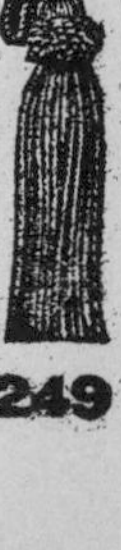

Colors: Black, white, medium brown, navy blue, gold, pink, cardinal, dark green, light blue or old rose. **State color and size.** Shipping wt., 2 oz.

25K3780

Length	Each
2 3/4 inches	8c
4 1/2 inches	12c
6 inches	15c
8 inches	21c

Order Blanks Are in Back of This Catalog

249

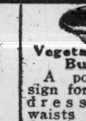

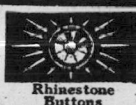

Sanitary Necessities

The fastidious woman of today demands correct fitting in gowns and dresses. The same is equally true about sanitary garments. The selection of sanitary goods that we sell has been created with that purpose in mind, so that we can always supply the exact size you want.

Kleinert's All Gum Rubber Sanitary Apron

Made of pure gum rubber. Easily cleaned. Will not cling to the body and will prevent wrinkles when worn under silk dresses. Width, about 20 in.; length, about 21 in. Colors: Natural rubber or flesh color with crossbar voile top. State color. Shpg. wt., 4 oz.
25K5045........**39c**

Kleinert's Sanitary Step-In

A very popular and serviceable sanitary garment. Made of a good grade cotton voile top and pure gum rubber. Has elastic at the waistline. A loose fitting, comfortable and light garment. Colors: Flesh or white. Sizes: Small, medium or large. State size and color. Shipping weight, 4 oz.
25K5054—Each............**45c**

Sanitary Bloomers

An ideal sanitary garment that will give you comfort, security and protection. Made of crossbar cotton voile top with pure gum rubber seat and elastic at waistline. The leg openings are trimmed with Valenciennes lace. A garment that we know you will like. Comes in sizes: Small, medium or large. State size. Flesh color only. Shpg. wt., 5 oz.
25K5055..............**89c**

Kleinert's Silk Sanitary Apron

Lightweight sanitary apron made of rubber coated silk. It affords proper protection and can be worn under the lightest weight garments. Will also prevent wrinkles when worn under silk dresses. Has crossbar Rayon voile top and well bound edges. Pink only. Width, about 20½ inches. Length, about 21 inches. Shipping wt., 2 oz.
25K5053.......**79c**

The sanitary goods shown on this and the opposite page are of standard quality. We do not handle inferior grades, but believe that the best is the least expensive.

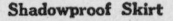

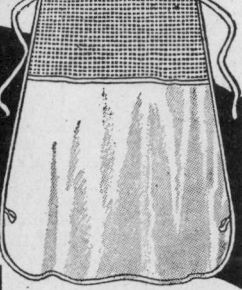

Kleinert's Sanitary Bloomers

Pure gum rubber with all seams cemented. Has rubber binding at knees and waistline which does away with renewing of elastic. Has openings at sides, making them more comfortable to wear. Easily cleaned. Natural rubber or flesh color, in sizes, small, medium or large. State size and color. Shipping weight, 8 ounces.
25K5062...........**98c**

Shadowproof Skirt

A shadowproof skirt that can be used as a sanitary garment, and will prevent wrinkles when worn under silk dresses. Made of a good quality crossbar voile, with gum rubber inserted in the back. Elastic at waistline. Comes in white or flesh color. Sizes: 24, 26, 28, 30 and 32 inches waist measure. Length, about 21 inches. State color and size. Shpg. wt., 5 oz.
25K5058............**65c**

Brassiere and Sanitary Princess Slip

A combination that serves as a brassiere and a sanitary garment and, at the same time, is shadowproof. The brassiere part is made of a good quality Rayon striped corset cloth. The slip of a fine quality voile. Trimmed with Valenciennes lace on the bottom. Lined in the back with pure gum rubber. Will prevent wrinkles when worn under silk dresses. Flesh color only. Comes in sizes: 32 to 44 inches bust measure. State size desired. Shipping weight, 6 oz. **$2.15**
25K5043—Each............

For Other Sanitary Articles for Women See Page 641.

Shadowproof Sanitary Skirt

Can be worn as a sanitary garment, will prevent wrinkles when worn under silk dresses and is shadowproof. Made of a high grade Rayon mixed mull with satin stripe. Has pure gum rubber inserted at the back and elastic at the waistline and trimmed with lace at the bottom. Length, about 21 inches. Sizes: Medium or large. Flesh color only. State size. Shipping wt., 4 ounces.
25K5051—Each.....**98c**

Kleinert's Rubberized Sanitary Apron

The rubber coating is a very fine grade and is the natural color of the rubber. Will stand boiling water for the purpose of sterilization. Has net top and loops for fastening to garters. We strongly recommend this apron. Width, about 22 inches; length, about 21 in. Shpg. wt., 4 oz.
25K5042.........**59c**

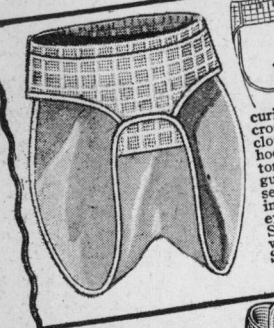

Sanitary Step-In

This tailored garment is form fitting and lends itself to the shape of the body, which gives you the most comfort and perfect security. The top is made of crossbar cotton cloth, which closes on the side with hooks and eyes. The bottom part is made of pure gum rubber with a cemented seam in the center. Fastens in front with hooks and eyes. Flesh color only. Sizes, from 24 to 34 inches waist measure. State size. Shpg. wt., 4 oz.
25K5040—Each **89c**

Kleinert's Santalette

An ideal sanitary garment. Made of a high grade mercerized marquisette top with pure gum rubber seat. Has rubber binding at waist and leg openings, which does away with renewing of elastic. Will not bind. Comes in flesh color or white with natural rubber. Sizes: Medium or large. State size and color. Shipping weight, 5 ounces.
25K5056
Each...........**85c**

NOBYND

"Nobynd" sanitary goods have been designed to meet the demand for comfortable, form fitting, hygienic garments. They are made of better quality materials and sold at very reasonable prices.

NOTE—Our Sanitary Articles Are Standard Quality. We Do Not Handle Inferior Grades. We Believe the Best Is the Most Economical.

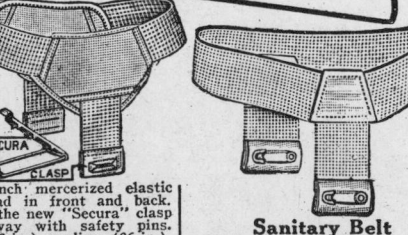

"Nobynd" Sanitary Belt

Made of a 2-inch mercerized elastic with a porous linen mesh pad in front and back. Sizes: Small (23 in.), medium (26 in.), large (30 in.), and extra large (34 in.). White or flesh color. Shpg. wt., 3 oz.
25K5031........**39c**

"Nobynd" Sanitary Belt

Sizes, 24 to 40 Inches Waist Measure.
A high grade well tailored belt. Made of 2-inch wide good grade mercerized elastic webbing with sateen inserted in front and back. Flesh color only. Sizes: 24, 26, 28, 30, 32, 34, 36, 38 and 40 inches waist measure. State size. Shipping wt., 3 ounces.
25K5038.................**55c**

"Nobynd" Sanitary Belt

Made of a 2-inch white elastic webbing with coutil inserted in front and back. Comfortable and well fitting with extra length tabs. Sizes: Small (23 in.), medium (26 in.), large (30 in.), and extra large (34 in.). State size. Shipping weight, 3 ounces.
25K5032.................**29c**

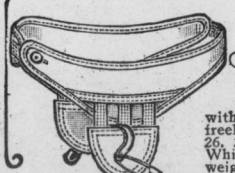

"Nobynd" Sanitary Belt

Made of good quality mercerized elastic with porous linen mesh pads in front and back. Buttons in front. Has sateen tabs and safety pins attached. Comfortable and well fitting. White or flesh color. Sizes: Small (23 in.), medium (26 in.), large (30 in.), and extra large (34 in.). State size and color. Shipping weight, 4 ounces.
25K5028.................**45c**

"Hickory" Sanitary Belt

Made of 2-inch mercerized elastic with sateen pad in front and back. Equipped with the new "Secura" clasp which does away with safety pins. Sizes: Small (23 in.), medium (26 in.), large (30 in.), and extra large (34 in.). Colors: White or flesh color. Shpg. wt., 3 oz.
25K5026.................**39c**

Sanitary Belt

Made of 2-inch good grade elastic webbing with extra long tabs. Comes in white or flesh. Sizes: Small (23 in.), medium (26 in.), large (30 in.), extra large (34 in.). State size and color. Shpg. wt., 3 oz.
25K5030.................**19c**

"Nobynd" Sateen Sanitary Belt

A well fitting belt made of a high grade sateen. The tabs are fastened to the belt with three strands of ⅝-inch elastic, so it gives freely to the movements of the body. Sizes, 24, 26, 28, 30, 32, 34 and 36 inches waist measure. White or flesh. State size and color. Shipping weight, 3 ounces.
25K5041.................**39c**

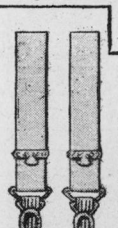

Save Money on Art Materials

Paintex gives you the rainbow to play with! Paintex—the wonderful new fabric paint, and Paintex liquid embroidery. At last—embroidery without a needle! Unlimited scope to express individuality.

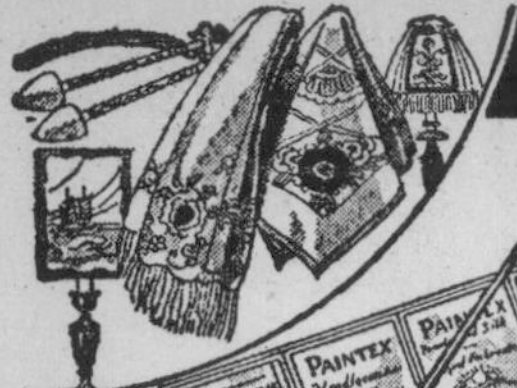

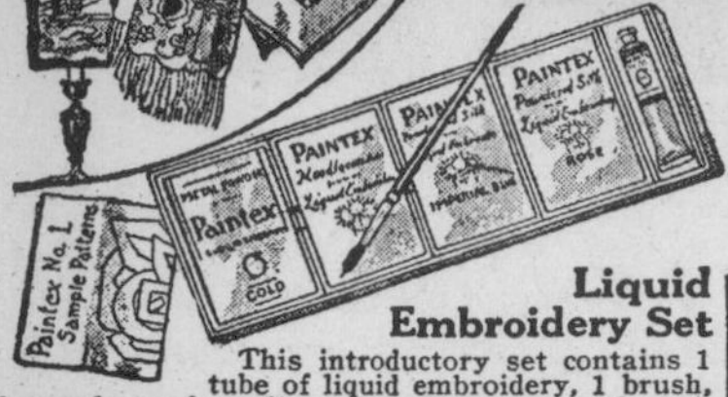

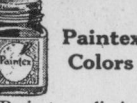

Paintex No. 1 Sample Patterns
Paintex

Liquid Embroidery Set

This introductory set contains 1 tube of liquid embroidery, 1 brush, 1 envelope of needle cones, 6 envelopes of powdered silk, rose, topaz, orange, imperial blue, emerald and purple; 2 envelopes of powdered metal, 1 gold and 1 silver. Sample pattern. Complete instructions. Shpg. wt., ¾ lb.
25K4762—Per set............... **$1.75**

Liquid Embroidery

Equally good on silks, linens, cottons and other fabrics of all shades. **White only.** Complete instructions. Shipping weight, 2 ounces.
25K4763
Per tube........ **43c**

Paintex Needle Cones

To be used with liquid embroidery. 1 envelope containing 6 cones. Shipping wt., 1 ounce.
25K4764
6 for............ **8c**

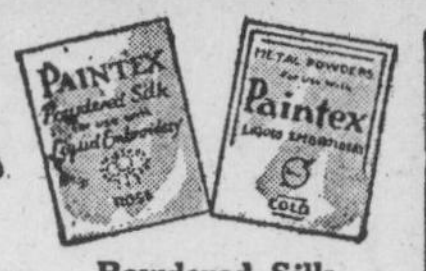

Paintex

Powdered Silk

Comes in colors same as 25K4765 at right, with white additional. **State color.** Shipping weight, 1 ounce.
25K4766
Per envelope... **17c**

Powdered Metal

Colors: Silver, gold, copper, steel, blue, red, green and purple. **State color.** Shipping weight, 1 ounce.
25K4767
Per envelope... **17c**

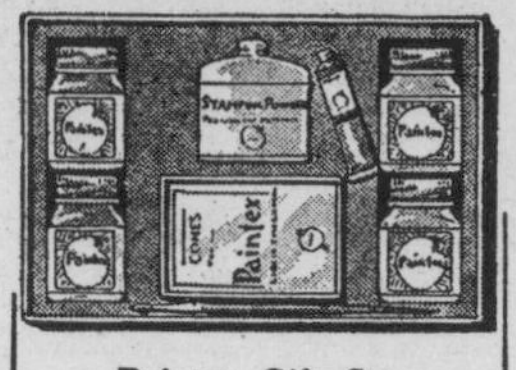

Paintex Gift Set

This set consists of three 1-ounce bottles of Paintex, 1 bottle of medium, which is used to lighten or thicken Paintex; 1 brush, 1 tube liquid embroidery, 2 envelopes powdered metal, 1 gold and 1 silver; 1 envelope needle cones, 1 perforated sample pattern, 1 box of stamping powder for use with pattern. Complete instructions. Shipping weight, 1¾ pound.
25K4761—Per set.............. **$2.60**

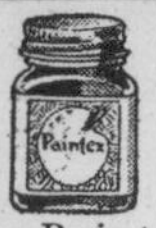

Paintex Colors

Paintex eliminates the necessity for any preparing of material either before or after color is applied. Colors: Lemon, topaz, orange, flame, scarlet, ruby, coral, rose, pink, lavender, heliotrope, purple, powder blue, light blue, turquoise, imperial blue, navy, dark green, emerald, light green, tan, brown, gray, black or medium (to lighten or thicken color). **State color.** Shpg. wt., 6 oz.
25K4765
Each, bottle... **29c**

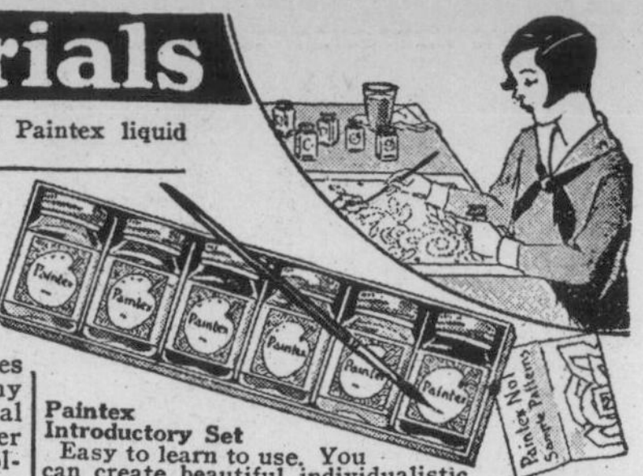

Paintex Introductory Set

Easy to learn to use. You can create beautiful individualistic apparel and many decorations so quickly it seems incredible. Set contains six 1-ounce bottles of Paintex, one each of the following colors: Orange, topaz, rose, emerald, imperial blue, and purple; one brush, one sample pattern and complete instructions included. Shipping weight, 1¾ pounds.
25K4760—Per set........ **$1.50**

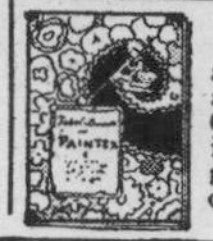

Paintex Instruction Book

(Fabric decorations with Paintex and liquid embroidery.) A remarkable book on color decorations. Color harmony chart. Over 85 illustrations in color. 100 gift suggestions, etc. Shipping weight, 2 ounces.
25K4768—Each..... **25c**

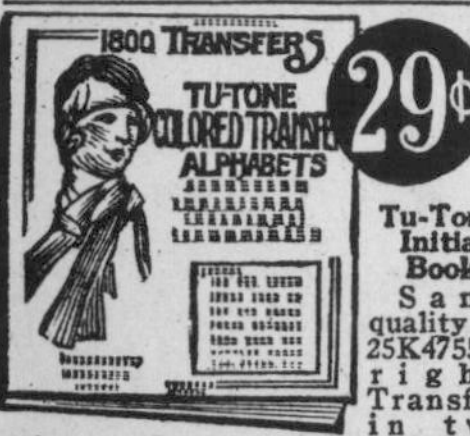

1800 TRANSFERS
TU-TONE COLORED TRANSFER ALPHABETS
29¢

Tu-Tone Initial Book

Same quality as 25K4755 at right. Transfers in two colors. Contains 12 alphabets: Old English, Italian, Floral and Script in five sizes, ½, ⅝, 1½ and 2 inches. Guaranteed to transfer six times; equal to 1,800 transfers. Also 1 page monogram brackets. Shpg. wt., 2 oz.
25K4753—Per book.... **29c**

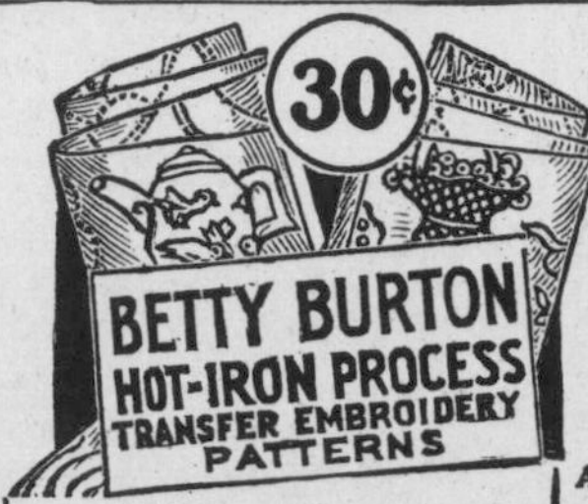

30¢
BETTY BURTON
HOT-IRON PROCESS
TRANSFER EMBROIDERY
PATTERNS

Embroidery Patterns

We believe this is the most comprehensive assortment ever offered at such a low price. Contains 230 designs, fourteen alphabets in Old English and Script, six alphabets in monograms, flowers, birds, fruit, towel and pillowcase ends, etc., and 30 dainty patterns for infants' wear. Shipping weight, 5 ounces.
25K4750—Per package.................. **30c**

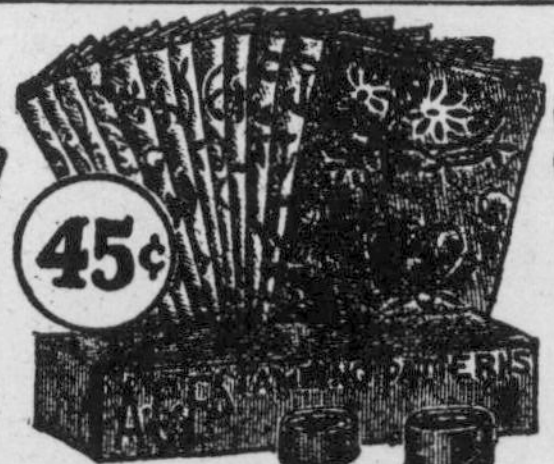

45¢

A. C. E. Stamping Pattern Outfit

Twelve large sheets. Over 100 latest patterns for stamping linens, etc. Two alphabets. One cake each of blue and white stamping wax with each set. Shpg. wt., 1 lb.
25K4744.......................... **45c**

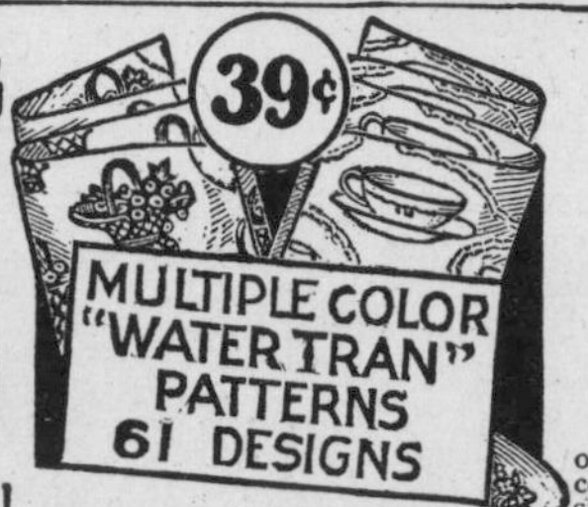

39¢
MULTIPLE COLOR
"WATER TRAN"
PATTERNS
61 DESIGNS

A new process that transfers in the colors in which they are to be embroidered. Simply use water and rub. Guaranteed to transfer six or more times. Contains designs of flower sprays, motifs, luncheon sets, handkerchief corners, etc. Two sheets for needle embroidery and two sheets for hand painting with Paintex or liquid embroidery. Shipping weight, 4 ounces.
25K4755—Per pkg...... **39c**

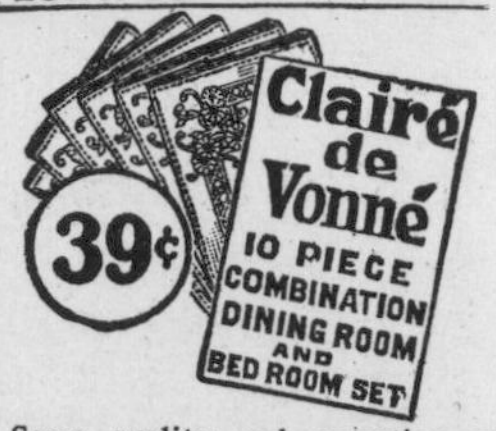

Clairé de Vonné
10 PIECE COMBINATION DINING ROOM AND BED ROOM SET
39¢

Same quality and execution as our Betty Burton Outfit 25K4750 consisting of 1 bedspread, 1 bolster, 1 comfort pillow, 1 bedside table cover, 4 curtain ends, 1 dresser scarf, 1 pincushion.
Will give individuality to your rooms. Full instructions. Shipping weight, 4 ounces.
25K4751—Set...... **39c**

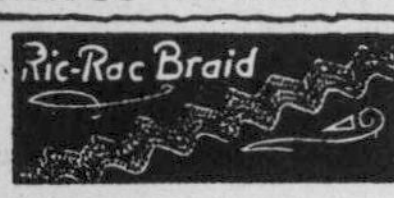

Ric-Rac Braid

Cotton Ric-Rac Braid

For trimming. **White only. State size.** Shipping weight, 2 ounces.

25K4738	12 Yds.
Width, about ⅜ in.	19c
Width, about ½ in.	21c
Width, about ⅝ in.	24c
Width, about ¾ in.	27c
Width, about 13/16 in.	30c
Width, about 14/16 in.	34c

Fine white cotton thread.

Mercerized Ric-Rac Braid

Measured from point to point. **State size.**

25K4743	12 Yds.
Width, about ⅜ in.	26c
Width, about ½ in.	28c
Width, about ⅝ in.	31c
Width, about ¾ in.	36c
Width, about 13/16 in.	40c
Width, about 14/16 in.	45c

Mercerized cotton colored Ric-Rac braid, 3 yards to piece. Size, ⅝ in. Black, light blue, pink, reseda, red, gold, lavender, old rose or delft. **State color.**
25K4745—Per piece..... **9c**

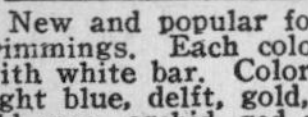

New and popular for dainty trimmings. Each color comes with white bar. Colors: Pink, light blue, delft, gold, orange, old rose, orchid, red or black. **State color.** Width, ⅝ inch. Three yards to piece. Shipping weight, 2 ounces.
25K4747—Per piece... **9c**

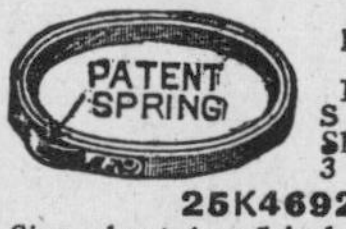

PATENT SPRING

Wooden Embroidery Hoops

Round shape, **State size.** Shipping wt., 3 ounces.
25K4692
Size, about 4 or 5 inches...... **12c**
Size, about 6 or 7 inches...... **14c**
Size, about 8 inches.......... **15c**
Oval shape. Sizes, 4½x9 inches or 6x12 inches. **State size.**
25K4694 .... **14c**

Embroidery Needles

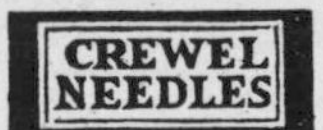

CREWEL NEEDLES

Good quality Crewel embroidery Needles. Twenty-five to the paper. Sizes, 3 to 9 or 5 to 10. **State size.** Shipping weight, 1 oz.
25K4690—Per paper..... **9c**

⅝ IN.

Imported Bone Rings

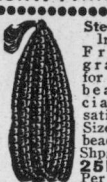

For bags, curtains, fancywork, etc. White or black. **State color and size.** Shipping weight, 2 ounces. Outside measurements.
25K4741
Size, about ⅝-in. Doz....... **8c**
Size, about ¾-in. Doz....... **10c**
Size, about 1-in. Doz....... **12c**

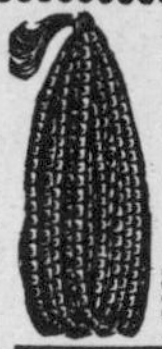

Steel Beads

Imported from France. Best grade. Desirable for all kinds of beadwork, especially handbags, satin slippers, etc. Size 8, about 1,200 beads to a hank. Shpg. wt., 2 ozs.
25K4684
Per hank.... **15c**

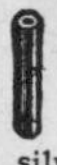

Bugle Beads

For trimming waists, dresses, hats, etc., as well as fancywork. Colors: White (satin), opal, black, gold, steel, silver, gunmetal, bronze, cherry red, periwinkle blue, iridescent purple, iridescent blue, iridescent brown or iridescent green. **State color.** Hanks consist of about 600 beads. Shpg. wt., 3 ozs.
25K4673—Per hank.................... **10c**

Colored Cut Glass Beads

Brilliant appearance, highest grade. Colors: White satin, crystal, canary, amethyst, bronze, nile green, amber, silver, gold, turquoise blue, steel, black, periwinkle blue, sand, wine red, cherry red, emerald green, medium pink, iridescent purple, iridescent brown, iridescent blue or iridescent green. About 1,000 beads to hank. **State color.** Shipping weight, 3 ounces.
25K4677—Per hank.................... **7c**

Rhinestones

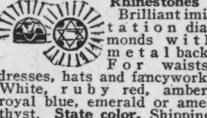

Brilliant imitation diamonds with metal back. For waists, dresses, hats and fancywork. White, ruby red, amber, royal blue, emerald or amethyst. **State color.** Shipping weight, 2 ounces.
25K4680
36 for.............. **20c**
Same as above, but put up 144 to the string. **State color.** Shipping weight, 2 ounces.
25K4681
144 for............. **69c**

English Cut Glass Beads

For trimming dresses, and other fancywork purposes. 600 to bunch. Colors: Black, bronze, iridescent blue, steel or cherry red. **State color.** Shipping weight, 3 ounces.
25K4675
Per bunch........... **39c**

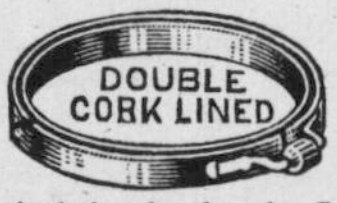

DOUBLE CORK LINED

Embroidery Hoops

Metal hoop has double cork lining and is especially practical for beadwork. Screw adjustment. Sizes, 4, 5, 6 or 7 inches. **State size.** Shipping weight, 3 ounces.
25K4696............ **18c**

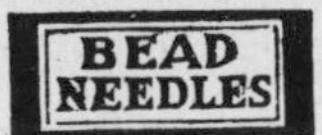

BEAD NEEDLES

Bead Needles

Correct size for all bead work. Package contains five long, fine needles. Shpg. wt., 1 oz.
25K4691—Per package.................... **8c**

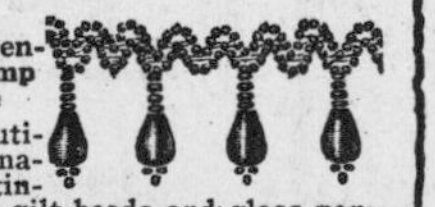

Glass Pendant Lamp Fringe

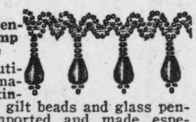

A beautiful combination of tinsel braid, gilt beads and glass pendants, imported and made especially for trimming lamps; colored pendants are assorted colors. Width, about 1¼ inches. Shipping weight, yard, 6 ounces.
25K3244
Per yard................ **39c**

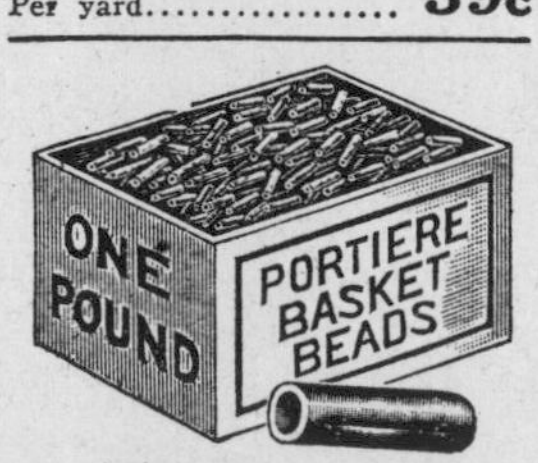

ONE POUND
PORTIERE BASKET BEADS

Portiere Basket Beads

Tubular glass beads, about ½ inch. Colors: White (satin), light blue, pink, emerald green, royal blue, red, navy blue, peacock green, black, gold or silver. **State color.** Shpg. wt., 1¼ lbs.
25K4676—Per lb..... **75c**
25K4678—Same as above, ¼ pound in envelope. **State color.** Shipping weight, 5 ounces.... **20c**

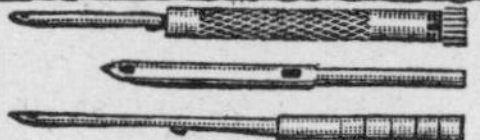

French Knot Embroidery and Rug Needle

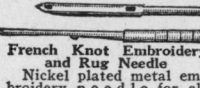

Nickel plated metal embroidery needle for all kinds of embroidery work, especially French knots, which it does very quickly. Has extra coarse brass point for rug making. Complete directions with every needle. Shipping wt., 2 ounces.
25K4689.......... **45c**

"Our Triumph," 12-Section Collapsible Dress Form With New Designed Waistline

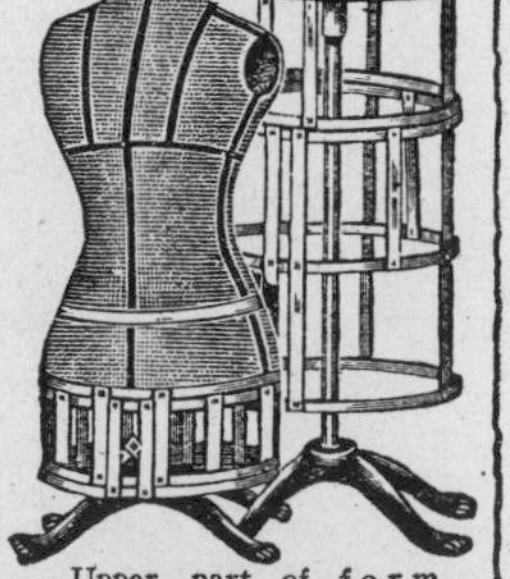

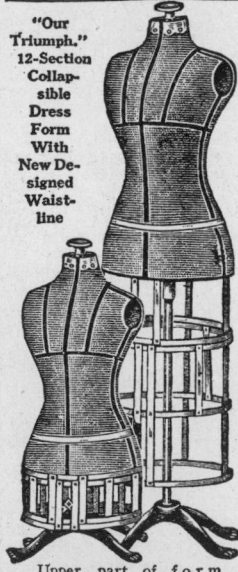

Upper part of form made of papier mache covered with black jersey cloth. Made in two styles, A and B. Style A when closed is 32 in. bust measure and extends to 48 in. Style B is 36 in. bust measure and extends to 52 in. **State style wanted,** A or B. Shipping weight, 35 pounds. **Cannot be shipped by parcel post.**
25K6080¼
Each.......... **$10.95**

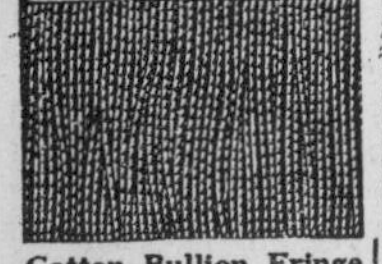

Cotton Bullion Fringe

For trimming bedspreads, curtains, scarfs, etc. Heading in two-tone effect: Ecru and old rose, ecru and delft, ecru and black; ecru and brown, or all light ecru. **State color.** Width, about 3½ in. Shipping weight, per yard, 3 ounces.
25K3242
Per yard....... **13c**

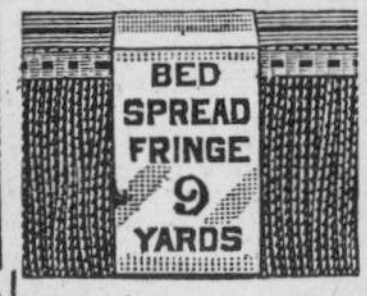

BED SPREAD FRINGE
9 YARDS

Cotton Bullion Fringe

Same fringe as 25K3242 at left, and same colors. Put up 9 yards to a piece. Just enough to trim your bedspread and at a saving. **State color.** Shipping weight, 1 lb.
25K3243 — Per piece of 9 yards... **$1.10**

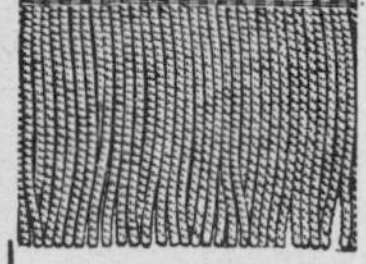

Rayon Bullion Fringe

For curtains, bedspreads and scarfs. Colors: Ivory (cream-white) or biege (light ecru). **State color.** Shipping weight, per yard, 3 ounces.
25K3234—Width, about 2 inches.
Per yard.......... **18c**
25K3233—Width, about 3 in. Yard.. **25c**

ALLSTATE TIRES

Are America's Greatest

8 Reasons Why

TIRE users everywhere ought to know the many reasons for the Superiority and Economy of ALLSTATE Tires. Only the best scientific principles, the finest workmanship and the highest quality of materials could produce this Super Mileage Maker. Study the details and you will appreciate your ALLSTATE Tires even more, and know how and why they resist wear, last longer and go farther — outliving their 12,000-mile guarantee.

Extra Miles

You men at the wheel actually *buy mileage in extra measure* when you choose ALLSTATE. Measure your tire value by "Most Miles Per Dollar" plus riding comfort and general satisfaction.

If you aren't enjoying maximum economy and superior service from your tires, it's because you have put off buying ALLSTATE.

1—*Quality* Only the finest materials are used in building ALLSTATE.

2—*Workmanship* ALLSTATE Tires are built by skilled mechanics with modern machinery under careful inspection and under the supervision of our engineers. They are built to measure up to the high standards of Sears, Roebuck and Co.

3—*Mileage* The real worth of any tire is the extra mileage above what you expect to get. ALLSTATE Tires have this extra mileage.

4—*Flexibility* In extra measure to give increased riding comfort and make maximum mileage possible. An unyielding tire has short life, because the cords and plies of fabric are pulled, strained and broken as the tire resists jolts. ALLSTATE Tires with the proper number of plies, of cords properly twisted to increase flexibility, avoid fabric breaks.

5—*Tread Design* Thick, sturdy and tough, built to give full road contact, insuring long, even tread wear.

6—*Protected Sidewalls* The tread design and extra ribs protect the sides against the wear of ruts, etc.

7—*Guarantee* Every ALLSTATE Tire is guaranteed against defects of workmanship and materials for a full 12,000 miles by the World's Largest Store. A responsible guarantee by a responsible firm.

8—*None Cheaper* There is no tire that is built better, quality considered, that can be purchased at ALLSTATE prices.

See for Yourself

Turn Now to Our Auto Supply Pages 458 to 497

12,000 Miles Guaranteed

Quick Shipment Anywhere in the United States

Within 24 hours after your orders reach us, your goods will be on their way to you from the Sears-Roebuck Store nearest you. The World's Largest Store gives you the quickest service as well as the lowest prices.

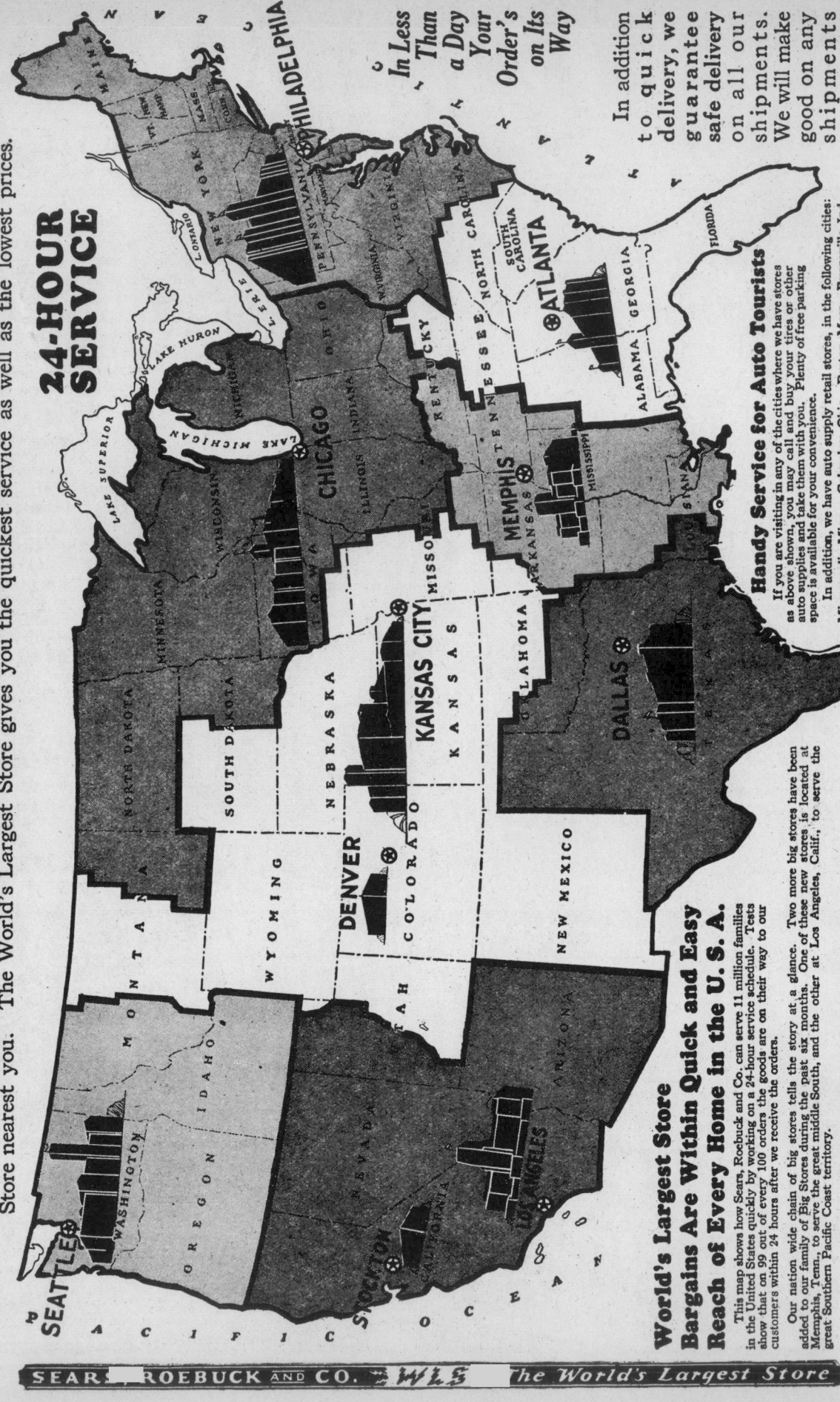

24-HOUR SERVICE

In Less Than a Day Your Order's on Its Way

In addition to quick delivery, we guarantee safe delivery on all our shipments. We will make good on any shipments that do not arrive in perfect condition.

World's Largest Store Bargains Are Within Quick and Easy Reach of Every Home in the U. S. A.

This map shows how Sears, Roebuck and Co. can serve 11 million families in the United States quickly by working on a 24-hour service schedule. Tests show that on 99 out of every 100 orders the goods are on their way to our customers within 24 hours after we receive the orders.

Our nation wide chain of big stores tells the story at a glance. Two more big stores have been added to our family of Big Stores during the past six months. One of these new stores is located at Memphis, Tenn., to serve the great middle South, and the other at Los Angeles, Calif., to serve the great Southern Pacific Coast territory.

All Our Stores Render the Same Efficient Service

Each of our great stores is a complete unit fully stocked with merchandise to meet practically all the requirements of everybody everywhere in the territory it serves. All our stores are served by the great Sears-Roebuck factory and warehouse organizations, and all our customers get the full benefit of the low prices made possible through our dealing with 11 million people throughout the country.

Handy Service for Auto Tourists

If you are visiting in any of the cities where we have stores as above shown, you may call and buy your tires or other auto supplies and take them with you. Plenty of free parking space is available for your convenience.

In addition, we have auto supply retail stores, in the following cities:

Minneapolis, Minn. Columbus, Ohio Boston, Mass. Evansville, Ind.

Another store will be opened in Camden, N. J. in August, and another in Milwaukee, Wis. in September, 1927. At all of these stores you can buy tires and other auto supplies and take them with you. Don't forget when you are touring that you can save money at the World's Largest Store. We quote the lowest prices for quality merchandise in the U. S. A. In entering any of the cities named any officer you ask will direct you to our stores.

SEARS, ROEBUCK AND CO. *The World's Largest Store*

Pilgrim Positive Wear
GUARANTEED Hosiery

Combed Cotton
4 Pairs for 85¢
Guaranteed to Wear 4 Months

Women's Combed Cotton Stockings
4 Pairs for 85¢
Guaranteed to Wear Four Months

86K432—Black.
86K436—White.
86K438—French tan.
Sizes, 8½, 9, 9½, 10 and 10½. State size. Shipping weight, 4 pairs, ¾ lb.
Knit of a very fine combed cotton yarn. An extra thread of combed cotton is knit into the soles, heels and toes and adds greatly to the life of the stockings. Double garter tops. These stockings are of medium weight. Very neat appearing. Fully seamless feet

Men's Combed Cotton Socks
4 Pairs for 85¢
Guaranteed to Wear Four Months

86K401—Black.
86K403—Dark brown.
86K405—Navy blue.
86K407—Light gray.
86K409—French tan.

Sizes, 9½, 10, 10½, 11, 11½ and 12. State size. Shipping weight, four pairs, ¾ pound.
Medium heavy weight, fine combed cotton socks that are soft and durable. The soles, heels and toes are reinforced with an extra thread of selected combed cotton. Elastic ribbed tops. Fully seamless.

Mercerized Cotton
3 Pairs for $1.00

Women's Mercerized Cotton Stockings
Guaranteed to Wear 3 Months
86K452—Black.
86K458—French tan.
86K459—Medium gray.
Sizes, 8½, 9, 9½ and 10. State size. Shipping weight, three pairs, ¾ pound.
A very fine gauge neat, appearing stocking, knit of an exceptionally high grade mercerized cotton yarn. A seam in the back of the leg gives the appearance of a fashioned stocking. Have double soles and high spliced heels. Extra reinforced heels and toes. Double garter tops. Seamless feet. Medium weight.

Extra Wide Tops for Stout Women
4 Pairs for $1.08

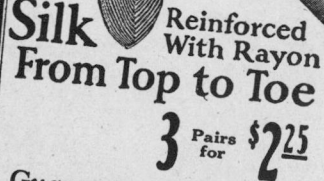

Guaranteed to Wear Four Months

86K483—Black.
86K487—White.
86K489—Nude.
Sizes, 8½ to 10½. State size. Shipping weight, four pairs, ¾ pound.
Knit of the same very fine quality combed cotton yarn as our 86K432. Full, wide double garter tops mean comfort and service for stout women. Fully seamless feet. Reinforced heels, toes and double soles.

Silk Reinforced With Rayon From Top to Toe
3 Pairs for $2.25

Guaranteed to Wear Three Months

86K475—Black, Dove gray, Blonde satin, Rose blonde, Champagne or Evenglow.
Sizes, 8½, 9, 9½ and 10. State size. Shipping weight, three pairs, ¾ pound.
Practical hose that lends smartness to your appearance. They look like all silk, yet they cost much less and are very serviceable. From top to toe the silk is knit on the outer surface and reinforced with Rayon on the inside, a wonderful combination for style and service. The seamed back has fashioned markings. Seamless feet for comfort. Mercerized cotton heels and toes. Ravel stop to prevent runs. These are exceptionally serviceable stockings and you make considerable saving by buying three pairs. Besides, we guarantee three pairs to wear three months.

Men's Mercerized Socks
3 Pairs for 78¢

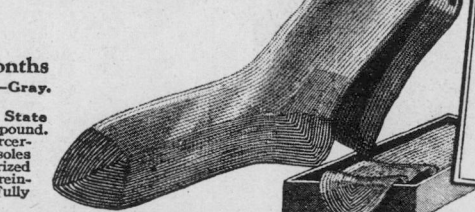

Guaranteed for Three Months
86K414—Black.   86K418—Gray.
86K416—Dark brown.
Sizes, 9½, 10, 10½, 11 and 11½. State size. Shipping weight, three pairs, ¾ pound.
Medium heavyweight, fine gauge mercerized cotton socks. The heels, toes and soles are reinforced with a two-thread mercerized cotton yarn. There is also an extra reinforcing in the toe to give extra wear. Fully seamless. Elastic ribbed tops.

Children's Winter Weight Hosiery

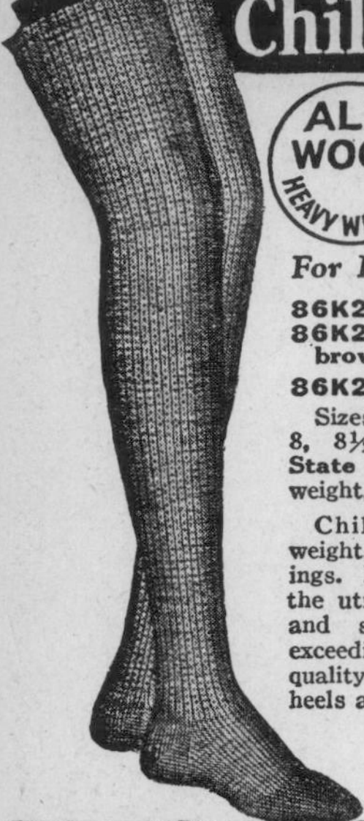

ALL WOOL HEAVY WEIGHT 68c

For Boys or Girls

86K2660—Black.
86K2661—Dark brown.
86K2662—Camel.
Sizes, 6, 6½, 7, 7½, 8, 8½, 9 and 9½. State size. Shipping weight, 5 ounces.

Children's heavy-weight, all wool stockings. Made to give you the utmost in warmth and service. Priced exceedingly low for this quality. Reinforced heels and toes. Finely knit, elastic ribbed legs. Flat knit feet. Fully seamless.

POPULAR FANCY ABOUT ONE-HALF WOOL 55c

86K2695—Heather brown.
86K2696—French tan.
86K2697—Dark gray.
86K2698—Powder blue.
Sizes, 6, 6½, 7, 7½, 8, 8½, 9 and 9½. State size. Shipping weight, 3 ounces.

Dress your children smartly with the season's latest fancy full length stockings. Knit of about one-half wool, balance fine quality cotton, these stockings combine style, service and warmth. Contrasting fast color yarns produce this neatly designed pattern, which is Guaranteed not to fade. Fully seamless flat knit feet. Reinforced heels and toes.

All Wool Socks With Red Tops 47c

86K2674—Light gray.
Sizes, 9 and 10. State size. Shpg. wt., 4 oz.
Ideal socks for skating or any winter sport. Knit of all-wool and are warm and comfortable. Heavy ribbed style with wide red stripe around the top. They can be worn as a long stocking or as a sport hose, as the tops can be rolled to come just below the knee. Flat knit seamless feet.

FANCY RIBBED ARTIFICIAL SILK AND WOOL 59c

This Season's Smartest Hosiery for Children

86K2681—Black.
86K2682—Dark brown.
86K2683—Champagne.
86K2684—French tan.
Sizes, 6, 6½, 7, 7½, 8, 8½, 9 and 9½. State size. Shipping weight, 3 oz.
Very dressy fancy ribbed stockings. Knit from the very finest soft yarns. About one-half wool; balance Rayon. Very pretty and well liked by every one.

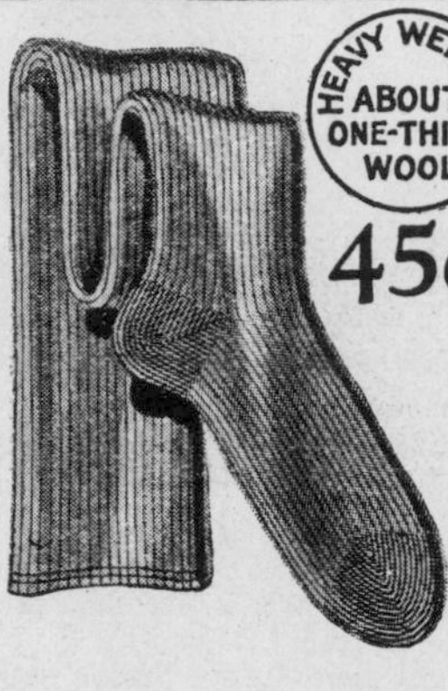

Rayon and Wool Stockings That Will Afford Style and Warmth

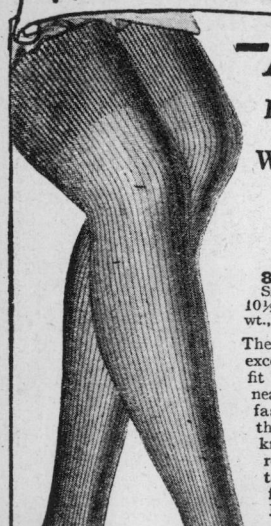

HEAVY WEIGHT ABOUT ONE-THIRD WOOL 45c

86K2680—Black.
86K2685—Dark brown.
Sizes, 5½, 6, 6½, 7, 7½, 8, 8½, 9 and 9½. State size. Shipping weight, 5 oz.
Good, serviceable, warm heavyweight stockings, about one-third wool, at a very moderate cost and much less than you can secure the same quality elsewhere. Finely ribbed elastic knit legs. Flat knit feet, reinforced heels and toes. Fully seamless.

Women's Winter Weight Hosiery

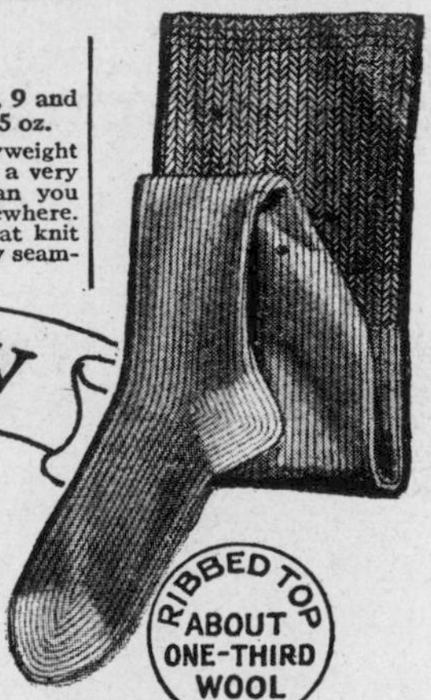

—ALL WOOL—

Heavy Weight Knit to Fit Without a Seam 67c

86K2504—Black.
Sizes, 8½, 9, 9½, 10 and 10½. State size. Shpg. wt., all sizes, 5 oz.

These stockings will give exceptional service and fit very comfortably and neatly. They are Pilgrim fashioned, which means they are shaped in the knitting and will always retain their shape. The toes and heels are reinforced with cotton. Double garter tops.

Extra Wide for Stout Women 77c

86K2505
Same quality as above in sizes 9, 9½, 10 and 10½. State size.

Extra Heavy Weight 65c

86K2537 Heather brown.
86K2538 Black.
Sizes, 9, 9½, 10 and 10½. State size. Shpg. wt., each pair, 6 ounces.

Wonderfully good big warm stockings for women. Lots of comfort and good service. Knit from good quality all wool yarn. Heavy ribbed legs. Flat knit seamless feet. good warm stockings that will give exceptional wear.

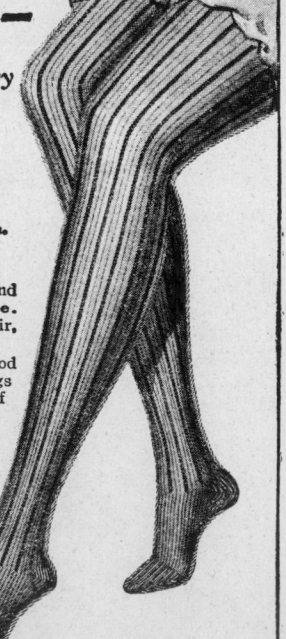

40c

One-Third Wool Elastic Ribbed Tops Medium Heavy Weight

86K2506—Black.
Sizes, 8½, 9, 9½ and 10. State size.
Good wearing medium heavy weight stockings. Reinforced heels and toes. Elastic ribbed tops. Fully seamless.

Extra Wide Tops for Stout Women 45c

86K2522—Black.
Sizes, 9, 9½, 10 and 10½. State size.
For stout women. Knit of the same yarn as our 86K2506. Fully seamless. Shipping weight, all sizes, 4 ounces.

RIBBED TOP ABOUT ONE-THIRD WOOL

Half Wool Stocking Feet

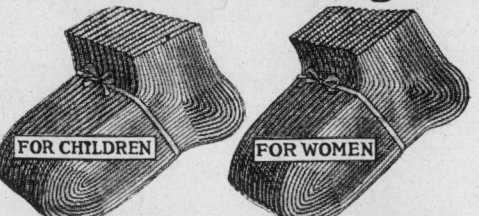

FOR CHILDREN — 3 Pairs for 55c

86K2672—Black.
Sizes, 6, 7, 8, 9 and 10. State size. Shipping weight, three pairs, 5 ounces.
These are extra stocking feet only. Knit from about one-half wool. Medium weight. Fully seamless.

FOR WOMEN — 3 Pairs for 65c

86K2367—Black.
86K2368—Oxford gray.
Sizes, 8½, 9, 9½ and 10. State size. Shipping weight, three pairs, ¾ pound.
Extra stocking feet. About one-half wool. Fully seamless.

FANCY WOOL HOSE

Silk and Wool Extra Fine Gauge

The Beauty of SILK and the Warmth of WOOL

$1.00
Our Leader Quality
PURE SILK AND WOOL
86K2570—Colors; Gray, French tan, Black, French nude, Flesh (on figure). Sizes, 8½ to 10. State size and color. Shipping weight, 3 ounces. Very fine gauge stockings, lightweight, but warm. Knit of about two-thirds soft virgin wool, balance pure thread silk. Toes and heels are mercerized cotton. Reinforced garter tops. Can be worn as underhose, too, as they are fine enough to be invisible under sheerest silk stockings. Seamless feet.

85c
Fancy Ribbed
RAYON AND WOOL
86K2541—Black.
86K2542—Sand.
86K2543—Medium gray.
86K2545—French tan.
86K2544—Black and silver.

Sizes, 8½, 9, 9½ and 10. State size. Shpg. wt., 3 oz. One of the season's most popular stockings. Special note should be made of the ribbed to the toe feature, which makes them especially fine for wear with low shoes. About two-thirds fine grade wool, balance Rayon. Fully seamless feet.

69c
A Big Value
86K2509—French tan.
86K2510—Black.
86K2511—Medium gray.
86K2512—Sand.
Sizes, 8½ to 10. State size. Shpg. wt., 3 oz. A very dressy fine gauge stocking. Knit from about one-half wool, balance Rayon. The double garter top is knit of mercerized cotton. Reinforced heels and toes. Fully seamless feet.

Underhose for wear Underneath Silk Stockings
75c
86K2546—Flesh. Sizes, 8½, 9, 9½ and 10. State size. Shpg. wt., 3 oz. Very fine gauge stockings, knit of one-half wool, balance mercerized cotton. Light weight, but warm. Fully seamless throughout. They come in flesh shade only, which is absolutely invisible when worn underneath the sheerest silk stockings. For style and comfort in cold weather buy these underhose.

48c
Fancy Dropstitch Effect—Half Wool
86K2555—Black.
86K2556—Dark brown.
86K2558—Medium gray.
Sizes, 8½ to 10. State size. Shpg. wt., 3 oz. A good warm stocking that will prove very dressy for wear with low shoes. Reinforced heels and toes. Fully seamless feet. This is one of our lowest priced stockings.

Rayon and Wool With Extra Wide Ribbed Tops for Stout Women
89c
86K2524—Black.
86K2526—Sand.
Sizes, 9 to 10½. State size. Shipping weight, 4 ounces.
Knit of about one-half wool, balance Rayon. Made full and wide with a real elastic ribbed top, insuring comfort and fit. Tops, heels and toes are knit of mercerized cotton yarn.

59c
Fancy Ribbed
HALF WOOL
86K2562—Black.
86K2564—Sand.
86K2565—French tan
Sizes, 8½, 9, 9½ and 10. State size. Shpg. wt., 4 oz. Knit of about one-half wool and balance good quality cotton. Offered in the latest popular shades with ribbed to the toe feature, making them very desirable to wear with low cut shoes. Double garter tops. Fully seamless feet. Reinforced heels and toes.

The Beauty of Silk From Top to Toe and the Warmth of Wool

FOR MISSES 70c

FOR WOMEN 79c

Stylish and Warm Stockings
Dressy fine gauge stockings knit of about half wool, balance Rayon. Will give plenty of service and absolute warmth. Reinforced garter tops. Heels and toes of mercerized cotton. Seamless feet. Shipping weight, 4 ounces.
FOR WOMEN
79c
86K2547—Black.
86K2548—Camel color.
86K2549—French tan.
86K2554—Medium gray.
Sizes, 8½, 9, 9½ and 10. State size.
FOR MISSES
70c
86K2571—Black, Camel color, French tan or Medium gray.
Sizes, 7½, 8, 8½, 9 and 9½. State size and color.
Same as above, but made narrower to fit the young girls.

Work Socks

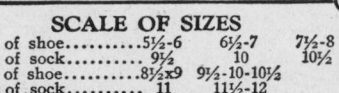

6 Pairs for 79c

6 Pairs for 79c
Famous Uncle Sam Socks
Actual Weight, 2 Lbs. Per Dozen

86K2004—Brown mixed.
Sizes, 9½, 10, 10½, 11 and 11½. State size. Shipping weight, six pairs, 1¼ lbs. You will profit in more ways than one if you choose these famous Uncle Sam Work Socks. You save money when you buy these socks here, and the comfort and service they afford are well worth considering. They are knit of good quality cotton yarn in medium heavy weight. Practical for farmers and workingmen. Very soft and comfortable. Reinforced heels and toes. Elastic ribbed tops. Fully seamless.

6 Pairs for 79c
Fine Gauge Work Socks That Will Stand a Lot of Wear

86K1938—Brown mixed.
86K1939—Blue mixed.
Come in one full size only. Shipping weight, six pairs, 1 pound.
These fine gauge work socks will stand up under the hard wear necessarily given them by workingmen. Very comfortable and serviceable. Knit from selected cotton. White toes, heels and elastic ribbed tops. Fully seamless.

SCALE OF SIZES			
Size of shoe	5½-6	6½-7	7½-8
Size of sock	9½	10	10½
Size of shoe	8½-9	9½-10-10½	
Size of sock	11	11½-12	

A Big Value

6 Pairs for 60c
Everyday Cotton Socks
86K1997—Dark brown.
86K1998—Black.
86K1999—Gray.
Sizes, 9½, 10, 10½, 11 and 11½. State size. Shipping weight, six pairs, ¾ pound.
Medium light weight, fully seamless cotton socks that are real bargains at our price and will give good service. Reinforced heels and toes and elastic ribbed tops.

23c Each Pair
Footease Socks Have Undyed Feet or Soles
86K2047 — Black with cream color soles, heels and toes.
86K2048 — Black with cream color feet.
Sizes, 9½ to 11½. State size. Shpg. wt., 3 oz.
There is no dye in the feet of these socks to irritate tender feet. They are made to give comfort. Knit of good quality cotton with elastic ribbed tops. Medium weight. Fully seamless.

Standard ROCKFORD Socks

6 Pairs for 60c
Actual Weight Per Dozen Pairs, 1½ Pounds
86K1958 Blue mixed
86K1959 Brown mixed.
One full size only. Shipping wt., 6 pairs, 1 lb. Men's Medium Weight Coarse Knit Cotton Rockford Socks. Elastic ribbed tops. Fully seamless feet.

6 Pairs for 72c
Actual Weight Per Dozen Pairs, 2 Pounds
86K1962—Blue mixed.
86K1963—Brown mixed.
One full size only. Shpg. wt., six pairs, 1¼ lbs. Men's Medium Heavy Weight Coarse Knit Cotton Rockford Socks. Elastic ribbed tops. Fully seamless feet.

6 Pairs for 64c
Medium Weight, Seamless Feet
86K1950—Black.
86K1951—Tan.
One full size only. Shpg. wt., six pairs, 1 lb. Men's Medium Weight Socks. Knit of a good quality cotton yarn. Black or tan with white heels, toes and elastic ribbed tops.

6 Pairs for 83c
Actual Weight, Per Dozen Pairs, 2½ Pounds
86K1964—Blue mixed.
86K1965—Brown mixed.
One full size only. Shpg. wt., six pairs, 1½ lbs. Men's Heavy Weight Coarse Knit Cotton Rockford Socks. Fully seamless feet.

6 Pairs for 65c
Actual Weight, Per Dozen Pairs, 1½ Lbs.
86K1966—Blue mixed.
86K1967—Brown mixed.
Boys' full size only. Shpg. wt., six pairs, 1 lb. Boys' Medium Weight Coarse Knit Cotton Rockford Socks. Elastic ribbed tops. Fully seamless feet.

6 Pairs for $1.10
Actual Weight, Per Dozen Pairs, 3 Lbs.
86K1968 Blue mixed.
86K1969 Brown mixed.
One full size only. Shipping weight, six pairs, 1¾ pounds. Men's Extra Heavy Weight Coarse Knit Cotton Rockford Socks. Elastic ribbed tops. Fully seamless feet.

For Boys

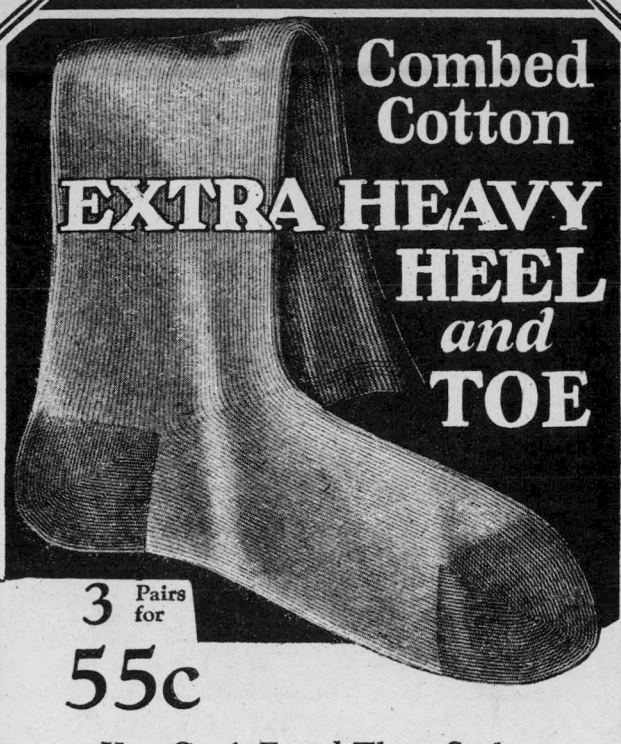

Combed Cotton
EXTRA HEAVY HEEL and TOE

3 Pairs for 55c

You Can't Equal These Socks for Wear

86K2012—Black.
86K2013—Dark brown.
86K2014—Medium gray.
86K2015—Champagne.

Sizes, 9½, 10, 10½, 11 and 11½. State size. Shipping weight, 3 oz. You will find these socks will give the most satisfactory service you have ever had, because the heels and toes have been so reinforced that it is almost impossible to wear them out. Neat appearing socks, knit of good quality combed cotton. Medium heavy weight. Fully seamless with comfortable fitting elastic ribbed tops. On account of their wonderful wearing qualities and our exceptionally low price, these socks have become very popular with our customers.

Socks *for* Dress

25c Each Pair

Just Look at This Low Price!

86K1942—Black.
86K1943—Dark brown.
86K1944—White.
86K1945—Navy blue.
86K1946—Medium gray.

Sizes, 9½, 10, 10½, 11 and 11½. State size. Shipping weight, 3 ounces. Socks that have exceptional wearing qualities. Knit of Rayon and cotton lisle yarns. Reinforced mercerized cotton heels and toes. Double soles and high spliced heels. Elastic ribbed mercerized tops. Medium weight. Fully seamless.

75c Each Pair

Our Best Quality —Full Fashioned Genuine Silk

86K1895—Black.
86K1896—Dark brown.
86K1897—Champagne.
86K1898—Medium gray.
86K1899—French tan.

Sizes, 9½, 10, 10½, 11 and 11½. State size. Shipping weight, 2 ounces. Socks that will please men who appreciate quality and fineness. Full fashioned. Mercerized cotton lisle heels, toes and elastic ribbed tops. Double soles. High spliced heels.

48c Each Pair

Genuine Silk Very Fine Quality

86K1889—French tan.
86K1890—Black.
86K1891—Dark brown.
86K1892—Navy blue.
86K1893—Medium gray.

Sizes, 9½, 10, 10½, 11 and 11½. State size. Shipping weight, 2 ounces.

Very popular, fine quality silk socks that are especially big values at our price. They look well and will wear extremely well. Reinforced cotton lisle soles and high spliced heels. Elastic ribbed tops. Seamless feet for comfort.

Popular FANCY Socks

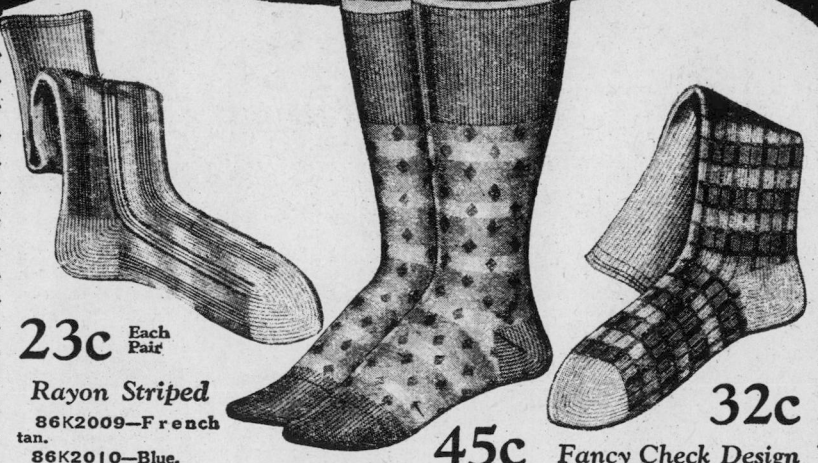

23c Each Pair

Rayon Striped

86K2009—French tan.
86K2010—Blue.
86K2011—Gray.

Sizes, 9½, 10, 10½, 11 and 11½. State size. Shipping weight, 2 oz.

Men will like these new fancy vertical striped socks. Knit of Rayon and combed cotton they will look well and wear well. Reinforced cotton toes, heels and elastic ribbed tops. Fully seamless.

45c

The Latest Diamond Pattern

86K2030—French tan.
86K2031—Gray.
86K2032—Blue.
86K2033—Brown.

Sizes, 9½, 10, 10½, 11 and 11½. State size. Shipping weight, 2 oz.

A high grade sock in the newest diamond pattern in contrasting colors. Knit of best grade Rayon and mercerized yarn. Reinforced heels and toes. Elastic ribbed tops. Fully seamless.

32c

Fancy Check Design

86K2005—Tan.
86K2006—Camel.
86K2007—Gray.
86K2008—Blue.

Sizes, 9½, 10, 10½, 11 and 11½. State size. Shipping weight, 2 ounces.

A neat but snappy sock in fancy check pattern of contrasting colors. Knit of Rayon reinforced with fine mercerized cotton yarn. Mercerized cotton tops and reinforced heels and toes. Fully seamless.

Fine Gauge Mercerized

25c Each Pair

The Finest Mercerized Socks Ever Sold at This Price

86K2090—Black.
86K2091—Dark brown.
86K2092—Navy blue.
86K2093—Medium gray.
86K2094—White.

Sizes, 9½, 10, 10½, 11 and 11½. State size. Shipping weight, 3 ounces.

We are sure you'll not find a bigger value in men's socks than we offer you here. These socks are knit from extra fine mercerized cotton yarn, silk-like in appearance. Elastic ribbed tops. Double soles. Reinforced toes and high spliced heels. Medium light weight.

See Index and Information Pages 542 to 570

Pilgrim BRAND
Cotton Shirts and Drawers

Heavy Flat-Knit Fleeced

Heavy Ribbed Cotton

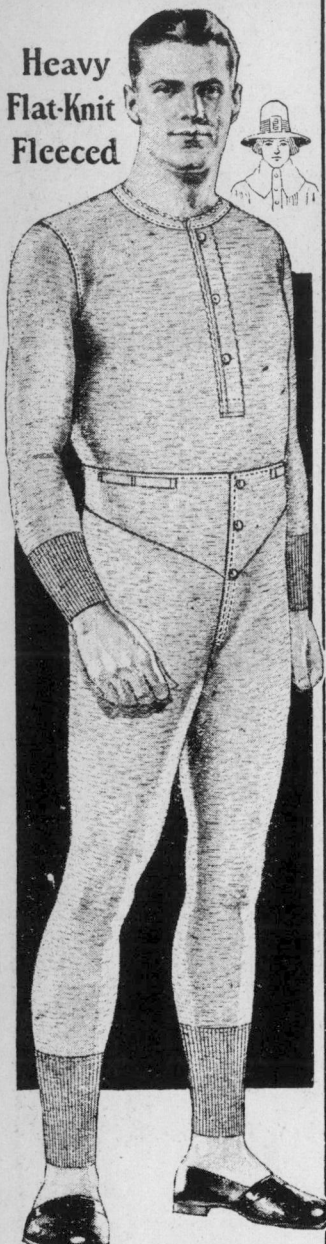

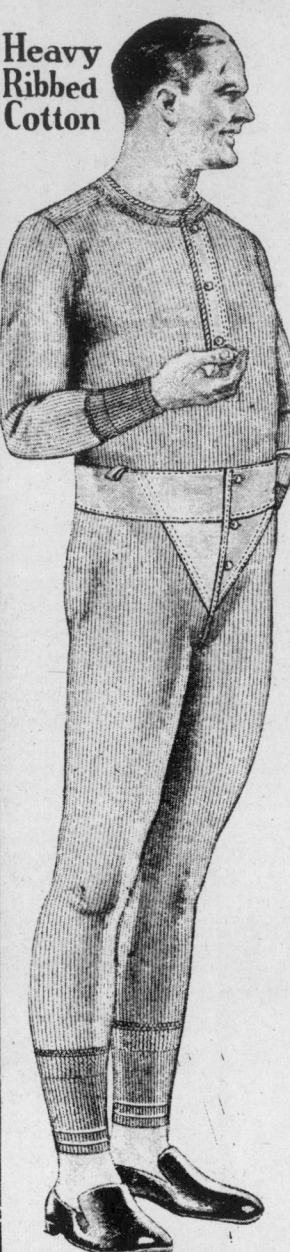

Double Breasted Double Seated

Each Garment 89c
CREAM COLOR
Flat Knit Heavy Fleece Lined Cotton

Inside has heavy, soft, thick nap fleecing.

UNDERSHIRTS
16K6052—Sizes, 34 to 46 in. chest measure. **State size.** Shipping weight, each, 1¼ pounds.
Each shirt........89c

DRAWERS
16K6053—Ankle length. Sizes, 30 to 44 in. waist measure. **State size.** Shipping weight, each, 1¼ pounds.
Each drawers.....89c

Each Garment $1.08
LIGHT BROWN
Flat Knit Cotton Double Front, Double Back

Shirts have double front and back, drawers have reinforced double seat. Heavy, soft, thick fleecing inside. Heavy weight.

UNDERSHIRTS
16K6074—Sizes, 34 to 46 in. chest measure. **State size.** Shipping weight, each, 1¼ pounds.
Each shirt........$1.08

DRAWERS
16K6075—Ankle length. Sizes, 30 to 44 inches waist measure. **State size.** Shipping weight, each, 1¼ lbs.
Each drawers......$1.08

Each Garment 74c
LIGHT BROWN
Flat Knit Heavy Fleece Lined Cotton

Inside of garment has a heavy, soft, thick nap fleecing. Heavy weight.

UNDERSHIRTS
16K6050—Sizes, 34 to 46 in. chest measure. **State size.** Shipping weight, each, 1¼ pounds.
Each shirt...... 74c

DRAWERS
16K6051—Ankle length. Sizes, 30 to 44 inches waist measure. **State size.** Shipping weight, each, 1¼ pounds.
Each drawers... 74c

Balbriggan Shirts and Drawers

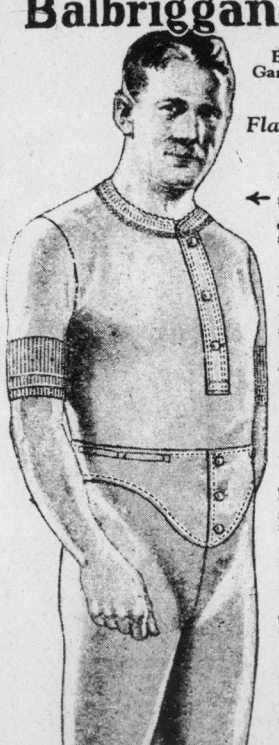

Each Garment 37c
CREAM COLOR
Flat Knit, Light Weight

UNDERSHIRTS
16K5006 — Short sleeves.
16K5008 — Long sleeves.
Sizes, 34 to 46 in. chest measure. **State size.**
Each shirt...37c

DRAWERS
16K5009 — Ankle length.
Sizes, 30 to 44 in. waist measure. **State size.**
Each drawers...37c
Shipping weight, each garment, 7 oz.

Each Garment 79c
Our Best Balbriggan
CREAM COLOR
Flat knit of selected cotton yarn. Exceptionally high grade garments in every respect.

UNDERSHIRTS
16K5062 — Short sleeves.
16K5032 — Long sleeves.
Sizes, 34 to 56 in. chest measure. **State size.**
Each shirt...79c

DRAWERS
16K5033 — Ankle length.
Sizes, 30 to 56 in. waist measure. **State size.**
Each drawers...79c
Shipping weight, each garment, ¾ lb.

Each Garment 79c
Flat Knit, Heavy Fleeced Lined Cotton
SILVER GRAY

Quality that is real quality. The satisfaction and long service this underwear gives are what make it the big value we claim it is. Flat knit, with a heavy, soft, cotton nap fleecing on the inside. Built for warmth and hard service. Heavy weight.

UNDERSHIRTS
16K6068—Sizes, 34 to 46 inches chest measure. **State size.** Shipping weight, each shirt, 1½ pounds.
Each shirt............79c

DRAWERS
16K6069—Ankle length. Sizes, 30 to 44 inches waist measure. **State size.** Shipping weight, each drawers, 1¼ pounds.
Each drawers...........79c

Each Garment 59c
Elastic Ribbed, Heavy Cotton
CREAM COLOR

Well made garments that are **real values at our especially low price.** They are knit from good quality cotton yarn and are slightly fleeced on the inside. Elastic ribbed.

UNDERSHIRTS
16K6028—Sizes, 34 to 46 inches chest measure. **State size.** Shipping weight, each, 1 pound.
Each shirt.............59c

DRAWERS
16K6029—Ankle length. Sizes, 30 to 44 inches waist measure. **State size.** Shipping weight, each, 1 pound
Each drawers.........59c

Men's SUMMER WEIGHTS

Pilgrim Leader
THE
UNION SUIT
with
7
Big
Points

Athletic Style Nainsook

16K5122—Fine checked pattern.
16K5123—Fancy striped pattern.

79c

White

Sizes, 34 to 46 inches chest measure. **State size.**
Shipping weight, 7 ounces.

One of the biggest values to be found anywhere in Men's Nainsook Suits. The following big features have made this our most popular Nainsook suit: 1—Nainsook cloth tested for strength. 2—Elastic band across back with special reinforcement in center. 3—Double stitched above and below band. 4—Full cut blouse for comfort and service. 5—Special tailored seat, will not gap. 6—Big, full cut sizes. 7—Closed crotch with double gusset for extra wear.

72c

Light Weight Cotton Ribbed Suit for Year Round Wear

16K5242 — Long sleeves.
16K5243 — Short sleeves.

Cream Color Ankle Length

Sizes, 34 to 46 inches chest measure. State size. Shipping wt., ¾ lb.

These light weight Union Suits are becoming more popular every year. They are just the right weight for between season's wear and are also preferred by many men for wear the year round. Knit of good grade cotton yarn in sizes that will fit correctly and comfortably. Smooth, flat locked seams throughout. Well made and carefully finished. You will find our price is very low for these suits.

Long or Short Sleeves

Four Styles

Combed Cotton Elastic Knit Union Suits

44c

Nainsook Suit

16K5215—White. →
Sizes, 34 to 46 inches chest measure. **State size.** Shipping weight, 7 ounces.
Athletic Style Union Suit made of a fine checked pattern nainsook. Designed and cut to full comfort giving dimensions. Will not bind. Elastic knit fabric in the back.

98c

Combed Cotton
16K5286
White.

Sizes, 34 to 46 inches chest measure. **State size.** Shipping weight, 8 oz.
Designed and made by one of the best manufacturers of men's underwear, from the finest soft combed cotton yarn, this elastic ribbed suit will fit comfortably and give excellent service.

Buttons on Shoulder Style

$1.50

Each Suit

Tall Slim

Long Sleeves

Stout

These Suits Will Fit You No Matter How You're Built

Cream Color
For Men of Average Build
16K5010—Short sleeves, ankle length.
16K5011—Long sleeves, ankle length.
Sizes, 34 to 50 inches chest measure. State size.

For Tall Slim Men
16K5012—Short sleeves, ankle length.
Sizes, 36 to 46 inches chest measure. State size.

For Short Stout Men
16K5037—Short sleeves, ankle length.
Sizes, 38 to 56 inches chest measure. **State size.** Shipping weight, each suit, ¾ lb.

Our Pilgrim Leader Quality Union Suits for wear the year round. We believe you will find these suits to be the finest combed cotton suits ever offered at anywhere near our price. Knit of long staple combed cotton yarn, carefully made and finished. Strongly sewed with smooth flat locked seams throughout. Of correct size and tailored to fit. Fine elastic ribbed. The tall, slim men will find comfort in the specially designed long body suit which eliminates all feeling of tightness in the crotch. The short, stout suit is made by a manufacturer who makes a specialty of correctly tailoring suits to fit short, stout men. No matter what suit you select, they are all real values made to give comfort and service.

Women's Cotton Union Suits

Just the Suit for Winter
They Have Satisfied Thousands of Our Customers

Can't Be Beat at This Price

68¢

Medium Winter Weight
Your Choice of Four Styles

68c Each Suit

COLOR, WHITE

16K6461—High neck, long sleeves, ankle length.
16K6462—Medium low (Dutch) neck, elbow sleeves, ankle length.
16K6463—Low neck, sleeveless. Tailored band top, ankle length.
16K6467—Medium low (Dutch) neck, elbow sleeves, knee length.
Sizes, 34, 36 and 38 inches bust measure. State size. Shipping weight, all sizes, ¾ pound.

Our biggest sellers in women's cotton union suits. They're popular because our immense purchasing power enables us to offer our customers a good quality, exceptionally well made suit at a price that can't be equaled anywhere. These suits are knit of a very good grade cotton yarn and are slightly fleeced on the inside. They will fit neatly and comfortably because the sides are tailored to fit the figure. Smooth, flatlocked seams throughout. Correctly made flap seat.

Extra Sizes 78c Each Suit

16K6464—High neck, long sleeves, ankle length.
16K6465—Medium low (Dutch) neck, elbow sleeves, ankle length.
16K6466—Low neck, sleeveless, tailored band top, ankle length.
16K6468—Medium low (Dutch) neck, elbow sleeves, knee length.
Same as above, in sizes, 40, 42 and 44 inches, bust measure. State size. Shipping weight, all sizes, ¾ lb.

Medium Heavy Weight Fine Elastic Ribbed

88c Each Suit

WHITE

16K6551—Low neck, sleeveless, knee length, tailored band top.
16K6552—High neck, long sleeves, ankle length.
16K6553—Medium low (Dutch) neck, elbow sleeves, ankle length.
16K6522—Medium low (Dutch) neck, elbow sleeves, knee length.
Sizes, 34, 36 and 38 inches bust measure. State size. Shipping weight, each suit, 1 pound.

This is one of our most popular suits. It is just the right weight and is knit from a good grade of selected cotton yarn. The inside has a soft brushed fleecing. All seams are flatlocked finished. We recommend these suits to you especially because they are so well made and nicely finished in every detail.

Extra Sizes $1.00 Each Suit

16K6555—High neck, long sleeves, ankle length.
16K6556—Medium low (Dutch) neck, elbow sleeves, ankle length.
16K6558—Low neck, sleeveless, knee length, tailored band top.
16K6523—Medium low (Dutch) neck, elbow sleeves, knee length.
Same as above, in sizes, 40, 42 and 44 inches bust measure. State size. Shipping weight, each suit, 1 pound.

An Outstanding Value!

A Very Low Price on a Popular Style—Medium Weight

63c Each Suit

63¢

16K6474—White.
Sizes, 34, 36 and 38 inches bust measure. State size. Knit of good quality cotton, slightly fleeced on the inside. Tailored band top, low neck, sleeveless, knee length style. Flap seat. Shaped sides.

Extra Sizes 73c Each Suit

16K6475—Sizes, 40, 42 and 44 inches bust measure. State size. Shipping weight, all sizes, ¾ lb.

Boys' Heavy Cotton Union Suits

All Suits on This Page Are Ankle Length

Pilgrim Brand
More and More Popular Every Year!

Very Soft   Very Warm

Flat Knit-Heavily Fleeced

Mottled Heliotrope   Light Brown   Cream Color

Boyville BRAND The Best Boys' Cotton Union Suit Made

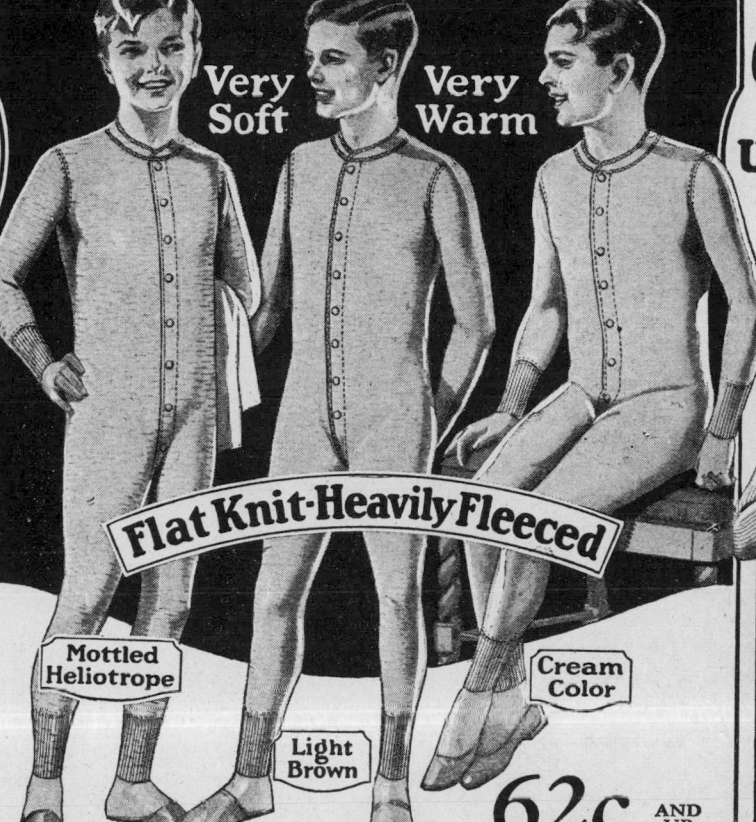

Heavy Weight Combed Cotton

59c AND UP
Silver Gray Extra Heavy Fleecing
Made of good quality cotton. Has a heavy, soft nap fleecing inside. State age. Shpg. wt., each suit, 1 lb.

Ages, Yrs. 16K7551	
3 and 4	$0.59
5 and 6	.66
7 and 8	.73
9 and 10	.80
11 and 12	.87
13 and 14	.94
15 and 16	1.00

75c AND UP
Mottled Heliotrope Color
Flat knit of extra good cotton with thick, heavy, soft nap fleecing inside. Elastic ribbed cuffs and anklets. State age. Shpg. wt., each suit 1¼ lbs.

Ages, Yrs. 16K7544	
3 and 4	$0.75
5 and 6	.85
7 and 8	.95
9 and 10	1.05
11 and 12	1.15
13 and 14	1.25
15 and 16	1.35

53c AND UP
Light Brown
Flat knit from good quality cotton. Thick, heavy, soft nap fleecing. Elastic ribbed cuffs and anklets. State age. Shipping weight, each suit, 1¼ lbs.

Ages, Yrs. 16K7557	
3 and 4	53c
5 and 6	60c
7 and 8	67c
9 and 10	74c
11 and 12	81c
13 and 14	88c
15 and 16	95c

62c AND UP
Cream Color
Flat knit of good quality cotton. Thick, heavy, soft nap fleecing. Elastic ribbed cuffs and anklets. State age. Shipping weight, each suit, 1¼ pounds.

Ages, Yrs. 16K7559	
3 and 4	$0.62
5 and 6	.69
7 and 8	.76
9 and 10	.83
11 and 12	.90
13 and 14	.97
15 and 16	1.04

48c AND UP
Medium Heavy Ribbed Cotton
Elastic ribbed. Slightly fleeced on the inside. State age. Shipping wt., each suit, 1 pound.

Ages, Yrs. 16K7556—Cream Color.	
3 and 4	48c
5 and 6	55c
7 and 8	62c
9 and 10	69c
11 and 12	76c
13 and 14	83c
15 and 16	90c

One of Our Best Sellers
57c AND UP
Heavy Ribbed Cotton
Exceptionally well made suit that has been tailored and finished with the same care used in the making of our men's suits. These suits have a soft nap fleecing on the inside and will not irritate the tenderest skin. Elastic ribbed. State age. Shipping weight, each suit, 1¼ pounds.

16K7564—Cream.

Ages, Yrs.		Ages, Yrs.	
3 and 4	57c	11 and 12	85c
5 and 6	64c	13 and 14	92c
7 and 8	71c	15 and 16	99c
9 and 10	78c		

57¢ AND UP

85c AND UP
Our Finest Cotton Suit for Boys
These Boyville suits have been carefully designed and strongly made to give excellent service. They are knit of fine combed cotton yarn and have a soft brushed fleecing inside. Correctly sized and the special Pilgrim seat gives extra fullness and will not bind. Elastic ribbed. Shpg. wt., each suit, 1 lb.

16K7530—Cream Color. Ages, Yrs.	
3 and 4	$0.85
5 and 6	.95
7 and 8	1.05
9 and 10	1.15
11 and 12	1.25
13 and 14	1.35
15 and 16	1.45

Parcel Post, Express and Freight Rates Are on Pages 542 to 545

The New Shoes for Fall~

On this page we portray two of the New Styles for Fall—one for men and one for women. They are representative of the newest of the season. After a glance at them we know you can't resist looking at every page, studying the hundreds of new styles we offer for your approval. No effort has been spared to make this the greatest, the most elaborate, the most stylish and practical collection of footwear ever shown by the World's Largest Shoe Store.

On these pages you will find shoes for the entire family and for practically every need, from the most formal dress shoe to the Greatest Work Shoe Money Can Buy. Footwear for all outdoor or indoor sports, footwear for any kind of weather, wet or dry, warm or cold, and several completely new lines as, for example, the fancy new galoshes for women, so beautifully displayed on page 336.

Throughout this Catalog we save you money! Our footwear is built to High Standards, from which we never waver. All our tremendous resources are employed for the purpose of offering you this quality at the lowest prices to be found anywhere.

$4.40

Tan
67K4401—D-E width.
67K4402—B-C width.

Black
67K4403—D-E width.
67K4404—B-C width.

Sizes, 5 to 11. Be sure to state size and width.
Shipping wt., 2½ lbs.

All the good looks a man could ask for—GOLD BOND quality, from its high grade tan or black genuine calfskin uppers to its oak tanned leather soles—are embodied in this model. GENUINE GOODYEAR WELT construction. Rubber heels. Fine stitching on tip, vamp and quarter indicate best style—that is found in all our dress shoes this season.

$3.69

15K2767
C-D-E width.

Sizes, 2½ to 8. Be sure to state size and width.
Shipping wt., 1½ lbs.

The very latest Four-Eyelet Oxford in one of the newest color combinations for the new season. Offered in gleaming black patent leather with contrasting black and white polka dot patent leather at tongue and as an underlay for cutouts on the saddle. Fashioned over the up to the minute Boulevard last. 1¾-inch military heel. Rubber top lift.

It's Easy to Fit You

We guarantee to fit you perfectly.
All the information we need to insure a fit is:

(1) **The size shoe you wear, or, if you do not know the size,**

(2) **All the numbers printed inside of a shoe that does fit.**

Our shoes are standard in size; so you will be certain to receive a pair of shoes the same size as those that do fit you perfectly.

EXPLANATION OF WIDTHS

A—*Very Narrow*   C—*Medium*   D—*Wide*
B—*Narrow*   E—*Very Wide*

Children's Shoes

In the case of children with growing feet it may be advisable to send us an outline of the *stockinged* foot. Use a plain piece of paper and pencil. This is necessary *only* if you do not know the exact size worn.

* * *

It is the purpose of the World's Largest Store to make ordering as simple as possible and yet to insure perfect satisfaction. You do not need to use any charts to determine the size shoe you want to buy from us. All we need to fit you satisfactorily is the simple information listed here.

ORDER BLANKS ARE IN BACK OF CATALOG

The Fashion Show

Vassar $4 45

Wellesley $2 98

Lorraine $3 45

Wellesley

15K2744—C - D - E width. Sizes, 2½ to 8.
15K2745—A - B width. Sizes, 3 to 8. $2 98

Be sure to state size and width.
Shipping wt., 1¾ lbs.

A new season has arrived. At the very outset the World's Largest Shoe Store presents the most elaborate Fashion Show in its history. Footwear from leading style centers of the world form the setting of the first act. Behind the scenes, as you turn the pages, you will find styles to suit every fancy and every need. The Wellesley—an adorable Three-Eyelet Tie—comes in lustrous black patent leather with black and white gingham leather underlay. Popular new Parisian last and 1¾-inch, patent leather covered wood heel.

Vassar

Tan Calfskin
15K3220—C - D - E width. Sizes, 2½ to 8.
15K3221—A - B width. Sizes, 3 to 8.
Patent Leather
15K3222—C - D - E width. Sizes, 2½ to 8.
15K3223—A-B width. Sizes, 3 to 8. $4 45

Be sure to state size and width.
Shipping wt., 1⅞ lbs.

The second celebrity of our Fashion Show—the Vassar—is brisk, alert and snappy, full of charm and youth. Four-Eyelet Ties of black patent leather or tan calfskin, both Paisley leather trimmed. Modern Boulevard toe. 1¾-inch heel with rubber top lift. GENUINE GOODYEAR WELT soles.

Ritz

15K2728—C - D - E width. Sizes, 2½ to 8.
15K2729—A - B width. Sizes, 3 to 8. $3 95

Be sure to state size and width.
Shipping wt., 1½ lbs.

And now we present the third favorite in Fashion's Review—the Ritz—a black patent leather Front Strap creation with fancy cutouts on the vamp skillfully trimmed in the latest morning glory color sunlight calf. Among its pleasing attributes is style that is authentic and so expressive of the mode, dainty, trim lines and all day comfort. Its toe is molded over the favorite new Parisian last. Poised on a slender 2-inch covered wood spike heel.

Lorraine

15K2734—C - D - E width. Sizes, 2½ to 8.
15K2735—A - B width. Sizes, 3 to 8. $3 45

Be sure to state size and width.

Before changing scenes allow us to introduce the fourth character—of foremost rank in Fashion's Parade, just as distinctive, just as appealing, just as well received by smartly dressed women as its companions—the Front Strap Slipper. Light color leather underlays in spider web design have been artistically wrought into strap, vamp and quarter of this black patent leather model. The toe is neatly fashioned over the round Parisian last. Patent leather covered wood heel, 1¾ inches high.

A Style Leader

15K2738—C-D-E width.
Sizes, 2½ to 8.
15K2739—A-B width.
Sizes, 3 to 8.
State size and width.
Shipping wt., 1¾ lbs.

$4.95

You can depend upon this Front Strap Model being right up to the minute. We present it here in black patent leather ornately trimmed on vamp, strap and quarter with iridescent rose blush patent leather. Same trimming covers the stylish 2½-inch wood spike heel. The toe is designed over the new Parisian last.

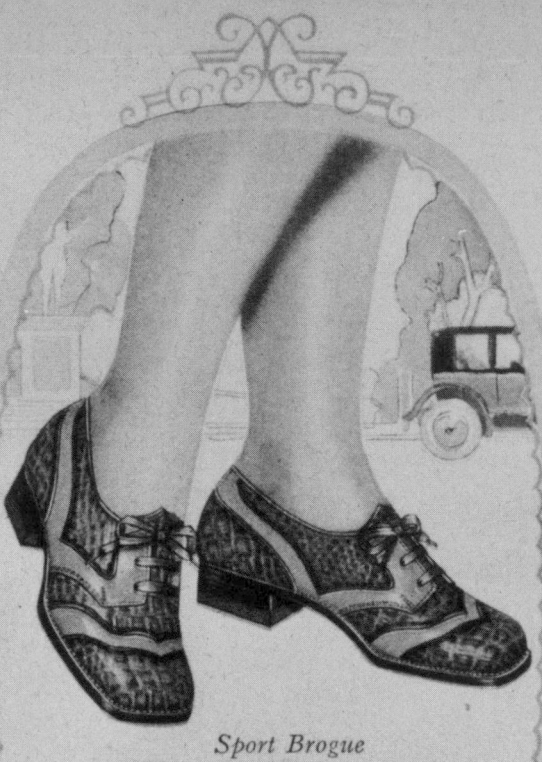

Sport Brogue

15K3228—C-D-E width.
Sizes, 2½ to 8.
15K3229—A-B width.
Sizes, 3 to 8.
State size and width.
Shipping wt., 1¾ lbs.

$4.45

We offer here another sporty three-eyelet brogue effect Oxford for fall and winter wear in brown alligator design leather with an underlay of rose blush calfskin. The nobby new collegiate square toe and 1-inch heel with rubber top lift make it an ideal walking model. Soles are easy bending GENUINE GOODYEAR WELT sewed.

Very Fashionable

15K2742—C-D-E width.
Sizes, 2½ to 8.
15K2743—A-B width.
Sizes, 3 to 8.
Be sure to state size and width.
Shipping wt., 1¾ lbs.

$3.95

Indicative of the style trend is this black patent leather Two-Eyelet Tie Model, with polka dot patent leather quarter. The covered wood spike heel, 2 inches high, and the attractive new modified Parisian shape toe lend an air of style distinction that you will be proud of.

Latest Sport Shawl Pump

15K3224—C-D-E width.
Sizes, 2½ to 8.
15K3225—A-B width.
Sizes, 3 to 8.
Be sure to state size and width. *Shipping wt., 1¾ lbs.*

$4.95

In shopping centers, on campus and on the boulevards of our big cities, where one may casually observe the best and latest creations of fashionable footwear, will be found a goodly assortment of sport styles. This brand new "Collegiate" sport shawl Pump comes in tan calfskin with shawl tip and quarter in brown Scotch design leather. New round boulevard last, 1-inch heel and GENUINE GOODYEAR WELT soles. Elastic front goring under bow insures perfect fit.

If you are in doubt about the size you require, see page 300.

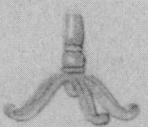

Unique Model

15K2736—C-D-E width. Sizes, 2½ to 8.
15K2737—A-B width. Sizes, 3 to 8.
State size and width.
Shipping wt., 1½ lbs.

$4.48

Beautiful daisy Paisley leather One-Eyelet Sport Style with black patent leather trimming. Strap runs through eyelets with metal buckle which fastens in front. Its low 1¼-inch patent covered wood heel and round new boulevard last impress you as undeniably collegiate.

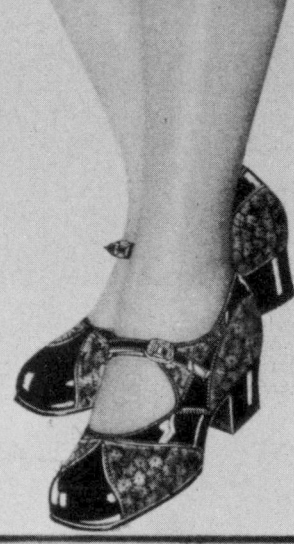

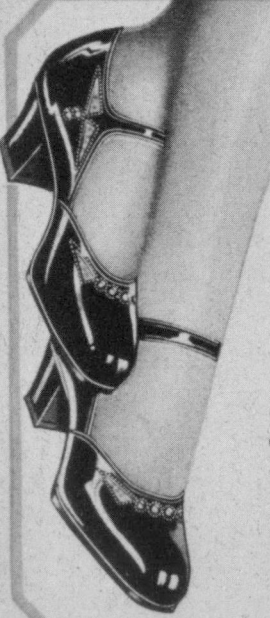

Charming, Indeed!

15K3226
C-D-E width. Sizes, 2½ to 8.

$3.89

15K3227
A-B width. Sizes, 3 to 8.
Be sure to state size and width. *Shpg. wt., 1½ lbs.*

The fact that it's patent leather marks the One-Strap above as an aristocrat in footwear. But fashion has contributed its very latest design of cutouts on vamp and quarter with embossed leather underlay, together with a new modified Parisian last and a 1¾-inch covered wood military heel. GENUINE GOODYEAR WELT soles furnish walking comfort and real wear.

Authentic Style

15K2687—Patent Leather.
15K2618—Rose Blush.
C-D-E width. Sizes, 2½ to 8.
Be sure to state size and width.
Shipping wt., 1½ lbs.

$3.59

Ultra-fashionable Tie in exquisite rose blush calf or glowing black patent leather. Beautiful Paisley trims vamp and lace stay where a pretty silk lace ties through two eyelets. Dainty new Parisian last. 1¾-inch covered wood military heel.

In Keeping With the Mode

15K2740—C-D-E width. Sizes, 2½ to 8.
15K2741—A-B width. Sizes, 3 to 8.
Be sure to state size and width. *Shipping wt., 1½ lbs.*

$3.95

This Three-Eyelet Tie illustrates how exceedingly attractive brown alligator leather can be made by applying a bit of rose blush gingham leather as trimming at proper points. Certainly an harmonious blending of colors. In addition there is a covered wood military heel, 1¾ inches high. New Parisian shape toe.

Isn't It Attractive?
15K2713—C-D-E width. Sizes, 2½ to 8.
15K2714—A-B width. Sizes, 3 to 8.
Be sure to state size and width.
$3.98
Shipping wt., 1½ lbs.
You can always rely on patent leather being in good style. When made up in a front strap model that sets smoothly over the instep you may be sure that your feet are becoming to the most critical observer. Black and white leather enhances the vamp and front and side straps. Shapely new Parisian last. 1¾-inch covered wood military heel. It is sure to win favor.

Trim—Dainty
15K2707—C-D-E width. Sizes, 2½ to 8.
Be sure to state size and width.
$2.48
Shipping wt., 1½ lbs.
Black patent leather One-Strap Slipper with decorative underlay on vamp. 1¾-inch heel with rubber top lift. The toe, built over the favored new Parisian last, offers style that is authentic, daintiness and walking comfort. A model to be proud of.

So Intriguing!
Rose Blush
15K2717—C-D-E width. Sizes, 2½ to 8.
15K2718—A-B width. Sizes, 3 to 8.
Patent Leather
15K2719—C-D-E width. Sizes, 2½ to 8.
15K2720—A-B width. Sizes, 3 to 8.
$3.98
State size and width. *Shipping wt., 1½ lbs.*
Charming front strap Slipper in rose blush calfskin or black patent leather with sunlight calfskin on vamp and front strap. Latest New York last. Wood covered 1¾-inch military heel.

Of Foremost Style
15K3230—C-D-E width. Sizes, 2½ to 8.
15K3231—A-B width. Sizes, 3 to 8.
$4.39
State size and width. *Shipping wt., 1¾ lbs.*
Isn't it neat? Blue and orange stitching is wrought into the saddle, tip and quarter of the tan calfskin Four-Eyelet Oxford here illustrated. Fashioned over the new boulevard last. 1-inch, rubber topped walking heel. Soles are GENUINE GOODYEAR WELT.

Always Appropriate
15K2688—C-D-E width. Sizes, 2½ to 8.
Be sure to state size and width.
$3.69
Shipping wt., 1½ lbs.
There's a bit of Paisley on so many of the models this season because it blends in so harmoniously with all leathers. How well it shows up with black patent leather, as on this One-Strap, at vamp, strap and quarter. Dainty cutouts on sides emphasize the completeness of design, while other style features are the new Parisian modeled toe and covered wood military heel, 1¾ inches high.

If You Are in Doubt About the Size You Require See Page 300

High in Fashion's Favor
15K2708—C-D-E width. Sizes, 2½ to 8.
15K2709—A-B width. Sizes, 3 to 8.
Be sure to state size and width.
$3.98
Shipping wt., 1¼ lbs.
Pastel parchment (a very light tan color) calfskin, embellished by a modish cutout quarter with tan Paisley underlay. So colorful, so vivid, so expressive of the style trend is the One-Strap model here offered. No wonder you admire it! Your friends will, too, when they observe how slender and trim its new Parisian last and 2½-inch covered wood spike heel make your feet appear. Very stylish, indeed.

Novel and Stylish
Black Kid
15K2746—C-D-E width. Sizes, 2½ to 8.
15K2747—A-B width. Sizes, 3 to 8.
Patent Leather
15K2748—C-D-E width. Sizes, 2½ to 8.
15K2749—A-B width. Sizes, 3 to 8.
$4.59
State size and width. *Shipping wt., 1½ lbs.*
All the style of the well liked three-eyelet tie and the softness of genuine black kid or patent leather are embodied in this alluring Oxford. Add to that a stylish cut-out vamp, fancy stitching on quarter and a shield tip. Comfortable medium toe and a rubber top lift on the 1½-inch heel make walking a pleasure. The soles are HAND TURNED—flexible and easy bending.

Portrays Grace and Beauty
15K2702—C-D-E width. Sizes, 2½ to 8.
15K2703—A-B width. Sizes, 3 to 8.
Be sure to state size and width.
$3.98
Shipping wt., 1½ lbs.
Wear this two-eyelet tie Oxford with confidence that it embraces all the best style of today. Black patent leather with Paisley trimmed cutouts on the quarter, a 2-inch covered wood spike heel and the new Parisian shape toe will be sure signs that you show good taste in the selection of your dress footwear.

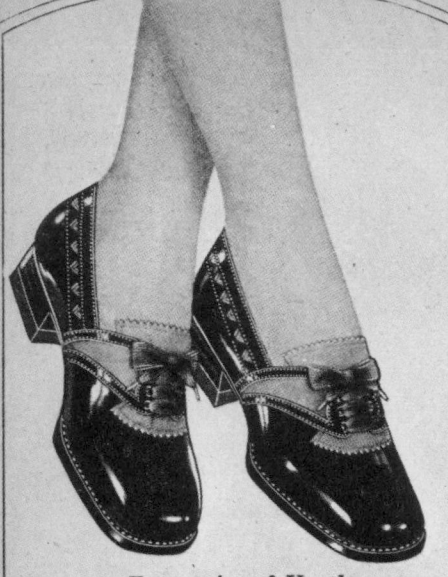

Expressive of Youth

15K2773—C-D-E width.
Sizes, 2½ to 8.
Be sure to state size and width.
Shipping wt., 1¾ lbs.

$2.98

Ranking high in style and good looks is the Four-Eyelet Tie here featured. Its gleaming black patent leather is attractively adorned with parchment calfskin tongue and underlay of same material on quarter and saddle strap. Its new Boulevard shaped toe and 1-inch heel with rubber top lift make it a model particularly suited to young women of today.

Inexpensive Sport Oxford

15K3011—Women's.
Sizes, 2½ to 8......**$1.88**
15K1011—Girls'.
Sizes, 11½ to 2.....**$1.48**
Wide widths only. State size.
Shipping wt.: Women's, 1¾ lbs.; Girls', 1½ lbs.

Economical Sport Oxford for knockabout wear. Full of service from its sturdy stitchdown soles to the very top of its brown leather uppers. Rubber heels.

Striking Contrast

15K2701
C-D-E width.
Sizes, 2½ to 8.
Be sure to state size and width.
Shipping wt., 1¾ lbs.

$2.95

Always in favor, we know this One-Strap will appeal to you. Black and white gingham leather—just a touch on the quarter and vamp—and black patent leather. Popular new Parisian last and 1¼-inch walking heel with rubber top lift.

Very Latest

15K2774
C-D-E width.
Sizes, 2½ to 8.
State size and width.
Shipping wt., 1¾ lbs.

$3.89

Medium tan color, fancy embossed, leather Three-Eyelet Tie, with lighter tan color tongue, pinked at vamp, and fancy perforations. 1¼-inch heel with rubber top lift. New Boulevard last, square toe.

Direct From Fashion Centers

15K2694—Rose Blush.
15K2695—Patent Leather.
C-D-E width. Sizes, 2½ to 8.
State size and width.
Shipping wt., 1¾ lbs.

$2.69

One-Strap, in rose blush or glossy patent leather, with the smart new black and white gingham leather underlay, cleverly introduced on vamp, as illustrated. A shoe no one can help but admire. Medium round toe, 1¼-inch walking heel with rubber top lift.

Indicative of the Style Trend

15K2772—C-D-E width. Sizes, 2½ to 8. State size and width.
Shipping wt., 1¾ lbs.

$2.45

Another dainty One-Strap style that will instinctively win admiring glances and merit style approval. Comes in lustrous black patent leather with light tan Paisley trimming on vamp and strap. Observe its trim new Parisian shaped toe, the 1¼-inch heel with rubber top lift and the fancy cutouts on the quarter.

Snappy Brogue

Women's. Sizes, 2½ to 8.
15K2776—Tan Leather. **$2.39**
15K2777—Black Leather.
Girls'. Sizes, 11½ to 2.
15K1171—Tan Leather. **$1.98**
15K1172—Black Leather.
Wide widths only. State size.
Shipping wt.: Women's, 1¾ lbs. Girls', 1½ lbs.

Appropriate for street or sport wear is the black or tan leather Blucher Oxford here pictured. Square toe, Boulevard last, fancy eyelets and low 1-inch heel with rubber top lift.

Nobby Sport Style

15K3238—C-D-E width. Sizes, 2½ to 8.
Be sure to state size and width.
Shipping wt., 1¾ lbs.

$3.45

Specially adaptable for sports wear or for anyone who does a great deal of walking is this Blucher Oxford, because of its foot form shaped medium round toe. Goodyear Superflex Welt soles of chrome leather and 1-inch heel with rubber top lift. Medium stone color leather with dark tan leather applique on quarter.

At the Peak of Popularity

15K2775—C-D-E width. Sizes, 2½ to 8. State size and width.
Shipping wt., 1¾ lbs.

$1.98

At no time has the One-Strap held greater sway in popularity than this season. It always fits so nicely at the sides and over the instep. We offer it in dressy black patent leather charmingly trimmed with dull embossed leather on strap and quarter. For neat lines notice the Parisian last and 1¼-inch walking heel. Rubber top lift.

Style and Quality

15K1610
Tan Calfskin.
15K1611
Black Calfskin.
C-D-E width.
Sizes, 2½ to 8.
State size and width.
Shipping wt., 2 lbs.

$2.98

For colder weather you will want a pair of these neat Lace Boots either in tan color calfskin with light tan applique at top or in black calfskin with patent leather applique. Swagger new collegiate round toe last with low, 1-inch heel. Rubber top lift.

If You Are in Doubt About the Size You Require, See Page 300

and Girls Will Admire

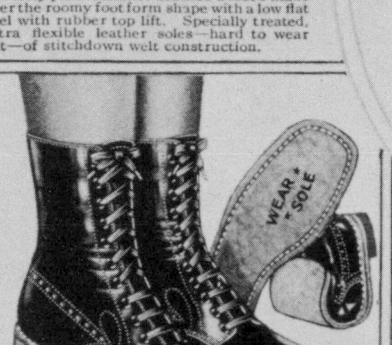
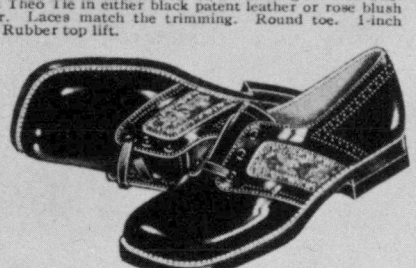

Sheep Wool

Serviceable and Pretty
15K916 — Girls' or Boys'. Sizes, 9 to 2. **98c**
15K917 — Tots'. Sizes, 5 to 8. **89c**
Shipping wt., ¾ lb.
Santa Claus, if you want to please the children, give them these pretty, blue felt Everetts. Round toe. Padded chrome leather soles.

49c
15K923
Sizes, 1 to 6.
Shipping wt., 8 oz.
Tots' comfort Slippers. Red felt with soft padded chrome leather sole. An ankle tie fastens them securely.

59c
15K906 — Pink. 15K907 — Baby Blue. Sizes, 1 to 6. State size.
Shipping wt., 6 oz.
Fur trimmed Bootees. Pink or baby blue felt. White fur trimming. Padded chrome leather soles. Foot form last.

98c
15K932 — Infants'. Sizes, 1 to 6.
Shipping wt., 8 oz.
Little toes will be cozy and comfortable in these pretty white sheepskin Slippers. The soft sheep lining and collar keep baby's feet warm as a toast. Red trim. Fine value.

We Are Proud of Our Sears Slippers

Sheep Wool

Cozy and Warm
15K930 — Girls' or Boys'. Sizes, 12 to 2. . . . . **$1.39**
15K931 — Small Girls' or Boys'. Sizes, 6 to 11. Shipping wt., ¾ lb. **1.19**
Natural sheepskin Hi-Los with sheep wool lining. The warm collar can be turned up to protect their ankles. Comfy soles. Colorful and attractive red pompon on front. Little folks are bound to like them.

Favorite With Santa
15K935 **69c**
Girls' or Boys'. Sizes, 9 to 2.
15K936 **59c**
Tots'. Sizes, 5 to 8.
Shipping wt., ¾ lb.
Better write Santa to leave you a pair. They're warm, red felt Everett style with soft padded chrome leather sole. Protect the children's health by keeping their feet warm when they get up in the morning and before they go to bed at night.

These Make a Practical Gift
15K927 — Girls' or Boys'. Sizes, 9 to 2. **69c**
15K928 — Tots'. Sizes, 5 to 8. **59c**
Shipping wt., ¾ lb.
Pretty red felt Everett, with hair felt sole. It is not expensive and will give surprisingly long service. At Christmas time little slippers like these are always a welcome gift for your own children and those of relatives or friends.

All Slippers on this page are wide widths and do not come in half sizes, unless otherwise stated. State size wanted.

Children Like These
15K919 — Girls' or Boys'. Sizes, 9 to 2. **98c**
15K920 — Tots'. Sizes, 5 to 8. **89c**
Shipping wt., ¾ lb.
These cute little red felt Slippers have sheep wool collars and fleece lining throughout. Very warm and serviceable and exceptionally well made.

89c
Aren't They Pretty?
15K905 — Girls' or Boys'. Sizes, 9 to 2. State size. **89c**
Shipping wt., ¾ lb.
These fawn color felt Everetts with brown tongue and gray plush trimming around the top are popular with children. Leather cushion comfy soles.

These Are Nice, Also
15K908 — Girls' or Boys'. Sizes, 9 to 2. **85c**
15K909 — Tots'. Sizes, 5 to 8. **75c**
Shipping wt., ¾ lb.
Very popular Copenhagen blue felt Bootee with bunny design on collar. Soft padded chrome leather soles.

Leather Slippers

Ask Santa to Bring This Hi-Lo
15K901 — Girls' or Boys'. Sizes, 9 to 2. **89c**
15K902 — Tots'. Sizes, 5 to 8. **79c**
Shipping wt., ¾ lb.
One of the nicest Slippers in old St. Nick's workshops. Red felt with red velvet turnup collar to keep the ankles warm. Soft padded chrome leather soles. Big savings!

Be Sure to State Size

95c
"Heap Big Chief"
15K918 — Girls' or Boys'. Sizes, 9 to 2. State size. Shipping wt., ¾ lb.
Real Indian Moccasins of tan suede leather. Red felt lined. Embossed Indian head on the vamp. Leather cushion comfy sole.

98c
Very Serviceable
15K929 — Girls' or Boys'. Sizes, 9 to 2. State size. Shipping wt., ¾ lb.
Like regular grown-ups. Felt lined blue leather Slippers with neat perforations on vamp and quarter. Leather comfy sole.

Restful Juliet for Children
15K914 — Girls' or Boys'. Sizes, 9 to 2. State size. **98c**
Shipping wt., 1 lb.
The children will look for a pair of these on the tree Christmas morning. Red felt Juliet trimmed with black fur. Stitchdown welt leather sole. Rubber heel.

Rayon

Satin

Satin
Dainty French Mules
15K3678 — Copenhagen Blue.
15K3679 — Nell Rose. Women's. Sizes, 2½ to 8, including half sizes. State size.
$1.79
Delicate pastel shades of silk thread embroider the toes of these lovely satin Mules. Smart satin covered 1½-inch heel, and the sock lining is quilted satin. Soft padded chrome leather soles.

Attractive Boudoir Slippers
15K3682 — Old Gold.
15K3683 — Turquoise Blue. Women's. Sizes, 3 to 8. No half sizes. **98c**
Shipping wt., 1 lb.
Made of quilted Rayon prettily trimmed with gold braid and charming ornament at side. Soft padded chrome leather sole.

So Charmingly Embroidered
15K3680 — Nell Rose.
15K3681 — Black. Women's. Sizes, 2½ to 8, including half sizes. **$1.59**
Shipping wt., ¾ lb.
Made of fine satin with gold color embroidered vamp and lace braid. Very smart. Soft padded chrome leather soles.

Velvet
The Very Newest
15K3665 — Old Rose.
15K3666 — Blue. Women's. Sizes, 3 to 8. No half sizes. **$1.49**
Shipping wt., ¾ lb.
Velvet is the latest note in Boudoir Slippers. The rich plain colors are trimmed with fancy braid and dainty ornament. Soft padded chrome leather soles.

80 **SEARS ROEBUCK AND CO.** WLS *The World's Largest Store*

Your Feet Will Never Know it's Winter

Popular Warm Lined Oxford

No Need to Have Cold Feet
15K3409—Sizes, 3 to 9. No half sizes. Wide widths only. Be sure to state size. **$1 95**
Shipping wt., 1½ lbs.

One of our customers suggested the design of this fleece lined Oxford. We appreciate that suggestion because it gives us an opportunity to offer the kind of shoes our customers want. Made of soft black genuine kid leather, fleece lined. Roomy, round toe, low 1-inch heel with rubber top lift.

Warm Feet on Winter Days

15K2415—Sizes, 3 to 9. No half sizes. Wide widths only. Be sure to state size. **$1 89**
Shipping wt., 1¾ lbs.

Good looking, comfortable and economical fleece lined Shoe. Comes in black genuine kid leather with a black felt top. Has rubber heel. At this remarkably low price it is a real bargain and a wise investment in health protection.

Fleece Lining for Warmth
"Compo-Soles" for Wear

15K2400—Sizes, 3 to 9. No half sizes. Wide widths only. Be sure to state size. **$2 98**
Shipping wt., 2 lbs.

If you want long wear with absolute comfort and warmth this fleece lined Shoe is the one to buy. Made of soft black genuine kid leather. "Compo-Soles", which are much more durable than leather soles, give them wearing strength. The wide toe, the blucher style and the low, 1-inch heel with rubber top lift provide the comfort. And for warmth you have the fleece lining.

Genuine Sheep Wool Lined
Great Shoe for Cold Weather

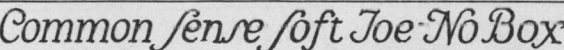

15K2405—Sizes, 3 to 9. No half sizes. Wide widths only. Be sure to state size. **$3 98**
Shipping wt., 2¼ lbs.

Your feet will be comfortable on coldest days this winter in these fine quality, soft, black genuine kid Shoes. Heavily lined with sheep's wool, they are the warmest shoes procurable for those troubled with cold feet. Higher cut than the ordinary shoe and has an extra wide ball. Rubber heel. Considering the fine quality, we're sure you will admit that $3.98 is a very low price for such a splendid shoe.

Common Sense Soft Toe No Box

Fits Closely and Snugly

15K2401 — Sizes, 3 to 9. No half sizes. Wide widths only. State size. **$1 95**

Shipping wt., 1½ lbs.

Neither the cold nor the cost is noticeable in a pair of these black genuine kid leather Shoes with black felt top. Fleece lined. A common sense shoe. Roomy, broad toe without any stiffening and the rubber heel for comfort. Get your pair today and be prepared for cold weather.

So Warm! So Comfortable!

15K2411—Sizes, 3 to 9. No half sizes. Wide widths only. Be sure to state size. **$2 69**
Shipping wt., 1¾ lbs.

Forget the cold and realize the joy of supreme foot comfort on the very coldest days of winter! It's the easiest thing imaginable in the black genuine kid common sense Shoe pictured at the left. Fleece lined throughout. The plain soft toe, the low heel, with rubber top lift, and the low price are three most comforting features. Typical of Sears great shoe values.

Stylish Winter Model

Snugly Smart
15K3424—Sizes, 2½ to 8, including half sizes; also 9. Wide widths only. State size. **$2 95**
Shipping wt., 1½ lbs.

Now you can have neat dress shoes that are just as warmly lined as those you have found so practical for daily wear. These two-button Shoes of black kid have comfortable round toes and 1½-inch military heels with rubber top lifts. The warm fleece lining will make your feet happy on cold days, and the trim lines will keep them looking smart.

Warm, Neat, Comfortable

15K2417—Sizes, 2½ to 8, including half sizes; also 9. Wide widths only. State size. **$2 98**
Shipping wt., 1¾ lbs.

So neat and dressy that you'd never suspect it had a warm fleece lining to protect your feet from the cold. Soft genuine black kid with sewed sole and 1¾-inch heel with rubber top lift. The blucher style and the plain toe insure comfort and plenty of foot room.

Built for Warmth and Foot Support

15K2404—Sizes, 2½ to 8, including half sizes; also 9. Wide widths only. Be sure to state size. **$2 98**
Shpg. wt., 1¾ lbs.

Sears special steel arch supporting shank and a long arch supporting counter are entirely new features in warm lined shoes. We know many women will favor it because it combines the advantages of comfort, warmth and proper support to the feet. Made of black genuine kid leather, fleece lined. Roomy round toe. 1-inch heel with rubber top lift.

For Little Girls

Fancy Color Trimming

Goodyear Welt

15K1337—Small Girls' Sizes, 8½ to 11. Wide widths only. Be sure to state size. *Shipping wt., 1¼ lbs.* **$2.65**

All the style of a trimly fitting lace boot and the dressy quality of sparkling black patent leather with a fancy black and white gingham leather applique on the top. Neatly perforated design finishes it off nicely. Thoughtfully built over the wide roomy foot form last with long wearing GENUINE GOODYEAR WELT soles and a spring rubber heel.

Drill Lined

Paisley Trim

Warm Lined

15K624 Fleece lining. **15K625** Drill lining. **98c** Tots'. Sizes, 3 to 8. Wide widths only. State size. *Shipping wt., ¾ lb.*

Serviceable, soft and comfortable genuine black kid shoes for fall and winter wear — one with warm fleece lining for the colder, more severe weather and the other drill lined for the occasional warm days. Flexible hand turned soles. Foot form last.

Extra Reinforced Toe

Red "Compo Sole"

One of Our Very Prettiest

15K1335—Small Girls' Sizes, 8½ to 11. Wide widths only. Be sure to state size. **$2.39**

Shipping wt., 1¼ lbs.

Not only one of **our** very prettiest shoes but we can safely venture just about the prettiest shoe you will find anywhere this season no matter where you go to select your little girls' shoes. Nowadays parents are demanding that their children's dress footwear be just as stylish, just as neat appearing, just as well fitting as their own, with quality and long wear in addition. This black patent leather lace shoe with its two-tone iridescent patent leather saddle embodies all the features you desire. Its foot form shape, easy bending stitchdown welt leather soles and spring rubber heel assure proper fit and good service.

Long Wear at Little Cost

15K1324—Black Leather. **15K1318**—Patent Leather. Small Girls' Sizes, 8½ to 11. Wide widths only. State size. **$1.85**

Shipping wt., 1¼ lbs.

Keeping little girls in everyday shoes won't be such a problem nor nearly so hard on your pocketbook if you fit them out with these good grade black leather or patent leather boots. Nice enough for dress wear, too. Their red "Compo Soles" will outwear almost two pairs of shoes with leather soles and will not mark floors. Notice the extra thickness at the toe where a lot of wear comes. Foot form last, of course, and flexible, stitchdown welt sole construction.

15K603 Tots'. Sizes, 3 to 8. Wide widths only. **$1.59** *Shipping wt., ¾ lb.*

Charming black patent leather Roman Slipper. Flexible hand turned sole and wide roomy toe for comfort.

15K635 Tots'. Sizes, 3 to 8. Wide widths only. State size. **$1.75** *Shpg. wt., ¾ lb.*

Shiny black patent leather blucher model with Paisley leather trimming at lace stay. Foot form shape. Turn sole.

Gingham Leather Trim

$1.98 **15K1312** Small Girls'. Sizes, 8½ to 11. Wide widths only. State size. *Shpg. wt., 1¼ lbs.*

Little girls will be proud of this black patent leather high shoe with its contrasting black and white gingham leather trimming. Stitchdown welt soles. Foot form last. Spring rubber heels.

15K1315 Small Girls'. Sizes, 8½ to 11. Wide widths only. State size. **$1.95** *Shpg. wt., 1¼ lbs.*

Equally attractive is the black calf boot at the right with black patent leather applied at lace stay and side. Foot form shape. Flexible stitchdown welt soles and spring rubber heels.

Wide Widths Only Be Sure to State Size

Wide Widths State Size

Gingham Leather Trim

Paisley Underlay

15K375 Tots'. Sizes, 3 to 8. **$1.45** *Shpg. wt., ¾ lb.*

How attractive! Black patent leather One-Strap underlaid with Paisley leather on vamp and strap! Wide roomy foot form shape. Flexible stitchdown welt soles.

15K378 Tots'. Sizes, 4 to 8. **$1.45** *Shipping wt., ¾ lb.*

Blucher oxford, well fitting at toe and instep. Black patent leather with four eyelets. Stitchdown welt soles. Foot form last.

15K374 Tots'. Sizes, 3 to 8. **$1.69** *Shipping wt., ¾ lb.*

So dressy a One-Strap model for little folks. Black patent leather with black and white gingham leather at front. Hand turned soles. Foot form last.

First Steps

Paisley Trim

15K821 Babies'. Sizes, 2 to 6. Wide widths only. State size. **$1.59** *Shipping wt., ¾ lb.*

Black patent leather with Paisley leather trimming. Flexible stitchdown welt chrome leather soles. Foot form last.

15K515—Babies'. Sizes, 1 to 5. Wide widths only. State size. **$1.29** *Shipping wt., ¾ lb.*

Three-strap Roman Sandal of exceptional quality and striking appearance. Made of patent leather. Foot form last. Flexible turn leather sole.

15K535 Babies'. Sizes, 2 to 6. Wide widths only. State size. **95c** *Shipping wt., ¾ lb.*

Dainty Blucher Oxford for babies' first steps. Comes in black patent leather. Modeled over nature's foot form last with bend easy stitchdown welt soles.

Black and Patent Leather

15K809—Black Kid. **15K810**—Patent Leather. Babies'. Sizes, 2 to 6. Wide widths only. Be sure to state size. **98c** *Shipping wt., ¾ lb.*

So soft and comfortable, so neat and dressy are these black kid or patent leather shoes in a blucher lace style. Wide and roomy all over, allowing your youngsters' feet natural development. Foot form shape. Flexible, easy bending stitchdown welt soles.

15K520 Babies'. Sizes, 1 to 5. Wide widths only. State size. **85c** *Shipping wt., ¾ lb.*

Nice looking black patent leather One-Strap. Flexible hand turned soles and wide, round and roomy foot form last — room for all five toes.

First Steps

15K813—Babies'. Sizes, 1 to 5. Wide widths only. State size. **89c** *Shipping wt., ¾ lb.*

This baby Shoe will give you lasting satisfaction. Made of soft, black kid leather over the foot form last with extra flexible turned sole.

Gingham Leather Trim

15K534 Babies'. Sizes, 1 to 5. Wide widths only. State size. **98c** *Shpg. wt., 8 oz.*

How effectively black and white gingham leather adorns this alluring little black patent leather One-Strap model! How extremely easy bending are the hand turned soles! And how proper for first steps is the foot form shape!

15K536 Babies'. Sizes, 2 to 6. Wide widths only. State size. **95c** *Shipping wt., ¾ lb.*

Baby's feet look just as stylish and well dressed in this model as your own when you wear those new shoes of yours. Black patent leather with attractive cutouts underlaid with colorful Paisley leather. Stitchdown welt soles. Foot form last.

Paisley Underlay

Babies' Pride

15K816—Babies'. Sizes, 1 to 5. Wide widths. State size. **98c** *Shipping wt., ¾ lb.*

Sturdiness, as well as neatness, make this shoe mothers' favorite. Extra flexible hand turned sole. Black patent leather with dull leather tops.

TOTTER
Travelers for Tots

15K608 $1.79
Sizes, 4 to 8.
Shpg. wt., 1 lb.
Moccasin vamp, blucher style of golden color, chrome tanned leather (called elkskin). Foot form last. Stitchdown welt leather soles. Extra flexible.

15K607 $1.69
Sizes, 3 to 8.
Shpg. wt., 1 lb.
Shiny black patent leather with stone color kid top. Attractive underlays on vamp. Hand turned sole. Roomy foot form last.

15K615 $1.98
Sizes, 5 to 8. Wide widths only. Be sure to state size.
Shipping wt., ¾ lb.
Patent leather high Shoe with bird design cutout at top underlaid with Paisley color leather. GENUINE GOODYEAR WELT sole. Foot form last. Spring heel.

Wide Widths Only Be Sure to State Size

15K648—Tan.
15K649—Patent. $1.69
Sizes, 4 to 8. Wide widths. State size.
Shipping wt., 1 lb.
Neat, stylish and sturdy Bluchers of either tan calfskin or glossy black patent leather. Correct in every way for active, growing feet. Roomy wide toes built over the foot form last and long wearing, flexible stitchdown welt chrome leather sole.

15K617—Sizes' 3 to 8. Wide widths only. State size. $1.98
Shipping wt., ¾ lb.
Pretty, indeed! Glistening black patent leather with stone color leather top. Patent leather lace stay. Foot form last. Extra flexible hand turned sole. A fine bargain.

15K646—Tan.
15K647—Patent. $1.98
Sizes, 4 to 8. Wide widths only. Be sure to state size.
Shipping wt., 1 lb.
What tot wouldn't like these? And mothers, too! Tan calfskin or black patent leather. Flexible stitchdown sole. Spring heel. Foot form shape.

15K645—Sizes, 4 to 8. Wide widths only. State size. $1.98
Shipping wt., 1 lb.
How dressy this pretty Shoe will look on your little one's feet. Made of parchment color calf with attractive cutouts on vamp underlaid with Paisley embossed leather. Easy bending stitchdown welt chrome tanned leather sole, sturdy and serviceable. Spring heel. Foot form last.

Wide Widths Only Be Sure to State Size

15K643—Sizes, 4 to 8. $1.89
Shipping wt., 1 lb.
Embossed stone color leather. Two-tone water wave effect. Chrome leather stitchdown welt sole. Spring heel.

15K609—Sizes, 4 to 8. $1.98
Shipping wt., ¾ lb.
Patent leather with black and white gingham leather trimmings. Chrome leather stitchdown welt sole.

Infants' Soft Soled Shoes

No Half Sizes

15K227—Pink trim.
15K228—Blue trim.
15K229—White trim. 65c
Sizes, 0 to 3. *Shipping wt., 6 oz.*
Two-button Moccasins of white leather.

15K223—Sizes, 0 to 3. 3 Pairs 98c
Shpg. wt., 6 oz.
Assorted colors; White and blue; brown and white, or all white. Only one size to box.

For Tiny Tots

Wide Widths
15K804—Parchment color.
15K805—Tan color.
15K806—Patent leather. **State Size** $1.69
Sizes, 2 to 6. *Shpg. wt., ¾ lb.*
Paisley leather underlay. Stitchdown welt sole. Foot form last.

15K807—Sauterne color.
15K808—Tan color. 98c
Sizes, 2 to 6. Wide widths only. State size.
Shpg. wt., ¾ lb.
Tiny tots' First Step blucher shoes. Uppers are sauterne color soft chrome tanned leather (called elkskin), or tan calfskin. Flexible stitchdown welt sole. Wide, roomy foot form last.

15K221 Blue
15K220 Pink. Sizes, 1 to 6. 69c
Shpg. wt., 6 oz.
Infants' quilted artificial silk Moccasins with warm furlike trimming. Nice for cold mornings and evenings. Soft padded chrome leather sole.

No Half Sizes State Size Shpg. wt., 6 oz.

15K232 59c
Sizes, 0 to 3. *Shpg. wt., 6 oz.*
Black patolite (softer than patent leather) with black and white gingham leather cuff on tops.

15K204 69c
Sizes, 0 to 3.
White leather with dainty pompon on front. Soft, padded leather sole. Comes packed in a gift box.

No Half Sizes
15K224 Pink trimmed.
15K225—Blue trimmed. Sizes, 0 to 3. State size. 59c
Shipping wt., 6 oz.
White leather with pink or blue buttons and underlays on the front. Will look very dressy on baby's feet.

15K811 98c
Sizes, 1 to 5. State size.
Shpg. wt., 8 oz.
Patent leather with dull kid top. Orange stitching and embossed leather applique on vamp. Foot form last. Hand turned sole.

15K818 $1.49
Sizes, 1 to 5.
Shpg. wt., 8 oz.
Patent leather with parchment color kid top. Bronze leather underlay on toe. Handturned sole. Foot form last.

No Half Sizes

No Half Sizes State Size Shpg. wt., 6 oz.

No Half Sizes

15K812 $1.39
Sizes, 1 to 5. State size.
Shpg. wt., 8 oz.
Tan kid leather with pastel parchment color kid top. Foot form shape. Turn sole. Applique on vamp.

15K815 $1.59
Sizes, 1 to 5. State size.
Shpg. wt., 8 oz.
Charming pastel parchment color kid with cutouts on vamp underlaid with fancy tan Paisley leather. Foot form last. Hand turned sole.

15K226 69c
Sizes, 0 to 3. State size.
Shpg. wt., 6 oz.
Pastel parchment color soft leather shoe with soft padded soles. Pompon on front.

15K230 Sauterne color leather.
15K231—Black leather. Sizes, 0 to 3. 53c
Shpg. wt., 6 oz.
Sauterne or black color leather. Chrome leather sole. Black model has white buttons and stitching.

15K234 Black and white.
15K235 — Black and parchment. Sizes, 0 to 3. 53c
Black patolite (softer than patent leather) with white or parchment color leather top.

15K233—Sizes, 0 to 3. State size. 59c
Shipping wt., 6 oz.
So dressy. Pure white soft chrome tanned leather. Looks so nice with all of baby's white dresses.

for Mail Carriers Policemen Firemen Railroad Men

① Sewed Heel Seat
② Arch Support
③ Weather Protection Storm Welt
④ 2 Full Soles
⑤ Goodyear Welt
⑥ Wear Proof Lining

$4⁶⁵

67K4001
Sizes, 5 to 12. D-E width. Be sure to state size.

Shipping wt., 3¾ lbs.

We say they're for Policemen—Firemen—Railroad Men—Mail-Carriers. But they're really for every man, especially for men who are on their feet hours at a time and who don't want to be buying new shoes every month or so. They are the standard of value. Because only the **best** of everything goes into them. Fine quality black boxed calf uppers. Extra selected double oak soles. First quality rubber heels. But why go on? Study the illustration. Note the features. And then understand that they are made by one of the best factories in America. **Men, this is a shoe.**

Genuine Australian Kangaroo

Oxfords
67K4480 D-E width.
67K4481—B-C width.

$5⁹⁵

Shoes
67K4220—D-E width.
67K4221—B-C width.

Sizes, 5 to 11. State size and width.
Shipping wt., 2½ lbs.

Soft as kidskin, yet tough as horsehide. That's GENUINE Australian kangaroo leather. The new special narrow shank makes these shoes hug the arch just as a glove does your hand. All the way through in construction and materials you'll find nothing but the very best. Kangaroo leather will not peel or scuff and has a luster you'll find in no other material. Takes a very high polish. Tests made by our Government prove kangaroo leather is the toughest known. Buy these shoes for looks, for comfort, for long wear, for economy. GENUINE GOODYEAR WELT. Rubber heels.

The Most Flexible Shoe in the World

$5⁹⁵

Tan Calfskin Oxfords
67K4370—D-E width.
67K4371—B-C width.
Sizes, 5 to 11.

Black Calfskin Oxfords
67K4470—D-E width.
67K4471—B-C width.
Sizes, 5 to 11.

$5⁹⁵

Black Kid Shoes
67K4164—D-E width.
67K4174—B-C width.
Sizes, 6 to 12.

$5⁹⁵

State size and width. *Shipping wt.: Oxfords, 2½ lbs., Shoes, 2¾ lbs.*

So famous, they need no introduction, these nationally known and nationally advertised shoes and oxfords. These are the new styles which embrace that patented feature found only in Soft Walks—extreme flexibility which allows your foot muscles and bones to work naturally. strengthens weak arches and aids even those whose feet are extremely tender to walk in comfort. Only the best materials and the finest workmanship in these splendid GENUINE GOODYEAR WELTS with rubber heels.

Congress Style
67K4145—Black. Sizes, 5 to 12. D-E width. State size and width. **$3⁹⁸**

Shipping wt., 2½ lbs.
Genuine Dr. Johnson's Shoe, sold only by us. Soft kidskin. Cushion innersole. Sears special steel arch supports. ALL LEATHER. Rubber heels. GENUINE GOODYEAR WELT.

Bankers' Last
67K4158—Brown. **$3⁹⁸**
67K4159—Black.
Sizes, 5 to 12. D-E width. State size and width. *Shipping wt., 2½ lbs.*
Has all the features which have made these shoes famous. The kidskin leather is extremely soft and comfortable. Steel Arch Supports.

$3⁹⁸

Dr. Johnson's
Sears Special Steel Arch Supports
Dr. Johnson's shoes, famous the country over, are made of softest kidskin. Built-in cushion insoles and special steel arch supports are an aid to tired feet. ALL LEATHER. Rubber heels. GENUINE GOODYEAR WELTS.

$4⁹⁵

Extra Large
Sizes, 6 to 16.
67K4150 Black. Extra large sizes, 6 to 16. Wide widths only. Be sure to state size. **$4⁹⁵**
Shipping wt., 2¾ lbs.
Extra quality shoe. Furnished in all sizes from 6 to 16. Has all of the features found in Dr. Johnson's Shoes. Steel Arch Supports.

Extra Wide
67K4160—Black Kid. **$4⁹⁵**
67K4161—Brown Kid.
Sizes, 6 to 13. Wide widths only. Be sure to state size. *Shipping wt., 3 lbs.*
Dr. Johnson's Shoe made for men who need an extra wide shoe. All sizes from 6 to 13. Choice of black or brown soft kidskin. Steel Arch Supports.

Gold Bond

The new **GOLD BONDS!** And that means the newest of the new—the most favored of the season's styles in last, pattern and leather.

And while these are the new style **GOLD BONDS**—every one is built to the famous **GOLD BOND** quality, just as good as gold and *just as standard*.

We're proud of them—*mighty proud*. We know they set the pace in shoe values everywhere.

$4.00

Tan Calfskin
67K4387—D-E width.
67K4388—B-C width.
Black Calfskin
67K4389—D-E width.
67K4390—B-C width.
Sizes, 5 to 11. State size and width.
Shipping wt., 2¾ lbs.
Calfskins for wear and looks, too. Simplicity in style which bespeaks real class. You never bought as much Shoe for $4.00 elsewhere. Oak bend sole. Rubber heels! And Gold Bond, you know what that means. GENUINE GOODYEAR WELT.

$4.40

Tan Calfskin
67K4362—D-E width.
67K4363—B-C width.
Sizes, 5 to 11. State size and width.
Shipping wt., 2½ lbs.
Tan Scotch Grain calfskin! Blucher style! Oak bend sole! Rubber heel! All for $4.40. A man's fall and winter Oxford—Gold Bond in every respect. A value extraordinary, because Scotch grain calfskin leather is very costly. GENUINE GOODYEAR WELT assures long wear.

$4.40

Tan Calfskin
67K4364—D-E width.
67K4365—B-C width.
Black Calfskin
67K4366—D-E width.
67K4367—B-C width.
Sizes, 5 to 11. Be sure to state size and width.
Shipping wt., 2¾ lbs.
Have you ever seen a "Snappier" Shoe in your life? It's the choice of thousands and we selected it after visiting all of the shoe centers of America. Real calfskin upper. Alligator trimmed, oak bend sole, Rubber heel. Gold Bond, too. And GENUINE GOODYEAR WELT.

$4.40

Tan Calfskin
67K4391—D-E width.
67K4392—B-C width.
Black Calfskin
67K4393—D-E width.
67K4394—B-C width.
Sizes, 5 to 11. Be sure to state size and width.
Shipping wt., 2½ lbs.
The season's most popular leather is alligator. Certainly you'll find it in the highest priced shoes. Gold Bond construction throughout. That means calfskin upper, oak bend sole, rubber heel. And, of course they are GENUINE GOODYEAR WELT construction.

$4.00

Patent Leather
67K4358—D-E width.
67K4359—B-C width.
Tan Calfskin
67K4360—D-E width.
67K4361—B-C width.
Sizes, 5 to 11. Be sure to state size and width.
Shipping wt., 2¾ lbs.
Here's the Gold Bond patent leather for real dress wear and a new grain trimmed tan calfskin for business use. Both styles are up to the minute and both are real values. GENUINE GOODYEAR WELT. Rubber heels for comfort.

$4.40

Tan Calfskin
67K4100—D-E width.
67K4101—B-C width.
Black Calfskin
67K4102—D-E width.
67K4103—B-C width.
Sizes, 5 to 11. Be sure to state size and width.
Shipping wt., 2¾ lbs.
Gold Bonds wouldn't be complete for fall and winter without this appealing high Shoe. In either tan or black calfskin it's in splendid taste. We believe this is the lowest priced all Calfskin Shoe on the market. Oak bend sole. GENUINE GOODYEAR WELT construction Rubber heel for comfort.

$4.00

Tan Trimmed
67K4466—D-E width.
67K4467—B-C width.
Black Trimmed
67K4468—D-E width.
67K4469—B-C width.
Sizes, 5 to 11. Be sure to state size and width.
Shipping wt., 2¾ lbs.
Here's the Gold Bond Sport Oxford, stylish with its tan or black alligator trimming contrasting the lighter color sport leather. Made like all Gold Bonds—as real shoes should be. Oak sole. Rubber heel. GENUINE GOODYEAR WELT.

★ The Greatest Work Shoe Money Can Buy ★

The Nation's Favorite

SMOOTH SIDE OF LEATHER TO THE FEET

Tongue Gusset Sewed to Upper to Keep Out Dirt and Water

$2⁷⁹ A PAIR

Genuine Goodyear Welt

One-Piece Full Vamp With Toe Cap Stitched Four Times

Full Grain Heavy Oak Tanned Leather Innersoles

Eyelets Heavy Brass

Two Full Grain Leather Heavy Outersoles

Triple Stitched With Waxed Thread

Canvas Packing Between Inner and Outer to Keep Shoe From Creaking

Solid Leather Counters Made of Best Sole Leather

Heels 5-Ply Solid Leather

67K4756—E-D Widths (Wide). Sizes, 8½ to 11.
67K4766—C Width (Medium Wide). Sizes, 9 to 11½.
Be sure to state size and width.
Shipping wt., 4 lbs.

$2⁷⁹

This Shoe is one of the greatest values in the whole catalog of big values. It stands out among other work shoes like steel does over iron. It is **The Shoe** for the workingman regardless of the kind of work! No matter whether you are looking especially for foot comfort, for foot protection or shoe service or shoe saving, we still say "It's the Greatest Work Shoe Money Can Buy," and here's the reason: This shoe was made for exactly the sort of service we recommend it, and it cost the United States Government $6 to $7 a pair! Built to stand up day after day, week after week and month after month under all sorts of conditions, and in all kinds of weather. Look at the illustration above and study the different good points of the shoe, then judge for yourself if it has an equal at $2.79.

67K4635—Sizes, 6 to 12. Wide widths only. Be sure to state size.
Shipping wt., 3¼ lbs.

$2⁹⁸

DOUBLE OAK TANNED LEATHER SOLE

STORM WELT

BLACK CHROME LEATHER WATER REPELLANT

This Shoe, with moccasin style toe, is always popular because it combines unusual comfort with unusual durability. Made of fine, soft chrome tanned (elkskin) water repellant black leather, with a soft but strong LEATHER LINING IN THE VAMP, furnishing additional comfort. It has two full solid leather soles with a special weatherproof welt between the uppers and the soles to keep out moisture. Priced unusually low for a shoe of this quality.

67K4816—Men's and Big Boys'. Sizes, 6 to 12..........**$1.98**
67K5316—Boys'. Sizes, 1 to 5½.......... **1.89**
Wide widths only. Be sure to state size.
Shipping wt.: Men's and Big Boys', 3 lbs.; Boys', 2½ lbs.

If you are looking for Comfort, Durability and Economy you will be pleased with this fine lightweight Work Shoe. Uppers are of genuine chrome tanned mustard color tan leather (called elkskin). Made with a medium weight "Wearflex" sole for added lightness, and an extra leather middle sole sewed to it with heavy thread. Heels are of live, springy rubber. Easy on the feet and low in price.

SOFT CHROME TANNED LEATHER (ELKSKIN UPPERS)

EXTRA LEATHER SOLE

WEARFLEX SOLES

RUBBER HEEL

67K4862—Men's and Big Boys'. Sizes, 6 to 12.......................**$1.65**
67K5305—Boys'. Sizes, 1 to 5½....................... **1.49**
67K5905—Small Boys'. Sizes, 9 to 13½....................... **1.29**
Wide widths. State size.
Shipping wt.: Men's and Big Boys', 2¾ lbs.; Boys', 2½ lbs.; Small Boys', 2 lbs.

Easy on your feet as a house slipper, and not much heavier in weight either. But for wear—what a shoe! The uppers are dark brown, soft, suede-like split leather, known generally as "muleskin," because it's so tough, and the soles are medium heavy all leather, with leather heels. For a "Featherweight" work shoe, these can't be beat for comfort and wear.

CHROME TANNED (ELKSKIN) SOFT LEATHER UPPERS

RUBBER HEEL

SURE-GRIP "COMPO-SOLE"

67K4651—Men's. Sizes, 5 to 12. Wide widths only. Be sure to state size.

$2⁴⁸

Shipping wt., 3 lbs.

The up to date work shoe is an oxford. Men, there's nothing like it for comfort, because it lets your feet "breathe." Here's our work oxford leader. Sturdy and comfortable, lasting and low priced. Its soft, full chrome tanned brown leather (called elkskin) uppers are good looking and easy on your feet. Its famous, "Compo Soles" will wear like iron. Heels are of good quality, live, springy rubber. An oxford carefully made in every detail, one that will stand the strain of hard wear.

Work Shoes

Mighty Fine Buy!

BELLOWS TONGUE

SOFT SMOOTH LEATHER UPPERS

WEARFLEX SOLE

$1.98

Men's and Big Boys' Sizes

67K4616—Men's and Big Boys'. Sizes, 6 to 12. **$1.98**
67K5216—Boys'. **1.89**
Sizes, 1 to 5½.
Wide widths only. Be sure to state size.
Shipping wt.: Men's and Big Boys', 3½ lbs.; Boys', 2¾ lbs.
Do not let the low Sears price mislead you. For this is a mighty good shoe in spite of the big saving it offers. The uppers are tan color, double tanned, smooth split leather, satisfactory both for looks and wear. Extra heavy, flexible "Wearflex" soles and rubber heels make for durability. Soles are nailed to uppers and "put on to stay." This is a real bargain shoe that we take pleasure in recommending to our customers.

$1.65
A PAIR

67K4817 Men's and Big Boys'. Sizes, 5 to 12. Wide widths only. Be sure to state size.
Shipping wt., 3 lbs.
Grab this bargain! The leader of leaders in value—an outstanding example of the buying power of the World's Largest Shoe Store. And how it wears! The brown chrome tanned (elkskin) uppers are soft as gloves, yet unbelievably strong. Soles are of double thickness at greatest points of wear. Leather heels. A real piece of merchandise, all the way through! Try a pair. Then you'll say they're **worth twice our price!**

67K4630—Men's and Big Boys'. Sizes, 6 to 12. **$1.89**
67K5267—Boys'. **1.69**
Sizes, 1 to 5½.
Wide widths only. Be sure to state size.
Shipping wt.: Men's and Big Boys', 3¼ lbs.; Boys', 3 lbs.
Surprisingly long wear and amazingly big saving were the two points we had in mind when selecting this work shoe. So if that's what you are looking for, it's the shoe to order. The stout, double tanned, brown split leather is not made for dressy looks, but nothing can be said against it for SERVICE. The oak tanned leather soles (two thicknesses where the wear comes) are stoutly nailed to the uppers and won't pull loose, nor will the leather heel. Guaranteed to give satisfaction, and priced within the reach of all.

BELLOWS TONGUE

$1.89
Men's and Big Boys' Sizes

THE HEEL THAT WON'T COME OFF

CHROME LEATHER SOLE

The Canvas Work Shoe Built Like a Tire! Gives Miles and Miles of Wear!

EXTRA HEAVY MAIL BAG CANVAS

EXTRA RUBBER TAP SOLE FOR LONGER WEAR

76K9632—Men's and Big Boys'. Sizes, 6 to 12. **$1.89**
76K9633—Boys'. **1.79**
Sizes, 1 to 5½.
Wide widths only. Be sure to state size.
Shipping wt.: Men's and Big Boys', 2¼ lbs.; Boys', 2¼ lbs.
This work shoe, with its extra heavy mail bag canvas uppers and extra tap sole for longer wear, is ideal for either work or play and is popular with both men or boys. Flexible, yet medium heavy to stand the gaff of hard wear. The sort of shoe you wear for comfort—and economy. Compare this shoe only with the best shoes of its kind and you will see that the low prices we are asking are nowhere near equaled anywhere else. Boys' sizes come in Bal pattern only.

$2.39
Men's and Big Boys' Sizes

Lowest Priced Dress Oxford in Years

Men's and Big Boys'. Sizes, 6 to 11.
67K4425—Brown. **$2.39**
67K4426—Black.
Boys'. Sizes, 1 to 5½.
67K6025—Brown. **1.89**
67K6026—Black.
Wide widths only. State size. Shpg. wt.: Men's, 2½ lbs.; Boys', 2¼ lbs.

In our last Midsummer Sale Book our sales on this low priced dress oxford were overwhelming—'way beyond our expectations. So we are offering it again this season in this new Fall and Winter Catalog, giving you men and boys the opportunity to "get in on a good thing." Made of brown or black smooth, glossy split leather, with sewed soles and rubber heels. Good quality throughout. Get your pair today! Wear them! After you've put them to what you consider a fair test, tell us what you think of them. If you aren't completely satisfied that they are the best dress oxford you ever bought for so little money, we want you to send them back and tell us why.

Here You Are, Boys!

67K5294—Boys'. Sizes, 1 to 5½. Wide widths only. **$2.59**
Be sure to state size.
Shipping wt., 2¾ lbs.

Boys, here's a school and work shoe that will stick to you through the toughest going. It's as good looking as you'd want for everyday; it's easy on your feet and its cost is very little. And as for wear, few come up to it. Whether you want them for hunting, hiking, work or school wear, these shoes will please you equally well. Uppers are of double tanned, double strength brown leather. "Compo-Soles" with extra leather middle sole, sewed together with heavy thread and nailed to the uppers so they can't come loose. Rubber heels.

BELLOWS TONGUE

"COMPO-SOLE"

RUBBER HEEL

TRIPLE STITCHED

It's Easy to Order From the World's Largest Store. See Page 546

327

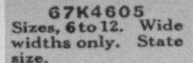

67K4605
Sizes, 6 to 12. Wide widths only. State size.

$2.98

Shipping wt., 3½ lbs.

Every man likes his work shoes to be soft and flexible, giving him that "easy feel," "bend easy" sensation in his feet throughout every working hour. We know of none that will do it any better than these mahogany color, chrome tanned leather (called elkskin) Shoes with their sure grip "Compo-Soles" and rubber heels. And they'll stand good hard wear, too. Double stitched soles of stitchdown construction. Illustration shows their extreme flexibility. Moccasin style toe.

Sure Grip
Compo Sole
Double
Sole Fastening

$3.98

Grizzly Bear Sole

67K4720 **$3.98**
Sizes, 6 to 12. Wide widths. State size.
Shipping wt., 3½ lbs.

These wonderfully soft, full chrome tanned leather, known as "Golden Elk," Shoes will tackle any kind of hardest work with all the brute strength and endurance of the fiercest grizzly bear. There's comfort, also, in the moccasin toe, in the flexible "Grizzly Bear" sole and heel of same composition, and more than ordinary wear.

The New Idea in Work Shoes

Strong Drill Lining

White
Waterproof
Caulk Welt

$3.25 Men's and Big Boys'. Sizes, 6 to 12.
67K4602—Brown.
67K4603—Black.

Boys.' Sizes, 1 to 5½.
67K5202—Brown.
67K5203—Black. **$2.85**

Small Boys'. Sizes, 11 to 13½.
67K5502—Brown.
67K5503—Black. **$2.45**

Wide widths only. State size.
Shpg. wt.: Men's and Big Boys', 3 lbs.; Boys', 2¾ lbs.; Small Boys', 2 lbs.

The New Idea in Work Shoes with us this season was a work shoe light in weight, full of comfort, long wearing yet good enough looking for dress wear when necessary. This is the one we selected because it embodies all those qualities and, by utilizing our tremendous buying power, we were able to get it at a bargain price. Here's your chance to make a big saving on your shoe bill. The uppers are soft, durable black or brown chrome tanned leather (commonly called elkskin) with strong drill lining and soft toes for inside comfort. Two full double soles add many miles of wear and much foot comfort in all weather. White weatherproof welt keeps out moisture. Full rubber heel.

The Shoe With More Than a Million Friends

Sure Grip
Compo Sole

Men's and Big Boys'. Sizes, 6 to 12.
67K47I4—Tan.
67K47I5—Black. **$2.98**

Boys.' Sizes, 1 to 5½.
67K52I4—Tan.
67K52I5—Black. **2.59**

Small Boys'. Sizes, 11 to 13½.
67K55I4—Tan.
67K55I5—Black. **$1.98**

Wide widths only. State size.
Shipping wt.: Men's and Big Boys', 3¾ lbs.; Boys', 3 lbs.; Small Boys', 2 lbs.

A work shoe, to make and keep More Than a Million Friends, must be dependable, go "through thick and thin" clear to the finish. This one does. Its soft, double tanned leather uppers stay soft even in barnyard work and they wear, too. Solid leather counters, innersoles and extra middle sole. "Compo-Soles" nailed and sewed to uppers. Rubber heels.

67K4826—Men's and Big Boys'. Sizes, 6 to 12. **$2.85**
67K5326—Boys.'. Sizes, 1 to 5½. **2.48**
67K5926—Small Boys.' Sizes, 9 to 13½. **1.98**

Wide widths only.
Be sure to state size.
Shipping wt.: Men's and Big Boys', 2¾ lbs.; Boys', 2½ lbs.; Small Boys', 1¾ lbs.

Here's the Shoe that greatly helps men and boys keep down their work shoe costs and keep up their appearance. Light and comfortable, but strong and sturdy. Uppers are smoke color, full chrome tanned (elkskin) leather with dark chocolate color leather trimmings. Sport tread "Compo-Soles" indicate that their wear is almost unlimited. One of our best values. Rubber heel.

Sport Tread
Compo Sole

Cowboy Headquarters - Finest Quality Boots and Shoes

We know that you fellows take pride in your cowboy boots and shoes—that when you buy a pair you want them to fit properly and show their good looks. You insist that they also come up to highest standards of quality. You know how absolutely essential it is that you can depend upon them at every point in every emergency. Nothing but the best goes into our cowboy boots and shoes. They are absolutely **All Leather**, best quality materials and workmanship, and correct in all details. The counter or spur piece is heavy, top quality, sole leather. Soles are heavy, oak tanned leather and GENUINE GOODYEAR WELT construction. Made in the southwest by foremost cowboy boot and shoe makers. Our low prices for standard quality leads you to make the World's Largest Store your Cowboy Headquarters for new purchases.

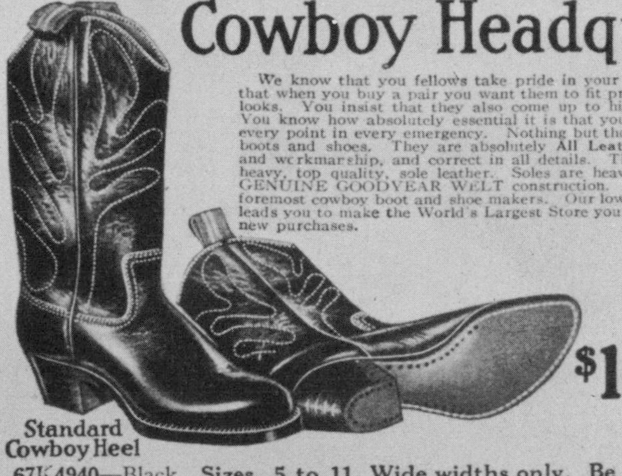

$10.95
Standard
Cowboy Heel

67K4940—Black. **Sizes, 5 to 11. Wide widths only. Be sure to state size.** Height, about 12 inches. *Shipping wt., 4 lbs.*

$7.75
Standard
Cowboy Heel

67K4121—Black. **Sizes, 5 to 11.**
67K4122—Brown. **Sizes, 5 to 11.**
Wide widths only. Be sure to state size. *Shipping wt., 2½ lbs.*

Men's and Boys' Leather House Slippers

$1.98

67K4501—Brown Kid.
67K4502—Black Kid.
Sizes, 5 to 12, including half sizes. Wide widths. State size.
Shipping wt., 1½ lbs.
Good looking, and priced for a saving. Made of soft brown or black kid leather over a comfortable, wide toe last. Sewed, all leather sole and rubber heel.

Suede Lining

$2.19

67K4500—Sizes, 5 to 12, including half sizes. Wide widths. State size.
Shipping wt., 1½ lbs.
A little better quality than ordinary—and worth every penny of the extra cost. You can't beat them for wear, warmth or worth! SOFT SUEDE LINED dark brown kidskin—so easy and restful to your feet. All leather soles. Rubber heels. We know they'll please you and that you'll agree our price makes a saving for you—one that you will appreciate.

$1.98

67K4506—Sizes, 5 to 12, including half sizes. Wide widths only. Be sure to state size.
Shipping wt., 2¼ lbs.
When the workday ends, there's nothing like being able to rest in comfort. These fine, soft leather House Slippers assure you of complete footease. Good for outdoors, too. Brown genuine kidskin uppers. Elastic gore at sides. Extra heavy flexible stitchdown sole and rubber heels.

Soft Felt Lined

98c **Brand New House Slippers** **$1.48**

67K3921
Sizes, 5 to 12, including half sizes.
Very newest brown and blue mottled leather. Soft padded chrome leather soles. Warm, soft felt lining for comfort.

67K3922
Sizes, 5 to 12. No half sizes.
Another brand new House Slipper of soft brown "Golden Elk" chrome tanned leather with contrasting leather cuff. Also lined with warm, soft felt.

Wide Widths Only
State Size
Shipping wt., 1 lb.

Genuine Sheep Wool
Wide Widths
State Size

67K4962—Men's and Big Boys'. Sizes, 6 to 12 ... **$1.69**
67K6703—Boys'. Sizes, 1 to 5 .... **1.49**
No half sizes. Shpg. wt., 1 lb.
Warm, genuine sheep wool lined House Slippers; think of how good they'll feel around the house on cold winter mornings; then make up your mind to order a pair at once.

Soft Felt Lining

67K4505—Sizes, 5 to 12, including half sizes. Wide widths. State size. **$1.79**
Shipping wt., 1¼ lbs.
Man! You'll get a lot of comfort and satisfaction from these soft, flexible, felt lined House Slippers. Brown genuine kid uppers. Easy bending, stitchdown leather sole, and rubber heel. Great for cold mornings when you get up to stir up the fire.

Fine Felt Slippers

95c

67K3919—Gray. **67K3920**—Brown.
Sizes, 5 to 12. No half sizes. Wide widths only. Be sure to state size. *Shipping wt., 1 lb.*
You just know there's all kinds of comfort and warmth in these brown or gray felt Slippers. Checked collar. Soft, padded chrome leather soles.

$1.39

67K3905—Blue. **67K3923**—Gray.
Sizes, 5 to 12. No half sizes. Wide widths only. Be sure to state size.
Shipping wt., 1 lb.
Good looking, aren't they? Gray felt with black and white checked velvet collar or blue felt with tan felt collar. Padded chrome leather soles. Practical, warm, comfortable.

$1.69

67K3901—Sizes, 5 to 12. No half sizes. Wide widths only. Be sure to state size.
Shipping wt., 1¼ lbs.
There's ease and comfort in these attractive brown felt Hi-Lo Slippers. Collar can be turned up and buttoned snugly around ankle. Flexible leather sole. Rubber heel. Service, warmth, economy.

$1.15

67K3915—Sizes, 5 to 12. No half sizes. Wide widths only. Be sure to state size.
Shipping wt., 1¼ lbs.
A plain, wide toed Slipper that appeals to men because of its neat, good looks, comfort and durability. Gray felt uppers; flexible, high grade, leather stitchdown sole and springy rubber heel. Our low price is typical of the savings you can always make at the World's Largest Shoe Store.

79c

67K3907—Sizes, 5 to 12. No half sizes. Wide widths only. Be sure to state size.
Shipping wt., 1 lb.
Durable, restful, and priced so low that they are within the reach of all. One of our most popular Slippers. Black felt, with hair felt soles. Slip into them in the evening and that tired feeling will vanish. Also a fine protection against cold floors on chilly winter mornings. Appropriate design on vamp.

Boys' Slippers

69c

67K3950—Boys'. Sizes, 1 to 6. No half sizes. Wide widths only. State size.
Shipping wt., 1 lb.
Here is a Slipper value we challenge anyone to beat! Practical, low priced black felt Everett for boys. Decorative design on vamp. Sole of thick warm hair felt. Remember, too, that slippers are always acceptable Christmas gifts.

98c

67K3953—Boys'. Sizes, 1 to 6. No half sizes. Wide widths. State size.
Shipping wt., 1 lb.
Boys, as well as men, like to have their feet comfy in the evening. Any boy will be pleased with these Hi-Los. Brown felt uppers, with brown velvet collar in a neat checkered pattern. Soft padded chrome leather sole.

Felt and Leather Sole

98c

67K3902—Sizes, 5 to 12. Wide widths. No half sizes. State size. Shpg. wt., 1¼ lbs.
You'll be astonished that only 98c buys as much genuine foot comfort as these warm durable black felt House Slippers furnish. Has two soles, the inner of hair felt and the outer of lightweight split leather. Heel of springy, live rubber. A slipper bargain.

69c

67K3924—Sizes, 5 to 12. No half sizes. Wide widths only. Be sure to state size.
Shipping wt., 1 lb.
Plain model in gray felt—just as warm, just as practical, just as comfortable as any felt Slipper on this page. Its padded chrome leather soles feel like soft cushions to your feet and they will wear well, besides. A mighty good buy at this unusual low price.

Best Rubber Footwear Made
FLINT Extra  ROCK Quality

Miners' Special
"FLINT ROCK"
(Extra Quality)

76K9325—Sizes, 5 to 12. No half sizes. Wide widths. State size. **$3.85**

Snag resister, duck interlined. Double sole, reinforced with rubber cleats and chafing strip to prevent laces wearing through full bellows tongue. **Worn over heavy socks.**

Wide Widths Only
No Half Sizes
State Size

"FLINT ROCK"
(Extra Quality)

76K9336—Men's. Sizes, 5 to 12. **$3.25**

Miners' black all rubber pac with sturdy soles and chafing strip to prevent laces wearing through the full bellows tongue. Duck lined and reinforced at all points where any strain comes. Worn over light or heavy socks.

Shpg. wt., 4¾ lbs.

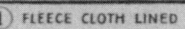

1. FLEECE CLOTH LINED
2. HEAVY CHAFING STRIP
3. EXTENSION EDGE
4. HIGH FOXING
5. FULL BELLOWS TONGUE
6. EXTRA HIGH GRADE RUBBER

76K9277—Men's. Sizes, 5 to 12. **$3.48**
76K9281—Boys'. Sizes, 3 to 6. **2.98**
No half sizes.
Shipping wt.: Men's, 5¾ lbs.; Boys', 4 lbs.
Red, all rubber, four-buckle Arctics (pressure cured process). Worn over shoes.

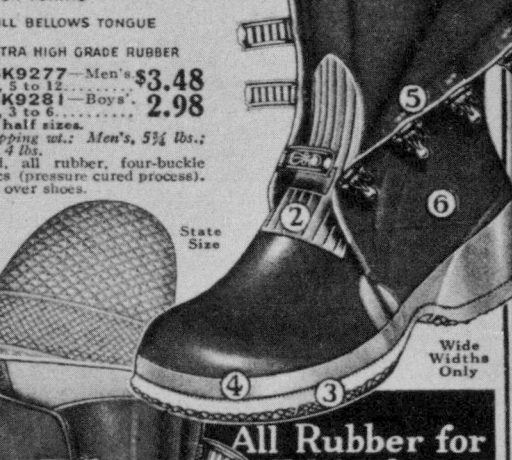

State Size

Wide Widths Only

All Rubber for All Weather

"FLINT ROCK"
(Extra Quality)
(Pressure Cured) **$3.98**

76K9274—Sizes 5 to 12. No half sizes. Wide widths. State size.

Shipping wt.: 6¼ lbs.

This high top five-buckle, red, all rubber Arctic will give more wear and protection than any other arctic on the market. Has a snow excluder and a heavy gray sole. Fleece cloth lined. Height, about 13 inches. **To be worn over shoes.**

Read About Rubber Quality on Page 337

Wide Widths No Half Sizes State Size Height, About 12 In. **$4.25**

"FLINT ROCK" *(Extra Quality)*
76K9359—Sizes, 5 to 12. *Shipping wt., 4¼ lbs.*
Lumbermen's and Hunters' red rubber Over (pressure cured process). Tough, springy vulcanized crepe sole and half heel give longer wear and lighter weight. Ribbed vamp. Best grade, soft, pliable, black horsehide top. Tan leather collar and backstay. Worn over socks or pacs.

For the Sportsman

"FLINT ROCK" *(Extra Quality)*
76K9335 **$4.45**
Sizes, 6 to 11. No half sizes. State size. Height, about 15 inches.
Shipping wt., 5¾ lbs.
An all rubber, high grade waterproof Over that can be used in place of leather Hi-Cuts for wading through snow and water while hunting, trapping or pursuing other outdoor sports. Full bellows tongue makes it a snow excluder to top. Made slim at the ankle to insure a good fit. Roomy moccasin vamp for comfort. Extra heavy gray sole for long wear. Worn over socks. Try a pair. You'll like them.

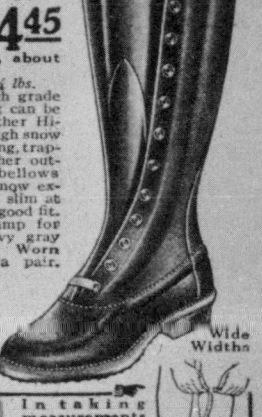

Wide Widths

In taking measurements for puttees, draw tape line snugly around largest part of calf as illustrated.

No Half Sizes

"FLINT ROCK"
(Extra Quality)

76K9452—Red Hip Boots. Men's. Sizes, 5 to 13.. **$5.75**
76K9402—Red Short Boots. Men's. Sizes, 5 to 13.. **3.75**
76K9403—Red Short Boots. Boys'. Sizes, 1 to 6... **3.25**

Wide widths only. State size.

Shipping wt.: Men's Short Boots, 6½ lbs.; Men's Hip Boots, 8½ lbs.; Boys' Short Boots, 4½ lbs.

Red boot with heavy gray sole. Highest grade rubber and other materials are perfectly vulcanized by the pressure curing process. Friction cloth lined and snag resister duck interlined.

"FLINT ROCK"
(Extra Quality)
Heavy Duty Work Rubbers
76K9123 **$1.65**
Sizes, 5 to 13.
Shpg. wt., 2½ lbs.
Our best heavy Rubbers for men. Extra high double vamp. Dull dark red finish; gray full double thick sole and heel. Specially constructed to fit close around the top to keep out water, snow and dirt. Fine for felt as well as leather shoes. (Fits shoes as shown in Figure 8, page 343.)

"FLINT ROCK"
(Extra Quality)
(Pressure Cured)
$2.50 **76K9200**
Sizes, 5 to 13. No half sizes. Wide widths only. Be sure to state size.

Shipping wt., 4 lbs.

One-buckle, red, all rubber Arctic with heavy gray sole for men and big boys! Has snow excluder and is fleece cloth lined. Just the thing for hard wear and is easy to keep clean. Others charge considerably more for this same quality. To be worn over shoes.

Wide Widths State Size

Full Grain Cowhide **$2.98**
76K9052 Brown.
76K9053 Black.
Sizes, 13 to 18 inches calf measurement. No half sizes. State size.
Shipping wt., 1¼ lbs.
Serviceable Puttee with strap and buckle fastener and is reinforced with a quarter lining.

Strap and Buckle Fastener
76K9056—Brown.
76K9057—Black.
Spring Fastener
76K9068—Brown.
76K9069—Black. **$3.95**
Men's. Sizes, 13 to 18 inches calf measurement.
Shipping wt., 2 lbs.
Strictly high grade Puttees. Made of full grain black or brown horsehide (sometimes called genuine cordovan). They are reinforced with quarter lining of genuine leather. Good looking and low priced.

No Half Sizes State Size

Extra Value!
76K9062 Men's. Sizes, 13 to 18 inches calf measurement. No half sizes. **$1.98**
76K9063 Boys'. Sizes, 10 to 13 inches calf measurement. No half sizes. State size. **$1.80**
Shipping wt.: Men's, 2 lbs.; Boys', 1¾ lbs.
This one-piece highly polished mahogany brown split leather Puttee is certainly SOME FINE VALUE. Fastens with a strap and buckle.

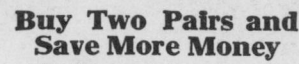

Keep Trim and Stylish in Bad Weather

Buy Two Pairs and Save More Money

This season the well dressed woman will have two pairs of galoshes — a low model for cold days when it is damp or there is not much snow on the ground, and a high model for severe winter weather when the snow is deep. It's a wise investment — your feet are always warm and look stylish in any weather; and look at the low prices we quote!

Popular Price Snap-on

$1.89 A PAIR

"GIBRALTAR" QUALITY

Black

76K9225—Designed to fit shoes as shown in Figures 3 and 4, page 342. Sizes, 2½ to 9.

76K9226—Designed to fit shoes as shown in Figures 1 and 2, page 342. Sizes, 2½ to 8.

Fawn

76K9227—Designed to fit shoes as shown in Figures 3 and 4, page 342. Sizes, 2½ to 8.

76K9228—Designed to fit shoes as shown in Figures 1 and 2, page 342. Sizes, 2½ to 8.

Wide widths only. Be sure to state size.

Shipping wt., 1½ lbs.

Just as stylish as the others is this "GIBRALTAR" QUALITY black or fawn color Snap On. made of a special gaiter cloth with pretty corduroy cuffs. Equally as practical, just a snap to close, unsnap the fastener and it's open. Fastener is adjustable for snug fit.

Tweed Jiffy

"GIBRALTAR" QUALITY

Tan

76K9230—Fits shoes as shown in Figures 3 and 4, page 342.

76K9231—Fits shoes as shown in Figures 1 and 2, page 342.

$2.95

Gray

76K9232—Fits shoes as shown in Figures 3 and 4, page 342..............

76K9233—Fits shoes as shown in Figures 1 and 2, page 342..............

$2.95

Sizes, 2½ to 8. Wide widths only. State size.

Shipping wt., 2 lbs.

This winter you will need a pair of low Jiffys as a complement to your wardrobe. None is more appropriate than this tan or gray tweed galosh with self cuff. The Jiffy fastener closes or opens in a flash. And look at our low price! Buy yours here with nice savings.

Silk and Wool Snap-on

$2.48 A PAIR

"PROFILE" (First Quality)

76K9235—Fits shoes as in Figures 3 and 4, page 342.

76K9236—Fits shoes as in Figures 1 and 2, page 342.

Sizes, 2½ to 8. Wide widths only. State size.

Shipping wt., 1¾ lbs.

Snap Ons are as necessary for afternoon and evening dress during bad, cold weather as a party pump. When they are of pure silk and wool tan tweed with Rayon striped cuff, like those featured above, you may be confident that your selection is beautiful, practical and decidedly in vogue. "PROFILE" QUALITY holds the attention that SNAP ON style attracts.

Popular Price Jiffy

All Wool Jiffy

$3.98

"PROFILE" (First Quality)

Fawn

76K9289—Fits shoes as in Figures 1 and 2 only, page 342. Sizes, 2½ to 8.

Black

76K9291—Fits shoes as in Figures 3 and 4, page 342. Sizes 2½ to 9.

76K9292—Fits shoes as in Figures 1 and 2, page 342. Sizes 2½ to 8.

Wide widths only. Be sure to state size.

Shipping wt., 2½ lbs.

For the more severe winter weather, with its deep snows, you will want Hi-Jiffys, of course. When you are satisfied with none but the best, these are the ones to purchase. They are made of all wool, double thread Jersey cloth in black or fawn color and are the highest grade gaiters made. "PROFILE" QUALITY sets a value for the dollar that cannot be equaled elsewhere.

"GIBRALTAR" QUALITY

76K9284—Fits shoes as shown in Figures 3 and 4, page 342.

76K9285—Fits shoes as shown in Figures 1 and 2, page 342.

Sizes, 2½ to 8. Wide widths only. Be sure to state size.

$3.45

Shipping wt., 2½ lbs.

There's no doubt whatsoever about the extreme popularity of tan tweed in this winter's galoshes. It glorifies the modern waterproof footwear with a new ideal of magnificence, giving grace and charm to all well dressed women. The aristocrat of our low priced Hi-Jiffys is the model pictured here. Its fleece lined tan tweed upper fits trimly all the way up the foot, protecting you from snow and cold. Well tailored and well built throughout. Just as practical as it is good looking. And such a bargain at $3.45!

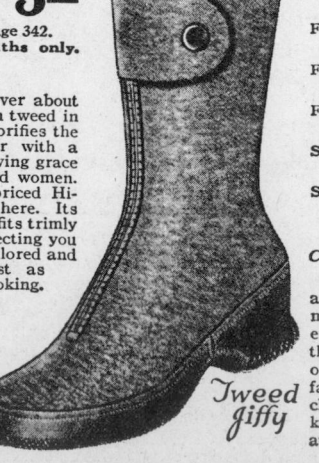

Tweed Jiffy

Order all Jiffys one-half size larger than shoe it is to be worn over. Order all Snap Ons the same size as shoe.

"GIBRALTAR" QUALITY

76K9286—Women's. Sizes, 2½ to 8. Fits shoes as in Figures 3 and 4, page 342.... **$2.88**

76K9287—Women's. Sizes, 2½ to 8. Fits shoes as in Figure 2, page 342......... **2.88**

76K9288—Women's. Sizes, 2½ to 8. Fits shoes as in Figure 1, page 342......... **2.88**

76K9296—Girls'. Sizes, 11 to 2............................. **2.65**

76K9297—Children's. Sizes, 6 to 10½.......................... **2.35**

Wide widths only. Be sure to state size.

Shipping wt.: Women's, 2½ lbs.; Girls', 2¼ lbs.; Children's, 2 lbs.

Our popular priced Jiffy—trim and elegant in appearance; comfortable, convenient and at a very moderate cost, made possible by our purchasing enormous quantities to supply the huge demand for this particular style. Jiffy is rightly named—on and off in a jiffy—just a touch to fasten, a touch to unfasten. It is made of a special, black high grade cloth which is rich looking and wears well. You know the popularity of this model and will appreciate its many advantages.

America's Biggest Value in Galoshes

"PROFILE"
(First Quality)

76K9258—To fit low heels. $2.65
76K9259—To fit high heels.
Women's. Sizes, 2½ to 8. Our best Four-Buckle Galosh. Made of high grade cashmerette cloth, finely and firmly woven. Fleece lined.

"GIBRALTAR" QUALITY

76K9263	76K9262
Children's. Sizes, $1.59 5 to 10½.........	Girls'. Sizes, $1.69 11 to 2......

76K9260—Women's. Sizes, 2½ to 8. To fit shoes with heels and toes as shown in Figure 3, page 342.............. $1.79
76K9261—Women's. Sizes, 2½ to 8. To fits shoes with heels and toes as shown in Figures 1 and 2, page 342.............. $1.79
76K9264—Women's. Sizes, 2½ to 9. To fits shoes with heels and toes as shown in Figure 4, page 342.............. $1.79

Wide widths only. Be sure to state size.
Shipping wt.: Women's, 2¼ lbs.; Girls', 1¾ lbs.; Children's, 1½ lbs.

America's Biggest Value. That's a broad statement, isn't it? Because this galosh has **so much quality at so little cost** to you, we have properly called it America's Biggest Value in Galoshes. We feel safely justified in saying that the four-buckle galosh, pictured at the right, is the biggest value that our customers will find anywhere in America. By buying in carload lots we are able to quote a much lower price and still maintain our high standard of quality, so you get first class merchandise at a big saving. That's what makes a value. Made of a special gaiter cloth and fleece cloth lined throughout. For the low price paid you will be surprised at the warmth and wear you will get out of it. **Order all these galoshes the same size as the shoes they are to be worn over.**

"GIBRALTAR" QUALITY
$1.79
PER PAIR
Women's Sizes

"PROFILE" *(First Quality)*
$2.65
PER PAIR
Women's Sizes

The Way to Tell Rubber Quality
is by the Trade Marks

10-karat gold is not as good as 14-karat, and 18-karat is better than either. All are gold—and look alike. So it is with rubber footwear. You can't tell which is best unless you know the brand, just as you can't tell the quality of gold unless you see the stamp. Reputable manufacturers trade mark their rubber products for your protection, so that you may know which quality you are buying.

We are the largest retailers of rubber footwear in the world. Because: Our customers have confidence in us; they know the quality of the goods they are buying; they know our footwear is honestly built; that the price is fixed by the quality; that we sell no low quality merchandise at any price.

Rubber footwear is produced in four standard qualities: Extra quality, first quality, second (or medium) quality and third quality. Many factories do not make third quality because it is not serviceable. For that reason you will not find third quality rubber footwear in any of our catalogs.

Here are examples of some of the best known brands of rubber footwear:

Extra Quality	First Quality	Medium Quality
FLINT ROCK	PROFILE	GIBRALTAR
AMERICAN SUPER	AMERICAN	PARA
CANDEE SUPER	CANDEE	FEDERAL
HUB MARK SUPER	HUB MARK	BAY STATE
LYCOMING SUPER	LYCOMING	KEYSTONE
WALES GOODYEAR SUPER	WALES GOODYEAR	CONNECTICUT
BULLSEYE	HOOD	YORK
ARROW		

Know the Quality You Are Buying!

For Women — Watertight Arctics — For Misses and Children

Well Known WASH-EZY Arctic "FLINT-ROCK" (Extra Quality)

76K9290—Women's. Sizes, 3 to 9. Wide widths only. Be sure to state size. No half sizes. *Shipping wt., 3¼ lbs.* **$3.25**

Absolutely watertight! No danger of wet feet in a pair of these WASH-EZY All Rubber Arctics for women. The very worst mud and slush wash right off with water, with hardly any effort at all. Chafing strip prevents buckles from wearing through full bellows tongue. Fleece cloth lined. Gray sole well reinforced where most wear comes.

"GIBRALTAR" QUALITY
Easy to Keep Clean

76K9272—Girls'. Sizes, 11 to 2........ **$1.98** | 76K9273—Children's. Sizes, 6 to 10½ **$1.89**

Wide widths only. Be sure to state size.
Shipping wt.: Girls', 2½ lbs.; Children's, 2¼ lbs.

You will find this lightweight, all rubber, flexible Galosh a great protection for the children against cold, damp weather. They are fleece lined throughout and have felt insoles which protect the feet from the cold, wet ground. Very practical and an economical investment in good health. Large bellows tongue makes them easy to put on or take off. Our low price makes them a value hard to duplicate anywhere.

Old Reliable "GIBRALTAR" QUALITY

76K9217—Women's. Sizes; 2½ to 8. To fit shoes as shown in Figures 3 and 4, page 342.................**$1.35**
76K9218—Girls'. Sizes, 11 to 2............ 1.19
76K9219—Children's. Sizes, 5 to 10½................. 1.09
Wide widths only. Be sure to state size.
Shipping wt.: Women's, 1½ lbs.; Girls', 1¼ lbs.; Children's, 1¼ lbs.

Heavy, black cashmerette top, one-buckle Arctic. It is fleece cloth lined for warmth. Plain edge. Durable rubber sole and heel. Great favorite with many of our customers because so economical. A bargain at these money saving prices made possible by carload purchases of rubber footwear from leading manufacturers.

Canvas Shoes

Our Very Best Sport Shoe

$2.50

76K9572—White. 76K9573—Brown. Men's and Big Boys'. Sizes, 6 to 11. Wide widths. State size. *Shipping wt., 2½ lbs.*

Made of the best canvas we can buy. White or brown duck uppers, black trimmed and fully lined. Specially constructed non-slip sole. Cushion heel and sponge rubber heel seat. Made snug fitting at the shank, which gives support for the arches. Lace to toe style, a shoe of superior quality and one that fits snugly. "Feltex" insole.

The All Around

76K9562—Men's and Big Boys'. Sizes, 6 to 12. **$1.95**
76K9563—Boys'. Sizes, 1 to 5½........... 1.79
Shipping wt.: Men's and Big Boys', 2½ lbs.; Boys', 2¼ lbs.

Wide Widths State Size

Going to play basket ball or take gym work this winter? These heavy lace to toe White Canvas Shoes are just the thing for all that kind of work. The neat rubber trimming, toe cap and double foxing which join uppers to vacuum style rubber soles give wear and appearance to the shoes as well. Uppers are unlined.

Quality Built-In

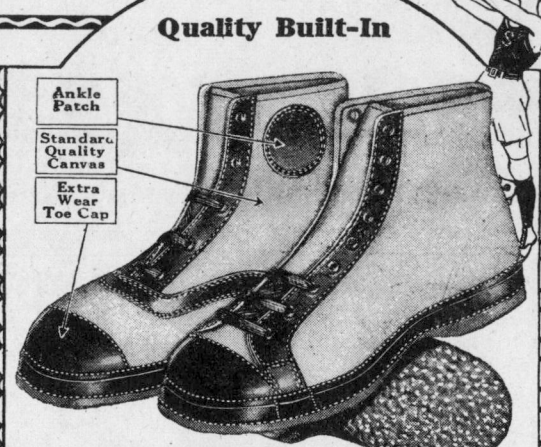

Ankle Patch
Standard Quality Canvas
Extra Wear Toe Cap

Bal Pattern
White Canvas
76K9525—Men's and Big Boys'. Sizes, 6 to 12. **95c**
76K9526—Boys'. Sizes, 1 to 5½........... **90c**
76K9527—Small Boys'. Sizes, 11 to 13½....... **85c**
76K9528—Women's. Sizes, 3 to 8........... **95c**

Brown Canvas
76K9534—Men's and Big Boys'. Sizes, 6 to 12. **95c**
76K9535—Boys'. Sizes, 1 to 5½........... **90c**
76K9536—Small Boys'. Sizes, 11 to 13½....... **85c**

Lace to Toe Pattern
White Canvas
76K9529—Men's and Big Boys' Sizes, 6 to 12. **95c**
76K9530—Boys'. Sizes, 1 to 5½........... **90c**
76K9531—Small Boys'. Sizes, 11 to 13½...... **85c**
76K9532—Children's. Sizes, 6 to 10½....... **80c**

Brown Canvas
76K9538—Men's and Big Boys'. Sizes, 6 to 12. **95c**
76K9539—Boys'. Sizes, 1 to 5½........... **90c**
76K9540—Small Boys'. Sizes, 11 to 13½. **85c**

Wide widths only. Be sure to state size.
Shipping wt.: Men's and Big Boys', 1¾ lbs.; Boys', 1½ lbs.; Small Boys', 1¼ lbs.; Women's, 1¼ lbs.

QUALITY BUILT IN! And the price put down to what you usually pay for greatly inferior Sport Shoes! But remember this—these shoes must not be confused with those cheap grades now on the market at about the same prices.
These are good grade, lightweight, white or brown canvas with rubber trimming. Have crepe-like rubber soles. Composition innersoles. Well reinforced.

Vulcanized Crepe Sole Sport Shoes

WHITE OR BROWN

Wide Widths Only State Size

White Canvas
76K9577—Men's and Big Boys'. Sizes, 6 to 12........ **$1.59**
76K9578—Boys'. Sizes, 1 to 5½........... **$1.49**

Brown Canvas
76K9567—Men's and Big Boys'. Sizes, 6 to 12........ **$1.59**
76K9568—Boys'. Sizes, 1 to 5½........... **$1.49**
Shipping wt.: Men's and Big Boys', 2¼ lbs.; Boys', 1¾ lbs.

Ever wear Sport Shoes with vulcanized crepe rubber soles? If you have, you know what they are, what they'll do. If you haven't, you've surely missed a lot of comfort and confidence of sure footing. Good grade white or brown canvas, unlined, rubber trimming. Lace to toe.

All White Shoe for Women

$1.00

76K9575—Sizes, 3 to 8. Wide widths only. Be sure to state size.
Shipping wt., 1½ lbs.

Neat appearance, extra quality and popular price are features of this white Canvas Shoe with a plain white closely woven canvas upper, composition insole and good grade rubber outsole. The lace to toe pattern makes it fit snugly all the way up the foot. Suitable for all indoor games and gymnasium.

"Flint Rock"
(Extra Quality)

76K9082
Shoe only.............. $2.35
76K9127
Rubber Over only........ 1.49
76K9500
Shoe and Over........... 3.75

Sizes, 5 to 12. No half sizes. Wide widths only. Be sure to state size.

Shipping wt.: Shoe and Over, 4½ lbs.; Shoe only, 2¼ lbs.; Rubber Over only, 2¾ lbs.

A wonderful cold weather combination for men. Black, part wool, part cotton, 9-inch knit Shoe with felt sole and heel, fitted with a "FLINT ROCK" (Extra Quality) rubber. High cut, close fitting and made with a double thick sole and heel.

76K9127 Rubber Over Only $1.49

76K9082 Shoe Only $2.35

76K9500 Shoe and Over $3.75

"Profile"
(First Quality)

76K9502 $4.69 Pac and Over

67K4956 $1.25 Pac Only

76K9382 $3.48 Over Only

76K9502 Pac and Over $4.69

67K4956 Pac Only $1.25

Sizes, 5 to 12. Be sure to state size.

Shipping wt.: Pac and Over, 5¼ lbs.; Over only, 5 lbs.; Pac only, ¾ lb.

An excellent combination consisting of a heavy rolled edge rubber over, with leather and light blanket lined stormproof arctic cloth top, together with a warm natural sheepskin wool Pac. Will keep your feet warm and dry in cold or wet weather. Inexpensive, too.

76K9382 Over Only $3.48

Rubber Overs With Black Full Grained Horsehide Tops
"PROFILE" (First Quality)

76K9365—Boys'. Sizes, 1 to 6. Height, about 10 inches.... $2.68
76K9366—Men's. Sizes, 5 to 12. Height, about 12 inches.. 3.48
76K9368—Men's. Sizes, 5 to 12. Height, about 16 inches.. 3.98

Wide widths only. No half sizes. Be sure to state size.

Shipping wt.: Boys' 3½ lbs.; Men's, 12-inch, 4½ lbs.; Men's, 16-inch, 4¾ lbs.

Rolled edge gum ribbed Over with black full grain horsehide top. Soft, pliable and strong. Heights measured over all. To be worn over socks or sheepskin pacs. Our low prices save you money.

Lumbermen's Socks
Boys' Waterproof Rubber Shoe
$2.69 Boys' Sizes

Wide Widths State Size

$1.85

PROFILE" (First Quality)
76K9350—Sizes, 5 to 12. No half sizes. *Shipping wt., 3½ lbs.*
First quality gum ribbed lumbermen's Over. Has rolled edge and cut low for attaching leather top. You thereby save about half the cost of a whole new pair. To be worn over socks.

"PROFILE" (First Quality)
$2.95 A PAIR

Red Rubber

Will Stand the Hardest Wear.
76K9362—Men's. Sizes, 5 to 12. No half sizes. Wide widths. State size. *Shipping wt., 4¼ lbs.*
First quality dark red rolled edge gum ribbed Over with dark brown durable horsehide leather top, which is securely fastened with four rows of heavy stitching. Height, over all, about 10 inches. Constructed to withstand the hardest kind of wear and, you will notice, they are priced especially low. Our immense buying power enables us to sell them to you at a considerable saving, compared with what this same quality costs you elsewhere.

Fleece Lined

79c
76K9088
Men's. Sizes, 6 to 12. No half sizes. State size.
Shipping wt., 8 oz.
Warm and comfortable heavy weight three-quarter length gray Socks. Soft tufted warm fleece lining. About two thirds wool, balance cotton. Order the same size as a shoe you wear.

76K9084
Men's. Sizes, 6 to 12. **$1.12**
76K9085
Boys'. Sizes, 1 to 6.. **.97**
No half sizes. Be sure to state size.
Shipping wt., ¾ lb.
Very warm lumbermen's Socks. Tufted. Black only. About one-half wool, balance cotton. Order same size as shoe you wear.

$1.49
Our Best Socks
76K9092—Men's. Sizes, 6 to 12. State size. *Shipping wt., 1 lb.*
There's a great deal of warmth and comfort on cold winter days in these Alaska Lumbermen's Socks. Tufted heavy foot. Black foot and gray leg. About two-thirds wool, balance cotton. Order same as shoe size.

"PROFILE" (First Quality)
76K9332—Boys'. Sizes, 1 to 6 .... $2.69
76K9333—Small boys'. Sizes, 11 to 13 .... 2.59
Wide widths. No half sizes. Be sure to state size.
Shipping wt.: Boys', 4½ lbs.; Small Boys', 3½ lbs.
Very popular favorite with boys is this black all rubber Hi-Cut. Sheds water like a rubber boot. Keeps the feet warm as any arctic will. Worn over light or heavy socks. Let your boys try them once. We know they'll like them.

To Be Worn Inside of Rubber Footwear

$1.98
BLUE FELT
76K9080—Men's. Sizes, 6 to 12. No half sizes. State size. *Shipping wt., 2 lbs.*
Our very best quality felt Boot. It is made of highest grade blue felt, that will keep your feet warm on the very coldest days. Has leather front, back and side stays. Order same size as the shoe you wear.

$1.59
76K9075
Sizes, 6 to 12. No half sizes. State size.
Shipping wt., 2 lbs.
Men's brown felt Boots. The kind you have always worn. Has leather front, back and sidestays. Order same as shoe you wear.
BROWN FELT

"GIBRALTAR" QUALITY
76K9314—One-Buckle. Men's. Sizes, 5 to 13 .... $1.98
76K9322—Two-Buckle. Men's. Sizes, 5 to 13 .... 2.45
No half sizes. Be sure to state size.
Shipping wt.: One-buckle, 3¾ lbs.; two buckle, 4¾ lbs.
One and two-buckle Overs. Have rolled edge and come in wide widths. To be worn over felt boots.

Send Sufficient Money for Postage on Parcel Post Shipments. Any Surplus Will Be Returned

341

Newest Fall Styles for Boys
Greatest Values in Years!

The curtain is up on the new styles for fall and winter. They are all here, the latest single and double breasted models in brand new fabrics of rich patterns. On this page and the pages that follow you'll find the cream of the season's output of mills famous the world over for the quality of their fabrics.

For Measuring Instructions See Page 548

We have tried to surpass even our own records of value giving this season and we believe we've accomplished it. We know that the young fellows want just about the same style lines and fabrics as their older brothers. We know that when you buy from this store you expect fabrics that will give the utmost wear, and prices that are honestly lower than they are anywhere else. And that's exactly what you get—plus the assurance that you will be completely satisfied with your purchase or your money will be returned without any trouble.

Clothing Order Blank Is on Page 1094

Popular Priced Two-Knicker Suit

It's not often that you find style, good looks and wear combined in a suit that sells at this remarkably low price. Stylish double breasted model with broad peak lapels. Very attractive herringbone pattern in a medium gray mixture. The cloth is all wool—sturdy, serviceable and good to look at. Extra knickers—every mother knows how much longer suits last with two pairs of lined knickers. Strongly sewed and made to stand hard wear. This is a mighty good value —you'll like it.

40K3196—Medium Gray Mixture. **$8.95**
Sizes, 7 to 16 years. State age size. Shipping weight, 4¼ pounds.

The New "Cloverleaf" Model for Boys

The "Cloverleaf" lapel and the high 3-button coat is just coming into its "own." We are one step ahead because we adapted this brand new style to boys' clothing. Here it is—made from an exceptionally strong, durable cloth. It is a nearly all wool twilled cassimere with a smooth surface and slow to show signs of wear. Note, too, that it is a pleasing pattern in the ever popular powder blue color. Extra good workmanship and strongly sewed and reinforced. Two pairs of lined knickers means added economy—because they double the wear at small additional cost.

40K3195—Powder Blue. **$8.65**
Sizes, 7 to 16 years. State age size. Shipping weight, 4¼ pounds.

The Invincible Hercules Worsted
King of Them All for Wear and Beauty

Regardless of price, you won't find a fabric that will wear as long as the all wool 18-ounce Hercules worsted in this stylish double breasted model. Quality is woven into every thread, shaped into every line of this suit. Even in old age, this suit will look like a thoroughbred. And the old age of this suit will be a good many months from the day you slip into it for the first time. No suit is free from the effects of weather conditions, nor will any suit wear forever. But this one comes closer to it than any of them. It is pre-shrunken and fast color. An occasional pressing will make it spring into the neat, crisp appearance of newness and it will hold a press remarkably well. Comes in dark gray or navy blue in the two-button, double breasted model with rolled lapels. Coat and vest are fully lined and pants are made with the popular wide bottoms and cuffs, regular pockets and belt loops. The Hercules is the King of Values as well as of wear.

40K3237—Navy Blue All Wool Worsted. **$11.95**
40K3193—Dark Gray All Wool Worsted. **11.95**
Sizes, 9 to 16 years. State age size; also give chest, waist and inseam measurements. Shipping weight, 4½ pounds.

You Boys Who Want the Best—You Mothers Who Want to Buy Wisely—Consider This Suit Before You Choose!

The difference between the best suit and the worst is not always something the unskilled eye can detect. Time alone can prove true superiority. And the test of time will point favorably to the superb quality in this suit. There is quality in the fabric, in the little hidden details of workmanship, and in the new style lines. The suit is made of a rich, durable all wool pure worsted in a new diamond weave, navy blue in color. This fabric has no superior when it comes to wear. The cut is the popular three-button double breasted with lapels, slightly rolled. The coat and vest are fully lined with a fine wool alpaca lining and the vest has five buttons and four pockets. The pants are wide at the bottoms and have cuffs. Excellently tailored down to the remotest detail. Your fit is assured. The real short cut to economy, after all, is by way of the best quality and that is just what you get in this suit. Remember, too, an extra pair of pants means extra wear for the whole suit.

40K3268—All Wool Navy Blue Diamond Weave Pure Worsted Long Pants Suit With Vest. **$12.95**
40K3293—Same Suit With Extra Pair of Long Pants. **$16.45**

Sizes, 9 to 16 years. State age size; also give chest, waist and inseam measures. Shipping weights: One-pants suit, 3¾ pounds; two-pants suit, 4¾ pounds.

Suits for Sturdy Lads Big Values!

Complete Outfit $1.39~

Complete Outfit $2.75~

All Wool $2.75~

All Wool $2.85~

Just Like Buffalo Bill
This dandy cowboy outfit will gratify his heart's desire and save his other clothes. It includes a shirt, cowboy style pants with fringe trimmings, bright bandana handkerchief, hat, lasso and toy cork pistol with holster and belt. Shirt, pants and hat are of good quality khaki.
Sizes, 4 to 14 years. State age size. Shpg. wt., 2 lbs.
40K3383
Complete Cowboy $1.39
Outfit..........

Ride 'Em Cowboy
Here is a khaki hat, a flannel shirt of red and black check with two breast pockets; washable khaki drill pants that have imitation leather trimmings with colored hand stenciled designs; bright bandana handkerchief, lasso, belt and holster, and large toy cork pistol.
Sizes, 4 to 14 years. State age size. Shpg. wt., 2¼ lbs.
40K3376
Complete Cowboy $2.75
Outfit..........

Sailor Style Suit
This dressy little suit gives you the most wear for your money. Made of an all wool, medium brown cassimere in the popular sailor style, with white mercerized braid trimming on collar, cuffs and bib. Bright color collegiate style belt. Fully lined knee pants that button to the waist. Side pockets. Black twill tie.
Sizes, 3 to 8 years. State age size. Shpg. wt., 2 lbs.
40K3321—All Wool
Brown $2.75
Cassimere..........

Sturdy Blazer Suit
Blazer blouse of all wool fabric in an attractive large plaid pattern of green, tan and dark blue. Two pockets with flaps to button. Sport style collar and cuffs. Sport style collar can be buttoned to the neck. All worsted jersey knit bottom. Straight style pants, all wool brown cassimere full lined.
Sizes, 3 to 8 years. State age size. Shpg. wt., 2 lbs.
40K3302—All Wool
Lumberjack $2.85
Suit..........

Flannel $1.25~

Flannel $1.79~

Genuine Tom Mix COWBOY OUTFIT

$1.95~

All Wool $2.50~

Dressy and Economical
This good looking, inexpensive, flannel suit will give lots of wear. Waist is made of cotton flannel in a tan and blue plaid with orange and lighter blue stripes. Pants are made of plain navy blue flannel, about one-fourth wool, and buttons to waist. Bright collegiate style belt, black twill tie, two chest pockets. Washable.
Sizes, 2 to 8 years. State age size. Shipping weight 1½ lbs.
40K3313—Flannel $1.25
Suit..........

Practical Middy Suit
This middy suit is neat, serviceable and very low in price. Made with trimmed sailor collar, black twill tie, sleeve emblem, patch pocket and straight pants. A good wearing flannel about one-third wool. Washable.
Sizes, 3 to 8 years. State age size. Shipping weight, 1½ pounds.
40K3329 — Dark Navy
Blue $1.79
Flannel..........

Here's a Boy's Dream Come True!
Every American youngster, at some time or another, has wished he could ride and throw a rope like Tom Mix. And along with that wish comes the desire to own a regular cowboy outfit. We'll back this one against all comers; in fact, Tom Mix himself has put his signature to the emblem on the shirt. The outfit includes: Twill flannel shirt in black, maroon and orange check with two patch pockets with flaps; pants of khaki drill with corduroy front and side trimmings and nickel plated spangles; large toy cork pistol, leather holster, belt, bandana handkerchief, lasso and large tan beaver felt hat. A splendid bargain!
Sizes, 4 to 14 years. State age size. Shpg. wt., 3 pounds.
40K3384—Tom Mix $3.75
Cowboy Outfit..........

Durable and Thrifty
Blazer style blouse of good quality flannel in handsome dark blue, orange and maroon plaid made with sport style collar and two chest pockets. Collar, cuffs and bottom of blouse made of navy blue corduroy. With either long or short straight style pants of navy blue corduroy. Dressy, serviceable and very economical.
Sizes, 3 to 8 years. State age size. Shpg. wt., 2 lbs.
40K3315—Long $1.95
Pants Suit..........
40K3314—Short 1.45
Pants Suit..........

Dressy, Warm and Serviceable
Waist is made of a jersey knit, all wool worsted material in a fancy tan and blue jacquard plaid. Laces down the front. Pants are made of jersey all wool worsted in a very attractive plain blue shade. They button to the waist. Bright color collegiate style belt. Pants have two side pockets and are full lined. A suit of high quality throughout.
Sizes, 2 to 8 years. State age size. Shpg. wt., 2¼ lbs.
40K3303 $2.50
Dressy Suit......

Suits *for* Play *and* Everyday

Indian Brave Suit

Inexpensive Indian suit, similar to the larger illustration at the right, in a lighter weight material and less trimmings. Smaller headdress. (See small illustration at the right.) Sizes, 2 to 10 years. State age size. Shpg. wt., 1¼ lbs.

40K3372
Light Weight Khaki Drill.

95c

$2.35~

$1.85~

95c

$1.89~

$2.75~

Good Suit for Little Fellows

Dark brown cassimere, about one-half wool, with fancy stripe decorations. Two lower patch pockets. Belt all around. Buttons down the front. Mercerized tassel tie. Fully lined. Straight style pants; two side pockets. Sizes, 3 to 8 years. State age size, Shpg. wt., 2¼ lbs.
40K3301—Dark Brown Cassimere. **$2.35**

Best of All for Wear

Here's a suit that will wear. Dark drab corduroy, warm and comfortable; Norfolk style with yoke and box plaits in front. Belt all around. Two pockets with flaps to button. Buttons down front. Straight style knee pants have side openings and buttonholes. Sizes, 3 to 8 years. State age size. Shpg. wt., 1¾ lbs.
40K3320—Dark Drab Corduroy..... **$1.85**

Big Chief—Ki, Yi!

He'll have lots of fun with this khaki drill coat with bright red front trimmings along the edges of sleeves; cuffs and bottom of coat with bright colored stenciled design, decorated with blue and gold fringe; khaki drill pants with blue and gold trimmings down the sides. Feathered headdress. Sizes, 4 to 14 years. State age size. Shpg. wt., 1¾ lbs.
40K3373—Good Weight Khaki Drill..... **$1.89**

Nifty Police Outfit

Police style coat with white braid trimmings on collar and cuffs. Police star and brass buttons. White braid down sides of pants. Good wearing dark blue drill. Leather belt with club and hat with chief's badge. Sizes, 4 to 14 years. State age size. Shipping weight, 1¾ pounds.
40K3381—Complete Policeman's Suit **$2.75**

Double Seat and Knee

69c

HERCULES 2.20 Weight Blue Denim

59c

85c

He Can't Wear These Out!

Made in the popular open front style with drop seat and shirt style collar. Seams are strongly stitched and buttonholes carefully made. Bar tacked at all points of strain. Double seat and knees for double wear. Riveted brass buttons will not come off or rust. Medium heavy weight, fast color, double and twist indigo blue denim or fast color fine weave khaki twill. Wash, wear well. Sizes, 3 to 8 years. State size. Shipping weight, 1 pound.
40K3631—Fast Color Indigo Blue Denim..... **85c**
40K3633—Fast Color Khaki Twill..... **85c**

Two Old Favorites

Blue or khaki, fast color. Both stand washing; wear well. Strongly stitched seams. Bar tacked at all points of strain. Open back, drop seat. Riveted brass buttons, don't come off or rust. Full and roomy. Sizes, 2 to 8 years. State age size. Shipping weight, ¾ pound.
40K3604—Fast Color Medium Heavy Weight Indigo Blue Stifel Drill..... **69c**
40K3606—Fast Color Khaki Twill..... **69c**

Our Best Play Suit

No matter how hard he plays, it will be almost impossible to wear through this improved Hercules suit. Made in the open front style with drop seat, two lower pockets and chest pocket. Seams are all carefully triple stitched. Side openings have continuous facings and cannot rip. Buttonholes securely stitched. Bar tacked at all points of strain. Covered fly front. Riveted brass buttons will not come off or rust. Made of the well known extra heavy 2.20 white back denim which is so popular in our men's high grade overalls. Cut full and roomy. Shaped sleeves and shoulders. Sizes, 3 to 8 years. State age size. Shipping weight 1¼ pounds.
40K3620—2.20 Weight White Back Indigo Blue Denim **$1.00**

Comfortable Rompers

Sturdy play suits. Fast color indigo blue stifel with white trimmings. Carefully stitched seams. Button back, with drop seat. Sizes, 2 to 7 years. State age size. Shpg. wt., ¾ lb.
40K3614—Fast Color Indigo Blue Stifel..... **59c**
Practical flannel romper, similar to above, but without the trimmings. Good wearing washable flannel, about one-third wool, in plain brown shade. Seams carefully stitched. Button back, with drop seat. Sizes, 2 to 7 years. State age size. Shpg. wt., 1 lb.
40K3615—Brown Flannel One-Third Wool **98c**

Handsome Sturdy and Thrifty

This little suit is very attractive and can be worn for dress or play, as it can be very easily washed. Waist is made of good weight, washable cotton material in a fancy brown and tan plaid with blue and green decorations. Brown twill tie. Plain, medium dark brown, washable twill flannel pants which button to waist. Collegiate style bright colored belt. Sizes, 2 to 8 years. State age size. Shpg. wt., 1 lb.
40K3300 Blazer Suit..... **85c**

Greater Coat Values
Enduring Quality and Thrifty Prices

Measuring Instructions Are on Page 548

Water Repellant Everdri

Genuine Horsehide

Two Great Favorites at New Low Prices

If you could really weigh the quality in these two coats with the price, you'd find a surprisingly large margin of value in your favor. The corduroy is thickset medium wale, specially made for long wear. The drab moleskin coat is heavy weight and sturdy. Both coats have excellent quality sheepskin lining, big beaverized sheepskin collar, warm sleeve lining and wristlets, arm shields, two muff pockets and two large lower pockets with flap. Style as illustrated. Here are two excellent coats at prices that will afford you a big saving! Sizes, 6 to 18 years. State age size. Shpg. wt., 5 lbs.

40K3868—Navy Blue Corduroy Sheepskin Lined Coat **$7.45**
40K3870—Drab Moleskin Sheepskin Lined Coat 7.45

The "Ace" of All Coats for Wear, Warmth, Quality and Economy

No coat anywhere will stand hard use like this one, and certainly there is no coat that will give its wearer more comfort in zero weather. It's made of dressy, tough, pliable black horsehide and lined with excellent quality sheepskin—a quality coat from start to finish and a big value at our low price. Made in single breasted style with facings of sturdy corduroy. Two muff pockets, two large lower pockets and belt all around. Sleeves lined and have adjustable tabs. Wide beaverized sheepskin collar.
Sizes, 8 to 18 years. State age size. Shipping weight, 6 pounds.

40K3853—Black Horsehide Sheepskin Lined Coat **$13.45**

Clothing Order Blank Is on Page 1094

Just Like Our Men's Famous Sheepskin Coat

Here is news for you! Boys' better quality sheepskin lined coats at lower prices. They are made of good weight drab moleskin, specially processed to repel water, and lined with choice pelts of sheepskin. The combination is a coat that is absolutely weatherproof. The collar is of beaverized sheepskin and turns up high, shawl style. Made in the double breasted style illustrated with two large lower pockets with flap, two muff pockets and belt all around. Five features place this coat in a class by itself. They are: Strong leather corners on the pockets to prevent ripping, sturdily reinforced armholes, closely knit sleeve wristlets, double moleskin thickness, the high quality of the sheepskin lining, and the water repellant moleskin. Still we keep the price down, actually lower than the price of an ordinary sheepskin coat.

State age size. Shipping weight, 4½ pounds.

40K3851—Drab Moleskin.
Sizes, 6 to 12 years **$5.45**
40K3852—Drab Moleskin.
Sizes, 14 to 18 years 6.45

Leather Coat—A Big Value!

Good quality cowhide leather coat in the popular mahogany shade and styled as illustrated. Body is lined with warm heavyweight blanket cloth and has two lower pockets and adjustable tab on sleeves. Leather affords greatest resistance against wear. Seams are strongly stitched. Size 18, 27 inches long. Smaller sizes are slightly shorter in proportion.
Sizes, 8 to 18 years. State age size. Shipping weight, 4 pounds.

40K3855—Split Cowhide Blanket Lined Coat **$5.85**

Genuine Horsehide

Here's Economy Without Sacrifice of Quality

There is as much warmth and protection against sub-zero winds in this coat as you find in the best of them, and it's made to give you much faithful service. This coat has always been a king of economy and the price this year is lower than ever. Sturdy moleskin is lined with sheepskin of excellent quality. Collar is made of beaverized sheepskin. Sleeves are lined with a good, fleecy cloth and have wristlets. Two lower pockets, substantially reinforced with leather tabs. Belt all around.
State age size. Shipping weight, 4½ pounds.

40K3862—Drab Moleskin Sheep Lined Coat. Sizes, 6, 8 and 10 years **$4.25**
40K3865—Drab Moleskin Sheep Lined Coat. Sizes, 12 and 14 years 5.25

Very Practical—Exceptionally Low in Price

This coat of genuine high quality black horsehide will keep son warm in the coldest weather and yet it's not too heavy to be worn during the milder days of fall and spring. It's lined with warm melton and made in the popular style illustrated with lapels that can be buttoned up close around the neck. Sleeves are fully lined and have adjustable tabs. Coat also has adjustable tab in back and two lower pockets with flaps. Size 18 coat measures 29 inches long and the smaller sizes are slightly shorter in proportion.
Sizes, 8 to 18 years. State age size. Shipping weight, 4½ pounds.

40K3859—Black Genuine Horsehide Melton Lined Coat **$8.50**

Here's Just the Suit He Needs for Play

40K3600—Fast Color Indigo Blue Stifel Drill.........................79c
40K3605—Fast Color Indigo Blue Denim.........................79c

Sizes, 2 to 8 years. State age size. Shipping weight, ¾ pound.

Play Ball! Those words mean his clothes are in for a rough time. It won't make any difference, though, if he is equipped with one of these sturdy play suits. The knees and seat, those places that usually get the worst of it, are of double thickness and the material itself will go through all kinds of abuse. Seams are double stitched and all points of strain are securely bar tacked. Open back and drop seat. Fast color red trimmings. Choice of two hard wearing materials that take a washing mighty well. Riveted brass buttons. Full cut.

DOUBLE Seat and Knees "Rufplay"

For Measuring Instructions See Page

Long Wear With Comfort and Economy

"Extra Heavy 220 Weight White Back Denim"

"Big Buddy" Invisible Drop Seat

A Favorite for Play—Inexpensive and Durable

40K3103—Little Fellow's Denim Overalls. Sizes, 3 to 8 years 45c

State age size. Shpg. wt., ¾ lb.
Don't worry about the wear and tear on son's clothes when these sturdy overalls of good, medium weight double and twist fast color indigo blue denim will solve the problem simply and inexpensively. All seams are triple stitched and won't rip. Side openings button. Large, roomy pockets, all strain points reinforced.

A Lot of Wear for a Little Money

Indigo Blue Denim

40K3108—Sizes, 3 to 8 years.........................59c
40K3110—Sizes, 9 to 14 years.........................69c
40K3114—Sizes, 15 to 18 years or 29 to 31 inches waist measure.........................79c

Jackets to Match
40K3112—Sizes, 9 to 14 years.........................69c
40K3116—Sizes, 15 to 18 years, or 32 to 36 inches chest measure.........................79c

State age size, waist or chest measure. Shipping weights: Sizes 3 to 8 years, 1 pound; sizes 9 to 18 years, 1¼ pounds.

In every respect these overalls and Jackets are like Dad's and they will give excellent service. The material is a good medium heavy weight double and twist indigo blue denim, fast color and very strong. The legs of the overalls have two triple stitched seams and are cut full size. Two swinging pockets, back and bib pocket. Adjustable suspenders. Jacket seams all triple stitched and pockets made roomy. Riveted buttons. Bar tacked at all strain points.

Our Sturdy Oak Jr. Boys' High Grade Overalls

40K3126—Sizes, 3 to 8 years.........................75c
40K3128—Sizes, 9 to 14 years.........................85c
40K3144—Sizes, 15 to 18 years or 29 to 31 inches waist measure.........................95c

Jacket to Match
40K3129—Sizes, 9 to 14 years.........................85c
40K3146—Sizes, 15 to 18 years or 32 to 36 inches chest measure.........................95c

State age size or waist or chest measure. Shpg. wt., each garment, 1¼ lbs.

One of the best overall buys you can find anywhere. Like men's high grade overalls, they're made of extra heavy 220 weight white back indigo blue denim, a wonder for wear. Side openings have two buttons. All the seams are triple stitched and will not rip. Two large pockets in back, swinging pockets in front and bib pocket. Continuous high back. Cut full. Wide suspenders will not bind. High wide bib. Jacket has three large pockets, triple stitched seams and open cuffs to button. Riveted buttons that will not come off and securely bar tacked at all strain points. Both jacket and overalls will stand many washings and will give good, hard, honest wear.

Don't Miss This Wide Choice of Allover Suits

40K3140—Fast Color Khaki Drill. Sizes, 6 to 14 years.........................$1.39
40K3142—Fast Color Indigo Blue Denim. Sizes, 6 to 14 years.........................$1.39
40K3148—Fast Color Khaki Drill. Sizes, 15 to 18 years or 32 to 36 inches chest measure.........................$1.59
40K3150—Fast Color Indigo Blue Denim. Sizes, 15 to 18 years or 32 to 36 in. chest measure.........................$1.59

State age size or give chest measure. Shipping weights: Sizes 6 to 14 years, 1¼ pounds; sizes 15 to 18 years, 1¾ lbs.

There's a solution to nearly every boy's overall needs among these numbers. The workmanship in each is exactly the same, which means that they're all made to stand lots of rough wear and many, many washings. Allover suits are mighty practical and they're becoming more and more popular. These button down the front and have a patented covered invisible drop seat. This is a convenient feature for there are no buttons in back to scratch the furniture. Side openings have two buttons. Riveted brass buttons that will not come off or rust. Cut full enough to be worn over other clothes. Bar tacked at all points of strain. Both the khaki and denim listed above are high grade, serviceable materials. **Real Sears Values.**

Parcel Post, Express and Freight Rates Are on Pages 542 to 545

SEARS "Great Store for Men"
Guides You to Correct Dress at Big Savings

WE ARE making clothing history right here! In our constant efforts to give you more for your money, this big new idea, Sears "Great Store for Men," was born. It's a new scheme, this "Great Store for Men," and it's the result of searching every nook and corner of the great clothing industry. We went from the mills to the big retail stores—from one coast to the other—to markets everywhere, to the world's foremost clothing experts, and then we analyzed our own 40 years' experience of selling clothing. From this tremendous mass of information, and you'll admit that it is huge, came this new idea—a "Great Store for Men."

And here is what it means:

1—Unusual values—big savings to you. (The spot cash we pay makes this possible.)
2—Finer materials than ever before.
3—Latest styles, selected models.
4—Far greater variety of colors and patterns.
5—Absolute guarantee of satisfaction.

On these five factors (things that interest you most) we have built this new scheme of merchandising and selling men's clothing. In other words, when you get nothing but strong, durable fabrics—the newest of new styles—rich, colorful patterns, big, honest values and a real guarantee of satisfaction, certainly you'll want to buy from Sears "Great Store for Men."

Look over every page of this men's section and see what this big new idea in retail merchandising brings you this season. It is well worth your while.

New Fall Colors and Fancy Weaves
High Quality Pure Wool Worsteds

It's pattern, men—new, colorful, rich looking—brand new, right from the style centers. And it's style, too. We've certainly gone one step ahead in these suits. Note the stylish lines of this fine "Clover Leaf" lapel coat and the three-button effect that college men and all well dressed men are demanding. The pattern is fancy weave with contrasting stripes—an altogether rich looking combination. Striped dark blue or the French (slate) gray, are the two new colors. The fabric is a weighty pure all wool worsted—strong, durable and slow to show signs of wear. Suit is well tailored and trim fitting. Coat full alpaca lined. Trousers have cuffs and are cut full. Regular vest. Yes, sir! We're proud of this suit and you will be, too. SIZES—34 to 42 inches chest, 29 to 40 inches waist and 29 to 34 inches inseam. State chest, waist and inseam measurements. Shipping weight, 5½ pounds.

45K8111—Striped Dark Blue $16.75
45K8112—Striped French (Slate) Gray 16.75

"Warm as Toast"
Heavy Winter Overcoat

Nothing finer has ever happened before. We are featuring this coat because it is a representative value from our new "Great Store for Men." By representative value, we mean one of a great many bargains that you will find throughout this clothing section. The material in this particular coat is heavyweight, a "Warm as Toast" fabric that will wear and give great service. In addition it is full twill lined. Snappy model with half belt in back. Tailored on stylish lines and strongly sewed. Two rich 1927 winter colors: Dark blue and dark brown. Length, about 44 inches. Big savings for you if you buy here. SIZES—34 to 44 inches chest. State chest measure taken over vest. Shipping weight, 7 pounds.

45K8367—Dark Blue $12.75
45K8368—Dark Brown 12.75

For Measuring Instructions See Page 548

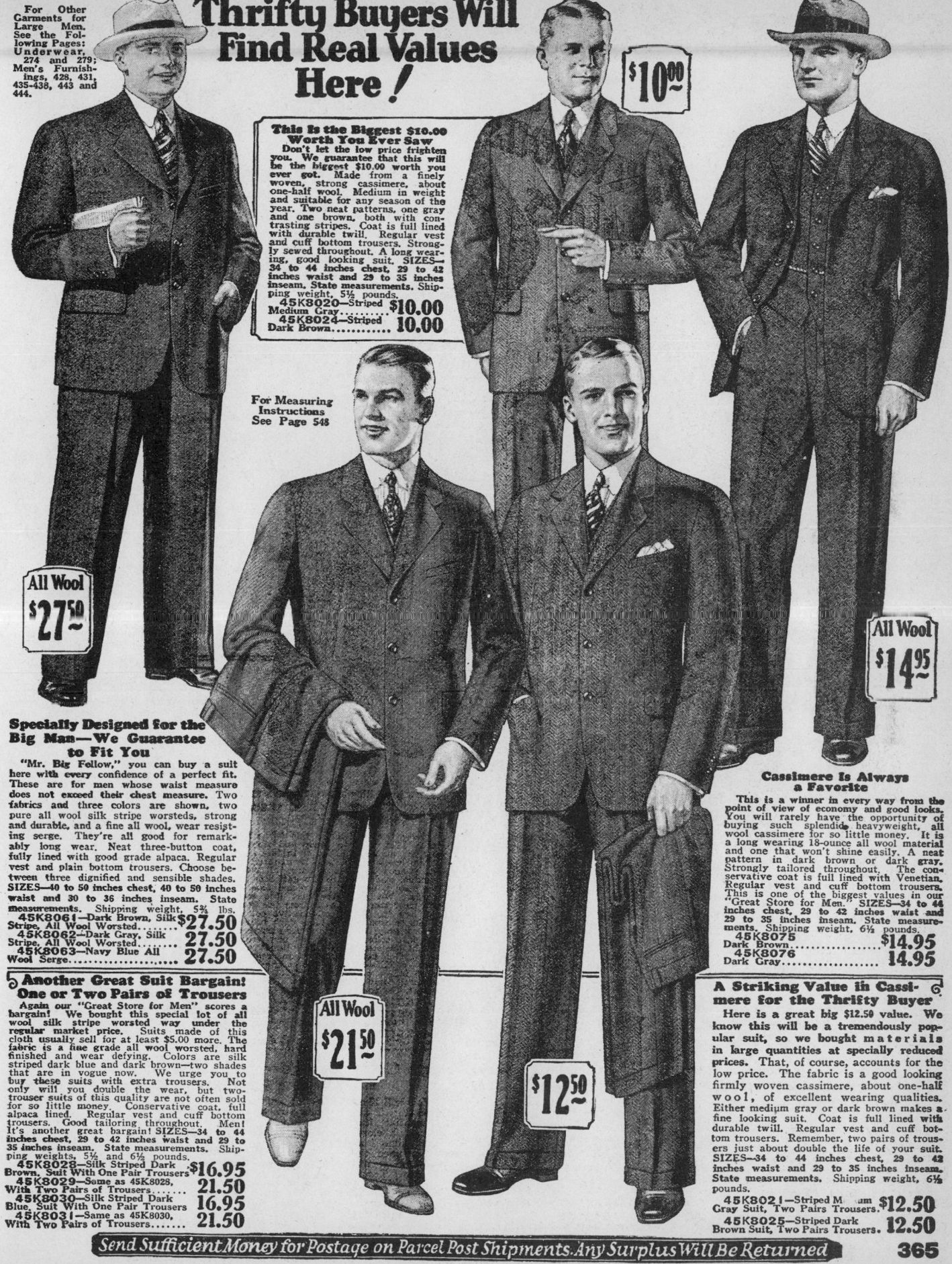

Convincing Proof of our Leadership in Values

We Guarantee Absolute Satisfaction

All Wool Glenurquhard Plaids Meeting Popular Demand

The beautiful rich shades in Glenurquhard plaids (two tones harmoniously blended) are the answer to their popularity. We are meeting this demand by listing here two plaids, medium gray or brown, both 1927 colors. The material is all wool cassimere a sturdy cloth that looks good and wears better. A strongly made suit. Coat is full lined with alpaca. Trousers have cuff bottoms. Regulation vest. Either color may be had with one or two pairs of trousers. SIZES—34 to 42 inches chest, 27 to 40 inches waist and 29 to 35 inches inseam. State measurements. Shpg. wts., 5½ and 6½ lbs.

45K8106—Medium Brown Glenurquhard Plaid **$14.75**

45K8107—Same as 45K8106, With Two Pairs of Trousers **$17.95**

45K8104—Medium Gray Glenurquhard Plaid **14.75**

45K8105—Same as 45K8104, With Two Pairs of Trousers **$17.95**

The "Clover Leaf"—Well Dressed Men Ask for It

Broad shoulders without being top heavy; trim waist and snug fit at the hips without being uncomfortable; "clover leaf" lapels, new and distinctive—that describes in a few words just what this brand new style is. Good quality pure all wool worsted is the fabric, and with it goes that popular contrasting striped pattern, with fancy weave effect. Two colors to choose from, striped dark blue or striped slate (French) gray. Coat has high three-button effect. Full alpaca lined. Cuff bottom trousers. Regular vest. Sturdy cloth for service, neat pattern for looks and low price for value. Sears "Great Store for Men is still forging ahead, always giving you more for your money. SIZES—34 to 42 inches chest, 29 to 40 inches waist and 29 to 35 inches inseam. State measurements. Shipping weight, 5½ pounds.

45K8109—Fancy Striped Dark Blue **$16.75**

45K8110—Fancy Striped Slate (French) Gray **$16.75**

The Diamond Weave Is Popular This Season

Most men look well in a double breasted coat—a slender man particularly so. This model is stylish in cut and is made well. Has wide lapels, slightly fitting waist and square shoulders. The diamond weave holds its popularity for both business and dress wear, because this unusual swagger pattern has an appeal to older men as well as young men. The fabric is pure all wool worsted, hard finished and will give extra good service. The color is dark blue—and don't forget that dark blue is very fashionable. The coat is full alpaca lined. Cuff bottom trousers. Regular vest. All in all this is an outstanding bargain at this price. SIZES—34 to 42 inches chest, 29 to 40 inches waist and 29 to 35 inches inseam. State measurements. Shipping weight, 5½ pounds.

45K8108—Dark Blue Diamond Weave **$17.95**

Two Materials—Two Prices— Never More for Your Money

We've succeeded in giving the young men the popular blue pencil stripe at a price they can well afford. Two materials at two different prices, cassimere or worsted. The lower priced suit is a cassimere, about one-half wool, strong, one that won't shine easily. The higher priced suit is made from pure all wool worsted, with silk stripes, a sturdy, durable fabric that will give excellent service. The color scheme is dark blue with lighter color pencil stripes. Both are well made. Coats are full lined with alpaca. Regular vest and cuff bottom trousers. For long wear and extra service we recommend our all wool worsted. In any case, whichever suit you buy you'll never get more for your money. SIZES—34 to 42 inches chest, 29 to 40 inches waist and 29 to 35 inches inseam. State measurements. Shipping weight, 5½ pounds.

45K8100—Striped Blue Cassimere (One-Half Wool) **$10.95**

45K8101—Striped Blue Worsted (All Wool) **16.75**

Quality ~Service Savings

Dashing Styles in Colorful Patterns

Style, Service and Good Looks at a Price You Can Afford

Dark colors are very appropriate for double breasted suits. That's why we chose these two fabrics. One a pure all wool worsted, is a very serviceable fabric and good for several seasons' wear. The dark blue color is relieved by silk stripes of silver color. The other material is a standard navy blue serge, fine twilled and has a hard wearing surface. A splendid model, too. Styled as it should be and tailored extremely well. Coat is one-half lined with alpaca. Trousers have cuff bottoms. Regular five-button vest. Style, service and good looks—that's only the beginning. Value at a price lower than usual is what we really want you to know about. SIZES—34 to 42 inches chest, 29 to 40 inches waist and 29 to 35 inches inseam. State measurements. Shipping weight, 5½ pounds.

45K8116—Silk Striped Blue All Wool Worsted.. **$22.85**
45K8117—Navy Blue All Wool Serge.......... **22.85**

Clothing Order Blank Is on Page 1094.

The Buyers Today Are Boosters Tomorrow!

No other suit value has been favored with such enthusiastic "word of mouth" advertising. Men, everywhere, who bought these quality suits, liked the fabric and make so well that they spread the good news. This is an unusually high quality fabric such as is found only in fine custom tailored suits. New patterns, marvelous colors and excellent tailoring, just right for fall, tell the story. This cloth is made by one of America's foremost woolen mills—it is a silk striped all wool pure worsted, hard twisted and great for long wear. Coat is one-half lined with alpaca. Regular vest. Cuff bottom trousers. Buyers today are boosters tomorrow. SIZES—34 to 42 inches chest, 29 to 40 inches waist and 29 to 35 inches inseam. State measurements. Shipping weight, 5½ lbs.

45K8136—Medium Gray With Silk Stripes... **$24.50**
45K8138—Medium Brown With Silk Stripes.. **24.50**

Fancy Weaves for Fall—Pure All Wool Worsted

Slowly but surely the fancy weave has made its way into men's clothes. It has arrived this season and you'll see fancy weaves everywhere. There are several soft tones of gray, attractive new shades, very neat but with enough "pep" and life to show the suit off to advantage. Or perhaps you'll like the brown combination better. Note the new "clover leaf" lapel. The fabric is an all wool pure worsted, durable and sure to give excellent service. Tailored well throughout. Trousers have cuff bottoms. Regular vest. Coat is half lined with alpaca. Buy and save, too, at our new "Great Store for Men." SIZES—34 to 42 inches chest, 29 to 40 inches waist and 29 to 35 inches inseam. State measurements. Shipping weight, 5½ pounds.

45K8113—Gray Fancy Weave........................ **$21.50**
45K8114—Brown Fancy Weave...................... **21.50**

Double Duty Two-Trouser Suits—Pure All Wool Worsted

Double duty means twice as much wear. The strong sturdy cloth and the extra trousers account for that. This two-trouser suit is made from a hard finished, twilled surfaced all wool pure worsted—with silk stripes—in other words, a tough cloth that is slow in showing signs of wear. Fall and winter colors, dark brown, blue and gray shades that most fine shops are showing. Tailored neatly and styled to hold its lines. Coat is one-half lined with alpaca. Regular vest and cuff bottom trousers. You can register this as another "knockout" value for our new "Great Store for Men." SIZES—34 to 42 inches chest, 29 to 40 inches waist and 29 to 35 inches inseam. State measurements. Shipping weight, 6½ pounds.

45K8118—Silk Striped Gray With Extra Trousers...................... **$25.00**
45K8120—Silk Striped Brown With Extra Trousers **25.00**
45K8122—Silk Striped Blue With Extra Trousers **25.00**

Order Blanks Are in Back of This Catalog

85 371

A Striking Display of Students' Styles

B $15.75~

A $11.45~

C $18.75~

See Opposite Page for Descriptions

Come in Sizes 31 to 36 Chest

D $15.85~
SUIT With Extra Trousers

E $16.95~

F $18.25~
SUIT With Extra Trousers

SIZE SCALE

These High School Suits are built and tailored the same as our young men's suits, but cannot be furnished larger than 36 inches chest.

Sizes of Suits on This and Opposite Page

Chest	31	32	33	34	35	36
Waist	26-29	26-29	27-30	28-31	29-32	30-33
Inseam	Ranges from 27 to 32 inches in proportion to the chest measure.					

Featuring Low Price New Novelty Weave

(A) 45K8206—Gray Fancy Weave
All Wool
Cassimere.......................... **$11.45**
State measurements. (See size scale at top of page.) Shipping weight, 5½ pounds. It's remarkable, this low price, and a better value would be hard to find. Sturdily made from an all wool cassimere fabric, good weight and serviceable. It is a snappy double breasted model in a new novelty weave pattern. Coat is full lined with alpaca. Regular vest and wide cuff bottoms. You are bound to know sooner or later that our "Great Store for Men." is chock full of bargains. You'll realize it when you unpack this suit.

Students, Attention! You Want A "Cloverleaf"

(B) 45K8212—Striped
Blue Fancy Weave........ **$15.75**
45K8214—Striped
French Gray Fancy Weave.. **15.75**
State measurements. (See size scale at top of page.) Shipping weight, 5½ pounds. You've seen the "Cloverleaf"—perhaps some of your friends wear it. At any rate it's brand new and from all appearances it is going to be a popular style this fall. Imagine the new effect—broad shoulders without being top heavy; trim waistline and snug hips without being uncomfortable. Note the three-button high cut and the "Cloverleaf" lapel—that's where the name comes from. Two pure all wool worsteds in striped blue fancy weave or striped French gray fancy weave. Splendid wearing cloth. Extra well tailored with coat full alpaca lined. Wide cuff bottoms and regular vest.

Style Notes Are Saying Gray and Brown Fancy Weaves

(C) 45K8224—Fancy
Gray Worsted............ **$18.75**
45K8226—Fancy
Brown Worsted............ **18.75**
State measurements. (See size scale at top of page.) Shipping weight, 5¼ pounds. Smart, ultrastylish fancy weaves are the latest development in students' clothes. Soft browns and medium grays are perhaps the most popular. While the color is important the cloth comes in for its share of praise. Pure wool worsted—a suiting that will wear and wear. Coat is a good looking two-button model and is full lined with alpaca. Trousers have wide cuffs. Regular vest. This is our best suit for students. You could rightfully expect to pay much more.

Setting the Pace for Style and Value

(D) 45K8208—Fancy
Brown Cassimere.......... **$12.50**
45K8209—Same as 45K8208 with
Two Pairs of
Trousers....................... **$15.85**
State measurements. (See size scale at top of page.) Shipping weights, 5¼ and 6 pounds. No doubt about it. This suit sets the pace for style and value. Take first the material—an all wool cassimere, good enough for suits selling for more money. Now as to style—well, it's a model that's being shown in all leading men's shops. Pattern? The new criss cross fancy weave—students everywhere like it. Coat is full lined with alpaca. Trousers have wide cuffs. Regular vest. Sure it's a big value. We are setting the pace for others.

Two Choice Patterns Students Are Demanding

(E) 45K8220—Blue
Diamond Weave Worsted... **$16.95**
45K8221—Brown
Diagonal Weave Worsted... **16.95**
State measurements. (See size scale at top of page.) Shipping weight, 5¼ pounds. Here's a pleasing pair! Style and pattern right together. Double breasted models are demanded by young fellows everywhere. Along with style goes diamond and diagonal weave fabrics. That's why we are showing this smart model in these two favorite patterns. The cloth is a pure worsted all wool—more than satisfactory from the "wear" point of view. Excellently made throughout with coat full alpaca lined. Regular vest and cuff bottom trousers. Savings? Certainly—we are famous for savings and honest values.

"Boyville" Senior Reaches New High Peaks in Value

(F) 45K8216—Striped
Dark Blue Cassimere....... **$14.95**
45K8217—Same as 45K8216 with
Two Pairs of
Trousers....................... **$18.25**
45K8218—Striped Dark
Gray Cassimere............ **14.95**
45K8219—Same as 45K8218
with Two Pairs of Trousers...... **18.25**
State measurements. (See size scale at top of page.) Shipping weights, 5½ and 6 pounds. Students! We want you to know that this all wool cassimere material is noted for strength and service. It has passed the same tests as our regular "Boyville" suits for boys. In other words, when a cloth will "hold" the average American boy—then you know it is strong and you know it will wear. Stylishly cut and strongly sewed. Two neat colors. Coat is full lined with alpaca. Wide cuff bottom trousers. Regular vest. The suit with one pair of trousers is a mighty fine "buy," but Boyville Senior two-trouser suits reach new high peaks in value.

Smart Collegiate Clothes

Popular Priced Fancy Cassimere

It's years since we have been able to offer a suit value of this kind. Fancy weaves are "the thing" but suits of that character have been expensive. We show here a fancy weave cassimere at an unusually low price. The material is one half wool, durable and neat looking. Attractive style and good quality tailoring. Brand new brown shade for fall and winter wear. Coat is full lined with alpaca. Regular vest and cuff bottom trousers. You'll be ahead if you buy this suit—especially so if you order it with two pairs of trousers. State measurements. (See size scale at left.) Shipping wts., 5½ and 6 lbs.
45K8200—Fancy Medium
Brown........................ **$ 8.95**
45K8201—Same as 45K8200
with Extra Trousers............ **11.50**

For Measuring Instructions See Page 548.

For Boys' Shoes and Oxfords See Pages 328 and 329.

Low Priced "Cloverleaf" Model

Style and quality at a low price. This brand new model known as the "Cloverleaf" priced within reach of all. Three-button coat with wide shoulders and snug fitting hips are the principal features, outside of the new shaped lapel which is called the "Cloverleaf." The material is a popular gray fancy weave all wool cassimere. Coat is full lined with alpaca. Wide cuff bottoms and regular vest. One or two pairs of trousers, whichever you prefer. State measurements. (See size scale above at left.) Shpg. wts., 5¼ and 6 lbs.
45K8202
Fancy Gray...... **$10.95**
45K8203—Same as 45K8202
with Two Pairs
of Trousers...... **$14.45**

One of Our Special Offers Double Breasted Suit

A blue pencil striped double breasted at a new low price. Suits in this popular pattern are usually sold for much more. Prudent and wise buying enables us to offer this splendid cassimere (half wool) suit at a big saving to you. The cloth is closely woven and sure to give the wear that you will expect. Handsome pattern with pencil stripes. Regular vest and wide cuff bottom trousers. It's a smart model for little money. State measurements. (See size scale above at left.) Shipping wt., 5¼ pounds.
45K8204
Striped Dark Blue. **$11.45**

An All Wool Melton Overcoat for Only $8.50

Although this is our lowest priced overcoat for high school students you'll find maximum value here. We are going after bigger business in our "Great Store for Men." That's why we built this coat up to a standard and not down to a price. Made of good quality heavyweight all wool melton overcoating—warm as well as long wearing. Strongly sewed and excellently tailored. Two 1927 winter colors. Worth much more in value, wear and style. SIZES—32 to 36 inches chest. State chest size taken over vest. Shpg. wt., 6 lbs.
45K8400—Medium Brown.......................... **$8.50**
45K8401—Dark Blue................................ **8.50**

Overcoats of Style and Distinction

For Men's Shoes and Oxfords See Pages 320 to 324

Clothing Order Blank Is on Page 1094

A Special Purchase Made This Low Price Possible

On the job as usual or we couldn't have stepped in and bought this fine cloth so we could sell it at this special low price. Watching the markets for bargains such as this is just one of the reasons we are able to give you such truly exceptional clothing values. Coats of this character and quality would regularly retail for many dollars more. You'll agree with us when you see the coat, feel the heavy warm fabric and note the exceptional tailoring. It's made from a thick, warm, heavy all wool overcoating—plaid back richly colored. Tailored in a popular style with half belt in back. Has wide French facings, deep yoke of self material and sleeves lined with Venetian. A word about color. It comes in three correct shades, snappy and good to look at—dark blue, gray or brown. Length of coat, about 44 inches. We saved money here, and we are passing the saving on to you.

SIZES—34 to 44 inches chest. State chest measure taken over vest. Shipping wt., 7 lbs.

45K8380—Dark Brown..............	$16.50
45K8381—Dark Gray................	16.50
45K8382—Dark Blue................	16.50

You'll See Chesterfields Everywhere You Go

Back come the Chesterfields! Once again the plain and straight lines of the Chesterfield model overcoat are in style. In contrast to the new and colorful patterns in men's suits is the somber blue shown in these dignified overcoats. This handsome garment is made from a warm and heavy all wool overcoating. Stylishly cut in a double breasted model, with medium wide lapels and a rich velvet collar. Full lined sleeves. Excellently made throughout. Abreast of the times with Style—that's one of the first things our "Great Store for Men" is noted for. Length, about 46 inches.

SIZES—34 to 44 inches chest. State chest measure taken over vest. Shpg. wt., 6¾ lbs.

45K8369—Dark Blue.................. $13.50

Description of Overcoats on Opposite Page

This Style Is a Great Favorite With Students

(A)
45K8402—Dark Brown................	$10.75
45K8403—Dark Blue.................	10.75

SIZES—32 to 36 inches chest. State chest measure taken over vest. Shipping weight 6¾ pounds.

This is a moderately priced coat, yet warm and comfortable, as it is made of a good quality, heavyweight, all wool, heather brown or blue melton. It is full lined with strong, durable twill. A dressy coat, with half belt. Cuffs on sleeves. Big, convertible, cold weather collar. Lengths, 39 to 42 inches. A favorite high school style.

The Students' Choice Fancy Weave Fabrics

(B)
45K8404—Bluish Gray Fancy Weave Mixture.......	$18.50
45K8405—Medium Brown Fancy Weave Mixture......	18.50

SIZES—32 to 36 inches chest. State chest measure taken over vest. Shipping weight, 6¾ pounds.

Just notice what students are wearing and you'll see fancy weave fabrics—and particularly in bluish gray or medium brown mixtures. They are the students' choice, so, to be in style, you'll want to wear one of these coats. The fabric is a closely woven heavyweight all wool material, warm and comfortable. Stylishly built double breasted model, with guaranteed satin yoke and sleeves, and strongly made throughout. Lengths, 39 to 42 inches. High school students should know that Sears "Great Store for Men" is the right place to buy and the right place to save.

Smartly Styled New Ulsterette Model

(C)
45K8406—Dark Brown..............	$15.75
45K8408—Navy Blue...............	15.75

SIZES—32 to 36 inches chest. State chest measure taken over vest. Shipping weight, 6¾ pounds.

Excellent taste has been shown in designing this new ulsterette model. It has all the dash and swagger of the best style winter coats. It would cost a great deal more at any other store. It is a splendid value. Made of fine, heavyweight, all wool, rich plaid back overcoating, and well made throughout. Sleeves are lined with genuine Venetian cloth. Lengths, 39 to 42 inches. Wide French facings, deep cloth yoke, cuff sleeves and belt at the back make this coat as handsome as it is lasting.

For Every Man's Wardrobe— Stylish Warm Overcoat

(D)
45K8372—Fancy Dark Brown Mixture............	$14.45
45K8373—Fancy Dark Gray Mixture............	14.45

SIZES—34 to 42 inches chest. State chest measure taken over vest. Shipping weight, 7 pounds.

This coat is one that deserves a place in every man's wardrobe. It has style and pattern; warmth and comfort, quality and low price. That's a combination that you can not afford to pass by. The fabric is a sturdy all wool overcoating in a neat fancy weave, dark brown or dark gray mixture. The coat is strongly sewed. Half belt in back. Double breasted model that is becoming to most men. Dollar for dollar, there is great value here.

Low Priced Overcoat—Heavyweight All Wool Melton

(E)
45K8365—Dark Brown..............	$8.95
45K8366—Dark Blue...............	8.95

SIZES—34 to 44 inches chest. State chest measure taken over vest. Shipping weight, 6¾ pounds.

"Moderate in price, but high in quality," tells this overcoat story. Made from a heavyweight, all wool melton—a material that looks well and wears well. Two dark shades, either brown or blue; colors that do not show soil easily. Stylish double breasted model. With half belted back. Strongly sewed throughout. Length, about 44 inches. One of our low priced overcoats, but one of our biggest values.

A Dressy Looking Coat — and a Good One

(F)
45K8370—Heather Brown Mixture.............	$11.50
45K8371—Medium Blue Mixture.............	11.50

SIZES—34 to 42 inches chest. State chest measure taken over vest. Shipping weight, 6¾ pounds.

Giving you the best that money can buy, we have even lowered the former low price on coats of this fabric. It is one of the best values in our clothing line. Snappy style, with its half belt and patch pockets with flaps, it is equally satisfying in warmth and long life. Nearly all wool, heavyweight overcoating. Popular heather brown or medium blue mixture with plaid back. Convertible collar. Length, 44 inches.

Style·Warmth·Comfort·Low Price

A $10.75~

B $18.50~

C $15.75~

D $14.45~

E $8.95~

F $11.50~

See Opposite Page
for Descriptions

We Guarantee to Save You Money!

8G 375

Dignified, Correctly Styled CHESTERFIELDS

For Measuring Instructions See Page 548

A Chesterfield Is Always Good Form

The Chesterfield is always stylish, always good looking. You can wear it on any occasion demanding an overcoat, with the assurance that you are neatly and correctly dressed. The material in this coat is medium weight melton cloth, three-quarters wool, with trim snug fitting collar of the same cloth. Lined throughout body and sleeves with a durable cotton twill. Two roomy lower pockets with neat flap. Medium vent in back. Length of coat, 43 inches. At our very low price this coat is a remarkable bargain. SIZES—34 to 44 inches chest. State chest measure taken over vest. Shipping weight, 6 pounds.

45K8300—Black...... $11.75
45K8302—Oxford Gray...................... 11.75

All Wool Melton
Style and Value Combined

Wherever well dressed men gather you will find Chesterfields worn. This type of overcoat has an air of smart dignity. And the one illustrated above will appeal instantly to the man who selects his clothes thoughtfully. Made from firmly woven all wool melton of a good, heavy weight. Body lining is of good quality serge; the sleeves are lined with satin. Especially well made and rightly tailored with a hand felled velvet collar. Has two generous lower pockets with flap. Medium length vent in back. Length of coat, 44 inches. REGULAR SIZES—34 to 44 inches chest. EXTRA SIZES—46 to 50 inches chest. State chest measure taken over vest. Shipping weight, 6 lbs.

45K8312—Black. Regular Sizes............... $19.95
45K8313—Black. Extra Sizes............... 21.95
45K8314—Oxford Gray. Regular Sizes............... 19.95
45K8315—Oxford Gray. Extra Sizes............... 21.95

Warmth—Style—Comfort
At a Low Price

A single breasted overcoat—one that combines good looks with extraordinary wearing qualities, perfect comfort and real warmth. Material is extra heavyweight all wool overcoating, closely and firmly woven—thick—it won't let the cold through. Length, 45 inches. Has cuff sleeves, wide french facings. Yoke facings and sleeves lined with venetian. Medium vent in back of coat. Two big patch pockets with flap. In either oxford gray or medium brown heather. SIZES—34 to 44 inches chest. State chest measure taken over vest. Shipping weight, 7½ pounds.

45K8306—Oxford Gray................... $17.50
45K8308—Medium Brown Heather....... 17.50

This Chesterfield Is for the Man Who Wants the Best

This is a splendid overcoat—a real big value—in looks and in high quality. It serves every need for everyday wear, besides answering the most strict requirements of dress wear. Made from heavy serviceable fine quality all wool melton in either black or dark oxford gray. Especially well tailored, with hand felled velvet collar and hand made buttonholes. Lined throughout with Skinner's satin. Length, 44 inches. This coat is our best Chesterfield. It is real economy to buy it. It will give splendid service and keep its dressy appearance for a long time. SIZES—34 to 44 inches chest. State chest measure taken over vest. Shipping weight, 6½ pounds.

45K8316—Black............................ $32.50
45K8318—Dark Oxford Gray............................ 32.50

For Other Garments for Larger Men See Following Pages: Underwear, 274, 279 and 285; Shirts, 435, 436 and 437; Nightshirts, 443 and 444.

For Men's Shoes and Oxfords See Pages 320 to 324

LET IT BLOW!
Storm Proof Overcoats

Sheep Lined Opossum Collar

A Serviceable and Inexpensive Ulster

We don't believe there is a better ulster anywhere for this low price. And you men, who are looking for the overcoat that most effectively combines durability, style, warmth and low price, will find this coat a source of lasting satisfaction to you. It's made of a good weight fabric, nearly three-fourths wool, in a rich dark brown that is very attractive. Lined throughout with a good grade of cotton twill. Large convertible collar. Adjustable sleeve tabs. Two big, roomy pockets with flaps and all around belt. Length, 48 inches. SIZES—36 to 48 inches chest. State chest measure taken over vest. Shpg. wt., 7½ lbs.

45K8319—Dark Brown............. **$11.95**

Dependable Style and Quality

This ulster will answer all your coat needs satisfactorily and at a small cost. You can depend on it for lots of wear and to keep you warm in the coldest weather. You can depend on the style to give you a well dressed appearance anywhere. And the price affords you a liberal saving. The coat is made of a heavy nearly all wool overcoating in a dark brown mixture or an oxford gray. Double breasted muff pocket style with half belt in back and two large lower patch pockets with flap. Upper half lined with quilted Venetian. Sleeves fully lined. Large convertible collar. Sleeve tabs. Length, 48 inches. SIZES—36 to 48 inches chest. State chest measure taken over vest. Shpg. wt., 8½ lbs.

45K8320 Dark Brown Heather....... **$14.95**
45K8321 Oxford Gray.............. **14.95**

Heavy All Wool Sheep Lined Ulster

Every man, at one time or another, has wanted a coat like this. It's stylish, good looking and very comfortable. Made of fine all wool dark brown mackinaw cloth, lined with first quality sheepskin, and has a large shawl style collar of Australian opossum fur. Made in the double breasted style illustrated with belt all around and two extra large, double stitched patch pockets with flap. Sleeves are lined with felted cloth and have double knit wristlets and arm shields. The coat will serve you well and prove a mighty good investment. The price is lower than ever. Length, 45 inches. SIZES—36 to 46 inches chest. State chest measure taken over vest. Shipping wt., 11 lbs.

41K581—Brown Mackinaw Cloth, Sheepskin Lining, Fur Collar..... **$29.95**

Heavyweight Wool Lined Black Dog Fur

Here at last, men, is your opportunity to buy a warm, good looking fur coat of excellent quality at a very modest price. Fur! It was man's first protection from the elements and today, more than ever before, its superiority is recognized everywhere. And of course, prices generally are pretty high. But every man can afford to buy this splendid coat for the simple reason that it's serviceable and low priced. Made of fine black dog fur. Has body lining of all wool blanket cloth and is lined in yoke and sleeves with Venetian. Has double knit wristlets, firmly sewed loops and olives, and a huge collar that can be fastened snugly around the neck. Small vent in the back. Length, 48 inches. It's a wonderful coat—a big value for your money! SIZES—36 to 48 inches chest. State chest measure taken over vest. Shipping weight, 11 pounds.

45K8350—Wool Lined Black Dog Fur Coat............. **$37.50**

Bargains
From Army Surplus

Leather Vest With Pockets

All Leather Wool Lined Vest
This is a little different from the ordinary leather vest, in that we have had it equipped with two big lower pockets. You will find this a great convenience. Like our number 41K627 at the right, it may be worn either under or over a coat. It is the regulation U. S. Army Jerkin, made of excellent quality tan glove leather and lined with heavy weight olive drab all wool melton. Splendid protection against cold. Cut roomy for solid comfort. SIZES—36 to 46 inches chest. State measurements. Shipping weight, 2½ pounds.
41K628—Tan Leather Vest......$2.49

Genuine U.S. Navy Pants All Wool - - - BLUE

U.S. Army All Wool Jacket

Leather Vest All Wool Lining

U. S. Army Jacket -- All Wool
Warm, Comfortable and Useful

Carefully tailored to U. S. Government specifications and standards out of all wool heavy weight finely woven olive drab melton. This is a splendid coat for knockabout use of every kind, sport, hunting, fishing or work in the open. It is snug fitting, warm and comfortable. The government paid three or four times as much for these coats as we are asking. It is one of the biggest bargains we have. You will never regret having one. State chest measure. Shpg. wt., 3½ lbs.
41K108—U. S. Army All Wool Olive Drab Jacket. SIZES—32 to 38 inches chest.......................... **$1.49**
41K115—U. S. Army All Wool Olive Drab Jacket. SIZES—40 and 42 inches chest.......................... **$1.69**

An All Leather Vest--Weather Proof and Wear Proof As Well

There is no better protection against cold than leather. Wind cannot get through this genuine U. S. Army leather vest. And the heavy weight olive drab all wool melton lining gives plenty of warmth and body comfort. The leather in this vest is an excellent quality heavy tan glove leather, with years of hard wear in it. It is flexible, comfortable and adjusts itself to the body so as to afford great freedom of movement. Will not bind anywhere. May be worn either over or under a coat. A very useful garment. First quality new vests approved by government inspectors. SIZES—36 to 46 inches chest. State chest measure. Shipping weight, 2½ pounds.
41K627—Army Leather Vest.......................... $2.19

For Measuring Instructions See Page 548

A Real Bargain
You'll Like These Pants!

Wear these genuine regulation U. S. Navy all wool blue pants for school, boating, camping or general wear around the house or on the farm. Have a marvelous capacity for long wear. We are selling quantities of them and they are getting more and more popular. They were carefully tailored under U. S. Government supervision out of standard Government inspected 16-ounce goods. Bell bottoms and thirteen-button front. Adjustable waist. An honest to goodness value! The cloth alone cost the Government much more than we are asking for the pants. SIZES—30 to 40 inches waist and 29 to 32 inches inseam measures. State waist and inseam measures. Shipping weight, 2½ pounds.
41K800—Genuine U. S. Navy All Wool Pants......**$2.25**

Genuine U. S. Government Army Breeches

Know real comfort in the outdoors, either for work or play, with a pair of these genuine U. S. Government Army Breeches. They give you a freedom of movement that ordinary trousers can never do. Cut full around the hips, they fit closely at the calves, where they are secured by lacing. There is a double knee reinforcement. All seams are double stitched and pocket corners bar tacked to prevent ripping. Comes in two materials—first quality olive drab khaki or olive drab all wool melton. Finest workmanship, all approved by government inspectors. SIZES—30 to 38 inches waist with inseams in proportion. State waist measurement.
41K883 — Olive Drab Khaki. Shipping weight, 2 pounds. **$1.45**
41K884—Olive Drab All Wool Melton. Shipping weight, 2¼ pounds.......**$2.89**

All Wool or Khaki Army Breeches

The World's Best Quality Overall

HERCULES

Extra Heavy 8 Oz. Pre-Shrunk Denim

$1.55 Each Garment

The Hercules Proves Its Own Claims

We say the HERCULES is the best overall made. We say it is the World's Biggest Overall Value. Those are pretty strong claims and they are not made thoughtlessly. The HERCULES bears them out every time. We have put it squarely up to the men who know overalls—men who wear them six days a week—and the HERCULES has never failed to make good. It has probably been compared one time or another with every overall on the market, and it has had the best of it every time. Every one we sell means more sales for us because other men see them and want them.

A man can get very enthusiastic over the HERCULES. It is a good looking overall. And it is so almighty comfortable—cut over roomy patterns to insure comfort and freedom of action to the wearer. For long wear it's like a suit of armor.

"Double Service" Denim—The Best Made

"Double Service" Denim is the only material that ever goes into a HERCULES Overall—the best denim that can be made. One of the world's famous denim mills makes it—specially and only for us—an extra heavy 8-ounce cloth with blue face and white back. This 8-ounce means exactly what it says, full 8 ounces to the yard, more threads to the inch and greater resistance to strain and general wear than ordinary denim can possibly give.

Before the material is cut every yard of this "Double Service" 8-ounce denim is shrunk both by water and steam. This is done to reduce the shrinkage which commonly follows the washing of the ordinary overalls. HERCULES Overalls are roomy and comfortable when you get them. They remain roomy and comfortable after their first washing or any washings that follow. HERCULES never binds anywhere.

Pockets, Pockets Everywhere!

Then, there is the immense convenience of the pockets—pockets everywhere, for general use and for special use, including pockets with guarded openings so that your watch, or your small tool, or your knife can't fall out.

We couldn't think of a thing to do to make the HERCULES Overall better this season except one; we added another pocket on the apron. It is a dandy big pocket, self faced and with button flap to prevent contents from falling out.

There are fifteen big features in the making of the HERCULES Overall—fifteen reasons why it is the most desirable work garment you can buy at any price. Here they are:

Fifteen Big Features

1 "Double Service" Blue Denim—Specially woven, full 8 ounces to the yard, More threads to the inch than usual.

2 Pre-Shrunken—Every piece thoroughly shrunk in water and steam.

3 Seams Guaranteed Not to Rip—New pair of overalls if they do.

4 Roomy—Big All Over—Mighty comfortable. Does not bind anywhere.

5 Pockets Double Stitched and Bar Tacked—Every pocket double stitched for greater strength and longer wear.

6 Overall pockets Self Faced—Longer life to the pocket edge.

7 Reinforced Jacket Pockets—Extra lined at bottom with long wearing heavy drill.

8 Guarded Pockets—Special guard for rule and watch pockets prevents contents from falling out.

9 Inside Jacket Pocket—A rare convenience, big and handy.

10 Hammer Strap—Broad and strong.

11 Adjustable Cuffs and Collar—Two sets of buttons allow loose or snug fit as desired.

12 Rustproof Buttons—Guaranteed not to come off.

13 Lined Suspenders—Lining holds suspenders flat—no twisting or curling.

14 Each Leg Has Two Seams—Hang better—fit better.

15 Big, Roomy Pocket—With buttoned flap on bib. New. Handy.

The HERCULES Overall, with these fifteen practical features, combines all the good points of every good overall made. Compare it with any other overall made. Compare it with overalls sold in your community at $2.00 to $2.50. If it isn't better than anything else you can find—send it back. We will, without question, return your money, including all transportation charges.

When ordering be sure to state waist and inseam measures of overalls and chest measure for jacket. See measuring instructions on page 548.

Regular sizes of jackets, 34 to 46 inches chest; overalls, 30 to 44 inches waist and 30 to 36 inches inseam. Shipping weight, 2¼ pounds. Extra sizes of jackets, 48 to 58 inches chest; overalls, 46 to 56 inches waist and 30 to 36 inches inseam. Shipping weight, 2½ pounds.

41K733—Coat Style Jacket. (See large illustration.) Regular sizes.	$1.55
41K731—High Back Apron Overalls. (Small illustration below shows back view.) Regular sizes.	1.55
41K732—Detachable Suspender Apron Overalls. (Small illustration below shows back view.) Regular sizes.	1.55
41K735—Pants Style Overalls Without Bib. Knees and Front are double thickness. (Small illustration below shows this overall.) Regular sizes.	1.55

Numbers listed below are furnished in extra sizes only.

41K753—Coat Style Jacket. (See large illustration.) Extra sizes.	1.85
41K751—High Back Apron Overalls. (Small illustration below shows back view.) Extra sizes.	1.85
41K752—Detachable Suspender Apron Overalls. (Small illustration below shows back view.) Extra sizes.	1.85

All Pockets Reinforced Double Stitched and Bar Tacked

Lined Suspenders

Triple Stitched Seams

Hammer Strap

Adjustable Collar and Cuffs

Safety Rule Pocket

Each Leg Has Two Seams

The World's Biggest Overall Value

Added Feature—New This Season Extra Handy Bib Pocket With Protective Flap

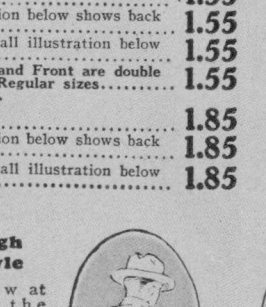

Pants Style—No Bib—Double Front

Small view at left shows the pants style, without bib (41K735). Both legs are double thickness in front. Any Hercules wears long and takes a lot of punishment. This one outwears 'em all.

Solid High Back Style

Small view at right shows the solid high back style which is both higher and broader than the ordinary kind (41K731 and 41K751). Observe the strong bar tacking at strain points and two large back pockets.

Detachable Suspender Style

Small view at left shows the detachable suspender style with elastic inserts that allow full play at the shoulders (41K732 and 41K752). A most comfortable style, preferred by many.

Front View

View at right shows front of both apron styles. Note high apron front, two deep and roomy swinging front pockets and two large bib pockets, one guarded, one with buttoned flap. Suspenders lined with same blue denim. Always comfortable.

Bigger Value Than Ever!
We've Improved the Coat
We've Lowered the Price
and We've Waterproofed It Too!

Full 36 inch Length

Now Only $7⁹⁸

Heavyweight Moleskin Cloth, Sheep Lined

Over 100,000 satisfied customers have worn and been pleased with our extra big value Sheep Lined Moleskin Coat. It is known from one end of the country to the other. It is made specially for us and sold only by us. It is made to our rigid specifications, under our direct supervision and carries our broad guarantee to satisfy you perfectly. The splendid materials are capable of the utmost in wear. The sturdy workmanship, the very unusual roomy comfort of this coat and its practicability will satisfy you thoroughly.

Now! A Better Coat for Less Money—and Waterproofed, Too!

We have always been way below the market in price for a coat of this quality, but now you actually pay less money than ever before—it's a bigger value than ever! On top of that you get a coat which protects you absolutely from wind, rain, sleet and snow. Because, fine as this coat has been, we have done the other thing necessary to place it above all other sheep lined coats in its class—we have treated the heavy moleskin cloth with a special process (no rubber used) to make it waterproof. Weatherproof! That's the word. It is proof against any and all kinds of bad weather.

Six Outstanding Features

The sheepskin lining is carefully selected from the finest to be had, generously soft, thick, woolly—warm! Soft knit worsted wristlets fit snugly around the wrists.

Heavy strips of leather reinforce the pocket corners, preventing them from ripping and tearing.

The armholes are specially reinforced to give longer wear and to permit free movement of the arms without ripping or tearing.

A seemingly small, but highly important, improvement are the guard buttons which, on the inside of the coat, back up every big button. No more buttons pulling off. Note the illustration of some of these features at the right.

The price is possible only because of the enormous quantities we buy. We believe confidently that no one but Sears can possibly give such genuine quality for so little money.

Sizes, 36 to 46 inches chest. Length, 36 inches. State chest measure taken over vest. Shipping weight, 7¼ pounds.

41K552 — Genuine Sheep Lined Waterproofed Drab Moleskin Coat. $7⁹⁸

Guard buttons—keep buttons from coming off.

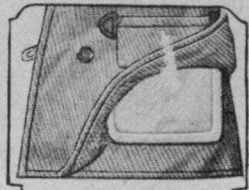

Genuine moleskin cloth specially processed—water proof.

Big, extra wide roomy swinging pockets between inside and outside lining—weatherproof — stormproof.

Real leather tacked at each end of pockets to prevent ripping and tearing.

Reinforced armholes prevent tearing of sleeves.

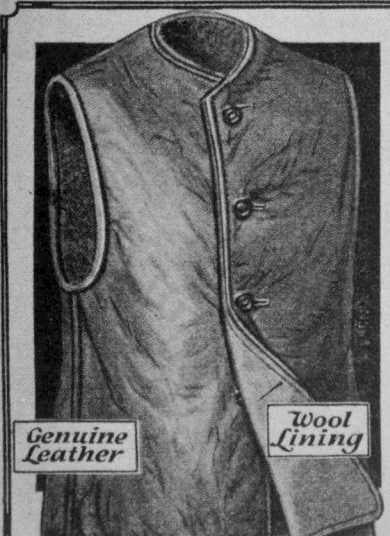

Genuine Leather
Wool Lining

Big Price Reduction on U.S. Army Jerkins
Wonderful for Warmth and Long Wear

THIS SEASON'S PRICE $2¹⁹

There is nothing quite equal to this Genuine U. S. Army Jerkin for wear and protection against wind and cold. Made of heavy selected quality tan leather. Soft and pliable and lined with heavyweight all wool melton cloth. It is an absolute defense against the elements, whether worn over or under your coat. And wear! Seems as if it never would wear out! Ask any army man or any other man who has ever worn one. We bought a huge lot of these jerkins at a fraction of their cost to the government. This saving we pass on to you. A splendid bargain. All first quality jerkins. All have passed the rigid government test.

Sizes, 36 to 46 inches chest measure. State chest measure. Shipping weight, 2¼ pounds.

41K5627—Tan Leather Only $2.19

Knit worsted wristlets grip the wrists snugly.

Four Special Values

For Easy Measuring Instructions See Page 548

Drab Thickset Corduroy

Gray and Black Striped Moleskin

Sheep Lined Mackinaw Overcoat

Waterproof and Weatherproof

New—And a Remarkable Value!
Complete Suit at $9.75

This is a different sort of work suit. We've made it well, of heavyweight gray and black striped moleskin cloth, and the linings and trimmings are of good quality. It is the sort of an outfit which any man might wear with complete satisfaction. Wears unusually well and looks unusually well. It does not easily show stain or soil. The coat is the regular 3-button style, with welt breast pocket and two lower set-in pockets with flap. Two buttons on sleeves. Good weight, strong, black cotton lining with striped sleeve lining. The vest is the regular 5-button single breasted no collar style with four pockets. Pants have cuff bottoms, and five big strong pockets. Suit is bar tacked and reinforced at all strain points. Strongly sewed. Guaranteed not to rip. You can buy the complete suit for the extraordinarily low price of $9.75, or you can buy coat, vest or pants separately.

Sizes—Coat and Vest, 34 to 44 inches chest; Pants, 30 to 44 inches waist and 30 to 36 inches inseam. State measurements. Shipping weights: Coat, 3½ pounds; Vest, 1½ pounds; Pants, 2 pounds.

41K420—Gray and Black Striped Coat	$5.25
41K417—Gray and Black Striped Vest	2.00
41K792—Gray and Black Striped Pants	2.50

Solid Comfort and Satisfaction

There is a sturdy quality to corduroy that you find in no other material. It is immensely comfortable in cold weather. And a quality like this, particularly, always looks natty and neat. This is a heavy, drab, thickset corduroy with the body and sleeves of the coat lined with khaki drill. There are flaps and buttons on all the pockets. All around corduroy belt with metal buckle. Five-button single breasted vest; also khaki drill lined. Cuff bottom pants with regular pockets of strong drill. A splendid corduroy suit at an equally splendid price. Service and satisfaction guaranteed.

Sizes—Coat and vest, 34 to 44 inches chest; pants, 30 to 44 inches waist and 30 to 36 inches inseam. State measurements. Shipping weights: Coat, 4 lbs.; Vest, 1½ lbs.; Pants, 2½ lbs.

41K413 Drab Corduroy Coat	$6.45
41K415 Drab Corduroy Vest	2.15
41K763 Drab Corduroy Pants	2.79

Comfort and Good Looks

About the last word in warmth and comfort and with a snappy style as well. Made of heavy all wool brown heather mackinaw cloth, body and ulster collar alike, with an all around belt of the same material. Lined with finest quality sheepskin to within 16 inches of the bottom. Below that there is a double thickness of the mackinaw cloth to the bottom of the coat. Sleeves are lined with warm fleeced moleskin cloth; double shields at the armpits. This is a splendid coat which you will find it hard to duplicate even at a much higher price than ours. The length of the coat is 44 inches.

Sizes, 36 to 46 inches chest. State chest measure taken over vest. Shpg. wt. 11 lbs.
41K578—Mackinaw Cloth, Sheepskin Lined.................. **$16.95**

Weatherproof and Waterproof

Good grade, attractive and serviceable, gray diagonal surface cotton cloth with heavy blanket lining and an interlining of rubber. Offers absolute protection against rain, wind and cold. To make it more completely a cold weather coat, there is added a warm, heavy beaverized sheepskin collar which turns up snugly about the ears. There are two handy muff pockets and two roomy lower patch pockets with flaps. All around belt with metal buckle. Length, 44 inches. We do not know where else you could secure such thorough protection in such a good looking coat for so little money.

Sizes, 34 to 46 inches chest. State chest measure taken over vest. Shipping weight, 6½ lbs.
41K145—Gray Diagonal Surface Submarine Coat **$6.50**

Send Sufficient Money for Postage on Parcel Post Shipments. Any Surplus Will Be Returned

393

For All-Around WEAR

All Weather Comfort in This Long Wearing Corduroy

This heavy weight, thickset drab corduroy Norfolk suit is about the most sensible outfit we know of if your work makes heavy demands on your clothing. There is nothing better. Workers, sportsmen—any man who needs clothing that will "stand the gaff" can buy nothing more practical. Body and sleeves of coat are full lined with khaki drill. Flaps on two large patch pockets. All around belt, with two buttons. Breeches sturdily reinforced at knees; lace at calves. All seams double stitched. SIZES—Coat, 34 to 44 inches chest; breeches, 30 to 42 inches waist and 25 to 27 inches inseam. State measurements. Shipping weights: Coat, 4 lbs; breeches, 2½ lbs.

41K419—Drab Corduroy Coat...... **$6.95**
41K882—Drab Corduroy Breeches...... **3.00**

How to Order Correct Inseams for Breeches

If your inseam measurement for regular pants is 31 inches or less, order 25 inches inseam for breeches; if your inseam measure for regular pants is 32 inches or more, order 27 inches inseam for breeches.

For Clothing Order Blank See Page 1094

Thickset Corduroy For Service

For Measuring Instructions See Page 548

Lace Bottom Breeches for Youths and Men

Men! Here they are! The breeches you've been looking for, at a big saving to you! These are wonderfully made. You can get them in either twilled moleskin (whipcord) or thickset drab corduroy. All seams are double stitched, knees are heavily reinforced and lace at the calves. You'll find these a really practical addition to your outdoor wardrobe. You'll appreciate the tremendous saving when you put these to the test of rough use. Our low prices make these breeches a mighty good buy. SIZES—26 to 42 inches waist and 25 to 27 inches inseam. State waist and inseam measures. Shipping wt. 2½ lbs.

41K879—Heavy Weight Olive Drab Moleskin (Whipcord). **$1.98**
41K882—Thickset Drab Corduroy...... **3.00**

Twilled Moleskin or Corduroy

Youths and Men's Sizes

Moleskin~ Bedford Cord or Corduroy

Button Bottom Breeches for Youths and Men

Breeches are the practical thing for the outdoor man, no matter what his job is. They're good for all the year round and in this particular model we offer you a choice of three splendid long wearing materials. Full cut, officers' model. Reinforced knees. Fastened with stout buttons and fit snugly at calf. Two slant pockets and a watch pocket in front and two hip pockets. All seams sturdily stitched. Belt loops. SIZES—26 to 42 inches waist and 25 to 27 inches inseam. State waist and inseam measures. Shpg. wt., 2¼ lbs.

41K885—Drab Moleskin Cloth...... **$2.65**
41K889—Laurel Bedford Cord...... **3.35**
41K890—Forest Green Corduroy...... **3.50**

An Amazingly Fine Suit in the Old Reliable Moleskin

Moleskin cloth was never more nicely made up in wearing apparel than in this popular belted model suit. The material is heavy weight gray and black striped moleskin—wonderful for wear as well as good looks. The style is pleasing. Coat has four pockets with flaps to button through, belt all around, plain back. Lined throughout with strong black cotton lining; the sleeves with a serviceable striped sleeve lining. There is one inside pocket. Five-button, no collar vest with four pockets. Breeches lace at the calves. Have knee patches and belt loops. This suit is a wonder for service as well as for looks. SIZES—Coat and vest, 34 to 44 inches chest; breeches, 30 to 42 in. waist and 25 to 27 in. inseam. State measurements. Shipping weights: Coat, 4 pounds; breeches, 2½ lbs.; vest, 8 ounces.

41K416—Gray and Black Striped Coat...... **$6.50**
41K417—Gray and Black Striped Vest...... **2.00**
41K888—Gray and Black Striped Breeches...... **2.85**

Striped Moleskin Neat and Durable

Gray Twill Cord or Blue Corduroy

Breeches You'll Like— Most Popular Fabrics

He is a hard man to please who will not like these breeches—made of the breeches cloths most popular for this fall season—a sturdy oxford gray diagonal weave twill cord of medium heavy weight or a handsome thickset blue corduroy of particularly long wearing quality. Both materials are excellently tailored; each has double seat and double knees. The legs lace at the calf. Bar tacked at all needed points and reinforced wherever needful. These are fine, comfortable, durable breeches for any kind of outdoor work or sport. A big value. SIZES—30 to 42 in. waist and 25 to 27 in. inseam. State waist and inseam measures. Shipping wt., 2¼ lbs.

41K886—Oxford Gray Twill Cord...... **$2.89**
41K881—Thickset Blue Corduroy...... **3.85**

Best Moleskin~ Leather Saddle Patches

Highest Quality— Good Looks—Best Value

These splendid breeches will please —will give complete satisfaction. They're our best heavy, firmly woven forest green moleskin cloth, with leather knee reinforcements. Correct style, fine appearing and will withstand the toughest wear, besides giving you perfect comfort. Double seat. Crotch seams specially reinforced and all points of strain bar tacked. Five pockets, two front and two hip, the left one with flap to button. SIZES—30 to 42 inches waist and 25 to 27 in. inseam. State measurements. Shipping weight, 2¼ pounds.

41K892—Forest Green Moleskin Cloth...... **$4.95**

Quality Mackinaws for Warmth and Comfort

Clothing Order Blank Is on Page 1094

Inexpensive and Serviceable

Exceptional Quality—Low Price

Mackinaws are favored universally for all winter wear. This one has just the right abundance of warmth and weight, is roomy, neat in design and has most all the practical mackinaw features you can think of. Made of a dark brown (plain) half wool mackinaw cloth. Double breasted style with large shawl style collar, two large lower pockets with flap, and belt all around. Length, 34 inches. Wonderfully made throughout. A mighty sound purchase.

Sizes, 34 to 46 inches chest. State chest measure taken over vest. Shpg. wt., 6¼ lbs.
41K630—Dark Brown Heather (Plain) Half Wool.................$5.95

All Wool Splendid Value

A Wonderful Coat for Service

Here is a mackinaw with a winning way! The minute you slip into it you'll feel that you have found a new friend; a friend that you'll regard as highly as you regard your favorite pipe or your dog. For there is a comfortable, snug warmth in this all wool coat that is utterly indifferent to the coldest weather.

Everything you want in a mackinaw, every detail of quality, is in this coat. It is made from fine quality heavy weight all wool mackinaw cloth, in a handsome oxford gray shade. Shawl collar, two extra large pockets with flap, all around belt and cuff effect with button are among the outstanding features. Collar has loop and button for fastening high around the neck. Wide facings of self material. 34 inches long. Sizes, 34 to 46 inches chest. State chest measure taken over vest. Shipping weight, 6¼ pounds.
41K634—Oxford Gray All Wool Mackinaw......... $7.95

For Measuring Instructions See Page 548

Attractive All Wool Plaid

Woodsman's Bright, All Wool Mackinaw

It's the kind that makes you think of frosted trails through the forest, of timber to be cut, and the satisfaction of being comfortably warm while in the open. It's an outdoor coat, all right, and a mighty good one! Made of fine all wool mackinaw cloth in a handsome maroon, brown and blue plaid. All seams securely sewed and all edges are neatly piped. Made in the double breasted style illustrated, with large shawl style collar that can be buttoned close to the neck, belt all around, one roomy breast pocket and two large lower pockets with flaps. Proper reinforcements and bar tacking. L'gth, 34 in.
Sizes, 34 to 46 inches chest. State chest measure taken over vest. Shipping weight, 6¼ lbs.
41K632—Maroon, Brown and Blue Plaid. $8.95

Extra Heavy 40 Ounce All Wool

Handsome Mackinaw of Enduring Quality

The best is usually the most economical in the long run. So it is with this mackinaw. It's undoubtedly one of the best we ever sold. For this price, you won't find as fine a coat anywhere. Conservative and handsome dark brown heather shade in one of the finest all wool mackinaw cloths we have ever seen; one that will wear wonderfully and keep you warm! Made in the double breasted style illustrated, with large shawl style collar, belt all around, adjustable cuffs, two large well made lower patch pockets with flap, and breast patch pocket. All seams double stitched, all edges neatly piped, proper bar tacking and reinforcements at all points of strain. A wonderful bargain! Full 36 inches long.
Sizes, 34 to 46 inches chest. State chest measure taken over vest. Shipping weight, 6¾ pounds.
41K635—Dark Brown Heather All Wool Mackinaw.................$10.00

Extra Heavy Extra Long Extra Warm

Extra Long All Wool Mackinaw—Our Best

Some men would rather wear a mackinaw than an overcoat; some men are partial to the overcoat. But there are a great many who seek a coat that combines all the good points of both, and for those men this coat was made. The extra length (about 40 in.) gives you all the advantages of an overcoat and yet facilitates all kinds of work in the open, with that easy fitting roominess that allows freedom of movement without being bulky. It's made of the most serviceable, practical and finest quality all wool extra heavy weight mackinaw cloth, in a rich shade of navy blue. Has shawl style collar, double breasted front with three-piece (fore parts detachable) belt all around, and two large lower pockets with flaps. It's positively the finest coat you can buy for this price!
Sizes, 34 to 46 inches chest. State chest measure taken over vest. Shipping weight, 7½ pounds.
41K636—Extra Weight All Wool Mackinaw $11.00

Best for Hunting

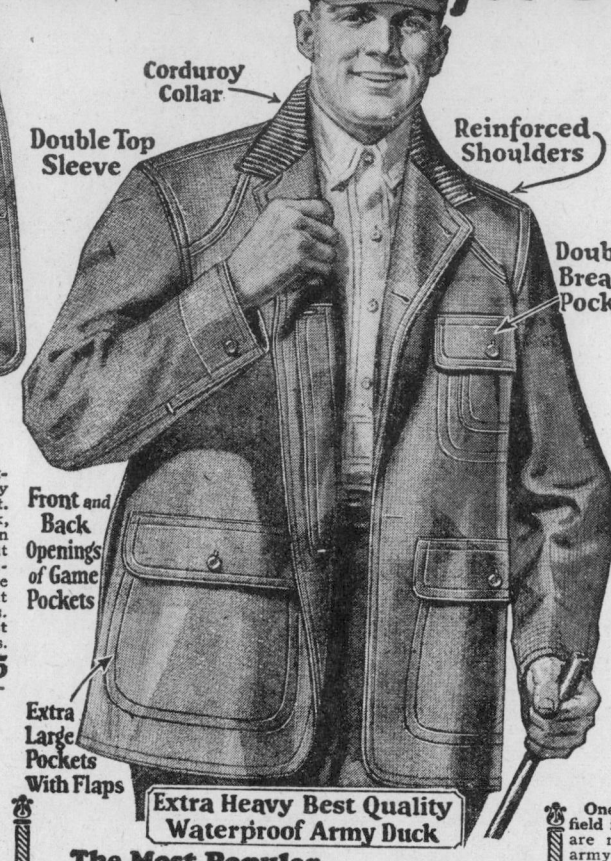

Corduroy Collar

Double Top Sleeve

Reinforced Shoulders

Double Breast Pocket

Front and Back Openings of Game Pockets

Extra Large Pockets With Flaps

Extra Heavy Best Quality Waterproof Army Duck

Guaranteed Waterproof Blanket Lined

Low Priced, Warm and Practical

This is a general purpose, all around knockabout hunting coat which, while priced very low, is serviceable and has a lot of wear in it. Heavy weight waterproofed khaki color duck, **blanket lined**. It is as warm and comfortable in bad weather as almost any coat you could put on. The sleeves are blanket lined, too. Corduroy collar, reinforced shoulders. Two large leather tipped game pockets with inside front openings. Large outside pockets with flaps. Sizes, 34 to 48 inches chest. State chest measure taken over vest. Shpg. wt., 5 lbs.

41K348—Blanket Lined Waterproof Duck Coat.................... **$4.25**

A Necessity for Every Hunter

Lightweight khaki color hunting vest; 32 to 36 shell loops of the same material. Every hunter knows the worth of this garment. Sizes, 34 to 48 inches chest measure. State chest measure. Shipping weight, 1¼ pounds.

41K344 — For 10 and 12-Gauge Shells **$1.08**

41K346 — For 16 and 20-Gauge Shells **1.08**

Leather Laughs at Cold

For additional protection, wear one of these genuine U. S. Army jerkins of glove leather and wool lined. May be worn over or under coat. Leather is of excellent quality; the lining is a heavy weight olive drab all wool melton. Cut roomy—free movement. Two generous size set-in pockets. Splendid for all outdoor winter sports as well as for hunting. Sizes, 36 to 46 inches chest. State chest measure. Shipping weight, 2¼ pounds.

41K628—Tan Leather................. **$2.49**

The Most Popular Hunting Coat We Sell
Snag Proof—Wear Proof—Waterproof

We doubt if you can find a better all around hunting coat than this at any price anywhere. We know you can't find one at anything like our price that will give you what this coat will. In the first place, it is made of the best quality heavyweight waterproofed army khaki color duck. It is full lined throughout body and top sleeves with the same cloth—a double thickness of this wonderful fabric. It is proof against wind, rain, cold, snags and the toughest kind of hard wear. Good quality corduroy collar. The corduroy faced cuffs are adjustable, buttoning snugly to the wrists when desired. Shoulders are heavily reinforced. There are ventilation eyelets under the arms. Handy match scratcher inside of lapel. All around blood proof game pockets, with both inside front and back opening. All outside pockets have flaps and button fast. All pocket openings are bar tacked—strengthening them. Every hunting fan will appreciate this splendid bargain and what a thoroughly complete and practical garment it is.
Sizes, 34 to 48 inches chest. State chest measurement taken over vest. Shipping weight, 6 pounds.

41K350—Best Quality Waterproof Army Duck..... **$5.25**

Genuine Leather

Wool Lining

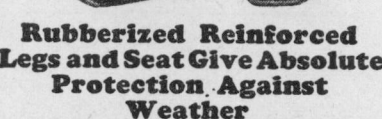

Waterproofed Duck With Rubberized Reinforced Seat and Legs

Rubberized Reinforced Legs and Seat Give Absolute Protection Against Weather

One of the most popular garments in the hunting field is a pair of tough weatherproof breeches. These are made of heavyweight waterproof khaki color army duck with large front and seat reinforcements of the same cloth, and with a rubber interlining. Will keep you dry. Bottoms lace. Sizes, 30 to 42 inches waist with regulation inseams. State waist measure. Shpg. wt., 3 lbs.

41K353—Army Duck With Rubber Interlining **$3.50**

A Mighty Handy Coat This—Protect Your Shells

This style of coat is highly endorsed by many sportsmen because of the outside shell loops protected by deep flaps from the weather, keeping the ammunition dry. Made of medium weight waterproofed khaki color army duck, lined throughout the body for additional warmth and protection. Reinforced shoulders. Ventilation gussets under arms. Corduroy faced cuffs are adjustable. Corduroy collar. Match scratcher. Large lower hand pockets and breast pocket all with flaps. All bar tacked to prevent tearing. Large game pockets run all around the back with both inside front and outside back openings. A dandy buy at our price.
Sizes, 34 to 48 inches chest. State chest measure taken over vest. Shipping weight, 5½ lbs.

41K335—Waterproof Duck Coat.... **$4.50**

Outside Shell Loops Feature This Coat

Great Values Too

Front Opening Game Pocket

Corduroy Collar

Reinforced Shoulders

Sage Green Shade Waterproofed Shelter Duck

Blood Proof Game Pocket

Low Priced Waterproofed and Durable

Made of Sage Green Duck to Blend With the Background

Sage green color for hunting coats is desirable anywhere. It is absolutely essential in some parts of the country. This coat is put up in a medium heavyweight waterproofed shelter duck at a price that puts it within every man's reach. It is proof against snagging or tearing. The body is full lined, for protection against the cold. Reinforced shoulders with ventilation eyelets under the arms. Corduroy collar and adjustable corduroy faced cuffs. Two lower double shell pockets and a double breast pocket, all with flaps. All around large game pockets with both front and back openings. SIZES—34 to 48 inches chest. State chest measure. Shipping weight, 4 pounds.

41K343—Sage Green Waterproof Shelter Duck..................... **$3.95**

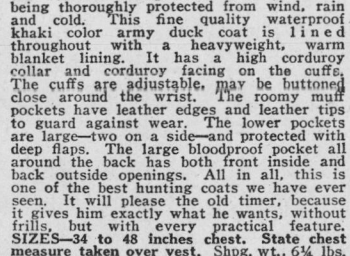

Heavy Waterproofed Duck Warm Blanket Lining

For Real Service—For All Kinds of Weather

This coat is made for the man who wants the best he can get and who insists on being thoroughly protected from wind, rain and cold. This fine quality waterproof khaki color army duck coat is lined throughout with a heavyweight, warm blanket lining. It has a high corduroy collar and corduroy facing on the cuffs. The cuffs are adjustable, may be buttoned close around the wrist. The roomy muff pockets have leather edges and leather tips to guard against wear. The lower pockets are large—two on a side—and protected with deep flaps. The large bloodproof pocket all around the back has both front inside and back outside openings. All in all, this is one of the best hunting coats we have ever seen. It will please the old timer, because it gives him exactly what he wants, without frills, but with every practical feature. SIZES—34 to 48 inches chest. State chest measure taken over vest. Shpg. wt., 6¼ lbs.

41K354—Blanket Lined Khaki Color Army Duck.......... **$5.65**

Don't Go Without a Hunting Coat When This One Costs So Little

No man need be deprived of a properly designed and well made hunting coat on account of price when he can buy this for $2.79. Made of medium weight khaki color waterproof duck with lined top sleeve and deep yoke in the back for wear, warmth and added protection against rain and weather. Has two large lower and breast pockets, all with flaps. Two large inside game pockets, with inside front openings. Reinforced shoulders. Corduroy collar. This is a smashing bargain—a big value. SIZES—34 to 48 inches chest. State chest measure. Shpg. wt., 3½ lbs.

41K334—Khaki Color Duck...... **$2.79**

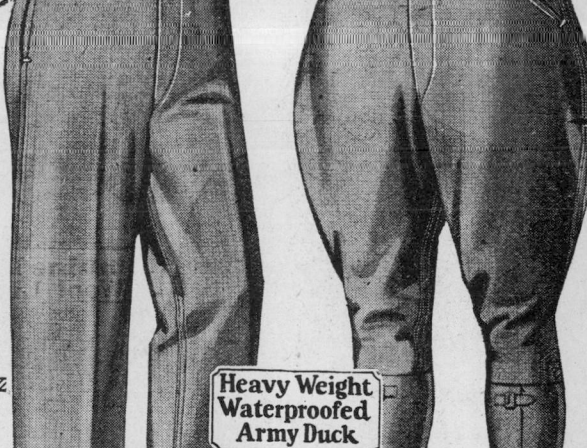

Heavy Weight Waterproofed Army Duck

This Coat Is Full Slicker Interlined

Body and Sleeves Slicker Lined—Absolutely Waterproof

Built for the man who insists upon thorough protection against rain and wind, this coat fills the bill completely. Wind cannot penetrate its slicker interlining in the body and sleeves —neither can rain. The outside material is a fine quality waterproof khaki color army duck. Collar and cuff facings are of good corduroy, the cuffs being adjustable for loose or snug fitting. Reinforced shoulders. Ventilation eyelets under arms. Match scratcher on inside of the lapel. Bloodproof game pockets all around in back with inside front and back openings. A most satisfactory coat, everything considered, including price. SIZES—34 to 48 inches chest. State chest measure. Shipping weight, 4 pounds.

41K352—Slicker Interlined Army Duck.......... **$5.45**

Snagproof and Long Wearing

Specially designed for hunters and those whose clothing is subjected to the wear and tear of rough country, these pants are made of heavyweight waterproof khaki color army duck and are guaranteed snagproof. They will wear and wear. Usual pockets, flaps to button on hip pockets. Belt loops and suspender buttons. Cuffs are pressed back but may be turned down when worn with boots or puttees. SIZES—30 to 44 inches waist, 30 to 36 inches inseam. State waist and inseam measures. Shipping weight, 2¼ pounds.

41K336—Khaki Color Army Duck:...... **$2.25**

These Make a Hit With the Outdoor Man

The fellow who prefers breeches for his outdoor sports, or for his work, finds here exactly what he wants. The heavyweight waterproof khaki colored duck of which they are made is snagproof, weatherproof and long wearing. Have usual pockets with flaps to button on hips. Belt loops and suspender buttons. Pants lace snugly at the calves. SIZES—30 to 42 inches waist, inseam in proportion. State waist measure. Shipping weight, 2¼ pounds.

41K338—Khaki Color Waterproof Duck. **$2.35**

Absolutely Waterproof

Let it Pour!

Practical Reversible Coat

Soft and Flexible Sou'-wester Waterproof Hat. Dull finish black rubber, lined with white sheeting. Stitched-down brim. Strapped and cemented seams. SIZES—6¾ to 7¾. State size. Shipping weight, 8 oz.
41K960 Black. **49c**

SIZES of Coats 41K940 and 41K899—34 to 48 inches chest. State chest measure taken over vest.

Dull Finish Black Rubber Coated Waterproof Nobby Hat. Soft, pliable brim may be worn turned up or down. Tan cotton lining. Band and seams are cemented, strapped and vulcanized. SIZES—6¾ to 7¾. State size. Shipping wt., 8 oz.
41K965 Black........ **79c**

Practical Two-In-One Reversible Waterproof Coat. Soft and flexible. One side is dull finish black rubber surfaced, other is drab cotton Asia cloth. Double back. Deep slash pockets and firmly cemented seams. Length, 52 inches. SIZES—34 to 48 inches chest. State chest measure taken over vest. Shpg. wt., 5½ lbs.
41K893—Black and Drab Reversible......... **$4.98**

Fireman's Coat
Fireman's Extra Heavy Double Coated Waterproof Coat of heavy cotton jeans cloth, thoroughly coated with dull finish black rubber on both sides. Long fly front. Large Corduroy faced collar, adjustable strap and buckle on sleeves. Seams are strongly sewed and vulcanized. Length, 48 inches. SIZES—34 to 48 in. chest. State chest measure. Shpg. wt., 7½ lbs.
41K935—Black. **$7.25**

Chicago Police Coat
Regulation model. Made of heavy weight cotton jeans cloth, heavily coated with dull finish black rubber. Tan jeans cloth inside body and sleeves. Has large double storm cape extending all around over shoulders and well down over arms. One large inside pocket and one club or billy pocket. Shield with loops for attaching star. Length, 54 inches. Shipping weight, 7½ lbs.
41K940—Black. **$7.89**

Black Rubber Coat
Soft and Pliable Dull Finish Black Rubber Surfaced Waterproof Coat. Lined throughout body and sleeves with good quality white sheeting. Has vulcanized one-seam back, two lower flap pockets and ventilation eyelets under arms. Length, 48 inches. Shipping weight, 5½ pounds.
41K899—Black. **$3.79**

Squam Waterproof Slicker Hat
Standard for years. Has chin strap and ear laps. Stitched-down brim. Soft cotton flannel lining. SIZES—6¾ to 7½. State size. Shpg. wt., ¾ lb.
41K970 Black. **48c**

Slicker Oil Compound
High quality. For recoating and preserving oiled slicker clothing. 1 pint can. Shpg. wt., 2½ lbs.
30K975 Black...... **28c**
30K976 Yellow..... **28c**

Waterproof Slicker Coat and Pants
Shoulders, elbows and fly front of jacket are triple thickness. Large cape around back. Pants made apron style with triple seat and triple front. Average length of jacket, 30 inches. Shpg. wt. of suit, 7 lbs.; jacket, 4½ lbs.; pants, 3½ lbs.
41K1030 Black Jacket...... **2.89**
41K1031 Black Pants...... **2.89**

Low Priced, Waterproof Slicker Suit
Jacket has triple fly storm front and double throughout balance of suit. Pants made apron front style with adjustable suspenders. Average length of jacket, 30 in. Shpg. wt. of suit, 6 lbs.; jacket, 3½ lbs.; pants, 3 lbs.
41K1000 Black Jacket...... **1.89**
41K1001 Black Pants...... **1.89**
SIZES—Jacket, 34 to 48 inches chest; pants, 32 to 44 inches waist. State chest measure of jacket, taken over vest, and waist measure of pants.

For Simple Measuring Instructions See Page 548

Extra Long
Extra Long Triple Fly Front Waterproof Slicker Coat. Made double throughout. Has rain excluding wristlets and high standing cloth faced collar with tab to button around throat. Two large patch pockets with flap. Length, 54 inches. SIZES—34 to 48 inches chest. State chest measure taken over vest. Shpg. wt., 5½ lbs.
41K1015 Black.............. **$3.75**

Pommel Riding Coat
Extra Long Triple Fly Front Waterproof Slicker Pommel Riding Coat. Extends over entire saddle and can easily be buttoned around legs, if desired. Average length, 58 inches. SIZES—34 to 48 inches chest. State chest measure taken over vest. Shpg. wt., 6½ lbs.
41K1025 Black.............. **$3.98**

Easy Walking Length Waterproof Slicker Coat
Made double throughout. Has fly front and rain excluding wristlets. High standing collar faced with serge to protect neck. Average length, 45 inches. SIZES—34 to 48 inches chest. State chest measure taken over vest. Shipping weight, 5 lbs.
41K1012—Black. **$2.89**

SEARS, ROEBUCK AND CO. WLS — The World's Largest Store

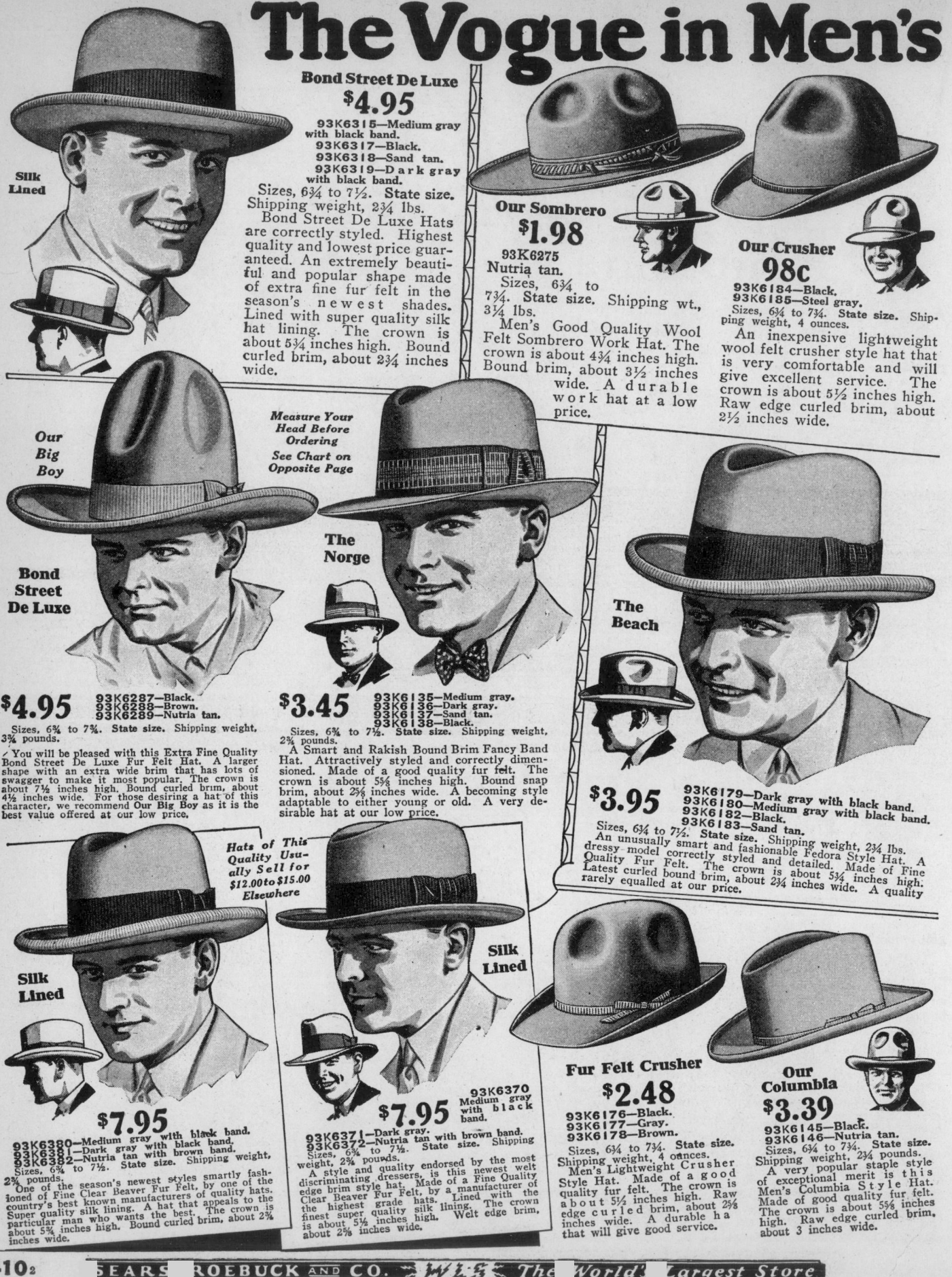

The Vogue in Men's

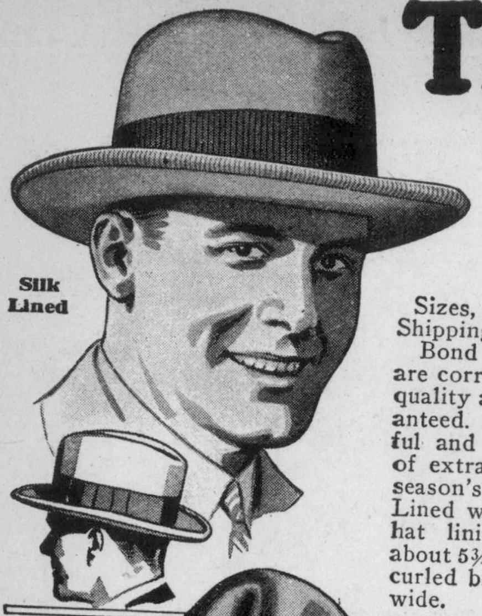

Silk Lined

Bond Street De Luxe

$4.95

93K6315—Medium gray with black band.
93K6317—Black.
93K6318—Sand tan.
93K6319—Dark gray with black band.

Sizes, 6¾ to 7½. State size. Shipping weight, 2¾ lbs.

Bond Street De Luxe Hats are correctly styled. Highest quality and lowest price guaranteed. An extremely beautiful and popular shape made of extra fine fur felt in the season's newest shades. Lined with super quality silk hat lining. The crown is about 5¾ inches high. Bound curled brim, about 2¾ inches wide.

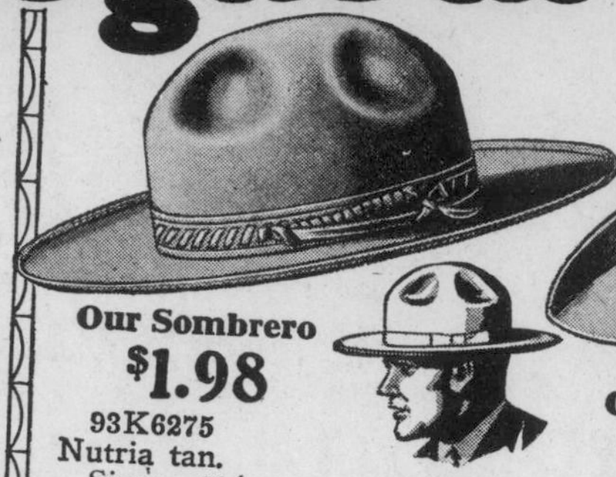

Our Sombrero

$1.98

93K6275
Nutria tan.

Sizes, 6¾ to 7¾. State size. Shipping wt., 3¼ lbs.

Men's Good Quality Wool Felt Sombrero Work Hat. The crown is about 4¾ inches high. Bound brim, about 3½ inches wide. A durable work hat at a low price.

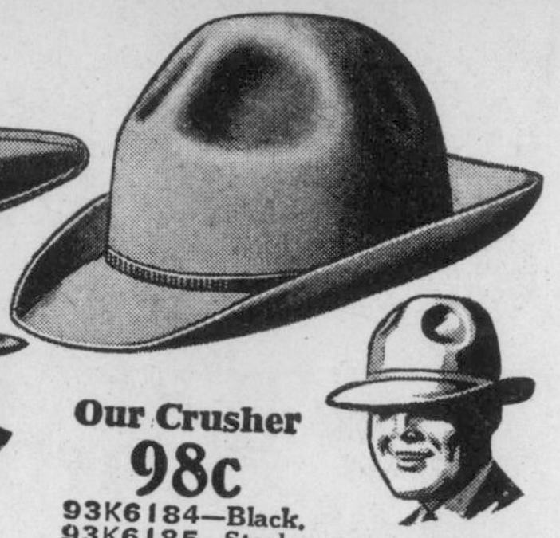

Our Crusher

98c

93K6184—Black.
93K6185—Steel gray.

Sizes, 6¾ to 7¾. State size. Shipping weight, 4 ounces.

An inexpensive lightweight wool felt crusher style hat that is very comfortable and will give excellent service. The crown is about 5½ inches high. Raw edge curled brim, about 2½ inches wide.

Measure Your Head Before Ordering
See Chart on Opposite Page

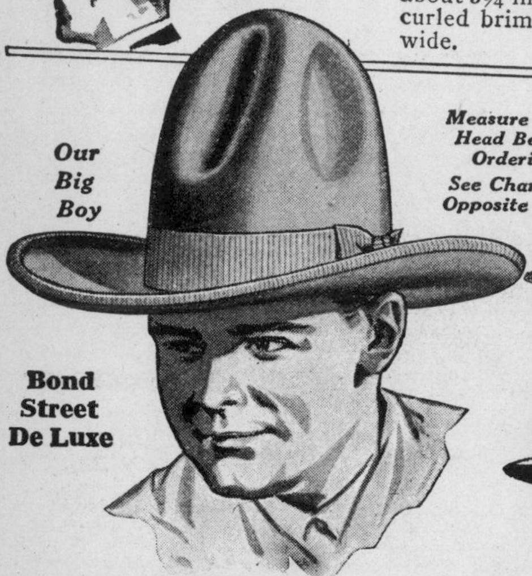

Our Big Boy

Bond Street De Luxe

$4.95

93K6287—Black.
93K6288—Brown.
93K6289—Nutria tan.

Sizes, 6¾ to 7¾. State size. Shipping weight, 3¾ pounds.

You will be pleased with this Extra Fine Quality Bond Street De Luxe Fur Felt Hat. A larger shape with an extra wide brim that has lots of swagger to make it most popular. The crown is about 7½ inches high. Bound curled brim, about 4½ inches wide. For those desiring a hat of this character, we recommend Our Big Boy as it is the best value offered at our low price.

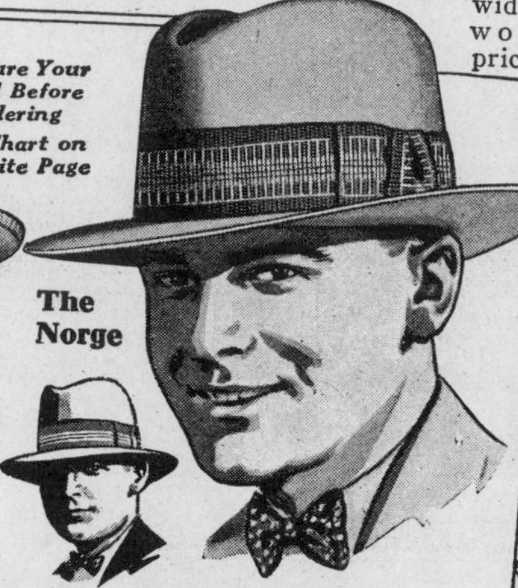

The Norge

$3.45

93K6135—Medium gray.
93K6136—Dark gray.
93K6137—Sand tan.
93K6138—Black.

Sizes, 6¾ to 7½. State size. Shipping weight, 2¾ pounds.

A Smart and Rakish Bound Brim Fancy Band Hat. Attractively styled and correctly dimensioned. Made of a good quality fur felt. The crown is about 5⅝ inches high. Bound snap brim, about 2⅝ inches wide. A becoming style adaptable to either young or old. A very desirable hat at our low price.

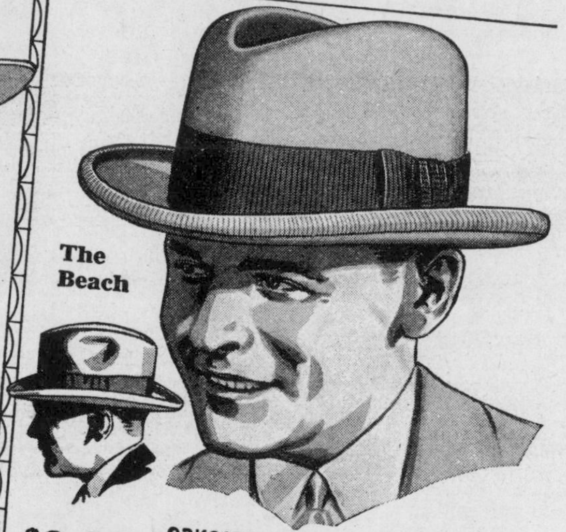

The Beach

$3.95

93K6179—Dark gray with black band.
93K6180—Medium gray with black band.
93K6182—Black.
93K6183—Sand tan.

Sizes, 6¾ to 7½. State size. Shipping weight, 2¾ lbs.

An unusually smart and fashionable Fedora Style Hat. A dressy model correctly styled and detailed. Made of Fine Quality Fur Felt. The crown is about 5¾ inches high. Latest curled bound brim, about 2¾ inches wide. A quality rarely equalled at our price.

Hats of This Quality Usually Sell for $12.00 to $15.00 Elsewhere

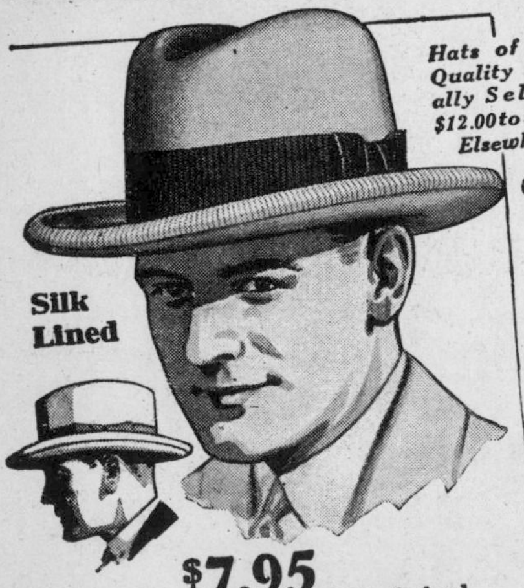

Silk Lined

$7.95

93K6380—Medium gray with black band.
93K6381—Dark gray with black band.
93K6382—Nutria tan with brown band.

Sizes, 6¾ to 7½. State size. Shipping weight, 2¾ pounds.

One of the season's newest styles smartly fashioned of Fine Clear Beaver Fur Felt, by one of the country's best known manufacturers of quality hats. Super quality silk lining. A hat that appeals to the particular man who wants the best. The crown is about 5¾ inches high. Bound curled brim, about 2¾ inches wide.

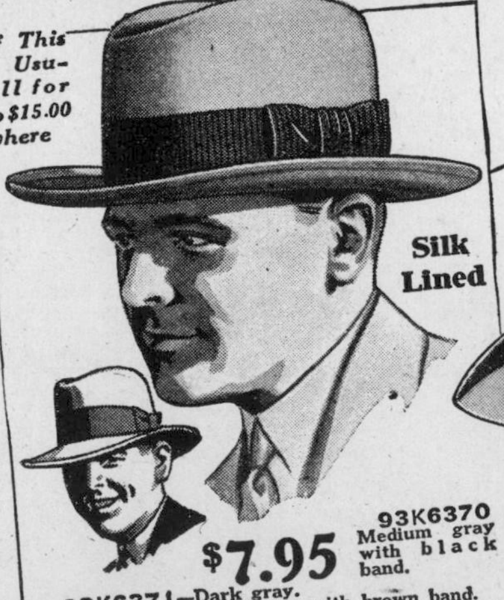

Silk Lined

$7.95

93K6370 Medium gray with black band.
93K6371—Dark gray.
93K6372—Nutria tan with brown band.

Sizes, 6¾ to 7½. State size. Shipping weight, 2¾ pounds.

A style and quality endorsed by the most discriminating dressers, is this newest welt edge brim style hat. Made of a Fine Quality Clear Beaver Fur Felt, by a manufacturer of the highest grade hats. Lined with the finest super quality silk lining. The crown is about 5½ inches high. Welt edge brim, about 2⅝ inches wide.

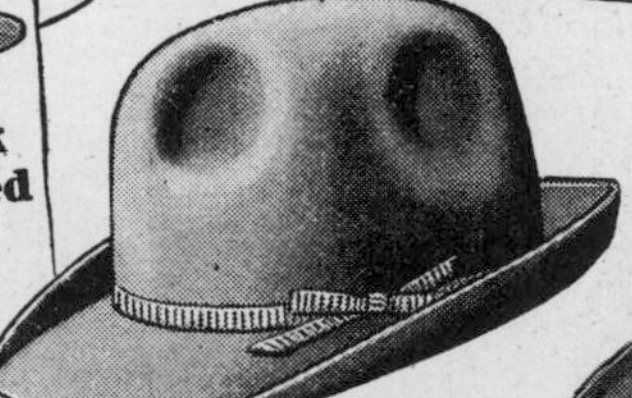

Fur Felt Crusher

$2.48

93K6176—Black.
93K6177—Gray.
93K6178—Brown.

Sizes, 6¾ to 7¾. State size. Shipping weight, 4 ounces.

Men's Lightweight Crusher Style Hat. Made of a good quality fur felt. The crown is about 5¼ inches high. Raw edge curled brim, about 2⅝ inches wide. A durable hat that will give good service.

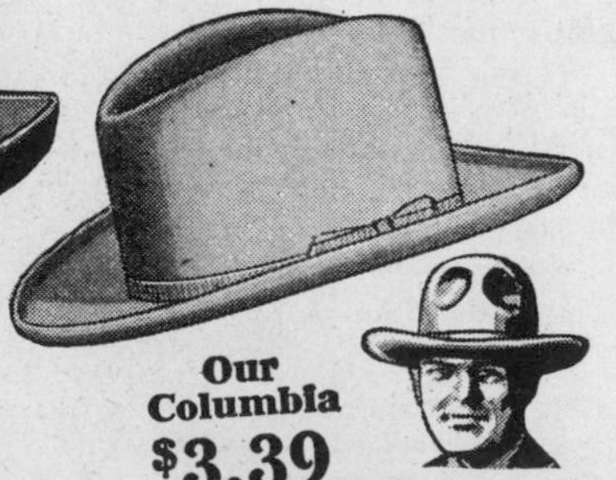

Our Columbia

$3.39

93K6145—Black.
93K6146—Nutria tan.

Sizes, 6¾ to 7¾. State size. Shipping weight, 2¾ pounds.

A very popular staple style of exceptional merit is this Men's Columbia Style Hat. Made of good quality fur felt. The crown is about 5⅝ inches high. Raw edge curled brim, about 3 inches wide.

Fall and Winter Hats

A Conservative Shape
$2.95

93K6165—Black.
93K6166—Brown.
93K6167—Dark gray.
Sizes, 6¾ to 7½. State size. Shipping weight, 2¾ pounds.
A fashionable, staple and popular Fedora Shape Hat. Made of a good quality fur felt. Attractively designed. The crown is about 5½ inches high. Raw edge brim, about 2⅝ inches wide. A combination of style and quality that will please you.

Bond Street De Luxe
Beaver Finish Silk Lined
$4.95
93K6390—Gray with black band.
93K6391—Nutria tan with brown band.
93K6392—Black.
Sizes, 6¾ to 7½. State size. Shipping weight, 2¾ pounds.
A new and distinctive shape in a Fine Quality Beaver Finished Fur Felt Hat. Carefully styled and correctly dimensioned. Elegantly lined with a super quality silk lining. The crown is about 5½ inches high. Raw edge brim, about 2⅝ inches wide.

Bond Street De Luxe
93K6340—Medium gray with black band.
93K6342—Sand tan with contrast band.
93K6343—Black with black band.
93K6345—Dark gray with black band.
Sizes, 6¾ to 7½. State size. Shpg. wt., 2¾ lbs.
$4.95
Bond Street De Luxe Snap Brim Hat. The season's most fashionable model. Has lots of style and character. Beautifully trimmed with fine quality band. Made of extra fine quality fur felt. Lined with super quality silk hat lining. The crown is about 5¾ inches high. Raw edge brim, about 2⅝ inches wide.

Silk Lined

The Wilton
Classy Model
$3.00
93K6110—Gray with black band
93K6111—Sand tan.
93K6112—Dark gray mixture.
Sizes, 6¾ to 7½. State size. Shipping weight, 2¾ lbs.
Ultra Stylish Snap Brim Hat. A handsome and fashionable model. Made of the finest quality fur and wool felt in the season's newest colors and trimmings. The crown is about 5½ inches high. Bound edge, snap brim, about 2⅝ inches wide. Attractively lined with silk hat lining.

Silk Lined

The Ritz
$3.95
93K6100—Gray with black band.
93K6101—Blue gray with blue band.
93K6102—Sand tan with brown band.
93K6103—Sand tan with maroon band.
Sizes, 6¾ to 7½. State size. Shipping weight, 2¾ pounds.
Our Snappiest Style Hat. An outstanding value made of a fine quality fur felt. The crown is about 5½ inches high. Raw edge, snap brim, about 2⅝ inches wide. A suitable style for either young or old.

Fur Felt Carlsbad
$3.95
93K6269—Brown.
93K6270—Black.
93K6271—Nutria tan.
Sizes, 6¾ to 7¾. State size. Shipping weight, 3½ pounds.
A hat of exceptional value and wear is our Fine Quality Fur Felt Carlsbad. A well proportioned hat for the outdoor man. The crown is about 7 inches high. Raw edge curled brim, about 4 inches wide.

Bound Brim Carlsbad
$2.29
93K6295 Brown
93K6296 Nutria tan.
Sizes, 6¾ to 7¾. State size. Shipping weight, 3½ pounds.
Men's Fine Quality Wool Felt Carlsbad Style Hat. A popular large shape suitable for the outdoor man. The crown is about 7 inches high. Bound brim about 4 inches wide. An inexpensive and serviceable work hat.

How to Measure
Measure all around head as illustrated, then refer to the table below to find the hat or cap size that corresponds to the number of inches your head measures and order that size.

Men's Hat and Cap Sizes, 6¾ to 7¾

If Head Measures as Follows in Inches	Order Following Size
19⅜	6⅛
19¾	6⅜
20⅛	6½
20½	6⅝
20⅞	6¾
21¼	6¾
21⅝	6⅞
22	7
22⅜	7⅛
22¾	7¼
23⅛	7⅜
23½	7½
23⅞	7⅝
23⅞	7¾

The Collegiate
Welt Edge · **Silk Lined**
$2.69
93K6125—Gray.
93K6128—Sand tan.
93K6129—Sand tan with solid color maroon band.
Sizes, 6¾ to 7½. State size. Shipping weight, 2¾ pounds.
A most effective and stylish hat. Made of a fine quality wool felt in the season's newest colors and fancy band effects. Handsomely lined with good quality silk hat lining. The crown is about 5½ inches high. The Rakish welt edge brim, about 2⅝ inches wide.

Men's Quality Caps

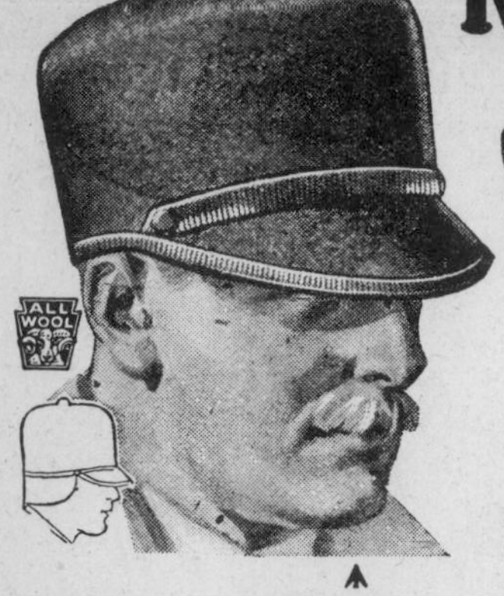

$1.00 93K4612—Dark blue.

Sizes, 6¾ to 7¾. **State size.** Shipping weight, 1¼ pounds.

Men's Scotch Style Cap. Made of all wool, closely woven, fully shrunk, knitted cloth. Felt lining. **Inside turndown band.** An extremely warm and comfortable cap priced exceptionally low.

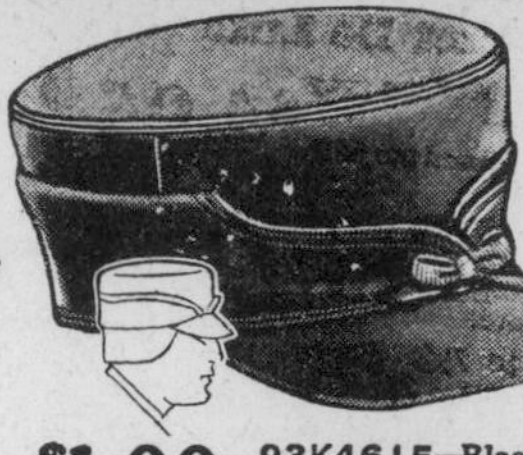

$1.00 93K4615—Black.
93K4616—Dark brown.
Sizes, 6¾ to 7¾. **State size.** Shipping weight, 1½ pounds.

We offer in this men's Havelock style an exceptionally good Cap at our low price. Made of a good quality wool mixed Thibet Cloth. Twill lining. Indestructible canvas visor. **Outside pulldown lined band.** The ideal cap for winter.

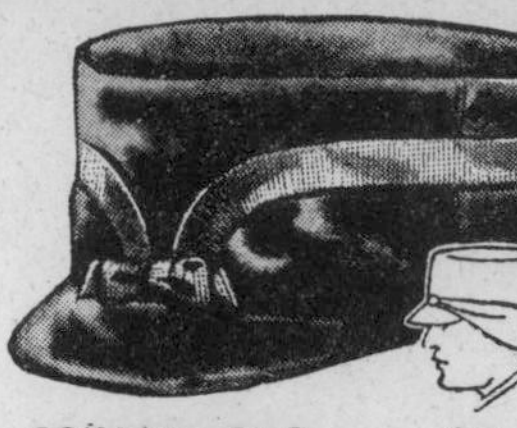

93K4602—Black. $1.39
Sizes, 6¾ to 7¾. **State size.** Shipping weight, 1¼ pounds.

Men's Judge Style Cap. Made of good quality silk plush and elegantly lined with durable twill. For comfort and hard wear this cap has no equal. Indestructible canvas visor. **Inside turndown lined band.**

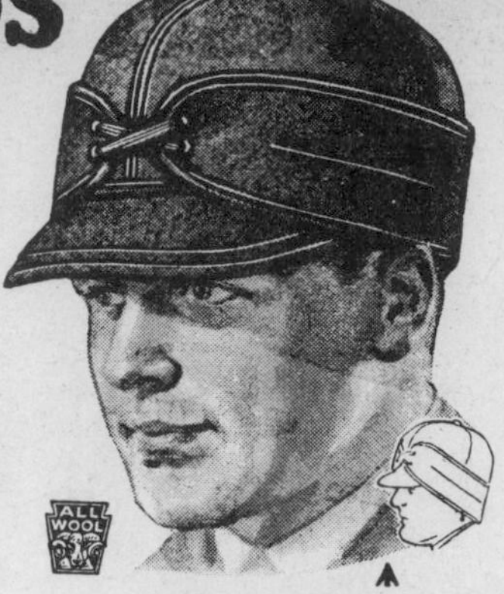

89c 93K4613—Oxford gray.
93K4614—Navy blue.

Sizes, 6¾ to 7¾. **State size.** Shipping weight, 1¼ pounds.

A style adaptable for warmth, service and durability is this Men's (railroader's style) Cap. Made of a good quality all wool cloth. Lined with splendid twill lining. Indestructible canvas visor. **Outside pulldown band.**

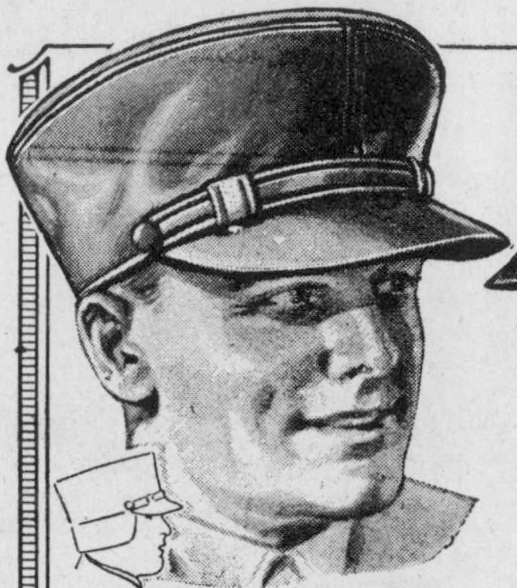

$1.59 93K4620 Brown.
93K4621 Black.

Sizes, 6¾ to 7¾. **State size.** Shpg. wt., 1¼ lbs.

Men's Judge Style Cap made of a good quality leather. Strong twill lining. Indestructible canvas visor. **Inside turndown lined band.** An excellent value.

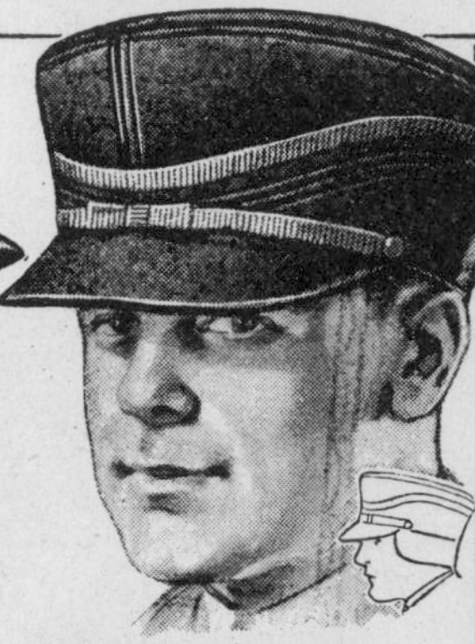

93K4630 Black.
93K4634 Dark brown. $1.39
Sizes, 6¾ to 7¾. **State size.** Shipping weight, 1¼ pounds.

Men's Popular Judge Style Cap, made of good quality wool mixed Thibet cloth. Good quality twill lining. Indestructible canvas visor. **Inside turndown lined band.**

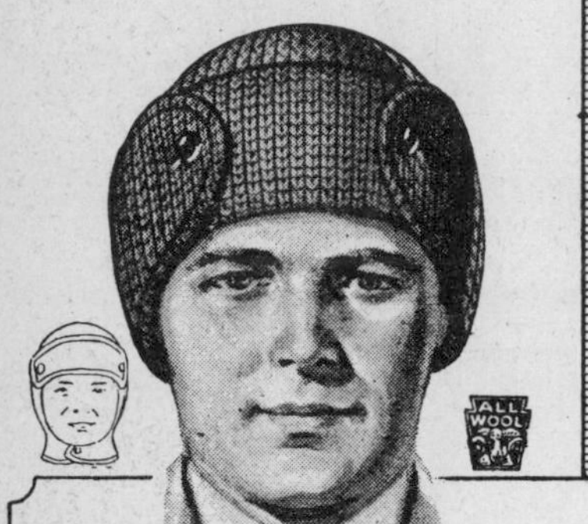

$1.60 83K4690—Brown.
83K4691—Navy blue.
83K4692—Maroon.
83K4693—Dark oxford.

Shipping weight, ¾ pound.

Tim's Hand Fashioned Knitted Cap for men. Made of 100 per cent pure wool worsted yarns of the finest grade. Each cap packed in a handsome gift box.

Men's Caps—Give Cap Size

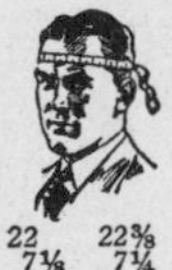

HOW TO MEASURE—Measure all around head as illustrated, then refer to the table below to find the cap size that corresponds to the number of inches your head measures and order that size.

Men's Cap Sizes, 6¾ to 7¾

If head measures, inches	20⅞	21¼	21⅝	22	22⅜
Order cap size	6¾	6⅞	7	7⅛	7¼
If head measures, inches		22¾	23⅛	23½	23⅞
Order cap size		7⅜	7½	7⅝	7¾

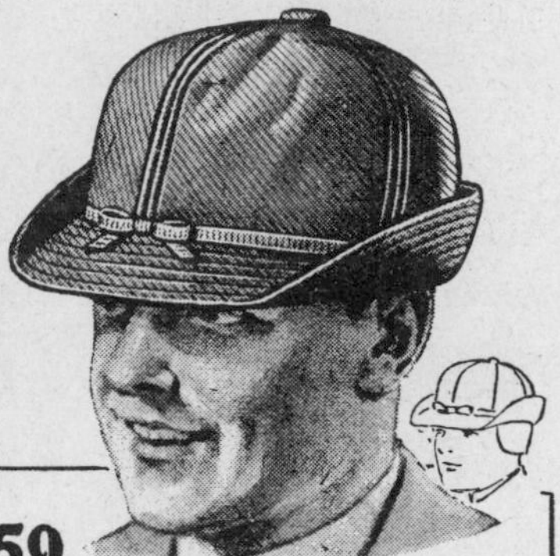

$1.59
93K4649—Khaki.

Sizes, 6¾ to 7¾. **State size.** Shipping weight, 1¼ pounds.

Men's All Weather Sport Hat. Made of a good quality twill cloth, rubberized and constructed so as to make it absolutely waterproof. Flannel lined and taped seams. **Inside turndown lined band.**

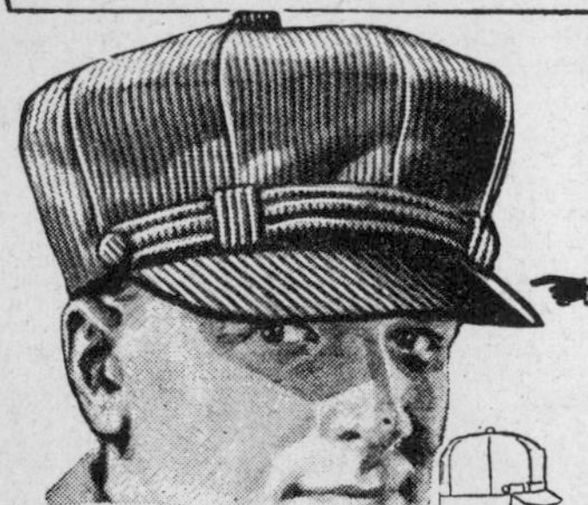

98c 93K4617—Army drab moleskin.
93K4622—Army drab corduroy.

Sizes, 6¾ to 7¾. **State size.** Shipping weight, 1¼ pounds.

A good all around serviceable Judge Style Cap. Made of a good quality moleskin cloth, or narrow ribbed corduroy. Good quality twill lining. Indestructible canvas visor. **Inside turndown lined band.** Warmth and service guaranteed.

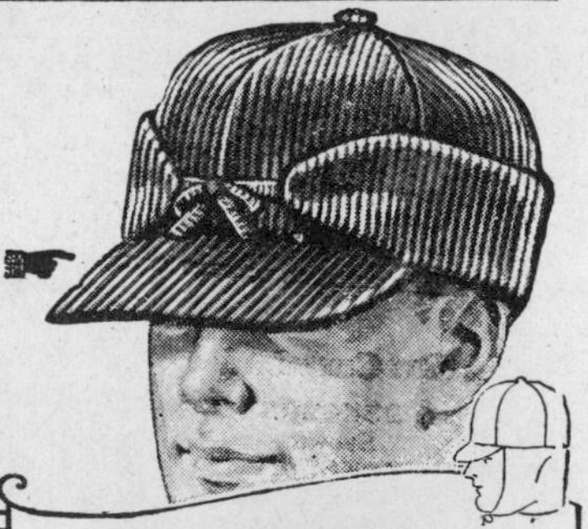

93K4635—Army drab. $1.39
Sizes, 6¾ to 7¾ **State size.** Shipping weight, 1½ pounds.

The ideal Sport or Hunter's Style Cap for men. Made of a good quality narrow ribbed corduroy. Strong and durable fleeced lining. Indestructible canvas visor. The Triple Outside Turndown Band insures protection against severe or stormy weather.

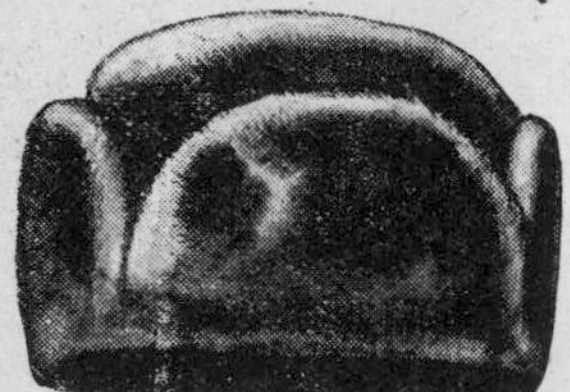

$7.95 93K4686—Black.
Sizes, 6¾ to 7¾. **State size.** Shipping weight, 1¼ pounds.

Men's extra fine quality Imported Sheared Coney Fur Cap commonly known as near seal. Detroit style. Finest quality satin lining. A well made and fine appearing cap. A splendid holiday gift.

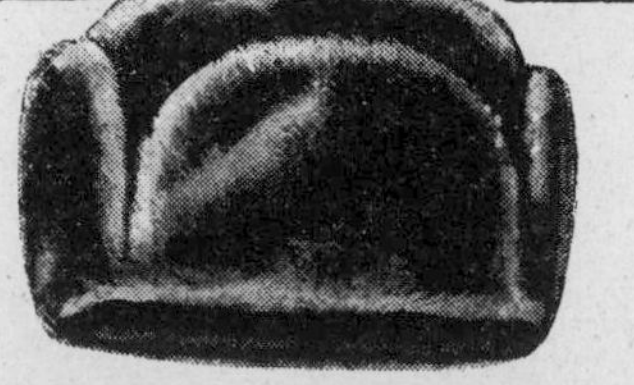

$2.98 93K4627—Black.
Sizes, 6¾ to 7¾. **State size.** Shipping wt., 1¼ pounds.

Men's Imported Sheared and Dyed Rabbit Fur Cap. Sateen lined. Detroit style.

93K4629—Black. $3.75
Same as above, but in a finer quality and satin lined.

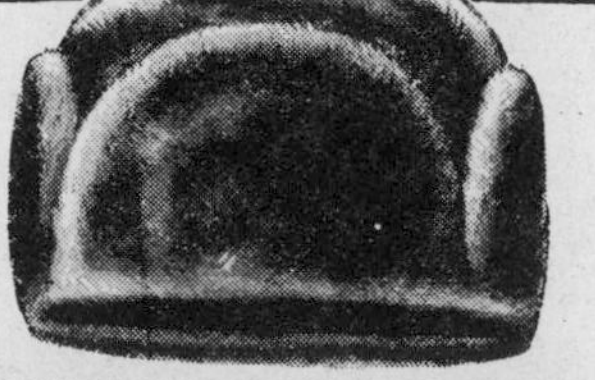

93K4684—Black. $5.98
Sizes, 6¾ to 7¾. **State size.** Shipping weight, 1¼ pounds.

Men's Selected Pieced Genuine Sealskin Fur Cap. Detroit style. Satin lined. A well made cap at a remarkably low price.

93K4685—Black. $16.95
Same style as above, but made of finest selected genuine sealskin.

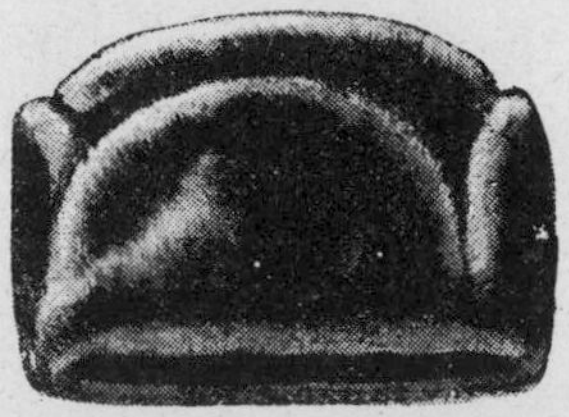

93K4628—Black. $4.95
Sizes, 6¾ to 7¾. **State size.** Shipping wt., 1¼ pounds.

Men's Imported Sheared Coney Fur Cap, commonly known as near seal. Detroit style. Excellent quality satin lining. A high grade cap that will give wonderful service.

Stylish Headwear

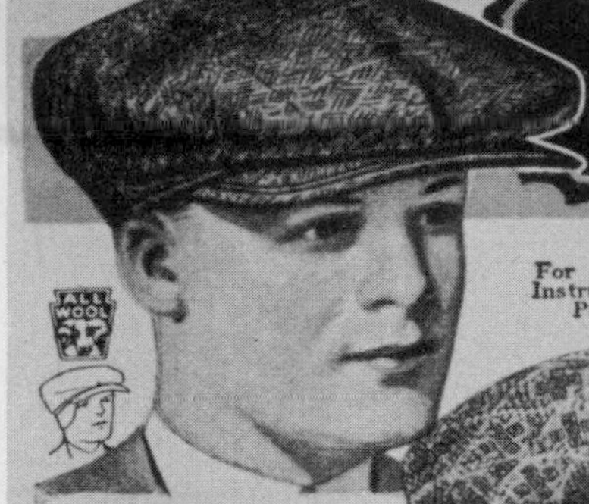

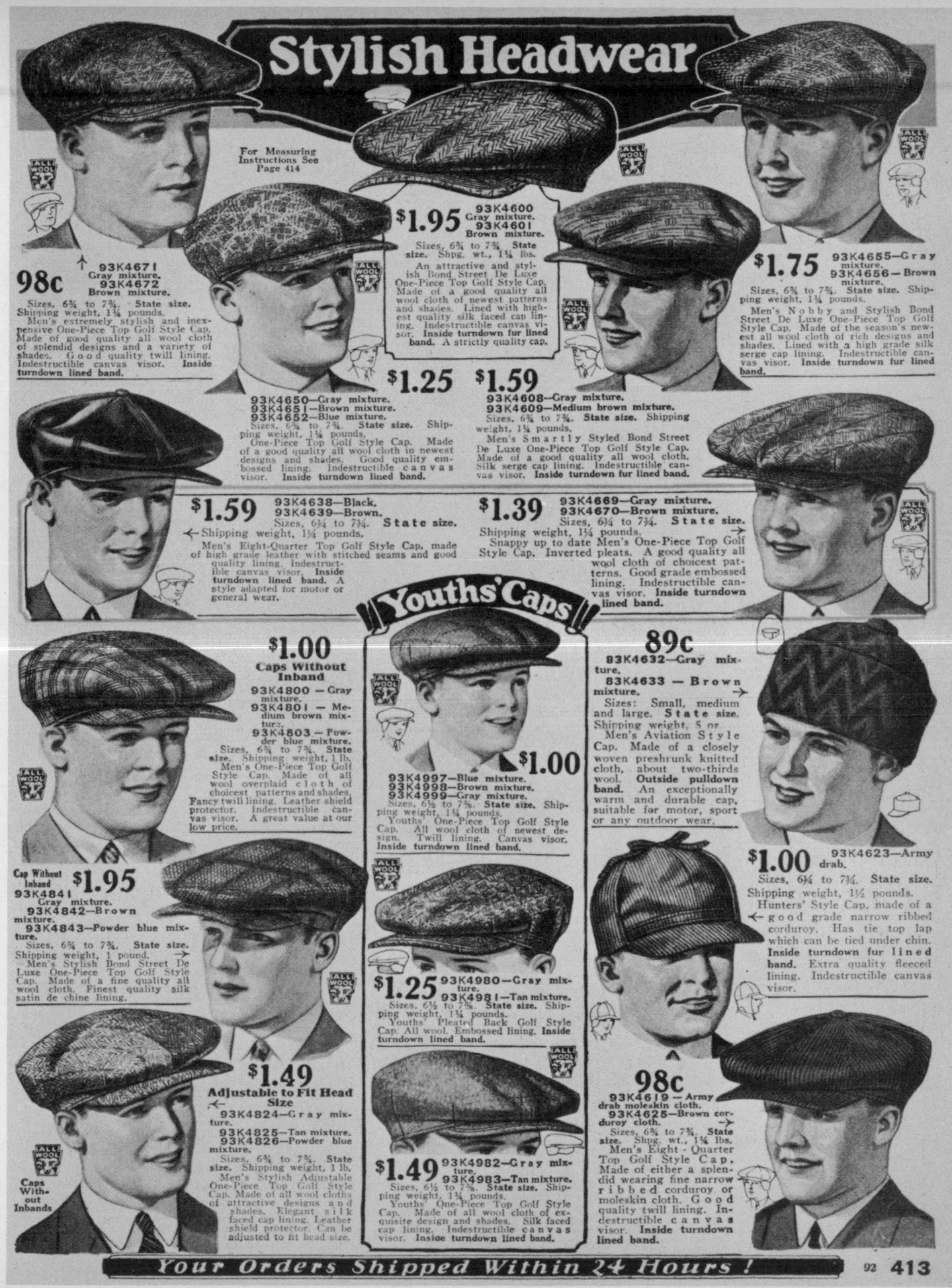

For Measuring Instructions See Page 414

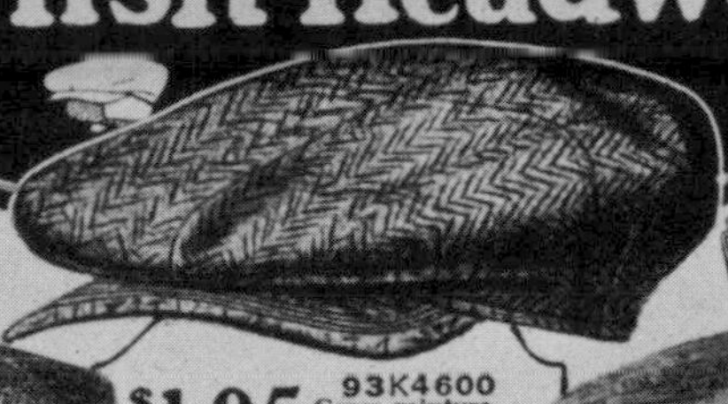

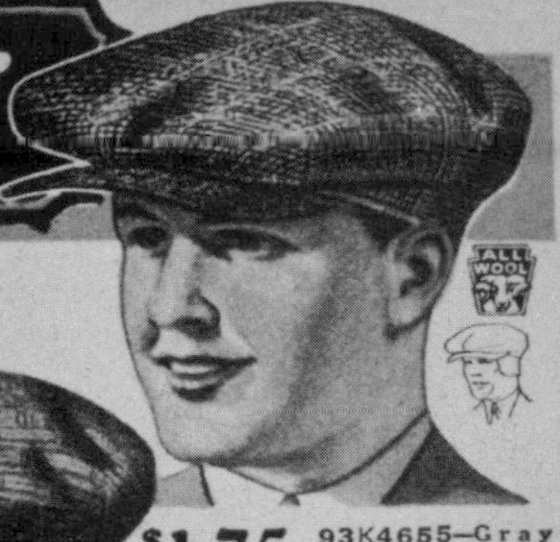

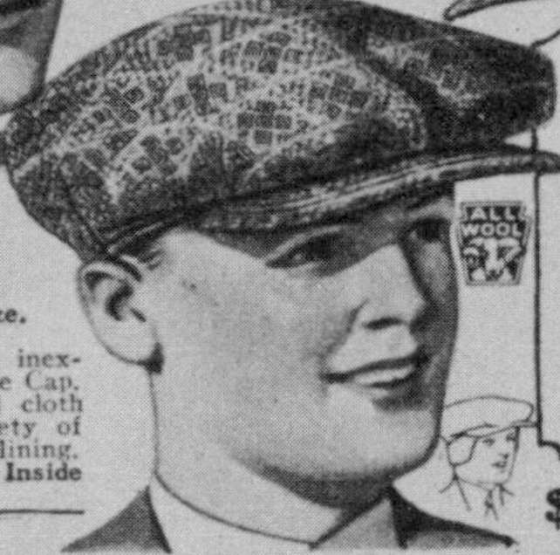

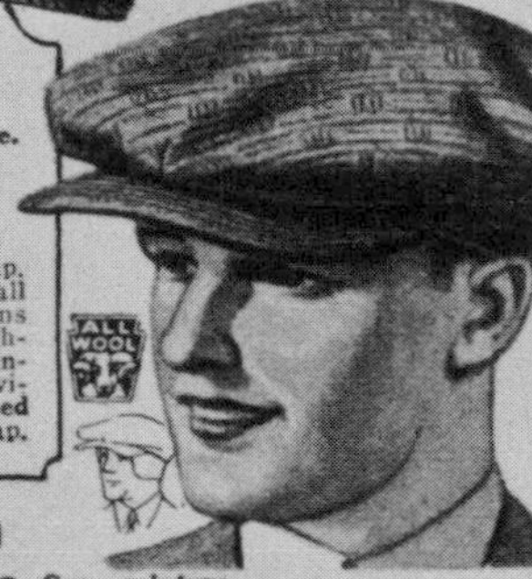

98c 93K4671 Gray mixture. 93K4672 Brown mixture.

Sizes, 6¾ to 7¾. State size. Shipping weight, 1¼ pounds.
Men's extremely stylish and inexpensive One-Piece Top Golf Style Cap. Made of good quality all wool cloth of splendid designs and a variety of shades. Good quality twill lining. Indestructible canvas visor. **Inside turndown lined band.**

$1.95 93K4600 Gray mixture. 93K4601 Brown mixture.

Sizes, 6¾ to 7¾. State size. Shpg. wt., 1¼ lbs.
An attractive and stylish Bond Street De Luxe One-Piece Top Golf Style Cap. Made of a good quality all wool cloth of newest patterns and shades. Lined with highest quality silk faced cap lining. Indestructible canvas visor. **Inside turndown fur lined band.** A strictly quality cap.

$1.75 93K4655—Gray mixture. 93K4656—Brown mixture.

Sizes, 6¾ to 7¾. State size. Shipping weight, 1¼ pounds.
Men's Nobby and Stylish Bond Street De Luxe One-Piece Top Golf Style Cap. Made of the season's newest all wool cloth of rich designs and shades. Lined with a high grade silk serge cap lining. Indestructible canvas visor. **Inside turndown fur lined band.**

$1.25 93K4650—Gray mixture. 93K4651—Brown mixture. 93K4652—Blue mixture.

Sizes, 6¾ to 7¾. State size. Shipping weight, 1¼ pounds.
One-Piece Top Golf Style Cap. Made of a good quality all wool cloth in newest designs and shades. Good quality embossed lining. Indestructible canvas visor. **Inside turndown lined band.**

$1.59 93K4608—Gray mixture. 93K4609—Medium brown mixture.

Sizes, 6¾ to 7¾. State size. Shipping weight, 1¼ pounds.
Men's Smartly Styled Bond Street De Luxe One-Piece Top Golf Style Cap. Made of a good quality all wool cloth. Silk serge cap lining. Indestructible canvas visor. **Inside turndown fur lined band.**

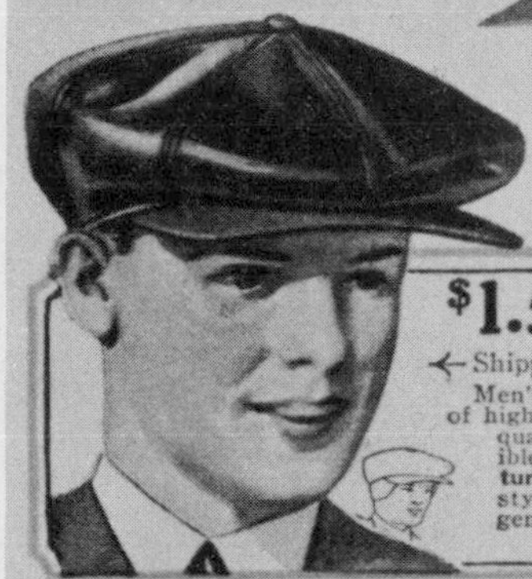

$1.59 93K4638—Black. 93K4639—Brown.

Sizes, 6¾ to 7¾. State size.
← Shipping weight, 1¼ pounds.
Men's Eight-Quarter Top Golf Style Cap, made of high grade leather with stitched seams and good quality lining. Indestructible canvas visor. **Inside turndown lined band.** A style adapted for motor or general wear.

$1.39 93K4669—Gray mixture. 93K4670—Brown mixture.

Sizes, 6¾ to 7¾. State size.
Shipping weight, 1¼ pounds. →
Snappy up to date Men's One-Piece Top Golf Style Cap. Inverted pleats. A good quality all wool cloth of choicest patterns. Good grade embossed lining. Indestructible canvas visor. **Inside turndown lined band.**

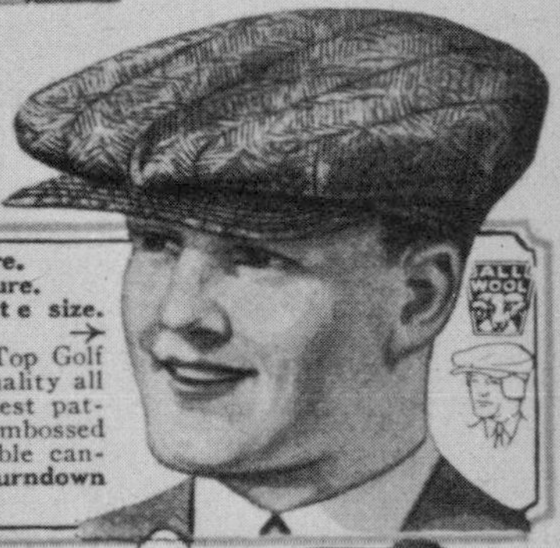

Youths' Caps

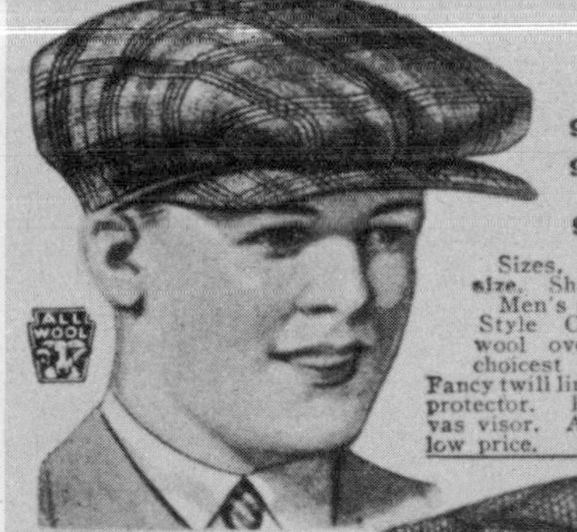

$1.00
Caps Without Inband

93K4800 — Gray mixture. 93K4801 — Medium brown mixture. 93K4803 — Powder blue mixture.

Sizes, 6¾ to 7¾. State size. Shipping weight, 1 lb.
Men's One-Piece Top Golf Style Cap. Made of all wool overplaid cloth of choicest patterns and shades. Fancy twill lining. Leather shield protector. Indestructible canvas visor. A great value at our low price.

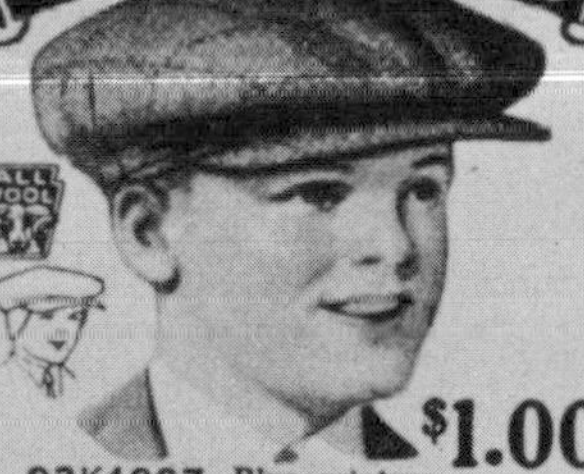

$1.00 93K4997—Blue mixture. 93K4998—Brown mixture. 93K4999—Gray mixture.

Sizes, 6½ to 7⅜. State size. Shipping weight, 1¼ pounds.
Youths' One-Piece Top Golf Style Cap. All wool cloth of newest design. Twill lining. Canvas visor. **Inside turndown lined band.**

89c 83K4632—Gray mixture. 83K4633 — Brown mixture. →

Sizes: Small, medium and large. State size. Shipping weight, 5 oz.
Men's Aviation Style Cap. Made of a closely woven preshrunk knitted cloth, about two-thirds wool. **Outside pulldown band.** An exceptionally warm and durable cap, suitable for motor, sport or any outdoor wear.

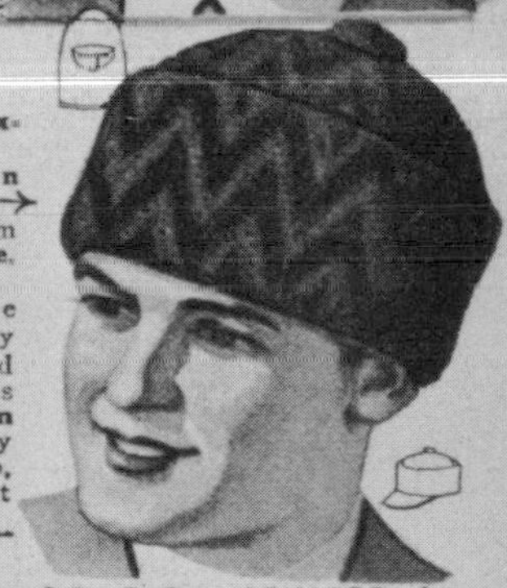

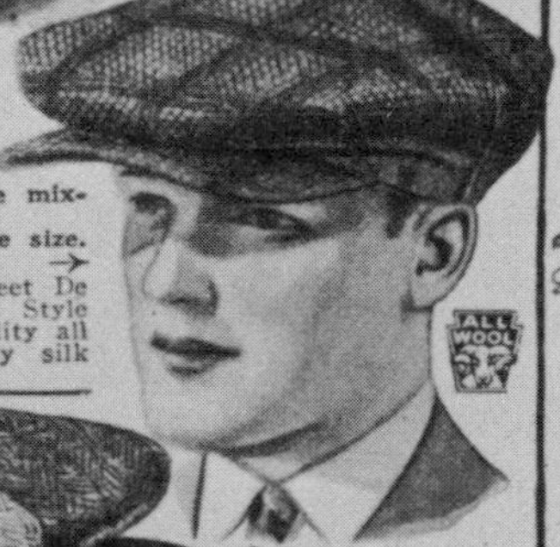

Cap Without Inband **$1.95**

93K4841 Gray mixture. 93K4842—Brown mixture. 93K4843—Powder blue mixture.

Sizes, 6¾ to 7¾. State size. Shipping weight, 1 pound. →
Men's Stylish Bond Street De Luxe One-Piece Top Golf Style Cap. Made of a fine quality all wool cloth. Finest quality silk satin de chine lining.

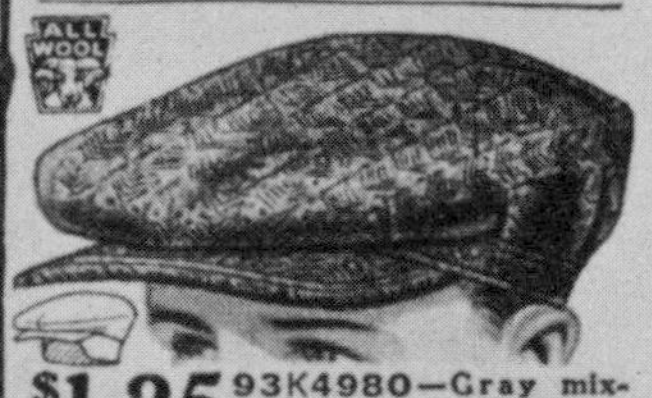

$1.25 93K4980—Gray mixture. 93K4981—Tan mixture.

Sizes, 6½ to 7⅜. State size. Shipping weight, 1¼ pounds.
Youths' Pleated Back Golf Style Cap. All wool. Embossed lining. **Inside turndown lined band.**

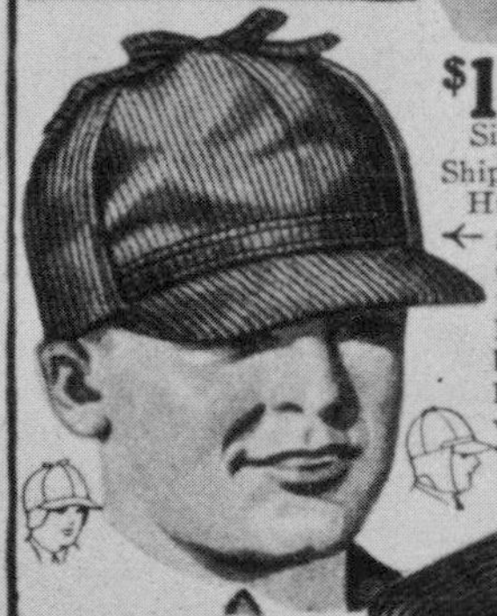

$1.00 93K4623—Army drab.

Sizes, 6¾ to 7¾. State size. Shipping weight, 1½ pounds.
Hunters' Style Cap, made of a ← good grade narrow ribbed corduroy. Has tie top lap which can be tied under chin. **Inside turndown fur lined band.** Extra quality fleeced lining. Indestructible canvas visor.

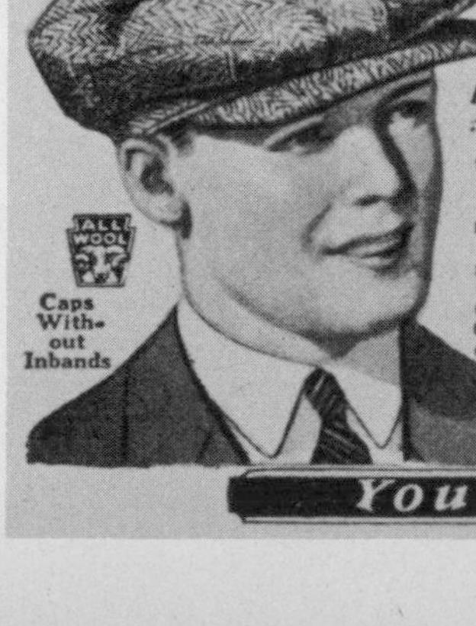

Caps Without Inbands

$1.49
Adjustable to Fit Head Size

← 93K4824—Gray mixture. 93K4825—Tan mixture. 93K4826—Powder blue mixture.

Sizes, 6¾ to 7¾. State size. Shipping weight, 1 lb.
Men's Stylish Adjustable One-Piece Top Golf Style Cap. Made of all wool cloths of attractive designs and shades. Elegant silk faced cap lining. Leather shield protector. Can be adjusted to fit head size.

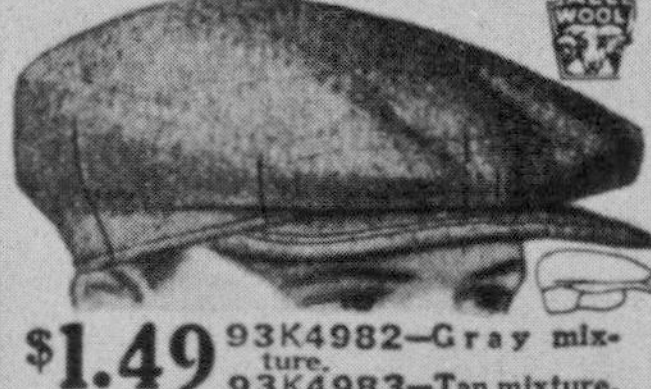

$1.49 93K4982—Gray mixture. 93K4983—Tan mixture.

Sizes, 6½ to 7⅜. State size. Shipping weight, 1¼ pounds.
Youths' One-Piece Top Golf Style Cap. Made of all wool cloth of exquisite design and shades. Silk faced cap lining. Indestructible canvas visor. **Inside turndown lined band.**

98c 93K4619 — Army drab moleskin cloth. 93K4625—Brown corduroy cloth. →

Sizes, 6¾ to 7¾. State size. Shpg. wt., 1¼ lbs.
Men's Eight-Quarter Top Golf Style Cap. Made of either a splendid wearing fine narrow ribbed corduroy or moleskin cloth. Good quality twill lining. Indestructible canvas visor. **Inside turndown lined band.**

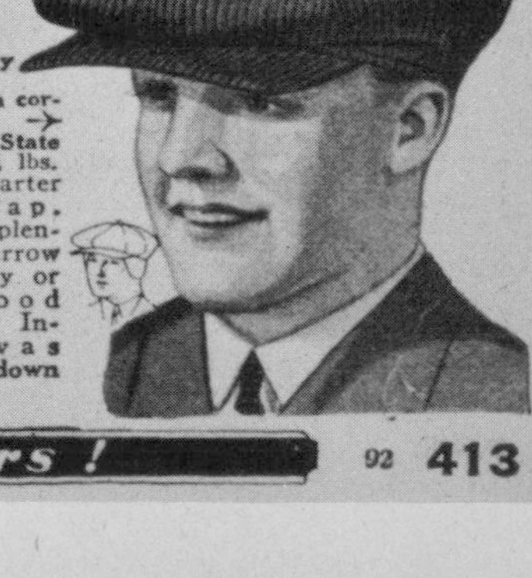

Your Orders Shipped Within 24 Hours!

The Newest *for* Boys' CAPS

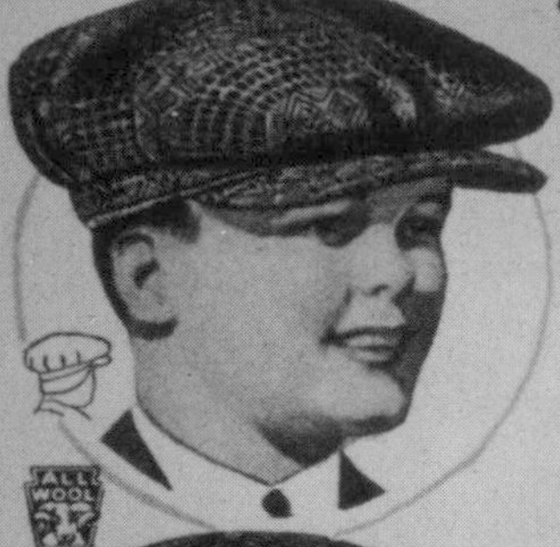

$1.39 93K4952 Gray mixture. 93K4953 Brown mixture.
Sizes, 6⅜ to 7⅛. **State size.** Shipping weight, 1 lb.
One of the smartest and classiest models. Boys' One-Piece Top Pleated Back Golf Style Cap. Made of a good quality all wool cloth of rich designs. Elegantly embossed lining. **Indestructible canvas visor. Inside turndown lined band.**

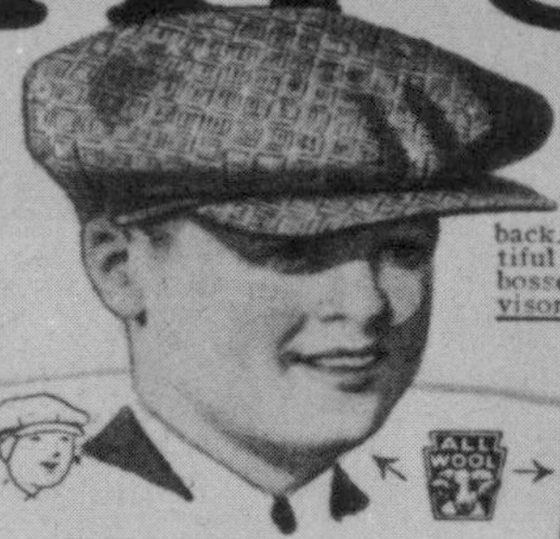

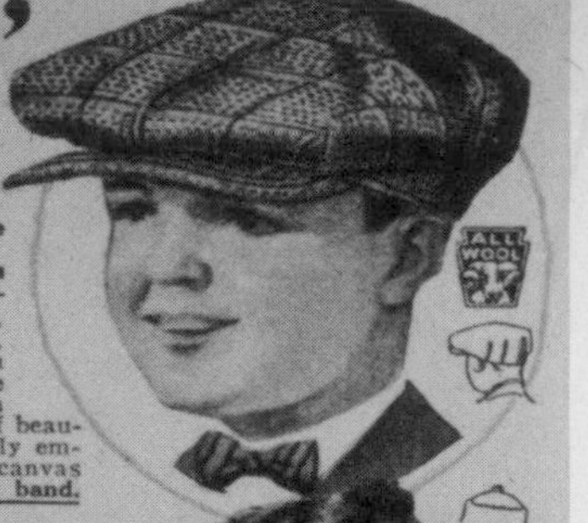

$1.15 93K4957 Powder blue mixture. 93K4958—Brown mixture.
Sizes, 6⅜ to 7⅛. **State size.** Shpg. wt., 1 lb.
A snappy and stylish One-Piece Top Golf Style Cap. Inverted pleats in back. Made of all wool cloth of beautiful designs and shades. Richly embossed lining. Indestructible canvas visor. **Inside turndown lined band.**

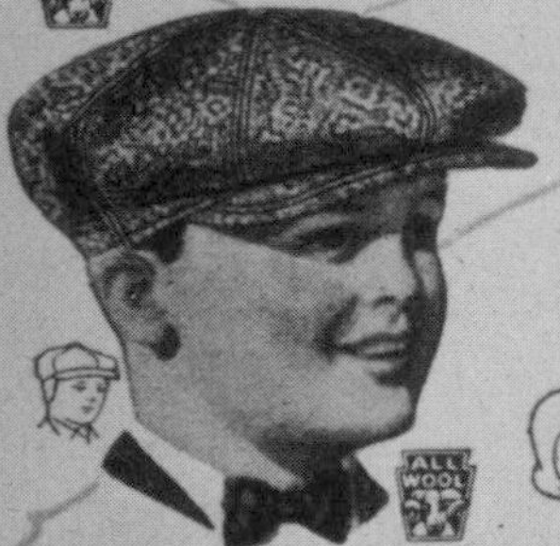

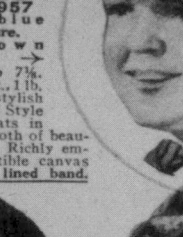

75c 93K4910 Brown mixture. 93K4911 Gray mixture.
Sizes, 6⅜ to 7⅛. **State size.** Shipping weight, 1 pound.
Very popular style Cap for boys made in Eight-Quarter Top Golf Style of all wool cloth in a variety of the latest patterns and shades. Good quality twill lining. Indestructible canvas visor. **Inside turndown lined band.**

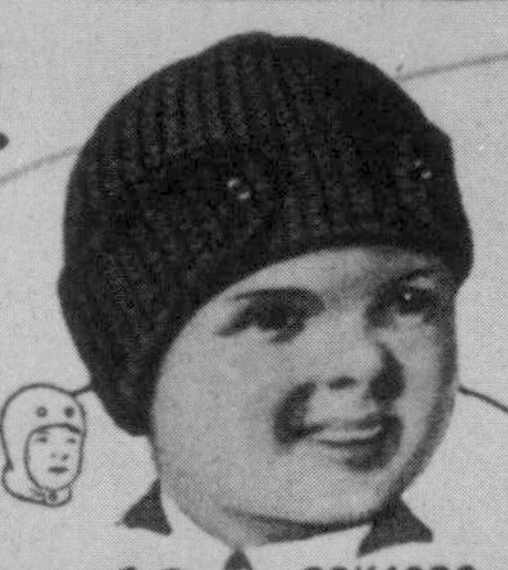

69c 83K4930 Brown. 83K4931 Navy Blue. 83K4932—Maroon.
Shipping weight, 4 ounces.
Boys' All Weather Knitted Cap of double thickness. Warm and durable and can be buttoned under chin. Made of about two-thirds wool. Priced very low for a cap of this quality.

89c 93K4967—Gray mixture. 93K4968—Tan mixture. 93K4969—Navy blue serge.
Sizes, 6⅜ to 7⅛. **State size.** Shipping weight, 1 pound.
Boys' Stylish One-Piece Top Golf Style Cap. Made of a fine quality all wool cloth of newest designs and shades. Twill lining. Indestructible canvas visor. **Inside turndown lined band.**

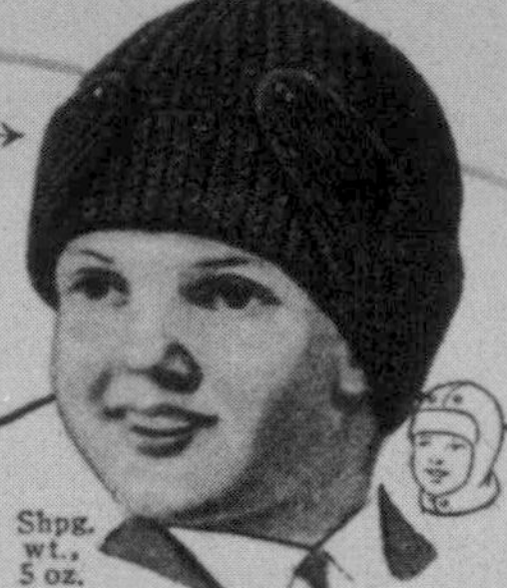

Shpg. wt., 5 oz.

98c 83K4943—Buff. 83K4944—Brown. 83K4945—Navy blue. 83K4946—Maroon.
Boys' All Wool Worsted Knitted Cap of double thickness. One of the greatest bargains offered in a quality cap. Can be turned down and buttoned under chin. Durability and warmth guaranteed. We defy competition at our low price.

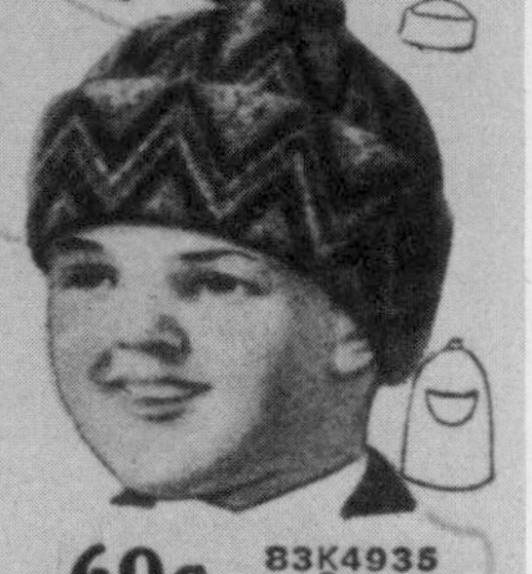

69c 83K4935 Gray mixture. 83K4936—Medium brown mixture.
Sizes: Small, medium or large. **State size.** Shipping weight, 7 ounces.
Boys' Aviation Style Cap. Made of a closely woven preshrunken knitted cloth, about two-thirds wool. Outside pulldown band. A popular style for sport or play.

For Little Men

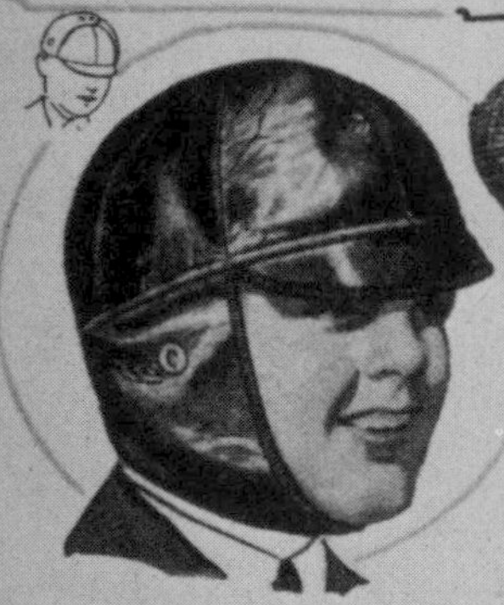

$1.48 93K4905—Brown. 93K4906—Black.
Sizes, 6⅜ to 7⅛. **State size.** Shipping weight, 8 ounces.
Boys' Leather Caps are extremely popular this season. Made of a good quality leather. Lined with a warm cloth lining and has a lined band that can be turned down and fastened under chin. A cap that is storm and weather proof.

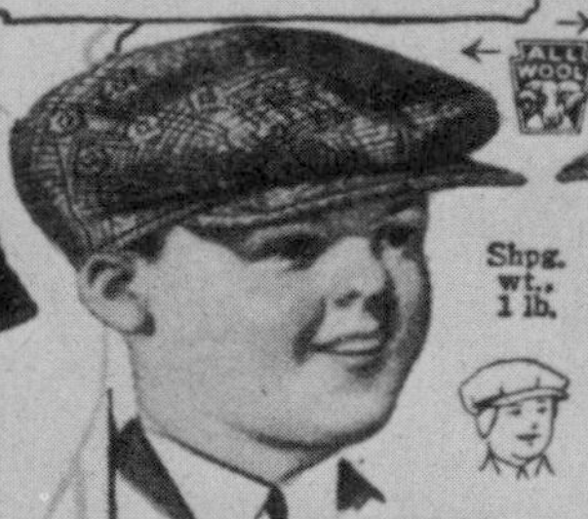

Shpg. wt., 1 lb.

75c 93K4940 Brown mixture. 93K4941 Gray mixture. 93K4913—Navy blue serge.
Sizes, 6¼ to 6⅞. **State size.**
One-Piece Top Golf Style Cap. Made of all wool and serge cloths. Good quality fancy twill lining. Indestructible canvas visor. **Inside turndown lined band.**

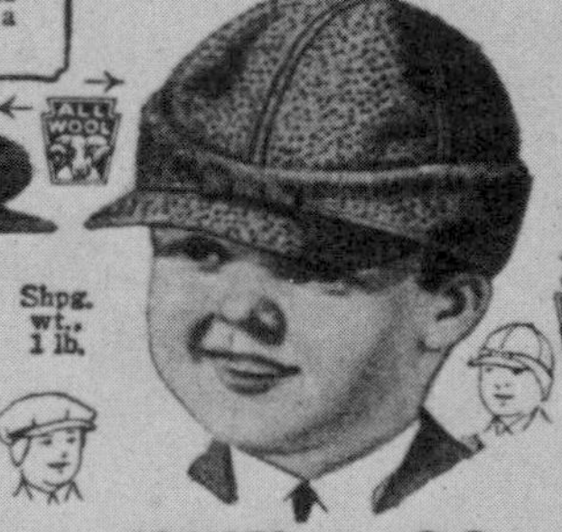

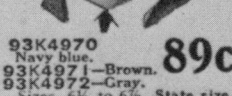

89c 93K4970 Navy blue. 93K4971—Brown. 93K4972—Gray.
Sizes, 6¼ to 6⅞. **State size.** Jockey style. All wool chinchilla. Twill lining. Canvas visor. **Outside pull down band.**

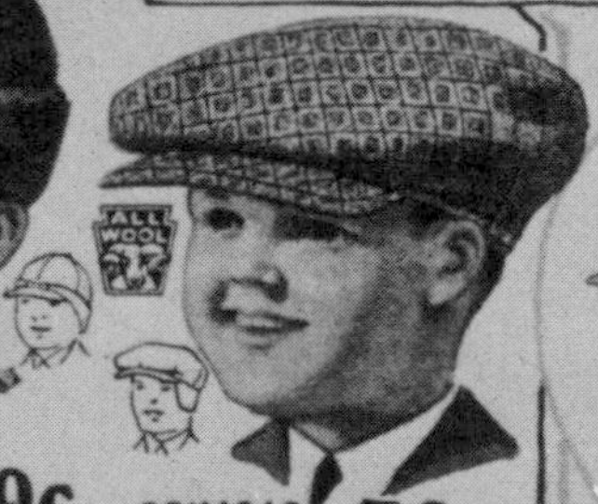

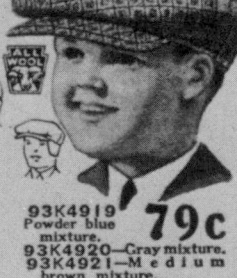

79c 93K4919 Powder blue mixture. 93K4920—Gray mixture. 93K4921—Medium brown mixture.
Sizes, 6¼ to 6⅞. **State size.** Shipping wt., 1 lb.
One-piece top golf style. Good quality all wool. Fancy twill lining. Indestructible canvas visor. **Inside turndown lined band.**

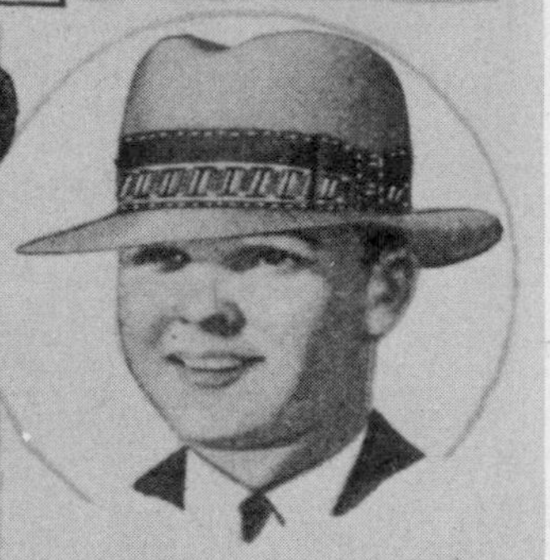

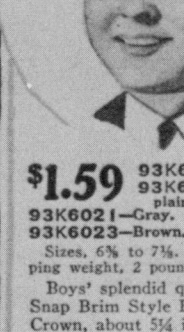

$1.59 93K6019—Sand tan. 93K6020—Black with plain black band. 93K6021—Gray. 93K6023—Brown.
Sizes, 6⅜ to 7⅛. **State size.** Shipping weight, 2 pounds.
Boys' splendid quality Wool Felt Snap Brim Style Hat. Fancy band. Crown, about 5¼ inches high. Raw edge brim, about 2⅛ inches wide. A very nobby and stylish hat.

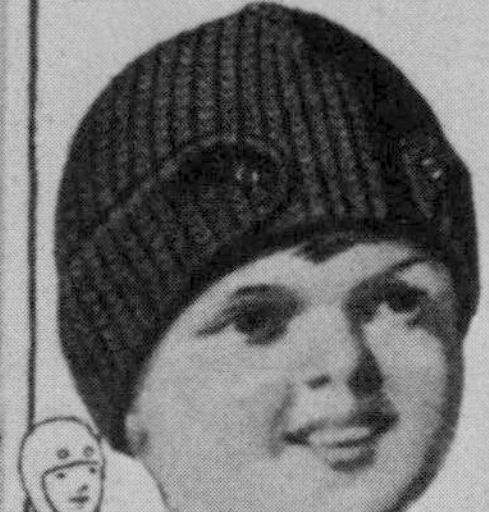

49c 83K4923—Buff. 83K4924—Brown. 83K4925—Navy blue. 83K4926 Maroon.
Shipping weight, 3 ounces.
Little Fellows' All Weather Knitted Hockey Cap of double thickness. Made of one-half wool yarns in four popular colors. A becoming style that will keep the little man warm and please him very much.

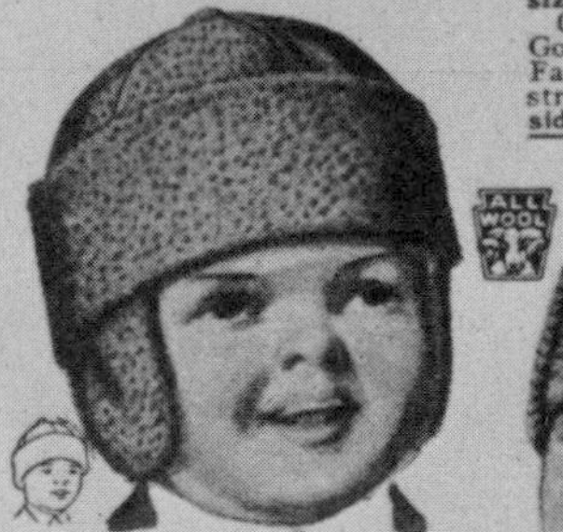

79c 93K4974—Navy blue. 93K4975—Brown. 93K4976—Gray.
Sizes, 6¼ to 6⅞. **State size.** Shipping weight, 1 pound.
Little Fellows' Turban. Made of a good quality all wool chinchilla cloth. Twill lining. **Inside turndown ear tabs.** A very warm and serviceable cap that will please the little man. Extremely low in price considering the quality.

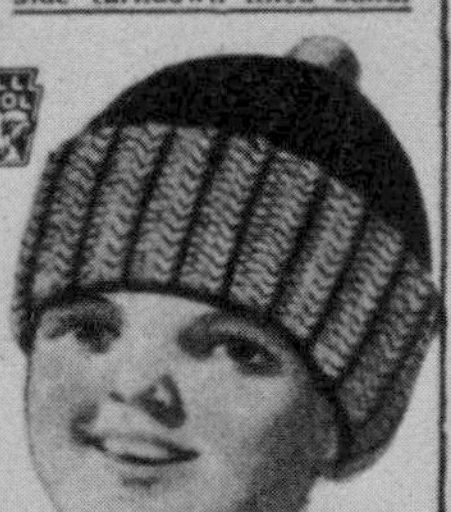

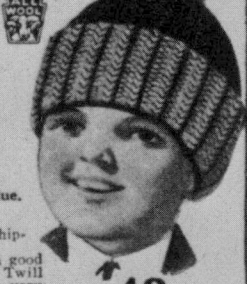

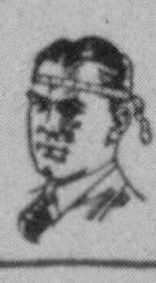

42c 83K4977—Brown and buff. 83K4978—Black and orange. 83K4979—Maroon and navy. 83K4984—Navy and red.
Shipping weight, 4 ounces.
Little Fellows' All Wool Knitted Hockey Cap of double thickness. This cap will give long service and at our low price is a wonderful value.

Men's, Boys' and Children's Hats and Caps

Give hat size after measuring head as below. In table below you will see hat size that corresponds to your measurements. **How to measure:** Measure head as illustrated, placing tape measure around head.

If Head Meas., Inches	Order Hat Size	If Head Meas., Inches	Order Hat Size
19⅜	6¼	22	7⅛
19¾	6⅜	22⅜	7¼
20⅛	6½	22¾	7⅜
20½	6⅝	23⅛	7½
20⅞	6¾	23½	7⅝
21¼	6⅞	23⅞	7¾
21⅝	7		

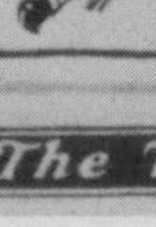

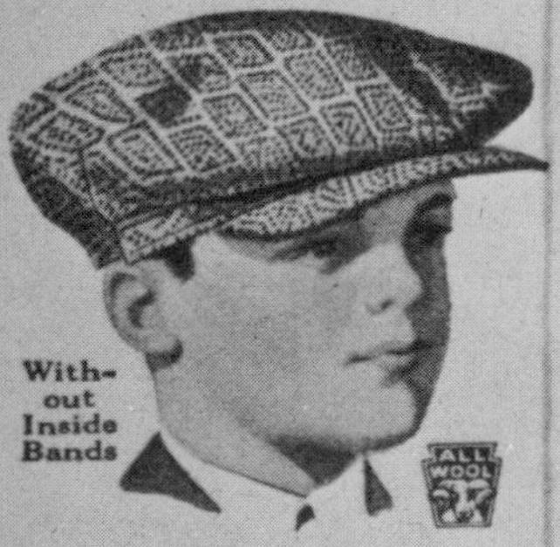

Without Inside Bands

Adjustable to Fit Head Size

$1.25 93K4782—Powder blue gray mixture. 93K4783—Tan mixture.
Sizes, 6⅜ to 7⅛. **State size.** Shipping weight, 1 pound.
Boys' One-Piece Top Golf Style Cap. Made of all wool cloths in newest designs and shades. Good quality **silk faced cap lining.** Leather shield protector. Indestructible canvas visor. Can be adjusted to fit head size.

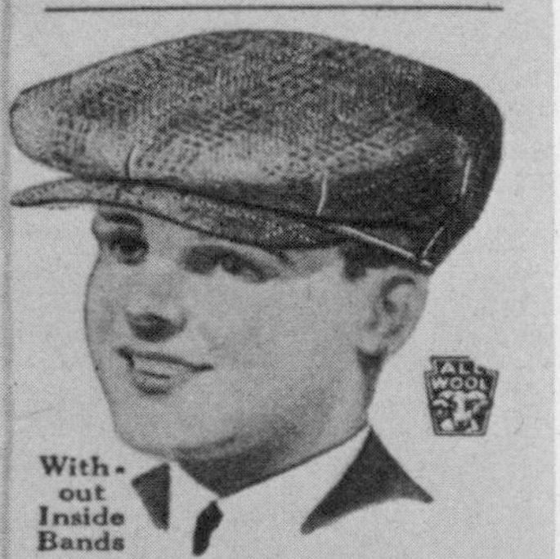

Without Inside Bands

75c 93K4779—Powder blue mixture. 93K4780—Gray mixture. 93K4781—Medium brown mixture.
Sizes, 6⅜ to 7⅛. **State size.** Shipping weight, 1 pound.
An exceedingly smart and stylish One-Piece Top Golf Style Cap for Boys. Made of a good quality all wool newest design cloth of elegant shades. Twill lining. Leather shield protector. Indestructible canvas visor.

Men's High Grade Dress Gloves

Unlined

How To Measure Your Hand for Size See Page 1095

Imported Heavy Duplex Chamoisuede
$1.15 33K4208—Beaver. 33K4209—Gray.
Sizes, 7½ to 10½. Half sizes. State size. Shipping weight, 3 ounces.
Very rich and stylish appearing are these Men's Imported Duplex (Double) Chamoisuede Fabric Gloves. Heavily embroidered fancy backs. Kip-Knot sewed seams and bolton thumbs. A quality glove that has never been priced so low.

Indestructo Saranac Buckskin
$2.98 33K4015—Yellowish tan.
Sizes, 7 to 10½. Half sizes. State size. Shipping weight, 8 ounces.
The finest quality Saranac Grain Buckskin Dress or Street Gloves we can offer you. Made of plumb weight chrome tanned grain buckskin which will remain soft and pliable under all conditions. Stitched backs. Half outseam sewed.

Imported Capeskin
$1.59 33K4009 Dark tan. 33K4010—Gray.
Sizes, 7 to 10½. Half sizes. State size. Shpg. wt., 4 oz.
One of our best values in Men's Unlined Dress Gloves. Made of an excellent quality chrome tanned imported capeskin. Stitched backs. Outseam sewed.

Unlined

Unlined Mocha
$2.98 33K4025 — Reindeer brown. 33K4026—Gray.
Sizes, 7 to 10½. Mocha Dress Gloves. Made of selected imported skins, desirable because of their velvety finish. Fancy embroidered backs. Outseam sewed.
Half sizes. State size. Shpg. wt., 4 oz.

Warm Fleece Lined Capeskin
$1.39 33K4206—Brown. 33K4207—Black.
Sizes, 7½ to 10½. Half sizes. State size. Shipping weight, 6 oz.
Another remarkable value in Men's Good Quality Fleece Lined Capeskin Gloves. Made of a good grade chrome tanned capeskin. Stitched backs. Half outseam sewed.

Fur Lined Imported Capeskin
$3.00 33K4236 Brown.
Sizes, 8 to 10½. Half sizes. State size. Shipping weight, 7 ounces.
Men's Fine Quality Capeskin Fur Lined Gloves. Made of a good quality chrome tanned capeskin with imported coney (rabbit fur) lining. Outseam sewed. Stitched backs. These gloves are well made in roomy sizes.

Warm Angora Brushed Wool Lining
$1.98 33K4223—Brown. 33K4224—Black.
Sizes, 8 to 10½. Half sizes. State size. Shipping weight, 7 ounces.
A wonderful value in Men's High Grade Dress or Street Gloves. Made of fine selected imported chrome tanned capeskin. Lined with warm Angora brushed wool lining. Adjustable strap fasteners at wrists. Half outseam sewed. Gloves that are well made in large and roomy sizes, which insure comfort as well as warmth.

Imported Capeskin

Silk Lined Capeskin
$2.45 33K4269—Dark tan. 33K4270—Gray.
Sizes, 7 to 10½. Half sizes. State size. Shipping weight, 4 ounces.
Our Finest Silk Lined Cape Gloves for men. Made of selected chrome tanned imported capeskin. Dressy and stylish gloves with fancy embroidered backs. Outseam sewed. Highest quality and lowest price. A style for the most discriminating dressers.

Lamb Lined Imported Capeskin
$4.39 33K4245 Brown. 33K4246—Black.
Sizes, 8 to 10½. Half sizes. State size. Shpg. wt., ¾ lb.
The finest glove value you can secure. Fine quality specially selected chrome tanned imported capeskin, with warm imported lambs' wool (fur) lining. Stitched backs. Adjustable strap fasteners at wrists.

Silk Lined Suede
$1.98 33K4267—Brown. 33K4268—Gray.
Sizes, 7 to 10½. Half sizes. State size. Shipping weight, 4 ounces.
Quality plus low price in Men's Silk Lined Suede Gloves. Stylish and popular. Embroidered backs. Half pique sewed.

Durable Unlined Capeskin
33K4002—Brown. **$1.00**
Sizes, 7 to 10½. Half sizes. State size. Shpg. wt., 4 oz.
A real value in Men's Unlined Capeskin Gloves. Made of a good quality chrome tanned capeskin. Stitched backs. Half outseam sewed.

Imported Unlined Capeskin
$1.98 33K3998—Gray. 33K3999—Dark tan.
Sizes, 7 to 10½. Half sizes. State size. Shipping weight, 4 ounces.
Our Men's Finest Unlined Capeskin Gloves. Made of selected chrome tanned imported capeskin that is soft and pliable. Newest fancy embroidered backs. Outseam sewed.

Fleece Lined Jersey
55c 33K4203—Black. 33K4204—Gray. 33K4205—Brown.
Sizes, 7½ to 10½. Half sizes. State size. Shpg. wt., 3 oz.
Men's Inexpensive Fleece Lined Closely Woven Jersey Fabric Gloves. Embroidered backs. Warm and comfortable.

Fleece Lined Suede
$1.75 33K4220 Brown. 33K4221 Gray.
Sizes, 7½ to 10½. Half sizes. State size. Shpg. wt., 6 oz.
Men's Excellent Quality Chrome Tanned Suede Gloves. Heavily fleeced lining. Embroidered backs. Half outseam sewed. A real value. Warm, long wearing gloves.

Seamless Wool Lined Imported Capeskin
$2.75 33K4213 Dark tan.
Sizes, 7½ to 10½. Half sizes. State size. Shipping wt., 5 ounces.
Fine quality imported chrome tanned selected capeskin. Lined with an excellent grade of all wool seamless knit lining. Heavily embroidered backs. Outseam sewed.

Angora Brushed Wool Lined Capeskin
33K4215—Dark tan. **$1.75**
Sizes, 7½ to 10½. Half sizes. State size. Shpg. wt., 8 oz.
Men's High Grade Angora Brushed Wool Lined Capeskin Gloves. Made of fine quality imported chrome tanned selected capeskin that will keep soft and pliable. Fancy embroidered back. Outseam sewed. Warm, dressy and serviceable gloves.

HERCULES JUNIOR WORK SHIRTS

69c
33K1025 — Blue chambray.
33K1026 — Gray chambray.
33K1027 — Khaki twill.
33K1028 — Fancy chambray.
Sizes, 12½ to 14 inches neck measure. Half sizes. State size. Shpg. wt. ¾ lb.
The Famous Hercules Junior Triple Stitched Work Shirts for boys. Have every well known Hercules feature. Big roomy sizes, interlined collar and cuffs, continuous non-rip sleeve facings, two large button-through pockets and genuine vegetable ivory buttons. Triple stitching on all principal seams.

GENUINE BROADCLOTH

79c
33K1418 — Tan.
33K1419 — Blue.
33K1420 — White.
Ages, 6, 7, 8, 9 and 10 years. State age. Shipping wt., 7 oz.
Genuine Cotton Broadcloth Dress Shirts for the little fellow. Made of good quality cotton broadcloth shirting with attached soft collar, faced sleeves, one pocket and soft single cuffs. Tie not included.

For Boys' Clothing See Pages 352 to 355

59c
33K990 — Blue chambray.
33K993 — Khaki tan shirting.
Ages, 6, 7, 8, 9 and 10 years. State age. Shipping weight, 7 oz.
Work Shirts for the little fellow. Made just like father's, of either good quality chambray or khaki tan shirting with interlined collar, faced sleeves and one pocket. Will give excellent service and will please the little fellow immensely.

69c
33K994 — Fancy patterns.
33K998 — Plain tan.
33K999 — Plain blue.
Ages, 6, 7, 8, 9 and 10 years. State age. Shpg. wt., 7 oz.
Dress Shirts for the little fellow. Made of good quality soft finish percale shirting with attached soft collar, faced sleeves and one pocket. Collar and cuffs are interlined. Dress-up shirts that will give good service. Tie not included.

$3.25
33K1935 — Navy blue.
33K1936 — Gray.
33K1937 — Light brown.
Ages, 8 to 16 years. State age. Shipping weight, 2½ pounds.
Boys' Cotton Blanket Cloth Bathrobe in a new design. A neat Indian pattern with bright, yet well blended colorings that boys like so well. Cord girdle and two pockets. A finely tailored garment with all seams reinforced.

33K1089 Fancy stripes. $1.39
Ages, 6 to 16 years. State age. Shipping weight, ¾ pound.
Boys' Shawl Collar Flannelette Pajamas. Made of excellent quality flannelette with collar, front, and pocket trimmed with fancy silk braid. One double frog loop and three buttons. Very attractive garments in a popular style that will give good service.

$1.29
33K1094 — Striped patterns.
Ages, 6 to 16 years. State age. Shipping weight, ¾ pound.
A New One-Piece Sleeping Suit for boys. Made of a very fine quality heavyweight flannelette in neat stripes. Braid and frog trimmed as illustrated. Flap seat. A garment that is bound to keep the boy warm and comfortable.

21c
33K8572 Fancy patterns.
Colors: Blue, red, brown, gray, green or plain black. State color. Shpg. wt., 1 oz.
Boys' Sport Bows in attractive fancy patterns. Made of good quality silk. Adjustable elastic band. Ties that will please any boy.

35c
33K8587 Fancy patterns.
Colors: Dark blue, red, brown, purple, gray or green. State color. Shpg. wt., 6 oz.
A silk mixed Four-In-Hand Tie in patterns real boys like. Comes in a neat box, making a very acceptable gift. A very good tie.

25c
33K8586 Fancy patterns.
Colors: Blue, red, brown, purple, gray or green. Shipping weight, 2 oz.
A Narrow Four-In-Hand Tie made of good quality neckwear silk in fancy patterns and colorings. Open end.

39c
33K8580
Comes in: Navy blue, red, brown, black or white; also Scotch plaid. State color. Shpg. wt., 1 oz.
Fine quality, heavyweight All Silk Windsor Tie.

33K8578
21c
Same as above, but in a lighter weight.

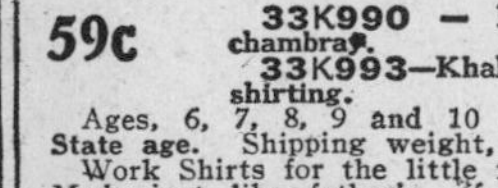

33K8895 — Black.
33K8896 — Gray.
33K8897 — Tan.
48c
Sizes, 24, 26, 28 and 30 inches waist. State size. Width, about 1⅜ inches. Shipping wt., 6 oz.
Genuine Cowhide Bridle Leather Belt for boys. Attractive embossed pattern. Nickel plated, self adjusting buckle.

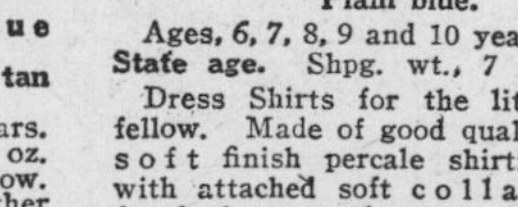

33K8881 — Black.
33K8882 — Brown.
33K8883 — Tan.
39c
Sizes, 24, 26, 28 and 30 in. waist. State size. Width, about 1⅜ in. Shpg. wt., 6 oz.
Boys' Fancy Wide Belt. Made of cowhide leather with fancy embossed grain. Nickel plated tongue buckle.

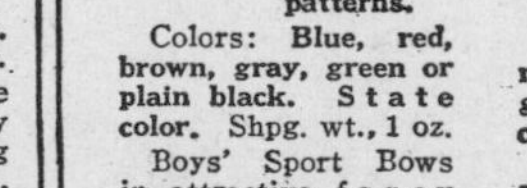

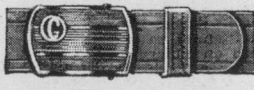

33K8888 — Black.
33K8889 — Brown.
39c
Sizes, 24 to 30 in. waist. State size and initial. Cannot furnish initials I, O, Q, U, V, X, Y or Z. Width, about 1 in. Shpg. wt., 3 oz.
Genuine Cowhide Bridle Leather Strap Belt. Smooth finish, stitched edge effect. Self adjusting nickel plated initial buckle.

All Wool Mufflers
98c
33K9305
Colors: Blue, gray or tan. State color. Shpg. wt., 8 oz.
Fine Quality Flannel or Cashmere Mufflers for boys. Imported from Europe and made of fine quality soft wool yarns. Ideal mufflers for boys, as they have plenty of warmth and are very attractive.

for Everyday Needs

89c
33K1085
Fancy stripes.
Ages, 6 to 16 years. State age. Shipping weight, ¾ pound.
A very practical Sleeping Garment for boys. One-piece pajama suit with big body dimensions insuring comfort. Made of good quality medium weight flannelette in neat patterns. Military collar and one pocket. Plain pearl button front to crotch. Drop seat.

79c 33K1001 Striped patterns.
Ages, 6 to 16 years. State age. Shipping weight, ¾ pound.
Our price is very low for this good quality Flannelette Nightshirt. Made large and roomy with flat collar and one pocket. Neat striped patterns. A garment that will give you much satisfaction.

39c 33K8765
Length, 30 in. Shipping weight, 3 ounces.
Boys' Dress Suspender equal, we think, to any 50-cent suspender on the market. Made of fancy elastic lisle webbing with colored leather ends to match. Gilted metal parts. A dressy and serviceable suspender that will please.

29c 33K8762
Length, 30 in. Shipping weight, 3 ounces.
Boys' Police and Firemen's Style Suspenders. Just like Dad's! Leather ends and nickel plated trimmings. Neat appearing suspenders, guaranteed to give long service. Our price is exceptionally low, quality considered.

25c 33K8571
Plain colors.
39c 33K8596
Fancy patterns.
Colors: Dark blue, red, brown, gray, purple or green. State color. Shpg. weight, 2 ounces.
Fine quality Four-In-Hand Tie. Made of silk mixed neckwear material.

23c
33K8575—Plain colors.
33K8573—Striped patterns.
Colors: Navy blue, red, brown, purple, gray or green. State color. Shipping weight, 2 ounces.
One of the finest ties you can buy at this price. Rayon and mercerized cotton knitted ties in fancy weaves. Comes in stripes or plain colors.

29c 33K8768
Length 30 inches. Shipping weight, 3 ounces.
Self Adjusting Sliding Cord Suspenders for boys. Good quality lisle webbing and nickel plated metal parts. Very serviceable suspenders, guaranteed to give satisfaction.

35c
33K8594—Plain colors.
33K8592—Fancy stripes.
Colors: Navy blue, red, brown, black or green. State color. Shipping weight, 4 oz.
An attractive gift for boys. Fine Quality All Rayon Knitted Ties in neat stripes or plain colors. Fancy crocheted weaves. Attractive neckwear that reflects value.

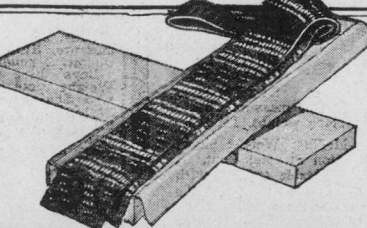

$1.29
33K1405—White.
33K1406—Tan.
33K1407—Blue.
Sizes, 12, 12½, 13, 13½ and 14 inches neck measure. State size. Shipping weight, 8 ounces.
Boys' Fine Quality Genuine Imported English Cotton Broadcloth Dress Shirts in plain colors. High grade dress shirts made in coat style with attached collar, soft single cuffs, and one pocket. The broadcloth is of a very fine count. Cannot be excelled for wearing qualities and appearance and makes beautiful shirts. Tie not included.

GENUINE English BROADCLOTH

For Boys' Clothing See Page 345 to 363

75c
33K1411
Plain tan.
33K1412
Fancy patterns.
33K1413—Plain blue.
Sizes, 11 to 14 inches neck measure. Half sizes. State size. Shipping weight, 8 oz.
Boys' Dress Shirts made of good quality soft finish percale with attached soft collar, soft single cuffs and one pocket. Serviceable shirts made over big, roomy patterns that will fit the boy in comfort. An exceptional value.

GENUINE BROADCLOTH

93c 33K1426—Fancy patterns.
Sizes, 12, 12½, 13, 13½ and 14 inches neck measure. State size. Shipping weight, ¾ pound.
Boys' Genuine Cotton Broadcloth Dress Shirts in attractive patterns. Made coat style with attached soft collar and soft single cuffs. Broadcloth shirts are famous for long wear and fine appearance. They are the most practical shirts on the market and are a real value. Tie not included.

GENUINE BROADCLOTH

85c
33K1423—White.
33K1424—Tan.
33K1425—Blue.
Sizes, 12, 12½, 13, 13½ and 14 inches neck measure. State size. Shipping weight, ¾ pound.
Boys' Genuine Cotton Broadcloth Plain Color Dress Shirts in coat style with attached soft collar and soft single cuffs. Neat durable shirts that will give real service, always look attractive and are comfortable fitting as they are made over big, roomy sizes. Tie not included.

55c
33K1019—Gray.
33K1021—Blue.
Sizes, 12½, 13, 13½, and 14 inches neck measure. State size. Shipping weight, ¾ pound.
Boys' Work Shirts. Made of a good quality chambray shirting in big, roomy sizes that will fit comfortably. Well made in every way and a wonderful value at this low price.

See Index and Information Pages 42 to 570

Sweaters for Boys and Youths

How to Order Sweaters for Boys and Youths

Boys' sizes are from 24 to 34 inches chest measure and are made to fit boys from 5 to 13 years old only.

Youths' sizes are 34 and 36 inches chest measure, and are made to fit boys 14, 15 and 16 years old only. **To get correct size, measure around chest under armpits when wearing a shirt or blouse and then order the next larger size; for instance, if chest measure is 30 or 31 inches, order size 32.** By following these instructions you will receive a sweater that will fit properly.

For Boys' Clothing See Pages 345 to 363

$1.69
83K1735 Maroon.
83K1736 Dark brown.
83K1737 Navy blue.

Sizes, 24 to 34 in. chest measure. **State size.** Shipping weight, 1½ pounds.

Boys' Wool and Cotton Shawl Collar Style Sweater Coat. Well made garment knitted of good cotton yarns with a small amount of wool. Will give good service. The price is low.

$1.59 83K1810—Seal brown. 83K1811—Leather tan.

Sizes, 24 to 34 inches chest measure. **State size.** Shpg. wt., 1¾ lbs.

Boys' Fine Quality Heavy Weight Fleeced Back Cotton Jersey Cloth Lumberjack Style Sweater Jacket. A good warm outdoor garment that will keep the boy comfortable in cold weather. Has regular shirt collar with snug fitting ribbed bottom and cuffs. Two pockets.

$1.75 83K1756—Brown. 83K1757—Leather tan.

Same as above, but in youths' sizes, 34 and 36 inches chest measure to fit boys 14, 15 and 16 years of age. **State size.** Shipping wt., 1¾ lbs.

89c 83K1860 Maroon. 83K1861 Brown.
83K1862—Navy blue.

Sizes, 24 to 34 inches chest measure. **State size.** Shipping weight, 1¼ pounds.

Boys' Medium Weight Cotton Pullover Style Shawl Collar Sweaters. Sturdy, serviceable garments designed for rough wear. Priced very low.

$1.39 83K1717 Dark gray. 83K1718 Brown.

Sizes, 24 to 34 inches chest measure. **State size.** Shpg. wt., 1½ lbs.

Boys' Fine Fleeced Back Cotton Jersey Sport Coat. Cut and tailored like a coat, with two pockets and regular coat cuffs. A low priced sport coat that is sturdy, serviceable and attractive.

89c 83K1712 Light oxford.

Sizes, 24 to 34 inches chest measure. **State size.** Shipping weight, 1¼ lbs.

Boys' Medium Weight Shawl Collar Cotton Sweater Coat. A low priced durable sweater with two pockets. Suitable for the rough wear boys usually give their clothes.

Descriptions of Bargains on Opposite Page

$2.75 EACH 83K1850 Navy with orange trim. 83K1851 Brown with buff trim. 83K1852—Maroon with navy blue trim.

Sizes, 24 to 34 inches chest measure. **State size.** Shipping weight, 1¾ pounds.

(A) Boys' Durable All Wool Medium Weight Pullover Style Sweater. Shawl collar. Has contrasting color cuffs, bottom and collar stripe. One of the best values on the market for those desiring service and durability.

$3.48 EACH 83K1815 Blue and green. 83K1816 Buff and green.

Sizes, 24 to 34 inches chest measure. **State size.** Shipping weight, 1¾ pounds.

(B) Boys' Heavy Weight All Wool Lumberjack Style Sweater Jacket. Has convertible collar and two buttoned pockets. A warm outdoor garment in a very attractive pattern that will please the boy immensely.

89c 83K4900 Blue and green. 83K4901 Buff and green.

(C) Shipping weight, 6 oz. All wool Caps to match Jackets listed above.

$4.59 EACH 83K1825 Navy with white trim. 83K1826 Maroon with white trim. 83K1827—Dark green with white trim.

Sizes, 24 to 34 inches chest measure. **State size.** Shipping weight, 2¼ pounds.

(D) The popular "Crew Neck V Type" Shaker Knit Pullover Sweater for boys. An attractive and up to date garment knitted of high grade wool and wool worsted yarns. Hand finished and fashioned throughout. Very suitable for all athletic wear.

89c EACH 83K4902 Navy with white trim. 83K4903 Maroon with white trim. 83K4904—Dark green with white trim.

(E) Shipping weight, 7 oz. Wool and wool worsted Caps to match Sweaters listed above.

$3.50 EACH 83K1855 Maroon. 83K1856 Navy Blue. 83K1857—Seal brown.

Sizes, 24 to 34 inches chest measure. **State size.** Shipping weight, 2¼ pounds.

(F) Boys' Durable All Wool Sweater Coat in a medium weight. Has shawl collar and two pockets. A warm, serviceable sweater at a very moderate price. You will find this garment very satisfactory.

$3.79 EACH 83K1880 Brown. 83K1881 Maroon. 83K1882—Navy.

Same as above, but in youths' sizes, 34 and 36 in. chest measure to fit boys 14, 15 and 16 years of age. **State size.** Shipping wt., 2½ lbs.

$4.98 EACH 83K1713 Seal brown with buff trim. 83K1719 Navy blue with orange trim. 83K1835—Plain maroon. 83K1836—Plain navy blue. 83K1837—Plain seal brown.

Sizes, 24 to 34 inches chest measure. **State size.** Shipping weight, 2 pounds.

(G) Boys' Fine Quality Heavy Weight Wool and Wool Worsted Shaker Knit Pullover Style Sweater. A full fashioned hand finish sweater with large shawl collar. Made of very fine wool and worsted yarns and can be had in plain colors, or with contrasting trim as quoted above.

$1.48 EACH 83K1838 Buff with brown check. 83K1839 Pearl gray with powder blue check.

Sizes, 24 to 34 inches chest measure. **State size.** Shipping weight, 1 pound.

(H) Boys' Checked Pattern V Neck Cricket Sweater. Made of a firm fabric knitted of wool worsted and cotton yarns. An attractive sweater that is very inexpensive.

$2.19 EACH 83K1791 Navy blue. 83K1792 Maroon. 83K1793—Dark brown.

Sizes, 24 to 34 inches chest measure. **State size.** Shipping weight, 2¼ pounds.

(J) Boys' Medium Weight Shawl Collar Sweater Coat. Knitted of good quality mixed yarns containing about one-third wool. Has two pockets and ribbed cuffs. A good serviceable coat at a very moderate price.

$2.19 EACH 83K1741 Silver gray. 83K1742 Powder blue. 83K1743—Tan.

Sizes, 24 to 34 inches chest measure. **State size.** Shipping weight, 1 pound.

(K) Fine Quality Fancy Pattern Cricket Style Sweater for boys. Made of fine wool worsted and cotton yarns with worsted and Rayon patterns. Very attractive and serviceable.

89c EACH 83K4959 Brown and buff. 83K4960 Navy and orange. 83K4961—Oxford and red.

Shipping weight, 7 oz.

(L) Boys' attractive sport Hockey Cap. Knit of fine quality yarn in double thickness with two-tone crown. A splendid cap that will give service as well as warmth.

$1.89 EACH 83K1895 Leather tan. Sizes, 24 to 34 inches chest measure. **State size.** Shipping wt., 2 pounds.

(M) Boys' Novelty Pattern Lumberjack Style Sweater jacket. Made of heavy weight fleeced back cotton Jersey cloth with regular shirt collar and snug fitting bottom and cuffs. The pattern is very attractive and every boy will certainly be delighted to wear one of these sweaters.

$2.98 EACH 83K1858 Fancy tan. 83K1859 Fancy gray.

Sizes, 24 to 34 inches chest measure. **State size.** Shipping weight, 1 pound.

(N) Fine Quality Wool Worsted Slipover Style Cricket Sweater. Knit of fine quality wool worsted and Rayon yarns, making a very bright and attractive pattern. Will please the boy immensely.

50c EACH 83K4937 Brown and buff. 83K4938 Navy blue and orange. 83K4939—Maroon and oxford gray. 83K4947—Maroon.

Shipping weight, 6 ounces.

(P) Boys' Jumbo Stitch Hockey Cap. Knit of a good quality all wool yarn in double thickness. A good serviceable cap that is priced very low.

Popular Styles
in Boys' Sports Wear

A $2.75 EACH

B Jacket $3.48

C Cap 89¢ EACH

D Sweater $4.59 EACH

E Cap 89¢ EACH

F $3.50 EACH

G $4.98

H $1.48

J $2.19 EACH

K $2.19 EACH

L 89¢ EACH

M $1.89

N $2.98 EACH

P 50¢ EACH

See Opposite Page for Descriptions

Men's Flannel Shirts

Pilgrim Brand BEST MAKE FLANNEL SHIRTS

Extra Value

$1.69 EACH

83K740—Blue.
83K741—Gray.
83K742—Khaki.

Sizes, 14 to 17 inches neck measure. Half sizes. **State size.** Shipping weight, 1½ pounds.

A real value in a Two-Flap Pocket Flannel Shirt. Made of a good quality, medium weight flannel containing about one-fourth wool, in big roomy dimensions that will fit comfortably. Has two large army style button-through flap pockets and interlined collar and cuffs. A serviceable flannel shirt at a very low price.

$1.85 83K748—Gray.
83K749—Khaki.

Same as above, but made with extra long body and sleeves to fit the tall slim man.

All Wool Broadcloth

$4.45 EACH

83K784—Slate (Gray).
83K785—Brown.
83K786—Tan.

Sizes, 14 to 17 inches neck measure. Half sizes. **State size.** Shpg. wt., 1¾ lbs.

Fine Quality All Wool Broadcloth Flannel Shirt. Made of one of the finest all wool broadcloths on the market, in coat style with two large button-through flap pockets and trimmed with fine vegetable ivory buttons. A high grade warm flannel shirt at a low price that represents a real saving.

All Wool

$3.69 EACH

83K732—Greenish gray.
83K733—Brown.
83K734—Tan.

Sizes, 14 to 17 inches neck measure. Half sizes. **State size.** Shipping weight, 1½ pounds.

High Grade All Wool Flannel Shirt in neat checked patterns. Medium heavyweight all wool in coat style, with two large button-through flap pockets. For the man who desires conservative patterns. Very warm and durable and made over roomy sizes.

Men's Lumberjacks

BUCKSKEIN JACKET

BUCKSKEIN

Army Serge

$3.98 EACH

83K850—Khaki tan.

Sizes, 14 to 17 inches neck measure. Half sizes. **State size.** Shipping weight, 1½ pounds.

Our Finest Quality Army Style Flannel Shirt made of a high grade half wool army serge flannel. Made coat style with two large button-through flap pockets and extra patch on elbow. A real army style flannel shirt that cannot be excelled for wear.

Buckskein Jacket

$4.95 EACH

83K802—Khaki.
83K803—Gray.

Sizes, 14 to 17 inches neck measure. Half sizes. Order same size as you would in a shirt. **State size.** Shipping weight, 1½ pounds.

The Famous "Buckskein" Lumberjack Style Shirt Jacket at a big saving. A practical outer garment made of double weight Buckskein fabric, a special cloth that has the appearance and feel of soft finish suede leather. Practically windproof.

All Wool Lumberjack

$4.69 EACH

83K757—Brown.
83K758—Green.

Sizes, 14 to 17 inches neck measure. Half sizes. Order same size as you would in a shirt. **State size.** Shipping weight, 2 pounds.

Heavyweight All Wool Flannel Lumberjack Style Shirt Jacket in attractive plaid patterns. A heavy and warm outdoor garment to be worn over shirt. Convertible collar and two large button-through flap pockets. Snug fitting wool worsted bottom.

Buckskein Shirt

$2.95 EACH

83K886—Khaki tan.
83K887—Gray.

Sizes, 14 to 17 inches neck measure. Half sizes. **State size.** Shipping weight, 1½ pounds.

The Nationally Advertised Genuine "Buckskein" Flannel Shirt at a big saving. Made of a soft medium weight cotton flannel that has the appearance and feel of soft suede leather and is practically windproof and very warm. Will not shrink after repeated washings and makes an unusually satisfactory shirt.

and Flannel Lumberjacks

Heavy Weight

$2.89 EACH

83K715—Khaki.
83K716—Gray.

Sizes, 14 to 17 inches neck measure. Half sizes. State size. Shipping weight, 1¾ pounds.

Heavyweight Standard Flannel Shirts in attractive plaid patterns. Heavyweight twilled flannel shirts with a cotton warp and wool and cotton mixed weighting. Coat style with two large button-through flap pockets. Big roomy sizes. Attractive shirts that will wear well and keep you warm.

Broadcloth Finish

$2.69 EACH

83K845—Khaki tan.
83K877—Gray.
83K878—Navy blue.
83K879—Green.

Sizes, 14 to 17 inches neck measure. Half sizes. Shipping weight, 1½ pounds.

Fine Quality Broadcloth Finish Flannel Shirts made of medium weight flannel containing about one-half wool. Made coat style with two large army style button-through flap pockets. High grade serviceable flannel shirts that will always give the best of satisfaction.

Regular and Extra Sizes

$3.85

83K855—Brown.
83K856—Gray.
83K858—Green.

Sizes, 14 to 17 inches neck measure. Half sizes. State size. Shipping weight, 1½ pounds.

High Grade All Wool Flannel Shirts in very attractive patterns and colorings. Made of a medium heavyweight all wool flannel that is warm and will give good service. These shirts are made in the convenient coat style with two large button-through flap pockets. They are big, roomy shirts that will fit comfortably.

$4.25

83K852—Brown.
83K853—Gray.

Same as above, but in extra sizes, 17½ to 20. Half sizes. State size. Shipping weight, 1½ pounds.

These shirts are designed to fit the extra large men in comfort.

Men's Lumberjacks

Corduroy Shirt

$2.89 EACH

83K896—Tan.
83K897—Gray.
83K898—Brown.

Sizes, 14 to 17 inches neck measure. Half sizes. State size. Shipping weight, 1¼ pounds.

Men's Good Grade Washable Corduroy Shirts in closed front style with two large button-through pockets. Matched buttons. Popular for school and college as well as for men who require shirts that will stand lots of hard wear.

Fine Wool Lumberjack

$5.95 EACH

83K796—Gray, black and red.
83K797—Tan and blue.

Sizes, 14 to 17 inches neck measure. Half sizes. Order same size as you would in a shirt. State size. Shpg. wt., 2 lbs.

Very High Grade Heavy Weight Fancy Lumberjack Style Shirt Jacket. Made of a fine virgin wool flannel in an unusually bright and attractive pattern. A snappy outdoor garment to be worn over your shirt. Has convertible collar and two large button-through flap pockets. Fine wool worsted knit bottom.

Heavy Lumberjack

$4.95 EACH

83K735—Gray plaid.
83K736—Brown plaid.

Sizes, 14 to 17 inches neck measure. Half sizes.

Order same size as you would in a shirt. State size. Shpg. wt., 2 lbs.

Extra Heavy Weight All Wool Lumberjack Style Shirt Jacket. The flannel is extra heavy and extra warm and the plaid patterns are exceptionally suitable for this style jacket. Has convertible collar and two large button-through flap pockets. Snug fitting wool worsted bottom. A heavy outdoor garment.

All Wool Broadcloth

$4.95 EACH

83K830—Tan and blue.
83K831—Gray and tan.

Sizes, 14 to 17 inches neck measure. Half sizes. State size. Shpg. wt., 1¾ lbs.

Very High Grade All Wool Broadcloth Flannel Shirts in beautiful patterns and colorings. One of the finest broadcloth flannels manufactured and has a very rich and attractive appearance. For those who prefer the finest in fancy flannel shirts. Made coat style with two large button-through flap pockets.

Broadcloth Dress Shirts
The Modern Shirting Modestly Priced

$1 59 33K410 — Blue figure.
33K411 — Lavender figure.
33K412 — Tan figure.
Sizes, 14 to 17 inches neck measure. Half sizes. **State size.** Shpg. wt., ¾ lb.
Genuine Broadcloth Dress Shirts in a fancy white dobby weave with colored figured pattern. Made with attached soft collar and soft single cuffs. Made in our very best style and dimensions. You will find the appearance and wearing qualities of these shirts unsurpassed.

95c 33K400 — White.
33K401 — Tan.
Sizes, 14 to 17 inches neck measure. Half sizes. **State size.** Shpg. wt., ¾ lb.
Genuine Plain Color Cotton Broadcloth Dress Shirts with attached soft collar and soft single cuffs. Made of a good quality American broadcloth shirting over our regular roomy, well fitting patterns. Well made, good wearing dress shirts at a money saving price. You cannot go wrong in buying broadcloth shirts if long wear and good appearance are desired. Made in the well liked coat style.

95c 33K404 — White.
33K405 — Tan.
Sizes, 14 to 17 inches neck measure. Half sizes. **State size.** Shpg. wt., ¾ lb.
Genuine Cotton Broadcloth Dress Shirts in neckband style with soft double cuffs. Made of a good quality American broadcloth shirting over our regular roomy dimensions that will fit you in comfort. At our low price these shirts are an exceptional value. Coat style.

It's a Real Economy to Buy Largely

$1 45 33K170 — White.
33K171 — Tan.
Sizes, 14 to 17 inches neck measure. Half sizes. **State size.** Shpg. wt., ¾ lb.
Fine Quality Imported English Cotton Broadcloth Dress Shirts in neckband style with soft double cuffs. High grade broadcloth dress shirts with unusual wearing qualities and fine appearance that are exceptional values. Coat style.

Double Cuffs

$1 89 33K125 — White.
33K126 — Tan.
33K127 — Blue.
Sizes, 14 to 17 inches neck measure. Half sizes. State size. Shipping weight, ¾ pound.
Attached Collar Shirts with soft double cuffs. Made of a fine full count imported English cotton broadcloth. For those who desire the comfort of an attached soft collar with the dressy appearance of the soft double cuffs. The broadcloth is one of the finest on the market and has a beautiful appearance and wonderful wearing qualities. Coat style.

Slim

$1 45 33K173 — White.
33K174 — Tan.
33K175 — Blue.
Sizes, 14 to 17 inches neck measure. Half sizes. **State size.** Shpg. wt., ¾ lb.
Fine Quality Imported English Cotton Broadcloth Dress Shirts with attached soft collar and soft single cuffs. A fine count imported shirting. Unusually fine appearance and wearing qualities. Will launder beautifully and always keep its fine finish. Coat style. Tie not included.

$1 57 33K509 — Gray stripe.
33K510 — Blue stripe.
33K512 — Tan stripe.
Sizes, 14 to 17 inches neck measure. Half sizes. **State size.** Shpg. wt., ¾ lb.
Genuine Cotton Broadcloth Fancy Pattern Dress Shirts with attached soft collar and soft single cuffs. Coat style. The broadcloth is of excellent quality and the patterns are the newest and most attractive. These shirts are very serviceable and we feel sure will please you in every way. Tie not included.

$1 79 33K440 — White.
33K441 — Tan.
Sizes, 14 to 18 inches neck measure. Half sizes. **State size.** Shpg. wt., ¾ lb.
Slim Size Dress Shirts made of genuine imported English cotton broadcloth with attached soft collar and soft single cuffs. Made with extra long body and extra long sleeves and carefully designed to fit the extra tall man. Coat style.

$1 89 33K527 — White.
33K528 — Tan.
Sizes, 17½ to 20 inches neck measure. Half sizes. **State size.** Shipping weight, ¾ pound.
Extra Large Size Dress Shirts made of genuine imported English cotton broadcloth with attached soft collar and soft single cuffs. Coat style. These shirts are made bigger in every way and are carefully designed to fit the large man in comfort.

Extra Large

OUR FAMOUS TRIPLE STITCHED WORK SHIRTS
HERCULES
Our Own Trade Mark

- LINED COLLAR
- DOUBLE YOKE
- FULL CUT ARM HOLES NO BINDING
- GENUINE VEGETABLE IVORY BUTTONS
- OVERSIZE BODY DIMENSIONS
- ONE PIECE NON-RIP SLEEVE FACING
- ALL PRINCIPAL SEAMS TRIPLE STITCHED
- EXTRA LONG SIDE SEAM WILL NOT PULL OUT
- EVERY SHIRT EXTRA LONG
- TWO LARGE POCKETS WITH BUTTONS
- CELEBRATED HERCULES HEAVYWEIGHT CHAMBRAY
- EXTRA LARGE LINED CUFFS

HERCULES GUARANTEED WORK SHIRTS. SOLD EXCLUSIVELY BY SEARS, ROEBUCK and CO. THIS LABEL IN EVERY SHIRT

89c 33K620—Blue. 33K624—Gray.
Sizes, 14½ to 17. Half sizes. **State size.** Shipping weight, 1 pound.
The Famous Hercules Triple Stitched Heavy Weight Chambray Closed Front Work Shirts. Made of one of the finest heavyweight chambrays manufactured, a cloth that has made many friends for Hercules shirts. With all the practical Hercules features it is absolutely the best work shirt value on the market today, and one of the most popular.

Slim Sizes

Extra Large Sizes

98c 33K636—Blue. 33K637—Gray.
Sizes, 14½ to 17. Half sizes. State size. Shipping weight, 1 pound.
Our Hercules Triple Stitched Heavyweight Chambray Shirts for the tall men who need shirts with longer body and longer sleeves. Made of our fine quality heavyweight chambray and carefully designed to fit the taller man in comfort.

98c 33K629—Blue. 33K630—Gray.
Extra sizes, 17½ to 20. Half sizes. State size. Shipping weight, 1 pound.
Our Hercules Triple Stitched Extra Size Work Shirts. Made of our fine quality heavyweight chambray in extra large neck sizes and extra large body dimensions that are carefully designed to fit the larger men in comfort. Coat style with center pleat all the way down.

Coat Style

98c 33K623—Black sateen.
Sizes, 14½ to 17. Half sizes. State size. Shipping weight, 1 pound.
Our Hercules Triple Stitched Sateen Work Shirts. Made of a fine quality lustrous sateen shirting, an excellent piece of cloth that will give unusually long service and makes exceptionally high grade work shirts.

93c 33K627—Blue with white polka dots.
Sizes, 14½ to 17. Half sizes. State size. Shipping weight, ¾ pound.
Our Hercules Triple Stitched Polka Dot Work Shirts. Made coat style of genuine Stifel polka dot shirting. The well known wearing qualities of Stifel cloth, with the practical Hercules features, make a shirt that is hard to excel for both wearing qualities and appearance.

HERCULES GUARANTEED WORK SHIRTS

89c 33K634—Gray plaid. 33K635—Tan plaid.
Sizes, 14½ to 17. Half sizes. State size. Shpg. wt., 1 lb.
Our Hercules Triple Stitched Fancy Chambray Work Shirts. Made of heavyweight Chambray in neat plaid patterns with all the practical and useful Hercules features.

98c 33K639—Tan sateen.
Sizes, 14½ to 17. Half sizes. State size. Shipping weight, 1 pound.
In these Hercules Triple Stitched Sateen Work Shirts are all the features pictured in the large illustration. Made of fine lustrous sateen shirting of an unusual quality that will give long, hard service. Fine, hard wearing work shirts.

93c 33K622 Khaki.
Sizes, 14½ to 17. Half sizes. State size. Shpg. wt., ¾ lb.
Our Hercules Triple Stitched Khaki Twill Work Shirts for good service. The cloth is an excellent piece of sulphur dyed khaki twill cut on a good fitting, comfortable pattern, with all the Hercules features. Makes very practical all around shirts. A good value at our low price.

93c 33K642 Blue. 33K643 Gray.
Sizes, 14½ to 17. Half sizes. State size. Shipping weight, 1 pound.
Our Hercules Triple Stitched Coat Style Work Shirts. Made of our fine quality heavyweight chambray in the popular and convenient coat style with center pleat all the way down. Fine for general everyday wear, in practical colors that wash well. For comfortable fitting and long wearing qualities these Hercules shirts cannot be excelled. Priced for a worth while saving.

A man doesn't buy a work shirt to be a good fellow. He buys the best he can get for his money. When he has found that he keeps on buying it. That's why our Hercules sales are higher every season. All the strong features in the big picture are found in every Hercules Shirt on this page.

Garments for Large Men
See also following pages:
Dress clothing .365, 378 and 384;
Work clothing .389, 391, 396 and 397;
Underwear .274 and 279.

Coat Style

SUPREME KNIT WEAR BEST MADE

Quality Sweaters
Moderately Priced

$2.29 EACH   83K1690—Maroon   83K1692—Navy blue   83K1693—Brown

Sizes, 34 to 46 inches chest measure. **State size.** Shipping weight, 2½ pounds.

Men's Medium Weight Half Wool V Neck Sweater Coats. Two pockets. Handy, serviceable sweater coats for all around wear at a very low price. You will find these coats to be very practical.

For Measuring Instructions on Men's Sweaters See Page 438.

$4.50 EACH   83K1637—Maroon   83K1638—Navy blue   83K1639—Seal Brown

Sizes, 34 to 46 inches chest measure. **State size.** Shpg. wt., 2¾ lbs.

Men's Serviceable All Wool Sweater Coat in a medium heavy weight, with large shawl collar and two pockets. These garments have always given very satisfactory service for many years, and at this low price are a most exceptional value. For all around service and warmth they cannot be excelled.

$3.98 EACH   83K1695—Navy blue   83K1696—Black   83K1697—Maroon

Sizes, 34 to 46 inches chest measure. **State size.** Shpg. wt., 3 lbs.

Fine All Wool V Neck Pullover Style Shaker Knit Sweaters at a real saving. Hand Finished and fashioned throughout. Made of all wool yarns. Everyone should have one of these practical, serviceable outdoor garments, which we are offering at an attractive low price, as he will find plenty of uses for it.

$4.98 EACH   83K1502—Navy blue   83K1503—Brown   83K1504—Maroon

Sizes, 34 to 46 inches chest measure. **State size.** Shpg. wt., 3½ lbs.

A wonderful value in an All Wool Hand Finished Shaker Knit Sweater Coat. A heavy coat made of all wool yarns and hand finished throughout. Large shawl collar and two knit-in pockets. Warm and serviceable and the price is exceptionally low.

$2.85 EACH   83K1614—Brown   83K1615—Maroon   83K1617—Navy

Sizes, 34 to 46 inches chest measure. **State size.** Shipping weight, 2¾ pounds.

Men's Medium Weight Sweater Coat made of mixed yarns containing about an equal amount of wool and cotton. Have ribbed cuffs and rack stitched bottom. Shawl collar and two pockets. Serviceable sweaters that have always given satisfaction.

$7.98 EACH   83K1571—Cardinal with black and white trim   83K1572—Navy blue with cardinal and gray trim   83K1573—Dark green with buff and cardinal trim

Sizes, 34 to 46 inches chest measure. **State size.** Shipping weight, 3½ pounds.

Fine Quality Wool and Wool Worsted Shaker Knit Sweater Coat. Full fashioned and hand finished throughout. Has large shawl collar and two pockets. Very attractive two-color stripings on collar, cuffs and bottom.

Shaker Sweaters
Full Fashioned ~ Hand Finished

$7.45 EACH
83K1508 Navy blue.
83K1509 Maroon.
83K1510—Black.

Sizes, 34 to 46 inches chest measure. State size. Shipping weight, 3 pounds.

High Grade Wool and Wool Worsted Shaker Knit "V" Neck Sweater Coat. Full fashioned and hand finished throughout. Two set-in pockets. A very fine quality shaker coat that is very practical and serviceable for the man who wants a heavy weighted sweater coat without a collar.

For Measuring Instructions See Page 438

$5.98 EACH
83K1580—Navy with orange trim.
83K1581—Gray with scarlet trim.
83K1582—Cardinal with white trim.
83K1583—Dark green with white trim.
83K1584—Old gold with black trim.
83K1585—Maroon with white trim.

Sizes, 34 to 46 inches chest measure. State size. Shipping weight, 2½ pounds.

The New Popular "Crew V" Shaker Pullover Sweater. Adopted by many colleges and high schools throughout the country. Made of high grade wool and worsted yarns and is hand fashioned and finished in the best manner possible. We can save you money on this practical garment.

$7.69
83K1630—Navy blue.
83K1631—Maroon.
83K1632—Black.
83K1633—Old gold.
83K1634—Cardinal.
83K1635—Dark green.

Sizes, 34 to 46 inches chest measure. State size. Shipping weight, 3½ pounds.

Very Fine Quality Heavyweight Shaker Knit Sweater Coat. Knitted from highest quality wool and worsted yarns. Has large shawl collar and knit-in pockets. Hand finished throughout. For appearance, warmth, and length of service a shaker knit sweater stands alone. This is a good shaker sweater. We carry in stock six popular and most wanted colors.

$5.98
83K1680—Navy blue.
83K1681—Maroon.
83K1682—Black.
83K1683—Old gold.
83K1684—Cardinal.
83K1685—Dark green.

Sizes, 34 to 46 inches measure. State size. Shipping weight, 2¾ pounds.

Very Fine Quality Heavyweight Wool and Wool Worsted Shaker Knit Pullover Sweater. An athletic sweater in "V" neck style that is very popular as an honor sweater throughout the schools and colleges of the country. A most handy and practical garment for all outdoor wear. Full fashioned and hand finished throughout.

$10.00 EACH
83K1545—Maroon.
83K1546—Seal brown.
83K1547—Navy blue.
83K1563—Buff.

Sizes, 34 to 46 inches chest measure. State size. Shipping weight, 3¼ pounds.

Our Finest Quality Heavyweight All Wool Worsted Shaker Knit Sweater Coat. A full fashioned, hand finished garment. Knit of a very fine quality yarn. Has large shawl collar and two knit-in pockets. As fine a shaker sweater as can be made, priced extremely low.

$9.85 EACH
83K1560—Seal brown.
83K1561—Navy blue.
83K1562—Maroon.

Sizes, 34 to 46 inches chest measure. State size. Shipping weight, 3¼ pounds.

Men's Lined Shaker Coat. A High Grade Heavyweight Wool and Wool Worsted Shaker Knit Sweater. Body is lined with contrasting color pure worsted knitted jersey cloth and makes a very warm outdoor garment. Is full fashioned and hand finished throughout. Has large shawl collar and two knit-in pockets.

Rich-Colorful-Handsome
Unusual Values

See Opposite Page for Descriptions

Quality Mufflers

A $4.98 EACH

B $3.98 EACH

C $3.39 EACH

D $2.35

E $7.95 EACH

F $2.19 EACH

G $1.89 EACH

H $3.98

J $2.98

K $1.45

L $1.25

M $1.79 EACH

Descriptions of Bargains on Opposite Page

$4.98 EACH
83K1591—Buff.
83K1592—Powder blue.
Sizes, 34 to 46 inches chest measure. State size. Shipping weight, 1¾ pounds.
(A) Men's Fancy All Wool Worsted Lumberjack Style Knitted Sport Jacket. Has convertible collar that can be worn open or closed, two pockets and snug fitting knitted bottoms. Very popular knockabout garments.

$3.98 EACH
83K1654—Powder blue mixture.
83K1655—Tan mixture.
Sizes, 34 to 46 inches chest measure. State size. Shipping weight, 1¼ pounds.
(B) A combination of snappy style and distinctive patterns and colorings are emphasized in this high grade All Worsted V Neck Cricket Sweater. Made of fine quality all wool worsted yarns with worsted and Rayon Jacquard patterns. The attractive blending of color and patterns will please you and we know our price represents a saving. One of the most attractive sweaters ever designed for sport wear.

$3.39 EACH
83K1646—Buff.
83K1647—Powder blue.
Sizes, 34 to 46 inches chest measure. State size. Shipping weight, 1¼ pounds.
(C) Men's All Wool Worsted V Neck Cricket Style Pullover Sweater. The fancy patterns and colors are very attractive.

$2.35 EACH
83K1590—Tan.
Sizes, 34 to 46 inches chest measure. State size. Shpg. wt., 2½ lbs.
(D) Men's Heavy Weight Fleeced Back Cotton Jersey Lumberjack Style Sweater Jacket in attractive pattern as illustrated. Has regular shirt collar and snug fitting ribbed cuffs and bottoms. An ideal garment for outdoor wear, as it is practically windproof.

$7.95 EACH
83K1686—White.
83K1687—Buff.
83K1688—Pearl gray.
Sizes, 34 to 46 inches chest measure. State size. Shipping weight, 2½ pounds.
(E) Something new in Shaker Sweaters. An all wool crew neck pullover style shaker knit sweater in attractive knitted-in Jacquard patterns. The contrasting colored Jacquard patterns and the warmth and wear of these serviceable garments, make them very attractive.

$2.19 EACH
33K9516—Plaid patterns.
33K9518—Jacquard patterns.
Colors: Blue, gray or tan. State color. Shipping weight, ¾ pound.
(F) Excellent Quality Cashmere or Flannel Mufflers in attractive plaid patterns or Jacquard designs. Imported from Europe. A high grade warm muffler woven of fine quality soft wool yarns.

$1.89 EACH
33K9509—Figured patterns.
33K9510—Polka dot.
Colors: Blue, white, gray or tan. State color. Shipping weight, 8 ounces.
(G) High Grade Washable Radium Silk Mufflers in the reefer or oblong style. Attractive printed figures or polka dots. Silk mufflers are very popular and the quality and patterns are sure to please you.

$3.98
33K9506—Fancy patterns.
Colors: White, blue or gray. State color. Size, about 34 inches square. Shipping weight, 8 ounces.
(H) A Beautiful All Silk Square Muffler in an attractive bordered design. This scarf is suitable for women as well as men. Made of a fine all silk crepe that is washable. One of the finest mufflers on the market. Square silk mufflers are new and very popular this season.

$2.98
33K9507—Fancy patterns.
Colors: Blue, white or gray. State color. Size, about 34 inches square. Shipping weight, 8 ounces.
(J) Washable Radium Silk Square Mufflers or Scarfs. Square mufflers are very fashionable this year and are worn by both men and women. Attractive figured design with border all around. A very suitable gift.

$1.45
33K9517
Colors: Blue, gray, tan or white. State color. Shipping weight, ¾ lb.
(K) A Fine Light Weight Wool Flannel and Rayon Muffler. Woven of good quality soft wool yarns with an attractive Jacquard pattern of Rayon. A sightly muffler that is very dressy.

$1.25
33K9508
Colors: Navy blue, pearl gray, black or white. State color. Shpg. wt., ¾ lb.
(L) Fine Weave Rayon Swiss Knitted Muffler. The weave of this muffler is such that it wrinkles very little, giving it a new and fresh appearance all the time. A high class dress muffler.

$1.79 EACH
83K1644—Gray with blue check.
83K1645—Buff with green check.
Sizes, 34 to 46 inches chest measure. State size. Shipping weight, 1¼ pounds.
(M) Men's V Neck Cricket Style Pullover Sweater made of wool worsted and cotton yarns in a neat checked pattern. The fabric is firm and makes a satisfactory sweater.

Men's Sleeping Garments

Well Made   **Full Sizes**

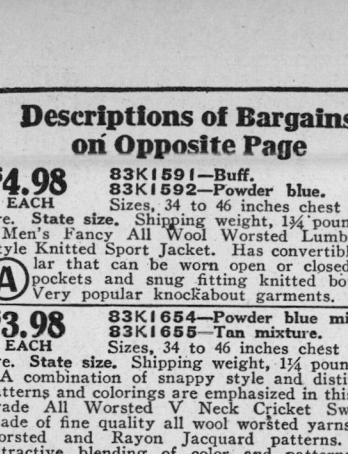

How to Order Pajamas

Neck Size	Chest Measure
15 inches	34-36 inches
16 inches	38-40 inches
17 inches	42-44 inches
18 inches	46-48 inches
19 inches	50 inches

$1.39
33K950—White.
33K951—Blue.
33K952—Tan.
Sizes, 15, 16, 17, 18 and 19. State size. See instructions on "How to Order" at top of page. Shipping weight, 1 lb.
Our popular plain color, light weight Cotton Pajamas. Made of excellent quality soft finish pajama cloth. Trimmed with four Rayon frog loops and pearl buttons. One pocket.

$1.29
33K960—White.
33K961—Blue.
33K962—Tan.
Sizes, 15 to 19. State size. See measuring instructions at top of page. Shipping weight, 1 pound.
Men's Slipover or Middy Pajamas. Made of excellent quality, plain color, soft finish cotton pajama cloth in large, roomy dimensions. Coat has one pocket. The buttonless pajama is becoming very popular. Try a suit now.

83c
33K905—White.
Sizes, 15, 16, 17, 18, 19 and 20. State size. Length, 50 inches. Shipping wt., ¾ lb.
Our Standard Quality White Muslin Nightshirt for men. Made collarless style and trimmed with fancy braid. One pocket. Full size dimensions and excellent workmanship make this, we think, the finest low priced garment on the market.

$2.25 Genuine Broadcloth
33K964 White broadcloth.
33K965 Blue broadcloth.
Mercerized Pongee
33K967 White cotton pongee.
33K968 Tan cotton pongee.
Sizes, 15 to 19. State size. See measuring instructions at top of page. Shipping weight, 1¼ pounds.
Men's High Grade Pajamas. Made either of fine count genuine broadcloth or of a soft mercerized cotton pongee, in plain colors. Have one pocket, Rayon frog loops and pearl buttons. These are quality pajamas and at our price you will be very well pleased with the savings.

$1.00
33K908—White.
Sizes, 15 to 20. State size. Length, 54 inches. Shipping weight, 1 pound.
Excellent Quality White Muslin Nightshirt. Made in large, roomy dimensions and trimmed with fancy braid, making a very attractive garment. This is a high grade nightshirt made bigger and better in every way and should be compared only with garments retailing at a higher price. An exceptional value.

Attractive Robes
Make Ideal Gifts

$10.98 33K1938 Blue and navy blue two-tone.
33K1939 Wine and blue two-tone.
Sizes, 34 to 48 in. chest measure. **State size.** Shipping weight, 2 pounds.
Men's Part Rayon Brocaded Lounging Robe made in a very neat pattern. The pocket trimming, collar, cuffs and underfacings are made of Skinners' satin. Rayon cord girdle. This robe would retail for a much higher price elsewhere and is a remarkable value at our price. Makes an appropriate gift for men.

33K1940 Navajo gray.
33K1941 Navy blue.
33K1942—Light brown.
$7.98
Sizes, 34 to 48 in. chest measure. **State size.** Shipping weight, 3½ pounds.
Men's Cord Trimmed Cotton Beacon Blanket Cloth Bathrobe in a new Indian pattern. This robe is offered in three popular ground colors with the typical Indian patterns of beautifully blended colorings. Has shawl collar and three pockets. Good quality cord girdle. All seams are reinforced.

$7.50 33K1920—Blue.
33K1921—Gray.
33K1922—Brown.
Sizes, 34 to 48 inches chest measure. State size. Shpg. wt., 4 lbs.
Men's Bathrobe and Slipper Set. Made of a fine quality cotton bordered blanket in a popular ombre or shaded pattern. Has large notch collar that can be worn two ways, as illustrated. Cord trimmings on collar, pockets, cuffs and front of robe. Rayon girdle and pearl buttons.

$5.79 33K1932—Blue.
33K1934—Brown.
Sizes, 34 to 48 inches chest measure. **State size.** Shipping weight, 3½ pounds.
A very low price for a Cotton Bordered Blanket Bathrobe. Made with large shawl collar and three pockets. Excellent quality Rayon cord girdle. A large and roomy garment, finely tailored. All seams are reinforced to prevent fraying.

$9.98 33K1950—Brown and tan double ombre.
33K1951—Blue and tan double ombre.
Sizes, 34 to 48 inches chest measure. State size. Shipping weight, 3¾ pounds.
Our Finest Shawl Collar Blanket Robe. Made of a heavyweight genuine Beacon double ombre cotton bordered blanket. The beautiful deep shaded pattern of well blended colors, cord trimming and fine Rayon cable and cord girdle make this a very rich looking robe. Finely tailored with all seams reinforced. Three pockets and pearl buttons. A high grade robe with plenty of warmth.

$3.98 33K1928—Blue and gray ombre.
33K1929—Brown and blue ombre.
Sizes, 34 to 48 inches chest measure. State size. Shipping weight, 3¼ pounds.
Men's Bathrobe made of good quality cotton blanket cloth in a very attractive new double ombre or shaded pattern. Has two large pockets and cord girdle. All seams reinforced. We believe this garment to be superior to any low priced robe on the market, as it is cut as large and tailored as well as the higher priced robes.

Do Your Christmas Shopping From This Catalog

445

The Latest Styles in Men's Collars

Semi-Soft Collars

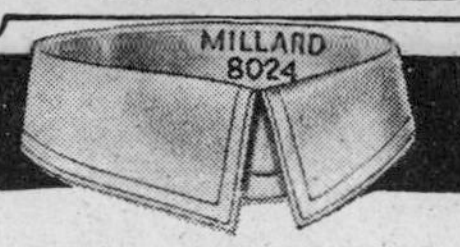
MILLARD
8024

69c FOR THREE 33K8024 Sizes, 12 to 17½. Half sizes. State size. Shipping wt. of three, 4 oz.
Semi-Soft Webbing Collar. Cotton inside band. Points, 2 inches; back, 1½ inches.

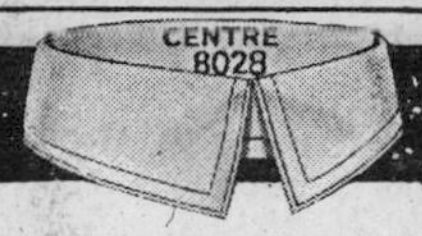
CENTRE
8028

69c FOR THREE 33K8028 Sizes, 14 to 17½. Half sizes. State size. Shipping wt. of three, 4 oz.
Semi-Soft Webbing Collar. Low inside band. Points, 2 inches; back, 1½ inches.

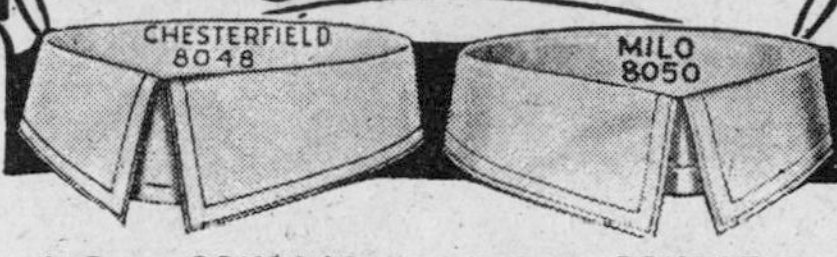
CHESTERFIELD
8048
MILO
8050

79c FOR THREE 33K8048 Sizes, 14 to 17½. Half sizes. State size. Shipping wt. three, 4 ounces.
Fine Webbing Semi-Soft Collar. Cotton inside band. Points, 2¼ inches; back, 1½ inches.

79c FOR THREE 33K8050 Sizes, 14 to 17½. Half sizes. State size. Shipping wt. three, 4 ounces.
Fine Webbing Semi-Soft Collar. Low cotton inside band. Points, 2 inches; back, 1½ inches.

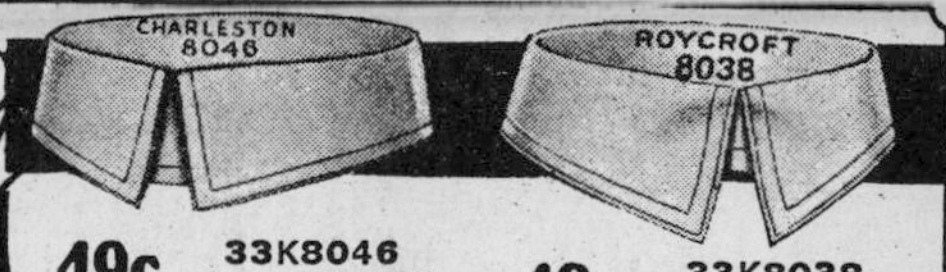
CHARLESTON
8046
ROYCROFT
8038

49c FOR THREE 33K8046 Sizes, 14 to 17½. Half sizes. State size. Shpg. wt. of three, 4 oz.
Semi-Soft Webbing Collar of good quality. Cotton inside band. Points, 2 inches; back, 1½ in.

49c FOR THREE 33K8038 Sizes, 12 to 17½. Half sizes. State size. Shpg. wt. of three, 4 oz.
Good Quality Semi-Soft Collar. Cotton inside band is low. Points, 2¼ in.; back, 1⅜ inches.

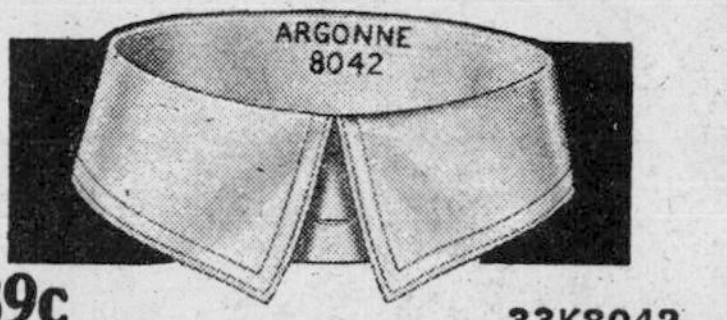
ARGONNE
8042

39c EACH 33K8042 Sizes, 14 to 17½. Quarter sizes to 15¾. State size. Shipping weight, 2 ounces.
Our Best All Webbing Semi-Soft Collar. One of the finest collars on the market. Points, 2 inches; back, 1½ inches.

Soft Collars

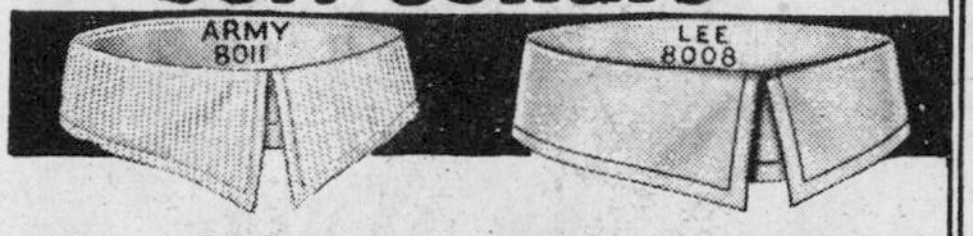
ARMY
8011
LEE
8008

65c FOR THREE 33K8011 Sizes, 14 to 17½. Half sizes. State size. Shpg. weight of three, 4 ounces.
Plain Pique Soft Collar. Front, 2½ inches; back, 1½ inches.

98c FOR SIX 33K8008 Sizes, 14 to 17½. Half sizes. State size. Shpg. weight of six, 6 ounces.
Quality Poplin Soft Collar. Points 2 inches; back, 1¼ inches.

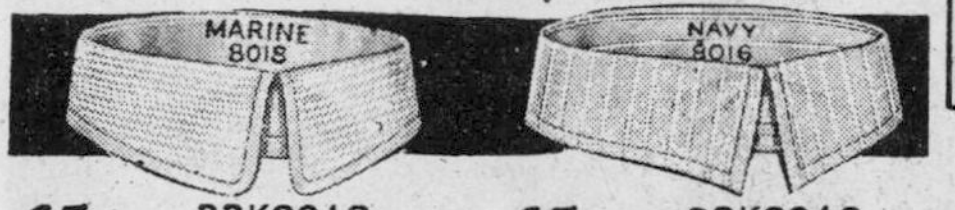
MARINE
8018
NAVY
8016

65c FOR THREE 33K8018 Sizes, 12 to 17½. Half sizes. State size. Shpg. weight of three, 4 ounces.
Plain Pique Soft Collar. Front, 2¼ inches; back, 1¾ inches.

65c FOR THREE 33K8016 Sizes, 14 to 17½. Half sizes. State size. Shpg. weight of three, 4 ounces.
Quality Pique Soft Collar. Points, 2 inches; back, 1¼ inches.

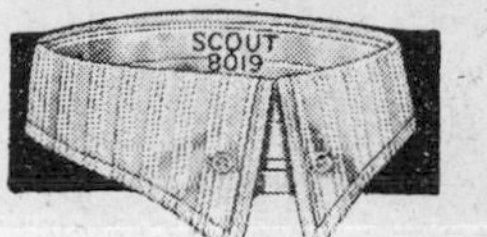
SCOUT
8019

65c FOR THREE 33K8019 Sizes, 14 to 17½. Half sizes. State size. Shpg. weight of three, 4 oz.
Good Looking Collar made of fine quality fancy pique. Buttons through to inside band. Points, 2½ inches; back, 1¾ inches.

Laundered Collars

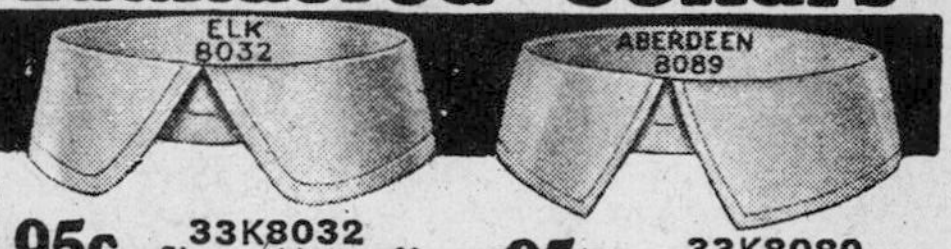
ELK
8032
ABERDEEN
8089

95c FOR SIX 33K8032 Sizes, 14 to 20. Quarter sizes to 15¾. State size. Shpg. wt. of six, ¾ lb.
Comfortable Collar. Low inside band. Front, 1¾ in.; back, 1½ inches.

95c FOR SIX 33K8089 Sizes, 14 to 20. Quarter sizes to 15¾. State size. Shpg. wt. of six, ¾ lb.
Stylish Collar with low inside band and medium points. Front, 2 inches; back, 1⅜ inches.

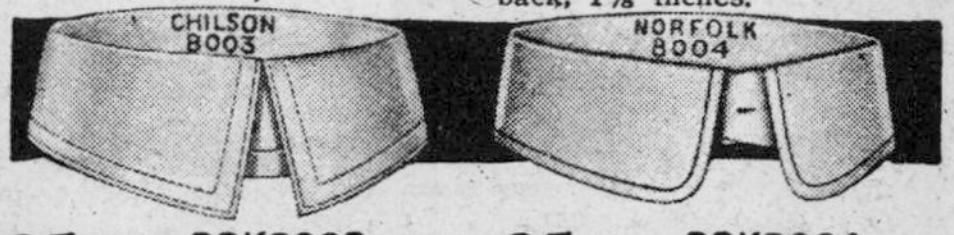
CHILSON
8003
NORFOLK
8004

95c FOR SIX 33K8003 Sizes, 14 to 18. Quarter sizes to 15¾. State size. Shpg. wt. of six, ¾ lb.
Neat Collar with lots of snap. Points, 2⅛ inches; back, 1⅝ inches.

95c FOR SIX 33K8004 Sizes, 14 to 18. Quarter sizes to 15¾. State size. Shpg. wt. of six, ¾ lb.
Dressy Collar of a popular shape. Low inside band. Points, 2 in.; back, 1½ in.

95c FOR SIX. 33K8077 Sizes, 14 to 19. Quarter sizes to 15¾. State size. Shpg. wt. of six, ¾ lb.
Our best selling Laundered Collar. A very neat, comfortable shape. Points, 2 inches; back, 1½ inches.

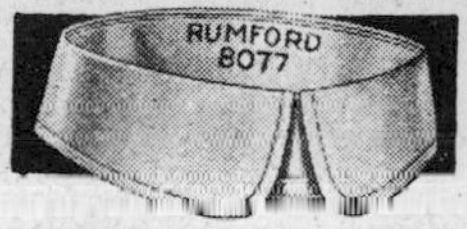
RUMFORD
8077

Semi-Stiff Collars

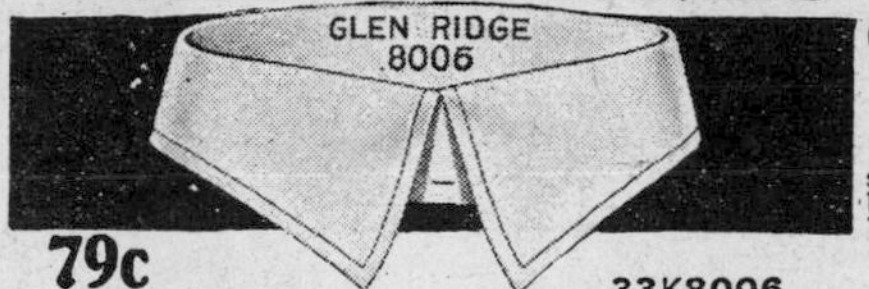
GLEN RIDGE
8006

79c FOR THREE 33K8006 Sizes, 14 to 18. Quarter sizes to 15¾. State size. Shpg. wt. of three, 4 oz.
Our "Super-Fine" quality light weight laundered collar. Will stand three times as much laundering as the ordinary starched collar. A comfortable shape. Points, 2⅜ inches; back, 1½ inches.

Silk Collars

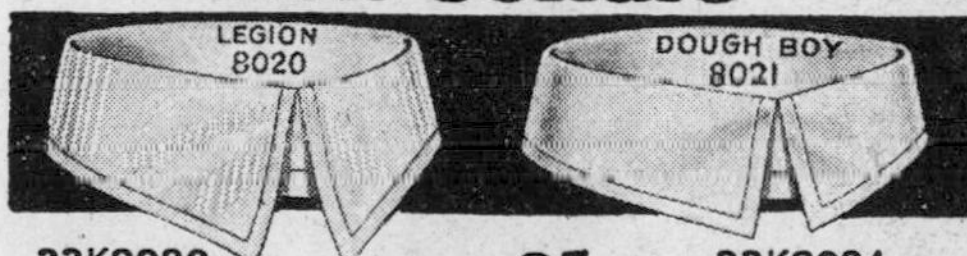
LEGION
8020
DOUGH BOY
8021

25c EACH 33K8020 Sizes, 14 to 17½. Half sizes. State size. Shpg. wt., 2 oz.
Fine Quality Self Striped Silk Mixed Soft Collar. Points, 2½ inches; back, 1½ inches.

25c EACH 33K8021 Sizes, 14 to 17½. Half sizes. State size. Shipping weight, 2 ounces.
Fine Quality Crepe Silk Soft Collar. Points, 2⅛ inches; back, 1⅜ inches.

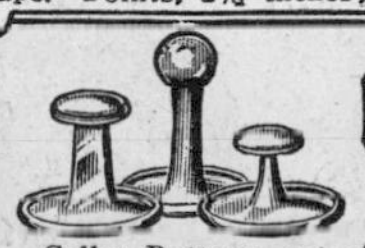

Collar Buttons, set of six. Shpg. wt., 2 oz.
4K9903—Rolled gold plate. 6 for......20c
4K9905—Gold filled. 6 for......30c

Illustrations show reduced size.

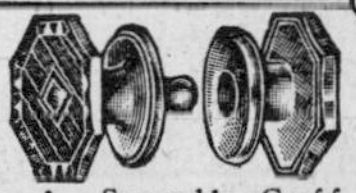

Separable Cuff Links, yellow color gold filled. Shpg. wt., 2 oz.
4K9909 Pair........40c

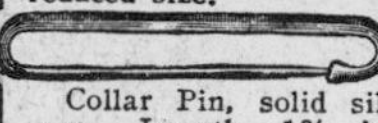

Collar Pin, solid silver. Length, 1¾ in. Shpg. wt., 2 oz.
4K9907........25c

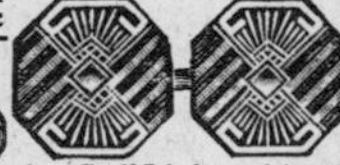

Cuff Links, white gold filled. Shpg. wt., 2 oz.
4K9901 Pair........40c

Rubber (Celluloid) Dull Linen Finish Collars

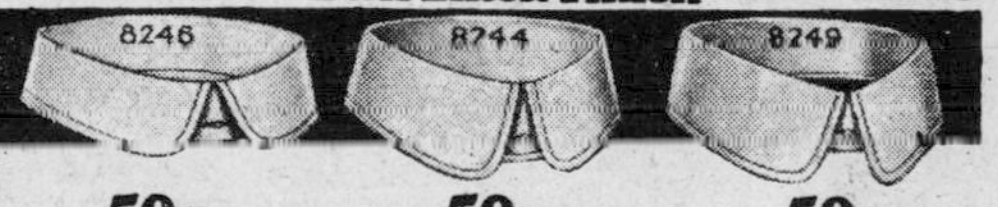
8246
8244
8249

59c FOR THREE 33K8246 Sizes, 12 to 18. Half sizes. State size. Shipping wt. of three, ¾ lb. Linen finish. Front, 1½ in.; back, 1¼ in.

59c FOR THREE 33K8244 Sizes, 14 to 18. Half sizes. State size. Shipping wt. of three, ¾ lb. Linen finish. Front, 2 inches; back, 1½ inches.

59c FOR THREE 33K8249 Sizes, 14 to 19. Half sizes. State size. Shipping wt. of three, ¾ lb. Linen finish. Low inside band. Front, 2 inches; back, 1⅛ inches.

Garters

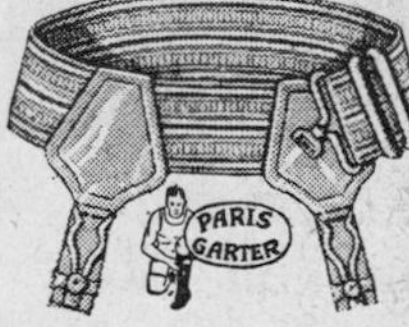
PARIS
GARTER

45c 33K9107 Assorted colors. Shipping weight, 5 ounces.
Genuine Paris Double Pad, Double Grip, Wide Weave Garters. About 1½-inch Rayon mixed elastic webbing with satin faced pads and rubber cushion loops. Non-rusting trimmings.

39c 33K9106 Assorted colors. Shipping weight, 4 ounces.
The Paris Single Grip Wide Weave Comfort Pad Garter at a reduced price. About 1½-inch fancy Rayon mixed elastic webbing with satin faced pad and rubber cushion loops. Non-rusting trimmings.

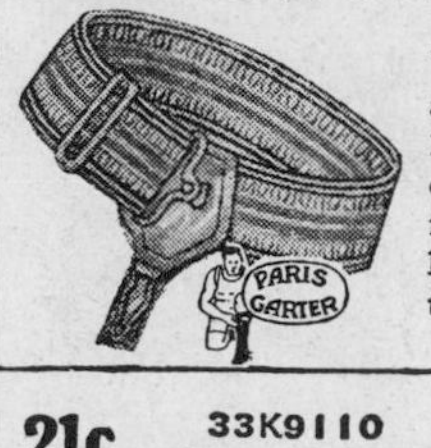
PARIS
GARTER

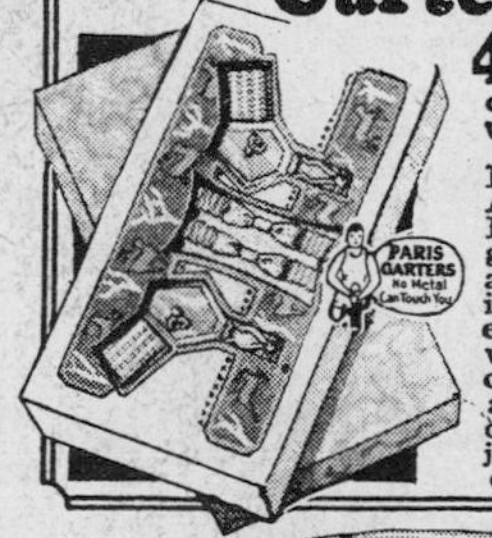
PARIS
GARTERS

48c 33K9116 Assorted colors. Shipping weight, 8 ounces.
Men's Genuine Paris Garter and Arm Band Set. Packed in a neat gift box. Garters are made of 1⅝-inch mercerized elastic webbing with single grip cotton moire pad and are very comfortable. Adjustable Rayon elastic arm bands.

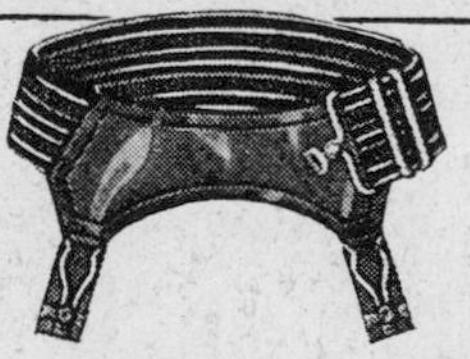

39c 33K9103 Assorted colors. Shipping weight, 5 ounces.
A New Double Grip Garter made of fine Rayon elastic webbing in an attractive design. Satin face pad and gold finish non-rusting brass trimmings.

27c 33K9108 Assorted colors. Shipping weight, 4 ounces.
Single Grip Garters with the popular "Long Stretch" web. This webbing has a long, easy stretch and will not bind the leg. Satin faced pad. Attractive patterns and colorings.

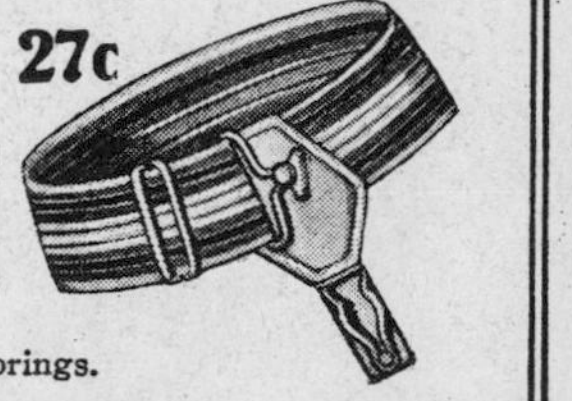

21c 33K9110 Assorted colors. Shipping weight, 4 oz.
Our most popular Single Grip Garters. Wide elastic bandage webbing with sateen pad. These garters were made to stand hard service.

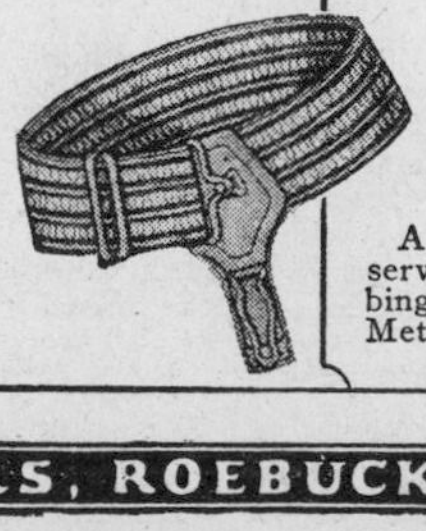

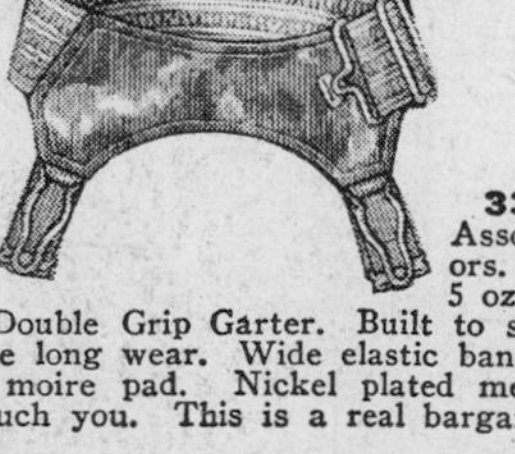

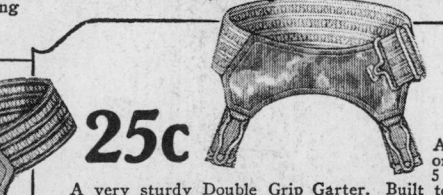

25c 33K9100 Assorted colors. Shpg. wt., 5 oz.
A very sturdy Double Grip Garter. Built to stand hard service and to give long wear. Wide elastic bandage webbing with cotton moire pad. Nickel plated metal parts. Metal does not touch you. This is a real bargain.

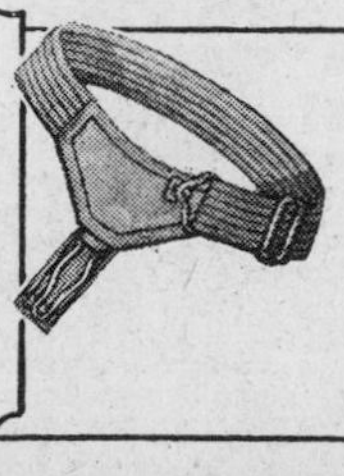

23c 33K9102 Assorted colors. Shipping weight, 4 ounces.
Single Grip Garters, made of about ⅞-inch Rayon webbing. Satin face pad. A very low price for a garter of this quality.

Men's Quality Ties!

$1.39
33K8331
Fancy patterns. Colors: Newer shades of blue, brown or gray. State color. Shpg. wt., 2 oz.
High grade neckwear in attractive patterns. Made of the better grade neckwear silks in the popular colorings. Non-wrinkable wool lining. This tie, we believe, is the finest on the market at our price.

89c
33K8380
Fancy patterns. Colors: Predominating shades of blue, brown or gray. State color. An attractive Silk Four-In-Hand Tie made with a wool lining which does not wrinkle. The patterns are very new. A very attractive bargain.

Shpg. wt. 2 oz.

$1.19
33K8333
Fancy patterns. Colors: Attractive blended patterns on ground colors of blue, gray or brown. State color. Newer designs and colorings. Made of good quality neckwear silk. Non-wrinkable lining and silk slip-easy band.

Shpg. wt., 2 oz.

$1.69
Hand Tailored
33K8330
Fancy patterns. Colors: Blue, purple, brown, gray or fancy black. State color. Shipping weight, 2 ounces.
Our Finest Four-In-Hand Tie, made either of high grade domestic or fine imported silks with an all wool non-wrinkable lining. A beautiful assortment of distinctive patterns. All hand tailored.

48c
33K8338
Fancy, gray or light brown.
Popular "Krinkle Crepe" Tie made of a silk mixed crepe. Attractive designs and colorings. Will give exceptional wear for a tie of this price.

79c
33K8337
Fancy patterns. Colors: Predominating shades of blue, gray or brown.
Fine assortment of the newest patterns and colors, made of fine quality neckwear silk. We are sure the quality and style will please you. A real neckwear value.

79c
33K8371 Plain colors
33K8379 Fancy patterns.
Colors: Blue, brown, gray or black. State color. Shipping weight, 2 ounces.
Genuine Silk and Wool Crepe Weave Ties in the latest patterns. Will not wrinkle and will always keep a fresh appearance. One of the finest wearing ties on the market, we believe.
For Boys' Ties refer to pages 422 and 423.

$1.00
33K8329
Fancy patterns. Colors: Blue, brown or gray. State color. Shipping weight, 2 ounces.
The Finest Dollar Tie on the market, we believe. This tie contains silks used only in higher priced ties, and the patterns are all new. It is, without doubt, the biggest neckwear value you can find.

Conservative Patterns

$1.00
33K8335
Fancy patterns. Ground colors: Dark blue, red, brown, gray, green or fancy black. State color. Shipping wt., 2 oz.
High grade open end Four-In-Hand Neckwear of heavy silk mixed materials. Non-wrinkable lining. You will be pleased with this tie.

48c
33K8328—Fancy patterns.
Ground colors: Dark blue, red, brown, purple, gray, green or fancy black. State color. Shipping weight, 2 ounces.
Our price is low on this fine quality Open End Tie. Attractive patterns. Slip-easy band.

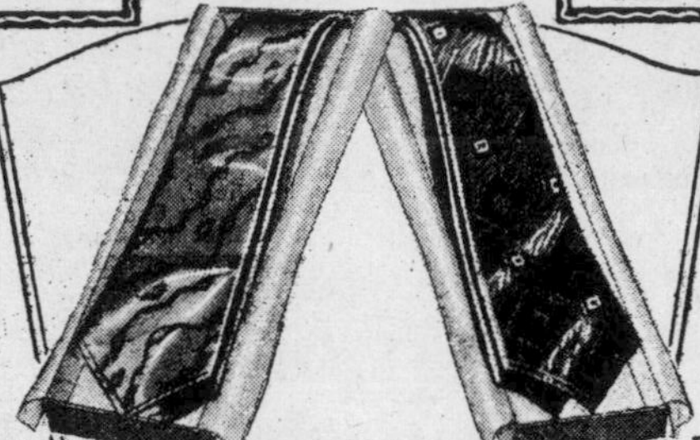

59c
33K8339
Fancy patterns. Colors: Blue, red, brown, purple, green or fancy black. State color. Shipping weight, 6 ounces.

89c
33K8346
Colors: Blue, gray, green or fancy black. State color. Shipping weight, 6 ounces.
Two different qualities in silk mixed Four-In-Hand Ties. Packed in a neat box, making a fine gift. A fine assortment of new and up to date patterns.

Knitted Ties

35c
33K8356—Plain colors.
33K8353—Fancy patterns.
Colors: Navy blue, brown, black, gray, green or maroon. State color. Shipping weight, 2 oz.
A very low price for an all Rayon Tie of this quality. Fancy patterns or plain colors. A very serviceable knit tie.

79c
33K8322—Plain colors.
33K8323 Fancy stripes.
Colors: Navy blue, brown, black, gray, green or maroon. State color. Shipping wt., 2 oz.
An All Silk Knitted Tie in fancy crocheted weaves. Comes in striped patterns or plain colors. Knitted ties are always popular.

59c
33K8359—Plain colors.
33K8358—Fancy stripes.
Colors: Navy blue, brown, black, gray, green or maroon. State color.
Attractive striped patterns or plain colors in a heavyweight Rayon Knitted Tie. Fancy crocheted weaves.

65c
33K8365 Fancy patterns
Today's most popular style in Knitted Neckwear. Has a new crochet stitch that brings out very attractive colorings. This tie is proving very popular at a higher price in exclusive haberdashers.

Colors: Blue, gray or brown. State color. Shpg. wt., 3 oz.

Shpg. wt., 2 oz.

45c
33K8306
Band teck.
Ground colors: Navy blue, red, brown, purple, gray, green or fancy black; also plain black or plain white. State color. Shipping weight, 2 ounces.

39c
33K8308
Shield teck.

Madeup Band or Shield Teck Ties of the better grade materials. Attractive patterns with conservative colorings.

Thousands of our customers praise our neckwear and are well pleased with the saving as well as the attractive patterns. Under each number at the top of the page are the latest patterns and colorings. At the left are neat and more conservative designs. Our ties are all made of standard neckwear silks, and we guarantee a saving to you. We also guarantee to send a tie that will be satisfactory, or return your money.

BOW TIES

23c
33K8315—Fancy patterns.
Colors: Navy blue, red, brown, fancy black, gray or green; also plain black. State color. Shipping weight, 1 ounce.
Sport Bows in attractive patterns. Adjustable elastic band that fits any size collar.

19c
33K8414
Plain colors.
Tricolette Sport Tie. Colors: Navy blue, brown or plain black. State color. Shpg. wt., 1 oz.

45c
33K8408—Length, 30 in.
33K8409—Length, 31 in.
33K8410—Length, 32 in.
Colors: Navy blue, red, brown, purple, gray, green, fancy black or plain black. State color. Shipping weight, 1 ounce.
Bat Wing Bow Ties of good quality neckwear silks. Attractive patterns and colorings.

55c
33K8425
Fancy patterns.
Colors: Newer shades of blue, gray or brown predominating; also black ground with black figure. State color. Shpg. wt., 2 oz.
Excellent Quality Madeup Band Bow Tie. Has appearance of hand tied bow. Adjustable band that will fit any size collar.

23c
33K8429—Plain colors.
Colors: Navy blue, red, brown, purple, gray, black or white. State color. Shipping weight, 1 ounce.
Good Quality Madeup Bow Tie. Made of silk mixed poplin. Poplin ties are always popular.

23c
33K8420—Figured patterns.
Colors: Navy blue, red, brown, purple, gray, green or fancy black; also plain black or plain white. State color. Shipping weight, 1 ounce.
Madeup Shield Bow Tie. Neat appearing patterns. Our price is very low. An attractive tie that will give good service.

The ELGIN Motor-Bike

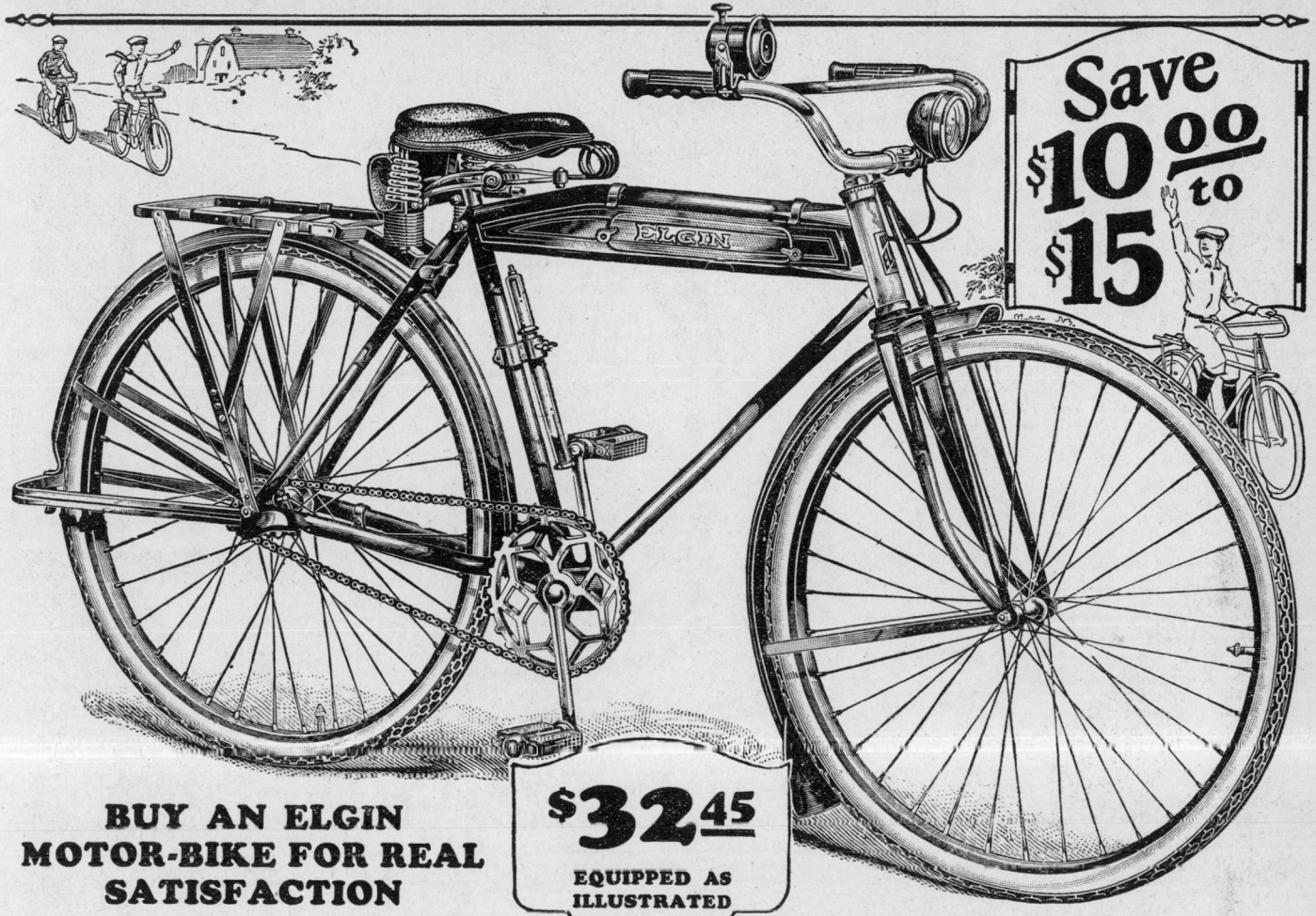

Save $10.00 to $15

$32.45 EQUIPPED AS ILLUSTRATED

BUY AN ELGIN MOTOR-BIKE FOR REAL SATISFACTION

Note These Features:

Frame

Up to date motor-bike frame of approved truss type. Made of 1-inch seamless steel bicycle tubing, with thoroughly reinforced flush joints. Patterned after standard motorcycle frame design.

Size

Furnished in 22-inch size only, with dip in top frame bar, making it practical to raise or lower the seat post to permit comfortable riding for practically anyone who can ride a 20, 22 or 24-inch diamond frame bicycle.

Mud Guards and Stand

Mud guards are of drop side style, front guard fitted with rubber splasher and rear guard with stand lock clip. Substantial motor-bike type stand fastening to clip on rear mud guard when bicycle is being ridden.

The Elgin Motor-Bike Leads All Others

You Would Pay $40.00 to $45.00 Elsewhere for a Bicycle of This Quality

The latest ideas in up to date bicycle manufacturing combined with sturdy reliable construction make the Elgin Motor-Bike one of the finest bicycles on the market today. The remarkably fine finish of this bike is quickly recognized and universally appreciated. We are offering this wonderful bicycle at a price easily $10.00 to $15.00 lower than you are usually asked elsewhere for a bicycle of similar type.

NO BICYCLE POSSESSES MORE REAL FEATURES

Note These Features:

Saddle

High grade comfortable riding Troxel saddle of motor-bike type, with good grade leather top. Has beehive type cushion springs, black finish. Size of top, length over all, about 10¾ inches; width, about 8¼ inches.

Wheels and Rims

Steel rims, enameled to match the frame, crescent cement type, for 28-inch tires. Both front and rear wheels have 36 spokes. Front hub is spindle type; rear hub, New Departure Coaster Brake Hub.

Tool Equipment

Heavy leather tool bag, reinforced with black metal ends. Has nickel plated clasp and ring. Equipment includes telescope type bicycle pump, bicycle wrench, tube of tire repair cement and oiler.

Other Features of ELGIN Motor-Bike Model Leadership

Tires

The famous U. S. Rubber Company's Chain Tread Tires. 28x1½-inch size. (See page 454 for detailed description and illustration of these splendid tires.)

Handle Bars

Famous De Luxe Motor-Bike Bars of forward extension type. Complete with substantial reinforcing bar with diamond tapered ends. Up to date type Gripwell grips, about 5 inches long.

Front Fork

Approved motor-bike type.

Headlight Battery Container

Attractive tank between two top bars for storing headlight battery.

Pedals

Motor-bike type corrugated rubber pedals, with pedal rubbers removable or adjustable.

Chain

⁵⁄₁₆x1-inch Diamond Roller Chain.

Hanger

One-piece drop forged crank with hanger lock ring.

Well designed sprocket, 26 teeth, of light weight. Has 7-inch tapering pedal crank.

Finish

An attractive cherry red with ivory head. Darts on bars and broad stripe down center of mud guard. Mud guards match frame finish.

The same finish is very widely used on many of the latest and best known makes of automobiles, being one of the best wearing finishes made. The many nickel plated metal parts complete a most attractive appearance.

28K1339¼—Our ELGIN Motor-Bike Model, equipped with New Departure Coaster Brake. Horn, Lamp and Luggage carrier, as illustrated. Shipping weight, 65 pounds..**$32.45**

28K1349¼—Our ELGIN Motor-Bike Model, equipped with New Departure Coaster Brake, but without horn, lamp or luggage carrier. Shipping weight, 65 pounds..**$29.95**

Three-cell flashlight batteries suitable for use with headlamp on 28K1339¼ bike, are shown on page 666 of this catalog.

ELGIN SPECIAL *Motor-Bike*

$25⁷⁵
COASTER MODEL

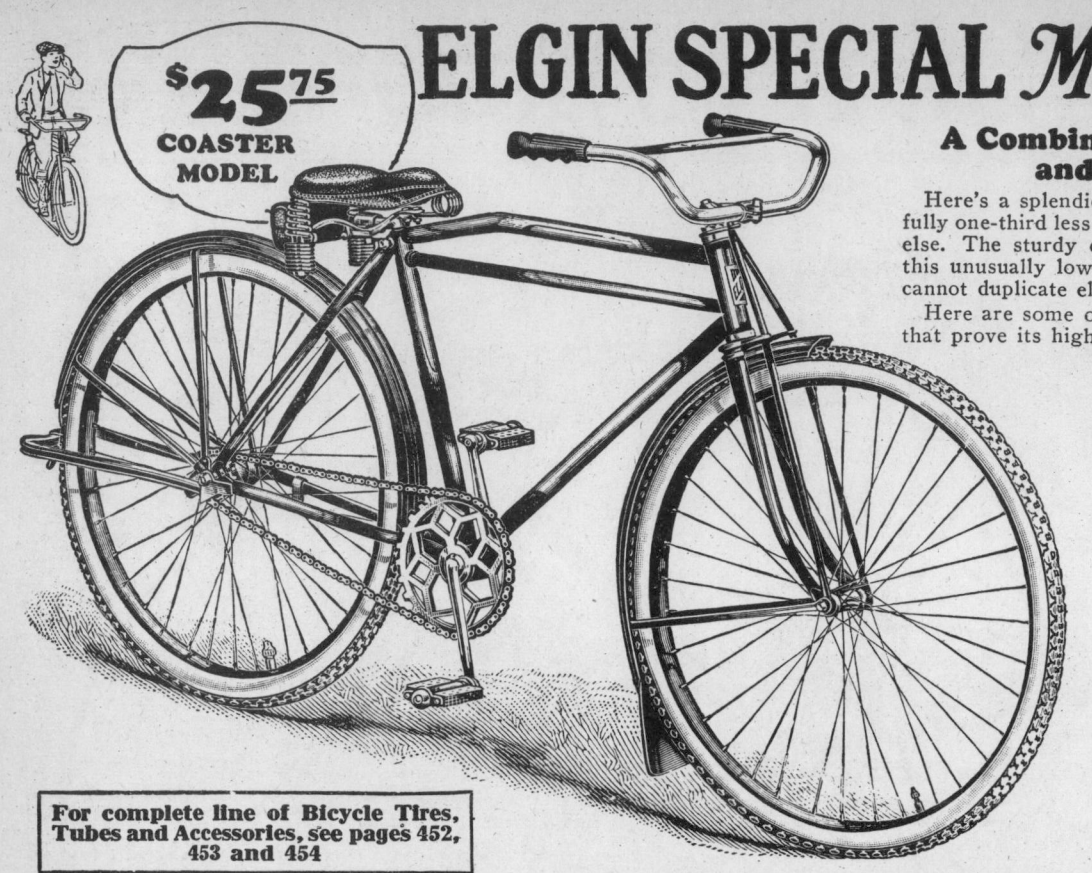

A Combination of Beauty and Strength

Here's a splendid, high grade Motor-Bike at fully one-third less than it would cost anywhere else. The sturdy construction, combined with this unusually low price, make it a value you cannot duplicate elsewhere.

Here are some of the features of this model that prove its high quality!

Motor-Bike frame is made of 1-inch seamless steel tubing, truss type. Furnished in 22-inch size. Equipped with the well known Red Studded Tread Tires, 28x1½ inches, single tube cement-on type.

Motor-Bike handle bars, complete with substantial reinforcing bar with diamond tapered ends; popular style rubber grips.

New Departure Coaster Brake.

Troxel Top Notch Saddle, with beehive type cushion springs.

Substantial Motor-Bike type stand.

Attractive cherry red finish, nickel plated metal parts.

Substantial tool bag, with bicycle wrench, hand pump, tube of tire repair cement and oiler.

28K1372¼—Our Elgin Special Motor-Bike Model, equipped with New Departure Coaster Brake. Shipping weight, 62 pounds..**$25.75**

For complete line of Bicycle Tires, Tubes and Accessories, see pages 452, 453 and 454

Single Bar Motor-Bike

A BIKE ANY BOY WOULD BE PROUD TO OWN

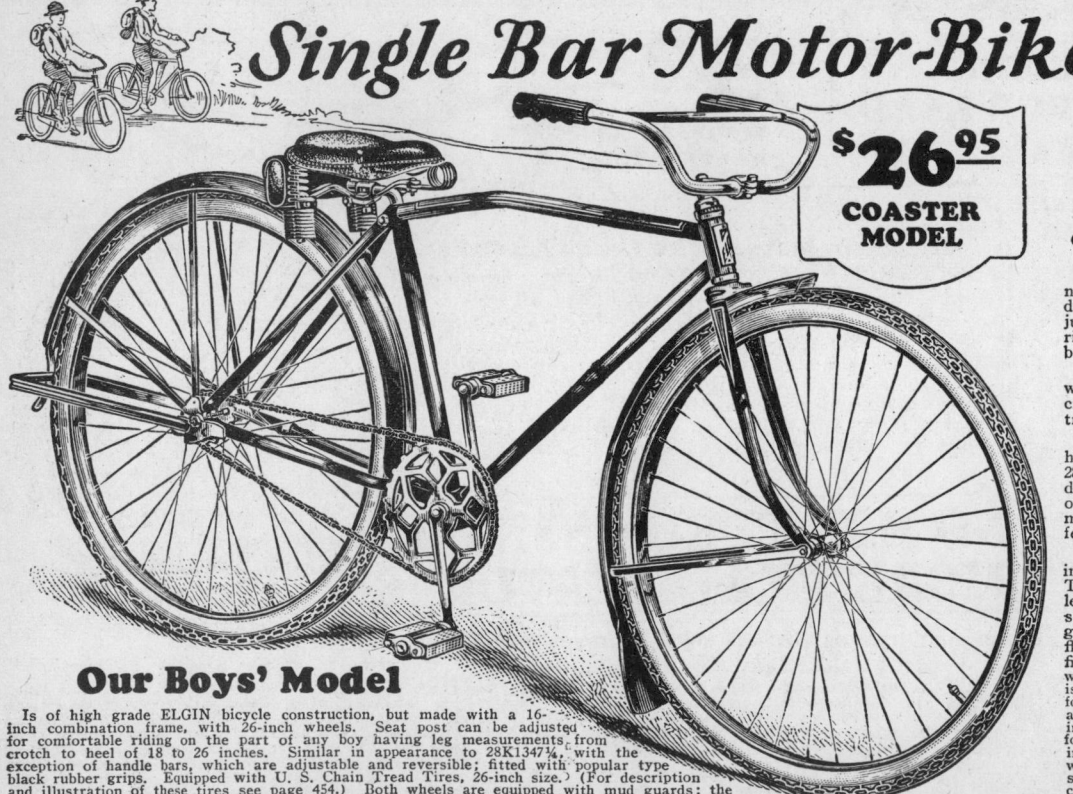

$26⁹⁵
COASTER MODEL

Our Price Saves You $10 or more on This Model

Others Generally Ask $37.50 for a Bike of This Quality

Our Single Bar Motor-Bike is furnished in 20-inch size only with a drop in the frame bar permitting adjusting the seat post for comfortable riding for all riders of 22-inch frame bicycles.

The frame is 1-inch bicycle tubing with flush joint reinforcements. Front crown is of up to date, late type, triple truss keystone arch design.

Tire equipment is the well known high grade U. S. Chain Tread Tires, 28x1½-inch size. (See page 454 for detailed description and illustration of these splendid tires.) The equipment includes the following excellent features:

De Luxe handle bars with reinforcing bar; 5-inch gripwell grips. Troxel Top Notch saddle with high grade leather top and beehive cushion springs, black finish. The mud guards are of drop side style, with flat braces. The front mud guard is fitted with splasher, the rear guard with clip for fastening stand, which is furnished in dull nickel finish. Comfortable, durable rubber pedals, with adjustable removable pedal rubbers, ¾-inch pitch Diamond Roller Chain, drop forged one-piece crank complete with 7-inch tapering pedal cranks and a light weight 26-tooth sprocket. Rims are steel, enameled to match the frame, of crescent cement type and laced with 36 spokes. A substantial leather tool bag with our regulation tool equipment. Furnished in cherry red and black finish, with darts on fork sides. Mud guards are enameled to match the frame.

28K1347¼—Our Single Bar ELGIN Motor-Bike, equipped with New Departure Coaster Brake. Shipping weight, 61 pounds...................**$26.95**

For Boys' Model see 28K1341¼ at left.

Our Boys' Model

Is of high grade ELGIN bicycle construction, but made with a 16-inch combination frame, with 26-inch wheels. Seat post can be adjusted for comfortable riding on the part of any boy having leg measurements from crotch to heel of 18 to 26 inches. Similar in appearance to 28K1347¼, with the exception of handle bars, which are adjustable and reversible; fitted with popular type black rubber grips. Equipped with U. S. Chain Tread Tires, 26-inch size. (For description and illustration of these tires see page 454.) Both wheels are equipped with mud guards; the front guard being fitted with splasher, the rear guard with stand lock clip. Stand comes in dull nickel finish. Equipped with Juvenile Troxel Saddle, with beehive cushion springs. Special rubber pedals, with adjustable pedal rubbers. Has a 1-inch pitch roller chain. Complete with tool bag, bicycle wrench, hand pump, tube of tire repair cement and oiler. Furnished in attractive cherry red and green. Steel rims enameled to match the frame. Mud guards match frame finish. Shipping weight, 55 pounds.

28K1341¼—Boys' Model ELGIN Bicycle, equipped with New Departure Coaster Brake.......**$25.75**
28K1320¼—Similar to 28K1341¼, but equipped with 24-inch wheels, Red Studded tread tires and finished in red enamel...**$23.45**
28K1314¼—Same as 28K1320¼, but without coaster brake..**20.45**

ELGINS *for* Girls *and* Women

$28⁹⁵

Junior Elgin Bicycles

$19⁴⁵ AND UP

It's a Beauty in Appearance and a Wonder for Endurance
Saves $8.00 to $15.00 Over Prices Asked by Others

A duplicate, on a smaller scale, of our regulation type ELGIN Bicycles. A real bicycle at little more than half the price of the slightly larger boys' model bicycles. This is a splendid model for little fellows with inseam measurement from crotch to heel of 16 to 23 inches. 14-inch frame of ⅞-inch steel tubing. Has metal rims with 20-inch single tube, red studded tread tires. Fitted with attractive type handle bars, complete with rubber grips and stand. Has brown leather saddle with triple coil easy riding spring and adjustable saddle clamp. Rubber pedals. Complete with front and rear mud guards with substantial braces. Sprocket has 20 teeth; high grade Diamond roller chain. Hubs are ball bearing, spindle type. Hubs, sprocket and spokes nickel plated; all other parts red enameled, matching frame finish. Frame is finished in red enamel with black stripings. Well made throughout and will stand lots of hard knocks. The finest bicycle made for small boys and priced far below its real value. Shipping weight, 38 pounds.

28K1309¼—Boys' Junior with 20-inch wheels	$19.45
28K1310¼—Same, with New Departure (Endee Brake)	22.45
28K1311¼—Girls' Junior, with 20-inch wheels	19.95
28K1312¼—Same, with New Departure (Endee Brake)	22.95

Girls' and Women's Models

We have left no stone unturned in making this a real honest to goodness bicycle in the true sense of the word. We have selected all the finest features in bicycle manufacturing and combined them in making this truly wonderful model. Its beauty of appearance and easy running qualities, combined with its sturdy construction, make this a bicycle anyone would be proud to own. Considering the quality and low price, this is truly a wonderful value.

This is a high grade well designed Women's Model Bicycle that is sure to give real satisfaction in every respect. The frame is made from 1-inch steel tubing, 20-inch size only. The equipment includes women's model Troxel saddle, 1-inch roller chain, metal chain guard, laced skirt guard, mud guards (splasher fitted to front guard and stand lock clip to rear guard), stand, rubber pedals, reversible handle bars with rubber motor-bike grips, tool bag and regulation tool equipment. The tire equipment is the famous U. S. Chain Tread Tires, 28-inch (see page 454). Furnished in attractive red with ivory head. Steel rims, enameled to match bicycle.

28K1345¼—Women's Model ELGIN Bicycle, equipped with New Departure Coaster Brake. Shipping weight, 63 pounds......**$28.95**

Genuine Sidewalk Bicycles

FOR FUN!

For Boys and Girls 4½ to 10½ Years of Age.

Girls' Model

Real "two-wheelers" to keep little folks safely off the streets. They are sure to be the envy of their friends. The small wheels and low construction insure safety. Made of the same quality materials, by the same skilled men, and with many of the stock parts of the regulation bicycle. Not a cheap make-shift, but a full fledged bike for the smaller youngsters. Heavy "balloon type" solid tires can't give trouble. Note these quality features, different only in a few dimensions: Lightweight, sturdy tubular construction throughout; light New Departure coaster brake; rubber pedals; regulation ball bearings; drop stand support and mudguard on rear wheel. Length over all, 32 inches. Wheel base, 28 inches. Seat to pedal adjustment ranges from 21 to 28 inches; crotch to heel measurement of children 4½ to 10½ years. Shpg. wt., 25 lbs.

28K1342¼—Boys' Sidewalk bicycle	$18.95
28K1344¼—Same, with New Departure (Endee Brake)	21.95
28K1346¼—Girls' Sidewalk Bicycle	19.45
28K1354¼—Same, with New Departure (Endee Brake)	22.45

Girls' Coaster Model

$25⁹⁵

As in the women's model shown above, we have spared no effort in making this Girls' Elgin Model a leader among girls' bicycles.

This model is of the same high grade construction as our Women's Elgin Model number 28K1345¼. It is beautiful in finish and as easy running and substantial as a bicycle can be made.

We are offering you this model at a price that will afford you a substantial saving and give you the service and satisfaction you have a right to expect. Satisfaction guaranteed or your money back.

Our Girls' Elgin Model is made with a 16-inch combination frame and 26-inch wheels. For comfortable riding the distance from the seat to lowest pedal is adjustable from 18 to 26 inches. Drop style frame equipped with laced skirt guard. The adjustable reversible handle bars are fitted with rubber motor-bike junior grips. The tire equipment is the well known U. S. Chain Tread Tires, 26-inch size. (For description and illustration of these tires, see page 454.) Both front and rear wheels are equipped with mud guards, the front guard being fitted with splasher, the rear guard with stand lock clip. Equipped with Juvenile Troxel Saddle, with beehive cushion springs. Special rubber pedals, comfortable and durable, with adjustable pedal rubbers. Has a 1-inch pitch roller chain. Complete with tool bag, with bicycle wrench, hand pump, tube of tire repair cement and oiler. Furnished in attractive cherry red and green. Steel rims, enameled to match bike. Mud guards match frame finish.

28K1343¼—Girls' Model ELGIN Bicycle, equipped with New Departure Coaster Brake. Shipping weight, 55 pounds......**$25.95**

28K1324¼—Same as 28K1343¼ but with 24-inch wheels, Red Studded tread tires and finished in red enamel **$23.95**

28K1322¼—Same as 28K1324¼ but without coaster brake 20.95

Save Money on Your

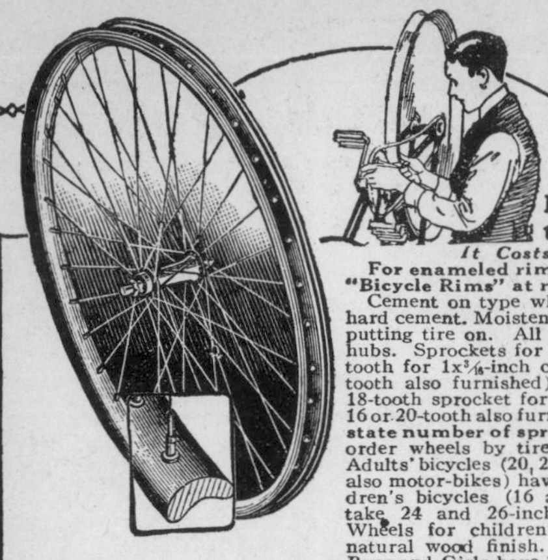

Fix Up the Old Bike

It Costs But Little

For enameled rims add 22 cents. See "Bicycle Rims" at right below.

Cement on type wheels have a coat of hard cement. Moisten with gasoline before putting tire on. All wheels have spindle hubs. Sprockets for rear wheels come 9-tooth for 1x3/16-inch chains (7, 8 and 10-tooth also furnished). Hubs come with 18-tooth sprocket for ½-inch chains (14, 16 or 20-tooth also furnished). **In ordering state number of sprocket teeth.** Always order wheels by tire size, not rim size. Adults' bicycles (20, 22 and 24-inch frames, also motor-bikes) have 28-inch tires. Children's bicycles (16 and 18-inch frames) take 24 and 26-inch tires respectively. Wheels for children's bicycles come in natural wood finish. Elgin Bicycles for Boys and Girls have 26-inch tires.

WHEELS FOR 28-INCH TIRES, CRESCENT CEMENT NATURAL WOOD RIMS

28K2141¼—Rear Wheel only. Crescent cement wood rim. Shipping weight, 3 lbs.........**$3.45**

28K2142¼—Front Wheel only. Crescent cement wood rim. Shipping weight, 2½ lbs...**$2.40**

BUILT-UP WHEELS FOR 28-INCH G. & J. STYLE CLINCHER TIRES. NATURAL WOOD RIMS

28K2143¼—Rear Wheel only. G. & J. style clincher wood rim. Shipping weight, 3½ lbs...**$3.60**

28K2144¼—Front Wheel only. G. & J. style clincher wood rim. Shipping weight, 2¾ lbs...**$2.55**

BUILT-UP WHEELS FOR 28-INCH TIRES, STEEL RIMS, BLACK

28K2152¼—Rear Wheel only. Equipped with Crescent cement steel rim. Shpg. wt., 4 lbs..**$3.25**

28K2153¼—Front Wheel only. Equipped with Crescent cement steel rim. Shipping weight, 3½ pounds.................**$2.20**

28K2154¼—Rear Wheel only. Equipped with clincher steel rim. Shpg. wt., 4¾ lbs.........**$3.30**

28K2155¼—Front Wheel only. Equipped with clincher steel rim. Shpg. wt., 3½ lbs...**$2.25**

BUILT-UP WHEELS FOR 24 AND 26-INCH TIRES, CRESCENT CEMENT NATURAL WOOD RIMS

28K2150¼—Rear Wheel only. **State size.** Shipping weight, 2½ pounds.................**$3.40**

28K2151¼—Front Wheel only. **State size.** Shipping weight, 2½ pounds.................**$2.40**

BUILT-UP WHEELS FOR 28-INCH TIRES, CRESCENT NICKEL PLATED STEEL RIMS

28K2162¼—Rear wheel, equipped with crescent cement nickel plated steel rim. Shipping weight, 4 lbs..............**$3.55**

28K2163¼—Front wheels, same type. Shpg. wt., 4 lbs.**$2.75**

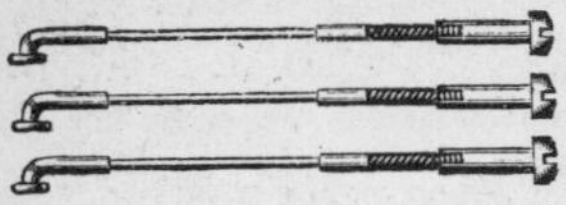

Spokes

Complete, with nipples and washers. Furnished in lengths listed below:

28K2185—Length, about 10⅛ inches. Per dozen.........**15c**

28K2186—Length, about 11⅛ inches. Per dozen.........**15c**

28K2187—Length, about 12⅛ inch. Per dozen.........**15c**

Shipping weight, above, any size, 8 ounces per dozen.

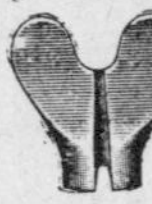

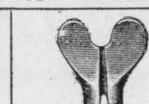

Nipple Grip

For tightening spoke nipples. Nickel plated. Shpg. wt., 3 oz.

28K2249 **9c**

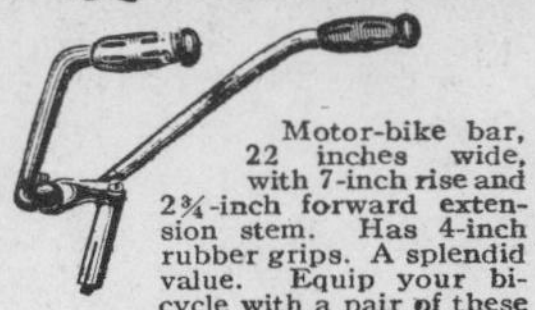

V-Type Handle Bar

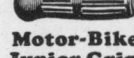

Motor-bike bar, 22 inches wide, with 7-inch rise and 2¾-inch forward extension stem. Has 4-inch rubber grips. A splendid value. Equip your bicycle with a pair of these bars and enjoy real comfort. Shipping weight, 3 pounds.

28K2139.........**$1.35**

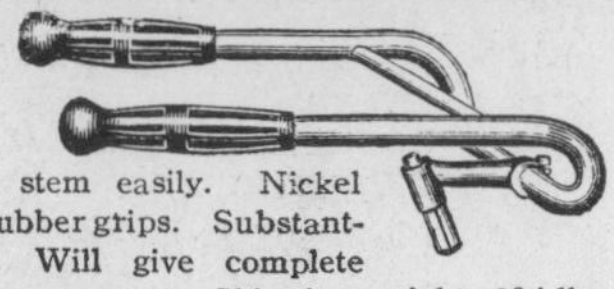

Elgin De Luxe Handle Bar

Our finest handle bar, 21½ inches wide. Has reinforcing bar with ends tapered to remove stem easily. Nickel plated, with 6-inch rubber grips. Substantial expander stem. Will give complete satistisfaction in every respect. Shipping weight, 3¾ lbs.

28K2085..............................**$1.68**

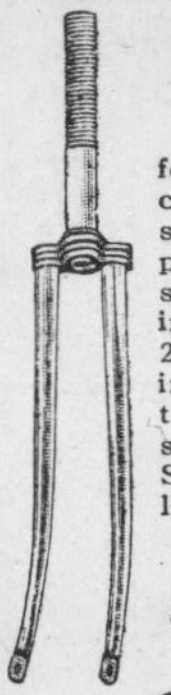

Bicycle Repair Fork

A splendid fork. Fork, crown and sides nickel plated. Long stem, 1 inch in diameter, 24 threads to inch. Triple truss keystone crown. Shpg. wt., 3 lbs.

28K2094

$1.98

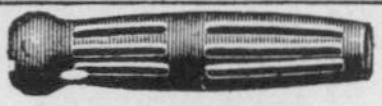

Motor-Bike Grips

Rubber; 6 in. long. Shipping weight, per pair, ¾ lb.

28K2116—Pair..**18c**

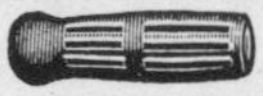

Motor-Bike Junior Grips

Black rubber, 4 inches long. Shipping weight, per pair, 4 oz.

28K2381
Per pair.......**13c**

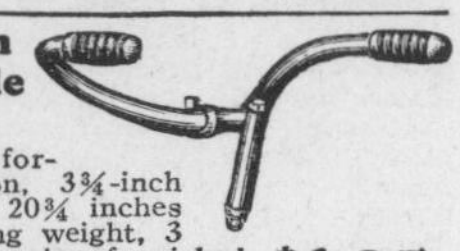

Extension Adjustable Bar

Has 2¾-inch forward extension. 3¾-inch drop. Bar is 20¾ inches wide. Shipping weight, 3 lbs. Leather grips furnished.

28K2086........................**$1.25**

Extra Stem, ⅞ inch diameter. Shipping weight, 1 pound.

28K2087..............................**45c**

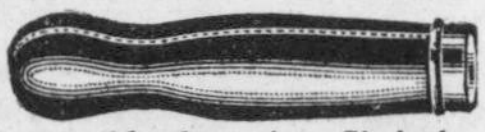

Good Quality Bulldog Grips

Good quality sewed leather grips. Six inches long, with wooden core shaped to fit hand. Open end has nickel plated ferrule. Shipping weight, per pair, 5 ounces.

28K2248—Pair..........................**27c**

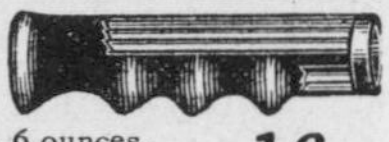

Gripwell

Knobs give better grip; 5 in. long, rubber. Shpg. wt., per pair, 6 ounces.

28K2352—Pair.............**16c**

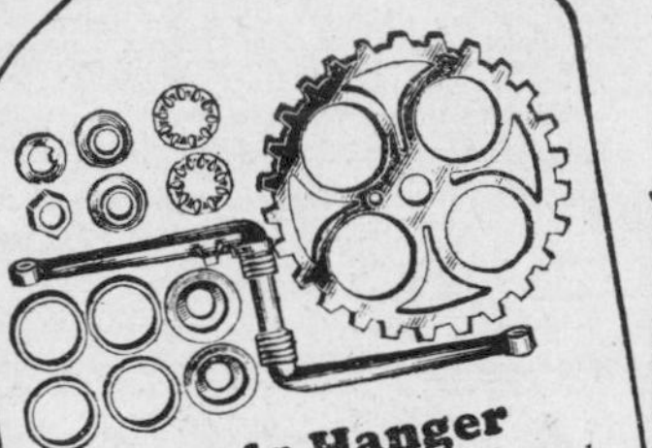

Repair Hanger

Comprises shaft and crank in one piece, cranks each 7 in. long, drilled and tapped for pedal shaft, 26-tooth sprocket complete with balls, ball retainers, key washer, locknut cups 25/32 inch in diameter and two sets of extra bushings to make cups 1 15/16 and 2 1/32 in. in diameter. Shpg. wt., complete outfit, 4¾ lbs.

28K2358—Complete. **$3.65**

Bicycle Rims

We do not furnish steel lined wood rims.

28-INCH MAPLE WOOD RIMS, NATURAL

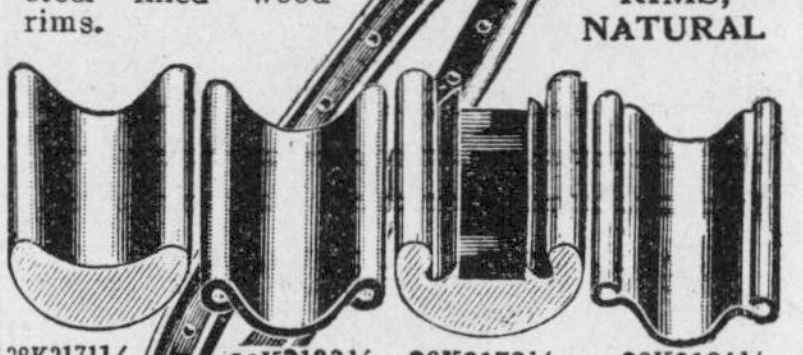

28K2171¼ 28K2193¼ 28K2178¼ 28K2184¼

NICKEL PLATED STEEL RIM

28K2193¼—Crescent Cement Rim, 36 holes, 28-inch size only. Shipping weight, 2¼ pounds......**90c**

28K2168—Cement Style Natural Wood Rim, 36 holes, 24-inch size. Shipping weight, 1 pound..............**85c**

28K2169—Cement Style Natural Wood Rim, 36 holes, 26-inch size. Shipping weight, 1½ pounds..............**85c**

28K2171¼—Crescent Cement Rim, 36 holes, 28-inch size. Shipping weight, 1½ pounds..............**80c**

28K2178¼—G. & J. Style Rim, 36 holes. 28-inch size. Shpg. wt., 1¾ lbs. **98c**

NOTE—Add 22 cents for enameled wood rims. Colors: Cherry red with ivory color center, or red with black stripes. **State color. Rims fitting 28x1½-inch tires also fit 28x1⅝-inch tires.**

STEEL RIMS, BLACK

28K2184¼—Clincher Rim, 36 holes, 28-inch size only. Shpg. wt., 2¾ pounds...**65c**

Roller Chains

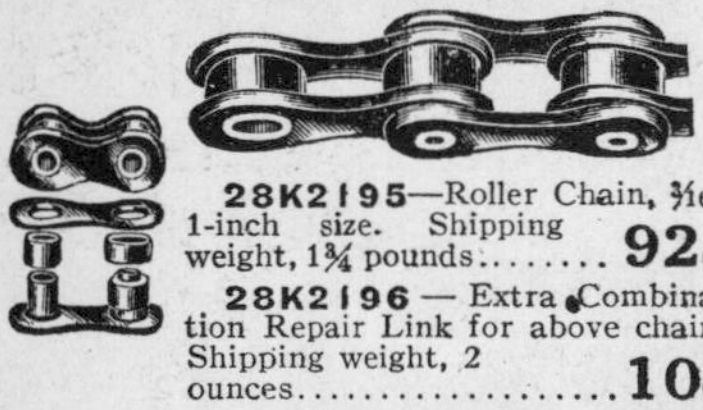

28K2195—Roller Chain, 3/16x1-inch size. Shipping weight, 1¾ pounds.......**92c**

28K2196—Extra Combination Repair Link for above chain. Shipping weight, 2 ounces..............**10c**

28K2197—Roller Chain, ⅛x½-inch size. Shipping weight, 1½ pounds..............**$1.10**

28K2199—Extra Combination Repair Link for above chain. Shipping weight, 2 ounces..............**10c**

"B" Block Chain

A well known block chain, a big value. Furnished 60 links, 3/16x1-inch size. Shipping wt., 1½ pounds.

28K2190.....**$1.58**

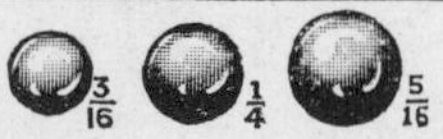

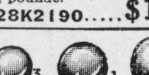

Steel Balls

3/16 ¼ 5/16

	Size	Shpg. Wt.	Per 100
28K2205	⅛-inch	4 oz.	8c
28K2206	3/16-inch	5 oz.	12c
28K2207	¼-inch	6 oz.	15c
28K2208	5/16-inch	7 oz.	18c
28K2209	⅜-inch	¾ lb.	24c

Trousers Guard

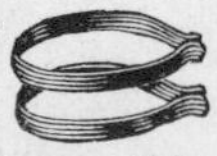

28K2232 — Shipping wt., 2 oz. Per pair...........**5c**

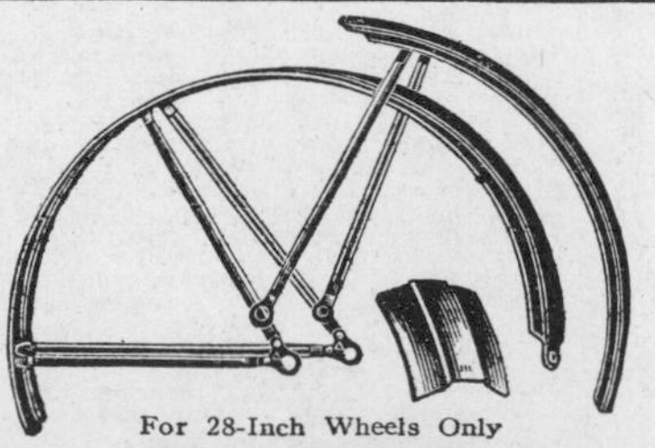

For 28-Inch Wheels Only

Mud Guards

Strong, light weight. Arched and corrugated. Black enameled finish. Shipping weight, per set, 4½ pounds.

28K2098—Per set, for front and real wheels..............**58c**

Mud Guard Attaching Outfit

Saves drilling or tapping frame. Outfit includes front bridge, necessary clamps, bolts and nuts. (Not illustrated.) Shipping wt., 3 oz.

28K2105—Per set..............**8c**

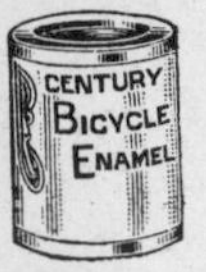

Century Enamel

No baking. Comes in colors of royal blue, jet black, Brewster green, carmine, bright vermilion, chrome yellow, French gray, cherry red, brown, cochin red, white or ivory. **State color wanted.** Shipping wt., ¾ lb.

28K2322—4-oz. can..............**18c**

Aluminum Enamel

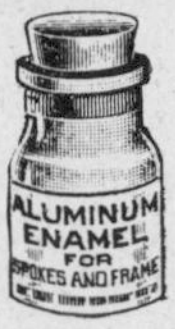

For rusty nickel plated parts. Shipping weight, 2 bottles, 1 pound.

28K2317

Two ½-ounce bottles..........**17c**

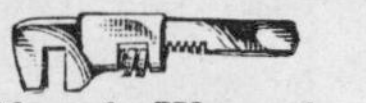

Bicycle Wrench

Dull nickel finish, 5 inches long. A handy, well made wrench that will give real satisfaction. Shpg. wt., 8 oz.

28K2242....**14c**

If you are in need of Spare Parts for your Bicycle you can supply your wants here and save money.

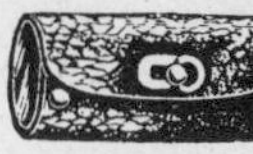

De Luxe Tool Bag

Black metal ends and nickel plated clasp and ring. Brown leather, 6 inches long. Shipping wt., ¾ pound.

28K2081....**30c**

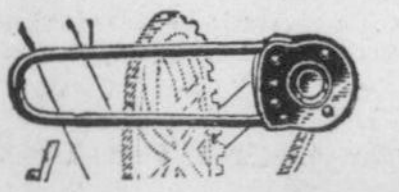

Sprocket Lock

Also fits rear hub. Keyless combination type. Shipping weight, 1 pound.

28K2354..........**72c**

Purchase your bicycle supplies at the World's Largest Store and be assured of real satisfaction.

Bicycle Equipment

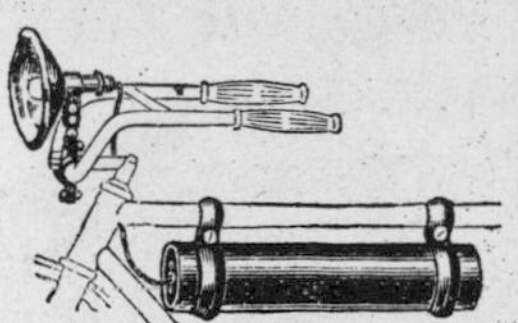

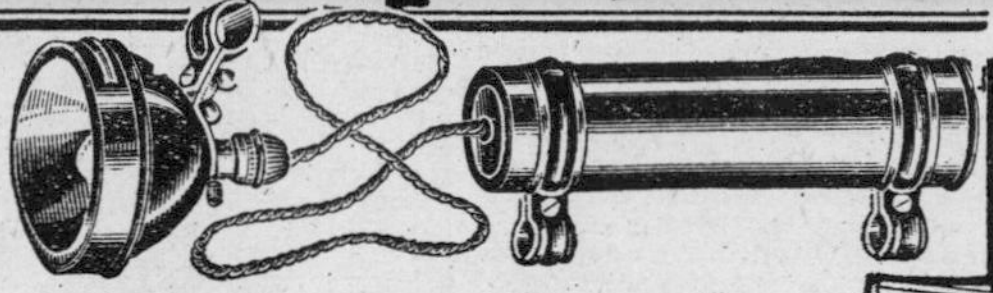

Electric Headlight Outfit

Every bicycle rider needs one of these splendid, up to date electric headlight outfits, priced for a special bargain.
Includes lamp with a 3½-inch front diameter, handy on and off switch at back, 1½-volt bulb, double contact Ediswan base, bracket for attaching lamp to handle bar stem. Single cell battery container, about 7 inches long, with clamps for attaching to bicycle frame and necessary wire. Without batteries. Lamp and single cell container come in black finish. Shipping weight, 2 pounds.

28K2126—Lamp outfit. $1.45

28K2135—Lamp with 2-cell container (13 inches long) and 2.8-volt bulb. Without batteries. Shpg. wt., 2½ lbs. 1.65

28K2017—Extra Headlight Bulbs, 2.8 volts for 28K2135 Lighting Outfit. Shpg. wt., 4 oz. .... .21

28K2137—Extra Headlight Bulbs, 1½ volts for 28K2126 Lighting Outfit. Shipping weight, 4 ounces.... .21

For Dry Cell Batteries see 57K3062 on page 666.

Popular Electric Headlight Outfit

Comprises up to date lamp with two-cell battery container (without battery), with necessary electric cord. Lamp has 1½-volt double contact bulb. On and off switch and bracket for attaching to front fork inside. Shipping weight, complete, 2 lbs.

28K2102... $2.10

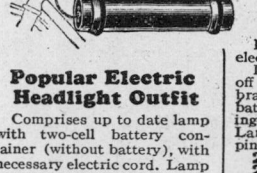

Equip Your Bicycle With Real Equipment

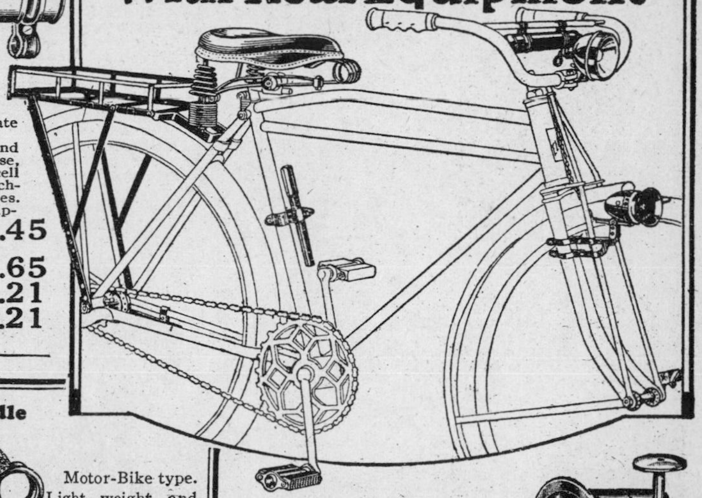

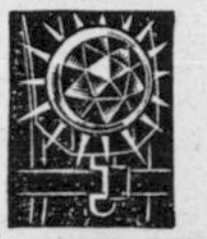

Reflex Tail Light

Up to date type signal to be attached to rear fender. Has about 2-inch ruby red cut-glass lens. Shows a strong red reflection when headlight rays strike it. Has nickel plated metal frame.

28K2223—Shpg. wt., 5 oz. 15c

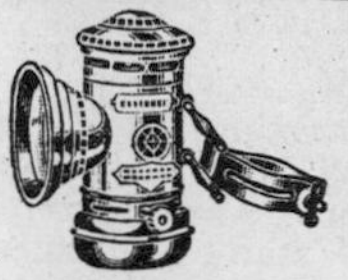

Kerosene Oil Lamp

A big value. Has 2½-inch lens, green and ruby color side lights. Nickel plated finish. Height, 5¾ inches. Rigid adjustable bracket. Shpg. wt., 1½ lbs.

28K2018..... 98c

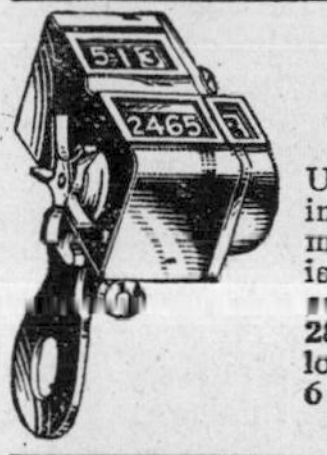

Veeder Trip Cyclometer

Trip and season cyclometer. Useful and interesting for keeping records of your trips, tire mileage, etc. Trip dial registers 99.9 miles and repeats; season dial, 9,999.9 miles. For **28-in. wheel only.** Specially low priced. Shipping weight, 6 ounces.

28K2225..... $2.48

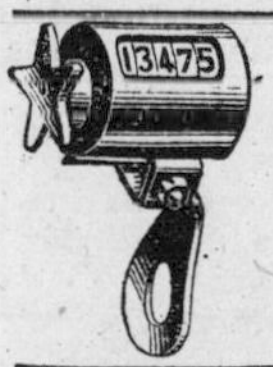

New Departure Cyclometer

Popular low priced model. Has 9,999.9 miles total register and repeats. **For 28-in. wheels only.** Shipping weight, 3 ounces.

28K2221........ 85c

Quick Action Telescope Pump

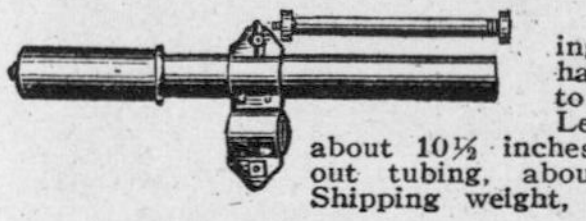

Quick working, well made, handy. Clamps to bicycle frame. Length, closed, about 10½ inches; open, without tubing, about 18 inches. Shipping weight, ¾ pound.

28K1954.......... 40c

Triumph Foot Pump

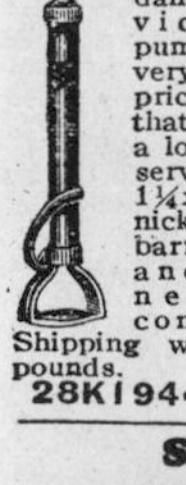

Here is a dandy, serviceable pump at a very low price and one that will give a lot of real service. Has 1¼x12-inch nickel plated barrel. Hose and connection complete. Shipping weight, 2 pounds.

28K1944 45c

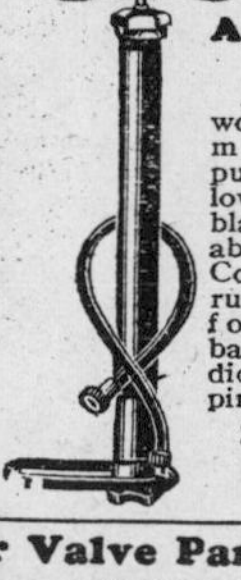

Quick Action Foot Pump

A splendid fast working, well made bicycle pump, unusually low priced. Has black cylinder, about 1¼x17 in. Complete with rubber hose and folding wire base. A splendid value. Shipping wt., 2½ lbs.

28K2278

65c

Schrader Valve Parts

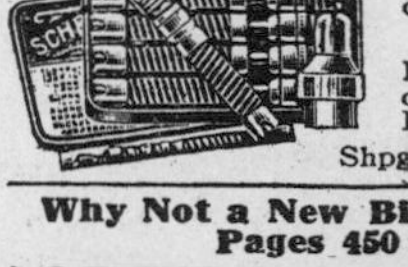

28K4539—Valve Caps only. Box of 5. .... 22c

28K4571—Valve Plungers or insides. Box of 5. Per box.......... 22c

Shpg. wt., either of above, 2 oz.

Why Not a New Bike This Year? See Pages 450 and 451

Troxel Top Notch Saddle

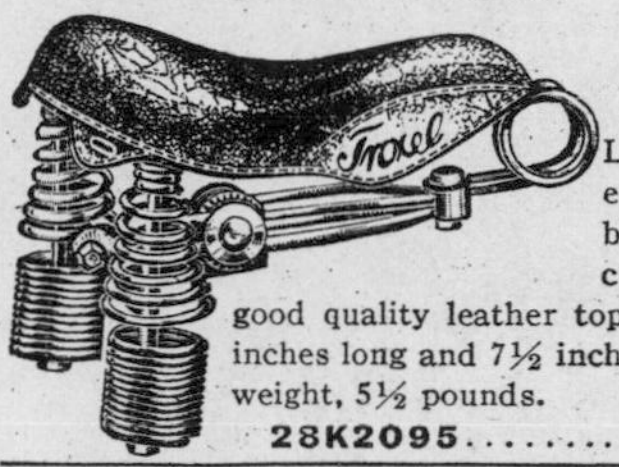

Motor-Bike type. Light weight and easy riding. Has black beehive type cushion springs, good quality leather top. Size of top, 10 inches long and 7½ inches wide. Shipping weight, 5½ pounds.

28K2095.............. $1.35

Favorite Juvenile Saddle

For boys' and girls' bicycles; popular beehive cushion spring type; black. A big value. Size of top, 6¾x9 in. (Not illustrated.) Shipping weight, 2¾ lbs.

28K2388.......................... $1.15

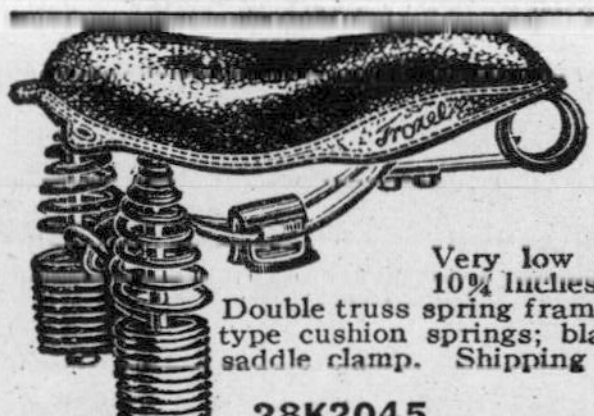

Troxel Motor-Bike Saddle

A splendid, large saddle of motorcycle type. Well padded and shaped leather top, neatly finished. Very low priced. Size of top, 10¾ inches long, 8¾ inches wide. Double truss spring frame and popular beehive type cushion springs; black finish. Universal saddle clamp. Shipping weight, 6½ pounds.

28K2045.......................... $1.58

New Departure Coaster Hub

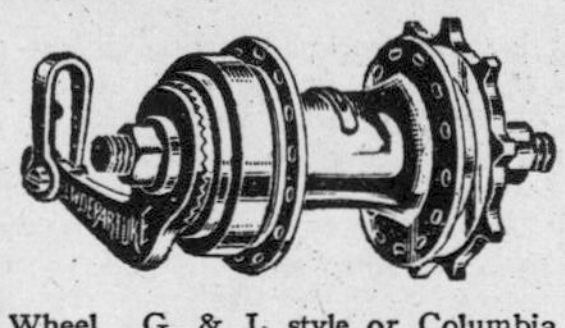

28K1986—New Departure Coaster Hub. Shpg. wt., 3 lbs. $4.25

28K1994¼ Built-Up Coaster Hub Wheel, Crescent Cement Natural Wood Rim. Size, 28 inches. Shpg. wt., 4¾ lbs. $6.45

28K1995¼ Built-Up Coaster Hub Wheel. G. & J. style or Columbia Clincher Natural Wood Rim. Shipping weight, 5 pounds. $6.55

28K1996¼—Built-Up Coaster Hub Wheel, Steel Crescent Cement Rim. Black. Shpg. wt., 5½ lbs. 6.35

28K1997¼—Built-Up Coaster Hub Wheel. Steel Clincher Rim. Black. Shpg. wt., 6 lbs. 6.40

NOTE—28K1994¼ and 28K1995¼ Rear Wheels can be furnished with enameled rims for 22 cents extra. For colors see note under 28K2178¼ on opposite page. All steel rims are furnished in black only. We do not furnish steel lined wood rims.

Unless otherwise specified, for 1x⅜-inch chain we will ship you a hub for thirty-six spokes with a 9-tooth sprocket (7, 8 or 10-tooth also furnished). When used with ½x⅛-inch chain we will ship you an 18-tooth sprocket unless 14, 16, 20 or 22-tooth is specified.

Spindle Hub

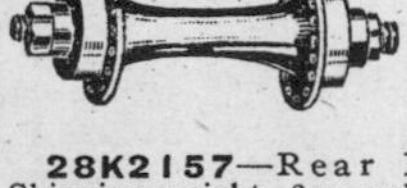

One-piece, nickel plated. Sprockets for rear hubs furnished 7, 8, 9 or 10-tooth and 14, 16, 18 or 20-tooth. **State sprocket size.** All hubs drilled 36 holes.

28K2157—Rear Hub and Sprocket. Shipping weight, 2 pounds.......... $1.50

28K2158—Spindle Front Hub only. Shipping weight, ¾ pound.......... .55

For Big Values in Real Bicycles turn to pages 449-450 and 451.

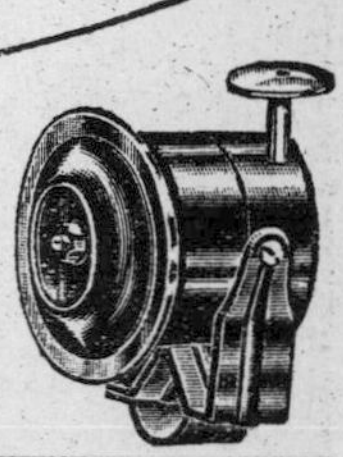

Classy Hand Horn

Up to date hand horn, a big value. Height, over all, 4½ inches; diameter at front, 3 inches. Clamps to handle bar. Shipping weight, 1½ pounds.

28K2335........... 60c

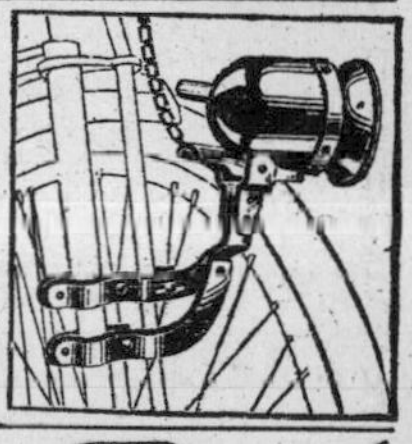

Wheel Horn

A beautifully finished wheel horn of the most improved type. Has strong, far reaching yet pleasant tone.

A finely finished product that you will be proud to put on your bicycle. Shipping weight, 1¾ pounds.

28K2133....... $1.25

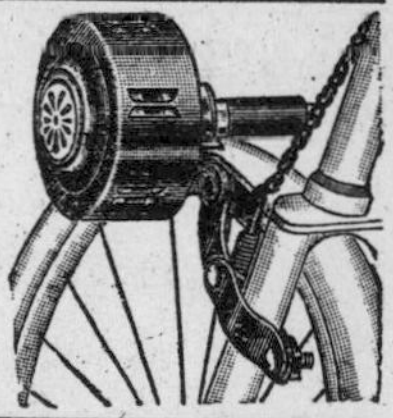

Favorite Siren

Gives the familiar siren warning. Roller is brought into contact with front tire by pulling chain. Has ball bearing construction. Outer drum nickel plated. Bracket furnished permits use on bicycle where front mud guard extends beyond fork. Shipping weight, 1¼ pounds

28K2132 75c

Luggage Carrier Stand

Carrier is 18⅜x12¼x4 in., taking standard market basket; light but strong. Stand attaches to rear axle pin. Carrier has stand lock clip. Black finish. Shpg. wt., 7¼ lbs.

28K2230 $1.55

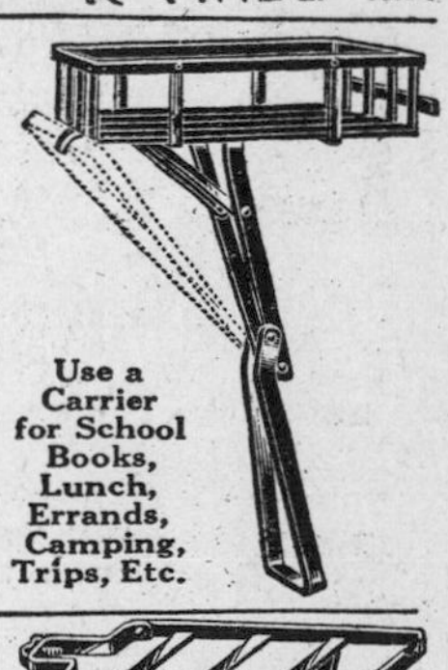

Use a Carrier for School Books, Lunch, Errands, Camping, Trips, Etc.

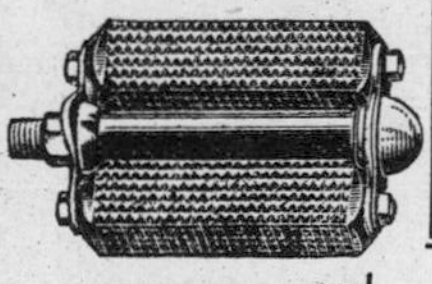

Triumph Rubber Pedals

Popular type, priced very low. Shpg. wt., per pair, 2¼ pounds.

28K2059 Pair.......... 98c

Pedal Rubbers for above. Shipping wt., per pair, 7 oz.

28K2073—Pair, for one pedal........ 14c

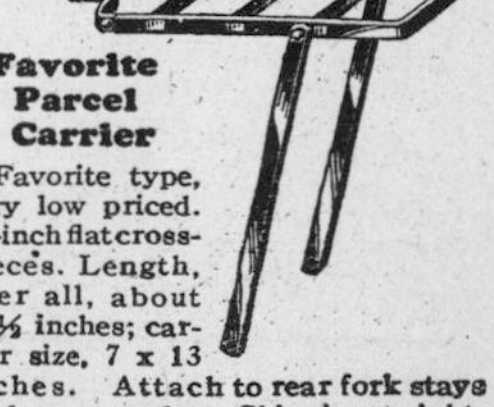

Favorite Parcel Carrier

Favorite type, very low priced. ½-inch flat cross-pieces. Length, over all, about 17½ inches; carrier size, 7 x 13 inches. Attach to rear fork stays and rear axle. Shipping weight, 3 pounds.

28K2227.......... 30c

Automobile ~Use Them for Many Purposes~
Robes

They Make Excellent Gifts

Motor Robes are so useful and practical that every household should have at least one. Use them for blankets, for the boys' den, for steamer rugs, for covers on couches or day beds, for camping, picnicking and all outdoor sports. As gifts, they are unsurpassed.

We carry an assortment of robes in unusually beautiful patterns and snappy colors in striking contrasts. All are exceptional values from the World's Largest Store.

All Wool Fringed Robe

All Wool Motor Robe at the price you would ordinarily pay elsewhere for part wool robes. You're getting the most for your money here at the World's Largest Store, for it is our tremendous buying power that enables us to combine such high quality and low price. Splendidly made of good grade all wool yarns with a smooth, soft finish. A robe can be beautiful as well as serviceable and, with this end in view, snappy colors and attractive plaids produce here a robe of smart, good looks. Color combination of red, green, and gray or combination of blue, green and gray. State color combination desired. Size, about 58x80 inches. Weight, about 3¼ pounds. Shpg. wt., 4 lbs.

24K8522—Each...........$4.98

Imported Italian Fringed Robe

$7.98

It is practically impossible to buy an All Wool Imported Robe elsewhere under $14.00 and here we are offering one for $7.98. The finest wool yarns, skillful weaving and the beauty of rich colors have all been combined to perfect a motor robe of exceptional beauty that is soft and luxurious and delightfully warm. It is double plaid, a different pattern on each side, in bright, snappy colors that create striking contrasts. Really two robes in one. It is wonderful quality and at our money saving price is a truly remarkable value. Comes on blue ground, brown ground, green ground or gray ground with plaids in harmonizing colors. State color combination desired. Size, about 60x80 inches. Weight, about 4¼ pounds. Shpg. wt., 5 lbs.

24K8551—Each................$7.98

All Wool Fringed Plaid Robe

There is real value in this All Wool Robe, for you couldn't buy a quality robe elsewhere at a price like this. It is firmly woven and will stand up under the most severe wear. The good grade of wool used, the splendid finish and soft wooly feel, combined with the exceptional beauty of the pattern and colors, make it a robe that will give complete satisfaction. The plaid pattern is reversible and comes in harmonizing shades of **dark blue ground with green and red stripes** or **dark blue ground with brown and gray stripes.** State color combination desired. Size, about 58x80 inches. Weight, about 4 pounds. Shipping weight, 4¾ lbs.

24K8530
Each....................$6.75

> It's Easy to Order From the World's Largest Store. See Order Blanks in Back of Catalog

Part Wool Robe

Low priced robe that is one of our biggest values. It is unexcelled for long, hard wear and is the type of robe you can use for radiator cover in winter. It is durably woven of cotton and a small amount of wool, and has a striped design in contrasting colors. It will give wonderful service and is unusual value at our amazingly low price. Comes on **gray ground with red stripes.** Size, about 53x72 inches. Wt., about 3¼ lbs. Shpg. wt., 4 lbs.

24K8502—Each...........................$1.98

All Wool Fringed Plain Back Robe

Our very best Imported All Wool Robe for those who desire better quality. The excellent grade of wool yarns and the soft texture give it that beautiful fluffy finish that is found only in the high grade robes. The fancy plaid in rich contrasting colors and the plain back harmonize to make a delightfully effective robe. Size, about 60x80 inches, including fringe. Predominating colors of **blue, brown or green.** State color. Weight, about 5 pounds. Shipping weight, 5¼ pounds.

24K8561
Each..........$11.50

Save Your Cushions   ALLSTATE Seat Covers

Lowest Prices $9.95 and Up

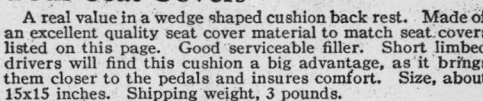

Cushions to Match Your Seat Covers

A real value in a wedge shaped cushion back rest. Made of an excellent quality seat cover material to match seat covers listed on this page. Good serviceable filler. Short limbed drivers will find this cushion a big advantage, as it brings them closer to the pedals and insures comfort. Size, about 15x15 inches. Shipping weight, 3 pounds.

28K8995—ALLSTATE Blue With Blue Trim Seat Cover Cushion................................. **85c**
28K8996—"Spic and Span," Tan With Red Trim Seat Cover Cushion......................... **85c**
28K8997—"Spic and Span" Blue With Blue Trim Seat Cover Cushion......................... **85c**

ALLSTATE DeLuxe Spanish Trim Seat Covers

Here is beauty and cleanliness for new cars and old ones. Our ALLSTATE seat covers are made of beautifully striped seat cover material the wearing edges reinforced with blue Spanish grain leatherette to harmonize with the material. Each set consists of covers for seats, backs, side panels, arm rests and doors, with large roomy pockets. Special fasteners make it possible to attach and detach ALLSTATE seat covers in a jiffy without marring the upholstery in the slightest. They need no tacking or sewing. Complete instructions in each box. Furnished in blue trim only which matches nearly all cars. When ordering be sure to mention make, year and model of your car. Shipping weight of Ford Sets, 6 pounds.

28K8942—Ford Tudor Coach, 1926-27. Per set.... **$9.95**
28K8943—Ford Fordor Sedan, 1926-27. Per set.... **$9.95**

28K8530—Chevrolet Sedan, 1925-26.
28K8536—Chevrolet Sedan, 1927.
28K8531—Chevrolet Landau Sed. 1925-26.
28K8532—Chevrolet Landau Sedan, 1927.
28K8533—Chevrolet Imperial Landau Sedan, 1926-27.
28K8534—Chevrolet Coach, 1926.
28K8535—Chevrolet Coach, 1927.

Any of the models listed above. Shipping weight, 6 lbs. Per set........ **$11.95**
28K8994½—For all 1925-26-27 four-passenger Coupes, four and five-passenger Coaches, Broughams, Sedans and Landau Sedans in makes as listed below. Shipping weight, 6 lbs. Per set.................. **$11.95**

Seat covers for the following makes of cars are shipped to you direct from the factory in NORTHEASTERN ILLINOIS: Ajax, Auburn, Buick, Cadillac, Chandler, Chrysler, Cleveland, Dodge, Durant, Erskine, Essex, Flint, Gardner, Gray, Hudson, Hupmobile, Jewett, Jordan, La Salle, Locomobile Jr. 8, Maxwell, Moon, Nash, Oakland, Oldsmobile, Overland, Packard, Paige, Peerless, Pontiac, Reo, Rickenbacker, Star, Studebaker, Velie, Willys-Knight, Whippet-Overland. When ordering under 28K8994½, be sure to give us the name of your car, year of your car, name of model, type of car (Coupe, Coach, Brougham, Sedan or Landau Sedan), model number, passenger (four or five), number of doors (two or four). Has your car wood panel on doors? It is very important that you give us all of this information, so that the seat covers furnished you will fit your car perfectly.

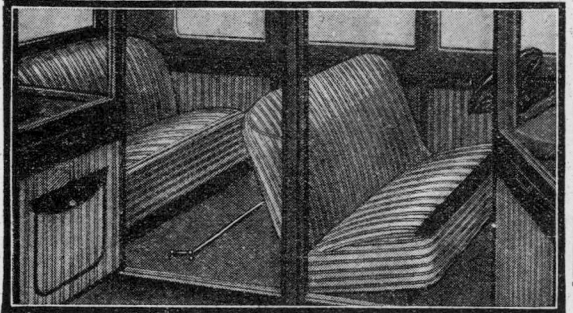

For FORD Tudor Coach and Fordor Sedan, 1926 and 1927 $6.95

For all Standard Cars $8.95

Spanish Trim *Spic and Span* Seat Covers

Fine quality striped Seat Covers trimmed in Spanish grain leatherette, and consisting of covers for seats, backs, side panels, arm rests and door covers with large buttoned flap pockets. Easy to attach. Special fasteners are provided so that they can be put on and taken off quickly and easily. No sewing necessary. Complete instructions with each set. Only because we buy them in such large quantities can we afford to quote these extremely low prices! Furnished in two color combinations—tan striped material with red Spanish trim or blue striped material with blue Spanish trim. State in your order which colors you wish. Shipping weight of Ford Sets, 5 pounds.

28K8634—Ford Tudor Coach, 1926-27. Per set.... **$6.95**
28K8630—Ford Fordor Sedan, 1926-27. Per set.... **$6.95**

28K8636—Chevrolet Sedan, 1925-26.
28K8644—Chevrolet Sedan, 1927.
28K8638—Chevrolet Landau Sedan, 1925-26.
28K8646—Chevrolet Landau Sed. 1927.
28K8648—Chevrolet Imperial Landau Sedan, 1927.
28K8640—Chevrolet Coach, 1926.
28K8642—Chevrolet Coach, 1927.

Any of the models listed above. Shipping weight, 5 lbs. Per set..... **$8.95**
28K8903½—For all 1925-26-27 four-passenger Coupes, four and five-passenger Coaches, Broughams, Sedans and Landau Sedans in makes as listed above under our ALLSTATE seat covers. Shipping weight, 5 lbs. Per set. **$8.95**

When ordering under 28K8903½, be sure to give us the name of your car, year of your car, name of model, type of car (Coupe, Coach, Brougham, Sedan or Landau Sedan), model number, passenger (four or five), number of doors (two or four). Has your car wood panels on doors? It is very important that you give us all of this information, so that the seat covers furnished you will fit your car perfectly.

ALLSTATE Spanish Trim Slip Covers

These beautiful Auto Slip Covers were made to supply the demand for coverings for seats and back rests only. Add beauty and give protection to the upholstery at small cost and can be quickly put on and taken off for cleaning purposes. Made of beautiful striped materials and reinforced with Spanish leatherette to match. Furnished in Blue only. Carefully designed and tailored, and easy to attach. Shipping weight, 5 pounds.

$3.95 and Up

28K8989—Ford Tudor Coach, 1926-27. Shpg. wt., 5 lbs. Per set.... **$3.95**
28K8990—Ford Fordor Sedan, 1926-27. Shipping weight, 5 lbs. Per set.... **$3.95**

28K8593—Chevrolet Sedan, 1925-26.
28K8597—Chevrolet Sedan, 1927.
28K8594—Chevrolet Landau Sedan, 1925-26.
28K8598—Chevrolet Landau Sed. 1927.
28K8599—Chevrolet Imperial Landau Sedan, 1927.
28K8595—Chevrolet Coach, 1926.
28K8596—Chevrolet Coach, 1927.

Any of the models listed above. Shipping weight, 5 lbs. Per set..... **$5.95**
28K8991½—For all 1925-26-27 four-passenger Coupes, Broughams, Sedans and Landau Sedans in makes as listed below. Shipping weight, 5 lbs. Per set. **$5.95**

Seat covers for the following makes of cars are shipped to you direct from the factory in NORTHEASTERN ILLINOIS: Ajax, Auburn, Buick, Cadillac, Chandler, Chrysler, Cleveland, Dodge, Durant, Erskine, Essex, Flint, Gardner, Gray, Hudson, Hopmobile, Jewett, Jordan, LaSalle, Locomobile Jr. 8, Maxwell, Moon, Nash, Oakland, Oldsmobile, Overland, Packard Paige, Peerless, Pontiac, Reo, Rickenbacker, Star, Studebaker, Velie, Willys-Knight, Whippet-Overland.

When ordering under 28K8991½ be sure to give us the name of your car, year of your car, name of model, type of car (Coupe, Coach, Brougham, Sedan or Landau Sedan), model number, passenger (four or five), number of doors (two or four). Has your car wood panels on doors?

It is very important that you give us all of this information, so that the seat covers furnished you will fit your car perfectly.

Car Awnings

Absolutely Theftproof

Every closed car owner should enjoy the distinction and comfort these attractive and useful theftproof awnings give, and at a very low cost. Let yourself and friends ride in cool comfort. These awnings keep out the heat, yet let in the breeze. Do not interfere with complete vision, but aid it by protecting you from the dangerous glaring sun and road reflections. Ingenious arrangement for attaching makes these awnings absolutely theftproof. Glass can be raised all the way without removing awning. Easily removed when not needed. Made of fancy waterproof awning canvas in two patterns: No. 1—Blue, gray, and white stripes; No. 2—Green and brown stripes, as in illustrations. Two-inch width adjustments. Be sure to state pattern number wanted.

Pattern 1 Catalog No.	Pattern 2 Catalog No.	Size	Shipping Weight
28K8864	28K8874	18½ in. extends to 20½ in.	2 lbs.
28K8865	28K8875	20½ in. extends to 22½ in.	2 lbs.
28K8866	28K8876	22½ in. extends to 24½ in.	2¼ lbs.
28K8867	28K8877	24½ in. extends to 26½ in.	2¼ lbs.
28K8868	28K8878	26½ in. extends to 28½ in.	2¾ lbs.
28K8869	28K8879	28½ in. extends to 30½ in.	2¾ lbs.
28K8870	28K8880	30½ in. extends to 32½ in.	3 lbs.
28K8871	28K8881	32½ in. extends to 34½ in.	3¼ lbs.
28K8872	28K8882	34½ in. extends to 36½ in.	3½ lbs.

Per pair............ **$1.69**

No. 1

No. 2

Lowest Prices

America's Best
DEARBORN SR

8,000

A TIRE that is *guaranteed for 8,000 miles* should have many, many more miles of steady service built into it to make the guarantee certain and worth while. This added mileage means an added saving to put back in your pockets. The economy of DEARBORN SR tires becomes more apparent the longer you use them. We designed DEARBORN SR Cords and Balloons to *SAVE YOU MORE MONEY* and *they will do it*. Tests have proved that.

Their Mileage Records Make New Friends Daily

Breaking their own mileage records daily, these money saving DEARBORN SR Cords and Balloons are proving their claim to the name "America's Best Low Priced Tires." Their fine performance is responsible for the number of repeat orders we are receiving daily, and makes it easy for DEARBORN SR Tires to make new friends everywhere. *Join the thousands who recognize a real tire bargain.*

BALLOON TIRES

Catalog No.	Size, Inches	Shpg. Wt. Lbs.	Rim Size	Each
28K243¼	29x4.40	17	21	$ 7.35
28K249¼	29x4.95	21	20	10.45
28K251¼	30x4.95	22	21	10.65
28K253¼	31x4.95	23	22	11.50
28K255¼	30x5.25	21	20	11.65
28K257¼	31x5.25	23	21	12.15
28K259¼	30x5.77	26	20	13.45

Possibly the tires now on your car are marked in this manner: 4.95/20, 5.25/21, 6.20/20, 7.30/20, or a similar marking. The last figures indicate your rim size. In our sizes listed above we have indicated the rim sizes, so you can be sure you are ordering the right size tire.

NOTE—ALLSTATE Tire Flaps are furnished with all DEARBORN SR Balloon Tires.

Heavy Gray Balloon Tubes

Catalog No.	Size, Inches	Shpg. Wt. Lbs.	Each
28K244	29x4.40	2¼	$1.49
28K250	29x4.95	2¾	1.85
28K252	30x4.95	3	1.95
28K254	31x4.95	3	2.07
28K256	30x5.25	3	2.25
28K258	31x5.25	3	2.45
28K260	30x5.77	3	2.65

TUBES WITH BENT VALVES

If your wheels require tubes with bent valves, we can furnish them. Add 20 cents to the price of each tube and be sure to state "bent valve" in your order in this manner—28K258-1-31x5.25 tube with bent valve, $2.65. Also give make, year and model of your car.

Remember, it is not easy to get tubes with bent valves while on the road. Better order a couple of spare tubes now.

All weights given on this page are approximate and may vary a trifle.

Order Your Tire and Tube Together

We offer the following combinations of casing and tube under a single number. Order under these numbers and you cannot "forget that tube."

Clincher Style Casing, With Gray Tube

Catalog No.	Size, Inches	Shpg. Wt., Lbs.	Each
28K603¼	30x3½ Reg.	16	$7.10
28K605¼	30x3½ Oversize	18	7.39

Straight Side Casing, With Gray Tube

Catalog No.	Size, Inches	Shpg. Wt., Lbs.	Each
28K613¼	32x4 S.S.	25	$12.25

Mail Your Orders for Tires, Tubes and Batteries to

CHICAGO — PHILADELPHIA — MINNEAPOLIS — BOSTON — COLUMBUS, OHIO or MEMPHIS

Whichever is nearest you

For EXTRA Miles USE OVERSIZE TIRES

The motorist is demanding more and more riding comfort. He knows that when his car is riding comfortably it is being saved the rack and hard wear of rough going.

It stands to reason, then, that the *larger your tires are the easier they will ride*, and they will contribute not only to your comfort but the long life of your car. That is why we recommend that you *use oversize tires*. You can make the change gradually if you wish—first change your rear tires and then, later on, your front ones.

We are always glad to sell you whatever tires you may want to buy, but if you want extra long service, extra economy, and extra comfort, equip your car with oversize tires. The chart across the bottom of page 463 shows the oversizes which we recommend.

In every instance the first tire listed is the size which we most strongly recommend, but the other sizes may also be used.

Low Priced Tires!
Cords and Balloons!

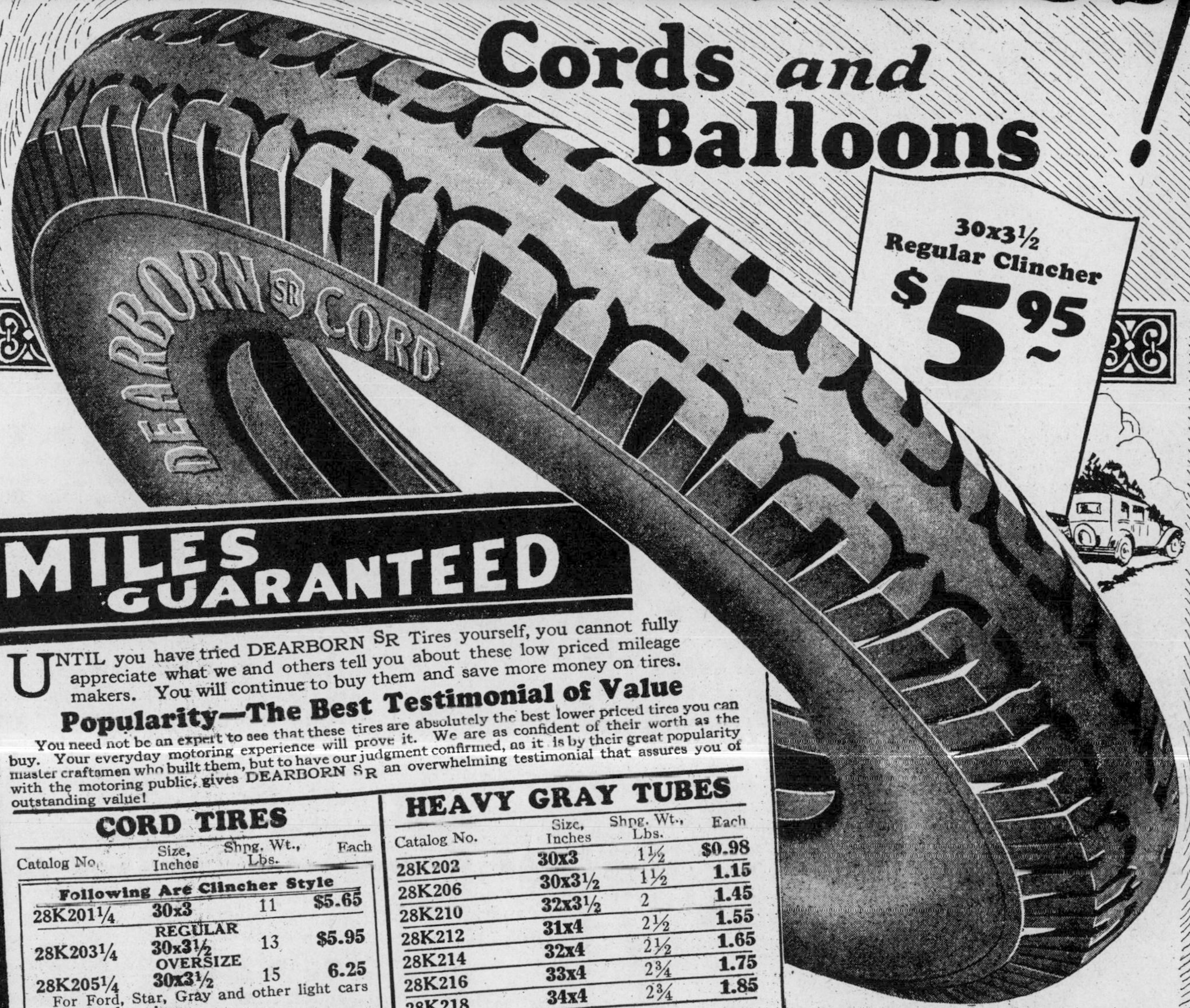

30x3½ Regular Clincher
$5.95

MILES GUARANTEED

UNTIL you have tried DEARBORN SR Tires yourself, you cannot fully appreciate what we and others tell you about these low priced mileage makers. You will continue to buy them and save more money on tires.

Popularity—The Best Testimonial of Value

You need not be an expert to see that these tires are absolutely the best lower priced tires you can buy. Your everyday motoring experience will prove it. We are as confident of their worth as the master craftsmen who built them, but to have our judgment confirmed, as it is by their great popularity with the motoring public, gives DEARBORN SR an overwhelming testimonial that assures you of outstanding value!

CORD TIRES

Catalog No.	Size, Inches	Shpg. Wt. Lbs.	Each
Following Are Clincher Style			
28K201¼	30x3	11	$5.65
28K203¼	REGULAR 30x3½	13	$5.95
28K205¼	OVERSIZE 30x3½	15	6.25

For Ford, Star, Gray and other light cars with clincher rims.

Catalog No.	Size, Inches	Shpg. Wt. Lbs.	Each
Following Are Straight Side Style			
28K207¼	30x3½ OVERSIZE	17	$7.65

Used principally on 1923, 1924 and 1925 models Chevrolet, Overland and 1924 Essex. Be sure your car has straight side rims.

Catalog No.	Size, Inches	Shpg. Wt. Lbs.	Each
	30x3½		$ 9.95
28K211¼	31x4	20	$ 9.95
28K213¼	32x4	21	10.65
28K215¼	33x4	22	11.45
28K219¼	32x4½	28	15.95
28K221¼	33x4½	29	16.25
28K223¼	34x4½	30	16.85
28K231¼	33x5	40	21.25

NOTE: ALLSTATE Tire Flaps are furnished with all straight side style DEARBORN SR Cords.

HEAVY GRAY TUBES

Catalog No.	Size, Inches	Shpg. Wt. Lbs.	Each
28K202	30x3	1½	$0.98
28K206	30x3½	1½	1.15
28K210	32x3½	2	1.45
28K212	31x4	2½	1.55
28K214	32x4	2½	1.65
28K216	33x4	2¾	1.75
28K218	34x4	2¾	1.85

Extra Heavy Oversize Red Tubes

Catalog No.	Size, Inches	Shpg. Wt. Lbs.	Each
28K120	32x4½	3½	$2.95
28K122	33x4½	3½	3.05
28K124	34x4½	3¾	3.19
28K132	33x5	4½	3.75

Tire and Tube prices are subject to change without notice. However, we guarantee that our prices on tires and tubes will always make you the same large saving they have in the past, when compared with prices on other tires and tubes of equal quality.

NOTE: Weights on this page are approximate and may vary a trifle.

We Guarantee

every DEARBORN SR TIRE against any defect in workmanship or material on a service basis of **8,000 Miles**

Mail Your Orders for Tires, Tubes and Batteries to
CHICAGO, PHILADELPHIA, MINNEAPOLIS, BOSTON, COLUMBUS, OHIO, MEMPHIS
Whichever is nearest you.

For MORE LUXURIOUS COMFORT and GOOD LOOKS USE OVERSIZE TIRES

High Pressure Regular Size	Recommended Oversize	High Pressure Regular Size	Recommended Oversize	Balloon Regular Size	Recommended Oversize	Balloon Regular Size	Recommended Oversize
30x3½	Cl.30x3½ Cl. oversize or 31x4.40 Cl. balloon	34x4½	35x4½	29x4.40	30x4.95, 31x5.00 or 30x4.75	29x5.25	31x6.00
30x3½	S.S.31x4 or 31x4.40 S. S. balloon	32x4½	33x5 or 33x5.77 balloon	27x4.40	28x4.75	30x5.25	32x6.00 or 32x6.20
32x3½	33x4	33x4½	34x5 Heavy duty or 34x5.77 balloon	26x4.75	30x5.25 or 29x4.95	31x5.25	33x6.00 or 33x6.20
31x4	32x4½ or 32x4.95 balloon	34x4½	35x5	30x4.75	31x5.00 or 31x5.25	30x5.77	32x6.75 or 32x6.00
32x4	33x4½ or 33x4.95 balloon	30x5	32x6 heavy duty	29x4.95	30x5.25 or 30x5.77	32x5.25	32x6.75 or 32x6.00
33x4	34x4½	31x5	36x6 heavy duty	30x4.95	31x5.25 or 31x5.00	33x6.00	32x6.75 or 33x6.20
		32x6	34x7 heavy duty	31x4.95	32x5.77	32x6.20	32x6.75
				28x5.25	30x6.00	32x6.20	32x6.75

NOTE—The first oversize tire listed IN ALL CASES is the SIZE WE RECOMMEND, but the other sizes may also be used.

For CATALOG NUMBERS and PRICES of OVERSIZE TIRE EQUIPMENT, turn to the page showing the tires in which you are interested.

Order Blanks Are in Back of This Catalog

463

ALLSTATE ⟨SR⟩
HEAVY DUTY
Truck and Bus Cords
Give More Mileage
They Are Built to Wear

RESULTS—That is what every truck and bus owner wants today from his tires.

MILEAGE—More mileage than you believed possible, is what you get from these heavy, hard working ALLSTATE Truck and Bus Cords. On every road they leave a trail of extra long mileage, going far beyond the *12,000 miles guaranteed* to prove their worth.

ALLSTATE are Profitable Truck Tires

Drivers relying on ALLSTATE Truck and Bus Cords don't worry about costly delays on the road. ALLSTATE Truck and Bus Cords are on the job with him and deliver the goods. Their sturdy road resisting strength, the broad flat road gripping tread, and the extra quality that means extra mileage are waiting to serve you profitably. *Longer mileage* is a part of your ALLSTATE purchase and you can't afford to spend money on anything else. These tires are built for business and mean business as you guide them over any road. Their business is to give service and save you money, and they do it well. Road tests prove it.

The Nation's Best Truck Tire Value

Every truck operator would be glad to read the many letters we have received praising these dependable, economical tires. But the best way to convince yourself that ALLSTATE Truck and Bus Cords *won't be outdistanced for value* is to buy one or a set today—and write your own testimonial..

Your Truck Needs These Tires!

This Guarantee Protects You!
These Famous ALLSTATE Truck and Bus Cords are guaranteed against any defects in workmanship or material on a service basis of

12,000 MILES
Many users of our truck tires tell us they run for 20,000 to 25,000 Miles.

6-Plies 30x3½ CLINCHER $10⁹⁵
The Best 30x3½ Tire Made at Any Price
Be Sure the Truck Tire You Buy Is a 6-Ply Tire

Get an extra rugged Heavy Duty Tire with six plies in a size which will fit Fords and other light cars with clincher rims.

This means that you can at last get a Ford size tire that will give real heavy duty service that has six plies to give extra endurance and an extra ¼-inch thickness of tough tread rubber to give extra wear.

These tires are suitable for all light truck service and we recommend them also for passenger sedans. The 30x3½ Heavy Duty Tire is THE tire for endurance and long service.

Mail Your Orders for Tires, Tubes and Batteries to
CHICAGO—PHILADELPHIA MINNEAPOLIS—COLUMBUS, OHIO MEMPHIS or BOSTON
Whichever is nearest you

Truck and Bus Cords

Catalog No.	Size, Inches	No. of Plies	Shpg. Wt., Lbs.	Each
28K305¼	30x3½Cl	6	19	$10.95
28K313¼	32x4 SS	6	25	16.95
28K319¼	32x4½SS	8	31	22.75
28K323¼	34x4½SS	8	33	24.85
28K329¼	30x5 SS	8	39	25.95
28K331¼	33x5 SS	8	43	28.85
28K333¼	34x5 SS	8	44	29.35
28K335¼	35x5 SS	8	46	29.65
28K337¼	32x6 SS	10	56	44.35
28K339¼	36x6 SS	10	62	48.50
28K343¼	34x7 SS	10	65	60.50

Note: ALLSTATE Tire Flaps are furnished with all Straight Side ALLSTATE HEAVY DUTY TIRES.

Tire and Tube prices are subject to change without notice. However, we guarantee that our prices on tires and tubes will always make you the same large saving they have in the past, when compared with prices on other tires and tubes of equal quality.

Extra Heavy Red Truck and Bus Inner Tubes

Catalog No.	Size, Inches	Shpg. Wt., Lbs.	Each
28K306	30x3½	2½	$1.85
28K314	32x4	3½	2.85
28K320	32x4½	4½	2.95
28K324	34x4½	4½	3.25
28K330	30x5	5¼	3.65
28K332	33x5	5½	3.85
28K334	34x5	5½	3.98
28K336	35x5	5¾	4.15
28K338	32x6	6	5.95
28K340	36x6	6¼	6.95
28K344	34x7	8	8.25

Tubes With Bent Valve

If your tubes require bent valves we can furnish them. Add 20c to the price of each tube and be sure to state "bent valve" in your order, in this manner (28K330—1—30x5 tube with bent valve—$3.85), also give make, year and model of your car. Remember, it is not easy to get tubes with bent valves on the road. Better order a couple of spare tubes now.

All weights given on this page are approximate and may vary a trifle

Puncture Proof TIRES

Note the Air Cells ↓

No More Tire Trouble

30 x 3½ COMPLETE WITH RIM **$16.45~**

30 x 3½ COMPLETE WITH RIM **$14.95~**

Guaranteed for 12 Months of Service

ALLSTATE CUSHION Truck Tires

For Ford, Chevrolet and Other Light Trucks

Keep your work car or light truck on the job! Install ALL-STATE Cushion Tires and *keep the job moving.*

Public Service Cars Use Them

Police Squad cars, and other public service cars in large cities use tires of this type because there is *never any doubt about the running dependability* at any time. ALLSTATE Cushion Tires are *absolutely puncture proof* and once installed will give no trouble.

These tires are *vulcanized to the rim* and can't slip. Absolutely the best tire of its kind on the road today, worthy to bear the same name and heavy safety tread as our famous ALLSTATE Cords.

Carry One as an Emergency Spare

Users of *pneumatic equipped* small cars in rough country will find this tire an excellent *emergency spare.*

Buy a set of these fine tires for your light work car or farm truck, for rural mail delivery, milk route service and other service where tire delays are costly, and you will enjoy absolute freedom from all tire worries for months and months.

Guaranteed For 12 Months of Service

We guarantee our new Cushion Tires for twelve full months against defects in material or workmanship. Join the Ever Growing Army of Users of ALLSTATE Cushion Tires.

28K277¼—Size, 30x3½, complete with rim which has four lugs, to fit Fords and Chevrolet, ready for mounting. Shpg. wt., 42 lbs............ **$16.45**

28K279¼—Size, 30x5, complete with rim which is flanged, ready for mounting. For Fords only. Shipping weight, 105 pounds.................. **$34.95**

Chevrolet Truck Owners

Our 30x5 ALLSTATE Cushion Tires will not fit Chevrolet wheels. We furnish special wheels for Chevrolets, at a very low price, on which our 30x5 ALLSTATE Cushion Tires will fit perfectly.

28K15240—Set of two 30x5 Truck Wheels, 12 bolts and 12 nuts. Shipping weight, 50 pounds............ **$9.95**

We do not recommend these tires where speeds of over 25 miles per hour are required. They are for HEAVY DUTY WORK ONLY.

AIR CELL Cushion Tires

For Fords and Chevrolet

Mr. Truck Owner:—

You will do well by your tire budget, MR. TRUCK OWNER, if you invest in a set of these convenient, trouble-free AIR-CELL Cushion Tires. Let them prove their economy over a period of extra long tire life. You spend no more money on tubes or spare casings. The air cells absorb the jolts and jars to a large degree, which no ordinary "solid" tire could do.

Twice The Mileage of a Pneumatic

These money savers look somewhat like a pneumatic tire, and will give at least *twice the mileage any pneumatic tire could possibly give*, with none of the worries. The hidden air cells in the center of these tires insure an added springiness or resiliency which rubber alone could not give.

They LOOK LIKE PNEUMATICS

Notice the *non-skid tread*, and the general resemblance in shape and style of the whole tire to the pneumatic type. When you substitute Air-Cell Cushion Tires on your truck, you save real money. *Cushion Tires MUST Be Practical and Economical—We Sell So Many of Them.*

28K275¼—Size, 30x3½, complete with rim ready for mounting. Shpg. wt., 38 lbs..... **$14.95**

Tire prices are subject to change without notice. However, we guarantee that our prices on tires will always make you the same large saving they have in the past, when compared with prices on other tires and tubes of equal quality.

Mail Your Orders for Tires, Tubes and Batteries to
**CHICAGO — PHILADELPHIA
MINNEAPOLIS — BOSTON
COLUMBUS, OHIO or MEMPHIS**
Whichever is nearest you

Peerless BATTERIES
18 MONTHS of

Assured Uninterrupted Battery Performance Guaranteed Battery Satisfaction

Over a period of years, hundreds of thousands of satisfied users of Peerless Batteries endorse their performance.

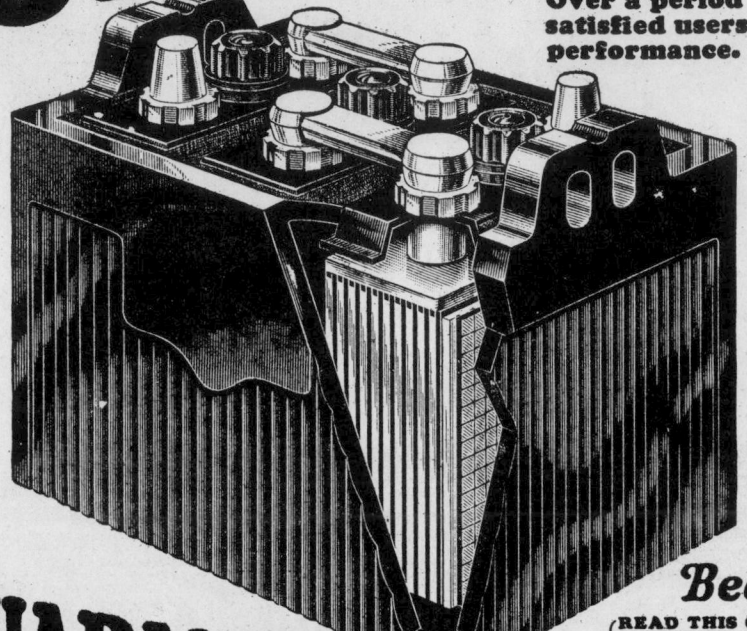

$8 35

For Ford-Chevrolet Overland Star-Gray

Never Before Have Batteries of "PEERLESS" Quality Been Sold at So Low a Price

GUARANTEED

READ THIS GUARANTEE—Every Peerless Battery is guaranteed 18 months to give satisfactory service, and will last much longer if given proper care. The resources and reputation of the World's Largest Store back up this guarantee. **YOU MUST BE SATISFIED.**

Catalog No.	Car	Description	Batteries	
28K7000½	Allen	1918-20 ALL	6-13	$ 9.95
28K7007½	Auburn	1920-25 Inc. 6-39, 6-43, 6-66	6-11	8.35
28K7008½	Auburn	1921-25 Inc. 6-51, 6-63, 6-88	6-13	9.95
28K7009½	Auburn	1926 ALL	6-11	8.35
28K7010½	Auburn	1927, 6-66, 8-77, 8-88	6-13	9.95
28K7012½	Ajax	1925-26 ALL	6-11	8.35
28K7018½	Briscoe (Wood)	1918-19-20 ALL	6-13	2.25
28K7019½	Briscoe (Wood)	1921 ALL	6-13	2.25
28K7024½	Buick (Wood)	1914 B-24, 25, 36, 37	6-13	2.25
28K7025½	Buick (Wood)	1914-15 B-36, 37, 54, 55, C-24, 25	6-13	2.25
28K7026½	Buick	1916 D-54, 55	6-11	9.95
28K7027½	Buick	1916 D-44, 45, 46, 47	6-13	8.35
28K7028½	Buick	1917-18 ALL 1921-24 Inc. 4 cyl.; 1925-26 Standard 6; 1927, 115	6-11	8.35
28K7029½	Buick	1919-24 Inc. 6 cyl.; 1925-26 Master 6; 1927-120, 128	6-13	9.95
28K7036½	Cadillac	1920-27 Inc. ALL	6-19	21.45
28K7044½	Case	1920-27 Inc. W. Y.	6-13	12.95
28K7045½	Case	1921-26 Inc. V. X., 1927 J. I. C.	6-13	9.95
28K7049½	Chalmers (Wd)	1916-17-18 ALL	6-13	2.25
28K7050½	Chalmers	1919-23 Inc. ALL	6-13	9.95
28K7051½	Chalmers	1924 ALL	6-13	9.95
28K7052½	Chandler	1916 Model 17	6-13	9.95
28K7053½	Chandler	1917-18 ALL to 24,000	6-11	8.35
28K7054½	Chandler	1919-20, 24,001 up	6-13	9.95
28K7055½	Chandler	1921-27 Inc. ALL	6-13	9.95
28K7059½	Chevrolet	1916-17-18 490	6-11	8.35
28K7062½	Chevrolet	1919-22 Inc. 490; 1923-27 Inc. Superior	6-11	8.35
28K7066½	Chevrolet	1917-18 Ser. F Baby Grand	6-13	9.95
28K7067½	Chevrolet	1919-20-21-22 FB, FB5, T	6-13	9.95
28K7069½	Chrysler	1924 ALL; 1927, 50	6-11	8.35
28K7070½	Chrysler	1925-27 Inc. 58, 60, 70	6-13	9.95
28K7071½	Chrysler	1926 Imperial 80	6-15	12.95
28K7072½	Chrysler	1927 Imperial 80	6-17	14.25
28K7073½	Cleveland	1919-24 Inc. ALL	6-13	8.35
28K7074½	Cleveland	1925-26 ALL	6-11	9.95
28K7075½	Cole	1918-19-20, 8-70 Aero 8	6-15	9.95
28K7079½	Cole	1921-22, 8-79	6-15	12.95
28K7080½	Cole	1923-25 Master	6-15	12.95
28K7081½	Columbia	1917-19 A. E.	6-13	8.35
28K7086½	Columbia	1920-23 Inc. 20 C, LS, 32, DT, 6V	6-11	8.35
28K7087½	Columbia	1924-25, 32, DT, 7U	6-11	8.35
28K7088½	Davis	1920-26 ALL; 1927, 92	6-11	8.35
28K7089½	Davis	1927, 93	6-13	9.95
28K7091½	Dodge	1915-21 Inc. ALL.	12-7	12.45
28K7092½	Dodge	1922-26 Inc. (12 volt)	12-7	12.45
28K7090½	Dodge	1926, Above Ser. A-518420; 1927 ALL (6-volt)	6-13	9.95
28K7093½	Dort	1916-20 Inc. ALL	6-13	8.35
28K7094½	Dort	1921-26 Inc. ALL	6-11	8.35
28K7098½	Durant	1921-26 Inc. 6 cyl	6-13	9.95
28K7099½	Durant	1922-26 Inc. 4 cyl	6-11	8.35
28K7102½	Earl	1923-24 ALL	6-13	9.95

Catalog No.	Car	Description	Batteries	
28K7707½	Elcar	1918-25 Inc. 4 cyl. 6 cyl.1927, 670,6-11		$8.35
28K7708½	Elcar	1925, 8 cyl. 1926 ALL; 1927, 8-82, 8-90	6-13	9.95
28K77113½	Elgin	1919-22 Inc. ALL	6-11	8.35
28K77106½	Erskine	1927, 6 cyl	6-11	8.35
28K77117½	Essex	1919-20-21 ALL	6-13	9.95
28K77118½	Essex	1922-26 Inc. ALL	6-11	8.35
28K77119½	Essex	1927 ALL	6-13	9.95
28K7720½	Flint	1923-27 Inc. 6-E, 80, B80	6-13	9.95
28K7721½	Flint	1924-27 Inc. 6-40, 60, Jr., Z18, B60	6-11	8.35
28K7724½	Ford	1919-27 ALL	6-11	8.35
28K77301½	Franklin	1916-17-18 Ser. 9; 1919-22 ALL	12-7	12.45
28K77731½	Franklin	1923-27 Inc. ALL	6-15	12.95
28K77734½	Gardner	1920-26 Inc. all but 8A; 1927, 6B	6-11	8.25
28K77735½	Gardner	1925-26, 8A; 1927; 8-90	6-17	14.25
28K77736½	Gardner	1927, 8-80	6-13	9.95
28K77738½	Grant	1917-18-19 K. G. H.	6-11	8.35
28K77739½	Grant	1920-22 Inc. ALL	6-13	9.95
28K77141½	Gray	1922-26 Inc. ALL	6-11	8.35
28K77144½	Haynes	1916-17-18, 36, 37, 38, 39, 40, 41, 44	6-15	12.95
28K77146½	Haynes	1920-25 Inc. ALL	6-15	12.95
28K77149½	Hudson	1916, 6-40	6-13	9.95
28K77150½	Hudson	1917-27 Inc. ALL	6-13	9.95
28K77152½	Hupmobile	1916-17 N1, N1, NO, NR, NU	6-13	9.95
28K77153½	Hupmobile	1918-19 ALL; 1920-21 AL	6-11	8.35
28K77157½	Hupmobile	1922-23-24 ALL	6-13	9.95
28K77159½	Hupmobile	1925-27, 4 cyl. 6 cyl	6-13	9.95
28K77160½	Hupmobile	1925-27 8 cyl	6-17	14.25
28K77166½	Jewett	1922-27 Inc. ALL	6-13	9.95
28K7770½	Jordan	1921-26 Inc. F, M, X, H, J; 1927, Line 8	6-13	9.95
28K77171½	Jordan	1925-26, 8 cyl.; 1927, Great Line 8	6-17	14.25
28K77179½	Kissel	1922-27 Inc. 45, 55, 65, 75	6-13	9.95
28K77182½	Lexington	1919-26 Inc. ALL	6-13	9.95
28K77184½	Liberty	1917-21 Inc. 10B, 10C Touring	6-11	8.35
28K77185½	Liberty	1921-26 Inc. 10D, 10C Coupe & Sedan	6-13	9.95
28K77186½	Lincoln	1920-27 Inc. ALL	6-19	21.45
28K77188½	Marmon	1920-26 ALL; 1927, 75	6-17	14.25
28K77189½	Marmon	1927 Little 8	6-13	9.95
28K77191½	Maxwell	1915-17 Inc. 25 (4 cables)	12-7	13.45
28K77192½	Maxwell	1918-20 Inc. ALL to 300,000 (2 cables)	12-7	13.15
28K77193½	Maxwell	1920-23 Inc. 300,001 up	6-13	10.50
28K77194½	Maxwell	1924-25 ALL	6-13	9.95
28K77197½	Mitchell	1917-19 Inc. D40	6-11	8.35
28K77199½	Mitchell	1919-21 Inc. E40, E42, F40; 1925, 6-40A	6-11	8.35
28K77200½	Mitchell	1922-24 ALL 1925, 50, 58	6-13	9.95
28K77204½	Moon	1919-22 Inc. ALL	6-13	9.95
28K77205½	Moon	1923-26 Inc. Spec. 6	6-13	9.95
28K77206½	Moon	1923-26 Inc. Light 6; 1927, 6-60, 6-80	6-13	8.35

Assure Continuous Service

BUY the right battery right now Choose the Peerless and be sure of long, continuous service and a big saving besides.

Compare The Peerless With Other Batteries

Thousands of others have, and have proved by purchase that they believe this dependable battery with the **18-Months' Guaranteed Service** is the ideal battery for them. **Full size and full capacity plates.** Genuine **Ebonine** container, **acid proof** and **practically unbreakable. Genuine Port Orford Cedar separators.** Only **new materials** are used, and all have been carefully tested and selected. Nothing but **absolute satisfaction** could result from a battery built to such high standards.

Save $5.00 to $15 on Your Battery Purchase

Tremendous popularity expressed in tremendous sales volume has proved the worth of the Peerless Battery in all cars, and this explains how we can save you from $5.00 to $15.00 on every battery you buy from us, as compared to prices often asked elsewhere for batteries of this quality.

Try a Peerless for 60 Days

So sure are we that the Peerless Battery will give you **absolute satisfaction** we invite you to try it in your car for **60 days.** If it does not satisfy you completely within that time send it back at our expense and we will return your money.

There's a Peerless Battery for Your Car—These wonderful batteries are made in sizes to fit all cars. Pick out the battery for your car from the list below. **If your car is not listed, send us the name, year and model and we will ship you the type of battery you require.**

Peerless Batteries Are Shipped Fully Charged

All Peerless Batteries are shipped fully charged, **ready for immediate installation** and service.

24 Hour Service

We ship all orders for batteries within twenty-four hours after they are received. If you are in urgent need of your battery, **telegraph your order,** and we will ship it C. O. D. the same day. The telegraph company will arrange this for you. **Be sure to give us your complete address in your telegram.**

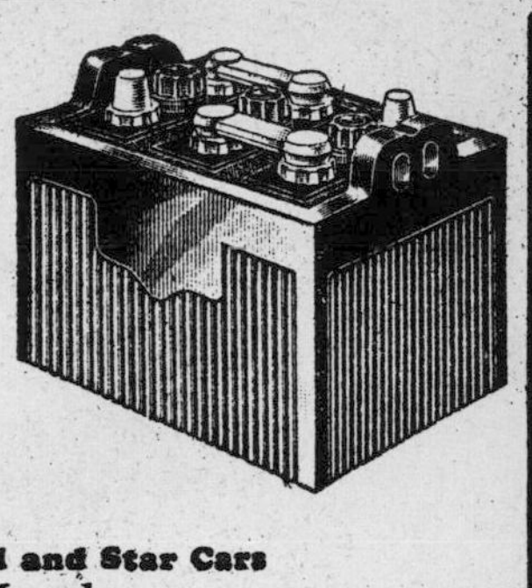

13-Plate Battery

Replacing STANDARD EQUIPMENT *On* FORD CARS

Also for Chevrolet, Overland and Star Cars

Guaranteed 18 Months

Here is a battery of the finest type for Ford owners who wish to duplicate the battery equipment which they bought with their cars. Furnished also for other cars as shown in table below.

This is a REAL Peerless Battery in all that the name implies—excellence of materials and workmanship, and ruggedness of construction. **Unmailable.** Shipping weight, 55 pounds.

28K17125⅓—6-volt, 13-plate battery for **Fords,** 1919-1927, Inc. ALL. . **$8.65**

28K17060⅓—6-volt, 13-plate battery for **Chevrolet,** 1916-17-18, Model 490. . . . . . **8.65**

28K17063⅓—6-volt, 13-plate battery for **Chevrolet,** 1919-22, Inc. Model 490; 1923-27, Inc. Superior. **8.65**

28K17236⅓—6-volt, 13-plate battery for **Overland,** 1916—75; 1917-18—90, 90B; 1919—90T, 90R, 90CC and Del.; 1920:23, Inc. ALL. **8.65**

28K17239⅓—6-volt, 13-plate battery for **Overland,** 1924-26 Inc. ALL; 1927, Whippet. **8.65**

28K17267⅓—6-volt, 13-plate battery for **Star,** 1922-27 Inc. ALL. **8.65**

NOTE—**Batteries are unmailable.** We recommend express shipments for all batteries.

Catalog No.	Car	Description	Batteries	
28K17209⅓	Nash	1917-18, 681, 682	6-11	$ 8.35
28K17211⅓	Nash	1919-24 Inc. 4 cyl	6-11	8.35
28K17212⅓	Nash	1919-26 Inc. 6 cyl. Big 6; 1927 Spec. 6, Adv. 6	6-13	9.95
28K17213⅓	Nash	1925-27 Inc. 4 cyl. Light 6	6-11	8.35
28K17217⅓	Oakland	1916, 32	6-11	8.35
28K17219⅓	Oakland	1917, 34	6-11	8.35
28K17220⅓	Oakland	1918-19, 34B, 34E	6-11	8.35
28K17221⅓	Oakland	1920, 34C	6-13	9.95
28K17222⅓	Oakland	1921-25 Inc. ALL	6-13	9.95
28K17223⅓	Oakland	1926-27 ALL	6-13	9.95
28K17225⅓	Oldsmobile	1916, 43, 44	6-11	8.35
28K17226⅓	Oldsmobile	1917-20, 45, 45A, 37A; 1919, 45B; 1924-25, 30B, 30C	6-11	8.35
28K17227⅓	Oldsmobile	1920, 45B; 1921-22-23 ALL; 1926, 30D	6-13	9.95
28K17230⅓	Oldsmobile	1927 ALL	6-11	8.35
28K17234⅓	Overland (Wood)	1915, 80, 81, 82; 1916, 86, 83, 83B, 83BOE 1917, 85, 85-6; Willys Six 1917-18, 86-B, 89-6	6-13	12.25
28K17235⅓	Overland	1916, 75; 1917-18, 90, 90B; 1919, 90T, 90R, 90CC and Del.; 1920-23 Inc. ALL	6-11	8.35
28K17238⅓	Overland	1924-27 Inc. ALL	6-11	8.35
28K17242⅓	Packard	1921-27 Inc. Single 6, 8 cyl. to 202,000	6-13	9.95
28K17243⅓	Packard	1924-27 Inc. 8 cyl. 202,001 up	6-17	14.25
28K17245⅓	Paige	1917, K-6-17, J-6-17; 1917-18, 6-39, 6-40, 6-51, 6-55; 1919-20 ALL	6-13	9.95
28K17246⅓	Paige	1921-22 ALL	6-13	9.95
28K17247⅓	Paige	1923-26 Inc. ALL	6-17	14.25
28K17232⅓	Paige	1927, 6-65, 6-75	6-13	9.95
28K17248⅓	Peerless	1918-22 Inc. ALL	6-15	12.95
28K17249⅓	Peerless (Wood)	1923-27 Inc. 8 cyl	6-17	16.25
28K17250⅓	Peerless	1924-27 Inc. 6 cyl	6-15	12.95
28K17253⅓	Pontiac	1926 ALL	6-13	9.95
28K17254⅓	Pontiac	1927 ALL	6-11	8.35
28K17251⅓	Reo	1916-20 ALL	6-13	9.95
28K17252⅓	Reo	1921-27 ALL	6-13	9.95
28K17255⅓	Rickenbacker	1922-27 Inc. ALL 6 cyl	6-13	9.95
28K17256⅓	Rickenbacker	1924-27 Inc. 8 cyl	6-17	14.25
28K17259⅓	Saxon	1915-16, S, S2	6-11	8.35
28K17260⅓	Saxon	1917-21 Inc. ALL	6-11	8.35
28K17263⅓	Scripps-Booth	1917-19, D, G, H, 6-39; 1920-22 Inc. ALL	6-11	8.35
28K17266⅓	Star	1922-27 Inc. ALL	6-11	8.35
28K17271⅓	Studebaker	1915, EC, SD	6-15	12.95
28K17272⅓	Studebaker	1916-18 Inc. ALL	6-13	9.95
28K17273⅓	Studebaker	1919 ALL	6-13	9.95
28K17274⅓	Studebaker	1920 ALL	6-13	9.95
28K17275⅓	Studebaker	1921-27 Inc. Big 6, Spec. 6	6-13	9.95
28K17276⅓	Studebaker	1921-27 Inc. Light 6, Standard 6	6-11	8.35
28K17279⅓	Velie	1917-18, 37, 39	6-13	9.95
28K17281⅓	Velie	1920-21, 38, 48	6-13	9.95
28K17282⅓	Velie	1922-25, 34, 48, 58, 60	6-11	8.35
28K17283⅓	Velie	1926, ALL; 1927, 60	6-13	9.95
28K17278⅓	Velie	1927, 50	6-11	8.35
28K17299⅓	Whippet	1927, 4 cyl	6-11	8.35
28K17298⅓	Whippet	1927, 6 cyl	6-13	9.95
28K17284⅓	Willys-Knight (Wood)	1915-17, 84, 88-4, 88-8; 1918, 88-8B; 1919 ALL	6-15	13.65
28K17285⅓	Willys-Knight	1924-27 Inc. 64, 65, 66, 66A, 67	6-17	14.25
28K17286⅓	Willys-Knight	1927, 70, 70A	6-15	12.95
28K17287⅓	Willys-Knight	1920-21 Model 20	6-17	14.25
28K17288⅓	Willys-Knight	1921-22-23 Model 20A	6-17	14.25

We ship batteries from factory in Chicago, Ill., Philadelphia, Pa., Kansas City, Mo., New York City, N. Y., Atlanta, Ga., Pittsburgh, Pa., Memphis, Tenn., Denver, Colo., Minneapolis, Minn., Boston, Mass., and Columbus, Ohio, whichever is nearest you. Send your order to Sears, Roebuck and Co., Chicago, Ill., Kansas City, Mo., Philadelphia, Pa., Atlanta, Ga., Memphis, Tenn., Minneapolis, Minn., Columbus, Ohio, or Denver, Colo. If you are in urgent need of your battery, telegraph your order and it will be shipped C. O. D. the same day. The telegraph company will arrange this for you. **Be sure to give your complete address in your telegram.**

NOTE—Unmailable. We recommend express shipments for all batteries.

Shipping weight, $8.35 and $8.65 batteries, 56 pounds; $12.25 batteries, 60 pounds; $9.95 and $10.50 batteries, 65 pounds; $12.45, $13.15 and $12.95 batteries, 73 pounds; $13.45 and $14.25 batteries, 79 pounds; $21.45 batteries, 91 pounds.

Universal Battery Terminal

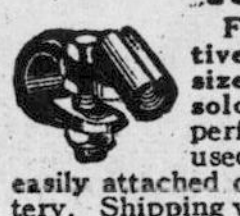

Fits positive or negative battery posts of any size or style without soldering. One-piece gives perfect contact, can be re-used and is quickly and easily attached or detached on any battery. Shipping weight, ¾ lb.

28K6669—Per pair. **29c**

Hard Rubber Cement

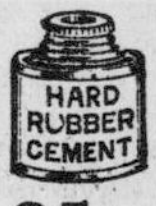

Permanently repairs broken storage battery jars, covers, etc. Use it, too, for repairing or replacing cracked celluloid curtains, for stopping gasoline leaks or as a gasket cement. Two-oz. can. Shipping wt., 4 oz.

28K8232 . . . . . . **35c**

For Radio Batteries, See Page 714

Mail Your Orders for Tires, Tubes and Batteries to

CHICAGO—PHILADELPHIA
MINNEAPOLIS—BOSTON
COLUMBUS, OHIO *or* **MEMPHIS**

Whichever is nearest you.

Our New Low Priced Battery

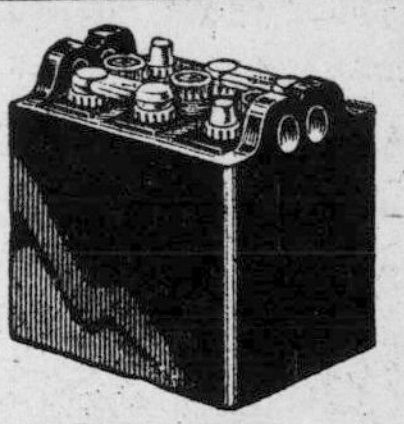

A very good battery for those who desire a lower price. Materials and workmanship equal our higher priced Peerless Battery, but the plate construction is somewhat lighter.

$7.65

Guaranteed for 12 months. **Unmailable.** Shipping weight, 53 pounds.

Catalog No.	Car	Year and Model		
28K17061⅓	Chervolet	1916-17-18, 490	6-11	$7.65
28K17064⅓	Chervolet	1919-22 Inc. 490; 1923-27, Inc. Superior	6-11	7.65
28K17126⅓	Ford	1919-27, Inc., ALL.	6-11	7.65
28K17237⅓	Overland	1916, 75; 1917-18, 90-90B; 1919, 90T 90R, 90CC and Del. 1920-23, Inc. ALL	6-11	7.65
28K17240⅓	Overland	1924-26, Inc. ALL; 1927, Whippet	6-11	7.65
28K17268⅓	Star	1922-27, Inc. ALL.	6-11	7.65

De Luxe Hydrometer Jar Outfit

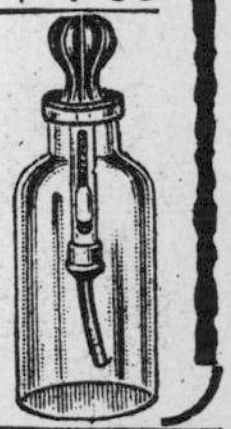

Inexpensive, popular type outfit. Comprises heavy glass one-half gallon jar for storing distilled water for battery and our 28K4851 De Luxe Hydrometer as listed on opposite page. Keep hydrometer in jar when not in use. Shipping wt., 4¾ lbs.

28K7168 . . . . . . **83c**

Rely on a RELIANCE RADIATOR

Winter and Summer Dependability for Fords

Guaranteed 18 months

NOTE
Measure from Bottom of Radiator to Bottom of Filler Neck as Shown in Illustration Below

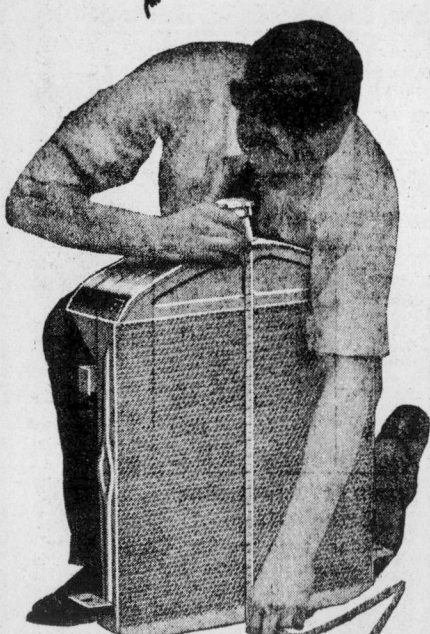

True radiator economy lies in its reliable, year round performance. Such dependability you buy in the Reliance Honeycomb Radiator. The Reliance is made of live brass, with 74 water channels and an increased number of air cells. The core is interchangeable with the standard Ford shell. It weighs only 30 pounds and is one of the best looking radiators sold. The Reliance will withstand motor vibration and the jarring and pounding of heavy road duty.

We guarantee the core 18 months against damage due to freezing

It is more economical to buy a new Reliance Honeycomb than it is to repair or patch your old and battered radiator.

This wonderful Reliance Honeycomb Radiator combines maximum cooling surface with large water channels, permitting free flow of water at all times.

We say, without hesitation, that the Reliance is the best buy for the money that you can buy anywhere because—

1—*Both honeycomb and extra large water channel features make this a radiator which combines the best points of other radiators.*

2—*It is interchangeable with standard Ford radiator and shell.*

3—*It is so constructed that motor vibration or jarring and pounding of heavy road duty will not cause any injury whatsoever.*

4—*Reliance Radiators are so constructed that we can guarantee the core for 18 months against damage due to freezing.*

RADIATOR WITH BLACK SHELL
$8.69
and Up

Radiator Without Shell

28K15198¼—1917-23 type. Height, 22¼ inches.................$7.95	28K15196¼—1924-27 type. Height, 23½ inches.................$8.39

Radiator With Black Enameled Shell

28K13255¼—1917-23 type. Height, 22⅝ inches.................$8.69 (See illustration.)	28K15194¼—1924-27 type. Height, 23⅞ inches.................8.98 (Not illustrated.)

Shipping wts: Radiator, complete with shell, 34 lbs.; radiators, without shell, 30 lbs. Unmailable.

Nickel Plated Radiator Shell

Bring your car up to date with an attractive nickel plated radiator shell exactly as used on the new closed model Ford cars. Two types, as listed below. Shipping weight, either style, 6 pounds.

28K13251¼—For 1917-23 Ford cars. (Not illustrated)...............$2.11	28K13253¼—For 1924-27 Ford cars. (Not illustrated)...............$2.19

Tubular Radiators and Water Pumps for Fords

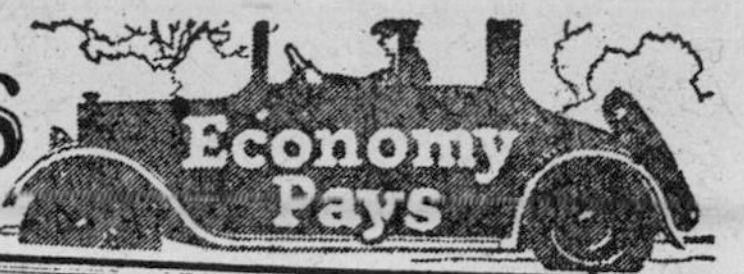

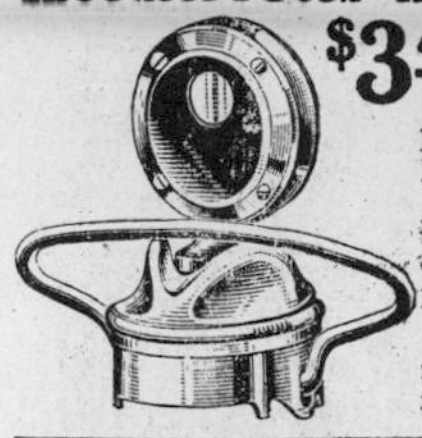

$3.45 Boyce Motometer

Warns you when motor is overheating from lack of water, oil, etc. Improved construction, having beveled crystals and easily readable broad thermometer tube. Offered considerably below regular retail price. Shipping weight, 1¼ pounds.

28K9423—Complete with ornamental nickel plated radiator cap............$3.45

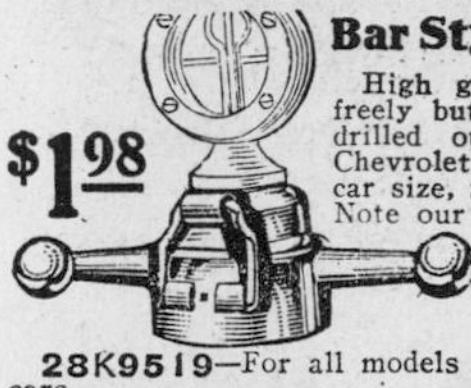

Bar Style Locking Radiator Cap

$1.98

High grade nickel plated cap. Cup turns freely but cannot be unscrewed. Hinged top drilled out for motometer use. Ford and Chevrolet size, about 7 inches long. Standard car size, about 8 inches long, with knob ends. Note our remarkably low prices. Motometer not included. Shipping weight, radiator caps, 1½ pounds.

28K9510 For Ford cars..........$1.98

28K9519—For all models of Chevrolet cars..........1.98

28K9518⅓—For all other cars except Willys-Overland. **Shipped from factory in Northeastern Illinois. In ordering be sure to state make, year and model of car**..........$3.15

Crystal-Onyx Automatic Locking Radiator Cap

$2.39 and Up

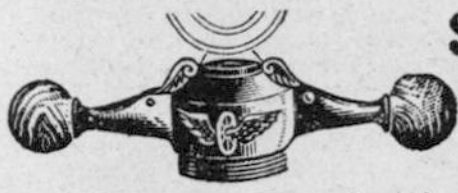

A real beauty. Crystal-onyx end balls; winged wheel front ornament. Improved cam type cover clamp. Tilt the cover to fill radiator. Cap is locked on. Complete instructions for attaching securely to car, with adequate motometer protection. Motometer not included. Shipping weight, 1½ pounds.

28K9574—For Ford or Gray cars..........$2.39

28K9575—For Chevrolet cars..........2.39

28K9576½—For cars other than those listed above. **Shipped from factory in NORTHEASTERN ILLINOIS. State make, model and year of car.** Shpg. wt., 2 lbs....$3.19

Radiator Moto-Wings

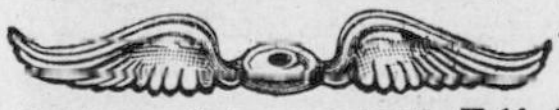

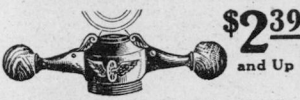

Popular radiator ornament. Held in place by any size motometer. (Motometer not furnished.) Nickel plated.

28K6071—10-inch size......34c

28K6073 14-inch size..........45c

Shipping weights, ¾ pound and 1¼ pounds.

Winged Radiator Cap for Fords

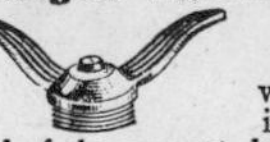

An all brass winged cap, heavily nickel plated and of the newest design. Gives your Ford a snappy, up to date appearance. A useful ornament of which you will be proud. Has special fitting for motometer. Shipping weight, 8 ounces.

28K6072..........65c

Eagle Radiator Cap

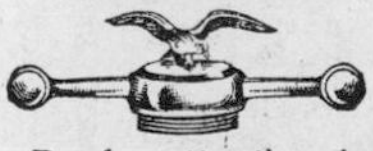

37c

Popular attractive, inexpensive radiator cap, with eagle ornament. Cap is about 6½ inches long, nickel plated, with ball ends. Furnished drilled with hole for inserting screw furnished to fasten ornament in place. Eagle is about 3¼ inches wide from tip to tip of wings. Shipping weight, ¾ pound.

28K6645..........37c

Fan Belt Guide for Fords

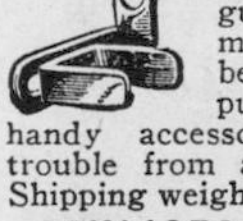

An efficient fan belt guide which bolts onto motor and keeps fan belt from slipping off its pulley. Buy one of these handy accessories and eliminate trouble from an overheated motor. Shipping weight, 4 ounces.

28K11056—Fits all model Fords..........9c

Finest Tubular Radiator for Fords

$8.95 and Up

This ***freeze-proof*** Tubular Radiator for FORDS is ***positively without equal*** for service on a Ford car. The radiator core is constructed of copper and is ***guaranteed against breakage due to freezing for 18 months.*** The water tubes are tinned inside and outside, making them impervious to the action of alkali water or acid. The upper and lower water tanks are made of brass, and ***will not corrode or rust.*** The connections are brass and bronze metal. The water capacity and the cooling surface are ***much greater than any others.*** They are equipped with our patented flexible brackets which eliminate excessive vibration. This is the ***only*** tubular radiator made that can be guaranteed against core breakage due to freezing.

Measure radiator from bottom of radiator to bottom of filler neck.

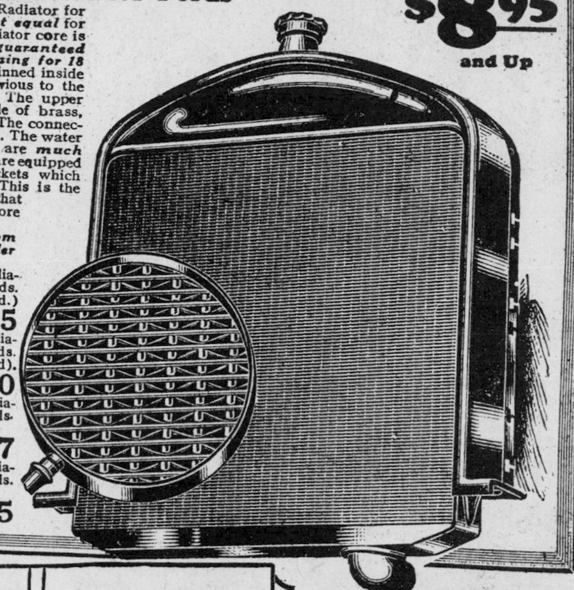

28K15700¼—Tubular Radiator, less Shell, for 1917-23 Fords. Height, 22¼ in. (Not illustrated.) Shipping weight, 29 pounds..........$8.95

28K15702¼—Tubular Radiator, less shell, for 1924-27 Fords. Height, 23½ in. (Not illustrated). Shipping weight, 30 pounds..........$9.40

28K15701¼—Tubular Radiator with Shell, for 1917-23 Fords. Height, 22⅝ in. Shipping weight, 30 pounds..........$9.87

28K15703¼—Tubular Radiator, with Shell, for 1924-27 Fords. Height, 23⅞ in. Shipping weight, 34 pounds..........$10.25

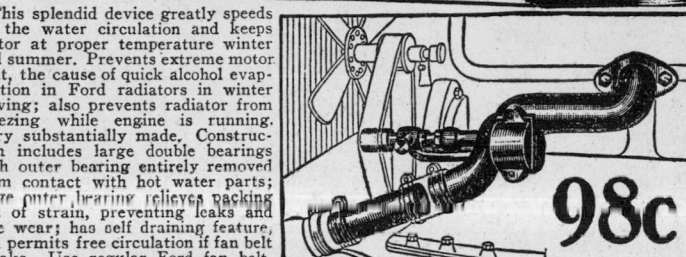

Triumph Circulating Water Pump

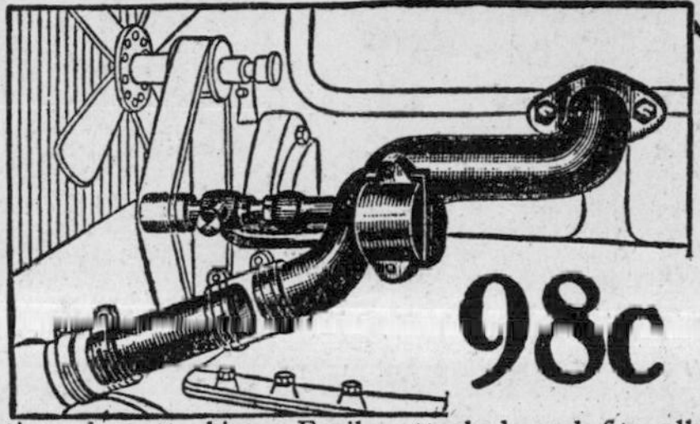

98c

This splendid device greatly speeds up the water circulation and keeps motor at proper temperature winter and summer. Prevents extreme motor heat, the cause of quick alcohol evaporation in Ford radiators in winter driving; also prevents radiator from freezing while engine is running. Very substantially made. Construction includes large double bearings with outer bearing entirely removed from contact with hot water parts; large outer bearing relieves packing nut of strain, preventing leaks and side wear; has self draining feature, and permits free circulation if fan belt breaks. Use regular Ford fan belt. Complete steel tube and full instructions for attaching. Easily attached, and fits all model Ford cars and trucks, including the new 1926 and 1927 models. Shipping weight, 6 pounds.

28K13053—Complete..........98c

Triumph De Luxe Water Pump

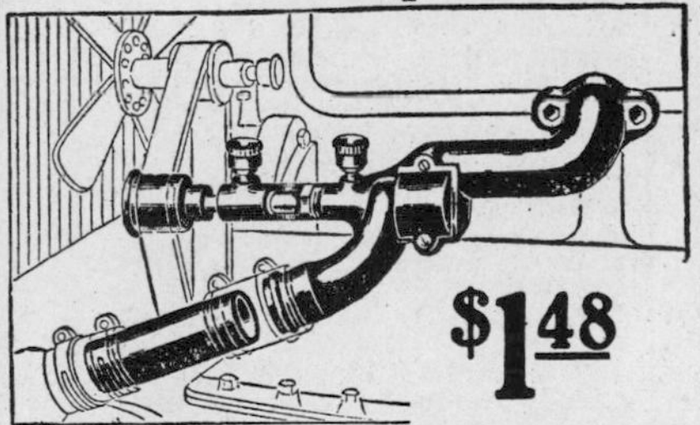

$1.48

A water pump of superior quality and construction, designed and built for long, hard service. It has large double bearings, with outer bearing entirely removed from contact with hot water parts. Leaks and side wear are prevented. Pump is self draining, permitting free circulation if fan belt breaks. Has **flanged pulley**, 2 grease cups, and outer bearing has bronze bushing and uses regular Ford fan belt. Complete with steel tube and full instructions for attaching. Fits all models Ford cars and trucks. Shipping weight, 6 pounds.

28K13153..........$1.48

Air Cleaner

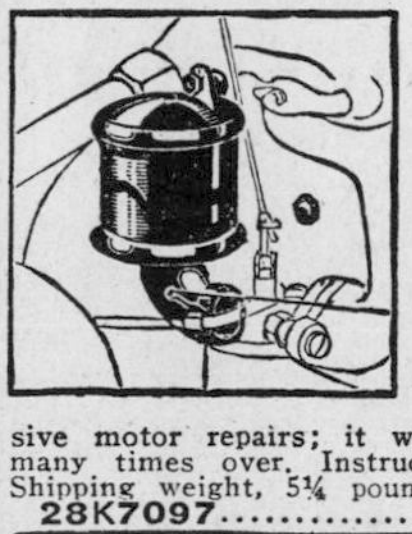

Removes all dirt from the air taken into motor through carburetor. Nearly six pounds of dust enters engine in 10,000 miles' driving on dirt roads. Some of this dust enters the oil, causing undue wear on all engine parts. This air cleaner will save expensive motor repairs; it will pay for its cost many times over. Instructions for installing. Shipping weight, 5¼ pounds.

28K7097..........$3.75

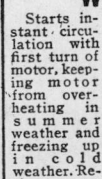

Water Circulator

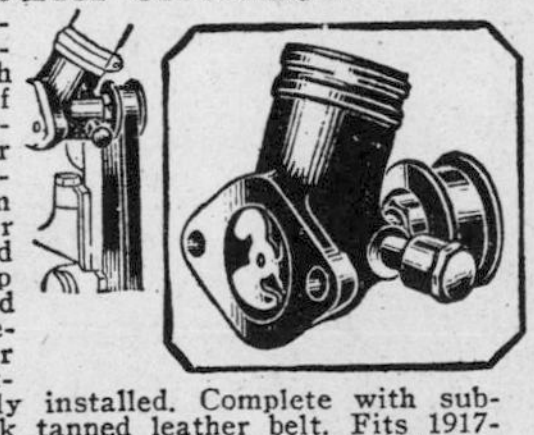

Starts instant circulation with first turn of motor, keeping motor from overheating in summer weather and freezing up in cold weather. Replaces upper water casting. Readily installed. Complete with substantial oak tanned leather belt. Fits 1917-1925 Ford cars. A splendid value. Shipping weight, 2½ pounds.

28K11097..........$1.35

Radiator Compound

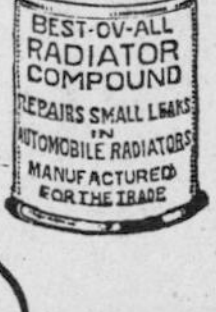

Permanently repairs all water leaks in radiators, cracked cylinders or water jackets, porous castings, sand holes or gaskets. Removes rust and lime incrustation in radiators; removes obstructions in plugged up radiators. Comes in ½-pint cans. Shipping weight, 8 oz.

28K11494 ½-pint can..........39c

Radiator Fluid

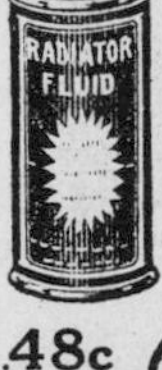

Furnished in two sizes, for cars with radiators up to 4 gallons capacity and for larger radiators or any size radiator which has a bad leak.

28K10883—About 4-oz. can. Shipping wt., 1¼ pounds..........30c

28K10885—About 8-oz. can. Shipping wt., 1¾ pounds..........48c

Mail Your Orders for all merchandise on this page either to

CHICAGO
PHILADELPHIA
MINNEAPOLIS
BOSTON
MEMPHIS

Whichever is nearest you.

Fan Belts

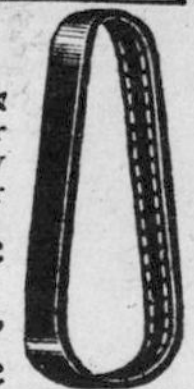

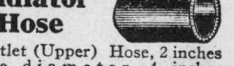

28K11621—Oak Tanned Leather Endless Belt. Very low priced. For 1917-25 Ford cars..........19c

28K9120 Leather Fan Belt, for 1926 and 1927 Fords...24c

28K9114—Fabric Fan Belt, for 1917-25 Ford Cars..........15c

28K9122—Fabric Fan Belt, for 1926 and 1927 Ford cars..........17c

Shipping weight of above fan belts, 4 ounces.

Radiator Hose

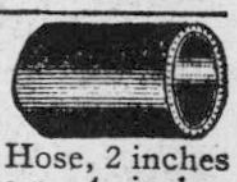

Outlet (Upper) Hose, 2 inches inside diameter, 4 inches long.

28K12086..........7c

Inlet (Lower) Hose, 1¾ in. inside diameter, 3¼ inches long.

28K11794..........4c

Shipping weights, ¾ pound and 7 oz. respectively.

Repacking for Water Pumps

Stop leaking pumps. Use this repacking. Semi-metallic for long life; packs tightly. Compressible. **Fits all pumps.** Supply sufficient for the life of your car. Simple to use. Shipping weight, ¾ pound.

28K8378..........48c

FOR BOOKS ON AUTOMOBILES SEE PAGE 785

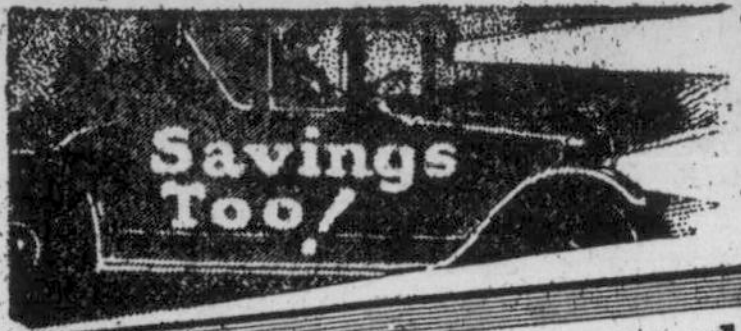

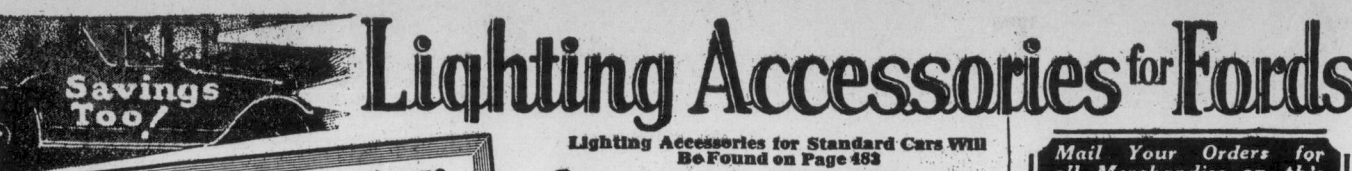

Lighting Accessories for Fords

Lighting Accessories for Standard Cars Will Be Found on Page 483

Standard Replacement Head Lamps for Fords

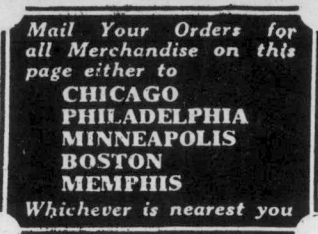

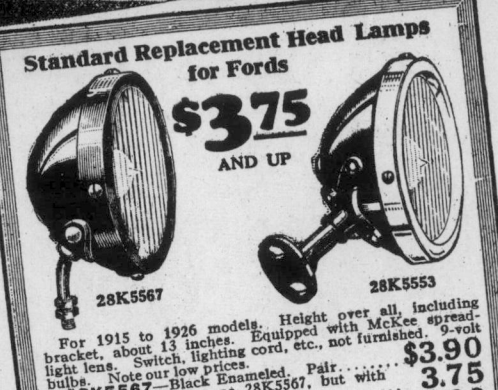

$3.75 AND UP

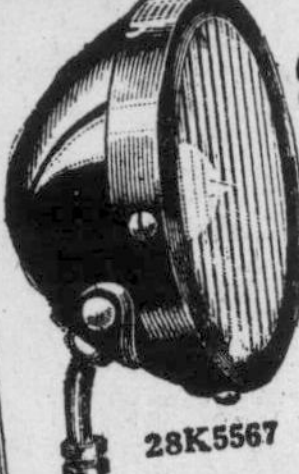

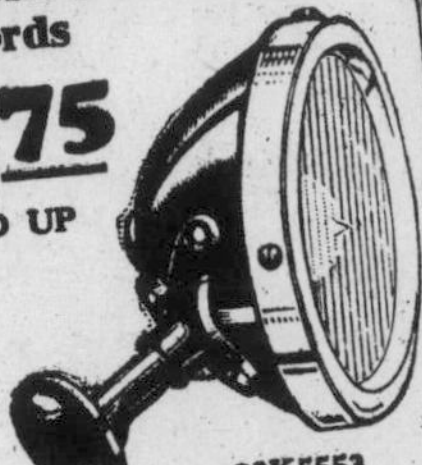

For 1915 to 1926 models. Height over all, including bracket, about 13 inches. Equipped with McKee spread-light lens. Switch, lighting cord, etc., not furnished. 9-volt bulbs. Note our low prices.
28K5567—Black Enameled. Pair........ $3.90
28K5559—Same as 28K5567, but with 6-volt Tulite Bulbs. Per pair........ 3.75
28K5553—For 1926 models. Without cross rod. Nickel door rim. Pair........ 3.90
28K2598—For 1926 models with cross rod. Pair........ 3.95
Shipping weight, either style, per pair, 10 pounds.

Electric Tail Lamp

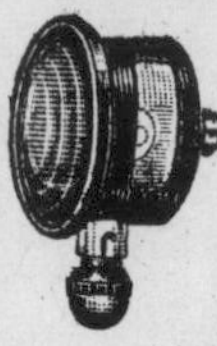

For 1915-25 models. Use with 6-volt battery. Regulation type.
28K5583 39c
Same, 18-24-volt bulb for magneto use.
28K7028 47c
Shpg. wt., either style, 1¼ lbs.

Tail Light License Bracket

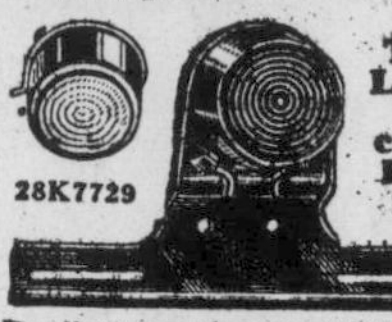

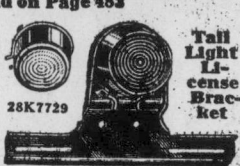

Duplicates equipment tail light—license holder. Lamp has 2-candle power, 6-8-volt single contact bulb. Shipping weight, 1¼ lbs.
28K7728........ 49c
28K7729—Lamp repair parts, including glass cup, metal cup, red celluloid and spring ring. Shipping weight, 1 pound........ 27c

Mail Your Orders for all Merchandise on this page either to
CHICAGO
PHILADELPHIA
MINNEAPOLIS
BOSTON
MEMPHIS
Whichever is nearest you

Automatic Guide Signal

The Light That Reads Your Mind

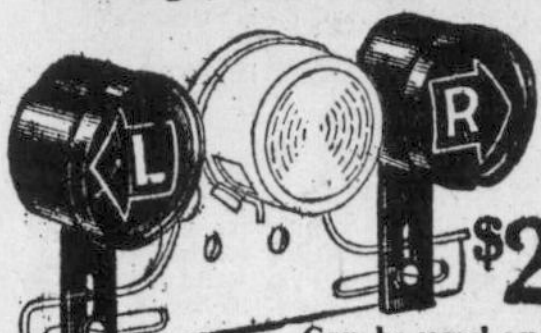

$2.98

Can be used on any car.

And now the World's Largest Store offers the newest in automobile safety lights. You may drive with ease of mind and with the utmost security, because every turn of your car flashes a message to those who drive behind you. Two strong lights attached to your license plate automatically signal the **right turn or the left turn.** Colored lenses of blue and canary actually read your mind, because you merely turn your wheel the slightest degree, and then, positive and sure, the automatic, high ratio switch contacts, and your direction light, with its arrow, charts your way to those behind. Very simple to install, no drilling; once adjusted there is no further tinkering and we guarantee that anyone can equip his or her car whether mechanically inclined or not. Causes no additional drain on storage battery. Detailed directions included. The Guide Signal is endorsed by experts everywhere. **Sold exclusively by Sears, Roebuck and Co.** Shipping weight, 2 lbs.
28K2588........ $2.98

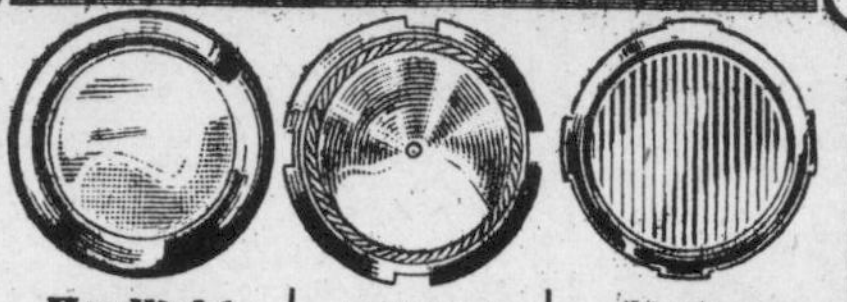

Headlight Door

(Part No. 6594X)

Headlight Door Rim with glass. Shipping weight, 2¾ pounds.
28K10312
Each.... 33c
28K10309
Door without glass, Shpg. wt., 1¾ lbs. Each.... 19c
28K10536
Nickel Plated Door Rim only. Shipping weight, 1¾ lbs. Each.. 37c

Reflector

(Part No. 6585X)

Reflector for 1915 to 1926 Ford Electric Headlights. Very low priced. Shipping weight, 1½ pounds.
28K14252
Each, 40c

McKee Spreadlight Lens

Well known efficient dimmer lens, approved in all states having anti-headlight glare laws. A splendid lens at a remarkably low price. Shipping weight, pair, 4½ pounds.
28K5356
For 1918-1926 Ford cars.
Per pair.... 34c

Stoplight for Fords

$1.35

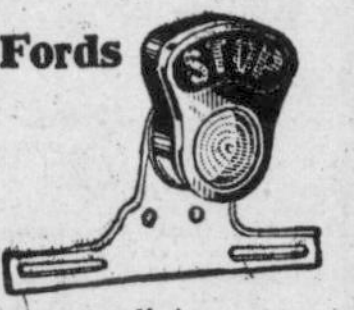

Tail Lamp Not Furnished

A new and better stoplight, which fits around regular Ford lamp. Black enamel finish, nickel plated removable face. Clear and distinct amber STOP lens. Complete with trouble-proof switch, which clamps around Ford Bendix Drive housing and **not** to your floor boards, 6-8-volt bulb, rubber insulated wire. Shpg. wt., 2 lbs.
28K2589........ $1.35

Practical Bright Light Socket

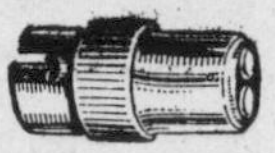

For use on Ford cars where lights are operated from magneto. Gives you bright light even when driving at a slow rate of speed. Easy to put on. One bulb continues to burn even if other burns out. Shpg. wt., 3 oz.
28K8190.... 24c

Under Hood Electric Motor Horn

$2.35

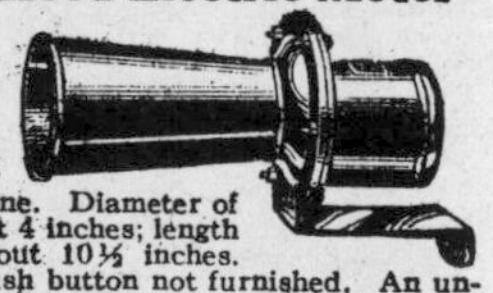

Adjustment at back for regulating tone. Diameter of mouth, about 4 inches; length over all, about 10½ inches. Cord and push button not furnished. An unusually big value. Shipping weight, 3 pounds.
28K2607—6-8-volt type, with bracket for mounting on engine having removable cylinder head........ $2.35

Dual System Electric Tail Lamp

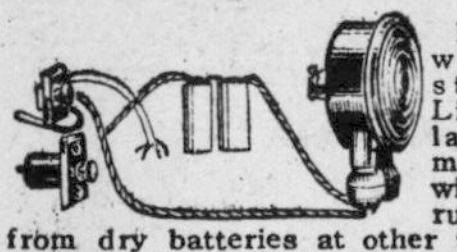

For models without starter. Lights tail lamp from magneto with engine running and from dry batteries at other times. Includes switch, wire, terminals, tail lamp with red semaphore lens and two bulbs, without dry cells. Wire one bulb to headlight switch and other to switch furnished, operating two dry cells, as per instructions. Priced very low. Shipping weight, 1¾ pounds.
28K11702........ $1.43

NATIONAL MAZDA Emergency Lamp Kit

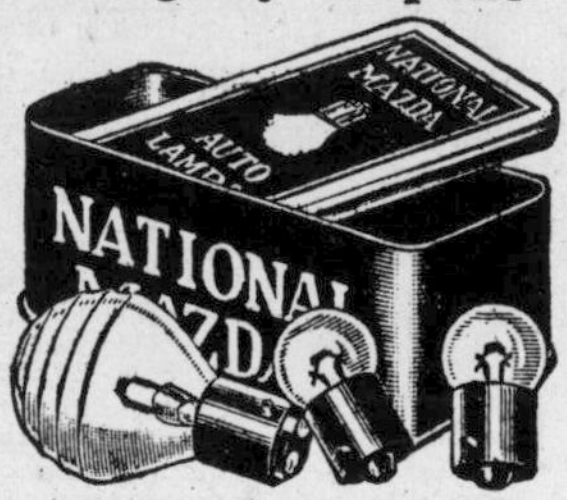

A compact and strong metal container which holds one 6-8-volts 21-2-candle power and two 6-8-volt 3-candle power single contact Mazda bulbs—complete lamp equipment for your Ford. May be stored under seat without fear of breakage. Shipping weight, 6 ounces.
28K747........ 73c

Standard Headlight Bulbs

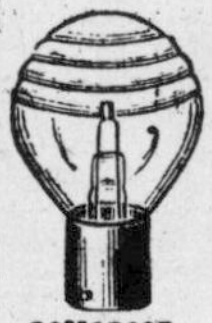

28K6076—Style S11, 21-C. P., 6-8-volt Nitrogen Headlight Bulb, single contact base.. 19c
28K5970—Style S11, Nitrogen Headlight Bulb, 21-C. P., 9-volt double contact base.... 21c
28K12037 — 6-8-volt style S11 Tungsten Tulite Bulb, double contact base, for late model Ford cars, equipped with Ford Liberty Starting Systems and Tulite bulbs. Gives 2-candle power light on dim switch, 21-candle power on bright light switch........ 24c
28K6515 — Style S11, Nitrogen Bulb, 27-C. P., 9-volt, double contact base........ 22c
Shipping weight, any of above, 6 oz.

Mazda Headlight Bulbs for Fords

Catalog No.	Mazda No.	Base	Volt	C.P.	
28K733	1138	DC	9	27	40c
28K734	1146	DC	18–24	27	60c
28K735	1158	DC	6–8	21–2	38c
28K732	1160	DC	9	21	35c

Blue Headlight Bulbs for Fords

Catalog No.	Mazda No.	Base	Volt	C.P.	
28K705	1160	DC	9	21	45c
28K707★	1158	DC	6–8	21–2	50c

★ Double Filament.
Shipping weight, any of above, 6 ounces.

Well Made Hand Horn

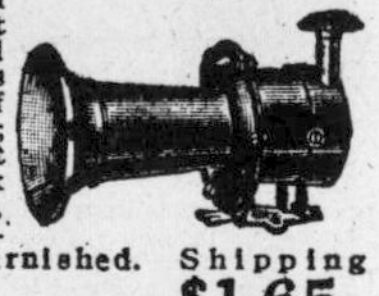

Sounds an alarm both when ratchet handle is pressed down and when it is released. Length of horn, about 9 in.; size of mouth, about 4½ inches. Black enameled finish, white metal trimmings. Bracket furnished. Shipping weight, 2½ pounds.
28K6704........ $1.65

Clamp-On Dash Lamp

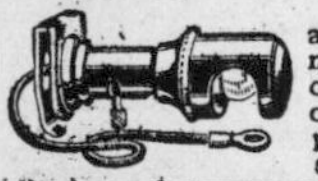

Handy dash lamp attached to instrument board of Ford cars, without screws or bolts. Loosen, panel containing switch and ammeter, slip lamp between panel and instrument board and tighten panel in place. Complete with insulated wire with terminal for quickly attaching to ammeter post. Black finish, on and off switch, 6-volt bulb. Shipping weight, 8 ounces.
28K8149—For all models up to (but not including) 1926...... 41c

Combination Horn Button and Light Switch

58c

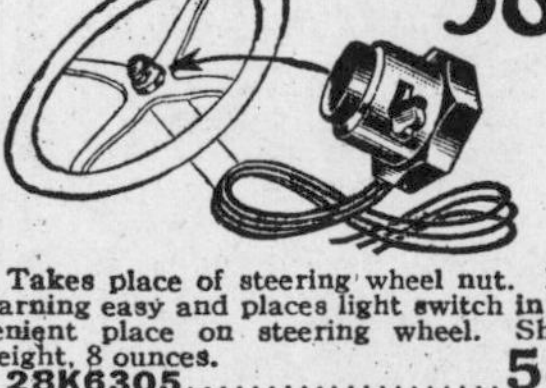

Takes place of steering wheel nut. Makes warning easy and places light switch in a convenient place on steering wheel. Shipping weight, 8 ounces.
28K6305........ 58c

A Real Current Regulator

98c and Up

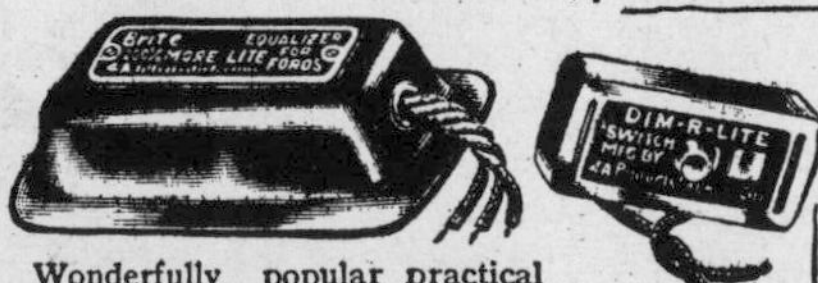

Wonderfully popular practical accessory, sold at real bargain prices. Gives you full clear driving light at slow engine speeds and acts as a choke coil at high engine speeds to prevent excess current from burning out bulbs. Use your regular bulbs. For 1915-17 Ford cars. Shpg. wt., 1¼ lbs.
28K8553—Without dimmer switch... 98c
Brite-Lite Coil complete with dimmer switch, as illustrated. Dimmer switch should be used when Brite-Lite Coil is used on 1918-24 models; can also be used on 1915-17 models. Shpg. wt., 1¼ lbs.
28K8252........ $1.65

Dash Lamp

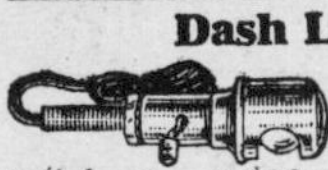

Nickel plated, 6-volt dash lamp; has on and off switch. Easily installed; only one ⅝-inch hole to drill. Fits either wood or metal dash. Fitted with insulated wire for attaching to switch. Single contact type; use as double contact lamp by grounding shank of lamp. Shipping weight, 6 ounces.
28K8211........ 39c

Four-Tone Chime Whistle

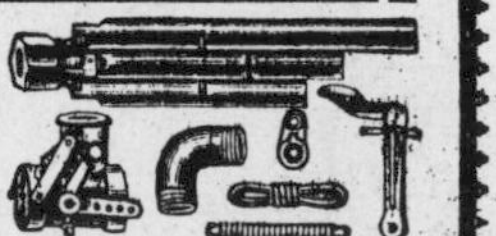

High grade well known chime whistle with four notes. Has cut-out pedal, cable, valve with double butterfly valve with 1½-inch opening, whistle, etc. Nickel plated; length of tubes, 13, 10½, 8⅞ and 6¾ inches. Shipping weight, 5¼ pounds.
28K10566
Complete.... $5.75

Jiffy Horn Button

24c

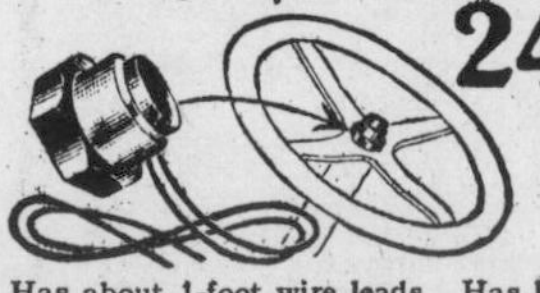

Has about 1-foot wire leads. Has hex nut base, replaces nut on top of steering wheel, the handiest place for your horn button. Shipping weight, 3 ounces.
28K1662........ 24c

Replace Your Dash Light

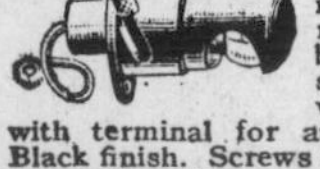

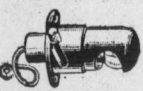

Duplicates dash light regularly furnished on closed models. Six-volt bulb, on and off switch, insulated wire lead complete with terminal for attaching to switch. Black finish. Screws for attaching. Shipping weight, 6 ounces.
28K8207........ 38c

Ignition Equipment for Fords

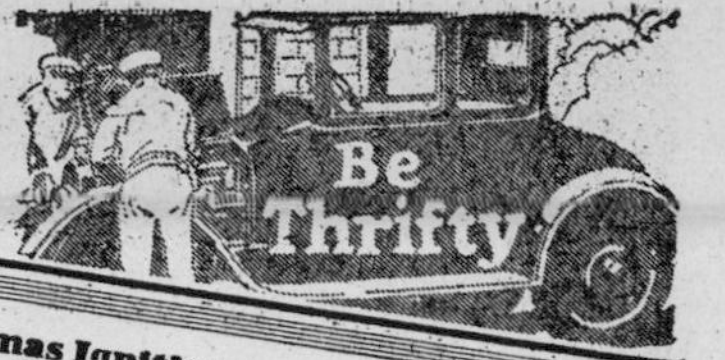

Be Thrifty

De Luxe Steering Wheel

$1.62

Here's a wonderful value in a high grade steering wheel of the popular 17-in. type. Has selected walnut finish rim, corrugated (see illustration) to give a secure grip. Spider is polished aluminum. Easily put on. This splendid oversize wheel adds greatly to the appearance of your car. Makes it easier to steer, too. Shipping weight, 3½ pounds.
28K6070.............$1.62

Lock Your Wheel and Ignition at the Same Time!

$8.95

This coincidental lock and wheel combination gives your car double protection. Every time you turn off your ignition, you lock your wheel so that it spins free. When you unlock your wheel you turn on the ignition. You can't forget! Good theft and safety insurance at this price. Complete outfit, including lock, wheel and horn button. Easily installed. Shipping wt., 6¼ pounds.
28K8396
Complete outfit.............$8.95
Coincidental Lock Only
28K8389
Shipping weight, 4 pounds $5.95

Reliable Semi-Spinning Lock

Ratchet lock approved by Underwriters' Laboratories. Strong and simply operated. Remove steering wheel post cap and screw lock case down until it stops. Drop forged case; case or lock mechanism cannot be cut, drilled or broken. Shipping weight, 2¾ pounds.
28K8205—For models up to and including 1924. $3.68
28K9558—For 1925 to 1927 Ford cars.............3.75

For Batteries for Ford Cars
See Pages 468 and 469

For Standard Ignition Equipment
See Page 482

Steering Gear

3519
3547
3517
3545

28K14208—(No. 3517) Steering Gear Pinion. Shipping weight, 2 ounces.............12c
28K14210—(No. 3519) Steering Gear Drive Pinion. Shipping weight, 8 ounces.............23c
28K14215—(No. 3545) Steering Post Bracket Bushing. Shipping wt., 6 ounces.
Per pair.............16c
28K14216—(No. 3547) Steering Gear Ball Arm. Shipping weight, 1 pound.............32c

Atwater Kent Ignition for Fords

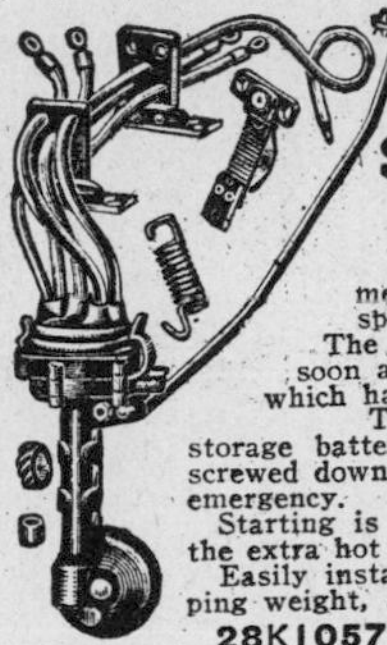

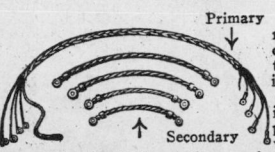

$8.95

Greatly increases the power, smooth running and flexibility of the engine. This is the same high quality Atwater-Kent ignition used as standard equipment on higher priced cars, furnished with special fittings to adapt it to the Ford car. The increase in power is readily noticeable as soon as installed on either a new Ford car or one which has been run thousands of miles.

This system for Fords is operated on the storage battery, using one Ford coil with vibrators screwed down tight. This leaves three spare coils for emergency.

Starting is easier even in cold weather, because of the extra hot spark at low speed. Easily installed. Complete direction furnished. Shipping weight, 5 pounds.
28K10573.............$8.95

Timing and Spark Plug Wires for Fords

Primary Wires cut correct length, and complete with terminals. Come in contrasting colors for identifying and replacing properly. Primary wiring set is protected by braid insulation against short circuiting due to oil, water, etc.

28K12363—Set of Four Primary Wires and Lighting Wire only. Shipping weight, ¾ pound.............31c
28K12364—Set of Four Secondary or Spark Plug Wires only. Shipping weight, 7 ounces.............17c
28K8326—Set of Four Spark Plug Wires for 1926-27 Fords. Shipping weight, ¾ lb.............17c
28K12088—Six-Wire Primary Set, for models equipped with regular Ford electric self starting system. Shipping weight, 1 pound.............39c
28K12094—Set of Four Timer Wires, One Generator Wire and Two Lighting Wires for 1923-25 models. Shipping weight, 1 pound.............55c
28K8559—Set of Four Timer Wires and Set of Four Spark Plug Wires for use on Fordson tractor. Shipping weight, 8 ounces.............48c
28K8325—Set of Four Timer Wires for 1926-27 Fords. Shipping weight, ¾ pound.............24c

Non-Corrode Battery Terminal

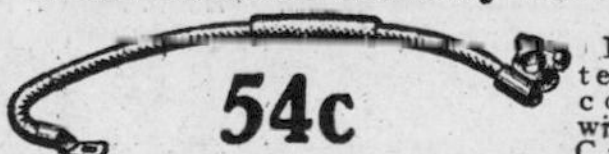

54c

Battery terminal, complete with cable. Cable is molded in lead terminal. Rubber insulation on cable is molded in lead terminal. No acid can eat into cable or terminal. A positive, permanent connection, which makes a good, clean contact even though post is dirty. Shipping wt., 8 oz.
28K7115.............54c

Short Proof Timer

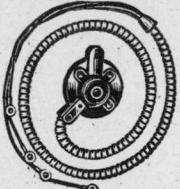

Substantial short proof timer with bakelite outer case and inner ring or race. Timer requires no oil or grease. Complete with substantial flexible metal conduit enclosing colored timer wires fitted with terminals. Construction prevents short circuits. Inner ring has copper inserts; timer terminals when properly connected under screws prevent loose connections; timer design prevents water entering timer. Guaranteed for 10,000 miles of service. Complete instructions for installing. Shipping weight, 1¼ pounds.
28K8318—Complete.............$1.69

Regulation Roller Contact Timer

Roller contact timer for Ford cars. A well made, inexpensive timer of regulation type.
Shipping weight, 1 pound.
28K5593.............39c

Genuine "Milwaukee" OIL-LESS Timer

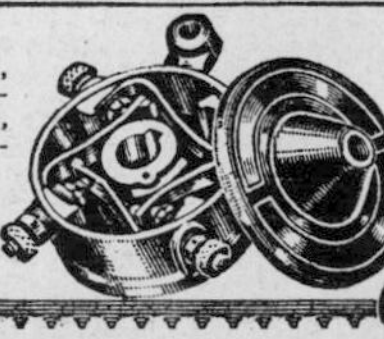

For smoother running motors install this famous oil-less, self-centering timer which maintains proper alignment and insures accurate contacts. Waterproof and oilproof. Self centering, self lubricating. Hardened steel cam bearing, large tungsten contact points; spring steel arms. No oiling, no cleaning. Operates on wipe and break principle. Attaches to cam shaft direct.
28K8324—Shpg. wt., ¾ lb.............$2.49

For Books on Automobile See Page 785

Thomas Ignition System

$5.75

Eliminates poor ignition by controlling timing of cylinder explosions much more closely than usual. Similar in type to the high priced distributor systems on standard cars. Distributor head rests on elevated bracket, away from oil, water, and dirt of drip pan or contact with fan belt. Operates with single Ford coil unit. Its use means a hotter spark, and a smooth, powerful easy running motor, giving easier starting, quicker acceleration and greater power. Complete with bakelite distributor case, elevated bracket, distributor supporting tube, hardened steel spiral gears and overhead wiring enclosed in supporting tube. Instructions furnished for installing. Shipping weight, 7 pounds.
28K10057—For magneto use.
28K10568—For battery use.............$5.75
For Special Coil Unit for Battery Type Thomas Ignition Outfit See 28K10818 Below.

Short Proof Timer Wire

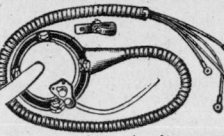

Prevents short circuits caused by oil, water and wear which rot ordinary timer wire insulation. Timer wires are protected by flexible metal conduit with substantial metal ring at one end fitting perfectly around any Ford timer, and metal strip for attaching flexible tubing to radiator rod. Complete instructions for installing. Guaranteed for 10,000 miles of service. Shipping weight, ¾ pound.
28K11568
Complete.............$1.27

Negative Battery Terminal

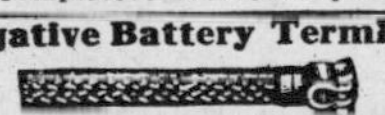

Non-corrosive ground terminal, consisting of fitting and about 6 inches of braided metal tape. Makes a strong and lasting ground for your battery. Shipping weight, 8 ounces.
28K7113—For 1924-27 Ford cars.............33c
28K7114—For 1920-27 Chevrolet cars (not illustrated).............45c

Genuine "Milwaukee" Roller Timer

$1.79

A well known, quality built timer following the Ford principle of operation. Short-proof, waterproof and oilproof. Assembled in attractive molded bakelite case. Bone-hard fiber race, welded studs, precision built brush assembly, best bronze castings, piano wire spring. Extra thick alloy steel contacts and special roller. Handy patented oil cup. Easily installed. Shipping weight, ¾ pound.
28K8323.............$1.79

De Luxe Dry Timer

For Fords and Fordson Tractor
Guaranteed, 10,000 Miles Service 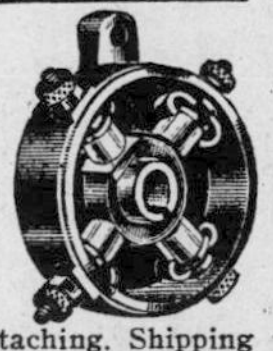
This high grade timer is a big favorite with Ford owners under its regular trade name. Very strongly made with bakelite case and positive working, long lasting spring contacts. Requires no oil or grease. Will give unusually long satisfactory wear, construction insuring positive contact and a rich hot spark, correctly timed. Full instructions for attaching. Shipping weight, ¾ pound.
28K8319.............$1.29

Special Coil Unit

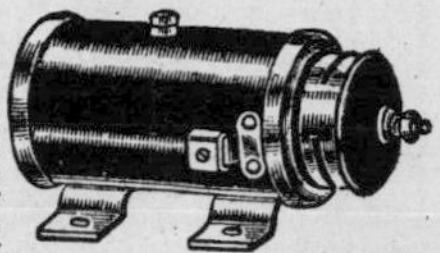

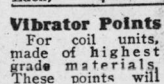

A coil unit especially designed for use with battery type Thomas Ignition System, described and illustrated above. Shipping weight 1 pound.
28K10818.............$2.95

Spark Coils

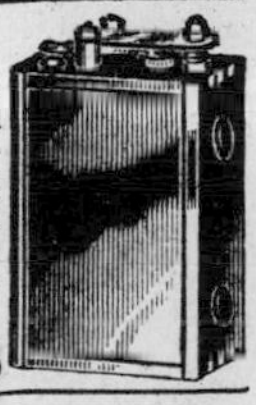

(No. 5007) Coil Unit
A splendid coil unit at a low price. Every coil is rigidly inspected during construction and is guaranteed to be in perfect electrical and mechanical condition. Shipping wt., 2¼ pounds.
28K14251
Each.............$1.15

Vibrator Points

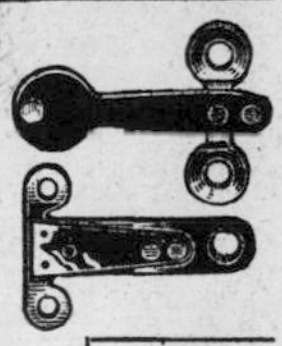

For coil units, made of highest grade materials. These points will give maximum service.
28K11934
Per pair, for all models, including new 1927 cars.............8c
Shipping weight, per pair, 2 ounces.

Horseshoe Extension Spark Plug

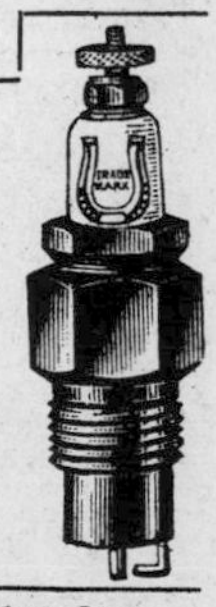

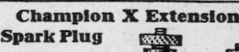

Same type as standard Ford equipment spark plug. Note our remarkably low price.
28K5214 — ½-inch size. Shipping weight, 5 ounces.
Each.............25c
28K5594—Same, in handy clip of four for convenient carrying. Shipping weight, 1 lb.
Per set of 4.............93c

Champion X Extension Spark Plug

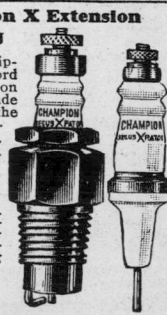

Regular equipment on the Ford car and Fordson tractor, and made especially for the Ford motor. ½-inch size only. Shpg. wt., 5 oz.
28K11818.............55c

Porcelains Champion X Spark Plug Extension Porcelains. Shipping weight, 2 oz.
28K7376.............25c

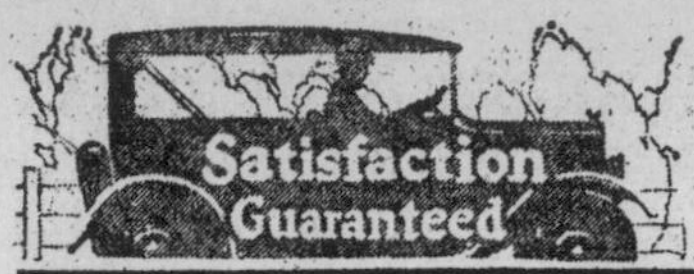

-Dress Up Your Ford Now-

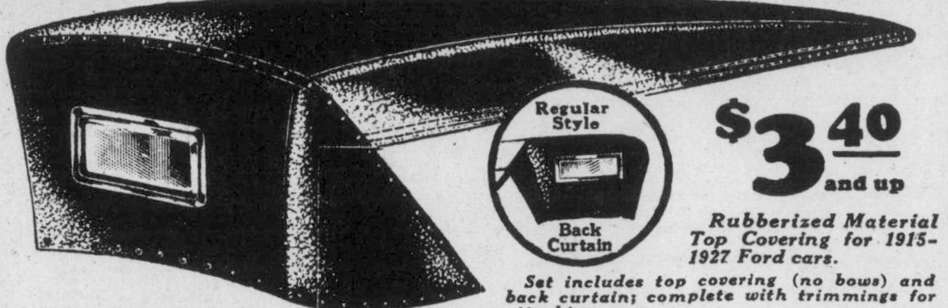

$3.40 and up

Rubberized Material Top Covering for 1915-1927 Ford cars.

Set includes top covering (no bows) and back curtain; complete with trimmings for attaching.

Don't Let Your Ford Look Shabby!

There is no need for anyone to be ashamed of the appearance of his car, when so few dollars will replace a worn, shabby or leaky top.

These top coverings come to you complete and ready to put on. They fit the frame exactly, slip easily into place and are permanently attached with very little effort and in a very short time. No expert help is needed. Full instructions with every top.

Cheer up your Ford with a new, snappy looking top. Nowhere can you do it as economically as here.

For Auto Paint and Enamel See Page 1035

Top Coverings for 1915-1922 Models, Regular Back Curtain

Catalog No.	Style Car	Back Curtain Lights	Shpg. Wt., Lbs.	Complete With Back Curtain
28K10269	Roadster	One Celluloid	6½	$3.40
28K10268	Touring	One Celluloid	10	4.90
28K13354	Roadster	Two Oval Glass	8½	3.95
28K13355	Touring	Two Oval Glass	12	5.55
28K5320	Roadster	One Oblong Glass, 6x18	8½	4.60
28K5322	Touring	One Oblong Glass, 6x18	12	6.15

Top Coverings for 1915-1927 Models, Gypsy Back Curtain

Catalog No.	Style Car	Back Curtain Lights	Shpg. Wt., Lbs.	Complete With Back Curtain
28K10264	Roadster, '15-'22	One Celluloid	7	$4.20
28K10263	Touring, '15-'22	One Celluloid	11	5.35
28K10252	Roadster, '15-'22	Two Oval Glass	9	4.50
28K10251	Touring, '15-'22	Two Oval Glass	12	6.20
28K10253	Roadster, '15-'22	One 6x18-In. Oblong Glass	9	4.75
28K10250	Touring, '15-'22	One 6x18-In. Oblong Glass	12	6.55
28K10261	Roadster, '23-'25	One Celluloid	7	3.90
28K10259	Touring, '23-'25	One Celluloid	11	5.35
28K5028	Roadster, '23-'25	Two Oval Glass	9	4.50
28K5026	Touring, '23-'25	Two Oval Glass	12	6.20
28K5013	Roadster, '23-'25	One 6x18-In. Oblong Glass	9	4.75
28K5008	Touring, '23-'25	One 6x18-In. Oblong Glass	12	6.60
28K10258	Roadster, '26-'27	One 6x18-In. Oblong Glass	9	4.90
28K10257	Touring, '26-'27	One 6x18-In. Oblong Glass	12	6.90

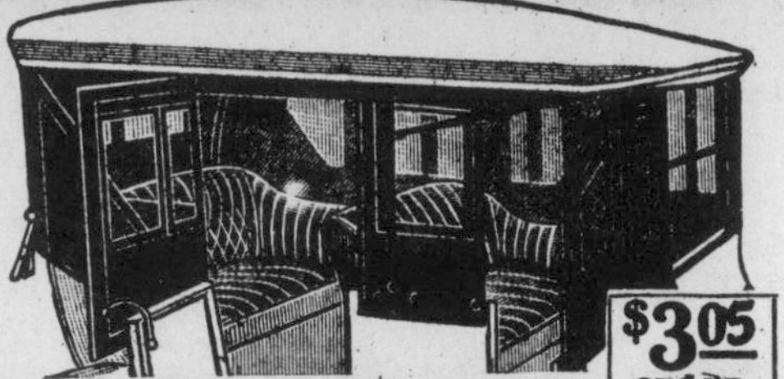

$3.05 and up

"Open With Door" Side Curtains

An up to date equipment that gives you the convenience of a closed car in getting in and out. Made of the same kind of materials as Ford car rubberized cloth curtains. Rods furnished for right doors so that curtains will open with door. Fit 1915-1927 models. Curtains complete with celluloid lights. A big value at our price. Furnished in two sizes, complete for attaching. Shpg. wts, per set: Touring models, 12 lbs; roadster models, 7 lbs.

28K7152¼—For 1915-22 roadsters. Per set...$3.50
28K10081¼—For 1923-25 roadsters. Per set... 3.10
28K14276¼—For 1926-27 roadsters. Per set.. 3.20
28K7154¼—For 1915-22 touring cars. Per set. 6.60
28K10082¼—For 1923-25 touring cars. Per set. 5.15
28K14275¼—For 1926-27 touring cars. Per set 6.20
28K14269¼—For right side 1915-22 touring cars. Shipping weight, per set, 3½ pounds. Per set........ 3.35
28K14270¼—For right side 1923-25 touring cars. Shipping weight, per set, 3½ pounds. Per set........ 3.35
28K14277¼—For right side of 1926-27 touring cars. Shipping weight, 3½ pounds. Per set.......... 3.05

Mail Your Orders for all Merchandise on this page either to
CHICAGO—PHILADELPHIA
MINNEAPOLIS—BOSTON
or MEMPHIS
Whichever is nearest you

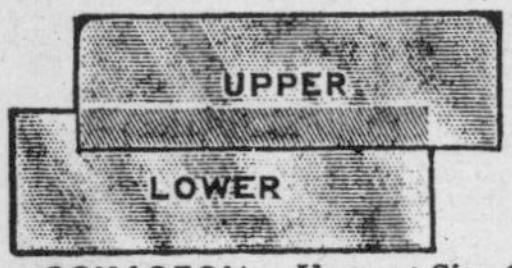

Fine, Clear Wind Shield Glass

Fits regular Ford wind shield frames. Comes 3/16 inch thick. Carefully packed.

28K4659¼—Upper Glass, about 10x38 inches. For 1915-1922 open models. Shipping wt., 13 lbs.......... $2.20

28K15174¼—Upper Glass, about 9⅝x35 11/16 in., for 1923-25 open car models. Shpg. wt., 13 lbs.......... $2.20

28K4661¼—Lower Glass, about 12x38 inches. For 1915-1922 touring models. Shpg. wt., 16 lbs.......... $2.60

28K15177¼—Upper Glass for Fordor (4-door) sedan and 1923-25 coupe, and Tudor (2-door) sedans. Size, 9¾x37 1/16 inches. Shipping weight, 13 pounds..... $2.10

28K15175¼—Lower Glass, for Fordor (4-door) sedan and 1923-25 coupe, and Tudor (2-door) sedans. Size, 7¾x37 3/16 inches. Shipping weight, 13 pounds........ $1.95

28K15172¼—Lower Glass, about 9⅝x37 3/16 in., for 1922-1925 roadsters and 1922-25 touring cars, upper and lower glass for 1916-1923 2-door sedans and 1919-1923 coupes. Shipping weight, 13 pounds..... $2.25

$1.35 per yard — Finest Quality Auto Top and Cushion Materials

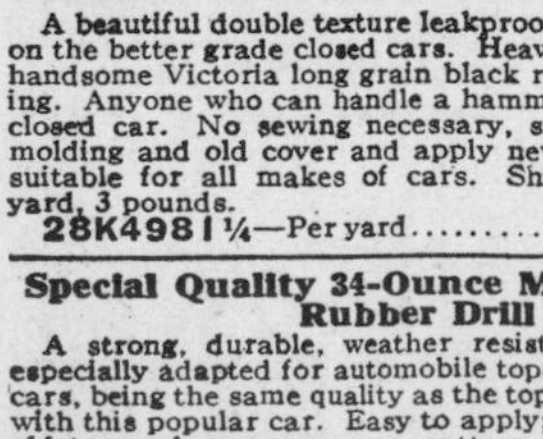

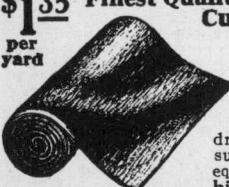

The Ideal Material for Auto Coverings

A double texture fabric, handsomely grained black rubber outside coating, rich drab back. Water and sun proof. Standard equipment on **America's highest grade vehicles and automobiles.** Nothing better made. 54 inches wide. Shipping weight, per yard, 2 lbs.

28K4982¼—Per yard.............. $1.35

Enclosed Car Deck Covering

A beautiful double texture leakproof fabric. Now used on the better grade closed cars. Heavy white twill back, handsome Victoria long grain black rubber outside coating. Anyone who can handle a hammer can re-cover his closed car. No sewing necessary, simply remove drip molding and old cover and apply new. 64 inches wide, suitable for all makes of cars. Shipping weight, per yard, 3 pounds.

28K4981¼—Per yard................ $1.65

Special Quality 34-Ounce Morocco Grain Rubber Drill

A strong, durable, weather resisting rubber fabric, especially adapted for automobile tops, particularly Ford cars, being the same quality as the top material furnished with this popular car. Easy to apply; simply remove the old top and use same as a pattern. Width, 54 inches. Black back. Shipping weight, per yard, 2¼ lbs.

28K4980¼—Per yard (not illustrated).... 85c

28K4973—Fabric Leather Trimming. Black roll of about 25 yards. Shpg. wt., 6 oz.... 28c

28K4975—Metalline nails. About 100 to a package. Shipping weight, 4 ounces........................ 9c

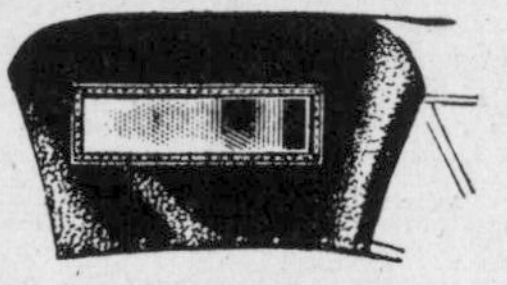

Special Back Curtains

Back curtains of substantial rubberized material. Wonderful bargains at our low prices. The back curtains with oval glass lights and the gypsy style back curtains are not illustrated.

Regular Back Curtains for 1915-1922 Models

Catalog No.	Style Car	Back Lights	Shpg. Wt., Lbs.	Each
28K13214	Touring	One Oblong Celluloid	2½	$1.35
28K13215	Roadster	One Oblong Celluloid	2½	1.35
28K13240	Touring	Two Oval Glass	4	1.70
28K13242	Roadster	Two Oval Glass	4	1.70

Gypsy Style Back Curtains for 1923-1927 Models

Catalog No.	Style Car	Back Lights	Shpg. Wt., Lbs.	Each
28K13216	Touring 1923-1925	One Oblong Celluloid	3	$1.80
28K13217	Touring 1926	One Oblong Celluloid	3	1.80
28K5034	Touring 1923-1925	Two Oval Glass	4½	2.15
28K5036	Roadster 1923-1925	Two Oval Glass	4	2.15
28K13210	Touring 1923-1925	One 6x18 Oblong Glass	4½	2.70
28K13213	Roadster 1923-1925	One 6x18 Oblong Glass	4½	2.70
28K13212	Touring 1926-1927	One 6x18 Oblong Glass	4	2.70
28K13211	Roadster 1926-1927	One 6x18 Oblong Glass	3	2.70

$2.90 and up

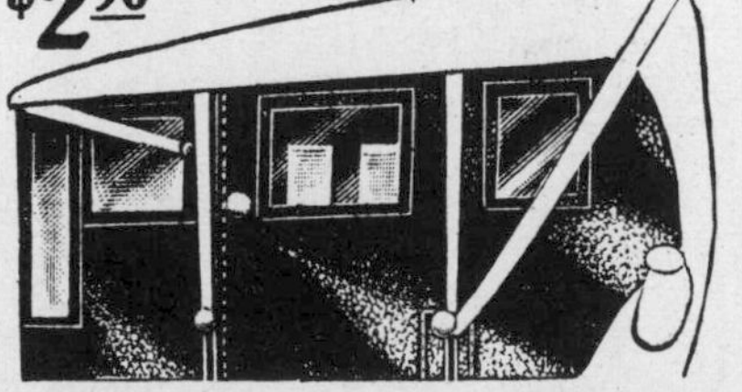

Furnished in same kind of material as Ford car rubberized cloth curtains, in set of four pieces. Complete for attaching. Remarkable values.

28K12910—Set of Side Curtains for 1915-1922 roadster. Shipping weight, per set, 5 pounds. Per set.......... $3.10

28K12909—For 1923-25 roadsters. Shipping weight, per set, 5 pounds. Per set.......... 2.90

28K12912—Set of Side Curtains for 1915-22 touring cars. Shipping weight, per set, 7¼ pounds. Per set.......... 5.20

28K12914—For 1923-25 touring cars. Shipping weight, per set, 7 pounds. Per set..... 5.20

28K14271—For right side 1915-22 touring cars. Shpg. wt., per set, 3½ lbs. Per set....... 2.95

28K14272—For right side 1923-25 touring cars. Shpg. wt., per set, 3½ lbs. Per set....... 2.95

Replace Curtain Lights

Glass Back Light Set

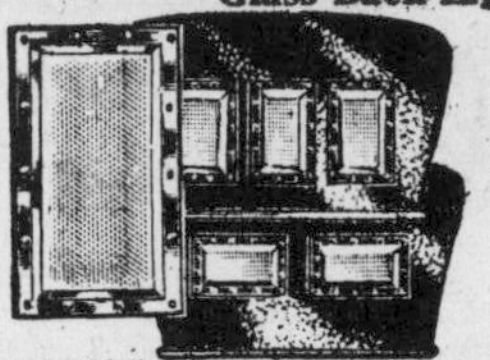

Complete in black enamel metal frames. Practical and very popular at our remarkable price. Replaces celluloid lights. Very durable.

28K10069—For 1917-22 Ford cars. Per set of 3.......... 51c

28K4667—Two-light oblong type, for 1923-24 Ford cars. Set of 2.................... 42c

28K10651—One oblong light type for 1925-27 Ford cars (glass is about 6x17 inches)....... 40c

Shipping weights, 3½, 3½ and 3¼ lbs., respectively.

Stick-Tite Back Curtain Light

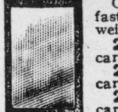

"Stick Them on Like a Postage Stamp"

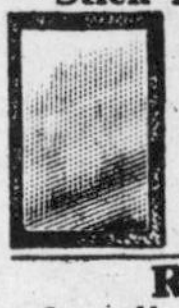

Cement into place, no sewing or metal fasteners. Complete with cement. Shipping weight, 6 ounces.

28K12958—For 1917-22 Ford cars. Each.......... 27c

28K1656—For 1923-24 Ford cars. (Not illustrated.) Each..... 28c

28K1708—For 1925-27 Ford cars. (Not illustrated.) Each..... 56c

Replace Curtain Lights

Installed Without Sewing. Furnished With Fasteners. Shipping weight, 6 ounces.

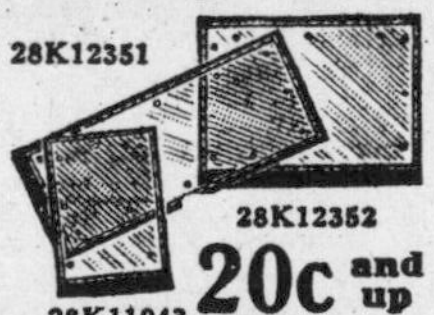

20c and up each

28K11041—Back Curtain Light for 1917-1922 cars. Size, about 6½x10½ inches. (Not illustrated.) Per single light 20c

28K9957—Back Light for 1923-24 cars. (Not illustrated.) Set of 2..... 39c

28K9221—Rear Light for 1925-1927 Ford cars. (Not illustrated.) Each............. 38c

28K12351—Replace Side Light for 1914-1924 cars. Size, about 7½x20½ inches. Each.. 36c

28K11043—Side Light for 1915-1924 cars. Size, about 10½x14½ inches. Each.......... 36c

28K12352—Side Light for 1914-1924 cars. Size, about 7½x10½ inches. Each........... 22c

Auto Top Pads

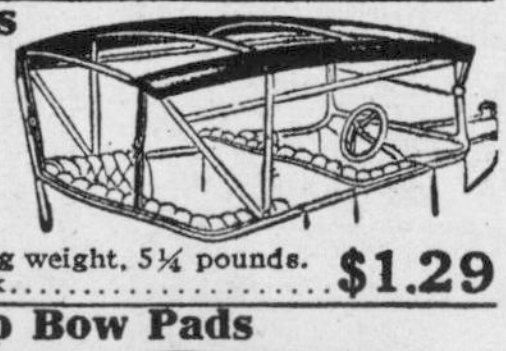

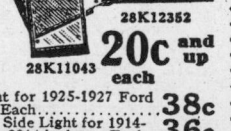

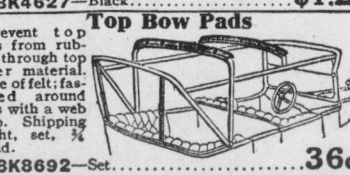

For Ford touring cars. Replace unsightly sagging misplaced top pads; it costs little and gives your car interior a neat appearance. Furnished in set complete for car. Shipping weight, 5¼ pounds.

28K4627—Black.................. $1.29

Top Bow Pads

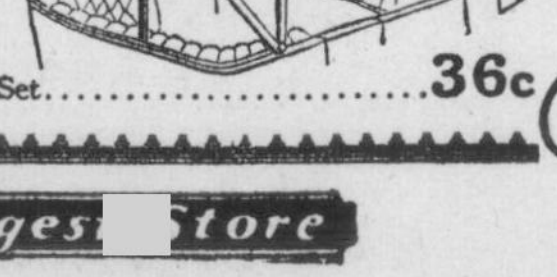

Prevent top bows from rubbing through top cover material. Made of felt; fastened around bows with a web strap. Shipping weight, set, ¾ pound.

28K8692—Set.................... 36c

Seat Covers for Fords

Mail Your Orders for all Merchandise on this page either to CHICAGO—PHILADELPHIA MINNEAPOLIS—BOSTON or MEMPHIS Whichever is Nearest You

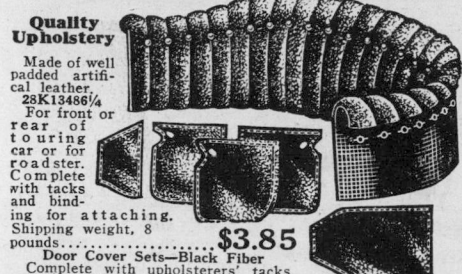

Quality Upholstery

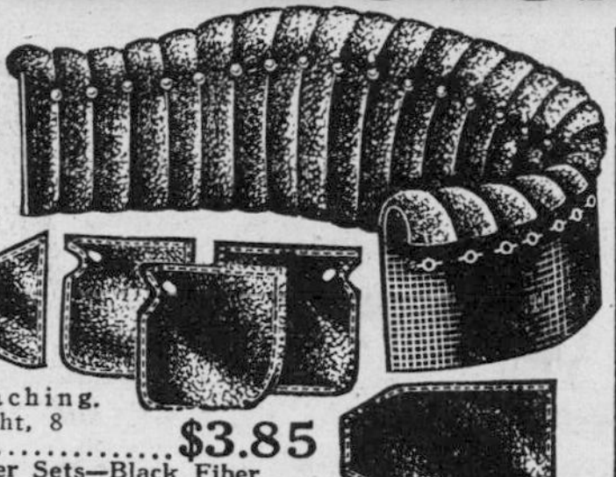

Made of well padded artificial leather. 28K13486¼ For front or rear of touring car or for roadster. Complete with tacks and binding for attaching. Shipping weight, 8 pounds...................... $3.85

Door Cover Sets—Black Fiber
Complete with upholsterers' tacks.
28K13235—Set of three pieces, complete for Ford 1917-25 roadster. Shipping wt., per set, 1½ lbs. Per set.............. 65c
28K13239—In set of five pieces, as illustrated, for Ford 1917-25 touring car. Shipping weight, per set, 3½ pounds. Set of 5.............. 95c

Door Hand Pad

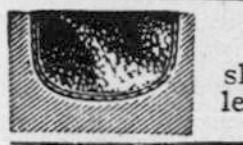

Prevents finger print marks or scratches showing on door. Metal body, artificial leather cover. Shpg. wt., 5 oz.
28K6981—Each.............................. 7c

Ball Grip Handles a Convenience

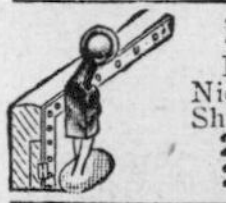

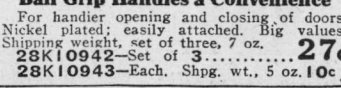

For handier opening and closing of doors. Nickel plated; easily attached. Big values. Shipping weight, set of three, 7 oz.
28K10942—Set of 3.............. 27c
28K10943—Each. Shpg. wt., 5 oz. 10c

Safety Mirror

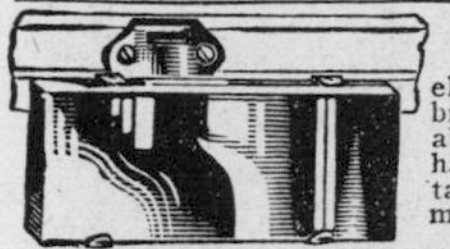

Size, 7x2⅝ inches. Has beveled edge; nickel plated top bracket; is completely adjustable to any angle desired; has additional bracket for attaching mirror on closed models. Shpg. wt., 1 lb.
28K9555.............. 42c

Ford and Standard Car Sun Curtains

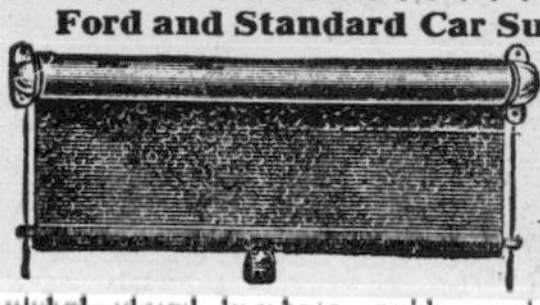

Heavy coated waterproofed fabric curtains, specially embossed finish. Will not fade or rot from sun's rays; will not tear. Cleaned with soap and water. Roller, nickel plated brackets, guide cords and screw eyes included. Pleasing slate color.

Catalog No.	Width, In.	Length, In.	
28K3990	13	24	$1.25
28K3991	20½	24	1.55
28K3992	20	24	1.55
28K3993	21	24	1.55
28K3994	21½	24	1.55
28K3995	25	24	1.55
28K3996	27	24	1.55
28K3997	31½	24	1.65

Shipping weight, any of the above, 1½ pounds.

Pedal Rubbers Aid Driving

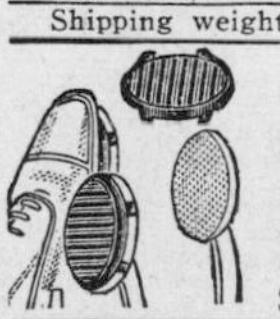

Give sure and more comfortable footing on pedals. Sets of three. Low priced, big value. Shipping weight, per set, ¾ lb.
28K11832
Set of 3.............. 30c

SPICK AND SPAN Striped Seat Covers for all Models of Ford Cars

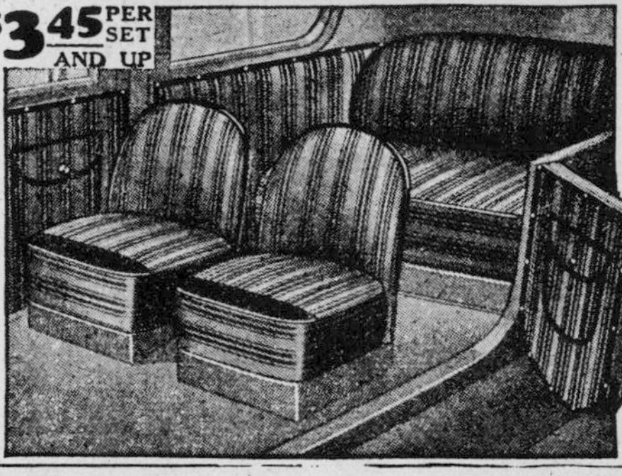

$3.45 PER SET AND UP

Attractive, durable, high grade striped seat covering material. Furnished for doors and car side panels also. One front and one rear door covering has pocket. Per Set

28K8908—For 1916-23 coupes.............. $3.95
28K8909—For 1924-25 coupes.............. 3.95
28K8910—For 1926-27 coupes.............. 3.95
28K8911—For 4-door (Fordor) sedans, 1923-24 and 25 models.............. 6.95
28K8912—For 1916-21 sedans (2-door).... 6.95
28K8913—For 1922-23 sedans (2-door).... 6.95
28K8914—For 1926 (Fordor) 4-door sedans 6.95
28K8915—For Tudor coach (1924-25)....... 6.95
28K8916—For 1926-27 Tudor coach......... 6.95
Shpg. wts.; Coupe and roadster, 3¾ lbs., others, 6 lbs.
28K8900—For 1916-21 roadster.............. $3.45
28K8901—For 1922-25 roadster.............. 3.45
28K8902—For 1926-27 roadster.............. 3.45
28K8906—For 1924-25 touring cars........ 6.95
28K8907—For 1926-27 touring cars........ 6.95

Allstate Spanish Trim Slip Covers for Fords

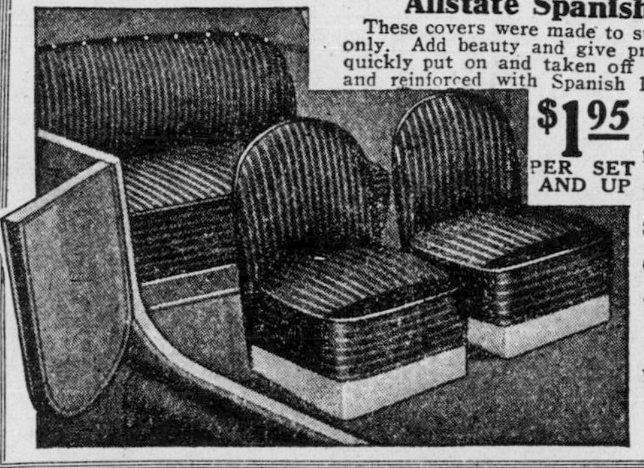

These covers were made to supply the demand for coverings for seats and backs only. Add beauty and give protection to the upholstery at small cost. Can be quickly put on and taken off for cleaning purposes. Made of striped materials and reinforced with Spanish leatherette to match. Easy to attach.

$1.95 PER SET AND UP

28K8917—For 1916-21 Ford roadsters. Shpg. wt., 1¼ lbs. Set... $1.95
28K8918—For 1922-25 Ford roadsters. Shipping weight, 1¼ pounds. Set.............. $1.95
28K8919—For 1926-27 Ford roadsters. Shipping weight, 1¼ pounds. Set.............. $1.95
28K8923—For Ford 2-door (1917-23) sedans, Shipping weight, 3½ pounds. Set.............. $3.95
28K8924—For Ford Tudor (1924-25 2-door) Coach. Shipping weight, 3½ pounds. Set... $3.95
28K8925—1926-27 Tudor Coach. Shipping weight, 3½ pounds.............. $3.95
28K8926—For 4-door (Fordor) Ford Sedans (1924-25). Shipping weight, 3½ lbs. Set.... $3.95
28K8927—1926-27 Fordor Sedan. Shipping weight, 3½ pounds.............. $3.95
28K8928—For 1916-23 Ford coupe.... 2.45
28K8929—For 1924-25 Ford coupe.... 2.45
28K8930—For 1926-27 Ford coupe.... 2.45
Shipping weight, per set, for coupes, 1¼ pounds.

Wind Shield Cleaner for 1926 and 1927 Closed Fords

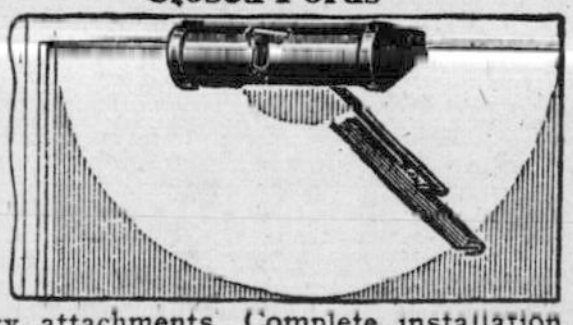

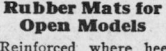

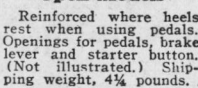

This high grade cleaner works from engine suction. Fits upper wind shield frame, using hole already drilled. Black enamel finish. Furnished complete with rubber hose and all necessary attachments. Complete installation instructions furnished with each wiper. Shipping weight, 1¾ pounds.
28K5016.............. $1.48

Rives Extension Pedal Pads

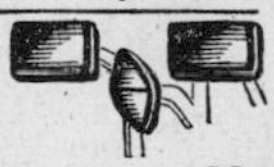

Two outside pads have flat rubber surface of about 2¼x3¼ in.; inner pad is corrugated. Clamps for attaching. For 1915-25 models.
28K5718—Set of 3.............. 69c
28K4647—Set of 3 (1926 and 1927).............. 69c
Shipping weight, 1¼ pounds.

Seat Cushions

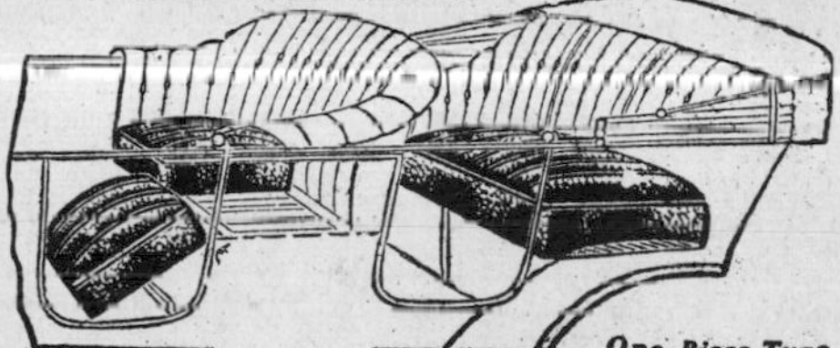

Divided Type

Well made artificial leather covered cushions of handy divided type for front touring seat or for roadsters. Permits raising right hand cushion handily for filling gas tank, etc. (Unmailable.) Shipping weight, 16 pounds.
28K13295¼—For 1915-21 models. Per pair.............. $4.45
28K13296¼—For 1922-25 models. Per pair.............. $4.45
28K13284¼—For 1926-27 models. Per pair.............. $4.70

One-Piece Type

One-piece high grade artificial leather covered seat cushion. Substantial inside burlap reinforcement for taking strains off leather covering of cushions. Spring construction includes wire trusses for holding spring in position. Has larger number of springs than generally used. (Unmailable.) A splendid value in a high quality cushion.
28K13278¼—For 1915-21 touring rear seat. Shipping wt., 21 pounds. Each.............. $4.50
28K13279¼—For 1922-25 touring rear seat. Shipping wt., 17½ lbs. Each.............. $4.50
28K13282¼—For 1926-27 Ford rear. Shipping weight, 18½ lbs. Each.............. $4.60
28K13276¼—For 1915-21 touring front seat or roadster. Shpg. wt., 18 lbs. Each. $4.20
28K13277¼—For 1922-25 touring front seat or roadster. Shpg. wt., 15½ lbs. Ea. $4.40
28K13286¼—For 1926-27 touring front seat. Shipping wt., 18 pounds. Each.............. $4.60

All Black Robe Rail

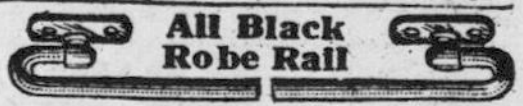

Length of crossbar, 28 in. Curved ends. An excellent value.
28K11836—Shipping weight, 3 pounds.............. 30c

Black and Nickel Robe Rail

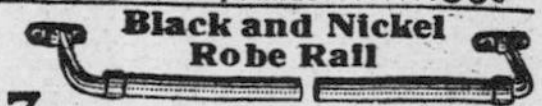

Folding black ends. Nickel plated bar, 27x⅝ inches. Shipping weight, 2¼ lbs.
28K11835.............. 57c

Carpets and Mats

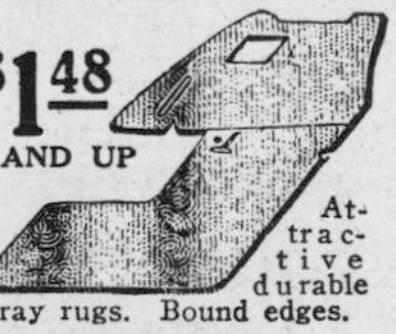

$1.48 AND UP

Attractive durable gray rugs. Bound edges.
28K4743—Coupe Carpet. For 1917-23 models. Shpg. wt., 3¼ lbs. Each.............. $1.49
28K9629—Coupe Carpet. For 1924-25 models. Shpg. wt., 3¼ lbs. Each.............. $1.48
28K9644—Carpet for 1926-27 Ford coupe. Shipping weight, 4 pounds.............. $1.48

28K4745 — Sedan Carpet, for 2-door sedans (1917-23). Two-piece.............. $2.94
28K9645 — Carpet for 1926-27 Ford Tudor coach.............. $3.10
28K9824 — Carpet for Tudor coach (1924-25). Two-piece.............. $3.10
Shipping weight, any of above, 4 pounds.
28K9364 — Carpet for four-door sedans (1924-25). Two-piece. Shpg. wt., 4 lbs.............. $2.63
28K9646 — Carpet for 1926-27 Ford four-door sedan. Shipping weight, 4 pounds.............. $2.63

Mat, two-piece, fits 2-door Ford sedans (1917-23). Shipping weight, 11 pounds.
28K15038.............. $1.70
Mat, one-piece for Ford coupe. (Not illustrated.)
28K15040 — 1916-23 models. Each.............. 83c
Mat, one-piece for 1924-25 Ford coupe. (Not illustrated.)
28K9627 Each.............. 83c
28K9641
Mat, for 1926-27 Ford coupe.............. 83c
Shipping weight, any of above, 5 pounds.
Two-piece rubber mat for 4-door Ford Sedans, 1924-25. (Not illustrated.)
28K4729.............. $1.69

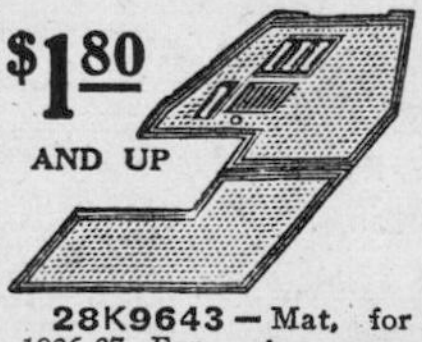

$1.80 AND UP

28K9643 — Mat, for 1926-27 Fordor sedan.............. $1.80
28K9820 — Mat, for Tudor coach (1924-5).............. $1.80
28K9642 — Mat, for 1926-27 Tudor coach.............. $1.93
Shipping weight, any of above, 11 pounds.

Replacement Dash Board

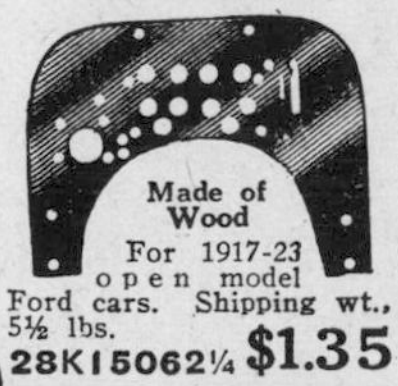

Made of Wood
For 1917-23 open model Ford cars. Shipping wt., 5½ lbs.
28K15062¼ $1.35

Rubber Mats for Open Models

Reinforced where heels rest when using pedals. Openings for pedals, brake lever and starter button. (Not illustrated.) Shipping weight, 4¼ pounds.
28K9640—For 1926-27 Ford touring 78c
28K9827 — Mat for 1917-23 Ford touring cars.............. 72c
28K9829 — Mat for 1924-25 Ford touring cars.............. 72c

Replace Your Old Footboards

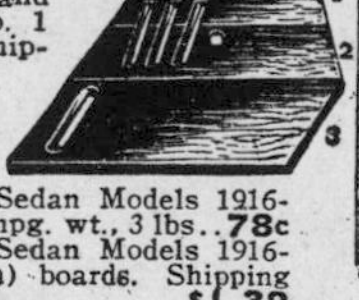

Hardwood. Unusually well made.
28K10066 — Touring and Roadster Models 1915-25, No. 1 and No. 2 boards together. Shipping weight, 4 pounds.. 60c
28K11713 — Touring and Roadster Models 1915-25, No. 3 board. Shipping weight, 5 pounds.............. 54c
28K11716—Coupe and Sedan Models 1916-25, No. 1 and No. 2 boards. Shpg. wt., 3 lbs.. 78c
28K11718—Coupe and Sedan Models 1916-25, No. 3 and No. 4 (bottom) boards. Shipping weight, 5 pounds.............. $1.32
28K11717—All Models 1926-27 No. 1 and No. 2 boards. Shipping weight, 3 pounds.. 84c
28K11719—All Models 1926-27 No. 3 and No. 4 (bottom) boards. Shpg. wt., 5 lbs.. $1.32

De Luxe Flower Vase

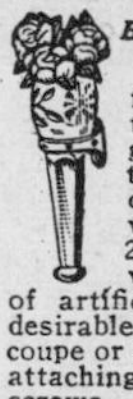

Beautifies Your Car

Inexpensive, neat flower vase of attractive pattern cut glass; anti-splash type. Over all height of vase, 7½ inches; width at top, about 2⅜ inches. Complete with small cluster of artificial roses. A most desirable ornament for your coupe or sedan. Nickel plated attaching brackets and set screws. Shipping weight, 1 pound.
28K6653.............. 75c

Attractive Flower Vase

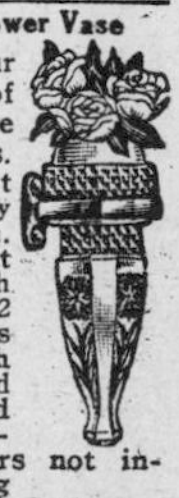

Beautify your car with one of these attractive flower vases. Made of cut glass in a very neat pattern. Height, about 7¼ inches; width at top, about 2 inches. Comes complete with nickel plated bracket and screws for attaching. Flowers not included. Shipping wt., 1¾ lbs.
28K6654 $1.15

Send Sufficient Money for Postage on Parcel Post Shipments. Any Surplus Will Be Returned

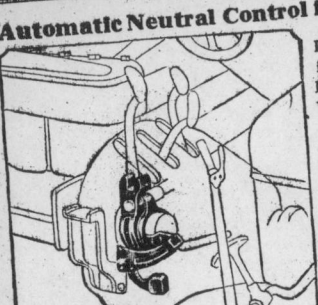

Thrift Is Always Safe — Ford Owners! Save on Gas and Oil

Automatic Neutral Control for Fords

Holds Pedal in Neutral Position Without Pulling Up Brake. Attached in five Minutes.

Gives All the Advantages of Gear Shift Cars

$3.98

Get gear shift convenience without sacrificing any of the advantages of the Ford method of operation. Don't guess at the neutral position. Why keep your foot on the pedal when you want to be in neutral? No slipping, no uncertainty! Start your motor in safety. Protect your starter from the strain that results when the car is accidentally in gear. Protect yourself from accident when you have to crank. Lengthen the life of your transmission bands, and the whole car. Have absolute confidence in driving whether forward or back. A real help for women drivers, as it simplifies the footwork. An ideal arrangement for the light delivery truck making frequent and hurried starts and stops. By absolutely preventing you from starting your motor with the clutch engaged, this device saves you in preventing accidents more than pays for the AUTOMATIC NEUTRAL CONTROL. Good insurance. Real comfort. Convenience and safety for only $3.98. Shipping weight, 4½ pounds.
28K8391 .... **$3.98**

$1.89

Saves You One-Fourth on Gas

Starts your motor instantly in any weather. Saving of one-fourth on gas guaranteed. Installed between carburetor and manifold. Follow instructions and you can easily install it yourself. Heats the mixture as it leaves the carburetor, thereby vaporizing the mixture completely before entering the cylinders. Converts low test into high test gas. Prolongs the life of your battery as current is drawn from generator only. Minimizes carbon deposits. A truly marvelous device. Try it and be convinced. Shipping wt., 8 oz.
28K9121—Model to fit Fords, Chevrolets and Star cars. **$1.89**
28K9577½—Model with dash switch makes starting even easier. Will fit Overland, Studebaker Light Six, Hupmobile Six 1927, Oldsmobile, Chrysler Four and Six, Jewett, Paige, Reo, Willys-Knight Four and 70, Rickenbacker Six, Kissel, Flint, Lexington, Mitchell Six, Chandler Six and Eight, and Pontiac. Shipped from factory in NORTHEASTERN WISCONSIN. **$2.89**

Gasoline Filter for 1926 Fords

The lower grades of gasoline, which are sold now, make gasoline filtering an absolute necessity. This remarkable device strains the gasoline through wire gauze, and all dirt and water settle to bottom of glass bowl. It will check expensive carbon deposits, avoid valve pitting and prevent hard starting and stalling. Install one now and add years to the life of your motor. Shipping weight, 1 pound.
28K11292. .... **95c**

Late Model L-4 Kingston Carburetor

$2.35 Complete

Has improved float, special metal fuel valve and durable bronze air valve. A remarkable value at this low price. Shipping weight, 3 pounds.
28K13272—Complete. **$2.35**

Late Model L-4K Kingston Carburetor

Same as above, but equipped with a good quality strainer. Shipping weight, 3¼ pounds.
28K13258 Complete. (Not illustrated.)
$3.25

Tel-Gas Gauge for 1926-27 Ford Cars

A gravity level instrument and most accurate gauge possible to build. Designed for Ford cars having cowl gasoline tanks, and shows accurately on instrument board the quantity of gasoline in the tank. It fits on the instrument board and is easy to install. It is a check on gasoline purchase. No moving parts to wear. Shipping weight, 2 ounces.
28K6662—For closed models 1926-27 .... **98c**
28K6672—For open models—1926-27 .... **98c**

Carburetor Choke Control

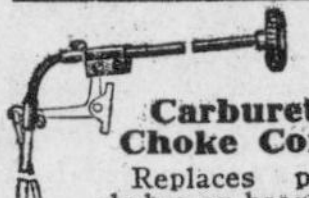

Replaces present choker on board. Use present carburetor rod; directions for installing. Use as choker when engine is cold. As motor warms up reduce richness of mixture, operating dial knob. Shipping wt., 1 lb.
28K5556. .... **58c**

Save Oil and Gas With This Device

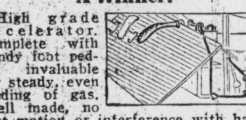

$2.95 Complete

Draws all oil vapor and unburnt gas from crankcase, drawing them into carburetor. Its use prevents waste of fuel and dilution of oil in crankcase. Lubricates valves and piston tops, creates partial vacuum in crankcase, stopping all oil leaks. Quickly installed without drilling holes. Shipping weight, 2 lbs.
28K1618 .... **$2.95**

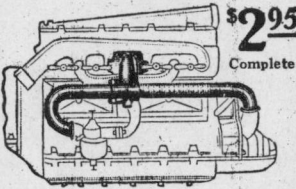

Handy Oil Gauge

Well made gauge with drain cock. Has glass tube protected by metal guard. Heavier construction than ordinary type. Replaces lower petcock. Shpg. wt., 7 oz.
28K11655 .... **45c**

Dash Oil Gauge
A Modern Necessity

Height of fluid in glass tube is regulated by air pressure in metal tube running from gauge to lower oil petcock to show exact oil supply. Complete with metal tubing and fittings. Shipping weight, 1 lb.
28K9420 .... **$1.25**

Force Feed Oiling Is the Thing!

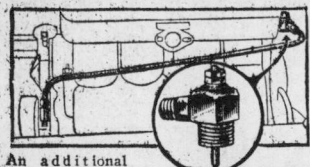

An additional oiling system on outside of motor, insuring oil supply to motor if regular oil line in motor becomes clogged. Special magneto plug with oil outlet, copper tubing and fitting for attaching at front of motor over timing gears. Instructions for installing. Shipping weight, ¾ lb.
28K6707—For all models up to and including 1925. .... **58c**
28K7098—For 1926-27 models. **58c**

Low Priced, Practical Accelerator

Well made, inexpensive foot accelerator; works smoothly under all driving conditions. Simply built and easily installed. Nickel plated finish. Full instructions for attaching. Will fit Fords up to and including 1925 model. Shipping wt., 1¼ lbs.
28K4623 .... **70c**

Get An OIL FILTER SYSTEM for Your Ford

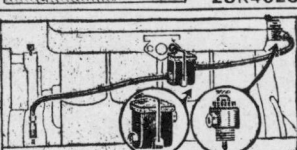

Keep the oil in your Ford motor clean and free flowing, and enjoy the full economy and efficiency you are entitled to. This practical yet inexpensive device filters the oil in your motor completely every 10 minutes, insuring clean, pure oil that does the job better, lasts longer, and keeps your oil system free and open at all times, besides adding to the running life of the motor itself. Similar devices are regular equipment on many makes of cars. Your Ford need not be without this money-saving refinement. Shpg. wt., 2 lbs.
28K6708 .... **$2.35**

Accelerator Foot Rest

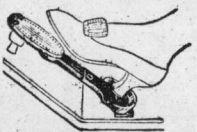

Permits holding foot in comfortable, desirable position and keeping even pressure on accelerator even on rough roads. Has collar at back to prevent heel slipping off foot rest. Adjustable for length. Oval rubber pedal pad at toe end. Shipping weight, 1 lb.
28K5730 .... **65c**

Springfield Accelerator— A Winner!

High grade accelerator. Complete with handy foot pedal; invaluable for steady, even feeding of gas. Well made, no lost motion or interference with hand throttle. Quickly installed; does not interfere with floor boards. Nickel finish. Instructions for attaching. Shipping weight, 1¼ pounds.
28K8203—Will fit all Fords up to and including 1925 model. **$1.15**
28K8204—For all Ford Cars equipped with Holly Carburetor and manifold. Shipping weight, 1¾ pounds. **$1.35**

Brass and Copper Tubing

Brass tubing ¼ inch in diameter. Shipping weight, 2 oz.
28K9572 Per foot **6c**
Copper tubing for piping gasoline or oil. Carried in ¼-inch size.
28K9578—Copper Tubing. Shipping weight, 2 ounces. Per foot **6c**

Universal Accelerator

No fumbling around or taking your hand from the wheel in a pinch. A slight pressure on the easily found pedal and your car hops ahead of the line. Makes driving easier. As easy to install as it is convenient. And it fits all Fords regardless of carburetor equipment. Don't put off owning this accelerator. Shpg. wt., 2 lbs.
28K8206—Fits Fords equipped with regular carburetor, Holley Hot Spot or Kingston Regenerator. **75c**

Mail your Orders for all merchandise on this page either to
CHICAGO PHILADELPHIA MINNEAPOLIS BOSTON MEMPHIS
Whichever is nearest you

Front Axle Parts

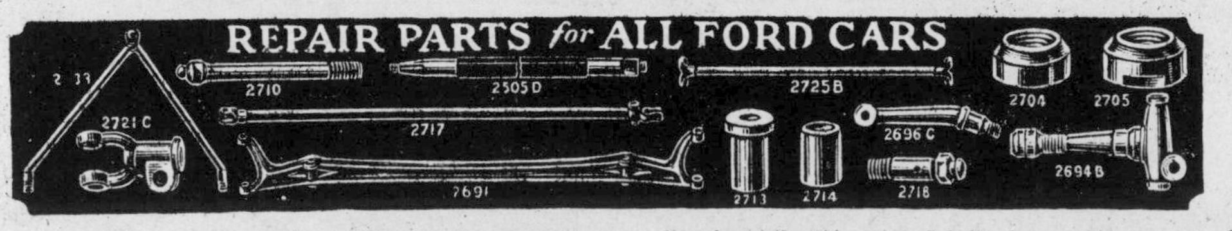

28K10124¼—(No. 2691) Front Axle only. Shipping wt., 19 lbs. **$6.38**
28K10634—(No. 2694B) Spindle Body, Right, 1911-1925 models. **95c**
28K10643—(No. 2695B) Spindle Body, Left, 1911-1925 models. (Not illustrated.) Shipping weight, either of above, 3½ lbs. **95c**
28K13494—(No. 2696C) Spindle Arm, Right, for 1920-1925 models. Shipping weight, 1 pound. **30c**
28K13495—(No. 2696D) Spindle Arm, Left, for 1920-1925 models. (Not illustrated.) Shipping wt., 1 lb. **30c**
28K11839—(No. 2704) Stationary Cone. Shipping weight, 5 ounces. **12c**

REPAIR PARTS for ALL FORD CARS

28K10954—(No. 2705) Adjusting Cone, Right Thread. Shipping weight, 3 ounces. **9c**
28K10956—(No. 2706) Adjusting Cone, Left Thread. (Not illustrated.) Shipping wt., 3 oz. **9c**
28K11892—(No. 2710) Spindle Bolt with Oiler. Shipping weight, ¾ pound. **11c**
28K14254—(No. 2713) Spindle Body Bushing (pair). Shipping weight, 5 ounces. **15c**

28K11658—(No. 2714) Spindle Arm Bushing. Shipping weight, 2 ounces. **3c**
28K10856¼—(No. 2717) Spindle Connecting Rod. Shipping weight, 3½ pounds. **$1.25**
28K11893—(No. 2718) Spindle Connecting Rod Bolt with Oiler. Shipping weight, 4 ounces. **9c**
28K14003—(No. 2721C) Spindle Connecting Rod Yoke. Shipping weight, 8 ounces. **28c**

28K11867—(No. 2725B) Steering Gear Connecting Rod. Shpg. wt., 2 lbs. **59c**
28K10076¼—(No. 2733) Front Radius Rod. (For models up to and including 1919.) **$1.25**
28K10062¼—(No. 2733B) Same for 1920-1925 models. (Not illustrated.) Shipping weight, 7¼ pounds. **$1.10**
28K9955¼—(No. 2505D) Rear Axle Shaft, replacing rear axle shaft. Shipping weight, 7 pounds. **85c**
28K13173¼—(No. 2595B) Drive Shaft only (tapered). (Not illustrated.) Shipping weight, 12 pounds. **$1.58**

480₃ — SEARS, ROEBUCK AND CO. W15 — The World's Largest Store

Equipment for FORDS and FORDSON Tractors

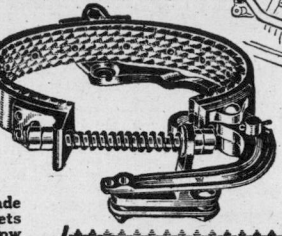

Handy Extra Parts

Positive Action Outside Rear Wheel Brake Set

$4.50 and Up

Do not confuse this high grade brake set with many inferior sets of similar appearance sold at low prices.

Gives your Ford car the smooth, positive braking action of high priced cars. Stops car without chattering or jarring. Uses regular foot brake pedal; easily attached over rear wheel brake drums. Replaces transmission foot brake. Made with bronze bushings, solid steel push rods, drop forgings and efficient equalizers having double adjustments. Lined with the highest quality woven brake lining. Black enamel finish. Instructions for installing. Shipping wt., 15 lbs.

28K12121—Per set. For models up to and including 1925. .... **$4.50**
28K12122—For 1926 and 1927 models... **7.65**
28K12123—For all models of Ford trucks... **7.98**

Steel Brake Shoes

Pressed from one piece. Flexible and efficient. Worn linings can be quickly replaced. Furnished in sets of two, complete with brake springs. An excellent value. Will fit all Ford cars up to and including 1925. Shpg. wt., per set, 3 lbs.
28K11710—Set....... **95c**

Fan Belts

Carry an Extra One With You

28K8390—Extra Heavy Oak Tanned Leather Endless Belt for Fordson Tractors. Will give satisfactory service. Very low priced. Shpg. wt., 6 ounces...... **93c**

See Pages 460 and 461 for the Famous ALLSTATE Tires

Rotating Radiator Ornament for All Cars

$1.49 Complete

The Rotascope is the most attractive radiator ornament on the market. It has beauty of design and finish and adds greatly to the appearance of any car, new or old. The four jeweled cups rotate easily on ball bearings, and will rotate with the slightest breeze. Made of brass, heavily nickel plated and highly polished. Very attractive.

28K9535—Rotascope, complete with highly nickeled cap to fit Ford cars. Shipping weight, ¾ pound.......... **$1.49**
28K9537—Rotascope, less radiator cap. For use on any other make of car. To attach remove radiator cap, drill ⅜₁₆-inch hole, insert screw and draw up nut against washer. Shipping weight, 8 ounces.......... **$1.33**

Pistons for Fordson Tractor

Very fine quality ground pistons with three rings. Pistons are ported for oil return. Complete with rings, bushings and wrist pins.

$2.48 Each

	Size	Shpg. Wt., Lbs.
28K1701	.010	5
28K1703	.005	5
28K1705	.0025	5
28K1707	4x4¼ in.	5

Oil Distributing Piston Rings

25c

Save oil and gasoline, stop oil pumping and spark plug fouling due to worn cylinders. Use one to each piston. To install, drill a few holes through piston at lower groove and put on ring. Knife edge of oil groove collects surplus oil on down stroke and drains it back through slots provided into crankcase. Instructions for installing. Shipping weight, 4 ounces.

28K1675	4x4¼ in.	25c
28K1677	.0025 oversize	25c
28K1679	.005 oversize	25c
28K1681	.010 oversize	25c
28K1683	.015 oversize	25c
28K1685	.025 oversize	25c

"Par Excellence" Tractor Core for Fordson

A most remarkable buy. The finest radiator core on the market. Famous cellular-tubular honeycomb construction. More efficient than other cores for Fordsons and much sturdier, although flexible enough to absorb road shocks. Beautiful in appearance, highest class workmanship. Guaranteed for 18 months against breakage due to freezing. Worth far more than our price.
28K15349¼. Shpg. wt., 50 lbs. **$14.95**

Real Protection for Your Fordson Radiator

"Wilson" Radiator Guard $2.45 and up

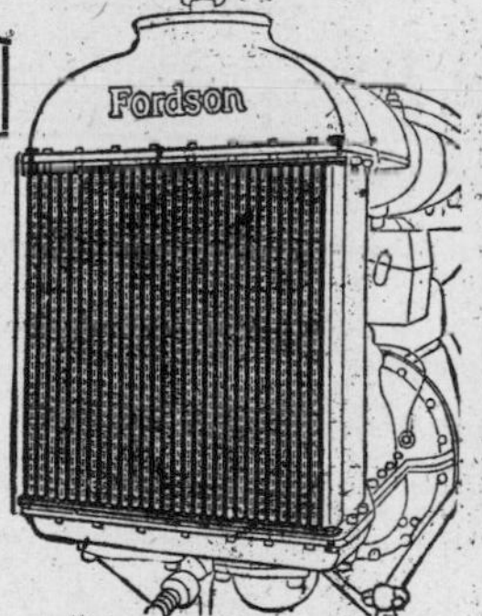

This self cleaning radiator guard is made entirely of steel and iron. Twenty-nine vertical rods are securely riveted into two heads. The rods are ¼ inch in diameter and spaced ⅝-inch from center to center, leaving ⅜-inch clearance between rods. This gives ample protection without checking the free air passage through the radiator.

The vertical parallel rods cause corn stalks or other obstructions to slide upward off the guard.
28K15126¼—Radiator Guard for Fordson. Shipping weight, 10 pounds. **$2.45**

McCormick-Deering Equipment
28K15128¼—McCormick-Deering, 10-20 Radiator Guard. Shipping weight, 12 pounds. **3.89**
28K15130¼—McCormick-Deering '15-30 Radiator Guard. Shipping weight, 12 pounds. **3.89**

Water Pump for Fordson Tractor

$6.85 Complete

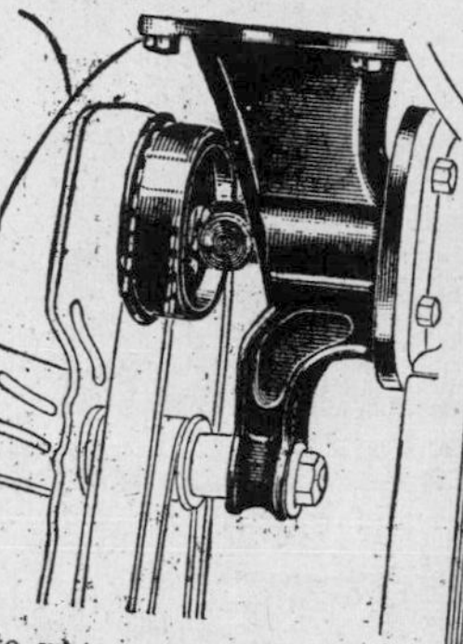

This splendid water pump is guaranteed to keep the Fordson tractor engine cool when operated in even the hottest weather. Pump is self contained, requiring no additional parts. Very simply installed; remove casting which serves as water passage between engine and radiator tank, remove fan and place it on bracket attached to water circulator and install circulator exactly as water inlet casting on tractor is installed. The drive belt fits around pulley on crankshaft directly over the fan belt as shown in illustration. Does not affect the use of governor. This is the simplest and most efficient water circulator made for Fordson Tractors. Shipping weight, 18 pounds.
28K15284¼—Complete................. **$6.85**

Mail Your Orders for all Merchandise on this page either to **Chicago, Philadelphia, Minneapolis, Boston, Memphis**. Whichever is nearest you.

Valves for Fordson Tractors

These high grade one-piece nickel chromium steel valves have a bright ground finish on seat and stem, with lower ends tempered and hardened to prevent flattening out. Perfect fitting. Shipping weight, 6 ounces.
28K1007—For 1917-24 Fordson, intake and exhaust. Each................. **59c**
28K1009—For 1924-26 Fordson, intake and exhaust. Each................. **59c**

De Luxe Dry Timers

Guaranteed for 10,000 Miles' Service

This high grade timer is a big favorite with Fordson owners under its regular trade name. Very strongly made with bakelite case and positive working, long lasting spring contacts. Requires no oil or grease. Will give unusually long satisfactory wear, construction insuring positive contact and a rich hot spark, correctly timed. Full instructions for attaching. Shipping weight, ¾ pound.
28K8319........ **$1.29**

Two Cars in One With This Truck Body for Ford or Chevrolet Roadster

$7.75 and Up

Here's a wonderful value! Put it on your Ford or Chevrolet roadster for hauling supplies quickly and cheaply. Excellently made of selected materials. Strong, durable hardware; substantially ironed and thoroughly braced. Over all size, 34x60 inches; 7½-inch side panels with three braces, 4-inch flare boards, hardwood sills. Has floor panel above battery. Ironed endgate, heavy duty hinges, drop forged fastener or catch, hooked tight on pivot bolts. Complete with body attaching bolts. Painted black. Shipping weight, 100 pounds.
28K2473⅓—For Ford roadster models up to and including 1925......................... **$7.75**
28K2474½—For Ford roadster model. 1926-27. 42 inches wide.....................**$8.75**
28K2475⅓—For Chevrolet roadster. All models up to and including 1927...... **8.95**

Body Irons for Slip-On Truck Body
A complete set of body irons or hardware as shown on the truck body at the right. You can make your own truck body if you prefer and secure this unusually substantial set of hardware forms at a low cost. Shpg. wt., complete set, 19 lbs. **$2.30**
28K11587⅓

Shipped from factory in NORTHEASTERN ILLINOIS, ST. PAUL, MINN., or EASTERN PENNSYLVANIA, whichever is nearest you.

We Guarantee Safe Delivery of All Our Shipments

481

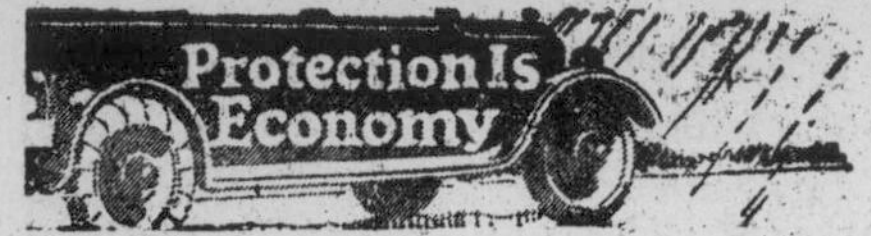

Drive in Safety

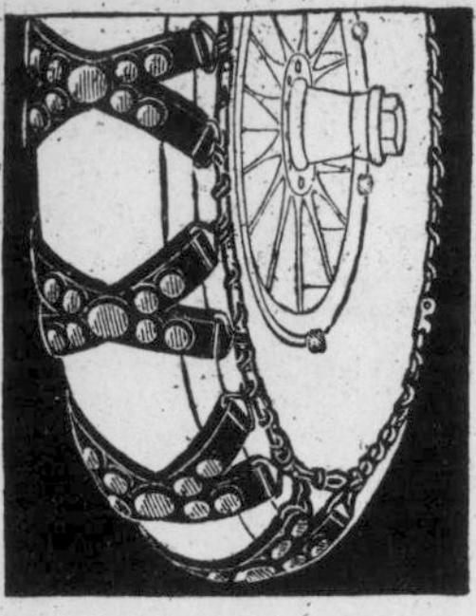

Rubber Chains—The Most Modern and Efficient Tire Chains Made

$9.45 PER PAIR AND UP

RUBBER CHAINS HOLD and KEEP QUIET about it. They don't penalize your tires and nerves for increased safety. These rubber cross links have a heavy button non-skid amplifying the principle of your regular non-skid tire. These chains HOLD TIGHT to the tire and hold the car tight to the road. They protect your tires from skid wear, without cutting or bruising. They are EASILY PUT ON, and can be left on without annoyance for real protection over mud, wet and dry pavements, or snow. Safety and Economy are secured Quietly with rubber chains. Don't wait! Be up to date. Buy your rubber chains today. Tomorrow you may need them.

Rubber Non-Skid Chains

Catalog No.	Fits Tire Size	Shipping Weight	Per Pair
28K4146	30x3½, also 29x4.95 Cords and Oversize	19 lbs.	$ 9.45
28K4151	31x4, also 31x4.40	21 lbs.	10.95
28K4157	32x4½, also 33x4. and 33x6.00	23 lbs.	11.25
28K4159	33x4½, also 32x5.77	23 lbs.	11.25

Rubber Non-Skid Chains (Balloon Size)

Catalog No.	Fits Tire Size	Shpg. Wt. Lbs.	Per Pair
28K4144	29x4.40, also 29x4.75	19	$ 9.45
28K4148	30x4.95, 30x5.25, 31x5.00	21	10.95
28K4155	31x4.95, 32x4., 31x5.25, 30x5.77, and 32x6.00	22	10.95
28K4153	31x5.25, 30x5.77, 30x5.00	22	10.95
28K4167	31x6.00	21	10.95
28K4161	33x5.77, 34x4., 34x4½, 33x5	23	12.25
28K4165	33x6.75, also 34x5.77	26	12.50

Rubber Cross Chains

Catalog No.	Fits Tire Size	Shpg. Wt. Lbs.	Per Set of 10
28K4132	Fits 3½ inches	3¼	$3.25
28K4134	4.40, and 4.75 and 4.95 in.	3¼	3.45
28K4136	5.00 inches	3¼	3.75
28K4138	5.25 and 5.77	4	3.75
28K4140	6.20 and 6.75 inches	4	3.95

Rubber Tire Chain Adjustors

Complete the efficiency of your rubber non-skid chains with a set of these specially designed adjusters to keep them taut and prevent rattling and side play. Tension secured by 6 extra thick rubber straps without interfering with the necessary progressive creeping of the chains that prevent tire wear. Shipping weight, 1 lb.

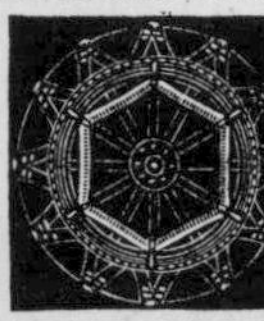

28K4324. **75c**

Finest Duo-Wear Chains

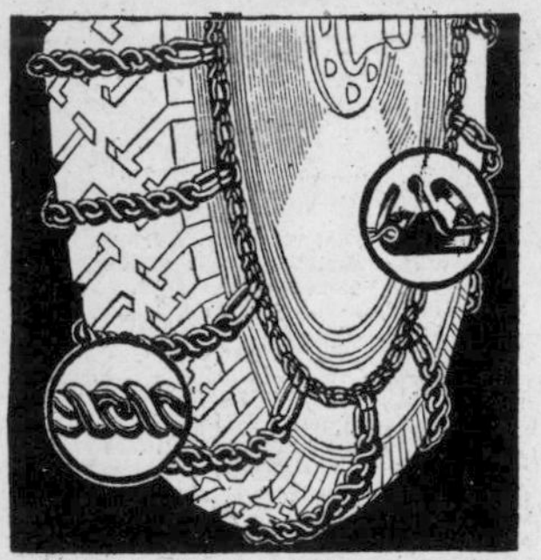

These tire chains wear longer, grab and hold on icy, wet or muddy roads quickly. Cross chains are casehardened and contain three doubly reinforced center links at the point of greatest wear. Note the illustration showing the excellent style fastener.

Order Same Size for Either Fabric or Cord Tires

Prices of Duo-Wear Tire Chains

Catalog No.	Size, Inches	Shpg. Wt., Lbs.	Per Pair
28K4185	30x3½	17	$3.25
28K4186	32x3½	18	3.85
28K4187	31x4	20	3.95
28K4188	32x4	20	3.95
28K4189	33x4	22	4.25
28K4190	34x4	22	4.65
28K4191	32x4½	22	4.65
28K4192	33x4½	22	4.75
28K4193	34x4½	24	4.95
28K4194	35x4½	25	5.65

Cross Chains for Duo-Wear Tire Chains

Sold in Sets of 10

Catalog No.	For Tire Size, In.	Shpg. Wt., Lbs.	Set of 10
28K4272	3½	3½	60c
28K4274	4	4¼	70c
28K4276	4½	4½	75c

Skid Chains for Balloon Tires

These skid chains for balloon tires are furnished in popular ballon tire sizes as listed below. They duplicate the construction of our Wear-Well Tire Chains at right above.

Prices of Balloon Wear-Well Tire Chains

Catalog No.	Size	Shpg. Wt.	Per Pair
28K4330	28x4.40	16	$2.85
28K4331	28x4.75	17½	3.25
28K4332	28x4.95	17½	3.35
28K4333	28x5.25	18	4.00
28K4177	29x4.40	15	2.95
28K4334	29x4.75	17½	3.30
28K4178	29x4.95	18	3.35
28K4335	29x5.25	19	4.05
28K4229	30x4.75	18	3.65
28K4230	30x4.95	18	3.65
28K4336	30x5.00	20	4.35
28K4180	30x5.25	22	4.20
28K4179	30x5.77	20	4.45
28K4337	30x6.00	23	4.75
28K4338	30x6.20	23	4.80
28K4339	30x6.75	25	5.30
28K4231	31x4.40	22	3.80
28K4182	31x4.95	21	3.90
28K4340	31x5.00	23	4.45
28K4181	31x5.25	22	$4.45
28K4236	31x5.77	21	4.95
28K4341	31x6.00	23	5.10
28K4342	31x6.20	23	5.20
28K4343	31x6.75	25	5.45
28K4237	32x4.95	21	4.35
28K4238	32x5.77	22	4.95
28K4239	32x6.00	22	5.45
28K4183	32x6.20	24	5.50
28K4344	32x6.75	26½	5.85
28K4240	33x4.90	20	4.55
28K4244	33x5.77	24	5.15
28K4245	33x6.00	24	5.75
28K4184	33x6.20	25	5.75
28K4246	33x6.60	25	6.45
28K4247	33x6.75	25	6.45
28K4248	34x5.77	25	5.35
28K4249	34x7.30	25	7.65
28K4345	34x7.50	28½	7.75

Mail Your Orders for all Merchandise on this page either to

CHICAGO
PHILADELPHIA
MINNEAPOLIS
BOSTON
MEMPHIS

Whichever is nearest you

Prices of Wear-Well Tire Chains

Catalog No.	Size, Inches	Shpg. Wt., Lbs.	Per Pair
28K5365	30x3½	14	$2.42
28K5366	32x3½	15	3.05
28K5367	31x4	14	3.10
28K5368	32x4	15	3.20
28K5369	33x4	15	3.30
28K5370	34x4	16	3.65
28K5371	32x4½	16	3.60
28K5372	33x4½	17	3.70
28K5373	34x4½	18	3.90
28K5374	35x4½	18	4.45

Cross Chains for Wear-Well Tire Chains

Catalog No.	Size, Inches	Shpg. Wt., Lbs.	Set of 10
28K4271	3½	3¼	52c
28K4273	4	3½	57c
28K4275	4½	3¾	65c

Sold in Sets of 10. Not Illustrated

Cross Chains for Balloon Wear-Well Tire Chains

Catalog No.	Size, Inches	Shpg. Wt., Lbs.	Set of 10
28K4277	4.40	3¼	$0.55
28K4278	4.75 and 4.95	3¼	.65
28K4279	5.25 and 5.77	3½	.82
28K4281	6.00 and 6.20	4½	1.10
28K4282	6.60	6	1.15
28K4283	6.75 and 7.30	6	1.25

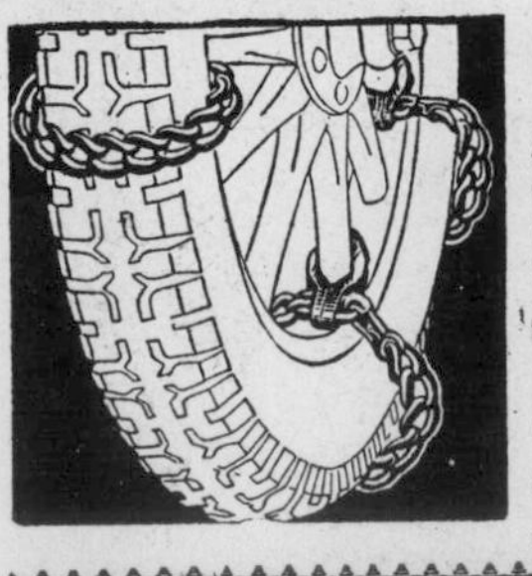

Emergency Mud and Snow Chains

These emergency tire chains are easily adjusted when you are in trouble. Clamp is placed around spoke and snap is hooked into loop holding chain securely. A set of four chains, packed in a bag, is cheap safety insurance.

28K4307—To fit 3 and 3½-inch tires. Per set of 4........**$2.65**

28K4308—To fit 4 and 4½-inch tires. Per set of 4.....**$2.95**

28K4309—To fit 5 and 5½-inch tires. Per set of 4.....**$3.75**

Shipping weights of above, 6, 8¼ and 9½ pounds, respectively.

Tire Chain Adjusters

Chain adjusters make the chain tighter around the tire and prevent noise and rattles which usually occur when chains are loose. Chains cannot slip off and become lost. Equalize tension and prevent undue wear. Do not interfere with creeping of the chains around tire. Shipping weight, 1¼ pounds.

28K4325—To fit 30 and 32-inch tires. Per pair..........**36c**

28K4327—For balloon tires. Per pair..........**36c**

28K4326—To fit 33 and 35-inch tires. Per pair.....**36c**

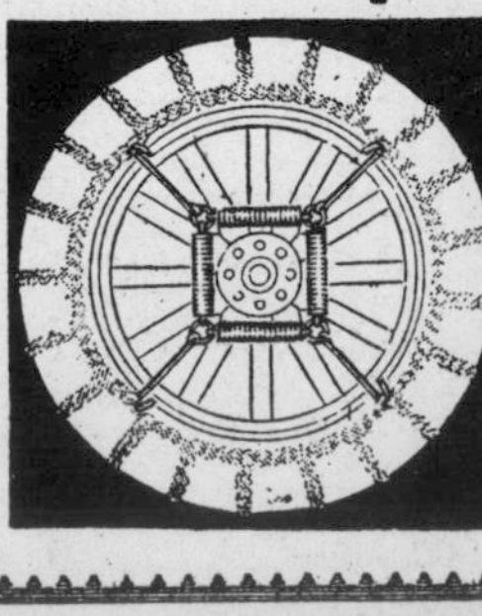

Play Safe! Carry a Spare Gallon

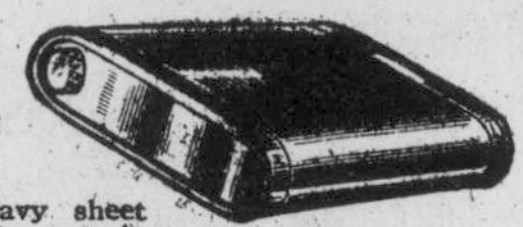

This heavy sheet metal reserve can is flat and compact. May be stored in very small space. Red lithograph finish. Holds 1 gallon of gas. Shipping weight, 2 pounds.

28K13192..................**78c**

Under Hood Electric Motor Horn

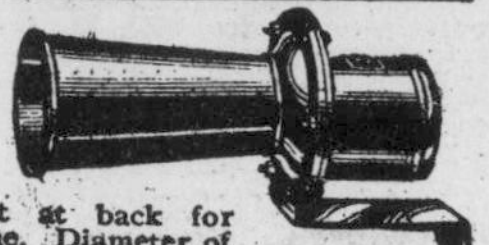

Adjustment at back for regulating tone. Diameter of mouth, about 4 inches; length, over all, about 10½ inches. Cord and push button not furnished. Shipping weight, any type, 3 lbs.

28K2607—6-8-volt type, with bracket for mounting on engine having removable cylinder head (bracket not illustrated)..........**$2.35**

28K2606—Horn, with dash bracket (as illustrated)..........**$2.45**

28K2608—12-16-volt type with bracket for mounting on engine (not illustrated)**$2.48**

Electric Motor Horn

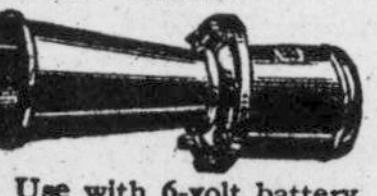

Large size electric motor horn. Length, over all, about 12½ inches; diameter at mouth, about 4¼ inches. Adjustment at back for regulating tone. Use with 6-volt battery. Cord and push button not furnished. Shipping weight, 4½ pounds.

28K2610—Under hood type, complete with dash bracket..........**$3.45**

Auto Siren

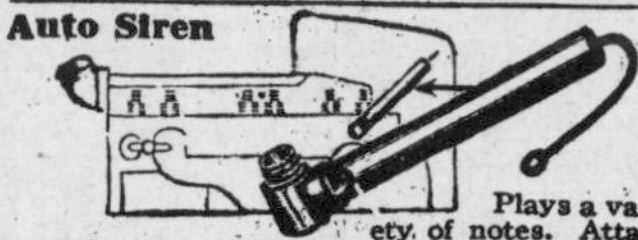

Plays a variety of notes. Attach to exhaust manifold. Operates by simply pulling cord. Attach cord to dash or steering wheel column.

28K9163—Shpg. wt., 1¼ lbs.....**75c**

Double Vision Non-Glare Rear Vision Mirror

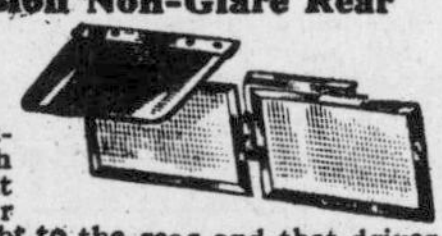

May be adjusted so that both driver and front seat passenger may look straight to the rear and that driver can see the rear and also cars attempting to pass from the left. A double insurance of safety. The non-glare colored night shield prevents dazzling glare of the headlight from the following car. Has nickeled bracket and beveled plate mirrors. Shpg. wt., 1¾ lbs.

28K9556..........**98c**

Safety Rear View Mirror

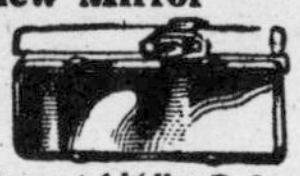

Size, 9x2¾ inches. Has beveled edge and nickel plated top bracket, fitting wind shield frame. Adjustable to any angle; has additional bracket fitting all closed standard cars. Shpg. wt. 1¼ lbs.

28K9557..........**84c**

Rear View Mirrors

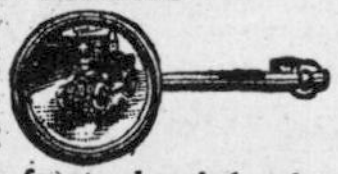

28K6795—5-inch front, reducing type, black. Attaches to wind shield frame. Shipping wt., 1½ lbs..........**75c**

28K6767—5-inch front, beveled edge glass, black. Adjustable. (Not illustrated.) Shipping weight, 1¾ pounds..........**$1.05**

Repair Links for Skid Chains

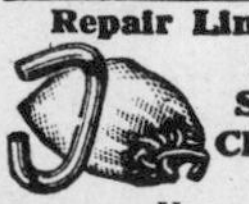

Use to repair broken links in your cross chains. 50 in bag. Shpg. wt., 1 lb.

28K11618 Bag.....**28c**

Chain Pliers

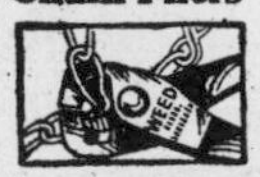

For removing and replacing broken cross chains. 12 inches long. Instructions for using. Shipping weight, 1¼ lbs.

28K4292 Per pair.....**48c**

License Plate Bolts

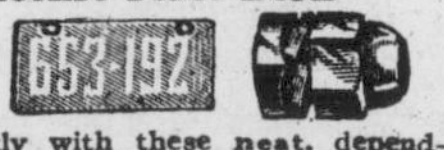

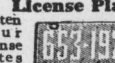

Fasten your license plates permanently with these neat, dependable, rustproof bolts that are specially designed for the purpose with a locking feature that holds. Shipping weight, 2 ounces.

28K8392—Set of 2......**18c**

at Low Cost —

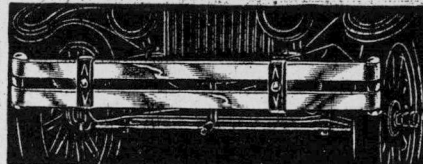 

Mail your orders for all merchandise on this page either to
CHICAGO — PHILADELPHIA
MINNEAPOLIS — BOSTON
or MEMPHIS
Whichever is nearest you

Sun Visors

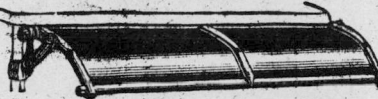

Made of heavy colored transparent celluloid, well adapted for softening sun or headlight glare for driver. Has rustproof aluminum frame. Strong and rigid. Has adjustable bracket fastening to open car wind shield frame; on closed cars screw bracket onto wind shield panel. One size, about 38 inches long. Fits any car, open or closed, except those with V type wind shields. Shipping weight, 5 pounds.
28K15156¼ $2.85

High grade metal visor at a remarkably low price. Black enameled finish. Has universal bracket fitting either open or closed cars, except with V shape wind shields. Adjustable to any angle desired. Size, about 10 inches wide and 40 inches long without brackets. Shipping weight, 9¾ lbs.
28K15162¼—Complete, with universal bracket $1.45

Well made sun visor at a bargain price. Made of black fiber board, leather grained, with metal frame that will not sag or rattle. Every car needs one at this time of year, and every car owner can afford one at this price. It has adjustable brackets in order that the visor may be set at any desired angle. Size of visor, about 8½x33¾ inches. Furnished complete with screws and brackets. Shipping weight, 4 pounds.
28K15155 .... $1.35

Bargain Wind Shield Wiper

You can't afford to drive in stormy weather without an automatic wind shield cleaner, when you can buy our splendid Standard Cleaner for little more than the price often asked elsewhere for many hand cleaners. You will have both hands free for steering, shifting gears, etc. You have a clear view of the road and traffic ahead, making driving safer and more pleasant.

This high grade cleaner works from engine suction. Install on upper wind shield frame, as illustrated, attach rubber hose furnished, drilling hole in intake manifold. Operates by turning button. Black enameled finish. Clips and screws for securely attaching hose to car body. Wiping arm has high grade rubber strip. Has attachment permitting using wiper as hand cleaner when only occasional stroke of wiping arm is needed to keep wind shield free from rain. Shpg. wt., 1¾ lbs.

28K5014 .... $1.48
28K7770—Wiping Arm only, for use with any automatic wind shield cleaner. Shipping wt., 2 oz. 20c
28K7768—Rubber Hose only, for use with any automatic wind shield cleaner. Shipping wt., 6 oz. 15c

Stampco Wind Shield Cleaner

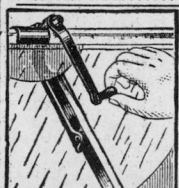

Well made, substantial, wonderfully low priced cleaner, fitting any open car wind shield. Has permanent spring pressure. Handy handle for operating, heavy rubber cleaning strip. Shpg. wt., ¾ lb.
28K6601 .... 24c

Have a First Aid Medical Kit in Your Car

First aid protection makes minor accidents harmless—in major accidents may save life. Be prepared—the next accident may happen to you! The Johnson and Johnson Auto Accident Case contains everything necessary to meet the unexpected emergencies of road or camp. Fits under the seat or in door pocket. Takes up little room. Shipping wt., 1½ lbs.
28K9750 ..... $2.57

(Illustration A)
Illustration shows bumper bar which fits FORD, CHEVROLET and OVERLAND Cars ONLY. Does not have bracket in rear as bumper at right.

(Illustration B)
Illustration shows bumper bar which fits all models listed below EXCEPT Ford, Chevrolet and Overland Cars.

Play Safe!   Buy Quality Bumpers!

You cannot afford to take chances on the road or in heavy traffic in the towns. GOOD bumpers have saved countless lives, to say nothing of material damage to automobiles.

A good, dependable bumper is worth whatever you have to pay for it. Those we list rank with the best in construction, efficiency and long life, although the prices are far below what you are ordinarily asked to pay for bumpers of as high quality.

These are of the latest popular type, made of high grade carbon, oil tempered, heat treated spring steel. Their great strength, together with the two-parallel bar construction and wide spread, insures greater protection to car and occupants in case of collision. Bars and small parts are nickel plated on copper and polished. Clamps have turnover tips and special bridge back block holding bumper bars absolutely tight and preventing shifting or rattling. Substantial flat brackets of 2¼-inch steel, readily attached.

$7⁴⁵ And Up

In Ordering, State Make, Year and Model of Car

We do not furnish universal brackets which give trouble when attaching bumpers. All bumpers bought from us are made to fit the car for which they are ordered.

1½-INCH BUMPER BARS (See Illustration A)

Standard Car Front

Standard Car Rear

Standard Car Rear Fender Guards

Make and Year of Car	Front Bumper Numbers	Shpg. Wt. Lbs.	Rear Bumper Numbers	Shpg. Wt. Lbs.	Fender Guard Numbers	Rear Shpg. Wt. Lbs.
Ford, up to and including 1925	28K15480¼	34	28K15481¼	43		
Ford, 1926-27	28K15582¼	35	28K15583¼	40	28K15584¼	40
Chevrolet, up to and incl. 1924	28K15482¼	39	28K15483¼	45		
Chevrolet, 1925-27	28K15500¼	30	28K15501¼	29	28K15674¼	25
Overland, 4-91, 1925-26	28K15502¼	39	28K15503¼	35	28K15594¼	37

Front or Rear Bumpers, each $7.45
Rear Fender Guards, per pair 7.45

(See Illustration B)

Make and Year of Car	Front Bumper Numbers	Shpg. Wt. Lbs.	Rear Bumper Numbers	Shpg. Wt. Lbs.	Fender Guard Numbers	Rear Shpg. Wt. Lbs.
Chrysler, 4-50, 1926-27	28K15599¼	44	28K15601¼	37	28K15800¼	23
Overland 4-96 Whippet	28K15596¼	40	28K15602¼	37	28K15802¼	27
Pontiac Coach	28K15597¼	42	28K15603¼	37	28K15806¼	25
Pontiac Coupe and Sedan	28K15598¼	42	28K15604¼	37	28K15804¼	25
Star 4 and 6, 1926-27	28K15595¼	41	28K15600¼	37	28K15808¼	25

For Front Bumpers, Rear Bumpers or Rear Fender Guards $8.25

Front Bumper for Fords

1¾-INCH BUMPER BARS (See Illustration B)

Make and Year of Car	Front Numbers	Shpg. Wt. Lbs.	Rear Bumper Numbers	Shpg. Wt. Lbs.	Rear Fender Guard Numbers	Shpg. Wt. Lbs.
Buick Standard Six, 1925-26	28K15606¼	46	28K15607¼	46	28K15816¼	44
Buick Standard Six, 1927	28K15627¼	46	28K15628¼	49	28K15810¼	45
Buick Master Six, 1924-27	28K15625¼	23	28K15626¼	51	28K15812¼	43
Cleveland Standard Six	28K15553¼	46	28K15554¼	46	28K15585¼	42
Cleveland Special Six	28K15629¼	44	28K15630¼	43	28K15818¼	44
Chrysler Six 60	28K15516¼	44	28K15517¼	44	28K15565¼	40
Chrysler 6-70, exc. Brougham	28K15631¼	47	28K15632¼	43	28K15814¼	46
Chrysler 6-70 Brougham	28K15633¼	47	28K15634¼	46	28K15816¼	48
Dodge, 1924 25 26 27	28K16490¼	45	28K15491¼	42	28K15566¼	43
Essex Six	28K15518¼	45	28K15519¼	45	28K15567¼	29
Falcon-Knight, 1927	28K15607¼	42	28K15608¼	41	28K15609¼	45
Hudson	28K15635¼	49	28K15636¼	42	28K15820¼	37
Hupmobile Six, 1926-27	28K15637¼	43	28K15638¼	45	28K15822¼	46
Jewett, 1927	28K15639¼	46	28K15640¼	48	28K15824¼	41
New Day Jewett, 1926 only	28K15555¼	50	28K15611¼	44	28K15588¼	40
Moon 6-60, 1927	28K15643¼	46	28K15644¼	42	28K15828¼	27
Moon Series A, 1926-27	28K15645¼	46	28K15646¼	42	28K15826¼	43
Nash Special Six, 1925-26	28K15647¼	46	28K15648¼	49	28K15830¼	45
Nash Special Six, 1927	28K15649¼	48	28K15670¼	41	28K15832¼	43
Nash Light Six, 1926-27	28K15672¼	46	28K15671¼	41	28K15673¼	41
Nash Advance Six, 1924-27	28K15611¼	46	28K15612¼	45	28K15834¼	47
Oakland	28K15492¼	45	28K15493¼	42	28K15575¼	44
Oldsmobile Six, 1925-26	28K15621¼	49	28K15622¼	41	28K15836¼	41
Oldsmobile Six, 1927	28K15623¼	47	28K15624¼	42	28K15838¼	26
Overland Six	28K15536¼	48	28K15537¼	46	28K15589¼	44
Paige, 1927 (115-in. W. B.)	28K15619¼	46	28K15620¼	42	28K15840¼	44
Studebaker Std. Six, 1925-26-27	28K15538¼	45	28K15539¼	45	28K15577¼	41
Studebaker Spec. Six, 1925-26-27	28K15540¼	46	28K15541¼	48	28K15578¼	36
Whippet Six, 1927	28K15605¼	42	28K15606¼	41	28K15610¼	45
Willys-Knight, 6-66, 1926-27	28K15617¼	41	28K15618¼	42	28K15842¼	44
Willys-Knight 6-70, 1926	28K15615¼	42	28K15616¼	43	28K15846¼	45
Willys-Knight 6-70, 1927	28K15613¼	42	28K15614¼	42	28K15844¼	45

Rear Bumper for Fords

Front Bumpers, Rear Bumpers or Rear Fender Guards $8.95

Bumpers listed below are shipped promptly from factory in NORTHEASTERN ILLINOIS.

28K15350½—Front Bumper, 1¾-inch bars for any car not listed above. In ordering be sure to state make, year and model of car. Complete. Shpg. wt., 53 lbs. $10.95

28K15352½—Rear Bumper, 1¾-inch bars, for any car not listed above. In ordering be sure to state make, year and model of car. Complete. Shpg. wt., 49 lbs. $10.95

Rear Fender Guards for Fords

Sets consisting of front bumper and rear fender guards for the following cars:
28K15850¼—Chevrolet 1925-26-27 Models .... Shipping Weight, 52 pounds
28K15852¼—Ford 1926-27 Models .... Shipping Weight, 74 pounds
28K15854¼—Pontiac 1926-27 Models .... Shipping Weight, 54 pounds
28K15856¼—Star 1926-27 Models .... Shipping Weight, 55 pounds
28K15858¼—Whippet 1926-27 Models .... Shipping Weight, 54 pounds
Per set for any of the above models $10.98
All Bumpers shipped from our store except when factory shipment is specified

---

Boyce Motometers at Cut Prices
(Do Not Fit Willys-Overland Cars)

Warn you when motor is overheating from lack of water, oil, etc. Furnished without radiator cap.

Standard Model. Has 3½-inch front, heavy beveled crystals both front and rear. Comes in nickel plated finish with black dial. A splendid model with latest improved features. Shipping weight, 1¼ pounds.
28K4828 .... $7.40

Universal Model. Of similar type to the above, but somewhat smaller. Comes in nickel plated finish with black dial, about 2¾ inches in diameter. (Not illustrated.) Shipping weight, 1 pound.
28K6319 .... $5.40

Boyce Midget Model. Front and rear beveled crystals; black and nickel plated dial, about 2¼ inches in diameter. Shipping weight, ¾ pound.
28K8199 .... $2.55

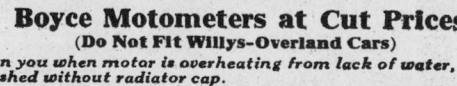
28K4828

28K8199

Parcel Post, Express and Freight Rates Are on Pages 542 to 545

Tops and Top Repairs

For Tops for Fords Cars and Top Repairs See Page 478

Prices of Standard Car Top Coverings
(5-Passenger Touring Models Only)

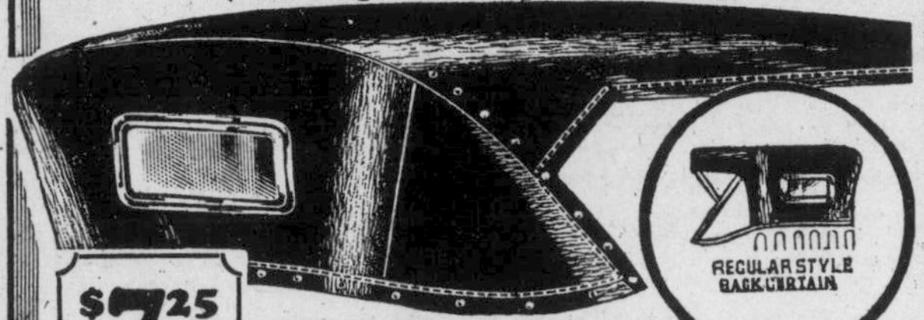

$7.25 AND UP

NOTE—Gypsy style back curtains furnished ONLY as stated.
Gypsy Style Back Curtain furnished only where original equipment top covering or back curtain includes Gypsy style back curtain.

Comes complete with top covering and back curtain for replacing present top covering and back curtain. Furnished in good quality imitation leather, with one 6x18-inch oblong flat glass in back curtain. Complete with necessary tacks and binding. We carry coverings in stock for the cars listed below and make prompt shipment.

Catalog No.	Make, Year and Model of Car	Each
28K1605	Buick D45, 1916-17, Gypsy Curtain	$ 8.45
28K1609	Buick D35, 1917	8.45
28K1611	Buick E45, 1918-19	8.45
28K1613	Buick E35, 1918	8.45
28K1615	Buick H45, K45, 1919-20, Gypsy Curtain	9.45
28K1617	Buick 45, 1921-22, Gypsy Curtain	10.25
28K1619	Buick 45, 1923, 6 Cyl., Gypsy Curtain	10.25
28K1621	Chevrolet 490, 1918-19	7.25
28K1623	Chevrolet 490, 1920-21	7.25
28K1625	Chevrolet 490, 1922, Gypsy Curtain	7.70
28K1627	Chevrolet Superior, 1923-24, Gypsy Curtain	7.70
28K1629	Dodge, 1915-16	8.20
28K1631	Dodge, 1917-18-19	8.20
28K1633	Dodge, 1920-21-22, Gypsy Curtain	8.40
28K1635	Dodge, 1923, Gypsy Curtain	8.40
28K1637	Dodge, 1924, Gypsy Curtain	8.40
28K1639	Maxwell 25, 1916-17	8.40
28K1641	Maxwell 25, 1918	8.40
28K1643	Maxwell, 1919-20-21	8.40
28K1645	Maxwell, 1922, Gypsy Curtain	8.40
28K1647	Maxwell, 1923-24, Gypsy Curtain	8.40
28K1649	Overland 83, 1916	8.30
28K1651	Overland 75, 1916-17	8.30
28K1653	Overland 90, 1917-18-19	8.30
28K1655	Overland 4, 1920-21	8.40
28K1657	Overland 4, 1922, Gypsy Curtain	8.40
28K1659	Overland 91, 1923-24, Gypsy Curtain	8.40

Shipping weight, any of above, 14½ pounds.

28K1673⅓—If you wish any of the above tops **without back curtain,** order under this number and **be sure to give the year and model of your car.** Deduct $3.90 from above prices. Shipping weight of top only, 6 lbs. **(Shipped from factory in NORTHEASTERN ILLINOIS in about 10 days' time.**

28K1661⅓—Top Covering and Back Curtain for all 5-passenger touring cars not shown above. **Gypsy style back curtain furnished ONLY when regular equipment on your car.** Shipping weight, 11 lbs. **(Shipped from factory in NORTHEASTERN ILLINOIS in about 10 days' time.) State make, year and model of car.** **$11.95**

28K1663⅓—Top Covering and Back Curtain made of 38-40-ounce **double texture imitation leather** with one 6x18-inch oblong beveled plate glass light mounted in brass nickel plated frame. **In ordering state make, year and model of car. Gypsy style back curtain furnished ONLY when regular equipment on your car.** (For 5-passenger touring models only.) Shipping weight, 15 pounds. **(Shipped from factory in NORTHEASTERN ILLINOIS in about 10 days' time.)** **$16.25**

28K2426⅓—Back Curtain for 5-passenger touring cars; made of **double texture imitation leather** with 6x18-inch oblong beveled plate glass light mounted in brass nickel plated frame. **In ordering be sure to state make, year and model of car. Gypsy style back curtain furnished ONLY when regular equipment on your car.** Shipping weight, 5 pounds. **(Shipped from factory in NORTHEASTERN ILLINOIS in about 10 days' time)** **$7.50**

For Auto Paint and Enamel See Page 1035

Celluloid

Replace broken, cracked or discolored side curtain or back curtain celluloid lights. It costs little and adds so much to the appearance of the car.
28K13155¼—Celluloid, in sheets about 20x50 inches. Shipping weight, 1½ pounds. Per sheet..... **98c**

"Stik-Tite" Celluloid Curtain Lights

Stick Them on Like a Postage Stamp

A bargain at our price. For Dodge rear or side curtains. Use cement furnished to make quick, satisfactory, permanent repair. Shipping weight, 6 ounces.
28K4294—Each..... **29c**

You Need Celluloid Cement

For repairing celluloid in auto curtains, or putting in celluloid lights with cement instead of sewing. Two-ounce can. Shpg. wt., 8 oz.
28K9387........ **18c**

Step Plates Protect Your Car
Rubber Insert Type

Up to date type with aluminum frame and mud scraper. Remarkably low priced. Rubber insert pad comes about 6½x8¼ inches between frame rims. Over all size of step plate, 9 inches deep by 9½ inches long. Bolt to running board. Bolts furnished. Shipping wt., per pair, 4¾ lbs.
28K9523—Pair.......... **$1.43**

Aluminum Step Plate With Scraper and Kick Plate

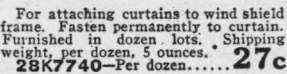

A fine quality step plate which has removable rubber mat and separate kick plate. A useful ornament to any car. Size, 7⅞ in. deep by 9⅛ inches wide. Complete with bolts for attaching.
28K9570—Plate and mat only (A). Shipping weight, 1¾ pounds..... **85c**
28K9568—Kick plate (B). Shipping weight, 6 ounces..... **39c**

Buy Step Plates for Safety

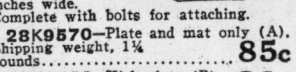

A very high grade cast aluminum step plate with kick plate and scrapercast in one piece with frame. Separate rubber mat. with frame. Separate rubber mat. Complete with bolts for attaching. Shipping weight, 1¼ pounds.
28K9569—Plate and rubber mat.......... **89c**

Cocoa Mats for Cleanliness

Two clips hold mat to running board. Size, about 14x8 inches. A bargain price. Shipping weight, 1¾ pounds.
28K13170.......... **62c**

Low Priced Rubber Mats

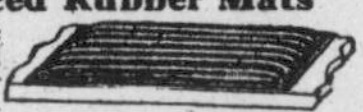

Well made corrugated black rubber mat for running board use. Size, about 7½x11 inches. No bolts furnished. Priced remarkably low. Shipping weight, 2 pounds.
28K10569.......... **15c**

Genuine "Stik-Tite" Roof Patch Strips

Repair holes or breaks in rubberized cloth or artificial leather tops before they leak or get larger. Your top will look much neater, too. Under surface has cement coating, protected by sheeting. Apply like an inner tube patch, following instructions given.
28K11047—"Stik-Tite" Roof Patch Strip, about 5x9 inches, for rubberized cloth tops..... **28c**
28K9636—Same, 6x18 inches, for rubberized cloth tops..... **73c**
28K9274—Same, 2x36 inches, for rubberized cloth tops..... **49c**
28K9630—"Stik-Tite" Roof Patch Strip, about 3x12 inches, for artificial leather tops..... **27c**
28K9634—Same, 6x18 inches, for artificial leather tops..... **73c**
28K9276—Same, 2x36 inches, for artificial leather tops..... **49c**
Shipping weight, any of above outfits, 5 ounces.

Handy "Lift the Dot" Curtain Fasteners

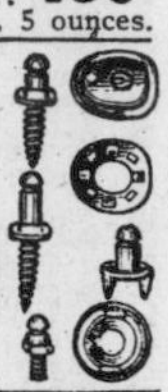

Handy repair package. Six sockets and clinch plates, one long and two short curtain studs for double and single thickness of curtains, two studs and washers and two wind shield studs. Nickel plated. Shipping weight, 4 ounces.
28K7590.............. **32c**

Standard Curtain Fasteners

For attaching curtains to wind shield frame. Fasten permanently to curtain. Furnished in dozen lots. Shipping weight, per dozen, 5 ounces.
28K7740—Per dozen...... **27c**

Two styles. Package contains six fasteners, two of style A and four style B (two each single and double ply curtains), complete with eyelets and washers. Furnished without screws. Shpg. wt., 4 oz.
28K7725—Brass finish. Per package..... **36c**
28K7760—Nickel plated..... **38c**

Auto Top Pads for All Cars

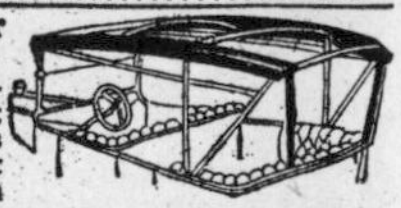

Replace unsightly sagging misplaced top pads; it costs little and gives your car interior a neat appearance. Come in complete set for car.
28K4625—Khaki, for all standard cars..... **$1.57**
28K4627—Black, for Ford cars..... **1.29**
Shipping weight, either set, 5¼ pounds.

Permanent Auto Top Cement

Use with top patching material to make a lasting waterproof patch on auto tops, cushions and seat covers; also on California style tops. Fills small holes in top. Two-ounce can. Shipping weight, 8 ounces.
28K9394..... **18c**

Complete Auto Top Mending Outfit

For repairing rubberized or mohair style tops, top boots, seat covers, side curtains, etc. Comprises 2-ounce bottle of cement, patching material and swab for applying. Shipping weight, ¾ lb.
28K9395—For rubberized tops..... **27c**
28K9397—For mohair style tops..... **27c**

Save on Cushion Re-Cover for Your Ford!

Seat cushion reupholstering costs you less and completely covers top and sides of your old worn out seat cushion. High grade artificial leather, padded, tufted. Fits snugly. Fastens with string ties. Shpg. wt., 2 lbs.
28K5190—1915-21 Touring Front and Roadster..... **$2.10**
28K5191—1922-27 Touring Front and Roadster..... **2.10**
28K5192—1915-21 Touring Rear..... **2.10**
28K5193—1922-27 Touring Rear..... **2.10**

Initials for the Car

Add individuality and beauty to your car with a set of these Super-Smart Beautygrams. They are very handsomely designed and made of solid German silver, sterling silver plated, bearing the owner's initials. Anyone can put them on in a few minutes with a special patented cement that holds them firmly. Beautygrams can be removed when car is repainted, or changed from car to car. You will never be satisfied with painted initials after seeing these Beautygrams. Put up in neat box in sets of two plates (one for each side of the car), and special cement for attaching. We can furnish any initial, except the letter "X." **Be sure to state initial wanted.** Shpg. wt., 4 oz.
28K8000—Set, complete with instructions for attaching. **$3.35**

Closed Car Window Anti-Rattlers

Rubber tip in end of set screw keeps steady even pressure on glass when screw is turned down. Lock-nut holds set screw in place. Nickel plated. Shipping wt., 3 ounces.
28K8702—Pair. **17c**

Attractive Seat Pads

Protect your clothes and seat cushions with these attractive, serviceable, two-piece straw seat covers bound and reinforced with strong khaki material. Pieces are fastened together to make combination back and seat pad. Clean them with sponge or damp cloth. Almost a necessity for hot weather, but valuable at all times, both for auto and for widespread outdoor use. Remarkably low priced. Shipping weight, 1¼ pounds.
28K6969.............. **69c**

Solid Comfort Back Cushion

A wonderful value in a V-shape cushion back rest. Artificial leather covering, good quality filler. Also brings short limbed drivers closer to pedals. Size, about 14x14½ inches. Black with white edging. Shpg. wt., 3 lbs.
28K13168.......... **83c**

Cleaning and Polishing Equipment

Ride in Comfort

Genuine Simoniz (Paste) Polish

44c EACH

Gives a lustrous finish that protects the car body surfaces splendidly against wind, rain and sun. You can remove dust, dirt and road splashes from a Simonized car without scratching finish or washing body surface. Apply Simoniz to a new car to keep the finish perfect.

Use Simon's Kleener to clean the car body before applying Simoniz. It removes greasy, dirty spots and stains. Simoniz is the finest polish for Duco finish cars. Preserves the dull luster peculiar to Duco and makes the car easy to clean.

28K13106—Simoniz (Paste Polish). Per 5-ounce can................**44c**
28K13107—Simon's Kleener. Per 9-ounce can................**44c**
Shipping weights, 1 and 1½ pounds, respectively.
For Automobile Paint and Enamel, See Page 1035

Fine Chamois Skins (Sheepskin)
$1.48 and up
24x27 in. Specially Priced

Excellent quality, low priced. Comes in pieces about 26x28 or 24x27 inches.
28K11858
Size, 24x27 inches............**$1.48**
28K10850
Size, 26x28 inches............**1.62**
Shipping weights, 6 and 8 ounces, respectively.
For Other Sizes of Chamois, See Page 646

Make Rough Roads Smooth

$5.95 PER PAIR

Front   Rear

Ride In Comfort With De Luxe Rebound Absorbers for Standard Cars

A highly efficient, unusually substantial shock absorber which smothers the rebound but does not interfere with downward spring action. Also checks side sway. Can be attached to channel frame of car at rear, usually without drilling frame. Illustrations clearly show method of attaching to either front or rear of car and principle of operation. Readily adjusted for weight of car, type of spring, or as driver desires. Comprises brake drum and splendid web strap, together with strong flexible spring. Furnished in black finish, in pairs, for either front or rear of car, complete with attachments for fitting to cars listed below. Splendidly adapted for use with balloon tires as well as regulation cord or fabric tires.

For all models Ajax, Anderson, Apperson, Auburn 1920-24, Buick, Cadillac, Case, Chambers, Chandler, Chevrolet 1925-1927, Cleveland, Cole, Columbia, Chrysler 4, Chrysler 50-60, Davis 1922-24, Diana, Dodge 1924-27, Dort, Durant except 1926, Elgin, Elcar 6, Essex 1924-27, 1926 Gray, HCS, Haynes, Hudson up to 1001, Hupmobile, Jewett (except 1925), Jordan, Lincoln, Maxwell, Moon, Nash 6, Oakland, Overland 6, Packard, Peerless, Pilot, Pontiac, Premier, Stephens, Studebaker, Velie 1925-27, Westcott, Willys-Knight.
In ordering be sure to state year and model of car.
28K15057—Front Absorbers. Shipping weight, per pair, 13 pounds. Per pair............**$5.95**
28K15061—Rear Absorbers. Shipping weight, per pair, 11 pounds. Per pair............**5.95**
28K15094½—Rebound Absorbers for all cars other than those listed above must be shipped from the factory in NORTHEASTERN ILLINOIS. Order under this number and be sure to state year and model of your car. Shipping weight, 24 pounds.
Per pair (two front or two rear absorbers). State which is wanted............**$5.95**

GREASE GUNS
Standard Pressure System
$3.05 AND UP

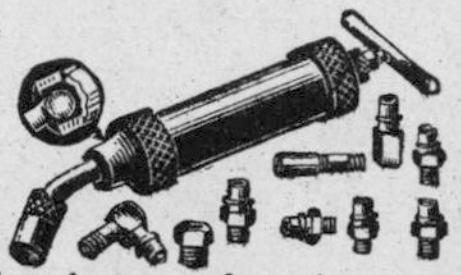

Everyone knows the importance of proper greasing for smooth, quiet running and lower repair bills. This system includes a gun operating with 2,000 pounds pressure, forcing in new grease to every part of the bearing and forcing out old grease, dirt, etc. Furnished as listed below complete with necessary fittings. In ordering be sure to state make, year, and model of car. All outfits, except 28K7864, are shipped from factory in NORTHEASTERN ILLINOIS.

28K7864—For all Ford, Gray and Star cars. Gun and eight fittings. Shipped from store. Shipping weight, 3½ lbs. Complete outfit............**$3.05**
28K7863½—For Chevrolet, 490 and Superior models, Flint and Maxwell cars. Shipping weight, 5½ pounds. Complete outfit............**$4.42**
28K7022½—For Case, Chandler, Chevrolet, except 490, Superior and K models; Cleveland, Dodge, Durant, Elgin, Essex, Franklin, Haynes, Hupmobile, Jordan, Nash, Oldsmobile, Overland 4-cyl., Studebaker and Velie cars. Shipping weight, 6 pounds. Complete outfit............**$5.68**
28K7862½—For Buick, Chalmers, Dort, Hudson, Jewett, Moon, Oakland, Overland 6-cyl., Reo and Willys-Knight cars. Shipping weight, 6½ pounds. Complete outfit............**$6.42**

High Pressure Grease Gun
$1.25

A splendid grease gun adapted for use with all high pressure greasing systems which use flexible metal tubing hose. If you have lost the grease gun from a high pressure system of the type stated, here is your opportunity to replace it at a slight expense. Has nonflexible nozzle for use as a regulation grease gun. Flexible tubing is not furnished with this gun. Diameter of barrel, 2 inches; length of barrel, 6 inches. Substantially made in white metal finish. Shpg. wt., 2 lbs.
28K7817............**$1.25**

Quick Action Oil Grease Gun
$1.18

Unusually substantial, all brass. About 9¼ inches long and 2 inches in diameter. Has positive spiral worm action. Small tip at spout is for oil use. Loosen thumbnut near handle to secure pushing action for plunger in oiling. Spout, about 5 inches long. Shipping weight, 2¼ pounds.
28K10930............**$1.18**

Flexible Spout Oiler

Comes in ½-pint size, with about 3¾-inch diameter. Flexible metal tubing spout with copper tip bent for conveniently reaching parts ordinarily difficult to oil. Length of spout, 7 inches. Shipping weight, 1¼ pounds.
28K9002............**35c**

Carshine Wax
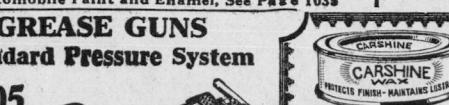

A high grade wax and cleaner, giving the car body surfaces a lasting, lustrous finish, proof against rain, wind and sun. Use cleaner to remove dirt and grease, then apply wax. Occasionally wipe waxed surface with a cloth to remove dust and mud without injuring finsh.
28K13104—Carshine Wax, about 5-ounce can............**30c**
28K13105—Carshine Cleaner, about 9-ounce can............**30c**
Shipping weights, 1 and 1½ pounds, respectively.
For White Cotton Waste, See Page 1016

Body Polish Is an Investment

A highly efficient body polish, well known under its trade name. Cleans soiled car surfaces without damaging car finish and leaves a dry, lustrous finish. Use also on highly varnished or enameled surfaces, such as pianos, furniture, etc. About 1-pint cans. Shipping weight, 2 pounds.
28K8091—Per can............**38c**

Keep the Car Looking Trim

This Rapid Repair Enamel is fine for touching up bumpers, fenders, radiators, rust spots, etc. One-half pint each quick drying black enamel with camel hair brush fastened to lid of can. Bristles rest in enamel, keeping brush in perfect condition. Shipping wt., 1 lb.
28K10912............**38c**

Auto Washer Brush

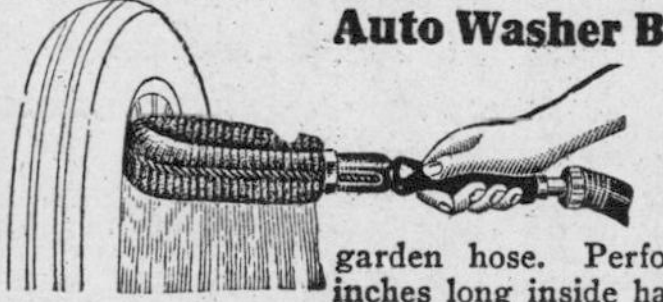

Has coupling for attaching to ordinary garden hose. Perforated brass tube, 13¾ inches long inside handle, carries water into brush. Has 1-inch soft durable bristles, set in circular form on twisted wire framework. 8-inch wood handle. Length over all, about 16½ inches. Shipping weight, 1¼ lbs.
28K5050............**$1.48**

Cuba Sheepswool Cut Sponges

A very good genuine Cuba Sheepskin Sponge at an extremely low price. This sponge will give excellent service.
28K10848 — Diameter, about 6½ inches. Shpg. wt., 5 oz.......**42c**

Genuine Rock Island Sheepswool Sponges

The finest of form sponges, this will give twice the wear that you would get from an ordinary sponge.
28K10855 — Diameter, about 5½ inches. Shipping weight, 6 ounces............**55c**
28K10849 — Diameter, about 7½ inches. Shipping weight, 7 ounces........**$1.78**

For Other Sponges, See Page 646

Dependable Metal Polish

An excellent polish for the polished metal parts on the car; used also for wind shield glass, lamp lenses, mirrors and windows. Not explosive or inflammable, will not injure hands or clothes. Comes in 1-pint can. Shipping wt., 1½ lbs.
28K8710—Per can... **36c**

Apex 1001 Oil

"The oil of 1001 uses." Use it for oiling automobile starters, generators, magnetos, electric motors. Invaluable, too, as a polish and rust preventive. 3-ounce can. Shipping weight, ¾ lb.
28K10342—Per can... **18c**

Measure Funnels
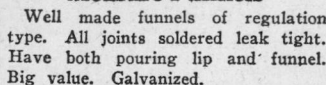

Well made funnels of regulation type. All joints soldered leak tight. Have both pouring lip and funnel. Big value. Galvanized.

Catalog No.	Size, Quart	Shpg. Wt.	
28K10088	1	2 lbs.	43c
28K10089	2	2¼ lbs.	56c
28K10090	4	4 lbs.	68c

Tin Funnels

28K7850
1-quart size............**12c**
28K7851
2-quart size............**14c**
28K7852
3-quart size............**15c**
Shipping weights, 1½, 1¾ and 2¼ pounds, respectively.

Handy Hand Dusting and Polishing Mitt

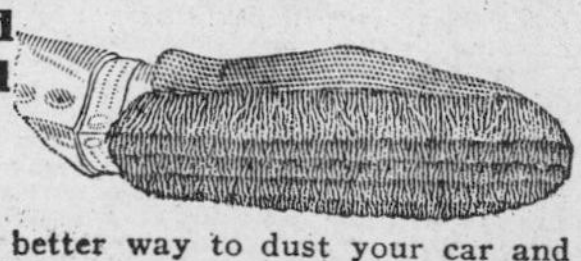

The easier and better way to dust your car and bring out the full, lustrous polish. Especially fine for the new lacquer finishes, and for brightening the windows and windshield. Pure silk nap over an inch thick, picks up dust without scratching. Easily washed; easily tucked away without scattering dust. Mittens are mulberry color, and fit either hand. Useful and necessary around the car and home. Shipping weight, 4 ounces.
28K8360............**35c**

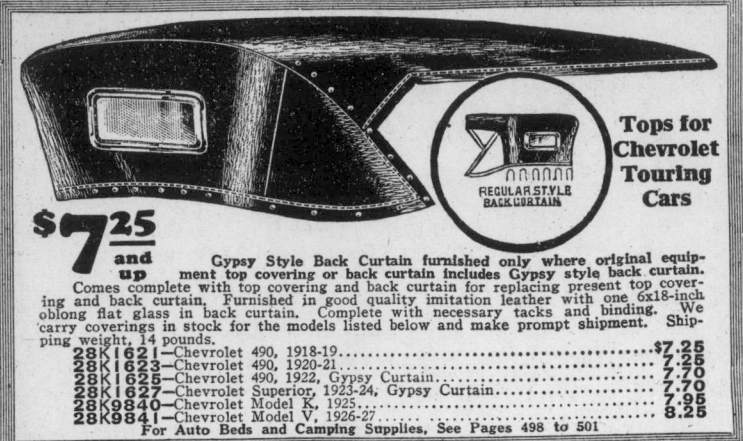

Mail Your Orders for All Merchandise on This Page Either to CHICAGO—PHILADELPHIA MINNEAPOLIS—BOSTON or MEMPHIS Whichever is nearest you

Equipment For

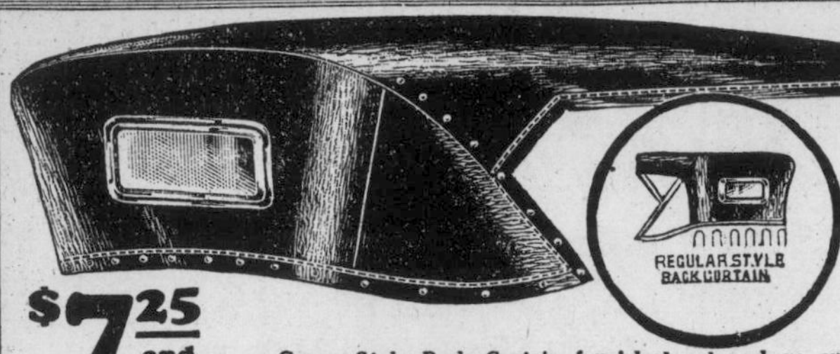

Tops for Chevrolet Touring Cars

$7.25 and up

Gypsy Style Back Curtain furnished only where original equipment top covering or back curtain includes Gypsy style back curtain.

Comes complete with top covering and back curtain for replacing present top covering and back curtain. Furnished in good quality imitation leather with one 6x18-inch oblong flat glass in back curtain. Complete with necessary tacks and binding. We carry coverings in stock for the models listed below and make prompt shipment. Shipping weight, 14 pounds.

28K1621—Chevrolet 490, 1918-19 .... $7.25
28K1623—Chevrolet 490, 1920-21 .... 7.25
28K1625—Chevrolet 490, 1922, Gypsy Curtain 7.70
28K1627—Chevrolet Superior, 1923-24, Gypsy Curtain 7.70
28K9840—Chevrolet Model K, 1925 .... 7.95
28K9841—Chevrolet Model V, 1926-27 .... 8.25

For Auto Beds and Camping Supplies, See Pages 498 to 501

Valve Covers

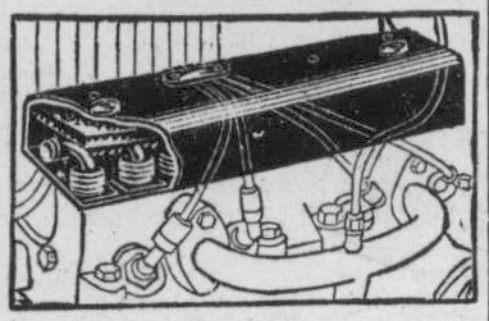

Black, baked enamel, heavy steel covers. Felt covers valves, muffling valve noise, and lubricates them. Keep felt saturated with oil, oiling through oil holes in cover. A popular, practical device. Easily installed. Shipping weight, 2½ pounds.
28K5543 .... 58c

Air Cleaner—Protects Your Engine

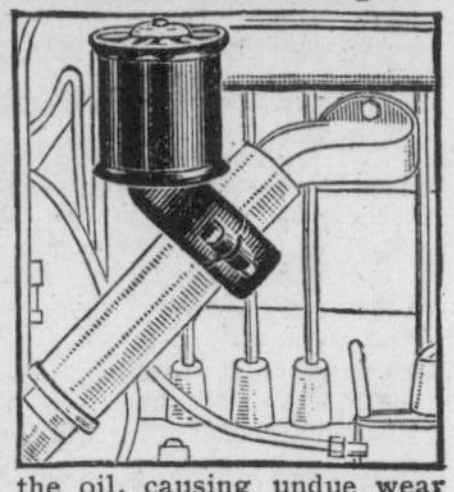

Splendid device recently added as regular equipment on many cars. It removes all dirt from the air taken into motor through carburetor. Nearly 6 pounds of dust enters engine in 10,000 miles' driving on dirt roads and a considerable amount even when driving on concrete roads. Some of this dust enters the oil, causing undue wear on all engine parts. This air cleaner will save expensive motor repairs; it will pay for its cost many times over. Complete instructions for installing. Shpg. wt., 5¼ lbs.
28K7096 .... $3.85

Pistons

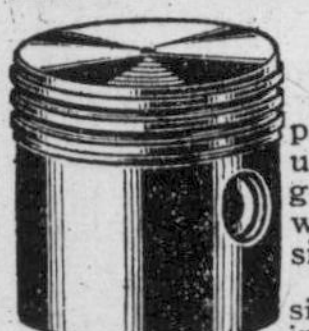

High grade, light weight pistons, fitted with regulation step-cut rings, together with excellent wrist pins. Furnished in sizes as listed below.
28K1628—Standard size, 3$^{11}/_{16}$ inches $1.79
28K1630—.0025 oversize 1.79
28K1632—.005 oversize 1.79
28K1634—.010 oversize 1.79
Shipping weight, any of above, 2¼ lbs.

Oil Regulating Piston Rings

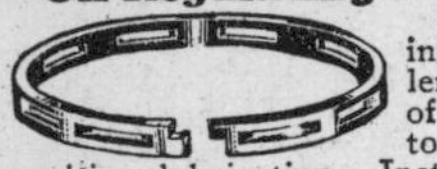

Stop oil pumping, save oil and lengthen the life of cylinders, pistons and rings by positive lubrication. Install these piston rings in your car and know the comfort of a smooth running motor. Shipping weight, 4 ounces.
28K1515—(3$^{11}/_{16}$x$^{3}/_{16}$) Standard size 40c
28K1517—(3$^{11}/_{16}$x$^{3}/_{16}$) .0025 oversize..40c
28K1519—(3$^{11}/_{16}$x$^{3}/_{16}$) .005 oversize...40c
28K1521—(3$^{11}/_{16}$x$^{3}/_{16}$) .015 oversize...40c
28K1526—(3$^{11}/_{16}$x$^{3}/_{16}$) .010 oversize...40c

Oil Distributing Piston Rings

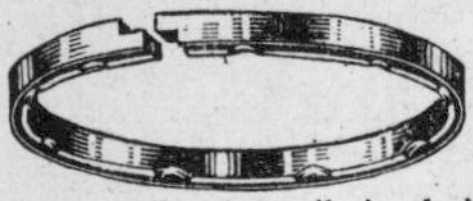

Save oil and gasoline, stop oil pumping and spark plug fouling due to worn cylinders. Use one to each piston. Surplus oil is drained back into crankcase. Instructions for installing. Shipping weight, 4 ounces.
28K1741—Standard, 3$^{11}/_{16}$x$^{3}/_{16}$-inch size 25c
28K1743—.0025 oversize 25c
28K1745—.005 oversize 25c
28K1747—.010 oversize 25c

Auto Top Pads for All Cars

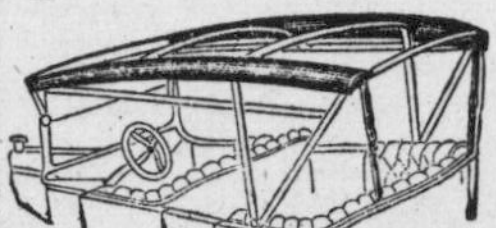

Replace unsightly sagging misplaced top pads; it costs little and gives your car interior a neat appearance. Come in complete set for car.
28K4625—Khaki, for all standard cars $1.57
28K4627—Black, for Ford cars $1.29
Shipping weight, either set, 5¾ pounds.

Front Fender Brace

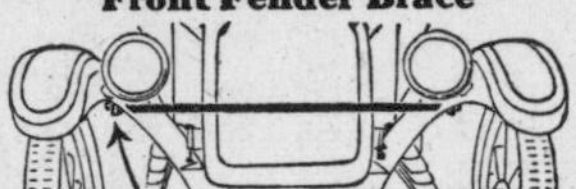

Tie rod to stiffen front fenders and prevent twisting of frame and side members, preventing fender and lamp vibration; also adapted for mounting license tags, etc. Instructions for installing.
28K15181¼—For Chevrolet 490 models, 1917 to May, 1923 .... 45c
28K15268¼—For Chevrolet Superior models, late 1923 to May, 1924 .... 45c
28K15288¼—For 1925 models, 1926 Model V 45c
Shipping weight, any type, 1½ pounds.

Non-Corrode Battery Terminal

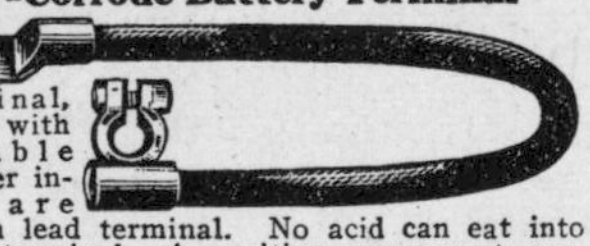

Terminal, complete with Cable and rubber insulation are molded in lead terminal. No acid can eat into cable or terminal. A positive, permanent connection, which makes a good, clean contact, even though battery contact post is dirty. Shipping weight, 8 ounces.
28K7116—For Chevrolet 1923-24-25.. 54c
28K7117—For Chevrolet 1926-27 (not illustrated) 57c

Balloon Wheels and Rims

$16.00 Per Set

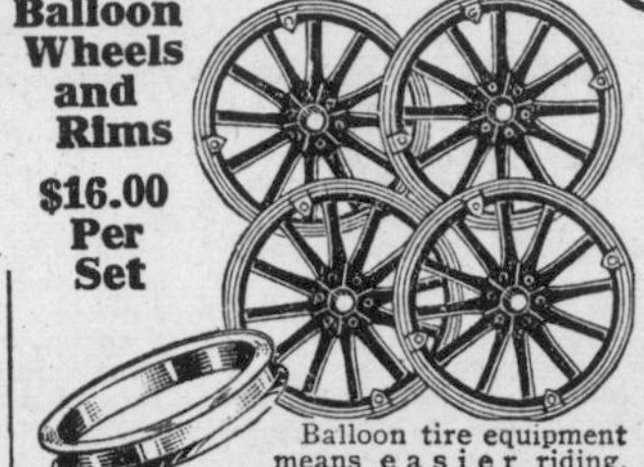

Balloon tire equipment means easier riding. Wheels are 21 inches in diameter, with bolt holes drilled; spokes are genuine hickory. Wheels are black finish. Rims are Jaxon, 28x3½-inch size for 29x4.40-inch straight side balloon tires. Extra rim is furnished. Shipping weight, complete set of four wheels, rims and extra rim, 125 pounds.
28K15311¼—Set complete $16.00

Fabrico Noiseless Timing Gear

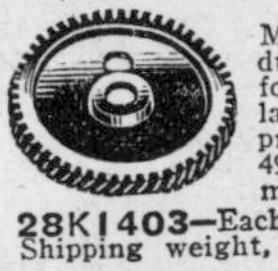

Made of Bakelite Macarti—best and most durable material known for gears. Will outlast metal gears if properly installed. For 490 and Superior models.
28K1403—Each $4.50
Shipping weight, 2½ pounds.

Handy Wrench Set

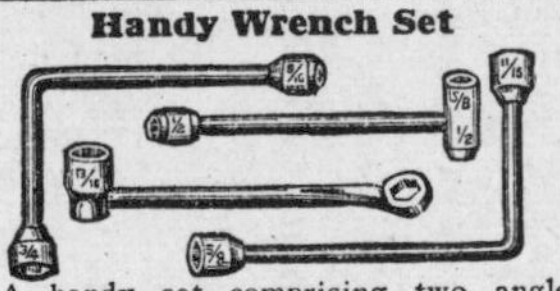

A handy set comprising two angle wrenches with hex socket opening sizes, $^{9}/_{16}$ and ¾ and ⅝ and $^{11}/_{16}$ inch; triple end wrench, opening sizes ½, ⅝ and ½ inch and double end wrench with $^{13}/_{16}$-hex nut opening and $^{13}/_{16}$-inch hex nut opening size. Fits practically every nut on Chevrolet cars. Nickel plated finish.
28K5319—Shpg. wt., 5½ pounds $1.48

Chevrolet Heater

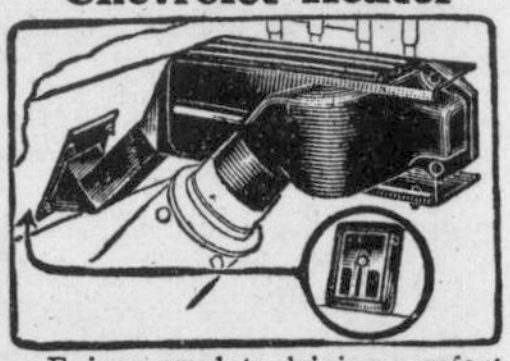

Enjoy complete driving comfort on the coldest days with this big heat producer! Its special cast iron manifold, housed in heavy sheet metal, replaces your regular manifold. A series of "heat ribs" along the sides increase the heating surface, and the entire construction is mechanically and scientifically correct to secure the greatest amount of heat possible. For all Chevrolets from 1923 to 1927 inclusive. Shpg. wt., 12 lbs.
28K9981 .... $3.98

Don't forget to order ALLSTATE Tires. They can be found on pages 460 and 461.

Gear and Pinion

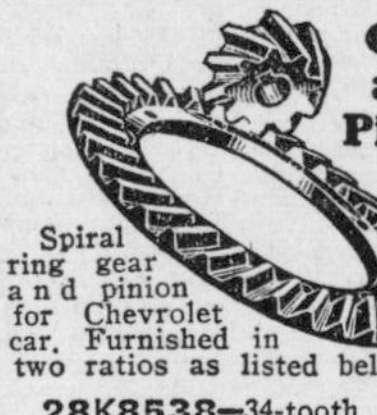

Spiral ring gear and pinion for Chevrolet car. Furnished in two ratios as listed below.
28K8538—34-tooth spiral ring gear and 9-tooth pinion. Shipping weight, 4 pounds. For Superior Model.
Per set of two gears $4.85
28K8539—33-tooth spiral ring gear and 9-tooth pinion. For 490 model. Shpg. wt., 5 lbs.
Per set of two gears $4.85

Radiators

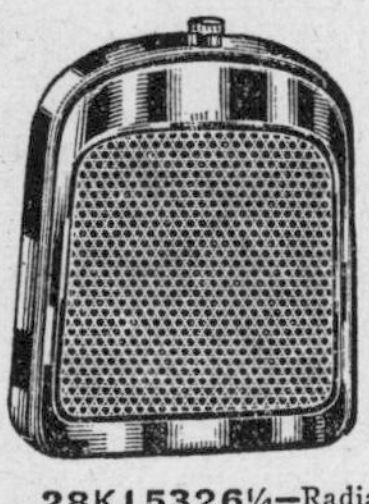

High grade radiators with brass cores and tanks. Connections are made of a rust and corrosion proof alloy. Shells are pressed steel and black enameled. IN ORDERING STATE YEAR OF CAR.
28K15326¼—Radiator, without shell, for 1918-22 model 490 Chevrolet, pump system $10.95
28K15328¼—Radiator without shell, for 1923-24 Superior model Chevrolet .. $11.95
28K15108¼—Radiator, without shell, for 1925 Model K Chevrolet $11.95
28K15704¼—Radiator, without shell, for 1926 Model V Chevrolet $12.25
Shipping weight, any of above, 40 lbs.
NOTE—Shells can be furnished for any of above radiators at $3.50 extra. Shells shipped promptly from factory in NORTHEASTERN ILLINOIS. In ordering be sure to state year of car.

Brake Band Outfits

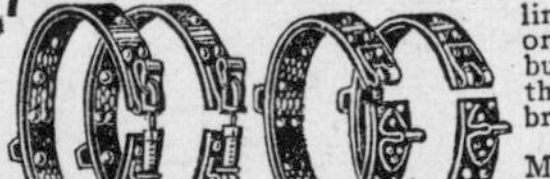

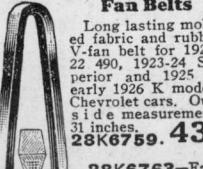

Best quality replacement lined brake bands, the same as original equipment. You can buy these sets for less than the cost of relining your old brakes.
28K8810—Chevrolet Model 490, 1922-23. Shipping weight, 5 pounds. Pair $2.45
28K8813—Chevrolet Series V, 1926-27, and Pontiac, 1926-27. Shipping weight, 6½ pounds. Pair $2.98
28K8811—Chevrolet Superior, 1924. Shipping weight, 6 pounds. Pair $2.45
28K8812—Chevrolet Series K, 1925 Superior. Shipping weight, 3½ pounds. Pair $2.45
28K8814—Dodge, 1922-24, serial numbers 715469 to A-173483. Shipping weight, 10 pounds. Pair $4.75
28K8815—Dodge, 1924-27, serial number A-173484 and higher models. Shipping weight, 10 pounds. Pair $4.75

Fan Belts

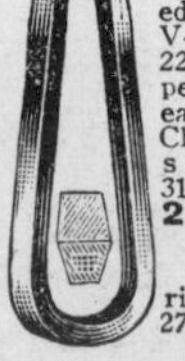

Long lasting molded fabric and rubber V-fan belt for 1920-22 490, 1923-24 Superior and 1925 to early 1926 K models Chevrolet cars. Outside measurement, 31 inches.
28K6759 .... 43c
28K6763—Fabric belt for late 1926-27 models 54c
28K6761 Leather fan belt for 1919 to early 1926 as above. 55c
28K6764—Leather belt for late 1926-27 models ... 69c
Shipping weight, each, ¾ lb.

Black and Nickeled Lamp Doors

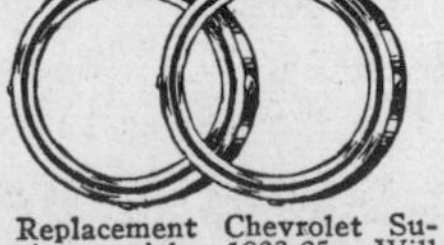

Replacement Chevrolet Superior models, 1923-25. Will also fit Oldsmobile Light Six. Made of steel, heavily copper plated, nickeled and handsomely striped in black, same as original equipment. Shipping weight, 1¼ pounds.
28K10323—For 1923-25 Chevrolet. Per pair 89c

McKee Spreadlight Lens

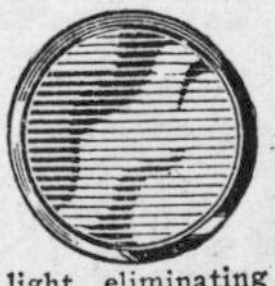

Project a light over a 12-foot wide road, giving 40 feet spread of light at 100 feet in front of the car. Give an ideal projection of light, eliminating glare and, at the same time, giving a wonderful night driving light.
28K10840—Size, 7¾ inches. Shpg. wt., 2½ lbs. Per pair. 31c
28K10842—Size, 8 inches. Shpg. wt., 2½ lbs. Per pair. 61c
28K10843—Size, 8⅛ inches. Shpg. wt., 2½ lbs. Per pair. 61c
28K10845—Size, 9 inches. Shpg. wt., 3 lbs. Per pair ... 61c

Starter Button Extension

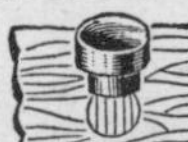

Metal collar fits over starter button. Has hard rubber, large button top which makes starter easy to reach with the foot. Will fit Ford, Chevrolet, Overland, Dodge, Whippet, Star, Pontiac, Paige, Jewett, Oldsmobile, Moon and Nash Light 6 cars. Shipping weight, 4 ounces.
28K9702 .... 24c

Chevrolet Floor Boards

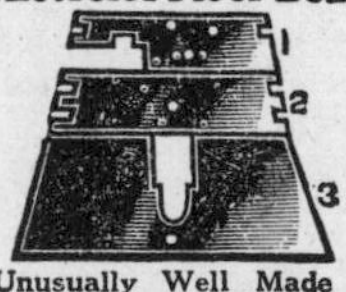

Unusually Well Made of Hardwood
28K11731—No. 1 Floor Board for all 1924-27 Chevrolet models. Shipping weight, 1¾ pounds 43c
28K11732—No. 2 Floor Board for all 1924-27 Chevrolet models. Shipping weight, 3 pounds 69c
28K11733—No. 3 Floor Board for all 1924-27 Chevrolet models. Shipping weight, 6 pounds $1.29

Winged Radiator Cap for Chevrolets

An all brass winged cap, heavily nickel plated and of the newest design. Gives your Chevrolet a snappy, up to date appearance. A useful ornament of which you will be proud. Has special fitting for motometers. Shipping wt., 8 ounces.
28K6074 .... 65c

Chevrolet Cars

Mail your orders for all merchandise on this page either to
CHICAGO, PHILADELPHIA MINNEAPOLIS, BOSTON or MEMPHIS
whichever is nearest you.

Top Deck Covers for Fords and Chevrolets

$2.35 AND UP

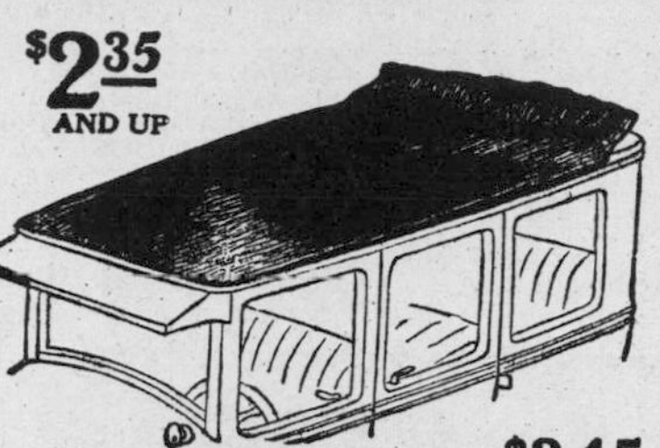

Be thrifty! Replace at low cost that leaky, shabby top deck of your closed car. This specially prepared heavy rubber cloth of long grain, finely woven and **waterproof**, will dress up your old closed car and will give long service. Tacks and welt are supplied with covers.

28K15716¼—Chevrolet Coupe. Shipping weight, 5 pounds.......**$2.45**
28K15718¼—Chevrolet Coach. Shipping weight, 8 pounds..........$3.65
28K15720¼—Chevrolet 4-Door Sedan. Shipping weight, 8½ lbs..... 3.85
28K15722¼—Chevrolet Landau Sedan. Shipping wt., 8 pounds..... 3.95
28K15710¼—Ford Coupe. Shipping weight, 5 pounds............ 2.35
28K15712¼—Ford Tudor Sedan. Shipping weight, 8 pounds........ 3.25
28K15714¼—Ford Fordor Sedan. Shipping weight, 8 pounds....... 3.35

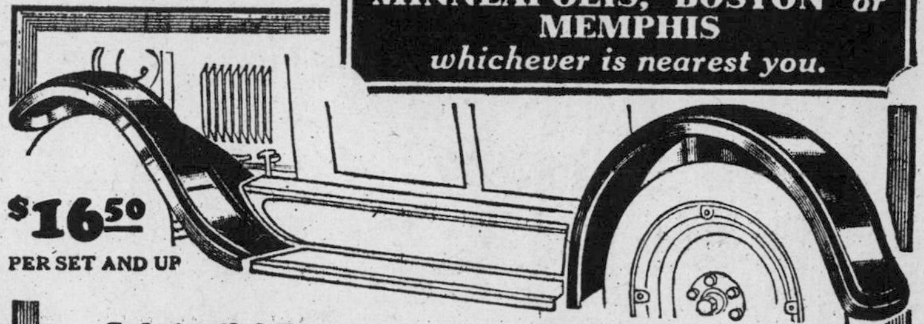

$16.50 PER SET AND UP

Substantial Duplicate Fenders for Chevrolet Cars

Well made and attractively finished in black baked enamel. (Running boards and shields not furnished with fenders.)

28K15675¼—Set of 4 for Touring and Sedan Superior (1923 after May)..........$16.50
28K15676¼—Set of 4 for Touring and Sedan Superior (1924)........ 16.50
28K15677¼—Set of 4 for Roadster and Coupe Superior (1923 after May)........ 19.95
28K15678¼—Set of 4 for Roadster and Coupe Superior (1924)...... 19.95
28K15679¼—Set of 4 for Touring, Sedan and 2-Pass. Coupe 1925-26, Series L........ 16.50
28K15680¼—Set of 4 for Coach 1925-26, Series K.............. 16.50
Shipping weight, any of the above, 68 pounds.

NOTE—If single fenders for either front or rear are wanted, write us and we will be glad to quote prices on same.

Side Curtains

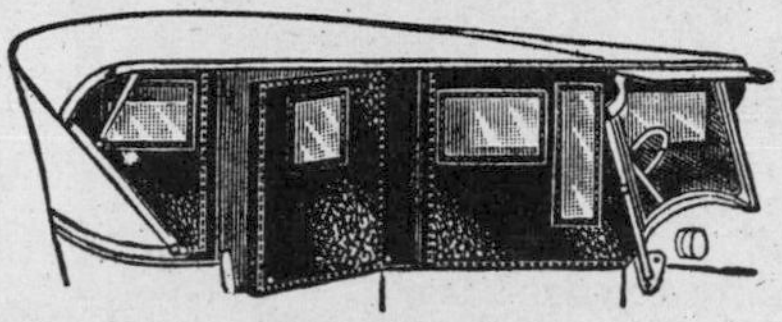

"Open With Door" Side Curtains for Chevrolets, in set of six pieces. Furnished in rubberized cloth as listed below. Complete with rods and fasteners. Gives you the convenience of a closed car in getting in and out. In ordering, **state year of car.** Shipping weight, 14 lbs.

28K9801—For 1918-19 490 touring models. Per set, complete.............**$7.25**
28K9803—For 1920-21 490 touring models..........................$7.25
28K9805—For 1922 490 touring models. Gypsy curtain style. Per set, complete.. 7.25
28K9807—For early 1923 Superior touring models. Lift the Dot fasteners, Per set, complete.......... 7.25
28K9809—For late 1923-24 Superior, 1925K touring models. Turnstile fasteners. Per set, complete.......... 7.25
28K9845—For 1925-26 Model V touring. Per set, complete............ 7.35

Nickel-Plated Hub Caps for Chevrolets

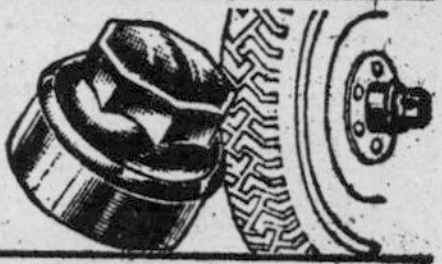

Hub caps add greatly to the appearance of your car. Made of highly polished nickel plated brass and are non-rusting. Keep the dust and grit from your wheel bearings. Quickly and securely installed. Shipping weight, 4 ounces.

28K8393—Fit all Chevrolets from 1923 to 1927, inclusive. Each........**18c**

STANDARD CAR EQUIPMENT

Full Vision Electric Wind Shield Cleaner

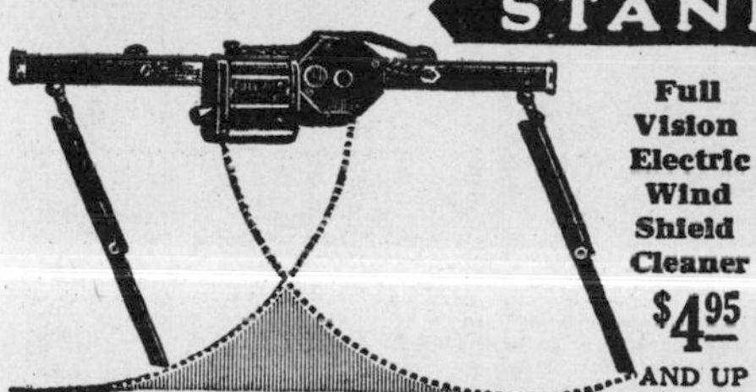

$4.95 AND UP

The entire mechanism of this cleaner is built in one compact unit with all moving parts enclosed and sealed against all possibility of damage. Mounted on outside of wind shield. Quickly attached with only two screws. Blades sweep complete half circles. Cannot drop to obstruct your view. Uses less current than a headlight bulb. Adjustable wiper arms. Fits all closed cars with either swinging or V. V. sliding wind shield. Brackets for open cars furnished only by request. Shipping weight, 4½ pounds.

28K5017—Complete....................**$6.75**
28K5018—6-volt. Same as above, but with single blade...................**4.95**
28K7394—For 1926 closed cars...................**4.95**
28K7397—For cars with one-piece Vertical Ventilating wind shields..........**4.95**
Shipping weight, 3 pounds.

Axle Shafts for Standard Cars

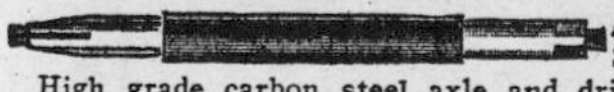

High grade carbon steel axle and drive shafts for the following cars. Carefully machined; will fit perfectly without further machining or cutting.

Axle Shafts

Catalog No.	Car and Model	Wt., Lbs.	Each
28K15069¼	Chevrolet 490, 1917-22 and early Sup. 1923..........	7½	$1.10
28K15063¼	Chevrolet Model F1923-24....	9	3.15
28K15064¼	Chevrolet Model K1925.......	9	3.38
28K15065¼	Chevrolet Model V1926......	9	3.38
28K15066¼	Chevrolet A. A. 1927.........	9	3.38
28K15077¼	Dodge, Models, 1915-1923....	11	1.45
28K15145¼	Dodge, late models, 1924-27..	12	2.70
28K15102¼	Essex Model 1923-26 Coach 6-cyl.	11	3.75
28K15103¼	Essex Model 1923-26 Sedan 6-cyl.	11	4.15
28K15101¼	Essex Model 1923-26 Coupe 6-cyl.	11	3.00
28K15098¼	Hupmobile Model R No. 1-2-3 1920-25 Right and Left.....	10	2.65
28K15139¼	Maxwell Model 1922-26, either R-L	11	3.15
28K15078¼	Maxwell, Model 1920-21. Fits either R-L	8½	1.10
28K15100¼	Nash Right and Left, 1923-26	14	4.15
28K15054¼	Overland Model 93, 6-cyl. 1925	12	3.00
28K15050¼	Overland Model Willys-Knight Model 66A, Great 6, 1925-27	13	4.50
28K15051¼	Overland Model Willys-Knight Model 70A, 6-cyl. 1925-27..	13	4.50
28K15052¼	Overland Model Whippet, 1926-27	12	3.15
28K15053¼	Overland Model 93A, 6-cyl. 1926-27	12	3.15
28K15055¼	Overland Little 4, Late Model No. 91, 1923-26..........	12	3.15
28K15059¼	Overland Little 4 Model 1920-22.	7½	1.25

Heavy Duty Luggage Carrier

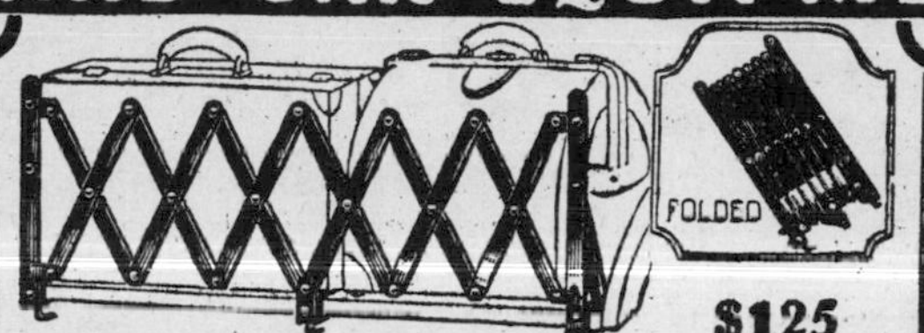

$1.25

A high grade, substantial luggage carrier, offered at about the price usually asked for the ordinary lighter weight, more cheaply made carriers. Everyone knows the value of a luggage carrier on trips, vacations, etc. Folds compactly for storing under rear seat, etc., when not in use. Adjustable, quickly clamped to running board. Greatest inside length, about 50 inches, about 15 inches high. Adjustable feature permits holding securely packages carried. Shipping weight, 9½ pounds.

28K15166¼...................................**$1.25**

CHALLENGE CARRIER—Regulation light weight luggage carrier, often sells elsewhere for $1.50 or more. A splendid value, second only to our Heavy Duty Carrier 28K15166¼, above. About 15 inches high and 50 inches greatest inside length. Has three clamping thumb fasteners. Complete with end brackets (Not illustrated.) Shipping weight, 8½ pounds.

28K14274.....................................**85c**

Disappearing Type Luggage Carrier

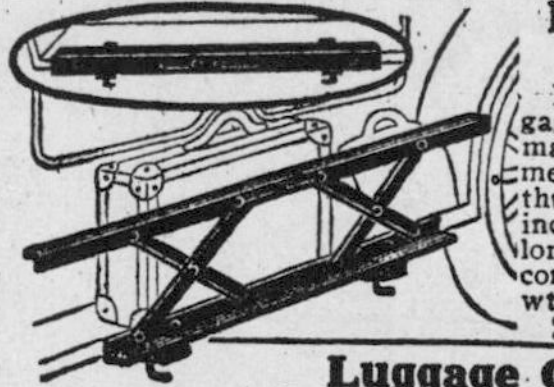

Popular type disappearing luggage carrier. Very substantially made, with angle iron frame members. Two substantial thumbscrew clamps. About 9 inches high (open). 5 inches long. Small illustration shows compact folding position. Shpg. wt., 11 lbs.

28K15148¼.....**$1.15**

Luggage Carrier Covers

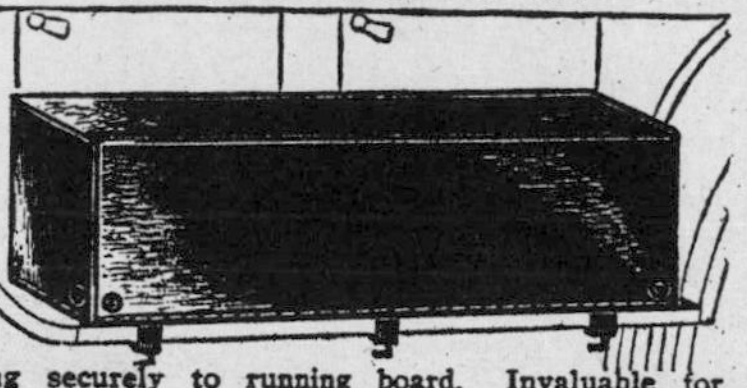

Finest waterproof material, cut and sewed to make a neat luggage carrier cover. 47½ in. long, 11 in. wide by 16 in. high. Made to completely and neatly cover luggage on running board. Brass eyelets at corners for fastening securely to running board. Invaluable for touring. Very low priced.

28K5448—Enameled Drill. Shpg. wt., 1 lb.......**$1.38**
28K5449—Waterproof Duck. Shpg. wt., 1¾ lbs......$2.35

Drive Shafts for Standard Cars

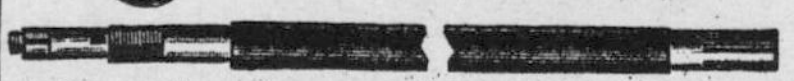

High grade carbon steel drive shafts for the following cars. Carefully machined; will fit perfectly.

Drive Shafts

Catalog. No.	Car and Model	Wt., Lbs.	Each
28K15071¼	Chevrolet 490, 1915-21............	15	$2.40
28K15072¼	Chevrolet 490, 1922-24............	10	2.40
28K15079¼	Maxwell, Model 25, 1914-17......	14	1.95
28K15081¼	Maxwell, Model 25, 1918-19......	15	2.05

Radiators for Standard Cars

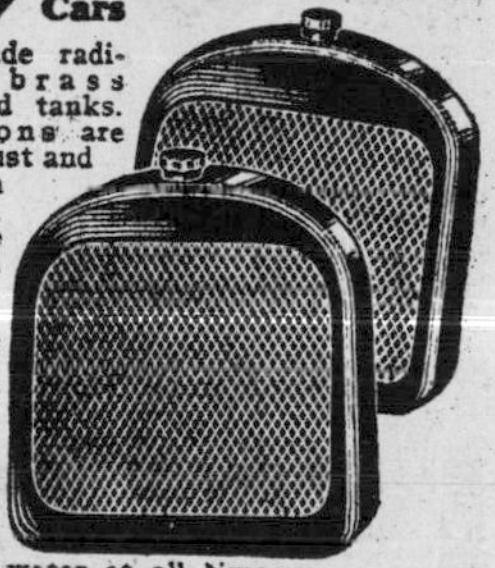

High grade radiators with brass cores and tanks. Connections are made of a rust and corrosion proof alloy. Shell are pressed steel and black enameled. These fine radiators combine maximum cooling surface with large water channels, permitting free flow of water at all times.

IN ORDERING STATE YEAR OF CAR.

28K15330¼—Radiator, without shell, for 1915-16 Dodge cars..........**$15.60**
28K15332¼—Radiator, without shell, for 1917 to early 1922 Dodge cars.$15.25
28K15334¼—Radiator, without shell, for late 1922 and 1923 Dodge cars.$15.60
28K15112¼—Radiator, without shell, for 1924-26 Dodge cars..........$15.60
28K15336¼—Radiator, without shell, for 1916-19 Maxwell cars.........$14.25
28K15338¼—Radiator, without shell, for 1920-21 Maxwell cars.........$17.40
28K15340¼—Radiator, without shell, for 1922-24 Maxwell cars.........$17.40
28K15341¼—Radiator, without shell, for 1925 Maxwell cars............$17.40
Shipping weight, any of above, 40 pounds.

Radiators listed below are shipped from factory in NORTHEASTERN ILLINOIS. IMPORTANT: Be sure to state make, year, model and serial number of your car.

28K15730⅓—For Buick, all 4-cylinder models, 1921-24, without shell. Shipping weight, 45 pounds..............$23.95
28K15731⅓—For Buick, all 6-cylinder models, 1920-27, without shell. Shipping weight, 50 pounds..............$28.95
28K15732⅓—For Chrysler, 4 and 6-cyl. models, 50-58-60-70, 1924-27, without shell. Shipping weight, 50 pounds........$28.45
28K15733⅓—For Essex, all 6-cylinder models, 1924-27, without shell. Shipping weight, 37 pounds..............$22.25
28K15734⅓—For Hudson Super-Six, all models, 1917-27, without shell. Shipping weight, 50 pounds..............$27.75
28K15735⅓—For Nash, all 4-cylinder models, 1921-24, without shell. Shipping weight, 38 pounds..............$18.25
28K15736⅓—For Nash, all 6-cylinder models, 1920-27, without shell. Shipping weight, 45 pounds..............$21.75
28K15737⅓—For Oakland, all models, 1920-27, without shell. Shipping weight, 45 pounds..............$24.85
28K15738⅓—For Studebaker Light 6 model, 1920-24, without shell. Shipping wt., 40 pounds..............$19.95
28K15739⅓—For Studebaker Special 6 model, 1920-27, without shell. Shipping wt., 50 pounds..............$29.35
28K15740⅓—For Studebaker Big 6 model, 1920-27, without shell. Shipping wt., 50 pounds..............$39.95

For Radiators for Ford Cars See Pages 470 and 471

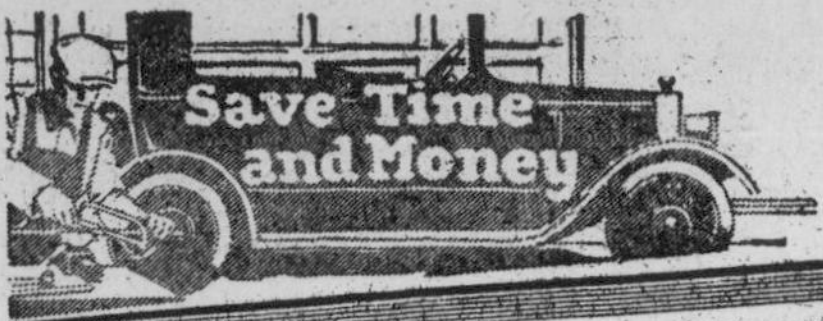

Garage Equipment

High Speed Electric Valve Grinder and Drill

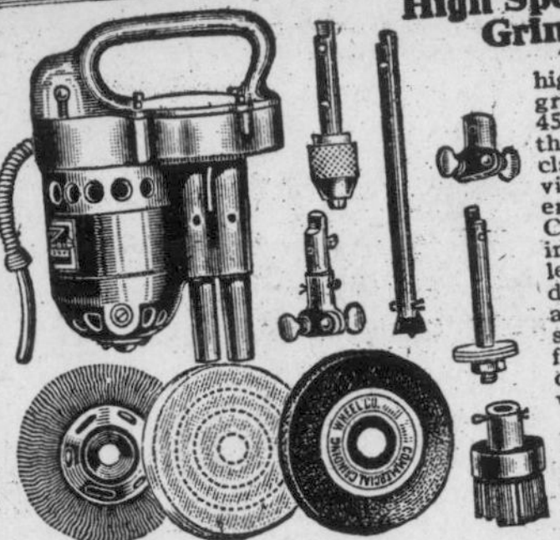

The only short oscillation high speed valve grinder which grinds all types of valves at 45-degree angle and will not throw compound. May be clamped in an ordinary bench vise for use as a bench grinder. Has many special uses: Carbon removing, bench grinding, buffing. Has one-fifth less parts than the ordinary drill. Fully guaranteed against defects in workmanship and materials. Works from either 110 or 120 A. C. or 110 or 120 D. C. Shipping weight, 11 pounds.

28K1777—Electric Drill, including all attachments except those listed below which are extra.... **$32.50**

Attachments to Fit Drill Listed Above

28K1772—Buffing Wheel, 12-ply, 4-inch diameter. Shpg. wt., 5 oz. 24c
28K1773—Emery Wheel, 4x¾-inch. Shipping weight, 1½ lbs... 58c
28K1774—Scratching Brush, 4-inch. Shipping weight, 7 oz..... 55c
28K1775—Carbon Brush. Shipping weight, ¾ lb.......... 98c
28K1776—Attachment for Grinding Overhead Valves. Shipping weight, ¾ pound.......... $1.48

Valve Refacing Lathe

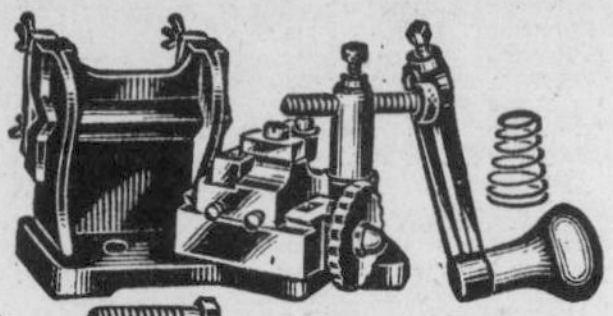

Hand Lathe Type designed to grind HARD, STEEL VALVES. Equipped with a special composition steel cutter that is set at a perfect 45-degree angle. Has a feed screw adjuster to move the circular cutter across the face of the valve, performing thereby a turning down operation. The stem of the valve is set into an accurate machined "V" groove and held in center with side clamps; also has a centering clamp for the valve head. Packed complete in a box. Shipping weight, 4½ pounds.

28K1376.......... **$4.95**

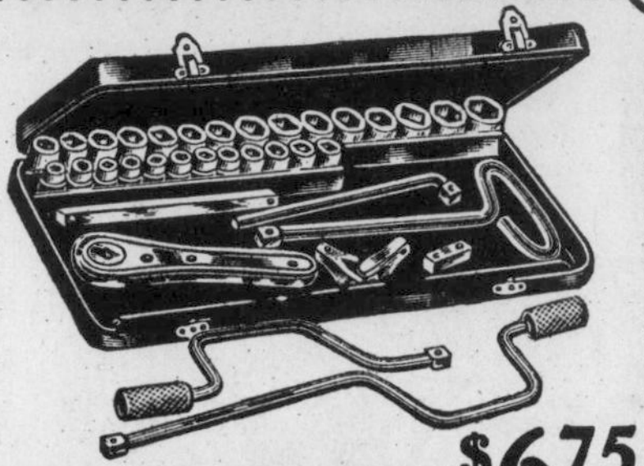

Complete Garage Man's Socket Wrench Set $6.75

A wonderful set which fits practically every nut and bolt on the car. Has complete equipment of 19 hex sockets ranging from 7/16 inches to 1¼ inches hex; 8 square sockets ranging from ⅜ inch to ⅞ inch square; 1 flat ratchet handle; 1 long speeder, square end, 20 inches long; 1 short speeder, square end, 12 inches long; 1 long T handle, square end, 9 inches long; 1 long extension, 9 inches long; 1 short extension, 2 inches long; 1 universal joint; 1 heavy steel box. Comes in a strong, black enameled metal case. A real friend to the garage man at an extremely low price.

28K1398—Shipping weight, 19 pounds.......... **$6.75**

"Double Use" Emery Wheels and Stand

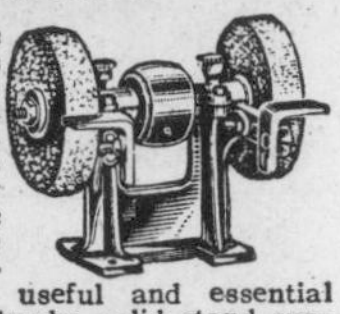

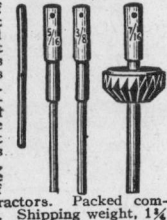

Our price is so low on this combined grinding and finishing outfit that there is no need for any garage to be without the many advantages of this useful and essential equipment. Sturdy, solid stand supports both grinding and finishing wheel, each measuring 6 inches in diameter and 1 inch thick, with ½-in. holes. Spindle measures ⅝ inch in diameter by 10½ inches long. Pulley is 4 inches wide by 3 inches in diameter. Shpg. wt., 20 lbs.

28K8387.......... **$5.18**

Samson Machinists' Vises

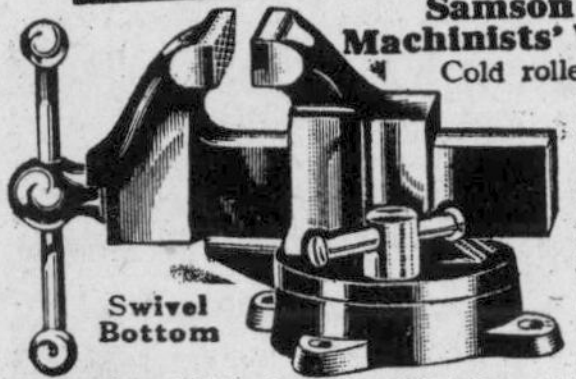

Swivel Bottom

Cold rolled steel screws and handles. Jaws faced with tempered steel. Bolts furnished for fastening vise to bench.

	Width Jaws, In.	Opens, In.	Shpg. Wt., Lbs.	
28K15132¼	3	4¼	28	$6.90
28K15134¼	3½	5	37	7.25
28K15136¼	4	6	51	9.15

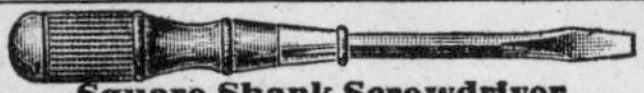

Square Shank Screwdriver

Made to stand hard service. Has large handle and square shank which makes it possible to use a wrench on it. Length, 11 inches. Blade, 5 inches. Weight, 6 ounces.

28K9720.......... **17c**

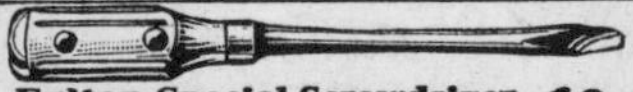

Fulton Special Screwdriver 60c 6-Inch

Shank and blade one solid forging of steel extending completely through handle. State length.

Length, blade, in...	4	6	8	10
Weight	6 oz.	¾ lb.	¾ lb.	1 lb.
28K9721	40c	60c	75c	90c

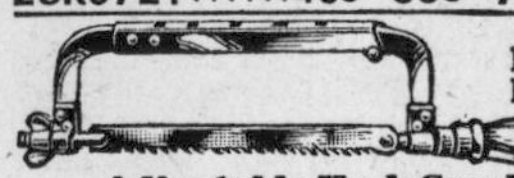

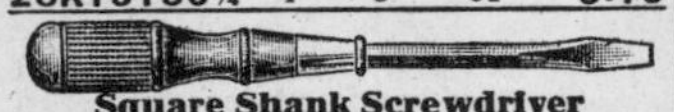

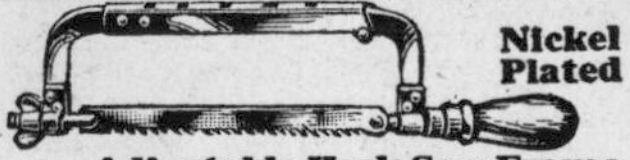

Adjustable Hack Saw Frame

Nickel Plated

Blade is adjustable to right angles with frame. Takes blade from 8 to 12 inches. Price includes one 8-in. blade. Wt., 1 lb.

28K9724.......... **25c**

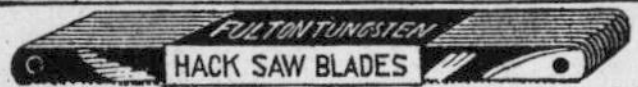

Tungsten steel, tempered hard all over, with medium teeth (18 to inch).

28K9725—Give length. We Do Not Sell Less Than a Full Package.

Length, inches	8	9	10	12
Weight, dozen, oz.	4	6	8	8
Per package of 1 doz.	33c	38c	42c	50c

Fulton Cold Chisel

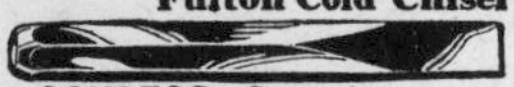

15c ½-In.

28K9722—State size.

Size, ½ in. Weight, 4 oz.......... 15c
Size, ⅝ in. Weight, ¾ lb.......... 19c
Size, ¾ in. Weight, 1 lb.......... 25c

Machinists' Ball Pein Hammer

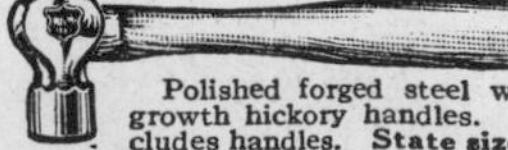

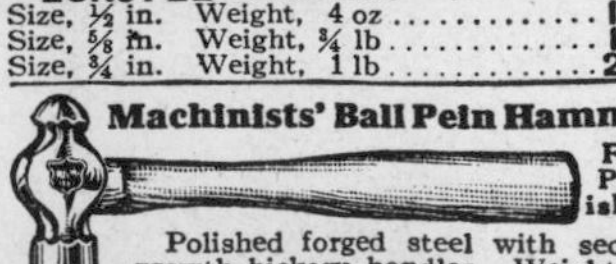

Full Polished

Polished forged steel with second growth hickory handles. Weight includes handles. State size.

Size No.	00	1	2	3	4
Weight, lbs.	1	1¼	1¾	2	2½
28K9719	50c	60c	64c	68c	72c

Sturdy Garage Hydrometer

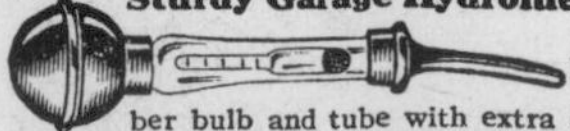

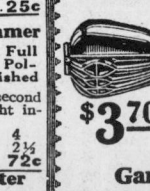

Has heavy rubber bulb and tube with extra strong glass tube and float which accurately registers cell gravity. Glass projections hold float away from walls of tube, insuring an accurate reading. Shipping weight, ¾ pound.

28K4853.......... **73c**

The Handy Garage Jack $4.75

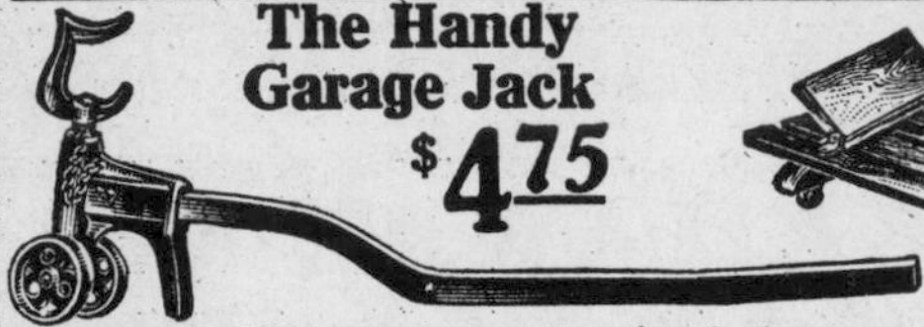

Does away with time and energy wasting drudgery. Simply wheel under, pull handle down and one wheel is lifted from three to five inches off the floor. Three point base of wheels and leg offers firm support. Length of handle, 68 inches. Will not tip over or slide out of position with load on. The quickest acting, most serviceable and economical jack for handling light cars and for tire service. Lowest height, 11½ inches; also adjusts to 15-inch height and 18½ inches highest point. Will lift a 3,000-pound load. Shipping weight, 31 lbs.

28K15005¼.......... **$4.75**

Sturdy Garage Creeper

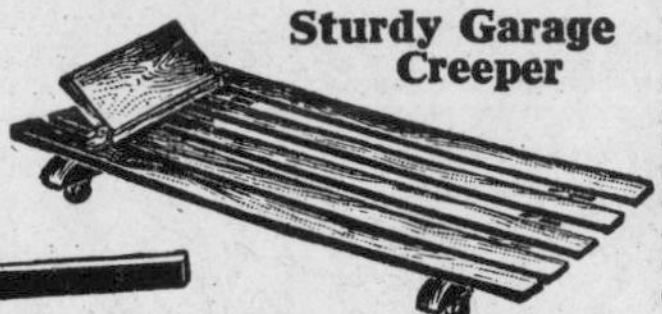

Made of hardwood, strongly reinforced. Has adjustable wood head rest and is built with hollow center, making it comfortable and easy to roll about under your weight. Sets low and slides under the lowest cars easily. Has strong ball bearing casters. Shipping weight, 9 pounds.

28K15150¼.......... **$1.48**

Don't Overlook This Great Value

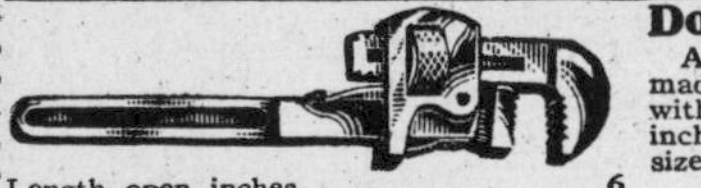

A standard high grade Stillson pattern wrench made of high grade steel. Parts interchangeable with any standard Stillson wrench. Sizes 6 and 8-inch have wood covered steel handles. All other sizes have solid steel handles. State size.

Length, open, inches	6	8	10	14	18	24	36
Takes pipe, inches	½	¾	1	1½	2	2½	3½
Shipping weight, pounds	½	¾	1¼	2½	4¼	8	14
28K9727	47c	60c	67c	85c	98c	$1.95	$3.70

Fulton Extra Grade Pliers Black Rubberoid Finish

15c 6-In.

Forged steel, properly tempered. 6-inch pliers will hold pipe up to ¾ inch; 8-inch and 10-inch will hold pipe up to 1 inch. Give length.

Length, inches	6	8	10
Weight	8 oz.	¾ lb.	1 lb.
28K9723	15c	25c	35c

These Pliers are drop forged and may vary a trifle in length.

Cotter Pin Puller

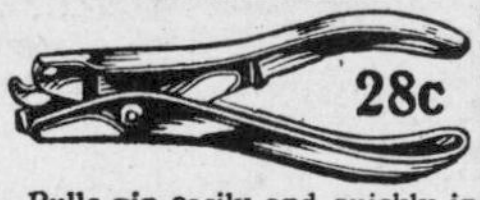

28c

Pulls pin easily and quickly in any location, from any position. Straightens pin as it pulls. Strongly made and has tempered steel hook. Shpg. wt., 6 oz.

28K9732.......... **28c**

"Pronto" Monkey Wrench

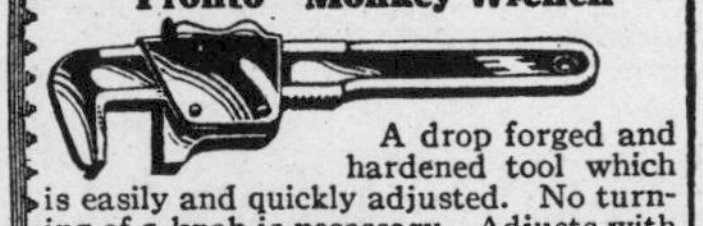

A drop forged and hardened tool which is easily and quickly adjusted. No turning of a knob is necessary. Adjusts with slight pressure of the thumb. Shipping weight, 1½ pounds.

28K9731.......... **72c**

"Pronto" Wrench for Pipes and Round Surfaces

72c

A drop forged and hardened tool which adjusts easily and quickly with slight pressure of the thumb. Jaws are set slightly at a slant and lower jaw has teeth to hold round surfaces.

28K9730—Shpg. wt., 1½ lbs.......... **72c**

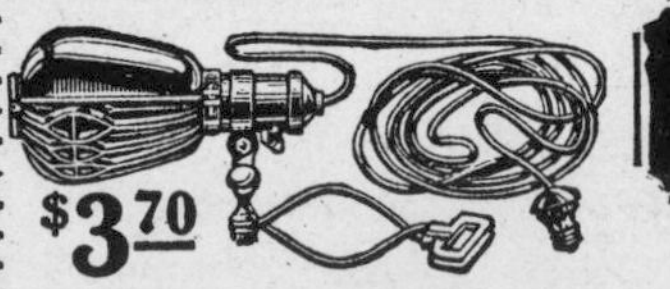

$3.70

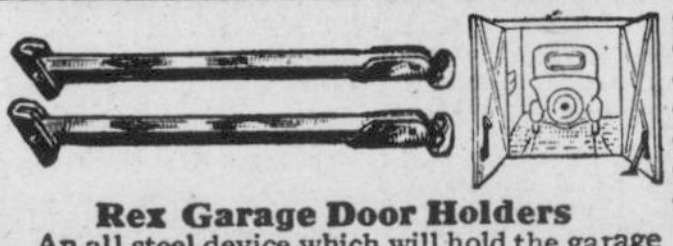

Garage Trouble Lamp

A strongly constructed lamp with 20-foot damage proof cord and heavy wire protector which has a non-glare shield. Handy clamp fastens easily and quickly anywhere. Ball joint makes instant adjustment to any position to suit your work. A convenient friend for the garage man. Shpg. wt., 2 lbs.

28K2602.......... **$3.70**

Mail Your Orders for All Merchandise on This Page Either to
CHICAGO—PHILADELPHIA
MINNEAPOLIS—BOSTON
or MEMPHIS
Whichever is nearest you

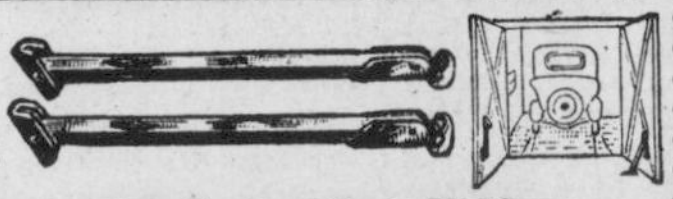

Rex Garage Door Holders

An all steel device which will hold the garage doors open at any desired position. Wind cannot swing doors shut and damage your car. Fold up out of the way when not in use. Shpg. wt., 2¾ lbs.

28K11553—Per pair.......... **58c**

Universal Type Valve Seat Reamer Set

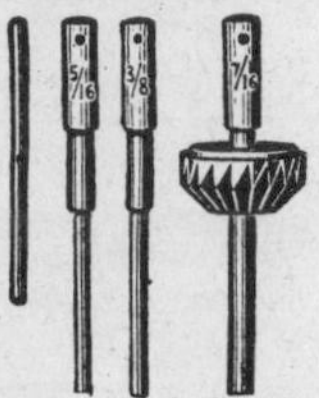

Consisting of one Valve Seat Reamer and the three most popular sizes of pilot stems—5/16, ⅜, 7/16. This combination set will handle more than 90 percent of all the makes of automobiles, as well as the majority of trucks and tractors. Packed complete in a box. Shipping weight, 1¾ pounds.

28K1374.......... **$3.75**

Gear Puller

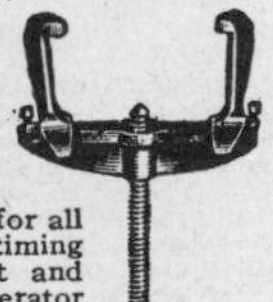

Takes diameters up to six inches. Equipped with one set of 3-in. arms. Screw, ⅝x8 inches. Specially designed for all light work such as timing gears, pump shaft and magneto gears, generator and starter repair work. Shpg. wt., 3 lbs.

28K1401 **$2.25**

Goodell-Pratt No. 6A Breast Drill

Full ball bearings reduce wear on spindle.

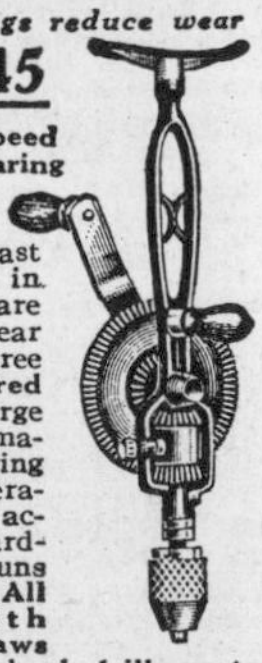

$4.45 Two Speed Ball Bearing

Steel pinions make heavy work easier and assure long life to drill. Malleable iron frame and adjustable iron breast plate are finished in black enamel, gears are red enameled. Gear ratio is even and three to one. Double geared steel pinions and large gear wheel have machine cut teeth, giving long life and easy operation. One end of accurately machined hardened steel spindle runs in ball bearing. All steel chuck with three hardened jaws for holding round shank drills up to ½ inch.

Two speeds. By turning shifter knob drill can be operated at fast or slow speed. Handles, polished hardwood. Length, 16 inches. Weight, 5 pounds.

28K9726.......... **$4.45**

Folding Harness or Garage Hooks

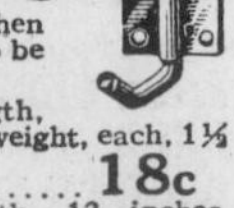

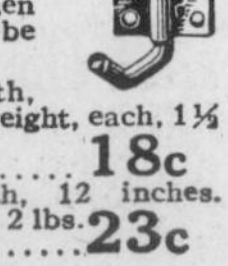

Made of steel. Black finish. A strong, serviceable article. Folds back when not in use. Locks automatically when swung into position to be used.

28K9728—Length, 10 inches. Shipping weight, each, 1½ pounds. Each.......... **18c**

28K9729—Length, 12 inches. Shipping weight, each, 2 lbs. Each.......... **23c**

Cold Weather Car Comfort

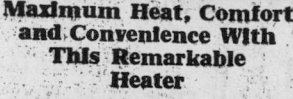

Mail Your Orders for All Merchandise on This Page Either to
CHICAGO—PHILADEL- PHIA—MINNEAPOLIS BOSTON or MEMPHIS
Whichever is nearest you

Cast Iron Forced Draft Heater for Fords

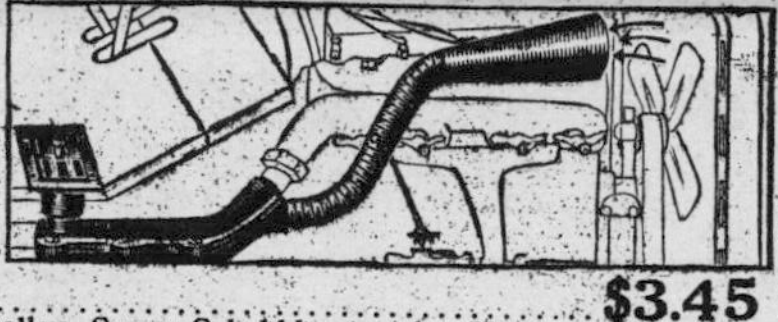

This efficient heat maker, which takes the sting out of winter driving is solidly constructed with a cast iron housing which attaches around the exhaust pipe. Note how the forced draft feature is increased by extending the horn toward the fan. Fits all model Ford cars, even those equipped with Holley, Swan, Schebler or other Hot Spot Vaporizers. Shipping weight, 12 pounds.

28K9991.................................. **$3.45**
28K10050—For Fords not equipped with Holley, Swan, Schebler or other Hot Spot Vaporizers. Not illustrated. Shipping weight, 3¼ pounds............... **3.45**

Taplex Charcoal Heater
For Automobiles and Winter Sport

This efficient heater occupies very little space, but gives enough heat with one filling to keep the car warm for twelve hours or longer. It is only necessary to ignite block of charcoal in center drawer and heater will give more than enough heat without the slightest inconvenience. Absolutely no smoke or fumes.

The bail handle and oval shape of this heater make it ideal to carry for use at football games and all winter sports. The Taplex Heater is especially good for keeping motor warm in an unheated garage. If placed under the hood, on side opposite to carburetor, it will keep cylinders and manifold warm and make starting easy in coldest weather.

For milk wagons, trucks, mail wagons and other commercial service wagons on the road all day, these heaters are unexcelled.

Order one today and make your winter driving comfortable.

28K9973—14-Inch Taplex Heater. Shipping weight, 6 pounds........ **$2.45**
28K9971—Charcoal for Taplex Heater, 13 bricks to the box. Per box. **90c**

Low Priced Triumph Heater for Fords

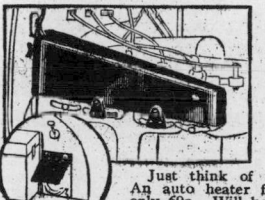

Just think of it! An auto heater for only 69c. Will heat your car comfortably and make winter driving a pleasure. Is well made and will give lots of real service. Inexpensive exhaust manifold heater. Delivers warm air into car through dash opening above floor boards. Has shut off register to install in dash. Quickly attached. Sheet steel, black finish. Will not fit 1926-27 Fords with Holley Carburetors. Shipping weight, 2½ pounds.
28K6610............................... **69c**

Anti-Draft Mats for Fords

Made of rubber and sheep's hide, wool lined to close pedal and brake lever slots for keeping out drafts in cold weather and engine heat in hot weather. A high grade set, made of excellent materials and very efficient. Installed without removing floor boards. Directions for attaching. Shipping weight, 1½ pounds.

28K7089—For Ford cars 1925 and earlier. Per set. **$1.32**
28K7072—For 1926-27 Fords. Per set....... **1.32**

Anti-Draft Mats

Heavy rubber slotted mats for 1925-26 Chevrolet models.

For Chevrolets

Slots are lined with draft tight sheep's wool, preventing passage of air through pedal and emergency brake openings. Can be put on in five minutes and you will ride in luxurious warmth and comfort. Shipping weight, 1 lb.
28K7074............................... **$1.32**

$2.25

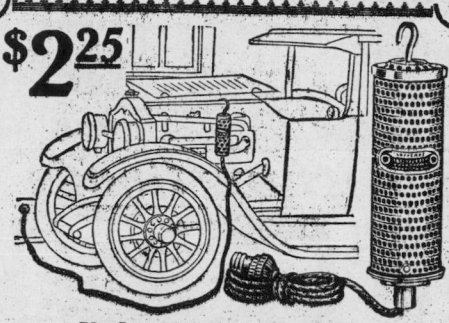

Under-Hood Motor Heater

A pierced metal cylinder, enclosing a resistance coil. This highly efficient heater hangs by a hook under the hood of your car. Has long wire and plug to attach to electric light socket in your garage. Keeps your motor warm and ready in the coldest weather at a very small cost. Strongly made and well finished for long service. This heater will pay for itself many times by keeping your motor safe from freezing and constantly ready for use. Shipping weight, 1½ lbs.
28K9972—115 Volts................. **$2.25**

For Chevrolet Heater See Page 494. Cold Weather Comfort at the Lowest Cost

$1.15 AND UP
Durable and Handsome Radiator and Hood Covers for Ford Cars

You will save considerable time and money by using a radiator and a hood cover in cold weather to keep water in radiator and oil in crankcase warm, when car is standing for some time out of doors, and to aid in easier starting.

These covers come complete with a curtain which can be regulated according to weather conditions. Will keep radiator from freezing. Both radiator and hood cover are well lined. Hood cover is entirely separate from radiator cover. High quality covers at remarkably low prices.
Enameled Cloth Covers. (Not illustrated.)
28K12925—Radiator Cover for 1917-1927 Ford cars. State year. Each..... **$1.15**
28K12926—Hood Cover for 1917-1925 Ford cars. State year. Each..... **1.35**
28K12923—Hood Cover for 1926-27 Fords. Each..... **1.35**
Artificial Leather Covers
28K13152—Radiator Cover, artificial leather, for 1917-1927 Ford cars. State year. Each..... **1.35**
28K13154—Hood Cover, artificial leather, for 1917-1925 Ford cars. State year. Each..... **1.85**
28K12924—Hood Cover, artificial leather, for 1926-27 Fords. Each..... **1.85**
Shipping weight, Radiator Covers, 1½ pounds; Hood Covers, 2½ pounds.

Radiator and Hood Covers for Standard Cars
28K5342½—Radiator Cover, imitation leather....... **$2.40**
28K5348½—Hood Cover, imitation leather....... **3.10**
Shipping weight: Radiator covers, 3 lbs.; Hood covers, 4 lbs.

In ordering Radiator or Hood Covers, be sure to state make, year and model of car. All covers are shipped from factory in NORTHEASTERN ILLINOIS in about 5 days' time.

$2.98 And Up

Finest Metal Radiator Shutters

Regulates the temperature of circulating system perfectly for the best driving conditions. Will keep radiator from freezing when driving. Is substantially made of cold rolled steel with a beautiful baked black enamel finish. Very conveniently operated from dash by means of a metal plunger control. Shutter attached by four bolts, to be inserted through the radiator core. Control clamps to dash. No holes to drill. These shutters are of the finest workmanship and finish and will give complete satisfaction in every respect. Equip your car with one and do away with the worry of freezing radiators. Shipping weight, 6 pounds.

Catalog No.	Name of Car	
28K15709¼	Buick Standard 6, 1926-27	$4.95
28K15711¼	Buick Master 6, 1926-27	4.95
28K15118¼	Chevrolet Superior	3.45
28K15120¼	Chevrolet "K," 1925-26	3.45
28K15713¼	Chevrolet, 1927	3.45
28K15715¼	Chrysler 58-60, 1925-26-27	4.95
28K15717¼	Chrysler 50, 1927	4.95
28K15116¼	Dodge, 1924-25-26-27	3.95
28K15171¼	Ford, 1917-23	2.98
28K15173¼	Ford, 1924-26-27	2.98
28K15719¼	Oakland, 1926-27	4.95
28K15721¼	Oldsmobile, 1925-26-27	4.95
28K15121¼	Overland 4, 1924-25-26	3.95
28K15124¼	Overland 6, 1925-26-27	3.95
28K15723¼	Pontiac, 1926-27	4.95
28K15724¼	Whippet 4, 1926-27	3.95
28K15725¼	Whippet 6, 1927	3.95

Maximum Heat, Comfort and Convenience With This Remarkable Heater

$5.45

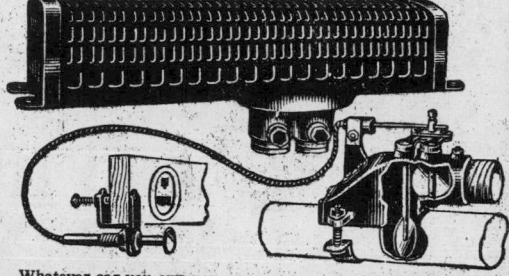

Whatever car you own you are sure to appreciate this wonderful, compact heater designed along the lines of those found on the highest priced cars and producing unusual warmth when and where you want it. Can be used as a rail, heelboard or toeboard heater, in front or back compartment, or both.

Heavy perforated sheet metal cover finished with two coats of high grade ovenbaked enamel. Heating element is of heavy cast iron in one piece with radiating fins and fingers for increasing heating surface and forcing heat where it belongs. Most heaters selling at this price have sheet metal elements which warp, rattle and cool quickly. Get this heater and get the best.

Superior quality control valve guides hot gases into heater where they belong and provides an absolute shut-off when desired, so that heater need not be removed in summer. Patent airtight adjustment fits all exhaust pipes without forcing. Nicely nickeled dash control clamps to dash; no holes necessary. Full and complete directions for quick, easy installation with each heater. Only one floorboard hole necessary. Shipping weight, 19 pounds.
28K9979—Heater, complete.......... **$5.45**

Low Priced Ford Heater

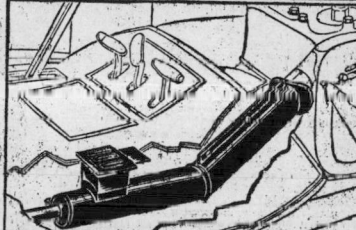

This one model fits all Fords regardless of manifold or special hot spot equipment. Heavy sheet metal construction fits around exhaust pipe, furnishing unusually large heating surface. Only clean, fresh air driven down deflector to register. No gases or dirt. Big volume of instant heat easily regulated by sliding register. Full, simple directions for quick, easy installation. A big value heat producer. Shipping weight, 3½ pounds.
28K9977............................... **$1.98**

Pedal Covers

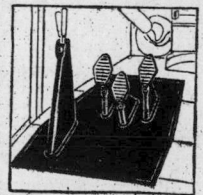

Protective mat which fits under rug or floor mat with sleeves that fit snugly around the pedals and emergency brake lever, closing all openings. Does not interfere with the operation of the car as the sleeves are flexible and work easily with the pedals. Made of strong, rubberized fabric material, waterproof, durable and very neat in appearance. Shipping weight, 1 pound.

28K10900—For Fords, 1911-25... **$0.87**
28K10901—For 1926-27 Fords..... **.87**
28K10902—For Chevrolet, 1917-24. **.98**
28K10903—For Chevrolet, 1925-26. **.98**
28K10904—For Overland 6, 1925-27 **.98**
28K10905—For Dodge, 1915-27... **1.39**
28K10906—For Star, 1922-27..... **.98**

Test Your Radiator With a Freezometer

Test the strength of the alcohol solution in your radiator this winter and avoid any danger of having your radiator freeze. The float indicates the freezing point of your solution accurately. Shipping weight, ¾ pound.
28K9208............................... **48c**

OVEN 10½ X 11 X 20½

CLOSED VIEW

Advertised Camp Needs at Cut Prices

$8⁴⁸

Super-Chef
Two - Burner Gasoline Camp Stove With Oven

Sold for $10.50 by Many Stores

Bakes, broils, boils, toasts, roasts and frys just like a kitchen range. Cooking surface; 11x20½ inches. Size, open, 11 inches wide, 21 inches long and 18 inches high. Burners spread the flames evenly without scorching; you have only to generate the one master burner. Iron grates and heavy gauge steel oven that may be used as a wind shield; tank of one-piece drawn brass. Tank and burners built as one unit; nothing to loosen or leak. Stove folds to 5x11x21 inches.
6K5472¼—Shipping weight, 24 pounds......... **$8.48**

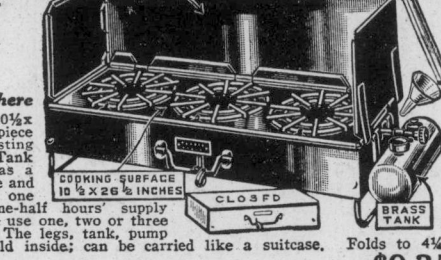

WINDSHIELD 9 INCHES HIGH

Prentiss Waber's
Three-Burner Gasoline Camp Stove for

$9³⁵

Usually Sells for $12.50 Elsewhere

Cooking surface, 10½ x 26½ inches; one - piece drawn brass, non-rusting gasoline tank. Tank and burners built as a unit; absolutely safe and clean. Tank holds one quart, two and one-half hours' supply for all burners. Can use one, two or three burners as desired. The legs, tank, pump and wind shield fold inside; can be carried like a suitcase. Folds to 4¼ x 10½x26 inches.
6K5458¼—Shipping weight, 24 pounds................**$9.35**

COOKING SURFACE 10½ X 26½ INCHES
CLOSED
BRASS TANK

UNBREAKABLE FUEL ROD GRATE

CLOSED

$3⁹⁸

Handy Chef
Two-Burner Gasoline Camp Stove

Cooking surface, 17x9 inches. The burners, tank and feed pipes are one solid unit and cannot leak or become loose. When not in use the stove folds up like a suitcase, with the gasoline box, measuring 17⅞x9½x5 inches and weighing only 12 pounds. Tank is of heavy gauge brass, box with wind shield of heavy gauge steel, heavily enameled. Flame can be regulated.
6K5459¼—Shipping weight, 14 pounds...... **$3.98**

ICY-HOT Vacuum Goods

"Icy Hot" School Lunch Kit

Metal carrying case, green finish. Dimensions, 8½x6¼x3 in. Leather handle. Equipped with ½-pint vacuum bottle, nickel plated screw-off top, enameled body. Removable filler. Case is partitioned so that bottle will stay in place and lunch can be kept clean. Shipping Weight, 3½ pounds.
6K4925 Complete kit...... **$1.89**

"Icy Hot" Lunch Kit Complete,

$1⁴³

Popular with factory, office and outdoor workers, school children and all who carry lunch. Black enameled metal case, leather handle, hinged lid, brass plated clasps. Good quality "Icy Hot" pint vacuum bottle, enameled body, aluminum cup and shoulder held in upper compartment, provides hot coffee or tea or cold drinks. Lower compartment keeps lunch clean and fresh.
6K4918—Complete lunch kit. Shipping wt., 4 pounds............... **$1.43**
6K4911—Pint vacuum bottle. Shipping wt., 2 pounds..................... **.89**
6K4910—Empty lunch kit. Shipping wt., 2 pounds............... **.55**

New Improved Model Gasoline Siphon

Draws gasoline from automobile tank for filling stoves, lamps, etc. Made of brass. Shipping weight, 8 ounces.
6K5454............**48c**

Safety Kerosene Oil Stove

No odor, smoke or soot. Tank or body is made of heavy brass, with steel legs and grate support. One quart of kerosene will burn 6 hours. Stove will boil a quart of water in about 3 minutes. Is 8 inches wide and 9 inches high when set up. Shipping weight, 4½ pounds.
6K5465......**$3.69**

Master Chef
Two-Burner Gasoline Camp Stove
Sells Up to $8.50 Elsewhere
With Grates

Made of extra heavy gauge steel. Has one-piece cast grate. Heavy gauge brass tank, telescope legs and combination wind shield and warming shelf. Burners and tank are one solid unit, which cannot leak. Can be used single or double and regulated to any size flame desired. Size of stove, when folded like a suitcase, is 18 inches long, 9 inches wide and 5¼ inches high. Complete with pump, funnel and directions. Shpg. wt., 16 lbs.
6K5460¼ **$5.85**

Folding Camp Stand
Two-Burner Size

One - piece metal construction, sliding joints. Will support a weight of 200 pounds. Brings top of stove about 27 inches from the ground. Stove attached to stand with patent fasteners, which hold stove rigidly. Folds to 1½x2¾x21 in. Fits stoves 6K5459¼, 6K5460¼ and 6K5472¼. Shipping wt., 3½ pounds.
6K5453............. **$1.28**

Large Size Stove Stand
To fit three-burner stove 6K5458¼. Shpg. wt., 4 lbs.
6K5452............. **$1.99**

Improved WLS Hot or Cold Jug

$1.89 This is without doubt one of our most startling 1927 values. So many people recognized this extraordinary value in 1926 that we sold practically 50,000 of these jugs. When you consider this and know that we have improved the quality and lowered the price for 1927 you will realize what a value you are getting.

The big 3¼-inch opening permits the insertion of bulky foods such as fried chicken, frankfurters and similar articles; also makes it easy to clean. The outside container is finished in dark green, aluminum cap and inside container is earthenware with cork insulation keeping contents hot or cold from 10 to 12 hours.
6K4930—Shipping weight, 12 pounds..... **$1.89**

"Icy Hot" Corrugated Vacuum Bottle

Corrugated seamless brass. Case highly polished and metal plated. Has removable filler and screw - off top. Will keep contents cold for 72 hours or hot for 24 hours.
Pint size. Standard list price, $2.50. Shipping weight, 2 pounds.
6K4903........**$1.69**
Quart size. Standard list price, $3.75. Shipping wt., 4 pounds.
6K4904............ **$2.48**

"Icy Hot" Vacuum Food Jar

Keeps solid foods hot for 24 hours or cold for 72 hours. Fine for picnics, etc. Black enameled heavy metal case with nickel plated cup and shoulder, with folding handle. Removable filler. Wide mouth to admit ice cream, etc. Shipping wts.: Pint, 3½ lbs.; quart, 5 lbs.
Pint size.
6K4934......**$2.39**
Quart size.
6K4935...... **3.39**

"Icy Hot" Green Enameled Vacuum Bottles

The popular low priced American made vacuum bottle.

89c

Green enameled case of heavy metal with aluminum shoulder and cup, with removable filler and screw-off top. Top serves as a drinking cup. Will keep liquids cold for 72 hours or hot for 24 hours.
Pint size.
6K4911—Shpg. wt., 2 lbs. **$0.89**
Quart size.
6K4912—Shpg. wt., 4 lbs. **1.69**

"Icy Hot" Vacuum Pitcher

A beautiful double utility pitcher that will enable you to have a convenient supply of hot or cold water or other beverages in the guest room or at the dining table. Suitable for hotel use also. Pitcher made of heavy, heavily nickel plated and highly polished, with nickel plated stopper. Will not leak. One-quart size. Shipping weight, 4 pounds.
6K4905....... **$6.75**

Extra Fillers or Inside Bottles

Will fit "Icy Hot" or any standard brand of vacuum bottle. Can easily be fitted by purchaser. Shipping weight, 2 pounds. 
6K4941—Pint size for Bottles 6K4903 and 6K4911............. **79c**
6K4942—Quart size, for Bottles 6K4904 and 6K4912...........**$1.29**
6K4947—Filler for pint size Food Jar 6K4934 .... **1.39**
6K4948—Filler for quart size Food Jar 6K4935............. **2.19**
6K4943—Filler for ½-pint size Bottle 6K4925................. **.79**
6K4944—Filler for Pitcher 6K4905....................... **3.39**

Extra Corks

To fit our Vacuum Bottles 6K4911, 6K4912, 6K4903 and 6K4904. Shipping weight, 3 ounces.
6K4922—Each **5c**

Campers' Cook Kit
31 or 43-Piece Aluminum Sets

Compact, complete cooking and serving outfit.

Four-Party Outfit
Four-Party Kit includes 31 essential utensils of solid aluminum; no seams, solder or joints. 3 cooking kettles, 1 coffee pot with cover, 4 coffee cups, 4 serving plates, 1 frying pan, 2 detachable handles, 1 pair non-leakable salt and pepper shakers, 4 each, nickel silver plated teaspoons, tablespoons, forks and knives. All pieces fit neatly into largest kettle, only 7 inches high with carrying bail.
6K5461¼—Shpg. wt., 10 pounds................. **$6.98**

Six-Party Outfit
Contains the same equipment with the addition of 2 cups, 2 plates, 2 teaspoons, 2 tablespoons, 2 forks and 2 knives.
6K5462¼—Shpg. wt., 12 pounds........... **$8.48**

Camp Cook Folding Fry Pan

Handle folds out of way when packed. Size, 9 inches in diameter. Made of sheet metal. Shipping weight, 2 lbs.
6K5463.................. **49c**

Drop the "STANLEY" It Won't Break

"Stanley" Unbreakable Vacuum Bottles

All steel, lined with flexible blue alamite with a porcelain-like surface. Easy to keep clean, sanitary. Guaranteed not to break. Makers claim it will keep liquids hot for 18 hours or cold for 24 hours. Body is nicely black finished with polished nickel plated cup.
6K4906—Pint size. Advertised price, $7.00. Shipping weight, 3 pounds................ **$5.98**
6K4907—One-quart size. Advertised price, $8.00. Shipping weight, 4 pounds......... **$6.79**
6K4908—Two-quart size. Advertised price, $10.00. Shipping weight, 6 pounds............. **$8.98**

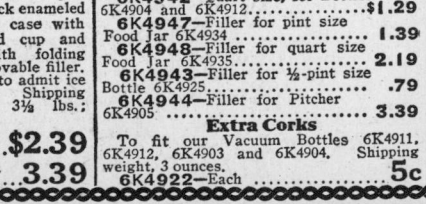

"Stanley" Lunch Kit With Unbreakable Pint Bottle

Keeps liquid hot for 18 hours or cold for 24 hours. Outside of bottle nicely finished in black with nickel plated cup, screw top. Kit is blue enameled metal, leather handle, hinged lid, nickel plated clasps.
6K4923—Complete, with one-pint bottle. Advertised price, $8.50. (Shipping weight, 5 pounds) **$6.98**
6K4924—Kit only. (Shpg. wt., 2 lbs.) **$1.23**

STANLEY GALLON JUG

"Stanley" Insulated Unbreakable Gallon Jug, Only $5.98
Advertised Price $7.50

Two polished aluminum cups nest into each other and fit over the stopper, enclosed in a polished aluminum screw top cap. Made of electrically welded steel with lining of blue porcelain-like enamel fused to the steel. Large mouth (3½ inches) to admit bulky food and will keep hot or cold for 10 hours. Cork insulation between container and outer steel shell. Strong handle.
6K4940—Shipping weight, 10 pounds........... **$5.98**

Camp and Tour in Comfort

$5.95 Actual Weight Only 35 Lbs.

Size when folded, 48 inches long, 6¼ inches wide and 4½ inches deep.

Double Size 48x78 Inches

Double Size 48x76 Inches

$9.98

Actual Weight Only 35 Lbs.

Size when folded, 48 inches long, 5 inches wide and 4½ inches deep.

Steel Folding Camp Bed
Wire Fabric Spring

A folding camp bed equipped with wire fabric springs that economically combines comfort with convenience. Steel frame construction makes it one of the most sturdy camp beds ever built. When in use, bed is 48 inches wide, 76 inches long and 15 inches high; when folded, 6¼ inches wide, 4½ inches deep and 48 inches long. Weight, about 45 pounds. This bed, used with a pad or mattress shown below, will be as comfortable as any bed in the home. Shipping weight, 40 pounds.

6K5439¼ **$5.95**

Improved Folding Camp Bed
Steel Frame With Canvas Top

FRAME—Made of special hardened steel, strongly reinforced. Has take-up tension brace so sagging of top may always be prevented. CANVAS TOP—Made of heavy 12-ounce khaki canvas, strongly reinforced with eleven strips of 2-inch webbing, attached to head rails with S hooks at one end and helical coil springs at other. When folded measures 48x5x4 inches. Shipping weight, 40 pounds.

6K5427¼ **$9.98**

This is the very latest style canvas top steel frame camp cot, which you will find very comfortable to sleep on.

Auto Bed

$7.98

Makes a comfortable full size bed for two persons. Easily set up. Bed consists of three parts; three wooden rails hinged in the center and covered with a heavy 12-ounce khaki duck, and two adjustable telescopic crossbars. Crossbars are adjustable for different widths of car bodies and are fitted with a simple device to insure proper tension of the canvas top at all times. Bed is full 6 feet long and about 50 inches wide at the head. Crossbars are of selected hardwood fastened together with galvanized iron fittings. When used in an automobile the bed rests on the body of the car, no strain on top or wind shield. Folded, occupies a space 3 feet long by 7 inches wide. Shpg. wt., 25 lbs.

6K5445¼—Fits any four, five and seven-passenger open or touring car. **$7.98**

6K5442¼—Two-door or two-door sedan of any size. Also suitable for the wide seven-passenger cars or narrow four-passenger sport models). Size, 69 inches long and 37 inches wide. Shipping weight, 25 pounds. **$7.98**

Well Known Camp Beds

King Folding Kamp Bed

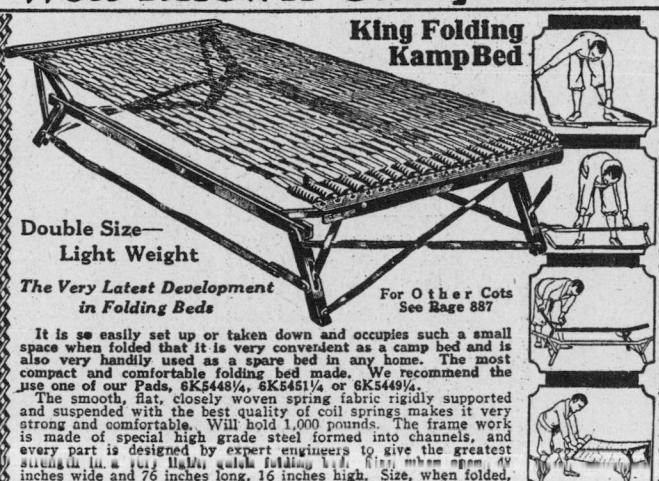

Double Size— Light Weight

The Very Latest Development in Folding Beds

For Other Cots See Page 887

It is so easily set up or taken down and occupies such a small space when folded that it is very convenient as a camp bed and is also very handily used as a spare bed in any home. The most compact and comfortable folding bed made. We recommend the use of one of our Pads, 6K5448¼, 6K5451¼ or 6K5449¼.

The smooth, flat, closely woven spring fabric rigidly supported and suspended with the best quality of coil springs makes it very strong and comfortable. Will hold 1,000 pounds. The frame work is made of special high grade steel formed into channels, and every part is designed by expert engineers to give the greatest strength in a soft light; each folding up flat when open, 69 inches wide and 76 inches long, 16 inches high. Size, when folded, 3x3½x48 inches. Shipping weight, 33 pounds.

6K5444¼ **$7.98**

Combined Mattress and Bed Roll

The feature of this mattress is the outside covering made of waterproof duck, so that when the mattress is rolled up the inside is protected from rain, dirt, etc. When mattress is used on bed, the outside waterproof duck tends to keep out dampness. Inside of mattress is covered with good quality khaki color denim, stuffed with white layer cotton felt. The flaps extend 12 inches on both sides. 5¼ inches at both the head and the foot end. Makes bundle of 10-inch diameter, 48 inches long, held securely by three heavy web straps. Size of mattress, 48x76 inches, Shipping wt., 15 lbs.

6K5449¼ **$6.79**

Waterproof Camp Blankets

Always remains soft and pliable. Made of very closely woven duck, dark color. Size, 54x84 inches. Treated with a waterproof solution, also windproof; has eyelets in corners and sides; double stitched.

6K5412—Shpg. wt. 4½ lbs..... **$1.79**

For Bed Blankets see pages 183 to 190

Kapok Cot Mattress

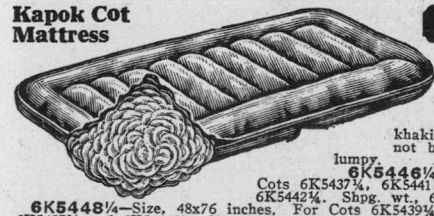

Filled with the finest prime Japan kapok, light in weight, well tufted and covered with khaki color denim; will not bunch or become lumpy.

6K5446¼—Size, 25x76 in. For Cots 6K5437¼, 6K5441¼ and 6K5442¼. Shpg. wt., 6 lbs..... **$4.25**

6K5448¼—Size, 48x76 inches. For Cots 6K5439¼, 6K5427¼ and 6K5444¼. Shipping weight, 10 pounds. **7.35**

Cotton Felt Mattress

Filled with good quality white layer felt and covered with heavy khaki denim.

6K5450¼—Size, 25x76 inches. For Cots 6K5441¼, 6K5437¼ and 6K5442¼. Shipping weight, 8 pounds. **$2.48**

6K5451¼—Size, 48x76 inches. For Cots 6K5439¼, 6K5427¼ and 6K5444¼. Shipping weight, 12 pounds. **4.48**

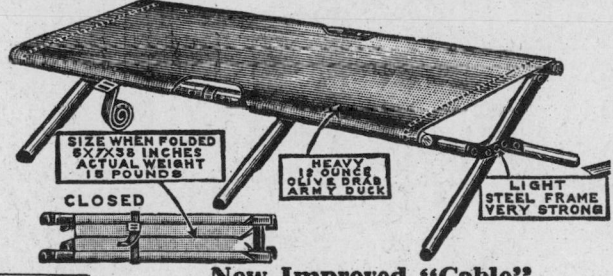

SIZE WHEN FOLDED 5X7X38 INCHES ACTUAL WEIGHT 18 POUNDS

CLOSED

Frame and Legs Steel, Light but Very Strong

HEAVY 18 OUNCE OLIVE DRAB ARMY DUCK

LIGHT STEEL FRAME VERY STRONG

New Improved "Cable" Folding Camp Cot

Steel Frame One-piece Construction

A new luxury for motoring or camping. Practically unbreakable; can hold the weight of four men at one time. This cot overcomes every one of the usual difficulties. Folds quickly and stands the hardest usage, even when placed on uneven ground. Very desirable, too, for the home. The fiber tipped legs prevent scratching of floors or wearing holes in rugs or carpets. Frame made of special U shape steel tubing with reinforced steel joints. Cannot split, warp or crack, and is not affected by weather. Finished in olive green enamel, with second coat baked on. Top is covered with 12-ounce khaki duck, tape bound and double sewed wherever strain comes. This covering is far superior to imported cloth or burlap used on other cots. Will not stretch or sag. Size, open, 6 feet 4 inches long, 26½ inches wide and 17 inches high. Folded, 38x7x5 inches.

6K5437¼—Shipping weight, 18 pounds. **$3.25**

High Quality at Low Prices

"Biltwell" Wood Folding Cot

Frame is made of selected hardwood, varnished natural finish, reinforced with steel braces. Covered with heavy, brown 12-ounce double filled duck. Made extra fine to give good service, and will hold 1,000 pounds. Size, when open, 27 inches wide and 78 inches long. Folds into small bundle, 4x6x39 inches. Shipping weight, 20 pounds.

6K5442¼ **$3.39**

"Excelsior" Folding Camp Cot

Frame of hardwood, reinforced by steel plates at joints. Cover is double filled white canvas. Cot measures 6 feet 4 inches long, 25 inches wide and 15 inches high. Folds into small bundle.

6K5441¼—Shipping weight, 18 pounds.. **$2.48**

Folding Camp Table

Made of selected varnished hardwood. Frame is braced with steel. Stands 27 inches high; top is 21x35 inches. When folded makes a package 6 inches in diameter and 27 inches long. Web straps for carrying. Shipping weight, 14 pounds.

6K5428¼ **$2.75**

"Cable" Folding Camp Chair
Steel Frame

Strong and durable, yet light in weight. Folds compactly. Seat made of heavy brown duck. Fiber tipped legs. Shpg. wt., 5 lbs.

6K5410¼ **95c**

Folding Camp Chair

Strong, hardwood frame. Seat of heavy duck. Legs reinforced by steel braces. Back rest. Shipping weight, 4½ pounds.

6K5429¼ **78c**

Folding Camp Stool

(Not illustrated.) As above, without back rest. Shpg. wt. 3 lbs.

6K5430¼ **59c**

Two-in-One Auto Crib

Can be used as a bed when baby is asleep or converted into a swing. Made of washable duck securely fastened to strong enameled steel frame, equipped at each end with adjustable double hangers. With two strong safety springs to act as shock absorbers. Size, 30 by 14 inches. Folds perfectly flat.

6K5401¼—Crib complete with cotton filled pad covered with figured material. Shipping weight, 6 pounds. **$2.59**

6K5402¼—Crib only, without pad. Shipping weight, 4 pounds. **$1.98**

All Our Tents are Standard Weight
Conforming with U.S. Gov't. Specifications

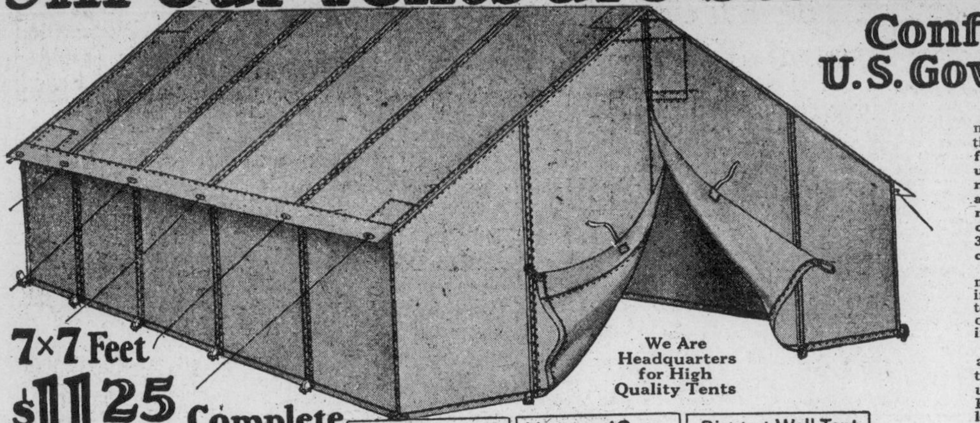

7×7 Feet
$11 25 Complete
All Waterproof

We Are Headquarters for High Quality Tents

Waterproofed Throughout	Heavy 12 oz. Khaki Duck	Biggest Wall Tent Value on the Market

Every inch of our tents is of standard weight and measures up to the right U. S. Government specifications in every detail. The standard weight of a tent fabric always, without exception, is weighed upon a 29-inch width scale. Tent buyers should not be misled by dealers who list their weights in a 36-inch width to give the impression that their material is of heavier weight. In reality an 8-ounce standard weight fabric and a 10-ounce 36-inch width are precisely the same. So you can make a comparison we list it both ways.

Compare our tents as to fabric, webbing reinforcements, size, waterproofing, convenience features, in fact, everything that is to be found in a desirable tent with any tent on the market at anywhere near our prices, and you will find ours greatly superior in every detail.

Twenty-five years as one of the largest manufacturers and retailers of tents have enabled us to build up such a tremendous volume of business that it is possible for us to sell tents far below the average retail price. From every section of the United States we are getting letters from thankful customers telling us how satisfactory our tents have been and what great savings they have made. Order any of the tents on these pages that suit your needs and know that you have the best value for the money obtainable.

"Superior" Heavy All Waterproofed Khaki Duck Wall Tent

Here is a genuine all waterproofed khaki duck wall tent, that we believe is superior to any wall tent on the market. The "Superior" is made in our own factory under the careful supervision of our own workmen. We have spared no expense in making every little detail of this tent in the most expert way and of the finest possible materials. Our special expensive process of waterproofing makes this tent absolutely rain and moisture proof. The finest closely woven strong fiber duck, weighing 12-ounces after waterproofing is used. Tent is also mildew-proof. The heavy waterproofed top eliminates the need for a fly with this tent.

Catalog No.	Width and Length	Height of Wall	Height of Tent	Complete	Without Poles	Shpg. Wt.
6K7714¼	7 x 7 ft.	3 feet	7 feet	$11.25	$10.45	47 lbs.
6K7715¼	8 x10 ft.	3 feet	7½ feet	14.98	13.98	56 lbs.
6K7716¼	9½x12 ft.	3 feet	7½ feet	17.95	16.85	72 lbs.
6K7717¼	12 x14 ft.	3½ feet	8 feet	23.95	22.75	90 lbs.

Popular "Builtwell" Duck Wall Tent Heavy Waterproofed Khaki Top (White Sides)

Our "Builtwell" wall tent is similar in every detail to our "Superior" tent, with the exception that the side walls are of closely woven white duck not waterproofed. The top, however, is of the same high grade, heavy khaki waterproofed duck. All size dimensions are the same as the "Superior." Buy the tent best suited for your needs. Because of the very slight difference in price we recommend that you buy an all waterproofed tent. Compare the quality, convenience, size and other desirable features of our tents with any other tents on the market, and you will choose from these pages.

Catalog No.	Width and Length	Height of Wall	Height of Tent	Complete	Without Poles	Shpg. Wt.
6K7720¼	7 x 7 ft.	3 feet	7 feet	$ 9.65	$ 8.85	40 lbs.
6K7721¼	8 x10 ft.	3 feet	7½ feet	12.65	11.65	50 lbs.
6K7722¼	9½x12 ft.	3 feet	7½ feet	15.98	14.88	64 lbs.
6K7723¼	12 x14 ft.	3½ feet	8 feet	21.65	20.45	82 lbs.

FULTON ALL WHITE DUCK WALL TENT (NOT WATERPROOFED)
In 8, 10, or 12-Ounce Standard 29-Inch Duck Closely Woven—Double Stitched

For Haying Tools, See Pages 998 and 1000.

$7 95 7x7 Feet Complete

ALL SEAMS DOUBLE STITCHED

Weights, 8, 10 and 12 ounces, measured upon the standard 29-inch width single filling duck. On 36-inch strip, weights would be 10, 12 and 15 ounces. Tent is sent you complete ready to set up. Included are additional top guy ropes, one for each end, with all tents listed 12x12-feet and larger. We give shipping weights of the 8-ounce tent only. The 10-ounce tent is one-quarter heavier than the 8-oz.; 12-oz. tent is one-half heavier than the 8-oz. Your tent will be on the way within 24 hours after the order is received.

Width and Length Feet	Ht. of Wall Feet	Ht. of Tent Feet	10-Oz. Duck 36-In. Width Same as 8-Oz. Duck 29-In. Width		12-Oz. Duck 36-In. Width Same as 10-Oz. Duck 29-In. Width		15-Oz. Duck 36-In. Width Same as 12-Oz. Duck 29-In. Width		If Poles Are Not Wanted Deduct	Shpg. Wt., 8-Oz. Tents
7 x 7	3	7	6K7725¼	$ 7.95	6K7726¼	$ 9.89			$0.80	33 lbs.
7 x 9	3	7	6K7728¼	9.85	6K7729¼	11.65	6K7730¼	$13.45	.90	41 lbs.
8 x10	3	7½	6K7731¼	11.45	6K7732¼	13.45	6K7733¼	15.60	1.00	44 lbs.
9½x12	3	7½	6K7734¼	13.85	6K7735¼	16.75	6K7736¼	19.45	1.10	55 lbs.
12 x14	3½	8	6K7737¼	18.85	6K7738¼	22.75	6K7739¼	26.50	1.20	68 lbs.
12 x16	3½	8	6K7740¼	21.65	6K7741¼	24.85	6K7742¼	27.95	1.75	82 lbs.
12 x18	3½	8	6K7743¼	22.95	6K7744¼	27.25	6K7745¼	31.45	1.90	94 lbs.
14 x16	4	9	6K7746¼	24.85	6K7747¼	29.95	6K7748¼	34.95	1.85	105 lbs.
14 x20	4	9			6K7750¼	33.95	6K7751¼	39.95	2.25	125 lbs.
14 x24	4	9			6K7753¼	37.95	6K7754¼	47.95	2.50	141 lbs.
16 x16	5	11	Not Made in This Weight		6K7756¼	35.95	6K7757¼	38.85	2.10	111 lbs.
16 x18	5	11			6K7759¼	37.45	6K7760¼	43.45	2.30	122 lbs.
16 x20	5	11			6K7762¼	43.95	6K7763¼	49.95	2.40	143 lbs.
16 x24	5	11			6K7765¼	48.45	6K7766¼	55.45	2.70	162 lbs.

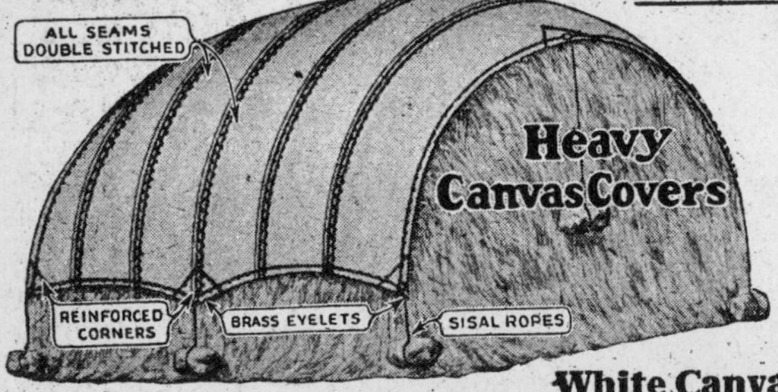

HEAVY CANVAS COVERS
Guaranteed Full Weight Duck

Heavy Canvas Covers

REINFORCED CORNERS **BRASS EYELETS** **SISAL ROPES**

Every man has realized the value of canvas covers as a protection to his crops. The small initial cost is returned tenfold each season in savings made through this needed protection. Through buying your covers from Sears, Roebuck and Co. you can get better values, better workmanship and an iron clad guarantee. We manufacture all covers in our own factories under the most careful supervision. Years of successful retailing have built up such an enormous volume that our prices are now lower than you can obtain at any other store. Wherever protection against the weather is desired, you will find the canvas cover listed here that will fulfill your requirements.

White canvas covers in woven single filling duck, standard weights in 29-inch widths. Finished around edge with brass eyelets and ropes. Strongly reinforced at all strain points. Seams double stitched throughout. All covers come in full sizes after seams, hems and reinforcements are taken care of. Whatever cover you may select you may be sure that you are getting full size, standard weight and the finest quality properly woven duck. If you wish any samples of material to make a price and quality comparison just write us and we will gladly send them to you.

White Canvas Covers

Made of Standard 29-In. Wide Single Filling Duck of 8-Oz. 10-Oz. or 12-Oz. Duck
6K7630¼—State size and weight wanted.
SHIPPING WEIGHTS—The shipping weights given are for 8-oz. covers. 10-oz. covers weigh one-fourth more and 12-oz. one-half more than 8-oz.

Size, Ft.	10-Oz. Duck 36-In. Width Same as 8-Oz. Duck 29-In. Width	12-Oz. Duck 36-In. Width Same as 10-Oz. Duck 29-In. Width	15-Oz. Duck 36-In. Width Same as 12-Oz. Duck 29-In. Width	Wt. of 8-Oz. 29-In. Wide
9½x16	$ 4.95	$ 5.98	$ 6.98	12 lbs.
9½x18	5.58	6.87	7.97	14 lbs.
12x14	5.59	6.79	7.98	14 lbs.
12x16	6.25	7.59	8.98	13 lbs.
12x20	7.79	9.48	10.98	17 lbs.
14x16	6.98	8.89	10.95	16 lbs.
14x20	8.98	10.98	12.98	20 lbs.
16x16	8.39	9.89	11.95	18 lbs.
16x20	9.98	12.59	14.79	23 lbs.
16x24	12.29	14.98	17.69	29 lbs.
18x20	11.89	14.59	16.98	26 lbs.
18x24	13.89	16.98	19.89	32 lbs.
18x30	17.89	21.75	25.85	40 lbs.
20x24	....	18.85	22.25	34 lbs.
20x36	....	27.95	32.98	51 lbs.
24x30	....	27.89	32.95	52 lbs.
24x36	....	33.25	39.35	60 lbs.

Brown Waterproof Covers

Made of Heavy Single Filling Duck Weighing About 18 Ounces to the Yard After Waterproofing
For the small difference in price we recommend that you buy waterproof covers.

Catalog No.	Size	Each	Weight
6K7659¼	8x10 feet	$ 4.98	14 pounds
6K7660¼	8x12 feet	5.98	17 pounds
6K7664¼	9x14 feet	7.95	22 pounds
6K7665¼	10x12 feet	7.69	21 pounds
6K7666¼	10x16 feet	9.98	28 pounds
6K7673¼	12x14 feet	10.59	29 pounds
6K7675¼	12x16 feet	11.95	33 pounds
6K7676¼	14x16 feet	13.95	41 pounds
6K7678¼	14x20 feet	17.95	50 pounds
6K7679¼	16x16 feet	16.39	47 pounds
6K7680¼	16x20 feet	20.40	56 pounds
6K7681¼	18x24 feet	27.45	75 pounds
6K7682¼	18x30 feet	33.95	91 pounds
6K7683¼	20x24 feet	29.95	82 pounds
6K7684¼	24x30 feet	44.95	115 pounds

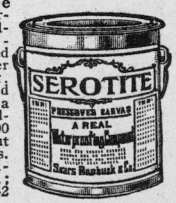

RANGER Hammerless Takedown Double Barrel Shotgun

$18.95

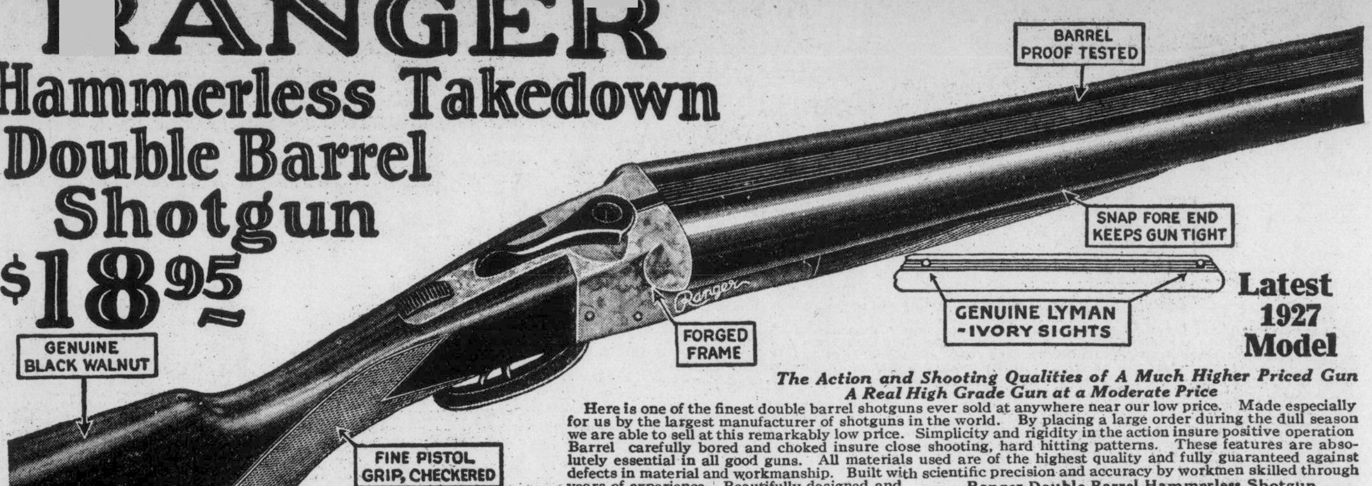

Latest 1927 Model

The Action and Shooting Qualities of A Much Higher Priced Gun
A Real High Grade Gun at a Moderate Price

Here is one of the finest double barrel shotguns ever sold at anywhere near our low price. Made especially for us by the largest manufacturer of shotguns in the world. By placing a large order during the dull season we are able to sell at this remarkably low price. Simplicity and rigidity in the action insure positive operation Barrel carefully bored and choked insure close shooting, hard hitting patterns. These features are absolutely essential in all good guns. All materials used are of the highest quality and fully guaranteed against defects in material and workmanship. Built with scientific precision and accuracy by workmen skilled through years of experience. Beautifully designed and finished.

BARRELS—The barrel and lug are forged in one piece. Blued steel, top rib matted, right barrel choke bored and left extra choke bored. Fitted with genuine Lyman ivory front and intermediate sights for sure alignment. Every barrel is proof tested.

STOCK AND FORE-END—Genuine black walnut, pistol grip, with extra fine quality of checkering. Hard rubber butt plate; length of stock, about 14 inches, with 3 to 3¼-inch drop. Fore-end has positive snap catch which keeps gun tight.

ACTION—All working parts are made of chrome vanadium steel, which will last a lifetime. Main spring and top lever spring are coiled piano wire and practically unbreakable. Has snap top lever, automatic thumb safety slide and takedown, casehardened frame. The action and shooting qualities of this gun compare with guns selling for much higher prices. Shipping weight, 15 pounds.

Ranger Double Barrel Hammerless Shotgun

Catalog No.	Gauge	Length of Barrel	Actual Weight	
6K 4¼	12	30 inches	7½ to 7¾ lb.	$8.95
6K 5¼	12	32 inches	7½ to 7¾ lb.	8.95
6K 6¼	16	30 inches	7¼ to 7½ lb.	8.95
6K 7¼	20	28 inches	6¼ to 6¾ lb.	8.95
6K 8¼	.410	26 inches	5½ to 6 lb.	8.95

Ranger Double Barrel Hammer Style Shotgun
Same as above, but hammer style instead of hammerless

Catalog No.	Gauge	Length of Barrel	Actual Weight	
6K58¼	12	30 inches	7½ to 7¾ lb.	$5.85
6K59¼	16	28 inches	7¼ to 7½ lb.	5.85

$25.95

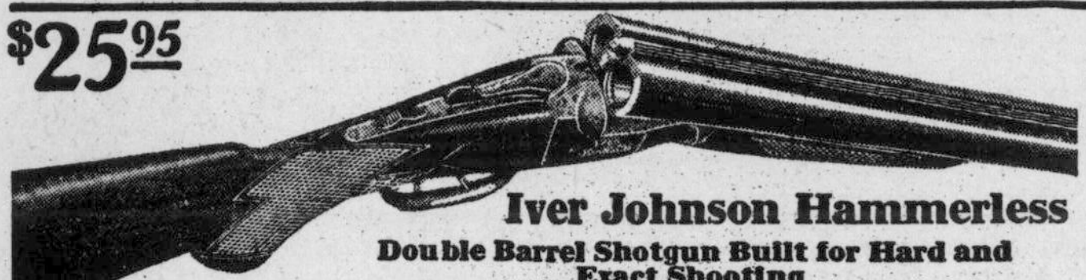

Iver Johnson Hammerless

Double Barrel Shotgun Built for Hard and Exact Shooting

Famous the World Over

This gun is made of strong tested material throughout, and is perfectly balanced. Has three-piece lightning lock, and the tension can be released without firing. The gun is beautifully designed and handsomely finished.

BARRELS—Barrel and half of lug and extension rib is forged of special steel in one piece. Right barrel is modified choke bored and left barrel full choke, with the exception of 12-gauge, 32-inch barrel and .410 bore, in which both barrels are extra full choke.

STOCK AND FORE-END—Selected black walnut, fully checkered and designed, not merely traced.

ACTION—All parts of the locks are dropped forged steel, accurately machined, highly polished and heat treated. Heat treated coil springs. Shipping weight, 14 pounds.

Catalog No.	Gauge	Length of Barrel	Actual Weight	
6K29¼	12	30 inches	7 lbs.	$25.95
6K30¼	12	32 inches	6¾ lbs.	25.95
6K32¼	20	28 inches	6½ lbs.	25.95
6K33¼	.410	26 inches	5¾ lbs.	25.95

$24.48

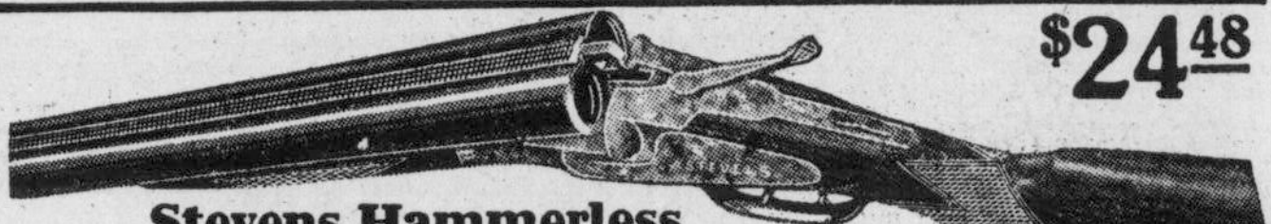

Stevens Hammerless

Double Barrel Shotgun No. 330 Noted for Its Hard Hitting Even Pattern

The Choice of Discriminating Sportsmen

Stevens latest model, designed to supply the popular demand for a gun of good appearance to sell at a low price. The action has all of the exclusive Stew features that insure a smooth working, reliable performance during years of hard usage.

BARRELS—High pressure compressed blued steel, tested with nitro powder. Matted rib. 12, 16 and 20-gauge right barrel choke bored, left barrel extra full choked. The .410 gauge has both barrels extra full choked. Action is beautifully polished and casehardened. Stock is of selected black walnut, finely checkered, full pistol grip capped, rubber butt plate.

ACTION—Hammerless. Top lever and bolt in one piece, coil springs. Large powerful extractors, automatic safety. Shipping weights, 12 pounds.

Catalog No.	Gauge	Length of Barrel	Actual Weight	
6K40¼	12	30 inches	7½ to 7¾ lbs.	$24.48
6K41¼	12	32 inches	7½ to 7¾ lbs.	24.48
6K42¼	16	28 inches	7¼ to 7½ lbs.	24.48
6K43¼	.410	28 inches	6¼ to 6¾ lbs.	24.48

$33.95

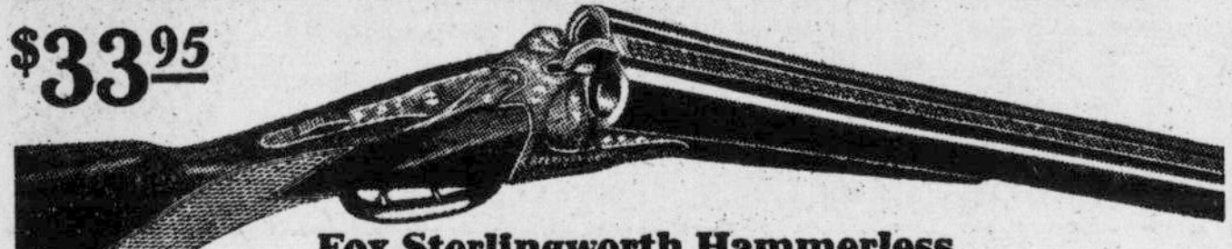

Fox Sterlingworth Hammerless

Double Barrel Shotgun

Theodore Roosevelt's Favorite

The Fox Sterlingworth gun is a plain, stanch, trustworthy gun at a reasonable price, that will make good all the time and under all conditions. Theodore Roosevelt, our famous former president and huntsman, used a Fox Sterlingworth gun on many of his big hunting trips.

BARRELS—Fluid compressed steel (Fox proof), thoroughly tested and guaranteed for strength and shooting qualities. Raised matted rib. Both barrels full choked.

STOCK AND FORE-END—Best quality American walnut, nicely checkered. Full pistol grip, with rubber cap and rubber butt plate. Stock, 14 inches long.

ACTION—Hammerless special action used by the Fox Manufacturing Company, with coil spring, which is guaranteed not to break. Shipping weight, 12 pounds.

Catalog No.	Gauge	Length of Barrel	Actual Weight	
6K36¼	12	30 inches	7¾ to 8 lbs.	$33.95
6K37¼	12	32 inches	7¾ to 8 lbs.	33.95
6K38¼	16	28 inches	6½ to 6¾ lbs.	33.95
6K39¼	20	26 inches	6 to 6½ lbs.	33.95

$28.25

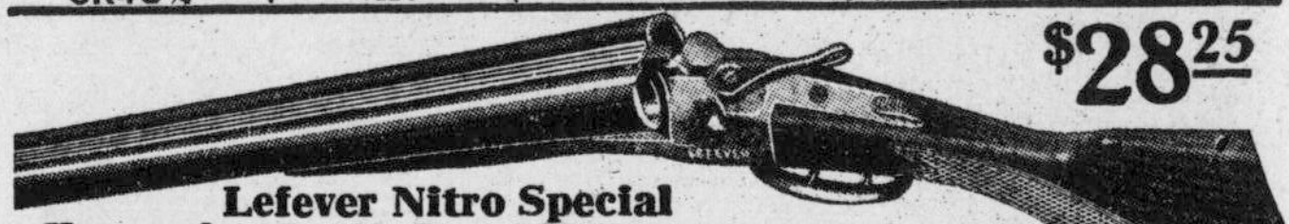

Lefever Nitro Special

Hammerless Double Barrel Shotgun

Price includes Good Quality Leather-trimmed Canvas, Can Rem-Oil, Good Cleaning Rods, Case and Complete Gun Cleaning Outfit.

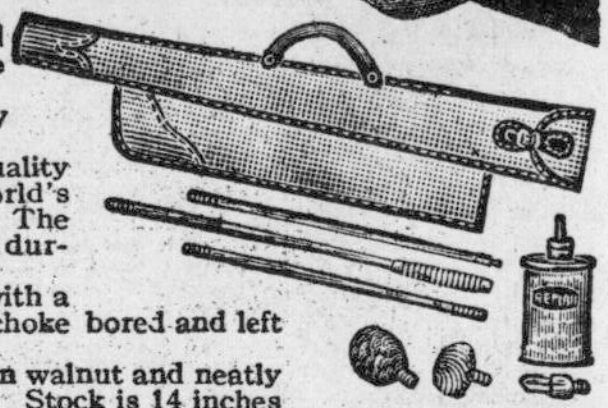

Recommended and purchased in large quantities by the United States Navy.

A dependable, hard hitting, well known high quality takedown model Shotgun. A Lefever gun won the World's championship at the Olympic Games in London. The name Lefever on a gun has stood for service and durability for more than fifty (50) years.

BARRELS—Made of special steel, proof tested with a double load. Raised matted top rib. Right barrel choke bored and left extra full choke bored.

STOCK AND FORE-END—Best grade American walnut and neatly checkered. Pistol grip and hard rubber butt plate. Stock is 14 inches long with 2⅞-inch drop at heel.

ACTION—The famous Lefever action, with non-breakable coil springs. The frame is a drop forging and will not crack. Has engraved bird on side of frame. Shpg. wt., 15 lbs.

Catalog No.	Gauge	Length of Barrel	Actual Weight	All for
6K44¼	12	28 inches	7½ lbs.	$28.25
6K45¼	12	30 inches	7½ lbs.	28.25
6K47¼	16	28 inches	6¾ lbs.	28.25
6K48¼	20	28 inches	6¼ lbs.	28.25

$16.95

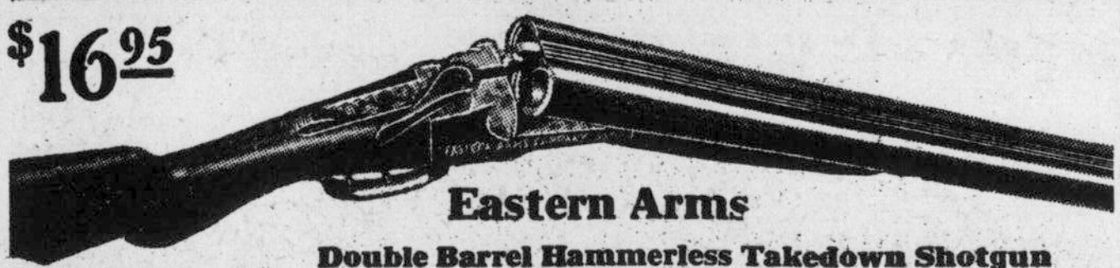

Eastern Arms

Double Barrel Hammerless Takedown Shotgun

This American shotgun is manufactured for us by a well known eastern firm of firearm manufacturers. While low in price, it is very dependable.

BARRELS—Blued steel, matted top rib, left barrel full choke, right barrel, slightly modified; positive extractor. Locking lug is solid extension from barrel.

ACTION—Hammerless, snap top lever; automatic thumb safety and casehardened frame.

STOCK—Walnut finish; rubber butt plate; length, 14 inches; drop, 3 to 3½ inches; snap fore-end. Shipping weight, 14 pounds.

Catalog No.	Gauge	Length of Barrel	Actual Weight	
6K24¼	12	30 inches	7½ to 8 lbs.	$16.95
6K25¼	12	32 inches	7½ to 8 lbs.	16.95
6K26¼	16	30 inches	7¼ to 7¾ lbs.	16.95
6K28¼	.410	26 inches	6 to 6¼ lbs.	16.95

$36.95

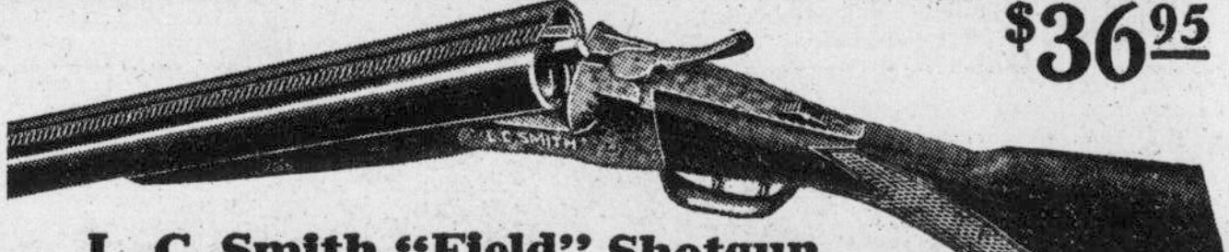

L. C. Smith "Field" Shotgun

The Gun Endorsed by All Discriminating Shooters

Fine Quality—Accurate—Dependable

Thousands of the "Field" models are in the hands of hunters who declare it a superior gun for hard shooting. Where such service is required in the timber and the brush, there the "Field" may be found, answering the trigger unfailingly. As to shooting powers, it hits as hard and accurately as its more expensive brothers.

BARRELS—Armor steel chosen because of its strength and uniformity, which has much to do with the popularity of this model.

STOCK AND FORE-END—Cut from a very fine grade of walnut, nicely checkered. Full pistol grip, with hard rubber cap and butt plate.

ACTION—The action is one that has made the L. C. Smith gun very popular. Guaranteed not to shoot loose. Shpg. wt., 14 lbs.

Catalog No.	Gauge	Length of Barrel	Actual Weight	
6K52¼	12	30 inches	7¼–7¾ lbs.	$36.95
6K53¼	12	32 inches	7½–8 lbs.	36.95
6K54¼	16	28 inches	6¼–7 lbs.	36.95
6K55¼	20	28 inches	5¾–6½ lbs.	36.95

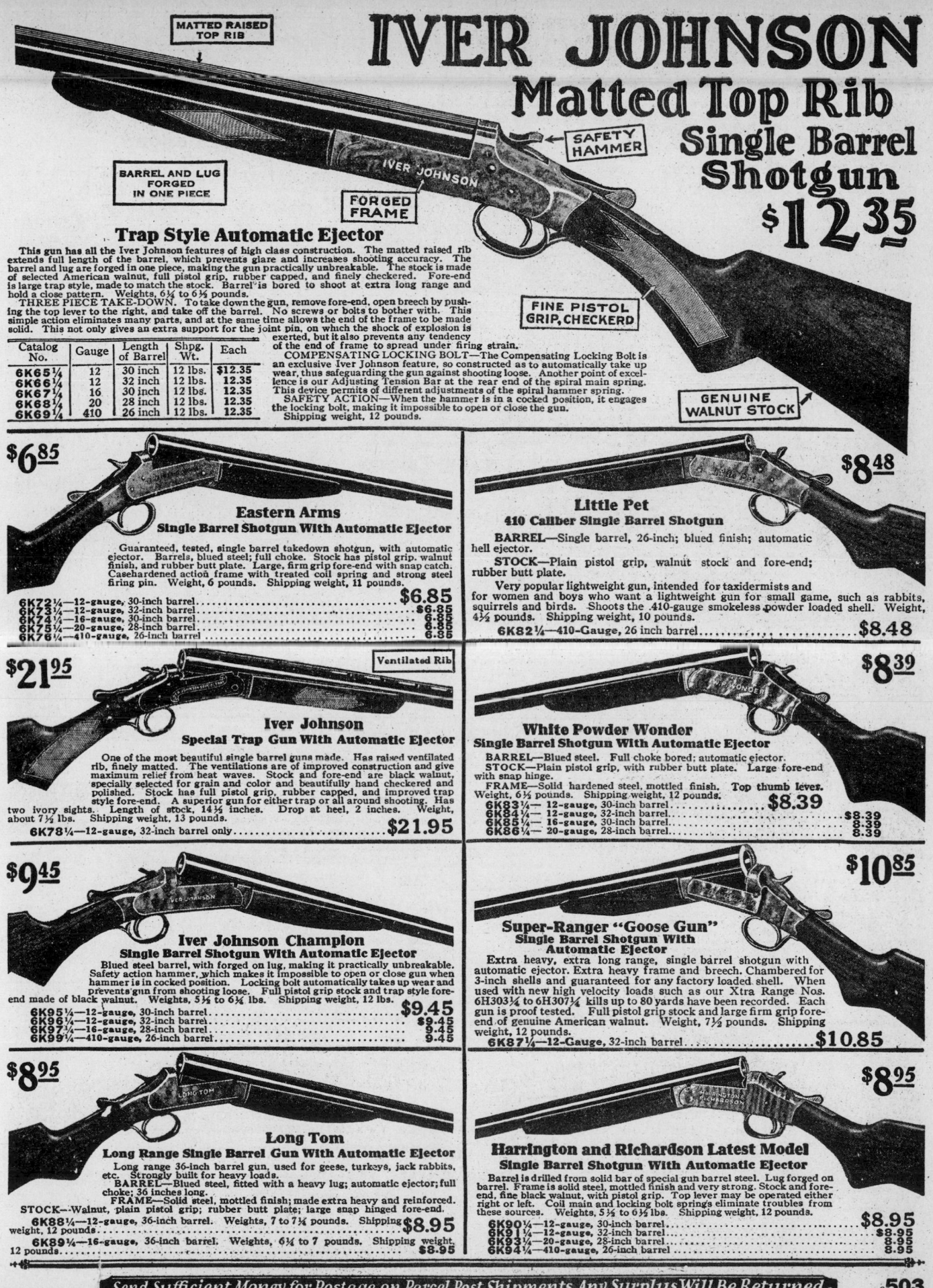

IVER JOHNSON
Matted Top Rib
Single Barrel Shotgun
$12³⁵

MATTED RAISED TOP RIB

SAFETY HAMMER

BARREL AND LUG FORGED IN ONE PIECE

FORGED FRAME

FINE PISTOL GRIP, CHECKERD

GENUINE WALNUT STOCK

Trap Style Automatic Ejector

This gun has all the Iver Johnson features of high class construction. The matted raised rib extends full length of the barrel, which prevents glare and increases shooting accuracy. The barrel and lug are forged in one piece, making the gun practically unbreakable. The stock is made of selected American walnut, full pistol grip, rubber capped, and finely checkered. Fore-end is large trap style, made to match the stock. Barrel is bored to shoot at extra long range and hold a close pattern. Weights, 6¼ to 6½ pounds.

THREE PIECE TAKE-DOWN. To take down the gun, remove fore-end, open breech by pushing the top lever to the right, and take off the barrel. No screws or bolts to bother with. This simple action eliminates many parts, and at the same time allows the end of the frame to be made solid. This not only gives an extra support for the joint pin, on which the shock of explosion is exerted, but it also prevents any tendency of the end of frame to spread under firing strain.

COMPENSATING LOCKING BOLT—The Compensating Locking Bolt is an exclusive Iver Johnson feature, so constructed as to automatically take up wear, thus safeguarding the gun against shooting loose. Another point of excellence is our Adjusting Tension Bar at the rear end of the spiral main spring. This device permits of different adjustments of the spiral hammer spring.

SAFETY ACTION—When the hammer is in a cocked position, it engages the locking bolt, making it impossible to open or close the gun. Shipping weight, 12 pounds.

Catalog No.	Gauge	Length of Barrel	Shpg. Wt.	Each
6K65¼	12	30 inch	12 lbs.	$12.35
6K66¼	12	32 inch	12 lbs.	12.35
6K67¼	16	30 inch	12 lbs.	12.35
6K68¼	20	28 inch	12 lbs.	12.35
6K69¼	410	26 inch	12 lbs.	12.35

$6⁸⁵

Eastern Arms
Single Barrel Shotgun With Automatic Ejector

Guaranteed, tested, single barrel takedown shotgun, with automatic ejector. Barrels, blued steel; full choke. Stock has pistol grip. walnut finish, and rubber butt plate. Large, firm grip fore-end with snap catch. Casehardened action frame with treated coil spring and strong steel firing pin. Weight, 6 pounds. Shipping weight, 11 pounds.

6K72¼—12-gauge, 30-inch barrel......................$6.85
6K73¼—12-gauge, 32-inch barrel......................$6.85
6K74¼—16-gauge, 30-inch barrel...................... 6.85
6K75¼—20-gauge, 28-inch barrel...................... 6.85
6K76¼—410-gauge, 26-inch barrel...................... 6.85

$8⁴⁸

Little Pet
410 Caliber Single Barrel Shotgun

BARREL—Single barrel, 26-inch; blued finish; automatic hell ejector.
STOCK—Plain pistol grip, walnut stock and fore-end; rubber butt plate.
Very popular lightweight gun, intended for taxidermists and for women and boys who want a lightweight gun for small game, such as rabbits, squirrels and birds. Shoots the .410-gauge smokeless powder loaded shell. Weight, 4½ pounds. Shipping weight, 10 pounds.

6K82¼—410-Gauge, 26 inch barrel.....................$8.48

$21⁹⁵

Ventilated Rib

Iver Johnson
Special Trap Gun With Automatic Ejector

One of the most beautiful single barrel guns made. Has raised ventilated rib, finely matted. The ventilations are of improved construction and give maximum relief from heat waves. Stock and fore-end are black walnut, specially selected for grain and color and beautifully hand checkered and polished. Stock has full pistol grip, rubber capped, and improved trap style fore-end. A superior form of either trap or all around shooting. Has two ivory sights. Length of stock, 14½ inches. Drop at heel, 2 inches. Weight, about 7½ lbs. Shipping weight, 13 pounds.

6K78¼—12-gauge, 32-inch barrel only...................$21.95

$8³⁹

White Powder Wonder
Single Barrel Shotgun With Automatic Ejector

BARREL—Blued steel. Full choke bored; automatic ejector.
STOCK—Plain pistol grip, with rubber butt plate. Large fore-end with snap hinge.
FRAME—Solid hardened steel, mottled finish. Top thumb lever. Weight, 6½ pounds. Shipping weight, 12 pounds.

6K83¼—12-gauge, 30-inch barrel......................$8.39
6K84¼—12-gauge, 32-inch barrel......................$8.39
6K85¼—16-gauge, 30-inch barrel...................... 8.39
6K86¼—20-gauge, 28-inch barrel...................... 8.39

$9⁴⁵

Iver Johnson Champion
Single Barrel Shotgun With Automatic Ejector

Blued steel barrel, with forged on lug, making it practically unbreakable. Safety action hammer, which makes it impossible to open or close gun when hammer is in cocked position. Locking bolt automatically takes up wear and prevents gun from shooting loose. Full pistol grip stock and trap style fore-end made of black walnut. Weights, 5⅛ to 6¼ lbs. Shipping weight, 12 lbs.

6K95¼—12-gauge, 30-inch barrel......................$9.45
6K96¼—12-gauge, 32-inch barrel......................$9.45
6K97¼—16-gauge, 28-inch barrel...................... 9.45
6K99¼—410-gauge, 26-inch barrel...................... 9.45

$10⁸⁵

Super-Ranger "Goose Gun"
Single Barrel Shotgun With Automatic Ejector

Extra heavy, extra long range, single barrel shotgun with automatic ejector. Extra heavy frame and breech. Chambered for 3-inch shells and guaranteed for any factory loaded shell. When used with new high velocity loads such as our Xtra Range Nos. 6H303¼ to 6H307¼ kills up to 80 yards have been recorded. Each gun is proof tested. Full pistol grip stock and large firm grip fore-end of genuine American walnut. Weight, 7½ pounds. Shipping weight, 12 pounds.

6K87¼—12-Gauge, 32-inch barrel.....................$10.85

$8⁹⁵

Long Tom
Long Range Single Barrel Gun With Automatic Ejector

Long range 36-inch barrel gun, used for geese, turkeys, jack rabbits, etc. Strongly built for heavy loads.
BARREL—Blued steel, fitted with a heavy lug; automatic ejector; full choke; 36 inches long.
FRAME—Solid steel, mottled finish; made extra heavy and reinforced.
STOCK—Walnut, plain pistol grip; rubber butt plate; large snap hinged fore-end.

6K88¼—12-gauge, 36-inch barrel. Weights, 7 to 7¼ pounds. Shipping weight, 12 pounds...................$8.95
6K89¼—16-gauge, 36-inch barrel. Weights, 6¼ to 7 pounds. Shipping weight, 12 pounds...................$8.95

$8⁹⁵

Harrington and Richardson Latest Model
Single Barrel Shotgun With Automatic Ejector

Barrel is drilled from solid bar of special gun barrel steel. Lug forged on barrel. Frame is solid steel, mottled finish and very strong. Stock and fore-end, fine black walnut, with pistol grip. Top lever may be operated either right or left. Coil main and locking bolt springs eliminate troubles from these sources. Weights, 5½ to 6½ lbs. Shipping weight, 12 pounds.

6K90¼—12-gauge, 30-inch barrel......................$8.95
6K91¼—12-gauge, 32-inch barrel......................$8.95
6K93¼—20-gauge, 28-inch barrel...................... 8.95
6K94¼—410-gauge, 26-inch barrel...................... 8.95

Repeating and Automatic Shotguns

One of the Most Popular Repeaters Ever Made

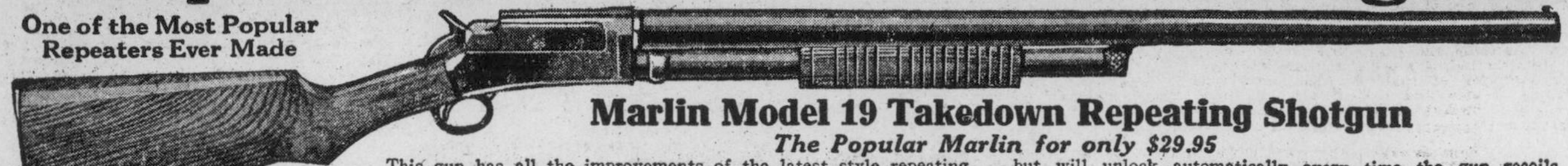

Marlin Model 19 Takedown Repeating Shotgun

The Popular Marlin for only $29.95

$29.95

This gun has all the improvements of the latest style repeating shotguns, and the well known Marlin solid top and side ejector. It has the simplest mechanism ever used in any repeating shotgun. The closed in breech block adds to the strength of the gun and also keeps out the snow, rain and dirt. The mechanism is entirely enclosed and will not clog or freeze up in cold weather. The visible hammer, always in sight, tells instantly whether the gun is cocked. Special design hammer prevents slipping off the thumb and accidental discharge. Automatic safety lock guarantees against hang fire shells

but will unlock automatically every time the gun recoils from the explosion. Barrel is made of special Marlin rolled steel. Chambers bored to accommodate shells up to 2¾ inches long. Stock and fore-end are made of black walnut. Stock is 13½ inches long, with full pistol grip and 2½-inch drop. Holds six shells. Full choke bored. Weighs about 7½ lbs. Shpg. wt., 12 lbs.

6K136¼—12-gauge, 30-inch barrel.............**$29.95**
6K137¼—12-gauge, 32-inch barrel.............**$29.95**

Stevens Improved No. 620 Model 1927 Hammerless Repeating Shotgun

Their Latest Model Repeating Shotgun

$38.39

Shotgun is takedown with hammerless action, visible locking bolt, safety firing pin and independent safety action and side ejection. Barrels are made of high pressure steel, full choke bored. The frame is of drop forging and solid breech, making it very strong. Stock and fore-end made of American walnut, nicely checkered, and with rubber butt plate. Every gun is tested with an excess load and will hold six shells. Chambered to take shells up to 2¾ inches long. Weight, 7¾ pounds. Shipping weight, 12 pounds.

6K124¼—12-gauge, 30-inch barrel. **$38.39**
6K131¼—12-gauge, 32-inch barrel.............**$38.39**
Stevens Improved No. 621 Model 1927
Same gun as above, but equipped with raised matted ribbed top.
6K132¼—12-gauge, 30-inch barrel.............**$41.59**
6K133¼—12-gauge, 32-inch barrel.............**$41.59**

Ranger Repeating Takedown Hammerless Shotgun

$29.95

This repeating shotgun has the same locking device as the automatic shotgun and is unlocked by the recoil of the discharge. This positively prevents accidents from hang fire shells. This action also makes it possible to operate gun with the greatest rapidity. Guaranteed to give service and satisfaction. Barrel is bored from a solid piece of high pressure steel, making it free of all defects, and is full choke bored for any load. Stock and slide handle are made of selected walnut. Full pistol grip stock, 13¾ inches long and with 2⅝-inch drop and hard rubber butt plate. Frame is made

from a solid drop forging. Safety is conveniently placed just in front of trigger. Safety firing pin and side ejection. Shipping weight, 12 pounds.

6K112—12-gauge, 30-inch barrel. **$29.95**
Weight, about 7¾ pounds.
6K113—12-gauge, 32-in. barrel. Weight, about 7½ lbs..$29.95
Same gun as above, but with matted top rib.
6K122—12-gauge, 30-inch barrel. **$34.95**
6K123—12-gauge, 32-inch barrel.............**$34.95**

Winchester Model 1912 Hammerless Repeating Takedown Shotgun

$42.95

Winchester Model 1912 Shotgun. Six-shot. Full pistol grip walnut stock and rubber butt plate. Positive safety trigger lock. Barrel of nickel steel and full choke bore. Has very smooth and easy working action. Weight, 7¼ pounds. Shipping weight, 12 pounds.

6K146¼—12-gauge, 30-inch barrel only....... **$42.95**
Winchester Model 1912 Shotgun, as above, but with raised matted rib on barrel.
6K145¼—12-gauge, 30-inch barrel only....... **$49.95**
Winchester Model 1912 Hammerless Takedown Shotgun.
6K157¼—Same as 6K145¼, but 16-gauge, with 28-inch full choke barrel. Weight, 6 pounds. Shpg. wt., 12 lbs......**$42.95**

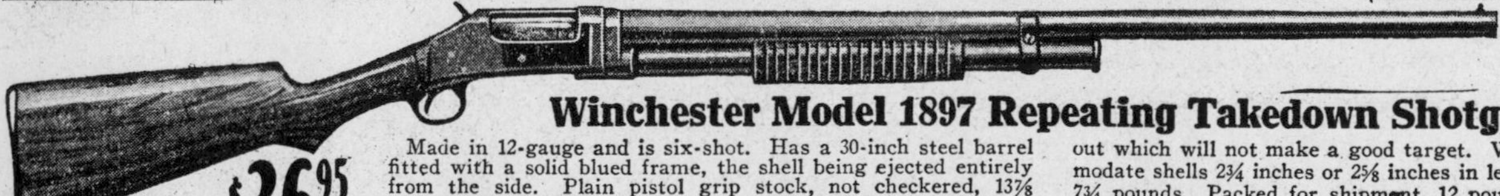

Winchester Model 1897 Repeating Takedown Shotgun

$36.95

Made in 12-gauge and is six-shot. Has a 30-inch steel barrel fitted with a solid blued frame, the shell being ejected entirely from the side. Plain pistol grip stock, not checkered, 13⅞ inches long, 1¾-inch drop at the comb and 2⅜-inch drop at heel. The takedown is strong and simple. It is made with a full choke bore barrel, great care being taken that none goes

out which will not make a good target. Will shoot and accommodate shells 2¾ inches or 2⅝ inches in length. Weight, about 7¾ pounds. Packed for shipment, 12 pounds.

6K148¼—Winchester 12-Gauge.
Repeating Shotgun................**$36.95**

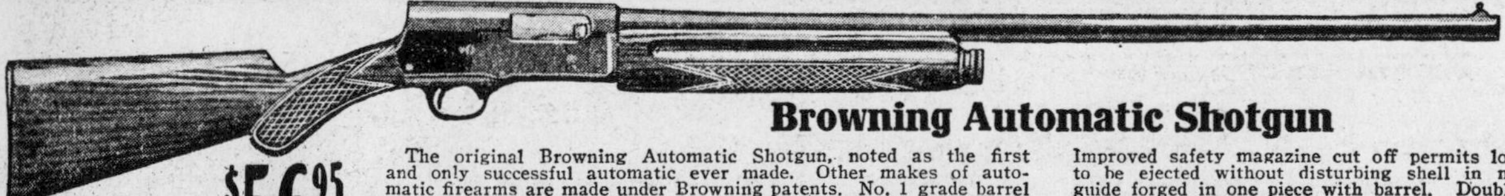

Browning Automatic Shotgun

$56.95
12-Gauge

The original Browning Automatic Shotgun, noted as the first and only successful automatic ever made. Other makes of automatic firearms are made under Browning patents. No. 1 grade barrel of high tensile strength cockerill steel, full choked, blued finish and matted receiver. English walnut stock and fore-end both nicely checkered. Pistol grip stock, 14¼ inches long with 2¼-inch drop.

Improved safety magazine cut off permits loaded shell in chamber to be ejected without disturbing shell in magazine. Barrel ring guide forged in one piece with barrel. Double extractor. Shipping weight, 12 pounds.
6K134—12-gauge, 30-inch barrel. Weight, 7¾ lbs. **$56.95**
6K135—16-gauge, 28-inch barrel. Weight, 7 lbs......**$68.95**

Marlin Model 42A Takedown Repeating Shotgun

$38.95

12-gauge only, with visible hammer, special Marlin rolled steel barrel, handsomely matted. Chambered for both 2¾ and 2⅝-inch shell. Black walnut pistol grip stock and slide handle. Length of stock, 13½ inches. Has improved automatic recoil block which holds the gun firmly locked until after the shell is discharged, then instantly automatically releases same. Full choke barrel, new style quick takedown. Six-shot. Weight, 7½ pounds. Shipping weight, 12 pounds.
6K138¼—12-gauge, 30-inch barrel.................**$38.95**
6K139¼—12-gauge, 32-inch barrel.................**$38.95**

Marlin Improved Model No. 43A Hammerless Repeating Shotgun

$45.95

The hammerless takedown 6-shot repeating shotgun. Solid steel breech, solid top, side ejecting with matted barrel and press button cartridge release. Has automatic recoil hangfire safety device and double extractors. Barrel made of special rolled steel and has a world wide reputation for hard hitting and uniform patterning, having won the world's championship at the Olympic Games of 1920. Gun will handle shells up to 2¾ inches long in both 12-

gauge and 20-gauge guns. Black walnut pistol grip stock and slide handle. Stock, 13½ inches long, 2½ inches drop. Weighs 8 pounds. Shipping weight, 13 pounds.
6K141¼—12-gauge, 30-inch barrel. **$45.95**
6K143¼—12-gauge, 32-inch barrel.................**$45.95**
Same gun as above, but in 20-gauge; full choke barrel. Weight, 5⅞ pounds.
6K144¼—20-gauge, 25-inch barrel.................**$45.95**

Sold in Every Country

The pioneer, long before the days of the covered wagon, had a great appreciation of the dependability of his Remington.

The sportsmen of today fully realize that there are no substitutes for Remington Rifles and Shotguns. Remington's recognized leadership and worldwide prestige in the firearms industry are the result of the high character of their product and the splendid service and satisfactory results obtained by owners of Remingtons.

Famous for a Century

Remington's methods of manufacturing, choosing and proving materials, boring, rifling, testing, inspecting, setting of sights, and working in the action, are scientific, modern and exclusive. The precision of manufacture of Remington firearms, their ease of operation, attractive, symmetrical lines, natural pointing qualities, perfect balance, the ease with which they swing to your shoulder, make you feel as though they were made to your order.

Fires 5 Shots in Rapid Succession

Remington Model 11A Autoloading Shotgun

A Hard Fast, Close Shooter $52.50 Without Rib on Barrel

$59.95 With Rib on Barrel

Remington Autoloading is unquestionably the most popular shotgun up to date. Unusually effective with a heavy load shell. Made to handle all loads of shells and guaranteed to give satisfactory results. The friction ring device acts as shock absorber and equalizes the recoil of the heavy loads. Stock and fore-end of best grade American walnut and nicely checkered. Full pistol grip. Stock is 14 inches long; 2½-inch drop. Barrel is full choke bored, 28 inches long. Wt. 8 lbs. Shpg. wt., 14 lbs. **$52.50**

6K191¼—12-gauge, 28-inch barrel.

Same gun as above, but with raised solid rib on barrel.

6K189¼—12-gauge, 28-inch barrel........................$59.95

Remington No. 10A Repeating Takedown Shotgun

$43.45 Without Top Rib

Recognized as one of the leading repeating shotguns. Is a hard, close shooter. For water fowl, upland game and at the traps. Has very smooth action. Adjustable bushing to take up any loose play that might develop from wear. Stock and fore-end of American walnut. Half pistol grip; 13¾ inches long; 2¾-inch drop. Full choke bored. Shipping weight, 12 pounds.

6K190¼—12-gauge, 30-inch barrel.....**$43.45**

Same gun as above, but with matted raised rib.

6K199¼—12-gauge, 30-inch barrel..........$51.10

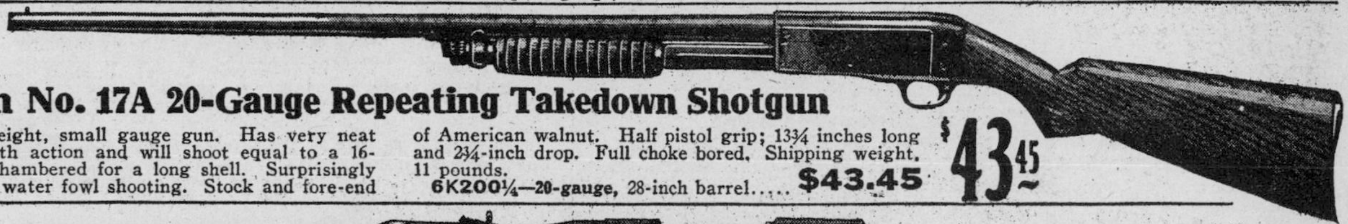

Remington No. 17A 20-Gauge Repeating Takedown Shotgun

$43.45

A wonderful lightweight, small gauge gun. Has very neat appearance and smooth action and will shoot equal to a 16-gauge gun, as it is chambered for a long shell. Surprisingly effective for field and water fowl shooting. Stock and fore-end of American walnut. Half pistol grip; 13¾ inches long and 2¾-inch drop. Full choke bored. Shipping weight, 11 pounds.

6K200¼—20-gauge, 28-inch barrel.....**$43.45**

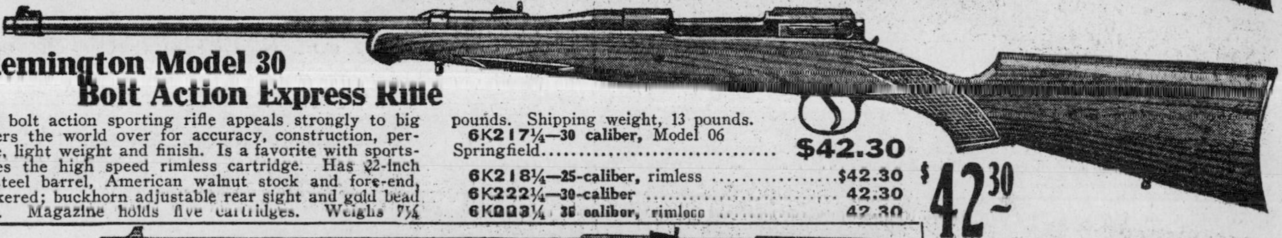

New Remington Model 30 Bolt Action Express Rifle

$42.30

This new bolt action sporting rifle appeals strongly to big game hunters the world over for accuracy, construction, perfect balance, light weight and finish. Is a favorite with sportsmen. Takes the high speed rimless cartridge. Has 22-inch Ordnance steel barrel, American walnut stock and fore-end, nicely checkered; buckhorn adjustable rear sight and gold bead front sight. Magazine holds five cartridges. Weighs 7½ pounds. Shipping weight, 13 pounds.

6K217¼—30 caliber, Model 06 Springfield....................**$42.30**

6K218¼—25-caliber, rimless $42.30

6K222¼—30-caliber 42.30

6K223¼—35-caliber, rimless..... 42.30

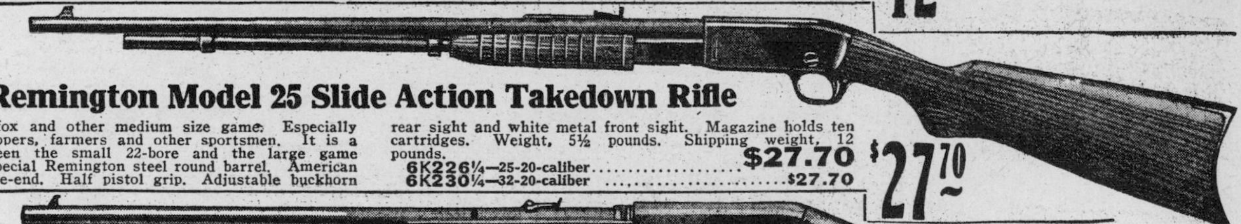

Remington Model 25 Slide Action Takedown Rifle

$27.70

Very suitable for fox and other medium size game. Especially recommended for trappers, farmers and other sportsmen. It is a happy medium between the small 22-bore and the large game rifles. Has 24-inch special Remington steel round barrel. American walnut stock and fore-end. Half pistol grip. Adjustable buckhorn rear sight and white metal front sight. Magazine holds ten cartridges. Weight, 5½ pounds. Shipping weight, 12 pounds.

6K226¼—25-20-caliber......................**$27.70**

6K230¼—32-20-caliber $27.70

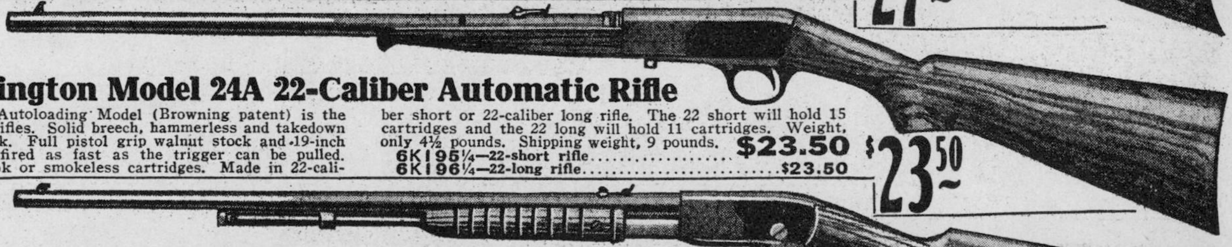

Remington Model 24A 22-Caliber Automatic Rifle

$23.50

The new Remington Autoloading Model (Browning patent) is the last word in automatic rifles. Solid breech, hammerless and takedown with positive safety lock. Full pistol grip walnut stock and 19-inch round barrel. Can be fired as fast as the trigger can be pulled. Will shoot either lesmok or smokeless cartridges. Made in 22-caliber short or 22-caliber long rifle. The 22 short will hold 15 cartridges and the 22 long will hold 11 cartridges. Weight, only 4½ pounds. Shipping weight, 9 pounds.

6K195¼—22-short rifle...................**$23.50**

6K196¼—22-long rifle....................$23.50

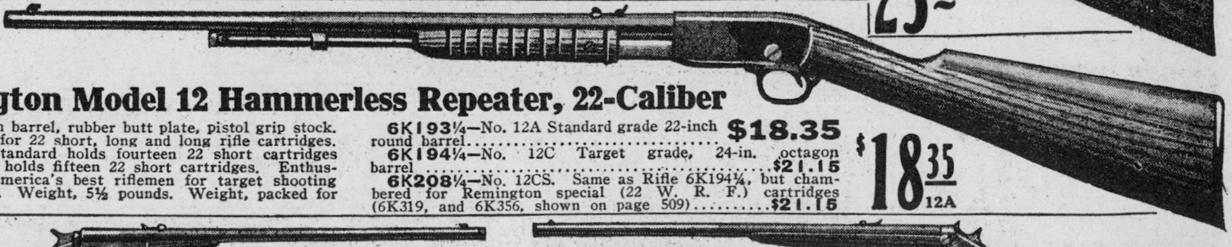

Remington Model 12 Hammerless Repeater, 22-Caliber

$18.35 12A

Has a round or octagon barrel, rubber butt plate, pistol grip stock. Both barrels chambered for 22 short, long and long rifle cartridges. Magazine of No. 12A Standard holds fourteen 22 short cartridges and the No. 12C Target holds fifteen 22 short cartridges. Enthusiastically endorsed by America's best riflemen for target shooting and small game hunting. Weight, 5½ pounds. Weight, packed for shipment, 10 pounds.

6K193¼—No. 12A Standard grade 22-inch round barrel....**$18.35**

6K194¼—No. 12C Target grade, 24-in. octagon barrel...........$21.15

6K208¼—No. 12CS. Same as Rifle 6K194¼, but chambered for Remington special (22 W. R. F.) cartridges (6K319, and 6K356, shown on page 509)........$21.15

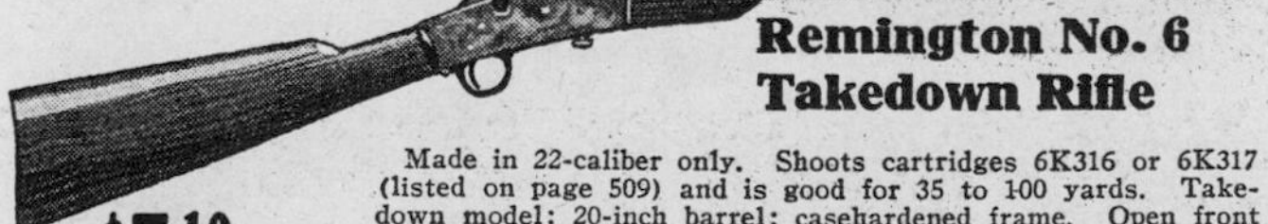

Remington No. 6 Takedown Rifle

$5.10

Made in 22-caliber only. Shoots cartridges 6K316 or 6K317 (listed on page 509) and is good for 35 to 100 yards. Takedown model; 20-inch barrel; casehardened frame. Open front and rear sights and folding peep sight fitted to tang. A reliable, lightweight rifle at a moderate price. Weight, 3¾ pounds. Packed for shipment, 8 pounds.

6K198¼ **$5.10**

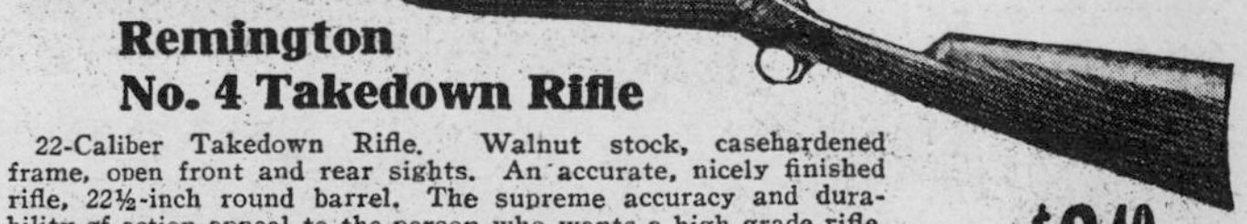

Remington No. 4 Takedown Rifle

$8.40

22-Caliber Takedown Rifle. Walnut stock, casehardened frame, open front and rear sights. An accurate, nicely finished rifle, 22½-inch round barrel. The supreme accuracy and durability of action appeal to the person who wants a high grade rifle. Rim fire. Shoots 22-caliber short, long or long rifle cartridges 6K316, 6K317 or 6K318 (listed on page 509). Weight, about 4½ pounds; packed for shipment, 8 pounds.

6K197¼ **$8.40**

It's Easy to Order From the World's Largest Store. See Page 546

505

Standard American Manufacturers

SMALL BORE RIFLES

Suitable for Hunting Crows, Hawks, Woodchucks and Small Game

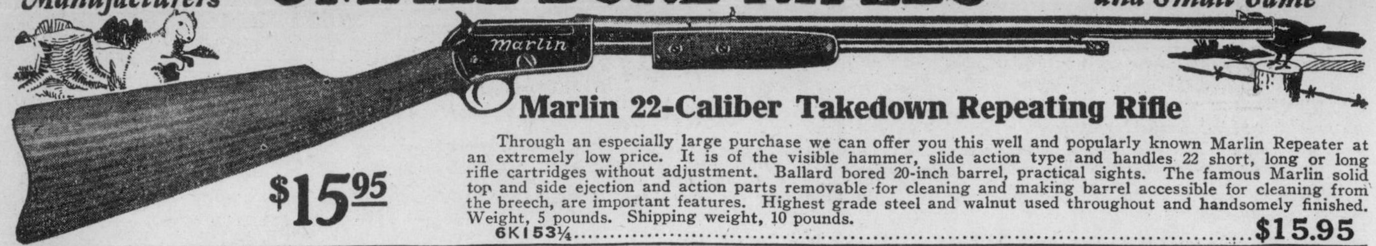

Marlin 22-Caliber Takedown Repeating Rifle

$15.95

Through an especially large purchase we can offer you this well and popularly known Marlin Repeater at an extremely low price. It is of the visible hammer, slide action type and handles 22 short, long or long rifle cartridges without adjustment. Ballard bored 20-inch barrel, practical sights. The famous Marlin solid top and side ejection and action parts removable for cleaning and making barrel accessible for cleaning from the breech, are important features. Highest grade steel and walnut used throughout and handsomely finished. Weight, 5 pounds. Shipping weight, 10 pounds.

6K153¼ $15.95

$20.35

The New Improved Marlin Model 37 Repeating Rifle, 22-Caliber

Similar to 6K153¼ in action, but is heavier. Has 24-inch round barrel with Ballard Rifling assuring accuracy and long life. Full magazine, holding 25 short, 20 long or 18 long rifle cartridges, all three being handled without adjustment. Simple takedown and by lifting out action parts—no tools necessary—these may be kept clean and barrel is made accessible for breech cleaning. Ivory bead front and Rocky Mountain rear sight. Handsomely finished rifle and splendid value. Shipping weight, 10 lbs.

6K154¼ $20.35

$19.85

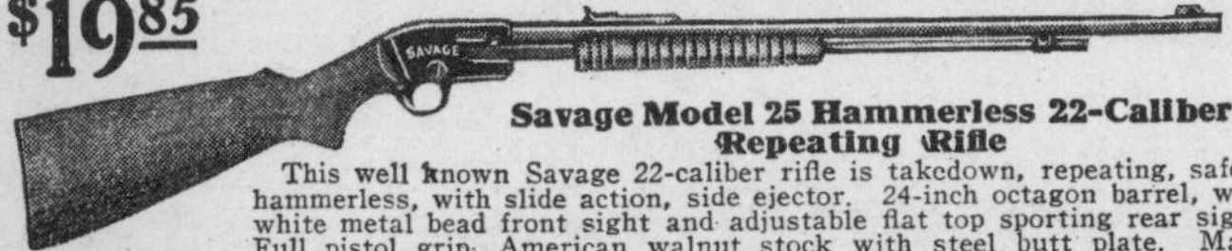

Savage Model 25 Hammerless 22-Caliber Repeating Rifle

This well known Savage 22-caliber rifle is takedown, repeating, safety hammerless, with slide action, side ejector. 24-inch octagon barrel, with white metal bead front sight and adjustable flat top sporting rear sight. Full pistol grip, American walnut stock with steel butt plate. Made to handle 22-caliber short, long or long rifle rim fire cartridges without adjustment. Weight, 5¾ pounds. Shipping weight, 8 pounds.

6K156¼ $19.85

$17.98

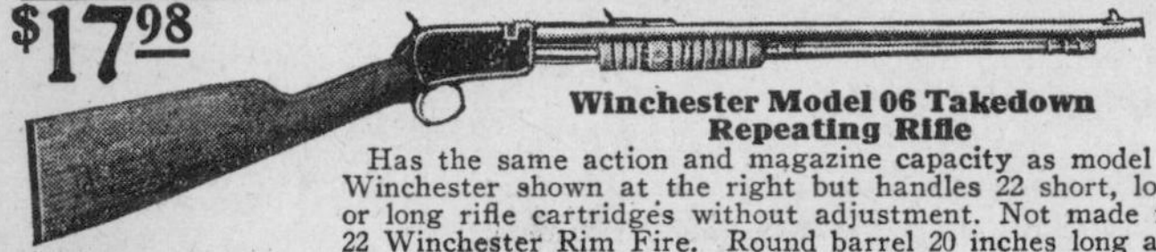

Winchester Model 06 Takedown Repeating Rifle

Has the same action and magazine capacity as model 90 Winchester shown at the right but handles 22 short, long or long rifle cartridges without adjustment. Not made for 22 Winchester Rim Fire. Round barrel 20 inches long and stock has shotgun butt plate. Good sights and is a thoroughly reliable and popular rifle. Weight, 5¾ pounds. Shipping weight, 10 pounds.

6K174¼ $17.98

$16.95

Savage "Sporter" 22-Caliber Repeating Rifle

New Savage model 23A Repeating Rifle. Bolt action. Pistol grip walnut stock, clip magazine to hold five cartridges. Bead front sight and adjustable open sporting rear sight. Metal butt plate. Weight, 6 pounds. Shipping weight, 16 pounds.

Cat. No.	Caliber	Barrel	Shoots Cartridges	Each
6K181¼	22	23 in.	22 Short, long or long rifle	$16.95
6K201¼	25-20	25 in.	25-20 Repeater, black or smokeless	20.95
6K202¼	32-20	25 in.	32-20 Repeater, black or smokeless	20.95

Extra Magazines for Savage Rifles

6K183—22-caliber ...45c
6K206—25-20 caliber..68c
6K207—32-20 caliber..68c
Shpg. wt., either style, 6 oz.

$12.50

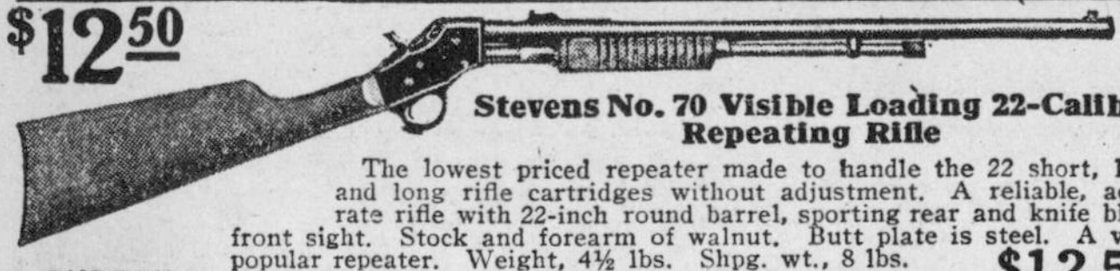

Stevens No. 70 Visible Loading 22-Caliber Repeating Rifle

The lowest priced repeater made to handle the 22 short, long and long rifle cartridges without adjustment. A reliable, accurate rifle with 22-inch round barrel, sporting rear and knife blade front sight. Stock and forearm of walnut. Butt plate is steel. A very popular repeater. Weight, 4½ lbs. Shpg. wt., 8 lbs.

6K205¼ $12.50

$8.98

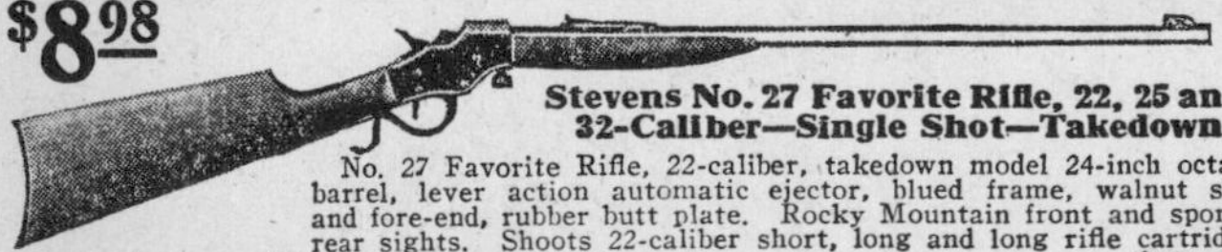

Stevens No. 27 Favorite Rifle, 22, 25 and 32-Caliber—Single Shot—Takedown

No. 27 Favorite Rifle, 22-caliber, takedown model 24-inch octagon barrel, lever action automatic ejector, blued frame, walnut stock and fore-end, rubber butt plate. Rocky Mountain front and sporting rear sights. Shoots 22-caliber short, long and long rifle cartridges. Weight, 4½ pounds. Shipping weight, 7 pounds.

6K212¼ $8.98
6K188¼—As above, but 25-caliber rim fire $8.98
6K192¼—As above, but 32-caliber rim fire 8.98
6K213¼—Stevens No. 17. Same as 6K212¼, but with round barrel 8.55

$6.35

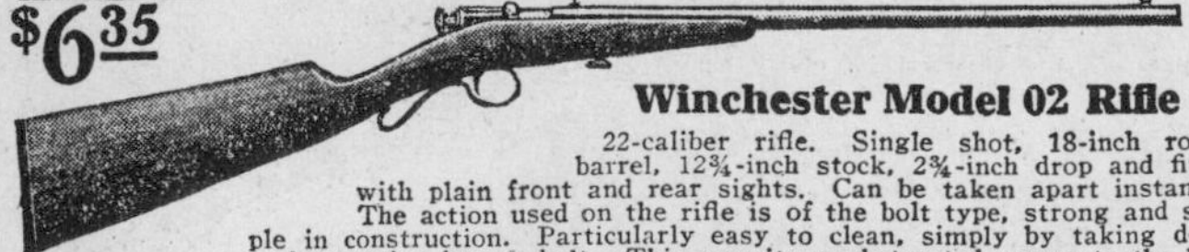

Winchester Model 02 Rifle

22-caliber rifle. Single shot, 18-inch round barrel, 12¾-inch stock, 2¾-inch drop and fitted with plain front and rear sights. Can be taken apart instantly. The action used on the rifle is of the bolt type, strong and simple in construction. Particularly easy to clean, simply by taking down and removing breech bolt. This permits unobstructed access to the barrel. Shoot cartridges 6K316 and 6K317. Weight, 3 lbs. Shpg. wt., 6 lbs.

6K178¼ $6.35

$2.55

Hamilton Single Shot Rifle, Model 27

Has 16-inch round tapered barrel. Adjustable rear and knife front sights. Will shoot 22 short, or 22 long rim fire cartridges. Walnut finish stock and fore-end. Length, over all, 30 inches. Weight, 2½ pounds. Shipping weight, 5 pounds.

6K233¼ $2.55

$24.30

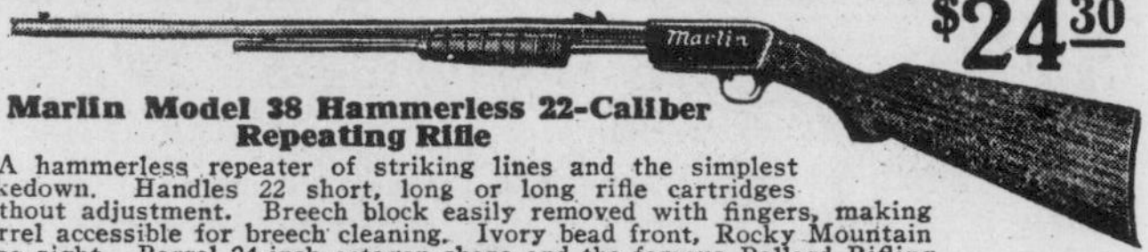

Marlin Model 38 Hammerless 22-Caliber Repeating Rifle

A hammerless repeater of striking lines and the simplest takedown. Handles 22 short, long or long rifle cartridges without adjustment. Breech block easily removed with fingers, making barrel accessible for breech cleaning. Ivory bead front, Rocky Mountain rear sight. Barrel 24-inch octagon shape and the famous Ballard Rifling assures accuracy and long life through depth and smoothness of grooves. Weight, 5½ pounds. Shipping weight, 10 pounds.

6K155¼ $24.30

$21.95

Winchester Model 57—Bolt Action Repeating Rifle

Military Style

Chambered for 22 long rifle cartridges only. Rifle is solid frame with 22-inch round blued steel barrel. One piece pistol grip stock and fore-end of selected walnut with steel butt plate. A consistent match winning rifle. The clip magazine holds five cartridges. Wide blade front sight. Rear sight capable of minute adjustment in both directions, windage and elevation. Weight, 5 pounds. Shipping weight, 10 pounds.

6K172¼ $21.95

$19.95

Winchester Model 90 Takedown Repeating Rifle

This rifle is fitted with 24-inch octagon blued barrel, adjustable rear sight and sporting front sight. Made in 22-caliber rim fire only, and although we can furnish rifles for three different sizes of 22-caliber rim fire cartridges, each style will chamber but one size cartridge. The rifle for 22-short cartridges will not take 22 long, 22 long rifle, or 22 Winchester rim fire.

Catalog No.	Model	Caliber	Barrel, Inches	Wt., Lbs.	Shpg. Wt.	Shoots Cartridges	Number of Shots	Each
6K175¼	90	22 Short	24 Octagon	6½	10 lbs.	6K316	15	$19.95
6K179¼	90	22 L. R.	24 Octagon	6½	10 lbs.	6K318	11	19.95
6K176¼	90	22 W.R.F.	24 Octagon	6½	10 lbs.	6K319	10	19.95

$9.75

Hamilton 22-Caliber Hammerless Takedown Repeating Rifle, Model 39

Chambered for 22 short only. Has round barrel, 21¼ inches long, with knife blade front sight and adjustable rear sight. American black walnut stock and fore-end. Bronze lined barrel accurately rifled and has solid steel breech. Will hold fifteen 22-caliber short rim fire cartridges, but will not chamber long or long rifle cartridges. Weight, 4 pounds. Shpg. wt., 6 lbs.

6K241¼ $9.75

$5.45

Stevens Crack Shot Rifle, 22 Caliber—Single Shot

No. 26 Crack Shot, 22-caliber, takedown model 20-inch round barrel, lever action, blued frame, knife blade front and open rear sights. Specially designed for smokeless powder ammunition. Shoots 22-caliber short, long and long rifle cartridges. Weight, 3¾ pounds. Shipping weight, 8 pounds.

6K211¼ $5.45

$4.50

Stevens Little Scout Rifle, 22-Caliber—Single Shot

No. 14¼ Little Scout, 22-caliber takedown model, 20-inch round barrel, casehardened frame, blued steel butt plate, nickel silver knife blade front and open rear sights. Shoots 22-caliber short, long and long rifle cartridges. Weight, 2¾ pounds.

6K210¼—Shipping weight, 8 pounds $4.50

$4.25

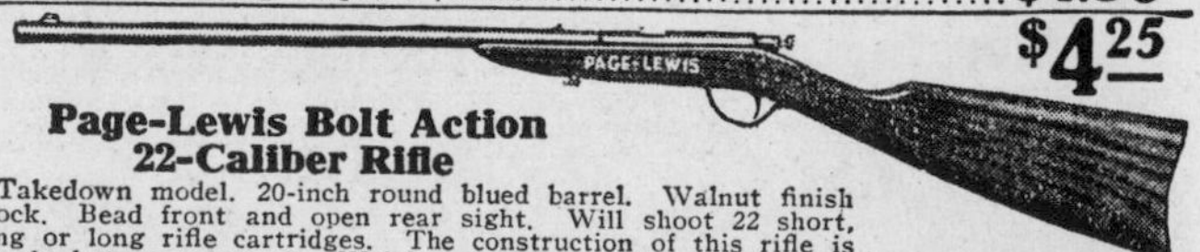

Page-Lewis Bolt Action 22-Caliber Rifle

Takedown model. 20-inch round blued barrel. Walnut finish stock. Bead front and open rear sight. Will shoot 22 short, long or long rifle cartridges. The construction of this rifle is simple but very strong. Weight, 3 pounds. Shipping weight, 5 pounds.

6K173¼ $4.25

$3.80

Stevens 22-Caliber Junior Rifle, No. 11 Single Shot

Has 20-inch round blued steel barrel, takedown model, positive extractor and one-piece military bolt. Bright metal knife front and flat top open rear sight. Will shoot 22 short, long or long rifle cartridges. Weight, 2¾ pounds. Shipping weight, 6½ pounds.

6K209¼ $3.80

HIGH POWER RIFLES

The Most Popular Models

Deer, Bear or Moose and all North American Big Game

FOR LARGE GAME **$39.95**

For 270 Winchester and 30 Gov't. 06 Centerfire Cartridges

Winchester Model 54 High Power Bolt Action Rifle

This Winchester rifle is simple, strong, and the very latest high power rifle made by the Winchester Company. Has 24-inch round tapered nickel steel barrel and one-piece selected walnut stock and fore-arm. Stock is handsomely checkered and has full pistol grip. Swivel eyes for sling strap attached to stock and forearm. The 270-caliber bullet has a very high velocity, and the 30-caliber is recognized as one of the finest cartridges for all around big game shooting. Rifle weighs 7¾ pounds. Shipping weight, 16 pounds.

6K165¼—270-caliber................................$39.95
6K166¼—30 Gov't. 06-Caliber.........................$39.95

$51.20

Remington Model 8A Autoloading Rifle, Takedown Style

A powerful rifle for big game and very popular with hunters. Has 22-inch ordnance steel barrel, straight grip stock of American walnut fitted with rifle style steel butt plate. Buckhorn adjustable step rear sight and white metal steel bead front sight. Magazine holds five cartridges. Length over all, 41½ inches; when taken down, 23 inches. Weight, 7¾ pounds. Shipping weight, 10 pounds.

6K224¼—30-caliber, rimless.......................$51.20
6K225¼—35-caliber, rimless........................$51.20

$46.15

Savage Model 99G High Power Takedown Repeating Rifle

Round barrel, of high pressure steel. Shotgun butt plate, full pistol grip, checkered stock and fore-end made of American walnut. Rifle has a rotary style magazine and indicator on top of receiver to show whether the rifle is cocked. White metal bead front sight and adjustable flat top sporting rear sight. 250-300 and 30-30 caliber have 22-inch barrel and weigh 6¾ pounds, and 300-caliber has 24-inch barrel and weighs 7 pounds. Shipping weight, 10 pounds. $46.15

6K185¼—30-caliber.................................$46.15
6K187¼—250-300-caliber............................$46.15
6K203¼—300-caliber................................46.15

$31.98

Winchester Model 94 Solid Frame Repeating Rifle

The well known lever action style, noted for its simple mechanism, accuracy and reliability. Has 26-inch solid frame octagon nickel steel barrel. Has sporting rear sight with sliding elevation, and sporting front sight. Stock and fore end of selected walnut. Full length magazine with capacity of nine cartridges. Straight grip and steel rifle butt plate. Weighs 7¾ pounds. Shipping weight, 12 pounds.

6K167¼—30-30-caliber..............................$31.98
6K168¼—32 Winchester Special Caliber...............$31.98

$23.65

Winchester Model 92 Carbine

A rifle for medium size game in standard calibers, shorter and lighter in weight, making it less burdensome to carry afield. Solid frame, with full magazine. 20-inch round barrel fitted with folding carbine rear sight and blade front sight. Lever action. Selected walnut stock and fore-end. Capacity, 12 shots. Weight, 5¾ pounds. Shipping weight, 11 pounds. $23.65

6K170¼—25-30-caliber..............................$23.65
6K171¼—32-20-caliber..............................$23.65

$40.95

Remington Model 14A Slide Action Repeating Rifle

The only high power slide action repeater on the market. Its smooth, dependable action, perfect balance and natural shooting qualities are outstanding features. Has 22-inch ordnance steel barrel, American walnut stock and fore-end, half pistol grip, rifle style steel butt plate. Buckhorn adjustable step rear sight and white metal bead front sight. Magazine holds five cartridges, and with one in chamber gives a capacity of six shots without reloading. Length over all, 41 inches; when taken down, 27½ inches. Weight, 6¾ pounds. Shipping weight, 10 lbs.

6K231¼—32-caliber, rimless........................$40.95
6K232¼—35-caliber, rimless........................$40.95

$34.85

Savage Carbine Model 99H

This well known carbine, of solid frame design, has 20-inch special round barrel. American walnut pistol grip stock and fore-end of plain design with steel butt plate, making a very serviceable firearm. Has all the well known Savage features and weighs 6½ pounds. Shipping weight, 10 pounds.

6K186¼—303-caliber................................$34.85
6K204¼—30-30-caliber..............................$34.85

$27.95

Winchester Model 94 Carbine

Made only in solid frame style, will full length magazine; capacity of 7 cartridges. 20-inch round nickel steel barrel, fitted with folding carbine rear sight and blade front sight, lever action. Selected walnut stock and fore-end. This carbine and these two cartridges are especially popular among deer and black bear hunters. Weight, 6½ lbs. Shipping weight, 11 pounds.

6K163¼—30-30-caliber..............................$27.95
6K164¼—32 Winchester Special......................$27.95

$38.95

Winchester Model 55 Lever Action Repeating Rifle. Takedown Model

A new model sporting rifle for deer and similar game. As dependable and has same action as Model 94, but lighter weight and takedown. Has 24-inch round tapered nickel steel barrel, selected American walnut stock and fore-end. Sporting rear sight with sliding elevation and Lyman gold bead sight. Lever action. Capacity, 5 shots. Weight, 6¾ pounds. Shipping weight, 10 pounds.

6K169¼—30-30-caliber..............................$38.95

Low Prices on High Quality Air Rifles

1 POUND DROP SHOT

Air Rifle Shot

One-pound box. For use in any of the air rifles on this page. Shipping wt., 1¼ pounds.

6K807
Per lb. 19c

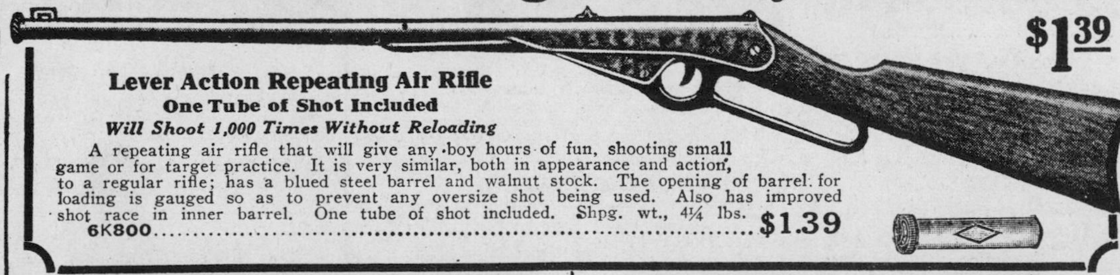

Lever Action Repeating Air Rifle
One Tube of Shot Included
Will Shoot 1,000 Times Without Reloading

$1.39

A repeating air rifle that will give any boy hours of fun, shooting small game or for target practice. It is very similar, both in appearance and action, to a regular rifle; has a blued steel barrel and walnut stock. The opening of barrel for loading is gauged so as to prevent any oversize shot being used. Also has improved shot race in inner barrel. One tube of shot included. Shpg. wt., 4¼ lbs.

6K800..$1.39

Air Rifle Shot

In tube container, patent top. Handy for loading magazines of repeating rifles. Contains 4½ oz. or about 250 pellets. Shpg. wt., 1 lb.

6K806
3 for 19c

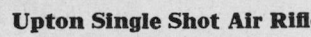

Upton Single Shot Air Rifle
One Tube of Shot Included

Single shot. Lever action. Shoots air rifle shot. The frame is gunmetal finished and strongly made. Walnut stock, nicely finished. Length of barrel, 19 inches; length over all, 31 in. Strongly made. Weight, 1¾ lbs. Shpg. wt., 3½ lbs.

6K804—With tube of shot.........................$1.00

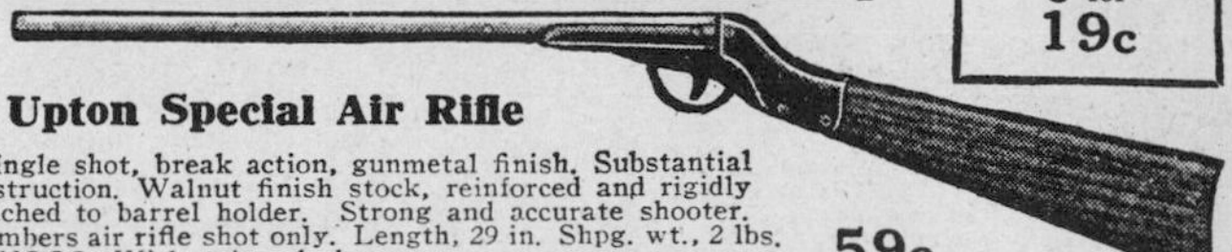

Upton Special Air Rifle

Single shot, break action, gunmetal finish. Substantial construction. Walnut finish stock, reinforced and rigidly attached to barrel holder. Strong and accurate shooter. Chambers air rifle shot only. Length, 29 in. Shpg. wt., 2 lbs.

6K802—With tube of shot.........................59c

$3.88

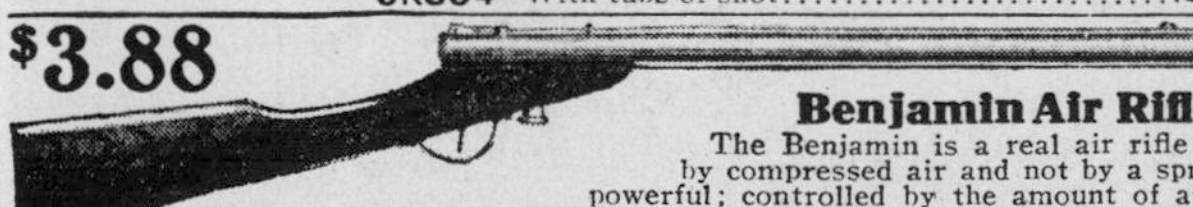

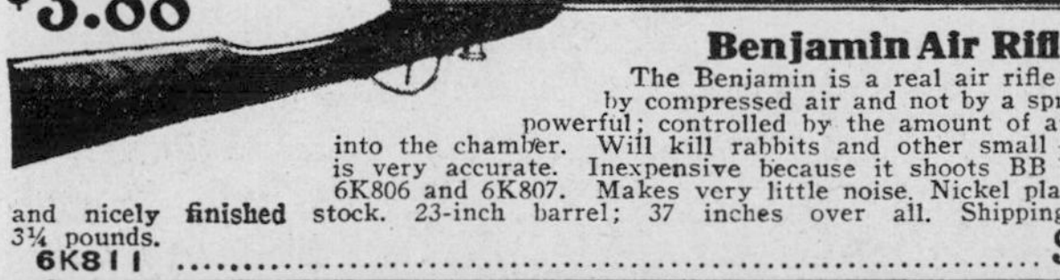

Benjamin Air Rifle

The Benjamin is a real air rifle operating by compressed air and not by a spring. Very powerful; controlled by the amount of air pumped into the chamber. Will kill rabbits and other small game and is very accurate. Inexpensive because it shoots BB shot, our 6K806 and 6K807. Makes very little noise. Nickel plated barrel and nicely finished stock. 23-inch barrel; 37 inches over all. Shipping weight, 3¼ pounds.

6K811...$3.88

$4.48

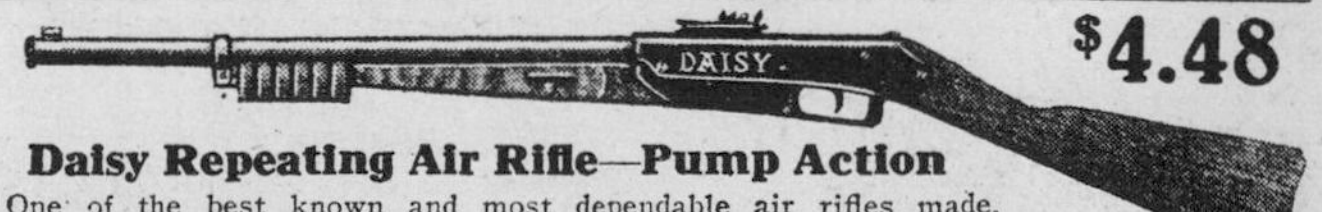

Daisy Repeating Air Rifle—Pump Action

One of the best known and most dependable air rifles made. Metal parts are blued finish and with genuine walnut stock. Has adjustable rear sight and stationary blade front sight. Holds 50 BB air rifle shot in magazine. Length over all, 38 inches. Weight, 3¼ pounds. Shipping weight, 5 pounds.

6K803¼..$4.48

See Index and Information Pages 542 to 570

P 2507

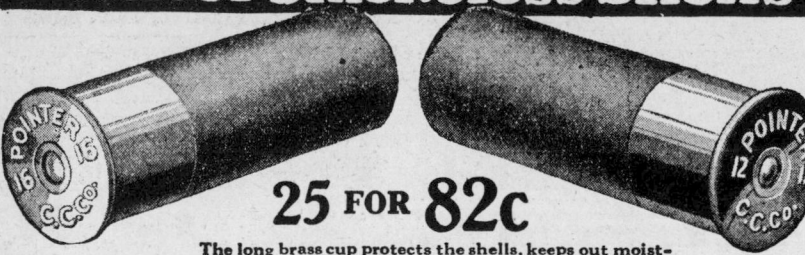

for Ammunition?

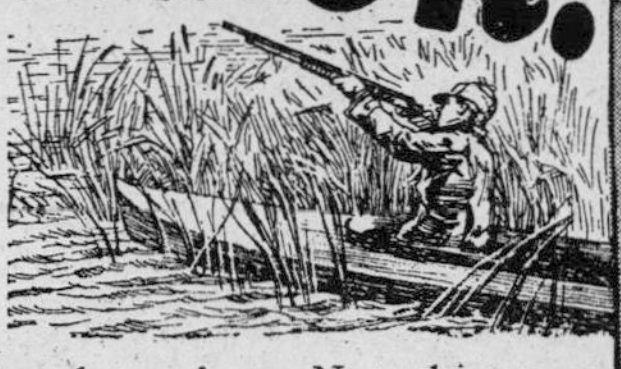

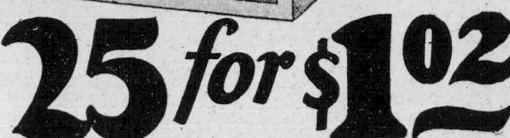

You Cannot Buy Better Shells

One of the largest, most prominent factories manufactures our ammunition. Our shells are exactly the same, loaded with the same powder and shot, and made in the same factory that makes one of the highest grade, nationally advertised shells which sell at prices much higher than ours. The enormous quantities we buy and slight margin of profit we add to our low factory cost make possible our low prices. Note the extra low prices on case lots. Sears guarantee backs every shell.

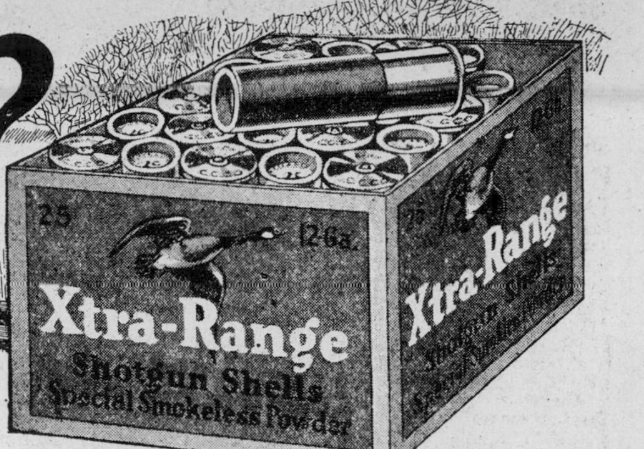

Xtra Range Smokeless Shells

Get Birds That Others Cannot Reach. For Range When You Need It.

As the result of the special progressive burning powder with which this shell is loaded it actually gives 15 to 20 yards greater range and holds a closer, uniform pattern even at the maximum distance. This special smokeless powder develops great energy with very low breech pressure and light recoil, making a fast, hard hitting, close shooting, extra long range load. Loaded in a special steel locked shell which represents the strongest and best type of construction known. Loaded with uniform size, selected **chilled** shot **only.**

25 for $1.02

12-Gauge Shells

2¾ Inches Long After Fired

Catalog No.	Oz. of Shot	Size of Chil'd Shot	Per Box 25 Shells	Per 100 Shells	Per Case, 500 Shells
6K475¼ 6K476¼ 6K477¼	1¼	2 4 5	$1.02	$4.04	$19.60
6K478¼ 6K479¼	1¼	6 7	1.02	4.04	19.60
6K480¼	1¼	B.B. Drop	1.02	4.04	19.60

16-Gauge Shells

2 9/16 Inches Long After Fired

Catalog No.	Oz. of Shot	Size of Chil'd Shot	Per Box, 25 Shells	Per 100 Shells	Per, Case 500 Shells
6K481¼ 6K482¼ 6K483¼	1⅛	4 6 7½	95c	$3.80	$18.20

20-Gauge Shells

2¾ Inches Long After Fired

Catalog No.	Oz. of Shot	Size of Chil'd Shot	Per Box, 25 Shells	Per 100 Shells	Per Case, 500 Shells
6K484¼ 6K485¼ 6K486¼	1	4 6 7½	93c	$3.72	$17.60

410-Gauge Shells

2½ Inches Long After Fired

Catalog No.	Oz. of Shot	Size of Chil'd Shot	Per Box, 25 Shells	Per 100 Shells	Per Case, 500 Shells
6K487¼ 6K488¼	⅜	6 7½	62c	$2.44	$11.60

Buy by the Case. You save in cost and you save in freight charges. Get your neighbor to join you in an order.

Loads Recommended for Game

KIND OF GAME	12-Gauge Dr. Powder	12-Gauge Oz. Shot	16-Ga'ge Dr. Powder	16-Ga'ge Oz. Shot	20-Ga'ge Dr. Powder	20-Ga'ge Oz. Shot	410-Gauge Dr. Powder	410-Gauge Oz. Shot	Sizes of Shot
Large Ducks, Geese, Turkey....	3¼	1⅛	2½	1	2¼	⅞			2, 4, 5, 6 BB
Medium Ducks, Prairie Chickens, Grouse, Pheasants, Crows...........	3 or 3¼	1¼ or 1⅛	2½	1	2¼	⅞	5/6	3/10	4, 5, 6 or 7½
Squirrels, Rabbits.	3	1⅛	2½	1	2¼	⅞	5/6	3/10	4, 5 or 6
Small Ducks, Pigeons..........	3	1¼ or 1⅛	2½	1	2¼	⅞	5/6	3/10	6 or 7½
Quail, Woodcock, Snipe, Shore Birds	3	1 or 1⅛	2½	1	2¼	⅞	5/6	3/10	7½
Trap Shooting..	3	1¼							
Long Range Shots for all above classes and for maximum loads in Smaller Gauges. Very effective at Short Ranges also, give close uniform patterns that mean clean kills.	Xtra Range	1¼	Xtra Range	1⅛	Xtra Range	1	Xtra Range	⅜	2, 4, 5, 6, 7 or 7½ B. B. for Large Birds, Foxes.

Do not be misguided in your selections by information from those of limited experience. Often times a good natural shooter is successful with a certain load and this influences less capable men to shoot that load. Both would be more successful with another load far more suitable. The best informed will usually choose smaller shot i. e. 6 or 7½ for all round use for all game except the larger species named in the first group.

Shipping weights: Box of 25 shells, 5 lbs.; box of 100 shells, 14 lbs.; box of 500 shells, 65 lbs.

Shells Cannot Be Shipped by Parcel Post

For Hunting Clothing See Page 400.

Metallic Cartridges

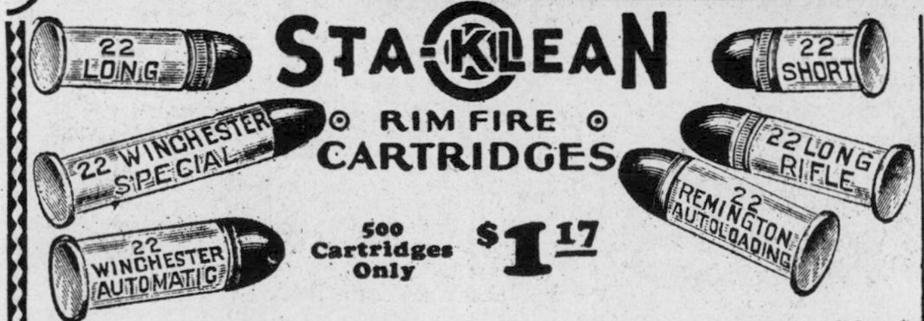

STA-KLEAN

RIM FIRE CARTRIDGES

500 Cartridges Only $1.17

Prevent corrosion and pitting. The Shooters' Delight. Prolongs life of your rifle. Buy a box of these new Sta-Klean cartridges on our recommendation. The trouble-free cartridge that, with the non-corrosive priming mixture, keeps your gun bore clean and free from rust or corrosion.

Catalog No.	Cannot be sent by Parcel Post — Caliber	For 50	For 100	For 500	Gr'ns Powder	Bullet Wt., Gr'ns	Wt., per 100
6K315	B. B. Caps..................	......	$0.25	$1.17	.....	20	7 oz.
6K316	22 Short....................	16c	.30	1.46	3	29	¾ lb.
6K317	22 Long.....................	22c	.41	2.00	5	35	1 lb.
6K318	22 Long Rifle...............	25c	.48	2.33	5	40	1¼ lbs.
6K328	22 Long Rifle Hollow Point....	28c	.53	2.53	5	38	1¼ lbs.
6K319	22 Spec. for Mod. 90 Win.....	36c	.70	3.47	7	45	1¼ lbs.
6K323	22 Rem. Auto. Loading.......	40c	.78	3.87	.....	45	1 lb.
6K324	22 Winchester Auto..........	40c	.78	3.87	.....	45	1 lb.
6K325	25 Stevens Rim Fire.........	55c	1.08	5.33	11	65	2 lbs.
6K326	32 Short Rim Fire...........	41c	.80	3.94	9	80	1¾ lbs.
6K327	32 Long Rim Fire............	47c	.92	4.52	13	90	2 lbs.

Black Powder Rifle Cartridges

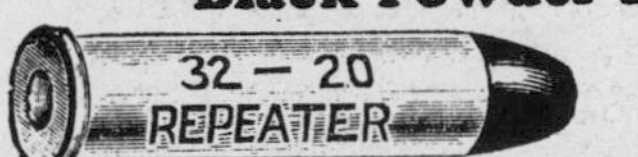

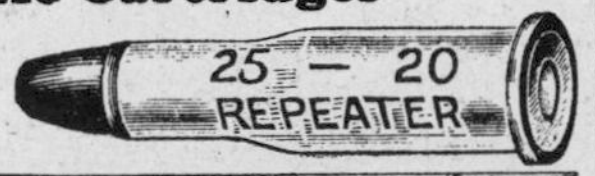

Catalog No.	Cannot be sent by Parcel Post — Caliber	For 50	For 100	For 500	Grn's Powder	Bullet Wt., Gr'ns	Wt., per 100
6K331	25-20 Repeating Rifles........	$1.05	$2.07	$10.28	17	86	2 lbs.
6K336	32-20 Repeating Rifles........	1.05	2.07	10.28	20	115	3 lbs.
6K340	38-40 Repeating Rifles........	1.26	2.49	12.38	40	180	4½ lbs.
6K342	44-40 Repeating Rifles........	1.26	2.49	12.38	40	200	5 lbs.
6K346	45-70 Caliber 405 Gr..........	For 20 $1.01	For 100 4.99		70	405	10 lbs.

Center Fire Smokeless Rifle Cartridges

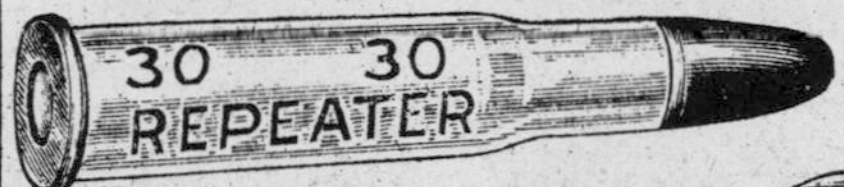

Cartridges Cannot Be Sent By Parcel Post.

If in doubt about caliber, send a sample shell that has been shot, or send the cover of the box.

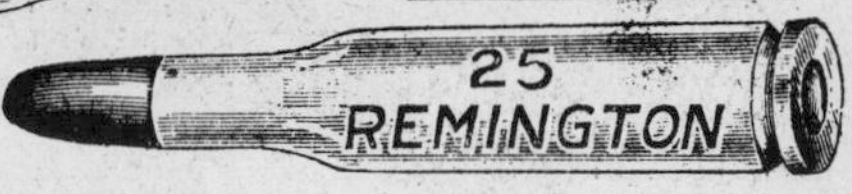

Center fire smokeless rifle cartridges

Catalog No.	Cannot be sent by Parcel Post — Kind of Bullet	Caliber	For 50	For 100	Bullet Wt., Grains	Weight, per 100
6K360	M. P.	25-20 for Repeating Rifles...	$1.31	$2.59	86	2¼ lbs.
6K361	S. P.	25-20 for Repeating Rifles...	1.31	2.59	86	2¼ lbs.
6K365	M. P.	32-20 for Repeating Rifles...	1.31	2.59	115	2½ lbs.
6K366	S. P.	32-20 for Repeating Rifles...	1.31	2.59	115	3 lbs.
6K373	S. P.	351 Self Loading...........	2.24	4.45	180	4½ lbs.

Sporting rifle cartridges, center fire, smokeless powder. If in doubt about caliber, send a sample shell that has been shot or send cover of box.

Catalog No.	Kind of Bullet	Cartridges cannot be sent by Parcel Post — Caliber	For 20	For 100	Gr'ns Powder	Bullet Wt., Gr'ns	Wt., 100, Lbs.
6K376	S. P.	22 Hi-Power for Savage Rifles	$1.06	$5.25	12	70	3¾
6K378	Expand'g	25-35 for Winchester Rifles..	.93	4.59	19	117	4¼
6K399	Expand'g	250-3000 for Savage Rifles...	1.18	5.84	..	100	4
6K379	M. P.	30-30 for Repeating Rifles...	1.07	5.28	23	170	5
6K380	S. P.	30-30 for Repeating Rifles...	1.07	5.28	23	170	5
6K398	Expand'g	300 Savage Repeating Rifles..	1.33	6.56	.....	150	4½
6K382	S. P.	303 Savage Repeating Rifles .	1.07	5.28	27	190	6¼
6K383	Expand'g	30 U. S. Army..............	1.41	6.95	35	180	7½
6K385	S. P.	32-40 for Repeating Rifles...	.90	4.46	24	165	5½
6K387	Expand'g	32 Winchester Special.......	1.06	5.26	.....	170	5¾
6K389	S. P.	38-55 for Repeating Rifles...	1.13	5.58	26	255	6½
6K400	Expand'g	270 Caliber................	1.53	7.61	.....	.....	.....

Rimless High Power Smokeless Cartridges

Catalog No.	Kind of Bullet	Cannot be sent by Parcel Post — Caliber	For 20	For 100	Bullet Weight	Weight, per 100
6K391	Expand'g	25 Remington Rimless........	$0.93	$4.59	100 grs.	4¼ lbs.
6K392	Expand'g	30 Gov't '06................	1.54	7.63	180 grs.	8 lbs.
6K393	S. P.	30 Remington Rimless........	1.07	5.28	170 grs.	6 lbs.
6K395	S. P.	32 Remington Rimless........	1.07	5.28	170 grs.	6 lbs.
6K397	Expand'g	35 Remington Rimless........	1.18	5.84	200 grs.	7 lbs.

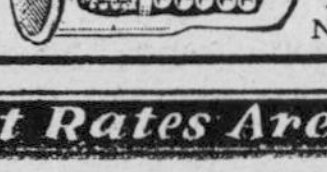

Shot Cartridges

22-caliber loaded with No. 12 shot.

Catalog No.	Caliber	For 50	For 100	Wt., 100
6K408	22 Long, R. F.	37c	72c	¾ lb.

Parcel Post, Express and Freight Rates Are on Pages 542 to 545.

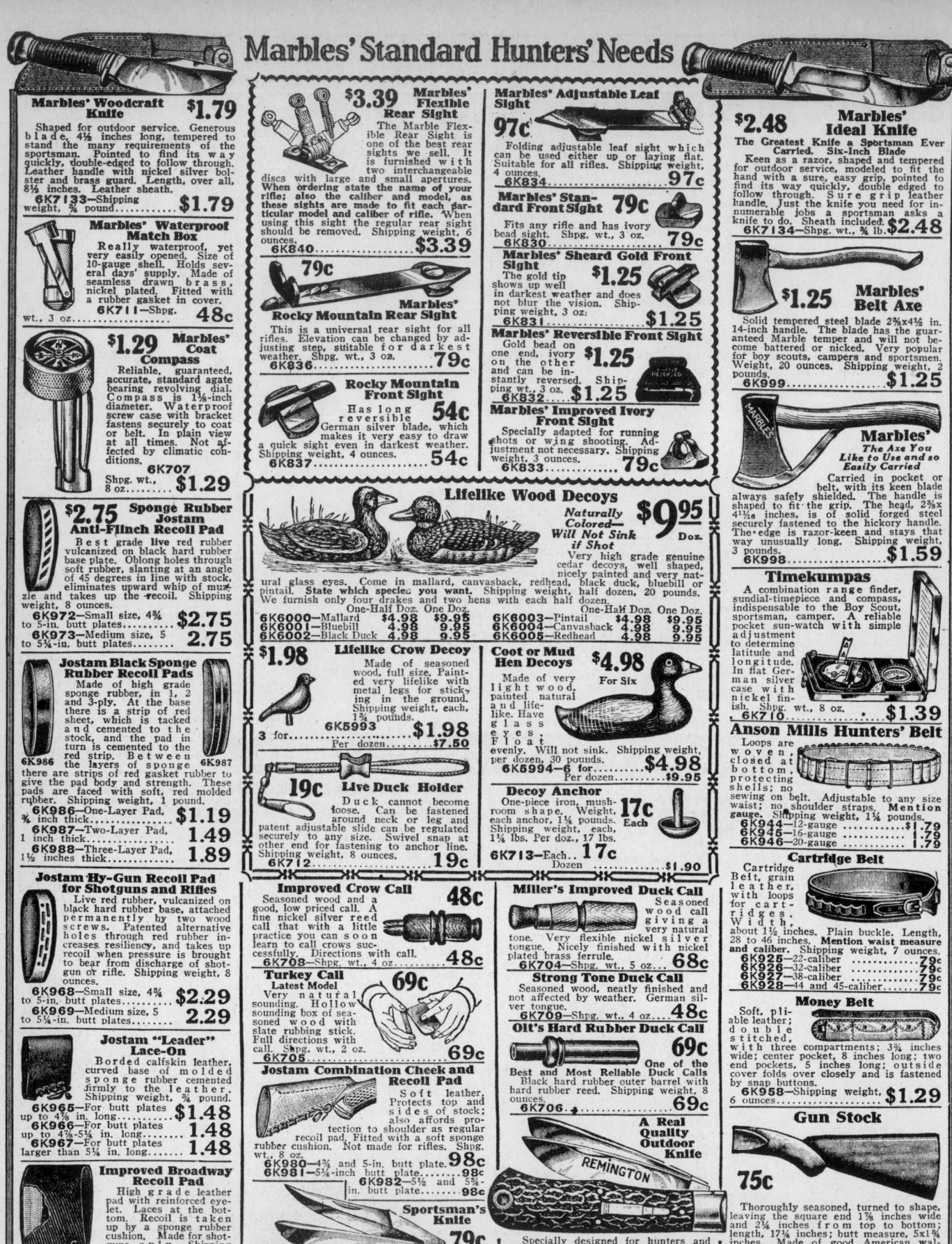

Marbles' Standard Hunters' Needs

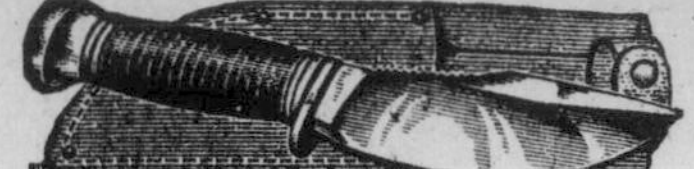

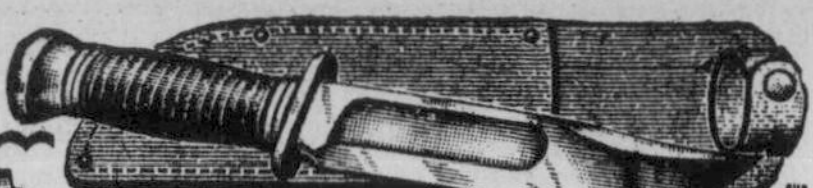

Marbles' Woodcraft Knife **$1.79**

Shaped for outdoor service. Generous blade, 4½ inches long, tempered to stand the many requirements of the sportsman. Pointed to find its way quickly, double-edged to follow through. Leather handle with nickel silver bolster and brass guard. Length, over all, 8½ inches. Leather sheath.
6K7133—Shipping weight, ¾ pound............ **$1.79**

Marbles' Waterproof Match Box

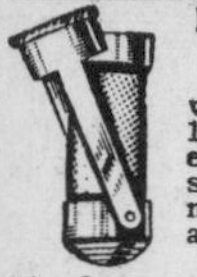

Really waterproof, yet very easily opened. Size of 10-gauge shell. Holds several days' supply. Made of seamless drawn brass, nickel plated. Fitted with a rubber gasket in cover.
6K711—Shpg. wt., 3 oz. **48c**

$1.29 Marbles' Coat Compass

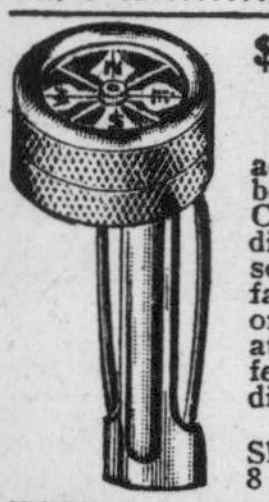

Reliable, guaranteed, accurate, standard agate bearing revolving dial. Compass is 1⅛-inch diameter. Waterproof screw case with bracket fastens securely to coat or belt. In plain view at all times. Not affected by climatic conditions.
6K707 Shpg. wt., 8 oz. **$1.29**

$2.75 Sponge Rubber Jostam Anti-Flinch Recoil Pad

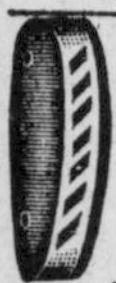

Best grade live red rubber vulcanized on black hard rubber base plate. Oblong holes through soft rubber, slanting at an angle of 45 degrees in line with stock, eliminates upward whip of muzzle and takes up the recoil. Shipping weight, 8 ounces.
6K972—Small size, 4¾ to 5-in. butt plates.......... **$2.75**
6K973—Medium size, 5 to 5¼-in. butt plates.......... **2.75**

Jostam Black Sponge Rubber Recoil Pads

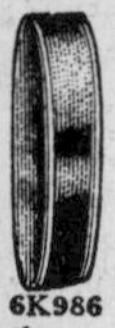
6K986

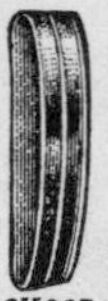
6K987

Made of high grade sponge rubber, in 1, 2 and 3-ply. At the base there is a strip of red sheet, which is tacked and cemented to the stock, and the pad in turn is cemented to the red strip. Between the layers of sponge there are strips of red gasket rubber to give the pad body and strength. These pads are faced with soft, red molded rubber. Shipping weight, 1 pound.
6K986—One-Layer Pad, ¾ inch thick.......... **$1.19**
6K987—Two-Layer Pad, 1 inch thick.......... **1.49**
6K988—Three-Layer Pad, 1½ inches thick.......... **1.89**

Jostam Hy-Gun Recoil Pad for Shotguns and Rifles

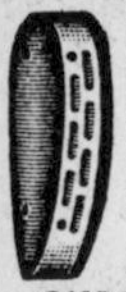

Live red rubber, vulcanized on black hard rubber base, attached permanently by two wood screws. Patented alternative holes through red rubber increases resiliency, and takes up recoil when pressure is brought to bear from discharge of shotgun or rifle. Shipping weight, 8 ounces.
6K968—Small size, 4¾ to 5-in. butt plates.......... **$2.29**
6K969—Medium size, 5 to 5¼-in. butt plates.......... **2.29**

Jostam "Leader" Lace-On

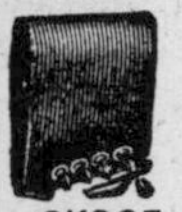

Borded calfskin leather, curved base of molded sponge rubber cemented firmly to the leather. Shipping weight, ¾ pound.
6K965—For butt plates up to 4⅞ in. long.......... **$1.48**
6K966—For butt plates up to 4⅞-5¼ in. long.......... **1.48**
6K967—For butt plates larger than 5¼ in. long.......... **1.48**

Improved Broadway Recoil Pad

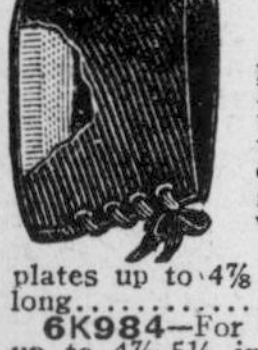

High grade leather pad with reinforced eyelet. Laces at the bottom. Recoil is taken up by a sponge rubber cushion. Made for shotguns only. Shipping weight, 8 ounces.
6K983—For butt plates up to 4⅞ inches long.......... **59c**
6K984—For butt plates up to 4⅞-5¼ inches long.......... **59c**
6K985—For butt plates larger than 5¼ inches long.......... **59c**

$3.39 Marbles' Flexible Rear Sight

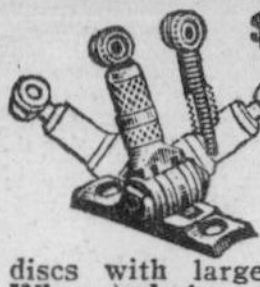

The Marble Flexible Rear Sight is one of the best rear sights we sell. It is furnished with two interchangeable discs with large and small apertures. **When ordering state the name of your rifle; also the caliber and model, as these sights are made to fit each particular model and caliber of rifle.** When using this sight the regular rear sight should be removed. Shipping weight, 6 ounces.
6K840.......... **$3.39**

79c Marbles' Rocky Mountain Rear Sight

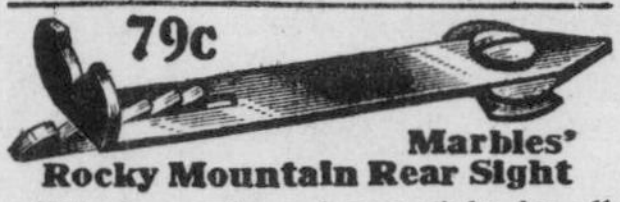

This is a universal rear sight for all rifles. Elevation can be changed by adjusting step, suitable for darkest weather. Shpg. wt., 3 oz.
6K836.......... **79c**

Rocky Mountain Front Sight **54c**

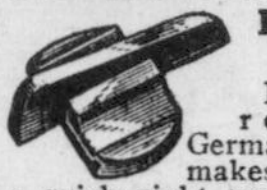

Has long reversible German silver blade, which makes it very easy to draw a quick sight even in darkest weather. Shipping weight, 4 ounces.
6K837.......... **54c**

Marbles' Adjustable Leaf Sight **97c**

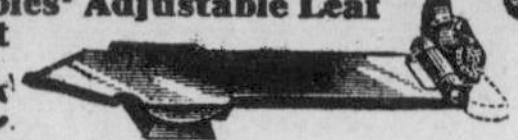

Folding adjustable leaf sight which can be used either up or laying flat. Suitable for all rifles. Shipping weight, 4 ounces.
6K834.......... **97c**

Marbles' Standard Front Sight **79c**

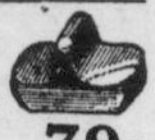

Fits any rifle and has ivory bead sight. Shpg. wt., 3 oz.
6K830.......... **79c**

Marbles' Sheard Gold Front Sight **$1.25**

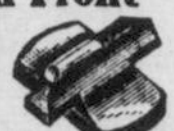

The gold tip shows up well in darkest weather and does not blur the vision. Shipping weight, 3 oz.
6K831.......... **$1.25**

Marbles' Reversible Front Sight **$1.25**

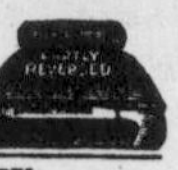

Gold bead on one end, ivory on the other and can be instantly reversed. Shipping wt., 3 oz.
6K832.......... **$1.25**

Marbles' Improved Ivory Front Sight

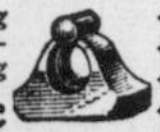

Specially adapted for running shots or wing shooting. Adjustment not necessary. Shipping weight, 3 ounces.
6K833.......... **79c**

$2.48 Marbles' Ideal Knife

The Greatest Knife a Sportsman Ever Carried. Six-Inch Blade

Keen as a razor, shaped and tempered for outdoor service, modeled to fit the hand with a sure, easy grip, pointed to find its way quickly, double edged to follow through. Sure grip leather handle. Just the knife you need for innumerable jobs a sportsman asks a knife to do. Sheath included.
6K7134—Shpg. wt., ¾ lb. **$2.48**

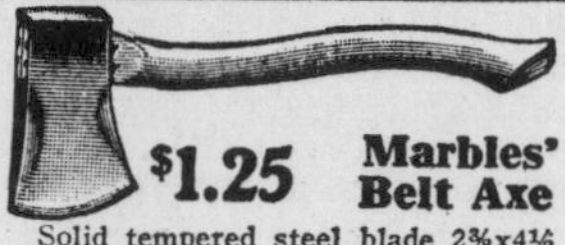

$1.25 Marbles' Belt Axe

Solid tempered steel blade 2⅝x4½ in. 14-inch handle. The blade has the guaranteed Marble temper and will not become battered or nicked. Very popular for boy scouts, campers and sportsmen. Weight, 20 ounces. Shipping weight, 2 pounds.
6K999.......... **$1.25**

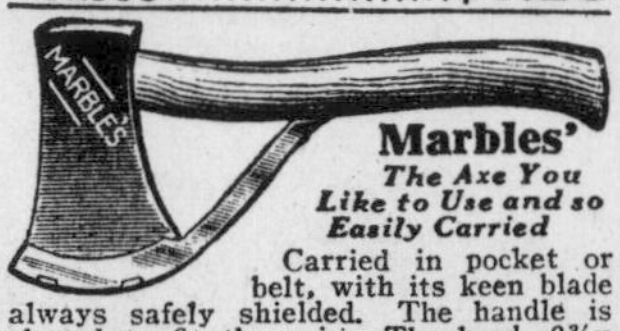

Marbles'
The Axe You Like to Use and so Easily Carried

Carried in pocket or belt, with its keen blade always safely shielded. The handle is shaped to fit the grip. The head, 2⅜x4[11/16] inches, is of solid forged steel securely fastened to the hickory handle. The edge is razor-keen and stays that way unusually long. Shipping weight, 3 pounds.
6K998.......... **$1.59**

Lifelike Wood Decoys **$9.95 Doz.**

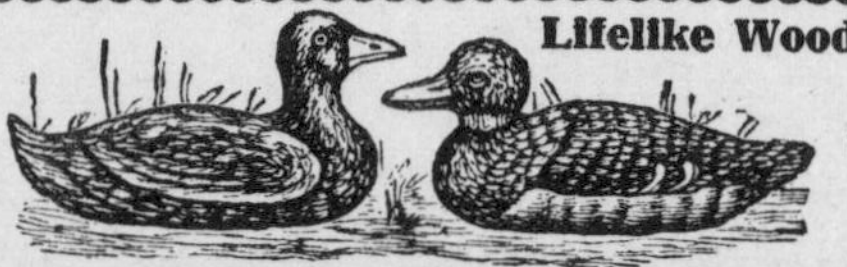

Naturally Colored—Will Not Sink if Shot

Very high grade genuine cedar decoys, well shaped, nicely painted and very natural glass eyes. Come in mallard, canvasback, redhead, black duck, bluebill or pintail. **State which species you want.** Shipping weight, half dozen, 20 pounds. We furnish only four drakes and two hens with each half dozen.

	One-Half Doz.	One Doz.
6K6000—Mallard	$4.98	$9.95
6K6001—Bluebill	4.98	9.95
6K6002—Black Duck	4.98	9.95
6K6003—Pintail	$4.98	$9.95
6K6004—Canvasback	4.98	9.95
6K6005—Redhead	4.98	9.95

$1.98 Lifelike Crow Decoy

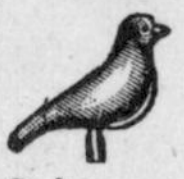

Made of seasoned wood, full size. Painted very lifelike with metal legs for sticking in the ground. Shipping weight, each, 1¾ pounds.
6K5993
3 for.......... **$1.98**
Per dozen.......... **$7.50**

Coot or Mud Hen Decoys **$4.98 For Six**

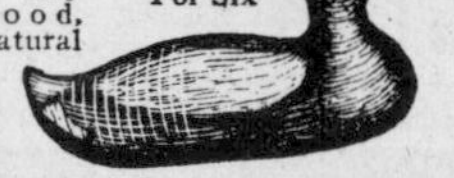

Made of very light wood, painted natural and lifelike. Have glass eyes. Float evenly. Will not sink. Shipping weight, per dozen, 30 pounds.
6K5994—6 for.......... **$4.98**
Per dozen.......... **$9.95**

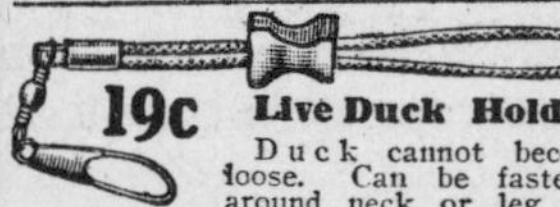

19c Live Duck Holder

Duck cannot become loose. Can be fastened around neck or leg and patent adjustable slide can be regulated securely to any size. Swivel snap at other end for fastening to anchor line. Shipping weight, 8 ounces.
6K712.......... **19c**

Decoy Anchor **17c Each**

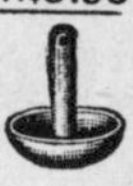

One-piece iron, mushroom shape. Weight, each anchor, 1¼ pounds. Shipping weight, each, 1¼ lbs. Per doz., 17 lbs.
6K713—Each.. **17c**
Dozen.......... **$1.90**

Timekumpas

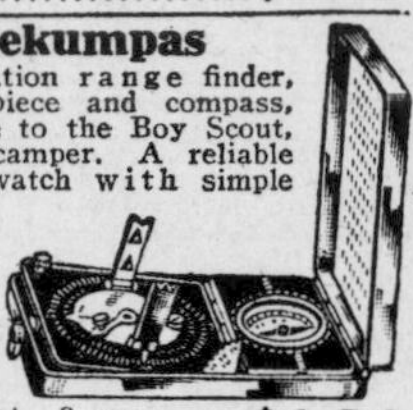

A combination range finder, sundial-timepiece and compass, indispensable to the Boy Scout, sportsman, camper. A reliable pocket sun-watch with simple adjustment to determine latitude and longitude. In flat German silver case with nickel finish. Shpg. wt., 8 oz.
6K710.......... **$1.39**

Anson Mills Hunters' Belt

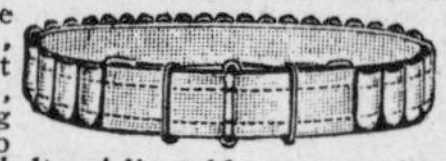

Loops are woven, closed at bottom, protecting shells; no sewing on belt. Adjustable to any size waist; no shoulder straps. **Mention gauge.** Shipping weight, 1¼ pounds.
6K944—12-gauge.......... **$1.79**
6K945—16-gauge.......... **1.79**
6K946—20-gauge.......... **1.79**

Cartridge Belt

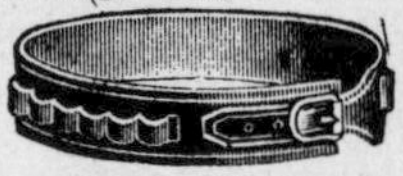

Cartridge Belt, grain leather, with loops for cartridges. Width, about 1½ inches. Plain buckle. Length, 28 to 46 inches. **Mention waist measure and caliber.** Shipping weight, 7 ounces.
6K925—22-caliber.......... **79c**
6K926—32-caliber.......... **79c**
6K927—38-caliber.......... **79c**
6K928—44 and 45-caliber.......... **79c**

Money Belt

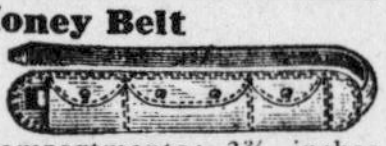

Soft, pliable leather; double stitched, with three compartments; 3¾ inches wide; center pocket, 8 inches long; two end pockets, 5 inches long; outside cover folds over closely and is fastened by snap buttons.
6K958—Shipping weight, 6 ounces.......... **$1.29**

Improved Crow Call **48c**

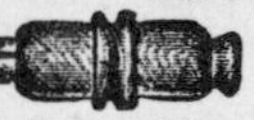

Seasoned wood and a good, low priced call. A fine nickel silver reed call that with a little practice you can soon learn to call crows successfully. Directions with call.
6K708—Shpg. wt., 4 oz.......... **48c**

Turkey Call **69c**
Latest Model

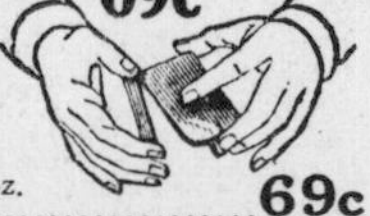

Very natural sounding. Hollow sounding box of seasoned wood with slate rubbing stick. Full directions with call. Shpg. wt., 2 oz.
6K705.......... **69c**

Jostam Combination Cheek and Recoil Pad

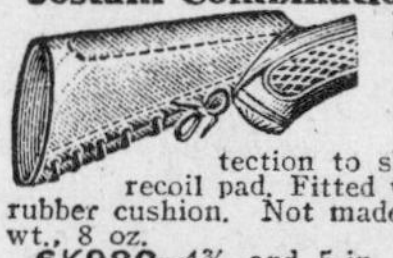

Soft leather. Protects top and sides of stock; also affords protection to shoulder as regular recoil pad. Fitted with a soft sponge rubber cushion. Not made for rifles. Shpg. wt., 8 oz.
6K980—4¾ and 5-in. butt plate.......... **98c**
6K981—5¼-inch butt plate.......... **98c**
6K982—5½ and 5¾-in. butt plate.......... **98c**

Sportsman's Knife **79c**

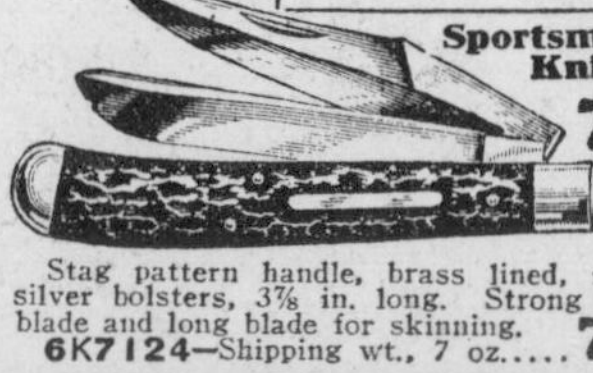

Stag pattern handle, brass lined, nickel silver bolsters, 3⅞ in. long. Strong saber blade and long blade for skinning.
6K7124—Shipping wt., 7 oz.... **79c**

Miller's Improved Duck Call

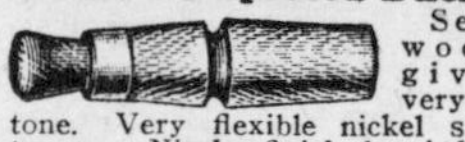

Seasoned wood call giving a very natural tone. Very flexible nickel silver tongue. Nicely finished with nickel plated brass ferrule.
6K704—Shpg. wt., 5 oz... **68c**

Strong Tone Duck Call

Seasoned wood, neatly finished and not affected by weather. German silver tongue.
6K709—Shpg. wt., 4 oz.... **48c**

Olt's Hard Rubber Duck Call **69c**

One of the Best and Most Reliable Duck Calls

Black hard rubber outer barrel with hard rubber reed. Shipping weight, 8 ounces.
6K706.......... **69c**

A Real Quality Outdoor Knife

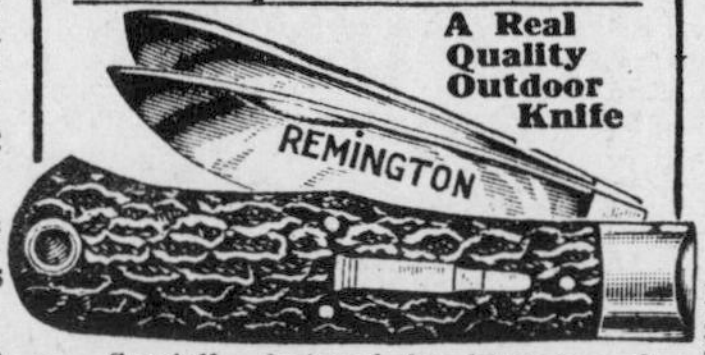

Specially designed for hunters and trappers. Blades are correctly shaped and have keen, durable cutting edges. Sticking blade and skinning blade, each 3⅝ inches long. Brass linings. Nickel silver bolster and shield. Stag pattern handle, 4½ inches long. Hole in end for thong or lanyard.
6K7123—Shpg. wt., ¾ pound.......... **$1.87**

Gun Stock

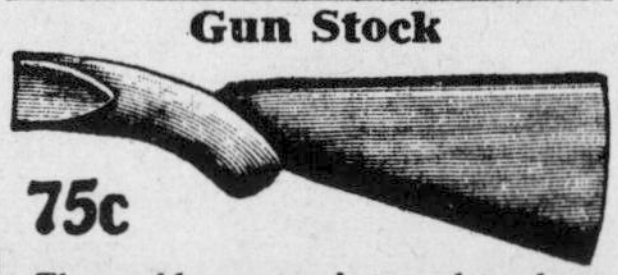

75c

Thoroughly seasoned, turned to shape, leaving the square end 1⅞ inches wide and 2¼ inches from top to bottom; length, 17¼ inches; butt measure, 5x1¾ inches. Made of good American walnut. Not fitted, just shaved. Suitable for double barrel breech loading guns.
6K687—Medium quality. Shpg. wt., 2¾ lbs.......... **75c**
6K688—Selected quality. Shpg. wt., 2½ lbs.......... **98c**
6K689—Extra fine grain, especially selected walnut stock. Shpg. wt., 2½ lbs.......... **$1.60**

The Things Hunters Really Need — The Choice of Experienced Hunters — Beat These Values if You Can

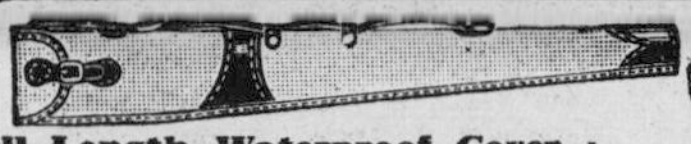

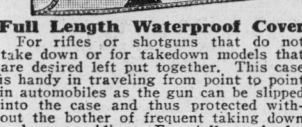

Full Length Waterproof Cover

For rifles or shotguns that do not take down or for takedown models that are desired left put together. This case is handy in traveling from point to point in automobiles as the gun can be slipped into the case and thus protected without the bother of frequent taking down and reassembling. Especially made for carbines and bolt action rifles and automatic shotguns.

Cover is tan heavy duck full canvas bound with heavy leather protector opposite the lock and also at muzzle. Leather handle and sling. Flannel lined. Always give manufacturer's name, model and length of barrel and the length over all of your gun or rifle. Shipping weight, 1 pound.

6K910 .... $1.48

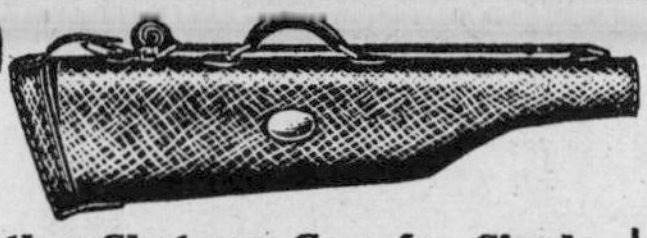

Leather Shotgun Case for Single, Double and Repeating Shotguns

Dark russet leather and fiber reinforced. Canton flannel lined, reinforced bottom seam, leather handle and sling, brass trimmings, inside rod pocket. For single, double and repeating shotguns only, 26, 28, 30 or 32-inch barrels. **State length.** Shipping weight, 4½ pounds.

6K905 .... $5.79

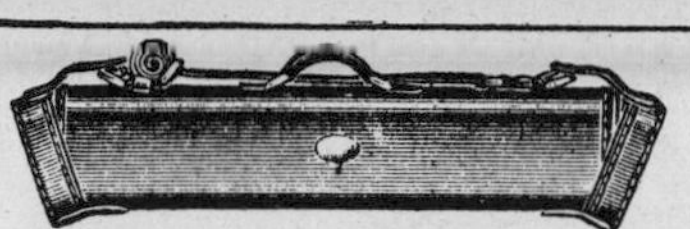

Leather Case for Single and Double Barrel or Repeating Shotgun

Good quality leather, fiber reinforced and lined. Brass trimmings, leather handle and shoulder sling. Furnished for 26, 28, 30 or 32-inch barrels. **State length of barrel, make and model of gun.**

6K919—Shpg. wt., 6¼ lbs.... $6.59

6K920—For Remington Automatic Shotguns. **State length of barrel** $6.79

6K921—For Winchester Automatic Shotgun $6.79

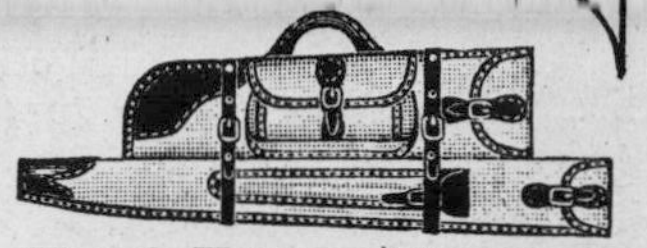

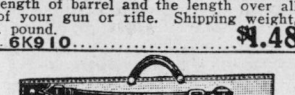

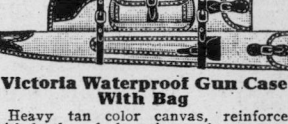

Victoria Waterproof Gun Case With Bag

Heavy tan color canvas, reinforced with leather, lock and muzzle protector and pocket for cleaning rod; also shell bag to hold fifty shells. For single, double or pump guns with 26, 28, 30 or 32-inch barrels. **State length of barrel.**

6K914—Shpg. wt., 1¾ lbs. $1.98

Same as 6K914, to fit Remington or Winchester Automatic Shotguns. **State length of barrel.**

6K915—Shpg. wt., 1½ lbs. $1.98

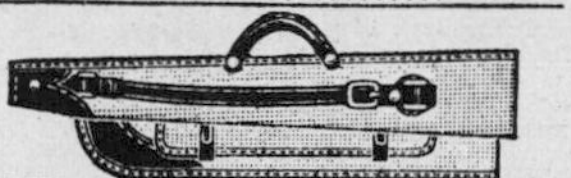

Folding Waterproof Gun Case

Tan color canvas, reinforced ends, leather muzzle protector, with sling strap and handle. Flannel lined. For single, double or pump guns with 26, 28, 30 or 32-inch barrels. **Mention length of barrel.** Shipping wt., 1¼ lbs.

6K917 .... $1.79

Flylock Automatic Safety Outdoor Knife

For Hunter, Fisherman, Trapper, Tourist and Camper

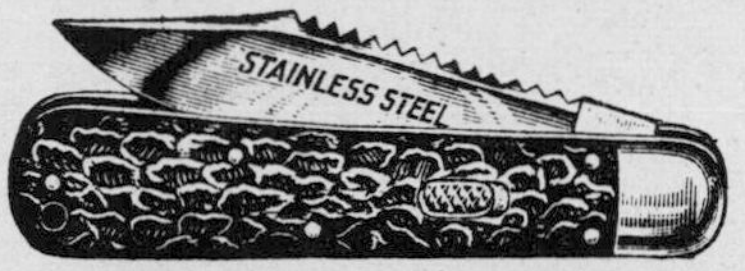

Operates with one hand by pressing and sliding button. Locks closed or open. 3¾-inch Crocus polished stainless steel blade, with serrated back for scaling fish. Nickel silver lining, bolster and back. Stag pattern handle, 5 inches long, with hole in end for thong or chain. Often sold elsewhere as high as $2.50. Shipping weight, 5 ounces.

6K7090 .... $1.98

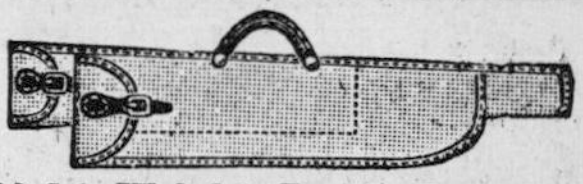

Light Weight Duck Gun Case

Tan color case for takedown shotgun. Has inside rod pocket. Lined throughout. For single, double or pump guns with 26, 28, 30 or 32-inch barrels. **Give length of barrel.**

6K916—Shpg. wt., 1 lb...... 79c

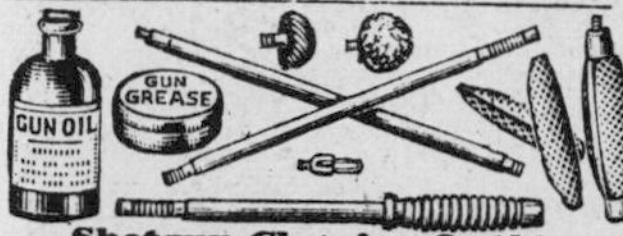

Shotgun Cleaning Outfit

Nine Articles

Outfit consists of one hardwood three-joint cleaning rod, one wool swab, one slotted wiper, one wire scratch brush, one Tomlinson wire gauze, spring center, gun cleaner, one bottle gun oil and one box of gun grease.

6K631—12-gauge. Shipping weight, 1¾ pounds.............. 69c

6K632—16-gauge 69c

6K633—20-gauge 69c

MARBLE'S GUN NEEDS

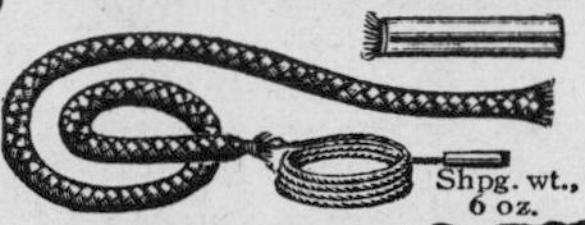

Shpg. wt., 6 oz.

Marble's Anti-Rust Rope

When saturated with oil this rope excludes air and moisture, preventing barrels from becoming rusted or pitted. Rope gives a constant pressure of oil against entire inner surface of barrel. One oiling will last a year.

6K551—12-gauge...49c	6K555—25-caliber....49c
6K552—16-gauge...49c	6K556—30 & 32-cal...49c
6K553—20-gauge...49c	6K557—35 & 38-cal...49c
6K554—22-caliber..49c	6K558—45 & 410-cal..49c

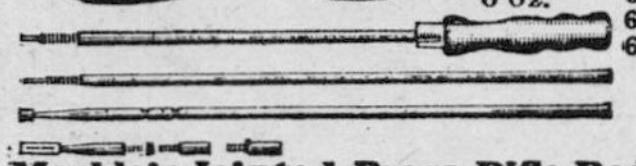

Marble's Jointed Brass Rifle Rod

Joints are reinforced steel. Strong and rigid as a one-piece rod. Has strong wood handle. Shpg. wt., 1 lb.

6K566—For 22 and 25-caliber.. 98c

6K567—For 30-caliber and larger. 98c

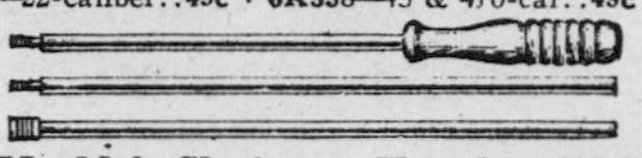

Marble's Shotgun Cleaning Rod

Made in three sections of ⅜-inch solid light metal. Has end for holding cleaning rag or brush. Strong wood handle. Put up in cloth bag.

6K560—Shpg. wt., 1 lb........ 87c

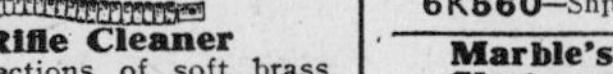

Marble's Rifle Cleaner

Made in eight sections of soft brass gauze, separated by fiber discs. Strung on spiral steel tempered wire. Will not injure rifle or barrel. Shpg. wt., 4 oz.

6K568 22-caliber............ 39c	
6K569 25-caliber..... 39c	6K572 38-caliber..... 39c
6K570 30 and 303-cal.. 39c	6K573 410 and 40-cal. 39c
6K571 32 caliber..... 39c	6K574 45-caliber.... 39c

Marble's Shotgun Cleaner

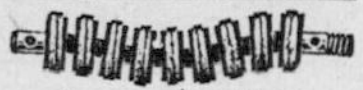

Made in sixteen sections of soft bras gauze, separated by fiber discs. Gives even pressure and will not injure inside of barrel. Cleaner lasts a lifetime. Shipping weight, 6 ounces.

6K562—12-gauge.............. 59c

6K563—16-gauge 59c

6K564—20-gauge 59c

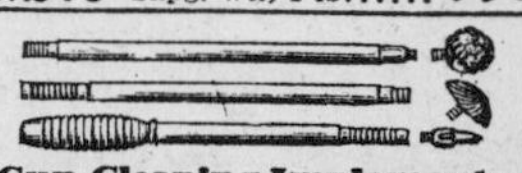

Gun Cleaning Implements

Made of seasoned hardwood. Brass joints and three implements consisting of swab, scratch brush and wiper. **State gauge.**

6K650—36 inches long. 10, 12 and 16-gauge. Shpg. wt., ¾ lb. Per set........................ 33c

6K651—36 inches long. 20 and 28-gauge. Shpg. wt., 7 oz. Per set. 33c

6K652—35 inches long. 410-caliber. Shpg. wt., 7 oz. Per set........ 33c

6K653—48 inches long. 10, 12 and 16-gauge. Shpg. wt., ¾ lb. Per set.. 39c

Tomlinson Cleaner

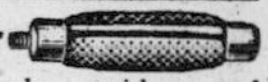

Removes lead and powder residue, and gives barrel thorough cleaning without injury. Shpg. wt., 3 oz.

6K639—12-gauge........... 25c

6K640—16-gauge 25c

6K641—20-gauge 25c

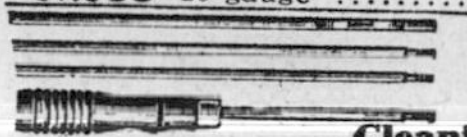

Four-Piece Brass Cleaning Rod

Each joint is about 8½ inches long and, when put together, the entire rod is about 33 inches long. Has swivel handle. Shipping weight, ¾ lb.

6K658—22 caliber............ 34c

6K659—For 25, 30, 32, 38, 44, 45 and 50-caliber. State caliber...... 39c

Brass Rifle Brush

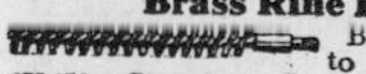

Brass Wire Brush to fit 6K658 and 6K659 Cleaning Rods. Brass shank. Especially made for cleaning rust and burnt powder out of rifles. Shipping weight, 2 ounces.

6K662—22-caliber..... 2 for 19c

6K663—25-caliber..... 2 for 19c

6K664—30-caliber..... 2 for 19c

6K665—32-cal. 2 for 19c

6K666—38-cal. 2 for 19c

Brass Wire Brush

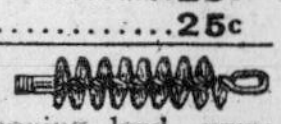

Wire brush for removing lead, powder caking and rust spots. Shipping weight, 3 ounces.

6K646—12-gauge........... 37c

6K647—16-gauge 37c

6K648—20-gauge 37c

Remington's Dependable Gun Needs

Rem Powder Solvent

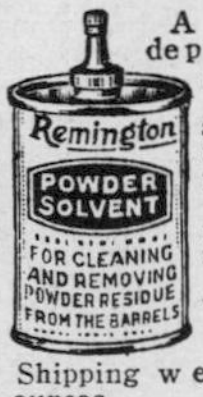

A superior dependable solvent for cleaning and removing powder residue from barrels of firearms. Very effective. Shipping weight, 8 ounces.

6K587...... 24c

Rem Oil

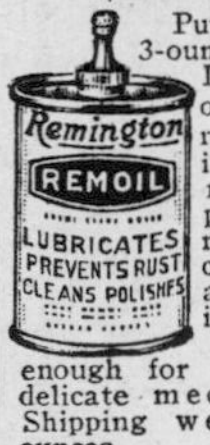

Put up in 3-ounce can. Light oil of superior quality. Lubricates, prevents rust, cleans and polishes. Light enough for the most delicate mechanism. Shipping weight, 8 ounces.

6K588...... 24c

Rem Gun Grease

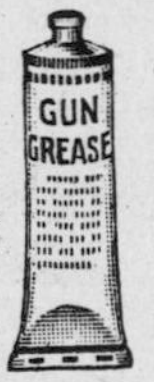

A most serviceable rust preventative for firearms and other metals. Put up in soft metal tube. Shipping wt., 4 oz.

6K586..... 12c

Rem Rust Remover

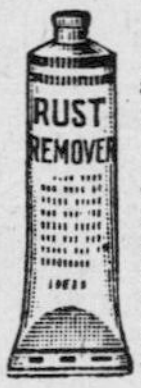

Removes rust from all metal surfaces. Specially recommended for firearms of all sorts and also good for other metal articles. Shpg. wt., 4 oz.

6K581.... 19c

Hoppe's Nitro Solvent No. 9

Keep Your Guns in the Finest Condition

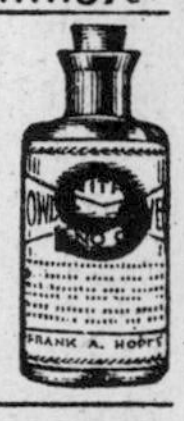

This well known solvent has been on the market for more than 22 years and is known everywhere for its dependability. It is the original solvent for removing burnt powder from gun barrels. Shpg. wt., 8 oz.

6K591........... 31c

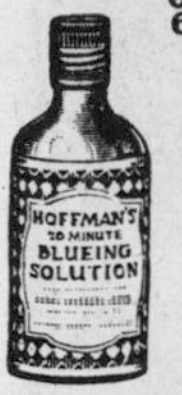

Hoffman's Gun Blueing Solution

Make your old gun barrels look like new. No experience required and only 20 minutes of your time in your own home will give surprising results. We have tried this blueing in our own gunshop with very satisfactory results. Put up in 4-ounce bottles. Shipping weight, 1 lb.

6K590......... $1.69

HUNTERS' CAPS

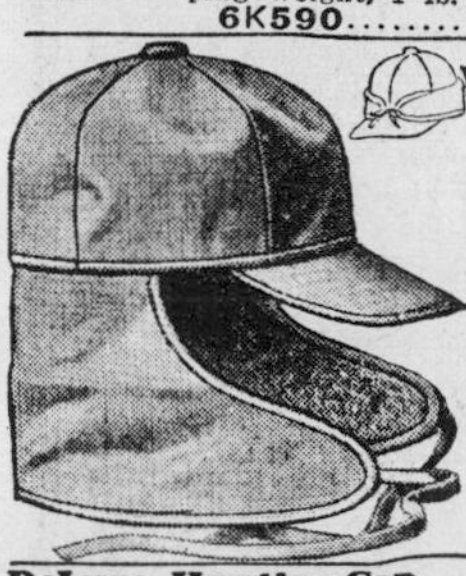

Duck Cap

Made of khaki color waterproof duck. Body of cap and large cape are warm flannel lined. Excellent rough or cold weather cap. Cape can be folded inside. **SIZES — 6¾ to 7¾. State size.** Shipping weight, ¾ pound.

6K5189.. 69c

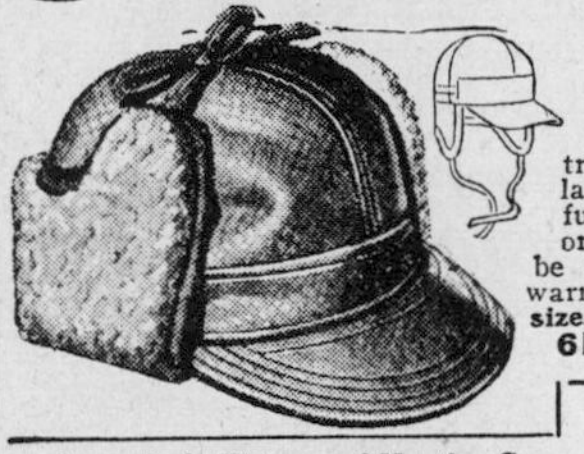

DeLuxe Sport Cap

A real quality cap for hunting and winter sport. Made of high grade mahogany glove leather and trimmed with the best heavy lambskin, closely resembling fur. Visor can be worn up or down. Ear protectors can be tied up when weather is warm. **Sizes, 6¾ to 7¾. State size.** Shpg. wt., 1 lb.

6K5192........ $2.48

Safety First DeLuxe Hunting Cap

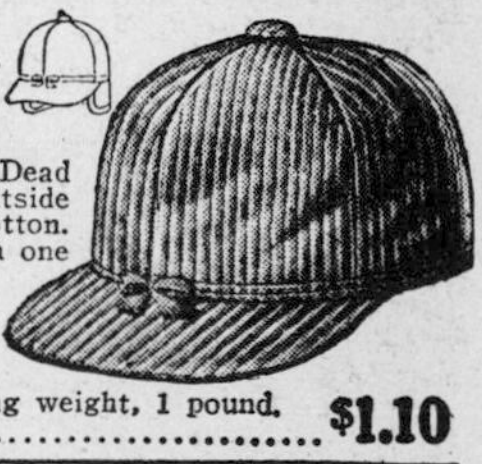

Reversible Red Lined Cap. Dead grass shade corduroy on outside and scarlet shade warm cotton flannel on inside. Opening on one side at bottom seam allows top part to be pulled over to cover the corduroy and bring scarlet side out. Inside turn-down lined band. **SIZES—6¾ to 8. State size.** Shipping weight, 1 pound.

6K5196.................................. $1.10

DeLuxe Hunting Cap

Made of best grade mahogany glove leather with sturdy eye shield and has warm earlaps, which can be let down in cold weather. A practical, fine quality and waterproof hunting cap. **Sizes, 6¾ to 7¾. State size.** Shipping weight, 1 lb.

6K5193
$1.98

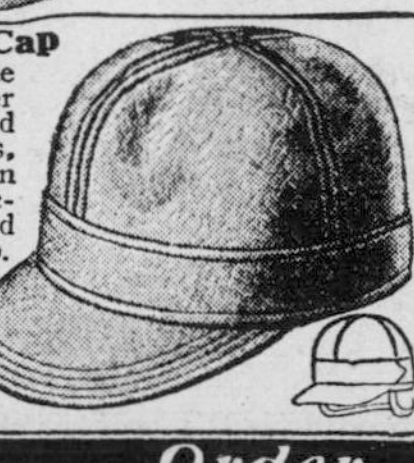

Jones Style Waterproof Hunting Cap

This cap is made of good grade waterproof khaki duck with extra strong reinforced brim and shield. Has corduroy lined earlaps, which can be folded back in cap when not in use. Cravat inner lining. **SIZES—6¾ to 7¾. State size.** Shipping wt., 1 pound.

6K5194.................. 98c

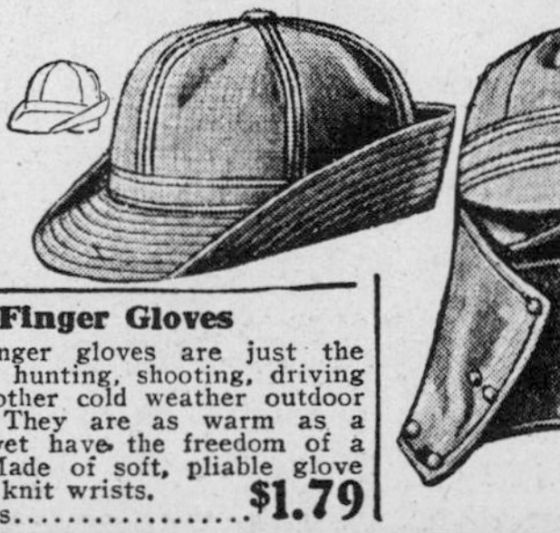

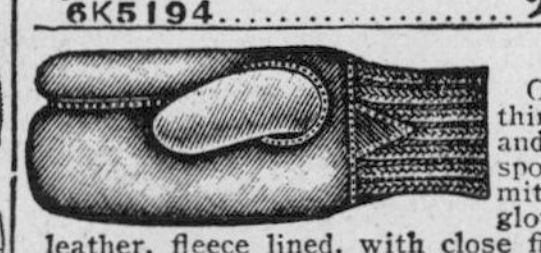

Finger Gloves

Our finger gloves are just the thing for hunting, shooting, driving and all other cold weather outdoor sports. They are as warm as a mitten, yet have the freedom of a glove. Made of soft, pliable glove leather, fleece lined, with close fitting knit wrists.

6K5188—Shipping weight, 8 ounces................ $1.79

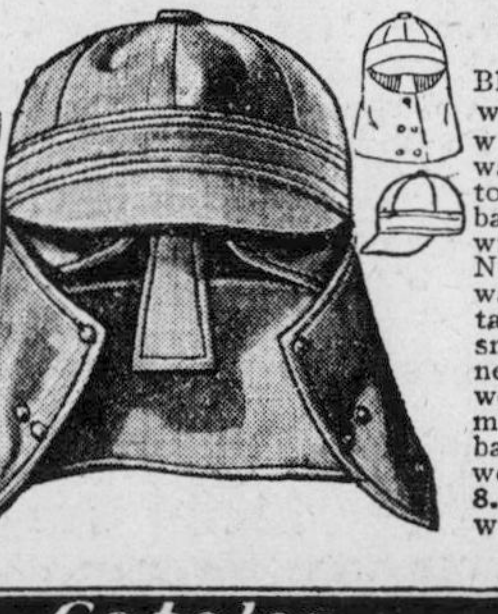

All Weather Cap

Improved Hunting and Blizzard Cap. Heavy weight khaki color waterproofed duck, warm, serviceable cotton lining. Has inside band to pull down, lined with warm material. Nosepiece. Detachable warm lined cape so attached that rain or snow cannot run down neck or back. Can be worn as ordinary cap in mild weather, with band over ears in cold weather. **SIZES—6¾ to 8. State size.** Shpg. wt., 1 lb.

6K5199.. $1.69

38c Spread Jaws 4⅝ In.

Simplicity Itself

3 for 35c Spread Jaws 3½ Inches

27c Spread Jaws 4⅞ Inches

For Teeth to Fit Traps on This Page see 6K5347 on Page 513.

THE SPRING'S THE THING

Double Spring Traps
Plain Jaws

Oneida Victor Traps are recognized as the world's standard. Made by one of the oldest and largest makers of animal traps. These new double spring traps are the latest, most dependable models of this company. While very low in price, they have the newest features, are very durable, efficient and are fully guaranteed. Will perform successfully any place, regardless of environment or climatic conditions.

Catalog No.	For Catching	Spread of Jaws	Price Each	Price Doz.	Shpg. Wt.,Lbs. Ea.	Shpg. Wt.,Lbs. Doz
6K5203 Size 2	Foxes, raccoons, etc.	4⅝ in.	38c	$3.91	1¾	23
6K5204 Size 3	Wildcats, coyotes, otters, etc.	5½ in.	61c	6.39	2½	28
6K5205 Size 4	Beavers, otters, wolves, etc.	5⅝ in.	75c	7.81	2¾	35

Victor Traps

Equipped with wide spreading double jaws. This type of jaw catches the animal high on the leg and special double construction prevents animal from gnawing or twisting free. Both sizes are shoulder catch types.

Single Spring—Double Jaws

Catalog No.	For Catching	Spread of Jaws	Price Ea.	Price Doz.	Shpg. Wt.,Lbs. Ea.	Shpg. Wt.,Lbs. Doz
6K5206 Size 91	Skunks, muskrats, mink, etc.	4⅞ in.	27c	$2.84	1	12
6K5207 Size 91½	Skunks, muskrats, fishers, etc.	5¼ in.	41c	4.26	1¾	19

Victor Traps

Catalog No.	For Catching	Spread of Jaws	Price 3 for	Price Doz.	Shpg. Wt.,Lbs. 3 traps	Shpg. Wt.,Lbs. Doz
6K5200 Size 0	House rats, pocket gophers, weasels, etc.	3½ in.	35c	$1.28	3	8
6K5201 Size 1	Muskrats, mink, opossums, skunks, etc.	4 in.	44c	1.59	3	8
6K5202 Size 1½	Skunks, raccoon, fishers, muskrats, etc.	4⅝ in.	78c	2.84	4	15

New Victor Giant Trap
Single Spring, Wide Spread Jaws, Firm, Tight Grip

Catalog No.	For Catching	Spread of Jaws	Price 3 for	Price Doz.	Shpg. Wt.,Lbs. 3 traps	Shpg. Wt.,Lbs. Doz
6K5211 No. 1 Giant	Skunks, muskrats, minks, etc.	4⅞ in.	63c	$2.27	4	15

Kompakt, Oneida's Latest Quick and High Catching Trap
Single Spring—Plain Jaws

With chain. A new lightweight trap with strong spring and sure grip jaws. Has a very wide jaw spread and lies very flat. Is quick and dependable.

Catalog No.	For Catching	Spread of Jaws	Price, Dozen	Shpg. Wt., Dozen
6K5242 Size 1	Muskrats, minks, opossums, skunks, etc.	4 in.	$1.15	9 lbs.

GIBBS TWO-TRIGGER TRAPS DO NOT INJURE THE PELT

$5.98 Dozen 55c Each

"Every Catch Stays Caught" Guaranteed Against Spring Breakage. Guaranteed to Prevent Wringing Off. Guaranteed Not to Injure Pelts.

Gibbs' "Two-Trigger" Trap

Two traps in one; the inner trap catches by the leg, the same as an ordinary trap and holds the animal while the outer trap gets the grip that keeps the animal tight. Lays very flat and is positive in action. One size only. Will catch and kill muskrat, mink and martin; catch and hold skunk, raccoon, opossum, woodchuck. Shpg. wt., each, 1¼ lbs.

6K5210—Each, 55c; dozen............$5.98

Oneida's Jump Traps
Single Spring—Single Jaws

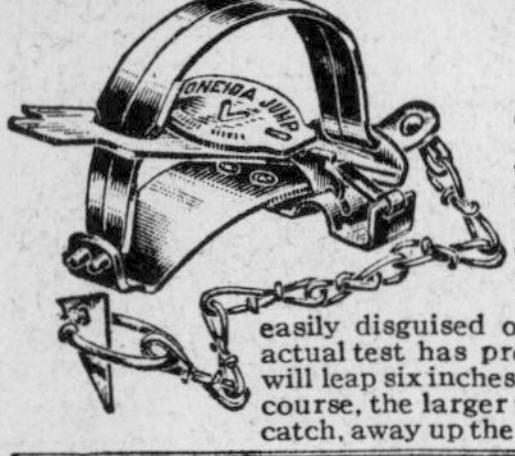

Oneida Jump Traps possess three distinct advantages: **1st.** Lightness; this means much to trapper who has to carry his traps long distances, and **2nd.** Compactness; this enables trapper to set them in small holes, dens and run ways. They lie very flat and are easily disguised or hidden, and **3rd.** Jump action; actual test has proved that the No. 1 Oneida Jump trap will leap six inches from ground when trap is sprung. Of course, the larger traps are even more active. This bound insures a good, high, secure catch, away up the animal's leg.

Catalog No.	For Catching	Spread of Jaws	Price 3 Traps	Price Doz.	Shpg. Wt.,Lbs. 3 Traps	Shpg. Wt.,Lbs. Doz
6K5244 Size 0	Gophers, rats, weasels, etc.	4 in.	51c	$1.84	2½	10
6K5245 Size 1	Muskrats, mink, opossums, skunks.	4¾ in.	59c	2.13	3½	12
6K5246 Size 1½	Skunks, fishers, raccoons, muskrats, etc.	5¼ in.	90c	3.26	4	15
6K5247 Size 2	Opossum, fishers, wildcat, raccoon, etc.	5⅝ in.	$1.41	5.11	5	18

Catalog No.	For Catching	Spread of Jaws	Price Each	Price Doz.	Shpg. Wt.,Lbs. Ea.	Shpg. Wt.,Lbs. Doz
6K5248 Size 3	Wildcats, coyotes, otters, etc.	6¾ in.	68c	$7.10	2	24
6K5249 Size 4	Beavers, wolves, otters.	7½ in.	82c	8.52	2½	35

Single Spring—Double Jaws

Catalog No.	For Catching	Spread of Jaws	Price Each	Price Doz.	Shpg. Wt.,Lbs. Ea.	Shpg. Wt.,Lbs. Doz
6K5251 Size 91	Muskrats, skunks, minks.	4¾ in.	33c	$3.41	1	10
6K5252 Size 91½	Muskrats, skunks, fishers	5¼ in.	44c	4.54	1¼	13

See 6K5347 Page 513 for Teeth to Fit These Traps

Gibbs' "SINGLE GRIP" Jump Type Traps

A coil spring type. They are smaller and lighter than the long spring type. Are easier to carry, set flatter, and are easier to place and hide. The springs are more flexible, and will last longer than flat springs. These traps can be set by hand without resting against the body. This saves getting wet and also having to pull up the trap stake to reset the trap. The springs are guaranteed against breakage for the life of the trap.

Catalog No.	For Catching	Spread of Jaws	Price Each	Price Dozen	Shpg. Wt. Lbs. Each	Shpg. Wt. Lbs. Dozen
6K5212 No. 1	Muskrats, mink, marten, etc.	5 Single Spring	20c	$1.98	1	8
6K5213 No. 2	Fox, raccoon, skunk, woodchuck, etc.	5½ Double Spring	35c	3.85	1½	12
6K5214 No. 3	Lynx, fisher, coyote, wildcat, etc.	6 Double Spring	59c	6.39	2	16
6K5215 No. 4	Beaver, wolf, otter, badger, etc.	6½ Double Spring	69c	7.80	2½	20

Oneida Genuine Newhouse Traps

Genuine Newhouse Traps
Single Spring—Plain Jaws

Catalog No.	For Catching	Spread of Jaws	Price Each	Price Doz.	Shpg. Wt.,Lbs. Ea.	Shpg. Wt.,Lbs. Doz
6K5220 Size 0	House rats, pocket gophers, weasels, etc.	3½ in.	34c	$3.55	1	10
6K5221 Size 1	Muskrats, skunks, mink, opossums, etc.	4 in.	41c	4.26	1¼	14
6K5222 Size 1½	Skunks, fishers, raccoons, muskrats, etc.	4⅝ in.	61c	6.39	1¾	16
6K5224 Size 2½	Otters, beavers	5⅛ in.	$1.50	15.62	2½	35
6K5226 Size 3½	Otters	6⅝ in.	1.63	17.04	3¾	45

Double Spring—Plain Jaws

Catalog No.	For Catching	Spread of Jaws	Price Each	Price Doz.	Shpg. Wt.,Lbs. Ea.	Shpg. Wt.,Lbs. Doz
6K5223 Size 2	Fox, raccoons, etc.	4⅝ in.	$0.92	$9.59	2	20
6K5225 Size 3	Wildcats, otters, coyotes.	5½ in.	1.23	12.78	3	35
6K5227 Size 4	Otters, wolves, beavers, etc.	5⅞ in.	1.50	15.62	3¾	43
6K5228 Size 4½	Wolves, panther	8⅛ in.	3.67		9	
6K5229 Size 14	Deer, otters, wolves, etc.	6¾ in.	1.57	16.33	4	44

Newhouse Double Jaw Traps
Single Spring—Double Jaws

Catalog No.	For Catching	Spread of Jaws	Price Each	Price Doz.	Shpg. Wt.,Lbs. Ea.	Shpg. Wt.,Lbs. Doz
6K5232 Size 91	Muskrats, skunks, minks.	4⅞ in.	54c	$5.08	1¼	13
6K5233 Size 91½	Muskrats, skunks, fishers	5¼ in.	72c	7.46	1¾	16

Newhouse Bear Trap

Catalog No.	For Catching	Spread of Jaws	Price Each	Price Doz.	Shpg. Wt.,Lbs. Ea.	Shpg. Wt.,Lbs. Doz
6K5230 Size 15	Bear	11¾ in.	$11.43		25	

Newhouse Webbed Jaw Traps
Single Spring—Webbed Jaws

Catalog No.	For Catching	Spread of Jaws	Price Each	Price Doz.	Shpg. Wt.,Lbs. Ea.	Shpg. Wt.,Lbs. Doz
6K5231 Size 81	Muskrats, opossums, skunks, etc.	4⅛ in.	49c	$5.11	1½	13

Improved Little Giant Self Setting Mole Trap

One of the Simplest and Surest Mole Traps Made. Very sensitive. No danger in setting; set by pulling up plunger rod. Trigger catches itself. Made of heavy tinned steel. Shipping weight, each, 3 pounds.

6K5320—Each.................**79c**
6 for...................$4.65

Trappers' Needs That Will Increase Your Catch

Bromwell Spring Floor Live Animal Trap

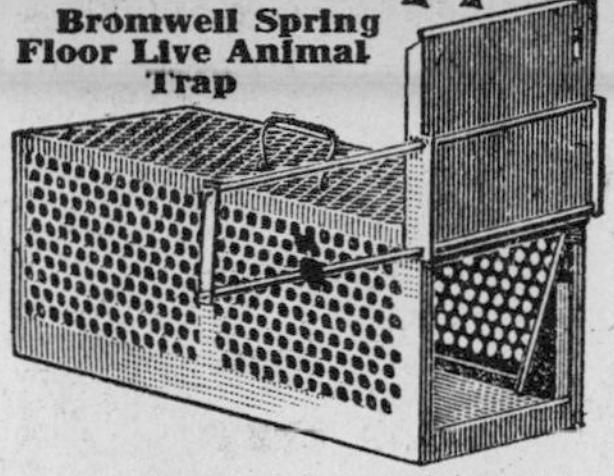

For catching muskrat, mink, rats and other small game alive without injuring them. Trap closes automatically when animal enters. Made of steel throughout. Size, 18x7¼x7¼ inches. Used in water or on land. Can be adjusted to close with light pressure, or with heavy pressure if more than one animal is to be caught at one setting. Shpg. wt., 7 lbs.
6K5343 .... $2.48

Victor's Improved Trap Setter

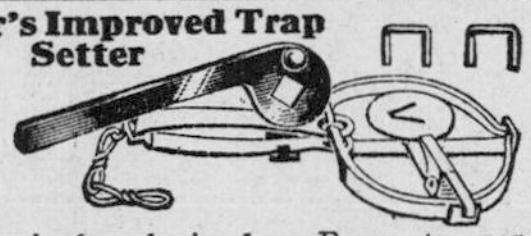

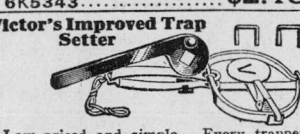

Low priced and simple. Every trapper should have one. Sets all traps up to Size 0. Two extra pieces for setting double spring traps. Shpg. wt., ¾ lb.
6K5336 .... 25c

Holdfast Jaws

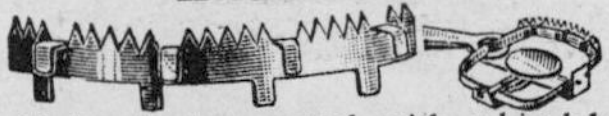

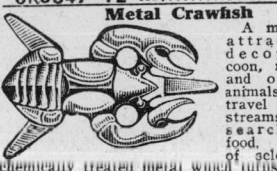

Made of strong steel with pliable clamps that fit on the jaw of any size trap up to number 4. Only one jaw needed on each trap. Will strengthen old traps. Will prevent animals from gnawing feet off. Shipping wt., 1½ lbs.
6K5347—12 for 48c

Metal Crawfish

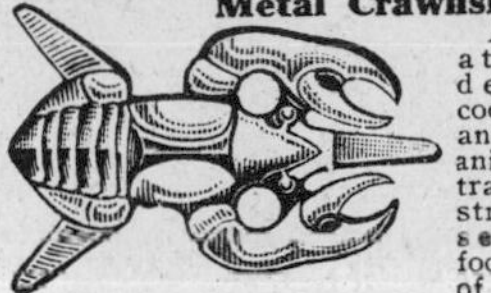

A most attractive decoy for coon, mink, and other animals that travel along streams in search of food. Made of selected, chemically treated metal which turns natural color when placed in water. Fits over pan of trap. Shpg. wt., 8 oz.
6K5338—Per half dozen 48c
Per dozen 83c

Glow Fish Shines in the Dark

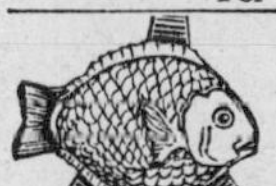

Coating of Eradium makes them attract the curious and inquisitive mink, coon and other fur bearing animals. The darker the night the more it glows. Shaped to fit pan of trap. Fasten to trap and animal will find it. Set trap along edge of stream and fasten chain to log or tree. Shipping weight, 8 ounces.
6K5337—Price, per dozen 79c

Tinfish Water Set

As above, only made of polished tin. Shpg. wt., per doz., 8 oz.
6K5335—Per dozen 21c

Sure Tan Tanning Powder

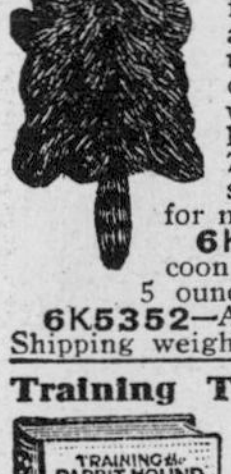

A proven compound for quick tanning of all small furs and skins; also land and water fowl. Easy to use without tanks, vats or other vessels. Does away with handling wet messy hides. Requires from 12 to 72 hours, depending upon skin. Raw furs intended for market should not be tanned.
6K5351—Enough for 5 raccoon skins. Shpg. wt., 5 ounces 25c
6K5352—About 1 pound. Shipping weight, 1½ pounds 69c

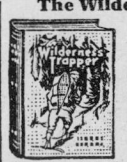

Burbank's Improved Animal Scents

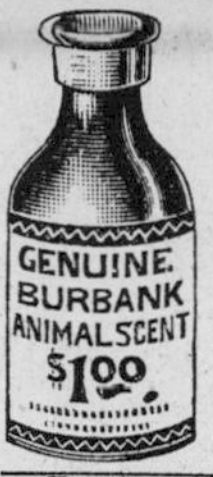

All standard $1.00 size packages. Increase your fur catch! Finish the season with a greater number of fine pelts than ever before. Go about it scientifically. You can do it with Burbank's new improved scents, the best attractors on the market. Each scent is scientifically prepared with best honey base and alcohol solution of pure glands and oils, and proven effective for the particular animal for which it is intended. Shipping weight, each bottle, 8 ounces.

Burbank's Mink Scent
Very latest improved scent. Very effective. Made from animal glands. 120 sets.
6K5371 .... 79c

Burbank's Coon Scent
For raccoons, weasels, etc. 120 Sets.
6K5372 .... 79c

Burbank's Muskrat Scent
A very effective new scent. One bottle for 120 sets.
6K5388 .... 79c

Burbank's Fox Scent
The formula of a famous trapper. Made from animal glands. One bottle for 120 sets.
6K5374 .... 79c

Burbank's Wolf and Coyote Scent
Very effective scent. One bottle for 50 sets.
6K5387 .... 79c

Burbank's Skunk and "Possum" Scent
A very popular and reliable scent. One bottle for 100 sets.
6K5394 .... 79c

Burbank's Triple Extract Beaver Castor
For Beaver, Bear and Lynx; also for making other scents. One bottle for 100 sets.
6K5389 .... 98c

Fur-Fame Trapping Needs

Paste—Bait and Trail Scent—Liquid

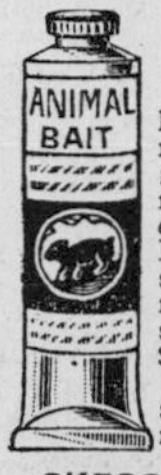

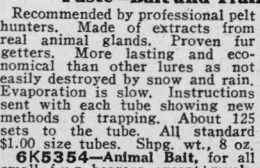

Recommended by professional pelt hunters. Made of extracts from real animal glands. Proven fur getters. More lasting and economical than other lures as not easily destroyed by snow and rain. Evaporation is slow. Instructions sent with each tube showing new methods of trapping. About 125 sets to the tube. All standard $1.00 size tubes. Shpg. wt., 8 oz.
6K5354—Animal Bait, for all small fur bearers except muskrat 69c
6K5353—Muskrat Bait .. 69c
6K5339—Trail Scent, for making trails to traps which animals follow. Tube .. 69c
6K5355—Three tubes of one kind or assorted. State kind wanted. Shipping weight, 1 pound $1.95

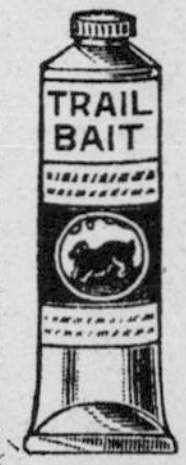

Preferred by many, as the best liquid decoy on the market. Made with extracts from real animal glands. Will not withstand the elements as well as the Paste Bait, but is an effective and successful lure. Comes in 4-ounce bottle sufficient for 250 sets. Shipping weight, 8 ounces.
6K5356—Animal Bait, for all small fur bearers except muskrat 69c
6K5357—Muskrat Bait 69c
6K5358—Trail Scent, for making trails to scattered set 69c
6K5359—3 bottles, any assortment. Shpg. wt., 1 lb. $1.95

Trap Scent Remover

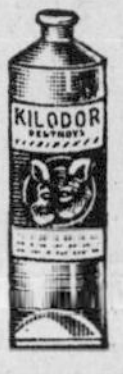

Kilodor destroys the "man smell" on your traps. Animals detect and avoid human scent. Cleaning your traps with Kilodor means more furs. Does away with all smoking and scouring. Pays for itself many times over. Tube lasts the average trapper a season. Shipping wt., 8 ounces.
6K5340—Regular 75c tube 49c

Skunk Scent Remover

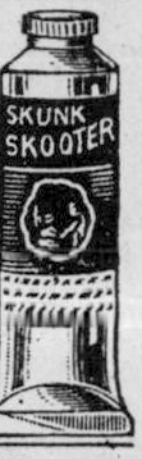

Have no fear of skunks. No need of burying the clothes with the odor. This magic preparation will remove the odor from your hands and clothes without fuss or bother. Every trapper should have several tubes in his outfit for emergencies. Simple to use and works almost instantly. Sold on money back guarantee. Shpg. wt., 8 oz.
6K5341—Regular 75c tube 49c

Amateur Skinning Outfit

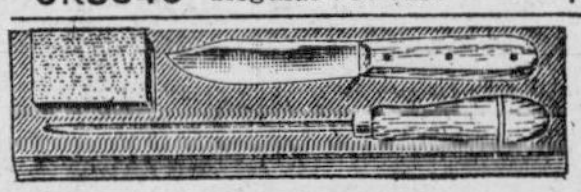

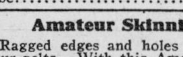

Ragged edges and holes lower the value of your pelts. With this Amateur Skinning Outfit you can do your work more thoroughly and efficiently. Removing tail bones becomes an easier task. A clean cut job makes your pelts more valuable. This outfit is a necessity to every young trapper and pays for itself several times over each season. Instruments made of good grade keen steel with varnished hardwood handles. Shipping wt., 2 lbs. Regular $1.00 size.
6K5344 .... 69c

Fur Stretcher

Approved by Fur Stretchers Generally as the Most Satisfactory

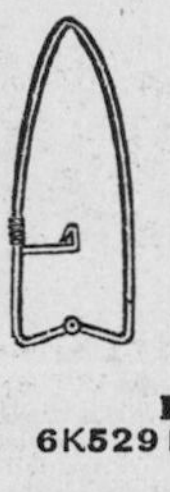

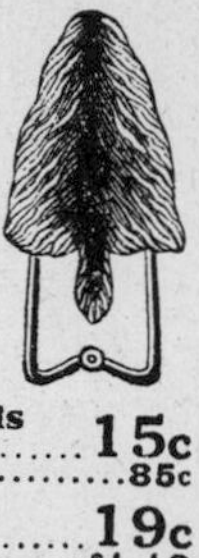

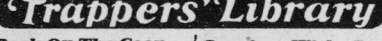

Get more money for your furs by drying them in the right shape. Many furs are ruined and much money is lost by careless handling, particularly by using fur stretchers with sharp edges which damage the fur. This stretcher has no sharp edges. Furs are dried in short time as air circulates through them thoroughly, and prevents molding. Made of steel wire and coated with tin to prevent rusting. Has adjustable hook to stretch fur lengthwise. This gives it perfect shape and higher market value. Can be used indefinitely. Shipping wt., each, 8 ounces.

For muskrat, small mink and other small animals 15c
6K5291—20½ inches long and 7¾ inches wide. Each
6 for 85c

For mink, coon and other larger animals 19c
6K5290—24 inches long and 9½ inches wide. Each
6 for $1.10

Model Game Smoker

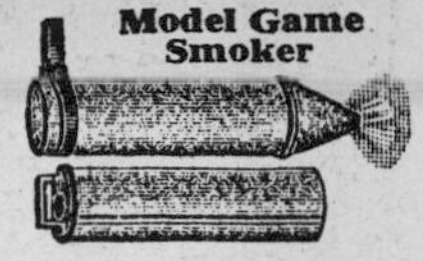

Drives animals out of dens, burrows and hollow trees. Shoots a powerful suffocating smoke produced from charcoal and sulphur compound. Made of galvanized steel. Operated by working two cylinders up and down. Box of compound and full directions sent with each.
6K5325—Shpg. wt., 5 lbs. $1.48
Extra boxes sulphur and charcoal compound. May be used with or without smoke gun. Shpg. wt., 8 oz.
6K5326—2 packages 23c
Per dozen boxes $1.30

Volcano Smokers

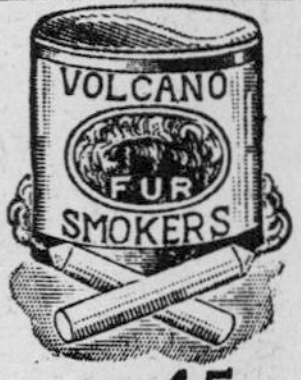

Will drive animals out during cold weather when fur is best. Made in form of candles. Completely fills den with powerful smoke gas and forces animals out. No metal to burn clothes or hands. Weigh only one ounce each. Widely used by coon and opossum hunters. Shpg. wt., 1 lb.
6K5345—Per package of 12 .45c
3 packages for $1.25

American Pedometer

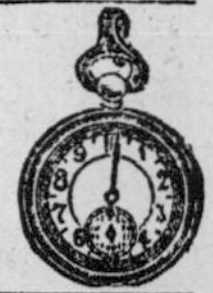

Shows how far you walk. Carry in watch pocket or on belt and every step registers. Figures on face indicate distance in miles you walk. Registers 100 miles and repeats.
6K5346—Shipping wt., 4 oz $1.98

Justrite Pocket Lighter

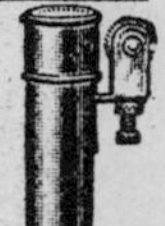

Brass, nickel plated, 2 inches long and ⅝-in. diam. Soak cotton in alcohol and turn wheel. Shipping weight, 2 oz.
6K4612 .... 19c
6K4628—½ Dozen Extra Flints. Shpg. wt., 1 oz 16c

Sharkskin Leather Waterproofing

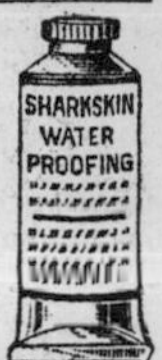

KEEP YOUR FEET DRY. SHARKSKIN LEATHER WATERPROOFING is a neatsfoot oil product that preserves and softens leather. Will more than save its cost in extra wear alone. Shipping weight, each tube, 8 ounces.
6K5349 .... 17c
3 tubes for 45c

Improved Rat Trap

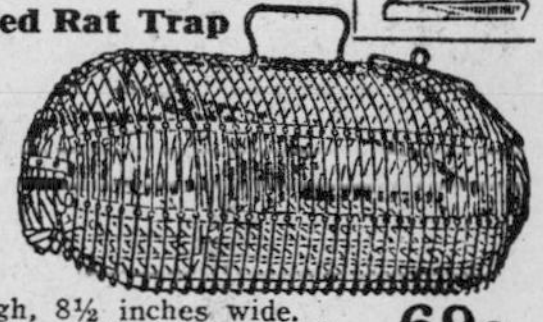

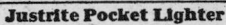

Heavy gauge non-rusting steel wire. Will not spread. 19 inches long, 7 inches high, 8½ inches wide.
6K5304—Shipping wt., 4 lbs ... 69c

Mouse Trap

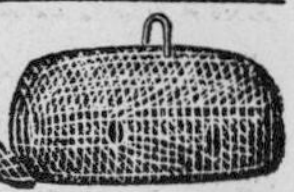

Rustproof wire. Holds many mice. 5 inches high, 8 inches long. Shipping weight, ¾ pound.
6K5303 ...... 39c

Four-Hole Wood Choker Mouse Trap

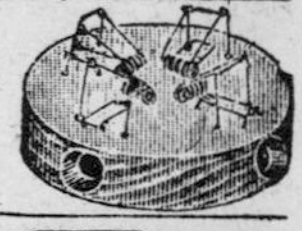

With improved loop trigger set. Shipping weight of three, 1¼ lbs.
6K5306—3 for 25c

Victor Rat Trap

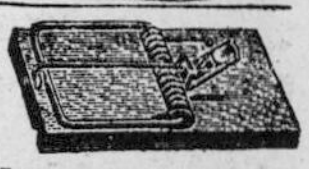

Extra thick hardwood base; short bait trigger; powerful spring. Shpg. wt. of three, 1¼ lbs.
6K5313—3 for. 19c
Victor Mouse Trap. Same as above, but smaller. Shpg. wt., dozen, 1¾ pounds.
6K5300—Per dozen 19c

Trappers' Library

Training The Rabbit Hound

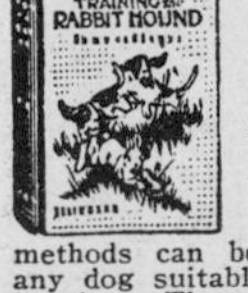

Carl Smith, the author, has had many years experience in the breeding and training of rabbit dogs. The training methods can be applied to any dog suitable for rabbit hunting. The same can be said of the chapter on diseases and remedies. No matter what kind of a dog you own you can't go wrong in buying this book. It is fully illustrated with famous rabbit hounds on the bench and also in action. Bound in cloth with front cover as illustrated. Shipping weight, 1½ pounds.
6K5261 .... 79c

The Wilderness Trapper

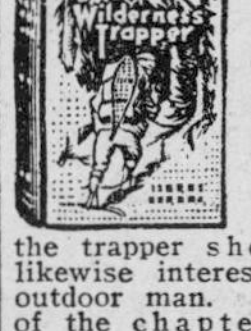

A book on trapping by Raymond Thompson, wilderness trapline expert. Contains sixteen chapters, everything the trapper should know, likewise interesting to the outdoor man. What some of the chapters contain: Outfitting the Wilderness Trapper; Getting Ready for the Fur Harvest; Fox Trapping; The Lynx; Marten and Fisher Trapping, etc. This book contains upward of 160 pages, with pictures and drawings of sets and tracks. Cloth bound. Shipping wt., 1½ pounds.
6K5262 .... 79c

A Book On The Coon Hound Exclusively

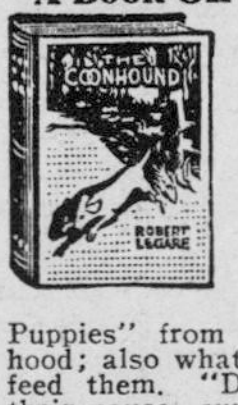

"Training a Coon Hound," several methods to meet conditions prevailing. "Care of Puppies" from birth to doghood; also what, and when to feed them. "Dog Diseases," their cause, cure and how to prevent them. Cloth bound, 5¼x7½ inches. 160 pages. Good readable type, fully illustrated with interesting pictures. Shipping weight, 1½ pounds.
6K5264 .... 79c

Cooning With Cooners

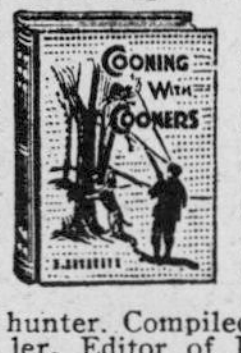

Packed with real coon hunting experiences. Illustrated from typical photographs. A favorite book for every coon hunter. Compiled by O. Kuechler, Editor of Hunter-Trader-Trapper, and containing many interesting stories of actual coon hunts with coon hunting dogs. This book should be in the home of every lover of the sport. Cloth bound. Shipping weight, 1½ pounds.
6K5260 .... 79c

Trap Lines and Trails

A Complete Manual on Trapping

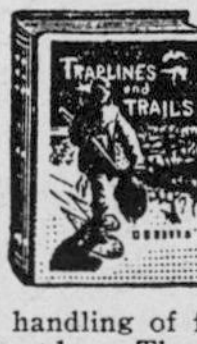

For both amateur and experienced trappers. Has 242 pp. of interesting information, latest methods and the general handling of fur bearing animals. The author, E. J. Dailey, has made a life study of trapping, and spent many years in the Adirondacks. Book is well bound in cloth. Has 54 illustrations. Chapter, "Caring and Marketing Furs" alone worth price of book. Shpg. wt., 1½ lbs.
6K5265 .... 79c

Practical Fur Ranching

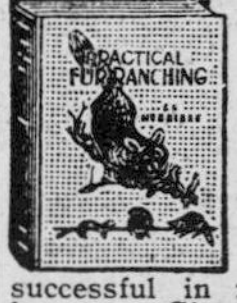

Just the book you want if interested in furs. Contains the most reliable information obtainable from those successful in raising fur bearers. Gives valuable, and practical, information. Has over 213 pages with illustrations and instructive drawings of pens and enclosures. Full description in detail of Silver Fox Raising, Mink, Muskrat, Skunk, Marten, Fisher and others. Just off the press. Shipping weight, 1½ pounds.
6K5263 .... $1.69

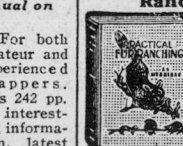

Send Sufficient Money for Postage on Parcel Post Shipments. Any Surplus Will Be Returned

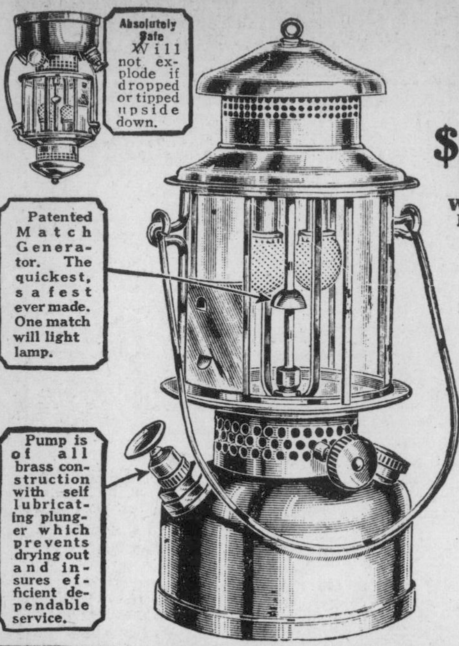

Absolutely Safe Will not explode if dropped or tipped upside down.
Patented Match Generator. The quickest, safest ever made. One match will light lamp.
Pump is of all brass construction with self lubricating plunger which prevents drying out and insures efficient dependable service.

WHITE-LITE Storm Proof Gas Lantern

400 Candle Power

$6.59 With Built In Pump

"A match a scratch and it's lit!"

$5.48 With Pump Separate

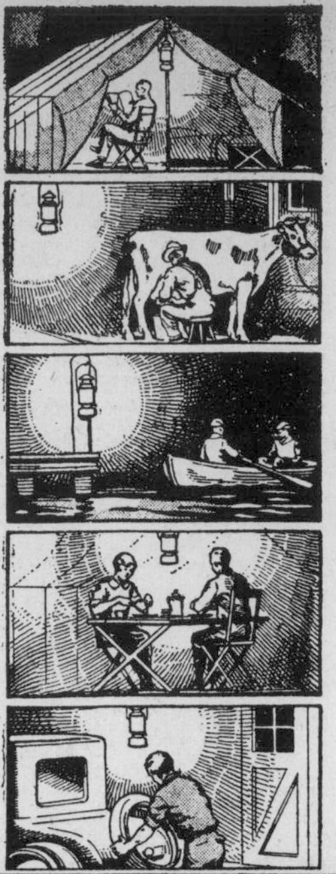

BRIGHTNESS OF 20 LANTERNS IN ONE

Always Ready for Use—Any Time—Anywhere—In Any Kind of Weather

A lighting marvel for out-of-door use in city, town and country. Unaffected by high wind, rain, snow and sleet, it can be carried right through the fiercest storm. This lantern is nationally advertised under a different name and sells for $9.00 with pump built in, $7.50 with separate pump.

Burning ordinary gasoline, the 2 mantles develop 400 candle power light or 20 times the candle power of an ordinary kerosene lantern. And with all this additional light it is very economical. Costs only one-third cent per hour to operate. It is safe and clean and will not explode if dropped or upset.

It has proved indispensable to every farmer, ranchman, planter, dairyman, poultryman and truck-gardener, for night and early morning choring. Used extensively by warehousemen, night-watchmen, liverymen, and hotel keepers; just the thing for campers, travelers, hunters and sportsmen; popular for chautauquas, camp meetings, shows and carnivals; splendid for street lighting in small towns and resorts.

Two outstanding features of the White-Lite are the very bright penetrating light and the patented cone shaded generator which lights very quickly and does not easily carbonize. Other gas lanterns sold elsewhere without this feature require much longer to light and clog more easily. Gasoline container made of heavy brass. Other parts of brass and metal, nickel plated. Mica globe. Lantern stands 13 inches high exclusive of handle and weighs 3½ pounds. Gasoline container holds one quart which will burn from 12 to 14 hours. Shipping weight, 6 pounds.

6K4601—Complete with pump built solid in tank, as illustrated...... **$6.59**

6K4600—As above, but with separate pump. Shipping weight, 6 pounds...... **$5.48**

6K4602—Extra mantles for above. Shpg. wt., 4 oz. Per half dozen.... **35c**

6K4604—Extra mica globes. Shipping weight, 8 ounces. Each...... **63c**

6K4606—Extra coal generator. Be sure to mention name of lamp generator is to be used in. Shpg. wt., 2 oz.. **27c**

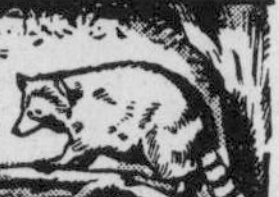

Justrite Powerful Carbide Gas Spot Lights

FOR HUNTING, TRAPPING, FISHING AND CAMPING

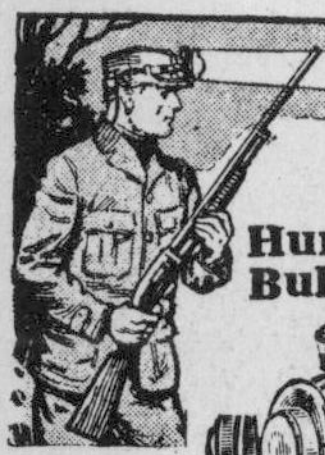

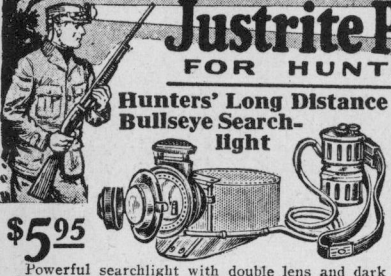

Hunters' Long Distance Bullseye Searchlight

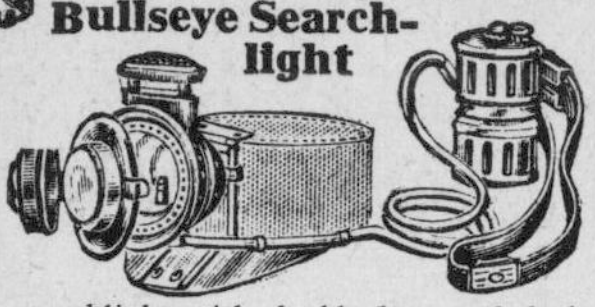

$5.95

Powerful searchlight with double lens and dark shutter. Deep concave 3-inch polished reflector and a 3-inch lens for flood light. Bullseye will throw light a long distance, dark shutter hides the light completely. Burns 5 to 6 hours on one filling. Soft rubber hose and strong belt. Cap not included. Shipping weight, 4 pounds.

6K4610...... **$5.95**

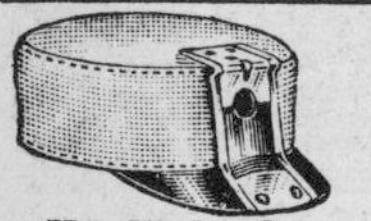

Headlight Cap

Plain brown canvas with a shield fitted in front. Sizes, 6½ to 7½. **State size.** Shpg. wt., ¾ lb.

6K4630...... **20c**

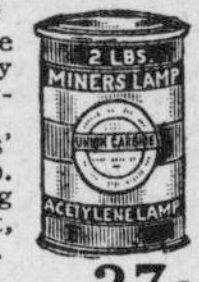

2 LBS.
MINERS' LAMP
ACETYLENE LAMP

Carbide

Can be used in any style carbide lamp. Miners' size, 2-lb. Shipping weight, 2½ pounds.

6K4640...... **27c**

Ten-pound can. Shpg. wt., 12 lbs.

6K4641 **$1.25**

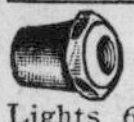

Carbide Light Tips

Made of metal outside with a lava center. Will not break or crack. For Lights 6K4643, 6K4645 and 6K4648 only. Shpg. wt., each, 2 oz.; half dozen, 4 oz.

6K4615—Each...... **4c**

Half dozen...... **19c**

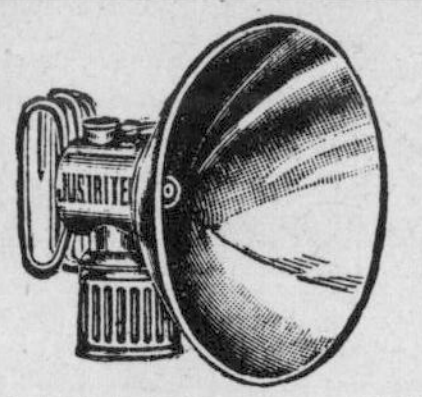

JUSTRITE

Large Reflector Carbide Lamp

$2.59

Folding handles and a large 7-inch highly polished nickel plated reflector which throws a powerful penetrating light over 300 feet. Burns 4 hours on one charge of carbide. Will not smoke, has non-clog water feed. Large reflector. Can be used by campers, hunters, etc., and will give a good reliable light. Shipping weight, ¾ lb.

6K4643...... **$2.59**

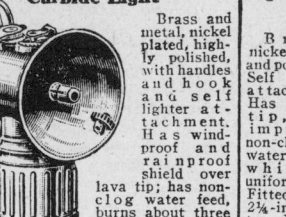

Campers', Hunters' and Sportsmen's Hand Carbide Light

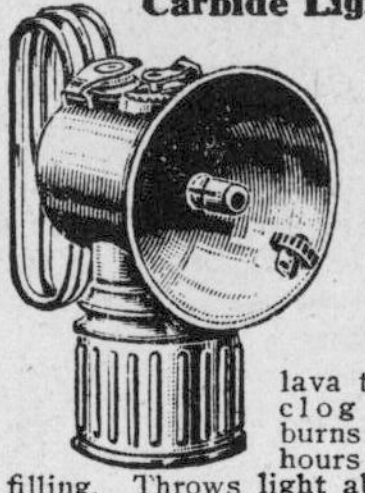

Brass and metal, nickel plated, highly polished, with handles and hook and self lighter attachment. Has windproof and rainproof shield over lava tip; has non-clog water feed, burns about three hours with one filling. Throws light about 75 feet. Height, 4¾ inches. Shipping wt., 2 pounds.

6K4645...... **$1.55**

Campers', Miners' and Sportsmen's Lightweight Carbide Lamp

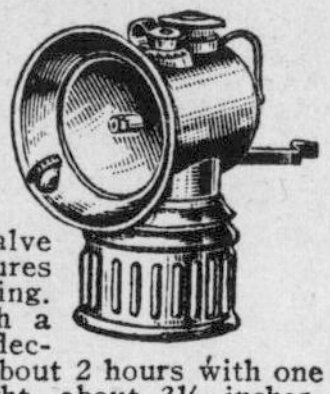

Brass, nickel plated and polished. Self lighter attachment. Has lava tip, also improved non-clogging water feed valve which insures uniform burning. Fitted with a 2¼-inch reflector. Burns about 2 hours with one filling. Height, about 3½ inches. Throws light about 50 feet. Shipping weight, 1 pound.

6K4648...... **89c**

Focusing Headlight

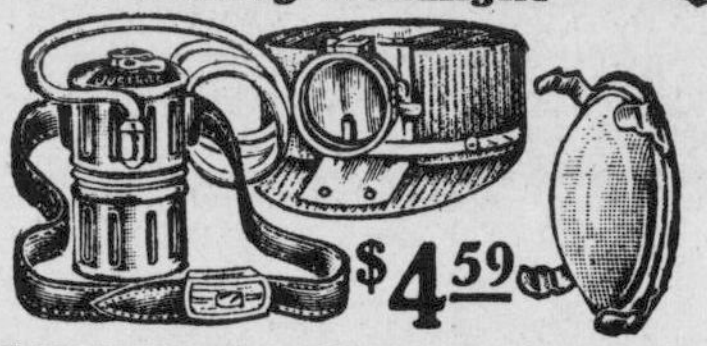

$4.59

Self Lighter Attachment, Extra Lens

Carbide container carried on belt, attached by rubber tube to burner. Headlight made of brass, nickel finish. Generator of steel, black finish. Strong glass lens, diameter, 2½ inches, will focus light about 300 feet. Headpiece weighs 5 ounces. Will not blow out. Burns 4½ to 5 hours. Extra No. 49 Concentrated Lens for spotlight purposes, which increases the power and distance.

6K4616—Complete lamp without cap. Shipping weight, 4 pounds...... **$4.59**

6K4619—Extra tip. Shpg. wt., 2 oz. 3 for **25c**

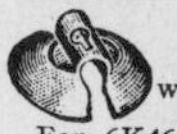

Felt Holders

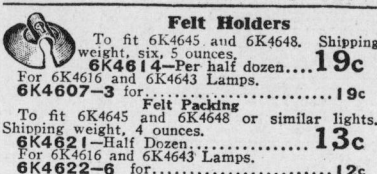

To fit 6K4645 and 6K4648. Shipping weight, six, 5 ounces.

6K4614—Per half dozen...... **19c**

For 6K4616 and 6K4643 Lamps.

6K4607-3 for...... **19c**

Felt Packing

To fit 6K4645 and 6K4648 or similar lights. Shipping weight, 4 ounces.

6K4621—Half Dozen...... **13c**

For 6K4616 and 6K4643 Lamps.

6K4622-6 for...... **12c**

SALT WATER TACKLE

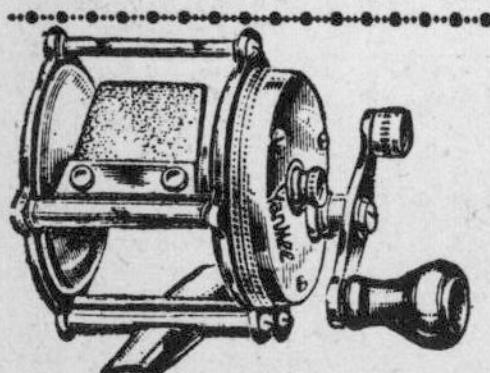

Montague's Yankee

Multiplying with bearing case for pivot. Adjustable click and drag. Special shaped black enamel handle. Fancy oil cups over pivot bearings.

6K4434—200 yds.; 2-in. pillar, 3¼-in. disc; wt., 14½ oz. Shpg. wt., 1½ lbs. **$3.39**

6K4435—250 yds.; 2-in. pillar, 3½-in. disc; wt., 1 lb. Shipping wt., 1½ lbs. **$3.59**

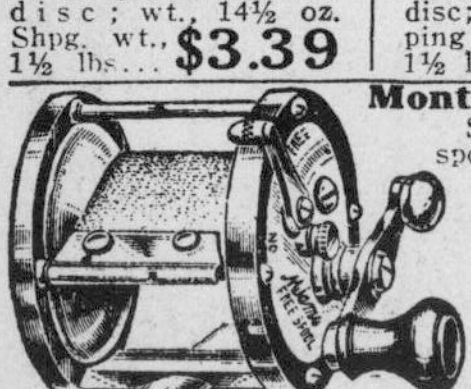

Montague's Miami

Steel pivots, free spool, double multiplying, adjustable click. Lever on side of top plate to adjust free spool action. Hard rubber plates reinforced with metal bands. Metal disc on top plate with gear bridge and pivot bearing. Fancy crank with special shaped rubber handle. Oil cups over pivot bearing.

6K4438—200 yds.; 2⅛-in. pillar, 3-in. disc; wt., 15 oz. Shipping wt., 1¼ lbs. **$7.39**

6K4439—300 yds.; 2⅛-in. pillar, 3¼-in. disc; wt., 16½ oz. Shpg. wt., 1¼ lbs. **$8.39**

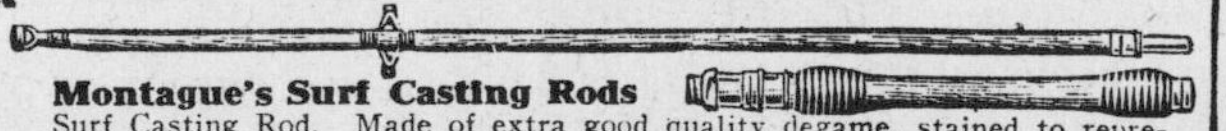

Montague's Surf Casting Rods

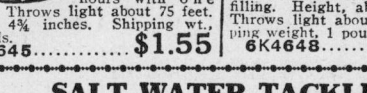

Surf Casting Rod. Made of extra good quality degame, stained to represent greenheart. One piece and detachable hickory spring butt. Nickel plated mountings, stirrup top, one pair large surf casting one ring guides, wound black, nicely varnished. Put up in canvas partition bag. Length of tip, 6 feet. Length of butt, 30 inches. Weight of tip, 13 oz.

6K4422......(Shipping weight, 4½ pounds)...... **$6.95**

Surf Casting Rod—Split Bamboo

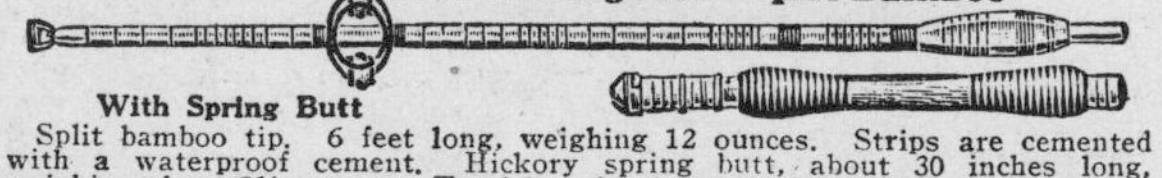

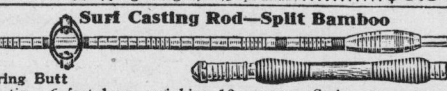

With Spring Butt

Split bamboo tip. 6 feet long, weighing 12 ounces. Strips are cemented with a waterproof cement. Hickory spring butt, about 30 inches long, weighing about 9½ ounces. Total length, about 8½ feet. Mounted with two large genuine agate guides and top. Colored cluster windings at short intervals. Heavy 1-inch reinforced reel seat. Shpg. wt., 4¼ lbs.

6K4402...... **$12.39**

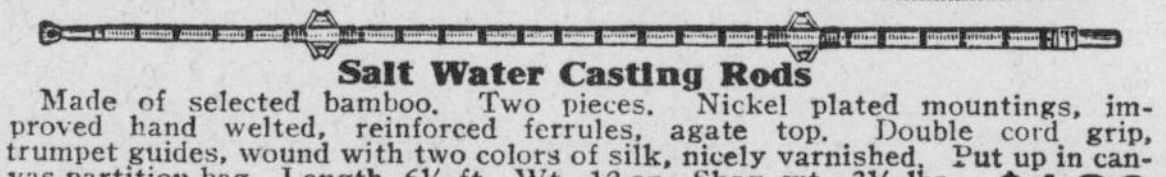

Salt Water Casting Rods

Made of selected bamboo. Two pieces. Nickel plated mountings, improved hand welted, reinforced ferrules, agate top. Double cord grip, trumpet guides, wound with two colors of silk, nicely varnished. Put up in canvas partition bag. Length, 6½ ft. Wt., 12 oz. Shpg. wt., 3½ lbs.

6K4409...... **$4.39**

Salt Water Rods

Made of extra good quality bamboo. Two pieces. Nickel plated mountings, improved hand welted double thick ferrules, double hole tops. Double black cord grip, trumpet guides, wound with two colors of silk, finely varnished. Put up in canvas partition bag. Length, 6½ feet. Wt., 20 oz.

6K4412......(Shipping weight, 1½ pounds)...... **$5.69**

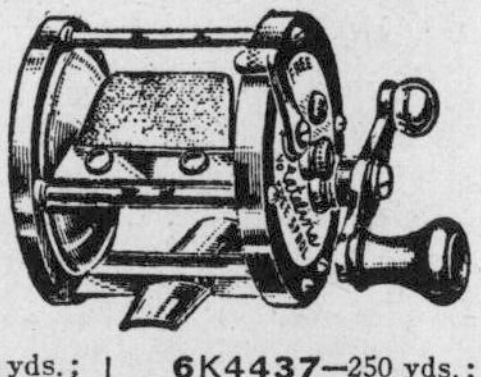

Montague's Catalina

Free Spool

Steel pivots, free spool, double multiplying. Adjustable click. Hard rubber plates reinforced with metal bands. Fancy crank with special shaped rubber handle.

6K4436—200 yds.; 2⅛-in. pillar, 3-in. disc; wt., 15¼ oz. Shpg. wt., 1¼ lbs. **$7.98**

6K4437—250 yds.; 2⅛-in. pillar, 3¼-in. disc; wt., 1 lb. Shipping wt., 1½ lbs. **$8.39**

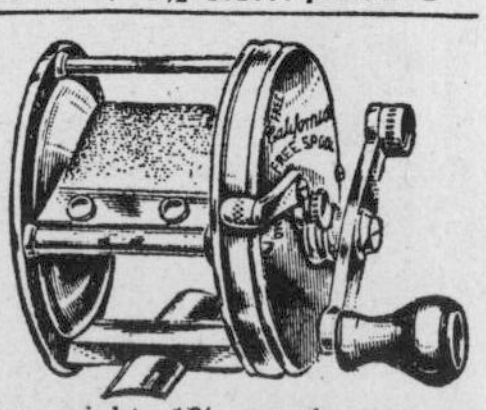

Montague's California

Steel pivots, free spool, double multiplying, adjustable click. Hard rubber plates reinforced with metal bands. Fancy crank with special shaped rubber handle. Oil cups over pivot bearing. Shipping weight, 1¾ pounds.

6K4432—California free spool reel. Nickel plated, has drag and click cap. 250 yards...... **$5.59**

6K4433—Same as above; only 300 yards.. **$5.98**

6K4431—Same as above; only 200 yards.. **$5.25**

Lowest Prices — Most Popular Rods and Tackle — Nationally Advertised

Horton's "Luckie" Casting Rod

Steel with genuine agate guides and agate offset tip, set in German silver mountings. Cork double grip handle with detachable finger hook. Shpg. wt., 1½ lbs. **$3.98**
6K4343—5 feet.......... $3.98
6K4344—5½ feet.......... $3.98

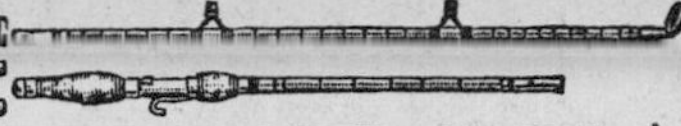

Heddon's Split Bamboo Rod

Genuine agate guides and tip, double solid cork grip. German silver reel seat. Nicely finished in silk windings in two colors. Weight, 5¾ ounces. Shpg. wt., 1½ lbs.
6K4268—5 feet.......... **$6.95**
6K4269—5½ feet.......... $6.95

Heddon's Favorite Split Bamboo Rod No. 6

Brown tone color. Solid double cork grip. Genuine agate mountings. German silver reel seat with locking reel band and ferrules. Closely wound with three colors of silk. In aluminum case. Weight, 5 oz. Shpg. wt., 2 lbs.
6K4288—4½ feet..... **$12.95**
6K4289—5 feet.......... $12.95

Homaco Double Grip Steel Casting Rods

Garnix guides and tip. It has a double cork grip handle with locking band and detachable finger hook. Shipping weight, 1½ pounds.
6K4322—5 feet.......... **$1.98**
6K4323—5½ feet.......... $1.98

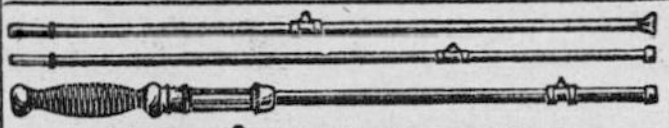

Kayo Steel Casting Rod

Three-joint steel casting rod with corrugated wood handle attached to first joint. Nickel plated reel bands. Metal frictionless guide and tip.
6K4319—5 ft. Shpg. wt., 1 lb... **58c**
6K4320—8 ft. Shpg. wt., 1½ lbs.. 58c

"Luckie" Telescopic Fly Rod with Reversible Handle

Solid cork handle with nickel plated reel seat and band; 28 inches long when telescoped. Shpg. wt., 1½ lbs.
6K4329—9 feet.......... **$1.79**
8½-ft. bait casting rod. Same as above, but with three-ring casting guides.
6K4327—Shpg. wt., 1½ lbs.. $1.79

One-piece Chrome Vanadium Steel Rod

Detachable double grip handle of solid cork and wood tip. Nickel plated brass reel seat with finger hook. Rod is black enameled and has two large agatine guides and large agatine tip. Shpg. wt., 2¼ lbs.
6K4340—5 feet long...... **$2.89**
6K4341—4 feet long.......... $2.89

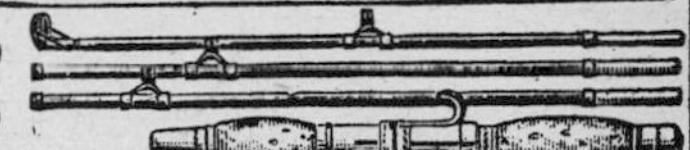

Genuine Bristol No. 27

Steel casting rod with locking reel band. Three genuine agate guides and offset tip. German silver mountings. Cork handle, detachable finger hook. Weight, 9¾ ounces. Shipping weight, 1½ pounds.
6K4304—4½ feet.......... **$8.98**
6K4307—5 feet.......... $8.98

Famous Reels at Low Prices

Shpg. wt., 1½ lbs.

Shakespeare Criterion Level Winding

100-yard capacity, full quadruple multiplying, correct, level winding, full nickel plated, double white celluloid handles, bronze bearings. Has click and adjustable drag.
6K4154... **$4.37**

Meisselbach's Okeh Level Winding Reel No. 600

Level winding attachment, fixed spool and closed line guide. Full 80-yard capacity. Seamless nickel brass tubing, full quadruple multiplying. Shpg. wt., ¾ lb.
6K4120..... **$3.98**

South Bend Level Winding Anti-Backlash

No thumbing required. Full quadruple gear ratio 4 to 1. Nickel silver, satin finish. Will hold 100 yards No.5 standard size silk line. Shpg. wt., 1 lb.
6K4185. **$14.85**

South Bend Oreno Level Winding Anti-Backlash

Same as above, but not as highly polished; plain bearings and one-piece set plate and supporting pillars. Shpg. wt., 1 lb.
6K4114...... **$7.65**

Heddon's No. 3-25 Level Winding Reel

Non-rusting nickel silver finish. Capacity, 100 yards of 15-lb. test line. Has double steady bar which takes the strain of the level winding attachment entirely off of the reel. Shpg. wt., 1 lb.
6K4103.. **$22.50**

Union Hardware Level Winding Reel

Full quadruple multiplying with positive level winding feature; nickel plated, white double handle, 80-yard capacity. Has adjustable drag click. Shpg. wt., ¾ lb.
6K4100... **$2.69**

Monarch Automatic Spring Hook

Bait is placed on small hook. When fish nibbles the gaff-like hooks snap shut and hold fish. Shipping weight, 3 ounces.
6K3611—For small fish like croppies, perch and sunfish **19c**
6K3612—For large fish (½ to 1 lb.)..... 24c

Heddon Basser

A near surface bait which gives an extreme limit of erratic side darting, dipping and sudden swerving action. Glass eyes. Shpg. wt., 4 oz.
6K3326—White body and red head.............. **87c**

The Heddon Vamp

Resembles a baby pike. Especially beautiful and deceptive in finish. Attractive diving and swimming movements. Shipping weight, 4 oz.
[illegible]—White body, red head...... **87c**

Heddon's Luny Frog

Travels through the water in a natural frog position. When retrieved, it dives and has a natural swimming movement. Length of body, 4¼ in. Shipping wt., 4 oz.
[illegible] Green Frog..... **$1.10**

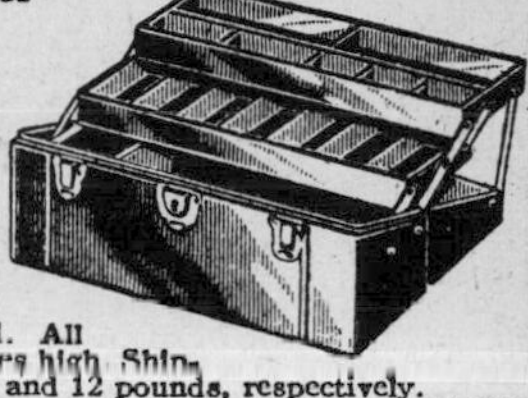

Outing's Cantilever Tackle Box

Electrically welded seams; rainproof. With the opening of the lid, trays automatically shift to position outside of box. Of heavy steel, enameled in a rich brown green color. Hinges, locks, snaps and handle loops are heavily brass plated. All [illegible] inches wide, 7 inches high. Shipping weights, 7¼, 9¼ and 12 pounds, respectively.
6K3552—12 in. long.......... $5.98
6K3553—16 in. long.......... 6.79
6K3554—21 in. long.......... 8.48

South Bend Wiz-Oreno

Practically weedless, single hook, swiveling spinner, hackle fly and pork rind snap. Shpg. wt., 4 oz.
6K3352—Red head, white body... **87c**

South Bend Dart-Oreno

Metal body with bright combination hackle and bucktail. Hook practically weedless. Shipping wt., 3 oz.
6K3394—Copper head.............. **87c**

South Bend Fish Oreno

Nickel plated head. Can be used for either surf or deep fishing. Shipping weight, 3 ounces.
6K3390—White body, red head.......... **$1.07**

South Bend Bass Orono Wabbler

Body of red cedar wood, 3½ inches long, enameled finish. Shipping wt., 4 oz.
6K3400—Hollow body spotted.... **87c**

Fishing Facts

It tells of fly fishing, bait casting and still fishing; where and how to fish. Fully illustrated. Over 200 pages and bound in cloth. Shpg., wt., 1 lb.
6K3508..... **79c**

Shpg. wt., 3 oz.

100 Assorted Hooks

Made up of all popular patterns and assorted sizes of each pattern. These hooks are all made from the best spring steel, sharpened to a very fine point and properly tempered.
6K3605—Box of 100. **21c**

Al. Foss Shimmy Wiggler

Nickel plated brass body and spinner with size 3-0 hook. Can use bucktail or pork rind. Rides upright. Shipping wt., 3 oz.
6K3250....... **79c**

Al. Foss Jazz Wiggler

Size 3-0 hook, tied with natural bucktail streamer. Used with or without pork rind. Shipping wt., 3 oz.
6K3339 White.............. **59c**

Genuine Skinner's Spoon Bait for Game Fish

Hollow point hooks. State size. Shpg. wt., 3 oz.
6K3245 Nos. 4½ and 4¾. Ea. **24c**

Natural Preserved Minnows

6K3436—Medium Shiners, about3 inches long. About 24 to the bottle. Shipping weight, 1¼ pounds.
Per jar..... **24c**

Linen Gill Nets

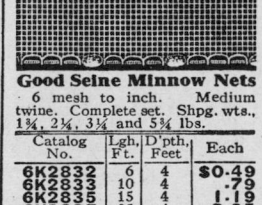

Can be set where it would be impossible to use a Seine, Hoop or Trap net. As a rule, Gill nets are fished on the bottom, floats hold them up like a fence, but they may be floated near the top with good results. Be sure to order mesh large enough for head of fish to be caught to enter. All our Gill Nets are hung on a one-half basis, that is, 200 yards of netting hung to make a net 100 yards long. **All sizes carried in stock.**

Catalog No.	Depth, Feet	Sq. Mesh, Inches	Size Twine No.	5 Yds. Long	10 Yds. Long	20 Yds. Long	30 Yds. Long	6K2996 Linen Gill Netting Only Per Yard
6K3039	3½	1½	30-3	0.95	1.89	3.68	$5.55	14c
6K3040	3½	2	30-3	.72	1.43	2.85	4.35	9c
6K3041	4	1	40-3	1.20	2.35	4.65	6.85	19c
6K3042	4	1¼	30-3	1.28	2.55	5.13	7.85	25c
6K3043	4	1½	30-3	.97	1.95	3.85	5.65	29c
6K3044	4	1¾	30-3	.85	1.65	3.25	4.98	13c
6K3045	4	2	30-3	.77	1.54	3.08	4.75	11c
6K3046	5	1	40-3	1.35	2.68	5.45	8.10	27c
6K3047	5	1¼	30-3	1.43	2.85	5.70	8.75	29c
6K3048	5	1½	30-3	1.17	2.34	4.67	6.95	21c
6K3049	5	1¾	30-3	1.00	1.98	3.95	5.95	17c
6K3050	5	2	30-3	.95	1.85	3.64	5.65	15c
6K3051	5	2¼	30-3	.89	1.75	3.60	5.25	13c
6K3052	6	1	40-3	1.65	3.25	6.40	9.60	32c
6K3053	6	1¼	30-3	1.76	3.50	7.05	10.80	37c
6K3054	6	1½	30-3	1.29	2.58	5.15	7.85	25c
6K3055	6	1¾	30-3	1.10	2.15	4.30	6.50	19c
6K3056	6	2	30-3	1.01	2.00	4.00	6.15	17c
6K3057	6	2¼	30-3	.97	1.90	3.75	5.65	15c

We carry only sizes listed. If longer nets are wanted, tie two together. Shpg. wt., per yd., 6 oz.

Good Seine Minnow Nets

6 mesh to inch. Medium twine. Complete set. Shpg. wts., 1¾, 2¼, 3¼ and 5¾ lbs.

Catalog No.	Lgh, Ft.	D'pth, Feet	Each
6K2832	6	4	$0.49
6K2833	10	4	.79
6K2835	15	4	1.19
6K2837	25	4	2.05

First quality. Put up in 1-pound skeins. We do not sell less than 1 pound of a size. **State size wanted.**
6K2814—Soft Laid Seine Twine. Sizes, 6, 9, 12. Per pound.......... **59c**
6K2815—Soft Laid Seine Twine. Sizes, 16, 20, 24, 28, 32. Per pound.......... **55c**
6K2816 — Medium Laid Seine Twine. Sizes, 6, 9, 12. Per pound.......... **64c**
6K2817 — Medium Laid Seine Twine. Sizes, 15, 18, 21, 24, 30, 36, 42. Per pound.. **56c**

Black Beauty Silk Waterproof Casting Line

Constructed of No. 1 Japan silk. Not affected by the action of alkali or salt waters. Two spools connected if desired. Shpg. wt., 6 oz.

Catalog No.	Breaking Strength	50-Yard Spool
6K3904	14 lbs.	$0.83
6K3905	18 lbs.	.98
6K3906	24 lbs.	1.19

South Bend Silk Casting Line

Color: White and black, striped lengthwise. Fifty-yard spool. Two spools connected if desired. Shpg. wt. 3 oz.

Catalog No.	Breaking Strength	50 Yards
6K3955	12 lbs.	$1.25
6K3956	19 lbs.	1.67
6K3957	25 lbs.	1.95

Brawn Mottled Beauty Silk Casting Line

Japan silk. Two spools connected if desired. Shpg. wt., 3 oz.

Catalog No.	Breaking Strength	50-Yard Spool
6K3911	14 lbs.	69c
6K3912	17 lbs.	79c
6K3913	20 lbs.	89c

Highest Quality Genuine Beaver Twisted Cuttyhunk Linen Line

The world's best grades of imported linen are used in the building of this sturdy line. Have the greatest possible strength and, at the same time, are properly twisted so that they are absolutely free from any imperfection. 50-yard spools Six spools connected if desired. Shipping weight, 4 ounces.

Catalog No.	No. of Strands	Breaking Strength	50-Yd. Spool
6K3975	9	18 lbs.	33c
6K3976	12	24 lbs.	39c
6K3977	15	30 lbs.	43c
6K3978	18	36 lbs.	49c
6K3979	21	42 lbs.	55c
6K3980	24	48 lbs.	63c
6K3981	27	54 lbs.	69c
6K3982	30	60 lbs.	77c
6K3983	36	72 lbs.	89c

Special Kingfisher Bait Casting Line

Grayish white with black check. 50-yard spools. Two spools connected if desired. Shpg. wt., 3 oz.

Catalog No.	Breaking Strength	50-Yard Spool
6K3935	12 lbs.	$0.89
6K3936	16 lbs.	1.15
6K3937	23 lbs.	1.27

To Find What You Want, See Index Pages 550 to 570

Quality Skis Developed by Skilled Ski Makers

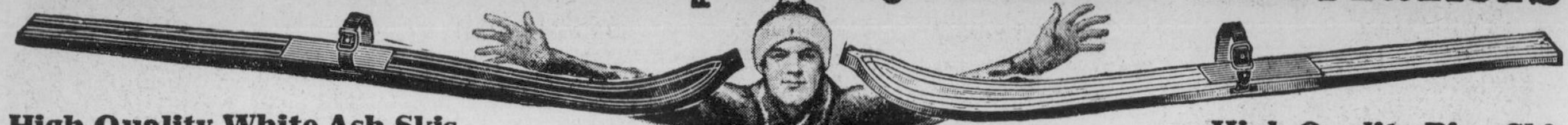
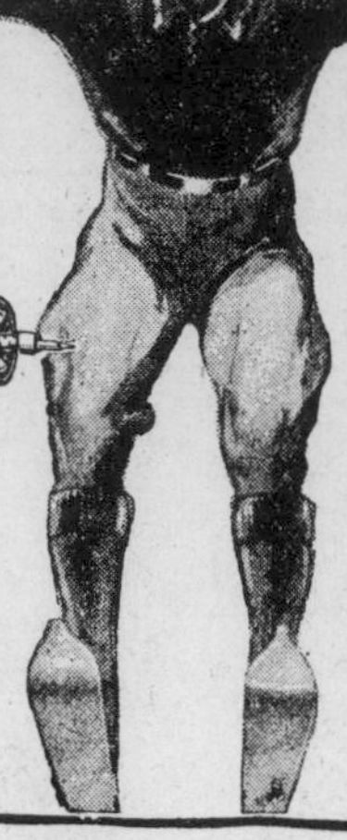

High Quality White Ash Skis

Made of a specially selected quarter sawed hard, tough ash. Finished in black with fancy grooved white stripes. Covered with several coats of waterproof varnish. Fitted with heavy leather toe straps and corrugated rubber foot rest. Nicely finished, well balanced.

	Wt., Abt.	Shpg. Wt.	Per Pair
6K5622¼—5 feet long	4 lbs.	6 lbs.	$2.98
6K5623¼—6 feet long	5 lbs.	7 lbs.	3.45
6K5624¼—7 feet long	8 lbs.	9 lbs.	3.95
6K5625¼—8 feet long	11 lbs. 6 oz.	13 lbs.	4.45

High Quality Pine Skis

First quality edge grained Norway pine, with strong, hard, smooth running surface. Several coats waterproof varnish, fancy stripes. Heavy toe straps and rubber foot rest.

	Wt., Abt.	Shpg. Wt.	Per Pair
6K5626¼—4 feet long	2 lbs. 12 oz.	3½ lbs.	$0.79
6K5627¼—5 feet long	3 lbs. 3 oz.	4 lbs.	1.29
6K5628¼—6 feet long	4 lbs. 11 oz.	6 lbs.	1.79
6K5629¼—7 feet long	7 lbs.	8 lbs.	1.98
6K5630¼—8 feet long	10 lbs.	11 lbs.	2.39

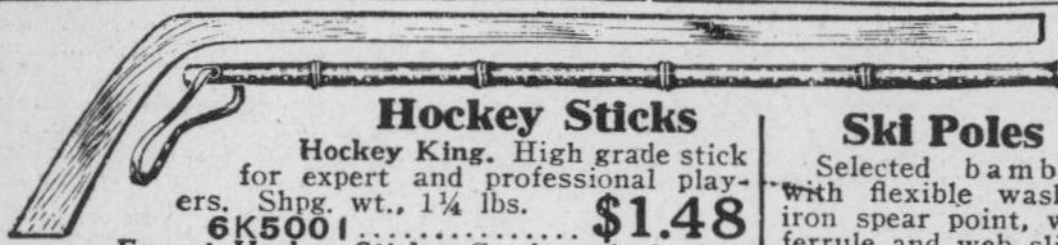
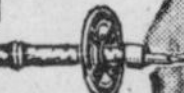

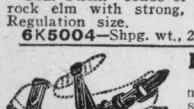

Hockey Sticks

Hockey King. High grade stick for expert and professional players. Shpg. wt., 1¼ lbs.
6K5001 .... $1.48

Expert Hockey Stick. Good grade hockey stick for the average player; full size and weight and properly shaped. Shpg. wt., 1¼ lbs.
6K5002 .... 79c

Youths' Hockey Stick. Not quite as long as the men's size, but made of good quality rock elm. Shpg. wt., ¾ lb.
6K5003 .... 28c

Goal Stick. Made of 2-piece selected rock elm with strong, straight grain. Regulation size.
6K5004—Shpg. wt., 2 lbs. $1.69

Ski Poles

Selected bamboo, with flexible washer, iron spear point, wire ferrule and web sling. 4½ feet long. Shipping weight, 1¼ lbs.
6K5643¼
Each 79c

Official Size Hockey Puck. Made of Pure rubber.
6K5005—Shipping weight, 3 oz. 28c

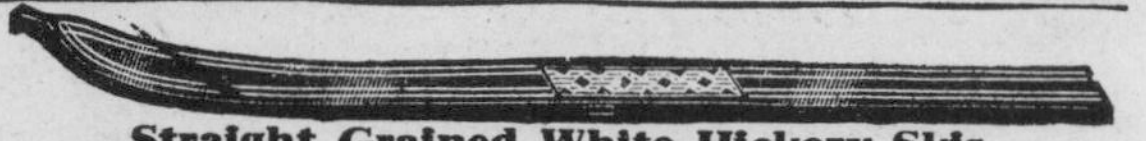

Straight Grained White Hickory Skis

Improved Model

Made of high quality selected white hickory, attractively finished in black with grooved white stripes. Running surface is double grooved. Leather toe straps and rubber foot rests. These skis are more particularly used as a leaping ski in contests.

	Wt. Abt.	Shpg. Wt.	Per Pair
6K5634¼—6 feet long	6 lbs. 3 oz.	7 lbs.	$3.95
6K5635¼—7 feet long	10 lbs.	11 lbs.	4.45
6K5636¼—7½ feet long	11 lbs.	12 lbs.	4.95
6K5637¼—8 feet long	12 lbs.	13 lbs.	5.65

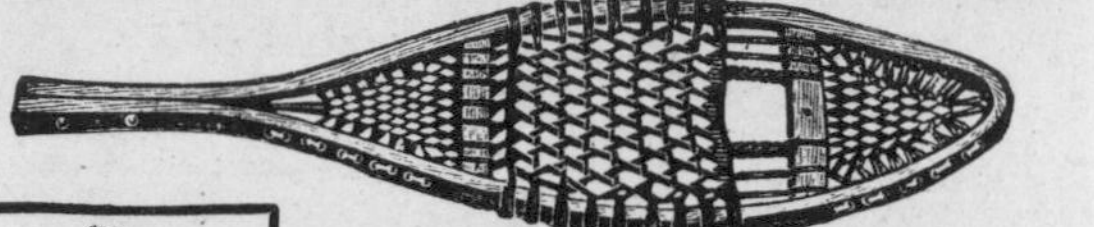

Selected Snowshoes

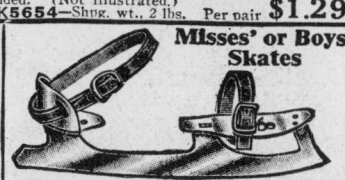

Made by one of the oldest and best snowshoe factories. Bows are handmade of selected one-piece, straight grain white ash butts; combining spring, lightness of weight and toughness of fiber. Strung with selected tanned cowhide. Slightly turned up at toe; neatly finished.

6K5659¼—Men's size, 14x42 inches. Weight, per pair, 4⅜ lbs. Shpg. wt., 5¾ lbs.
Per pair $5.98

6K5657¼—Women's size, 11½x36 in. Weight, per pair, 4⅜ pounds. Shpg. wt., 5¾ lbs.
Per pair $4.23

Snowshoe Sandals or Bindings

For Men and Women

Made of heavy leather, with soles riveted together. Rawhide laces for top and for lacing to snowshoes included. (Not illustrated.)
6K5654—Shpg. wt., 2 lbs. Per pair $1.29

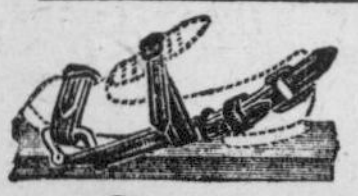

Expert Ski Bindings

Leather Ski Bindings, with metal side plates and bolts and solid leather straps with tightening clamp instead of buckle. Easy to put on and take off. Shpg. wt., 1½ lbs.
6K5647—Pair. $1.98

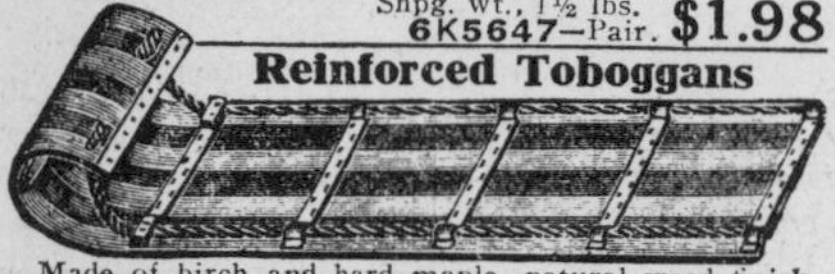

Reinforced Toboggans

Made of birch and hard maple, natural wood finish. The middle and two outside slats are thicker than the other four, adding to strength and speed. Very easy steering. Long, graceful bend, takes bumps easily, runs well in deep snow. Fitted with ½-inch cotton rope, fastened with leather loops.

6K5638¼—5 ft. long.	Shpg. wt., 15 lbs.	$5.79
6K5639¼—6 ft. long.	Shpg. wt., 17½ lbs.	6.98
6K5641¼—8 ft. long.	Shpg. wt., 23 lbs.	9.39
6K5642¼—10 ft. long.	Shpg. wt., 27 lbs.	10.95

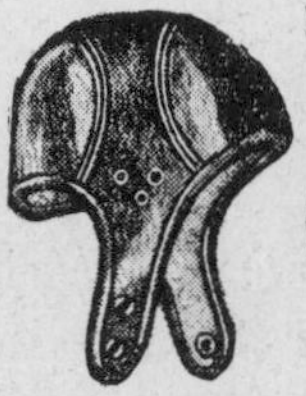

Skaters' Helmet

Also Adaptable for All Winter Sports

Finest black, soft pliable leather; triple stitched and felt lined. Adjustable chin fasteners. Will fit any size from 6¾ to 7½. Shipping wt., 8 oz.
6K5018 $1.48

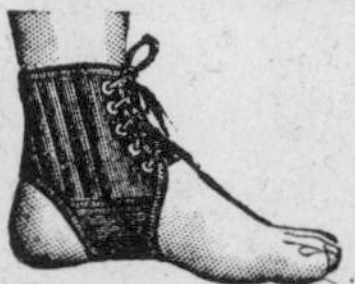

Leather Adjustable Ankle Support

Soft sheepskin, reinforced with removable stays. Gives extra strength. Give size shoe worn. Shipping wt., 8 oz.
6K1750—For men. Sizes, 6 to 10. Per pair....... $1.29
6K1751—For women and boys. Sizes 2 to 7 Per pair. $1.29

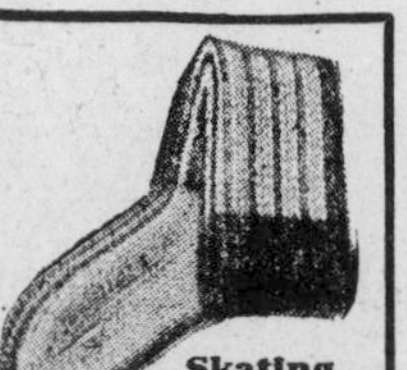

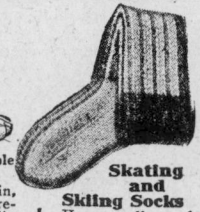

Skating and Skiing Socks

Heavy, all wool. For men and women. Sizes, 9, 10, 11. State size. Shpg. wt., 8 oz.
6K5021—6-inch high socks, gray with 3-inch green cuff... 69c
6K5020—17-in. high hose, white with green top........ 79c

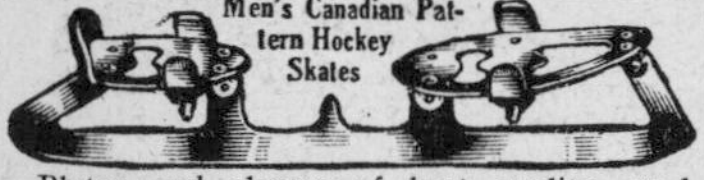

Men's Canadian Pattern Hockey Skates

Plates and clamps of best quality steel, nickel plated, polished. Sizes, 9½ to 12 inches. State length of shoe in inches.
6K5086—Shipping wt., 3 lbs. $1.33

Special High Grade Runners
As above, but hard tempered steel runners. State length.
6K5084 .... $1.69

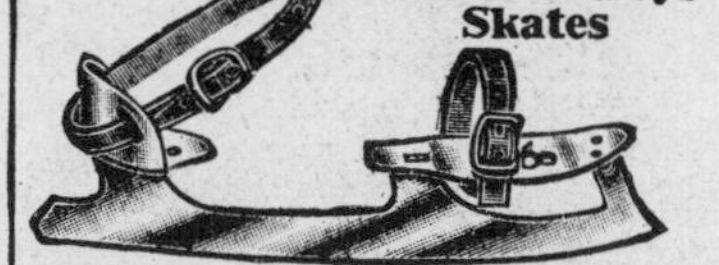

Misses' or Boys' Skates

Rocker runner, good quality polished steel skate. Adaptable where runners are worn. Leather straps. Sizes, 8 to 11 inches. State length of shoe in inches.
6K5090—Shpg. wt., 2½ lbs. $1.05

Improved Clamp Skates

Something New—An Adjustable Skate

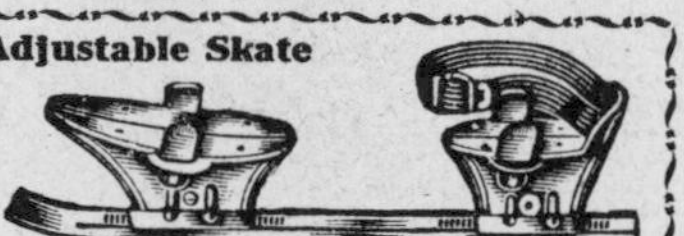

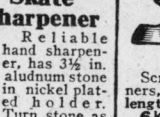

Always sure to fit. Clamp plates movable on runners by slight adjustment. Fits any size men's or women's shoe. Guaranteed to hold tight and not work loose. All parts steel, nicely finished and strongly constructed. Full size adjustable clamps and web straps. Shpg. wt., 2¾ lbs.
For Women 6K5097 .... 98c
For Men 6K5096 .... 98c

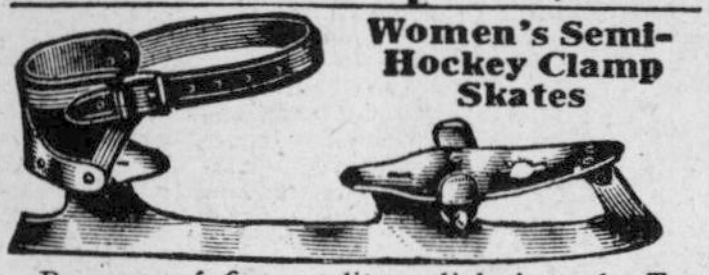

Women's Semi-Hockey Clamp Skates

Runners of fine quality polished steel. Top plates and clamps of best cold rolled steel. Sizes, 8 to 11 inches. State length shoe in inches.
6K5092—Shpg. wt., 2½ lbs. $1.29

Women's Nickel Plated Skates
Same as above, but highly nickel plated. State length.
6K5093 .... $1.59

Ice Skate Key
6K5033—Shpg. wt., 2 oz. 5c

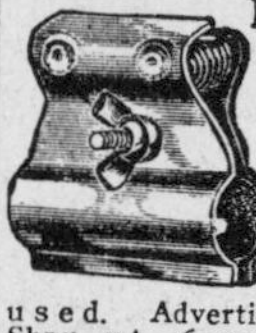

Berghman's Skate Sharpener

Reliable hand sharpener, has 3½ in. aludnum stone in nickel plated holder. Turn stone as used. Advertised price, $1.00. Shpg. wt., 6 oz.
6K5027 .... 69c

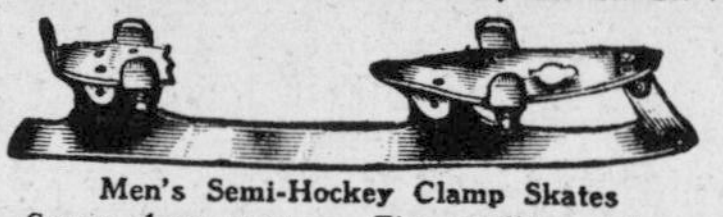

Men's Semi-Hockey Clamp Skates

Screw clamp pattern. Fine quality steel runners, well polished. Sizes, 9½ to 12 in. State length.
6K5087—Shpg. wt., per pair, 3 lbs. ... 89c
Same as above, but entire skate is nickel plated. State length.
6K5088 .... $1.29

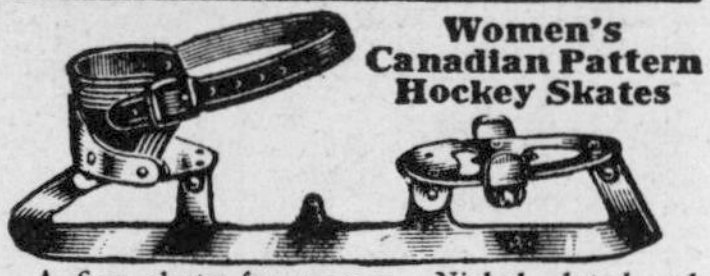

Women's Canadian Pattern Hockey Skates

A fine skate for women. Nickel plated and polished. Straight runners of good quality steel. Top plates of cold rolled steel. Strong russet heel straps, nickel plated heel bands. Sizes, 8½ to 11 inches. State length shoe in inches.
6K5091—Shpg. wt., 2¾ lbs. $1.59

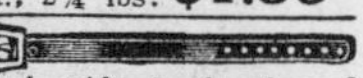

Skate Straps

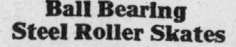

21 inches long, ⅝ inch wide, made of good heavy quality leather with buckle.
6K5030—Shpg. wt., 3 oz. Pair ... 12c

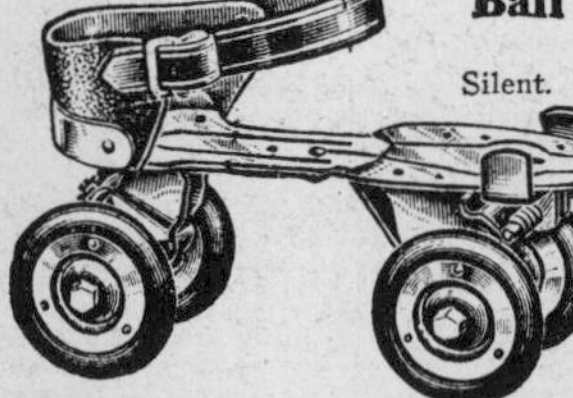

Ball Bearing Rubber Tire Skates

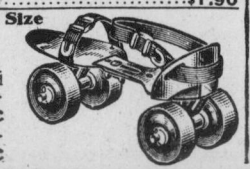

Silent. Speedy. Non-skid. Shock absorbing. Long wearing. Will extend to fit shoes 8½ to 11½ inches.
6K4817—Men's and boys' size. Shpg. wt., 5 lbs. Per pair $3.25
6K4818—Women's and girls' size, with high back strap.
Shipping weight, 5 pounds.
Per pair $3.25
6K4819—Juvenile size, to fit shoes 6 to 8 inches.
Per pair 3.25
6K4820—Extra rollers for above. Shipping weight, 1½ pounds. Each 24c
Per set of 8 .... $1.90

CHICAGO Roller Skates

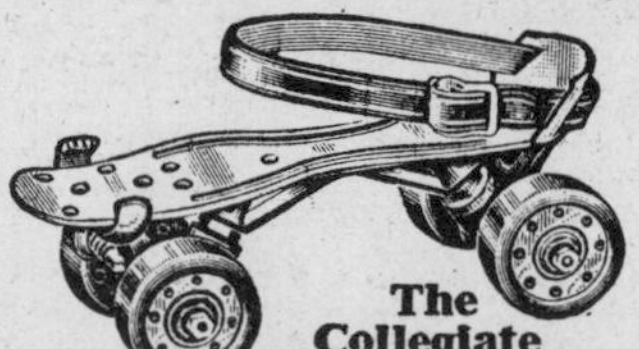

The Collegiate

For Men and Women

Advertised Price, $5.00.

Ball bearing skates, cold rolled steel rollers. Strongly constructed, rubber cushion shock absorbers. High speed, heavy duty ball bearing wheels. Sizes to fit shoes 6, 7, 8 and 9. State choice. Shipping wt., 6 lbs.
6K4826—Girls' sizes.... $3.98
6K4825—Boys' sizes....... 3.98

Roller Skate Keys
6K4850—Shipping weight, each, 2 oz. Each, 4c; per dozen 42c

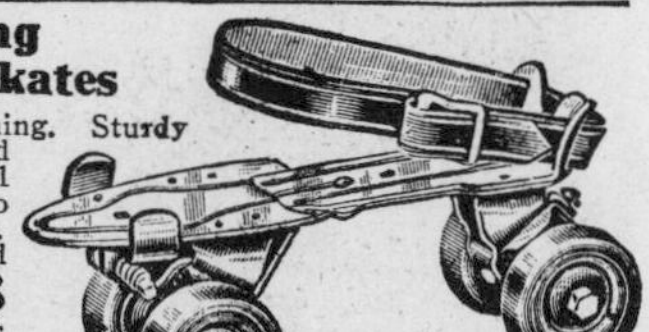

Ball Bearing Steel Roller Skates

Swift and easy running. Sturdy construction. Nickel plated and highly polished. Will extend to fit shoes 8½ to 11 in. Shipping wt., 5 lbs.
6K4828—Men's and boys' size. Per pair.... $1.68
6K4829—Women's and girls' size, with high back strap. Per pair.... $1.79
6K4830—Juvenile size. Fits shoes 6 to 8 inches. Shipping weight, 3 pounds. Per pair $1.79
6K4857—Extra rollers. Shipping wt., 5 oz. Each 14c

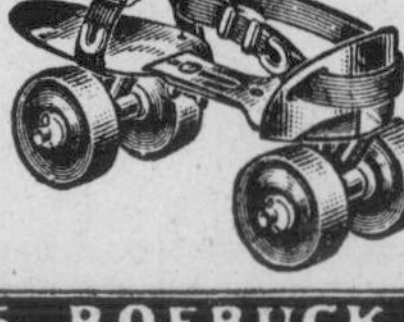

Extension Skates—Small Size

Plain Bearings—Pressed Steel Rollers

New improved sidewalk plates. Web heel and toe strap. Extend to fit shoes 6 to 9 inches long. Shpg. wt., 3 lbs.
6K4821—Per pair... 85c
6K4840—Rollis for above. Shipping wt., 5 lbs. Per set of 8 .... 34c

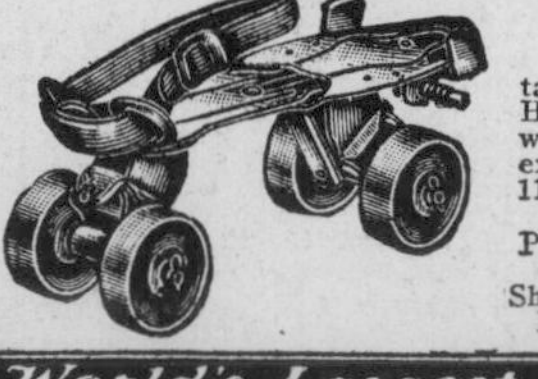

Extension Skates—Medium Size

Plain Bearings—Pressed Steel Rollers

Built with rubber cushions to take out the jar and vibration. Highest grade cold rolled steel, well finished and durable. Skates extend to fit shoes from 8½ to 11½ inches. Shpg. wt., 5 lbs.
6K4822
Per pair $1.29
6K4840—Rolls for above. Shipping weight, 1 lb. Per set of 8 .... 34c

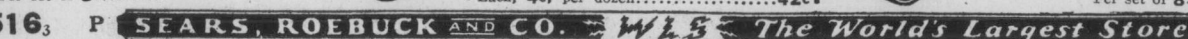

Prices Much Lower Than Elsewhere

Famous
Nestor Johnson's Hockey Skates

NESTOR JOHNSON NORTH STAR SKATES — NESTOR JOHNSON MFG CO. CHICAGO

Genuine
Planert's Hockey Skates

PLANERT'S NORTHLIGHT SKATES

$8.95 "They Go Like Lightning"
Regular Advertised Price, $11.00
Hockey Skates for Men and Women

Every skater knows Johnson's famous North Star Tubular Hockey Skates. For general skating, either on inside rinks or outdoor skating ponds, this is one of the easiest, safest and most completely satisfactory skates. A real help to the beginner and a joy to the expert. High carbon steel special runner tempered by Johnson's process, that insures speed, safety and firm grip. Shoes are made throughout of high grade leather, giving perfect comfort and real support to the foot when skating. Leather strap fits to skate itself, for additional ankle support. Latest non-rusting aluminum finish. Complete with shoes.

For Boys and Men. Full sizes, 5 to 11. Be sure to state size of shoe worn. Shpg. wt., 4¼ lbs.
6K5040—Per pair... **$8.95**

For Girls and Women. High top shoes. Full sizes, 3 to 8. Be sure to state size of shoe worn. Shipping weight, 4¼ pounds.
6K5041—Per pair... **$8.95**

The Popular "North Light" $8.67
Regular Advertised Price, $11.00
Hockey Skates for Men and Women

One of the most popular selling tubular hockey skates. Nationally advertised; used and endorsed by leading skating champions. Light in weight, yet extremely strong. Highly tempered crucible tool steel runners. A fine quality skate with a keen lasting edge. A superior skate for speed with safety, attached to a fine quality leather shoe designed for maximum skating comfort. Reinforced with tape straps and strong ankle strap. Wide padded tongue protects foot from tight lacing. Latest non-rusting aluminum finish. Complete with shoes.

For Boys and Men. Shoes come in full sizes only. Adult sizes, 3 to 11, inclusive. State size of shoe worn. Shipping wt., 4½ lbs.
6K5063—Per pair... **$8.67**

For Girls and Women. High top shoes. Adult sizes, 2, 3, 4, 4½, 5, 5½, 6 and 7. State size of shoe worn. Shipping wt., 4½ lbs.
6K5064—Per pair... **$8.67**

Johnson's "Flyer" Hockey Skates
"Swift as Wings"

Perfectly balanced, accurately fitted. A splendid skate for all around skating. A genuine Nestor Johnson product of the usual dependable Johnson quality. Welded throughout, seamless one-piece tubes and high carbon tempered steel blades. Shaped for easy turning on small radius. Shoes of genuine leather, comfortable, and properly shaped for utmost ease in skating. Aluminum finish, complete with shoes. Regular advertised price, $8.00.

For Women. High top shoes as illustrated. Full sizes, 3 to 8 (no half sizes). State size of shoe worn. Shpg. wt., 4¼ lbs.
6K5043 Per pair... **$6.48**

For Men. Full sizes, 5 to 11. State size of shoe worn. Shipping weight, 4¼ pounds.
6K5042 Per pair... **$6.48**

Planert's "Winner" Hockey Skates
"The Speed Demon"

Men and women both will find complete enjoyment in "Planert's Winner" for hockey, fancy or general skating, when quick skating and speed are required. Has an all leather, soft, black shoe, well padded and taped insuring comfort and warmth. The skate is the popular tubular model with a specially hardened steel runner with a keen edge. Latest aluminum finish and strongly riveted to the shoe.

For Women. High top shoes as illustrated. Full sizes, 3 to 8 (no half sizes). State size of shoe worn. Shpg. wt., 4 lbs.
6K5062 Per pair... **$6.48**

For Men. Shoe sizes, 5 to 11 (no half sizes). State size of shoe worn. Shpg. wt., 4¼ lbs.
6K5061 Per pair... **$6.48**

Be sure to state size of shoe worn

If you do not know the size of shoe worn, give us the number inside of a shoe that does fit.

The Champions Win With North Stars

Finest Racing Skates
Models Used by Professionals

Speed! Lightness! Durability!

If you do not know the size of shoe worn, give us the number inside of a shoe that does fit.

Johnson's North Star Racers

These same Johnson's with which world titles have been won, are offered to you for only $8.95. Their wonderful strength, style, quality, lightness and special features attract both professional and amateur skating stars. High carbon steel, strong, rigid runner. Cups and plate are of one piece, cold drawn, seamless steel and securely fastened to the comfortable all leather shoe. Patented rib on tube prevents runner from even the slightest springing or bending. Full men's sizes, 5 to 11. Be sure to state size of shoe worn. Nationally advertised price, $11.00.
6K5044—Per pair. (Shpg. wt., 4¼ lbs.)... **$8.95**

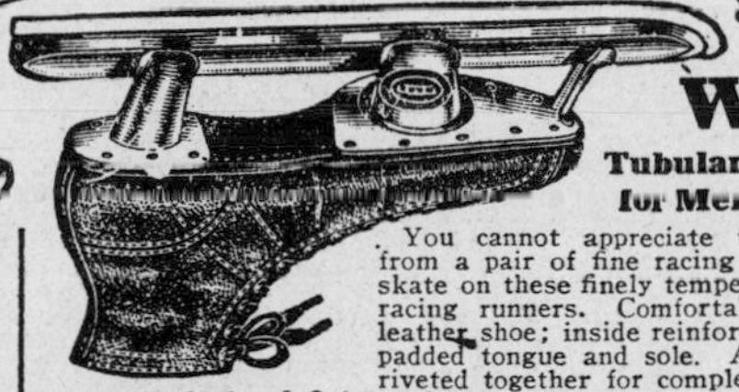

$6.68 WLS
Tubular Racing Skates for Men and Women

You cannot appreciate the real comfort from a pair of fine racing skates until you skate on these finely tempered tubular model racing runners. Comfortable fitting, black leather shoe; inside reinforced with tape and padded tongue and sole. All parts strongly riveted together for complete safety. Beautiful nickel plated finish. An exceptionally low price for these fine racing skates.

For Boys and Men. Shoe, full sizes, 5 to 11, inclusive. State size of shoe worn. Shipping weight, 4½ pounds.
6K5072—Per pair. **$6.68**

For Girls and Women. High top shoes. Full sizes, 3 to 8, inclusive. State size of shoe worn. Shpg. wt., 4 lbs.
6K5073—Per pair. **$6.68**

Planert's Northlight Racers

They're off! And if the racer does his part of the work, Northlights will carry him across the tape far in the lead. The championship racing skate used and endorsed by so many experts. Highly tempered, crucible steel runners, for a keen lasting edge. Fine quality leather shoes of soft black calf, with solid oak leather soles. Cups and sole plates are made of rustproof steel, and are soldered and riveted together giving double strength. Exceptionally light, giving the best possible results. Full men's sizes, 3 to 11. Be sure to state size of shoe worn. Beautiful nickel plated finish. Regular advertised price, $12.50. Shipping weight, 4½ pounds.
6K5060—Per pair... **$8.67**

$7.65 Popular Priced Shoe Skates $5.79
$3.89 For Men and Women $6.68

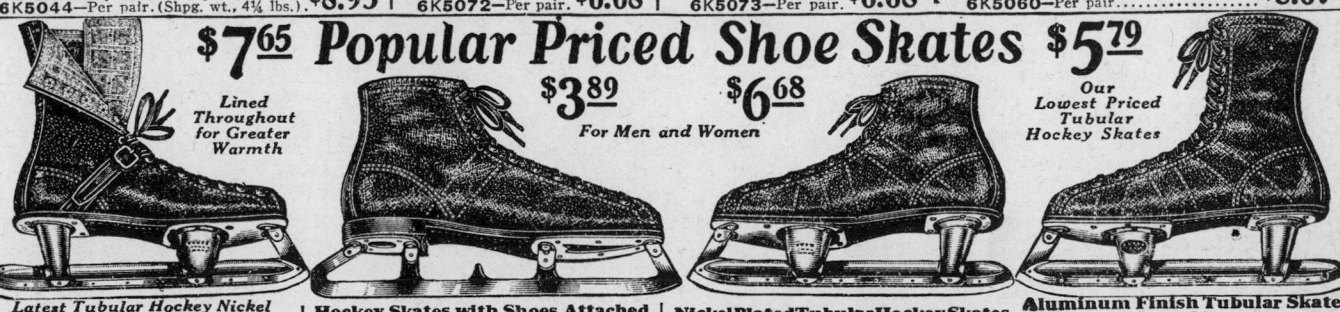

Lined Throughout for Greater Warmth

Our Lowest Priced Tubular Hockey Skates

Latest Tubular Hockey Nickel Plated Skates
Warm Fleecy Lined, Comfortable Shoes

Don't let cold weather prevent you from skating. In these skates additional protection against cold is furnished. Shoes are completely warm fleecy lined. The shoe itself is made of a soft pliable, black leather. Latest English welt, with durable leather sole riveted to skates. Equipped with leather strap, giving additional ankle support. Strong tubular highly tempered steel runners. Best workmanship throughout. Highly nickel plated.

For Men. High top shoes, come in full sizes only, 5 to 11. Give size of shoe worn. Shpg. wt., 4½ lbs.
6K5071 Per pair... **$7.65**

For Girls and Women. High top shoes. Come in full sizes only, 3 to 8, inclusive. State size of shoe worn. Shpg. wt., 4¼ lbs.
6K5070 Per pair... **$7.65**

Hockey Skates with Shoes Attached
An Unusual Value

Regular hockey skates with shoes attached! No more bother with clamps. Shoe and skate firmly riveted together. Canadian pattern with rounded head for fancy or backward skating. Shoes are made of a soft, black leather, reinforced with tape straps inside. Innersoles and tongues lined to give greater comfort and warmth. Solid hockey heels and strong counters. Runners of a high quality steel, properly tempered to keep a sharp edge for a long time. Nickel plated and polished to prevent rust.

For Boys and Men. Shoes come in full sizes only, 3 to 11, inclusive. Give size of shoe worn. Shpg. wt., 4¼ lbs.
6K5059 Per pair... **$3.89**

For Girls and Women. High top shoes. Come in full sizes only, 3 to 8, inclusive. State size of shoe worn. Shpg. wt., 4¼ lbs.
6K5057 Per pair... **$3.89**

Nickel Plated Tubular Hockey Skates
With Comfortable Good Quality Shoes

A sturdy, serviceable skate for inside rinks or outdoor skating. Both shoes and skates are made throughout of select high grade materials insuring long life and durability. Highly tanned, pliable black leather shoe. Inside reinforced with tape; tongue and innersole padded to protect foot. Runners carefully tempered of high carbon steel, highly nickel plated and polished.

For Boys and Men. Full sizes only, 5 to 11, inclusive. State size of shoe worn. Shipping weight, 4½ lbs.
6K5068 Per pair... **$6.68**

For Girls and Women. High top shoes. Come in sizes 3, 4, 5, 6, 7 and 8. State size of shoe worn. Shipping wt., 4½ lbs.
6K5069 Per pair... **$6.68**

Aluminum Finish Tubular Skates
A Special Bargain

If you want a low priced tubular hockey skate with proven strength and durability don't fail to get this bargain. Soft black all leather shoe with inside web strap reinforcements, and felt padded tongue and innersole. Firmly riveted to lightweight carbon steel frame. Runners, 7/64-inch thick, made of tool steel highly tempered, to insure sharp edges, aluminum finish. Well made, lightweight, yet strong and substantial.

For Girls and Women. High top shoes. Come in sizes 2, 3, 4, 4½, 5, 5½, 6, 7, and 8. State size of shoe worn. Shpg. wt., 4¼ lbs.
6K5067 Per pair... **$5.79**

For Boys and Men. Shoes come in full sizes only, 3 to 11, inclusive. State size of shoe worn. Shpg. wt., 4¼ lbs.
6K5066 Per pair... **$5.79**

Do Your Christmas Shopping Early

Leading Coaches Recommend

For Shoes See Page 542

Wilson's Official Double Lace Intercoll egiate Basket Ball

Their official ball, equipped with the valve type bladder, which permits inflating without lacing or unlacing the ball. Made of finest pebbled grain cowhide, specially tanned. Double lined with two-ply fabric which prevents stretching of leather and eliminates bulging, lopsided balls. Official as to shape, size and weight. Complete, with valve type bladder and instructions. Shpg. wt., 2½ lbs.
6K1826—Each.... **$12.40**
Two or more. Each......$12.00

"J. C. Higgins" Official Basket Ball **$9.98**
Ready Laced and Ready to be Inflated

Has the new rubber valve stemless bladder. The finest quality pebbled grain cowhide, from which all the stretch has been removed; backed with canvas lining. Guaranteed to be official in every respect. Complete with new rubber valve, stemless bladder, inflating and deflating tool and instructions. For indoor use only. Shipping weight, 2½ lbs.
6K1823............ **$9.98**

"Paddy" Driscoll
Famous Coach St. Mels Academy Says:
Sears, Roebuck and Co.
I have found the quality and price of your sporting goods and also the quick service that you give unequaled elsewhere.
I am glad to speak a good word to all of my friends in regard to the satisfaction I have had with this dependable athletic equipment.
Yours very truly,
J. L. "Paddy" Driscoll

$6.95 Official Size
"COLLEGE" Basket Ball
Ready Laced and Ready to Inflate

Improved with the rubber valve stemless bladder so ball can be inflated without disturbing the lace. Fine quality pebbled grain American cowhide leather, heavy canvas lined to insure proper shape. Sewed with heavy waxed lined thread. Official size. Made on the four-piece pattern. Guaranteed to give best results. For indoor use only. Complete with rubber bladder and instructions. Shipping weight, 2 pounds.
6K1816.......... **$6.95**

3.98
"Scholastic" Basket Ball
Official Size

A splendid practice ball of regulation size. Made of selected pebbled grain cowhide, backed with a heavy canvas lining, strongly stitched with thread. Made on the four-piece pattern, like the better grade balls. For indoor use only. Complete with pure gum rubber bladder, leather lace and lacing needle. Shipping weight, 2 pounds.
6K1825........ **$3.98**

Cotton Supporter Style Athletic Shirt

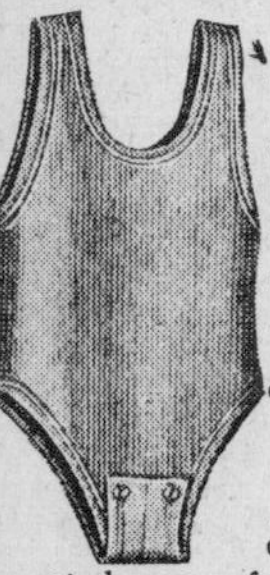

Made of finest quality, medium weight cotton yarns, white color only. The feature of this shirt is the supporter attachment which prevents shirt from pulling out of trunks. Even sizes, to fit 28 to 42 inches chest measure. **State size.**
6K2021—Shipping weight, ¾ lb.......... **44c**
Team lots of five or more, each.......... **42c**

All Wool Worsted Supporter Style Shirt

Solid colors. Made of medium heavyweight all wool worsted yarns, fast color. Athletic style, with neck and armpits cut extra low. Even sizes; to fit 28 to 42 inches chest measure. **State size.** Shipping weight, ¾ pound.
6K2017—Solid navy blue......... **$1.95**
6K2018—Solid white $1.95
6K2019—Solid purple 1.95
6K2020—Solid scarlet red.........1.95
Team lots of five or more, each.. **$1.90**

All Wool Worsted Shirts

Athletic style, with neck and armpits cut extra low. Made of medium heavy all wool worsted yarns, fast color, with the latest varsity striping. Even sizes, to fit 30 to 42 inches chest. **State size.** Shpg. wt., each, ¾ lb.
6K2000—Navy blue with white stripes............. **$1.95**
6K2001—Maroon with white stripes $1.95
6K2002—Black with burnt orange stripes $1.95
6K2003—Purple with old gold stripes $1.95
6K2006—Scarlet red with white stripes $1.95
6K2040—Kelly green with white stripes. 1.95
Team lots of five or more, each.......... 1.90

Cotton Striped Athletic Shirt

Same style and sizes as above.
6K2022—Navy blue, white stripes..... **79c**
6K2023—Maroon, white stripes.........79c
6K2024—Black, orange stripes.........79c
6K2036—Purple, old gold stripes.......79c
Team lots of five or more, each...........75c

All Wool Worsted Athletic Shirt

Medium heavyweight all wool worsted yarns. Athletic style with neck and armpits cut extra low. Solid colors. Even sizes, to fit 30 to 42 inches chest. **State size.** Shipping weight, each ¾ lb.
6K2033 Maroon.............. **$1.79**
6K2034—Navy blue $1.79
6K2038—White.... 1.79
6K2010—Purple ... 1.79
6K2025—Kelly green 1.79
Team lots of five or more, each........ **$1.75**

Cotton Athletic Shirts

Same style as 6K2033. Sizes to fit 26 to 44 inches chest. **State size.** Shipping wt., each, 8 oz.
6K2027—White **39c**
Team lots of five or more, each.........37c
6K2026—Navy blue 48c
Team lots of five or more, each..........46c

95c

Popular Basket Ball Pants

With Loose Hanging Pads

A value you will find hard to beat. The quality and workmanship is of the very best. Improved with the loose hanging hip pads, the same as used in better grade pants, far superior to those made with the sewed-in pads. Olive drab drill, fly front, strap and buckle at waist. Even sizes, to fit 26 to 42 in. waist measure. **State size.** Shpg. wt., ¾ lb.
6K2072.. **95c**
Team lots of five pairs or more, per pair..........89c

"Suede Cloth" Basket Ball Pants

Made of the latest material for basket ball pants known as "Suede" cloth. Short inseam with diagonally cut legs, with loose hanging hip pads. Prominent stripe of contrasting color on side seams. Fly front, strap and buckle at waist. Even sizes, to fit 28 to 38 in. waist measure. **State size.** Shpg. wt., 1 lb.
6K2041 Navy blue with white stripes........ **$1.88**
6K2044—Black and burnt orange stripes..........$1.88
6K2045—Purple with old gold stripes...............1.88
6K2046—Scarlet red with white stripes...............1.88
Team lots of five pairs or more, per pair 1.80

"Prep" All Wool Flannel Pants

Made of all wool flannel. Fast color, loose hanging hip pads. Short inseam, with diagonally cut legs. Stripes of contrasting color. Fly front, strap and buckle at waist. Sizes to fit 28 to 40 inches waist measure. **State size.** Shipping weight, 1 pound.
6K2042—Purple with old gold stripes...... **$2.59**
6K2047—Black with burnt orange $2.59
6K2048—Navy blue with white stripes $2.59
Team lots of five pairs or more, per pair...............$2.48

Colored Twill Basket Ball Pants

Fine quality twill, with loose hanging pad, fly front, strap and buckle. Short inseam with diagonally cut legs. Trimmed on side seams in contrasting colors. Even sizes, to fit 28 to 38-inch waist measure. **State size.** Shipping weight, 1 pound.
6K2079—Kelly green with white stripes........... **$1.59**
6K2084—Purple with old gold stripes $1.59
6K2080—Burnt orange with black stripes $1.59
6K2085—Scarlet red with white stripes $1.59
Team lots of five pairs or more, per pair...............$1.49

White Running or Gym Pants

Made of good quality material, either white muslin or white twill. Button fly front, adjustable back lace. Ideal for gymnasium or track. These pants and our white Athletic Shirt 6K2027, shown on this page, make an ideal suit of underwear. Sizes to fit 26 to 40 inches waist measure. **State waist measure.** Shipping weight, 5 ounces.
6K2089—White muslin... **43c**
Team lots of five or more................ **41c**
6K2086—White twill................ **69c**
Team lots of five or more per pair.......... **66c**

Official Basket Ball Goals

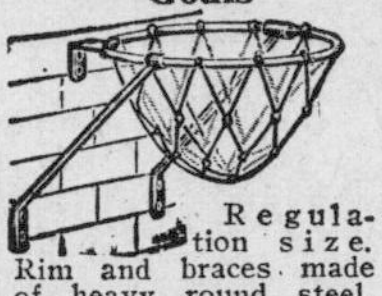

Regulation size. Rim and braces made of heavy round steel. Strong and durable. Far superior to goods sold elsewhere at higher prices. Complete with hand knotted seine twine net with draw string at bottom, which allows net to be used open or closed. Shipping weight, per pair, 14 pounds.
6K1832¼ Per pair.... **$3.95**
Extra net for above goals. Shpg. wt., 4 oz.
6K1848—Each.39c

Regulation Size Basket Ball Goals

Heavy steel frame. Rim is attached to iron casting, which is held rigid to wall or backstop. Fitted with hand knotted seine twine cotton net laced on frame. Draw string in bottom, which allows net to be used open or closed. These goals are not to be compared to cheaper goals sold elsewhere. Shpg. wt., pair, 12 lbs.
6K1828¼ Each.......... **$1.25**
Price, per pair....$2.45
Extra net for above goals. Shipping weight, 4 ounces.
6K1849—Each 28c

Footless Athletic Stockings

Has latest varsity striping (one wide and two narrow stripes). Generally used with sanitary socks shown below. Extra heavy ribbed cotton stockings. Colors: Navy blue, white stripes; maroon, white stripes; black, burnt orange stripes; purple, old gold stripes; Kelly green, white stripes; scarlet red, white stripes. **State color.** Shipping wt., 8 oz.
6K2055—Pair **62c**
Lots of five or more pairs, per pair........ **59c**

Heavyweight, worsted ribbed stockings with a backing of cotton yarns for reinforcement, which adds strength and long life. Same style as above. Navy blue with white stripes; black with burnt orange stripes; maroon with white stripes, or purple with old gold stripes. **State color.** Shipping weight, ¾ pound.
6K2057—Pair............ **98c**
Team lots of five or more, per pair........ **95c**

Athletic Stockings with Feet

Heavy ribbed cotton, adapted for basket ball or foot ball use. Size, 10 and 11. Colors: Navy blue with white stripes; maroon with white stripes, or purple with old gold stripes. Shpg. wt., ¾ lb. **State size and color.**
6K2065 Pair.......... **62c**
Same grade as 6K2065, solid colors (no stripes). Black, navy blue, maroon or purple.
6K2060 Pair.......... **60c**
Team lots of five pairs or more, per pair.......... **58c**

Our letters and numerals furnished only when shirts and jerseys are ordered from us. Made of wool felt. We will require seven to ten days to furnish. **When ordering, mark plainly lettering or numeral wanted; also style and color.**

H *B* **6**
Style No. 1 Style No. 2 Style No. 3

6K2056½

Style	Size, In.	Not S'w'd, Each	S'w'd, Each
Full Block Letters.. 1	3 or 4	10c	15c
	5 or 6	17c	24c
Plain Block Numerals.. 4	3 or 4	10c	15c
	5 or 6	17c	24c
Script Letters..... 3	3 or 4	15c	25c
	5 or 6	20c	30c

Referees' Whistle

Loud and shrill, full nickel plated, with ring for chain. Shipping wt., 4 ounces.
6K1873. **18c**

White Sanitary Socks

Worn with footless stockings or separately, for basket ball, tennis or gymnasium. Sizes, 10 and 11. **State size.** Shipping weight, 4 ounces.
6K2070—Cotton socks. Pair.. **15c**
Team lots of five pairs or more, per pair.........13c
6K2071—Wool socks. Pair...49c
Team lots of five pairs or more, per pair..........46c

Our Basketball Equipment

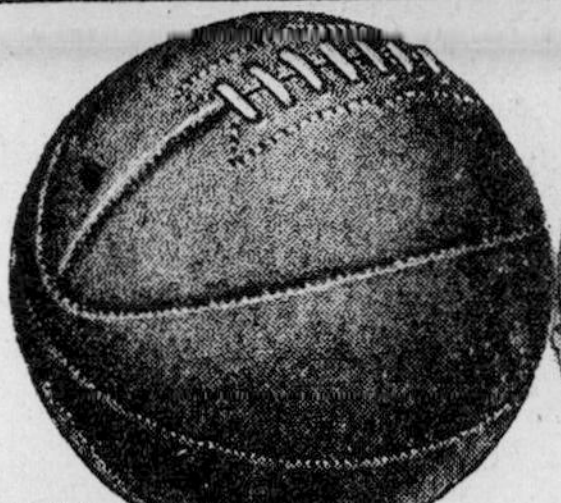

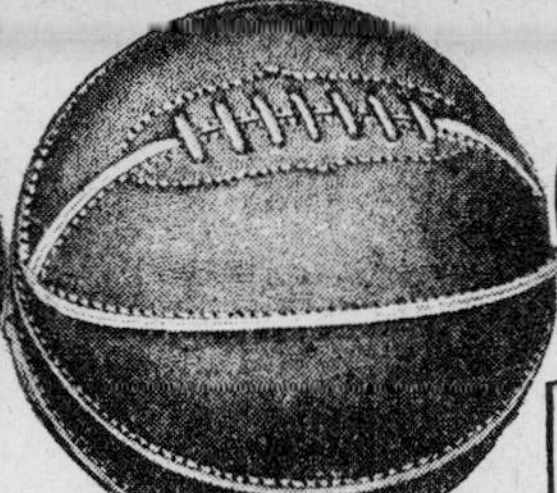

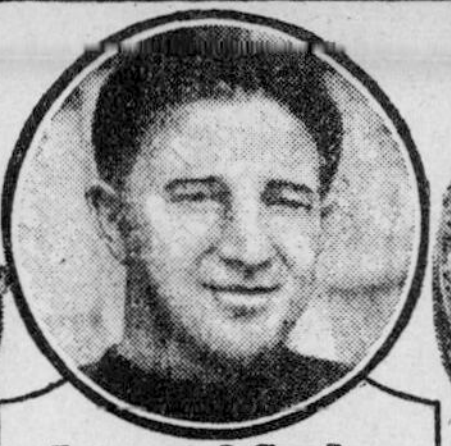

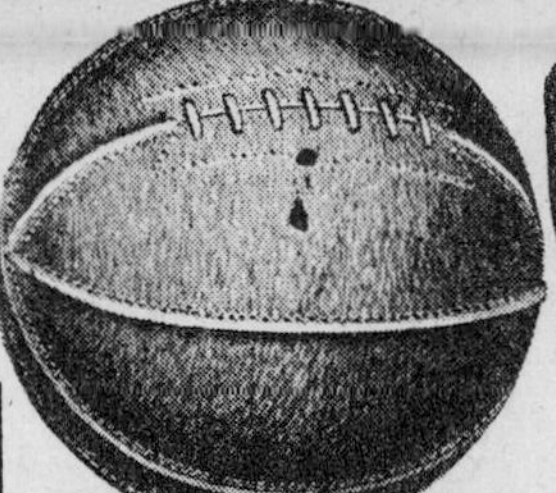

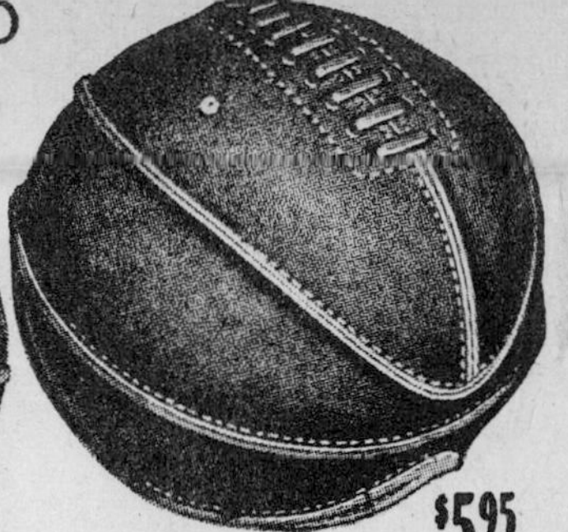

$2.69

"Amateur" Basket

For Indoor Use Only

Regulation size. Good grade pebbled grain split cowhide leather, full drill lined, sewed with strong thread. For indoor use only. Lace and rubber bladder included. Four-piece pattern same as our higher priced balls, which insures long wear. Far superior to similar balls offered by others at higher prices. Shipping weight, 1½ lbs.

6K1841........ **$2.69**

"Amateur" $2.69

Outseam Basket Ball

Good quality pebbled grain split cowhide leather, canvas lined, regulation size. Raised leather seams make it suitable for rough playgrounds. Four-piece pattern same as our higher priced balls, which insures long wear. Far superior to cheap balls made of sheepskin. Complete with rubber bladder and lace. Shpg. wt., 1¼ lbs.

6K1842........ **$2.69**

Leonard Sachs

Basket Ball Coach, Loyola University, says:

I certainly am glad that young fellows everywhere now have the opportunity to get dependable, standard, official equipment at your low prices. I have examined your official sporting goods and find the material and workmanship unusually good. They will, I believe, surely stand the gaff.

Very truly yours,

Leonard D Sachs

"Scholastic" $4.39

Outseam Basket Ball

Popular priced regulation size. Made of fine quality pebbled grain cowhide, heavy canvas lined, waxed thread sewed. Raised seams prevent wear on stitching. Four-piece pattern, which insures long wear. Complete with rubber bladder, leather lace and needle. Shipping weight, 1¾ pounds.

6K1817........ **$4.39**

$5.95

"J. C. Higgins" Official Playground Outseam Basket Ball

Especially constructed for outdoor use. Improved this year with the new rubber valve stemless bladder, making it unnecessary to lace or unlace the ball when ready to inflate. Made on the four-piece pattern of high quality American pebbled grain cowhide leather with raised seams, which will prevent wear on the stitching. Sewed with heavy waxed thread. Canvas lined. Complete with new rubber bladder, valve type, and instructions. Shipping weight, 2¼ pounds.

6K1818........ **$5.95**

Sweat or Training Shirt

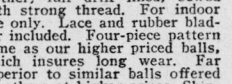

Boys' Sizes, 83c — Men's Sizes, 97c Ea.

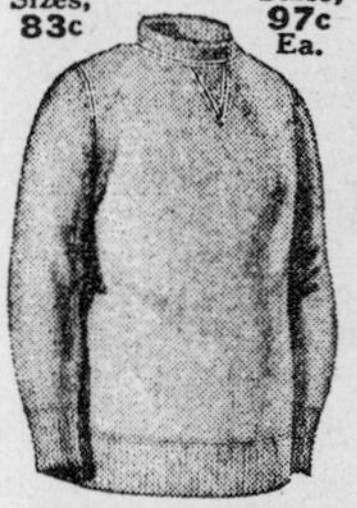

Good grade of cotton, fleece lined, gray color. Used extensively in all forms of sport. Helps the player to "warm up" before the game or for practice use. Even sizes. **State size.** Shipping wt., 2½ pounds.

6K2015—Men's sizes, 34 to 44 chest measure........ **97c**

Team lots of **5** or more. Each.. **92c**

6K2016—Boys' sizes, 26 to 32 chest measure........ **83c**

Team lots of **5** or more. Each.. **78c**

Printed Design Sweat Shirt

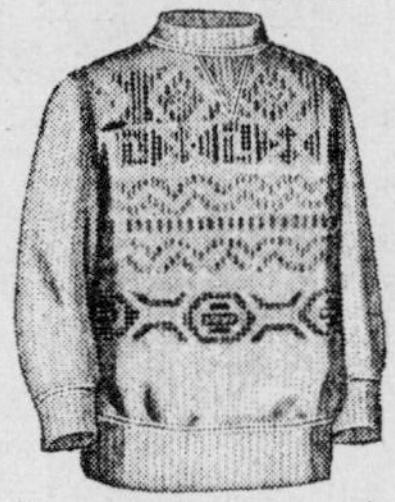

Made of good grade cotton, fleece lined. Color of body is white with printed design in contrasting fast colors. This garment is strictly for athletic wear. Worn with or without a top shirt. Even sizes. **State size.** Shipping weight, 2½ pounds.

6K2014—Men's sizes, 34 to 44 chest measure........ **$1.25**

6K2013—Boys' sizes, 26 to 32 chest measure........ **$1.10**

Knitted Middies

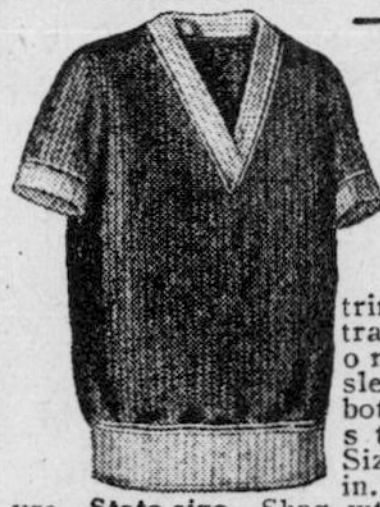

All wool worsted yarns. V-neck style, quarter stripe sleeves, trim in contrasting colors on neck, sleeves and bottom. Rib stitched. Sizes, 34 to 42 in. bust measure. **State size.** Shpg. wt., ea., 2 lbs.

6K2064—Scarlet red with white trimmings. Each........ **$2.69**

6K2063—Purple with old gold trimmings. Each........ **$2.69**

Team lots of **5** or more. **State color.** Each........ **$2.50**

6K2069½—Any other color combination can be furnished in 10 days' time in not less than team lots of 5 or more. Each........ **$2.69**

Cotton Gym Bloomers

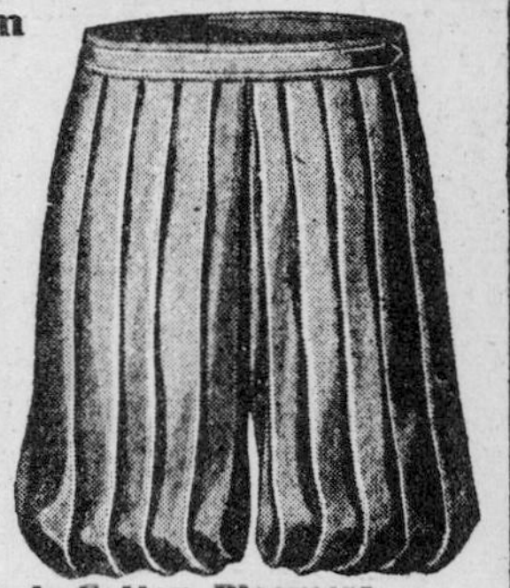

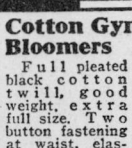

Full pleated black cotton twill, good weight, extra full size. Two button fastening at waist, elastic at knees, reinforced crotch. Black only. Sizes to fit, 26 to 36-in. waist measure. **State waist measure.** Shpg. wt., ¾ lb.

6K2083—Ea., **$1.18**

Team lots of 5 or more. Each.. **$1.13**

Children's Cotton Bloomers

Same style and material as 6K2083. Sizes, 8 to 14 years. State age. Shipping wt., ¾ pounds.

6K2096—Each........ **97c**

Team lots of **5** or more. Each........ **92c**

Serge Bloomers

University style. Fine quality, Whitman's all wool serge. Extra full pleated to knee, high grade well made garment. Two-button fastening at waist, elastic band around knees, reinforced crotch. Sizes to fit 26, 28, 30, 32, 34 to 36 inches waist measure. **State waist measure.** Shpg. wt., 1 lb.

6K2081—Black........ **$3.25**

6K2082—Navy blue........ **$3.25**

Team lots of 5 or more. Each........ **3.15**

Sweat Pants

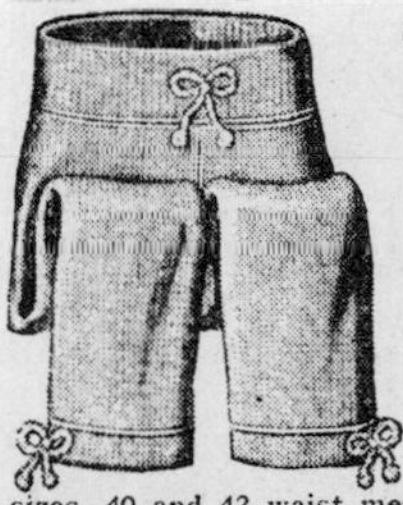

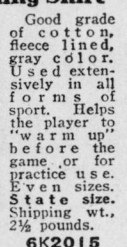

Made of fine quality cotton, fleece lined, same material as our 6K2016 and 6K2015 Sweat Shirts, gray color. Draw string at waist and ankles. Excellent for general training purposes. Small sizes, 32 and 34; medium sizes, 36 and 38; large sizes, 40 and 42 waist measure. **State size.** Shipping weight, 2 pounds.

6K2050........ **$1.20**

Colored Sweat Shirts

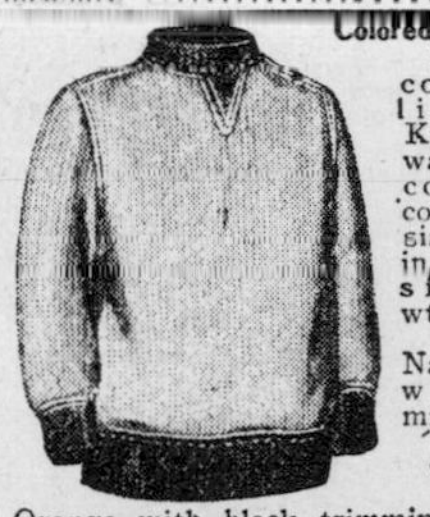

Fine quality cotton fleece lined fabric. Knit cuffs and waistband of contrasting color. Even sizes, 34 to 42 in. chest. **State size.** Shpg. wt., 2½ lbs.

6K2011 Navy blue with white trimming. **$1.29**

6K2012 Orange with black trimming........ **$1.29**

6K2008—Red with white trimming........ **$1.29**

Basket Ball Bladder

Pure gum rubber bladder.

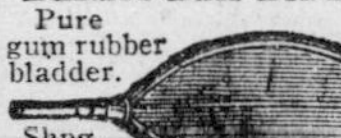

Shpg. wt., 5 oz.

6K1827—Four-piece stem bladder, regulation large size, heavy wt. **79c**

6K1834—Two-piece stem bladder. For balls 6K1841, 6K1842, 6K1825 and 6K1817........ **49c**

6K1845—Valve bladder, for basket ball 6K1823, 6K1816 and 6K1818. **$1.60**

6K1846—Valve bladder for basketball 6K1826........ **$1.39**

Gym Knickers

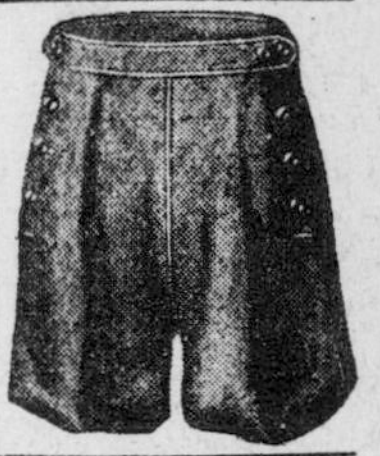

Displacing the pleated bloomer in many schools. Used with either middy blouse or knitted middy. Made of fine quality black cotton twill. Adjustable waistband opens on both sides; one pocket; elastic at knee. Full size throughout. Sizes to fit 26 to 36 inches waist measure. **State size.** Shipping wt., ¾ lb.

6K2078 Each........ **$1.15**

Team lots of **5** or more. Each........ **$1.10**

"Bike" Elastic Anklet

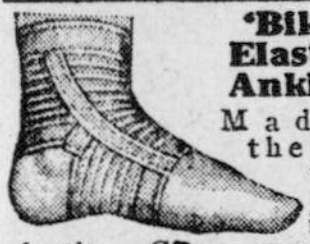

Made of the best mercerized elastic. Gives maximum support with the greatest comfort. Prevents strains and reduces swellings. Used for all kinds of sports. Shpg. wt., 4 oz.

6K2087........ **39c**

Supporter and Protector for Basket Ball, Football and Baseball

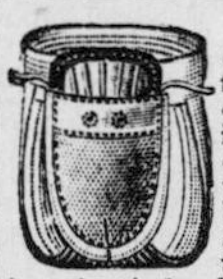

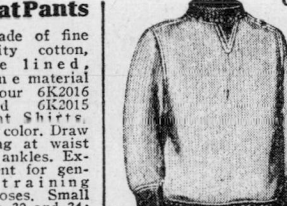

3-in. elastic abdominal elastic band and two 3-in. elastic leg bands. Jersey knit pouch contains a light aluminum guard. Waist, 26 to 42 inches. **Give waist measure.** Shipping weight, 7 ounces.

6K2099 **$1.89**

"Bike" No. 55 Elastic Supporter

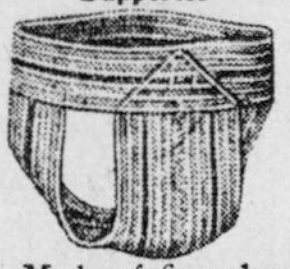

Made of fine elastic with attractive woven stripe. V seam front allows greater elasticity. Medium sizes, 30 to 38 in. waist measure. Large sizes, 40 to 44 in. **State size.** Shipping weight, 5 ounces.

6K2092 **34c**

"Bike" No. 77 Elastic Supporter

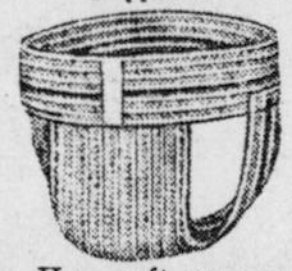

Has soft mercerized mesh, elastic front, 3-inch waistband, 2-in. leg band of fine quality elastic. Medium sizes, 30 to 38 in. waist measure. Large sizes, 40 to 44 in. **State size.** Shipping wt., 5 oz.

6K2093 **48c**

"Bike" Wide Waist Supporter

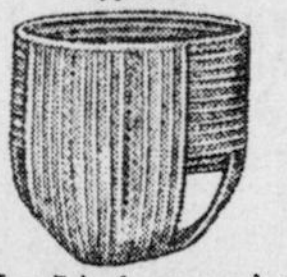

Has 7-inch mercerized special weave waistband and 3-in. leg bands. Excellent supporter, abdominal brace is desirable. Medium sizes, 30 to 38. Large sizes, 40 to 44 in. waist measure. **State size.** Shipping weight, 8 oz.

6K2091..... **62c**

For Other Athletic Supporters See Page 637

Girls' Basket Ball Pants

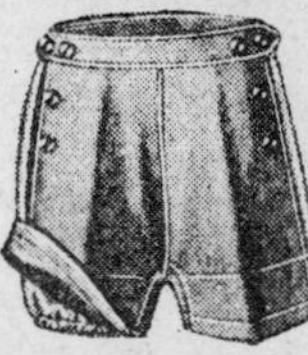

Popular suede cloth, elastic bottom shield sewed inside. Buttons on side. Even sizes, 26 to 36 inches waist measure. **State size.** Shpg. wt., 1 lb.

6K2061 Scarlet red........ **$2.59**

6K2062—Purple........ **$2.59**

Team lots of **5** pairs or more. **State color.** Pair........ **$2.47**

6K2054½—Any other color can be furnished in 10 days in not less than team lots of **5** or more. Each........ **$2.59**

Eyeglass Protector

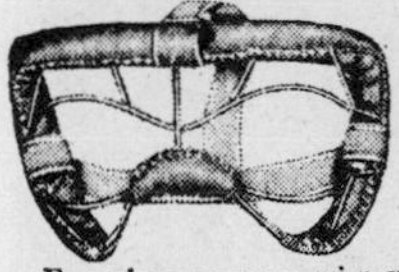

For players wearing glasses. Strong steel wire with electrically welded joints. Well padded leather covered elastic straps. Shpg. wt., 1 lb.

6K1879........ **$2.59**

Basket Ball Score Book

To score 20 games. Cloth covered cardboard cover. Shipping weight, 4 ounces.

6K1878........ **39c**

Basket Ball Rules

Rules for men and women; also includes volley ball, soccer and indoor rules. Shpg. wt., 2 oz.

6K1829........ **8c**

Leather Wrist Strap

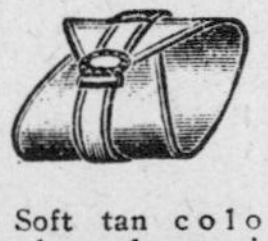

Soft tan color leather, chamois lined. Buckle allows adjustment to the smallest fraction. Shpg. wt., 5 oz.

6K2088—Double strap, 2¾ inches wide........ **39c**

Elastic Knee and Elbow Pads

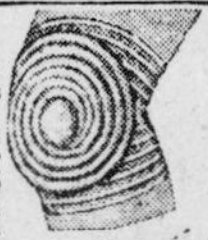

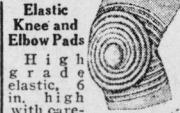

High grade elastic, 6 in. high with carefully sewed circular felt pad. Shpg. wt., 8 oz.

6K2095—Knee Pads. Per pair........ **69c**

6K2094—Elbow pads. Per pair........ **69c**

"Bike" Knee Pad

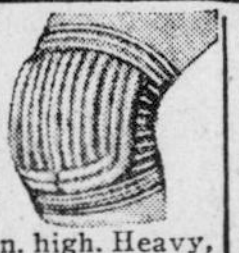

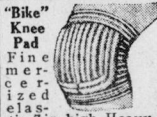

Fine mercerized elastic, 7 in. high. Heavy, firmly sewed felt pad. A comfortable knee pad that gives real support. Shpg. wt., 8 oz.

6K2098—Pair. **95c**

Roll Style Knee Pads

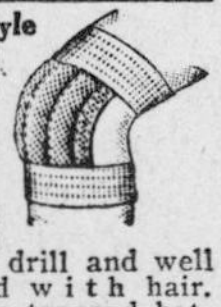

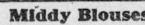

Covered with good grade khaki drill and well stuffed with hair. Elastic top and bottom. Shpg. wt., 8 oz.

6K2097 Pair........ **89c**

Medium Size Inflater

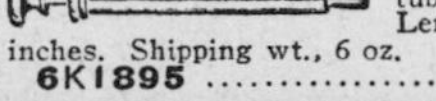

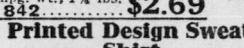

Polished tube brass. Length, 13 inches. Shipping wt., 6 oz.

6K1895........ **27c**

Lacing Needle

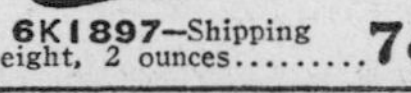

6K1897—Shipping weight, 2 ounces........ **7c**

Middy Blouses

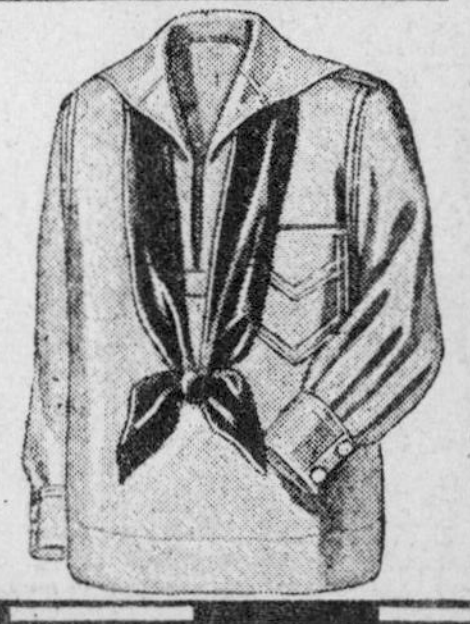

Excellent quality, heavy white cotton lonsdale twill cloth. Black middy tie. Square sailor collar, one pocket, 3-in. hem at bottom. Sloped form fitting sides which insure a better and snug fit. Sizes to fit 30 to 44 inches bust measure. **State size.** Shpg. wt., ¾ lb.

6K2058—With long sleeves.... **$1.39**

6K2059—With short sleeves... **$1.29**

Team lots of **5** or more, **5** cents less for blouse.

See Index and Information Pages 542 to 570

2519

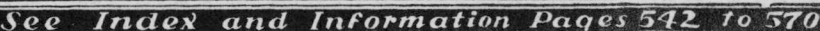

Endorsed by These Famous Players

Roger Kiley
Chuck Carney
Four Horsemen of Notre Dame

"Eddie" Hunsinger
Ralph "Moon" Baker
George Halas

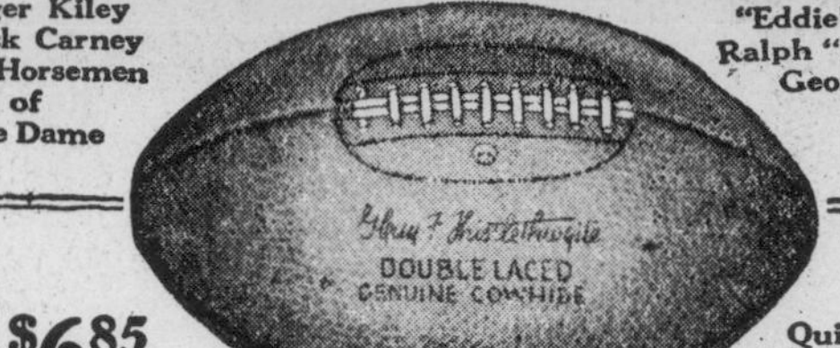

$3.95

"College" Rugby Football

Our new valve stemless bladder does away with tedious job of lacing. Simply inflate it. Made of fine quality genuine pebbled grain cowhide leather; stitched canvas lined. Fine for practice and used by many in regular games. Official size. Furnished with stemless rubber bladder and lace.

6K2301—Shpg. wt., 1¾ lbs....... **$3.95**

$6.85

Quickly Inflated

"Glenn F. Thistlewaite" Official Football

Stemless Bladder, Ready Laced and Ready to Be Inflated

Official football, no lacing. Has valve stemless bladder. Inflated in 2 or 3 minutes. Finest quality grain cowhide. Double canvas lining. Guaranteed official in weight, size and shape. Attachments for inflating and deflating are included with complete instructions.

6K2300—Shipping weight, 1¾ pounds............ **$6.85**

$5.48

Official Interscholastic Football

Ready Laced—Ready to Inflate

No lacing, no bladder stem to tie. Inflates quickly through valve. Finest pebbled grain cowhide. Patented double lining stitch holds ball in shape, prevents stretching. Official size and weight. Complete with stemless bladder and rawhide lace.

6K2302—Shipping weight, 1¾ lbs... **$5.48**

"Scholastic" Rugby Football

Official in Size

Made of fine quality genuine pebbled grain cowhide leather; stitched with heavy waxed thread with a locksitch. Canvas lined. Furnished with high quality rubber bladder, leather lace and lacing needle. Shipping weight, 1¾ pounds.

6K2303 **$2.98**

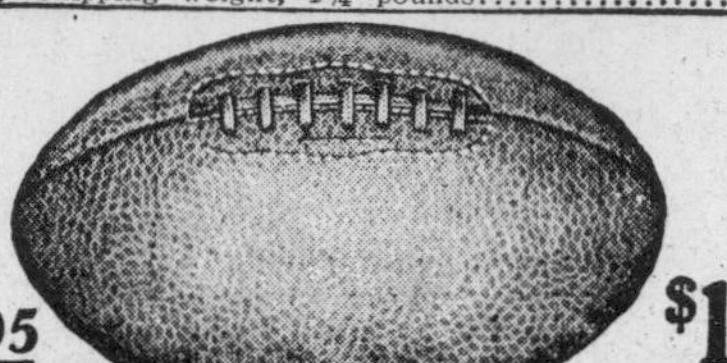

$1.95

Cowhide Rugby Football

Made of special grade genuine grain cowhide leather, canvas lined. Strongly stitched. Official size. Funrished complete with strong rubber bladder and lace. Shipping weight, 1½ pounds.

6K2308 **$1.95**

$1.15

"Practice" Rugby Football

Official Size

Big low priced football value. Made of chrome tanned pebbled grain split cowhide, canvas lined, strongly stitched. Furnished with pure rubber bladder and lace. Shipping weight, 1½ pounds.

6K2304 **$1.15**

Boys' Rugby Football

Pebble Grained Leather

A boys' size football, made of pebbled grain split cowhide leather, strongly sewed and well finished. A trifle smaller than regulation size, but well made. Generally called medium size football. A boy's joy! Complete with lace and pure rubber bladder. Shpg. wt., ¾ lb.

6K2305 .. **79c**

Extra bladder for above boys' football. Made of pure rubber. Shipping weight, 4 ounces.

6K2312 **25c**

Rugby and Soccer Football Rules

Containing rules of both games. Also basketball and indoor rules. Shpg. wt., 3 oz.

6K1829 **8c**

"College" Football Pants

Made in the latest college style, embodying every necessary feature for both protection and comfort. Fine quality heavy duck, olive drab color, felt hip and kidney pads, covered with white canvas. Sponge rubber spine protector, together with felt tailbone guard. Flexible fiber thigh protectors, felt covered. Felt knee pad with sponge rubber kneecap protector, reinforced on outside. Knee covered with split cowhide leather, adding double wear. Fly front with sewed eyelets, reinforced with heavy tape for added wear. Tapered form fitting leg, tunnel loops in back. Double stitched throughout and reinforced at all points of strain. Sizes to fit 28 to 40 inches waist measure. **State size.** Shpg. wt., 3 lbs.

6K2330—Per pair.... **$4.95**

Recommended by "Red" Grange

"Red" Grange Football **$2.79**

Regulation Size

Well made football of tough selected pebbled grained cowhide. Seamless rubber bladder. Strong rawhide lace. Wilson lacing needle and autographed picture of "Red" Grange included. Each ball certified with "Red" Grange's signature. Shipping weight, 1¾ pounds.

6K2310..... **$2.79**

"Red" Grange Varsity Football **$3.98**

Ready Laced

Genuine "Red" Grange football, certified with his signature. Patented air valve inflates bladder like a tire. No lacing or unlacing. Regulation size. Strong pebbled grained cowhide, fabric lined, with pure rubber bladder. Autographed picture of "Red" Grange with each football. Strong hand pump, rawhide lace and needle included. Shpg. wt., 1¼ lbs.

6K2309...... **$3.98**

"Red" Grange Scholastic Football **$1.69**

A genuine "Red" Grange ball within the price of every boy. Regulation size. Well made of split cowhide leather. Has seamless rubber bladder. Rawhide lace, Wilson lacing needle and autographed picture of "Red" Grange, all included at our low price. Shpg. wt., 1 lb.

6K2311..... **$1.69**

Rugby Football Bladder

Fine quality pure rubber bladder. Shpg. wt., 5 oz.

6K2320—Four-piece pattern. Regulation size and weight for 6K2303 Footballs............. **63c**

6K2321—Two-piece pattern. Suitable for footballs like 6K2308 and 6K2304............. **47c**

Metal valve rubber bladder for Rugby Footballs 6K2300, 6K2301 and 6K2302. Shipping weight, 6 oz.

6K2322.................. **$1.20**

"Varsity" Helmet

Solid, firm tan strap leather. Hand molded and fiber stiffened; inside top crown reinforced with shock absorbing construction; large cheek and ear protector. Heavily padded throughout with best grade white felt; elastic forehead adjustment and chin strap.

6K2345—Shpg. wt., 3 lbs. **$3.65**

Boys' Football Pants

Made of good quality olive drab color drill; heavy drill waistband. Front of pants padded with split reed thigh guards. Laced fly with sewed eyelets and tape reinforcement. Belt loops. Sizes to fit 24 to 34 in. waist measure. **State size.** Shipping wt., 2 pounds.

6K2331.............. **$1.79**

$3.89

"Red" Grange Boys' Football Pants

Made of good quality duck, felt pad at top, reinforced with tape. Flat fiber thigh guards, well padded. Complete with leather strap and buckle at waist. Autographed photograph of "Red" Grange furnished with each pair of pants. Sizes, 26 to 34 waist measure. **State size.** Shipping weight, 2 lbs.

6K2332......... **$3.89**

"Red" Grange Helmet

$2.79

Patterned after the helmet "Red" used in all his games and certified with his autograph. Made of heavy stiff leather, lined with white felt. Back extension piece for added protection; elastic forehead piece; large ventilated ear protectors. Autographed picture of "Red" Grange included. Shpg. wt., 2 lbs.

6K2347......... **$2.79**

$2.79

"Red" Grange Shoulder Pad

Each pad certified with "Red" Grange's signature. Made of good quality cowhide, lined throughout with white felt. Stiff leather shoulder caps; leather collarbone protector. Operated in the "ball and socket" fashion, giving complete protection with absolute freedom. Complete with autographed photograph of "Red" Grange. Shipping weight, 1½ pounds.

6K2352...................... **$2.79**

Boys' Helmet

An all leather helmet; ideal for boys, heavy black leather molded and stiffened. Lined with good quality white felt. Elastic forehead adjustment and chin strap. Shpg. wt., 1½ lbs.

6K2346 **$1.98**

Intercollegiate Shoulder Pad

Sanitary white felt lined pad, covered with finest strap leather. Molded leather hinged shoulder caps. Strongly reinforced at chest. Solid sole leather collarbone protector. Elastic arm band. Special "Adjusto" rapid lacer. Shipping weight, 2½ pounds.

6K2350..................... **$3.45**

All Wool Worsted Supporter Style Football Jersey

Has supporter attachment, a real feature which prevents jersey from pulling out. Made of heavyweight worsted yarn, plain colors. Double elbows. Regulation style collar. Sizes to fit 30 to 42 in. chest measure. State size. Shpg. wt., 1½ lbs.

6K2360—Navy blue. **$3.59**

6K2361—Scarlet red.......... **3.59**

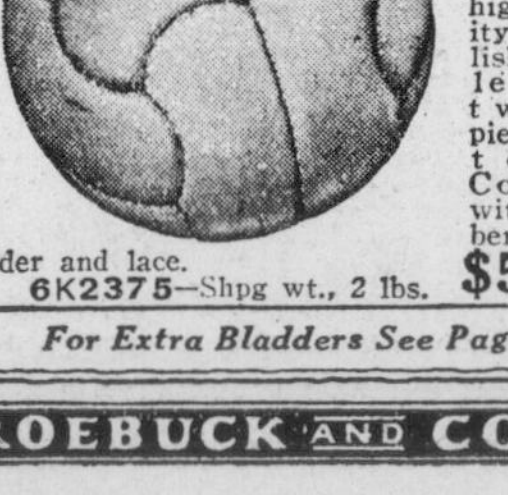

Imported English Soccer Ball

Hand sewed of high quality English tan leather, twelve piece pattern. Complete with rubber bladder and lace.

6K2375—Shpg. wt., 2 lbs. **$5.48**

For Extra Bladders See Page 519

"College" Soccer

Made of genuine cowhide leather, sewed with waxed thread, canvas lined. Regulation size. Can also be used as a volley ball. Furnished with leather lace, needle and good quality rubber bladder. Shipping wt., 1½ pounds.

6K2376. **$3.59**

"Practice" Soccer

Regulation size, made of good quality pebbled grain split cowhide leather, strongly sewed. Excellent value and will give much better service than balls made of cheaper leather. Good quality rubber bladder and lace. Shpg. wt., 1½ lbs.

6K2377.............. **$2.19**

Boys' Shoulder Pad

Good quality gray felt; leather collarbone reinforcements; molded and stiffened leather shoulder caps; adjustable at lacing. Shpg. wt., 1 lb.

6K2351.............. **$1.69**

Official Equipment at Bargain Prices
Says Sammy Mandell

Set of 4 $4.95

Corbett Pattern Boxing Gloves
High quality soft glove leather, dark red color, stuffed with excellent quality genuine hair. Double stitched; full drill lined; leather bound. Deep laced wrists, padded cuffs, finger grips. Excellent gloves for instructors. Weight, each about 8 ounces. Shipping weight, 3¼ pounds.
6K1408
Set of 4 gloves. **$4.95**

Set of 4 $5.95

Pupils' Double Cuff Style Boxing Gloves
Corbett pattern, with double length padded cuffs, finger grips and deep laced wrists. High quality tan color soft leather, drill lined and stuffed with excellent quality genuine hair. Made strong and durable to withstand the severe usage given boxing gloves by amateurs. Leather bound deep laced wrist. Designed with extra long cuffs to give all the protection possible. Weight, each, about 9 ounces. Shipping weight, 4½ pounds.
6K1409—Set of 4 gloves..... **$5.95**

World's LightWeight Champion

Wilson Official 6-Ounce Fighting Gloves
Set of 4 $6.75
Constructed to withstand the most severe championship use. Made according to professional specifications. Exactly the same as used by many fighters in the ring today. Plenty of room for bandages worn over the knuckles. Finest selected leather; rich wine color. Lined with best quality duck, and filled with highest grade curled hair. Leather welted seams. Each glove weighs 6 ounces. Shpg. wt., 3 lbs. 6K1410—Set of 4 gloves..... **$6.75**

Set of 4 $7.75

Special Gymnasium Model Boxing Gloves
Large Size Boxing Gloves for Friendly Bouts or Training Purposes
Made of finest selected glove leather, filled with highest grade curled hair. Lined with best quality duck. Large padded cuff, palm grip, laced wrist. Each glove weighs about 10 ounces. Shipping weight, 4½ pounds.
6K1412
Set of 4 gloves......... **$7.75**

Set of 4 $1.89

Juvenile All Leather Boxing Gloves
For youngsters, ages 3 to 6 years. Soft glove leather, stuffed with good quality hair, drill lined, laced wrist. Well stitched throughout. Standard pattern. Shipping weight, 2 lbs.
6K1401
Set of 4 gloves..... **$1.89**

Set of 4 $2.79

Boys' Standard Pattern Boxing Gloves
Made of good quality soft glove leather, padded with hair. Well stitched, drill lined; palm grip, laced wrist; fabric bound around edges. An ideal set for boys, ages 6 to 10 years. Shipping weight, 2 pounds.
6K1406
Set of 4 gloves......... **$2.79**

Set of 4 $3.25

Youths' All-Leather Corbett Pattern Boxing Gloves
Made of good quality soft glove leather. Weight, each, about 5 ounces. Stuffed with hair, full drill lined; finger grips, padded wrist. Laced wrist. Well stitched, fabric bound. For ages 8 to 14 years. Shipping weight, 2¾ pounds.
6K1404—Set of 4 gloves. **$3.25**

Set of 4 $3.87

Young Men's All Leather Corbett Pattern Boxing Gloves
Six-ounce all leather gloves. Made of fine quality soft glove leather. Stuffed with good quality hair, full drill lined, deep lacing, padded cuff, stitched finger grips, fabric bound edges, well stitched throughout. Shipping weight, 3 pounds.
6K1402
Set of 4 gloves **$3.87**

Striking Bags

Only $3.98

Double End Striking Bags
This style bag is used without platform, attaching to floor and ceiling.

Double End, Full Size Bell Shape Striking Bag
Black soft glove leather; full canvas lined; leather welted and taped seams. Triple stitched with strong thread. Can be used either as single or double end bag. Furnished complete with rubber bladder, elastic cord and rope. Shpg. wt., 2 lbs.
6K1441... **$3.98**

Striking Bag Bladders
For double end striking bag; also oval or bell shape. Fine quality pure rubber. Shipping weight, 7 ounces.
6K1453—Four-piece pattern, regulation size. For 6K1429 and 6K1441 bags...... **63c**
6K1452—Two-piece pattern for low price bags, like 6K1426.....**48c**

Only $2.59

Regulation Size, Double End Bag
Good quality tan color soft glove leather. Triple stitched, taped seams, leather bound. Leather loops at both ends, complete with rope, elastic cord and bladder. Shipping weight, 1¾ lbs.
6K1429... **$3.45**

Striking Bag Mitts
Soft glove leather, finger grip in center, hair padded over knuckles, laced wrists, fabric bound, giving ample protection to the knuckles. A necessity for the everyday puncher. Shipping wt., 8 oz.
6K1458 Per pair.. **$1.19**

Youths' Medium Size Double End Bag
Made of fine leather, full drill lined; leather loops at top and bottom. Excellent bag for youths. Complete with rope, elastic cord and rubber bladder. Shipping weight, 1½ pounds.
6K1426... **$2.59**

Youths' Medium Size Pear Shape Bag
Made of good quality soft glove leather, full drill lined, well sewed. Strong leather loop. Bladder included. Shpg. wt., 1¼ lbs.
6K1435 **$1.98**

Regulation Size Pear Shape Bag
Made of good quality soft glove leather in dark red color. Leather welted seams, full canvas lined, taped underseam, strong leather loop top; leather bound. Complete with rubber bladder and lace. Shipping weight, 1½ lbs.
6K1439... **$3.39**

Doorway Apartment Striking Bag Platform

Noiseless Striking Bag Platform With Shock Absorbing Springs
Constructed of hardwood, securely bolted. One-piece maple rim, 2¾ inches in diameter.
6K1449¼ Shpg. wt., 11 lbs. **$3.98**
Adjustable wall attachments for raising or lowering platform to any desired height. Shipping wt., 2½ lbs.
6K1451 **79c**

Can be put up without removing the door and without tools of any kind, but door must swing back all the way. Adjustable to any standard doorway. Rubber clamps hold it firmly in place. Cannot mar the finest finish. Four springs absorb the vibration and noise. Adjustable to any height. Made of hardwood, nicely finished. Shipping wt., 20 lbs.
6K1448¼ **$6.95**

Pear Shape Bags
This style is best when used with striking bag platform.

Heavy Gym or Police Bag
Regulation size, made of high quality light tan horsehide. Canvas lined with extra tape under seam. Leather welted seams, triple stitched; strong leather loop. Complete with heavy rubber bladder. Shipping weight, 2 pounds.
6K1438... **$4.48**

Striking Bag Swivel
Bag can be instantly removed or a new rope inserted by unscrewing the projecting stem. Nickel plated. Shipping wt., 1 lb.
6K1450.. **53c**

Elastic Floor Attachment
Elastic covered with braided cotton. Used for attaching the bottom of a double end bag to the floor. Shpg. weight, 3 ounces.
6K1442 **18c**

Only $5.39

Full Size Professional Bag
High quality selected calfskin tan color. Leather welted seams; full canvas lined; double stitched throughout. Leather loop top. Bladder included. Shpg. wt., 1½ lbs.
6K1440. **$5.39**

Striking Bag Bladders
For pear shape bag, fine quality pure rubber. Shipping weight, 7 ounces.
6K1454—Four-piece pattern, regulation size for 6K1440, 6K1438 and 6K1439 bags... **63c**
6K1455—Two-piece pattern for 6K1435 bags..... **49c**

Volley Balls and Net

"Wilson" Official Volley Ball
Made of special tanned pearl color horsehide. Canvas lined, well sewed. Official in size and shape. Complete with rubber bladder, lace and needle. Shipping wt., 1½ lbs.
6K1836 **$3.79**

Volley Ball Net
Regulation size, 27 feet long, 3 feet wide, made of heavy No. 12 white cotton twine. Full weight. Shpg. wt., 2 lbs.
6K1838... **$1.20**

Volley or Soccer Ball Bladder
6K1830—Four-piece bladder, heavy weight for Volley Ball 6K1836 and Soccer Ball 6K2375. Shpg. wt., 7 oz. **63c**
6K1833—Two-piece bladder for volley balls like 6K1835, 6K1837 and Soccer Balls 6K2376 and 6K2377.. **44c**

Practice Volley Ball
Made of good quality genuine cowhide, tan color. Canvas lined. Regulation size. Complete with rubber bladder, lace and needle. Shipping wt., 1½ pounds.
6K1835 **$2.69**

Amateur Volley Ball
Good quality tan color leather. Canvas lined. Regulation size. Complete with rubber bladder and lace. Shipping weight, 1¾ pounds.
6K1837.. **$1.98**

Parcel Post, Express and Freight Rates Are on Pages 542 to 545

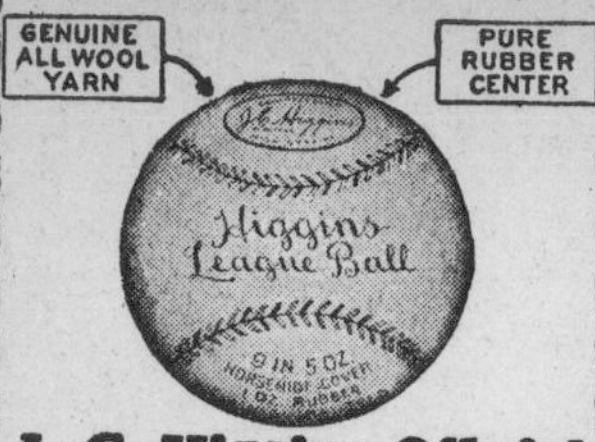

J. C. Higgins Official

Guaranteed for twenty-seven innings against ripping, tearing or losing its shape, if not played with when wet. Rubber center, all wool yarn wound, specially tanned selected horsehide covering, sewed with strong thread. Guaranteed to be the equal of any official baseball on the market. Each ball wrapped in tissue paper and tinfoil and packed in individual sealed box. Shpg. wt., each, 8 oz.
6K1600—Each........$1.19
Per dozen, $13.95; per half dozen........$7.05

Wilson Official League Ball

The cork and rubber center insures balance and accurate flight. Wound with best grade genuine all wool yarn. Selected horsehide cover sewed with best linen thread. Shpg. wt., 8 oz.
6K1602—Each
$1.39
Dozen...$15.00

Professional League Ball

Guaranteed for nine innings against ripping, tearing or losing its shape. Fine quality horsehide cover strongly sewed by hand; rubber center, yarn wound. Size, 9 in. Wt., 5 oz. Shpg. wt., 8 oz.
6K1605
85c

Pitchers' Pride Baseball

Good grade horsehide cover; strongly stitched with linen thread; rubber center. An excellent, lively ball for boys. Size, 9 inches. Regulation weight. Shipping weight, 8 ounces.
6K1607
49c

Boys' Winner Baseball

Genuine leather covered, strongly stitched with linen thread. Rubber center. Regulation size. A splendid ball for small boys. Shipping weight, 7 ounces.
6K1609
36c

Outseam Playground Ball

A splendid low priced outseam ball with good quality genuine horsehide leather cover, strongly stitched; 12 inches in circumference. Shpg. wt., ¾ lb.
6K1610 63c

J.C.Higgins Official Indoor Ball

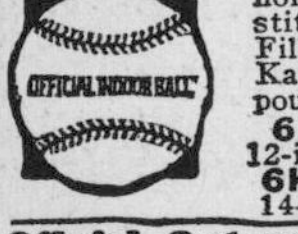

Excellent quality horsehide cover, well stitched, hand sewed. Filled with genuine Kapok. Shpg. wt., 1 pound.
6K1613 12-inch........95c
6K1612 14-inch........$1.19

Official Outseam Playground Ball

Finest quality horsehide cover. Filled with genuine Kapok. Well made, hand sewed. Will stand lots of hard use. Shpg. wt., 1 lb.
6K1615 12-inch ball........95c
6K1608 14-inch ball...$1.27

Official Playground Ball

Genuine horsehide leather cover, well sewed. About 10½ inches in circumference. Shipping wt., 8 oz.
6K1614........39c

Regulation Indoor Bat

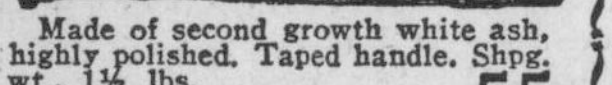

Made of second growth white ash, highly polished. Taped handle. Shpg. wt., 1½ lbs.
6K1717........55c

Famous World's Series Pitcher Says Your Baseball Equipment is Standard in Every Respect

Virgil Barnes Model

Approved and autographed by Virgil Barnes, star pitcher for the New York "Giants". Genuine horsehide, oil rubbed. Full leather lining. Strongly stitched. Thumb and forefinger connected with leather lacing. Shpg. wt., 1½ lbs.
6K1664—To wear on left hand........$1.98
6K1665—To wear on right hand; for left-handed throwers.$1.98

Wm. Southworth Model

Endorsed and autographed by the star St. Louis National outfielder. Professional model. Constructed of genuine horsehide, properly oiled to prevent cracking. All leather lined. Leather welted seams. Leather laced at wrist. Wet thumb connection. Shpg. wt., 1¼ lbs.
6K1688—To wear on left hand........$2.35
6K1689—To wear on right hand; for left-handed throwers...$2.35

G. C. Alexander

Endorses this glove. Professional league model. Diverted seams prevent ripping. Made of high grade dark tan color oil treated horsehide; lined throughout with soft leather. Laced between thumb and forefinger. Reinforced with ⅝-inch strip over thumb welt. Leather welted seams. Laced at wrist with leather. Shpg. wt., 1½ lbs.
6K1676—To wear on left hand....$3.39
6K1677—To wear on right hand; for left-handed throwers.......$3.39

G. C. Alexander "Junior" Model

For the young ball player. Endorsed by the great pitcher, G. C. Alexander. Good quality horsehide, tan color, leather lined and correctly padded. Welded seams; laced at wrist. Shipping weight, 1¼ lbs.
6K1662—To wear on left hand........$1.57
6K1663—To wear on right hand; for left-handed thrower..$1.57

Youths' Full Size Glove

Good quality tan color horsehide, strongly stitched. Properly padded. Leather palm. Webbed thumb and forefinger. Shipping weight, 1 pound.
6K1680—To wear on left hand........$1.15
6K1681—To wear on right hand; for left-handed thrower.$1.15

Catchers' Mitts

Youths' Semi-Pro Model

Good quality horsehide leather palm and fingers; well padded; deep pocket; laced all around edge; well stitched. Strap and buckle at wrist. Shpg. wt., 1¾ lbs.
6K1648—To wear on left hand.$1.75
6K1649—To wear on right hand; for left handed thrower....$1.75

"Gabby" Hartnett, Jr. Model

Good quality genuine light tan cowhide palm and fingers; leather back. Well padded, deep pocket; full bound, laced edge. Patented, protected adjustable wrist strap. Will give excellent service. Shpg. wt., 1¾ lbs.
6K1640—To wear on left hand.....$2.45
6K1641—To wear on right hand; for left-hand thrower. $2.45

"Bob O'Farrell" Scoop Model

Endorsed and autographed by the famous catcher of the St. Louis Nationals. A real scoop model many stores would sell at $6.00. High quality dark tan color cowhide leather throughout. Special felt padding, deep pocket, leather laced edge, double stitched. Wrist strap with patented non-interfering buckle. Shpg. wt., 2½ lbs.
6K1638—To wear on left hand........$3.87

"C. Leo 'Gabby' Hartnett" Model

Endorsed by "Gabby" Hartnett, Chicago "Cub" catcher. The leather used in this mitt is of the finest quality golden brown cowhide. Hand molded palm with specially constructed asbestos felt padding, hand formed and hand stitched. Ready broken with deep, natural ball pocket. Leather bound and leather laced edge. Patented protected adjustable wrist strap. Shipping weight, 2¾ pounds.
6K1634—To wear on left hand.........$5.48

First Baseman's Mitts

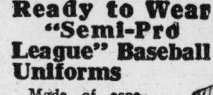

Youths' Model

Good quality soft and pliable horsehide leather; well padded finger back; laced edge. A good serviceable mitt for youths. Shipping weight, 1¼ pounds.
6K1660—To wear on left hand$1.75
6K1661—To wear on right hand; for left-handed thrower. $1.75

Professional Model

Exceptional Value in Design and Material. High quality oiled tan horsehide throughout, soft and flexible. Full leather lined, leather bound and well stitched. Special felt padding, giving mitt a ready broke pocket. Leather laced edge. Shipping wt., 1¾ pounds.
6K1658—To wear on left hand$2.95
6K1659—To wear on right hand; for left handed thrower...$2.95

WLS Big League Baseball Bats

Made of selected second growth mountain ash. Perfectly balanced. Shipping weight, 2½ pounds.
6K1706—Similar in size and balance to the bat used by Babe Ruth........$1.18
6K1708—Similar in size and balance to the bat used by Rogers Hornsby........$1.18
6K1709—Similar in size and balance to the bat used by Eddie Collins........$1.18
6K1705—Similar in size and balance to the bat used by Ty Cobb........$1.18

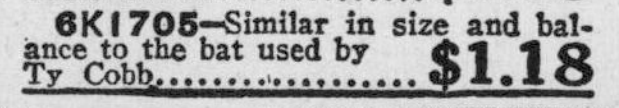

W L S League Bat

Selected second growth ash. Professional model. Shipping weight, 2½ lbs.
6K1712—With tape wound grip........95c

WLS Youths' Professional Bats

Good quality ash, light brown burnished finish. Tape wound grip.
6K1714—Shipping weight, 2½ pounds........57c

W L S Junior League Bat

Hardwood, flame burnt, yellow finish, highly polished. Length, about 32 inches.
6K1715—Shipping weight, 2¼ pounds........34c

Boys' Specials

Fielder's Glove

Leather, felt padding; palm, leather lined. Bound edge. Shpg. wt., 8 oz.
6K1684—To wear on left hand. 76c
6K1685—To wear on right hand; for left handed throwers 76c

Catchers' Mitt

Soft glove leather throughout; well padded. Shpg. wt., 1¼ lbs.
6K1650—To wear on left hand 95c
6K1651—To wear on right hand; for left handed throwers 95c

Fielder's Glove

Leather, felt padding; palm, leather lined. Shpg. wt., 6 oz.
6K1686 To wear on left hand.. 49c
6K1687 To wear on right hand; for left handed throwers... 49c

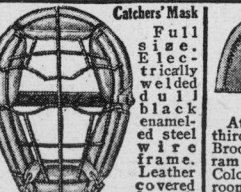

Catchers' Mask

Full size. Electrically welded dull black enameled steel wire frame. Leather covered head, cheek and chin pads, padded with hair. Elastic head strap.
6K1695 Shpg. wt., 1½ lbs. $1.89
6K1699 Youths' size........$1.25

Amateur Baseball Cap

Athletic flannel one-third wool. Deep crown, Brooklyn style. Buckram unbreakable visor. Colors. Gray with maroon trimmings, gray with navy blue trimmings; plain navy blue or plain black. Sizes, 6¾ to 7½. State size and color. Shipping wt., 4 ounces.
6K1777.....59c

Ready to Wear "Semi-Pro League" Baseball Uniforms

Made of especially woven athletic flannel, one-third wool, with woven stripe. Made strictly along professional lines, embodying every feature needed to insure comfort. Sizes, 34 to 42 inches chest measure. Give chest measure and size of cap.

Shirt—V neck with trimmed insert, two rows cordage on front and elbow sleeves. Pants—Tunnel loops, peg style. Cap—Deep crown, Brooklyn style, corded seams, with unbreakable buckram visor. Footless Cotton Hose—Gray with stripe to match trimmings. Belt—Stationary. Shpg. wt., 3½ lbs.
6K1797—Blue-gray with green stripes. Each....$5.95
6K1798—Gray with navy blue stripes. Complete 5.95
Nine uniforms or more in any of above colors. Each.. 5.50

Boys' Ready to Wear Baseball Uniforms

Made of a special cotton athletic flannel, strong and durable. Gray with navy blue stripes. Consists of shirt, pants, stationary belt, footless hose and cap. Sizes, 28 to 36 inches chest measure. State chest measure and size of cap. Shipping weight, 2½ lbs.
6K1791—Complete......$3.45
Nine uniforms or more. Each..$3.00

Big Savings at these LOW PRICES on Equipment of Such Good Quality

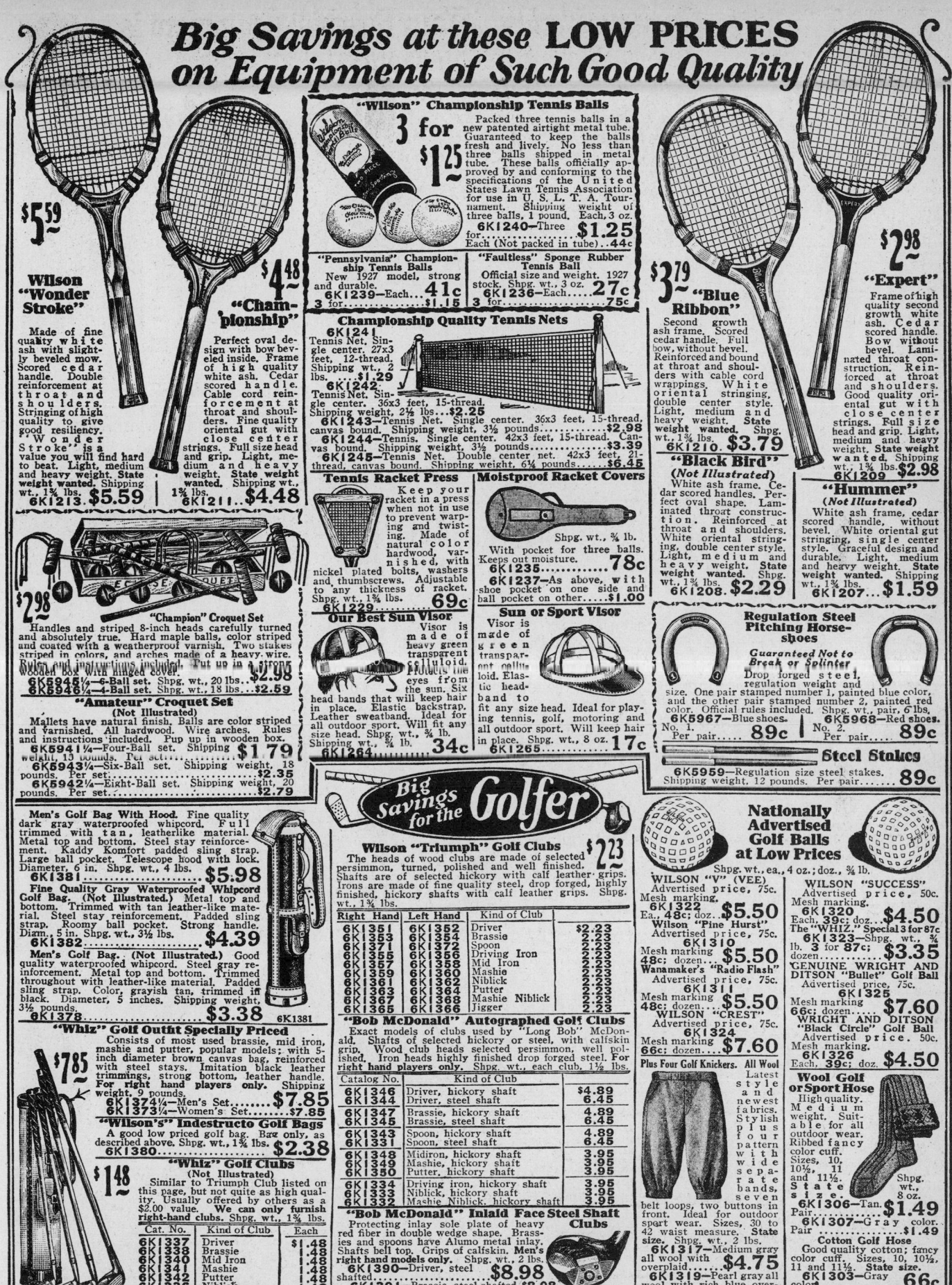

$5.59

Wilson "Wonder Stroke"

Made of fine quality white ash with slightly beveled mow. Scored cedar handle. Double reinforcement at throat and shoulders. Stringing of high quality to give good resiliency. "Wonder Stroke" is a value you will find hard to beat. Light, medium and heavy weight. **State weight wanted.** Shipping wt., 1¾ lbs.
6K1213..**$5.59**

$4.48

"Championship"

Perfect oval design with bow beveled inside. Frame of high quality white ash. Cedar scored handle. Cable cord reinforcement at throat and shoulders. Fine quality oriental gut with close center strings. Full size head and grip. Light, medium and heavy weight. **State weight wanted.** Shipping wt., 1¾ lbs.
6K1211...**$4.48**

"Wilson" Championship Tennis Balls

3 for $1.25

Packed three tennis balls in a new patented airtight metal tube. Guaranteed to keep the balls fresh and lively. No less than three balls shipped in metal tube. These balls officially approved by and conforming to the specifications of the United States Lawn Tennis Association for use in U. S. L. T. A. Tournament. Shipping weight of three balls, 1 pound. Each, 3 oz.
6K1240—Three for.................. **$1.25**
Each (Not packed in tube)..**44c**

"Pennsylvania" Championship Tennis Balls
New 1927 model, strong and durable.
6K1239—Each...**41c**
3 for...............**$1.15**

"Faultless" Sponge Rubber Tennis Ball
Official size and weight. 1927 stock. Shpg. wt., 3 oz.
6K1236—Each.....**27c**
3 for....................**75c**

Championship Quality Tennis Nets

6K1241—Tennis Net. Single center. 27x3 feet, 12-thread. Shipping wt., 2 lbs. **$1.29**
6K1242—Tennis Net. Single center. 36x3 feet, 15-thread. Shipping weight, 2½ lbs...**$2.25**
6K1243—Tennis Net. Single center. 36x3 feet, 15-thread, canvas bound. Shipping weight, 3½ pounds..............**$2.98**
6K1244—Tennis. Single center. 42x3 feet, 15-thread. Canvas bound. Shipping weight, 3½ pounds..............**$3.39**
6K1245—Tennis Net. Double center net. 42x3 feet, 21-thread, canvas bound. Shipping weight, 6¼ pounds......**$6.45**

$3.79

"Blue Ribbon"

Second growth ash frame. Scored cedar handle. Full bow, without bevel. Reinforced and bound at throat and shoulders with cable cord wrappings. White oriental stringing, double center style. Light, medium and heavy weight. **State weight wanted.** Shpg. wt., 1¾ lbs.
6K1210. **$3.79**

$2.98

"Expert"

Frame of high quality second growth white ash. Cedar scored handle. Bow without bevel. Laminated throat construction. Reinforced at throat and shoulders. Good quality oriental gut with close center strings. Full size head and grip. Light, medium and heavy weight. **State weight wanted.** Shipping wt., 1¾ lbs.
6K1209..**$2.98**

"Black Bird"
(Not Illustrated)

White ash frame. Cedar scored handles. Perfect oval shape. Laminated throat construction. Reinforced at throat and shoulders. White oriental stringing, double center style. Light, medium and heavy weight. **State weight wanted.** Shpg. wt., 1¾ lbs.
6K1208. **$2.29**

"Hummer"
(Not Illustrated)

White ash frame, cedar scored handle, without bevel. White oriental gut stringing, single center style. Graceful design and durable. Light, medium and heavy weight. **State weight wanted.** Shipping wt., 1¾ lbs.
6K1207...**$1.59**

$2.98

"Champion" Croquet Set

Handles and striped 8-inch heads carefully turned and absolutely true. Hard maple balls, color striped and coated with a weatherproof varnish. Two stakes striped in colors, and arches made of a heavy wire. Rules and instructions included. Put up in a strong wooden box with hinged cover.
6K5945¼—6-Ball set. Shpg. wt., 20 lbs.. **$2.98**
6K5946¼—4-Ball set. Shpg. wt., 18 lbs...**$2.59**

"Amateur" Croquet Set
(Not Illustrated)

Mallets have natural finish. Balls are color striped and varnished. All hardwood. Wire arches. Rules and instructions included. Pup up in wooden box.
6K5941¼—Four-Ball set. Shipping weight, 15 pounds. Per set.................. **$1.79**
6K5943¼—Six-Ball set. Shipping weight, 18 pounds. Per set..............................**$2.35**
6K5942¼—Eight-Ball set. Shipping weight, 20 pounds. Per set..............................**$2.79**

Tennis Racket Press

Keep your racket in a press when not in use to prevent warping and twisting. Made of natural color hardwood, varnished, with nickel plated bolts, washers and thumbscrews. Adjustable to any thickness of racket. Shpg. wt., 1¾ lbs.
6K1229........... **69c**

Moistproof Racket Covers

Shpg. wt., ¾ lb.

With pocket for three balls. Keeps out moisture.
6K1235............. **78c**
6K1237—As above, with shoe pocket on one side and ball pocket on other.....**$1.00**

Our Best Sun Visor

Visor is made of heavy green transparent celluloid. Protects the eyes from the sun. Six head bands that will keep hair in place. Elastic backstrap. Leather sweatband. Ideal for all outdoor sport. Will fit any size head. Shpg. wt., ¾ lb. Shipping wt., ¾ lb.
6K1264............. **34c**

Sun or Sport Visor

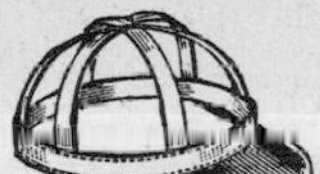

Visor is made of green transparent celluloid. Elastic headband to fit any size head. Ideal for playing tennis, golf, motoring and all outdoor sport. Will keep hair in place. Shpg. wt., 8 oz.
6K1265............ **17c**

Regulation Steel Pitching Horseshoes

Guaranteed Not to Break or Splinter

Drop forged steel, regulation weight and size. One pair stamped number 1, painted blue color, and the other pair stamped number 2, painted red color. Official rules included. Shpg. wt., pair, 6 lbs.
6K5967—Blue shoes. No. 1. Per pair..... **89c**
6K5968—Red shoes. No. 2. Per pair..... **89c**

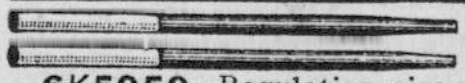

Steel Stakes

6K5959—Regulation size steel stakes. Shipping weight, 12 pounds. Per pair....... **89c**

Big Savings for the Golfer

Men's Golf Bag With Hood. Fine quality dark gray waterproofed whipcord. Full trimmed with tan, leatherlike material. Metal top and bottom. Steel stay reinforcement. Kaddy Komfort padded sling strap. Large ball pocket. Telescope hood with lock. Diameter, 6 in. Shpg. wt., 4 lbs.
6K1381.................. **$5.98**

Fine Quality Gray Waterproofed Whipcord Golf Bag. (Not Illustrated.) Metal top and bottom. Trimmed with tan leather-like material. Steel stay reinforcement. Padded sling strap. Roomy ball pocket. Strong handle. Diam., 5 in. Shpg. wt., 3½ lbs.
6K1382................... **$4.39**

Men's Golf Bag. (Not Illustrated.) Good quality waterproofed whipcord. Steel gray reinforcement. Metal top and bottom. Trimmed throughout with leather-like material. Padded sling strap. Color, grayish tan, trimmed in black. Diameter, 5 inches. Shipping weight, 3½ pounds.
6K1378.............................. **$3.38**

6K1381

"Whiz" Golf Outfit Specially Priced

$7.85

Consists of most used brassie, mid iron, mashie and putter, popular models; with 5-inch diameter brown canvas bag, reinforced with steel stays. Imitation black leather trimmings, strong bottom, leather handle. **For right hand players only.** Shipping weight, 9 pounds.
6K1374¼—Men's Set........ **$7.85**
6K1373¼—Women's Set........**$7.85**

"Wilson's" Indestructo Golf Bags

A good low priced golf bag. Bag only, as described above. Shpg. wt., 1¾ lbs.
6K1380.......................... **$2.38**

$1.48

"Whiz" Golf Clubs
(Not Illustrated)

Similar to Triumph Club listed on this page, but not quite as high quality. Usually offered by others as a $2.00 value. **We can only furnish right-hand clubs.** Shpg. wt., 1¾ lbs.

Cat. No.	Kind of Club	Each
6K1337	Driver	$1.48
6K1338	Brassie	1.48
6K1340	Mid Iron	1.48
6K1341	Mashie	1.48
6K1342	Putter	1.48
6K1336	Niblick	1.48
6K1335	Mashie Niblick	1.48

Wilson "Triumph" Golf Clubs $2.23

The heads of wood clubs are made of selected persimmon, turned, polished and well finished. Shafts are of selected hickory with calf leather grips. Irons are made of fine quality steel, drop forged, highly finished, hickory shafts with calf leather grips. Shpg. wt., 1¾ lbs.

Right Hand	Left Hand	Kind of Club	
6K1351	6K1352	Driver	$2.23
6K1353	6K1354	Brassie	2.23
6K1371	6K1372	Spoon	2.23
6K1355	6K1356	Driving Iron	2.23
6K1357	6K1358	Mid Iron	2.23
6K1359	6K1360	Mashie	2.23
6K1361	6K1362	Niblick	2.23
6K1363	6K1364	Putter	2.23
6K1367	6K1368	Mashie Niblick	2.23
6K1365	6K1366	Jigger	2.23

"Bob McDonald" Autographed Golf Clubs

Exact models of clubs used by "Long Bob" McDonald. Shafts of selected hickory or steel, with calfskin grip. Wood club heads selected persimmon, well polished. Iron heads highly finished drop forged steel. **For right hand players only.** Shpg. wt., each club, 1½ lbs.

Catalog No.	Kind of Club	
6K1346	Driver, hickory shaft	$4.89
6K1344	Driver, steel shaft	6.45
6K1347	Brassie, hickory shaft	4.89
6K1345	Brassie, steel shaft	6.45
6K1343	Spoon, hickory shaft	4.89
6K1331	Spoon, steel shaft	6.45
6K1348	Midiron, hickory shaft	3.95
6K1349	Mashie, hickory shaft	3.95
6K1350	Putter, hickory shaft	3.95
6K1334	Driving iron, hickory shaft	3.95
6K1333	Niblick, hickory shaft	3.95
6K1332	Mashie Niblick, hickory shaft	3.95

"Bob McDonald" Inlaid Face Steel Shaft Clubs

Protecting inlay sole plate of heavy red fiber in double wedge shape. Brassies and spoons have Alumo metal inlay. Shafts bell top. Grips of calfskin. **Men's right hand models only.** Shpg. wt., 2 lbs.

6K1390—Driver, steel shafted.......................... **$8.98**
6K1391—Brassie, steel shafted.**$8.98**
6K1392—Spoon, steel shafted...................**$8.98**

Nationally Advertised Golf Balls at Low Prices

Shpg. wt., ea., 4 oz.; doz., ¾ lb.

WILSON "V" (VEE)
Advertised price, 75c. Mesh marking.
6K1322
Ea., 48c; doz...**$5.50**

Wilson "Pine Hurst"
Advertised price, 75c.
6K1310
Mesh marking 48c; dozen... **$5.50**

Wanamaker's "Radio Flash"
Advertised price, 75c.
6K1311
Mesh marking 48c; dozen.... **$5.50**

WILSON "CREST"
Advertised price, 75c.
6K1324
Mesh marking 66c; dozen.... **$7.60**

WILSON "SUCCESS"
Advertised price, 50c. Mesh marking.
6K1320
Each, 39c; doz... **$4.50**

The "WHIZ." Special 3 for 87c
6K1323—Shpg. wt., ¾ lb. 3 for 87c; dozen........... **$3.35**

GENUINE WRIGHT AND DITSON "Bullet" Golf Ball
Advertised price, 75c.
6K1325
Mesh marking 66c; dozen..... **$7.60**

WRIGHT AND DITSON "Black Circle" Golf Ball
Advertised price. 50c. Mesh marking.
6K1326
Each, 39c; doz. **$4.50**

Plus Four Golf Knickers. All Wool

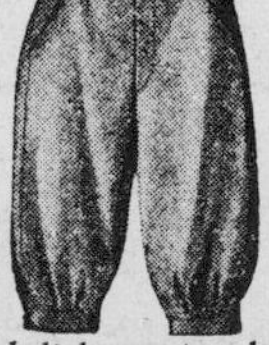

Latest style and newest fabrics. Stylish plus four pattern with wide separate bands, seven belt loops, two buttons in front. Ideal for outdoor sport wear. Sizes, 30 to 42 waist measure. **State size.** Shpg. wt., 2 lbs.
6K1317—Medium gray all wool with overplaid....... **$4.75**
6K1319—Pearl gray all wool with rich blue overplaid decoration....**$5.85**

Wool Golf or Sport Hose

High quality. Medium weight. Suitable for all outdoor wear. Ribbed fancy color cuff. Sizes, 10, 10½, 11 and 11½. **State size.** Shpg. wt., 8 oz.
6K1306—Tan. Pair............... **$1.49**
6K1307—Gray color. Pair **$1.49**

Cotton Golf Hose

Good quality cotton; fancy color cuff. Sizes, 10, 10½, 11 and 11½. **State size.**
6K1303—Gray color............... **66c**
6K1304—Tan color. **66c**

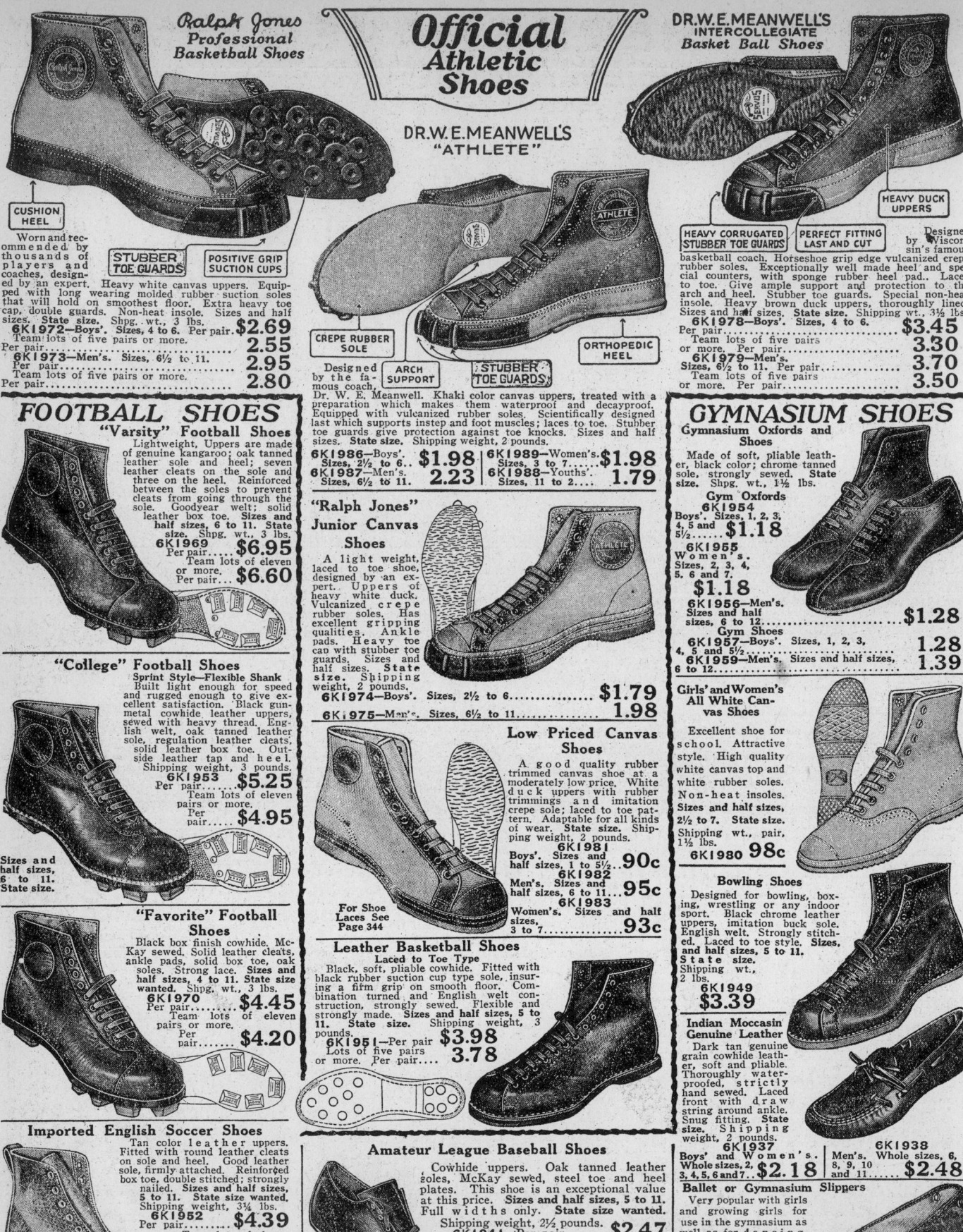

Ralph Jones Professional Basketball Shoes

Official Athletic Shoes

DR. W. E. MEANWELL'S "ATHLETE"

DR. W. E. MEANWELL'S INTERCOLLEGIATE Basket Ball Shoes

CUSHION HEEL

STUBBER TOE GUARDS

POSITIVE GRIP SUCTION CUPS

Worn and recommended by thousands of players and coaches, designed by an expert. Heavy white canvas uppers. Equipped with long wearing molded rubber suction soles that will hold on smoothest floor. Extra heavy toe cap, double guards. Non-heat insole. Sizes and half sizes. State size. Shpg. wt., 3 lbs.

6K1972—Boys'. Sizes, 4 to 6. Per pair.... **$2.69**
Per pair............................ **2.55**
6K1973—Men's. Sizes, 6½ to 11.
Per pair............................ **2.95**
Team lots of five pairs or more.
Per pair............................ **2.80**

CREPE RUBBER SOLE

ARCH SUPPORT

STUBBER TOE GUARDS

ORTHOPEDIC HEEL

Designed by the famous coach Dr. W. E. Meanwell. Khaki color canvas uppers, treated with a preparation which makes them waterproof and decayproof. Equipped with vulcanized rubber soles. Scientifically designed last which supports instep and foot muscles; laces to toe. Stubber toe guards give protection against toe knocks. Sizes and half sizes. State size. Shipping weight, 2 pounds.

6K1986—Boys'. Sizes, 2½ to 6.. **$1.98** | 6K1989—Women's. Sizes, 3 to 7.... **$1.98**
6K1987—Men's. Sizes, 6½ to 11. **2.23** | 6K1988—Youths'. Sizes, 11 to 2.... **1.79**

HEAVY CORRUGATED STUBBER TOE GUARDS

PERFECT FITTING LAST AND CUT

HEAVY DUCK UPPERS

Designed by Wisconsin's famous basketball coach. Horseshoe grip edge vulcanized crepe rubber soles. Exceptionally well made heel and special counters, with sponge rubber heel pad.. Laces to toe. Give ample support and protection to the arch and heel. Stubber toe guards. Special non-heat insole. Heavy brown duck uppers, thoroughly lined. Sizes and half sizes. State size. Shipping wt., 3½ lbs.

6K1978—Boys'. Sizes, 4 to 6.
Per pair............................ **$3.45**
Team lots of five pairs or more. Per pair............ **3.30**
6K1979—Men's. Sizes, 6½ to 11. Per pair............ **3.70**
Team lots of five pairs or more. Per pair............ **3.50**

FOOTBALL SHOES

"Varsity" Football Shoes

Lightweight. Uppers are made of genuine kangaroo; oak tanned leather sole and heel; seven leather cleats on the sole and three on the heel. Reinforced between the soles to prevent cleats from going through the sole. Goodyear welt; solid leather box toe. Sizes and half sizes, 6 to 11. State size. Shpg. wt., 3 lbs.

6K1969
Per pair..... **$6.95**
Team lots of eleven or more. Per pair... **$6.60**

"College" Football Shoes

Sprint Style—Flexible Shank Built light enough for speed and rugged enough to give excellent satisfaction. Black gunmetal cowhide leather uppers, sewed with heavy thread. English welt, oak tanned leather sole, regulation leather cleats, solid leather box toe. Outside leather tap and heel. Shipping weight, 3 pounds.

6K1953
Per pair....... **$5.25**
Team lots of eleven pairs or more. Per pair..... **$4.95**

Sizes and half sizes, 6 to 11. State size.

"Favorite" Football Shoes

Black box finish cowhide. McKay sewed. Solid leather cleats, ankle pads, solid box toe, oak soles. Strong lace. Sizes and half sizes, 4 to 11. State size wanted. Shpg. wt., 3 lbs.

6K1970
Per pair........ **$4.45**
Team lots of eleven pairs or more. Per pair....... **$4.20**

Imported English Soccer Shoes

Tan color leather uppers. Fitted with round leather cleats on sole and heel. Good leather sole, firmly attached; strongly nailed. Reinforced box toe, double stitched; strongly nailed. Sizes and half sizes, 5 to 11. State size wanted. Shipping weight, 3½ lbs.

6K1952
Per pair........ **$4.39**
Team lots of eleven or more pairs. Per pair....... **$4.15**

"Ralph Jones" Junior Canvas Shoes

A light weight, laced to toe shoe, designed by an expert. Uppers of heavy white duck. Vulcanized crepe rubber soles. Has excellent gripping qualities. Ankle pads. Heavy toe cap with stubber toe guards. Sizes and half sizes. State size. Shipping weight, 2 pounds.

6K1974—Boys'. Sizes, 2½ to 6.................. **$1.79**
6K1975—Men's. Sizes, 6½ to 11.................. **1.98**

Low Priced Canvas Shoes

A good quality rubber trimmed canvas shoe at a moderately low price. White duck uppers with rubber trimmings and imitation crepe sole; laced to toe pattern. Adaptable for all kinds of wear. State size. Shipping weight, 2 pounds.

6K1981 Boys'. Sizes and half sizes, 1 to 5½. **90c**
6K1982 Men's. Sizes and half sizes, 6 to 11... **95c**
6K1983 Women's. Sizes and half sizes, 3 to 7.............. **93c**

For Shoe Laces See Page 344

Leather Basketball Shoes

Laced to Toe Type Black, soft, pliable cowhide. Fitted with black rubber suction cup type sole, insuring a firm grip on smooth floor. Combination turned and English welt construction, strongly sewed. Flexible and strongly made. Sizes and half sizes, 5 to 11. State size. Shipping weight, 3 pounds.

6K1951—Per pair **$3.98**
Lots of five pairs or more. Per pair.... **3.78**

Amateur League Baseball Shoes

Cowhide uppers. Oak tanned leather soles, McKay sewed, steel toe and heel plates. This shoe is an exceptional value at this price. Sizes and half sizes, 5 to 11. Full widths only. State size wanted. Shipping weight, 2½ pounds.

6K1941—Per pair.................. **$2.47**
Team lots of nine pairs or more. Per pair.......................... **$2.29**

GYMNASIUM SHOES

Gymnasium Oxfords and Shoes

Made of soft, pliable leather, black color; chrome tanned sole, strongly sewed. State size. Shpg. wt., 1½ lbs.

Gym Oxfords
6K1954 Boys'. Sizes, 1, 2, 3, 4, 5 and 5½. **$1.18**
6K1955 Women's. Sizes, 2, 3, 4, 5, 6 and 7. **$1.18**
6K1956—Men's. Sizes and half sizes, 6 to 12................ **$1.28**

Gym Shoes
6K1957—Boys'. Sizes, 1, 2, 3, 4, 5 and 5½. **1.28**
6K1959—Men's. Sizes and half sizes, 6 to 12............... **1.39**

Girls' and Women's All White Canvas Shoes

Excellent shoe for school. Attractive style. High quality white canvas top and white rubber soles. Non-heat insoles. Sizes and half sizes, 2½ to 7. State size. Shipping wt., pair, 1½ lbs.

6K1980 **98c**

Bowling Shoes

Designed for bowling, boxing, wrestling or any indoor sport. Black chrome leather uppers, imitation buck sole. English welt. Strongly stitched. Laced to toe style. Sizes and half sizes, 5 to 11. State size. Shipping wt., 2 lbs.

6K1949 **$3.39**

Indian Moccasin Genuine Leather

Dark tan genuine grain cowhide leather, soft and pliable. Thoroughly waterproofed, strictly hand sewed. Laced front with draw string around ankle. Snug fitting. State size. Shipping weight, 2 pounds.

6K1937 Boys' and Women's. Whole sizes, 2, 3, 4, 5, 6 and 7. **$2.18** | 6K1938 Men's. Whole sizes, 6, 7, 8, 9, 10 and 11... **$2.48**

Ballet or Gymnasium Slippers

Very popular with girls and growing girls for use in the gymnasium as well as for dancing. Made of black kid leather, very soft and pliable; soft toe. State size. Shipping weight, 1 pound.

6K1936—Growing girls'. Sizes and half sizes, 2½ to 7.............. **$1.98**
6K1935—Girls'. Sizes, 12, 12½, 13, 13½, 1, 1½ and 2.............. **1.88**

A Complete Playground at a Low Price

A Slide, Teeter Totter, and Merry-Go-Round, All in One

Three popular "playtime" features at a lower cost than the usual price for one.

The same fine construction and quality of the Merremaker is usually found only in much higher priced equipment. The Merremaker is rigidly constructed of clear selected wood and the strongest steel. Easily set up or changed to any of the three features shown in illustrations. Finished in a bright red enamel with weatherproof spar varnish. Board for slide, teeter totter and merry-go-round is a solid piece of smooth, fine grained wood, 9 feet long by 14 inches wide. Strong ladder is 6 feet long, hinged in center to form support for teeter totter and merry-go-round. Steps, solidly bolted. Take advantage of this splendid value and keep your children a home with healthful muscle-building play. Shipping weight, 50 pounds.

6K1560¼ Merremaker. $18.95

Slide

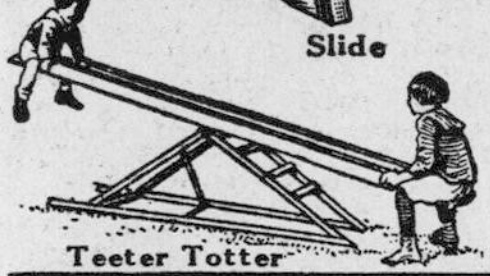

Teeter Totter

Merry-Go-Round $18.95

Popular Merremaker Gym

Trapeze, Rings, Horizontal Bar and Swing

As a muscle and health builder, source of constructive fun for the kiddies, and as an unusual value, there is nothing finer that we can recommend than the Merremaker. The four features, as illustrated below, and to the right, offer so much variety of play that the children never tire of this apparatus. They can play on the swing one week, the rings the next and the trapeze the next and so on. The Merremaker gym can be used all the year round. Is rubber padded, for wintertime use in the playroom, basement or attic. Is 7 ft. high and 5 ft. wide. Finished in an attractive red enamel with a weatherproof spar varnish finish. Strongly constructed of clear selected wood and steel at the points of greatest strain. Tested to hold 700 pounds. Heavy chain swing is securely bolted to top beam. Seat, trapeze and horizontal bar made of fine grain selected wood. Smooth finish iron flying rings. Easy to set up in 10 minutes. Shpg. wt. 40 lbs.

6K156¼—Merremaker Gym...... $10.95

MERREMAKER GYM

TRAPEZE RINGS BAR

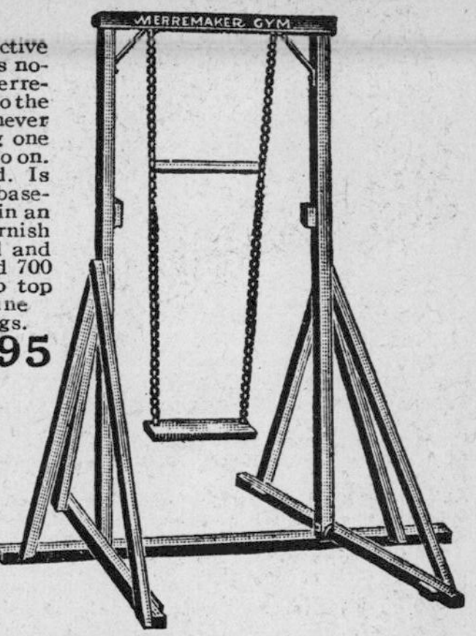

Portable Slide

Constructed throughout of well seasoned hardwood, well painted and varnished. The ladder is built with steps of hardwood strongly put together, and provided with a steel pipe railing. The bottom or bed of the slide is of galvanized "Armco" iron. The type of slide is "fast" and will withstand the weather. Shipped direct from factory in NORTHERN INDIANA.

Catalog No.	Height to Top of Ladder	Length of Slide, Feet	Shpg. Wt. Lbs.	Each
6K6100½	5 feet	10	90	$17.95
6K6101½	6 feet	12	100	21.45
6K6102½	7 feet	14	105	24.95

Send for Free Catalog

For complete selection of playground equipment send for Sporting Goods Catalog 568K.

All Wool Felt

All wool, 72 in. wide. Navy blue, black, white, purple, maroon, orange, red, green, old gold or tan. State color. No less than ½ yd. sold. Shipping weight, per yd., 1¼ pounds.

6K2625—Any color listed, except white. Per yard... **$2.75**
6K2626—White only. Per yard **$3.20**

Home Excercising Apparatus — For Men and Women

Elastic Cord Chest Pull

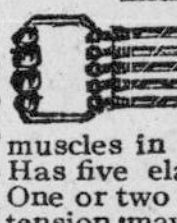

Has strong tension for developing the muscles in shoulders, chest, back and arms. Has five elastic cables attached to hand grips. One or two cables may be removed so that the tension may be varied. An excellent way to keep fit. Shpg. wt., 1½ lbs.

6K1569...... $1.69

Giant 10-Cable Chest Pull

One of the strongest and best chest pull made. Has ten elastic spring cables fitted into rubberoid hand grips. You can regulate resistance as you wish by simply detaching the cables. Not illustrated. Shipping weight, 2½ pounds.

6K1568...... $2.98

"Peerless" 5-In-1 Wire Exerciser

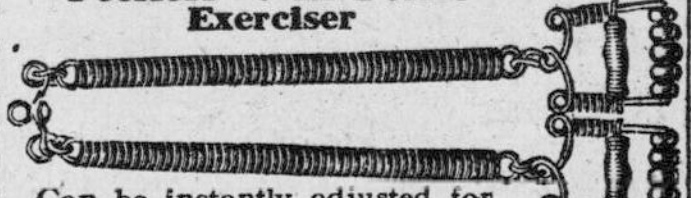

Can be instantly adjusted for use as a wall exerciser, chest pull, combination grip and massage roller handles. All metal parts nickel plated. Chart of instructions included. Shpg. wt., 2½ lbs.

6K1564—Medium tension... **$2.39**
6K1563—Heavy tension... **2.55**
6K1565—Extra heavy tension... **2.79**

Black Iron Dumbbells

If only one dumbbell is wanted, send one half of the price. Excellent values at these low prices. Shpg. wt., 3 lbs.

6K1516—State weight wanted.

Wt. Each	Shpg. Wt.	Per Pr.	Wt. Each	Shpg. Wt.	Per Pr.
1 lb.	2 lbs.	21c	10 lbs.	12 lbs.	$1.89
2 lbs.	3 lbs.	39c	15 lbs.	20 lbs.	2.79
3 lbs.	4 lbs.	59c	20 lbs.	25 lbs.	3.60
5 lbs.	7 lbs.	99c	25 lbs.	30 lbs.	4.40

Complete Home Gym Outfit

For the Men And Boys Who Want to Keep Fit

Affords an almost complete training of the muscles. Outfit includes elastic five-cable chest pull with rubberoid handles; quality spring exerciser for back, arm and chest muscles; pair of heavy tension grips, steel wrist and forearm developers; three illustrated charts giving complete courses in physical training. Packed in attractive box. Shipping weight, 5 pounds.

6K1567...... $3.48

Swinging Rings and Trapeze Bars

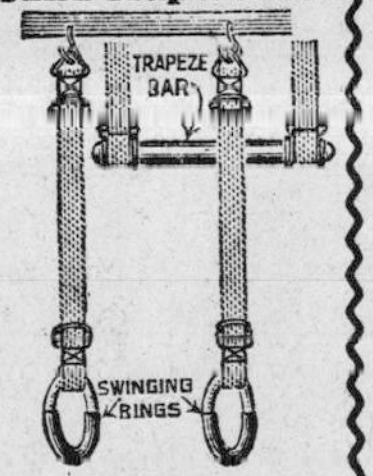

Good quality webbing, very strong. Adjustable steel buckles, hooks. All wood parts nicely smoothed and well finished. Simple to set up. For adults as well as youngsters. Can be used outdoors. These are low prices. Shpg. wt., 3 lbs.

6K1558 Swinging Rings with rubber clips. Per pair... **$2.79**
6K1559—Trapeze bar... **$2.39**

Health Swing

The Home Gymnasium

For Men, Women and Children

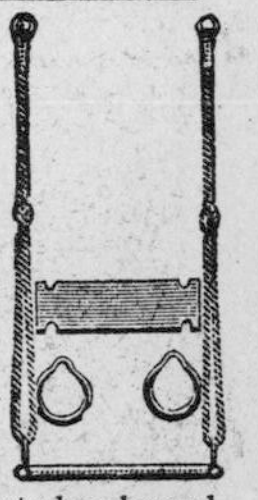

Successfully combines three needed exercises. May be used as a swing, with trapeze bar, or with rings. The finest, and easiest way for keeping physically fit. Makes an excellent swing for the children. The ropes are about 68 inches long, ½-inch thick. Has strong malleable iron hooks to hold the bar, rings or swing. Trapeze bar is perfectly turned from finest beechwood. Swing board made of smooth fine grained wood. Rings are cushioned, with soft pliable leather. Shpg. wt., 6 lbs.

6K1566...... $3.79

Unmounted United States Wool Flags

ALL WOOL BUNTING FLAGS

U. S. War Department Standard Guaranteed Fast Colors

Sewed bunting flags. Forty-eight stars, sewed on both sides of field, and placed according to Government regulation. Stripes sewed with double seams. Size recommended for average schoolhouse flag is 5x8 feet.

Catalog No.	Size, Feet	Each	Shpg. Wt.
GK2600	2½ x 4	$2.25	6 oz.
6K2601	3 x 5	3.20	¾ lb.
6K2602	4 x 6	4.58	1 lb.
6K2603	5 x 8	6.85	1½ lbs.
6K2604	6 x10	9.25	2 lbs.
6K2605	8 x12	13.85	3 lbs.
6K2606	10 x19	28.75	7 lbs.

Dog Collars — Leads — Medicines

How to Measure for Dog Collars

Draw a tape measure closely around your dog's neck and get the exact measurement. The measurements of our collars are from the first hole to the side hole. Two extra holes allow about 1½ inches to 2 inches room for growing dogs. Prices do not include locks. Names engraved on collars 5 cents a letter. Write name to be engraved plainly.

Leather Muzzles

Russet strap leather. Buckles for adjustment. Give number nearest to measurement around dog's neck.

Catalog No.	Neck, In.	Shpg. Wt.	
6K4730	12	3 oz.	19c
6K4731	14	3 oz.	23c
6K4732	16	4 oz.	29c
6K4733	18	4 oz.	39c
6K4734	21	5 oz.	49c

Black Braided Leather Lead

Length, 54 in. Shipping weight, 6 ounces.

6K4786. 27c

Kennel Dog Chains

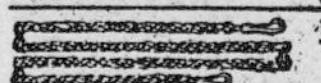

Polished steel round wire.
6K4790—Medium links, length 4½ ft. Shpg. wt., ¾ lb... **27c**
6K4791—Heavy links, length, 6 ft. Shipping weight, 1¼ lbs... **35c**

Dog Collar Lock

Padlock, 1 x ¾-inch, all nickel plated, with key. Shipping wt., 3 oz.
6K4784...... 25c

Braided Leather Dog Whip

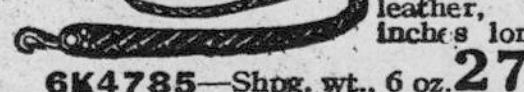

Black four-plait leather, 36 inches long.
6K4785—Shpg. wt., 6 oz... **27c**

Dog Call

Heavy Metal Whistle, 2¾ in. long; also suitable as police or referee's signal. Shpg. wt., 3 oz.
6K4787...... 25c

Combination Dog Collar and Harness

Black heavy leather. Large brass plated studs. Name plate and "D" ring. Collars not needed with this harness. Give number nearest to measurement around body at back of front legs.

Catalog No.	Body Measure	Width Straps	Shpg. Wt.	
6K4720	14 in.	½ in.	5 oz.	$1.39
6K4721	16 in.	⅝ in.	6 oz.	1.48
6K4722	18 in.	⅝ in.	7 oz.	1.59
6K4723	20 in.	¾ in.	8 oz.	1.79
6K4724	22 in.	¾ in.	¾ lb.	1.98
6K4725	24 in.	1 in.	¾ lb.	2.25
6K4726	26 in.	1¼ in.	1 lb.	2.67
6K4727	28-32 in.	1¼ in.	1¼ lb.	2.98

Nickel Plated Studded Collars

Sturdy and attractive. Heavy oak tanned russet leather, double thickness, with large and small studs. Give number nearest to measurement around neck. Shipping weight, each, 6 oz.

Catalog No.	Neck Measure, In.	Width of Collar, In.	
6K4690	13	1¼	69c
6K4691	15	1¼	79c
6K4692	17	1¼	89c
6K4693	19	1¼	98c

Leather Spike Collars

Heavy black leather lined, 13 and 15-inch collars each have a single row of pointed brass spikes, and a double row of brass plated studs. 17 and 19-inch collars each have a double row of spikes and a triple row of studs. Give number of collar nearest to measurement wanted. Shipping weight, each, 1 lb.

Catalog No.	Neck Measure	Width, Collar	
6K4650	13 in.	1½ in.	$1.39
6K4651	15 in.	1½ in.	1.59
6K4652	17 in.	2 in.	1.69
6K4653	19 in.	2 in.	1.89

Jewel Studded Collar

Black grain leather, double row of round brass plated studs with imitation turquoise studs; sheepskin lined. Give number nearest to measurement around neck.

Catalog No.	Neck Measure	Width Collar	Shipping Wt.
6K4680	9 in.	½ in.	29c
6K4681	11 in.	⅝ in.	37c
6K4682	13 in.	¾ in.	43c
6K4683	15 in.	1 in.	55c
6K4684	17 in.	1 in.	67c
6K4685	19 in.	1 in.	79c

Dr. McGinty's Wonder Preparations for Dogs and Cats

The Wonder Preparations for dogs and cats are one of the most popular brands. The formulas used are the same Dr. McGinty has found to be most effective in his practice, and if you follow directions closely you are sure to obtain good results. Directions with each package.

Mange Soap
Regular $1.00 Size
6K4660—Shipping wt., 1½ pounds... **69c**

Tape Worm Capsules
Regular $1.00 Size
6K4661—Shpg. wt., 6 oz... **69c**

Cankered Ear Treatment
Regular $1.25 Size
6K4662—Shpg. wt., 6 oz... **89c**

Flea Powder
Regular $1.00 Size
6K4663—Shpg. wt., 6 oz... **69c**

Hook Worm Capsules
Regular $1.00 Size
6K4664—Shpg. wt., 4 oz... **69c**

Worm Syrup for Puppies
Regular $1.25 Size
6K4665—Shpg. wt., 6 oz... **89c**

Bresko Dog Food
Keep Your Dog in Good Condition 
A carefully prepared ration of pure lean meat, washed wheat cereals, cod liver oil and mineral salts. It contains every essential element for the growth and health of the dog. Suitable for all sizes and breeds. Dogs need not be coaxed to eat Bresko—they like it from the first taste. Directions on package.
6K4666—5-pound package... **59c**
6K4667¼—25-pound package... **$2.69**

A Small Investment for Happy Evenings

Indoor Games for the Grown-Up

Lowest Prices on Most Popular Games

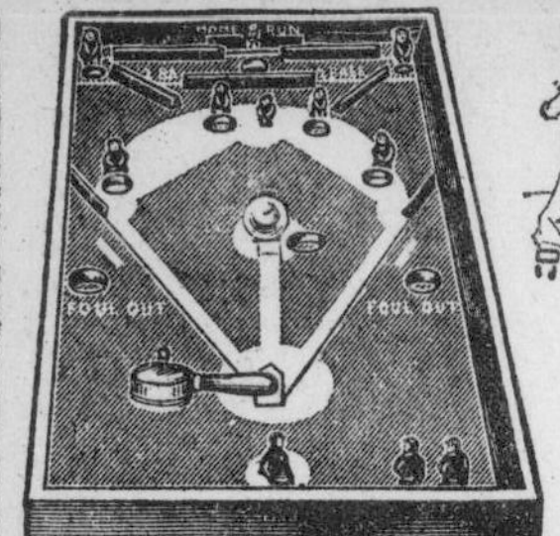

The All-Fair Baseball Game
A Real Game of Skill

Exciting fascinating game for baseball enthusiasts. Played the same as real baseball. Fast or slow balls can be pitched. Batter will strike out, fly out or get a hit, depending upon his ability. Metal base is used to insure a level playing field. Has mahogany finish wooden frame, metal baseball players, composition ball, wooden bat and strong, unbreakable springs. Size of game, 17½x24½ inches and 1¾ inches high. Shpg. wt., 5 lbs. Advertised price, $7.50.
6K1042¼ **$6.59**

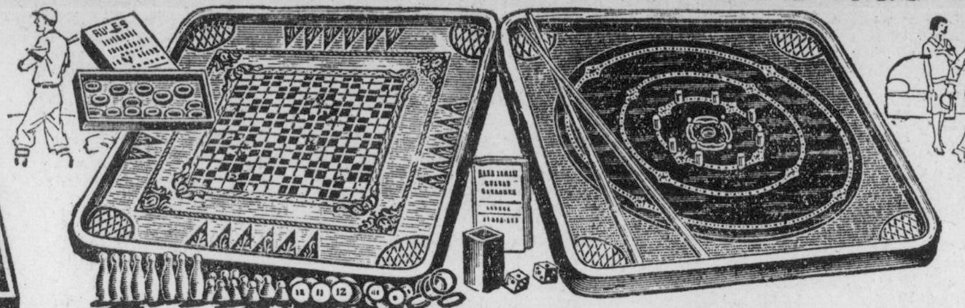

De Luxe Carrom Board
67 Games On One Board
$8.87

Youngsters and grownups both find a world of fun in a Carrom Board. Includes carrom, crokinole, checkers and many others—67 games in all—an equipment of 120 pieces and a book of instructions. Beautiful mahogany crokinole panel, and green felt lined ditch. Carrom side and rim made of selected white maple. Diagrams in a beautiful transfer resembling inlaid wood. Measures 29 inches square. This is one of the best carrom boards made and notice our low price. Shipping weight, 12 pounds. Advertized price, $10.00. Unmailabe.
79K488 .... **$8.87**

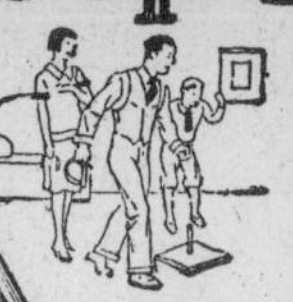

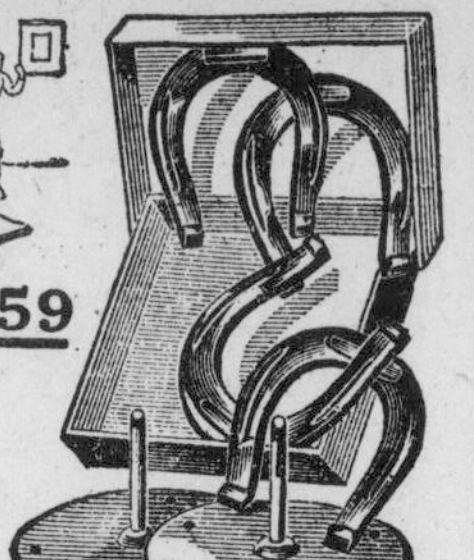

$1.59

For Other Games See Pages 576 to 605

"Gym" Rubber Horseshoes

A rubber horseshoe set that can be played anywhere. Used in gymnasiums, homes, or out of doors. Women play this game as well as men. Set consists of four horseshoes made of flexible rubber, and reinforced on the inside with steel to give added strength and durability; two nickel plated steel pegs and metal bases with screws for holding base to floor if desired. Shipping weight, 4 pounds.
6K1040 .... **$1.59**

PING PONG

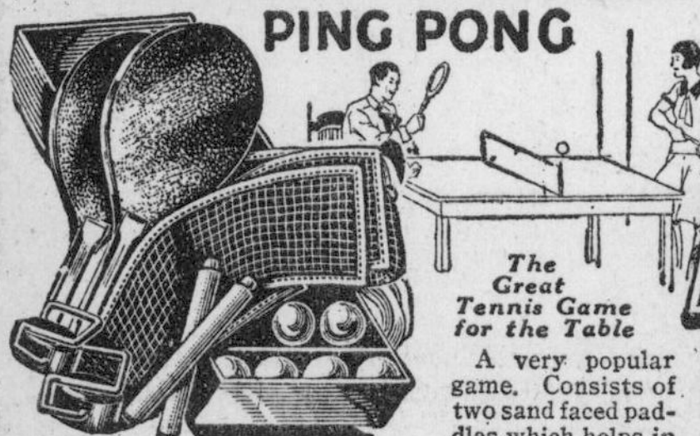

The Great Tennis Game for the Table

A very popular game. Consists of two sand faced paddles which helps in "cutting" the ball; a good quality net, bound with tape, and standards made of wood with adjustable table clamps; also six ping pong balls. Set of rules included with each set. Lots of fun for little money. Shpg. wt., 3 lbs.
6K1044 .... **$2.48**

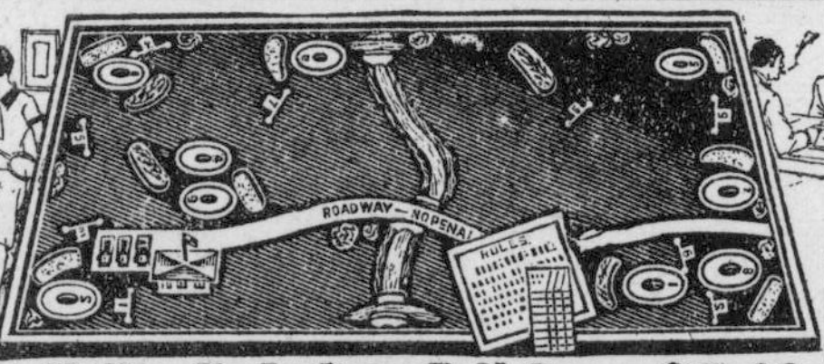

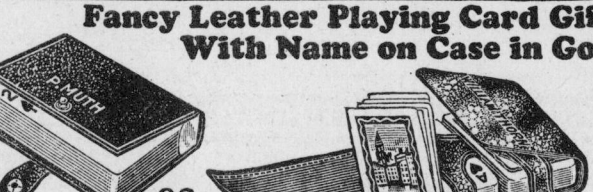

Holland's Indoor Golf Game **$2.48**
For Every Member of the Family

Golf! Nine holes of it in the coldest winter months. But you don't have to stop at nine. Thirty-six holes won't exhaust you and the longer you play the more fascinating this indoor golf becomes. Its fairways and greens, bunkers and hazards attract the most particular golfer. Little discs are used for clubs and balls. The course is laid out on a durable cardboard—oil processed in three fast colors. Will not crack. Size of course, 35x24½ inches. Shipping weight, 3 pounds.
6K1043¼ **$2.48**

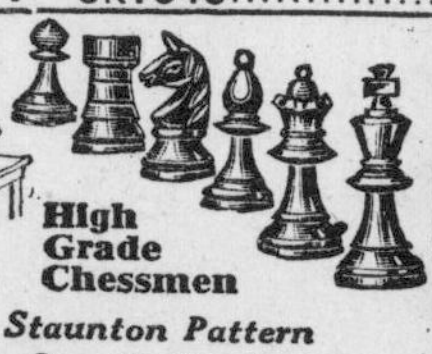

High Grade Chessmen
Staunton Pattern
Our $2.69 Set

Stunton Pattern. Felt bottoms, weighted. Nicely varnished finish. Height of king, about 3 inches. Hinged covered wood box. Shipping wt., 1½ pounds.
6K1051 .... **$2.69**

Our $1.29 Set

Staunton Pattern. Natural finish. Height of king, 2⅞ in. Wood box. Shipping weight, ¾ pound.
6K1052 .... **$1.29**

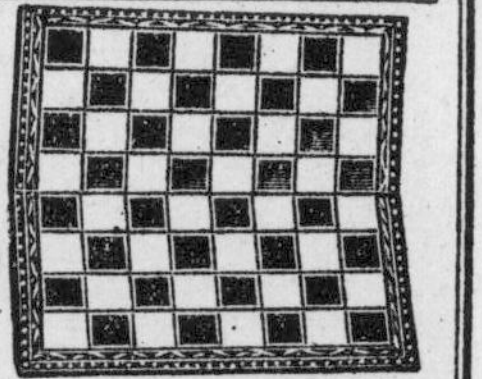

Chess Board

Double hinged extra heavy board. Lithographed paper playing surface in red, black and gold and varnished. Back covered with blue pebbled leatherette paper, stamped with the word "Chess." Size, 16¼ inches square. Shpg. wt., 1 lb.
49K123 .... **39c**

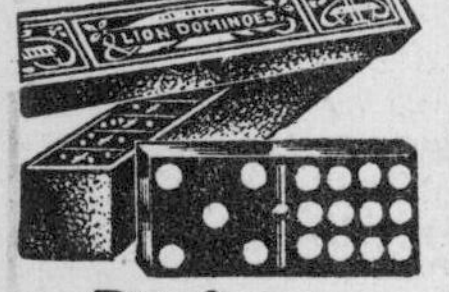

Dominoes

Double Twelve. Hardwood, wax luster, ebony finish; embossed. Size, 1¾x⅞x⅜ inches. In wood frame box. Rules included with each set. Shpg. wt., 2¼ lbs.
49K231—Per set. **98c**

Double-Nine Dominoes. Cardboard box. Size, 1⅝x 13/16x¼ in. Embossed wood. Shpg. wt., 1½ lbs.
49K230—Per set. **69c**

Fancy Leather Playing Card Gift Sets With Name on Case in Gold

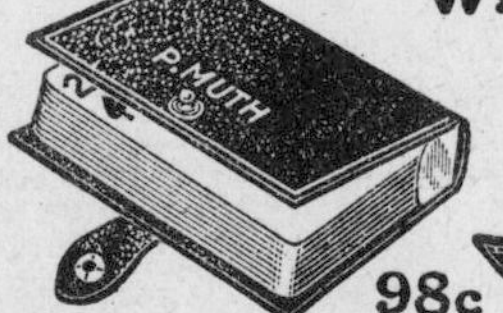

98c

Real Leather Case and Cards
An Ideal Christmas Gift

High grade black genuine leather case, also a deck of gold edged playing cards. (Not picture back.) Size, when closed, 2¾x3¾ inches. **Write plainly name wanted on case.** Shipping weight, 6 ounces.
6K1015 .... **98c**

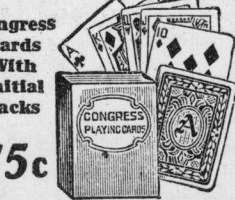

Double Deck Cards in Genuine Leather Case

Case made of genuine leather, two-tone brown Norwood finish with snap fastener; two decks of gold edge Congress playing cards. Whist size. An ideal gift outfit. **Print plainly name wanted on case.** Size, when closed, 3¾x4¾ inches.
6K1017—Shpg. wt., ¾ lb. **$2.25**

Single Deck Case **$1.29**

A very attractive set. Case is made of genuine leather, beautiful blue morocco finish. Snap fastener. One deck Whist size Congress fancy back playing cards, gold edged. Size, closed, 2¾x3¾ inches. **Print plainly name wanted on case.**
6K1016—Shipping wt., ¾ lb. **$1.29**

89c

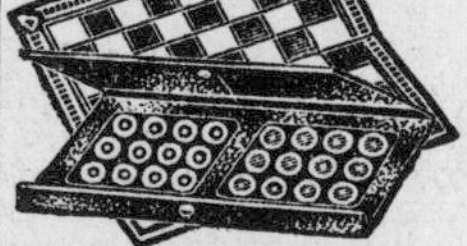

Checkerboard in Case

Cloth covered portfolio case with a 14-inch flat, cloth covered board and two sunken compartments holding composition checkers. When through just fasten snap on case and you have package only 14x7x½ inches. Shpg. wt., 1½ lbs.
49K118 .... **89c**

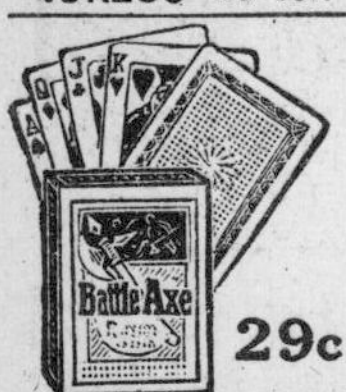

29c

Battle Axe Cards Standard Size

Linen finish cards with plain edge. A good card for so low a price. Shpg. wt., 4 oz.
6K1005 .... **29c**

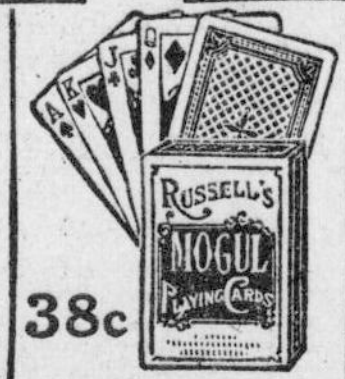

38c

Mogul Standard Size

High grade linen finish playing cards. Plain edge. Shpg. wt., 4 oz.
6K1006 .... **38c**

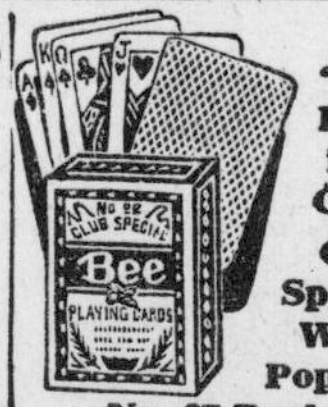

'Bee' Playing Cards Club Special With Popular No. 67 Back

One of the most popular playing cards. Linen finish; plain edges, red or blue, all over design backs. Regular size. Shipping weight, 4 oz.
6K1009 .... **49c**

Congress Cards With Initial Backs

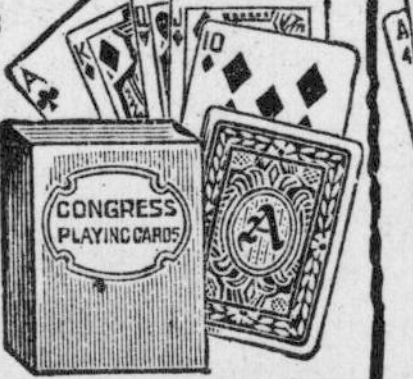

75c

Whist size, with your initial on the back of each card. Be a step ahead of your neighbors. **Be sure to print plainly the initial you want.** Shpg. wt., 4 oz.
6K1011 .... **75c**

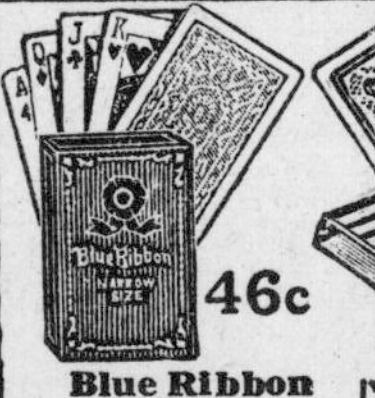

46c

Blue Ribbon

Good quality linen card. Perfect clip, noncurling. Shipping wt., 4 oz.
6K1007 Whist Narrow size **46c**
6K1012 Poker size **46c**

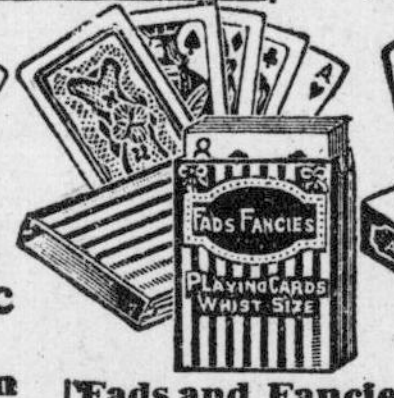

Fads and Fancies

Narrow size Whist cards with gold edges. Highly finished linen stock. Put up in elegant embossed telescope case.
6K1013 Shpg. wt., 6 oz. **59c**

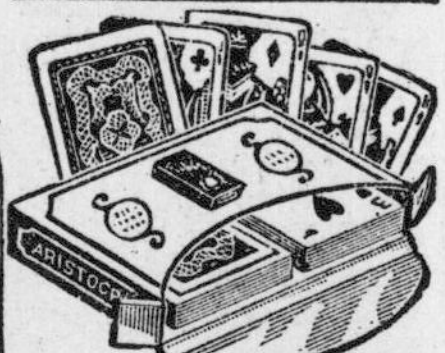

Aristocrat Twin Decks **98c**

Narrow Whist size, highly finished linen stock, superb quality. Nothing like it for quality and beauty of design. Shpg. wt., ¾ lb.
6K1014 Two Decks **98c**

Big Poker Chip Rack Value

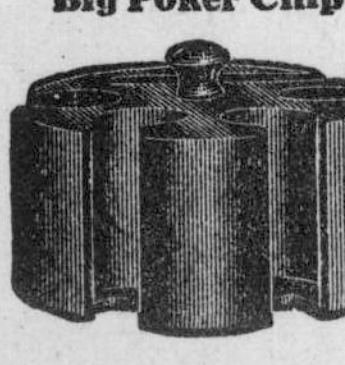

It pays to keep your chips and cards in a rack. Made of good grade wood in mahogany finish and has compartments for 100 chips and one deck of cards. Size, 6 inches in diameter, and 3¼ inches in height. Chips and cards are not included. Shipping weight, 1¼ pounds.
6K1023 .... **$1.27**

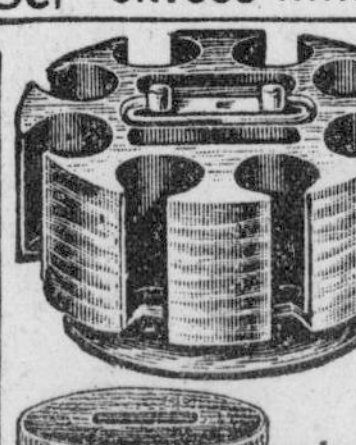

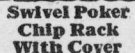

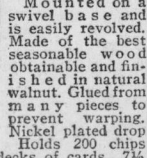

Swivel Poker Chip Rack With Cover

Mounted on a swivel base and is easily revolved. Made of the best seasonable wood obtainable and finished in natural walnut. Glued from many pieces to prevent warping. Nickel plated drop handle. Holds 200 chips and 2 decks of cards. 7½ in. diameter. Height, 4½ in. Shpg. wt., 3 lbs.
6K1024 .... **$2.98**

Poker Chips

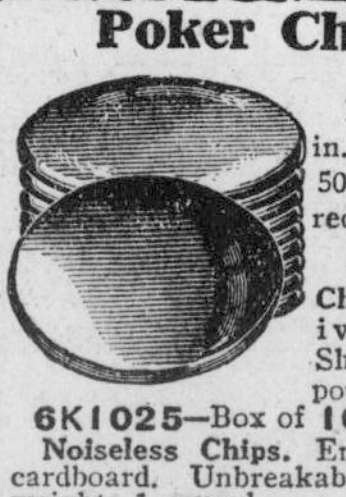

Diam., 1½ in., 100 to box; 50 white, 25 red and 25 blue.

Composition Chips. Plain ivory finish. Shpg. wt., 2½ pounds.
6K1025—Box of 100. **67c**

Noiseless Chips. Enamel finish cardboard. Unbreakable. Shipping weight, 1 pound.
6K1026—Box of 100. **46c**

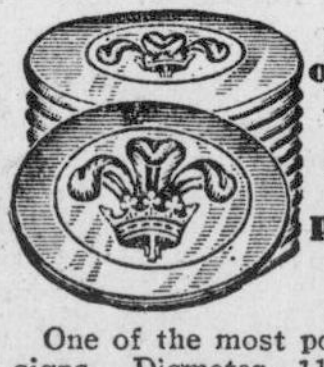

Prince of Wales Design Engraved Composition Poker Chips

One of the most popular designs. Diameter, 1½ inches. 100 to a box, 50 white, 25 red and 25 blue. Shipping wt., 2½ lbs.
6K1022—Box of 100 .... **$2.28**

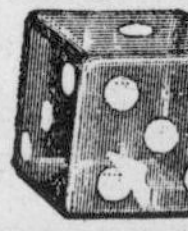

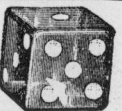

Celluloid Dice

Transparent red celluloid dice with white spots. ⅝-in. square. Will roll perfectly. Five to set. Shpg. wt., 3 oz.
6K1027 Set of 5 .... **34c**

Practical Christmas Suggestions

$4.98

Adjustable Shaving Stand With Gillette Razor

Beautifully nickel plated and polished frame. Fancy rectangular base with pierced filigree containers for porcelain cup, and bottle for shaving lotion. 7-inch beveled mirror on strong nickeled rod, adjustable from 16 to 21 inches high. Good bristle shaving brush with black enameled handle and standard Gillette safety razor with one blade included. Shipping weight, 4 pounds.
6K6335........ $4.98

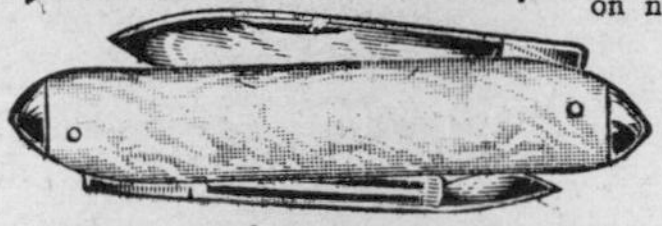

Genuine Pearl Handle Pocket Knife

Beautiful fancy shape handle 3 inches long, with nickel silver tips and brass linings. Full polished, best quality steel blade 2¼ inches long, and combination nail file and cleaner. Shipping weight, 5 oz.
6K7092........ $1.69

Our Finest Badger Shaving Brush

This excellent brush has large, full, beautifully rounded knot of high quality silver tip badger hair, 2 inches long. White celluloid ferrule and dark red mottled bakelite fancy shape handle. Length, over all, 4½ inches. In satin lined gift box. Usually offered by others as a $5.00 to $6.00 value. Shipping weight, 8 ounces.
6K6817........ $3.87

Wade and Butcher Stainless Steel

Shpg. Wt. 2¼ Lbs.

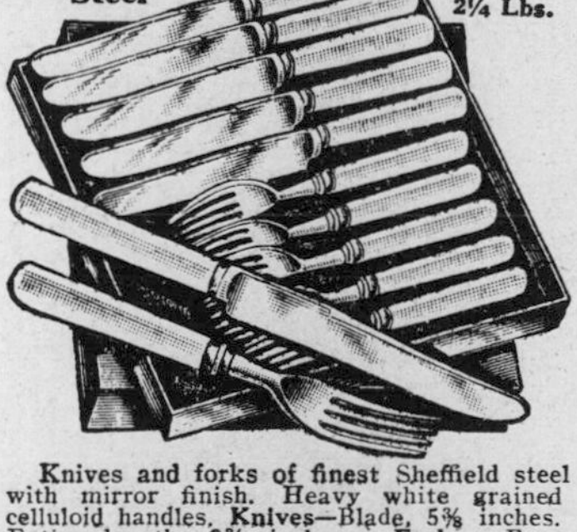

Knives and forks of finest Sheffield steel with mirror finish. Heavy white grained celluloid handles. Knives—Blade, 5⅝ inches. Entire length, 9⅜ inches. Forks — Four prong. Entire length, 7½ in.
6K7228—Six knives and 6 forks.......... $11.98
6K7229—Knives only, set of 6,.......... 5.98

A Useful Bread Knife and Board

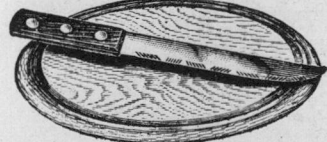

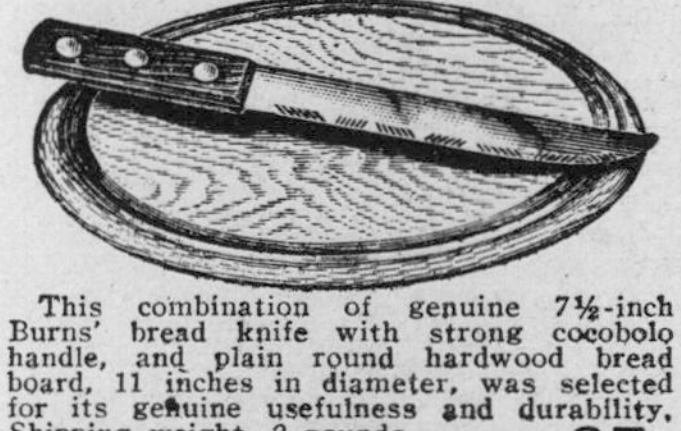

This combination of genuine 7½-inch Burns' bread knife with strong cocobolo handle, and plain round hardwood bread board, 11 inches in diameter, was selected for its genuine usefulness and durability. Shipping weight, 2 pounds.
6K7211—Both for.......... 87c

Gift Shaving Outfit

A beautiful imported porcelain mug, with rose and gold edge decoration, standard nickel plated Gem safety razor with one blade and good white bristle shaving brush with white celluloid ferrule and black enameled handle. Complete in bottom tufted lined gift box. Shipping weight, 5 pounds.
6K6338....... $1.00

Adjustable Shaving Mirrors

Shaving Mirror, mounted on nickel plated brass frame. Fine 7-inch French beveled glass. Can be set on table with glass at any angle, or used as a hand mirror. Shpg. wt., 2 lbs.
6K6678........ 98c
6-inch mirror, otherwise same as above. Shpg. wt., 1½ lbs.
6K6677 79c

Ever-Ready

For Other Shaving Brushes See Page 529

Auto Strop Parisian Gold Safety Razor

This beautiful outfit made up of a genuine gold plated Auto Strop Safety Razor, gold plated blade box containing 10 Auto Strop blades, gold plated strop holder hinged to inside of case and genuine Auto Strop leather strop. Complete in brown seal grain leather covered metal case, silk and velvet lined. Shipping weight, 1 lb.
6K6333........ $4.98

Auto Strop Parisian Silver Safety Razor

Similar to above, but razor, blade box and strop holder are silver plated, and put up in black leather case, Shpg. wt., 1 lb.
6K6334........ $3.98

Gold Plated Ever Ready Safety Razor

A new handsome gift set composed of one genuine gold plated Ever Ready razor and gold plated blade box containing five Ever Ready blades, in satin lined silver plated flat metal case, size, 3x3x⅝ inches, with 24-karat gold plated inlay design on top of case. Shipping weight, 1 pound.
6K6325........ $3.59

Popular Priced Pure Badger Shaving Brush

Beauty and durability will be found in this brush with its soft, high grade badger hair, 1⅞ inches long, and all white celluloid handle and ferrule. Length, over all, 4½ inches. In satin lined gift box.
6K6813—Shipping weight, 8 ounces.................. $1.89

$2.98

$1.59

Popular 3-Piece Carving Sets

Northampton Quality

Genuine stag handles. Knife has 8-inch blade of best carbon steel. Spring guard fork and steel to match. All with nickel silver bolsters. Complete in cloth lined box. Shipping weight, 2 pounds.
6K7318—Per set........ $2.98
6K7319—Same as above, of stainless steel.......... 3.98

Special at $1.59

Stag pattern handles with white celluloid caps and nickel plated bolsters. Knife has 9-inch carbon steel blade. Spring guard fork and steel to match. Complete in cloth lined box. Shipping weight, 2 lbs.
6K7317—Per set.......... $1.59

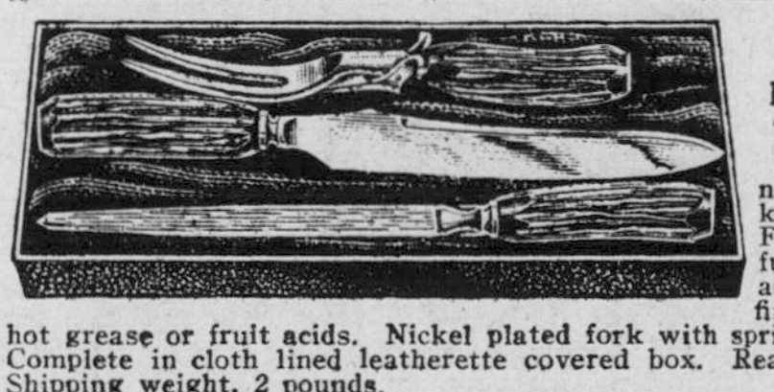

Genuine Wade and Butcher

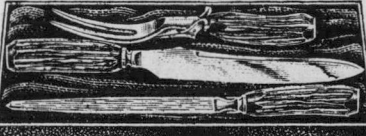

Beautiful Mirror Finish
The One We Recommend

Genuine stag handles with nickel silver caps. 8-inch knife blade forged from Firth stainless steel, carefully ground, heat treated and polished to a mirror finish. Unaffected by rust, hot grease or fruit acids. Nickel plated fork with spring guard; Steel to match. Complete in lined leatherette covered box. Real quality and satisfaction. Shipping weight, 2 pounds.
6K7316—Per set.......... $6.59

For Other Carving Sets see page 759

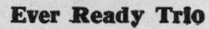

Ever Ready Trio

A handsome gift box containing standard Ever Ready nickel plated razor with one blade, regular 75c Ever Ready shaving brush with 2-inch bristles, black celluloid ferrule and white celluloid handle and 35c tube of Safetee shaving cream. A useful gift. Shipping wt., 1 lb.
6K6337.......... 98c

Circular Extension Mirror

A French bevel glass, 8 inches in diameter, set in solid burnished nickel plated frame with metal back. Frame can be attached to the wall and extended to 24 inches; also adjustable to any angle desired. An unusually handy, convenient article for general household use, but specially suitable for attaching near window, where plenty of light is available. Shipping wt., 3 lbs.
6K6675. $1.98

$2.79

Ever-Ready

Selected Badger Shaving Brush

A quality brush having dandy full knot of fine, soft badger hair, 1⅞ inches long, white celluloid ferrule and black and white striped drawn celluloid handle with white celluloid base. Length over all, 4½ inches. In satin lined gift box. Shipping weight, 8 ounces.
6K6816........ $2.79

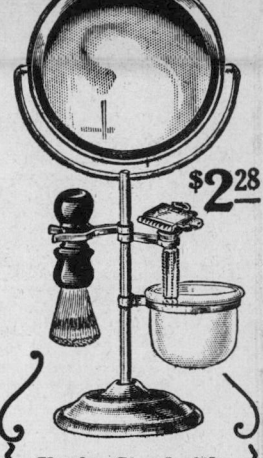

$2.28

Shaving Stand with Gem Razor

Fine nickel plated frame, round base and bracket, supporting porcelain cup. 6-inch round beveled mirror. Good bristle shaving brush with black enameled handle, and standard nickel plated Gem safety razor with one blade included. Height, 14 inches. Shipping weight, 3½ lbs.
6K6336..... $2.28

STAINLESS STEEL

Two-Blade Stainless Steel Pearl Handle Knife

Genuine pearl handle, 3⅛ inches long. German silver tips and linings. 1¾-inch and 1½-inch blades.
6K7100—Shpg. wt., 4 oz. $1.39

Three-Blade Knife

Same as above, but with extra stainless combination file blade.
6K7061—Shpg. wt., 5 oz. $1.79

Handy Scissors Set

A convenient set for traveling or home use, consisting of one 6-inch scissors and one 4-inch embroidery scissors, both made of fine quality solid steel, carefully ground, accurately fitted and highly nickel plated. Complete in fancy tan color genuine leather case, satin lined, with clasp. Shipping wt. ¾ pound.
6K6974—Per set.......... $2.79

Ladies' Fancy Pattern Scissors Set
Imported from Germany

$1.98

This set consists of a 3½-inch sharp pointed embroidery scissors, a 4½-inch scissors and a 5½-inch scissors, all with fancy gilt pattern handles. Put up in alligator grained genuine leather case. Makes a very handsome and desirable gift. Shipping weight, ¾ lb.
6K6973—Per set.......... $1.98

Send Sufficient Money for Postage on Parcel Post Shipments. Any Surplus Will Be Returned

527

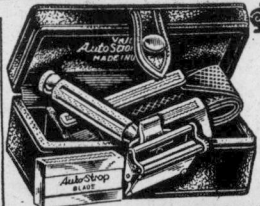

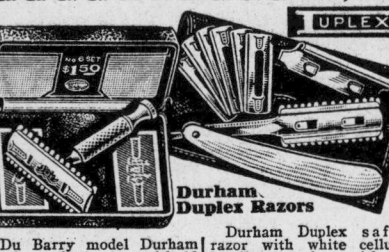

You Can Pay More But You Can't Buy Better Razors

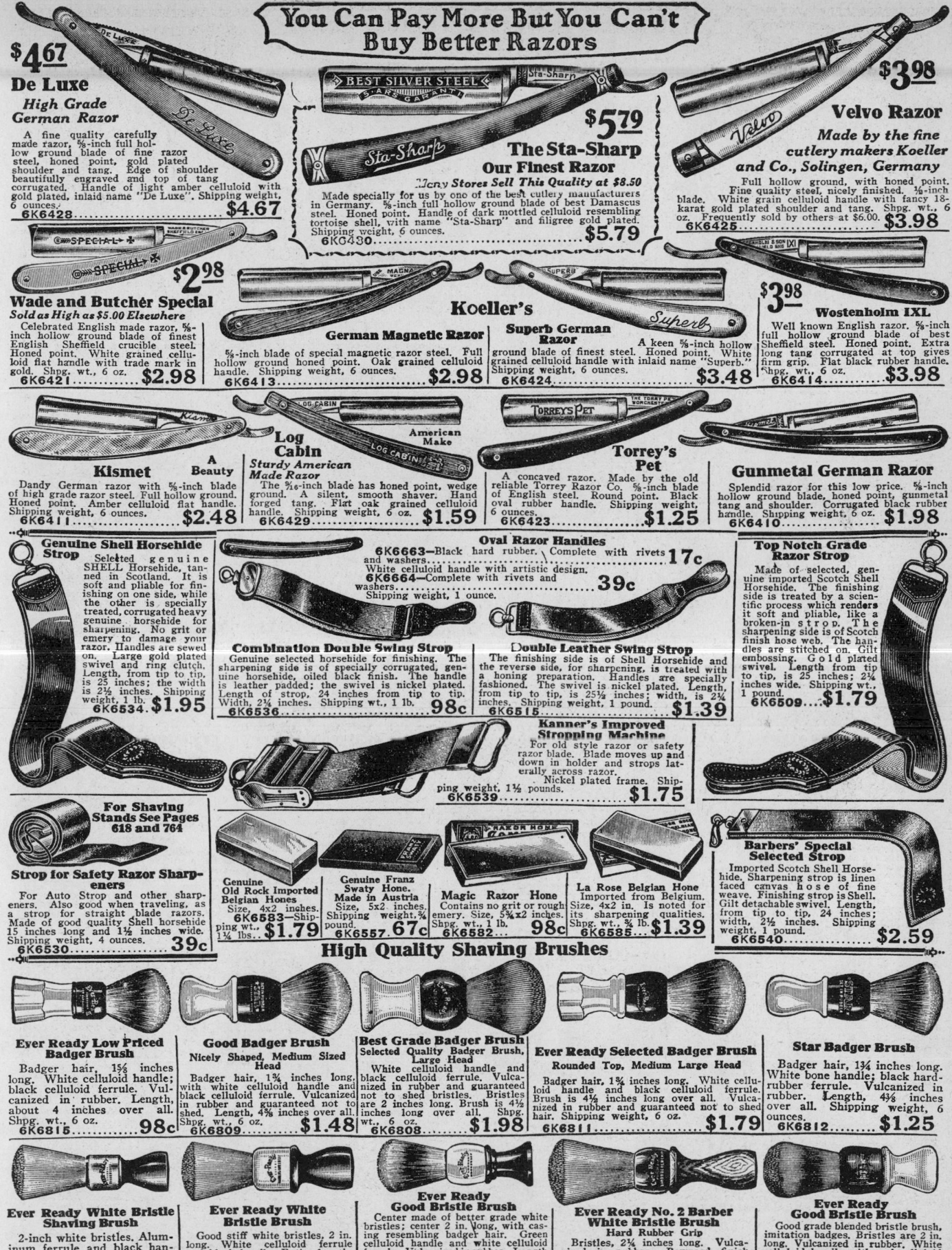

$4.67

De Luxe
High Grade German Razor

A fine quality carefully made razor, 5/8-inch full hollow ground blade of fine razor steel, honed point, gold plated shoulder and tang. Edge of shoulder beautifully engraved and top of tang corrugated. Handle of light amber celluloid with gold plated, inlaid name "De Luxe". Shipping weight, 6 ounces.

6K6428 .... **$4.67**

$5.79

The Sta-Sharp
Our Finest Razor
Many Stores Sell This Quality at $8.50

Made specially for us by one of the best cutlery manufacturers in Germany. 5/8-inch full hollow ground blade of best Damascus steel. Honed point. Handle of dark mottled celluloid resembling tortoise shell, with name "Sta-Sharp" and filigree gold plated. Shipping weight, 6 ounces.

6K6430 .... **$5.79**

$3.98

Velvo Razor
Made by the fine cutlery makers Koeller and Co., Solingen, Germany

Full hollow ground, with honed point. Fine quality steel, nicely finished. 5/8-inch blade. White grain celluloid handle with fancy 18-karat gold plated shoulder and tang. Shpg. wt., 6 oz. Frequently sold by others at $6.00.

6K6425 .... **$3.98**

$2.98

Wade and Butcher Special
Sold as High as $5.00 Elsewhere

Celebrated English made razor, 5/8-inch hollow ground blade of finest English Sheffield crucible steel. Honed point. White grained celluloid flat handle with trade mark in gold. Shpg. wt., 6 oz.

6K6421 .... **$2.98**

Koeller's
German Magnetic Razor

5/8-inch blade of special magnetic razor steel. Full hollow ground honed point. Oak grained celluloid handle. Shipping weight, 6 ounces.

6K6413 .... **$2.98**

Superb German Razor

A keen 5/8-inch hollow ground blade of finest steel. Honed point. White grained celluloid handle with inlaid name "Superb." Shipping weight, 6 ounces.

6K6424 .... **$3.48**

$3.98

Wostenholm IXL

Well known English razor. 5/8-inch full hollow ground blade of best Sheffield steel. Honed point. Extra long tang corrugated at top gives firm grip. Flat black rubber handle. Shpg. wt., 6 oz.

6K6414 .... **$3.98**

Kismet
A Beauty

Dandy German razor with 5/8-inch blade of high grade razor steel. Full hollow ground. Honed point. Amber celluloid flat handle. Shipping weight, 6 ounces.

6K6411 .... **$2.48**

Log Cabin
Sturdy American Made Razor

The 9/16-inch blade has honed point, wedge ground. A silent, smooth shaver. Hand forged tang. Flat oak grained celluloid handle. Shipping weight, 6 oz.

6K6429 .... **$1.59**

Torrey's Pet

A concaved razor. Made by the old reliable Torrey Razor Co. 5/8-inch blade of English steel. Round point. Black oval rubber handle. Shipping weight, 6 ounces.

6K6423 .... **$1.25**

Gunmetal German Razor

Splendid razor for this low price. 5/8-inch hollow ground blade, honed point, gunmetal tang and shoulder. Corrugated black rubber handle. Shipping weight, 6 oz.

6K6410 .... **$1.98**

Genuine Shell Horsehide Strop

Selected genuine SHELL Horsehide, tanned in Scotland. It is soft and pliable for finishing on one side, while the other is specially treated, corrugated heavy genuine horsehide for sharpening. No grit or emery to damage your razor. Handles are sewn on. Large gold plated swivel and ring clutch. Length, from tip to tip, is 25 inches; the width is 2½ inches. Shipping weight, 1 lb.

6K6534 .... **$1.95**

Oval Razor Handles

6K6663—Black hard rubber. Complete with rivets and washers. **17c**

6K6664—White celluloid handle with artistic design. Complete with rivets and washers. Shipping weight, 1 ounce. **39c**

Combination Double Swing Strop

Genuine selected horsehide for finishing. The sharpening side is of specially corrugated, genuine horsehide, oiled black finish. The handle is leather padded; the swivel is nickel plated. Length of strop, 24 inches from tip to tip. Width, 2¼ inches. Shipping wt., 1 lb.

6K6536 .... **98c**

Double Leather Swing Strop

The finishing side is of Shell Horsehide and the reverse side, for sharpening, is treated with a honing preparation. Handles are specially fashioned. The swivel is nickel plated. Length, from tip to tip, is 25½ inches; width, is 2¼ inches. Shipping weight, 1 pound.

6K6515 .... **$1.39**

Top Notch Grade Razor Strop

Made of selected, genuine imported Scotch Shell Horsehide. The finishing side is treated by a scientific process which renders it soft and pliable, like a broken-in strop. The sharpening side is of Scotch finish hose web. The handles are stitched on. Gilt embossing. Gold plated swivel. Length from tip to tip, is 25 inches; 2¼ inches wide. Shipping wt., 1 pound.

6K6509 .... **$1.79**

Kanner's Improved Stropping Machine

For old style razor or safety razor blade. Blade moves up and down in holder and strops laterally across razor. Nickel plated frame. Shipping weight, 1½ pounds.

6K6539 .... **$1.75**

For Shaving Stands See Pages 618 and 764

Strop for Safety Razor Sharpeners

For Auto Strop and other sharpeners. Also good when traveling, as a strop for straight blade razors. Made of good quality Shell horsehide 15 inches long and 1½ inches wide. Shipping weight, 4 ounces.

6K6530 .... **39c**

Genuine Old Rock Imported Belgian Hones

Size, 4x2 inches.

6K6583—Shipping wt., 1¼ lbs. **$1.79**

Genuine Franz Swaty Hone

Made in Austria. Size, 5x2 inches. Shipping weight, ¾ pound.

6K6557 .... **67c**

Magic Razor Hone

Contains no grit or rough emery. Size, 5¾x2 inches. Shpg. wt., 1 lb.

6K6582 .... **98c**

La Rose Belgian Hone

Imported from Belgium. Size, 4x2 in. Is noted for its sharpening qualities. Shpg. wt., ¾ lb.

6K6585 .... **$1.39**

Barbers' Special Selected Strop

Imported Scotch Shell Horsehide. Sharpening strop is linen faced canvas hose of fine weave. Finishing strop is Shell. Gilt detachable swivel. Length, from tip to tip, 24 inches; width, 2½ inches. Shipping weight, 1 pound.

6K6540 .... **$2.59**

High Quality Shaving Brushes

Ever Ready Low Priced Badger Brush

Badger hair, 1⅝ inches long. White celluloid handle; black celluloid ferrule. Vulcanized in rubber. Length, about 4 inches over all. Shpg. wt., 6 oz.

6K6815 .... **98c**

Good Badger Brush
Nicely Shaped, Medium Sized Head

Badger hair, 1¾ inches long, with white celluloid handle and black celluloid ferrule. Vulcanized in rubber and guaranteed not to shed. Length, 4⅝ inches over all. Shpg. wt., 6 oz.

6K6809 .... **$1.48**

Best Grade Badger Brush
Selected Quality Badger Brush, Large Head

White celluloid handle and black celluloid ferrule. Vulcanized in rubber and guaranteed not to shed bristles. Bristles are 2 inches long. Brush is 4½ inches long over all. Shpg. wt., 6 oz.

6K6808 .... **$1.98**

Ever Ready Selected Badger Brush
Rounded Top, Medium Large Head

Badger hair, 1¾ inches long. White celluloid handle and black celluloid ferrule. Vulcanized in rubber and guaranteed not to shed hair. Shipping weight, 6 oz.

6K6811 .... **$1.79**

Star Badger Brush

Badger hair, 1¾ inches long. White bone handle; black hard-rubber ferrule. Vulcanized in rubber. Length, 4⅛ inches over all. Shipping weight, 6 ounces.

6K6812 .... **$1.25**

Ever Ready White Bristle Shaving Brush

2-inch white bristles. Aluminum ferrule and black handle. Length, 4¼ in. over all. Shpg. wt., 6 oz.

6K6801 .... **19c**

Ever Ready White Bristle Brush

Good stiff white bristles, 2 in. long. White celluloid ferrule and black handle. Entire length, 4¾ inches. Vulcanized. Shipping weight, 6 ounces.

6K6806 .... **37c**

Ever Ready Good Bristle Brush

Center made of better grade white bristles; center 2 in. long, with casing resembling badger hair. Green celluloid handle and white celluloid ferrule. Vulcanized in rubber. Length over all, 4½ inches. Shipping weight, 6 ounces.

6K6804 .... **59c**

Ever Ready No. 2 Barber White Bristle Brush
Hard Rubber Grip

Bristles, 2¼ inches long. Vulcanized in rubber. Boxwood finish handle, black rubber ferrule. Length, 5¾ inches. Shpg. wt., 6 oz.

6K6807 .... **49c**

Ever Ready Good Bristle Brush

Good grade blended bristle brush, imitation badges. Bristles are 2 in. long. Vulcanized in rubber. White celluloid handle with red celluloid ferrule. Entire brush, 4½ in. long. Shipping wt., 6 oz.

6K6803 .... **79c**

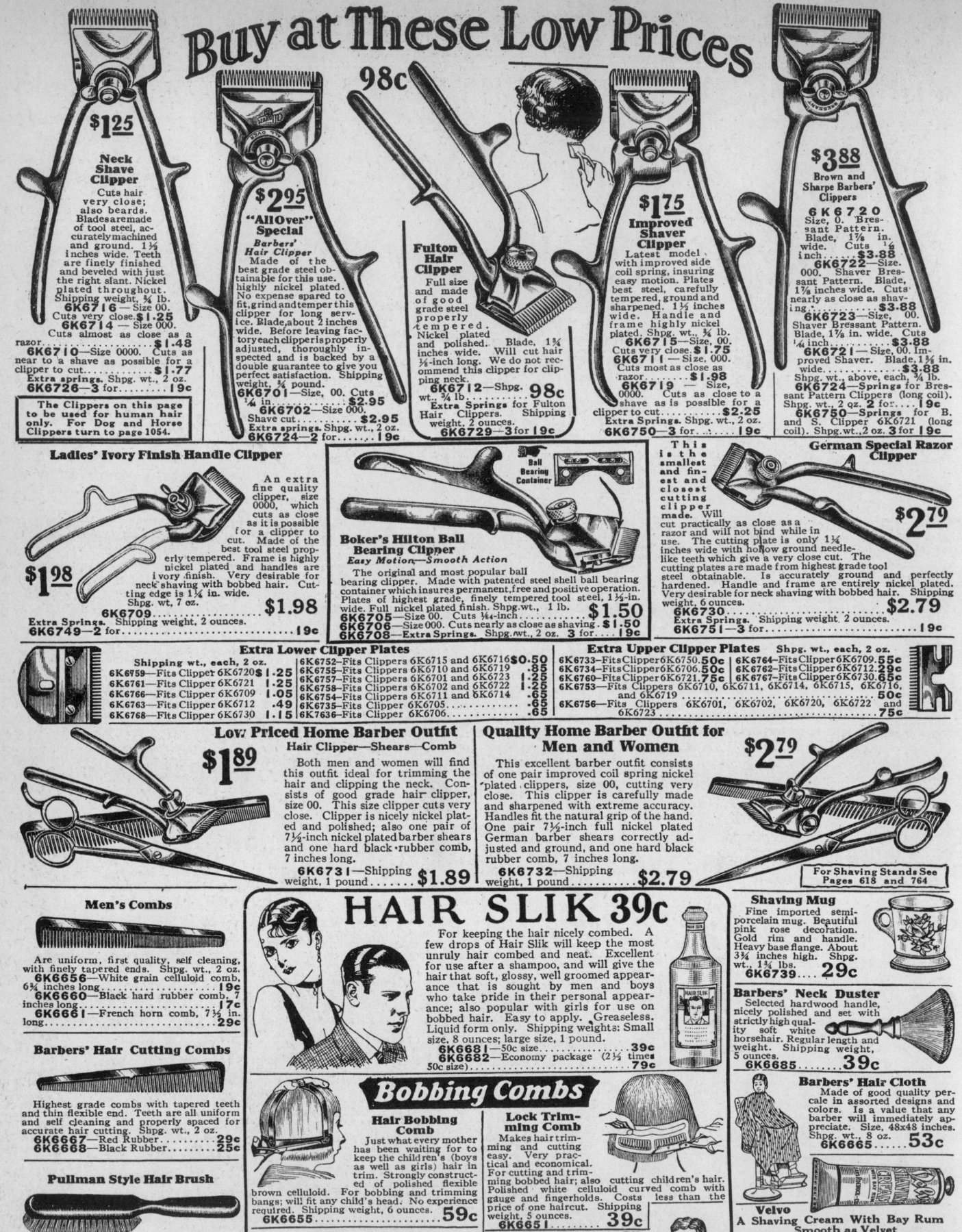

STA-SHARP Shears and Scissors That STA-SHARP
LOW PRICES MADE POSSIBLE BY OUR GREAT VOLUME!

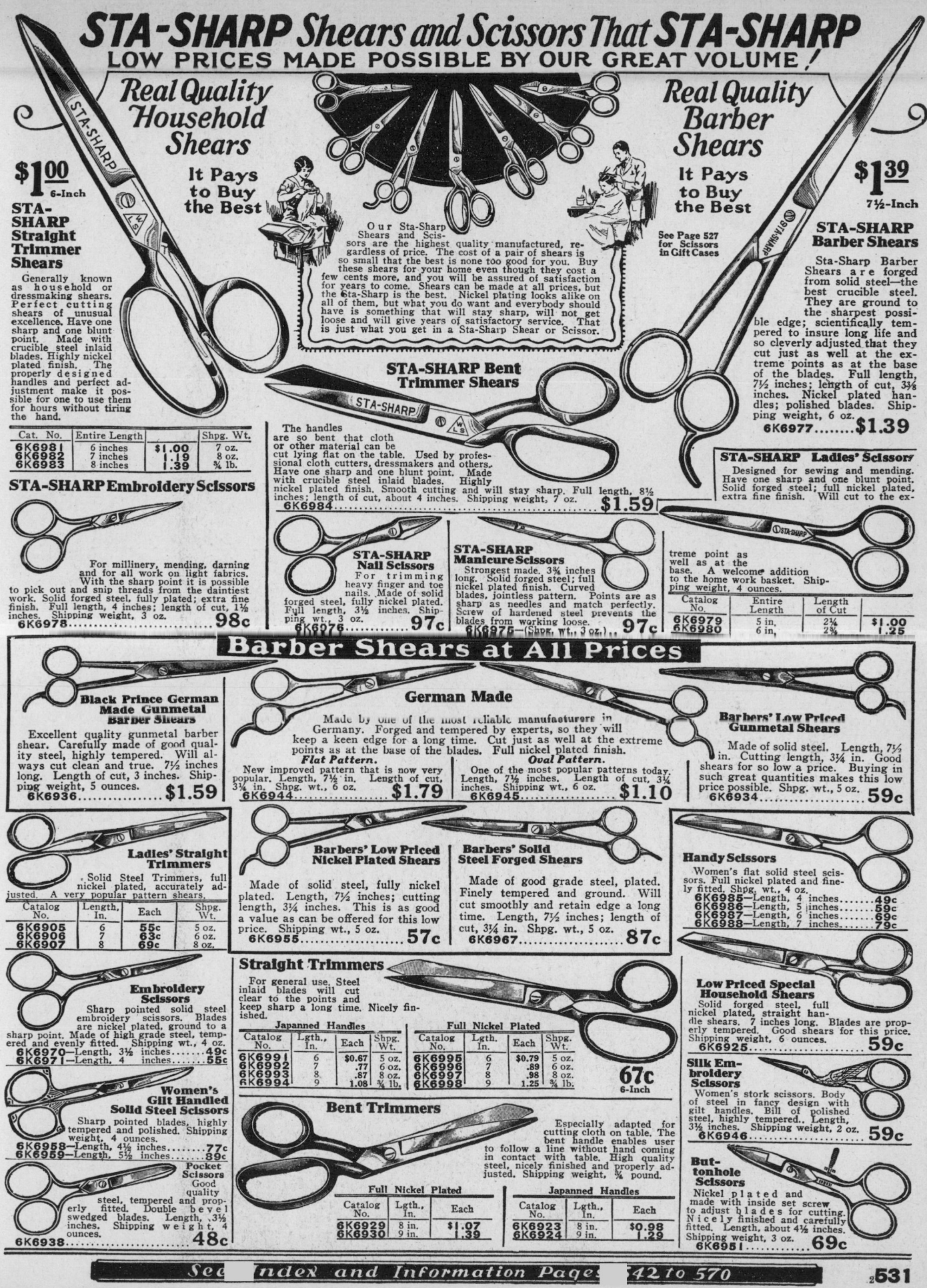

Real Quality Household Shears
It Pays to Buy the Best

$1.00 6-Inch

STA-SHARP Straight Trimmer Shears

Generally known as household or dressmaking shears. Perfect cutting shears of unusual excellence. Have one sharp and one blunt point. Made with crucible steel inlaid blades. Highly nickel plated finish. The properly designed handles and perfect adjustment make it possible for one to use them for hours without tiring.

Cat. No.	Entire Length		Shpg. Wt.
6K6981	6 inches	$1.00	7 oz.
6K6982	7 inches	1.19	8 oz.
6K6983	8 inches	1.39	¾ lb.

STA-SHARP Embroidery Scissors

For millinery, mending, darning and for all work on light fabrics. With the sharp point it is possible to pick out and snip threads from the daintiest work. Solid forged steel, fully plated; extra fine finish. Full length, 4 inches; length of cut, 1½ inches. Shipping weight, 3 oz.
6K6978 ...... **98c**

STA-SHARP Bent Trimmer Shears

The handles are bent so that cloth or other material can be cut lying flat on the table. Used by professional cloth cutters, dressmakers and others. Have one sharp and one blunt point. Made with crucible steel inlaid blades. Highly nickel plated finish. Smooth cutting and will stay sharp. Full length, 8½ inches; length of cut, about 4 inches. Shipping weight, 7 oz.
6K6984 .... **$1.59**

Our Sta-Sharp Shears and Scissors are the highest quality manufactured, regardless of price. The cost of a pair of shears is so small that the best is none too good for you. Buy these shears for your home even though they cost a few cents more, and you will be assured of satisfaction for years to come. Shears can be made at all prices, but the Sta-Sharp is the best. Nickel plating looks alike on all of them, but what you do want and everybody should have is something that will stay sharp, will not get loose and will give years of satisfactory service. That is just what you get in a Sta-Sharp Shear or Scissor.

See Page 527 for Scissors in Gift Cases

Real Quality Barber Shears
It Pays to Buy the Best

$1.39 7½-Inch

STA-SHARP Barber Shears

Sta-Sharp Barber Shears are forged from solid steel—the best crucible steel. They are ground to the sharpest possible edge; scientifically tempered to insure long life and so cleverly adjusted that they cut just as well at the extreme points as at the base of the blades. Full length, 7½ inches; length of cut, 3⅜ inches. Nickel plated handles; polished blades. Shipping weight, 6 oz.
6K6977 .... **$1.39**

STA-SHARP Nail Scissors

For trimming heavy finger and toe nails. Made of solid forged steel, fully nickel plated. Full length, 3½ inches. Shipping wt., 3 oz.
6K6976 ...... **97c**

STA-SHARP Manicure Scissors

Strongest made. 3¾ inches long. Solid forged steel; full nickel plated finish. Curved blades, jointless pattern. Points are as sharp as needles and match perfectly. Screw of hardened steel prevents the blades from working loose.
6K6975—(Shpg. wt., 3 oz.) .. **97c**

STA-SHARP Ladies' Scissors

Designed for sewing and mending. Have one sharp and one blunt point. Solid forged steel; full nickel plated, extra fine finish. Will cut to the extreme point as well as at the base. A welcome addition to the home work basket. Shipping weight, 4 ounces.

Catalog No.	Entire Length	Length of Cut	
6K6979	5 in.	2¼	$1.00
6K6980	6 in.	2¾	1.25

Barber Shears at All Prices

Black Prince German Made Gunmetal Barber Shears

Excellent quality gunmetal barber shear. Carefully made of good quality steel, highly tempered. Will always cut clean and true. 7½ inches long. Length of cut, 3 inches. Shipping weight, 5 ounces.
6K6936 .... **$1.59**

German Made

Made by one of the most reliable manufacturers in Germany. Forged and tempered by experts, so they will keep a keen edge for a long time. Cut just as well at the extreme points as at the base of the blades. Full nickel plated finish.

Flat Pattern.
New improved pattern that is now very popular. Length, 7½ in. Length of cut, 3¼ in. Shpg. wt., 6 oz.
6K6944 .... **$1.79**

Oval Pattern.
One of the most popular patterns today. Length, 7½ inches. Length of cut, 3¼ inches. Shipping wt., 6 oz.
6K6945 .... **$1.10**

Barbers' Low Priced Gunmetal Shears

Made of solid steel. Length, 7½ in. Cutting length, 3¼ in. Good shears for so low a price. Buying in such great quantities makes this low price possible. Shpg. wt., 5 oz.
6K6934 .... **59c**

Ladies' Straight Trimmers

Solid Steel Trimmers, full nickel plated, accurately adjusted. A very popular pattern shears.

Catalog No.	Length, In.	Each	Shpg. Wt.
6K6905	6	55c	5 oz.
6K6906	7	63c	6 oz.
6K6907	8	69c	8 oz.

Barbers' Low Priced Nickel Plated Shears

Made of solid steel, fully nickel plated. Length, 7½ inches; cutting length, 3¼ inches. This is as good a value as can be offered for this low price. Shipping wt., 5 oz.
6K6955 .... **57c**

Barbers' Solid Steel Forged Shears

Made of good grade steel, plated. Finely tempered and ground. Will cut smoothly and retain edge a long time. Length, 7½ inches; length of cut, 3¼ in. Shpg. wt., 5 oz.
6K6967 .... **87c**

Handy Scissors

Women's flat solid steel scissors. Full nickel plated and finely fitted. Shpg. wt., 4 oz.
6K6985—Length, 4 inches...... 49c
6K6986—Length, 5 inches...... 59c
6K6987—Length, 6 inches...... 69c
6K6988—Length, 7 inches...... 79c

Embroidery Scissors

Sharp pointed solid steel embroidery scissors. Blades are nickel plated, ground to a sharp point. Made of high grade steel, tempered and evenly fitted. Shipping wt., 4 oz.
6K6970—Length, 3½ inches...... 49c
6K6971—Length, 4 inches...... 55c

Straight Trimmers

For general use. Steel inlaid blades will cut clear to the points and keep sharp a long time. Nicely finished.

Japanned Handles				Full Nickel Plated			
Catalog No.	Lgth., In.	Each	Shpg. Wt.	Catalog No.	Lgth., In.	Each	Shpg. Wt.
6K6991	6	$0.67	5 oz.	6K6995	6	$0.79	5 oz.
6K6992	7	.77	6 oz.	6K6996	7	.89	6 oz.
6K6993	8	.87	8 oz.	6K6997	8	.98	8 oz.
6K6994	9	1.08	¾ lb.	6K6998	9	1.25	¾ lb.

67c 6-Inch

Low Priced Special Household Shears

Solid forged steel, full nickel plated, straight handle shears. 7 inches long. Blades are properly tempered. Good shears for this price. Shipping weight, 6 ounces.
6K6925 .... **59c**

Women's Gilt Handled Solid Steel Scissors

Sharp pointed blades, highly tempered and polished. Shipping weight, 4 ounces.
6K6958—Length, 4½ inches....... 77c
6K6959—Length, 5½ inches....... 89c

Pocket Scissors
Good quality steel, tempered and properly fitted. Double bevel swedged blades. Length, 3½ inches. Shipping weight, 4 ounces.
6K6938 .... **48c**

Bent Trimmers

Especially adapted for cutting cloth on table. The bent handle enables user to follow a line without hand coming in contact with table. High quality steel, nicely finished and properly adjusted. Shipping weight, ¾ pound.

Full Nickel Plated			Japanned Handles		
Catalog No.	Lgth., In.	Each	Catalog No.	Lgth., In.	Each
6K6929	8 in.	$1.07	6K6923	8 in.	$0.98
6K6930	9 in.	1.39	6K6924	9 in.	1.29

Silk Embroidery Scissors

Women's stork scissors. Body of steel in fancy design with gilt handles. Bill of polished steel, highly tempered. Length, 3½ inches. Shipping weight, 2 oz.
6K6946 .... **59c**

Buttonhole Scissors

Nickel plated and made with inside set screw to adjust blades for cutting. Nicely finished and carefully fitted. Length, about 4½ inches. Shipping weight, 3 oz.
6K6951 .... **69c**

Built to Give Years of Service

$11⁹⁵ 18-In.

Black or Brown Color

Genuine Top Grain Cowhide

$9⁷⁵ 18 In. Lg.

Black or Brown Color

Genuine Top Grain Cowhide

Heavy genuine full top grain 4-ounce cowhide leather, hand boarded grain, large three-piece pattern. Leather covered heavy steel frame, with highly polished solid brass lock and end catches. Leather handle. Sewed reinforced leather corners. Lined throughout with genuine leather. Shipping wts., 9 and 11 lbs. **$9.75**

6K9380¼—Black. 18 inches long........ $9.75
6K9382¼—Black. 20 inches long......... $10.45
6K9381¼—Brown. 18 inches long.......... 9.75
6K9383¼—Brown. 20 inches long.......... 10.45

$14⁹⁵ 18-In.

For Brief Cases See Page 705

$7⁴⁵ 16-In.

Black or Brown Color

Genuine Top Grain Cowhide

Made of smooth full grained cowhide leather in three-piece style. Leather covered steel frame, riveted in. Leather handle, with brass plated inside lock and lift catches. Welted seams. Soft leather lining, with two short and one long pockets. Sewed padded leather corners.

6K9352¼—Black. 16 in. Shpg. wt., 7 lbs. **$7.45**
6K9353¼—Black. 18 in. Shpg. wt., 8 lbs. $8.25
6K9354¼—Black. 20 in. Shpg. wt., 9 lbs. 8.95
6K9355¼—Brown. 16 in. Shpg. wt., 7 lbs. 7.45
6K9356¼—Brown. 18 in. Shpg. wt., 8 lbs. 8.25
6K9357¼—Brown. 20 in. Shpg. wt., 9 lbs. 8.95

Your initials in gold leaf letters put on bags and suitcases for 25c extra. Two or three letters. Print letters wanted.

Genuine Top Grain Cowhide

A large size attractive bag. Extra heavy 4-ounce genuine hand boarded top grain cowhide leather, three-piece style, welted seams. Black or brown color. Hand stitched in leather covered English steel frame; reinforced with stitched-on leather corners. Solid brass lock and catches; double leather handles. Lined throughout with soft leather. Three pockets. Shipping weights, 10 and 11 pounds. **$14.95**

6K9375¼—Black. Length, 18 inches........ $14.95
6K9376¼—Black. Length, 20 inches........ $15.95
6K9377¼—Brown. Length, 18 inches........ 14.95
6K9378¼—Brown. Length, 20 inches........ 15.95

Genuine Top Grain Cowhide Bag

Two leather straps all around. Full grain genuine cowhide in rich dark brown color, with double stitched edges, stitched-on leather corners. Leather covered steel frame riveted in. Two leather straps all around, with stitched-on strap loops. Leather handle, brass lock and catches. Leather lined, with one long pocket. Corners reinforced with leather.

6K9373¼—Length, 18 inches. Shipping weight, 9 pounds........ **$10.45**
6K9374¼—Length, 20 inches. Shipping weight, 10 pounds........ $11.45

Genuine Top Grain Cowhide

Large, strong three-piece bag. Made of extra heavy 4-ounce genuine cowhide leather, hand boarded grain finish. Hand sewed English steel frame covered with leather. Solid brass inside lock and lift catches. Welted seams. Padded leather corners stitched on. Strong leather handle. Leather lined, three pockets.

6K9386¼—Black. 18 inches.
Shipping weight, 9½ pounds........... **$11.95**
6K9387¼—Black. 20 inches.
Shipping weight, 11 pounds.................... $12.95
6K9388¼—Brown. 18 inches.
Shipping weight, 9½ pounds............. 11.95
6K9389¼—Brown. 20 inches.
Shipping weight, 11 pounds................. 12.95

$10⁴⁵ 18-In.

$9⁹⁵ 24-In.

Genuine Top Grain Cowhide Leather

Made of heavy genuine smooth or cobra grain cowhide, with reinforced edges, riveted-on cowhide corners. Cowhide leather straps all around, with leather loops riveted on with bell rivets. Leather handle. Brass plated lock and end catches. Loose turned-in cloth lining with improved single piece shirt fold, leather straps inside. 13 inches high, 7¼ inches wide. Shipping weights, 11 and 12 pounds.

Finish	Length	
6K9431¼—Brown, smooth.	24 in.	**$9.95**
6K9432¼—Brown, smooth.	26 in.	$10.95
6K9433¼—Black cobra.	24 in.	9.95
6K9434¼—Black cobra.	26 in.	10.95

New Lift Catches ↓

Shark Grained Split Cowhide

Our low price for this Southmore Suitcase makes this one of our outstanding values. Neat pattern brown shark grained embossed split cowhide, with stitched ends. Reinforced at all edges to stand hard knocks. Good steel frame, with substantial lock and catches. Riveted-on leather corners; cloth lining, with one long shirt fold or pocket. 12½ inches high and 7½ inches wide.

	Length	Shpg. Wt.	
6K9435¼	24 in.	11 lbs.	**$5.45**
6K9436¼	26 in.	12 lbs.	$5.95

New Lift Catches ←

$13⁴⁵ 24-In.

Genuine Top Grain Cowhide Leather

Made of heavy boarded grain, genuine cowhide leather, with stitched-on cowhide leather corners lined with fine quality leather. Two leather straps all around and stitched-on leather strap loops. Sewed leather hinge full length of case; strong leather handle with stitched-on handle loops. Single piece drop shirt fold, brass lock and catches. 13 inches high and 7½ inches wide. Shipping weights, 12 and 13 pounds. **$13.45**

6K9437¼—Brown. Length, 24 in... $13.45
6K9438¼—Brown. Length, 26 in........$14.45
6K9439¼—Black. Length, 24 in. 13.45
6K9440¼—Black. Length, 26 in......... 14.45

$1⁷⁹ 24-In.

Brown Fiber Suitcase

Keep one on hand for all purposes. In an emergency one of these cases often proves valuable. Made over steel frame, reinforced with chip board. Two leather straps all around. Leather corners, riveted; brass plated lock and catches. Lined inside. Shipping weights, 8 and 9 pounds. **$1.79**

6K9413¼—Length, 24 inches.............. $1.79
6K9408¼—Length, 26 inches.............. $1.98

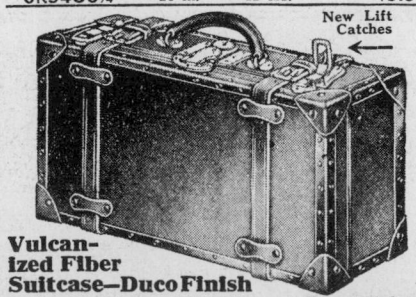

Vulcanized Fiber Suitcase—Duco Finish

A very strong and durable case. Has steel bound edges and metal corners. Frame is extra strong pressed steel with edges bound and riveted. Black finish steel corners, brass plated lock and catches. Leather handle and two leather straps. Cloth lined. Equipped with shirt folds.

	Length	Height	Width	Shpg. Wt.	
6K9470¼	24 in.	13 in.	7½ in.	13 lbs.	**$5.45**
6K9471¼	26 in.	13 in.	7½ in.	14 lbs.	$5.95
6K9472¼	28 in.	13 in.	7½ in.	15 lbs.	6.35
6K9473¼	30 in.	13 in.	7½ in.	16 lbs.	6.85

$3⁴⁵ 26-In.

"Savoy" Hard Fiber Suitcase

Sells in most stores at $5.00. Steel frame and metal reinforced corners. Heavy brass plated hardware, strong lock, two drawbolts and two outside straps. Cloth lined, fitted with shirtfold and full set of straps. Size, 26x13x8 inches. Shipping weight, 11 pounds.

6K9418¼—Black. 26 inches........... **$3.45**
6K9419¼—Brown. 26 inches........... $3.45

Choose From the Latest Styles in Women's Guaranteed Cases

$4.75 $5.75

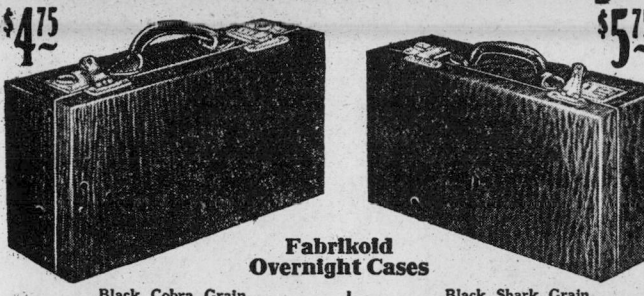

Women's Fitted Cases

Fabrikoid Overnight Cases

Black Cobra Grain
Lightweight wood sides; fiber bottom and lid. Sateen lining, with shirred pocket. Leather handle, strong locks and catches. Matches Hat Box 6K9428¼. Shipping weight, 7 pounds.
6K9442¼—Length, 22 in.; height, 12¾ in.; width, 6¼ in... **$4.75**

Smooth Black Enamel Duck Covering
Matches Hat Box 6K9426¼. Sateen lining.
6K9400¼—Length, 22 in.; height, 12 in.; width, 6¼ in.... **$4.75**

Black Shark Grain
An attractive overnight case covered with the popular shark grain Dupont fabrikoid. Lined throughout with fine quality silkoline. Two brass plated locks. Leather handle; shirred pocket in lid and pocket at end. In four popular sizes. Shpg. wts.: 5, 6, 7 and 8 lbs. respectively.
6K9443¼—Length, 16 inch **$5.75**
6K9444¼—Length, 18 inches..**$6.25**
6K9445¼—Length, 20 inches.. 6.75
6K9446¼—Length, 22 inches.. 7.45

Genuine Grain Cowhide Leather

Black Cobra Grain   With Folding Tray
Round edge case covered with genuine cowhide leather, black cobra grain, same on folding tray. Padded top lid. Leather handle; two good satin finish solid brass locks. Shirred lid pocket. Tray equipped with ten pieces good quality beautiful fancy shaped white pearl on amber toilet fittings. Tray can be folded and carried separately (see small illustration). Tray and case lined with best quality silk moire. Size of case, 22x12x7 inches. Shipping weight, 10 pounds.
6K9447¼.............**$24.95**

Genuine Grain Cowhide Leather

Black Cobra Grain   With Folding Tray
Made of genuine black grain cowhide leather over light wood sides and ends; silk moire lined, with pocket in the lid, two brass locks and leather handle. Equipped with extra folding tray containing eight useful and beautiful white pearl on amber toilet pieces. This tray (see small illustration) is fitted with lock and handle and can easily be removed and folded, making it unnecessary to carry case to the washroom. Size of case, 22x12½x6½ inches. Shipping weight, 10 pounds.
6K9448¼.............**$19.45**

Women's Overnight Cases

$9.75

Genuine Cowhide
Black Cobra Grain
Made of cowhide leather over a steel frame. Leather handle with stitched-on handle loops. Very attractive silkoline lining with shirred pocket in lid and end of case. Two brass locks.
6K9415¼—Length, 23 inches; height, 12 inches; width, 6 inches. Shipping weight, 9½ pounds..... **$9.75**

$11.95

Genuine Cowhide
Black Cobra Grain
Reinforced with light veneer and fiber boards. Leather handle, and full length sewed leather hinge. Two brass locks. Attractive silk moire lining. Three shirred pockets. Padded top.
6K9403¼—Length, 20 inches; height, 12¾ inches; width, 6¼ in. Shipping weight, 7 pounds... **$11.95**
6K9404¼—Length, 22 inches; height, 12 inches; width, 6¼ inches. Shipping weight, 8 pounds... **$12.95**
6K9405¼—Length, 24 inches; height, 13 inches; width, 6½ inches. Shipping weight, 9 pounds... **$13.95**

Special Values in Hat Boxes
Shpg. Wt., 9 Lbs.

Black Enamel Duck
Black Fabrikoid Binding
Leather handle. Double stitched. Neat sateen lining. Brass plated lock and catches.
6K9425¼—Diameter, 18 inches........ **$3.45**

Black Enamel Duck
Genuine Tan Leather Binding
Double stitched. Removable hat form. Attractive sateen lining.
6K9426¼—Diameter, 18 inches........ **$4.95**

Black "Dupont" Fabrikoid
Cobra Grained
Bound with genuine leather. Sateen lining; removable hat form, all black.
6K9428¼—Diameter, 18 inches........ **$4.95**

Better Grade Fabrikoid
Black Cobra Grained
Bound with genuine leather. Lined in silkoline. Brass plated lock and bolts. Leather handle. Removable hat form.
6K9429¼—Diameter, 18 inches........ **$5.95**

Dupont Fabrikoid Hat Box
Black Color—Cobra Grain
Bound with genuine leather. Brass lock and catches. Leather handle. Removable hat form. Attractive lining.
6K9421¼—Diameter, 18 inches, bound with tan leather binding................ **$7.45**
6K9423¼—Diameter, 18 inches, bound with black leather binding............... **$7.45**

Genuine Split Cowhide
Baby Elephant Grain
Genuine leather. Bound. Silkoline lining. Leather handle. Removable hat form.
6K9463¼—Black, Diameter, 18 inches.... **$9.75**
6K9464¼—Brown, Diameter, 18 inches.... 9.75

Genuine Black Cowhide
Cobra Grained
Silk moire lining. Padded top. Leather handle, all black.
6K9430¼—Diam. 18 in. **$12.95**

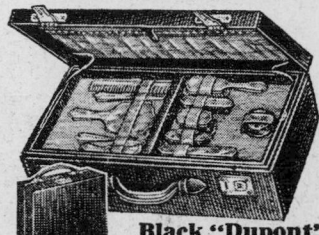

Women's Fitted Case

Black "Dupont" Fabrikoid
Cobra Grained
Folding tray covered with same material as outside of case and equipped with eleven attractive and useful fancy rose color on amber toilet fittings. Small illustration shows tray folded into small case with handle for carrying. Lined with high quality silkoline; shirred lid pocket. Two satin finish brass locks; sewed-in leather handle. Size, 22x12½x6½ inches. Shipping weight, 10 pounds.
6K9441¼.............. **$13.65**

Black "Dupont" Fabrikoid
Cobra Grained
Our low priced overnight case with fittings in lid. The case is covered with Dupont fabrikoid, black cobra grain finish. Equipped with eight attractive and useful toilet fittings held in lid. Lined throughout with a fine quality silkoline; shirred pockets in ends. Two brass locks; leather handle. Size, 22x12x6 in. Shpg. wt., 8 lbs.. **$9.95**
6K9449¼.............. **$9.95**

Your initials in gold leaf letters put on bags and suitcases for 25c extra. Two or three letters. Print letters wanted.

Hand or Auto Trunks
Steel Covered Wood Box Trunk
Very handy for the tourist or autoist. Steel covered wood box reinforced with steel runners; all black finish. Leather handle; brass plated draw bolts and spring lock. All edges bound with steel angle iron. Brass plated steel corners. Size, 28x15½x9½ inches.
6K9507¼—Shipping wt., 20 lbs.,.... **$4.75**

Fiber Covered Wood Box Trunk
Made of black hard rolled fiber over a strong wood box, fiber binding closely tacked, good corner bumpers. Brassed combination bolt and locks. Leather handle at end and front. Very neat pattern cloth lining, with removable tray. Size, 28x16½x8½ inches.
6K9508¼—Shipping wt., 15 lbs..... **$9.95**

Steamer Trunk
Black metal covered steamer trunk over good wood box, bound with fiber, with two of the new metal skids of runners across top and front, two real leather straps, good lock and bolts.
6K9503¼—Size, 32x19x12 in. Shpg. wt., 43 lbs... **$10.95**
6K9504¼—Size, 36x21x12¾ inches. Shpg. wt., 45 lbs... **$11.95**
6K9505¼—Size, 40x22x13½ inches. Shpg. wt., 54 lbs... **12.95**

Vulcanized Fiber Steamer Trunk
Five-ply vulcanized fiber construction, round edges, heavy hardware partly hand riveted. Full cloth lined, with deep top tray. Three double nailed fiber center bands, which make it very strong. Black body, with center band blue color. Has high grade lock and draw bolts of superior quality. Matches our Box Trunks 6K2524¼, 6K9525¼ and 6K9526¼, on opposite page.
6K9500¼—Size, 30x20x13 in. Shpg. wt., 55 lbs... **$13.95**
6K9501¼—Size, 40x21¼x13 inches. Shpg. wt., 65 lbs... **$14.95**

$4.95

Small Metal Covered
Camp Trunk or Army Locker
A roomy case suitable for many purposes, such as packing and storing out of season clothing. Very handy for the autoist making a week-end trip or for camping. Box of well seasoned lumber, covered with heavy black steel sheeting. Corner bumpers. Slides on front and top. Good lock and draw bolts. Leather handle on front so it can be carried as suitcase; also handle on end. Equipped with divided tray. Size, 31x16x13 in. Shpg. wt., 33 lbs.
6K9541¼—Black................. **$4.95**
6K9542¼—Olive drab................. $4.95

$29.95

Belber's
Guaranteed TRUNKS as Low as $19.75

Belber's Wardrobe
$53.95
Equipped with Belber's Patented Safelock

$41.95

"Stratford" Wardrobe Trunk
Made by Belber

Box of three-ply veneer wood covered and interlined with vulcanized fiber. Open top. Wide vulcanized fiber binding. Four drawers including large bottom drawer with removable hat form. Shoe box, laundry bag, eight hangers, steel drawer locking bar.

6K9514¼—Size, 40x21½x20 inches. Shipping weight, 82 pounds.......... **$29.95**

Steamer Size Trunk

Same style as above, excepting it has three drawers including one large tumbler drawer, shoe pockets, no locking bar. Six hangers.

6K9515¼—Size, 40x21½x14 inches. Shipping weight, 68 pounds.......... **$24.85**

"Cadillac" Box Trunk

$12.95   32-In.

Vulcanized Fiber Covered Five-Ply Construction

Five-ply construction. This means three-ply basswood veneer covered and interlined with vulcanized fiber. Popular round edge style with metal skids which run lengthwise of the trunk, on the top and front. Deep top tray, full covered, and an extra dress tray. Brass plated lock and draw bolts. The body and binding are black. Lining is a neat pattern of good quality. Will positively give a great deal of service, as the construction is of the best.

6K9560¼—Size, 32x19x21 inches. Shipping weight, 55 pounds......... **$12.95**
6K9561¼—Size, 36x20½x23 inches. Shipping weight, 60 pounds......... **13.95**
6K9562¼—Size, 40x22x24¼ inches. Shipping weight, 65 pounds......... **14.95**

For Package Carrying Straps, See Page 1056

Large Size
Special Features

1. Good patented safe tumbler lock which locks or unlocks trunk in one operation, and does away with the draw bolts.
2. Has ten hangers with new patented soft curtain follower which holds the clothing absolutely rigid. Washable fabrikoid lining.
3. Five drawers including convertible hat drawer.

with removable hat form. Nickel trimming on drawers, and two large nickel drawer pulls. Steel bar drawer locking rod.

4. Removable ironing board, iron holder.
5. Sateen laundry bag with silk cord.
6. Patented shoe box which works in channel.

Box constructed of three-ply veneer wood covered and interlined with vulcanized fiber. All round edged, covered with wide closely-nailed vulcanized fiber binding, steel runner on sides. Open solid dome top with plush facing, with nickel stay hinge. Substantial brass plated steel hardware including two heavy hinges in open top and three heavy hinges in back.

6K9513¼—Size, 43x21x22 inches. Shipping weight, 106 pounds.......... **$53.95**

Same as above, but not tacked as closely. Two steel runners on sides, 8 hangers and has open dome top. Patented clothes retainer which holds the clothes in place without any hard pressure.

6K9512¼—Size, 43x21½x20 inches. Shipping weight, 95 pounds.......... **$46.95**

Same as 6K9512¼, but has four drawers with neat pattern cloth lining. Patented clothes retainer which holds the clothes in place without any hard pressure, 8 hangers.

6K9511¼—Size, 42x21½x20 inches. Shipping weight, 94 pounds.......... **$38.95**

$24.45   Regular Size
"Waldorf" Wardrobe Trunk
Made by Belber

Box of three-ply veneer wood with wide vulcanized fiber binding. Closed top with all round edges. Substantial brass plated steel hardware including snap lock, draw bolts, and three hinges in back. Neatly cloth lined, with shoe pockets and laundry bag to match. Extension clothes trolley, four drawers with removable hat form in large bottom drawer. Eight hangers.

6K9517¼—Regular size, 40x21½x20 inches. Shipping weight, 75 pounds.......... **$24.45**

As above, with three drawers including one large tumbler drawer. Six hangers.

6K9518¼—Size, 40x21½x14 inches. Shipping weight, 60 pounds.......... **$19.75**

Wardrobe Trunk
Made by Belber

Five-ply construction, which means three-ply veneer wood with vulcanized fiber covering and inter lining. Fitted with Belber patented massive hardware; riveted throughout. Patented new dustproof valances which prevent the dust from getting into the trunk. Soft curtain clothes retainer, ironing board, iron holder. Drawer locking device. This comprises all the necessary fittings to make a high grade wardrobe trunk. Lined with blue cloth with gold figures. An extremely durable as well as beautiful trunk. Size, 43x21½x22 inches. Shipping weight, 90 pounds. **$41.95**

6K9506¼.......... **$41.95**

"Sherman" Box Trunk

$14.95   32-In.

Vulcanized Fiber Five-Ply Construction

Our best quality box trunk of five-ply construction, which means three-ply basswood veneer covered and interlined with vulcanized fiber. Round edges. Heavy hardware, partly hand riveted. Full cloth lined. Deep top tray with division for hat box. Extra dress tray. Has three double nailed fiber center bands which make it very strong and beautiful. Black body with blue center band, forming a beautiful contrast. Has high grade lock and draw bolts of superior quality. Leather handle at each end. Any traveler or tourist will be proud of this trunk.

6K9524¼—Size, 32x19x21 inches. Shipping weight, 52 pounds......... **$14.95**
6K9525¼—Size, 36x20½x23 inches. Shipping weight, 58 pounds......... **15.95**
6K9526¼—Size, 40x22x24½ inches. Shipping weight, 68 pounds......... **16.95**

For Trunk Straps, See Page 1057

$9.75   32-In.
Lincoln Box Trunk, Metal Covered

Box of well seasoned lumber and covered with strong metal covering. Has two iron bands riveted at hinges and draw bolts, these bands completely encircle the trunk when draw bolts are fastened. The corners and all edges are protected with iron angles. Heavy brass plated draw bolts and spring lock. Has four hardwood slats on top and bottom and two all around body. Two leather handles. Fancy pattern paper lining, one tray, one end of which forms covered hat compartment.

6K9545¼—Size, 32x19½x21½ inches. Shipping weight, 58 pounds......... **$9.75**
6K9546¼—Size, 36x21½x23½ inches. Shipping weight, 70 pounds......... **10.85**
6K9547¼—Size, 40x22x24 inches. Shipping weight, 80 pounds......... **11.95**

$7.48   28-In.
"Harvey" Low Priced Trunk
Metal Covered—Leather Straps

Strong enough for all practical purposes. Box made of well seasoned lumber with metal covering, and bindings, with one slat all around body and three slats on top, leather handles at each end. The feature of this trunk is the two leather straps all around. Brass plated hardware including corners, lock and end catches. Very neatly lined. One dress tray and covered hat box at one end of tray. Especially suitable for home use to store wearing apparel and linens.

6K9551¼—Size, 28x17½x21 inches. Shipping weight, 43 pounds......... **$7.48**
6K9552¼—Size, 32x19x22 inches. Shipping weight, 55 pounds......... **7.95**
6K9553¼—Size, 36x20½x23 inches. Shipping weight, 65 pounds......... **8.95**

It's Easy to Order

You can be sure it is easy to order from the World's Largest Store, for in a single year we receive more than 35 million orders from men, women and children in all walks of life, in rural communities, towns and cities, in every part of the United States. We in turn find their orders easy to understand and we guarantee satisfaction to all.

Be Sure to Come and See Us

WHEN you are visiting in Philadelphia be sure to come and see us. Our store is located in the northeast part of Philadelphia on Roosevelt Boulevard, and is easily reached by elevated train, surface car, automobile or bus. Any officer or trainman will gladly direct you how to get here. The bus lines from the city pass our door.

If you come by auto, you can park your car here as we have ample free parking space.

We will gladly show you through the Philadelphia home of the World's Largest Store. If you wish to order while here, you will be free to do so. At our retail store here you can buy over the counter and take your purchases with you if you so desire. Most of the articles shown in our catalog are on display.

WRITE IN ANY LANGUAGE. We can read it. There will be no delay on this account. You may use either pencil or ink, whichever is handy. It is better to use one of our order blanks which you will find in the back of this catalog. We also enclose order blanks in your shipments and you can keep those in your catalog for use when needed. In addition, we will mail you more order blanks free on request. If at any time you have no order blank, it will be all right to use any plain paper. The suggestions on this page will help you to write up your order.

Name and Address

We like to have you write or print your name and address on your orders VERY PLAINLY. It enables us to avoid mistakes in addressing packages or letters.

Always Write Your Name the Same Way

For example, if your name is Richard T. Jones, write the first name, middle initial and last name every time just that way; or if you write it R. T. Jones, always write it that way. If you have no middle initial, please write the first name in full.

The Family Should Order Under One Name

If possible, have all the members of the family order under The Name of the Head of the Family. This simplifies our records.

When Changing Your Address

If you have moved since you sent us your last order, be sure to give us your former complete address, as well as your new address. We can then send your catalogs and other mail to your new address.

Necessary Information on Orders

Put down the number of each article you select; the names of the articles and the sizes and colors where necessary; and fill in the price.

How to Send Money

We require payment in full with orders, unless otherwise stated. You are perfectly safe in sending payment since our guarantee protects you. You can send the money to us in any of the following ways:

1—Postoffice money order. 4—Cash by registered mail.
2—Express money order. 5—Personal check.
3—Bank draft. 6—By telegraph.

Your order and money may be sent by telegraph when YOU ARE IN A SPECIAL HURRY. The telegraph company will arrange this for you. Be sure to give your complete address in your telegram.

If you live on a rural route you can give the letter containing your order and money to your carrier and he will buy a money order for you at the postoffice and enclose it in the envelope with your order and mail it to us. This is a ruling of the Postoffice Department and you are protected by the carrier's receipt.

Shipping Information and Charges

All transportation charges are to be paid by our customers. In the description of each article in the catalog we give the approximate shipping weight.

Parcel Post

By adding up the weights of the articles you order and referring to pages 542 and 543, you can tell what the postage will be. Add this amount to your order in case you are asking us to ship by parcel post. If too much is sent for postage, we will return the balance. **Do not send stamps for this purpose, but include the proper amount in your remittance.**

Express

When goods are to be shipped by express, and there is no agent at your railroad station, please tell us the nearest convenient station at which there is an agent and where you can get the shipment and pay the charges.

It is not necessary to include with your order additional money to pay charges. You may pay charges to express agent when shipment arrives. Charges are the same either way.

See pages 544 and 545 for express and freight rates.

Freight

When goods are to be shipped by freight, it is best to pay your agent the charges when the shipment reaches you. If there is no freight agent at your shipping point, you should send additional money to prepay the freight charges. It is only necessary to prepay freight charges when there is no agent at your station. Charges are the same either way. When goods are shipped from a factory or warehouse you pay the freight from the town where the factory or warehouse is located instead of from Philadelphia.

Freight Is the Cheapest

Parcel post and express rates are low, but the cheapest way of shipping is by freight. While we welcome all orders, large or small, for parcel post, express or freight shipment, we find the biggest savings are made by our customers who plan their purchases in advance and order them all at once shipped by freight.

If You Order Goods Sent by Freight or Express—Be Sure to Give Your Shipping Point—If It Is Different From Your Postoffice.

When You Do Not Tell Us How to Ship

In this case we will consider that you have left it to our judgment and we will ship your goods the way it will be to your best advantage.

Factory Shipments Save You Money

We can save you money on some of our heavier and bulkier articles by shipping them direct from the various factories where they are made or from a warehouse. That saves freight and cartage to our store, double handling and other expenses. The descriptions tell you when goods are to be shipped from factory or warehouse. If you have any of these articles on your order, the fact THAT THEY WILL BE SHIPPED SEPARATELY should be considered in deciding whether the remainder of the order should be shipped by parcel post, express or freight. Of course, by far the greater part of our merchandise is shipped direct from our store.

We ship promptly from all our factories as they usually carry a large stock of finished articles. Shipments in most cases are ready to go as soon as orders arrive. There is practically no delay. Where extra time is required, our descriptions state it, or if a delay is necessary, you are promptly notified.

Eleven Million Families Buy From the World's Largest Store

That Tells the Story of Our *Big Values*—*Prompt Service* and *Fair Dealing* Better Than Anything Else We Can Say.

Our Bargains Are Within Quick and Easy Reach of Every Home in the U. S. A. See the Map on Page 258—Showing Locations of The Big Stores in Our Great Chain.

If Necessary to Return Goods Please Follow These Simple Directions

If you ever have occasion to return any merchandise, we can give you **better service** if you follow these instructions:

Please tell us WHY the goods you are returning are unsatisfactory. We ask this because we are anxious to still further improve our merchandise and our service in any possible way. If you give the REASON WHY you are not pleased it may help us to prevent similar faults in other shipments.

To Return by Parcel Post

If you return goods by parcel post, paste an envelope containing your letter and the bills to the outside of the package and put a 2-cent stamp on the envelope in addition to the postage on the package. In this way we will receive your letter and the package at the same time and can attend to your wishes promptly.

This Shows You How a Package Should be Wrapped and Addressed When Returning Goods to Us by Parcel Post

DO NOT ENCLOSE YOUR LETTER INSIDE THE PACKAGE AS THIS IS CONTRARY TO POSTAL LAWS

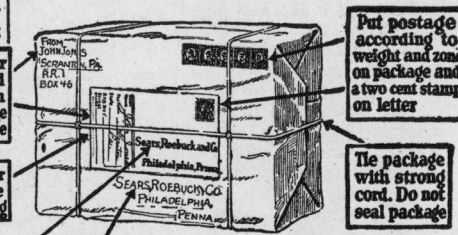

Write your name and address on both package and envelope

Paste letter to package under string

Put postage according to weight and zone on package and a two cent stamp on letter

Tie package with strong cord. Do not seal package

Address both package and letter to us

Notice to Customers on Rural Routes—Postage on packages mailed on a rural route is 2c a package less than if mailed from a postoffice, but to secure this advantage the words "MAILED ON RURAL ROUTE" must be written on package.

To Return by Express

Packages which cannot be returned by parcel post and which are not heavy enough to move by freight should be packed securely, addressed to us and shipped by express.

To Return by Freight

BEFORE RETURNING GOODS SHIPPED FROM A FACTORY please write us. We ask this. so we can tell you whether we want the goods sent to our store or back to the factory. If we have asked you to return merchandise by freight see that it is packed securely and addressed to us.

When returning merchandise by either express or freight, your full name and address should be placed on the inside or outside of the package. Place the word "FROM" in front of your name. Your agent will give you a receipt and this should be mailed to us at once with your letter explaining your reason for returning the merchandise. If your postoffice is different than the town from which the goods are returned, be sure to tell us.

See Page 543 About Our Quick Service in Auto Supplies From Columbus, Ohio, and Boston, Mass.

35 Million Orders
RECEIVED IN ONE YEAR
PROVE

It's Easy to Order From the World's Largest Store

It is so easy that a child can order from Sears! All you have to do is to pick out the things you want and write them down on the order blank, as shown on the sample order. If you haven't an order blank, plain paper will do. Write with either pen or pencil, whichever is handier for you, and write in any language you wish, we can translate them all.

The more you order by mail, the more convinced you will be that the mail order way is the easiest way to order the necessities of life.

Simply give correct catalog number, quantity wanted, the name of the article and, wherever necessary, state size and color. Figure up the total cost of the articles ordered and enclose amount required. Should you desire to have the goods shipped by parcel post include enough to pay postage according to weight. Should there be more than necessary we always return the balance.

Here is a sample order written on one of our order blanks just to show you how easy it is to order from Sears.

Order Blank · Sears, Roebuck and Co.

See Order Blanks in back of this catalog. Information on Parcel Post, Freight and Express rates on pages 542 to 545. Additional information about ordering on opposite page.

The best ways to send money are by Postoffice Money Order, Express Money Order, Bank Draft, or Personal Check. If you send cash, be sure to have the letter registered at the postoffice. You take no risk. We guarantee satisfaction and safe delivery of the goods you order.

Write in Any Language

It's Easy to Measure for Clothing

Our clothing is carefully made according to correct size standards. You do not need to order larger sizes than we specify. Our descriptions tell you the size range and you can order with the assurance that, if your size is listed, we guarantee the garment will fit you. Our sizes are obtained by securing the average of thousands of men, women and children in each size, and we believe are the most accurate standards in the country.

We Guarantee to Fit and Please You

Figure 1

Men's, Young Men's and Youths' Clothing

How to Take the Measurements

Stand in your natural way, breathe regularly and do not expand chest; also take everything bulky out of your pockets.

Chest. Take measurement over vest. Measure all around body at chest, close up under arms, snug but not tight. Tape measure should be over shoulder blades at the back. See line marked A on Figure 1.

Waist. If you wear a belt, take it off and take your measure over pants all around body at waist. Your waistline is just above hip bones. Feel sides for location of hip bones. See line marked B on Figure 2.

Inseam. This is to show length of pants leg. Stand straight and draw pants well up in crotch. Measure from close up in crotch to bottom of trousers, at length desired. See line marked C on Figure 2. For cuff bottom trousers measure 1 inch shorter than for plain bottom pants.

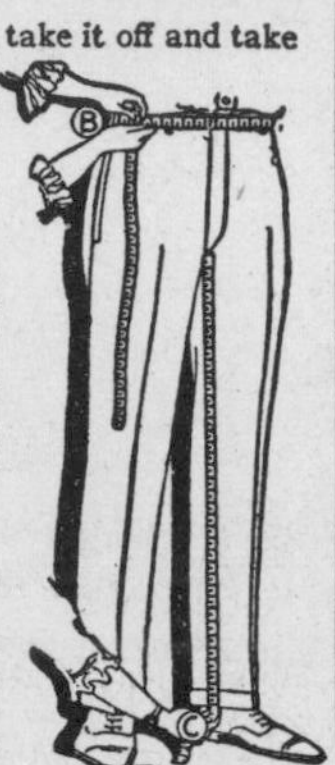

Figure 2

What Measurements to Give in Your Order

Suits. Give chest and waist measures and length of inseam; also height, weight and age.

Coats of All Kinds, Jackets, Raincoats and Overcoats. State chest measure taken over vest; also height, weight and age.

Vests. Give chest and waist sizes; also height, weight and age.

Pants (Both Dress and Work Pants) and Overalls. Give waist size and length of inseam; also height, weight and age.

WOMEN'S, MISSES' and JUNIORS'

Coats, Dresses, Knickers, Blouses, Raincoats, etc.

HOW TO TAKE MEASUREMENTS:

Always Pull Tape Close but Not Tight.

Do Not Allow. We Will Make All Necessary Allowances.

Give Each Measurement as Stated in Description of Garment You Are Ordering.

Actual Bust Measurement
For any garment, be sure to measure over very largest part of bust with dress or blouse on. Tapeline in back must run on shoulder blades and not below them.

Actual Waist Measurement
This measurement is very important when ordering knickers and skirts. Please do not allow *extra.* Give actual tape measurement, over dress or blouse.

Actual Lower-Hip Measurement
This means very *largest* part of figure below waist. Do not "allow." We will make all necessary allowances. Measure over dress or skirt.

Length Garment Desired
For dresses, coats or raincoats, measure down back from neckline to hem, as shown in small diagram, N to L.
For skirts measure down front from waist, as shown (W to S).

Height
Knowing your height, we can use the very best judgment in sending you the proper dress, coat, suit or knicker. Give weight, also, if you desire best possible fit

Tell Us This—Do you like to wear your garments loose-fitting or close-fitting? See space for answer on order blank.

Use Clothing Order Blank in Back of This Catalog

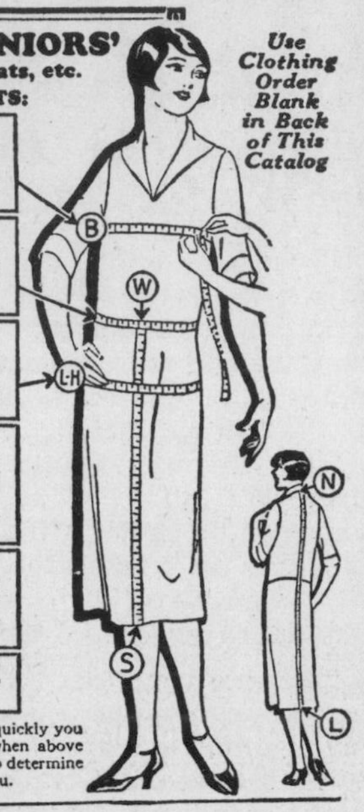

You Will Be Delighted! To learn how easily and quickly you can be correctly fitted when above information is given to us. Our years of experience enables us to determine from these measurements exactly what size garment will fit you.

Sweaters

A roomy sweater will give better service. Your proper sweater size is 2 inches larger than actual measure.

Women's Sweaters: Measure all around body at bust over blouse or dress. To your actual bust measure add 2 inches. For example, if your actual bust measure is 38 inches, order size 40 sweater.

Men's Sweaters: Take measurement around body at chest over vest and order sweater 2 inches larger than your chest measure. For example, if your chest measure is 40 inches, order size 42.

For children's and misses' sweaters, give age size.

To Measure for Boys' Long Trousers and Long Trousers Suits

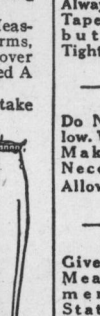

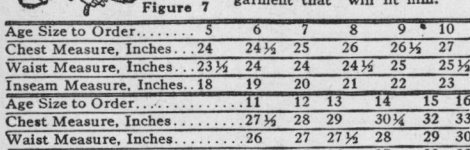

Figure 7

For suits, measure boy's chest, waist and inseam, as shown in figure 7 at N, P and R. For trousers, measure waist and inseam only as in figure 7 at P and R. Our boys' long trousers and long trousers suits are sold according to age, size and measurements. The table below shows you the measurements of the different age sizes. For example: If your boy's chest measure is 27 inches, waist measure 25½ inches and inseam 23 inches, order size 10. If you find that your boy's measurements do not agree with age sizes given in the table, send us the boy's chest, waist and inseam measurements and state his height and weight and we will send a garment that will fit him.

Age Size to Order	5	6	7	8	9	10
Chest Measure, Inches	24	24½	25	26	26½	27
Waist Measure, Inches	23½	24	24	24½	25	25½
Inseam Measure, Inches	18	19	20	21	22	23
Age Size to Order	11	12	13	14	15	16
Chest Measure, Inches	27½	28	29	30¼	32	33
Waist Measure, Inches	26	27	27½	28	29	30
Inseam Measure, Inches	24	25	26	27	28	29

Men's Underwear

Union Suits and Undershirts. Give chest size. Take off your vest. Measure all around body over your shirt.

Underdrawers. Give waist size.

Men's Dress, Work and Nightshirts. State neck measure.

Gloves

HOLD HAND OUT FLAT WITH FINGERS TOUCHING, THUMB RAISED; draw tape close around hand but not tight, as shown in illustration (do not include thumb). The number of inches shown by this measurement is your correct glove size.

Women's Sizes in Silk Fabric, Knitted Yarn and Fleece Lined Kid Gloves: 6, 6½, 7, 7½, 8, 8½.

Women's Sizes in Unlined Kid Gloves: 5¾, 6, 6¼, 6½, 6¾, 7, 7¼, 7½, 7¾, 8, 8½.

Men's Sizes: 7, 7½, 8, 8½, 9, 9½, 10, 10½.

For gloves for infants and children from 6 months to 14 years of age, give age of child.

Boys' and Girls' Clothing

GIVE AGE SIZE. To find AGE SIZE, take the boy's or girl's chest measure, then consult boys' or girls' scale of sizes below.

Before ordering a boys' or girls' garment it is necessary to know the chest measure in order to know the proper AGE SIZE to order, as boys of the same age will vary very greatly in size, and the same with girls. For example, a boy only 10 years of age may be as large as the average boy of 12; or, on the other hand, he may be as small as the average boy of 9 years. Girls of the same age also vary in size. The size scales herewith show the average chest measure of boys and girls of each age. These have been compiled from the measurements of many thousands of boys and girls of each age.

HOW TO MEASURE CHEST. For a boy, see "D" on Figure 5. Measure all around body at chest over his shirt or blouse. For a girl, see "L" on Figure 6. Measure all around body at chest over her dress or blouse. In either case, see that the tape measure is well up under arms, and that it is over shoulder blades at the back. After you have the measurement, see boys' or girls' scale to find what age size to order.

Boys' or Little Fellows'

Knee Pants, Suits, Overcoats, Raincoats, Mackinaw Coats, Blouses and Underwear

How to Use Size Scale

For example: If your boy's chest measure is 24 inches, order age size 5, or if your boy's chest measure is 30¼ inches, order age size 14.

In case your boy's chest measure is between two of the measurements given below, order the age size for the next larger chest measure.

For example: If your boy's chest measure is 28½ inches, order age size 13.

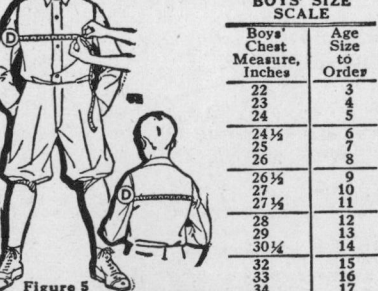

Figure 5

BOYS' SIZE SCALE

Boys' Chest Measure, Inches	Age Size to Order
22	3
23	4
24	5
24½	6
25	7
26	8
26½	9
27	10
27½	11
28	12
29	13
30¼	14
32	15
33	16
34	17

Girls' or Children's

Dresses, Blouses, Middies, Raincoats and Underwear

How to Use Size Scale

For example: If your girl's chest measure is 22 inches, order age size 3, or if your girl's chest measure is 31 inches, order age size 12.

In case your girl's chest measure is between two of the measurements given below, order the age size for the next larger chest measure.

For example: If your girl's chest measure is 26½ inches, order age size 8.

GIRLS' SIZE SCALE

Girls' Chest Measure Inches	Age Size to Order	Lgth. of Dress, In.
21	2	20
22	3	22
23	4	23
24	5	24
25	6	26
26	7	27
27	8	28
29	10	32
31	12	36
33	14	40

Figure 6

Hats and Caps

Men's and Boys' Hats and Caps. Measure all around head, as illustrated; then refer to the table below.

Children's Hat Sizes, 6¼ to 6⅞. Boys' Hat Sizes, 6⅜ to 7⅛. Men's Hat Sizes, 6¾ to 7¾.

If Head Measures, In.	19⅜	19¾	20⅛	20½	20⅞	21¼	21⅝	22	22⅜	22¾	23⅛	23½	23⅞
Order Hat Size	6¼	6⅜	6½	6⅝	6¾	6⅞	7	7⅛	7¼	7⅜	7½	7⅝	7¾

Names of COLORS and Their MEANING

A
AIREDALE—medium dark tan, the color of an Airedale dog.
ALICE BLUE—medium blue.
ALMOND—light tan.
ALMOND GREEN—medium light green with grayish cast.
ALOMA—medium tan.
AMBER—golden yellow.
AMBER ONYX—amber color in marble effect.
AMERICAN BEAUTY—the color of a deep red rose.
AMERICAN VERMILION—brilliant red.
AMETHYST—bluish purple.
ANTIQUE GOLD—deep orange yellow.
ANTIQUE IVORY—very deep cream, pale yellow.
ANTIQUE SPANISH BRASS—Deep golden orange.
ANTIQUE VERDIGRIS BRONZE—greenish bronze.
ANTWERP BLUE—dark blue.
APPLE GREEN—light green.
ARMY DRAB—medium shade of tan with greenish cast.
ASHES OF ROSES—soft shade of medium rose color.
ATHENIA—medium to dark old rose.
ATMOSPHERE—a very light tan, lighter than champagne.
AUTUMN BROWN—dark brown with a grayish cast.
AZURE BLUE—light blue (sky blue).

B
BABY BLUE—very light blue.
BABY PINK—very light pink.
BAMBOO—a medium tan.
BATTLESHIP GRAY — medium gray.
BEAVER—brownish gray.
BEGONIA—medium yellowish rust.
BEIGE—light tan, slightly darker than ecru.
BLANCHE—white.
BLOND SATIN—a medium light tan.
BLUE GRAY—medium gray with bluish cast.
BLUE HEATHER—heather mixture, blue predominating.
BLUE IRIDESCENT—rainbow blue.
BLUSH PINK—flesh color with pink tint.
BOIS DE ROSE—dark rose color.
BRIAR ROSE—bright rose.
BRICKDUST—slightly lighter than red-brown brick.
BRISTOL BROWN—dark copper color.
BRONZE—color of bronze.
BROWN HEATHER—heather mixture brown predominating.
BROWN SUGAR—color of brown sugar.
BRUNETTE—dark cream.
BUFF—medium tan, with yellow cast.
BURNT BRASS—dull unpolished brass finish.
BURNT ORANGE—natural orange with reddish cast.
BURNT SIENNA—rich reddish brown.
BURNT UMBER—dark brown.

C
CADET BLUE—medium grayish blue.
CAFE AU LAIT—rich coffee cream color.
CAMEL—medium tan as the color of a camel.
CANARY—bright yellow.
CANNA—light henna.
CARDINAL—bright red.
CARMINE—brilliant red.
CARROT—light orange.
CELESTIAL BLUE—very light blue.
CERISE—light red with purple cast.
CHAMPAGNE—light creamy tan.
CHANEL RED—dark red (garnet).
CHERRY—a fairly bright red.
CHERRY BLOOM—a bright rose pink.
CHEVREUSE—dark old rose color.
CHIN CHIN BLUE—a light Copenhagen blue.
CHINESE RED—bright red.
CHINESE WHITE—white without any yellows or blues.
CHOCOLATE BROWN—rich dark brown.
CINNAMON HEATHER—tan and brown mixture.
CLARET RED—medium wine.
COCOA BROWN—medium brown, the color of cocoa.
COBALT BLUE—dark blue.
COPENHAGEN BLUE—medium blue.
CORDOVAN—dark reddish brown.
CHROME GREEN—mixed shades of green.
CHROME LEMON—mixed shades of yellow.
CHROME ORANGES—mixed shades of oranges.
CHROME YELLOW—mixed shades of yellow.
CLARET WINE—medium wine.
COPPER—the color of copper.
COPPER GREEN POLYCHROME—natural copper background, with green sheen and red and green decorations.
COPPERLEAF—similar in color to a new copper penny.
CORAL—the color of coral, deep rose pink.
CORN—a light yellow.
CRAB APPLE—the average color of the ripe fruit, a reddish orange.
CRANBERRY—color of cranberries, a rich dark red.
CREAM—the color of cream.
CREAM WHITE—white with yellow cast.
CREMNITZ WHITE—pure white.
CRIMSON LAKE—deep transparent red.
CRYSTAL WHITE—transparent white.

D
DAHLIA—dark orchid.
DEAD GRASS—greenish brown.
DELFT—medium blue.
DOVE GRAY—gray with rose tint, one shade lighter than shadow.
DRAB—dark shade of grayish brown.

E
EBONY BLACK—deep dull black.
EBONY—black.
ECRU—light tan, slightly lighter than beige.
EMERALD GREEN—bright green.
EMPIRE GREEN—medium light green.
ENGLISH OAK—a reddish medium brown.
EVENGLOW—medium gray with a rose tint.

F
FAWN—light tan, the color of a fawn.
FIRE—color of fire.
FIREFLY—deep bright pink.
FLAKE WHITE—pure white.
FLAME—bright orange red, the color of flame.
FLESH—pale pink, skin color.
FOREST GREEN—a medium green.
FRENCH BEIGE—medium pinkish tan.
FRENCH BLOND—medium shade of tan.
FRENCH BLUE—medium blue.
FRENCH GRAY—medium gray.
FRENCH NUDE—a shade darker than flesh.
FRENCH TAN—dark tan.
FUCHSIA—maroon tinged with purple.

G
GAMBOGE—yellow.
GARNET—dark red.
GENDARME BLUE—dark peacock blue.
GERANIUM—brilliant red, the color of the geranium flower.
GOLD—the color of gold, deep yellow.
GOLDEN—light khaki.
GOLDEN AMBER—golden yellow.
GOLDEN BROWN—medium brown, gold cast.
GOLDEN IRIDESCENT—rainbow amber.
GOLDEN ROD—the color of the goldenrod flower.
GOLDEN TAN—dark tan with yellow cast.
GOLF GREEN—dark green.
GOOSEBERRY GREEN—light green.
GRACKLEHEAD BLUE—rich medium blue, darker than Copenhagen, lighter than navy.
GRAIN—as the name implies, the color of ripened yellow grain.
GRASS GREEN—color of grass.
GREEN GOLD—yellow green.
GULL GRAY—light gray.
GUNMETAL—very dark gray.
GYPSY RED—medium dark red.

H
HEATHER BLUE—medium blue, brown cast.
HEATHER BROWN—heather mixture, brown predominating.
HEATHER TAN—tan mixture.
HELIOTROPE—lavender.
HENNA—reddish brown.
HOLLY GREEN—green with a black tone.
HOLLY RED—red.
HONEYDEW—light pinkish yellow.
HOOKER'S GREEN—medium green.
HORSE CHESTNUT—a reddish brown.

I
IMPERIAL BLUE—very light blue.
INDIGO—dark blue.
INDIAN RED—deep red.
IRIDESCENT BLUE—dark blue with bright luster.
IRIDESCENT BROWN—dark brown with bright luster.
IRIDESCENT GREEN—dark green with bright luster.
IRIDESCENT PURPLE—dark purple with bright luster.
IRIDESCENT WHITE—white with opal cast.
IVORY—cream color.
IVORY WHITE—white with slight cream or ivory cast.
IVORY BLACK—clear jet black.
IVY GREEN—soft shade of medium green.

J
JADE—bright medium green.
JAPANESE RED—bright red.
JASPE TAUPE—two-tone taupe.
JOCKEY RED—bright red.
JUNGLE GREEN—dark rich forest green.

K
KELLY GREEN—bright green.
KHAKI—regular army tan.
KING'S YELLOW—bright medium yellow.
KIT FOX—a medium gray.

L
LAMPBLACK—a true black.
LAUREL—dark green shade.
LAUREL OAK—a reddish brown.
LAVENDER—light purple.
LEAF BROWN—light golden brown.
LEAF GREEN—light green.
LEATHER TAN—brownish tan.
LEMON—yellow.
LEOPARD—the color of a leopard's fur—tawny yellow with black markings.
LILAC—very light purple.
LINEN—natural tan.

M
MAGENTA—dark purple red.
MAHOGANY—dark reddish brown.
MAHOGANY BROWN—brown with maroon cast.
MAIZE—light yellow (corn).
MAIZE PEARL—light yellow (corn).
MANDARIN—orange.
MAROON—dark red.
MAUVE—deep lilac, or lavender.
MEGILP—transparent and colorless.
MEMPHIS—medium blue.
MINK—the color of mink fur, medium brown with darker markings.
MINK BROWN—medium brown.
MODE—medium shade of tan.
MOLE GRAY—the color of Mole fur, dark gray.
MONKEY SKIN—light tan with pinkish tint.
MORNING GLORY—iridescent silver.
MOSAIC BLUE—medium blue, darker than Copenhagen.
MOSS GREEN—soft medium green.
MOTHER GOOSE—medium tan.
MULBERRY—reddish purple.
MYRTLE GREEN—dark green.

THE NAMES OF COLORS Used in Our Descriptions Are Here Alphabetically Arranged and Their Meaning Made Clear

There is a saying that "there is nothing new under the sun," and that may be true as to colors, for multitudes of colors have always existed. But it has been left to modern artists to finely distinguish the different shadings and make them available for our abundant use.

Now every season ushers in a new array of shades, or some variation of their names, because color is the leading way to portray new styles.

After all there is little confusion because most of the names are descriptive; that is, they suggest the shades. Names of common objects such as animals, flowers, vegetation, the landscape, or other features furnish the suggestions. Tangerine, flesh, chocolate brown, sand and reindeer tan readily bring to mind the idea of the shades.

In this catalog we list the newest shades as well as the widest range of colors. The World's Largest Store gives you complete service in bringing you the new shades as they are introduced.

About variations in shades. It is important to remember that dyes for the different shades do not produce exactly the same effect or tone in all the different materials. That is, a certain shade of color will not have just the same tone in silk, wool and cotton. Finish in fabrics also produces a difference in tone. A lustrous finish will not have the identical cast of color as the rough surfaced fabric.

Paint colors are not included in this list. See pages 1023 and 1024.

N
NAPLES YELLOW—bright deep yellow.
NAPOLEON BLUE—very bright blue.
NATIONAL BLUE—dark blue.
NATIONAL RED—bright red.
NATURAL—flesh.
NATURAL GRAY—dark cream with gray cast.
NATURAL LINEN—tan, the color of undyed linen.
NATURAL STRAW—natural straw color (tan).
NATURAL TAN—light tan.
NAVAJO GRAY—light gray with Indian designs.
NAVY BLUE—dark blue.
NELL ROSE—medium rose.
NATURAL TINT—half way between black and white.
NEW BLUE—rich medium blue.
NICKEL GRAY—medium light shade of gray.
NILE GREEN—soft medium green.
NUDE—light tan, a shade darker than champagne.
NUT BROWN—light golden brown.
NUTRIA TAN—medium tan.

O
OAK BROWN—medium golden brown.
OAKWOOD BROWN—medium brown.
OLD BURGUNDY—a very dark wine.
OLD GOLD—as the name implies, a dull gold.
OLD IVORY—yellow cream.
OLD ROSE—soft rose with grayish cast.
OLIVE—dull brown green.
OLIVE DRAB—regular U. S. Army olive drab shade.
OLIVE GRAY—dark gray with green cast.
OLIVE GREEN—medium green of yellow tint.
OLIVE TAN—greenish tan.
OPAL—white with reddish cast.
ORCHID—a delicate light lavender.
OXFORD GRAY—dark gray.
OYSTER WHITE—white with cream cast.

P
PALMETTO GREEN—soft shade of medium grayish green.
PANSY—the color of a pansy blossom, a deep purple.
PARCHMENT—deep cream color.
PASTEL PARCHMENT—very light cream color.
PAYNES' GRAY—medium gray tinged with blue.
PEA GREEN—pale grayish green with yellow cast.
PEACH—as the name implies, a light yellowish pink.
PEACOCK BLUE — medium blue with greenish cast.
PEARL BLUSH—shade darker than flesh.
PEARL GRAY—light gray.
PENCIL BLUE—clear bright blue, slightly darker than Copenhagen.
PERMANENT BLUE—medium dark blue.
PERIWINKLE BLUE—medium blue with lavender cast.
PERSIAN ROSE—a slightly brighter shade than rose.
PETUNIA—plum color.
PIGEON GRAY—medium gray.
PIPING ROCK—gray.
PIRATE RED—bright red.
PLATINUM—light gray, as the color of the metal.
POLYCHROME—mixed colors.
PONGEE—light tan.
POPCORN—light yellow (canary).
POWDER BLUE—light grayish blue.
PRUSSIAN BLUE—rich dark blue.
PURPLE LAKE—rich transparent purple.

Q
QUEEN BLUE—medium light blue.

R
RACHEL—dark cream, lighter than brunette.
RAW SIENNA—bright brownish yellow.
RAW UMBER—dark greenish brown.
REINDEER BROWN—dark tannish brown.
REINDEER TAN—a dark tan, slightly lighter than Reindeer brown.
RESEDA GREEN—medium grayish green.
ROSE—deep pink.
ROSE BEIGE—medium tan with rose cast.
ROSE BLONDE—dark gray with rose tint, a shade lighter than rose taupe.
ROSE BREATH—light rose.
ROSE PEARL—deep pink.
ROSE PINK—pink with rose cast.
ROSEWOOD—deep rose, soft brownish tone.
ROSE BLUSH—light sand shade with brick cast.
ROSE TAUPE—dark gray with rose cast.
ROYAL BLUE—bright blue.
ROYAL PURPLE—bright purple.
RUBY—deep rich red.
RUBY PINK—dark pink.
RUBY RED—same as ruby.
RUST—as the name implies, the color of rust.
RUSSET—reddish brown.
RUSTIC BROWN—medium reddish brown.
RUSSIAN VIOLET—purple.

S
SABLE—dark tan.
SAILOR BLUE—a deep rich blue, lighter than navy.
SALMON—medium yellowish pink.
SAND—light tan.
SAP GREEN—vivid light green.
SAPPHIRE BLUE—bright blue.
SAUTERNE—very light tan.
SCARLET—a bright red.
SCARLET LAKE—bright red.
SEAL BROWN—dark brown.
SEDGE—a dark reddish tan.
SEPIA—brown.
SHARON—deep bright rose.
SHELL GRAY—similar to pearl gray.
SHELL PINK—deep yellowish pink.
SILVER—very light gray.
SILVER GRAY—light gray, the color of silver.
SILVER MOON—gray.
SILVER MUSKRAT—dark and light gray markings resembling fur.
SILVER WHITE—white with a silver cast.
SLATE—medium light gray.
SNOW WHITE—pure white like snow.
SPANISH GOLD—deep orange gold.
SPRING GREEN—light bright green.
STEEL—medium light gray.
STEEL GRAY—medium light gray.
STONE—light tan (sand).
STONE MARTEN — brown with white tinge.
SUNRISE—silver with pink cast.
SWEETPEA—shade between a pink and orchid.

T
TAMARACK TAN—a medium tan.
TAN—light brown.
TAN-YELLOW—yellow brown.
TANGERINE—bright reddish orange.
TAUPE—brownish gray.
TAUPE GRAY—gray with a brownish cast.
TERRE VERTE—dull dark green.
TIGER LILY—like flower, a deep salmon shade.
TOPAZ—yellow.
TORTOISE—medium tan.
TURKEY RED—bright red.
TURQUOISE—a light blue with greenish cast.

V
VANDYKE BROWN—deep rich brown.
VELVET BROWN—soft brown.
VERDIGRIS—medium green.
VENETIAN RED—bright light red.
VIOLET—as the name implies, bluish lavender.
VIRGIN WHITE—pure white.

W
WILD HONEY—light brown.
WINE—a very dark rich red.
WOOD BROWN—medium brown.

Y
YELLOW OCHRE—medium light yellow.

Z
ZINC WHITE—pure bright white.

...this INDEX
Makes It Easy to Find Any of Our 35,000 Bargains

A | al | ar | au | au | au | au

"A" Batteries....714
"A" Power Units.712
Abdominal Bands,
Accouchement ..146
Abdominal Bands,
Babies' 148, 151
Abdominal Belts..638
Abdominal Supports (Corsetry)
108-112, 116-120, 143
Absorbent Cotton.641
Absorbers, Shock
.......477, 493
Accelerators 480
Accelerator Foot
Rests 480
Accordions .678-679
Accordions, Blow..702
Accouchement
Bands 146
Acids, Photo......800
Acid Gloves......640
Acid Measures...974
Acid Recharges,
Extinguisher ...1016
Adapters
Cord Tip 717
Film Pack.......800
Radio Tube 717
Adding Machines..794
Address Books....794
Address Cards,
Mailing 535
Adhesive Plasters.641
Adjusters
Casement 978
Tire Chain 484
Violin Support ..670
Adzes and Handles.985
Aerators, Milk...974
Aerials and Supplies, Radio......716

Agricultural
Boilers 1066
Foundation 706
Implements and
Repairs .1060-1065
Machinery.1036-
1044, 1062 -1063
Tools 998-1000
—Also see "Farm."
Air Cleaners,
Motor....471, 494
Air Cushions.....641
Air Ferns......921-922
Air Filters......772
Air Gauges, Tire..467
Air Moisteners...962
Air Rifles, Shot..507
Air Valves, Siphon.962
Airizers, Vacuum
Cleaner 660
Alarm Clocks
.........767, 769
Alaskas 342-343
Albums 801
Albums, Record..696
Album Leaves....801
Alcohol, Rubbing.643
Alcohol, Solidified 646
Alcohol Lamps...718
Alcoves, Breakfast 1086
Alfalfa Forks....1000
Allover Laces....248
Almonds 606
Almond Cream...631
Almond Lotions..631
Alpacas 214
Altar Candlesticks.766
Altar Services....765
Alto Horns.......681
Alum 642
Aluminum Cleaners 964

al

Aluminum Letters
and Figures.....977
Arithmetic Books.788
Aluminum Paint..1025
Aluminum Powder 1025
Aluminum Ware
..964-965, 967, 969
Aluminum Ware,
Campers 498
Amber Goggles...
.........491, 771
Ammeters..468, 715
Ammoniac 997
Ammunition
.........508-509
Ammunition Belts.510
Amplifier Panels..717
Amplifier Tubes..713
Analgesic Balm..643
Anchors
Decoy 510
Embroidered ...249
Guy Wire 716
Stanchion 1068
Anchor Loops,
Track 1068
Andirons 1084
Angel Food Cake
Pans......928, 965
Angelus Toilet
Preparations ...717
Angle Valves....1012
Angular Boring
Attachments 988
Animal Baits.....513
Animal Cookies...606
Animal Scents...513
Animal Smokers..513
Animal Traps.512-513
Ankle Boots
Horse 1052
Ankle Supports..
...516, 519, 636
Announcements,
Birth 639, 776
Annunciator Wire.716
Ant Killers......646
Antenna Equipment 716
Anti-Cow Kickers.974
Anti-Rattlers.477, 490
Antiphlogistine ..643
Antiseptics 643
Antonyms 788
Anvils
.............993
Anvils, Jewelers'.718
Anvil, Vise and
Drill 992
Anvil Saw Sets...984
Anvil Tools......993
Apple Parers....968

Aprons
Babies' Bib......155
Blacksmiths' ...993
Clothespin 970
Girls'.76-83, 141, 158
Mechanics'..387, 993
Sanitary 252
Stamped 245
Storekeepers' ..387
Waterproof, Children's.141, 155, 158
Waterproof,
Men's 381, 800
Waterproof,
Women's 141
Women's.
...81-82, 88, 141
Apron Ginghams..
.........166-168
Aquariums...922, 927
Arch Supports...636
Arch Support
Shoes, Men's...
....320-321, 333
Arch Support
Shoes, Women's
....307, 313-314
Architects' Instruments and Supplies....797, 986

ar

Arctics 335, 338, 340
Arms, Tone, Phonograph 696
Arm Bags....104-106
Arm Bands.......446
Arm Chairs
...848-849, 852-
857, 867 - 869, 908
Arm Rests, Banjo.676
Arm Shields.....253
Army Goods
Breeches 385
Carrying Cases..536
Coats..385, 402-403
Jacks 1001
Leggings 541
Lockers 536
Puttees ...335, 541
Shoes..324, 333, 541
Socks 272
Vests 385
Arnica, Tincture of.643
Arresters, Lightning 666, 716
Art Linens.......223
Art Needle Work
See "Fancywork"
Art Ticking......181
Art Toweling.223, 228
Artgum 797
Artificial
Flowers, Plants.
239-240, 572, 921-922
Flowers, Hat....103
Fruits 921
Leather...813, 1003
Silk—See "Rayon"
Artists' Materials 795-797
Artists' Smocks... 88
Asafetida Pills....643
Asbestos
Furnace Cement.962
Gaskets 482
Joint Runners..1016
Lighting Rings..955
Pads, Table...
....224, 230-231
Paper 961
Pipe Covering
...........961-962
Roof Cement...1020
Aseptic Gauze...641
Ash Dumps......1084
Ash Trays, Stands
238, 615, 618,
764, 766, 904,921-923
Asphalt Paint...1021
Asphalt Roofing..
.........1078-1081
Asphalt Shingles.1080
Aspirin 643
Astrakhans 211
Athletic Goods
.........516-525
Athletic Supports
...........519, 637
Athletic Trophies.765
Atlases 784
Atomizers.614, 630, 641
Attic Sash......1086
Augers, Closet..1016
Augers, Hollow..988
Augers, Post Hole
.........999, 1014
Augers, Well....1014
Auger Bits......988
Austrian Cloths..815
Autograph Albums
...........801
Auto Strop Razors 527-528
Automatic
See Name of Article Wanted.
Automobiles, Children's 605
Automobiles, Toy
..594, 595, 597, 605

au

Automobile Accessories
Accelerators ...458-497
Accelerators 480
Accelerator Foot
Rests 480
Air-Cleaners.471, 494
Anti-Rattlers 477,490
Awnings 458
Axle Parts......
....476, 480, 495
Baby Cribs......499
Balloon Tires.460-463
Balloon Tire
Wheels....476, 494
Batteries..468-469
Battery Chargers 714
Battery Terminals..469, 473, 494
Battery Testers....468-469, 496
Bearing Caps....474
Bearing Scrapers.486
Beds 499
Bendix Drives...475
Blowout Boots..466
Bodies, Truck...481
Body Irons,
Truck 481
Books 785
Brakes 481
Brake Bands
and Sundries..
.....475, 489, 494
Brushes 493
Brushes, Paint.1029
Bumpers 485
Bushings..474, 480
Bushing Tools...475
Buttons, Horn..472
Camp Equipment
.498-501, 513, 536
Carbon Removers...486, 488, 496
Carburetors and
Controls 480
Carrying Cases..536
Celluloid 490
Celluloid Cement
...........469, 490
Celluloid Cement
...........469, 490
Chains 467, 484
Chamois...493, 646
Cheesecloth ...177
Cigar Lighters..482
Circulators.471, 481
Clocks 491
Clutch Facings..486
Clutch Release..494
Coils..472-473, 482
Coil Parts......473
Connecting Rods
.......474, 480
Connecting Rod
Bolts....474, 480
Cotter Pins.....488
Cotter Pin Extractors....488, 496
Cotton Waste..1016
Covers (Canvas).501
Crank Holders..476
Crakshafts 474
Creepers 496
Cribs, Babies'...499
Cup Grease.....457
Current Regulators 472
Curtains
..478-479, 490, 495

au

Auto—Cont'd
Curtain Fasteners 490
Curtain Lights..
........478, 490
Cushions
....458, 479, 490
Cut-Outs...477, 491
Cut-Out Controls 491
Cylinder Heads..475
Cylinder Head
Gaskets 474
Dash Boards....479
Dash Lamps....472
Differential Lubricants 457
Distributor Parts.482
Door Covers....479
Door Hand Pads.479
Door Handles...479
Drive Shafts....480
Dusters....646, 973
Emblems ....
471, 481, 494, 787
Enamels 1024, 1035
Fan Belts.......
....471, 481, 494
Fenders....476, 495
Fender Braces..
.......477, 494
Fender Guards..485
Flashlights 667
Floor Boards....494
Foot Boards....479
Freezometers ..497
Funnels 493
Garages
(Special Catalog)570
Garage Supplies
.........493, 496
Gas Savers.....480
Gaskets...474, 482
Gasoline Cans..
.......484, 941
Gasoline Filters..
.......486, 496
Gasoline Gauges.480
Gear Pullers....496
Gears 473-
474, 476, 489, 494
Gloves 126,
415, 420, 432-433
Goggles...491, 771
Greases 457
Grease Guns.475, 493
Grease Retainers.476
Guide Signals...472
Hammers 985
Headlights 472
Heaters....494, 497
Hoists 1000
Hoods, Women's 127
Hood Covers....497
Horns..472, 474, 484
Hub Parts.476, 495
Hydrometers ...
....468-469, 496
Ignition...473, 482
Inner Casings...466
Inner Tubes
.......459-464
Inner Tube Repairs ...466-467
Iron Cement....474
Jacks 487, 496,1001
Lacquer 1035
Lamps and Accessories ....
.472, 482-483, 496
Lathes, Valve
Refacing..488, 496
Luggage Carriers 495
Magneto Files...990
Magneto Parts..482
Main Bearing
Caps 474
Manifold Heaters 494
Maps 491

au

Auto—Cont'd
Mats ....
..479, 490-491, 497
Mirrors...479, 484
Mittens 419-420
Motometers.471, 485
Mufflers 477
Neutral Control.480
Nuts 488
Oils and Greases
..456-457, 492-493
Oil Cans.......996
Oil Gauges.....480
Oil Guns...475, 493
Oiler Cans......493
Oiling Systems..
.........475, 480, 493
Packing, Sheet..995
Packing, Valve..474
Paints 1035
Pedal Pads.....479
Pistons.474, 481, 494
Piston Parts....474
Piston Rings....
474, 481, 486, 494
Pliers 989
Polish and Wax.493
Power Pulleys..995
Power Saws....1041
Polishing Mitts.493
Radiators
..470-471, 494-495
Radiator Accessories 470-
471, 481, 494, 497
Reamers ....
..474-475, 488, 496
Rebabbitters ...474
Refinishing Outfits 1035
Reflectors..472, 491
Repacking,
Pump 471
Rim Tools.......
...467, 475, 487
Robes 455
Robe Rails......479
Running Boards
and Sundries
.........476-
477, 487, 490-491
Running Board
Coops 1074
Running Board
Trunks 536
Saws 984
Scales, Truck..1076
Scarfs 243
Screwdrivers.488,988
Seat Covers
....458, 479, 490
Seat Cover Materials....181, 478
Seat Cushions..
....458, 479, 490
Seat Dressing..1035
Seat Pads......490
Shades 479
Shafts.480, 489, 495
Shim Stock.....486
Shock Absorbers
.........477, 493
Shoes, Men's...330
Silicate of Soda.491
Sockets, Lamp..472
Sockets, Steel...488
Socket Wrenches
....475, 488, 496
Spark Plugs and
Sundries..473, 482
Speedometers and
Parts 489
Sponges...493, 646
Spotlights.....483
Springs ....
..476-477, 492-493
Spring Covers..476
Spring Parts....476
Steering Attachments 477
Steering Column
Braces 477

au

Auto—Cont'd
Steering Wheels,
Locks and
Covers...473, 491
Step Plates.....490
Stoplights..472, 483
Sun Shields.479, 485
Switches....472, 482
Tail Lamps.....
....472, 483, 491
Tents 501
Timers....473, 481
Timer Wire Sets.473
Tires, Repairs,
Sundries...460-467
Tires, Inner.....466
Tire Chains.....484
Tire Covers.....491
Tire Pumps.....487
Tire Reliners....466
Tire Tools..467, 487
Tool Boxes......491
Tool Kits..482, 488
Top Coverings
...478, 490, 494
Top Dressing...1035
Top Repairs....
478, 490, 494, 1003
Tow Rope,
Chains 467
Transmission
Lubricants.456-457
Transmission
Parts 475
Truck Bodies...481
Truck Tires and
Tubes ....
..459-460, 464, 465
Truck Wheels...465
Trunks 536
Tubing....480, 487
Underslung
Parts 477
Upholstery 479
Valves 474,
477, 481, 487, 491
Valve Covers....494
Valve Tools
474, 486, 488, 496
Valve Tools,
Electric 496
Varnish 1035
Vases.....479, 491
Vibrator Points.473
Vises 992
Visors 485
Vulcanizers.....467
Washers.474, 476, 488
Water Pumps
.........471, 481
Wax 493
Wheels....476, 494
Wheel Parts....
...476, 480, 488
Wheel Pulls.476, 488
Whistles..472, 484
Windshield Sundries ....
..478-479, 485, 495
Wiring Sets.....473
Wraps 127
Wrenches ..475,
482, 488, 496, 989
Awls, Harness..1054
Awls, Sewing...1057
Awl Blades 1054
Awl Handles....1054
Awl Needles....1057
Awl Thread.....1057
Awnings, Auto...458
Awning Cloth...177
Awning Pulleys..1000
Axes 510, 982
Ax Handles.....982
Axles......1001, 1003
Axle Grease.....457
Axle Parts......
....476, 480, 495
Axminster Rugs..
831-832, 834-837, 839

"B" Batteries.....715
"B" Power Units.712
Babbitt Metal.....997
Babbitting Jigs....474

Baby Goods 144-161
Aprons, Bib......155
Bags 146
Bands......148, 151
Banks 639
Baskets 639
Bassinets 588, 880-882
Bath Tubs..639, 883
Beds....588, 880-881
Bed Clothes Fasteners 147
Bibs 150-151
Binders 151
Birth Announcements 639, 776
Blankets 146, 150, 186, 190
Blanket Cloth....209
Bloomers 146
Bonnets 153
Books..776, 778, 801
Bootees 144
Bottles, Nursing.639
Bottle Brushes...639
Bottle Nipples....639
Bracelets 748
Brush and Comb Sets 639
Buggies 899
Buntings 150
Caps 144, 150, 152-153, 161
Capes.......152, 161
Carriages 899
Carriage Robes...161
Carts 899
Chairs...587, 882-883
Chambers 976
Christening Garments 155
Closet Seats......883
Coats........152, 161
Commode Chairs.883
Costume Slips....245
Creepers 154-155
Cribs........880-881
Cribs, Auto.......499
Crib Blankets... ....186, 190
Crib Comforters.182
Crib Mattresses 880-881
Crib Pads.......147
Crib Sheets......147
Crib Sheets, Rubber...147, 639
Crib Sheeting... ....176, 179-180
Cups...583, 764, 922
Diapers....146
Diaper Bags....146
Diaper Cloth 165,173
Diaper Covers....146
Diaper Linings...146
Dishes......764, 922
Dolls 584-585, 588, 629
Drawers 146
Dresses ..154-155, 158-159
Dresses, Stamped 245
Dress Yokes....249
Dressing Tables.883
Drying Frames..147
Ear Caps....150
Eiderdown 209
Exercisers 588-589, 882
Feeder Clocks....639
Flannels 172-173
Foods....639
FoodPusher Sets 754-755
Fork and Spoon Sets.754, 756, 764
Gates 882
Ginghams ..166-168
Go Carts 899
Guards, Sled....602
Hats....152-153, 161
Helmets 153
High Chairs 882-883
Hose Supporters 147, 156
Hosiery 149
Hot Water Bottles 639
Infants' Cloth. 165, 172-173, 176, 209
Jackets.144, 150-151
Jewelry....748
Kimonos 150
Lap Pads....147

Baby Goods—Cont'd
Layettes....145
Leggings 144
Marguerites 151
Medicines 639
Mittens.....124, 144
Moccasins...150, 317
Mugs.......583, 764
Navel Bands.....151
Necklaces 748
Nightgowns..150-151
Nipples, Bottle..639
Nursery Chairs..883
Nursing Bottles.639
Overalls 155
Overcoats..152, 161
Pads, Crib..880-881
Pants, Rubber....146
Pillows.147, 880-881
Pillowcases 147
Pinning Blankets 150
Pins, Gold...748-749
Pins, Safety....255
Plates..583, 764, 922
Powder 639
Quilts 182-183
Rattles 589
Receiving Blankets* 150
Record Books... ....776, 801
Ribbon 241
Rings 748
Rockers 882-883
Rompers — See "Creepers."
Romper Cloth... 165-168, 170, 175, 177
Sacques....144, 151
Safety Pins....255
Sandals 316
Scales 972
Shawls 142
Sheets, Crib....147
Sheets, Crib Rubber...147, 639
Shirts 148
Shoes 150, 316-317
Skirts 150-151, 154-155
Sleeping Garments 150-151
Slips 155
Slippers 150
Soaps.....635, 639
Soap Boxes....639
Sponges 639
Spoons 764
Stockings....149
Sulkies 899
Suppositories 639
Sweaters....144, 160
Swings.....588, 882
Syringes 639
Talcum Powder.639
Teething Rings..589
Thermometers, Bath 146
Toilet Sets....639
Towels 146
Toys...588-589, 629
Tubs, Bath 639, 883
UmbilicalTrusses 637
Underskirts 150-151, 154-155
Underwear 146-148, 156
Vests 148
Walkers..588, 882
Wardrobes 882
Wash Cloths....146
Wrappers ...150-151
Yards, Folding..882
Yokes 249
Bachelor Buttons..249
Backs, Sink.......1007
Backs, Stove, Fire.976
Back and Hip Straps 1054
Back Bands.......1054
Back Bands (Millwork) 1087
Back Combs....121
Back Curtains.478, 490
Back Pads, Harness 1054-1055
Back Saws....984
Backgammon 576

Bags
Airizer, Vacuum Cleaner 660
Arm 104-106
Band Instrument 683-684
Banjo 676
Beaded....104, 106
Bicycle Tool....452
Boston....104, 106
Brief 705
Children's....90, 106
Clothes 254

Bags—Cont'd
Collar 619
Diaper 146
Douche 640
Drum 683
Garment 254
Golf 523
Guitar 676
Hand 104-106
Hat 121
Hot Water..639-640
Mandolin 676
Mason's Tool....999
Mesh.....736, 739
Music 705
Music Stand....703
Sachet 233
School 705, 796
Shopping 104
Sleeping, Babies' 150-151
Snare Drum....683
Striking 521
Striking, Boys'..579
Tobacco 618
Traveling104,534-536
Ukulele 676
Urinal 641
Vanity 104-105,736-737,739
Violin 671
Bag and Hat Sets 90
Bag Frames....254
Bag Seeders....1063
Bag Snaps....1058
Bag Trucks....998
Baggage Holders..495
Bait, Fish....515
Baits, Animal....513
Bait Swivels....515
Baking Dishes 763, 921, 928
Baking Pans...964-967
Balances, Sash....978
Balances, Spring...974
Balance Caps and Staffs, Watch....718

Balls
Ball Bearing....452
Baseballs 522
Basket..518-519, 579
Beach 579
Bibb 1012
Christmas Tree..574
Closet Tank....1005
Footballs 520
Footballs, Boys' 520, 579
Gear Shift....491
Golf 523
Indoor 522
Moth 646
Play 579
Playground 522
Rubber 589
Soccer 520
Tea 765
Tennis 523
Volley 521
Ball Bats....522
Ball Bearings, Bicycle 452
Ball Bearings, Hub....474, 476
Ball Cocks....1005
Ball Fringes....815
Ball Pein Hammers985
Ball Sockets, Auto.477
Ball Watches....720
Ballet Slippers....524
Balloons 588
Balloon Tires..460-463
Balloon Wheels and Rims..476, 494
Balms....631, 643
Baluster Stock....1087

Bands
Abdominal 146, 151, 638
Accouchement ...146
Arm 446
Babies'....148, 151
Back 1054
Belly 1054
Brake 475, 494
Breast 146
Hat 241
Head 121
Lumberjack 209
Nose 1052
Poultry Leg....1075
Rubber 794
Shirt Collar....254
Sweat 523
WristWatch.720,723

Band Instruments .680-683
Band Instruments, Jazz 592
Band Linings, Brake 475, 489
Band Saws....983
Band Saw Blades.983
Band Wheels, Sewing Machine 197
Bandages, Elastic.636
Bandages, Gauze..641
Bandage Cloth.177, 636
Bandanas 235
Bandeaux, Bust136-137
Bandeaux, Corset 108-113, 116, 119-120, 143
Bandeaux, Hat....103
Bandeaux, Head...121
Banjos....673
Banjo Supplies.... ....672, 676, 703
Banjo-Ukes....674
Banks 596, 639

Bars
Bicycle Repair...452
Clothes Hanger.254
Handle 452
Towel 1010
Trapeze 525
Wrecking 997
Bar Iron 980
Bar Pins 733, 738, 741, 749
Barbed Wire....1072

Barbers' Supplies ..229, 527, 531, 635
Baritone Horns...681

BARNS
See Page 1089
—Or Write for Barn Catalog

Barn Equipment 1068
Barn Hardware... ....980, 998, 1000
Barn Outfits, Hay 1000

Barn Paint.1021, 1023
Barn Sash....1086
Barn Ventilators.1082
Barometers 772
—Also see page 596
Barrels, Oak....968
Barrels, Oil, Steel.456
Barrel Bolts 978
Barrel Carts 1064
Barrel Churns....974
Barrel Faucets....456
Barrel Pumps.... ....456, 1014-1015
Barrel Spigots....968
Barrel Sprayers....1015
Barrel Trucks....998
Barrettes 121, 749
Barrows 999, 1064
Barrow Sprayers.1015
Basco Cloth....180
Bases, Lamp.240, 657
Base Boards....1087
Base Knobs....978
Base Receptacles..659
Base Shoes....1087
Baseball Games... ....526, 577-578
Baseball Goods 522, 524
Baseball Outfits, Boys' 579
Basins, Wash (Lavatories)... 1006-1007
Basins, Wash (Pans) 964, 976
Basin Cocks....1012

Baskets
Babies' 639, 882
Basket Ball....518
Bonbon 920
Bread, Silver....763
Cake, Silver.762, 765
Feed 998
Flower, Glass...920
Flower Filled....572
Fruit, Silver....762
Household 970
Magazine 902
Wire Nest 1074
Basket Balls, Boys'.579

Basket Ball Goods .518-519
Basket Ball Shoes.524
Bass Drums and Supplies 683-684
Bass Horns....681
Bassinets.588, 880-882
Basting Thread....251
Bats, Ball....522
Bath Blankets....146
Bath Brushes.616, 1010
Bath Cabinets....641
Bath Cocks....1012
Bath Curtains, Shower 254
Bath Heaters....1009
Bath Rugs.230-231, 831
Bath Salts....632
Bath Showers....1009
Bath Sponges....639
Bath Stools....1010
Bath Thermometers 146
Bath Towels 224, 229-232
Bath Towels, Babies' 146
Bath Towelings...228

Bathrobes
Boys' 422
Children's 159
Girls' 85
Men's 445
Women's 84-85
Bathrobe Blankets.190
Bathroom
Cabinets 845-846
Hardware 978-979, 1010
Heaters 660
Lights 653-654
Mirrors 1010
Outfits 1004
Scales 972
Trimmings 1010

Bathtubs
Babies'....639, 883
Folding.641,883,1009
Porcelain 1008
Steel 1009
Bathtub Enamel.1026
Bathtub Seats....1010
Batiste....165, 204

Batteries
Auto 468-469
Dry....665-666, 714
Farm Light Plant 665
Flash Light....666
Lantern 666
Medical 664
Multiple 665
Radio 714-715
Battery Cable....715
Battery Chargers. 714-715
Battery Clips....715
Battery Eliminators.....712, 715
Battery Meters... ....468, 714-715
Battery Switches. 666, 716
Battery Syringes..714
Battery Terminals... ....469, 473, 494
Battery Testers... 468-469, 496, 714-715
Batting 191
Bay Rum....635
Beach Balls....579
Beads
Children's 590
Christmas Tree. 574-575
Portiere 256
Prayer 750
Trimming 256
Bead Craft Sets...802
Bead Necklaces... ....239, 735, 739
Bead Needles....256
Bead Thread....250
Beaded Bags.104, 106
Beading, Lace....248
Beams, Lumber..1088
Beams, Scale....972
Beam Scales.972, 1076
Bean Pots....926
Bears 586
Bearings, Ball....452
Bearings, Hub.474, 476
Bearing Caps....474
Bearing Scrapers..486
Beaters, Cream...969
Beaters, Cymbal...683
Beaters, Drum....683
Beaters, Egg....969
Beauty Clay....631
Beaver Shawls....142

Beds
Auto 499
Auto, Babies'....499
Babies' Swing...588
Bow End.... 858-866, 896-897
Camp 499
Children's ..880-881
Cot 887
Cot, Outdoor....499
Couch 888-889
Davenport 868-872, 888
Day....872, 888-889
Doll 580
Steel....887, 896-898
Wood 858-866
Bed Blankets..183-190
Bed Casters....977
Bedclothes Fasteners 147
Bed Comforters182-183
Bed Lamp Shades.656
Bed Mattresses... 867, 887, 892-895, 898
Bed Mattress Protectors 193-194
Bed Pans....641
Bed Pillows....885
Bed Sheets.184, 192-193
Bed Sheets, Babies'147
Bed Sheets, Waterproof.147, 639
Bed Sheetings... ...176, 178-180, 223
Bed Sheetings, Rubber.147, 194, 639

Bedspreads 168-169, 194-195
Hand Painted...244
Stamped 245
Bedspread Materials 169, 195, 815
Bedspread Sets... ....168-169, 194-195
Bed Springs.... ....890-891, 898
Bed Ticking 181
Bed Warmers..639-640
Bedbug Killers....646
Bedroom Chambers 976
Bedroom Furniture 858-866, 875-876, 880-881, 884-898, 903, 906-907
Bedroom Lamps..655
Bedroom Slippers ...310-312, 315, 334
Bedroom Ware 921, 925, 976
Beef, Iron and Wine 642
Bee Keepers' Supplies....1069

Bells
Church 1063
Cow 974
Door, Electric...665
Drummers' 683
Factory 1067
Farm 1063
Paper 572
Schoolhouse 1063
Sheep 974
Sleigh 1057
Turkey 974
Bell Ringing Transformers 665
Bell Straps....974
Bell Wire....716
Belladona Plasters 643
Bellybands 1054

Belts
Abdominal 115-116, 119-120, 638
Boys' 422
Cartridge 510
Corset 114-116, 119-120
Fan...471, 481, 494
Gun Shell 510
Health 116
Hunters' 510
Linemen's 666
Machine 994-995
Maternity 143
Men's 447, 740
Money 510
Pump Jack....1044
Reducing 638
Sanitary 252-253
Sewing Machine.197
Women's 121
Belt and Hose Supporters 253
Belt Buckles....249
Belt Chains, Men's 727-728
Belt Countershafts 996
Belt Dressings....995
Belt Hooks....994
Belt Lacers....994
Belt Lacing....995
Belt Pulleys....994

Belting
Canvas 994
Leather 995
Link Chain....994
Rubber 995
Woven 994-995
Benches
Piano 705
Vanity 858-864
Wash 971
Work 984
Bench Cushions, Piano 705
Bench Grinders....996
Bench Planes....987
Bench Screws....992
Bench Vises....992
Bench Wringers...971
Bends, Closet....1012
Bends, Pipe.1012-1013
Bendix Drives and Parts 475
Bengalines 219
Berry Crushers...1069
Berry Dishes.... ....922-925, 927
Berry Spoons.... ....754-759, 761
Bevels, Sliding T..986
Beverages 646
Beverage Bottles..968
Beverage Straws.. ....646, 802
Bias Cutting Gauges 197
Bias Seam Tape....254
Bibs, Babies'..150-151
Bibs, Barbers'....530
Bib Aprons, Babies' 155

Bibbs, Plumbing.1012
Bibb Balls.......1012
Bibb Seat Dresses.1012
Bibb Washers....1012
Bibles.......786-787
Bible Stories....
..........778-779, 786

Bicycles 449-451
Bicycles, Children's
.........451, 604
Bicycle Supplies..
.........452-454
Bill Files.......794
Billfolds....622-623
Bins, Grain.....1062
Binders
Abdominal..146, 151
Babies'.........151
Breast 146
Loose Leaf......796
Binder Canvas (By
the Yard).......177
Binder Covers....500
Binding
Blanket 254
Carpet 841
Linoleum 824
Matting 841
Oilcloth 824
Seam 254
Ski 516
Snowshoe 516
Binding Braids...254
Binding Posts....717
Binoculars 770
Birds, Books on..784
Birds, Xmas Tree.574
Bird Cages
......233, 239, 970
Bird Cage Hooks.
Springs and
Stands 970
Bird Calls......510
Bird Grit.......646
Bird Remedies....646
Bird Seed 646
Birth Announce-
ments 639, 776
Birthday Books...776
Birthday Cake
Decorations 607
Birthday Jewelry
...741-742; 748-750
Bissell's Carpet
Sweepers 973

Bits
Auger 988
Brace 988
Countersink 988
Drill......988, 991
Drill, Jewelers'..718
Expansion 988
Gimlet 988
Horse 1051-1052
Mule 1051
Reamer 988
Screwdriver 988
Ship Auger Car.988
Bit Braces 988
Bit Brace Drills..988
Bit Snaps......1058
Bit Stock Drills..991
Blackboards ....
.......590-591, 794
Blackboard Eraser.794
Blackhead Remov-
ers.530, 617, 631, 640
Blacking, Shoe...344
Blacking, Stove...938
Blacking Boxes...903
Blackleg Medi-
cines 645
Blackleg Syringes.645
Blacksmiths'
Aprons 993
Blacksmiths' Tools
....985, 990-993
Blacksmithing
Books 785
Bladders
Basket Ball.....519
Football 520
Striking Bag....521
Volley Ball.....521
Bladder Inflaters..519

Blades
Band Saw.......983
Bracket Saw....984
Buck Saw.......982
Butchers' Saw..533
Coping Saw.....984
Dehorning Saw..975
Drag-Saw......1041
Floor Scraper...987
Hack Saw.......984
Harness Awl...1054
Harrow 1060
Hoof Shear.....993
Jewelers' Saw...718
Kitchen Saw....533

Blades—Cont'd
Leather Knife..1054
Mouth Float....645
Paint Scraper..1029
Safety Razor....
.........528, 634
Tree Pruner.....999

Blankets
Babies' Bath...146
Babies' Pinning..150
Babies'Receiving.150
Bath Robe......190
Bed 183-190
Camp 183, 499
Comforter ..182-183
Crib 186, 190
Horse 1056-1057
Saddle 1051
Stable 1056
Waterproof 499
Blanket Bindings.254
Blanket Cloth....209
Blanket Lined
Clothing.347, 357-
359, 379, 381, 393,
400-402, 404, 406-407
Blanket Pins,
Horse 1058
Blast Furnaces..1016
Blazer Coats—See
"Lumberjacks."
Bleached Goods..
.....165, 173, 176-
180, 192-193, 227-228
Blinds (Shades)
Window 819-821
Blocks
Aerial Connector.716
Drummers' 683
Pillow 994
Post 994
Pulley 1000
Saw Setting....984
Toy 588-591
Block Machines,
Cement 1084
Blood Purifiers..642
Blood Purifiers,
Stock 645

Bloomers
Babies' Rubber..146
Children's ..156-157
Girls'...156-157, 164
Gymnasium 519
Knit 292
Sanitary 252
Women's ...132-
133, 135, 290, 292
Bloomer Cloths
Cotton
165, 171-175, 177
Rayon 214-215
Sateen.170-171, 175
Silk 212-219
Bloomer Dresses..
.........80, 158-159
Blotters, Roller...764

Blouses
Army Style.359, 385
Boys'....346, 362
Flannel — See
"Lumberjacks."
Girls' 72-75
Gymnasium.75, 519
Knitted ....
.....72-73, 128-
129, 160, 162 - 163
Leather 403-404
Lumberjack—See
"Lumberjacks."
Middy 75, 519
Misses' 72-75
Women's 72-75
Blouse Bands,
Lumberjack 209
Blouse Flannels..
.....168, 205, 209
Blouse Lacers...249
Blouse Linens...223
Blow Accordions..702
Blow Pipes, Jewel-
ers' 718
Blow Torches...1016
Blowers, Black-
smiths' 993
Blowout Boots..466
Blueing, Gun Bar-
rel 511

Boards
Base 1087
Blackboards ....
.......590-591, 794
Bread 614
Clapboards ...1088
Dash 479
Drawing...795, 797
Floor, Auto.....494
Foot, Auto.....479
Game..526, 576-578
Ironing 970
Ironing, Built-In1086

Boards—Cont'd
Lumber 1088
Mounting 716
Ouija 576
Plaster 1077
Print Trimming.800
Running, Auto..476
Sink, Drain...1007
Spelling 590
Stove 976
Wagon, Sand...1003
Wall 1077
Wash 971
Weather 1088
Boats; Sauce..914-919
Boat Engines....1045
Boat Engine Cov-
ers 1045
Boat Motors....1045
Bob Sleds......1064

Bobbed Hair
Brushes.....530, 616
Clippers 530
Combs
121, 530, 616, 737

**Bobbed Hair
—Cont'd**
Curlers
121, 123, 634, 664
Dressing 634
Nets 122-123
Bobbins 197
Bobbin Winder
Rubbers 197
Bodies, Auto
.............481
Bodies, Breeching.1058
Bodies,Stock Rack1064
Body Braces....638
Body Irons, Auto
Truck 481
Body Protectors..519
Bohemian Ticking.181

Boilers
Agricultural ...1066
Coffee 966
Dairy 1066
Double 964-966
Ham 966-967
Range 1009
Steam Heat.962-963
Stock Feed....1066
Wash......967, 971
Water Heat.962-963
Boiler Compounds1016
Boiler Heaters,
Range 1009
Bolsters, Wagon..
........1002-1003
Bolster Cushions..
..884, 886, 888-889
Bolster Springs..1002
Bolster Stakes...1002

Bolts
Carriage 981
Connecting Rod
..........474, 480
Door 978
Eye 1000
Foot 978
Ironwork 981
License Plate..484
Machine 981
Rod Track.....1068
Stall Hook....1068
Stove 981
Tire 981

Wagon Box....1002
Bolt Clippers...981
Bolt Nuts 981
Bolt Snaps.....1058
Bolt Tongs 993
Bolt Washers...981
Bonbon Dishes...
.....765, 920-921
Bone, Steamed..645
Bone Builders,
Stock 645
Bone Buttons....249
Bone Rings 256
Boning Knives....533
Bonnets..89-91, 153

Books
773-789, 794-796, 801
Accounting 788
Address 794
Adventure.......
....773-775, 781-782
Albums 801
Algebra 788
Amusements.779, 783

**Rely on Reliance
Radiators**
*Guaranteed for
18 Months
Against Damage
Due to Freezing*
All Year 'Round
Radiators.
For all Ford cars
from 1917-26.
**See Page 470 for Prices
Big Values for Auto Owners**
Buying for eleven million
customers, we have built up a
tremendous business in Auto-
mobile Accessories. Our ALL-
STATE Tires (pages 460 and
461) have literally "taken the
country by storm." Every car
owner will find big values
in our Auto Supply sec-
tion, pages 458 to 497.

Books—Cont'd
Animal Stories..
..774, 778-779, 782
Antonyms 788
Arithmetic 788
Armature Wind-
ing 785
Astronomy 773
Atlases 784
Auction Bridge..783
Auto Trail Guide.491
Automobiles 785
Babies' Record..
..........776, 801
Basketball Rules.519
Batteries, Care
and Repairs....785
Bed Time Sto-
ries 778-780
Bibles 786-787
Bible Stories—
......778-780, 786
Biographies.773, 782
Birds 784
Birthday 776
Blank Books....794
Bookkeeping 788
Boys'...776, 779-782
Building 785
Butterfly Guides.784
Calculators 788
Campfire Stories.780
Caponizing 644
Cards 783
Card Writing...785
Care of Children.783
Carpentry 785
Cartoons 782
Cash Books....794
Catholic 787
Cements 785
Checkers 783
Chemistry 788
Chess 783
Children's Books
773, 778 - 782, 786
Chord Books...703
Christmas...776, 778
Civil Service...788
Classics.773, 776, 788
Composition 794
Conundrums 783
Cooking 784

Books—Cont'd
Correspondence
.........783, 788
Cut-Out Dolls...779
Dancing 783
Day 794
Designing and
Decorating....
.....785, 795, 1017
Detective Stories
....773, 775, 782
Devotional...786-787
Dictionaries 784
Dramas 773
Drawing.779,788,795
Dreams 783
Educational ....
........784-785, 788
Electrical 785
Encyclopedias....
.....409, 783-785
Engines 785
Engineering 785
Entertainment....
......779, 782-783
Etiquette 783
Fairy Tales.....
....773, 778-780
Fancywork 250
Fiction ....
...773-775, 778-782
Fishing 515
Flowers 784
Football Rules..520
Foreign Lan-
guages...784, 788
Fortune Telling..783
French 784, 788
Frontier Stories
.......775, 782
Furniture Finish-
ing 785
Games.....779, 783
Geometry 788
German...784, 788
Gift 776
Girls'...776, 779-780
Graduation Rec-
ords 776
Grammar 788
Hair Style......122
Health 783
Heating Systems.785
History 782
Home Study.785, 788
Humor.773, 776, 782
Hygienics 783
Indians 781-782
Interior Decorat-
ing..785, 795, 1017
Italian 784
Jiu Jitsu 783
Jokes 782
Journal 794
Keys of Heaven.787
Keys of the Bible.787
Knitting 250
Latin 784, 788
Law 788
Ledgers 794
Letter Writing
.........783, 788
Lettering 785
Life of Christ...779
Loose Leaf Books
and Fillers.796, 801
Love Letters....783
Love Making....783
Machinists'
Books 785
Made Easy Series
......783, 788, 795
Magic 783
Manners 783
Manuals of De-
votion 787
Maps (Atlas)....784
Mathematics 788
Mechanics .781, 785
Medical 783
Memoranda.239, 794
Memory ...776, 801
Mixing of Colors
and Paints.....785
MotherGoose778-780
Motors 785
Movies 774-775
Music Instructors
...677, 682,702-703
Mystery.773-775, 782
Nature Lovers'..784
New Books......773
New Testaments.786
Note Books.....
.....789, 794, 796
Novels ....
...773-775, 780, 782
Nursery 778-780
Operas 773
Paint 785
Painting.256, 785,795
Palmistry 783
Parliamentary
Rules 784
Penmanship 788

Books—Cont'd
Personality.773, 788
Photoplay ...774-775
Picture.778-779, 782
Poems 773, 776
Prayer Books786-787
Public Speaking.788
Questions Games.788
Radio 785
Rapid Calculator.788
Readings 783
Receipt 794
Recipes 784
Recitations 783
Religious 774,
776,778-780,786-787
Riddles 783
Roof Framing...785
Santa Claus....778
School Day Rec-
ords 776, 801
Score Books....519
Scrap Books.....794
Sex Hygiene....783
Shakespeare ...776
Sheet Metal....785
Short Cuts in
Figures 788
Shorthand 788
Sign Painting...785
Sketch 779
Songs...677, 702-703
Spanish 784, 788
Speakers 783
Speechmaking ..788
Spelling 788
Steam Boilers...785
Steel Square....785
Stump Speeches.788
Swedish 784
Synonyms 788
Telephony 785
Testaments 786
Toasts 782-783
Toy 778-779
Tractors 785
Translations ...788
Travel 773
Tree Guides ...784
Tricks 779, 783
Volleyball Rules.519
Welding 785
Western Stories
....774-775, 781-782
Will Power 788
Wireless Teleg-
raphy 785
Wiring 785
Witty Stories...782
Wood Finishing.785
Writing Courses.788
Book Bags and
Satchels.705, 796
Book Ends ......
..766, 794, 922, 925
Book Racks...879, 902
Bookcases......905
Bookmarks 238

Boots
Ankle 1052
Blowout, Auto..466
Boys'.......335-339
Children's 339
Cowboys' 332
Felt 341
Girls' 339
Men's
332, 335, 339, 341
Rubber 335, 339
Women's ...319, 339
Boot Hooks 319
Boot Socks...339, 341
Boot Top Patches.344
Bootees, Babies'..
........144, 312, 317
Borders, Rug....828
Boric Acid......643
Boring Attach-
ments, Angular.988
Boring Outfit,
Well 1015
Boston Bags.104, 106

Bottles
Babies' 639
Cream 974-975
Crown Cap.....968
Hot Water..639-640
Insulated 498
Milk 975
Milk Tester....974
Nursing 639
Perfume...612, 925
Refrigerator ...927
Vacuum 498
Water...921, 927
Bottle Brushes..975
Bottle Brushes,
Babies' 639
Bottle Caps, Metal.968
Bottle Caps, Milk.975
Bottle Cappers..968
Bottle Corks....646
Bottle Fillers..968

Bottle Linings,
Vacuum 498
Boudoir Caps.....242
Boudoir Clocks.766-767
Boudoir Lamps 655-656
Boudoir Pillows233,244
Boudoir Slippers
.........310-312
Bouquets, Bridal,
Confirmation ...121
Bouquets, Corsage
.........242-243
Boutonnieres ...
..103, 233, 242-243
Bows and Arrows.600
Bows and Repairs,
Violin......670-671
Bow End Beds....
....858-866, 896-897
Bow Ties....422, 448
Bowie Knives....510

Bowls
Berry...922-925, 927
Bulb (Flower)..
.....240, 614, 923
Candy 239
Cereal..914-919, 921
China.........
.914-919, 921, 924
Closet 1005
Cut Glass......920
Enameled 966
Fish 927
Flower.240, 921, 925
Fruit.........239,
762, 921 - 922, 925
Lavatory .1006-1007
Mixing....926, 964
Nut 614
Oyster. 914-917, 921
Salad.........238,
914 - 920, 922 - 925
Silver 762
Soup..914-917, 921
Stock Watering.1068
Sugar..765, 914-919
Wash (Pans) 964,976
Bowl and Pitcher
Sets 976
Bowl Rings, Sep-
arator 1040
Bowling Games...577

Boxes
Candy..575, 609, 925
Cash......789, 977
Cedar 906-907
Cigarette..238, 923
Collar 619
Cut-Out 658
Deed......789, 977
Dresser 615
Egg 1074
Fiber 535
Grain Truck...1064
Grit 1074
Hand Cart.....1064
Handkerchief ..615
Hat 536
Honey 1069
Jewel.........
.238, 612, 764, 766
Lunch.........
.498, 796, 965, 967
Mail 998
Match 510
Miter 985
Outlet 658
Paint......591, 797
Parasol 106
Pencil......794, 796
Powder ....
238, 632, 736-
737, 739, 922-923
Powder Puff.240,
612, 922-923, 925
Recipe.....784, 846
Salt 926
Sewing 615
Shirt Waist....
.....903, 906-907
Shoe Shining...903
Skirt 903
Soap 639
Switch 658
Tackle 515
Tool......985, 990
Tool, Auto.....491
Tool, Boys'....600
Truck 1065
Umbrella 106
Vanity......104-105
238, 240, 612,
632, 736 - 737,
739, 922-923, 925
Wagon 1064-1065
Box Carts......1064
Box Hardware.977, 979
Box Nails 977
Box Rods, Wagon.1002
Box Trucks 998
Box Trunks....536-537

Take a **PORTOLA**
to the Party!

See
Page
690

Music and Fun for All
Any Place
Any Time
Any Where

Feeds
—For Stock and Poultry ..644-645
Feed Baskets......998
Feed Cookers....1066
Feed Cooker Covers and Grates..1066
Feed Cutters and Attachments ...1062
Feed Grinders....1063
Feeders, Hog1066-1067
Feeders, Poultry 926, 1074
Feeder Clocks, Baby 639
Feeding Troughs 1066-1067, 1074
Feeler Gauges.....990
Feet, Stocking... ....260, 266, 268
Felloe Boring Machines 983
Felt, Builders' ...1077
Felt, Table........224
Felt, Tarred......1077
Felt, Wool........525
Felt, Base Floor Coverings 826, 828, 830
Felt Boots........341
Felt Letters.......518
Felt Packing......514
Felt Roofing.....1077
Felt Slippers 310, 312, 334
Felt Washers.474, 476
Felt Weatherstrips.977
Fence Gates...... ....1070, 1072, 1073
Fence Making Tools....1000, 1072
Fence Posts, Steel 1072
Fence Post Preservers 1020
Fence Staples ...1073

Fencing 1070-1073
Fencing Shoes....524
Fencing Wire....1072
Fenders, Auto 476, 495
Fenders, Stirrup.1051
Fender Braces.477, 494
Fender Guards....485
Fender Lacquer..1035
Fender Repairs....477
Ferns 921-922
Ferneries.877-879, 902
Ferrules, Neckyoke, Singletree.1002
Ferrules, Pipe...1012
Fertilizer Sowers.1065
Fever Thermometers 641
Fiber Furniture 878-879, 883
Fiber Gears 489
Fiber Rugs...... ......823, 825, 831
Fiction 773-775, 778-782
Fiddles 668-670
Field Glasses 770-771
Fifes 682
Fife Instructors 682, 703
Fife Mouthpieces.682
Figs 606
Fig Bars..........606
Fig Syrups 642
Figures
Aluminum 977
Steel 986
Stock Marking..975
Filament Switches.716
Filberts 606

Files
Bastard 990
Bill 794
Desk 909
Hand Saw.......990
Jewelers' 718
Letter 794
Magneto 990
Mill 990
Nail....612, 617, 764
Rat Tail..........990
Saw Filer.........984
Taper 990
Veterinary 645
File Handles.......990
Filers, Saw.......984
Filet Nets.....810-811
Filing Guides.....984
Fillers
Battery 468-469, 714-715
Bottle (Siphon) .968
Bottle, Vacuum.498

Fillers—Cont'd
Crevice 1027
Egg Carrier....1074
Wood 1027
Filletster Planes..987
Films 798
Films, Moving Picture 799
Film Developers..800
Film Packs and Adapters 800
Filters, Air.......772
Filters, Gasoline 480, 486
Fin Cutters, Plow.1060
Fine Tooth Combs 616
Fingerboards and Charts, Musical Instrument 670, 676
Finials 1083
Finishing Braids.249
Finishing Lumber 1088
Finishing Nails....997
Fire Extinguishers 1016
Fire Extinguisher Recharges 1016
Fire Lighters.....513
Fire Sets........ ....930-931, 1084
Fire Shovels, Stove 976

Firearms 502-507
Firebacks 976
Fireless Cookers 969
Firemen's Coats...408
Firemen's Shoes..320
Fireplace Furnishings 1084
Fireplace Furnishings, Electric....665
First Aid Kits....485
Fish Bowls....922, 927
Fishing, Books on.515
Fishing Boots.335, 339
Fishing Coats.....408

Fishing Equipment 514-515
Fishing Equipment, Salt Water.514
Fishing Hats......408
Fishing Lights.... ....514, 666-667

Fixtures
Aerial Mast.....716
Bathroom 1010
Built-In House.1086
Curtain 822
Electric Lighting 648-654
Stable 1068
Toilet Paper....1010
Fixture Studs.....658
Flags 525
Flagons 765
Flanges, Roof....1012
Flanges, Stall Floor 1068
Flange Unions...1013

Flannels
Babies' 172-173
Cotton 168, 172-173, 177
Diaper 173
Lumberjack.168, 209
Outing.....172, 177
Shirting....168, 209
Wool 173, 204-206, 209
Flannel Shirts.426-433
Flannelette Wear 135, 138-139, 150-151, 156-157
Flaps, Auto Rim..466
Flashings, Chimney 1080
Flashlights 667
Flashlight Batteries 666
Flashlight Bulbs..666
Flat Crepes..216, 218
Flatirons 970
Flatirons, Electric 662
Flatiron Handles..970
Flaxons 165
Flinch Cards......578
Flints, Lighter....618
Floats, Tank.....1066
Floats, Veterinary.645
Float Blades.......645
Float Valves...... ....1005, 1066

Floor
Boards, Auto....494
Brushes 972

Floor—Cont'd
Coverings ...823-841
Drains 1013
Hooks 1000
Lamps 657
Mops 972
Mop Oil........1027
Oil 1027
Paint.....1023, 1027
Polish 1027
Registers 976
Scrapers and Blades 987
Tile 1086
Trays, Stove.... 930-933, 934A, 976
Varnish 1031
Wax 1027
Waxing Brushes 1027
Flooring 1088
Flooring Clamps.985
Flooring Nails.....997
Floss, Dental......635
Floss, Embroidery.250
Floss, Knitting....250
Flouncing....248-249
Flour, Paste.....1032
Flour Mills.......1063
Flour Sifters......967

We are headquarters for lowest prices on dependable *Woodworking Machinery*. Whether your needs are large or small, be sure to send for our Woodworking Machinery Catalog, 528KA.

Flowers
Artificial ...239-240, 572, 921 - 922
Boutonnieres 103, 233, 242-243
Bulbs (in Bowls).614
Cake 607
Corsage 242-243
Hat 103
Table 921-922
Wax 121
Flower Baskets...920
Flower Baskets, Electric 572
Flower Bowls..... ....240, 921, 925
Flower Making Supplies 802
Flower of the Flax Linens...223, 226-227
Flower Vases
Auto............479, 491
Bronze Finished.766
Dutch Silver.....238
Electric 656
Glass...921-923, 925
Japanese 240
Silver 765
Flue Cleaners......961
Flush Plates.......659
Flutes 682
Flute Cleaners.....684
Fobs 728
Folds, Music.......705
Folders, Birth Announcement 639
Folders, Photo.....800

Folding
Bathtubs 641, 883, 1009
Benches 971
Cameras 798-799
Chairs.......499, 849
Cots.........499, 887
Couches 888-889
Crates 1074
Dressing Tables, Babies' 883

Folding—Cont'd
Go-Carts 899
Ladders 1034
Screens 903
Stands, Stove....498
Stepladders 1034
Stools 499
Stoves 498
Tables 902-903
Tables, Camp....499
Tables, Radio....712
Yards, Babies'..882
Folios (Bags).....705
Folios, Music...... ....677, 682, 702-703

Foods
Babies' 639
Birds' 646
Dog 525
Invalids'....639, 646
Poultry 644
Stock 645
Food Choppers and Accessories. 968-969
Food Cookers, Stock 1066
Food Jugs..........498
Food Pusher Sets. 754-755
Foot
Boards, Auto....479
Bolts 978
Pumps 453
Remedies....636, 643
Rests, Auto.......480
Scrapers 979
Tubs 976
Valves, Pump..1014
Warmers 639-640
Wheels, Jewelers'718
Footings, Net......248

Football Goods 520, 524
Footballs, Boys'... ....520, 579
Footwear —See Shoes, Oxfords, etc.
Force Cups.......1016
Force Pumps...... 1014-1016
Forceps, Veterinary 645
Foreign Languages.....784, 788
Forges 993
Forge Blowers......993

Forks
Alfalfa 1000
Bicycle Repair..452
Cake 756
Coke 998
Cold Meat....... ....754-759, 761
Crupper 1054
Grapple 1000
Harpoon Hay...1000
Hay.......998, 1000
Lemon 238
Manure 998
Olive 761
Oyster..754-755, 757
Pickle 238, 754-759, 761

Forks—Cont'd
Salad 754-757, 759, 761
Scoop 998
Spading 998
Table, Silver....... 754-761
Fork and Knife Sets.527, 533, 754-761
Fork and Spoon Sets, Babies'.... ....754, 756, 764
Fork, Knife and Spoon Sets...... ....533, 754-760, 765
Fork, Knife and Spoon Sets, Children's 754-759, 764
Fork Handles, Farm 998
Forms, Dress.......256
Formaldehyde Candles 641
Fortune Tellers... ....576, 578
Foulards 171
Foundations, Hair.122
Foundations, Wax Comb 1069
Founts, Holy Water 766
Fountains, Hog.1066
Fountains and Heaters, Poultry 926, 1075
Fountain Combs..634

Fountain Pens751-753, 793
Fountain Pen and Stand Sets..751, 793
Fountain Pen Inks 752, 792
Fountain Syringes 640

Frames
Door 1087
Drying......147, 970
Handbag 254
Honey 1069
Jewelers' Saw ..718
Photo 612, 614, 800
Printing 800
Saw 983
Window 1086
Franklin Sewing Machines ...198-201
Fraternity Jewelry 732-733, 744-745, 747
Freezers 969
Freezometers 497

Freight Rates 544-545
French Books.784, 788
French Fryers.....965
French Serges.....204
French Window Hardware ...978-979
Frets, Guitar......676
Friction Hoists .1076
Friction Pulleys 1040, 1043
Friction Tape......482
Friendship Spoons.761
Fringes
Curtain 815
Dress 249
Fancywork 249, 256
Rug 824
Shade 820-821
Frocks—See Dresses.
Frock Prints...... 169, 171, 213-215, 218
Frogs, Artificial..515
Frogs, Violin Bow 670
Fronts, Bridle...1052
Fronts, Nest......1074
Fronts, Water, Stove 945
Fruits, Artificial..921
Fruits, Candied...606
Fruits, Dried.....606

Fruit
Baskets 762
Bowls, Chinese.239
Bowls, Glass 921-922, 925
Bowls, Silver....762
Cake 606
Canning Outfits.969
Crushers 968
Jars 927
Jar Caps, Rings. 646, 927
Jar Holders.......969
Knives ....754, 756 - 757, 759, 761
Parers 968
Presses 968-969
Slicers 968

Frying Pans 498, 965, 967
Fudge 608
Fudge Aprons....245
Fuel, Carbide Lamp 514
Fulton Saws...982-984
Fumigators 641
Funnels 493, 968
Funnels, Conductor 1083

Fur Goods
Caps, Men's.....412
Cloth 210-211
Coats, Men's ...379
Coats, Women's, Misses' 18-20
Collars 246-247
Cuffs 246-247
Gloves 416, 419
Mittens, ..416, 419
Scarfs and Chokers 19-20
Trimmings...246-247
Fur Stretchers....513
Fur Tanners 513

Furnaces
Butchers' 1066
Heating 958-961
Parlor 930-934
Soldering 1016
Furnace Cement....962
Furnace Pipes.....961
Furnace Regulators 963
Furnace Scoops ...998
Furnishings, Home, Books on1017
Furnishings, Men's, Boys' 126, 410-448

Furniture
Bedroom ....858-866, 875 - 876, 880 - 881, 884-898, 903, 906-907
Breakfast Room 848, 851
Camp 499
Dining Room ...847-849, 852-857
Fiber...878-879, 883
Kitchen ...842-846, 848-851
Lawn...849, 877-879
Library .... 865, 873 - 879, 900 - 905, 908 - 909
Living Room .... 867-879, 900 - 904, 908
Nursery 880-883
Office...846, 908-909
Porch..849, 877-879
Reed 877-883
School .... 647, 849, 908 - 909
Toy....580, 582-584
Furniture Casters.977
Furniture Cover Cloth 181
Furniture Enamels 1024, 1026
Furniture Finishing and Repairing, Books on...785
Furniture Gimp.. ....812-813, 1003
Furniture Glides..977
Furniture Lacquer 1024-1025, 1030
Furniture Polish.1027
Furniture Varnish 1024, 1030-1031
Furniture Wax..1027
Furniture Webbing.812
Fuses, Electric.658, 666

G

Gag Swivels......1058
Gaiters 342-343
Galena 716
Galoshes 336-338
Galvanized Pipe...961
Galvanized Steel.1082
Galvanized Wire.1072
Games..526, 576-579
Game Books...779, 783
Game Calls........510
Game Shears.533, 759
Game Smokers.....513
Game Traps...512-513

GARAGES
Write for Sectional Garage Catalog

Garage Aprons 381, 387
Garage Equipment 493, 496
Garage Hardware 496, 980
Garage Stoves 937
Garage Tanks......456
Garage Tents......501
Garage Tools..... ....496, 992, 996
Garden Hose.......998
Garden Implements and Tools 998-999, 1063
Garlands.572, 575, 802
Garment Bags.....254
Garment Hangers 233, 254, 978
Garment Mending Tissue 255

Garters
Babies' 147, 156
Boys'..233, 253, 446
Girls'........233, 253
Men's 446
Women's ...233, 253
Garter Elastic.....255
Garter Sets....233, 241
Garter Waists.253, 293

Gas
Fitters' Tools... 984, 989, 997, 1016
Heaters 939
Hot Plates..942-943
Lamps, Carbide.514
Logs 1084
Pipe 1013
Stoves 942-946
Stove Lighters...944
Stove Ovens.956-957
Tubing 939
Water Heaters.1009
Gaskets
Asbestos 482
Copper 482
Cork 474
Cylinder Head..474
Pipe Union 1013
Gasket Cement.469, 474

Gasoline
Cans........484, 941
Engines...1041-1043
Engine Books.....785
Engine Oils.....457
Filters......480, 486
Funnels....493, 968
Furnaces 1016
Gauges 480
Lamps 929
Lamp Generators.929
Lanterns 514
Mantles......514, 929
Measures 493
Pumps....456, 1014
Savers, Auto.....480
Siphons 498
Storage Tanks...456
Stoves.....498, 941
Torches 1016
Tubing 480
Gates, Driveway..1070
Gates, Porch.......882
Gates, Walk.1072-1073
Gate Castings....1072
Gate Hooks.......980
Gate Steels......1070
Gate Valves......1012
Gateleg Tables.....902

Gauges
Bias Cutting....197
Butt 986
Feeler, Metal...990
Gasoline 480
Jointer 987
Mainspring 718
Oil, Auto........480
Plane 987
Pressure..1011, 1013
Saw Tooth.......984
Tire, Auto........467
Water....1011, 1013
Gauge Cocks.....1013
Gauge Knives....1054
Gauge Tubes.....1013
Gauge Wheels, Plow 1060

Gauntlets
Boys' 416
Girls' 416
Men's 418-421
Riding 1051

For Information About the Names of Colors See Page 549

Hind's Honey and Almond Creams.631

Hinges
Cupboard 979
Door 978-980
Spring 978
Strap 980
T 980
Hinge Hasps........980
Hip and Back Straps 1054
Hip Boots.. 335, 339
Hip Reducers.........113, 116-119
Histories 782
Hitches, Rope....1000
Hitch Attachments, Plow....1002
Hitching Straps..1054

Hives and Accessories..1069
Hobbles, Cow.....974
Hobbles, Horse...1052
Hobby Horses.....587

Hockey Caps
Babies' 161
Boys' ...414-415, 424-425
Girls' ..131, 161, 415
Men's.......412, 415
Women's ..131, 415
Hockey Pucks......516
Hockey Skates.516-517
Hockey Sticks......516
Hods, Coal.........976
Hoes 998
Hoe Attachments, Cultivator 1063
Hog Dips...........645
Hog Feeds..........645
Hog Feeders........1066
Hog Fencing........1071
Hog Houses.......1066
—Or See Special Catalog 570
Hog Markers.......975
Hog Oil..............1066
Hog Oilers..........1066
Hog Remedies......645
Hog Ringers and Rings 975
Hog Scalders.......1066
Hog Tamers.........975
Hog Troughs.........1066-1067
Hog Waterers.........1066-1067
Hohner Musical Instruments 677-679, 702
Hoists......1000, 1076
Hoisting Rope...1000

Holders
Baggage 495
Cake Candle.......607
ChristmasCandle.575
Christmas Tree..574
Cigar 621
Cigarette....491, 621
Clarinet Reed....684
Cymbal 683-684
Dental Floss.....635
Dictionary 784
Door 977-978
Door, Auto.........479
Drum 683
Duck, Hunters'..510
Felt Packing......514
Fruit Jar............969
Garage Door..........496, 980
Harmonica 677
Horse Tail..........1058
Ladder Rung....1034
License......472, 483
Moth Ball..........646
Pen 238, 794
Pipe 1015
Post Card..........800
Pot 245
Rope Sling.....1000
Sash 978
Seed Corn..........998
Shoe 344
Silverware 245
Spoon 765
Starting Crank..476
Toilet Paper....1010
Tooth Brush.....1010
Toothpick...765, 920
Towel 1010
Tumbler 1010
Violin 703
Watch Movement 718
Holdbacks 1002
Holdback Straps.1054
Hole Diggers.......999, 1014-1015
Hollow Augers......988
Hollow Punches...981

Holly Paper.......573
Hollywood Bags 104-106
Holy Bibles...786-787
Holywater Founts.766

Homes .1090-1091
Home Decorating Suggestions.785, 1017
Homestudy Books and Courses.785, 788
Hondas 1052
Hones 529
Honey and Almond Creams....631
Honey Cough Syrups 643
Honey Dishes......927
Honey Making Supplies 1069
Hoods, Women's.........90, 103, 127
Hood Clamp Silencers 477
Hood Covers, Auto.497
Hoof Cutters......993
Hoof Dressing.....457
Hoof Parers........993
Hoof Rasps........990

Hooks
Bathroom 1010
Belt 994
Bird Cage.........970
Boot 319
Button 612
Cant 982
Chain 982
Clothesline..970, 977
Coat 978
Conductor Pipe.1083
Crochet.....250, 254
Cup 977
Curtain Rod.....822
Fish 515
Floor 1000
Gate 980
Grab Chain.......982
Hame 1058
Harness 1058
Hat 978
Husking 998
Ladder 1034
Picture 822
Screw 977
Singletree 1002
Spoon 515
Tassel 822
Track Hanging.1000
Hooks and Eyes....977
Hooks and Eyes, Dress 255
Hooks and Staples.980
Hook Bolts.......1068
Hoops, Fancywork.256
Hope Chests..906-907
Hoppers, Poultry Feed 1074
Hopper Closets...1005
Horehound...608, 643

Horns
Auto...472, 474, 484
Band 681
Bicycle 453
Hearing 770
Shoe...233, 615, 764
Toy 593
Horn Buttons, Auto 472
Horses, Rocking.............587, 589
Horses, Stitching.1054

Horse
Bits 1051-1052
Blankets ..1056-1057
Blanket Pins....1058
Bridles 1051-1052
Brushes 1056
Clippers..1054, 1056
Collars 1049
Collar Pads.........1049, 1055
Combs 1056
Covers 1057
Halters 1053
Harness 1046-1048, 1054
Hobbles 1052
Liniments 643
Mouth Floats......645
Rasps 990
Shears 1053-1054
Speculums 645
Tail Clasps........1058
Ties 1053
Whips 1057
Horseradish Graters 969

Horseradish Jars..765
Horseshoes.........993
Horseshoes, Pitching.....523, 526, 576
Horseshoe Calks...993
Horseshoe Nails...993
Horseshoeing Tools 990, 993

Hose
Garden 998
Gas Stove.........939
Pump, Auto........487
Radiator, Auto..471
Spray 1015
Suction 995
Hose Bibbs........1012
Hose Extensions..1015
Hose Nozzles 998
Hose Supports
Babies'.......147, 156
Children's....156, 253
Women's 253

All Leather Vest
Weatherproof Wearproof

There is no better protection against wind and cold than leather. This genuine U. S. Army leather vest, new and first quality, has a heavy-weight olive drab all wool melton lining to give plenty of warmth and body comfort.
Full size. Will not bind anywhere. May be worn either over or under a coat. A very useful garment for outdoor work or sport. Every man should have one.

For Complete Details See Page 385

Hosiery
..........149, 259-273
Hosiery, Athletic........516, 518, 523
Hosiery Feet.........260, 266, 268
Hosiery Guards, Splash 254
Host Chairs.........848-849, 852-857
Hot Air Furnaces.................958-961
Hot Dish Trays....928
Hot Plates, Electric 662
Hot Plates, Gas.................942-943
Hot Plates (Stove).967
Hot Water Bags 639-640
Hot Water Boilers 962-963
Hot Water Bottles 639-640
Hot Water Coils...961
Hot Water Heating, Books on...785

Hot Water Heating Plants 962-963
Hot Water Tanks.1009
Hotbed Coverings..177
Hotbed Glass.......977
Hotel Glassware....926
Hotel Tableware..............914, 921
Houbigant's Preparations 630
Hounds, Wagon.............1002-1003

Houses
Already Cut....1090
Garages (Special Catalog).........570
Hog 1066
—Or See Special Catalog 570
Poultry (Special Catalog) 570
Ready Made.........1089-1090

House Dresses 81-83, 86-88
House Dress Goods 165-171, 174-176
House Numbers...977
House Paints.................1022-1023
House Paint Color Suggestions 1017
House Slippers.......310-312, 315, 334
House Wiring Supplies 658-659
Housing, Harness.1053
Housing Letters.1053

How to Order 546
How to Take Measurements ..548
Hubs, Bicycle......453
Hub Covers.........476

Hub Parts, Auto.........474, 476, 495
Huck Towels..230-231
Huck Toweling....228
Hug-Me-Tights ...127
Humidifiers 962
Humidors.....615, 618
Humorous Books.......773, 776, 782

Hunters'
Ammunition.508-509
Axes........510, 982
Belts 510
Boots, Shoes......335
Caps....412-413, 511
Clothing 400-401
Duck Holders....510
Flashlights 667
Game Calls.......510
Gloves 511
Guns, Rifles.502-507
Hats 412
Hatchets...510, 982
Knives..510-511, 532
Lamps.......514, 666
Overs 335
Tents 501
Husking Hooks, Pins 998
Hydrant Clamps.1012
Hydrant Cocks...1012
Hydrogen Peroxide 643
Hydrometers 468-469, 496, 714-715
Hygeia Nursers....639
Hygiene, Books on 783
Hypo 800

I

Ice Box Dishes...926
Ice Cream Freezers 969
Ice Cream Glasses 921, 926
Ice Cream Slicers 755-757, 761

Ice Creepers.......344
Ice Skates and Supplies.516-517
Ice Skates, Kiddies'579
Ice Tongs...........982
Iced Tea Pitchers.927
Iced Tea Sets.920, 925
Iced Tea Spoons.........754-757, 759
Iced Tea Tumblers.920-921,925-926
Ignition Dry Cells...665-666, 714
Ignition Goods, Auto........473, 482
Illusion, Bridal....243
Imitation Diamonds 740
Imitation Leather 813, 1003

Implements and Farm Machinery 1036-1044, 1060-1061, 1063-1065
Implement Paints 1021
Implement Repairs 1060-1061, 1063
Incense Burners and Incense.239, 630
Increasers, Pipe..1012

Incubators 1074-1075
Indelible Inks......797
Indelible Pencils..792
Indian Blankets...187
Indian Head Cloth 174, 178
Indian Play Suits.355
Indian Stories.781-782
Indicators, Speed.990
Indoor Ball Goods.522
Indoor Ball Shoes.524
Induction Coils....666

Infants'
—See "Baby Goods."
Inflaters, Bladder.519
Ingram's Creams..631
Initial Plates, Auto.490
Initial Rings.......733, 742, 748, 750

Inks
Drawing 797
Fountain Pen752,792
Indelible 797
Waterproof 797
White 801
Ink Erasers.792, 794
Inkstands 751, 766, 793
Inkwells..751, 766, 793
Inlets 181
Inner Casings.....466

Inner Tubes
Auto Tire...459-464
Bicycle Tire........454
Inner Tube Repairs....454, 466-467
Insecticides 644-646
Insertions.. 248-249
Insoles.......339, 344
Instruction Books, Music 677, 682, 702-703

Instruments
Band 680-683
Drawing 797
Leveling 986
Poultry Raisers'.644
Telegraph 666
Veterinary 645
Insulated Wire..........658, 666, 716
Insulating Staples.666
Insulating Tape....658
Insulators, House Wiring 658-659
Insulators, Radio..716
Insulators, Phone.666
Interior Decorating 785 1017

INVALID CHAIRS
See Page 641
—Or Write for Invalid Chair Catalog

Invalids' Cushions.641
Invalids' Foods....639

Iodent Tooth Paste.635
Irish Mails 602
Iron, Bar 980

Irons
Body, Truck.....481
Curling.....123, 664
Electric 662
Neckyoke 1002
Plane 987
Sadirons....662, 970
Singletree 1002
Soldering 997
Soldering, Electric 716
Tire 467
Waffle.........663, 967
Yarning 1016
Iron Cement.......474
Iron Kettles.967, 1066
Iron Pegs, Tent....501
Iron Pipe and Fittings 1012-1013
Iron Tonics...642, 645

Ironing Machines 913
Ironing Boards....970
Ironing Boards, Built-In 1086
Ironing Board Covers and Pads....177
Ironwork Bolts.....981
Ironwork Paints..1021
Irregular Curves...797
Irrigation Pumps.1015
Isinglass 938
Italian Dictionaries 784
Ivory Pyralin Toilet Articles.......612-613, 616-617

J

Jacks
Auto..487, 496, 1001
Garage 496
Ladder 1034
Pump 1044
Radio 717
Wagon 1001
Jack Screws 1001

Jackets
Babies'..144, 150-151
Cardigan 127
Chamois 638
Cooker 1066
Overall 360-361, 386-389
Slicker 408
Women's, Girls'.127
Work 403, 406
—Also See Lumberjacks and Sweaters.
Jackknives 532
Jam Jars 920, 924-925, 927
Jambs, Door......1087
Jap Rose Soap.....635
Japanese Gift Items 232, 238-241, 244
Japanese Rugs.....823

Jars
Candy......921, 927
Cereal 926
Cigar.........618, 766
Cooky 927
Food, Vacuum...498
Fruit 927
Horseradish 765
Jam.920, 924-925, 927
Marmalade.920, 925
Puff 764
Refrigerator 926
Slop 976
Spice 926
Tobacco 766
Jar Caps 646
Jar Cap Rubbers..646
Jar Holders, Fruit.969
Jardiniers 921
Jardiniere Stands..903
Jazz Bands 592
Jazz Banjos 673
Jazz Bells 683
Jazzbo 702
Jelly Dishes..765, 927
Jelly Glasses.........926
Jelly Presses........968
Jelly Servers..756, 761
Jerkins....385, 402-403
Jerseys, Athletic...520
Jersey Cloth..175, 206

Jews' Harps........702
Jewels, Watch....718
Jewel Boxes.......238, 612, 764, 766
Jewelers' Tools and Supplies 718

Jewelry.719-750
Babies' 748
Birthday ..741-742, 748-750
Diamond.730-733,743
Fraternity ..732-733, 744-745, 747
Imitation Diamonds 740
Jigs, Rebabbitting.474
Jiggers, Golf.......523
Jobbing Stones, Jewelers' 718
Jock Straps...519, 637
Joints, Swivel......489
Joint Finishers...1077
Joint Runners ...1016
Jointers, Plow.....1060
Jointers, Saw.....984
Jointer Gauges....987
Jointer Planes.....987
Joists 1088
Joke Books..........782
Joke Goods..........596
Journals 794
Journal Grease....457
Jugs, Communion.765
Jugs, Food..........498
Jugs, Syrup 762
Jugs, Water..498, 926
Juice Extractors.............968-969
Juliets .310-312, 315
Jump Spark Coils.665
Jumpers, Overall........360-361, 386-389
Junior Lamps......657
Junket Powders...646

K

Kalsomines 1024, 1032
Kalsomine Brushes ..1028-1029
Kalsomine Sizing.1032
Kalsomine Sponges 1032
Kasha Cloth........205
Kegs 968
Keg Spigots.........968
Kennel Chains.....525
'Kerchiefs, Cold Cream 631
Kerosene
Barrels 456
Cans 976
Heaters(Water)1009
Lamps 929
Lamps, Bicycle..453
Lanterns 976
Pumps 456, 1015
Stoves 498, 938-939, 955-957

Kettles
Caldron 1066
Cooking.498,964-967
Copper 967
Iron 967, 1066
Lard 967, 1066
Preserving...964-967
Steamer 257, 965-966, 969
Strainer 965
Tea 964-967
Kettle Cleaners.646,964
Kettle Covers.964, 967
Kettle Menders....646
Kewpie Kameras..798
Keys, Banjo........676
Keys, Skate.........516
Keys, Telegraph...666
Keys, Ukulele......676
Keys, Watch........718
Keys, Wireless.....666
Key Pads, Clarinet.684
Key Purses... 622-623
Keyhole Saws.......984
Khaki Cloth.........166
Kid Gloves ...125-126, 415-417, 432-433
Kidney Plasters....643
Killers, Vermin 644-646
Kimonos.......84-85
Kimonos, Babies'..150
Kimono Cloth.165, 172-173, 210, 215-219

Kits
Camp Cooking..498
Clarinet Repair..684
First Aid........485
Saxophone Repair 684
Tool, Auto.482, 488
Tool, Household.985
Vacuum Lunch.498
Violinists' 670

Kitchen
Cabinets 842-845
Chairs 848-851
Clocks......767, 769
Cupboards ..845-846
Curtains 807-809
Cutlery.....527, 533
Furniture 842-846, 848-851
Heaters 945-946
Lights 653-654
Rugs...823, 829-830
Saws, Blades....533
Sinks 1006-1007
Spoons 533
Stools 846
Stoves 940-957
Tables..846, 850-851
Towels, Towelings...223, 228-230
Utensils.527,533, 926, 928, 964-969
Kleinert's Goods.. ....146-147, 252-253
Kneaders, Bread..967
Knee Bandages...636
Knee Caps.........636
Knee Length Hosiery 260
Knee Pads..519, 1052

Knickers
Boys' 363
Girls'.......74, 519
Men's 523
Misses' 72-74
Women's..72-74, 519

Knives
Blacksmiths' 993
Boning 533
Bread.......527, 533
Butchers' 533
Butter 754-761
Butter Spreaders [illegible]
Cake....755-757, 761
Carving Sets.527, 759
Castrating 645
Cattlemen's 532
Cheese 761
Cobblers' 344
Cuticle......612, 764
Dehorning 975
Drawing 987
Drop 794
Fingernail 617
Food Chopper...968
Fruit 754, 756-757, 759, 761
Glaziers' .1028-1029
Harness Makers'1054
Hay 999
Horseshoers' 993
Hunting.510-511,532
Kitchen.....527, 533
Painters' 1029
Paperhangers'...1028
Paring 533
Penknives..527, 532
Penknives, Gold.747
Pie.....755-757, 761
Pocket 510-511, 527, 532
Putty 1028-1029
Skinning.510,532-533
Slicing 533
Steak.......533, 759
Sticking 510
Table, Silver.754-761
Table, Stainless Steel.......527, 533
Table, Steel.527, 533
Tool 532
Tree Pruning.....999
Knife and Chain Sets 532, 747
Knife and Fork Sets 527, 533, 754-761
Knife, Fork and Spoon Sets...... ....533, 754-760, 765
Knife, Fork and Spoon Sets, Children's 583, 754-759, 764
Knife Grinders.996-997
Knife Steels........533
Knife Switches....666
Knit Goods
—See "Sweaters, Caps, Gloves, Etc."
Knitting, Books on.250
Knitting Cotton...251
Knitting Needles..250
Knitting Yarns....250

Knobs
Base 978
Brass 979
Dial 717
Door 978-979
Furniture 979
Glass 979
House Wiring...658
Insulating, Radio716
Percolator 964
Kodaks 799
Kotex Napkins....253
Kraut Cutters.....969

L

"LL" Sheeting...178
Labels, Stock Marking 975
Laces and Embroideries....248-249
Laces, Shoe.......344
Lace Collars and Cuffs 242-243
Lace Curtains 803-806
Lace Curtain Materials 810-811
Lace Leather......995
Lace Panels... ....803-804, 806, 811
Lace Vestees......242
Lacers, Middy.....249
Lacing, Belt.......995
Lacing Machines..994
Lacing Needles....519
Lacquer, Auto...1035
Lacquer, Furniture.1024-1025, 1030
Lacquer Brushes.1029
Lacquer Thinners.1025
Ladders 1034
Ladder Hooks, Jacks, Rung Replacers.1034
Ladles
Cream 754-755, 758-759, 761
Gravy..[illegible], 761
Plumbers' 1016
Salad Dressing.. ....757, 759
Soup 966
Lady Janis' Toilet Preparations.630-633
Lambrequins 803

Lamps
Alcohol 718
Auto 472, 482-483, 496
Bicycle 453
Boudoir 655-656
Camp 514, 666
Carbide 514
Christmas Tree..575
Desk, Electric....655
Electric House..659
Flashlight 666
Floor, Electric...657
Gasoline 929
Girandole 656
Night 929
Oil 929
Radio Cabinet...713
Sanctuary 766
Sewing 197, 929
Table....655-656, 929
Therapeutic 664
Tungsten 659
Vigil 766
Lamp Bases..240, 657
Lamp Bulbs
Auto 472, 483
Bicycle 453
Flashlight 666
House 659
Lamp Burners.....929
Lamp Chimneys...929
Lamp Cords.......659
Lamp Cords, Auto.482
Lamp Extensions..929
Lamp Generators..929
Lamp Globes......929
Lamp Guards 659
Lamp Lacquer, Auto 1035
Lamp Mantels.....929
Lamp Parts, Auto 472, 483, 494
Lamp Pulls 233
Lamp Regulators..472
Lamp Shades...... ....239, 655-657, 929
Lamp Shade Painting Outfits..256, 795
Lamp Shade Trimmings......249, 256

Lamp Wicks.......929
Lampblack..1032, 1035
Lanterns
Electric.649, 654, 666
Gasoline 514
Oil 976
Lantern Batteries..666
Lantern Bulbs.....666
Lantern Globes 514, 976
Lap Protectors....147
Lard Kettles.967, 1066
Lard Presses 968
Lariats 1052
Lariat Rope......1000
Larvex 646
Lashes, Whip....1057
Lasts, Shoe Repair 344
Latches
Barn Door.......980
Casement 978
Door 979
Night 979
Lath, Wood......1088
Lathes and Accessories......983, 996
Lathes, Jewelers'..718
Lathes, Valve.488, 496
Lathing Hatchets.985
Lathing Nails.....997
Latigos 1051
Latigo Straps....1051
Latin Books..784, 788
Launderite Bed Linens......179, 192

Laundry
Benches 971
Mailing Cases....535
Stoves 937, 942-943, 953-954
Tubs.......913, 1010
Tub Bibbs......1012
Utensils 970-971
Lavatories 1006-1007
Lavatory Faucets.1012
Lavoris 635
Law, Books on...788
Lawns 223
Lawn Fencing ...1077
Lawn Furniture.. ....849, 877-879
Lawn Mowers.....998
Lawn Mower Sharpeners 996
Lawn Sprinklers..998
Laxatives.642-643, 645
Layettes 145
Lazy Straps......1054
Leads, Bull......1053
Leads, Cattle......974
Leads, Dog........525
Lead, Pencil.......793
Lead, Pig.........1012
Lead, Sheet.....1012
Lead Joint Runners1016
Lead Melting Pots and Ladles.......1016
Lead Pencils 792, 794
Lead Pencils, Magazine.....751, 793-794
Lead Pipe and Fittings 1012-1013
Lead Solvents.....511
Lead-Ins, Radio...716

Leather
Artificial..813, 1003
Harness 1053
Lace 995
Shoe 344
Leathers, Pump...1015
Leather Aprons....993
Leather Bags.104-106
Leather Belt Lacing 995
Leather Belting....995
Leather Blouses403-404
Leather Cement...344
Leather Cleaners..344
Leather Coats.... ....347, 358, 402-405
Leather Drapes...818
Leather Dressing. 344, 456-457, 513, 1035
Leather Dyes......344
Leather Gimp....1003
Leather Jackets...405
Leather Knives... ....344, 1054
Leather Punches..981
Leather Shoestrings344
Leather Tanners...513
Leather Vests.... ....385, 400, 402
Leather Washers..658
Leaves, Album....801

Leaves, Loose Paper..........796, 801
Ledgers 794
Legs, Sewing Machine 197
Leg Bands, Poultry 1075
Leg Rests, Stove 934B

Leggings
Army 541
Boys'........335, 343
Children's..144, 342
Elastic 636
Girls' 342
Men's.335, 343, 541
Women's 342
Lemon Dishes.....765
Lemon Face Creams631
Lemon Forks.....238
Lemonade Sets 920, 925
Lemonade Tumblers 920-921, 925-926
Lenses, Headlight...472, 483, 494
Le Page's Cement.646
Le Page's Glue... ....646, 1032
Letters
Aluminum 977
Harness 1053
Rubber Type.....792
Steel 986
Stock Marking..975
Uniform 518
Letter Files.........794
Letter Openers... ....233, 238
Letter Paper....... ....776, 790-791
Letter Writing, Books on...783, 788
Lettering, Books on 785
Levels 986
Level and Square.986
Leveling Instruments 986
Library Furniture 873-879, 900-901, 905, 908-909
Lice Killers.......644
License Holders 472, 483

License Plate Bolts 484
Licorice Sticks...642
Lids, Kettle..964, 967
Lifts, Safety.....1000
Lifts, Sash........978
Lift Pumps......1014
Lifters, Valve.474, 486

Lights
Auto 472, 482-483, 496
Bicycle 453
Campers' 514, 666-667
Cap 514
Carbide 514
Curtain, Auto... ....478, 490
Fishing 514
Flash 667
Hunters' 514, 667

Lights—Cont'd
Miners' 514, 667
Panel, Radio.....713
Sewing Machine.197
Tent 666
Light Tips, Carbide 514
Lighters, Cigar... ..482, 618, 662, 746
Lighters, Fire.....513
Lighters, Gas Stove 944
Lighter Flints 618

Lighting Fixtures 648-654
Lighting Outfits, Christmas Tree..575
Lighting Plant Batteries 665
Lighting Rings.....955
Lighting Rings, Brooder 1075
Lightning Arresters.......666, 716
Lightning Rods and Fittings....1076
Lime Sowers.....1065
Limestone Grit...644
Lines
Chalk 986
Clothes 970
Fishing 515
Harness..1051, 1053
Plow 1053
Tow 467
Wire 970
Line Buckles.....1058
Line Rings.........1058
Lineman's Gloves.418
Linemen's Tools... ..658, 666, 989, 1000

Linens
By the Yard
Art 223
Bed 223
Dress 223
Handkerchief ...223
Lingerie 223
Table ......[illegible], 228
Toweling...223, 228

Linen Goods
Collars, Men's...446
Collars and Cuffs.242
Doilies 226
Fancywork .244-245
Handkerchiefs 234-237
Pillowcases 223
Tablecloths and Napkins 225-227, 230-232
Thread 251
Towels.228, 230-232
Linen Testers......771
Linene..170, 174, 180
Lineshafts...994, 1041

Lingerie
...132-137, 164, 290
Lingerie Braid....254
Lingerie Clasps... ....254, 749

Lingerie Cloth
Cotton 165, 170-171, 174-176
Linen 223
Rayon 214-215
Silk 212-213, 215-219
Lingerie Ribbons..241
Lingerie Tape.....254
Liniments 643

Linings
Brake Band.475, 489
Carpet 824
Coat, Dress.171, 175, 210-214, 217
Diaper 146
Hat 103
Linoleum 824
Transmission Band 475, 489
Vacuum Bottle...498
Links
Cable Chain......982
Chain, Bicycle...452
Cuff 446, 732, 746-747
Skid Chain.......484
Speedometer 489
Link Chain Belting 994

Linoleums
.........823, 826-830
How to Order...826
Linoleum Binding.824
Linoleum Cement.824
Linoleum Linings.824
Linoleum Paste....824
Linoleum Varnish 1031
Linseed Oil.......1022
Lipsticks 632
Liquid Embroidery.256
Liquid Face Powder 633
Liquid Glue.789, 1032
Liquid Paste.....789
Liquid Porcelain.1026
Liquid Smoke.....646
Listerine 635
Lithia Tablets.....643
Litters (Cots).....499
Litter Carriers and Attachments ...1000
Little Women's Coats 22-25
Liver Pills.........642
Living Room Furniture 867-879, 900-904, 908
"LL" Sheeting....178

Locks
Box 979
Cupboard 979
Dog Collar........525
Door 978-979
Drawer 979
Mail Box..........998
Padlocks....979, 998
Rope Sling.....1000
Screen Door......978
Sprocket 452
Steering Wheel..473
Tire Cable.........467
Trunk 979
Window 978
Lock Chains, Wagon 1064
Lock Washers.488, 981
Lockers, Army.....536
Lockers, Kitchen..845
Lockets 748
Locknuts 658
Lodge Emblems (Jewelry) ..732-733, 744-745, 747
Logs, Gas........1084
Log Chains........982
Log Hooks........982
Log Saws.....982-983
Log Saw Outfits.1041
Log Wedges.......982
Longcloth 176
Looking Glasses—See Mirrors.
Loom, Electric.....658
Looms, Carpet....196
Loom Fasteners...658
Loops, Curtain....804
Loops, Harness... ....1054, 1058
Loops, Portiere...804
Loops, Track Anchor 1068
Loose Leaf Books and Fillers.796, 801
Loose Pin Butts...979
Lotions........631, 635
Lotto Games......578
Loud Speakers 712-713

Lounges—See "Couches."
Lounge Covers....817
Lounging Robes... ....84-85, 445
Love, Books on...783
Loving Cups.......765
Low Boys.........862
Low Boy Mirrors.862
Lozenges.......608, 642
Lubricants, Phonograph 696
—For Other Lubricants See "Oils" and "Greases."
Lubricators, Auto Spring.........476, 493
Lubricators, Engine 1013
Luggage 535-537
Luggage Carriers, and Covers, Auto.495
Luggage Carriers, Bicycle 453

Lumber ... 1088

Lumberjacks
Boys' .158-160, 350, 362, 424-427
Girls' 72-73, 160, 162-163
Men's ..403-404, 428, 430-431, 438-439, 442-443
Misses' 72-73
Women's 72-73, 128-129
Lumberjack Bands 209
Lumberjack Flannels....168, 209
Lumberjack Outfits, Boys'... 354-355
Lumbermen's
Mittens 419
Overs.........335, 341
Sawing Outfits.1041
Socks........339, 341
Tools 982-983
Lunch Boxes, Pails ...498, 796, 965, 967
Lunch Cloths... ....230-232, 244
Lunch Kits.......498
Lunch Paper.......802
Luncheon Sets.... ..223, 232, 245, 802
Lysol 643

M

Machines
—See Name of Machine Wanted.
Machine Belts and Belting 994-995
Machine Bolts.....981
Machine Covers...501
Machine Oil....... ....456-457, 1032
Machinery, Concrete 1084
Machinery, Wood Working 983
Machinists' Books.785
Machinists' Tools and Supplies.... ..984-990, 992, 1016
Mackinaw Clothing.....359, 362, 379, 393, 399, 403

Made to Order CLOTHING
Men's—Young Men's
Mail Post Card on Page 540 for Free Book of Actual Cloth Samples

Madras 211
Magazines, Rifle..506
Magazine Baskets and Stands..879, 902
Magazine Pencils. 793-794
Magazine Racks...794
Magnesia 642
Magnets 666
Magnet Wire.......716

The Greatest Work Shoe Money Can Buy
Cost the Government Between $6.00 and $7.00

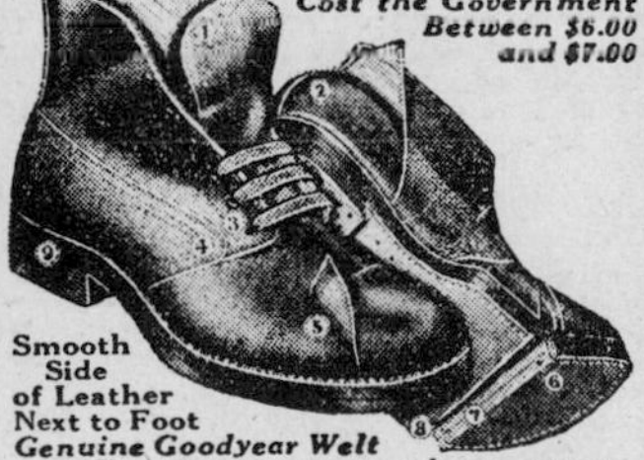

Smooth Side of Leather Next to Foot
Genuine Goodyear Welt

1—Tongue gusset sewed to upper; keeps out dirt and water. 2—Solid sole-leather counters. 3—Heavy brass eyelets. 4—Triple stitched with wax thread. 5—One-piece full vamp; cap stitched four times. 6—Full grain heavy oak tanned leather innersoles. 7—Two full grain leather heavy outersoles. 8—Canvas packing between inner and outer soles keeps shoe from creaking. 9—Five-ply leather heels.
Sewed-on soles; strongly reinforced.

See Page 326 for Complete Details.

Simoniz 493
Singletrees ....
.....1002-1003, 1063
Singletree Irons..1002
Sinks and Fittings
.....1006-1007, 1013
Sink Pumps.......1014
Siphons, Gasoline..498
Siphon Air Valves.962
Sizing, Burlap....1032
Sizing, Glue......1032
Sizing, Kalsomine.1032
Sizing, Painters'.1032
Sizing, Wallpaper.1032

Skates .516-517, 579
Skate Supplies.....516
Skating Cap Sets
...........131, 161
Skating Shoes
With Skates......517
Skating Socks.....516
Skeins, Wagon...1001
Sketch Books......779
Sketching Canvas..795
Skid Chains, Auto.484
Skid Chain Links..484
Skis and Supplies.516
Skiing Socks.......516
Skillets 967
Skin Stretchers....513
Skin Tanners.......513
Skinning Tools.....
....510, 513, 532-533

Skirts
Babies' ....
...150-151, 154-155
Girls' 75
Middy 75
Misses' 74
Sanitary 252
Women's 74
Skirt Boxes.......903
Skirt Fasteners....255
Skirt Hangers......254
Skirtings.. 166,
168, 177, 204-205,
207, 209-211, 214-215
Skunk Odor Removers 513
Slate Surfaced Roofing ..1078-1080
Slaw Cutters......969
Sleds 1064
Sleds, Children's...602
Sled Runners.....1064
Sledges 985
Sledge Handles....985

Sleeping Outfits
Babies' 150-151
Boys' 422-423
Children's ..156-157
Girls'...139, 156-157
Women's 139
Sleeves, Georgette.242
Sleigh Bells......1057
Sleigh Gear.......1064
Slicers, Fruit......968
Slicers, Ice Cream
.........755-757, 761
Slicers, Vegetable.969
Slicing Knives.......533

Slickers
Boys' 357
Girls' 21
Men's.......381, 408
Misses' 21
Women's 21
Slicker Aprons....381
Slicker Hats..21, 408
Slicker Oil.........408
Slicker Suits.......408
Slides, Harness...1058
Slides, Playground.525
Slides, Shuttle.....197
Slide Sets, Microscope 771
Slide Trombones..680
Sliding Door Hangers and Track....980
Sliding T Bevels..986
Slings, Wagon...1000
Sling Pulleys......1000

Slips
Babies' 155
Girls' 139,
141, 156-157, 164
Misses'.....139, 164
Pillow, Babies'...147
Pillow, Bed.192-
193, 223, 232, 244
Pillow, Stamped.244
Princess — See "Costume Slips."
Sanitary 252
Women's
132-134, 139-140
Slip Harness.......1054
Slip-On Bodies....
Auto 481

Slippers
Babies'......150, 316
Boudoir 310-312
Boys' 334
Children's 316
Dancing 524
Felt.....310-312, 334
Girls'.......309, 318
Gymnasium 524
Men's 334
Women's ....
301-309, 313-315
Women's, House
.......310-312, 315
Slipper Buckles...
121, 249, 738-739, 749
Slipper Fasteners..249
Slipper Soles.......344
Slop Jars..........976
Smelling Salts.....632

Smocks...... 88
Smock Cloths.....
169-170, 174-176, 180
Smoke Liquids,
Meat 646
Smokepipe and
Fittings 961
Smokers, Animal..513
Smokers, Bee....1069
Smoking Pipes....621
Smoking Stands..
...........618, 904
Smoking Tobacco.620
Smoothing
Brushes 1029
Snaps, Bag.......1058
Snaps, Harness..1058
Snaps, Rope.....1058
Snap Fasteners....255
Snap Fastener Tape255
Snares, Drum.....684
Snare Drums......683
Snare Drum Bags.683
Snaths, Scythe.....999
Snips, Tinners.....996
Saw Chains, Auto.484
Snow Shovels.....998
Snowshoes 516

Soaps
Babies'......635, 639
Harness ....[illegible]
Pumice 635
Shampoo 634
Shaving 635
Toilet 635
Soap Boxes.......639
Soap Dishes......1010
Soap Kettles.......967
Soccer Goods 520, 524
Society Emblems.
732-733, 744-745, 747

Socks
Army 272
Athletic.516, 518, 523
Boot.........339, 341
Boys'........260, 272
Children's 260
Guaranteed 259
Lumbermen's ..
...........339, 341
Men's ....
..259, 264, 270-273
Polar........339, 341
Rockford 272
Silk 273
Skating 516
Work 272

Sockets
Anti-Rattler 477
Curtain Pole......822
Electric 659
Headlight 472
Hex 488
Radio Tube.......717
Socket Finders.....659
Socket Wrenches,
Auto..475, 488, 496
Soda, Phosphate...642
Soda, Silicate of...491
Soda Mints.........642
Soda Recharges,
Extinguisher ...1016
Sodium Fluoride....644
Sodium Salicylate.643
Sofas..............884, 886
Sofa Covers........817
Sofa Pillows.......
..233, 244, 884, 886
Sofa Pillow Tops..239
Soft Collars 446
Soft Collar Cases..619
Soft Collar Pins...728
Softeners, Water.1010
Softener Salts.....1010
Soilpipe and Fittings 1012-1013
Soiesette 174

Solder
Household 997
Jewelers' 718
Plumbers' 1012
Radio 716
Silver 983
Solderine 646
Tinners' 997
Wire..........658, 997
Soldering Coppers
..............716, 997
Soldering Coppers,
Jewelers' 718
Soldering Fluid.....718
Soldering Furnaces 1016
Soldering Irons,
Electric 716
Soldering Outfits..997
Soldering Paste....
.............658, 997
Soles, Shoe..........344
Soles, Slipper.......344
Sole Plates.........344
Sole Leather........344
Solidified Alcohol..646
Solvents, Lead......511
Solvents, Nitro.....511
Solvents, Drain..1016
Sombreros 410
Song Books........
........677, 702-703
Song-O-Phones ...592
Song Restorers,
Bird 646
Song Whistles......684
Sounders, Wireless.666
Soundpost Setters.670
Soup Bowls, Plates
.....914-919, 921, 966
Soup Ladles........966
Soup Spoons........
.......754-759, 761
Soutache Braids....249
Souvenir Spoons...761
Sou'westers....357, 408
Sowers, Fertilizer.1065
Sowers, Lime......1065
Spades 998
Spading Forks......998
Spaghetti Tubing..716
Spanish Books.784, 788
Spark Coils....473, 665
Spark Guards......1084
Spark Plugs and
Sundries....473, 482
Spark Plug
Wrenches 475
Spats 342-343
Speakers, Loud.712-713
Speculums, Horse.645
Speed Indicators..990
Speedometers 489
Speedometer Parts.489
Spelling Boards.....590
Spelling, Books on.788
Spice Jars..........926
Spiders 967
Spigots, Keg.......968
Spindle Hubs.......453
Spinet Chairs.......905
Spinet Desks........905
Spirits Camphor...643
Spirits Peppermint.642
Spirits Turpentine.642
Spittoons.....926, 976
Splash Guards,
Hosiery 254
Splices, Trace......1058
Splicing Clamps....989
Spokes, Bicycle.....452
Spokes, Wagon...1003
Spoke Repairers...1002
Sponges, Bath......639
Sponges; Cleaning ..
....493, 646, 1032

Spoons
Babies' 764
Berry...754-759, 761
Dessert.......755, 760
Friendship 761
Golf 523
Grape Fruit......
......754-757, 759
Iced Tea.754-757, 759
Jelly 756, 761
Kitchen 533
Orange.754-757, 759
Soup....754-759, 761
Sugar 754-761
Table, Aluminum 533
Table Silver.754-761
Table, Steel.........533
Tea, Aluminum....533
Tea, Silver..754-761
Tea, Steel...........533
Spoon Holders.......765
Spoon Hooks........515
Spoon Trays.........924
Sport Clothing — See Lumberjacks, Knickers, Breeches, Hunters,' etc.

Sporting Goods .498-525
—Or See Special
Catalog 570
Spotlights.....483, 667
Spouts, Gutter...1083
Spout Strainers..1083
Spray Bath Brushes 1010
Spray Carts 1064
Spray Hose and
Fittings 1015
Spray Syringes....640

Sprayers
Barrel Pump...1015
Bucket 1015
Compressed Air.1015
Hand.......646, 1015
Medicine 641
Perfume 614, 630
Shower Bath...1010
Wheelbarrow 1015
Spraying Gloves....640
Spraying Materials
...........646, 1032
Spreads, Bed..168-
169, 194-195, 244-245
Spread Rollers....1058
Spreaders, Butter
...754-757, 759, 761
Spreaders, Harness1054
Spreaders, Manure1065
Spreaders, Toe.....636
Spreader Straps..1055

Springs
Auto 476, 492
Babies' Swing....588
Beds....890-891, 898
Bird Cage.........970
Bolster 1002
Clock 718
Door 978
Hair Clipper......530
Horse Clipper..1054
Phonograph 696
Shock Absorbers
...........477, 493
Steering, Auto...477
Tree Pruner.......999
Wagon 1002
Watch 718
Spring Balances...974

DAUNTLESS

Warm Air Circulator

Looks Like a Phonograph

Heats Like a Furnace

See Page 931

$5.00 DOWN

Spring Cotters 488
Spring Covers,
Auto 476
Spring Hinges.....978
Spring Lifters.474, 486
Spring Lubricators 476, 492
Spring Parts, Auto.476
Spring Punches....981
Spring Scales.972, 974
Spring Seats,
Wagon 1065
Spring Shackles...476
Spring Wagons...1044
Sprinklers, Lawn..998
Sprocket Chains,
Bicycle 452
Sprocket Locks....452
Sprouters, Oats..1075
Spurs, Drum..683-684
Spurs, Linemen's..666

Spurs, Riding....1051
Spur Straps......1051
Spyglasses 770-771
Squares, Halter..1058
Squares, Steel....986
Squares, T.........797
Squares, Try.......986
Square and Level..986
Squibbs' Tooth
Pastes 635
St. Christopher's
Medals 787
Stable Blankets..1056
Stable Brooms....1056
Stable Fittings...1068
Stable Sheets.....1056
Stable Ventilators.1082
Stack Covers......500
Stack Cover Cloth.177
Stackers, Cob....1062
Stackers, Hay....1000
Stacomb 634
Staffs, Bull.......1053
Stag Coats........403
Stains, Hair........634
Stains, Shingle...
...........1020, 1023
Stains, Varnish....
...........1024, 1030
Stains, Wood Dye.1030
Stainless Steel Cutlery.....527, 533,
754-756, 758-759, 761
Stair Carpets
.............840-841
Stair Corners.....822
Stair Nosing......822
Stair Pads.........841
Stair Rods.........822
Stair Treads.......824
Stakes, Bolster....1002
Stakes, Horseshoe.523
Stakes, Riveting...718
Stalls and Fittings.1068
Stamps, Rubber...792
Stamps, Tool......986
Stamp Pads.......792

Stamped Goods
.... 244-245
Stamping Machines 792
Stamping Outfits 256
Stanchions and
Fittings, Cattle.1068

Stands
Bicycle 453
Bird Cage.........970
Book 879
Christmas Tree..574
Coat and Hat....903
Cobblers' 344
Dictionary 784
Drum 683
Ink....751, 766, 793
Jardiniere 903
Living Room......903
Magazine ....
......794, 879, 902
Music 703
Plant...877-879, 902
Shaving ....
.....527, 618, 764
Shoe Polishing..903
Smokers'....618, 904

Stands—Cont'd
Stove 498
Telephone 904
Wash 976
Standards, Lamps
..............240, 657
Standards, Pump.1014
Staples
Carpet 977
Fence 1073
Gate or Door.....980
Hame 1058
Insulating 666
Netting 1073
Screen 977
Stars, Middy......249
Starrett's Tools....990
Starter Button Extensions 494
Starter Drives,
Auto 475
Starting Batteries,
Auto 468-469
Starting Handle
Holders 476
Stationery
.....776, 789-794, 796
Stationery, Children's 791
Statuary.614, 766, 769
Statues, Religious
...........787, 921-923
Statuettes ....
.....239, 574, 921-923
Steak Knives.533, 759
Steam Boilers.962-963
Steam Cabinets.....641
Steam Cocks......1012
Steam Cookers.257,
965-966, 969, 1066
Steam Engines,
Toy 596
Steam Gauges....
..........1011, 1013

Steam Heating Plants
..............962-963
Steam Pipe and
Fittings 1013
Steam Radiators..962
Steamed Bone.....645
Steamer Kettles..
257, 965-966, 969
Steamer Rugs.....455
Steamer Trunks..
..............536-537
Steamfitters' Tools
..984, 989, 997, 1016
Steel, Sheet......1082
Steels, Gate......1070
Steels, Guitar.....676
Steels, Knife......533
Steel Squares.....986
Steel Wheels.....1001
Steel Wool and
Shavings 987
—For Other Steel Articles See Name of Article Wanted.
Steering Column
Braces, Auto....477
Steering Gears....473
Steering Rod Silencers 477
Steering Wheels
and Locks.......473
Steering Wheel
Covers 491
Stems, Handlebar.452
Stencils, Fancywork 256
Stencils, Wall....1032
Stencil Brushes..1032
Stencil Sets.......590
Stenographers'
Supplies 789
Step-Ins, Sanitary.252
Step-Ins, Women's
....132-133, 136, 290
Step Plates, Auto.490
Stepladders ...1034
Sterling Silverware 761
Sterilized Gauze...641
Stereoscopes 596
Stereoscopic Views.596
Sterno Canned
Heat 646
Stevens Shotguns
and Rifles.....
........502, 504, 506
Stew Pans.........965
Sticks, Drum......684
Sticks, Golf........523
Sticks, Hockey.....516
Sticking Knives....510
Stickpins.728, 732, 741
Stifel Cloth........166
Stiffeners, Heel....344
Stirrups, Saddle..1052
Stirrup Straps and
Fenders 1051
Stitching Horses.1054

Stocks
Gun 510
Jewelers' Drill...718
Pipe Threading.1016
Screw Cutting.....990
Whip 1057
Stock, Baluster...1087
Stock Feeds.......645
Stock Feed Cookers 1066
Stock Markers.....975
Stock Medicines...645
Stock Pots.........966
Stock Scales......1076
Stock Troughs...
..........1066-1067
Stock Waterers...
..........1066-1068

Stockings
Athletic.....516, 518
Babies' 149
Boys' ....
260, 264, 268, 272
Christmas...571, 588
Elastic 636
Girls' ..260-261,
264-265, 268-269
Golf 523
Guaranteed .....
.........259, 268-269
Rayon..149, 260-
261, 264-265, 269
Rockford 266
Silk.259, 261-263, 265
Women's ....
259-263, 265-267
Stocking Drying
Frames 147
Stocking Feet.....
.......260, 266, 268
Stogies 620

Stones
Corundum ..996-997
Grindstones .996-997
Jewelers' Jobbing 718
Oil 987
Pumice 1035
Sickle Grinder...996
Stone Boat Heads.1076
Stone Monuments.1045
Stonemasons' Tools
............986, 999
Stoners, Cherry...968
Stools
Bath 1010
Folding 499
Kitchen 846
Office 909
Stepladder 1034
Stops, Door.240, 1087
Stops, Pipe.......1012
Stops, Window...1087
Stop Cocks.......1012
Stoplights......472, 483
Stoppers, Vacuum
Bottle 498

Storage Batteries
Auto 468-469
Radio 714
Storage Tanks.....
.....456, 1011, 1067
Store Lights........653
Storm Alaskas.342-343
Storm Doors.......1085
Storm Glasses......772
Storm Sash........1085
Storm Sash Hangers 977
Storm Serges......204

Stout Sizes
—For Men
Coats.........391, 407
Collars 446
Nightshirts ..443-444
Overalls, Jumpers 389
Overcoats 378
Pants...384, 396-397
Raincoats 408
Rubber Footwear.335
Shirts 428-
429, 431, 435-437
Shoes 320
Suits 365
Suspenders 447
Sweaters 438-439
Underwear ....
...274-275, 279-285

Stout Sizes
—For Women
Aprons.......88, 141
Bloomers 135
Brassieres 136-137

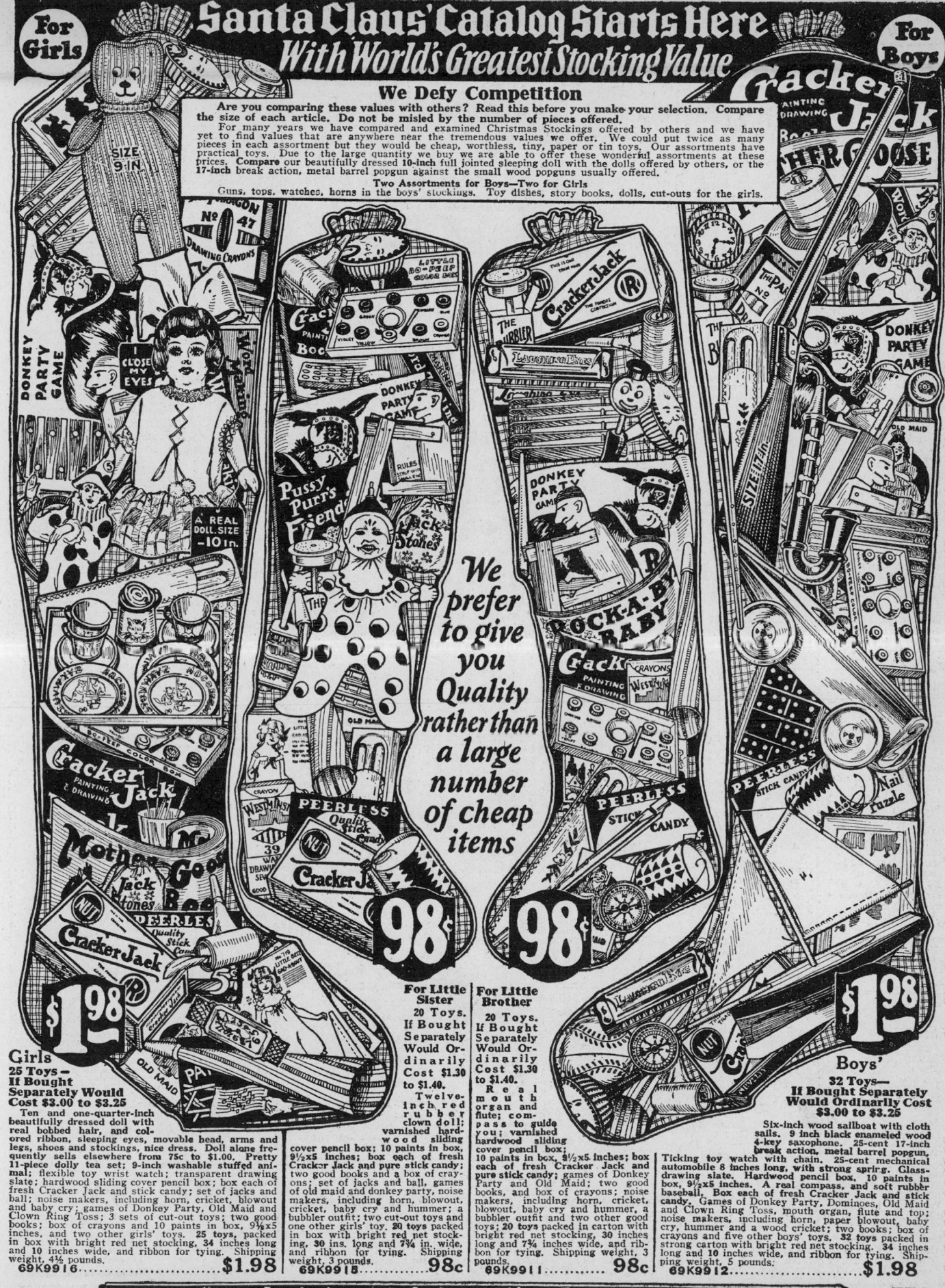

Everything for the

Artificial Christmas Trees

These Beautiful Trees Are Made of the Finest Quality Materials

Folding Everlasting

Easy to Put Up and Take Down. Preferred by Many to Regular Evergreens

Clean, Sanitary, Economical

Do Not Be Misled By Lower Prices. It Pays to Buy Quality.

When comparing prices, we want to remind you that our trees are made by the acknowledged finest manufacturer in the world, and have from 10 per cent to 25 per cent more large and small main branches and a greater quantity of smaller side branches than those offered by others. They very closely resemble the natural tree, and when trimmed will make a much better appearance than the skimpy, inferior trees offered at slightly lower prices. These trees are made of material that does not shed. More popular each year and rapidly replacing the evergreen tree; less expensive, as they can be used season after season. Each tree has a white enameled wood pot, similar to one shown. The larger sizes are in sections for easy packing. Candle holders on each tree.

Seven-Foot Tree
72 large and 140 small branches. Width, 45 inches.
79K6607—(Shpg. wt., 12 lbs.)........ **$7.98**

Six-Foot Tree
Sixty-seven large and 90 small branches. Width, about 38 inches. Shipping weight, 9 lbs.
79K6606..**$5.98**

Three-Foot Tree
Thirty-one large and 15 small branches. Width, about 21 inches. Shipping weight, 2 lbs.
79K6603..**$1.29**

Five-Foot Tree
Fifty-five large and 66 small branches. Width, about 34 inches. Shipping weight, 6 lbs.
79K6605..**$3.98**

Two-Foot Tree
Twenty branches. Width, 13 inches. Shipping weight, 1 lb.
69K6602....**59c**

Four-Foot Tree
Forty-five large and 30 small branches. Width, about 26 inches. Shipping weight, 3 lbs.
79K6604..**$2.39**

19-Inch Tree for Your Dinner Table
Nineteen branches. Width, 10 inches. Shipping wt., ¾ lb.
69K6601... **39c**

Beautiful Imported Hand Decorated Glass Ornaments

We have selected the four most popular sizes of glass ornaments. Each box a wonderful value for the price. Each assortment has fancy reflectors and round balls with pretty hand decorations and many attractive colors.

Biggest Value Ever Offered
Reflectors are the more expensive pieces in any assortment. Even in our lowest priced box, there are six pretty 1⅝-inch brilliant reflectors with colors in center; six hand decorated fancy clusters, acorns and cones. Diameter, about 2 inches. Shpg. wt., 1 lb.
69K6626
Per box of 12.....**29c**

This Assortment Sold Elsewhere for Considerably More Money
Six new style deep reflectors; four hand decorated round balls and two fancy clusters. Diameter, about 2 inches. Shpg. wt., 1¼ lbs.
69K6627
Per box of 12...**49c**

You'll Appreciate the Extra Fine Quality of These Latest Style Beauties
Six new style oval and round reflectors, with gorgeous colored centers; the others are expensive hand decorated crimped and round balls. Diameter, 2¼ inches. Shpg. wt., 1½ lbs.
69K6628
Per box of 12....**79c**

Our Best and Largest Ball Assortment
Really a Gorgeous Assortment
The many colors and expensive hand decorations make this an outstanding value beyond comparison. New color combinations on the six new style deep reflectors and extra fancy handwork on the six round balls. Diameter, 3½ in. Shpg. wt., 2 lbs.
69K6629
Per box of 12.......**98c**

Sixteen Unusually Beautiful Fancy Glass Ornaments
The Assortment We Recommend

Five-inch red, white and blue boat with gilt mast; two pretty balloons, 6 inches and 4 inches in height; basket with handle has green imitation fern; 4-inch trumpet and 3⅛-inch saxophone; bird and parrot with glass tail mounted on spring snap; large Santa Claus face and tinkling bell; closed umbrella, with glass hanger; five fancy oblongs and reflectors, hand decorated in beautiful colors and with tinsel wire and cord. Shpg. wt., 1¾ lbs.
69K6630—Per box of 16.................... **$1.00**

Big Variety for a Low Price
Medium Small Ornaments

A Special Bargain

Twelve Fancy Glass Ornaments

42c

Box Size 9¼x5¾

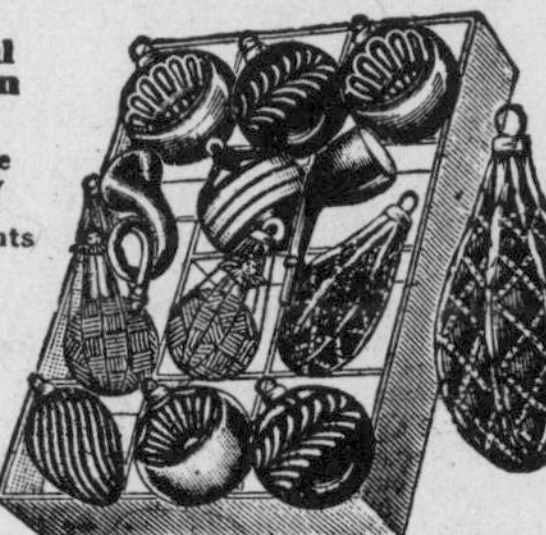

Such fancy tinsel and chenille hand decorated fancy ornaments are found usually only in much higher priced assortments, but we are making an extra special bargain offer of this set. All pretty colors, 4-inch pipe, 3¼-inch trumpet and three fancy balloons, three 1½-inch size colored reflectors and four hand decorated, 1½-inch balls. Shipping weight, 1¼ pounds.
69K6631—Per box of 12........ **42c**

Fancy Colored Cardboard Village 89c

Eight Different Houses You Can Have a Light In Each

Under the tree or among the branches, they will give a pretty colored effect. Opening in each for electric light or a small candle. Colored transparent windows. Average size, each house, 3⅝x3¼x1⅞ inches, mounted on cardboard base. Each roof has imitation snow. Shpg. wt., 2 lbs.
69K6636... **89c**

Fancy Waxed Angels With Trumpets

A box of these beautifully hand decorated angels should be on every tree. Each with mohair wig and glistening spun glass, movable wings, suspended by rubber band that moves them up and down. Length, 4½ inches. Shpg. wt., 1 lb.
69K6516—Box of 6........ **59c**

One Large Angel, 25c
Length, 6¼ inches. Beautiful in every detail. Shipping weight, ¾ pound.
69K6517—Each.. **25c**

12 for 79c

These Perky Little Glass Birds and Parrots With Spun Glass Tails Will Look So Cute Perched on Your Tree
No tree is complete without a box of these beautiful birds. Fasten on branches with patent snap. Assorted colors; about 5 inches long. Shpg. wt., ¾ lb.
69K6634—Per box of 12..... **79c**

Popular, Effective Trimmings

100 Round Beads 39¢

100 Beads, ½-Inch Diameter
Ten on each string, assorted colors. Gold, silver, red, blue and green. Each string 10 in. long. Shpg. wt., ¾ lb.
69K6637
Box of 10 strings........ **39c**

10 Strings of Beautifully Colored Glass Beads

100 Beads, Six Pretty Colors
Fine quality, satin finish; ovals, 1½ to 1¾ inches in length, with silvery color round beads, ⅝ inch in diameter; length of each string, 12 in. Shpg. wt., 1 lb. 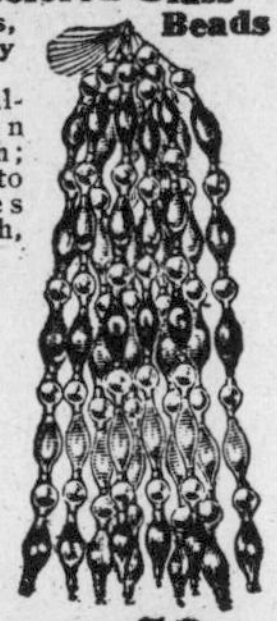
69K6638.... **59c**

Daddy Do Your Duty
$3.79

A Real Value in Santa Claus Suit
Make this a real Christmas for your beloved ones. Mask of excellent quality cloth, starched and waxed. Has soft wool beard, mustache and eyebrows, and red cloth hood with white trimming. The coat and trousers are of red cotton cloth with white trimming. Belt can be adjusted to fit any ordinary size person. Complete in box. Shpg. wt., 1¾ lbs.
69K6620
$3.79

Santa Claus Mask

For a simple makeup, use a bed sheet and this large, roomy Santa Claus mask with hood. The youngsters enjoy that happy jovial expression. White wool beard, eyebrows, mustache, etc. Red cloth hood, white trimmed. Mask of excellent quality stiff cloth, waxed. Shipping wt., 1 lb.
69K6506...... **67c**

67c

Tree Stand That Holds Water
Keeps the Tree Fresh

79c

Stand is heavy sheet steel with three metal braces. Enameled dark green. For trees up to 8 feet high. Diameter of pan, 14½ inches. Deep enough to hold several quarts of water. Shipping wt., 6 lbs. **79c**

Religious Figures

Each set consists of Babe in the Crib, Mary, Joseph; Three Wise Men; Shepherd and Animals. Also green imitation grass.

Our 98c Set, Similar to Picture Above
Tallest figure, about 4⅞ inches. Assorted standing and kneeling figures in proportion. Shipping weight, 2¾ lbs.
69K6675—Box of 12 pieces............ **98c**

Our $2.39 Set Similar to Illustration
Tallest figure, about 5⅞ inches. Others in proportion. Standing and kneeling figures. Shipping weight, 5 pounds.
69K6676—Box of 12 pieces.... **$2.39**

Very Fine Quality and Elaborate Figures $4.98
Features, detail and coloring very attractive; animals have natural looking glass eyes. Tallest figure, 8¼ inches. Others in proportion. Kneeling and standing figures. Shipping weight, 8 pounds.
79K6678—Set of 12 pieces........ **$4.98**

Christmas Tree

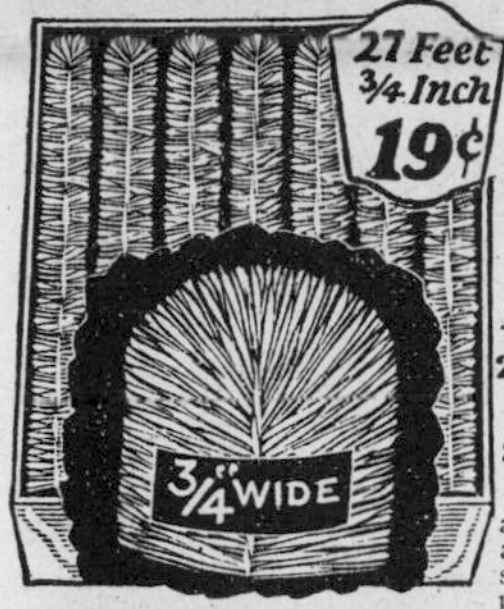
27 Feet
3/4 Inch
19¢
3/4" WIDE

Beautiful and Brilliant Silvery Sparkling Tinsel

Our tinsel is very closely woven, fluffy and exceptionally brilliant. Silvery tinsel always beautifies any tree. No tree is completely trimmed without this tinsel to drape over the branches. It fills the open spaces between ornaments. Has fully 10 per cent more tinsel per yard than tinsel offered elsewhere at or about the price we ask.

27 Ft. of Full Round ¾-Inch Width
Silver Color Tinsel, 19c

All one piece. Will go a long way in decorating a tree. Fine quality sparkling tinsel. Shipping weight, 5 ounces.

69K6576—Box of **27** feet for........... **19c**

45 Feet of ½-In. Width Silver Color Tinsel, 25c
Will Drape Tree Several Times Around

A wonderful space filler. Shipping wt., 6 ounces.

69K6574—Box of **45** feet for................ **25c**

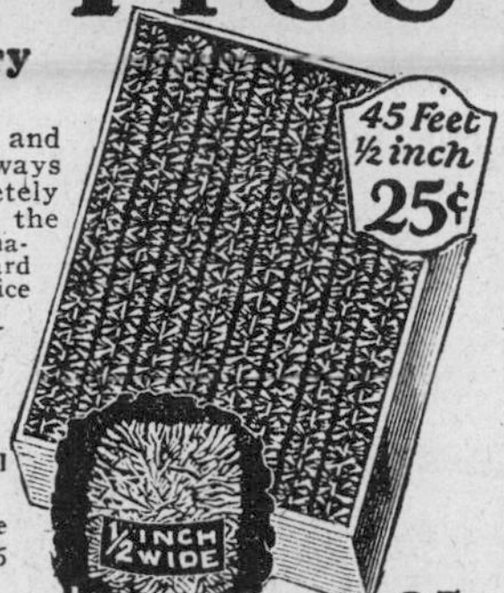
45 Feet
½ inch
25¢
½ INCH WIDE

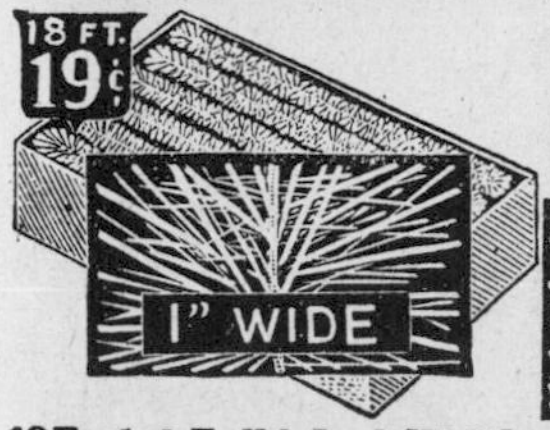
18 FT.
19¢
1" WIDE

18 Feet of Full 1-Inch Width
Extra Heavy Silver Color Tinsel, 19c

All one piece. Bright and very attractive. Greatly beautifies any tree. Shipping weight, 5 ounces.

69K6575—Box of **18** feet for.............. **19c**

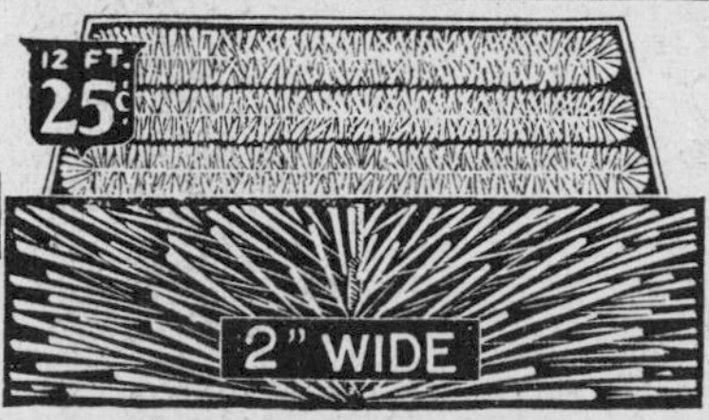
12 FT.
25¢
2" WIDE

Our De Luxe Silver Color Tinsel Garland

12 Feet of 2-Inch Width Fine Quality Tinsel

For those wishing extra wide tinsel. Exceptionally beautiful. Shpg. wt., 6 oz.

69K6586—Box of **12** feet for.... **25c**

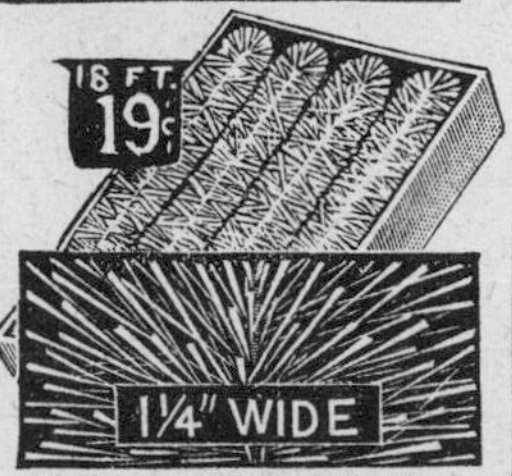
18 FT.
19¢
1¼" WIDE

18 Feet of Fine Quality 1¼-Inch Width
Will Delight Everyone

All one piece. Fine quality; very attractive. Shpg. wt., 6 oz.

69K6584—Box of **18** feet for......... **19c**

6 Fine Quality Candy Boxes 33c

Made of cardboard, red, green and gold color paper. Trimmed with tinsel. Cornucopias, 9 in. long; mandolin and guitar, 7⅝ in. long; basket and bucket paper lined. Shpg. wt., 1 lb.

69K6571. **33c**

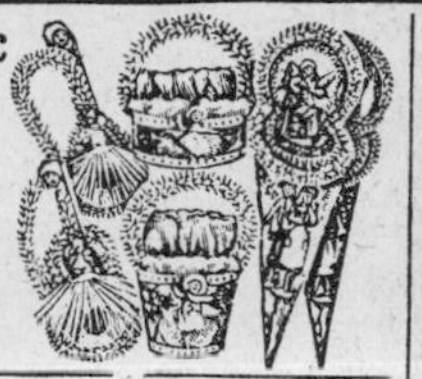

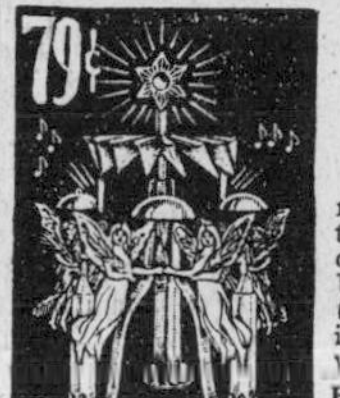
79¢

Revolving Musical Tinkling Chime Tree Tops
For Electric or Candle Lighted Trees
Also Placed on Table

Made from brilliant nickeled metal. Six metal angels uphold three differently tuned bells. Upper part revolves and the strikers attached to it play the bells. Shpg. Wt., 1¼ lbs.

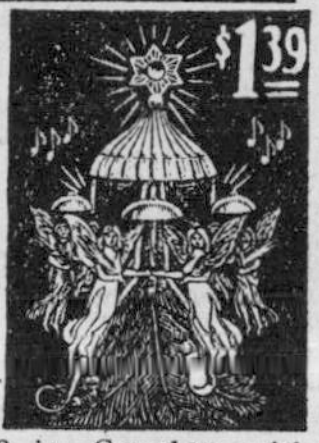
$1.39

For Candle Lights

Height, 10½ in. The heat from the candles causes fan to revolve and the strikers attached to it play soft, tinkling music. Complete with three 4⅛-in. candles.

69K6526.............. **79c**

Electric Tree Top

Height, 8 in. Complete with cord and plug to attach to tree lights. When lights are turned on, dome revolves and the strikers attached to it play the bells.

69K6525....... **$1.39**

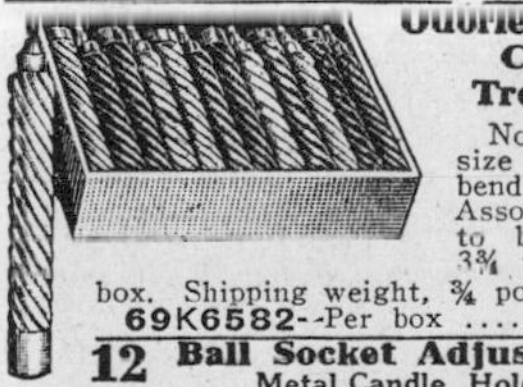

Odorless, Dripless Christmas Tree Candles

Not thin, flimsy size candles that bend so easily. Assorted colors to box. Length, 3¾ inches. 36 to box. Shipping weight, ¾ pound.

69K6582--Per box **9c**

12 Ball Socket Adjustable Metal Candle Holders 17c

Candles always straight. Clip holder to branch and adjust ball socket.

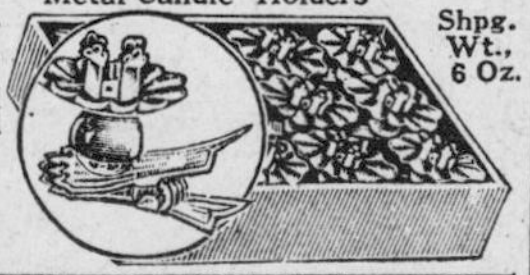

Shpg. Wt., 6 Oz.

69K6537
Per box of **12**
17c

12 Beautifully Colored Unbreakable Ornaments

39¢

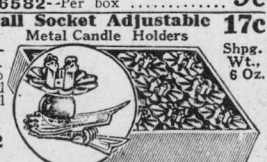

Twelve brilliantly colored 3-layer fireproof metal ornaments, 3½ in. in diameter. Reflect many bright colors. Silvery tinsel rosette in center; assorted designs and colors.

69K6569—Shipping weight, 7 oz.... **39c**

120 Wire Hangers for Tree Ornaments 23c

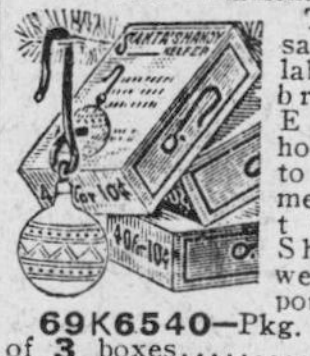

They save time, labor and breakage. Easily hooked on to ornament and tree. Shipping weight, ¾ pound.

69K6540—Pkg. of **3** boxes......... **23c**

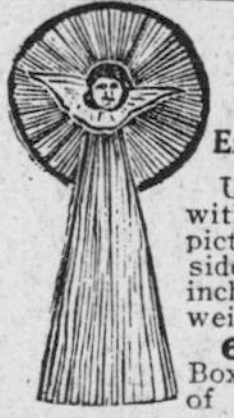

Snow White Spun Glass Ornaments Will Show Up Exceedingly Well

Unbreakable, with pretty angel picture on each side. Length, 6 inches. Shipping weight, 4 oz.

69K6635
Box of **12**.. **59c**

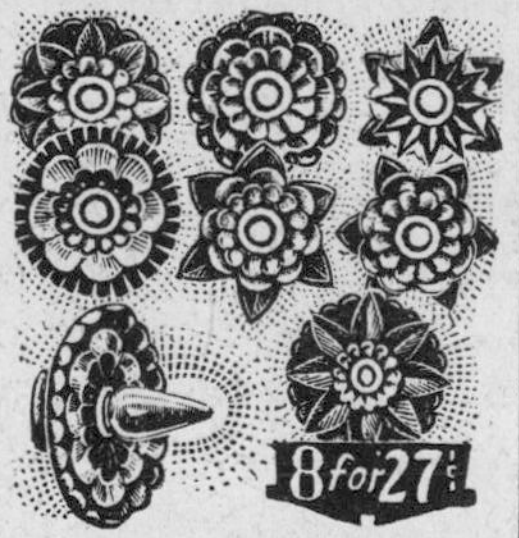
8 for 27¢

Increase the Brilliance of Your Tree Lights

These reflectors produce a wonderful effect. Assorted designs and colors. Three layers of colored metal foil; diam., 3½ in. Properly insulated, will not short circuit. Lights not included. Shipping weight, 6 oz.

69K6600
Box of **8**.............. **27c**

We Buy Only from the Most Reliable Makers of Tree Outfits

Quality Christmas Tree Lights

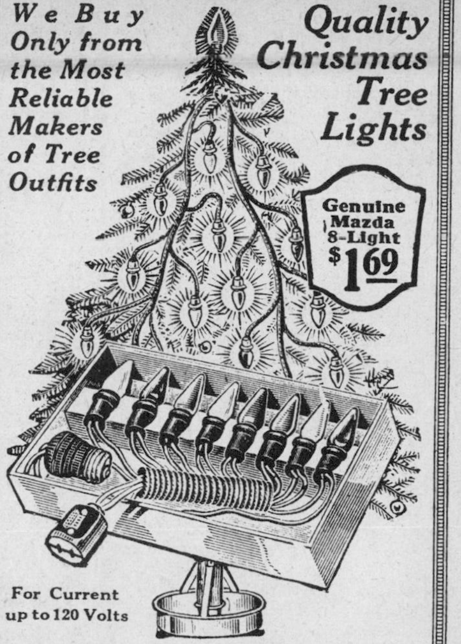
Genuine Mazda 8-Light $1.69

For Current up to 120 Volts

Genuine Mazda Electric Light Outfits for the Christmas Tree

Add More Lights to Your Lighting Outfit—Make Your Tree More Beautiful. It Is Simple With This New "Tachon" Outfit

No Transformer Necessary. Not to Be Used With Battery Current

Add strings of lights as you desire; it makes no difference whether your old outfit is a carbon lamp set or Mazda. These new outfits have an extra connector and you simply attach plug from your old outfit into the new outfit. This will enable you to build up your set, using only one electric light socket. Connector can also be used for attaching to transformer to run toy electric trains, an electric fan, heater or any electric appliance that takes up to 110 volts. For decorating the porch, room, hall or lawn.

69K6593—New complete outfit. (8 lights.) Shpg. wt., 1¼ lbs. **$1.69**

69K6543—New complete outfit. (16 lights.) Shpg. wt., 3 lbs. **$3.27**

69K6597 — New complete outfit. (24 lights.) Shpg. wt., 3½ lbs.. **$4.85**

69K6588—Box of 3 colored Mazda lamps for Mazda sets only. Shpg. wt., 8 oz.. **29c**

3 Large Boxes Silver Color Tinsel Icicles

A Real Value

Others Usually Ask 10c a Box

These Sparkling Artificial Icicles Will Make Your Christmas Tree Gleam With Radiance

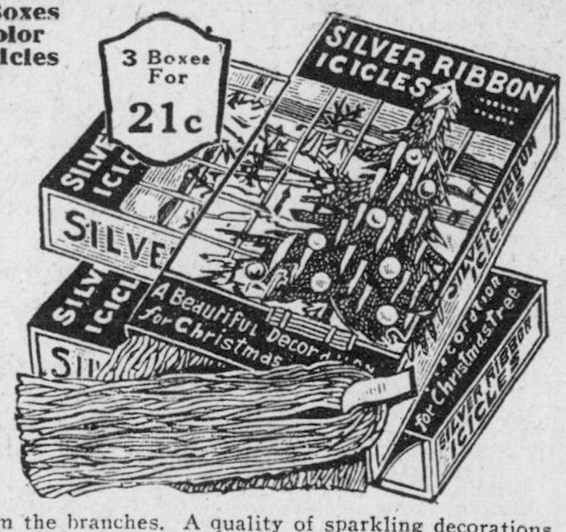
3 Boxes For 21c
SILVER RIBBON ICICLES
A Beautiful Decoration for Christmas

Beautiful tinfoil tinsel in loose strands for decorating the tree. They look very pretty dangling from the branches. A quality of sparkling decorations at a low price. Merely throw it on the tree in small amounts and let it hang. Shipping weight, 8 ounces.

69K6500—Package of **3** boxes................. **21c**

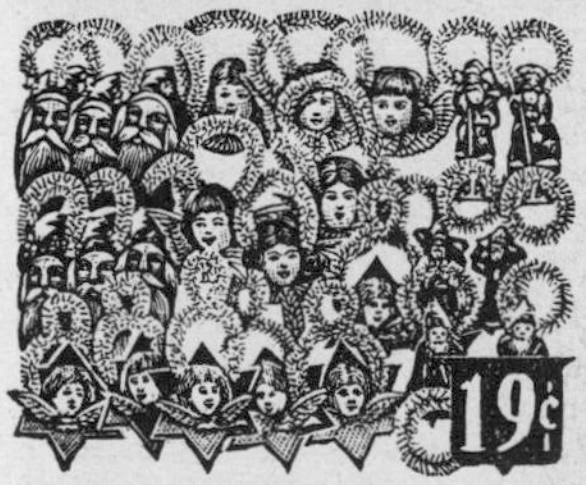
19¢

24 Colored Pictures Trimmed With Silver Color Tinsel

Assorted Angel and Santa Claus designs from 5 to 6 inches long. Shipping weight, 6 ounces.

69K6552—Box of 24..... **19c**

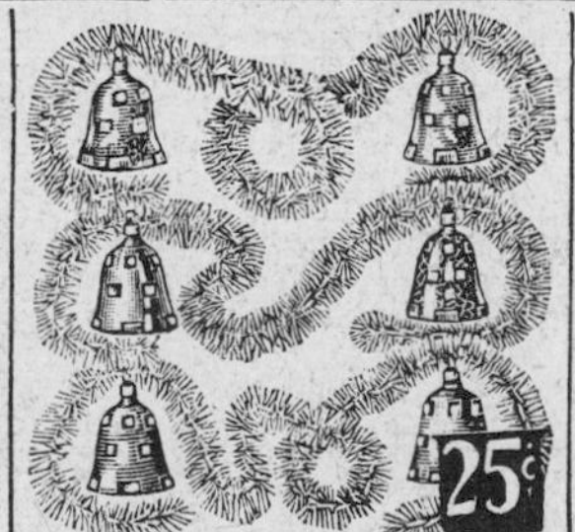
25¢

3 Tinsel Garlands With Glass Bells

Each a yard long, of ⅞-inch closely woven tinsel. Two 1½-inch bells on each. Will add immensely to a tree. Shpg. wt., 8 oz.

69K6550—Box of 3 for... **25c**

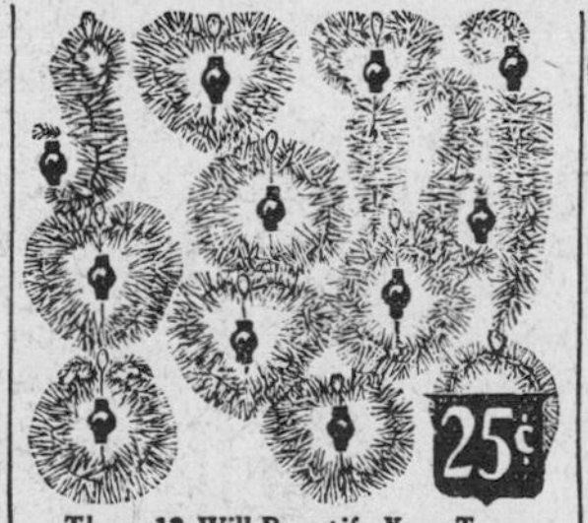
25¢

These 12 Will Beautify Your Tree Very Brilliant—Each Piece Has a Pretty Colored Glass Bead

Six and 7-inch pendants; hearts and ovals in proportion. Shipping weight, 8 ounces.

69K6534—Box of **12** for **25c**

38¢

36 Glittering Tinsel Ornaments, 38c

Pretty silvery pendants, icicles and other fancy shapes. Average size, about 3½ inches. Eighteen have colored glass bead. These scattered in the tree will add considerable sparkle to it. Big value assortment. Shipping weight, 8 ounces.

69K6535—Box of 36... **38c**

Tinsel Tree Top

Height 13½ in 25c

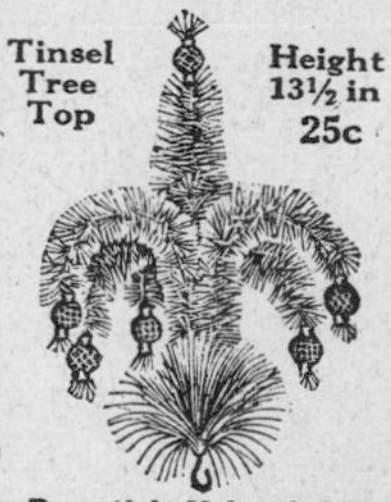

Beautiful—Unbreakable

Wide, bushy, brilliant silver color tinsel. Each branch has colored glass bead. Width, 6½ inches.

69K6511
Shpg. wt., ¾ lb. **25c**

Order Blanks Are in Back of This Catalog

Fun the Year 'Round

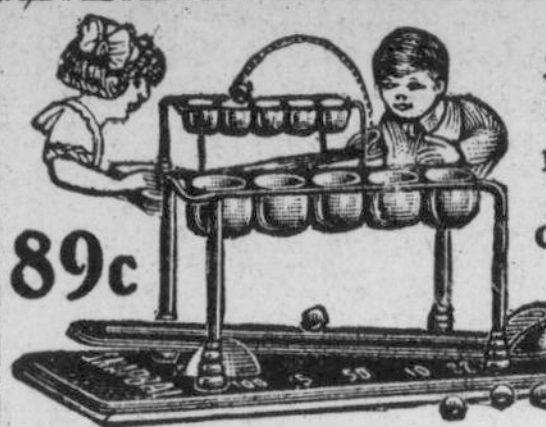

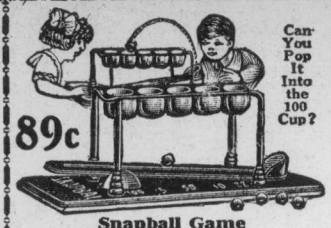

Can You Pop It Into the 100 Cup?
89c

Snapball Game

A game for the whole family. After dinner, treat mamma and daddy to a real exciting time. Made entirely of metal finished in bright colors. Put ball on one end of the lever, press the other end down quickly and watch the ball fly into one of the cups. These are numbered so you can keep score. Five balls and five cups. Cups, 2¼x1¾ inches; base, 20x5⅝ inches; height, over all, 7¼ inches. Shpg. wt., 2 lbs.
49K159 .... 89c

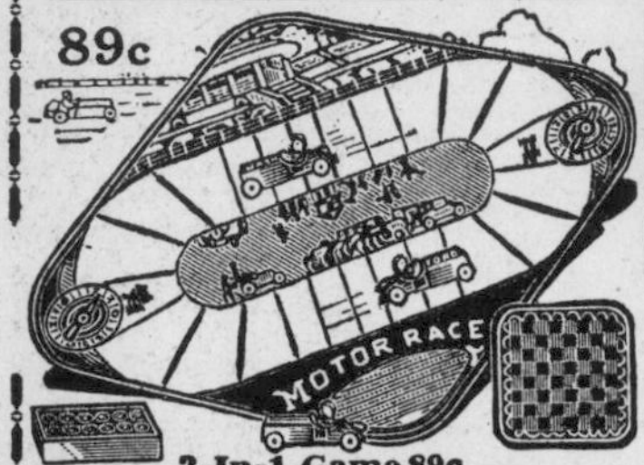

89c
MOTOR RACE

2-In-1 Game 89c
Motor Race, Metal Checkerboard and Checkers

A beautifully lithographed metal board having a race track on one side and a 13-inch checkerboard on the other side. Full set of checkers. The motor race has two spinners and 4 differently colored racing cars, such as Stutz, Buick, etc. Board measures, over all, 16⅝ in. square. Shipping weight, 3 lbs.
79K102 .... 89c

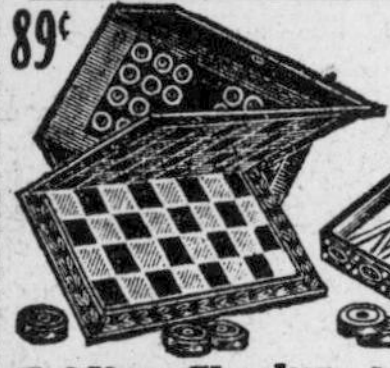

89¢

Folding Checker-board in Case

Cloth covered portfolio case with a 14-inch flat cloth covered board and two sunken compartments holding composition checkers. When through, just fasten snap on case and you have package only 14x7x½ inches. Shpg. wt., 2 lbs.
49K114... 89c

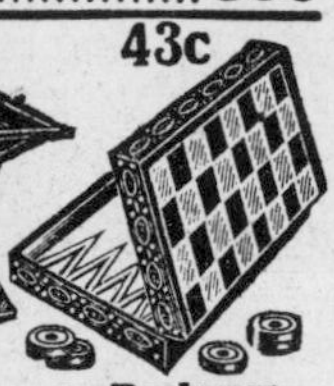

43c

Backgammon and Checker-board

Finished in red, gold and black. Book type, 15x15 in., with set of checkers. Wood frame. Shpg. wt., 1¼ lbs.
49K116
43c

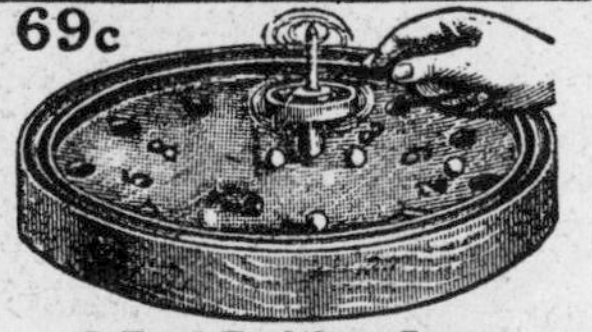

69c

A Real Exciting Game
Frequently Sells for $1.00 Elsewhere

Bowl made of nicely varnished hardwood and has overhanging rim to keep marbles from jumping out. Spin the square spindle top in center of bowl in which the balls are placed and then watch the fun. Largest score wins. Bowl, 7⅞ inches in diameter, 1 inch deep. Shipping weight, 2¼ lbs.
49K214 .... 69c

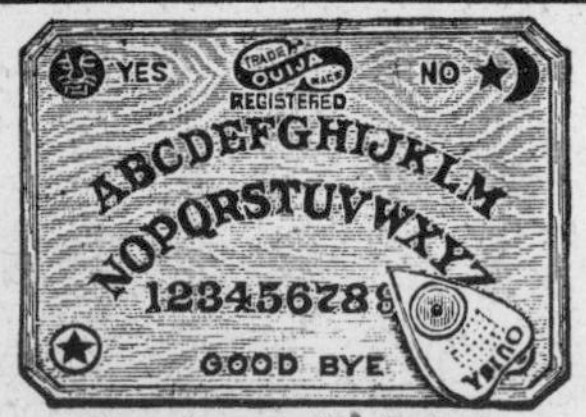

YES
NO
OUIJA
REGISTERED
ABCDEFGHIJKLM
NOPQRSTUVWXYZ
1234567890
GOOD BYE

Genuine Ouija Board

Apparently answers questions concerning your past, present and future. Manufactured by the originators of the famous ouija board and equipped with Fuld's new patented transparent indicator, found on no other boards. Size, 22x15 in. Shpg. wt., 3⅜ lbs.
49K112 .... 98c

57 Games on One Board Only $4.69

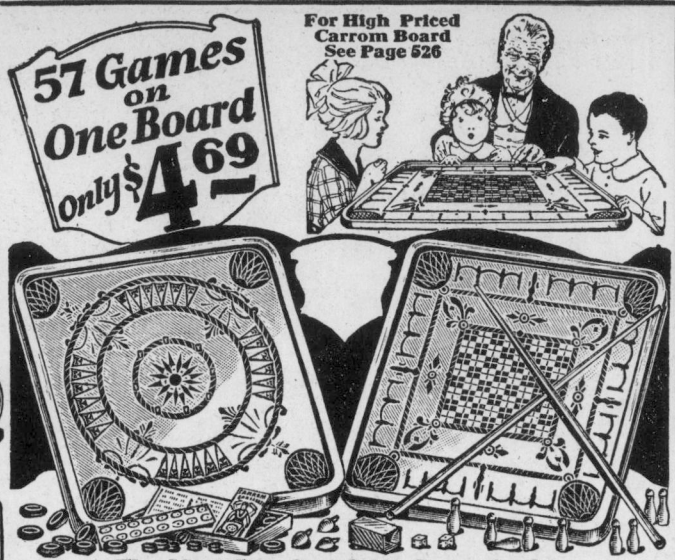

For High Priced Carrom Board See Page 526

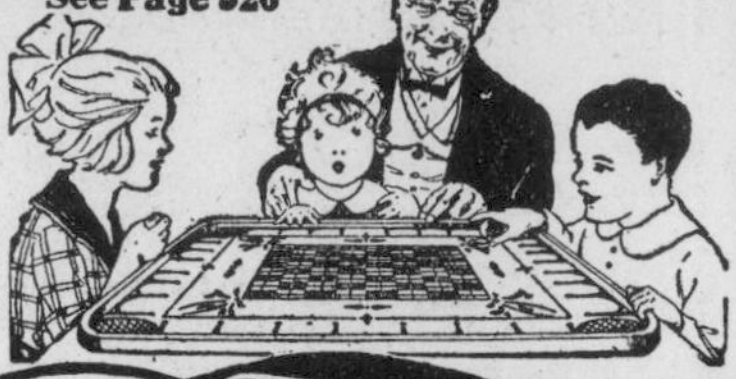

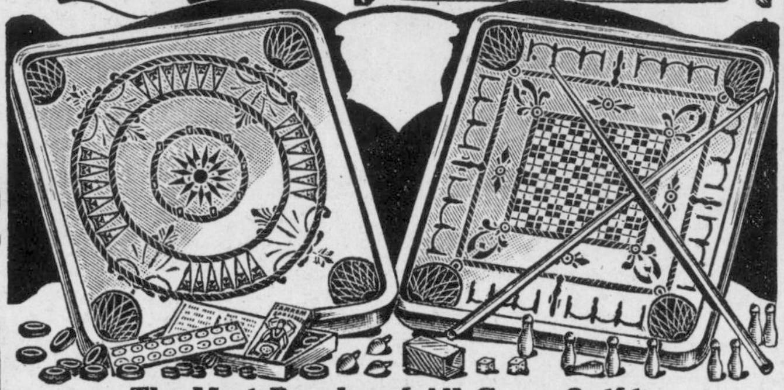

The Most Popular of All Game Outfits
A Famous Carrom Archarena Board

A household is not complete without one of these boards. The entire family can thoroughly enjoy itself playing all the various games. Games are played on both sides. This is a flat board and can be laid away in a corner.

Well made standard combination game board. Complete with seventy-one men and pieces for playing, including two 26-inch tapered cues. For playing fifty-seven games, such as crokinole, carroms, checkers, etc. Full instruction for playing all of them. The panel is made of three-ply maple veneer, natural wood finish. Crokinole and checker markings are artistically stenciled on the polished surface of wood. Size, 28½ inches square. Shipping weight, complete outfit, 11 pounds. Unmailable.
79K489—Complete $4.69

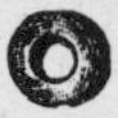

Crokinole and Carrom Rings

Complete set of thirty assorted white, green and red crokinole and carrom rings, made of hardwood, in pasteboard box. Shipping weight, 7 oz.
49K480 .... 29c

A Popular Game

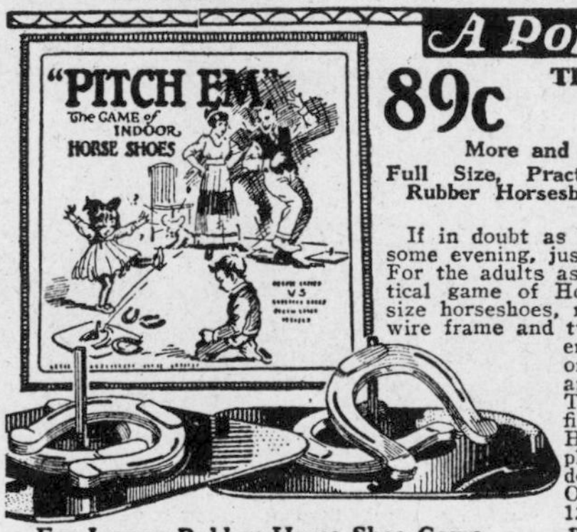

"PITCH EM"
The GAME of INDOOR HORSE SHOES

For Larger Rubber Horse Shoe Game See Page 528

89c **The Nationally Advertised "Pitch-Em" Indoor Horseshoes**

More and More Popular Every Year

Full Size, Practically Indestructible, Reinforced Rubber Horseshoes—Will Not Injure Furniture or Floors

If in doubt as to how to entertain your friends some evening, just bring out your horseshoe game. For the adults as well as the youngsters. A practical game of Horseshoes, consisting of four full size horseshoes, made of rubber mounted on steel wire frame and two pegs firmly fastened in nicely enameled broad metal plates to set on floor. You can get "ringers" and "leaners," just like outdoors. The rubber shoes will not injure the finest furniture should they strike. Have a jolly good time this winter playing this old familiar game indoors. Can also be used outdoors. Outfit packed in neat box. Size, 12x12 inches. Shipping weight, 2¾ pounds.
49K128—Per set 89c

All Steel Pool Table With the Popular Spring Cues

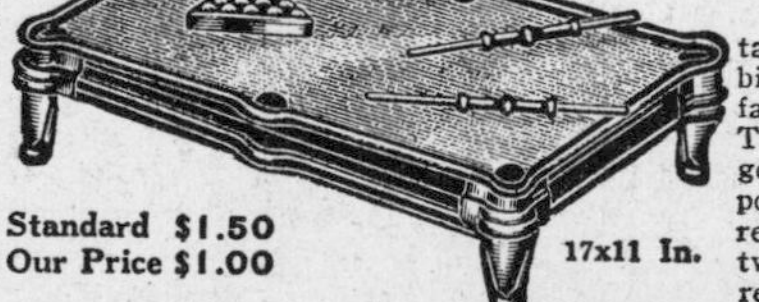

Standard $1.50
Our Price $1.00

17x11 In.

At last we have found a real pool table for you. Made as solidly as the big fellows. All sheet steel legs so fashioned that they cannot come off. Table finished in bright red and green; good quality felt playing bed. Has six pocket holes which lead to a well made return rack under the table bed. Has two spring cues, 7⅝ inches long, which requires real skill in handling, making the game interesting. Has metal triangle and sixteen ⅝-inch assorted color glass marbles. Size of table, over all, 17x11⅝x4 inches. Shpg. wt., 5 lbs.
79K160 .... $1.00

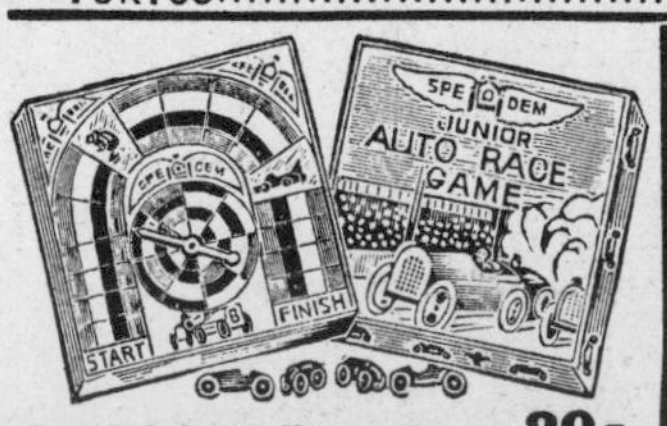

SPEEDEM
JUNIOR
AUTO RACE GAME
START
FINISH

Special Auto Race Game 39c

No more exciting game. Each kiddie has his own little metal racer. Spins the dial in his turn and advances or sets back his car on the attractively lithographed track according to his "break of luck." Big value for the price. Box, 11½ inches square. Two to four can play. Shipping weight, 1¼ pounds.
49K144 .... 39c

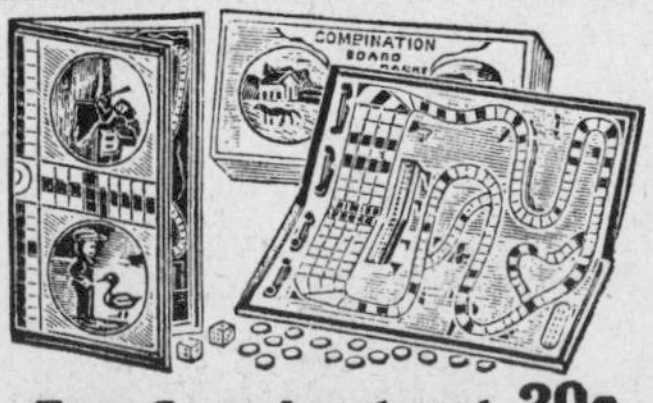

COMBINATION

Four-Game Assortment 39c

Two folding boards, each 12 inches square; one has Indian Home game on one side and Army and Navy game on the other. The second board has Auto Race and Animal and Bird game. Nicely lithographed. Two wood dice and discs to play with. Box, 13¼x6¼ inches. Directions included. Shipping weight, 1½ pounds.
49K164—Both boards 39c

Loads of Fun Shooting These Crows

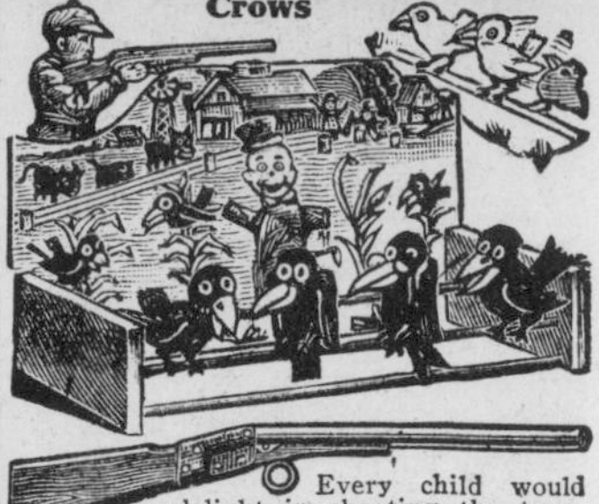

Every child would delight in shooting the troublesome old crows. With new 17-inch blue steel barrel gun the kiddie can shoot at the four heavy cardboard crows who sit so peacefully on the fence. If you hit a crow he topples backward, showing you what score you've made; can be set up again. In attractive box, 12⅝x13x2¾ inches. Cork ammunition included. Shipping weight, 1¾ pounds.
49K181 .... 79c

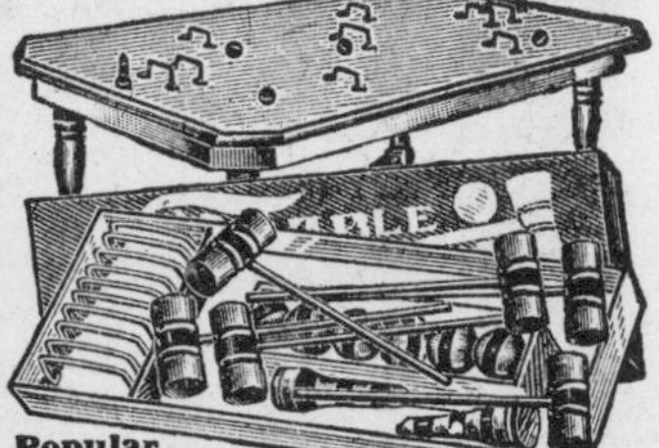

Popular 6-Mallet Croquet Set

A real game for the whole family. Six mallets, each 9 inches long with 2⅝-inch head, and six 1¼-inch balls, each in distinguishing colors; wire arches. Box, 14x6 inches. Shipping weight, 1¾ lbs.
49K111 .... 98c

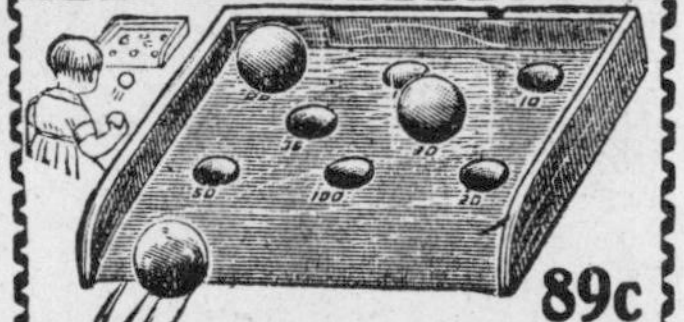

89c

The Exciting Ball Rolling Game

A great game for parties. Roll the balls into the holes, the largest score wins. Strongly made of varnished wood, with eight numbered depressions in base of frame and three nicely enameled 3-inch wood balls. Board, 11½x11⅛x1¾ inches. Shipping wt., 2¾ pounds.
49K185 .... 89c

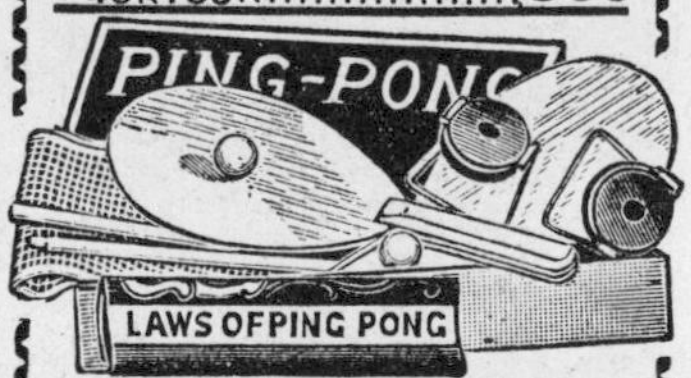

PING-PONG
LAWS OF PING PONG

Famous Ping Pong Game

Speed and quick thinking. Played like tennis. Can be played by adults and children. Adjustable to any size table. Fasten the 40 x 5½-inch well bound cotton net. Two smooth 3-ply paddles, 11⅜x5¼ inches and two genuine "Match" ping pong balls. In box, 12⅛x6⅞x2 inches.
49K156—Shipping weight, 1½ pounds $1.79

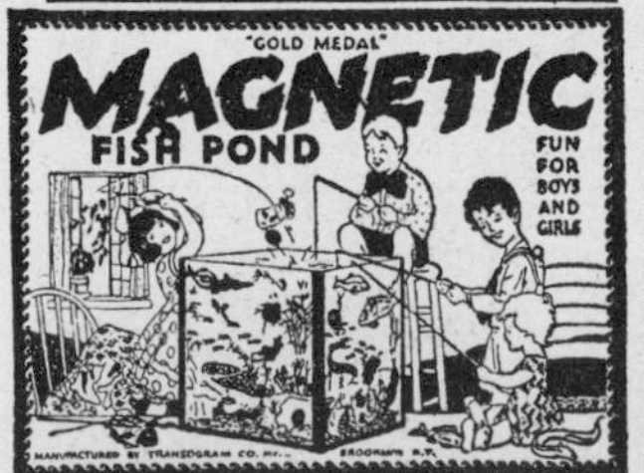

"GOLD MEDAL"
MAGNETIC
FISH POND
FUN FOR BOYS AND GIRLS

4-Pole Magnetic Fish Pond, 39c

Pretty colored box, 11½x8½ inches. Folding pond, 6¾ inches square. Four poles, equipped with magnets and twenty colored fish and objects, like tin can, old shoes, etc., included. Shipping weight, 1 pound.
49K172 .... 39c

for the Whole Family

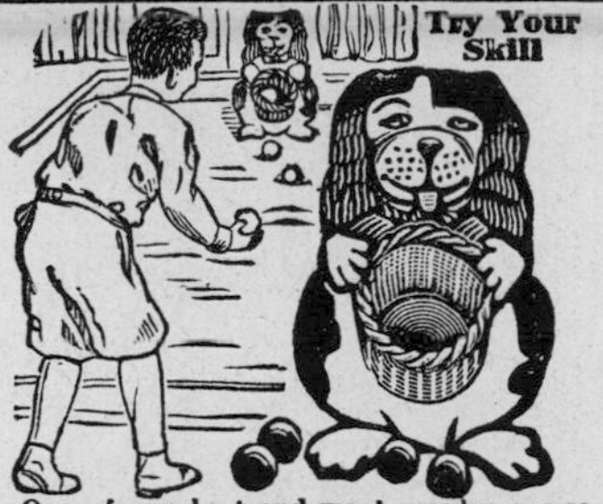

One of our best and most popular games of skill. Looks simple, but just try it. A real family game for the long, winter evenings. "Lucky Pup" is his name. Heavy fiber board with a metal frame support. Finished in genuine washable oil colors. One of these games will afford unlimited entertainment and excitement. Size, 13½x9 inches. Four rubber balls included. Shipping weight, 1 pound.
49K105....................39c

PARCHEESI

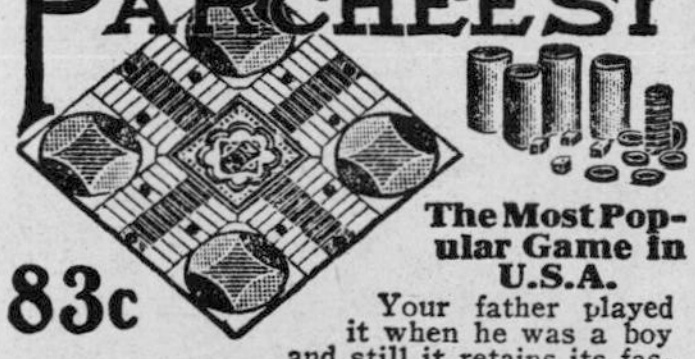

The Most Popular Game in U.S.A.

83c

Your father played it when he was a boy and still it retains its fascination. 18¾x18¾-inch folding board, dice, four cups, four sets of colored counters and directions. Shipping weight, 1¾ pounds.
49K100....................83c

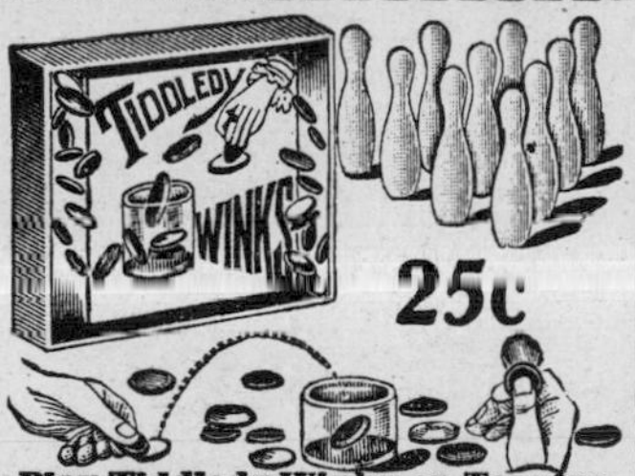

Play Tiddledy Winks or Tenpins

Two games in one. Play tiddledy winks with the glass cup and then tenpins, trying to make a "strike" with your shooting disc. 16 small winks, 4 large winks, 10 well shaped tenpins and glass tumbler. Box, 6x4¾ inches. Shpg. wt., 1 lb.
49K154....................25c

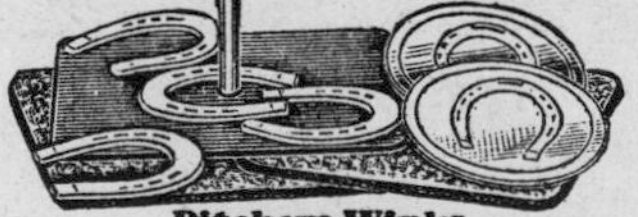

Pitchem Winks

Played like Tiddledy Winks. 2-inch square metal plate with nickel plated stake in center. Two pieces of felt for shooting; two embossed discs and four pressed 1⅛-inch metal shoes. Shipping weight, 8 ounces.
49K174....................19c

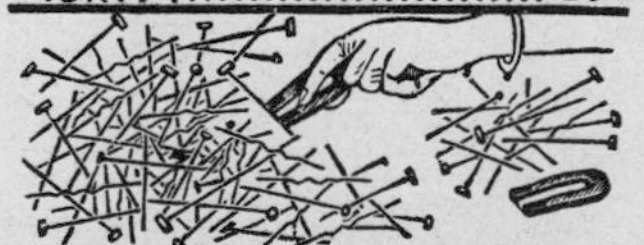

Magnetic Metal Jack Straws
The Test for Eye and Steadiness

Throw the steel straws in a heap and try to remove one straw at a time with your magnet without moving any of the others. Two magnets included. Box, 9¼x5⅝ in. Shpg. wt., 8 oz.
49K195....................39c

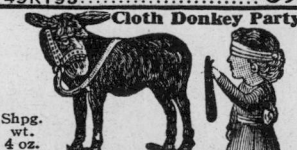

Cloth Donkey Party

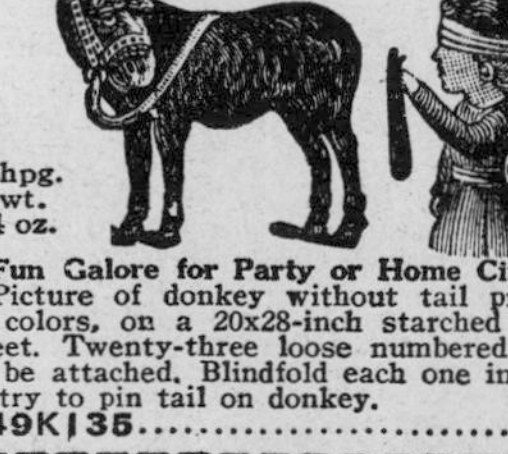

Shpg. wt. 4 oz.

Fun Galore for Party or Home Circle

Picture of donkey without tail printed in colors, on a 20x28-inch starched cloth sheet. Twenty-three loose numbered tails to be attached. Blindfold each one in turn to try to pin tail on donkey.
49K135....................19c

BURROWES

Pool Tables $8.98 to $29.95

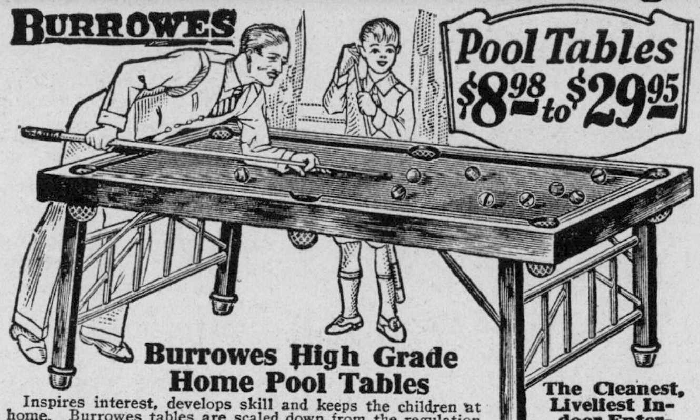

Burrowes High Grade Home Pool Tables

The Cleanest, Liveliest Indoor Entertainment

Inspires interest, develops skill and keeps the children at home. Burrowes tables are scaled down from the regulation size. Beds are smooth and level and covered with good quality cloth. The rubber cushions are live and give a quick, accurate return. Four corner and two side pockets. Tables are of selected grain birchwood, mahogany finish. With each table is a complete outfit of balls, two cues, triangle and a Book of Rules.

This Fine Burrowes Table With Folding Legs for $29.95

Size, 65x32½ inches between cushions. High grade. Has folding legs, rigidly braced and leveled by means of screw ball feet. These are collapsible so table can be put away. High grade rubber cushions covered with good quality green felt. Pool balls, 1⅞ in. in diameter. Shipping wt., 82 lbs. Unmailable.
79K481....................$29.95

Table With Folding Legs for $13.67

Measures 50x26½ inches, outside rail, and 28 inches high. Stand is collapsible so table can be put away. Balls, 1½ inches in diameter. Shipping weight, 26 pounds.
79K479....................$13.67

Table With Folding Legs for $8.98

Measures 43½x23½ inches outside rail, and 25½ inches high. Legs can be folded underneath. Balls, 1¼ inches in diameter. Shipping weight, 17 lbs.
79K477....................$8.98

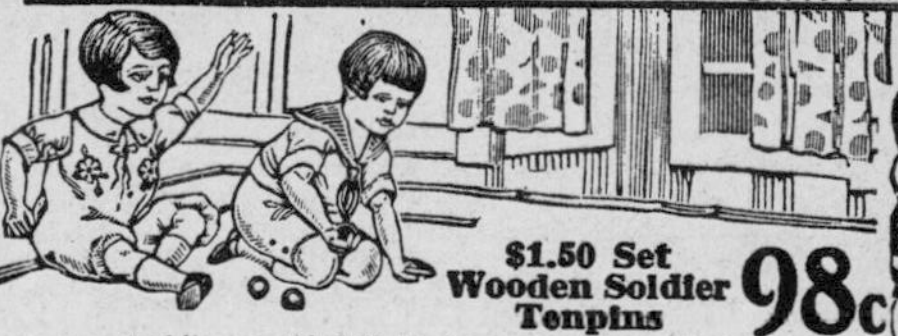

Ten Pins

$1.50 Set Wooden Soldier Tenpins 98c

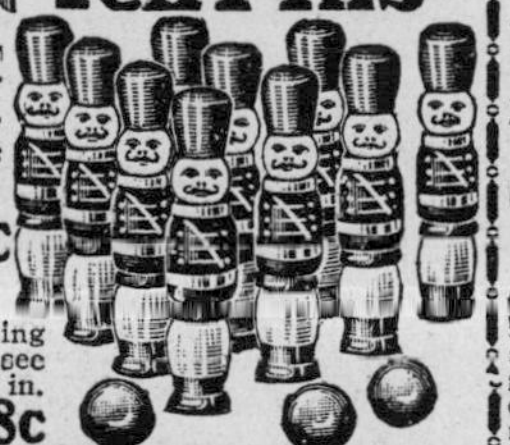

Any kiddie would delight in seeing these little wooden soldiers in their brightly colored uniforms standing at attention. Each is 5½ in. tall and the nicely colored bowling balls are 1½ in. in diameter. Set the soldiers up and see what score you can get. In attractive box, 15⅝x5¾ in. Shipping weight, 1½ pounds.
49K119....................98c

4 Big Games for 39¢

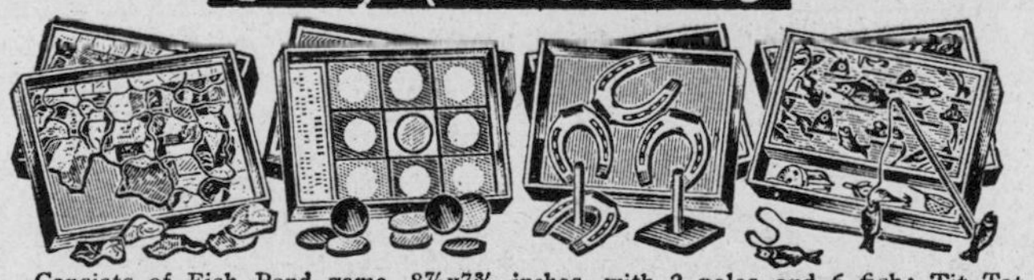

Consists of Fish Pond game, 8⅞x7¾ inches, with 2 poles and 6 fish; Tit Tat Toe Tossing game, 9x7¾ inches; Indoor Horseshoe game, 7⅝x6¼ inches with cardboard shoes and wood standards; Cardboard Puzzle Map of U. S., 8x6¼ inch. Shipping weight, 2 pounds.
49K194—All Four Games for....................39c

Dominoes

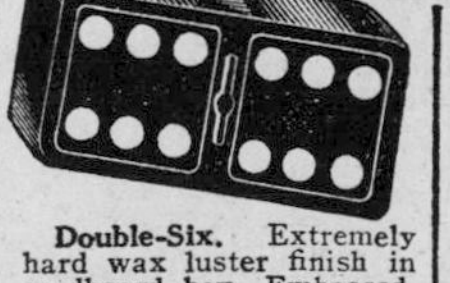

Double-Six. Extremely hard wax luster finish in cardboard box. Embossed. Size, 2x1x5/16 inches. Shipping weight, 1 pound.
49K124
Per set.......... 37c

Double-Six in cardboard box. Size, 1⅝x⅞x5/16 in. Embossed. Shipping wt., ¾ pound.
49K233
Per set.......... 19c

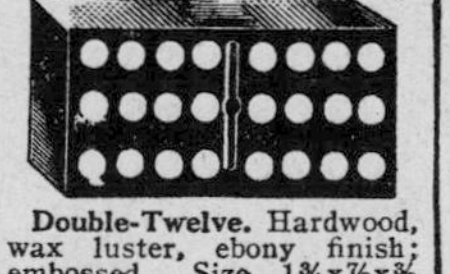

Double-Twelve. Hardwood, wax luster, ebony finish; embossed. Size, 1¾x⅞x⅜ in. In wood frame box. Shipping weight, 2¼ lbs.
49K166
Per set.......... 98c

Double-Twelve Dominoes. Cardboard box. Size, 1⅝x15/16x¼ in. Embossed wood. Shipping weight, 1½ lbs.
49K165
Per set.......... 67c

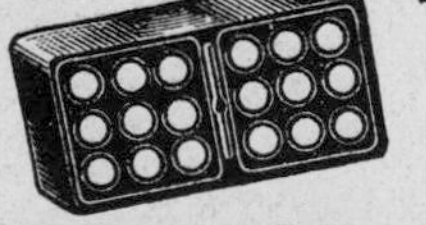

Double-Nine. Embossed hardwood, wax luster, ebony finish. Size, each, 1⅝x15/16x⅜ in. Shipping weight, 1¼ pounds.
49K162—Set..... 42c

Double-Nine. Embossed wood. Size, 1⁷⁄₁₆x¾x¼ in. Shipping wt., ¾ lb.
49K232—Set..... 21c

All Steel Automatic Pin Setting Bowling Alley $1.69
Regular $2.00 Size
24x5⅜x4 Inches

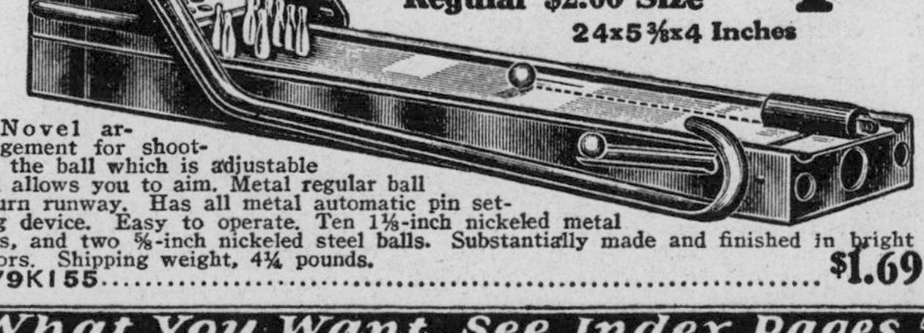

Novel arrangement for shooting the ball which is adjustable and allows you to aim. Metal regular ball return runway. Has all metal automatic pin setting device. Easy to operate. Ten 1⅛-inch nickeled metal pins, and two ⅝-inch nickeled steel balls. Substantially made and finished in bright colors. Shipping weight, 4¼ pounds.
79K155....................$1.69

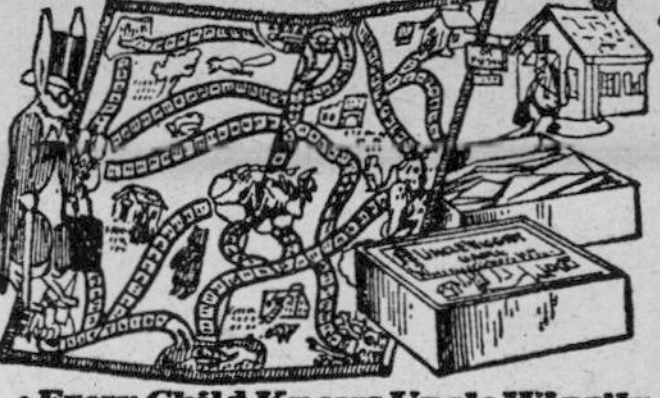

Every Child Knows Uncle Wiggily

From two to four can play and each has a wooden Uncle Wiggily. Uncle Wiggily wants to get to Doctor O'Possum's office. 140 cards tell, with funny verses and directions, how many hops forward or backward Uncle Wiggily can take. There are many traps and pitfalls. The first Uncle Wiggily to reach Doctor O'Possum's wins. Size of board, 16 in. square. Shpg. wt., 1½ lbs.
49K104....................59c

Baseball and Football Games
Real Action! More Popular Each Year

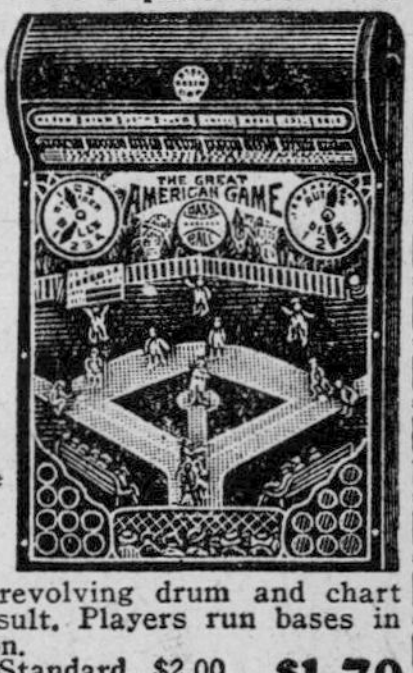

Only crack of the bat and the thud of the tackle are missing. These games are sturdily built. Real action. Size, 13½ x 8⅞ in. Wood and steel frame. Shipping wt., 2¾ lbs.

Baseball Game

Place player in batter's box, press lever; revolving drum and chart shows the result. Players run bases in regular fashion.
49K133—Standard $2.00 value....................$1.79

Football Game

An exciting game where players can use judgment. Ball advances same as real game. Endorsed by college coaches.
49K132—Standard $2.00 value....................$1.79

The Famous Pollyanna

98¢

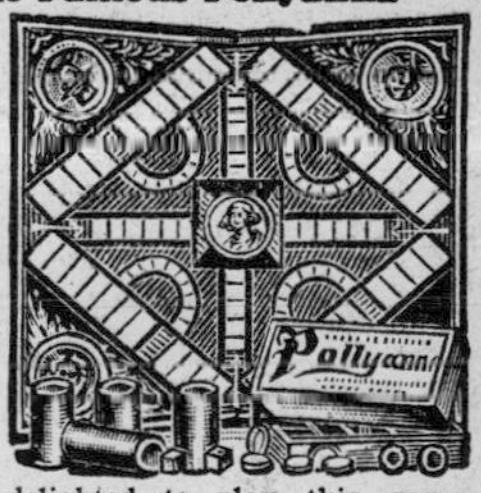

One of the largest selling games on the market. Most every kiddie will love the Pollyanna characters and will be delighted to play this game. Two to four people can play. A fine quality folding board, 19 inches square, beautifully lithographed. Four wood dice cups. Colored discs and dice to play with. Shipping wt., 2 lbs.
49K161....................98c

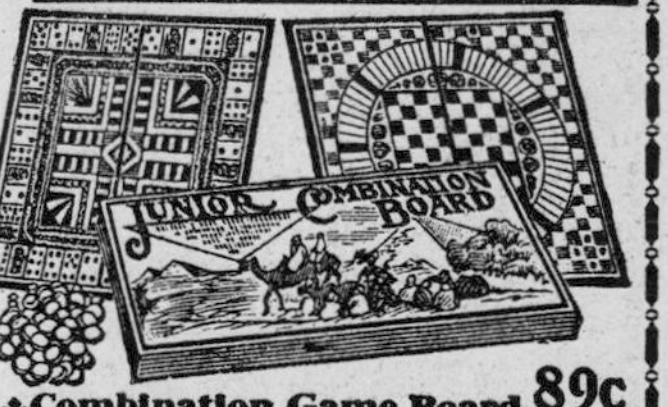

Combination Game Board 89c

Twelve dandy games can be played on it. Board is 16¼ inches square. Made of thick cardboard with linen center hinge. Highly colored playing surface. Directions for playing included. Fifty-nine pieces and metal spinner for playing. Box, 16¾x8½ inches. Shipping weight, 2¼ pounds.
49K177....................89c

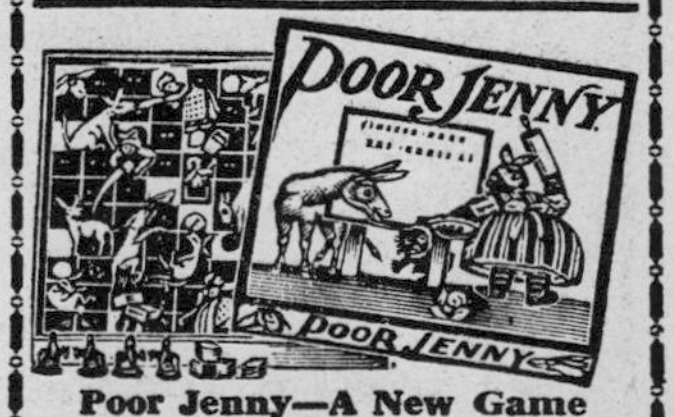

Poor Jenny—A New Game

Attractively lithographed board showing Jennie the donkey in her troubles. From two to four can play, each taking a mule (each one has a different name) and then throwing the cubes which also have names on them. Box, 11½x11½x1½ inches. Shipping wt., 1¼ lbs.
49K117....................39c

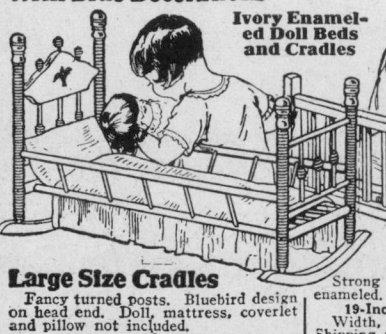

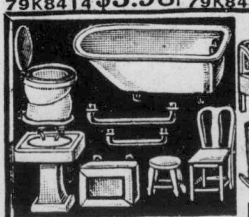

DOLL BUGGIES

Beauty-Style Class-Quality TREMENDOUS VALUES

$2.59

Just Think of It!

Cute Little Fiber Reed Buggy, $2.59

A dandy for the little tot. Hood and body of flat fiber reed, trimmed with braid and metal to withstand hard knocks. **Will hold a doll 16 inches tall.** Body, 17x7¾ inches; handle, 21½ inches from floor. 6-inch strong wire wheels with ¼-inch rubber tires; shiny metal hub caps. Body and hood enameled light tan; steel running gear, wheels and handle are black. Shpg. wt., 8 lbs.

79K8254........................**$2.59**

$4.98

A New, Popular, Dainty Perambulator

Right Up to the Minute

Any doll up to 20 inches tall would look cute in it. Body made from 3-ply veneer wood and has turquoise blue enameled fiber reed roll over front; hood of tan enameled full round fiber reed with graceful roll enameled turquoise blue. Body, 17⅜x9⅝ inches, enameled rich cream color with pencil stripe decorations in black; entire seat and hood lined with pretty cloth. Back reclines. Strong 7-inch wheels with 5/16-inch rubber tires. Bright metal hub caps. Gearing and handle enameled tan. Push bar, 23 inches from floor. Shipping weight, 12 lbs.

79K8260...........**$4.98**

Sold up to $6.50 Elsewhere

$4.98

Our Leader Value

Beautifully shaped body for **dolls up to 20 inches tall.** The back reclines; body and hood made of full round fiber reed. Hood has a graceful roll over front; body has inverted roll; both trimmed with pretty braid and beautifully enameled. 8-inch wheels with ⅜-inch rubber tires; nickel plated hub caps. Handle, 25¾ inches from floor. Body, 20¾x10¼ inches. Adjustable hood. Entire seat lined with pretty cloth. Shpg. wt., 13 lbs.

Royal Blue Enameled body and hood; balance cream color.
79K8258 **$4.98**

Rich Tan Enameled body, hood and wheels; balance black.
79K8257 **$4.98**

Only **$2.98**

A Pretty Buggy for Small Dolls

Is made of full round fiber reed—the kind that little sister will be proud to own. **Will hold a 16-inch doll.** Is reinforced around the top with metal binding. Body, 17¾x7⅞ in.; handle, 21½ inches from floor; 7-inch wire wheels with ¼-inch rubber tires; shiny metal hub caps. Body and hood enameled tan and trimmed with fiber braid; steel running gear and handle are black. Adjustable hood. Shpg. wt., 8 lbs.

79K8255........................**$2.98**

Here's a Dandy

$3.98

Sold by Many Stores at $5.00

Large Roll on Hood and Body

Shpg. wt., 9 lbs.

Adjustable Hood

Any little girl would be "tickled" to take her dolly out in this stylish buggy. **It will hold a doll as large as 18 inches tall.** Body and hood made of full round fiber reed and trimmed with braid, enameled in a rich royal blue color; cream enameled 7-inch strong wire wheels equipped with ¼-inch rubber tires. Steel running gear and handle enameled black. Body, 18⅛x9½ inches; handle, 22 inches from floor; shiny metal hub caps.

79K8256.............................**$3.98**

$1.67

See This Stylish, Baby Blue Color, Enameled Doll Stroller

For All Size Dolls

Made of closely woven round fiber reed with fancy roll and braid around top, beautifully enameled baby blue, cream and black. Very attractive for kiddies. Nicely varnished. Natural finish curved wood handles. 6-inch strong wire wheels with ¼-inch rubber tires; shiny metal hub caps. Seat, over all, 9¼x9 in. Large enough to hold large size Ma-Ma doll. Shipping weight, 4 pounds.

79K8277... **$1.67**

Here's a Beauty With Balloon Tires

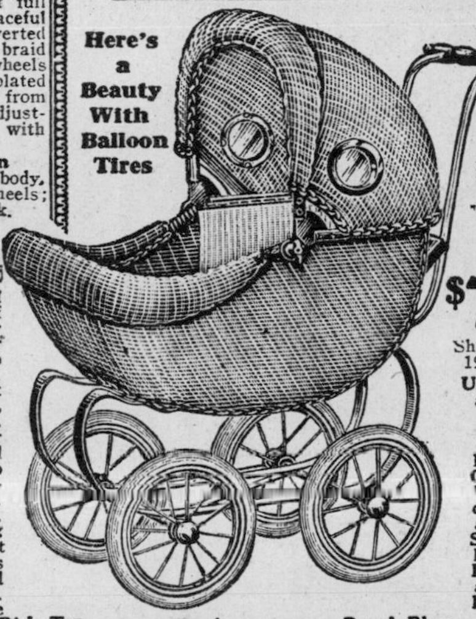

Sold Up to $12.00 Elsewhere

$7.98

Shpg. wt. 19 lbs.

Unmailable.

Plate Glass Windows and Stylish Roll on Hood and Body

Body and hood of round fiber reed, for dolls up to 22 inches. Body, 21x11½ inches, 8-in. wheels, ¾-in. rubber tires. Nickel plated hub caps. Handle, 20 in. from floor. Reclining back, seat and sides of seat lined with cloth. Adjustable hood.

Rich Tan Enameled body, hood and wheels; balance black.
79K8263.......**$7.98**

Royal Blue Enameled body and hood; balance, cream color.
79K8262.......**$7.98**

Metal Carts

Beautiful Royal Blue Enameled Perambulator With Yellow Enameled Rubber Tire Wheels

For 16-In. Doll

Doll not Included

$1.98 Special

Strong metal body, 16¾x7⅝ inches, with turned edges. Bright yellow 6-in. wheels with ¼-inch rubber tires. Wood handle, 24½ in. high. Three-bow folding hood covered with artificial leather. Shpg. wt., 7 lbs.

79K8216.........................**$1.98**

All Steel Doll Sulky

Only **89c**

For All Size Dolls. All steel, enameled black with yellow wheels and yellow striping on seat. 6-inch wheels, ¼-inch rubber tires. 20½-in. folding handle. Seat, 8x6¾ inches. Shpg. wt., 4 lbs.

79K8250 **89c**

Popular Folding Metal Go-Cart

$1.19

Sunshade, seat and back made from glossy black with blue stripe artificial leather, black enameled steel frame. Holds an 18-inch doll. Push bar, 22 in. from floor, 6-inch wheels; ¼-inch rubber tires. Shipping weight, 5 pounds.

79K8253 **$1.19**

Pullman Special at $9.98

Sold Up to $15.00 Elsewhere

These Two Beauties Have Tubular Steel Handles and Balloon Tires

Our De Luxe Model

$12.98

Sold Up to $18.00 Elsewhere

Unmailable.

Shpg. wt., 40 lbs.

Artillery Wheels

With balloon tires, tubular steel handle rods, reclining back. Hood and seat lined with genuine corduroy. Large graceful roll on body and hood, real glass windows in hood. Will hold doll up to 24 inches tall. Body and hood made of round fiber reed trimmed with braid. 9-inch wheels with ⅝-inch rubber tires. Handle, 28½ inches from floor. Body, 25½x11½ inches, adjustable hood. Nickel plated hub caps. Shpg. wt., 33 lbs. **Unmailable.**

Royal Blue Enameled body and hood; entire running gear, cream color.
79K8264... **$9.98**

Rich Tan Enameled body, hood and wheels; balance black.
79K8265... **$9.98**

If you are looking for the best fine quality doll buggy value on the market, this is it. Just like a baby buggy. Strong, 10-inch artillery wheels with ¾-inch balloon type rubber tires. Entire body and hood lined with genuine corduroy. Real glass windows. Fancy tubular steel handle rods. Will hold doll, 28 inches tall. Strong brake. Body and hood made from full round fiber reed, with large size roll on each. Body, 27x13¼ inches. Adjustable hood, leather strap. Nickel plated hub caps. Handle, 29 inches from floor.

Rich Tan Enameled body, hood and wheels; running gear black.
79K8275... **$12.98**

Royal Blue Enameled body and hood. Running gear cream color.
79K8276. **$12.98**

It's Easy to Order From the World's Largest Store. See Page 546

Selected Toys for Girls

Chain Stitch $3.98

Some Beauty

Little Girls Love to Sew
Sews easily and well. Made of heavy metal. Fancy gilt decoration on black enamel; nickel plated wheel and trimmings. Makes four chain stitches at each turn of the driving wheel. Size, 7⅝x5⅝x7¼ inches. Shipping weight, 8¼ pounds.
49K5800.................$3.98

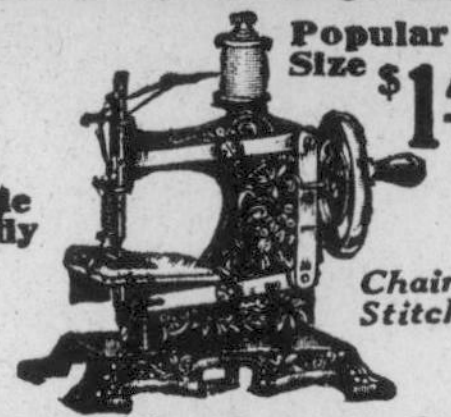

Popular Size $1.48

A Little Dandy

Chain Stitch

Make the little girl happy. Black enamel metal. Nickel plated trimmings. A little machine that sews chain stitches smoothly. Size, 6x3½ x6¼ inches. Each packed complete in box. Shpg. wt., 2¼ lbs.
49K5802.................$1.48

Little Dandy $2.69

Chain Stitch

Right Size for Little Girls

Solid and substantial. Made of heavy metal. Thread tension and raising foot. Makes fine stitches. Enameled black with gilt decorations. Nickel plated sewing top. Size, 6½x6x4 inches. Shipping weight, 3¾ pounds.
49K5809.................$2.69

$5.98

Chain Stitch

Our Finest Toy Sewing Machine. Handy Little Machine for Around the House

Has many attachments. Can be used for many practical purposes. All metal construction. Automatic tension, drop foot, shuttle, nickel plated sewing top, thread tension and heavy flywheel with handle. Base, black with gilt decoration. Size, 11x6½x8½ inches.
79K5810.................$5.98

Shpg. wt., 14 lbs.

Girls' Dresser Sets

Our Best Set
Beautifully hand decorated, pearl on amber filled pyralin. Just like mother's set. 8-inch beveled glass, mirror with brush and comb. In plain gift box. Shpg. wt., 2 pounds.
87K6133
$2.98

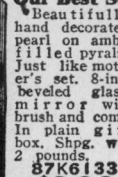

A Dainty Set
Pink and white grained filled pyralin. Gilt border and head decorated in colors. 8-inch beveled glass mirror, brush and comb. In plain gift box. Shipping wt., 2 lbs.
87K6132
$1.98

A Beauty
Attractive, ivory grained, filled pyralin pieces. 7-inch mirror, 5¾-inch brush and 5-in. comb, each hand decorated in pretty colors. In plain gift box. Shpg. wt., 1½ lbs.
87K6130
98c

All 5 for 98c

The Biggest Toy Cleaning Set We Have Ever Offered

Mothers! Here Is a Real Practical Toy House Cleaning Set for Little Girls.

Every little girl likes to play house, to sweep and help mother with her work.
(1) A real colored yarn mop with 24-inch varnished round wood handle. (2) 11-inch colored cotton yarn duster. (3) A good grade 32-inch broom with varnished wood handle. (4) A real Bissell toy sweeper with revolving brush and round wood handle, 24 in. long. It actually sweeps and has two dumping dust pans. (5) A nicely enameled corrugated metal dust pan. Size, 9x5⅛ inches, with 5-inch gilt lacquered metal handle. All five packed in box. Shipping weight, 5½ pounds.
79K9185.........98c

79c

Complete Sewing Basket for Little Girls
Cute, complete set any girl will enjoy. Made of bright red rafia interwoven with fancy straw braid. Hinged cover with fastener. Inside padded and covered with colored sateen. Six spools and two balls of colored thread, bodkin, thimble, celluloid tatting shuttle and three needles. Size, 5½x4x2 in. Neatly packed complete in box. Shipping weight, 1 pound.
69K9163.....79c

Often Sold Elsewhere at From $4.00 to $4.50

Something Out of the Ordinary for the Little Girl
Made of wood, enameled in pretty ivory with blue trimming, two pretty transfer pictures, one on each side of cabinet. Two hinged covers. Height, 23¾ inches. Shipping wt., 8 pounds.
79K9164.....$2.98

DOLLY DEAR

Dolly Dear Family
Make Your Own Cloth Dolls, 21c
Three dolls lithographed in colors on cloth, 35x21 inches, with full instructions how to cut out, sew and stuff. Makes ideal unbreakable rag dolls for the youngster. Large doll when stuffed measures 24½ in. in height and can wear real baby size clothes. The two little dolls are about 7¼ in. in height. Shpg. wt., 4 oz.
69K7212...21c

Every little girl loves to play cook for her dollies. All high parts highly polished.

Fancy Large Nickel Plated Cast Iron Stoves
Each stove has a fancy back, grate, water reservoir, removable back and front apron, lined oven, stove pipe, removable lids, hinged doors, dinner pot, skillet, coal scuttle, shovel and lid lifter.

A Dandy, Only $2.39
Size: Length, 12½ in.; height, 11⅝ in.; depth, 6 in. Complete with draft damper; real warming oven with two hinged doors, 1½-inch lids. Shipping weight, 9 pounds.
69K7311..$2.39

A Beauty, $1.59
Size: Length, 11⅝ in.; height, 10⅜ in.; depth, 5 in. Similar to one shown. Has dummy warming oven and only four 1½-inch lids. No draft damper. Shpg. wt., 7 lbs.
69K7310.$1.59

Combination Toy Gas Range and Stove
White With Blue Trimmings
A new stove, just like Mother's. Top of stove measures 9x5⅝ inches; has four lids and four imitation gas burners. Total height, 10½ in. Complete with cast iron skillet, dinner kettle and lid lifter. Shpg. wt., 8 lbs.
69K7307
$1.79

Everything for Dolly's Laundry

Here's a Complete Set at Low Price $1.00

Consists of a strong wood ironing board 20½x 5⅝x13⅜ in., a nickel plated sadiron, 4⅛x2½ inches, a basket, 11½x 7¼ inches, 12 feet of clothesline, 2 iron pulleys, 6 tiny clothespins in bag, 7-inch metal tub, and 6⅝x3⅜-inch metal washboard. Exceptional value. Shpg. wt. 5¾ lbs.
79K1704.................$1.00

Everything for Dolly's Laundry $1.98

Rubber Roll Wringers

10-Inch Metal Wash Tub

Glass Surface Washboard

Girls! When Mamma does her washing you can do yours. 10-inch metal tub, finished in blue enamel with white enamel inside. Metal wringer with 3¾-inch rubber rollers which actually wring clothes. Wood frame, heavy glass surface washboard, 11x5⅛ in., a collapsible clothes rack, a wash basket, 11½x7 in. and 12 girlie clothespins.
79K1701—Shipping weight, 5¾ lbs.................$1.98

25c

Girls' Octagon Shape Toy Wrist Watch
A little beauty. Every little girl loves to wear a wrist watch just like Mother's. Ten pretty sparkling imitation diamonds set in around the dial; colored stone in stationary crown, heavy glass crystal; adjustable grosgrain ribbon wristlette with clasp for fastening. Shipping weight, 3 ounces.
69K9113.................25c

Baby Betsy Ironing Boards
You can actually iron on these. Made by same workmen who build ironing boards for grownups. Nice smooth lumber, no nasty splinters, easy to set up.
79K1775
For important business of ironing doll clothes, handkerchiefs and lots of other things. Top, 35x10⅜ in. Height adjustable from 20 to 25 inches. Shipping wt., 6¼ lbs.....$1.00

Large Size

Will You Need a Toy Sadiron? See Them Below. The One We Recommend

For the Tiny Tot
49K1777—Very strong. Looks just like Mother's. Size top, 20½x5½ in. About 13½ in. high. Shipping weight, 1¾ pounds.....42c

Nickel Plated Toy Sadirons
These actually iron. Like Mamma's. Detach the bottom, heat and when hot attach handle and iron away. Polished wood handles. Two sizes. 
Our Small Iron 4⅛x2½ in. Shipping weight, 1¼ pounds.
49K1797.................22c
Our Large Iron 5x3½ inches. Shipping wt., 2¾ lbs.
49K1798.................45c

Animals *for the* Little Folks

Compare These Wonderful Values

The kiddies will love, cuddle and squeeze these little pals. They certainly are lovable with their cunning faces, pudgy bodies and fat arms and legs. Each has lifelike glass eyes. Heads, arms and legs are jointed so baby can turn their heads and arms into all sorts of positions. Their bodies are covered with short pile, brown plush. All bears have squeaker voices.

16-Inch Bear 49K4304 Shipping wt., 1½ lbs. $1.39	12-Inch Bear 49K4302 Shipping wt., 1 lb. 79c	9½-Inch Bear 49K4301 Shipping wt., 1 lb. 59c

Our Best Quality Mohair Bears Cannot Be Duplicated at Our Prices

Beautifully shaped, realistic looking teddies. Made (by a high grade maker) of extra fine grade fluffy, long pile mohair plush. Have natural looking glass eyes, and movable head, arms and legs. Each has squeaker voice and pretty ribbon around its neck.

Sells Up to $2.50 Elsewhere 13-in. bear. Shipping wt., 1⅛ lbs. 49K4318 $1.98	Sells Up to $3.50 Elsewhere 14½-inch bear. Shpg. wt., 1¼ lbs. 49K4319 $2.79

Our Leader 14-Inch Size 98c

A nicely made 14-inch bear which has many points of quality as well as size; really exceptional for this price. Made by a very fine teddy bear manufacturer. Any baby would go wild over this cunning fellow. He will play with it all day and then sleep with it at night. The two will be pals. Has movable head, arms and legs, glass eyes and a squeaker voice. Made of good grade short pile plush. Comparison will prove the big value of our bear against competition. Shipping weight, 1⅛ pounds.
49K4314 .... 98c

Our Medium Grade Bears With Voices

See these perky little faces, fat, soft, roly-poly bodies. Heads, arms and legs move. Have lifelike glass eyes. Bodies are covered with soft, long pile, brown color plush, and all have voice in the back. The bodies are better shaped than our lower priced bears, and the arms are longer and more shapely.

10-Inch Bear 49K4308 Shipping wt., 1¼ pounds. 98c	12-Inch Bear 49K4309 Shipping wt., 1¼ pounds. $1.29	14-Inch Bear 49K4310 Shipping wt., 1¾ pounds. $1.69

Three Dandy Teddies

Beautiful White Fur Kitty

98c Real Fur

Cute, and surprisingly natural looking. The baby will love this white fur Angora kitten with its yellow glass lifelike cat eyes and pretty pink mouth. Very natural looking. Meows when small ring is pulled. 6 in. high. Shpg. wt., 7 oz.
49K4097 .... 98c

Fluffy White Spitz Dog

$1.19

Bow-wow; that is what he says when he opens his mouth as you stroke his back. Looks like a Spitz dog. Has fluffy coat of white fur. Has long, bushy tail and glass eyes. Length, 7 inches. Shipping weight, 1 pound.
49K4035 .... $1.19

29c Washable Soft Stuffed Toy

Cute, soft and cuddly. Baby can roll on it without hurting himself. Knit cloth in attractive colors with hand painted face in fast colors. Ribbon of same material around its neck. Kapok stuffed. Height, 9 in. Shpg. wt., 5 oz.
49K4022 .... 29c

Soft, Lovable Plush Kitty

Made of good quality white plush. Ribbon around its neck with bow and bell; also fluffy little ball between paws, catlike glass eyes and squeaker voice. Length, 7 in. Shipping weight, ¾ pound.
49K4000 .... 79c

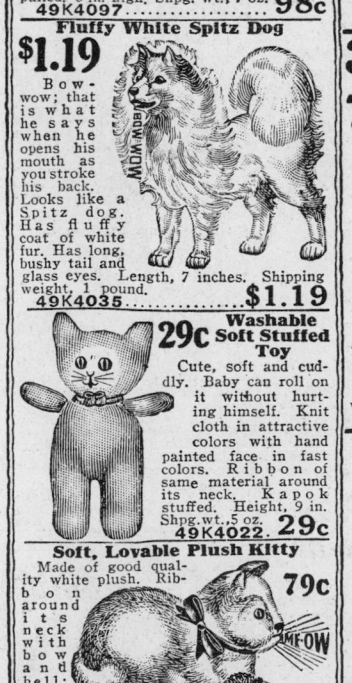

Child Can Actually Ride This Beautiful Plush Bear on Wheels

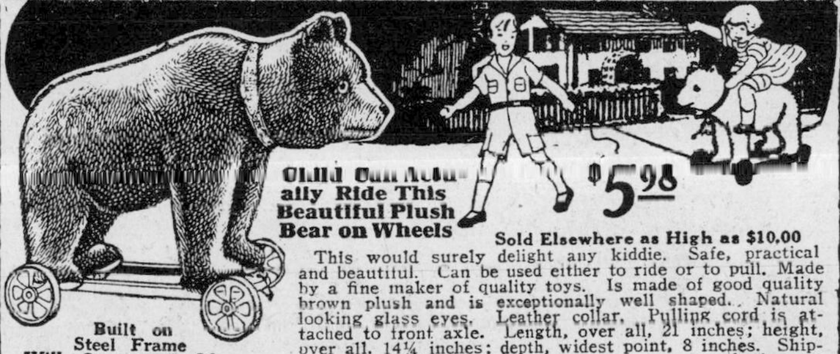

$5.98 Sold Elsewhere as High as $10.00

This would surely delight any kiddie. Safe, practical and beautiful. Can be used either to ride or to pull. Made by a fine maker of quality toys. Is made of good quality brown plush and is exceptionally well shaped. Natural looking glass eyes. Leather collar. Pulling cord is attached to front axle. Length, over all, 21 inches; height, over all, 14¼ inches; depth, widest point, 8 inches. Shipping weight, 7¼ lbs.
79K4030 .... $5.98

Built on Steel Frame Will Support 150 Lbs.

39c and 79c Famous Cartoon Characters

The kiddies will just love them. Washable, made of imitation leather, stenciled in bright, fast, harmless colors. Stuffed with soft material.

Popular Skeezix $1.00 Size Height, 13½ in. Shipping wt., 1 lb. 49K4042 ..... 79c
Standard 50c Size Height, 9¾ in. Shipping weight, 8 ounces. 49K4047 ..... 39c

59c Skeezix' Doggy Made to stand upright. Size, 8¼x6½. Shipping weight, 8 ounces. 49K4046 59c

79c Little Orphan Annie's Sandy Legs made so he can stand up alone. Size, 9x8⅜. Shipping wt., 8 ounces. 49K4041 ... 79c

Orphan Annie Made to stand upright. Size, 13⅝x3⅞. Shipping weight, 1 pound. 49K4040 79c

Dapple Gray—Pull Metal Ring and Hear His Voice

98c Voice

Natural Shape—Cloth Covered

This sturdy lifelike horse mounted on strong, hardwood platform, 11¼x4¾ inches, holds first prize in babyland. Saddle, bridle and trappings in artificial leather and has cloth saddle blanket. Height, 9¾ inches. Shpg. wt., 3 lbs.
69K7513 .... 98c

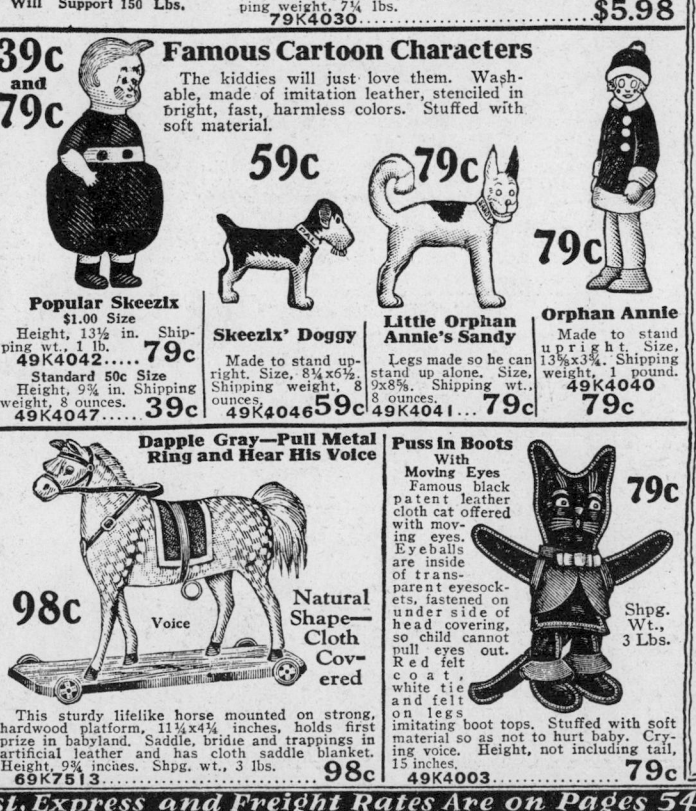

Puss in Boots With Moving Eyes

79c

Famous black patent leather cloth cat offered with moving eyes. Eyeballs are inside of transparent eyesockets, fastened on under side of head covering, so child cannot pull eyes out. Red felt coat, white tie and felt on legs imitating boot tops. Stuffed with soft material so as not to hurt baby. Crying voice. Height, not including tail, 15 inches.
49K4003 .... 79c

Barking Dog for Baby

25c

Baby size bow-wow with baby size bark. He's small and light in weight. Opens his mouth every time he barks. White with brown spots. Length, about 8 in., 6¾ in. high. Shipping wt., 8 oz.
49K4075 ...... 25c

Famous "Steiff" Molly Dog

$3.48

Finest Money Can Buy. Materials and workmanship are of the best. Made of silky long pile white plush with brown markings. Natural looking glass eyes. Silk ribbon bow around neck and squeaker voice. 8½ inches tall, 8¼ inches long. Shpg. wt., ¾ lb.
49K4044 .... $3.48

Soft Cuddly Featherweight Puppy With Voice

59c

Made Especially for the Tiny Baby. Made of white washable imitation leather, nicely painted in fast colors. Kapok stuffed. Height, 12 inches. Shipping wt., ¾ lb.
49K4014 .... 59c

Cute Plush Pup for 98c

Very nicely shaped. Made of good quality brown color plush. Has glass eyes and little doggy collar. Measures 8 in. long and 7½ in. high. Shpg. wt., ¾ lb.
49K4017 .... 98c

Toys to Delight the Kiddies

35c

See the Dog Wiggle

Body is so made up that, as the dog is pulled along the floor, it wiggles and sways back and forth. Strong cardboard, reinforced with cloth and lithographed in natural colors. Length, 23¾ inches; height, 6¼ inches. Shipping weight, 1 lb.
49K5467 .... 35c

89c

The Teddy Speed Racer

Here's a little speed racer made of solid, nicely enameled wood with nickeled and brass engine trimmings. As car is piloted along by the two little speed drivers with little brass caps, you can hear the imitation engine noise. Very strongly made; has cord to pull. Size, over all, 9½x3⅝x4 inches. Shipping weight, 1½ lbs.
49K5469 .... 89c

69c

A CrackerJack Value for 69c

Happy Ham, who is 9½ in. long, in his gay attire sits back in his bright wood auto like a king. As car is pulled along he bobs back and forth. **Giddap Jockey,** who is 9 in. long, races his horse along pulling the lines and bobbing back and forth as he goes along with you. **Tom Turno,** snappy cardboard clown tumbles over his bar and hits the bell on the platform as he is pulled along. Wood platform and wheels in bright colors. 7 in. long, 10¾ in. high. Shipping wt., 2¼ lbs.
49K5480—All 3 for 69c

ALL KIDDIES LOVE ANIMALS 98¢

A Stock Farm Complete With Barn

Here is real sport and lots of play value. Children play for hours putting the animals into the stalls and feeding them imaginary hay. A box of toothpicks makes an ideal rail fence. With old spools, cut in half, and twigs inserted for fence posts and mother's thread a fence can be built. The barn measures 12¾ inches long; 9 inches high. In it are fourteen wooden farm animals. The barn is made of good grade wood, nicely decorated. Fence materials shown not included. Shipping weight, 6 pounds.
79K9125 .... 98c

This Jack Is Some Kicker

The Peppiest Action Toy of This Year

79¢

As mule is pulled along. Oh Boy! Just see him kick. Up and out, high and low, bucking, kicking and stamping. Substantially made of wood attractively decorated. Donkey has cord tail and leather ears. Front wheels have rubber tires. Cord for pulling. Size, over all, 9⅜x 5¾x3⅞ inches. Shipping wt., 1⅜ lbs.
49K5463 .... 79c

Doc Hustler---Extra Quality

$1.29

14½-In. Long Has Rubber Tires

A beautiful floor toy for those who want something exceptionally nice. See Doc turn his head when his car turns. Made of wood and metal beautifully enameled. All metal parts nickel plated; has bumper, dummy headlight, motometer and running boards. Size, over all, 14½x 6½x4½ inches. Shipping wt., 2½ pounds.
49K5461 ...... $1.29

98¢

25-Inch Tractor Set

Made of sheet steel, lithographed in natural colors. Consists of tractor with strong spring motor which pulls the harrow, rake and grain wagon. Tractor can be set to run straight or in circle. Shipping weight, 2½ pounds.
49H5748 .... 98c

The Whirling Twins

89c

As toy is pulled along, the enameled wood twins whirl around holding hands; mounted on nicely lithographed metal frame; nothing to go wrong. Size, over all, 8¼x 5⅞ x 4½ in. Cord for pulling. Shipping wt., 1½ lbs.
49K5460
89c

Hustler Pup This Dog Walks and Barks

89c

Strong hardwood, handsomely finished and enameled in black and white. Imitation leather ears and collar, strong leash about a yard long with rubber bulb on end which, when squeezed, imitates dog bark. Mechanism on rear axle causes legs to move backward and forward when dog is pulled. Height of dog, 8 inches. Length, 8 inches. Wood wheels. Shpg. wt., 1½ lbs.
49K5462 .... 89c

Red Metal Wagon for 29c

Plenty big for the little tot to pull around. Front wheels turn under when turning corner like big wagon. 10¼ x 6¼ in. Twisted wire handle. Shipping weight, 1¾ pounds.
49K5457 .... 29c

4 for $1.00

Some Value for Little Tots---Beat This If You Can

1—All Steel Wagon. Front wheels turn under body. Size, 10¼x 6¼ inches. 3-inch wheels, wire handle.

2—21-In. Wheelbarrow, red enameled sheet steel body, 8x7x2⅝ inches, round wood handles, 4½-inch double disc steel wheel.

3—Nicely Colored Metal Sand Pail With Handle; shovel 10⅝ inches long.

4—All Steel Sand Crane. Turn crank and scoop will do the rest. Size, 8½x 7¾x3½ inches.

Shipping weight, 6 pounds.
79K9136—All 4 toys for. $1.00

Schoenhut's Humpty Dumpty Circus

What Fun! Just Like Real Circus

Animals will stand on one leg, sit up or lie down. Clowns can balance on ladder, and figures will do stunts. Figures, made of wood, are full jointed and dressed. Almost unbreakable. Finished in bright enamel colors.

7-Piece Outfit, $1.79 Including 7-in. clown, donkey and elephant; ladder, chair, barrel and tub. Shipping wt., 1¾ lbs.
69K9135
$1.79

Canvas Tent and Sawdust Ring

Collapsible canvas tent, 30 in. high, decorated with flags and equipped with wire trapeze and rings. Red curtain in back on gilt pole trimmed with gold fiber fringe. Base, 24x18 in., with sawdust glued to it and 16½-inch painted wood ring in center. Shipping weight, 5¼ pounds.
79K9145 .... $2.98

12-Piece Outfit, $4.98
6½-in. circus girl and ringmaster, Brown bear, poodle dog, horse and 7 pieces in 69K9135. Shpg. wt., 2¼ lbs.
69K9144
$4.98

89c

Gray Beauty Pacers

Horses are lifelike, legs moving back and forth when pulled along. This toy is well made and durable. Wheels, legs and all moving parts are made of metal. Red painted slat style hay wagon. Size, over all, 18⅝x6½ inches. Shipping wt., 2¾ lbs.
79K5454 ..... 89c

Pacing Pony 43c

Horse has a lifelike pacing movement when drawn along, legs moving back and forth. Wheels, legs and all moving parts made of metal, balance of wood, nicely decorated. Size, over all, 13½ inches long, 6½ inches high. Shpg. wt., 1½ lbs.
49K5455 .... 43c

Fairy Hay Wagon

43c

Painted bright red. Wood, with metal wheels; 24-inch twisted wire handle. Size of wagon, 10¼x5½x5⅝ inches. Big enough for blocks and small toys. Shipping wt., 1¾ pounds.
49K5458 .... 43c

The Kiddie Choo Choo With Bell

89c

Bell rings as choo choo is pulled along floor. Made of wood, nicely enameled with stenciled engine details. Has nickeled boiler rods and nickel plated bell. Has cord for pulling. Size, over all, 10¾x4⅝x2⅞ inches. Shipping weight, 2 pounds.
49K5465 .... 89c

89c

Watch Girl Jump Rope

As she is pulled along the little girl jumps in the most lifelike fashion. Strongly made of wood and metal, nicely enameled in bright colors. Will make any kiddie happy who owns it. Cord for pulling. Size, over all, 7¾x7⅞x4¼ inches. Shpg. weight, 2 pounds.
49K5464 .... 89c

Teddy Jockey

89c

See jockey drive the comical little black wooden horse with heavy cord legs. Gallops with funny motion when pulled along. Beautifully finished. Metal platform with pulling cord. 7⅝ in. high, 6½ inches long. Shipping weight, 1¾ pounds.
49K5474 .... 89c

For Strength and Health

HERE'S VALUE $1.98

Baby's First Pedal Car

For Tots 2 to 4 Years

Rubber pedals and grips. So easy to handle, parents need not worry about their children's safety. 8-inch double disc steel front wheel with ½-inch rubber tire and 6-inch double disc steel rear wheels with ⅜-inch rubber tires; rubber pedals and grips, curved steel handle bars, nicely finished wood seat. 11 inches high. Shpg. wt., 9 lbs.

79K8361

Very special value at. **$1.98**

Our Two Leaders

Sold Elsewhere as High as $7.50

For Youngsters 2 to 4 Years

Our Price Only $4.98

$3.89

High Class Full Tubular Kidobike

Plain Bearing Wheels

Sells Up to $5.00 Elsewhere

Easy to handle and pedal. Tubular steel frame and curved steel fork enameled bright red; wood seat and wheels enameled green. Front wheel, 9½ in. dia.; rear wheels, 7½ in. dia., all with ¾-inch rubber tires; handle bars finished with non-rusting tin finish. Shipping weight, 14 pounds.

79K8367.......... **$3.89**

$4.98

Ball Bearing Kiddies' Tubular Velocipede With Coil Spring Bicycle Saddle

This classy Kidobike with its tubular steel frame, genuine leather saddle on double coil nickel plated springs, and nickel plated and polished curved steel handle bars, is as substantial, easy running and cute as it can be. Equipped with fine quality bicycle bell, 9½-inch ball bearing front wheel, 7½-inch rear wheels and ¾-inch rubber tires. Rubber grips on handle bars, rubber pedals, polished aluminum hub caps. Frame and fork enameled bright red, wheels a pretty grass green. Shpg. wt., 16 lbs.

79K8368.......... **$4.98**

$2.89

Kiddies' Bike With Ball Bearing Front Wheel

Adjustable Saddle Shape Wood Seat

Smooth running, ball bearing front wheel 8½ inches in diameter with ¾-inch rubber tire; rear wheels 6¼ inches in diameter with ⅝-inch rubber tires and nickel plated hub caps. Curved steel handle bars with jingle bell attached and rubber grips; wide rubber pedals. Saddle shape wood seat enameled a deep orange color and steel frame a pretty grass green color. Shpg. wt., 12 lbs.

79K8366.......... **$2.89**

Special $1.00

18¼x8 in.

Sold by Many Stores at $1.50

Special Play Wagon for Little Tots Only $1.00

Hardwood bottom, heavy sheet steel sides with rolled top to reinforce body, 6-inch metal wheels and gears; hardwood tongue. Body, 18¼x8¼ inches, nicely enameled in snappy colors. Shpg. wt., 5 lbs.

79K7623.......... **$1.00**

59¢

Giddap, Stick Horsie

One of the Most Popular Toys

The Kind All Youngsters Want

A New Greatly Improved High Class Stick Horse

Nicely cut-out horsie's head beautifully finished and enameled in black and white, with yellow and red decorations. Well made throughout. The youngster trots along, guiding the horse with real [illegible] strong, nicely blue enameled round wood stick and two 4-inch double disc red enameled steel wheels. Shipping weight, 2 pounds.

69K9112.......... **59c**

Beautifully Finished Spinaway Coasters

In New Colors

Quality Throughout

Finished in high gloss orange and grass green color enamels. Double disc 5¼-inch steel wheels, ½-inch rubber tires; wood seat, handle and underpinning. Shipping wt., 6 lbs.

For Tots Up to 2 Years	For Tots 2 to 3 Years
79K7500	79K7504
Height to seat, 9⅛ in.	Height to seat, 10 in.
$1.98	**$2.69**

$1.98

$2.69

Real Riding Horses Extra Fine Quality

Horsie's Head and Front Legs Hinged for Easy Steering—Head Turns With Wheels

$2.98 $3.59

Hardwood reinforced with dowels. Will withstand hard knocks and rough usage. Saddle shape brown enameled wood seat. Steel axles and nickel plated hub caps. Finished chip-proof enamel; red, yellow, gray and black.

Double Disc Steel Wheels ½-Inch Rubber Tires

79K7506 — For children 2 to 3 yrs. 5-inch wheels. Shpg.wt., 9 lbs.... **$2.98**	79K7507 — For children 3 to 4 yrs. 6-inch wheels. Shpg.wt., 11 lbs.... **$3.59**

Every Youngster Loves a Horsie

$7.98

$9.98

Nicely shaped wood head and legs. Finished dapple gray with black enameled hoofs, red enameled nostrils and mouth. Metal stirrups and swing rods, hardwood arch and frame enameled red and striped in yellow. Leatherette padded saddle, bridle and breast band.

Full Size Beauty

As illustrated, with glass eyes, large saddle and corduroy blanket. Total height, 33 inches; length, 36 inches. Shpg. wt., 30 lbs.

79K7536 **$9.98**

Smaller body, hair mane, tail, saddle and black bead eyes; no blanket under saddle. Total height, 30 inches; length, 31½ inches. Shipping weight, 28 pounds.

79K7535 **$7.98**

Swinging Horse at a Low Price

Oh Boy! This Is Some Galloper Height, 23¼ In. Length, 33 Inches

$3.69

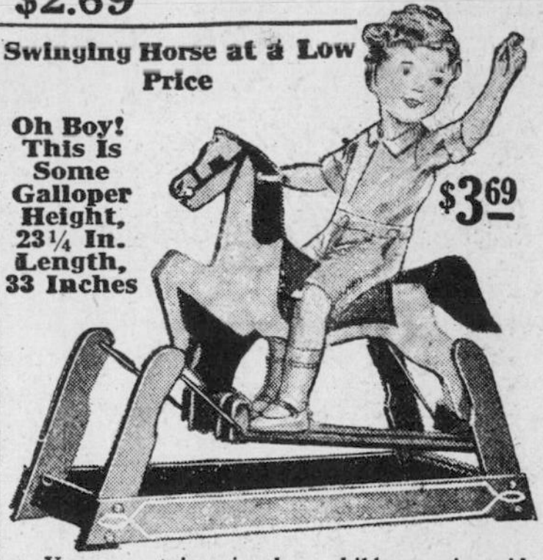

You cannot imagine how children enjoy riding a horse that has an even and gentle gallop. Here's one that will suit the youngster in every respect. Strong wood frame with metal swing rods. Quality horse finished in five snappy colors. Chip-proof enamels. Shpg. wt., 17 lbs.

79K7544—Unmailable.......... **$3.69**

Chairs and Rockers for the Little Ones

Latest Style Windsor Chair or Rocker

Every child wants to be up to date. All the rage this year. For the larger youngsters. Beautifully enameled in ivory with blue striping.

Rocker

Fancy oval shape seat, 13x12 inches, 10¾ inches from floor. Height, over all, 22½ in. Shpg. wt., 9 lbs.

79K8569.......... **$2.19**

Chair

Same as above. Seat stands 10 inches from floor. Total height, 22¼ inches. Shpg. wt., 8 lbs.

79K8568.......... **$1.89**

Bright Red Rocker

Without Arms

The little child will enjoy rocking dolly to sleep in her own little rocker. Bright red enameled hardwood with black and yellow striping.

Medium Size. Size of seat, 10 inches square; height of seat from floor, 10¾ inches; total height at back from floor, 21¾ inches. Shipping weight, 5 pounds.

79K8559

$1.10

Bright Red Chairs

The little youngster will be pleased with one of these. Bright red enameled hardwood with yellow and black neat striping.

For the Little Tot

Seat, 9⅜x9 inches. Height, seat from floor, 8½ inches; total height at back from floor, 19 inches. Shipping weight, 4 pounds.

79K8556..... **73c**

For Medium Size Child

Seat, 10 inches square. Height, seat from floor, 9¾ inches; total height at back from floor, 21½ inches. Shipping weight, 5 pounds.

79K8558..... **95c**

Bright Red Rockers With Arms

Bow back rockers with arm rests for large youngsters, strong hardwood, enameled red with black and yellow striping. Seat, 13x12½ in. Height of seat from floor, 11¾ in. Total height, 25½ in. Fancy spindle back. Nicely beveled seat. Shipping weight, 9 pounds.

79K8567 **$2.19**

Medium Size

Seat, 12x12¼ Inches

Height of seat from floor, 11¼ in. Total height, 25 in. Plain spindle back. Shpg. wt., 6 lbs.

79K8565

$1.59

World's Largest 3-in-1 Stroller Value
Sold Up to $6.00 Elsewhere. Our Price, **$3.98**

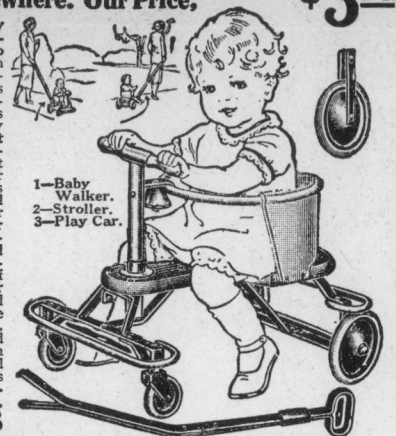

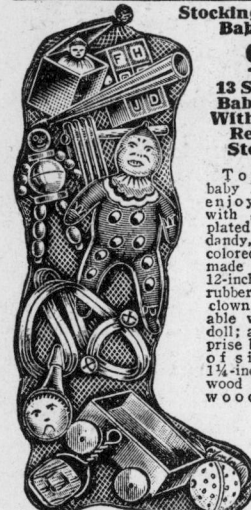

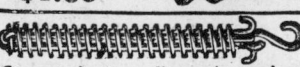

the Baby

Soft Rubber Bouncing Balls

Sanitary Washable   Lively Quality

Miller Rubber Balls Known From Coast to Coast

Colored Rubber Balls
The Color and Picture Is in the Rubber (Not Painted)
Retain their bouncing quality and keep fully inflated indefinitely if not badly abused. Assorted designs.

6-in. diameter.
Shpg. wt., 1¼ lbs.
69K7732 **87c**

4-in. diameter.
Shpg. wt., ¾ lb.
69K7734 **39c**

5-in. diameter.
Shpg. wt., 1 lb.
69K7733 **59c**

3-in diameter.
Shpg. wt., 7 oz.
69K7739 **21c**

Educational White Rubber Balls
By playing with an educational ball baby soon learns the A B C's, numbers and animals. The designs are raised, so that each subject is distinct. The larger the ball, the better the designs.

3-inch diam.
Shpg. wt., 8 oz.
69K7735 **10c**

4-inch diam.
Shpg. wt., ¾ lb.
69K7715 **25c**

6-inch diam.
Shpg. wt., 1¼ lbs.
69K7703 **59c**

Colorful Balls for Baby
The strong sateen covers are made in bright, snappy color combinations. When the rubber bladder is blown up to fill the cover you have a very attractive ball. If bladder breaks, new one can be inserted. Shipping weight, 3 ounces.

Diam., 7 in.
69K7712 **29c**

Diam., 9 in.
69K7711 **39c**

Every Baby Loves a Whistle Ball
When squeezed it whistles. Good grade heavyweight rubber, in assorted designs. Diameter, about 2¾ inches. Shpg. wt., 4 oz.
69K7710 **10c**

Shooflys for Baby

$2.59   Regular $3.50 Values   **$2.79**

Shpg. Wt., 12 lbs.

These Galloping Ponies, $2.59
Flat arc rockers permit gentle swaying motion. Made of 3-ply hardwood, beautifully enameled in white, red and black. Can be washed without injury to finish. Red enameled wood play box for baby's toys. Height to tip of ears, 19¼ inches. Length, 36 inches. Width, 11¾ inches.
79K7551.........$2.59

This Beautiful Swan Shoofly, $2.79
Baby will enjoy the gentle swaying motion of this pair of white swans. Made from 3-ply veneer wood, beautifully enameled in white with yellow and black beak and light green trimmings. Complete with play box for baby's toys. Length, over all, 31¾ inches. Height, 15¾ inches. Width, 11¾ inches.
79K7556.........$2.79

A Special Chime Value for 48c
48c
The best chime value we have ever offered. Plays real music as it is pushed or pulled along. The metal chime barrels are shaped like the well known choral tops and are finished in red, yellow and natural white metal color. Width of chime barrels, over all, 8 inches; length of entire chime, over all, 22 in.; diameter, chime barrel, 4 in. Shpg. wt., 1 lb.
49K2400 **48c**

The Waddling Daddy Ducky 42c
Wood beautifully enameled. Head can be moved from side to side. Top of head and wings are red and his wheels black. The single front wheel is set off center, making him waddle. He stands 7½ in. high and is 9¼ in. long. A cord to pull is attached. Shipping weight, 1½ pounds.
49K5470 **42c**

Here's Value
$1.10

Rockie Toddler $1.10
Ideal Nursery Toy for Tots
Every Baby Wants to Ride
Baby Can't Get Hurt
Low, broad wood seat and wide arc rockers of substantial wood beautifully enameled in white with red, yellow and black decorations. Seat, 4¼ inches high; total height, 14½ inches; length, 21½ inches. Shipping weight, 7 lbs.
79K7554—Special at **$1.10**

ROUND CORNER SAFETY BLOCKS

40 BLOCKS 1¾ in cubes 98c   **36 BLOCKS 1¼ in cubes 39c**

The Biggest Values We Have Ever Offered
By a special exclusive arrangement we are able to offer to you at the same price (as last year), a larger quantity than ever, of the new fancy decorated, brightly colored, round cornered, safety A B C block. A big improvement over the old style. While playing the child becomes familiar with the alphabet and different types of animals and objects printed on the blocks. Made of lightweight wood two sides embossed with letters in the center of the new filigree design, and enameled in colors. The other four sides have printed pictures, letters and numerals in colors. The child can build with these blocks also, so you have a combination of building blocks and A B C blocks. Two sizes:

Forty 1¾-Inch Blocks, 98c
We recommend this set for those who want larger blocks. Box, 9¼x7¼x3⅝ inches. Shpg. wt., 4 lbs.
49K3663 **98c**

Thirty-Six 1¼-Inch Blocks, 39c
Value possible because of our huge purchasing power. Box, 8⅞x8¾x1½ inches. Shpg. wt., 1¾ lbs.
49K3662 **39c**

ABC Teacher. 47c
Smooth Finish Wood
Will teach a child to spell and recognize words. Made of wood. Many are only one piece, making them stronger than those of more than one piece. Average 2½ inches high and ⅛ inch thick. Complete alphabet. Shipping weight, 2 pounds.
49K3655 **47c**

Rattle Blocks for Baby
39c
One of these blocks held up to baby and shaken will make the little eyes sparkle with pleasure. A very nice toy for a baby, as each block has a rattle in it, as well as attractive pictures on each side. The blocks are hollow wood cubes. In box, 5¾ in. square. Shpg. wt., 2 lbs.
49K3671 **39c**

Bell Reins for Baby to Play Horsie
Nickel plated 1-inch bells on decorated oilcloth. Well made; pretty colors. Brother or sister or even mother will drive as baby trots along like a pony, making music with the bells.

20-Bell Reins
Shipping weight, 1 pound.
49K2353 **39c**

8-Bell Reins
Shipping weight, 7 ounces.
49K2454 **25c**

Unlatch the Door and Hear Him Crow 
59c
Cage is wood with printed imitation tile roof and brick sides. Size, over all, 7x6¼x 4¾ inches. Shpg. wt., 1¼ lbs.
69K9126 **59c**

6 Brightly Colored Celluloid Toys
Will keep baby amused when bathing. Two pretty swans, 2⅜ inches long; two ducks, 2¾ inches long, and two gold fish, 3⅝ inches long. Fast colors. Shpg. wt., 8 oz.
69K9178—Box of 6 **39c**

Celluloid Teething Toys—Colors Will Not Come Off
Cute doll, in assorted characters, 4½ inches high, barrel shape red rattle, 2¾ inches diameter with twisted handle, 2¼-inch teething ring with cord and tassel. Shipping weight, 8 ounces.
69K9153 **29c**

What's Inside Surprise Box
Unhook the lid, quick as a wink up it comes with a funny squeak. Assorted figures, wood box covered with paper. Size, 4¼x4¼ inches. Shpg. wt., ¾ lb.
69K7020 **25c**

Chick in Egg
15c
Three in one. Rattle, whistle and teething ring. White rubber. Height, over all, 4½ in. Shpg. wt., 2 oz.
49K4400 **15c**

The Ever Popular Rubber Rattle

12c
Seven-Bell Rattle
All babies like the sound of bells. Six ¾-inch and one 1½-inch bell, fastened on a black wood handle. Height over all, 5 inches. Shipping weight, 8 ounces.
49K2480 **12c**

39c
Has Smiling and Crying Faces
The better quality red rubber rattle. Length over all, 7 inches. Shpg. wt., 3 oz.
49K4403 **39c**

Low Prices on Playthings

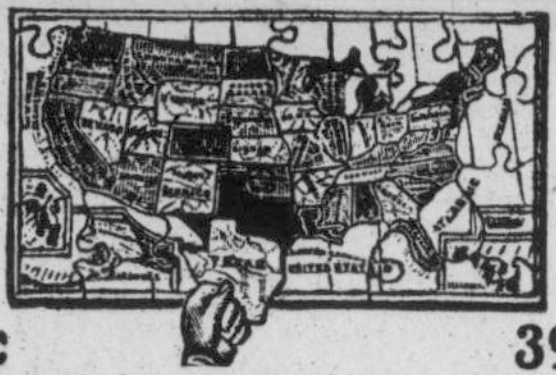

79c 39c

U. S. Maps Cut on State Lines

Easy way of teaching the shapes and locations of States. Principal cities, rivers, mountains, and lakes shown. Make maps 20x12 in. Box, 12½x11⅛ inches.

Our Best Seller

Compare this value. Made of 3-ply wood, smoothly cut. Shpg. wt., 1¾ lbs.
49K3871 .... 79c

For the Smaller Child

Made of heavy cardboard with the additional puzzle feature of a farm scene on back of map. Regular 50c value. Shpg. wt., 1¼ lbs.
49K3870 .... 39c

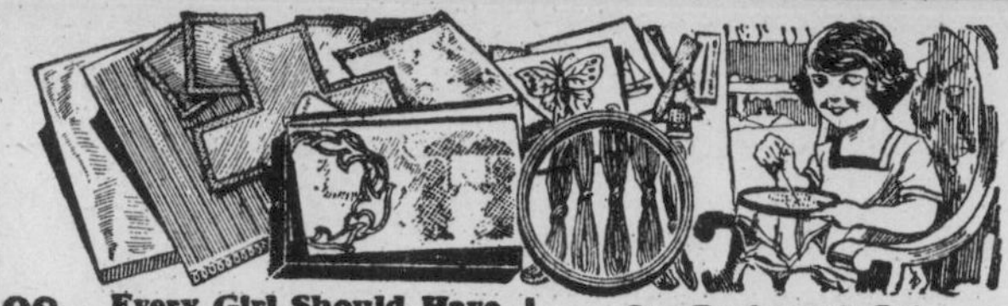

98c Every Girl Should Have These Embroidery Sets

Set for Older Girls

Complete as illustrated. Two good quality, colored border guest towels, 14x7½ inches; glass towel, centerpiece, and 4—5⅝-inch doilies. All hemmed and ready to embroider. Also tools, designs, etc. Shipping weight, 7 oz.
49K3818 .... 98c

Our Beginner's Set 39c

A Real Bargain

Consists of 5-inch hoops, 5 skeins of embroidery cotton, 4 doilies, thimble, needle and design sheets with letters, numbers and patterns to transfer to cloth. Box, 10⅞x7⅝ inches. Shipping weight, 5 ounces.
49K3816 .... 39c

Colored Wood Beads for Stringing

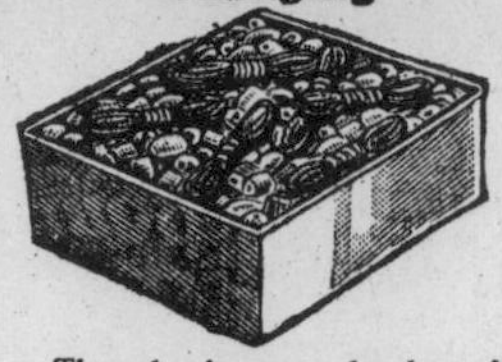

23c Up

Very Popular With Kiddies

These beads are made of wood in different shapes, some cylindrical, some square, some round, all nicely colored and varnished. Necklace, designs, etc., can be made with them. Three different size packages, each in heavy cardboard boxes.

450-Bead Box, 79c

An exceptionally good value. Has 6 tipped cords. Shipping weight, 1⅛ lbs.
49K3810 .... 79c

185 Beads in This Box, 42c

A lot of beads for this price. Has 4 cords. Shipping weight, ¾ pound.
49K3813 .... 42c

Beginners' Bead Set, 23c

A big value, with 2 cords. Shipping weight, 7 ounces.
49K3831 .... 23c

39c

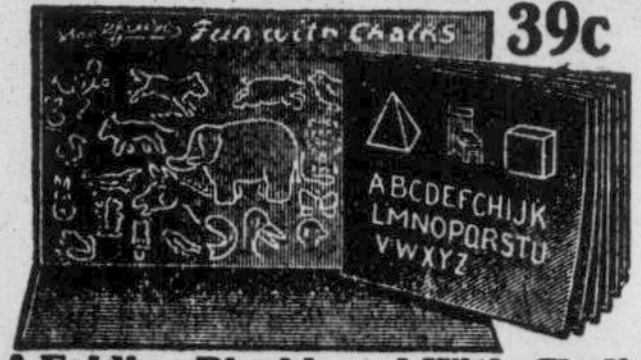

A Folding Blackboard With Chalk

Stout cardboard covers. Opens like a book, lower half being a blackboard. 14 pages of figures, animals and objects to copy. Size, open, 18x15⅛ in. Shpg. wt., 1½ lbs.
49K3809 .... 39c

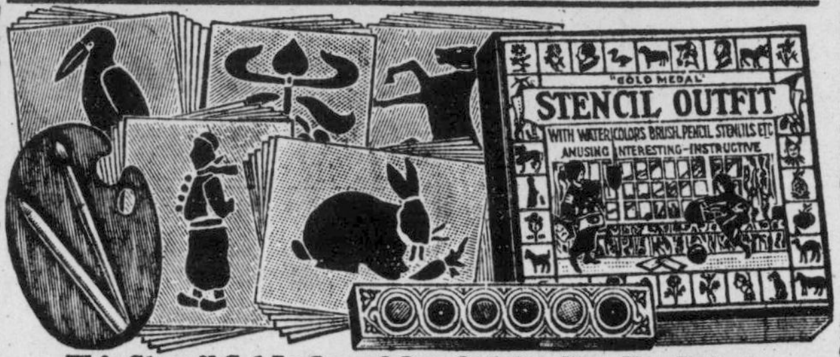

This Stencil Set Is One of Our Outstanding Toy Values

Easy for children to use. Teaches them to concentrate. Thirty interesting stencils, 6x4¾ inches, in the following designs: 12 animals, 6 figures, 6 fruits and 6 flowers. Small pencil, brush, cardboard palette and 6 good quality water colors set in box. Attractive box, 9½x9¼ inches. Shpg. wt., 1 lb.
49K3827 .... 39c

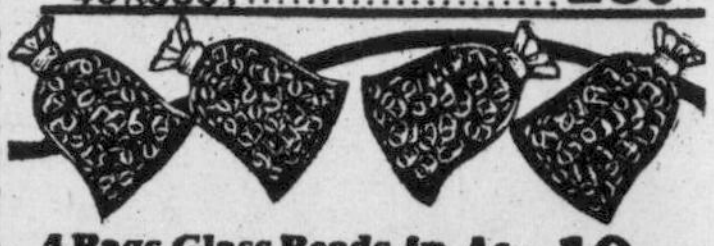

4 Bags Glass Beads in Assorted Colors and Shapes 19c

About 225 assorted color glass and clay beads; each bag about 2x2¼ inches; different size beads. Shpg. wt., 7 oz.
49K3815 .... 19c

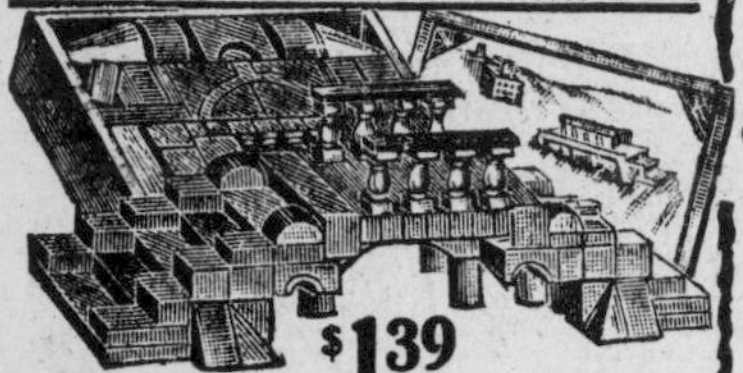

$1.39

Architectural Building Blocks

The Nicest Set of Building Blocks We Could Find

All kiddies love to build bridges, houses and structures of their own imagination. Smooth hardwood blocks in attractive shapes. About 90 blocks, packed two layers in wooden box with slide cover. Size of box, 10⅛x7¾ inches. Shipping weight, 4¾ pounds.
49K3641 .... $1.39

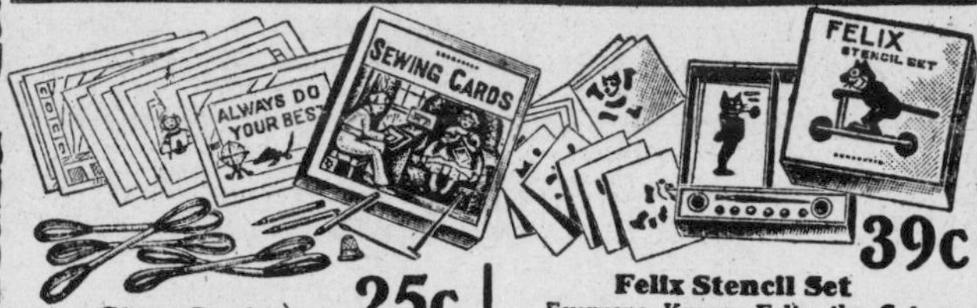

Story Sewing 25c

Very Special Value

Sew motto on the cards, color, and then frame your handiwork. Ten combination sewing and coloring cards, 9¼x7¼ inches; 5 skeins colored embroidery floss, thimble, needle, perforator and 3 colored wax crayons. Shipping weight, ¾ pound.
49K3841 .... 25c

39c

Felix Stencil Set

Everyone Knows Felix the Cat

The kiddies will surely enjoy drawing the funny antics of Felix. Twelve 5½x3½-inch waxed stencils, 2 cakes black paint, good brush and thumb tacks included in set so that the different pictures can be painted through the stencil. Attractive box, 8¼ inches square. Shipping weight, 1 pound.
49K3840 .... 39c

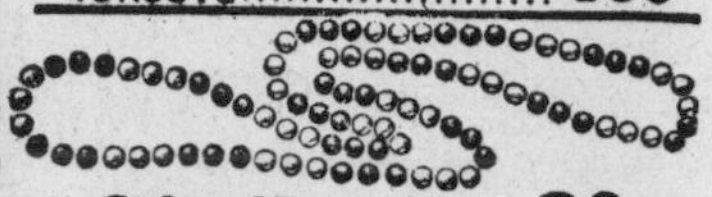

String of Heavy Glass Beads 29c

Watch your youngster play with the smooth nicely colored glass beads. A variety of bright colors. Can be used for stringing, identifying colors, or as necklaces. String of about 84—⅝-inch beads. Shipping weight, 1 pound.
49K3825 .... 29c

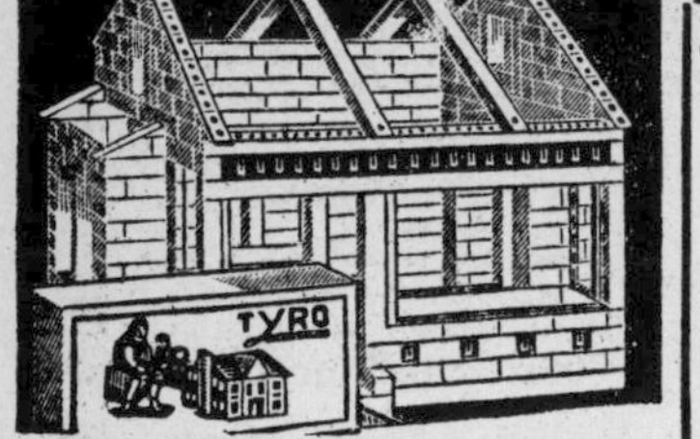

Models Really Hold Together

The blocks are held together by wood rods so that objects made will not fall apart. A wren house you can make can actually be placed on a post for use by birds. Instruction books included.

$5.00 Set for $4.49

Over 500 pieces. Builds endless number of complicated models. Box, 14x11x2¼ inches. Shipping weight, 9½ pounds.
79K4711 .... $4.49

$2.00 Set for $1.69

About 220 pieces. Builds more complicated models than cheaper set. Box, 12x8¾x1¾ in. Shipping weight, 4¼ pounds.
49K4710 .... $1.69

$1.00 Set for 83c

About 130 pieces. Builds many models. Box, 10x7x1¼ inches. Shpg. wt., 2¼ lbs.
49K4709 .... 83c

39c 79c and $1.19

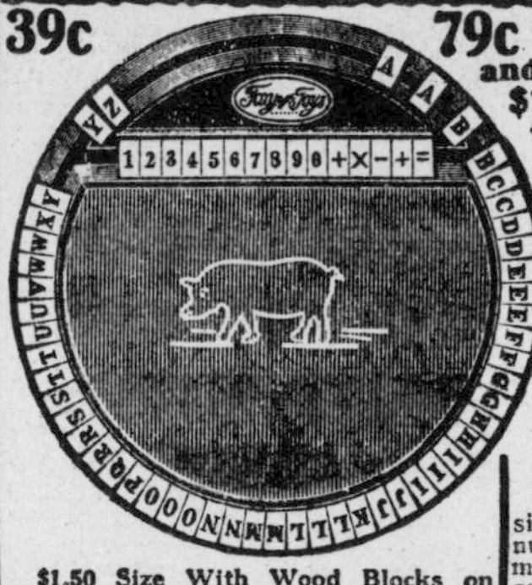

The Genuine Fox All Steel Combination Slate and Educational Boards

A Toy to Instruct as Well as Amuse

These boards have complete alphabets and provide a simple way of teaching the child his A B C's, how to spell, write words, short sentences and simple arithmetic. Large letters on varnished wood blocks fit into grooves so they cannot fall out, but still can very easily be slid around into the center groove to form words and short sentences. Slate pencil included. Slate surface on both sides.

3 Sizes

$1.00 Size for 79c

The most popular size; 65 letters, numerals and arithmetical characters on one side. Slate surface on other side. 13-inch size. Shipping wt., 2¼ lbs.
49K3842 .... 79c

50c Size for 39c

Forty-eight letters, numerals and arithmetical characters on one side. Slate surface on other side. 9⅝-in. size. Shipping weight, 1¼ pounds.
49K3801 .... 39c

$1.50 Size With Wood Blocks on Both Sides $1.19. One side has 65 letters, figures and mathematical signs. The other side has 45 words and pictures taken from "Teachers' Manual of Sight Reading." 13 inches in diam. Shpg. wt., 2¾ lbs.
49K3863 .... $1.19

Pictures Appear Just Like Magic

Surprise Pictures

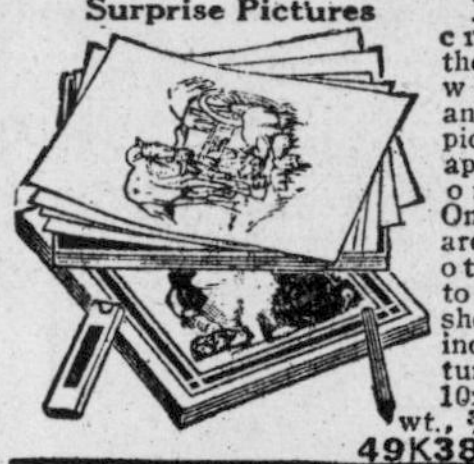

Rub the hard crayon over these blank white sheets and, presto! a picture to color appears. Crayons included. On opposite side are printed other pictures to color. 16 sheets, 9¼x7¾ inches; 32 pictures. In box, 10x8¾ in. Shpg. wt., ¾ lb.
49K3845 .... 25c

Well Known Diamoblox Set

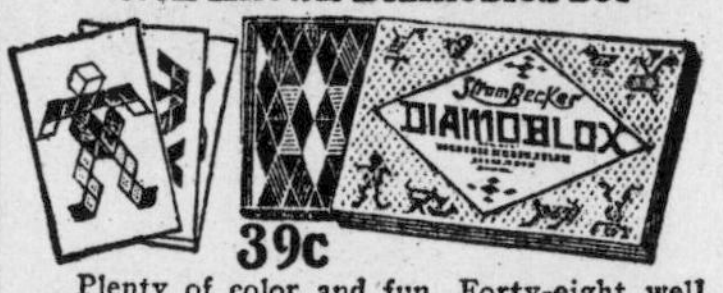

39c

Plenty of color and fun. Forty-eight well sanded diamond shaped wood blocks, in attractive cardboard box, 9⅝x6⅝ inches. Blocks nicely enameled in white, green, yellow, blue, red and brown from which you can make beautiful color designs, and also build objects if you wish. Helps develop the child's imagination. With each set is included two sheets of designs and booklet for working puzzles. A very good mind builder. Shipping weight, 1¼ pounds.
49K3656 .... 39c

Kiddies' Picture Blocks 98c

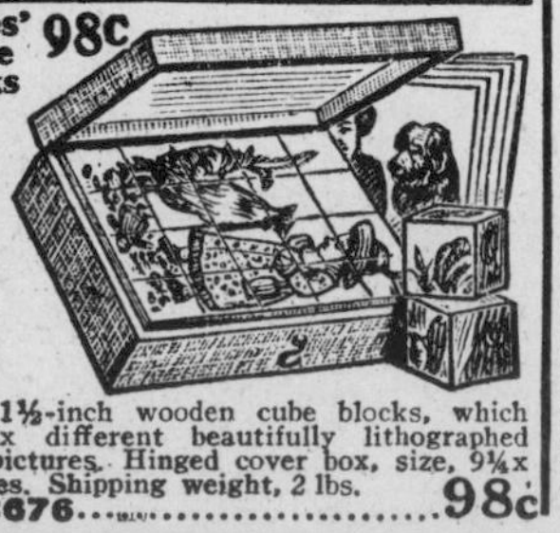

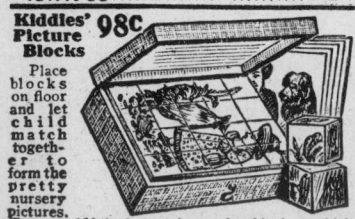

Place blocks on floor and let child match together to form the pretty nursery pictures. Twenty 1½-inch wooden cube blocks, which make six different beautifully lithographed colored pictures. Hinged cover box, size, 9¼x7¾ inches. Shipping weight, 2 lbs.
49K3676 .... 98c

Wagon and Load of Blocks $1.98

Well constructed, attractively colored wood wagon box with contrasting color molding, measuring 17x10½x3⅝ inches, and full of various shaped, smoothly finished blocks, about 156 in all. Has real turntable wagon axle which can be swung around when wagon is pulled along. Also 15-in. tongue handle. Actual front and rear axle to hold wheels, which have painted spokes. Easy to put away. Just remove wheels, tongue, lower front axle and place in box with blocks. Shpg. wt., 9 lbs. Chart of Models included.
79K3632 .... $1.98

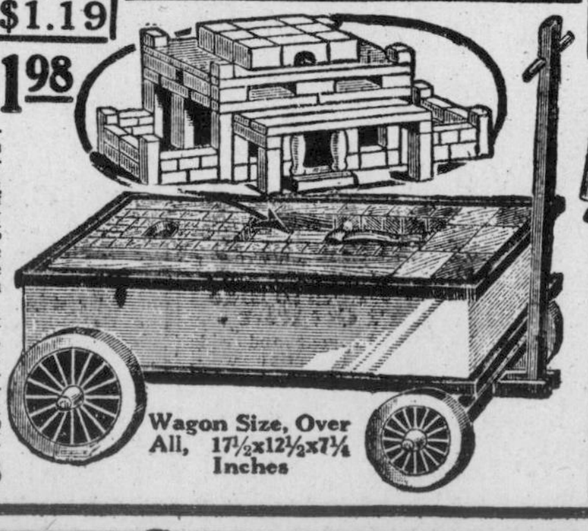

Wagon Size, Over All, 17½x12½x7¼ Inches

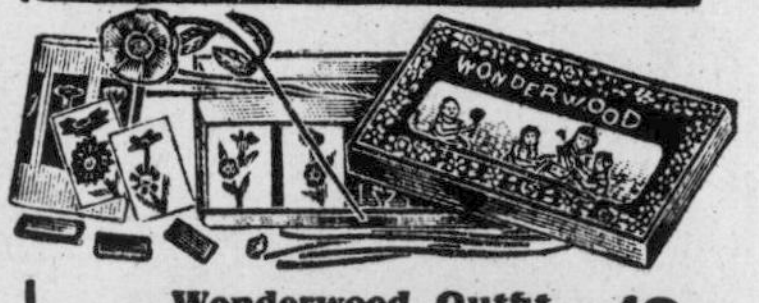

Wonderwood Outfit Makes Realistic Flowers 42c

Realistic, yet simple enough for tiny tots. They will sit for hours making pretty flowers with the colored wood flower petals, colored clay and stems. Set consists of 10 green fiber stems, 4 envelopes of thin colored wood flower petals and leaves, and enough colored plastic clay to hold flower petals and leaves in position. Packed in attractive box, 11⅛x7⅝ inches. Full instructions. Shipping weight, 1 pound.
49K3848 .... 42c

That Instruct and Amuse

Make a Train With These Blocks

89c

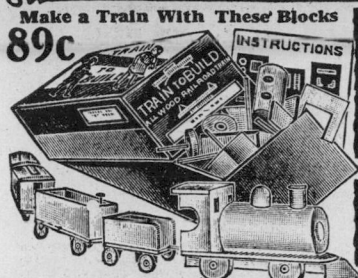

A new, entertaining and instructive toy. Made of wood blocks and wood pins. First the engine, then the coal car, and the gondola, the freight car with moving doors, and the observation car. And then, best of all, when constructed, train can be pulled around like the big fellows. Train, when completed, is 27½ inches long. Packed in lithographed box, 11¾x4⅝x3¼ inches. Directions included. Shpg. wt., 2¼ lbs.
49K3659 .... **89c**

36½-Inch, 3-Drawer Roll Top Desk

$17.67

Here's just the roll top desk for the children. Convenient for keeping school books, pencils and paper, and also to help interest the child in his work. Made of hardwood, in golden oak finish. Has panel sides, extension writing board, and three large drawers on right side, the top one having lock and key. Four pigeonholes and drawer in center. Revolving swivel type chair is adjustable from 13 to 17 inches. The chair legs are fastened with iron brackets, which prevent splitting. Desk, over all, 36½x31x16½ inches. Shipping weight, 88 pounds. Unmailable.
79K3852 .... **$17.67**

Popular Flat Top Desk

$16.98

The newest and most popular desk. Made of hardwood with golden oak finish. Big roomy top, 31x22 inches, beautifully finished and varnished. Has one row of pigeon holes 4⅜ inches high on back of top. Three drawers on right hand side of desk. 32 inches high, 31 inches long and 22 inches wide. Swivel chair to match, adjustable from 14 to 18 inches. Shipping weight, 88 pounds. Unmailable.
79K3819 .... **$16.98**

Medium Size 2-Drawer Desk

$9.98

Made of same material as our higher priced set s in golden oak finish, but built smaller to suit the little child. 32 inches high, 22 inches wide and 14⅞ in. deep. Has four pigeonholes, two drawers on right side, the top one having lock and key. Straight back chair, seat 12 inches from floor. Shipping wt., 51 lbs. Unmailable.
79K3851 .... **$9.98**

Foundation of an Education
THE GENUINE HOME EDUCATOR, DESK & BLACKBOARD
MADE ESPECIALLY FOR US, AND WE PRIDE OURSELVES THAT THIS IS THE FINEST, MOST COMPLETE BOARD OFFERED ANYWHERE AT THIS PRICE. WELL WORTH THE DIFFERENCE IN PRICE OVER CHEAPER BOARDS.

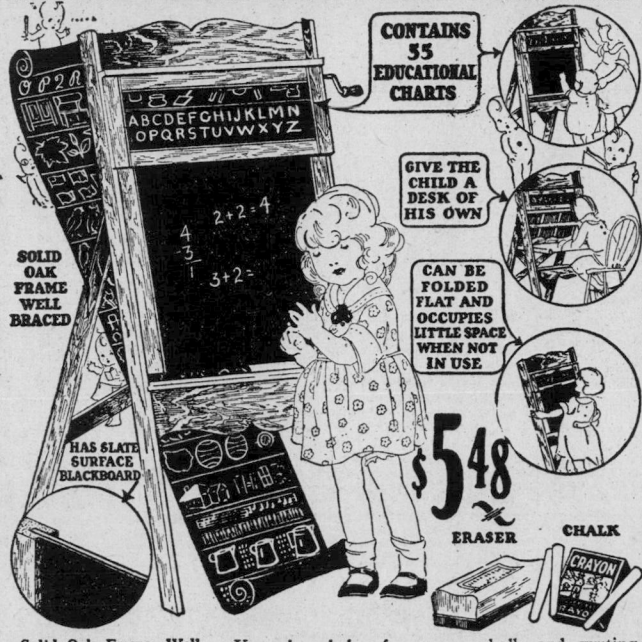

CONTAINS 55 EDUCATIONAL CHARTS

GIVE THE CHILD A DESK OF HIS OWN

CAN BE FOLDED FLAT AND OCCUPIES LITTLE SPACE WHEN NOT IN USE

SOLID OAK FRAME WELL BRACED

HAS SLATE SURFACE BLACKBOARD

$2+2=4
4
3
1
3+2=

$5 48

ERASER   CHALK

Solid Oak Frame. Well Braced. Appropriate for Play or Home Work.

Has pigeonholes for paper, chalk and writing materials. Has 55 charts which were approved by Chicago educators and are to be found in no other blackboard, as they are printed for us exclusively. There are simple charts devoted to A B C's, elementary drawing, leaves, vegetables, first steps in reading music, geography, how to tell time, etc. Fifteen charts give simple, effective ideas for teaching arithmetic; colored charts of American birds, flowers, fruits; also tables of weights and measures, and the Declaration of Independence. To change to desk turn button and pull blackboard down. Pigeonhole cabinet work for tablets, crayons, etc. finished in ebony color with a frame in golden oak with two coats of varnish. Slate surfaced blackboard (not painted), eraser and box of crayons. Height, 46 inches, set for use; width, 21⅝ inches. Shipping wt., crated, 17 lbs. Unmailable.
79K3811 .... **$5 48**

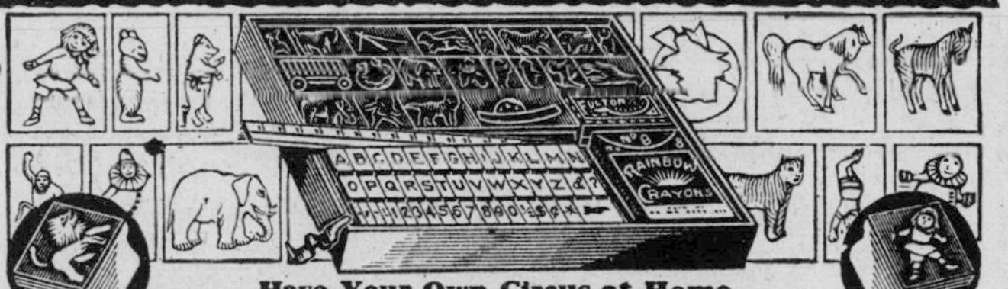

Have Your Own Circus at Home

Every boy loves a circus. When you give your own show you can print your own signs and invitations with this set. Has 66 stamps; animals, clowns, alphabet, etc. Circus wagon stamp, 1¾x1½ inches. Letters, ½ inch high, 8 crayons, ink stamp pad and 8-inch wood rule. Box, 10x8⅞ inches. Shipping weight, 1 pound.
49K3828 .... **79c**

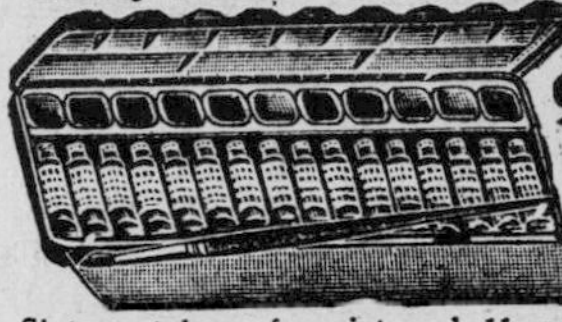

Brand New Farm and Jungle Set

The little boys and girls will enjoy making pictures of their own creation with the 70 farm animal, jungle beast and sign marker rubber stamps. The stamps are of good quality rubber, being cut deeper than the average toy set sold by other stores, thus making clear, distinct, fine cut impressions. There is also a complete alphabet of ½-inch capital letters and numerals; 2⅝x1⅞-inch self inking stamp pad, and 8-inch rule, box of good size crayons and small block of stamp paper. Full set of directions included. All packed in nicely lithographed box, 10x8⅞ inches. Shipping weight, 1 pound.
49K3834 .... **79c**

First Printing Lesson

27c

About 248 pieces; box, 6¼x5 inches. Three capital and four small letter alphabets, ink pad, 3-row type holder and tweezer. Capitals, ⁷⁄₁₆ inch high. Shpg. wt., 7 oz.
49K3824 .... **27c**

80 Characters for Sign Making

You can print your own signs and invitations just the way you want them. Complete alphabet of capitals, small letters, numerals, etc., ink pad and 8-inch wood ruler. Box, 12⅝x4½ inches. Shipping weight, 1 pound.
49K3829 .... **79c**

The Popular Toy Saxophones

We believe these are the best toy saxophone values now offered. All nickel plated metal, practically unbreakable. Much classier looking than the old style wood and metal horns. All have 8 keys or more, so simple tunes can be played. Sheet music included. Compare with others on the market at these prices. We have them in four different qualities.

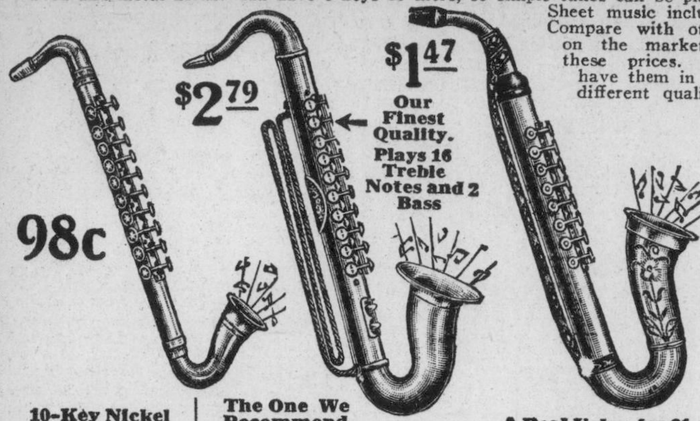

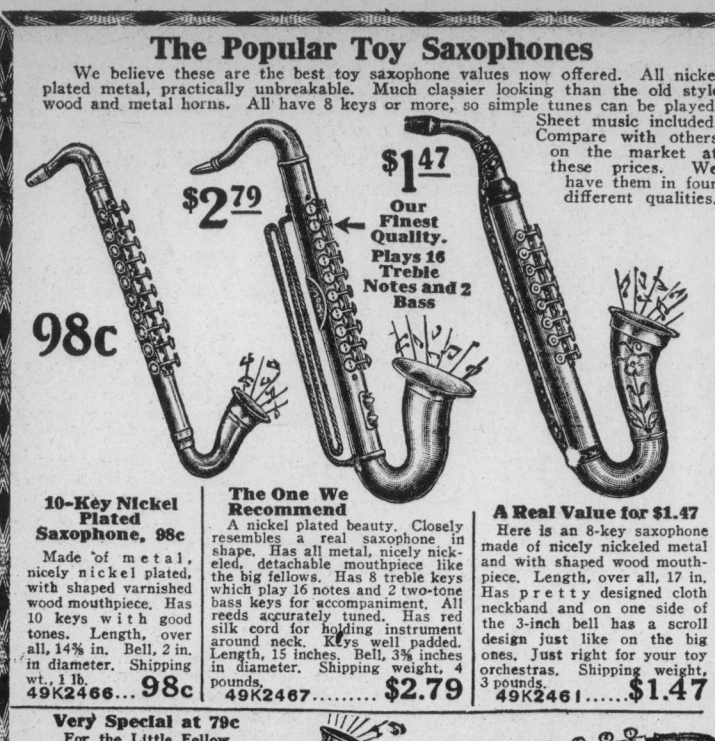

$2.79 — Our Finest Quality. Plays 16 Treble Notes and 2 Bass

$1.47

98c

10-Key Nickel Plated Saxophone, 98c

Made of metal, nicely nickel plated, with shaped varnished wood mouthpiece. Has 10 keys with good tones. Length, over all, 14⅝ in. Bell, 2 in. in diameter. Shipping wt., 1 lb.
49K2466... 98c

The One We Recommend

A nickel plated beauty. Closely resembles a real saxophone in shape. Has all metal, nicely nickeled, detachable mouthpiece like the big fellows. Has 8 treble keys which play 16 notes and 2 two-tone bass keys for accompaniment. All reeds accurately tuned. Has red silk cord for holding instrument around neck. Keys well padded. Length, 15 inches. Bell, 3⅜ inches in diameter. Shipping weight, 4 pounds.
49K2467......... $2.79

A Real Value for $1.47

Here is an 8-key saxophone made of nicely nickeled metal and with shaped wood mouthpiece. Length, over all, 17 in. Has pretty designed cloth neckband and on one side of the 3-inch bell has a scroll design just like on the big ones. Just right for your toy orchestras. Shipping weight, 3 pounds.
49K2461...... $1.47

Very Special at 79c
For the Little Fellow

Eight-key, turned wood saxophone with nickel plated metal horn and mouthpiece; nice tone. Length, over all, 14 inches. Shpg. wt., 1 lb.
49K2460........ 79c

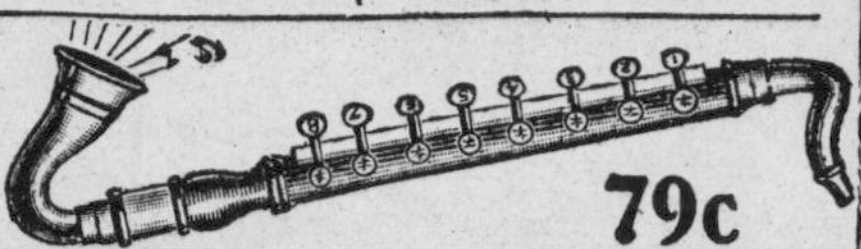

79c

Miniature Banjo Uke with Resonator Back

Can be used as pocket uke. Measures 16¾ in. long by 5½ in. wide.

98c

Every child has wanted to own a banjo uke. Surprisingly fine tone. Can be played same as full size uke. Has genuine calfskin head, accurate fretting, four good quality strings, nickel plated flesh ring and tailpiece. Nicely finished light color hardwood frame. Shpg. wt., 1¼ lbs.
49K2442.. 98c

Boys' Dandy Drums and Violins

The two better drums are priced very special and considering the quality, are exceptional values. The all metal drum is low priced and fits the need of those who want an extra durable drum at a bargain.

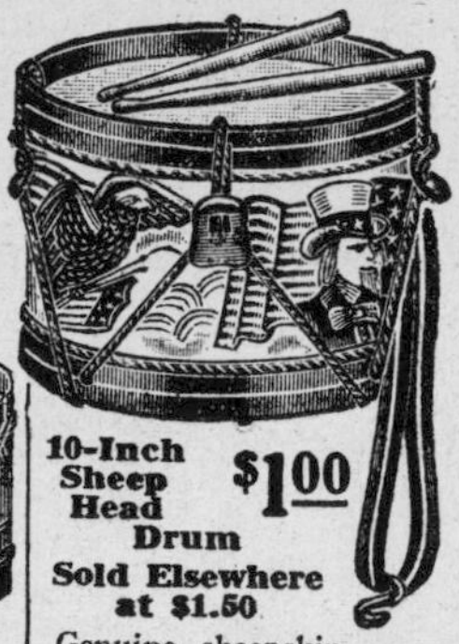

12-In. Calf Head Drum. $1.98 Sold as High as $3.00 Elsewhere

Genuine calf head and sheep bottom. Golden oak, solid hardwood shell, gut snares and leather ear fasteners. A pair of drumsticks and web shoulder strap included. Ht., 6 inches. Shipping weight, 2½ pounds.
79K2484.......... $1.98

10-In. All Metal Drum for... 48c

Nicely lithographed sturdy drum. Height, 4¾ inches. Shpg wt., 3¾ lbs.
49K2472........ 48c

10-Inch Sheep Head Drum $1.00 Sold Elsewhere at $1.50

Genuine sheepskin head and fiber bottom. Beautifully lithographed metal sides with leather ear fasteners, gut snares and pair of good sticks. Height, 7¼ in. Shpg. wt., 2½ lbs.
79K2483...... $1.00

$1.48

19⅝ in. long

Imported Toy Wood Violin

Here's a dandy little toy fiddle for the child. Imagine the fun drawing the bow back and forth over the gut strings. Made of well seasoned wood with swelled back and front, mahogany stained and varnished. Violin has extension sides like real ones, and is 19⅝ inches long by 5⅞ inches wide. Has shaped tailpiece and fingerboard, four gut strings, wood bridge and black keys. Has adjustable horsehair bow, 17½ inches long. Resin included. Shipping weight, 1¾ pounds.
49K2332.. $1.48

Musical Toys

Musical Tops

59c

These tops have always been popular. The sight of rainbow colors revolving around at a rapid pace while different organlike chords are playing, always charms a child. Chords change when handle is tapped with finger or hand as top spins. Light weight metal beautifully finished in bright red, white, blue and yellow. Strings included. Two qualities.

39c

Extra Fine Quality 3-Chord Top

Stronger metal and better colors than generally used. Heavy metal balance ring built in top, which prolongs spinning. Beautiful chords, full and harmonious. Height, 8½ inches; diameter, 5¼ inches. Shipping weight, 1½ pounds.
49K2375........................ 59c

Special 2-Chord Top Value

An excellent top at this price. Not as heavy metal as 49K2375 and has only two chords, but a dandy top and a big value. Shipping weight, ¾ pound.
49K2396........ 39c

ACCORDIONS
You Can Actually Play on These

98c

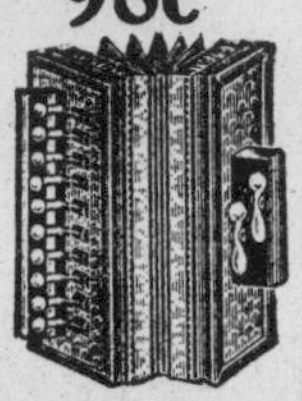

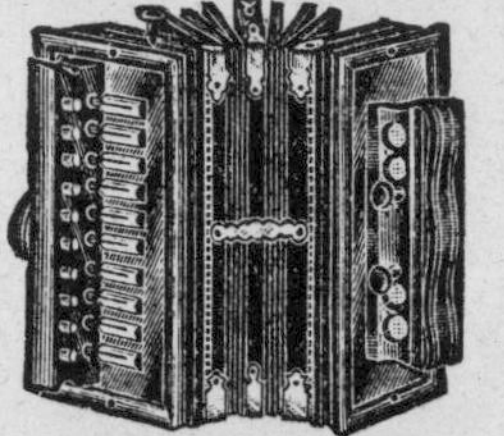

59c

10-Key Accordion

An enameled metal frame, 10 double reed metal keys. Two bass keys, single bellows. Size, closed, 8¾ x 6¾ x 4⅛ in. Shipping weight, 1¼ lbs.
49K2364 98c

Exceptional Accordion Value

Black enameled wood frame braced with nickel plates on top and bottom. Double bellows with metal corners. 20 treble notes and two bass keys. Size, closed, 9¼x 8x4½ inches. Shipping weight, 3¼ pounds.
49K2371.......... $1.98

8-Key New Model Accordion for Baby

Heavy cardboard frame, covered with attractively colored paper; 8 nickel plated metal treble keys, 16 notes, and one bass. Single bellows. Size, 8⅛x4x3⅜ in. Shpg. wt., 1½ lbs.
49K2344 59c

Genuine nickel plated patented playphones. The only ones on which the receiver hook rings bell like real phone

89¢

The All Nickel Plated "Silver Chime" Talking Phone

Pull down receiver hook and hear the tinkle, tinkle of the two bells. Cord to use for talking from one room to another. Nickel plated base, felt bottom. Special receiver, 9¼ in. high. Shipping wt., 1½ pounds.
49K2464........ 89c

47¢

All Nickel Plated Phone. Wonderful Value

Smaller than others offered at about this price, but much better quality. Nickel plated. 1⅝-inch bell. 6¾-inch high. Shpg. wt., 1 pound.
49K2463. 47c

Has Real Ma-Ma Voice

When receiver is worked up and down, the chimes tinkle and the "ma-ma" voice is heard. Nickel plated, felt bottom. A quality phone. Height, 9¼ in. Shipping wt., 1¾ pounds.
49K2465.. $1.00

Unbreakable Metal Horse and Bell Chime

42c

Just Right for Baby

A toy that will last, being practically unbreakable. Just see this stately metal horse draw the 2½-in. heavily nickeled plated bell set between two 3½-in. nickeled steel wheels. Substantially constructed. Length, over all, 8¾ inches. Shpg. wt., 2 lbs.
49K2314.................. 42c

89¢

Two-Horse Bell Chimes

Sight of this on Christmas morn would make any child's eyes pop. Two shiny metal gray iron horses are hitched to 3-inch nickel plated bell set between two nickel plated 5¼-in. steel wheels. Measures 11¼-in. long. Very sturdily built and also appealing. Shpg. wt., 2¾ lbs.
49K2313.................. 89c

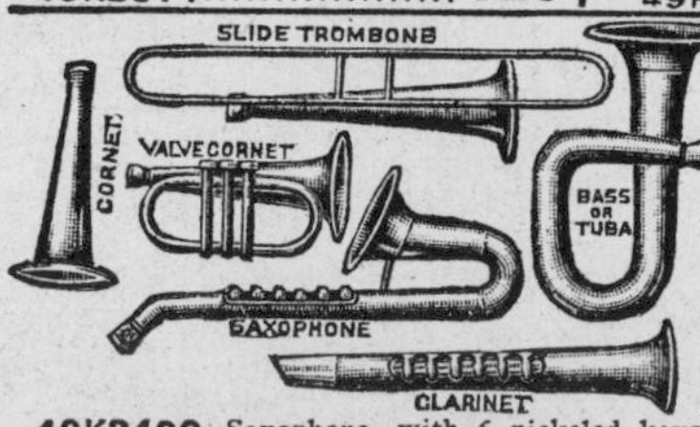

Song-o-Phones

Organize a song-o-phone band and have the time of your life. Anyone who can sing or hum a tune can play without studying. Remember singing through a comb covered with paper? This is just as easy. All instruments, except Clarinet, are brass plated metal, highly polished and have aluminum mouthpieces. Clarinet made of metal, finished in black baked-on enamel. Keys nickel plated. Full directions included.

49K2490—Saxophone, with 6 nickeled keys. 17 inches long; 4½-inch bell. Shpg. wt., 2 lbs.......... $2.69
49K2491—Trombone, with working slide open, 24 inches long; 4½-inch bell. Shipping weight, 2½ pounds.......... $2.29
49K2492—Cornet, 9 inches long; 4½-inch bell. Shpg. wt., 1¼ lbs. .79
49K2493—Valve Cornet. Like the big ones. 9 inches long; 4½-inch bell. Shipping weight, 1¾ pounds.......... 1.67
49K2494—Tuba. 12 inches long; 6-inch bell. Shpg. wt., 2 lbs.... 2.39
49K2495—Clarinet. Black finish. 15½ inches long; 3⅝-inch bell. Shipping weight, 2¾ pounds.......... 1.69
49K2496—Extra Vibrators, 12 to pkg. Shpg. wt., 1 oz.......... .06

for the Youngster
Horns and Trumpets

25c
Little Boy Blue's Cow-horn

Attention!

39c

Pretty Nickel Plated Horn, 25c
The kiddies love to strut around with one of these pretty two-tone horns trimmed with chenille gilt trimmed cord and tassels. Loads of fun, blowing and blowing. Length, 12 inches, and has 3½-inch bell. Shpg. wt., ¾ lb.
49K2390... 25c

25c
Shpg. wt. 1 lb.
Every kiddie knows how Little Boy Blue blew his horn. Attractive, nicely made, metal, two-tone horn, with cord for hanging over your shoulder. Bell, 2⅞ in. diameter. Length, about 8¼ in. Wood mouthpiece. Shpg. wt., ¾ lb.
49K2385........25c

Exceptional Trumpet Value
Make your pals stand at attention when you blow your brass finish trumpet. This is a nice loud sounding one, with green cord around it, trimmed with gilt tinsel, and two heavy green tassels. Has bugle mouthpiece. Is 11 inches long, and the bell measures 3⅝ inches in diameter. Shipping weight, ¾ lb.
49K2394....39c

$1.19

Imported Cathedral Pipe Tone Organ
A very fine imitation of a real pipe organ. Merely turn crank. All metal, handsomely lithographed in colors. Crank operates fan which drives air over reeds. Turning crank changes chords. Size, 6½x4x4 inches. Shpg. wt., 1¾ lbs.
49K2351........$1.19

Music and Action

79c

Surprising Tone Combinations

Every Child Loves a Merry-Go-Round
The music plays as the horses, pigs and their riders fly around. Wind up the strong spring and watch the little man turn the crank. Made of metal, finished in very snappy, attractive color enamels. Like the ones you see at the fairs. Flag on top. Height, including flag pole, 7 inches. Diameter, 5⅞ inches. Most other stores charge $1.00 for this size.
49K2356........79c

19c
Pretty Metal Music Box for Baby
The combination of colors and the tinkling music will make any baby's eyes sparkle. Metal, finished in red, blue and yellow. About 4½ inches high and 4½ inches in diameter. Shipping weight, 1 lb.
49K2376........19c

$4.98
See Our Phonograph Department for Records. Pages 691-696. Plays 10-inch Records.

Wonderful Toy Phonograph
Well constructed of heavy metal (still light enough to carry around). Good motor. Start and stop lever and speed regulator. Good nickel plated rim reproducer. Horn, nickel plated on inside, gives maximum tone. Base with enameled kiddie design is 10½ inches in diameter. Horn, 7¾ inches long and record plate, 7½ inches in diameter. Shipping wt., 7¼ lbs.
79K2421........$4.98

Musical Chicks for 39c
Turn crank and watch the colored wood chicks peck in time with music. Made of wood, finished in red and has cardboard with colored pictures on front; also wood cage effect around chicks. Size, 6⅛x5⅞ inches.
49K2373—Shipping wt., 1¼ lbs.....39c

Here's a Toy Uke to Strum

33c
Reinforced neck. Four wire strings. Wood tuning keys. Length, 14 in.; diameter, 3¾ in.
49K2432 Shpg. wt., ¾ lb....33c

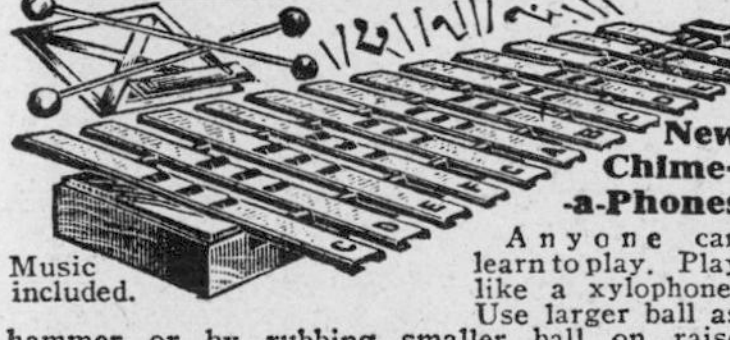

New Chime-a-Phones
Anyone can learn to play like a xylophone. Use larger ball as hammer or by rubbing smaller ball on raised surfaces you can get a beautiful tremolo effect. Metal music stand to attach to frame. Music included.
12-Key Size 16⅜ in. long. Shpg. wt., 2 lbs. 49K2452 $1.69
10-Key Size 13⅞ in. long. Shpg. wt., 1¼ lbs. 49K2451 $1.29

Bird Whistles

3 for 19c
Fill with water, blow and hear imitation of singing canaries. Decorated metal, 3½ in. long. Shipping weight, 8 ounces. Package of 3 for.
69K8050........19c

For Your Brass Band

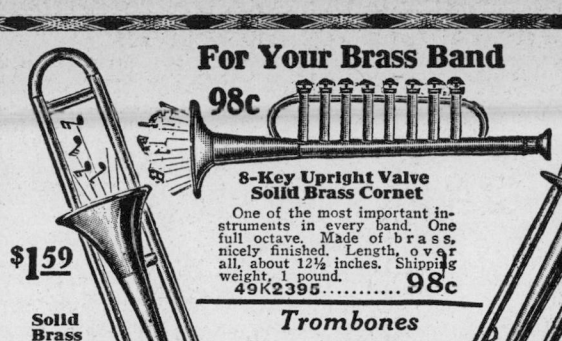

98c
8-Key Upright Valve Solid Brass Cornet
One of the most important instruments in every band. One full octave. Made of brass, nicely finished. Length, over all, about 12½ inches. Shipping weight, 1 pound.
49K2395............98c

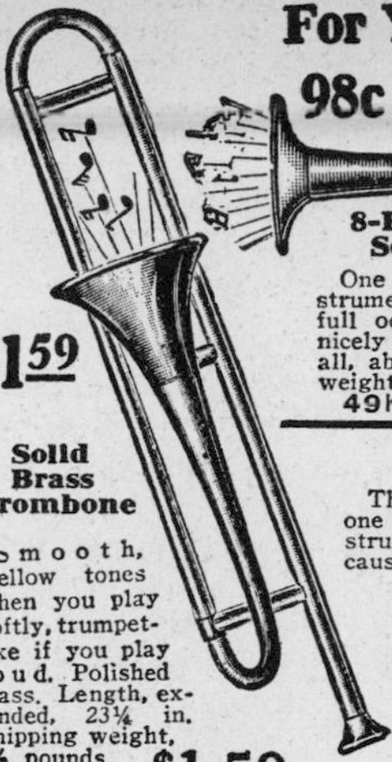

$1.59
Solid Brass Trombone
Smooth, mellow tones when you play softly, trumpet-like if you play loud. Polished brass. Length, extended, 23¼ in. Shipping weight, 1½ pounds.
49K2318 $1.59

Trombones
The trombone has become one of the most popular instruments of the day, because of the effects that are obtained by running the slide up and down. Produces all kinds of weird tones. Each plays eight notes, making it possible to play simple melodies. Easy to play. Well tuned.

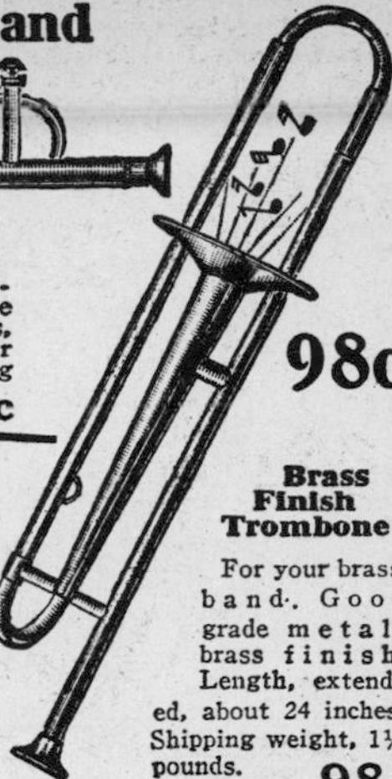

98c
Brass Finish Trombone
For your brass band. Good grade metal brass finish. Length, extended, about 24 inches. Shipping weight, 1¼ pounds.
49K2340 98c

12-Key Clarinet
Tremolo Clarinet

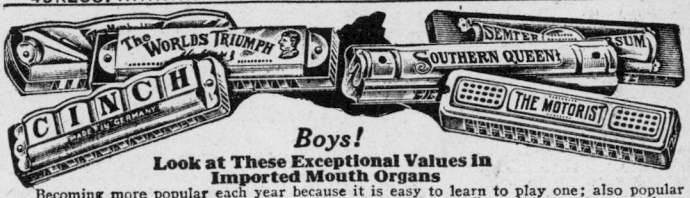

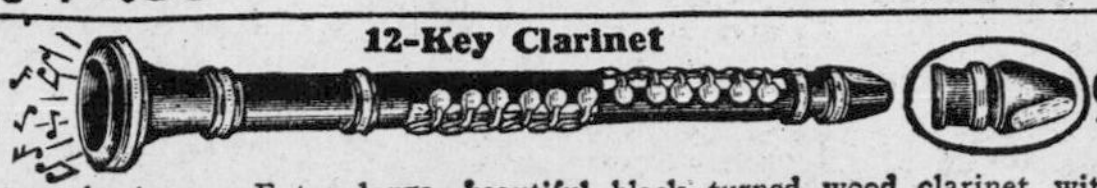

98c
Sweet tremolo tones. Extra large, beautiful black turned wood clarinet with gilt trimmings. Has duckbill mouthpiece. 12 nickel plated snap spring padded keys arranged on both sides. 18⅝ inches long. Bell top measures 2⅜ inches. Shpg. wt., 1½ lbs.
49K2337........98c

Boys!
Look at These Exceptional Values in Imported Mouth Organs

Becoming more popular each year because it is easy to learn to play one; also popular on radio. We take great pride in the values we are able to offer. An enormous purchase permits us to offer these wonderful values in harmonicas, made by the foremost manufacturers in Europe. Two different qualities. Both exceptional values at the prices we ask.

24-Reed Tremolo Harmonicas, 16c
Exceptionally good quality. Have full clear tones because of high grade reeds. Different titles. Average length, about 4⅛ inches. Shipping weight, 4 ounces.
49K2348............16c

Special 20-Reed Harmonicas, 10c
Bargains! Not as good quality nor quite as large as 49K2348, but good tone and good looking. Assorted designs. Average length, about 4 inches. Shpg. wt., 4 oz.
49K2345............10c

Schoenhut's Quality Pianos

Do not confuse with cheaper pianos. Schoenhut pianos cost a little more, but it pays to buy them because they are the best toy pianos sold. They are real quality, beautifully finished and accurately tuned.

These pianos are all carefully tuned so that simple melodies can be played and the child actually taught the rudiments of music. Wood frames shaped like ordinary upright piano, stained to represent rosewood and nicely varnished. Wood keys painted white with black markings to represent the black keys of a real piano. Instruction book included with each. Each piano packed in strong shipping carton. Furnished in five sizes as described below. No bench included.

22 Keys	18 Keys	15 Keys	12 Keys	8 Keys
Size, over all, 22¾ x 9⅝ x 12½ inches. Shipping weight, 12¾ lbs.	Size, over all, 19 x 12¼ x 8¼ inches. Shipping weight, 8½ lbs.	Size, over all, 15¾ x 9⅝ x 7½ inches. Shipping weight, 5⅝ lbs.	Size, over all, 13⅛ x 7¼ x 8⅝ inches. Shipping weight, 4¼ lbs.	Size, over all, 9¼ x 6¼ x 7½ inches. Shipping weight, 2¼ lbs.
79K2428	79K2427	79K2413	79K2411	49K2408
$4.98	$3.98	$2.69	$1.89	98c

Schoenhut's Better Grade Upright Pianos

$4.98 and $10.98
For the person wanting a better quality piano. Made in mahogany finish with the added details of regular piano legs, paneled front, music rack, hinged top and dummy foot pedals. Have steel notes which are accurately tuned. Two sizes. Music included.

VERY WELL MADE PIANO
18-key size, over all, 19⅜x16½x8¾ in. wide. Shpg. wt., 13½ lbs.........$4.98
79K2430

Exceptionally Fine Toy Piano
Made by Cabinet Makers
22-key size, over all, 22¾x21⅛x11¼ inches. Heavier and larger frame, better finish, better key construction and tone quality than 79K2430. Shipping weight, 35 pounds.
79K2433—Unmailable........$10.98

Marx Guaranteed Mechanical Toys

Hobo Train

45c

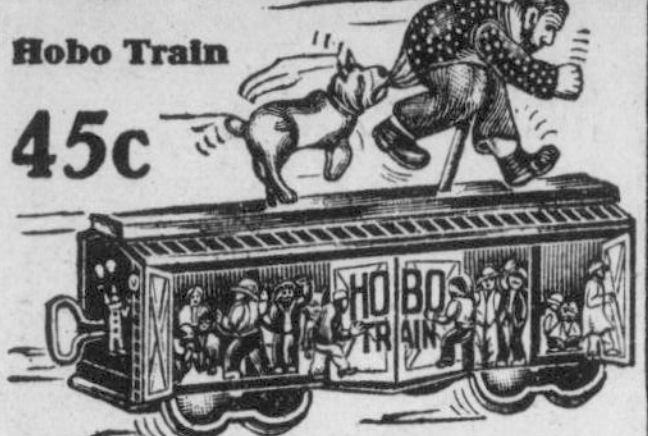

Real action! See the ferocious bull-dog jerk at the coat tails and pull the scared, fleeing hobo back each time, while the car goes steadily on in a wide circle. 7½-inch metal box car, lithographed with scene showing hobos in box car. Fun galore. Size, over all, 7½x6⅝ in. Strong spring motor. Shipping weight, 1 pound.

49K5731 .... 45c

$1.00

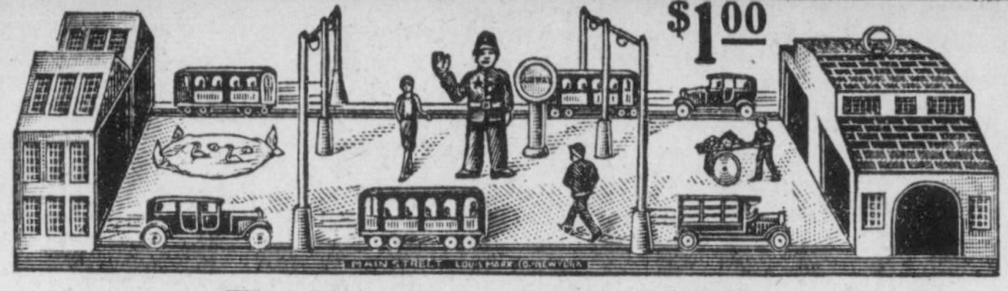

Main Street 24 In. Long — **The Newest Sensation—A Whole Town In Itself** — **Standard $1.50 Toy**

One of the biggest mechanical toy sensations this year. A little town in itself. Just wind the strong spring motor, then release the brake, and see street cars, autos and trucks, hurry back and forth, some one way and some the other. Lithographed in attractive colors. Real enjoyment for the kiddies. Made of metal and measures 24x3¾x2¾ inches. Shipping weight, 2 pounds.

49K5732 .... $1.00

See Circus Animals Do Their Tricks

Monk Climbs Pole — Clown Turns on Bar

87c

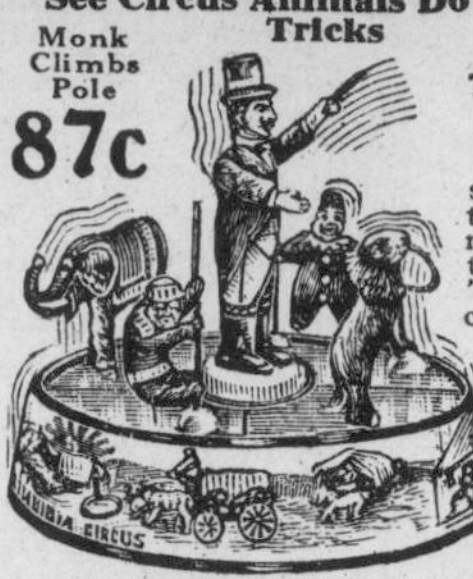

Wind spring; the ring-master turns round, cracking his whip, making the animals and clown in their turn do their stunts. Made of metal, lithographed in circus colors. Good spring motor. Diameter, base, 7½ inches; height, over all, 8 inches. Shpg. wt., 1½ lbs.

49K5717 .... 87c

87c

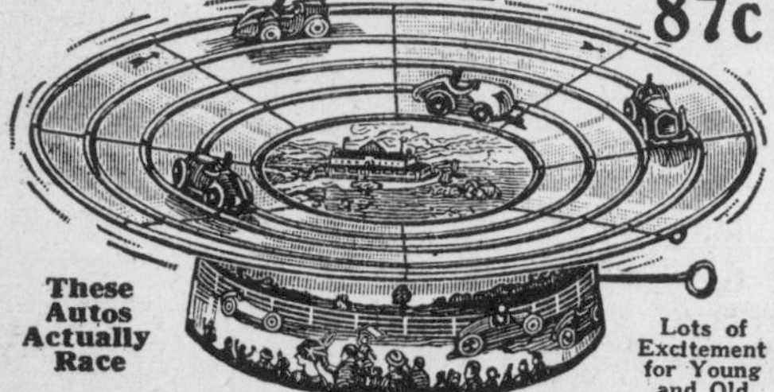

These Autos Actually Race

Lots of Excitement for Young and Old

One of the Most Popular Toys Made

After motor is wound, the cars whirl round in their individual courses by the peculiar up and down rocking motion of the track, which makes it very uncertain as to the progress of the racers, any car being likely to win. Track, 13 in. in diameter, made of metal and beautifully lithographed. Cars, 2 inches long, are made of metal and finished in distinguishing snappy colors. Good spring motor. Height, over all, 3½ inches. Shipping weight, 1½ pounds.

49K5713 .... 87c

HeeHaw—The Balky Mule 42c

Real Action — *He Balks He Kicks*

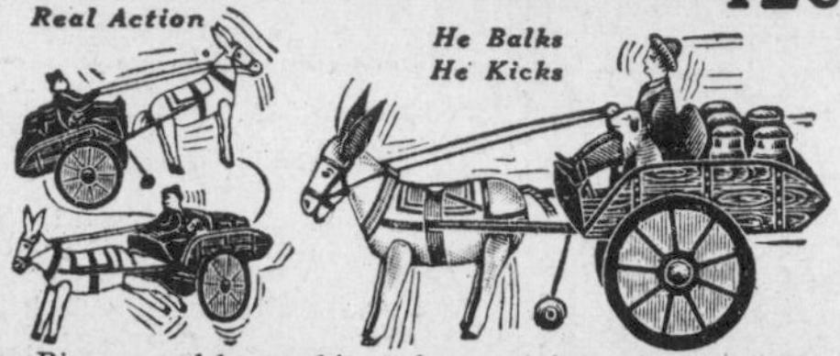

Bigger and better hit each year. A comical toy. Uncanny how it operates. This mule has real pep and is some kicker. He backs up when he should go forward and rears up on his hind legs so that the poor driver doesn't know what to do. Metal, and finished in attractive natural colors. Assorted designs. Strong spring. Average length, about 9 inches; 5¾ inches high. Shipping weight, 1 pound.

49K5747 .... 42c

Real Clever — Brand New 87c

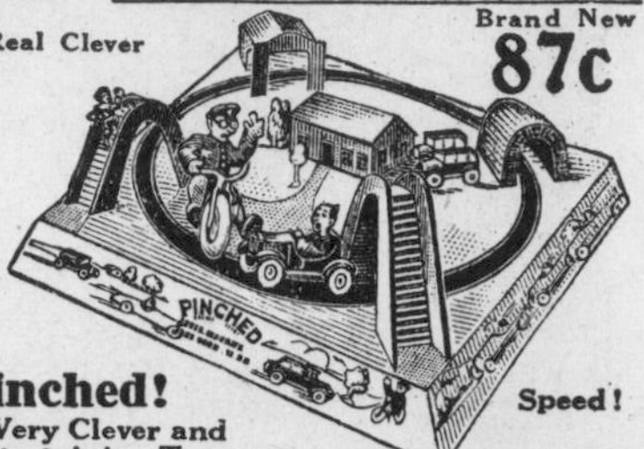

Pinched!

A Very Clever and Entertaining Toy — **Speed!**

See this speedy little roadster shoot round and round, through the bridges and tunnels, and all of a sudden, the motorcycle cop shoots out from behind the station, stops him and "pinches" him. When cop is pushed back behind station again, the auto starts away automatically, only to be "pinched" over and over again. Made of metal, lithographed in bright natural colors. Size, over all, 10 inches square, 3½ inches high. Shpg. wt., 1¼ lbs.

49K5738 .... 87c

Here You Are, Fellers! The Very Latest Airplane Kite

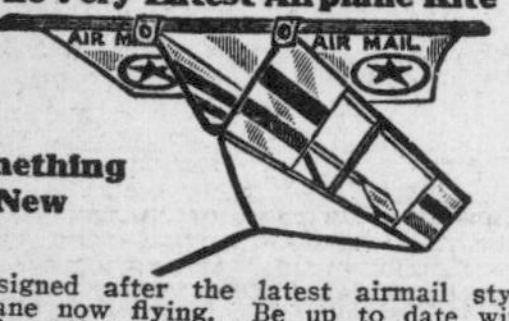

Something New

Designed after the latest airmail style airplane now flying. Be up to date with this beautiful red, white and blue large size flier, measuring 34x34 inches. Made of strong, flexible wood sticks and tough paper nicely decorated to resemble mail plane. Full directions for assembling. Shipping weight, 1 pound.

69H7791 .... 25c

Brand New Action—The Funniest Car Made 48c

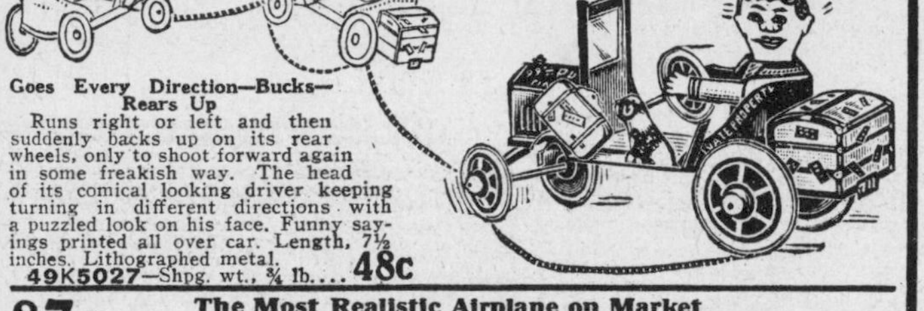

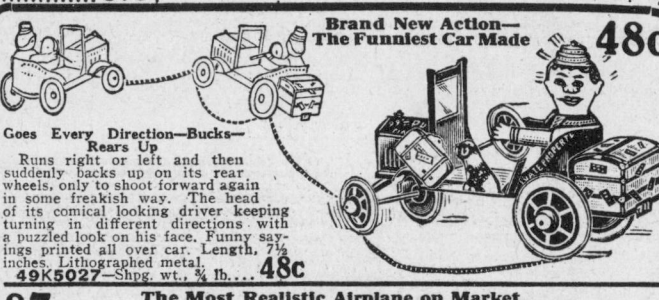

Goes Every Direction—Bucks—Rears Up

Runs right or left and then suddenly backs up on its rear wheels, only to shoot forward again in some freakish way. The head of its comical looking driver keeping turning in different directions with a puzzled look on his face. Funny sayings printed all over car. Length, 7½ inches. Lithographed metal.

49K5027—Shpg. wt., ¾ lb. 48c

New Two-Propeller Biplane

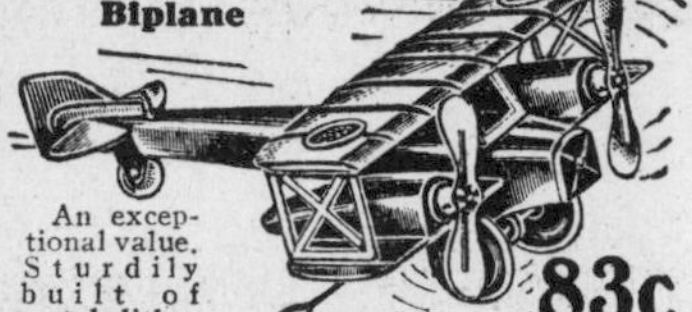

83c

An exceptional value. Sturdily built of metal, lithographed in bright colors. Has two propellers which revolve when plane is in action, and an adjustable rudder so plane can run straight or in circle. Man driver in cockpit. Just see it whiz along the floor. 12 inches long; a 9⅞-inch wing spread and 4½ inches high. Strong spring motor. Shipping weight, 2 pounds.

49K5739 .... 83c

87c — The Most Realistic Airplane on Market

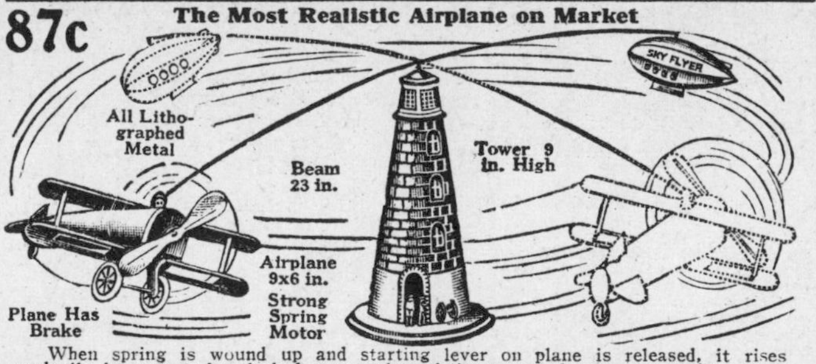

All Lithographed Metal — Beam 23 in. — Tower 9 In. High — Airplane 9x6 in. — Strong Spring Motor — Plane Has Brake

When spring is wound up and starting lever on plane is released, it rises gradually from ground and circles a number of times around tower; as spring motor stops, the plane volplanes downward until it lands gracefully on ground. Parts all metal and lithographed in attractive colors. Shipping weight, 1½ pounds.

49K5765 .... 87c

The Famous Climbing Monkey, 19c

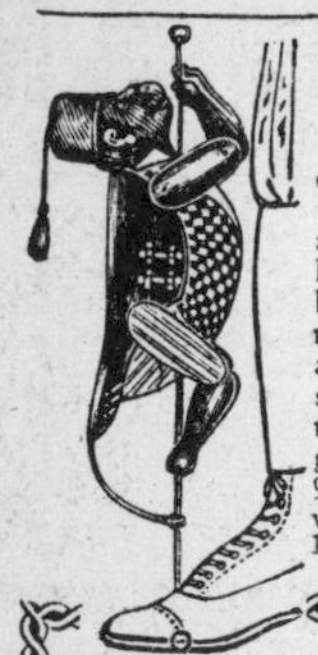

Watch monk climb up and down the string. There are cheaper monkeys on the market, but performance is not as satisfactory as this one. Large size, quality monk made of lithographed sheet metal. 9½ in. long and 3 in. wide. Shipping weight, 1 pound.

49K5723 .... 19c

Charleston Trio

45c

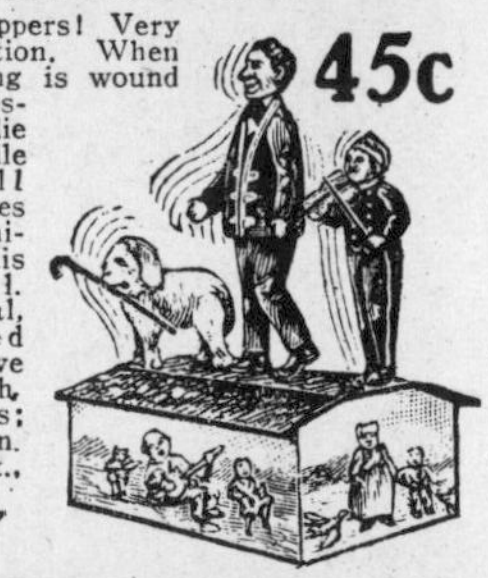

Some steppers! Very snappy action. When strong spring is wound up Charleston Charlie dances while the small negro fiddles and the animal nods his approval. Made of metal, lithographed in attractive colors. L'gth, 4⅝ inches; height, 9 in. Shipping wt., 1 pound.

49K5727 45c

49c — Famous Honeymoon Express, 49c

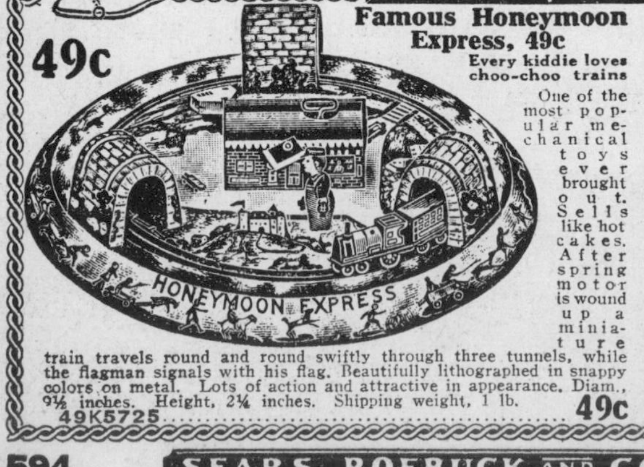

Every kiddie loves choo-choo trains

One of the most popular mechanical toys ever brought out. Sells like hot cakes. After spring motor is wound up a miniature train travels round and round swiftly through three tunnels, while the flagman signals with his flag. Beautifully lithographed in snappy colors on metal. Lots of action and attractive in appearance. Diam., 9½ inches. Height, 2¼ inches. Shipping weight, 1 lb.

49K5725 .... 49c

25c

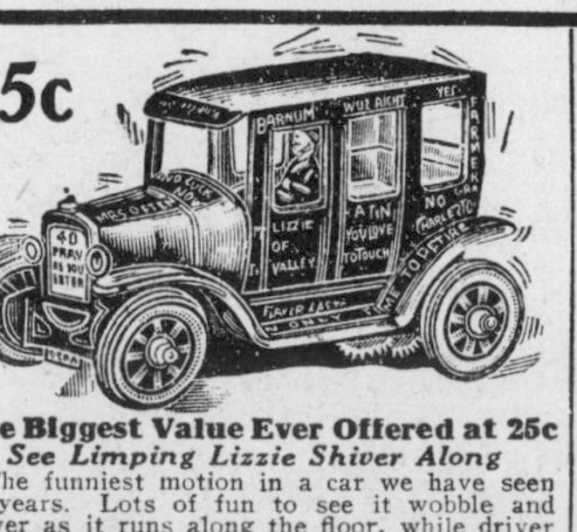

The Biggest Value Ever Offered at 25c

See Limping Lizzie Shiver Along

The funniest motion in a car we have seen in years. Lots of fun to see it wobble and shiver as it runs along the floor, while driver in front seat holds on for dear life. Such sayings as: "Mrs. Often;" "99 44/100% pure tin;" "Thanks for the Buggy Ride;" "Four Wheels, No Brakes," and many other funny, popular remarks printed all over the car. Shipping weight, ¾ lb.

49K5009 .... 25c

$1.00 Stop! Look! and Listen!

Brand New and a Wonderful Toy

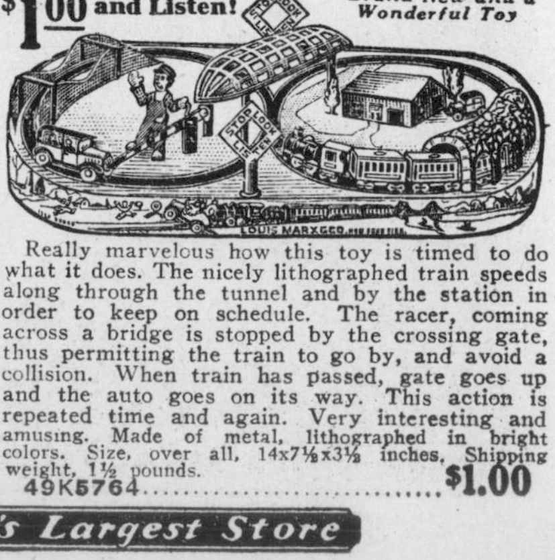

Really marvelous how this toy is timed to do what it does. The nicely lithographed train speeds along through the tunnel and by the station in order to keep on schedule. The racer, coming across a bridge is stopped by the crossing gate, thus permitting the train to go by, and avoid a collision. When train has passed, gate goes up and the auto goes on its way. This action is repeated time and again. Very interesting and amusing. Made of metal, lithographed in bright colors. Size, over all, 14x7½x3½ inches. Shipping weight, 1½ pounds.

49K5764 .... $1.00

Other Action Toys of Quality

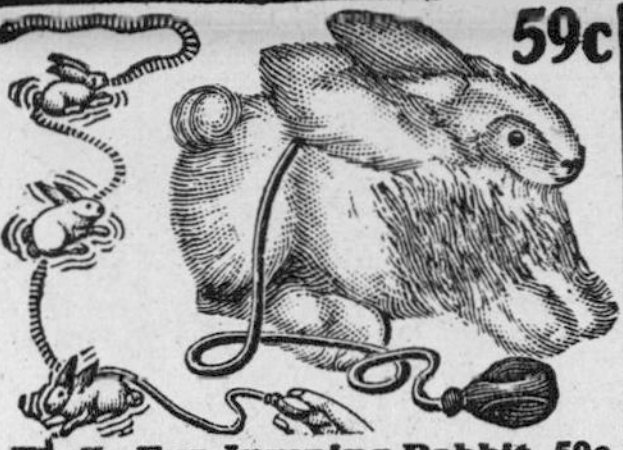

59c

Fluffy Fur Jumping Rabbit, 59c

For the tiny tot or for the older kiddie because of its "peppy" action. Size of a baby cottontail. Glass eyes. Press rubber bulb and rabbit jumps and moves its ears. Size, over all, about 6 in. Shipping weight, 1 pound.
49K5769..................59c

4 in 1 98c

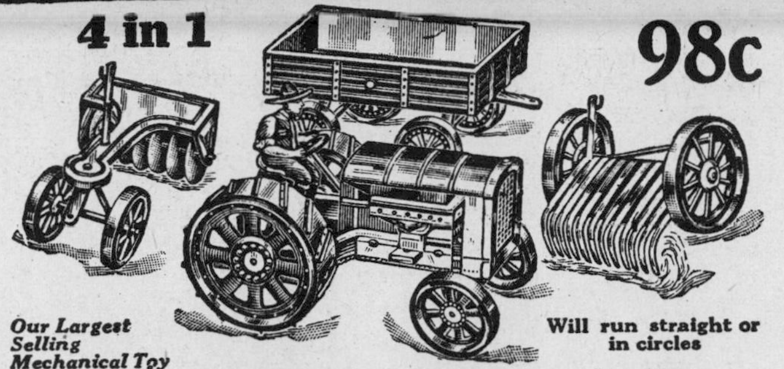

Our Largest Selling Mechanical Toy

Will run straight or in circles

A 4-In-1 Tractor Set, 27 Inches Long, for 98c

We offer here the outstanding tractor value on market this year. This is our largest selling mechanical toy, and one of our biggest values for the money. It is made of metal, lithographed in bright colors. Each set consists of tractor with a man driver, a four-wheel wagon, two-wheel rake and a seven-disc harrow. Tractor has strong spring motor. Measures 27 inches long, over all. Tractor, 7⅞ inches long, with other three pieces in proportion. Shipping weight, 3¼ pounds.
49K5748..........98c

Steam Shovel and Dump Truck 48c

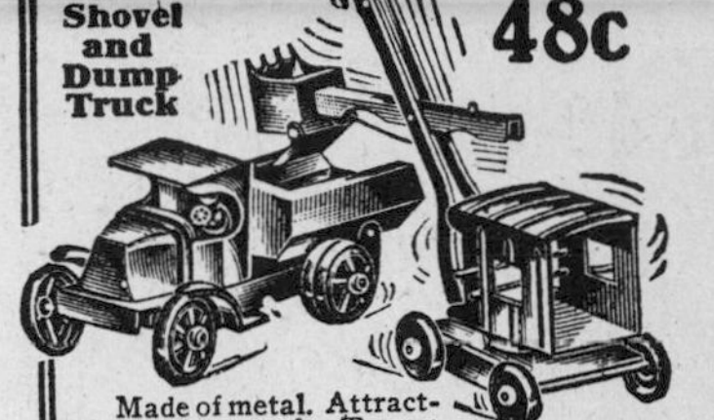

Made of metal. Attractively decorated. Turn crank, and shovel will scoop up dirt or sand and place it where you wish. Measures, 8½x7¼ inches. Truck has strong spring motor and will actually dump. Measures, 9¼ inches long and 4¼ in. high. Shpg. wt., 1½ lbs.
49K5070—Both for.......48c

Two-Car Garage 89c

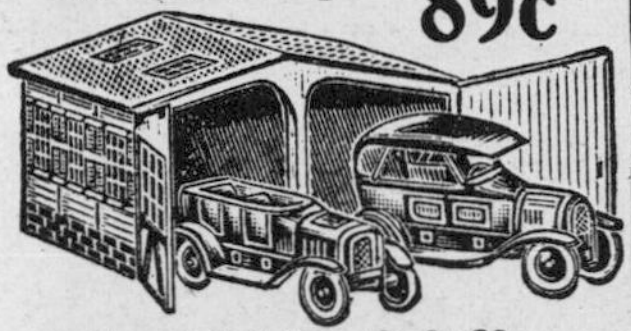

Special Value, Only 89c

Metal garage and two up to date mechanical automobiles with strong spring motors. It stands 4⅝ in. high by 8¼ in. wide. Lithographed windows and skylight. Roadster, 6x2¼x2⅝ in. and a touring car, 6x2⅝x3 in. Autos run straight or in circle. One of our most popular toys. Shipping weight, 2 pounds.
49K5019..................89c

One-Car Garage With Racer

29c

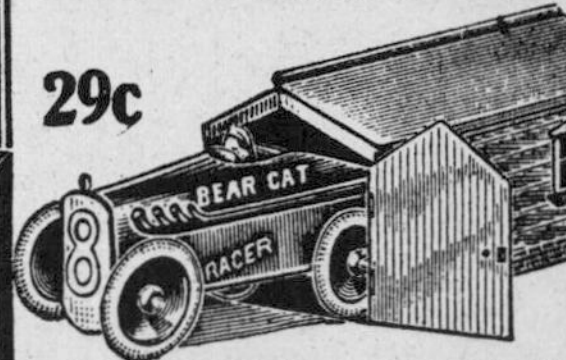

Made especially for the little fellows. The metal garage, very nicely lithographed, is 6¾x3⅜x3¼ in. The classy little metal racer with the driver measures, 6¾x2⅝x3 inches. Car has strong spring motor and can be set to run either straight or in a circle. Garage has floor and hinged door. Shpg. wt., 3 lbs.
49K5023..................29c

Four Remarkable Values for 25c Each

These Cars Can be Set to Run Straight or in Circles

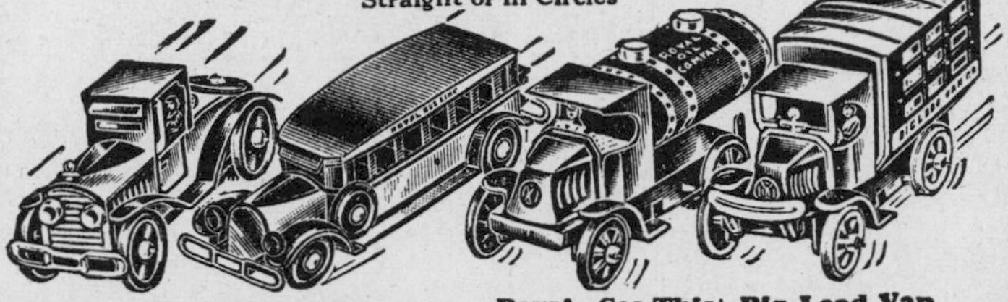

9-Inch Roadster

Complete with bumper, imitation headlights, motometer, disc wheels, extra wheel and sport top. Metal, finished in bright colors. Good spring. Length, 8¾ inches; 3⅞ inches high. Shipping weight, ¾ pound.
49K5031...25c

10-Inch Mechanical Bus

Made of metal, attractively lithographed. Has front bumper, dummy headlights, visor and spare wheel; strong spring motor. Length, 10 inches, height, 3 inches. Shipping weight, ¾ lbs.
49K5035...25c

Boys! See This Tank Truck

All metal oil tank truck, lithographed in bright colors; the kind used by the big companies. Has strong spring motor. Complete your garage with one of these. Size, 8¾x4⅝x3 in. Shpg. wt., 1 lb.
49K5050...25c

Big Load Van

Watch this van haul the load of toy grocery packages around the room. Strongly made of metal, nicely lithographed. Rear doors actually open. Has strong spring motor. Size, 9½x5 inches. Shipping weight, 1 pound.
49K5051...25c

59c

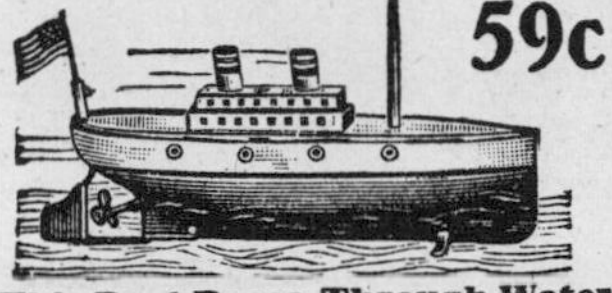

This Boat Races Through Water

Cranks like a racing auto. Friction motor spins propeller, driving boat through the water. Adjustable rudder. Steel, finished in attractive colors. Two rows of cabins. Two smokestacks. Height, 3½ inches; length, 9 inches. Shipping weight, 1½ pounds.
49K5743..................59c

$1.79

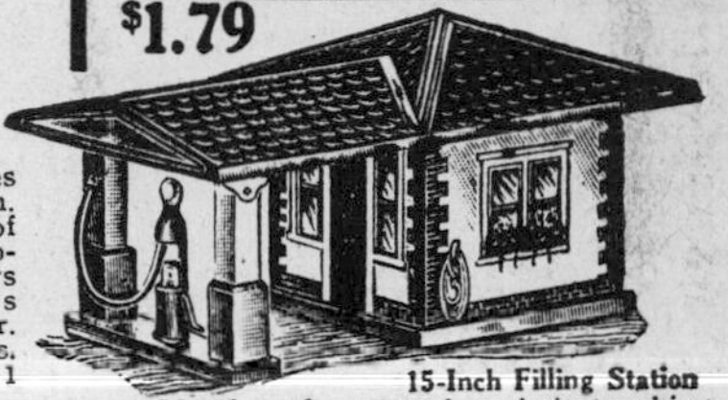

15-Inch Filling Station

Metal roof, stamped to imitate shingles; free water, free air illustrations. Has a gas tank, 4 inches high, with rubber tube and crank which, when turned, registers up to five gallons. Pillars are wood and house is metal. Size, over all, 15⅞x8⅞x7¼ inches. Shipping weight, 4¾ pounds.
79K5010..............$1.79

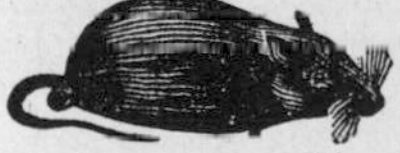

19c

Looks Like a Real Mouse

When it runs along the floor the girls runs like mad. Made of metal, friction motor. 2¾ inches long, not including tail. Shipping weight, 3 ounces.
49K5716..................19c

3 Tremendous Values for 47c Each

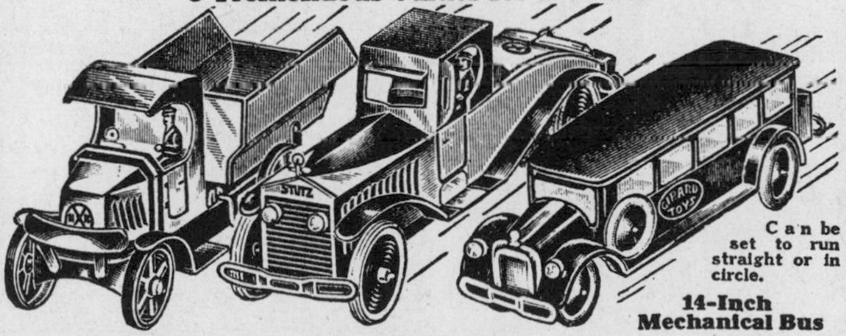

Can be set to run straight or in circle.

13-Inch Dump Truck

Patterned after big Mack Trucks you see. Substantially made of metal, lithographed in bright colors. Has bumper. Good spring motor. Size, over all, 13⅛x6x4⅝ inches. Shpg. wt., 1½ lbs.
49K5053......47c

16-Inch Stutz Racer

The biggest roadster ever offered at this price. Metal nicely lithographed, with front bumper, dummy headlights and motometer, rear fender bumpers and spare wheel. Has strong spring motor. 16¼x5⅜x4 in. Shpg. wt., 1½ lbs.
49K5052.......47c

14-Inch Mechanical Bus

This is a duplicate of the big busses; made of metal lithographed in bright colors. Has front and rear bumpers, spare tire, visor, dummy motometer, headlights and dummy baggage carrier. Has strong spring motor. Size, 14¼x4½x4½ inches. Shipping weight, 1 pound.
49K5054..........47c

25c

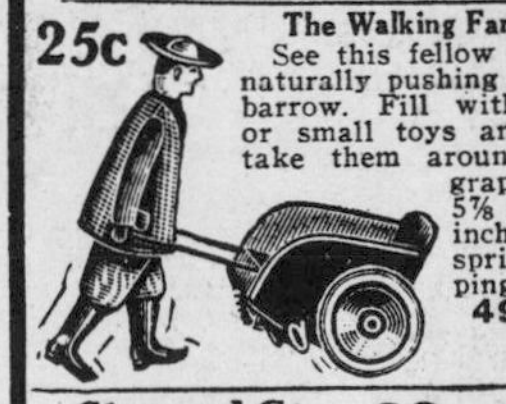

The Walking Farmer Boy

See this fellow walk very naturally pushing his wheelbarrow. Fill with marbles or small toys and let boy take them around. Lithographed metal, 5⅞ x 5½ x 2½ inches. Good spring. Shipping wt., 1 lb.
49K5749
25c

The New Loop The Loop

Put 2½x1½-inch metal auto in tower. Push to start it, and auto shoots down, making a loop in the air, and lands on lower track to race off on to the floor. Made of metal. 27½ in. long, 12⅝ in. high and 3 in. wide. Shipping weight, 1¾ pounds.

49K5055
25c

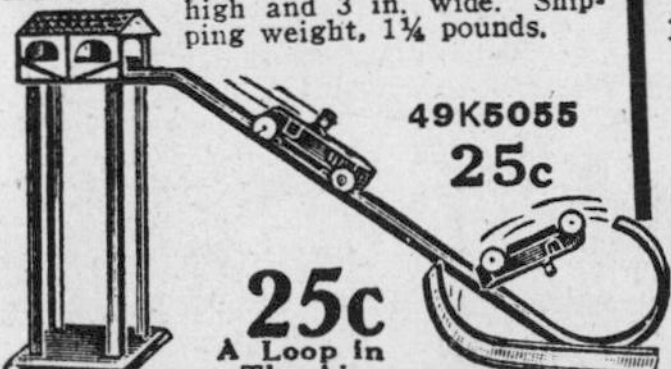

25c
A Loop In The Air

Stop and Go Station 39c

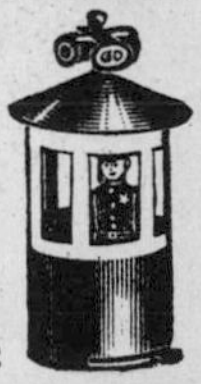

Just what you need to complete your toy town. A round house, 7⅛x3 inches, in which is an officer who turns around when you operate the stop and go signal by means of lever. Strongly made of sheet steel. Lithographed in bright colors. Shipping weight, 1¾ pounds.
49K5056.......39c

Wolverine Sandy Andy Toys

Automatic Sand Crane

An exceptionally clever toy. See the sand car load up. When filled it swings around in a big circle and the little man dumps contents. All steel, enameled in bright colors. Size, 13⅜x14 inches. Can of sand included. Shipping weight, 3¾ pounds.
49K5782.........$1.00

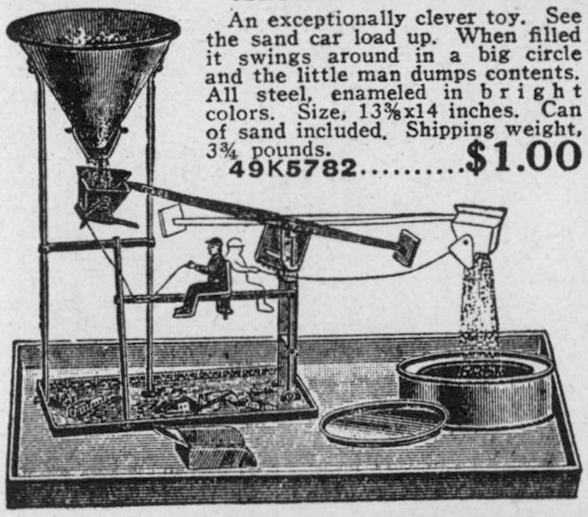

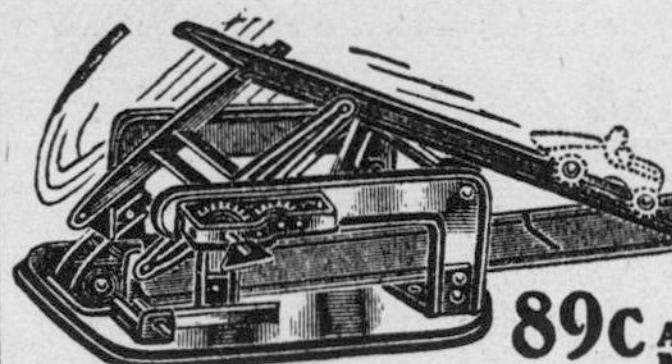

89c

Over and Under—The Long Running Toy

Forward on upward incline, backward on lower. Then automatically up and over again. Sheet steel, nicely decorated. Place the 2½-inch racer on upper track and after it reaches lower end of bottom track the motor starts; carrier picks up auto and carries it to the upper track. Size, about 25x3 inches. Shipping weight, 1¾ pounds.
49K5832.....................89c

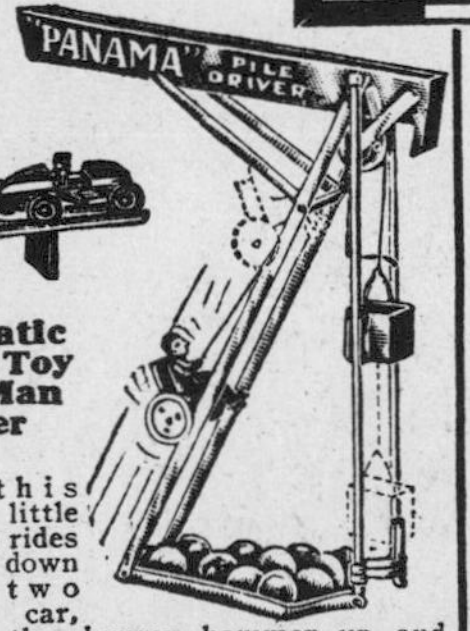

Automatic Marble Toy With Man Driver

See this busy little man. He rides up and down in his two wheel car, working the dummy hammer up and down as long as marbles are kept in hopper above. Complete with eight metal balls. Size, over all, 16¼x12¼ inches. Shpg. wt., 2¼ lbs.
49K5822............98c

Famous Sandy Andy

Light gauge sheet steel, attractively painted. Simply pour sand in the hopper and the car starts going up and down the incline, carrying sand to the bottom. This operation is continued automatically as long as there is sand in the hopper. Size, over all, 9¼x10¾ inches. Can of sand included. Shpg. wt., 2 lbs.
49K5742
59c

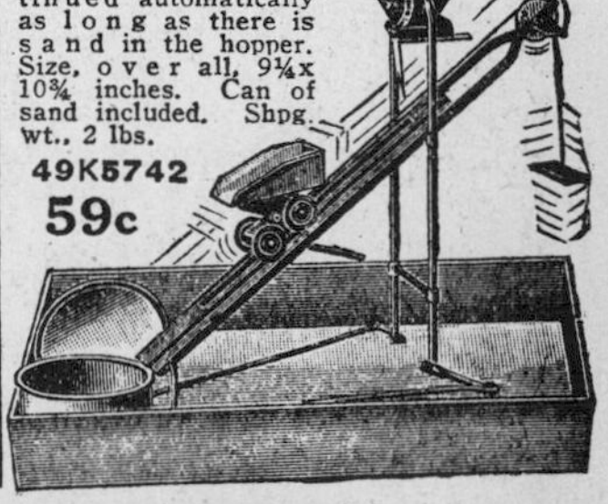

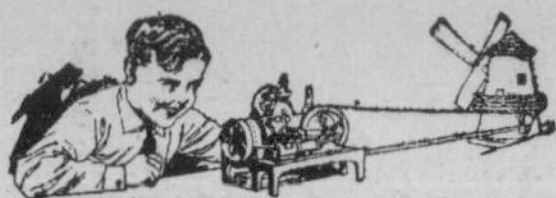

Dandy Little Steam Engines

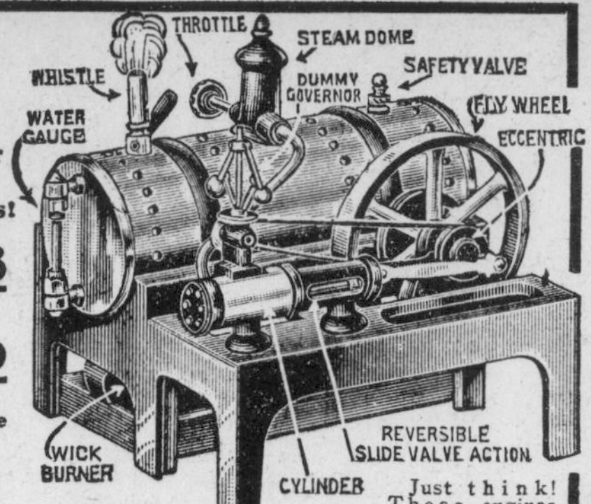

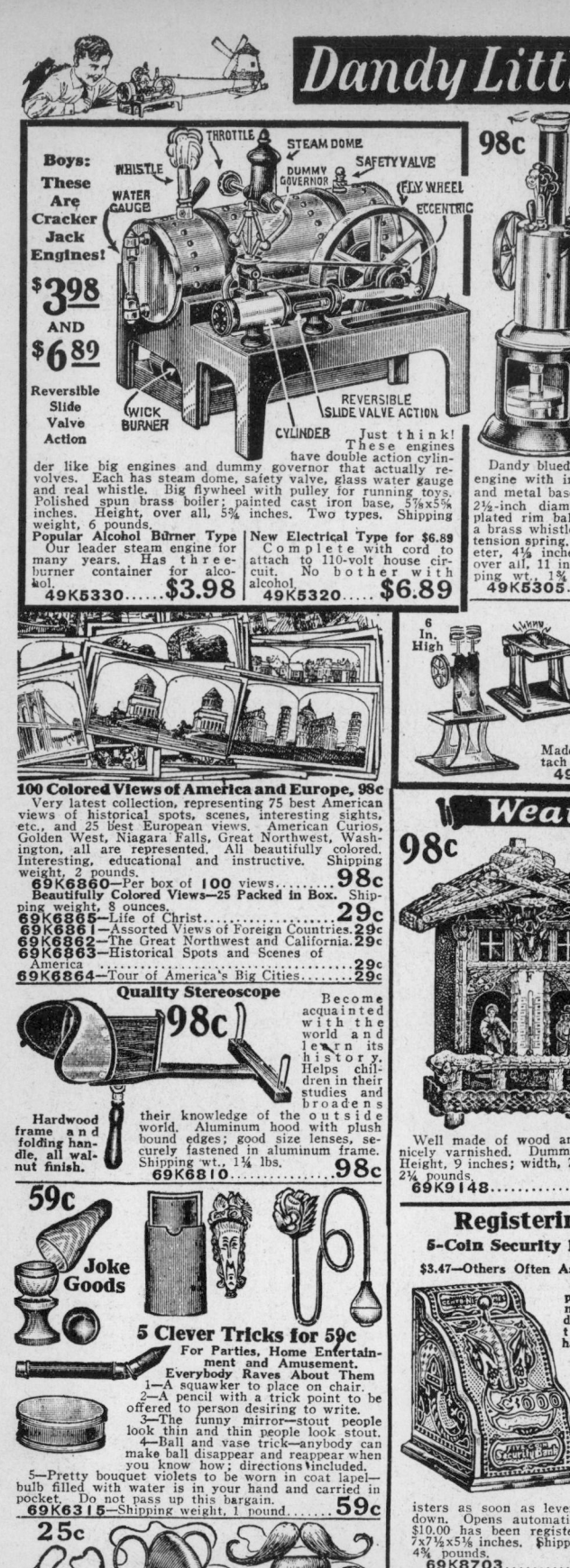

Boys: These Are Cracker Jack Engines!

$3.98 AND $6.89

Reversible Slide Valve Action

Just think! These engines have double action cylinder like big engines and dummy governor that actually revolves. Each has steam dome, safety valve, glass water gauge and real whistle. Big flywheel with pulley for running toys. Polished spun brass boiler; painted cast iron base, 5⅞x5⅝ inches. Height, over all, 5¾ inches. Two types. Shipping weight, 6 pounds.

Popular Alcohol Burner Type
Our leader steam engine for many years. Has three-burner container for alcohol.
49K5330......**$3.98**

New Electrical Type for $6.89
Complete with cord to attach to 110-volt house circuit. No bother with alcohol.
49K5320......**$6.89**

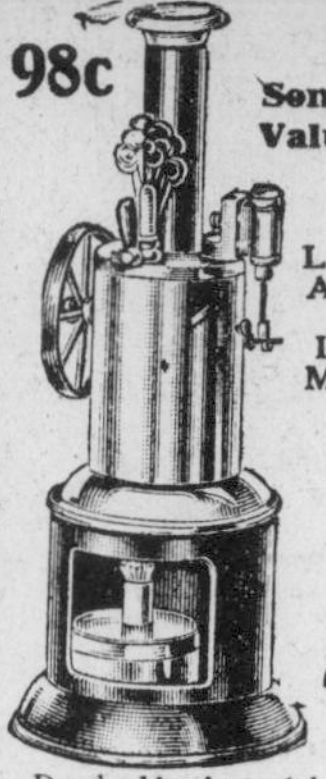

98c Some Value

Lots of Action for Little Money

Dandy blued steel boiler engine with iron fire box and metal base. It has a 2½-inch diameter, nickel plated rim balance wheel, a brass whistle and safety tension spring. Base diameter, 4½ inches. Height, over all, 11 inches. Shipping wt., 1¾ lbs.
49K5305......**98c**

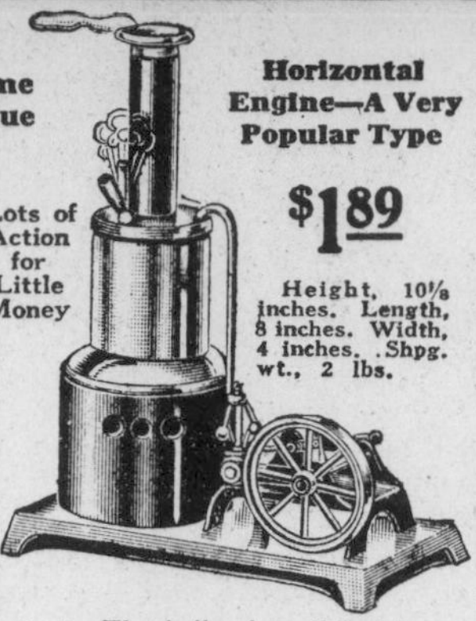

Horizontal Engine—A Very Popular Type

$1.89

Height, 10⅛ inches. Length, 8 inches. Width, 4 inches. Shpg. wt., 2 lbs.

The boiler is polished brass finish, the fire box and base are steel, decorated in gray and rich red. It has a rotating governor; also a filler, brass whistle and spring safety valve. Balance wheel has turned finish face, and the shaft carries a small pulley for belt to run small toys.
49K5306......**$1.89**

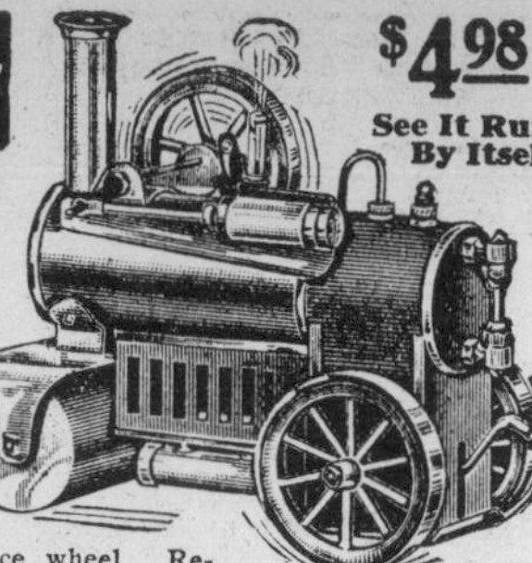

$4.98
See It Run By Itself

Combination Steam Roller and Tractor

Brass roller and chain drive. Nickel plated 2¼-inch balance wheel. Remove chain and you have a stationary engine. Nickel plated brass boiler; whistle, water gauge, safety valve. Fuel box fits into rear end. Length, 6¾ in. Height, 6½ in. Width, 3½ in. Shipping weight, 2¾ pounds.
49K5309......**$4.98**

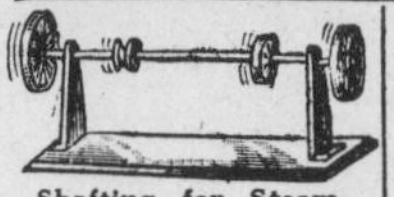

Shafting for Steam Engines

Four-pulley shafting for steam engine, mechanical or electric motor. All metal. Four toys can be operated at one time. Base, 6½x3⅛ in.; height, 2¾ in. Shipping wt., 1 lb.
49K5408......**25c**

Windmill for Your Engine

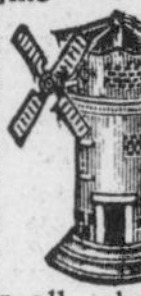

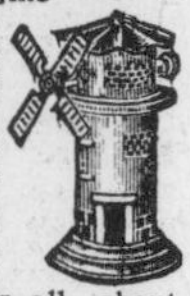

When attached to your engine its arms will fly around at a great rate. Made of metal, finished in attractive colors. Height, over all, about 6½ in.; width arms, over all, 4½ in. Shpg. wt., 1 lb.
49K5405......**39c**

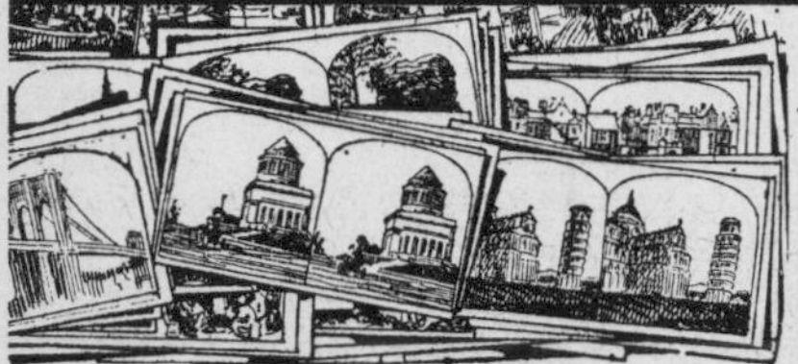

100 Colored Views of America and Europe, 98c

Very latest collection, representing 75 best American views of historical spots, scenes, interesting sights, etc., and 25 best European views. American Curios, Golden West, Niagara Falls, Great Northwest, Washington, all are represented. All beautifully colored. Interesting, educational and instructive. Shipping weight, 2 pounds.
69K6860—Per box of 100 views......**98c**

Beautifully Colored Views—25 Packed in Box. Shipping weight, 8 ounces.
69K6865—Life of Christ......**29c**
69K6861—Assorted Views of Foreign Countries..**29c**
69K6862—The Great Northwest and California..**29c**
69K6863—Historical Spots and Scenes of America......**29c**
69K6864—Tour of America's Big Cities......**29c**

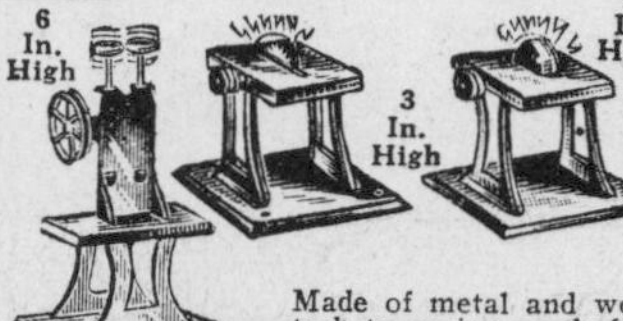

3 for 59c
Boys: See These Accessories

Imitation grindstone, 3 in. high; a saw on platform, measuring 3 in. high and a dandy stamp mill, 6 in. high. Made of metal and wood, each with pulley to attach to engine or shafting. Shpg. wt., 1 lb.
49K5407–3 for......**59c**

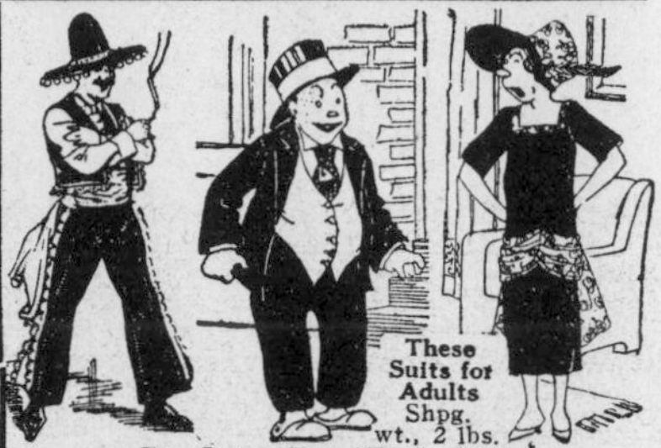

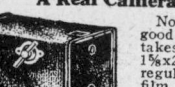

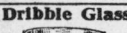

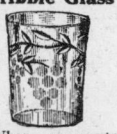

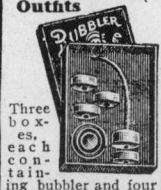

These Suits for Adults Shpg. wt., 2 lbs.

Good Quality Cloth Suits

Mexican
Our most popular Suit. Real snappy. Dark blue hat, jacket, pants with imitation gold fringe, yellow sash.
49K4534 **$2.39**

Jigg's Suit
Black coat and trousers, red vest, fancy tie, white spats and black hat with white band Irish mask.
49K4541 **$2.39**

Maggie, Jigg's Wife
Jaunty hat with feather, striking brown dress with gaudy ruffled trimming. Good material. Irish mask.
49K4540 **$2.39**

Weather House

98c

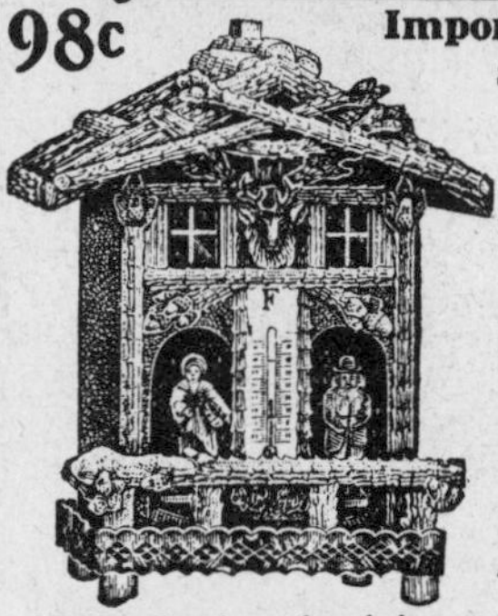

Imported Weather Prophet

Sold Elsewhere as High as $1.50
Our Price, Only 98c
Tell Tomorrow's Weather

Popular, attractive little weather prophet forecasts the weather eight to twenty-four hours in advance. Merely hang up outside on the window frame, on the side of the house or even put on mantel in the house and the cute little figures will do the rest. When the weather is going to be fine the woman comes out and the man stays in, but if a storm is brewing or rain threatens, the man comes out and the woman stays in. Will do a fair job of forecasting.

A Curio as Well as a Weather House

Well made of wood and decorated with pine twigs, cones, etc. All nicely varnished. Dummy windows and thermometer. Reindeer head. Height, 9 inches; width, 7½ inches; depth, 4½ inches. Shipping weight, 2¼ pounds.
69K9148......**98c**

Quality Stereoscope

98c

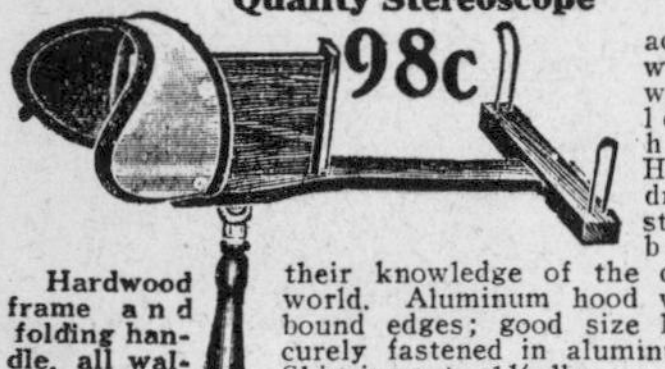

Hardwood frame and folding handle, all walnut finish.

Become acquainted with the world and learn its history. Helps children in their studies and broadens their knowledge of the outside world. Aluminum hood with plush bound edges; good size lenses, securely fastened in aluminum frame. Shipping wt., 1¼ lbs.
69K6810......**98c**

A Real Camera for 79c

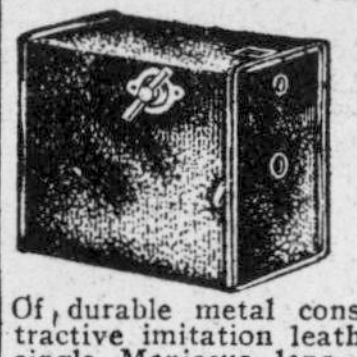

Not a toy but a handy, good looking camera that takes real pictures, size 1⅝x2½ inches, from any regular vest pocket size film roll. Buy one for yourself and another for your children. Enjoy amateur photography with this practical little camera. It measures 2¼ x 3 x 3½ in. Of durable metal construction, covered with attractive imitation leather. Has one view finder—single Meniscus lens. Takes instantaneous pictures only. No adjustment necessary. Shipping weight, 1 pound.
3K42665......**79c**
3K42709—Film for the above, eight exposures......**22c**

59c

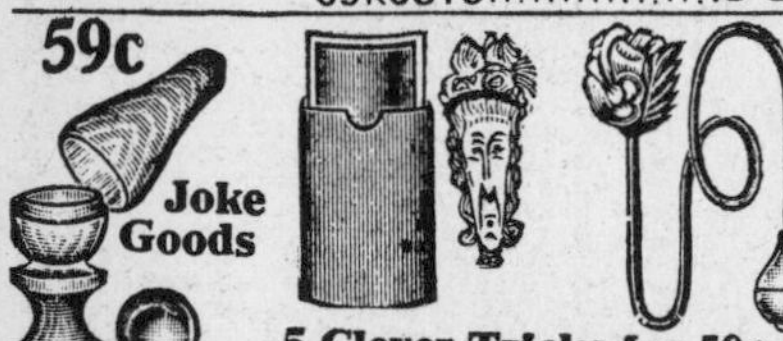

Joke Goods

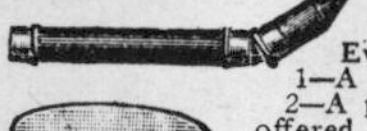

5 Clever Tricks for 59c
For Parties, Home Entertainment and Amusement.
Everybody Raves About Them

1—A squawker to place on chair.
2—A pencil with a trick point to be offered to person desiring to write.
3—The funny mirror—stout people look thin and thin people look stout.
4—Ball and vase trick—anybody can make ball disappear and reappear when you know how; directions included.
5—Pretty bouquet violets to be worn in coat lapel—bulb filled with water is in your hand and carried in pocket. Do not pass up this bargain.

69K6315—Shipping weight, 1 pound......**59c**

25c

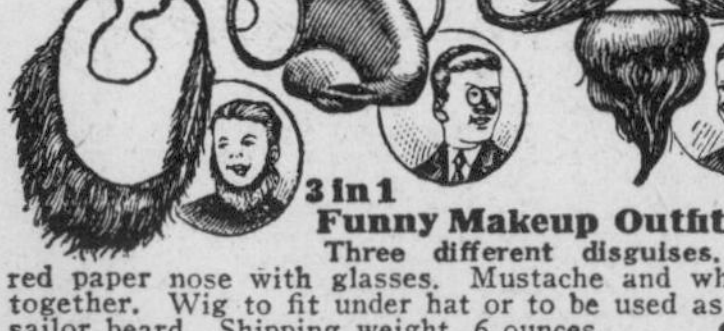

3 in 1 Funny Makeup Outfit, 25c
Three different disguises. Big red paper nose with glasses. Mustache and whiskers together. Wig to fit under hat or to be used as funny sailor beard. Shipping weight, 6 ounces.
49K4501......**25c**

Registering and Adding Banks

5-Coin Security Bank
$3.47—Others Often Ask $4.00

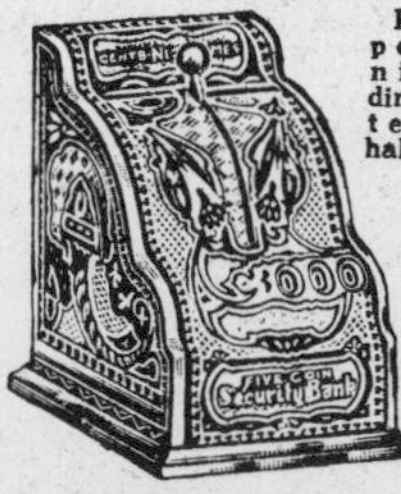

Registers pennies, nickels, dimes, quarters and halves. All steel, beautifully lithographed in an etchkraft finish in five colors. Each coin registers as soon as lever is pulled down. Opens automatically when $10.00 has been registered. Size, 7x7½x5¼ inches. Shipping weight, 4¾ pounds.
69K8703......**$3.47**

The American 3-Coin Bank

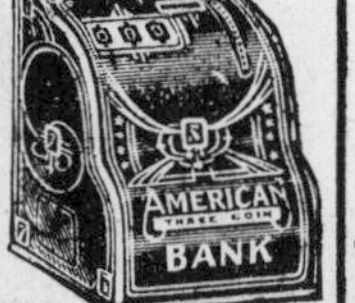

Registers and adds pennies, nickels and dimes. Opens at $5.00. Decorated in black and gold. Size, 5½x5⅝x4⅛ inches. Shipping weight, 2¾ pounds.
69K8711......**$1.79**

The New Lucky 3-Coin Bank
When nickel is deposited bell rings once, twice for a dime and five times for a quarter. Opens at $10.00. All steel lithographed in five colors. Size, 5⅛x5x4 inches. Shipping weight, 2¾ pounds.
69K8701......**$1.79**

Dribble Glass

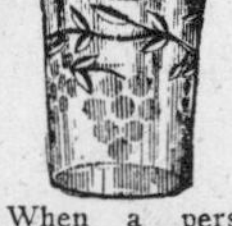

When a person drinks, contents drip down chin. Victim usually thinks fault his own. Shpg. wt., 1 lb.
69K6303......**39c**

Metal Crawling Bugs

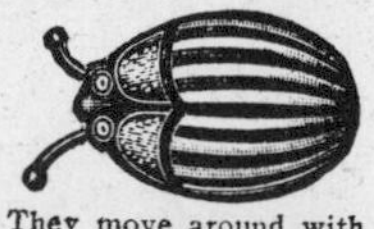

They move around with a slow, almost weird motion. True to life colors. About 2 inches long. Will do clever tricks. Shpg. wt., 3 oz.
69K9121
Package of 2 for..**29c**

Home Savings Bank

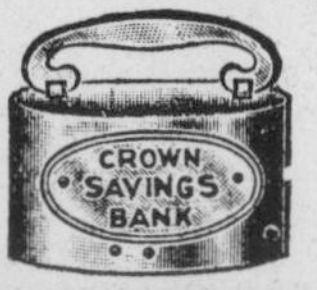

Heavily nickel plated steel bank. Height, 2¼ inches. Length, 3⅞ inches. Opening for coins and paper money. Key furnished. Shipping weight, 1 pound.
69K8708......**79c**

Three-Bubbler Outfits

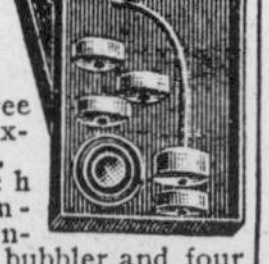

Three boxes, each containing bubbler and four small cakes of pure castile soap. Shpg. wt., ¾ lb.
69K9152—Per package of 3 boxes......**23c**

The Original Cum-Bac Toy

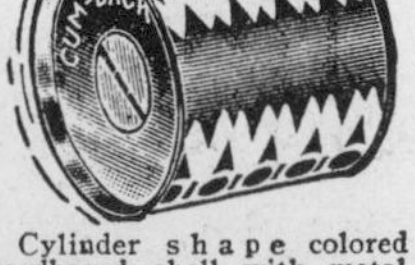

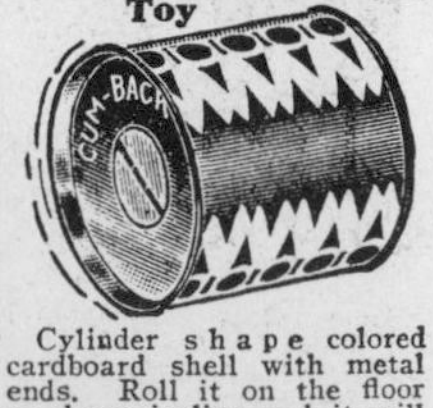

Cylinder shape colored cardboard shell with metal ends. Roll it on the floor or down incline and it will come back to you. Size, 2¼ x 2⅝ inches. Shipping weight, 8 ounces.
69K9123......**8c**

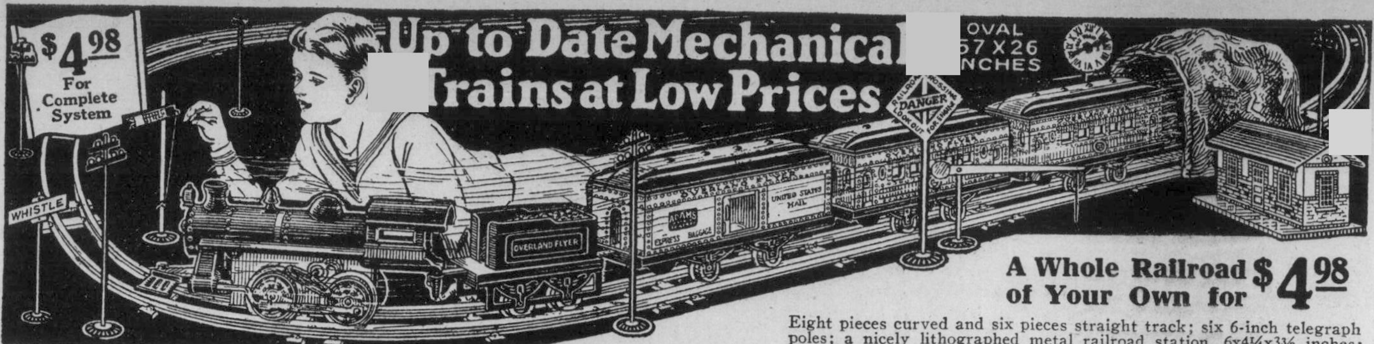

$4.98
For
Complete
System
WHISTLE
DANGER
OVAL
57X26
INCHES
OVERLAND FLYER
UNITED STATES MAIL

Up to Date Mechanical Trains at Low Prices

A Whole Railroad of Your Own for $4.98

This 32-inch train has dandy 7-inch, black enameled, iron locomotive with guaranteed clockwork motor, nickel plated piston rods, brake, lithographed tender with imitation coal and three beautifully lithographed cars (each car 6 inches long, one a baggage car).

Eight pieces curved and six pieces straight track; six 6-inch telegraph poles; a nicely lithographed metal railroad station, 6x4¼x3⅜ inches; 6-inch tunnel; 9½-inch double movable arm semaphore; 7-inch crossing signal; 6-inch whistle signal; 6-inch clock with moving hands and 7-inch railroad gate with dummy lantern. Shpg. wt., 7 lbs.
79K5101—All for.. **$4.98**

$4.98

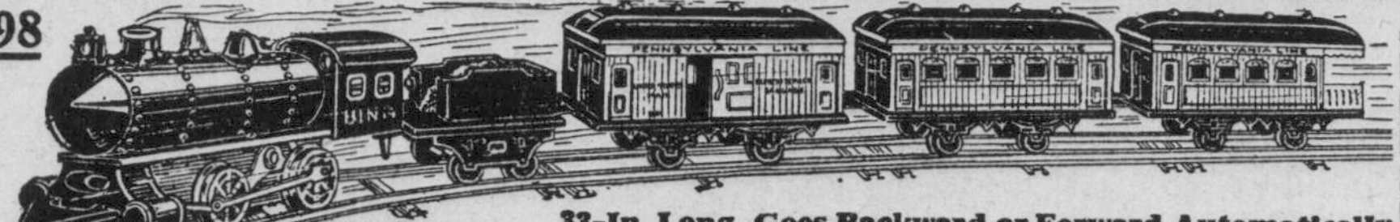

PENNSYLVANIA LINE

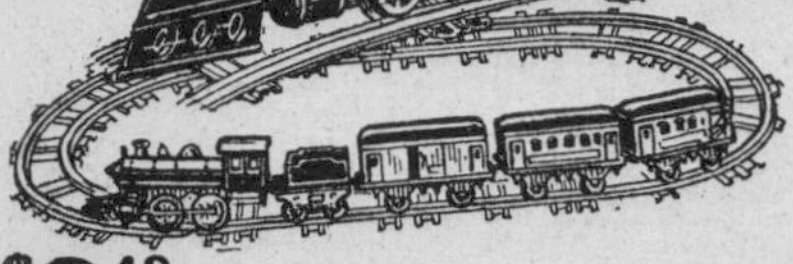

33-In. Long. Goes Backward or Forward Automatically

Baggage car with sliding doors, Pullman and observation cars. Eight pieces of curved and four straight track form an oval 10 feet in circumference. One piece has automatic device for reversing or stopping train without touching it. Levers in engine can be used for reversing, starting and stopping. Eight-inch engine, enameled metal, has nickel plated steel pistons. Tempered steel clockwork motor and speed control. Cars, 5⅝ inches long, lithographed in natural colors.
49K5135—Train, complete (Shpg. wt., 4½ lbs.).... **$4.98**

$2.48

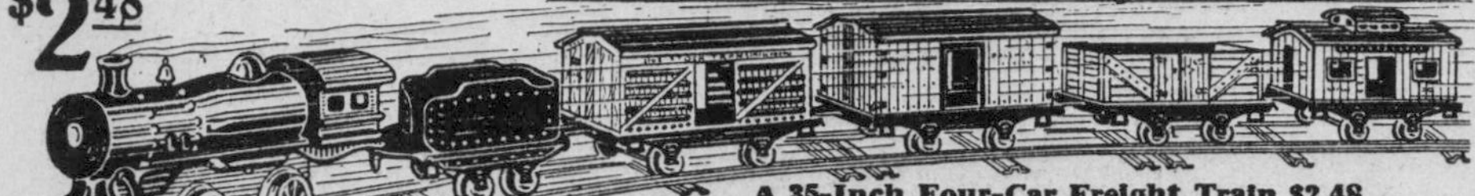

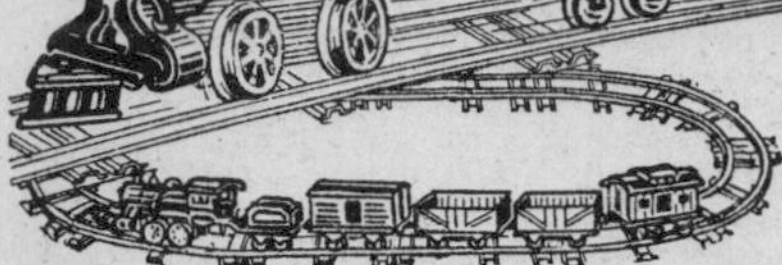

A 35-Inch Four-Car Freight Train $2.48

This is a real value, boys. Measures 35 inches long, has 6¼-inch camel back type locomotive with strong clockwork motor; coal tender; a 4½-inch gravel car; 5-inch freight car, 5-inch latticed stock car and a 5-inch caboose with cutout doors and windows. All attractively lithographed. Has eight pieces of curved and two pieces of straight track, forming an oval 100 inches in circumference. You can't miss this set to complete your train yard. Shipping weight, 5¼ pounds.
49K5108.. **$2.48**

$2.98

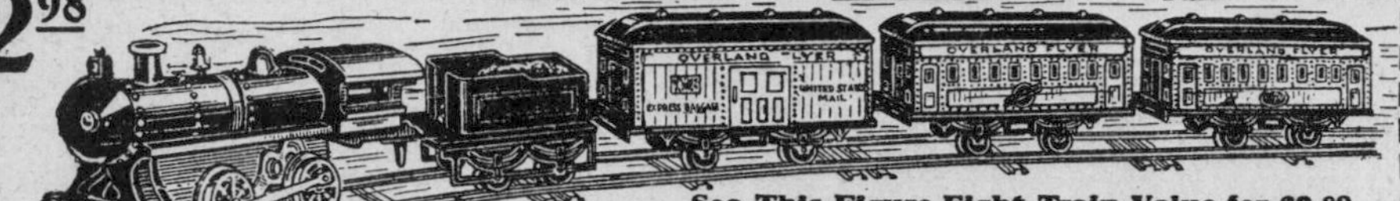

OVERLAND FLYER

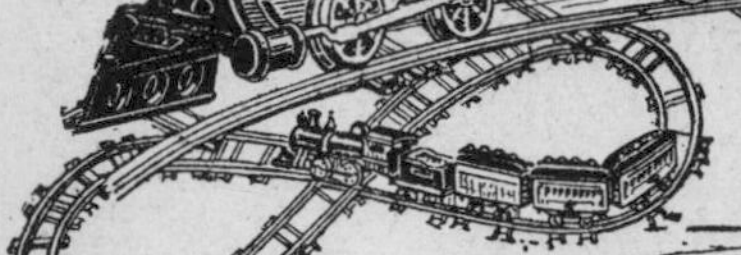

See This Figure Eight Train Value for $2.98

A dandy value! **This train measures about 26½ inches long,** has a 6½-inch nicely finished iron locomotive with strong clockwork motor and nickel plated piston rods and brake. A lithographed tender with imitation coal; three nicely lithographed metal cars, one a baggage car, each 5⅜ in. long. Fourteen pieces of curved track and crossover, making figure eight 54x26 in. Shpg. wt., 5 lbs.
49K5103.. **$2.98**

$1.98 Track 102 Inches Around

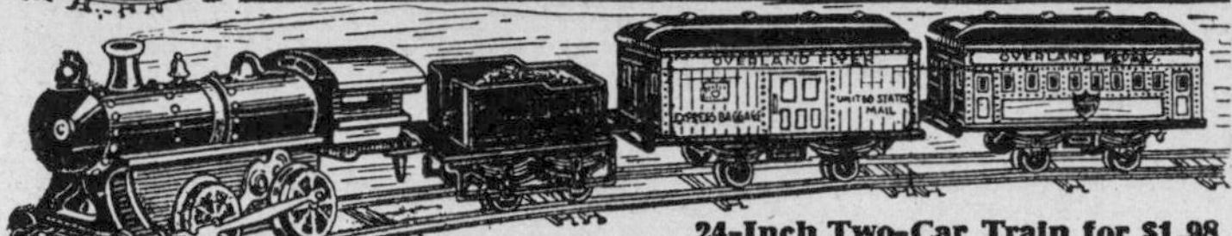

OVERLAND FLYER

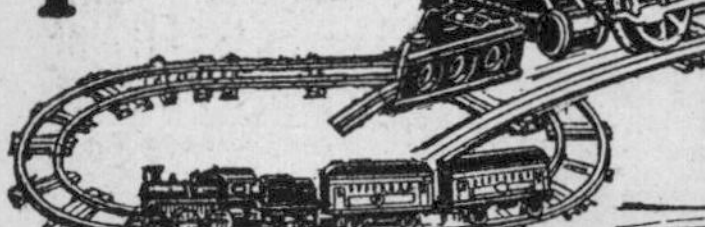

24-Inch Two-Car Train for $1.98

6½-inch cast iron locomotive, with pistons and brake, a lithographed coal car, two lithographed 5¼-inch cars, one a baggage car; eight pieces curved track and two pieces of straight track, all for this price. Track forms oval about 102 inches in circumference. An unprecedented value. Shipping weight, 4 pounds.
49K5104.. **$1.98**

$1.48 Track 84 Inches Circumference

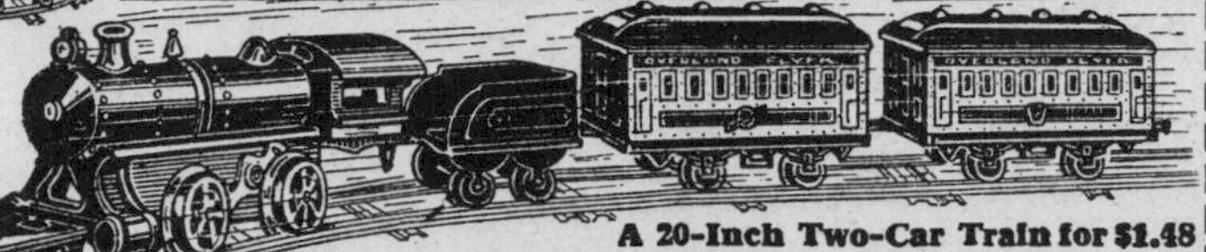

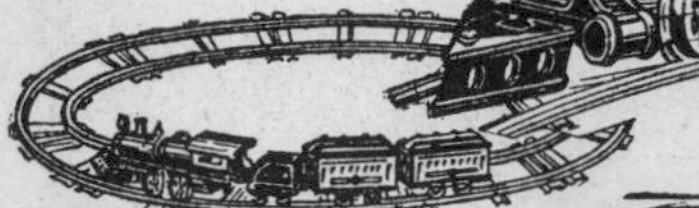

A 20-Inch Two-Car Train for $1.48

A 20-inch train with a 6½-inch cast iron locomotive, lithographed tender, two 5½-inch heavy metal fine quality lithographed passenger cars with metal floors, 8 pieces curved track, making circle 84 inches in circumference. Compare this value. Shpg. wt., 3 lbs.
49K5107.. **$1.48**

98c Circle 60-Inch Circumference

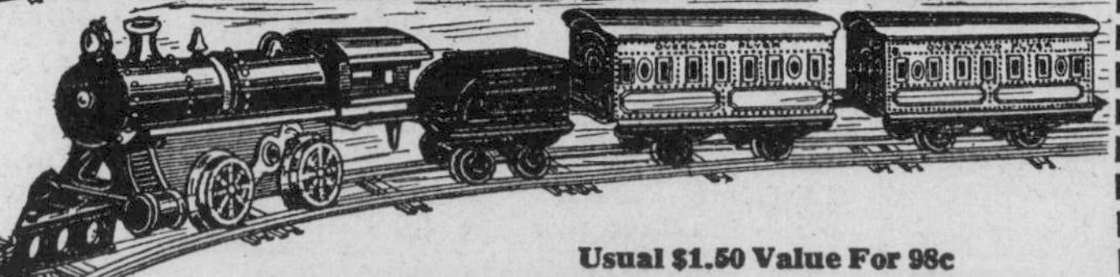

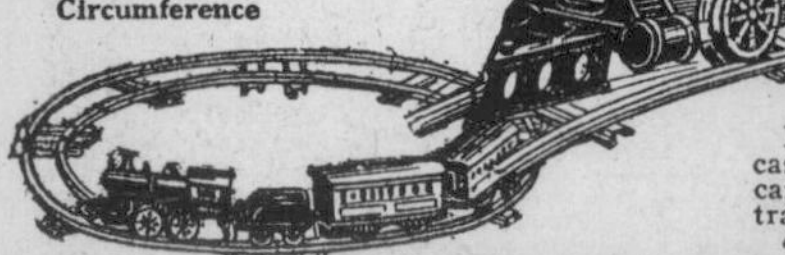

Usual $1.50 Value For 98c

Here's a real value for the little fellow. A 19-inch train with a 6-inch cast iron locomotive. A lithographed tender, two 4¼-inch lithographed cars, light in weight so kiddie can handle easily, and four pieces curved track, making circle 60-inch circumference. Shpg. wt., 2¾ lbs.
49K5105.. **98c**

Real Action Hand Car on Track

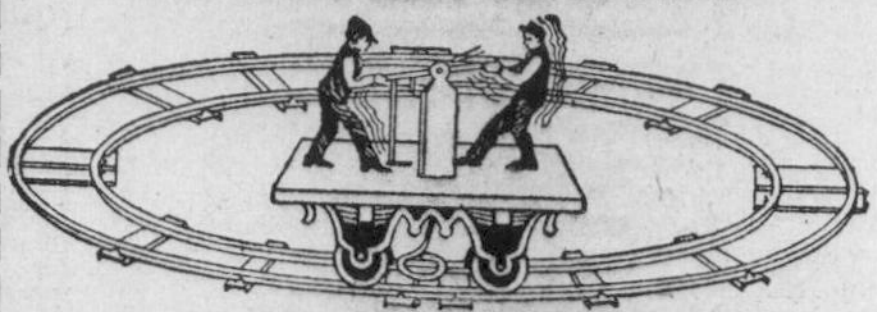

See the two little men work naturally, bending up and down as the little hand car spins around the complete oval track. The car measures 4⅜x3½ in. and is made of steel lithographed in natural colors. There are four pieces of curved track, forming a circle 56 inches in circumference. Equipped with strong clockwork motor. Shpg. wt., 1 lb.
49K5700.. **59c**

RAILWAY EQUIPMEN

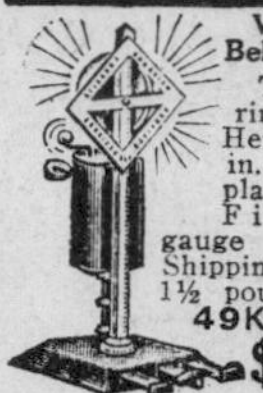

Warning Bell Signal

Train rings bell. Height, 7¼ in. Nickel plated bell. Fits any gauge track. Shipping wt., 1½ pounds.
49K5225 **$1.19**

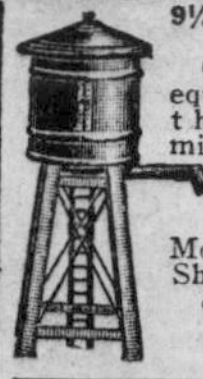

9¼-Inch Water Tank

Complete your equipment with this dandy miniature tank. Painted in attractive colors. Movable spout. Shpg. wt., ¾ lb.
49K5244 **59c**

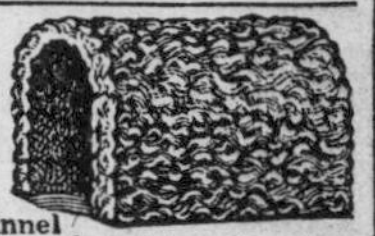

Tunnel

Rough finish, attractively colored metal tunnel. 6¼x5½x5⅝ inches. Shpg. wt., 1 lb.
49K5206..... **23c**

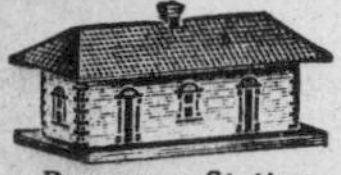

Passenger Station

Windows and doors are cut out. Lithographed in colors. Size, 10¼x5⅜x4⅞ inches. Shpg. wt., 1½ lbs.
49K5207... **98c**

Mechanical Track

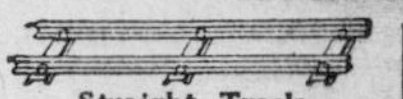

Straight Track

Each piece, 10¼ inches long. Shpg. wt., 1 lb.
49K5202
Set of **6** pieces..... **37c**

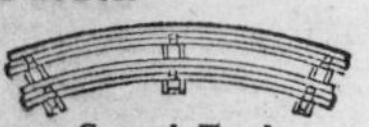

Curved Track

Eight sections make circle. Shpg. wt., 1 lb.
Set of **6** pcs.
49K5201 **37c**

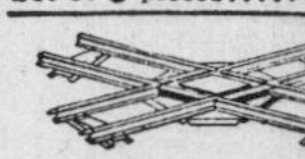

Crossover

49K5203
Shpg. wt., 1 lb..... **39c**

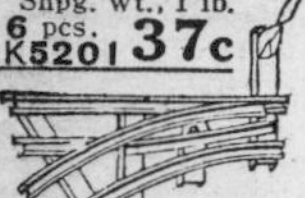

Switches

Shpg. wt., 1 lb.
49K5204 **89c**
Per pair........

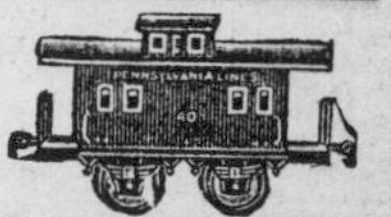

PENNSYLVANIA LINES

5½-Inch Freight Caboose

Hand rail back and front. Shpg. wt., 1 lb.
49K5220..... **39c**

Shpg. wt., 2 lbs

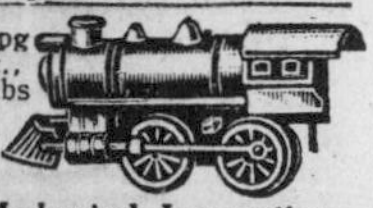

Mechanical Locomotive

Cast iron. Nickel plated piston rods. 6½ in. long. No tender.
49K5222 **$1.29**

Loading Derrick

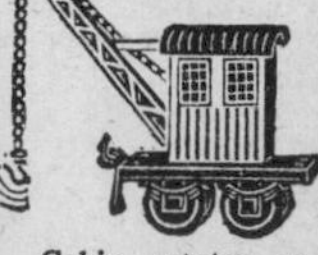

Cabin rotates so actual lifting can be done from any angle. 5 inches high over all. Shpg. wt., ¾ lb.
49K5243. **43c**

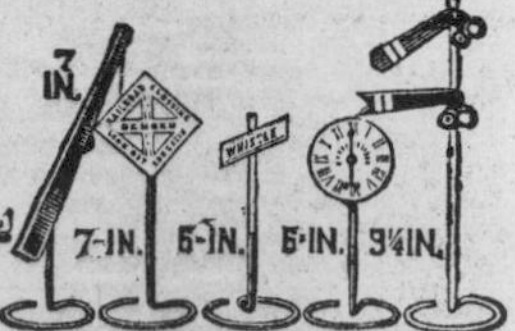

7 IN.
7-IN.
5-IN.
5-IN.
3¼IN.
WHISTLE

5 Parts for the Price of 1

Semaphore, crossing gate and clock have moving signal parts. Strong steel, enameled in railway colors. Shpg. wt., 1 lb.
49K5226-5 pieces **48c**

LIONEL ELECTRIC TRAINS

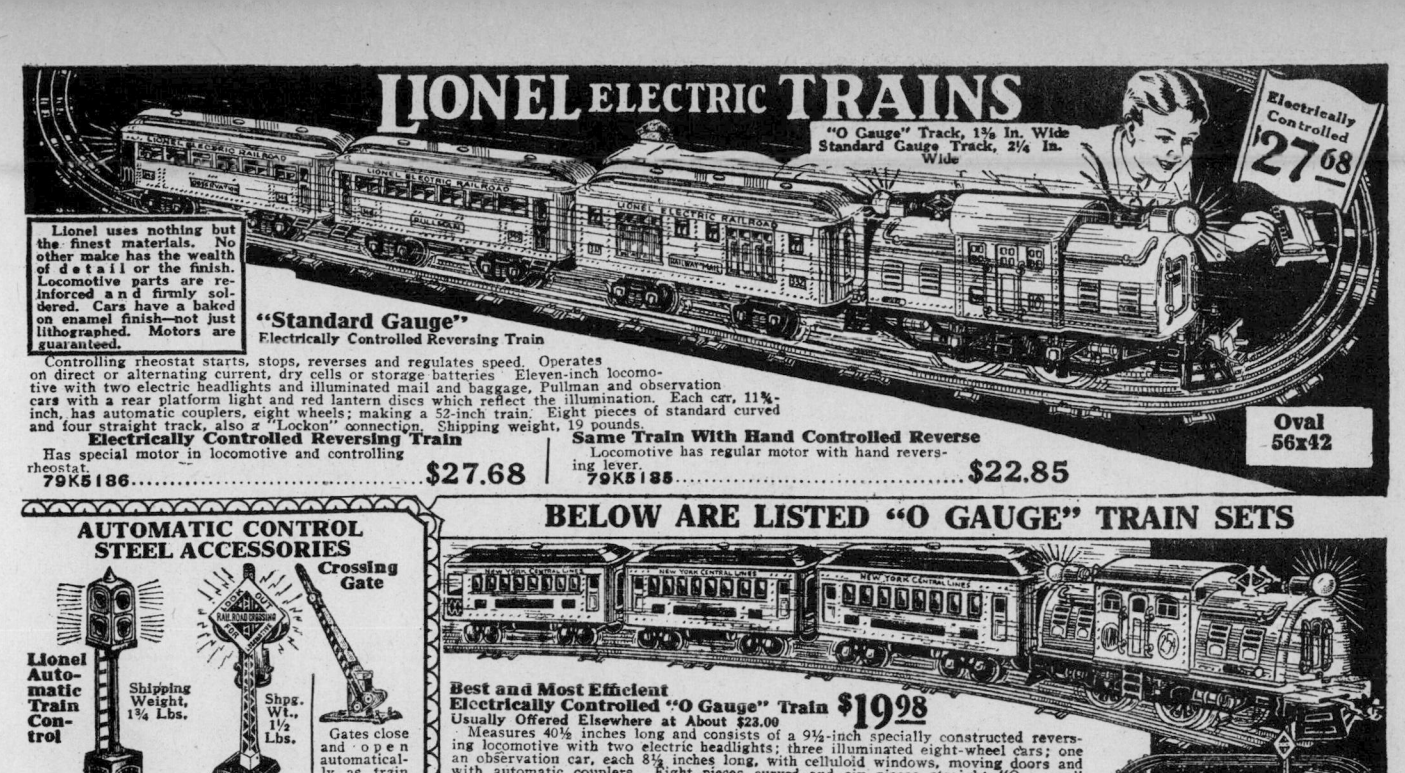

"O Gauge" Track, 1⅜ In. Wide
Standard Gauge Track, 2¼ In. Wide

Electrically Controlled $27.68

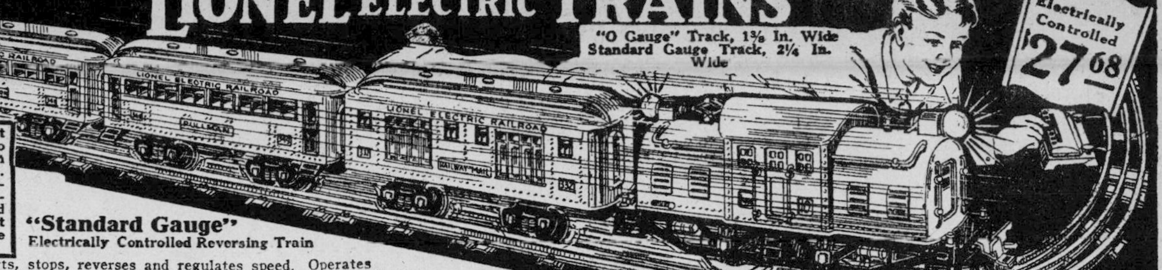

Lionel uses nothing but the finest materials. No other make has the wealth of detail or the finish. Locomotive parts are reinforced and firmly soldered. Cars have a baked on enamel finish—not just lithographed. Motors are guaranteed.

"Standard Gauge"
Electrically Controlled Reversing Train

Controlling rheostat starts, stops, reverses and regulates speed. Operates on direct or alternating current, dry cells or storage batteries. Eleven-inch locomotive with two electric headlights and illuminated mail and baggage, Pullman and observation cars with a rear platform light and red lantern discs which reflect the illumination. Each car, 11¾-inch, has automatic couplers, eight wheels; making a 52-inch train. Eight pieces of standard curved and four straight track, also a "Lockon" connection. Shipping weight, 19 pounds.

Oval 56x42

Electrically Controlled Reversing Train
Has special motor in locomotive and controlling rheostat.
79K5186..**$27.68**

Same Train With Hand Controlled Reverse
Locomotive has regular motor with hand reversing lever.
79K5185..**$22.85**

AUTOMATIC CONTROL STEEL ACCESSORIES

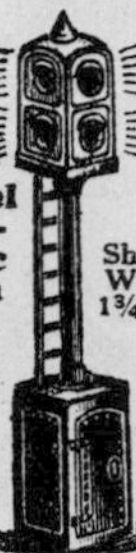

Lionel Automatic Train Control
Shipping Weight, 1¾ Lbs.

Train approaches! Red signal lights up. Train stops. After a few seconds, red light goes out and green signal lights up. Train starts automatically. Signal 10⅝ in. high. Can be placed anywhere in track formation.
49K5251—For "O gauge" track..........**$4.48**
49K5247—For "Standard gauge" track..........**$4.48**

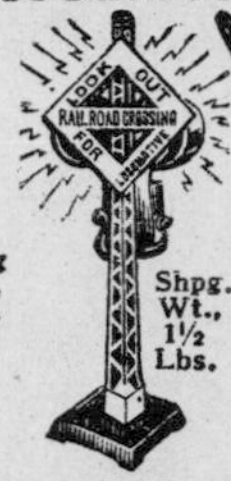

Bell Warning Signal
Shpg. Wt., 1½ Lbs.
Nicely enameled. Nickel plated bells. Bells ring while train is passing. Sign is brass.
For "O Gauge" 49K5250 $2.69
For Standard Gauge 49K5246 $2.98

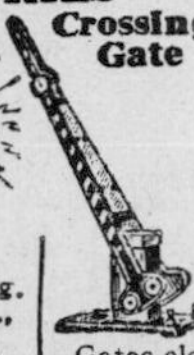

Crossing Gate
Gates close and open automatically as train passes. Gate, 10⅞ inches long, enameled black.
49K5252 For O gauge. Shpg. wt., 1½ lbs. $3.59
49K5248 For Standard gauge. Shpg. wt., 1¾ lbs. $3.79

Lamps

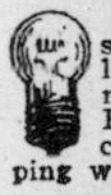

For general use such as in headlights, illuminated cars, etc. Packed in wood container. Shipping wt., 5 oz.
49K5254 14-volt..........**25c**
49K5255 8-volt..........**25c**

Illuminated Lamp Post

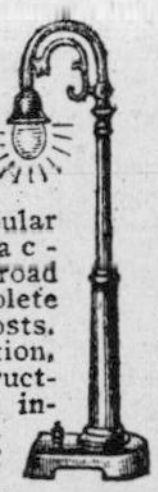

The most popular electric train accessory. No railroad system is complete without lamp posts. A real reproduction, carefully constructed. Light globe included. Height, 7⅝ in. Shipping wt., ¾ lb.
49K5253 **$1.10**

Electrical Straight Track

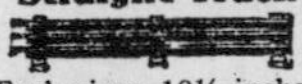

Each piece, 10¼ inches. "O gauge" track. Shpg. wt., ¾ lb.
49K5235 Set, 2 pieces.......**36c**
"Standard gauge" track. Shipping weight, 1¼ pounds.
49K5231 Set, 2 pieces...**54c**

Electrical Curved Track

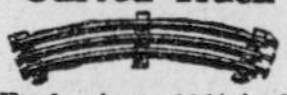

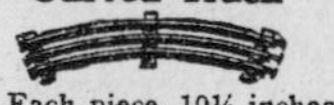

Each piece, 10¼ inches long. "O gauge" track. Shpg. wt., ¾ lb.
49K5236 Set, 2 pieces....**36c**
"Standard gauge" track. Shpg. wt., 1½ lbs.
49K5232 Set, 2 pieces....**54c**

Switches

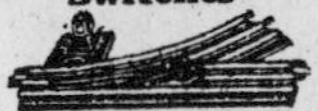

"O gauge" track. Shipping weight, 2 lbs.
49K5200 Per pair.....**$3.39**
"Standard gauge" track. Shpg. wt., 3½ lbs.
49K5234 Per pair.....**$4.48**

Crossover

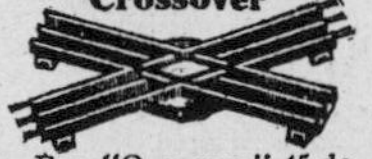

For "O gauge," 45 degrees. Sh. wt. 1 lb.
49K5216....**89c**
For "Standard gauge," 90 degrees. Shpg. wt., 1½ lbs.
49K5233....**$1.10**

BELOW ARE LISTED "O GAUGE" TRAIN SETS

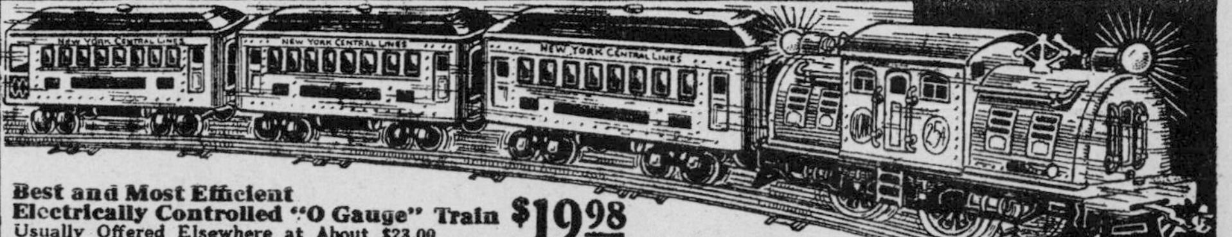

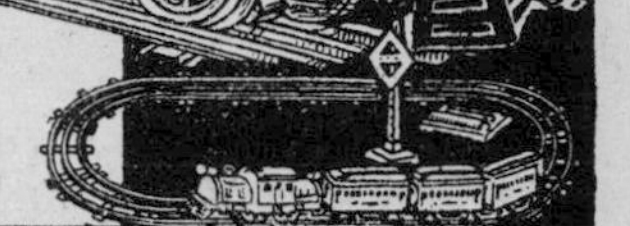

Best and Most Efficient Electrically Controlled "O Gauge" Train $19.98
Usually Offered Elsewhere at About $23.00

Measures 40½ inches long and consists of a 9½-inch specially constructed reversing locomotive with two electric headlights; three illuminated eight-wheel cars; one an observation car, each 8½ inches long, with celluloid windows, moving doors and with automatic couplers. Eight pieces curved and six pieces straight "O gauge" track, making oval 59x30 inches. "Lockon" connection, track clips, automatic reversing rheostat and a 6¾-inch warning signal.
79K5190—Shipping weight, 11 pounds........................**$19.98**

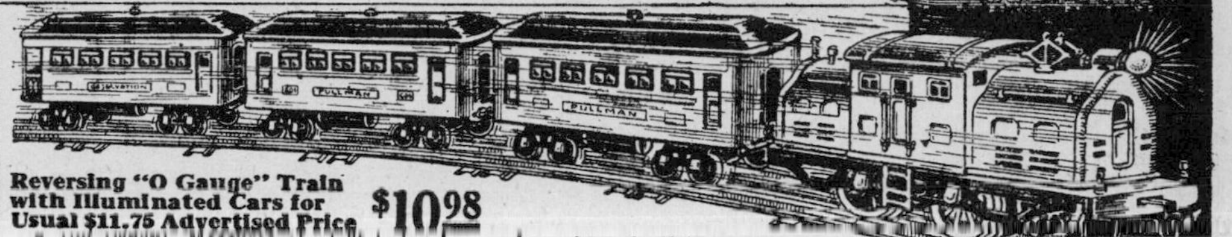

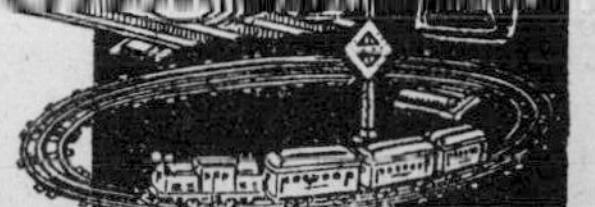

Reversing "O Gauge" Train with Illuminated Cars for Usual $11.75 Advertised Price $10.98

A Jim Dandy! Measures about 36 inches long and consists of a 7-inch reversing locomotive with one headlight, two illuminated Pullman cars, one illuminated observation car, each 7½ inches long, and each with eight wheels and automatic couplers. Outfit has eight pieces of "O gauge" curved and four pieces straight track, "Lockon" connection, track clips, battery rheostat and a 6¾-inch warning signal. Track forms oval, 50½x30 inches.
49K5188—Shipping weight, 9¾ pounds........................**$10.98**

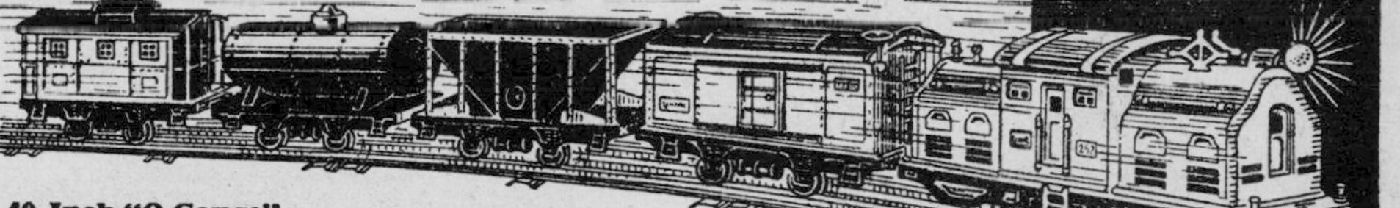

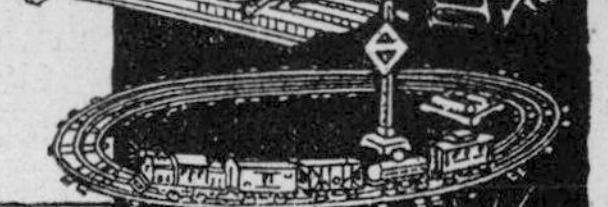

40-Inch "O Gauge" Reversing Four-Car Freight Train $9.67
Usual $10.75 Advertised Price

O Boy! What you need to complete your train yard. A 7-inch reversible locomotive with electric headlight; 6¾-inch box car; 6½-inch coal car with real chute dump; 6½-inch oil car; 6½-inch caboose; eight pieces "O gauge" curved and two pieces straight track, forming oval 39x30 inches. "Lock-on" connection, track clips, rheostat and 6¾-inch warning signal included.
49K5191—Shipping weight, 10 pounds........................**$9.67**

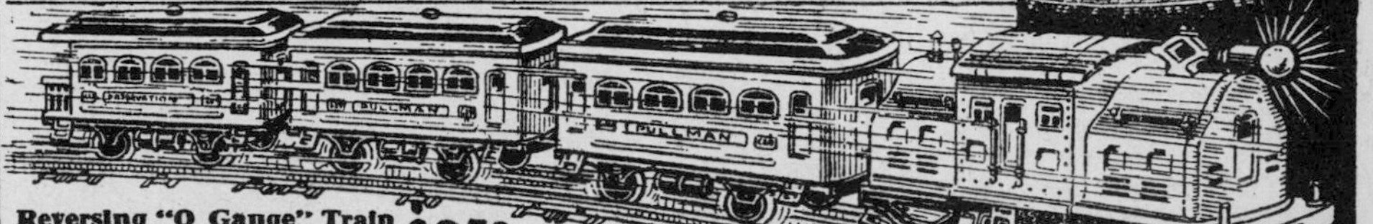

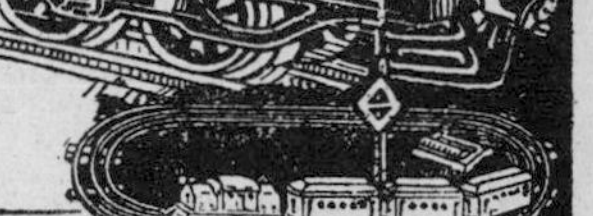

Reversing "O Gauge" Train $8.79
Usual $9.75 Advertised Price

Measures about 33¾ inches long and consists of 7-inch reversing locomotive with headlight, two Pullman cars and one observation car, each measuring 6½ inches long and each with mottled celluloid windows and automatic couplers. Eight pieces of "O gauge" curved, two pieces of straight track, "Lockon" connection, track clips, battery rheostat and 6¾-inch warning signal. Track forms oval. 40x31 inches.
49K5189—Shipping weight, 8½ pounds........................**$8.79**

TRANSFORMERS

$4.79 $2.98

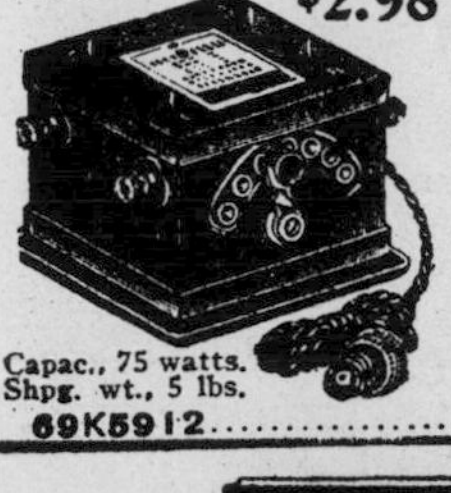

Capac., 75 watts. Shpg. wt., 5 lbs.

For Toy Trains and Motors

For reducing lighting current in your home to suitable voltage for toy trains and motors. If your house lighting current is an alternating 100 to 120 volts, it is more economical, safe and simple to use a transformer. Each with cord and plug to connect to your light socket; also switch to govern speed of trains. **Cannot Be Used on Direct Current.** Directions with each.

For all small and medium size trains running on "O gauge" track and requiring 7 to 10 volts.
69K5912..........................**$2.98**

For larger train outfits requiring 12 to 15 volts, or where additional cars or accessories are used. Capacity, 100 watts. Shipping weight, 7 pounds.
69K5913....**$4.79**

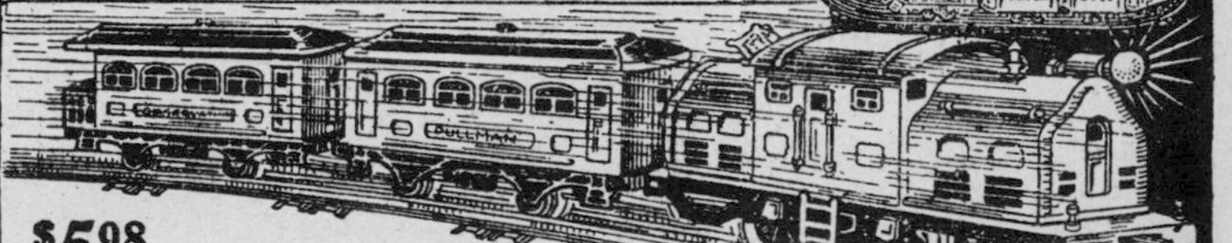

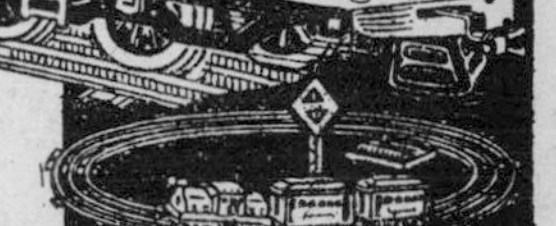

$5.98 24-Inch Two-Car Train

As good quality throughout as our higher priced sets, but made to fit need of smaller boy. Locomotive, not reversible, 7¾ inches long. Two 6½-inch passenger cars, one an observation car, celluloid windows, opening doors and automatic couplers. Eight pieces "O gauge" curved track. "Lockon" connection, battery rheostat; track clips and a 6¾-inch warning signal included.
49K5192—Shipping weight, 8½ pounds......**$5.98**

Order Blanks Are in Back of This Catalog

Daddy I want This Big Tool Chest

$5.98 $3.48

Parents! Give your boy the chance he deserves. Encourage and help develop his constructive ability. He is eager for it! It will keep him happy and busy at constructive play and will make him a more capable man in later years.

Boys! We have scoured the entire country to give you the best outfits for your use. Not a lot of cheap, small pieces of metal and wood to make a big display, but outfits consisting of real tools, just the right size for your use.

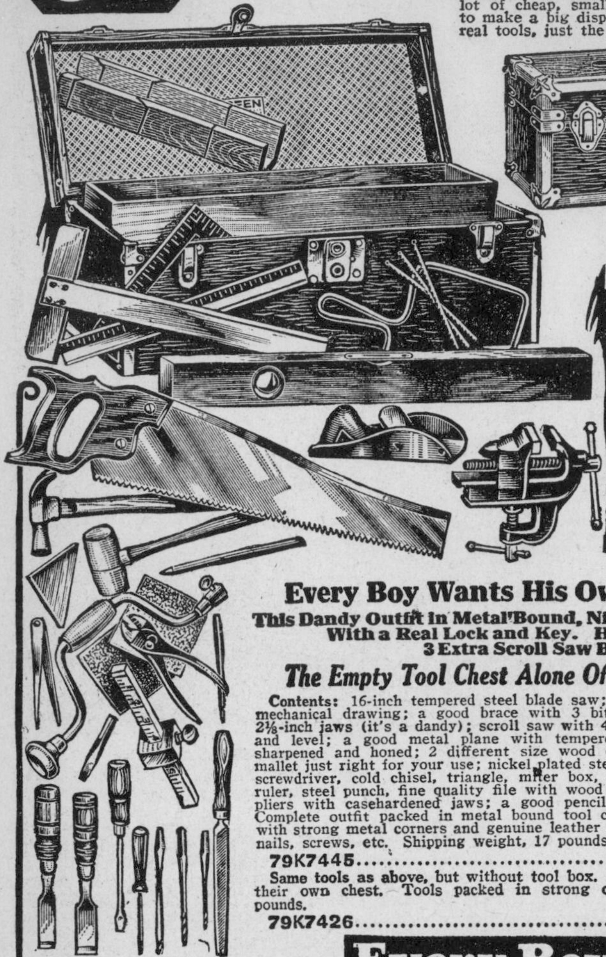

BOYS! DON'T OVERLOOK THIS DANDY BIG CHEST For only $5.98

17 Tools in a Beautiful
Hardwood Chest for the Younger Carpenter

Lots of fun making toys and novelties. Wood handle saw with 12-inch steel blade; a real 12-inch level made of hardwood; a steel plane with tempered steel blade; a useful brace and bit; tempered steel blade wood chisel; a dandy scroll saw with a blade; nickel plated metal angle square and bright metal compass; a hammer and mallet to fit your hand, screwdriver, awl, miter box, triangle, pencil and ruler all packed in nicely varnished hardwood chest, 16½x8⅜x5⅞ inches, with tray for nails and screws. Shipping weight, 10 pounds.
79K7432 .... **$3.48**
Same tools as above, but without chest, for boys who wish to make their own. Tools packed in carton.
79K7437—Shipping weight, 6 pounds **$1.98**

10 Pieces for $1.00

Fine quality brace and bit, 12-inch steel blade saw, nickel plated metal angle square. A good grade hammer and screwdriver, wood miter box, varnished 12-inch ruler, metal compass and pencil. Shpg. wt., 4 lbs.
69K7436 .... **$1.00**

Boys! Make Your Own Toys

Draw Them—Saw Them—Make Them—Paint Them

With this outfit you can make a great variety of small wooden toys and novelties. Contains a nickel plated scroll saw with blades, a wood bench with metal clamp to fasten to table, full size toy designs ready for tracing, 1 sheet of carbon paper, thumb tacks, several pieces of thin wood, a brad awl, sandpaper and ruler. Cotter pins, crayons and paints to color them. Complete "Manual of Instructions." Shipping wt., 3½ lbs.
69K7444 .... **$1.79**

Every Boy Wants His Own Tool Chest
This Dandy Outfit In Metal Bound, Nicely Covered Tool Chest With a Real Lock and Key. Has 27 Tools and 3 Extra Scroll Saw Blades

The Empty Tool Chest Alone Often Sells for $2.50

Contents: 16-inch tempered steel blade saw; 14¼-inch wood T square for mechanical drawing; a good brace with 3 bits; a regular iron vise with 2⅛-inch jaws (it's a dandy); scroll saw with 4 blades; a real 19-inch plumb and level; a good metal plane with tempered steel blade that may be sharpened and honed; 2 different size wood chisels; a good hammer and mallet just right for your use; nickel plated steel angle square and compass; screwdriver, cold chisel, triangle, miter box, awl, 12-inch varnished wood ruler, steel punch, fine quality file with wood handle; wood scratch gauge; pliers with casehardened jaws; a good pencil and 2 pieces of sandpaper. Complete outfit packed in metal bound tool chest, size 20x7¾x7¾ inches, with strong metal corners and genuine leather handle. Wood tray inside for nails, screws, etc. Shipping weight, 17 pounds.
79K7445 .... **$5.98**
Same tools as above, but without tool box. For boys who want to make their own chest. Tools packed in strong carton. Shipping weight, 13 pounds.
79K7426 .... **$3.98**

Every Boy Wants a Gun

The Largest Selling Shooting Game on the Market

69c

An exceptional value at this price. Aim straight! Bang! Down they go. It's dandy practice and real sport. A first class 17-inch steel barrel, wood stock, break action popgun with a nicely lithographed target printed in colors to represent a real jungle, in which three little colored celluloid birds are sitting. Jungle is printed on good grade cardboard and has folding arrangement permitting target to stand up or fold flat when not in use. Requires real skill and creates pleasant rivalry. Cork ammunition included. Target measures 16 inches long, 10⅝ inches high and 3 inches deep when set up. In neat box. Shipping weight, 1¾ pounds.
49K5663 .... **69c**

79c
Famous "King" Rapid Fire Pump Popgun

Absolutely harmless. Loads automatically; loud popping noise with both forward and backward movement of the handpiece; no flying corks; beautiful blue finish on all metal parts; stock and handpiece walnut stained hardwood. 27 inches long. Shpg. wt., 1½ pounds.
49K5648—$1.00 size. **79c**

Think of a 21-Inch King Popgun for 39c
Standard 50c Gun.
39c

Real "King" Popgun for 21c

A new type gun, not the old cumbersome kind. Has blued steel barrel and walnut stained hardwood stock. New type round trigger. Break action with strong spring like air rifle. Cork attached to string. Length, over all, 21 inches.
49K5604—Shpg. wt., 1½ lbs. **39c**

A new style 17-inch popgun with blued steel barrel, new style easy operating trigger and strong spring. Walnut stained hardwood stock. Cork attached to string; shoots with loud report. Harmless. Length, over all, 17 inches.
49K5603—Shpg. wt., 8 oz. **21c**

69c
29-Inch Nicely Finished Break Action Popgun

Here's a dandy. Shoots cork with loud "Bang." The blued steel barrel alone is 17 inches long. The stock is made of natural finish walnut. Has break action like a real air rifle. Has a good steel spring that does not get out of order easily. Length, over all, 29 inches. Shipping weight, 1¾ pounds.
49K5600 .... **69c**

One of Our Most Popular Toys

Here's the Gun Every Boy Wants. Every time you pull the trigger a big red flash shoots out. A real repeater. You don't have to cock it; just pull the trigger. You can shoot 5,000 flashes before reloading. Strongly made of steel. For extra Reloads see below. Length, 4½ inches.
49K5657—Shipping weight, 6 ounces. **21c**
Reloads for Ronson Repeater, each reload good for 5,000 shots. Shipping weight, 1 ounce.
49K5658—3 reloads **13c**

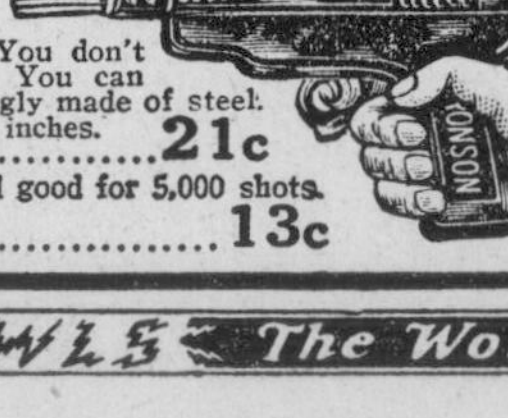

59c
2-in-1 Combination Bow and Arrow and Parachute Set for 59c

A special value. Very popular with the kiddies. Think of a 28-inch real hickory bow, 3 suction rubber tip arrows, a bright color cloth parachute with cardboard trapeze artist and 18½-inch stick to shoot it with; also 27¾-inch heavy cardboard Sitting Bull target with three targets printed on it, all for this price. Unprecedented value.
49K5664—Shipping wt., 1¾ lbs... **59c**

Exceptional Value in Shooting Game

The equal of many $1.00 values elsewhere. With this dandy 17-inch steel barrel, break action, popgun and corks included, you can shoot the lion, tiger, bear, elephant or the war painted Indians. 12 cardboard figures in all, each one in beautiful natural colors. Shipping weight, 1¾ pounds.
49K5661 .... **49c**

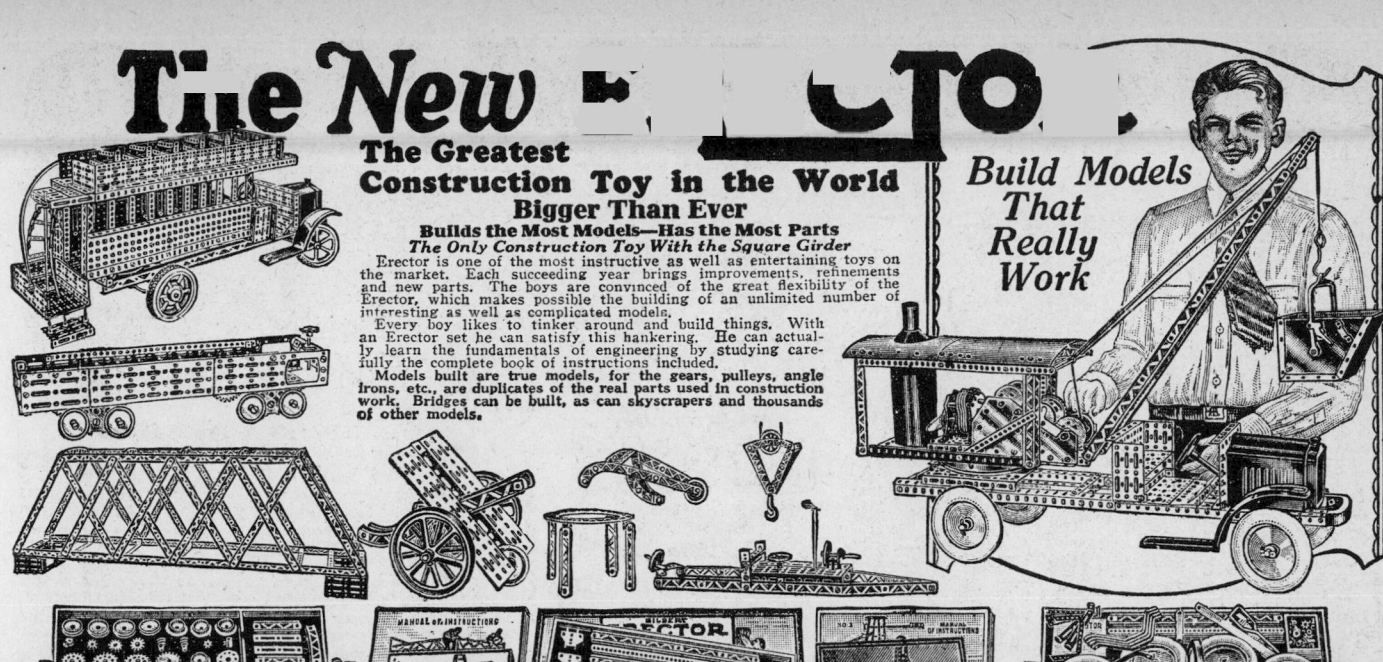

The New E CTO

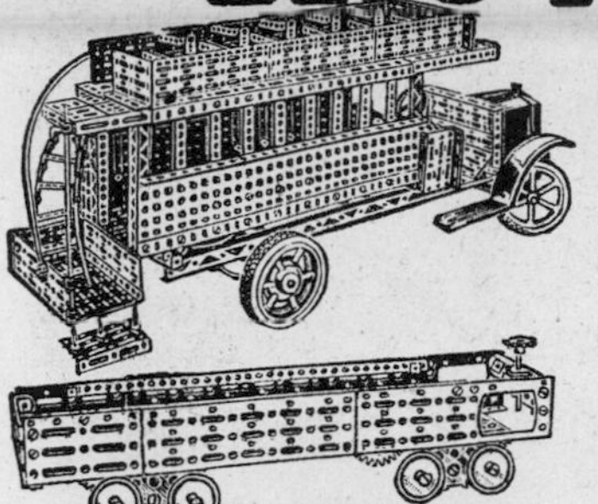

The Greatest Construction Toy in the World

Bigger Than Ever

Builds the Most Models—Has the Most Parts

The Only Construction Toy With the Square Girder

Erector is one of the most instructive as well as entertaining toys on the market. Each succeeding year brings improvements, refinements and new parts. The boys are convinced of the great flexibility of the Erector, which makes possible the building of an unlimited number of interesting as well as complicated models.

Every boy likes to tinker around and build things. With an Erector set he can satisfy this hankering. He can actually learn the fundamentals of engineering by studying carefully the complete book of instructions included.

Models built are true models, for the gears, pulleys, angle irons, etc., are duplicates of the real parts used in construction work. Bridges can be built, as can skyscrapers and thousands of other models.

Build Models That Really Work

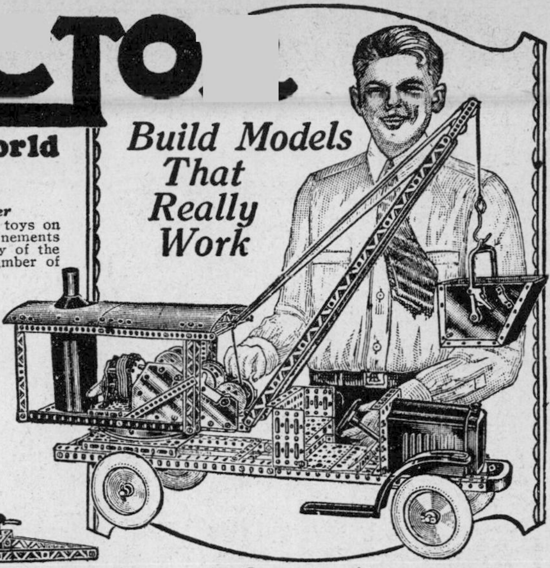

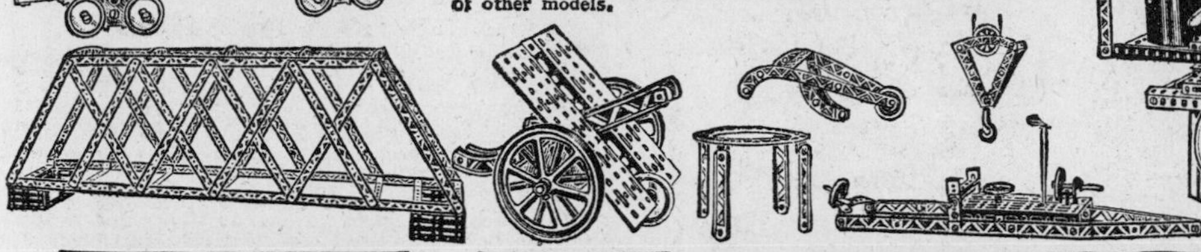

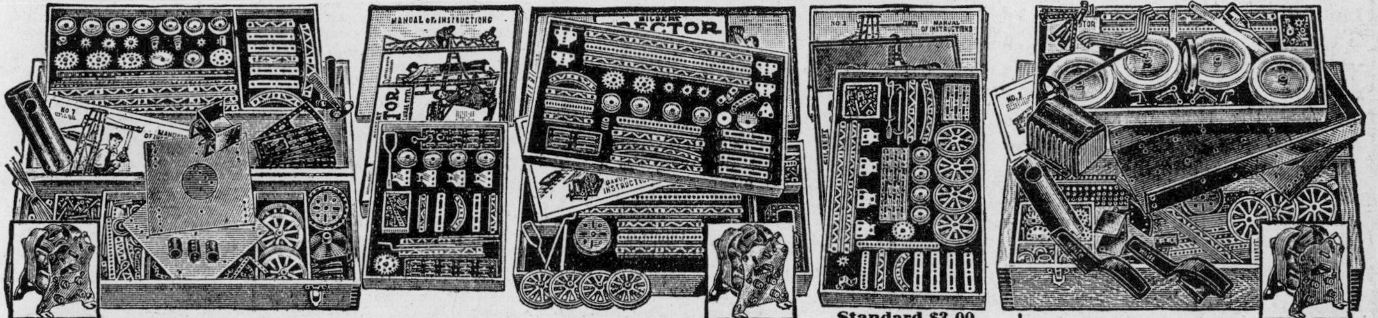

Standard $10.00 Erector, $8.98

473 Parts—Builds 533 Models

Here's a dandy set. It has a powerful, already assembled motor. Furthermore, it is assembled in a heavy, stained and varnished wood box with brass side grips and suitcase catches. **It has many parts not in the smaller sets, which make it possible to build such models as a miniature steam engine, steam shovel, crane, derrick and Ferris wheel.** A wonderful collection of girders, pulleys, boiler, digger, scoop, etc. Wood box, 21½x8¼x3¼ inches. Shipping weight, 13 pounds.

79K4716............... **$8.98**

Standard $1.00 Erector Only 89c

104 Parts—Builds 278 Models

Just the set to start out with. Although it has less parts than the other sets, you can build many models with it. If you buy a larger size, just add these parts to your new set, for they are interchangeable. In attractive cardboard box, 12⅝x8⅞x¾ inches. Shipping wt., 1¾ pounds.

49K4717....... **89c**

Standard $5.00 Erector, With Motor, $4.47

235 Parts—Builds 500 Models

A very popular size which will make any boy happy. Builds bridges, airplanes, anything you wish. Then attach your model to the already assembled motor and watch it work. In attractive, strong cardboard box, 18x10x2½ inches. Shpg. weight, 6 pounds.

79K4720. **$4.47**

Standard $3.00 Erector, $2.69

169 Parts—Builds 380 Models

A barrel of fun to be had with this set. The square, girder-like structural steel enables you to build about 380 models. This is a dandy set, and any boy will find plenty of thrill in making all the models shown in the instruction book. In attractive, strong cardboard box, 18x10x1¼ inches. Shipping weight, 3 pounds.

49K4715. **$2.69**

Standard $15.00 Erector, $12.98

Motorized Erector Set With Chassis

627 Parts—Builds 554 Models.

Oh Boy! With this new set you can build all models shown on this page. A strong steel frame dump truck, hook and ladder, bus, steam boiler and also many other models that cannot be built with smaller sets. Included are rubber tired wheels, boiler plate, steering knuckle, bumper, fenders and electric motor. In strong wood box, stained and varnished, with hinged lid, brass side grips and snap catches. Size, over all, 21⅝x8¼x4¾ inches. Shpg. wt., 20 lbs.

79K4718............. **$12.98**

TINKERTOY

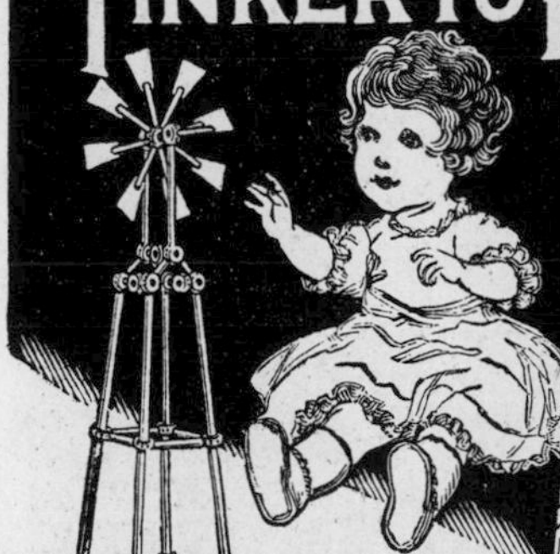

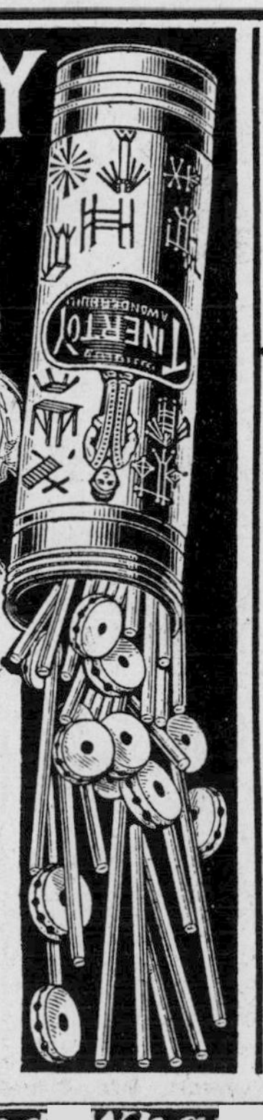

Tinker Toy Wonder Builder

Will Build Operating Models

An ideal wood construction toy for the younger child. Very simple in principle, being based on the old adage, "A stick and a spool will amuse a child." Seventy pieces of different shapes packed in a neat cylindrical box. One set will build many models, but two or three will build more complicated and interesting models.

1 Set for 63c

For building simple models. Shipping weight, 1¼ pounds.

49K4760—Per set......... **63c**

2 Sets for $1.21

To build larger models. Shipping weight, 2½ pounds.

49K4761—2 sets for.... **$1.21**

3 Sets for $1.75

For building still larger and more complicated models. Shipping weight, 3¾ pounds.

49K4768—3 sets for.... **$1.75**

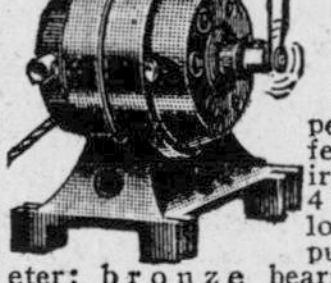

Polar Cub Motor

Biggest Selling Universal Motor in the World For Direct or Alternating Current of 110 Volts

Runs about 2,700 revolutions per minute. With plug and 5 feet of cord. Black enameled iron base 2¾x4 inches. Stands 4 inches high. Shaft, 4 inches long, has a detachable grooved pulley about ⅝ inch in diameter; bronze bearings. Shipping weight, 2¾ pounds.

69K5906.......................... **$4.59**

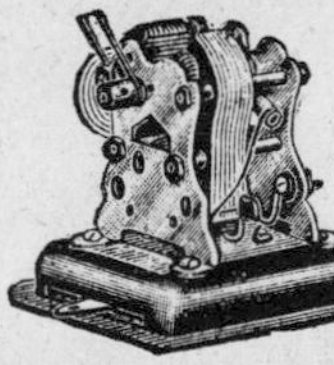

Powerful Battery Motors

Runs on 2 to 4 dry batteries. Book showing 48 experiments included with each motor. Will operate Tinker Toy, Erector and small accessories. Mounted on steel base; size, 4x4 inches.

With Reverse Lever

69K5940

Shpg. wt., 2 lbs.... **$1.79**

Without Reverse Lever and Metal Base

69K5942

Shpg. wt., 1¼ lbs.... **89c**

Bilt E-Z, the Popular Construction Toy

Bilt-E-Z

"The BOY Builder"

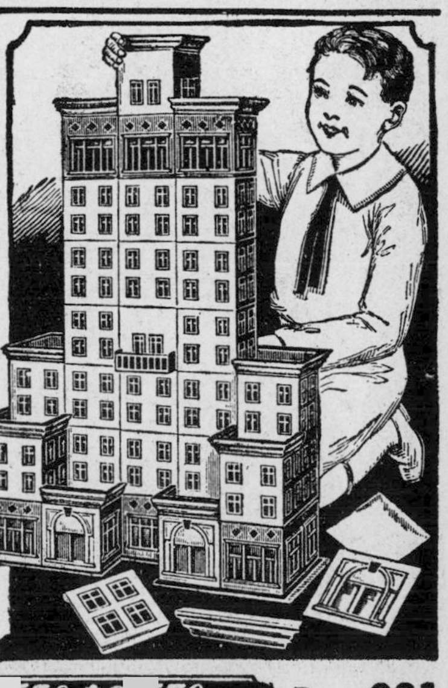

Just as the Child Builds the Toy, So the Toy Builds the Child. For Both Boys and Girls.

Boys! Build beautiful skyscrapers or accessories for your train sets, such as stations, trestles and then forts, castles, etc., besides.

Girls! Think of the thrill of building your own doll house to order, with as many stories, rooms and porches as you want.

Complete models are not flimsy things, but substantial structures which you can carry about. When you tire of one building, pull it apart in a jiffy and start another.

All parts are interchangeable, buy as many sets as you like, for you just add that many more parts. All parts are sheet steel, enameled in white and gray. Each set in heavy cardboard box, covered with neat imitation leather effect paper. In each set are floors, windows, walls, friction pieces, cornices and balconies in varying quantities, depending on size of set. Four different sizes.

No. 0

Standard $1.00 Set 83c

Builds more than 100 models. 70 parts in this set. Size of box, 10x6¾x1⅛ in. Shpg. wt., 1¾ lbs.

49K4705....... **83c**

No. A

With this set you can

Standard $3.50 Set $2.95

build about 300 models. Has 259 parts and comes packed in cardboard box, 10x7x2¼ inch. Shipping weight, 3½ pounds.

49K4703... **$2.95**

No. 00

Standard $2.00 Set $1.69

Builds more than 200 models. Has 146 parts. Box, 10¼x6¾x1½ inches. Shpg. wt., 2¾ lbs.

49K4706... **$1.69**

No. B

Standard $5.00 Set $4.35

Can build over 400 models with this popular set. Has 363 parts. Heavy cardboard box, 11x9x2¼ inch. Shpg. weight, 6 lbs.

49K4707... **$4.35**

98¢ 32-Inch — FLYING ARROW Steering Sleds — $2.69 56-Inch

It Pays to Buy a good Sled

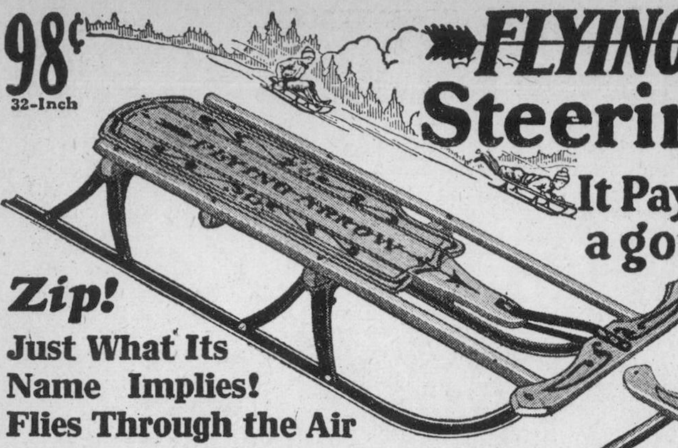

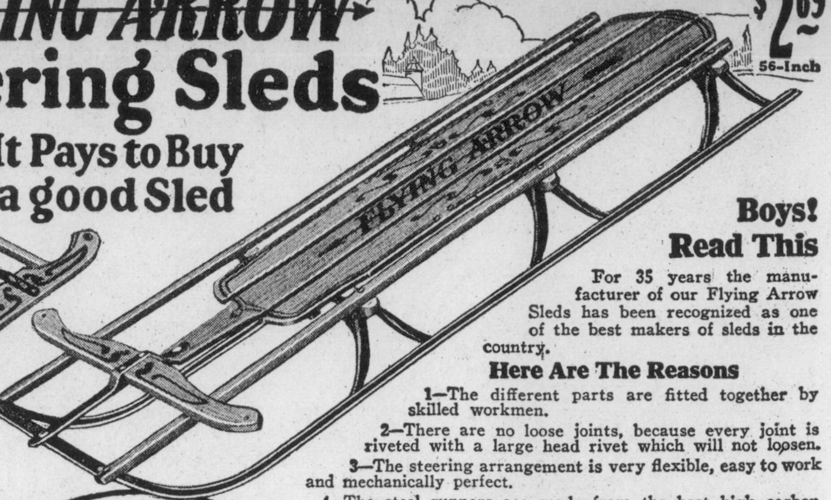

Zip!

Just What Its Name Implies! Flies Through the Air

Flying Arrow Sleds are popular with boys everywhere. Wood parts nicely varnished and decorated. There are cheaper sleds on the market, but how long do they last and will the boy be perfectly satisfied? Our sturdy, well constructed Flying Arrow Sleds have made a real reputation; any proud owner of one can tell you. They steer easily around curves, because the runners curve up abruptly in front, leaving a greater part of the long flat runners on the ground, and because the runners are made of first quality tempered spring steel. The knees or braces are heavy gauge stamped steel, securely riveted to top and runners. The sound and solid hardwood lumber used for top will not split or warp.

32-Inch Sled
79K8300
Shpg. wt., 7 pounds... **98c**

36-Inch Sled
79K8301
Shpg. wt., 8 lbs..... **$1.39**

40-Inch Sled
79K8302
Shpg. wt., 10 lbs... **$1.67**
Unmailable.

Baby Guard

79c

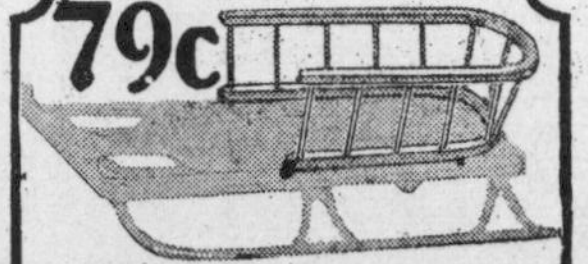

Fasten to Any Sled

Just the thing for baby; later guard may be removed and youngster can have a regular sled. Hardwood throughout, natural finish varnished. Complete with screws for fastening. Sled not included. Shpg. wt., 1¼ lbs.
79K8310 **79c**

Boys! Read This

For 35 years the manufacturer of our Flying Arrow Sleds has been recognized as one of the best makers of sleds in the country.

Here Are The Reasons

1—The different parts are fitted together by skilled workmen.

2—There are no loose joints, because every joint is riveted with a large head rivet which will not loosen.

3—The steering arrangement is very flexible, easy to work and mechanically perfect.

4—The steel runners are made from the best high carbon spring steel, which gives them extreme durability and wonderful steering quality. Best steel now used for sled runners.

5—The steel supports or knees are the best money can buy and are riveted to runners, not welded.

6—The wood tops and side rails are made from selected hardwood which is smoothly machined, all edges rounded and sanded, making them free from slivers and sharp ends.

7—All wood parts are carefully finished and varnished with durable varnish to withstand weather exposure and hard use; they are attractively decorated in red and blue.

We Repeat—Flying Arrow Sleds are made from the best materials, by good workmen, will withstand the roughest treatment on ice or snow and will steer easier than any other sleds on the market.

These Two Have Double Crossbars for Steering.

45-Inch Sled
But four stout knees.
79K8303—Room enough for yourself and two of your friends. Shpg. wt., 11 lbs.
Unmailable.......... **$1.98**

56-Inch Sled
And six stout knees, as illustrated.
79K8311—Plenty big for anybody. Stronger crossbars and braces. Shipping weight, 12 pounds.
Unmailable........ **$2.69**

Toy Farm Wagons

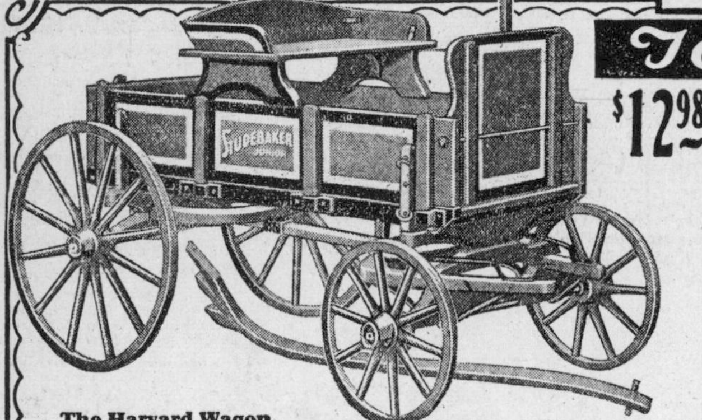

The Harvard Wagon

Similar to the Studebaker Junior, but with plainer gears and less trimming and details. Front wheels, 14 inches; rear wheels, 20 inches. Shipping weight, 64 pounds. Unmailable.

Harvard Senior
Body, 40x18 inches.
79K7676......... **$11.48**

Harvard Junior
Body, 36x18 inches.
79K7675.............. **$9.98**

$12.98

Beautiful Studebaker Jr. Toy Farm Wagon, Only $12.98

No Other Mail Order House Sells This Beautiful Wagon

The original boys' size farm wagon. A perfect miniature of dad's Studebaker. The sides and ends are removable, leaving bed and stakes when lumber wagon is wanted; gearing is made like that on large farm wagons with bent hounds and adjustable reach; all parts strongly ironed and braced; steel bushings in hubs to take up wear. Wheels have steel tires, 3/32 inch thick, welded together by hydraulic pressure; staggered spokes; steel axles, 9/16 inch in diameter. All wood parts are kiln dried hardwood, beautifully enameled in green and red, neatly striped and trimmed with black and yellow. Complete with tongue and seat.

Studebaker Junior

As Illustrated—The One We Recommend

An especially high class, strong and substantial wagon well worth the difference in price over lower priced farm wagons. Body, 36x17 inches. Front wheels, 12 inches; rear wheels, 18 in. Shipping weight, 66 lbs.
79K7685—Unmailable. **$12.98**

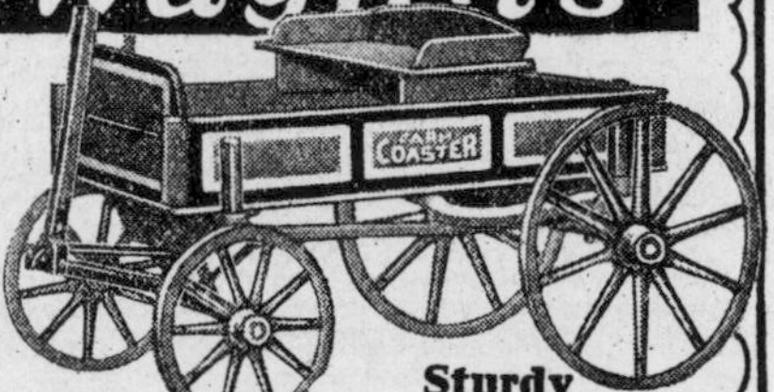

Sturdy Farm Coaster

Bargain Especially Built **$7.48**
Not a Flimsy Play Wagon

Has the strength in construction of our other farm wagons, but is not as fancily decorated or trimmed; rear hound and regular coaster wagon tongue with strong braces to front bolster. Body enameled green, wheels are red. Body and seat are removable. Wheels, 12 inches and 18 inches in diameter. Body is deep enough to hold big loads and measures 36x16 inches. Can be used as coaster or for hauling. Shipping weight, 52 lbs. Unmailable.
79K7673......................... **$7.48**

For Playground Equipment see page 525

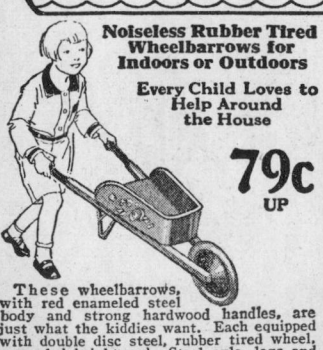

Noiseless Rubber Tired Wheelbarrows for Indoors or Outdoors

Every Child Loves to Help Around the House

79c UP

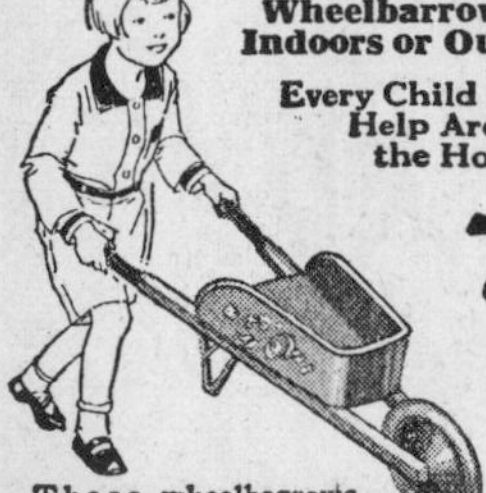

These wheelbarrows, with red enameled steel body and strong hardwood handles, are just what the kiddies want. Each equipped with double disc steel, rubber tired wheel, enameled bright red. Steel axle, legs and cross brace. **Two sizes.**

Body, 11x8½x4 inches. Handles, 26½ inches long. 6-inch wheel with ⅜-inch rubber tire. Shipping wt., 4 lbs.
79K7628...................... **79c**

Heavier Gauge Steel Body and Braces

Body, 13x10x4½ inches. Handles, 29½ inches long. 6-inch wheel; ½-inch rubber tire. Shpg. wt., 8 lbs.
79K7629................. **$1.00**

$6.98 Shpg. Wt., 28 Lbs.

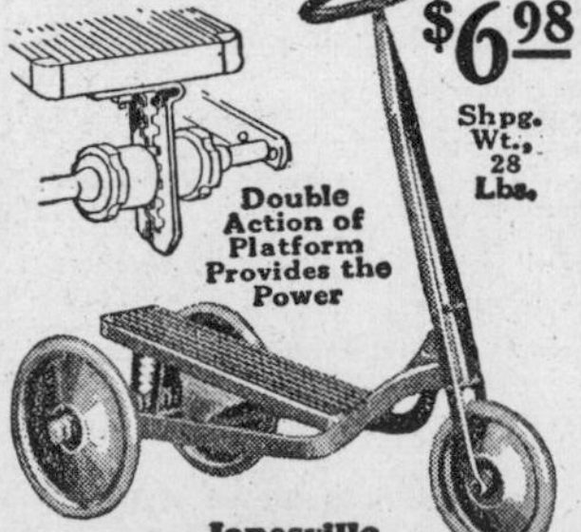
Double Action of Platform Provides the Power

Janesville Scudder Car

The 18½x4½-inch rubber covered wood platform works on a center fulcrum. By throwing the weight of the body first on one foot and then on the other, the platform is tilted up and down, driving the car forward. Ten-inch roller bearing, double disc steel rear wheels and 8¼-inch front wheel equipped with ¾-inch rubber tires. All steel frame and wheels enameled red and striped in black.
79K8805................ **$6.98**

Genuine Irish Malls

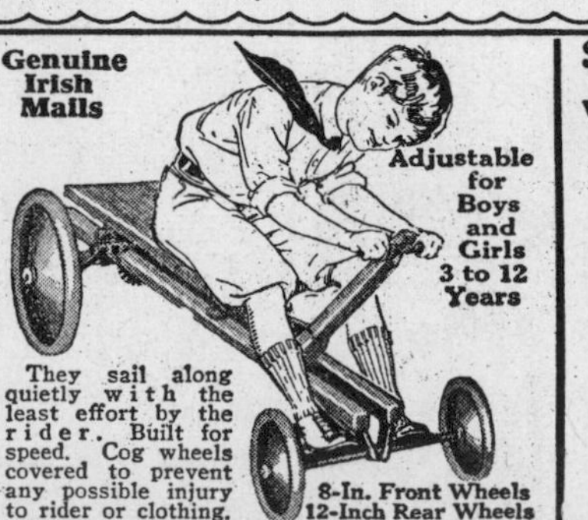
Adjustable for Boys and Girls 3 to 12 Years

They sail along quietly with the least effort by the rider. Built for speed. Cog wheels covered to prevent any possible injury to rider or clothing.

8-In. Front Wheels
12-Inch Rear Wheels

De Luxe Model With Roller Bearing Disc Steel Wheels—⅝-Inch Rubber Tires

Encased roller bearings. Green enameled seat and wheels; frame, lever rod bright red enamel, neatly striped. Lgth. over all, 41 in.
79K8800—Shpg. wt., 32 lbs... **$9.98**

The Irish Mail Special

Spoke wheels equipped with ½-inch rubber tires. Beautifully enameled in green, red and black. Length, over all, 41 in.
79K8802—Shpg. wt., 25 lbs... **$5.89**

$10.00 VALUE **$6.98**

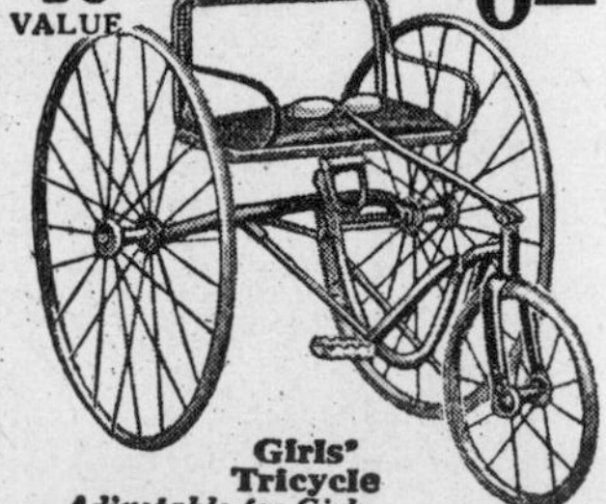

Girls' Tricycle

Adjustable for Girls From 4 to 10 Years

The large quantity we buy, enables us to offer this exceptional bargain. Not a cheap, flimsy tricycle made to fit a certain price, but one that will give good service. Frame is tubular steel beautifully enameled and striped. Seat upholstered with artificial leather. 12-inch front and 20-inch rear wheels with ½-inch rubber tires. One size only, adjustable by raising or lowering seat. Shpg. wt., 38 lbs. Unmailable.
79K8371.................. **$6.98**

$4.48 All Steel One-Piece Body
OLYMPIC FLYER

Curved Steel Tongue

The Best All Steel Wagon Made
If You Want the Best Steel Coaster—Here It Is!
The One We Recommend

$5.98

Body is all one piece— not a removable top that buckles, warps and is almost impossible to replace when once taken off, but a strong substantial body that is always satisfactory.

Curved Tubular Steel Tongue.

Strong Enough to Hold 4 Men Total Weight 600 lbs

To Meet Competition

These All Steel Wagons are not as strongly built as our De Luxe Wagon, but are offered to meet price competition and also the demand for less expensive wagons. Made in the same factory as our De Luxe All Steel Wagon and by the same skilled workmen who have demonstrated that they know how to make real wagons. Slightly lighter weight undergear construction, but a far superior wagon to many offered at similar prices. Body made from automobile steel, has roll top and beaded sides, enameled in red (baked on). Wheels are of the double disc steel type. Curved tubular steel tongue and channel steel bolsters enameled black; classy nickel plated hub caps.

Sold Up to $6.00 Elsewhere.
Our Price, $4.48
Body 33x13¾ inches. Red enameled double disc steel, 9½-inch diameter roller bearing wheels with gilt striping; ¾-inch rubber tires.
Shpg. wt., 33 lbs. **$4.48**
79K7638....

For the Youngster too Small to Handle a Large Size Coaster. Body 28x12 inches.
Handy for Mother to haul her child around in when shopping. 8-inch double disc steel plain bearings wheels, enameled red striped in gilt, with ⅝-inch rubber tires. Shipping weight, 30 pounds.
79K7637............. **$3.59**

Riveted 10-Inch Double Disc Steel Wheels
Extra Large Roller Bearings
Every Boy Wants One of These Beautiful Wagons. Every Part Well Made—A Wagon You Will Be Proud Of

Note Strong Steel Gears Balloon Style 1-Inch Rubber Tires

Body size, 14½x33½ inches. Made of strong, heavy gauge automobile steel with large roll rim at top and beaded sides for strength, beauty and massive appearance. No sharp edges or corners. The entire body is beautifully bright red enameled, baked-on, not painted. Gears and axles are of strong steel construction which will not break or wear. Ten-inch double disc steel wheels with large size casehardened steel roller bearings. Wheels enameled in bright red with gilt striping. Fancy, nickel plated, large size hub caps. One-inch size balloon type rubber tires.
79K7648—Shipping weight, 37 pounds......... **$5.98**

$4.89 Our Latest Improved Flyaway Coaster
Ball Bearing

$4.48
Roller Bearing

CURVED STEEL TONGUE

←BRAKE

Every Part Fully Guaranteed

Only the finest materials are used, and the construction is of the highest type. The body is kiln dried hardwood and nicely finished in every detail; tight joints and both front and back end boards are mortised into the sides, making a high class wagon body. There's a strong steel bumper to which the tongue is fastened, that will protect your wagon. Channel steel running gears with strong steel braces to body. The most vital part of a wagon is the wheel; our wagons have the highest quality wide hub double disc steel wheel, stamped from extra heavy gauge steel with interlocking flange at rim forming a positive lock. (No chance for the wheel to come apart.) Body, 36x16 inches. Varnished natural finish; top rails enameled red; ½-inch steel axles; nickel plated hub caps. Each with steel brake. Shipping weight, 34 pounds.

Strong Steel Gears, Axles and Braces ¾-Inch Rubber Tires

Boys! You Cannot Go Wrong With a Flyaway Coaster

Roller Bearing
Others Usually ask $10.00.
10-inch wheels, ¾-inch rubber tires. **$4.48**
79K7660

Ball Bearing
10-inch wheels, ¾-inch rubber tires. **$4.89**
79K7670

The Faultless Light Sheet Steel Wagon

Rolled sheet steel beaded body; hardwood tongue and bottom. Enameled red, green and black.

79K7024—Size of body, 10½x22½ inches; 7½-inch diameter strong steel wheels. Shpg. wt., 8 lbs......... **$1.59**

79K7632—Size of body, 12½x26½ inches; 9¾-inch diameter strong steel wheels. Shpg. wt., 14 lbs......... **$2.25**

Well Braced Steel Under Pinning

Flying Arrow Junior

$3.39

For the Child too Small to Handle a Large Wagon. Body 28x12½ inches Steel Gears ⅝-Inch Rubber Tires

Handy for Mother to Haul Her Youngster Around In When Shopping.

Just the right size for the girl or boy desiring a wagon, but not yet big enough to handle a standard size coaster. Selected hardwood body and tongue, finished in natural color with durable varnish; top rails and all edges trimmed with bright red enamel. Red enameled 7¼-inch double disc steel wheels with black striping; ⅝-inch rubber tires. Strong steel axles, braces and gears; nickel plated hub caps. Body, 28x12½ in.
79K7634 **$3.39**
Shpg. Wt., 16 Lbs.

Special Strong Curved Handle for Easy Steering

$7.67 Our De Luxe Model Wood Coaster With Curved Tongue, Ball Bearing Wheels, 1-Inch Balloon Type Rubber Tires — in a Class by Itself

GOULD'S COASTER

1-Inch Rubber Tires. Ball Bearing 10-Inch Double Disc Wheels

The highest type wood coaster of extreme beauty and sturdy construction. Large body, 38x16 inches, made from clean, first class hardwood, ½ inch thick throughout; beautifully finished natural color with two coats of durable coach varnish and enameled red. Top rails nicely beveled and enameled. Special curved 5-ply wood tongue nicely beveled and practically unbreakable. Extra heavy hardwood bolsters with strong steel braces; patented axle clamps place the pulling strain on the axles close to the wheels, making it unusually sturdy and easy steering. 10-inch double disc steel, high quality ball bearing wheels enameled red with black striping and equipped with 1-inch rubber tires. Complete with brake and nickel plated hub caps. It pays to buy the best. Shipping weight, 41 pounds.
79K7669............. **$7.67**

The Flying Arrow Playmate, $2.25

Cute, shiny coaster designed for the little tots. Same high class materials and construction. Hardwood body, 10¾x24 inches. Top of body without rails, but finished with bright red enamel. Steel axles, braces and gears enameled black. 6-inch red enameled double disc steel wheels with ½-inch rubber tires. Nickel plated hub caps, hardwood tongue. Shipping weight, 11 pounds.
79K7633............. **$2.25**

Beautiful Columbia
Ball Bearing
Velocipedes

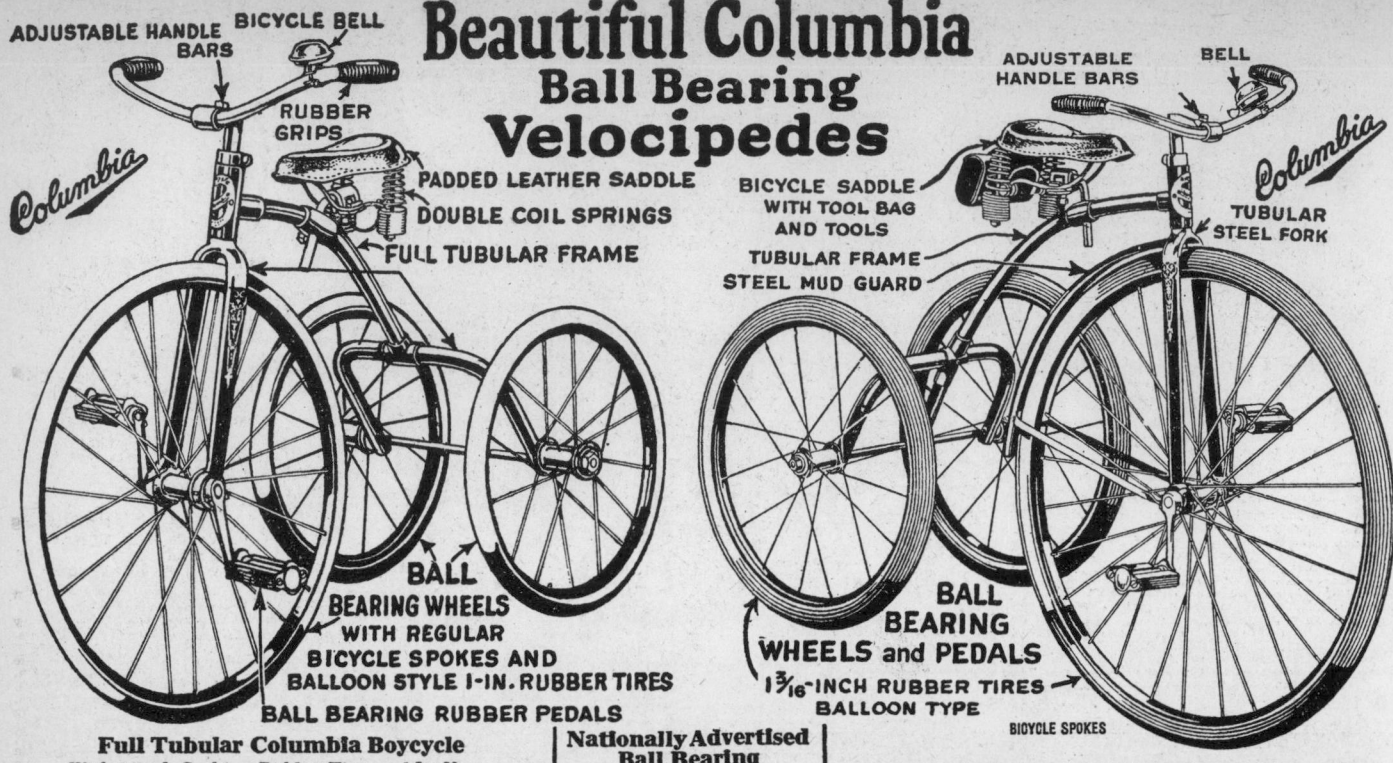

ADJUSTABLE HANDLE BARS · **BICYCLE BELL** · **RUBBER GRIPS** · **PADDED LEATHER SADDLE** · **DOUBLE COIL SPRINGS** · **FULL TUBULAR FRAME** · **BALL BEARING WHEELS WITH REGULAR BICYCLE SPOKES AND BALLOON STYLE 1-IN. RUBBER TIRES** · **BALL BEARING RUBBER PEDALS**

ADJUSTABLE HANDLE BARS · **BELL** · **BICYCLE SADDLE WITH TOOL BAG AND TOOLS** · **TUBULAR FRAME STEEL MUD GUARD** · **TUBULAR STEEL FORK** · **BALL BEARING WHEELS and PEDALS** · **1 3/16-INCH RUBBER TIRES BALLOON TYPE** · **BICYCLE SPOKES**

Full Tubular Columbia Boycycle
With 1-inch Cushion Rubber Tires and Its New Berkshire Blue Enamel

Can you picture your youngster when being presented with this dandy velocipede? Built just like brother's large bicycle; sturdy, best in construction and most practical. Heavy tubular steel frame and fork with nickel plated crown. Selected from many different types and, in our opinion, supreme in quality and up to date in every detail. Classy nickel plated tangent bicycle spokes with nipples for tightening. Ball bearing rubber pedals; nickel plated cranks; tubular steel handle bars with large size rubber grips; fine quality padded leather seat with resilient nickel plated double coil springs. Complete, with bicycle bell. Rims of wheel enameled red with two black stripes same as on large bicycles. Neat nickel plated Columbia monogram on head. Sizes given below are shortest measurements. Measure child from crotch to heel. Seat may be raised 3½ inches. **Two largest sizes unmailable.**

Catalog No.	Diam., Front Wheel	Seat to Lower Pedal	Shpg. Wt., Lbs.	Each
79K8337	14 in.	17 in.	22	$ 8.98
79K8338	16 in.	19 in.	25	9.98
79K8339	20 in.	21 in.	29	11.48
79K8340	24 in.	23 in.	32	12.48

Standard Tubular Ball Bearing Velocipedes
Red Enamel finish. Not as fancily decorated as the Columbia.

Catalog No.	Diam., Front Wheel	Seat to Lower Pedal	Shpg. Wt., Lbs.	Each
79K8317	14 in.	17 in.	22	$ 7.98
79K8318	16 in.	19 in.	25	8.98
79K8319	20 in.	21 in.	29	10.79
79K8320	24 in.	23 in.	32	11.98

Nationally Advertised Ball Bearing Velocipedes
It Pays to Buy a Columbia Boycycle

Made in the Same Factory and by the Same Skilled Workmen as Are the Large Size Columbia Bicycles, Famous for 50 Years.

You Cannot Go Wrong With a Columbia

Graceful in Appearance Comfortable and Extremely Durable

The Full Tubular Columbia Superb Boycycle

The Finest Velocipede Made—With Mud Guard and Large Corrugated 1 3/16-Inch Cushion Rubber Tires. Resemble Bicycle Tires—Finished in the New Berkshire Blue Enamel and Red Rims—Tool Bag on Saddle Contains Wrench and Oil Can.

Built of same materials as finest bicycle; tubular steel fork with nickel plated crown. Brightly enameled mud guard on front wheel with nickel plated brace to axle. Ball bearing wheels and rubber pedals. Nickel plated bicycle style cranks and tangent spokes. Tubular steel frame with three-brace backbone. Rims of wheels enameled Berkshire blue and red. Very pretty combination. The motor-bike type saddle on nickel plated double coil springs has tool bag containing oil can and wrench. Nickel plated tubular steel handle bars with large nickel plated bicycle bell and rubber grips; shiny nickel plated Columbia monogram on head. Sizes given below are shortest measurements. Measure child from crotch to heel. Seat may be raised 3½ inches. **Two largest sizes unmailable.**

Catalog No.	Diam., Front Wheel	Seat to Lower Pedal	Shpg. Wt., Lbs.	Each
79K8392	16 in.	19 in.	29	$11.98
79K8393	20 in.	21 in.	32	13.48
79K8394	24 in.	23 in.	35	14.98

The New Two-Wheel Ball Bearing Speed Cycles

Adjustable for Children from 6 to 12 Years

NICKEL PLATED TUBULAR STEEL HANDLE BARS · **MOTOR BIKE STYLE SADDLE DOUBLE COIL SPRINGS** · **STRONG 1-INCH DIA. TUBULAR STEEL FRAME** · **ADJUSTABLE BICYCLE CHAIN AND SPROCKET** · **COASTER BRAKE** · **1-INCH RUBBER TIRES** · **PARKING STAND**

With Coaster Brake $15.98

No Brake $10.98

Built just like the larger bicycle with high grade heavy tubular steel frame, 1 inch in diameter and finished in high gloss bicycle enamel (baked on). Highly nickel plated and polished curved tubular steel handle bars; equipped with adjustable leather saddle mounted on coil springs; best grade adjustable bicycle roller chain; ball bearing sprocket axle and wheels; rubber pedals and grips; parking stand with quick action spring, nickel plated tangent spokes, hubs and trimmings. Length, over all, 41 inches; height, to handle bars, 32 inches. Shipping weight, 28 pounds.

De Luxe Model With New Departure Coaster Brake on Rear Wheel for Only $15.98

12-inch ball bearing wheels with 1-inch balloon type rubber tires; motorcycle type seat, beautifully enameled in red and striped in black; nickel plated trimmings.
79K8377.. **$15.98**

Special Bargain Without Coaster Brake, $10.98

Same cycle, but without brake 12-inch ball bearing wheels with 1-inch rubber tires. Enameled bright red and striped in black; trimmings nickel plated.
79K8376.. **$10.98**

Rubber Tired Velocipedes

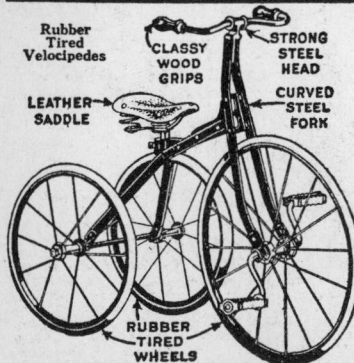

CLASSY WOOD GRIPS · **STRONG STEEL HEAD** · **LEATHER SADDLE** · **CURVED STEEL FORK** · **RUBBER TIRED WHEELS**

Dependable and Low Priced

Nicely curved, black enameled handle bars with enameled wood grips. Frame is wide and made of heavy half oval steel, enameled black. Wheels are enameled bright red and equipped with ½-inch non-skid rubber tires. One-piece steel crank and pedals enameled red. Leather seat is adjustable and may be raised 3 inches. Sizes below give shortest measurements. **Measure child from crotch to heel. Largest size unmailable.**

Catalog No.	Diam., Front Wheel	Seat to Lower Pedal	Shpg. Wt., Lbs.	Each
79K8332	14 in.	16 in.	17	$2.98
79K8333	16 in.	18 in.	18	3.48
79K8334	20 in.	20 in.	21	3.98

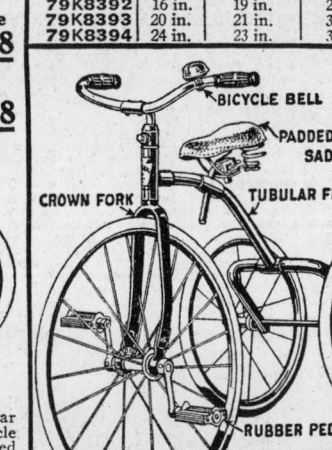

BICYCLE BELL · **PADDED LEATHER SADDLE** · **CROWN FORK** · **TUBULAR FRAME** · **RUBBER PEDALS** · **1-IN. RUBBER TIRES**

Low Priced Tubular Velocipede With Bell—Plain Bearing Wheels With Bright Tin Plated Straight Spokes. Note Full 1-Inch Rubber Tires.

Heavy seamless bicycle tubing frame. Crown fork; 1-inch rubber tires; nickel plated 5⁄8-inch tubular steel handle bars with rubber hand grips; rubber on pedals. Leather saddle mounted on coil springs. Frame and wheels finished in brilliant bicycle enamel, neatly striped. Sizes given are with seat as low as it will go. Seat can be raised 3½ inches. Measure child from crotch to heel. **Two largest sizes unmailable.**

Catalog No.	Front Wheel Diam.	Seat to Lower Pedal	Shpg. Wt., Lbs.	Each
79K8362	14 in.	17 in.	23	$6.98
79K8363	16 in.	19 in.	25	7.47
79K8364	20 in.	21 in.	27	8.98
79K8365	24 in.	23 in.	29	9.98

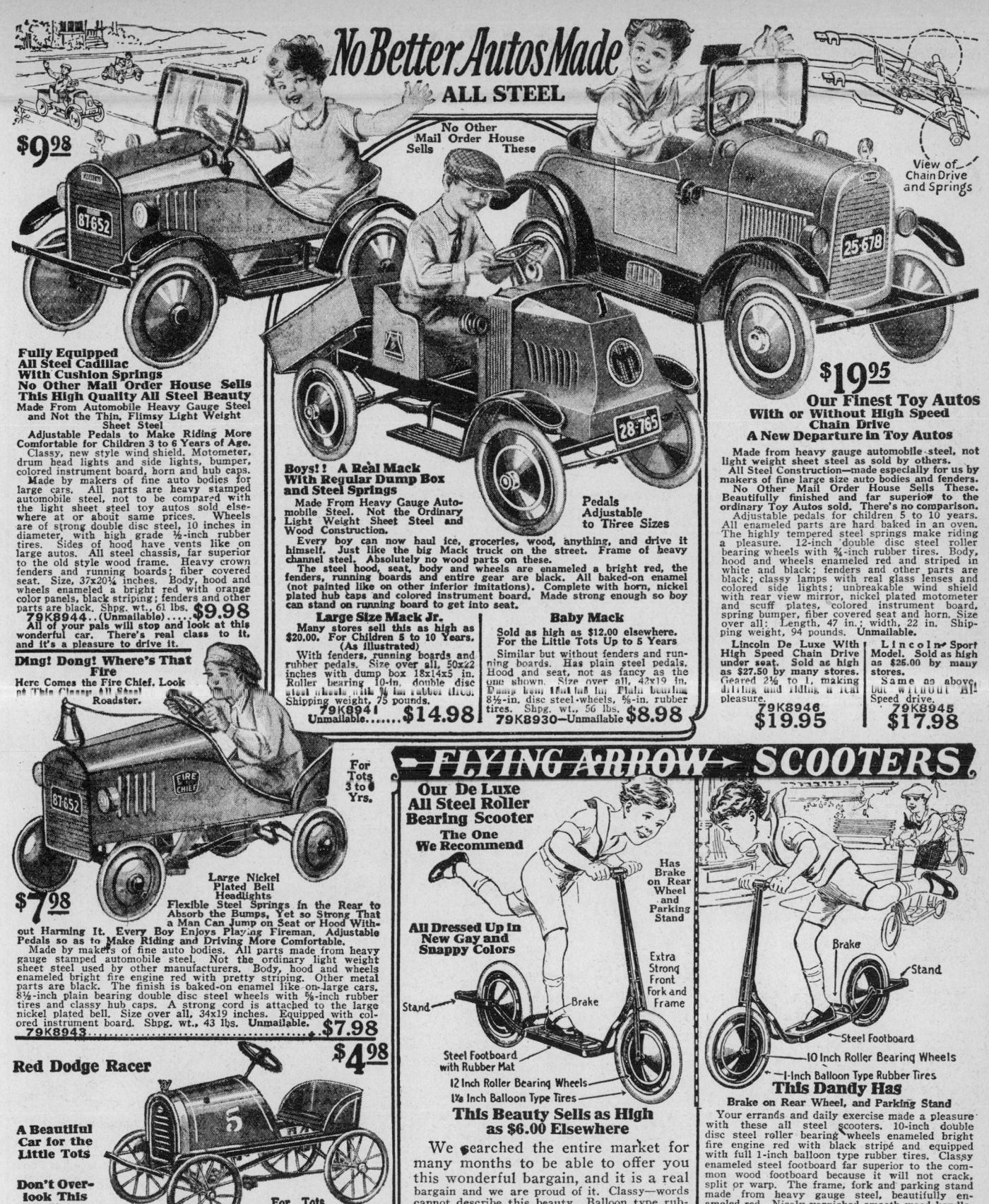

No Better Autos Made
ALL STEEL

No Other Mail Order House Sells These

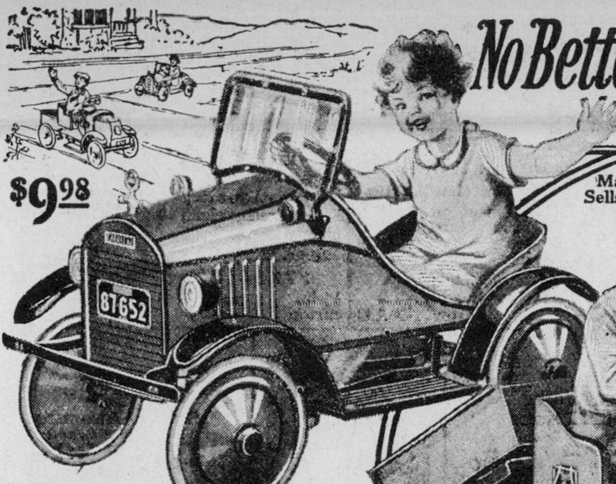

$9.98

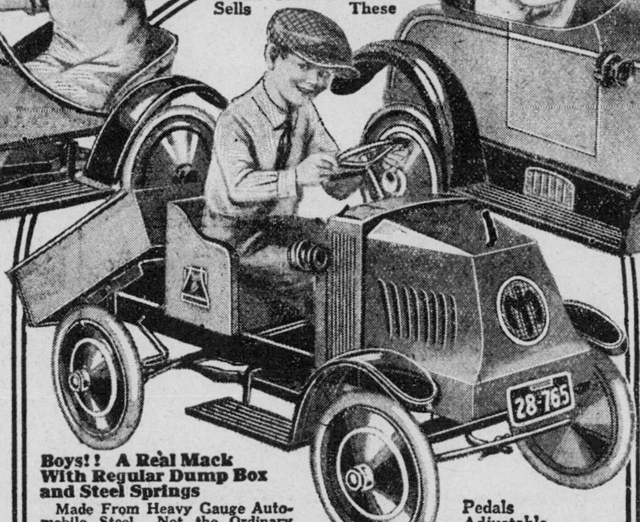

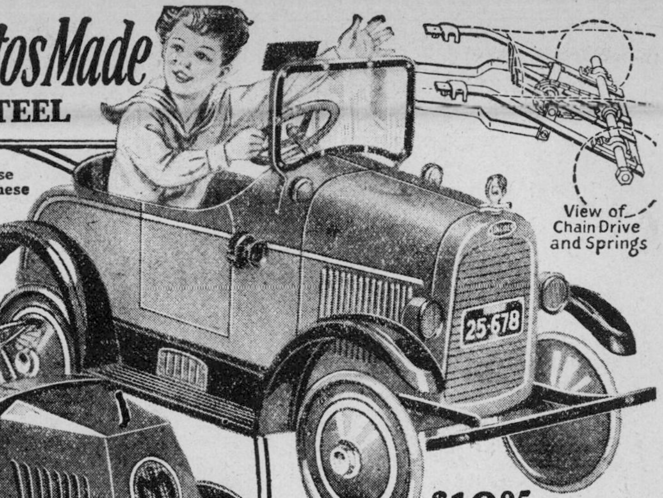

Fully Equipped All Steel Cadillac With Cushion Springs
No Other Mail Order House Sells This High Quality All Steel Beauty

Made From Automobile Heavy Gauge Steel and Not the Thin, Flimsy Light Weight Sheet Steel

Adjustable Pedals to Make Riding More Comfortable for Children 3 to 6 Years of Age.

Classy, new style wind shield. Motometer, drum head lights and side lights, bumper, colored instrument board, horn and hub caps.

Made by makers of fine auto bodies for large cars. All parts are heavy stamped automobile steel, not to be compared with the light sheet steel toy autos sold elsewhere at or about same prices. Wheels are of strong double disc steel, 10 inches in diameter, with high grade ½-inch rubber tires. Sides of hood have vents like on large autos. All steel chassis, far superior to the old style wood frame. Heavy crown fenders and running boards; fiber covered seat. Size, 37x20¼ inches. Body, hood and wheels enameled a bright red with orange color panels, black striping; fenders and other parts are black. Shpg. wt., 61 lbs.

79K8944..(Unmailable)..... **$9.98**

All of your pals will stop and look at this wonderful car. There's real class to it, and it's a pleasure to drive it.

Boys!! A Real Mack With Regular Dump Box and Steel Springs

Made From Heavy Gauge Automobile Steel. Not the Ordinary Light Weight Sheet Steel and Wood Construction.

Pedals Adjustable to Three Sizes

Every boy can now haul ice, groceries, wood, anything, and drive it himself. Just like the big Mack truck on the street. Frame of heavy channel steel. Absolutely no wood parts on these.

The steel hood, seat, body and wheels are enameled a bright red, the fenders, running boards and entire gear are black. All baked-on enamel (not painted like on other inferior imitations). Complete with horn, nickel plated hub caps and colored instrument board. Made strong enough so boy can stand on running board to get into seat.

Large Size Mack Jr.

Many stores sell this as high as $20.00. For Children 5 to 10 Years. (As illustrated)

With fenders, running boards and rubber pedals. Size over all, 50x22 inches with dump box 18x14x5 in. Roller bearing 10-in. double disc steel wheels with ¾-in. rubber tires. Shipping weight, 75 pounds.

79K8941 Unmailable....... **$14.98**

Baby Mack

Sold as high as $12.00 elsewhere. For the Little Tots Up to 5 Years

Similar but without fenders and running boards. Has plain steel pedals. Hood and seat, not as fancy as the one shown. Size over all, 42x19 in. Dump box [illegible] in. Plain bearing 8½-in. disc steel wheels, ⅝-in. rubber tires. Shpg. wt., 56 lbs.

79K8930—Unmailable **$8.98**

$19.95

Our Finest Toy Autos
With or Without High Speed Chain Drive
A New Departure in Toy Autos

Made from heavy gauge automobile steel, not light weight sheet steel as sold by others.

All Steel Construction—made especially for us by makers of fine large size auto bodies and fenders.

No Other Mail Order House Sells These. Beautifully finished and far superior to the ordinary Toy Autos sold. There's no comparison.

Adjustable pedals for children 5 to 10 years. All enameled parts are hard baked in an oven. The highly tempered steel springs make riding a pleasure. 12-inch double disc steel roller bearing wheels with ¾-inch rubber tires. Body, hood and wheels enameled red and striped in white and black; fenders and other parts are black; classy lamps with real glass lenses and colored side lights; unbreakable wind shield with rear view mirror, nickel plated motometer and scuff plates, colored instrument board, spring bumper, fiber covered seat and horn. Size over all: Length, 47 in.; width, 22 in. Shipping weight, 94 pounds. **Unmailable.**

Lincoln De Luxe With High Speed Chain Drive under seat. Sold as high as $27.50 by many stores. Geared 2½ to 1, making driving and riding a real pleasure.

79K8946 **$19.95**

Lincoln Sport Model. Sold as high as $25.00 by many stores.

Same as above, but without Hi-Speed drive.

79K8945 **$17.98**

Ding! Dong! Where's That Fire

Here Comes the Fire Chief. Look at This Classy All Steel Roadster.

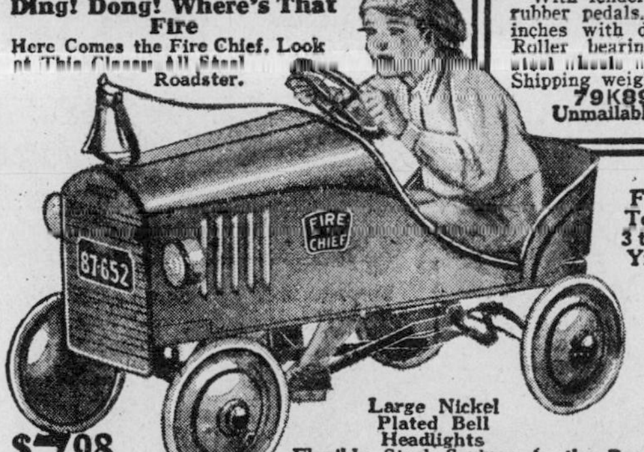

For Tots 3 to 6 Yrs.

$7.98

Large Nickel Plated Bell Headlights

Flexible Steel Springs in the Rear to Absorb the Bumps, Yet so Strong That a Man Can Jump on Seat or Hood Without Harming It. Every Boy Enjoys Playing Fireman. Adjustable Pedals so as to Make Riding and Driving More Comfortable.

Made by makers of fine auto bodies. All parts made from heavy gauge stamped automobile steel. Not the ordinary light weight sheet steel used by other manufacturers. Body, hood and wheels enameled bright fire engine red with pretty striping. Other metal parts are black. The finish is baked-on enamel like on large cars. 8½-inch plain bearing double disc steel wheels with ⅝-inch rubber tires and classy hub caps. A strong cord is attached to the large nickel plated bell. Size over all, 34x19 inches. Equipped with colored instrument board. Shpg. wt., 43 lbs. **Unmailable.**

79K8943.. **$7.98**

Red Dodge Racer

$4.98

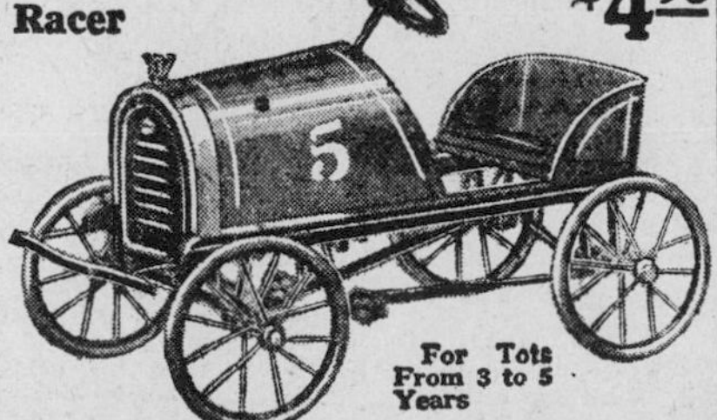

A Beautiful Car for the Little Tots

Don't Overlook This Big Value

For Tots From 3 to 5 Years

Strong 10-inch wheels with ½-inch rubber tires; 7-inch metal steering wheel with dummy gas control. Up to date motometer and steel bumper; comfortable and roomy seat; nickel plated hub caps. Figure 5 stenciled on each side of hood just like on the big racers. Size, over all, 34x21½ inches. Bright red enameled body, seat and wheels with yellow striping and black enameled gear. **Unmailable.** Shipping weight, 32 pounds.

79K8925.. **$4.98**

FLYING ARROW SCOOTERS

Our De Luxe All Steel Roller Bearing Scooter

The One We Recommend

All Dressed Up in New Gay and Snappy Colors

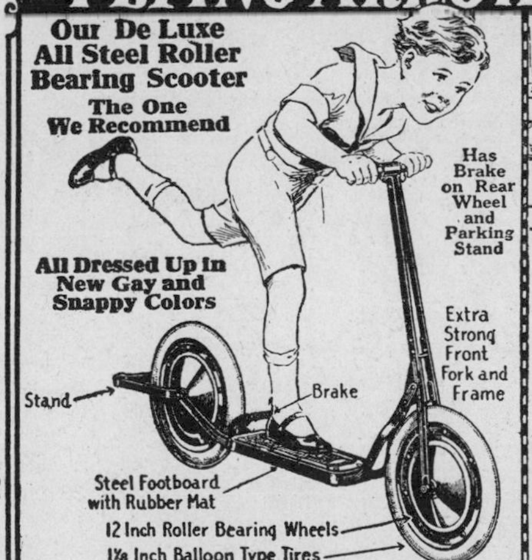

This Beauty Sells as High as $6.00 Elsewhere

We searched the entire market for many months to be able to offer you this wonderful bargain, and it is a real bargain and we are proud of it. Classy—words cannot describe this beauty. Balloon type rubber tires, 1⅛ inches in diameter; high class 12-inch double disc steel orange color enameled wheels with grass green stripe near outer edge and green bullseye center on each side; large size roller bearings. Oh! how easy they run. Heavy rubber mat on black enameled steel footboard and a good brake for sudden stops. All steel strong frame and parking stand enameled gray. Smooth wood handle. If you want quality, here it is. Shpg. wt., 19 lbs.

79K8817........................ **$3.98**

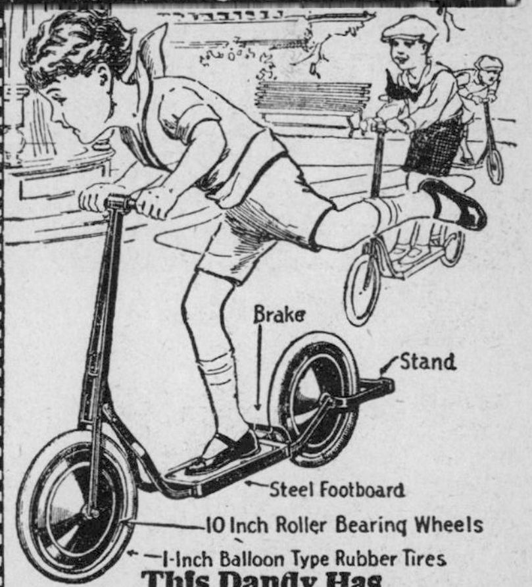

This Dandy Has

Brake on Rear Wheel, and Parking Stand

Your errands and daily exercise made a pleasure with these all steel scooters. 10-inch double disc steel roller bearing wheels enameled bright fire engine red with black stripe and equipped with full 1-inch balloon type rubber tires. Classy enameled steel footboard far superior to the common wood footboard because it will not crack, split or warp. The frame, fork and parking stand made from heavy gauge steel, beautifully enameled red. Nicely varnished smooth wood handle. Shipping weight, 15 pounds.

79K8818......................... **$2.98**

Our Special at $1.98

Little Boys and Girls Can Handle With Ease

Beautiful in finish and construction, with 8-inch red enameled double disc steel roller bearing wheels, striped in gilt and equipped with ¾-inch rubber tires; steel footboard; parking stand on rear wheel, but no brake. Strong steel frame enameled bright red. Shpg. wt., 15 lbs.

79K8819......................... **$1.98**

See Index and Information Pages 542 to 570

Everybody Likes Candy

Delicious Chocolate Coated Cherries

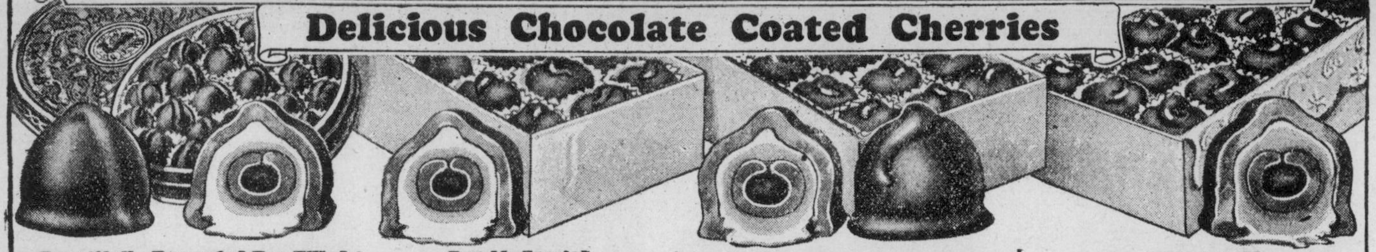

Beautifully Decorated Box Filled With Delicious Chocolate Cherries
A Splendid Gift
Contains one pound fine quality hand dipped chocolate cherries in cream. Carefully packed in red and green decorated metal box. A gift long to be remembered. Size box, 7½ inches. Shipping weight, 2 pounds.
87K8045—Complete.......... 69c

Our 44c Special
Twenty-four whole cherries in flowing cream, hand dipped in dark sweet vanilla chocolate coating. One pound of these fine cherries are packed in an attractive box. We feel sure you will agree with us that it is a remarkable value at this low price. Shipping wt., 1½ lbs.
87K8056—1-lb. box....... 44c

Our Best Quality Delicious Chocolate Coated Cherries in Cordial
Delicious whole red cherries in liquid. Dark sweet vanilla chocolate coating. Luscious eating cherries, that melt in your mouth. A treat for lovers of high grade chocolate covered cherries. Packed in beautifully colored cherry designed box. Shpg. wts.: 1-lb. box, 1½ lbs.; 2-lb. box, 2¾ lbs.
87K8003 1-lb. box.... 69c | 87K8042 2-lb. box...$1.29

Special Value, 57c
Twenty-four big, whole, luscious cherries in a rich liquid cream, hand dipped in dark sweet vanilla chocolate coating. A very fine, juicy, delicious eating chocolate covered cherry. Neatly and attractively packed in an appropriate gift box. One pound box, net weight. Shpg. wt., 1½ lbs.
87K8000—1-pound box....... 57c

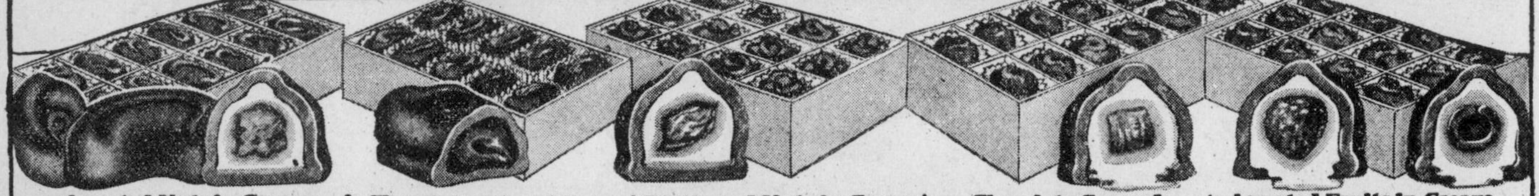

Assorted Nuts in Cream
Nut caramels, pecans, almonds, walnuts and filberts in cream. Covered with a rich dark sweet chocolate coating. A wonderful assortment of 24 pieces. Shipping weight, 1½ pounds.
87K8009
Box of 24 pieces..... 57c

Chocolate Covered Dates
A wonderful eating confection. Delicious pitted dates, heavily covered with a rich chocolate coating. Exceptionally high quality dates and chocolate. Shpg. wt., 1½ lbs.
87K8052—One-pound box............ 55c

Fruits and Nuts in Cream
A candy that grows more popular every day. Assortment includes whole cherries, hazel nuts and raisins in cream, heavily coated with dark vanilla chocolate. Shipping weight, 1½ pounds.
87K8019..........55c
1-lb. Box

Chocolate Covered Pineapple
Dark vanilla chocolate covered true fruit pineapple in cordial. A confection that will satisfy and please. Shipping weight, 1½ pounds.
87K8018—Twenty-four pieces per box..... 55c

Assorted Fruits in Cream
A fruit assortment of whole cherries, crushed pineapple and crushed strawberries, in a rich cream. Dark sweet vanilla chocolate coating. Shipping weight, 1½ pounds.
87K8020
1-pound box......... 48c

EVERYBODY LOVES CANDY BARS!

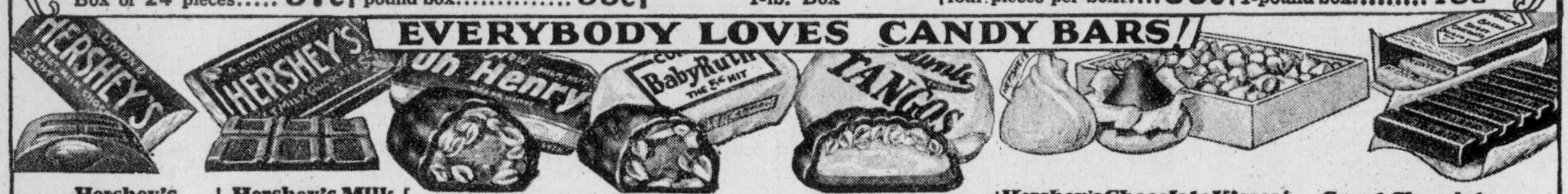

Hershey's Almond Bars
24 regular 5c almond bars to box. Shpg. wt., 3 lbs.
87K8531
Per box.... 98c

Hershey's Milk Chocolate Bars
24 regular 5c bars to box. Shipping wt., 3 lbs.
87K8530
Per box..... 98c

New Oh Henry Bars
12 regular 10c size bars to box. Shpg. wt., 3 lbs.
87K8581 98c

Baby Ruth Bars
24 regular 5c size bars to box. Shpg. wt., 3 lbs.
87K8588. 98c

Bunte's Tango Bar
A splendid eating bar. 24 regular 5c size bars to box. Shpg. wt., 3 lbs.
87K8569 98c

Hershey's Chocolate Kisses
Very fine flavor and real quality. A very delightful foil wrapped pure milk chocolate confection. Shpg. wt., 1½ lbs.
87K8032
Per 1-lb. box.......... 54c

Sweet Chocolate
Montclair Brand
Finest quality. Delicious for eating in place of candy. Fine for icings, candy making, etc. Two ½-lb. cakes to pkg. Shpg. wt., 1¼ lbs.
77K388—1 lb... 36c

And Here's Candy to Make the Kiddies Happy!

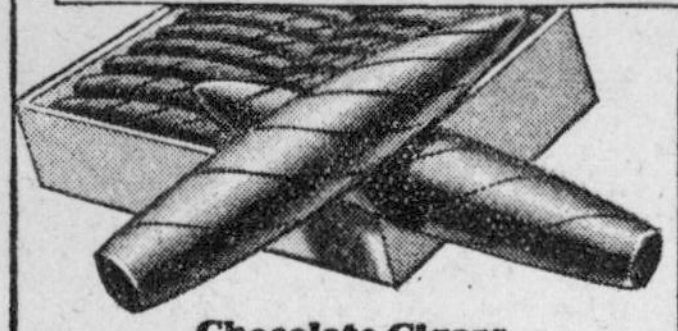

Chocolate Cigars
Solid chocolate cigars are always such a delight to the kiddies. Packed fifty cigars to a box. Shpg. wt., 2 lbs.
87K8265—Per box of 50...39c

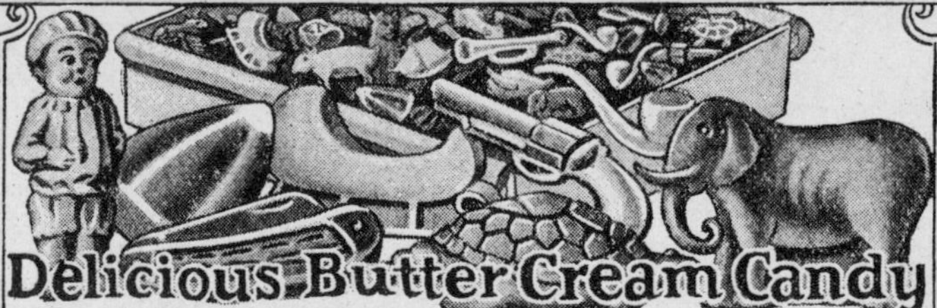

Delicious Butter Cream Candy

The Popular Soft Creamy Kiddie Candy
The eating qualities, purity and genuine goodness of this assortment for the little ones cannot be beaten. Little bears, lions, dolls, corn, vegetables, pigs and other fancy shapes made of pure, wholesome, creamy, delicious butter cream candy, distinctively colored and very appetizingly flavored. Candy that is as healthful as it is delicious. Fine for children's parties at any time, and especially suitable for the filling of Christmas stockings. This mixture is a very popular kiddie confection, and it will give the kiddies many happy surprises. When you give the child a box of these little candies you give him many happy hours.

Shipping weight, 1½ lbs.
87K8293
1-pound box........ 25c

Shipping weight, 2¼ lbs.
87K8292
2-pound box...... 43c

Shipping weight, 3¾ lbs.
87K8304
3-lb. fancy box...... 59c

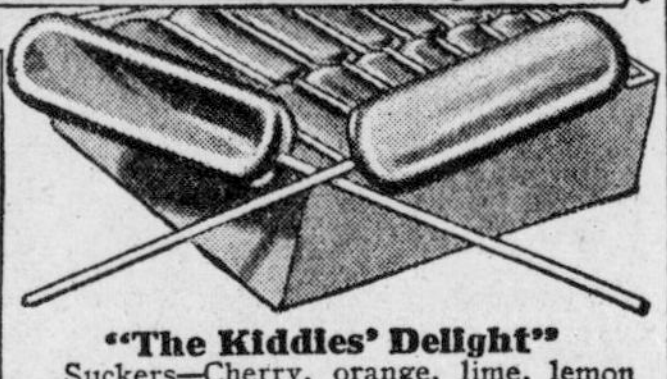

"The Kiddies' Delight"
Suckers—Cherry, orange, lime, lemon and butterscotch flavors. 50 penny suckers to box. Shpg. wt., 2 lbs.
87K8165—Per box of 50... 39c

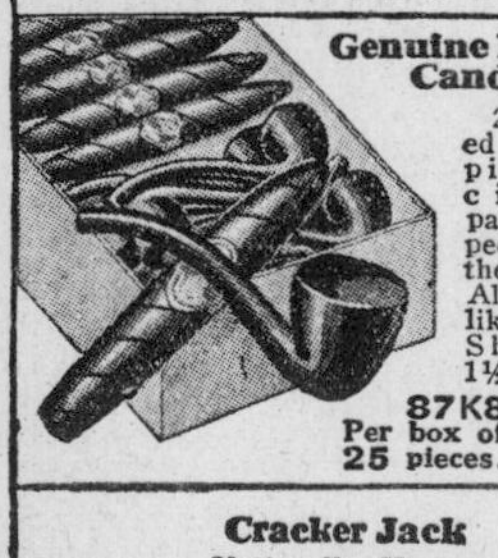

Genuine Licorice Candies
25 assorted licorice pipes and cigars, packed especially for the kiddies. All kiddies like licorice. Shpg. wt., 1½ lbs.
87K8210
Per box of 25 pieces... 21c

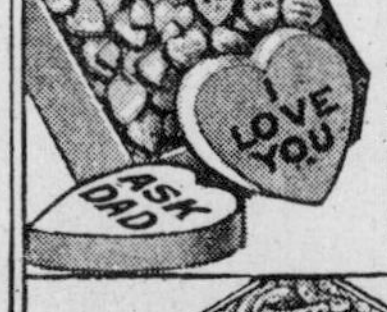

Candy Motto Hearts
No kiddies' party is complete without "Motto Hearts." Small size. Shipping weight, 1½ lbs.
87K8244
Per box of 1 pound.... 25c

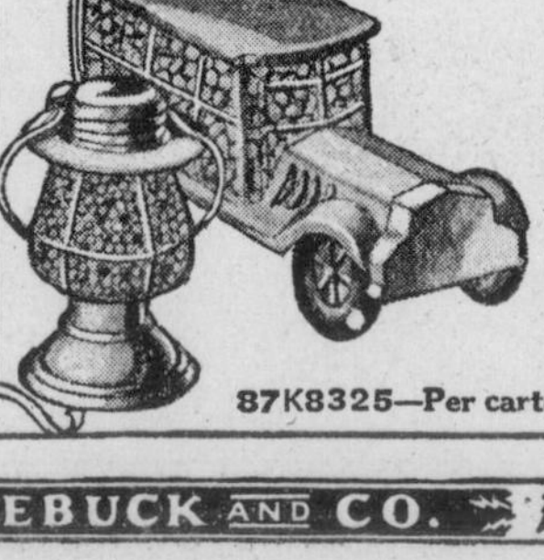

Glass Novelties Filled With Candy
4 Best Sellers
Kiddies enjoy playing with these novelty glass toys filled with dainty sugar candies. A glass lantern, automobile, radio and telephone. Shipping weight, 4 pounds.

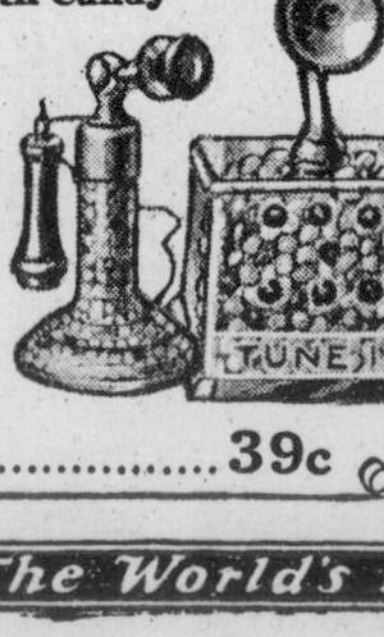

87K8325—Per carton of 4 toys..................... 39c

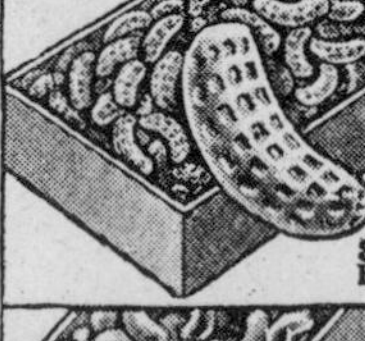

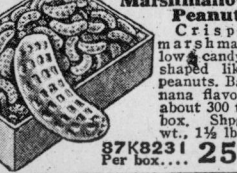

Marshmallow Peanuts
Crispy marshmallow candy, shaped like peanuts. Banana flavor. about 300 to box. Shpg. wt., 1½ lbs.
87K8231
Per box.... 25c

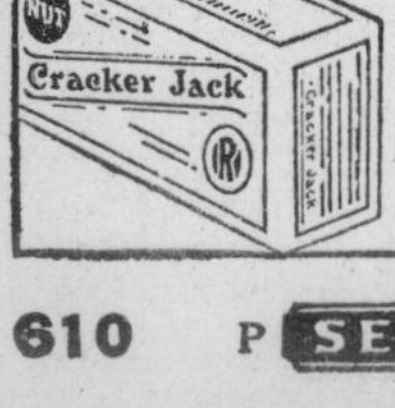

Cracker Jack
Nationally Known
Delicious popcorn and peanut confection. Shipping wt., 2¼ lbs.
87K8251
Per carton of 6 regular packages 25c

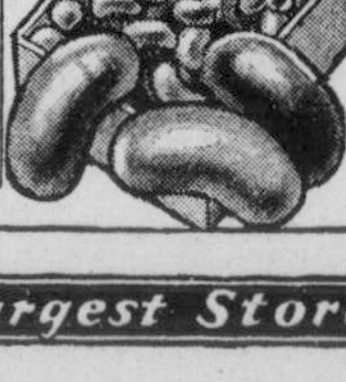

Jelly Beans
Snappy Colors
Candies with fresh, chewey centers. Shipping weight, 1½ lbs.
87K8199
Per 1-lb. box.... 19c

~ *Complete* PYRALIN *Gift Sets* ~

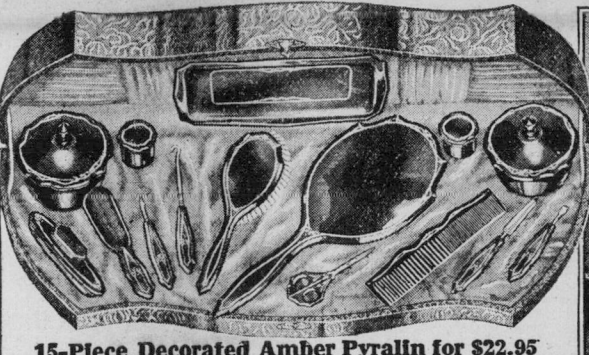

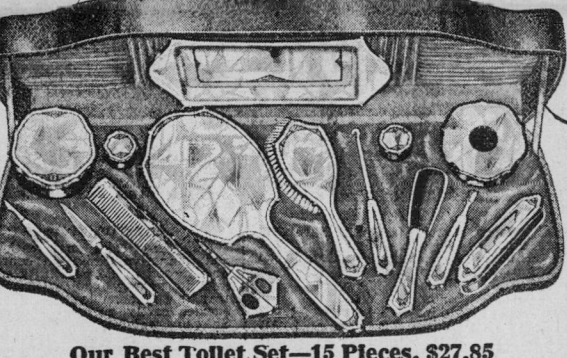

15-Piece Decorated Amber Pyralin for $22.95
The Rainbow, this season's newest pattern, is offered in beautiful, transparent, genuine amber pyralin. Exquisitely decorated in gilt and black enamel outlines. All pieces fine quality, heavy weight. Mirror is 14½ in. long, other pieces in proportion. A set like this sells elsewhere at much higher prices. Fifteen useful pieces. The beautiful, hinged cover gift case lined throughout with fine quality satin forms a splendid setting for this set. Size of case, 30x11½x3¾ inches. Shipping weight, 10 pounds. **$22.95**
8K6120¼

Our Best Toilet Set—15 Pieces, $27.85
Here is a beautiful gift that will make its owner happy. Beautiful white pearl on amber pyralin, each piece decorated with 22-karat gold and inlaid with black enamel. The white pearl closely resembles genuine mother of pearl. The rich transparent amber beveled edge effectively brings out the harmony embodied in the combination of pearl and amber. Set consists of mirror, 15¼ inches long, and 14 other useful articles, as illustrated, in a handsome case, 30x 11½x3½ inches. Generously lined with a fine quality satin. This beautiful gift set frequently sells for $35.00 to $40.00. Shpg. wt. 10 lbs.
8K6121¼.................................**$27.85**

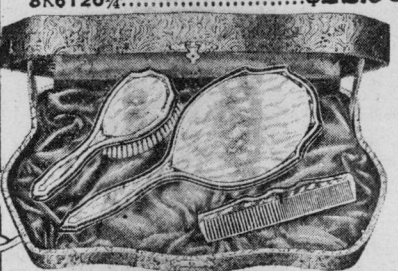

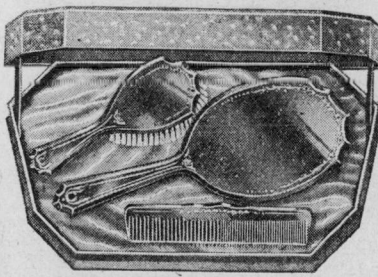

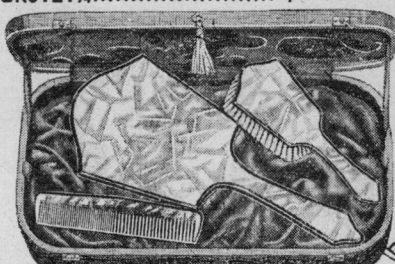

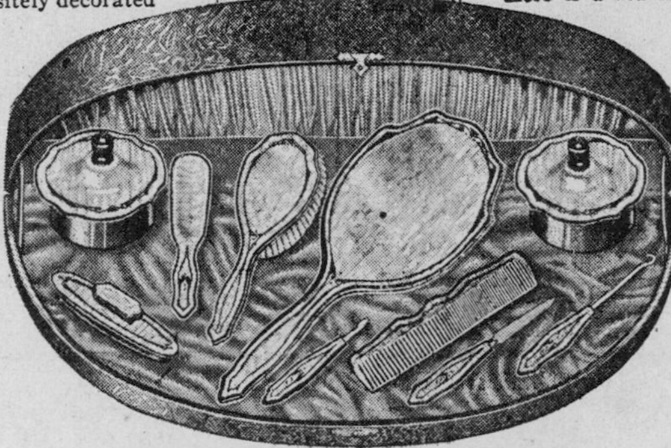

Pearl on Amber Pyralin Sets, $9.98
The beautiful coloring of mother of pearl have been duplicated in these wonderful sets. This white pearl on amber is beautifully decorated in gilt color and black, as illustrated. Maize (corn color) on amber and rose (a dainty pink) on amber do not have decorations. Mirror is 14½ inches long. Each set in beautiful case, lined with fine heavy satin. Shipping weight, 5 pounds.
87K6128—White pearl on amber, decorated as illustrated..................**$9.98**
87K6129—Maize pearl on amber, not decorated.$9.98
87K6140—Rose pearl on amber, not decorated. 9.98

10-Piece Pearl on Amber Pyralin
This fine quality decorated pyralin set in beautiful half moon shape, elaborate case, makes a wonderful gift suggestion. White pearl, with amber background, daintily decorated in gilt color and black. Fine quality heavyweight pieces. All high grade. (10 pieces in all.) Mirror is about 14½ in. long. Complete in beautiful hinged half moon shape gift case with inside top and bottom lined with fine quality satin. Size of case, 20¼x11¼x3¾ in. Shipping weight, 9 pounds.
8K6117¼.................................**$16.98**

[For Silver Plated Toilet Articles, See Page 764]

Mayflower Pearl on Amber Set
In Fancy Sewing Box
The soft tone beauty of pearl pyralin, which resembles mother of pearl, is well brought out by the rich transparent amber edge. Classic mirror, 15½ inches long, quality brush and comb. Complete in gorgeous hinged case, covered with gold color embossed paper and lined with oriental pattern cloth. When empty, case becomes a sewing box, with dainty pincushion and three brass posts for spools. Size of case, 18x9 inches. Shipping weight, 6 pounds.
87K6111.................................**$13.69**

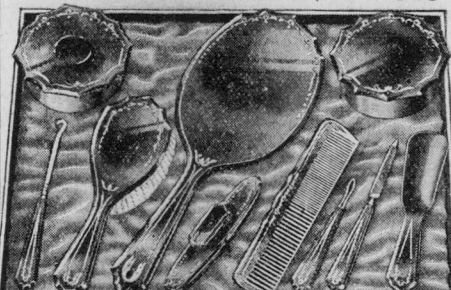

3-Piece Decorated Amber Pyralin Set
Handsome gilt color decorations with black enamel inlay on heavy transparent amber pyralin. An exceptionally good looking set. Fine quality comb and mirror. Mirror is 13½ inches long. Complete in fancy gift box. Top and bottom satin lined. Shipping weight, 5 pounds.
87K6124.................................**$6.98**

10-Piece Decorated Amber Pyralin
The beauty of gilt color and black decoration on transparent amber pyralin is well brought out in this attractive set. All high grade pieces that match perfectly. Classic mirror, 13½ inches; also other useful pieces as illustrated. Well packed in gift box, bottom sateen lined. Shpg. wt. 7 lbs. **$12.67**
87K6114.

10-Piece Decorated Pyralin Set
A fine quality 10-piece decorated genuine pyralin set at a real bargain price. A charming ivory pyralin pattern, decorated in gilt color and black. Mirror is 13½ inches long, nine other first quality useful pieces, sizes in proportion. Complete in gift box, bottom sateen lined. Shipping weight, 7 pounds.
87K6115.................................**$9.98**

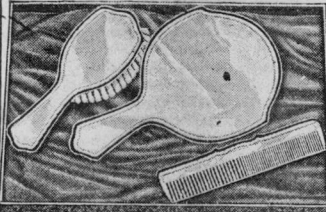

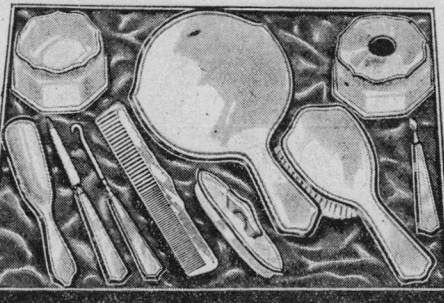

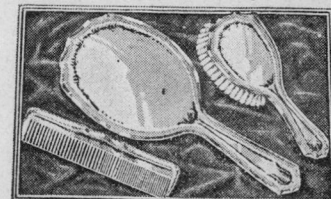

3-Piece Ivory on Amber Set, $2.98
This is an exceptionally good value. Filled ivory on amber brush, comb and mirror at illustrated. Mirror is 15½ inches long. Complete in gift box, bottom sateen lined. Shipping weight, 5 pounds.
87K6105.................................**$2.98**

10-Piece Ivory on Amber Set for $6.98
Our lowest priced 10-piece set. Complete set of useful pieces as illustrated. Good quality filled ivory on amber in attractive pattern. Mirror is 10½ inches long, nine other pieces in proportion. Complete in gift box with bottom sateen lined. Shipping weight, 7 pounds.
87K6112.................................**$6.98**

Decorated Ivory Pyralin, $4.98
Beautiful white ivory pyralin, decorated in gilt and black enamel. A 3-piece quality set that will please. Mirror is 13½ inches long, comb and brush to match. In gift box, bottom sateen lined. Shipping weight, 5 pounds.
87K6102.................................**$4.98**

Appropriate Gift Suggestions

Swinging Picture Frame

Gold color bronze finish. Burnished edges. Embossed designs. Has glass front and felt base. Picture not included. Good frames at low prices.

	Size Glass	Shpg. Wt.	
8K5700	4x 6 in.	1½ lbs.	$0.98
8K5701	6x 8 in.	2 lbs.	1.25
8K5702	8x10 in.	2½ lbs.	1.48

Glass Top Serving Trays
Conventional Pattern

Mahogany color mat with fancy border and attractive design in center. Mahogany finish wood frame, skillfully embossed. Good looking, strong handles. A well constructed tray at a reasonable price. Felt base. Glass surface easily washed. Size, 17x11 inches. Shipping weight, 3¾ lbs.
8K5751¼ ... $1.79

Picture Serving Tray

A beautiful picture, "June Roses," in mahogany finish wood frame. Substantial handles. Well constructed throughout. Felt base. Glass surface. This tray will add to the attractiveness of any room. Size, 17¼x 11¼ inches. Shpg. wt., 3½ lbs.
8K5752¼ ... $1.39

Hand Carved Swinging Picture Frame

Antique silver bronze frame, hand burnished. Artistic hand carvings in very latest style, popular designs. Has glass front and felt base. Picture not included.

	Size Glass	Shpg. Wt.	
8K5703	4x 6 in.	1½ lbs.	$1.59
8K5704	6x 8 in.	2 lbs.	1.79
8K5705	8x10 in.	2½ lbs.	1.98

"Narcisse de Jerri" Perfume

A beautiful gift package of quality perfume. Large size 9-oz. bottle, with frosted black glass stopper. Wrapped in transparent cellophane and put in a black paper box trimmed with gold color. Thousands of packages were sold last year at a much higher price. A charming gift. Shpg. wt., 2 lbs.
8K2904
$3.98

Girls' Bobby Set

Pearl amber pyralin in popular maize color. For the girl with bobbed hair. Fine quality military style brush with selected white bristles. Comb, 4½ inches long, all fine teeth. In attractive gift box. Bottom lined and tufted. A quality set throughout. Shipping wt., 1 lb.
87K6134 ... $1.98

Atomizer Dresser Set

A splendid gift. Attractive perfume atomizer with perfume dropper to match. Each has brass fittings, gold plated. Bowls are frosted glass, with dainty hand painted flower decorations. Complete in beautiful gift box. Atomizer, 4½ inches high. Shipping weight, 1½ pounds.
8K4250 ... $2.98

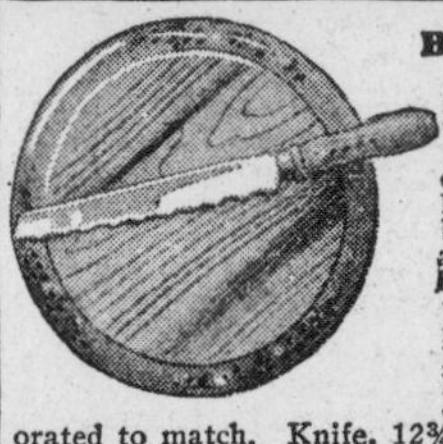

Decorated Bread Board

A useful gift. Hardwood board, 11 inches in diameter, polished, with beautiful enameled border, hand decorated with pretty flower design. Handle of knife enameled and decorated to match. Knife, 12¾ inches long. Complete in gift box. Shipping weight, 2 pounds.
8K5780 ... $1.59

Polychrome Nut Bowl

Shipping wt., 1½ lbs.

A useful gift for the home. Polychrome finish over wood with burnished gilt and blue decorations. Diam., 8⅛ in. Has felt bottom. Complete with six picks and cracker.
8K5795 ... $2.39

Nut Bowl Set $1.29

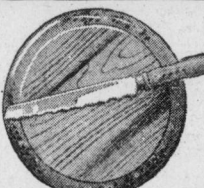

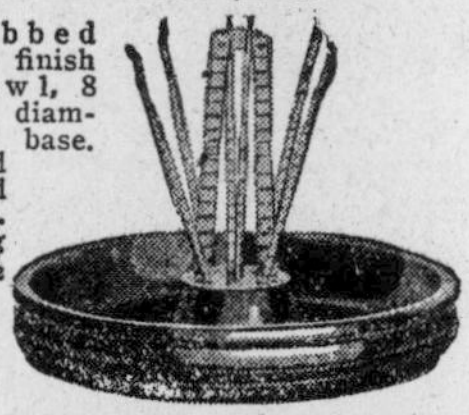

Hand rubbed mahogany finish wooden bowl, 8 inches in diameter. Felt base. Nickel plated cracker and six picks. Shipping weight, 1½ pounds.
8K5794 ... $1.29

Narcissus Bulbs in Bowls

Each Bowl furnished in attractive gift box. Moss for planting included. Bulbs flower in about 8 weeks. Shipping wt., 2½ lbs.

Crumb Sweeper

A gift that is sure to please. Neatly constructed, heavy nickel plated with fancy design. Black enameled wood handle. Sweeps up the crumbs and can be cleaned as easily as a carpet sweeper. Width, 5½ in. Each in box. Shipping wt., 1 lb.
8K5793. $1.48

Florentine Bowl

A beautiful piece of graceful pottery, richly embossed in bold relief. Diameter of bowl, 7 in. Four bulbs are furnished with bowl. Packed complete in gift package.
8K5789 ... $1.98

Paper White Narcissus Bulbs Only

The importation of paper white narcissus has been forbidden, and all bulbs offered for sale are now American grown. We cannot guarantee flowers from each bulb, but we assure you we offer the best bulbs procurable. Shipping weight, 8 oz.
71K2575 Package of 6 ... 49c

Bowl and Bulbs 69c

A 6-inch imported Japanese earthenware bowl, enameled black with green leaves and red roses. Complete with three bulbs in gift box.
8K5786 ... 69c

A Beautiful Gift

A 7½-inch imported Japanese earthenware bowl enameled black, with raised flowers in colors with gilt outlines, in gift box with 4 bulbs.
8K5787 ... $1.29

Shell Chips for Bulbs

Small size shell chips in assorted colors that will not fade. Add to beauty of flowers and bowl and keep bulbs in place. Shipping weight, package, 2½ pounds.
8K5796 Pkg. of 2 lbs. ... 21c

A Gift Elephant

This splendid statue makes a unique gift. The Japanese bronze antique finish permits use anywhere as an attractive ornament. Made of metal, 8 inches long, 5 inches high. Each in gift box. Shipping weight, 3 pounds.
8K5799 ... $1.59

Pretty Landscape Picture

Rustic scenes of nature in all its wonderful colorings. Assorted subjects in octagon shape artistic frames in colors that harmonize with picture. Has a glass front. Size, 22½x18½ inches. Shipping weight, 7 pounds.
8K5710¼ ... $1.89

Genuine Imported Tapestry
A Beautiful Gift for the Home

Not an imitation or print, but real heavy, imported woven tapestry. Beautiful colorings interwoven in designs copied from life. Assorted artistic subjects. Beautiful wood frame, hand colored in harmony with general color scheme, brings out the beauty of the tapestry. No glass. A gift suitable for the finest home. Size, over all, 25x 41½ inches. Packed carefully. Shipping weight, 18 pounds.
8K5717¼ ... $6.25

The Garden Gate Picture

One of the popular garden flower scenes. Beautiful colorings that stand out like real flowers. Garden gate in center and majestic mountains in background. Fancy shape artistic frames in harmonizing colors. Complete with glass. Size, over all, 22½x18½ inches. Shipping weight, 6 pounds.
8K5716¼ ... $1.89

Beautify Your Home With These Pictures

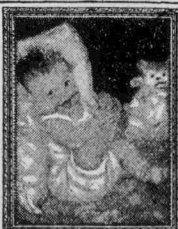

Spring Song

A favorite picture of youth. Beautiful colors. Antique gilt frame with glass. Size, 17¾x13¾ in. Shpg. wt., 5½ lbs.
8K5711 ... $1.08

Poppies

Brings out the natural color of beautiful poppies. Antique frame with glass front. Size, 17¾x13¾ in. Shipping wt., 5 lbs.
8K5719 ... $1.08

The Lone Wolf

Our best selling picture, noted for simplicity and depth of coloring. A gilt frame with glass front. Size, 17¾x13¾ inches. Shipping weight, 5 pounds.
8K5712 ... $1.08

The End of the Trail

A popular subject in beautiful colorings. Antique gilt frame with glass front. Size, 17¾x13¾ inches. Shipping weight, 5 pounds.
8K5706 ... $1.08

Marine

A delightful and popular subject. Artistic frame harmonizes with picture. Glass front. Size, 17¾x13¾ inches. Shpg. wt., 5 lbs.
8K5720 ... $1.08

Both Ends Meet

A wonderful baby picture. Delicate colorings. Fancy frame, with glass. Size, 17¾x13¾ in. Shpg. wt., 5 lbs.
8K5718 ... $1.48

For All Occasions

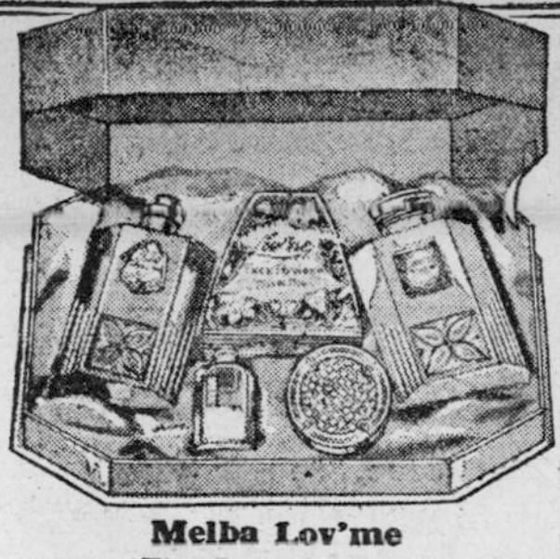

Melba Lov'me
Five-Piece Gift Set
Beautiful gift box, bottom lined and tufted, containing regular size bottle of Lov'me toilet water, face powder, talcum powder in glass bottle, party compact and ½-ounce bottle of perfume. Regular $5.25 size set. Shipping wt., 2 pounds.
8K3383 .... **$4.39**

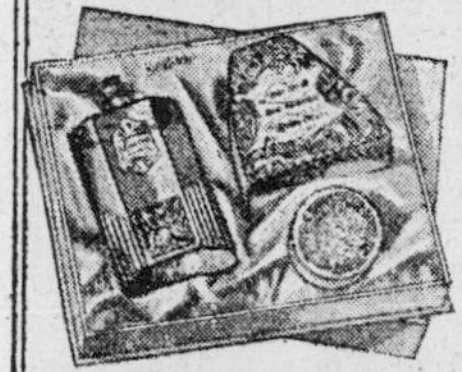

Melba Lov'me Three-Piece Gift Set
Gift box, bottom lined, and tufted, containing regular size Lov'me toilet water, face powder and Melba rouge. Regular $2.75 size set. Shipping weight, 1½ pounds.
8K3384 .... **$2.39**

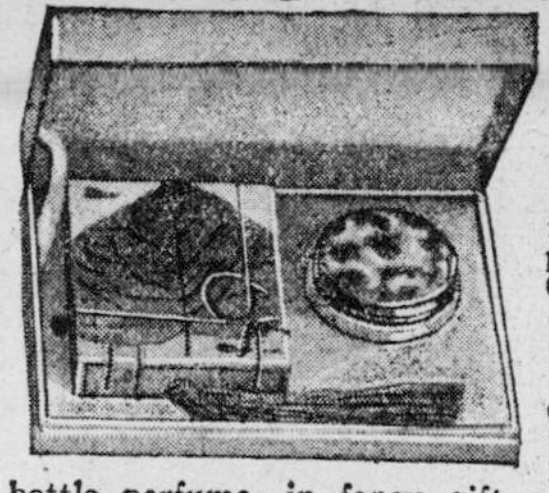

Coty Gift Sets
Three most popular Coty odors. Gift boxes, containing 2-oz. bottle perfume, in fancy gift package, and standard $1.00 size powder compact, in dainty brass box with enameled cover. Beautiful gifts. Shpg. wt., 1¼ lbs.

L'Origan.	$8.00 size—8K3385..	$7.19
Paris.	$7.75 size—8K3387..	6.98
Chypre.	$7.75 size—8K3388..	6.98

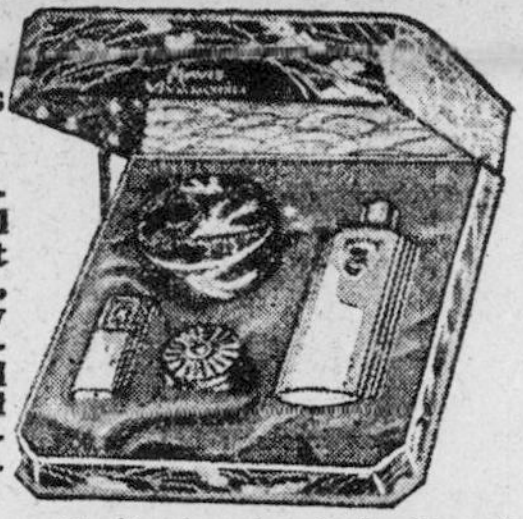

Mavis Gift Set
Beautiful gift box, richly embossed and lithographed. Bottom satin lined and tufted. Contains regular size packages of Mavis toilet water, face powder, purse size perfume and rouge. Regular $3.75 size set. Shipping weight, 2 pounds.
8K3377 .... **$2.98**

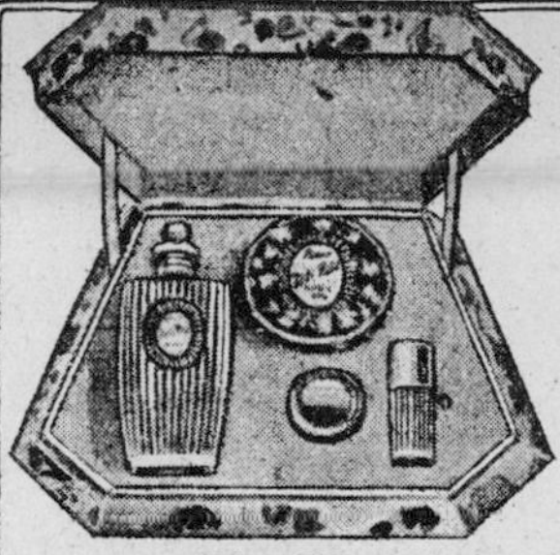

Djer Kiss
Four-Piece Gift Set
Elaborate gift box; cover has fancy embossing and decorations. Hinged back. Botton plush lined. Contains regular size packages Djer Kiss toilet water, face powder, rouge and $1.00 size perfume. Regular $5.00 size set. Shpg. wt., 2 lbs.
8K3382 .... **$3.98**

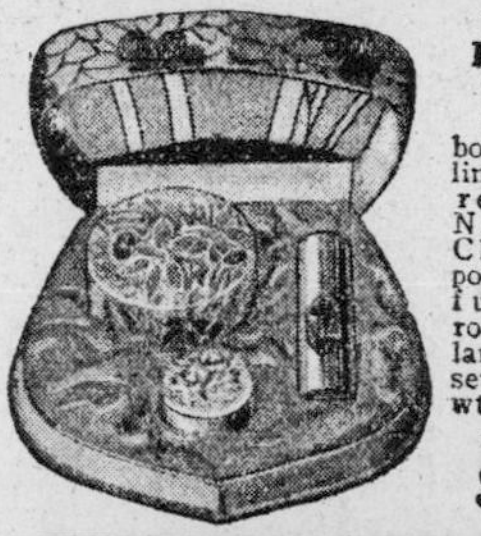

Narcisse De Chine Gift Set
Fancy gift box, bottom lined. Contains regular size Narcisse de Chine face powder, perfume and rouge. Regular $2.75 size set. Shipping wt., 1½ lbs.
8K3397
$2.39

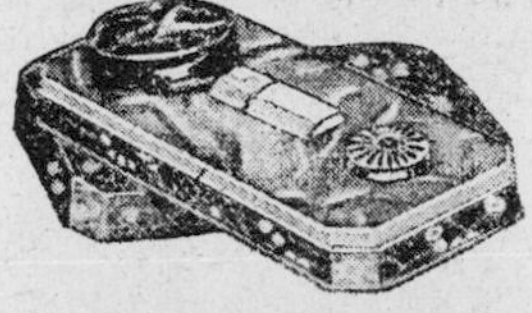

Mavis Three-Piece Gift Set
Beautifully decorated gift box, bottom lined and tufted satin. Contains regular size package of Mavis face powder, rouge, small size perfume. Regular $2.25 size set. Shpg. weight, 1½ pounds.
8K3391 .... **$1.89**

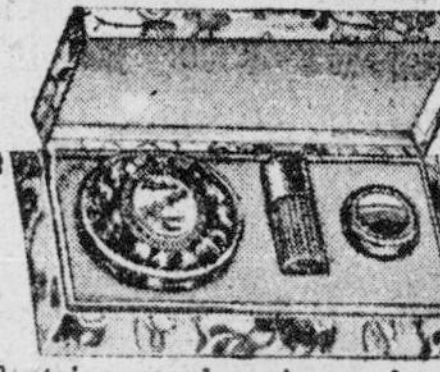

Djer Kiss Three-Piece Gift Set
Fancy hinged box, bottom plush lined. Contains regular size packages of Djer Kiss face powder, rouge and $1.00 size perfume. Regular $2.75 size set. Shipping weight, 1½ pounds.
8K3381 .... **$2.39**

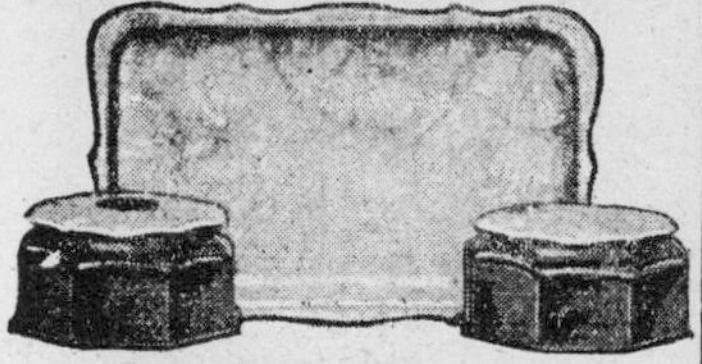

Pearl Pyralin Dresser Set
Beautiful, popular maize color pearl on transparent amber pyralin. A quality set that will make a wonderful gift. Size of tray, 8¾x5½ inches. Puff box and hair receiver, each, 4 inches in diameter. Shipping weight, 8 ounces.
8K5729 .... **$1.98**

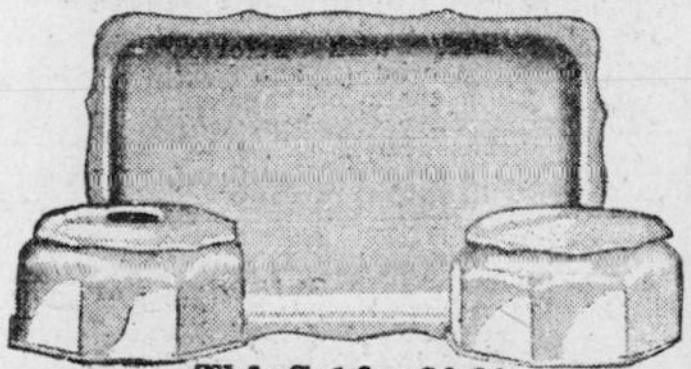

This Set for $1.39
Good quality pyralin ivory, fancy pattern, three-piece dresser set. Tray is 9x5¾ inches. Puff box and hair receiver 4 inches in diameter. Shpg. wt., 6 oz.
8K5725 .... **$1.39**

Beautiful Hand Painted Dresser Boxes

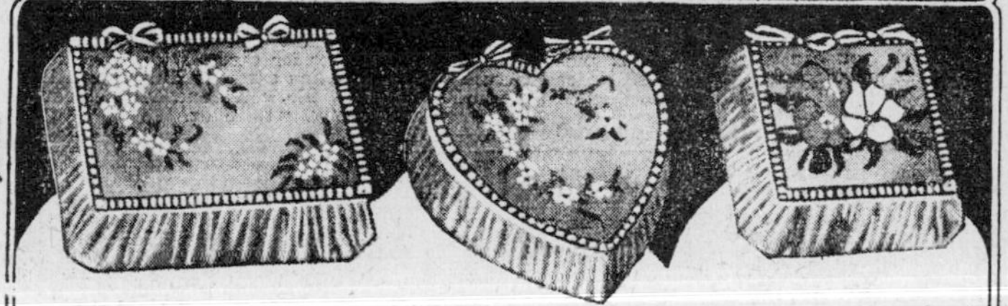

Dainty holiday gifts. The charm and daintiness of hand painted gifts are always appreciated. Hand painted designs, on semi-transparent tops, which are fastened with ribbon bows to light blue satin side boxes. Shipping weight, ¾ pound.

Forget-Me-Not
Size, 8x7x2 inches. Lined with mull.
87K1732 .... **79c**

Heart Shape
Lined with mull. Size, 7¼x7¼x2 inches.
87K1736 .... **98c**

Forget-Me-Not
Size, 6½x6½x2 inches. Not lined.
87K1712 ..... **59c**

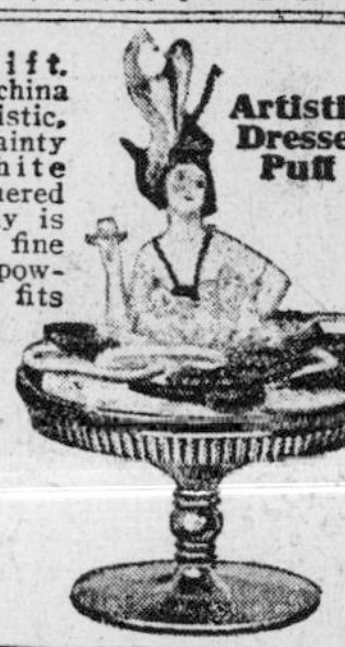

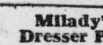

Artistic Dresser Puff
A quality gift. The charming china lady, so realistic, is dressed in dainty black and white skirt with feathered headpiece. Body is fastened to fine quality velour powder puff which fits in dainty white frosted glass dish with black trimming. A distinctive dresser ornament. About 6 in. high. Shpg. wt., 1 lb.
8K5745
$1.48

Burnt Wood Boxes
In Attractive Designs
Inexpensive boxes, always popular. May be used for sewing or for keeping little nicknacks.

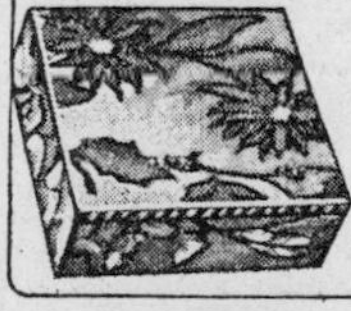

Handkerchief Box
6¼x6¼x1¾ in. Shpg. weight, ¾ pound.
87K1721. **17c**

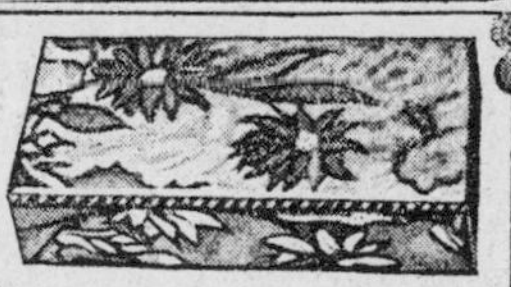

Utility Box
12x5x1¾ inch. Shpg. weight, ¾ pound.
87K1722. **19c**

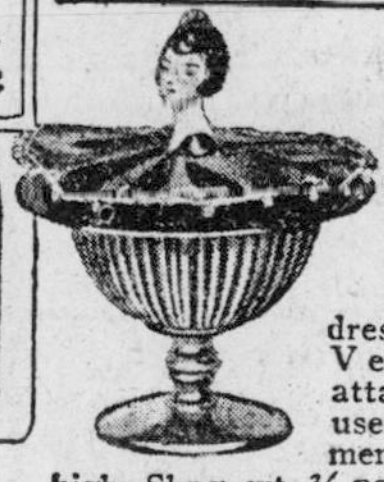

Milady's Dresser Puff
Fancy tangerine color glass bowl, trimmed in black. For face powder. A dainty tangerine color silk skirt, fancy ruffle dresses the china lady. Velour powder puff attached makes it a useful dresser ornament. About 5 inches high. Shpg. wt., ¾ pound.
8K5744 .... **98c**

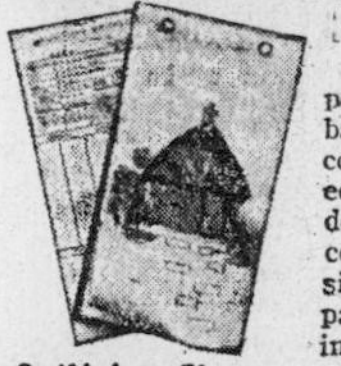

Bridge Score Pad
A beautiful and inexpensive gift. Front and back cover made of gold color cloth. Hand painted, conventional design decoration on top. Set contains two standard size regulation score pads, each pad containing about 40 sheets. Size, 8x4½ in. Shpg. wt., 4 oz.
8K5746 .... **79c**

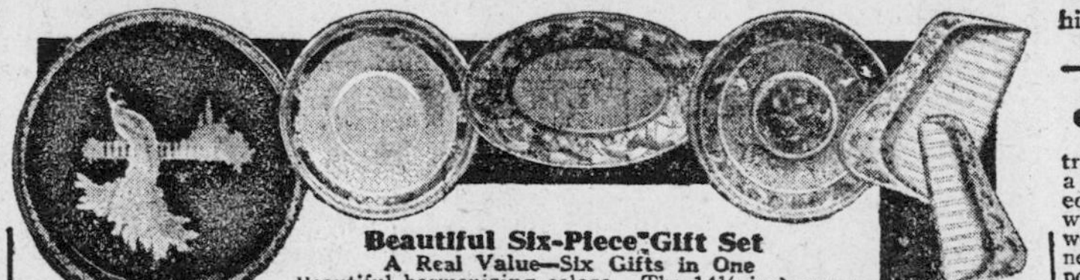

Beautiful Six-Piece Gift Set
A Real Value—Six Gifts in One
Beautiful harmonizing colors. The 14¼-inch serving tray with peacock design generally retails at this price alone. In addition, you will find a floral bread tray, 12x7⅜ inches; a 10-inch fruit bowl; a 10-inch cake dish, and a floral crumb set, each made of unbreakable metal and lithographed in natural colors. Easily kept clean. Shipping weight, 4 pounds.
8K5792¼ **98c**

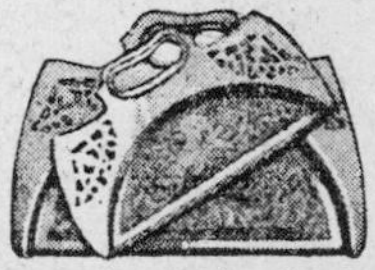

Fancy Crumb Set
A most attractive set. Has a hand hammered effect design with filigree work in the corners. Highly polished solid brass. Tray, 8½x6 inches. Scraper to match. In gift box.
8K5778—Shpg. wt., 8 oz.... **98c**

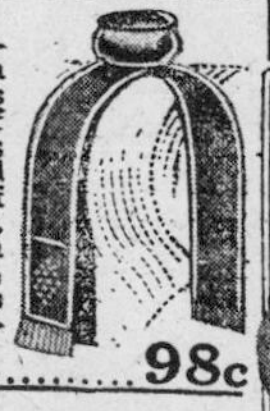

Arm Chair Ash Tray
A popular style ash receiver, simply hang over arm of chair. Polished brass ash tray snaps on and off for easy cleaning. Weights in ends keep it in place, and prevent tipping. Made of genuine leather, wine color, decorated in gilt with fringed ends. Length, 18½ inches. Bowl, 2¼ inches square. In gift box. Shipping weight, 8 ounces.
8K5747 .... **98c**

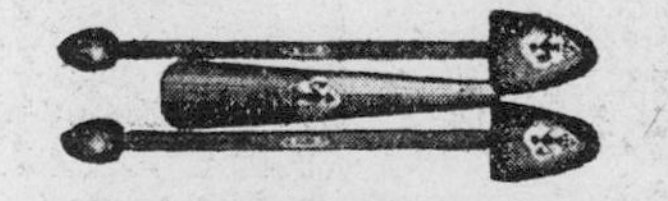

Shoe Trees and Horn Set
A splendid, inexpensive gift. Attractively decorated on Chinese red enamel over hardwood. Each set in gift box. Shipping wt., 8 ounces.
8K5798 .... **59c**

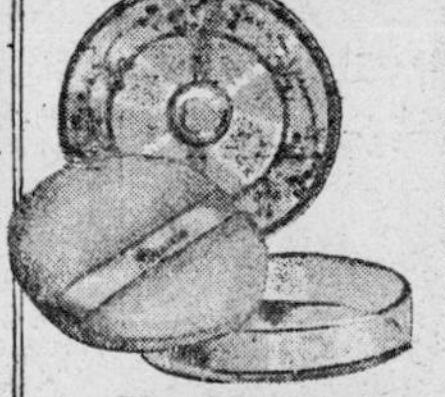

Hand Painted Face Powder Dish
A dainty gift. Beautifully hand painted clear glass container with quality velour powder puff. Size of dish, 4 in. wide; 1 in. high. Shpg. wt., 1 lb.
8K5749 .... **98c**

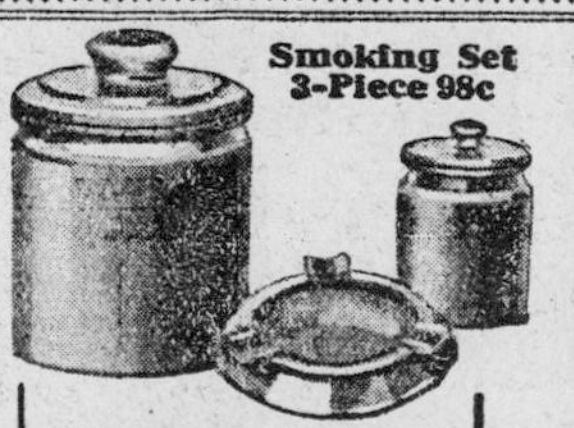

Smoking Set 3-Piece 98c
A wonderful value. Deep red, colored frosted glass, black trimmed. Cigar humidor, 5x7 inches, holds about 25 cigars. Cigarette jar, 3x4 inches, and ash tray, 5 inches in diameter. Shipping weight, 4 pounds.
8K6689 .... **98c**

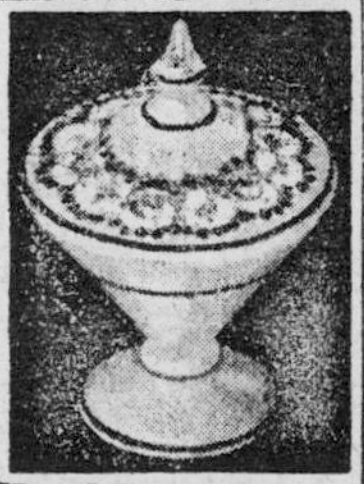

Hand Painted Fancy Candy Jar
Frosted glass, hand painted floral designs. A quality gift. 8 in. high and 5½ in wide. Shpg. wt., 2 lbs.
8K5748 ..... **$1.69**

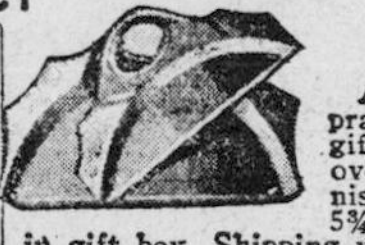

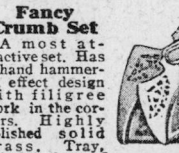

Crumb Tray and Scraper
Artistic design. A practical and useful gift set. Nickel plated over brass, cannot tarnish. Size of tray, 5¾x8½ inches. Each in gift box. Shipping wt., 8 oz.
8K5788 .... **79c**

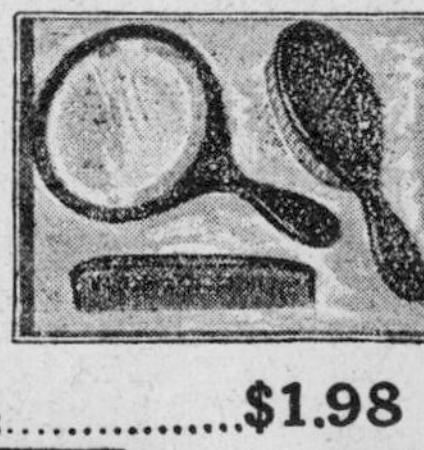

Ebony Finish Toilet Set
Good quality beveled edge mirror, with brush and comb to match. Size of mirror, about 10½ inches long. In plain gift box. Shipping weight, 2½ pounds.
87K6198 .... **$1.98**

Send Sufficient Money for Postage on Parcel Post Shipments. Any Surplus Will Be Returned

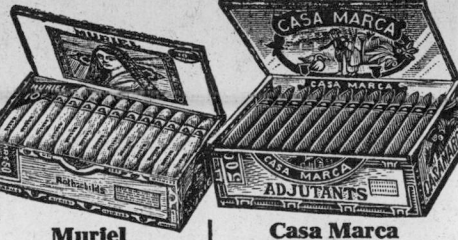
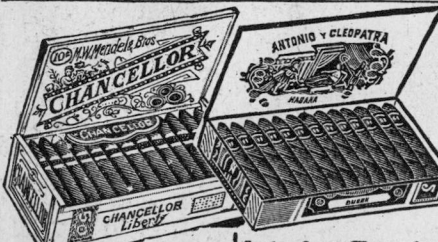
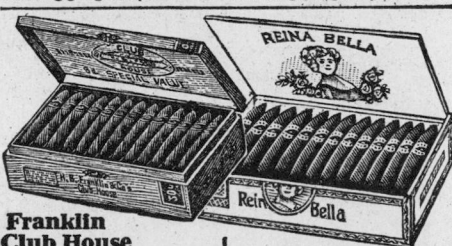

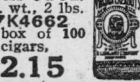

Just the Things Men Like—Wonderful Gifts!

Genuine Pyralin Sets Decorated in Gold — Each in Gift Box

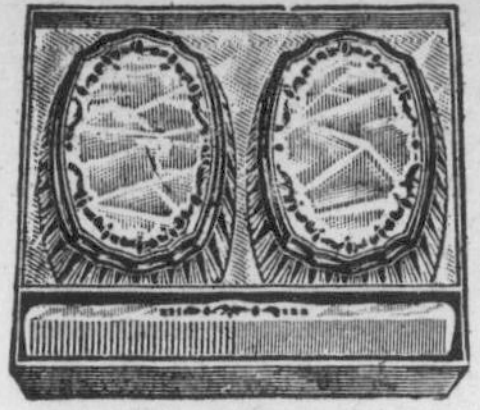

Pearl on Amber Pyralin Military Set

A popular gift suggestion. A pair of good brushes with long white bristles and 7-inch comb to match. Made of beautiful white pearl on amber pyralin, decorated in gilt color with black enamel inlay. Each set in plain gift box. Shpg. wt., 2 pounds.
87K6160........**$3.98**

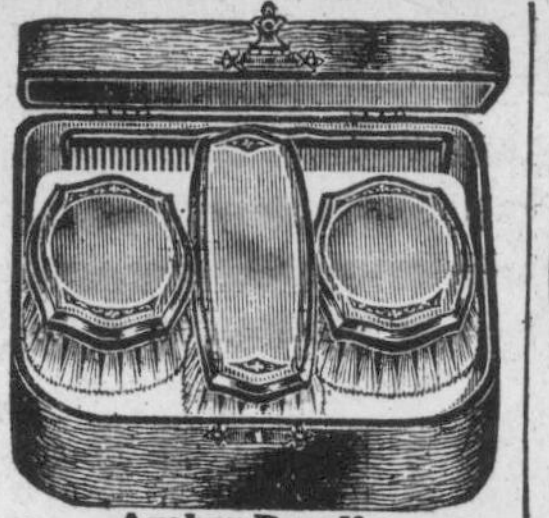

Amber Pyralin
Gold Decorated

Clear, transparent amber color pyralin with beautiful 22-karat gold decoration, black enameled inlay. Cloth brush, two military brushes and comb in hinged cover, fancy utility box. Bottom lined and tufted. Shpg. wt., 3 lbs.
87K6163
Four-piece set........**$6.98**

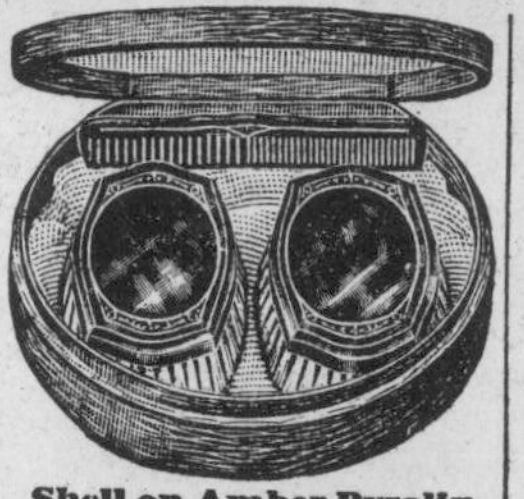

Shell on Amber Pyralin
Gold Decorated

The 22-karat gold decoration shows to advantage on dark tortoise shell on amber color pyralin. Good quality white bristle brushes and comb to match. In beautiful utility gift box, bottom lined and tufted. Shipping wt., 2 pounds.
87K6161........**$4.98**

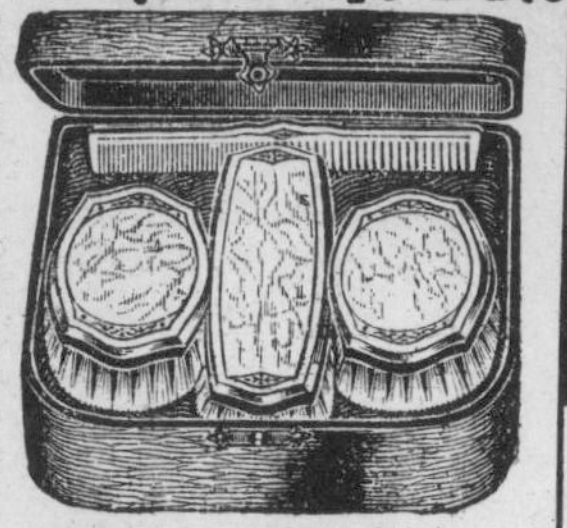

Our Finest Military Set

Beautiful white pearl on amber pyralin. Each piece richly decorated in 22-karat gold and black enamel. Two fine quality hair brushes, cloth brush and comb to match, in unusually pretty hinged utility gift box. Bottom lined and tufted. Shpg. wt., 3 lbs.
87K6164........**$8.98**

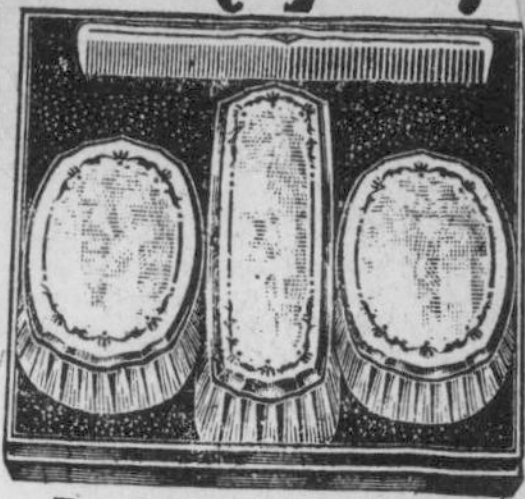

Pearl on Amber Pyralin

White pearl on amber pyralin, decorated in gilt with black enamel inlay. Two popular style military brushes; also cloth brush and comb. This is an exceptionally good value at price offered. Complete in plain gift box. Shipping weight, 3 pounds.
87K6165.....**$5.69**

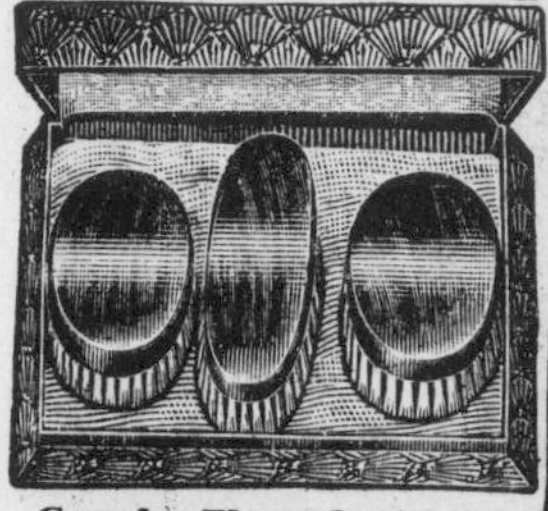

Genuine Ebony for $4.98

A rich 4-piece military set fitted with two natural color, genuine ebony hair brushes and cloth brush to match. Each has long white bristles; also 7-in. black hard rubber comb. Most any man would be pleased with this set for a Christmas present. In beautiful hinged gift box, bottom lined. Shpg. wt., 3 lbs.
87K6155..........**$4.98**

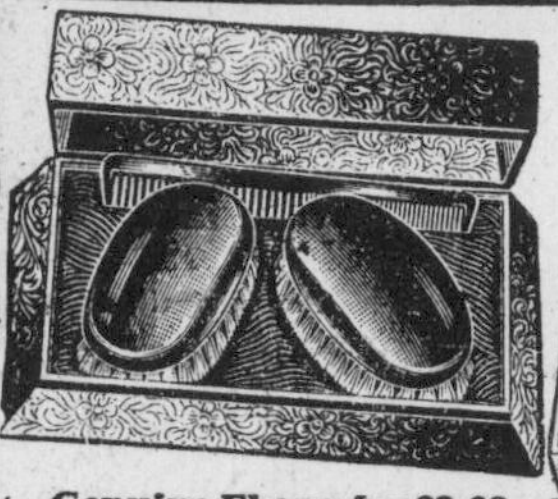

Genuine Ebony for $3.98

A real quality set. Brushes have natural color, genuine ebony back. Long, white, selected bristles, firmly set. 7-inch comb. Complete in beautiful hinged gift box, that can also be used as a utility box. Shpg. wt., 2 lbs.
87K6154........**$3.98**

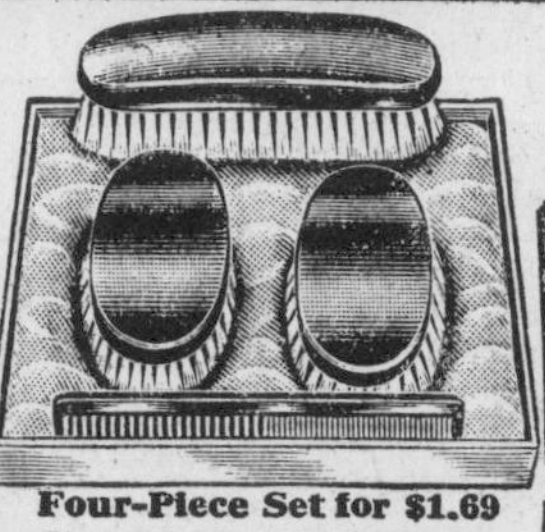

Four-Piece Set for $1.69

Ebony finish hair brushes and cloth brush with white bristles firmly fastened. 7-inch comb. In plain gift box.
87K6151........**$1.69**
Three-Piece Set............**98c**
Similar to above set, but without cloth brush.
87K6150..........**98c**
Shpg. wt., each set, 2½ lbs.

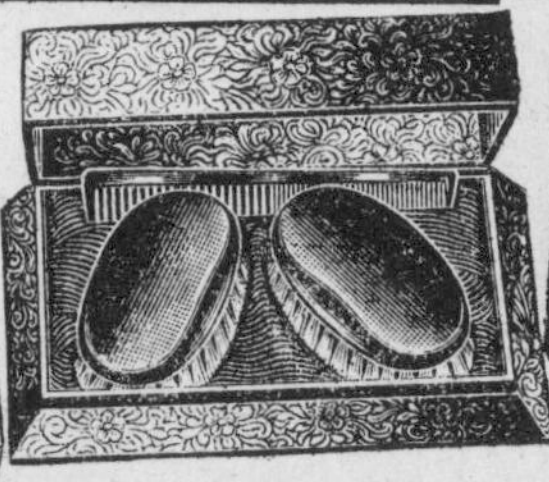

Ebony Finish Three-Piece Military Set

Good quality ebony finish, solid back military hair brushes with selected stiff white bristles, firmly set. 7-inch black hard rubber comb. Complete in fancy hinged gift box, bottom lined and tufted. Shpg. wt., 2 lbs.
87K6152........**$2.39**

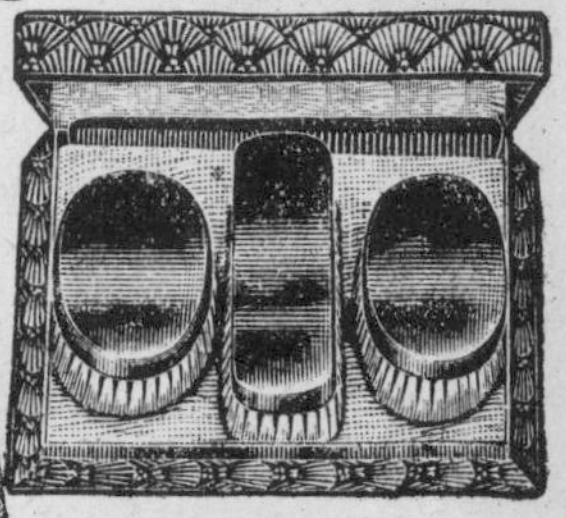

Four-Piece Set

Pair of good quality ebony finish, solid back military brushes with selected stiff white bristles, firmly set. Comb is 7 inches long, made of black, hard rubber. Four pieces complete in fancy, hinged gift box. Bottom lined and tufted. Shpg. wt., 3 lbs.
87K6153.......**$2.98**

Gifts That Make Traveling More Pleasant

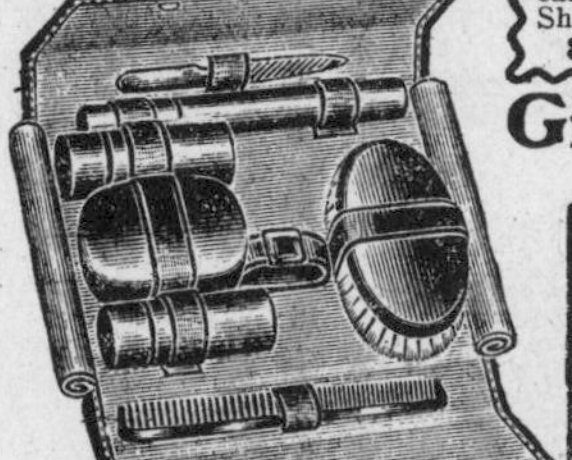

A Special for $4.98

Genuine black leather, fancy grained case, leather lined. Case contains the most used articles, including military brush, comb, file, soap box, tooth brush holder, tooth paste holder and tubes for shaving soap or other articles, such as buttons, pins, etc.; also space for safety razor. Size, closed, 3½x6¾ in. Shpg. wt., 2 lbs.
87K6181..........**$4.98**

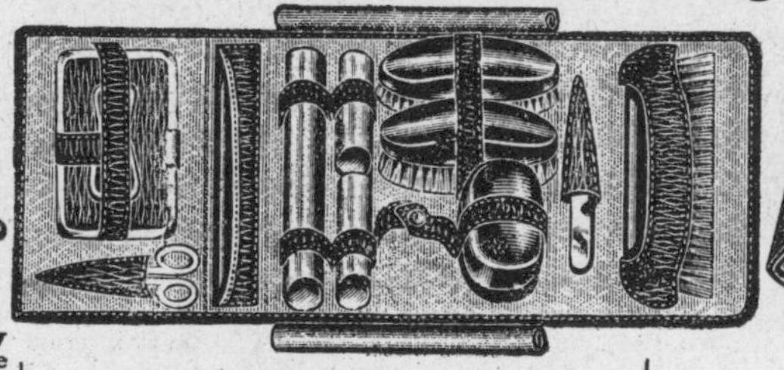

Our Finest Quality Set, $9.98

Beautiful, black grained leather case, leather lined. Each article is of good quality and will give you maximum service and satisfaction. Set contains military brushes, cloth brush, nail file, soap box, tubes for tooth brush, tooth paste, etc.; also a comb, scissors, swinging handle mirror and a space for a safety razor. Folded, case measures 8½x8½ inches. Shipping wt., 3 lbs.
87K6183..........**$9.98**

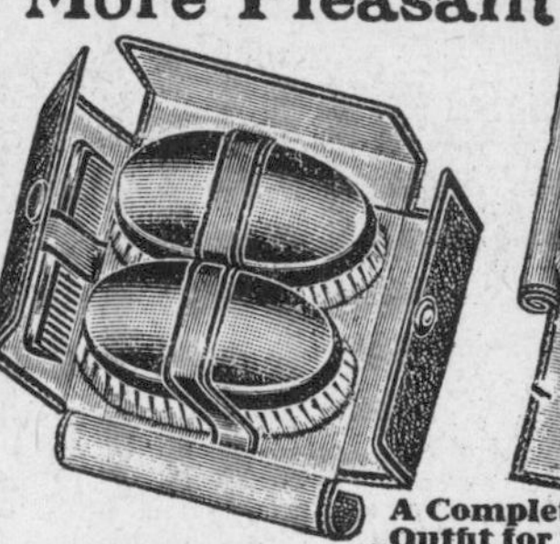

Compact Military Set

Genuine leather case with pair of genuine natural color ebony military brushes with stiff white bristles, and a black hard rubber comb. Size of case, closed, 5½x5½ inches. Shipping weight, 1⅛ lbs.
87K6177.........**$4.98**

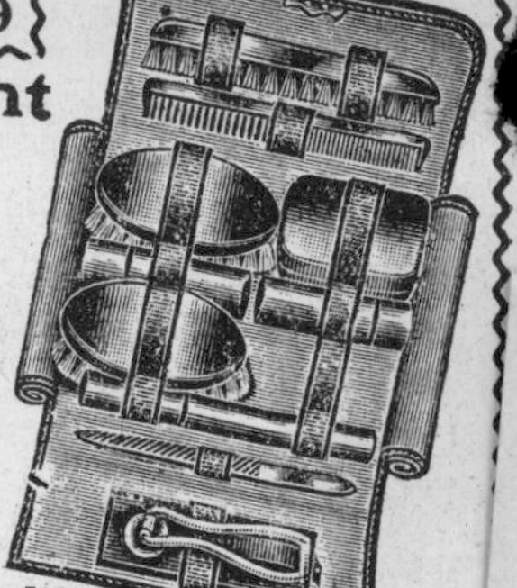

A Complete Outfit for $7.67

Genuine black leather case with tan leather lining. Set contains ebony finish military brushes, hat brush, comb, soap box, file, mirror with back rest, and other articles as shown; also a loop for safety razor. Case, folded, measures 9¾x7¾ in. Shpg. wt., 2¾ lbs.
87K6182..........**$7.67**

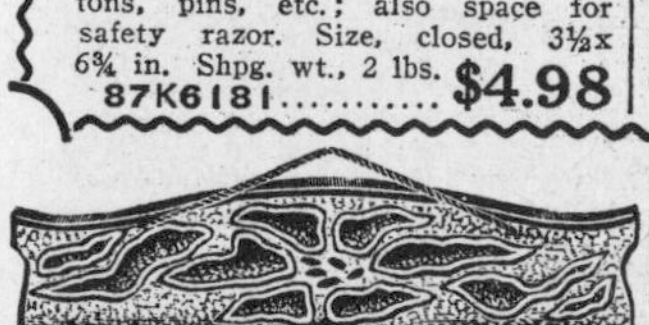

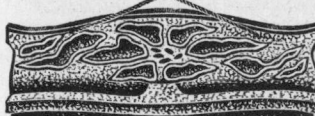

Artistic Tie Rack

A useful gift in a design that is exceptionally attractive. Beautiful polychrome effect in green, red, gold and black colors on wood. Has silk cord for hanging. Length, 14 inches. Ties easily slipped on over end of bar. Each in box. Shipping weight, 1 pound.
8K5777..........................**69c**

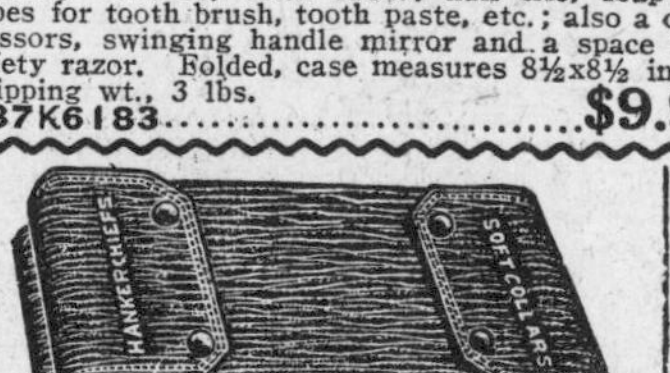

Soft Collar and Handkerchief Case

Beautifully grained leather case, turned edge as in most expensive cases, with silk moire lining. A wonderful gift. One article serves the purpose of two or more. Although especially designed for collars and handkerchiefs, one or two ties may also be carried. Case is 22½ inches long, when open. When closed, measures 10x5½ inches. Shipping weight, ¾ pound.
87K1564..........**$3.98**

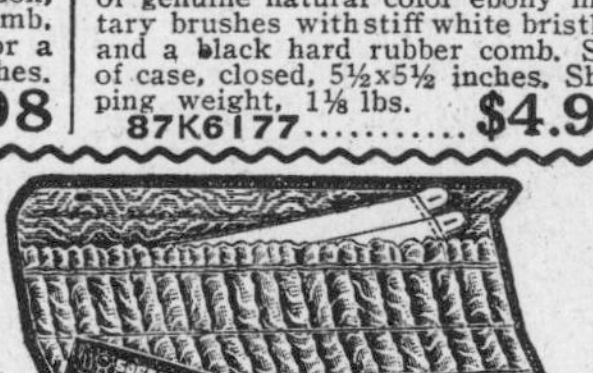

Soft Collar and Tie Case

A combination case that keeps soft collars or ties compact and clean. Fancy, genuine black leather case, attractively lined with silk moire. Size, closed, 13½x4½ inches. Shpg. wt., 10 oz.
87K1563..........**$2.59**

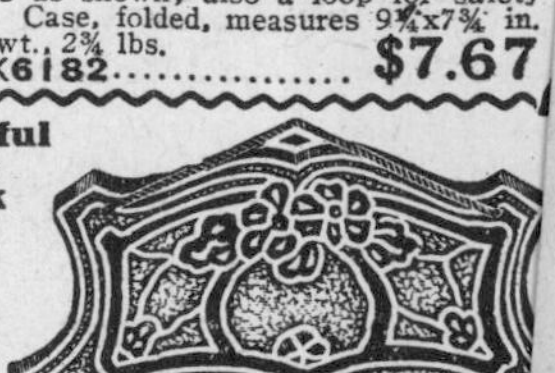

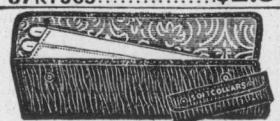

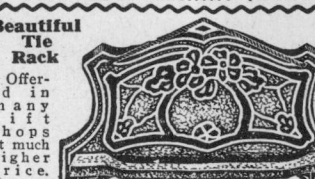

Beautiful Tie Rack

Offered in many gift shops at much higher price. Every man needs a tie rack and this one is a be... Pretty blue polychrome effect background, tied with silver color, decorated in fancy c... Silk cord for hanging. Size, 12½x6 in. 9...
8K5779—Shipping weight, 1 lb.

Genuine Leather Collar Bag

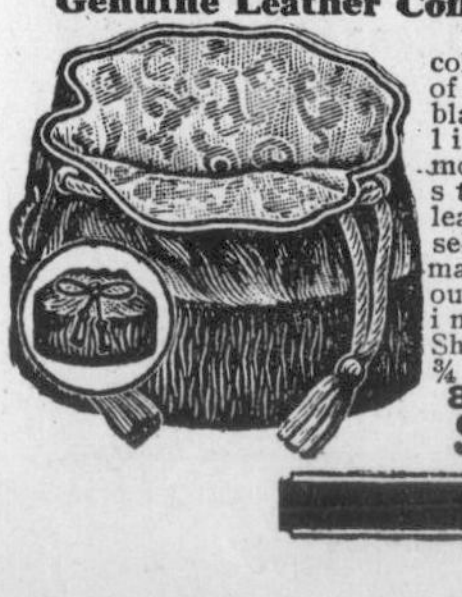

For stiff collars. Made of genuine black leather, lined with moire. Draw string has leather tassels. Well made throughout. 7 inches in diameter. Shipping wt., ¾ lb.
87K1579
$1.59

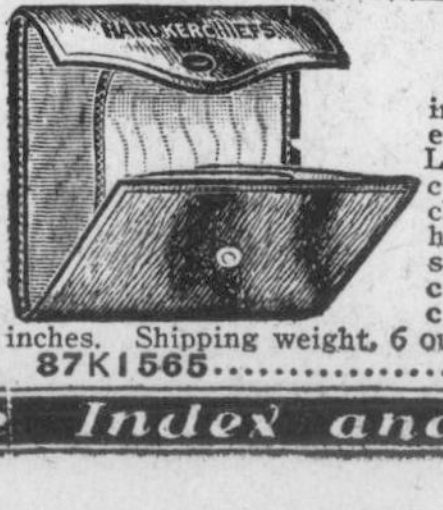

Handkerchief Case

Made of genuine black leather, fancy grain. Lined with pretty cotton moire cloth. Keeps handkerchiefs smooth and clean. Size, closed, 6x5⅝ inches. Shipping weight, 6 ounces.
87K1565..........**98c**

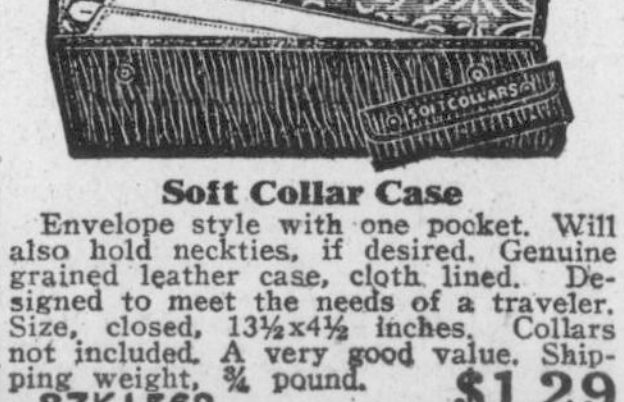

Soft Collar Case

Envelope style with one pocket. Will also hold neckties, if desired. Genuine grained leather case, cloth lined. Designed to meet the needs of a traveler. Size, closed, 13½x4½ inches. Collars not included. A very good value. Shipping weight, ¾ pound.
87K1562..........**$1.29**

Fancy Shape Collar Box

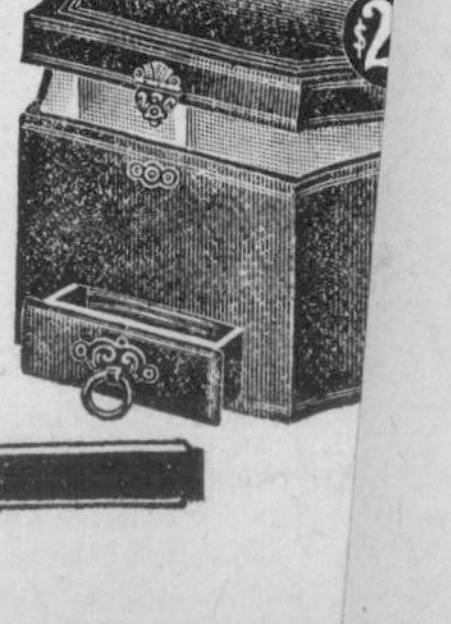

Covered with black leatherette (closely resembles leather). Drawer for collar buttons, cuff links and stick pins. Satin lined throughout. Size, 9x6½x5¾ in. Shpg. wt., 2½ lbs.
87K1513
$2.39

See Index and Information Pages 542 to 570

MEN'S PIPES

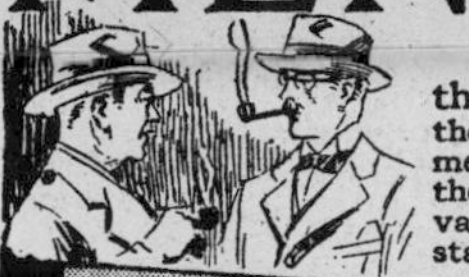

Men everywhere are telling their friends about the new Sears-Roebuck Pipes. They have found they smoke better. This is because of our scientific methods of treating. No pipe smoker has too many pipes, they are ideal gifts. We have long been famous for values in meerschaum pipes in fitted cases on which we stamp any name in gold, a real personal gift.

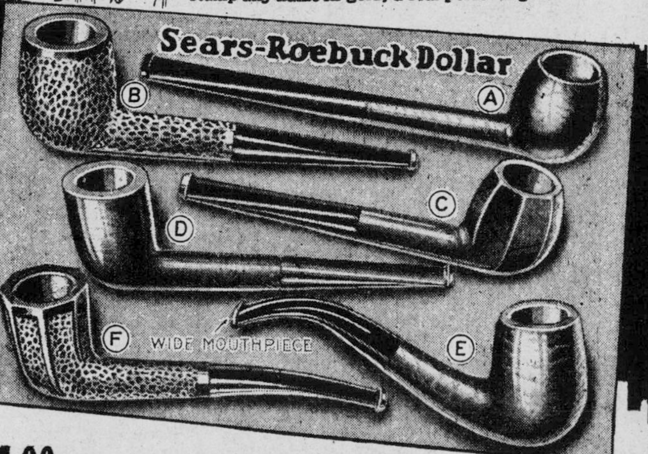

Sears-Roebuck Dollar
A
B
C
D
E
F
WIDE MOUTHPIECE

$1.00 EACH State Letter Indicating Choice

Shpg. wt., each, 5 oz.
18K4003—Try these remarkable "Sears-Roebuck Dollar" Pipes. Skillfully made of selected genuine briar roots scientifically oil treated to make them porous. Porous briar smokes sweet and mellow right from the start. No varnish in these bowls. No distasteful breaking-in. A choice of the most popular styles in the handsome dark Italian finish. All bowls are full size and fitted with black vulcanite mouthpieces. We guarantee these pipes to give absolute satisfaction.

Sears, Roebuck "Drinkless"

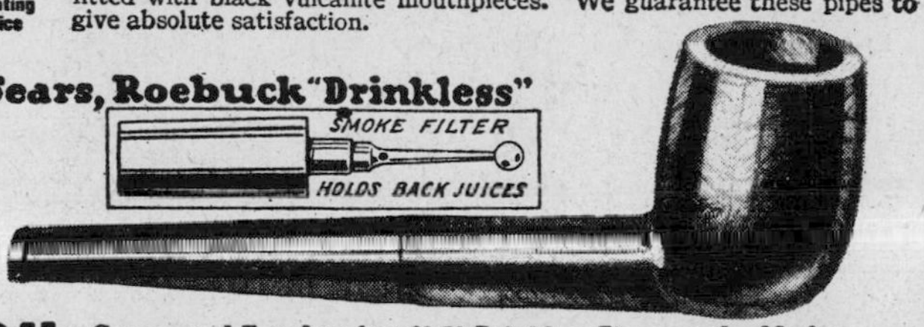

SMOKE FILTER
HOLDS BACK JUICES

$2.75

Guaranteed Equal to Any $3.50 Drinkless Pipes on the Market.
18K4027—Length, 5½ in. Shipping weight, 6 ounces. The New Sears-Roebuck Drinkless Pipe of fine Italian briar, scientifically treated to give a cool sweet smoke. Smooth, highly polished full size bowl with special "setter" feature. We use the original improved aluminum drinkless attachment which is patented. Do not confuse with similar devices that are worthless. Each in special box.

Genuine Steel's

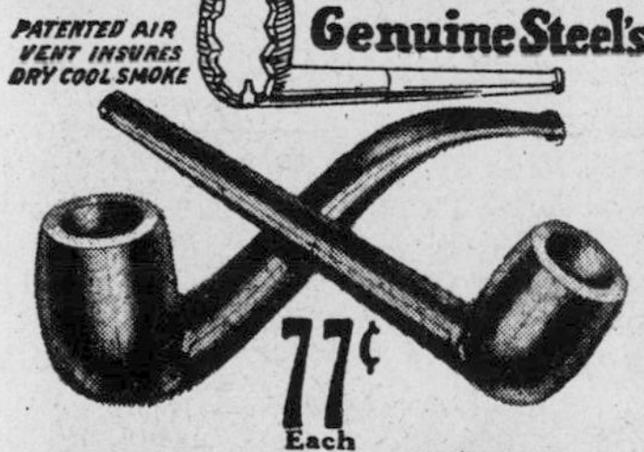

PATENTED AIR VENT INSURES DRY COOL SMOKE

77¢ Each

18K4035 Bent Style. **18K4033** Straight Style.

Length, straight pipe, 5½ inches. Shipping weight, 5 ounces. Low price on the "Steels" Imported Italian Briar Pipe with patented aluminum air valve at bottom of bowl. Prevents pipe from becoming wet or foul. Keeps the pipe dry and insures slow even combustion of tobacco, resulting in a drier, cooler and sweeter smoke. Full size bowls. Black vulcanite bits.

W.L.S. Broken-in Pipes

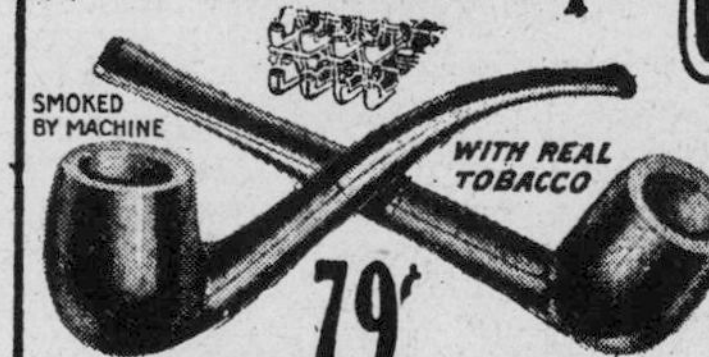

SMOKED BY MACHINE
WITH REAL TOBACCO

79¢ EACH

18K4092 Bent. **18K4090** Straight.

Length of straight pipe, 5¾ inches. Shipping weight, 5 ounces. High grade pipe of selected Italian briar, already broken-in, at a very low price. These pipes have been smoked by the new mechanical smoking machine. Guaranteed absolutely sanitary. A cake of choice tobacco is formed in the bowl, giving a sweet mellow smoke from the start. Handsome highly polished full size bowls. Aluminum cleaner. Flat dry smoker mouthpiece of tasteless black vulcanite.

Meerschaums
The Ideal House Pipes

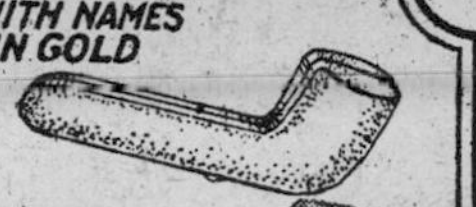

IN FITTED CASES WITH NAMES IN GOLD

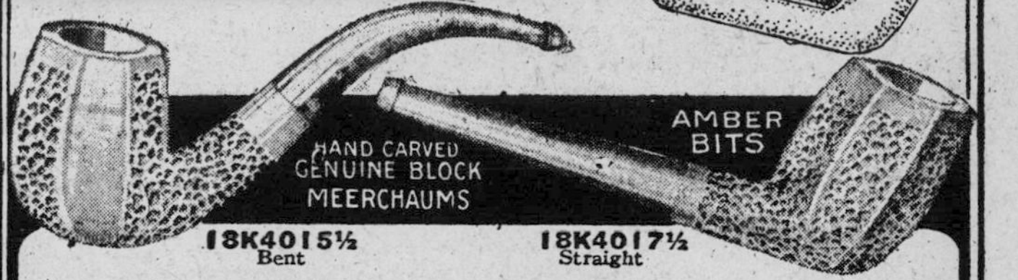

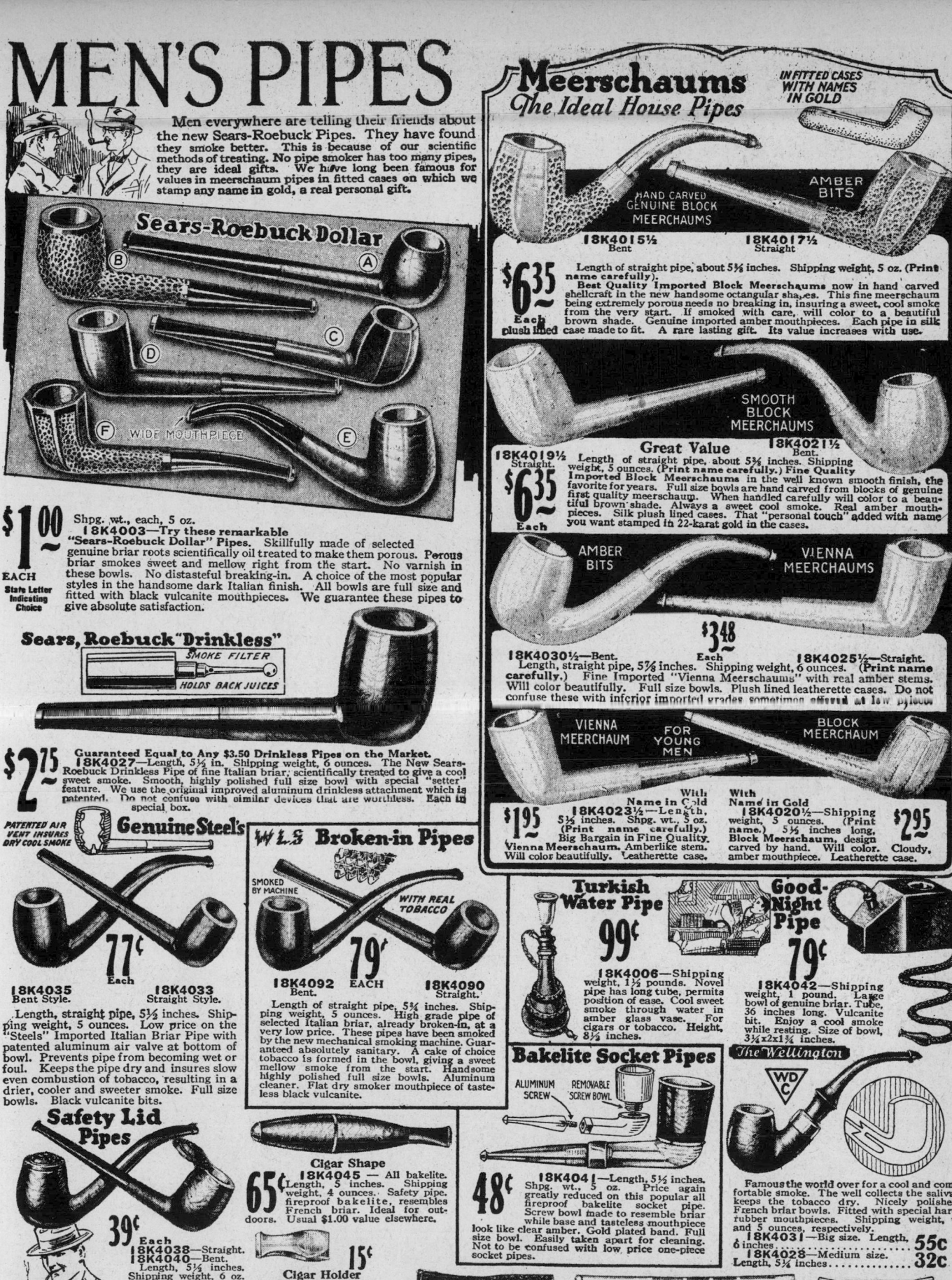

HAND CARVED GENUINE BLOCK MEERCHAUMS
AMBER BITS

18K4015½ Bent **18K4017½** Straight

$6.35 Each plush lined

Length of straight pipe, about 5⅜ inches. Shipping weight, 5 oz. **(Print name carefully).**
Best Quality Imported Block Meerschaums now in hand carved shellcraft in the new handsome octangular shapes. This fine meerschaum being extremely porous needs no breaking in, insuring a sweet, cool smoke from the very start. If smoked with care, will color to a beautiful brown shade. Genuine imported amber mouthpieces. Each pipe in silk case made to fit. A rare lasting gift. Its value increases with use.

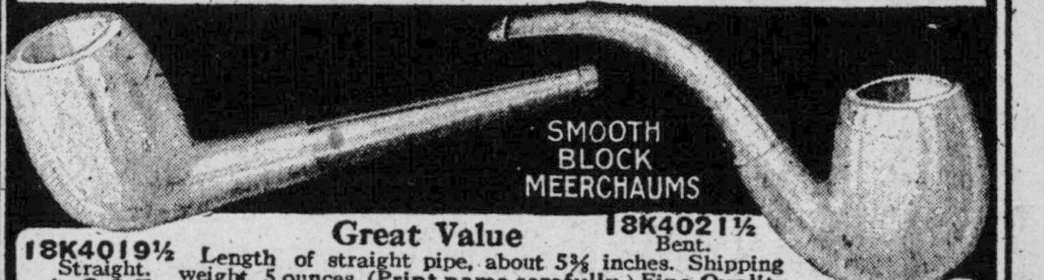

SMOOTH BLOCK MEERCHAUMS

Great Value

18K4019½ Straight. **18K4021½** Bent.

$6.35 Each

Length of straight pipe, about 5⅜ inches. Shipping weight, 5 ounces. **(Print name carefully.) Fine Quality Imported Block Meerschaums** in the well known smooth finish, the favorite for years. Full size bowls are hand carved from blocks of genuine first quality meerschaum. When handled carefully will color to a beautiful brown shade. Always a sweet cool smoke. Real amber mouthpieces. Silk plush lined cases. That "personal touch" added with name you want stamped in 22-karat gold in the cases.

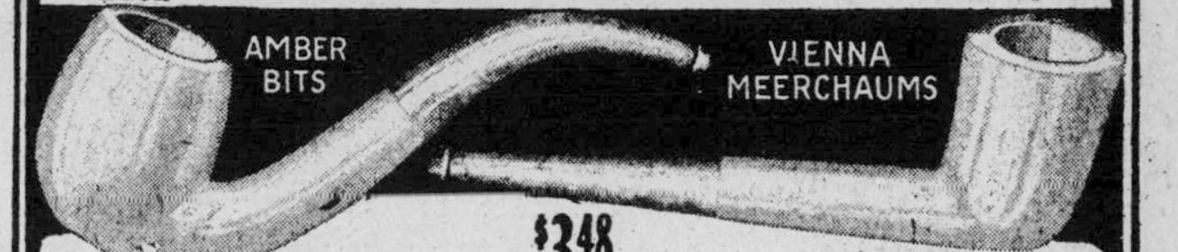

AMBER BITS
VIENNA MEERCHAUMS

$3.48 Each

18K4030½—Bent. **18K4025½**—Straight.
Length, straight pipe, 5⅝ inches. Shipping weight, 6 ounces. **(Print name carefully.)** Fine Imported "Vienna Meerschaums" with real amber stems. Will color beautifully. Full size bowls. Plush lined leatherette cases. Do not confuse these with inferior imported grades sometimes offered at low prices.

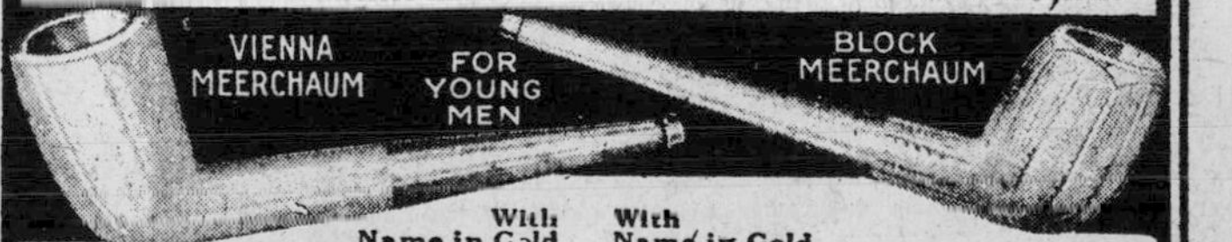

VIENNA MEERCHAUM
FOR YOUNG MEN
BLOCK MEERCHAUM

$1.95 With Name in Gold **18K4023½**—Length, 5½ inches. Shpg. wt., 5 oz. **(Print name carefully.)** Big Bargain in Fine Quality Vienna Meerschaum. Amberlike stem. Will color beautifully. Leatherette case.

$2.95 With Name in Gold **18K4020½**—Shipping weight, 5 ounces. **(Print name.)** 5½ inches long. Block Meerschaum, design carved by hand. Will color. Cloudy, amber mouthpiece. Leatherette case.

Turkish Water Pipe

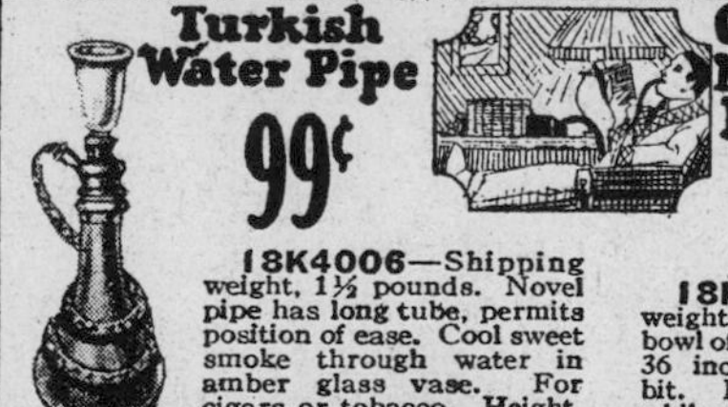

99¢

18K4006—Shipping weight, 1½ pounds. Novel pipe has long tube, permits position of ease. Cool sweet smoke through water in amber glass vase. For cigars or tobacco. Height, 8½ inches.

Good-Night Pipe

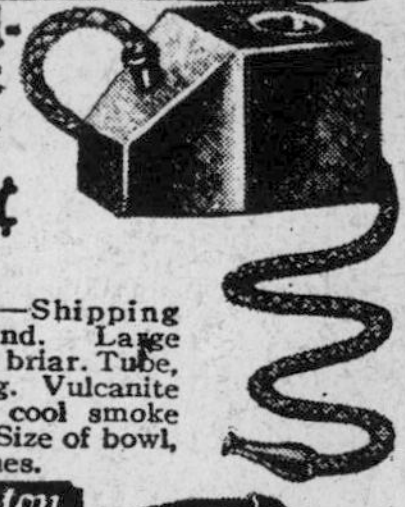

79¢

18K4042—Shipping weight, 1 pound. Large bowl of genuine briar. Tube, 36 inches long. Vulcanite bit. Enjoy a cool smoke while resting. Size of bowl, 3¼x2x1¾ inches.

Safety Lid Pipes

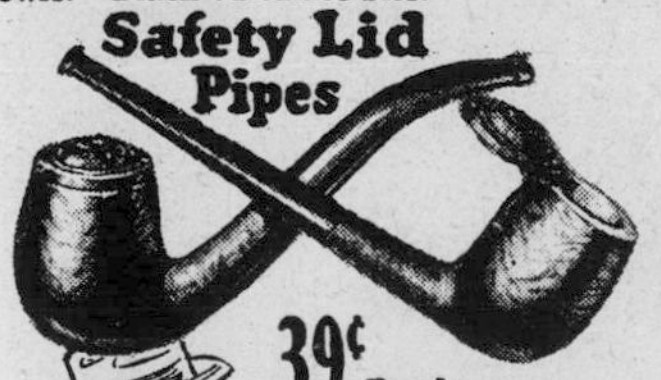

39¢ Each
18K4038—Straight. **18K4040**—Bent. Length, 5¼ inches. Shipping weight, 6 oz. New sparkless pipe of Italian briar with fireproof bakelite lid. Sparks cannot fly, ashes cannot spill. Full size bowl. Aluminum cleaner. Vulcanite mouthpiece. Smoke anywhere with safety.

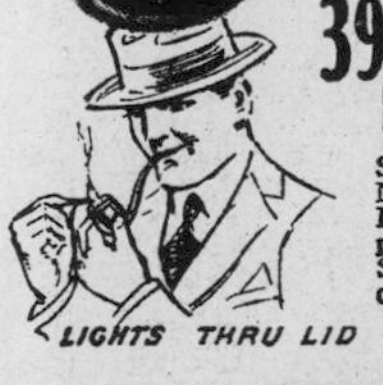

LIGHTS THRU LID

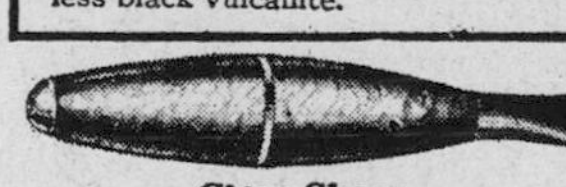

Cigar Shape
65¢ **18K4045** — All bakelite. Length, 5 inches. Shipping weight, 4 ounces. Safety pipe. fireproof bakelite, resembles French briar. Ideal for outdoors. Usual $1.00 value elsewhere.

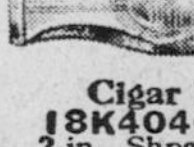

15¢ **Cigar Holder**
18K4046—Length, 2 in. Shpg. wt., 2 oz. Improved Cigar Holder. Special threads to hold cigar securely. Made of a tasteless fireproof composition to resemble clear amber.

Bakelite Socket Pipes

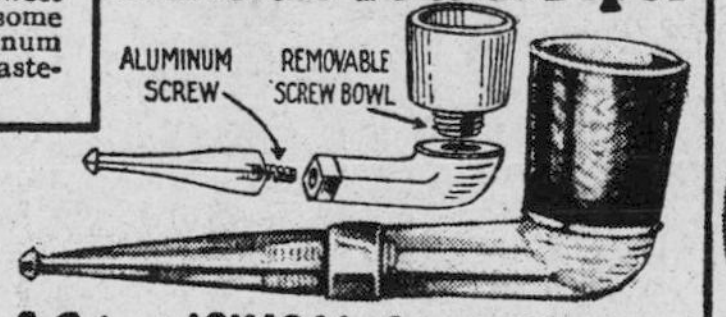

ALUMINUM SCREW
REMOVABLE SCREW BOWL

48¢ **18K4041**—Length, 5½ inches. Shpg. wt., 5 oz. Price again greatly reduced on this popular all fireproof bakelite socket pipe. Screw bowl made to resemble briar while base and tasteless mouthpiece look like clear amber. Gold plated band. Full size bowl. Easily taken apart for cleaning. Not to be confused with low price one-piece socket pipes.

The Wellington

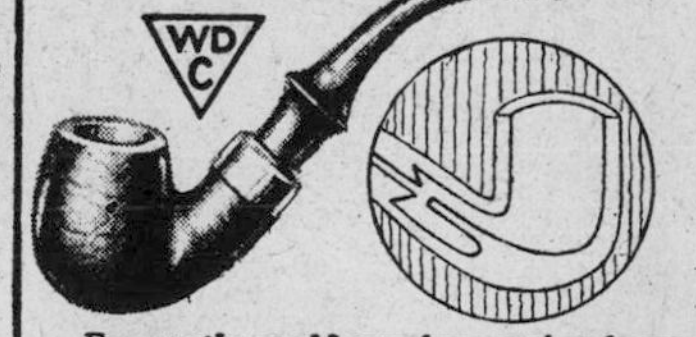

WDC

Famous the world over for a cool and comfortable smoke. The well collects the saliva, keeps the tobacco dry. Nicely polished French briar bowls. Fitted with special hard rubber mouthpieces. Shipping weight, 4 and 5 ounces, respectively.
18K4031—Big size. Length, 6 inches **55c**
18K4028—Medium size. Length, 5¼ inches **32c**

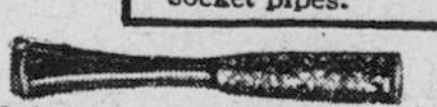

39¢ **18K4053** Length, 3⅛ inches. Shipping weight, 2 ounces. Patented Twisto Cigarette holder. Ejects cigarette butt with a twist. Rough briar holder. Black rubber mouthpiece.

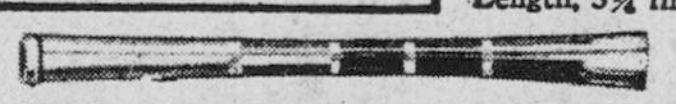

79¢ **18K4050**—Length, 5¾ in. Shipping weight, 2 ounces. Cigarette holder. New long style. Beautiful transparent colorings. Resembles bakelite.

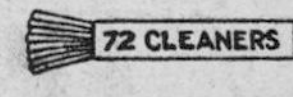

72 CLEANERS

Pipe Cleaners For 9¢
18K4259—Package of 72 cleaners. Shpg. wt., 2 ounces. "The Best" Pipe Cleaners. Covered wire.

Parcel Post, Express and Freight Rates Are on Pages 4[illegible] to [illegible]45

SUNSHINE - the New Happy Baby

So Pleased Over Being Able to Stand All Alone

These 3 Sunshine Photos Sent With Each Doll

REGISTERED U.S. PATENT OFFICE

Each Doll Has Rubber Panties

SUNSHINE Is Without Doubt the Real Prize Baby of the Year

SMILING faced, dimpled baby doll, sure to bring Sunshine and Happiness to your little daughter. Darling, childlike head and kiddie legs, enabling doll to stand or sit, have been beautifully modeled from a happy one-year old. High grade, strong, composition head, fitted with go-to-sleep eyes and with open mouth showing tongue and teeth. Full composition kiddie arms and legs, cotton stuffed body and babylike crying voice. Adorable dress and bonnet of very sheer, dainty, white organdy, trimmed with Valenciennes lace and silk ribbon. Each doll with rubber panties, and there are three pretty Sunshine photos included as shown above. We carefully examined the best baby dolls in the world's markets and decided Sunshine was the most charming and at our low prices the greatest value by far.

	Height	Shpg. Wt.	
18K2932¼	23 inches	4½ lbs.	$6.48
18K2930¼	18 inches	3 lbs.	4.75
18K2928	14 inches	2¼ lbs.	2.98

Fine Glass Eyes ~ New Art Celluloid Unbreakable Heads

"Sunny Girl" Fine "Madame Hendren" doll with beautiful, bright, fixed glass eyes and the new, "Art Celluloid," unbreakable head, having the most natural complexion ever produced. Slender body, composition arms and legs, Ma-Ma voice, painted molded hair. Beautiful dress and bonnet of colored voile with dotted Swiss ruffling. Silk socks. 18K2939¼ Height, 20 in. Shpg. wt., 3¼ lbs. $4.89 18K2937 Height, 14 in. Shpg. wt., 1¾ lbs. $2.98

2 Sizes

Lovely Double Curls of Real Hair

Special Feature Value

Real Hair

Our Largest and Finest

22½ Inches Tall

Splendid Value

29 Inches Tall

A Perfect Beauty Fine Wig of Real Hair Sleeping Eyes With Eyelashes Ma-Ma Voice Fine Shoes With Snap Fasteners

25 Inches of Beauty

$6.95 18K2942¼ Shipping wt., 5¼ lbs. We examined thousands of dolls and just had to buy this beauty. Your little girl will love it, too. New slender arms and legs of durable composition; slender body, go-to-sleep eyes, eyelashes, Ma-Ma voice, silk stockings. Also has high grade, real hair wig and an exquisite party style dress of silk mull with lace and ribbon trim. Buy this doll on our recommendation.

$3.95 Big Sears Value 18K2944¼ — Shipping weight, 4½ lbs. Dolls of this quality and size usually sell for at least $5.00, even in "Sales" in the big city stores. Lovely French style, marcelled wig of real human hair with fancy silk ribbon headband. Composition head, go-to-sleep eyes; eyelashes, open mouth showing teeth and tongue, and Ma-Ma voice. Soft, cuddly body, composition legs. Colored organdy dress with lace and ribbon rosette trimming.

$1.48 In Her Pretty Dress 18K2947—15½ in. Shipping wt., 2¼ lbs. Not as big as her sisters on this page, but very sweet looking just the same. Has newly bobbed neatly brushed, mohair wig, strong composition head and legs, sleeping eyes and Ma-Ma voice. Dress and bonnet of colored, silky Rayon. A splendid value for this low price.

She Looks Just Like a Fairy Princess!

$7.98 18K2949¼—Shipping weight, 7 pounds. It would be difficult indeed to find a Ma-ma doll as lovely as this one. Large, perfectly modeled head is framed by a superb quality wig of real human hair, having bangs and a double row of long curls all kept neatly in place by a silk ribbon headband. Her dress is charmingly fashioned of shimmering, silky Rayon, daintily trimmed with fancy lace and ribbon streamers. Lifelike sleeping eyes with eyeglasses, open mouth showing tongue and teeth, large composition head, arms and legs, and silk stockings. Little girls will adore this doll and we also highly recommend it as a "last doll" for the child who is fast growing up.

"Please, Santa, Bring Me One of Those Lovely Dolls From Sears!"

Our Great Special $4.95

It's Simply Marvelous Value!

Does your little girl, like most little girls the world over, want to play mother? This is the expression of a wish to be like her own mother and is a high ideal that should be encouraged. Why not give your daughter a really fine big doll now, like the one here pictured, with go-to-sleep eyes, hair eyelashes and fine Ma-Ma voice? The beautiful dress of colored, silky Rayon has a low neck, short sleeves and real wide lace edging with ribbon trim. Natural looking fine mohair wig with neat part and silk ribbon bow. New slender type composition legs and arms and fine body. Truly a wonderful purchase.

18K2952¼
Shpg. wt., 5¼ lbs....$4.95

26 Inch Size

Smiling "Happytot" Babies—2 Sizes

Holds her (very natural looking) glass nursing bottle just like a real live baby. Strong head, sleeping eyes, painted hair. Composition arms, baby shape body and legs, crying voice.

$3.98 — 18K2954 Height, 16 in. Shpg. wt., 2¾ lbs. "Happytot" with hand knitted jacket and bonnet. Organdy dress.

$1.98 — 18K2955 Height, 12½ in. Shpg. wt., 1¾ lbs. Smaller "Happytot" with white organdy dress and bonnet but without knitted outfit.

MA-MA MA-MA

Just Wind the Handle of the Bassinette and Away It Rolls by Itself —At the Same Time You Hear the Call, "Ma-Ma! Ma-Ma! Ma-Ma!" One of the cleverest novelties of the season, sure to delight the kiddies. Fancy wicker basket is mounted on brightly colored, sturdy disc wheels and contains a bisque head, moving eye baby doll and a lace edged pillow and cover. Bassinette is 10¾ inches long and doll is 8½ inches tall. Splendid value.
18K2957
Shipping wt., 2¾ lbs.......... $1.98

WHISTLE WHISTLE

"Madame Hendren" Novelty Dolls

Has Eye Lashes

$1.69 Cowboy Whistler 18K2961 Height, 13½ in. Shipping weight, 1½ lbs. A favorite, especially with boys. Good costume; felt fringe on pants; felt hat. Whistles when legs are pressed on table, or any flat surface. Composition head, painted features.

"Nize Baby" 18K2965 Height, 15½ inches. Shipping weight, 1½ lbs. Everyone loves "Nize Baby" made famous by Milt Gross. Fancy bloomer style, baggy costume, big felt shoes. $1.27 Crying voice, painted features, cotton stuffed.

NIZE BABY

I SAY MA-MA I GO TO SLEEP

I SAY MA-MA

21 Inches Tall

Finely Made 20-Inch Doll

Big Sears Value
Pretty Moving Eye Doll
$2.48 — 18K2959¼—Shpg. wt., 4¼ pounds. Smartly styled dress and bonnet of colored organdy with fancy braid trimming. Calls Ma-Ma, has go-to-sleep eyes, hair eyelashes, open mouth, tongue and teeth. Large composition head and forearms, full composition legs, cotton stuffed body, bobbed style mohair wig and silk stockings are other good features.

Charmingly Dressed Ma-Ma Doll
New Slender Type
$1.89 — 18K2967¼ — Shipping weight, 3½ pounds. An unusually pretty Ma-Ma voice doll at a very low price. Dress of fine voile in a very attractive print design is cut low at the neck and shows the pretty chest. Bonnet to match dress. Natural looking mohair wig; painted eyes and features and beautifully proportioned slender legs and arms of durable composition. Has cotton stuffed body and is very well made throughout. An excellent value.

Strong Metal Head Dolls

Our Famous WEARWELL Brand For Rough Play

TRADE MARK REG., U.S. PAT. OFF

Popular "Wearwell" Dolls to Dress Now Fitted With Crying Voice

Guaranteed unbreakable "Minerva" Metal Heads, parted and curled mohair wig and bright, fixed glass eyes. Strong, pink Silesia cloth covered body; stuffed plump. Forearms and hands of carved wood, nicely enameled.

	Ht., In.	Shpg. Wt., Lbs.	
18K2970	15	1¾	$0.89
18K2973	17	2	1.25
18K2975¼	20	2¾	1.59

We Americans play hard and our children do likewise, therefore dolls are sometimes pretty roughly handled and the head gets broken. Our Metal Head Dolls fill a long felt want, because the heads cannot break and are so guaranteed. The go to sleep dollies with metal heads are guaranteed unbreakable, too, and the eyes have been put in to stay. We are headquarters for Metal Head Dolls and can offer you dolls of better quality for less money.

$2.98

Our Largest and Best Quality Metal Head Doll

18K2993¼—Height, 20 inches. Shipping weight, 3¼ pounds.

Special Value. This beauty has a dainty flowered organdy dress and her hair is held neatly in place by a silk ribbon headband. Go to sleep eyes, Ma-Ma voice, composition legs, cotton stuffed body and guaranteed unbreakable metal head and metal arms and hands.

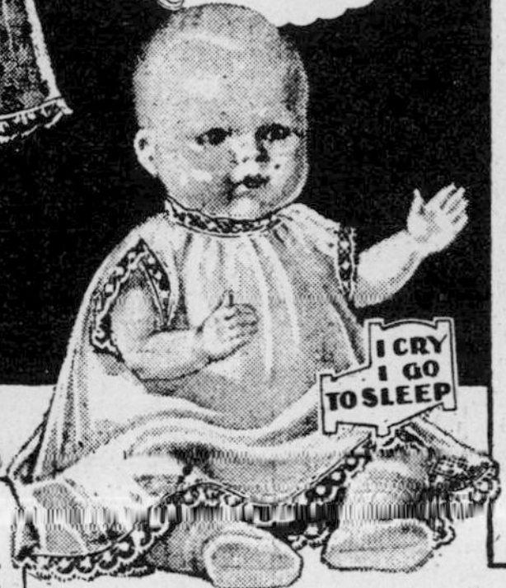

79c

18K2981—Height, 14 inches. Shipping weight, 1½ pounds.

Character doll has cry voice, a colored romper dress and cap to match. Guaranteed unbreakable metal head; painted eyes and features.

98c

18K2984 — Height, 14 inches. Shipping wt., 1½ pounds.

Ma-Ma doll, has guaranteed unbreakable metal head, sleeping eyes, painted hair, stuffed body. Brightly colored dress and hood of nicely colored cotton materials.

$1.65

18K2988—Height, 15½ inches. Shpg. wt., 2¼ pounds.

A larger and better quality Ma-Ma voice doll with mohair wig, sleeping eyes, composition legs and guaranteed unbreakable metal head. Charming dress and bonnet of printed organdy edged with Valenciennes lace.

Cunning Little Baby

99c **18K2991**—Height, 12 in. Shipping weight, 2 pounds.

She's young, but can stand hard knocks. Head, arms and bent baby legs all of strong metal. Will sleep; also cry. White lawn dress.

Women everywhere will rejoice with us over our being able to offer this widely known "Vanta Baby" at special low prices. We consider these to be the finest babies to dress that have ever appeared in the market.

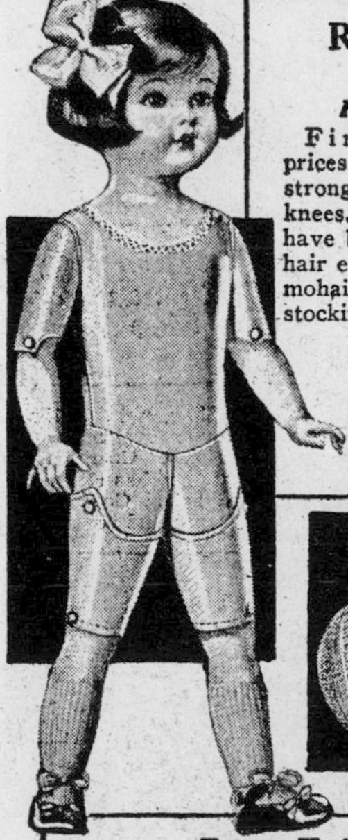

Ready to Be Dressed Kid Body Dolls

Famous "Sunshine" Grade

Fine quality imported dolls, low prices. Bodies of fine white kid leather strongly jointed at hips, elbows and knees. The beautiful bisque heads have bright lifelike moving glass eyes, hair eyelashes and dainty, bobbed style mohair wigs with ribbon bow. Neat stockings and slippers.

	Ht., In.	Shpg. Wt., Lbs.	
18K3015	15¾	1½	$1.98
18K3017¼	21¼	2¾	2.95
18K3019¼	23¼	3¾	3.75

Fancy Knitted Sweater and Cap to Match

59¢

18K2996—Shipping weight, 6 ounces. For Ma-Ma or Baby Dolls. Closely knit of silky mercerized cotton and wool yarns in dainty colors trimmed with white. Mention height of doll and we will send a size to fit. For dolls 10 to 20 inches tall.

"Vanta Baby" Doll Clothes

Set consists of dress and bonnet of dainty white organdy trimmed with lace and silk ribbon; white lawn underslip, celluloid rattle on silk ribbon. Note small view showing how Vanta Baby looks when dressed. Prices below are for clothes only with Vanta twistless fastening tape. No pins or buttons. Shipping weight, ¼ pound.

Set No.	Will Fit Doll No.	Per Set
18K2945	18K2977	$0.79
18K2946	18K2978¼	1.10
18K2950	18K2982¼	1.59

Vanta

DRESSING BABIES

"The Perfect Treasures" With the Widely Known Vanta Baby Garments Without Pins or Buttons

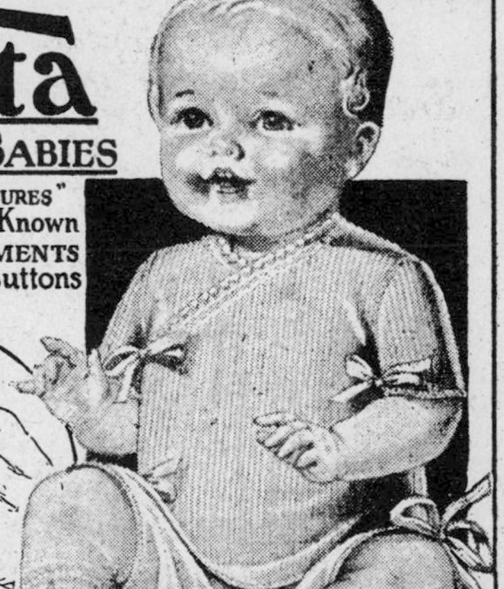

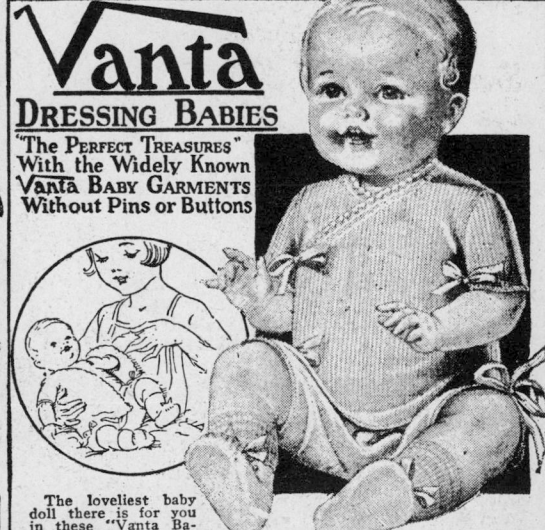

The loveliest baby doll there is for you in these "Vanta Babies." They cry and go to sleep just like real children, and you can dress them without pins or buttons just as mother does her baby. You can buy dainty doll clothes for her, too, as shown at left or perhaps mother will make them if you are real good. Genuine Vanta Baby vest and pantie of fine non-shrinkable white material has dainty little bows of twistless tape. This style garment worn by thousands of real babies. Beautiful smiling baby head; arms and legs are all of strong composition tinted in a delicate flesh pink color. Cotton stuffed body, neat socks and moccasins.

	Height	Shipping Weight	
18K2982¼	21½ inches	4 pounds	$5.95
18K2978¼	19 inches	3 pounds	4.85
18K2977	14 inches	2¼ pounds	3.48

"Santa and Sears" For a Merry Christmas
The Happy Combination

Has Eyelashes

95¢
95¢
$1.00

Ma-Ma Voice Doll
18K3020—Height, 16 inches. Shpg. wt., 1¾ lb. Dandy play doll with dress and bonnet, good cotton material printed with attractively colored kindergarten figures. Strong head, painted features.

Sleeping Doll
18K3022 Height, 15½ in. Shpg. wt., 1½ lb. Strong head, go-to-sleep eyes, crying voice, pretty organdy dress and bonnet. Big value.

"Happy Tot" with Bottle
18K3024 Height, 13 in, Shpg. wt., 1½ lbs. Crying voice, composition head, arms, romper dress. Cotton stuffed.

Wonder Value, 24½ In. Tall $2.98
18K3027¼ Shipping wt., 4½ lbs. A great big beautiful doll with go-to-sleep eyes, mohair wig and crying voice. Exquisite dress and bonnet of colored organdy with lace trim. Child-like composition head and legs; also large composition forearms and hands.

Infant Doll 95¢
18K3134—Over all, 14½ in.; doll, 11¾ in. Shpg. wt., 1¼ lb. Strong head; sleeping eyes, crying voice, soft body. Neat pillow and blanket.

Extra Value Fine Baby
18K3051 Height, 14 in. Shpg. wt., 1¾ lb. Baby doll, painted features, crying voice; composition head and legs; voile dress.

$1.00

Bisque Head

98¢

Infant Doll
18K3039 Length, over all, 17½ in. Shpg. wt., 1¾ lb. Fine Value Imported Doll. Bisque head, go-to-sleep eyes, crying voice, long white infant dress, cotton stuffed body; also open mouth and pacifier.

Rubber Hands That Feel so "Real"

$1.79 "Suck-a-Thumb" Baby
18K3033 Height, 13½ in. Shpg. wt., 1¾ lb. A lifelike darling with soft, flexible rubber arms and hands which are as pleasant to touch as a living baby's chubby arm. Open mouth just large enough for her thumb, finger or pacifier. Strong head, go-to-sleep eyes, crying voice, white organdy dress. Soft and cuddly.

I am a Big, Big Baby

Fine Little Baby Doll In Our Best Box Bag With Those "Goo-Goo" Eyes

Every Kiddie Wants This Set
18K3043 Shpg. wt., 1¾ lbs. "Hollywood" bag is our best grade Kiddies' size, has metal hinges, catch lock. Clever colored picture on cover with moving eyes. See small view. Little newborn dolly inside the bag has bisque head, clever go-to-sleep eyes, long white dress and is wrapped in a colored blanket.

98¢

$1.95 Blanket Baby
18K3035 — Doll, 16½ in. tall; over all, 21 in. Shpg. wt., 2½ lbs. Special value. Lovable, new smiling face baby in a long white infant dress and wrapped in a fancy blanket. Cries when tilted. Has sleeping eyes and composition head.

Big Special Metal Head Doll

$1.48

20 Inch Size

18K3041¼—Shpg. wt., 3 lbs. A Bargain Offer. Built to stand hard knocks and rough play. Guaranteed unbreakable metal head has sleeping eyes and painted hair. Good Ma-Ma voice; pretty dress and bonnet.

See My Eyes Roll!

"Flossy Flirt" Bargain

$2.98 A 19½ Inch Size

Dependable Quality
A Grade Below Those Listed on Page 624
18K3045¼ Shpg. wt., 3½ lbs. This is the doll with those marvelous "Flirty" eyes which roll gayly from side to side, wink and blink mischievously and also go to sleep. She says Ma-Ma, too, and her strong head will not break even if she should fall out of her bed or carriage. Has mohair wig, composition legs and pretty, colored organdy dress and bonnet.

$1.19 Basinette Baby
18K3055 — Shpg. wt., 1¼ lb. Well made of natural wicker, contains an 8-in. bisque head, sleeping eye baby doll with white dress. Basinette, 10 in. long, 7 in. high.

39¢ Bisque Babe in Basket
18K3146—Jointed dolly in white flannel dress is neatly tucked in a clever little wicker basket. Length, over all, 8 in. Shpg. wt., ¾ lb.

45¢ Pretty Dolly Set
18K3049 — Shpg. wt., ¾ lb. A 6-in. celluloid doll, a brightly colored child's necklace, a bracelet and a metal vanity case. All neatly put up in attractive, colored box.

19½ Inch

Big Dolls for Small Prices

$1.65
New Smiling Face Baby
18K3003 ¼ Height, about 20 inches. Shpg. wt., 3 lbs. Bargain Value. Crying voice baby doll with large, smiling character head having painted hair and features. Head of strong composition. Dress of white organdy with sweet lace edged ruffle; bonnet to match. Body and bent baby shaped legs—are cotton stuffed. Long white stockings.

55c
Ma-Ma Doll
18K3005 — Height, 13½ in. Shpg. wt., 1 lb. Well made doll at a low price. Has strong composition head and arms and a neatly made two-piece dress of good cotton material. Dependable Ma-Ma voice. A favorite with young children.

45c
Crying Voice Baby Doll
18K3008 — 15½ inches over all; doll itself is 12 inches. Shpg. wt., 1¼ lbs. New infant doll. Strong head; crying voice; long white dress; stuffed body. Composition hands.

23c
Character Doll
18K3012
Height, 12 inches. Shpg. weight, ¾ pound. Has strong composition head and arms and neat costume of colored cotton materials. Stuffed body and legs. No voice.

99c 20-Inch Doll with Mohair Wig
18K3018
Shipping weight, 2¾ pounds. This pretty dolly is wearing a neatly made romper of good color cotton material. Her head, forearms and hands are of durable composition and she has a most natural looking wig of soft mohair. Fitted with good crying voice. A big doll for a small price.

Rubber Dolls
19c EACH

18K3461
Girl Doll

18K3459
Boy Doll

High grade, sanitary red rubber doll, with whistle. Height, 5 inches. Shpg. wt., 3 oz.

Nursery Doll
39c
18K3037
Shipping wt., 1 lb. Height, 11½ inches. Soft nursery doll, stockinet material stuffed with cotton. Very light, sanitary; easily washed. Painted features. Bright colors.

Wonder Value
25-Inch Play Doll
18K3016 **99c**
Shipping wt., 4½ lbs. Has large child-like head, forearms and hands of strong composition, and well shaped, plump stuffed body and legs. Romper of good cotton material printed with attractively colored animal figures and alphabet letters. Fine crying voice; painted features, a doll that will surely make children happy.

10c
Rubber Pants
18K3063—Shpg. wt., 4 oz. Doll pants, bloomer style. Neatly made of elastic gum rubber. Shirred at waist and knees. Measure doll around body at waist and state inches.

Doll Slippers
15c A Pair
18K3585
In ordering give length of foot from heel to toe. Sizes 1¾ in. to 3¾ in. Shipping weight, 3 oz. Special low price on good quality, artificial black patent leather slippers.

Doll Stockings
10c A Pair
18K3574
In ordering give length of foot from heel to toe. Fancy openwork white cotton doll stockings. Come in sizes from 1¾ inches up to 3¾ inches. Shipping weight, 2 ounces.

Real Hair Doll Wigs

How to Measure for Wigs
Measure the circumference of the doll's head and state the inches. Use strong glue in fastening wig.

Ringlet Wigs, Real Hair
Good quality wig with ringlet curls. Thoroughly sanitary and well made on a net foundation. Medium brown, dark brown or blonde. State size and color wanted. Shipping wt., 4 oz.
18K3554—9, 10, 11 and 12 in..$0.97
18K3555—13, 14, 15 and 16 in. 1.45

Bobbed Style Wig
Nicely made on a net foundation of thoroughly sanitary human hair. Easily kept looking neat. Medium brown, dark brown or blonde. State color and size wanted. Shipping weight. 4 oz.
18K3560—9, 10, 11 and 12 in. $0.79
18K3562—13, 14, 15 and 16 in. 1.15

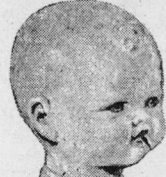

Baby Type—Strong Composition Heads —Moving Eyes

18K	Height, In.	Will Fit Body	Shpg. Wt., Lbs.	
18K3556	3¼	9 in. tall	¾	59c
18K3557	4¼	11 in. tall	1	69c
18K3558	5	13 in. tall	1¼	88c

Very fine quality beautifully finished. Lifelike moving eyes, painted hair. Round neck with groove. Body sizes given are for body alone, without head.

Pretty Doll Heads

FROM HERE TO HERE
HOW TO ORDER DOLL HEADS

Measure the body from shoulder to shoulder across the top and then order the head that is nearest to the measure.

Fine Composition Heads with Sleeping Eyes, Eyelashes and Mohair Wigs

18K	Ht. In.	Across Shldr. In.	Shpg. Wt.	
18K3511	4½	2½	6 oz.	$0.88
18K3513	5¾	3	¾ lb.	1.15
18K3515	7	3½	¾ lb.	1.49
18K3517	7¾	4¼	1 lb.	1.75
18K3519	8½	4½	1½ lbs.	1.98

Best quality; fine, smooth, lifelike finish; also have eyelashes. Three largest sizes have open mouth, showing teeth and tongue.

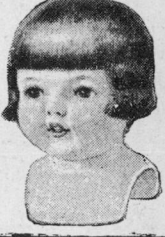

Famous Unbreakable "Minerva" Metal Heads

18K	Height, In.	Across Shldr. In.	Shpg. Wt.	
18K3432	3¼	2½	6 oz.	16c
18K3434	3⅝	2¾	6 oz.	21c
18K3438	4½	3¼	7 oz.	27c
18K3440	5¼	3½	8 oz.	38c
18K3442	6	4¼	¾ lb.	75c
18K3468	6¼	5	1 lb.	88c

Celebrated "Minerva" heads at low prices. Finish is baked onto the metal base. Two largest sizes have glass eyes, other sizes have painted eyes. Molded painted hair.

Extra High Grade Imported Bisque Heads

18K	Ht. In.	Across Shldr. In.	Shpg. Wt.	
18K3404	4¼	3	7 oz.	0.50
18K3405	4¾	3¼	8 oz.	.65
18K3406	5¼	3¾	¾ lb.	.88
18K3407	5¾	4¼	¾ lb.	1.27
18K3408	6¾	4¾	¾ lb.	1.89
18K3410	7¼	5¾	1¼ lbs.	2.39

Lifelike features, moving glass eyes, fine bobbed style mohair wig.

Composition Heads with Painted Features

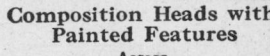

18K	Ht. In.	Across Shldr. In.	Shpg. Wt.	
18K3541	4½	2½	4 oz.	19c
18K3543	5¾	3	7 oz.	27c
18K3547	7	3½	¾ lb.	48c
18K3547	7¾	4¼	1 lb.	55c
18K3549	8½	4½	2 lbs.	63c

Best American make at very low prices. Painted hair and features. Breast plate style. Handsome durable heads.

IMPORTED and DOMESTIC PERFUMES and TOILET WATERS

Djer-Kiss

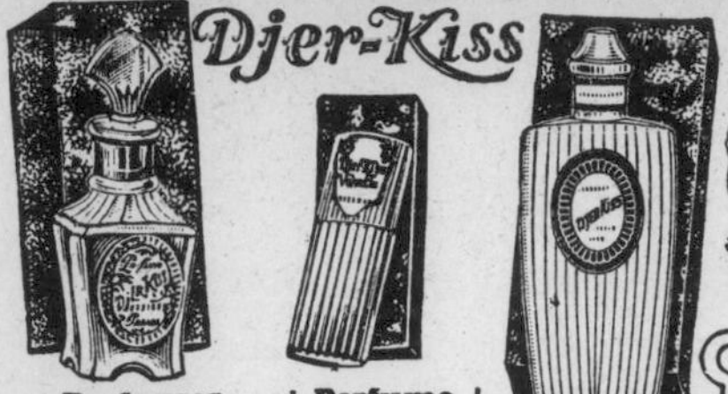

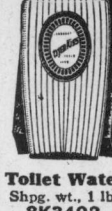

Perfumes
Shpg. wt., 1 lb.
8K2916
$2.00 size.
$1.69
8K2917—$3 size.
$2.59

Perfume Vanette
Shpg. wt., 6 oz.
8K2918
$1.00 size. **85c**

Toilet Water
Shpg. wt., 1 lb.
8K3402
$2.00 size.
$1.69

Coty

L'Origan

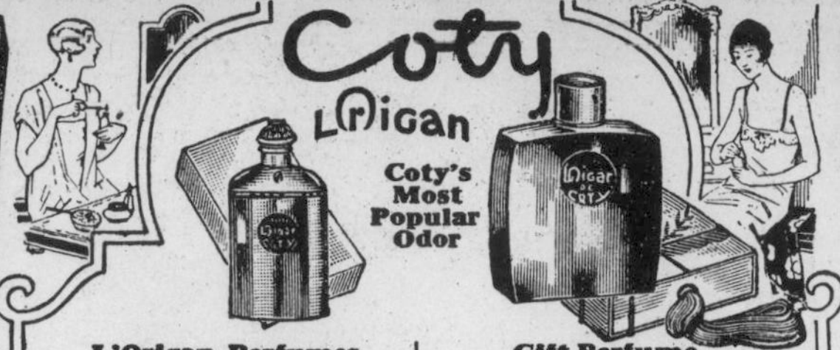

Coty's Most Popular Odor

L'Origan Perfumes
Shipping wt., each, 8 oz. **89c**
8K2921—$1.00 size.
8K2947—$2.00 size. **$1.76**
8K2948—$3.75 size. **3.39**

Gift Perfume
Beautiful imported bottle in fancy gift box, with silk tassel. 2 oz. Shpg. wt., ¾ lb.
8K2961—$7 size. **$6.49**

L'Origan Toilet Water, 4 oz. $4.00 size—8K3437 ... **$3.49**

Mavis

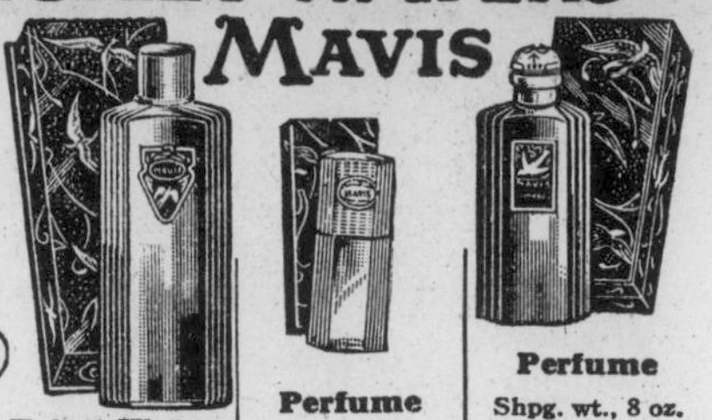

Toilet Water
Shpg. wt., 1¼ lbs.
8K3411
$1.00 size.
83c

Perfume
Shpg. wt., 6 oz.
8K2939
Purse size.
42c

Perfume
Shpg. wt., 8 oz.
8K2931
$1.25 size.
$1.09

Narcisse

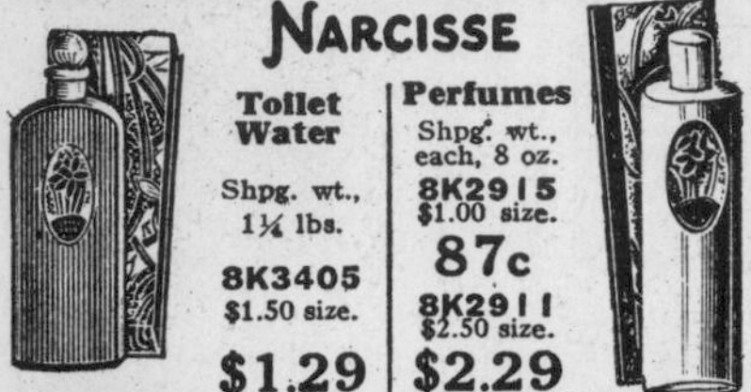

Toilet Water
Shpg. wt., 1¼ lbs.
8K3405
$1.50 size.
$1.29

Perfumes
Shpg. wt., each, 8 oz.
8K2915
$1.00 size.
87c
8K2911
$2.50 size.
$2.29

EMERAUDE

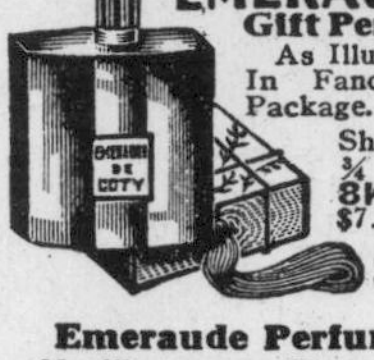

Gift Perfume
As Illustrated. In Fancy Gift Package.
Shpg. wt., ¾ lb.
8K2963
$7.25 size.
$6.59

Emeraude Perfumes
Not illustrated. Shpg. wt. 8 oz.
8K2983—$1.00 size.... **89c**
8K2974—$2.00 size. **$1.76**
8K2969—$3.75 size. **3.39**

Emeraude Toilet Water
Shpg. wt., 1¾ lbs.
8K3420—$4.00 size. **$3.49**

Chypre

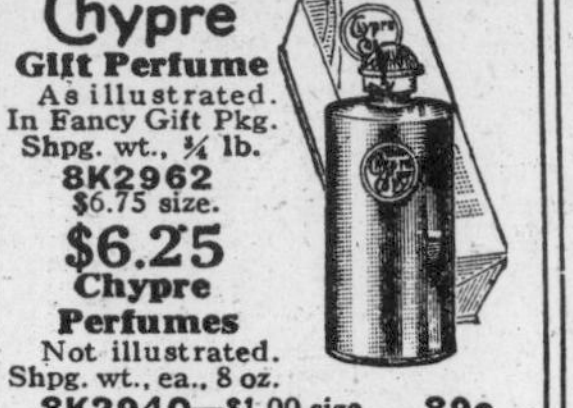

Gift Perfume
As illustrated. In Fancy Gift Pkg. Shpg. wt., ¾ lb.
8K2962
$6.75 size.
$6.25

Chypre Perfumes
Not illustrated. Shpg. wt., ea., 8 oz.
8K2940—$1.00 size.... **89c**
8K2944—$2.00 size. **$1.76**
8K2964—$3.75 size. **3.39**

Chypre Toilet Water
Shipping weight, 1¾ lbs.
8K3431—$4.00 size. **$3.49**

Melba

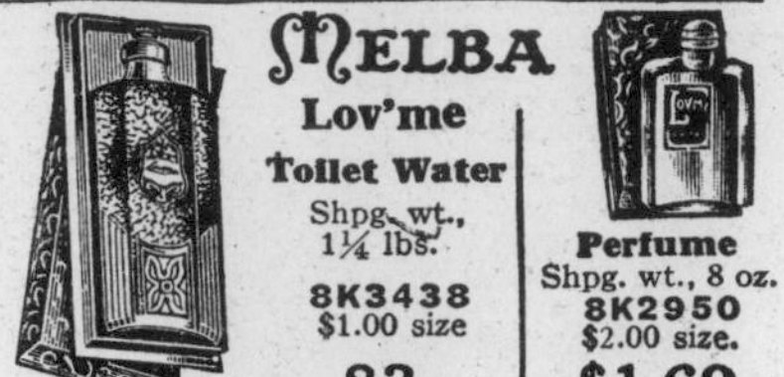

Lov'me

Toilet Water
Shpg. wt., 1¼ lbs.
8K3438
$1.00 size
83c

Perfume
Shpg. wt., 8 oz.
8K2950
$2.00 size.
$1.69

DOMESTIC PERFUMES

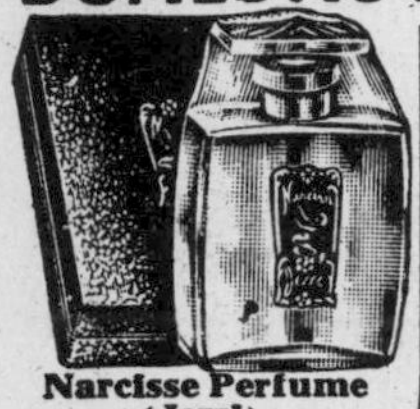

Narcisse Perfume (Jerri)
An exceptional offer. Those who like Narcisse will appreciate this wonderful value. In beautiful gift package. Shpg. wt., large size, 2 lbs.; small, ¾ lb.
8K2913—9 oz... **$3.98**
8K2910—1 oz...... **.69**

Popular Priced Perfumes
For those desiring a medium quality perfume. Four popular flower odors. No money spent for fancy packages.

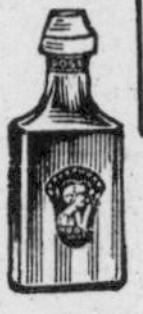

Plain bottles. Contents, 1 oz. Exceptional value at the price offered. Shpg. wt. ¾ lb.

Lily of the Valley
8K2942.......... **39c**
White Rose
8K2943.......... **39c**
Trailing Arbutus
8K2951.......... **39c**
Sweet Pea
8K2954.......... **39c**

PARIS

Perfumes and Toilet Water

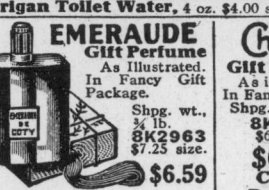

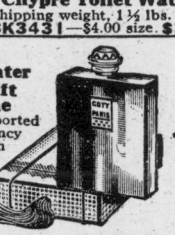

Paris Perfumes
Not illustrated. Shpg. wt., each, 8 oz.
$1.00 size.
8K2922 ... **89c**
$2.00 size.
8K2926 **$1.76**
$3.75 each.
8K2965 **3.39**

Paris Gift Perfume
Beautiful imported bottle and fancy gift box with silk tassel. 2 oz. $6.75 size. Shpg. wt. ¾ lb.

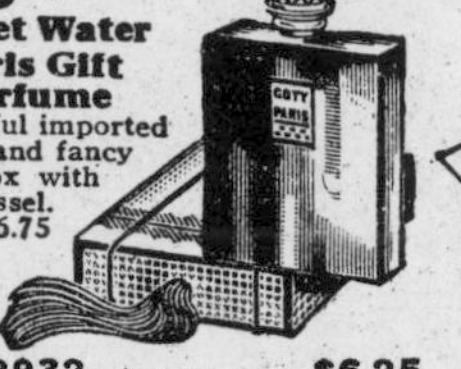

8K2932............ **$6.25**

Paris Toilet Water
8K3444—Shpg. wt. 1½ lbs., $4.00 size. **$3.49**

IMPORTED PERFUMES

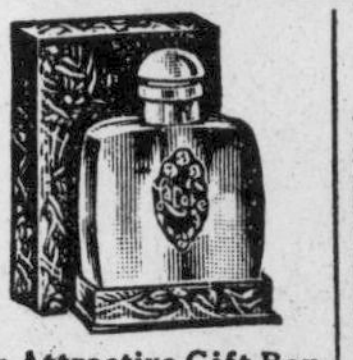

In Attractive Gift Box
Quality French perfume, in popular flower odors. In fancy 1 oz. bottles, each in gift box. Shpg. wt., ¾ lb.

Narcissus
8K2987.......... **98c**
Lily of the Valley
8K2988.......... **98c**
White Rose
8K2989.......... **98c**

For Home Use
In plain bottles. Each in box. No money spent for fancy packages. Fine quality perfumes, imported from France. Four popular odors. Net contents, 1 oz. Shipping weight, ¾ pound.

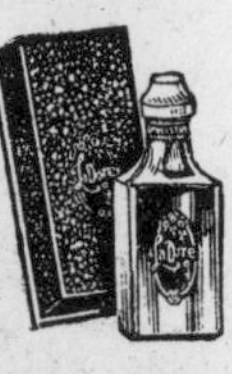

Narcissus
8K2977.......... **79c**
Trailing Arbutus
8K2978.......... **79c**
Lily of the Valley
8K2979.......... **79c**
Rose
8K2980.......... **79c**

SACHETS

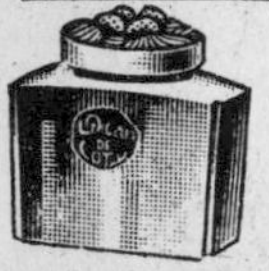

Coty's L'Origan
8K3276—$1.90 size jar........... **$1.69**
Djer Kiss
8K3284—$1.00 size jar........... **85c**
Lady Janis Envelope Sachets Rose
8K3282.......... **19c**
Lily of the Valley—8K3285..... **19c**
Oriente—8K3286.......... **19c**
Shpg. wts.: Jars, 8 oz.; envelopes, 2 oz.

CARON

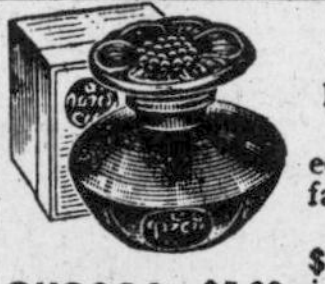

Black Narcissus
A popular imported perfume. Each in fancy gift package.
8K2924
$3.00 size.... **$2.69**
8K2920—$7.00 size....... **6.39**
Shipping weight, ¾ pound.

HOUBIGANT

Quelques Fleurs

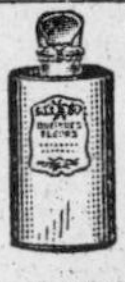

8K2984—1 oz. size.. **$3.79**
Add 21c for postage.
8K2903—Purse size.... **89c**
Add 11c for postage.
Toilet Water—
8K3422—$3.50 size.......... **$3.29**
Add 21c for postage.

DRALLE

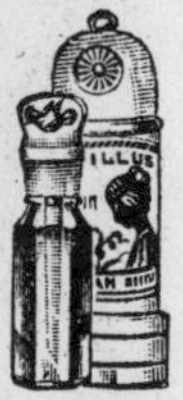

Dralle's Illusion is the original imported concentrated perfume. Popular Lily of the Valley odor. $1.00 size. One drop will retain its fragrance for a long time. Each little vial in polished wood box. Shipping weight, 5 ounces.
8K2975.......... **79c**

PERFUME ATOMIZERS

Fine quality atomizers that give satisfaction. Shipping weight, each, ¾ pound.

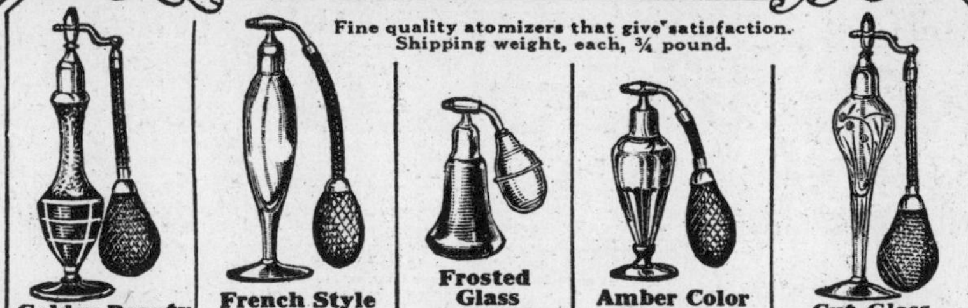

Golden Beauty
Rich black bowl with beautiful 22-karat gold encrusting and etching. Height, about 7½ inches.
8K4259. **$4.67**

French Style Amber Color
A beautiful design. Transparent amber color glass bowl. About 6½ inches high.
8K4257. **$1.98**

Frosted Glass
Dainty blue frosted bottle. Gold plated brass top fittings. About 3½ inches high.
8K4255. **89c**

Amber Color
Popular amber color bowl with gold plated brass top fittings. About 5¼ inches high. $2.00 size.
8K4256. **$1.69**

Cut Glass
Beautiful canary color cut glass bowl. Gold plated, brass top fittings. 7¾ in. high. $4.00 value.
8K4258
$2.98

HUDNUT

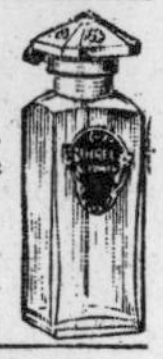

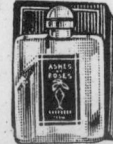

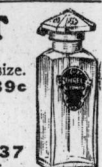

Three Flowers
Perfume. Purse size.
8K2994.......... **89c**
Toilet Water
$1.50 Size.
Not illustrated
8K3408.... **$1.37**
Postage, each, 11c.

Colgate

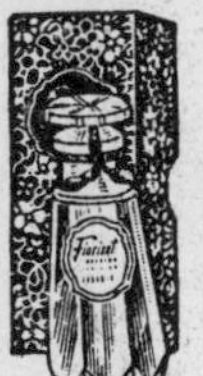

Florient
Perfume, 1 oz.
8K2996... **89c**
Toilet Water
8K3440. **$1.37**
Cashmere Bouquet
Perfume
8K2997. **$1.37**
Toilet Water
8K3439... **89c**
Postage, each, 11c.

L·T·Piver

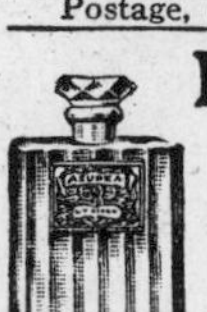

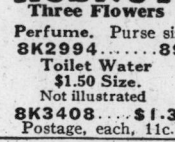

Azurea
Perfume. 1 oz.
8K2929. **$1.59**
Vegetal. 4 oz.
8K3403. **$1.39**
Le Trefle
Perfume, 1 oz.
8K2928.......... **$1.59**
Vegetal. 4 oz.
8K3404.......... **$1.39**
Shipping weight, 1 lb.

GoLLiwoGG

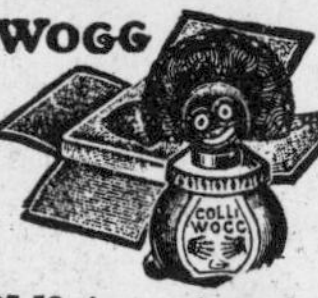

Imported Perfume
The Lucky Little Fellow
Fur Head—$7.50 size.
8K2966.......... **$6.79**
Fur Head—$4.50 size.
8K2967.......... **$3.98**
8K2968—Purse size, not illustrated. $2.25 size.......... **$1.98**
Shpg. wt., above perfumes, ¾ lb.

INCENSE BURNERS

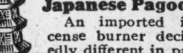

Japanese Pagoda
An imported incense burner decidedly different in pattern to most styles. Japanese earthenware. Decorated in natural colors. Incense burns readily in this pagoda. Use cone incense. 6½ in. high.
Shipping weight, 1 lb.
8K4181.......... **39c**

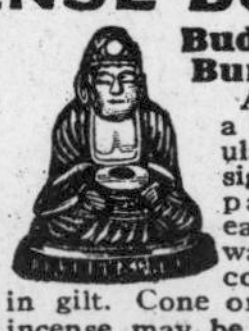

Buddha Burner
Always a popular design. Japanese earthenware; decorated in gilt. Cone or stick incense may be used. Height, about 4½ in. Ship. wt. 1 lb.
8K4176.... **25c**

Antique Finish Incense Burner
A splendid copy of a favorite Grecian urn made of metal antique finish. This beautiful ornament makes an appreciated gift. Use cone incense.
About 6 in. high
Shpg. wt., 1 lb.
8K4182.......... **98c**

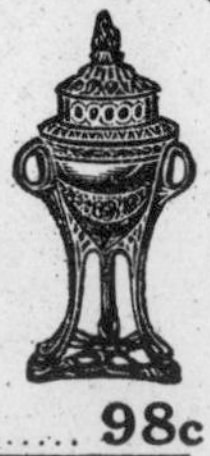

Rajah Cone Incense
Highly perfumed fragrant odors. Rose or Oriental. State choice. 40 large cones to box. This is real quality incense and will give satisfaction.
8K4179.......... **39c**

Hindoo Incense
Distinctive odors, Rose, Oriental and Wistaria. State choice. 20 large cones to box. Reg. 25c size. Shpg. wt., 4 oz.
8K4180.......... **19c**

Mary Garden

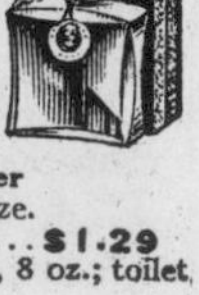

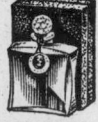

Perfumes
½ oz. Reg. $1.50 size.
8K2957... **$1.29**
1 oz. Reg. $2.75 size.
8K2958... **$2.39**
Toilet Water
Reg. $1.50 size.
8K3417.......... **$1.29**
Shpg. wt., perfumes, 8 oz.; toilet waters, 1 lb.

ASHES OF ROSES

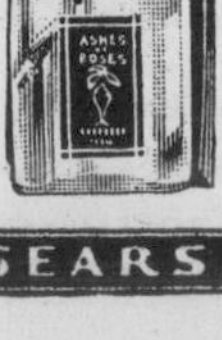

Imported Perfume
Vanity size
8K2900. **89c**
Postage, 6c.
$3.50 size
8K2990. **$3.29**
Postage, 11c.

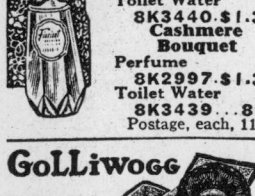

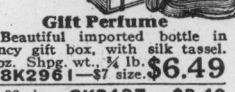

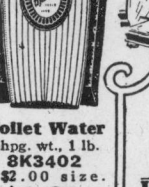

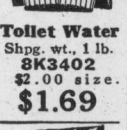

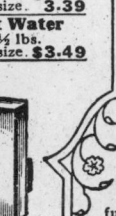

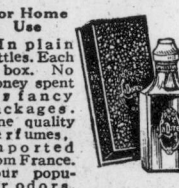

FINE IMPORTED and DOMESTIC FACE POWDERS

La Dore
A fine quality imported French face powder. Noted for its adherent qualities and its delicate fragrance. Colors: White, flesh and brunette. State choice. In fancy box. Shipping weight, 7 oz. **79c**
8K2833

Lisbeth
A popular imported Parisian face powder. Nicely perfumed. Exceptional value at this price. Colors: White, flesh and brunette. State choice. Shipping weight, 7 ounces. **69c**
8K2831

Coty
Four Popular Odors
Well known face powders. Delightfully perfumed. Each in attractive box. Regular $1.00 size. Colors: White, flesh and brunette. State choice. Shipping wt., each, 7 ounces.

L'Origan 8K2880	Paris 8K2893	Chypre 8K2802	Emeraude 8K2808
89c	89c	89c	89c

Royal Veloutine
Our finest quality face powder. Exquisitely perfumed. Made by Chas. Fay, Paris, France. In large fancy embossed box. Regular $2.50 size. Colors: White, flesh and brunette. Shipping wt., 8 oz. **$1.98**
8K2814

L'Avalon
An unusually fine quality adherent Parisian face powder. Has a charming fragrance and velvety smoothness. Fancy box. Flesh, white and brunette. Shpg. wt., 8 oz. **98c**
8K2801

Lady Janis Liquid Face Powder

For shiny skin. Very adherent. Blends with the skin. Apply with finger tips or soft cloth. Flesh or white. Shpg. wt., 1 lb.
8K2860
59c

Pompeian
The well known beauty powder. Regular 60c size.
8K2800 ....**49c**

Lady Janis
A fine adherent powder imported from France. Nicely perfumed.
8K2809 ....**59c**

Lady Janis De Luxe
An exceptionally fine quality imported adherent powder. Delightfully perfumed. Large fancy box.
8K2868 ....**98c**

Anita
A popular imported face powder, especially low priced.
8K2807 ....**48c**

Mavis
Vivaudou's well known face powder. Regular 50c size. **42c**
8K2869

Narcisse de Chine	Princess Pat	Lov'me	Melba	Melba Bouquet	Melbaline	Djer Kiss	
Delightfully perfumed.	Regular $1.00 size.	Regular 75c size.	Regular 50c size.	Regular 50c size.	Regular 25c size.	Regular $1.00 size.	Regular 60c size.
8K2818..66c	8K2845..89c	8K2829..63c	8K2825..39c	8K2826..39c	8K2828..19c	8K2804..85c	8K2803..47c

All face powders carried in white (blanche), flesh (natural) and brunette (rachel). State choice. Shpg. wt., per box, 7 oz.

Azurea	Le Trefle	Manon Lescault	Bourjois Java	Java Cold Cream Powder	Peaches	Ashes of Roses	Luxor	Mary Garden
Regular $1.00 size.	Regular $1.00 size.				One shade only.		Regular 50c size.	Regular $1.00 size.
8K2841	8K2840	8K2811	8K2806	8K2867	8K2834	8K2827	8K2812	8K2830
83c	83c	$1.37	42c	87c	$1.37	$1.37	39c	83c

Gardenia	Three Flowers	Kissproof	Harriet Hubbard Ayer's Powders			Golliwogg	Quelques Fleur	Lady Esther
8K2847	8K2887	Regular $1.00 size.	Ayeristocrat	Luxuria	Medallion	Regular $1.25 size.	8K2844	Regular 50c size.
89c	66c	8K2866 83c	8K2852 66c	8K2876 89c	8K2832 66c	8K2819 98c	$1.37	8K2823
Postage, 11c.	Postage, 9c.		Postage, 9c.	Postage, 11c.	Postage, 9c.		Postage, 13c.	39c

Tetlow's Pussywillow
Regular 50c size.
8K2836
39c

Powder Puffs

Colgate's Florient
8K2846
42c
Postage, 8c.

Carmen
Regular 50c size.
8K2853
39c

Tetlow's Swan Down
Regular 35c size.
8K2837
28c

Hygienol Wool Puff
Widely advertised washable wool puff. Regular 25c. 3¼-in. size. Shpg. wt., 2 oz.
8K4150 **19c**

Finest Quality Velour Puffs
3½-inch diameter. Peach or flesh colors. State color. Shpg. wt., 2 oz.
8K4163 Each .. **19c**

Rose Bud Gift Puff
Fine quality velour puff. 3½-in. diameter. Each in gift package. Regular 50c value. Peach or flesh colors. State color. Shpg. wt., 2 oz.
8K4171 Each .. **33c**

Lady Janis Velour Puffs
Big Value. Two puffs, 3¼-in. size. One flesh and one peach color, per envelope. Shpg. wt., 3 oz.
8K4166 Pkg. of 2 for .. **17c**

Velour Puff
In Rubber Pouch. Keeps the puff clean. 3¼-inch peach color puff in dainty rubber pouch. Shipping weight, 3 ounces.
8K4161 Each .. **19c**

La Blache
Regular 50c size.
8K2854
39c

Colgate's Cashmere Bouquet
8K2817
19c
Postage, 6c.

Parcel Post, Express and Freight Rates Are on Pages 542 to 545

633

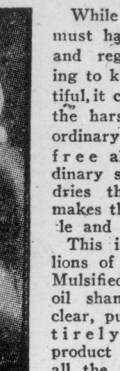

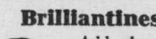

68 Chances to Save

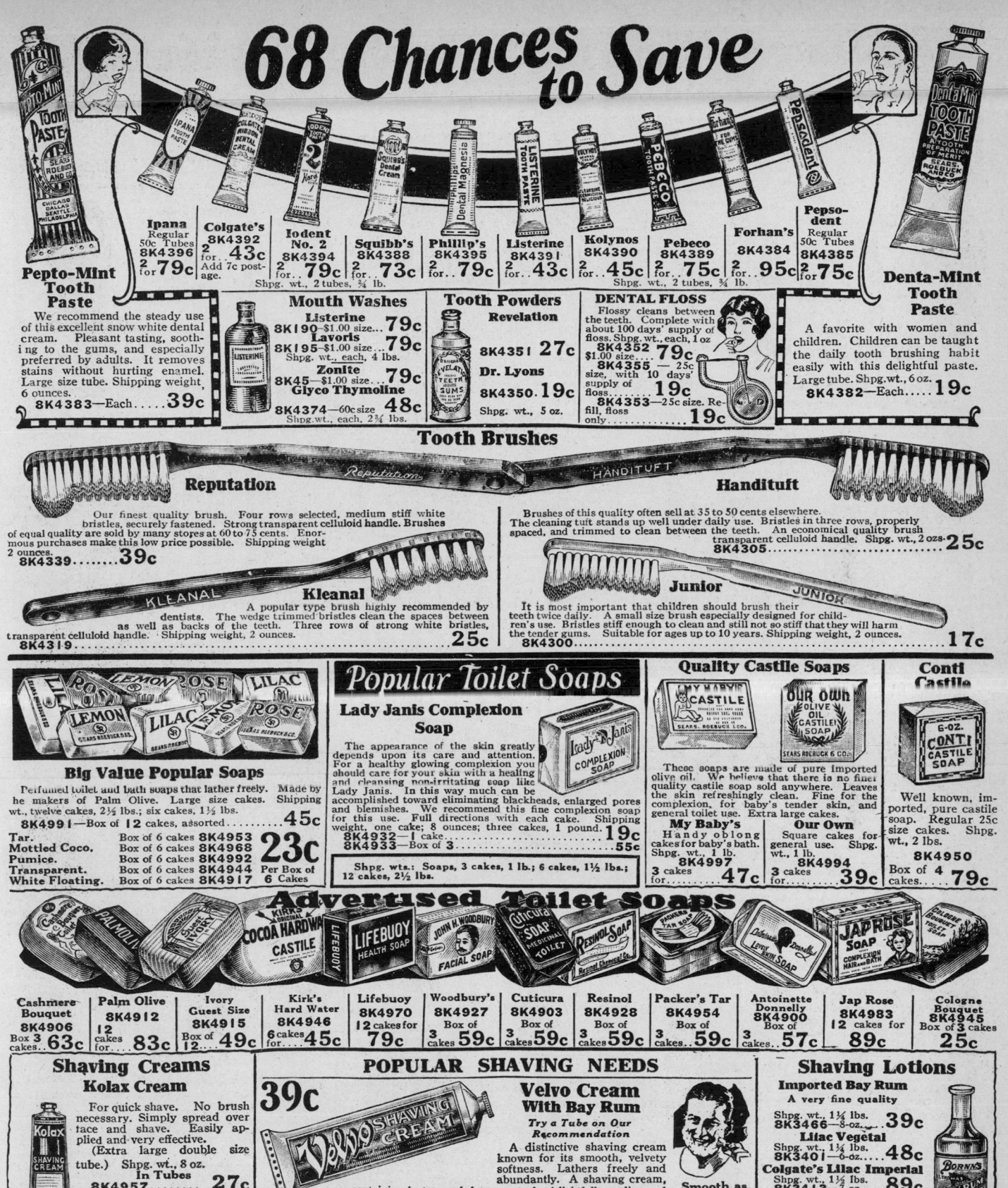

Pepto-Mint Tooth Paste

We recommend the steady use of this excellent snow white dental cream. Pleasant tasting, soothing to the gums, and especially preferred by adults. It removes stains without hurting enamel. Large size tube. Shipping weight 6 ounces.
8K4383—Each.....39c

Tooth Pastes

Ipana Regular 50c Tubes	8K4396	2 for 79c
Colgate's	8K4392	2 for 43c (Add 7c postage)
Iodent No. 2	8K4394	2 for 79c
Squibb's	8K4388	2 for 73c
Phillip's	8K4395	2 for 79c
Listerine	8K4391	2 for 43c
Kolynos	8K4390	2 for 45c
Pebeco	8K4389	2 for 75c
Forhan's	8K4384	2 for 95c
Pepsodent Regular 50c Tubes	8K4385	2 for 75c

Shpg. wt., 2 tubes, ¾ lb.

Mouth Washes
- Listerine 8K190—$1.00 size... 79c
- Lavoris 8K195—$1.00 size... 79c — Shpg. wt., each, 4 lbs.
- Zonite 8K45—$1.00 size... 79c
- Glyco Thymoline 8K4374—60c size 48c — Shpg.wt., each, 2¾ lbs.

Tooth Powders
- Revelation 8K4351 27c
- Dr. Lyons 8K4350 19c

Shpg. wt., 5 oz.

DENTAL FLOSS
Flossy cleans between the teeth. Complete with about 100 days' supply of floss. Shpg. wt., each, 1 oz
- 8K4352 $1.00 size... 79c
- 8K4355 — 25c size, with 10 days' supply of floss.... 19c
- 8K4353—25c size. Refill, floss only.... 19c

Denta-Mint Tooth Paste

A favorite with women and children. Children can be taught the daily tooth brushing habit easily with this delightful paste. Large tube. Shpg.wt., 6 oz.
8K4382—Each.....19c

Tooth Brushes

Reputation — Our finest quality brush. Four rows selected, medium stiff white bristles, securely fastened. Strong transparent celluloid handle. Brushes of equal quality are sold by many stores at 60 to 75 cents. Enormous purchases make this low price possible. Shipping weight 2 ounces.
8K4339.......39c

Handituft — Brushes of this quality often sell at 35 to 50 cents elsewhere. The cleaning tuft stands up well under daily use. Bristles in three rows, properly spaced, and trimmed to clean between the teeth. An economical quality brush transparent celluloid handle. Shpg. wt., 2 ozs.
8K4305 25c

Kleanal — A popular type brush highly recommended by dentists. The wedge trimmed bristles clean the spaces between as well as backs of the teeth. Three rows of strong white bristles, transparent celluloid handle. Shipping weight, 2 ounces.
8K4319 .....25c

Junior — It is most important that children should brush their teeth twice daily. A small size brush especially designed for children's use. Bristles stiff enough to clean and still not so stiff that they will harm the tender gums. Suitable for ages up to 10 years. Shipping weight, 2 ounces.
8K4300 17c

Popular Toilet Soaps

Lady Janis Complexion Soap
The appearance of the skin greatly depends upon its care and attention. For a healthy glowing complexion you should care for your skin with a healing and cleansing non-irritating soap like Lady Janis. In this way much can be accomplished toward eliminating blackheads, enlarged pores and blemishes. We recommend this fine complexion soap for this use. Full directions with each cake. Shipping weight, one cake; 8 ounces; three cakes, 1 pound.
- 8K4932—1 cake 19c
- 8K4933—Box of 3 ..... 55c

Shpg. wts.: Soaps, 3 cakes, 1 lb.; 6 cakes, 1½ lbs.; 12 cakes, 2½ lbs.

Big Value Popular Soaps
Perfumed toilet and bath soaps that lather freely. Made by the makers of Palm Olive. Large size cakes. Shipping wt., twelve cakes, 2½ lbs.; six cakes, 1½ lbs.
8K4991—Box of 12 cakes, assorted 45c

Tar.	Box of 6 cakes 8K4953	
Mottled Coco.	Box of 6 cakes 8K4968	23c
Pumice.	Box of 6 cakes 8K4992	Per Box of
Transparent.	Box of 6 cakes 8K4944	6 Cakes
White Floating.	Box of 6 cakes 8K4917	

Quality Castile Soaps
These soaps are made of pure imported olive oil. We believe that there is no finer quality castile soap sold anywhere. Leaves the skin refreshingly clean. Fine for the complexion, for baby's tender skin, and general toilet use. Extra large cakes.
- **My Baby's** — Handy oblong cakes for baby's bath. Shpg. wt., 1 lb. 8K4997 3 cakes for 47c
- **Our Own** — Square cakes for general use. Shpg. wt., 1 lb. 8K4994 3 cakes for 39c

Conti Castile
Well known, imported, pure castile soap. Regular 25c size cakes. Shpg. wt., 2 lbs.
8K4950 Box of 4 cakes 79c

Advertised Toilet Soaps

Cashmere Bouquet	8K4906	Box 3 cakes.. 63c
Palm Olive	8K4912	12 cakes for 83c
Ivory Guest Size	8K4915	Box of 12 49c
Kirk's Hard Water	8K4946	6 cakes for 45c
Lifebuoy	8K4970	12 cakes for 79c
Woodbury's	8K4927	Box of 3 cakes 59c
Cuticura	8K4903	Box of 3 cakes 59c
Resinol	8K4928	Box of 3 cakes 59c
Packer's Tar	8K4954	Box of 3 cakes 59c
Antoinette Donnelly	8K4900	Box of 3 cakes 57c
Jap Rose	8K4983	12 cakes for 89c
Cologne Bouquet	8K4945	Box of 3 cakes 25c

Shaving Creams

Kolax Cream
For quick shave. No brush necessary. Simply spread over face and shave. Easily applied and very effective. (Extra large double size tube.) Shpg. wt., 8 oz. In Tubes
8K4957 27c
Economical Size One-half pound jar. Shpg. wt., 1½ lbs.
8K4958 ....39c

Advertised Shaving Creams
- Ingram's 8K4934 39c
- Palm Olive 8K4935 27c
- Mennen's 8K4960 39c
- Williams' 8K4940 39c
- Colgate's 8K4904 29c

Shpg. wt., creams, each, 8 oz.

POPULAR SHAVING NEEDS

39c — Velvo Shaving Cream

Velvo Cream With Bay Rum
Try a Tube on Our Recommendation

A distinctive shaving cream known for its smooth, velvety softness. Lathers freely and abundantly. A shaving cream, containing just enough bay rum to be delightfully cooling and refreshing. Extra large double size tube. 50c size. Shipping weight, 8 ounces.
8K4902 — Smooth as Velvet 39c

Shaving Sticks
- Colgate's 8K4910 ..... 29c
- Williams' 8K4913 ..... 29c

Shpg. wt., each 6 oz.

Styptic Pencil — Quickly stops bleeding. Shipping weight, 2 ounces. 8K4905—Pkg. of 3 sticks 10c

Bars
- Colgate's 1 lb. (8 cakes) 8K4925 49c
- Williams' 1 lb. (6 cakes.) 8K4919 48c — Shipping weight, 1¼ lbs.

Shaving Lotions

Imported Bay Rum
A very fine quality. Shpg. wt., 1¼ lbs. 8K3466—8-oz... 39c

Lilac Vegetal
Shpg. wt., 1¼ lbs. 8K3401—6-oz... 48c

Colgate's Lilac Imperial
Shpg. wt., 1½ lbs. 8K3413—7-oz... 89c

Pinaud's Lilac Vegetal
Shpg. wt., 1¼ lbs. 8K3410—6-oz... 98c

Eau de Coty (Cologne)
$1.00 size. Shpg. wt., 1 lb. 8K3452... 89c

Melba Lilac Vegetal
75c size. Shpg. wt., 1½ lbs. 8K3453... 63c

Mennen's Talc for Men
8K3064—Shpg. wt., 7 oz... 19c

For Razors and Shaving Brushes, See Page 527

We Guarantee to Satisfy You and Save You Money

Best Quality Elastic Stockings Seamless

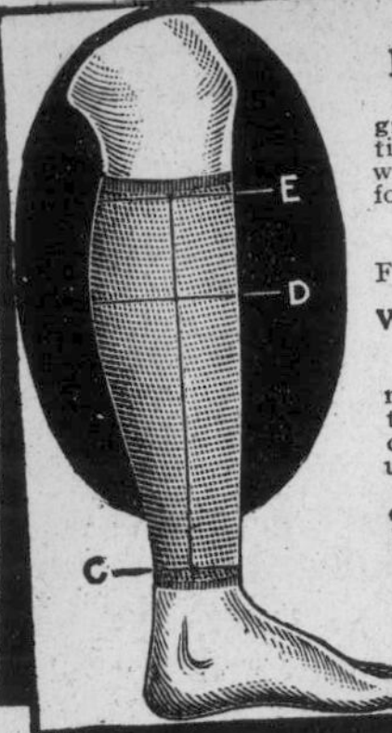

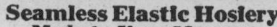

Garter Leggings

Made to your measure from best grade elastic webbing. Prices on elastics vary depending upon the quality; we sell only the best. Prices shown are for single legging.

Seamless Leggings

8K3639⅓—Silk Woven. Flesh color only............ **$3.79**
8K3629⅓—Cotton Woven. Cream color...... **2.98**

Seamed Leggings

A less expensive elastic garment, machine made, of cotton covered elastic webbing with seam at back. Especially recommended for temporary use.
8K3631—Flesh color only................................ **97c**

How to Measure for a Legging

With a tapeline measure around leg at C, D and E; also distance C to E on vertical line. Give exact measurements. **State if for right or left leg.** Average length of legging, 12 inches. Shipping wt., 4 oz.

Seamless Elastic Hosiery
Made to Your Measure

We sell the best quality seamless elastics at prices you have been paying for those made with seams. Seamless elastics have an even support at all points, giving correct pressure where needed most. For this reason they are especially adapted to the relief of varicose veins, weak, ulcerated, swollen or sprained limbs. Seamless elastics fit better, are more comfortable and are less noticeable on the leg than those with seams.

All Seamless Elastics shipped from factory in Massachusetts.
Seamed Elastics shipped from factory in Northeastern Illinois.

Important Notice

All articles on this page where lettered measurements are requested, are specials and require from six to ten days to make, depending upon the item.

Elastic stockings can be readily cleaned with any good cleaning fluid or with lukewarm water and castile soap. Rinse only, do not wring out water. Let stocking dry slowly, away from fire or radiator.

How to Measure

All measurements should be taken with leg in position illustrated, and in the morning before the limbs have had an opportunity to swell. It is advisable whenever possible to have someone else take your measurements, as they can probably get them more exact. We allow for stretching so give exact measurements. Be very careful to have your measurements correct, as when elastics are once made according to special size we cannot accept their return. Prices shown on elastics are for one garment only. If a pair is desired send double amount. **State whether for right or left leg.** If possible consult a physician before ordering.

Garter Stockings

Our seamless stockings are made to fit your own particular case. The tension throughout all seamless garments is designed to exert the proper pressure where most needed. It pays to buy quality merchandise.

Seamless Stocking

8K3638⅓—Silk Woven. Flesh color only.......... **$5.98**
8K3618⅓—Cotton Woven. Cream color.......... **3.98**

Seamed Stocking

A machine made stocking, with seam at back. Made of cotton covered elastic webbing. Ideal for temporary use.
8K3630½—Flesh color only................................**$2.25**

How to Measure for a Garter Stocking

Measure around the leg and foot at A, B, C, D and E; also distance from floor to E on vertical line. Give exact measurements. **State if for right or left leg.** Shpg. wt., 7 oz.

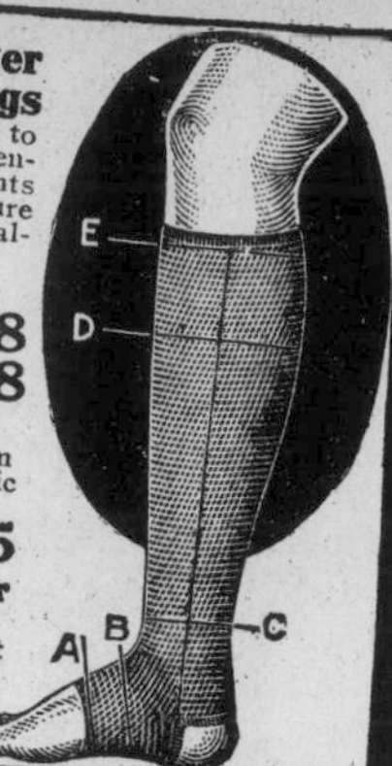

Seamless Thigh Stocking
Silk Woven. Flesh Color Only

Made to measure from the best quality covered elastic. Carefully woven.
8K3632⅓................................ **$10.98**

How to Measure for Thigh Stocking

With a tapeline measure around leg and foot at A, B, C, D, E, F, G, H and I; also distance separately from floor to F and from F to I on vertical line indicated by arrow. Distance from F to I should not be more than 10 inches. **State if for right or left leg.** Shipping weight, 1 pound.

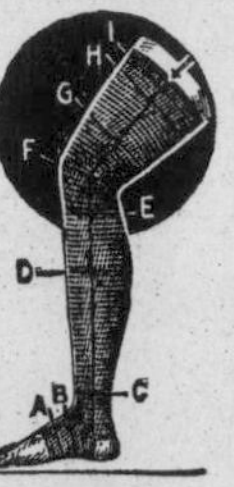

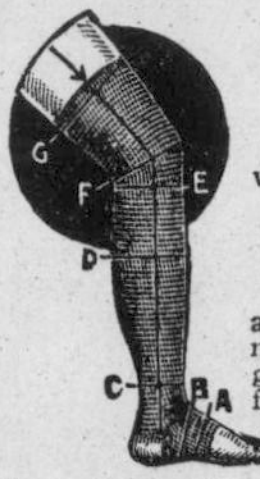

Seamless Knee Stocking
Silk Woven. Flesh Color Only

Made to measure from good quality elastic webbing. Carefully woven.
8K3635⅓................................ **$7.98**

How to Measure for Knee Stocking

With a tapeline measure around leg and foot at A, B, C, D, E, F and G (take G measurement about 4 inches above the knee); also give the distance separately from floor to F and from F to G on vertical line indicated by arrow. **State if for right or left leg.** Shipping weight, 8 ounces.

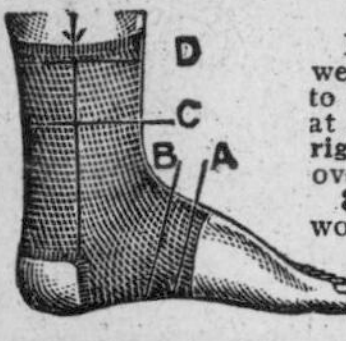

Cotton Woven Anklet

For athletes or anyone with weak or sprained ankles. Made to measure. Measure around foot at A, B, C and D and **state if for right or left foot.** Height, not over 8 in. Shpg. wt., 3 oz.
8K3634⅓—Seamless (hand woven). Cream color only.............. **$2.59**
8K3626—Seamed (machine made). Flesh color.............. **59c**

Elastic Bandages Carried in Stock

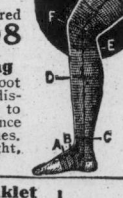

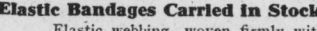

Elastic webbing, woven firmly with soft cotton thread, making a bandage that is light, strong and porous. Especially good for preventing swelling in the leg caused by varicose veins. May be used for support about other parts of the body. Used by athletes after a strain. Will not shift out of position. Shipping weight, 4 ounces.
8K3623—2½ in. wide; length, stretched, 15 feet..... **59c**
8K3625—3 in. wide; length, stretched, 15 feet..... **69c**

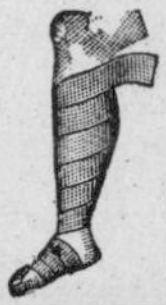

Cotton Woven Knee Cap

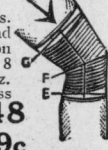

For weak or swollen knees. Measure around leg at G, F and E. The distance from G to E on line shown by arrow is about 8 inches. Shipping weight, 3 oz.
8K3637⅓—Quality seamless (hand woven). Cream color.............. **$2.48**
8K3627—Seamed (machine made). Flesh color.......... **59c**

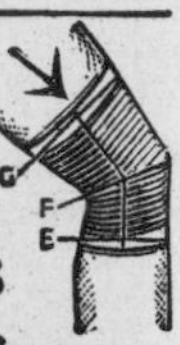

Arch Supports

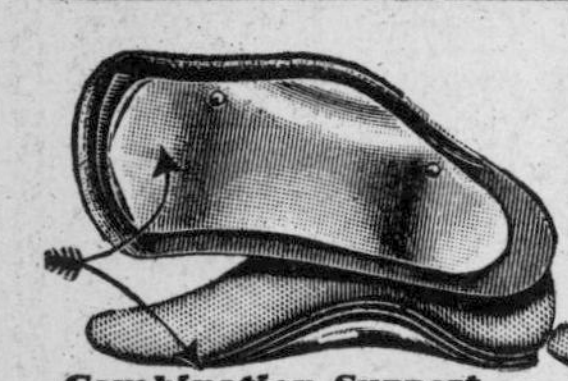

Combination Support

Especially designed to raise the bones slightly and relieve the ligaments causing metatarsalgia or Morton's toe (sharp pains under the ball of the foot, generally accompanied with callouses). Genuine nickel plate with grain leather top. See "How to Order."
8K2701
Per pair.......... **$2.98**

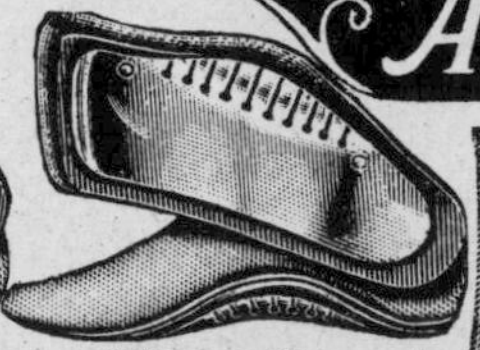

"Harvard" Arch Support

Reinforced, light weight support. The metal plate is made from non-rusting nickel silver, reinforced to give additional support. Smooth grain leather top. See "How to Order."
8K2702
Per pair....... **$1.39**

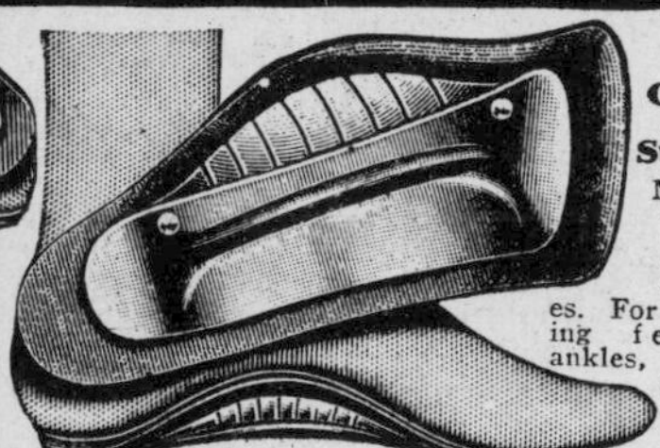

Cooper Arch Support

Made to relieve broken down or fallen arches. For tired, aching feet, weak ankles, pains up and down the legs and callouses brought about by fallen arches. Gradually raises and strengthens the arch. Made of grain leather and nickel silver plates. See "How to Order."
8K2708—Per pair........................... **$1.89**

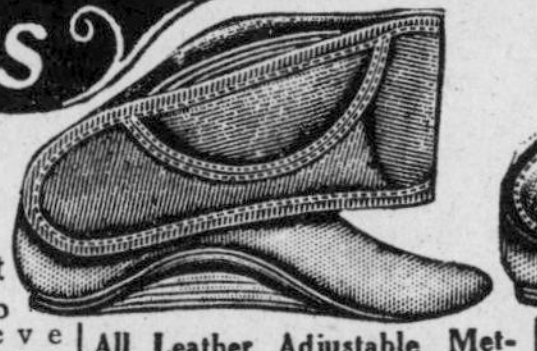

All Leather Adjustable Metatarsal and Arch Support

No metal, light weight, easy to adjust and comfortable to wear. The adjustable feature is simple and enables one to raise or lower the arch correction to the comfort of the wearer. Good quality grain leather. See "How to Order."
8K2729
Per pair....... **$1.39**

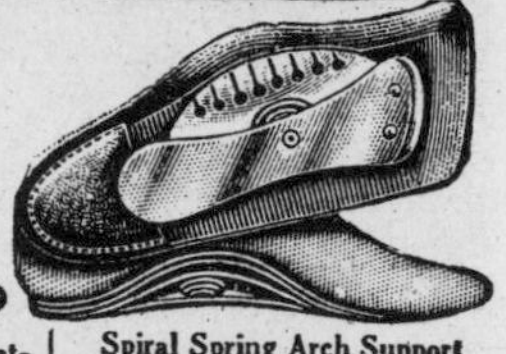

Spiral Spring Arch Support

Especially designed for heavy people. Two strong non-rusting nickel silver plates, separated by a heavy spring. As you walk the spring expands and contracts with the weight of the body, giving elasticity to the support. It has also a cushion under the heel. Wear one and enjoy that "walking on air" feeling. See "How to Order."
8K2703—Pair **$2.39**

Walter's Liquid Corn Remover

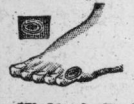

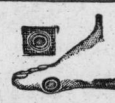

Throw away your corn knives and razors. Use the safe, easy way and avoid bleeding feet. One trial will convince you. A few drops applied to the corn four or five nights, a good soaking and the corn may be removed, roots and all. Shpg. wt., 7 oz.
8K2760—Per bottle... **19c**

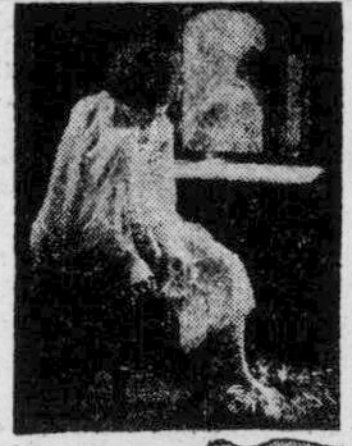

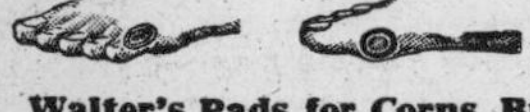

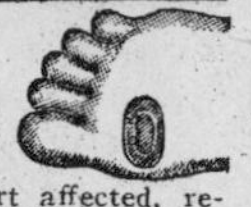

Walter's Pads for Corns, Bunions and Callouses

The pad is placed directly over the part affected, removing the immediate pressure, affording relief in a short time. Simple and efficient. The tremendous sale of these pads proves their worth. Shipping weight, 2 ounces.

For Corns	For Bunions	For Callouses
8K2761 12 pads.. **25c**	8K2762 6 pads.... **25c**	8K2763 6 pads.... **25c**

Fisher Bunion Protector

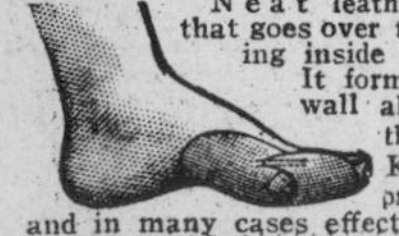

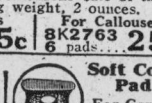

Neat leather device that goes over the stocking inside the shoe. It forms a firm wall all around the bunion. Keeps it protected and in many cases effects a cure. Shipping weight, 4 ounces.
Women's Size Only.
8K2720—Right........ **67c**
8K2721—Left......... **67c**

Soft Corn Pad
For Corns Between the Toes

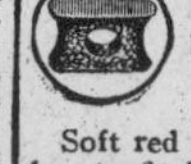

Soft red sponge rubber to fit between the toes. Hole allows for corn, thus relieving the pressure. Shipping wt., 1 oz.
8K2773... **17c**

How to Order Foot Supplies

Place your foot on a piece of paper and with a pencil held perfectly upright draw the outline of each foot. Mail us the drawing with your order. **State size of shoe and if for man or woman.**

How to Wear Arch Supports

Your arches will gradually conform to the shape of the support, but until the bones resume their normal, healthy position, you may suffer a little soreness. Wear supports an hour or so the first day, gradually increasing the time each day. After a week your feet should be free from soreness. We suggest for pains of any kind in your feet you first consult your physician. Shpg. wt., Arch Supports, ¾ lb.

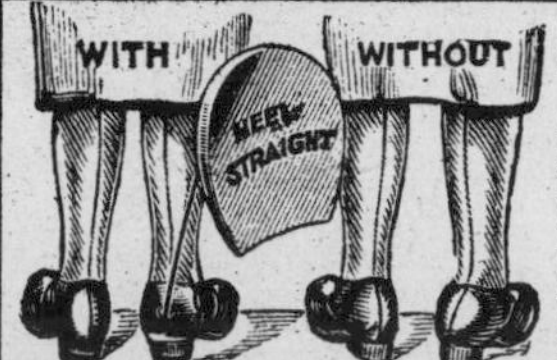

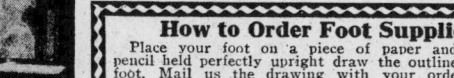

Keep Your Heels Straight

Worn inside shoe. Levels foot and prevents heels wearing down on side. **State whether for man or woman and size of shoe.** Shipping wt., 2 oz.
8K2759
Per pair... **19c**

Toe Spreader
For Bunions or Overlapping Toes

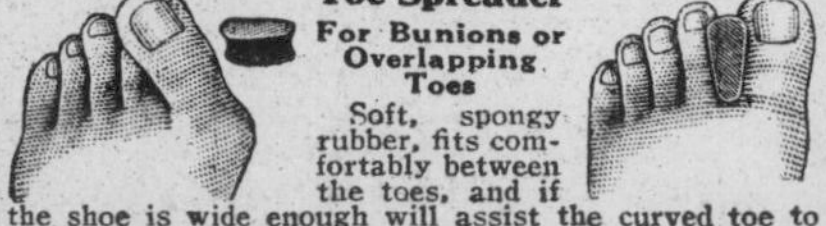

Soft, spongy rubber, fits comfortably between the toes, and if the shoe is wide enough will assist the curved toe to its natural position. Shipping wt., 1 oz.
8K2770—Each......................... **16c**

Ankle Supports

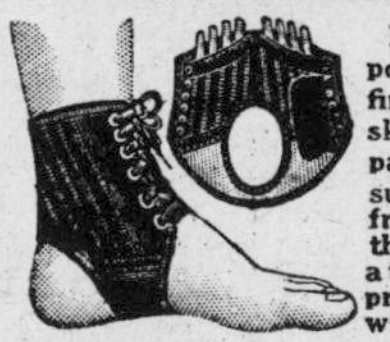

NOTE—These supports are made from first grade sheepskin. Do not compare with inferior supports made from split leathers offered at lower prices. Shpg. wt., 6 oz.

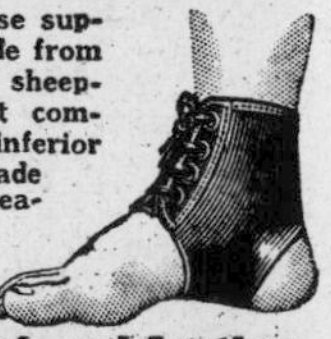

Adjustable Support

Reinforced with removable stays over both sides of ankles, giving extra strength. Any one stay can be removed to ease pressure at any point. **Give size shoe worn.**
8K2780 — For men. Sizes, 6 to 10. Per pair......... **$1.29**
8K2781 — For women and boys. Sizes, 2 to 7. Per pair. **$1.29**

Reinforced Leather

Fits ankle perfectly and has no seams at back to chafe or bind. Good quality. Not made in children's sizes. **Mention size shoe you wear.**
8K2787 — For men. Sizes 6 to 10 shoe. Per pair..... **98c**
8K2788 — For women and boys. Sizes, 2 to 7 shoe. Per pair..... **98c**

Dr. Simm's Ankle and Arch Support

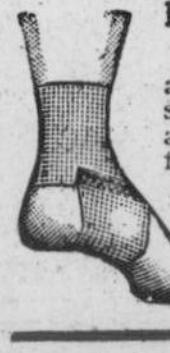

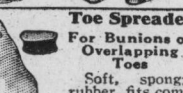

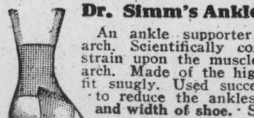

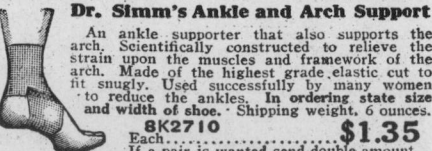

An ankle supporter that also supports the arch. Scientifically constructed to relieve the strain upon the muscles and framework of the arch. Made of the highest grade elastic cut to fit snugly. Used successfully by many women to reduce the ankles. **In ordering state size and width of shoe.** Shipping weight, 6 ounces.
8K2710
Each.......................... **$1.35**
If a pair is wanted send double amount.

Spring Trusses

Our Best Scrotal Truss

For regular or scrotal rupture. Strong steel spring easily adjusted to the shape of the body. Spring padded on side next to body and covered with double stitched, with roll at edges. Soft velvo pad, leather covered with soft cloth understraps. **State size and side wanted.** Shipping weight, 1¼ pounds.

8K3541—Single. Even sizes, 32 to 42 .... **$4.89**

8K3543—Double. Even sizes, 34 to 38 inches. **7.98**

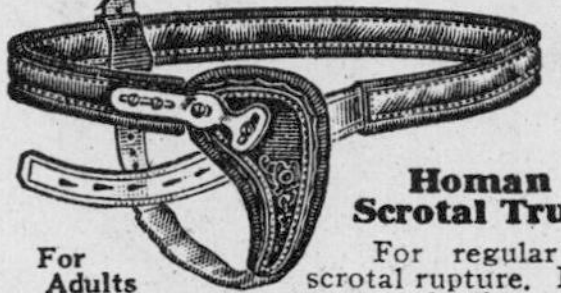

Homan Scrotal Truss

For Adults and Children

For regular or scrotal rupture. Has strong leather covered spring, adjustable, soft velvo pad and soft cloth understrap. Single only, sizes 30 to 40, carried in stock. Sizes under 30 shipped from factory require about 10 days' time. **State size and side wanted.** Shipping weight, 1 pound.

8K3568 .... **$3.67**

Chase Style Spring Truss

Leather covered soft composition pad fitted with patent ball socket. Adjustable to left or right side. Strong spring padded and covered, with soft leather. Even sizes, 32 to 42. **State size.** Shipping weight, 1¼ pounds.

8K3545 Single **$3.67** | **8K3546** Double **$4.95**

French Style Improved Truss

An exceptionally good truss for ordinary rupture. Has strong springs, padded on the inside and covered with fine, soft leather, with rolled edges. Adjustable composition pad, no understraps. Single only. Sizes 32 to 42. **State size and side.** **$2.79**

8K3562—Shipping weight, 1 pound.

Rubber Covered Spring Truss

Strong steel springs covered with rubber tube. Two black enameled hard rubber discs in back. Even sizes, 34 to 38 inches. **State size and side wanted.** Shpg. wt., 1½ lbs.

Single — One leather covered soft front pad and one hard rubber blind front pad. **$4.98**

Double — With two leather covered soft velvo front pads. **8K3588** .... / **8K3589** **$5.47**

Hood's Truss

Leather covered strong springs. Fitted with soft leather covered composition pads. Even sizes, 32 to 38 inches. **State size and side.** Shipping weight, 1¼ pounds.

8K3548 Single **$3.89** | **8K3549** Double **$4.69**

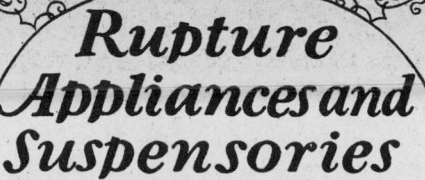

Rupture Appliances and Suspensories

Non-Slip Rubber Pad Trusses

Used for Scrotal as Well as Ordinary Ruptures

We offer you our most popular style spring or elastic truss with a pad that will not slip. This washable pad has a red corrugated rubber cover, with a spongy rubber center. It can easily be adjusted to give the support where needed, and will keep its position, holding rupture firmly in place. The understrap is partly covered with rubber tube, which tends to eliminate much of the chafing often caused by understraps. We have either spring or elastic belt. All metal fittings nickel plated. Both trusses exceptionally well made throughout. Sizes 32 to 42. **State size wanted and side on which rupture is located.** Shipping weight, 1¼ pounds.

Spring Truss — With non-slip pad. Spring padded and covered with soft fine quality leather with wide roll edges. **8K3542** **$5.67**

Elastic Truss — With non-slip pad. Fine quality elastic webbing belt, easily adjusted. **8K3529** **$3.98**

How to Measure for a Truss

Take measurement around body on line with rupture, holding the tape line snugly, 1 inch below hip joints. The truss to fit correctly should fit snugly around body slightly above the fleshy part of the buttock. **Carried in even sizes only.**

NOTE—Consult a physician before ordering a truss, to be sure you obtain the correct style.

Leeland Elastic Truss

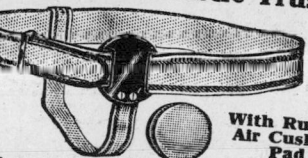

With Rubber Air Cushion Pad

Here Are Some Reasons Why This Truss Has Always Been so Popular

It can be worn by many people who will not wear ordinary spring or elastic trusses. The air cushion pad clings to the body and can easily be adjusted to the desired position and, when once set, the pad will stay firmly in place without disity comfort. Belt and understrap made of good quality elastic webbing. It can be worn without being noticed through the clothing. When once adjusted it can be worn at work or at play without having to be readjusted. We recommend the rupture appliance and feel sure it will give satisfaction, as it is easily adjusted, comfortable to wear and a very popular truss. Sold in single and double. We carry these trusses in stock in nine sizes from 30 to 42 inches, and therefore are prepared to fill any orders promptly. **State size and side.** Shipping weight, ¾ pound.

8K3503 Single .... **$2.98** | **8K3504** Double **$3.98**

High Grade Suspensories

Adjustable for All Sizes

Shipping Weight, Each, 3 ounces.

J. P. Style

Requires no understraps to hold pouch in place. The edge of pouch is elastic, providing comfortable adjustment. Sack is made of silk and mercerized cotton, close mesh.

8K3768 .... **39c**

Army and Navy Style

Light, strong and made to fit. Easily washed.

8K3761—Cotton thread sack, elastic understrap **39c**

8K3762—Good open mesh, elastic bands **69c**

8K3764—Fine light weight, extra quality silk sack, with elastic bands **98c**

Our Best Suspensory

Light, clean, durable. Open mesh sack is made of fine quality heavy silk, nicely finished. Cool and comfortable. Easily washed.

8K3774 .... **$1.39**

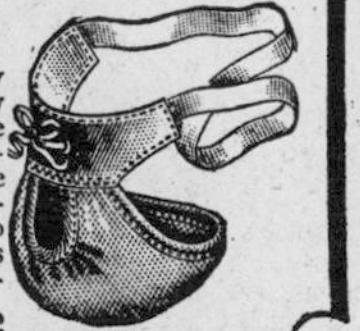

Draw String Suspensory

A satisfactory style, the draw string taking the place of understraps. Good grade cotton sack. Easily washed, no elastic in bands and very serviceable.

8K3753 .... **39c**

Athletic Elastic Supporters

Improved Chicago Snap Front

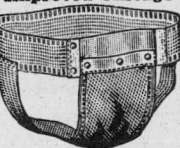

Can be put on without removal of garments. Snap fasteners for securing sack and waistband opening. Elastic web waistband and understraps; open mesh sanitary cotton linen front. May be washed in warm water without injury. Medium and large sizes. **State size.** Shpg. wt., 4 oz.

8K3607 .... **79c**

The Strap Supporter

Recommended for athletes and swimmers. Light, cool and comfortable. Fits well, no buckles or narrow bands to cause discomfort. Made of good quality elastic webbing. **State size.** Medium and large sizes. Shipping weight, 5 ounces.

8K3610 .... **39c**

For other Athletic Supporters, see Page 519.

Elastic Trusses

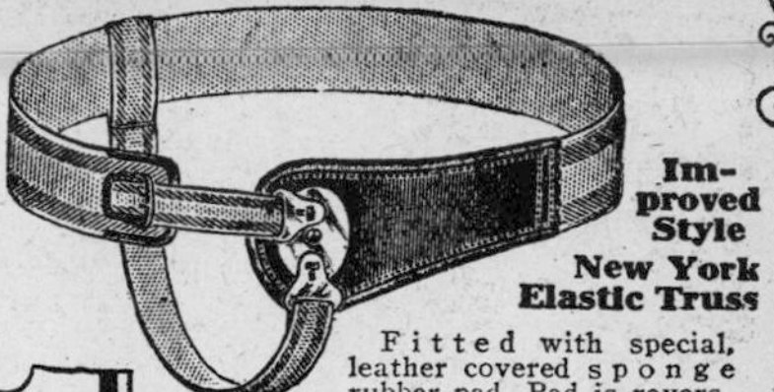

Improved Style New York Elastic Truss

Fitted with special leather covered sponge rubber pad. Pad is reversible for right or left side. Elastic web belt and understraps. Even sizes, 30 to 42 inches. **State size.** Shipping wt. 8 ounces.

8K3510 .... **$1.39**

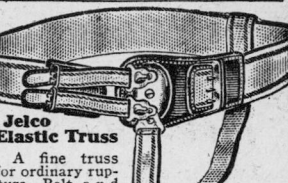

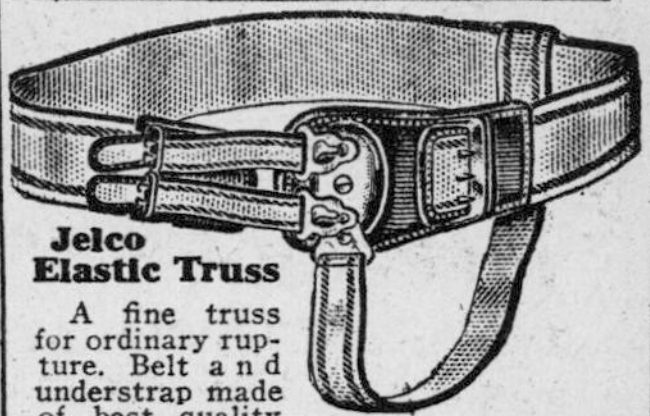

Jelco Elastic Truss

A fine truss for ordinary rupture. Belt and understrap made of best quality elastic webbing. Oval leather covered velvo hernia pad with slide buckle. Easily adjusted for either right or left side rupture. **State size wanted.** Shipping weight, ¾ pound.

Single—Even sizes, 30 to 42 in. **8K3501** **$2.79**

Double—Even sizes, 32 to 38 in. **8K3502** **$3.87**

Boston Elastic Truss

A good, low priced truss for ordinary rupture. Elastic webbing belt and understrap easily adjusted. Soft, leather covered velvo pad. Used for right or left side. Even sizes 30 to 42 inches. **State size.** Shipping weight, ¾ pound.

8K3514 .... **$1.75**

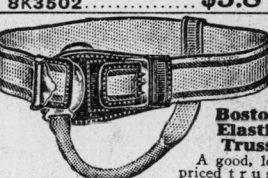

Lever Elastic Truss

Worn for either double or single rupture. The lever appliance affords extra support in case of severe rupture. Belt and understraps made of best quality elastic webbing, easily adjusted. Even sizes, 32 to 40 inches. **State size.** Shipping weight, 1 lb.

Black Enameled Hard Pads. **8K3525** **$3.35**

Leather Covered Soft Pads. **8K3526** **$3.79**

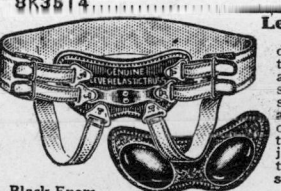

Elastic Scrotal Truss

For scrotal or ordinary rupture. Soft leather covered composition pad holds rupture in place. Belt and understrap made of fine quality elastic webbing. Even sizes, 32 to 40 inches. **State size and side on which rupture is located.** Shipping weight, ¾ pound.

8K3527 .... **$3.79**

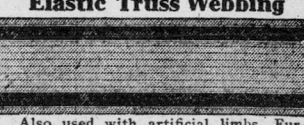

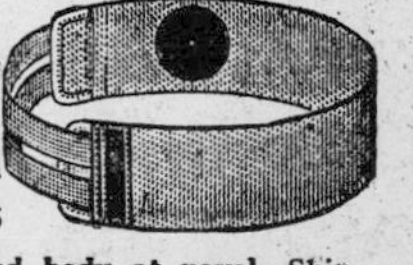

Umbilical Truss

For youths and infants. Elastic belt buckles at side. Polished hard rubber pad. Even sizes, 16 to 26 inches. Give size around body at navel. Shipping weight, 2 ounces.

8K3522 .... **$1.79**

Elastic Truss Webbing

Also used with artificial limbs. Furnished in any length desired. We sell the better grade truss webbing. Shipping weight, per yard, 3 ounces.

8K3530—Width, ¾ inch. Per yard	**17c**
8K3531—Width, 1 inch. Per yard	**21c**
8K3532—Width, 1¼ inches. Per yard	**35c**
8K3533—Width, 1¾ inches. Per yard	**45c**
8K3534—Width, 2 inches. Per yard	**55c**

For other Elastics See Page 255.

Abdominal Supporters, ~ Shoulder Braces ~ and Chamois Vests

Don't Be Round Shouldered

Quality Unlined Chamois Vest
For Men and Women

Fine quality white chamois. Warm, yet not bulky. Protects wearer from winds and cold. When ordering give chest or bust measurement, over or under clothing according to the way you intend wearing the vest. Even sizes, 32 to 46. State size. Shpg. wt., ¾ lb.

8K3793
For women............$3.98
8K3794—For men.....$3.98

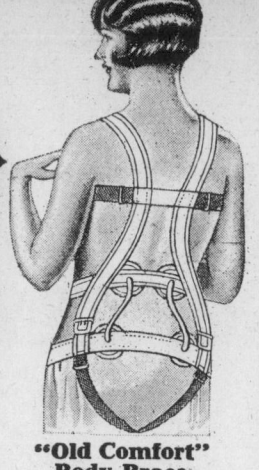

"Old Comfort" Body Brace

A combination shoulder brace and abdominal supporter. The shoulder straps and waist belt are elastic, but the hip belt and understraps are non-elastic. The nickel plated brass plates are large and comfortable. Extra set of understraps furnished. Even sizes, 30 to 46 inches only. State size around body 2 inches below top of hip bones. Shipping weight, 1¼ pounds.
8K3700.......$4.59

"Perfect Form" Brace
Made of extra strong white gabardine cloth with adjustable lacing. Keeps the shoulders, back and head erect; expands the lungs, compelling deep breathing. Can be worn without discomfort. Even sizes, 26 to 42 inches. State size. Shpg. wt., 8 oz.
8K3728.......$1.39

"Ideal" Brace
Permits deep, easy breathing. Straightens round shoulders, and expands the chest. Helps you to stand, sit and grow erect. Made of white strong twill. Easily washed. Even sizes, 24 to 42 inches. State size. Shipping weight, 8 ounces.
8K3730.......98c

Mesh Cloth Brace
Expands the chest—reduces the abdomen. Scientifically made of white ventilated open mesh linen cloth, the same as furnished in all high priced surgical garments. Strong, but lightweight, cool and comfortable in summer. Even sizes, 26 to 42 in. State size. Shpg. wt., 8 oz.
8K3736.......$1.79

NOTE—Have another person take your chest measure over the underwear, up under the arms." Carried in even sizes only. Corset laces in back easily adjusted. Held in place by belt which fastens by buckle in front. These shoulder braces can be worn by men, women and children.

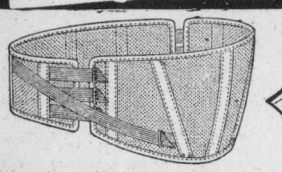

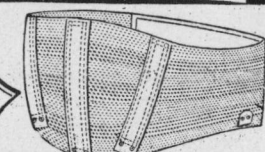

Walter's Linen Mesh Cloth Supporter for Men and Women
Made of fine quality woven open mesh white linen cloth, the same as generally used only in the highest priced surgical garments. Strong, light, cool and comfortable. Made to fit the form and support the abdomen. Reinforced with corset stays, covered with fine quality soft leather. Washable. Adjustable lift-up straps on each side give extra support. Sizes, 30 to 52 inches only; widths in proportion. See "How to Order," center of page. Shipping weight, ¾ pound.
8K3657.........................$2.98

"Higgins" Elastic Supporter
Popular style abdominal supporter for men and women. In many cases has helped reduce surplus fat. Made of good quality elastic webbing, fashioned to fit the form. Laces in back. Easily adjusted to fit. Women can wear it with or without corset. Has front leather covered corset stays for extra support. See "How to Order," center of page. The belt furnished will be slightly smaller, for we allow for stretching to give proper support. Shipping wt., 1 lb.
8K3698—Even sizes, 30 to 38 in. $2.67
8K3699—Even sizes, 40 to 52 inches. $2.98

How to Order
Abdominal supporters, to give most satisfactory results, must fit correctly. Great care should be taken to give correct measurements, at places indicated. If possible, it is better to have someone else take the measurements. The tape measure should be fitted snugly, neither too tight nor too loose. Take measurements as stated below and as shown on figure above. Be sure to include measurements, A. B. C., with your order as well as the size of belt you now wear. We will send you correct size, making full allowances for stretch of material, and reduction of abdomen.
A. Measure around body 1 inch below waistline where top of belt should be worn.
B. Measure around body just above hips and around largest part of abdomen.
C. Measure around the lowest part of abdomen, back at an angle over hips just above buttocks where bottom of belt should be worn.

"Front Clasp" Elastic Lift-Up Supporter
Excellent supporter for men and women. Can be removed without disturbing adjustment. Good quality mercerized elastic webbing. Has strong, pliable front corset stays, covered with fine leather. Lacing and lift-up strap adjustment on each side. See "How to Order," center of page. We allow for stretching. Shipping weight, 1 pound.
8K3681—Even sizes, 30 to 38 inches only............$4.98
8K3682—Even sizes, 40 to 50 inches only............$5.98

"Hoffman" Elastic Abdominal Supporter
Will Also Help in Reducing Surplus Fat
For men and women. Made of best quality elastic webbing. Fashioned to fit the form, making it more comfortable and practical. Laces in back. See "How to Order," center of page. Belt sent you will be smaller to allow for stretching to give proper, permanent support. Shipping weight, 8 ounces.
8K3658—Even sizes, 30 to 38 inches..............$1.97
8K3659—Even sizes, 40 to 52 inches..................$2.25

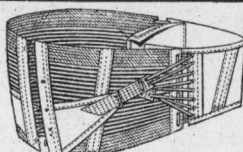
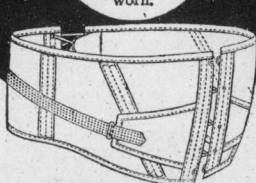
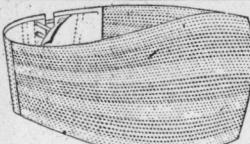

"Faust Understrap" Supporter
Our Best Non-Elastic Supporter
For men and women. Made of fine quality linen mesh cloth. Light, strong, cool and comfortable. Easily washed. Laces in back. Has corset stays covered with fine soft leather. Bottom at front and understrap padded with chamois. Even sizes, 30 to 50 inches. See "How to Order," center of page. Shipping weight, ¾ pound.
8K3694............$3.98

Wrap-Around Supporter
For Men and Women
Practical non-elastic abdominal lift-up supporter for everyday use. Exceptionally well suited for anyone desiring a low priced supporter for temporary or everyday use. Made of white twill cloth, which is washable. Easily adjusted. Even sizes, 30 to 52 inches. See "How to Order," center of page. Shipping wt., ¾ pound.
8K3666..........$1.59

"Front Clasp" Non-Elastic Supporter
For men and women. Made of fine quality white gabardine cloth. Comfortable to wear and is washable. Strong front clasps easily fastened. Reinforced with corset stays and lift-up straps. Laces in back. Even sizes, 30 to 52 inches. See "How to Order," center of page. Shipping weight, ¾ lb.
8K3651............$2.98

Moleskin Cloth Supporter
For Men and Women
Made of fine quality, soft moleskin cloth. Fits the form and supports the abdomen. Reinforced with leather covered corset stays, adjustable lift-up straps on each side. Fits well and is comfortable. Sizes, 30 to 52 inches See "How to Order," center of page. Shipping weight, ¾ pound.
8K3669............$2.59

Uterine Supporter
Supports the abdomen and aids in holding abdominal organs in place. Complete with rubber tubing understraps and hard rubber cup pessary. Even sizes, 28 to 48 inches only. See "How to Order," center of page. Shpg. wt., ¾ lb.

8K3660.........$2.25

Pessaries	Understraps
Shpg. wt., 4 oz.	Shpg. wt., 2 oz.
8K3674	8K3687
Each,	Per pair
44c	22c

Comfort and Health for Ba

Hand Decorated Baby Sets

Dainty designs, beautifully hand decorated in delicate shades of pink and blue combination. Suitable for either boy or girl. A splendid gift that is always appreciated. The brushes are of good size with soft hair to protect baby's tender scalp. The other pieces are of good weight, designed for satisfactory service. All articles are ivory color pyralin material. Attractive presentation card included in each set.

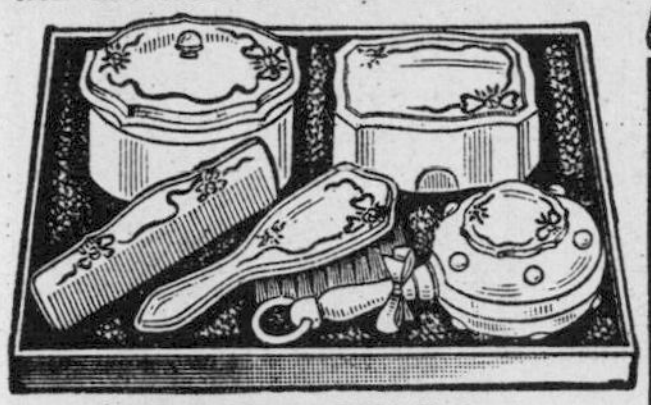

Our Best Gift Set

Five useful articles offered in an attractive cloth lined gift box. Comb, brush, rattle, soap box and powder box. Shipping weight, 1 pound.
8K2106.............. **$1.39**

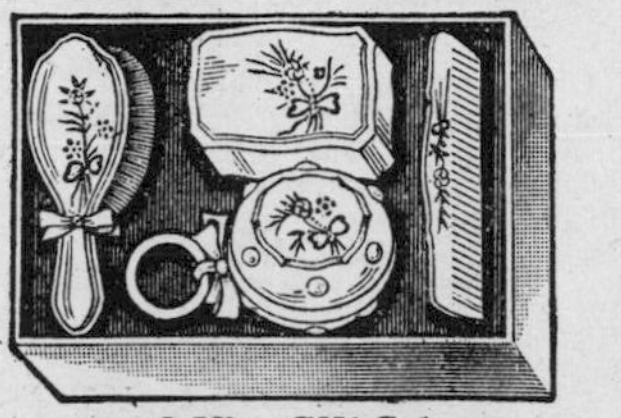

A Nice Gift Set

Comb, brush, rattle and soap box in an inexpensive gift box. Shipping weight, 8 ounces.
8K2109...................... **98c**

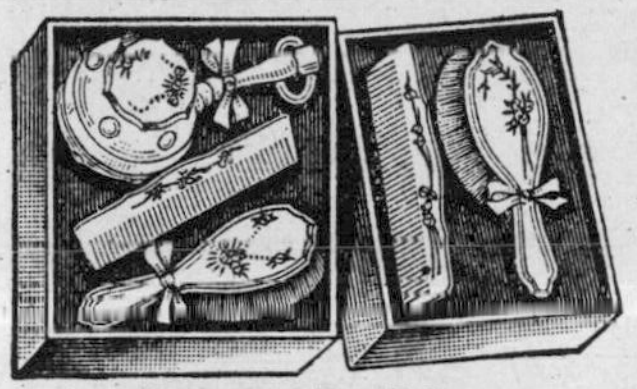

Inexpensive Sets

Comb, brush, and rattle in a display box. A very low price for this set. Shipping weight, 8 ounces.
8K2108. **67c**

A dainty comb and brush set. Would be an appreciated gift. Shipping weight, 3 oz.
8K2107. **45c**

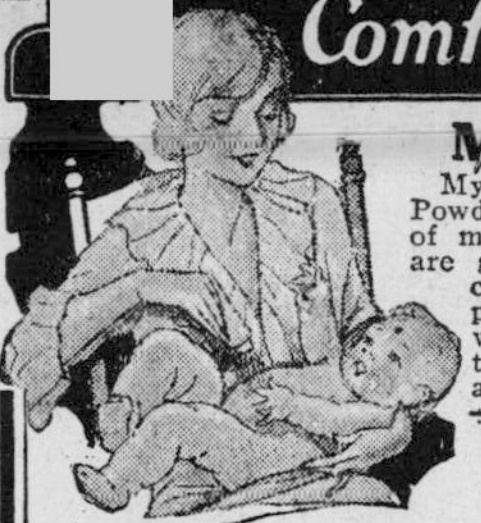

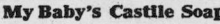

My Baby's Products

My Baby's Talcum, Medicated Dusting Powder and Castile Soap are the results of many tests to give you articles that are guaranteed absolutely pure and that can be used without fear. For the protection of your baby's tender skin, we do not hesitate to recommend these, My Baby's Products, as pure and harmless articles.

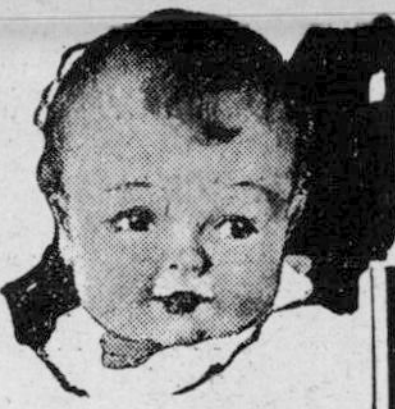

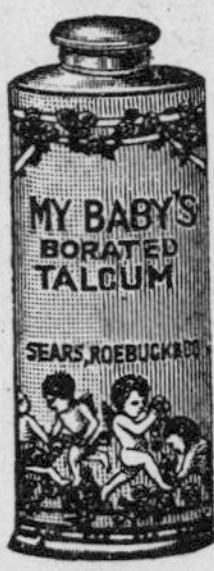

My Baby's Borated Talcum

Snow white, made from finest grade imported talcum powder. Delightfully perfumed, borated and with just the right quality of other ingredients to make it a soft, fluffy hygienic powder for toilet and nursery use. Shpg. wt., 7 oz.
8K3061—Per can **19c**

My Baby's Castile Soap

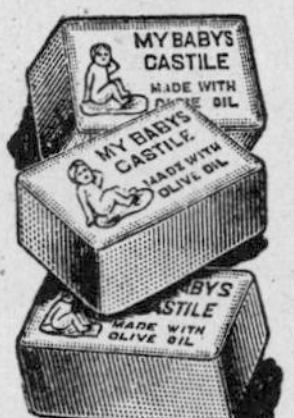

An exceptionally fine white castile soap. Made with pure imported olive oil. In our opinion the finest castile soap made for baby use. Will not chafe nor irritate. Large cakes. Shipping weight, three cakes, 1 pound.
8K4997
Pkg. of 3 cakes..... **47c**

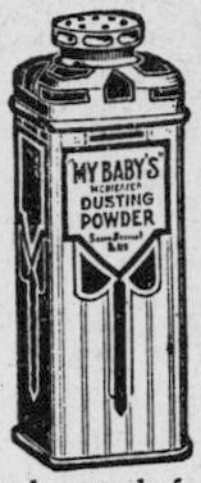

My Baby's Medicated Dusting Powder

Cooling, soothing and healing. Used as a preventive and also for general nursery uses as a relief for baby skin irritations, such as chafing, prickly heat, diaper and teething rash, etc. Contains no zinc stearate. Shpg. wt., 8 oz.
8K3059....... **39c**

Quality Sponges

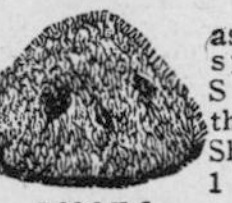

Known as silk sponges. Softer than cloth. Shpg. wt., 1 oz.
8K454
Large.......... **39c**

Other Talcum Powders

Mennen's Borated Talcum
Shipping wt., 1 lb.
8K2120—2 cans for. **39c**

Johnson and Johnson Baby Powder
Shipping wt., 8 oz.
8K2157—2 cans for. **39c**

Soap Box

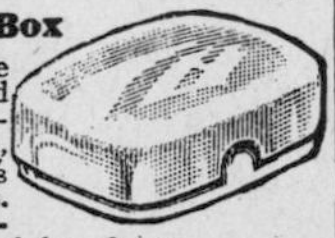

White grained celluloid, 2½ x 3⅝ inches. Shipping weight, 2 oz.
8K2240......... **19c**

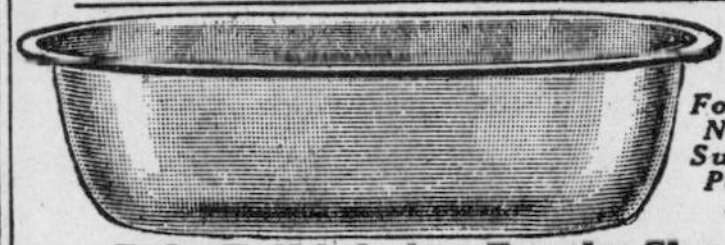

For Other Nursery Supplies see Pages 145 and 883

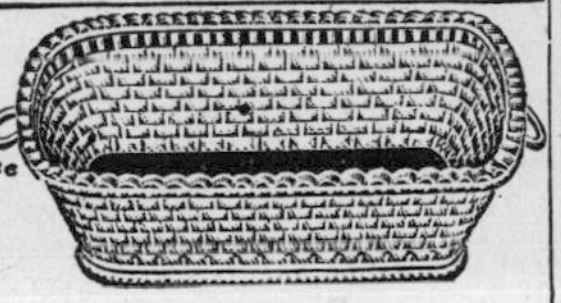

Baby Bathtubs in a Popular Size

It Pays to Buy a Good Tub

An extra large bathtub for baby. Oval. 17½x7 inches. Heavily coated with glistening white enamel, over steel. Blue trimmed. Rolled edge, leaving no sharp surface. Shipping weight, 10 pounds.
8K2167¼........................ **$3.69**

Oval Shape (Not Illustrated)

A popular size. White enamel with blue trim. Size, 20x15¾x5 inches. Shipping weight, 8½ pounds.
8K2168¼........................ **$1.98**

For Nursery Scales See Page 972

Baby Basket

Keep baby's bath requisites in one handy place. Straw chip and willow basket. Size, 16x13x4½ in. Shipping weight, 2¾ lbs.
8K2131.................. **98c**

For Bassinets, see page 881

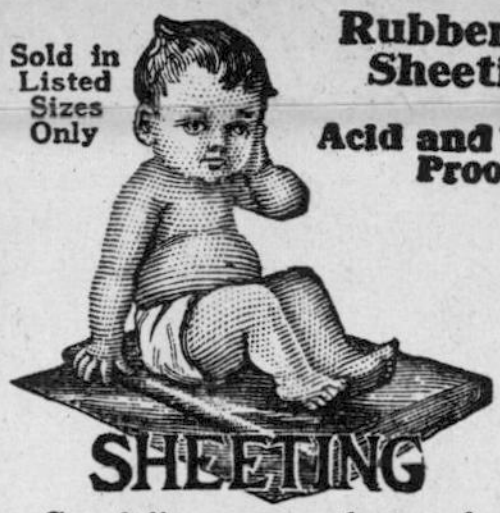

Sold in Listed Sizes Only

Rubberized Sheeting

Acid and Water Proof

Carefully cut so that ends do not fray and require hemming. We do not recommend the use of cheap sheeting, for it will not give satisfactory service. Here are two grades, both good quality. One a standard sheeting, the other a superior sheeting. We recommend the superior sheeting, which is steam cured and, though slightly higher in price, will more than make up the difference in durability and long service. Shipping weight, per square yard, ¾ pound.

Our Superior Sheeting Steam Cured

8K2610—27 inches square.......................... **59c**
8K2611—36 in. square..**$0.89**
8K2612—36x72 inches... **1.75**
8K2613—45 in. square... **1.59**
8K2614—54 in. square... **1.89**

Standard Sheeting

8K2621—36 in. square..... **59c**
8K2623—45 in. square..... **98c**

Soft All Rubber Sheeting

First quality all white color rubber sheets. These sheets are very popular, due to their softness and the fact that they are easily cleaned. (Not illustrated.) Shipping weight, per square yard, ¾ pound.
8K2616—36x36 inches.... **63c**
8K2617—36x45 inches...... **79c**

Pure Gum Crib Sheet

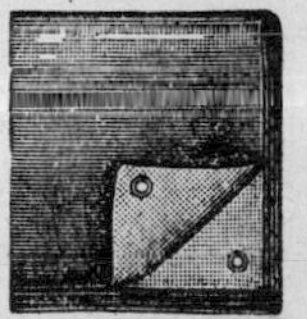

All rubber, yellow in color, can be washed without danger of spoiling. Does not wrinkle. May be put over or under regular sheet to protect mattress. Size, 27x36 inches. Shipping weight, ¾ pound.
8K2618... **59c**

For rubber sheeting by the yard, see page 194.

Baby Foods

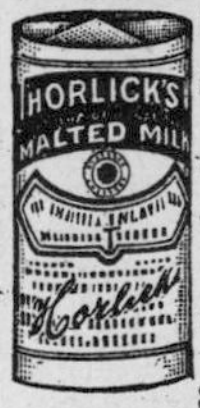

Horlick's Malted Milk

Hospital size, 5 pounds. Shpg. wt., 11 lbs.
8K2220...... **$2.98**
Large. Contents, 1 pound. Shpg. wt., 3¼ lbs.
8K2221.............. **79c**

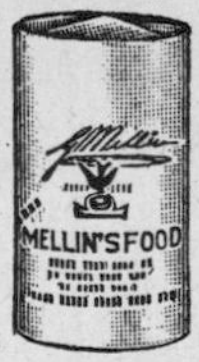

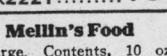

Mellin's Food

Large. Contents, 10 oz. Shpg. wt., 2¾ lbs.
8K2233.............. **65c**
Case of 12 bottles. Shpg. wt., 25 lbs.
8K2239¼... **$7.69**

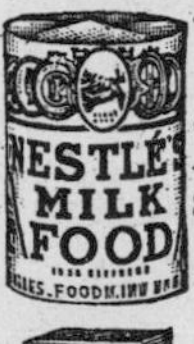

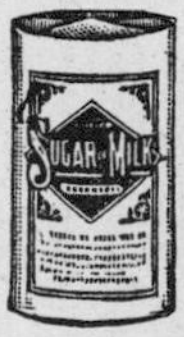

Nestle's Food

Hospital size, 4½ lbs. Shpg. wt., 6½ lbs.
8K2222........ **$2.87**

Sugar of Milk, U. S. P.

Mallinckrodt's, 1-lb. size. Shpg. wt., 1¾ lbs.
8K2232............ **55c**

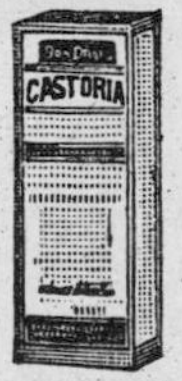

Dextri-Maltose

No. 1. 1-pound size.
8K2243—Shpg. wt., 1½ lbs.. **65c**
No. 3. 1-pound size.
8K2245—Shpg. wt., 1½ lbs.. **65c**

Fletcher's Castoria

Laxative for children. Shipping weight, 2 pounds.
8K55—2 bottles....... **59c**

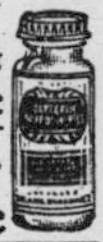

Glycerin Suppositories

One dozen to bottle. Infants' size. Shpg. wt., 8 oz.
8K196.................. **19c**

Breast Pump

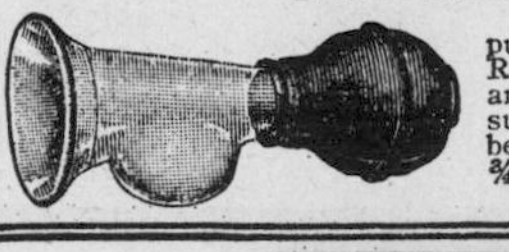

A popular style pump. Large size. Red rubber bulb guarantees steady, strong suction. Clear glass bell. Shipping weight, ¾ pound.
8K2466... **48c**

Birth Announcements

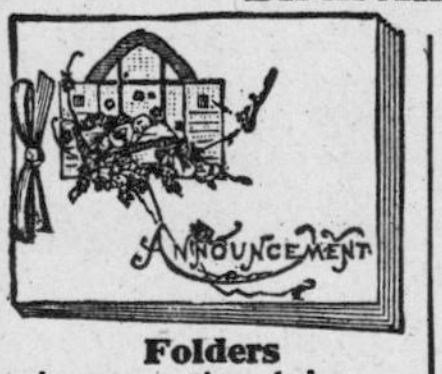

Folders

Announce the glad news. Assorted designs; combination pink or blue colorings, making them suitable for either boy or girl. Size, 4⅛x2⅞ inches. Envelopes for each. Shpg. wt., 2 oz.
8K2176
Pkg. of 6 folders... **39c**

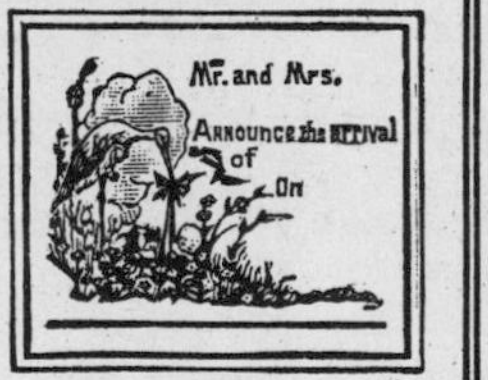

Cards

Tell them about your baby. When born, name, etc. All ready to be filled in. Genuine steel die engraved. Size, 3⅝x4⅛ in. Envelopes for each card. Shipping weight, 2 ounces.
8K2175—Package of 10 cards............ **25c**

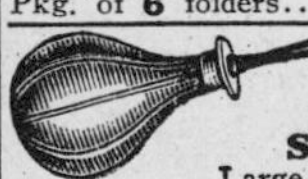

Large Infant Syringe

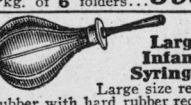

Large size red rubber with hard rubber rectal pipe. Capacity, 5 oz. Shpg. wt., 6 oz.
8K2114......... **39c**

Infant's Syringe

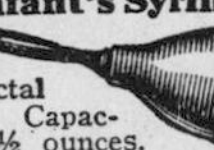

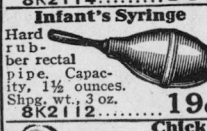

Hard rubber rectal pipe. Capacity, 1½ ounces. Shpg. wt., 3 oz.
8K2112......... **19c**

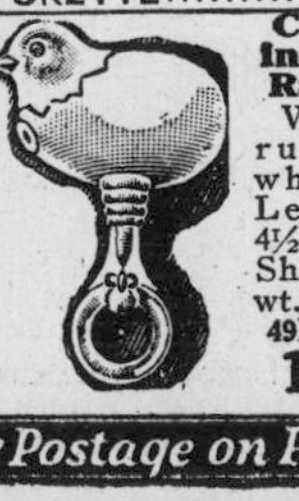

Chick in Egg Rattle

White rubber whistle. Length, 4½ in. Shipping wt., 3 oz.
49K4400
15c

Baby's Own Hot Water Bottle

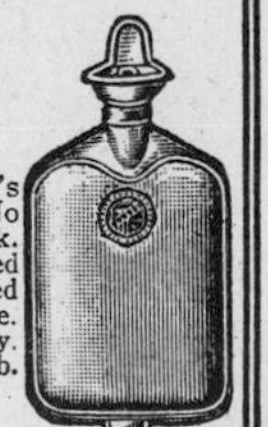

Keeps baby's crib warm. No seams to leak. Good grade red rubber. Also used as a face bottle. 1-pint capacity. Shpg. wt., ¾ lb.
8K2124
79c

Baby's Own Bank

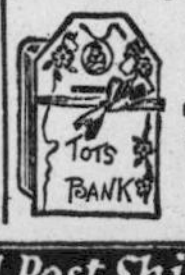

A splendid gift for the new baby. Heavy white ivory pyralin delicately hand decorated bank. Height, about 4 in. Shpg. wt., 4 oz.
8K2141. **49c**

Nursing Needs

Pyrex Nursing Bottles

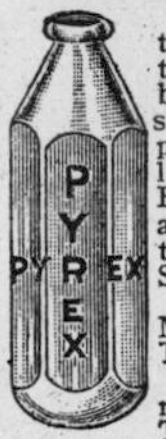

Boil them, keep them on ice, reheat them, they will not break. They are slightly higher in price, but they outlast all other types. Full 8-ounce, graduated, with flat sides to prevent rolling. Shpg. wt., 1¼ lbs.
8K2152—Wide Mouth Type....... **21c**
8K2154—Narrow Mouth Type....... **21c**

Hygeia Wide Mouth Nursing Bottles

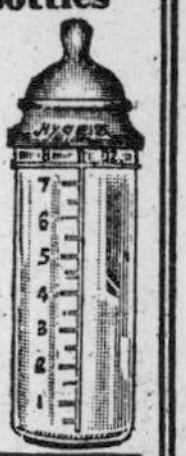

Hygeia Nurser
Complete 8 oz. size. Shpg. wt., 1¼ lbs.
8K2150
25c

Hygeia Breast Nipples
8K2153
Package of 2 for
25c
Shpg. wt., nipple, 2 oz.

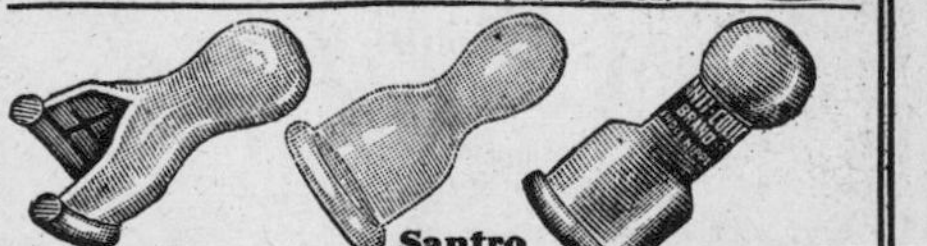

Feed-Rite
Red Rubber

The cross prevents nipple's collapsing. Shpg. wt., 2 oz.
8K2128
Package of 5..... **29c**

Santro
Transparent Rubber

The widely used transparent nipple. Standard for years. Household shape. Shpg. wt., 2 oz.
8K2125
Package of 3 for... **23c**

Anti-Colic
Black Rubber

Well known popular nipple. Pure gum. Shpg. wt., 2 oz.
8K2127
Package of 3 nipples. **17c**

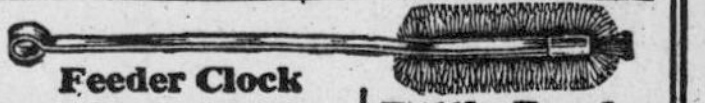

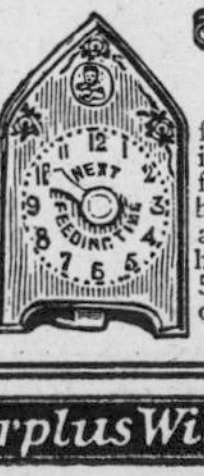

Feeder Clock

Indicates the time for baby's next feeding. Easel back clock face with movable hand. Grained green and white pyralin, hand decorated. Height, 5 inches. Shpg. wt., 4 ounces.
8K2140... **49c**

Bottle Brush

The tuft of stiff bristles on end cleans corners. Length, 11 inches. Shipping weight, 4 oz.
8K2123
10c

Trustworthy Rubber Goods

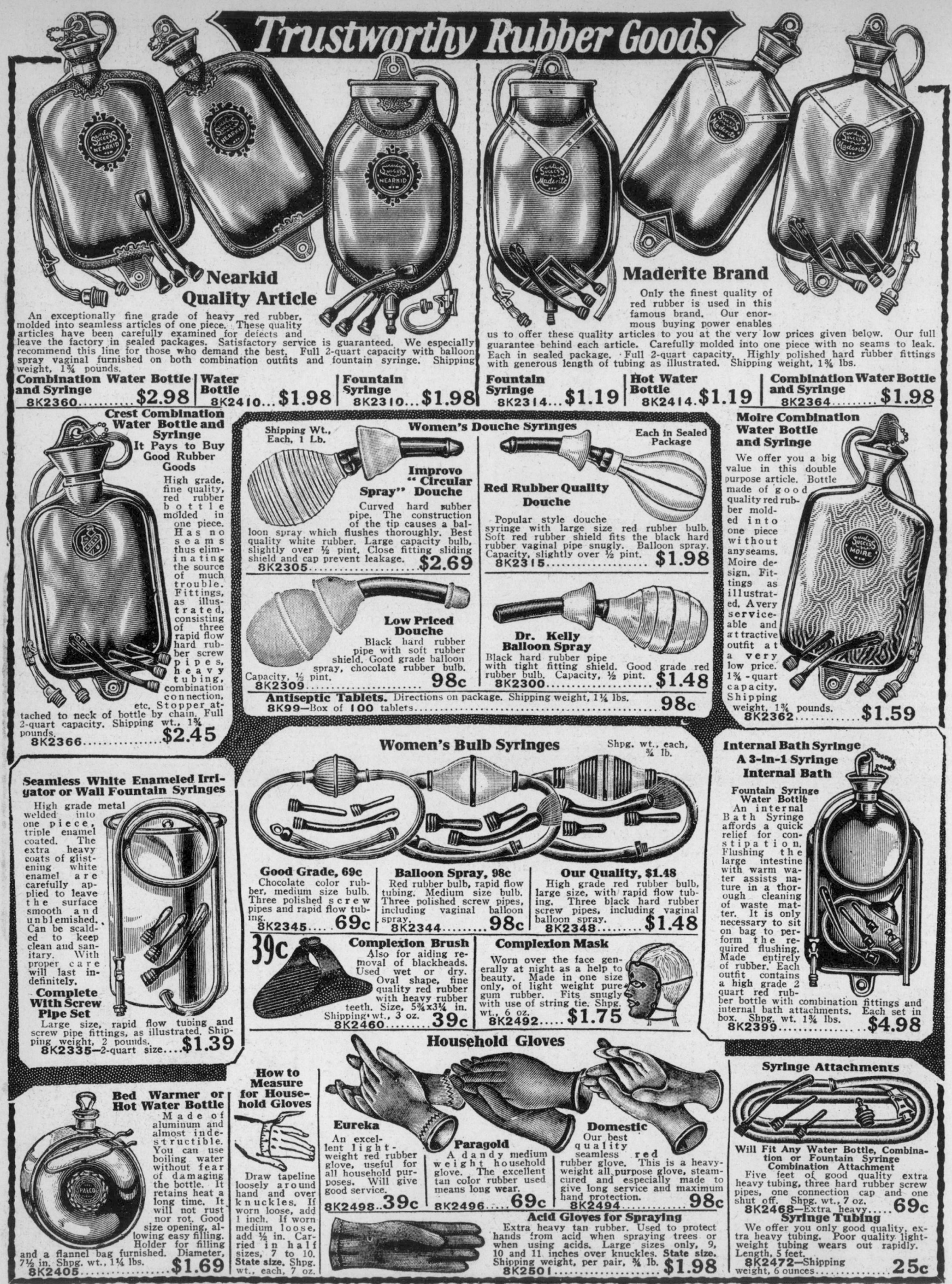

Nearkid Quality Article

An exceptionally fine grade of heavy red rubber, molded into seamless articles of one piece. These quality articles have been carefully examined for defects and leave the factory in sealed packages. Satisfactory service is guaranteed. We especially recommend this line for those who demand the best. Full 2-quart capacity with balloon spray vaginal furnished on both combination outfits and fountain syringe. Shipping weight, 1¾ pounds.

Combination Water Bottle and Syringe 8K2360 .... **$2.98**	**Water Bottle** 8K2410 ... **$1.98**	**Fountain Syringe** 8K2310 ... **$1.98**

Maderite Brand

Only the finest quality of red rubber is used in this famous brand. Our enormous buying power enables us to offer these quality articles to you at the very low prices given below. Our full guarantee behind each article. Carefully molded into one piece with no seams to leak. Each in sealed package. Full 2-quart capacity. Highly polished hard rubber fittings with generous length of tubing as illustrated. Shipping weight, 1¾ lbs.

Fountain Syringe 8K2314 ... **$1.19**	**Hot Water Bottle** 8K2414 ... **$1.19**	**Combination Water Bottle and Syringe** 8K2364 .... **$1.98**

Crest Combination Water Bottle and Syringe

It Pays to Buy Good Rubber Goods

High grade, fine quality, red rubber bottle molded in one piece. Has no seams thus eliminating the source of much trouble. Fittings, as illustrated, consisting of three rapid flow hard rubber screw pipes, heavy tubing, combination connection, etc. Stopper attached to neck of bottle by chain. Full 2-quart capacity. Shipping wt., 1¾ pounds.
8K2366 .... **$2.45**

Women's Douche Syringes

Shipping Wt., Each, 1 Lb.

Each in Sealed Package

Improvo "Circular Spray" Douche
Curved hard rubber pipe. The construction of the tip causes a balloon spray which flushes thoroughly. Best quality white rubber. Large capacity bulb, slightly over ½ pint. Close fitting sliding shield and cap prevent leakage.
8K2305 .... **$2.69**

Red Rubber Quality Douche
Popular style douche syringe with large size red rubber bulb. Soft red rubber shield fits the black hard rubber vaginal pipe snugly. Balloon spray. Capacity, slightly over ½ pint.
8K2315 .... **$1.98**

Low Priced Douche
Black hard rubber pipe with soft rubber shield. Good grade balloon spray, chocolate rubber bulb. Capacity, ½ pint.
8K2309 .... **98c**

Dr. Kelly Balloon Spray
Black hard rubber pipe with tight fitting shield. Good grade red rubber bulb. Capacity, ½ pint.
8K2300 .... **$1.48**

Antiseptic Tablets. Directions on package. Shipping weight, 1¼ lbs.
8K99—Box of 100 tablets. **98c**

Moire Combination Water Bottle and Syringe

We offer you a big value in this double purpose article. Bottle made of good quality red rubber molded into one piece without any seams. Moire design. Fittings as illustrated. A very serviceable and attractive outfit at a very low price. 1¾-quart capacity. Shipping weight, 1¾ pounds.
8K2362 .... **$1.59**

Seamless White Enameled Irrigator or Wall Fountain Syringes

High grade metal welded into one piece; triple enamel coated. The extra heavy coats of glistening white enamel are carefully applied to leave the surface smooth and unblemished. Can be scalded to keep clean and sanitary. With proper care will last indefinitely.

Complete With Screw Pipe Set
Large size, rapid flow tubing and screw pipe fittings, as illustrated. Shipping weight, 2 pounds.
8K2335—2-quart size **$1.39**

Women's Bulb Syringes

Shpg. wt., each, ¾ lb.

Good Grade, 69c
Chocolate color rubber, medium size bulb. Three polished screw pipes and rapid flow tubing.
8K2345 .... **69c**

Balloon Spray, 98c
Red rubber bulb, rapid flow tubing. Medium size bulb. Three polished screw pipes, including vaginal balloon spray.
8K2344 .... **98c**

Our Quality, $1.48
High grade red rubber bulb, large size, with rapid flow tubing. Three black hard rubber screw pipes, including vaginal balloon spray.
8K2348 .... **$1.48**

39c

Complexion Brush
Also for aiding removal of blackheads. Used wet or dry. Oval shape. Best quality red rubber with heavy rubber teeth. Size, 5⅝x3¼ in. Shipping wt., 3 oz.
8K2460 .... **39c**

Complexion Mask
Worn over the face generally at night as a help to beauty. Made in one size only, of light weight pure gum rubber. Fits snugly with use of string tie. Shpg. wt., 6 oz.
8K2492 ..... **$1.75**

Internal Bath Syringe
A 3-in-1 Syringe
Internal Bath

Fountain Syringe Water Bottle
An internal Bath Syringe affords a quick relief for constipation. Flushing the large intestine with warm water assists nature in a thorough cleaning of waste matter. It is only necessary to sit on bag to perform the required flushing. Made entirely of rubber. Each outfit contains a high grade 2 quart red rubber bottle with combination fittings and internal bath attachments. Each set in box. Shpg. wt. 1¾ lbs.
8K2399 .... **$4.98**

Bed Warmer or Hot Water Bottle

Made of aluminum and almost indestructible. You can use boiling water without fear of damaging the bottle. It retains heat a long time. It will not rust nor rot. Good size opening, allowing easy filling. Holder for filling and a flannel bag furnished. Diameter, 7½ in. Shpg. wt., 1¾ lbs.
8K2405 .... **$1.69**

How to Measure for Household Gloves

Draw tapeline loosely around hand and over knuckles. If worn loose, add 1 inch. If worn medium loose, add ½ in. Carried in half sizes, 7 to 10. State size. Shpg. wt., each, 7 oz.

Household Gloves

Eureka
An excellent light weight red rubber glove, useful for all household purposes. Will give good service.
8K2498 .... **39c**

Paragold
A dandy medium weight household glove. The excellent tan color rubber used means long wear.
8K2496 ..... **69c**

Domestic
Our best quality seamless red rubber glove. This is a heavy weight all purpose glove, steam-cured and especially made to give long service and maximum hand protection.
8K2494 ..... **98c**

Acid Gloves for Spraying
Extra heavy tan rubber. Used to protect hands from acid when spraying trees or when using acids. Large sizes only, 9, 10 and 11 inches over knuckles. State size. Shipping weight, per pair, ¾ lb.
8K2501 .... **$1.98**

Syringe Attachments

Will Fit Any Water Bottle, Combination or Fountain Syringe Combination Attachment
Five feet of good quality extra heavy tubing, three hard rubber screw pipes, one connection cap and one shut off. Shpg. wt., 7 oz.
8K2468—Extra heavy. **69c**

Syringe Tubing
We offer you only good quality, extra heavy tubing. Poor quality light-weight tubing wears out rapidly. Length, 5 feet.
8K2472—Shipping weight, 6 ounces. **25c**

DeVilbiss No. 16 Atomizer
Widely used by doctors. Adjustable for reaching upper or lower parts of nose and throat. Suitable for either oil or water. Nickel plated fittings. Complete with two bottles and special tip for nasal spraying.
8K2551—Shpg. wt., 1 lb. **$1.39**

Non-Spill Atomizer
Special locking device prevents leakage and evaporation and permits adjustment of spray to any volume desired. Suitable for oil and water. Easily cleaned. Nickel plated.
8K2555—Shpg. wt., 1 lb. **98c**

Air Cushions
For Invalids' Use or as a Seat Cushion
Will prevent bed sores for invalids; also adaptable as a restful cushion on chairs or boats. **16-In. Size**

All Rubber
A soft pliable air cushion for which there has been a great demand. Shipping wt., 1 lb.
8K2520 **$1.98**

Cloth Inserted
Red rubber, double coated on strong cloth with reinforced edges. Will withstand long, hard usage. Shpg. wt., 1 lb.
8K2522 **$2.35**

Formaldehyde Torch
For fumigation purposes about the home. One candle sufficient to thoroughly disinfect 700 cubic feet. Directions on package. Shipping wt., ¾ lb.
8K652 **33c**

Popular Cabinet for Taking Vapor or Turkish Baths
Chair Not Included

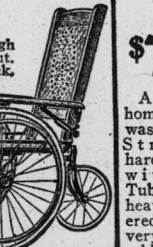

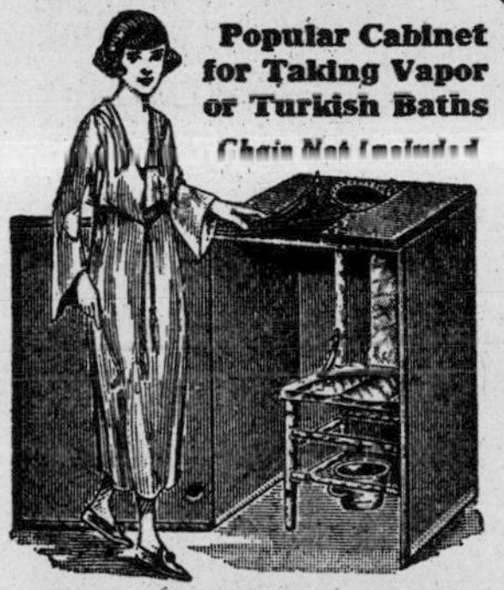

Turkish Bath Cabinet
Used to reduce weight; also very helpful in cleansing pores of skin. A quality cabinet of full steel support construction, covered with heavy waterproof black sheeting. Alcohol heater and vaporizer included. Heats quickly. Uses very little alcohol. Size, set up, 26⅝x29½x41 in. Folds compactly. Shipping weight, 22 pounds. Unmailable.
8K4005¼ **$9.39**

Absorbent Cotton and Gauze

Reliable Cotton
A good quality absorbent cotton is one of the first needs after an accident. Always be prepared and have a roll of Reliable Cotton handy. This grade is superior to ordinary qualities. Packed in 1 pound aseptic rolls. Shipping wt., 1¼ lbs.
8K2662 **48c**

Reliable Gauze
Absorbent gauze is extensively used as the proper aseptic dressing of wounds and should be available for all emergencies. Leaves no lint. Highly absorbent. Width, 36 inches; length, 5 yards. Packed in 1 pound aseptic rolls. Shipping wt., 6 oz.
8K2665 **39c**

Johnson & Johnson Red Cross Gauze
Clean, aseptic and thoroughly sterilized. Comes in a sealed package. Each length, 5 yards long, 36 inches wide. Shipping weight, 5 ounces.
8K2666 **43c**

Johnson & Johnson Red Cross Cotton
Well known advertised brand at a very low price. Each roll in sealed box. Highly absorbent. Shipping weight, 1¼ pounds.
8K2663 **69c**

Bed and Douche Pans

Heavy coated glistening white enamel ware, odorproof and extremely durable.

Bed and Douche Pan
Convenient shape and comfortable. Easy to keep clean and sanitary. Fine quality steel pan, enameled with best quality white enamel, smoothly and evenly finished. This style is widely used in hospitals. Size, 12x14½ inches. Each in sanitary carton. Shipping weight, 4 pounds.
8K2691 **$2.48**

Bed or Douche Pan
A shining white enameled pan for sick room use. The flat shape and wide opening make it simple to use and easy to clean. All parts nicely enameled and finished for perfect sanitation. Size, 12x16 inches. Shipping wt., 4¾ pounds.
8K2694 **$1.59**

Family Bed Pan
Spout at one end for use as male urinal and large opening in middle for use as bed pan. Opening allows easy cleaning. Separate cover fits snugly. Well coated with first quality white enamel, blue trimmed. Size, 12½x16 in. Shpg. wt., 5 lbs.
8K2695 **$1.79**

High Grade Soft Rubber Urinal Bags
Each in Sealed Package
Have special valves which prevent return flow of urine to upper part. Are equipped with non-leaking screw plugs at base, which allows bag to be easily emptied without detaching. Can be cleaned and sterilized with little trouble. Consult your physician before ordering to be sure you purchase the correct article for your needs. For sanitary reasons bags cannot be returned. Shipping weight, 1 pound.

Male Day or Night Style
Long rubber tube enables wearer to place lower bag outside of bed at night. Long tube may be detached during the day.
8K2536 **$4.98**

Boys' Size
Similar to above, but smaller.
8K2537 **$3.69**

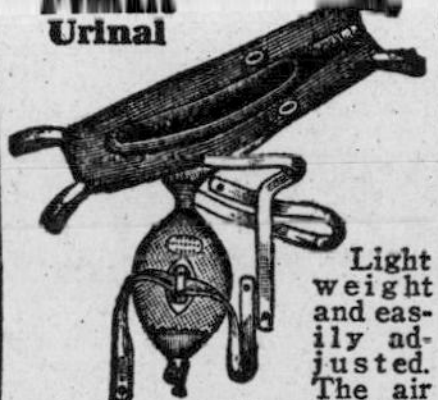

Female Urinal
Light weight and easily adjusted. The air cushion provides a snug fit and is very desirable to wear.
8K2532 **$4.98**

Male Large Top Style
Endorsed by many as the ideal male urinal. Topholds the entire scrotum without chafing. Patented shield prevents any return flow when reclining. Designed for day or night use.
8K2533 **$5.67**

Maplewood Crutches
Shipped From Stock
Each crutch carefully selected from clear grained rock maple to insure strength and safety. Hardwood shaped top and hand grip. Fitted with rubber tips. Take measure from armpit to floor in standing position and add 2 inches. Even sizes only, 36 to 60 inches. Shipping weight, 4 pounds.
8K2699¼—Pair **$1.69**

Rubber Tips for Crutches
Bailey's Won't Slip. Construction of bottom tends to reduce the danger of slipping on smooth or polished surfaces. Size given is diameter end of crutch. Shipping wt., 3 oz.
8K2697—Pair, ⅞ in. **22c**

Adhesive Plaster

A neat and secure way to hold a bandage in place on cuts and burns. Has many home uses. Sticks to anything dry. Shpg. wt., 4 oz.
8K409—5 yards by 1 inch **29c**

Gauze Bandages
Should Always Be on Hand for Emergency Use
Ten yards of plain gauze bandage, 2 inches wide, for dressing wounds. Thoroughly sterilized and ready for instant use. Shipping weight, 1 ounce.
8K2672—2 bandages for **19c**

Rubber Catheter
Sizes, 12, 14, 16, 18, 20 and 22. French scale. Send size in American or English scale, and corresponding size will be shipped. If no size is given, 18 will be sent. Shpg. wt., 1 oz.
8K2510 **19c**

Hard Rubber Syringes
Shpg. wt., 3 oz.

Male style, Soft Rubber Tip
8K2505—Capacity, ⅝ oz. **29c**
Female Style, Blunt End
8K2504—Capacity, 2 oz. **79c**

Clinical Thermometers
Our Best Thermometers
The Bureau of Standards at Washington, D. C., has tested each thermometer and has attached a certificate of accuracy. Popular one-minute style. Wide scale; large figures, easily read. Shipping weight, 5 ounces.
8K2605—In hard rubber case **$1.39**

Popular Thermometers
While these have not been tested by the Bureau of Standards the manufacturer guarantees them to be accurate. Popular one-minute style. Each in hard rubber case. Shipping weight, 5 ounces.
8K2600 **87c**
NOTE—Thermometers, although marked to register in one minute, are best left in mouth two or three minutes to record the accurate temperature.

Durabulb Infant Thermometer
Indispensable in the care of the child. It gives the mother an accurate and reliable indication of the baby's condition. Adapted for either rectal or oral use. Made with extra heavy bulb end to prevent snapping due to sudden twisting. Large figures, easily read. Certificate of accuracy accompanies each one. Packed in hard rubber case. Shipping weight, 5 ounces.
8K2604 **$1.19**

Invalid Chairs Ready for Shipment

Reed Rolling Chair
A popular chair for those desiring firm, easy riding qualities, good appearance and low price. Especially constructed for use on streets. Equipped with jar absorbing elliptical springs. Shipping weight, 95 pounds.
8K5005¼—¾-in. rubber tires **$33.30**
Dimensions:
Height of back, 27 in. Height of seat from floor, 22 in. Width, between arms, 17 in. Large wheels, 26 in.; small wheels, 10 in. Narrowest doorway through which chair will pass, 27 inches.

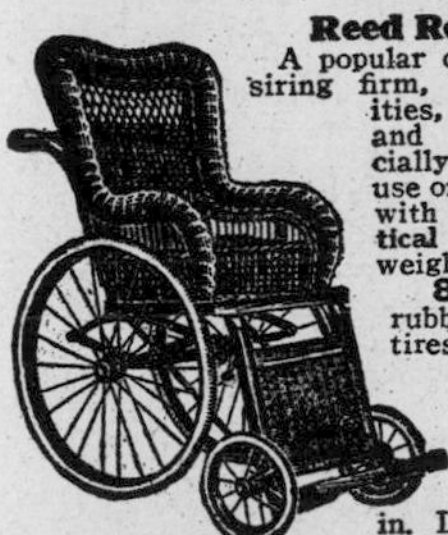

Reclining Rolling Chair
Adjustable Back 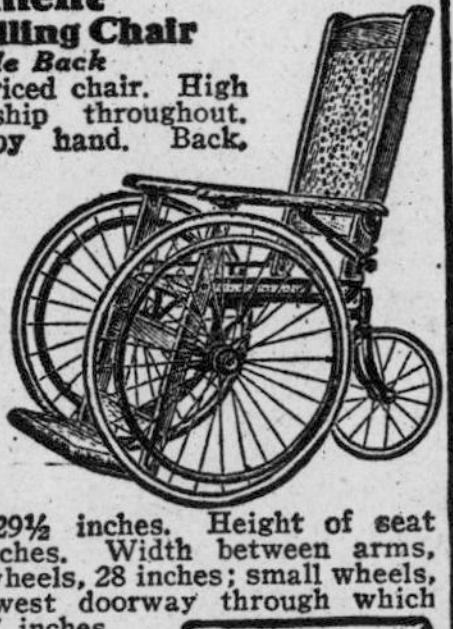
A popular low priced chair. High class workmanship throughout. Easily propelled by hand. Back, seat and leg rest are filled with 3-ply veneer, nicely finished in oak. Has rear swivel wheel. Shipping weight, 95 pounds.
8K5001¼
With ¾-inch rubber tires **$27.30**
Dimensions:
Height of back, 29½ inches. Height of seat from floor, 20 inches. Width between arms, 17 inches. Large wheels, 28 inches; small wheels, 14 inches. Narrowest doorway through which chair will pass, 27 inches.

This Catalog Mailed Free on Request—Ask for 537PK
Our complete line of Invalid Chairs is too large to show in this limited space. Realizing the need for special equipment on chairs, such as commode attachments, divided leg rests, self propelling attachment, upholstering and several other requirements of invalids, we have made arrangements to have most of our chairs made to order to satisfy our customers' specification. We will be pleased to send you our Invalid Chair Catalog 537PK, postpaid on your request. Allow three weeks for delivery of all special chairs, although generally shipments are made much quicker.

Portable Folding Bathtubs
$7.98
$6.45
Convenient Large Size for Farm, Homes, Cottages and Camps

A convenience as well as a necessity for many homes. Does away with the need of old fashioned wash bowls or tubs. Strong, varnished hardwood frame with steel braces. Tub material is a heavy rubber covered canvas duck, very tough and durable. The bottom of the tub rests on the floor, taking most of the weight off the frame. No danger of tipping over. Inside is smooth, soft and silky. Hot water does not shrink or rot it. The tub dries very quickly. Roll it up and stand it behind the door in your closet. It occupies very little room. Full size tub: 5 feet long, 24 inches wide, 16 inches deep, measured inside. Shipping weight, carefully crated, 21 pounds. Mailable.

Made in Two Qualities
The One We Advise You to Buy
Heavy weight canvas duck. Both sides covered with a thick coating of rubber.
8K4025¼ **$7.98**

Single coated, thick, rubber covered canvas duck. The tub generally sold elsewhere at a higher price than
8K4026¼ **$6.45**

Poultry and Farm Needs

Poultry Minerals for Laying Hens

The necessary minerals are usually lacking in winter feed, and, when shortage occurs the hen stops laying. Reputation minerals supply this deficiency. Formula: High calcium limestone, 1,000 lbs.; spent bone black, 740 lbs.; epsom salts, 20 lbs.; sulphur, 120 lbs.; iron oxide, 20 lbs.; meat meal, 100 lbs.

100 LBS. POULTRY MINERALS

8K978½—100-lb. bag. **$2.65**
Shipped from INDIANAPOLIS, IND.
8K981¼—25-lb. bag. **$1.15**
Shipped from stock.

Egg Mash—Protein, 20 Per Cent

Increase your egg production by feeding hens the reliable, economical and well balanced ration with egg producing ingredients. Increase the yield without lowering vitality of hen. It pays to buy a good mash for all year around maximum egg production.
Make your hens pay.

SILVER QUILL EGG MASH WITH BUTTERMILK (Protein)

8K969¼—100-lb. bag. **$3.40**
8K968¼—25-lb. bag. **90c**

Growing Mash—Protein, 16%

For quick, uniform growth. For firm, heavy, tasty broilers. It is rich in bone, blood and muscle building elements and brings chicks to maturity in the quickest possible time. Produces good, heavy broilers and gets pullets in best condition for heavy egg production. It pays to buy the best.

SILVER QUILL GROWING MASH FOR QUICK GROWTH

8K973¼—100-lb. bag. **$3.79**
8K972¼—25-lb. bag. **$1.05**

Chick Mash—Protein, 14 Per Cent

A safe and complete food for baby chicks. Contains the essential ingredients of both animal and vegetable proteins in correct proportions. One pound of this food will raise a baby chick past the dangerous period.

SILVER QUILL CHICK MASH WITH BUTTERMILK

8K977¼—100-lb. bag. **$4.39**
8K976¼—25-lb. bag. **$1.29**
8K975¼—10-lb. bag. **57**
All Mashes Shipped From Stock.

100 LBS. OYSTER SHELLS

Give your hens plenty of oyster shells for good hard shelled eggs. These shells are clean, odorless and ground to the right size for your hens. Contain 98% of calcium carbonate (lime). Free from clam shells.
8K961¼.
100-lb. bag... **79c**
Shipped from stock.

100 LBS. POULTRY GRIT

The kind of grit every poultry raiser wants. Clean, hard, sharp limestone grit crushed to right size so fowls take it greedily. Contains 95 per cent calcium carbonate (lime).
8K960⅓— 100 lbs. medium,
coarse....... **67c**
Shipped from factory in MARYLAND.

100 LBS. MEAT SCRAPS

Protein, 50%
Increase your egg production. Furnishes the protein necessary for a full egg yield. Should be fed to poultry for health, growth and economical egg production.
8K980⅓
100 lbs. **$3.98**
Shipped from factory in NORTHEASTERN ILLINOIS.

50 LBS. GRANULAR CHARCOAL

Absorbs gases and aids digestion. Keeps fowls in better health. Poultry charcoal is in small granules, for both old and young fowls. Cannot be shipped by express.
8K963¼
50-lb. bag. **$1.39**
Two 50-lb. bags. **2.55**
Shipped from stock.

It Pays to Caponize!

SEE THE DIFFERENCE

CAPONIZED

NOT CAPONIZED

Caponize the young roosters you intend to market. Caponized roosters quickly put on additional weight and bring high prices. Caponizing is practiced and endorsed by leading poultry men and is easy for anyone to do. It enables you to market birds at a season when most other fowl are off the market. Due to the scarcity of fowl at off seasons and because of their added size and firm choice quality of meat, capons bring fancy prices and are always in great demand.

Our "E-Z" set is of simple design and was designed for us by an expert. It is well made of good materials. Complete instructions clearly and simply written and illustrated are packed with each set. With these instructions, even the most inexperienced can safely use this simple "E-Z" set and caponize his own roosters. Shipping weight, ¾ pound.
8K1940—Caponizing Set and Directions. **$2.89**
Capon for Money—A 40-page book of full instructions and pictures, giving diagrams, when and how to caponize. Do not miss it. Shipping weight, 7 ounces.
8K1942—Each. **15c**

Cod Liver Oil for Poultry

Poultry raisers are fast learning the value of Cod Liver Oil when freshly mixed with other feeds. Do not mix ahead but always add the oil just before feeding. Greatly increases resistance to disease and speeds the recovery of rundown flocks. High in vitamin content. Every lot tested to insure an abundance of vitamins "A" and "D." Directions on each can. Shipping weight, per gallon, 10 pounds.
8K950¼—1-gallon can. **$1.98**
8K951¼—5-gallon can. **9.60**
Above shipped from stock.
8K952⅓—30-gallon drum. **$38.75**
Shipped from warehouse in EASTERN MASSACHUSETTS.

Semi-Solid Buttermilk

Creamy buttermilk, condensed to a thick semi-solid paste, in which form it contains its maximum feed and tonic value. Abounds with proteins and digestible minerals. Baby chicks thrive on it. Develops pullets for heavy fall and winter egg production without impairing their vitality, and greatly increases resistance to disease. Directions with each can. Shipping weight, per can, 8 lbs.
8K955¼—1-gallon can. **85c**
8K956¼—6 1-gallon cans. **$4.89**
Above shipped from stock.

Improved Nest Eggs

These quality eggs should not be compared with ordinary powder eggs. They serve every purpose of the porcelain or the common enameled wood eggs and, in addition, serve as a lice exterminator. Made of insect powder, lime and binder. Hens moving over eggs force powder on nest, as well as feet and feathers. 12 eggs to box. Shipping wt., 2½ lbs.
8K903—Box of 12 eggs for. **29c**

Whiticide

A disinfecting white water paint to be used in poultry house, stables, cellars, etc. It is non-poisonous. Spray or paint everything in the poultry house from the floor to the ceiling with Whiticide. Mix with water and put on easily with brush or spray. Does not scale or rub off.
8K647—5-pound package. **69c**

Odorless Indoor Closet

Install a "Handee" and enjoy real comfort. No flies in summer, no exposure in the winter. Can be put in anywhere and is always ready for use. Saves embarrassment in avoiding public gaze. Saves the danger of diseases and pestilence arising from outhouses.

$5.98 Complete

Easily and Quickly Installed

Many state boards of health recommend this kind of toilet for its convenience, accessibility, privacy, comfort, ventilation, germ destruction and fly prevention. It abolishes the outdoor privy in schools, country hotels, summer resorts, camps, etc.

Closet of sheet steel. Has snug fitting hardwood, not easily split, mahogany finish seat with hinged cover. Outside container nicely enameled. Has inner removable galvanized container of 6 gallons capacity. Contents are disinfected by the action of the chemical. Furnished complete with six 11-inch lengths of 3-inch enameled ventilating pipe, two elbows, one wall collar, one toilet paper holder, one roll toilet paper and one gallon of "Handee" Improved Liquid Chemical. Simply add ¼ cup of chemical to 2 gallons of water, and closet is ready for use. One gallon of chemical sufficient for an average family for about six months.

"Handee" Indoor Toilet
8K4050¼—"Handee" Closet. Complete with one gallon of "Handee" Improved Liquid Chemical. Unmailable. Shpg. wt., 40 lbs. **$5.98**

"Handee" Improved Liquid Chemical
A quality product superior to those generally offered. Will keep your closet clean and help kill disease germs. Packed in 1-gallon containers. Shipping weight, 11 pounds. Not mailable. Chemical only.
8K4054¼
Per gallon. **$1.39**

For Water Closet Outfits See Page 1005

LICE POWDER

Sodium Fluoride Compound
Recommended by U. S. Department of Agriculture as most successful exterminator of lice on poultry. 1 pound applied dry by "pinch" method will treat 100 fowls. Directions on package.
8K633—1-pound carton. **33c**
8K634—5-pound package. **$1.39**
Above shipped by express only

POULTRY REMEDIES

Beebe's Avian Bacterin
A Government Inspected Chicken Vaccine
Keep your flock free from disease. Used for prevention of roup, cholera, etc. Shipping weight, 8 ounces.
8K1861—40-dose vial. **$1.15**

Roup Remedy
Also recommended for colds, canker and bowel complaints in fowls and pigeons.
8K914—Shipping weight, ¾ pound. **34c**

White Diarrhea Remedy

Safe, reliable remedy every poultryman should have on hand at all times. Forty tablets in package makes about 10 gallons.
8K915—Shipping weight, 4 ounces. **34c**

for Greater Profits

100 LBS.
POWDERED
SULPHUR

A good blood purifier and conditioner. Used with regular feeds or in combination with other minerals. **Cannot be shipped by express.**
8K807⅓ 100 pounds.. **$2.79**
Shipped from factory near PHILADELPHIA, PA.

100 LBS.
GLAUBER
SALTS

A fine laxative and regulator for stock generally, not only acts as an eliminant but keeps stock in much better condition. Nice, white salts.
8K785⅓ 100-lb. bag.. **$1.98**
Shipped from factory near PHILADELPHIA, PA.

100 LBS.
GRANULAR
COPPERAS

A good iron tonic to tone up the system. Used either alone or in mixtures. Every stock raiser should keep a supply on hand.
8K762⅓ 100 pounds.. **$2.25**
Shipped from factory near PHILADELPHIA, PA.

100 LBS.
EPSOM
SALTS

U. S. P. Quality
A good laxative and bowel regulator. Keeps indefinitely. Added to feed keeps stock in good condition.
8K758¼ 100 pounds **$2.79**
Shipped from stock.

Reputation
CALF
MEAL

Protein, 25%; Fat, 5%; Fiber, 6¾%
Raising calves on whole milk is neither profitable nor necessary. Take the young calf away from the mother at five or six days of age and feed it Reputation Calf Meal—the ideal baby calf food. In this way you can save the calf and still sell the cow's milk.
Reputation Calf Meal is made to produce results. Its quality is uniform, inexpensive and reliable. Directions in every bag. **Shipped from stock.**
8K801¼—100 pounds........ **$4.39**
8K800¼—25 pounds........ **$1.20**

Reputation
PIG
MEAL
FOR QUICK GROWTH

Protein, 20%; Fat, 5%; Fiber, 4½%
A concentrated food, fed the same as milk, containing just the right percentage of vegetable protein, fat, starch, etc., to be a real milk substitute and fit the particular needs of infant pigs.
Reputation Pig Meal is not an experiment, but a reliable, inexpensive food, easily prepared at a moment's notice. Full directions in every bag. **Shipped from stock.**
8K806¼ 100 pounds.... **$4.39**
8K805¼—25 lbs. **$1.20**

STOCK
FEEDING
MOLASSES

When used with roughages or in a slop, these feeds are made more palatable and digestible. Increases the milk flow in cows. Hogs and steers gain weight more rapidly.
It has been found that when replacing not more than half the corn in a ration, molasses has slightly more feeding value, pound for pound, than corn alone. **Shipped from PHILADELPHIA, PA., at prices quoted for that point only. Each barrel, about 54 gallons. Shipping wt., per barrel, 700 pounds.**
8K842⅓—Philadelphia, Pa.................. **$9.98**

Veterinary Instruments

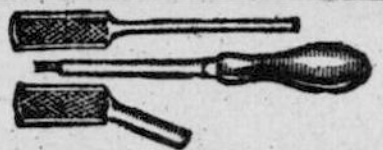

Dependable Combination Horse Mouth Float
Easy to operate. Has straight attachment for lower molars and angle head for uppers. Nickel plated steel shanks. Black enameled wooden handle. Shipping wt., 2 lbs.
8K1862..... **$2.79**

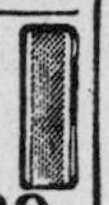

Extra Steel Blades
For Above
Rasp on one side, file on the other. Length, 3¼ in. Shipping wt., 3 oz.
8K1863........ **29c**

Cattle Trocar and Canula

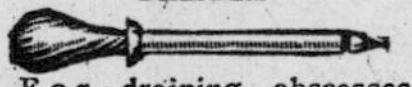

For draining abscesses and reducing bloat. Good grade steel, heavily nickel plated. Shipping weight, ¾ pound.
8K1973........ **67c**
8K1974—Extra Canula. Shpg. wt., 2 oz........ **45c**

Castrating Knife

Strong metal handle, high grade steel blade and hook; spring back. Shpg. wt., 3 oz.
8K1893......... **$1.39**

Eclipse Emasculator
Made of quality steel, polished and nickel plated. Handles, dull finish.
8K1891—Curved. Shpg. wt., 1½ lbs.. **$6.98**

Dr. Edwards' Improved Emasculator
Double crushing attachment which crushes cord and tends to prevent hemorrhage. Shpg. wt., 1¾ lbs.
8K1878........ **$9.98**

Self Retaining Milk Tubes

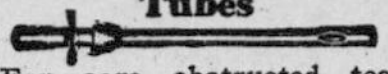

For sore obstructed teats and hard milkers. Nickel plated. Shipping weight, 2 oz.
8K1975—Set of 4 tubes........ **39c**

Self Retaining Teat Dilator

For hard milkers. Non-corrosive alloy. Shipping weight, 1 ounce.
8K1977......... **19c**

Syringes

Made of seamless brass tubing, nickel plated. A necessity on every farm. Tight fitting plunger; two pipes. Shpg. wt., 1 lb.
8K1918 Capacity, 2 ounces..... **98c**
8K1919 Capacity, 4 oz. **$1.69**

Our Best Horse Speculum

A strong hand forged steel speculum, nickel plated, dull finish. Provides safety for the operator, coupled with every advantage offered in a speculum. A single pull on chain closes it. Can be taken apart and carried in grip. Shipping wt., 7½ lbs.
8K1886.. **$11.67**

Milk Fever Outfit
For Sterilized Air Treatment

Milk fever is an acute disease, and very often fatal unless treatment is given at once. Simply inject sterilized air into the udder. Shipping weight, 1 pound.
8K1895......... **$2.39**

Pig Extractors

The "Old Reliable" Pig Forceps
Cast steel, nickel finish. Use on large or small sows. Shipping weight, 2 pounds.
8K1965......... **$1.67**

Improved Style

Drop forged steel, nickel plated, dull finish. Will not injure sow. Shpg. wt., 1¾ lbs.
8K1963........ **$3.59**

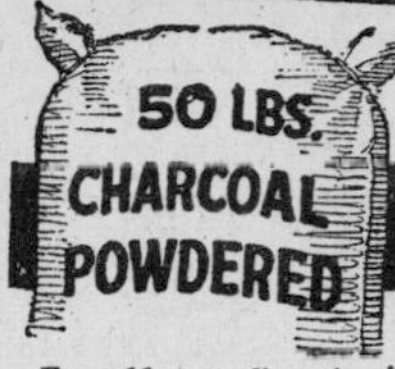

50 LBS.
CHARCOAL
POWDERED

Excellent digestive stock conditioner. A valuable addition to the feed.
8K772¼ 50-lb. bag.... **$1.25**
Two 50-lb. bags. **$2.30**
Shipped from stock.

100 LBS.
ODORLESS
STEAMED
BONE

A purified product for feeding. Stock eat it readily and benefit profitably. Contains 65% bone phosphate lime.
8K808⅓ 100 lbs........ **$2.85**
Shipped from NORTHEASTERN ILLINOIS.

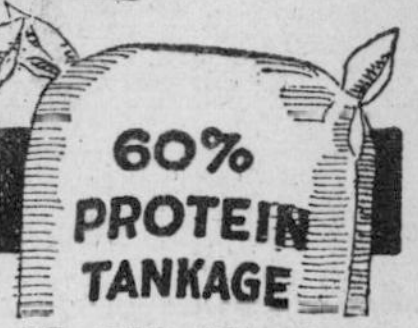

60%
PROTEIN
TANKAGE

Meat Meal Tankage
Growing pigs must have rations balanced with a protein to build muscle, flesh and bone. Tankage is the most economical source of protein, is appetizing, nourishing and greatly relished. Write for prices.

SANTONIN TABLETS

With Areca Nut, Aloin and Oil of Wormseed
Santonin has been recommended by state and government authorities as the best product to get rid of worms. Tablets contain 3 grains Santonin, 3 grains Calomel and 6 grains Soda Bicarbonate. Supplants the old dangerous balling gun and capsules. Shpg. wt., 6 oz.
8K883—Box of **25** tablets........ **$3.98**

Reputation Deworming Oil
A sure and safe treatment for worms. Made from oil chenopodium and castor oil. Give with dose syringe. Directions on package.
8K857—Pint bottle.......................... **$1.05**
8K858—Quart bottle.......................... **1.98**
8K859¼—1-gallon can.......................... **6.98**
Shipping weight, above, 2 lbs. per quart.

Two-Oz. Brass Syringe for Giving Oil
8K1920—Graduated piston bar and one long pipe. Shipping weight, 1 pound.......................... **87c**

Beebe's Blackleg Aggressin Government Inspected Serum
A germ free vaccine for the prevention of blackleg. Satisfactorily administered by any herdsman, and will produce a high degree of lasting immunity. Pellets and filtrate give only temporary relief. Shipping weight, 8 ounces.
8K1867—Vial. 10-dose.......................... **$1.15**

Quitman's Syringe
For administering vaccine and bacterins, 5 c. c. capacity. Shipping weight, 1 lb.
8K1860.......................... **$1.25**

Reputation Dip

A dip and disinfectant for the extermination of parasites, lice, ticks, fleas and many other insects. One gallon makes 70 gallons of dip. Directions on package.
8K610½ 1 gallon. Shpg. wt., 12 lbs...... **$1.19**
8K611¼—5 gallons. Unmailable.
Shipping weight, 48 pounds.......................... **$ 4.39**
8K613⅓—50 gallons. Shpg. wt., 450 lbs.. **19.95**
Fifty-gallon steel drums shipped from factory in NORTHEASTERN ILLINOIS.

Reputation Minerals
for Hogs, Cattle and Sheep

Mineral Mixtures of Leading Agricultural Colleges

These mixtures are the result of careful experimentation, carefully and accurately made. Priced as low as possible, using proper quality ingredients—we believe by actual feeding test will give as good results as any on the market.

10 Reasons Why You Should Feed Minerals

1—**Your stock needs minerals**—for bone, flesh, blood, hoofs and hair—minerals are absolutely essential for successful growth.
2—**Most pastures and yards** have been more or less depleted of minerals and it now becomes necessary to supply the minerals in this form.
3—**Actually proved results.** Not some patented stock tonic or somebody's guess, but a mixture of minerals balanced in the proportions found after thousands of experiments to give the best results.
4—**Greater gains.** It has been proved that mineral feeding means less food necessary per 100 pounds gain. Ask your agricultural college or county agent.
5—**Bigger profits.** These mixtures aid growth of pigs and stock generally, enabling them to be sold at higher prices on the earlier markets.
6—**Quicker markets and shorter feeding period.** Grows stock faster, uses less feed, saves many days bringing to market sizes, and costs less to raise.
7—**Better and bigger hogs and stock generally** in less time with less disease and, by supplying necessary minerals, prevents objectionable eating habits.
8—**Necessary** to hogs of all ages from shotes to motherhood—hogs should have minerals before them at all times. Also very beneficial to cattle and sheep.
9—**Endorsed** by leading agricultural colleges and feed experts as absolutely essential for successful hog and stock raising.
10—**Real results count.** Do not be influenced entirely by price. Our mineral mixtures are the results of careful experiments by experts and are in our opinion the best on the market.

All minerals shipped from factory near INDIANAPOLIS, IND.

Hog Minerals

Complex Mixture
Iowa Modified
This is one formula above all others that we can recommend. It contains all the essential elements, together with the tonics, laxatives and potassium iodide so essential for preventing hairless animals and goitre. The 5 per cent meat meal is a later improvement on the Iowa complex mixture, making it more palatable and more easily eaten.

Formula: Spent bone black, 25 per cent; high calcium limestone, 34.97 per cent; common salt, 11 per cent; sulphur, 4 per cent; copperas, 2 per cent; glauber salts, 6 per cent; epsom salts, 2 per cent; hardwood ashes, 10 per cent; meat meal, 5 per cent; potassium iodide, .03 per cent.
8K775⅓
100 pounds.......................... **$2.69**
300 pounds.......................... **$ 7.89**
1,000 pounds.......................... **24.69**

Backbone Mixture
Iowa Simple Formula
It is really surprising what good results can be obtained even from this simple mixture. This formula carries the principal elements in which ordinary feeds are deficient.
Formula: Common salt, 15 per cent; high calcium limestone, 49.97 per cent; spent bone black, 35 per cent; potassium iodide, .03 per cent.
8K750⅓
100 pounds... **$1.79**
300 lbs... **$ 4.98**
1,000 lbs... **15.98**

Dairy Minerals

Improved Formula
Insures more milk, healthier herds, stronger calves, less abortion, better growth, greater profit.
The need for proper minerals in the daily rations of cattle cannot be overestimated. Iodides are essential to prevent big losses of new born calves through goitre or weakness.
Formula: High calcium limestone, 34.97 per cent; spent bone black, 25 per cent; common salt, 20 per cent; hardwood ashes, 9 per cent; tobacco dust, 3 per cent; glauber salts, 4 per cent; epsom salts, 1 per cent; copperas, 1 per cent; iron oxide, 1 per cent; sulphur, 1 per cent; potassium iodide, .03 per cent.
8K754⅓
100 pounds.......................... **$2.69**
300 pounds.......................... **$ 7.89**
1,000 pounds.......................... **24.69**

Sheep Minerals

Authorities have endorsed our Improved Dairy Minerals as the ideal mineral for sheep. Experiments have proved that the correct ingredients are included to act as a tonic and to insure rapid growth. See prices above.

Parcel Post, Express and Freight Rates Are on Pages 542 to 545

Home Needs

CHAMOIS SKINS

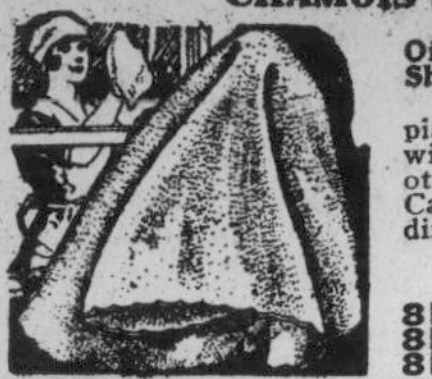

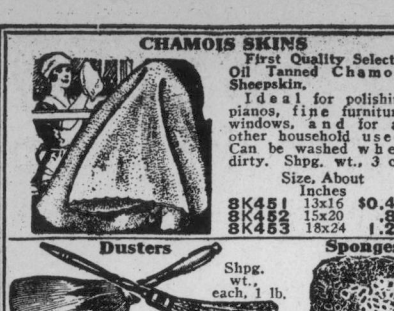

First Quality Selected Oil Tanned Chamois Sheepskin.

Ideal for polishing pianos, fine furniture, windows, and for all other household uses. Can be washed when dirty. Shpg. wt., 3 oz.

	Size, About Inches	
8K451	13x16	$0.45
8K452	15x20	.87
8K453	18x24	1.25

Dusters / Sponges

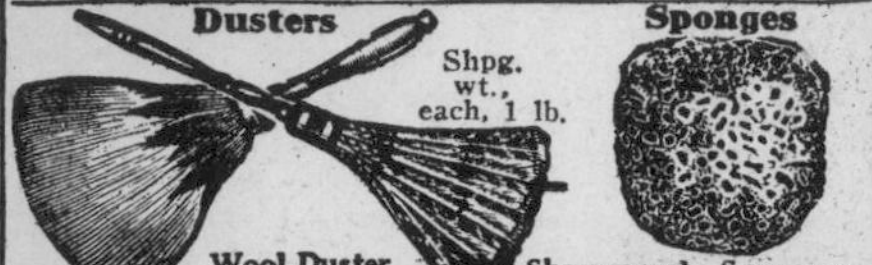

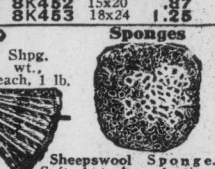

Shpg. wt., each, 1 lb.

Wool Duster Does not scratch. Easily washed. About 12 inches long.
8K1386—$1.25 size. 98c

Feather Duster. 29 inches long over all.
8K1390 .... 43c

Sheepswool Sponge. Soft but long lasting. Diameter, wet, 5½ in.
8K459 .... 69c

Popular Sponge. For household needs. Diameter, wet, 6 in.
8K457 .... 27c
Shpg. wt., 3 oz.

Tint or Dye With Diamond Package Dyes

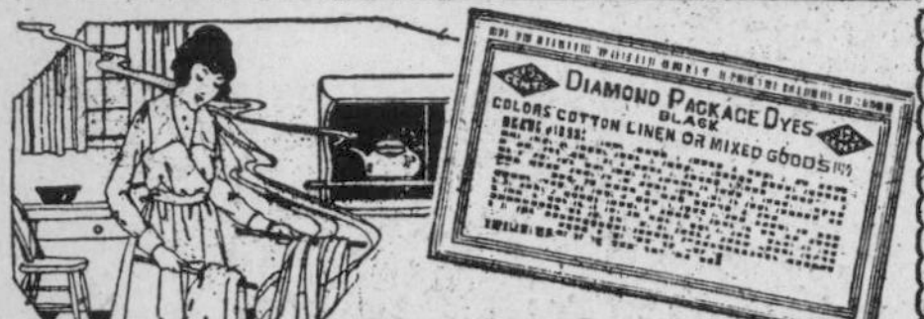

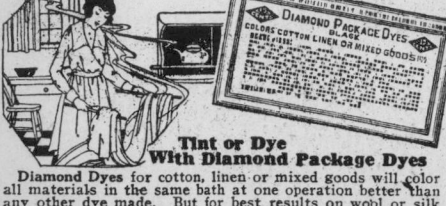

Diamond Dyes for cotton, linen or mixed goods will color all materials in the same bath at one operation better than any other dye made. But for best results on wool or silk use "Diamond Dye for wool or silk." Diamond Dyes furnished as: Light blue, dark blue, navy blue, brown, seal brown, green, dark green, pink, cardinal red, turkey red, garnet, black, purple, yellow, orange or gray. Combine colors to form popular shades. **Specify color and material to be dyed.** Shipping weight, package, 2 ounces.

8K333—For cotton, linen or mixed goods 11c
8K334—For wool or silk 11c

Liquid Meat Smoke

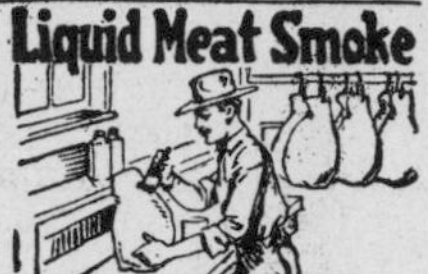

A quality product. Not only gives the meat that mild, tasty flavor, such as given by a slow hickory smoke, but aids in preserving as well. One quart will cure 250 pounds of meat. Shipping weight, 5 pounds.
8K464—1-qt. bottle 65c

Sterno Kitchenette Set

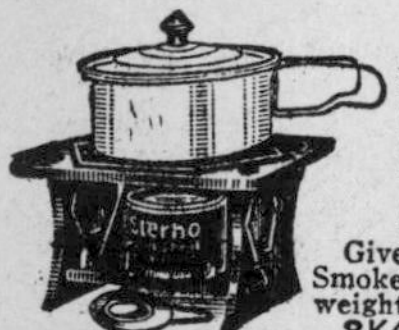

Useful indoors and outdoors the year around. Includes polished aluminum boiler, 1-pint capacity, a folding stove, a can of Canned Heat and extinguisher. Shipping wt., 1½ lbs.
8K462—Complete 39c

Sterno Canned Heat
Gives quick, steady, intense heat. Smokeless and odorless. Shipping weight, 8 ounces.
8K463—3 regular 10c cans. 25c

KEEP YOUR BIRD IN SONG

Big Combination Offer

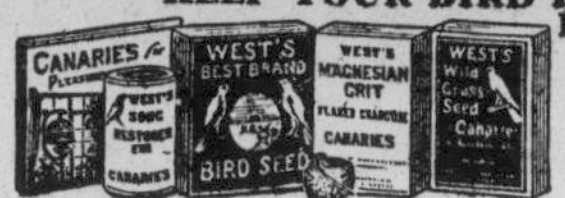

A well selected assortment, suited for every canary, containing articles that are essential to the bird's welfare. One package each of Bird Seed, Magnesian Grit, Song Restorer, Bird Nip and one 8-ounce package of Wild Grass Seed, to furnish a change of diet and give your bird a taste of freedom; also a booklet, "Canaries for Pleasure and Profit." Shipping weight, 3½ lbs.
8K495—All 5 packages 59c

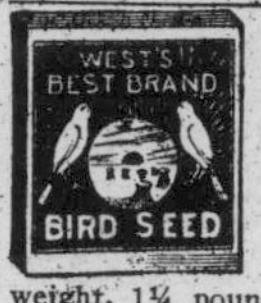

A high grade combination of selected seeds, the choice of noted bird breeders. Composed of canary, rape and millet seed only. Does not contain red millet. Shipping weight, 1¼ pounds.
8K490—1-lb. package .. 19c

Bird Nip

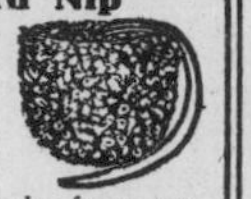

Furnishes food and amusement for your bird. Made from assorted bird seeds. Shpg. wt., 3 pkgs. 6 oz.
8K493
3 for 23c

Mendets

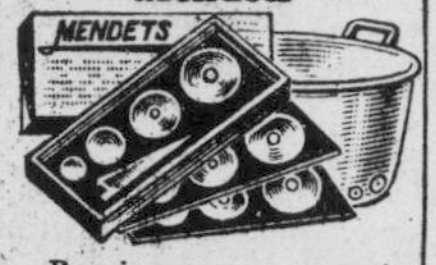

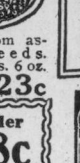

Repair your own pots and pans easily and quickly. Complete outfit including rivets and small hand wrench for applying. Enough for twelve repairs. Shpg. wt., 4 oz.
8K320—Reg. 25c pkg. for 19c

Household Mender 18c

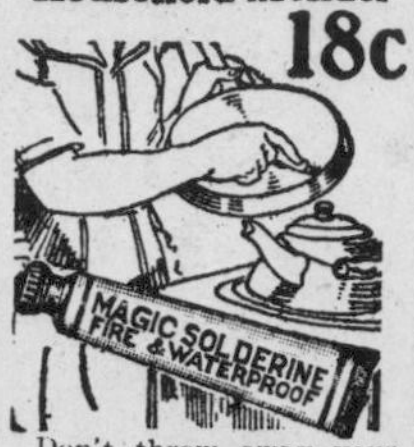

Don't throw away your kitchen utensils because they leak. Magic Solderine mends pipes, radiators, pots, etc., without heat and makes a waterproof and fireproof repair job. Shpg. wt., 4 oz.
8K324—Large tube, 25c size 18c

Du Pont's Household Cement

The Universal Mender

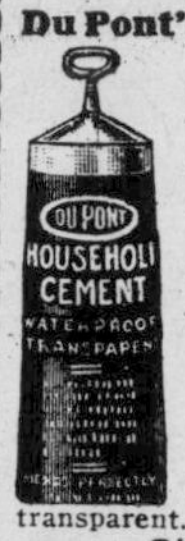

Mends anything that is broken or torn. Glass, china, cloth, bone, wood, ivory or leather. When once cemented together will not break again in the same place. It is waterproof and transparent. Shpg. wt., 3 oz.
8K318
25c size, only 19c

Le Page's Glue
8K319—1-oz. tube .. 16c

Le Page's China Cement
8K321—1-oz. tube .. 17c

Solvo Closet Bowl Cleaner

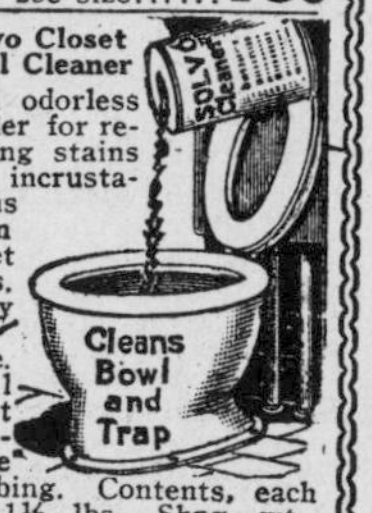

An odorless powder for removing stains and incrustations from toilet bowls. Easy to use. Will not injure plumbing. Contents, each can, 1⅛ lbs. Shpg. wt., each can, 1¾ lbs.
8K323—3 cans for .. 49c
1 can for 17c

BEVERAGES

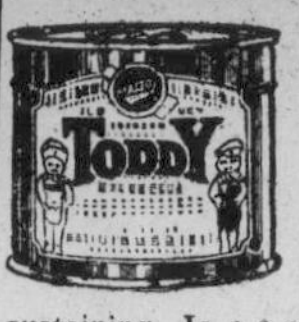

Toddy A Malt Food A Meal in a Glass Refreshing, invigorating and sustaining. Is easily digested. Serve at meals or between if you become tired; also before retiring for instant and restful sleep. Shpg. wts., 2 and 7¼ lbs.
8K428—1 pound 45c
8K427—5 lbs $1.98

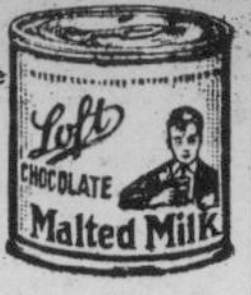

Loft's Chocolate Malted Milk A refreshing drink for the entire family. Blended from rich full cream dairy milk. Malt made from ripe grains and Loft's delicious breakfast cocoa. Builds muscle. Shipping weights, 2 and 7¼ pounds.
8K426—1 lb. 45c
8K425—5 lbs. $1.98

Junket Powder

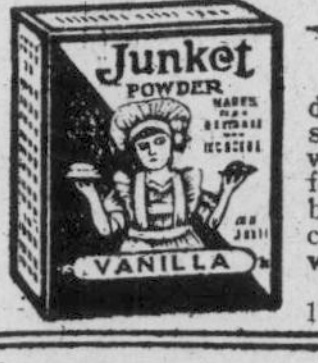

Attractive, delicious custardlike desserts are easily made with this sweetened and flavored powder without eggs or cooking; also used for making rich ice cream. Raspberry, orange, lemon, vanilla or chocolate flavors. **State flavors wanted.** Shipping weight, 1 lb.
8K460—3 regular 15c packages 30c

TOILET PAPERS

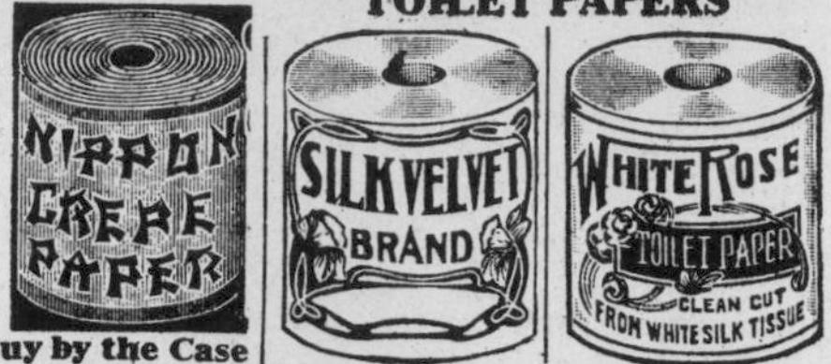

Buy by the Case
Good quality crepe paper in 4-oz. rolls. Strong and tough. Not to be confused with cheaper grades. Shpg. wt., 11 lbs.
8K438¼
1 case, 24 rolls .. 83c

High grade white tissue, soft and non-irritating, yet strong. The rolls contain the full number of sheets, perforated; each sheet, 4½x5 inches.

Silk Velvet 600 sheets per roll. Shpg. wt., twelve rolls, 8 lbs.
8K440
12 rolls .. 68c

White Rose 1,000 sheets per roll. Shpg. wt., 6 rolls, 5 lbs.
8K442
6 rolls .. 55c

Imported French Olive Oil

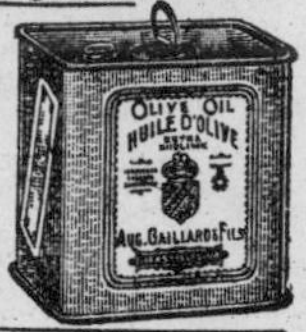

An extra fine quality, especially recommended for salads and cookery. Inspected, tested and filtered, and may be used for medicinal purposes. Full, rich, natural olive flavor, smooth, pleasant taste and good color.

	Size	Shpg. Wt.	
8K223	8-oz. can	¾ lb.	$0.39
8K224	1-pt. can	1½ lbs.	.69
8K226	½-gal. can	4½ lbs.	2.39
8K221	1-gal. can	8¾ lbs.	4.48

Canning Needs

Jar Rings

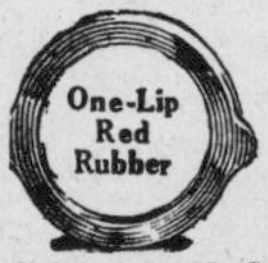

The one-lip ring with the extra large lip for easy opening. Made heavy to insure a perfect seal. Guaranteed to meet requirements specified by the U. S. Dept. of Agriculture for hot, cold pack and steam pressure canning. Shipping weight, ¾ pound.
8K402—3 dozen rings 23c

Jar Caps Genuine Mason Caps

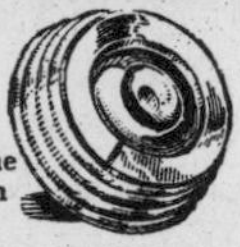

Made of zinc with white porcelain lining. Shpg. wt., 1¾ lbs.
8K405
1 dozen caps. 27c

For Other Canning Needs See Page 969

Bug Killers

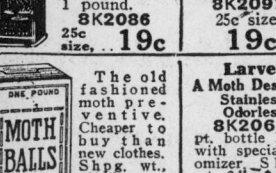

Peterman's kills bedbugs and their eggs in one application. May be applied on mattresses and bedding. Shpg. wts., 1¾ and 8¾ lbs.
8K2085—14-oz. can, patent spout. 24c
8K2087¼
1-gallon can .. $1.59

Insect Powder

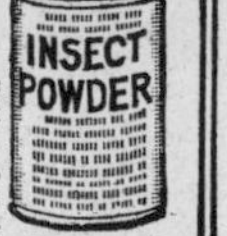

This is one of the most popular powders used to kill insects such as roaches, ants, waterbugs, etc. Very effective. Shipping weight, 1¾ pounds.
8K2035
1-lb. carton 69c

Roach Food

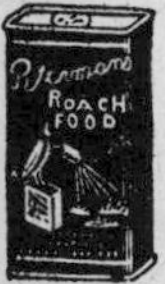

Effective against roaches and waterbugs. Shipping wt., 1 pound.
8K2086
25c size .. 19c

Ant Food

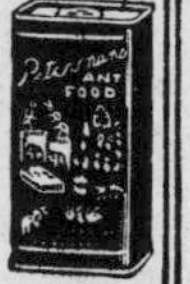

An effective method of destroying ants. Shpg. wt., 1 lb.
8K2097
25c size.
19c

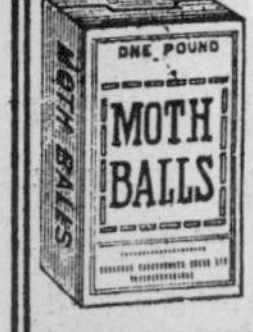

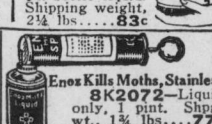

The old fashioned moth preventive. Cheaper to buy than new clothes. Shpg. wt., 1¼ lbs.
8K2083
Per pound 13c

Larvex
A Moth Destroyer Stainless, Odorless

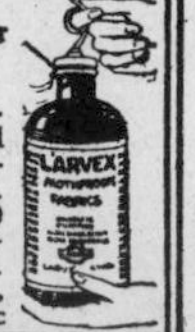

8K2063—1-pt. bottle liquid with special atomizer. Shpg. wt., 3 lbs. $1.29
8K2064—1-pt. bottle liquid. Shipping weight, 2¼ lbs 83c

Moth Ball Holders

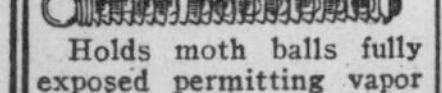

Holds moth balls fully exposed permitting vapor to reach all parts of clothes closet. Shpg. wt., 2¼ lbs.
8K2082—6 holders and 1 lb. moth balls. 48c

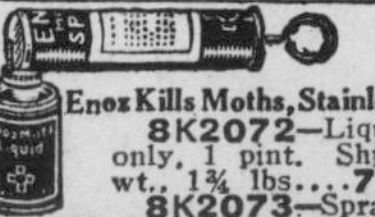

Enoz Kills Moths, Stainless
8K2072—Liquid only, 1 pint. Shpg. wt., 1¾ lbs 77c
8K2073—Sprayer with 5 oz. liquid, Shpg. wt., 8 oz 39c

Paper Towels

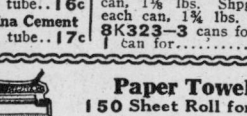

150 Sheet Roll for 18c

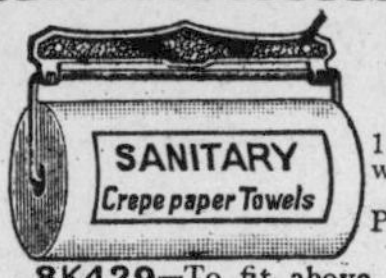

Highly absorbent. Size, 11½x15 inches. Handy in kitchen or wash room. Shpg. wt., 2 lbs.
8K430
Per roll 18c

Paper Towel Rack
8K429—To fit above towels. Shipping weight, 1 pound 39c

Paper Plates—Cups—Straws

Paper Plates

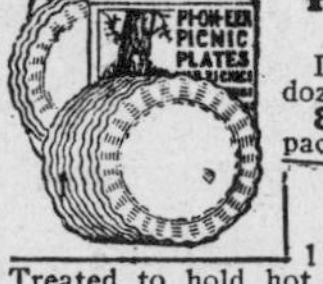

Ideal for parties and picnics. One dozen 8-inch plates to the package.
8K411—Regular 10c package. Shpg. wt., 2 lbs 8c

Dixie Paper Cups

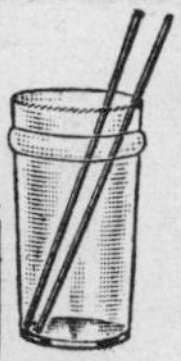

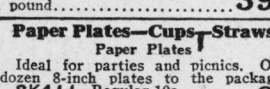

Ideal way to serve liquid refreshments. Treated to hold hot or cold drinks. Eight cups per package. Shpg. wt., three pkgs., 1¾ lbs.
8K407—3 regular 10c packages for 22c

Sanitary Beverage Straws
The kind used at soda fountains. Adds a touch of daintiness to home service. Shpg. wt., 5 oz.
8K410—Pkg. of about 65 straws 8c

Parchment Paper in Wall Cartons

Packed in handy packages for ready use. A necessity in every home. High quality white vegetable parchment, 30-pound basis. For wrapping cheese, butter, meat or sandwiches. When wet, parchment paper becomes exceedingly strong. Contains no wax, grease or paraffin.

Carton of 250 Sheets

	Size	Wt., Lbs.	
8K420	9x12	2¼	63c
8K421	8x11	2	55c

Carton of 500 Sheets

	Size	Wt., Lbs.	
8K422	9x12	4½	$1.10
8K423	8x11	4½	.89

Chris Hansen's Dairy Products

Cheese Color Tablets
Convenient and economical for coloring cheese. Shpg. wt., 6 oz.
8K340—Vial, 12 tablets 27c

Rennet Tablets
Indispensable for making cheese. Directions furnished. Shipping weight, 6 ounces.
8K341—Box of 24 tablets 79c

HANDY HOUSEHOLD BRUSHES

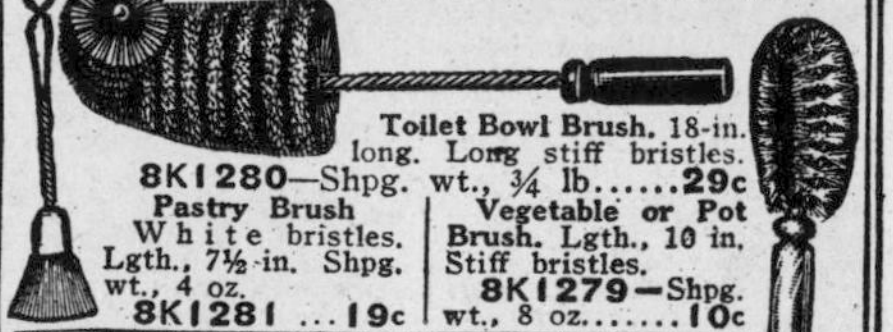

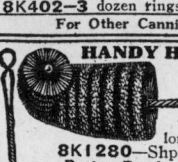

Toilet Bowl Brush. 18-in. long. Long stiff bristles.
8K1280—Shpg. wt., ¾ lb 29c

Pastry Brush
White bristles. Lgth., 7½ in. Shpg. wt., 4 oz.
8K1281 .... 19c

Vegetable or Pot Brush. Lgth., 10 in. Stiff bristles.
8K1279—Shpg. wt., 8 oz 10c

White Cotton Twine

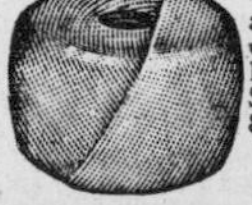

Extra Strong
Useful article for every home. Shpg. wt., 8 oz.
8K477
2 balls, 17c

Toothpicks

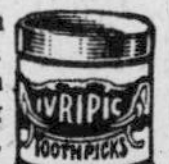

Useful in every home. Quality picks, in cans, containing about 750 picks. Shpg. wt., 8 oz.
8K469—3 cans for .. 14c

Household Corks

About 35 assorted corks. Shipping weight, 4 ounces.
8K481—Box of assorted corks 15c

Quart Size Corks
Diam., 1⁵⁄₁₆ inch at top.
8K483—Package of 150 .... 79c

Pint Size Corks
Diam., 1³⁄₁₆ inch at top.
8K482—Package of 150 .... 59c
Shpg. wt., above, 8 oz.

Carpet Cleaner

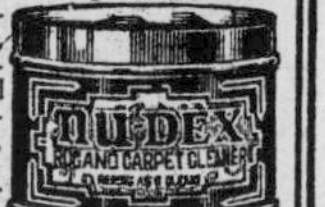

Use on tapestries, overstuffed furniture, draperies or portieres. Enough for two 9x12-foot rugs. Shpg. wt., 2¼ lbs.
8K498—1 large can Nu-Dex 39c

Adhesive Tape

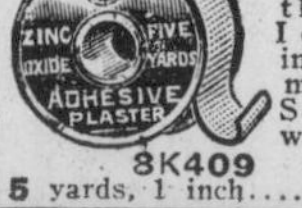

Sticks to anything. Ideal instant mender. Shpg. wt., 4 oz.
8K409
5 yards, 1 inch 29c

Three-in-1 Oil

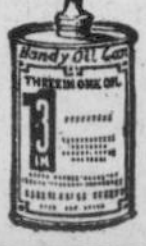

Lubricates, Cleans and Polishes
The genuine widely known oil in handy oil can with spout. Shpg. wt., ¾ lb.
8K470
30c size 24c

SAFES

Fireproof

An Indispensable Necessity for the Home and Office

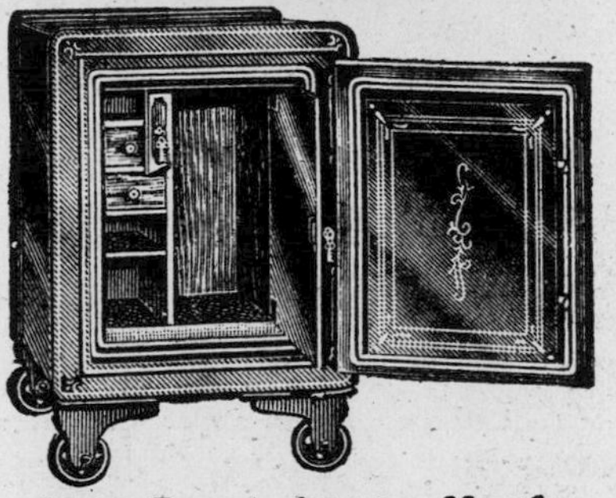

$5.00 Down—$5.00 a Month

No household or business man can afford to be without a safe and run the risk of losing important papers and other valuables by fire or theft when you can buy one of these fireproof safes at such a low price. These safes give you full protection at much lower prices than you would have to pay elsewhere for standard safes of equal value. Be sure to buy a safe large enough to hold all your valuables and allow for growing business.

Made of tough steel with double bottom for greater strength. Fireproof filling in walls; has stood many fire tests. Tongue and groove door construction absolutely excludes heat, smoke and flames from contents of safe in case of fire. Three-tumbler combination locks furnished on all sizes. Our best safe, 22K1882 has Yale O. B. B. combination lock. Other sizes have our own special combination lock. Oak finish cabinet. These safes are built with an Inner Door, an additional safeguard.

Your name put on safe without extra charge when so ordered. Packed carefully in burlap. **Shipped from our factory in NEWARK, OHIO.**

Specially arranged cabinet can be made to your order. Changes in measurements of safe bodies cannot be made.

MEASUREMENTS AND PRICES	Arrangements of Cabinets
Our best safe. Fireproof walls, 5½ inches thick, withstand a fiercer prolonged fire than the lighter 4-inch walls of our other safes. Yale O. B. B. combination lock. Height, with wheels, 35½ inches. Inside measures 19 inches high, 10[illegible] inches wide, 11 inches deep. Shipping weight, 972 lbs. **22K1882 — With inner door.** Cash price...... **$62.50** Time payment price **$68.50.**	6½x5-inch cash box having steel door with key lock. 2¾x4½-inch cash drawer in cash box. 3x5[illegible]-inch drawer with knob. Two 4¼x5⅛-in. pigeonholes. 19x8⅜-inch book space.
Fireproof walls, 4 inches thick. Height, including wheels, 29½ inches. Inside measures 15 inches high. 11 inches wide. 10 inches deep. Shipping weight, 485 lbs. **22K1874 With inner door.** Cash price...... **$46.50** Time payment price.. **$51.50**	5x4-inch lock cash box. 2¼x3½-in. cash drawer. 3x4-inch drawer with knob. 3x4-inch pigeonhole. 3¼x4-inch pigeonhole. 15x6¾-inch book space.
Fireproof walls, 4 inches thick. Height, including wheels, 26 inches. Inside measures 13 inches high, 10 inches wide, 10 inches deep. Shipping weight, 390 lbs. **22K1872 — With inner door.** Cash price...... **$42.50** Time payment price.. **$46.50**	5x4-inch lock cash box. 2¼x3½-in. cash drawer. 3x4-inch drawer with knob. 4¼x4-inch pigeonhole. 13x5¾-inch book space.
Fireproof walls, 4 inches thick. Height, including wheels, 25 inches. Inside measures 12 inches high, 8 inches wide, 9 inches deep. Shipping weight, 316 pounds. **22K1870 — With inner door.** Cash price...... **$39.50** Time payment price.. **$43.50**	5x4-inch lock cash box. 2¼x3½-in. cash drawer. 3x4-inch drawer with knob. 3½x4-inch pigeonhole. 12x3½-inch book space.

TERMS $5.00 down, and $5.00 a month. When ordering on Easy Time Payments use Time Payment Order Blank on page 1092.

Small Safes for the Home and Small Offices

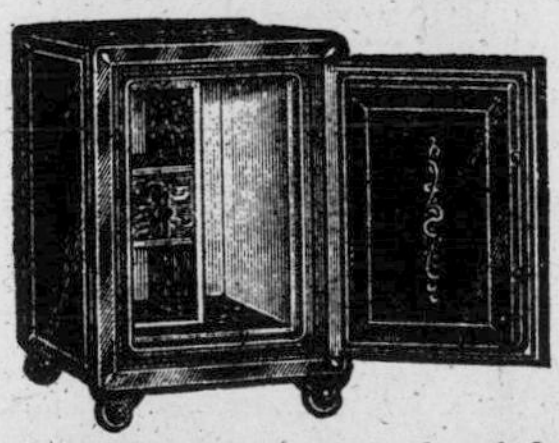

Anyone Can Afford a Safe at Our Low Price

More convenient than a safe deposit box. Lock drawer, 2¾x3-inch; two pigeonholes, 3x3½-inch; book space, 11x3½ inches. Walls, 2 inches thick. Height, including wheels, 16½ inches. Inside measures 11x7x10 inches. Shipping weight, 125 pounds.

22K1867—Without cabinet................................ **$17.50**

22K1868—With cabinet.............. **18.50**

These two safes sold for cash only.
Will pack in a wooden box for $1.60 extra.

SCHOOL DESKS

Factory to You Prices

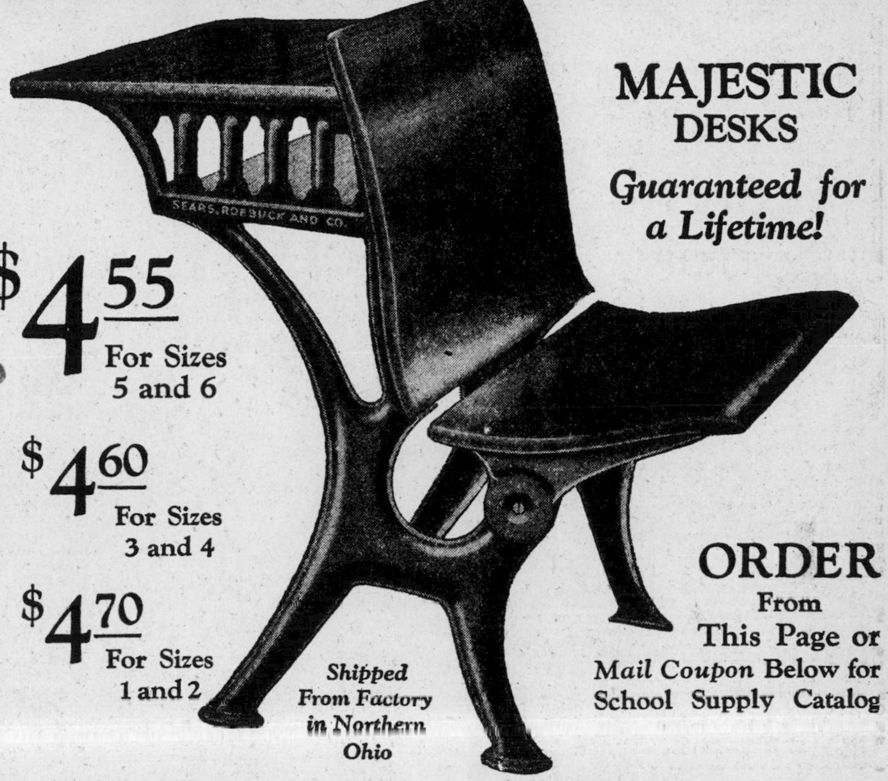

MAJESTIC DESKS

Guaranteed for a Lifetime!

$4.55 For Sizes 5 and 6

$4.60 For Sizes 3 and 4

$4.70 For Sizes 1 and 2

Shipped From Factory in Northern Ohio

ORDER From This Page or *Mail Coupon Below for* School Supply Catalog

1.— **Genuine semi-steel standards,** graceful and attractive.

2.— Greater tested strength, due to half-round casting.

3.— Guaranteed semi-steel castings. The best castings money can buy. There is a great difference in school desk castings offered as "semi-steel;" some are only ordinary cast iron.

4.— Noiseless seat hinge. For forty years the Majestic seat hinge has been the most satisfactory one in use.

5.— Woods. Scientifically designed, form fitting back and seat woods insure correct seating posture.

6.— **Inclination of desk top** conforms to approved standards.

7.— **The Michigan hard maple** selected for the Majestic Desk is recognized as the best possible wood for school desk construction. Because of its close, tough texture or grain, maple makes an ideal writing surface.

8.— **Finish.** On woods genuine lacquer, the toughest and longest wearing finish known. On castings, genuine Japan enamel baked on.

9.— **Inkwell.** The Tannewitz has for years been recognized as the standard school desk inkwell. Impossible to accidentally spill ink. The only truly foolproof inkwell.

10.— **Sanitary features.** No sharp corners or pockets to accumulate dust. Inner surfaces of the feet are filled in. Book box is well lighted and ventilated.

11.— **Installation.** School desks are shipped knocked down in order to reduce the freight charges. The Majestic Desk is so constructed that it is easy to assemble. The most inexperienced person can easily set up our desks. At the same time, the construction is such that, when installed, it is the most solidly rigid desk obtainable.

Majestic Desk—46M24.

Size No.	Ages Accommodated	Height of Top, Inches	Length of Top, In., Single	Floor Space, Inches	Single Desks			Double Desks		
					Shpg. Wt., Lbs.	Desks	Front or Rear, All Sizes	Shpg. Wt., Lbs.	Desks	Fronts or Rears
1	14 to Adults	29	24	28	55	$4.70	$4.48	76	$6.75	$5.95
2	13 to 14	27½	24	27	55	4.70	4.48	76	6.75	5.95
3	11 to 12	26	21	26	45	4.60	4.48	65	6.70	5.95
4	9 to 10	24	21	24	45	4.60	4.48	65	6.70	5.95
5	7 to 8	22½	19	22	35	4.55	4.48	53	6.65	5.95
6	5 to 6	21	19	21	35	4.55	4.48	53	6.65	5.95

Shipping weights of Fronts and Rears are ⅜ the weight of the complete desk.

Mail This Coupon for Free Catalog

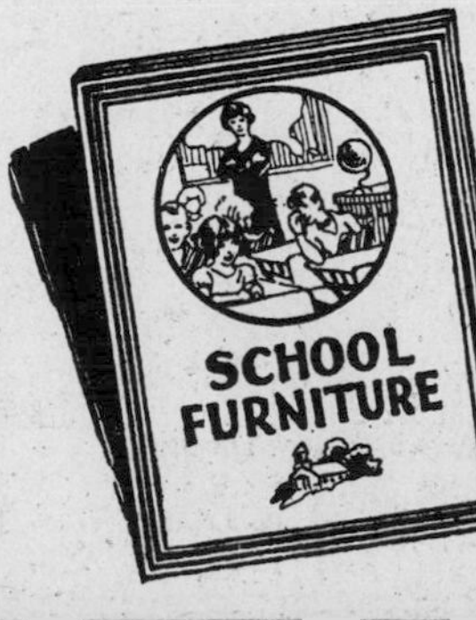

SEARS, ROEBUCK AND CO.,
Philadelphia

Send me your Special School Furniture Catalog 550K

Name..

Postoffice..

Rural Route.................... Box No.....................

State...

Street and No...

Sparkling Crystal Prisms *of* Light

34K5419
3-Light
$23.00

34K5400
6-Light
$28.00

34K5421
1-Light
$8.00

34K5402
2-Light
$19.00

34K5417
5-Light
$31.50

34K5415
5-Light
$31.50

34K5096
2-Light
$5.65

34K5095
1-Light
$3.89

CRYSTAL fixtures are different from any other type of lighting. They are always in style. You never get tired of looking at their glittering beauty. Not so long ago they were used only in palaces and in the homes of the very wealthy. At our prices they are within the reach of all. They are made of beautiful metal castings, richly embossed. Finished in genuine silver plate, shaded with rich black. Don't you want one or more of these sparkling beauties in your home?

The round lamps shown are not included in the price. Use our lamp 34K6825 on 34K5095, 34K5417, 34K5096 and 34K5400; and lamp 34K6878 on 34K5415. Lamps shown on page 659.

34K5415—36 inches long, 24 inches wide. Has 169 glittering glass prisms. 5 lights. **Not mailable.** Shipping weight, 35 lbs. Less lamps......**$31.50**

34K5419—23 inches long, 13 inches wide. Has 169 glittering glass prisms. 3 lights. **Not mailable.** Shipping weight, 20 lbs. Less lamps.....**$23.00**

34K5417—36 inches long, 22½ inches wide. Has 193 glittering glass prisms. 5 lights. **Not mailable.** Shipping weight, 23 lbs. Less lamps......**$31.50**

34K5421—11 inches long, 10 inches wide. Has 68 glittering glass prisms. 1 light. Shipping weight, 7 lbs. Less lamp........**$8.00**

34K5400—36 inches long, 23½ inches wide. Has 203 glittering glass prisms. 6 lights. **Not mailable.** Shipping wt., 35 lbs. Less lamps.....**$28.00**

34K5402—17 inches long, 17½ inches wide. Has 201 glittering glass prisms. 2 lights. **Not mailable.** Shpg. wt., 25 lbs. Less lamps..........**$19.00**

34K5095—Extends 6 in. Wall plate, 4¼x8¼ inches. 1 light. Shpg. wt., 4 lbs. Less lamps.**$3.89**

34K5096—Extends 4¼ in.; width, 9½ inches. Wall plate, 8½x4¼ inches. 2 lights. Shipping weight, 5 lbs. Less lamps......**$5.65**

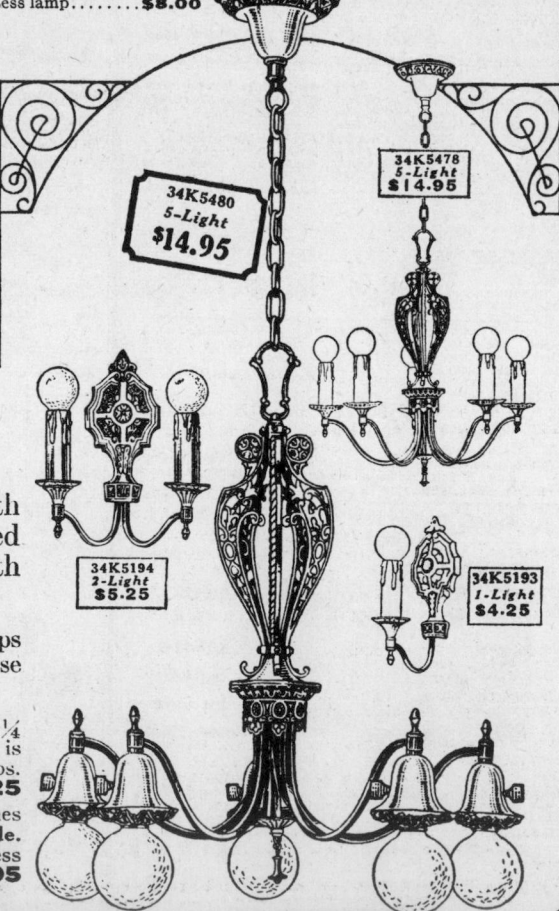

34K5478
5-Light
$14.95

34K5480
5-Light
$14.95

34K5194
2-Light
$5.25

34K5193
1-Light
$4.25

Polychrome Gold Finish

These fixtures are made of brass, beautifully finished with background of antique gold color and very neatly decorated with polychrome colors of red and green; also equipped with old ivory color drip candles.

The ball lamps shown are not included in the price. Use lamps 34K6878 on 34K5480, and on 34K5478. 34K5194 and 34K5193 use lamp 34K6825. Lamps are shown on page 659.

34K5193—1 light. Extends 6 inches. Wall plate is 4¼x8¼ inches. Shpg. wt., 4 lbs. Less lamp....**$4.25**

34K5478—5 lights. 36 inches long; 20 inches wide. **Not mailable.** Shipping weight, 30 pounds. Less lamps.....................**$14.95**

34K5194—2 lights. Extends 4¼ inches; 9¼ inches wide. Wall plate is 4¼x8¼ inches. Shipping weight, 5 lbs. Less lamps.................**$5.25**

34K5480—5 lights. 36 inches long; 20 inches wide. **Not mailable.** Shipping weight, 30 pounds. Less lamps.....................**$14.95**

Unusual Fixture Values

Beautiful Aluminum Fixtures

Aluminum lighting fixtures are very popular at the present time. These fixtures are made of genuine cast aluminum, finished in a soft satin dull silver color background, with polychrome decorations of dull gold, red and green. A very attractive and lasting finish. The round frosted lamps shown are not included in the price. Use our 34K6888 Lamp on 34K5336, 34K5121 and 34K5120; and 34K6889 Lamp on 34K5334, 34K5326, 34K5332, 34K5299, 34K5266, 34K5215 and 34K5122. Lamps shown on page 659.

34K5330—5 lights, 36 inches long, 16 inches wide. Fitted with keyless sockets. Shipping weight, 20 lbs. Not mailable. Less lamps.....**$7.85**

34K5334—4 lights, 36 inches long, 14½ inches wide. Fitted with keyless sockets. Shipping weight, 15 pounds. Less lamps.....**$6.98**

34K5326—3 lights, 36 inches long, 12½ inches wide. Fitted with keyless sockets. Shipping weight, 12 pounds. Less lamps.....**$6.35**

34K5336—5 lights, 36 inches long, 16 inches wide. Fitted with keyless sockets. Shipping wt., 20 lbs. Not mailable. Less lamps.....**$7.75**

34K5332—5 lights, 10 inches long, 16 inches wide. Fitted with keyless sockets. Shipping weight, 15 pounds. Less lamps.....**$7.75**

34K5122—1 light. Wall plate, 8½x4½ inches. Shipping weight, 4 pounds. Less lamp.....**$2.25**

34K5299—3 lights, 5 inches long, 12½ inches wide. Fitted with keyless sockets. Shipping weight, 8 pounds. Less lamps.....**$3.90**

34K5266—2 lights, 4 inches long. Oval shape, 11½x5½ inches. Fitted with keyless sockets. Shpg. wt., 6 lbs. Less lamps.....**$2.75**

34K5215—1 light, 5 inches long, 6 inches wide. Fitted with keyless socket. Shipping weight, 3 pounds. Less lamps.....**$1.70**

34K5121—2 lights. Wall plate, 8½x4½ inches. Extends 4½ inches. Equipped with switch. Shpg. wt., 5 lbs. Less lamps.....**$3.00**

34K5120—1 light. Wall plate, 8½x4½ inches. Extends 4½ inches. Equipped with switch. Shipping weight, 4 pounds.....**$2.25**

Extends 5 inches. Equipped with switch. Shipping weight, 4 pounds.....**$2.25**

"How to Choose Colors and Furnishings for the Home." See page 1017 about this wonderful book at a bargain price.

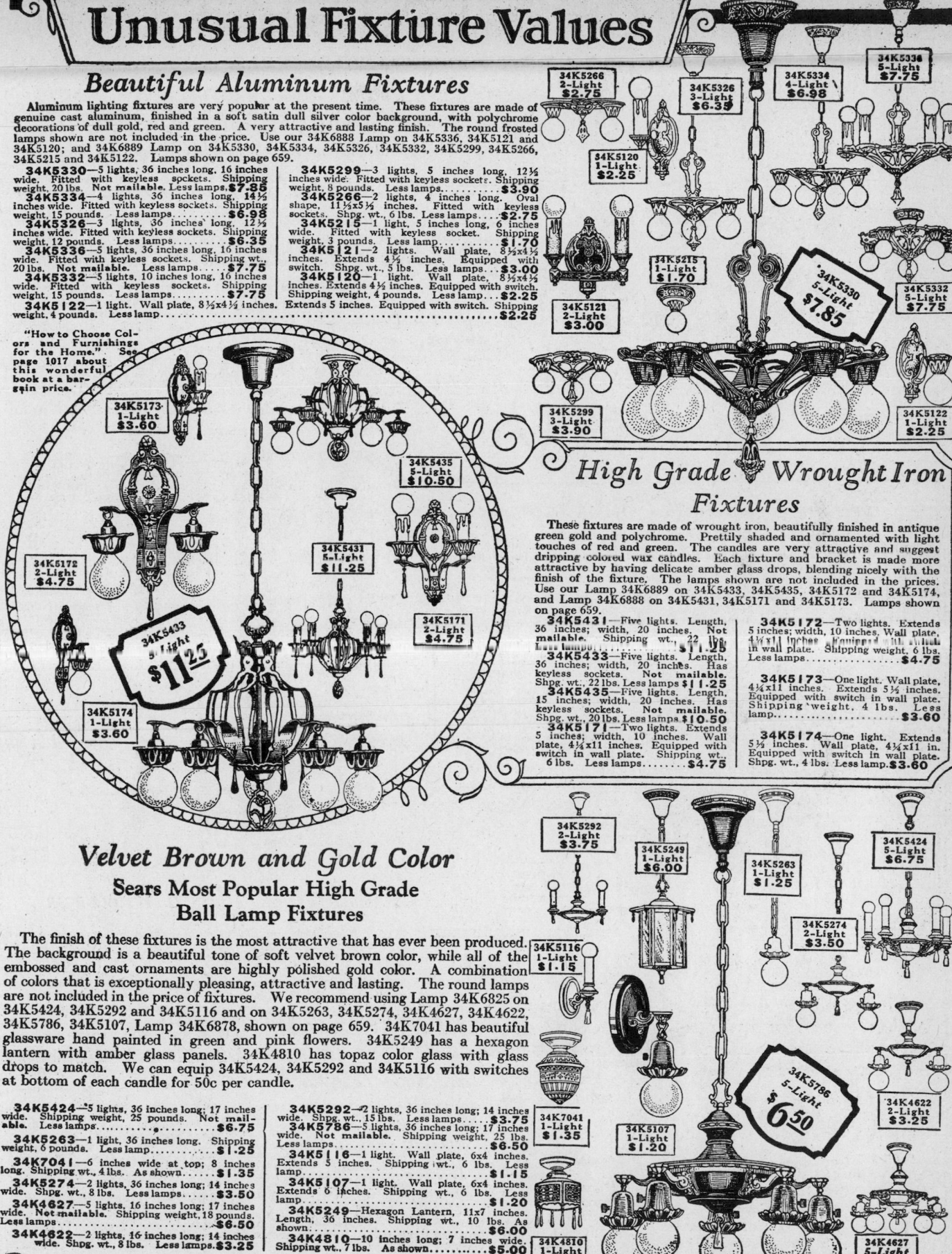

High Grade Wrought Iron Fixtures

These fixtures are made of wrought iron, beautifully finished in antique green gold and polychrome. Prettily shaded and ornamented with light touches of red and green. The candles are very attractive and suggest dripping colored wax candles. Each fixture and bracket is made more attractive by having delicate amber glass drops, blending nicely with the finish of the fixture. The lamps shown are not included in the prices. Use our Lamp 34K6889 on 34K5433, 34K5435, 34K5172 and 34K5174, and Lamp 34K6888 on 34K5431, 34K5171 and 34K5173. Lamps shown on page 659.

34K5431—Five lights. Length, 36 inches; width, 20 inches. Not mailable. Shipping wt., 22 lbs. Less lamps.....**$11.25**

34K5433—Five lights. Length, 36 inches; width, 20 inches. Has keyless sockets. Not mailable. Shpg. wt., 22 lbs. Less lamps.....**$11.25**

34K5435—Five lights. Length, 15 inches; width, 20 inches. Has keyless sockets. Not mailable. Shpg. wt., 20 lbs. Less lamps.....**$10.50**

34K5171—Two lights. Extends 5 inches; width, 10 inches. Wall plate, 4½x11 inches. Equipped with switch in wall plate. Shipping wt., 6 lbs. Less lamps.....**$4.75**

34K5172—Two lights. Extends 5 inches; width, 10 inches. Wall plate, 4½x11 inches. Equipped with switch in wall plate. Shipping weight, 6 lbs. Less lamps.....**$4.75**

34K5173—One light. Wall plate, 4½x11 inches. Extends 5½ inches. Equipped with switch in wall plate. Shipping weight, 4 lbs.....**$3.60**

34K5174—One light. Extends 5½ inches. Wall plate, 4½x11 in. Equipped with switch in wall plate. Shpg. wt., 4 lbs. Less lamp.....**$3.60**

Velvet Brown and Gold Color
Sears Most Popular High Grade Ball Lamp Fixtures

The finish of these fixtures is the most attractive that has ever been produced. The background is a beautiful tone of soft velvet brown color, while all of the embossed and cast ornaments are highly polished gold color. A combination of colors that is exceptionally pleasing, attractive and lasting. The round lamps are not included in the price of fixtures. We recommend using Lamp 34K6825 on 34K5424, 34K5292 and 34K5116 and on 34K5263, 34K5274, 34K4627, 34K4622, 34K5786, 34K5107, Lamp 34K6878, shown on page 659. 34K7041 has beautiful glassware hand painted in green and pink flowers. 34K5249 has a hexagon lantern with amber glass panels. 34K4810 has topaz color glass with glass drops to match. We can equip 34K5424, 34K5292 and 34K5116 with switches at bottom of each candle for 50c per candle.

34K5424—5 lights, 36 inches long; 17 inches wide. Shipping weight, 25 pounds. Not mailable. Less lamps.....**$6.75**

34K5263—1 light, 36 inches long. Shipping weight, 6 pounds. Less lamp.....**$1.25**

34K7041—6 inches wide at top; 8 inches long. Shipping wt., 4 lbs. As shown.....**$1.35**

34K5274—2 lights, 36 inches long; 14 inches wide. Shpg. wt., 8 lbs. Less lamps.....**$3.50**

34K4627—5 lights, 16 inches long; 17 inches wide. Not mailable. Shipping weight, 18 pounds. Less lamps.....**$6.50**

34K4622—2 lights, 16 inches long; 14 inches wide. Shpg. wt., 8 lbs. Less lamps.....**$3.25**

34K5292—2 lights, 36 inches long; 14 inches wide. Shpg. wt., 15 lbs. Less lamps.....**$3.75**

34K5786—5 lights, 36 inches long; 17 inches wide. Not mailable. Shipping weight, 25 lbs. Less lamps.....**$6.50**

34K5116—1 light. Wall plate, 6x4 inches. Extends 5 inches. Shipping wt., 6 lbs. Less lamp.....**$1.15**

34K5107—1 light. Wall plate, 6x4 inches. Extends 6 inches. Shipping wt., 6 lbs. Less lamp.....**$1.20**

34K5249—Hexagon Lantern, 11x7 inches. Length, 36 inches. Shipping wt., 10 lbs. As shown.....**$6.00**

34K4810—10 inches long; 7 inches wide. Shipping wt. 7 lbs. As shown.....**$5.00**

Labels within the illustration:

- 34K5266 2-Light $2.75
- 34K5326 3-Light $6.35
- 34K5334 4-Light $6.98
- 34K5336 5-Light $7.75
- 34K5120 1-Light $2.25
- 34K5215 1-Light $1.70
- 34K5121 2-Light $3.00
- 34K5299 3-Light $3.90
- 34K5330 5-Light $7.85
- 34K5332 5-Light $7.75
- 34K5122 1-Light $2.25
- 34K5173 1-Light $3.60
- 34K5435 5-Light $10.50
- 34K5431 5-Light $11.25
- 34K5172 2-Light $4.75
- 34K5433 5-Light $11.25
- 34K5171 2-Light $4.75
- 34K5174 1-Light $3.60
- 34K5292 2-Light $3.75
- 34K5249 1-Light $6.00
- 34K5263 1-Light $1.25
- 34K5424 5-Light $6.75
- 34K5116 1-Light $1.15
- 34K5274 2-Light $3.50
- 34K5786 5-Light $6.50
- 34K5107 1-Light $1.20
- 34K7041 1-Light $1.35
- 34K4810 1-Light $5.00
- 34K4622 2-Light $3.25
- 34K4627 5-Light $6.50

Fixtures of Beauty

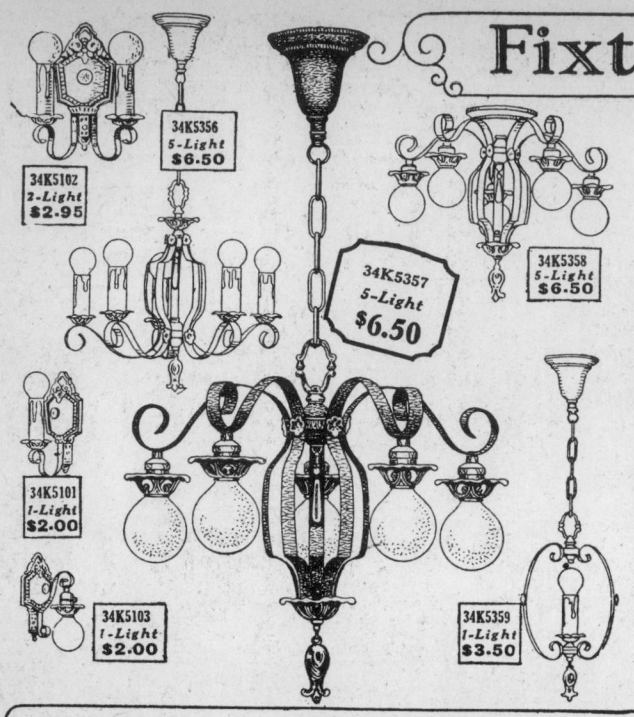

The Newest in Wrought Iron Fixtures

These wrought iron fixtures are very modern in design, and are as attractive as they are modern. The finish is Spanish gold, a beautiful shade of antique mottled green gold with a delicate touch of polychrome in the fancy ornaments. The special color of finish is not only warm and attractive, but also wonderfully adapted to any room, as it will blend well with practically all color schemes. The candles have the effect of dripping wax and are of antique ivory color.

The lamps shown are not included in the prices. Use our 34K6888 Lamps on 34K5102, 34K5356, 34K5101 and 34K5359; and 34K6889 Lamps on 34K5358, 34K5357 and 34K5103. Lamps shown on page 659.

New lighting fixtures will make a wonderful difference in the appearance of your home.

34K5357—5 lights. 36 inches long, 19 inches wide. Has key sockets. Shipping weight, 16 pounds. Not mailable. Less lamps....**$6.50**

34K5356—5 lights. 36 inches long, 19 inches wide. Has keyless sockets. Shipping weight, 16 pounds. Not mailable. Less lamps....................**$6.50**

34K5358—5 lights. 16 inches long, 19 inches wide. Has keyless sockets. Shipping weight, 16 pounds. Not mailable. Less lamps....................**$6.50**

34K5359—1 light. 36 inches long, 8½ inches wide. Shipping weight, 7 pounds. Less lamp.............................**$3.50**

34K5102—2 lights. Extends 4 inches. Width, 8¼ inches. Wall plate, 9x4½ inches. Equipped with switch. Shipping weight, 6 pounds. Less lamps............**$2.95**

34K5101—1 light. Extends 5 inches. Wall plate, 9x4½ inches. Equipped with switch. Shipping weight, 4 pounds. Less lamp.**$2.00**

34K5103—1 light. Extends 5 inches. Wall plate, 9x4½ inches. Equipped with switch. Shipping weight, 4 pounds. Less lamp.**$2.00**

Brown Tone and Gold Color

When you purchase lighting fixtures from Sears, Roebuck and Co. you get the best there is and at prices so low that they cannot be duplicated anywhere considering, of course, the high grade quality of our finish, material and workmanship. The fixtures shown are finished in a pretty shade of brown color, with the embossed and cast ornaments in a highly polished gold color. All fixtures, except candle type, have key sockets for turning on and off the light.

The round lamps are not included in the price. Use our 34K6825 Lamps on 34K5468 and 34K5469; and 34K5183, 34K6878 Lamps on 34K4639, 34K4643, 34K4641, 34K5253, 34K5233, 34K5777, 34K5182 and 34K5298. Lamps shown on page 659.

34K5777—4 lights. 36 inches long; 18 inches wide. Shipping weight, 20 pounds. Not mailable. Less lamps........**$4.75**

34K5468—5 lights. 36 inches long; 17 inches wide. Shipping weight, 20 pounds. Not mailable. Less lamps......**$5.25**

34K5469—Same as above, but 4 lights. Shipping weight, 18 lbs. Not Mailable. Less lamps................**$4.50**

34K5253—2 lights. 36 inches long; 15 inches wide. Shipping weight, 8 pounds. Less lamps............**$2.75**

34K5298—3 lights. 36 inches long; 18 inches wide. Shipping weight, 15 pounds. Less lamps..............**$3.75**

34K5233—1 light. 36 inches long. Shipping weight, 4 pounds. Less lamp.. **1.15**

34K5182—1 light. Oval back, 6x4 inches. Extends 5 inches. Shipping weight, 3 pounds. Less lamp...........**$1.20**

34K4641—4 lights. 13 inches long; 18 inches wide. Shipping weight, 18 pounds. Less lamps.............**$4.35**

34K4639—3 lights. 12 inches long; 16 inches wide. Shipping weight, 10 pounds. Less lamps..............**$3.75**

34K4643—Like above, but 2 lights. Shipping weight, 9 lbs. Less lamps....**$2.45**

34K5183—1 light. Oval wall back, 6x4 inches. Extends 5 inches. Shipping weight, 3 pounds. Less lamp.............**$1.20**

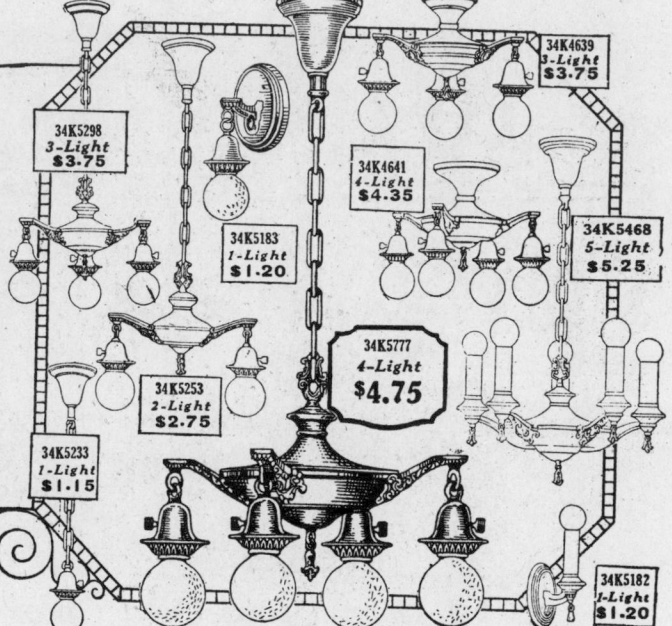

Genuine Gold Plated Fixtures

GOLD PLATED! Immediately you think of one of the most precious metals on earth. You associate it with something beautiful, something worth while. GENUINE GOLD PLATE with beautiful polychrome relief is used throughout as the finish of these fine lighting fixtures. They are magnificent, and the only GENUINE GOLD PLATED AND POLYCHROME set on the market sold at these remarkably low prices. Under this gold plate the structure is of *genuine solid brass*, especially cast in French molding sand to better bring out the beautiful designs. The beauty of their design and workmanship, when combined with the gold finish, will make your home a place of loveliness. Remember, heretofore gold plate has been used only on the most expensive and elaborate fixtures. Notice OUR prices.

The lamps shown are not included in our prices. Use our 34K6825 Lamps on 34K5128, 34K5129, 34K5282 and 34K5477; and 34K6878 Lamps on 34K5479, 34K5289, 34K5281, 34K4629 and 34K4638. Lamps shown on page 659.

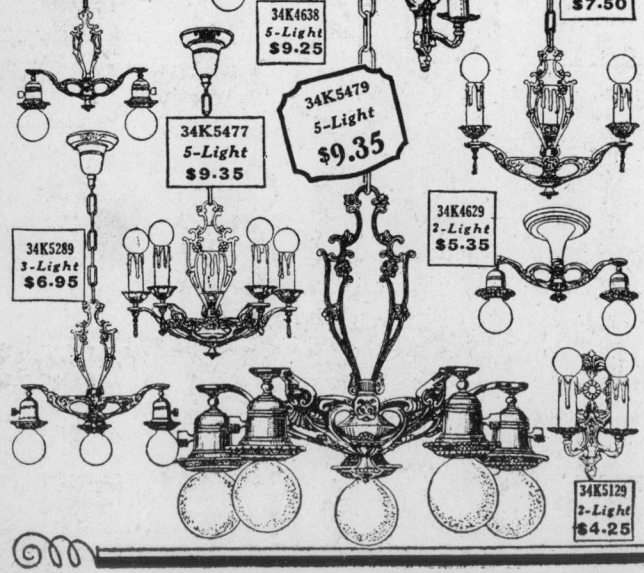

34K5479—5 lights. Has key switches. Length, 36 inches; width 17 inches. Not mailable. Shipping weight, 20 pounds. Less lamps...........................**$9.35**

34K4638—5 lights. Length, 12 inches; width, 17 inches. Not mailable. Shipping weight, 20 pounds. Less lamps......**$9.25**

34K4629—2 lights. Length, 12 inches; width, 14½ inches. Shipping weight, 8 pounds. Less lamps.................**$5.35**

34K5281—2 lights. Has key switches. Length, 36 inches; width, 14½ inches. Shipping weight, 9 pounds. Less lamps.......**$5.60**

34K5128—1 light. Wall plate, 10x4½ inches. Width, 7 inches. With switch on candle. Shipping weight, 4 pounds. Less lamp.................................**$2.95**

34K5289—3 lights. Has key switches. Length, 36 inches; width 14½ inches. Shipping weight, 19 pounds. Less lamps....**$6.95**

34K5282—3 lights. Length, 36 inches; width, 13½ inches. Shipping weight, 18 pounds. Less lamps...............**$7.50**

34K5477—5 lights. Length, 36 inches; width, 17 inches. Shipping weight, 25 pounds. Less lamps....................**$9.35**

34K5129—2 lights. Wall plate, 10x4½ inches. Width, 7 inches. Extends 5 inches. Has switch on each candle. Shipping weight, 5 lbs. Less lamps.............**$4.25**

for Every Home

The Latest
in Spanish Design Fixtures

Wonderful reproductions of real Spanish designs. Everything about these fixtures is suggestive of the peculiarities of Spanish art. They are made of solid cast bronze, in hammered effect, giving the appearance of being wrought by hand, as was done by the metal-mongers in olden times. The finish is antique Spanish brass color, with the Spanish shields in polychrome colors. The round frosted lamps are not included in the price of fixtures. Use our Lamps 34K6888 on 34K5401, 34K5066 and 34K5067; and Lamps 34K6889 on 34K5404, 34K5411, 34K5208 and 34K5360. Lamps shown on page 659.

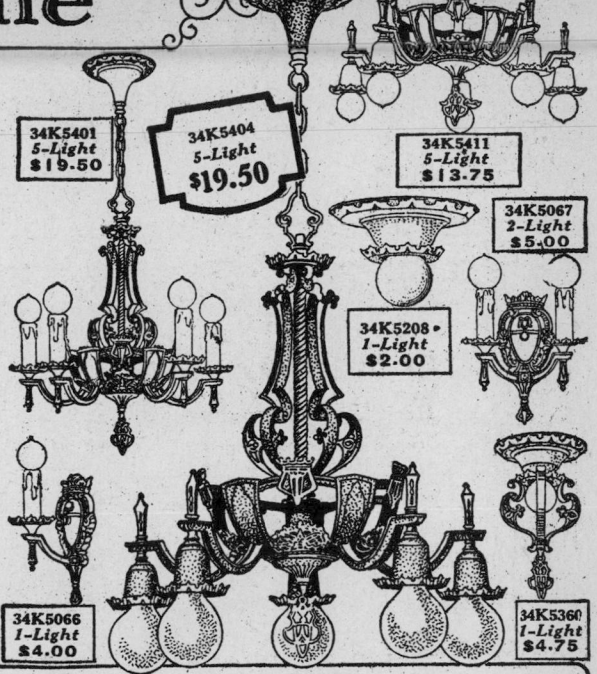

34K5401—5 lights. 36 inches long, 20 inches wide. Shipping weight, 25 pounds. **Not mailable. Less lamps $19.50**
34K5404—5 lights. Key sockets. 36 inches long, 20 inches wide. Shipping weight, 25 lbs. **Not mailable. Less lamps ..$19.50**
34K5411—5 lights. Keyless sockets. 13 inches long, 20 inches wide. Shipping weight, 25 pounds. **Not mailable. Less lamps...........................$13.75**
34K5208—1 light. 6½ inches wide, 8 inches long. Shipping wt., 6 lbs. Less lamp..$2.00

34K5360—1 light. 11 inches long, 6½ inches wide. Shipping weight, 10 pounds. Less lamp $4.75
34K5066—1 light. Wall plate, 10x4½ inches. Extends 4½ inches. Equipped with switch. Shpg. wt., 5 lbs. Less lamp..$4.00
34K5067—2 lights. Wall plate, 10x4½ inches. Width, 7½ in. Equipped with switch. Shipping wt., 8 lbs. Less lamps $5.00

Solid Aluminum Fixtures

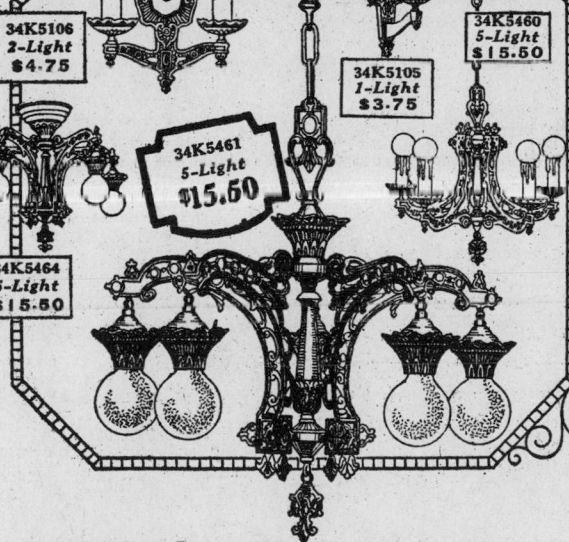

All the beauty, grandeur and charm of the finest are yours if you select these massive solid aluminum fixtures for your home. The finish is a dull gold matt color with applied burnished trimmings, with just a touch of color. The beautiful designing and exquisite workmanship is of a quality that you expect to find only in fixtures costing much more. Elsewhere you would generally pay twice as much for fixtures as high a grade as these. The lamps shown are not included in the prices. Use our 34K6825 Lamps on 34K5197, 34K5198 and 34K5437; and Lamps 34K6878 on 34K5443, 34K5199, 34K5474, 34K5441, 34K5202, 34K5204 and 34K5203. Lamps shown on page 659.

34K5437—5 lights. Length, 36 inches; width, 16½ inches. Shipping weight, 20 pounds. Not mailable. Less lamps...................**$8.75**
34K5202—1 light. Length, 6½ inches; width, 8 inches. Shipping weight, 4 lbs. Less lamp......**$1.75**
34K5441—5 lights. Length, 36 inches; width, 16½ inches. With turn button sockets. Shipping weight, 18 lbs. Not mailable. Less lamps.**$8.75**
34K5443—5 light. Length, 8½ inches; width, 16½ inches. With keyless sockets. Shipping weight, 15 pounds. Not mailable. Less lamps....**$7.95**
34K5198—2 lights. Wall plate, 12½x4¼ inches. Extends 5 inches. Width, 9 inches. With switch. Shpg. wt., 5 lbs. With lamps...**$3.40**

34K5197—1 light. Wall plate, 12½x4¼ inches. Extends 5½ inches. With chain pull switch. Shpg. wt., 4 lbs. Less lamp........**$2.65**
34K5199—1 light. Wall plate, 12½x4¼ inches. Extends 5½ inches. With turn button socket. Shpg. wt., 4 lbs. Less lamp......**$2.38**
34K5474—3 lights. Length, 36 inches; width, 14 inches. With turn button key socket. Shipping weight, 12 lbs. Not mailable. Less lamps.**$5.25**
34K5204—3 lights. Length, 9 inches; width, 14 inches. With keyless sockets. Shipping weight, 12 pounds. Not mailable. Less lamps...**$5.25**
34K5203—2 lights. Length, 9 inches; width, 12 inches. With keyless sockets. Shipping weight, 8 pounds. Less lamps.................**$3.75**

Genuine Cast Brass

We recommend these beautiful electroliers for beautifying and supplying that quality of highest elegance in the home. They are made of solid cast brass, finished in antique gold color. Their general make-up is very ornate and massive. The design is a combination of French and Italian with the French pattern more in evidence. You will be surprised at the beauty of these fixtures. The round lamps shown are not included in the price. For 34K5460, 34K5105 and 34K5106 use Lamps 34K6888; and for 34K5461 and 34K5464 use Lamp 34K6889. Lamps shown on page 659.

34K5460—5 lights. Length, 36 inches; width, 20 inches. Shipping weight, 22 pounds. Not mailable. Less lamps...................**$15.50**
34K5461—5 lights. Length, 36 inches; width, 20, inches. Shipping weight, 22 pounds. Not mailable. Less lamps...................**$15.50**
34K5106—2 light. Wall plate, 11x4½ inches. Equipped with switch. Shipping weight, 5 pounds. Less lamps **$4.75**

34K5464—5 lights. Length, 18 inches; width, 20 inches. Shipping weight, 22 pounds. Not mailable. Less lamps...................**$15.50**
34K5105—1 light. Wall plate, 11x4½ inches. Extends 6 inches. Equipped with switch. Shipping weight, 4 pounds. Less lamp.............**$3.75**

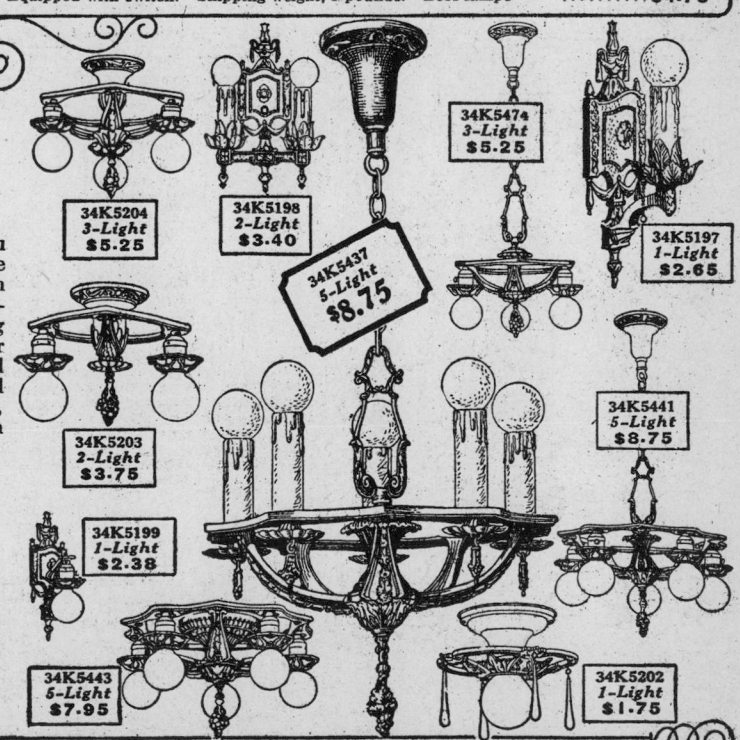

Graceful Fixtures Beautify Your Home

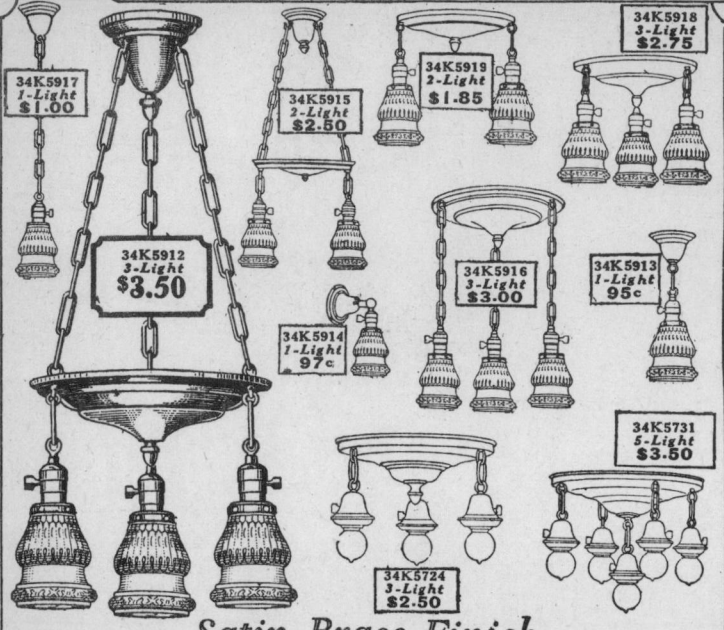

Satin Brass Finish

These fixtures are very appropriate for those who desire neat appearing, serviceable fixtures at extremely low prices.

The pans and ceiling canopies are made of heavy weight brass nicely finished in brush satin brass color and heavily coated with lacquer to preserve the finish. All of these fixtures are equipped with key switches.

Like all of our fixtures they are assembled and wired ready to install in accordance with the requirements of the National Board of Fire Underwriters (the acknowledged highest authority for the proper construction of all electrical material). Lamps not included in price.

Satin brass finish. Length, 36 inches. Width of round pan, 12 inches. Frosted fancy glassware. Shipping weight, 18 pounds.
34K5912—3 lights...............$3.50

Satin brass finish. Length, 14 inches. Top canopy, 4½ inches wide. Fancy frosted glassware. Shipping weight, 3 pounds.
34K5913—1 light...............95c

Satin brass finish. Length, 10 inches. Round pan, 14 inches wide. Use our 34K6825 Lamps shown on page 659. Shipping weight, 12 lbs.
34K5731—5 lights. Without Lamps..................$3.50

Satin brass finish. Extends from wall 6 inches. Frosted fancy glassware. Shipping weight, 3 pounds.
34K5914—1 light..................97c

Satin brass finish. Length, 36 inches. Oval pan, 12 inches long, 6 inches wide. Frosted glassware. Shipping wt., 12 lbs.
34K5915—2 lights...........$2.50

Satin brass finish. Length, 36 inches. Round pan, 14 inches wide. Frosted fancy glassware. Shipping weight, 18 pounds.
34K5916—3 lights...............$3.00

Satin brass finish. Length, 10 inches. Round pan, 12 inches wide. Use our 34K6825 Lamps shown on page 659. Shipping weight, 8 lbs.
34K5724—3 lights. Without lamps.....................$2.50

Satin brass finish, 36 inches long. White frosted glassware. Shipping weight, 6 pounds.
34K5917—1 light..................$1.00

Satin brass finish. Length, 14 inches. Round pan, 12 inches wide. Frosted glass. Shipping weight, 15 pounds.
34K5918—3 lights............$2.75

Satin brass finish, 12 inches wide. Oval pan, 12x6 inches. Frosted glass. Shipping weight, 10 pounds.
34K5919—2 lights...........$1.85

Genuine Silver and Black

Silver and black have always been effective in the decorative scheme of the room, not only for its beauty, but also because of its appropriateness. Genuine silver plate, combined with the effect of embossed parts brought out in black, give to these fixtures a strikingly rich, distinctive appearance. Indeed, the long, graceful curves, the scroll designing and the clever embossing, will more than please you. You can rest assured you are offered a real bargain and, as usual, Sears quality is of the best. Length, 36 inches; width, 20 inches. Lamps not included in price. Use our Lamp 34K6825 on 34K5466, 34K5163 and 34K5164 and 34K6878 on 34K5463. Lamps shown on page 659. The fixtures cannot be shipped by parcel post. The brackets match the fixtures. Height, 10 inches; width of wall plate, 4½ in. Each bracket is equipped with a switch.

34K5164—2-Light Bracket. Shipping weight, 5 pounds.........$3.00

34K5163—1-Light Bracket. Shipping weight, 4 pounds............$2.25

34K5463—5-Light Ball Lamp Fixture. Shipping weight, 30 pounds..$8.50

34K5466—5-Light Candle Fixture. Shipping weight, 30 pounds.....$7.95

Glass Bowl Fixtures

Metal parts satin brass finish. Length, 36 inches. Frosted glass, fancy design 14x16-inch bowl, and side lights to match.

34K5946—Has one keyless socket inside of bowl, but no side lights.
Shipping weight, 15 pounds.....................$3.00

34K5947—Has one keyless socket inside of bowl, and three side lights with key sockets.
Shipping weight, 25 pounds.....................$5.00

Bedroom Lighting Fixtures

These fixtures have been specially designed for the lighting of bedrooms. They are also very appropriate for sun parlors and breakfast rooms. Beautifully embossed cast metal, finished in old ivory, with dainty decorations of green leaves and pink flowers. The ball lamps are not included in the price. Use our lamps 34K6825 on 34K5155, and lamp 34K6878 on 34K5325, 34K5327 and 34K5216. For lamps see page 659.

34K5155—1-light bracket. Wall plate, 9½x4¾ inches. Extends 4½ inches. Equipped with switch. Shpg. wt., 5 lbs. Less lamps..........$2.00

34K5216—1-light ceiling fixture. Length, 5 inches; width, 7 inches. Keyless socket. Shipping weight, 3 pounds. Less lamps...........$1.15

34K5325—2-light. Length, 5 in. Oval cast plate, 11¾x5¼ inches. Keyless socket. Shipping weight, 5 pounds. Less lamps...............$2.00

34K5327—3-light. Length, 5 in.; width, 10¾ inches. Triangular shaped cast plate. Keyless socket. Shipping weight, 5 lbs. Less lamps...$2.75

Genuine Silver Plate Fixtures

You have only to look at the illustration to see the grace and charm of the designing of these fixtures, and you can easily imagine the soft and lovely effect of Genuine Silver Plate. These fixtures are very popular, as their simple lines harmonize with the majority of homes, and add to the loveliness of the room.

These fixtures are 36 inches long and 19 inches wide. Lamps not included in price. 34K5472 and 34K5473 take 34K6878 lamps and 34K5444 and 34K5445 take 34K6825 lamps, shown on page 659. *These fixtures are not mailable.* Shipping weight, 17 pounds.

34K5472—4 lights.....................$7.45
34K5473—Same as above, but 5 lights.... 8.79
34K5444—4 lights..................... 6.75
34K5445—Same as above, but 5 lights.... 8.25

Fixtures for Kitchens, Bathrooms, Bedrooms, Halls

Hall or Bedroom Brackets

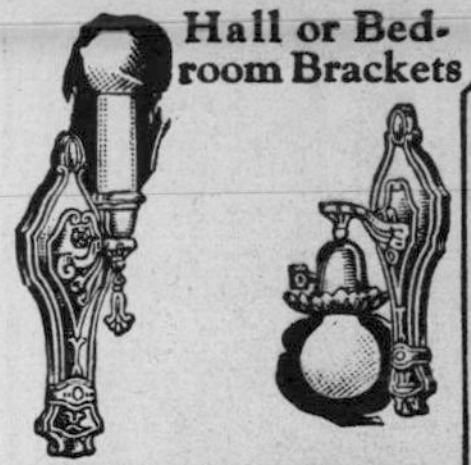

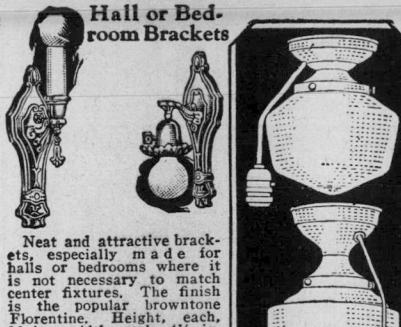

Neat and attractive brackets, especially made for halls or bedrooms where it is not necessary to match center fixtures. The finish is the popular browntone Florentine. Height, each, 12 in.; width, each, 4½ in. Extends from wall, 4½ in. Shpg. wt., ea., 5 lbs.

34K5110 — Candle Bracket, without lamp. Use our 34K6825 Lamp on page 659.... **$1.89**

34K5111—Drop Ball Lamp Bracket, without lamp. Use our 34K6878 Lamp on page 659 .... **$1.89**

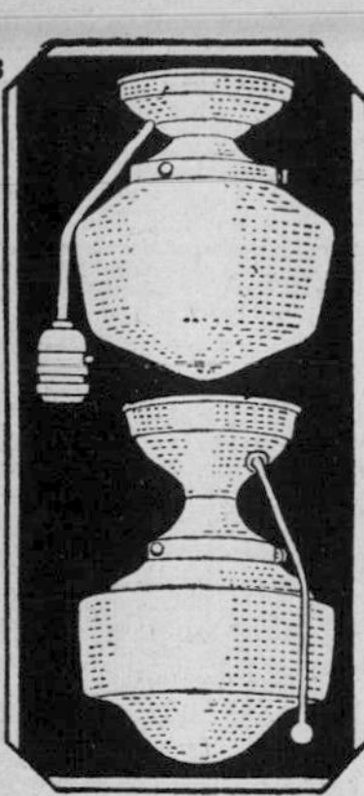

Low Priced Kitchen Light

Has combination switch and utility socket. Glass shade is 8 inches wide. Length of entire fixture, 9 inches. Takes 75-watt nitrogen Lamp. Shpg. wt., 6 lbs.

34K7094 As shown.. **$1.89**

White Enameled Kitchen Unit

Same unit as 34K7071, shown at right with pull switch but without utility socket. Shipping weight, 8 pounds.

34K7073 As shown... **$1.75**

34K7063—Same as 34K7073 but without pull switch....... **$1.39**

Wonderful Kitchen Light

You are offered this large, high grade kitchen light at a price that means a real saving. Truly a light that will make work in your kitchen easier and more pleasant. Throwing a powerful white light, it may be likened to a bright, sunny day—yet it does not glare. Do not compare this unit with units of similar design but smaller size which sell for less. It is equipped with a combination switch, and utility socket which drops within easy reach to attach an electric iron. The utility socket, being in the center of the room, permits you to place your ironing board anywhere you desire in the kitchen. A 100-watt nitrogen lamp gives the best results. White enamel finish. The glass is 9 in. wide; length of entire fixture, 11 in. Shipping weight, 8 pounds.

34K7071—As shown, with switch and utility socket, but without lamp **$2.30**

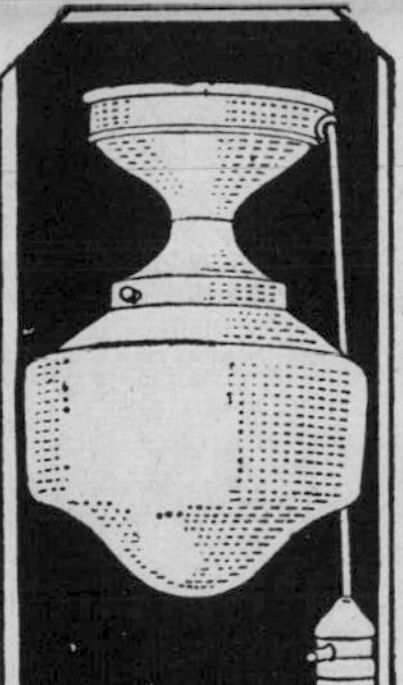

Store Fixtures

For attaching close to the ceiling. Made of brass, in bronze finish. Length, 10 in. Glass bowl, 12 in. wide. Will take 150-watt nitrogen lamp. Fitted with keyless socket. Shpg. wt., 20 lbs.

34K4540 **$2.65**

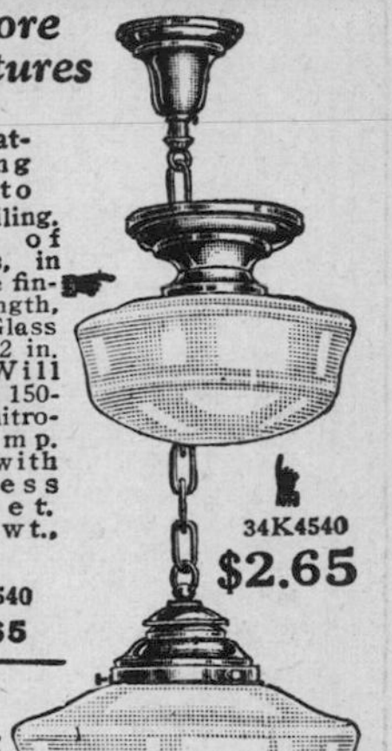

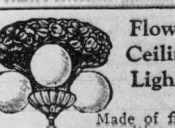

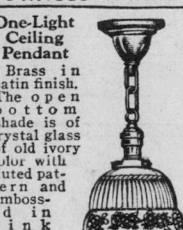

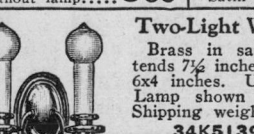

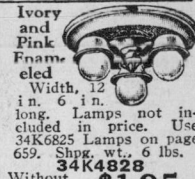

Brass, bronze finish. Length, 36 in. Powerful reflecting glass bowl, 14 in. wide. Takes 200-watt nitrogen lamp, fitted with keyless socket. Shipping weight, 22 pounds.

34K4539 .... **$4.25**

Ivory and Blue Ceiling Fixture

Length, 7½ in. Width, 12 in. Finished in old ivory and tinted in blue. Has keyless sockets. Use our 34K6878 Lamps, shown on page 659. Shpg. wt., 8 lbs.

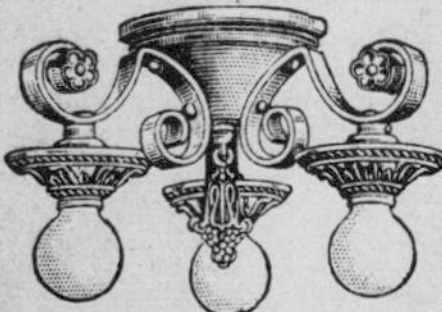

34K4831—3 lights, without lamps **$4.35**

34K4830—As above, but 2 lights, without lamps **$3.45**

Attractive Ceiling Fixtures

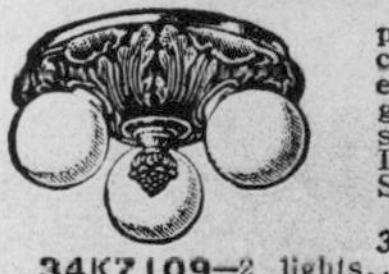

Very effective and inexpensive. Made of fiber composition in heavy leaf effect. Finished in a dull gold color. Has keyless sockets. Use our 34K6878 Lamps, shown on page 659. Shipping weight, 5 pounds.

34K7054... 3 lights........ **$3.25**

34K7109—2 lights........................ $2.85

34K7110—4 lights........................ 6.45

34K7056—6 inches wide, 1 light........ 1.20

Flower Ceiling Lights

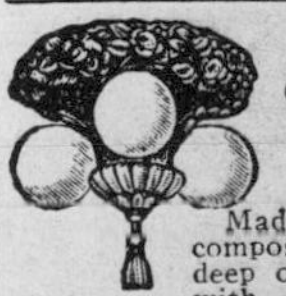

Made of fiber composition in deep old ivory with a pretty background of raised painted flowers in their natural colors. Has the simplicity and beauty of nature. It is about 9 in. long and 9 in. wide. Use 34K6878 Lamps shown on page 659. Shipping weight, 5 pounds.

34K7057 Without lamps... **$5.95**

Attractive Ceiling Light

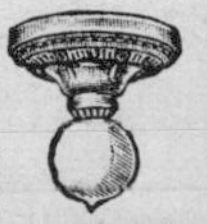

Made of brass. Ivory tinted background with dainty roses and leaves. A pale blue ribbon encircles the entire fixture. Length, 5 in. Has keyless socket. Use 34K6878 Lamp shown on page 659. Shpg. wt., 2 lbs.

34K7053 Without lamp... **$1.95**

Decorated Glass

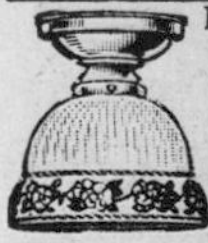

Brass, satin finish, 5½ in. at top. Shade is in ribbed effect with floral embossed bottom in pink and green. Keyless socket. Height, 8 in. Shpg. wt., 4 lbs.

34K7052 As shown... **$1.19**

One-Light Ceiling Fixture

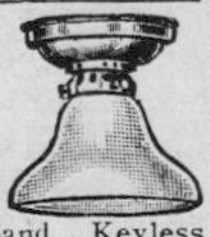

Length, 6½ inches. Brass, satin finish, 5¼-in. ceiling band. Keyless socket. Frosted glass reflector, 6 in. in diameter. Shpg. wt., 4 lbs.

34K7020 As shown **69c**

Same as above, but with chain pull switch.

34K7045..... **$1.19**

Hand Painted Ceiling Light

Brass finished in old ivory tinted in blue. Length, 13 inches. Width, 8 inches. Glass bowl is hand painted in pink and blue flowers, and has 5 blue glass crystals at bottom. Has keyless socket. Shipping weight, 6 lbs.

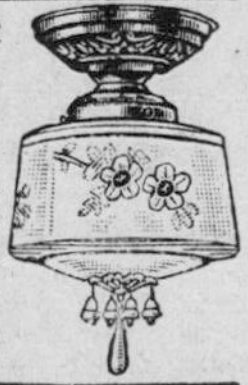

34K4801 As shown............ **$3.29**

Hand Painted Kitchen Light

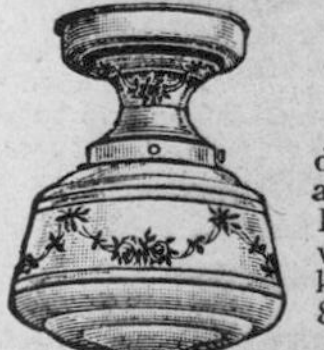

Finished in white enamel, decorated with blue borders and garlands of flowers. Length, over all, 11 inches; width of glass, 9 inches. Has keyless socket. Shipping wt., 8 lbs.

34K7097....... **$2.25**

Bathroom Fixtures

One-Light Bracket

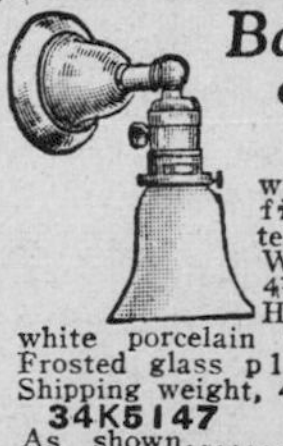

Brass in white enamel finish. Extends 6 inches. Wall canopy, 4½ in. wide. Has insulated white porcelain key socket. Frosted glass plain shade. Shipping weight, 4 pounds.

34K5147 As shown....... **$1.35**

Round Enamel Pendant

Length, 15½ in. Brass in white enamel finish. Canopy, 5 inches wide. Frosted glass reflector. Keyless socket. Shpg. wt., 5 lbs.

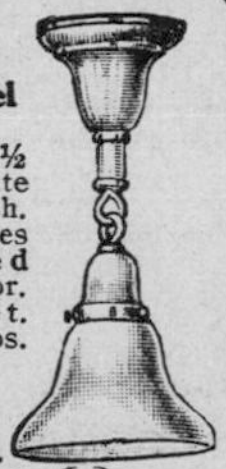

34K4923 As shown. **$1.65**

Brick Pattern Glass

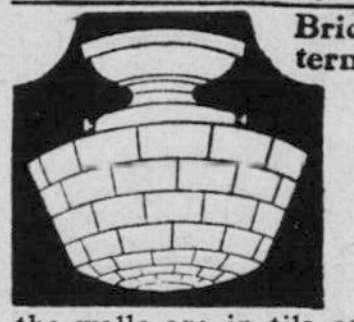

The glassware will match all rooms where the walls are in tile or imitation brick pattern. Length, 8½ in.; width, 9 in. Finished in white enamel. Fitted with keyless socket for electric light. Shpg. wt., 8 lbs.

34K4533 As shown...... **$1.75**

Ivory Enameled Bracket

Finished in ivory enamel, oval back 4x6 in. We recommend our 34K6825 Lamp shown on page 659. Shipping weight, 3 pounds.

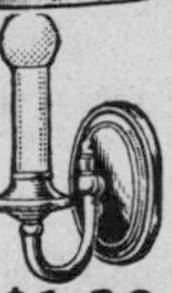

34K5176 Without lamp..... **$1.89**

Tile Design Mirror Bracket

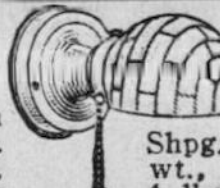

Brass in white enamel. Extends 9 in. Wall plate is 4½ in. wide. Oval glass shade in tile design and opal color resembling porcelain. Has pull chain socket. Shpg. wt., 4 lbs.

34K5063 As shown........ **$1.95**

Enameled Mirror Bracket

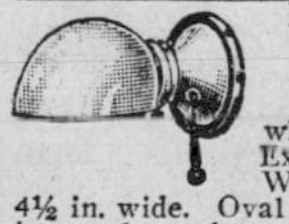

Brass in white enamel. Extends 9 in. Wall plate is 4½ in. wide. Oval glass shade in opal color, resembling porcelain. Has chain pull socket. Shpg. wt., 4 lbs.

34K5061 As shown....... **$1.29**

Latest for Bathrooms

This bracket closely resembles porcelain. It is made of white metal, finished in porcelain white enamel. The little knob turns the light on or off. **At the base it is equipped with a receptacle for use with electric curling irons, vibrators, etc.** The round lamp is not included in the price. See 34K6825 Lamp on page 659. Shpg. wt., 6 lbs.

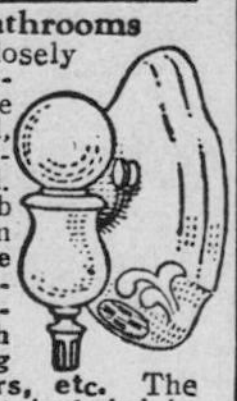

34K5057 Without lamp.... **$2.35**

Same as above, but without extra plug outlet at bottom.

34K5065 .... **$1.85**

White Enamel Ceiling Light

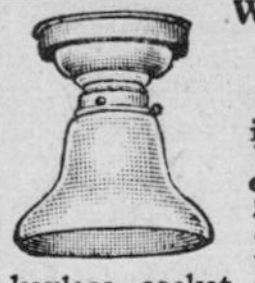

Length, 6½ in. Genuine brass in white enamel finish. 5¼-inch round ceiling band fitted with keyless socket for one electric light. Frosted glass, 6 inches in diameter. Shpg. wt., 4 lbs.

34K7064 As shown...... **75c**

Genuine Porcelain

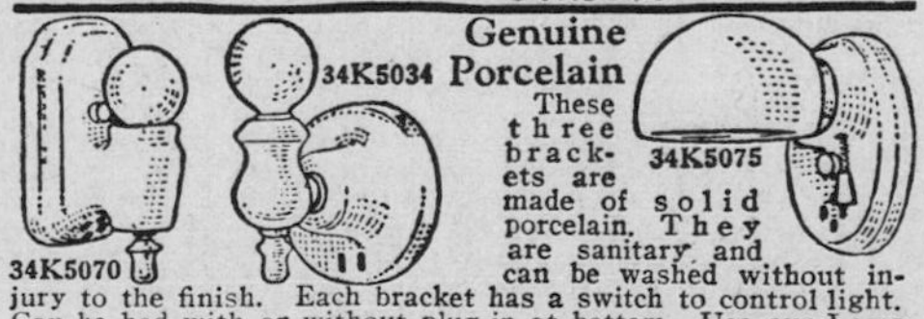

These three brackets are made of solid porcelain. They are sanitary and can be washed without injury to the finish. Each bracket has a switch to control light. Can be had with or without plug-in at bottom. Use our Lamp 34K6825 shown on page 659. Shipping weight, 4 pounds.

34K5070—6¾ in. high, 4 in. wide, less lamp..... $3.00

34K5071—Same as 34K5070, but without plug..... 2.50

34K5034—4½ in. wide, less lamp.................... 2.98

34K5033—Same as 34K5034, but without plug..... 2.69

34K5075—6½ in. high, 4 in. wide, less lamp..... 2.50

34K5076—Same as 34K5075, but without plug..... 2.25

Old Ivory Finish

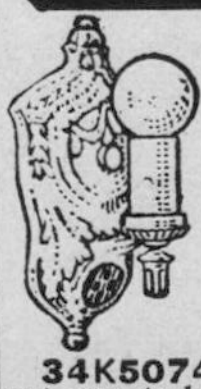

Old ivory color. Measures 9¼x5 in. Has a receptacle at bottom. Is turned on or off with knob at bottom. Use our 34K6825 Lamp shown on page 659. Shipping weight, 4 pounds.

34K5072 Without lamp **$2.85**

34K5074—Same as above, without receptacle.................. $2.45

White Enamel Finish

Made of brass, finished in white enamel. Is 5¾ in. long, 5½ in. wide. An ideal and inexpensive bathroom fixture. Equipped with chain pull socket. Use our 34K6878 Lamp shown on page 659. Shipping weight, 3 pounds.

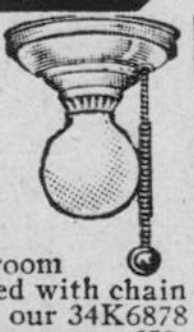

34K5210 .... **89c**

One-Light Ceiling Pendant

Brass in satin finish. The open bottom shade is of crystal glass of old ivory color with fluted pattern and embossed in pink flowers and green leaves. Round ceiling canopy, 4½ inches wide. Length, 16 inches. Fitted with keyless socket for one electric light. Shpg. wt., 5 lbs.

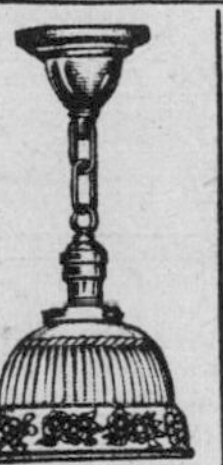

34K4913 As shown.... **$1.75**

One-Light Pendant

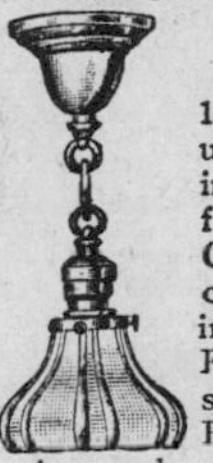

Length, 16 in. Genuine brass in satin finish. Ceiling canopy, 4½ in. wide. Keyless socket. Frosted glass, clear crystal ribbed shade. Shipping weight, 4 pounds.

34K4908 As shown. **$1.25**

Fancy Ball Ceiling Light

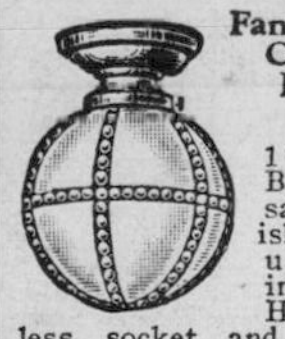

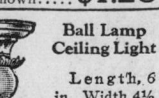

Length, 10¾ in. Brass in satin finish. Measures 5¼ in. at top. Has keyless socket and frosted glass 8-in. ball. Shpg. wt., 6 lbs.

34K7023 As shown..... **$1.25**

Ivory and Pink Enameled

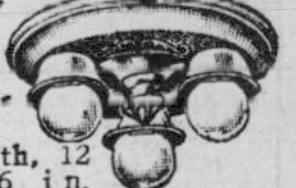

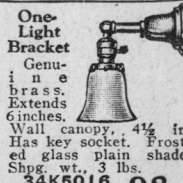

Width, 12 in. 6 in. long. Lamps not included in price. Use 34K6825 Lamps on page 659. Shpg. wt., 6 lbs.

34K4828 Without lamps...... **$1.95**

34K4829 Same as above, but 2-light $1.75

Ball Lamp Ceiling Light

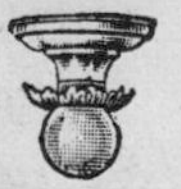

Length, 6 in. Width 4½ in. Brass finished in ivory color. Use our Lamp 34K6878 shown on page 659. Shpg. wt., 2 lbs.

34K5211 Without lamp..... **50c**

One-Light Bracket

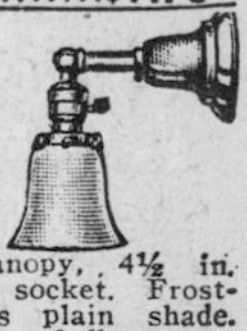

Genuine brass. Extends 6 inches. Wall canopy, 4½ in. Has key socket. Frosted glass plain shade. Shpg. wt., 3 lbs.

34K5016 Satin brass.... **98c**

Two-Light Wall Bracket

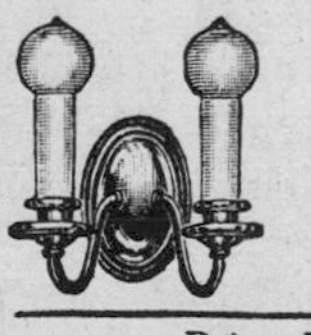

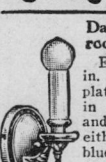

Brass in satin finish. Extends 7½ inches. Oval canopy, 6x4 inches. Use our 34K6825 Lamp shown on page 659. Shipping weight, 5 pounds.

34K5139 Without lamps............ **$1.89**

Dainty Bedroom Bracket

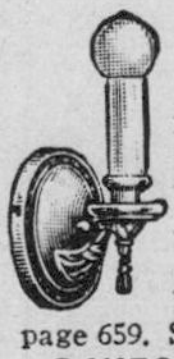

Embossed 4x6-in. oval wall plate. Finished in cream color, and tinted in either pink or blue color. Use our 34K6825 Lamp shown on page 659. Shpg. wt., 5 lbs.

34K5020—Pink tint. Without lamp **$1.35**

34K5021—Blue tint. Without lamp..... $1.35

Candle Brackets

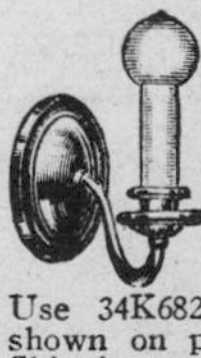

Brass in satin finish. Extends 7½ in. Oval canopy, 6x4 in. Use 34K6825 Lamp shown on page 659. Shipping wt., 4 lbs.

34K5138 Without lamp....... **$1.49**

Save ONE-HALF on Wall Paper. See Pages 1018-1019

Pendants *for* Bedrooms, Halls, Kitchens *and* Bathrooms

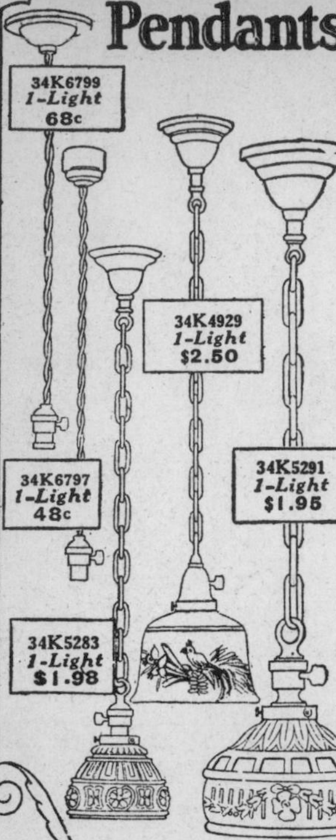

34K6799
1-Light
68c
34K4929
1-Light
$2.50
34K6797
1-Light
48c
34K5291
1-Light
$1.95
34K5283
1-Light
$1.98

4-foot twisted cotton covered cord, 5-inch satin brass ceiling plate and brass key socket. Shipping weight, 2 pounds.
34K6799—Each............**68c**
5 for.............................$3.35

4-foot twisted cotton covered cord with porcelain rosette for concealed wiring. Brass key socket. Shipping weight, 2 pounds.
34K6797—Each..............**48c**
5 for.............................$2.35

One-Light Enameled Pendant
Length, 36 inches. Made of genuine brass in ivory enamel finish. Round ceiling canopy, 4½ inches wide. Has key socket and ivory tinted glass shade with bird design. Shipping weight, 5 pounds.
34K4929—Each...........**$2.50**

One-Light Chain Pendant
Length, 36 inches. Genuine brass in satin finish. Canopy, 4½ inches wide. Fancy embossed design 7-inch open bottom frosted glass shade. Brass key socket. Shipping weight, 5 pounds.
34K5283—As shown.
Each........................**$1.98**

Pink Tinted Shade
Made of brass, 36 inches long over all, finished in satin brass. 7-inch white satin finish glass shade, tinted pink with garlands of pink flowers and green leaves. Brass key socket. Shipping weight, 5 pounds.
34K5291—As shown.
Each.............................**$1.95**

Made of brass. Finished in ivory and blue trimming or ivory and pink trimming. Length, 34 inches. Has keyless socket. Shade is 8 inches, and hand painted in blue and pink flowers with five glass crystals to match. Shpg. wt., 7 lbs.
34K4832—Pink **$3.95**
34K4833—Blue 3.95

Double Duty Pendant
Length, 36 inches. Genuine brass in satin finish. Has chain pull socket with side outlet for attaching electrical devices. Plain frosted glass shade. Shipping weight, 4 pounds.
34K5223—As shown.**$2.69**

Reflector Pendant
Length, 36 inches. Genuine brass, satin finish. Ceiling canopy, 4½ inches wide. Frosted glass 7-inch 60-watt reflector. Brass key socket. Shipping weight, 5 pounds.
34K4916—As shown.
Each..........................**$1.35**
5 for..........................$6.50

4-foot weatherproof cord with 4-inch cover for iron ceiling box. Porcelain key socket. Shipping wt., 2 pounds.
34K6774—Each..........**50c**
5 for...........................$2.25
34K6755—Same as above, but with 3¼-inch cover. Each.....55c
5 for...........................$2.50

4-foot cord with porcelain cleat rosette for open wiring. Twisted cotton covered lamp cord and brass key socket. Shpg. wt., 2 lbs.
34K6777—Each..........**48c**
5 for.........................$2.15

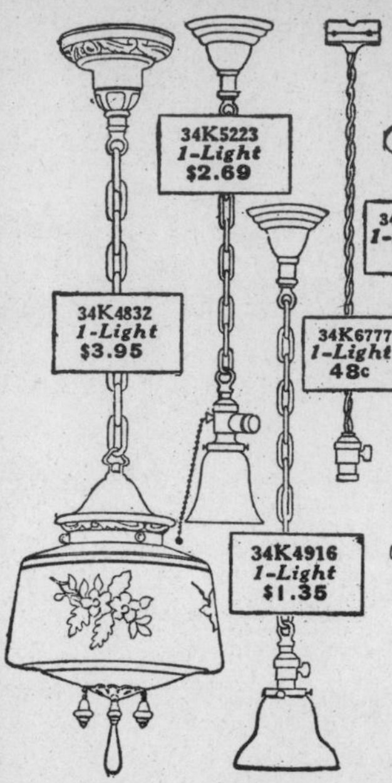

34K5223
1-Light
$2.69
34K6774
1-Light
50c
34K4832
1-Light
$3.95
34K6777
1-Light
48c
34K4916
1-Light
$1.35

Porch Lights

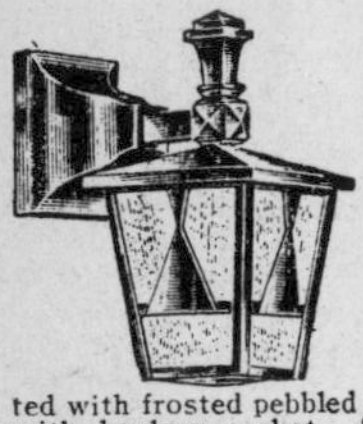

Porch Lantern
Iron in black finish. Extends 8½ in. 5-inch square wall canopy. Lantern, 7x6 in., fitted with frosted pebbled glass. Wired with keyless socket. Shipping wt., 8 pounds.
34K7107—As shown. **$2.85**

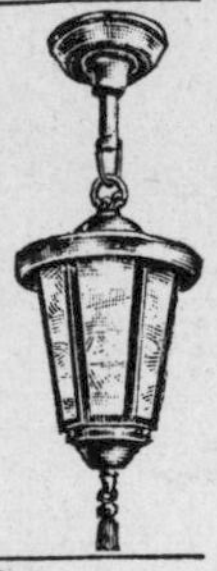

Amber Glass Lantern
Made of sheet iron in black finish. Length, 22 inches over all. Lantern is 8 inches wide and 13 inches long. Has six panels of amber color glass. Keyless socket. Shpg. wt., 8 pounds.
34K5297
As shown,
$4.45

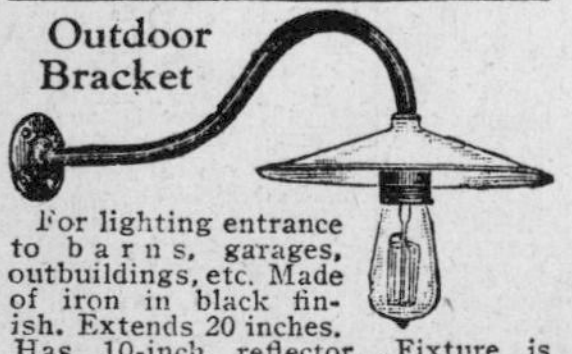

Outdoor Bracket
For lighting entrance to barns, garages, outbuildings, etc. Made of iron in black finish. Extends 20 inches. Has 10-inch reflector. Fixture is equipped with weatherproof keyless socket. Shipping weight, 9 pounds.
34K7062—Without lamp...............**$2.00**

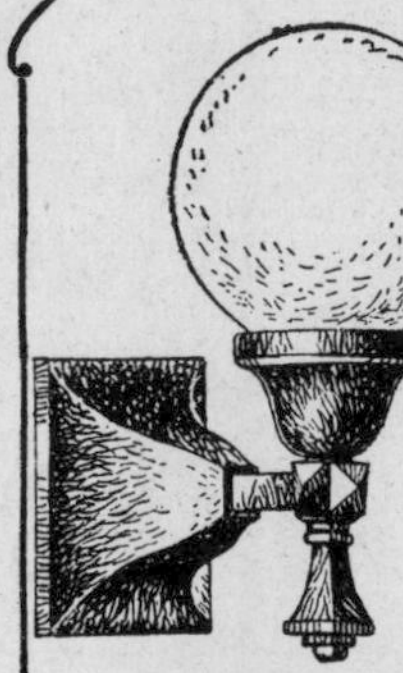

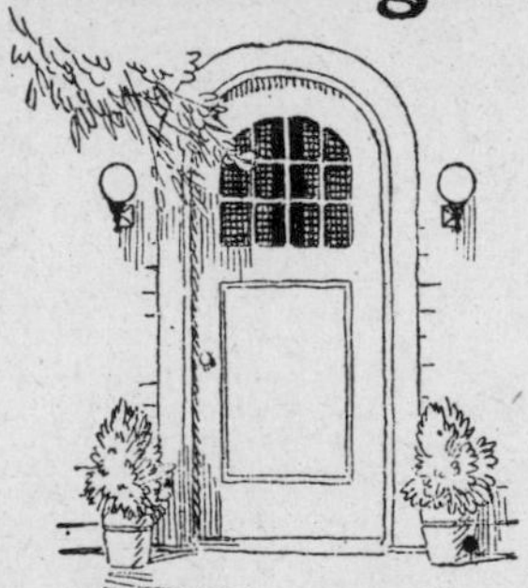

Porch Bracket
A popular type of porch light, of neat and attractive appearance. Extends 7 inches. Made of iron in black finish. Has 5-inch square canopy. The fixture is wired to a keyless socket. Frosted glass 6-inch ball. Shpg. wt., 8 lbs.
34K7076—As shown.........**$1.95**

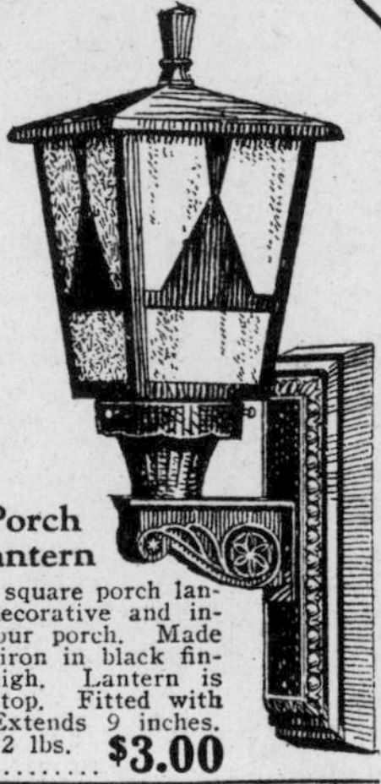

Porch Lantern
This ornamental square porch lantern will give a decorative and inviting effect to your porch. Made of cast and sheet iron in black finish. 16 inches high. Lantern is 6 inches wide at top. Fitted with keyless socket. Extends 9 inches. Shipping weight, 12 lbs. **$3.00**
34K7105

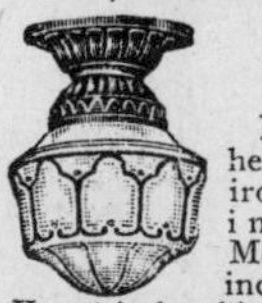

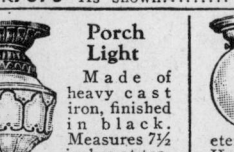

Porch Light
Made of heavy cast iron, finished in black. Measures 7½ inches at top. Has 8-inch white satin finish glass ball, with black ribbing. Wired with keyless, porcelain socket. Shipping weight, 8 pounds.
34K7072
As shown...... **$2.35**

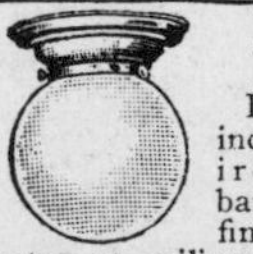

Porch Light
Length, 7¼ inches. Cast iron ceiling band in black finish. Diameter at ceiling, 6 inches. Has porcelain keyless socket. Frosted glass 6-inch ball. Can be used for open wiring only. Shipping weight, 5 pounds.
34K7017
As shown.......... **65c**

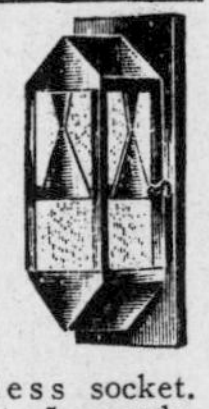

Iron Porch Lantern
Attached alongside of door. Height, 12 in. Extends 4½ in. Made of black sheet iron. Has frosted glass. Wired with porcelain keyless socket. Shipping weight, 5 pounds.
34K7101—As shown.............. **$3.25**

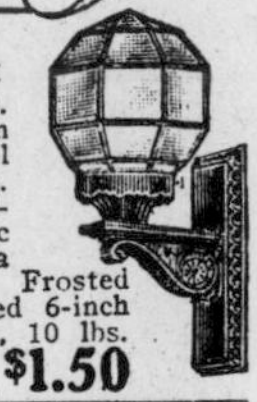

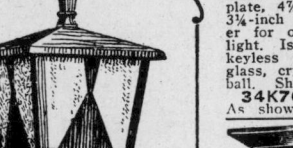

Porch Bracket
Extends 9 inches. Made of iron in black finish. Wall plate, 4⅞x9 inches. 3¼-inch globe holder for one electric light. Is wired to a keyless socket. Frosted glass, crystal ribbed 6-inch ball. Shipping wt., 10 lbs.
34K7013
As shown......... **$1.50**

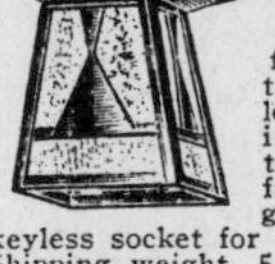

Porch Lantern
Iron in black finish. Square lantern, 7½ in. in length and 6½ in. in width across top. Fitted with frosted pebbled glass panels. Has keyless socket for one electric light. Shipping weight, 5 lbs.
34K7103 **$2.00**

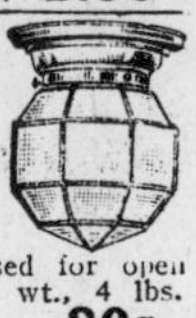

Porch Light
Length, 7¼ inches. Cast iron in black finish. Diameter at ceiling, 6 in. Has porcelain keyless socket. Frosted glass ball, crystal ribbing. Mission style. Can be used for open wiring only. Shipping wt., 4 lbs.
34K7016
As shown................ **89c**

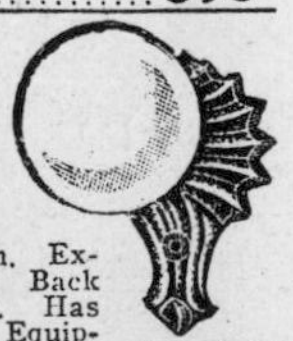

New Design
The very newest idea in porch lighting. Made of cast iron in verde green finish. Extends 8 inches. Back plate, 8x5 inches. Has keyless socket. Equipped with 6-inch frosted glass ball. Shipping weight, 7 lbs.
34K7066—As shown. **$1.80**

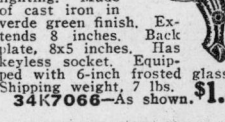

Genuine Solid Copper Fixtures

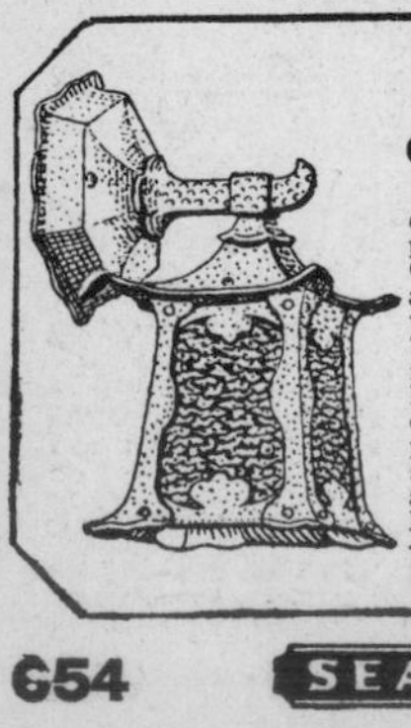

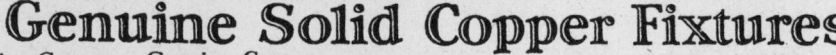

Genuine Copper
Of hammered solid copper in natural polished copper finish. Copper mellows with age, producing a beautiful finish. Extends 7 in. Lantern is 5¼ in. square and 6½ in. high with light amber color crackled glass panels. Has keyless socket. Can be used anywhere. Has one light. Shipping wt., 4 lbs.
34K7102. **$5.25**

Genuine Copper
Made of hammered solid copper in natural polished copper finish. Height, 10½ inches. Lantern is 5¼ in. square and 6½ in. high and has light amber color crackled glass panels. Has keyless socket. Can be used anywhere. Has one light. Shipping weight, 4 lbs.
34K7104
$5.25

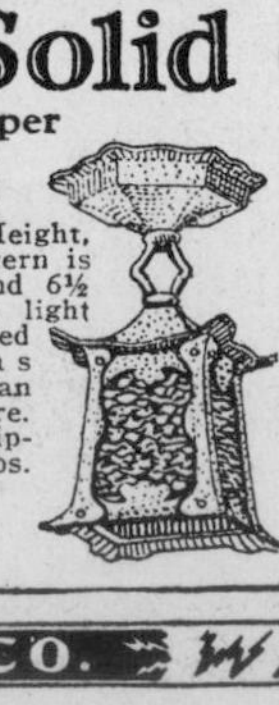

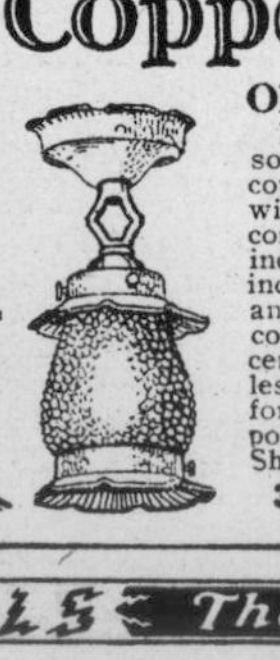

Old Lantern Style
Made of hammered solid copper in natural copper color. Copper will withstand climatic conditions. Height, 11½ inches. Lantern is 7½ inches high, 5 in. wide and has a dark amber colored crackled glass center. Fitted with keyless socket. Is adapted for either inside or on porches. Has one light. Shipping weight, 6 lbs.
34K7108 **$4.95**

Old Lantern Style
Made of hammered solid copper in natural copper color. Exceedingly attractive and inexpensive. Extends 7 inches. Lantern is 7½ in. high and 5 inches wide and has a dark amber color crackled center. Fitted with keyless socket. Is adapted for either inside or porches. Has one light. Shpg. wt., 4 lbs.
34K7106
$4.95

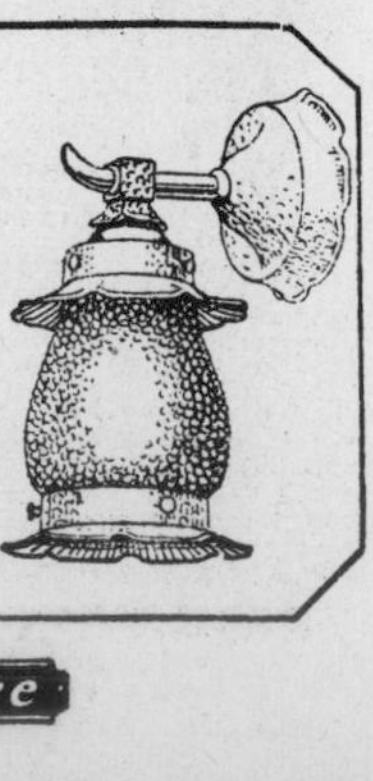

FLOOR LAMP SHADES
AT UNHEARD OF PRICES

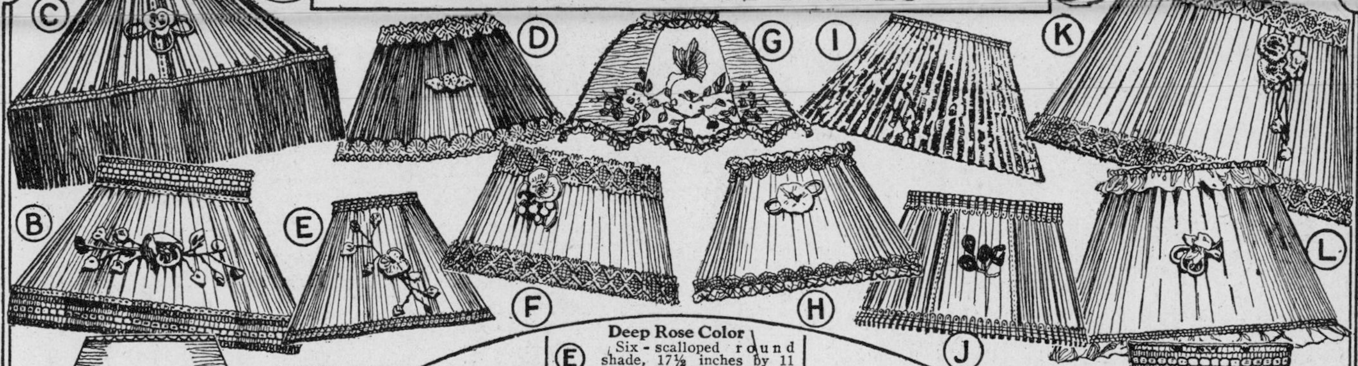

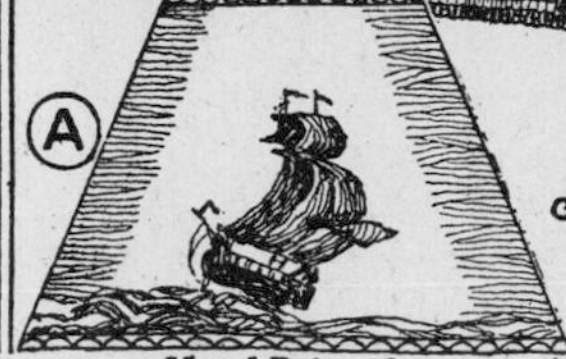

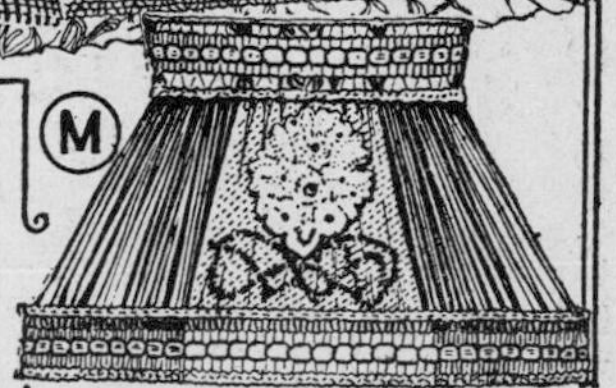

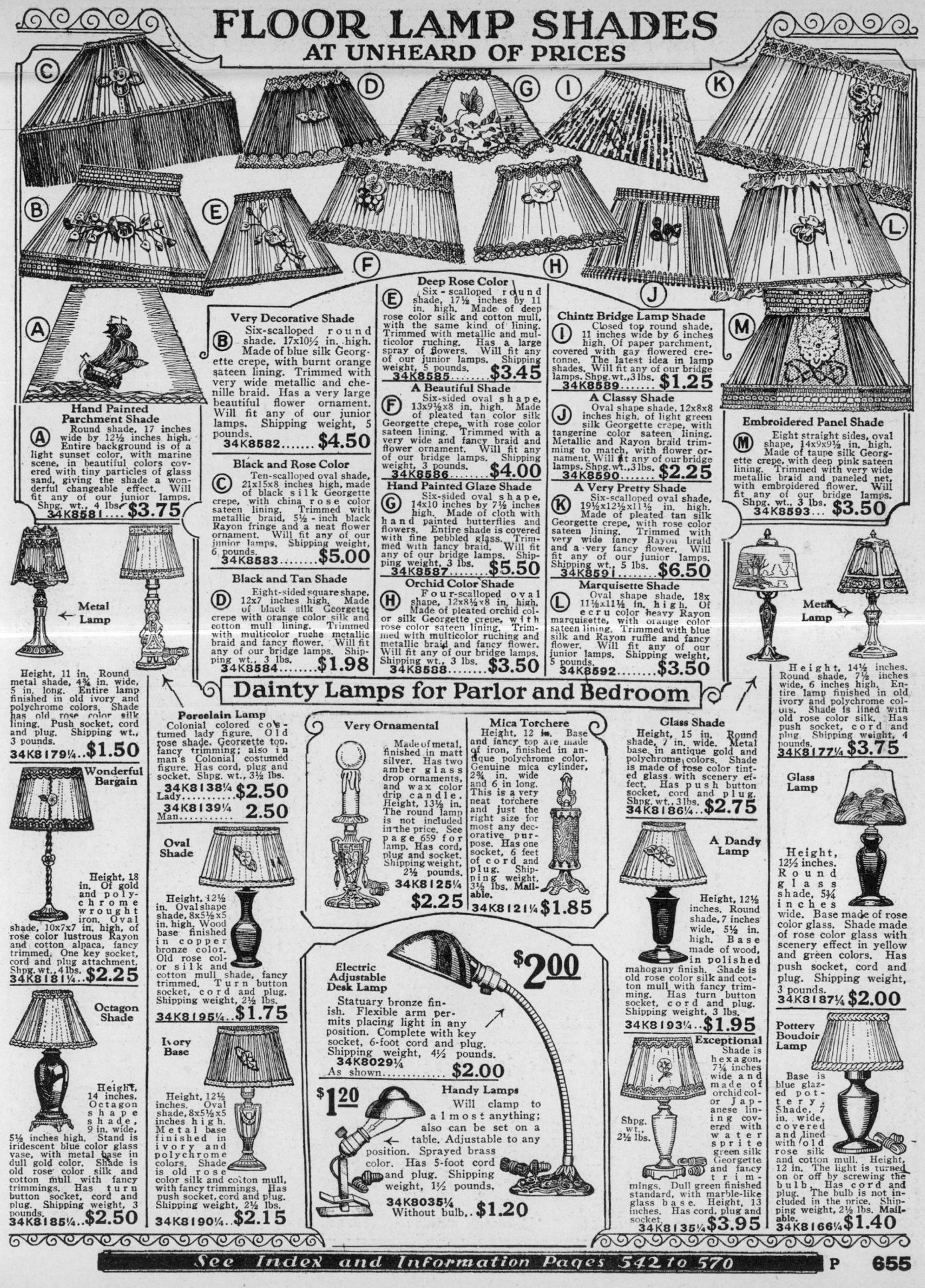

Hand Painted Parchment Shade
(A) Round shade, 17 inches wide by 12½ inches high. Entire background is of a light sunset color, with marine scene, in beautiful colors covered with tiny particles of glass sand, giving the shade a wonderful changeable effect. Will fit any of our junior lamps. Shpg. wt., 4 lbs.
34K8581....$3.75

Very Decorative Shade
(B) Six-scalloped round shade. 17x10½ in. high. Made of blue silk Georgette crepe, with burnt orange sateen lining. Trimmed with very wide metallic and chenille braid. Has a very large beautiful flower ornament. Will fit any of our junior lamps. Shipping weight, 5 pounds.
34K8582.......$4.50

Black and Rose Color
(C) Ten-scalloped oval shade, 21x15x8 inches high, made of black silk Georgette crepe, with china rose color sateen lining. Trimmed with metallic braid, 5½-inch black Rayon fringe and a neat flower ornament. Will fit any of our junior lamps. Shipping weight, 6 pounds.
34K8583.........$5.00

Black and Tan Shade
(D) Eight-sided square shape, 12x7 inches high. Made of black silk Georgette crepe with orange color silk and cotton mull lining. Trimmed with multicolor ruche metallic braid and fancy flower. Will fit any of our bridge lamps. Shipping wt., 3 lbs.
34K8584.........$1.98

Deep Rose Color
(E) Six-scalloped round shade, 17½ inches by 11 in. high. Made of deep rose color silk and cotton mull, with the same kind of lining. Trimmed with metallic and multicolor ruching. Has a large spray of flowers. Will fit any of our junior lamps. Shipping weight, 5 pounds.
34K8585........$3.45

A Beautiful Shade
(F) Six-sided oval shape, 13x9½x8 in. high. Made of pleated tan color silk Georgette crepe, with rose color sateen lining. Trimmed with a very wide and fancy braid and flower ornament. Will fit any of our bridge lamps. Shipping weight, 3 pounds.
34K8586...........$4.00

Hand Painted Glaze Shade
(G) Six-sided oval shape, 14x10 inches by 7½ inches high. Made of cloth with hand painted butterflies and flowers. Entire shade is covered with fine pebbled glass. Trimmed with fancy braid. Will fit any of our bridge lamps. Shipping weight, 3 lbs.
34K8587.........$5.50

Orchid Color Shade
(H) Four-scalloped oval shape, 12x8½x8 in. high. Made of pleated orchid color silk Georgette crepe, with rose color sateen lining. Trimmed with multicolor ruching and metallic braid and fancy flower. Will fit any of our bridge lamps. Shipping wt., 3 lbs.
34K8588.........$3.50

Chintz Bridge Lamp Shade
(I) Closed top round shade, 11 inches wide by 6 inches high. Of paper parchment, covered with gay flowered cretonne. The latest idea in lamp shades. Will fit any of our bridge lamps. Shpg. wt., 3 lbs.
34K8589..........$1.25

A Classy Shade
(J) Oval shape shade, 12x8x8 inches high, of light green silk Georgette crepe, with tangerine color sateen lining. Metallic and Rayon braid trimming to match, with flower ornament. Will fit any of our bridge lamps. Shpg. wt., 3 lbs.
34K8590.......$2.25

A Very Pretty Shade
(K) Six-scalloped oval shade, 19½x12½x11½ in. high. Made of pleated tan silk Georgette crepe, with rose color sateen lining. Trimmed with very wide fancy Rayon braid and a very fancy flower. Will fit any of our junior lamps. Shipping wt., 5 lbs.
34K8591.........$6.50

Marquisette Shade
(L) Oval shape shade, 18x11½x11½ in. high. Of ecru color heavy Rayon marquisette, with orange color sateen lining. Trimmed with blue silk and Rayon ruffle and fancy flower. Will fit any of our junior lamps. Shipping weight, 5 pounds.
34K8592.......$3.50

Embroidered Panel Shade
(M) Eight straight sides, oval shape, 14x9x9½ in. high. Made of taupe silk Georgette crepe, with deep pink sateen lining. Trimmed with very wide metallic braid and paneled net, with embroidered flower. Will fit any of our bridge lamps. Shpg. wt., 3 lbs.
34K8593...$3.50

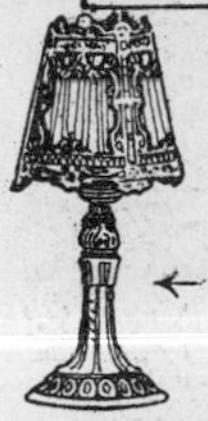

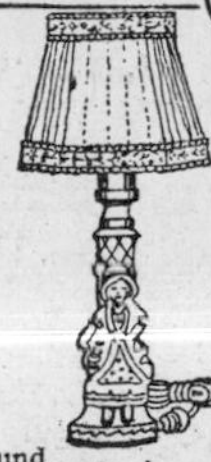

Metal Lamp

Height, 11 in. Round metal shade, 4¾ in. wide, 5 in. long. Entire lamp finished in old ivory and polychrome colors. Shade has old rose color silk lining. Push socket, cord and plug. Shipping wt., 3 pounds.
34K8179¼..$1.50

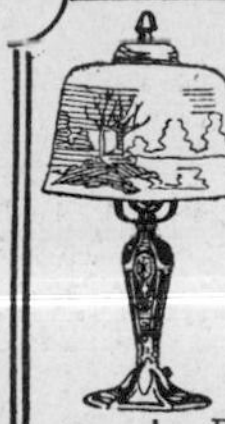

Metal Lamp

Height, 14½ inches. Round shade, 7½ inches wide, 6 inches high. Entire lamp finished in old ivory and polychrome colors. Shade is lined with old rose color silk. Has push socket, cord and plug. Shipping weight, 4 pounds.
34K8177¼ $3.75

Dainty Lamps for Parlor and Bedroom

Porcelain Lamp
Colonial colored costumed lady figure. Old rose shade. Georgette top, fancy trimming; also in man's Colonial costumed figure. Has cord, plug and socket. Shpg. wt., 3½ lbs.
34K8138¼ Lady..........$2.50
34K8139¼ Man..........2.50

Wonderful Bargain

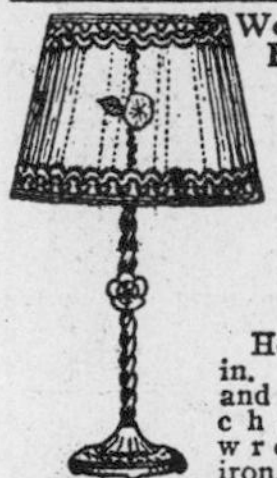

Height, 18 in. Of gold and polychrome wrought iron. Oval shade, 10x7x7 in. high, of rose color lustrous Rayon and cotton alpaca, fancy trimmed. One key socket, cord and plug attachment. Shpg. wt., 4 lbs.
34K8181¼..$2.25

Octagon Shade

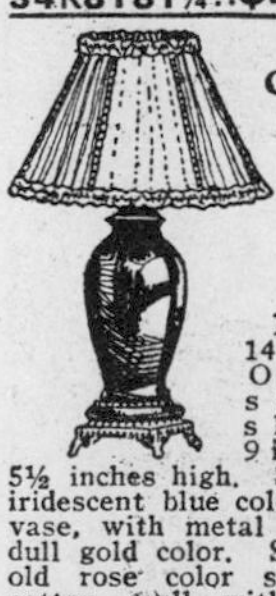

Height, 14 inches. Octagon shape shade, 9 in. wide, 5½ inches high. Stand is iridescent blue color glass vase, with metal base in dull gold color. Shade is old rose color silk and cotton mull with fancy trimmings. Has turn button socket, cord and plug. Shipping weight, 3 pounds.
34K8185¼..$2.50

Oval Shade

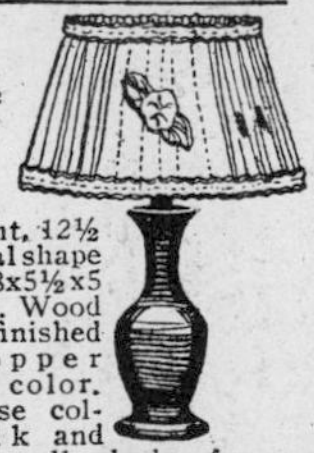

Height, 12½ in. Oval shape shade, 8x5½x5 in. high. Wood base finished in copper bronze color. Old rose color silk and cotton mull shade, fancy trimmed. Turn button socket, cord and plug. Shipping weight, 2½ lbs.
34K8195¼..$1.75

Ivory Base

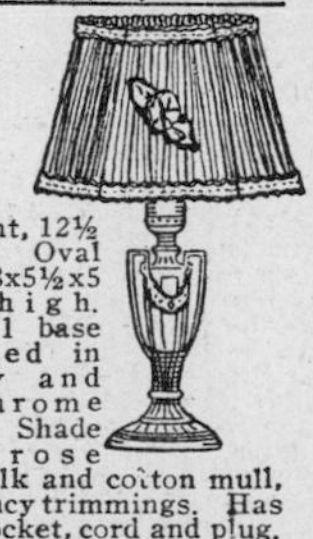

Height, 12½ inches. Oval shade, 8x5½x5 inches high. Metal base finished in ivory and polychrome colors. Shade is old rose color silk and cotton mull, with fancy trimmings. Has push socket, cord and plug. Shipping weight, 2½ lbs.
34K8190¼..$2.15

Very Ornamental

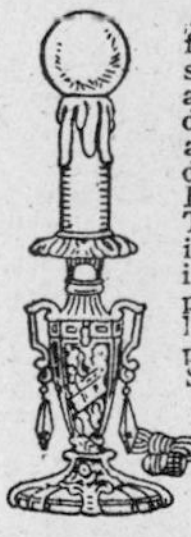

Made of metal, finished in matt silver. Has two amber glass drop ornaments, and wax color drip candle. Height, 13½ in. The round lamp is not included in the price. See page 659 for lamp. Has cord, plug and socket. Shipping weight, 2½ pounds.
34K8125¼
$2.25

Mica Torchere
Height, 12 in. Base and fancy top are made of iron, finished in antique polychrome color. Genuine mica cylinder, 2¾ in. wide and 6 in long. This is a very neat torchere and just the right size for most any decorative purpose. Has one socket, 6 feet of cord and plug. Shipping weight, 3½ lbs. Mailable.

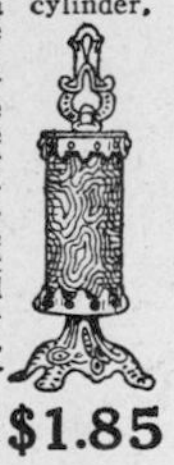

34K8121¼ $1.85

Electric Adjustable Desk Lamp

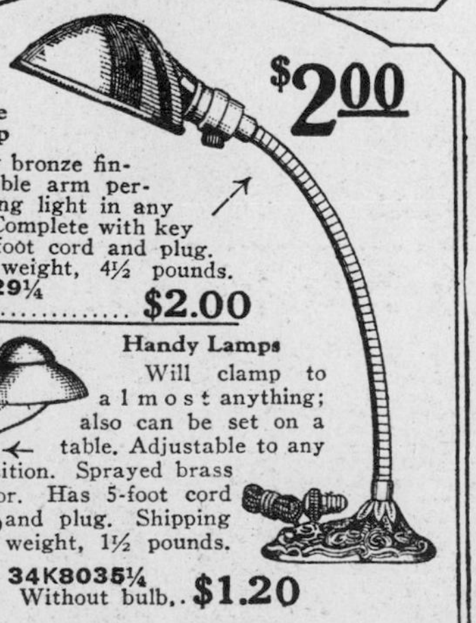

$2.00

Statuary bronze finish. Flexible arm permits placing light in any position. Complete with key socket, 6-foot cord and plug. Shipping weight, 4½ pounds.
34K8029¼
As shown........... $2.00

$1.20

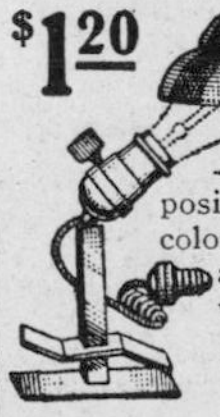

Handy Lamps
Will clamp to almost anything; also can be set on a table. Adjustable to any position. Sprayed brass color. Has 5-foot cord and plug. Shipping weight, 1½ pounds.
34K8035¼
Without bulb..$1.20

Glass Shade
Height, 15 in. Round shade, 7 in. wide. Metal base in antique gold and polychrome colors. Shade is made of rose color tinted glass with scenery effect. Has push button socket, cord and plug. Shpg. wt., 3 lbs.
34K8186¼..$2.75

A Dandy Lamp

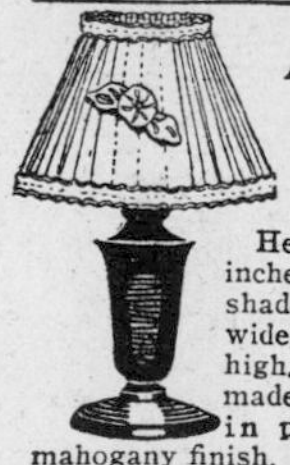

Height, 12½ inches. Round shade, 7 inches wide, 5½ in. high. Base made of wood, in polished mahogany finish. Shade is old rose color silk and cotton mull with fancy trimming. Has turn button socket, cord and plug. Shipping weight, 3 lbs.
34K8193¼..$1.95

Exceptional

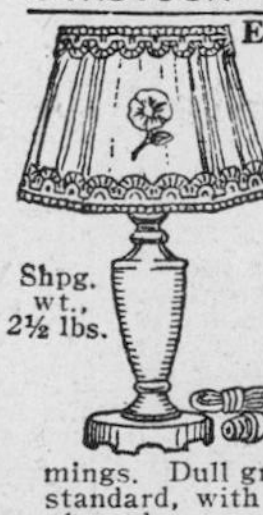

Shade is hexagon, 7¼ inches wide and made of orchid color or Japanese lining covered with water sprite green silk Georgette and fancy trimmings. Dull green finished standard, with marble-like glass base. Height, 13 inches. Has cord, plug and socket. Shpg. wt., 2½ lbs.
34K8135¼$3.95

Glass Lamp

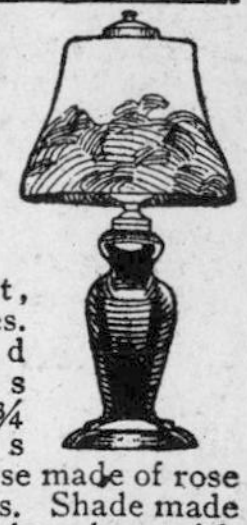

Height, 12½ inches. Round glass shade, 5¾ inches wide. Base made of rose color glass. Shade made of rose color glass with scenery effect in yellow and green colors. Has push socket, cord and plug. Shipping weight, 3 pounds.
34K8187¼ $2.00

Pottery Boudoir Lamp

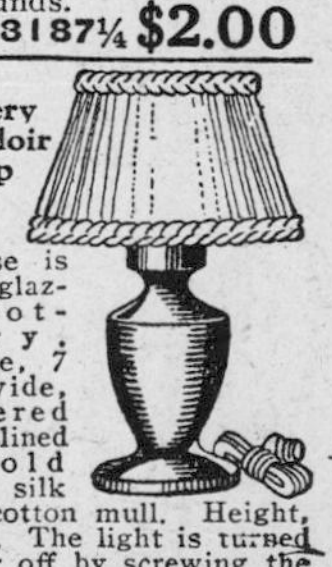

Base is blue glazed pottery. Shade, 7 in. wide, covered and lined with old rose silk and cotton mull. Height, 12 in. The light is turned on or off by screwing the bulb. Has cord and plug. The bulb is not included in the price. Shipping weight, 2½ lbs. Mailable.
34K8166¼$1.40

See Index and Information Pages 542 to 570

Special Priced Table Lamps

$2.75 to $18.00

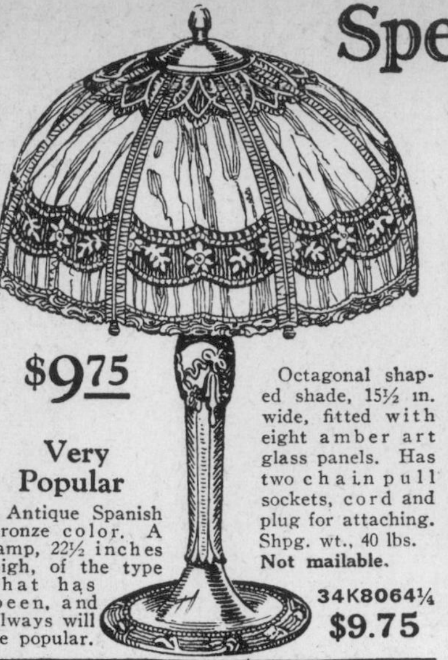

$9.75

Very Popular

Antique Spanish bronze color. A lamp, 22½ inches high, of the type that has been, and always will be popular.

Octagonal shaped shade, 15½ in. wide, fitted with eight amber art glass panels. Has two chain pull sockets, cord and plug for attaching. Shpg. wt., 40 lbs. **Not mailable.**

34K8064¼ **$9.75**

Genuine Silver and Black

$18.00

There isn't a lovelier combination than silver and black. This entire lamp is finished in genuine silver plate and black relief.

Square shaped 16-in. shade, having eight large amber art glass panels, top and sides with small pink color corner panels. Has two chain pull sockets, cord and plug. Height, 24 in. Shpg. wt., 45 lbs. **Not mailable.**

34K8108¼ **$18.00**

$10.50

A Wonderful Value

Stand made of iron in antique gold and black finish. Height, 26 in.

Oval shaped shade, 16 x 11 inches, made of blue silk georgette crepe with burnt orange color sateen lining. Has metallic braid, velveteen strips and silk flower ornament. Has two chain pull sockets, 6-foot cord and plug. Shipping weight, 12 lbs.

34K8216¼ **$10.50**

Fancy Torchere

$1.75

Height, 12½ inches; width of base, 4½ in. Made of metal, finished in gold bronze with flowers and leaves in natural colors. This is a new type of torchere. It can be used on dressers and anywhere a small decorative light is needed. See page 659 for round lamps. Shpg. wt., 4 lbs.

34K8142 Without lamps...... **$1.75**

34K8146

Beautiful Girandoles

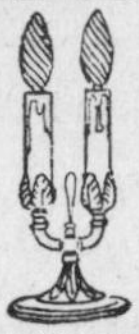

34K8144

Girandoles are the most effective of decorative lighting. They can be used anywhere. 34K8146 is 13 inches high and 8 inches wide. 34K8144 is 9½ inches high and 4½ inches wide. Made of cast brass, finished in natural gold color, with flowers and leaves in natural colors. The lamps are not included in the price.

34K8144—Without lamps. Shipping weight, 4 pounds.... **$4.75**

34K8146—Without lamps. Shipping weight, 5 pounds..... **6.75**

Twisted flame lamp for above girandoles and candelabra base.

34K6952—Each.......... **45c**

$7.25

Very Attractive

Metal lamp in a very attractive copper green polychrome finish. Height, 21 inches. Hexagonal 14¾ in. shade with amber glass panels. Has one push button socket, six feet of cord and plug for attaching. Shpg. wt., 40 pounds. **Not mailable.**

34K8069¼ **$7.25**

Paper Parchment

$5.75

Height, 23½ inches. Round shade, 16 inches wide, 9 inches high. Metal stand finished in dull gold and polychrome colors. Shade is made of paper parchment, with bird and pink and green flower design, with multicolor ruching. Has push button socket, cord and plug. Shipping weight, 10 pounds.

34K8051¼.... **$5.75**

Bed Shade

Made of blue silk Georgette with old rose silk and cotton mull lining. Trimmed with fancy metallic braid and flowers. Oval shape, 10x5½x6 inches high. Has key socket and cord and plug. Shpg. wt., 2 lbs.

34K8241 **$1.90**

Bed Shade

Made of rose color silk Georgette crepe, with old rose color sateen lining. Trimmed with fancy braid and flower. Measures 10x3½x7½ inches high. Has key socket, cord and plug. Shipping wt., 2 lbs.

34K8232 **$3.00**

Bed Shade

Made of lavender silk and cotton crepe with American beauty color sateen lining. Trimmed with fancy wide braid and flowers. Has key socket, cord and plug. Measures 8¾x4x4¾ in. high. Shipping weight, 2 pounds.

34K8237 **$1.49**

Splendid Value

$11.50

Finished in antique gold. Height, 22 in. Diameter of shade, 16 inches. The shade has six amber onyx color glass panels at top and six border panels in blended red at bottom. It is made of metal and is complete with two chain pull sockets, 6 feet of cord and plug. Shpg. wt., 40 lbs.

34K8067¼ **$11.50**

An Impressive Lamp

$2.75

Beautiful in design and style. Yet we offer it at an astonishingly low price. Base is made of glass in dark olive green mottled effect, with fancy decorations of red and gold. Shade is of old rose color cotton mull with fancy braid and applied flower. Has one chain pull socket, cord and plug. Height, 19 in. Shade, 13 inches. Shpg. wt., 12 lbs.

34K8112¼ **$2.75**

A New Type Lamp

$7.50

Iron stand in antique dull gold. Oval shade, 15 x 11 in. Made of garnet color silk Georgette, lined with Persian rose color, mercerized sateen, trimmed with multicolor ruffled Rayon ribbon, black velvet stripes and novelty flowers. Height of lamp, 28 inches. Has two chain pull sockets, cord and plug for attaching. Shipping weight, 20 lbs.

34K8074¼... **$7.50**

An exceedingly attractive low priced lamp. Base is made of glass, decorated with bluebird and red flower design on green gold mottled luster background. Ht., 22 inches.

$4.65

Decorated Luster Glass Vase

Has 15-inch round scalloped shade made of burnt orange colored silk and cotton mull trimmed with metallic braid and fancy silk spray. Has one light, 6-foot cord and plug. Shpg. wt., 10 lbs.

34K8122¼ **$4.65**

Pink Silk Shade

$6.50

Height, 24 in. Six-sided scalloped oval shade, 16x13x10 in. high. Metal stand finished in dull gold and polychrome colors, with ebony black center. Shade is made of rose color silk and cotton mull, with fancy trimmings. Has two pull chain sockets, cord and plug. Shipping wt., 12 lbs.

34K8056¼ **$6.50**

Electric Flower Vase

$9.25

Genuine silver plated Three lights A wonderful ornament for the dining room table. Height, without flowers, 17 in.; width, 15 in. Lamps not included. Use lamp 34K6825 shown on page 659. Shipping weight, 18 pounds.

34K8080¼ As shown with artificial flowers.... **$9.25**

Hand Painted Lamp

Lamp base made of ornamental cast iron, finished in dull antique gold color. Height of lamp, 24½ in. Has 12½x9½-inch oval paper parchment shade, hand-decorated in bird and flower design. The entire shade is covered with glass particles, giving a beautiful sparkling effect. Has one light, 6-foot cord and plug. Shipping weight, 7 lbs.

34K8083¼........ **$5.50**

An Exceptional Bargain

Stand is made of wood, attractively finished in dull gold and ebony black. Height of lamp, 24 inches. Has two chain pull sockets, cord and plug attachment. Oval shade, 16x10 inches, is made of rose color sateen, trimmed with fancy metallic braid and novelty flower. Shipping weight, 15 lbs.

34K8078¼.... **$4.95**

Ebony Color Pottery Vase Lamp

$13.50

Round 18-in. shade with black silk Georgette crepe over pink color silk and cotton tussah. Lining and flounces of golden color mercerized sateen. Rayon trimmed; fancy gold color metal braid. Height, 25 inches. Two chain pull sockets, 6 feet of cord and plug. Shipping wt., 18 lbs.

Mailable.

34K8101¼ As shown. **$13.50**

Big Bargains in Floor Lamps
$4.50 to $12.50

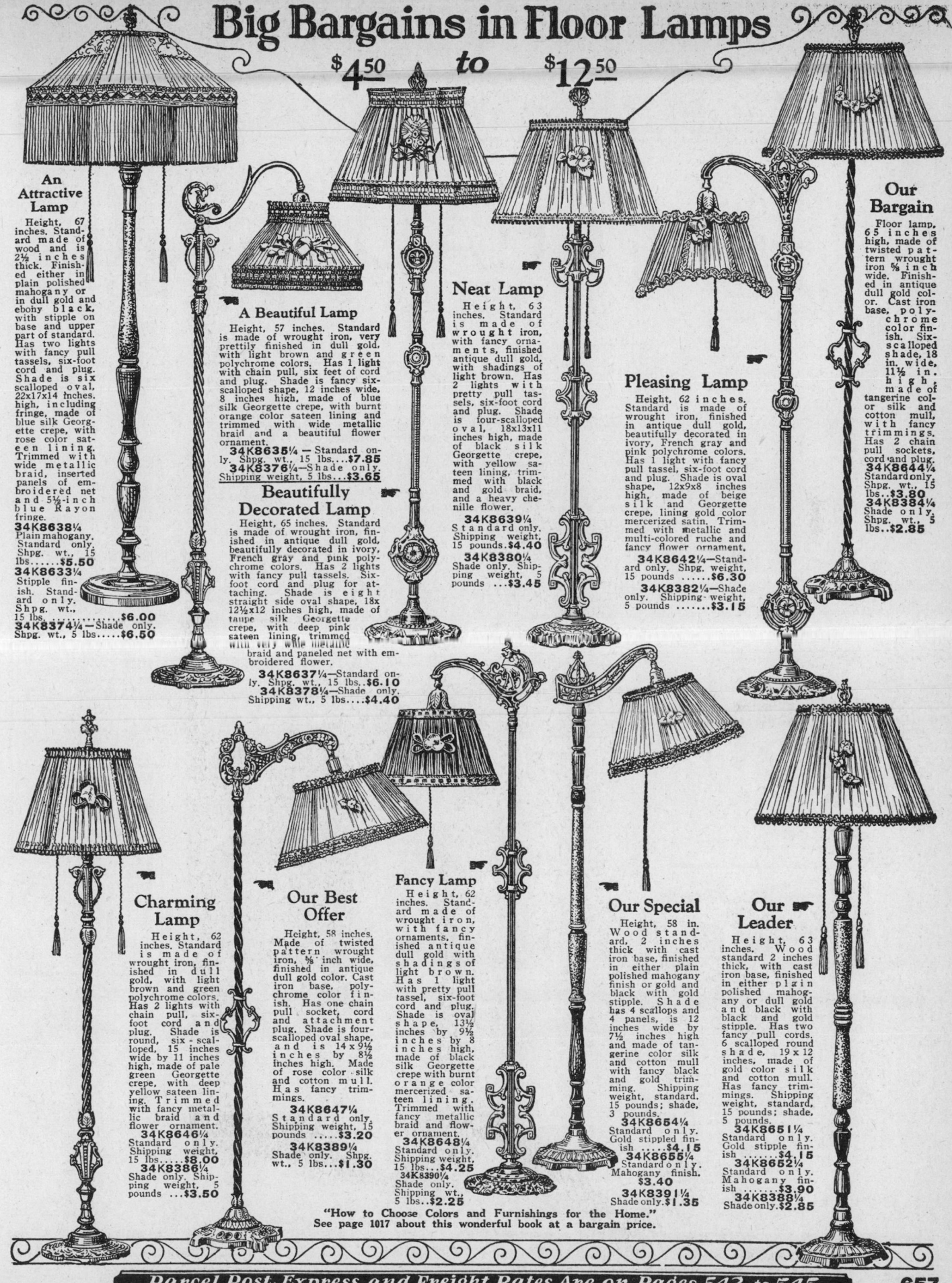

An Attractive Lamp

Height, 67 inches. Standard made of wood and is 2½ inches thick. Finished either in plain polished mahogany or in dull gold and ebony black, with stipple on base and upper part of standard. Has two lights with fancy pull tassels, six-foot cord and plug. Shade is six scalloped oval, 22x17x14 inches high, including fringe, made of blue silk Georgette crepe, with rose color sateen lining. Trimmed with wide metallic braid, inserted panels of embroidered net and 5½-inch blue Rayon fringe.

34K8638¼ Plain mahogany. Standard only. Shpg. wt., 15 lbs......$5.50
34K8633¼ Stipple finish. Standard only. Shpg. wt., 15 lbs......$6.00
34K8374¼—Shade only. Shpg. wt., 5 lbs.....$6.50

A Beautiful Lamp

Height, 57 inches. Standard is made of wrought iron, very prettily finished in dull gold, with light brown and green polychrome colors. Has 1 light with chain pull, six feet of cord and plug. Shade has fancy six-scalloped shape, 12 inches wide, 8 inches high, made of blue silk Georgette crepe, with burnt orange color sateen lining and trimmed with wide metallic braid and a beautiful flower ornament.

34K8635¼ — Standard only. Shpg. wt. 15 lbs...$7.85
34K8376¼—Shade only. Shipping weight, 5 lbs...$3.65

Beautifully Decorated Lamp

Height, 65 inches. Standard is made of wrought iron, finished in antique dull gold, beautifully decorated in ivory, French gray and pink polychrome colors. Has 2 lights with fancy pull tassels. Six-foot cord and plug for attaching. Shade is eight straight side oval shape, 18x12½x12 inches high, made of taupe silk Georgette crepe, with deep pink sateen lining trimmed with very wide metallic braid and paneled net with embroidered flower.

34K8637¼—Standard only. Shpg. wt., 15 lbs...$6.10
34K8378¼ — Shade only. Shipping wt., 5 lbs...$4.40

Neat Lamp

Height, 63 inches. Standard is made of wrought iron, with fancy ornaments, finished antique dull gold, with shadings of light brown. Has 2 lights with pretty pull tassels, six-foot cord and plug. Shade is four-scalloped oval, 18x13x11 inches high, made of black silk Georgette crepe, with yellow sateen lining, trimmed with black and gold braid, and a heavy chenille flower.

34K8639¼ Standard only. Shipping weight, 15 pounds..$4.40
34K8380¼ Shade only. Shipping weight, 5 pounds ...$3.45

Pleasing Lamp

Height, 62 inches. Standard is made of wrought iron, finished in antique dull gold, beautifully decorated in ivory, French gray and pink polychrome colors. Has 1 light with fancy pull tassel, six-foot cord and plug. Shade is oval shape, 12x9x8 inches high, made of beige silk and Georgette crepe, lining gold color mercerized satin. Trimmed with metallic and multi-colored ruche and fancy flower ornament.

34K8642¼—Standard only. Shpg. weight, 15 pounds $6.30
34K8382¼—Shade only. Shipping weight, 5 pounds $3.15

Our Bargain

Floor lamp, 65 inches high, made of twisted pattern wrought iron ⅝ inch wide. Finished in antique dull gold color. Cast iron base, polychrome color finish. Six-scalloped shade, 18 in. wide, 11½ in. high, made of tangerine color silk and cotton mull, with fancy trimmings. Has 2 chain pull sockets, cord and plug.

34K8644¼ Standard only. Shpg. wt., 15 lbs..$3.80
34K8384¼ Shade only. Shpg. wt., 5 lbs..$2.85

Charming Lamp

Height, 62 inches. Standard is made of wrought iron, finished in dull gold, with light brown and green polychrome colors. Has 2 lights with chain pull, six-foot cord and plug. Shade is round, six-scalloped, 15 inches wide by 11 inches high, made of pale green Georgette crepe, with deep yellow sateen lining. Trimmed with fancy metallic braid and flower ornament.

34K8646¼ Standard only. Shipping weight, 15 lbs.....$8.00
34K8386¼ Shade only. Shipping weight, 5 pounds ...$3.50

Our Best Offer

Height, 58 inches. Made of twisted pattern wrought iron, ⅝ inch wide, finished in antique dull gold color. Cast iron base, polychrome color finish. Has one chain pull socket, cord and attachment plug. Shade is four-scalloped oval shape, 14 x 9½ inches by 8½ inches high. Made of rose color silk and cotton mull. Has fancy trimmings.

34K8647¼ Standard only. Shipping weight, 15 pounds ...$3.20
34K8389¼ Shade only. Shpg. wt., 5 lbs...$1.30

Fancy Lamp

Height, 62 inches. Standard made of wrought iron, with fancy ornaments, finished antique dull gold with shadings of light brown. Has 1 light with pretty pull tassel, six-foot cord and plug. Shade is oval shape, 13½ inches by 9½ inches by 8 inches high, made of black silk Georgette crepe with burnt orange color mercerized sateen lining. Trimmed with fancy metallic braid and flower ornament.

34K8648¼ Standard only. Shipping weight, 15 lbs...$4.25
34K8390¼ Shade only. Shipping wt., 5 lbs...$2.25

Our Special

Height, 58 in. Wood standard, 2 inches thick with cast iron base, finished in either plain polished mahogany finish or gold and black with gold stipple. Shade has 4 scallops and 4 panels, is 12 inches wide by 7½ inches high and made of tangerine color silk and cotton mull with fancy black and gold trimming. Shipping weight, standard, 15 pounds; shade, 3 pounds.

34K8654¼ Standard only. Gold stippled finish $4.15
34K8655¼ Standard only. Mahogany finish. ...$3.40
34K8391¼ Shade only..$1.35

Our Leader

Height, 63 inches. Wood standard 2 inches thick, with cast iron base, finished in either plain polished mahogany or dull gold and black with black and gold stipple. Has two fancy pull cords. 6 scalloped round shade, 19 x 12 inches, made of gold color silk and cotton mull. Has fancy trimmings. Shipping weight, standard, 5 pounds; shade, 5 pounds.

34K8651¼ Standard only. Gold stipple finish $4.15
34K8652¼ Standard only. Mahogany finish $3.90
34K8388¼ Shade only..$2.85

"How to Choose Colors and Furnishings for the Home." See page 1017 about this wonderful book at a bargain price.

$19⁹⁵
Cash Without Attachments

VACUUM
SAVE TIME ···· SAVE WORK

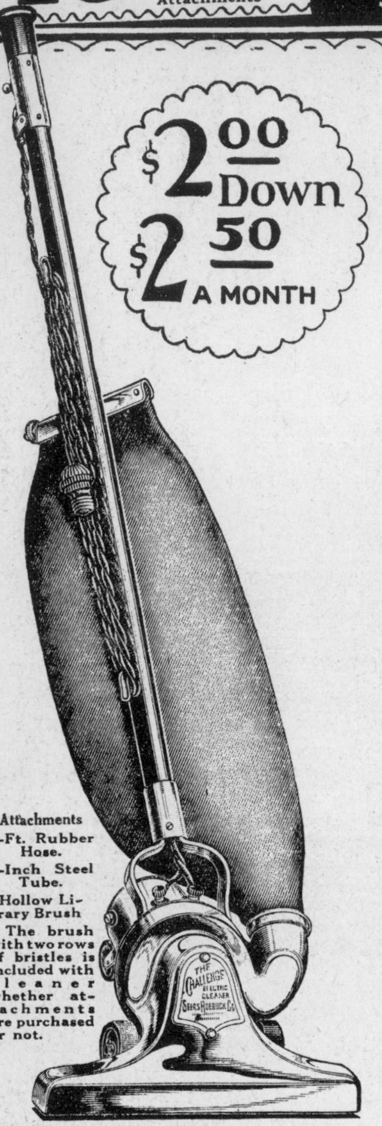

$2⁰⁰ Down $2⁵⁰ A MONTH

The Bronze Bearing
CHALLENGE
A GREAT CLEANER

THOUSANDS of housewives insist that the CHALLENGE CLEANER banishes "house cleaning day."
You wanted to put off the heavy work, content to do light cleaning until that later day of reckoning when rugs, carpets, drapes and all went on the line for a thorough cleaning. Now, the CHALLENGE does it all so easily and thoroughly every day that housewives are forever freed of that postponed day of drudgery.

The sturdy construction of the CHALLENGE CLEANER, its mechanical perfection and the ease with which it works, place it at the top of the list of essential home equipment. It carries our absolute, ironclad guarantee of first class materials and workmanship and satisfactory performance.

Test the CHALLENGE CLEANER in your home. Take advantage of our liberal home trial offer and convince yourself of its many superior features. If it does not satisfy you in every way you are at liberty to send it back and we will return every cent you have paid. Use Time Payment Order Blank on page 1092, if ordering on Easy Payments.

Specifications of the Challenge

NOZZLE AND FRAME: Made of highly polished cast aluminum. Nozzle is 13½ inches long.
MOTOR: 110-volt, universal type (operates on A. C. or D. C.), fan cooled, phosphor bronze bearings. Low current consumption. Requires little care. Housing is cast aluminum.
FAN: Attached direct to motor shaft. Six blades, accurately balanced. Made of cast aluminum.
HANDLE AND SWITCH: Ebonized wood handle with trigger switch, easy grip ball knob. Furnished with a 22-foot mercerized cord and plug.
DUST BAG: Heavy vacuum cleaner cloth. Retains all dirt and grit. Easily disconnected for removal of dirt.
BRUSH: New principle. Two rows of stationary bristles on either side of suction opening loosens imbedded dirt and lint more effectively than a revolving brush. Shipping weight, 19 pounds.

57K215 5¼—Without attachments. Cash price	$19.95	57K216 6¼—With attachments. Cash price...... $23.70
57K217 7¼—Without attachments. Easy Payment price ($2.00 down and $2.50 per month)...... $21.95		57K218 8¼—With attachments. Easy Payment price ($2.00 down and $2.50 per month)...... $26.10

Special Offer

57K226 6¼—With attachments, complete, and with AIRIZER DEVICE. Shipping weight, 23 pounds. Cash price...... $28.65
57K227 7¼—With attachments, complete, and with AIRIZER DEVICE. Shipping weight, 23 pounds. Easy Payment price ($2.00 down, $2.50 per month)...... 31.50

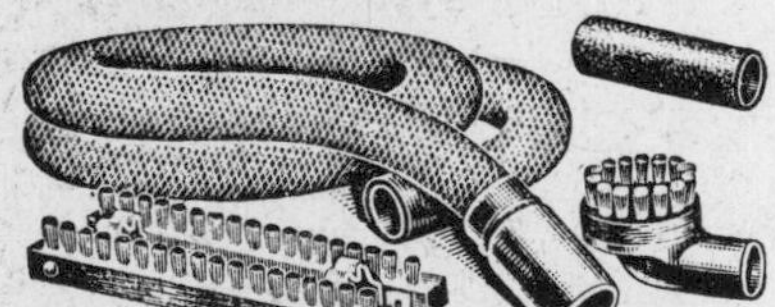

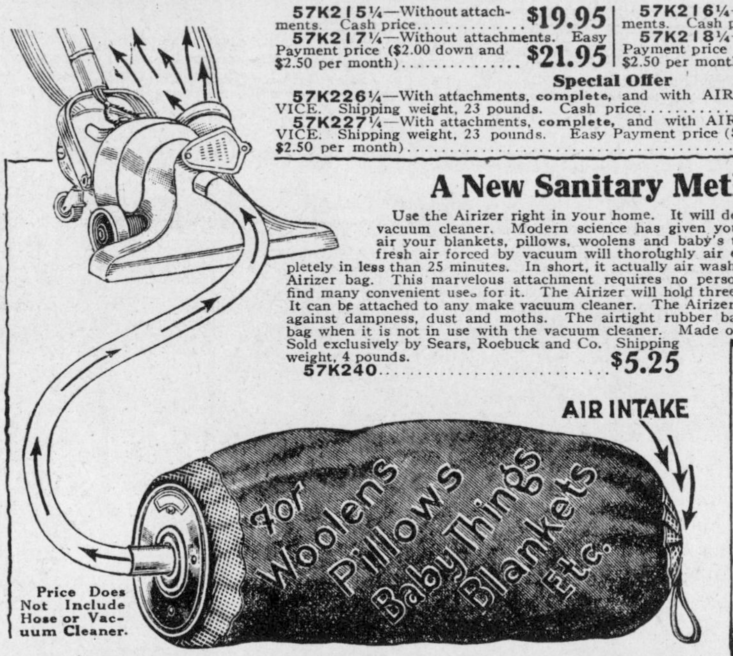

Attachments
8-Ft. Rubber Hose.
5-Inch Steel Tube.
Hollow Library Brush
The brush with two rows of bristles is included with cleaner whether attachments are purchased or not.

Price Does Not Include Hose or Vacuum Cleaner.

For Woolens Pillows Baby Things Blankets Etc.

AIR INTAKE

A New Sanitary Method

Use the Airizer right in your home. It will double the usefulness of your vacuum cleaner. Modern science has given you a new way to thoroughly air your blankets, pillows, woolens and baby's things. Volumes of filtered fresh air forced by vacuum will thoroughly air every thread and fiber completely in less than 25 minutes. In short, it actually air washes the entire contents of the Airizer bag. This marvelous attachment requires no personal attention, and you will find many convenient use for it. The Airizer will hold three double blankets or pillows. It can be attached to any make vacuum cleaner. The Airizer insures your furs and silks against dampness, dust and moths. The airtight rubber bag affords a perfect storage bag when it is not in use with the vacuum cleaner. Made of durable rubberized fabric. Sold exclusively by Sears, Roebuck and Co. Shipping weight, 4 pounds. $5.25
57K240......

USED AS MOTHPROOF STORAGE BAG

Challenge Radiator

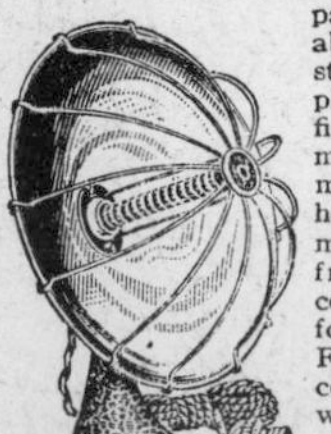

The Challenge is compact and handy to move about. It has a 10-inch steel bowl heavily copper plated. Stand is neatly finished in a serviceable mottled green enamel. Best materials are used. A heavy guaranteed element mounted on a porcelain frame insures you an exceptional amount of heat for a radiator of this size. Fitted with standard 6-foot cord and plug. Shipping weight, 8 pounds.
57K3708—For 110-volt city current only...... $1.98

Energex Radiator

The Energex has a solid copper bowl 12 inches in diameter. The guard and fittings are heavy, durable and nicely finished. The base is of cast iron sturdily designed and easy to keep clean. The radiator is perfectly balanced so as to prevent tipping. Best element mounted on a cone type porcelain frame. Complete with standard 6-foot cord and plug. Shipping weight, 10 pounds.
57K3345—For 110-volt city current only...... $2.98

Quality Radiator

This highly perfected radiator furnishes a desirable addition for any home. It has the popular searchlight adjustment. The bowl is of heavy copper, 14 inches in diameter. The stand is of cast iron, beautifully designed. The cone type element offers heat radiation over a wide area. The radiator also makes an efficient hair dryer and bathroom heater. Complete with 6-foot cord and durable plug. Shipping weight, 14 pounds.
57K3347—For 110-v. city current only...... $4.65
Cone type element to be used on any of the radiators shown here. Shpg. wt., 1 lb.
57K3369...... 69c

ELECTRIC IRONS

World's Largest

FAVORITE
No-Burn-Out Iron

The Favorite iron employs the embedded element, which is guaranteed to last a lifetime. Has a heavy nickel plated finish, which retains its luster and will not easily tarnish. The iron is graceful in design and has a broad ironing surface with perfect heat control. The handle is highly insulated and will not heat. The strong stand is an additional Favorite feature. This iron is to be compared with similar styles selling at $5.50 and $6.00, and represents a wonderful value, with all of the finest ironing qualities. Weighs full 6 pounds, complete with table stand and six-foot detachable cord. Shipping weight, 9 pounds.

57K3567—For 110-volt city current only...... **$3.65**

Supreme
The Aristocrat Iron

For the discriminating purchaser who demands the ultimate in beautiful design, ease of work and perfect ironing convenience, we offer this Supreme iron. The very latest and most graceful body design with a guaranteed embedded element. The extreme slope of sides and rear, with a long point, gives you complete visibility from all ironing edges; a feature which will not be found in many irons. Perfectly balanced and easily controlled. The toggle switch in the bakelite plug is another added convenience, as it eliminates removing the cord. The Supreme is built as fine as any iron can be. It is equal to the advertised irons selling for $7.00 and $7.50. You cannot find a more beautiful iron at a greater saving. Complete with table stand, 6-foot cord and plug, equipped with switch. Full weight, 6½ lbs. Shipping weight, 9½ pounds.

57K3385—For 110-volt city current only.... **$4.95**

For Sadirons See Page 970

CHALLENGE

A full weight, guaranteed, two-piece iron. Best mica element. Built along graceful lines. Nicely nickel plated and a fine ironing arrangement. The Challenge is our own iron, designed by us. With standard cord and plug and featured tip-up stand. Shipping weight, each, 9 pounds.

57K3313—For 110-volt city current only...... **$1.89**

ENERGEX
A Beveled Edge Iron

The new Energex embodies all of the features which make for perfect ironing service. The new beveled edge is an outstanding feature, as it adds perfect balance to the iron and presents a greater heat surface at the edge, where it is most needed. You will be more than delighted with this super Energex value. Full 6-pound iron, complete with cord and plug. Shipping weight, each, 9 pounds.

57K3312—For 110-volt city current only..... **$2.55**

TABLE STOVES

Challenge Stoves

Constructed of the best heavy sheet steel. Dull black enamel finish, with nickel plated legs. Rotary single heat switch. Best heat resisting porcelain plates. Bottom is protected by strong sheet steel. The single burner stove measures 8x8x5 inches. The double burner stove measures 18x8x5 inches.

57K3536¼—Single Burner Stove, for 110-volt city current only. Shipping weight, 8 pounds......... **$2.69**

57K3524¼—Double Burner Stove, for 110-volt city current only. Shipping weight, 12 pounds. **4.25**

These Challenge stoves are exactly the same style and dimensions as those shown above, except for the fact that they are equipped with the new two-heat elements. Stoves may be used for toasting and warming purposes.

57K3338—Challenge Single Burner Stove, with two-heat element. For 110-volt city current only. Shipping weight, 8 pounds. **$3.75**

57K3339—Challenge Double Burner Stove, complete with two-heat element. For 110-volt city current only. Shipping weight, 12 pounds................. **5.45**

Energex Table Stoves

Heavy cast stoves for kitchenette use. Beautiful black enamel finish. Best porcelain element. The single burner stove has a three-heat switch, which provides full, medium and low heat. The double stove has a switch which provides for heat on either burner or both burners at once. The stoves are 5½ inches high. Equipped with a 6-foot cord and plug.

57K3320¼—Single Burner Stove, for 110-volt city current only. Shipping weight, 12 pounds. **$5.25**

57K3379¼—Double Burner Stove, for 110-volt city current only. Shipping weight, 22 pounds. **8.45**

Flat Top Toaster

$1⁷⁹

This toaster is beautifully designed. Highly nickel plated and will toast two slices of bread at one time. Has best grade element, imitation ebony handles and comes complete with 6-foot cord. Shipping weight, 4 pounds.

57K3701—For 110-volt city current only........................ **$1.79**

Energex Stove

This strong stove has cast metal frame, a porcelain element with coils held firmly in place. We recommend this well made Energex appliance. Shpg. wt., 6½ lbs.

57K3374—For 110-volt city current only........................ **$1.98**

CORN POPPER

Enjoy fresh popped corn, right on your living room table, without the inconvenience of heavy pans over the fire. This handy appliance will make popcorn a daily habit. Contains enough for a large batch, and the corn may be stirred while popping without moving the popper or burning the operator. Equipped with the best heating element and detachable 6-foot cord and plug. Also full directions for making popcorn. Shipping weight, each, 6 pounds.

57K3387—For 110-volt city current only........... **$1.75**

ELECTRIC GRILLS

Energex Grill

Broils, steams, fries or toasts. Broils steaks, bakes biscuits, muffins or cup cakes. Pans and cups of heavy aluminum. The stove is highly nickel plated. The three-heat switch permits the used of full, medium or low current, giving any desirable temperature for cooking. You could not purchase a finer table appliance than the Energex Grill. Shipping weight, 10 pounds.

57K3317—For 110-volt city current only......... **$9.45**

Table Grill

You can prepare a whole meal on the table with this handy electric grill. Has a deep pan for broiling, a shallow pan for frying, a griddle plate and a rack of three separate cups. The cooking may be done either above or below the element. All parts are rustproof and highly nickel plated. The grill is very attractive in appearance and is an exceptional value at this remarkably low price. Furnished with a 6-foot separable cord. Shipping weight, 9 pounds.

57K3543—For 110-volt city current only......... **$4.45**

Energex Griddle

This new Energex appliance will be a useful and ornamental addition to your table. It will fry three eggs at a time. It has a heavy, indestructible element, highly nickel plated body, heatproof legs and special heatproof handles so that it may be easily moved about the table. Fitted with a convenient 6-foot cord and plug. Has a deep aluminum grid which is easy to keep clean. Shpg. wt., 6 lbs.

57K3705—For 110-volt city current only......... **$4.75**

CIGAR LIGHTER

This new electric convenience is neatly molded in a mahogany tinted porcelain, which will perfectly match your radio set or furniture. Has push-button contact and removable element. Convenient silk cord, which may be permanently connected to a nearby fixture. Does away with unsightly matches and offers a novelty for your home. Shipping weight, 1½ lbs.

57K3388—For 110-volt city current only.......... **85c**

Appliance Store

Challenge Percolator

Strong reliable percolator for everyday use. Makes eight cups of coffee. A real convenience at this remarkable price. Comes furnished with detachable 6-foot cord. Shipping weight, 4 pounds.

57K3372—For 110-volt city current only............ $2.69

Energex Percolator

Fine nine-cup percolator, built to give long and satisfactory service. Fancy handle and best aluminum polish. This percolator is a quality product throughout. Shipping weight, 4 pounds.

57K3584—For 110-volt city current only.... $3.89

For other Coffee Percolators see pages 964 and 965.

PERCOLATORS

Supreme Percolators.

Made of heavy copper, body beautifully designed and nickel plated. No-Burn-Out heating element will give unlimited service. Designed at the direction of coffee experts. The perfect element arrangement used produces the best that may be obtained from the coffee. The heavy embedded element retains the heat for some time after the current is turned off. Fitted with black rubberoid handle, unbreakable glass top and silk cord. Shipping weight, each, 7 pounds.

57K3599—Six-Cup Size. For 110-volt city current only......... $6.40

57K3383—Nine-Cup Size. For 110-volt city current $7.95

Colonial Party Set

An Ideal Gift

Beautiful four-piece percolator set that makes an ideal wedding or Christmas gift. It is made of the sparkling Nicalume ware, highly polished and easy to clean. This new wonder metal is formed by coating aluminum with heavy nickel which has a permanent silver-like brilliancy that will always have a new appearance. Nickel finished tray, with colonial creamer and sugar bowl, gold plated inside. Nicely finished with insulated feet and loving cup handles. Nine-cup capacity. Shipping weight, for complete set, 12 pounds.

57K3382—For 110-volt city current only.. $15.75

TOASTERS

EAT MORE TOAST
Perfect Service with the Ideal table appliance. Always delicious, brown toast without trouble or delay, on any of these four attractive toasters.

Challenge Toaster

We have this remarkable Challenge Toaster at the lowest price ever offered on an upright toaster. The element is suspended in a porcelain frame. The frame and all metal parts are highly nickel plated. The toaster is guaranteed to give perfect satisfaction. Shipping weight, 4 pounds.

57K3516—For 110-volt city current only............$1.73

MIXER

A strong, efficient mixer for general use in the home. Well made, black enameled frame and stand to hold the mixer. May be used either on the stand or separately. Furnished with strong 6-foot cord and plug, complete with stand. Shipping wt., 7 lbs.

57K3376—For 110-volt direct or alternating current only.................. $4.35

CORD and PLUG

Always have one on hand. Will fit any standard appliance.
57K3328 Cord Set, complete. Shipping wt., ¾ lb. 46c
57K3704 Cord Set, complete with switch in plug. Shipping weight, 1 pound 89c
57K3329—Attachment plug only. Shipping weight, 6 ounces........10c

Popular Toaster

Makes two pieces of toast at a time. The bread is evenly and quickly toasted. Heavy nickel plated frame, designed to give long service. Best grade heating element mounted in porcelain insulation. Six-foot cord and plug. Shipping weight, 5½ pounds.

57K3700—For 110-volt city current only........ $2.49

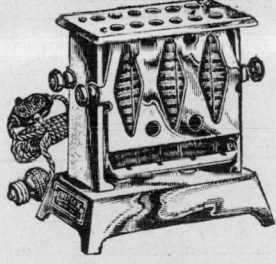

Energex Toaster

For those who desire the very best in time and labor saving appliances, we recommend this fine Energex Toaster. A heavy cast, nickel plated base. Turns the toast easily and quickly. Equipped with heatproof handles. Furnished with a 6-foot cord and plug. Shipping weight, 4 pounds.

57K3309—For 110-volt city current only........... $4.49

Giant "Flip Flop"

It Turns the Toast

Designed to meet the present day needs for a large, speedy toaster. Combines beauty with those sturdy qualities necessary to withstand everyday service. The patented toast turning doors enable the user to turn the toast quickly without touching it. The doors and handles are heat insulated to provide for ease of operation. All parts are heavily nickel plated and highly polished. Makes two slices of toast at a time and is large enough to contain the largest slices of bread. This toaster, at this exceptional price, is a real value. Shipping weight, each, 5 lbs.

57K3321—For 110-volt city current only...................... $2.98

ELECTRIC WAFFLE IRONS

Challenge

A fine, full size waffle iron. The grid measures 7¼ inches in diameter. The body is made of steel, beautifully nickel plated. The grids are of pure die cast aluminum. The feet are equipped with fiber tips. Best element arranged to give satisfactory service. We also furnish a recipe booklet with full instructions for making waffles. Shipping weight, 10 lbs.

57K3702—For 110-volt city current only........... $4.95

Waffle Mold

This mold is carefully designed and beautifully finished. It has a special groove around the grid to catch any batter overflow. The grids are made of pure die cast aluminum; the body is of steel, beautifully nickeled. The slotted hinge provides for the proper expansion. Guaranteed heating elements and perfect heat control. An exceptional value at this price. Shipping wt., each, 11 lbs.

57K3717—For 110-volt city current only.......... $7.95

Energex

A neat, convenient design that will add charm to the most exclusive table. Its high grade aluminum grids require no greasing. The perfected indestructible porcelain unit used is an exclusive Energex feature, which insures proper heat distribution. Complete with aluminum tray, cord and plug. Shipping weight, 11 pounds.

57K3703—For 110-volt city current only........... $9.45

Electrical Aids To Health and Beauty

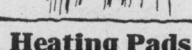

Bandage Pad

$3.10

A newly designed pad which adapts itself for many home uses. The pad makes a perfect bandage and will provide heat applications for the arms and limbs, as it may be securely tied in place by means of the attached ribbons. Gives perfect results where a larger pad or hot water bottle would be too heavy or slip out of place. A perfect pad for warming the baby's crib. Measures 5½x19 inches, has two 18-inch ribbons and a 9½-foot cord with a detachable plug connection so that the entire cord is not connected when the pad is being applied to the patient. Shipping weight, 2 lbs.
57K3389—For 110-volt city current only **$3.10**

Comfort Warming Pad

$4.29

Special rubber insulation makes pad safe and reliable. A three-heat switch controls temperature of the pad to high, medium or low heat. Size, 12x15 inches, with 10-foot cord. Shipping weight, 2½ pounds.
57K3353—For 110-volt city current only **$4.29**

The Energex

$5.45

Full and soft as a pillow. Proper temperature at all times. A double layer of heavy flannel and best wool eiderdown. Size, 12x15 inches, with 10-foot cord. Shipping wt., 2½ lbs.
57K3322—For 110-volt city current only **$5.45**

Heating Pads

Physicians everywhere are advising the use of a heating pad in the home. Hospitals are taking on this safe electric application as standard equipment. Our new assortment of low priced pads offers you the best in quality pillow effect and perfect heat control. The heat is clean and dry, and the eiderdown pillow rests as lightly as a feather upon the body.

Violet Rays

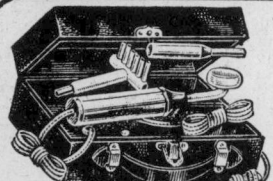

Challenge Ray

Comes in a neat imitation leather case. Furnished with the general applicator, a scalp applicator, and a metal applicator. Often offered as a $12.50 outfit elsewhere. Shipping wt., 5 pounds.
57K3706—For 110-volt city current only **$7.95**

Energex Violet Ray

May be used for massaging, scalp treatments, and as a remedy for pains and aches. Throat applicator is very effective for treating colds and bronchial trouble. Eye and face electrode is used for facial massage. Usually offered by others as a $25.00 value professional machine. Shipping weight, 7 pounds.
57K3707—For 110-volt city current only **$12.75**

Ozone Generator Set

This complete violet ray set includes the popular Ozone generator complete. This generator adapts the violet ray for a complete new series of cures and benefits. It is effective in curing catarrh, bronchitis, hay fever and many other respiratory ailments. A heavy duty professional set which is especially designed to give best results with the Ozone generator and also contains all of the advantages found in the other violet ray machines. Complete with all attachments and liquid inhalant. Shipping weight, each, 8 pounds.
57K3716—For 110-volt city current only **$18.75**

Motor Driven Vibrator

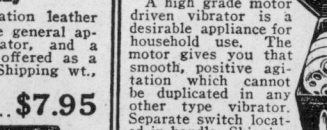
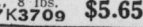

A high grade motor driven vibrator is a desirable appliance for household use. The motor gives you that smooth, positive agitation which cannot be duplicated in any other type vibrator. Separate switch located in handle. Shipping wt., 8 lbs.
57K3709 .... **$5.65**

Medical Batteries

Has pair of conducting cords, one pair wooden handles, one pair of metal handles, one pair of sponge electrodes and one nickel plated foot plate. The triple and double cell batteries also include hair brush. **Triple Cell Medical Battery.** Shipping wt., 20 lbs.
57K3340 Complete with accessories and three dry cells **$12.45**
Double Cell Medical Battery. Shpg. wt., 13 lbs.
57K3341—Complete with accessories and two dry cells. (Not illustrated.) **$8.42**
Single Cell Medical Battery. Opening top and bottom. Shipping weight, 7¾ pounds.
57K3342—Complete with accessories and one dry cell. (Not illustrated.) **$6.45**

Therapeutic Lamp

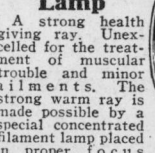

A strong health giving ray. Unexcelled for the treatment of muscular trouble and minor ailments. The strong warm ray is made possible by a special concentrated filament lamp placed in proper focus with the highly polished reflector. The switch is conveniently located at the top of the handle. The 6-foot cord extends through the handle, permitting a greater ease of operation. Complete with 110-volt concentrated bulb. Shipping weight, 5 lbs.
57K3380—For 110-volt city current only **$2.98**

Vapolite

This new appliance has many uses. May be used to heat one tablespoonful of any liquid preparation. The vaporizing process enables this small appliance to be used for driving away mosquitoes and summer insects. May be installed in clothes closets or chests to destroy moths. A convenient fumigator after illness. For medicated salves used for coughs and colds, it gives very satisfactory results when used with Vick's Vapo Rub, Mentholatum and other inhalants. Shipping weight, 2 pounds.
57K3315—For 110-volt city current only **$1.55**

HAIRDRESSING STYLES!

For Other Curling Irons, See Page 123

Challenge Waver

A waver gives the soft effect which is becoming so fashionable. The Patricia wave shown here is a natural looking style and very becoming to business women. To make the prettiest waves use our Challenge Waver. Shipping weight, 1 pound.
57K3579—For 110-volt city current only **98c**

Hair Beauty Set

Marcel at Home

An electric set for the complete care of the hair at the price of a single visit to the hairdresser. Complete as shown. Shpg. wt., 1 lb.
57K3358—For 110-volt city current only **98c**

Annette Waver

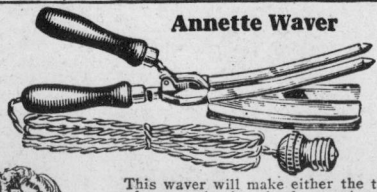

This waver will make either the tight or loose curls, by simply varying the pressure on the handle. A heavy professional type waver which may be adapted to any style of hairdress. Will not overheat or scorch the hair. Shipping weight, 3 pounds.
57K3581—For 110-volt city current only **$1.98**

With each hair waving appliance on this page we furnish a complete instruction sheet, giving full information regarding the use of a curling iron or waver; also important suggestions as to waving hair of different qualities.

De Luxe Waver Set

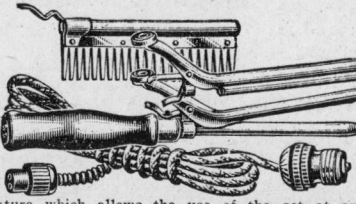

Each set is so adjusted that it comes to just the proper temperature for best waving results. The detachable cord is an additional feature which allows the use of the set at any distance from the fixture. Each iron contains our new style hints in a complete set of instructions for the curler. Shipping weight, 1 pound.
57K3343—For 110-volt city current only **$1.45**

Hair Dryer

A Clean Warm Current of Air

Frame is heavy metal, baked in black enamel finish. Fan is connected direct to motor shaft. Fitted with a high quality element, wound on a specially treated frame. Strong, high speed motor. Gives a strong, warm current of air. Shipping weight, 5 pounds.
57K3377—For 110-volt direct or alternating current **$4.35**

Challenge Curling Iron

Our Challenge curling iron has a small barrel and is very effective in making the tight waves which are so becoming in the Cluster Bob. An ideal iron for students and for traveling purposes. Shpg. wt., 1 lb.
57K3569—For 110-volt city current only **49c**

Curler and Marcel Waver

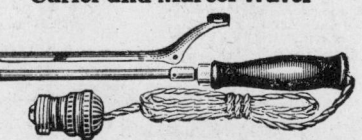

A most charming style of hair dressing is the popular side wave effect. The marcel rod produces the loose waves desired, and the iron with clamp is most effective in turning the ends under. Shipping weight, 1 pound.
57K3577—For 110-volt city current only **69c**

Quality Curling Iron

This beautiful iron has a mahogany handle and a fine silk cord which is detachable. It is furnished in a neat dresser box. Makes heavier waves than the ordinary iron. It is very effective in producing the popular Diana wave as shown at the right. Shipping weight, 3 pounds.
57K3578—For 110-volt city current only **$1.75**

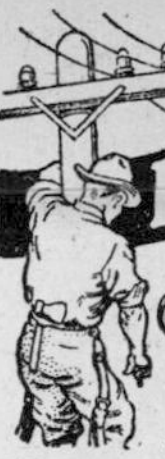

Linemen's Equipment — Telephone and Telegraph Supplies — Insulators and Wire

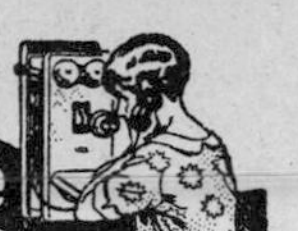

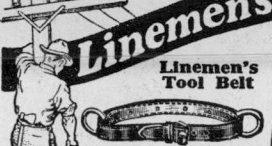

Linemen's Tool Belt

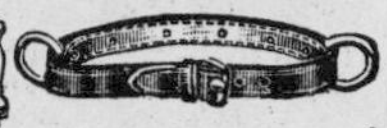

Made of high grade leather. Width of strap, 2 in. Length, 46 in. Shipping weight, 1½ pounds.
57K3464....... **$1.75**

Climber Straps

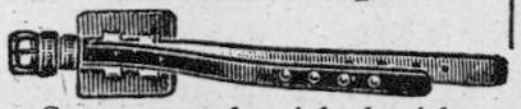

Straps are furnished with a leather pad which prevents the climber from digging into the knee. Can be used with any style of climber, either eastern or western. Shipping weight, 2 pounds.
57K3465—Per set of four, 2 upper, 2 lower............ **$1.59**

Linemen's Safety Straps

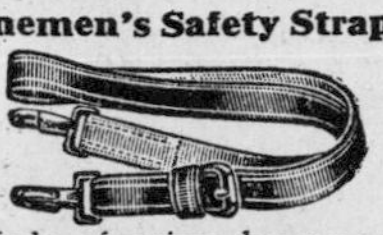

Made of prime harness leather, single strap, 5 feet 6 inches long, 1¾ inches wide. Shpg. wt., 2 lbs.
57K3463....... **$1.98**

Linemen's Climbers

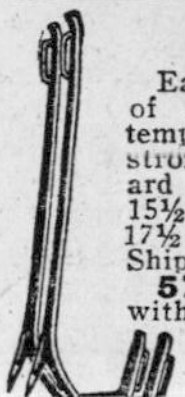

Eastern pattern. Made of high grade steel, tempered, finely finished, strong and safe. Standard length namely, 15, 15½, 16, 16½, 17 and 17½ inches. State length. Shipping weight, 4 lbs.
57K3466 — Pair, without straps. **$1.98**

Ground Rod

Iron Ground Rod, 6 feet long, ½ inch in diameter. Galvanized. Shipping weight, each, 3½ pounds.
57K3467¼—Each.. **39c**
Dozen $4.60

Iron Guy Rod

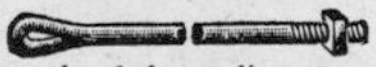

Length, 6 feet; diameter, ⅝-inch. Galvanized with square nut. Shipping weight, each, 6¼ pounds.
57K3468¼—Each... **67c**
Dozen $7.95

Staples (Not Illustrated)

¾-inch (No. 3). Shipping weight, 1 pound.
57K3461—Package of 100............ **17c**
Copper plated, ½ inch.
57K3462—1-pound package.............. **23c**
Shipping weight, 1½ pounds.

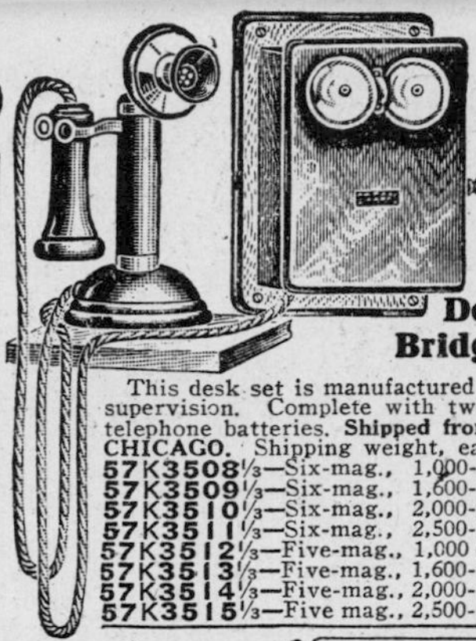

Desk Phone Bridging Type

This desk set is manufactured under our own supervision. Complete with two WLS special telephone batteries. Shipped from factory near CHICAGO. Shipping weight, each, 33 pounds.

57K3508⅓—Six-mag.,	1,000-ohm..	$15.10
57K3509⅓—Six-mag.,	1,600-ohm..	15.20
57K3510⅓—Six-mag.,	2,000-ohm..	15.25
57K3511⅓—Six-mag.,	2,500-ohm..	15.30
57K3512⅓—Five-mag.,	1,000 ohm..	14.95
57K3513⅓—Five-mag.,	1,600-ohm..	15.10
57K3514⅓—Five-mag.,	2,000-ohm..	15.20
57K3515⅓—Five mag.,	2,500-ohm..	15.25

Service

We are in a position to give you figures on a switchboard ranging from six to three hundred lines. Send in your requirements. We will forward an estimate, showing necessary equipment at lowest prices.

Chicago DeLuxe Bridging Telephones

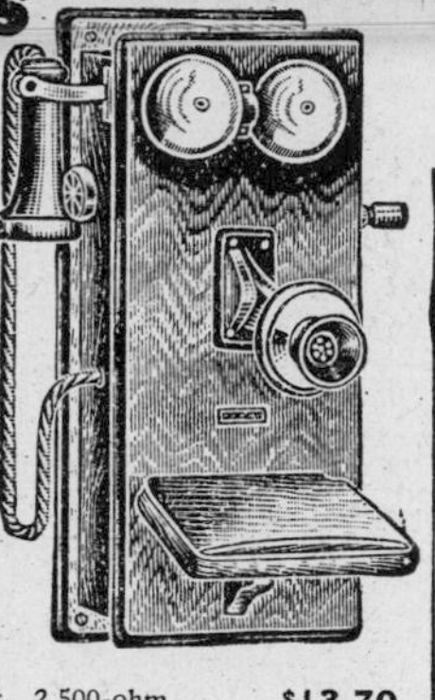

The finest manufactured country line telephones. Prices below include telephone and set of two special WLS telephone batteries. Phones are shipped from factory near CHICAGO. Shpg. wt., each, 36 lbs.
57K3500⅓—Six-magnet, 1,000-ohm. $13.35
57K3501⅓—Six-magnet, 1,600-ohm. $13.45
57K3502⅓—Six-magnet, 2,000-ohm. $13.60

57K3503⅓—Six-magnet,	2,500-ohm........	$13.70
57K3504⅓—Five-magnet,	1,000-ohm........	13.30
57K3505⅓—Five-magnet,	1,600-ohm........	13.35
57K3506⅓—Five-magnet,	2,000-ohm........	13.45
57K3507⅓—Five-magnet,	2,500-ohm........	13.75

Insulators

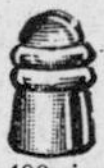

No. 9 for telephone, telegraph work, 400 in barrel. Weight, 300 lbs.
57K3456¼
400 insulators............... **$21.24**
Each..(Shpg. wt., 4 oz.)..6c

Insulators

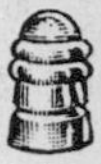

Double groove for telephone transposition work, 400 in barrel. Weight, barrel, 300 pounds.
57K3457¼
400 insulators... **$25.35**
Each.(Shpg. wt., 4 oz.).7c

Pins

Size, 1¼x8 inches. For use on crossarms. Painted. Weight, each, 8 ounces.
57K3459¼—Per sack, 250 pins. (Shipping weight, 62 pounds). **$5.60**
Each, in less than sack lots 3c

Brackets

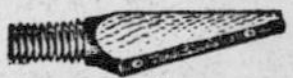

For telephone and telegraph line construction. Can be fastened to side of pole. Painted. Weight, each, ¾ pound.
57K3458¼—Each..... **3c**
20 for 52c   100 for $2.30

Malleable Iron Brackets

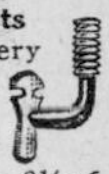

Insulator Bracket. Very strong, well made malleable casting, japanned.
57K3460 — Short Arm Wall Bracket. Size, 2½x6 inches. Shipping wt., each, ¾ lb. Dozen. **$1.85**
Each 16c

Powerful Electro Magnet

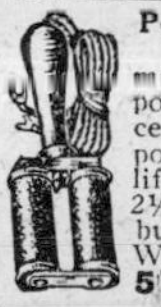

With one dry cell magnet has a lifting power of 2 pounds, two cells will lift about 5 pounds, four cells will lift over 10 pounds. Two 2½-foot conducting cords, but without batteries. Wt., 1 lb.....
57K3483. **$2.25**

Telephone Accessories

Receiver

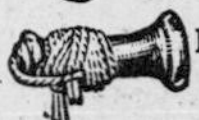

Bi-Polar Receiver. Can be used on any telephone.
57K3405—Shipping weight, 1½ lbs. **$1.28**

Receiver Cords

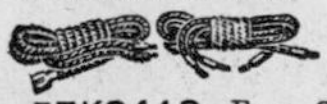

36-inch. Three types. Shipping weight, 2 oz.
57K3412—Spade and Straight terminals....... **27c**
57K3413—Four Straight terminals 27c
57K3414—Four Spade terminals..27c

Fuses

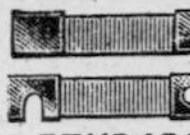

Shipping weight, per dozen, 4 oz.
57K3433—Western Union. Copper tip. Per 100, $2.76; per doz.... **35c**
57K3434—Postal Copper Tip. Per 100 ....$2.85
Per dozen .... .36

Wall Telephones S. H. Couch

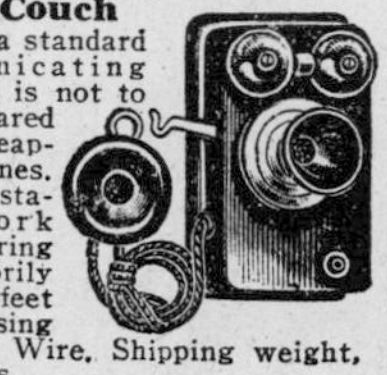

This is a standard communicating phone and is not to be compared with the cheaper toy phones. For two-station work only. Will ring satisfactorily over 600 feet of wire, using 57K2590¼ Wire. Shipping weight, 5½ pounds.
57K3401—Per Pair, without batteries or wire................ **$13.95**

Transmitter

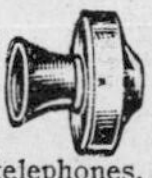

Solid Back Transmitter. Button type granular carbon transmitter, fits both old and new type telephones. Shpg. wt. 1¼ lbs.
57K3409... **$1.87**

Mouthpiece

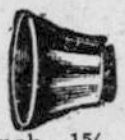

Composition mouth-piece. For Bell and Automatic, having thread size 30 per inch, ¹⁵⁄₁₆ in. in diam. Shpg. wt., 5 ounces.
57K3407 .... **9c**

Protector and Cut-out

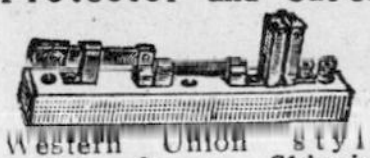

Western Union style, porcelain base. Shipping weight, ¾ pound.
57K3430....... **79c**

Lightning Arrester

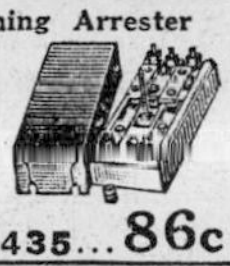

Air gap protector. Shpg. wt., 1½ lbs.
57K3435... **86c**

Baby Knife Switches

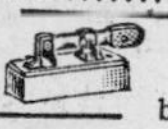

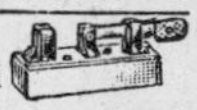

Porcelain base telephone, telegraph and battery switches.
57K3439—Single Pole Throw Switch. Shipping weight, 6 oz.................... **13c**
57K3440—Single Pole Double Throw Switch. Shipping weight, ¾ lbs............. **21c**
57K3441—Double Pole Single Throw Switch. Shipping weight, ¾ lbs.............. **23c**

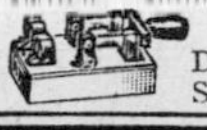

57K3442—Double Pole Double Throw Switch. Shipping weight, 1 lb... **32c**

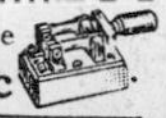

Telegraph Instruments

4-Ohm Private Line Set

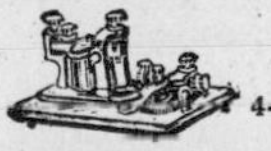

Consists of our Aluminum Lever Giant Sounder 57K3555 and a Bar Standard Steel Lever Key. Shipping weight, 4 pounds.
57K3557....... **$4.85**

4-Ohm Giant Sounder

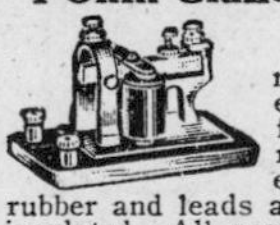

Rapid aluminum sounder, with brass frame. Magnets are covered with hard rubber and leads are thoroughly insulated. All parts are adjustable. Shpg. wt., 1½ lbs.
57K3555 **$2.50**
20-Ohm Giant Sounder
57K3556—Shpg. wt., 1½ lbs........ **$2.75**

Beginners' Outfits

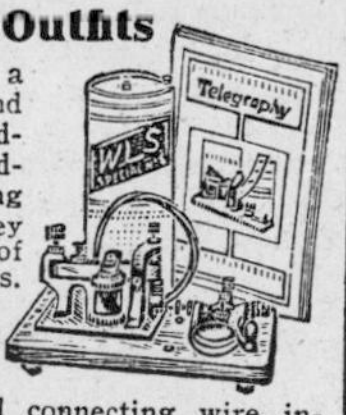

Consists of a full size key and sounder on hardwood base. Sounder lever, binding posts and key switch lever are of lacquered brass. Key lever is nickel plated and buffed. Instruction book, dry battery and connecting wire included. Shpg. wt., 5 lbs.
57K3564............. **$4.25**
Same as above, except with buzzer for wireless practice work.
57K3561—Wireless practice set........... **$2.78**

Superior Wireless Key

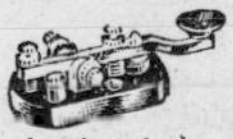

Provided with large hardened contact points. Knob is of hard rubber composition. Shipping weight, 1 pound.
57K3562............. **$2.48**

Steel Lever Key

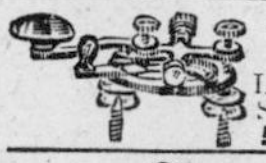

Standard Steel Lever Key with legs. Shpg. wt., ¾ lb.
57K3559 $2.00

20-Ohm Standard Relay

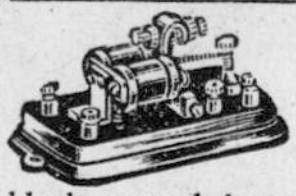

Polished base with sub-base of black enameled cast iron. For telegraph lines up to 10 miles; also burglar and alarm systems. Shipping weight, 2¼ pounds.
57K3554............. **$3.45**

Rubber Covered Twisted Pair

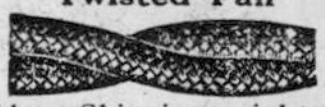

For outside work. No. 19 copper wire with insulation of black rubber. Shipping weight, per 100 feet, 3½ lbs.
57K2590¼
Per 100 feet......... **$1.29**
Same as above, but for inside work. Shpg. wt., per 100 feet, 3½ lbs.
57K2589¼
Per 100 feet......... **$1.29**
Neither of the above is suitable for lighting circuit use.

Induction Coil

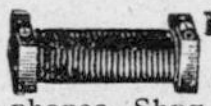

Suitable for all style magneto telephones. Shpg. wt., 6 oz.
57K3420........ **79c**

Lanterns and Flashlight Supplies

The Light for Every Purpose!

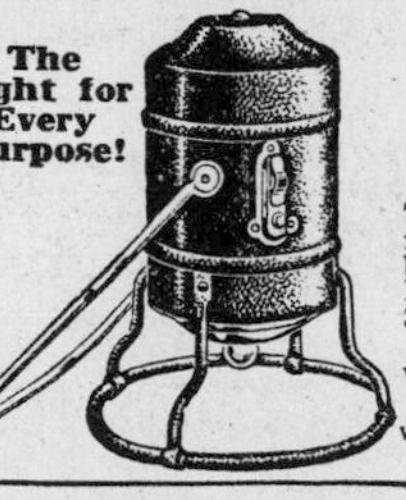

Campers' Lantern

A new light for the camp or farm. Safe and convenient. Throws a bright, concentrated spot, and also produces a flood of light upward at a 45-degree angle. The large base and protected bulb are other convenient features. Especially designed for boating and night traveling. Shipping weight, each, 6 pounds.
57K3098—Campers' Lamp, complete with bulb and battery........................ **$3.12**
57K3099—Extra Battery for lantern above. Shipping weight, 1 pound.................................... **52c**
For extra Lamp see 57K3044 shown at right.

Utility Lanterns

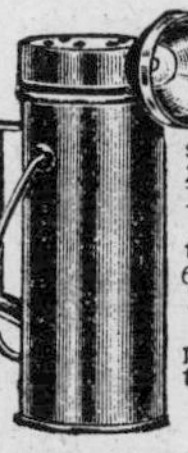

A strong, handy light for the farm. Always ready and requires little attention. Uses standard dry cell batteries. The double cell lantern is 7½x6¼x4 in., and requires two W L S Batteries, 57K3062, shown at right. The single cell lantern is 2⅞ inches in diameter and 8 inches high. Requires one W L S Battery 57K3062.
57K3029—Complete with bulb and battery: Shipping weight, 6 pounds............................. **$1.35**
For extra bulb see 57K3040, shown at right.
57K3025—Double Cell Lantern, complete with bulb and two batteries. Shpg. wt., 9½ lbs... **$2.25**
For extra bulb see 57K3045 at right.
For Oil Lanterns see page 976

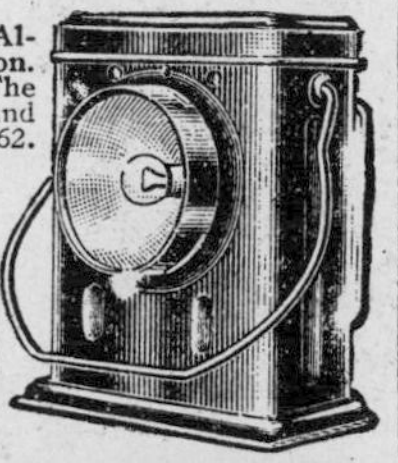

Shurlite Flashlight Batteries

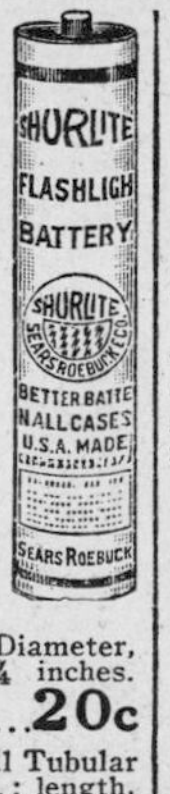

A strong and reliable source of power for your flashlight. You can buy no better.
57K3049—Three-Cell Tubular Battery. Diameter, 1⅜ inches; length, 7 inches. Shipping weight, ¾ pound...... **27c**
57K3051 — Five-Cell Tubular Battery. Diameter, 1⅜ inches; length, 11¾ in. Shipping weight, 1¼ pounds.... **49c**
57K3052 — Two-Cell Tubular Battery. Diameter, 1⅜ inches; length, 4¾ inches. Shipping weight, 8 ounces.................. **20c**
57K3053—Two-Cell Tubular Battery. Diameter, 1 in.; length, 3¾ inches. Shipping weight, 4 ounces....... **16c**

W L S Special Dry Cell

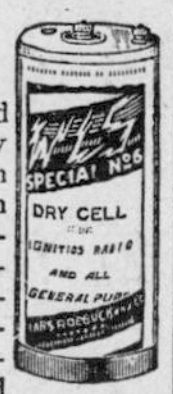

Designed especially for lantern and ignition work. Suitable for stationary gasoline engines, automobiles and launches. Guaranteed to test at least 25 amperes. Size, 2½x6 in. Shipping weight, 3 pounds.
57K3062. **30c**
Battery connection for lighting and ignition work. Shpg. wt., 3 ounces.
57K3455 Package of 10.. **15c**

Eveready Mazda Lamps

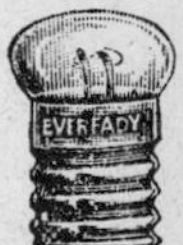

Genuine Eveready Mazda Flashlight Lamps. They give the maximum light with the least amount of battery consumption. Shipping weight, pkg. of 2, 4 oz.

Catalog No.	Mazda No.	Rating	Eveready No.	Pkg. of 2
57K3032	1	2.2	1180	21c
57K3033	2	3.3	1181	21c
57K3036	17	3.8	1193	21c
57K3037	3	2.3	1182	21c
57K3038	16	2.5	1198	21c
57K3039	18	4	1199	27c
57K3040	19	1.25	1451	21c
57K3041	31	6	1195	27c
57K3042	13	3.8	1162	27c
57K3043	14	2.5	1161	27c
57K3044	G4½	5	Lantern	37c
57K3045	35	2.4	1117	21c

Quality VIOLINS Guaranteed

"Music self played is happiness self made"

Shipping weight of Violins, 6 pounds

Adjusted for Easy Playing

Maple back and sides and straight grained spruce top. Ebony fingerboard, tailpiece and pegs. Color illustrations sent on request. See "Note" below.

12K160¼—Guarnerius model, imitation old....... **$9.95**

12K180¼—Stradivarius model, pearl inlaid pegs and tailpiece, carved scroll and chin rest, orange color.

$9.95

12K190¼ Amati model, reddish brown, shaded to natural.

$9.95

Old Seasoned Wood Used

Selected maple back and sides and seasoned spruce top. Fine ebony fingerboard, tailpiece and pegs. Excellent quality spirit varnish. Color illustrations sent free on request. See "Note" below.

12K175¼—Stradivarius model, fine imitation of old.. **$19.95**

12K185¼—Amati model, one-piece back. Scroll hand carved on back and sides. Fluted tailpiece and pegs. Reddish color, shaded to the natural.

$19.95

12K195¼ Stradivarius model, rich reddish color.

$19.95

Shpg. wt. 6 lbs.

NOTE

We furnish on request illustrations of actual color and shading of any violin on this page. Simply say, "Send me color plate of violin No. ......" and mention catalog number of violin.

Choice of Three Finishes

All modeled after Stradivarius, the most famous of all makers, but different in color and in type. All have two-piece backs with ebony fingerboard, tailpiece and pegs. Flamed maple neck and scroll. Color illustrations sent on request. See "Note" to left.

12K161¼—Reddish brown, shaded to the natural color of the wood............. **$12.45**

12K181¼—Imitation old.................. 12.45

12K191¼—Dark orange finish.............. 12.45

Alfred Dolling

Three Fine Stradivarius Models

Accurately proportioned Stradivarius models. Finely flamed maple back and sides, selected spruce top. Ebony fingerboard, tailpiece and pegs. Color illustrations sent on request. See "Note" at right.

12K174¼—Imitation of old (well marked) ... **$14.95**

12K184¼—Golden shaded to the natural color of the wood.. 14.95

12K194¼—Chocolate brown................ 14.95

Robert Berger

NOTE

We will furnish on request illustrations showing actual color and shading of any violin on this page. Simply say, "Send me color plate of violin No. ....." and mention catalog number of violin.

Master Made

The value of a violin depends upon two things—workmanship and material. The purchase of a violin from us guarantees your receiving an instrument which cannot be duplicated anywhere near the prices we ask. And remember, a well made violin is always an investment, as its value increases with age.

Shipping weight, Violins, 6 lbs.

Scientifically Constructed for Tone Quality

A group of fine violins all patterned after measurements of the old masters. Beautiful in appearance, pleasing in tone and so carefully made that they will last indefinitely. Fine figured maple and seasoned spruce used in their construction. Extra quality ebony fingerboard, tailpiece and pegs. Color illustrations sent free on request. See "Note" above.

12K153¼—Casper Da Salo model with fancy double purfling. Reddish gold in color...... **$24.95**

12K163¼—Stradivarius model in a fine copy of the old master even to the marks of age.... **$24.95**

12K173¼—Stradivarius model in a rich reddish brown color.. **$24.95**

This famous maker duplicates the old masters perfectly, not only in appearance, but in similarity of tone quality. He uses beautifully figured old garret seasoned maple and spruce and works it with the most exacting care. The trimmings are of the finest ebony. Will please the most critical player. Color illustrations sent on request. See "Note" above.

12K177¼—Stradivarius model, perfectly copied, showing marks of age and wear. Reddish gold color shaded to natural where marks of age appear... **$38.50**

12K187¼—Stradivarius model, new finish in light golden brown color.......... **$38.50**

It is difficult to improve on these violins at any price. We have testimonials comparing them favorably even with the famous violins over 200 years old. Their fine mellow tone has that penetrative quality which soloists and orchestra players seek, and which is usually found only in violins that have been played for years. Color illustrations sent on request. See "Note" above.

12K158¼—Stradivarius model, orange color.... **$50.00**

12K179¼—Beautiful and faithful reproduction of a famous Stradivarius. Golden in color. Marks of age as natural as though the instrument were 200 years old.. **$50.00**

Pleasing and Responsive in Tone

Two violins perfectly proportioned according to their respective models. Both are excellent in tone, and so well constructed are they that the tone will improve with age and use. None but old, thoroughly seasoned maple and spruce used for the body. Figured maple neck and scroll. Very fine ebony fingerboard, pegs and tailpiece. Color illustrations sent on request. See "Note" above.

12K166¼ — Guarnerius model, golden brown in color....... **$29.95**

12K176¼ — Copy of a famous Stradivarius, showing marks of age........ **$29.95**

Learn to Play a Violin

"Music self played is happiness self made"

The earning capacity of a proficient violinist often exceeds $100.00 per week. To learn is easy—it's just a question of getting started. Our better outfits are used by many professionals. Our less expensive ones are ideal for the beginner and amateur.

NOTE—Excepting where particularly stated, all violins are full size.

Complete Violin Outfits

Learn to Play on This Violin

You'll be astonished at the remarkable quality of this violin at this price. Stradivarius model. Maple back and sides. Spruce top and maple neck. Inlaid purfling around edges. Ebonized fingerboard, pegs and tailpiece. Brownish color shaded to natural. Outfit consists of: One violin as described, one marbleized cardboard case, one Brazil wood bow, one piece rosin, one instruction book, one fingerboard chart, one extra set of steel strings. Shipping wt., 7 lbs.

12K100¼—Full size................... **$4.95**
12K101¼—Same as above, but in three-quarter size, for children from 8 to 12 years of age........................... **$4.95**
12K102¼—Same, but half-size, for children from 6 to 8 years old............. **4.95**

Maggini Model **$14⁹⁵**

Flamed two-piece maple back. Maple neck and scroll. Selected, spruce top. Double inlaid purfling around edges. Ebony fingerboard, tailpiece and pegs. Brilliant red, shaded to natural color of wood. Good tone. Includes: Violin shape case, covered with artificial leather, felt lined and with lock and clasps; Brazil wood bow with whalebone grip; ½ doz. steel "E" strings; rosin, chin rest, extra set of gut strings, tuner, "E" string adjuster, fingerboard chart, two books. Shipping weight, 10 pounds.
12K114¼..................... **$14.95**

Stradivarius Model

Favorite of many players. Broad proportions give it a powerful tone. Two-piece flamed maple back. Maple sides. Spruce top. Ebony fingerboard, tailpiece and pegs. One of our best sellers. Brownish, shaded to natural color. Outfit includes imported violin shape case with nickel plated clasps and lock, full felt lined; Brazil wood bow with pearl eye in frog; full nickel silver lined; chin rest; rosin; extra set of gut strings; fingerboard chart; four-pipe tuner and Guckert's "Self Instructor." Shipping weight, 10 pounds.
12K113¼
$12.45

Stradivarius Model

A value that should not be overlooked. Well constructed Stradivarius model with two-piece maple back and spruce top. Maple sides and neck. Inlaid purfling. Ebonized hardwood fingerboard, tailpiece and pegs. Brownish color shaded to the natural. Full size. There is no question of value being here. Outfit includes Brazil wood bow with ebony frog, imported violin shaped case with lock, rosin, extra set steel strings, chin rest, fingerboard chart, "A" tuning pipe and instruction book. Shipping wt., 8 pounds.
12K103¼..... **$7.45**

We particularly recommend this outfit for those who want everything needed to start them on their studies. The violin is a Stradivarius model exceptionally well made. Two-piece flamed maple back and straight grained spruce top. Maple neck and sides. Neatly inlaid purfling. Ebonized hardwood fingerboard, tailpiece and pegs. Pegs are fitted so they will not slip. Bridge also fitted. Rich reddish color covered with spirit varnish. You'll wonder how we can sell this outfit for so little, as all articles included are of unusual quality. Ordinarily the violin alone would cost a great deal more than we ask for the entire outfit. With it we include: One imported violin shaped case with nickel plated lock and clasps, half lined with felt; one Brazil wood bow, ebony nickel silver lined frog, pearl eye, leather grip; one piece rosin; one extra set of gut strings; one four-pipe tuner; one chin rest; one fingerboard chart; one Guckert's Instruction Book; one "Young Violinist's Favorites"; one japanned music stand. Equal value would cost $15.00 to $18.00 elsewhere. Shipping weight, 14 pounds.

12K105¼—Full size................... **$9.95**
Same as above, but in three-quarter size for children from 8 to 12 years old.
12K109¼..................... **$9.95**

Stradivarius Model

Slightly smaller than the ordinary model. Slender neck. Figured two-piece maple back and sides, spruce top. Genuine ebony fingerboard, tailpiece and pegs. Dark amber finish covered with a transparent spirit varnish. Includes: Case, covered with artificial leather, felt lined, nickel plated lock; Brazil wood bow, whalebone grip; ebony chin rest; rosin; one set Acme gut strings; six Bell brand "E" strings; adjuster and inset bridge for steel "E" strings; fingerboard chart; ebony mute; four-pipe tuner; Wichtl's Instruction Book and "Most Popular Violinist's Pieces." Shipping weight, 13 pounds.
12K115¼............................ **$19.95**

Guarnerius Model

Figured two-piece maple back and seasoned spruce top. Figured maple neck and scroll. Ebony fingerboard, tailpiece and pegs. Chocolate brown in color. Responsive in tone. Includes: Pernambuco wood bow, nickel silver lined; case, covered with artificial leather, full velveteen lined; Bernadel rosin; ebony chin rest; fingerboard chart; Wichtl's Instruction Book; "Most Popular Violin Pieces"; extra set of Verona gut strings; one dozen Black Diamond steel "E" strings; adjuster and inset bridge for steel "E" strings; Wolf tone mute; four-pipe tuner; shoulder pad; nickel plated music stand. Shipping weight, 15 pounds.
12K117¼
$24.95

SUPERTONE TENOR BANJOS

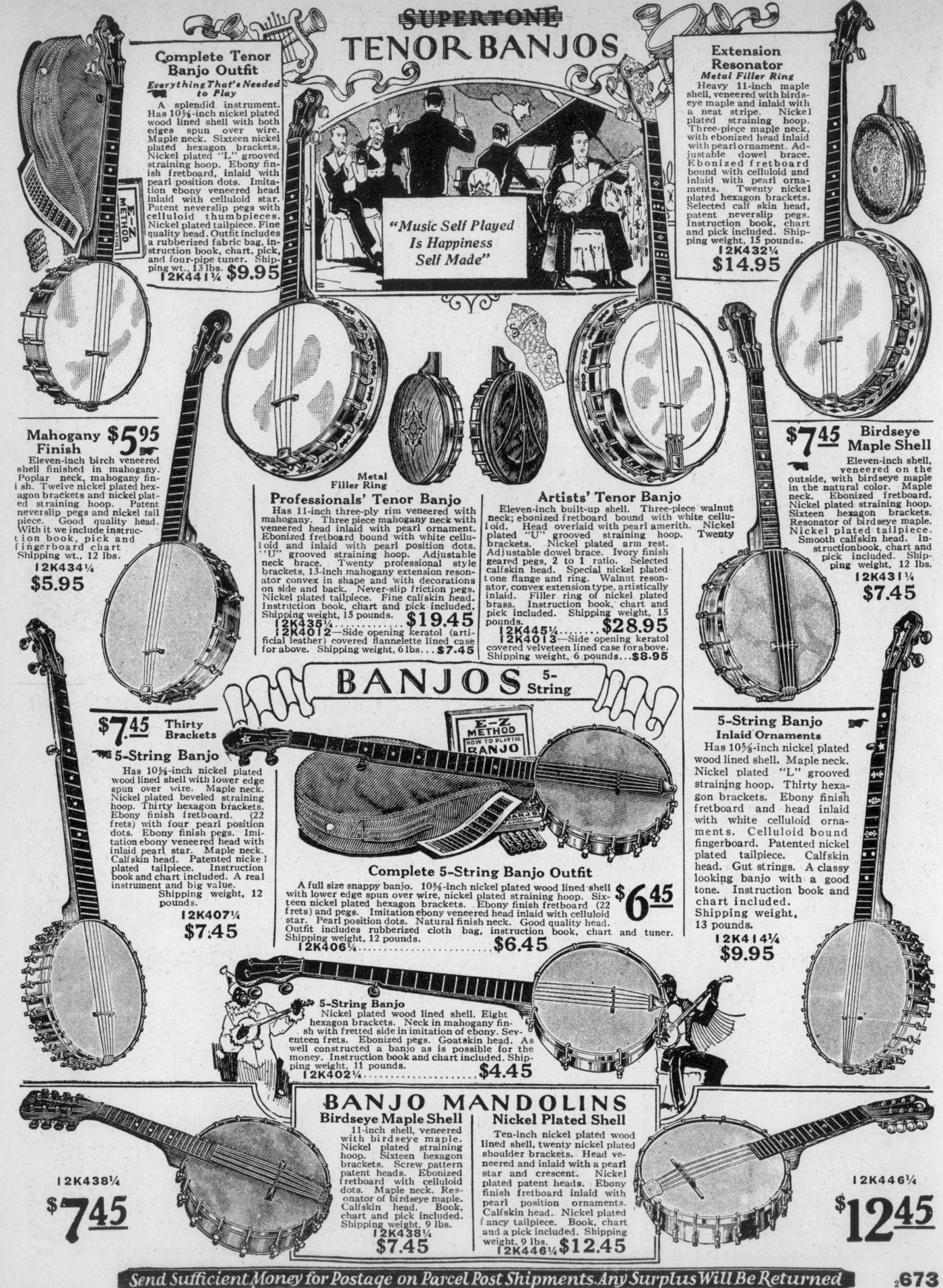

"Music Self Played Is Happiness Self Made"

Complete Tenor Banjo Outfit
Everything That's Needed to Play

A splendid instrument. Has 10⅝-inch nickel plated wood lined shell with both edges spun over wire. Maple neck. Sixteen nickel plated hexagon brackets. Nickel plated "L" grooved straining hoop. Ebony finish fretboard, inlaid with pearl position dots. Imitation ebony veneered head inlaid with celluloid star. Patent neverslip pegs with celluloid thumbpieces. Nickel plated tailpiece. Fine quality head. Outfit includes a rubberized fabric bag, instruction book, chart, pick, and four-pipe tuner. Shipping wt., 13 lbs.
12K441¼ $9.95

Extension Resonator
Metal Filler Ring

Heavy 11-inch maple shell, veneered with birdseye maple and inlaid with a neat stripe. Nickel plated straining hoop. Three-piece maple neck, with ebonized head inlaid with pearl ornament. Adjustable dowel brace. Ebonized fretboard bound with celluloid and inlaid with pearl ornaments. Twenty nickel plated hexagon brackets. Selected calf skin head, patent neverslip pegs. Instruction book, chart and pick included. Shipping weight, 15 pounds.
12K432¼ $14.95

Mahogany Finish $5.95

Eleven-inch birch veneered shell finished in mahogany. Poplar neck, mahogany finish. Twelve nickel plated hexagon brackets and nickel plated straining hoop. Patent neverslip pegs and nickel tailpiece. Good quality head. With it we include instruction book, pick and fingerboard chart. Shipping wt., 12 lbs.
12K434¼ $5.95

Metal Filler Ring
Professionals' Tenor Banjo

Has 11-inch three-ply rim veneered with mahogany. Three piece mahogany neck with veneered head inlaid with pearl ornament. Ebonized fretboard bound with white celluloid and inlaid with pearl position dots. "U" grooved straining hoop. Adjustable neck brace. Twenty professional style brackets, 13-inch mahogany extension resonator convex in shape and with decorations on side and back. Never-slip friction pegs. Nickel plated tailpiece. Fine calfskin head. Instruction book, chart and pick included. Shipping weight, 15 pounds.
12K435¼ $19.45
12K4012—Side opening keratol (artificial leather) covered flannelette lined case for above. Shipping weight, 6 lbs... **$7.45**

Artists' Tenor Banjo

Eleven-inch built-up shell. Three-piece walnut neck; ebonized fretboard bound with white celluloid. Head overlaid with pearl amerith. Nickel plated "U" grooved straining hoop. Twenty nickel brackets. Nickel plated arm rest. Adjustable dowel brace. Ivory finish geared pegs, 2 to 1 ratio. Selected calfskin head. Special nickel plated tone flange and ring. Walnut resonator, convex extension type, artistically inlaid. Filler ring of nickel plated brass. Instruction book, chart and pick included. Shipping weight, 15 pounds.
12K445¼ $28.95
12K4013—Side opening keratol covered velveteen lined case for above. Shipping weight, 6 pounds...**$8.95**

$7.45 Birdseye Maple Shell

Eleven-inch shell, veneered on the outside, with birdseye maple in the natural color. Maple neck. Ebonized fretboard. Nickel plated straining hoop. Sixteen hexagon brackets. Resonator of birdseye maple. Nickel plated tailpiece. Smooth calfskin head. Instruction book, chart and pick included. Shipping weight, 12 lbs.
12K431¼ $7.45

BANJOS 5-String

$7.45 Thirty Brackets
5-String Banjo

Has 10⅝-inch nickel plated wood lined shell with lower edge spun over wire. Maple neck. Nickel plated beveled straining hoop. Thirty hexagon brackets. Ebony finish fretboard. (22 frets) with four pearl position dots. Ebony finish pegs. Imitation ebony veneered head with inlaid pearl star. Maple neck. Calfskin head. Patented nickel plated tailpiece. Instruction book and chart included. A real instrument and big value. Shipping weight, 12 pounds.
12K407¼ $7.45

Complete 5-String Banjo Outfit

A full size snappy banjo. 10⅝-inch nickel plated wood lined shell with lower edge spun over wire, nickel plated straining hoop. Sixteen nickel plated hexagon brackets. Ebony finish fretboard (22 frets) and pegs. Imitation ebony veneered head inlaid with celluloid star. Pearl position dots. Natural finish head. Good quality head. Outfit includes rubberized cloth bag, instruction book, chart and tuner. Shipping weight, 12 pounds.
$6.45
12K406¼ $6.45

5-String Banjo Inlaid Ornaments

Has 10⅝-inch nickel plated wood lined shell. Maple neck. Nickel plated "L" grooved straining hoop. Thirty hexagon brackets. Ebony finish fretboard and head inlaid with white celluloid ornaments. Celluloid bound fingerboard. Patented nickel plated tailpiece. Calfskin head. Gut strings. A classy looking banjo with a good tone. Instruction book and chart included. Shipping weight, 13 pounds.
12K414¼ $9.95

5-String Banjo

Nickel plated wood lined shell. Eight hexagon brackets. Neck in mahogany finish with fretted side in imitation of ebony. Seventeen frets. Ebonized pegs. Goatskin head. As well constructed a banjo as is possible for the money. Instruction book and chart included. Shipping weight, 11 pounds.
12K402¼ $4.45

BANJO MANDOLINS

Birdseye Maple Shell

11-inch shell, veneered with birdseye maple. Nickel plated straining hoop. Sixteen hexagon brackets. Screw pattern patent heads. Ebonized fretboard with celluloid dots. Maple neck. Resonator of birdseye maple. Calfskin head. Book, chart and pick included. Shipping weight, 9 lbs.
12K438¼ $7.45
$7.45
12K438¼

Nickel Plated Shell

Ten-inch nickel plated wood lined shell, twenty nickel plated shoulder brackets. Head veneered and inlaid with a pearl star and crescent. Nickel plated patent heads. Ebony finish fretboard inlaid with pearl position ornaments. Calfskin head. Nickel plated fancy tailpiece. Book, chart and a pick included. Shipping weight, 9 lbs.
12K446¼ $12.45
12K446¼
$12.45

SUPERTONE UKULELES

Very Fine Outfit
Mahogany Ukulele

Natural color mahogany body and neck, carefully made and finished. The top edge, fretboard and soundhole are bound with white and black celluloid which, in contrast to the brownish finish of the body, gives a rich and dignified effect. Extension fretboard. Patent neverslip pegs. Sweet tone. Canvas case, instruction book and pick included. Shipping weight, 5 pounds.

12K464¼ **$4.85**

The Latest in Ukes
Colored lacquer finish in crackle effect over ivory color background. Top edge and soundhole bound with celluloid. Poplar neck colored to match body. Patent friction pegs. Instruction book and pick included. For players who prefer something original. Shpg. wt., 4 lbs.

12K453¼—Green finish **$2.69**
12K454¼—Red finish $2.69

Handcraft Ukulele

Same as our No. 12K465¼ on opposite side, excepting that this instrument is made with top and back edge, and fretboard bound with white celluloid. Fretboard inlaid with six position ornaments. An instrument the greatest ukulele player will be proud to own. Side opening keratol (artificial leather) covered and flannel lined, and has nickel plated lock and clasps included. Instruction book and pick also included. Shpg. wt., 6 lbs.

12K466¼ **$9.75**

Ukulele Outfit
Very Popular With Boy and Girl Scouts

Body finished in walnut color. Fingerboard is accurately fretted. With this ukulele we include one fitted bag of rubberized fabric with metal snap fasteners, an instruction book and felt pick. Shipping weight, 4 pounds.

12K461¼ **$1.75**

Music self played is happiness self made.

Birchwood Ukulele

Birch body and poplar neck carefully made and finished. Top edge and soundhole bound with white celluloid, which makes a contrast to the brownish finish. Neverslip friction pegs. A better instrument than the price would indicate. Instruction book and pick included. Shpg. wt., 4 lbs.

12K451¼ **$1.95**

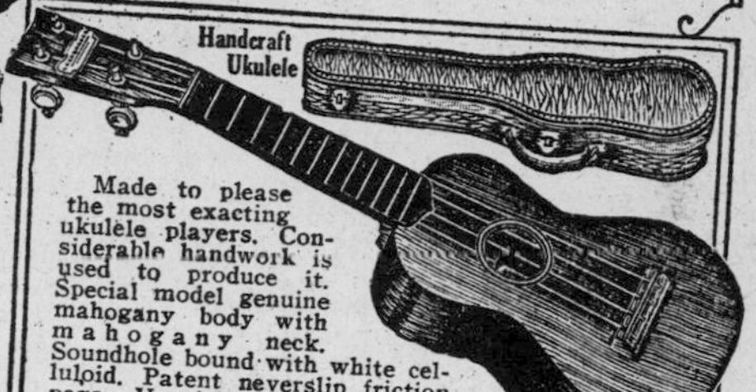

More Fun When You Have a Uke Along

Complete Outfit

Everything that's needed to play the ukulele. The ukulele is made of selected birchwood. Celluloid bound soundhole. Shaped back. Brownish color. Substantially built and of good tone. Neverslip friction pegs. With this ukulele we include one rubberized fabric bag, one instruction book and one felt pick. Shipping weight, 5 pounds.

12K458¼ **$2.39**

Mahogany Ukulele

Body of mahogany. Mahogany finish neck and head. Patent neverslip pegs. Edge of top and soundhole inlaid with purfling and wood in corded effect. Finished in the natural color. Accurately fretted. Excellent tone. Instruction book and pick included. Shpg. wt., 4 lbs.

12K456¼ **$3.35**

Handcraft Ukulele

Made to please the most exacting ukulele players. Considerable handwork is used to produce it. Special model genuine mahogany body with mahogany neck. Soundhole bound with white celluloid. Patent neverslip friction pegs. Varnished and hand rubbed. Side opening keratol (artificial leather) covered and flannel lined, nickel plated lock and clasps included; also instruction book and pick. Shipping weight, 6 pounds.

12K465¼ **$7.75**

Banjo Ukes

All Metal Body

Rim and extension resonator made of brass nickel plated. Mahogany finish neck with silveroid position dots. Twelve nickel plated brackets. Nickel plated tailpiece and fine calfskin head. Patent neverslip friction pegs. Instruction book and pick included. A wonderful value. Shipping weight, 6 pounds.

12K492¼ **$7.45**
12K4401—Keratol covered, side opening case to fit $2.59

Mahogany
With Extension Resonator

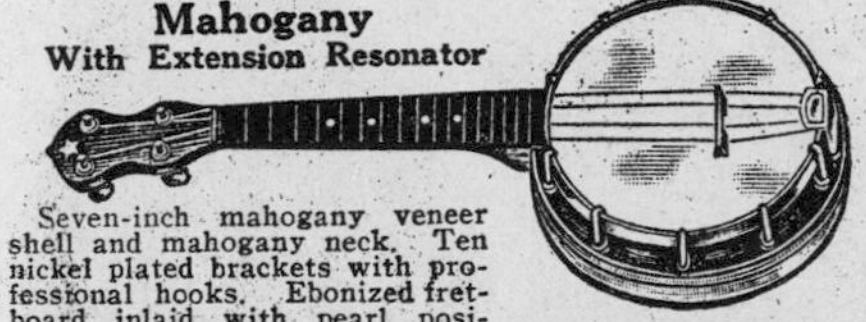

Seven-inch mahogany veneer shell and mahogany neck. Ten nickel plated brackets with professional hooks. Ebonized fretboard inlaid with pearl position dots. Ebonized veneered head inlaid with pearl star. Three-ply mahogany veneered extension resonator, convex shape and inlaid with black and white celluloid binding around edge. Nickel plated tailpiece and straining hoop. Calfskin head. Patent neverslip friction pegs. Instruction book and pick included. Shipping weight, 5 pounds.

12K495¼ **$7.75**

California Style

Seven-inch shell veneered with genuine walnut. Poplar neck in natural color. Neverslip friction pegs. Resonator on back. Calfskin head is decorated with a canoe scene in many colors. Instruction book and felt pick included. A very popular style. Shpg. wt., 5 lbs.

12K474¼ **$3.45**

Complete Banjo Uke Outfit
A Big Value

Eight-inch three-ply shell veneered with birdseye maple. Ebonized veneered fretboard with three position dots. Nickel plated straining hoop, twelve nickel plated hexagon brackets. Calfskin head, nickel plated tailpiece. Patent neverslip friction pegs. Keratol covered, felt lined, side opening case, instruction book and pick included. Shipping weight, 6 pounds.

12K491¼ **$7.75**

Birdseye Maple Veneered

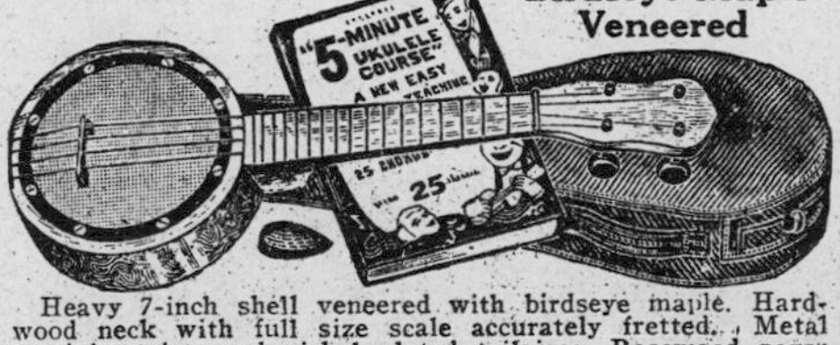

Heavy 7-inch shell veneered with birdseye maple. Hardwood neck with full size scale accurately fretted. Metal straining ring and nickel plated tailpiece. Rosewood pegs; calfskin head. Entire instrument finished in the natural color. Rubberized fabric bag, instruction book and felt pick included. Shipping weight, 5 pounds.

12K472¼ **$2.45**

Low Priced Good Banjo Uke

Our price is positively the lowest at which such a good instrument can be sold. It has a 7-inch rim of hardwood in the natural finish, highly polished. Poplar neck. Full banjo ukulele scale. Japanned metal adjustable straining ring. Calfskin head; nickel plated tailpiece; good quality gut strings. Instruction book and pick included. Shipping weight, 5 pounds.

12K473¼ **$1.73**

Professional Banjo Uke
New Type Extension Resonator

Eight-inch genuine walnut veneered shell. Walnut neck with head overlaid with pearl amerith. Extension resonator of walnut, convex in shape and inlaid. Metal filler ring of nickel plated brass. "U" style straining hoop of brass, nickel plated. Ebonized fretboard with four pearl position dots. Black neverslip pegs. Instruction book, pick and wrench included with instrument. Shipping weight, 6 pounds.

12K496¼ **$12.45**
12K4402—Keratol covered side opening case to fit $2.65

Walnut Finish
10 Brackets

Seven-inch laminated shell finished in walnut. Nickel plated straining hoop, ten nickel plated hexagon brackets. Fine quality calfskin head, nickel plated tailpiece. Patent neverslip friction pegs. Instruction book and pick included. Shipping weight, 5 pounds.

12K476¼ **$4.45**

With Resonator
**Mahogany Shell
California Style**

Seven-inch shell, genuine mahogany veneer. Inlaid stripe on side of shell. Convex resonator with fancy soundholes on back. Mahogany neck with inlaid stripe on fingerboard. Patent friction pegs. Calfskin head. Special japanned metal straining ring. Instruction book and pick included. Shipping weight, 5 pounds.

12K478¼ **$4.25**

SUPERTONE GUITARS

Instruction Book and Chart Included with These Guitars

Music Self Played is Happiness Self Made

Combination Guitar Outfit

Can be Played in Regular or Hawaiian Style

Instruction Book and Chart Included with These Guitars

Mahogany Finish

Imitation mahogany body. White birch top. Mahogany finish neck. Ebonized fretboard with celluloid position dots. The top edge and soundhole are bound with black celluloid. Guard plate of decalcomania in many colors. Decalcomania stripe in back. Patent heads with steel plates and brass gears. Nickel plated tailpiece. Standard size. Shipping wt., 14 lbs.

12K231¼.....**$4.79**

12K232¼—Same as above, but in three-quarter or women's size..............**$4.79**

Birchwood Brown Finish

Figured birchwood back and sides. Finished in a brownish color. Natural birch top with decalcomania stripes around soundhole. Hardwood fretboard inlaid with three position dots. Screw patent heads with brass gears and steel plates. Nickel plated tailpiece. Standard size. A well made guitar. Good finish, workmanship and tone. Shipping weight, 14 pounds.

12K230¼ (Standard size).....**$3.95**

Genuine Mahogany

This outfit includes everything that is needed to start playing. The guitar itself is a handsome instrument, well made of seasoned materials. The body is of genuine mahogany. Top of white spruce. Mahogany neck and head. Ebonized fretboard inlaid with three position dots. The top edge and soundhole are inlaid with a beautiful colored block design and bound with white celluloid. Ebonized bridge with pearl inlaid bridge pins. Brass screw pattern patent heads. With it we include rubberized cloth bag, instruction book, fingerboard chart, extra set of Bell brand steel strings, tuner with pipe for each string, thumb pick and steel nut for playing Hawaiian style. Standard size.

12K240¼—Shpg. wt., 16 lbs.....**$9.95**

12K241¼—Guitar only. Shipping wt., 14 pounds.......................**$7.95**

Genuine Mahogany
Beautifully Figured

Back and sides of selected genuine mahogany. Spruce top and mahogany neck. Head veneered and inlaid with pearl ornament. Ebonized fretboard inlaid with pearl ornaments and bound with white celluloid. Bone nut: Edges of top, soundhole and back inlaid with black and white wood inlay artistically arranged. Ebonized bridge and bridge pins. Nickel plated patent heads. Standard size. Shpg. wt., 14 lbs.

12K247¼ **$14.95**

Our Finest A Beauty

Body of beautifully figured koa wood with top of selected spruce. Mahogany neck with veneered head inlaid with pearl. Ebony finish fretboard, bound with tortoise shell celluloid and inlaid with pearl. Bone nut. The edge of the top is inlaid with pearl and bound with celluloid imitation of tortoise shell. Soundhole inlaid and bound to match. Rosewood and holly stripe inlaid down the middle of the back. Ebonized bridge with bone fret and imitation ivory bridge pins, celluloid end pin. Nickel plated patent heads. Shipping wt., 15 pounds.

12K275¼ Standard size, **$19.75**

12K277¼ Grand Concert size ...**$23.45**

Exceptional Tone Quality

Guitar made of genuine figured mahogany. Top and back edges are inlaid with black and white purfling and bound with alternating black and white celluloid blocks in a corded effect which gives the instrument a very striking appearance.

Music Self Played is Happiness Self Made

HAWAIIAN GUITARS

The Hawaiian (sometimes called the steel) Guitar, with its beautiful quavering and sharp staccato tones, has done much to make the Hawaiian music so extremely popular. Owing to the fact that the strings when open, or when barred, form natural chords, it is comparatively easy to learn to play this instrument. Steel bar, picks and instruction book, as illustrated, included with 12K489¼, 12K485¼ and 12K488¼.

Genuine Mahogany

Back and sides of selected genuine mahogany. Spruce top mahogany grained. Mahogany neck and head. Ebony finish fretboard inlaid with three position dots. Fancy colored wood mosaic inlaying around soundhole and edge of top. Top and soundhole bound with white celluloid. Brass screw pattern patent heads with composition buttons. Ebony finish bridge and nickel plated fancy tailpiece. Patented removable nut. (By removing nut it can be played in regular style.) Canvas case, instruction book, steel bar, fingerboard chart and three picks included. Shipping weight, 16 pounds.

12K499¼.....................**$9.75**

Ebonized fretboard with pearl position ornaments. Head veneered with koa wood and inlaid with pearl. Ebonized bridge and bridge pins, the bridge pins being inlaid with pearl. Nickel plated patent heads. This instrument has a full round tone, with plenty of volume. Book, picks, etc., shown above at right, included. Shipping weight, 14 pounds.

12K488¼ **$14.25**

Top, sides and back of figured birch, finished in koa wood. Beautiful colored decalcomania design on sides and top. Ebony finish fretboard inlaid with white celluloid position dots. Edges of top, back and soundhole bound with black and white celluloid in corded effect. Patent heads with composition buttons. Articles (books, picks, etc.), shown above included. Shipping weight, 14 pounds.

12K489¼.......**$7.25**

Selected Birchwood

Top, sides and back of figured birch. Ebony finish fretboard inlaid with white celluloid position dots. Edges of top and soundhole bound with white celluloid. Ebony finish bridge with metal fret. Nickel plated tailpiece. Patent heads with composition buttons. Body, including top and neck, is finished in brownish color, slightly shaded at center of top and back. A well made instrument at a low price. Articles (books, picks, etc.), shown above at left, included. Shpg. wt., 14 lbs.

12K485¼.................**$4.95**

It's East to Order From The World's Largest Store. See Page 540

675

MOUTH ORGANS
MUSICAL PALS

Hohner Up to Date Tremolo
Two harmonicas in one, in different keys. Forty-eight double holes, ninety-six reeds, brass plates, nickel plated covers. Comes in handsome case with metal hinges and clasps. Length, 9 inches. Shipping wt., 1 lb.
12K5144................$2.19

"Marine Band" Tremolo
8⅝ Inches Long
A double sided harmonica in two different keys. Forty double plates, eighty tremolo tuned reeds, brass plates, fancy nickel plated covers, nicely ornamented; mahogany finish frame with gilt decorations. Shipping weight, ¾ pound.
12K5141................$1.49

HOHNER BRAND
Order Book 12K1645, below, sold only with Harmonicas.

Hohner "Goliath"
7½ Inches Long
A large tremolo harmonica. Twenty-four double holes, forty-eight reeds, brass plates. Case of imitation alligator skin with metal clasp and hinges.
12K5140—Shpg. wt., ¾ lb...$1.23

Hohner "Sportsman"
Sixteen double holes, thirty-two tremolo tuned reeds, brass plates, nickel plated covers. 5¼ inches in length. Shipping wt., 6 ounces.
12K5137................59c

Hohner "Trumpet Call"
Ten double holes, forty reeds, producing an organ-like tone; brass plates. Has wind saving device. Five brass trumpet horns. Length, 4⅞ in. Shipping wt., 1 pound.
12K5148 $2.19

Hohner Vest Pocket Chimes
Double sided with twelve double holes and twenty-four reeds on each side. Brass plates. Nickel plated rounded covers. 4¼ inches long and 2 inches wide. Shipping weight, 7 ounces.
12K5130................83c

Hohner "Marine Band"
Ten holes and twenty reeds; brass plates. Nickel plated covers. Hardwood frame, nicely varnished. 4 inches long. Shipping weight, 4 ounces.
12K5133................44c

Hohner Chromonica
Twenty holes and forty powerful reeds with wind saving device. Brass plates and heavy nickel plated covers. Mouthpiece is nickel plated, with a slide for producing the half tones. Length, 4¾ inches. Shipping wt., ¾ lb. $2.37
12K5150

Hohner Full Concert
Ten double holes, forty reeds, brass plates. Covers, finely nickel plated and have overlapping ends. 4⅝ inches long. Shipping weight, 5 ounces.
12K5131................63c

Hohner "Auto Valve"
Has a wind saving arrangement making it as easy blowing as any single reed mouth organ. Ten double holes, forty reeds, brass plates, nickel plated covers; 4⅝ inches long. Shipping weight, 5 ounces.
12K5139................88c

Hohner "Harmonette"
Fourteen double holes, twenty-eight reeds, genuine brass plates and nickel plated covers. Resonator or sound box of wood, reinforced with metal back. A beautiful effect can be produced with it. Length, 4⅝ inches. Shipping wt., ¾ pound.
12K5147......83c

Harmonica Holder
Will fit harmonica not more than 4⅝ inches in length. When not in use it may be folded into small compass. Shipping weight, 5 ounces.
12K5124......48c

Hohner "Echophone"
Finest tone effect can be produced. Horn is 4½ inches long, and made of heavy solid brass. Ten single holes, twenty reeds, brass plates, nickel plated covers. Shpg. wt., 8 oz.
12K5101......83c

BEAVER BRAND
Order Book 12K1645 with your Harmonicas

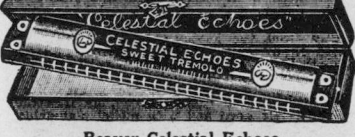

Beaver Concert Tremolo
Large double sided harmonica with 30 double holes on each side and 120 tremolo tuned reeds. Heavily nickel plated covers perforated in beautiful design. Hardwood frame with decorated extension ends. 10 inches long. Fancy imitation alligator box. Shipping weight, 1¼ pounds.
12K5125................$1.65

Play the Harmonica at Sight
Shows how to obtain half-tones, trills, tremolos and all kinds of variations. Thirty-two pages. Shipping weight, 2 ounces.
12K1729..23c

Beaver Regimental Band
A favorite with ten holes and twenty reeds. Brass plates. Nickel plated covers. A dandy; 4 in. long Shpg. wt., 4 oz.
12K5121 21c

New Standard Harmonica Course 200 Songs
Sixty-four pages with playing instructions and collection of 200 songs such as "Turkey in the Straw," "Old Black Joe," "When You and I Were Young, Maggie," "Aloha Oe," "Home, Sweet Home," etc. Simple and easy and anybody with little practice can play any song in this book. Shipping weight, 2 ounces.
12K1645—Sold only with mouth organs....12c

Beaver University Chimes
9¼ Inches Long, Two Bells
Double Harmonica, tuned in two harmonizing keys. Decorated frame, forty-eight holes on each side. Twenty-four reeds on each of four plates or ninety-six reeds in all. Four separate nickel plated covers. Two bells on a special bridge-like frame. Shpg. wt., 1¼ lbs.
12K5118................$1.45

Beaver Celestial Echoes
Tremolo Tuned—7 Inches Long
Brass plates, twenty-four double holes, forty-eight reeds. Handsome paper covered wood box with metal clasp. Sweet, powerful tone. An exceptional value. Shipping weight, ¾ pound.
12K5114................65c

Concert Regimental Band
Brass plates, ten double holes, forty fine reeds. Heavy nickel plated covers. 4⅝ inches long. Shpg. wt., 5 oz.
12K5122................43c

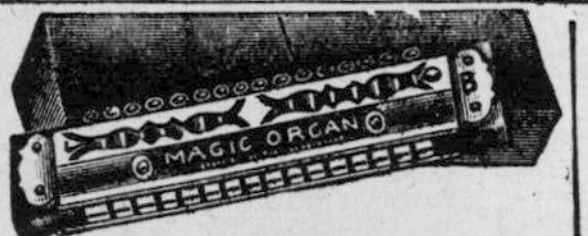

Beaver Magic Organ
Length, 5⅞ Inches
Double covers with imitation organ pipes. Tremolo or wavy effect in tone. Sixteen double holes, thirty-two reeds. Brass plates. Shipping weight, 5 oz.
12K5126................35c

Silvery Sounds Double Sided
7 Inches Long
Forty-eight holes and forty-eight reeds on each side. Brass plates. Covers are nickel plated and neatly chased and perforated. Tremolo tuned.
12K5116—Shipping wt., ¾ lb.........95c

LOWEST PRICES
Send for Book 12K1645 above.

Loud Speaker Harmonica
Brand new. With it even a beginner can easily get the same effects a professional does. Easy blowing, full toned harmonica with a detachable loud speaker horn. The horn is nickel plated with gilt inside bell. Ten holes and 20 reeds. Four inches long. Shipping weight, 1 pound.
12K5154................42c

Fourteen Trumpets
Sixteen double holes and thirty-two reeds. Nickel plated covers, fancy design. One of our best sellers. Length, 4¼ inches. Shpg. wt., 5 oz.
12K5152 23c

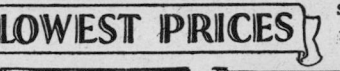

Savoy Band
Double sided, with 14 double holes and 28 reeds on each side. Brass plates and nickel plated covers. Mahogany finish frame. Length, 4½ inches long. Shipping weight, ¾ pound.
12K5127.....39c

The Espera
Ten holes, twenty reeds, genuine brass plates and nickel plated covers. Priced as low as most with imitation brass plates, 4 in. long. Shpg. wt., 3 oz.
12K5101......17c

Reed-o-Phone
Ten-hole, twenty-reed harmonica with a horn attachment which is an extension of the covers. Brass plated plates. 4 inches long. Shipping weight, ¾ lb.
12K5128......33c

Compass Harp
The favorite with Boy Scouts as it has an accurate compass mounted in the top. 14 double holes and 28 reeds. Hardwood frame, nickel plated covers. Length, 4⅝ inches. Rich in tone and easy to blow. Shipping weight, 6 ounces.
12K5153...65c

See Index and Information Pages 4 to 570

P 677

Accordions of

PIANO KEYBOARD STYLE
SUPERTONE

Size, 7x17 in.

Similar in construction to the $300.00 and $400.00 instruments used by professionals. Ebonized hardwood frame with a high piano polish. Edges inlaid in black and white wood mosaic. Treble panel is of metal in fancy design. Genuine steel reeds individually mounted on leather and screwed to removable blocks. Thirty-four piano style treble keys and forty-eight bass keys operated through sunken metal panel. Deep bellows of 16 folds bound with leatherette. Metal Stradella style corners. Size, 7x17 inches. We include with it a wood case, as illustrated, covered with imitation leather and lined with felt. Nickel plated lock and clasps and strong handle. Shipping wt., 52 lbs.

12K663¼............................. **$75.00**

Same as above, but with 24 basses. Shpg. wt., 49 lbs.

12K662¼............................. **59.45**

Piano Keyboard Accordion

25 piano keys tuned chromatically. Twelve basses producing four groups of chords. Ebony finish frame. Edges inlaid with wood mosaic. Bellows of 18 folds. Strong leather shoulder, hand and thumb straps. Stradella style metal corners. Four sets of steel reeds on individual reed plates. Size, 7x13⅜ inches. Wood carrying case, covered with leatherette and lined with felt, nickel plated lock. Shpg. wt., 30 lbs.

12K661¼.. **$31.95**

Size, 7x13⅜ in.

Two-Stop German Styles
Beaver Brand

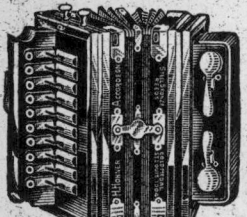

Three-Ply Panels. Two Stops, Two Basses—Size, 5½x10¼ inches. Extra well made, nicely finished and accurately tuned.

Frame, ebony finish, with shaped moldings. Three-ply panels (which eliminates splitting). Double bellows of eight folds with metal corner protectors. Two sets of bronze reeds, ten keys with nickel plated buttons, two spoon shape basses, nickel plated ornaments. Shipping weight, 7 pounds.

Size, 5½x10¼ in.

12K601¼...................... **$2.69**

Hohner
Ten Keys, Two Basses

Highly polished ebonized frames and keyboard. Double bellows of six folds with metal corner protectors, patent self acting spring clasps. Pearl buttons. Nickel plated corner trimmings. Ten nickel plated button keys, two basses, two sets of bronze reeds, two metal stops. Size, 5¾x10½ inches. Shipping weight, 8 pounds.

12K605¼...................... **$4.95**

Size, 5¾x10½ inches

Size, 6x11 in.

Milano Organetto

Frame, imitation rosewood, decorated with white stripes and bound with Stradella style corners. Steel reeds. Pearl buttons. Lyre shape thumb screw clasps, permitting the instant tightening or removal of frame. Nickel plated trimmings. Felt lined hand and thumb straps. Instruction book included.

Has four sets of steel reeds on removable reed blocks. Bellows of fourteen folds. Twenty-one keys. Eight basses arranged in both major and minor chords. Shipping weight, 12 pounds.

12K651¼............... **$13.85**

Supertone

Panels are decorated with decalcomania in imitation of wood blocks. Frames are rosewood finish and have Stradella metal corners. Bellows of 16 folds. Genuine steel reeds; leather shoulder, hand and thumb strap. Twenty-one treble keys and twelve basses with pearl buttons. Imitation leather covered felt lined case included, as illustrated at top of page, with nickel plated lock and clasps. Shpg. wt., 17 lbs.

12K656¼............... **$19.95**

Two-Row Styles
Beaver Brand

Ebonized frame and keyboard highly polished. Treble and bass panels in the natural maple finish. Bellows of fourteen folds with metal corner protectors. Nickel plated trimmings. Twenty-one treble keys and eight basses with glass buttons. Four sets of bronze reeds. Shipping weight, 12 lbs.

12K621¼............... **$7.95**

Hohner
Twenty-One Keys, Eight Basses

Italian style. Frames, keyboard and panels in mahogany finish, with impressed color stripes. Stradella style metal corners on frames. Leather hand and thumb straps. Bellows of fourteen folds, with metal corner protectors, double row open keyboard, nickel plated metal trimmings. Twenty-one pearl melody keys, eight pearl bass keys, four sets of bronze reeds mounted on individual reed plates and removable blocks. Shipping weight, 14 pounds.

12K638¼ **$12.95**

Size, 6⅛x11½ in.

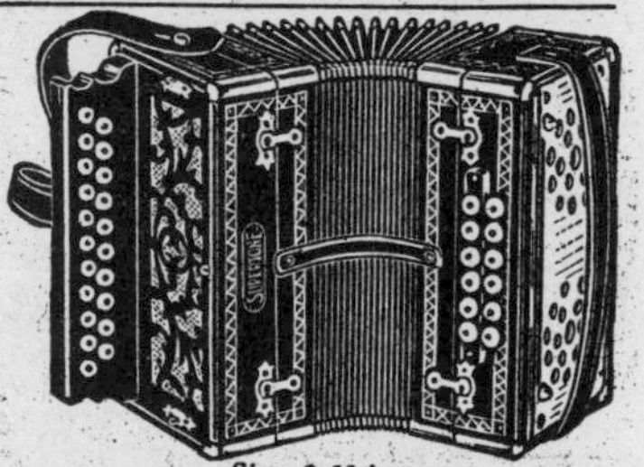

Size, 6x11 in.

Supertone De Luxe

Genuine walnut veneered frame and panels, highly polished. Panels and keyboard are inlaid with wood mosaic in harmonizing colors, the front panel sloping gracefully from the keyboard. Frame is artistically decorated on all sides and fitted with metal corners. Deep, cloth bound bellows. Front panel is cut in fancy grill work. Enclosed key action. Rounded pearl buttons on keys. Leather shoulder strap. Imitation leather cloth covered case included, as illustrated at top of page, felt lined and with nickel plated lock and clasps with Supertone accordions. Also instruction book. Twenty-one treble keys, four sets of genuine steel reeds mounted on removable blocks. Sixteen basses, bellows of eighteen folds. Size, 6x11 inches. Shipping weight, 17 pounds.

12K658¼...................... **$29.95**

GERMAN STYLE
FOUR STOPS

Size, 6¾x12½ in.

Beaver Brand
21 Keys—4 Basses
Four Sets of Reeds

Frame, imitation ebony. Panels, three-ply (which eliminates splitting), bright color, stamped with gilt decorations. Bellows, double style of ten folds with corner protectors. Four sets of bronze reeds, twenty-one keys, four stops, four spoon basses. Nickel plated keys and trimmings. This instrument is large and powerful in tone. Shipping weight, 10 lbs.

12K609¼....................................... **$7.95**

Hohner
Stradella Corners
Four Sets Genuine Steel Reeds

Ebonized frames and keyboard. Mahogany finish panels. Nicely decorated. Corners of frame reinforced with nickel plated protectors. Triple bellows of nine folds with metal corners, self-acting spring clasps. Ten long metal keys, two basses, four sets genuine steel reeds, four stops. Size, 7x12¼ inches. Shipping weight, 12 pounds.

12K610¼...................... **$8.95**

Same, but with three sets of steel reeds and three stops. Size, 6¾x11½ inches.

12K613¼—Shipping weight, 12 pounds........................ **$7.95**

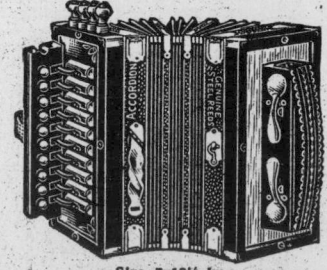

Size, 7x12¼ in.

Superior Quality

Supertone—Italian Model
Considering beauty, quality of workmanship and tone there are no accordions that we know of superior to our Supertones.

Milano Organetto—Italian Model
The name of Milano Organetto has been given to these accordions because of their organ-like tone. They are superior in construction and tone to most other accordions of similar style.

Beaver Brand—Italian and German Style
They are extra well made, nicely finished and accurately tuned. Instruction Book included with all Accordions.

Case Included with 12K657¼ and 12K659¼

Three-Row Styles

Milano Organetto
Thirty-One Keys, Twelve Basses
Frame, imitation rosewood decorated with white stripes and bound with Stradella style corners. Bellows of 14 folds with metal corners and bound with oilcloth. Steel reeds. Pearl buttons. Lyre shape thumbscrew clasps, permitting the instant tightening or removal of frame. Nickel plated trimmings. Felt lined hand and thumb straps. Has six sets of melody reeds on removable reed blocks. Basses in major and minor chords. Shipping weight, 15 pounds.
12K652¼ $22.45

Size, 6¾x11¾ Inches

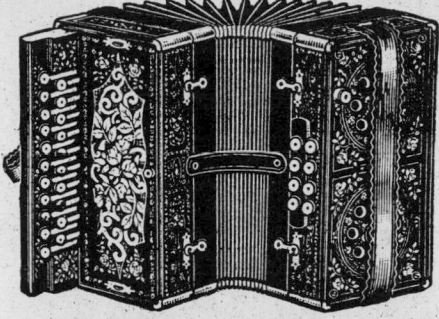

Size, 6x11 Inches **$9⁴⁵**

Richly Designed—Impressed Gilt Decorations
Twenty-One Keys—Eight Basses
Never before have we or anyone else sold an accordion of this kind at so low a price. No sacrifice has been made in the quality to produce such a handsome instrument.
Walnut finish frames, size 6x11 inches, with full metal bound corners. Olive green bellows of 16 folds with nickeled corner protectors. Twenty-one treble keys and eight bass keys, all with pearl buttons. Very beautiful scroll work on front panel in impressed rose design with leaves and flowers covered with gilt. The design is overlaid on the entire instrument with gilt which richly brings out the flowers and leaves. **Genuine steel reeds.** Shipping weight, 12 pounds.
12K630¼........................$9.45

Size, 6⅝x11¾ Inches

Supertone
Superior Tone Quality
Same high quality as our Supertone De Luxe listed below without elaborate marquetry. Panels are decorated with decalcomania in imitation of wood blocks. Frames are rosewood finish and have Stradella style metal corners. Bellows of 18 folds bound with maroon colored leatherette. Straight model keyboard; genuine steel reeds; leather shoulder strap. Thirty-one treble keys and sixteen basses. Imitation leather covered felt lined case included; as illustrated at top of page, with nickel plated lock and clasps. Shipping weight, 22 pounds. **$26.45**
12K657¼..............

Single Row Styles

Beaver Brand
Ebonized frame and keyboard highly polished. Treble and bass panels in the natural maple finish, the treble cut in fancy grill work. Bellows of ten folds with metal corner protectors. Nickel plated clasps and trimmings. Ten treble keys and four basses with glass buttons. Bronze reeds.
12K620¼
Shpg. wt., 9 lbs. **$4.35**

Size, 5½x10¼ Inches

Hohner Stradella Model
Italian style. Walnut finished frames and keyboard. Edges of top frame inlaid with fancy black and white wood. Sloping panel. Frames reinforced with nickel plated Stradella corners. Nickel plated die cut panel with fancy perforations. Bellows of sixteen folds, with metal corner protectors. Triple row closed keyboard, nickel plated metal trimmings, leather clasps and leather shoulder strap. Heavy metal finger plate. Thirty-one imitation bone melody keys, six sets of steel treble reeds and four sets of steel bass reeds mounted on removable blocks. Size, 7⅛x13 inches. Carrying case clothlined, with hinged cover, lock and handle included. Shipping weight, 26 pounds.
12K641¼..............$36.95

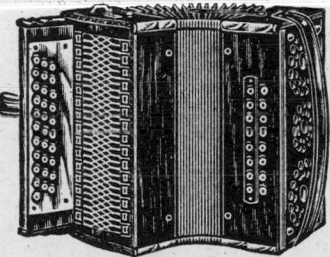

Size 7⅛x13 Inches

Milano Organetto
Ten Keys, Four Basses
Frame, imitation rosewood decorated with white stripes and bound with Stradella style corners. Bellows of 10 folds with metal corners and bound with oilcloth. Steel reeds. Pearl buttons. Lyre shape thumbscrew clasps, permitting the instant tightening or removal of frame. Nickel plated trimmings. Felt lined hand and thumb straps. Has two sets of steel reeds on individual plates, ten keys, four basses. Size, 6x11 inches. Shipping weight, 10 pounds.
12K650¼.... $7.45

Size, 6x11 Inches

Supertone DeLuxe Italian Style—Genuine Steel Reeds
Genuine walnut veneered frames inlaid with colored wood marquetry and reinforced with Stradella style corners. Thirty-one treble keys, six sets of genuine steel reeds, mounted on removable blocks. Rounded pearl finger buttons. Twenty basses, bellows of twenty folds bound with black leatherette. Leather shoulder strap. Size, 7x12½ inches. Case illustrated at top of page included. Our Supertone instruments are as good as any made. Shipping weight, 28 pounds. **$39.95**
12K659¼............

Hohner
**Ten Keys, Four Basses
Invisible Key Action**
Italian style. Walnut finished frames decorated with impressed colored stripes and reinforced with metal corners. Top panel scroll cut in fancy design. Bellows of twelve folds, with metal corner protectors, closed keyboard, nickel plated metal trimmings. Ten imitation bone button keys, four bass keys, two sets of bronze reeds. Shipping weight, 11 pounds.
12K636¼........$7.75
Same as above, but with steel reeds. Shipping weight, 11 lbs.
12K637¼........$8.75

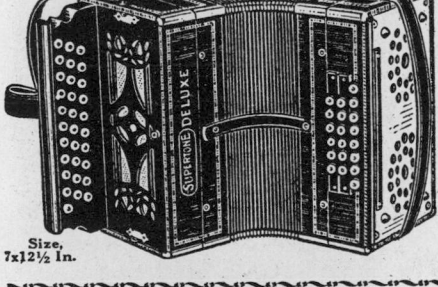

Size, 7x12½ In.

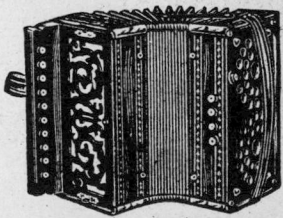

Size, 5¾x10¼ Inches

THREE STOP BEAVER BRAND

Size, 6x12 Inches

Large Size
Frame, ebony finish, with shaped moldings. Panels, three-ply (which eliminates splitting); finished in very bright colors with impressed gilt decorations. Bellows, triple style, in two colors, with nine folds fully protected by metal corners. Three full sets of bronze reeds. Three stops, ten nickel plated keys with metal buttons, nickel plated clasps and trimmings. Two spoon bass keys. Shipping weight, 9 lbs.
12K606¼............$4.75

Fancy Model—Octave Tuning
Frame, ebony finish with treble panel of the sunken type. Extra deep bellows made of ten wooden ribs, each rib covered by nickel plated band of metal surmounted by a gilt ornament and held in place by fancy gilt studs. Three sets of steel reeds, three fancy metal stops, ten ebony finish and fancy decorated keys with brass rods. Two basses. Pearl buttons. Nickel plated trimmings. Size, 7x13½ inches. Shipping weight, 13 pounds.
12K617¼............$12.45

Size, 7x13½ Inches

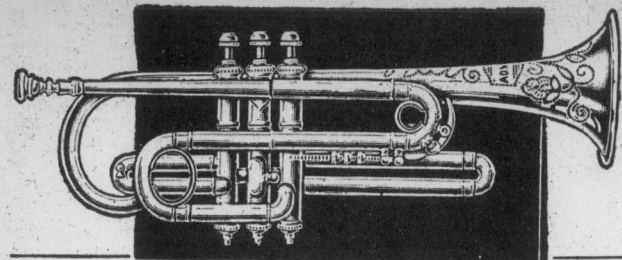

B Flat CORNET With Quick Change to A

ADVANCE Engraved bell and pearl buttons. Fitted with water key. Length, 16½ inches. Low pitch. For band or orchestra playing. Shipping weight, 7 pounds.

12K704¼—Brass........................... **$8.55**
★12K705½—Nickel plated................. $ 9.75
★12K706½—Silver plated, satin finish; gold plated bell............ 13.95

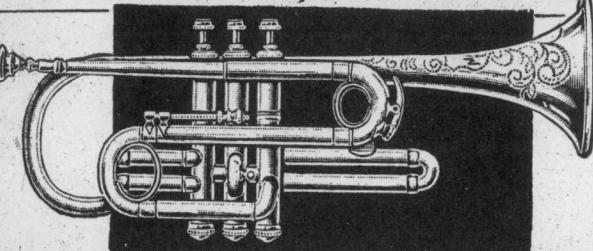

B Flat CORNET With Quick Change to A

MARCEAU Low pitch. Fitted with water key. Engraved bell and pearl buttons. Length, 16½ inches. For band or orchestra playing. Shipping weight, 7 pounds.

★12K708¼—Brass....................... **$11.45**
★12K709½—Nickel plated............... $12.95
★12K710½—Extra quality silver plate, satin finish; gold plated bell. 20.80

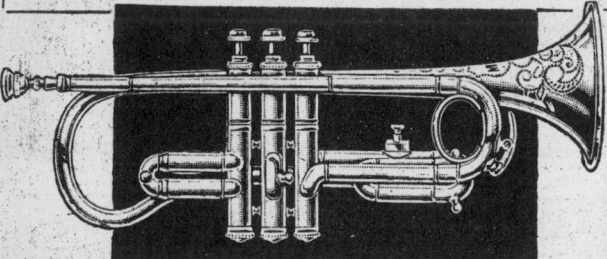

CORNET IN C, B Flat and A

MARCEAU By simply changing the slides you can play either C, B flat or A. Low pitch. Engraved bell and pearl buttons. Length, 15¼ inches. Shipping weight, 8 pounds.

★12K721¼—Brass, polished............. **$14.95**
★12K722½—Nickel plated, polished....... $16.45
★12K723½—Extra quality silver plate, satin finish; gold plated bell. 24.30

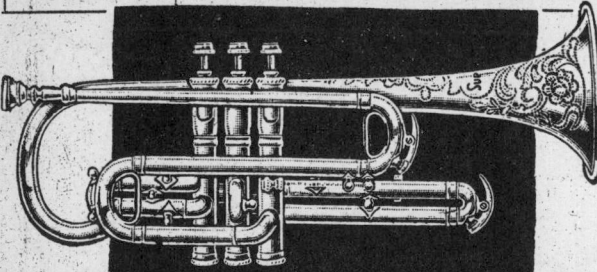

B Flat CORNET With Quick Change to A

SUPERTONE Adjustment rod on quick change slide. Engraved wreath on bell. Box spring valves. Pearl buttons. Low pitch. Length, 16½ inches. Shipping weight, 8 pounds.

★12K731¼—Brass, polished............. **$19.45**
★12K732½—Nickel plated, polished........ $20.95
★12K733½—Extra quality silver plate, satin finish; gold plated bell. 27.45

CORNET IN C, B Flat and A. Low Pitch
Same as above, but in C, B Flat and A. Length, 14½ inches. Shipping weight, 8 pounds.

★12K734¼—Brass, polished............. **$24.75**
★12K735½—Nickel plated, polished........ $26.25
★12K736½—Extra quality silver plate, satin finish; gold plated bell. 34.00

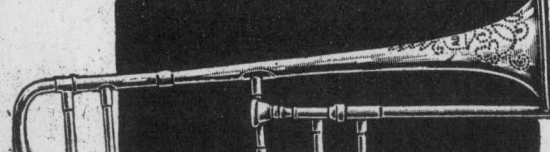

B Flat Tenor Slide Trombone Low Pitch

ADVANCE Smooth, positive slide action. Responsive tone. Length, 45 inches. 7-inch bell. Low pitch. Shipping weight, 12 pounds.

12K765¼ **$8.55**
Brass....
★12K766½
Nickel plated. $9.95
★12K767½—Silver plated, satin finish; gold plated bell.
$14.75

Brass Band

B Flat Tenor Slide Trombone Low Pitch

SUPERTONE Low pitch. Total length, about 45 inches. Bell, 7 inches. Shipping weight, 12 lbs.

12K744¼ **$17.45**
Brass....
★12K745½—Nickel plated............ **$19.40**
★12K746½—Extra quality silver plate, satin finish; gold plated bell............**$28.40**

B Flat Tenor Slide Trombone Low Pitch

MARCEAU Length, 45 inches. Engraved bell, 7 inches in diameter. Shipping weight, 12 pounds.

12K784¼ **$11.45**
Brass....
★12K785½—Nickel plated............**$13.40**
★12K786½—Extra quality silver plate, satin finish; gold plated bell............**$21.90**

Marceau INSTRUMENTS, AMERICAN MODELS

Made according to the models and measurements of the most expensive American instruments. They are silver soldered (not soft, like inferior instruments), and have nickel silver pistons. They are carefully braced and reinforced. All handsomely engraved and the valve instruments fitted with pearl buttons. Mouthpiece, music lyre and instruction book included with all instruments.

*NOTE—Plated instruments are not carried in stock. They are specially plated upon receipt of order, insuring you a bright, clean horn. On all orders for plated instruments allow ten to twelve days' time.

ADVANCE INSTRUMENTS
The Lowest Priced Good Band Instruments

Far better in material, workmanship and tone than our prices denote. They are particularly suitable for beginners and amateurs who want to invest as little as possible. However, for those who care to spend a little more, they will find in our Marceau and Supertone brands the greatest values in brass band instruments. Mouthpiece, music lyre and instruction book included.

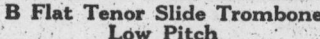

Instruments

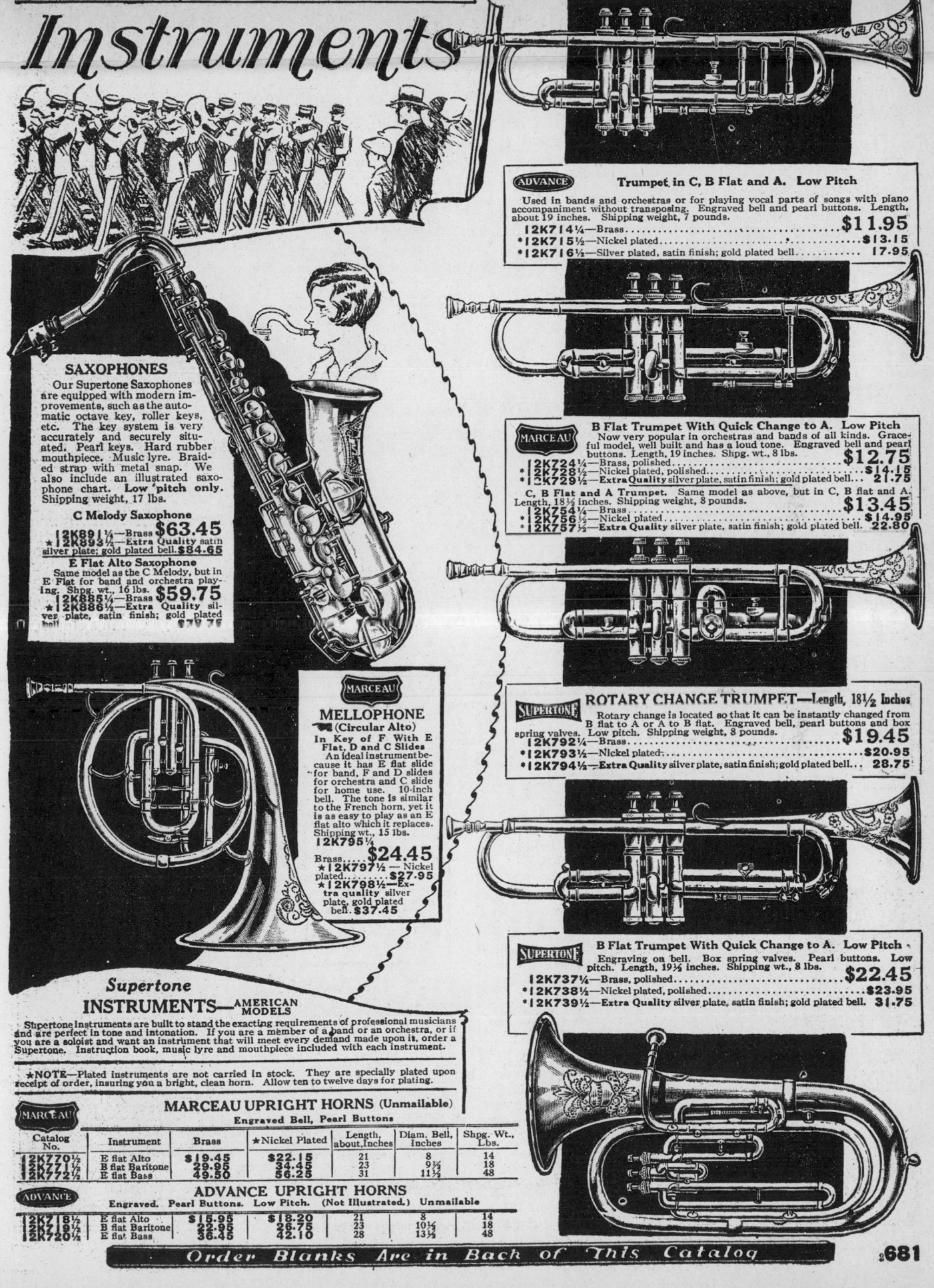

CLARINETS
GRENADILLA WOOD · EBONITE

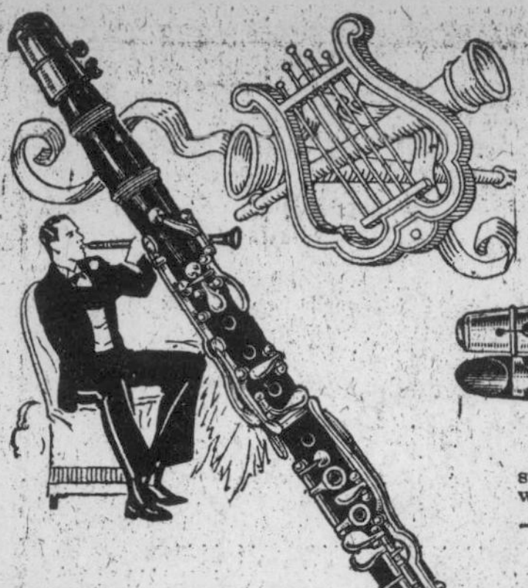

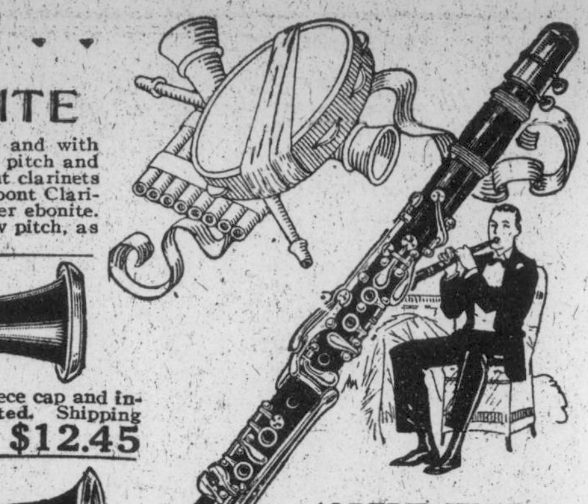

Our wood clarinets are made from thoroughly seasoned grenadilla wood and with proper care will not check or split. Our Lafayette clarinets are accurate in pitch and intonation and much better than our low prices would indicate. Our Dupont clarinets acknowledge no superior and, at our prices, become a value unequaled. Dupont Clarinets are carried in both wood and ebonite. Many professional players prefer ebonite. Ours are of rod ebonite which is superior to cast. All clarinets tuned to low pitch, as adopted by all musical organizations in America.

ALBERT SYSTEM—13 KEYS—2 RINGS

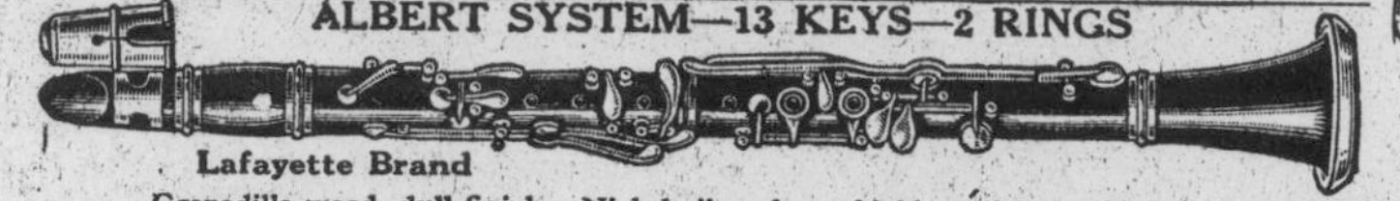

Lafayette Brand

Grenadilla wood, dull finish. Nickel silver keys, highly polished. Mouthpiece cap and instruction book included. Low pitch. Key of B flat or C. State key wanted. Shipping weight, 4 pounds.

12K800¼—Lafayette Brand **$12.45**

DUPONT BOEHM SYSTEM CLARINETS

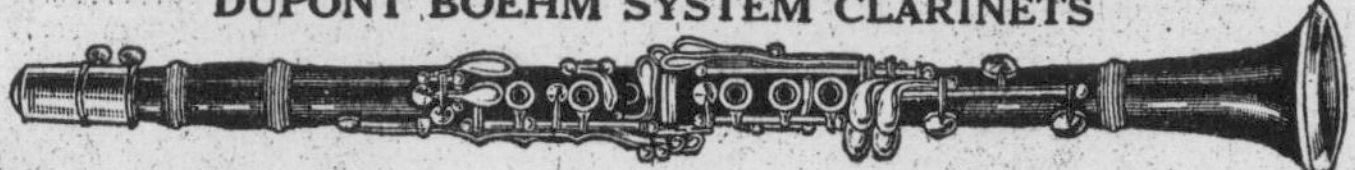

It is the ambition of nearly all clarinet players to own a Boehm System clarinet, but a player of ordinary means is unwilling to pay $65.00 to $90.00. At our remarkably low price we offer an instrument that will meet all professional requirements. Fitted with nickel silver keys, ferrules and rings. Shipping weight, 4 pounds.

12K809¼—Grenadilla wood, 17 keys, 6 rings, key of B flat low pitch only. Mouthpiece cap and instruction book included **$34.25**

12K810¼—Same as above, but made of ebonite (see note above) $39.25

12K811¼—Same as 12K810¼, but in key of C (C Melody) 39.25

ALBERT SYSTEM 15 KEYS—2 RINGS

Lafayette Brand

Grenadilla wood, dull finish. Nickel silver keys, highly polished. Mouthpiece cap and instruction book included. Low pitch. **Key of B flat or C. State key wanted.** Shipping weight, 4 pounds.

12K801¼ $13.75

ALBERT SYSTEM
15 Keys-4 Rings-4 Rollers

Mouthpiece cap and instruction book included. Shipping weight, 4 pounds. **Key of B flat or C.** Low pitch. **State key wanted.**

Lafayette Brand—Grenadilla Wood
12K802¼ $17.45

DUPONT—Grenadilla Wood
12K807¼ $22.45

Dupont, made of ebonite.
12K813¼ $24.95

FIFES

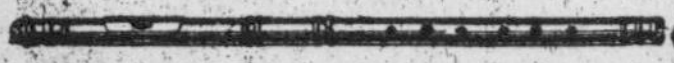

Brass, nickel plated, for professional players. Key of C or B flat. **State key.** Shipping weight, ¾ pound.

12K5091 .... **$1.25**

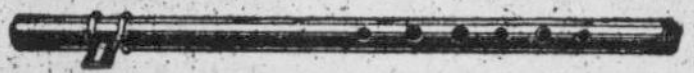

Nickel plated metal, with mouthpiece adjusted all ready for playing Key of B flat or C. **State key.** Shipping weight, ¾ pound.

12K5082 .... **19c**

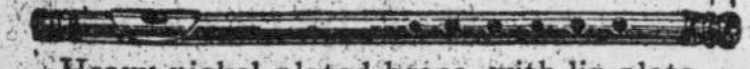

Heavy nickel plated brass, with lip plate and fancy ends. B flat or C. **State key.** Shipping weight, ¾ pound.

12K5088 .... **69c**

Fife Instruction Book

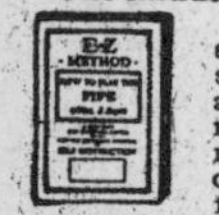

Contains simple instructions; also rudiments of music and chart for fingering exercises and a number of selections for the fife. Shpg. wt., 2 oz.

12K1725 .... **14c**

Fife Mouthpiece

Composition metal, adjustable, 2⅜ to 2⅝ inches in circumference. Shipping weight, 2 ounces.

12K5099 **9c**

ALL METAL M. DUPONT ARTIST MODEL

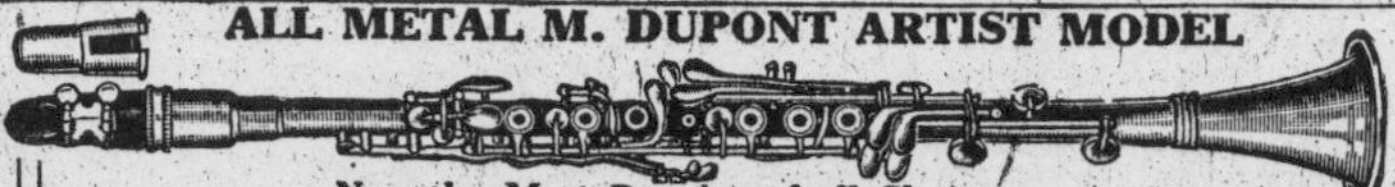

Now the Most Popular of all Clarinets

Leading clarinetists have found this instrument to be exactly what they want. Being of metal it will not check or split. It is subject to a minimum of expansion, therefore the keys and rings will always fit properly and the action will be positive and lightning fast. It is fitted with a simple and effective tuning adjustment. Made of cast nickel silver and highly polished. Seventeen keys and six rings, all adjusted with careful precision. In B♭ low pitch only. Shipping weight, 7 pounds.

12K817¼—Nickel silver **$65.00**

12K818¼—Same, but silver plated $72.75

12K8006—Case for same, keratol covered, silk plush lined, nickel plated lock and clasps. Shipping weight, 6 pounds $7.95

CLARINET OUTFIT
Low Pitch, B Flat Only

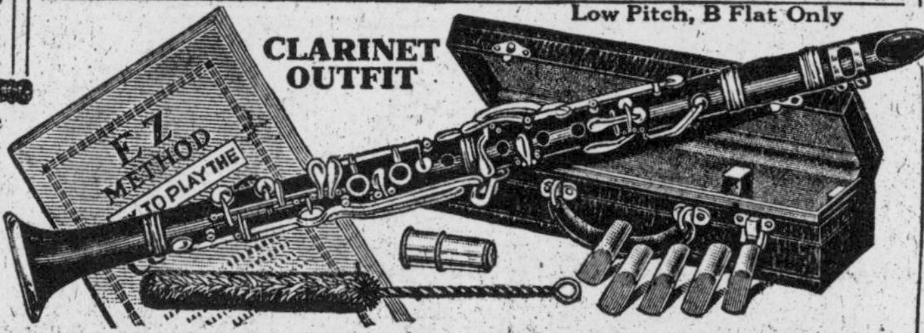

Complete outfit for the beginner and the amateur. Everything that is needed to play and care for the clarinet is included. Clarinet made of seasoned grenadilla wood. Is fitted with nickel silver keys, rings and ferrules. Very carefully made and accurately tuned and also responsive in tone. The outfit consists of clarinet as described, one keratol covered flannelette lined case with nickel plated clasps, six reeds, one cleaner, mouthpiece cap and one instruction book. Shipping weight, 7 pounds.

12K804¼—15 keys, 2 rings, B flat, low pitch. Outfit complete **$16.45**

BUGLES

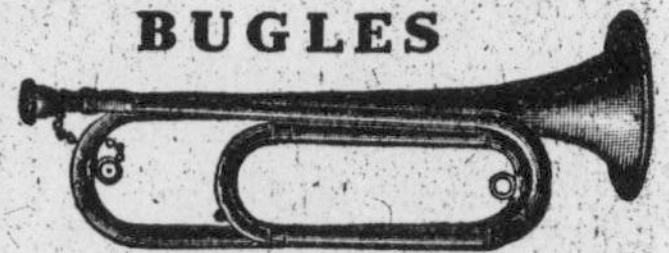

Attention! Scout Masters and Parents

Cavalry Trumpet

U. S. Army Specifications

Brass polished. Key of G with F slide, complete with mouthpiece and chain. Weight, boxed, 5 pounds.

12K5070¼ **$2.79**

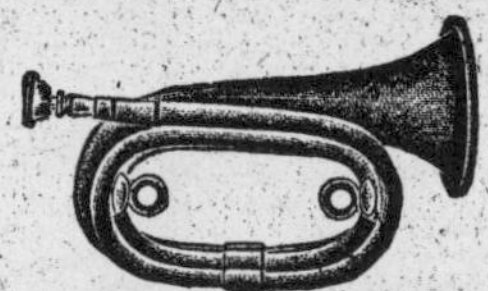

Lowest Prices on Good Bugles for Boy Scouts

B Flat Army Bugle

U. S. Government specifications. Made of high grade brass, highly polished. Loud tone and easy blowing. Shipping weight, 3½ pounds.

12K5069¼ **$2.95**

PICCOLOS

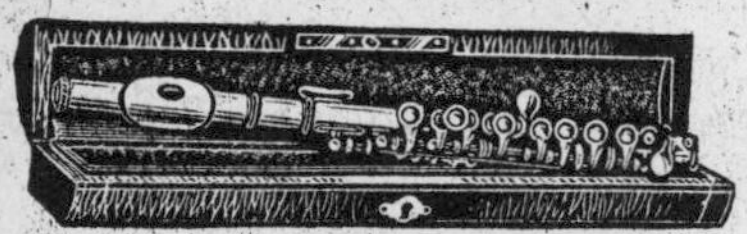

Supertone Boehm System Piccolo

Made in two sections of nickel silver and silver plated. Raised metal lip plate, thumb and finger supports. Keratol covered wood case lined with velveteen with lock and key. Shipping weight, 1¼ pounds.

12K860—Key of C. Low pitch, for orchestra **$39.95**

12K861—Key of D flat. Low pitch, for band $39.95

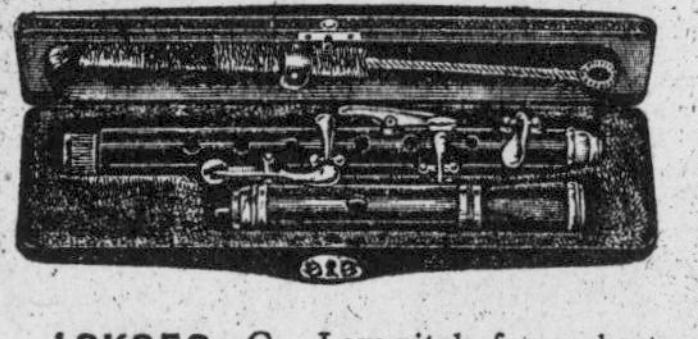

Supertone Meyer System Piccolo

Grenadilla wood. Ebonite head which will not check or split, six nickel silver keys, tuning slide and cork joints. Velveteen lined cloth covered case, with lock and key. Swab and instruction book included. Very fine quality. Shipping weight, 1 pound.

12K858—C. Low pitch, for orchestra **$4.69**

12K859—D flat. Low pitch, for band. Each $4.69

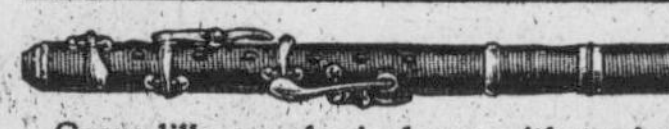

Meyer System Piccolo

Grenadilla wood, six keys, with tuning slide, cork joints and nickel silver. Shipping weight, 1 pound.

12K854—C. Low pitch, for orchestra **$3.25**

12K857—D flat. Low pitch, for band $3.25

NOTE—OUR FLUTES AND PICCOLOS are carefully inspected and the keys adjusted before leaving our store. The wooden instruments are made of as thoroughly seasoned material as can be procured and with proper care will not check or split.

Ebonite heads are guaranteed not to check or crack.

FLUTES

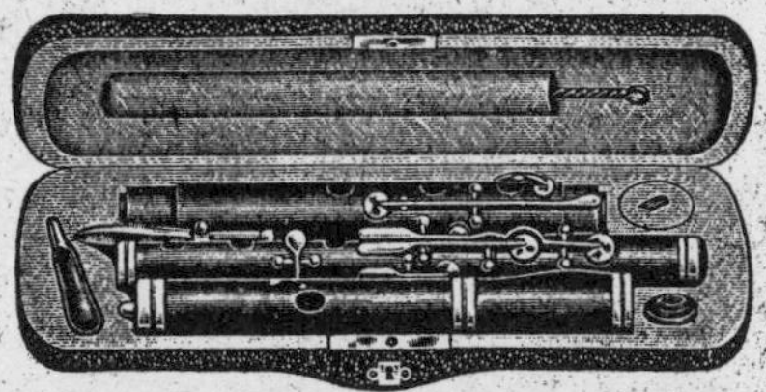

Supertone Flutes, Meyer System, in Cases Key of C. Low Pitch

Selected grenadilla wood, ebonite head, which is guaranteed against splitting or checking; cork joints; ten nickel silver keys, kid pads. Fine lined case, with greasebox, screwdriver, swab, pads, lock and key.

12K841—Shipping weight, 4 pounds **$14.95**

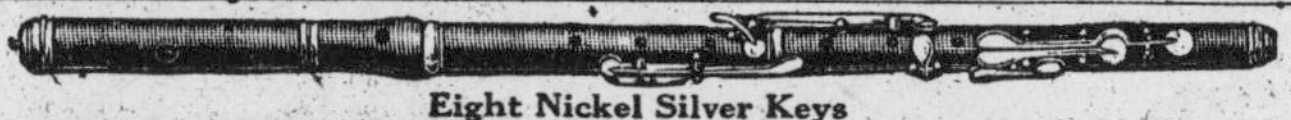

Eight Nickel Silver Keys

12K834—Grenadilla wood. Eight nickel silver keys. Tuning slide. Key of C. Shipping weight, 1¾ pounds **$8.95**

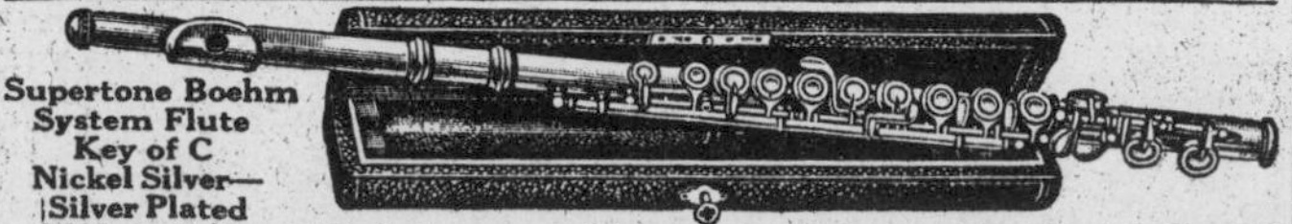

Supertone Boehm System Flute Key of C Nickel Silver—Silver Plated

Made entirely of nickel silver and silver plated. Has raised lip plate. Closed G sharp key. Roller on C key. In three sections. Shaped wood case covered with artificial leather and lined with velveteen; nickel plated lock. This style flute often sells for $75.00 or more elsewhere.

12K849—Shipping weight, 5 pounds **$53.75**

DRUMS

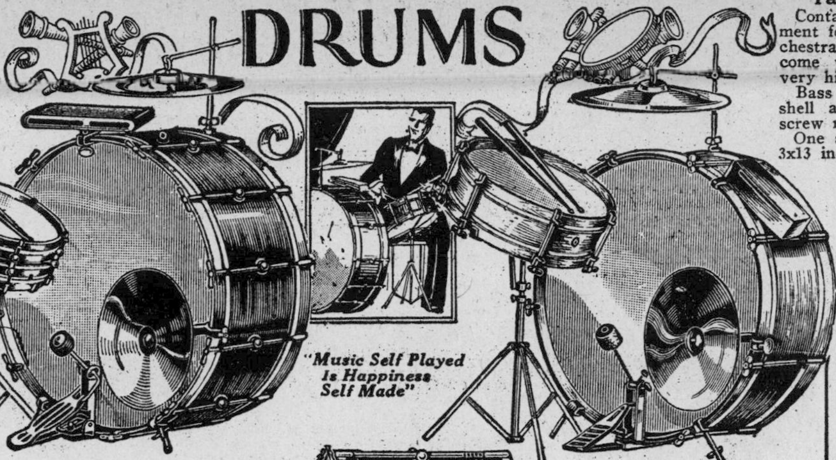
"Music Self Played Is Happiness Self Made"

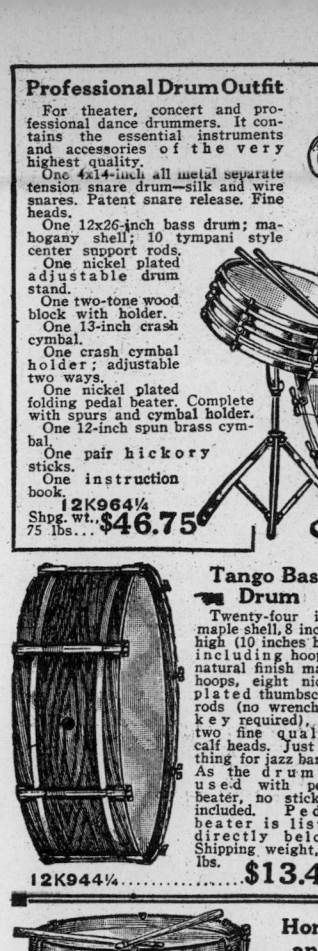

Professional Drum Outfit

For theater, concert and professional dance drummers. It contains the essential instruments and accessories of the very highest quality.

One 4x14-inch all metal separate tension snare drum—silk and wire snares. Patent snare release. Fine heads.

One 12x26-inch bass drum; mahogany shell; 10 tympani style center support rods.

One nickel plated adjustable drum stand.

One two-tone wood block with holder.

One 13-inch crash cymbal.

One crash cymbal holder; adjustable two ways.

One nickel plated folding pedal beater. Complete with spurs and cymbal holder.

One 12-inch spun brass cymbal.

One pair hickory sticks.

One instruction book.

12K964¼
Shpg. wt., 75 lbs... **$46.75**

Tango Drum Outfit

Contains all necessary equipment for the dance or home orchestra. The drums and all that come with them are made of very high grade materials.

Bass drum, 8x24 inches. Maple shell and hoops, eight thumbscrew rods. Fine calf heads.

One snare drum. Maple shell, 3x13 inches. Maple hoops. Six thumbscrew rods, eight snares.

One adjustable drum stand.

One 12-inch crash cymbal.

One crash cymbal holder.

One wood block with clamp.

One pedal beater with spurs and cymbal holder.

One 12-inch brass cymbal.

One pair of hickory sticks.

One instruction book.

12K961¼—Shpg. wt., 60 pounds.......**$27.95**

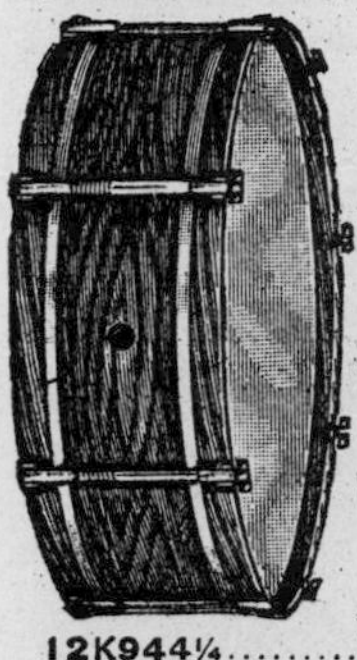

Tango Bass Drum

Twenty-four inch maple shell, 8 inches high (10 inches high including hoops), natural finish maple hoops, eight nickel plated thumbscrew rods (no wrench or key required), and two fine quality calf heads. Just the thing for jazz bands. As the drum is used with pedal beater, no stick is included. Pedal beater is listed directly below. Shipping weight, 45 lbs.

12K944¼............**$13.45**

Bass Drums With Tympani Rods

Mahogany shell, 10x24 inches, varnished finish. Natural maple hoops, ten nickel plated tympani style rods with strong center support. (No key or wrench required.) Two fine white calfskin heads. A drum with a big tone. Stick and instruction book included. Shipping wt., 50 lbs.

12K946¼.. **$18.45**

Same as above, but with shell size, 12x26 inches. Shipping weight, 55 lbs.

12K950¼. **$20.95**

Same as above, but with shell size, 14x28 inches. Twelve rods. Shipping wt., 65 pounds.

12K952¼.. **$22.95**

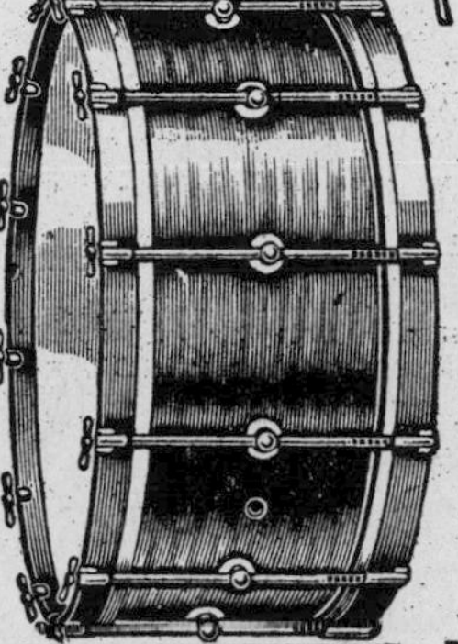

Junior Drum Outfit

Outfit consists of: One snare drum, nickel plated shell, 3x12 inches, six thumbscrew rods, two calfskin heads, hickory sticks; one bass drum, 6x22-inch maple shell with two heads, six thumbscrew rods; one drum and cymbal beater, one nickel plated folding snare drum stand; one 10-inch brass cymbal; one 8-inch brass cymbal; cymbal clamp; one cymbal arm; one pair spurs, one instruction book. Shipping weight, 55 pounds.

12K959¼............**$19.45**

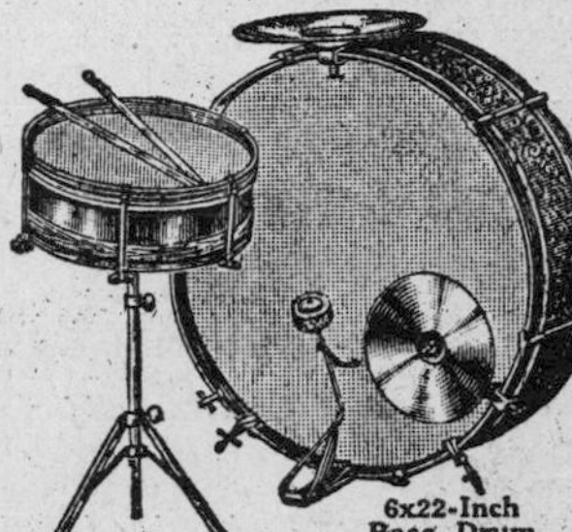

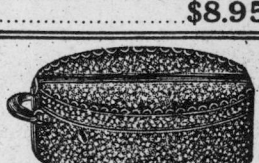

6x22-Inch Bass Drum

SNARE DRUMS

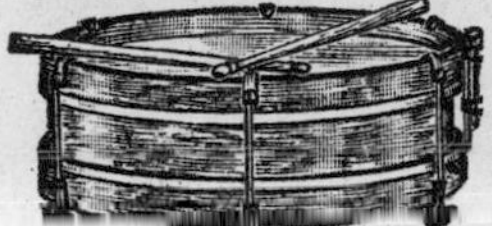

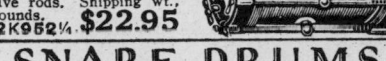

Home and Orchestra Snare Drum

Maple shell, size, 3x13 inches. Adjustable snare strainer. Six thumbscrew rods. Two calfskin heads, eight snares. Includes a pair of sticks and instruction book. Shpg. wt., 8 lbs.

12K902¼............**$5.95**

Junior Snare Drum

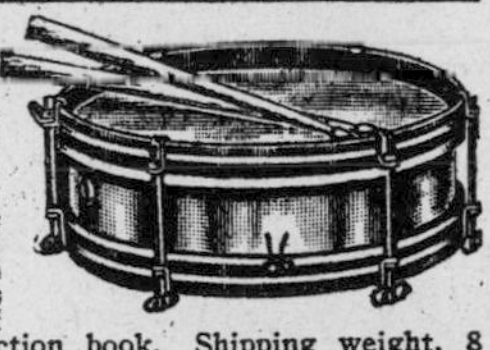

Nickel plated shell, size, 3x12 inches. Hoops with metal bands, six thumbscrew rods, adjustable snare strainer. Two calfskin heads. Includes sling, a pair of sticks and instruction book. Shipping weight, 8 pounds.

12K901¼............**$4.45**

The Very Highest Quality Snare Drum

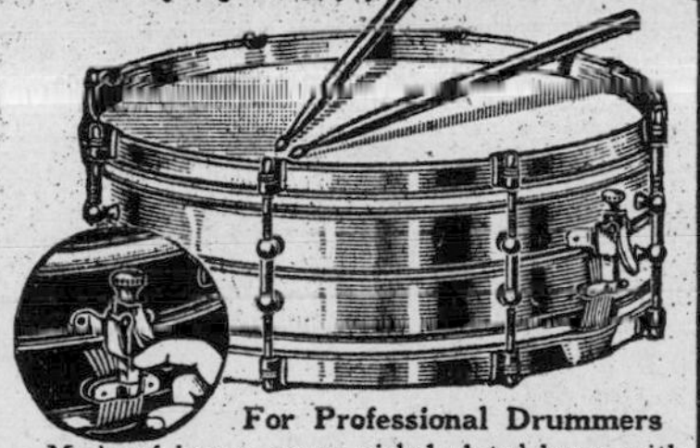

For Professional Drummers

Made of heavy gauge nickel plated brass with double thickness center reinforcement. Flanged counter hoops of nickel plated brass with rounded edges. Snare bed is graded and beveled to insure correct centering. Eight separate tension lugs. Wire and silk snares. Snare throw-off quick and positive. Size of shell, 5x14 inches. Instruction book and sticks included. Shipping weight, 13 pounds.

12K923¼............**$23.95**

Separate Tension Snare Drum

Patent snare release for tom-tom effect. Nickel plated shell of spun brass with center reinforcement, fine quality heads. Six separate tension lugs. Wrench, hickory sticks and instruction book included. Size of shell, 4x14 inches (about 5½x14 inches, including hoops). Shpg. wt., 12 lbs.

12K920¼..... **$13.75**

12K921¼—Same as above, but 5x14 inches............**$13.95**

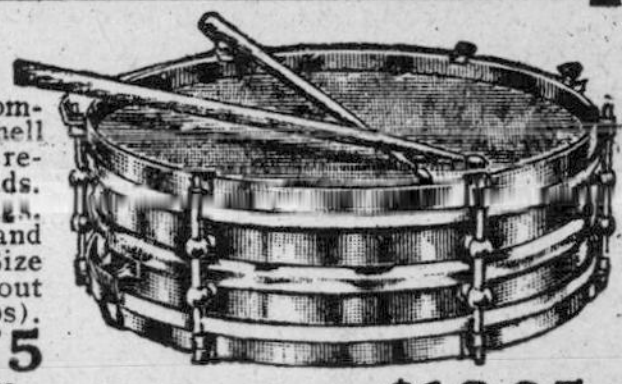

Orchestra Snare Drum

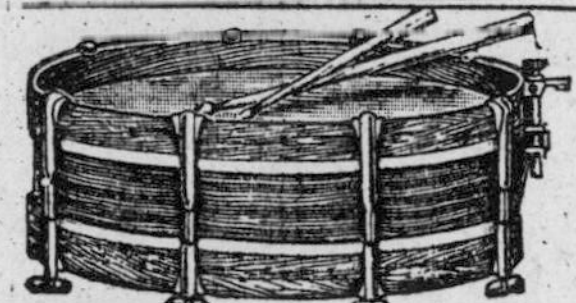

Mahogany shell, size 4x15 inches. Ten wire and silk snares, nickel plated snare strainer with patent snare release for tom-tom effect. Fine calfskin heads. Instruction book and hickory sticks included. Shpg. wt., 9 lbs.

12K908¼.... **$12.45**

Same as above, but with shell size, 3x13 inches, 6 rods and 8 snares. Shipping weight, 8 pounds.

12K903¼............**$8.95**

Drum and Cymbal Beaters

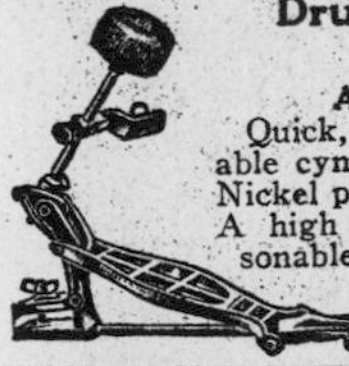

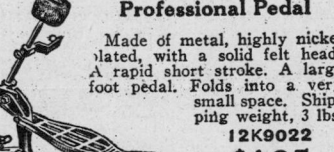

A Direct Stroke

Quick, sure action. Adjustable cymbal striker and beater. Nickel plated metal. Felt head. A high class pedal at a reasonable price. Folds into small space. Shpg. wt., 3 pounds.

12K9021.. **$3.95**

Professional Pedal

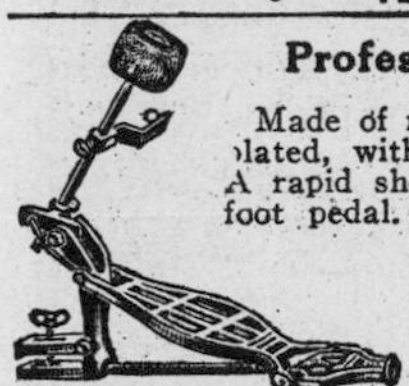

Made of metal, highly nickel plated, with a solid felt head. A rapid short stroke. A large foot pedal. Folds into a very small space. Shipping weight, 3 lbs.

12K9022
$4.95

Chinese Wood Block

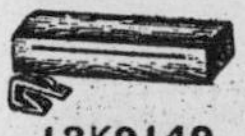

Chinese redwood, very loud. Size, 7x2¼ inches. Shipping weight, 1¼ pounds. Without holder.

12K9149............**49c**

12K9153—Nickel Plated Holder for same. Shpg. wt., 3 ounces............**39c**

Two-Tone Wood Block and Holder

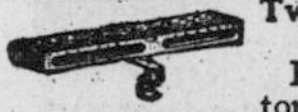

Resonant. Two different tones. Nickel plated holder with strong clamp.

12K9148—Shpg. wt., 2 lbs..... **$1.19**

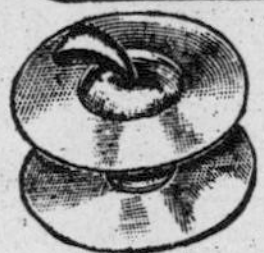

Cymbals (Brass)

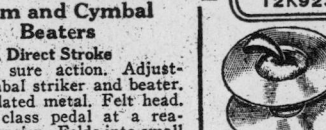

Twelve-inch spun brass, good tone with lasting vibrations. Shpg. wt., 4 lbs.

12K9041
12-inch, per pair
$2.49

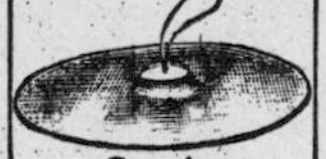

Genuine Chinese Crash Cymbals

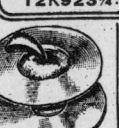

Hammered gong metal. Has very loud and penetrating tone. Shpg. wt., each, 2½ lbs.

12K9046
12-inch. **$1.98**

12K9047
13-inch .. **$2.49**

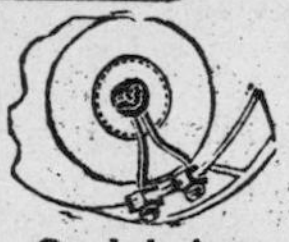

Cymbal Arm

For side of drum. Sure clamp. Cymbals not included. Shpg. wt., ¾ lb.

12K9052
75c

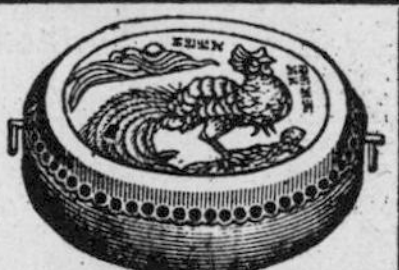

Genuine Chinese Drum or Tom-Tom

Nine-inch shell of a special composition with decorated skin heads. Shipping weight, 2½ pounds.

12K9151.. **$2.39**

Holder for Chinese Drum. Nickel plated. Shipping weight, ¾ lb.

12K9150.... **59c**

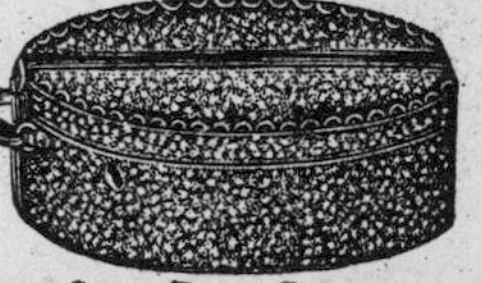

Snare Drum Case

Made of hard fiber, which will give long service. Round telescope style, with flat bottom. Will hold any snare drum up to 15 inches. Shipping weight, 10 pounds.

12K9010¼............**$2.90**

"Jazerup" Bells

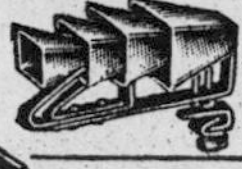

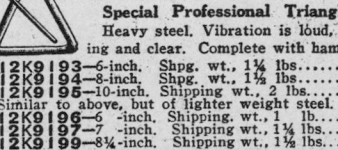

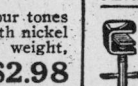

Bronze finish metal. Four tones tuned in chime effect. With nickel plated holder. Shipping weight, 3 lbs.

12K9172. **$2.98**

Drum Stand

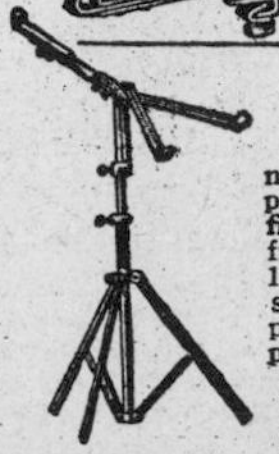

Steel, nickel plated. Will fit any drum from 12 to 16 inches in size. Shipping wt., 2 pounds.

12K9120
$1.39

Drum Spurs

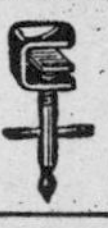

Thumbscrew to fasten to hoop. Shipping weight, 6 ounces.

12K9115
Per pair..... **65c**

Special Professional Triangles

Heavy steel. Vibration is loud, lasting and clear. Complete with hammer.

12K9193—6-inch. Shpg. wt., 1¼ lbs......**65c**
12K9194—8-inch. Shpg. wt., 1½ lbs......**78c**
12K9195—10-inch. Shipping wt., 2 lbs.....**89c**

Similar to above, but of lighter weight steel.

12K9196—6 -inch. Shipping. wt., 1 lb....**38c**
12K9197—7 -inch. Shipping wt., 1¼ lbs...**45c**
12K9199—8¼-inch. Shipping wt., 1½ lbs...**55c**

Drum Bags

State size of shell, not including hoops. Rubberized cloth with bound edges. Handle and patent snap fasteners.

	Diam.	Ht.	Shpg. Wt.	
12K9005	22 in.	6 in.	2 lbs.	$2.95
12K9006	24 in.	8 in.	2 lbs.	3.25
12K9001	24 in.	10 in.	2¼ lbs.	3.35
12K9004	26 in.	12 in.	2¼ lbs.	4.25
12K9012	12 in.	3 in.	1 lb.	1.35
12K9013	13 in.	3 in.	1 lb.	1.39
12K9007	15 in.	4 in.	1 lb.	1.49
12K9008	14 in.	4 in.	1 lb.	1.48

Drummers' Tambourine

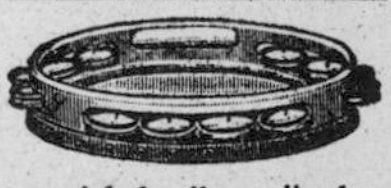

Ten-inch reinforced shell of highly polished maple, twelve sets of heavy nickel silver jingles. Head waterproofed by special process for professionals. Shipping weight, 1¼ pounds.

12K5391............**$2.45**

To Find What You Want, See Index Pages 550 to 570

BRASS INSTRUMENT SUPPLIES

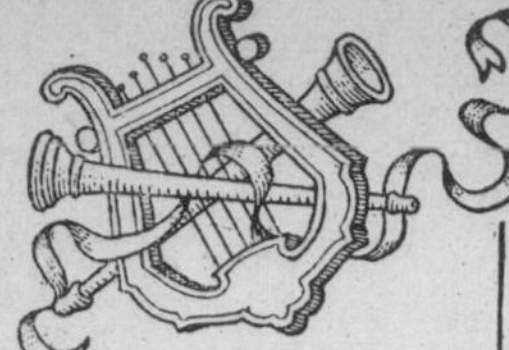

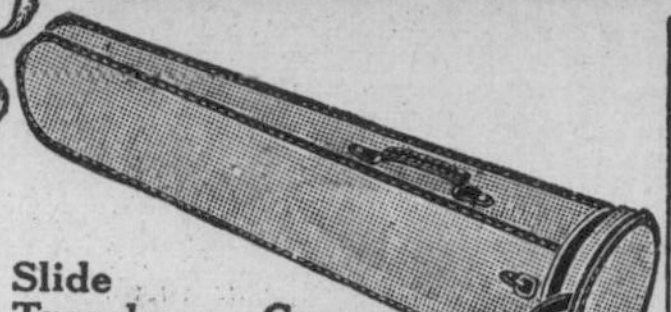

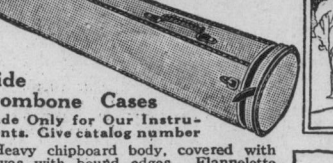

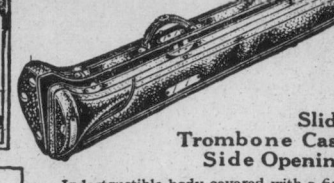

Slide Trombone Cases

Made Only for Our Instruments. Give catalog number

Heavy chipboard body, covered with canvas with bound edges. Flannelette lined. Nickel plated buckles. End opening. Shpg. wt., 7 lbs.

12K7002¼—Canvas....**$3.30**

12K7012¼—Same as 12K7002¼, but covered with keratol (artificial leather)....**$4.30**

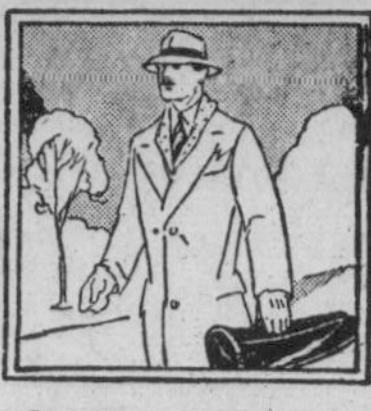

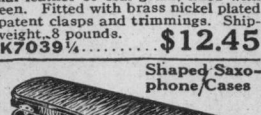

"Music self played is happiness self made."

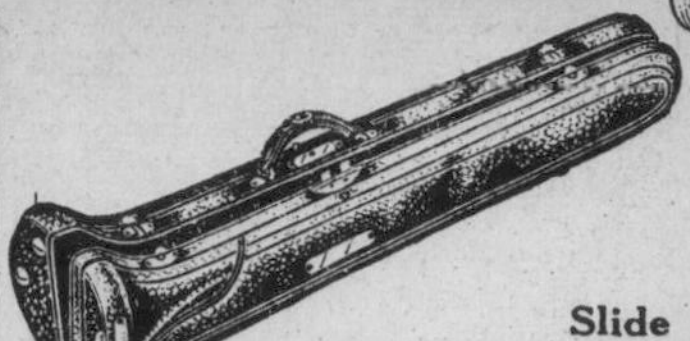

Slide Trombone Case Side Opening

Indestructible body covered with a fine artificial leather or seal grain, lined with velveteen. Fitted with brass nickel plated lock, patent clasps and trimmings. Shipping weight, 8 pounds.

12K7039¼....**$12.45**

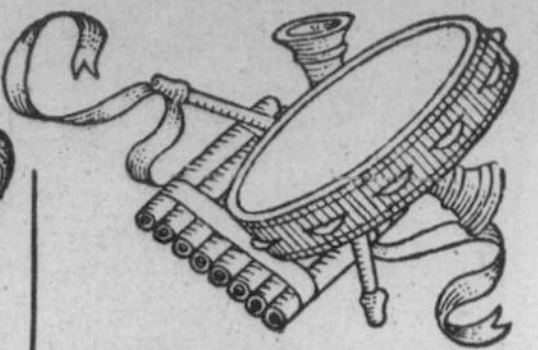

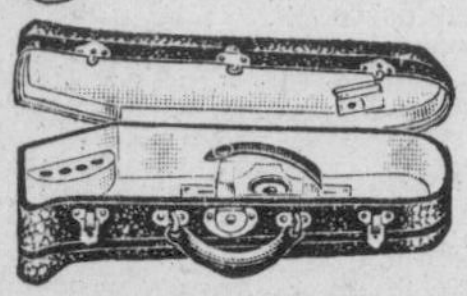

Cornet Cases

Covered with seal grain keratol (artificial leather). Lined with flannel. Trimmings, lock and clasps are nickel plated. Adjustable jaw for holding the cornet. For cornets up to 16 inches long. Shipping wt., 6 lbs.

12K7036....**$4.49**

12K7038—Same, but for trumpet cornets up to 19½ inches long....**$4.98**

Saxophone Cases

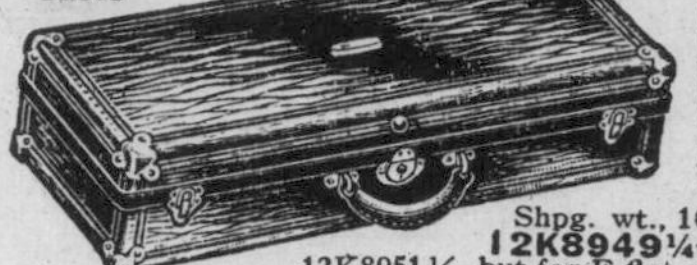

12K8951¼ Oblong shape. Covered with keratol (imitation leather). Lined with flannelette, nickel plated trimmings. For C melody. Shpg. wt., 10 lbs..**$6.69**

12K8949¼—Same as 12K8951¼, but for E flat alto saxophone. Shipping weight, 10 pounds....**$6.39**

12K8948¼—Same as 12K8951¼, but for B flat soprano saxophone. Shipping weight, 9 pounds....**$5.95**

Shaped Saxophone Cases

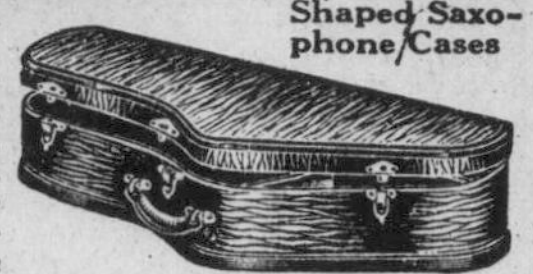

Body made of heavy chipboard, covered with high grade keratol (imitation leather), nickel plated trimmings. Large compartment. Flannel lined. Shipping wt., 10 pounds.

12K8952—For C melody saxophone....**$4.95**

12K8953—For Eb alto saxophone....**$4.45**

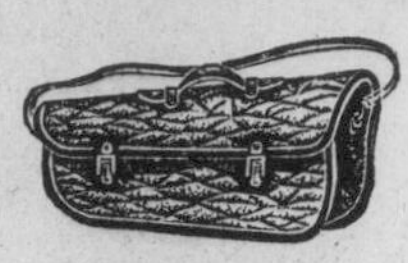

Cornet Cases

12K7021 — Canvas covered, flannelette lined, shoulder strap. For cornets up to 17 inches long. Shpg. wt., 2 lbs....**$1.49**

12K7022 — Split leather sides and top, flannelette lined, Shoulder strap. For cornets up to 17 inches long. Shipping weight, 2¾ pounds..**$2.45**

12K7026 — Same as 12K7022, but 21 inches long, to fit trumpet cornet. Shipping weight, 3¾ pounds..**$2.49**

FOR THE SAXOPHONE

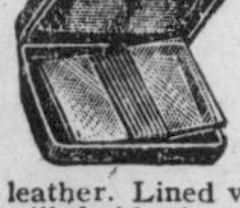

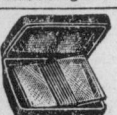

Saxophone Reed Case

12K8964—Covered with artificial leather. Lined with velveteen. Glass plate will hold six reeds. Shipping weight, 6 ounces....**55c**

Saxophone Mouthpieces

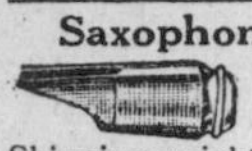

12K8956—Solid rubber. For C melody saxophone. Shipping weight, 5 ounces....**$1.75**

12K8959 — Same as 12K8956, but for E flat alto saxophone..**$1.69**

12K8955 — Same as 12K8956, but for B flat soprano saxophone....**$1.55**

Saxophone Cord

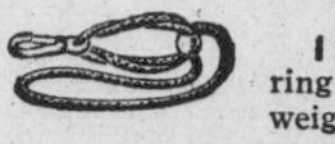

12K8958—Black silk with ring and snap. Shipping weight, 3 ounces....**42c**

C Melody Saxophone Reeds

12K8960—Fine quality. For C melody saxophone only. Shipping wt., 3 oz. One-half dozen....**69c**

Alto Saxophone Reeds

12K8961—Fine quality for alto saxophones only. Shipping weight, 3 ounces. One-half dozen....**63c**

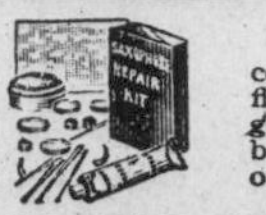

Saxophone Repair Kit

Consists of a tube of glue, cork cement, seven pads, ten assorted flat and round springs, cork for goose neck, cork grease and felt bumpers. Shipping weight, 4 ounces.

12K8965....**75c**

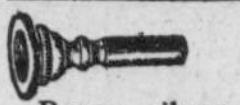

Ideal B Flat Cornet and Trombone Mouthpieces

Brass, silver plated. Wide rim. For severe playing. Shipping weight, 3 ounces.

12K7050....**69c**

For Slide Trombones.

12K7051....**95c**

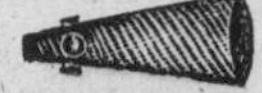

Cornet and Trombone Mutes

Fiber Cornet Mute, finished in gilt. Shpg. wt., 4 oz.

12K7055....**35c**

12K7057—Same as above but for trombone....**49c**

Aluminum Cornet Mute. Shpg. wt., 5 ounces.

12K7058....**$1.10**

Same as above but for slide trombone.

12K7059....**$1.95**

Music Racks for Band Instruments

Shipping Weight, 5 Ounces	Catalog No.	Brass	Nickel Plated
For Cornets, All Upright Horns and Saxophones	12K7070	23c	33c
For Clarinet	12K7074	....	73c
For Slide Trombone	12K7080	49c	58c

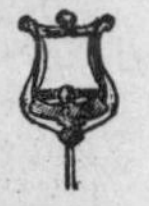

DRUMMERS' SUPPLIES

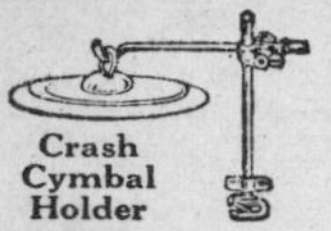

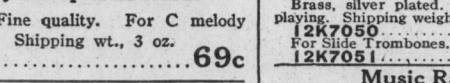

Crash Cymbal Holder

12K9056 — Two adjustments. Cymbal not included. Shipping weight, ¾ pounds....**95c**

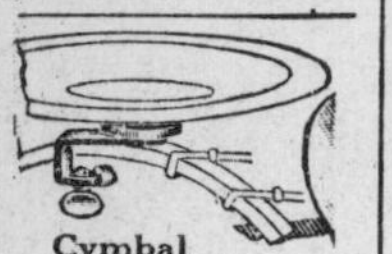

Cymbal Holder

12K9054 — For top of drum. Plated metal. Shpg. wt., 4 oz....**49c**

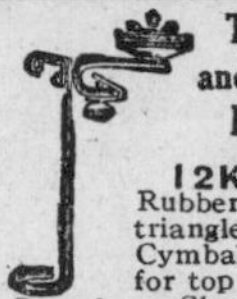

Triangle and Cymbal Holder

12K9198 Rubber covered triangle holder. Cymbal holder for top of drum. Sureclamp. Shpg. weight, 6 ounces....**69c**

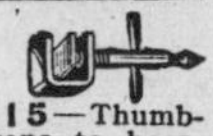

Drum Spurs

12K9115—Thumbscrew fastens to hoop. Shipping weight, 6 oz. Per pair....**65c**

Head Tucker

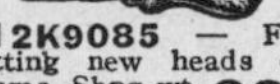

12K9085 — For putting new heads on drums. Shpg. wt., 3 oz....**23c**

Snare Drum Sticks

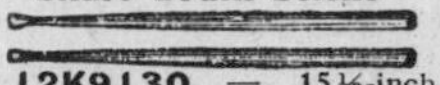

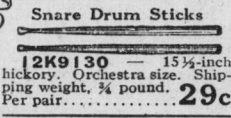

12K9130 — 15½-inch hickory. Orchestra size. Shipping weight, ¾ pound. Per pair....**29c**

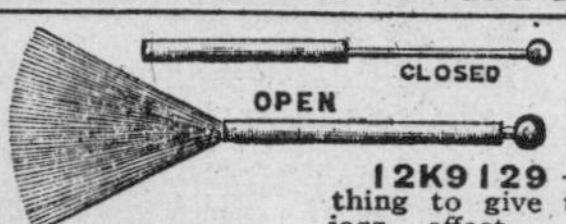

Jazz Drum Sticks

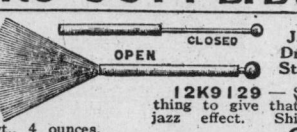

12K9129 — Something to give that real jazz effect. Shipping wt., 4 ounces. Per Pair....**69c**

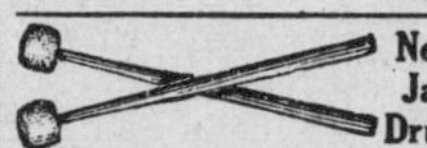

New Jazz Snare Drum Sticks

Heads made of live material covered with a good grade of felt. A jazz drummer cannot afford to be without these. Shpg. wt., 7 oz.

12K9128—Per pair....**$1.49**

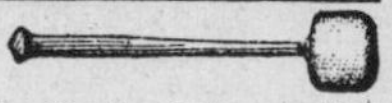

Bass Drum Sticks

12K9127—Head of live rubber material covered with felt, hardwood stick. Extra fine quality. Shpg. wt., ¾ lb....**$1.49**

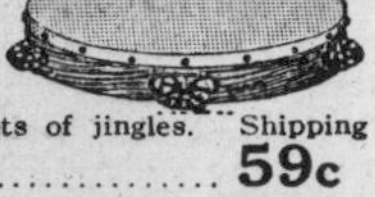

Dancers' Tambourines

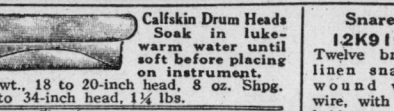

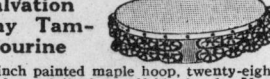

7-inch maple rim, with tacked head and three sets of jingles. Shipping weight, 8 ounces.

12K5384....**59c**

Same as 12K5384, but with six sets of jingles. Shipping weight, ¾ lb.

12K5385....**69c**

Same as 12K5384, but has 8-inch rim with twelve sets of jingles. Shipping weight, ¾ pound.

12K5386....**98c**

Maple rim, 10-inch tacked calfskin head, twelve sets of jingles. Shipping weight, 1 pound.

12K5388....**$1.35**

Tympani Style Drum Rods

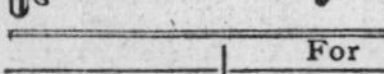

Light and strong. Nickel plated metal. **Measure shell only.**

	For	Shpg. Wt.	Each
12K9095	10-in. shell	4 oz.	67c
12K9096	12-in. shell	7 oz.	68c
12K9097	14-in. shell	8 oz.	69c

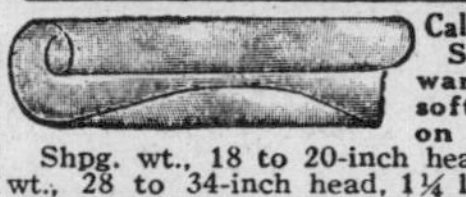

Calfskin Drum Heads

Soak in lukewarm water until soft before placing on instrument.

Shpg. wt., 18 to 20-inch head, 8 oz. Shpg. wt., 28 to 34-inch head, 1¼ lbs.

No.	Size		
12K9072	18	15-inch drum	$1.60
12K9073	19	16-inch drum	1.80
12K9074	20	17-inch drum	1.95
12K9076	28	24-inch bass drum	3.95
12K9078	32	28-inch bass drum	5.25
12K9079	34	30-inch bass drum	6.25

Snares

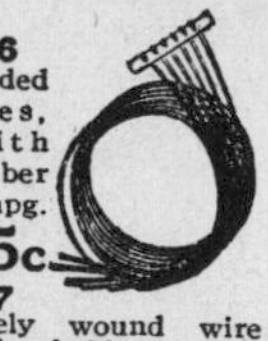

12K9106 Twelve braided linen snares, wound with wire, with fiber holder. Shpg. weight, 3 oz....**85c**

12K9107 Twelve closely wound wire snares with fiber holder. Shpg. wt., 3 oz....**75c**

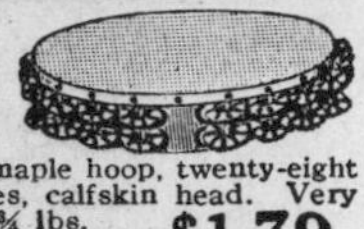

Salvation Army Tambourine

10-inch painted maple hoop, twenty-eight sets of metal jingles, calfskin head. Very loud. Shpg. wt., 1¾ lbs.

12K5390....**$1.79**

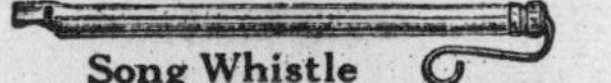

Song Whistle

May be used with all instruments and voice. Heavy nickel plated brass. Shipping weight, 1 pound.

12K5368....**$1.35**

CLARINET SUPPLIES

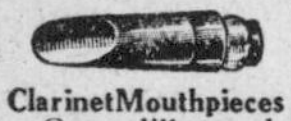

Clarinet Mouthpieces

Grenadilla wood, cork joint. B flat or C. State key. Shpg. wt., 4 oz.

12K8014....**79c**

Hard rubber, with cork joint. B flat or C. Shipping wt., 4 oz.

12K8015....**$1.45**

Reed Holder

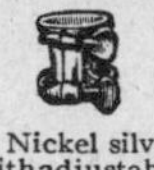

Nickel silver with adjustable screws. Shipping weight, 3 ounces.

12K8037 **27c**

Clarinet Case

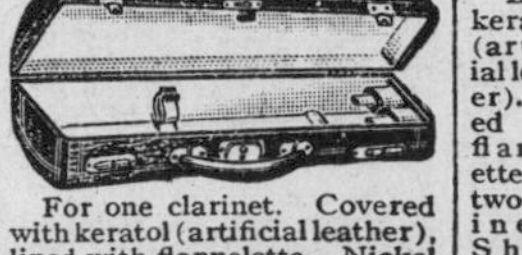

For one clarinet. Covered with keratol (artificial leather), lined with flannelette. Nickel plated trimmings. Shpg. wt., 3 lbs.

12K8002....**$4.89**

Case for Two Clarinets

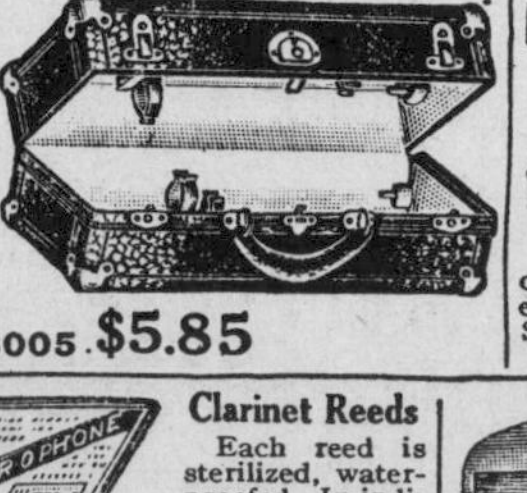

Black keratol (artificial leather). Lined with flannelette. For two clarinets. Shipping wt., 6 lbs.

12K8005 **$5.85**

Clarinet Case

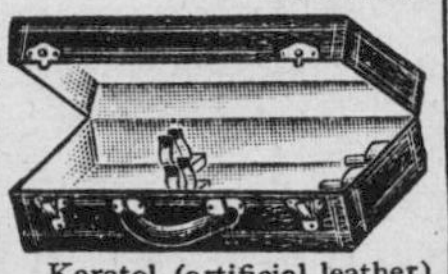

Keratol (artificial leather) covered. Lined with flannelette. Nickel plated trimmings. Shpg. wt., 3 lbs.

12K8003....**$2.25**

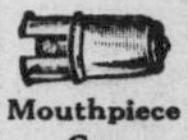

Mouthpiece Cap

Nickel plated. Shipping weight, 3 ounces.

12K8016 **39c**

Clarinet Repair Kit

(Not Illustrated)

Consists of tube of glue, cork cement, seven most necessary pads, ten assorted springs, cork grease and felt bumpers. Shipping weight, 4 ounces.

12K8017 **75c**

Clarinet Reed Case

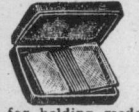

Velveteen lined. Keratol (artificial leather). Glass plate for holding reeds. Will hold 8 reeds. Shpg. wt., 4 oz.

12K8032....**45c**

Clarinet Reeds

B flat and C. Shpg. wt., 8 oz.

12K8021—Marceau. Each..**4c**

12K8023—Lafayette. Each.**6c**

12K8024 — Dupont Superior Quality. Each....**9c**

12K8025 — Carl Schubert Waterproof. Each....**15c**

12K8027—Carl Schubert "Artist." Each....**18c**

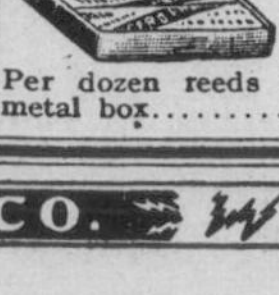

Clarinet Reeds

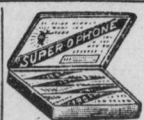

Each reed is sterilized, waterproofed. In individual envelopes. B flat or C. Shpg. wt., 3 oz.

12K8029 Per dozen reeds in sealed metal box....**$1.25**

Clarinet Reed Trimmer

12K8033 Metal. Does clean and accurate work. Shipping weight, 2 ounces....**49c**

Clarinet, Flute and Piccolo Cleaners

12K8010—Clarinet or Flute Cleaner. Wool. Shpg. wt., 2 oz....**19c**

12K8048—Piccolo Cleaner. Wool. Shpg. wt., 2 oz....**12c**

Clarinet Key-Pads

Fifteen pads to set. (Not illustrated.) Shipping weight, 2 ounces.

12K8012—Per set....**23c**

TRUPHONIC
Has Won the
NATION'S APPROVAL

An avalanche of popular approval has followed in the wake of the Truphonic! Our customers have bought the Truphonic by the thousands, and our factories are busy night and day to ship their orders on time. A year ago Truphonic was new. Today it has taken its place at the head of the finest phonographs made. This supremacy was achieved because of its perfection in tone, the beauty of the cabinet designs and our unparalleled values.

Truphonic is the marvel of all phonographs! It is magic! Listeners who hear it for the first time are amazed at the perfect tone. **Customers who have bought it write to tell us that never have they listened to anything like it.** Here is a tremendous advancement; a long, long step ahead of all former phonograph construction. Developed and perfected in our own big factories by our own acoustic engineers, the Truphonic is unlike all old time phonographs. When placed side by side with the finest phonographs made today, even those costing twice as much, the Truphonic has been pronounced by experts to be the best in beauty of tone. The boom of the bass, the resonance of a fine piano, the sweetness of an old violin, the pure melody of a famous voice—these the Truphonic conveys to you naturally; without effort, without distortion. Flawless music!

The Imperial

It is fitting that the most realistic reproduction of music the world of science has ever discovered should be housed in this beautiful cabinet. Massive, dignified, impressive, the Imperial is a true work of art, a masterpiece in design. Its value and beauty will be appreciated more and more with the passage of time. You will enjoy the incomparable music and the exquisite appearance of this Truphonic for a lifetime. Here is not only music at its best but furniture craftsmanship such as has never been offered before at the price. Here is natural pure tone in every note; here is unmistakable quality in every line and every detail. Genuine Mahogany or Walnut woodwork, gold plated metal parts; 12-inch velvet covered turntable, the famous triple spring Silvertone motor, powerful and silent running; new improved reproducer and tone arm and, of course, the exclusive Truphonic method of reproduction. These are a few of the quality features. 46 inches high, 31½ inches wide, 23½ inches deep. **Shipped from our PHILADELPHIA store.** Five Silvertone records (our selection) and assortment of steel needles included. Shipping weight, 300 pounds.

46K4899—In Mahogany.
46K4900—In Walnut. **$152.00**

$12.00 with order, balance $12.00 a month. When ordering use Time Payment Order Blank on page 1092.
Price does not include ship model.

The Truphonic Phonograph is certainly a great contribution to the art of music. Notes and tone shadings, which have scarcely been touched in phonographs of the past, seem to be perfectly reproduced in this wonderful instrument. It has my personal endorsement and recommendation.

Yours truly,
PATRICIA ANN MANNERS
Star in "The Student Prince"

IMPERIAL

Open View of the Imperial. Record books are not included.

30 DAYS' FREE TRAIL—EASY PAYMENTS

We invite you to try the Truphonic in your home for 30 days before you decide whether you wish to keep it. Order the model of your choice and send only the required first down payment. Then after you have had the opportunity of putting the Truphonic to every test, if it is not satisfactory you may return it and we will gladly return your money including any transportation charges you have paid.

If you keep the instrument you can pay for it according to the easy payment terms specified. In this way you can enjoy the incomparable music and entertainment of this supreme phonograph while you are paying for it in monthly amounts so small you will scarcely notice them.

The Argyle

No one ever dreamed that such a remarkable, such an exquisite musical instrument as the Argyle could be purchased at a price so amazingly low. Never before has there been the volume, the rhythm, the absolutely perfect, realistic tones that are produced by this Truphonic phonograph. You will be just astounded at the utmost exactness to the original rendition as you will be at the extraordinary beauty of the design and the exceptionally big value. A Spanish type highboy cabinet with the appeal of the Argyle would cost a great deal more elsewhere! And then you would not be getting the same true, delightful music. For only in the Truphonic can you obtain such perfection, and the Truphonic is our own exclusive development. No other phonograph can excel the Truphonic, because in this new instrument there is absolutely no difference between the original artist's selection and the Truphonic's re-creation of it. Actual tests have proved this. Prove it yourself by taking advantage of our thirty days' trial offer. Try it in your own home. Unless you have heard a Truphonic you have not heard the finest musical instrument of the age. Real workmanship, real quality is built into the Argyle, inside and out. It is made of **genuine, selected mahogany or walnut**, with contrasting decorations. The antique metal pulls lend charm and grace. Silent and powerful triple spring Silvertone motor, 12-inch felt covered turntable, new improved reproducer and tone arm and complete Truphonic interior construction. 42½ inches high, 35 inches wide, 21½ inches deep. **Shipped from our PHILADELPHIA store.** Five Silvertone records (our selection) and needle assortment included. Shipping weight, 215 pounds.

46K4897—In Mahogany.
46K4898—In Walnut. **$118.00**

$10.00 with order; balance $8.50 a month. When ordering use Time Payment Order Blank on page 1092.

ARGYLE

TRUPHONIC
Silvertone

It is marvelous! Decidedly superior to anything I have heard. Truphonic rendition is human—such fidelity is amazing! To those who are about to purchase a phonograph, it is my belief that the Truphonic will more than please the most critical.

Sincerely yours,
CHARLES H. THOMAS, B. M.
Popular Concert Organist

ARAGON

The very latest idea in modern cabinet design is developed in this new Truphonic Silvertone. We are offering the Aragon model at a price which represents a sensational saving. That an instrument of such striking beauty, such apparent originality in line and finish and such inherent good workmanship should be offered at such a low price as $80.00 is one of the greatest merchandising feats of a decade!

In the opinion of expert judges of fine furniture, the Aragon is, without question an outstanding leader among all phonographs of the better quality. A semi-console type of cabinet, inspired by an exclusive and artistic French pattern, it has a beautiful two-tone front with rich, inlaid effect. Luxurious, sumptuous, expressive of value far beyond what we are asking. And like a jewel which sparkles in a perfect setting, the pure, clear, flawless Truphonic tone pours out in magnificent melody, to hold you breathless with wonder.

The Truphonic principle of true reproduction is probably the greatest achievement of the entire industry! As true to life as the original, as natural as the voice itself. As The big, extra size tone chamber, the special acoustic construction, the newest approved mechanical equipment and the big, powerful Silvertone motor, complete the appointments which make this new Aragon a leading favorite.

We can furnish the Aragon in **mahogany** or **walnut**, beautifully shaded and polished to bring out all the artistic graining of the selected woods. The instrument measures 35¼ inches high, 26 inches wide, 21½ inches deep. Price includes five Silvertone records (our selection) and an assortment of steel needles. Shipped from PHILADELPHIA store. Shipping weight, 125 pounds.

46K4866—Mahogany.
46K4867—Walnut.

$80.00

$5.00 with order; balance $6.00 per month. Use Time Payment Order Blank on page 1092.

Open view of the Aragon. Record Books illustrated not included.

Open View of the Fairfax Showing Record Compartments.

FAIRFAX

To bring the Truphonic within the reach of everyone, we have designed this superb, low priced cabinet, the Fairfax, It has the new, genuine Truphonic construction. It has the same marvelous true tone as our more expensive cabinets. We have successfully built into this most delightfully designed upright model all the Truphonic characteristics which make this modern phonograph so desirable for the up to date home. The quality of its music will delight and surprise you here just as it does in any of our other models. Well made throughout, from interior mechanical equipment to exterior of **genuine mahogany, walnut** or **fumed oak**. The Fairfax is one of our feature bargains, a value so extraordinary, so sensational that it will astound you when you see and hear it in your own home. There it will be a constant source of pleasure and a pleasant reminder in the years to come of the outstanding savings offered by Sears, Roebuck and Co. Cabinet is 41 inches high, 18 inches wide, 19 inches deep. Equipped with the same durable double spring Silvertone motor, powerful and silent running, as well as all other mechanical fittings which are used in every one of our models regardless of price. Price includes five Silvertone records (our selection) and assortment of steel needles. Shipped from PHILADELPHIA store. Shipping weight, 90 pounds.

46K4874— Mahogany.
46K4875— Walnut.
46K4876— Fumed Oak.

$45.00

$4.00 with order; balance $3.00 a month. Use Time Payment Order Blank on page 1092.

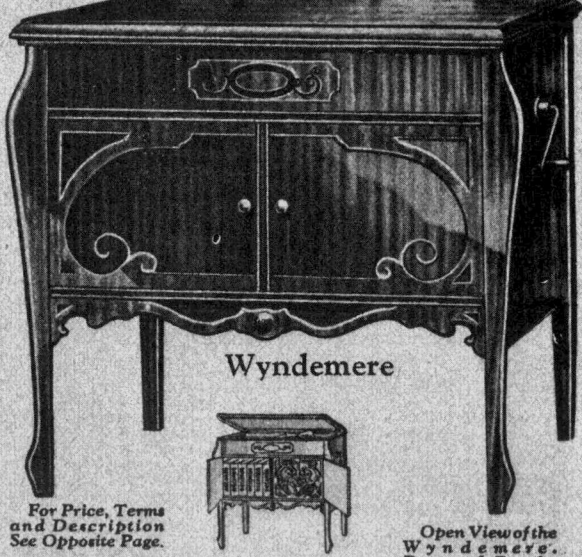

Wyndemere

For Price, Terms and Description See Opposite Page.

Open View of the Wyndemere. Record Books Are Not Included.

The New Musical Triumph

Silvertone

KENMORE

A great orchestra is playing a beautiful symphony. A hundred instruments blend in throbbing, thrilling harmony. Stillness—and then the clear, pure strains of a violin, sweet as the call of a thrush to its mate, rise and fall to hold you breathless with wonderment. That is the Truphonic! Never before such music—its only counterpart the original. There is a new experience awaiting you. Unless you have listened to the Truphonic you cannot imagine the tremendous improvement that has been made in the reproduction of music. You will be astonished at the new beauty of tone. It compares with the old type phonograph as a mighty pipe organ compares with the hand organ. The Truphonic tone is resonant, vibrant and clear as crystal. Never before has there been such beauty in cabinet design as the Kenmore. New, graceful, convenient, imposing, dignified, one of the most pleasing our skilled cabinet makers have ever produced. A semi-console type, it has been acclaimed by critics as the perfectly proportioned cabinet. Only the World's Largest Store could offer such an outstanding quality product at such a sensationally low price. This beautiful Queen Anne period cabinet is made of genuine selected mahogany or walnut in two-tone finish. It stands 36 inches high, 32½ inches wide and 21 inches deep. 12-inch felt covered turntable. Famous double spring Silvertone motor, powerful and silent running. All exposed parts are attractively nickel plated, in keeping with the other appointments of this luxurious appearing model. Shipped from our PHILADELPHIA store. Price includes five Silvertone records (our selection) and an assortment of steel needles. Shipping weight, 163 pounds.

46K4880—In Mahogany.
46K4881—In Walnut.

$102.00

$10.00 with order, balance $7.50 a month.
Use Time Payment Order Blank on Page 1092

Open View of the Kenmore showing Grille and Record Book Compartments

WYNDEMERE

(Illustrated on Opposite Page)

The exclusive, perfected Truphonic method of sound reproduction, incorporated in this striking console, is a never failing source of satisfying pleasure and enjoyment. Truphonic is no longer an experiment, but a proved, finished invention which neither subtracts from nor adds to the original rendition of voice or musical instrument. Why not take advantage of our 30-day FREE TRIAL offer as explained on page 685 so you can have the opportunity of actually hearing this astounding new improvement in musical reproduction? Nothing else is like it. No other phonograph ever built has such beauty of tone, such pure, sweet, natural music as the Truphonic. In the Wyndemere console, the Truphonic construction assures absolute fidelity to every note; every chord is exactly as played when the master record was made. A new era in musical reproduction demands an accompanying improvement in cabinet design. The Wyndemere is a worthy model to house such a marvelous acoustic development as the Truphonic. The front of the Wyndemere is beautifully two-toned, adding to the rich effect produced by the curved outline. Still further emphasizing the luxuriousness of its appearance is the handsomely grained and rubbed genuine mahogany or walnut. Only $5.00 down and $4.00 a month permits you to own and enjoy this greatest musical instrument of the age. Guaranteed mechanical equipment. Measures 32 inches wide, 32 inches high and 20 inches deep. Shipped from our PHILADELPHIA store. Price includes five Silvertone records (our selection) and steel needle assortment. Shipping weight, 120 pounds.

46K4889—In Mahogany.
46K4890—In Walnut.

$57.75

$5.00 with order, balance $4.00 a month.
Use Time Payment Order Blank on Page 1092

VICTORIA

Only a year ago the Truphonic ushered in the new era of phonograph construction. Until the arrival of Truphonic a phonograph was, after all, just a phonograph. But because this new creation is a real musical instrument, because it brings to the home the same perfection you hear when listening to the actual artists themselves, it revolutionized all former conceptions of reproduced music. The success of the Truphonic was instantaneous. Already we have sold thousands. Truphonic is a proved fact, a proved success. The Victoria is exquisite in its proportions and its craftsmanship, a delight to the eye and a fitting home for the flawless music which it reproduces. The beauty of the cabinet and the beauty of the tone are in perfect harmony. You would expect, after seeing this magnificent instrument, to hear such music as you never heard before. We promise you that all your anticipations will be realized. Nothing has been spared in the materials or the appointments of the Victoria to make it a superb masterpiece, as a cabinet as well as a phonograph. Made of genuine mahogany or walnut. Note the delicate tracery of the contrasting two-tone panels, inset in doors of exactly matched woods. From the extended top to the graceful Queen Anne legs, the Victoria has every characteristic associated with high quality furniture. 12-inch felt covered turntable and nickel plated metal parts. Silent double spring motor. Cabinet is 45 inches high, 22 inches wide and 20 inches deep. Shipped from our PHILADELPHIA store. Price includes five Silvertone records (our selection) and an assortment of steel needles. Shipping weight, 135 lbs.

46K4855—In Mahogany.
46K4856—In Walnut.

$76.00

$6.00 with order, balance $6.00 a month.
Use Time Payment Order Blank on Page 1092

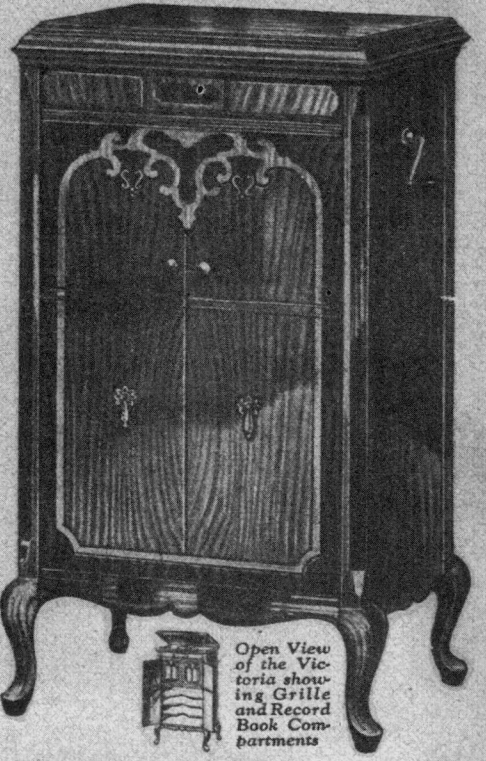

Open View of the Victoria showing Grille and Record Book Compartments

A New CONSOLETTE
The Worlds Biggest Value

Price includes five Silvertone records (our selection) and an assortment of steel needles.

Open View shows grille and record compartments.

The Waldorf

In a class by itself, distinguished for its unparalleled quality, its unequaled value, its matchless tone! No silver throated songster ever warbled a melody more sweet and intriguing than this new Truphonic. The meadow lark, gayly trilling his message of happiness on a sparkling, crisp, sunshiny morning, has met his rival. Here is remarkable compass and variety, here is full volume, crystal clear, and throbbing, vibrant resonance that will thrill you with its incomparable music. It will entertain you as you have never been entertained before. It will sing for you, play for you, give you all that you can ask of any musical instrument. The Waldorf is our favorite, the leader value in our showing of new Truphonics. On it we have concentrated our great buying power and manufacturing facilities to bring you the biggest phonograph bargain ever known! We want to prove it. We want to send you this consolette, to try in your home where you can compare it, hear it. If you are not convinced of its tremendous value you can return it. The Waldorf is made of selected woods, mahogany or walnut, beautifully finished. All metal parts are nickel plated. It is equipped with our finest double spring silvertone motor, powerful and silent running. Size, 34 inches high, 18 inches wide, 18 inches deep. It has our exclusive Truphonic construction and appointments. Shipped from Philadelphia Store. Shipping weight, 90 pounds.

46K4851 Mahogany.
46K4852 Walnut. **$47⁵⁰**

$4.00 with order
$3.00 a month
Use Time Payment Order Blank on Page 1092

VALENCIA
An Improved Silvertone Table Model

"In Valencia we found our Paradise." There's a Paradise of Happiness for you in this marvelous musical instrument, a Paradise of Gaiety, of Dancing, of Music, of Dreams, of Joy, of Entertainment. Magic, you will say when you hear it! Every listener wonders at the pure, natural, truly beautiful tone. In no other table model phonograph will you find tone superior to this. And the Valencia is a genuine Silvertone, the phonograph with a million friends. It is new, improved, better! That is why the Valencia, at our low money saving price, represents a value without equal, a bargain so sensational, it sweeps aside all comparison. There is no comparison except with the very highest priced instruments on the market. The Valencia table model is a full size phonograph. It will do everything any other phonograph will do, regardless of how much more you pay. Furnished in Mahogany, Walnut or Oak. Equipped with the famous silvertone double spring motor, 12-inch felt covered turntable; nickel plated metal parts. Size, 20⅜ inches deep, 18 inches wide, 15¾ inches high. Shipping weight, 50 pounds. Steel needles included. **Not mailable.**

46K4862—Mahogany.
46K4863—Walnut. **$36⁰⁰**
46K4864—Oak.

$3.00 with order, $3.00 a month
Use Time Payment Order Blank on Page 1092

Amazing Bargains!
8 BIG FEATURES

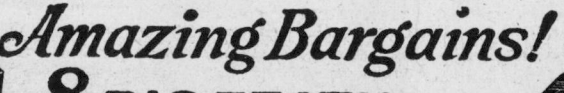

1—Best portable motor on the market.
2—Dovetailed corners—far superior to the usual nailed construction.
3—Ready to play, instantly.
4—Convenient record compartment.
5—Self contained tone chamber.
6—Riveted hardware—handle, needle cup and hinges can't come off.
7—Genuine Dupont Keratol covering.
8—Non-rust brass trimmings, nickel plated.

The marvelous tone of the genuine Silvertone Phonograph in a portable model! A wonderful companion for your playtime hours. Take it with you anywhere! Dancing parties, every entertainment is many times more enjoyable when a portable Silvertone instrument is along. Convenient, easy to carry, it brings life and laughter and the magic of melody wherever it goes.

$18²⁵
Master Portable

$14⁹⁵
The Portola

This is far more than just a portable phonograph. Here is the new, amazing master construction that makes the perfect phonograph. The most delicate shades of tone are reproduced with the startling fidelity and truthfulness that only the Master Silvertone can attain. There is no comparison between this fine instrument and portable phonographs sold elsewhere for much more than our low price. Here is the portable without an equal, the last word in excellence, worthy in every way of the name Silvertone.

Enjoy this instrument for 30 days under our free trial offer. Notice the special features shown above. Compare this phonograph with any other portable sold. We know you will be more than delighted with its extraordinary and beautiful performance.

Every single detail emphasizes the high quality of the materials and workmanship. The Silvertone tone arm, sound chamber and special reproducer are housed in a strongly built keratol covered case. 11½ inches wide, 15 inches long, 7½ inches high, strengthened by triple leather corners. The needle cup has spring top, preventing needles falling out. 10-inch felt covered turntable plays all 10 and 12-inch records (except Edison). Steel needles included. Can be sent by mail. Shipping weight, 18 pounds.
46K4603—The Master Portable. (No records included.) Sold for cash only. **$18.25**

Our own factories have solved the problem of building a good Portable Phonograph at a low price! In the Portola we offer a splendid instrument of excellent tone and real workmanship for less money than you would have to pay for the same quality elsewhere.

This remarkable phonograph plays all 10 and 12-inch standard disc records and plays them with a beautiful tone. Just lift the cover and there it is, ready to play, nothing to take apart or put together, and it weighs only 14 pounds. We have equipped it with a genuine Silvertone single spring motor which will play two 10-inch selections with one winding. It is not to be compared with the average cheap motor ordinarily used in portable phonographs that usually sell at or near our price.

The Portola has a suspended tone chamber. It is equipped with a nickel plated brass tone arm, a 10-inch felt covered turntable and a keratol holder for 10-inch records. Covered with black wear and weather resisting genuine Dupont keratol. The needle cup has a spring cover to prevent needles from falling out. It is 14¾ inches long, 11½ inches wide, 7½ inches high. Steel needles are included. Thirty days trial. See also eight big features listed above. **Can be sent by mail.** Shipping weight, 16 pounds.
46K4602—The Portola (no records included). Sold for cash only...... **$14.95**

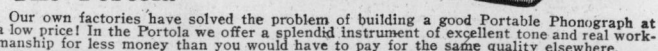

24¢ Challenge Records — 10 for $2.29 Each

If you want the best, we recommend the Silvertone. For those who want a lower priced record we offer the Challenge, which is better than those usually sold at 35c and equally as good as most sold at 50c. Order by catalog number and selection number. Shipping weight, 1 record, 1½ pounds; 10 records, 5½ pounds.

12K6301—Each, 24c; 10 for..............................$2.29

Descriptive Selections

152 Barney McCoy. Ernest Stoneman. Pretty Snow Dear. Ernest Stoneman.

149 Billy Richardson's Last Ride. Vernon Dalhart. An Old Fashioned Picture. Vernon Dalhart.

162 In the Baggage Coach Ahead. Vernon Dalhart. The Runaway Train. Vernon Dalhart.

167 Just Tell Them That You Saw Me. Vernon Dalhart. Mother's Grave. Vernon Dalhart.

153 May I Sleep in Your Barn Tonight, Mister? Ernest Stoneman. Silver Bell. Ernest Stoneman.

150 Papa's Billy Goat. Vernon Dalhart. Puttin' On Style. Vernon Dalhart.

154 Put My Little Shoes Away. Vernon Dalhart. The Old Fiddler's Son. Vernon Dalhart.

155 The Engineer's Child. Vernon Dalhart. The Great Titanic. Vernon Dalhart.

156 The Freight Wreck at Altoona. Vernon Dalhart. The Ship That Never Returned. Vernon Dalhart.

166 The John T. Scopes Trial. Vernon Dalhart. Bryan's Last Fight. Vernon Dalhart.

160 The Letter Edged in Black. Vernon Dalhart. The Death of Floyd Collins. Vernon Dalhart.

165 The Lightning Express. Vernon Dalhart. The New River Train. Vernon Dalhart.

164 The Little Rosewood Casket. Vernon Dalhart. Blue Ridge Mountain Blues. Vernon Dalhart.

163 The Prisoner's Song. Vernon Dalhart. Mother and Home. Vernon Dalhart.

161 The Wreck of the Southern Old '97. Vernon Dalhart. A Boy's Best Friend Is His Mother. Vernon Dalhart.

157 The Unknown Soldier's Grave. Vernon Dalhart. Zeb Turney's Gal. Vernon Dalhart.

159 Thrills That I Can't Forget. John Ferguson. Railroad Daddy. John Ferguson.

158 Wild Bill Jones. John Ferguson. I Wish I Was Single Again. John Ferguson.

Popular Vocal

203 Always. Challenge Trio. Someone to Love. Challenge Trio.

196 Any Ice Today, Lady? Kaufman and Campbell. Hi-Ho the Merrio. Jack Kaufman.

260 Blue Skies. Geo. De Wees. Play Gypsies—Dance Gypsies. Geo. De Wees.

261 Coronado Nights. Harold Charles. Me. Harold Charles.

262 Everything's Made for Love. The Jolly Bakers. Thinking of You. The Jolly Bakers.

263 Hello, Bluebird. Irving Kaufman. Lonely Eyes. Irving Kaufman.

222 Hello, Swanee, Hello. Robbins and Uke. Jersey Walk. Robbins and Uke.

264 High-High-High Up in the Hills. The Jolly Bakers. If Tears Could Bring You Back to Me. Harold Charles.

197 Hi-Diddle-Diddle. Jack Kaufman. What! No Spinach? Kaufman and Campbell.

190 How Many Times? Madge Thompson. It Won't Be Long Now. Billy Jones.

205 I Don't Believe It, But Say It Again. Jack Malone and His Uke. Gimme a Little Kiss, Will Ya, Huh? Jack Malone and His Uke.

200 I Wish I Had My Old Gal Back Again. Wilson Bros. Drifting and Dreaming. Wilson Bros.

226 I Want to Be Known as Susan's Feller. Johnnie Wilson. Make Him Feel at Home. Johnnie Wilson.

265 I Wonder How I Look When I'm Asleep. (Vocal.) Mae Thompson. If I Didn't Know Your Husband. Mae Thompson.

207 Let Me Call You Sweetheart. Harry Robbins. Blue Eyed Sally. Wilson Bros.

206 Let the Rest of the World Go By. Harris and Smith. That Tumble Down Shack in Athlone. Rollins Trio.

202 Moonlight and Roses. Harley Thomas. Just a Cottage Small. Harley Thomas.

208 Oh, How I Miss You Tonight. Wilson Bros. All Alone. Wilson Bros.

194 Put Your Arms Where They Belong. Charles Hart. My Dream of the Big Parade. Charles Hart.

189 She Put a Little Powder on Her Nose. Billy Jones. Me Too. Billy Jones.

198 Show That Fellow the Door. Lucky Wilson and His Uke. The Pump Song. Jack Kaufman.

192 Sleepy Head. The Pullman Four. Baby Face. Arthur Fields.

188 The Miami Storm. Vernon Dalhart. There's a New Star in Heaven Tonight (Rudolph Valentino). Vernon Dalhart.

267 Thinking of You. The Jolly Bakers. Everything's Made for Love. The Jolly Bakers.

266 When I First Met Mary. Challenge Quartet. Sam, the Old Accordion Man. (Quartet.) Challenge Quartet.

227 Where Do You Worka, John? Jack Kaufman. Cock-A-Doodle, I'm Off My Noodle. Jack Kaufman.

191 Where'd You Get Those Eyes? Madge Thompson. Who Wouldn't? Madge Thompson.

Dance Selections

253 Ain't She Sweet? (Fox Trot.) Lou Gold With The Melody Men. You Should See My Tootsie. (Fox Trot.) Lou Gold With The Melody Men.

127 Black Bottom. (Fox Trot.) Joe Candullo and His Everglades Orchestra. Messin' Around. (Slow Drag.) Joe Candullo and His Everglades Orchestra.

238 Blue Skies. (Fox Trot.) (Vocal Chorus.) Mandel's Melody Men. One Alone. (Fox Trot.) (Vocal Chorus.) Fenwick's Dance Orch.

130 Breezin' Along With the Breeze. (Fox Trot.) (Vocal Chorus.) The Hoosier Radio Boys. Cry Baby. (Fox Trot.) (Vocal Chorus.) Joe Candullo and His Everglades Orchestra.

140 Bye, Bye, Blackbird. (Fox Trot.) (Vocal Chorus.) The Hickory Knoll Dance Orchestra. Blue Bonnet—You Make Me Feel Blue. (Fox Trot.) (Vocal Chorus.) Nathan Glantz and His Orchestra.

256 Don't Take That Black Bottom Away. (Fox Trot.) Fred Rich and His Times Square Orchestra. Mother Dear. (Fox Trot.) Elmer Grosso's Greenwich Village Orch.

132 For My Sweetheart. (Fox Trot.) (Vocal Chorus.) Hoosier Radio Boys. Only You and Lonely Me. (Fox Trot.) (Vocal Chorus.) Joe Candullo and His Everglades Orchestra.

147 Gimme a Little Kiss, Will Ya, Huh? (Fox Trot.) (Vocal Chorus.) Twin City Dance Orchestra. I'm in Love With You, That's Why. (Fox Trot.) (Vocal Chorus.) The Kentucky Cardinals.

114 Give Me a Ukulele and a Ukulele Baby. (Fox Trot.) (Vocal Chorus.) Fenwick's Novelty Dance Orchestra. Sunday. (Fox Trot.) (Vocal Chorus.) Royal North West Collegians.

146 Good-Night, I'll See You in the Morning. (Fox Trot.) (Vocal Chorus.) The Atlanta Serenaders. A Cup of Coffee, a Sandwich and You. (Fox Trot.) (Vocal Chorus.) Nathan Glantz and His Orchestra.

209 Hello, Bluebird. Challenge Dance Orchestra. Just a Little Longer. Challenge Dance Orchestra.

148 I Certainly Could. (Fox Trot.) (Vocal Chorus.) Twin City Dance Orchestra. I Don't Believe It, But Say It Again. (Fox Trot.) (Vocal Chorus.) Twin City Dance Orchestra.

145 I'd Climb the Highest Mountain If I Knew I'd Find You. (Fox Trot.) (Vocal Chorus.) Royal Northwest Collegians. But I Do—You Know I Do. (Fox Trot.) (Vocal Chorus.) Twin City - Dance Orchestra.

135 I'm Just Wild About Animal Crackers. (Fox Trot.) The Memphis Bell Hops. It's Breaking My Heart To Keep Away From You. (Fox Trot.) (Vocal Chorus.) The Memphis Bell Hops.

257 I'm Looking Over a Four Leaf Clover. (Fox Trot.) Twin Cities Dance Orchestra. Sunny Hawaii. Twin Cities Dance Orchestra.

212 In a Little Spanish Town. (Waltz.) Royal Northwest Collegians. Gigolo. (Fox Trot.) Royal Northwest Collegians.

142 Just a Cottage Small. (Fox Trot.) (Vocal Chorus.) The Alabama Entertainers. Lonesome and Sorry. (Fox Trot.) (Vocal Chorus.) Nathan Glantz and His Orchestra.

131 Lay My Head Beneath a Rose. (Waltz.) Golden Gate Waltz Players. Sleepy Bye. (Waltz With Vocal Chorus.) Miami Beach Orchestra.

126 Looking at the World Thru Rose Colored Glasses. (Fox Trot.) (Vocal Chorus.) The Golden Gate Serenaders. Nothing Else Matters but Love. (Fox Trot.) (Vocal Chorus.) Fenwick's Novelty Dance Orchestra.

233 Mary Lou. (Fox Trot.) (Vocal Chorus.) Challenge Dance Orchestra. Song of the Wanderer. (Fox Trot.) (Vocal Chorus.) Memphis Melody Players.

115 Meadow-Lark. (Fox Trot.) (Vocal Chorus.) Fenwick's Novelty Dance Orchestra. Because I Love You. (Fox Trot.) (Vocal Chorus.) Challenge Dance Orchestra.

258 She Looks Like Helen Brown. (Fox Trot.) Miami Garden Orchestra. Come Day—Go Day. (Fox Trot-Shuffle.) Miami Garden Orchestra.

119 Stars Are the Windows of Heaven. (Fox Trot.) (Vocal Chorus.) Challenge Dance Orchestra. Why Do Ya Roll Those Eyes? (Fox Trot.) (Vocal Chorus.) Challenge Dance Orchestra.

DANCE TO THE LATEST HITS

A list of the latest hits in Challenge Records is released every month and will be sent you on request. Put your name on mailing list now. Write for Challenge Record List 9506K.

137 That's Why I Love You. (Fox Trot.) Joe Candullo and His Everglades Orchestra. I May Be Dancing With Somebody Else. (Fox Trot.) (Vocal Chorus.) The Cuban Dance Kings.

239 There Ain't No Maybe in My Baby's Eyes. (Fox Trot.) (Vocal Chorus.) Fenwick's Dance Orchestra. Forgive Me. (Fox Trot.) (Vocal Chorus.) Blue Diamond Orchestra.

211 There's a Little White House. (Fox Trot.) The Cuban Dance Kings. If Tears Could Bring You Back to Me. Memphis Melody Players.

234 Thinking of You. (Fox Trot.) (Vocal Chorus.) Northwest Collegians. A Blues Serenade. (Fox Trot.) Memphis Melody Players.

141 Tonight's My Night With Baby. (Fox Trot.) (Vocal Chorus.) Nathan Glantz and His Orchestra. Hello, Aloha! How Are You? (Fox Trot.) (Vocal Chorus.) Nathan Glantz and His Orchestra.

129 Valencia. (Fox Trot.) The Cuban Dance Kings. I'm Lonely Without You. (Fox Trot.) (Vocal Chorus.) The Cuban Dance Kings.

116 When You Waltz With the One You Love. (Waltz With Vocal Chorus.) Fenwick's Novelty Dance Orchestra. Why Did You Say Goodbye? (Waltz With Vocal Chorus.) Challenge Dance Orchestra.

254 You Can't Cry Over My Shoulder. (Fox Trot.) Golden Gate Serenaders. I'm Gonna Meet My Sweetie Now. (Fox Trot.) Golden Gate Serenaders.

255 You're the One for Me. (Fox Trot.) Miller's Music Makers. Sunday Girl. (Fox Trot.) Miller's Music Makers.

136 Where'd You Get Those Eyes? (Fox Trot.) (Vocal Chorus.) Nathan Glantz and His Orchestra. I Love a Ukulele. (Fox Trot.) (Vocal Chorus.) Nathan Glantz and His Orchestra.

Old Time Fiddlin' and Dance Selections

501 All I've Got Is Done Gone. Dock Roberts and Edgar Boaz. And the Cat Came Back the Very Next Day. Dock Roberts.

109 Arkansas Traveler. Uncle Jim Hawkins. Turkey in the Straw. Uncle Jim Hawkins.

504 Behind Those Gray Walls. Dalhart. Wreck of "1256." Dalhart.

232 Frankie's Gamblin' Man. Clarence Adams. The Golden Willow Tree. Clarence Adams.

101 Hell Broke Loose in Georgia. Uncle Jim Hawkins. And the Cat Came Back the Very Next Day. Uncle Jim Hawkins.

224 Just a Melody. Dalhart and Robison. When You're Far Away. Dalhart and Robison.

229 Roving Gambler. Clarence Adams. In the Shadow of the Pine. Carl Harris.

503 Miami Storm. Dalhart. Jesse James. Dalhart.

112 My Baby Loves Shortenin' Bread. Uncle Jim Hawkins. Billy in the Low Grounds. Uncle Jim Hawkins.

104 Ocean Waves (With Calls). Tom Owens W L S Barn Dance Trio. Buffalo Girls. Tom Owens W L S Barn Dance Trio.

108 Party Quadrille (With Calls). The Barnstormers. Circle Waltz (With Calls). The Barnstormers.

504 Railroad Daddy. Welby Toomey. Thrills That I Can't Forget. Welby Toomey.

102 Seneca Square Dance. Fiddlin' Dave Neal. Listen to the Mocking Bird. Fiddlin' Dave Neal.

505 The Dream of the Miner's Child. Dalhart. Life of Tom Watson. Dalhart.

110 The Old Hen Cackled and the Rooster Crowed. The Three Howard Boys. Down in Tennessee Blues. The Three Howard Boys.

244 The Poor Tramp Has to Live. Uncle Ben Hawkins. When the Roses Bloom Again. Uncle Ben Hawkins.

243 Wreck of Number Nine. Dalhart. Wreck of Royal Palm. Dalhart.

506 Wreck of the Shenandoah. Dalhart. Stone Mountain Memorial. Dalhart.

Vocal Standard Selections or Songs of Yesterday

171 Home, Sweet Home. The Challenge Quartet. On the Banks of the Wabash. The Challenge Quartet.

172 When You're Gone I Won't Forget. Russell and Myrick. Till We Meet Again. Vernon Dalhart.

Only Silvertone 39¢

Made of the best suitable materials for the purpose. Will surprise and please by the purity and faithful reproduction of tones. Of as lasting a quality and as free from surface noises as it is possible to make them. Musically, scientifically and mechanically correct.

12K6201—Order by catalog number 12K6201, and give selection number of each record. All are 10-inch records. Shpg. wt., 2 lbs. **39c**

Popular Vocal Selections

3308 Ain't She Sweet.
My Idea of Heaven. Both by Jane Gray.

2690 Always. Irving Combs.
Down by the Winegar Woiks. Frank Howard.

3835 Baby Face. Arthur Fields.
Who Wouldn't? Arthur Fields.

2293 Barney Google. (Tenor and Baritone.) Jones and Hare.
I Love Me. (Tenor.) Clarke.

2902 Bye-Bye Blackbird. Irving Combs.
My Dream of the Big Parade. Curt Phillips.

2226 Call Me Back, Pal o' Mine. (Tenor.) Lewis James.
While the Years Roll By. (Tenor and Baritone.) Lewis James and Elliott Shaw.

2117 Casey Jones. (Male Quartet.) Shannon Four.
Steamboat Bill. (Baritone.) Ernst Hare.

2577 Collegiate. (Male Duet.)
The Farmer Took Another Load Away. (Male Duet.) Both by Jones and Hare.

3236 Could I? I Certainly Could.
Gimme a Little Kiss, Will Ya, Huh? Both by Confidential Charley.

2814 Hello, Aloha! How Are You? James and Raymond.
I'm Just Wild About Animal Crackers. Phillips and Moore.

3836 Hi Diddle Diddle. Jack Kaufman.
The Pump Song. Jack Kaufman.

3831 Hi Ho the Merrio. Jack Kaufman.
So's Your Old Man. Black Kids of Harmony.

2409 How Do You Do? (Comedy.) (Tenor and Baritone Duet.) Jones and Hare.
Go 'Long Mule. (Comedy.) Harry Raymond.

2806 How Many Times?
Lonesome and Sorry. Both by Irving Combs.

3813 I'd Climb the Highest Mountain If I Knew I'd Find You.
I've Found a Round About Way to Heaven. Both by Wilson Bros.

5043 If Tears Could Bring You Back to Me. Harold Charles.
Hush a Bye. (Quartet.) The Cardinal Quartet.

3305 I'm Looking Over a Four-Leaf Clover. The Harmonizers.
My Connecticut Gal. The Harmonizers.

3237 I'm Gonna Let the Bumble Bee Be.
Hooray for the Irish. Both by Honey Duke and His Uke.

2551 I'm Knee Deep in Daisies. (Baritone.) Arthur Fields.
I Wonder If We'll Ever Meet Again. (Tenor.) Tom Moore.

3306 I've Never Seen a Straight Banana. Jane Gray.
Hello, Cutie. Jane Gray.

4001 It Ain't Gonna Rain No Mo'.
Red Headed Music Maker. Both by Wendell Hall With His Ukulele.

2799 I Wish You Were Jealous. Arthur Fields.
When the Sun Goes Down on the Lonesome Pine. Harry Raymond.

3208 Just a Cottage Small.
Someone to Love. Both by Irving Kaufman.

3829 Lay My Head Beneath a Rose. Dalhart.
The Old Fiddler's Song. Dalhart.

3234 Let's Talk About My Sweetie.
So Does Your Old Mandarin. Both by Confidential Charley.

2123 Little Ford Rambled Right Along. (Tenor.) Jones.
Si's Been Drinking Cider. (Tenor and Baritone.) Bernard and Hare.

2060 Love Nest. (Tenor.) Hart.
Let the Rest of the World Go By. (Tenor and Contralto.) Hart and Terrell.

2582 Let Me Call You Sweetheart. (Tenor.) Lewis James.
New York Ain't New York Any More. (Tenor.) Tom Moore.

3278 Mary Lou.
Pretty Cinderella. Both by Honey Duke and His Uke.

2810 My Cutie's Due at Two to Two Today.
Thanks for the Buggy Ride. Both by Dave Landis.

3309 My Sunday Girl.
You'll Never Be Missed a Hundred Years From Now. Both by Jack Kaufman.

2040 Oh! What a Pal Was Mary. (Tenor.) Charles Hart.
Beautiful Ohio. (Tenor.) George Wilton Ballard.

2526 Oh! How I Miss You Tonight. (Tenor.) Sidney Mitchell.
Pal of My Cradle Days. (Tenor.) Charles Harrison.

3212 Sitting on Top of the World.
Don't Be Afraid to Come Home. Both by Irving Kaufman.

3214 Sleepy Time Gal.
Then I'll Be Happy. Both by West and Thomas.

2813 So's Your Old Lady.
As Long as the Gas Holds Out. Both by Phillips and Moore.

2262 Swanee River Moon. (Soprano and Contralto.) Nair and Williams.
Old Pal Why Don't You Answer Me? (Tenor.) Ballard.

3268 Thanks for the Buggy Ride.
It Don't Do Nothing But Rain. Both by West and Thomas.

2316 Ten Thousand Years From Now. (Tenor Solo.) Dalhart.
Just a Girl That Men Forget. (Tenor Solo.) Lewis James.

3277 That's Why I Love You. Jack Kaufman.
I'd Love to Meet That Old Sweetheart of Mine. Jack Kaufman.

5046 Thinking of You. (Quartet.) The Silvertone Four.
Take in the Sun, Hang out the Moon. (Quartet.) Belmont Garden Quartet.

2816 There's a New Star in Heaven Tonight, Rudolph Valentino. Fern Holmes.
Where Does She Live? Arthur Fields.

2355 That Old Gang of Mine. (Tenor Duet.)
Mickey Donohue. (Tenor Duet.) Both by Dalhart and Smalle.

2411 The Pal That I Loved Stole the Gal I Loved. (Tenor Solo.) George Wilton.
Jealous. (Tenor Solo.) Tom Moore.

2120 The Trail of the Lonesome Pine. (Contralto.) Amy Ellerman.
Little Bunch of Shamrocks. (Tenor and Baritone.) Ballard and Wheeler.

3209 Too Many Parties, Too Many Pals. Irving Kaufman.
You're Always a Baby to Mother. Billy West.

3500 The Old Brown Pants.
Stand Up and Sing for Your Father. Both by Frank Morris.

2692 Tie Me to Your Apron Strings Again.
That Certain Party. Both by Phillips and Moore.

2013 Till We Meet Again. (Tenor Duet.) Hart and James.
That Wonderful Mother of Mine. (Tenor.) Burr.

3529 Tonight's My Night With Baby.
Red Wine and Brew. Both by Harry Geis.

3830 Valencia. The Four Hooligans.
Where'd You Get Those Eyes? Vaughn Deleath.

2439 Way Out West in Kansas. Dalhart.
Oh, You Can't Fool An Old Hoss Fly. Hare.

3207 What Can I Say After I Say I'm Sorry?
Five Foot Two, Eyes of Blue. Both by Jane Gray.

2900 When the Red, Red Robin Comes Bob, Bob, Bobbin' Along. Irving Combs.
In the Middle of the Night. Wesley Davis.

2226 While the Years Roll By. (Tenor and Baritone Duet.) James and Shaw.
Call Me Back, Pal o' Mine. (Tenor Solo.) James.

2336 When Clouds Have Vanished and Skies Are Blue.
Pal of My Dreams. (Tenor Solo.) Both by Ballard.

2458 Yearning. (Tenor.) Moore.
Without You, Dear. (Tenor.) Ballard.

2557 Yes Sir, That's My Baby. (Male Duet.)
Every Little While. (Male Duet.) Both by Phillips and Moore.

Latest Vocal Selections

5044 Blue Skies. George DeWees.
Lonely Eyes. Harold Charles.

5045 Hello, Swanee, Hello. Jack Lane and His Uke.
I Can't Get Over a Girl Like You. Jack Lane and His Uke.

5042 High, High, High Up in the Hills. (Quartet.) The Silvertone Four.
I've Got the Girl. (Quartet.) The Cardinal Quartet.

2893 I Never See Maggie Alone. Phillips and Moore.
Bridget O'Flynn. Phillips and Moore.

2889 I'm Tellin' the Birds, How I Love You. Radio Kings.
Give Me a Ukulele. Radio Kings.

2886 In a Little Spanish Town. Radio Kings.
'Deed I Do. Radio Kings.

5047 Sam, the Old Accordion Man. Belmont Garden Quartet.
Everything's Made for Love. The Silvertone Four.

2895 What Does It Matter? Irving Combs.
Pal of My Heart. Chas. Wheeler.

2894 When I First Met Mary. Phillips and Moore.
She Said and I said. Radio Kings.

2888 Where Do You Worka, John? Radio Kings.
If My Baby Cooks (as Good as She Looks). Phillips and Moore.

Selections by W L S Radio Stars

We have now made it possible for you to hear your favorite W L S radio star on your phonograph. A record is always at hand; ready to play when you so desire.

BY CHUBBY PARKER (VOICE WITH BANJO)

5012—I'm a Stern Old Bachelor.
Bibalollie Boo.

5011 Nickety, Nackety, Now, Now, Now. Whoa, Mule!

5013 Oh, Suzanna.
Little Brown Jug.

BY WALTER PETERSON (HARMONICA AND GUITAR)

5009 Medley of Old Timers. No. 1:
{ Sidewalks of New York.
Let Me Call You Sweetheart.
Sweet Rosie O'Grady.

Medley of Old Timers. No. 2:
{ After the Ball.
In the Good Old Summer Time.
Peek-a-Boo.

BY W L S PLAYERS (VIOLIN, PIANO AND CELLO)

5010 The Old Timers (Waltz.)
Songs of the South.

BY TOMMY DANDURAND AND HIS BARN DANCE FIDDLERS WITH CALLERS

5039 Big Town Fling.
Larry O'Gaff.

5014 Haste to the Wedding.
Campbells Are Coming.

5015 Two-Step Quadrille.
Devil's Dream.

BY RALPH WALDO EMERSON (WLS STUDIO ORGAN)

5038 At the End of the Sunset Trail.
Swanee River, Old Kentucky Home.

5037 Silver Threads Among the Gold.
When You and I Were Young, Maggie.

5026 The World Is Waiting for the Sunrise.
Indian Love Call.

BY GRACE WILSON

5041 Carry Me Back to Old Virginia.
Honey Stay in Your Own Back Yard.

5040 Forget Me Not Means Remember Me.
Promise That You Won't Forget Me.

WALTER PETERSON,
The Kentucky Wonder Bean

Ralph Emerson

SEARS, ROEBUCK AND CO. WLS The World's Largest Store

Sensational Price Reductions
on These New BECKWITHS

46K382

$398.00

THINK OF IT! A genuine Beckwith player piano, famous for its tone quality, for less than $400.00, and a genuine Beckwith straight piano for only $275.00. **Here's real value for you, a genuine bargain such as is not equaled elsewhere in America today.** To sell Beckwiths at these prices is like offering United States Treasury Certificates at 75c on the dollar. These are New Instruments, new from the smallest screw to the last coat of varnish and made by master craftsmen who have been building Beckwiths for a quarter of a century. Constructed with all the faithful adherence to the ideals which from the first we have incorporated in every Beckwith. Guaranteed for 25 years with the same confidence in their promise of utmost satisfaction and offered with the knowledge that there is nothing finer, nothing better in tone, materials or workmanship for the money. These instruments are superior in their class, triumphs of successful manufacturing plans which we started many months ago to bring you the **greatest piano bargains that were ever offered.** Our tremendous cash resources, our unexcelled manufacturing facilities, our long experience in piano building are responsible for these huge savings we can now offer you. This is your opportunity! **Resolve today that you will have one of these splendid instruments in your home.** Our liberal, easy payment plan, our one price policy with no interest or extras to add, our 30-day free trial offer, our unqualified guarantee of satisfaction or your money back make the Beckwith the ideal instrument to buy.

$10.00 DOWN
$10.20 per Month

30-Day Free Trial   No Interest To Add

THE MODEL shown above is made in our most popular size, 4 feet 4 inches high and 5 feet wide. This player is fully equipped with all the latest improvements, containing every necessary attachment for reproducing the finest music by roll. Has a transposing device which will enable anyone instantly to change the key—indispensable for singing. Automatic sustaining pedal at just the right moment removes the dampers from the strings, giving that full loud pedal effect so noticeable in hand playing. Automatic tracking device keeps the roll running evenly over the tracker bar at all times. The scale is even and well balanced. The tonal quality is identical with our larger instruments. The case is double veneered, made in either genuine mahogany or American walnut, dull satin finish. Copper wound bass strings. Brass finish trimmings. Ivory keys. Here is a piano you will be proud to own. Shipping weight, 875 pounds. Shipped from factory in SOUTHERN INDIANA only.

46K382—Player piano, with player bench and 20 music rolls. $10.00 with order, balance $10.00 a month. In mahogany................ **$398.00**

For ukulele attachment add $10.00 to the price.
For walnut add $10.00 to the price.
Use Time Payment Order Blank on Page 1092.

YOU WILL like this new model Beckwith. It is 4 feet 4 inches long and 5 feet wide. This is the most popular size now and in great demand. It has the same rich, clear tone as our larger Concert size instruments. It is made just exactly like our Concert pianos with full length metal plate and quick repeating piano action. Spruce sounding board. Copper wound bass strings and ivory keys. Like the player above, the case is double veneered throughout and can be had in either genuine mahogany or walnut. Finish dull satin. Shipped from factory in SOUTHERN INDIANA. Shipping weight, 750 pounds.

46K381—Beckwith piano, including bench and instruction book, $10.00 with order, $10.00 a month. Mahogany...................... $275.00

For Walnut add $10.00 to the price.
Use Time Payment Order Blank on Page 1092.

$275.00

BECKWITH Pianos and Players Sold Only by Sears, Roebuck and Co.

46K381

If You Are Interested in Used Piano Bargains

Write for our complete list. These rebuilt instruments have all been reconditioned in our own factory, by the same expert piano makers who built them originally. They have been put in first class condition, inside and out, and bear the same 25-year guarantee as we place on our new Beckwiths. Except for slight evidence of use they are good as new. Write today and see how much you can save. We have some exceptionally attractive bargains.

BECKWITH *Challenges*

To Furnish BECKWITH
Buy Direct From the Factory and Save ⅓

BETWEEN the daylight and the dark, there is an hour that only music can fill. Nothing will take the place of song.

Turn to the Beckwith and release its clear, golden tones. In an instant the house that you have kept all day is home.

No musical training is necessary to play the New Era Beckwith; it plays by roll. Yet throughout its playing your hand is on the keyboard controlling its every tone. Here every mood is gratified. You can soften it to a whisper or raise it to a crescendo of glorious harmony. You can play it fast or slow, accompany voices or instruments.

Guaranteed 25 Years

Every Beckwith Piano is guaranteed for twenty-five years against any possible defect in material or workmanship. It is more than a guarantee. It is your assurance of absolute musical satisfaction, a quarter century of musical happiness. Not only is our guarantee a pledge of highest quality, but a symbol of the confidence that we, as manufacturers and designers, place in the performance, durability, and perfection of the Beckwith Piano.

Thirty-Day Trial

We do not want you to spend one cent in trying the New Era Beckwith in your home. After thirty days' trial, if not fully satisfied we will take the instrument back and return all your money, including freight and drayage charges. No matter where you buy, you will have to pay freight, for the charges are always added to the price by the dealer who sells the instrument. The freight from our factory to your station, however, is very little compared with the big saving you make.

Easy Monthly Payments

The small down payment is all you need send us for thirty days, and then only easy monthly payments that you can well afford. **You can play while you pay.**

There is no interest to add; no extra charge of any kind for this convenience. You pay only the price shown in the catalog description, plus the transportation charges and no more. Those prices are the World's Lowest for instruments of the **Beckwith's** Unchallenged Superiority.

$10.⁰⁰ DOWN $12.⁰⁰ A MONTH

For those of our customers who want something a little better than the average, for discriminating people who demand and appreciate the very latest in design, we offer the distinctive model shown above. With its many improvements and refinements it is one of the finest and most artistic player pianos we have ever offered. We do not hesitate to ask you to compare it with the highest priced player pianos of the day. Although it is the same size and construction throughout as the other two instruments shown on these pages, it is more expensive to make because of the carved trusses and pilasters. This makes a very handsome design, which is distinctive in appearance and will be a constant source of pleasure to any purchaser. As a piece of furniture, it can take its place in the most elaborate home. As a player piano, we know of nothing better from the standpoint of appearance, durability or performance. We highly recommend it to those who want something a little different. Has full length metal plate, highest grade player action, genuine ivory keys and other features found only in the most expensive instruments on the market. Comes in dull satin finish only. Size: 4 feet 4 inches high, 5 feet 1½ inches long, and 2 ft. 4 inches deep. Shipping weight, 875 pounds. **Shipped from factory in SOUTHERN INDIANA or NEW YORK CITY, NEW YORK.**

46K407—Player Piano in Mahogany With Player Bench and Twenty Music Rolls. $10.00 with order; balance, $12.00 a month.

For Walnut, add $10.00 to the price.
For Ukulele Attachment, add $10.00 to the price.
Use Time Payment Order Blank on Page 1092.

$465.⁰⁰

A special Piano Catalog has been printed to show our large selection of Beckwith Pianos. Every size, from the concert to the midget that stands only 3 feet 8 inches high, is represented. If you prefer a piano or player piano of a different type from those illustrated on these pages, send for this special Beckwith Piano Catalog 561K.

All COMPETITION
QUALITY at BECKWITH PRICES

WE always have built the Beckwith so well that it would give a generation of service—the kind of service that we can stand squarely back of with our written guarantee of satisfaction. We would never jeopardize our reputation for honest dealing by making a piano that would not, for years and years, give you the enjoyment, the pleasure, the pride of ownership that should be yours when you buy this finest of musical instruments.

The New Era Beckwith

This is the day of changed conditions in the home. Rooms are oftentimes not as large, or there is more demand for space to be used for other furnishings. The big, bulky, cumbersome piano that consumed a large part of the room and required a half dozen men to move from place to place, has gone. But its passing occasions no regrets. For in its place we have designed a new and finer instrument, the New Era Beckwith. New grace, new beauty, new pleasing lines in the case and new compactness in the construction make the New Era Beckwith the most modern, up to the minute piano on the market today. It is only 4 feet 4 inches high—takes up less room, is easier to move around, harmonizes better with other furnishings. Yet, notwithstanding the smaller size, nothing has been lost in the construction because of the more compact, more efficient use of space in the piano itself. **Neither does the reduced size affect the wonderful tone quality or the famous Beckwith durability.** We know from our own long experience in piano manufacturing and the exhaustive tests we have made in our own factory, that the New Era Beckwith is the counterpart in every particular, except weight and dimensions, of the old Beckwith. The apartment size piano or player is the favorite wherever pianos are now sold. Once you have seen it, once you have it installed in your home, you would have no other.

We can now offer the Apartment Size Beckwith at a lower price than asked anywhere for a really fine piano. We have cut size, **we have cut price**—the fine tone and the splendid workmanship which insure lifetime durability, are left in the new Beckwith. The standards of twenty years have not been altered. The Beckwith today, as yesterday, holds all honors as **the premier piano value of the world.**

No dealer has ever competed with us in fineness of tone quality. The Apartment Size Beckwith now has no rivals in price. No other store in the world can sell you a piano approaching the Beckwith at these low prices.

Full Length Metal Plate

It takes a well constructed back, supported by a full length cast iron plate, to stand the strain of about 20 tons' tension exerted by the strings of a piano. In the Beckwith, the plate runs the length and width of the piano and weighs approximately 155 pounds. You are gambling with the future when you buy a piano which does not have a full length heavy iron plate or a strong, well constructed back. Tone quality depends upon sufficient physical strength.

$10.00 DOWN $12.00 A MONTH
46K435

THE popular demand for a good player piano at a moderate price finds its answer in this New Era Beckwith. Here is a lifetime investment in happiness for all the family; here is the best player piano at the lowest price.

This latest, improved model in the new apartment size is thoroughly equipped to give you the greatest pleasure. A transposing device enables anyone to change the key instantly, an indispensable aid to singing. The automatic sustaining pedal removes the dampers from the strings at just the right moment to give that full, loud, pedal effect so noticeable in hand playing, while an automatic tracking device keeps the music roll running evenly over the tracker bar at all times. Only genuine ivory keys are used. Every advantage possessed by the most expensive instrument is here.

A well designed, well made case in the new apartment size of double veneer genuine mahogany or American walnut, dull satin finish, holds the full length metal plate. Double wound brass strings, selected to give the finest tone, and brass finish fittings make this the player piano without equal.

Size, 4 feet 4 inches high, 5 feet 1½ inches long, and 2 feet 4 inches deep. Shipping weight, 875 pounds. **Shipped from factory in NEW YORK CITY.**

46K435—Player Piano in Mahogany, with Player Bench and Twenty Music Rolls, $10.00 with order; balance, $12.00 a month. No interest to add **$450.00**

For Walnut, add **$10.00** to the price. For Ukulele Attachment, add **$10.00** to the price. **Use Time Payment Order Blank on page 1092.**

$10.00 DOWN $10.00 A MONTH

HERE is the piano for your home. Its sterling worth, its enduring goodness and its mellow, liquid tone quality will be constant sources of gratification to you in the years to come. With the knowledge gained from long experience, our designers have developed this fine piano for you. Expect from it the same tonal quality, the same durability and the same fine appearance of a more expensive instrument.

Made in the apartment size only, 4 feet 4 inches high, which is now so popular. Because of its small size, it is lighter in weight, easier to handle and more readily takes its place in the interior decorating scheme of your home.

Every feature of modern piano construction to improve the appearance, tone quality and durability has been incorporated in the two instruments on this page. The cases are veneered inside and out, the outer veneer being genuine figured mahogany, quarter sawed oak or American walnut. Comes only in dull satin finish. Pedals and exterior metal trimmings finished in brass.

Size, 5 feet 1½ inches long, 4 feet 4 inches high, 2 feet 1 inch wide. Shipping weight, 775 pounds. **Shipped from factory in SOUTHERN INDIANA or NEW YORK CITY.**

46K401—With Duet Bench and Instruction Book. In mahogany, $10.00 with order, $10.00 a month. No interest to add. **$324.00**

For Quarter Sawed Oak or Walnut, add $10.00 to the price. For Ukulele Attachment, add $10.00.
Use Time Payment Order Blank on Page 1092.

46K401

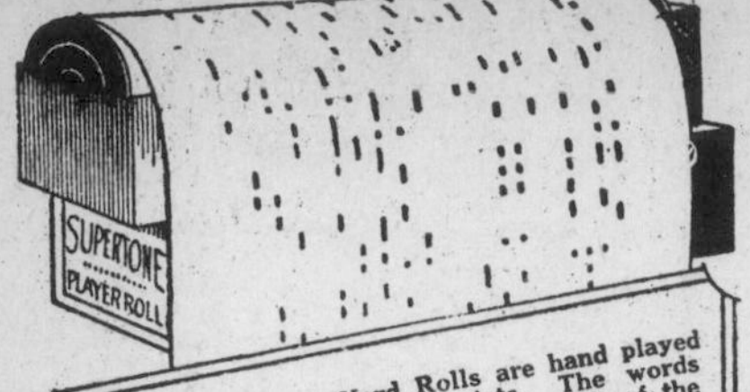

SUPERTONE WORD ROLLS

For latest hits send for special list 9506K.

43c EACH

Supertone Player Word Rolls are hand played reproductions by famous pianists. The words are plainly printed on the right hand side of the rolls. All popular rolls contain two verses and two choruses.

All Supertone Player Rolls are mechanically perfect and musically correct. They are put up in neat and serviceable strawboard boxes covered in imitation of leather.

SUPERTONE PLAYER ROLL

12K5905—Order by Catalog No. 12K5905 and Roll Number
Shipping Weight, Each, ¾ Pound

Always Give a Few Extra Titles as Second Choice

FOX TROTS

Roll No. Title
5959 A Lane in Spain
5895 **Ain't She Sweet?**
5862 A Little Music in the Moonlight
5929 All I Want Is You
5623 Alone at Last
5643 Angry
5651 Are You Sorry?
5801 As Long As I Have You
5930 **At Sundown**
5794 **Baby Face**
5630 Bam Bam Bammy Shore
5811 Barcelona
5635 Because of You
5842 **Beside a Garden Wall**
5855 Black Bottom
5887 **Blue Skies**
5790 Breezin' Along With the Breeze
5775 **Bye, Bye, Blackbird**
5679 Clap Hands Here Comes Charlie
5756 Could I—I Certainly Could
5831 Cover Me Up With the Sunshine
5896 **Crazy Words, Crazy Tune**
5903 Deed I Do
5812 Deep Henderson
5709 Dinah
5832 Don't Be Angry
5819 Don't Sing Aloha When I Go
5770 **Drifting and Dreaming**
5904 **Everything's Made for Love**
5681 Five Foot Two, Eyes of Blue
5829 For My Sweetheart
5909 **Forgive Me**
5722 Gimme a Little Kiss, Will Ya, Huh?
5962 **Gonna Get a Girl**
5789 Hello, Aloha, How Are You?
5866 Hello, Bluebird
5958 **Hello, Cutie**
5910 Hello, Swanee, Hello
5774 **Hi Ho the Merrio**
5760 Hi Diddle Diddle
5892 **High, High Up in the Hills**
5518 Honest and Truly
5912 **Hoosier Sweetheart**
5870 How Could Red Riding Hood?
5779 How Many Times?
5815 I Don't Want Nobody But You
5694 I Love My Baby
5913 I Love You, But I Don't Know Why
5934 I Love the College Girls
5894 I Never See Maggie Alone.
5834 I Never Knew What the Moonlight Could Do
5856 I Wanna Be Known as Susie's Feller
5723 I Wish You Were Jealous of Me
5935 I Wonder How I Look When I'm Asleep
5749 I'd Climb the Highest Mountain
5835 **I'd Love to Call You My Sweetheart**
5924 Idolizing
5641 If I Had a Girl Like You
5595 If You Knew Susie
5914 **If You See Sally**
5839 I'm Gonna Park Myself in Your Arms
5780 I'm in Love With You, That's Why
5897 **I'm Looking Over a Four-Leaf Clover**
5791 I'm Lonely Without You
5682 I'm Sittin' on Top of the World
5860 I'm Telling the Birds, Tellin' the Bees How I Love You
5902 I've Never Seen a Straight Banana
5932 I've Gotta Get Myself Somebody to Love
5803 In a Little Garden
5558 Indian Love Call
5805 In My Gondola
5400 It Ain't Gonna Rain No Mo'
5915 **It All Depends on You**
5874 **It Made You Happy When You Made Me Cry**
5820 It's a Happy Old World After All
5854 Just a Birdseye View of My Old Kentucky Home
5828 Just a Little Dance
5846 Keep a Little Sunshine in Your Heart
5654 Kinky Kid's Parade
5848 Lay Me Down to Sleep in Carolina
5696 Let's Talk About My Sweetie
5916 Lonely Eyes
5742 Lonesome and Sorry
5776 Looking at the World Through Rose Colored Glasses
5852 **Mary Lou**
5824 **Meadow Lark**
5530 Me and the Boy Friend
5764 Meet Me Tonight in Dream Land
5851 **Me, Too (Ho-Ho! Ha-Ha!)**
5898 **Moonbeams, Kiss Her for Me**
5613 Moonlight and Roses
5877 **Moonlight on the Ganges**
5519 Morning
5821 My Cutie's Due at Two to Two Today
5865 My Girl Has Eye Trouble
5937 **My Idea of Heaven (Is Being in Love With You)**

Roll No. Title
5936 Muddy Waters
5938 Nesting Time
5940 Night Time in Picardy
5946 Oh! Baby, Don't We Get Along
5650 Oh Boy, What a Girl
5631 Oh Say Can I See You Tonight
5807 Only You and Lonely Me
5818 On the Riviera
5700 Paddlin' Madeline Home
5719 Poor Papa
5939 Positively, Absolutely (Does She Love Me)
5816 Precious
5729 Pretty Little Baby
5947 Red Lips, Kiss My Blues Away
5961 Rio Rita
5676 Roll 'Em Girls
5792 Roses
5920 **Sam the Old Accordion Man**
5701 Shake That Thing
5843 Shanghai Honeymoon
5849 She Knows Her Onions
5678 Show Me the Way to Go Home
5670 Sleepy Time Gal
5685 Smile a Little Bit

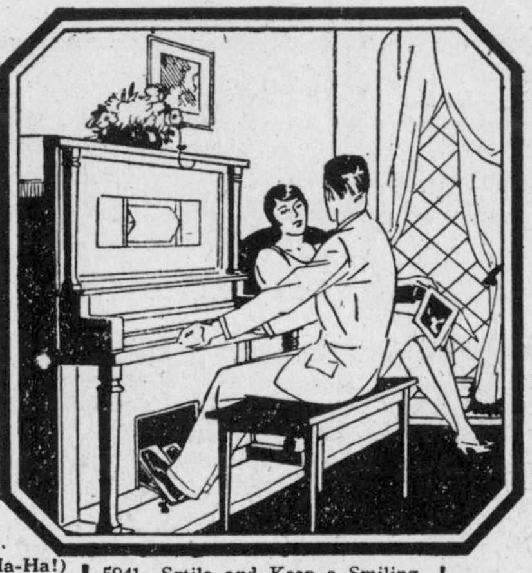

5941 Smile and Keep a Smiling
5762 Somebody's Lonely
5806 **Someone Is Losin' Susan**
5922 **Song of the Wanderer**
5634 Sonya
5617 Summer Nights
5864 Sunday
5850 Sweet Little Mammy
5885 Take in the Sun, Hang Out the Moon

Roll No. Title
5943 Take Your Finger Out of Your Mouth
5717 Talking to the Moon
5951 Tenderly Think of Me
5889 Tell Me Tonight
5693 Thanks for the Buggy Ride
5659 That Certain Party
5845 That Night in Araby
5825 That's My Girl
5900 **That's My Hap, Hap, Happiness**
5954 That's What I Think of You
5772 **That's Why I Love You**
5810 The Little Black Mustache
5687 Then I'll Be Happy
5813 The Pump Song
5884 There Ain't No Maybe in My Baby's Eyes
5859 There's a Little White House Where the Red, Red Roses Grow
5957 There's Something Nice About Everyone
5879 Thinking of You
5688 Tie Me to Your Apron Strings
5838 Trudie
5837 Trying to Forget
5766 Ting-a-Ling
5823 Turkish Towel
5773 **Valencia**
5691 What Can I Say After I Say I'm Sorry?
5933 When Day Is Done
5888 **When I First Met Mary**
5781 When the Red, Red Robin Comes Bob, Bob, Bobbin' Along
5928 **When You're in Love**
5785 Where Did You Get Those Eyes
5883 **Where Do You Worka, John?**
5956 Where the Wild, Wild Flowers Grow
5514 Where's My Sweetie Hiding?
5817 While the Years Go Drifting By
5901 **Yankee Rose**
5572 Yearning Just for You
5610 Yes, Sir, That's My Baby
5925 You Can't Cry Over My Shoulder
5782 You Gotta Know How to Love
5890 **You're the One for Me**

WALTZES

5731 A Night of Love
5716 A Coal Miner's Dream
5692 Always
5769 **At Peace With the World**
1010 Beautiful Ohio
5847 Because I Love You
5833 Blame It on the Waltz
5826 Cherie I Love You
5918 Dawn of Tomorrow

Roll No. Title
5948 **Falling in Love With You**
5011 Hawaiian Dreams
5012 Hawaiian Nights
5911 **Honolulu Moon**
5949 I Could Waltz Forever With You, Sweetheart
5927 I'll Take Care of Your Cares
5882 **In a Little Spanish Town**
5533 Let Me Call You Sweetheart
5640 Let Us Waltz as We Say Goodbye
5960 **Lonesome Waltz**
5917 May God Bless You Mother for All That You've Done for Me
1066 Missouri Waltz
5029 My Isle of Golden Dreams
5577 Oh How I Miss You Tonight
1078 One, Two, Three, Four
5536 Only a Weaver of Dreams
5589 Pal of My Cradle Days
5919 **Put Your Arms Where They Belong**
5899 **Rock Me to Sleep In an Old Rocking Chair**
5950 **Russian Lullaby**
5861 School Day Sweethearts
5804 Sleepy Head
5942 So Blue
5620 Sometime
5083 Sweet Hawaiian Moonlight
5952 That Saxophone Waltz
5953 That's What I Call a Pal
5964 The Night of Love
5761 The Prisoner's Sweetheart
5797 The Good Bad Girl
5209 Three o'Clock in the Morning
1099 Till We Meet Again
5891 **Tonight You Belong to Me**
5689 Too Many Parties and Too Many Pals
5827 Trail of Dreams
5822 There's a New Star in Heaven Tonight (Rudolph Valentino)
5893 **What Does It Matter**
5535 When You and I Were Seventeen
5945 Who Are You Fooling Tonight
5672 Wreck of the Shenandoah
5886 Yesterday

BALLADS

5225 Call Me Back, Pal o' Mine
5705 Convict and the Rose
5673 Death of Floyd Collins
5727 Dream of the Miner's Child
5944 Far Away Bells, The
5809 I Want a Pardon for Daddy
5711 Just a Cottage Small (By a Waterfall)
5955 Just an Ivy Covered Shack
5857 Loney Acres in the West
5830 My Heart Will Tell Me So
5795 Song of the Volga Boatman
5618 **The Prisoner's Song**
5600 The Wreck on the Southern Old '97
5704 **The Letter Edged in Black**
5713 The Little Rosewood Casket
5131 When I'm Gone You'll Soon Forget
5130 When You're Gone I Won't Forget
5863 Within the Prison of My Dreams

12K5905—Standard and Sacred 43c Each

Roll No. Title
168 A Dream
1001 A Perfect Day
161 Abide With Me
163 Adeste Fidelis
5438 After the Ball
101 All Hail the Power of Jesus Name
104 Aloha Oe
102 America
1141 America Forever
184 American Heart Songs (Darling Nellie Gray, Home Sweet Home, Etc.)
1134 At Dawning (I Love You)
5648 **Beautiful Isle of Somewhere**
169 Blue Bells of Scotland
1013 Break the News to Mother
170 Calm as the Night
5246 **Carry Me Back to Old Virginny**
5006 Casey Jones
145 Columbia the Gem of the Ocean
128 Coming Thro' the Rye
132 Darling Nellie Gray
191 Deep River (Old Negro Melody)
5101 **Down the Trail to Home, Sweet Home**
5585 Drowsy Waters
1142 Entrance of the Gladiators
106 **Face to Face**
5638 From the Land of the Sky Blue Water
1139 God Be With You Till We Meet Again
164 Hark, the Herald Angels Sing
192 He Leadeth Me
1035 Holy City, The
107 Home, Sweet Home
172 How Firm a Foundation
157 I Know That My Redeemer Liveth
5583 I Love You Truly
108 I Need Thee Every Hour
167 I'll Take You Home Again, Kathleen
5923 I'm a Stern Old Bachelor
1045 In the Baggage Coach Ahead
109 In the Evening by the Moonlight
173 In the Garden
5019 In the Shade of the Old Apple Tree
5020 It's a Long Way to Tipperary
155 Jesus, Lover of My Soul
189 Jingle Bells
141 Juanita
142 Just Before the Battle Mother
5022 Keep the Home Fires Burning
175 Killarney
151 Lead, Kindly Light
165 Let the Lower Lights Be Burning
5025 **Let the Rest of the World Go By**
160 Love's Old Sweet Song
139 Marching Through Georgia.
1145 Midnight Fire Alarm
5584 **Mighty Lak' a Rose**
5027 Mother Machree.
112 My Old Kentucky Home
1073 My Wild Irish Rose
5931 Nickity, Nockity, Now Now, Now
148 Nearer, My God, to Thee
162 Nursery Rhymes—By Baby Buntin', Three Blind Mice, Mary Had a Little Lamb, etc.)
1077 Oh, How I Hate to Get Up in the Morning.

FOREIGN WORD ROLLS

We have a very fine collection of word rolls in the Italian, German, Polish and Bohemian languages. If interested write for our Special Circular 6813K. Sent postpaid on request.

195 Oh Susanna
130 Oh, Promise Me
144 O Sole Mio (My Sunshine)
138 Old Black Joe
5103 Old Pal, Why Don't You Answer Me?
185 Old Southern Songs (Old Kentucky Home, Old Black Joe, etc.)
194 Olden Time Melodies (Sweet Rosie O'Grady, Sidewalks of New York)
1079 On the Banks of the Wabash
115 Onward Christian Soldiers
183 **On Wisconsin**
177 Over the Stars There Is Rest
1146 Paul Revere's Ride
5041 Red Wing
152 Rock of Ages
111 Rosary, The—Nevin
188 Sacred Roll (Worship the King, Hail the Power of Jesus' Name, etc.)
190 Safe in the Arms of Jesus
166 Saviour, Like a Shepherd Lead Us
187 Sidewalks of New York
117 Silent Night
5044 Silver Bell
1086 **Silver Threads Among the Gold**
1140 Softly and Tenderly Jesus Is Calling
1147 Soldiers of the Sea
5072 Somewhere a Voice Is Calling
5046 **Star of the East**
113 Star Spangled Banner, The
118 Swanee River
159 Sweet Adeline
5077 Sweet Bunch of Daises
5250 Sweet Bye and Bye
120 Sweet Hour of Prayer
197 Sweetest Story Ever Told
179 The Church in the Wildwood
180 The Lost Chord
181 The Message of the Violet
5586 **The Old Rugged Cross**
1149 The Rainbow Division
1148 The Stars and Stripes Forever
5051 There's a Long, Long Trail
1131 There's a Mother Old and Gray
1100 Trail of the Lonesome Pine
1101 Turkey in the Straw
137 Way Down Yonder in the Cornfield
121 What a Friend We Have in Jesus
1138 When the Roll Is Called Up Yonder
182 When They Ring the Golden Bells
122 **When You and I Were Young, Maggie**
123 Where Is My Wandering Boy Tonight?
1121 Where the River Shannon Flows
158 Where the Silvery Colorado Wends Its Way
1104 Where the Sunset Turns the Ocean's Blue to Gold
149 Whispering Hope
140 Yankee Doodle
198 You'll Never Miss Mother 'Till She's Gone

Powerful Pump for Player Piano

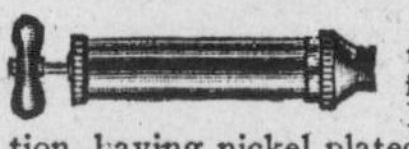

This pump is very valuable to piano tuners in locating defective notes caused by dirt. Made of very heavy construction, having nickel plated brass cylinder. Length, about 9 inches; diameter, 1½ inches.

12K5294—Shipping weight, 1¼ pounds **$2.10**

33c EACH

SUPERTONE INSTRUMENTAL ROLLS

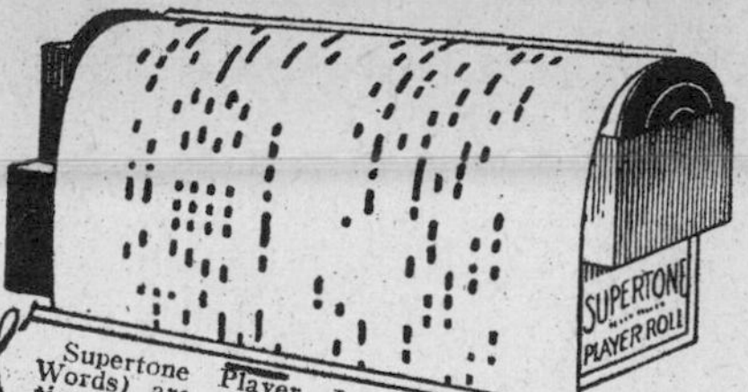

Supertone Player Instrumental Rolls (No Words) are played from the original composition as written.

All Supertone Player Rolls are mechanically perfect and musically correct. They are put up in neat and serviceable strawboard boxes covered in imitation of leather.

We especially recommend titles listed in heavy type.

Always give a few extra titles as second choice.

SUPERTONE PLAYER ROLL

For 88-Note Player Pianos

12K5921—Order by Catalog No. 12K5921 and Roll Number
Shipping Weight, 3/4 Pound

Marches

Roll No.	Title
10042	Across the Border
10090	American Patrol
10044	Army and Navy March
10197	Boy Scouts of America
10094	Clayton's Grand March
10012	Creole Belles
10015	**Dixie Darling**
10150	El Capitan (Sousa)
10152	General Grant's March
10103	Hands Across the Sea
10178	Heaven's Artillery
10105	High School Cadets
10203	Italian Royal March
10110	King Cotton (Sousa)
10170	La Sorella
10205	Lincoln Centennial March
20076	Lohengrin Wedding March, Part 1
20077	Lohengrin Wedding March, Part 2
10158	Manhattan Beach March
10207	Midnight Flyer
10244	Military March
10160	Military Parade
10031	**National Emblem March**
10163	**Our Director's March**
10179	Palace of Peace
10032	Panama-Pacific March
10210	Paul Revere's Ride
10184	Rapid Fire March
10165	**Repasz Band March.** Very harmonious and stirring
10064	Seventh Regiment March I. N. G.
20058	Sousa March Medley
10066	Spirit of Independence
10119	**Stars and Stripes Forever**
10213	Thunderer, The
10214	Tipperary Guards
10255	Under the Double Eagle
10040	U. S. Field Artillery
10141	Washington Post (Sousa)
20078	Wedding March (Mendelssohn), Part 1
20079	Wedding March (Mendelssohn), Part 2

Waltzes for Dancing

Roll No.	Title
10043	American Waltzes—Containing Swanee River, Old Kentucky Home, etc.
10215	Autumn Leaves
10216	Bride's Waltz
10089	Cecile
20070	Dream of Heaven (A Pretty and Dreamy Melody), Part 1
20071	Dream of Heaven, Part 2
10016	**Drowsy Waters** (Wailana) Hawaiian Waltz
10124	Floreine (Syncopated)
10020	**Hawaiian Dreams** With imitations of the Hawaiian Guitar
10226	Hawaiian Hula
10227	Hawaiian Nights
10021	Hawaiian Waltz Medley
10056	Hesitation Waltz
10026	Just a Night in Dreamland
10237	**Kiss of Spring**
10220	La Spagnola (Wonderful Spanish Waltz)
10221	Lost Hope (Speranze Perdute, Mandolin and Guitar arrangement)
10229	Merry Widow Waltz
10058	Missouri Waltz
10059	Moonlight Waltz
20068	My Treasure (Tesoro Mio) Italian Waltz, Part 1
20069	My Treasure (Tesoro Mio) Italian Waltz, Part 2
10228	Myona (Hawaiian)
10230	Nights of Gladness
10067	Sweet Luana (Hawaiian)
10037	Those Hawaiian Melodies
10069	Venetian Nights
10070	Waters of Venice
20072	Wedding of the Winds, Part 1
20073	Wedding of the Winds, Part 2
10086	Whispers of Love

Concert Waltzes

Roll No.	Title
10144	**Amoureuse**
10081	Inamorata Beloved
10148	Black Hawk
10149	Edelweiss Glide
10151	Frolic of the Frogs
20805	Grand Canyon of Arizona
20054	Love's Dreamland Waltz
20080	Over the Waves, Part 1
20081	Over the Waves, Part 2

Reveries

Roll No.	Title
10131	Apple Blossoms
10093	Beautiful Star of Heaven
10185	**By the Fireside.** Very Beautiful Melody
10224	Chapel Chimes
10098	Convent Bells
20084	Evening Chimes, Part 1
20085	Evening Chimes, Part 2
10100	Falling Waters
10113	Meditation (Morrison)
10122	Midnight Chimes
10115	Monastery Bells
10161	**Moonlight on the Ocean**
10162	Old Cathedral Chimes
10116	Robin's Return
10117	Sabbath Chimes
10118	Shadows on the Water
10167	Star of the Sea
10078	**Woodland Echoes**

Rags

Roll No.	Title
10004	At a Georgian Camp Meeting (Cake Walk)
10005	Black and White Rag
10013	**Dill Pickles** (Very Raggy)
10029	Maple Leaf Rag
10286	Nola
10034	Red Pepper
10035	Smoky Mokes (Cake Walk)
10036	ThatGoshDarnTwo-StepRag

Blues

Roll No.	Title
10257	All Star Jazz Band Blues
10258	Arkansas Blues
10259	Baby Won't You Please Come Home?
10265	Crazy Blues
10274	Lonesome Lovesick Blues
10276	Missouri Blues
10284	Whistling Blues

Descriptive

Roll No.	Title
10087	**Barcarolle** (Tales of Hoffman)
10091	Battle of Waterloo
10079	Ben-Hur Chariot Race
10006	Blue Bells of Scotland
10080	Burning of Rome
10235	**Dance of the Demons**
10088	Jolly Blacksmith
10132	Jolly Coppersmith
10027	Just as the Ship Went Down
10114	Midnight Fire Alarm
10245	Moonlight on the Hudson
10076	Napoleon's Last Charge
10120	The Storm
10077	**Twittering of the Birds**
10072	Wreck of the Titanic

Standard and Light Classics

Roll No.	Title
10002	All Hands 'Round
10145	**Angels' Serenade**
10146	Anvil Chorus
10147	Ave Maria (Bach-Gounod)
10293	By the Waters of Kalula (Hawaiian)
10048	Chicken Reel
20053	Chimes of Normandy
10014	Dixie
10051	Dream of the Shepherdess
10292	Elegie
10019	Glow Worm
10073	Good Old Fashioned Reels
20082	Hearts and Flowers. (A Flower Song), Part 1
20083	Hearts and Flowers, Part 2
10022	Hiawatha
10106	Hornpipes
10154	Humoreske Op. 101
10107	Hungarian Dances, No. 6
10291	La Golondrina
10111	La Paloma (Mexican)
10156	**Longing for Home**
10112	Maiden's Prayer
10288	Melody in F
10287	Melody (Dawes)
10290	Minuet in G
10082	Mocking Bird (Paraphrase) With bird imitations
10159	Mighty Lak a Rose (Nevin)
10123	Narcissus (Water Scene)
10171	Rustic Dance
10289	Souvenir
10068	Too Much Ginger
10039	Turkey in the Straw

Operatic

Roll No.	Title
20040	**Bohemian Girl**
10249	Carmen
20042	Cavalleria Rusticana
20063	Firefly Musical Comedy
20074	Il Trovatore, Part 1
20075	Il Trovatore, Part 2
10250	La Traviata
10157	Lucia di Lammermoor

Overtures

Roll No.	Title
20064	Poet and Peasant, Part 1
20065	Poet and Peasant, Part 2
20066	William Tell, Part 1
20067	William Tell, Part 2

SHEET MUSIC

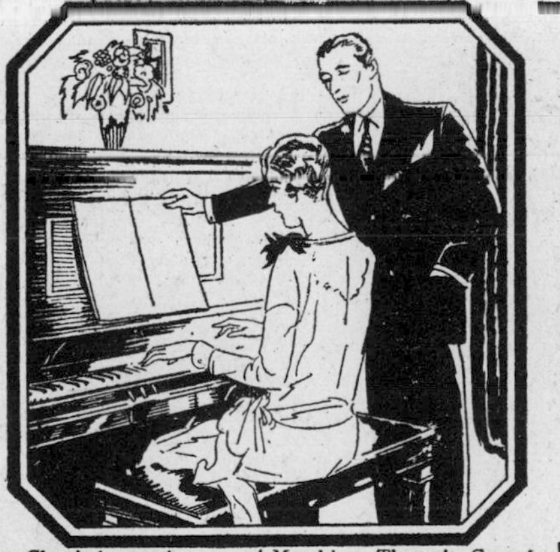

Standard, Operatic and Classic

Give catalog number and names of selections desired. Always give a few extra titles as second choice.

12K0000—SONGS WITH PIANO ACCOMPANIMENT. 15 copies for.......... **79c** Each.......................... **6c**

Shipping weight, 15 copies, 1¼ pounds.

Adeste Fidelis
Aloha Oe—Liliuokalani
Alone—Newman
Anchored—Watson
Angels' Serenade—Braga
Anvil Chorus
Ave Maria—Bach-Gounod
Barcarolle—From Tales of Hoffman—Offenbach
Battle Cry of Freedom
Beauty's Eyes—Tosti
Believe Me If All Those Endearing Young Charms
Calvary—medium voice
Ciribiribin
Columbia, the Gem of the Ocean—Shaw
Come Back to Erin
Dixie Land—Emmett
Dream of Paradise—Gray
Eili, Eili
Eyes So Tender—Kemble
Flower of the Everglade
Good-Bye—Tosti
Home, Sweet Home
How Can I Forget You?
Humoreske
I Think of You by Day and Dream of You by Night
If I Only Had a Sweetheart Just Like You
In Old Madrid—Trotere
In the Valley of Tears
Jerusalem—Parker
Just Before the Battle, Mother
Kathleen Mavourneen
Last Rose of Summer
Longing—Burke
Lost Chord—low voice
Love's Old Sweet Song
Marching Through Georgia
My Country, 'Tis of Thee
Massa's in the Cold, Cold Ground
My Darling Nellie Gray
My Genevieve—Verona
My Old Kentucky Home
Nearer, My God, to Thee
'Neath the Pines of Vermont
Old Black Joe—Foster
Old Folks At Home
On the Farm in Old Missouri
One Sweetly Solemn Thought
O Sole Mio
O That We Two Were Maying
Rock of Ages
Rocked in the Cradle of the Deep
Sextette From Lucia
Silent Night, Holy Night
Song of the Volga Boatmen
Spring Song—Mendelssohn
Star Spangled Banner
Still as the Night
Take Me Back to My Own Little Home, Sweet Home
Tenting on the Old Camp Ground
The Light That Failed
The Palms—high voice—Faure
The Palms—low voice—Faure
The Rosary—Welles
Way Down South in Dixie
When You and I Were Young, Maggie
Whispering Hope
Yankee Doodle, Guard Your Coast

Instrumental Piano Music—(No Words)

12K0650—15 copies for......(Shpg. wt., 15 copies, 1¼ lbs.).... **79c Each.. 6c**

Across the Hot Sands
Adoration Meditation
After Dark on Broadway
Alpine Hut
An Arabian Scout—Two-Step
Angel's Dream—Lange
Anvil Chorus—Krausse
Arkansaw Traveler
Bashful Betty—Two-Step
Battle of Waterloo
Beautiful Blue Danube Waltzes—Strauss
Birds of Paradise
Birth of Love Waltzes
Black Hawk Waltzes
Bohemian Girl—Balfe
Bridal Chorus (Lohengrin)
Camp of the Gypsies
Cavalleria Rusticana
Chapel in the Forest
Charge of the Uhlans
Citizen's Galop—Volti
Colonial Guards March
Con Amore—Beaumont
Consolation—Mendelssohn
Consuela March
Convent Bells—Spindler
Corn Flower Waltzes
Dancing in the Barn—Schottische
Danube Wave Waltzes
Devoted Hearts
Dorothy—S. Smith
Dream of the Shepherdess
Dying Poet—Gottschalk
Edelweiss Glide
Edelweiss Pure as Snow
Elegie—Massenet
Esmeralda Waltz
Evening Star—Liszt
Evergreen Waltz
Fairy Wedding Waltz
Falling Star—Reverie
Falling Waters—Truax
Farewell to the Piano—Beethoven
Faust—Gounod
FifthNocturne,Op.52-Leybach
Flatterer, The
Flower Song—Lange
Frolic of the Frogs
Funeral March—Chopin
General Grant's March
General Smith's March
Gertrude's Dream Waltz
Good Evening Schottische
Gun Powder Rag
Gypsy Dance
Haymaker's Barn Dance
Heather Bells—Lange
Heather Rose—Lange
Heavenward March
Hidden Charms
Highland Fling
Home, Sweet Home (variations)
Huckleberry Finn
Humoreske—Dvorak
Hungarian Dance No. 5
Il Trovatore—Verdi—Dorn
I Wish I Were in Dixie (variations)
Invitation to the Dance
Irish Washer Woman
Jolly Fellows Waltz
La Fountaine, Op. 221
La Paloma (The Dove)
La Sorella March
Last Hope—Gottschalk
Le Secret—Intermezzo
Light Cavalry Overture
Lily of the Valley Mazurka
Listen to the Mocking Bird
Little Moonshine Two-Step
Longing for Home
Love's Dreamland Waltz
Love's Greeting
Lustspiel Overture
Maiden's Prayer
Marching Through Georgia
Martha—Selections
Melodies of Scotland
Melody in F—Rubinstein
Memories of the South
Merry Widow Waltzes
Mignonette (or Pink)
Minuet—Paderewski
Monastery Bells—Wely
Moonlight Meander
Morning Prayer
Mountain Bell—Schottische
Murmuring Zephyrs
Music Box—Liebich
My Old Kentucky Home
Nearer, My God, to Thee
Old Black Joe—Foster
Old Folks at Home
OldOaken Bucket (variations)
Orange Blossom Waltzes
Orvetta Waltzes—Spencer
Over the Waves Waltzes
Overture Patriotic
Overtures of Irish Melodies
Peaceful River Waltzes
Pearly Dewdrops Mazurka
Peri Waltzes
Poet and Peasant Overture—Suppe
Polish Dance
Prince Imperial Galop
Princeton Tiger—March
Qui Vive Galop
Rank and File—Lange
Recess Time—March—Powell
Remember Me (Far Away)
Return of the Conqueror
Rippling Waves—Milward
Romance of Love—Engelmann
Roses and Thorns—Waltz
Rustic Dance—Howell
Rustle of Spring
Salut a Pesth March
Salute the Flag—March and Two-Step
Scarf Dance—Chaminade
Schubert's Serenade—Liszt
Second Mazurka—Godard
Second Waltz—Godard
Serenata—Moszkowski
Sextette from "Lucia"
Shepherd Boy—Wilson
Silver Stars—Bohm
Silvery Thistle (L'Argentine)
Silvery Waves—Wyman
Simple Confessions—Thome
Song of India
Sounds From the Ringing Rocks
Souvenir—Drdla
Spring Song—Mendelssohn
Starlight Waltz
Storm, The—Weber
SweetBye andBye (variations)
Tales of Hoffman
Tam o' Shanter
Tannhauser March
Tarantelle—Heller
The Angel of Love
The City Troop March
The Drum Major—March
The Elks Carnival March
The Old Cathedral Chimes
The Palms—Leybach
Thine Own—Lange
Thunder and Lightning
Traumerei—Schumann
Tulip, Op. 111
Twentieth Century March
Under the Double EagleMarch
Valse Bleue—Margis
Valse, Op. 83—Durand
Voice of Long Ago
Warblings at Eve
Water Lilies, Novelette
Waves of the Ocean Galop
Wayside Rose—Fischer
Wedding March — Mendelssohn
When You and I Were Young, Maggie (variations)
Whisperings of Love
William Tell Overture
Woodland Echoes
Zampa Overture

Children's Piano Pieces

Chopsticks
Cinderella March
Dinner Party Waltz
Evening Schottische
Garland of Roses—Waltz
Hey, Diddle, Diddle Galop
Jack and Jill Polka
Little Bo Peep
Little Dancer's Mazurka
Little Dancer's Polka
Little Dancer's Waltz
Little Fairy March
Little Fairy Schottische
Little Fairy Waltz
Love Song
Polka Joyeuse
Primrose Waltz
Robinson Crusoe
Rondino
Sack Waltz
Twilight Valse
You and I Waltz

Parcel Post, Express and Freight Rates Are on Pages 542 to 545

Methods and Folios

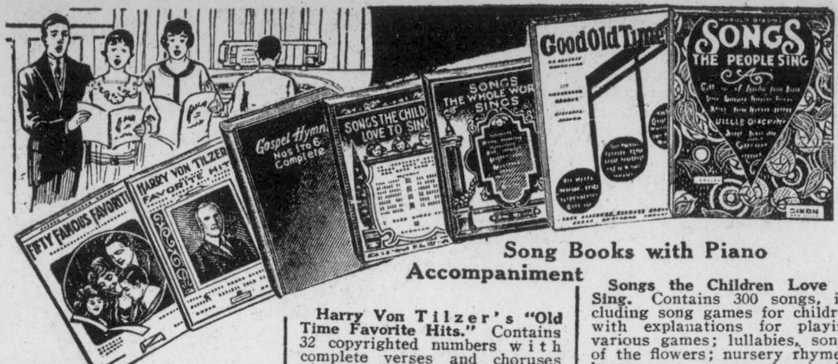

Song Books with Piano Accompaniment

Fifty Famous Favorites. Contains fifty songs complete with words and music, such as "Banks of the Wabash," "In the Good Old Summertime," "The Sidewalks of New York," etc. Shipping weight, 5 ounces.
12K1601.......... 35c

For Books on Entertainment See Page 783

Harry Von Tilzer's "Old Time Favorite Hits." Contains 32 copyrighted numbers with complete verses and choruses of each. The kind Mother and Dad used to sing. It will make them happy to sing these old favorites with you again. Such selections as: "Wait Till the Sun Shines Nellie," "Down on the Farm," "Where the Morning Glories Twine Around the Door," "The Green Grass Grew All Around," etc. Shipping weight, 8 ounces.
12K1623.......... 39c

Gospel Hymns Nos. 1 to 6. Complete with words and music. Bound in cloth. 739 hymns. Shipping weight, 2 pounds.
12K1608.......... $1.79

Songs the Children Love to Sing. Contains 300 songs, including song games for children with explanations for playing various games; lullabies, songs of the flowers; nursery rhymes, home songs, songs of animals, songs of birds, sacred songs, songs of Christmas, songs of our country, etc. 256 pages. Shpg. wt., 1½ lbs.
12K1611.......... 98c

Songs the Whole World Sings. Contains 204 songs, 254 pages. Children's songs, home songs, love songs, operatic songs, patriotic songs, etc. It is arranged so that the songs can be sung or played as piano solos. It is printed from engraved plates and bound so that it lies flat when opened. Shipping weight, 1¼ pounds.
12K1600.......... 98c

Good Old Timers. 75 songs you can't forget. Contains "Darktown Strutters' Ball," "Farmer in the Dell," "Turkey in the Straw," etc. Shipping weight, 8 ounces.
12K1605.......... 35c

Harold Dixon's "Songs the People Sing." A collection of world famous songs. Such musical gems as "Whispering Hope," "Song of the Volga Boatman," "O Sole Mio," "In the Gloaming," and about 50 others equally as good. Arranged for either instrumental or vocal with Uke diagrams; also instructions on how to play the Uke. 95 pages. Shipping weight, 8 ounces.
12K1621.......... 39c

Haviland's Good Old Songs. (Not illustrated.) A collection of 25 copyrighted songs that never grow old, such as "Blue Bell," "Good Old U. S. A.," "College Life March," "Down in Jungletown," etc. All with Uke accompaniment in diagram form with instructions on how to play. 43 pages. Shipping weight, 8 ounces.
12K1622.......... 39c

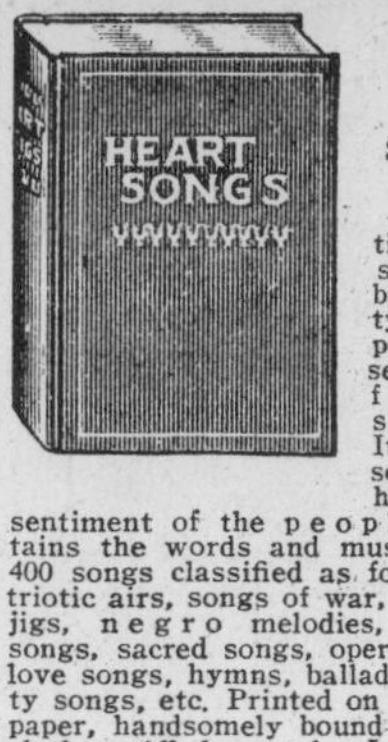

Heart Songs
512 Pages
Size, 9x6½ Inches

A collection of music compiled by twenty thousand people who sent in their favorite songs. It represents the history and sentiment of the people. Contains the words and music of over 400 songs classified as follows: Patriotic airs, songs of war, sea songs, jigs, negro melodies, children's songs, sacred songs, operatic songs, love songs, hymns, ballads, fraternity songs, etc. Printed on clear white paper, handsomely bound in maroon cloth, stiff board. Lettering is stamped in gold. Shipping weight, 2¼ pounds.
12K1690.......... 89c

Organ Instructors

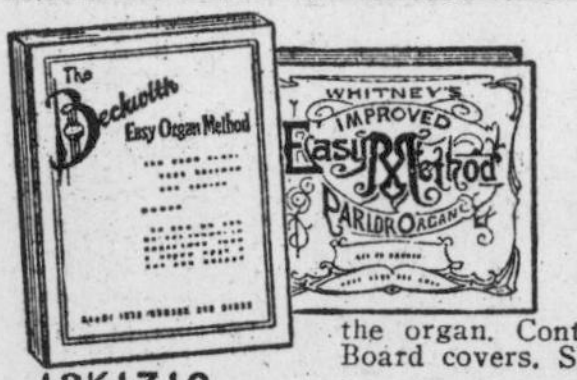

The Beckwith Easy Organ Method. Contains regular instructions besides a study of all the chords simply explained by illustrations of the organ keyboard, showing the fingers used in each chord. 104 pages. Shpg. wt., 1¼ lbs.
12K1703.......... 59c

Whitney's Improved Easy Method. For the parlor organ. An attractive system by which the pupil learns to play the organ. Contains also a choice collection of pieces. Board covers. Shipping weight 1¾ pounds.
12K1710.......... 69c

Cornet and Clarinet

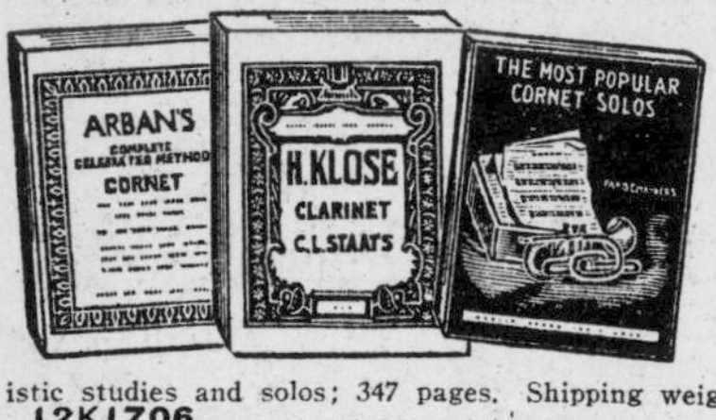

Arban's Complete Celebrated Method for the Cornet or E Flat Alto, E Flat Tenor, Baritone, Euphonium and B Flat Bass in the Treble Clef. Every variety of articulation, tonguing, staccato, breathing, etc., is thoroughly treated and explained. Contains studies, 150 songs and operatic airs, sixty-eight duets for two cornets, 14 characteristic studies and solos; 347 pages. Shipping weight, 2½ lbs.
12K1706.......... $2.85

H. Klose Clarinet Method. 259 pages of studies, exercises and fifty duets for clarinets. Chart for the fifteen-key Albert system and chart and descriptive table for the Boehm System. Shipping weight, 2½ pounds.
12K1707.......... $2.85

The Most Popular Cornet Solos
Twenty-eight selections with piano accompaniments, by famous composers. Cornet and piano parts bound separately. 126 pages. Shpg. wt., 1 lb.
12K1660.......... 98c

Saxophone Pieces the Whole World Plays

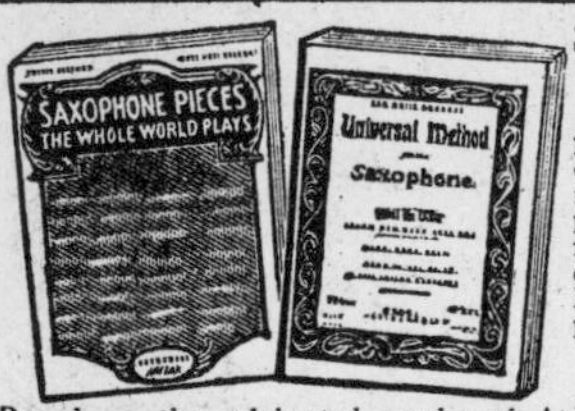

Contains fifty melodious pieces with piano accompaniment, by such great composers as Beethoven, Brahms, Gounod, Mendelssohn, Schubert, etc. Saxophone and piano parts are bound separately. Published for C Melody, Eb Alto or Bb Tenor saxophone. **State for which key book is wanted.** 160 pages. Shipping weight, 1¾ pounds.
12K1694.......... $1.59

Universal Method for Saxophone
Based on the celebrated works of A. Mayeur, H. Klose and others. Complete in every detail. Contains 320 pages of exercises and studies explaining all the technical points of saxophone playing; also a chart showing the complete scale for all saxophones, twenty operatic melodies, sixteen duets for 2Eb and 2Bb saxophones, and a number of solos. Shipping weight, 3½ lbs.
12K1711.......... $2.85

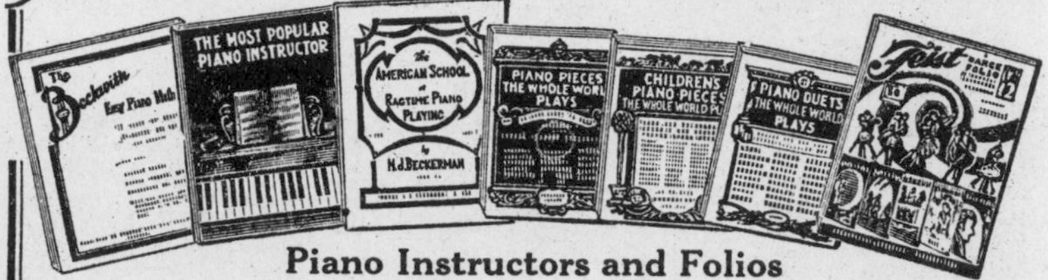

Piano Instructors and Folios

The Beckwith Easy Piano Method. Contains a complete method of instruction, besides a very elaborate study of all the chords, easily explained by illustrations of the piano keyboard, showing the fingers used in each chord. There are also many other valuable illustrations and instructions for the beginner or advanced pupil. This book will teach you how to play chords and accompaniments without the aid of a teacher. 104 pages. Shipping weight, 1 lb.
12K1700.......... 59c

The Most Popular Piano Instructor. You will find in this book an instructor that replaces the old methods by presenting the theories of music in a manner that continually keeps the interest of student. 126 pages. Shipping weight, 1¾ pounds.
12K1702.......... 85c

American School of Ragtime Piano Playing. A simple and concise method which teaches the principal features of ragtime and popular piano playing. You can learn how to "rag" any straight melody, such as ballads, waltzes, marches, etc. Contains fundamental principles of music exercises and catchy ragtime pieces. Shipping weight, 6 ounces.
12K1701.......... 39c

Piano Pieces the Whole World Plays. A collection of seventy compositions as follows: Classical, modern, light and operatic piano pieces. 256 pages. Shipping weight, 1¾ pounds.
12K1661.......... 98c

Children's Piano Pieces the Whole World Plays. 150 compositions especially arranged for the little ones. 253 pages.
12K1662—Shipping weight, 1¼ pounds.......... 98c

Piano Duets the Whole World Plays. 255 pages of famous compositions arranged as piano duets. Classical, modern, light, sacred and operatic.
12K1657—Shipping weight, 1¾ pounds.......... 98c

DANCE FOLIOS FOR PIANO

Feist Dance Folio No. 12
Contains "In a Little Spanish Town," "It Made You Happy," "Thinking of You," "Sunday," "Just a Birdseye View," and about 25 others.
12K1644—Shipping weight, 8 ounces.......... 35c

Universal Dance Folio No. 13
Contains over 30 dance tunes such as "I Never See Maggie Alone," "Song of Shanghai," "Yankee Rose," "Because I Love You," "How I Love You," etc.
12K1640—Shipping weight, 8 ounces.......... 35c

Universal Dance Folio No. 12
Contains over 30 great tunes such as "When the Red, Red Robin Comes Bob, Bob, Bobbin' Along," "Always," "How Many Times," "At Peace With the World," etc.
12K1624—Shipping weight, 8 ounces.......... 35c

Star Dance Folio No. 29
Contains 30 great dance tunes such as "Looking Over a Four Leaf Clover," "Moonbeams Kiss Her for Me," "Hello Bluebird," "All I Want Is You," etc.
12K1642—Shipping weight, 8 ounces.......... 35c

Gem Dance Folio 1927 No. 2
Contains about 30 tunes such as "Me Too," "Where Do You Worka John," "In a Little Garden," "Sleepy Head," etc.
12K1641—Shipping weight, 8 ounces.......... 35c

Blow Accordions

Length, About 14 Inches

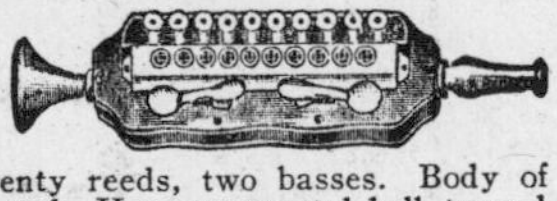

Ten keys, twenty reeds, two basses. Body of wood nicely painted. Has ornamental bell, turned mouthpiece and metal trimmings. Length, 14 in. An accurately tuned blow accordion. Shipping weight, 1¾ pounds.
12K6000.......... 98c

Hohner's Organette

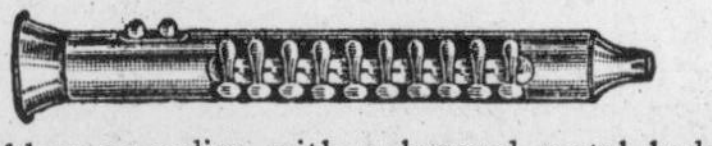

A blow accordion with a brassed metal body, cylindrical in shape. Has metal mouthpiece and bell. Ten nickel plated keys and two basses; also a nickel plated plate with numbers of keys stamped thereon. Length, 13 inches. Shipping weight, 1½ pounds.
12K6010.......... $1.85

Ocarinas

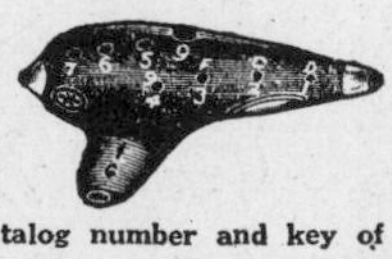

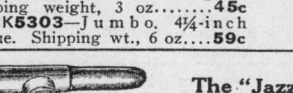

Ocarinas are not toys, they are real instruments capable of producing beautiful harmonies. They are very easy to learn to play. Our Ocarinas are imported and made of special clay. We guarantee them to be in perfect tune, easy to blow and birdlike in tone. A sheet of instructions with each instrument. **Be sure to give catalog number and key of instrument desired.**

12K5222

Key of	Sopranos	Shpg. Wt.
C	15c	4 oz.
B flat	16c	4 oz.
A	17c	4 oz.
G	18c	4 oz.
F	19c	6 oz.
E	19c	6 oz.
E flat	19c	6 oz.

12K5223

Key of	Altos	Shpg. Wt.
C	28c	¾ lb.
B flat	29c	¾ lb.
G	31c	2½ lbs.

12K5224

Key of	Basses	Shpg. Wt.
C	89c	3 lbs.

12K5225
QUARTET. Key of C. Consists of 1st and 2d Tenor, 1st and 2d Bass. These are carefully selected instruments and accurately tuned to harmonize with each other. Shipping weight, 2¼ lbs. Quartet of four ocarinas.......... $1.10

12K5227—Same as 12K5225, but in the key of G. Shipping weight, 2½ pounds. Quartet of four ocarinas.......... $1.49

Jews' Harps

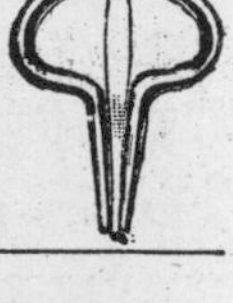

12K5300—2-inch tongue. Shipping weight, 1 ounce. 19c
12K5301—2¼-inch tongue. Shipping weight, 2 oz.......... 38c
12K5302—3½-inch tongue. Shipping weight, 3 oz.......... 45c
12K5303—Jumbo. 4¼-inch tongue. Shipping wt., 6 oz.... 59c

The "Jazzbo"

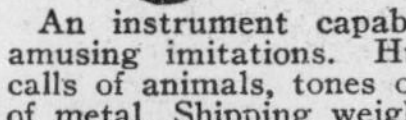

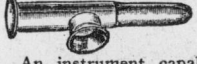

An instrument capable of producing many amusing imitations. Hum, talk or imitate the calls of animals, tones of instruments, etc. Made of metal. Shipping weight, 4 ounces.
12K5145.......... 7c

It's Easy to Order From the World's Largest Store. See Page 546

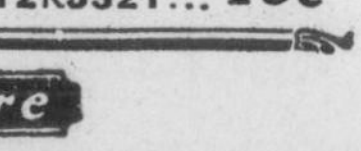

Chromatic Tuning Pipe
Low pitch harmonica style. Shipping weight, 3 ounces.
12K5321... 19c

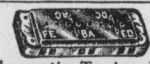

for Musical Instruments

Carl Fischer's Tutors

Complete in every detail so that a beginner using it, with practice, can easily learn any instrument. Published for:

Alto Horn, Banjo, Baritone Horn, Bass Clef; Baritone Horn, Treble Clef; Bass E flat Horn (or Tuba), Bass Viol (or Double Bass), BBb Bass, Flute, Clarinet, Mandolin, Cornet, Guitar, Drums, Tympany; Orchestra Bells, Xylophone, Piano, Fife, Piccolo, Saxophone, Violoncello, Tenor Banjo, Violin, Tenor Valve Trombone, Bass Clef; Tenor Valve Trombone, Treble Clef; Tenor Slide Trombone, Bass Clef; Tenor Slide Trombone, Treble Clef. State for which instrument instructor is wanted. Shpg. wt., 1 lb.
12K1720..........79c

Guckert's Self Instructor for Violin. All the scales, chords and exercises in every major and minor key are fully illustrated in this book by diagrams of the fingerboard, showing the positions of the fingers. It shows correct fingering and bowing and many other features. 48 pages. Shpg. wt., ¾ lb.
12K1705..........59c

Wichtl's Young Violinist. An excellent book for beginners, including 100 progressive exercises in the first position through all intervals and keys, with the second violin part for the teacher. It contains also Pleyel's celebrated violin duets. 135 pages. Shipping weight, 1½ pounds.
12K1704..........65c

Violin Pieces the Whole World Plays. Sixty musical compositions with piano accompaniment. Practically every noted composer from Bach to Tschaikowsky is represented here and the performer has the choice of classic, modern and light compositions. Violin and piano parts are bound separately. Violin part written in small notes above piano score as guide to pianist. 303 pages. Shipping weight, 2¼ pounds. **$1.59**
12K1650......$1.59

The Violinists' Book of Songs. A collection of 200 standard songs arranged for violin (or mandolin) with piano accompaniment, with an obligato part for second violin (or mandolin), such as concert songs, opera songs, sacred songs, hymns, love songs, home songs, college songs, sea songs, folk songs, southern songs, patriotic songs, foreign national songs. 294 pages. Shipping weight, 2 pounds.
12K1653......$1.59

Violin Instructors and Folios

The Most Popular Violin Pieces, with piano accompaniment. Twenty-nine selections, all arranged in the first position. Violin and piano parts bound separately. 96 pages. Shipping weight, 1 pound.
12K1654..........85c

The Young Violinists' Favorite No. 1. Fifty pages of overtures, quadrilles, polkas, waltzes, mazurkas, jigs, etc. Violin only. Shipping weight, 6 ounces.
12K1652..........39c

Drawing Room Collection for Violin and Piano. 122 pages of standard selections, which include nearly every kind of music from quadrille to operatic music. Shipping weight, 1 pound.
12K1655......49c

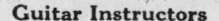

Uke, Banjo Uke and Hawaiian Guitar

Peterson Ukulele Method. A self instructor, thorough and easily understood. Contains the following essentials: Rudiments of music, explanation of diagrams, how to hold and tune uke, how to transpose from "C" to "D" tuning, the various strokes, exercises and scales on all strings, diagrams of chords in all keys, etc. Also 14 uke solos. 66 pages. Shipping weight, 6 ounces.
12K1734..........29c

The Ukulele and How to Play It. A complete, practical method with notation (playing by note) and diagram (playing by ear) systems. Profusely illustrated. 49 pages. Shipping wt., 8 oz.
12K1716..........59c

Smith's 200 Songs for Ukulele. The biggest collection of ukulele songs ever published. Contains words and music of over 200 songs, such as: Comic songs, home songs, southern songs, college songs, children's songs, sacred songs, etc. The simple uke diagrams are set directly over the music. Each diagram chord as it appears in the accompaniment is labeled with its name or title, making it adaptable for guitar, mandolin, banjo-uke and tenor banjo. Shipping weight, ¾ pound.
12K1689..........39c

Remick's Popular Songs With Uke and Banjo Uke Accompaniment. Contains besides instructions for playing 15 popular hits such as "Looking Over a Four-Leaf Clover," "Moonbeams Kiss Her for Me," "Blame It on the Waltz," "Hello Bluebird," "All I Want Is You," etc. Shipping weight, 8 ounces.
12K1643..........35c

Smith's Comic Songs for the Uke and Banjo-Uke. (Not illustrated.) Contains twelve of the funniest songs ever written. The ukulele acompaniments are written in simple diagram chords directly under the songs. Anyone can play them at sight. Shipping weight, 3 oz.
12K1699..........23c

The Steel (Hawaiian) Guitar and How to Play It. A complete, practical method with notation (playing by note) and diagram (playing by ear) systems. Profusely illustrated. 40 pages. Shipping weight, 6 ounces.
12K1717..........59c

Chords and Accompaniment for the Hawaiian Guitar. By William J. Smith. A complete and easily understood method showing how to play chords and accompaniments on the Hawaiian Guitar. Written in both musical notation and diagram. 30 pages. Shpg. wt., 5 oz.
12K1736..........39c

Smith's Songs for Hawaiian Guitar. A splendid collection of songs, including many of the old favorites such as "Aloha Oe," "Home Sweet Home," "When You and I Were Young, Maggie," etc. Arranged for voice with Hawaiian guitar accompaniment. Can be used for 1st and 2d Hawaiian Guitar by transposing the melody parts an octave higher than written. 72 pages. Shpg. wt., ¾ lb.
12K1616..........69c

Guitar Instructors

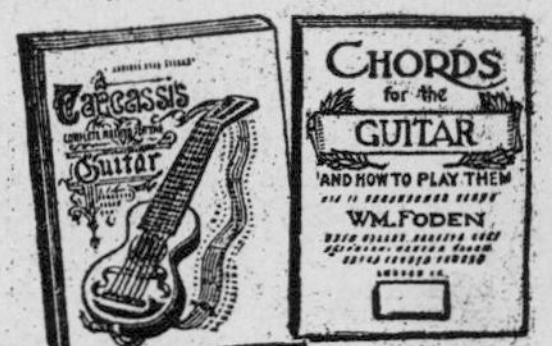

Carcassi's Method for the Guitar. Contains much valuable matter not found in other books. The number of popular songs in each of the different keys, together with the masterly instructions of Carcassi makes this a desirable method for both teacher and pupil. 112 pages. Shipping weight, 1¼ pounds.
12K1708..........75c

Chords for the Guitar. By William Foden. Written in both musical notation and diagram. Includes the necessary rudiments of music, explanation of diagrams and many other valuable features. Shipping wt., 7 oz.
12K1737..........29c

Tenor Banjo and Banjo

Chords for the Tenor Banjo by Wm. Foden. Learn to play by note with this combination diagram and notation method. Very simple. 48 pages. Shipping wt., 7 oz.
12K1714..........29c
A diagram chord book arranged for banjo in C notation. Instructions are very simple. No teacher required. 11 pages. Shipping weight, 7 ounces.
12K1712..........29c

Scheidlmeier's Tenor Banjo Method

This book has been instantly acclaimed and endorsed by the foremost banjoists of the leading orchestras. Contains the following essentials: How to read notes, form, play and transpose chords, rag and jazz, play full harmony, play from orchestra and piano parts, etc. 101 pages. Can be used as a self instructor. Shipping weight, 1 pound.
12K1735..........79c

Note Speller

Spaulding's Note Speller. If you are learning to sing or play any musical instrument, the Note Speller will teach you how to read the notes quickly and accurately without interfering with your present routine of practice and study. Shipping weight, 5 ounces.
12K1723..........59c

Mandolin

Contains many beautiful solos and duets. Special attention is devoted to tuning, shifting, memorizing, sight reading, tremolo playing, double note playing, etc. 144 pages. Shipping weight, 1 pound.
12K1719..........79c

Stand Bags

12K5376 Rubberized cloth for stands not over 17½ inches long. Shipping weight, 2 ounces.........**27c**
12K5379—For stands not over 21 inches long. Shipping wt., 2 oz.........**32c**

Stand Cases

12K5380 Flat style, smooth cowhide. For stands not over 17 inches long. Shipping weight, 1 pound.........**$0.97**
12K5381—For stands not over 21 inches long. Shpg. wt., 1 lb.........**1.48**
Same as 12K5388C but with patented easy lock. Pull the tab and your case is opened. No straps or buckles to bother with. For stand not over 17 inches long. Shipping weight, 1 pound.
12K5382..........$1.49

Music Stands
Automatic

Nickel plated steel; tubing of nickel plated brass. Patent friction spring action. No thumbscrews. Light, strong and evenly balanced and has a large desk. A superior stand in every way. Length, folded, 16 inches. Extends to 4 feet 10 inches in height. Shipping weight, 2½ pounds.
12K5375..........$1.49

12K5375 **$1.49**

Ordinary Quality Stands

Japanned Thumbscrew Stand. Length when folded, 21 inches. Shpg. wt., 6 lbs.
12K5371..........59c
Steel, nickel plated; light, strong and durable. Length when folded, 21 inches. Shipping weight, 2½ pounds.
12K5374..........85c

Violin Holder

Nickel plated. Can be attached to any music stand. A necessity to every violinist. Shipping wt., ¼ pound.
12K5370..........49c

Directors' Stand

Orchestra and Band Stand. Cast iron with pedestal in claw design, enameled and gilded. Adjustable indestructible metal desk in imitation oak. Extends to 5 feet 2 inches in height. Shipping wt., 15 lbs.
12K5373¼ **$2.98**

12K5373¼ **$2.98**

AT YOUR SERVICE~

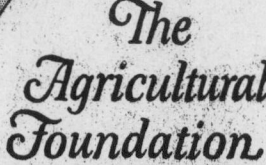

WLS
World's Largest Store

SERVICE is the keynote of WLS—a service rendered in your behalf. And there are many kinds of service. If our market broadcast enabled you to catch a peak price for the products of your flock or farm—that was a service. If our Homemaker's Broadcast brought to your easy chair information by which a step could be saved, or a short cut made, that was another service. And if our musical programs, brought to your fireside through the long evenings, gave you a fleeting hour of pleasant entertainment, or a bit of happiness, that was a service of the highest order.

Constant service is our watchword. WLS was conceived in your interests, is operated in your behalf and is dedicated to your service. It is your station. Write us frequently. If we broadcast a feature that you like, write and tell us about it. It is our way of knowing that we are pleasing you. If certain phases of our broadcasting do not appeal to you, tell us about them. That is the way we can give you what you want.

Tune in on WLS
344.6 meters

The Agricultural Foundation

The Sears-Roebuck Agricultural Foundation is entering upon its fourth year of service to the farmer—and the farmer's wife. It has sought since its beginning to be an active, helpful force in the Nation's Agriculture. Through its association with WLS, and its excellent cooperation with all the agricultural agencies in the field, it has rendered a definite service to hundreds of thousands of farm people. It has become in effect a veritable clearing house for farm problems.

The services of trained farm people, people who through study and experience have qualified themselves are at your constant disposal.

The Farm Service Department will answer any question on farm practices, poultry, marketing, live stock problems and insect pests. Every question receives immediate personal attention.

Our Home Service Department renders a similar service for the housewife. Problems concerning the home, the wardrobe, the daily menu, the baby and the thousand and one other little perplexities about the home come to this deparment daily.

We are interested in your accomplishments on the farm and concerned with your success. Keep in touch with our Agricultural Foundation. Help us help you.

Sears, Roebuck and Co.
The World's Largest Store

SO EASY TO SET UP

A Silvertone Radio Receiver

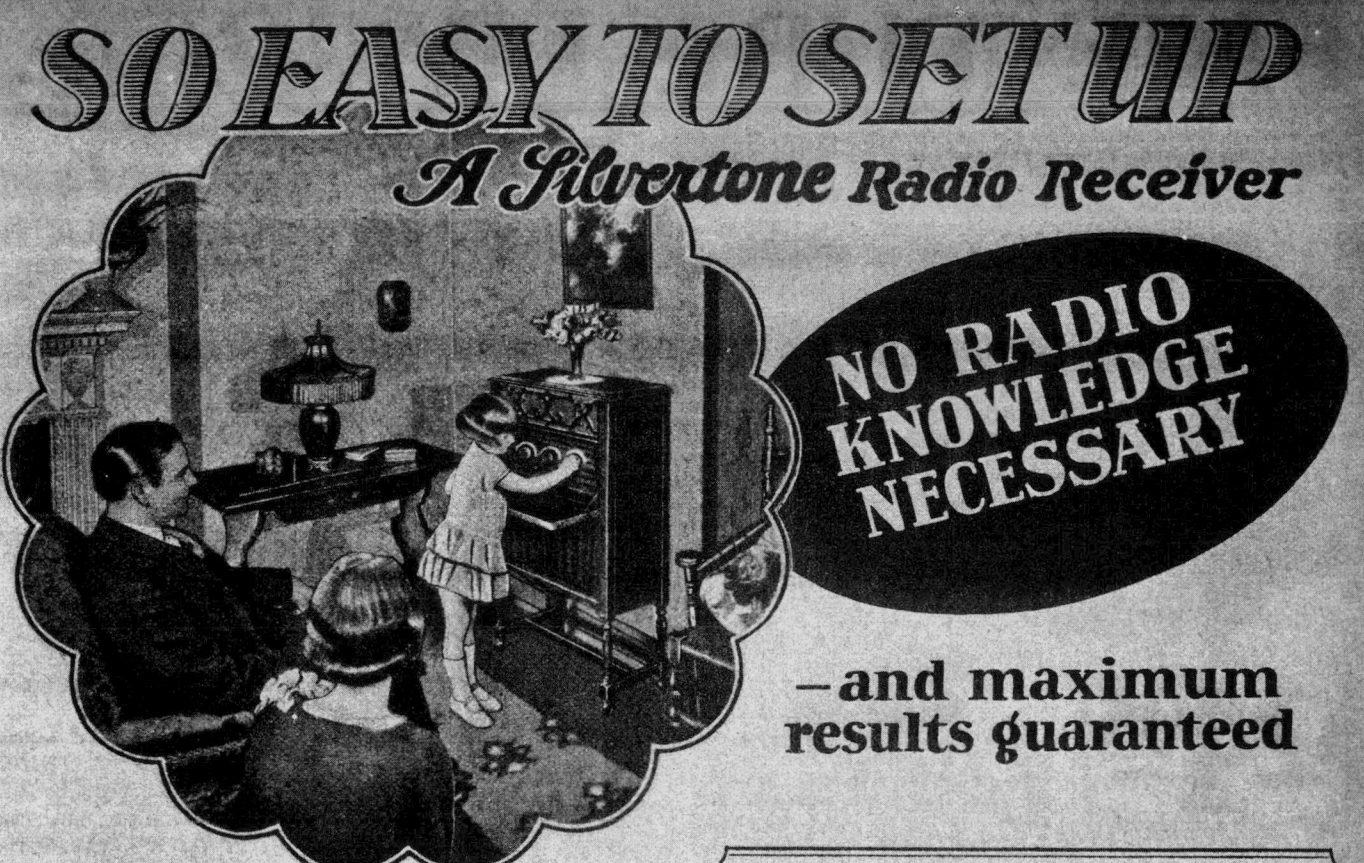

NO RADIO KNOWLEDGE NECESSARY

—and maximum results guaranteed

So Easy to Install

In a very short while you are on the air, for it is simple to set up a Silvertone Receiver. No radio knowledge necessary. Silvertone Receivers are paramount in simplicity and free from any complicated features. We guarantee that anyone, no matter how uninformed in such matters, by following our simple instructions and diagrams, can readily install a Silvertone Receiver and get perfect results. Thousands of people annually buy radio sets from us, install them themselves and tell us of results that are truly marvelous.

A Home Necessity

Radio has become an almost indispensable part of homelife. It brings to the fireside, from points far and near, the world's most inspiring music, the voices of great singers and the words of our country's most notable men and women. It brings the news of the day; many things of interest to the housewife; entertainment and education to the young, and comfort to the old. It keeps the family together; no roaming around seeking entertainment. Radio is the most marvelous gift of the present age, and no family should be without its untold advantages.

A Great Farm Asset

Radio enters our economic life; particularly the everyday business affairs of the farm. Live stock quotations, commodity prices, weather reports and agriculture talks are just a few of the numerous advantages radio affords the farmer. Many purchasers of Silvertone Receivers tell us they were able to make enough money in a short time by keeping posted on daily markets to pay for their sets. No farm today should be without a radio.

You Take No Chances

You can set up a Silvertone easily and quickly, and any member of your family can operate it. Every set is thoroughly tested before being shipped. We guarantee that it will reach you in proper condition; that it will be exactly as we describe it and that it will perform to your entire satisfaction. If for any reason you are not completely satisfied and do not want to keep your set we will return your money and all transportation charges. If you want to save money and have guaranteed satisfaction, buy a Silvertone Receiver.

We Save You ¼ to ½

We are the world's largest distributors of radio receivers direct to the customer. We completely manufacture our own product. We have our own large modern radio factory; employ our own staff of engineers and technical experts and design and manufacture all of our own cabinets and consoles. Our low manufacturing costs mean a saving to you. We also save you the wholesale distributor's profit, salesmen's commissions and high advertising costs. Buy a Silvertone from us, set it up yourself and save one-fourth to one-half of the usual retail price for a set of this quality.

We Sell on Time

If you prefer to pay on the installment plan why not take advantage of our liberal terms? You will find that the enjoyment derived will far exceed your monthly payments and, in practically no time, you will have your radio paid for. Thousands of purchasers are enjoying the advantage of easy payments.

For Quality and Performance

We guarantee you maximum results. We guarantee our five-tube sets to have a range equal to any five-tube set manufactured the world over, notwithstanding our lower prices. Our six-tube set is a peer among radio receivers and defies all comparison. Aside from range, Silvertone Receivers are unexcelled in tone quality and simplicity of operation. Attention has been given to mechanical sturdiness in such a pronounced way that you are assured of continuous, dependable performance. You do not have to be afraid of anything going wrong with a Silvertone Receiver.

What to Buy

This depends on what the purchaser prefers and how much he feels he can afford. For all around satisfaction and dependability at the lowest possible cost, you will be well pleased with any one of our five-tube models. Our six-tube sets have more amplification, render more volume, and also bring in distance to a greater degree. Further, they embrace single control, a feature that makes it possible to tune in stations by merely turning one knob. While necessarily adding to the cost, it is a convenience many purchasers prefer.

FIVE TUBE *Silvertone*

Manufactured and SEARS, ROEBUCK

Silvertone Five-Tube Receivers will give you the range you want, the tonal quality you appreciate and the dependability you expect for complete, continuous satisfaction. Our prices are lower than ever, and represent a standard of value that should be instantly recognized. Buy a Silvertone Receiver and be dollars ahead. Presented in four models of cabinets.

A Silvertone is easy to install. No radio knowledge is necessary.

$400 Down
$400 Monthly

$2495 CASH WITHOUT ACCESSORIES

Model XIV

Here is an opportunity for you to enjoy, at a minimum cost, the advantages of the Silvertone five-tube set. You pay a low price, but are assured of performance and range. Cabinet of simple, but neat design, carefully made of selected gumwood veneer, dark mahogany finish. Size, 21 inches long, 10¾ inches deep and 8¾ inches high. At our low price on this model you cannot afford to be without the great advantages of radio reception.

Model XIV Silvertone Receiver, without accessories. Shipping weight, 29 pounds.

57K2788¼—Cash price.........................$24.95
57K2789¼—Easy payment price, **$4.00** cash with order and **$4.00** per month until paid.....................$27.50

Model XIV Silvertone Receiver, complete with all accessories (ready to set up and operate), including five detector-amplifier storage battery tubes, one 57K2267¾ guaranteed cone speaker, shown on page 713, two large heavy duty 45-volt "B" batteries, one voltmeter (for testing "B" batteries), one 100-ampere-hour storage battery, one battery tester (for testing storage battery), complete aerial and ground equipment, Shipping weight, 130 pounds.

57K2790¼—Cash price.........................$54.95
57K2791¼—Easy payment price, **$9.00** cash with order and **$9.00** per month until paid.....................$59.95
When ordering on Time Payments use Time Payment Order Blank on page 1092.

Model XVI

A very striking value for those interested in a console receiver at a low price. Has a built-in reproducer, hinged top and a removable front. Provides easy access to tubes and all batteries. The cabinet is made of gumwood with a genuine mahogany top and front; dark mahogany finish; neat two-tone trim. Size, 37 inches high, 30½ inches wide across the front and 13½ inches deep.

Model XVI Silvertone Radio Console, without accessories. Shipping weight, 90 pounds.

57K2796¼—Cash price.........................$49.95
57K2797¼—Easy payment price, **$8.00** cash with order and **$8.00** per month until paid.....................$54.95

Model XVI Silvertone Radio Receiver, complete with all accessories (ready to set up and operate), including five detector-amplifier storage battery tubes, two large heavy duty 45-volt "B" batteries, one voltmeter (for testing "B" batteries), one 100-ampere-hour storage battery, one battery tester (for testing storage battery), complete aerial and ground equipment. Shipping weight, 195 pounds.

57K2798¼—Cash price.........................$74.95
57K2799¼—Easy payment price, **$12.00** cash with order and **$12.00** per month until paid.....................$81.00
When ordering on Time Payments use Time Payment Order Blank on page 1092.

$4995 CASH, Without Accessories
$800 Down
$800 Monthly

RADIO RECEIVERS

Sold Exclusively by and CO.

The radio assembly embraces the Tuned Radio Frequency Circuit. It is strong, rugged and reflects symmetry and precision in engineering. Contains no parts likely to get out of order. All sockets for the five tubes are mounted on a heavy, floating type subbase. Solid steel panel to match cabinets. Three neatly decorated tuning dials, volume control and switch. Easy to set up and operate. No radio knowledge necessary. We guarantee complete satisfaction.

$6.00 Down
$6.00 Monthly

$34.95 CASH WITHOUT ACCESSORIES

Model XV

You may prefer this receiver, as the use of a separate loud speaker is not required. The built-in sound chamber is of ample size and is designed along lines that make for remarkable results. It is fitted with a heavy metal throat to which is attached a large modern type reproducing unit that will stand heavy volume with wonderful tone quality. We guarantee you complete satisfaction. The cabinet is made of selected gumwood, dark mahogany finish. It measures 30½ inches long, 10¾ inches deep and 9 inches high. Equipped with our regular Silvertone five-tube radio assembly.

Model XV Silvertone Receiver only, without accessories. Shipping weight, 40 pounds.
57K2792¼—Cash price $34.95
57K2793¼—Easy payment price, **$6.00** cash with order and **$6.00** per month until paid $38.50

Model XV Silvertone Receiver, complete with all accessories (ready to set up and operate), including five detector-amplifier storage battery tubes, two large heavy duty 45-volt "B" batteries, one voltmeter (for testing "B" batteries), one 100-ampere-hour storage battery, one battery tester (for testing storage battery), complete aerial and ground equipment. Shipping weight, 145 pounds.
57K2794¼—Cash price $59.95
57K2795¼—Easy payment price, **$9.00** cash with order and **$9.00** per month until paid $65.95

When ordering on Time Payments use Time Payment Order Blank on page 1092.

$59.95 CASH, Without Accessories

$9.00 Down
$9.00 Monthly

Model XVII

Console type cabinet with a complete built-in sound chamber set above the radio assembly. Made of genuine mahogany, which has a rich, hand rubbed finish. Two-tone trim. Removable panel in front of battery compartment. Radio assembly mounted on a pull-out slide, affording ready access to the tubes. Height of console, 44½ inches; width, across the front, 25 inches; depth, 13¼ inches.

Model XVII Silvertone Radio Console only, without accessories. Shipping weight, 100 pounds.
57K2800¼—Cash price $59.95
57K2801¼—Easy payment price, **$9.00** cash with order and **$9.00** per month until paid $65.95

Model XVII Silvertone Receiver, complete with all accessories (ready to set up and operate), including five detector-amplifier storage battery tubes, two large heavy duty 45-volt "B" batteries, one voltmeter (for testing "B" batteries), one 100-ampere-hour storage battery, one battery tester (for testing storage battery), complete aerial and ground equipment. Shipping weight, 205 pounds.
57K2802¼—Cash price $84.95
57K2803¼—Easy payment price, **$13.00** cash with order and **$13.00** per month until paid $92.95

When ordering on Time Payments use Time Payment Order Blank on page 1092.

SIX TUBE *Silvertone*

Manufactured and by SEARS

Get the day's events on a big six-tube Silvertone. You will be impressed with its precision, simplicity and sturdiness of design. You are assured more amplification, greater range, more volume and better tone quality.

$6.00 down $6.00 Monthly

$39.95 CASH WITHOUT ACCESSORIES

Model XVIII

Only from the World's Largest Store can you buy a powerful six-tube, single control Radio at such a low price. The beauty, simplicity and efficiency of this model places it foremost among America's leaders.

Genuine walnut top, dark walnut finish throughout. Dimensions: 21¾ inches long, 9½ inches high and 11 inches deep.

Model XVIII Silvertone Receiver only, without accessories. Shipping weight, 35 pounds.

57K2804¼—Cash price.................................$39.95
57K2805¼—Easy payment price, **$6.00** cash with order and **$6.00** per month until paid........................$43.95

Model XVIII Silvertone Receiver, complete with all accessories (ready to set up and operate), including six detector-amplifier storage battery tubes, two large heavy duty 45-volt "B" batteries, one voltmeter (for testing B batteries), one 100-ampere-hour storage battery, one battery tester (for testing storage battery), one large Silvertone loud speaker 57K2207¼ (or one Silvertone cone speaker 57K2240¼, if preferred instead of 57K2207¼), complete aerial and ground equipment. Shipping weight, 165 pounds.

57K2806¼—Cash price.......................$79.49
57K2807¼—Easy payment price, **$12.00** cash with order and **$12.00** per month until paid.............$86.95

When ordering on Time Payments use Time Payment Order Blank on page 1092.

$11.00 down $11.00 monthly

Model XX

So that all may enjoy the profound advantages of a six-tube Silvertone console, we have purposely designed this receiver. It is new, it is individual and it is well made. Genuine mahogany, hand rubbed finish. Fitted with two doors on the battery compartment, and a pull-out slide for the radio assembly. Height of console, 44½ inches; width, across front, 26 inches; depth, 13½ inches.

Model XX Silvertone Receiver only, without accessories. Shipping weight, 100 pounds.

57K2812¼—Cash price...........................$72.50
57K2813¼—Easy payment price, **$11.00** cash with order and **$11.00** per month until paid..............$79.75

Model XX Silvertone Receiver, complete with all accessories (ready to set up and operate), including six detector-amplifier storage battery tubes, two large heavy duty 45-volt "B" batteries, one voltmeter (for testing "B" batteries), one 100-ampere-hour storage battery, one battery tester (for testing storage battery), complete aerial and ground equipment. Shipping weight, 205 pounds.

57K2814¼—Cash price..............$99.95
57K2815¼—Easy payment price, **$16.00** cash with order and **$16.00** per month until paid...........$109.75

When ordering on Time Payments use Time Payment Order Blank on page 1092.

$72.50 CASH WITHOUT ACCESSORIES

RADIO RECEIVERS

Sold Exclusively ROEBUCK and Co.

Our one-dial control enables you to bring in one station after another with just the turn of one hand. Station wave lengths and graduations appear, in an illuminated window. Tube sockets all spring mounted. Three heavy low ratio transformers that insure perfect amplification. The same radio assembly is used in each Silvertone model presented herein. Anyone can easily set up and operate a Silvertone receiver. No radio knowledge necessary.

$9.00 down $9.00 Monthly

Model XIX

Table type cabinet with built-in reproducer. Sound chamber is correctly proportioned for both artistic and acoustic requirements, and is equipped with a high quality reproducing unit. Dome is hinged to cabinet, which can be raised to give ready access to the radio assembly. Made of genuine walnut, dark walnut finish. Size of cabinet, over all, 21¾ inches long, 15½ inches high and 11 inches deep.

$54.95 CASH WITHOUT ACCESSORIES

Model XIX Silvertone Receiver, without accessories. Shipping weight, 43 pounds.
57K2808¼—Cash price................ $54.95
57K2809¼—Easy payment price, $9.00 cash with order and $9.00 per month until paid........ $59.95

Model XIX Silvertone Receiver, complete with all accessories (ready to set up and operate), including six detector-amplifier storage battery tubes, two large heavy duty 45-volt "B" batteries, one voltmeter (for testing "B" batteries), one 100-ampere hour storage battery, one battery tester (for testing storage battery), complete aerial and ground equipment. Shipping weight, 148 pounds.
57K2810¼—Cash price................ $82.95
57K2811¼—Easy payment price, $13.00 cash with order and $13.00 per month until paid.... $91.00

When ordering on Time Payments use Time Payment Order Blank on page 1092.

$14.00 down $14 monthly

Model XXI

It is difficult to picture the beauty and massive qualities of a console such as this striking piece of furniture. Made of genuine walnut, set off by an attractive routed design in three-tone effect, hand rubbed and highly polished. Large sound chamber complete with a heavy, high quality reproducing unit. Radio assembly mounted on a pull-out slide. Size of cabinet, 46 inches high, 30 inches wide and 15½ inches deep.

Model XXI Silvertone Receiver only, without accessories. Shipping weight, 118 pounds.

57K2816¼—Cash price.................... $87.50

57K2817¼—Easy payment price, **$14.00** cash with order and **$14.00** per month until paid.....$95.95

Model XXI Silvertone Receiver, complete with all accessories (ready to set up and operate), including six detector-amplifier storage battery tubes, two large heavy duty 45-volt "B" batteries, one voltmeter (for testing "B" batteries), one 100-ampere-hour storage battery, one battery tester (for testing storage battery), complete aerial and ground equipment. Shipping weight, 220 pounds.

57K2818¼—Cash price. $115.50
57K2819¼—Easy payment price, **$18.00** cash with order and **$18.00** per month until paid............ $127.00

When ordering on Time Payments use Time Payment Order Blank on page 1092.

$87.50 CASH WITHOUT ACCESSORIES

Parcel Post, Express and Freight Rates Are on Pages 542 to 545

Your RADIO Deserves Its Own Table

Console Table With Built-In Speaker

Our highest quality radio table, fitted with a soundbox or horn placed behind the left front grille panel. Top of table is made of genuine walnut veneer; ends selected gumwood finished in dark walnut, highly polished. It will harmonize well with almost any radio set. Has small drawer in front, yet ample room is provided for all batteries. Reproducing unit not included. Size of top, 38x18 inches; height, about 30½ inches. The soundbox is fitted with a ⅞-inch threaded metal coupling. If unit is wanted see our 57K2219 shown on page 713. Shipping weight, 80 pounds. **Shipped from factory in SOUTHERN MICHIGAN or EASTERN PENNSYLVANIA.**

57K2943⅓.............................. **$19.95**

Large Console Table

Provides room for both receiver and speaker. A table that ordinarily retails for $18.00 to $20.00, yet our price is only $11.95. A real quality table. Selected gumwood top, highly finished in dark mahogany. Back is entirely open, permitting access to a large charger and battery compartment. Attractively decorated; legs fluted. Top measures 38 inches long by 18 inches wide. Height of table, 30 inches. Shipping weight, 75 pounds. **Shipped direct from factory in CENTRAL INDIANA or EASTERN PENNSYLVANIA.**

57K2944⅓.............................. **$11.95**

Small Console Table

A small, neat, low priced table that meets many needs. The front is removable, permitting instant access to batteries. Nicely finished; neat routed design in front. Suited for our receivers, Models XIV, XVII and XIX. Gumwood veneer top, 23½ inches long by 13 inches deep. Height of table, 30 in. Shipping weight, 40 pounds.

57K2927¼—Mahogany finish............. **$9.65**
57K2928¼—Walnut finish.............. **9.68**

New Console Table

One of the most popular types of radio tables now before the public. Well proportioned, attractively designed and sturdily built. Selected gumwood veneer top; highly finished in walnut or mahogany. Two panel effect doors in front, fitted with metal drop pulls. Back of table is closed. An ideal piece for parlor or living room. Will harmonize with your radio set. Size of top, 31¾ inches long, 15 inches deep. Height, 30 inches. Shipping weight, 50 pounds.

57K2929¼
Mahogany finish.......... **$12.95**
57K2930¼
Walnut finish............ **12.98**

Utility Radio Table

Construction is of thoroughly seasoned wood, strongly built throughout. Designed along simple lines and is neat, and well appearing. Dark mahogany finish. Has a built-in battery compartment, measuring 32 inches long by 9¾ inches deep. Buy a Utility Radio Table and keep your batteries and connections out of sight. Top of table measures 36 inches long by 18 inches wide; height, 30 inches. Shipping weight, 55 pounds.

57K2945¼.............................. **$9.48**

Folding Radio Table

The top and shelf are of heavy fiber board and the supporting side rails are seasoned hardwood, 1½ inches deep by ¾ inch thick. The covering is genuine waterproof leatherette, dark green in color, on both top and shelf. Legs have a mahogany finish; corners on top and shelf are protected by heavy metal trunk type corner plates. The top measures 15⅝x28 inches; the shelf, 12x28 inches; 26 inches high. Shipping weight, 14 pounds. **Unmailable.**

57K2933¼.................. **$3.59**

Walnut Radio Cabinet

A new, attractive design, heavier in material and construction than the ordinary cabinet. Rich two-tone genuine walnut, selected stock, stained, shellacked and rubbed. All sizes are 10 inches deep, to accommodate any style set. The measurements given below are exact panel sizes:

57K2338¼—7x18 inches. Shipping weight, 21 pounds............. **$5.98**
57K2339¼—7x21 inches. Shipping weight, 29 pounds............. **6.49**
57K2340¼—7x24 inches. Shipping weight, 31 pounds............. **6.80**
57K2341¼—7x26 inches. Shipping weight, 34 pounds............. **7.95**

WLS POWER UNIT

Carefree and Economical Socket Power

Consists of two devices: Storage battery eliminator and "B" battery eliminator. Operates from light socket and can be instantly installed by any set owner. Always ready for instant use and will operate any size set up to ten six-volt tubes with the utmost satisfaction. With the use of this unit power is automatically turned on or off from the filament switch on the panel of your radio set. The W L S power unit contains no delicate parts, it is noiseless in operation and guaranteed to give you complete socket power satisfaction. Not to be confused with many lower priced units which do not give proper service.

$56.95 COMPLETE

Always Ready for Instant Use

The "A" eliminator contains no battery, bulb, acid or moving parts; current rectification is accomplished by means of a new and proved scientific principle of dry metallic plates that will last indefinitely. Furnishes constant "A" power for any set up to ten six-volt tubes. May be used separately if desired. Assembled in a nicely finished steel case that matches "B" unit. Size, 5¾x13 inches; height, 9¾ inches.

The "B" unit is the same as unit 57K2456¼ described on page 715. No taps are provided for "C" battery elimination. Where receiver calls for "C" voltage, best results are obtained by the use of a regular "C" battery. Shipping weight, 45 pounds.

57K2451¼—Complete "A" and "B" unit as described..... **$56.95**
57K2455¼—"A" unit only as described. Shpg. wt., 24 lbs... **27.95**

$1.29 Nationally Famous WLS Tubes

We Guarantee Them

W L S Tubes are superior tubes. They are tubes for those who want the very best; those who want the maximum in signal audibility, sensitiveness and uniformity of performance over a long life period. W L S Tubes represent the highest type of tubes that modern science and manufacturing skill have been able to produce. Detector-amplifier 6-volt type. Draws ¼ ampere. New type base, 1⅜ inches in diameter; long prongs.

57K2976—Shipping weight, 1 pound.................. **$1.29**

Solartron Vacuum Tubes

Equal to many tubes sold elsewhere at higher prices. The Solartron Tube carries our full guarantee. It is constructed in a very substantial manner; possesses volume and tone quality, and is not to be confused with the many poor, short lived tubes on the market offered at around our low price of 85c. Such tubes we refuse to handle. Detector-amplifier 6-volt type. Draws ¼ ampere. New type base, 1⅜ inches in diameter; long prongs.

57K2970—Shipping weight, 1 pound.................. **85c**

Power Tubes

Where provision is not made in a radio receiver for the use of a power tube, a change in receiver wiring is necessary. Also, power tubes require 135 volts of "B" battery and 9 to 27 volts of "C" battery. 57K2977 is the higher amplifier of the two types quoted below and is best suited, especially for a five-tube set, where volume is wanted with no sacrifice in range. 57K2968 is particularly suited for six-tube sets. While its amplification factor is less than 57K2977, it draws more current in the plate circuit, thus rendering a more pronounced fullness and quality of tone preferred by many critics. Both tubes are 6-volt type; filament draws ½ ampere; diameter of base, 1⅜ inches. Power tubes, however, are not required for the proper performance of Silvertone Receivers. Shipping weight, 1 pound.

57K2977—W L S 512.................. **$2.59**

57K2968—W L S 571.................. **2.59**

Special Detector Tube

A special, fully guaranteed, highly sensitive tube for use in the detector socket only. Increases volume and makes set more sensitive, especially noticeable on distance reception. Equal to other makes of tubes selling at much higher prices. Proper use does not require any change in wiring of set. Has new type base, 1⅜ inches in diameter, with long prongs. Draws ¼ ampere. 6-volt type.

57K2950—Shipping weight, 1 pound.................. **$2.59**

Dry Battery Tubes

Detector-amplifier 4½-volt tube, used for dry cell sets; also portable sets. Base, 1 inch in diameter; short terminals. Draws .06 ampere. Three 1½-volt dry batteries connected in series are generally used as the "A" battery for this tube.

57K2951—Shipping weight, 1 pound.................. **$1.37**

Detector-amplifier 4½-volt dry battery tube, similar to above, but fitted with the new type base having long prongs. Diameter of base, 1³⁄₁₆ inches. Draws .06 ampere. Requires same battery arrangement as 57K2951.

57K2952—Shipping weight, 1 pound.................. **$1.37**

Detector-amplifier 1½-volt dry battery tube, fitted with new type base having long prongs. Diameter of base, 1⅜ inches. Draws ¼ ampere. One 1½-volt dry cell for each tube gives good results for the "A" battery.

57K2953—Shipping weight, 1 pound.................. **$1.63**

Hi-Mu Tube

For resistance coupled sets or units. Has amplification factor of 30, and is best suited for first and second audio stages; can also be used as a detector. Fully guaranteed, 6-volt type; draws ¼ ampere. Maximum plate voltage 1.80. Diameter of base, 1⅜ inches. Shipping weight, 1 pound.

57K2969.................. **$1.39**

Guarantee

When you order W L S Tubes you do so with the assurance that the tubes you receive have been tested first and have proved highly efficient. Built in the latest and most scientific manner with the best of materials, these tubes are subject to rigid tests before being packed for shipment.

We guarantee W L S Tubes to have long life, high amplification and select tone quality. Should a W L S Tube fail to give the service you expect, we will immediately replace it or return your money without question.

W L S Silvertone Speaker

Silvertone Model 1 Speaker is fitted with a large unit having a heavy magnet and substantial coils which, coupled with fine workmanship and precision, have produced a unit of the very highest order. This Silvertone Speaker assures full enjoyment of the wonders of radio reception. Fitted with a substantial cast aluminum base and gooseneck, having a beautiful brown crystalline finish which harmonizes with almost any radio cabinet. Top or bell part of speaker is made of solid bakelite, highly polished. Height, over all, 21¼ inches. Width across top opening, 13 inches. Shipping weight, 10 pounds.

57K2207¼.................. **$11.75**

Silvertone Speaker Model No. 2

This speaker is similar to Silvertone Speaker 57K2207¼ above, except that it is of smaller dimensions. Brown crystalline finish. The polished bakelite top measures 11 inches across opening. Height of speaker, over all, 18¼ inches. Represents a very substantial value. Shipping weight, 12 pounds.

57K2208¼.................. **$9.95**

Silvertone Cone Speaker $11.75

Unquestionably one of the greatest values of the season in radio. Big reproducers of similar quality often sell for $20.00 to $25.00, yet we ask only $11.75. Equipped with a large, heavy magnet which has a sensitive, floating type armature that assures the utmost in clarity and realism throughout the entire musical scale. Built to handle the higher voltage of power tubes and is guaranteed to handle volume without any sacrifice of true tone quality. Made of a heavy russet brown parchment in both front and back; neatly decorated and reinforced around outer edge of cone. Mounted on a strong metal frame and pedestal; bronze finish. Diameter, 19 inches. Height, over all, 21¼ inches. Shipping weight, 23 pounds.

57K2241¼.................. **$11.75**

Smaller cone, same as above in both design and construction. Diameter, 14 inches. Height, over all, 16½ inches. Shpg. wt., 13 lbs.

57K2240¼.................. **$7.95**

Howl Arrester

A heavy rubber cap that shields tubes and reduces microphonic noises. Generally used on the detector tube but may be used on other tubes in set. For regular 6-volt detector or detector-amplifier tubes. Shipping weight, 8 ounces.

57K2444.................. **59c**

Tube Tester

To insure best results at all times your radio tubes must operate at highest possible efficiency. Poor reception and performance can usually be traced to poor tubes. To know the condition of each tube is but a simple matter with this dependable tube tester. Takes any 6-volt tubes shown on this page. Size 5x3 inches; 2 in. high. Shpg. wt., 2¾ lbs.

57K2416.................. **$5.62**

Tube Rejuvenator

Radio tubes that have become paralized, or partially so, may be restored to new life. Use only on alternating current, 110-volt, 60 cycles. (Ordinary city current.) Shpg. wt., 3 lbs.

57K2428.................. **$2.75**

Head Phones

Meteor phones, guaranteed for sensitivity, tone quality and durability. Low in price but highly efficient. Built to withstand the rough handling to which phones are generally subjected. Aluminum backs, polished composition screw-off caps. Headband covered with heavy webbing. Shipping weight, 1½ pounds.

57K2198.................. **$1.49**

Receiver Cords

Worn cords often short circuit, and it is well to replace them before they cause trouble.

57K2172

Single type having two pin tips at each end. Shpg. wt., 3 oz.......... **19c**

57K2173

Double type having two pin tips at one end and four at the other. Shpg. wt., 3 oz.......... **27c**

57K2174

Brandes Superior type having two pin tips at one end and four spade tips at the other. Shipping weight, 3 ounces.......... **35c**

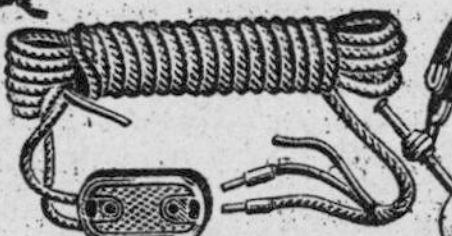

Extension Cords

Permits locating your loud speaker or reproducing unit some distance from receiving set. Double heavy black cord with two tips at each end; connector included. Furnished only in lengths listed below.

57K2211 — 20 feet. Shpg. wt., 3 oz.......... **79c**

57K2213—50 ft. Shipping wt., ¾ lb.......... **$1.15**

Head Phones

Enjoy true, clear reproduction. Bi-polar type, substantial coils and heavy silicon steel magnets. Fitted with a canvas covered adjustable headband; substantial, highly polished, screw-off black caps; strong aluminum backs. Shipping weight, 2 pounds.

57K2169.................. **$2.45**

Popular Cone Speaker

A reproducer that has enjoyed national success and ranks high in performance and reliability. Has a very heavy magnet, fitted with armature and stylus bar, a superior principle not generally incorporated in speakers selling under $10.00. Handles volume without blasting, and is clear and distinct in its reproduction. Exceptionally strong construction throughout. Has a metal frame entirely around the outer edge of the parchment. Mounted on a bronze finished metal stand; a very remarkable value. Diameter, 12 inches; height, 14 inches. Shipping weight, 7 pounds.

57K2267¼.................. **$4.98**

Quick Change Plug

Insert phone or cord tips and plug into your set. No screws or tools necessary. Shpg. wt., 4 oz.

57K2202.................. **23c**

Panel Light

Miniature lamp to set on radio cabinet. Weighted felt lined base. Gold finish. Operates from storage or "A" battery circuit of set. Four feet of double cord and a regular 6-volt electric light bulb included. Height, 5½ in. Shipping weight, 1½ lbs.

57K2242.................. **$1.39**

Ear Pads

Soft springy sponge rubber. Fit snugly over phones and protect ears. You will be surprised at how much comfort they give. Shipping weight, 5 ounces.

57K2170 Per pair.................. **37c**

Reproducing Unit

Designed to embody simplicity, sturdiness and sensitiveness; also good tonal quality. Especially well suited for phonograph or radio console use. Has a ⅞-inch threaded nipple. Fitted with a 30-inch cord with regular phone cord metal tips. Shipping weight, 1¼ pounds.

57K2219.................. **$2.85**

Order Blanks Are in Back of This Catalog

Watchmakers' Tools and Materials

Should you desire to order balance staffs, hole jewels, cap jewels, mainsprings, hairsprings, etc., send a sample to us and state name of watch. Enclose in your letter or package your name and address. When ordering hairsprings state size and strength.

Old gold accepted by us at the highest market price in exchange for any article in our jewelry department. We allow 72c for 18-karat, 56c for 14-karat, 40c for 10-karat, per pennyweight. In all cases we hold gold until we are advised by customers that estimate of value is satisfactory.

SHIPPING WEIGHTS—We give the weights of the articles on this page. Where no weight is given, the shipping weight is 4 ounces.

We repair watches that have been purchased from us. We maintain a completely equipped watch repair department operated by skilled watchmakers. All work guaranteed. Should you send your watch, write your name plainly on a tag, together with your address, and attach same to watch. Pack watch carefully in Cotton Batting or Tissue Paper in a substantial box and address package to us. Mail your watch to us by insured mail. An estimate will be sent you immediately before work is begun. Two weeks are required, after we receive your answer, to properly complete the work. Lowest prices for expert workmanship.

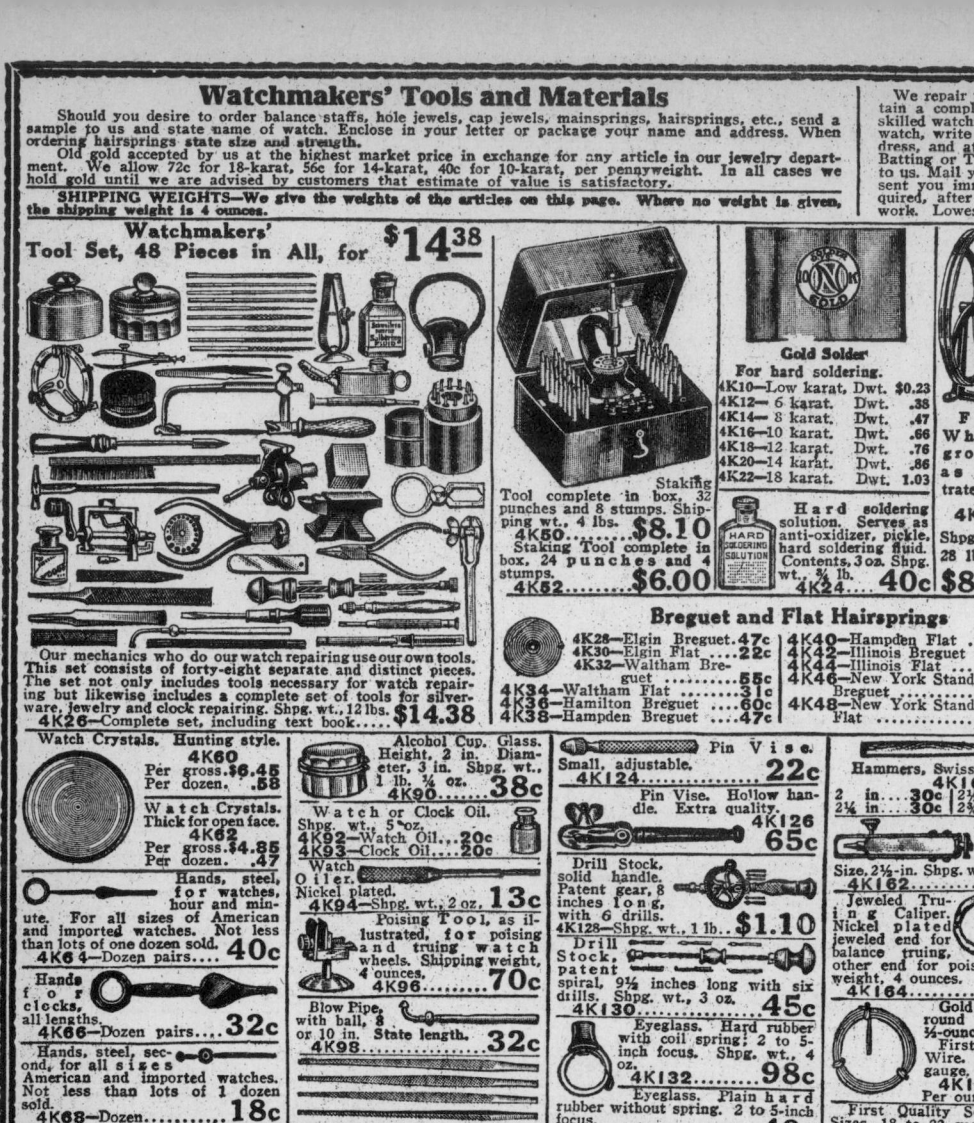

Watchmakers' Tool Set, 48 Pieces in All, for $14.38

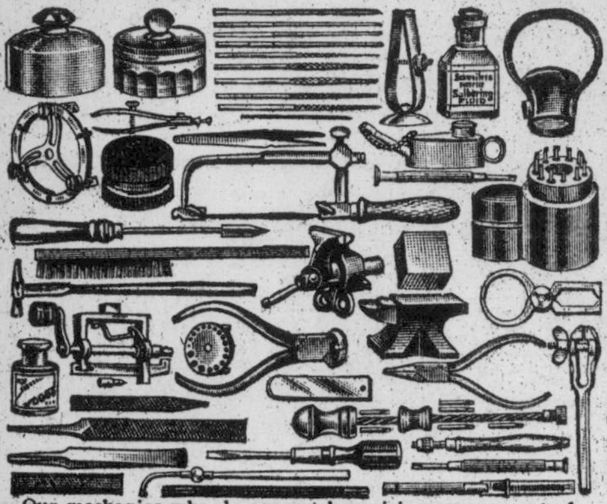

Our mechanics who do our watch repairing use our own tools. This set consists of forty-eight separate and distinct pieces. The set not only includes tools necessary for watch repairing but likewise includes a complete set of tools for silverware, jewelry and clock repairing. Shpg. wt., 12 lbs.
4K26—Complete set, including text book.... $14.38

Staking Tool complete in box, 32 punches and 8 stumps. Shipping wt., 4 lbs.
4K50........ $8.10
Staking Tool complete in box, 24 punches and 4 stumps.
4K52........ $6.00

Gold Solder
For hard soldering.

4K10—Low karat.	Dwt.		$0.23
4K12—6 karat.	Dwt.		.38
4K14—8 karat.	Dwt.		.47
4K16—10 karat.	Dwt.		.66
4K18—12 karat.	Dwt.		.76
4K20—14 karat.	Dwt.		.86
4K22—18 karat.	Dwt.		1.03

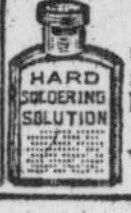

Hard soldering solution. Serves as anti-oxidizer, pickle, hard soldering fluid. Contents, 3 oz. Shpg. wt., ¾ lb.
4K24........ 40c

Foot Wheel, grooved, as illustrated.
4K54
Shpg. wt., 28 lbs.
$8.50

Watchmakers Lathe

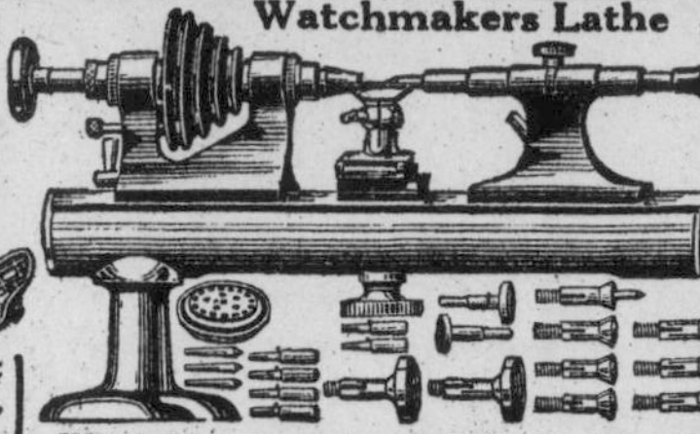

Watchmakers' genuine G. Boley Lathe, with tip over hand rests, as illustrated, including 10 wire chucks, 10 brasses on wooden stand with glass cover, and 9 feet of belting complete.
4K56—Shipping wt., 20 lbs.... $34.75
Watchmakers' imported lathe, similar to the above, with 14 wire chucks, 5 brasses and 9 feet of belting complete. Chucks will interchange with Webster-Whitcomb.
4K58—Shipping wt., 15 lbs.... $23.50

Breguet and Flat Hairsprings

4K28—Elgin Breguet. 47c
4K30—Elgin Flat 22c
4K32—Waltham Breguet 55c
4K34—Waltham Flat 31c
4K36—Hamilton Breguet 60c
4K38—Hampden Breguet 47c
4K40—Hampden Flat 30c
4K42—Illinois Breguet 55c
4K44—Illinois Flat 25c
4K46—New York Standard Breguet 28c
4K48—New York Standard Flat 24c

Counter Shaft, Nickel plated, wood pulley, with metal speed wheel.
4K192
Shpg. wt., 4 lbs.
$3.06

Watch Crystals. Hunting style.
4K60
Per gross. $6.45
Per dozen. .58

Watch Crystals. Thick for open face.
4K62
Per gross. $4.85
Per dozen. .47

Hands, steel, for watches, hour and minute. For all sizes of American and imported watches. Not less than lots of one dozen sold.
4K64—Dozen pairs.... 40c

Hands for clocks, all lengths.
4K66—Dozen pairs.... 32c

Hands, steel, second, for all sizes American and imported watches. Not less than lots of 1 dozen sold.
4K68—Dozen........ 18c

Roller Jewels or Ruby Pins for Elgin, Waltham, Hampden or New York Standard. All sizes. Not less than lots of 1 dozen sold.
4K70—Dozen........ 50c

A
B
C

Mainsprings for watches. All styles and sizes. Not less than ¼ dozen sold.
4K72—Dozen....... $1.34

Mainsprings for clocks.
4K74—1 day.... 12c
4K76—8 day.... 28c
Mention width wanted.
Shipping weight, 1 lb.

Elgin Balance Staffs. All sizes. Not less than ¼ dozen sold.
4K78—Dozen....... $1.06

Waltham Balance Staffs. All sizes. Not less than ¼ doz. sold.
4K80—Dozen....... $1.06

Hampden, Springfield, Seth Thomas, Plymouth, New York Standard, Trenton or Rockford Balance Staffs. All sizes.
4K82—Dozen....... $1.06

Balance Hole Jewels, cock and foot, for Elgin, Waltham, Hampden or New York Standard, for all sizes. Not less than ¼ dozen sold.
4K84—Dozen....... $1.02

Balance Cap or End Stones for Elgin, Waltham, Hampden or New York standard. All sizes. Not less than ¼ doz. sold.
4K86—Dozen....... 70c

Alcohol Cup. Glass. Height, 2 in. Diameter, 3 in. Shpg. wt., 1 lb. ¼ oz.
4K90........ 38c

Watch or Clock Oil. Shpg. wt., 5 oz.
4K92—Watch Oil.... 20c
4K93—Clock Oil.... 20c

Watch Oiler. Nickel plated.
4K94—Shpg. wt., 2 oz. 13c

Poising Tool, as illustrated, for poising and truing watch wheels. Shipping weight, 4 ounces.
4K96........ 70c

Blow Pipe, with ball, 8 or 10 in. State length.
4K98........ 32c

Files, Needle. Length of file complete, 4 inches. Shipping weight, 3 ounces.
4K100—Set of 6... 76c

Watch Brush, 3-row. Shpg. wt., 5 oz.
4K102........ 36c

4-row. Shipping weight, 5 ounces.
4K104........ 40c

Pliers, flat. Swiss make, 4-in. Shpg. wt., 3 oz.
4K106. 38c

Pliers, round. Swiss make, 4-in. Shpg. wt., 4 oz.
4K108... 38c

Pliers, end cutting. Swiss make, 4-in. Shpg. wt., 4 oz.
4K110........ 67c

Pliers, side cutting. Swiss make. 4-inch. Shipping weight, 3 oz.
4K112..... 67c

Alcohol Spheric Lamp, glass bulb, nickel plated base. Height, 5½ in. Shpg. wt., 6 oz.
4K114. 76c

Alcohol Lamp, glass bulb and cover, 4 in. high. Shipping weight, 8 ounces.
4K116........ 37c

Pendant Sleeve Driver, with nine prongs. Fits all sizes and styles of pendant sleeves. Shpg. wt., 3 oz.
4K118........ 94c

One doz. assorted Clock Drills. Shpg. wt., 2 oz.
Not less than 1 doz. sold.
4K120—Dozen........ 28c

Pin Vise. Small, adjustable.
4K124........ 22c

Pin Vise. Hollow handle. Extra quality.
4K126
65c

Drill Stock, solid handle. Patent gear, 8 inches long, with 6 drills.
4K128—Shpg. wt., 1 lb... $1.10

Drill Stock, patent spiral, 9¼ inches long with six drills. Shpg. wt., 3 oz.
4K130........ 45c

Eyeglass. Hard rubber with coil spring; 2 to 5-inch focus. Shpg. wt., 4 oz.
4K132........ 98c

Eyeglass. Plain hard rubber without spring. 2 to 5-inch focus.
4K134........ 40c

Eyeglass. Double lens. Very powerful, for very accurate work. Shpg. wt., 4 oz.
4K136........ 98c

English Cutting Broaches. Set of 4. Shpg. wt., 2 oz.
4K138........ 30c

Blow pipe, plain, 8 or 10 inches. State length. Shipping weight, 4 ounces.
4K140
Each..... 16c

Files, half round or flat. State choice and length. Shpg. wt., 4 oz.
4K142
3-inch cut 3........ 30c
4-inch cut 3........ 34c
5-inch cut 3........ 44c

Files, Screw Head. For filing slots in screw heads. Length, 3½ inches.
4K144—Shpg. wt., 5 oz. 30c

Pivot Files. Conical pivots for balance staffs or square for pinions. State choice. Length, 2 inches.
4K146........ 40c

Tweezers. Medium points, nickel plated.
4K148........ 15c

Tweezers with hand remover on opposite end.
4K150........ 25c

Tweezers, hand remover.
4K152........ 46c

Tweezers. Fine points, nickel plated.
4K154........ 15c

Tweezers, hollow handle, Boley make, fine points, for hairsprings and other fine work.
4K156........ 27c

Hammers, Swiss. State size.
4K160
2 in.... 30c | 2½ in.... 35c
2¼ in.... 30c | 2¾ in.... 35c

Adjustable roller remover. Nickel plated. Size, 2½-in. Shpg. wt., 4 oz.
4K162........ 98c

Jeweled Truing Caliper. Nickel plated jeweled end for balance truing, other end for poising. Shipping weight, 4 ounces.
4K164........ $1.58

Gold plated wire, round or square; in ½-ounce coils.
First Quality Round Wire. Sizes, 16 to 21 gauge.
4K166
Per ounce........ 85c

First Quality Square Wire. Sizes, 18 to 22 gauge.
4K168........ 85c

Saw Frame. Extra quality. Shpg. wt., 7 oz.
4K170.. 63c

Saw Blades. (Not less than 1 dozen sold.)
4K172........ 14c

Jobbing Stones assorted. Containing all colors and sizes in imitation of genuine.
4K174........ 90c

Anvil with hub. Nickel plated. ⅝x1¾-in. Shpg. wt., 8 oz.
4K176. 94c

Gauge for watch mainsprings, with gauge for measuring thickness. Length, 4¼ inches.
4K178........ $1.20

Silver Solder, for hard soldering or brazing. Shpg. wt., 2 oz.
4K180
Per oz.... $1.18

Soft Solder. 4K182.... 13c

Soldering Copper, small for jewelers. Shpg. wt., 6 oz.
4K184........ 22c

Soldering Fluid. Shipping wt., 7 oz.
4K186........ 18c

Staking and Punching Set, 24 punches and hollow steel stake in boxwood box. Shpg. wt., ¾ lb.
4K188
Set.... $1.25

Drills, set of forty-eight drills, assorted sizes, with drill stock in boxwood box. Shpg. wt., ¾ lb.
4K190
Set........ $1.40

Jewel Chucks, adjustable. Set of eight, used for holding jewels when reducing thickness of setting.
4K194—Shipping weight, 6 ounces.. $2.10

Vise, 1½-inch steel jaws, clamp vise, handy to adjust to any work bench. Shipping wt., 3 lbs.
4K196.. 90c

Screwdrivers. Set of seven, nickel plated. Shipping wt., 5 oz.
4K198
Set of 7.... 90c

Metal Head Screwdriver, in small, medium or large size. State size.
4K200........ 13c

Screwdriver. Adjustable, pull off top for extra blades, four different sizes.
4K202—Complete........ 24c

Winder, mainspring. Swiss. Length, 3½ inches.
4K204
98c

Oil stone Slips, hard, three-corner or square, 3-in. State choice. Shpg. wt., 1 oz.
4K206........ 38c

Roller Jewel Setter, nickel plated. Shipping weight, 2 oz.
4K208........ 23c

Screw Plate, single notched, 24 holes. Shpg. wt., 3 oz.
4K210........ $1.40

Gravers. Set of four. Square. Shpg. wt., 4 oz.
4K212... 85c

Movement Holder, brass. Adjustable for all size watch movements.
4K214........ 70c

Patent key. Fits any key wind watch.
4K216—Set........ 18c

Jewelers' Cement. For cementing china, glass, ivory, beads, pearls and jewelry. Shpg. wt., 5 oz.
4K218
Bottle........ 24c

Granite Hold Fast Cement. Shpg. wt., 5 oz.
4K220—Bottle. 18c

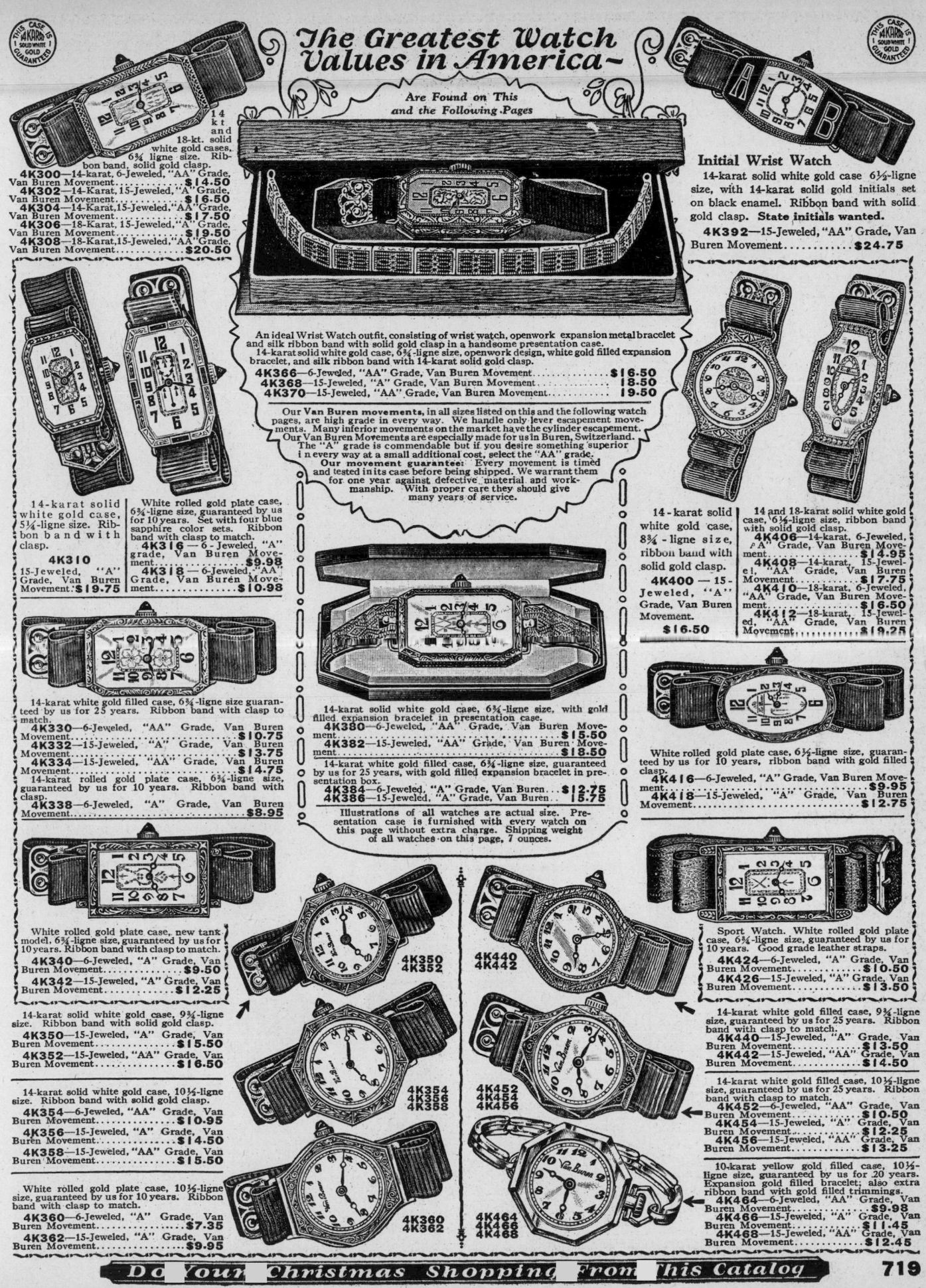

The Greatest Watch Values in America~

Are Found on This and the Following Pages

14 kt and 18-kt. solid white gold cases, 6¾ ligne size. Ribbon band, solid gold clasp.

4K300—14-karat, 6-Jeweled, "AA" Grade, Van Buren Movement..........$14.50

4K302—14-Karat, 15-Jeweled, "A" Grade, Van Buren Movement..........$16.50

4K304—14-Karat, 15-Jeweled, "AA" Grade, Van Buren Movement..........$17.50

4K306—18-Karat, 15-Jeweled, "A" Grade, Van Buren Movement..........$19.50

4K308—18-Karat, 15-Jeweled, "AA" Grade, Van Buren Movement..........$20.50

Initial Wrist Watch

14-karat solid white gold case 6½-ligne size, with 14-karat solid gold initials set on black enamel. Ribbon band with solid gold clasp. **State initials wanted.**

4K392—15-Jeweled, "AA" Grade, Van Buren Movement..........$24.75

An ideal Wrist Watch outfit, consisting of wrist watch, openwork expansion metal bracelet and silk ribbon band with solid gold clasp in a handsome presentation case.

14-karat solid white gold case, 6¾-ligne size, openwork design, white gold filled expansion bracelet, and silk ribbon band with 14-karat solid gold clasp.

4K366—6-Jeweled, "AA" Grade, Van Buren Movement..........$16.50

4K368—15-Jeweled, "A" Grade, Van Buren Movement..........18.50

4K370—15-Jeweled, "AA" Grade, Van Buren Movement..........19.50

Our Van Buren movements, in all sizes listed on this and the following watch pages, are high grade in every way. We handle only lever escapement movements. Many inferior movements on the market have the cylinder escapement. Our Van Buren Movements are especially made for us in Buren, Switzerland. The "A" grade is commendable but if you desire something superior in every way at a small additional cost, select the "AA" grade.

Our movement guarantee: Every movement is timed and tested in its case before being shipped. We warrant them for one year against defective material and workmanship. With proper care they should give many years of service.

14-karat solid white gold case, 5¼-ligne size. Ribbon band with clasp.

4K310 15-Jeweled, "A" Grade, Van Buren Movement: $19.75

White rolled gold plate case, 6¾-ligne size, guaranteed by us for 10 years. Set with four blue sapphire color sets. Ribbon band with clasp to match.

4K316—6-Jeweled, "A" grade, Van Buren Movement..........$9.98

4K318—6-Jeweled, "AA" Grade, Van Buren Movement..........$10.98

14-karat white gold filled case, 6¾-ligne size guaranteed by us for 25 years. Ribbon band with clasp to match.

4K330—6-Jeweled, "AA" Grade, Van Buren Movement..........$10.75

4K332—15-Jeweled, "A" Grade, Van Buren Movement..........$13.75

4K334—15-Jeweled, "AA" Grade, Van Buren Movement..........$14.75

14-karat rolled gold plate case, 6¾-ligne size, guaranteed by us for 10 years. Ribbon band with clasp.

4K338—6-Jeweled, "A" Grade, Van Buren Movement..........$8.95

14-karat solid white gold case, 6¾-ligne size, with gold filled expansion bracelet in presentation case.

4K380—6-Jeweled, "AA" Grade, Van Buren Movement..........$15.50

4K382—15-Jeweled, "AA" Grade, Van Buren Movement..........$18.50

14-karat white gold filled case, 6¾-ligne size, guaranteed by us for 25 years, with gold filled expansion bracelet in presentation box.

4K384—6-Jeweled, "A" Grade, Van Buren..........$12.75

4K386—15-Jeweled, "A" Grade, Van Buren..........15.75

Illustrations of all watches are actual size. Presentation case is furnished with every watch on this page without extra charge. Shipping weight of all watches on this page, 7 ounces.

14-karat solid white gold case, 8¾-ligne size, ribbon band with solid gold clasp.

4K400—15-Jeweled, "A" Grade, Van Buren Movement. **$16.50**

14 and 18-karat solid white gold case, 6¼-ligne size, ribbon band with solid gold clasp.

4K406—14-karat, 6-Jeweled, "A" Grade, Van Buren Movement..........$14.95

4K408—14-karat, 15-Jeweled, "AA" Grade, Van Buren Movement..........$17.75

4K410—18-karat, 6-Jeweled, "AA" Grade, Van Buren Movement..........$16.50

4K412—18-karat, 15-Jeweled, "AA" Grade, Van Buren Movement..........$19.25

White rolled gold plate case, 6½-ligne size, guaranteed by us for 10 years, ribbon band with gold filled clasp.

4K416—6-Jeweled, "A" Grade, Van Buren Movement..........$9.95

4K418—15-Jeweled, "A" Grade, Van Buren Movement..........$12.75

White rolled gold plate case, new tank model, 6¾-ligne size, guaranteed by us for 10 years. Ribbon band with clasp to match.

4K340—6-Jeweled, "A" Grade, Van Buren Movement..........$9.50

4K342—15-Jeweled, "A" Grade, Van Buren Movement..........$12.25

14-karat solid white gold case, 9¾-ligne size. Ribbon band with solid gold clasp.

4K350—15-Jeweled, "A" Grade, Van Buren Movement..........$15.50

4K352—15-Jeweled, "AA" Grade, Van Buren Movement..........$16.50

14-karat solid white gold case, 10½-ligne size. Ribbon band with solid gold clasp.

4K354—6-Jeweled, "AA" Grade, Van Buren Movement..........$10.95

4K356—15-Jeweled, "A" Grade, Van Buren Movement..........$14.50

4K358—15-Jeweled, "AA" Grade, Van Buren Movement..........$15.50

White rolled gold plate case, 10½-ligne size, guaranteed by us for 10 years. Ribbon band with clasp to match.

4K360—6-Jeweled, "A" Grade, Van Buren Movement..........$7.35

4K362—15-Jeweled, "A" Grade, Van Buren Movement..........$9.95

4K350
4K352

4K440
4K442

4K354
4K356
4K358

4K452
4K454
4K456

4K360
4K362

4K464
4K466
4K468

Sport Watch. White rolled gold plate case, 6¾-ligne size, guaranteed by us for 10 years. Good grade leather straps.

4K424—6-Jeweled, "A" Grade, Van Buren Movement..........$10.50

4K426—15-Jeweled, "A" Grade, Van Buren Movement..........$13.50

14-karat white gold filled case, 9¾-ligne size, guaranteed by us for 25 years. Ribbon band with clasp to match.

4K440—15-Jeweled, "A" Grade, Van Buren Movement..........$13.50

4K442—15-Jeweled, "A" Grade, Van Buren Movement..........$14.50

14-karat white gold filled case, 10½-ligne size, guaranteed by us for 25 years. Ribbon band with clasp to match.

4K452—6-Jeweled, "AA" Grade, Van Buren Movement..........$10.50

4K454—15-Jeweled, "A" Grade, Van Buren Movement..........$12.25

4K456—15-Jeweled, "AA" Grade, Van Buren Movement..........$13.25

10-karat yellow gold filled case, 10½-ligne size, guaranteed by us for 20 years. Expansion gold filled bracelet; also extra ribbon band with gold filled trimmings.

4K464—6-Jeweled, "AA" Grade, Van Buren Movement..........$9.98

4K466—15-Jeweled, "A" Grade, Van Buren Movement..........$11.45

4K468—15-Jeweled, "AA" Grade, Van Buren Movement..........$12.45

Ladies' Wrist Watches in 18-K 14-K Solid Gold

The greatest Watch values in America are offered by Sears, Roebuck and Co. If you wish to buy a good wrist watch and save money, you can easily select it from these pages. Every movement we sell is timed and tested in the case before being shipped. We warrant each movement for one year against defective material and workmanship. With proper care it should give many years of service. Illustrations show actual size of each watch. Presentation case is included with each watch. Shipping weight of all Watches on this page, 7 ounces.

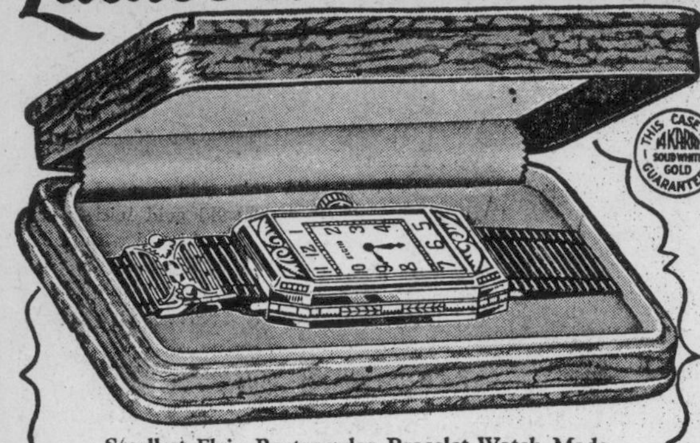

Smallest Elgin Rectangular Bracelet Watch Made Cased and Timed at the Factory

14-Karat Solid White Gold Case, hand engraved, fitted with 15-jeweled Elgin movement. Ribbon band with solid gold clasp.
4K500—Regular retail price, $60.00
Our price....................**$49.50**

18-Karat Solid White Gold Case, hand engraved, similar to the above, fitted with 17-jeweled Elgin movement, ribbon band with solid gold clasp.
4K502—Regular retail price. $85.00.
Our price....$67.50

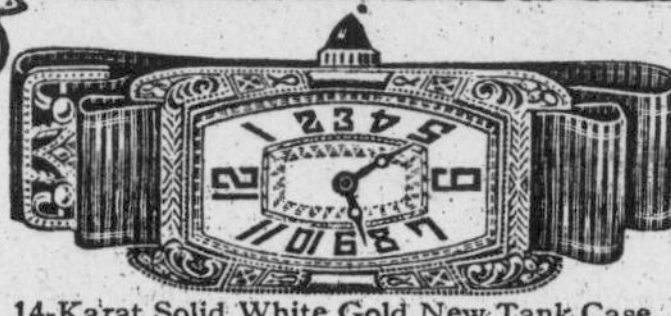

14-Karat Solid White Gold New Tank Case, 6¾-ligne size, ribbon band with solid gold clasp.
4K508—15-Jeweled, "A" Grade, Van Buren Movement..............**$18.50**
4K510—15-Jeweled, "AA" Grade, Van Buren Movement..............**$19.50**

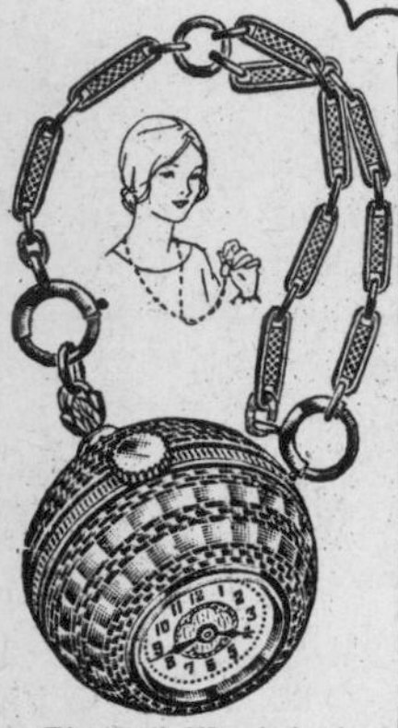

The Ball Watch is the new idea for ladies' timepiece. Illustration shows actual size. Consists of solid silver ball beautifully enameled in colors, pink, blue and green, with 16-inch enameled chain to match. Fitted with high grade 8¾-ligne size, 15-jeweled imported movement. Price is for complete watch with chain.
4K514—Pink.. **$24.50**
4K516—Blue... **24.50**
4K518—Green. **24.50**

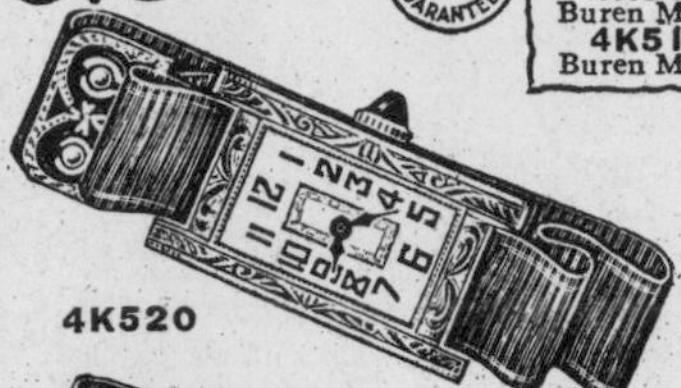

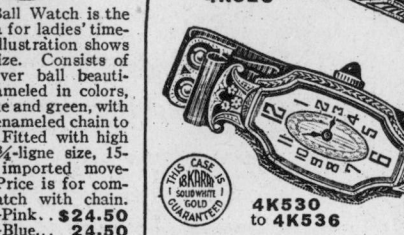

4K520

14-Karat Solid White Gold Tank Shape Case, 5¼-ligne size, ribbon band with solid gold clasp.
4K520—15-Jeweled, "A" Grade, Van Buren Movement..............**$21.75**

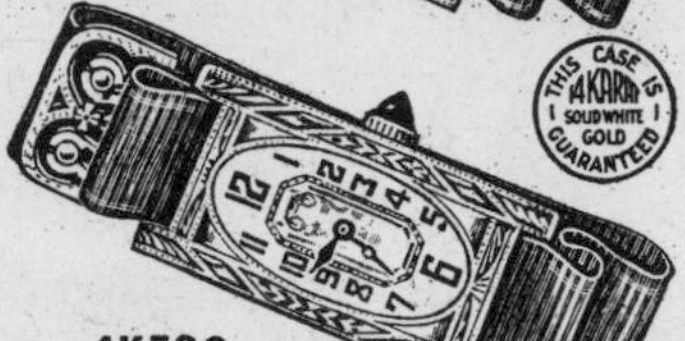

4K526

14-Karat Solid White Gold New Style Case, 5½-ligne size, ribbon band with solid gold clasp.
4K526—15-Jeweled, "AA" Grade, Van Buren Movement..............**$25.00**

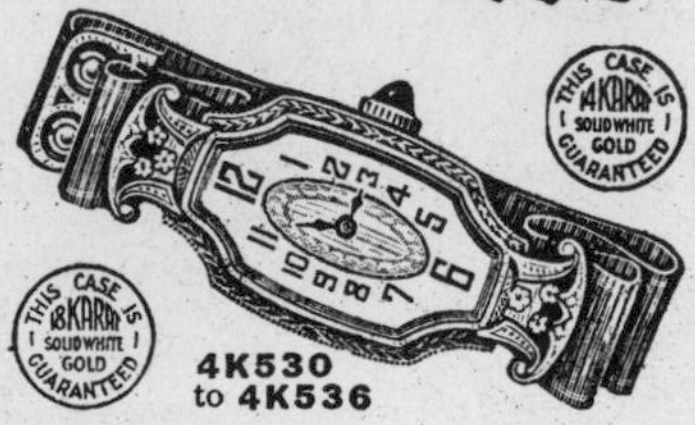

4K530 to 4K536

14 or 18-Karat Solid White Gold Case, 6½-ligne size, ribbon band with solid gold clasp.
4K530—14-Karat, 15-Jeweled, "A" Grade, Van Buren Movement..........**$17.75**
4K532—14-Karat, 15-Jeweled, "AA" Grade, Van Buren Movement..........**$18.75**
4K534—18-Karat, 15-Jeweled, "A" Grade, Van Buren Movement..........**$19.75**
4K536—18-Karat, 15-Jeweled, "AA" Grade, Van Buren Movement..........**$20.75**

Elgin and Waltham

14-Karat Solid White Gold Case, 10/0 size, ribbon band with solid gold clasp.
4K590—7-Jeweled Elgin..............**$27.35**
4K592—7-Jeweled Waltham..............**27.35**
4K594—15-Jeweled Elgin..............**32.95**
4K596—15-Jeweled Waltham..............**32.95**

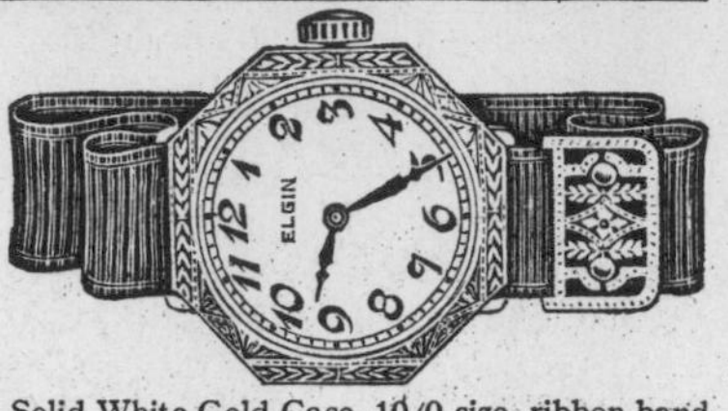

14-Karat Solid White Gold Case, 10/0 size, ribbon band with solid gold clasp.
4K600—7-Jeweled Elgin..............**$26.75**
4K602—7-Jeweled Waltham..............**26.75**
4K604—15-Jeweled Elgin..............**32.50**
4K606—15-Jeweled Waltham..............**32.50**

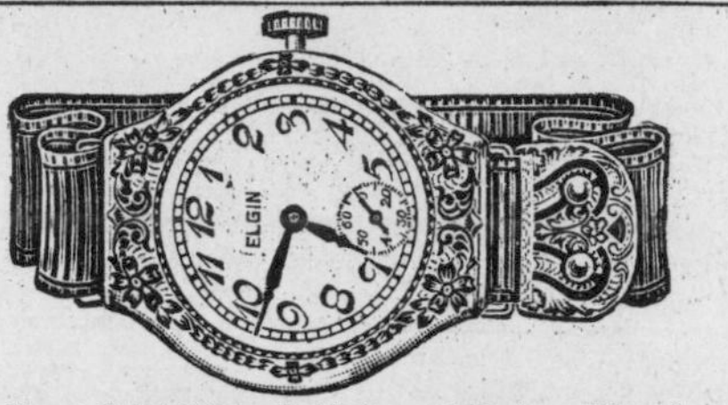

14-Karat Solid White Gold Case, 6/0 size, ribbon band with solid gold clasp. **State movement wanted.**
4K610—7-Jeweled, Elgin or Waltham....**$21.40**
4K612—15-Jeweled, Elgin or Waltham...**27.25**

14-Karat White Gold Filled Case, 6/0 size. Case guaranteed by us for 25 years. Ribbon band with clasp to match. **State movement wanted.**
4K614—7-Jeweled, Elgin or Waltham....**$18.45**
4K616—15-Jeweled, Elgin or Waltahm...**24.75**

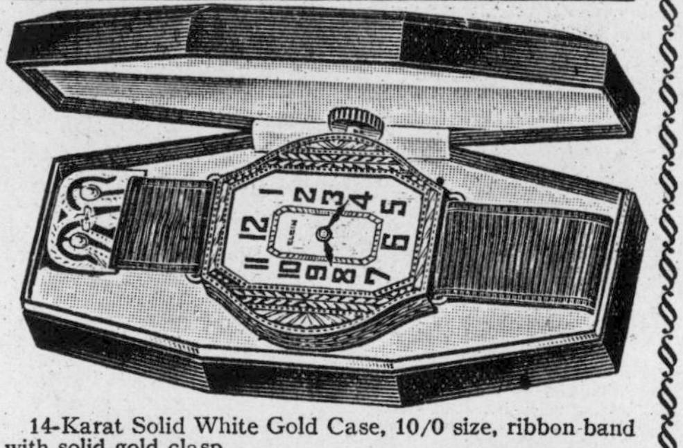

14-Karat Solid White Gold Case, 10/0 size, ribbon band with solid gold clasp.
4K620—7-Jeweled Elgin..............**$29.95**
4K622—15-Jeweled Elgin..............**34.90**

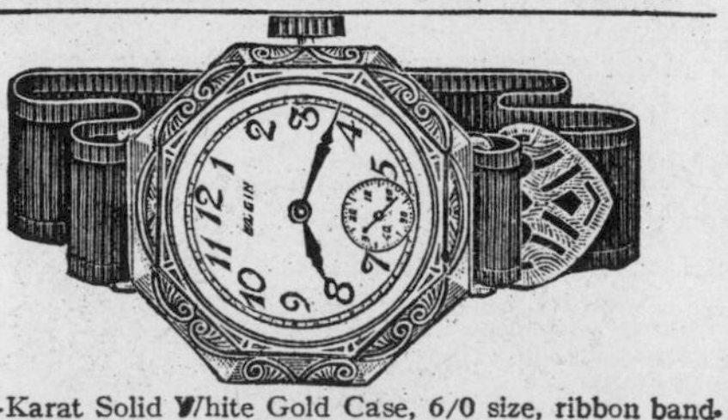

14-Karat Solid White Gold Case, 6/0 size, ribbon band with solid gold clasp. **State movement wanted.**
4K630—7-Jeweled Elgin or Waltham.....**$21.40**
4K632—15-Jeweled Elgin or Waltham....**27.25**

14-Karat White Gold Filled Case, 6/0 size, case guaranteed by us for 25 years. Ribbon band with clasp to match. **State movement wanted.**
4K634—7-Jeweled Elgin or Waltham.....$18.45
4K636—15-Jeweled Elgin or Waltham.....24.75

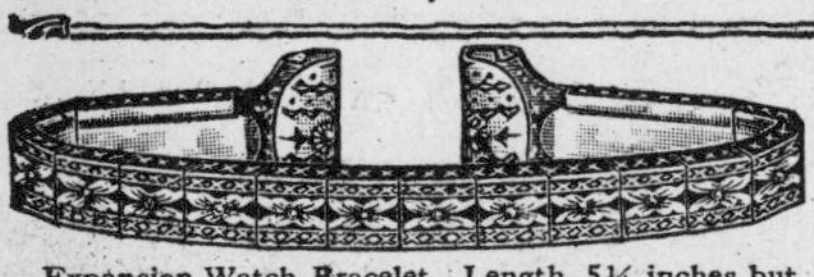

Expansion Watch Bracelet. Length, 5¼ inches but expands to 6½ inches. Furnished in ⅜ and ⁷⁄₁₆-inch end hooks. **State size wanted.**
4K540—Yellow gold filled..............**$1.75**
4K542—White gold filled..............**1.75**

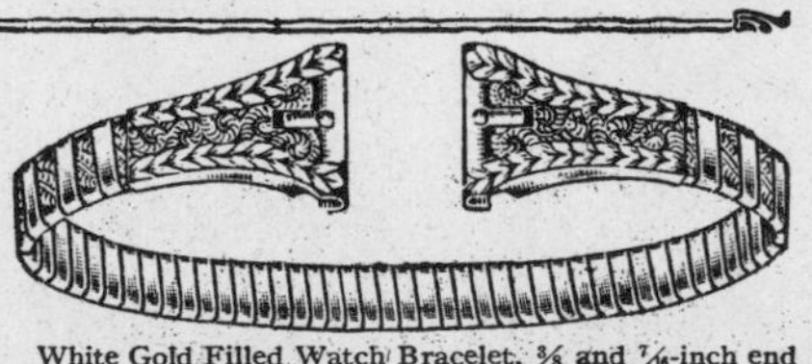

White Gold Filled Watch Bracelet, ⅜ and ⁷⁄₁₆-inch end hooks. **State size wanted.**
4K550—Length, 4¾ inches, expands to 5¾ in. **$2.85**
4K552—Length, 5 inches, expands to 6 in.. **2.85**
4K554—Length, 5¼ inches, expands to 6¼ in. **2.85**

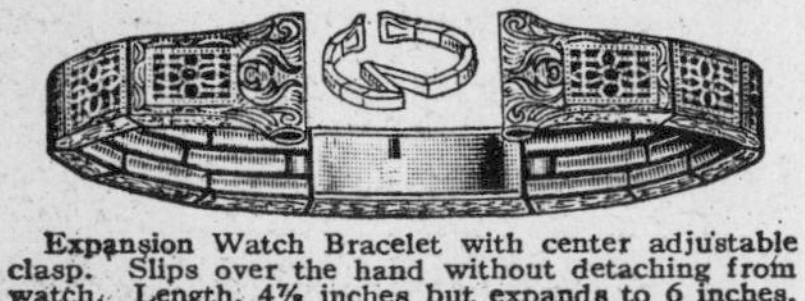

Expansion Watch Bracelet with center adjustable clasp. Slips over the hand without detaching from watch. Length, 4⅞ inches but expands to 6 inches. ⅜-inch end hook, open work design.
4K544—White gold filled..............**$2.50**

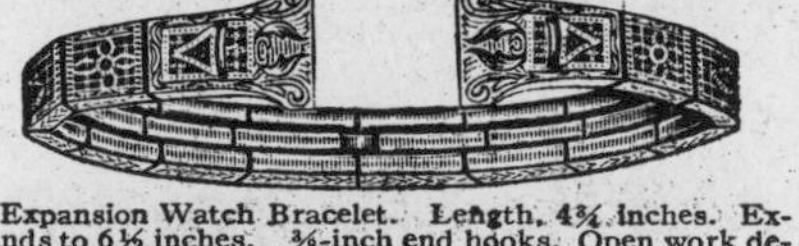

Expansion Watch Bracelet. Length, 4¾ inches. Expands to 6½ inches. ⅜-inch end hooks. Open work design. Four sapphire blue sets.
4K560—White gold filled..............**$2.25**

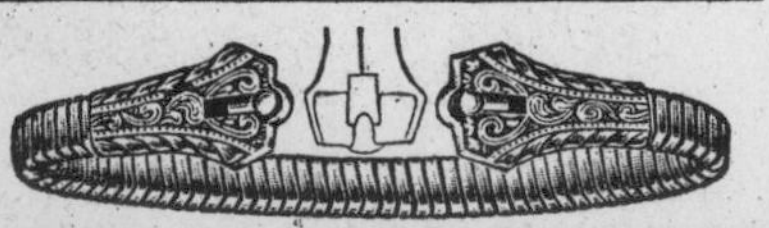

Expansion Watch Bracelet for 4K464 on page 719. Length, 5 inches. Expands to 6 inches.
4K546—Yellow gold filled..............**$1.75**

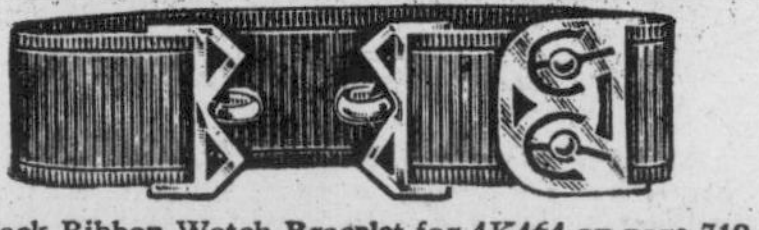

Black Ribbon Watch Bracelet for 4K464 on page 719.
4K566—Yellow gold filled trimmings.......**$0.38**
4K568—14-karat yellow solid gold trimmings. **1.35**

Shipping weight of all watch bracelets, 3 ounces.

Diamond Set Wrist Watches

14 and 18 Karat Solid White Gold

The watches on this page were designed by Master Craftsmen. If you desire beauty, dependability and up to the minute styles, select one of the splendid watches shown on this page.

Our "A" grade movement is commendable. We know it will give satisfaction, but if you desire something better, finer finished superior in every way but at a small additional cost, then select our "AA" grade.

We warrant our "A" and "AA" movements for one year against defective material and workmanship. With proper care they should give many years of service. Illustrations are actual sizes. Shipping weight of all Watches on this page, 7 ounces.

14-Karat Solid White Gold Case, 6½-ligne size. Set with two genuine brilliant regular cut diamonds and four blue synthetic sapphires. Ribbon band with solid gold clasp.

4K700—6-Jeweled, "AA" Grade, Van Buren Movement....................................**$24.50**

4K702—15-Jeweled, "A" Grade, Van Buren Movement....................................**$28.50**

4K704—15-Jeweled, "AA" Grade, Van Buren Movement....................................**$29.50**

14-Karat Solid White Gold Case, 6½-ligne size, set with two genuine brilliant regular cut diamonds and four blue synthetic sapphires. Ribbon band with solid gold clasp.

4K712—15-Jeweled "AA" Grade, Van Buren Movement....................................**$32.50**

14-Karat Solid White Gold Case, 6½-ligne size, set with two genuine brilliant regular cut diamonds and four blue synthetic sapphires. Ribbon band with solid gold clasp.

4K718—15-Jeweled, "A" Grade, Van Buren Movement....................................**$32.50**

4K720—15-Jeweled, "AA" Grade, Van Buren Movement....................................**$33.50**

14-Karat Solid White Gold Case, 6¾-ligne size, set with two genuine brilliant regular cut diamonds and two blue synthetic sapphires. Ribbon band with solid gold clasp.

4K726—15-Jeweled, "A" Grade, Van Buren Movement....................................**$29.50**

4K728—15-Jeweled, "AA" Grade, Van Buren Movement....................................**$30.50**

Platinum Trimmed Wrist Watch

18-Karat Solid White Gold Genuine Platinum Trimmed Case, 6½-ligne size, set with four genuine brilliant regular cut diamonds and four blue synthetic sapphires. Ribbon band with solid gold clasp.

4K734—15-Jeweled, "A" Grade, Van Buren Movement....................................**$36.50**

4K736—15-Jeweled, "AA" Grade, Van Buren Movement....................................**$37.50**

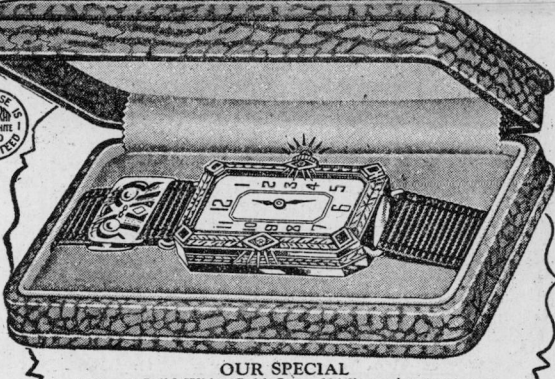

OUR SPECIAL

14-Karat Solid White Gold Case, 6¾-ligne size, two genuine brilliant regular cut diamonds and four blue synthetic sapphires (one in each corner). Ribbon band, solid gold clasp.

4K748—6-Jeweled, "AA" Grade, Van Buren Movement....................................**$23.75**

4K750—15-Jeweled, "A" Grade, Van Buren Movement....................................**$28.00**

4K752—15-Jeweled, "AA" Grade, Van Buren Movement....................................**$29.00**

14-Karat Solid White Gold Case, 5½-ligne size, set with two genuine brilliant regular cut diamonds and four emerald green color sets.

4K740—15-Jeweled, "AA" Grade, Van Buren Movement....................................**$35.50**

18-Karat Solid White Gold Case, 5½-ligne size, set with six genuine brilliant regular cut diamonds and two blue synthetic sapphires. Ribbon band with solid gold clasp.

4K754—15-Jeweled, "AA" Grade, Van Buren Movement....................................**$58.00**

18-Karat Solid White Gold Case, 6½-ligne size, set with four genuine brilliant regular cut diamonds and four blue synthetic sapphires. Ribbon band with solid gold clasp.

4K760—15-Jeweled, "A" Grade, Van Buren Movement....................................**$44.00**

4K762—15-Jeweled, "AA" Grade, Van Buren Movement....................................**$45.00**

18-Karat Solid White Gold Case, 5½-ligne size, set with eight genuine brilliant regular cut diamonds. Ribbon band with solid gold clasp.

4K766—15-Jeweled, "AA" Grade, Van Buren Movement....................................**$61.50**

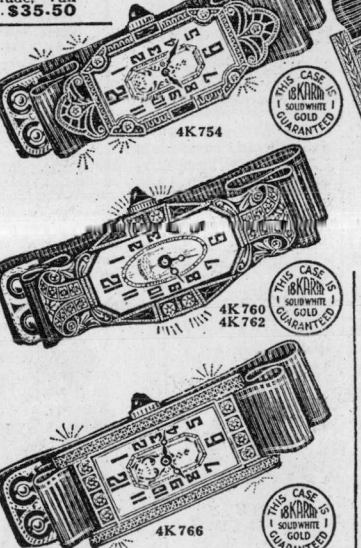

4K754

4K760
4K762

4K766

18-Karat Solid White Gold Case, 5¼-ligne size, set with two genuine brilliant regular cut diamonds and four blue synthetic sapphires. Ribbon band with solid gold clasp.

4K770—15-Jeweled, "A" Grade, Van Buren Movement....**$37.50**

Genuine Platinum and Platinum-Trimmed Diamond Set Watches

18-Karat Solid White Gold Genuine Platinum Trimmed Case, 5½-ligne size, set with six genuine brilliant regular cut diamonds and four blue synthetic sapphires. Ribbon band with solid gold clasp.

4K776—15-Jeweled, "AA" Grade, Van Buren Movement....................................**$63.50**

18-Karat Solid White Gold Genuine Platinum Trimmed Case, 5½-ligne size, set with six genuine brilliant regular cut diamonds and four emerald green color sets. Ribbon band with solid gold clasp.

4K786—15-Jeweled, "AA" Grade, Van Buren Movement.................**$69.50**

18-Karat Solid White Gold Genuine Platinum Trimmed Case, 6½-ligne size, set with twenty-two genuine brilliant regular cut diamonds. Ribbon band with solid gold clasp. Usually sells for $125.00 elsewhere.

4K782—15-Jeweled, "AA" Grade, Van Buren Movement....................................**$89.50**

Very Beautiful Genuine Platinum Case, 5½-ligne size, set with 32 genuine brilliant regular cut diamonds, total weight, about ½ carat or 59/100 carat. Ribbon band with 18-karat clasp. Usually sells for $250.00 elsewhere. A special Sears value.

4K790—15-Jeweled, "AA" Grade, Van Buren Movement.......................**$175.00**

See Index and Information Pages 542 to 570

Railway Watches

Hamilton Railway Watch

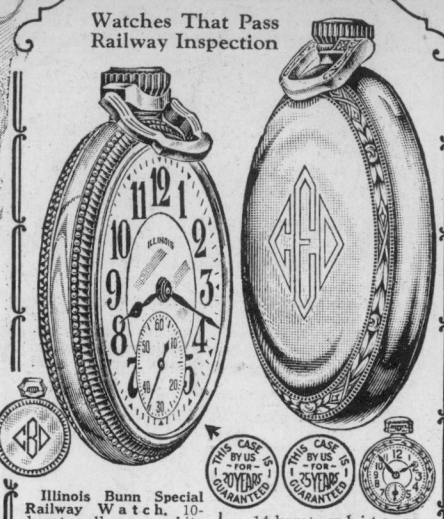

Mention Letters Wanted

This Hamilton Railway Watch is generally known as the "No. 992," manufacturer's list price, $60.00. Our price is $49.50, including any two or three-letter monogram. The case is 10-karat yellow gold filled, 16-size, guaranteed by us for 20 years. The movement has 21 jewels, adjusted to 5 positions, temperature and isochronism. Will pass railroad inspection. The bows on these watches vary slightly. These watches are cased and timed at the factory.

4K1278....$49.50

Our movement guarantee: Every movement we sell is timed and tested in its case before being shipped. With proper care any movement will give you entire satisfaction for many years. We warrant them for one year against defective material and workmanship. Illustrations show actual size of the watches. Presentation case with every watch without charge. Shipping weight, 8 ounces.

Special railway model, nickel composition case. Constructed with an extra inside cap, insuring absolute protection against dust and dampness. 16-size, screw back and bezel, dustproof pendant and new rigid squat bow. Fitted with following movements which pass railway inspection:

4K1308—19-J. Riverside Waltham $34.30
4K1312—21-J. Crescent St. Waltham.$36.75
4K1314—23-J. Vanguard Waltham.. 41.00
4K1316—23-J. Spec. Railway Hampden 43.50

Also fitted with following movements, which will not pass railway inspection:

4K1320— 7-J. Waltham or Elgin...$10.45
4K1322—15-J. Waltham or Elgin.. 15.25
4K1324—17-J. Waltham or Elgin.. 18.10
4K1326—17-J. P. S. Bartlett Waltham 18.95
4K1328—19-J. Railway Hampden.. 33.75

Exactly forty-one years ago, Richard W. Sears, founder of Sears, Roebuck and Co., began selling watches to railroad men. Since that time Sears, Roebuck and Co. have sold over four million watches. We believe that many of the watches sold many years ago are still serving their owners in a faithful way. If you have one of our watches that has given you many years of service, we would like you to write us a letter telling us about your experience.

The Howard Railway Watch. Our price is only $52.25. Standard list price, $80.00. The case is 16-size, gold filled, extra quality, new heavy duty model, guaranteed by us for 25 years. Dustproof with non-pullout bow. The 21-jewel movement is adjusted to 5 positions, temperature and isochronism, and lever setting only. Will pass railroad inspection. Furnished in a special velvet lined case. Price includes engraving any two or three letters. **State letters wanted.**

4K1332—White.$62.25
4K1334—Green $62.25

Illinois Bunn Special Railway Watch. 10-karat yellow or white gold filled, plain back, open face, 16-size case, guaranteed by us for 20 years. New model especially designed for railroad watch; has extra heavy pendant and bow. Fitted with 21 or 23 jewels, 60-hour movement, adjusted to 6 positions, temperature and isochronism. Pass railroad inspection. Cased and timed at the factory. Engraved with any two or three letter monogram. **State letters wanted.**

4K1390—21-J. yellow gold filled. Standard list price, $60.00. Our price is...$42.50
4K1392—21-J., white gold filled. Standard list price, $65.00. Our price is........$47.50
4K1394—23-J. yellow gold filled. Standard list price, $70.00. Our price is....$49.50
4K1396—23-J., white gold filled. Standard list price, $75.00. Our price is........$54.50

14-karat white or green gold filled, 16-size, open face, dust and dampproof, swing ring case, guaranteed by us for 25 years. Engraved with any two or three letter monogram. **Mention letters, color of gold and movement wanted.** The following movements pass railway inspection:

4K1400—19-Jeweled Riverside Waltham. $42.90
4K1404—21-Jeweled Crescent St. Waltham $45.75
4K1408—23-Jeweled Vanguard Waltham $51.00

Also fitted with following movements which will not pass railway inspection:

4K1412—15-Jeweled Waltham or Elgin $23.75
4K1414—17-Jeweled Waltham or Elgin $26.75
4K1416—17-Jeweled P. S. Bartlett, adjusted, Waltham $27.50

Heavy double protective Railway watch. 10-karat yellow gold filled, 16-size case, guaranteed by us for 20 years. This case is constructed to meet the most severe requirements. Popular with railroad men. Very sturdy. It is fitted with a new type of rigid pendant and extra strong bow. The illustration shows the back and the front of the watch. Small sectional view shows its construction, the front bezel unscrewed, the center holding the movement, and the inside protecting cap, thus giving double protection. Engraved with your name. Prices quoted include engraving. **Give catalog number and movement wanted and write plainly the name to be engraved.**

The following movements pass railway inspection:

4K1420—19-Jeweled Riverside Waltham. $37.75
4K1424—21-Jeweled Crescent St. Waltham $41.00
4K1428—23-Jeweled Vanguard Waltham. 50.00

Also fitted with following movements which do not pass railway inspection:

4K1432— 7-Jeweled Waltham or Elgin.$15.85
4K1434—15-Jeweled Waltham or Elgin. 20.95
4K1436—17-Jeweled Waltham or Elgin. 24.50
4K1438—17-Jeweled P. S. Bartlett Waltham 25.50

Monogrammed Watches

Style A   Style B

12-size, 10 and 14-karat, yellow gold filled, plain polished case. Open face, screw back and screw bezel. Either style engraving, "A" or "B," included in price. **Mention letters, style of engraving and movement wanted.** 10-karat cases are guaranteed by us for 20 years. 14-karat cases for 25 years.

4K1340—15-J. Van Buren Movement, 10-karat....$11.75
4K1342—15-J. Van Buren Movement, 14-karat.........$14.75
4K1344— 7-J Waltham, Elgin or Hampden Movement, 10-karat............ 12.85
4K1346— 7-J. Waltham, Elgin or Hampden Movement, 14-karat............ 16.15
4K1348—15-J. Waltham, Elgin or Hampden Movement, 10-karat............ 16.65
4K1350—15-J. Waltham, Elgin or Hampden Movement, 14-karat............ 19.85
4K1352—17-J. Waltham, Elgin or Hampden, 10-karat......... 19.50
4K1354—17-J. Waltham, Elgin or Hampden, 14-karat......... 22.35
4K1356—19-J. P. S. Bartlett Waltham, 10-karat.... 23.00
4K1358—19-J. P. S. Bartlett Waltham, 14-karat.... 26.25
4K1360—17-J. O. F. Elgin Movement, adj., 10-karat.. 25.75
4K1362—17-J. O. F. Elgin Movement, adj., 14-kt.. 30.70

16-size, 10 and 14-karat, yellow gold filled, plain polished case. Open face, screw back and screw bezel. Any style engraving, "A" or "B," included in price. (For style of engraving see 4K1340.) **Mention letters, style of engraving and movement wanted.**

4K1370—15-Jeweled Van Buren Movement, 10-karat, 20-year case.$13.25
4K1372—15-Jeweled Van Buren Movement, 14-karat, 25-year case.......$16.40
4K1374— 7-Jeweled Waltham or Elgin Movement, 10-karat, 20-year case....$13.50
4K1376— 7-Jeweled Waltham or Elgin Movement, 14-karat, 25-year case....$16.65
4K1378—15-Jeweled Waltham or Elgin Movement, 10-karat, 20-year case....$18.15
4K1380—15-Jeweled Waltham or Elgin Movement, 14-karat, 25-year case....$21.25
4K1382—17-Jeweled Waltham or Elgin Movement, 10-karat, 20-year case....$20.80
4K1384—17-Jeweled Waltham or Elgin Movement, 14-karat, 25-year case....$23.95

Famous Watches - Greatly Reduced Prices

Gold Filled Open Face Watches

The engraving on the watches may vary slightly from the illustrations shown, because our stock is replenished daily with the latest designs. Understand, however, that the model, shape, general appearance and quality are as described.

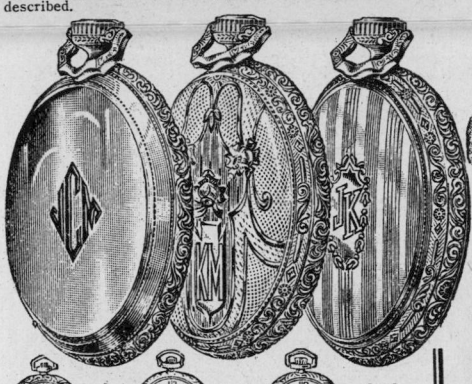

We warrant all movements for one year against defective material and workmanship. With proper care they should give many years of service. Illustrations show actual size. Presentation case with every watch without charge. Shipping weight, watches, 8 ounces.

Elgin Streamline 17-Jewel Monogram Watch **$32.50** All our watches are timed and tested before leaving our store.

Style A Style B Style C

10-karat white or green gold filled, 12-size, open face. Cases guaranteed by us for 20 years. Your choice of the three styles, A, B and C, illustrated above at the same price. **When ordering be sure to mention style wanted.** Price includes engraving with any two or three letters. **Mention catalog number, letters, movement, color of gold and style wanted.**

4K1450—15-Jeweled Van Buren	$14.25
4K1452—7-Jeweled Elgin or Waltham	14.50
4K1454—15-Jeweled Elgin or Waltham	18.35
4K1456—17-Jeweled Elgin or Waltham	20.85
4K1458—17-Jeweled Elgin, Adjusted	25.50
4K1460—19-Jeweled P. S. Bartlett Waltham	28.75

10-karat white or green gold filled, 12-size, open face, hinge back, quindecagon shape case. Prices include engraving with any two or three-letter monogram. State letters, catalog number, movement and color of gold wanted.

4K1504—15-Jeweled Van Buren	$15.00
4K1506—7-Jeweled Waltham, Elgin or Hampden	15.75
4K1508—15-Jeweled Waltham, Elgin or Hampden	20.50
4K1510—17-J. Waltham, Elgin or Hampden	22.50
4K1512—17-Jeweled Elgin, Adjusted	25.50
4K1514—17-Jeweled P. S. Bartlett Waltham	29.95

WALTHAM

Waltham Colonial, 12-size, open face, monogram watches. Extra thin model, white or green gold. Gold filled and solid gold. Fitted with 17-jeweled adjusted movement. Exposed winding wheels and patent regular prices include cost of monogram. **State color of gold and letters wanted.**

14-karat white or green gold filled case is guaranteed by us for 25 years. Frequently sells elsewhere for $40.00. Our price is only $32.50.

4K1554—White gold filled	$32.50
4K1556—Green gold filled	32.50

14-karat white or green gold solid gold. Others often ask $60.00. Our price is only $47.50.

4K1558—White solid gold	$47.50
4K1560—Green solid gold	47.50

Elgin Streamline, 12-size, open face, monogram watch. Furnished in white or green color solid gold or gold filled. Very thin model. Fitted with 17-jewel movement, 3 adjustments. Exceptional timekeepers. Special silver dial. Prices include cost of monogram. **Mention letters wanted.** 14-karat white or green gold filled case is guaranteed by us for 25 years. Others often ask $40.00. Our price is only $32.50.

4K1564—White gold filled	$32.50
4K1566—Green gold filled	32.50

14-karat white or green solid gold. Others often ask $60.00. Our price is only $47.50.

4K1568—White solid gold	$47.50
4K1570—Green solid gold	47.50

Because Sears-Roebuck have for years offered the lowest prices on the finest watches obtainable, we have become America's largest watch merchants. This fine model in 14-karat solid white or green gold is an example of our great values. This is an open face case with plain back and hand engraved edge. Our price includes engraving with two or three letters. State catalog number, letters and color of gold wanted.

4K1574—7-Jeweled Waltham, Elgin or Hampden	$25.00
4K1576—15-Jeweled Waltham, Elgin or Hampden	$29.50
4K1578—17-Jeweled Waltham, Elgin or Hampden	$32.00
4K1580—17-Jeweled Elgin, Adjusted	$35.00
4K1582—19-Jeweled P. S. Bartlett Waltham	$38.50

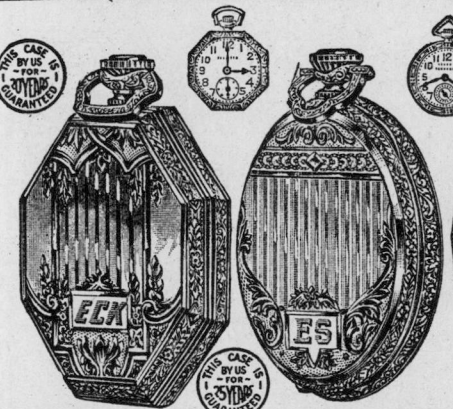

10-karat white or green gold filled, 12-size, open face, octagon shape. Price includes engraving with any two or three letters. Mention catalog number, color of gold and letters wanted.

4K1520—15-Jeweled Van Buren	$15.25
4K1522—7-Jeweled Waltham, Elgin or Hampden	$16.50
4K1524—15-Jeweled Waltham, Elgin or Hampden	$20.50
4K1526—17-Jeweled Waltham, Elgin or Hampden	$23.50
4K1528—17-Jeweled Elgin, Adjusted	$26.00
4K1530—19-Jeweled P. S. Bartlett Waltham	$29.75

14-karat white or green gold filled, 12-size, open face case guaranteed by us for 25 years. Price includes engraving with any two or three letters. **Mention catalog number, color of gold and letters wanted.**

4K1540—15-Jeweled Van Buren Movement	$15.00
4K1542—7-Jeweled Waltham or Elgin Movement	$16.25
4K1544—15-Jeweled Waltham or Elgin Movement	$20.50
4K1546—17-J. Waltham or Elgin	$22.85
4K1548—17-Jeweled Elgin Movement, Adjusted	$26.85
4K1550—19-Jeweled P. S. Bartlett Waltham Movement	$29.50

14-karat white or green gold filled, 12-size, open face, quindecagon shape case, guaranteed by us for 25 years. Prices include engraving with any two letters. **State catalog number, letters and color of gold wanted.**

4K1590—7-Jeweled Waltham, Elgin or Hampden	$18.85
4K1592—15-Jeweled Waltham, Elgin or Hampden	$22.75
4K1594—17-Jeweled Waltham, Elgin or Hampden	$25.15
4K1596—17-Jeweled Elgin, Adjusted	$26.85
4K1598—19-Jeweled P. S. Bartlett Waltham	$30.00

14-karat white or green gold filled, 12-size, open face, octagon shape case, guaranteed by us for 25 years. Prices include engraving with any two letters. **State catalog number, letters and color of gold wanted.**

4K1606—7-Jeweled Waltham, Elgin or Hampden	$18.85
4K1608—15-Jeweled Waltham or Elgin	$22.75
4K1610—17-Jeweled Waltham, Elgin or Hampden	$25.15
4K1612—17-Jeweled Elgin, Adjusted	$26.85
4K1614—19-Jeweled P. S. Bartlett Waltham	$30.00

Hamilton

A genuine Hamilton Watch which usually sells elsewhere for $50.00 for only $44.00. This famous movement is supplied in either a white or green gold filled case, guaranteed by us for 25 years. This is the popular 12-size model. The case is beautifully engraved. The dial is of silver metal with an attractively engraved center. Our prices include engraving of a two or three letter monogram. State letters wanted. The 17-jeweled movement is of the finest type, timed and tested before leaving the factory.

4K1620—White gold filled	$44.00
4K1622—Green gold filled	44.00

The Popular Dueber-Hampden Watches

$10.98

Engraved with any 2 or 3 Letter Monogram—State Letters

Dueber-Hampden

Illustrations are actual size. Shipping weight of all watches on this page, 8 ounces. All our watches are timed and tested before leaving our store.

The Dueber-Hampden Co. for a generation has made high class watches which have become famous throughout the world for accuracy and soundness of construction. They are dependable timekeepers and will give a lifetime of service—and for comparatively little money, too. Here is an opportunity to buy one of them for about one-third less than the usual retail price. It is without question one of the greatest values ever offered in a good watch made by one of the leading American watchmakers.

It is one of the always popular 12-size, open face, screw back, and screw bezel, thin model, plain highly polished, monogrammed watches. The case is 10-karat yellow gold filled, guaranteed by us for 20 years. The movement is 7-jeweled, has nickel plates and exposed winding wheels. Accurate and sound in every way. Timed and tested at the factory. **State initials wanted.**

4K1630......$10.98

Rolled Gold Plate

We guarantee Our Rolled Gold Plated Cases to give you 10 years of service. We warrant our movements for one year against defective material and workmanship.

A watch of beauty and distinction, with all the grace and dependability of a true aristocrat. This watch is for the man who discriminates—who recognizes fine workmanship and who demands quality and accuracy. Patterned after a very expensive watch, this quindecagon, 12-size, open face, thin model is an outstanding value!

Note These Remarkable Features

You may select either a white or green rolled gold plated case, guaranteed by us for 10 years. Note the French bow, usually supplied only on the finest of watches. Examine the beautifully engraved case, which we furnish in a variety of up to the minute designs. The silvered dial is such as is only found in the finest watches.

The movement is our own high grade Van Buren, guaranteed by us for one year against defective material and workmanship. This fine watch should give you many years of splendid service.

Remember: This is a watch that we give our highest recommendation. Dollar for dollar, we know of no watch that is its equal. Only because Sears-Roebuck are the world's largest dealers in watches are we able to offer this astonishing value! State color of gold desired. Shpg. wt., 8 oz.

4K1660—6-Jeweled................**$7.75**
4K1662—15-Jeweled................**$9.75**

Where can you duplicate this beautiful Dueber-Hampden Watch at our price, $8.50?

It is a 12-size, open face thin model. The case is a copy from one of the latest high priced watches, exquisitely engraved design made of a solid white metal known as silverine, a nickel compound resembling white gold. The movement is 7-jeweled, with nickel plates and winding wheels. Attractive dial with gold finish fancy center.

4K1632...$8.50

Genuine Dueber-Hampden

15-jeweled movement in 20-year case for only $14.50.

We suggest this watch for the man who wants the medium grade and price Dueber-Hampden. We are certain you cannot equal the value elsewhere.

12-size, 10-karat white or green gold filled, open face, beautifully hand engraved in a variety of designs, case guaranteed by us for 20 years. Either 15 or 7-jeweled, and cased and tested at the factory. Has nickel plates, exposed winding wheels and patent regulator. Silver metal with gold finish engraved center.

4K1638—15-Jeweled, white gold filled........**$14.50**
4K1640—15-Jeweled, green gold filled...**$14.50**
4K1642—7-Jeweled, white gold filled...**$11.50**
4K1644—7-Jeweled, green gold filled...**$11.50**

Genuine Dueber-Hampden

17-jeweled movement in 20-year case for only $15.98.

Here is your opportunity to buy a real high grade, beautiful, 17-jeweled watch at a price far below the prices asked elsewhere for watches of similar grade.

12-size, open face, beautifully hand engraved in a variety of designs. 10-karat gold filled case, guaranteed by us for 20 years. The movement is 17-jeweled, adjusted, patent regulator, exposed winding wheel. Fancy gold finish engraved center silver metal dial. Initial engraved without extra cost. State initial wanted.

4K1646—White gold filled........................**$15.98**
4K1648—Green gold filled.........................**$15.98**

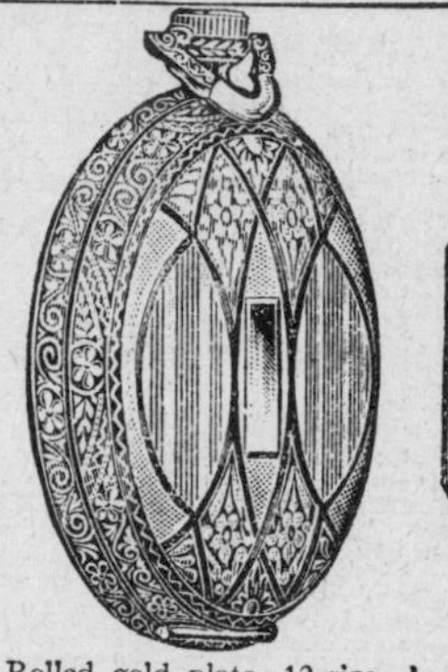

Genuine Dueber-Hampden

17-jeweled adjusted movement in 25-year case for only $19.75.

For the man who wants the best Dueber-Hampden Watch, we have this fine reliable timekeeper. It is really a remarkable watch, high grade in every way, with a splendid movement which will keep accurate time. In fact, a watch you will be thoroughly satisfied with. Now consider our price—only $19.75 against the usual retail price, $32.50. 12-size, thin model, open face, beautifully hand engraved in a variety of new designs. 14-karat white or green gold filled case, guaranteed by us for 25 years. Fitted with 17-jeweled adjusted movement, safety pinion, patent regulator, exposed winding wheel, breguet hair springs and cut expansion balance. Dial in silver metal with gold finished beautiful center design. Initial engraved without extra cost. State initial wanted.

4K1652—White gold filled........**$19.75**
4K1654—Green gold filled.**$19.75**

Rolled gold plate, 12-size, open face, white or green gold engraved case, guaranteed by us for 10 years. Mention catalog number, color of gold and movement.

4K1670—6-Jeweled Van Buren Movement, with raised gold figured dial....... **$7.50**
4K1672—15-Jeweled Van Buren Movement, with raised gold figured dial..........**$9.50**
4K1674—7-Jeweled Waltham, Elgin or Hampden........**$12.25**
4K1676—15-Jeweled Waltham or Elgin....**$16.00**

Rolled gold plate, 12-size, open face, octagon shape, white or green gold color, engraved case, guaranteed by us for 10 years. Mention catalog number and color of gold.

4K1680—6-Jeweled Van Buren, with raised gold figured dial. **$8.00**
4K1682—15-Jeweled Van Buren, with raised gold figured dial.........**$10.00**
4K1684—7-Jeweled Waltham, Elgin or Hampden.......**$12.80**
4K1686—15-Jeweled Waltham, Elgin or Hampden.....**$16.85**

12 and 16-Size Hunting Style

Rolled gold plate, yellow color, hunting style, engraved case, guaranteed by us for 10 years. Mention catalog number and movement.

4K1690—12-Size, 6-Jewel Van Buren Movement....**$9.50**
4K1692—12-Size, 15-Jeweled Van Buren...**$12.75**
4K1694—12-Size, 7-Jeweled Waltham or Elgin....**$14.00**
4K1696—12-Size, 15-Jeweled Elgin.......**$17.75**
4K1710—16-Size, 6-Jeweled Van Buren Movement....**$9.85**
4K1712—16-Size, 15-Jeweled Van Buren Movement.....**$13.10**
4K1714—16-Size, 7-Jeweled Waltham or Elgin....**$13.35**
4K1716—16-Size, 15-Jeweled Waltham or Elgin....**$17.95**

For Everyday Use

Luminous Numerals and Hands Plain Numerals and Hands

BACK VIEW OF WATCH

We warrant our movements for one year against defective material or workmanship, thus giving you ample protection. With proper care they should give many years of service. Shipping weight of any watch on this page, 8 oz.

We wanted a watch to defy competition, and here it is! After months of intensive search, we offer the greatest watch value in years. Think of it! Only $4.75 for this 12-size, open face, thin model. In appearance it is similar to watches selling for many times our price. The case is of solid white metal but it looks like white gold. The beautiful silvered dial is patterned after dials that are used only on very expensive watch movements. We fitted this case with our own high grade 6-jeweled Van Buren movement, with lever escapement, such as is used only in the better grade of watches. This fine watch should give you many years of splendid service. We guarantee movement against defective material and workmanship for one year.
4K1860. $4.75

Only $1.40 or $1.98 for this new Laddie Watch, especially designed for us. Has unbreakable crystal. Sold nowhere else. Is guaranteed for one year against defective material and workmanship. A good timekeeper. Will run 30 hours with one winding. The case is of a metal resembling silver in appearance. The dial is silvered metal. Any initial engraved on the shield without charge. **Order by number and state initial wanted.**

4K1800—Plain numerals and hands.............................$1.40
4K1802—Luminous numerals and hands........$1.98

92c
Plain Dial

The newest 16-size thin model nickel plated watch. It is American made, stem wind and stem set. Plain polish with non-breakable crystal. These watches are thoroughly regulated before leaving our establishment. Will run from 24 to 30 hours with one winding. Guaranteed for one year. The plain dial has plain numerals and hands, the luminous dial has luminous numerals and hands. **Order your choice by catalog number.**

4K1806 Plain dial **92c**
4K1808 Luminous dial.....$1.55

Nickel composition, 12-size screw back and screw bezel with fancy new style bow. Mention catalog number and movement wanted.

4K1840—6-J. Van Buren....$5.85
4K1844—15-Jeweled Van Buren.....................$9.25
4K1848—7-J. Waltham, Elgin or Hampden....$10.25
4K1850—15-J. Waltham, Elgin or Hampden....$13.95
4K1852—17-J. Waltham, Elgin or Hampden....$15.85
4K1854—17-J. Elgin Movement, adjusted......$19.75

Octagon Shape Watch

A very popular octagon shape, low priced, American made watch. Antique pendant and easy winding crown. Silvered metal dial. Timed and tested at the factory. Will run from 24 to 30 hours with one winding. Guaranteed for one year.

4K1930 Plain dial.... $1.40
4K1932 Luminous dial.......$2.15

Solid silver, 12-size, open face, screw back and screw bezel, bright polish case fitted with following movements. State movements.
4K1892—15-Jeweled Van Buren Movement....$11.25
4K1894—7-Jeweled Waltham, Elgin or Hampden....$13.50
4K1896—15-Jeweled Waltham, Elgin or Hampden..$17.50
4K1900—17-Jeweled Elgin, adjusted............$22.50
4K1902—19-Jeweled P. S. Bartlett Waltham $25.75

Illustrations Show Actual Size

Nickel composition, 12-size, screw bezel swing ring solid back case with dustproof screw nut pendant. **Mention catalog number and movement wanted.**

4K1910 6-J. Van Buren.......$6.25
4K1914—15-J. Van Buren.....................$9.35
4K1918—7-Jeweled Waltham or Elgin....$10.65
4K1920—15-Jeweled Waltham or Elgin....$14.25
4K1922—17-Jeweled Waltham or Elgin....$16.75
4K1924—17-Jeweled Elgin, adjusted...........$20.15

Nickel composition, 16-size, screw bezel, solid back, swing ring case. Dust and damp proof with screw nut pendant. Mention catalog number and movement.

4K1952 6-J. Van Buren.....$6.35
4K1954 15-J. Van Buren.....$9.50
4K1956 7-J. Waltham or Elgin....$9.55
4K1958 15-J. Waltham or Elgin...$13.95
4K1960 17-J. Waltham or Elgin....$16.15
4K1962 19-J. Railway Hampden...$33.50
4K1964 19-J. Riverside Waltham...$34.25

Nickel composition, bright polish, 16-size with the new rigid fancy antique style bow and stem. Screw back and screw bezel, dust and damp proof. Mention catalog number and movement.

4K1940 6-Jeweled Van Buren.....$5.75
4K1942 15-Jeweled Van Buren.....$8.90
4K1944 7-J. Waltham or Elgin.....$9.50
4K1946 15-J. Waltham or Elgin.....$13.85
4K1948 17-J. Waltham or Elgin....$16.98

4K1816 4K1818 4K1820

Nickel plated chain adapted for nickel watches. 13 inches long. Shipping wt. 2 oz.
4K1816 **20c**

Same style as above, only sport model, large ring. Length, 7 in. Shipping wt., 2 oz.
4K1818 **15c**

Leather strap, 13 inches long. Shipping wt. 2 oz.
4K1820 **15c**

The Pathfinder Watch with compass in top of crown. Made in America. Nickel finished case, attractive shield design on back, stem wind and pendant set, lever escapement, unbreakable crystal. Dependable compass in crown. Will run from 24 to 30 hours with one winding. Guaranteed for one year.

4K1830—Plain............$1.45
4K1832—Luminous........$1.92

Chains to Be Proud of

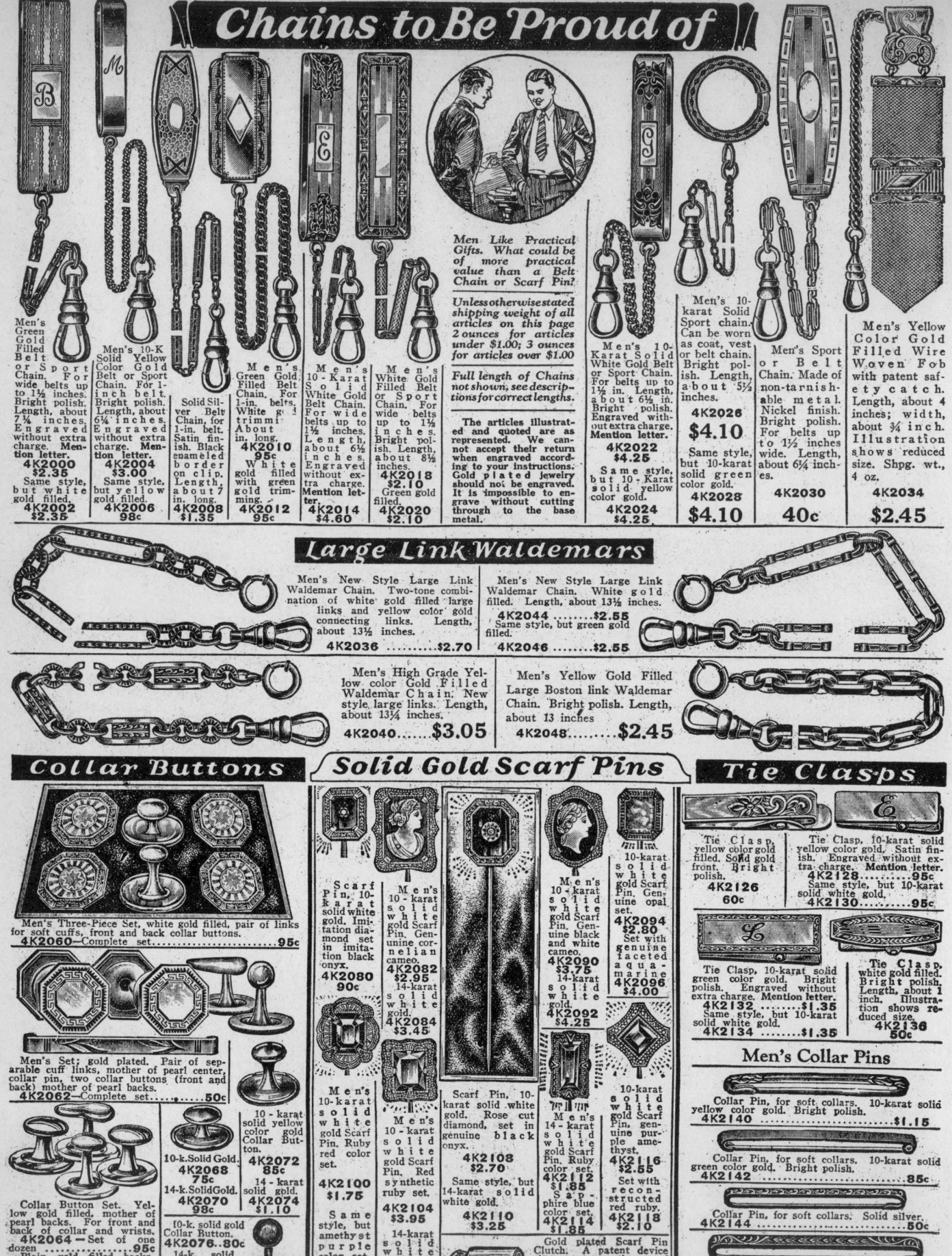

Men's Green Gold Filled Belt or Sport Chain. For wide belts up to 1½ inches. Bright polish. Length, about 7¼ inches. Engraved without extra charge. Mention letter.
4K2000 ......$2.35
Same style, but white gold filled.
4K2002 ....$2.35

Men's 10-K Solid Yellow Color Gold Belt or Sport Chain. For 1-inch belt. Bright polish. Length, about 6¼ inches. Engraved without extra charge. Mention letter.
4K2004 ....$3.00
Same style, but yellow gold filled.
4K2006 ......98c

Solid Silver Belt Chain, for 1-in. belt. Satin finish. Black enameled border on clip. Length, about 7 in. long.
4K2008 ....$1.35

Men's Green Gold Filled Belt Chain. For 1-in. belts. White gold trimmed. About in. long.
4K2010 ......95c
White gold filled with green gold trimming.
4K2012 ....95c

Men's 10-Karat Solid White Gold Chain. For wide belts up to 1½ inches. Length, about 6½ inches. Engraved without extra charge. Mention letter.
4K2014 ....$4.60

Men's White Gold Filled Belt or Sport Chain. For wide belts up to 1½ inches. Bright polish. Length, about 8½ inches.
4K2018 ....$2.10
Green gold filled.
4K2020 ......$2.10

Men Like Practical Gifts. What could be of more practical value than a Belt Chain or Scarf Pin?

Unless otherwise stated shipping weight of all articles on this page 2 ounces for articles under $1.00; 3 ounces for articles over $1.00

Full length of Chains not shown, see descriptions for correct lengths.

The articles illustrated and quoted are as represented. We cannot accept their return when engraved according to your instructions. Gold plated jewelry should not be engraved. It is impossible to engrave without cutting through to the base metal.

Men's 10-Karat Solid White Gold Belt or Sport Chain. For belts up to 1½ in. Length, about 6½ in. Bright polish. Engraved without extra charge. Mention letter.
4K2022 ......$4.25
Same style, but 10-karat solid yellow color gold.
4K2024 ......$4.25

Men's 10-karat Solid Sport chain. Can be worn as coat, vest or belt chain. Bright polish. Length, about 5½ inches.
4K2026 ....$4.10
Same style, but 10-karat solid green color gold.
4K2028 ......$4.10

Men's Sport or Belt Chain. Made of non-tarnishable metal. Nickel finish. Bright polish. For belts up to 1½ inches wide. Length, about 6¼ inches.
4K2030 ......40c

Men's Yellow Color Gold Filled Wire Woven Fob with patent safety catch. Length, about 4 inches; width, about ¾ inch. Illustration shows reduced size. Shpg. wt., 4 oz.
4K2034 ......$2.45

Large Link Waldemars

Men's New Style Large Link Waldemar Chain. Two-tone combination of white gold filled large links and yellow color gold connecting links. Length, about 13½ inches.
4K2036 ......$2.70

Men's New Style Large Link Waldemar Chain. White gold filled. Length, about 13½ inches.
4K2044 ......$2.55
Same style, but green gold filled.
4K2046 ......$2.55

Men's High Grade Yellow color Gold Filled Waldemar Chain. New style, large links. Length, about 13¼ inches.
4K2040 ......$3.05

Men's Yellow Gold Filled Large Boston link Waldemar Chain. Bright polish. Length, about 13 inches.
4K2048 ......$2.45

Collar Buttons

Men's Three-Piece Set, white gold filled, pair of links for soft cuffs, front and back collar buttons.
4K2060—Complete set 95c

Men's Set; gold plated. Pair of separable cuff links, mother of pearl center, collar pin, two collar buttons (front and back) mother of pearl backs.
4K2062—Complete set 50c

Collar Button Set. Yellow gold filled, mother of pearl backs. For front and back of collar and wrists.
4K2064—Set of one dozen 95c
Plain gold filled backs, without mother of pearl.
4K2066—Set of one dozen 70c

10-karat solid yellow color gold Collar Button.
4K2068
10-k. Solid Gold. 75c
14-K. Solid Gold. 4K2070 ......98c

10-k. solid gold Collar Button.
4K2076 ......80c
14-k. solid gold.
4K2078 ......$1.00

10-karat solid yellow color gold Collar Button.
4K2072 ......85c
14-karat solid gold.
4K2074 ......$1.10

Solid Gold Scarf Pins

Scarf Pin, 10-karat solid white gold. Imitation diamond set in imitation black onyx.
4K2082 ......90c

Men's 10-karat solid white gold Scarf Pin. Genuine cornelian cameo.
4K2084 ......$3.45

Men's 10-karat solid white gold Scarf Pin. Ruby red color set.
4K2100 ......$1.75
Same style, but amethyst purple color set.
4K2102 ......$1.75

Men's 10-karat solid white gold Scarf Pin, Red synthetic ruby set.
4K2104 ......$3.95
14-karat solid white gold.
4K2106 ......$4.45

Scarf Pin, 10-karat solid white gold. Rose cut diamond, set in genuine black onyx.
4K2108 ......$2.70
Same style, but 14-karat solid white gold.
4K2110 ......$3.25

Men's 10-karat solid white gold Scarf Pin. Genuine opal set.
4K2094 ......$2.80
Set with genuine faceted aquamarine.
4K2096 ......$4.00

Men's 10-karat solid white gold Scarf Pin. Genuine black and white cameo.
4K2090 ......$3.75
14-karat solid white gold.
4K2092 ......$4.25

Men's 14-karat solid white gold Scarf Pin. Ruby red color set.
4K2112 ......$1.85
Sapphire blue color set.
4K2114 ......$2.10

10-karat solid white gold Scarf Pin, genuine purple amethyst.
4K2116 ......$2.55
Set with reconstructed red ruby.
4K2118 ......$1.85

Gold plated Scarf Pin Clutch. A patent device that prevents the scarf pin from slipping out of the tie.
4K2122 ......15c

Tie Clasps

Tie Clasp, yellow color gold filled. Solid gold front. Bright polish.
4K2126 ......60c

Tie Clasp, 10-karat solid yellow color gold. Satin finish. Engraved without extra charge. Mention letter.
4K2128 ......95c
Same style, but 10-karat solid white gold.
4K2130 ......95c

Tie Clasp, 10-karat solid green color gold. Bright polish. Engraved without extra charge. Mention letter.
4K2132 ......$1.35
Same style, but 10-karat solid white gold.
4K2134 ......$1.35

Tie Clasp, white gold filled. Bright polish. Length, about 1 inch. Illustration shows reduced size.
4K2136 ......50c

Men's Collar Pins

Collar Pin, for soft collars. 10-karat solid yellow color gold. Bright polish.
4K2140 ......$1.15

Collar Pin, for soft collars. 10-karat solid green color gold. Bright polish.
4K2142 ......85c

Collar Pin, for soft collars. Solid silver.
4K2144 ......50c

Collar Pin, for soft collars. Yellow color gold filled.
4K2146 ......28c

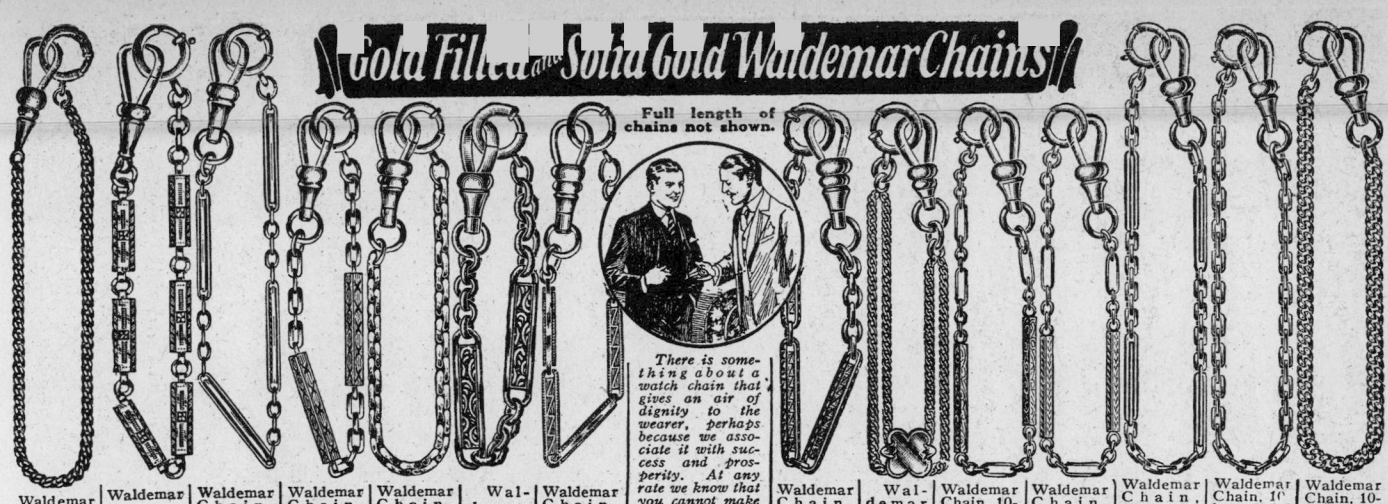

Gold Filled and Solid Gold Waldemar Chains

Full length of chains not shown.

There is something about a watch chain that gives an air of dignity to the wearer, perhaps because we associate it with success and prosperity. At any rate we know that you cannot make a mistake when you present a man with a watch chain.

Shipping weight of vest chains, 4 oz.; all other chains, 3 oz.

All Waldemar chains, fitted with spring rings and swivel; all vest chains with bar, toggle and swivel

Waldemar Chain. Rolled gold plate, soldered flattened curb links. Length, about 13½ inches.
4K2200
65c

Waldemar Chain, non-tarnishable white metal, platinum finish. Length, about 13 inches.
4K2206
$1.20

Waldemar Chain, yellow color gold filled, soldered links. 13 inches.
4K2210 **$1.20**
Same style, but white gold filled.
4K2212 **$1.20**

Waldemar Chain, white gold filled. Soldered links. About 13¼ inches.
4K2214 **$1.60**
Same style, but green gold filled.
4K2216 **$1.60**

Waldemar Chain, white gold filled, flat links. Length, about 13¼ inches.
4K2218 **$1.75**
Same style, but green gold filled.
4K2220 **$1.75**

Waldemar Chain, yellow color rolled gold plate. Length about 13 inches.
4K2222
$1.35

Waldemar Chain, green gold filled. Heavy wt. Length, about 13¼ inches.
4K2226 **$2.45**
Same style, but white gold filled.
4K2228 **$2.45**

Waldemar Chain, green gold filled, heavy wt. Length, about 13 inches.
4K2230 **$2.40**
Same style, but white gold filled.
4K2232 **$2.40**

Waldemar Chain, yellow color gold filled, double strand soldered curb links. Length, about 13½ in.
4K2234 **$2.30**

Waldemar Chain, 10-karat solid white gold. Length, about 13 inches.
4K2238 **$3.30**
Same style, but 10-karat solid green gold.
4K2240 **$3.30**

Waldemar Chain, two-tone, 10-karat solid white and green gold. Length, about 13 inches.
4K2242 **$3.65**
Same style, but 14-karat green gold.
4K2244 **$5.05**

Waldemar Chain, 10-karat solid yellow color gold, soldered links. About 13 inches.
4K2246 **$4.35**
Same style, but 14-karat solid green gold.
4K2248 **$6.15**

Waldemar Chain, 10-karat sol'd yellow color gold soldered links. About 12½ inches.
4K2250 **$4.55**
Same style, but 10-karat solid green gold.
4K2252 **$4.55**

Waldemar Chain, 10-karat solid white gold, Flattened curb links soldered. Length, about 13 inches.
4K2254 **$4.45**
4K2256 14-karat solid white gold: **$5.85**

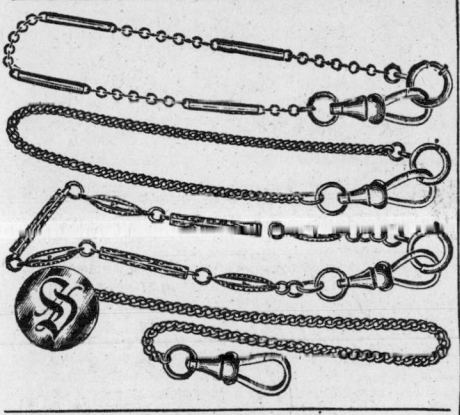

Waldemar Chain, two-tone 14-karat solid white and yellow color gold links. Very attractive. Length, about 13 inches.
4K2258 **$4.85**
4K2260 — Same style but 10-karat. **$3.50**

Waldemar Chain, 14-karat solid yellow color gold, soldered curb links. Length abt. 12½ inches. **$4.75**
4K2262
4K2264 — 10-karat solid yellow color gold. **$3.40**

Waldemar Chain. 10-karat solid white gold. Lgth. abt. 13 in. **$5.40**
4K2266
4K2268 — Same style, but 14-karat solid white gold. **$7.30**

◄ Men's Coat Chain, 10-karat solid yellow color gold. Curb links soldered. Length, about 8¼ inches. Bright polish. Engraved with any letter without extra charge. Mention letter.
4K2270 **$2.75**

Waldemar Chain, 14-karat solid white gold, soldered links. Length, about 13 inches. **$5.75 ►**
4K2274
4K2276 — 10-karat solid white gold. **$5.00**

Waldemar Chain, 14-karat solid yellow color gold. Soldered links. Length, about 12¼ inches. **$7.20**
4K2278
4K2280 — 10-karat solid yellow color gold. **$5.15**

Waldemar Chain, 14-karat solid yellow color gold, flattened curb soldered links. Length, about 12½ inches. **$9.70**
4K2282
4K2284 — Same style but 10-karat solid yellow color gold. **$6.00**

Men's Coat Chain, yellow color gold filled. Flattened curb soldered links. Length, about 8½ inches. Bright polish.
4K2286 **80c**

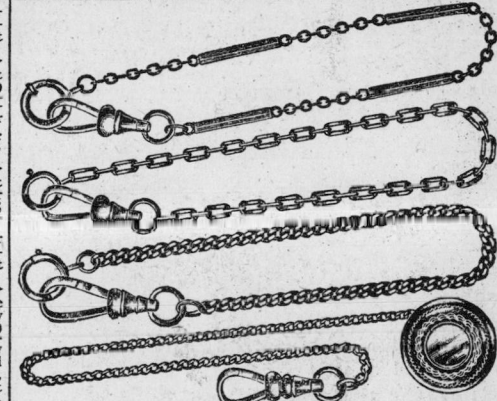

Vest Chains

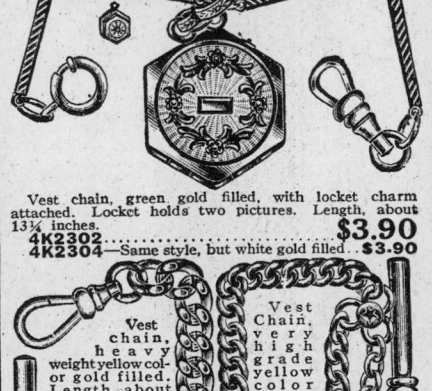

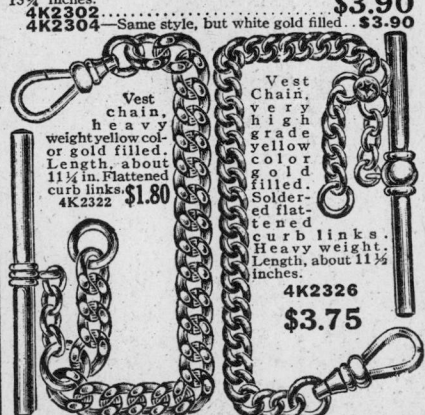

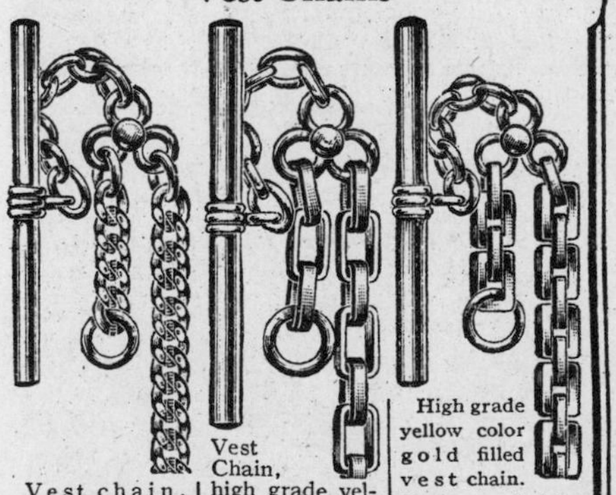

Vest chain, yellow color gold filled. Soldered flattened curb links. Length, about 10½ inches.
4K2290
$1.35

Vest Chain, high grade yellow color gold filled, large Boston links. Length, about 11½ inches.
4K2294
$1.80

High grade yellow color gold filled vest chain. Heavy weight. Length, about 10½ inches.
4K2298
$3.25

Vest chain, green gold filled, with locket charm attached. Locket holds two pictures. Length, about 13¼ inches.
4K2302 **$3.90**
4K2304 — Same style, but white gold filled. **$3.90**

Vest chain, heavy weight yellow color gold filled. Length, about 11¼ in. Flattened curb links.
4K2322 **$1.80**

Vest Chain, very high grade yellow color gold filled. Soldered flattened curb links. Heavy weight. Length, about 11½ inches.
4K2326
$3.75

Vest Chain, 10-karat solid yellow color gold. Dickens style. Soldered flattened curb links. Length, about 13 in.
4K2306 **$5.00**
4K2308 — Same style, but 14-karat solid yellow color gold. **$7.00**

Vest Chain, 10-karat solid yellow color gold. Length, about 15 inches. Dickens style. Soldered curb links.
4K2310 **$5.25**
4K2312 — Same style, but 14-karat solid yellow color gold. **$7.25**

Vest Chain, high grade yellow color gold filled. Curb links. Locket holds two pictures, colored ornamented top. Length, about 13¼ inches.
4K2314
$3.45

Vest Chains

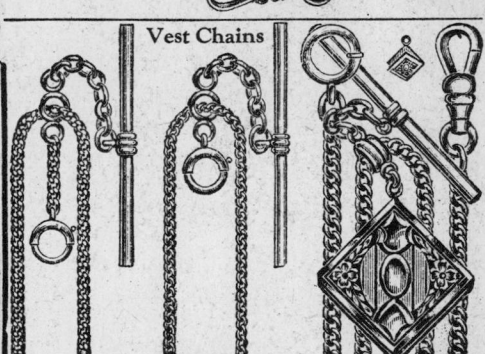

Vest Chain, 14-karat solid yellow color gold. Soldered flattened curb links. Length, about 10¼ inches.
4K2318 **$9.20**
4K2320 — Same style, but 10-karat solid yellow color gold. **$8.50**

Vest Chain, 14-karat solid yellow color gold. Dickens style. Soldered flattened curb links. Length, about 15 inches.
4K2330 **$11.00**
4K2332 — Same style, but 10-karat solid yellow color gold. **$8.50**

Send Sufficient Money for Postage on Parcel Post Shipments. Any Surplus Will Be Returned

729

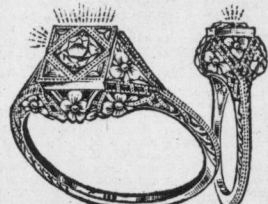

GENUINE DIAMONDS

See Page 732 for Men's Diamond Set Rings

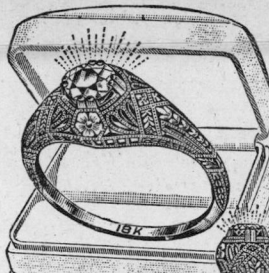

See Page 732 for All Platinum Diamond Set Rings

Betty Jane

Solid 18-karat white gold, fancy pierced design, with our first quality diamonds, as quoted below. Small illustration shows size of ring. Certificate "A" sent.

Catalog No.	Carat	Price
4K2720	1/8 or 13/100 carat	$28.25
4K2722	1/4 or 19/100 carat	$36.00
4K2724	1/4 or 19/100 carat	$44.25
4K2726	1/4 or 25/100 carat	$67.25
4K2730	1/3 or 33/100 carat	$95.75
4K2732	3/8 or 37/100 carat	$107.25
4K2734	1/2 or 44/100 carat	$141.75
4K2736	1/2 or 50/100 carat	$170.25

See Page 721 for Diamond Set Wrist Watches

When you invest in a fine diamond you invest in beauty eternal, passing years do not mar or dull its splendor, indeed they enhance its worth.

Weight for weight, grade for grade, we save you a large amount on each purchase. Our representatives make their selections direct from the great diamond markets of Amsterdam and Antwerp. The saving made by the quantities purchased and the cash discount together with the fact that we sell for cash—no credit losses and no interest charges—enables us to quote the lowest prices in the world on high grade diamonds.

Our broad guarantee sent with every ring purchased (see reprint of certificate "A" on opposite page), is backed by capital exceeding one hundred million dollars. Safeguard yourself by purchasing your diamond from a house of undoubted integrity. You do not have to guess at size or quality. Every diamond we sell is expertly analyzed, graded according to quality and sold by weight.

What is desirable in a diamond?

First: It should be very brilliant. Second: It should be white in color, because being most commercial, is most desirable. Third: Perfect in cutting, in proper proportions, with full number of facets. Fourth: Free from conspicuous flaws, cracks and blemishes.

All rings on this and opposite page furnished in sizes 5 to 8. Be sure to give ring size. See page 745 for ring measuring chart.

Beulah

Solid 18-karat white gold mounting, lacy pierced design, set with our first quality diamonds, as quoted below. Small illustration shows size of ring. Enlarged picture shows design of ring in detail. Certificate "A" sent.

Catalog No.	Carat	Price
4K2740	1/8 or 5/100 carat	$13.25
4K2742	1/8 or 5/100 carat	14.75
4K2744	1/8 or 5/100 carat	17.75
4K2746	1/4 or 19/100 carat	21.50
4K2748	1/8 or 13/100 carat	25.75
4K2750	1/4 or 16/100 carat	34.50
4K2752	1/4 or 19/100 carat	$42.75

Irene

Solid 18-karat white gold mounting, fancy pierced design, set with our first quality diamonds, as quoted below. Certificate "A" sent.

Catalog No.	Carat	Price
4K2760	1/8 or 13/100 carat	$27.00
4K2762	1/4 or 19/100 carat	$43.00
4K2764	1/4 or 26/100 carat	$66.00
4K2766	3/8 or 37/100 carat	$106.00

Marilyn

Solid 18-karat white gold, prong setting, beautifully engraved, set with our first quality diamonds, as quoted below. Certificate "A" sent.

Catalog No.	Carat	Price
4K2860	1/8 or 12/100 carat	$27.50
4K2862	1/4 or 16/100 carat	$34.25
4K2864	1/4 or 19/100 carat	$43.75
4K2866	1/4 or 25/100 carat	$56.00
4K2868	1/3 or 33/100 carat	$66.50
4K2870	3/8 or 37/100 carat	$82.50
4K2872	1/3 or 43/100 carat	$94.50
4K2874	3/8 or 47/100 carat	$106.25
4K2876	1/2 or 44/100 carat	$141.00
4K2878	1/2 or 50/100 carat	$166.00

Genevieve

Four Prong Ring. Gives the effect of square cut diamond. Solid 18-karat white gold, with either blue synthetic sapphires or imitation emeralds. **Be sure to state choice.** Set with our first quality diamonds as listed below. Certificate "A" sent.

Catalog No.	Carat	Price
4K2890	1/4 or 25/100 carat	$68.75
4K2892	1/3 or 33/100 carat	$96.75
4K2894	3/8 or 37/100 carat	$113.50
4K2896	1/2 or 44/100 carat	$171.50
4K2898	5/8 or 63/100 carat	$249.25
4K2900	3/4 or 75/100 carat	$321.25
4K2902	7/8 or 87/100 carat	$415.95
4K2904	1 carat	488.50
4K2906	1 1/4 carat	633.75
4K2908	1 1/2 carat	758.50

Inez

Solid 18-karat white gold, four prongs, giving the effect of a square cut diamond, fancy pierced design, with our first quality diamonds, as quoted below. Certificate "A" sent.

Catalog No.	Carat	Price
4K2920	1/4 or 25/100 carat	$67.35
4K2922	1/4 or 29/100 carat	$83.50
4K2924	1/3 or 33/100 carat	$95.75
4K2926	3/8 or 37/100 carat	$111.25
4K2928	1/2 or 44/100 carat	$141.75
4K2930	1/2 or 50/100 carat	$170.25
4K2934	5/8 or 63/100 carat	$248.25
4K2936	3/4 or 75/100 carat	$319.50
4K2938	1 carat	487.50

Eleanor

Your choice of solid 18-karat white or natural color gold engraved solitaire mounting, set with our first quality diamonds, as quoted below. Enlarged illustration shows ring in detail. Small illustration shows size of ring. Certificate "A" sent.

Natural gold	White gold	Carat	Price
4K2950	4K2970	1/8 or 12/100 carat	$23.75
4K2952	4K2972	1/4 or 16/100 carat	$41.75
4K2954	4K2974	1/4 or 20/100 carat	$63.75
4K2956	4K2976	1/4 or 25/100 carat	$80.00
4K2958	4K2978	1/3 or 33/100 carat	$94.00
4K2960	4K2980	3/8 or 37/100 carat	$108.75
4K2962	4K2982	1/2 or 44/100 carat	$167.00
4K2964	4K2984	5/8 or 63/100 carat	$244.75

Angela

Very fine solid white gold, four-prong mounting, gives the effect of a square cut diamond. Set with fine regular cut brilliant diamond on each side and our first quality diamonds, as listed below. Enlarged illustration shows design in detail. Small illustration shows size. Certificate "A" sent.

Catalog No.	Carat	Price
4K2986	1/4 or 25/100 carat	$77.25
4K2988	1/3 or 33/100 carat	$105.75
4K2990	3/8 or 37/100 carat	$122.25
4K2992	1/2 or 44/100 carat	$180.25
4K2994	5/8 or 63/100 carat	$258.75
4K2996	3/4 or 73/100 carat	$330.00
4K2998	7/8 or 87/100 carat	$424.85
4K3000	1 carat	$497.25
4K3002	1 1/16 carat	$548.50
4K3004	1 1/3 carat	$579.75
4K3006	1 1/4 carat	$642.25
4K3008	1 1/2 carat	$767.25

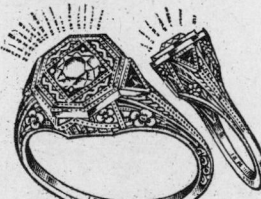

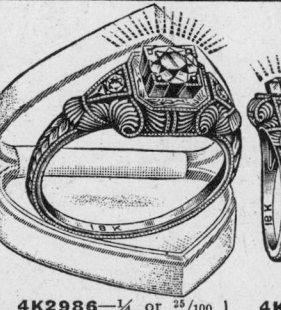

Elaine

Solid 18-karat white gold, fancy pierced design, with our first quality diamonds. Small illustration shows size of ring. Certificate "A" sent.

Catalog No.	Carat	Price
4K2770	1/8 or 5/100 carat	$9.45
4K2772	1/4 or 5/100 carat	12.00
4K2774	1/4 or 6/100 carat	13.50
4K2776	1/4 or 9/100 carat	16.50
4K2778	1/8 or 13/100 carat	21.25
4K2780	1/8 or 17/100 carat	25.50
4K2782	1/4 or 18/100 carat	33.50
4K2784	1/4 or 19/100 carat	41.50
4K2788	1/4 or 26/100 carat	64.75

Pauline

Solid 18-karat white gold, floral pierced design, with blue synthetic sapphire on each side and our first quality diamonds, as listed below. Enlarged illustration shows design in detail. Small illustration shows size of ring. Certificate "A" sent.

Catalog No.	Carat	Price
4K2800	1/8 or 13/100 carat	$27.50
4K2802	1/4 or 16/100 carat	36.25
4K2804	1/8 or 19/100 carat	45.25
4K2806	1/4 or 33/100 carat	57.00
4K2808	1/4 or 33/100 carat	68.00
4K2812	1/2 or 44/100 carat	95.50
4K2814	3/8 or 47/100 carat	109.50
4K2818	1/2 or 63/100 carat	169.50

Clarice

Solid 18-karat white gold, pierced design with our first quality diamonds, as listed below. Certificate "A" sent.

Catalog No.	Carat	Price
4K2830	1/8 or 13/100 carat	$28.00
4K2832	1/4 or 16/100 carat	35.75
4K2834	1/4 or 19/100 carat	44.25
4K2836	1/4 or 25/100 carat	67.00
4K2838	1/3 or 33/100 carat	95.75
4K2840	3/8 or 37/100 carat	112.50
4K2842	1/2 or 44/100 carat	170.25
4K2844	5/8 or 63/100 carat	248.50
4K2846	3/4 or 75/100 carat	320.25
4K2848	1 carat	487.50

Mildred

Very fine all platinum, heavy weight fully engraved; pierced bowknot design, with our first quality diamonds as quoted below. Certificate "A" sent.

4K3012—12/100	carat....	$ 53.25
4K3014—19/100	carat....	69.25
4K3016—25/100	carat....	92.25
4K3018—29/100	carat....	108.50
4K3020—33/100	carat...	121.00
4K3022—37/100	carat....	132.25
4K3024—50/100	carat....	195.50

Our First Quality

Alice

Solid platinum prong mounting, pierced floral design, set with our first quality diamonds. Certificate "A" sent.

4K3028—37/100	carat...	$140.75
4K3034—50/100	carat....	204.00
4K3036—57/100	carat....	242.75
4K3038—63/100	carat....	281.50
4K3040—75/100	carat....	355.00
4K3042—87/100	carat....	449.75
4K3044— 1	carat....	523.75

Platinum-Diamond Set Rings

Our Diamond Certificate

With most diamonds quoted on this and the other pages, we send either our "A" or "B" certificate. See page 730 for reprint of our "A" certificate. Our "B" certificate, besides being a guarantee of quality and weight, guarantees that if, after wearing and comparing or having it valued, or for any reason whatsoever, you are not satisfied, any time within thirty days from date of purchase, you may return it for exchange or have your money refunded, together with transportation charges. This gives you a long time to prove our statement and the value you have received by comparison and expert advice.

Ring measuring chart on page 745.

Shipping weight, any article on this page, 4 ounces.

Honora

Very latest pattern in all Platinum Dinner Ring. Beautiful lacy design fully engraved with your choice of blue synthetic sapphires or emerald color stones and nine brilliant diamonds; our first quality; total weight, about 50/100 carat. Certificate "B" sent.

4K3046 Diamonds and blue synthetic sapphires..... $150.00

4K3048 Diamonds and emerald color stones............ 150.00

Solid platinum mounting, beautifully engraved, with four blue synthetic sapphires, six brilliant regular cut diamonds and our first quality diamonds as quoted below. Certificate "A" sent.

4K3050—1/8 or 12/100	carat..	$ 61.50
4K3054—3/16 or 19/100	carat..	77.50
4K3056—1/4 or 25/100	carat..	100.50
4K3062—3/8 or 37/100	carat..	140.25
4K3066—1/2 or 50/100	carat..	203.75

Solid platinum, four-prong mounting, gives the effect of square cut diamond. Finely pierced bowknot design, fully engraved, set with our first quality diamonds. Certificate "A" sent.

4K3074—37/100	carat.	$134.75
4K3076—50/100	carat.	198.25
4K3078—63/100	carat.	275.75
4K3080—75/100	carat.	347.75
4K3082—87/100	carat.	442.50
4K3084— 1	carat.	514.75

Very Latest Wedding Ring. Also makes an ideal wedding anniversary or Christmas gift. Solid platinum, set all around with twenty brilliant regular diamonds. Be sure to give exact ring size desired. Enlarged illustration shows ring in detail.

4K3086 ....$84.25

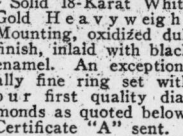

Very fine solid platinum, fully engraved, an exceptionally beautiful ring, set with blue synthetic sapphires, four brilliant white diamonds and our first quality diamonds as quoted below. Certificate "A" sent.

4K3088—75/100	ct.	$378.75
4K3090—87/100	ct.	473.75
4K3092—94/100	ct.	516.00
4K3094— 1	ct.	546.00
4K3100— 1¼	ct.	691.00
4K3102— 1½	ct.	816.00

Ladies' 14 and 18-Karat White Gold Fancy, Diamond Set Rings

14-Karat Solid White Gold Mounting, lacy pierced design, set with brilliant regular cut diamond. Certificate "B" sent.

4K3104.......$6.45

$6.95 for this dainty 18-Karat Solid White Gold Ring, set with fine regular cut diamond. Certificate "B" sent.

4K3106.......$6.95

$7.75 for this 18-Karat Solid White Gold Openwork Mounting, set with brilliant regular cut diamond weighing 3/100 carat. Certificate "B" sent.

4K3108.......$7.75

Solid 18-Karat White Gold Mounting, pierced design, set with brilliant regular cut diamonds as listed below. Certificate "B" sent.

4K3110—3/64 or 5/100	ct.	$10.35
4K3112—1/16 or 6/100	ct.	11.75
4K3114—5/64 or 8/100	ct.	14.45
4K3116—3/32 or 10/100	ct.	18.75

Dainty 18-Karat Solid White Gold Mounting, set with brilliant regular cut diamonds as quoted below. Certificate "B" sent.

4K3118—3/64 or 5/100	ct.	$11.00
4K3120—1/16 or 6/100	ct.	12.45
4K3122—5/64 or 8/100	ct.	15.15
4K3124—3/32 or 10/100	ct.	19.50
4K3126— 1/8 or 12/100	ct.	23.25

Solid 18-Karat White Gold, pierced design, set with two blue synthetic sapphires and fine regular cut diamonds as quoted below. Certificate "B" sent.

4K3128—1/16 or 6/100	ct.	$13.95
4K3130—5/64 or 8/100	ct.	16.65
4K3132—3/32 or 10/100	ct.	20.95
4K3134 — 1/8 or 12/100	carat	$24.75
4K3136 — 5/32 or 16/100	carat	$31.75
4K3138 — 3/16 or 19/100	carat	$39.25

Men's 14 and 18-Karat Diamond Set Rings

14-Karat Green Gold With White Gold Top. Mounting, black enamel inlaid. A fine heavyweight ring set with our first quality diamonds as quoted below. Certificate "A" sent.

4K3140—19/100	ct.	$52.75
4K3142—25/100	ct.	78.75
4K3144—33/100	ct.	104.15
4K3146—37/100	ct.	115.75
4K3148—50/100	ct.	178.95
4K3150—75/100	ct.	328.50

Solid 18-Karat White Gold, satin finish, set with our first quality diamonds as quoted below. Certificate "A" sent.

4K3164 — 3/32 or 10/100	carat...	$26.65
4K3166 — 1/8 or 12/100	carat...	$30.85
4K3168 — 5/32 or 16/100	carat...	$38.65
4K3170 — 3/16 or 19/100	carat...	$46.95
4K3172 — 7/32 or 22/100	carat...	$59.50
4K3174 — 1/4 or 25/100	carat...	$69.75

18-Karat Solid White Gold set with our first quality diamonds as listed below. Certificate "A" sent.

4K3188—25/100	ct.	$73.00
4K3190—33/100	ct.	101.50
4K3192—37/100	ct.	113.00
4K3194—50/100	ct.	176.50
4K3196—75/100	ct.	325.75
4K3198— 1	ct.	493.00

Solid 18-Karat White Gold, Heavyweight Mounting, set with two blue synthetic sapphires and our first quality diamonds as quoted below. Certificate "A" sent.

4K3200—1/8 or 12/100	carat........	$35.85
4K3202—1/4 or 25/100	carat........	$74.85
4K3204—3/8 or 37/100	carat........	$114.75
4K3206—1/2 or 50/100	carat........	$177.75
4K3208—5/8 or 63/100	carat........	$255.75

Solid 18-Karat White Gold Heavyweight Mounting, oxidized dull finish, inlaid with black enamel. An exceptionally fine ring set with our first quality diamonds as quoted below. Certificate "A" sent.

4K3214—37/100	ct.	$111.75
4K3216—50/100	ct.	175.25
4K3218—63/100	ct.	252.75
4K3220—75/100	ct.	324.75
4K3222— 1	ct.	495.75
4K3224—1½	ct.	761.75

Cluster Rings

Seven Fine Diamonds Set to Look like One

18-Karat White Gold, Platinum Top. Seven brilliant diamonds set in four prongs so as to give the effect of one large square cut diamond.

4K3226 $59.75

Seven Fine Diamonds Set to Look like One

Solid 18-Karat White Gold Mounting, fancy pierced design, platinum top set with seven fine brilliant regular cut diamonds, giving the appearance of one large diamond.

4K3228.. $67.75

Solid 14-Karat White Gold Tie Clasp, 1⅛ inches long, set with brilliant regular cut diamond.

4K3230.......... $4.75

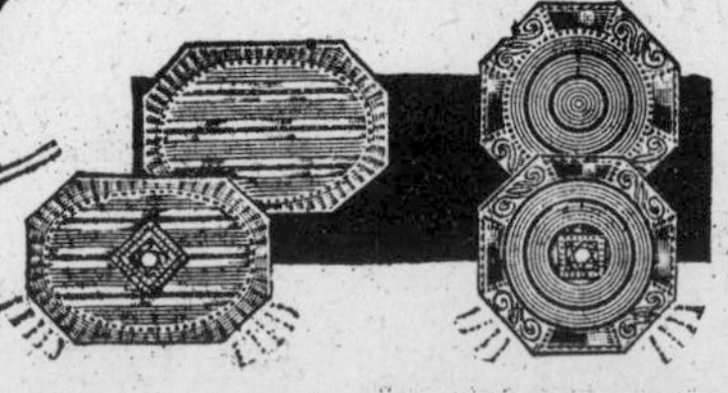

Platinum on 14-Karat Yellow Gold Cuff Links for soft cuffs, set with small brilliant regular cut diamonds.

4K3232 $16.75

14-Karat Solid White Gold Cuff Links for soft cuffs, black enamel inlaid, set with brilliant regular cut diamonds, 3/100 each; total weight, 6/100.

4K3234..... $21.50

Solid 18-Karat White Gold, raised Masonic emblem, with blue synthetic sapphires and diamond weighing 5/100 carat.

4K3236 $24.50

Solid 18-Karat White Gold Consistory Ring, with blue synthetic sapphires and brilliant diamond weighing 12/100 carat.

4K3240 $44.25

Diamond Set Scarf Pins

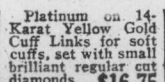

18-Karat White Gold on 14-Karat Green Gold Scarf Pin, set with small regular cut diamond.

4K3244 $4.50

Solid 14-Karat White Gold Scarf Pin, set with genuine black onyx and fine, brilliant, regular cut diamond.

4K3246 $6.15

Solid 18-Karat White Gold Scarf Pin, set with small blue synthetic sapphire and brilliant diamond weighing 10/100 carat.

4K3248 $20.75

Unusual in Quality Moderate in Price

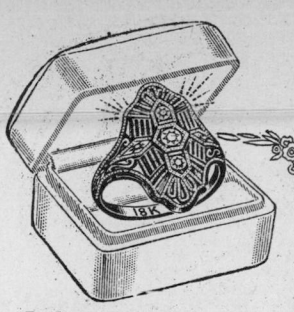

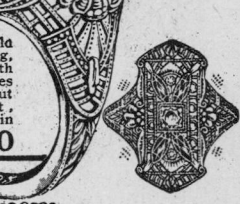

Ladies' Fine Dinner or Small Finger Ring

18-karat white gold, platinum top, lacy pierced design, set with three brilliant diamonds, weighing 12/100 carat. Furnished in sizes 3 to 7.
4K3250 .... $33.65

Under no circumstances do we sell poor grade diamonds that lack brilliancy or are not properly cut.

No refund certificate is sent with the beautiful diamond set jewelry shown on this page. Every stone shown is really a splendid specimen; which, while not quite as good as our fine First Quality, are very beautiful.

Our broad guarantee applies to every article here the same as on any of the diamond line. If, after you receive the jewel and after having compared it with others, you do not find a splendid saving, or if for any reason whatsoever you wish to return the jewel to have your money returned together with transportation charges, you may do so within thirty days. You assume no risk whatsoever.

Solid 18-karat white gold, pierced design, beautifully engraved, set, with two blue synthetic sapphires and three brilliant regular cut diamonds; total weight, 18/100 carat. Furnished in sizes 3 to 8.
4K3252. $37.50

An exceptional bargain. Solid 18-karat white gold dinner or little finger ring, lacy pierced design, set with four blue synthetic sapphires and three fine regular cut diamonds; total weight, 10/100 carat. Furnished in sizes 3 to 7.
4K3254. $27.50

Solid 18-karat white gold, beautifully engraved, set with two blue synthetic sapphires and brilliant regular cut diamond, weighing 6/100 carat. Furnished in sizes 3 to 7.
4K3256 .... $17.95

Solid 18-karat white gold, fancy pierced design, set with two brilliant regular cut diamonds; total weight, 20/100 carat. Furnished in sizes 3 to 7.
4K3258 .... $42.00

Solid 18-karat white gold dinner ring, very finely pierced, set with four emerald color stones and three brilliant regular cut diamonds; total wt., 24/100 carat. Furnished in sizes 3 to 7.
4K3260 .... $52.45

Diamond Set Onyx Rings

Solid 14-karat white gold, pierced design, set with genuine black onyx and fine regular cut diamond. Furnished in sizes 3 to 7.
4K3262 ..... $7.65

Solid 14-karat white gold mounting, pierced design, set with encrusted genuine black onyx and brilliant regular cut diamond. Furnished in sizes 3 to 8.
4K3264 ..... $9.25

Solid 14-karat white gold mounting, set with concave encrusted border genuine black onyx and fine regular cut diamond. Furnished in sizes 3 to 8.
4K3266 ,, $10.25

Eastern Star Ring

Solid 14-karat gold mounting, enameled Eastern Star emblem, and brilliant regular cut diamond set on genuine black onyx. Furnished in sizes 3 to 8.
4K3268 ..... $8.25

Ladies' Diamond and Initial Onyx Ring

14-karat solid white gold, fancy pierced design, with initial and small brilliant diamond set on genuine black onyx. Furnished in sizes 3 to 7. Be sure to give size and initial desired.
4K3270 .. $11.00

DIAMOND SET BRACELETS

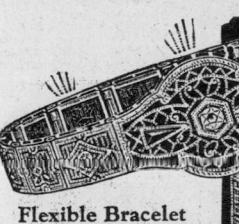

Shipping weight, any article on this page, 3 oz.

Flexible Bracelet

Platinum on 14-karat white gold, flexible bracelet, fancy pierced design, set with two blue synthetic sapphires and three brilliant regular cut diamonds; total weight, 15/100 carat.
4K3282 .. $55.75

Solid 14-Karat White Gold Bracelet
Dainty filigree pattern, set with four blue synthetic sapphires and brilliant regular cut diamond.
4K3284 .... $15.50

Fashion's latest note — the flexible bracelet.
Solid 14-karat white gold bracelet, with three fine regular cut diamonds set on genuine black onyx.
4K3286 $18.00

Double stone rings, set with brilliant regular cut diamond in center. The mountings are 14-karat solid white gold, fancy pierced design. The double stones in colors quoted below. Furnished in sizes 3 to 7. Be sure to give size and stone desired.
4K3272 — Synthetic Ruby and diamond **$8.75**
4K3274 — Genuine Amethyst and diamond **$9.00**
4K3276 — Synthetic blue sapphire and diamond **$11.00**
4K3278 — Genuine Aquamarine and diamond **$13.50**
4K3280 — Emerald (green color) and diamond **$14.00**

Platinum and 14-Karat Solid White Gold Bar Pins

Bar Pin

Dainty and lovely — it adds a very charming decorative touch to the Lady of Fashion. Platinum and 14-karat white gold bar pin, lacy pierced design, set with two blue synthetic sapphires and brilliant white diamond, weighing 5/100 carat.
4K3288 ..... $25.00

Ladies' Bar Pin

An exquisite and fashionable Bar Pin that will give life to a dark frock. Platinum on 14-karat solid white gold, very fine lacy pierced design, set with three fine brilliant white diamonds, weighing about 14/100 carat.
4K3290 .... $38.75

Combination Pendant and Brooch

The bow at top may be folded back out of sight when worn as a brooch. Small illustration shows reduced size of brooch. Platinum on 14-karat white gold, dainty pierced design, set with brilliant white diamond, weighing 5/64 or 8/100 carat. Black silk guard, 30 inches long, with platinum top slide.
4K3294 .... $35.00

For Ring Chart See Page 745

18-karat solid white gold earscrews. Beautiful earrings that are always stylish and in good taste, for pierced ears, set with brilliant regular cut diamonds, weighing 6/100 each; total weight, 12/100 carat.
4K3292 .... $22.25

Solid 18-karat white gold earscrews, for pierced ears, set with blue synthetic sapphires and brilliant regular cut diamonds in top and pendant; total weight, 26/100 carat.
4K3296 .... $47.00

A typical example of the bargains offered by our diamond department.
Solid 14-karat white gold bar pin, dainty pierced design, set with brilliant regular cut diamond.
4K3298 .... $5.75

Beautiful presentation case sent with every diamond illustrated on these pages

Bracelets
Are in Vogue

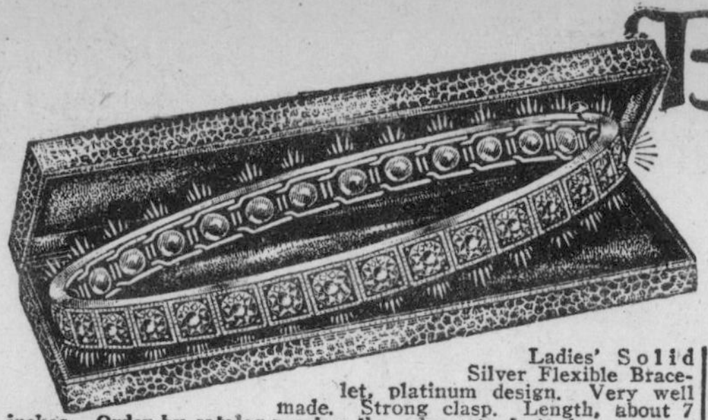

Ladies' Solid Silver Flexible Bracelet, platinum design. Very well made. Strong clasp. Length, about 7 inches. Order by catalog number the color sets desired.

4K3300—Brilliant imitation diamond sets............$2.98
4K3302—Ruby red color sets............................2.98
4K3304—Sapphire blue color sets......................2.98
4K3306—Amethyst purple color sets....................$2.98

Unless otherwise stated illustrations show actual Size. All Bracelets sent in neat presentation cases.

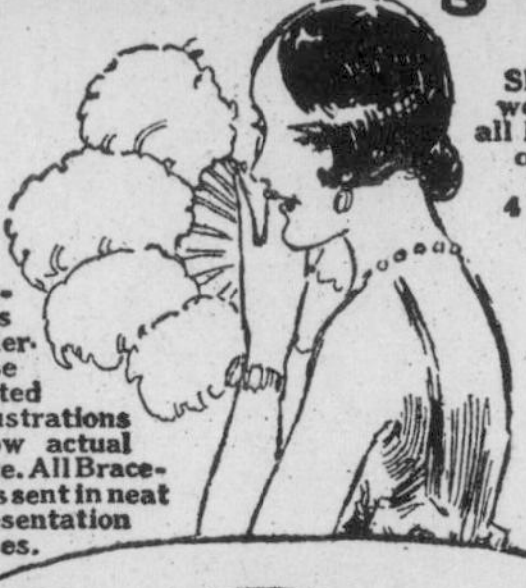

Shipping weight of all Bracelets on this page, 4 ounces

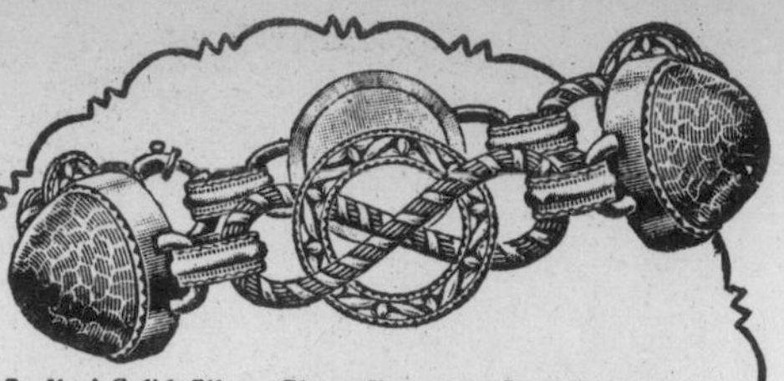

Ladies' Solid Silver Slave Bracelet. Length, about 7½ inches. Just the thing for the well dressed up to date young lady. Loose link slave braclets are all the vogue. We are listing a complete selection in the newest styles with the most popular color settings (to match your outfits) at prices considerably lower than you could purchase them elsewhere. **Order by catalog number given below the color sets desired.**

4K3362—Jade green color sets......$2.98
4K3364—Cherry red color sets...... 2.98
4K3366—Imitation black onyx...... 2.98

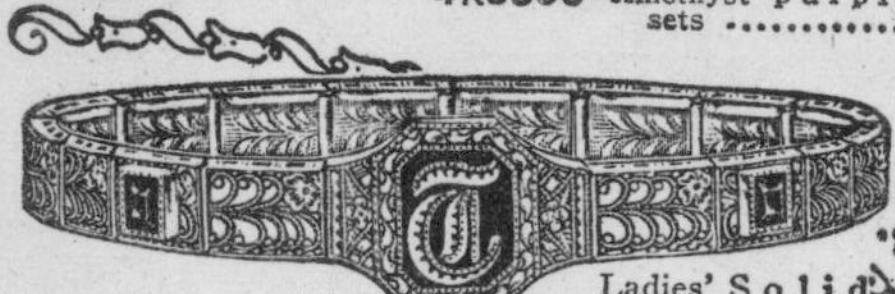

Ladies' Solid Silver Initial Bracelet, something new and attractive. Any initial in solid silver set on imitation black onyx. Openwork links. Length, about 7¼ inches. **Mention letter wanted.**

4K3308 ....$3.98

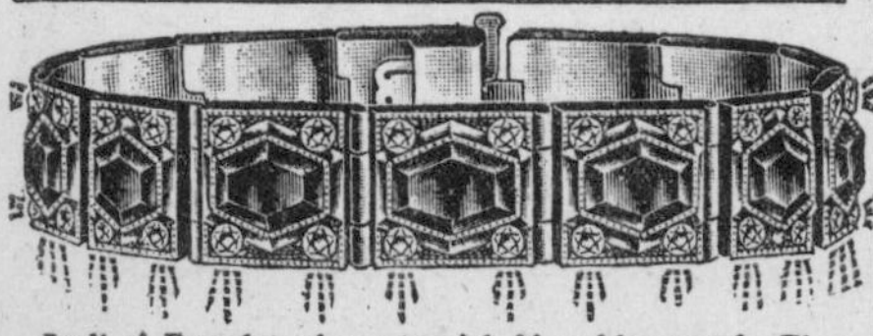

Ladies' Bracelet of non-tarnishable white metal. Fine brilliant imitation diamonds and large emerald green color set in each link. Very attractive and rich in appearance. Length, about 7 inches.

4K3310 ....$4.00
Same style, but imitation diamonds and rose color sets.
4K3312 ....$4.00
Same style, but imitation diamonds and sapphire blue color sets.
4K3314 ....$4.00
Same style, but imitation diamonds and topaz (amber color sets).
4K3316 ....$4.00

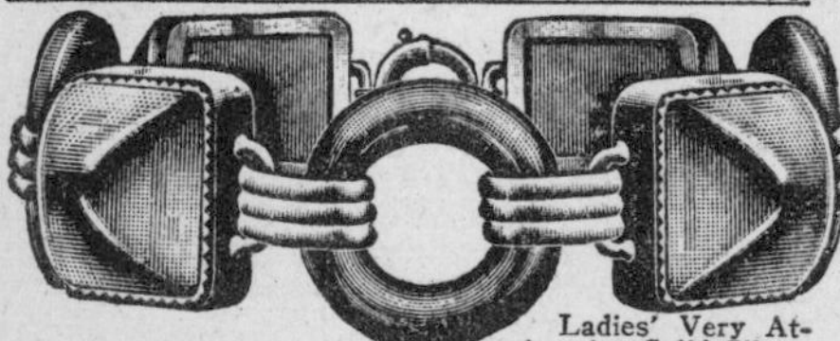

Ladies' Very Attractive Solid Silver Slave Bracelet. Length, about 8 inches. Jade green color circles with cornelian (light reddish brown) sets.

4K3318 ....$4.25
Same style, but jade green color circles and sets.
4K3320 ....$4.25

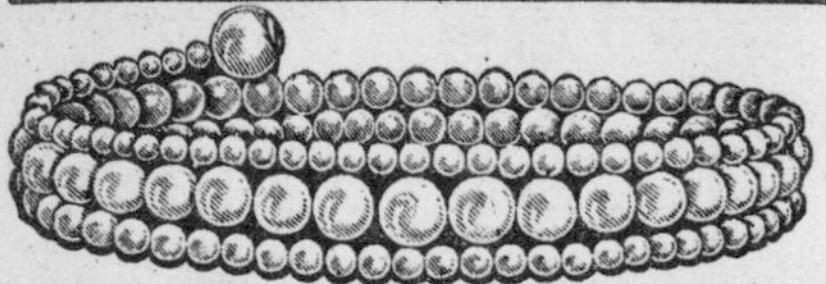

Ladies' Good Quality Indestructible Pearl Bracelet. Graduated style. Spiral effect, winds around the wrist. Illustration shows slightly reduced size of pearls.

4K3322 ....$1.98

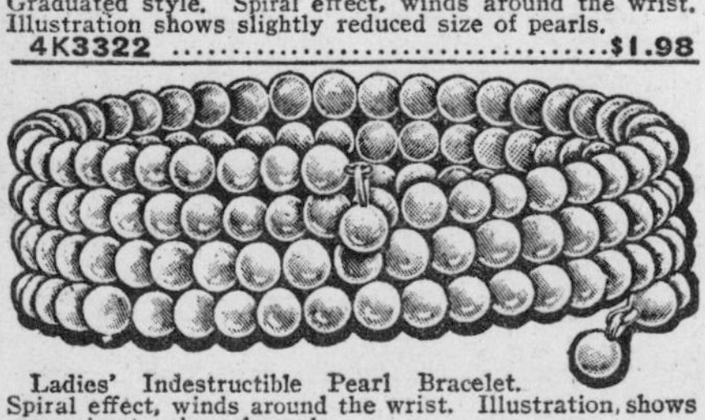

Ladies' Indestructible Pearl Bracelet. Spiral effect, winds around the wrist. Illustration shows approximate size of pearls.

4K3324 ....50c

Ladies' High Grade Indestructible Pearl Bracelet with fancy solid silver clasp. Length, about 7¾ inches.

4K3326 ....$3.98

Where we describe a setting as ruby color, sapphire color, etc., we wish it understood that these are the finest artificial stones made to imitate the gem mentioned.

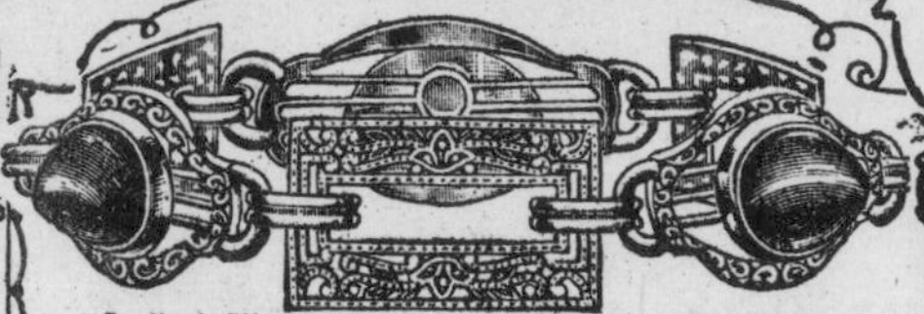

Ladies' Silver Plated Slave Bracelet. Length, about 8 inches. **Order by catalog number given below the color sets desired.**

4K3328—Ruby red color sets..............$1.65
4K3330—Sapphire blue color sets.......... 1.65
4K3332—Amethyst purple color sets........ 1.65

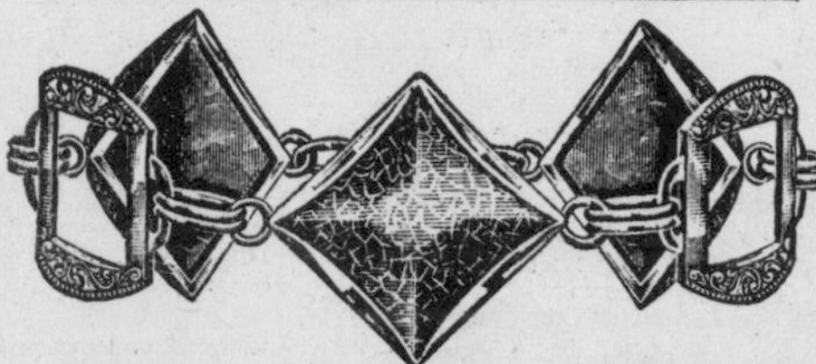

Ladies' Silver Plated Bracelet. Length, about 7¼ inches. **Order by catalog number below the color stone sets desired.**

4K3334—Jade green color sets..............$1.45
4K3336—Cherry red color sets.............. 1.45
4K3338—Lapis (dark blue) color sets....... 1.45

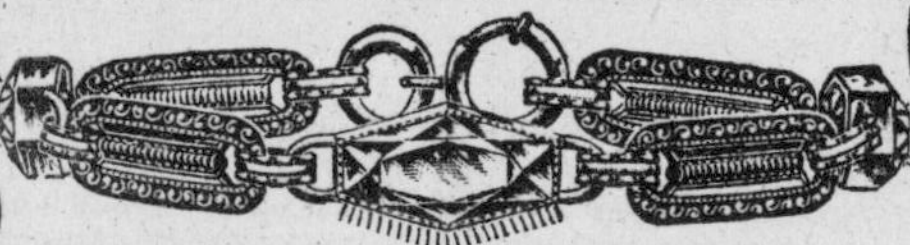

Ladies' Solid Silver Bracelet. **Order by catalog number the color sets desired.** Length, about 7¼ inches.

4K3340—Aquamarine color sets (light bluish green)..............$3.50
4K3342—Rose color sets.............. 3.50
4K3344—Imitation diamond sets....... 3.50

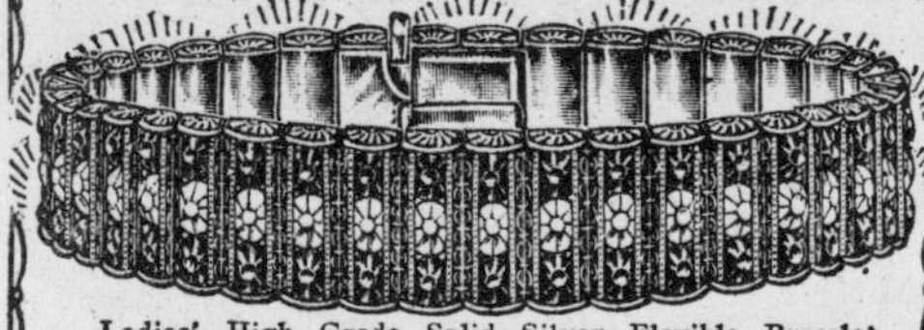

Ladies' High Grade Solid Silver Flexible Bracelet. Very well made. Length, about 6½ inches. **Order by catalog number below the color sets desired.**

4K3346—All imitation diamond sets..........$3.85
4K3348—Ruby red and imitation diamond sets.......... 3.85
4K3350—Sapphire blue and imitation diamond sets.......... 3.85
4K3352—Aquamarine (bluish green) and imitation diamond sets.......... 3.85

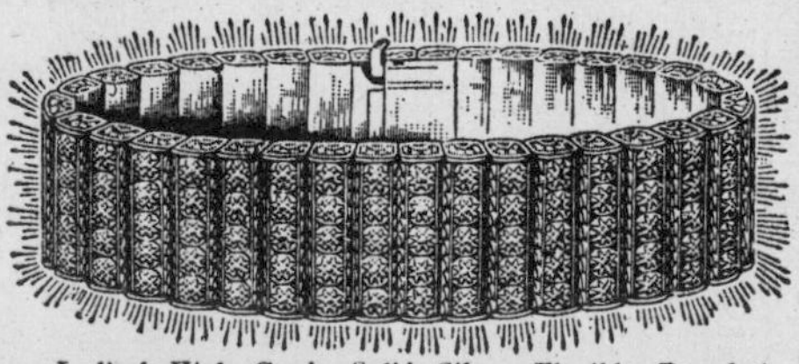

Ladies' High Grade Solid Silver Flexible Bracelet. Very attractive and well made. Length, about 6¾ in. Width, about ¾ in. Illustration shows reduced size. **Order by catalog number the color sets desired.**

4K3354—All imitation diamond sets.......$7.98
4K3356—Ruby red and imitation diamond sets.......... 7.98
4K3358—Sapphire blue and imitation diamond sets.......... 7.98
4K3360—Emerald green and imitation diamond sets..........$7.98

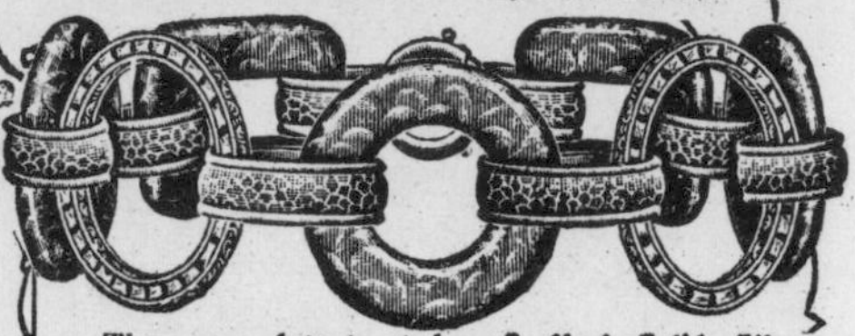

The very latest style. Ladies' Solid Silver Slave Bracelet. Combination of silver and jade green color circles. Length, about 7½ inches.

4K3368 ....$2.98

Ladies' Solid Silver Slave Bracelet. Engraved links. Length, about 7½ inches.

4K3376 ....$2.98
4K3378—Same, green, but gold filled .. 2.98

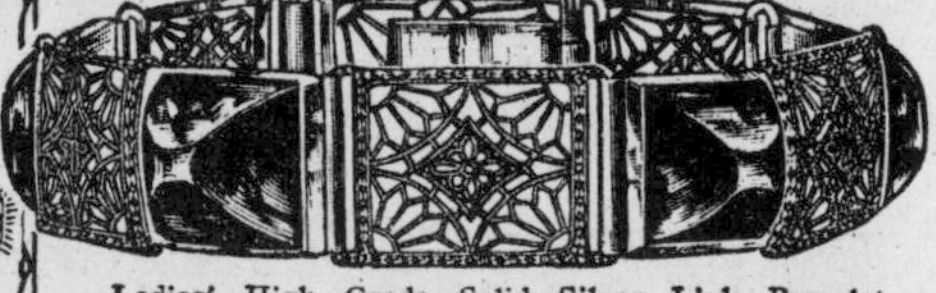

Ladies' High Grade Solid Silver Link Bracelet. Very attractive openwork pattern. **Order by catalog number the color sets desired.** Length, about 6¾ in.

4K3380—Sapphire blue color sets........$3.75
4K3382—Ruby red color sets.............. 3.75

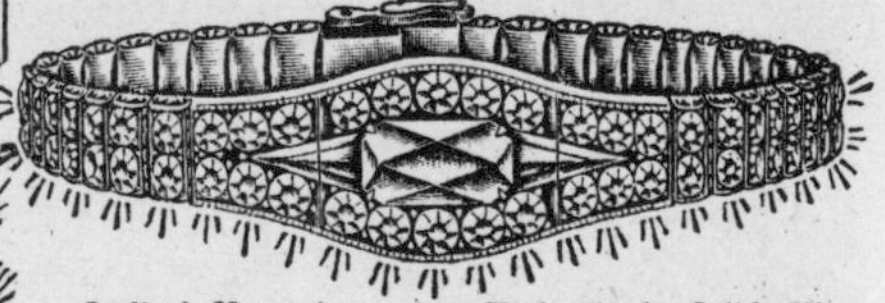

Ladies' Very Attractive High Grade Solid Silver Flexible Bracelet. Length, about 6¾ inches. Patent safety catch. **Order by catalog number the color sets desired.**

4K3384—All imitation diamond sets....$5.98
4K3386—Ruby red and imitation diamond sets.......... 5.98
4K3388—Sapphire blue and imitation diamond sets.......... 5.98
4K3390—Aquamarine (bluish green) and imitation diamond sets.......... 5.98

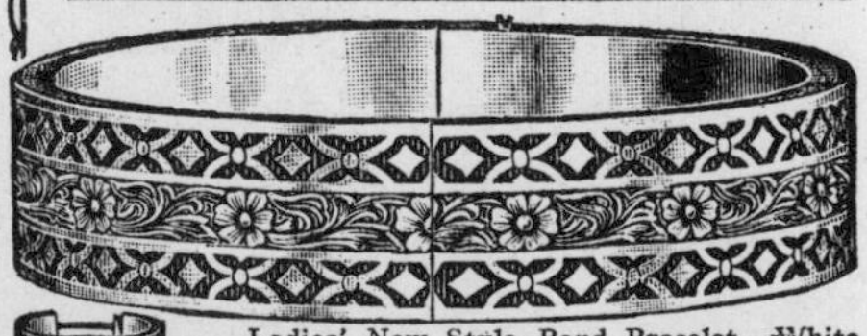

Ladies' New Style Band Bracelet. White gold filled. Measures about 2½ inches in diameter when closed. Opens to slip on wrist easily. Engraved pattern.

4K3392 ....$3.48
Same style as above, but green gold filled.
4K3394 .... 3.48

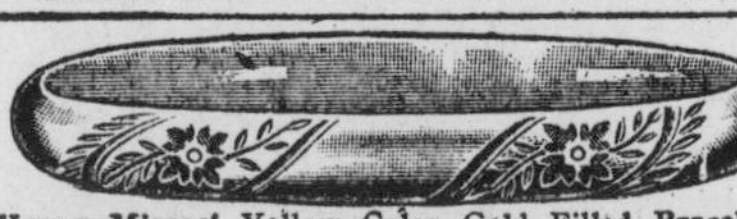

Young Misses' Yellow Color Gold Filled Bracelet. Bright polish. About 1⅞ inches in diameter.

4K3396—Engraved design..........$1.45
4K3398—Plain gold filled bracelet, not engraved 1.45

Senorita Pearls with Real Pearl Lustre

Select with care the pearls that are to adorn Milady. **Senorita Pearls,** in luster and beauty almost rivaling the Oriental, are solid and indestructible. We list **Senorita Pearls** in four grades "A," "B," "C" and "D," according to quality. The higher the cost, the more perfectly matched are the pearls and the higher the luster. Our "A" grade compares favorably with the finest imitation pearls made, which are sold by exclusive jewelers at much higher prices. Our "B," "C" and "D" grades are all unusual values. **All pearls are furnished in attractive presentation cases.**

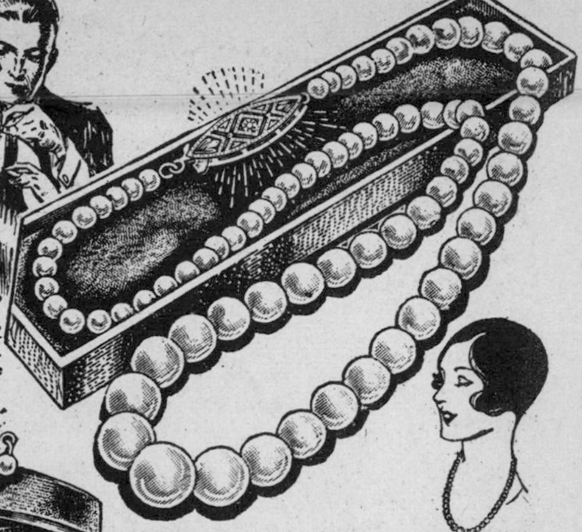

Our Senorita Fine Quality Indestructible Pearl Necklace "B" luster. Festoon style. Very attractive. The festoon is set with brilliant imitation diamonds and large sapphire blue color set in center. 10-karat solid white gold clasp. Length, about 15 inches, not including festoon. The pearls are small and dainty; illustration shows size. Comes in beautiful rose color genuine leather satin lined folding case, as illustrated. Shipping weight, 8 ounces.
4K3400 ....$7.50
As above, but emerald green color setting in festoon.
4K3402 ....$7.50

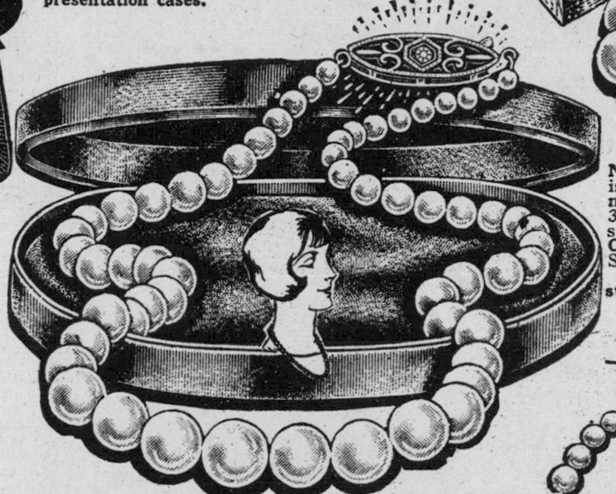

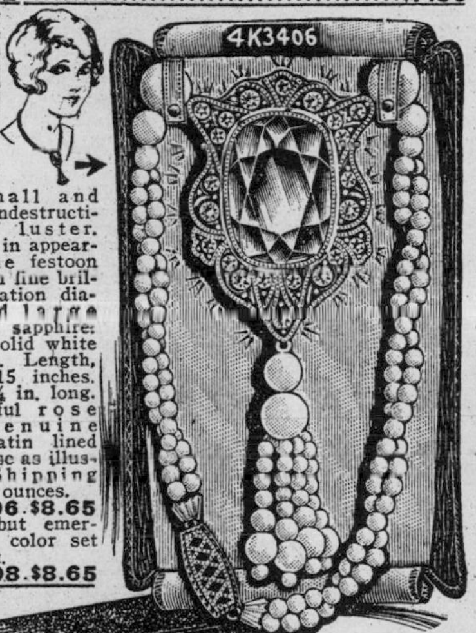

New Style Senorita Double Strand Twisted Pearl Necklace, known as "Seed Pearls" very small and dainty; indestructible. "B" luster. Very rich in appearance. The festoon is set with five brilliant imitation diamonds and large blue color sapphire; 10-karat solid white gold clasp. Length, about 15 inches. Tassel, 2¼ in. long. In beautiful rose color, genuine leather satin lined folding case as illustrated. Shipping weight, 8 ounces.
4K3406 .$8.65
Same, but emerald green color set in festoon.
4K3408 .$8.65

Very Dainty Festoon Style Pearl Necklace. Small indestructible pearls; sizes as illustrated. "D" luster. White gold filled clasp. Fine brilliant imitation diamonds set in square effect tassel. Length, about 15 in. tassel, about 1¾ inches long. Comes in neat presentation box. Shpg. wt., 6 oz.
4K3412
$3.50

The Very Latest
Every woman and girl will want one of these 60-inch necklaces of Indestructible Pearls. This is indeed an unusual value. Pearls of equal luster and brilliancy frequently retail at two and three times our price. "D" luster. The beads are a uniform size. Small illustration shows actual size of the pearls. Shpg. wt., 8 oz.
4K3488 ....98c

Our Senorita Superior Quality Necklace. "A" luster. Our highest grade indestructible Pearl Bead Necklace. Graduated style. 14-karat solid white gold clasp, set with regular genuine cut diamond. Illustration shows size of pearls in our 36 inch strand. Shorter strands have slightly smaller pearls, graduated in proportion to length. Furnished with plush presentation case, as illustrated. Shipping weight, ¾ pound.
4K3424—15-inch length (Choker style)........$13.50
4K3426—18-inch length......................14.25
4K3428—24-inch length......................15.65
4K3430—30-inch length......................17.00
4K3432—36-inch length......................18.45

Three-Strand Senorita Indestructible Pearl Necklace, "B" luster. Length of strands, 18, 20 and 24 inches. Clasp is solid silver set with large indestructible pearl. Illustration of section in center shows approximate size of larger pearls in necklace. Shpg. wt., 8 oz.
4K3436—Three-strand $6.80
Same style but two-strand necklace; 18 and 24-inch lengths.
4K3438 ....$5.00

Good Quality Indestructible Pearl Necklace; choker style; very pretty bowknot tassel effect. Length, about 15 inches; tassel, about 3 inches long. Spring ring clasp. Illustration shows pearls slightly reduced in size. Shipping weight, 4 ounces.
4K3446 ....55c

Three-Strand Indestructible Pearl Necklace. Length of strands, 14½, 15 and 16 inches. Silver plated colored stone set clasp. Illustration of section in center shows approximate size of larger pearls in necklace. Shipping weight, 6 ounces.
4K3442 ....75c

Senorita Fine Quality Indestructible Pearl Necklace. "C" luster. Graduated style. Clasp is 14-karat solid white gold, set with chip diamond. Illustration shows size of pearls in our 36-inch strand. Shorter strands have slightly smaller pearls, graduated in proportion to length. **Order by catalog number the length desired.** Shipping weight, 8 ounces.
4K3450—15-inch length (Choker style).......$3.45
4K3452—18-inch length 3.85
4K3454—24-inch length 4.65
4K3456—30-inch length 5.45
4K3458—36-inch length 6.25

Choker Style Good Quality Indestructible Pearl Necklace. Length, about 15 in. Solid silver clasp set with colored sets as listed below. Illustration shows reduced size of clasp. Illustration of section shows approximate size of pearls, graduated in proportion. Shipping weight, 5 oz.
4K3460—Ruby red color clasp........$1.35
4K3462—Sapphire blue color clasp........$1.35
4K3464—Emerald green color clasp...$1.35
4K3466—Topaz (amber color) clasp...$1.35

24-inch String Indestructible Pearls. Unusual value. Bright luster. Imitation diamond set in non-tarnishable metal clasp. Illustration of section shows approximate size of pearls, graduated in proportion. Shpg. wt., 4 oz.
4K3470—24-inch length 55c
4K3472—Same quality, but 15-inches, (Choker style) ...55c

The Very Popular "Queen Style" 60-in. Indestructible Pearl Necklace. Small pearl between each large pearl. "D" luster. Uniform size. Illustration of section above shows size of pearls. Shipping weight, 8 ounces.
4K3476 .....$2.98

Fine Quality Indestructible Pearl Necklace. "D" luster. Solid silver clasp set with brilliant imitation crystal. Illustration of section shows size of center pearls in 20-inch strand. The center pearls in the shorter strands are slightly smaller. Shipping weight, 4 ounces.
4K3480—16-inch length $1.75
4K3482—18-inch length $1.95
4K3484—20-inch length $2.25

60-inch Length

Exquisite Compacts

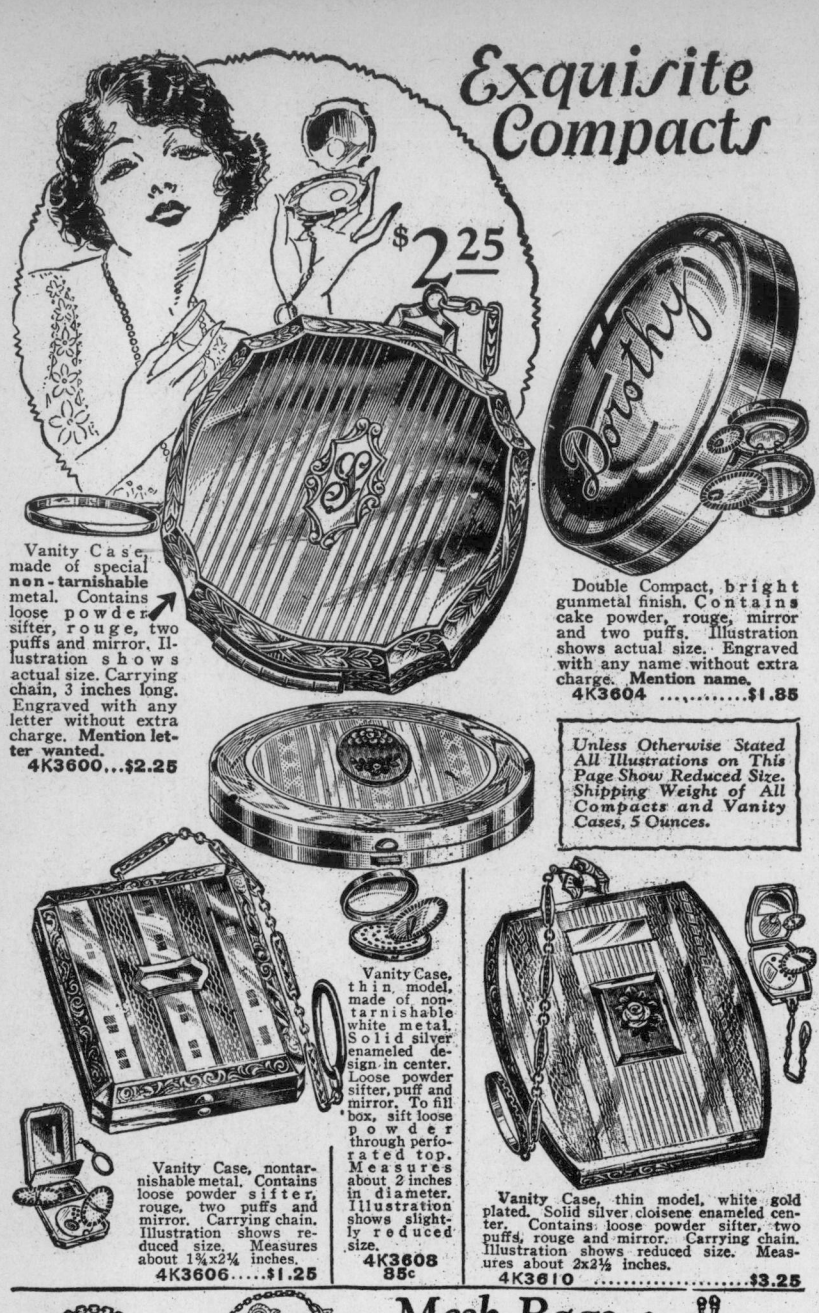

2^{25}

Vanity Case, made of special non-tarnishable metal. Contains loose powder sifter, rouge, and two puffs and mirror. Illustration shows actual size. Carrying chain, 3 inches long. Engraved with any letter without extra charge. Mention letter wanted.
4K3600...$2.25

Double Compact, bright gunmetal finish. Contains cake powder, rouge, mirror and two puffs. Illustration shows actual size. Engraved with any name without extra charge. **Mention name.**
4K3604...........$1.85

Unless Otherwise Stated All Illustrations on This Page Show Reduced Size. Shipping Weight of All Compacts and Vanity Cases, 5 Ounces.

Vanity Case, thin, model, made of non-tarnishable white metal. Solid silver enameled design in center. Loose powder sifter, puff and mirror. To fill box, sift loose powder through perforated top. Measures about 2 inches in diameter. Illustration shows slightly reduced size.
4K3608 85c

Vanity Case, nontarnishable metal. Contains loose powder sifter, rouge, two puffs and mirror. Carrying chain. Illustration shows reduced size. Measures about 1¾x2¼ inches.
4K3606.....$1.25

Vanity Case, thin model, white gold plated. Solid silver cloisene enameled center. Contains loose powder sifter, two puffs, rouge and mirror. Carrying chain. Illustration shows reduced size. Measures about 2x2½ inches.
4K3610...........$3.25

Mesh Bags

High Grade Silver Plated Mesh Bag. Pierced frame. Fish scale mesh, which is practically indestructible. Jeweled catch. Bag about 6 in. deep. Carrying chain. Shpg. wt., ¾ lb.
4K3640.....$3.25

Very New and Attractive Mesh Bags. Made of indestructible mesh enameled in colors. Light green background with gold and darker green color design. Enamel guaranteed not to chip. Gold plated frame. Illustrations show reduced sizes. Order by catalog number the size desired. Shpg. wt., ¾ lb.
4K3642 — 3½x6½ inches, including fringe $3.25
4K3644 — 4¼ x 7 inches, including fringe $4.50

Mesh Bags made of indestructible mesh enameled in colors. Light blue background with gold and darker blue color design. Enamel guaranteed not to chip. Gold plated frame. Order by catalog number the size desired. Shipping wt., ¾ pound.
4K3646 — 3½x5¾ inches $3.50
4K3648 — Pattern similar to above, same color scheme. 4½ x 6 inches $4.75

High Grade Silver Plated Mesh Bag. Piccadilly style. Fine mesh. Jeweled catch. Contains mirror and puff and place for powder as shown in small illustration. Bag about 7¼ inches deep. Carrying chain. Shipping wt., ¾ pound.
4K3650...........$8.50

Shipping Weight of Compacts and Vanity Cases, 5 Ounces.

Vanity Case, silver plated. A compact attractive as it is useful. Contains loose powder sifter, rouge, two puffs and mirror. Carrying chain. Illustration shows reduced size. Measures about 2 inches square. Any name engraved without extra charge. Mention name wanted.
4K3616
$2.65

Vanity Case silver plated. Beautiful enameled design in center. Contains mirror, loose powder sifter, rouge, two puffs and coin holder. Measures about 2x2 inches. Illustration shows reduced size. Carrying chain.
4K3620
$2.25

Vanity Case, made of non-tarnishable white metal, with solid silver enameled center. Contains loose powder sifter, rouge, two puffs and mirror. Carrying chain. Illustration shows reduced size. Measures about 2 inches square.
4K3622
$1.65

Vanity Case. One of our newest compacts that will appeal instantly to the woman of fashion. Made of non-tarnishable white metal, with solid silver enameled center. Contains cake powder, rouge, two puffs and mirror. Utility space for cards, etc. Carrying chain. Illustration shows reduced size. Measures about 1¾x2¾ in.
4K3624
$2.50

Vanity Case, silver plated. An unusually beautiful vanity that is sure to gain wide approval this season and is fully as useful as it is attractive. Contains cake powder, rouge, lipstick, two puffs and mirror. Lipstick rises automatically when box is opened. Carrying chain. Illustration shows reduced size. Measures about 2x3 inches.
4K3628
$4.25

Vanity Case, silver plated. A compact that lends a decorative touch as well as being decidedly useful. Contains cake powder, rouge, two puffs, mirror and comb. Carrying chain. Measures about 1¾ x3 inches. Illustration shows reduced size.
4K3630
$1.75

Vanity Case, silver plated. Beautiful color design. Contains loose powder sifter, rouge, two puffs and mirror. Carrying chain. Measures about 2 in. in diameter. Illustration shows reduced size.
4K3632
$1.75

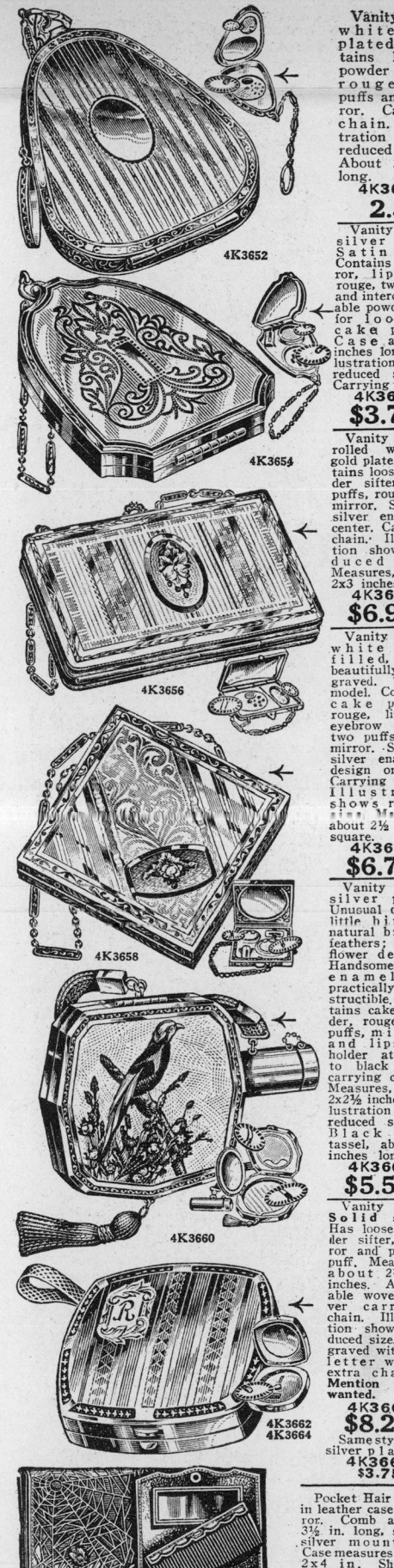

Vanity Case, white gold plated. Contains loose powder sifter, rouge, two puffs and mirror. Carrying chain. Illustration shows reduced size. About 2½ in. long.
4K3652
2.50

4K3652

Vanity Case, silver plated. Satin finish. Contains mirror, lipstick, rouge, two puffs and interchangeable powder box for loose or cake powder. Case about 3 inches long. Illustration shows reduced size. Carrying chain.
4K3654
$3.75

4K3654

Vanity Case, rolled white gold plate. Contains loose powder sifter, two puffs, rouge and mirror. Solid silver enameled center. Carrying chain. Illustration shows reduced size. Measures, about 2x3 inches.
4K3656
$6.98

4K3656

Vanity case, white gold filled, very beautifully engraved. Thin model. Contains cake powder, rouge, lipstick, eyebrow pencil, two puffs and mirror. Solid silver enameled design on top. Carrying chain. Illustration shows reduced size. Measures about 2½ inches square.
4K3658
$6.75

4K3658

Vanity Case, silver plated. Unusual design, little bird in natural bright feathers; also flower design. Handsomer than enamel and practically indestructible. Contains cake powder, rouge, two puffs, mirror and lipstick holder attached to black braid carrying cord. Measures, about 2x2½ inches. Illustration shows reduced size. Black fringe tassel, about 2 inches long.
4K3660
$5.50

4K3660

Vanity Case, Solid silver. Has loose powder sifter, mirror and powder puff. Measures, about 2¼x2¼ inches. Adjustable woven silver carrying chain. Illustration shows reduced size. Engraved with any letter without extra charge. **Mention letter wanted.**
4K3662
$8.25
Same style, but silver plated.
4K3664
$3.75

4K3662
4K3664

Pocket Hair Comb in leather case; mirror. Comb about 3½ in. long, solid silver mounting. Case measures about 2x4 in. Shipping weight, 3 ounces.
4K3682 $1.75

A Modern Essential

Shipping weight of Vanity Cases and Compacts, 5 oz. Unless otherwise stated, illustrations on this page show reduced size.

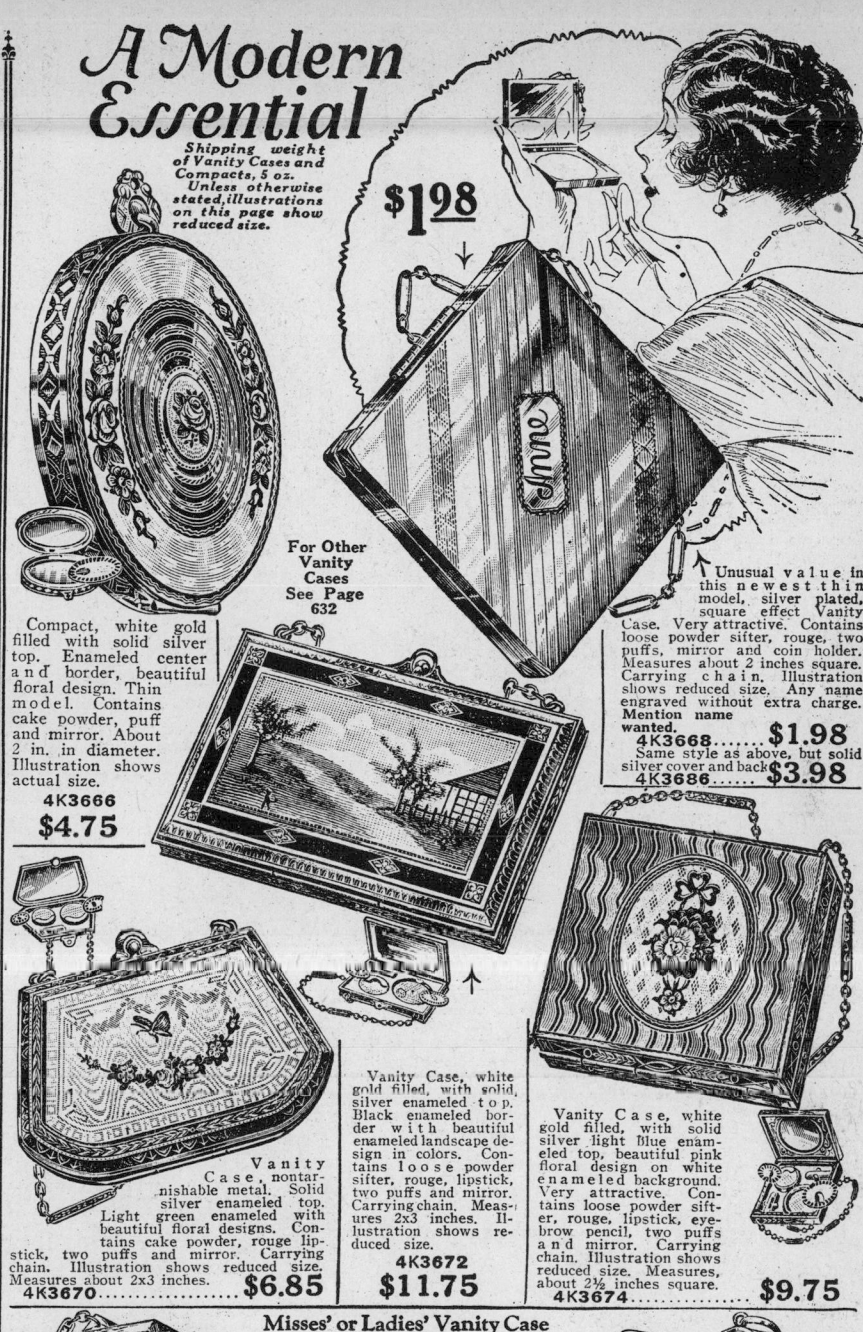

$1.98

Compact, white gold filled with solid silver top. Enameled center and border, beautiful floral design. Thin model. Contains cake powder, puff and mirror. About 2 in. in diameter. Illustration shows actual size.
4K3666
$4.75

For Other Vanity Cases See Page 632

Vanity Case, nontarnishable metal. Solid silver enameled top. Light green enameled with beautiful floral designs. Contains cake powder, rouge lipstick, two puffs and mirror. Carrying chain. Illustration shows reduced size. Measures about 2x3 inches.
4K3670................**$6.85**

Vanity Case, white gold filled, with solid silver enameled top. Black enameled border with beautiful enameled landscape design in colors. Contains loose powder sifter, rouge, lipstick, two puffs and mirror. Carrying chain. Measures 2x3 inches. Illustration shows reduced size.
4K3672
$11.75

Unusual value in this newest thin model, silver plated, square effect Vanity Case. Very attractive. Contains loose powder sifter, rouge, two puffs, mirror and coin holder. Measures about 2 inches square. Carrying chain. Illustration shows reduced size. Any name engraved without extra charge. **Mention name wanted.**
4K3668......**$1.98**
Same style as above, but solid silver cover and back.
4K3686......**$3.98**

Vanity Case, white gold filled, with solid silver light blue enameled top, beautiful pink floral design on white enameled background. Very attractive. Contains loose powder sifter, rouge, lipstick, eyebrow pencil, two puffs and mirror. Carrying chain. Illustration shows reduced size. Measures, about 2½ inches square.
4K3674................**$9.75**

Misses' or Ladies' Vanity Case

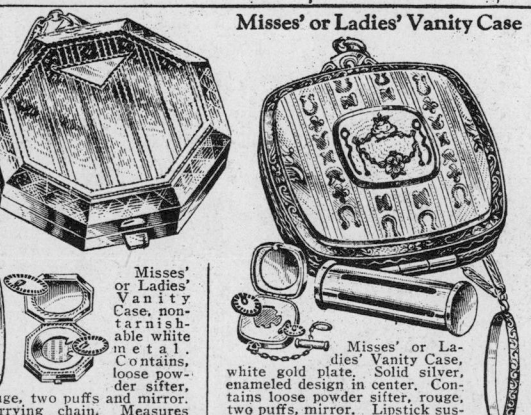

Misses' or Ladies' Vanity Case, nontarnishable white metal. Contains, loose powder sifter, rouge, two puffs and mirror. Carrying chain. Measures about 1¾ inches in diameter. Illustration shows reduced size.
4K3676................**$1.75**

Misses' or Ladies' Vanity Case, white gold plate. Solid silver, enameled design in center. Contains loose powder sifter, rouge, two puffs, mirror. Lipstick suspends from the carrying chain. Measures about 1¾ in. square.
4K3678................**$6.75**

Misses' or Ladies' Vanity Case, two-tone white gold plate with green gold border and carrying chain. Solid silver enameled center. Contains loose powder sifter, rouge, two puffs and mirror. Illustration shows reduced size. Measures about 1¾ inches square.
4K3680..........**$5.50**

Ladies' Handy Comb in silver plated case. About 2¾ inches long. Black cord guard attached, about 32 inches long. Illustration shows reduced size. Cord is detachable, can be used as pocket comb. Shipping weight, 3 oz.
4K3684................**50c**

Essentials for the Well Dressed Woman

Ladies' Solid Silver Imitation Diamond Set Festoon, very elegant and rich in appearance. The chain is solid silver, about 16 inches long.
4K4000 .... $4.50

Ladies' Attractive Festoon. Brilliant imitation diamonds, with indestructible pearl drops. Chain is of solid silver, very well made. Stones are set in silver plated metal. Length, about 15 inches. Choker style. Spring ring clasp.
4K4002 .... $1.39

Ladies' Festoon Necklace. Gives the effect of platinum, set with diamonds. Solid silver chain, soldered links. Length, about 15 inches. Choker style. Pendant, about 2¼ inches long. Illustration shows slightly reduced size.
4K4004 $6.25

Solid Silver Ring, imitation diamonds and blue sapphire. Sizes, 4 to 9.
4K4042 $1.15

Ladies' Solid Silver Ring, set with large imitation square diamond in center and imitation diamonds all around the center stone. Sizes, 4 to 9. State size.
4K4044 ... $1.05

Solid Silver Ring, three square imitation diamonds in center, six imitation diamonds in shank. Sizes, 4 to 9. State size.
4K4046 98c

Ladies' Solid Silver Ring, set with brilliant imitation diamonds. Sizes, 4 to 9. State size.
4K4048 ..... 50c

Ladies' Solid Silver Ring, set with imitation diamond in center and two blue sapphires set in center. Sizes, 4 to 9. State size.
4K4050 ...... 98c

Illustrations on this page show actual size, unless otherwise stated. Shipping weight of all articles on this page, 3 oz., unless otherwise stated.
All articles in neat presentation case.

Very Attractive Festoon, Silver Plated. Large brilliant imitation diamond in center, surrounded by smaller imitation diamonds. Chain, about 21 in. long.
4K4008 .... $4.25

Very Attractive Festoon, made of white metal, set with brilliant imitation diamonds. Length, about 15 in. Choker style.
4K4010 ..... $1.05

Earrings, for unpierced ears. Silver plated, with imitation diamond sets.
4K4012 .. 48c

New Style Long Effect Earrings, for unpierced ears. Silver plated, with imitation diamond sets. Chain connection.
4K4014 .... $1.65

Earrings, for unpierced ears. Solid silver. Large imitation diamond, set in knot and drop, and smaller imitation diamonds in connecting chain. Very attractive.
4K4024 $4.75

Ladies' Snake Bracelet, the very newest style spiral effect, winds around the wrist. Solid silver, set with brilliant imitation diamonds. Will fit almost any wrist.
4K4054 .... $5.98

Ladies' Bracelet, Silver plated. Center design set with brilliant imitation diamonds. Openwork links set with four imitation diamonds. Length, about 7 in.
4K4056 .... $1.60

Ladies' Very Attractive Bracelet of non-tarnishable white metal. Very well made. Set with brilliant imitation diamonds and blue sapphires.
4K4058—Length, about 7 inches $3.95

Ladies' New Style Slave Bracelet. Solid silver, set with brilliant imitation diamonds. Very attractive.
4K4060—Length, about 6½ inches $4.50

Ladies' Solid Silver Slave Bracelet, set with brilliant imitation diamonds. The large sets are sapphire blue color. Very neat and attractive.
4K4062—Length, about 6¾ inches $4.75

Silver Plated Brooch, set with brilliant imitation diamonds. Very attractive. Safety catch.
4K4018 .... $1.95

Ladies' Brooch. Silver plated, set with imitation diamonds and three blue sapphires. Safety Catch. Bowknot effect.
4K4020 .... $2.98

Ladies' Shoe Buckles, Silver plated, set with imitation diamonds. Illustration shows reduced size. Measures about 1⅛ x1¾ inches.
4K4022—Pair .. $3.45

Initial Brooch. Silver plated, set with imitation diamonds. Furnished with any initial. Mention letter wanted.
4K4026 .... $1.25

Attractive Bowknot Brooch. Ribbon effect. Silver plated, set with imitation diamonds. Safety catch.
4K4028 .... $2.30

Ladies Brooch. Solid silver, set with imitation diamonds. Bird design in center enameled in colors. Safety catch.
4K4030 .... $1.45

Ladies' Solid Silver Bar Pin, set with fine imitation diamonds. Safety catch.
4K4032 .... 90c

Ladies' Solid Silver Bar Pin, set with fine imitation diamonds. Safety catch.
4K4034 .... 85c

Ladies' Solid Silver Bar Pin, set with fine imitation diamonds. Length, about 3 inches. Illustration shows reduced size.
4K4036 .... $1.45

Ladies' Solid Silver Bar Pin, set with fine imitation diamonds. Length, about 2½ in. Illustrations shows reduced size.
4K4038 .... 75c

Silver Plated Bracelet, set with fine imitation diamonds. About 2¾ inches in diameter.
4K4064 .... $1.25

Fashion Requires Costume Jewelry

...s' Solid Silver Ring. Sizes, 4... **State size.** Shipping wt., 3 oz.
4K4200—Jade green color....$1.15
4K4202—Light...ine (star sapphire ...lor set)....$1.15
4K4204—Alexandrite (iridescent red color set).$1.15

Ladies' Solid Silver Ring. Sizes, 4 to 9. **State size.** Shipping wt., 3 oz.
4K4206—Aquamarine (bluish green color set)....$1.25
4K4208—Ruby red color set..$1.25
4K4210—Sapphire blue color set....$1.25

Ladies' Solid Silver Ring. Sizes, 4 to 9. **State size.** Shpg. wt., 3 oz.
4K4212 Jade green color.75c
4K4214 Cherry red color....75c
4K4216 Lapis (dark blue) 75c

Ladies' Solid Silver Ring. Order by catalog number the color setting. Sizes, 4 to 9. State size. Shipping weight, 3 ounces.
4K4218—Sardonyx color set (reddish brown).$1.35
4K4220—Imitation black onyx $1.35
4K4222—Lapis blue color (dark mottled blue)..$1.35

GENUINE SETS

Ladies' 10-Karat Solid White Gold Ring. Pierced design. Order by catalog number the setting wanted. All genuine stones. Sizes, 4 to 9. State size. Shpg. wt., 3 oz.
4K4226—Genuine amazinite (jade green color) ..$5.75
4K4228—Genuine sardonyx (reddish brown color)..$5.75
4K4230—Genuine black onyx $5.75

Ladies' Loose Link Slave Bracelet. Solid silver. Length, about 7½ inches. Order by catalog number the color sets desired. Shipping weight, 3 oz.

4K4232—Jade green color sets, jet black circles.....$4.25
4K4234—Cornelian (light brown sets), jet black circles 4.25
4K4236—Lapis (mottled blue sets), jet black circles. 4.25

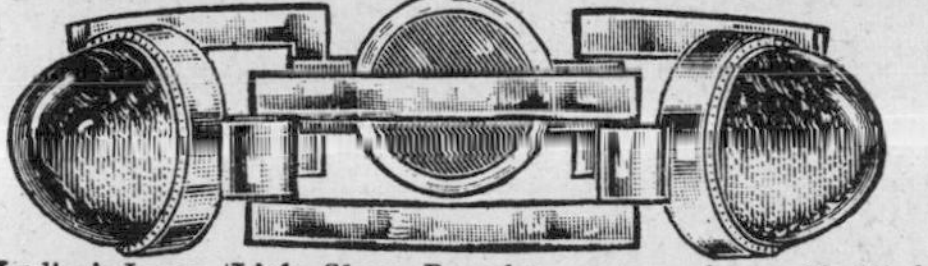

Ladies' Loose Link Slave Bracelet, green color gold filled. Length, about 7 inches. Shipping weight, 3 ounces.
4K4238—Jade green color sets...$3.98
4K4240—Cherry red color sets..................3.98
4K4242—Rose color sets...............3.08

Ladies' Slave Bracelet. Gold plated. Length, about 7½ inches. Shipping weight, 3 ounces.
4K4244—Ruby red color sets....................$1.65
4K4246—Sapphire blue color sets...................1.65
4K4248—Amethyst purple color sets....................1.65

14-Karat Solid Gold   Genuine Stone Sets

Ladies' Very High Grade Loose Link Slave Bracelet. 14-karat solid yellow color gold with genuine sets. Bright polish. Length, about 7½ inches. Shipping weight, 3 ounces.
4K4250—Genuine black onyx.......................$19.50
4K4252—Genuine chrysophrase (dark green, resembles jade)................19.50
4K4254—Genuine sardonyx (reddish brown color).. 19.50

Ladies' Very Attractive Solid Silver Brooch, large jade green color set. Illustration shows reduced size. Measures, about 1x1⅜ inches. Matches earrings 4K4320, on this page. Shipping weight, 3 ounces.
4K4256—Jade green color set...............$1.35
Same style, but cherry red color set, matches earrings 4K4322, on this page.
4K4258 ....$1.35

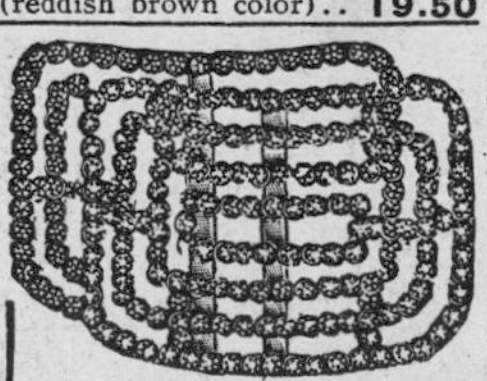

Ladies' Imported Genuine Cut Steel Shoe Buckles at a very low price. Illustration shows reduced size. Measures about 1½x2¼ inches. Adds style to the appearance of Milady's slipper. Shipping wt., 4 oz. 
4K4260—Pair $3.50

Italian Jet (Black) Necklace. Length, about 30 inches. Jet screw clasp. Illustration shows size of largest beads in graduation. Shpg. wt., 4 oz.
4K4262 ....$2.50
Same quality, but 15-inch length (choker style). Beads slightly smaller than illustrated.
4K4264 ....$1.50

This attractive festoon comes in three colors: Light green, rose color and amber color. Length, about 15 inches. Choker style. Spring ring clasp. Star design in center drop. Order by catalog number the color desired. Shipping weight, 4 ounces.
4K4278—Light green..........$1.00
4K4280—Rose color 1.00
4K4282—Amber color 1.00

GENUINE AMBER
Genuine Imported Amber Bead Necklace. Length, about 25 inches. The beads are graduated and faceted, bringing out all the soft lights. Clasp is of amber, screw style. Illustration shows size of largest beads. Shpg. wt., 4 oz.
4K4294 ....$6.95
16 inches long (choker style). Beads in this length are slightly smaller than illustrated.
4K4296 ....$3.85

Genuine Clear Cut Crystal Necklace at an unusually low price. Length, about 28 inches. Graduated style. Solid silver spring ring clasp. Illustration shows size of largest beads in graduation. Shpg. wt., 8 oz.
4K4266..............$9.50
Same quality, but 15-inch length (choker style): Shipping weight, 5 ounces.
4K4268..............$4.75

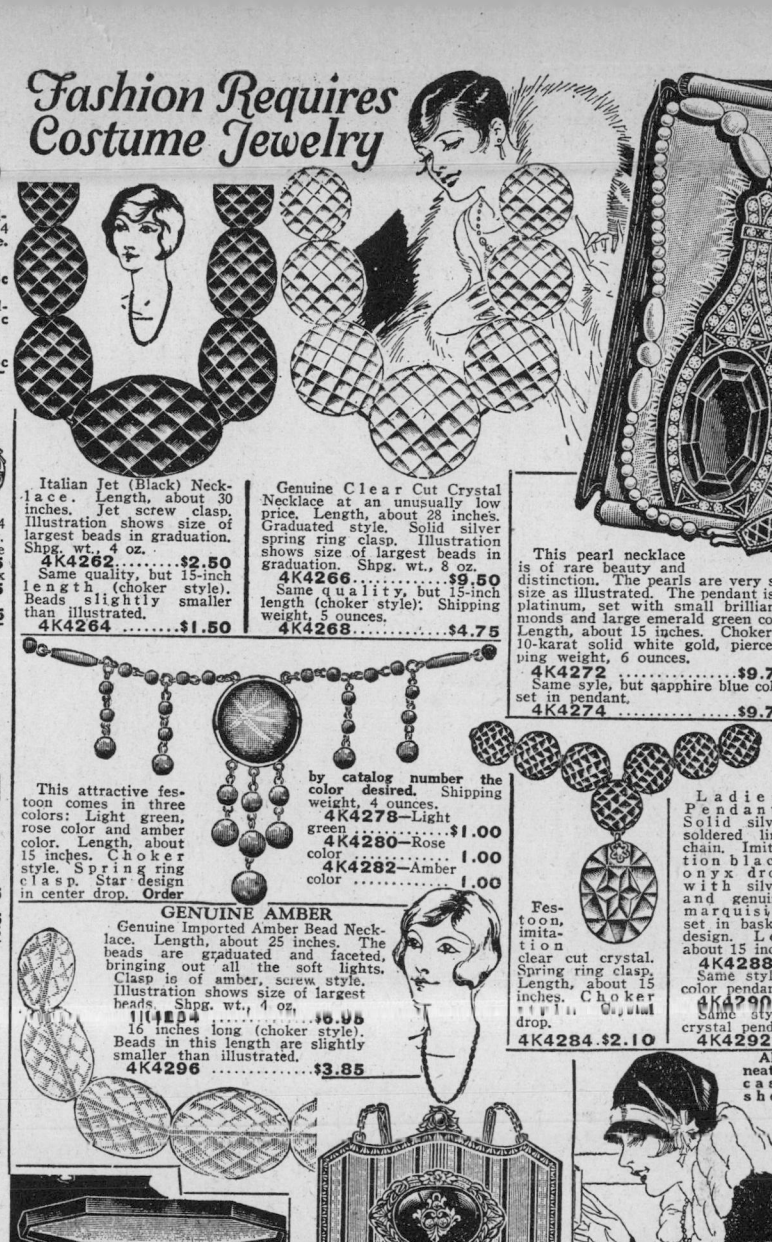

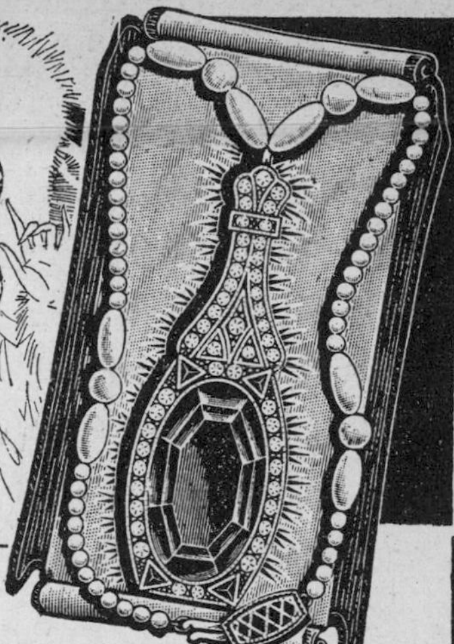

This pearl necklace is of rare beauty and distinction. The pearls are very small and dainty, size as illustrated. The pendant is made to imitate platinum, set with small brilliant imitation diamonds and large emerald green color set in center. Length, about 15 inches. Choker style. Clasp is 10-karat solid white gold, pierced design. Shipping weight, 6 ounces.
4K4272 ....$9.75
Same style, but sapphire blue color set in pendant.
4K4274 ....$9.75

Ladies' Pendant. Solid silver soldered link chain. Imitation black onyx drop with silver and genuine marquisite set in basket design. Length of chain, about 15 inches. Choker style.
4K4284..$2.10
Same style, but jade green color set.
4K4288.........$1.95
Same style, but imitation crystal pendant.
4K4292.........$1.95

Festoon, imitation clear cut crystal. Spring ring clasp. Length, about 15 inches. Choker style. Crystal color drop.
4K4286...........$1.95
Same style, but jade green color pendant.
4K4290..........$1.95

All articles sent in neat presentation cases. Illustrations show size unless otherwise stated.

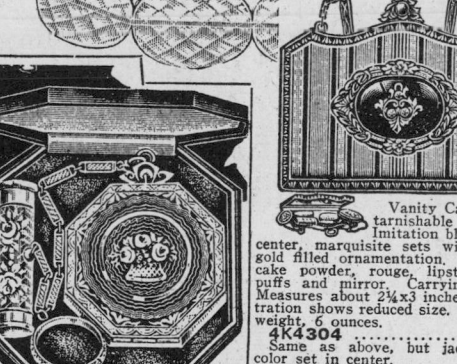

Vanity Case, non-tarnishable metal. Imitation black onyx center, marquisite sets with green gold filled ornamentation. Contains cake powder, rouge, lipstick, two puffs and mirror. Carrying chain. Measures about 2¼x3 inches. Illustration shows reduced size. Shipping weight, 6 ounces.
4K4304 ....$7.00
Same as above, but green color set in center.
4K4306...........$7.00

Vanity Case and Lipstick Holder 1½ inches long, attached to carrying chain. Solid silver. Light green enameled top, floral design in center, Lipstick enameled with rose design. Contains loose powder, sifter, rouge, two puffs, mirror and lipstick. Case, about 1⅞x1⅜ inches. Plush presentation case. Shpg. wt., 8 oz.
4K4300 ...$10.98

Ladies' Combination Mesh Bag and Vanity Case. Indestructible mesh enameled in colors, background light blue. Vanity case attached to the mesh bag is silver plated with beautiful enameled design on top in colors to harmonize with the mesh. Contains powder, rouge, two puffs, mirror and comb. Carrying chain. Bag measures about 3x5½ inches, including vanity case. Shipping weight, ¾ pound.
4K4308 ...$10.50

Ladies' Button Effect Earrings, for unpierced ears. Light green color imitation pearl. Gold filled mountings. Shipping weight, 3 oz.
4K4310 ......$1.25
Same as above, but gunmetal color imitation pearl.
4K4312 ......$1.25

Ladies' Very Fashionable Drop Earrings for unpierced ears. Gold plated (antique finish) jade color sets. Length, about 2 inches. Shpg. wt., 3 oz.
4K4314 ....$1.10

Drop Earrings for unpierced ears. Jade green color sets, imitation black onyx connection. Gold plated trimmings. Length, about 1¾ in. Shpg. wt., 3 oz.
4K4316 ....$1.98

Ladies' Fashionable Drop Earrings for unpierced ears. Gold plated (antique dull finish). Cherry red color sets. Length, about 1¾ in. Shpg. wt., 3 oz.
4K4318 ......95c

Jade Green Color Ladies' Button Effect Earrings for unpierced ears. Silver plated trimmings. Shpg. wt., 3 oz.
4K4320..55c
Cherry red color.
4K4322......55c

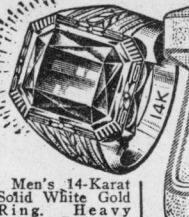
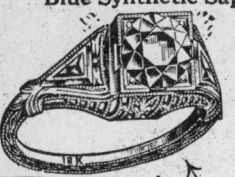

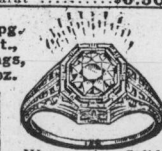

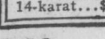

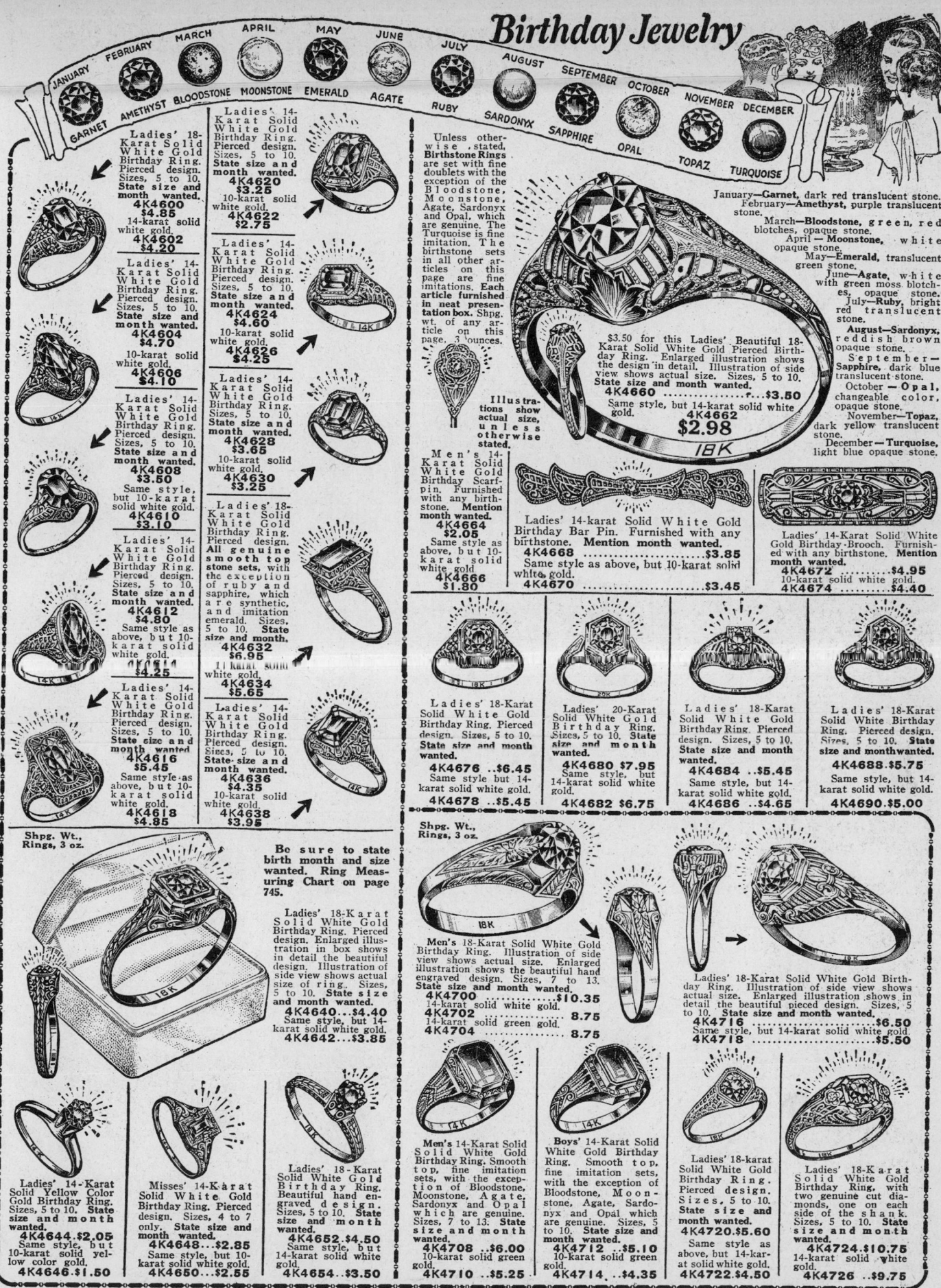

Ladies' 10 and 14-Karat Solid Gold Set Rings

Ladies' 14-Karat Solid White Gold Ring, set with genuine cultured pearl. Sizes, 5 to 10. **State size.**
4K4800
$3.85

Ladies' 14-Karat Solid White Gold Ring, set with genuine aquamarine (bluish green color). Sizes, 5 to 10. **State size.**
4K4806..$9.25
Same style, but 10-karat solid white gold.
4K4808..$8.75

Ladies' 14-Karat Solid White Gold Ring, set with genuine topaz (amber color). Sizes, 5 to 10. **State size.**
4K4834..$6.25
Same style, but set with reconstructed red ruby.
4K4836..$5.25

Ladies' 14-Karat Solid White Gold Ring, set with genuine green agate (jade color). Sizes, 5 to 10. **State size.**
4K4838 $5.65
Same style, but 18-karat solid white gold.
4K4840 $6.85

Shipping Weight, Rings, 3 Ounces

Ladies' 10-Karat Solid White Gold Ring, yellow color gold floral design. Fine imitation diamond set in imitation black onyx. Sizes, 5 to 10. **State size.**
4K4842 ....$3.35

Ladies' 14-Karat Solid White Gold Ring, **genuine and synthetic sets.** Sizes, 5 to 10. **State size.**
4K4810—Synthetic ruby...**$4.50**
4K4812—Genuine Amethyst (purple) **4.50**
4K4814—Genuine Aquamarine (very light bluish green) **4.50**
4K4816—Garnet (dark red) **4.50**
4K4818—Topaz (amber)... **4.50**
4K4820—Synthetic Pink sapphire **4.50**

Ladies' 14-Karat Solid White Gold Ring, **genuine and synthetic sets.** Sizes, 5 to 10. **State size.**
4K4822—Synthetic ruby...**$4.25**
4K4824—Genuine Amethyst **4.25**
4K4826—Genuine Aquamarine (very light bluish green) **4.25**
4K4828—Genuine Garnet (dark red) **4.25**
4K4830—Topaz (amber color) **4.25**
4K4832—Synthetic pink sapphire **4.25**

Ladies' 10-Karat Solid White Gold Ring, set with genuine light purple amethyst. Smooth top stone, faceted back. Sizes, 5 to 10. **State size.**
4K4864
$4.95
Same style, but set with reconstructed red ruby.
4K4866..............................$4.95

Ladies' 10-Karat Solid White Gold Ring, set with genuine Cornelian cameo, light brown background. Sizes, 5 to 10. **State size.**
4K4856..$3.95

Ladies' 14-Karat Solid White Gold Ring, set with genuine Cornelian cameo, light brown background. Sizes, 5 to 10. **State size.**
4K4858..$6.25

Ladies' 10-Karat Solid White Gold Ring, set with genuine black and white cameo. Black background with white head. Sizes, 5 to 10. **State size.**
4K4860..$9.85

Ladies' 10-Karat Solid White Gold Ring, set with genuine Cornelian cameo (light brown background). Sizes, 5 to 10. **State size.**
4K4862..$4.25

Ladies' 14-Karat Solid White Gold Ring, set with genuine changeable color opal. Sizes, 5 to 10. **State size.**
4K4844..$5.35
Same style, but 10-karat solid white gold.
4K4846..$4.85

Ladies' 14-Karat Solid White Gold Ring, emerald green doublet set. Sizes, 5 to 10. **State size.**
4K4848.....$4.65
Same style, but sapphire blue doublet set.
4K4850.....$4.65
Same style, but ruby red doublet set.
4K4852.....$4.65

Ladies' 14-Karat Solid White Gold Ring, genuine purple amethyst set. Sizes, 5 to 10. **State size.**
4K4870...$4.75
Same style, with genuine garnet (dark red).
4K4872...$4.75
Same style, with reconstructed red ruby.
4K4874...$4.35
Same style, set with genuine aquamarine (bluish green color).
4K4876....$8.50

Ladies' 14-Karat Solid White Gold Ring. Sizes, 5 to 10. **State size.**
4K4878—Synthetic ruby (red color) set **$4.25**
4K4880—Genuine Amethyst (purple color) set...**$4.25**
4K4882—Genuine Aquamarine (very light bluish green color) set...**$4.25**
4K4884—Genuine topaz (amber color) set **$4.25**
4K4886—Synthetic sapphire (pink color) set **$4.25**

Misses' 10 and 14-Karat Solid Gold Rings

Misses' 14-Karat Solid White Gold Ring, set with cultured pearl, two blue sapphires set in shank. Sizes, 5 to 10. **State size.**
4K4854..........$4.95

Birthday Ring. Misses' 10-Karat Solid Yellow Color Gold Birthday Ring set with any birthstone. Sizes, 4 to 7. **Mention size and month wanted.**
4K4900.......................$1.15
14-Karat solid gold.
4K4902................... 1.65

Misses' 10-Karat Solid White Gold Ring, amethyst purple color set. Sizes, 4 to 7. **State size.**
4K4914..$3.10
Ruby red color set.
4K4916..$3.10
Aquamarine (bluish green) set.
4K4918..$3.10

Misses' 10-Karat Solid White Gold Ring, with aquamarine (light bluish green) set. Sizes, 4 to 7. **State size.**
4K4930..$2.10
Same style, but 14-karat solid white gold.
4K4932..$2.50

Misses' 14-Karat Solid White Gold Ring, amethyst purple color set. Sizes, 4 to 7. **State size.**
4K4934
$1.80
Same style, but sapphire blue color set.
4K4936
$1.80

Misses' or Boys' 10-Karat Solid Yellow Color Gold Seal Ring. Engraved with any letter without extra charge. Sizes, 4 to 8. **State size and letter to be engraved.**
4K4920...............$1.75

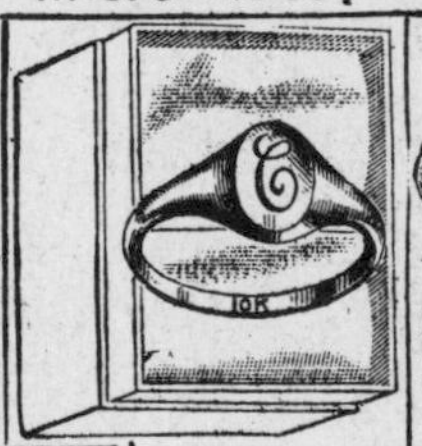

Misses' or Boys' 10-Karat Solid Yellow Color Gold Ring. Bright polish. Engraved with any letter. Sizes, 4 to 8. **State size and letter.**
4K4922
$2.00

Ladies' 14-Karat Solid White Gold Ring, set with reconstructed red ruby. Sizes, 5 to 10. **State size.**
4K4890..$4.25
Set with genuine topaz (amber color).
4K4892..$4.25
Set with genuine aquamarine (very light bluish green).
4K4894..$6.75

Misses' 10-Karat Solid White Gold Ring. Ruby red color set. Sizes, 4 to 7. **State size.**
4K4926
$1.65
Amethyst purple color.
4K4928.........$1.65

Misses' 10-Karat Solid White Gold Ring, ruby red color set. Sizes, 4 to 7. **State size.**
4K4940
$2.60

Amethyst purple color set.
4K4942 ....$2.60
Aquamarine (bluish green color) set.
4K4944 ....$2.60

Misses' 14-Karat Solid White Gold Ring, set with genuine changeable color opal. Sizes, 4 to 7. **State size.**
4K4906
$4.00

Misses' 10-Karat Solid White Gold Ring, 18-karat solid white gold floral design. Sapphire blue color setting. Sizes, 4 to 7. **State size.**
4K4908 ..$1.95

Misses' 10-Karat Solid White Gold Ring, sapphire blue color setting. Sizes, 4 to 7. **State size.**
4K4910
$1.65

Misses' 14-Karat Solid White Gold Ring, dark red garnet color setting. Sizes, 4 to 7. **State size.**
4K4912
$2.90

Misses' 14-Karat Solid White Gold Ring, ruby color set. Sizes, 4 to 7. **State size.**
4K4946
$1.85

Misses' 10-Karat Solid Yellow Color Gold Ring. Ruby red color set. Sizes, 4 to 7. **State size.**
4K4948
$1.50

Misses' 14-Karat Solid White Gold Ring, genuine opal set. Sizes, 4 to 7. **State size.**
4K4952..$2.95

Misses' 10-Karat Solid White Gold Ring, genuine dark red garnet set. Sizes, 4 to 7. **State size.**
4K4954..$3.65

Misses' 10-Karat Solid White Gold Ring, ruby color set. Sizes, 4 to 7. **State size.**
4K4956
$2.10

Misses' 10-Karat Solid Yellow Color Gold Ring, Roman satin finish. Genuine rose diamond set. Any letter engraved. Sizes, 4 to 7. **Mention size and letter wanted.**
4K4970..$3.65

Misses' or Boys' 10-Karat Solid White Gold Seal Ring. Sizes, 4 to 7. Engraved with any letter without extra charge. **State size and letter wanted.**
4K4972 ....$2.65

Misses' or Boys' 10-Karat Solid Yellow Color Gold Seal Ring. Sizes, 4 to 7. Engraved with any letter. **State size and letter wanted.**
4K4974 ....$1.55

Misses' 10-Karat Solid White Gold Initial Ring. Pierced design. Any letter set on genuine black onyx. Sizes, 4 to 7. **State size and letter wanted.**
4K4976.......................$4.25

Misses' 10-Karat Solid White Gold Ring, ruby color set. Sizes, 4 to 7. **State size.**
4K4958
$2.50

Misses' 10-Karat Solid White Gold Ring, set with genuine rose diamond and two blue sapphires. Sizes, 4 to 7. **State size.**
4K4960....$3.98

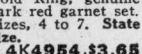

Misses' 10-Karat Solid Yellow Color Gold Band Ring. Sizes, 5 to 8. **State size.**
4K4964
$1.35

Misses' 14-Karat Solid White Gold Ring, genuine rose diamond in genuine black onyx. Sizes, 4 to 7. **State size.**
4K4966....$3.98

Misses' 14-Karat Solid White Gold Ring, reconstructed ruby set. Sizes, 4 to 7. **State size.**
4K4968
$3.25

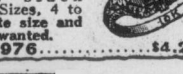

Shipping weight of all Rings on this page, 3 ounces. Each ring sent in neat Presentation Case. **Regarding the Stones in Our Jewelry.** Where stones are described as ruby color or amethyst color, etc., they are the finest imitations. Described as doublets, these are also fine imitations made by joining a hard genuine crystal to the front of fine colored glass. The hard crystal front makes it impervious to scratches and wear. Where the gems are genuine they are so described. **Mention ring size wanted. See Ring Measuring Chart on page 745.** Illustrations show actual size.

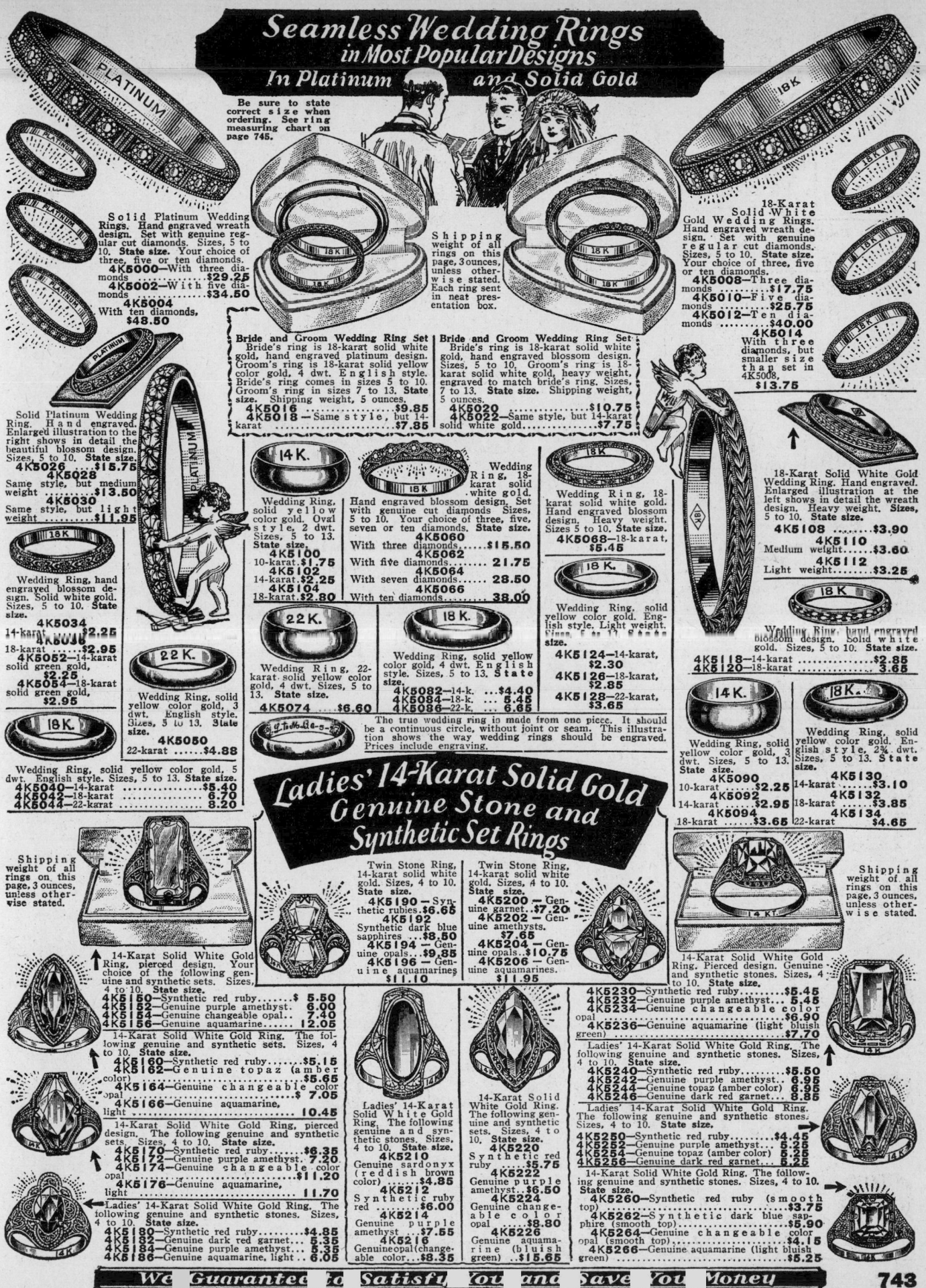

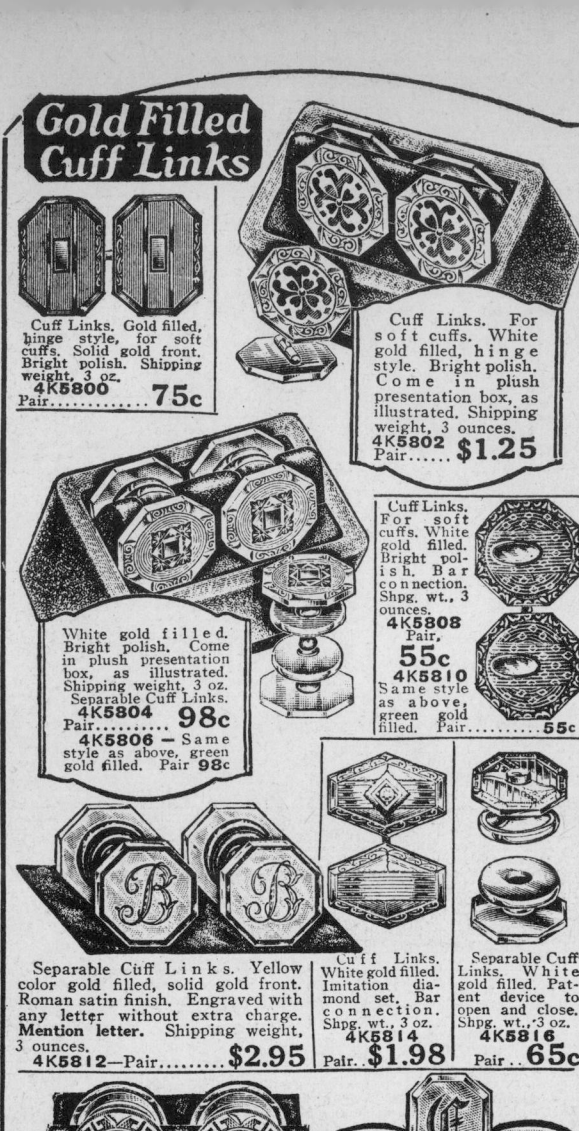

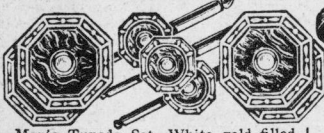

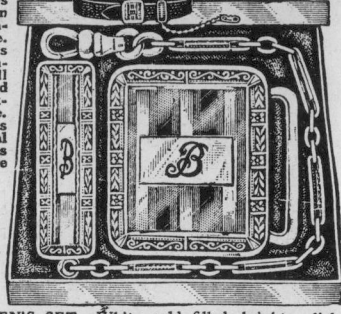
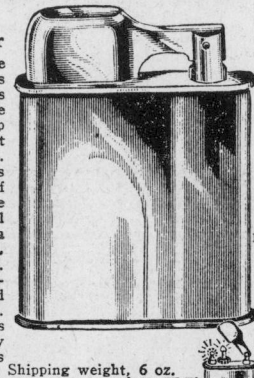
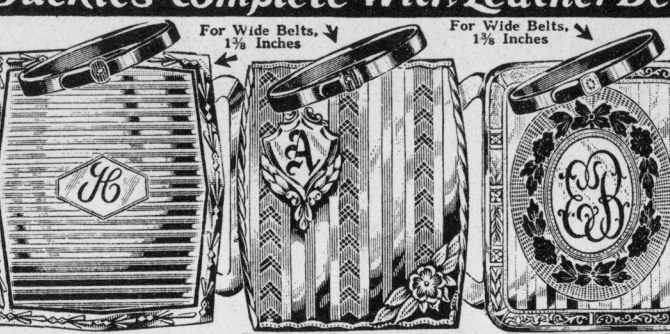

Men's Dress Sets

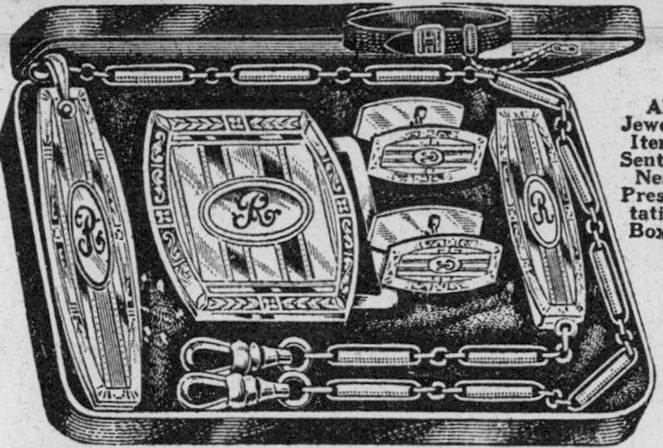

Men's Dress Set. Two-tone combination of white and green gold filled. Consists of knife, about 2½ inches long; Waldemar chain, about 13½ inches long; belt chain (for 1⅜-inch belt), about 8 inches long; pair of hinge style cuff links; buckle, about 1⅜ inches wide, together with **black cowhide fine seal grain leather belt**, sizes, 30 to 44. Engraved with any letter without extra charge. Comes in neat presentation case. **Mention letter to be engraved and size of belt wanted.** Shipping weight, ¾ pound.
4K5900—Complete set, with belt......... **$8.50**

All Jewelry Items Sent in Neat Presentation Boxes

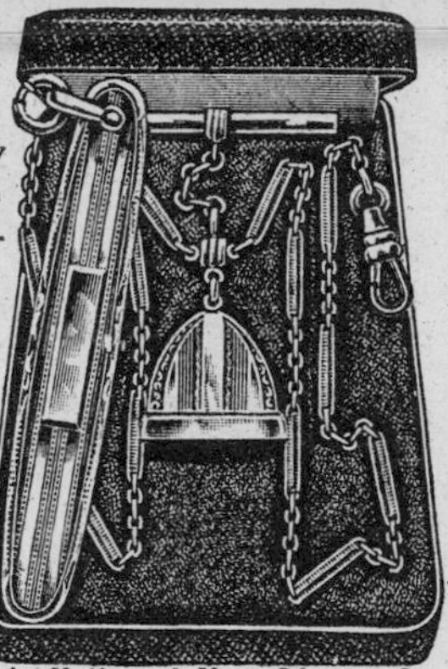

Men's Knife and Vest Chain Set. White gold filled. Bright polish. Knife, about 2¼ inches long, has one blade. Length of chain, about 15 inches, charm attached. Comes in neat presentation box. Shipping weight, 6 oz.
4K5902.............. **$4.95**

Cigarette Cases and Sets

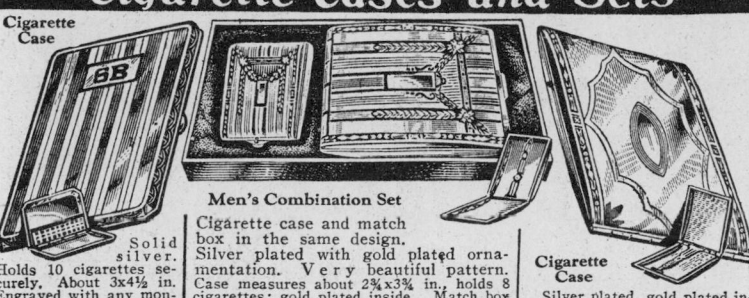

Cigarette Case

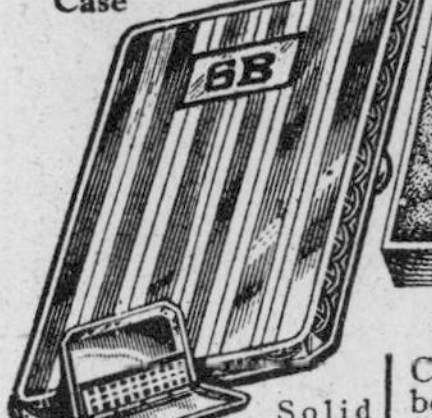

Solid silver. Holds 10 cigarettes securely. About 3x4½ in. Engraved with any monogram. **Mention letters wanted.** Shpg. wt., 8 oz.
4K5904 ......$9.25
4K5906—Silver plated $2.98

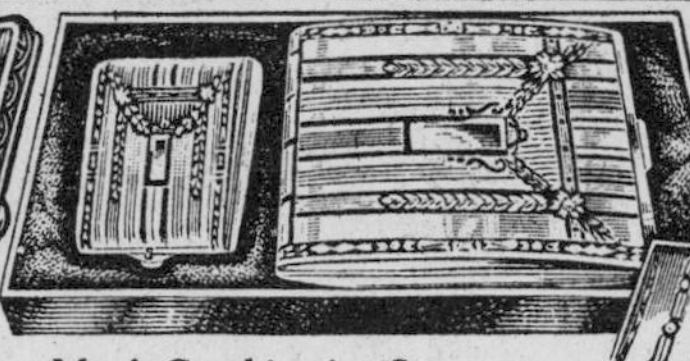

Men's Combination Set

Cigarette case and match box in the same design. Silver plated with gold plated ornamentation. Very beautiful pattern. Case measures about 2¾x3¾ in., holds 8 cigarettes; gold plated inside. Match box measures about 1⅜x2¼ in.; gold plated inside. Comes in neat presentation case. Illustration shows reduced size. Shipping weight, 8 ounces.
4K5908.............. **$4.50**

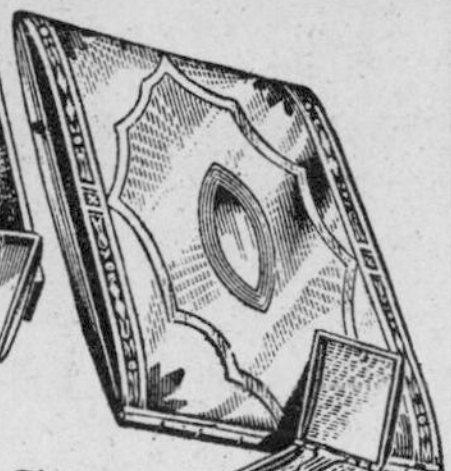

Cigarette Case

Silver plated, gold plated inside. Holds 9 cigarettes. Measures 2¾x3¾ inches. Illustration shows reduced size. Shpg. wt., 8 oz.
4K5910....... **$1.90**

Knives and Knife Sets

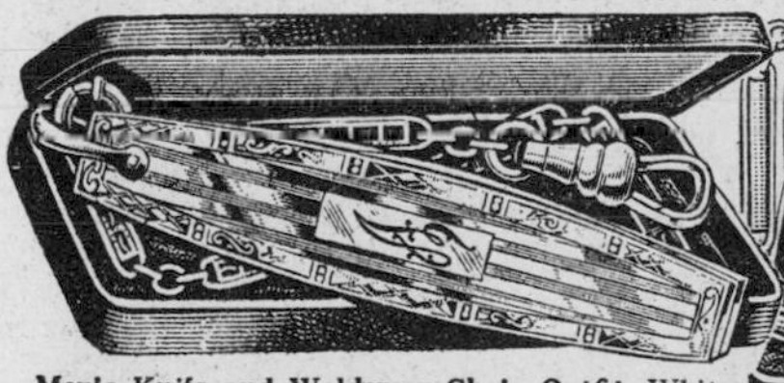

Men's Knife and Waldemar Chain Outfit. White gold filled. Chain, about 13 inches long. Knife, about 2¼ inches long, has two blades. Engraved with any letter without extra charge. **Mention letter wanted.** Comes in neat presentation case. Illustration shows reduced size. Shipping weight, 5 ounces.
4K5914 **$3.45**

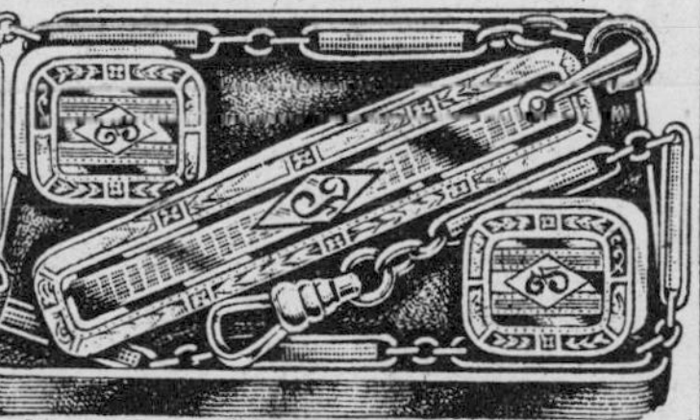

Men's Set. White gold filled. Waldemar chain, about 13¾ in. Knife, about 2¼ in. long, has one blade. Pair of cuff links for soft cuffs, hinge style. Illustration shows reduced size. **Mention letter to be engraved.**
4K5916—Shipping weight, 6 oz.. **$4.65**

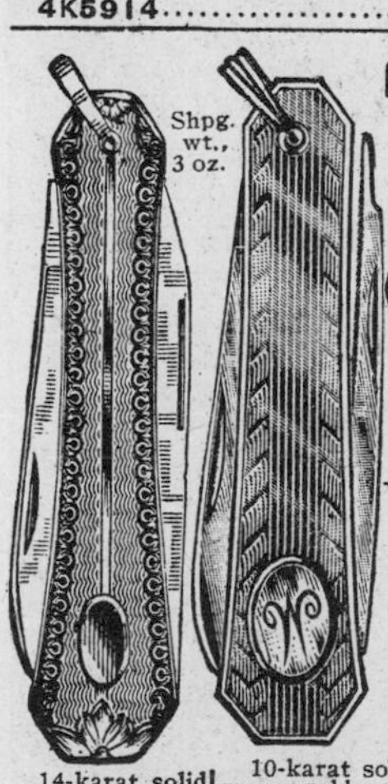

Shpg. wt., 3 oz.

14-karat solid white gold; one blade, one nail file. 4K5918 **$3.35**
4K5920—14-kt. solid green gold, **$3.35**

10-karat solid green gold, one blade and nail file. **State initial.**
4K5922..**$2.50**
10-karat solid white gold.
4K5924..**$2.50**

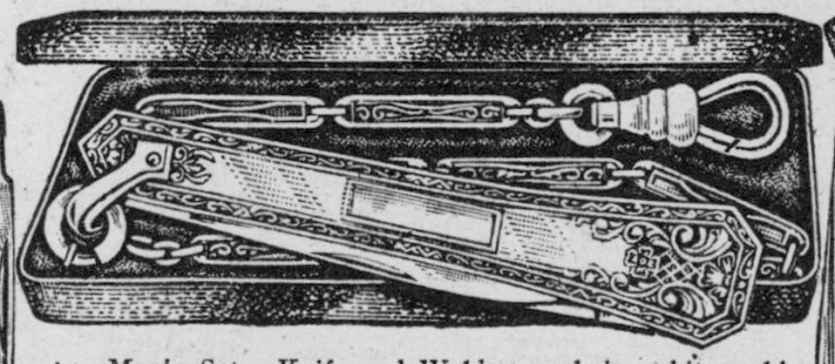

Men's Set. Knife and Waldemar chain, white gold filled. Illustration shows actual size of knife; has two blades. Chain, about 13 inches long. Comes in neat presentation case. Shipping weight, 6 oz.
4K5928 **$3.98**

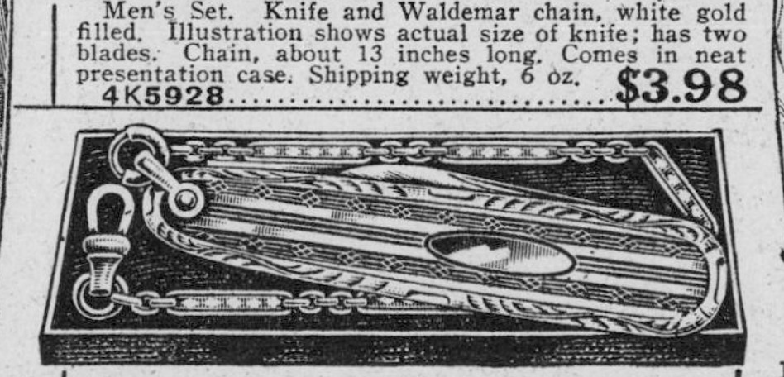

Men's Knife and Chain Set. Two-tone white and green rolled gold plate. Knife, about 2¼ inches long, has two blades. Waldemar chain, about 13 inches long. Illustration shows reduced size. Comes in neat presentation box. Shipping weight, 4 ounces.
4K5930.............................. **$1.75**

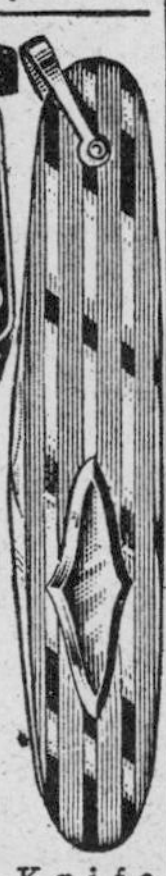

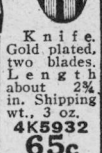

Knife. Gold plated, two blades. Length about 2¾ in. Shipping wt., 3 oz.
4K5932 **65c**

Solid Gold Cuff Links

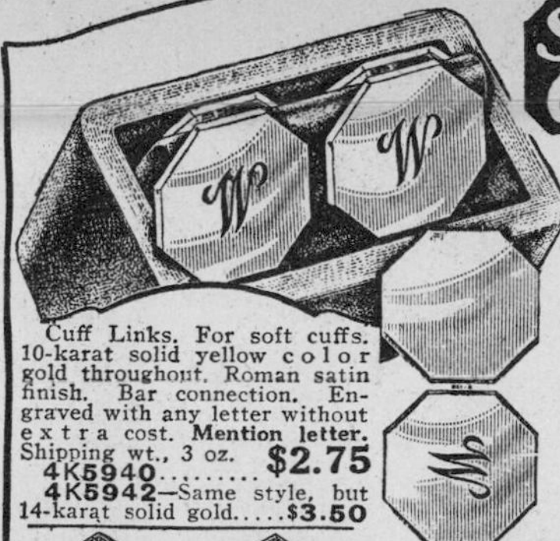

Cuff Links. For soft cuffs. 10-karat solid yellow color gold throughout. Roman satin finish. Bar connection. Engraved with any letter without extra cost. **Mention letter.** Shipping wt., 3 oz.
4K5940.......... **$2.75**
4K5942—Same style, but 14-karat solid gold.....**$3.50**

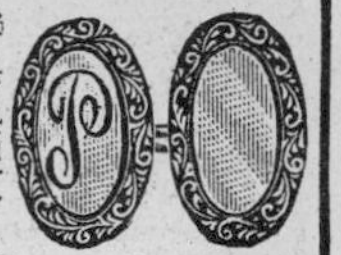

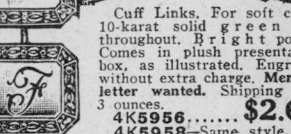

Cuff Links. For soft cuffs. 10-karat solid yellow color gold. Alloyed bar connection. Satin finish. Engraved with any letter without extra charge. **Mention letter wanted.** Shpg. wt., 3 oz.
4K5944..... **$1.40**

Articles showing engraving will be engraved without extra charge. The articles illustrated here are as represented. We cannot accept their return when engraved according to your instructions.

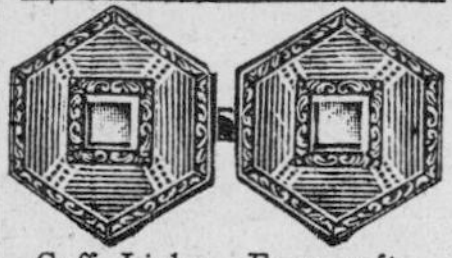

Cuff Links. For soft cuffs. 10-karat solid white gold throughout. Bar connection. Bright polish. Shpg. wt., 3 oz.
4K5948.... **$2.20**
4K5950—Same style, but 14-karat solid white gold **$2.70**

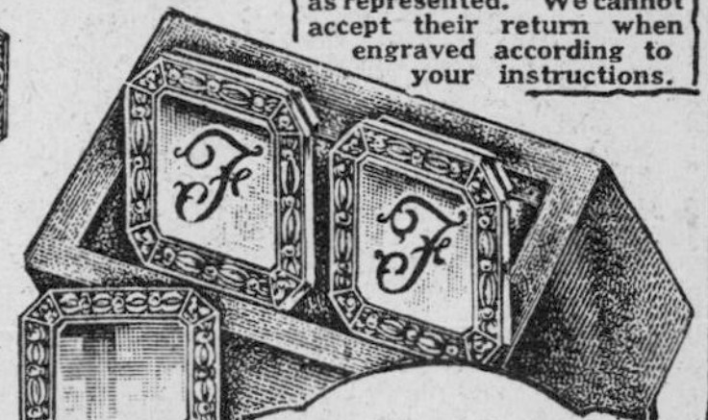

Cuff Links. For soft cuffs. 10-karat solid green gold throughout. Bright polish. Comes in plush presentation box, as illustrated. Engraved without extra charge. **Mention letter wanted.** Shipping wt., 3 ounces.
4K5956...... **$2.65**
4K5958—Same style, but 10-karat solid white gold **$2.65**

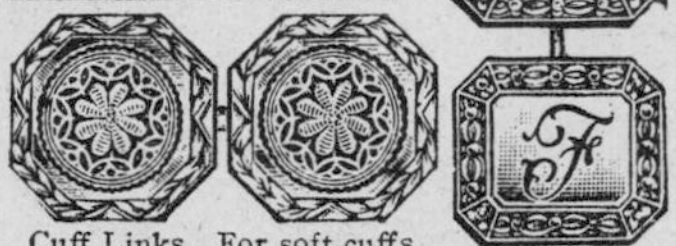

Cuff Links. For soft cuffs. 10-karat solid gold throughout, green gold center white gold border, bar connection. Shpg. wt., 3 oz.
4K5952..... **$3.35**

Illustrations of Cuff Links Show Actual Size.

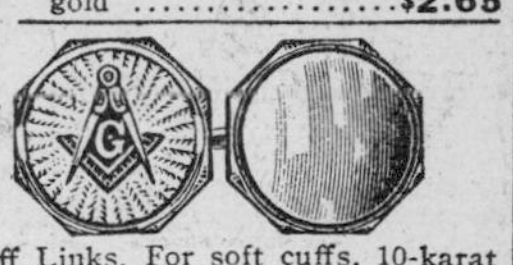

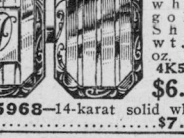

Cuff Links. For soft cuffs. 10-karat solid green gold throughout. Bar connection. Bright polish. Shipping wt., 3 ounces.
4K5962—Masonic emblem **$4.25**
4K5964—Same style, but Odd Fellow's emblem **$4.25**

Cuff Links. For soft cuffs. 10-karat solid yellow color gold. Alloyed bar connection. **Mention letter wanted.** Shipping weight, 3 ounces.
4K5960.......... **$2.75**

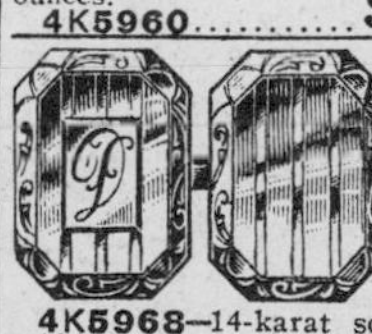

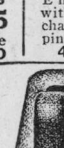

10-kt. solid white gold. Shpg. wt., 3 oz.
4K5966 **$6.25**
4K5968—14-karat solid white gold **$7.50**

Cuff Links. For soft cuffs. 10-karat solid yellow color gold, Roman satin finish. Alloyed bar connections. Engraved without extra charge. **Mention letter wanted.** Shipping weight, 3 ounces.
4K5970 **$1.80**

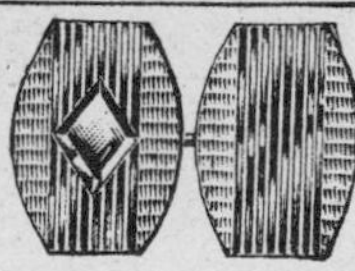

Cuff Links. For soft cuffs, 14-karat solid white gold throughout. Bright polish. Bar connection. Shipping wt., 3 ounces.
4K5974 **$4.40**
4K5976 — Same style, but 10-karat solid white gold **$3.30**

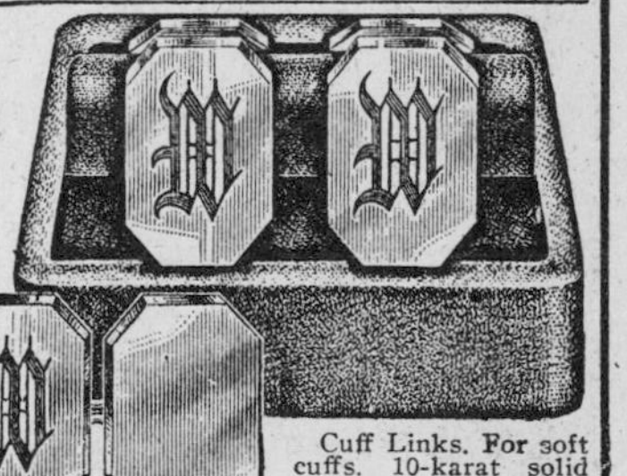

Cuff Links. For soft cuffs. 10-karat solid yellow color gold. Roman satin finish. Bar alloyed connection. In plush presentation box. **Mention letter.**
4K5980—Shpg. wt., 3 oz.... **$2.15**

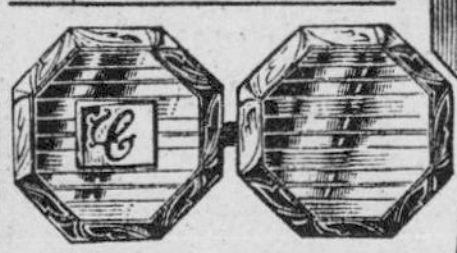

Cuff Links. For soft cuffs. Heavy weight, 10-karat solid white gold throughout. Bright polish. Engraved without extra charge. **Mention letters.** Shipping wt., 3 ounces.
4K5984..... **$5.75**
4K5986—Same style, but 14-karat solid white gold **$7.00**

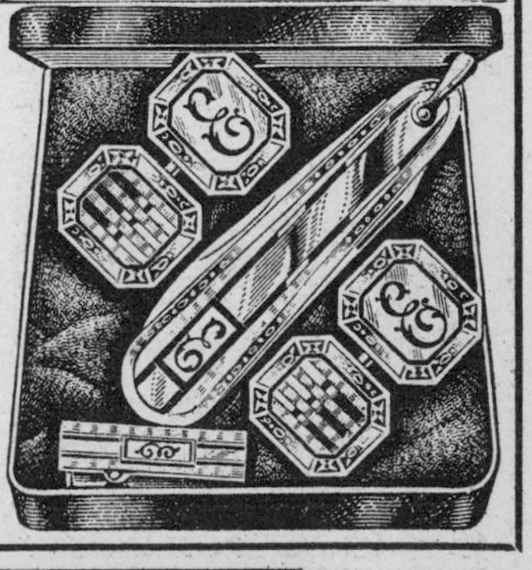

Men's Set. 10-karat solid white gold throughout. Bright polish. Knife, about 2¼ inches long, has one blade and nail file. Pair of gold links for soft cuffs. Bar connection. Tie clasp. Engraved without extra charge. **Mention letter wanted.** Illustration shows slightly reduced size. Shipping weight, 4 ounces.
4K5990....... **$6.95**

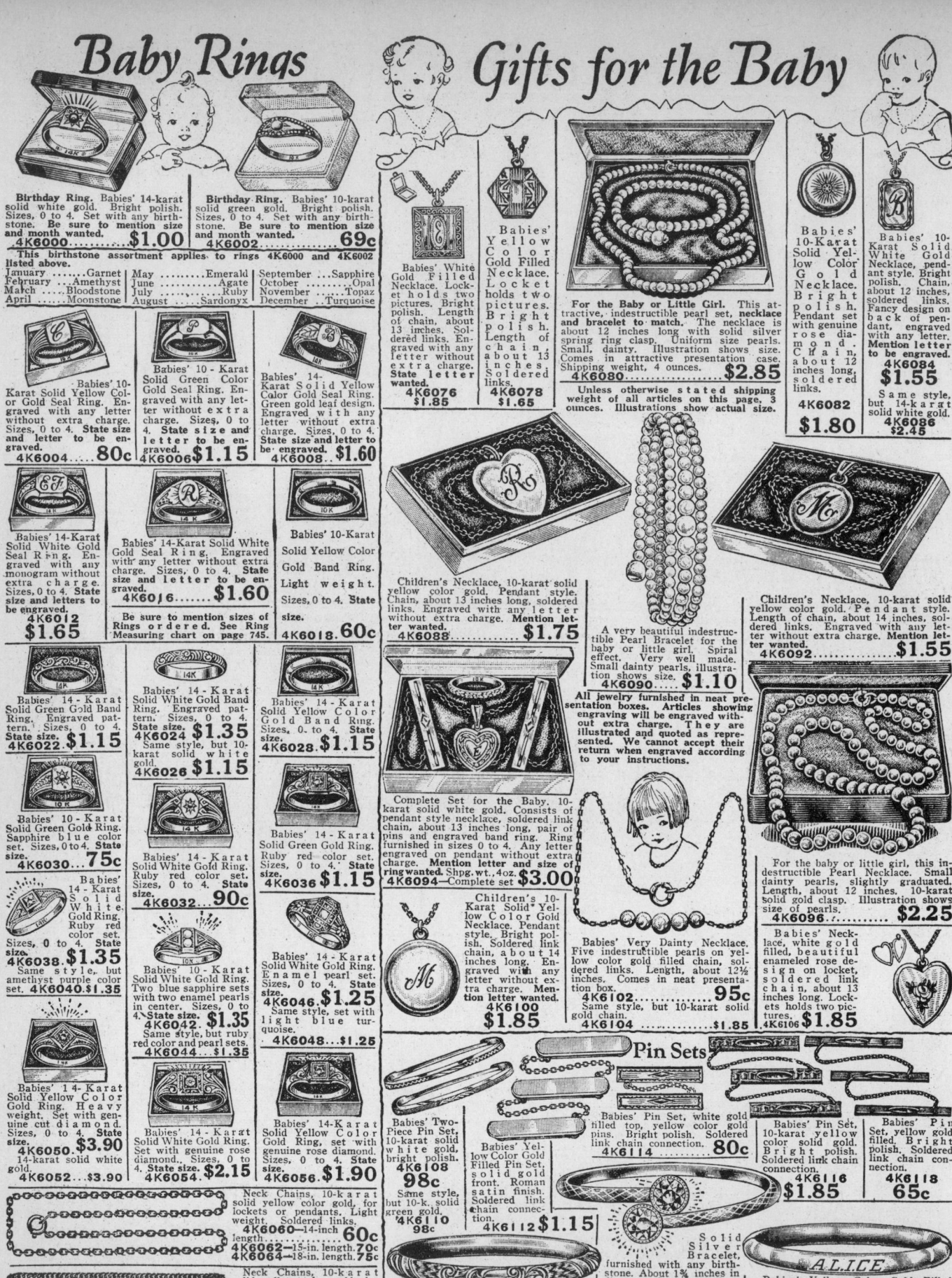

Birthday Ring. Babies' 14-karat solid white gold. Bright polish. Sizes, 0 to 4. Set with any birthstone. Be sure to mention size and month wanted. 4K6000 .... **$1.00**

Birthday Ring. Babies' 10-karat solid green gold. Bright polish. Sizes, 0 to 4. Set with any birthstone. Be sure to mention size and month wanted. 4K6002 .... **69c**

This birthstone assortment applies to rings 4K6000 and 4K6002 listed above.

January ...... Garnet	May ...... Emerald	September ... Sapphire
February ...... Amethyst	June ...... Agate	October ...... Opal
March ..... Bloodstone	July ...... Ruby	November ...... Topaz
April ..... Moonstone	August ...... Sardonyx	December ... Turquoise

Babies' 10-Karat Solid Yellow Color Gold Seal Ring. Engraved with any letter without extra charge. Sizes, 0 to 4. State size and letter to be engraved. 4K6004 ..... **80c**

Babies' 10-Karat Solid Green Color Gold Seal Ring. Engraved with any letter without extra charge. Sizes, 0 to 4. State size and letter to be engraved. 4K6006 .... **$1.15**

Babies' 14-Karat Solid Yellow Color Gold Seal Ring. Green gold leaf design. Engraved with any letter without extra charge. Sizes, 0 to 4. State size and letter to be engraved. 4K6008 .. **$1.60**

Babies' 14-Karat Solid White Gold Seal Ring. Engraved with any monogram without extra charge. Sizes, 0 to 4. State size and letters to be engraved. 4K6012 **$1.65**

Babies' 14-Karat Solid White Gold Seal Ring, Engraved with any letter without extra charge. Sizes, 0 to 4. State size and letter to be engraved. 4K6016 .. **$1.60**

Babies' 10-Karat Solid Yellow Color Gold Band Ring. Light weight. Sizes, 0 to 4. State size. 4K6018. **60c**

Be sure to mention sizes of Rings ordered. See Ring Measuring chart on page 745.

Babies' 14-Karat Solid Green Gold Band Ring. Engraved pattern. Sizes, 0 to 4. State size. 4K6022 **$1.15**

Babies' 14-Karat Solid White Gold Band Ring. Engraved pattern. Sizes, 0 to 4. State size. 4K6024 **$1.35**
Same style, but 10-karat solid white gold. 4K6026 **$1.15**

Babies' 14-Karat Solid Yellow Color Gold Band Ring. Sizes, 0 to 4. State size. 4K6028 **$1.15**

Babies' 10-Karat Solid Green Gold Ring. Sapphire blue color set. Sizes, 0 to 4. State size. 4K6030 ... **75c**

Babies' 14-Karat Solid White Gold Ring. Ruby red color set. Sizes, 0 to 4. State size. 4K6032 .... **90c**

Babies' 14-Karat Solid Green Gold Ring. Ruby red color set. Sizes, 0 to 4. State size. 4K6036 **$1.15**

Babies' 14-Karat Solid White Gold Ring. Ruby red color set. Sizes, 0 to 4. State size. 4K6038 **$1.35**
Same style, but amethyst purple color set. 4K6040 **$1.35**

Babies' 10-Karat Solid White Gold Ring. Two blue sapphire sets with two enamel pearls in center. Sizes, 0 to 4. State size. 4K6042 **$1.35**
Same style, but ruby red color and pearl sets. 4K6044 **$1.35**

Babies' 14-Karat Solid White Gold Ring. Enamel pearl set. Sizes, 0 to 4. State size. 4K6046 **$1.25**
Same style, set with light blue turquoise. 4K6048 **$1.25**

Babies' 14-Karat Solid Yellow Color Gold Ring. Heavy weight. Set with genuine cut diamond. Sizes, 0 to 4. State size. 4K6050 **$3.90**
14-karat solid white gold. 4K6052 **$3.90**

Babies' 14-Karat Solid White Gold Ring. Set with genuine rose diamond. Sizes, 0 to 4. State size. 4K6054 **$2.15**

Babies' 14-Karat Solid Yellow Color Gold Ring, set with genuine rose diamond. Sizes, 0 to 4. State size. 4K6056 **$1.90**

Neck Chains, 10-karat solid yellow color gold, for lockets or pendants. Light weight. Soldered links.
4K6060—14-inch length. **60c**
4K6062—15-in. length. **70c**
4K6064—18-in. length. **75c**

Neck Chains, 10-karat solid yellow color gold, for lockets or pendants. Heavy weight. Soldered links.
4K6066—14-in. length. **$1.20**
4K6068—18-in. lth. **$1.50**
4K6070—22-in. lth. **$1.85**

Babies' White Gold Filled Necklace. Locket holds two pictures. Bright polish. Length of chain, about 13 inches. Soldered links. Engraved with any letter without extra charge. State letter wanted. 4K6076 **$1.85**

Babies' Yellow Color Gold Filled Necklace. Locket holds two pictures. Bright polish. Length of chain, about 13 inches. Soldered links. 4K6078 **$1.65**

For the Baby or Little Girl. This attractive, indestructible pearl set, **necklace and bracelet to match.** The necklace is about 12 inches long with solid silver spring ring clasp. Uniform size pearls. Small, dainty. Illustration shows size. Comes in attractive presentation case. Shipping weight, 4 ounces. 4K6080 .... **$2.85**

Unless otherwise stated shipping weight of all articles on this page, 3 ounces. Illustrations show actual size.

Babies' 10-Karat Solid Yellow Color Gold Necklace. Bright polish. Pendant set with genuine rose diamond. Chain, about 12 inches long, soldered links. 4K6082 **$1.80**

Babies' 10-Karat Solid White Gold Necklace, pendant style. Bright polish. Chain, about 12 inches, soldered links. Fancy design on back of pendant, engraved with any letter. Mention letter to be engraved. 4K6084 **$1.55**
Same style, but 14-karat solid white gold. 4K6086 **$2.45**

Children's Necklace, 10-karat solid yellow color gold. Pendant style. Chain, about 13 inches long, soldered links. Engraved with any letter without extra charge. Mention letter wanted. 4K6088 .... **$1.75**

A very beautiful indestructible Pearl Bracelet for the baby or little girl. Spiral effect. Very well made. Small dainty pearls, illustration shows size. 4K6090 ..... **$1.10**

All jewelry furnished in neat presentation boxes. Articles showing engraving will be engraved without extra charge. They are illustrated and quoted as represented. We cannot accept their return when engraved according to your instructions.

Children's Necklace, 10-karat solid yellow color gold. Pendant style. Length of chain, about 14 inches, soldered links. Engraved with any letter without extra charge. Mention letter wanted. 4K6092 **$1.55**

Complete Set for the Baby. 10-karat solid white gold. Consists of pendant style necklace, soldered link chain, about 13 inches long, pair of pins and engraved band ring. Ring furnished in sizes 0 to 4. Any letter engraved without extra charge. **Mention letter and size of ring wanted.** Shpg. wt., 4 oz. 4K6094—Complete set **$3.00**

Children's 10-Karat Solid Yellow Color Gold Necklace. Pendant style. Bright polish. Soldered link chain, about 14 inches long. Engraved with any letter without extra charge. Mention letter wanted. 4K6100 **$1.85**

Babies' Very Dainty Necklace. Five indestructible pearls on yellow color gold filled chain, soldered links. Length, about 12½ inches. Comes in neat presentation box. 4K6102 **95c**
Same style, but 10-karat solid gold chain. 4K6104 **$1.85**

For the baby or little girl, this indestructible Pearl Necklace. Small dainty pearls, slightly graduated. Length, about 12 inches. 10-karat solid gold clasp. Illustration shows size of pearls. 4K6096 **$2.25**

Babies' Necklace, white gold filled, beautiful enameled rose design on locket, soldered link chain, about 13 inches long. Lockets holds two pictures. 4K6106 **$1.85**

Pin Sets

Babies' Two-Piece Pin Set, 10-karat solid white gold, bright polish. 4K6108 **98c**
Same style, but 10-k. solid green gold. 4K6110 **98c**

Babies' Yellow Color Gold Filled Pin Set, solid gold front. Roman satin finish. Soldered link chain connection. 4K6112 **$1.15**

Babies' Pin Set, white gold filled top, yellow color gold pins. Bright polish. Soldered link chain connection. 4K6114 **80c**

Babies' Pin Set, 10-karat yellow color solid gold. Bright polish. Soldered link chain connection. 4K6116 **$1.85**

Babies' Pin Set, yellow gold filled. Bright polish. Soldered link chain connection. 4K6118 **65c**

Babies' Bracelet, yellow color gold filled. Bright polish. Fancy engraved design. Measures about 1½ inches in diameter. 4K6120 .... **$1.60**

Solid Silver Bracelet, furnished with any birthstone. About 1⅜ inches in diameter. Spiral effect, slips on and off easily. Will fit little girls up to five years of age. Be sure to mention month wanted. 4K6122 **$1.85**

Babies' Yellow Color Gold Filled Bracelet. Bright polish. Measures about 1½ inches in diameter. Engraved with any name without extra charge. Mention name wanted. 4K6124 **$1.50**

For the Woman of Taste

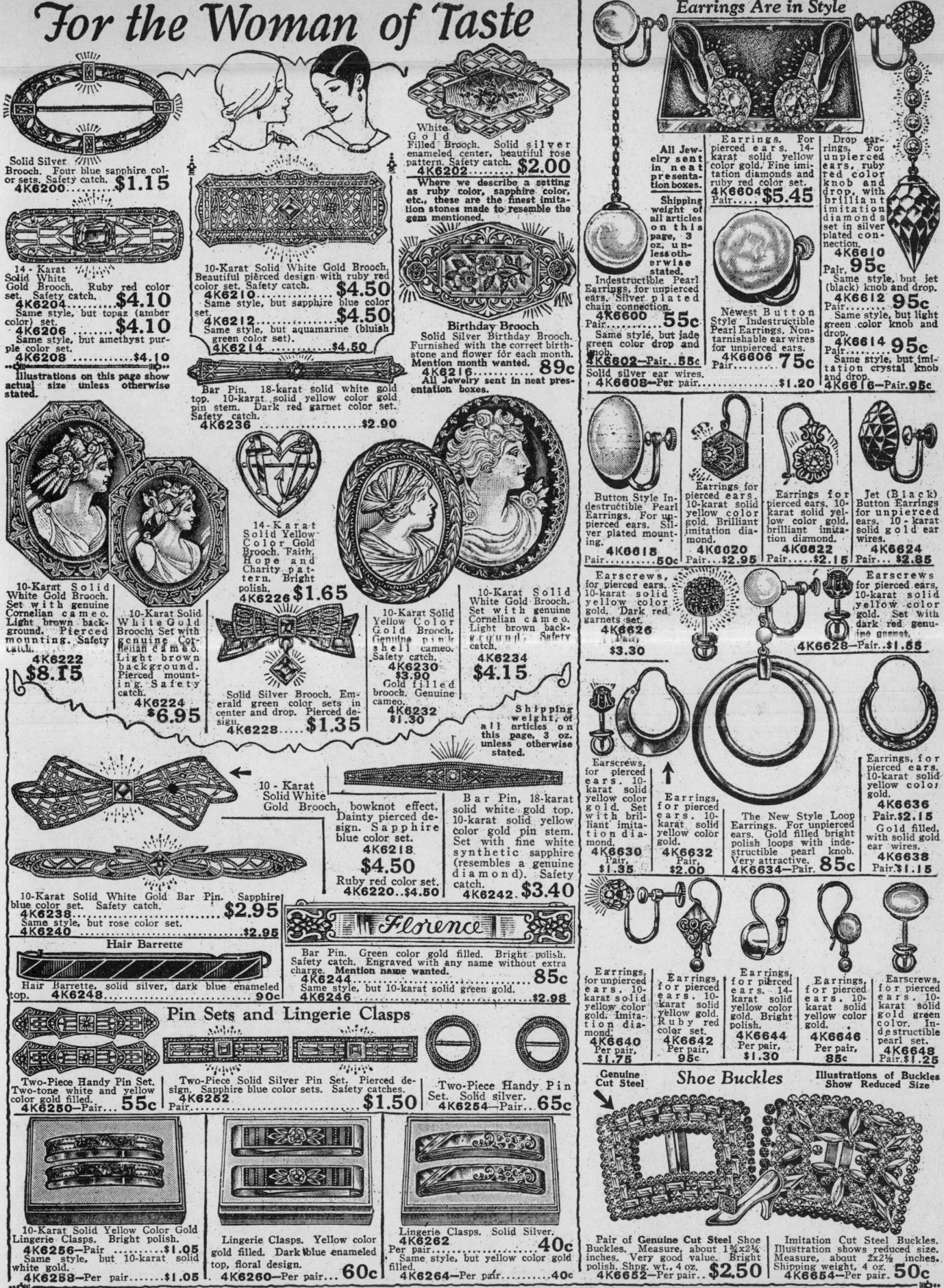

Solid Silver Brooch. Four blue sapphire color sets. Safety catch.
4K6200...... **$1.15**

14-Karat Solid White Gold Brooch. Ruby red color set. Safety catch.
4K6204............ **$4.10**
Same style, but topaz (amber color) set.
4K6206............ **$4.10**
Same style, but amethyst purple color set.
4K6208............ **$4.10**
Illustrations on this page show actual size unless otherwise stated.

10-Karat Solid White Gold Brooch. Beautiful pierced design with ruby red color set. Safety catch.
4K6210............ **$4.50**
Same style, but sapphire blue color set.
4K6212............ **$4.50**
Same style, but aquamarine (bluish green color set).
4K6214............ **$4.50**

Bar Pin. 18-karat solid white gold top. 14-karat solid yellow color gold pin stem. Dark red garnet color set. Safety catch.
4K6236............ **$2.90**

White Gold Filled Brooch. Solid silver enameled center, beautiful rose pattern. Safety catch.
4K6202............ **$2.00**
Where we describe a setting as ruby color, sapphire color, etc., these are the finest imitation stones made to resemble the gem mentioned.

Birthday Brooch
Solid Silver Birthday Brooch. Furnished with the correct birthstone and flower for each month. Mention month wanted. **89c**
4K6216............
All Jewelry sent in neat presentation boxes.

10-Karat Solid White Gold Brooch. Set with genuine Cornelian cameo. Light brown background. Pierced mounting. Safety catch.
4K6222 **$8.15**

10-Karat Solid White Gold Brooch Set with genuine Cornelian cameo. Light brown background. Pierced mounting. Safety catch.
4K6224 **$6.95**

14-Karat Solid Yellow Color Gold Brooch. Faith, Hope and Charity pattern. Bright polish.
4K6226 **$1.65**

Solid Silver Brooch. Emerald green color sets in center and drop. Pierced design.
4K6228..... **$1.35**

10-Karat Solid Yellow Color Gold Brooch. Genuine pink shell cameo. Safety catch.
4K6230 **$3.90**
Gold filled brooch. Genuine cameo.
4K6232 **$1.30**

10-Karat Solid White Gold Brooch. Set with genuine Cornelian cameo. Light brown background. Safety catch.
4K6234 **$4.15**

Shipping weight of all articles on this page, 3 oz. unless otherwise stated.

10-Karat Solid White Gold Bar Pin. Sapphire blue color set. Safety catch.
4K6238............ **$2.95**
Same style, but rose color set.
4K6240............ **$2.95**

Hair Barrette
Hair Barrette, solid silver, dark blue enameled top.
4K6248............ **90c**

10-Karat Solid White Gold Brooch, bowknot effect. Dainty pierced design. Sapphire blue color set.
4K6218 **$4.50**
Ruby red color set.
4K6220..**$4.50**

Bar Pin, 18-karat solid white gold top. 10-karat solid yellow color gold pin stem. Set with fine white synthetic sapphire (resembles a genuine diamond). Safety catch.
4K6242. **$3.40**

Florence
Bar Pin. Green color gold filled. Bright polish. Safety catch. Engraved with any name without extra charge. Mention name wanted.
4K6244............ **85c**
Same style, but 10-karat solid green gold.
4K6246............ **$2.98**

Pin Sets and Lingerie Clasps

Two-Piece Handy Pin Set. Two-tone white and yellow color gold filled.
4K6250—Pair.. **55c**

Two-Piece Solid Silver Pin Set. Pierced design. Sapphire blue color sets. Safety catches.
4K6252 Pair.... **$1.50**

Two-Piece Handy Pin Set. Solid silver.
4K6254—Pair.. **65c**

10-Karat Solid Yellow Color Gold Lingerie Clasps. Bright polish.
4K6256—Pair **$1.05**
Same style, but 10-karat solid white gold.
4K6258—Per pair.......**$1.05**

Lingerie Clasps. Yellow color gold filled. Dark blue enameled top, floral design.
4K6260—Per pair... **60c**

Lingerie Clasps. Solid Silver. Per pair............**40c**
4K6262
Same style, but yellow color gold filled.
4K6264—Per pair.... **40c**

Earrings Are in Style

All jewelry sent in neat presentation boxes.
Shipping weight of all articles on this page, 2 oz., unless otherwise stated.

Indestructible Pearl Earrings, for unpierced ears. Silver plated chain connection.
4K6600 Pair.... **55c**
Same style, but green color drop and knob.
4K6602—Pair.. **55c**
Solid silver ear wires.
4K6608—Per pair.............. **$1.20**

Earrings. For pierced ears. 14-karat solid yellow color gold. Fine imitation diamonds and ruby red color set.
4K6604 Pair..... **$5.45**

Newest Button Style Indestructible Pearl Earrings. Non-tarnishable ear wires for unpierced ears.
4K6606 Pair..... **75c**

Drop earrings. For unpierced ears, ruby red color knob and drop, with brilliant imitation diamonds set in silver plated connection.
4K6610 Pair.... **95c**
Same style, but jet (black) knob and drop.
4K6612 Pair.... **95c**
Same style, but light green color knob and drop.
4K6614 Pair.... **95c**
Same style, but imitation crystal knob and drop.
4K6616—Pair.**95c**

Button Style Indestructible Pearl Earrings. For unpierced ears. Silver plated mounting.
4K6618 Pair....**50c**

Earrings for pierced ears. 10-karat solid yellow color gold. Brilliant imitation diamond.
4K6620 Pair....**$2.95**

Earrings for pierced ears. 10-karat solid yellow color gold, brilliant imitation diamond.
4K6622 Pair....**$2.15**

Jet (Black) Button Earrings for unpierced ears. 10-karat solid gold ear wires.
4K6624 Pair....**$2.85**

Earscrews, for pierced ears. 10-karat solid yellow color gold. Dark red garnets set.
4K6626 Pair... **$3.30**

Earscrews for pierced ears. 10-karat solid yellow color gold. Set with dark red genuine garnet.
4K6628—Pair. **$1.55**

Earrings, for pierced ears. 10-karat solid yellow color gold. Set with brilliant imitation diamond.
4K6630 Pair.. **$1.35**

Earrings, for pierced ears. 10-karat solid yellow color gold.
4K6632 Pair.. **$2.00**

The New Style Loop Earrings. For unpierced ears. Gold filled bright polish loops with indestructible pearl knob. Very attractive.
4K6634—Pair.. **85c**

Earrings, for pierced ears. 10-karat solid yellow color gold.
4K6636 Pair.**$2.15**
Gold filled, with solid gold ear wires.
4K6638 Pair.**$1.15**

Earrings, for unpierced ears. 10-karat solid yellow color gold. Imitation diamond.
4K6640 Per pair. **$1.75**

Earrings, for unpierced ears. 10-karat solid yellow color gold. Ruby red color set.
4K6642 Per pair, **95c**

Earrings, for pierced ears. 14-karat solid yellow color gold. Bright polish.
4K6644 Per pair, **$1.30**

Earrings, for pierced ears. 10-karat solid yellow color gold.
4K6646 Per pair, **85c**

Earscrews, for pierced ears. 10-karat solid gold green color. Indestructible pearl set.
4K6648 Pair.**$1.25**

Shoe Buckles

Genuine Cut Steel

Illustrations of Buckles Show Reduced Size.

Pair of **Genuine Cut Steel** Shoe Buckles. Measure, about 1¾x2¼ inches. Very good value. Bright polish. Shpg. wt., 4 oz.
4K6652—Per pair.. **$2.50**

Imitation Cut Steel Buckles. Illustration shows reduced size. Measure, about 2x2½ inches. Shipping weight, 4 oz.
4K6654—Per pair.. **50c**

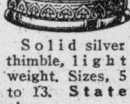

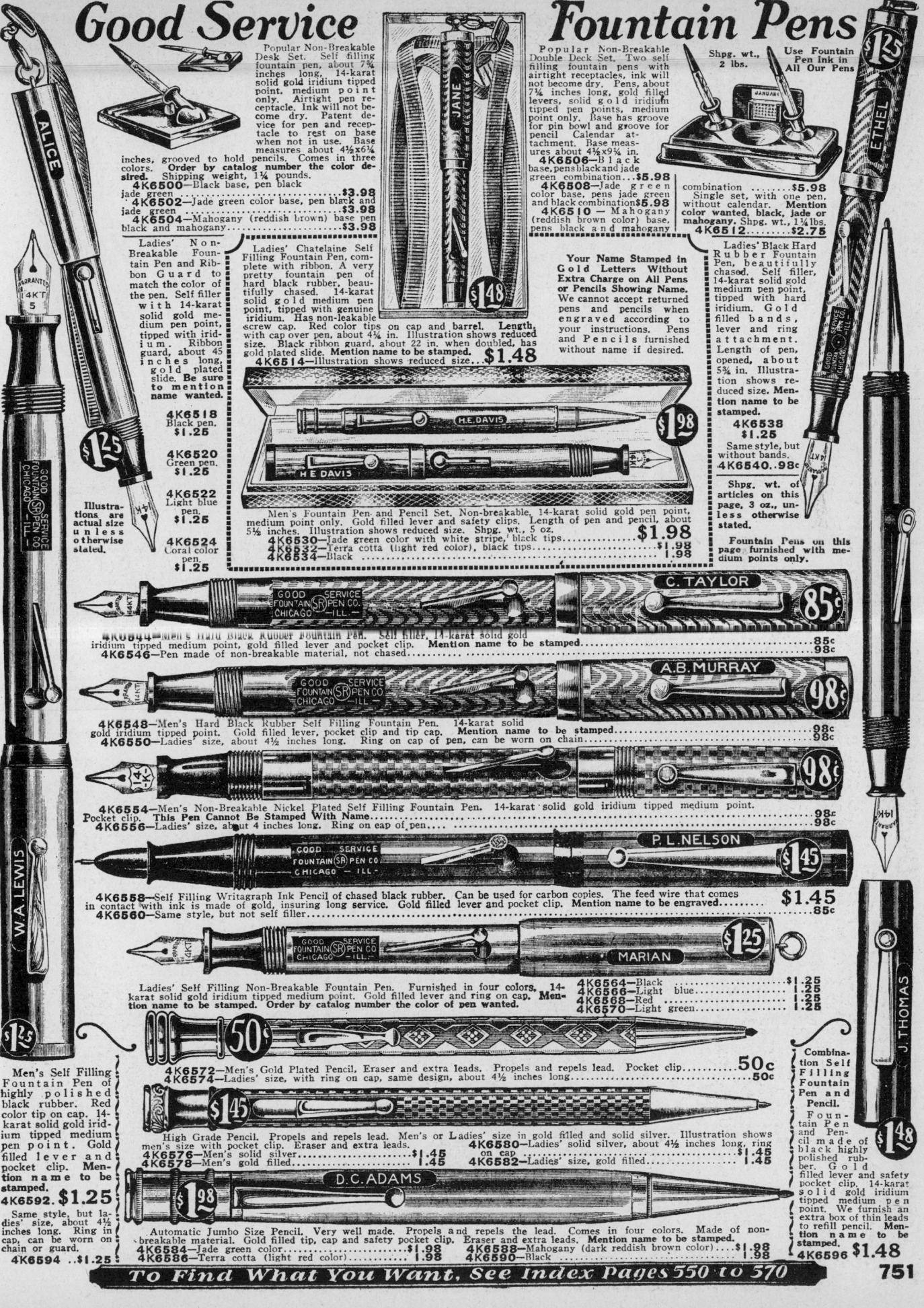

Good Service Fountain Pens

Popular Non-Breakable Desk Set. Self filling fountain pen, about 7¾ inches long, 14-karat solid gold iridium tipped point, medium point only. Airtight pen receptacle. Ink will not become dry. Patent device for pen and receptacle to rest on base when not in use. Base measures about 4½x6¾ inches, grooved to hold pencils. Comes in three colors. **Order by catalog number the color desired.** Shipping weight, 1¼ pounds.
4K6500—Black base, pen black jade green..................$3.98
4K6502—Jade green color base, pen black and jade green..................$3.98
4K6504—Mahogany (reddish brown) base pen black and mahogany..................$3.98

Popular Non-Breakable Double Deck Set. Two self filling fountain pens with airtight receptacles, ink will not become dry. Pens, about 7¼ inches long, gold filled levers, solid gold iridium tipped pen points, medium point only. Base has groove for pin bowl and groove for pencil Calendar attachment. Base measures about 4½x9¾ in.
4K6506—Black base, pens black and jade green combination..................$5.98
4K6508—Jade green color base, pens jade green and black combination $5.98
4K6510—Mahogany (reddish brown color) base, pens black and mahogany combination..................$5.98
Single set, with one pen without calendar. **Mention color wanted, black, jade or mahogany.** Shpg. wt., 1¼ lbs.
4K6512..................$2.75

Shpg. wt., 2 lbs. Use Fountain Pen Ink in All Our Pens

Ladies' Non-Breakable Fountain Pen and Ribbon Guard to match the color of the pen. Self filler with 14-karat solid gold medium pen point, tipped with iridium. Ribbon guard, about 45 inches long, gold plated slide. **Be sure to mention name wanted.**
WARRANTED 14KT 5
4K6518 Black pen. $1.25
4K6520 Green pen. $1.25
4K6522 Light blue pen. $1.25
4K6524 Coral color pen. $1.25

$1.25 Illustrations are actual size unless otherwise stated.

Ladies' Chatelaine Self Filling Fountain Pen, complete with ribbon. A very pretty fountain pen of hard black rubber, beautifully chased. 14-karat solid gold medium pen point, tipped with genuine iridium. Has non-leakable screw cap. Red color tips on cap and barrel. **Length,** with cap over pen, about 4¼ in. Illustration shows reduced size. Black ribbon guard, about 22 in. when doubled, has gold plated slide. **Mention name to be stamped.** $1.48
4K6514—Illustration shows reduced size. $1.48

Your Name Stamped in Gold Letters Without Extra Charge on All Pens or Pencils Showing Name. We cannot accept returned pens and pencils when engraved according to your instructions. Pens and Pencils furnished without name if desired.

Ladies' Black Hard Rubber Fountain Pen, beautifully chased. Self filler, 14-karat solid gold medium pen point, tipped with hard iridium. Gold filled bands, lever and ring attachment. Length of pen, opened, about 5¾ in. Illustration shows reduced size. **Mention name to be stamped.**
4K6538 $1.25
Same style, but without bands.
4K6540..98c

Shpg. wt. of articles on this page, 3 oz., unless otherwise stated.

Fountain Pens on this page furnished with medium points only.

H.E. DAVIS — H E DAVIS — $1.98

Men's Fountain Pen and Pencil Set. Non-breakable. 14-karat solid gold pen point, medium point only. Gold filled lever and safety clips. Length of pen and pencil, about 5½ inches. Illustration shows reduced size. Shpg. wt., 5 oz. $1.98
4K6530—Jade green color with white stripe, black tips..................$1.98
4K6532—Terra cotta (light red color), black tips..................1.98
4K6534—Black..................1.98

GOOD SERVICE FOUNTAIN PEN CO. CHICAGO—ILL. — C. TAYLOR — 85c
4K6544—Men's Hard Black Rubber Fountain Pen. Self filler, 14-karat solid gold iridium tipped medium point, gold filled lever and pocket clip. **Mention name to be stamped**..................85c
4K6546—Pen made of non-breakable material, not chased..................98c

GOOD SERVICE FOUNTAIN PEN CO CHICAGO—ILL — A.B. MURRAY — 98c
4K6548—Men's Hard Black Rubber Self Filling Fountain Pen. 14-karat solid gold iridium tipped point. Gold filled lever, pocket clip and tip cap. **Mention name to be stamped**..................98c
4K6550—Ladies' size, about 4½ inches long. Ring on cap of pen, can be worn on chain..................98c

98c
4K6554—Men's Non-Breakable Nickel Plated Self Filling Fountain Pen. 14-karat solid gold iridium tipped medium point. Pocket clip. **This Pen Cannot Be Stamped With Name.**..................98c
4K6556—Ladies' size, about 4 inches long. Ring on cap of pen..................98c

GOOD SERVICE FOUNTAIN PEN CO CHICAGO—ILL — P.L. NELSON — $1.45
4K6558—Self Filling Writagraph Ink Pencil of chased black rubber. Can be used for carbon copies. The feed wire that comes in contact with ink is made of gold, insuring long service. Gold filled lever and pocket clip. **Mention name to be engraved.**..................$1.45
4K6560—Same style, but not self filler..................85c

GOOD SERVICE FOUNTAIN PEN CO CHICAGO—ILL. — MARIAN — $1.25
Ladies' Self Filling Non-Breakable Fountain Pen. Furnished in four colors. 14-karat solid gold iridium tipped medium point. Gold filled lever and ring on cap. **Mention name to be stamped.** Order by catalog number the color of pen wanted.
4K6564—Black..................$1.25
4K6566—Light blue..................1.25
4K6568—Red..................1.25
4K6570—Light green..................1.25

50c
4K6572—Men's Gold Plated Pencil. Eraser and extra leads. Propels and repels lead. Pocket clip..................50c
4K6574—Ladies' size, with ring on cap, same design, about 4½ inches long..................50c

$1.45
High Grade Pencil. Propels and repels lead. Men's or Ladies' size in gold filled and solid silver. Illustration shows men's size with pocket clip. Eraser and extra leads.
4K6576—Men's solid silver..................$1.45
4K6578—Men's gold filled..................1.45
4K6580—Ladies' solid silver, about 4½ inches long, ring on cap..................1.45
4K6582—Ladies' size, gold filled..................1.45

D.C. ADAMS — $1.98
Automatic Jumbo Size Pencil. Very well made. Propels and repels the lead. Comes in four colors. Made of non-breakable material. Gold filled tip, cap and safety pocket clip. Eraser and extra leads. **Mention name to be stamped.**
4K6584—Jade green color..................$1.98
4K6586—Terra cotta (light red color)..................1.98
4K6588—Mahogany (dark reddish brown color)..................$1.98
4K6590—Black..................1.98

ALICE

W.A. LEWIS — $1.25
Men's Self Filling Fountain Pen of highly polished black rubber. Red color tip on cap. 14-karat solid gold iridium tipped medium pen point. Gold filled lever and pocket clip. **Mention name to be stamped.** $1.25
4K6592. $1.25
Same style, but ladies' size, about 4½ inches long. Ring in cap, can be worn on chain or guard.
4K6594..$1.25

ETHEL — $1.25

J. THOMAS — $1.48

Combination Self Filling Fountain Pen and Pencil. Fountain Pen and Pencil made of black highly polished rubber. Gold filled lever and safety pocket clip. 14-karat solid gold iridium tipped medium pen point. We furnish an extra box of thin leads to refill pencil. **Mention name to be stamped.**
4K6596 $1.48

To Find What You Want, See Index Pages 550 to 570

Guaranteed for 25 Years

ROGERS Silverware

Guaranteed for 25 Years

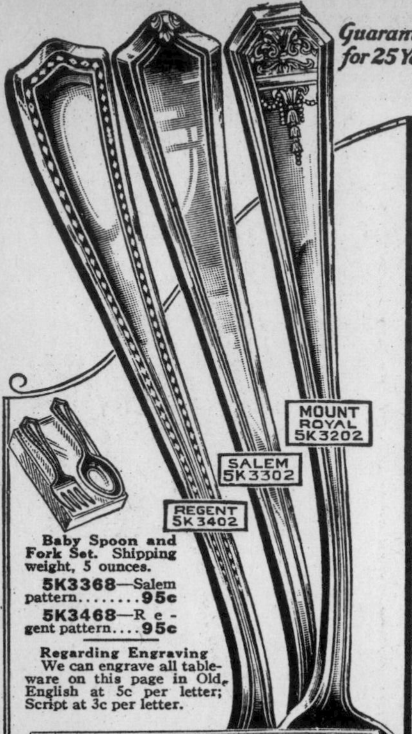

Baby Spoon and Fork Set. Shipping weight, 5 ounces.
5K3368—Salem pattern........**95c**
5K3468—Regent pattern....**95c**

Regarding Engraving
We can engrave all tableware on this page in Old English at 5c per letter; Script at 3c per letter.

Teaspoons, Tablespoons and Forks have extra plating on parts that receive the most wear.	Regent Pattern, Bright Finish	Salem Pattern, Gray Finish	Mount Royal, Dull Finish	Shpg. Wt.	
Teaspoons. Set of six....	5K3402	5K3302	5K3202	8 oz.	$1.15
Tablespoons. Set of six..	5K3414	5K3314	5K3214	1 lb.	2.30
Forks, medium. Set of six.	5K3418	5K3318	5K3218	1 lb.	2.30
Knives. Solid handle. Set of six..............	5K3419	5K3319	5K3219	1¾ lbs.	2.60
Knives. Hollow handle. Set of six..............	5K3421	5K3321	5K3221	1½ lbs.	6.65
Knives. Hollow handle. Stainless steel. ½ doz.	5K3422	5K3322	5K3222	1¾ lbs.	7.20
Knives. Solid handle. Stainless steel. ½ doz.	5K3423	5K3323	5K3223	1¾ lbs.	4.50
Sugar Shell. Each.......	5K3424	5K3324	5K3224	4 oz.	.43
Butter Knife. Each......	5K3426	5K3326	5K3226	4 oz.	.45
Oyster Forks. Set of six..	5K3436	5K3336	5K3236	¾ lb.	2.35
Six Silver Plated Hollow Handle Knives and Six Medium Forks. Set....	5K3435	5K3335	5K3235	3 lbs.	8.95
Cream Ladle. Each.....	5K3446	5K3346	5K3246	6 oz.	.78
Fruit Knives. Set of six..	Not made	5K3360	5K3260	1¼ lbs.	2.00
Children's Set. Three-piece	Not made	5K3376	5K3276	¾ lb.	1.35
Butter Spreaders. ½ dozen	5K3481	5K3381	5K3281	¾ lb.	3.00

Teaspoons, Tablespoons and Forks have extra plating on parts that receive the most wear.	Victory Pattern, Dull Finish	Lincoln Pattern, Bright Finish	La France Pattern, Dull Finish	Shpg. Wt.	
Teaspoons. Set of six....	5K3502	5K3102	5K3002	8 oz.	$1.35
Tablespoons. Set of six..	5K3514	5K3114	5K3014	1 lb.	2.70
Forks, medium. Set of six.	5K3518	5K3118	5K3018	1 lb.	2.70
Knives. Solid handle. Set of six................	5K3519	5K3119	5K3019	1¾ lbs.	2.65
Knives. Hollow handle. Set of six..............	5K3521	5K3121	5K3021	1½ lbs.	6.75
Knives. Hollow handle. Stainless steel. ½ doz.	5K3522	5K3122	5K3022	1¾ lbs.	7.25
Knives. Solid handle. Stainless steel. ½ doz.	5K3523	5K3123	5K3023	1¾ lbs.	4.55
Sugar Shell. Each.......	5K3524	5K3124	5K3024	4 oz.	.46
Butter Knife. Each......	5K3526	5K3126	5K3026	4 oz.	.48
Oyster Forks. Set of six..	5K3536	5K3136	5K3036	¾ lb.	2.55
Six Silver Plated Hollow Handle Knives and Six Medium Forks. Set ...	5K3535	5K3135	5K3035	3 lbs.	9.45
Cream Ladle. Each......	Not made	5K3146	5K3046	6 oz.	.85
Fruit Knives. Set of six..	5K3560	5K3160	5K3060	1¼ lbs.	2.20
Children's Set. Three-piece	5K3576	5K3176	5K3076	¾ lb.	1.50
Butter Spreaders. ½ doz.	Not made	5K3181	5K3081	¾ lb.	3.35

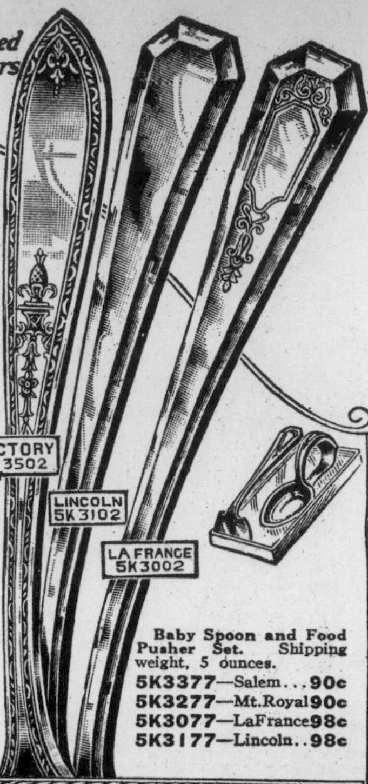

Baby Spoon and Food Pusher Set. Shipping weight, 5 ounces.
5K3377—Salem...**90c**
5K3277—Mt.Royal**90c**
5K3077—LaFrance**98c**
5K3177—Lincoln..**98c**

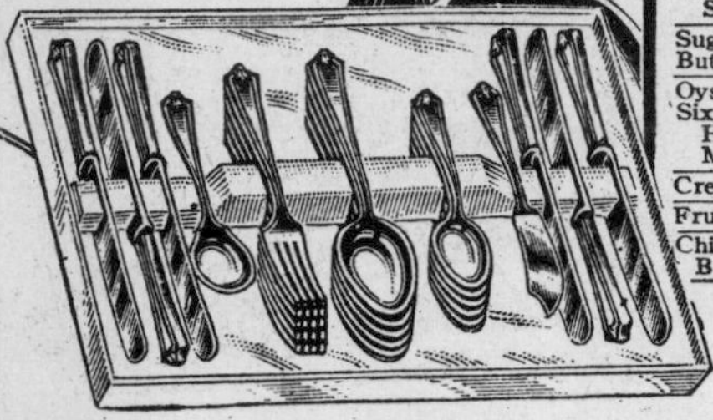

Twenty-Six Piece Set. Complete in Tray Box, consisting of 6 teaspoons, 6 tablespoons, 6 medium forks, 6 hollow handle knives, sugar shell and butter knife.

Twenty-Six Piece Set, with solid handle, silver plated knives in Presentation Box. Shipping weight, 5¾ pounds.
5K3382—Salem........................$8.98
5K3482—Regent........................ 8.98
5K3282—Mt. Royal..................... 8.98
5K3582—Victory........................ 9.95
5K3082—La France..................... 9.95
5K3182—Lincoln........................ 9.95

Twenty-Six Piece Set, with solid handle, **stainless steel** knives, in Presentation Box. Shipping weight, 5¾ pounds.
5K3395—Salem........................$1 .79
5K3495—Regent........................ 10.79
5K3295—Mt. Royal..................... 10.79
5K3595—Victory........................ 11.85
5K3095—La France..................... 11.85
5K3195—Lincoln........................ 11.85

Twenty-Six Piece Set with hollow handle, **stainless steel** knives, in Tray Box. Shipping weight, 5¾ pounds.
5K3398—Salem........................$13.45
5K3498—Regent........................ 13.45
5K3298—Mt. Royal..................... 13.45
5K3598—Victory........................ 14.50
5K3098—La France..................... 14.50
5K3198—Lincoln........................ 14.50

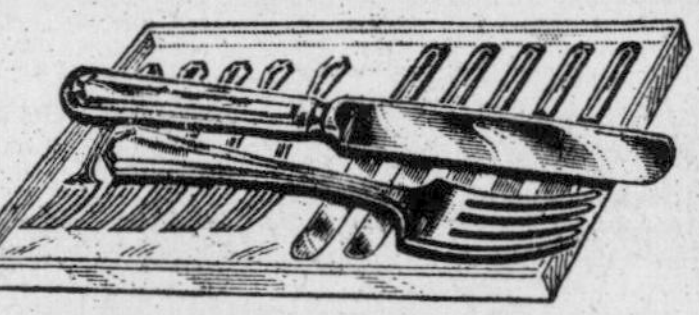

Knife and Fork Set

Six silver plated solid handle knives and six medium forks. Shpg. wt.. 3 lbs.
5K3340—Salem............**$4.85**
5K3440—Regent........... **4.85**
5K3240—Mt. Royal........ **4.85**
5K3540—Victory........... **5.25**
5K3040—La France........ **5.25**
5K3140—Lincoln........... **5.25**

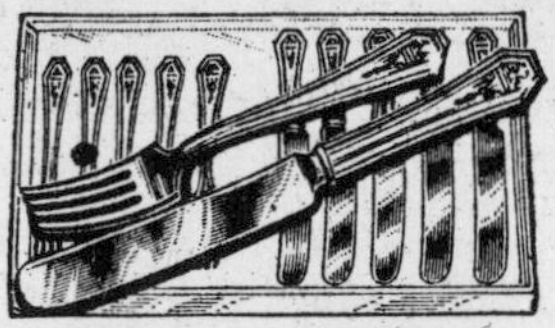

Knife and Fork Set

Six hollow handle knives with **stainless steel blades,** and six silver plated medium forks. Shipping weight, 3 pounds.
5K3333—Salem............**$9.45**
5K3433—Regent........... **9.45**
5K3233—Mt. Royal........ **9.45**
5K3533—Victory........... **9.89**
5K3033—La France........ **9.89**
5K3133—Lincoln........... **9.89**

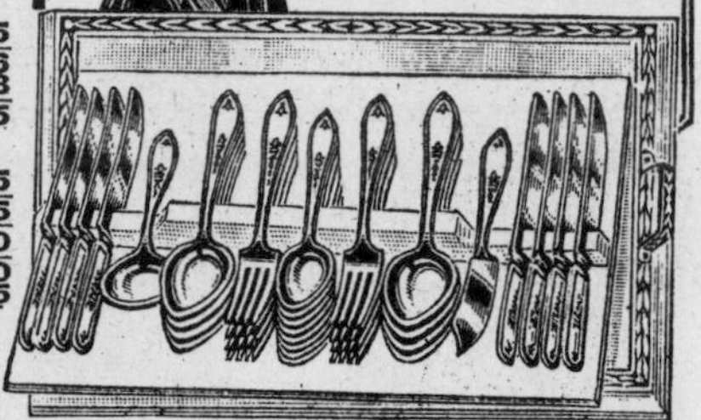

The Ideal Set—Pieces of Eight. 34 pieces—in attractive Presentation Tray, a combination silverware container and glass lined Serving Tray with handles.

Set consists of 8 teaspoons. 8 tablespoons, 8 medium forks, 8 medium knives, sugar shell and a butter knife.

Thirty-Four Piece Set with solid handles, silver plated knives in Presentation Tray. Shpg. wt., 6¾ lbs.
5K3383—Salem........................$13.35
5K3483—Regent........................ 13.35
5K3283—Mt. Royal..................... 13.35
5K3583—Victory........................ 14.75
5K3083—La France..................... 14.75
5K3183—Lincoln........................ 14.75

Thirty-Four Piece Set with hollow handles, **stainless steel** knives. Shipping weight, 6¾ pounds.
5K3399—Salem........................$19.30
5K3499—Regent........................ 19.30
5K3299—Mt. Royal..................... 19.30
5K3599—Victory........................ 20.65
5K3099—La France..................... 20.65
5K3199—Lincoln........................ 20.65

Thirty-Four Piece Set with solid handles, **stainless steel** knives in Presentation Tray. Shpg. wt., 6¾ lbs.
5K3393—Salem........................$15.75
5K3493—Regent........................ 15.75
5K3293—Mt. Royal..................... 15.75
5K3593—Victory........................ 17.15
5K3093—La France..................... 17.15
5K3193—Lincoln........................ 17.15

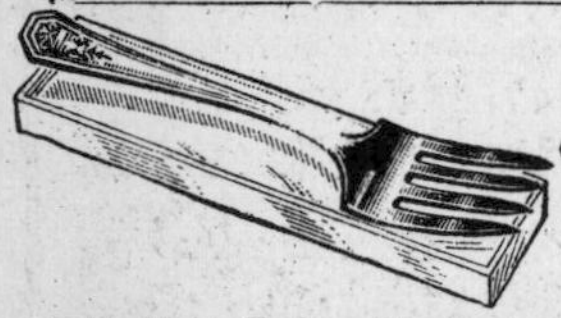

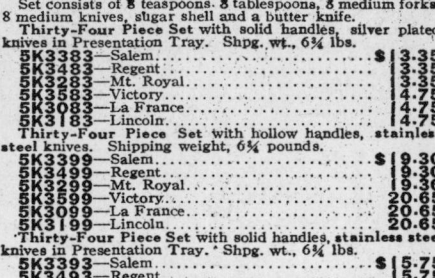

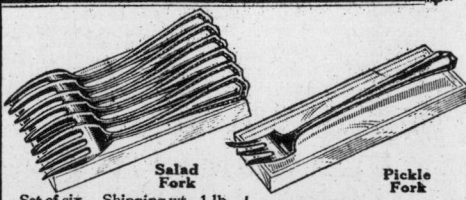

Cold Meat Fork. Shipping weight, 7 ounces.
5K3364—Salem.......**83c**
5K3464—Regent......**83c**
5K3264—Mount Royal **83c**
5K3564—Victory......**90c**
5K3064—La France...**90c**
5K3164—Lincoln......**90c**

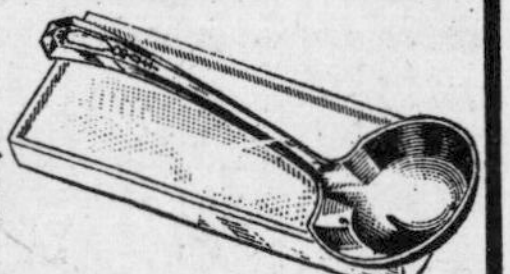

Gravy Ladle. Shipping weight, 8 ounces.
5K3348—Salem....**$0.96**
5K3448—Regent... **.96**
5K3248—Mount Royal.................. **.96**
5K3548—Victory... **1.10**
5K3048—La France. **1.10**
5K3148—Lincoln. **1.10**

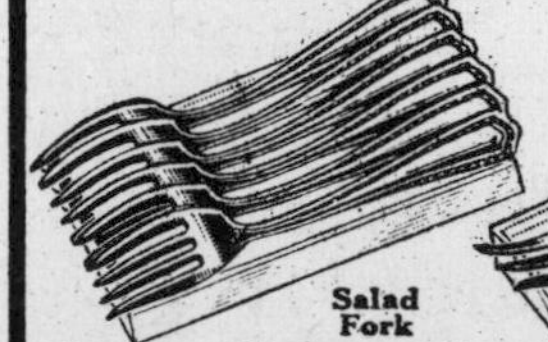

Salad Fork

Set of six. Shipping wt., 1 lb.
5K3337—Salem...**$3.35**
5K3437—Regent.. **3.35**
5K3237—Mount Royal........... **3.35**
5K3537—Victory....**3.65**
5K3037—La France **3.65**
5K3137—Lincoln...**3.65**

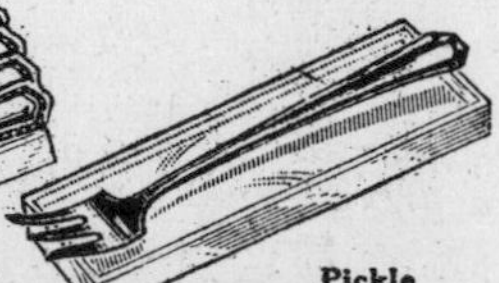

Pickle Fork

Shipping weight, 4 ounces.
5K3352-Salem....**54c**
5K3452-Regent...**54c**
5K3252-Mt. Royal.**54c**
5K3552-Victory...**57c**
5K3052-La France.**57c**
5K3152-Lincoln...**57c**

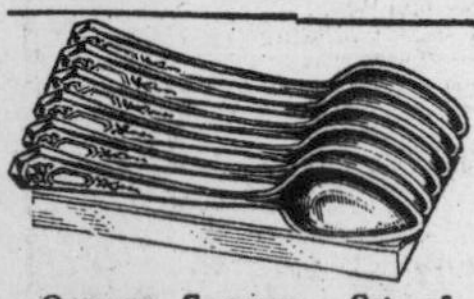

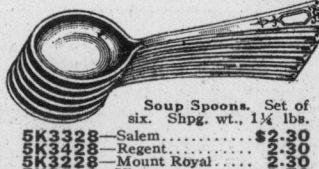

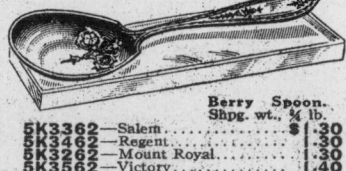

Orange Spoons. Set of six. Shipping weight, ¾ pound.
5K3342—Salem....................**$2.15**
5K3442—Regent.................... **2.15**
5K3242—Mount Royal............ **2.15**
5K3042—La France............... **2.25**
5K3142—Lincoln.................. **2.25**

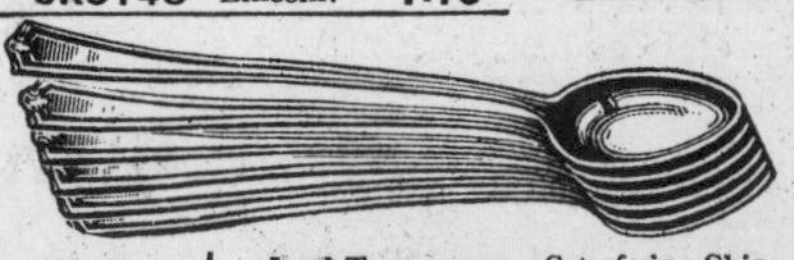

Iced Teaspoons. Set of six. Shipping weight, 1 pound.
5K3371—Salem........**$2.35**
5K3471—Regent....... **2.35**
5K3271—Mt. Royal.... **2.35**
5K3571—Victory....... **2.60**
5K3071—La France.... **2.60**
5K3171—Lincoln....... **2.60**

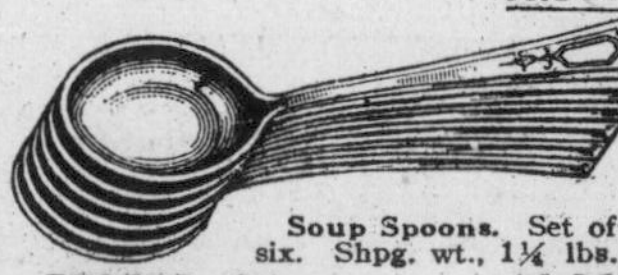

Soup Spoons. Set of six. Shpg. wt., 1¼ lbs.
5K3328—Salem..............**$2.30**
5K3428—Regent.............. **2.30**
5K3228—Mount Royal....... **2.30**
5K3528—Victory.............. **2.70**
5K3028—La France.......... **2.70**
5K3128—Lincoln.............. **2.70**

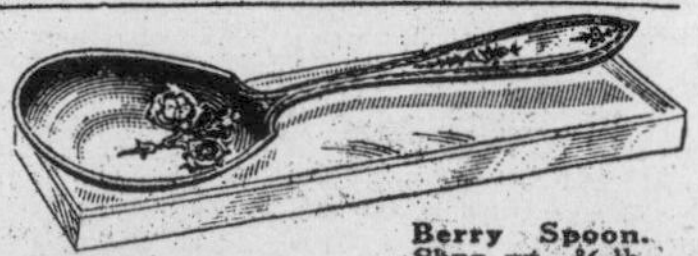

Berry Spoon. Shpg. wt., ¾ lb.
5K3362—Salem....................**$1.30**
5K3462—Regent.................... **1.30**
5K3262—Mount Royal............ **1.30**
5K3562—Victory.................... **1.40**
5K3062—La France............... **1.40**
5K3162—Lincoln.................. **1.40**

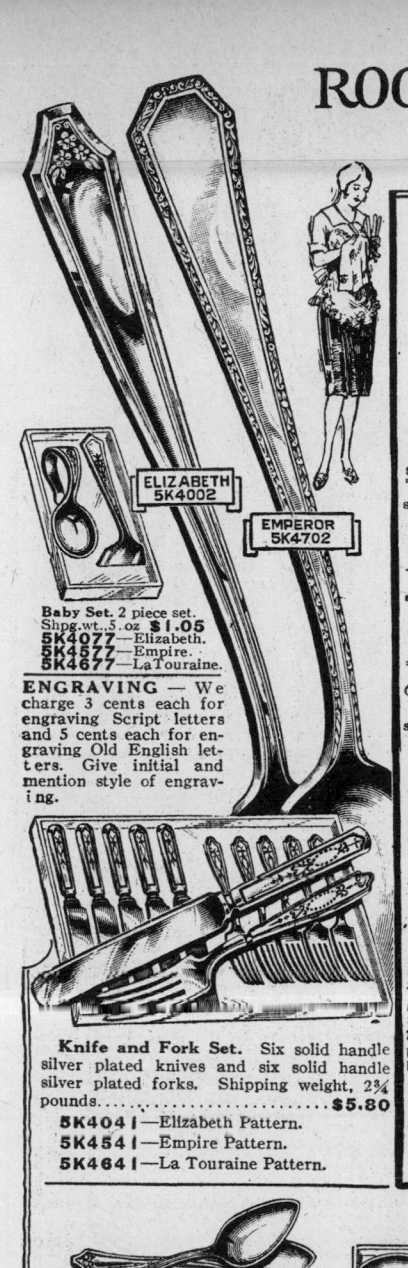

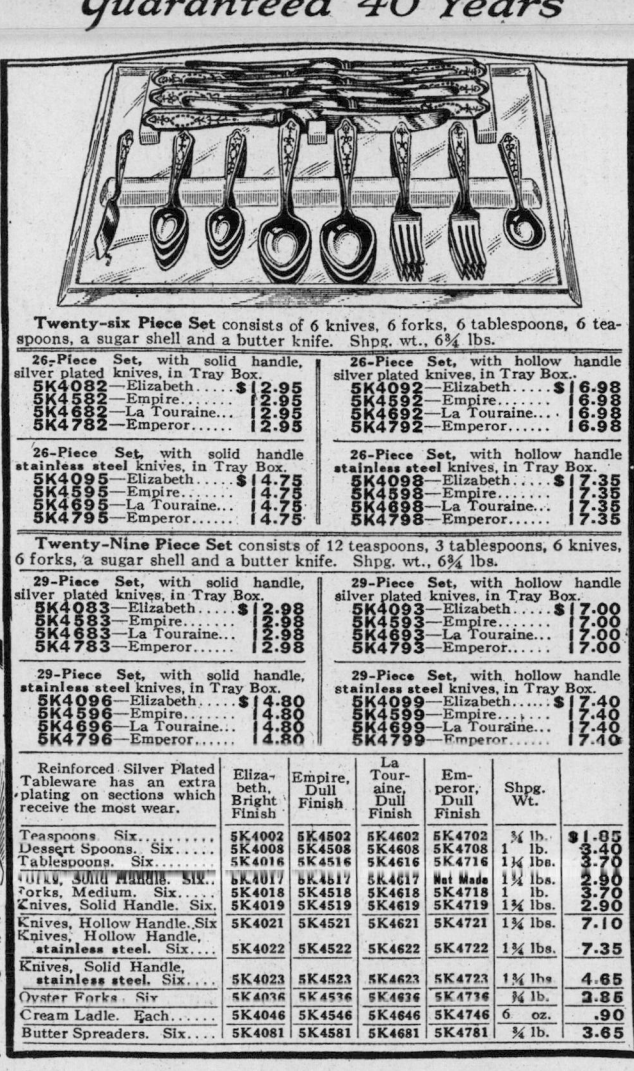

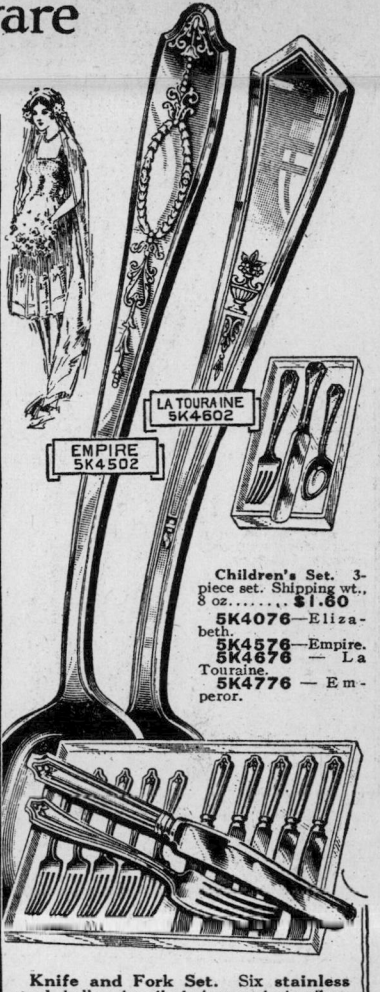

ROGERS Silver Plated Tableware

Guaranteed 40 Years

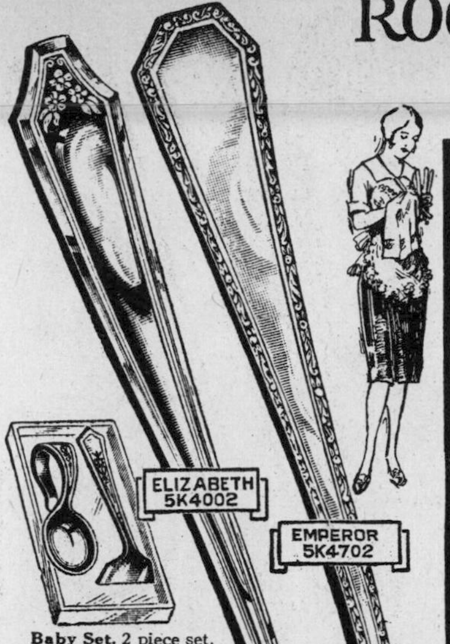

Baby Set. 2 piece set. Shpg. wt., 5 oz. **$1.05**
5K4077—Elizabeth.
5K4577—Empire.
5K4677—La Touraine.

ENGRAVING — We charge 3 cents each for engraving Script letters and 5 cents each for engraving Old English letters. Give initial and mention style of engraving.

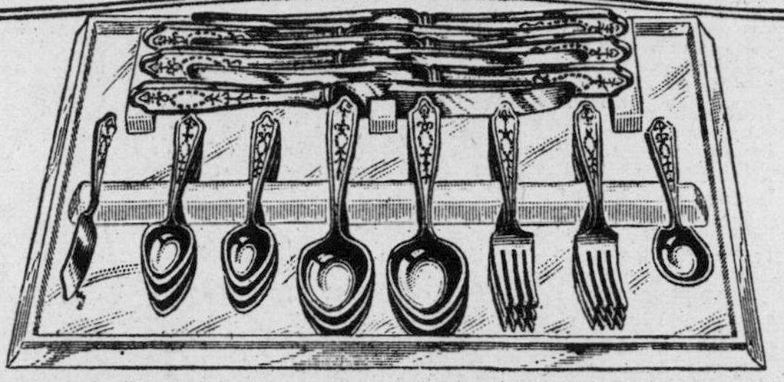

Twenty-six Piece Set consists of 6 knives, 6 forks, 6 tablespoons, 6 teaspoons, a sugar shell and a butter knife. Shpg. wt., 6¾ lbs.

26-Piece Set, with solid handle, silver plated knives, in Tray Box.
5K4082—Elizabeth.....$12.95
5K4582—Empire.......12.95
5K4682—La Touraine...12.95
5K4782—Emperor......12.95

26-Piece Set, with hollow handle silver plated knives, in Tray Box.
5K4092—Elizabeth.....$16.98
5K4592—Empire.......16.98
5K4692—La Touraine...16.98
5K4792—Emperor......16.98

26-Piece Set, with solid handle **stainless steel** knives, in Tray Box.
5K4095—Elizabeth.....$14.75
5K4595—Empire.......14.75
5K4695—La Touraine...14.75
5K4795—Emperor......14.75

26-Piece Set, with hollow handle **stainless steel** knives, in Tray Box.
5K4098—Elizabeth.....$17.35
5K4598—Empire.......17.35
5K4698—La Touraine...17.35
5K4798—Emperor......17.35

Twenty-Nine Piece Set consists of 12 teaspoons, 3 tablespoons, 6 knives, 6 forks, a sugar shell and a butter knife. Shpg. wt., 6¾ lbs.

29-Piece Set, with solid handle, silver plated knives, in Tray Box.
5K4083—Elizabeth.....$12.98
5K4583—Empire.......12.98
5K4683—La Touraine...12.98
5K4783—Emperor......12.98

29-Piece Set, with hollow handle silver plated knives, in Tray Box.
5K4093—Elizabeth.....$17.00
5K4593—Empire.......17.00
5K4693—La Touraine...17.00
5K4793—Emperor......17.00

29-Piece Set, with solid handle, **stainless steel** knives, in Tray Box.
5K4096—Elizabeth.....$14.80
5K4596—Empire.......14.80
5K4696—La Touraine...14.80
5K4796—Emperor......14.80

29-Piece Set, with hollow handle **stainless steel** knives, in Tray Box.
5K4099—Elizabeth.....$17.40
5K4599—Empire.......17.40
5K4699—La Touraine...17.40
5K4799—Emperor......17.40

Reinforced Silver Plated Tableware has an extra plating on sections which receive the most wear.	Elizabeth, Bright Finish	Empire, Dull Finish	La Touraine, Dull Finish	Emperor, Dull Finish	Shpg. Wt.	
Teaspoons. Six..........	5K4002	5K4502	5K4602	5K4702	¾ lb.	$1.85
Dessert Spoons. Six.....	5K4008	5K4508	5K4608	5K4708	1 lb.	3.40
Tablespoons. Six........	5K4016	5K4516	5K4616	5K4716	1¼ lbs.	3.70
Forks, Solid Handle. Six..	5K4017	5K4517	5K4617	Not Made	1¼ lbs.	2.90
Forks, Medium. Six.....	5K4018	5K4518	5K4618	5K4718	1 lb.	3.70
Knives, Solid Handle. Six.	5K4019	5K4519	5K4619	5K4719	1¾ lbs.	2.90
Knives, Hollow Handle. Six	5K4021	5K4521	5K4621	5K4721	1¾ lbs.	7.10
Knives, Hollow Handle, **stainless steel.** Six....	5K4022	5K4522	5K4622	5K4722	1¾ lbs.	7.35
Knives, Solid Handle, **stainless steel.** Six....	5K4023	5K4523	5K4623	5K4723	1¾ lbs.	4.65
Oyster Forks. Six	5K4036	5K4536	5K4636	5K4736	¾ lb.	3.85
Cream Ladle. Each......	5K4046	5K4546	5K4646	5K4746	6 oz.	.90
Butter Spreaders. Six....	5K4081	5K4581	5K4681	5K4781	¾ lb.	3.65

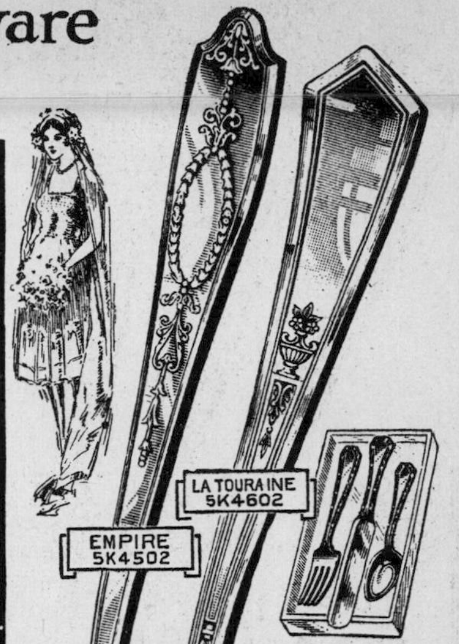

Children's Set. 3-piece set. Shipping wt., 8 oz........**$1.60**
5K4076—Elizabeth.
5K4576—Empire.
5K4676 — La Touraine.
5K4776 — Emperor.

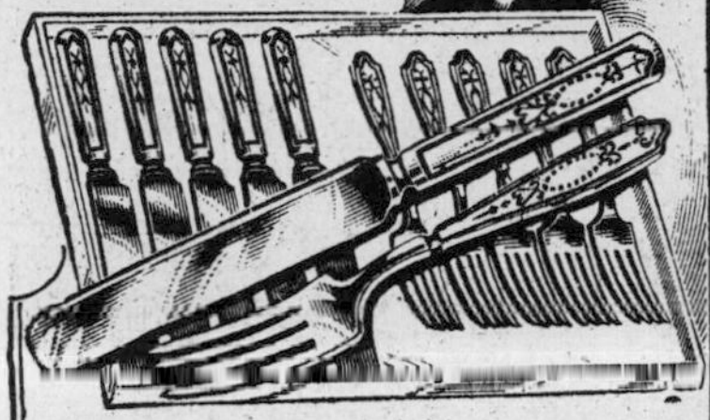

Knife and Fork Set. Six solid handle silver plated knives and six solid handle silver plated forks. Shipping weight, 2¾ pounds..........**$5.80**
5K4041—Elizabeth Pattern.
5K4541—Empire Pattern.
5K4641—La Touraine Pattern.

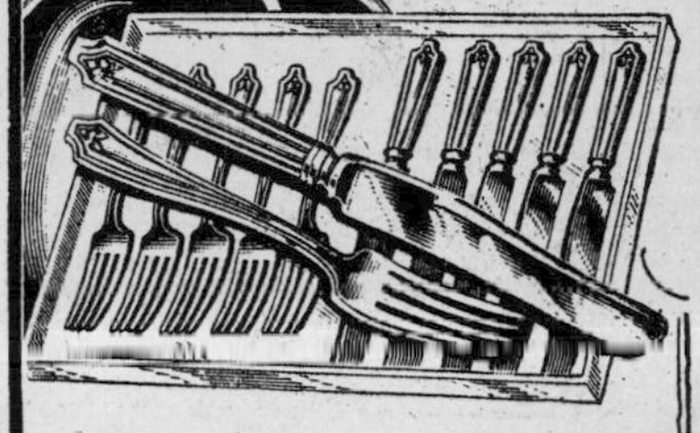

Knife and Fork Set. Six **stainless steel,** hollow handle knives and six silver plated medium forks. Shipping weight, 3 pounds..........**$11.00**
5K4031—Elizabeth Pattern.
5K4531—Empire Pattern.
5K4631—La Touraine Pattern.
5K4731—Emperor Pattern.

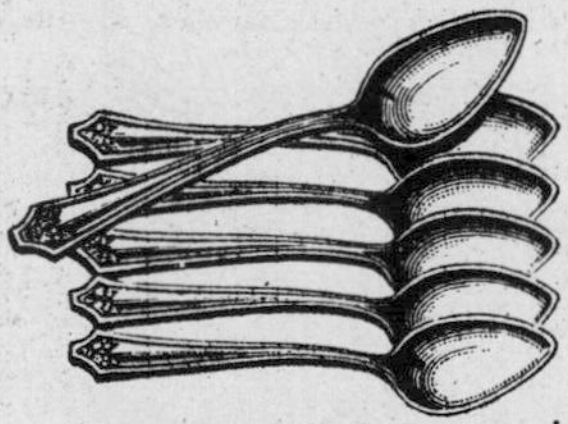

Teaspoons. Shpg. wt., ¾ lb. Set of six..........**$1.85**
5K4002—Elizabeth.
5K4502—Empire.
5K4602—La Touraine.
5K4702—Emperor.

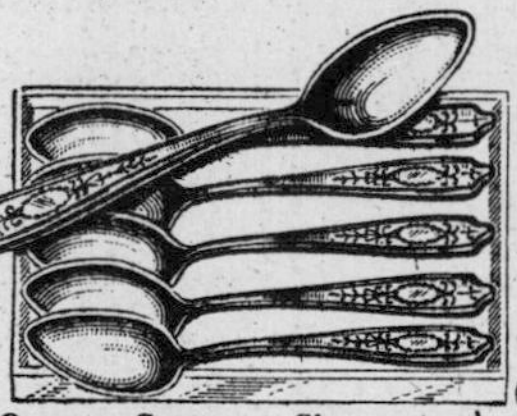

Orange Spoons. Shpg. wt., 1 lb. Set of six........**$2.50**
5K4042—Elizabeth.
5K4542—Empire.
5K4642—La Touraine.
5K4742—Emperor.

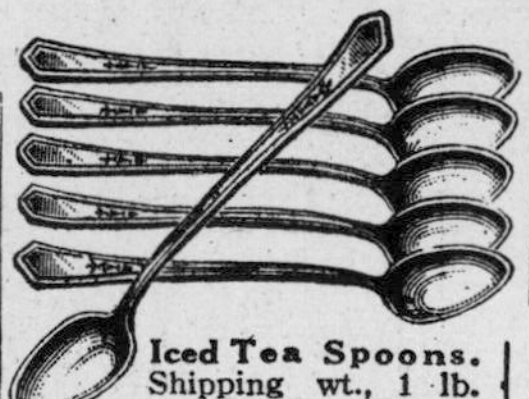

Iced Tea Spoons. Shipping wt., 1 lb. Set of six ...**$2.75**
5K4071—Elizabeth.
5K4571—Empire.
5K4671—La Touraine.
5K4771—Emperor.

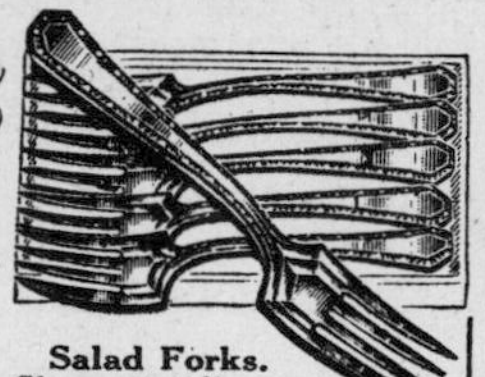

Salad Forks. Shpg. wt., 1 lb. Set of six..........**$3.75**
5K4037—Elizabeth.
5K4537—Empire.
5K4637—La Touraine
5K4737—Emperor.

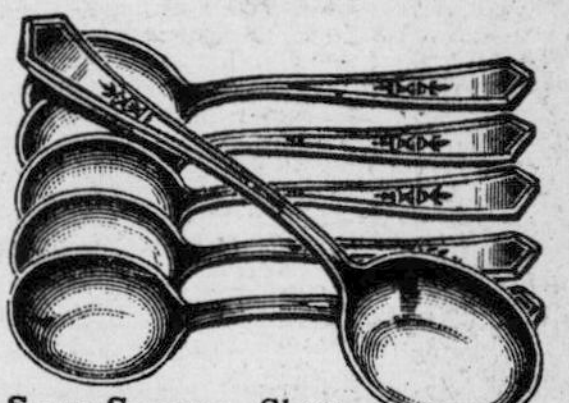

Soup Spoons. Shpg. wt., 1¼ lbs. Set of six...**$3.70**
5K4028—Elizabeth.
5K4528—Empire.
5K4628—La Touraine.
5K4728—Emperor.

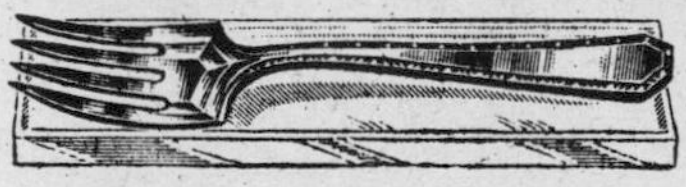

Cold Meat Fork. Shpg. wt., 7 oz. Each..........**93c**
5K4064—Elizabeth.
5K4564—Empire.
5K4664—La Touraine.
5K4764—Emperor.

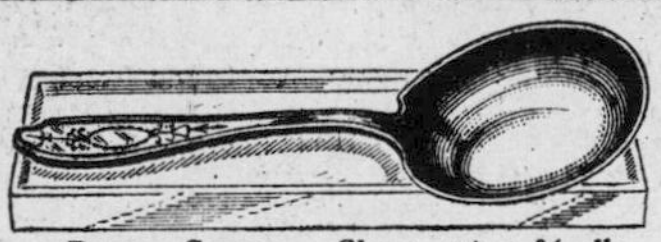

Berry Spoon. Shpg. wt., ¾ lb. Each..........**$1.60**
5K4062—Elizabeth.
5K4562—Empire.
5K4662—La Touraine.
5K4762—Emperor.

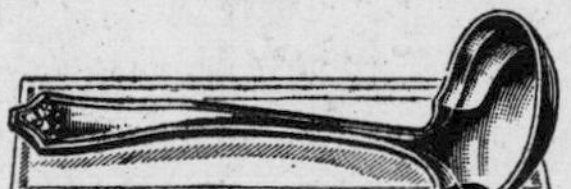

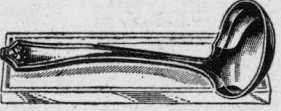

Gravy Ladle. Shpg. wt., 7 oz. Each..........**$1.25**
5K4048—Elizabeth.
5K4548—Empire.
5K4648—La Touraine.
5K4748—Emperor.

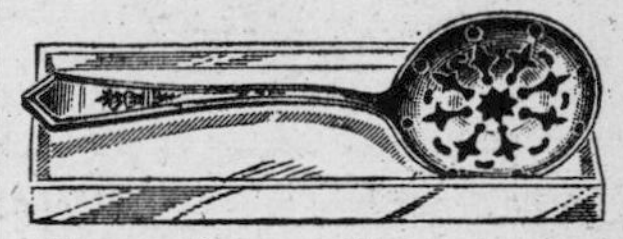

Tomato Server. Shpg. wt., 8 oz. Each..........**$1.69**
5K4055—Elizabeth.
5K4555—Empire.
5K4655—La Touraine.
5K4755—Emperor.

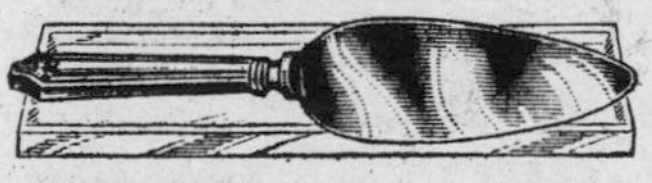

Pie Server. Hollow Handle. Shpg. wt., 8 oz. Each..........**$2.90**
5K4047—Elizabeth.
5K4547—Empire.
5K4647—La Touraine.
5K4747—Emperor.

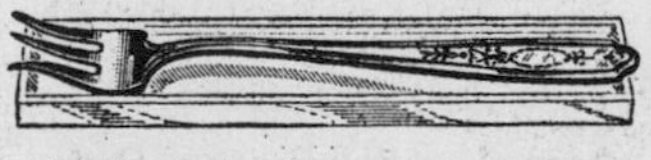

Pickle Fork. Shpg. wt., 4 oz. Each..........**58c**
5K4052—Elizabeth.
5K4552—Empire.
5K4652—La Touraine.
5K4752—Emperor.

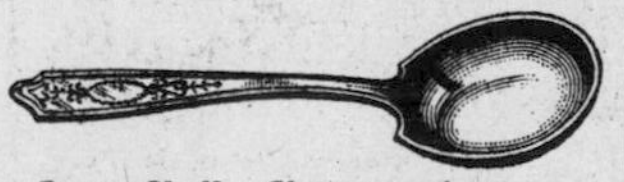

Sugar Shell. Shpg. wt., 4 oz. Each..........**58c**
5K4024—Elizabeth.
5K4524—Empire.
5K4624—La Touraine.
5K4724—Emperor.

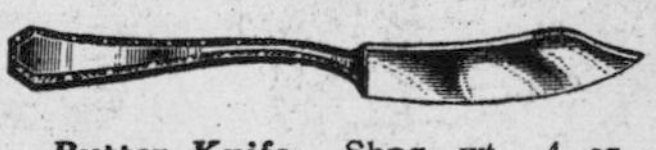

Butter Knife. Shpg. wt., 4 oz. Each..........**68c**
5K4026—Elizabeth.
5K4526—Empire.
5K4626—La Touraine.
5K4726—Emperor.

COMMUNITY PLATE

Guaranteed For 50 Years

The finest brand of silverware manufactured by the Oneida Community Silverware Co. is known as "Community Plate." This is the brand that they guarantee for fifty years of satisfactory service. They manufacture other brands, guaranteed for shorter terms of years. Remember: There is but one "Community Plate," each piece so stamped on the back of the handles. Illustrations of teaspoons show actual size.

We supply with any 26-piece set on this page, or each piece, without extra charge, a beautiful costly Buffette of soft, pliable suede leather, lined with special non-tarnish cloth, in addition to their regular presentation box. See illustration of Buffette for the single pieces. A Sterling Name Plate on the 26-Piece Buffette is supplied for engraving your initials or your full name. We engrave each piece of silverware on this page, with any one initial and your full name on the name plate without extra charge. State initial and style of engraving desired; also write plainly the name for the name plate.

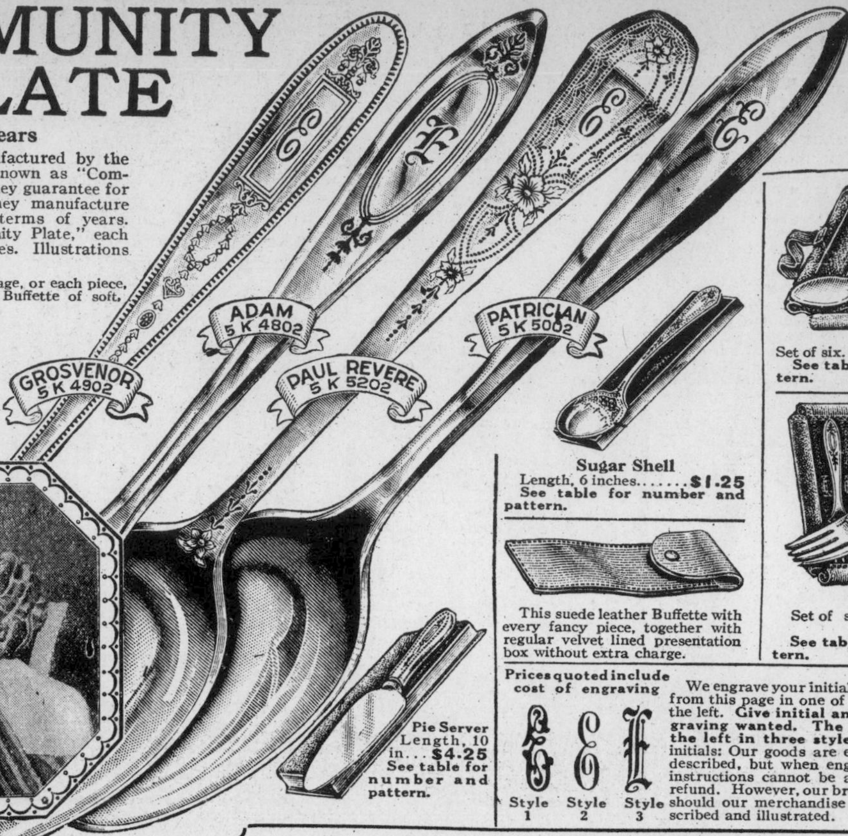

GROSVENOR 5 K 4902
ADAM 5 K 4802
PAUL REVERE 5 K 5202
PATRICIAN 5 K 5002

Iced Tea Spoons
Set of six. Length 7⅝ in. **$6.00**
See table for number and pattern.

Sugar Shell
Length, 6 inches......**$1.25**
See table for number and pattern.

This suede leather Buffette with every fancy piece, together with regular velvet lined presentation box without extra charge.

Salad Forks
Set of six. Length, 6⅛ inches. **$7.50**
See table for number and pattern.

Pie Server
Length, 10 in.. **$4.25**
See table for number and pattern.

Prices quoted include cost of engraving

Style 1 Style 2 Style 3

We engrave your initial on all silverware selected from this page in one of the three styles shown to the left. Give initial and mention style of engraving wanted. The initial (E) is shown to the left in three styles. Regarding engraving initials: Our goods are exactly as illustrated and described, but when engraved according to your instructions cannot be accepted for exchange or refund. However, our broad guarantee holds good, should our merchandise prove different than described and illustrated.

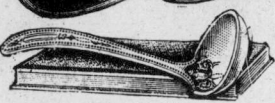

Gravy Ladle
Length, 7⅛ inches......**$2.75**
See table for number and pattern.

Jelly Server
Length 7 inches......**$1.50**
See table for number and pattern.

Cold Meat Fork
Length, 8⅜ inches......**$2.50**
See table for number and pattern.

Leather Buffette

Orange or Grape Fruit Spoons
Set of six. Length, 5½ inches......**$5.75**
See table for number and pattern.

Butter Knife
Length, 7½ inches. **$1.25**
See table for number and pattern.

Read Our Special Offer Below

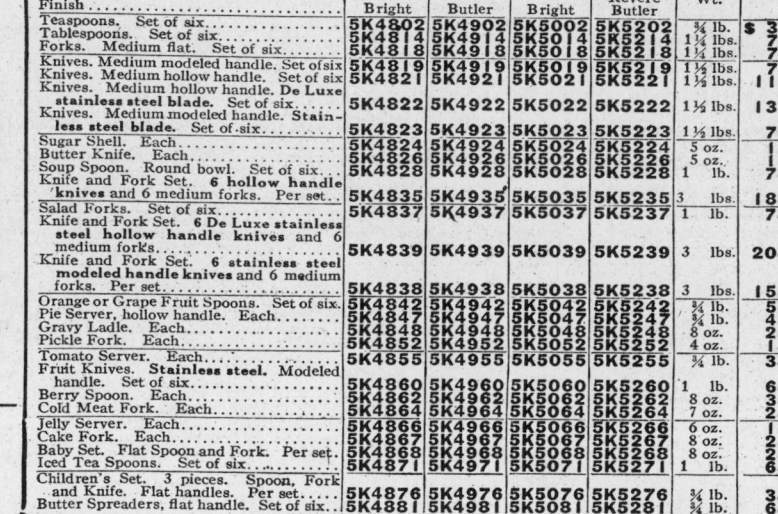

Pattern	Adam	Grosvenor	Patrician	Paul Revere	Shpg. Wt.	
Finish	Bright	Butler	Bright	Butler		
Teaspoons. Set of six	5K4802	5K4902	5K5002	5K5202	¾ lb.	$ 3.75
Tablespoons. Set of six	5K4814	5K4914	5K5014	5K5214	1¼ lbs.	7.50
Forks. Medium flat. Set of six	5K4818	5K4918	5K5018	5K5218	1¼ lbs.	7.50
Knives. Medium modeled handle. Set of six	5K4819	5K4919	5K5019	5K5219	1½ lbs.	7.00
Knives. Medium hollow handle. Set of six	5K4821	5K4921	5K5021	5K5221	1½ lbs.	11.00
Knives. Medium hollow handle. De Luxe stainless steel blade. Set of six	5K4822	5K4922	5K5022	5K5222	1½ lbs.	13.00
Knives. Medium modeled handle. Stainless steel blade. Set of six	5K4823	5K4923	5K5023	5K5223	1½ lbs.	7.50
Sugar Shell. Each	5K4824	5K4924	5K5024	5K5224	5 oz.	1.25
Butter Knife. Each	5K4826	5K4926	5K5026	5K5226	5 oz.	1.25
Soup Spoon. Round bowl. Set of six	5K4828	5K4928	5K5028	5K5228	1 lb.	7.50
Knife and Fork Set. 6 hollow handle knives and 6 medium forks. Per set	5K4835	5K4935	5K5035	5K5235	3 lbs.	18.50
Salad Forks. Set of six	5K4837	5K4937	5K5037	5K5237	1 lb.	7.50
Knife and Fork Set. 6 De Luxe stainless steel hollow handle knives and 6 medium forks	5K4839	5K4939	5K5039	5K5239	3 lbs.	20.50
Knife and Fork Set. 6 stainless steel modeled handle knives and 6 medium forks. Per set	5K4838	5K4938	5K5038	5K5238	3 lbs.	15.00
Orange or Grape Fruit Spoons. Set of six	5K4842	5K4942	5K5042	5K5242	¾ lb.	5.75
Pie Server, hollow handle. Each	5K4847	5K4947	5K5047	5K5247	¾ lb.	4.25
Gravy Ladle. Each	5K4848	5K4948	5K5048	5K5248	8 oz.	2.75
Pickle Fork. Each	5K4852	5K4952	5K5052	5K5252	4 oz.	1.50
Tomato Server. Each	5K4855	5K4955	5K5055	5K5255	¾ lb.	3.25
Fruit Knives. Stainless steel. Modeled handle. Set of six	5K4860	5K4960	5K5060	5K5260	1 lb.	6.75
Berry Spoon. Each	5K4862	5K4962	5K5062	5K5262	8 oz.	3.50
Cold Meat Fork. Each	5K4864	5K4964	5K5064	5K5264	7 oz.	2.50
Jelly Server. Each	5K4866	5K4966	5K5066	5K5266	6 oz.	1.50
Cake Fork. Each	5K4867	5K4967	5K5067	5K5267	8 oz.	2.75
Baby Set. Flat Spoon and Fork. Per set	5K4868	5K4968	5K5068	5K5268	8 oz.	2.00
Iced Tea Spoons. Set of six	5K4871	5K4971	5K5071	5K5271	1 lb.	6.00
Children's Set. 3 pieces. Spoon, Fork and Knife. Flat handles. Per set	5K4876	5K4976	5K5076	5K5276	¾ lb.	3.00
Butter Spreaders, flat handle. Per six	5K4881	5K4981	5K5081	5K5281	¾ lb.	6.25

Twenty-six pieces, complete, in our beautiful Duo-Service Tray for only $28.25 and up. Each set consists of six knives, six forks, six tablespoons, six teaspoons, a sugar shell and butter knife. One of these splendid 26-piece sets, complete with our beautiful Duo Service Tray, will make a worthy gift for any bride. Shipping weight, 26-piece set, 8 pounds.

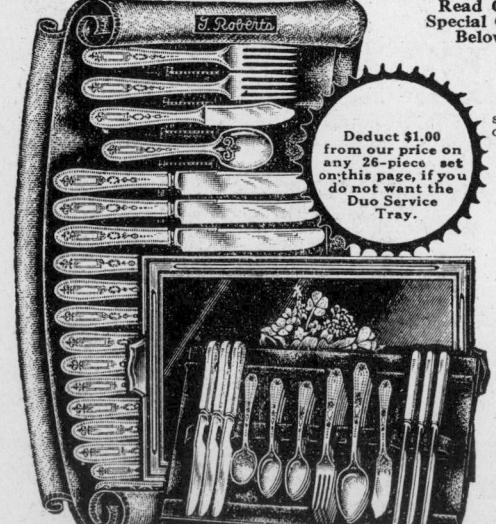

Deduct $1.00 from our price on any 26-piece set on this page, if you do not want the Duo Service Tray.

Our Special Offer

With every 26-Piece Set of Community Plate we include the Duo-Service Tray.

Finished in smart black lacquer with gilt trimmings and glass lined with a colorful decorated background.

The silver rack fits inside the tray. We also include our Leather Buffette with every 26-piece set. If you do not wish the tray, deduct $1.00 from our prices on any 26-piece set on this page.

Duo Serving Tray

Adam Pattern—26-Piece Set Bright Finish

5K4880—With Duo Serving Tray and modeled handle knives, silver plated blades......**$28.25**
5K4894—With Duo Serving Tray and stainless steel, modeled handle knives......**$28.75**
5K4898—With Duo Serving Tray and De Luxe stainless steel, hollow handle knives......**$34.25**
Deduct $1.00 from our price on any 26-piece set on this page if you do not want the Duo Serving Tray.

Grosvenor Pattern—26-Piece Set Butler Finish

5K4980—With Duo Serving Tray and modeled handle knives, silver plated blades......**$28.25**
5K4994—With Duo Serving Tray and stainless steel, modeled handle knives......**$28.75**
5K4998—With Duo Serving Tray and De Luxe stainless steel, hollow handle knives......**$34.25**
Deduct $1.00 from our price on any 26-piece set on this page if you do not want the Duo Serving Tray.

Patrician Pattern—26-Piece Set Bright Finish

5K5080—With Duo Serving Tray and modeled handle knives, silver plated blades......**$28.25**
5K5094—With Duo Serving Tray and stainless steel, modeled handle knives......**$28.75**
5K5098—With Duo Serving Tray and De Luxe stainless steel, hollow handle knives......**$34.25**
Deduct $1.00 from our price on any 26-piece set on this page if you do not want the Duo Serving Tray.

Paul Revere—26-Piece Set Butler Finish

5K5280—With Duo Serving Tray and modeled handle knives, silver plated blades......**$28.25**
5K5294—With Duo Serving Tray and stainless steel, modeled handle knives......**$28.75**
5K5298—With Duo Serving Tray and De Luxe stainless steel, hollow handle knives......**$34.25**
Deduct $1.00 from our price on any 26-piece set on this page if you do not want the Duo Serving Tray.

Oneida Community PAR PLATE

Guaranteed for 20 Years

The Par Plate brand illustrated on this page, manufactured by the Oneida Community Silverware Co., is guaranteed by them for twenty years of satisfactory service. Their aim was to furnish beautiful silverware at a price so low that it would supply a great popular demand, yet produce a silverware that they could conscientiously recommend for durability, beauty of design, and excellence of finish. Twenty years of actual service represents a generation of wear. The patterns probably are the acme of perfection in silverware designing for these grades.

ENGRAVING

We charge 3 cents each for engraving Script letters, and 5 cents each for engraving Old English letters. Regarding engraving initials: Our silverware is exactly as illustrated and described, but when engraved according to your instructions cannot be accepted for exchange or refund. However, our broad guarantee holds good should our merchandise prove different in any way than described and illustrated. **If engraving is wanted give initial and mention style.**

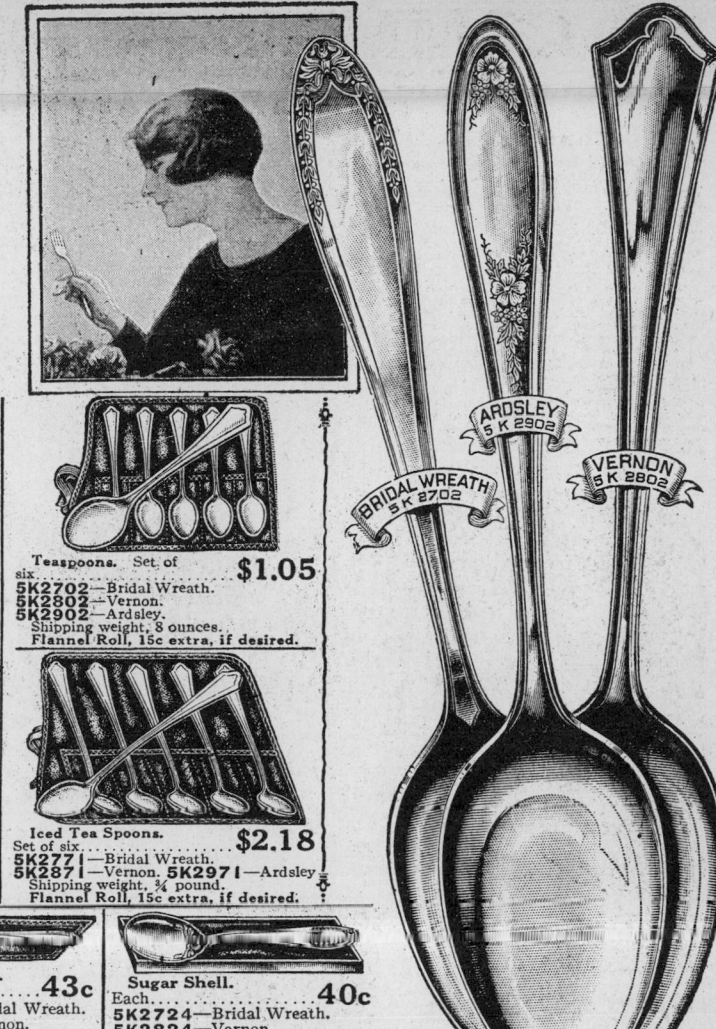

A flannel container with every piece of silverware on this page if you so desire, at a very small extra cost.	Bridal Wreath Pattern, Gray Finish	Vernon Pattern, Bright Finish	Ardsley Pattern, Dull Finish	Shpg. Wt	Without Roll	With Canton Flannel Roll
Teaspoons. Set of six	5K2702	5K2802	5K2902	8 oz.	$1.05	$1.20
Tablespoons. Set of six	5K2714	5K2814	5K2914	1 lb.	2.10	2.35
Medium Forks, regular size. Set of six	5K2718	5K2818	5K2918	1 lb.	2.10	2.35
Solid Handle Knives. Set of six	5K2719	5K2819	5K2919	1¾ lbs.	2.65	2.90
Hollow Handle Knives. Set of six	5K2721	5K2821	Not Made	1½ lbs.	6.50	6.75
Sugar Shell. Each	5K2724	5K2824	5K2924	6 oz.	.40	.50
Butter Knife. Each	5K2726	5K2826	5K2926	6 oz.	.43	.53
Oyster Forks. Set of six	5K2736	5K2836	Not Made	¾ lb.	2.00	2.15
Orange Spoons. Set of six	5K2742	5K2842	Not Made	¾ lb.	1.98	2.13
Salad Dressing or Cream Ladle. Each	5K2746	5K2846	5K2946	6 oz.	.72	.82
Pie Server. Each	5K2749	Not Made	Not Made	¾ lb.	1.27	1.37
Fruit Knives. Set of six	5K2760	5K2860	Not Made	1 lb.	2.42	2.57
Children's 3-Piece Set, Knife, Fork and Spoon	5K2776	5K2876	Not Made	¾ lb.	1.28	1.38
Butter Spreaders. Set of six	5K2781	5K2881	5K2981	¾ lb.	2.50	2.65

Teaspoons. Set of six $1.05
5K2702—Bridal Wreath.
5K2802—Vernon.
5K2902—Ardsley.
Shipping weight, 8 ounces.
Flannel Roll, 15c extra, if desired.

Iced Tea Spoons. $2.18
Set of six
5K2771—Bridal Wreath.
5K2871—Vernon. 5K2971—Ardsley
Shipping weight, ¾ pound.
Flannel Roll, 15c extra, if desired.

Cold Meat Fork.
Each 78c
5K2764—Bridal Wreath
5K2864—Vernon.
5K2964—Ardsley.
Shipping weight, 7 ounces.
Flannel Roll, 10c extra, if desired.

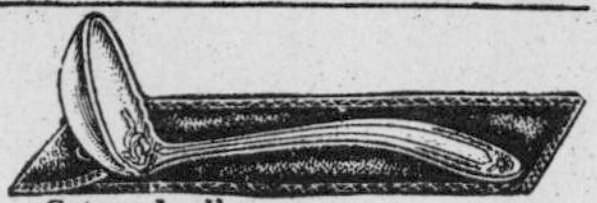

Gravy Ladle.
Each 98c
5K2748—Bridal Wreath.
5K2848—Vernon.
5K2948—Ardsley.
Shipping weight, 8 ounces.
Flannel Roll, 10c extra, if desired.

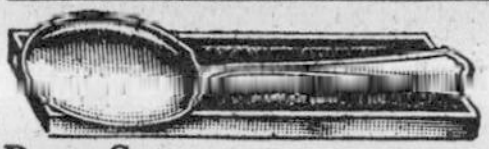

Berry Spoon.
Each $1.30
5K2762—Bridal Wreath.
5K2862—Vernon.
5K2962—Ardsley.
Shipping weight, ¾ pound.
Flannel Roll, 10c extra, if desired.

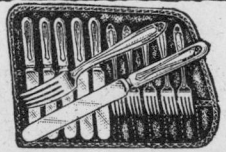

Pickle Fork.
Each 70c
5K2752—Bridal Wreath.
5K2852—Vernon.
Not made in Ardsley pattern.
Shipping weight, 5 oz.
Flannel Roll, 10c extra, if desired.

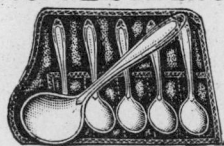

Butter Knife.
Each 43c
5K2726—Bridal Wreath.
5K2826—Vernon.
5K2926—Ardsley.
Shipping weight, 6 ounces.
Flannel Roll, 10c extra, if desired.

Sugar Shell.
Each 40c
5K2724—Bridal Wreath.
5K2824—Vernon.
5K2924—Ardsley.
Shipping weight, 6 ounces.
Flannel Roll, 10c extra, if desired.

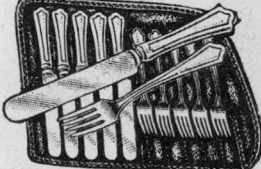

Butter Spreaders. Set of six ... $2.50
5K2781—Bridal Wreath.
5K2881—Vernon.
5K2981—Ardsley.
Shipping weight, ¾ pound.
Flannel Roll, 15c extra, if desired.

Knife and Fork Set. 6 solid handle knives and 6 medium forks.
Per set $4.75
5K2740—Bridal Wreath.
5K2840—Vernon.
5K2940—Ardsley.
Shipping weight, 3 pounds.
Flannel Roll, 30c extra, if desired.

Soup Spoons.
Set of six $2.10
5K2728—Bridal Wreath.
5K2828—Vernon.
Not made in Ardsley pattern.
Shipping weight, 1 pound.
Flannel Roll, 25c extra, if desired.

Salad Forks.
Set of six $2.95
5K2737—Bridal Wreath.
5K2837—Vernon.
5K2937—Ardsley.
Shipping weight, 1 pound.
Flannel Roll, 15c extra, if desired.

Knife and Fork Set. 6 hollow handle knives and 6 medium forks. Per set ... $8.60
5K2735—Bridal Wreath.
5K2835—Vernon.
Not made in Ardsley pattern.
Shipping weight, 3 pounds.
Flannel Roll, 30c extra, if desired.

Silverware, tremendously smart and inexpensive. Patterns of distinction, created by the makers of Community Plate. In selecting a silver service, choose one of these patterns in the 26-piece set. A complete service for six covers. Six knives, six forks, six tablespoons, six teaspoons, a sugar shell and a butter knife are included. Knives are furnished with **solid** or **hollow** handles with silver plated blades. To protect your silver service, a neat Presentation Box lined with blue velvet, can be included at a slight additional cost.

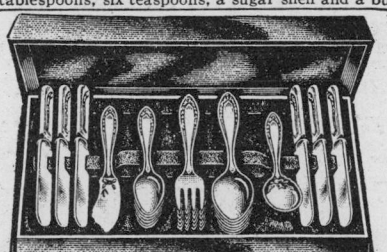

26-Piece Set With Solid Handle Knives $ 7.75
5K2780—Bridal Wreath Pattern, Without Box. Shipping weight, 3½ pounds.
5K2782—Bridal Wreath Pattern, With Box.. 8.35
Shipping weight, 5½ pounds.
26-Piece Set With Hollow Handle Knives 11.60
5K2790—Bridal Wreath Pattern, Without Box. Shipping weight, 3½ pounds.
5K2792—Bridal Wreath Pattern, With Box. 12.20
Shipping weight, 5½ pounds.

26-Piece Set With Solid Handle Knives
5K2980—Ardsley Pattern, Without Box. $7.75
Shipping weight, 3½ pounds.
5K2982—Ardsley Pattern, With Box..... 8.35
Shipping weight, 5½ pounds.

26-Piece Set With Solid Handle Knives $ 7.75
5K2880—Vernon Pattern, Without Box...
Shipping weight, 3½ pounds.
5K2882—Vernon Pattern, With Box....... 8.35
Shipping weight, 5½ pounds.
26-Piece Set With Hollow Handle Knives 11.60
5K2890—Vernon Pattern, Without Box...
Shipping weight, 3½ pounds.
5K2892—Vernon Pattern, With Box....... 12.20
Shipping weight, 5½ pounds.

1865 Wm Rogers Silver Plated Tableware 1865

Guaranteed for 45 Years

LA SALLE PATTERN

BUTLER DULLED   SILVER FINISH

Guaranteed for 45 Years

TEA SPOON 5K4102

TABLE SPOON 5K4114

MEDIUM FORK 5K4118

HOLLOW HANDLE KNIFE 5K4121

CREAM LADLE 5K4146

PICKLE FORK 5K4152

COLD MEAT FORK 5K4164

BERRY SPOON 5K4162

SOLID HANDLE KNIFE 5K4119

GRAVY LADLE 5K4148

SUGAR SHELL 5K4124

SOLID HANDLE FORK 5K4117

SOUP SPOON 5K4128

BUTTER KNIFE 5K4126

Engraving

We charge 3 cents each for engraving Script letters, and 5 cents each for engraving Old English letters. Mention initial and style. Regarding engraving initials: Our silverware is exactly as illustrated and described, but when engraved according to your instructions cannot be accepted for exchange or refund. However, our broad guarantee holds good should our merchandise prove different in any way than described and illustrated.

Knife and Fork Set. Six hollow handle knives, 16-pennyweight quality, and six medium spoon handle forks. La Salle Pattern. Shpg. wt., 3 lbs.
5K4134—Set, without roll . . . **$11.50**
5K4135—With roll **$11.75**

Children's Three-Piece Set. Silver plated. Regular size. Shpg. wt., 8 oz.
5K4176—La Salle Pattern. Per set . . . **$1.75**

GUARANTEE

We guarantee this silverware to satisfy you perfectly. We will replace with new goods of the same pattern at any time within 45 years any piece of 1865 Rogers silverware which fails to give satisfactory everyday service.

No finer plated silverware can be obtained for the money than the Celebrated Wm. Rogers 1865 Tableware. The beauty of the La Salle pattern has aroused the admiration of thousands throughout the country. No finer gift can be made than this splendid silver service. Guaranteed by the manufacturer for 45 years of family service.

Knife and Fork Set. Six solid handle knives and six solid handle forks. 12-pennyweight quality. La Salle Pattern. Shipping weight, 2¾ pounds.
5K4141—Set, without roll . . . **$6.00**
5K4143—With roll **$6.25**

Order by Number	La Salle Pattern Dull Silver Finish	Shpg. Wt.	
Teaspoons. Set of six	5K4102	¾ lb.	$2.00
Tablespoons Set of six	5K4114	1 lb.	4.00
Solid Handle Forks. Set of six . .	5K4117	1¼ lbs.	3.00
Medium Forks Set of six	5K4118	1 lb.	4.00
Solid Handle Knives Set of six . . .	5K4119	1¾ lbs.	3.00
Hollow Handle Knives Set of six . .	5K4121	1¾ lbs.	7.50
Hollow Handle Knives with stainless steel blades. Set of six . .	5K4122	1¾ lbs.	8.75
Sugar Shell. Each	5K4124	4 oz.	.70
Butter Knife. Each	5K4126	4 oz.	.80
Round Bowl Soup Spoons. Set of six . .	5K4128	1 lb.	4.00
Cream Ladle in Box. Each	5K4146	6 oz.	.95
Gravy Ladle in Box. Each	5K4148	8 oz.	1.35
Pickle Fork in Box. Each	5K4152	5 oz.	.90
Berry Spoon in Box. Each	5K4162	¾ lb.	1.75
Berry Spoon, gold plated bowl. Each . .	5K4163	¾ lb.	2.15
Cold Meat Fork in Box. Each . . .	5K4164	7 oz.	1.10
Cold Meat Fork, gold plated tines. In Box. Each	5K4165	7 oz.	1.30

The Ideal Set Pieces of Eight

The Pieces of Eight Set consists of 8 teaspoons, 8 tablespoons, 8 knives, 8 forks, a sugar shell and butter knife. 34 pieces in all, with a beautiful tray container, a combination silverware container and glass lined serving tray with handles. Ship. wt., 7½ lbs.
5K4187—34-Piece Set, with silver plated solid handle knives. La Salle Pattern **$18.35**
5K4189—34-Piece Set, with stainless steel hollow handle knives. La Salle Pattern **$25.98**

THE SET FOR SIX

Consists of 6 knives, 6 forks, 6 tablespoons, 6 teaspoons, a sugar shell and butter knife. La Salle Pattern. The attractive Presentation Tray is furnished without extra charge. Shipping weight, 6½ pounds.
5K4182—26-Piece Set, with solid handle knives, silver plated blades **$14.00**
5K4184—26-Piece Set, with hollow handle knives, silver plated blades **18.45**
5K4186—26-Piece Set, with hollow handle knives, stainless steel blades . . **19.70**

Silver Plated Tableware

MANUFACTURED BY
WM. ROGER'S MFG. CO.

Guaranteed 15 Years

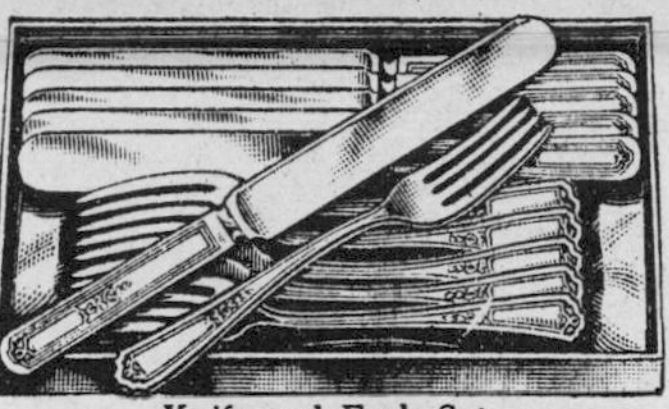

Knife and Fork Set
Six solid handle knives, 9¼ inches long, and six flat handle medium forks, 7½ inches long. Shipping weight, 2¾ pounds.
5K1735—Chatham Pattern.
Per set (without box).......... **$3.55**

Berry Spoon

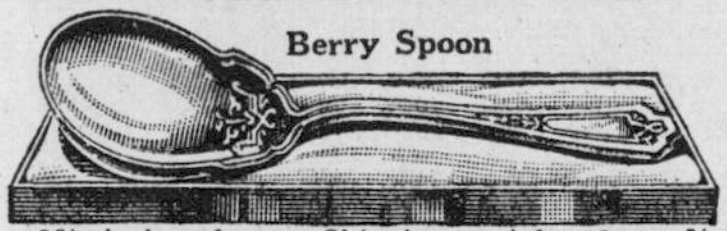

8¾ inches long. Shipping weight, 8 oz.
5K1762—Chatham pattern.
Each.......................... **85c**

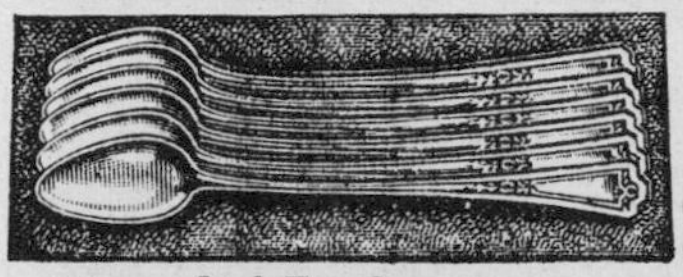

Iced Tea Spoons
7⅝ inches long. Shipping weight, 1 lb.
5K1771—Chatham Pattern.
Per set of six............ **$1.40**

Gravy Ladle

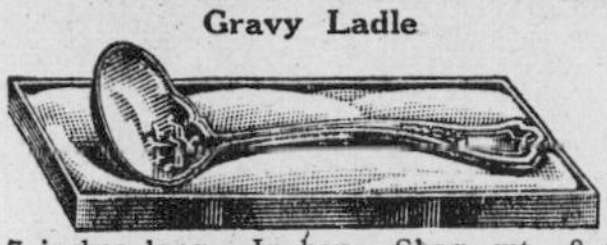

7 inches long. In box. Shpg. wt., 8 oz.
5K1748—Chatham Pattern.
Each.......................... **72c**

Chatham Pattern Dull Finish

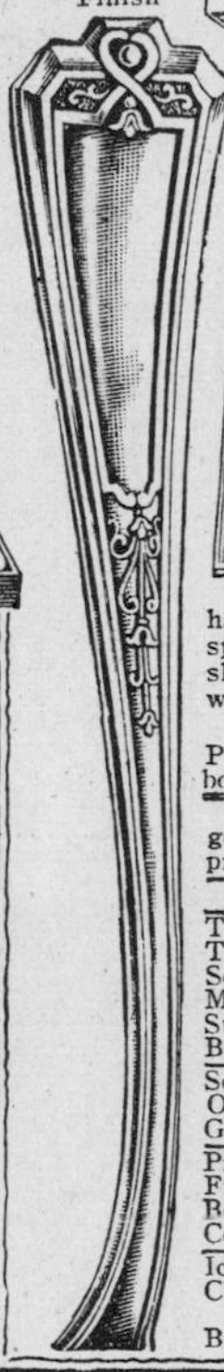

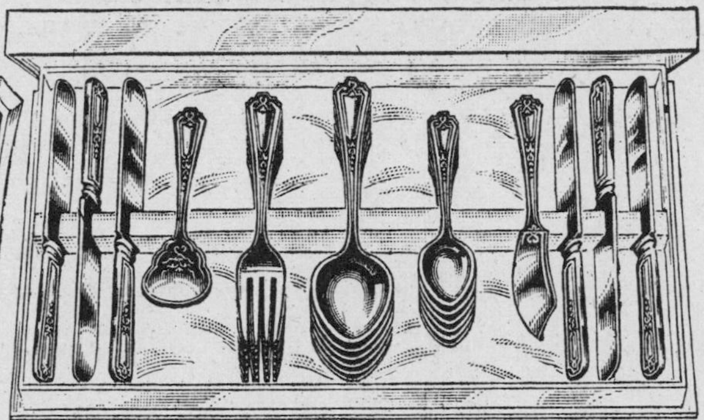

Twenty-Six Piece Set. Six solid handle knives, six forks, six teaspoons, six tablespoons, sugar shell and butter knife. Shipping weight, 3½ pounds.
5K1780 — Chatham Pattern.
Per set (without box).................. **$6.32**

A Twenty-Six Piece Set. Six teaspoons, six tablespoons, six solid handle knives, six medium spoon handle forks, one sugar shell and butter knife. In tray box. Shipping weight, 5½ pounds.
5K1789 — Chatham Pattern.
Per set (with box)...................... **$6.92**

A Silver Plated Ware that will give you good service, far beyond what our low prices may lead you to expect. Order by Number	Chatham Pattern Dull Finish		Shpg. Wt.
Teaspoons. Set of six	5K1702	$0.80	8 oz.
Tablespoons. Set of six	5K1714	1.60	1 lb.
Solid Handle Knives. Set of six	5K1719	1.95	1¾ lbs.
Medium Forks. Set of six	5K1720	1.60	1 lb.
Sugar Shell. Each	5K1724	.26	4 oz.
Butter Knife. Each	5K1726	.29	5 oz.
Soup Spoons. Round Bowl. Set of six	5K1728	1.60	1 lb.
Orange and Grape Fruit Spoons. Set of six.	5K1742	1.65	¾ lb.
Gravy Ladle. Each	5K1748	.72	8 oz.
Pickle Fork. Each	5K1752	.45	5 oz.
Fruit Knives. Set of six	5K1760	1.60	¾ lb.
Berry Spoon. Each	5K1762	.85	8 oz.
Cold Meat Fork Each	5K1764	.65	6 oz.
Iced Tea Spoons. Set of six	5K1771	1.40	1 lb.
Children's Set. 3 pieces. Knife, fork and spoon	5K1776	.75	¾ lb.
Butter Spreaders. Set of six	5K1781	1.75	¾ lb.

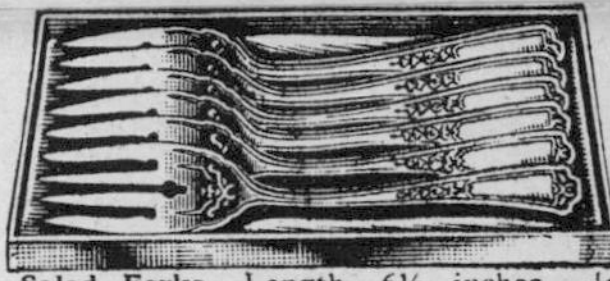

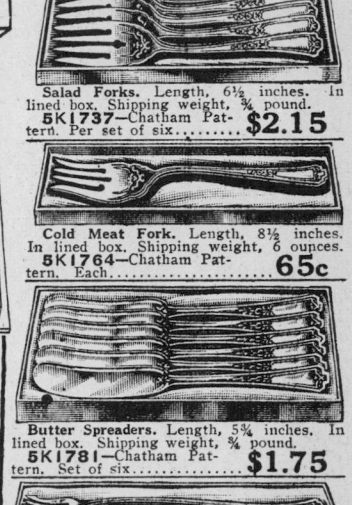

Salad Forks. Length, 6½ inches. In lined box. Shipping weight, ¾ pound.
5K1737—Chatham Pattern. Per set of six........ **$2.15**

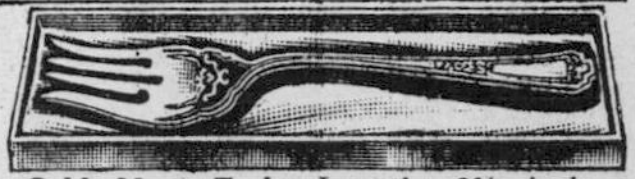

Cold Meat Fork. Length, 8½ inches. In lined box. Shipping weight, 6 ounces.
5K1764—Chatham Pattern. Each...................... **65c**

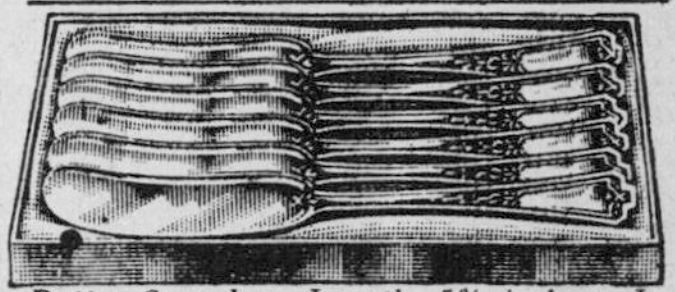

Butter Spreaders. Length, 5¾ inches. In lined box. Shipping weight, ¾ pound.
5K1781—Chatham Pattern. Set of six.................. **$1.75**

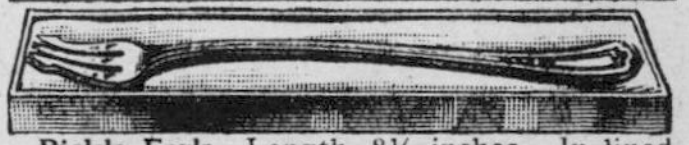

Pickle Fork. Length, 8¼ inches. In lined box. Shipping weight, 5 ounces.
5K1752—Chatham Pattern.
Each.............................. **45c**

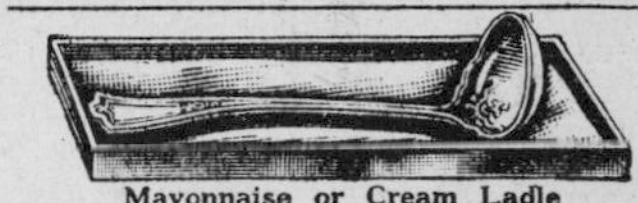

Mayonnaise or Cream Ladle
Length, 6 inches. In box. Shpg. wt., 5 oz.
5K1746—Chatham Pattern.
Each............................ **59c**

SILVER PLATED
and Stainless Steel Cutlery

The stainless, steel blades on the sets we show here are guaranteed not to rust or stain from any cause whatsoever. Unlike silver plate on steel blades, these knives can be sharpened without destroying them. No unsightly black edges ever occur. Stainless steel blades cannot be silver plated.

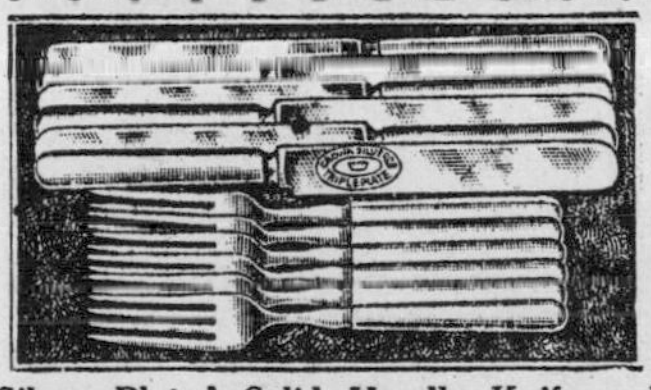

Silver Plated Solid Handle Knife and Fork Set
Knives are 9¼ inches long. Forks are 7⅝ inches long. Shipping wt., 2½ lbs.
5K525—6 knives and 6 forks.................. **$1.35**

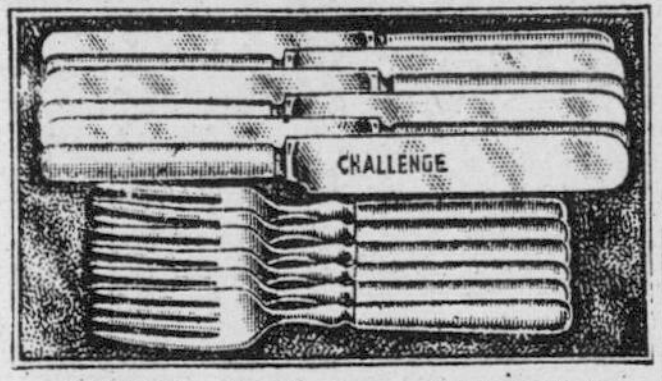

Solid Handle Knife and Fork Set
Silver Plated 4-Pennyweight quality. Shipping weight, 2½ pounds.
5K527—Set of six knives and six forks.................. **$1.59**

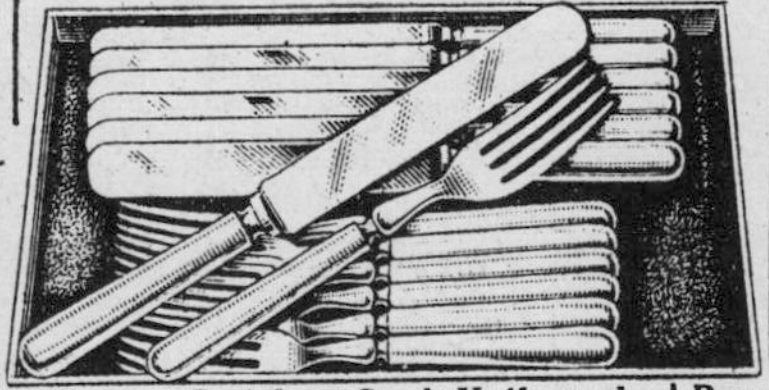

Rogers Stainless Steel Knife and Fork Set
Six solid handle **stainless steel** knives, straight blade, with silver plated handles, and six silver plated medium forks. Shipping weight, 2¾ pounds.
5K514............................ **$6.30**

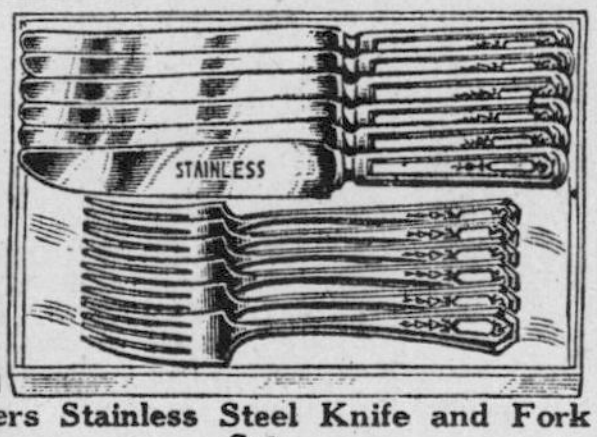

Rogers Stainless Steel Knife and Fork Set
Six solid handle French blade **stainless steel** knives and six silver plated dull finish spoon handle forks. Shipping weight, 2¾ pounds.
5K505—La France Pattern... **$7.25**

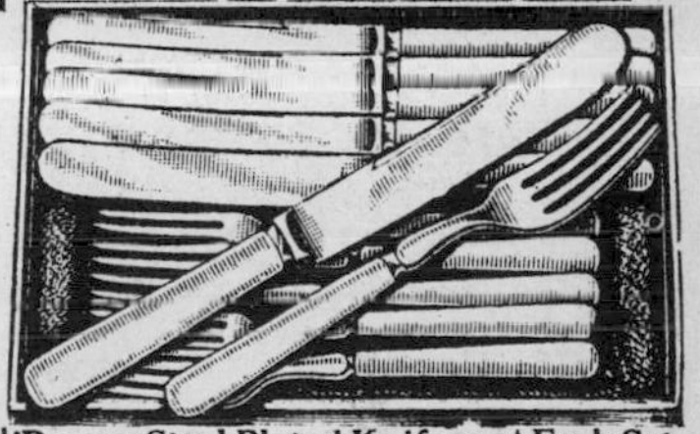

'Rogers Steel Plated Knife and Fork Set
12-pennyweight quality. Knives, 9¼ inches long. Forks, 7½ inches long.
5K561—Set of 6 knives and 6 forks. Shpg. wt., 2¾ lbs.... **$4.68**

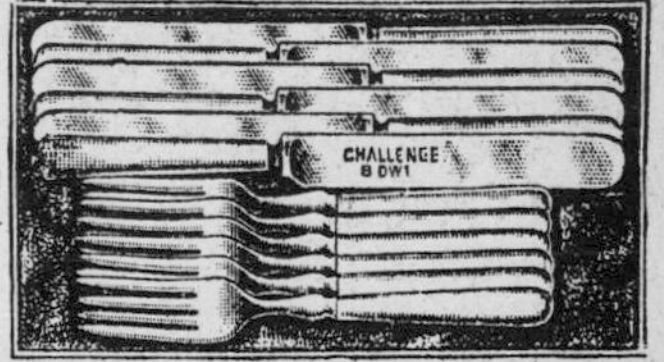

Silver Plated Knife and Fork Set
8-pennyweight quality. Six knives, 9¼ inches long; six forks, 7⅝ inches long. Shipping wt., 2½ pounds.
5K520—Per set............ **$2.49**

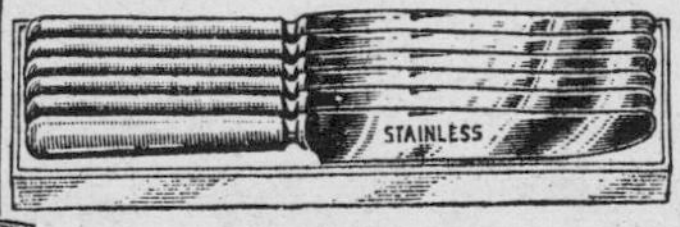

Steak Knives
Stainless steel with silver plated handle. Knives are both useful and ornamental. Length, 9¼ inches. Shipping weight, 1½ pound.
5K533—Set of six.......... **$3.25**

Silver Plated Nut Pick and Cracker Set

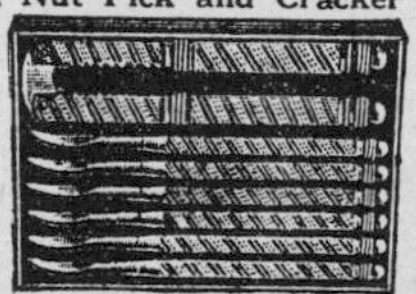

Six picks and one cracker, in glazed paper covered, cloth lined box. Shipping wt., 12 ounces.
5K577—Silver Plated Nut Set... **65c**

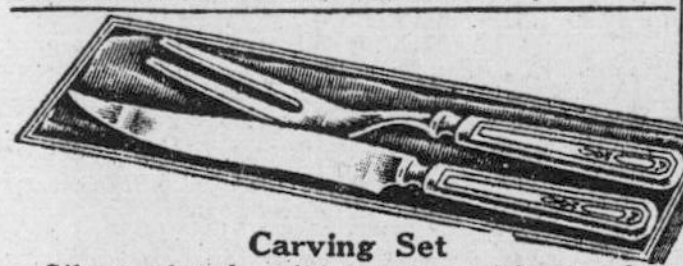

Carving Set
Silver plated solid handle with **stainless steel** blade and tines. Blade, 6⅝ inches long. Entire length of knife, 10⅝ inches. Shipping weight, 1¼ pounds.
5K550........................ **$2.65**

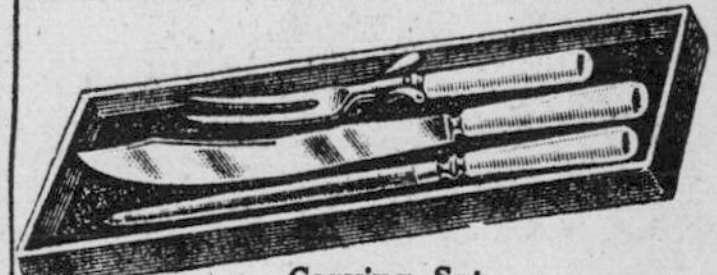

Carving Set
Silver plated, dull finish, hollow handle. Handle and blade are welded together. The blade is fine **stainless steel**, 9 inches long. Entire length of knife, 13¾ inches. Other pieces in proportion. Shpg. wt., 2¼ lbs.
5K558.................... **$4.20**

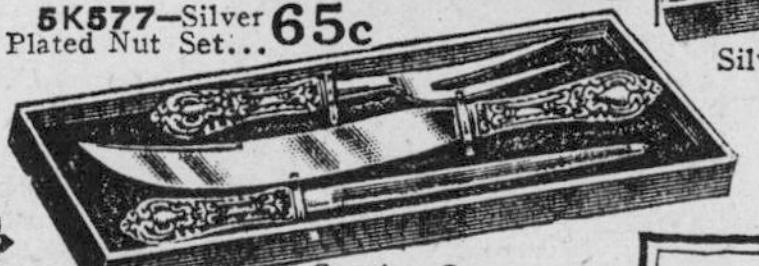

Carving Set
Silver plated hollow handle with **stainless steel knife.** The knife blade is 8 inches long. Entire length of knife, 13 inches long. Other pieces in proportion. Shpg. wt., 2½ pounds.
5K556........................ **$3.00**

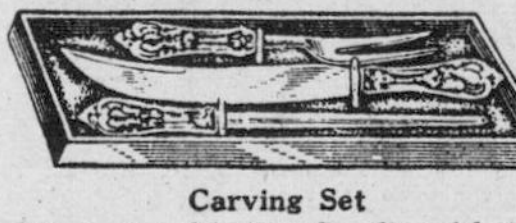

Carving Set
Silver plated hollow handle with **steel** knife. Entire blade, 9 inches long; entire length of knife, 13¾ inches. Shipping weight, 2½ pounds.
5K554.................... **$2.45**

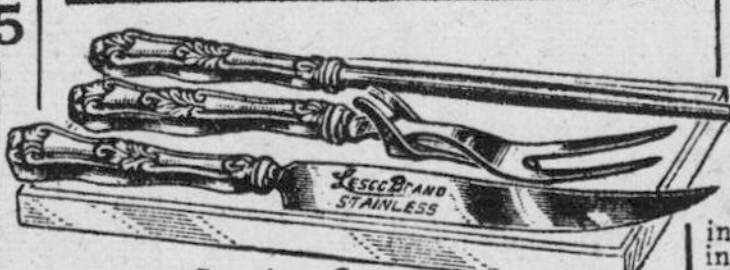

Carving Set
Nickel plated hollow handle with **stainless steel** blade and tines. The knife blade is 8¼ inches long. Entire length of knife, 13¼ inches long and the other pieces in proportion. Shpg. wt., 2½ lbs.
5K552.......................... **$1.95**

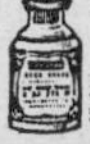

Electroline Polish
Cleaner, preserver and renovator for silverware. Paste form. Shipping weight, 1 pound.
5K500.................. **19c**

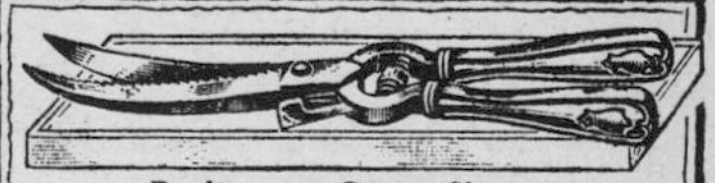

Poultry or Game Shears
Nickel plated bright polish throughout. The handle is hollow, and shears are very strong and durable. Entire length, 11 inches. Shipping wt., 1½ lbs.
5K560.................. **$3.75**

GENUINE ROGERS
NICKEL SILVER TABLEWARE

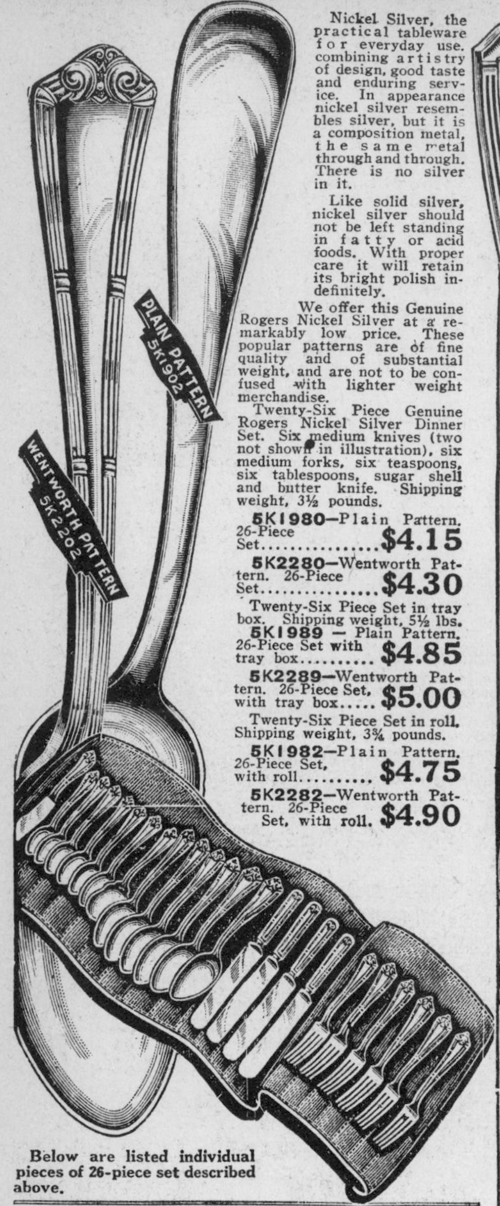

Nickel Silver, the practical tableware for everyday use, combining artistry of design, good taste and enduring service. In appearance nickel silver resembles silver, but it is a composition metal, the same metal through and through. There is no silver in it.

Like solid silver, nickel silver should not be left standing in fatty or acid foods. With proper care it will retain its bright polish indefinitely.

We offer this Genuine Rogers Nickel Silver at a remarkably low price. These popular patterns are of fine quality and of substantial weight, and are not to be confused with lighter weight merchandise.

Twenty-Six Piece Genuine Rogers Nickel Silver Dinner Set. Six medium knives (two not shown in illustration), six medium forks, six teaspoons, six tablespoons, sugar shell and butter knife. Shipping weight, 3½ pounds.

5K1980—Plain Pattern. 26-Piece Set............ **$4.15**
5K2280—Wentworth Pattern. 26-Piece Set......... **$4.30**

Twenty-Six Piece Set in tray box. Shipping weight, 5½ lbs.
5K1989—Plain Pattern. 26-Piece Set with tray box......... **$4.85**
5K2289—Wentworth Pattern. 26-Piece Set with tray box..... **$5.00**

Twenty-Six Piece Set in roll. Shipping weight, 3¾ pounds.
5K1982—Plain Pattern. 26-Piece Set, with roll........... **$4.75**
5K2282—Wentworth Pattern. 26-Piece Set, with roll. **$4.90**

PLAIN PATTERN 5K1902
WENTWORTH PATTERN 5K2202

Below are listed individual pieces of 26-piece set described above.

Order by Number	Plain Pattern		Wentworth Pattern		Shpg. Wt.
Teaspoons. Set of six	5K1902	$0.48	5K2202	$0.50	8 oz.
Dessert Spoons. Six.	5K1908	.90	5K2208	.95	¾ lb.
Tablespoons. Set of six	5K1914	1.00	5K2214	1.05	1 lb.
Medium Forks. Set of six	5K1918	1.00	5K2218	1.05	1 lb.
Sugar Shell. Each..	5K1924	.15	5K2224	.16	3 oz.
Butter Knife. Each..	5K1926	.16	5K2226	.17	3 oz.
Medium Knives. Set of six	5K1932	1.45	5K2232	1.50	1½ lbs.

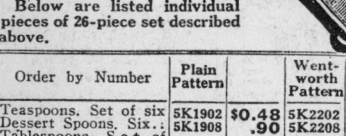
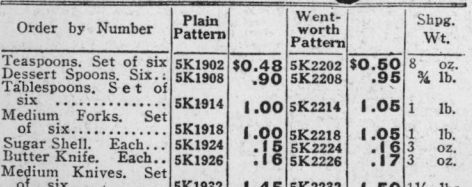
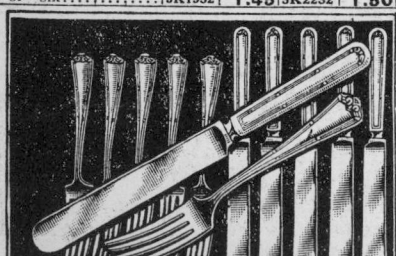

Knife and Fork Set
Rogers Nickel Silver. Six solid handle knives and six medium forks. Knives, 9½ inches long; forks, 7½ inches long. Shipping weight, 2½ pounds.
5K1907—Plain pattern. Per set......... **$2.39**
5K2207—Wentworth Pattern. Per set...... **2.45**

ALASKA
Silverlike Tableware

Alaska Extra Heavy Weight Tableware

The need for an extra heavy weight tableware induced us to have made this new pattern extra heavy weight Alaska Silverlike set.

You can expect this tableware to last the term of your natural life. It is of the same white silverlike metal through and through, but contains no silver. It will show only the slightest effects of wear.

The weight of metal is great in each piece. It cannot be bent or distorted in shape by severe use.

You can keep each piece clean by scouring it with any cleaning polish.

Restaurants, hotels and boarding house owners will find this ware ideal if long, continued hard service is demanded.

Alaska Silverlike Metal is easily kept clean, but it should not be left in vinegar or acids or salt for long periods of time; this is also true of solid silverware.

PRUDENCE PATTERN

> **Knife and Fork Set.** Alaska extra heavy weight. Six knives and six forks, the same metal throughout. Shipping weight, 2½ lbs.
> **5K1355**—Prudence pattern. **$2.90**

> **Regarding Engraving**
> We can engrave all tableware on this page in Old English at 5c per letter. Script at 3c per letter.

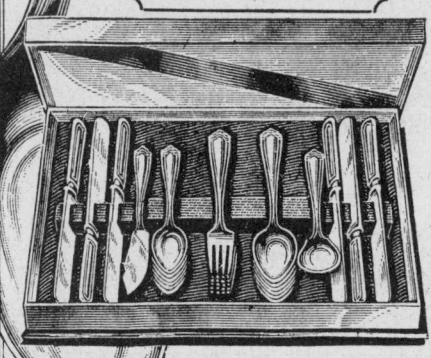

The set consists of 26 pieces; 6 knives, 6 forks, 6 teaspoons, 6 tablespoons, a sugar shell and butter knife, all regulation size. You may order it with or without box.

5K1376—26-Piece Set, without box. Shpg. wt. 3¾ lbs......... **$5.10**
5K1378—26-Piece Set, complete with box. Shpg. wt., 5½ lbs. **5.80**

Following are individual pieces of 26-piece set shown above.

Alaska Heavy Weight	Prudence Pattern		Shpg. Wt.
Teaspoons. Set of 6	5K1370	$0.65	¾ lb.
Tablespoons. Set of 6	5K1371	1.30	1 lb.
Medium Forks. Set of 6	5K1372	1.30	1 lb.
Medium Knives. Set of 6	5K1373	1.60	1¾ lbs.
Sugar Shell. Each..	5K1374	.19	4 oz.
Butter Knife. Each..	5K1375	.20	4 oz.

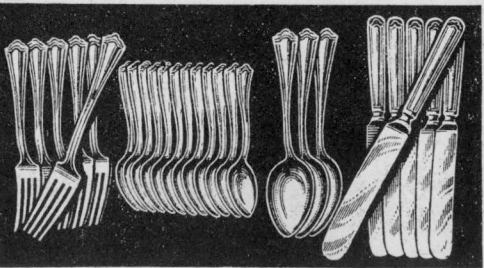

Our 27-Piece Special
Alaska Silverware
We have prepared a special outfit in the Prudence Pattern (listed directly above) which is complete in every respect, but without box or the flannel roll. Set consists of 6 knives, 6 forks, 12 teaspoons and 3 tablespoons. Shipping weight, 4 pounds.
5K1379—Special Set, 27 Pieces Alaska Silverware............ **$4.72**

In color and appearance Alaska Silverlike Metal Tableware is difficult to distinguish from solid silver. Yet it contains no silver. It is not plated. It is made of the same metal throughout and, with ordinary use and care, will last a lifetime.

GUARANTEE—We guarantee Alaska Silverlike Metal Tableware for the term of your natural lifetime.

We furnish these 26-Piece Tableware Sets in either pattern, with cloth lined box or roll, or without box or roll. Set consists of 6 teaspoons, 6 tablespoons, 6 knives, 6 forks, 1 sugar shell, 1 butter knife. Shipping weight, without box or roll, 3½ pounds; with box, 5½ pounds; in roll, 3¾ lbs.

5K1306—26-Piece Set. Laval Pattern, without box or roll...... **$4.40**
5K1316—26-Piece Set. Colonial Pattern, without box or roll....... **$4.88**
5K1309—26-Piece Set. Laval Pattern, with box.......... **$5.10**
5K1319—26-Piece Set. Colonial Pattern, with box........... **$5.58**
5K1338—26-Piece Set. Laval Pattern, with roll.................. **$5.00**
5K1339—26-Piece Set. Colonial Pattern, with roll............ **$5.48**

LAVAL PATTERN 5K1300
COLONIAL PATTERN 5K1310

Knife and Fork Set
Alaska Silverlike Metal
Six medium knives and six medium forks. Silverlike Metal Tableware. Shipping weight, 2 pounds.
5K1352—Laval Pattern........... **$2.58**
5K1354 Colonial Pattern... **2.80**

Below are listed individual pieces of 26-piece set described above.

Article	Laval Pattern		Shpg. Wt.
Teaspoons. Set of six..	5K1300	$0.52	8 oz.
Tablespoons. Set of six..	5K1301	1.04	1 lb.
Med. Forks. Set of six	5K1302	1.04	1 lb.
Med. Knives. Set of six	5K1303	1.55	1½ lbs.
Sugar Shell. Each.....	5K1304	.17	3 oz.
Butter Knife. Each.....	5K1305	.18	3 oz.

Article	Colonial Pattern		Shpg. Wt.
Teaspoons. Set of six..	5K1310	$0.59	8 oz.
Tablespoons. Set of six..	5K1311	1.18	1 lb.
Med. Forks. Set of six..	5K1312	1.18	1 lb.
Med. Knives. Set of six	5K1313	1.65	1½ lbs.
Sugar Shell. Each.....	5K1314	.19	3 oz.
Butter Knife. Each.....	5K1315	.20	3 oz.

Our Special 14-Piece Set
We have prepared a special set of 6 teaspoons, butter knife, sugar shell and 6 tablespoons. The patterns are the beautiful Colonial and Laval, listed above. Our price does not include the presentation box or flannel roll. Shipping weight, 1½ pounds.
5K1356—Laval Pattern................ **$1.88**
5K1358—Colonial Pattern.............. **$2.10**

SOLID SILVER TABLEWARE

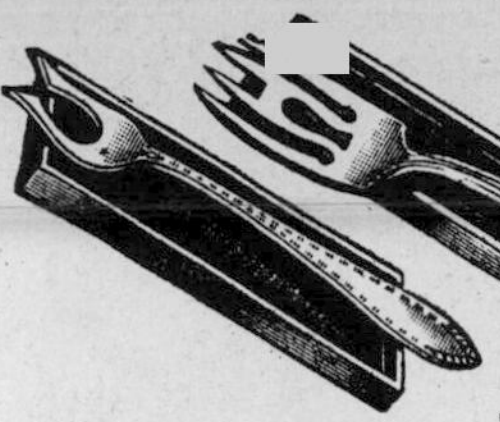

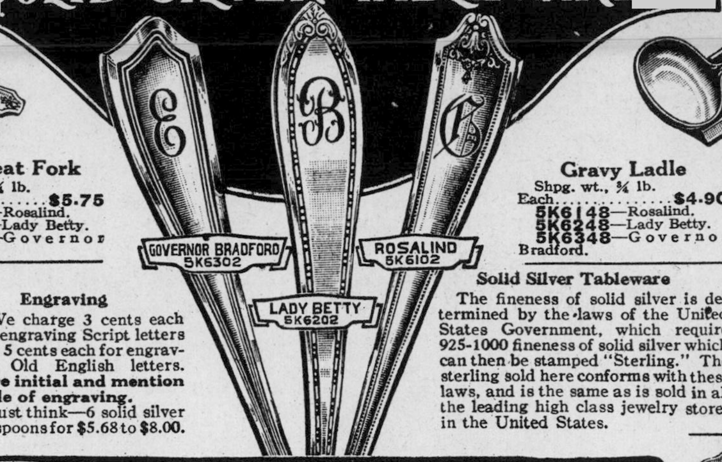

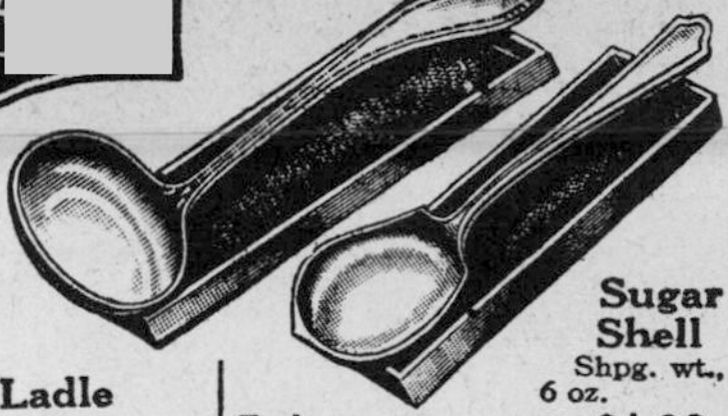

Pickle Fork
Shpg. wt., 5 oz. Each. **$2.00**
5K6152—Rosalind.
5K6252—Lady Betty.
5K6352—Governor Bradford.

Cold Meat Fork
Shpg. wt., ¾ lb.
Each......... **$5.75**
5K6164—Rosalind.
5K6264—Lady Betty.
5K6364—Governor Bradford.

GOVERNOR BRADFORD 5K6302
ROSALIND 5K6102
LADY BETTY 5K6202

Gravy Ladle
Shpg. wt., ¾ lb.
Each........ **$4.90**
5K6148—Rosalind.
5K6248—Lady Betty.
5K6348—Governor

Sugar Shell
Shpg. wt., 6 oz.
Each......... **$1.90**
5K6124—Rosalind.
5K6224—Lady Betty.
5K6324—Governor Bradford.

Friendship Spoons
5K6300
5K6100
5K6200

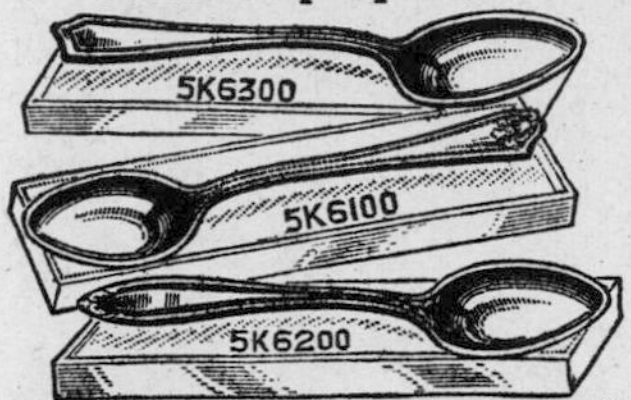

A Friendship or Souvenir Spoon is a gift that is always appreciated. Shpg. wt., 5 oz.
Each.................... **98c**
5K6100—Rosalind.
5K6200—Lady Betty.
5K6300—Governor Bradford.

Engraving
We charge 3 cents each for engraving Script letters and 5 cents each for engraving Old English letters.
Give initial and mention style of engraving.
Just think—6 solid silver teaspoons for $5.68 to $8.00.

Solid Silver Tableware
The fineness of solid silver is determined by the laws of the United States Government, which require 925-1000 fineness of solid silver which can then be stamped "Sterling." The sterling sold here conforms with these laws, and is the same as is sold in all the leading high class jewelry stores in the United States.

Salad Forks
Shpg. wt., ¾ lb.
Set of six............ **$13.50**
5K6137—Rosalind.
5K6237—Lady Betty.
5K6337—Governor Bradford.

Butter Knife
Shpg. wt., 6 oz. Each...... **$3.20**
5K6126—Rosalind.
5K6226—Lady Betty.
5K6326—Governor Bradford.

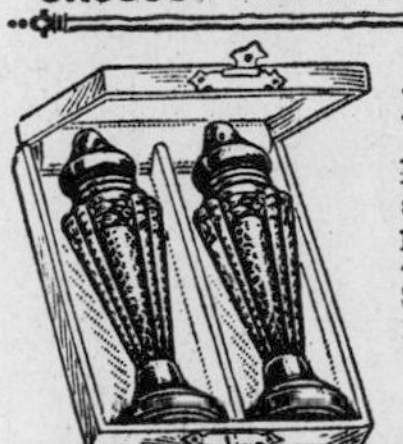

Salt and Pepper Set
Solid silver. Hammered design. Bright polish. Height, 4¾ inches. Shipping wt., 1¼ lbs.
5K6030
Pair **$4.50**

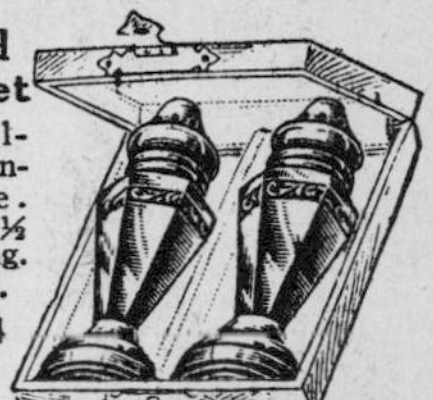

Buy Solid Silver and Have It Forever.	Rosalind. Gray Finish	Lady Betty. Bright Finish	Governor Bradford. Bright Finish	Shipping Weight	
Teaspoons, light weight. Set of six..	5K6102	5K6202	5K6302	8 oz.	$5.68
Teaspoons, medium weight. Set of six.	5K6104	5K6204	5K6304	¾ lb.	6.50
Teaspoons, heavy weight. Set of six.	5K6106	5K6206	5K6306	¾ lb.	8.00
Tablespoons. Set of six.	5K6116	5K6216	5K6316	1 lb.	16.20
Forks, medium. Set of six.	5K6118	5K6218	5K6318	1 lb.	16.20
Knives, hollow handle, stainless steel blades. Set of six.	5K6122	5K6222	5K6322	1½ lbs.	18.20
Soup spoons, round bowl. Set of six.	5K6128	5K6228	5K6328	1 lb.	16.20
Cream Ladle. Each	5K6146	5K6246	5K6346	7 oz.	2.90
Cake Server or Ice Cream Slicer, hollow handle. Each	5K6147	5K6247	5K6347	¾ lb.	3.75
Berry Spoon. Each	5K6162	5K6262	5K6362	¾ lb.	6.50
Butter Spreaders. Set of six.	5K6181	5K6281	5K6381	¾ lb.	10.00

Salt and Pepper Set
Solid silver. Octagonal shape. Height, 3½ inches. Shpg. wt., 1½ lbs.
5K6044
Pair **$3.75**

SOLID SILVER

Salt and Pepper Set
Solid silver. Bright finish, substantial weight. In attractive paper box. Shpg. wt., ¾ lb.
5K6032—Pair.. **79c**

Individual Salt and Pepper Set
Solid silver. Three salt and three pepper shakers. Bright finish, very substantial. Height, 1⅝ inches. Packed in attractive paper box. Shipping weight, 1 pound.
5K6034—Set of 6............ **$2.25**

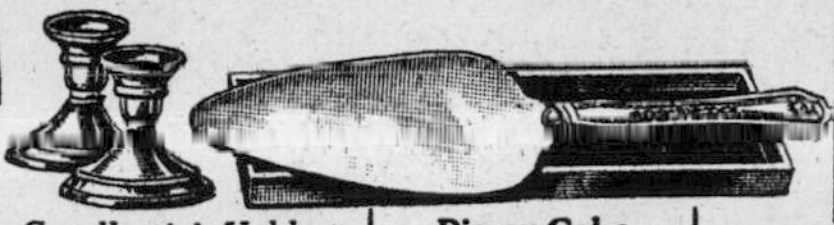

Candlestick Holders
Solid silver, except inside of base which is filled, as usual, with composition to increase stability. Bright polish. Height, 2¾ in. Shpg. wt., 2½ lbs.
5K6036—Pair. **$4.50**

Pie or Cake Server
Solid silver. Hollow handle with plated blade. Length, 10 inches. Shipping wt., in box, 1 lb.
5K6038. **$2.25**

Salt and Pepper Set
Solid silver. Bright finish. Height, 3¾ in. Shpg. wt., 1¼ lbs.
5K6040
Pair....... **$2.75**

Individual Salt and Pepper Set
Solid silver. Three salt and three pepper shakers. Hammered effect. Height, 1½ inches. In attractive paper box. Shipping wt., 1 lb.
5K6042—Set of six **$1.50**
Salt and Pepper Set
Same as above, in paper box. Shipping weight, 8 ounces.
5K6043—Per pair.... **62c**

Salt and Pepper Set
Solid silver. Hammered effect. Height, 1¾ inches. Shipping weight, ¾ pound.
5K6050—Per pair.... **$1.98**

PEARL HANDLE FANCY TABLEWARE

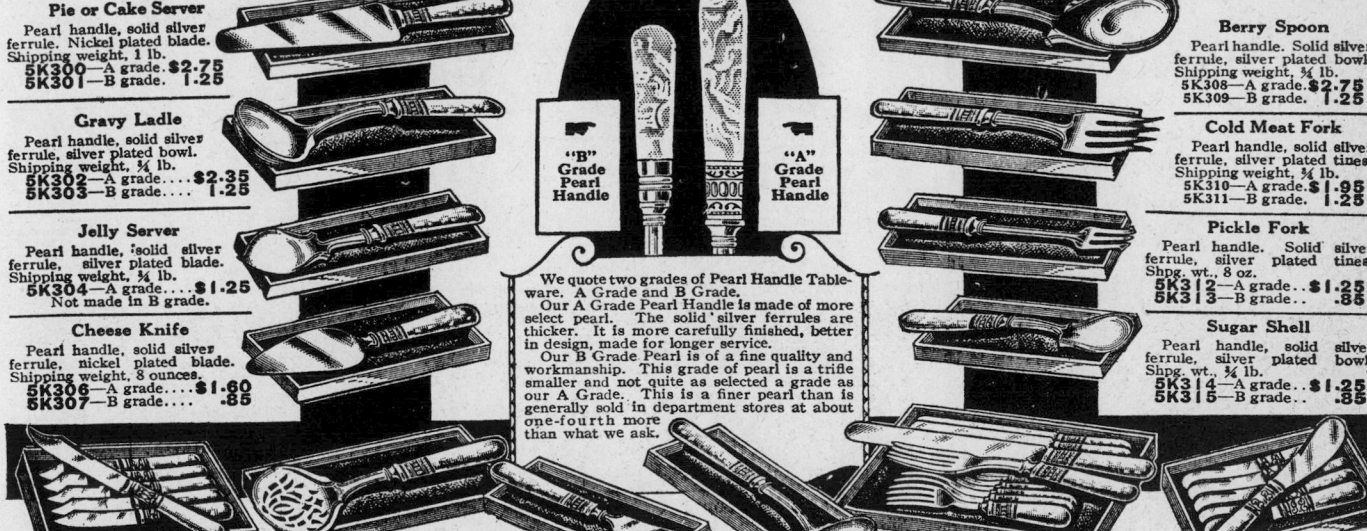

Pie or Cake Server
Pearl handle, solid silver ferrule. Nickel plated blade. Shipping weight, 1 lb.
5K300—A grade.. **$2.75**
5K301—B grade.... **1.25**

Gravy Ladle
Pearl handle, solid silver ferrule, silver plated bowl. Shipping weight, ¾ lb.
5K302—A grade.... **$2.35**
5K303—B grade.... **1.25**

Jelly Server
Pearl handle, solid silver ferrule, silver plated blade. Shipping weight, ¾ lb.
5K304—A grade.... **$1.25**
Not made in B grade.

Cheese Knife
Pearl handle, solid silver ferrule, nickel plated blade. Shipping weight, 8 ounces.
5K306—A grade.... **$1.60**
5K307—B grade.... **.85**

"B" Grade Pearl Handle
"A" Grade Pearl Handle

We quote two grades of Pearl Handle Tableware. A Grade and B Grade.
Our A Grade Pearl Handle is made of more select pearl. The solid silver ferrules are thicker. It is more carefully finished, better in design, made for longer service.
Our B Grade Pearl is of a fine quality and workmanship. This grade of pearl is a trifle smaller and not quite as selected a grade as our A Grade. This is a finer pearl than is generally sold in department stores at about one-fourth more than what we ask.

Berry Spoon
Pearl handle. Solid silver ferrule, silver plated bowl. Shipping weight, ¾ lb.
5K308—A grade.. **$2.75**
5K309—B grade.... **1.25**

Cold Meat Fork
Pearl handle, solid silver ferrule, silver plated tines. Shipping weight, ¾ lb.
5K310—A grade.. **$1.95**
5K311—B grade.... **1.25**

Pickle Fork
Pearl handle. Solid silver ferrule, silver plated tines. Shpg. wt., 8 oz.
5K312—A grade.. **$1.25**
5K313—B grade.. **.85**

Sugar Shell
Pearl handle, solid silver ferrule, silver plated bowl. Shpg. wt., ¾ lb.
5K314—A grade.. **$1.25**
5K315—B grade.. **.85**

Fruit Knives
Pearl handle, solid silver ferrules, silver plated blades. Shpg. wt., 1 lb. Set of six.
5K316—A grade.. **$4.45**
Not made in B grade.

Tomato Server
Pearl handle, solid silver ferrule, silver plated server. Shipping wt., ¾ pound.
5K318—A grade.... **$2.75**
5K319—B grade........ **1.25**

Butter Knife
Pearl handle, solid silver ferrule, silver plated blade. Shipping weight, 8 ounces.
5K320—A grade.... **$1.25**
5K321—B grade........ **.85**

Cream Ladle
Pearl handle, solid silver ferrule, silver plated bowl. Shipping weight, ¾ pound.
5K322—A grade. **$1.95**
5K323—B grade. **1.15**

Knife and Fork Set
Pearl handle, solid silver ferrules, silver plated blades and tines. Shipping weight, 3½ pounds. Set of 6 knives and 6 forks.
5K324—A grade.... **$15.98**
Not made in B grade.

Butter Spreaders
Pearl handle, solid silver ferrule, silver plated blades. Shpg. wt., 1 lb. Set of six.
5K326—A grade **$4.45**
Not made in B grade.

Order Blanks Are in Back of This Catalog

High Grade Silver Plated Tableware

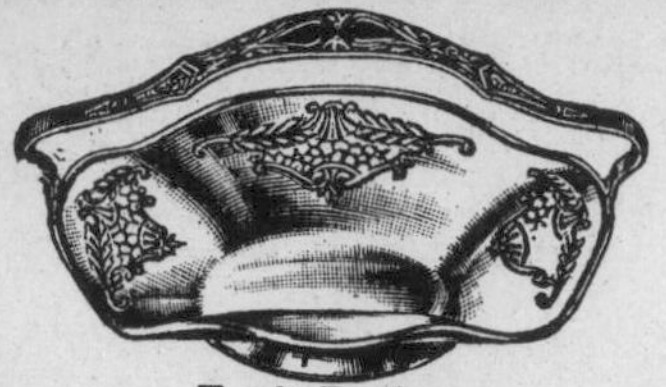

Fruit Basket

Silver plated, "A" quality, Butler dull finish. Engraved design ornamentation, with applied border. Diam. 9¾ in. Shpg. wt., 4 lbs.
5K7600 .... **$4.69**

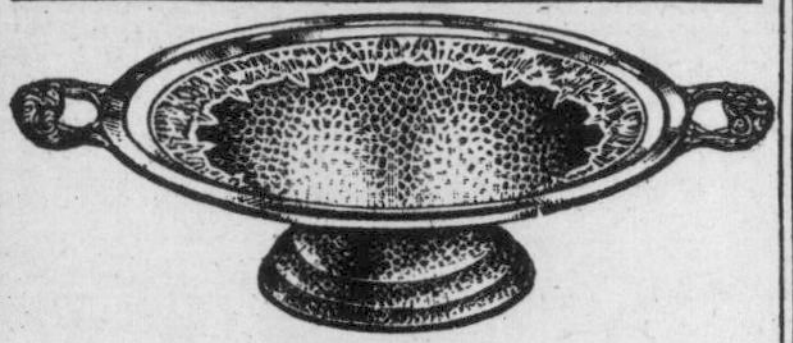

Fruit Bowl

Silver plated, "A" quality, Butler dull finish; hammered design. Pierced ornamentation. Diam., 10⅝ inches; height, 3 inches. Shipping weight, 4 pounds.
5K7602 .... **$3.85**

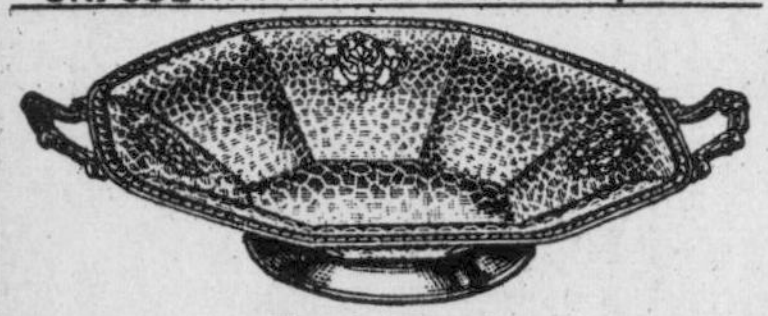

Fruit Bowl

Silver plated, "A" quality, dull finish, hammered design. Octagonal shape. Diam., 10 in.; height, 2 in. Fluted border. Shpg. wt., 4 lbs.
5K7604 .... **$5.45**

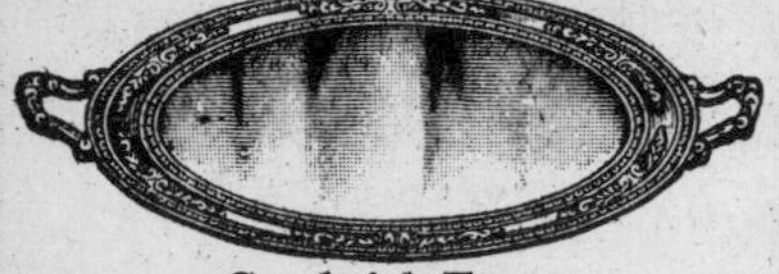

Sandwich Tray

Round. Silver plated, "A" quality, dull finish. Embossed design border. Diameter, 10¼ inches. Shipping weight, 3½ pounds.
5K7606 .... **$4.00**

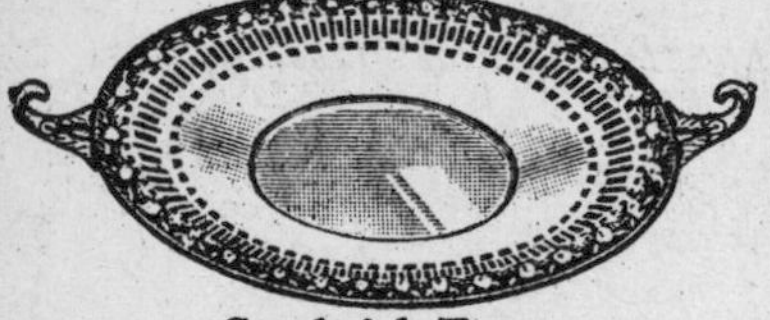

Sandwich Tray

Round. Silver plated, "B" quality, bright finish. Pierced design. Diameter, 10 inches. Shipping weight, 3 pounds.
5K7608 .... **$3.45**

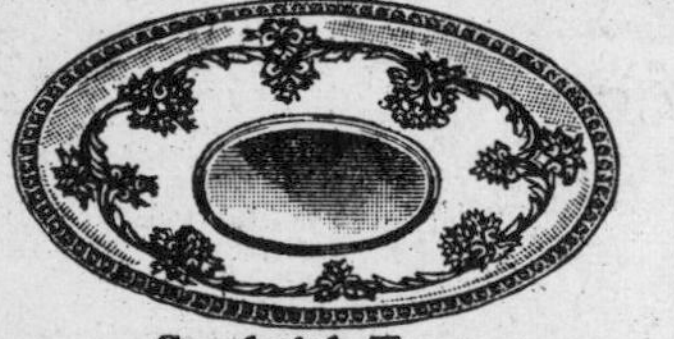

Sandwich Tray

Silver plated, "A" quality, Butler finish. Embossed design. Diameter, 10 inches. Shipping weight, 2¾ pounds.
5K7610 .... **$2.95**

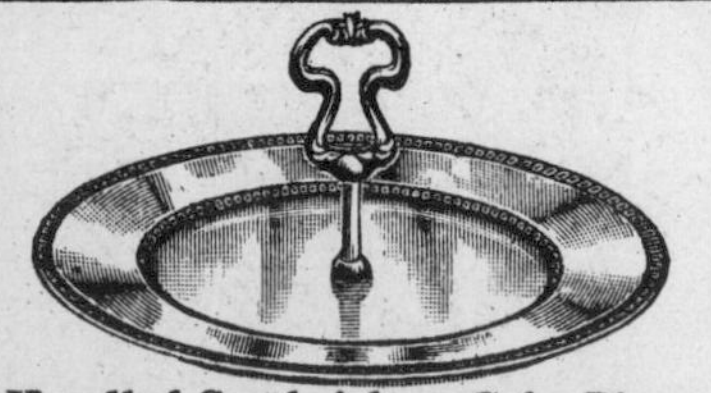

Handled Sandwich or Cake Plate

Silver plated, "A" quality, bright polish. Ornamented border. Diameter, 10½ inches; height, including handle, 5⅞ inches. Shipping weight, 4½ pounds.
5K7612 .... **$4.75**

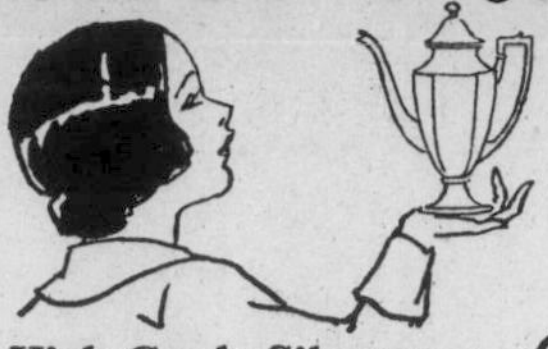

High Grade Silverware

We sell two grades of silverware. Our "A" quality, heavily silver plated on fine nickel silver, compares favorably with that generally carried by exclusive jewelers. Our "B" quality, plated on genuine Britannia Metal to insure lasting service, while not as fine as our "A" grade, will give excellent satisfaction. We do not carry low grade, cheaply made silverware. Every article, regardless of its price, has been selected with the idea of producing a beautiful and serviceable article.

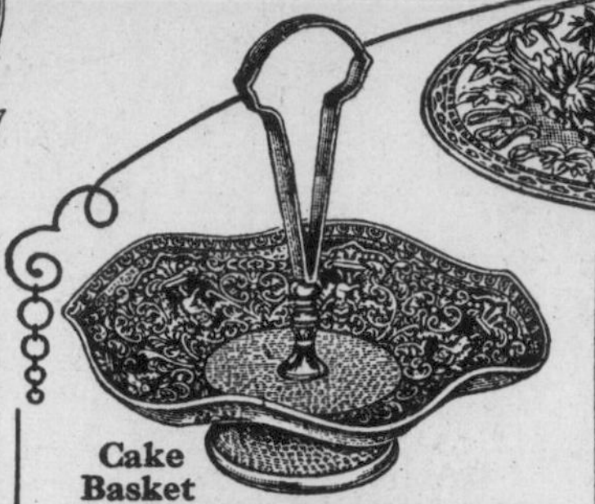

Cake Basket

Silver plated, "A" quality, dull finish. Dutch design. Diameter of tray, 10⅞ inches. Shpg. wt., 6½ lbs.
5K7614 .... **$8.50**

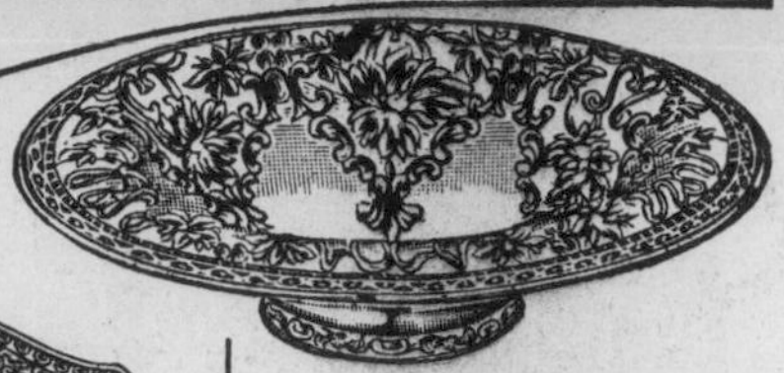

Fruit Bowl or Centerpiece

Silver plated, "B" quality, bright finish. Fancy engraved design. Diameter, 14¼ in. Height, 3⅜ in. Shipping weight, 6½ pounds.
5K7616 .... **$5.25**

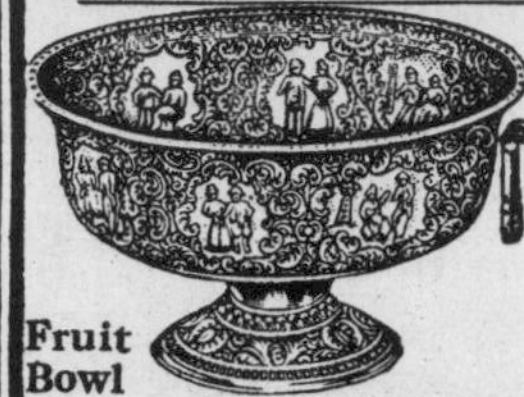

Fruit Bowl

Silver plated, "B" quality, dull finish. Dutch design. Gold plated inside. Diameter, 9⅝ in. Height, 5⅝ in. Shipping weight, 6 lbs.
5K7618 .... **$6.15**

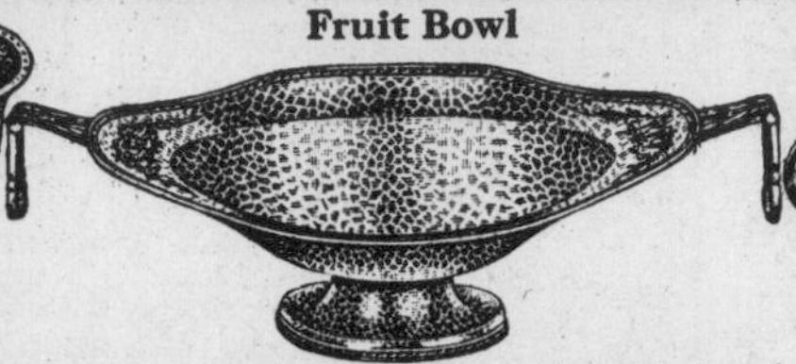

Fruit Bowl

Silver plated, "A" quality, dull finish. Hammered design. Ornamented applied border. Bowl measures 12¾x9½ inches; height, 4½ inches. Shipping weight, 5 pounds.
5K7620 .... **$6.65**

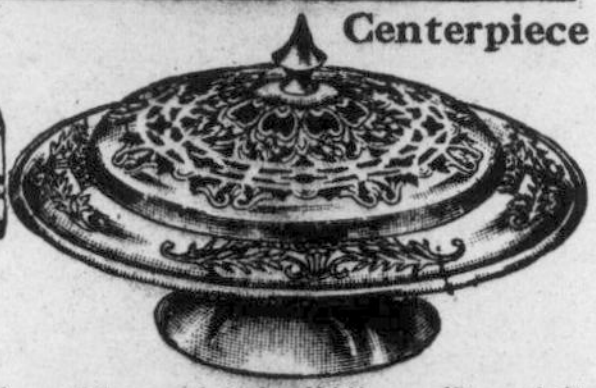

Centerpiece

Silver plated, "A" quality, dull finish. Engraved design. Pierced cover for flowers. Diameter, 10¼ inches; height, 6 inches. Shipping weight, 5 pounds.
5K7622 .... **$7.75**

TEA OR COFFEE SETS

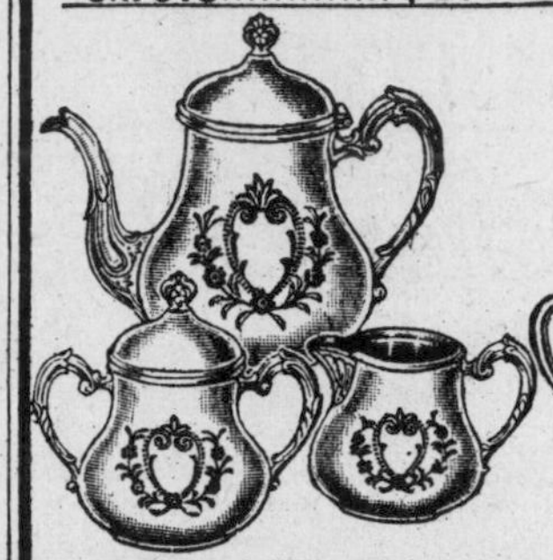

Silver plated, "B" quality, Butler dull finish, with engraved ornamentation. Teapot is 7⅝ inches high and holds 2 pints. Sugar bowl is 6 inches high. Cream pitcher is gold plated inside. Shipping weight, 6 pounds.
5K7632
Three-Piece Set **$8.48**

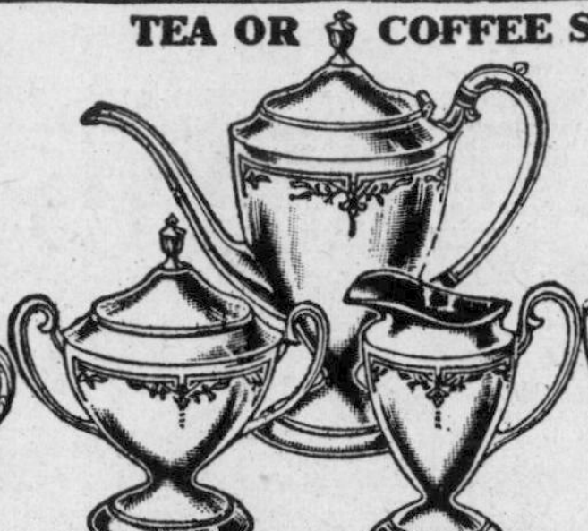

Bright polish, "B" quality, dainty engraved ornamentation. Pot is 9 inches high and holds 1⅜ pints. Sugar bowl is 7 inches high. Cream pitcher, gold plated inside. Shipping weight 7¾ pounds.
5K7624
Three-Piece Set **$12.75**

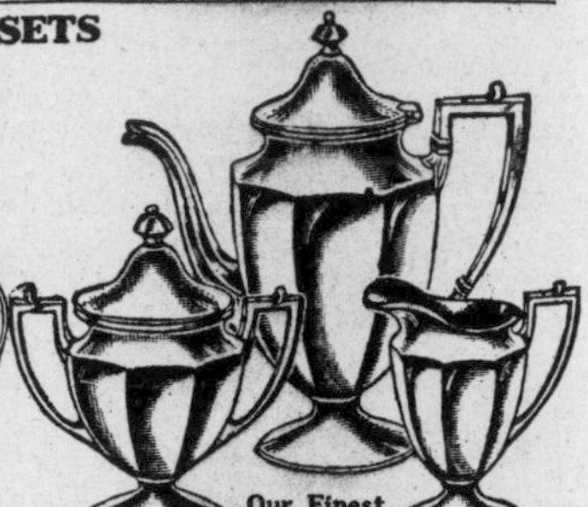

Our Finest Tea Set

Silver plated, bright polish, "A" quality. Pot, 10 inches high. Cream pitcher gold plated inside. Sugar bowl, 7¼ inches high. Shipping weight, 7 pounds.
5K7640 .... **$23.00**

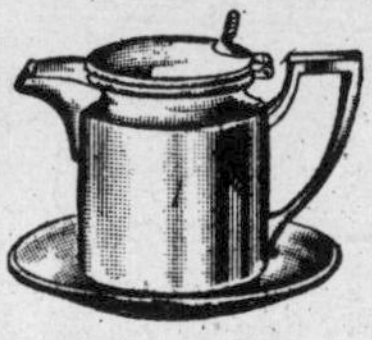

Syrup Pitcher

Silver plated, "B" quality, Butler finish. Height, 3¾ inches. Diameter of tray, 5 inches. Shipping weight, 2¼ pounds.
5K7648 **$3.95**

Coffee Set

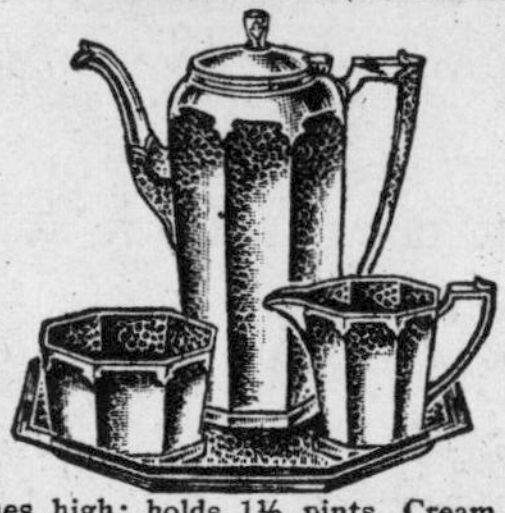

Four-Piece Coffee or Chocolate Set. Silver plated, "B" quality. Hammered design. Pot is 7½ inches high; holds 1½ pints. Cream pitcher is 2⅝ inches high. Sugar bowl and cream pitcher are gold plated inside. Octagonal tray is 8⅝ inches in diameter. Shipping weight, 7 pounds.
5K7650 .... **$8.45**

Tea or Coffee Set

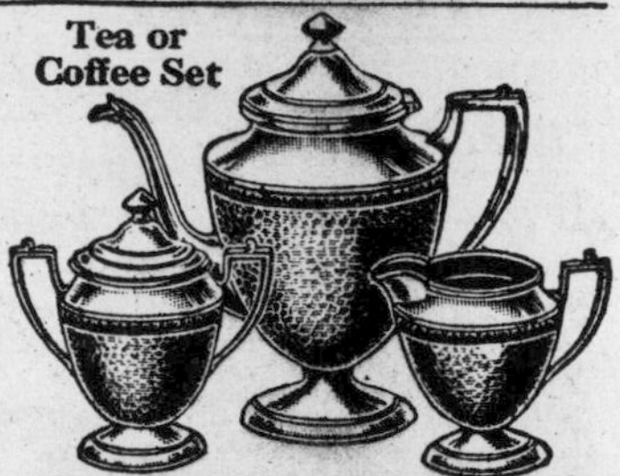

Silver plated, "A" quality. Hammered design. Pot is 8½ inches high. Cream pitcher is gold plated inside. Shipping weight, 6 pounds.
5K7652 .... **$11.85**

Crumb Set

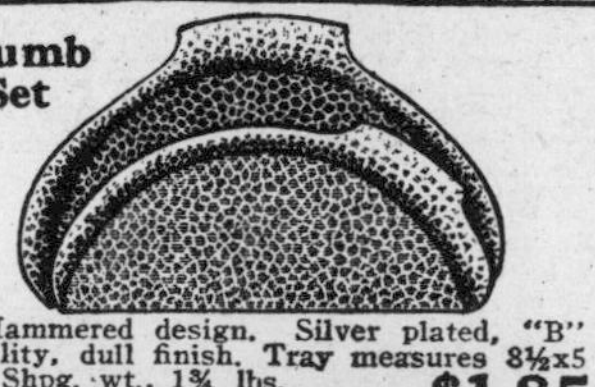

Hammered design. Silver plated, "B" quality, dull finish. Tray measures 8½x5 in. Shpg. wt., 1¾ lbs.
5K7660 .... **$1.85**

Crumb Sweeper

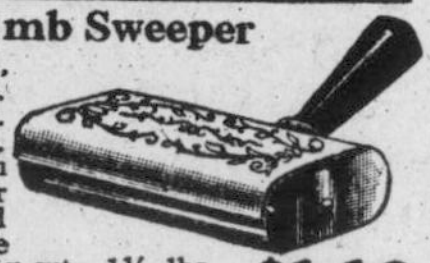

Silver plated, "B" quality. Etched design. Wood handle. Bristle brush sweeper. Cover can be raised to remove the crumbs. Shipping wt., 1½ lbs.
5K7662 .... **$1.19**

Candlesticks

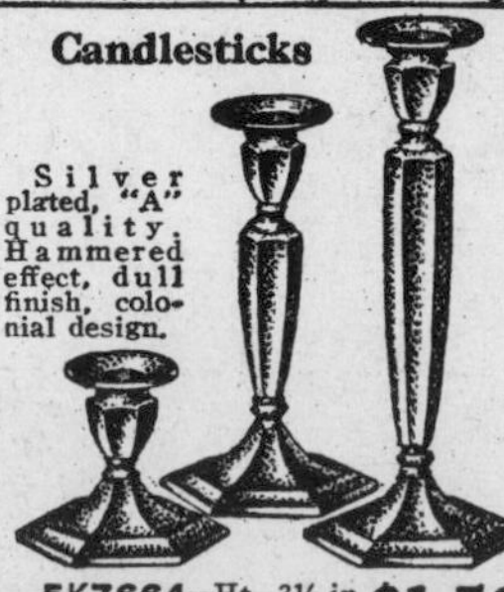

Silver plated, "A" quality. Hammered effect, dull finish, colonial design.

5K7664—Ht., 3½ in. Shpg. wt., 1¾ lbs. Each **$1.58**
5K7666—Ht., 7¼ in. Shpg. wt., 2½ lbs. Each **1.90**
5K7668—Ht., 10¾ in. Shpg. wt., 3 lbs. Each **2.60**

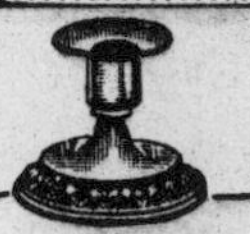

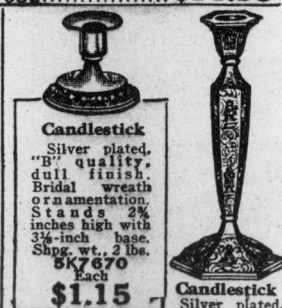

Candlestick

Silver plated, "B" quality, dull finish. Bridal wreath ornamentation. Stands 2⅝ inches high with 3⅛-inch base. Shpg. wt., 2 lbs.
5K7670
Each
$1.15

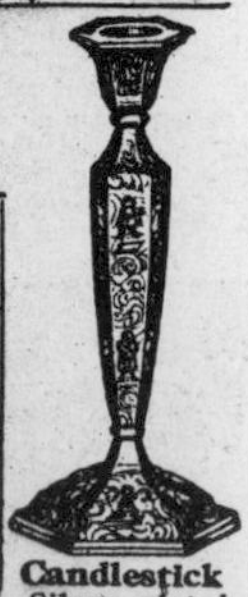

Candlestick

Silver plated, "B" quality, dull finish. Dutch design. Height, 10 inches. Shipping weight, 3½ pounds.
5K7672—Each..... **$2.75**

Patterns of Distinction and Beauty

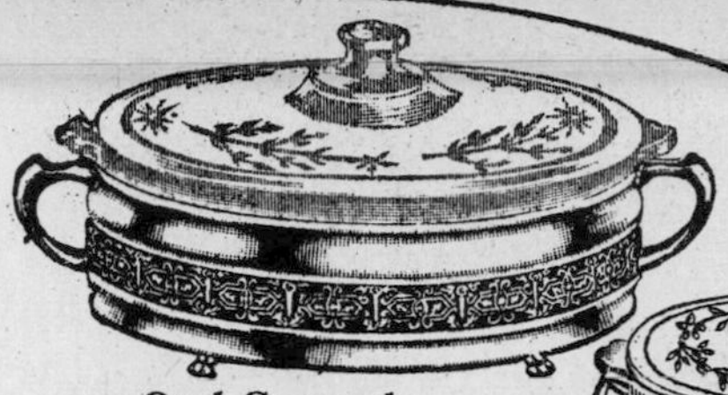

Oval Casserole
Silver plated "A" quality, bright finish with dull finish etched band design. Pyrex glass lining holds 3 pints. Measures 10¼x7¼ inches. Has floral cut cover. Shpg. wt., 9 lbs.
5K7701 .... $5.65

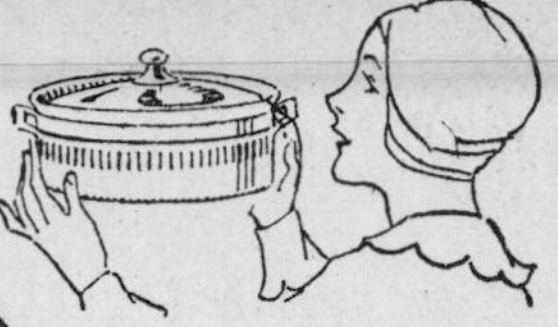

You will be proud to have our Silverware grace your table. Each piece was selected by our buyers after months of careful consideration. Each piece will fit gracefully into the decorative scheme of your table. We have selected the biggest values, the most artistic and latest designs on the market and we have priced them at a substantial saving to you.

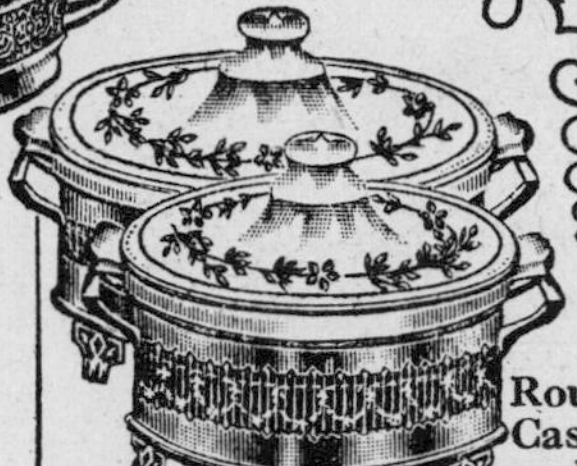

Round Casseroles
Silver plated, "A" quality frames, dull finish, pierced design with Pyrex linings. Floral decorated covers.
5K7703—6¾ inches in diameter, holds 2 pints. Shpg. wt., 6 lbs. $4.25
5K7705—7¾ inches in diameter, holds 3 pints. Shpg. wt., 7½ lbs. $4.90

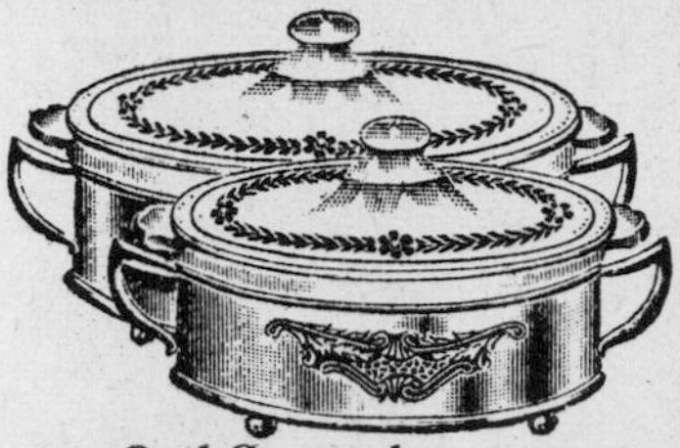

Oval Casserole
Silver plated, "A" quality, dull etched design ornamentation with Pyrex glass lining, cut ornamented cover. Shipping weight, 6 pounds.
5K7707—Measures 7¾x5¾ inches. Holds 2 pints $4.50
"A" quality, same as above, but measures 9x6½ inches. Holds 3 pints. Shipping weight, 7½ pounds.
5K7709 .... $5.35

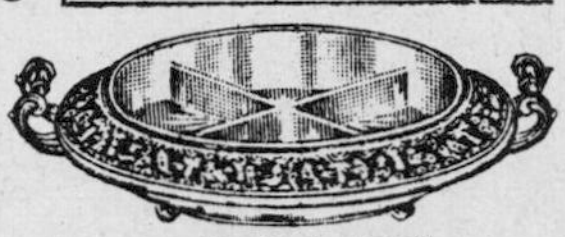

Relish Dish
Silver plated, "A" quality, Dutch design, dull finish frame with four compartments. Clear glass container, 7 inches in diameter. Frame is 9 inches in diameter. Shipping weight, 5½ pounds.
5K7713 .... $5.95

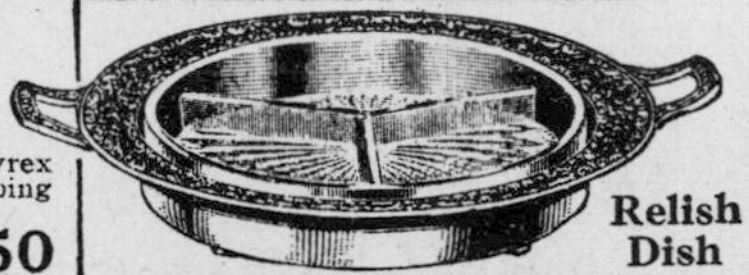

Relish Dish
Silver plated, "A" quality, dull finish, with three compartments, glass lining. Diameter of frame, 10⅝ inches. Lining, 8 inches in diameter. Shipping weight, 6¼ pounds.
5K7711 .... $5.50

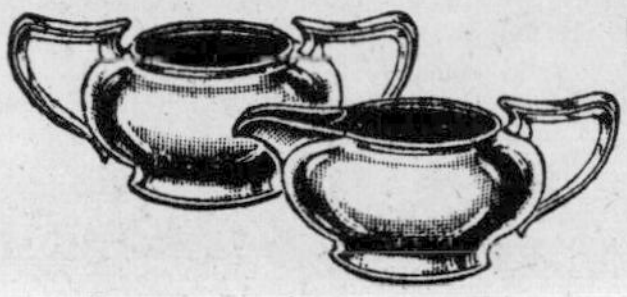

Sugar and Cream Set
Silver plated, "B" quality, bright finish, gold plated inside. Height of sugar bowl, 2½ inches. Diameter, 4½ inches. Shipping weight, 3 pounds.
5K7715 .... $4.72

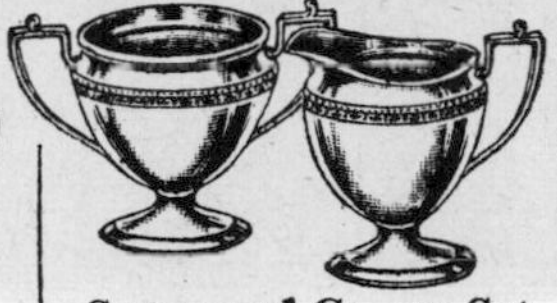

Sugar and Cream Set
Silver plated, "A" quality, dull finish, gold plated inside. Embossed ornamentation. Sugar bowl, 3¾ inches high. Shipping wt., 3 lbs.
5K7717 .... $5.95

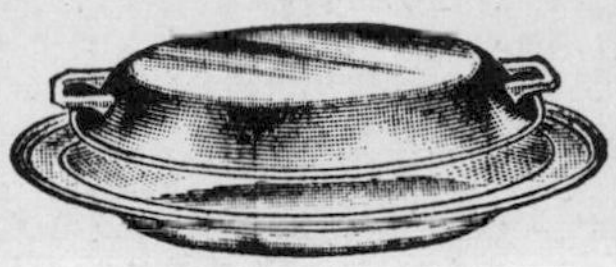

Vegetable Dish
Silver plated, "A" quality, Butler dull finish, plain pattern. Cover can also be used as a separate dish. Shpg. wt., 4 lbs.
5K7719 .... $4.89

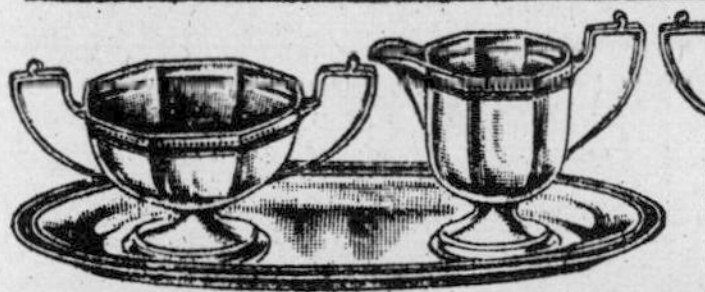

Sugar and Cream Set with Tray
Silver plated, "A" quality, dull finish tray. Measures 11x5½ inches. Cream pitcher is 3⅜ inches high. Sugar bowl and cream pitcher, gold plated inside. Shipping weight, 3 pounds.
5K7721 .... $8.25

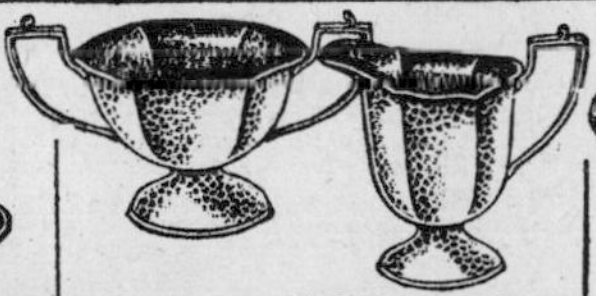

Sugar and Cream Set
Silver plated, "A" quality, dull finish, hammered design. Height, 6¾ inches. Capacity, 4 pints. Shipping weight, 5 pounds.
5K7723 .... $5.45

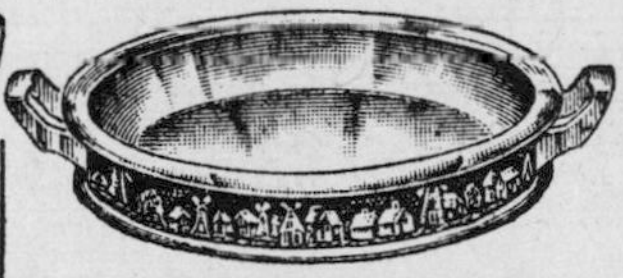

Pie Plate
Silver plated, "A" quality frame, Dutch design, dull finish with Pyrex glass lining 9⅝ inches in diameter. Shipping wt., 5 lbs.
5K7725 .... $2.95

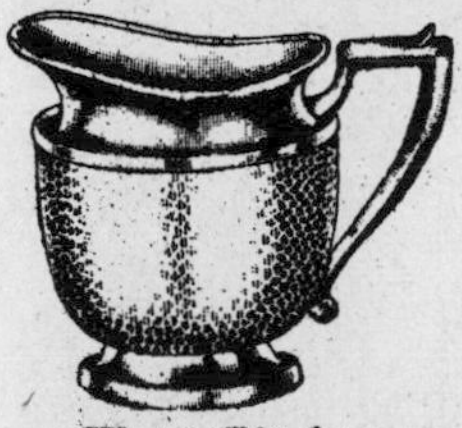

Water Pitcher
Silver plated, "A" quality, dull finish hammered design. Height, 6¾ inches. Capacity, 4 pints. Shipping weight., 5 pounds.
5K7729 .... $4.35

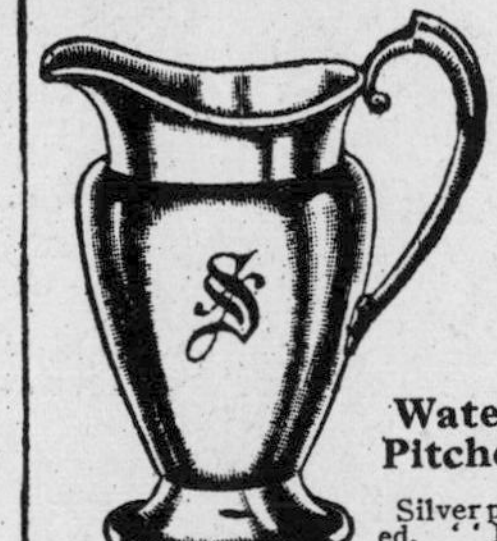

Water Pitcher
Silver plated, "B" quality, dull finish, engraved with one Old English initial if desired. **State initial wanted.** Height, 9¾ inches. Holds 4 pints. Shipping weight, 6 pounds.
5K7731 .... $6.60

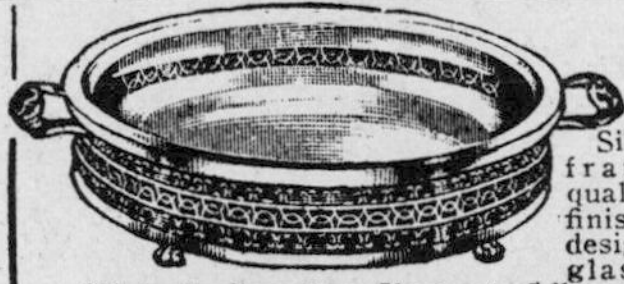

Pie Plate
Silver plated frame, "B" quality, dull finish, pierced design. Pyrex glass lining, 9⅝ in. in diameter. Shpg. wt., 5 lbs.
5K7727 .... $2.25

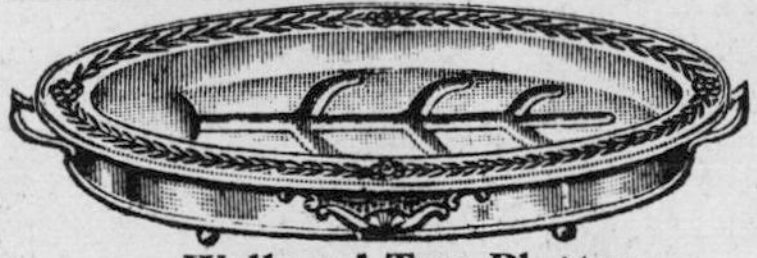

Well and Tree Platter
Silver plated, "A" quality frame, dull finish with Pyrex glass lining. Cut floral ornamentation. Measures, 15x11 inches. Shipping weight, 7 pounds.
5K7739 .... $5.85

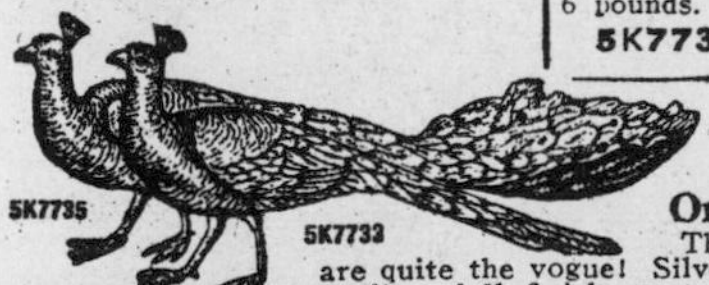

Table Ornaments
These Peacocks are quite the vogue! Silver plated, "B" quality, dull finish, protected from tarnish by a heavy lacquer. Eyes are set with bright color stones. We supply these birds in two sizes.
5K7733—Peacock, 4¼ inches high and 10¼ inches long. Shipping weight, 2¾ pounds $2.95
5K7735—Peacock has fan shape tail. 4¾ inches high, 13 inches long. Shpg. wt., 3½ lbs. 3.38

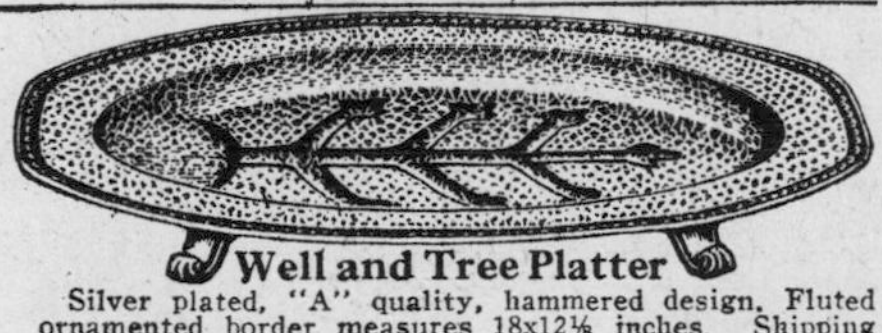

Well and Tree Platter
Silver plated, "A" quality, hammered design. Fluted ornamented border measures 18x12⅛ inches. Shipping weight, 8 pounds.
5K7737 .... $6.98

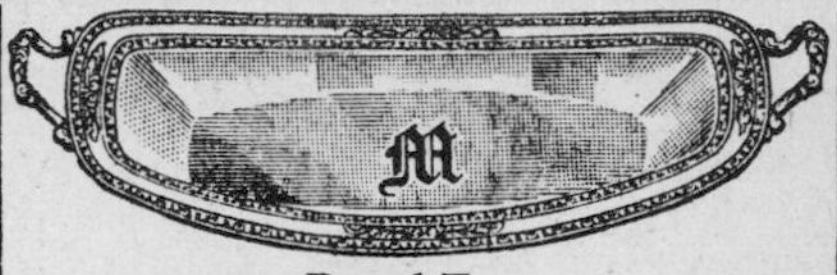

Bread Tray
Silver plated, "A" quality, Butler dull finish. Tray measures 13¾x6⅝ inches, including handles. Engraved with one Old English initial. **State initial desired.** Shipping wt., 3 lbs.
5K7741 .... $4.25

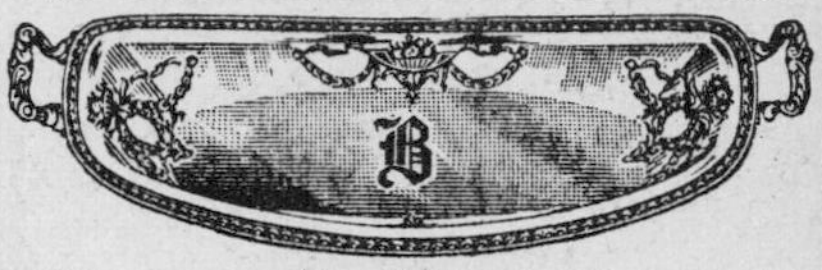

Bread Tray
Silver plated, "A" quality, dull finish, beautifully embossed design. Engraved with one Old English initial. **State initial desired.** Tray measures 13¼x6¼ inches, including handles. Shipping weight, 3 pounds.
5K7743 .... $3.75

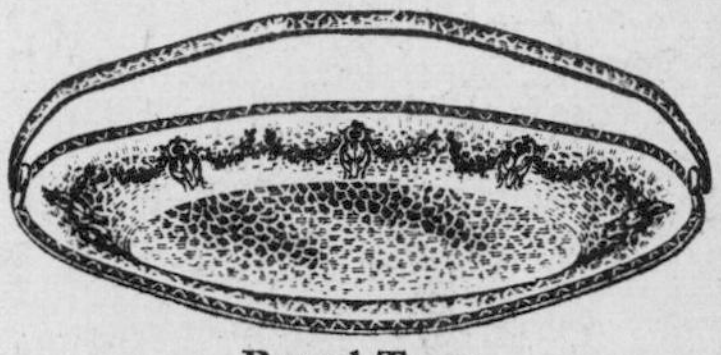

Bread Tray
Silver plated, "B" quality, hammered design with applied border, Butler dull finish. Tray measures 12x7 inches. Shpg. wt., 3 lbs.
5K7745 .... $2.90

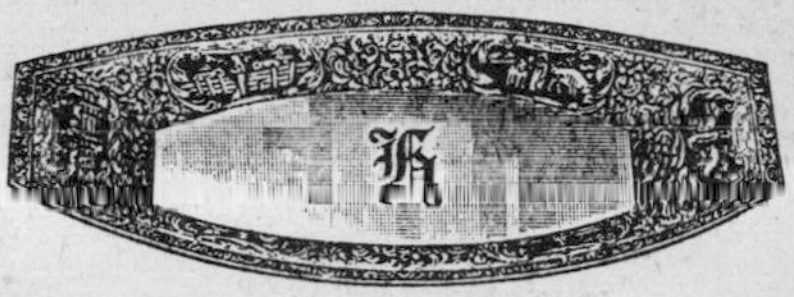

Bread Tray
Silver plated, "B" quality, Dutch design, dull silver finish. Engraved with one Old English initial. **State initial desired.** Tray measures 13x7½ inches. Shipping wt., 3 lbs.
5K7747 .... $2.75

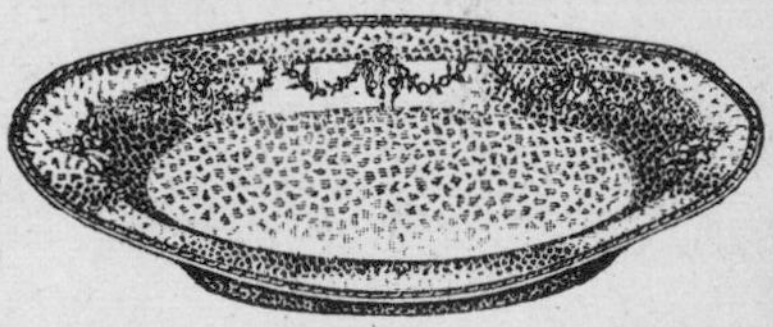

Bread Tray
Silver plated, "B" quality, hammered design, dull finish with applied border. Measures, 12x7 inches. Shipping weight, 2½ lbs.
5K7749 .... $2.25

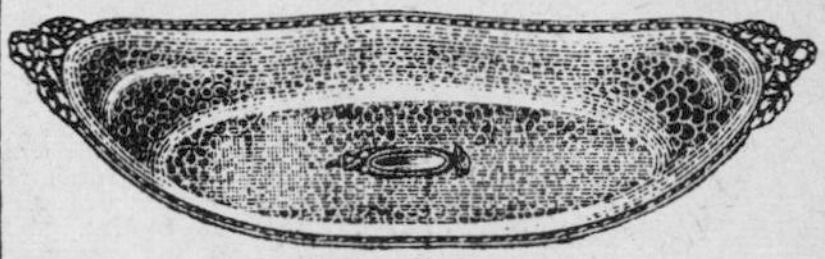

Bread Tray
Silver plated, "A" quality, hammered design, dull finish. Fluted border. Extreme length, 14 inches; width, 6⅝ inches. Shipping weight, 3 pounds.
5K7751 .... $3.30

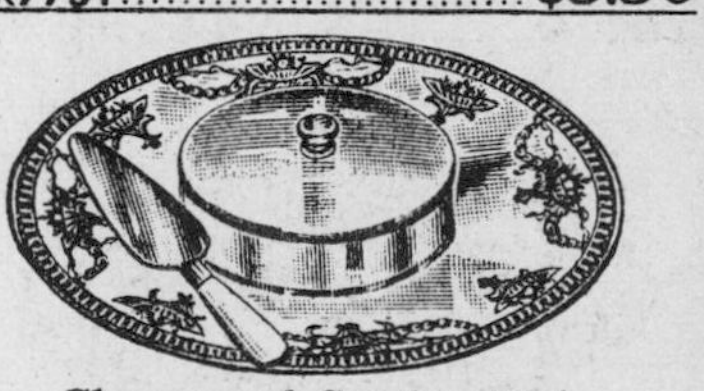

Cheese and Cracker Dish
Silver plated, "A" quality, dull finish, tray and cover. Tray has fluted ornamentation. Diameter of tray, 10 inches. Glass cheese container, 4½ inches in diameter. Complete with pearl handle cheese server. Shipping weight, 3½ lbs.
5K7753 .... $3.95

To Find What You Want, See Index Pages 550 to 570

Gifts for Milady

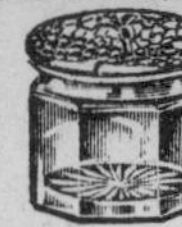

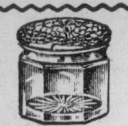

Puff Jar. Gilt finish top; hammered effect. Ornamentation with spray of flowers. Clear glass container. Height, 3¼ inches. Diameter, 3 in. Shpg. wt., 2 lbs.
5K8800 ....98c

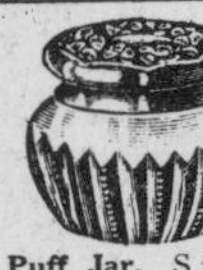

Puff Jar. Silver plated cover. Floral ornamentation. Bright finish. Has clear glass container. Height, 3⅜ inches. Diameter, 3¾ in. Shpg. wt., 2 lbs.
5K8802 ....85c

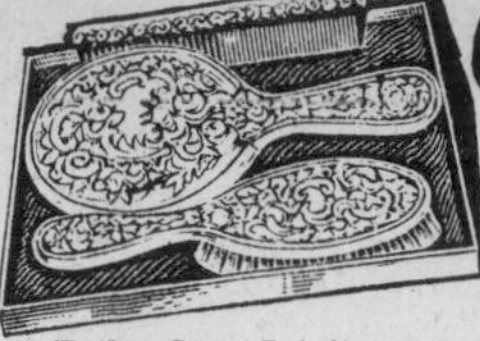

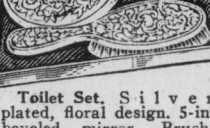

Toilet Set. Silver plated, floral design. 5-in. beveled mirror. Brush, 8¾ in. Comb, 7 inches. Shpg. wt., 3¼ lbs.
5K8804 ....$2.75

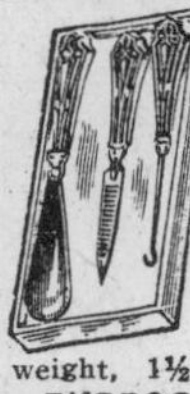

Manicure Set. Silver plated hollow handles, dull finish, embossed design. Consists of file, shoe horn and button hook. File is 7½ in. Other pieces in proportion. Shipping weight, 1½ pounds.
5K8806 ....$1.85

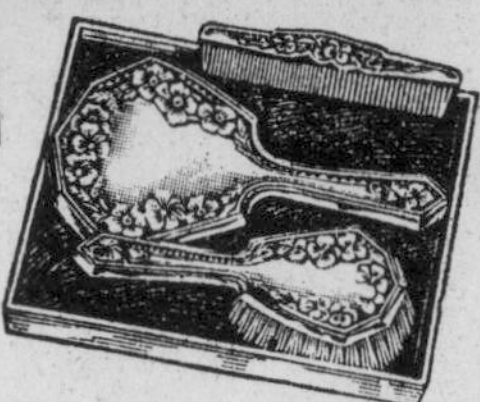

Toilet Set. Silver plated, dull finish, embossed design. Mirror, 11½ inches long with 5-inch beveled glass. Brush 9 inches long. Shipping weight, 4 pounds.
5K8808
$5.45

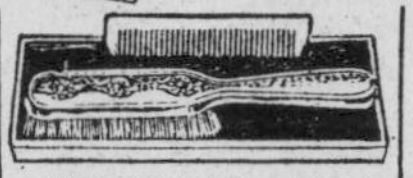

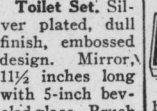

"Miss Bob" Set. Brush has silver plated back and white bristles. Brush is 8 inches long and 1½ inches wide. White celluloid comb, 4½ inches long. Shpg. wt., 1½ lbs.
5K8810 ....$3.25

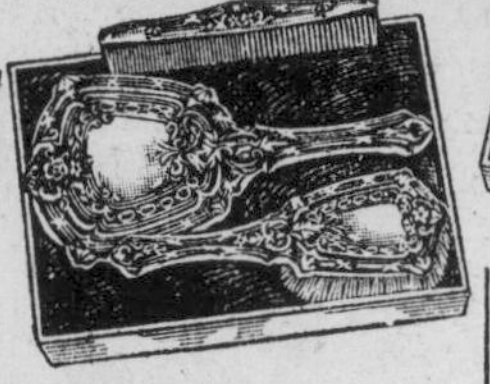

Toilet Set. Three-piece, silver plated, dull finish. Embossed design. 11¼-inch mirror with 5-inch beveled glass. Shpg. wt., 4 pounds.
5K8812
$6.00

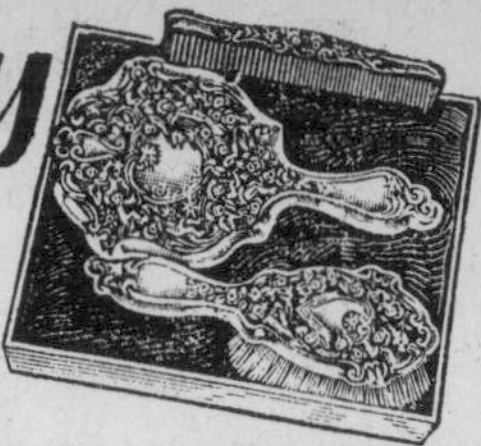

Three-Piece Toilet Set. Silver plated, dull finish. Beautifully embossed with figures. Mirror is 10⅜ inches long and has 4½-inch beveled glass. Brush is 8¾-inches long. Shipping weight, 4 pounds.
5K8814 ....$4.75

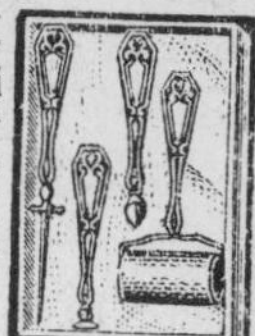

Writing Set. Silver plated, letter opener, eraser, roll blotter and seal. Seal engraved with one Old English letter. **State initial.** Shpg wt., 1¾ lbs.
5K8816
$2.25

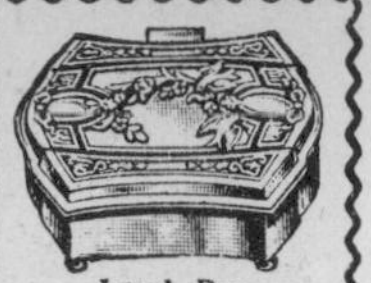

Jewel Box
Silver plated, dull finish. Silk lined. Measures about 4x2¾ inches. Shipping wt., 3 pounds.
5K8890 **$3.89**

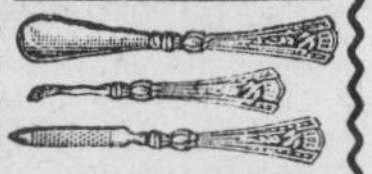

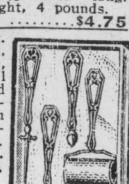

Toilet Articles
Silver plated, hollow handles, length, about 7 in. Shipping weight, each, 8 ounces.
5K8892
Nail File........69c
5K8894
Cuticle Knife....69c
5K8896
Shoe Horn.......69c

Children's and Babies' Sets

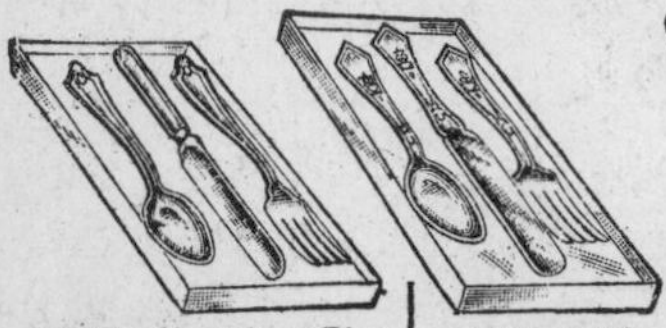

Children's Three-Piece Set. Silver plated gray finish. 25-year quality. Consists of knife, fork and spoon in box. Shipping weight, 8 ounces.
5K8822—Per set.$1.35

Children's Three-Piece Set. Silver plated. Dull finish. 40-year quality. Standard size. Shpg. wt., ¾ lb.
5K8824
Per set...$1.60

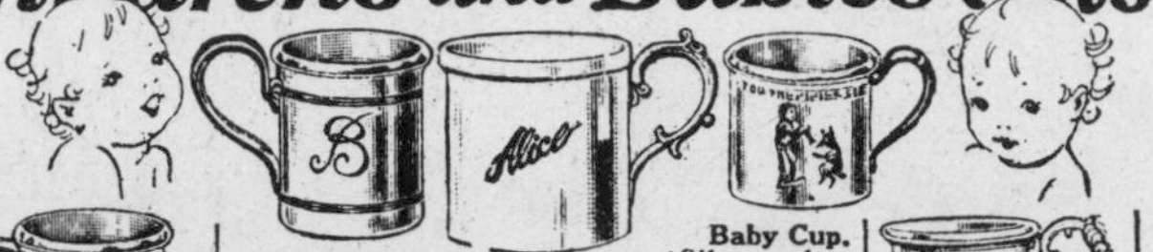

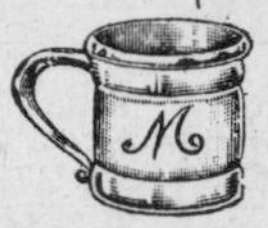

Baby Cup. Silver plated, dull finish, gold plated inside. Height, 2½ inches. Engraved with one initial. **State initial wanted.** Shpg. wt., 1 lb.
5K8826.$1.35

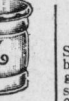

Baby Cup. Silver plated, bright polish, gold plated inside. Height, 2⅞ in. Engraved with one initial. **State initial. wanted.** Shipping wt., 1 lb.
5K8828
$1.50

Baby Cup. Silver plated, dull finish, gold plated inside. Height, 2⅝ inches. Engraved with baby's first name in script letters. **State name.** Shpg. wt., ¾ lb.
5K8830
$1.25

Baby Cup. Silver plated, dull finish, gold plated inside. Ornamented with Tom, the Piper's Son. Height, 2¼ inches. Shpg. wt., 1 lb.
5K8832
$1.00

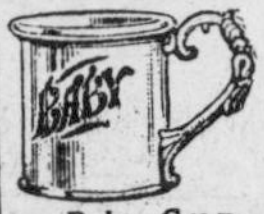

Baby Cup. Silver plated, dull finish, gold plated inside. Engraved "Baby". Height, 3 in. Shpg. wt.,1 lb.
5K8834...79c

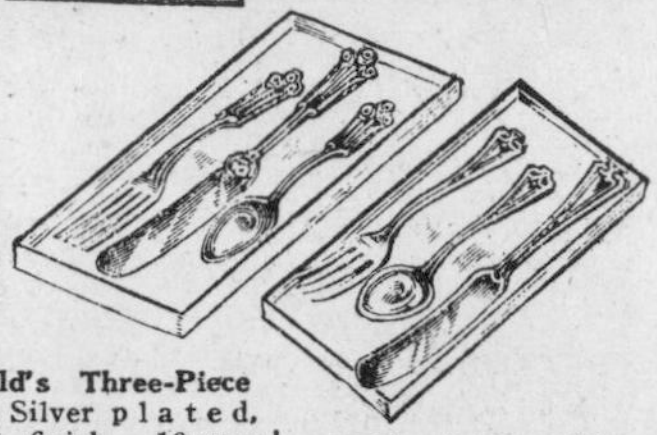

Child's Three-Piece Set. Silver plated, gray finish. 10-year quality. Knife is 7½ inches long, fork is 6 inches long. In box. Shpg. wt., ¾ lb.
5K8836
Per set.......**50c**

Children's Three-Piece Set. Silver plated, dull finish. 15-year quality. Consists of knife, fork and spoon. In box. Shipping wt., ¾ lb.
5K8838
Per set **75c**

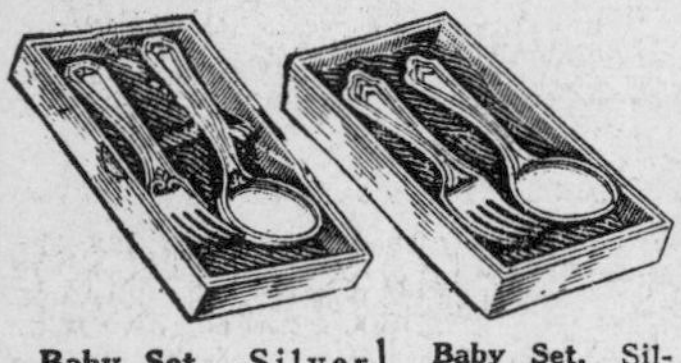

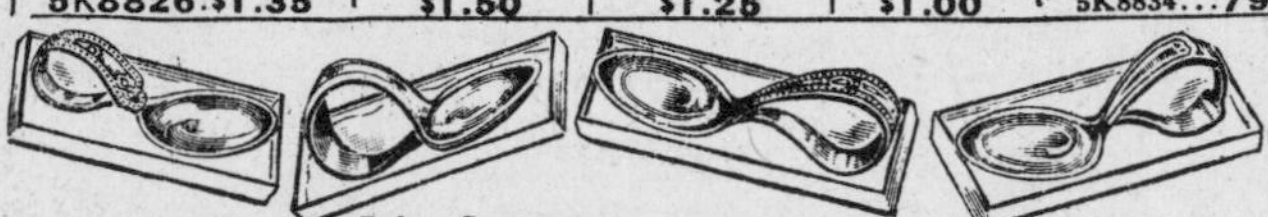

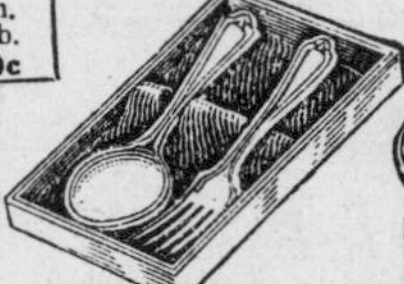

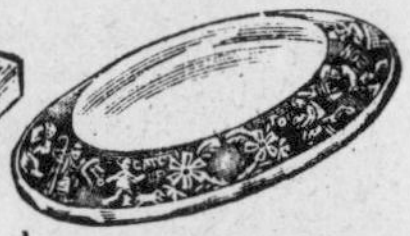

Baby Set. Silver plated spoon and fork, flat handle, dull finish. 15-year plate. Length of spoon, 4½ inches. In box. Shpg. wt., 6 oz.
5K8840—Set **75c**

Baby Set. Silver plated spoon and fork, flat handle, bright finish. 15-year quality. Length of spoon, 4 inches. In box. Shipping weight, 6 ounces.
5K8842
Per set... **60c**

Baby Spoon. Solid silver, dull finish, curved handle. Length, 3 inches. In box. Shpg. wt., 3 oz.
5K8846
$1.40

Baby Spoon. Silver plated, curved handle, dull silver finish. 25-year plate. Length, 3¼ in. In box. Shipping weight, 4 ounces.
5K8848
Per set... **60c**

Baby Spoon. Silver plated guaranteed 50 yrs. Curved handle; dull silver finish. Length, 3½ in. In box. Shpg. wt., 3 oz.
5K8850 **$1.00**

Baby Spoon. Silver plated, dull finish. 15-year quality. Lgth., 3¾ in. In box. Shpg. wt., 3 oz.
5K8852.....**45c**

Baby Fork and Spoon Set. Silver plated, dull finish. 25-year quality. Shpg. wt., 5 oz.
5K8854
Per set...... **95c**

Baby Plate. Silver plated, dull finish border, bright center. Ornamented with embossed nursery rhymes. Diameter, 7¾ inches. Shipping weight, 1½ pounds.
5K8856 **$2.65**

Appropriate Gifts for Men

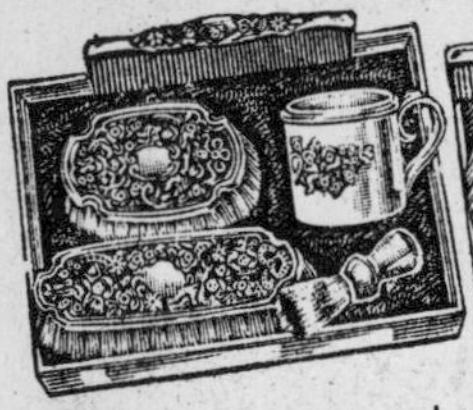

Shaving Outfit. Silver plated. Dull finish. Military brush, 4½x3 inches. Clothes brush, comb, mug glass lined, shaving brush. Shipping weight, 6 pounds.
5K8858... **$6.35**

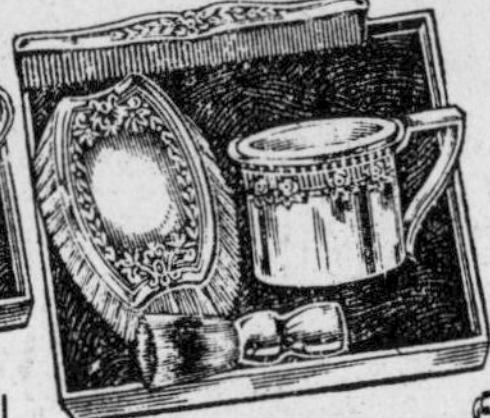

Shaving Outfit. Silver plated, dull finish, embossed floral design. Military brush measures 4½x3 inches. Comb is 7½ inches long. Mug has glass lining. Silver plated handle shaving brush. Shipping weight, 5 pounds.
5K8860..... **$4.95**

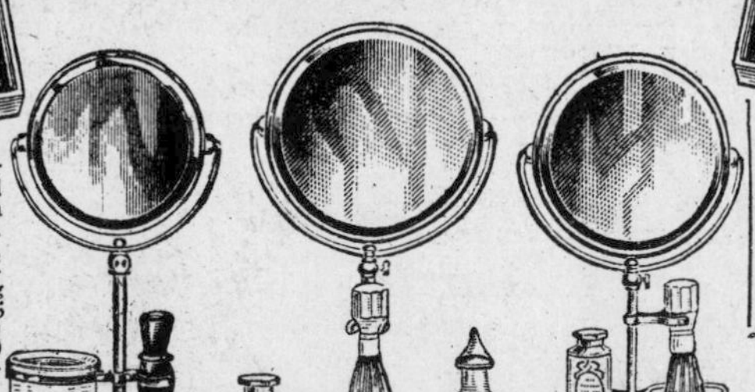

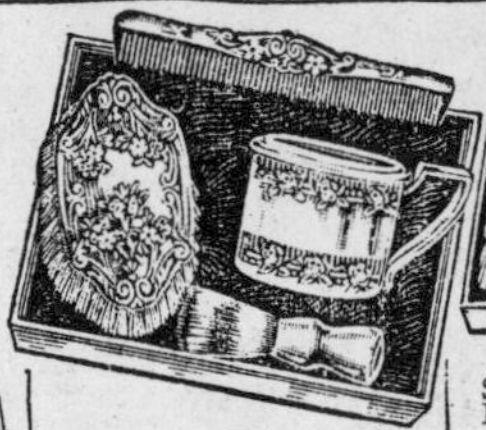

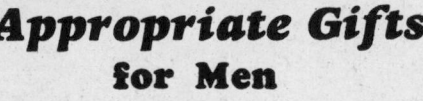

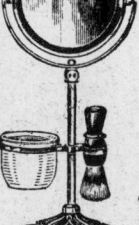

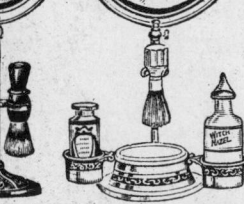

Shaving Outfit. Silver plated. Dull finish. Embossed design. Military brush, 4¾x3 inches. Comb; mug with glass lining, shaving brush. Shipping weight, 5 pounds.
5K8862... **$4.57**

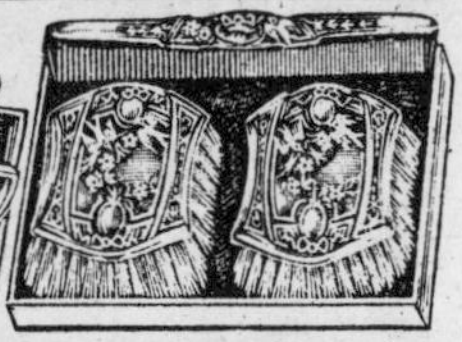

Military Set. Three-piece. Silver plated, dull finish. Floral design. Brush measures 4½x3 inches. Comb, 7½ inches long. Shpg. wt., in box, 2 lbs.
5K8864.... **$5.00**

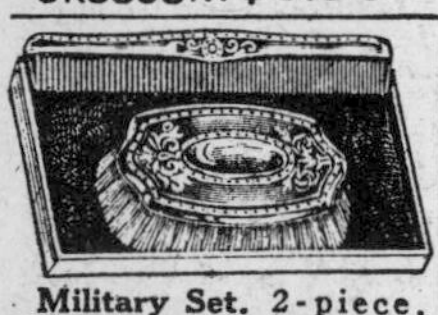

Military Set. 2-piece. Silver plated. Dull finish. Brush, 4¾x3 inches. Comb, 7½ inches. Shipping wt., 1¾ pounds.
5K8872..... **$3.18**

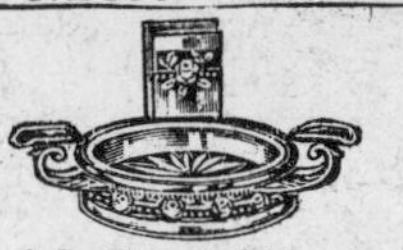

Ash Tray. Silver plated, bright finish frame. Diameter, 4¼ inches. Glass lined ash tray. Shipping weight, 2 pounds.
5K8876... **$1.65**

Shaving Stand. Silver plated, dull finish. Fluted design. Height, extended, 24 in. Has 6-inch beveled mirror. White glass container and shaving brush. Shipping wt., 5 lbs.
5K8866
$3.00

Shaving Stand. Silver plated. Dull finish. Height, extended, 21½ inches. 7-inch beveled mirror. Powder and bottle for toilet water. Good shaving brush. Shpg. wt., 7 lbs.
5K8868
$5.75

Shaving Stand. Silver plated. Hammered design. Height, extended, 21½ in. 7-inch beveled mirror. Shaving powder; shaving brush with white celluloid handle. Shpg. wt., 5 lbs.
5K8870
$4.78

For Razors and Shaving Brushes See Pages 527 to 529

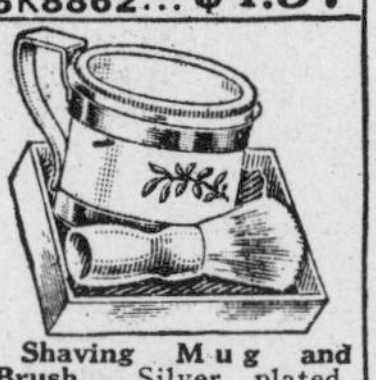

Shaving Mug and Brush. Silver plated. Satin finish mug, with glass container. Silver plated handle brush. Shipping weight, 3 pounds.
5K8888. **$2.00**

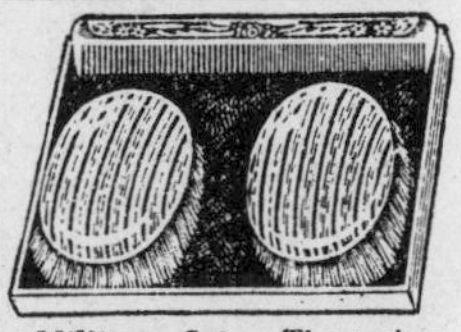

Military Set. Three-piece. Silver plated, bright finish. Engine turn design. Brush measures 4¼x2¾ inches. 7½-inch comb. Shipping weight, in box, 2 lbs.
5K8886..... **$3.65**

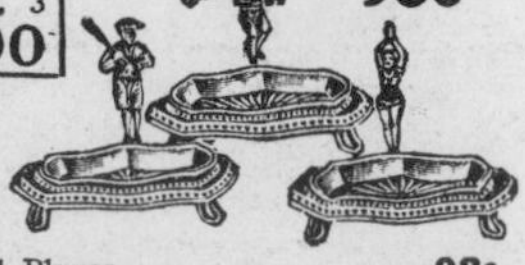

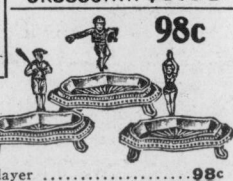

98c

Ash Trays. Silver plated frames, dull finish with colored glass ash container. Container measures 3⅞x2¾ in. Shpg. wt., 1¾ lbs.
5K8880—Baseball Player 98c
5K8882—Football Player 98c
5K8884—Bathing girl 98c

Shaving Mug and Brush. Silver plated. Dull finish mug, glass container. Silver plated handle shaving brush. Shipping wt., 3 lbs.
5K8874......... **$2.25**

Gifts That Add to the Table's Charm

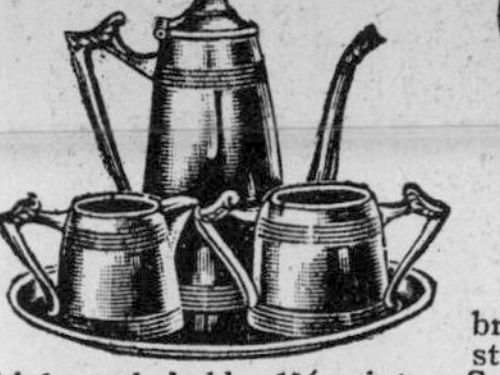

Tea or Coffee Set

Silver plated, bright finish. Pot stands 7½ inches high and holds 1¼ pints. Sugar bowl, 2¾ inches high. Tray measures 9⅜ inches in diameter. Shipping wt., 6¼ lbs.
5K7700..............................**$4.65**

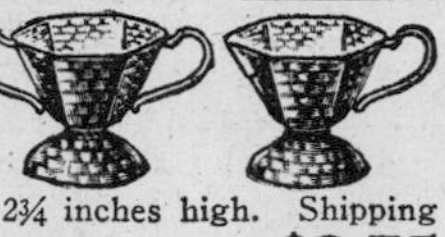

Sugar and Cream Set. Silver plated, hammered design. Gold plated inside. Sugar bowl, 2¾ inches high. Shipping weight, 2 pounds.
5K7702..............................**$3.75**

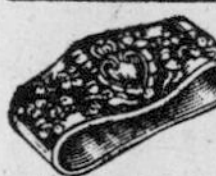

Napkin Ring. Silver plated, bright finish. Top measures 2⅞x1¾ in. In lined box. Shipping wt., 8 ounces.
5K7704
70c

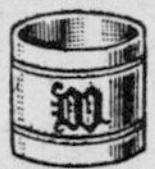

Napkin Ring. Silver plated, bright finish. 1½ in. high. Engraved with one Old English initial. State initial. Shipping wt., 8 oz.
5K7706
42c

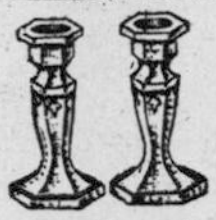

Candlesticks. Silver plated, hammered design. Height, 4 inches. Shipping weight, 1½ lbs.
5K7708
Per pr. **$1.25**

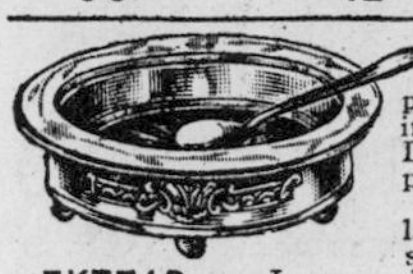

Marmalade or Lemon Dish. Silver plated frame. Glass lining. Cut ornamentation. Diameter, 5⅛ in. Shipping weight, 1¾ lbs.
5K7710 — Marmalade dish with spoon..........**98c**
5K7712 — Lemon dish with fork..........**98c**

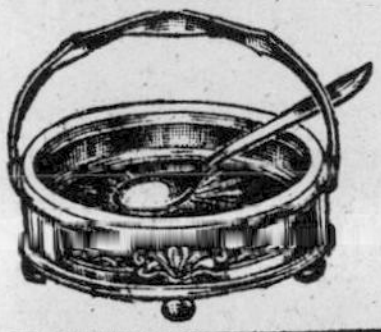

Marmalade or Lemon Dish. Silver plated, satin finish frame. Glass lining, 4¼ inches in diameter. Shipping wt., 1¾ lbs.
5K7714—Marmalade dish and spoon...**$1.25**
5K7716—Lemon dish with fork.......**$1.25**

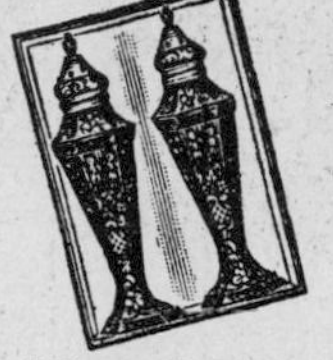

Salt and Pepper Set. Silver plated, Dutch design, satin finish. Height, 6 in. Shpg. wt., 1¾ lbs.
5K7718
Per pair......**$2.25**

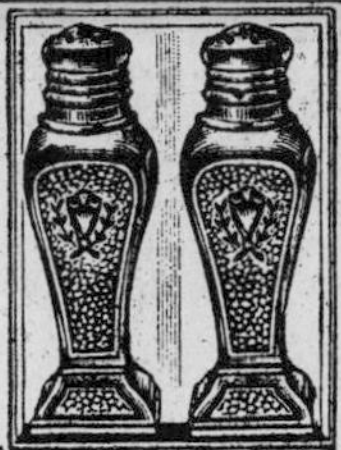

Salt and Pepper Set. Silver plated. Hammered design with shield ornamentation. Ht., 4¾ in. Shpg. wt., 2 lbs.
5K7720
Pair **$1.00**

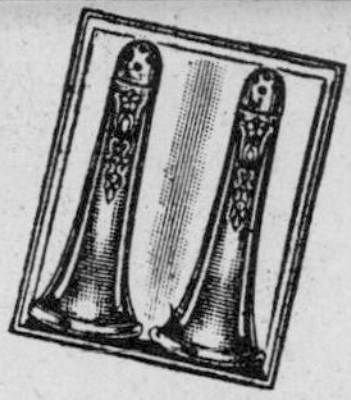

Salt and Pepper Set. Silver plated. Bright finish. Fluted design. Height, 5½ inches. Shpg. wt., 1¾ lbs.
5K7722
Pair **$2.00**

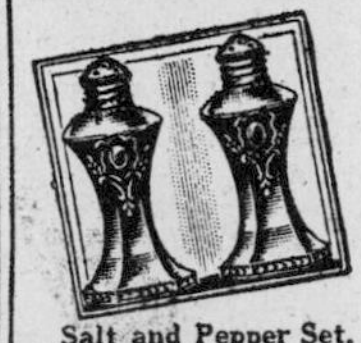

Salt and Pepper Set. Silver plated, dull finish. Shield design ornamentation. Ht., 3⅝ inches. Shipping weight, 1½ pounds.
5K7724
Pair **92c**

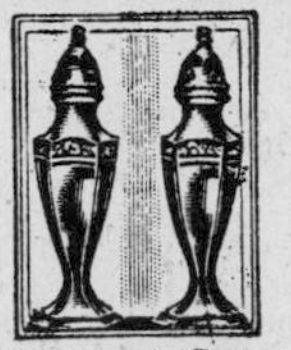

Salt and Pepper Set. Silver plated, dull finish. Ht., 4½ inches. Shipping weight, 1½ pounds.
5K7726
Pair **$1.25**

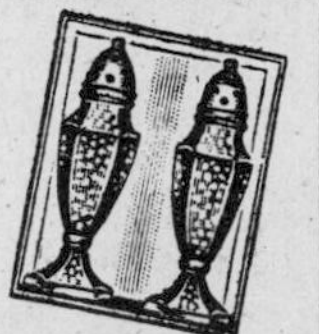

Salt and Pepper Set. Silver plated, hammered design. Ht., 4 inches. Shipping wt., 1½ pounds.
5K7728
Pair **$1.50**

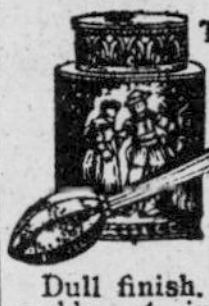

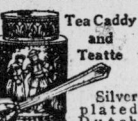

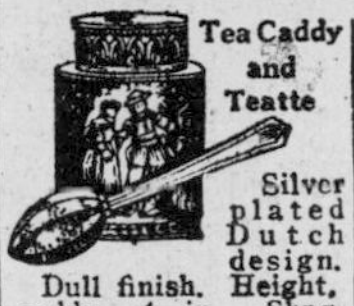

Tea Caddy and Teatte

Silver plated Dutch design. Dull finish. Height, caddy, 4 in. Shpg. wt., 1½ lbs.
5K7730...**$2.20**
Teatte only. Silver plated; length, 5¼ in. Shpg. wt., 8 oz.
5K7732
48c

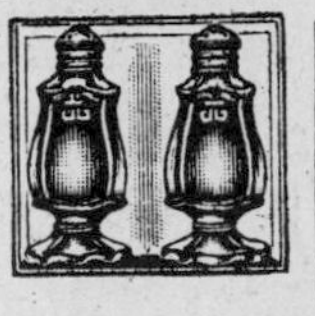

Salt and Pepper Set. Silver plated, dull finish. Height, 5¼ inches. Shipping wt., 1¼ lbs.
5K7734—Pair.**87c**

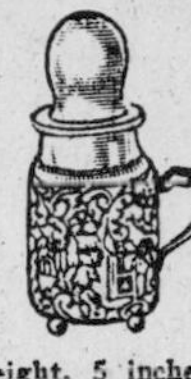

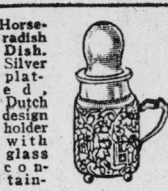

Horseradish Dish. Silver plated, Dutch design holder with glass container. Height, 5 inches. Shipping weight, 1½ pounds.
5K7736
$1.45

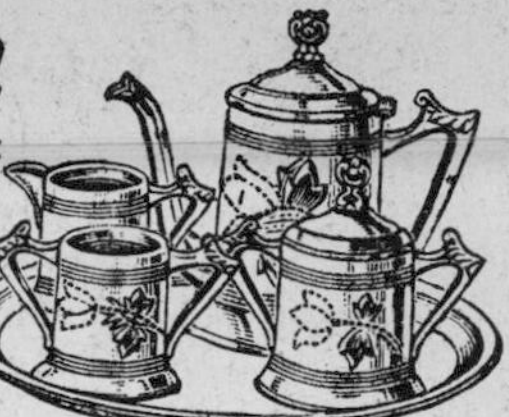

Tea or Coffee Set

Teapot, sugar bowl, cream pitcher, spoon holder, tray. Silver plated. Bright finish. Diameter of tray, 12 inches. 2-pint teapot. Shpg. wt., 9½ lbs.
5K7738..............................**$6.75**

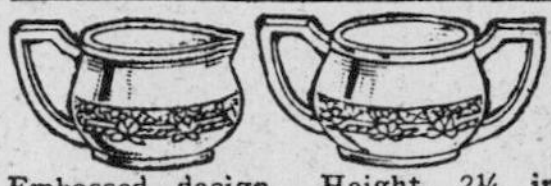

Sugar and Cream Set. Silver plated. Slightly dulled finish known as Butler. Embossed design. Height, 2¼ inches. Gold plated inside. Shipping weight, 2 pounds.
5K7740..............................**$3.00**

Toothpick Holders

Shipping weight, ¾ pound.

Silver plated, satin finish, gold plated inside. Height, 2⅛ inches.
5K7742..**85c**

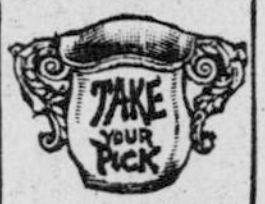

Silver plated, gold plated inside. Height, 2 inches.
5K7744..**$1.45**

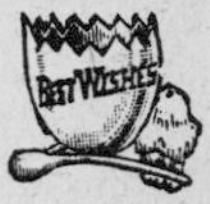

Silver plated, gold plated inside. Height, 2½ inches.
5K7746...**75c**

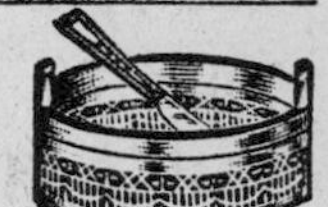

Butter Tub and Knife. Silver plated. Bright polish. Glass container. Holds ½ lb. Shipping wt., 1½ lbs.
5K7748 ....**$1.20**

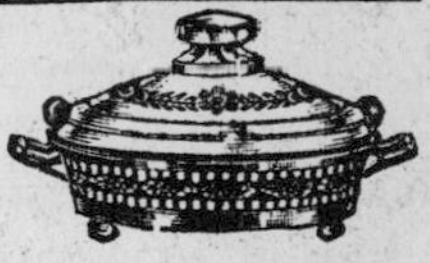

Butter Dish. Silver plated frame with handles. Pierced design, satin finish; has 5-inch clear glass lining with cut floral glass cover. Shipping weight, 3 pounds.
5K7750 ....**$1.95**

Gift Suggestions

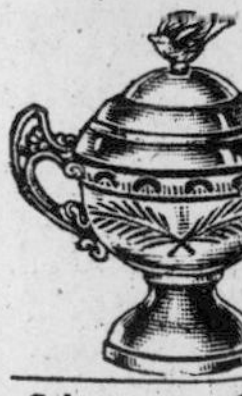

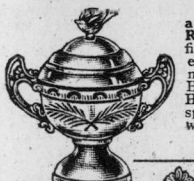

Sugar Bowl and Spoon Rack. Satin finish. Bright engraved ornamentation. Ht., 8½ in. Holds 12 spoons. Shpg. wt., 4 lbs.
5K7752
$2.25

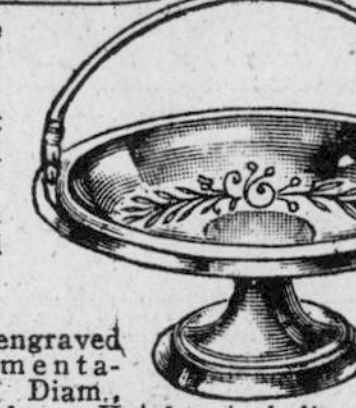

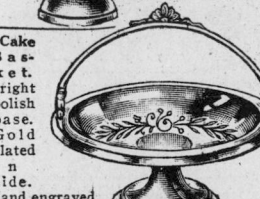

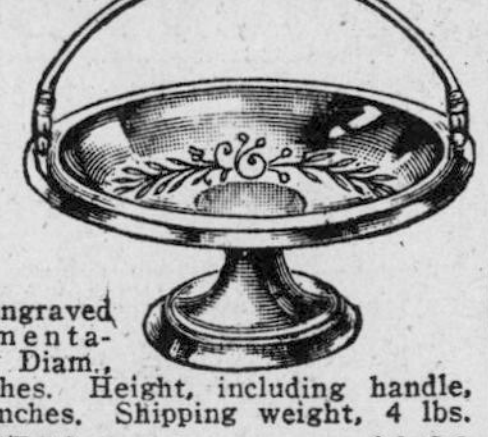

Cake Basket. Bright polish base. Gold plated inside. Hand engraved ornamentation. Diam., 10 inches. Height, including handle, 10⅝ inches. Shipping weight, 4 lbs.
5K7754 ....**$4.00**

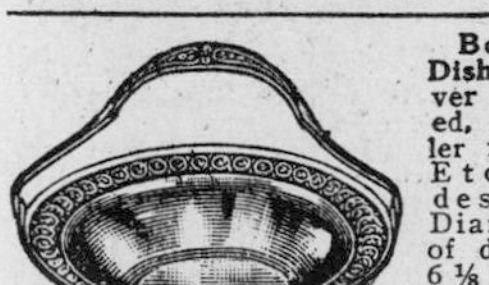

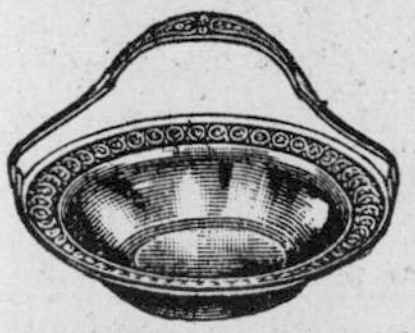

Bonbon Dish. Silver plated, Butler finish. Etched design. Diameter of dish, 6⅛ in.; height, including handles, 4½ inches. Shipping weight, 1½ lbs.
5K7756 ....**$1.78**

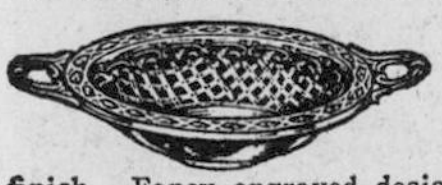

Bonbon Dish. Silver plated, bright finish. Fancy engraved design. Oval shape. Size, 6½x8⅝ inches, including handle. Shipping weight, 2 lbs.
5K7758 ....**$1.96**

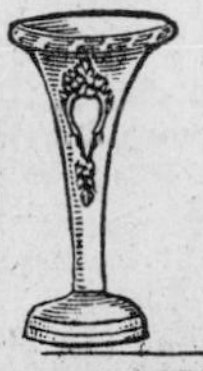

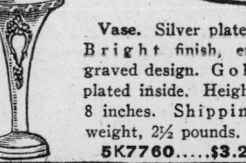

Vase. Silver plated. Bright finish, engraved design. Gold plated inside. Height, 8 inches. Shipping weight, 2½ pounds.
5K7760.....**$3.25**

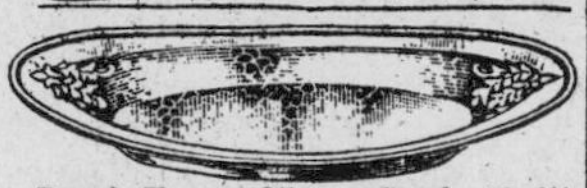

Bread Tray. Silver plated, 12x6¼ inches. Dull finish. Hammered effect. Engraved design. Applied border.
5K7762—Shpg. wt., 2½ lbs.**$1.95**

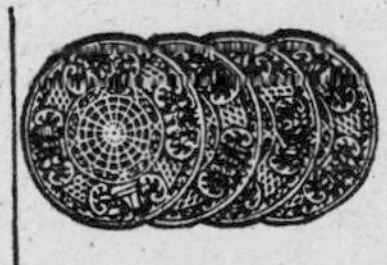

Table Mats. Silver plated. Dutch design with felt bottoms. Used for hot dishes. Diameter, 6 inches. Shipping wt., 1½ lbs.
5K7764
Set of 4..........**$1.00**

Prize or Loving Cups

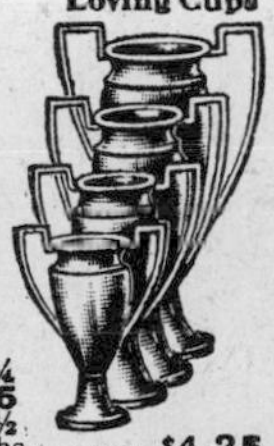

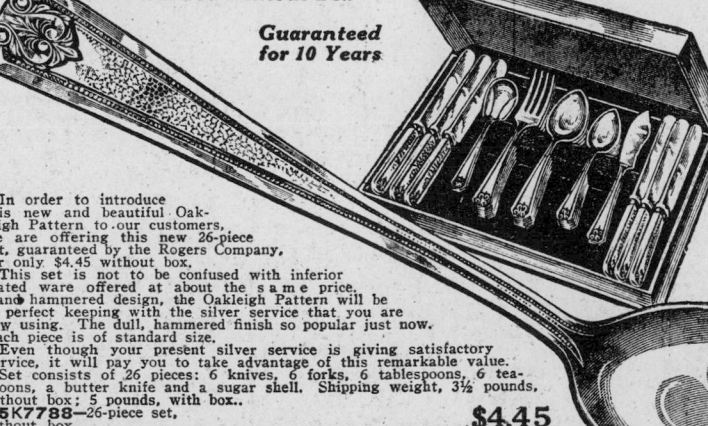

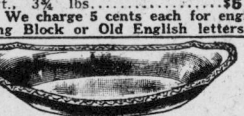

Silver plated, dull finish. Gold plated inside.
5K7766—Ht., 5¾ in. Shpg. wt., 1½ lbs......**$2.70**
5K7768—Ht., 7 in. Shpg. wt., 2¼ lbs. **$3.65**
5K7770—Ht., 8½ in. Shpg. wt., 3 lbs..........**$4.25**
5K7772—Height, 9¾ in. Shpg. wt., 3¾ lbs....................**$5.15**
We charge 5 cents each for engraving Block or Old English letters.

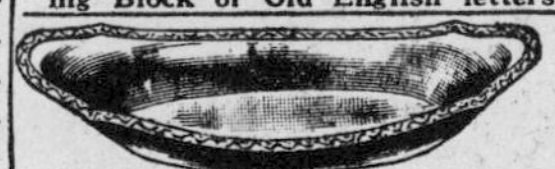

Bread Tray. Silver plated, bright finish. Floral applied border. Measures 12x6⅝ inches. Shipping weight, 2½ pounds.
5K7774 ....**$2.64**

COMMUNION SERVICE

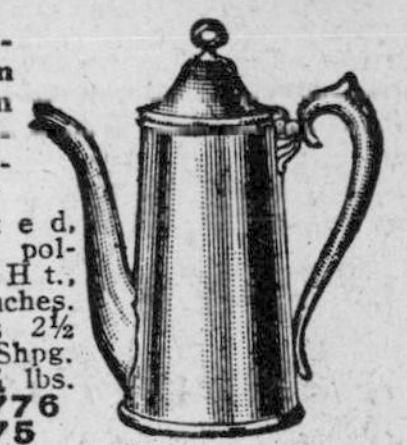

Communion Flagon or Filler. Silver plated, bright polish. Ht., 8⅝ inches. Holds 2½ pints. Shpg. wt., 2¾ lbs.
5K7776
$6.75

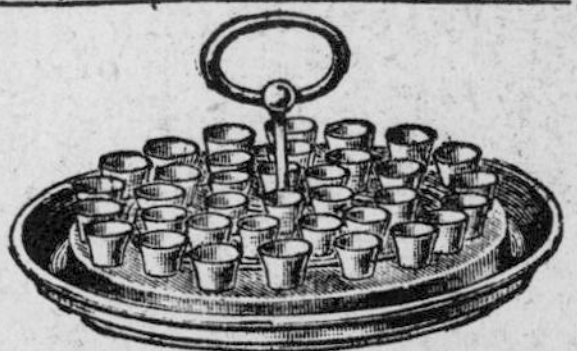

Individual Communion Service. Silver plated, bright polish. Thirty-six glasses in rack. Diameter, 13½ inches. Height of handle, 9¼ inches.
5K7778—Tray with 36 glasses. Shipping wt., 9½ lbs.......**$17.85**
Extra Glasses. Shpg. wt., doz. 1½ lbs.
5K7780—Per dozen **$1.45**

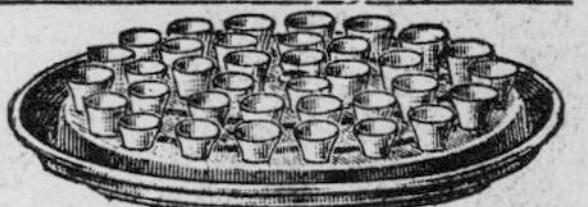

Individual Communion Set. Silver plated, bright polish, 36 glasses in rack. Height, 2 inches. Diameter, 13½ inches. Shipping weight, 9 lbs.
5K7782—Complete **$15.25**

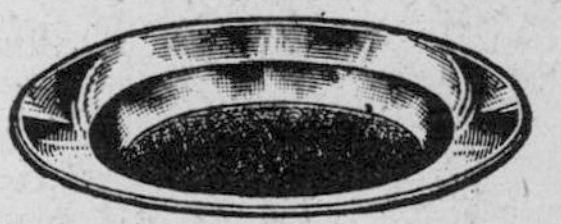

Collection Plate. Silver plated, bright polish. Cloth lined center. Diameter, 9¼ inches. Shipping wt., 2 pounds.
5K7784 ....**$3.50**

A Stupendous Value!

$4.45 for This Complete 26-Piece Set Without Box

Guaranteed for 10 Years

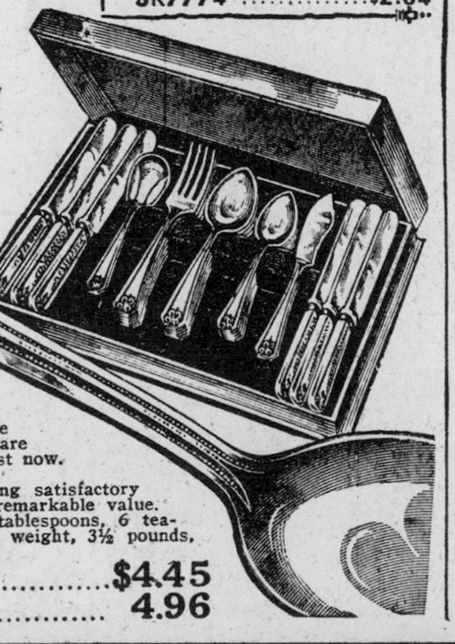

In order to introduce this new and beautiful Oakleigh Pattern to our customers, we are offering this new 26-piece set, guaranteed by the Rogers Company, for only $4.45 without box.

This set is not to be confused with inferior plated ware offered at about the same price. Hand hammered design, the Oakleigh Pattern will be in perfect keeping with the silver service that you are now using. The dull, hammered finish so popular just now. Each piece is of standard size.

Even though your present silver service is giving satisfactory service, it will pay you to take advantage of this remarkable value.

Set consists of 26 pieces: 6 knives, 6 forks, 6 tablespoons, 6 teaspoons, a butter knife and a sugar shell. Shipping weight, 3½ pounds, without box; 5 pounds, with box.

5K7788—26-piece set, without box..............................**$4.45**
5K7790—26-piece set, with box..............................**4.96**

Bronze Finished—Artistic and Useful

The House Beautiful deserves only the finest furnishings. There is no place for that which is ornate or out of harmony with the general decorative scheme. Finished in fine bronze, these Novelty Sets will harmonize with the furnishings of any home. Whether it be a gift for Milady or a present for the Man of the House, some article from this fine assortment will be sure to please.

Book Ends
Bronze finish. Ornamented with Sheep and Shepherd Dog. Height, 5½ inches; width, 4¾ inches. Shpg. Wt., 8 lbs.
5K8900 Per pair..... **$2.89**

Three-Piece Clock Set
Bronze finish. Clock is 7⅞ inches wide at base, stands 5½ inches high. Octagonal shape, gold finish dial. Measures 3¼x2 in. 30-hour movement. Candlesticks are 6⅛ in. high. Shipping weight, 8½ pounds.
5K8901 Three-piece set.......... **$6.45**
5K8902—Clock only. Shipping weight, 4½ lbs.... **4.59**
5K8903—Candlesticks. Shipping weight, 5 pounds. Per pair.......... **$1.90**

Three-Piece Clock Set
Bronze finish floral decoration. Clock is 4 inches high, 7 inches wide and has 2-in. gold finish dial. 30-hour movement. Candlesticks, 4⅞ in. high. Shipping weight, 6 pounds.
5K8904—Three-piece set. **$4.65**
5K8905—Clock only. Shipping weight, 4¼ pounds. **3.75**
5K8906—Candlesticks. Shipping weight, 3 pounds. Per pair.......... **95c**

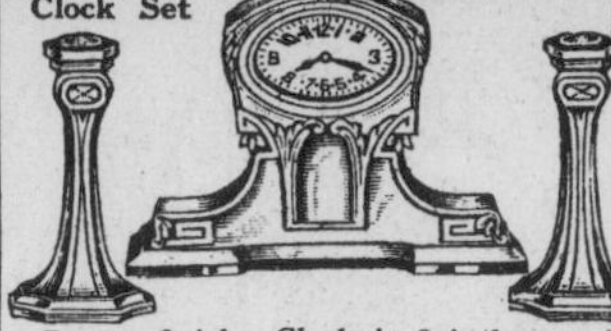

Three-Piece Clock Set
Bronze finish. Clock is 9 inches at base. Stands 7⅛ inches high. Has oval dial, 3¼x2⅞ in. 30-hour movement. Candlesticks are 6⅛ in. high. Shipping weight, 10 pounds.
5K8907—Three-piece set.......... **$7.25**
5K8908 Clock only. Shpg. wt., 6 lbs. **$5.45**
5K8909 Candlesticks. Shpg. wt., 5 lbs. Per pair, **$1.90**

Book Ends
Bronze finish Dancing girl, 7 inches high. Base, 3½x3⅞ in. Shpg. wt., 10 lbs.
5K8910 Per pair..... **$4.38**

Ink Stand and Pen Holder
Bronze finish. Stand measures 9¼ inches long, 5 inches deep and 4¼ inches high. Hinged cover inkwell with removable glass container. Shipping weight, 6½ pounds.
5K8911 **$2.88**

Cigarette and Ash Tray
Bronze finish. Cigarette container lined with cedar. Ash holder glass lined. Tray measures 5x7 inches. Height, 3½ inches. Shipping wt., 5 lbs.
5K8914.......... **$2.90**

Ash Tray
Bronze finish with glass Ash Tray. Five inches in diameter. Measures 7x6 in. at base. Stands 6 inches high. Shipping weight, 5½ pounds.
5K8922.......... **$2.90**

Flower Vase
Bronze finish. Stands 6½ inches high. Very artistic and ornamental. Shpg. wt., 2½ pounds.
5K8926 **97c**

Inkwell
Bronze finish with hinged cover, and glass ink container. Measures 5¼x5½ inches at base. Shipping wt., 3½ lbs.
5K8912 **$1.00**

Cigar or Tobacco Jar
Bronze finish top with glass container. Height, 7½ in. Shpg. wt., 5 lbs.
5K8916 **$1.25**

Ash Tray and Match Holder
Bronze finish Tray and Holder, with glass removable ash container. Measures 5½x5½ at base and is 4¾ inches high. Shpg. wt., 5 lbs.
5K8918.. **$2.00**

Ash Tray and Pipe Holder
Bronze finish. Removable glass ash container. Tray measures 4x7 inches. Shpg. wt., 4 lbs.
5K8920... **$2.15**

Ash Tray and Match Holder
Bronze finished Tray and Match Holder. Tray measures 4x6 in. and is 3⅞ in. high. Shpg. wt., 2¾ lbs.
5K8924 **89c**

Flower Vase
Bronze finish, 8⅝ in. high. Diameter of base, 3 in. Shpg. wt., 4½ lbs.
5K8928 **$2.00**

24-Karat Ormolu Gold Plated Articles

Pincushion. Gold plated frame. Cloth top. 3½x2¼x2-inch. Shpg. wt., 1 lb.
5K8930 **50c**

Jewel Case. Gold plated. 4½ x 3¼ x 3 inches.
5K8932 Shipping wt., 2 pounds. **90c**

Jewel Case Gold plated. Cloth lined. Measures, 3⅝x2¼x2¾ inches. Shipping wt., 1½ pounds.
5K8934 **65c**

Jewel Case Goldplated. Cloth lined. 4½x4¼x3½ inches. Shipping wt., 2½ lbs.
5K8936 **$1.18**

Jewel Case Gold plated. Cloth lined. 4¾x3x4½ in. Shpg. wt., 3 lbs.
5K8938 **$1.39**

Jewel Case Gold plated. Cloth lined. Measures 6⅛x4x2¾ inches. Shipping weight, 4 pounds.
5K8940... **$1.65**

Jewel or Handkerchief Case Gold plated. Cloth lined. Measures, 7½ x 3½ x 3¼ in. Shpg. wt., 4 lbs.
5K8942....... **$1.85**

Jewel Case Gold plated. Cloth lined. Measures 6¼x4½x4½ in. Shpg. wt., 5¼ lbs.
5K8944..... **$2.00**

24-Karat Ormolu Gold Plated Religious Articles

Crucifix, Candelabra and Holy Water Fount
Gold plated, satin finish. Height, 11¾ in. Complete with candles. Shpg. wt., 6 pounds.
5K8946... **$3.00**

Candlestick
Floral design, gold plated. Height, 5¾ in. Shipping wt., 1½ lbs.
5K8948 **65c**

Crucifix
Gold plated, satin finish. Ht., 10 inches. Shipping wt., 3 lbs.
5K8950 **$1.45**

Crucifix
Gold plated, satin finish. Ht., 11 inches. Shipping wt., 3½ lbs.
5K8952 **$1.98**

Crucifix
Gold plated, satin finish. Ht., 9½ inches. Shpg. weight, 2½ lbs.
5K8954 **$1.20**

Crucifix
Gold plated, satin finish. Height, 7⅝ inches. Shpg. weight, 2 lbs.
5K8956 **72c**

Holy Water Fount Hanging. Gold plated. Height, 5½ in. Shpg. wt., 1¼ lbs.
5K8958 **54c**

Crucifix and Candlestick Set
Gold plated, satin finish. Crucifix, 9 in. high. Candlesticks, each, 5⅛ in. high. Shpg. wt., 5 lbs.
5K8960—3-piece set.......... **$2.35**

Gold Plated Placques

Measures 6x4⅜ in. Shpg. wt., 1½ lbs.
5K8962—Saint Theresa.......... **85c**
5K8964—Sacred Heart of Jesus.......... **85c**
5K8966—Saint Anthony and child.......... **85c**

Vigil or Sanctuary Lamp
Gold plated base with removable ruby glass candle holder. Height, 5⅝ inches. Shipping weight, 1¾ pounds.
5K8968.......... **95c**

CANDLESTICKS

Gold finish. Ht., 9¼ inches. Shpg. wt., 3¾ lbs.
5K8970 Each, **$1.45**

Gold finish. Height, 4½ inches. Shipping weight, 3 pounds.
5K8972 Each, **98c**

Gold finish. Height, 7⅛ inches. Shpg. wt., 3⅛ lbs.
5K8974 Each **$1.00**

Holy Statues
Gold plated. Satin finish. Height, 5⅛ in. Shipping wt., 1¼ lbs.
5K8976—Sacred heart of Jesus...... **50c**
5K8978—Statue of the Blessed Virgin **50c**
5K8980—Saint Anthony and Child... **50c**

Bust of Our Lord
Gold plated. Height, 5⅝ in. Shpg. wt., 2 lbs.
5K8982.......... **98c**

The NATIONAL CALL

$3.50 **$2.50**

Quality 8-Day Alarm Clocks

The Alarm Clock With a Conscience

The first requisite in an alarm clock is absolute reliability. It must not—cannot fail.

The National Call has won its name as "the clock with a conscience," because of its unerring faithfulness. It is always to perform. Just set the alarm and you can rest in ease—free of worry—knowing that when the moment arrives, to the exact second, the gentle but imperative summons of The National Call will insist that you awaken.

From coast to coast its cheery "Good Morning" starts the daily punctual activity of thousands of families. It is the positive assurance of breakfast on time, work on time, school on time. It is as inevitable as the dawn itself.

This sturdy eight-day clock is built for lasting, dependable service. All it requires is that you wind it only once a week. It is the equal of any alarm clock made. Because of the tremendous volume of our business we offer this wonderful bargain to our customers at a price even lower than is ordinarily asked by others for common one-day clocks. The National Call is sold only by Sears, Roebuck and Co.

"Let the "clock with a conscience" start your day right."

Shows the Time at Night

The luminous dial and hands enable you to see the time as clearly by night as by day. Runs eight days with only one winding. Alarm is clear and loud and is easily controlled by small button at the top of clock. Solid brass and steel parts. Case is nickel plated. Dial, 4½ in.; height, 6 in.
5K8538—Shipping weight, 2¾ lbs..... **$3.50**

For Long and Reliable Service

Attractively nickel plated case with white face and black numerals and hands so you can read the hours and minutes easily. Well made of solid brass and steel parts. Gives the correct time for eight days with only one winding. Good clear ring. Stands 6 inches high and has a 4½-inch dial.
5K8560—Shipping weight, 2¾ pounds...... **$2.50**

Big Built ~ Soundly Constructed Fine Running

Reliable One-Day Alarm Clock

Nickel plated. Made by one of the most responsible and reliable clock manufacturers. Height, 5¾ in.; 3¾-in. dial; alarm rings for ½ minute. Shipping wt., 2 pounds.
5K8520 Plain dial.... **$0.79**
5K8511 Luminous dial **1.29**

White Enamel Kitchen Clock

8-day lever movement. White enamel wood case. Does not alarm. 6¾ in. high, 5-in. silver finished dial. Shipping wt., 3½ pounds.
5K8503...... **$3.98**

One-Day Alarm Clock

Nickel plated case with stem shut off. Alarm bell enclosed in case. Clock is 4½ in. high and has 3¾-in. dial. Shpg. wt., 2 lbs.
5K8522—Plain dial **79c**
5K8524—Luminous dial **$1.29**

A Great Big Clock 6 Inches High

Ting-a-ling-a-ling! Now, open your eyes to two more first rate alarm clock values. These are really exceptional "buys" at the prices we quote; were it not for our huge purchasing and selling power such clocks would cost you considerably more. Designed by clockmakers of long and successful experience and built throughout of substantial materials to give you reliable, accurate service for years. Cases are heavily nickel plated. Just wind once in 30 hours, set the alarm to the hour desired, and you'll be there at roll call every morning! This clock stands 6 inches high and has a 4¼-inch dial. Shipping weight, 2½ pounds.
5K8555—Plain dial, **$1.89**   5K8557—Luminous dial, **$2.50**

One-Day Back-Bell Alarm Clock

Height, 5¼ in. and has a 3⅞-in. dial. Case nickel plated with 4-inch alarm bell on back. Continuous alarm. Plain white dial; or black dial with luminous numerals and hands, easily read in the dark. Shipping weight, 3 pounds.
5K8510—Plain dial...... **$1.08**
5K8512—Luminous dial.... **$1.60**

Pedestal Alarm Clock

Enameled in imitation old ivory, beautifully grained. Alarm shut-off switch on top of the clock, with enclosed alarm bell. Clock is 5¾ inches high and 4 inches wide at base and has 3½-inch dial. Runs 30 hours with one winding. Shipping weight, 2¾ lbs.
5K8525 Plain dial...... **$1.45**
5K8527—Luminous dial...... **$1.95**

Celluloid Clocks

Boudoir Alarm Clock

Imitation ivory alarm clock. Ornaments, columns and top are finished in robin's egg blue. 6½ inches high; 3-inch dial. Runs 30 hours with one winding. Shipping wt., 5¼ pounds.
5K8563... **$3.25**

Boudoir Clock

Amber color celluloid, with green color front. Dial, 3⅓x 1⅞ in.; length, 7⅞ in.; ht., 4¾ in. 30-hour movement. Not an alarm clock. Shipping wt., 2 pounds.
5K8567...... **$3.75**

Desk or Boudoir Clock

This attractive desk or boudoir clock is furnished in old ivory. Columns and panel above the dial are finished in light green. Clock is 7¾ in. wide and 4⅝ in. high, and has a 1¾-in. dial. This clock does not sound alarm. Runs 30 hours with one winding. Shpg. wt., 3¼ lbs.
5K8565...... **$2.35**

Desk or Dresser Clock

A beautiful little dresser or boudoir clock. Imitation pearl and amber case. Dial is oval shape, 2¾x2 in. Reliable one-day movement, without alarm. 8 in. long and 4½ in. high. Shpg. wt., 2 lbs.
5K8569...... **$2.89**

Mahogany Finish 8-Day Dresser or Desk Clock

Runs 8 days with one winding. Does not alarm. 9⅝ inches wide at base, 4 inches high, 2⅜-inch silvered dial with black numerals and hands. Shipping weight, 3 pounds.
5K8550...................... **$3.98**

De Luxe Bungalow Clock

Here's the newest clock on the market. The case represents a beautiful bungalow, in natural colors; even the foliage is colored to represent nature.

It is practically indestructible; made of highly compressed wood pulp compound, carefully enameled in natural colors.

The clock runs 30 hours with one winding. Length, 9¾ inches; 5½ inches high. Shipping weight, 5 pounds.
5K8500...... **$2.95**

The Homestead Clock

You'll like the Homestead clock. Practically indestructible. Made of highly compressed wood pulp, beautifully enameled in natural colors. The Homestead is a modern house, with attached garage and tile roof. Does not alarm. Reliable 30-hour movement, with an attractive rectangular dial, 1⅞x 1½ inches. Clock stands 6⅝ inches high and is 10 inches long. Shipping weight, 5 pounds.
5K8508... **$3.45**

Boudoir Clocks

Green Metal Desk Clock

Green cracked finish. Trimmed with brass. 2-inch dial. Clock stands 3¼ inches high and is fitted with reliable 30-hour movement. Without alarm. Shipping wt., 2 lbs.
5K8541. **$1.75**

A Reliable Traveling Clock

Genuine blue crinkled leather cover. Drop front and back. Clock is only 3½ in. high and 2¾ in. wide when closed; 1⅞-inch dial and reliable 30-hour movement. Does not alarm. Shipping wt., 1½ lbs.
5K8545. **$2.79**

Novelty Clock

Just the clock for the desk or boudoir! Wooden frame, finished in antique gold, with just a touch of color on the ornaments. One-day movement. Not an alarm clock. 7 inches high and 3⅞ in. wide at base. The octagonal shape dial is 3¼x2⅜ inches. Shipping weight, 2 pounds.
5K8543 **$3.19**

The Radio Clock

As beautiful as it is compact. A metal clock, finished in old ivory. 3½-inch base with a 2-inch dial. Reliable 30-hour movement. This is not an alarm clock. Shipping wt., 1¼ lbs.
5K8547. **$1.18**

We Guarantee Safe Delivery of All Our Shipments

Clocks of Charm

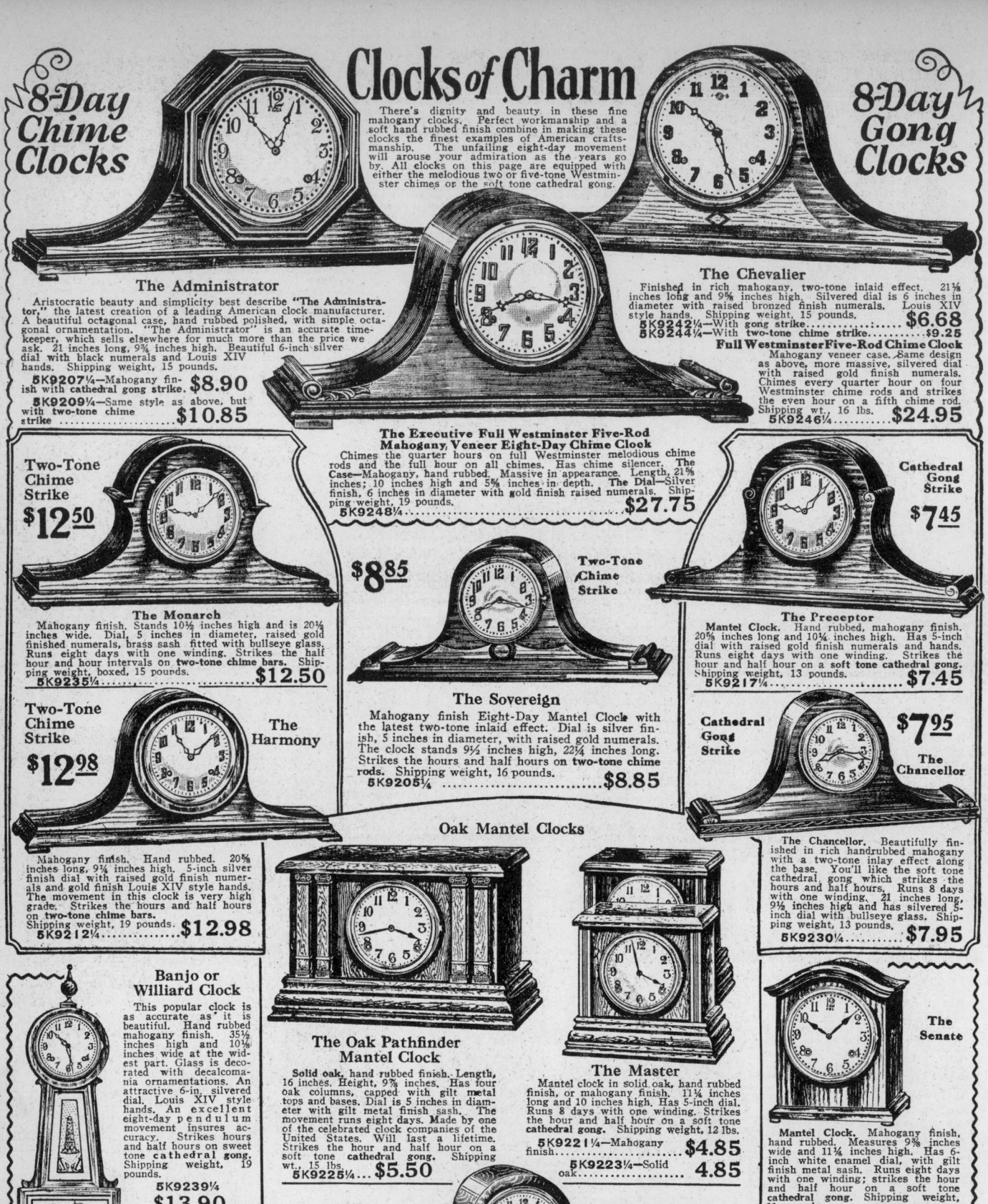

Mantel Clocks
Beauty-Accuracy

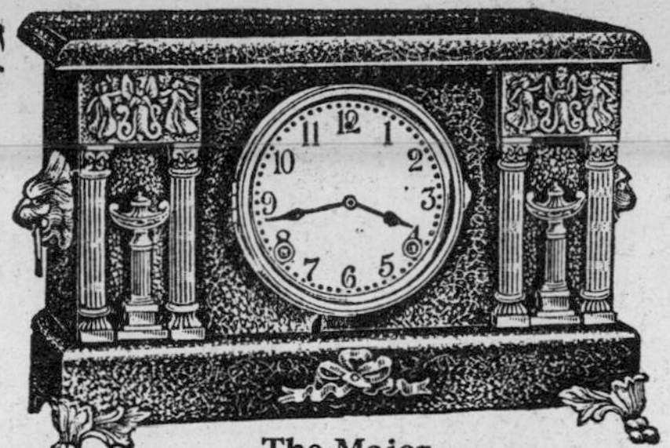

The Major

Mantel Clock. The new Florentine russet finish, so popular just now. This russet (golden brown) finish, with a novel and exceedingly attractive crystallized effect, is not only soft and pleasing in appearance but contrasts splendidly with the handsome gilt metal trimmings. It will neither be affected by dust nor moisture. Clock runs eight days with one winding. It is 15 inches long and 10 inches high. Has a 5-inch dial, with clean cut numerals and hands and is protected by a fine bullseye glass. Strikes hours and half hours on deep cathedral gong. Shipping weight, 15 pounds.
5K9101¼ **$5.50**

Select with care the clock that is to grace your mantel. On these pages you will find guaranteed clocks made by the foremost clockmakers of America. They have reliable movements that will give unfailing service. Each case is splendidly finished with exceptional care even to minute details. Unless specified otherwise, these clocks strike the hours and half hours on a soft tone cathedral gong. With ordinary care any of our clocks should give years of satisfaction. It will pay you to purchase one of these fine mantel clocks from the World's Largest Store.

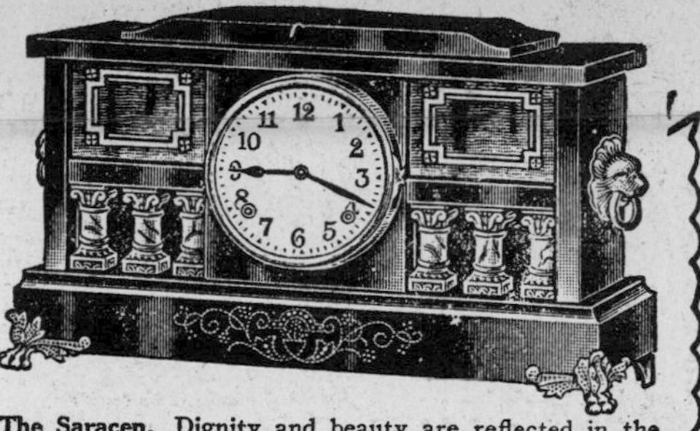

The Saracen. Dignity and beauty are reflected in the Saracen, one of the finest examples of American craftsmanship. Although the case represents a departure from the conventional black enameled wood clock, it will harmonize with the furnishings of any living room. This handsome blackwood clock with its high polish finish is sure to win your approval. Side ornaments, feet, columns, caps and bases are finished in gilt. The columns are marble-like in appearance. Above the columns are two mahogany finish panels with two-tone inlay effect. Hours and half hours are struck on a cathedral gong. The 8-day movement is reliable. The 5-inch porcelain dial with a bullseye glass is especially easy to read. Clock is 20 in. long, 10¾ inches high. Shpg. wt., 17 lbs.
5K9105¼ **$6.90**

$8.40

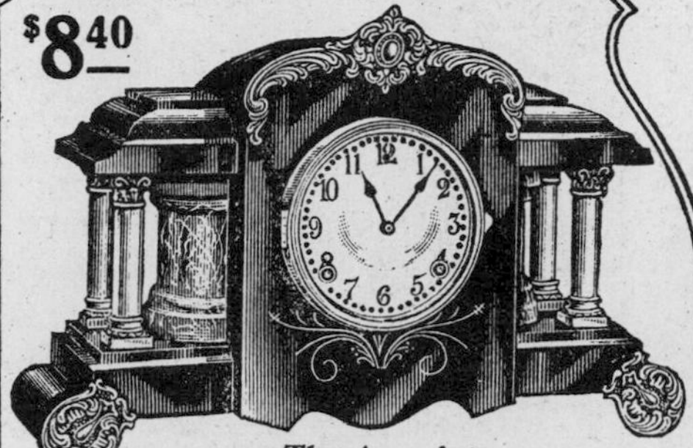

The Associate

Mantel Clock. The most popular pattern on the market and our highest grade black enameled clock. Highly polished, 18¼ inches long and 12 inches high. The 5-inch dial is covered with an exceptionally clear bullseye glass, framed with a gilt metal sash. Front is decorated with gilt metal ornamentations and engraved scroll. Sides are attractively finished with variegated red ornamentation and fine imitation (white) onyx columns, set in gilt metal caps and bases. The movement, the most important part of the clock, runs 8 days with one winding. Strikes hours and half hours on a cathedral gong. We recommend **The Associate** as one of the best values offered in clocks. Shipping weight, 19 lbs.
5K9104¼
$8.40

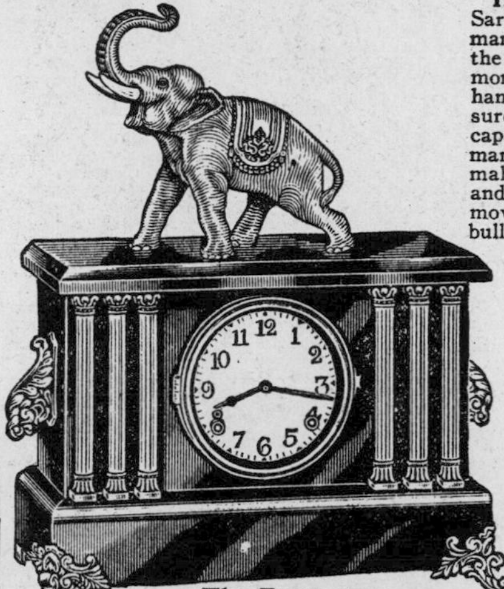

The Protector

Mantel Clock. Black enameled wood, polished to a high finish. 16¾ inches wide, 10½ inches high and has 5-inch dial. Bullseye glass with gilt finish metal sash. Has six silver finish columns, capped with gilt metal tops and bases, gilt metal side ornaments and feet. The movement runs 8 days with one winding. Strikes the hour and half hour on a soft tone cathedral gong. Shipping weight, 15 pounds.
5K9107¼—Clock only **$5.38**

An Ornament for Your Clock

The attractive silver plated Elephant, shown on the clock above, will enhance the beauty of any Blackwood Mantel Clock. Heavily lacquered to prevent tarnishing. The elephant stands 8¼ inches high and is 9¾ inches long. Shipping weight, 7 pounds.
5K9000—Ornament only **$3.65**
5K9002¼—Clock and Ornament, complete **8.95**

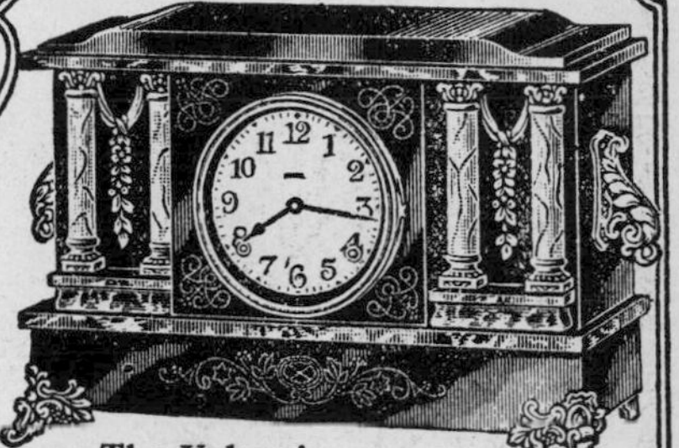

The Valencia

A popular black enameled wood clock attractively decorated with green top and bottom moldings. Four ivory-like columns. Has gilt metal feet, side ornaments and trimming. The 5-inch dial is protected by a bullseye glass. Reliable 8-day movement. Beautiful cathedral gong strikes hours and half hours. 16¾ inches long, 11¾ inches high. Shipping weight, 15 pounds.
5K9108¼ **$6.35**

Kitchen Clocks of Quality at Unusually Low Prices

$5.00 AND UP

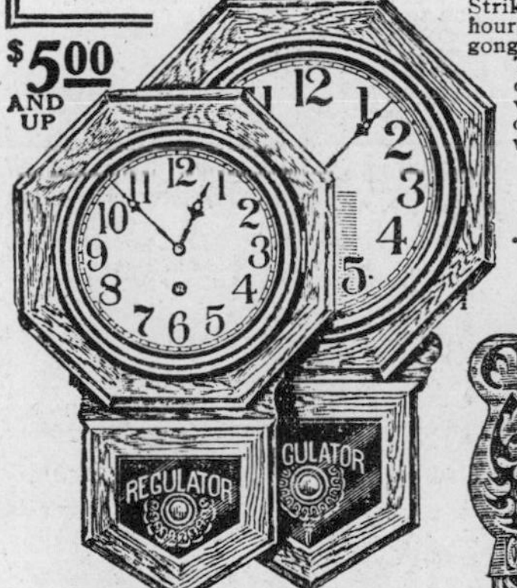

Oak Wall Clock for Church, School, Shop or Factory

Runs 8 days. 22¾ inches high, 10-inch dial. Shipping weight, 16 lbs.
5K9135¼—Time only **$5.00**
5K9137¼—Time with calendar $5.55
5K9139¼—Time with strike on wire gong $6.20
Same as above with 12-inch dial; height, 26 inches. Shipping weight, 20 pounds.
5K9140¼—Time only..... $5.80
5K9142¼—Time with calendar $6.35
5K9144¼—Time with strike on wire gong $6.70

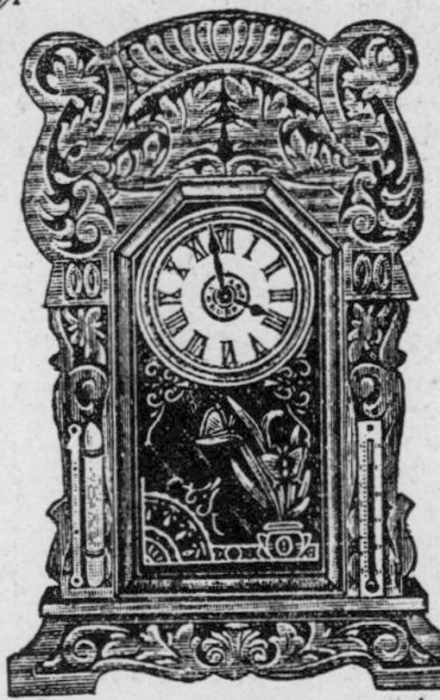

Oak Front Eight-Day Kitchen Clock

Strikes the hour and half hour. Has alarm attachment. Fancy embossed case. Stands 22½ inches high and 15 inches wide. 5¼-inch dial. Fitted with thermometer to tell temperature; also a barometer that predicts the changes in the weather. Shpg. wt., 15 lbs.
5K9121¼. **$5.35**

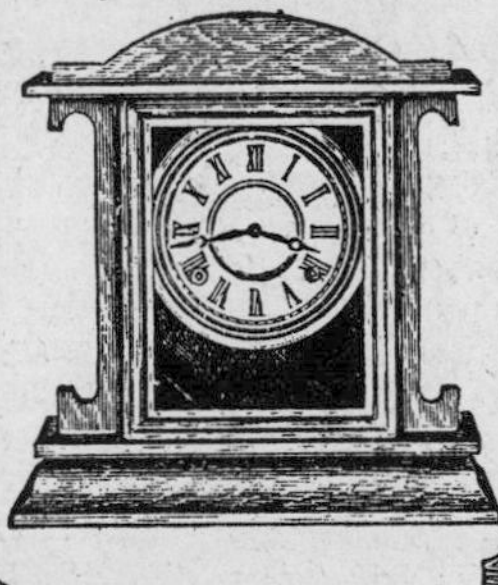

Oak Kitchen Clock

One of the latest models from the factory. It is a small but beautifully designed and accurate kitchen clock. Is 13⅜ inches wide. Stands 13¾ inches high. Has an 8-day movement. Strikes the hours and half hours on a wire gong. Shpg. wt., 10 lbs.
5K9129¼ **$3.30**

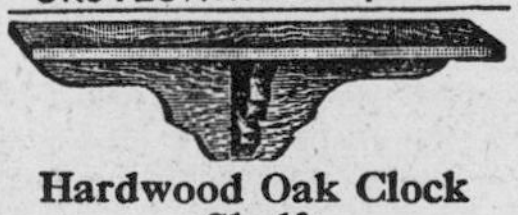

Hardwood Oak Clock Shelf

Fits shelf clocks only; 16½ inches long and 5 inches wide. Shipping wt., 2 lbs.
5K8595 .... **75c**

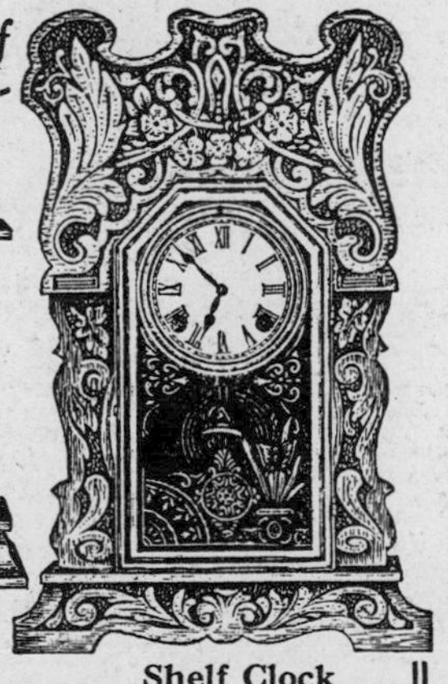

Shelf Clock

Oak finish. Embossed in beautiful scrolls and leaves. Light oak with heavy varnish finish. Runs 8 days with one winding; 22¼ inches high and 15⅛ inches wide; 5¼-inch dial. Shipping wt., 16 lbs.
5K9123¼—Wire bell strike....... **$3.65**
5K9125¼—Wire bell strike with alarm.. **$4.15**
5K9127¼—Gong bell strike with alarm. **$4.60**

Regulator Clock for Office, Factory or Store

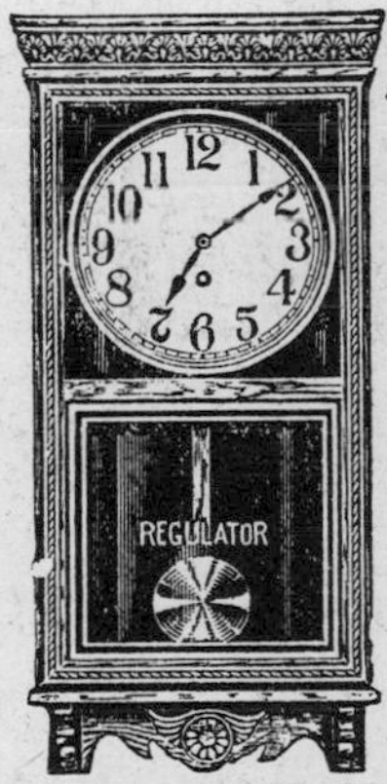

Hanging Wall Regulator Clock

Oak. Runs 8 days with one winding. 35 inches high; 12-inch dial. Shipping weight, 30 pounds. **Not mailable.**
5K9232¼—Time only **$7.15**
5K9234¼—Time and strike **$8.00**
5K9236¼—Time, strike and calendar attachment.... **8.50**

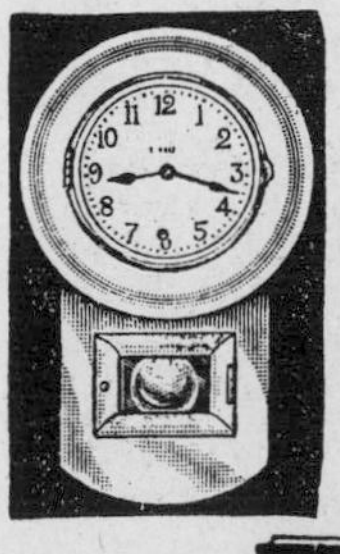

White Enamel Kitchenette Eight - Day Wall Clock. Every home should have one. White enamel with nickel - plated trimmings makes the most pleasing appearance. 13¼ inches high, 8 inches wide; 5-inch dial. Shpg. wt., 7 lbs.
5K9115¼
$5.25

Kitchen, School or Hall Clock

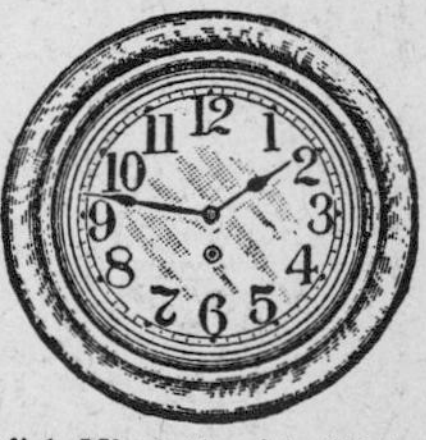

A clock for church, school, factory, shop or home. 17½ in. in diameter and finished with a front of hand rubbed oak. Has 12-inch dial. Minute hand is 5½ in. long. We guarantee the 8-day pendulum movement for accuracy under almost any conditions. This clock registers the time only. Ideal for public or domestic use. Shipping weight, 15 pounds.
5K9111¼
Oak front **$5.98**

See Index and Information Pages 542 to 570

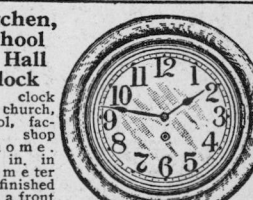

For Field and Theater

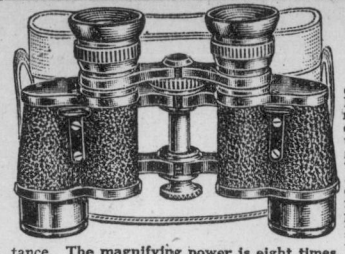

Eight-Power French Made Prism Binoculars

Made by one of the best known French manufacturers of Prism Binoculars. Prisms give an exceptionally clear and wide field of vision, the field being approximately 115 yards across at 1,000 yards distance. The magnifying power is eight times. The right hand eyepiece is adjustable for separate focusing for people of unequal vision. Shipping wt., 4½ lbs.
5K9548¼—With genuine leather case..... **$22.98**

Eight-Power Dr. F. A. Woehler Binoculars

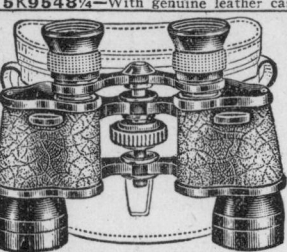

Made of the best materials obtainable, and has all the well known superior qualities of Prism binoculars. Glasses have center focusing arrangement, allowing exceedingly rapid adjustment, as in the case of moving objects. Right hand eyepiece is made movable, allowing an adjustment to equalize the difference in strength of the two eyes. Diameter of object glass, 1¼ inches. Size, closed, 4¾ inches high. Field of vision, 115 yards across at 1,000 yards distance. Magnifying power, 8 times. Covering, black leather. Shipping weight, 4½ pounds.
5K9560¼—Complete in genuine leather case. **$28.00**

Eight-Power Prism Binoculars

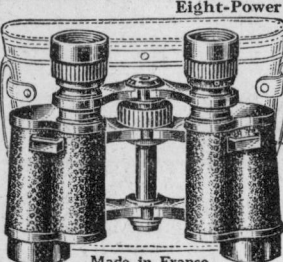

Black enamel finish, body covered with leather. Has adjustment to equalize differences in strength of the two eyes; also can be adjusted for pupillary distance. Magnifying power, 8 times. Field of vision, 90 yards at 1,000 yards distance. Shpg. wt., 4 lbs.
5K9552¼ With leather case and shoulder strap.
$15.95

Made in France

Chevalier Field Glass

Magnifying Power—3½ times. Width of field, 70 yards at 1,000 yards distance. Size—Extended, 5⅝ inches; closed, 4⅜ inches. Object Glasses—19 lignes or 1¹¹⁄₁₆ inches in diameter. Finish—Glossy black enamel; covering, black pebble grain leather. Case—Artificial leather, with shoulder strap. Instrument is of the tourist type, with short bodies and long draw tubes. Shpg. wt., 3 lbs.
5K9612¼
$5.95

Grammont Field Glass

Magnifying Power—5½ times. Size—Extended, 7⅜ inches; closed, 6⅝ inches. Wt., 1⅞ lbs. Object Glasses—26 lignes or 2⅜ inches in diameter. Finish—Glossy black enamel; covering, fine quality smooth tan leather.
Case—Covered with smooth tan leather, velveteen lined, with shoulder strap. Shipping wt., 4½ lbs.
5K9606¼
$9.85

High Power Field Glass

Magnifying Power—6½ times. Width of field, 40 yards at 1,000 yards distance.
Size—Extended 9 in.; closed, 7½ in. Weight, 1¾ lbs.
Object Glasses—21 lignes or 1⅞ in. in diam.
Finish—All metal parts, glossy black enamel; covering, black genuine morocco leather.
Case—First quality leather with shoulder strap. An ideal instrument for use where the distances are great. Shpg. wt., 4½ lbs.
5K9602¼ **$12.50**

Chevalier Field Glass

Magnifying Power—4 times. Width of field, 76 yards at 1,000 yards distance. Size—Extended, 6¾ inches; closed, 5½ inches. Weight, 1½ lbs. Object Glasses—24 lignes or 2⅛ inches. Draw tubes, glossy black enamel; other metal parts, glossy black enamel and nickel plated; covering, black pebble grained leather. Case—Covered with artificial leather with shoulder strap. Shpg. wt., 4 lbs.
5K9604¼ **$8.50**

Handy Standard Field Glass

Magnifying Power—6 times. Width of field, 55 yards at 1,000 yards distance. Size—Extended, 7⅜ inches; closed, 6 inches. Weight, 2 pounds. Object Glasses—26 lignes or 2⅜ inches in diameter. Finish—All metal parts, glossy black enamel; covering, black genuine morocco leather. Case—Good quality leather with shoulder strap. In both optical qualities and mechanical construction this instrument is beyond criticism. Shipping weight, 5 pounds.
5K9600¼ **$13.98**

Chevalier Field Glass

Magnifying Power—3½ times. Width of field, 76 yards at 1,000 yards distance. Size—Extended, 5⅝ in.; closed, 4⅛ in. Weight 12½ ounces. Object Glasses—19 lignes or 1¹¹⁄₁₆ inches in diameter. Finish—Draw tubes, dead black enamel; other metal parts, glossy black enamel, with two narrow gold plated bands; black pebble grained leather covering. Case—Artificial leather, with shoulder strap. Extra large eyepieces make this an exceptionally effective glass.
5K9620¼—Shpg. wt., 2½ lbs....... **$5.95**

Extra Brilliant Field Glass

Magnifying Power—3½ times. Width of field, 113 yards at 1,000 yards distance. Size—Extended, 4½ in.; closed, 3¾ in. Wt., 1½ lbs. Object Glasses—24 lignes or 2⅛ inches in diameter. Finish—All metal parts, glossy black enamel; covering, black genuine morocco leather. Case—First quality leather with shoulder strap. Has extreme brilliancy of illumination, very large field and fine definition.
5K9618¼—Shpg. wt., 3½ lbs.... **$11.50**

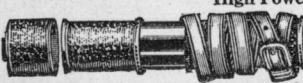

Clamp for Telescopes or Binoculars

For best results a support for the instrument is essential. This clamp is adjustable for any size telescope we list. Works fine on a camera tripod. Shpg. wt., 1 lb.
5K9516¼
$6.00

Extra High Grade Telescope, $24.50
45-Magnifying Power

Made in France

The most powerful terrestrial telescope we handle. It is the lenses which make this instrument a very superior telescope, these lenses being ground from the finest optical glass, very carefully centered and accurately adjusted. For astronomical work the celestial eyepiece listed at the right is a necessary addition to the telescope. For observation of the sun a dark glass is mounted on the slide cover of the eyepiece. Magnifying power, 45 times. Draw tubes, trimmings and all exposed metal parts made with black finish, the very best and most expensive finish known for optical instruments. This fine black finish will never tarnish nor rust, and the draw tubes always work smoothly and easily. Body of instrument covered with fine leather, morocco grained. This telescope is made with sunshade, and instead of the ordinary cap it is provided with hinged metal cover which affords perfect protection to the object glass. Length, extended, about 41½ in.; closed, about 12½ in. Weight, 3½ lbs. Diameter of object glass, 25 lignes or 2⅛ in. Magnifying power, 45 times.
5K9518¼—Shipping weight, 6 pounds..... **$24.50**

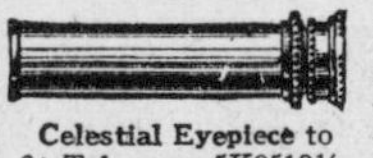

Celestial Eyepiece to fit Telescope 5K9518¼ for astronomical work, increasing power to 68 times. With all celestial eyepieces, the image is seen inverted, a matter of no consequence in astronomical observations, but which, of course, renders such eyepieces unsuitable for terrestrial work. Shipping wt., 2 lbs.
5K9520¼ **$6.85**

High Power Double Achromatic Telescope, $18.95
40-Magnifying Power

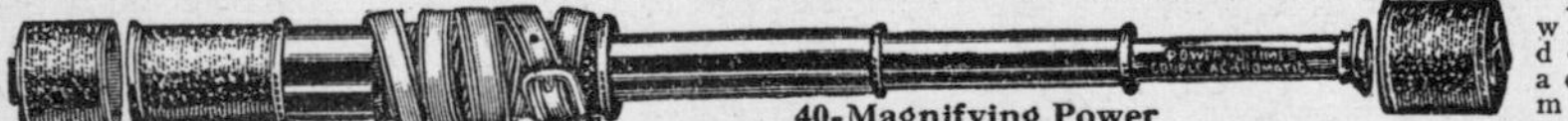

Made with double achromatic eyepiece and double achromatic object glass. Special construction of objective and eyepiece makes possible an extraordinary high magnifying power in a comparatively small and compact instrument. Although object glass measures only 19 lignes (1¹¹⁄₁₆ inches) in diameter, and total length of instrument, extended, is only about 20¾ inches, the magnifying power is forty times. Width of field, 17 yards at 1,000 yards distant. Length, when closed, about 8 inches. Draw tubes furnished in dead black. Body covered with fine leather, morocco grained. Provided with leather caps for each end and shoulder strap with loop for attaching to the body of the instrument. Shipping weight, 3 pounds.
5K9522¼ **$18.95**

Achromatic Telescope

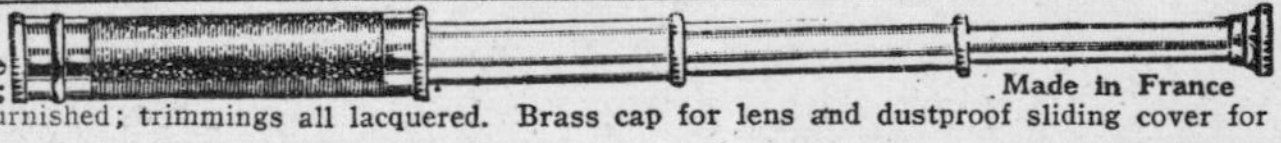

Bodies covered with fine leather, morocco grained; brass draw tubes, highly burnished; trimmings all lacquered. Brass cap for lens and dustproof sliding cover for eyepiece.

Made in France

5K9502¼—Achromatic Telescope. Diameter, object glass, 10 lignes or ⅞ inch; length, extended, about 14½ inches; closed, about 5¼ inches; magnifying power, ten times. Width of field, 30 yards at 1,000 yards distance. Shipping weight, 1 pound. **$3.45**

5K9504¼—Achromatic Telescope. Diameter, object glass, 12 lignes or 1⅛ inches; length, extended, about 16½ inches; closed, about 6 inches; magnifying power, 12 times. Width of field, 35 yards at 1,000 yards distance. Shipping weight, 1¾ pounds. **$3.85**

5K9506¼—Achromatic Telescope. Diameter, object glass, 14 lignes or 1¼ inches; length, extended, about 17¾ inches; closed, about 6¾ inches; magnifying power, 15 times. Width of field, 30 yards at 1,000 yards distance. Shipping weight, 2 pounds. **$4.50**

5K9508¼—Achromatic Telescope. Diameter, object glass, 16 lignes or 1⅞₆ inches; length, extended, about 23¾ inches; closed, about 8¼ inches; magnifying power, 20 times. Width of field, 22 yards at 1,000 yards distance. Shipping weight, 2¼ pounds. **$5.95**

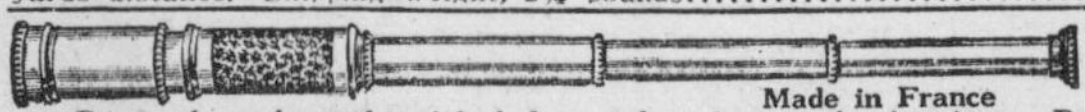

Achromatic Sunshade Telescopes, $8.50 and $14.90

Made in France

Brass throughout, burnished draw tubes, lacquered trimmings. Provided with sunshade, which can be extended forward to shade the object glass. Bodies covered with fine leather, morocco grained.

5K9512¼—Object glass, 19 lignes or 1¹¹⁄₁₆ inches; length, extended, about 29½ inches; closed, about 9¾ inches; magnifying power, 2? times. Width of field, 17 yards at 1,000 yards distance. Shipping weight, 4½ pound. **$8.50**

5K9514¼—Object glass, ? lignes, or 1¹⁵⁄₁₆ inches; length, extended, about 36½ inches; closed, about 10⅞ inches; magnifying power, 30 times. Width of field, 16 yards at 1,000 yards distance. Shipping weight, 5¼ pounds. **$14.90**

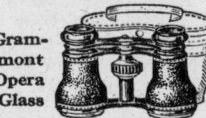

Chevalier Opera Glass

Size—Closed, 2⅜ inches. Object Glasses—1⅛ inches in diameter. Draw tubes, gold plated; other metal parts, glossy black enameled; covering, black pebbled leather. Achromatic lenses. Shpg. wt., 1½ lbs.
5K9622¼...... **$3.25**

Grammont Opera Glass

Size—Closed, 2⅜ inches. Object Glasses—1⅛ inches in diameter. Draw tubes, gold plated; other metal parts, glossy black enamel. Leather covering, with two ornamental beaded gold plated bands. Achromatic lenses. Shpg. wt., 1½ lbs.
5K9636¼—With black leather case. **$3.98**

Folding Field or Opera Glass

This glass can be used for indoor or outdoor sport and is a high grade instrument. Size, closed, 2⅜x4⅛ inches, ¾ inch deep. Object glass, 1 inch in diameter. All metal parts black enamel. Case covered with black leather. Shipping weight, 1 pound.
5K9610¼...... **$8.45**

Dr. Fossgate's Vibro-Phone

An improved form of conversation Tube, with an internal diaphragm for dividing and intensifying the sound waves. Spiral spring lining, hard rubber earpiece and special metallic mouthpiece finished in black enamel. Length, over all, 40 inches. Diameter of mouthpiece, 2½ inches. Weight, 9 ounces. Shipping weight, 1½ pounds.
5K9734—Vibro-Phone, covered with black mohair. **$3.25**
5K9736—Vibro-Phone, covered with black silk. **3.90**

London Hearing Horns

Made throughout of metal and finished in dead black. Sounds coming from a distance may be heard and understood, as in churches, public halls, etc. Is particularly adapted to those who are only moderately deaf, but for those who are very deaf we recommend the Vibro-Phones.
5K9740—2½ in. high. Shipping weight, 1 pound. **$1.35**
5K9742—4 inches high. Shipping weight, 1½ pounds. Each. **1.65**

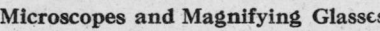

Magnifying Glasses for Reading and Work

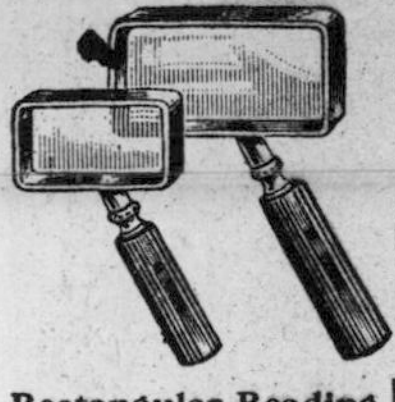

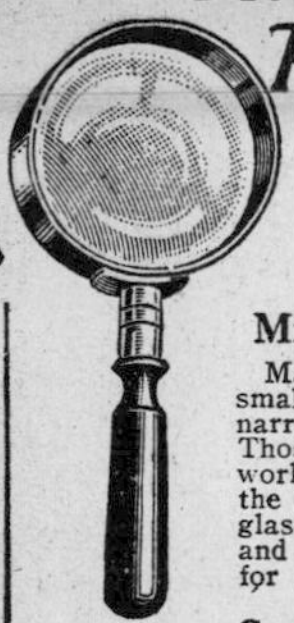

Make it easy to read, convenient for examining any small object. The smaller sizes have the highest magnifying power, but with the larger sizes a greater area can be seen at one time. AS BURNING GLASSES these instruments are very powerful.

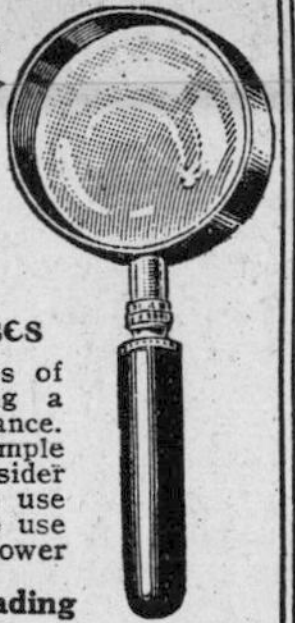

Rectangular Reading Glass

Made by Bausch and Lomb Optical Company. The offset handle makes this the most practical glass for reading we know of. Frame is heavily nickel plated, wood handle. Glass is made in such a way the magnifying power at the end of the glass is the same as the center. Shipping weight, 1 pound.

5K9760 3⅜x1¾ in.... **$2.95**
5K9762 3⅞x2 inches. **3.25**

Microscopes and Magnifying Glasses

Magnifiers of high power are made with lenses of small diameter and short focal lengths, giving a narrow field of view with narrow working distance. Those with low power have a wide field with ample working distance. In making your choice consider the character of the work in which you wish to use glass. The glasses with low power are easier to use and generally more satisfactory than the high power for ordinary purposes.

Good Reading Glasses at Very Low Prices

Imported reading glasses. Nickel plated rims. Black wood handles. Remarkably inexpensive, yet very serviceable reading glasses.

	Diam., In.	Shpg. Wt.	
5K9724	2	¾ lb.	$0.45
5K9726	2½	1 lb.	.55
5K9728	3	1¼ lbs.	.75
5K9730	4	1½ lbs.	1.15
5K9732	5	2 lbs.	1.80

Extra Quality Reading Glasses

Best grade reading glasses, very powerful lenses. Strong nickel plated rims. Black wood handles. Finely made and finished throughout. We can highly recommend them.

	Diam., In.	Shpg. Wt.	
5K9714	2	¾ lb.	$0.70
5K9716	2½	1 lb.	.75
5K9718	3	1¼ lbs.	.95
5K9720	4	1½ lbs.	1.75
5K9722	5	2 lbs.	2.75

Triple Lens Magnifier

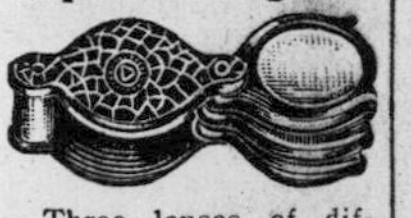

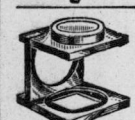

Three lenses of different foci, mounted in imitation rubber bellows shape folding pocket case. The lenses may be used singly or in various combinations, thus affording seven different magnifications. Diameters of lenses, ½, ⅝ and ¾ inch. Magnifying power, 6 to 20 times. Shipping weight, 3 ounces.
5K9712.. **$1.60**

Tripod Microscope

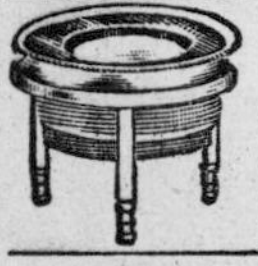

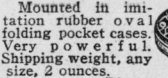

Two extra quality double convex lenses, separated by a diaphragm ring, forming a powerful double magnifier. Diameter of lenses, 1¾ inches; diaphragm opening, ¾ inch. Magnifying power, 3 times. Lacquered brass mounting. Made in France. Shipping weight, 8 ounces.
5K9758............................ **62c**

Linen Tester

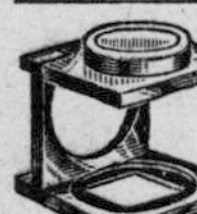

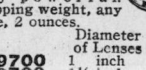

Nickel plated folding style. Easily carried in the pocket. Diameter of glass 1⅟₁₆ in. Magnifying power, five times. Shipping wt., 8 oz.
5K9755.. **$3.82**

Pocket Magnifier

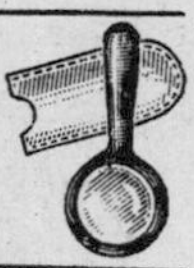

Demi-amber frame. Flat handle in neat leather container. Diameter of lens, 1⅟₁₆ inches. Entire length of reader 2¾ inches. Shipping wt., 4 ounces.
5K9763..... **50c**

Double Lens Magnifiers

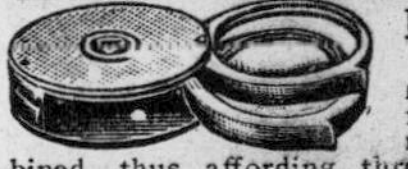

Two lenses of different foci, mounted in imitation rubber oval folding pocket cases. The lenses may be used separately or combined, thus affording three degrees of magnifying power. Shipping weight, any size, 3 ounces.

	Diameter of Lenses	Magnifying Power	
5K9706	⅞ and 1 inch	4 to 8 times	$1.25
5K9708	1 and 1¼ inches	3½ to 7 times	1.60
5K9710	1¼ and 1½ inches	3 to 6 times	2.10

Single Lens Magnifiers

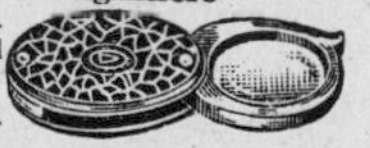

Mounted in imitation rubber oval folding pocket cases. Very powerful. Shipping weight, any size, 2 ounces.

	Diameter of Lenses	Magnifying Power	
5K9700	1 inch	4 times	$0.89
5K9702	1¼ inches	3½ times	1.00
5K9704	1½ inches	3 times	1.25

Fine Compasses

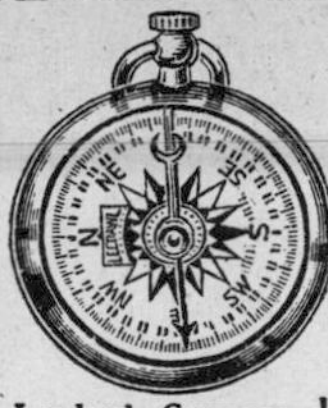

Leedawl Compass

Made by the Taylor Instrument Company. Polished white metal case, 1⅝-in. dial, untarnishable silver-like metal, tempered steel points on which the needle operates; screw top. Beveled crystal glass. Shpg. wt., 6 oz.
5K9743.$1.20

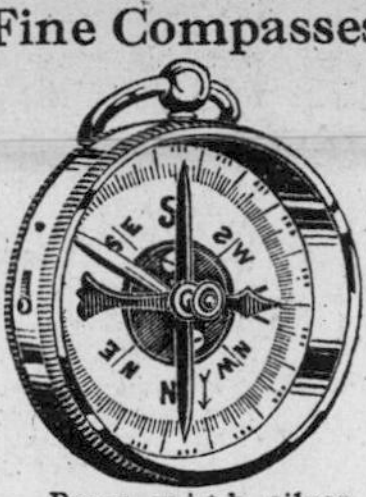

Brass with silver finish dial. Full circular division. Jeweled cap to needle and sliding stop. A special hand points exactly in the direction the user wishes to go by merely revolving bottom of the compass after the bearings have been determined. Dial, 1⅞ in. Shipping weight, 4 oz.
5K9746... **92c**

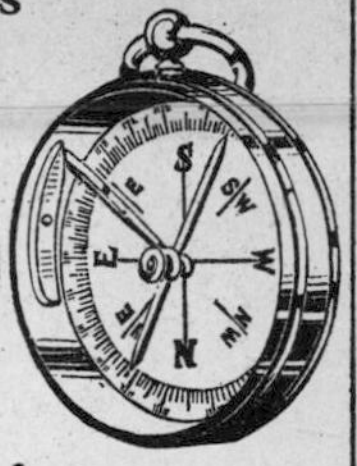

Watch Style Pocket Compass,

silver finish metal dial, bevel edge glass, brass case and provided with sliding stop. Diam., 1¾ inches. Shipping weight, 3 ounces.
5K9756. **55c**

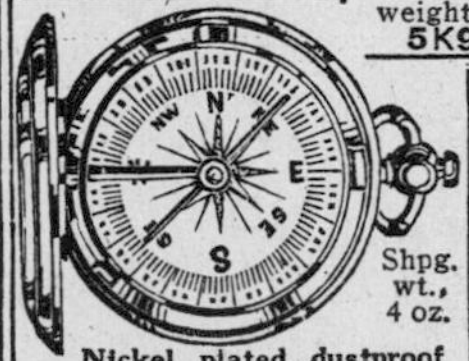

Shpg. wt., 4 oz.

Nickel plated dustproof case spring hinged cover, opened by pressing on stem; best jewel mounted English bar needle; automatic stop and beveled glass. The full circle divisions are engraved on a silver finish metal dial. Diam., 2 in.
5K9751.... **$2.75**

Compass, similar to above. This instrument is not as fine in quality as 5K9751, but will prove satisfactory. Diameter, 1¾ inches.
5K9752... **$1.45**

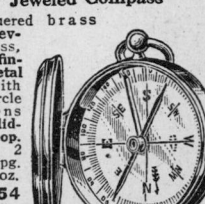

Jeweled Compass

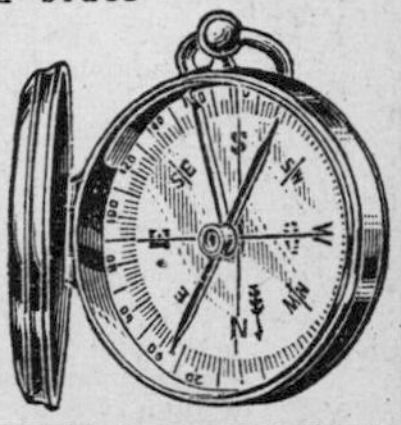

Lacquered brass case, **beveled glass, silver finish metal dial** with full circle divisions **and sliding stop.** Diam., 2 in. Shpg. wt., 5 oz.
5K9754 **92c**

Fine Jeweled Compass

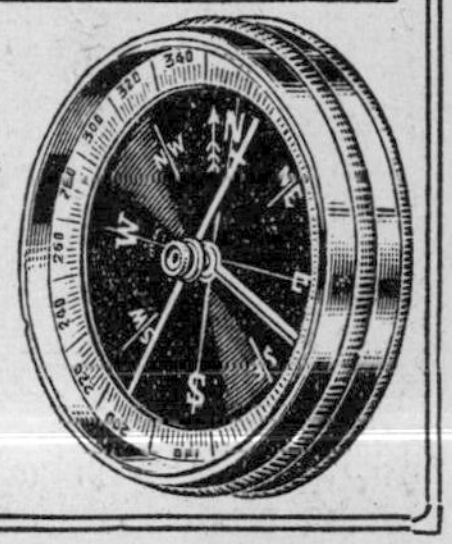

High Grade Pocket Compass, Brass case, 2⅝ in. in diameter, with cap cover; heavy beveled glass, automatic stop, **jewel mounted English bar needle.** Bottom of compass is oxidized in black with white lettering, and the full circle divisions are engraved on a silver finish metal dial **raised to level of needle.** Shpg. wt., 6 oz.
5K9748.............. **$2.45**

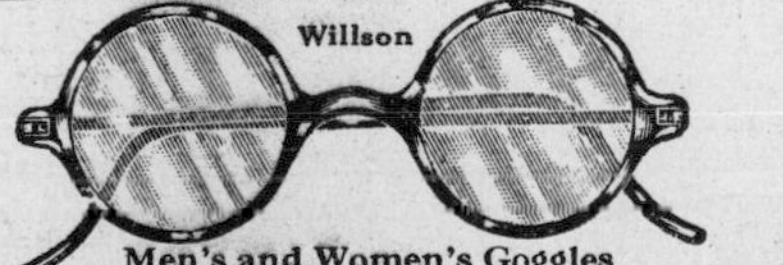

Willson

Men's and Women's Goggles

High Grade Imitation All Shell Goggles with straight temples. 1¾-inch lenses in amber, smoke or clear glass. Protect your eyes against sun glare and dust. Fine for motoring. May be worn for hours without discomfort. Shipping weight, ¾ pound.
5K9785—Amber glass............................ 50c
5K9786—Smoked glass............................ 50c
5K9791—Clear glass............................ 50c

Wide Vision Goggles

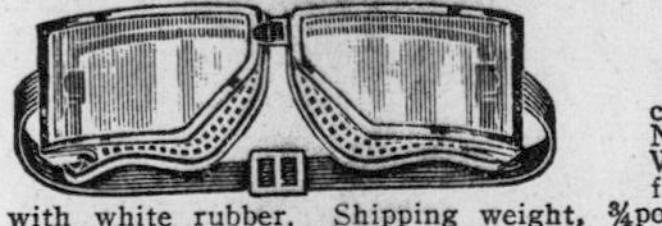

Double strength curved glass. Nickel plated. Well ventilated frame. Trimmed with white rubber. Shipping weight, ¾pound.
5K9776—Clear glass............................ .75c
5K9777—Amber glass............................ .75c

Wind, Dust and Sun Glasses

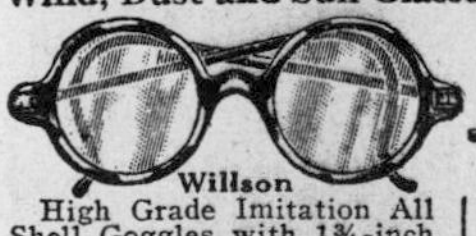

Willson

High Grade Imitation All Shell Goggles with 1¾-inch lenses in amber, smoke or clear glass. Shpg. wt., ¾ lb.
5K9781—Smoked glass.... **45c**
5K9783 Amber glass......... 45c
5K9784 Clear glass......... 45c

Drop Eye Goggles

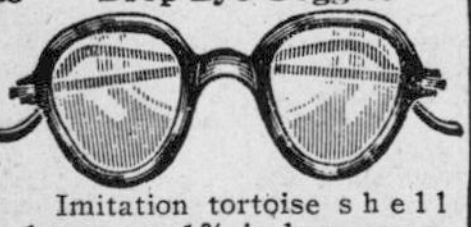

Imitation tortoise shell lenses are 1¾ inches across. Shipping weight, ¾ pound.
5K9792 Clear glass.......... 40c
5K9793 Amber glass.......... 40c
5K9794 Smoked glass.......... 40c

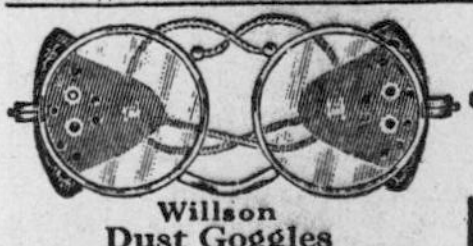

Willson

Dust Goggles

Rustproof White Metal Goggles, with ventilated leather side shields, flexible cable ear bows and the adjustable bridge. 1⅞-inch lenses. With metal case. Shipping weight, ¾ pound.
5K9787—Amber glass.......... **75c**
5K9788 Clear glass.......... 75c

Willson

Tight Fitting Ventilated Goggles

All metal frame and screen guards. Lens measure 1¾x1½ inches. Goggles every farmer, thresher or anyone who must work in dusty places should have. Shipping weight, ¾ pound.
5K9795—Smoked glass.......... **32c**
5K9797 Clear glass.......... 32c

American Made Pockescopes, Field Glasses and Microscopes

Buy one of these high grade, inexpensive Field Glasses or Pokescopes. Instruments of similar size and same quality usually sell for one-fourth to one-third more elsewhere

For small instruments, the power is unusual, about six times magnification, the same as demanded of Field Glasses used by the United States Army Officers.

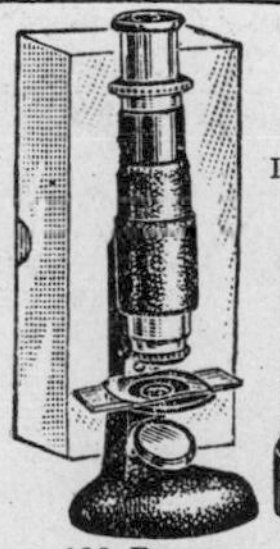

100-Power Microscope

This microscope is American made and has an achromatic optical system which magnifies objects 100 diameters distinctly and brilliantly over the entire field. It is extremely simple to operate and made of high grade material and workmanship. Height, 6 inches; diameter at base, 2¼ in. Packed in a substantial plush lined case and supplied with one prepared slide and complete instructions. Shpg. wt., 2¼ pounds.
5K9532 **$6.25**

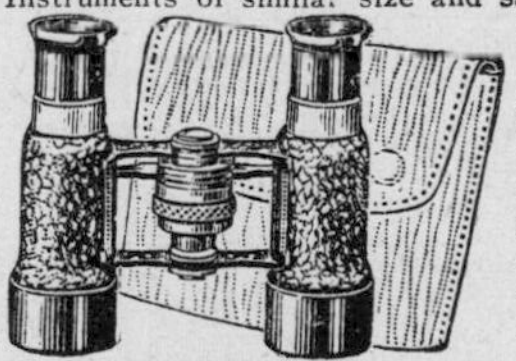

Magnifying Power, 6 Times

Adjustable for pupillary distance. Screw-focusing system. Fine definition. Objective lenses are 25 M. M. in diameter. Black finish. Shipping weight, 2 lbs.
5K9625¼ Complete.......... **$4.75**

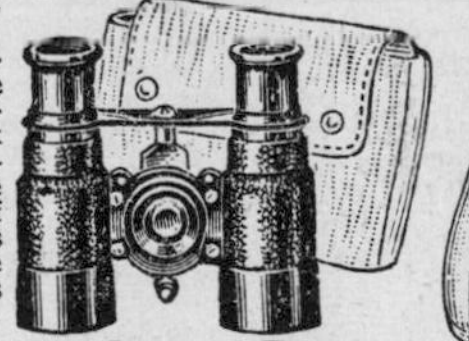

Magnifying Power, 6 Times

Can be conveniently carried in pocket. Objective lenses are 25 M. M. in diameter. Lever focusing arrangement. Measurements in case are 4x3½ inches. Shipping weight, 2 pounds.
5K9626¼ Complete.......... **$3.65**

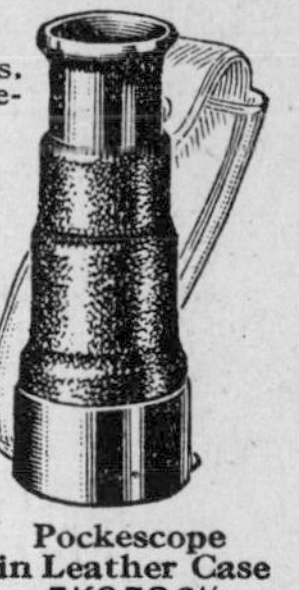

Pockescope in Leather Case

5K9526¼ Length, closed, 2⅝ in. Maximum diam., 11/16 inch. Magnifying power, 3 times. Shpg. wt., 8 ounces.. **82c**

5K9528¼ Length, closed, 3 in. Maximum diam., 11/16 in. Magnifying power, 4½ times. Shipping weight, 8 ounces. **$1.20**

5K9530¼ Length, closed, 3¼ in. Maximum diam., 1 3/16 in. Magnifying power, abt. 6 times. Shipping weight, ¾ pound.. **$1.60**

Pocket Microscope

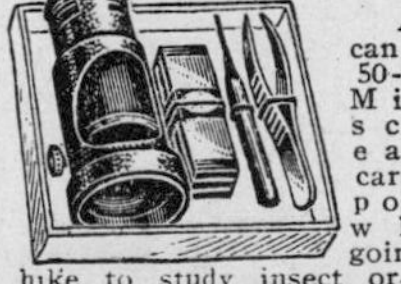

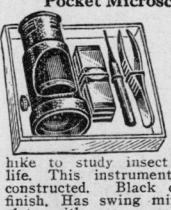

American Made 50-Power Microscope easily carried in pocket when going on hike to study insect or plant life. This instrument is well constructed. Black crystalline finish. Has swing mirror complete with one prepared slide, two glass slides, one dissecting needle, and one pair of tweezers. Complete instruction how to use sent with each instrument. Shipping weight, 1½ lbs.
5K9533........ **$1.98**

Microscope Slide Sets

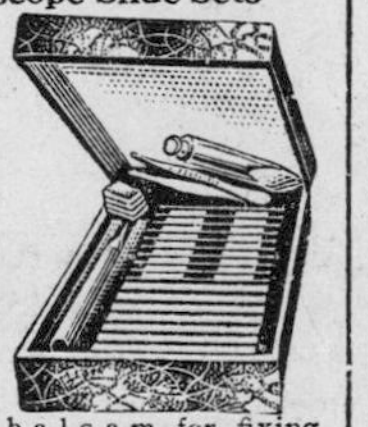

Ten prepared slides with ten plain slides with glass covers. One dissecting needle, one pair of tweezers, a tube of Canada balsam for fixing cover glasses. Shipping weight, 1 pound.
5K9535........ **$2.50**
5K9537—20 each plain glass slides with cover glasses in rack box. Shipping weight, 1 lb........ **65c**

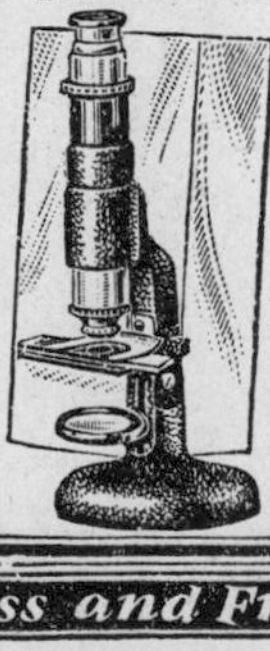

250-Power Microscope
Made in America

A compact microscope which has all of the advantages of the more expensive instruments.

A carefully corrected achromatic optical system with a large field of view. Variable magnification from 100 to 250 diameters. Tilting stand. Adjustable mirror for substage or top illumination. Finger spring clips for holding slides. Height, 7⅛ inches; diameter at base, 3 inches; stage, 2 inches square. Finish, black and crystallized lacquer, with nickel trim. One prepared slide; complete instructions. Shipping weight, 4 pounds.
5K9538.................. **$11.98**

Compound Microscope

Made in Paris. **Constructed of brass. Is 6½ inches high** when focused. Swinging mirror for the illumination of objects; **triple lens** can be separated. **When all three lenses are used the magnifying power is 70 times;** with two lower lenses, 50 times, and with single lens, 30 times. In wood case. Brass tweezers, two plain glass slides and one prepared object. Shipping weight, 2 pounds.
5K9778......... **$3.35**

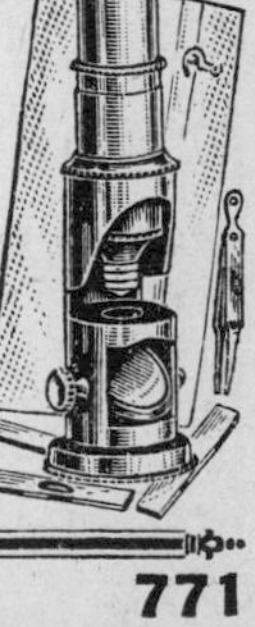

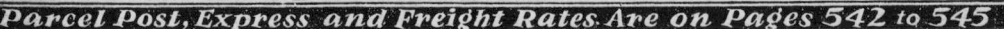

Parcel Post, Express and Freight Rates Are on Pages 542 to 545

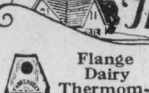

THERMOMETERS
The Correct Temperature Means Better Health

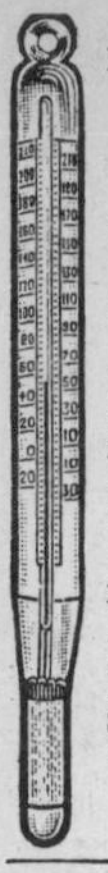

American Made Floating Dairy Thermometer

Mercury. All glass. Very accurate. Extra large figures; red lettering for scalding cheese, churning and freezing points. Weighted with shot, stands upright in cream. Extreme length, 10¼ in. Not to be compared with the cheap imported thermometer. Shipping wt., 1 pound.

5K9454 **54c**

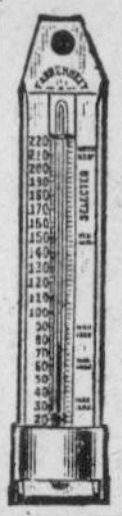

Flange Dairy Thermometer

Made by the Taylor Instrument Co. Spirit Nickel plated brass scale with stamped figures and lines. Sliding guard for bulb. Length, 8 in. Shipping weight, 1 lb.

5K9452 **65c**

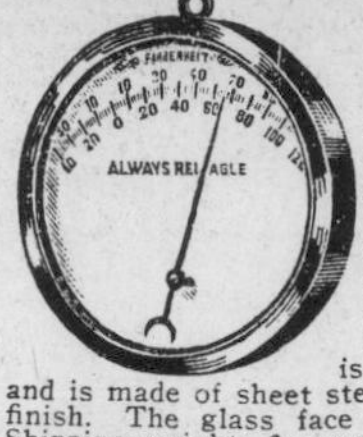

Easy Reading Thermometer

Has needle indicator, 4 in. long. The graduations rise from 40 degrees F. below to 120 degrees F. above zero, thereby making it an ideal thermometer for inside or outside use. The case is 7 in. in diameter and is made of sheet steel with a japanned finish. The glass face protects the dial. Shipping weight, 3 pounds.

5K9544 **$1.60**

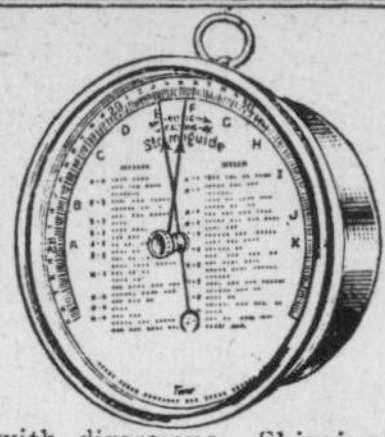

Tycos Stormoguide

Made by the Taylor Instrument Co. Gives a 12 to 24-hour weather forecast. Complete forecasts plainly shown on the dial. Round brass case, blue bronze finish. For use from sea level to an altitude of 3,500 feet. Complete with directions. Shipping weight, 3½ pounds.

5K9545 **$14.50**

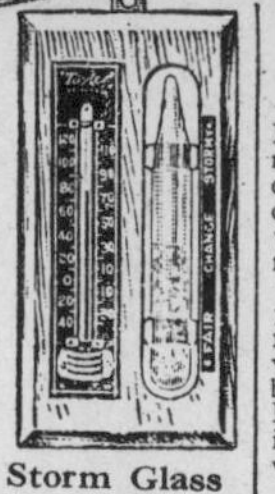

Storm Glass and Thermometer

Made by the Taylor Instrument Co. Oak back, 3¾x7¾ in. Good spirit thermometer with black scale and white figures. Extra large storm glass. Shipping weight, 1½ pounds.

5K9410 **$1.30**

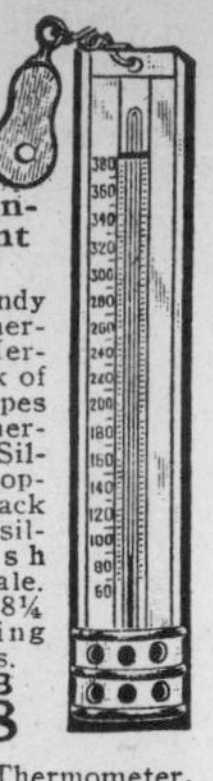

Candy Thermometer Made by the Taylor Instrument Co.

Home Candy Making Thermometer. Mercury. Book of candy recipes with each thermometer. Silver finish copper case. Black figures on silver finish brass scale. Length, 8¼ in. Shipping wt., 1½ lbs.

5K9478 **$1.68**

Candy Thermometer, similar to the above, made by a different manufacturer. Length, 9 inches.

5K9477 **$1.35**

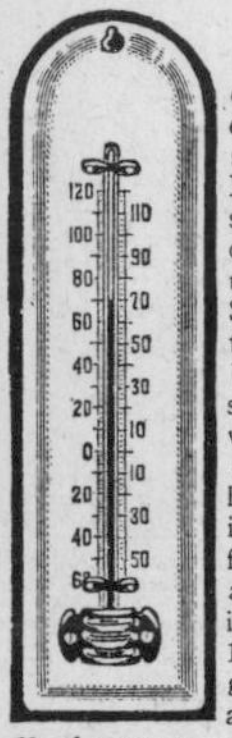

Distance Reading Thermometer

White enameled on steel. For inside or outside use. Spirit tube, black scale on white enamel. Registers from approximately 120 degrees above to 60 degrees below zero. Length over all, 9 in. Shpg. wt., 1½ pounds.

5K9438... **79c**

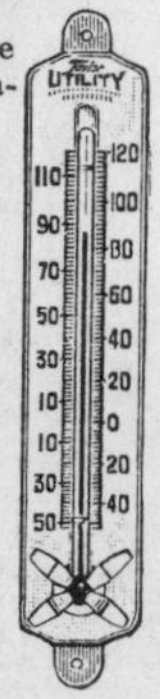

White Enamel Window or Outside Thermometer

Made by the Taylor Instrument Co. Distant reading scale. Permacolor (non-fading) filled tube. Length, 8⅜ in. Shipping weight, 1¼ lbs.

5K9405.. **85c**

Same as above, but with brackets for window use.

5K9407.. **85c**

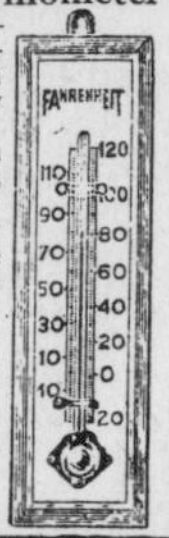

Outdoor Thermometer

Solid Mahogany Back Thermometer, 9⅛ in. in length by 2⅜ in. in width. Registers from 120 degrees above to 50 degrees below zero. Large black scale and figures on white. Metal background, 7-inch magnified red spirit tube. Shpg. wt., 1¼ lbs.

5K9421 **43c**

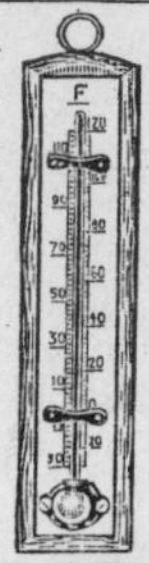

Indoor Thermometer

Light oak back, nicely finished. Scale and numerals black on gold finish background. Registers from about 110 degrees above to 30 degrees below. Has magnifying red spirit tube. Length, 6¼ in. Shpg. wt., ¾ lb.

5K9423 **45c**

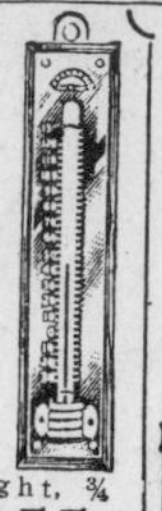

Indoor or Outdoor Thermometer

8½ in. high. Manufactured by the Taylor Instrument Co. and has magnifying mercury glass tube. Generally sold elsewhere at $1.00. Shipping weight, ¾ pound.

5K9409... **55c**

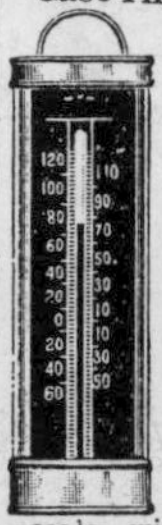

Taylor's Metal Case Thermometer

Popular thermometer for all around service. A good thermometer because of its wide copper plated case, wide scale with large easy reading white figures and graduations on black oxidized background. Magnifying tube filled with red spirit. Scale range, 20 to 60 below to 120 F. above. Length, 7⅛ in. Shipping weight, 1¼ lbs.

5K9415 **90c**

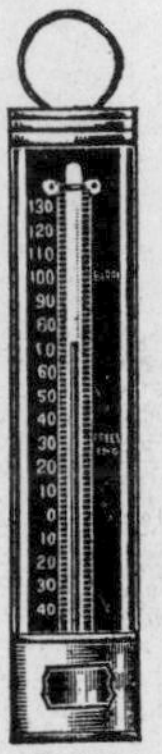

Tycos Thermometer

Made by the Taylor Instrument Co. Heavily enameled, thoroughly baked, weather resisting case, 9¾ in. long. Non-fading fluid in tube. White, plain and distinct figures. Registers about 50 below to 120 above zero. Shpg. wt., 1¾ lbs.

5K9401 **$1.55**

As above, but with mercury. 40 degrees below to 120 degrees above.

5K9400 **$1.65**

Dustite Respirators

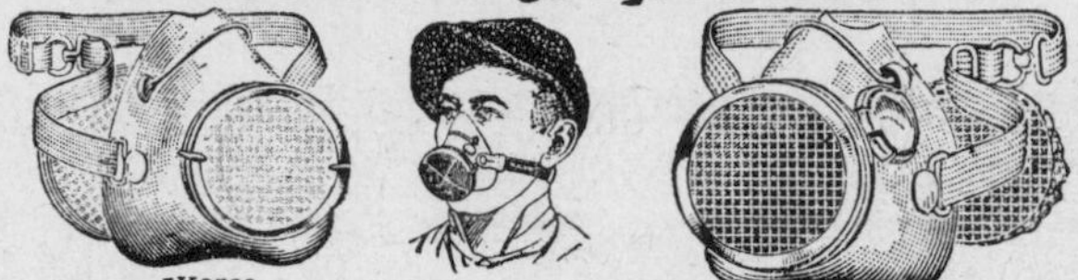

5K9766 5K9769

In Our Opinion the Best Made

Have passed the test and secured the approval of the UNDERWRITERS' LABORATORIES for the protection of workers in dusty conditions. No thresherman, miller or farmer should be without one. Filter and clean the air you breathe. Light, comfortable and easily cleaned. All parts interchangeable. Made of high grade rubber. Complete, as illustrated. Shipping weight, 1 pound.

5K9766—Respirator, with 12 filters **$1.45**

5K9768—Extra Cotton Filters. Shpg. wt., 2 oz. Per pkg. of 50.. **35c**

5K9769—Respirator, as illustrated above, wet sponge type with relief valve. Shipping weight, 1 pound **$1.95**

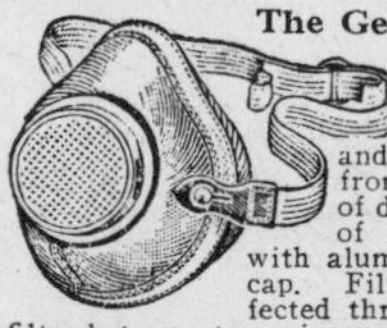

The Gem Respirator

Protects nose and mouth from intrusion of dust. Made of leather, with aluminum nose cap. Filtration effected through cloth filter between two wire mesh screens. Interchangeable filters, adjustable to anyone. Complete with 1 dozen cloth filters, two extra wire screens and elastic band to hold it on. Shipping weight, 1 pound.

5K9770 **97c**

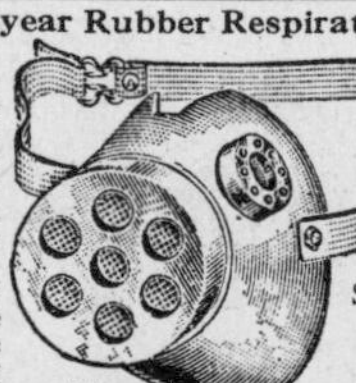

Goodyear Rubber Respirator

For those whose duties take them in dusty places. Made of white pliable rubber with elastic band. Has metal breathing relief valve complete with sponge for filtration. Shpg. wt., 1¼ lbs.

5K9773 **89c**

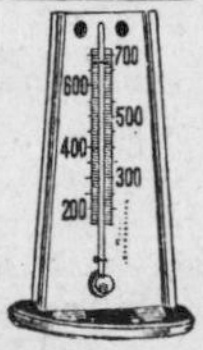

Oven Thermometer

White porcelain. Made by the Taylor Instrument Co. The Taylor book of recipes with each order gives the proper temperature for bread, roasts, etc. Mercury tube filled by nitrogen pressure to prevent separation. Approximately 200 to 600 degrees Fahrenheit. Easily read. Height, 5 inches. Shipping weight, 1⅛ pounds.

5K9444 **$1.75**

Oven Thermometer Made by Different Manufacturer

White scale and figures on black finish, metal back. Mercury tube registers from 100 degrees to 600 degrees Fahrenheit. Height, 5½ inches. Book of recipes with each thermometer. Shipping wt., 1¼ lbs.

5K9441 **$1.40**

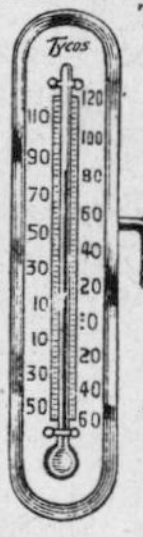

Tycos Extra High Grade White Enameled Thermometer for Window or Porch

Made by the Taylor Instrument Co.

Stands all weather conditions. It will not corrode or deteriorate. Sturdily constructed. Tube mounted on pure white watch dial porcelain scale. The entire back is made of metal. First selection, red Permacolor (non-fading) easily read fluid filled tube. Registers approximately 60 degrees below zero to 120 degrees Fahrenheit above. Magnifying tube plain and distinct. 10¼ inches long and 2⅜ inches wide. Shipping wt., 2¼ lbs.

5K9440 **$2.65**

IMPORTED CUCKOO CLOCKS

Our imported Cuckoo Clocks are selected from the best designs and best values to be found. The fronts or carvings are all handwork, walnut finish, perfectly seasoned and kiln dried. These clocks are operated by weights that insure good time keeping. We inspect every clock by setting it up and running it. Directions for adjusting and striking sent with each clock. We do not carry cheaper Cuckoo Clocks, because we found them **not dependable.**

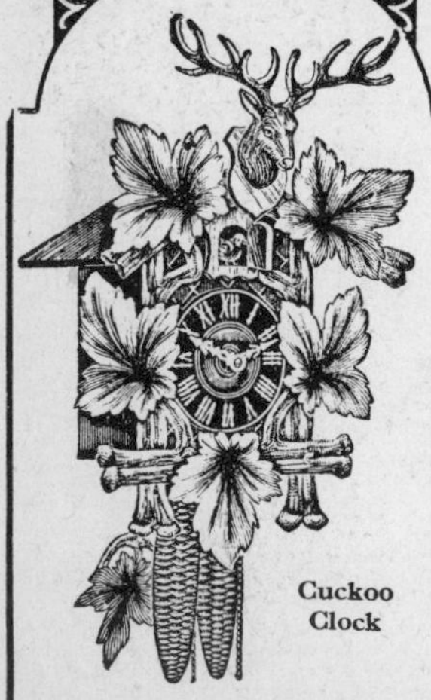

Cuckoo Clock

Ornamented with deer head and oak leaves. Extreme **height, 19½ inches;** width, 13 inches. Dial is 5 inches in diameter. Runs one day. Strikes on a wire gong, at the same time cuckoo appears and calls the hour and half hour. Shipping weight, 21 pounds.

5K9314¼ **$13.45**

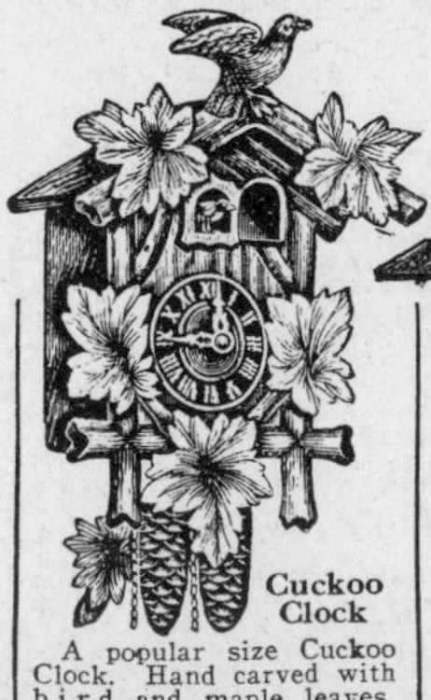

Cuckoo Clock

A popular size Cuckoo Clock. Hand carved with bird and maple leaves. Cuckoo appears and calls hours and half hours and strikes wire gong simultaneously. 3-inch dial and white numerals. Extreme height, 12 inches. Width, 8¾ inches. Shipping wt., 8 lbs.

5K9300¼ **$5.65**

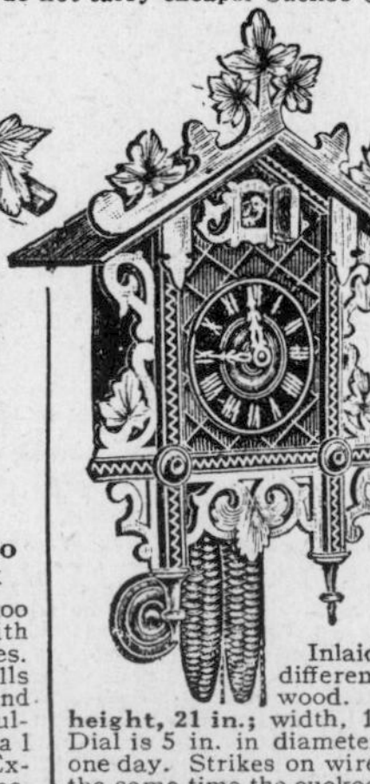

Cuckoo Clock

Inlaid with different colored wood. Extreme **height, 21 in.;** width, 13 inches. Dial is 5 in. in diameter. Runs one day. Strikes on wire gong at the same time the cuckoo appears and calls the hours and half hours. Shipping wt., 21 lbs.

5K9304¼ **$10.98**

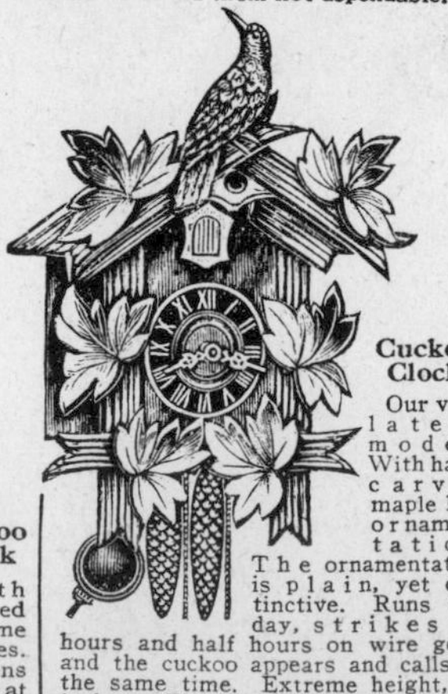

Cuckoo Clock

Our very latest model. With hand carved maple leaf ornamentation. The ornamentation is plain, yet distinctive. Runs one day, strikes the hours and half hours on wire gong and the cuckoo appears and calls at the same time. Extreme height, 19 inches. Extreme width, 14 inches. Has 4½-inch dial. Shipping weight, 19 pounds.

5K9316¼ **$12.25**

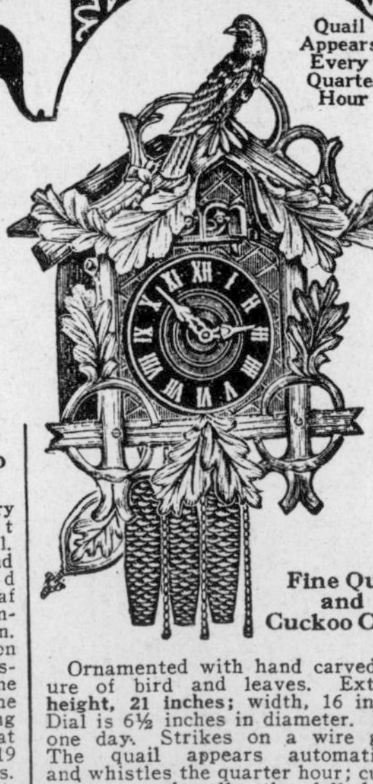

Quail Appears Every Quarter Hour

Fine Quail and Cuckoo Clock

Ornamented with hand carved figure of bird and leaves. Extreme **height, 21 inches;** width, 16 inches. Dial is 6½ inches in diameter. Runs one day. Strikes on a wire gong. The quail appears automatically and whistles the quarter hour; cuckoo appears and calls the full hours. Shipping wt., 35 lbs.

5K9318¼ **$19.50**

The Best Sellers!

$1.69 Each

Have your name and address printed on your writing paper. See page 791.

Usually Retail at $2.00

Here they are! The finest fiction of the year by authors internationally known for the vividness and gripping interest of their novels. Many fascinating hours for you are bound within the covers of the books listed below. Shipping weight, 1¼ pounds.

3K664—God and the Grocery Man. Harold Bell Wright
3K665—Forlorn River. Zane Grey (Ready November 1st)
3K669—The Mating Call. Rex Beach
3K89—Bellarion, the Fortunate. R. Sabatini
3K90—Under the Tonto Rim. Z. Grey
3K1212—The Understanding Heart. P. B. Kyne
3K1251—The Black Hunter. J. O. Curwood

3K91—Cherry Square. G. S. Richmond
3K92—Black Pearls. R. W. Alexander
3K99—The Chinese Parrot. E. D. Biggers
3K180—The Incredulity of Father Brown. G. K. Chesterton
3K181—Not Afraid. D. Coolidge
3K189—Preface to a Life. Z. Gale
3K192—The Flame of Courage. G. Gibbs
3K93—Lucky Numbers. M. Glass
3K95—Hand and Ring. A. K. Green
3K132—Confession. C. Hamilton
3K135—The Unearthly. R. Hichens
3K137—The Pope of the Sea. B. V. Ibanez

3K138—Michael Forth. M. Johnston
3K139—St. Michael's Gold. B. H. Jones
3K140—The Blood of Kings. W. R. Kauffman
3K141—The Big Mogul. J. C. Lincoln
3K142—Perella. J. W. Locke
3K143—This Mad World. H. MacGrath
3K144—Kindling and Ashes. G. B. McCutcheon
3K145—The Blue Castle. L. M. Montgomery
3K148—Hearts of Hickory. J. T. Moore
3K153—Harvey Gerrard's Crime. E. P. Oppenheim

Intrigue, romance, breath taking adventure, heart stirring love, are portrayed as only master creators can portray them. Look over the titles—notice the authors—every book shown herewill appeal to you and every one is a great value at the low price we ask. Average 300 pages. Bound in cloth. Size 5½x7¾ inches.

3K156—The Magic Garden. G. S. Porter
3K163—Pandora. A. B. Reeve
3K171—The Master of the Microbe. R. W. Service
3K173—Folly's Gold. L. Scott
3K175—Far End. M. Sinclair
3K176—Page Mr. Tutt. A. Train
3K178—The Corbin Necklace. H. K. Webster
3K85—The Red-Haired Girl. C. Wells
3K86—Here and Beyond. E. Wharton
3K87—Beau Sabreur. C. P. Wren.

Any one of the above titles................$1.69

Biography, Humor, Travel, Drama, Art

Here is published for the first time a series of popular priced non-fiction books that sold in original editions for $2.50 to $5.00. Printed from the original plates, without abridgment. Bound in cloth. Average 300 pages. Size, 5⅜x8 inches, on a fine quality of white-wove book paper.

3K1357—Bird Neighbors. Blanchan.
3K1332—Mirrors of Washington. Anonymous.
3K1333—A Short Life of Mark Twain. Albert Bigelow Paine
3K1334—Woodrow Wilson As I Know Him. Joseph P. Tumulty
3K1335—Science Remaking the World. Otis W. Caldwell and Edwin E. Slosson
3K1336—The Autobiography of Benjamin Franklin
3K1338—A Book of Operas. Henry Edward Krehbiel
3K1339—Barnum. M. R. Werner
3K1340—Cleopatra. Claude Ferval
3K1342—In Brightest Africa. Carl E. Akeley
3K1343—Brain and Personality. W. Hanna Thomson

3K1344—Jeanne D'Arc. M. O. Oliphant
3K1345—Progress and Poverty. Henry George
3K1346—Astronomy for Everybody. Prof. Simon Newcomb
3K1347—My Life and Work — Henry Ford. Samuel Crowther
3K1348—Lincoln's Own Stories. Anthony Gross
3K1352—Edge of the Jungle. William Beebe
3K1353—Recollections and Letters of General Robert E. Lee. Captain Robert E. Lee
3K1354—Second Book of Operas. Henry Edward Krehbiel
3K1355—Faery Lands of the South Seas. Hall and Nordhoff
3K1364—Shandygaff. Morley.

Any one of the above books. (Shipping weight, 1½ pounds).................89c

---

The Famous Readers' Library

29¢ each   **American Home Classics**   **2 for 55¢**

Any Two Books, 25c
Any Five Books, 55c

Bound in rich red cloth; beautiful ornamental design stamped in full gilt on side and back. Measures 4½x6¾ inches. Average 225 to 300 pages.
Never before has anyone offered such wonderfully well made books at so low a price. Printed from brand new plates, with large, easily read type on a fine quality of white paper. Fancy pictorial end sheets.

Inez. Augusta J. Evans
Ishmael. Mrs. Southworth
Ivanhoe—Vol. I. Scott
Ivanhoe—Vol II. Scott
Last Days of Pompeii. Bulwer Lytton
Self Raised. Mrs. Southworth
Thelma. Marie Corelli
The Spy. J. Fenimore Cooper
Andersen's Fairy Tales.
Grimms' Fairy Tales.
Hans Brinker. Dodge
Lena Rivers. Mary J. Holmes
Jane Eyre. Charlotte Bronte
Treasure Island. Robert Louis Stevenson
Dr. Jekyll and Mr. Hyde and Kidnapped. Stevenson
Homestead on the Hillside. Mary J. Holmes
Sherlock Holmes Detective Stories. Doyle
Thorns and Orange Blossoms. Bertha M. Clay

Alice in Wonderland and Alice Through the Looking Glass. Lewis Carroll
Last of the Mohicans. J. Fenimore Cooper
Black Rock. Ralph Connor
Uncle Tom's Cabin. Harriet Beecher Stowe
Plain Tales From the Hills. Rudyard Kipling
File No. 113. Emile Gaboriau
Murders in the Rue Morgue. Edgar Allan Poe
Little Minister. J. M. Barrie
English Orphans. Holmes
Capitola's Peril. Mrs. E. D. E. N. Southworth
Black Beauty. Anna Sewell
Scarlet Letter. Hawthorne
Under Two Flags. "Ouida"
Marion Grey. Mary J. Holmes
Pilgrim's Progress. John Bunyan
Tom Brown's School Days. Thomas Hughes
Tanglewood Tales. Hawthorne

3K84—Any two. 25c
Shipping weight, 1 lb...25c
Any five. Shipping weight, 2½ lbs........55c
Any ten. Shipping weight, 5 lbs............$1.00

THEIR LOW PRICE brings these good books within the reach of all. Bound in a fine quality of linen weave pattern book cloth. Set off by an ornamental gilt stamping on side and back in a rich dignified design. Printed entirely from new plates in large easily read type on a high grade white book paper. Size, 5x7¼ inches. Average 250 pages.

Marble Faun. Hawthorne
Merry Men and Other Stories, The. Stevenson
Mill on the Floss, The—Vol. I. Eliot
Mill on the Floss, The—Vol. II. Eliot
New Arabian Nights. Stevenson
Oliver Twist—Vol. I. Dickens
Oliver Twist—Vol. II. Dickens
Pathfinder, The. Cooper
Pere Goriot. Balzac
Phantom 'Rickshaw and Other Stories, The. Kipling
Picture of Dorian Gray, The. Wilde
Pioneers, The. Cooper
Prince Otto. Stevenson
Sappho. Daudet
Soldiers Three and Other Stories. Kipling
Twenty Years After — Vol. I. Dumas
Twenty Years After — Vol. II. Dumas
Vicar of Wakefield, The. Goldsmith
Autocrat of the Breakfast Table. Holmes
Treasure Island. Stevenson
Little Minister, The. Barrie
Scarlet Letter, The. Hawthorne
Tale of Two Cities. Dickens
Three Musketeers, The—Vol. I. Dumas
Three Musketeers, The—Vol. II. Dumas
Lena Rivers. Holmes
Under Two Flags. Ouida
Light That Failed, The. Kipling
Master of Ballantrae, The. Stevenson
Two Orphans, The. D'Ennery
Capitola's Peril. Southworth
Study in Scarlet. A. Doyle
Spy, The. Cooper
Homestead on the Hillside. Holmes

Sherlock Holmes Detective Stories. Doyle
David Copperfield—Vol. 1 Dickens
David Copperfield—Vol. II. Dickens
Hunchback of Notre Dame, The —Vol. I. Hugo
Hunchback of Notre Dame, The —Vol. II. Hugo
House of Seven Gables, The. Hawthorne
Christmas Stories. Dickens
Plain Tales From the Hills. Kipling
Jane Eyre. Bronte
Last of the Mohicans, The. Cooper
Ishmael. Southworth
Self Raised. Southworth
Last Days of Pompeii, The. Bulwer Lytton
Tempest and Sunshine. Holmes
Ivanhoe—Vol. I. Scott
Ivanhoe—Vol. II. Scott
Dr. Jekyll and Mr. Hyde and Kidnapped. Stevenson
Marion Grey. Holmes
Uncle Tom's Cabin. Stowe
Thorns and Orange Blossoms. Clay
Old Curiosity Shop — Vol. I. Dickens
Old Curiosity Shop — Vol. II. Dickens
Old Mam'selle's Secret. Marlitt
Courting of Dinah Shadd and Other Stories, The. Kipling
Child's Garden of Verses and Other Poems, A — Stevenson
Vanity Fair—Vol. I. Thackeray
Vanity Fair—Vol. II. Thackeray
Wonder Book. Hawthorne
File No. 113. Gaboriau
Tragedy of the Sea, A. Balzac
Prairie, The. Cooper
Pride and Prejudice. Austen
Lamplighter, The. Cummins

Tales from Shakespeare. Lamb
Pinocchio. Collodi
Thelma. Corelli
Inez. Evans
Murders in the Rue Morgue. Poe
Deerslayer, The. Cooper
Pilgrim's Progress, The. Bunyan
In His Steps. Sheldon
Tanglewood Tales. Hawthorne
Robinson Crusoe. Defoe
Tom Brown's School Days. Hughes
Hans Brinker. Dodge
Black Beauty. Sewell
Alice in Wonderland. Carroll
Grimm's Fairy Tales. Grimms
Andersen's Fairy Tales. Andersen
Swiss Family Robinson. Wyss
Gulliver's Travels. Swift
Barrack Room Ballads, Etc. Kipling
Black Rock. Connor
Blithedale Romance. Hawthorne
English Orphans, The. Holmes
First Violin, The. Fothergill
Man Who Laughs, — Vol. I. Hugo
Man Who Laughs, — Vol. II Hugo

3K199—Any one of the above books. (Shipping weight, each, 1 pound)................29c
Any two for....................55c   Any five for....................$1.35

Order Blanks Are in Back of This Catalog

63¢

A GENTLEMAN of COURAGE!
James Oliver CURWOOD

These pages contain practically all the "Best Sellers" and only books that have made good find a place here. Consequently you are always sure of securing a worth while novel. Shipping weight, each, 1½ pounds.

Today's Best Books

The UNKNOWN Quantity By Ethel M. Dell AUTHOR OF TETHERSTONES

RED OF THE REDFIELDS By GRACE S. RICHMOND

MOTHER of GOLD EMERSON HOUGH

A SON OF HIS FATHER HAROLD BELL WRIGHT

THE KEEPER OF THE BEES GENE STRATTON-PORTER

James Oliver Curwood

Epic tales of the great northwest, the land of snow, of romance, of heroism and loyalty. Curwood has made it a land of enchantment for his readers. His characters, filled with the spirit of adventure and romance, cannot fail to fascinate and thrill. His popularity is growing steadily, and soon he will be the most widely read American author.

3K318—Isobel
3K381—God's Country and the Woman
3K466—Kazan
3K1282—Grizzly King, The
3K811—Baree, Son of Kazan
3K809—Valley of Silent Men, The
3K890—Honor of the Big Snows
3K209—Courage of Marge O'Doone
3K211—Back to God's Country
3K127—Gentleman of Courage, A
3K812—Alaskan, The
3K772—Flaming Forest, The
3K792—River's End, The
3K740—Golden Snare, The
3K220—Wolf Hunters
3K631—Danger Trail
3K217—Courage of Captain Plum
3K206—Flower of the North
3K1123—Nomads of the North
3K2366—Hunted Woman, The
3K881—Gold Hunters, The
3K1061—Country Beyond, The
3K261—Steele of the Royal Mounted
Any one of the above books 63c
3K1215—Ancient Highway.$1.69
3K1251—Black Hunter..... 1.69

Ethel M. Dell
3K1286—Desire of His Life, The
3K1270—Bars of Iron
3K60—Keeper of the Door
3K61—Knave of Diamonds
3K668—Charles Rex
3K402—Greatheart
3K936—Rocks of Valpre
3K943—Tetherstones
3K1043—Top of the World, The
3K259—Unknown Quantity, The
3K944—Way of an Eagle
Any one of the above books 63c

Grace S. Richmond
3K902—Red of the Redfields
3K1182—Rufus
3K218—Brown Study
3K014—Red and Black
3K022—Second Violin
3K041—Strawberry Acres
3K050—Twenty-Fourth of June
3K057—Under the Country Sky
3K216—Mrs. Red Pepper
3K296—Red Pepper Burns
3K015—Red Pepper's Patients
Any one of the above books .63c

Emerson Hough
3K172—Mother of Gold
3K459—Covered Wagon, The
3K230—54:40 or Fight
3K657—Girl of the Half-Way House, The
3K745—Heart's Desire
3K656—Mississippi Bubble, The
3K612—North of 36
3K258—Ship of Souls
3K933—Story of the Cowboy
3K161—Way of a Man
Any one of the above books 63c

Christmas Cards
See Page 777

Harold Bell Wright
3K1213—Son of His Father
3K1144—Mine With the Iron Door
3K716—Helen of the Old House
3K2499—Re-Creation of Brian Kent, The
3K335—Eyes of the World, The
3K271—Shepherd of the Hills, The
3K395—Winning of Barbara Worth
3K1236—When a Man's a Man
Any one of the above books 63c
3K725—Uncrowned King, The..........95c

Gene Stratton Porter
3K1216—Keeper of the Bees, The
3K1130—White Flag
3K1129—Her Father's Daughter
3K895—Daughter of the Land
3K518—At the Foot of the Rainbow
3K170—Freckles
3K470—Girl of the Limberlost
3K782—Harvester
3K1304—Laddie
3K2377—Michael O'Halloran
3K2378—Song of the Cardinal (140 pages)
Any one of the above books 63c

Clarence E. Mulford
3K1318—Bar 20-Three
3K663—Cottonwood Gulch
3K146—Bar 20
3K297—Man From Bar 20
3K168—Buck Peter's Ranchman
3K269—Johnny Nelson
3K147—Bar 20 Days
3K226—Coming of Cassidy
3K1266—Black Buttes
3K212—Rustler's Valley
3K212—Bring Me His Ears
3K223—Tex
3K281—Orphan, The
3K257—Hopalong Cassidy
3K660—Hopalong Cassidy Returns
Any one of the above books 63c
3K198—Corson of the J. C.$1.69
3K455—Bar 20 Rides Again. 1.69

The MAID of the MOUNTAIN By Jackson Gregory

MEADOWLARK BASIN By B. M. Bower Author of DESERT BREW

LITTLE SHIPS KATHLEEN NORRIS This NOVEL has never appeared in any magazine

COTTONWOOD GULCH CLARENCE E. MULFORD

Jackson Gregory
3K264—Maid of the Mountain, The
3K64—Under Handicap
3K714—Timber Wolf
3K1371—Desert Valley
3K1277—Joyous Trouble Maker, The
3K1283—Judith of Blue Lake Ranch
3K393—Man to Man
3K1252—Daughter of the Sun
3K1032—Everlasting Whisper, The
3K1104—Outlaw, The
Any one of the above books.......... 63c
3K197—Desert Thoroughbred, The..........$1.69

B. M. Bower
3K265—Meadow Lark Basin
3K65—Cabin Fever
3K66—Lonesome Land
3K1214—Desert Brew
3K251—Eagle's Wing
3K1254—Belle Helen Mine
3K1148—Voice of Johnny Water
3K2165—Chip of the Flying U
3K917—Flying U Ranch
3K2196—Flying U's Last Stand
3K1132—Cow Country
3K646—Lonesome Trail
3K638—Star of the Desert
3K2277—Ranch at the Wolverine
3K1026—Jean of the Lazy A
Any one of the above books............ 63c
3K120—Van Patten....$1.69
3K907—White Wolves.... 1.69

Kathleen Norris
3K124—Beloved Woman, The
3K202—Butterfly
3K203—Certain People of Importance
3K496—Callahans and the Murphys, The
3K204—Harriet and the Piper
3K207—Lucretia Lombard
3K589—Rose of the World
3K682—Little Ships
Any one of the above books ... 63c

WE WILL PUT ANY BOOK on this page or page 775 in a Colored Holly Covered Box for 5 Cents Extra.

Edgar Rice Burroughs

Moon Maid

3K370 Girl From Hollywood, The
3K1288 Moon Maid, The
3K900 Tarzan and the Ant Men
3K1146 Tarzan and the Golden Lion
3K954 Tarzan of the Apes
3K834 Return of Tarzan

3K2307—Beasts of Tarzan
3K1220—Son of Tarzan
3K451—Tarzan and the Jewels of Opar
3K2470—Jungle Tales of Tarzan
3K610—Tarzan, the Untamed
3K699—Tarzan, the Terrible
3K1145—Mucker, The
3K164—Chessmen of Mars, The
3K353—At the Earth's Core
3K354—Pellucidar. A sequel to "At the Earth's Core"
3K1255—Bandit of Hell's Bend
3K1263—Cave Girl, The
3K856—Thuvia, the Maid of Mars
3K768—Princess of Mars, The
3K851—God of Mars, The
3K048—Warlord of Mars, The
3K715—Land That Time Forgot
3K1289—Eternal Lover, The
Any one of the above books 63c
3K1284—Mad King, The....$1.69
3K115—Outlaw of Torn, The.. 1.69

63¢

BEAU GESTE B. C. WREN'S

Great Novels Dramatized for the Movies

3K1268—Amateur Gentleman. J. Farnol.
3K128—America. R. W. Chambers.
3K71—Barrier, The. Rex Beach.
3K1269—Bat, The. M. R. Rinehart.
3K1300—Beau Geste. Wren.
3K101—Ben-Hur. Gen. Lew Wallace.
3K1066—Beverly of Graustark. McCutcheon.
3K1065—Black Pirate. Gates.
3K263—Call of the Wild. London.
3K266—Camille. Dumas.
3K68—Drusilla With a Million. E. Cooper.
3K758—East of the Setting Sun. McCutcheon.
3K1285—Four Horsemen of the Apocalypse, The. V. B. Ibanez.
3K267—General, The. Warren.
3K794—Green Archer, The. Wallace.
3K67—Green Goddess. L. J. Miln.
3K401—Happy Warrior. Hutchinson.
3K077—Heart of the Hills. John Fox, Jr.
3K958—Hunchback of Notre Dame. V. Hugo.
3K2184—If Winter Comes. Hutchinson.
3K979—Iron Horse, The. E. C. Hill.
3K372—Janice Meredith. P. L. Ford.
3K1074—La Boheme. M. Rash.
3K73—Lost World. C. Doyle.
3K357—Main Street. S. Lewis.
3K814—Mare Nostrum. V. B. Ibanez.
3K683—Mr. Wu. L. J. Miln.
3K1274—Moby Dick. (Sea Beast.) Melville.
3K386—Mother. Norris.
3K285—Music Master, The. Klein.
3K298—Nervous Wreck, The. Rath.
3K1075—Old Ironsides. Wright.

3K268—One Increasing Purpose. Hutchinson.
3K72—Passionate Quest. E. P. Oppenheim.
3K982—Phantom of the Opera. G. Lerous.
3K262—Plastic Age, The. P. Marks.
3K980—Pony Express, The. H. J. Forman.
3K275—Resurrection. Leo Tolstoy.
3K272—Return of Peter Grim. Belasco.
3K428—Riding Kid From Powder River. Knibby.
3K338—Sandra. Bell.
3K274—Scarlet Letter. Hawthorne.
3K1265—Seven Keys to Baldpate. Biggers.
3K103—Shadow of the East. E. M. Hull.
3K1275—She. H. R. Haggard.
3K969—So Big. E. Ferber.
3K1267—Sons of the Sheik. E. M. Hull.
3K83—Sorrows of Satan. M. Corelli.
3K273—Sparrows. Rask.
3K985—Stella Dallas. Olive H. Prouty.
3K160—Ten Commandments, The. McMahon.
3K469—Trail of the Lonesome Pine, The. John Fox, Jr.
3K339—Valentino as I Knew Him. Ullman.
3K308—Virginian, The. O. Wister.
3K1273—Volga Boatman. K. Bercovici.
3K225—Whispering Smith. F. H. Spearman.
3K69—Winds of Chance. Rex Beach.
3K070—Woman Thou Gavest Me. Hall Caine.

Famous Authors !

Each book is bound in cloth. Size, 5½ x 7¾ inches. Average from 250 to 500 pages. Most of the books have attractive colored pictorial jackets. Shipping weight, each, 1½ pounds.

63¢

Charles Alden Seltzer
3K95—Channing Comes Through
3K1293—Ranchman
3K896—Way of the Buffalo, The
3K219—West
3K594—Drag Harlan
3K214—"Firebrand" Trevison
3K2365—Range Boss
3K2286—Boss of the Lazy Y, The
3K1308—Last Hope Ranch
3K227—Coming of the Law, The
3K956—Vengeance of Jefferson Gawne
3K407—"Beau" Rand
3K957—Square Deal Sanderson
3K045—Trail to Yesterday
3K053—Two-Gun Man
3K1176—Brass Commandments
Any one of the above books **63c**
3K438—Gentleman From Virginia, The $1.69

William MacLeod Raine
3K1294—Roads of Doubt
3K190—Desert's Price
3K1147—Ironheart
3K561—Man Size
3K733—Tangled Trails
3K644—Bucky O'Connor
3K040—Crooked Trails and
3K662—Daughter of the Dons
3K237—Ridgeway of Montana
3K2242—Steve Yeager
3K174—Texas Ranger
3K038—Vision Splendid
3K376—Sheriff's Son
3K493—Man Four Square, A
3K1093—Big Town Round-Up
3K556—Oh, You Tex
3K1324—Gunsight Pass
3K535—Wyoming
Any one of the above books........**63c**
3K918—Bonanza ..$1.69
3K439—Judge Colt. 1.69

3K1088—Sandy. Meherin.
3K1087—Road to Love, The. Meherin.
3K689—Nora Pays. Lucile Van Slyke.
3K707—Bread and Jam. Nalbro Bartley.
3K1295—Her Man (Stolen Love). Burton.
3K1086—Love Bound. Burton.
3K1089—Footloose. Burton.
3K722—Honey Lou, or The Love Wrecker. Burton.
3K723—Petter. Burton.
3K425—Flapper Wife, The. Burton.
3K1296—Good Bad Girl, The. Van Duzer.
3K724—Golden Roads. Van Duzer.
3K1297—Joanna. Gates.
3K727—Love's Greatest Mistake. Kummer.
3K728—Sonia. Hurst.
3K746—Mollie. Ball.
Any one of above books........ **63c**

LOVE'S GREATEST MISTAKE
by FREDERIC ARNOLD KUMMER
Modern Romances
3K502—Chickie. Meherin.
3K993—Sequel to Chickie. Meherin.

Rafael Sabatini
3K116—St. Martin's Summer
3K484—Bardelys The Magnificent
3K96—Captain Blood
3K158—Sea Hawk, The
3K458—Scaramouche
3K1292—Fortune's Fool
3K688—Snare, The
3K1211—Mistress Wilding
Any one of the above books **63c**
3K89—Bellarion, The Fortunate ..$1.69
3K580—Carolinians, The $1.69

POLLY ANNA
THE GLAD BOOK
ELEANOR H. PORTER

Eleanor H. Porter
3K74 Money, Love and Hate
3K75 Turn of the Tide
3K500—Pollyanna
3K719—Sister Sue
3K453—Dawn
3K2436—Just David
3K1291—Road to Understanding
3K1310—Hustler Joe
3K429—Six-Star Ranch
3K415—Oh Money, Money
3K552—Mary Marie
3K150—Cross Currents
3K208—Miss Billy
3K210—Miss Billy's Decision
3K215—Miss Billy Married
Any one of the above books **63c**

Sax Rohmer
3K815—Bat Wing
3K816—Brood of the Witch Queen
3K817—Dope
3K818—Dream Detective
3K819—Fire Tongue
3K820—Golden Scorpion
3K821—Gray Face
3K822—Green Eyes of Bast
3K839—Hand of Fu-Manchu
3K846—Insidious Dr. Fu-Manchu
3K857—Quest of the Sacred Slipper, The
3K858—Return of Dr. Fu-Manchu
3K859—Tales of Chinatown
3K861—Tales of Secret Egypt
3K862—Yellow Claw, The
Any one of the above books **63c**

Three Weeks
Elinor Glyn's
IMMORTAL ROMANCE
Illustrations from the Photoplay a Goldwyn Picture

Elinor Glyn
3K670 His Hour
3K200 Six Days
3K803 Three Weeks
3K671—Love's Blindness
3K672—The Man and the Moment
3K677—The Philosophy of Love
3K678—The Price of Things
3K679—The Reason Why
3K681—This Passion Called Love
3K1307—Beyond the Rocks
3K704—Great Moment, The
3K744—Man and Maid
Any one of the above books. **63c**

Grace Miller White
3K994—From the Valley of the Missing
3K891—Judy of Rogue's Harbor
3K995—Rose o' Paradise
3K1250—Secret of the Storm Country, The
3K996—Shadows of the Sheltering Pines, The
3K997—Storm Country Polly
3K2233—Tess of the Storm Country
3K992—Marriage of Patricia Pepperday, The
Any one of above books. **63c**

The VANISHING AMERICAN
Zane Grey
Harper & Brothers Publishers

Zane Grey
These tales of the desert, the forest and the mountains overflow with exciting situations.
3K986—Vanishing American, The
3K1119—Thundering Herd
3K1175—Call of the Canyon, The
3K1106—Wanderer of the Wasteland
3K1112—To the Last Man
3K906—U. P. Trail, The
3K1073—Wildfire
3K871—Betty Zane
3K676—Heritage of the Desert, The
3K021—Riders of the Purple Sage
3K283—Desert Gold
3K685—Light of the Western Stars, The
3K2271—Last of the Plainsmen, The
3K2294—Lone Star Ranger, The
3K306—Rainbow Trail, The
3K1260—Last of the Great Scouts
3K1184—Border Legion, The
3K1082—Mysterious Rider, The
3K605—Young Forester
3K606—Ken Ward in the Jungle
3K152—Spirit of the Border
3K2589—Desert of Wheat, The
3K696—Man of the Forest, The
3K737—Last Trail, The
3K607—Red Headed Outfielder
3K1001—Short Stop, The
3K1000—Day of the Beast, The
3K999—Young Pitcher, The
3K632—Young Lion Hunter
3K1298—Roping Lions in the Grand Canyon
Any one of the above books **63c**
3K90—Under the Tonto Rim $1.69
3K665—Forlorn River (Ready November 1st) $1.69

Personalize Your Books
With the purchase of any five books shown on these two pages (774 and 775) we will print your name in neat gold letters on the covers free of charge. State in your order whether you wish this done. Only one individual's name on any five books purchased at one time.

Popular Fiction

Any book listed below 63c

3K130—Ann's House of Dreams. Montgomery.
3K584—Arrowsmith. Sinclair Lewis.
3K134—At the Mercy of Tiberius. Wilson.
3K723—Barbarian Lover. M. Pedler.
3K310—Barriers Burned Away. E. P. Roe.
3K1300—Beau Geste. P. C. Wren.
3K1311—Black Hood, The. T. Dixon.
3K557—Blue Blood. Owen Johnson.
3K94—Blue Window, The. Bailey.
3K1317—Brass. C. G. Norris.
3K1313—Bread. C. G. Norris.
3K2472—Chevrons. Leonard Nason.
3K243—Chicken Wagon Family. Benefield.
3K2217—Clansman, The. T. Dixon, Jr.
3K555—Clouded Pearl, The. Berta Ruck.
3K424—Coast of Folly. Dawson.
3K130—Constant Nymph. M. Kennedy.
3K642—Corporal Cameron of the Northwest Mounted Police. Ralph Connor.
3K1312—Creeping Jenny. K. D. Wiggins.
3K306—Crisis, The. W. Churchill.
3K79—Crystal Cup. G. Atherton.
3K194—Daddy Long Legs. J. Webster.
3K221—Days of '49. Young.
3K563—Deep in the Hearts of Men. Waller.
3K1328—Desert Love. Joan Conquest.
3K11—Enemies of Women. V. B. Ibanez.
3K1325—Father Abraham. I. Bacheller.
3K681—Fourteenth Key. Carolyn Wells.
3K1303—Fourth Norwood, The. Pinkerton.
3K241—Gabriel Samara, Peacemaker. Oppenheim.
3K547—Gaspards of Pine Croft. Ralph Connor.
3K98—Go-Getter Gary. Bennet.
3K076—Heart of the Desert. Willsie.
3K252—His Official Fiancee. Berta Ruck.
3K236—Hoosier Schoolmaster. Eggleston.
3K609—House of Dreams Come True. Pedler.
3K110—Illiterate Digest. Will Rogers.
3K114—In a Shantung Garden. Miln.
3K246—Iron Chalice, The. Cohen.
3K989—Kingdom Around the Corner. Dawson
3K222—Kneel to the Prettiest. Ruck.
3K976—Land of Forgotten Men. E. Marshall.
3K378—Leap Year Girl. Berta Ruck.
3K653—Life Everlasting. Corelli.
3K1056—Lamp of Fate. Pedler.
3K1309—Little French Girl. Anne Sedgwick.
3K187—Little Shepherd of Kingdom Come. John Fox, Jr.
3K224—Loudon from Laramie. Ames.

3K1314—Lucky in Love. B. Ruck.
3K596—Maid-at-Arms. Robt. W. Chambers.
3K78—Miracle. C. B. Kelland.
3K597—Money to Burn. R. W. Kauffman.
3K2364—Nan of Music Mountain. Spearman.
3K527—Night Hawk. A. Stringer.
3K228—Nina. Ertz.
3K645—North of Fifty-Three. Sinclair.
3K248—Pollyanna of the Orange Blossoms. Smith.
3K742—Rebecca of Sunnybrook Farm. K. D. Wiggins.
3K598—Reckless Lady, The. P. Gibbs.
3K526—Red Ashes. M. Pedler.
3K747—Red-Headed Kids. A. M. Chisholm.
3K721—Red Lamp, The. M. R. Rinehart.
3K748—Red Ledger, The. F. L. Packard.
3K1734—Romeo in Moon Village. McCutcheon.
3K512—Rosary, The. Florence Barclay.
3K964—Roughneck, The. R. W. Service.
3K749—Ruben and Ivy Sen. L. J. Miln.
3K205—Sea Wolf. London.
3K2253—Selwood of Sleepy Cat. Spearman.
3K231—Settlers of the Marsh. Grove.
3K108—Seven Sleepers. F. Beeding.
3K1026—Sheik, The. E. M. Hull.
3K766—Shield of Silence. H. Comstock.
3K249—Skookum Chuck. White.
3K1327—Slave Ship. M. Johnston.
3K968—Soul of Abe Lincoln. B. Babcock.
3K863—Soul of Ann Rutledge. B. Babcock.
3K113—Soundings. Gibbs.
3K767—Spaniard, The. Juanita Savage.
3K255—Stolen Idols. Oppenheim.
3K33—Story Girl, The. L. M. Montgomery.
3K516—Sundown Slim. H. B. Knibbs.
3K185—Test of Donald Norton. R. W. Pinkerton.
3K232—Tomorrow's Tangle. Pedler.
3K72—Treading the Winepress. Connor.
3K1315—Twisted Foot, The. W. P. White.
3K335—Valley of the Voices. Geo. Marsh.
3K845—Virgin of the Sun. H. R. Haggard.
3K923—Vision of Desire. M. Pedler.
3K254—We Must March. Morrow.
3K773—West of Dodge. Ogden.
3K289—White Fang. Jack London.
3K1329—Wild Geese. Martha Ostenso.
3K947—Without Gloves. J. B. Hendryx.
3K838—Woman He Desired, The. L. Gerard.
3K838—Wrath to Come, The. Oppenheim.
3K408—Yolanda. Chas. Major.

63¢

GABRIEL SAMARA PEACEMAKER
By E. PHILLIPS OPPENHEIM

Christmas Cards, see page 777

THE ENCHANTED HILL
By PETER B. KYNE

Peter B. Kyne
Gripping tales of the sea, the great woods, the tropics and the Northland.
3K126—Enchanted Hill, The
3K1142—Never the Twain Shall Meet
3K1064—Cappy Ricks Retires
3K1110—Pride of Palomar, The
3K705—Kindred of the Dust
3K037—Valley of the Giants, The
3K706—Cappy Ricks
3K1143—Captain Scraggs
3K709—Long Chance, The
3K720—Webster-Man
Any one of the above books **63c**
3K1212—Understanding Heart, The $1.69

To Find What You Want, See Index Pages 550 to 570

The LITTLE FOLKS

BOOKS LITTLE TOTS WILL ENJOY

The Child's Delight

A striking set of toy books that every little one will love. Each has 16 colored pages. Size, 6x11 in. Shpg. wt. of set, 1 lb.
Little Froggie Green
Our Jungle Friends
The Owl and the Bee
Topsy Tabbykins
3K1337—Per set of 4 books...39c

Set of 8 Cut-Out Books

Beautifully illustrated with colored pictures. Size, 5¼x7½ in. Shpg. wt., ¾ lb.
A Apple Pie A-B-C   Story of Aladdin
Three Little Kittens   Old Woman in the
Henny Penny   Shoe
Red Riding Hood   Three Bears
                                   Animal Book
3K1377—Set of 8 books..49c

Set of Shaped Books

Attractively colored paper covers. Each book has 15 pages and is pictured. Size, 4⅞x7½ in. Shipping weight, per set, ¾ pound.
3K1417—Per set of 4 books......27c

Peter Rabbit Set

Each book contains 16 pages in colors and in black and white. Colored covers. Size, 8¾x11½ inches. Shipping weight, 1 pound.
The Tale of Peter Rabbit
Peter Rabbit and His Pa
Peter Rabbit and His Ma
Peter Rabbit Goes to School
3K1456—Per set of 4 books....59c

Old Favorites

Colored 10-page books. Fully illustrated in color and outline. Four page color illustrations in each book. Size, 7⅛x9½ in. Shipping weight, set of four, 8 ounces.
Red Riding Hood   The Three Bears
Jack and the Bean The Night Before
  Stalk   Christmas
3K1607—Set of 4 books..23c

Set of 4 Little Tots' Cloth Books

Six pages of pictures (some colored) in each book. Size, 6x8⅝ inches. Shipping weight, set, ¾ pound.
3K1413—Per set of 4 books......47c

Little Bo-Peep Books

Inexpensive toy books. Twenty-four pages each, half of which are full page color pictures, the other half the story. Light board covers in colors. Size, 3½x5¼ in. Shpg. wt., per set, 6 oz.
Little Bo-Peep, Mother Goose Rhymes, The Night Before Christmas, The Three Bears.
3K1446—Per set of 4.....19c

Linen Toy Books

Here is an 8-page, brightly colored linen toy book, 2 pages of which are in colors, the other 6 in black and white. Just the thing to buy for the little tots. Size, 6x8¾ inches. Shpg. wt., set of three, 6 oz.
Toyland A B C, Animal Book, Mother Goose.
3K1452—Set of 3 books......39c

INTERESTING for LITTLE READERS

Santa Claus Big Picture and Story Book

Told with large pictures. 96 pages. Colored board covers. Size, 7⅞ x 9¾ in. Shpg. wt., 1¼ lbs.
3K1376 29c

Colored pictures on every page. Size, 10x12 in. 14 pages. Beautifully colored board cover. Shpg. wt., 6 oz.
Our Farm Friends
Night Before Xmas
Big ABC Book
Big Circus Book
A Day at the Zoo
Robinson Crusoe
Puss in Boots
Mother Goose Rhymes
3K1453   Each 23c   2 for....43c

Mother Goose Favorites

Includes all the well known rhymes and jingles. Fully illustrated. Bound in boards, in colors, cloth back. Indexed, 288 pages. Size, 7x9 in. Shipping weight, 2 pounds.
3K1541 ......79c

A set of four Bible Stories written in a simple, easily understood way. Size, 3½x7 inches. Illustrated in colors. Shipping weight, 8 ounces.
3K1623—Per set of 4 books 49c

Tell Me a Story

With color plates and numerous illustrations in black and white. Size, 7¼x9¾ in. 128 pages. Colored boards covers. Shpg. wt., 1¼ lbs.
3K1374 59c

Mother's Story Book.
3K1404 59c

Set of Six Toy Books

Each book has 10 pages printed with large type. A picture on every page and 4 of them are in full colors. Colored cover. Size, 6½x8¾ in. Shpg. wt., per set, 6 oz.
The Tale of Peter Rabbit
Peter Rabbit Runs Away
Peter Rabbit Goes to the Market
Little Black Sambo
The Little Red Hen
Wee Peter Pug
3K1411   Per set (6 books)..39c

Mother Goose

Contains 96 pages of pictures and verse. Each page has pictorial border. Contains 168 pictures. Paper covers. Cover design in colors. Size, 6⅞x8¼ inches. Shipping weight, 1 pound.
3K1395 29c

Cloth Toy Books

When soiled, wash with the clothes. These books are printed on a soft cloth, and every page is completely covered and decorated in exceedingly bright and variegated colors. Clear print. Untearable. 
3K1427—12 pages. Shpg. wt., each, 2 oz. Size, 4¼x7 in.
Farm Yard Pets Birds' Picnic
Darlings' A B C Five Little Pigs
Any 2 for 35c; complete set of 4 for.....69c
3K1426—6 pages. Shpg. wt., each, 3 oz. Size, 4⅞x7¾ in.
Little Boy Blue The Frog Who
Circus A B C   Would a-Woo-
Puss in Boots   ing Go
Any 2 for 25c; complete set of 4 for.....49c

Children's Favorites

Colored board covers, cloth back. Average, 48 pages. Size, 7½x9¾ in. Shpg. wt., each, 8 oz.
Mother Goose   Palmer Cox's
  A B C   Brownies
Natural History Mother Goose
Night Before   Nursery
  Christmas   Rhymes
Jolly Santa   Mother Goose
  Claus   Melodies
St. Nicholas'   Black Beauty
  Visit   Young Folks'
Palmer Cox's   Bible Stories
  Queer People   Uncle Tom's
Palmer Cox's   Cabin
  Funny An-   Hans Brinker
  imals
3K1408—Each, 14c; 3 for.39c

The Children's Library

Bound in cloth. Size, 7x9 inches. Average, 125 pages. Illustrated. Shipping weight, each, 1¼ pounds.
Santa Claus   Story of Jesus
  Story Picture   Black Beauty
  Book   Child's Garden
Alice's Adven-   of Verses
  tures in Won-   Robinson Crusoe
  derland   Mother Goose
The Night Be-   Favorite Fairy
  fore Christ-   Tales
  mas   Grimms' Fairy
Puss in Boots   Tales
Robin Hood
3K1479—Each, 49c; 2 for.95c

Grimms' or Andersen's Fairy Tales

Cloth. Size, 5¼x7½ inches. Shipping wt., each, 1¼ lbs.
3K1378 Grimms' Fairy Tales. 258 pages. 59 stories. 49c
3K1363 Andersen's Fairy Tales. 256 pages. 38 stories. 49c

Mother Goose Nursery Rhymes

The Night Before Christmas

Peter Rabbit Series

57 pages each. Full page illustrations in colors and black and white. Board covers. Size, 5½x7¾ in. Shpg. wt., each, 7 oz.
The Tale of Peter Rabbit
Peter Rabbit and Sammy Squirrel
Peter Rabbit and Jimmy Chipmunk
Peter Rabbit and His Pa
Peter Rabbit and His Ma
Peter Rabbit Goes to School
3K1547—Each......26c
Any 2 for............49c

Story Hour Books

Bound in colored board covers. Illustrations on almost every page. 32 pages. Size, 7½x9¾ in. Shpg. wt., ¾ lb.
Bed Time Story Hour
Sand Man Story Hour
Sleepy Time Story Hour
3K1606 29c

LOVE THESE FAVORITES

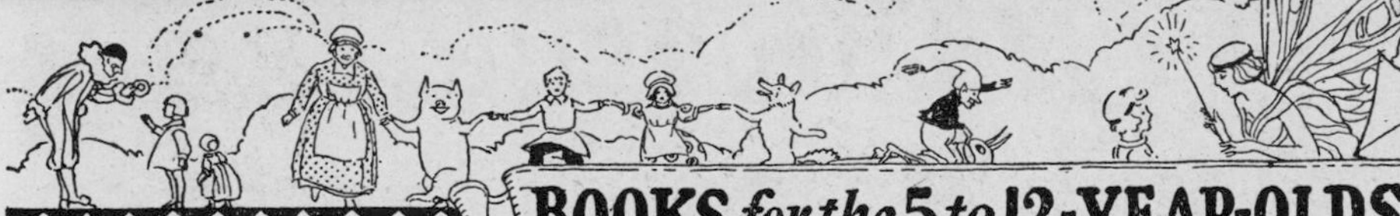

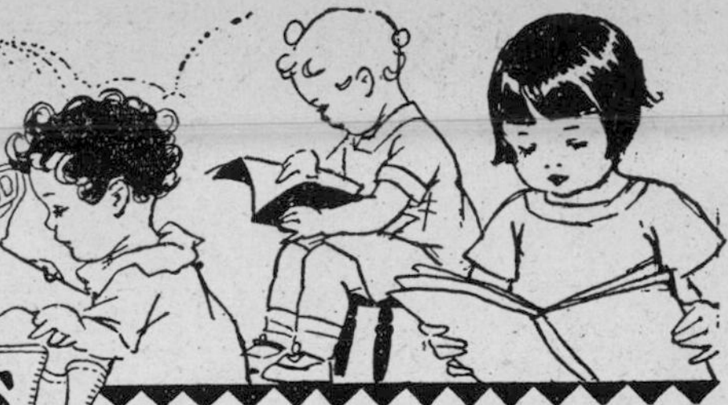

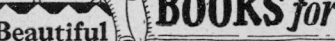

BOOKS *for the* 5 to 12-YEAR-OLDS

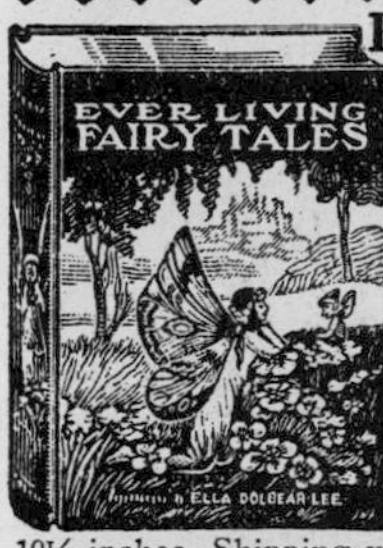
EVER LIVING FAIRY TALES

Beautiful Books Wonderfully Illustrated

By Ella Dolbear Lee

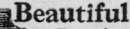

Books the child will treasure for years to come.

Handsomely bound in cloth. 24 colored pictures and many others in black and white. Average 250 pages. Size, 7¾x10⅛ inches. Shipping weight, 3 pounds.

3K1772—Ever Living Fairy Tales.
3K1358—Mother Goose.
3K1410—Grimms' Fairy Tales.
3K1493—The Adventures of Robinson Crusoe.

Each............................**$1.48**

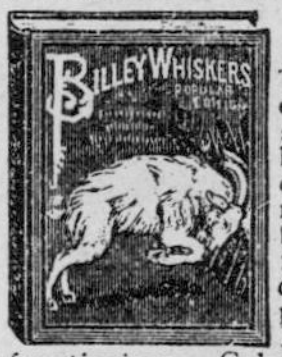
BILLY WHISKERS

Billy Whiskers

By Frances Trego Montgomery. Every child should read this book. The story of a fun-loving, mischief - making frolicsome goat. A favorite with all children. 158 pages, illustrated. Full page colored frontispiece. Colored board covers. Size, 6½x7¾ inches. Shipping weight, 1 pound.

3K1373..................**29c**

Sleepy-Time Tales and Tuck-Me-In Tales

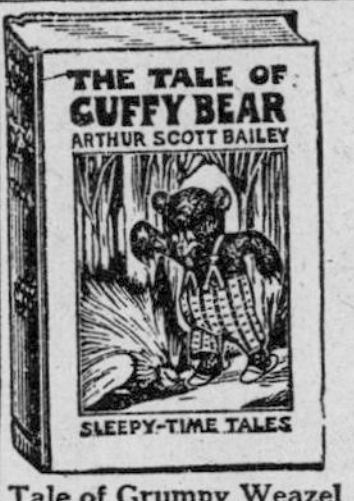
THE TALE OF CUFFY BEAR
ARTHUR SCOTT BAILEY
SLEEPY-TIME TALES

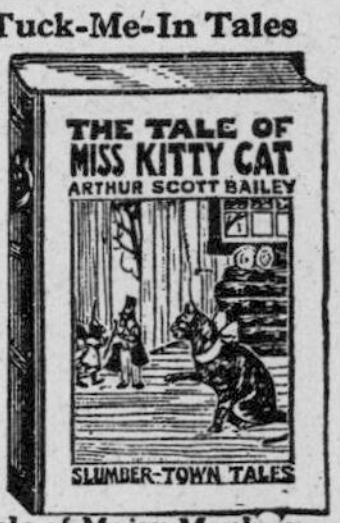
THE TALE OF MISS KITTY CAT
ARTHUR SCOTT BAILEY
SLUMBER-TOWN TALES

These books for little people of 3 to 8 years old tell of the adventures of the two and four-footed creatures of our American woods and fields and farmyard in an amusing way, which delights small two-footed human beings and brings forth the plea, "Mother, please read me again 'bout Cuffy Bear and the time he stuck his foot in the hot maple syrup." Average 110 pages. Full page colored illustrations. Bound in cloth. Size, 5x7 in. Shipping weight, each, 1 pound.

- The Tale of Grandfather Mole
- The Tale of Cuffy Bear
- The Tale of Fatty Coon
- The Tale of Nimble Deer
- The Tale of Frisky Squirrel
- Tale of Billy Woodchuck
- Tale of Grumpy Weazel
- The Tale of Master Meadow-mouse
- The Tale of Peter Mink
- The Tale of Jimmy Rabbit
- The Tale of Sandy Chipmunk
- The Tale of Brownie Beaver
- The Tale of Paddy Muskrat
- The Tale of Dickie Deer Mouse
- The Tale of Miss Kitty Cat
- The Tale of Ferdinand Frog
- The Tale of Tommy Fox
- The Tale of Timothy Turtle
- The Tale of Major Monkey
- The Tale of the Muley Cow
- The Tale of Old Dog Sport
- The Tale of Grunty Pig
- The Tale of Henrietta Hen
- The Tale of Pony Twinkleheels

3K1556—Any one of the above titles..........................**33c**
Any three for..........................**95c**

Prudy Series

By Sophie May

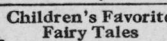

For the smaller girls this series is ideal. Every story of Prudy's doings will please and interest from start to finish. Bound in cloth. Size, 5⅛x6⅝ inches. Average 150 pages. Shipping wt., each, 1¾ lbs.

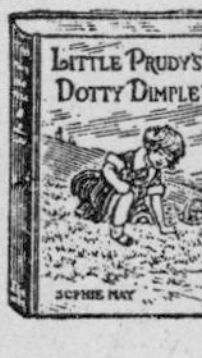
LITTLE PRUDY'S DOTTY DIMPLE
SOPHIE MAY

- Little Prudy
- Little Prudy's Story Book
- Little Prudy's Cousin Grace
- Little Prudy's Dotty Dimple
- Little Prudy's Sister Susie
- Little Prudy's Captain Horace

3K1735
Each..........................**29c**
Set of 6 books in box **$1.69**

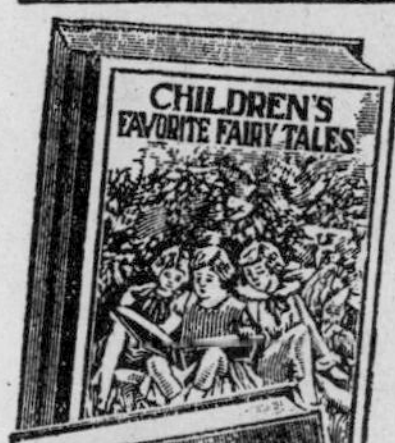
CHILDREN'S FAVORITE FAIRY TALES

Children's Favorite Fairy Tales

All the old favorites, the kind that never grow old. Bound in colored boards. Fully illustrated. Colored frontispiece. 122 pages. Size, 7⅝x9⅝ in. Shipping weight, 1½ pounds.

3K1387
Each..........**59c**

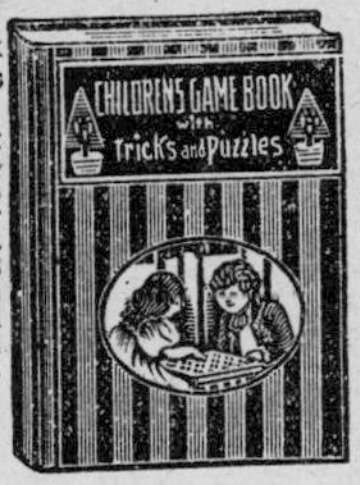
CHILDREN'S GAME BOOK with Tricks and Puzzles

Children's Game Book With Tricks and Puzzles

Just the thing for children to have for parties and outdoor amusements. Contains 128 pages, bound in highly colored board covers. Shipping weight, 1 pound.

3K3116
39c

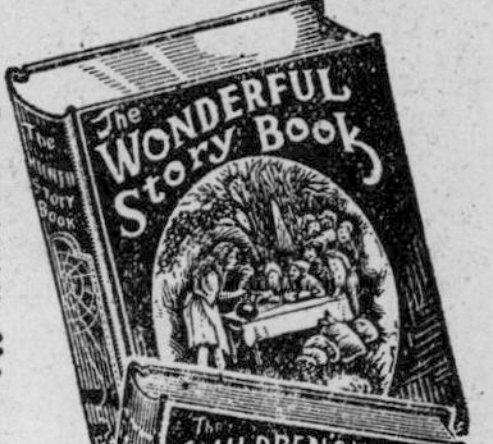
The WONDERFUL Story Book

The Wonderful Story Book

A Great Book

65 stories with 150 illustrations. Colored frontispiece. Board covers with beautiful illustration on cover. Size, 7¾x9¾ inches. 384 pages. Shpg. wt., 2 pounds.

3K1546 **95c**

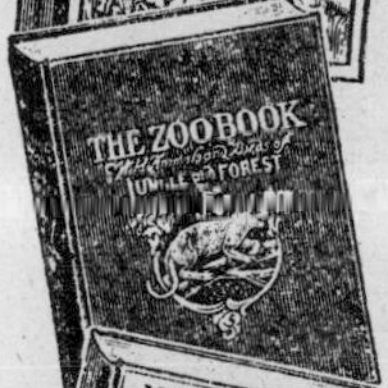
THE ZOO BOOK

The Zoo Book

Wild Animals of the Jungle and Forest. Their habits, modes of life and peculiar traits. 100 illustrations, of which 36 are full page. Cloth. Size, 7⅛x9⅞ in. 248 pages. Shipping wt., 1¾ pounds.

3K1554 **89c**

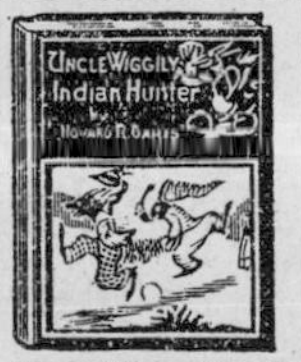
UNCLE WIGGILY'S Indian Hunter
HOWARD R. GARIS

Uncle Wiggily Books

By Howard R. Garis

Beautiful cloth bound edition with colored picture on cover. Colored illustration on every page. 30 pages. Size, 6¼x7½ inches. Shpg. wt., each, 8 oz.

- Uncle Wiggily's Water Spout
- Uncle Wiggily's Laughing Gas Balloon
- Uncle Wiggily's Empty Watch
- Uncle Wiggily's Radio
- Uncle Wiggily and Beaver Boys
- Uncle Wiggily and Turkey Gobbler
- Uncle Wiggily's Auto Sled
- Uncle Wiggily's Snow Man
- Uncle Wiggily's Holidays
- Uncle Wiggily's Apple Roast
- Uncle Wiggily's Picnic
- Uncle Wiggily's Fishing Trip
- Uncle Wiggily's June Bug Friends
- Uncle Wiggily's Visit to the Farm
- Uncle Wiggily's Silk Hat
- Uncle Wiggily, Indian Hunter
- Uncle Wiggily's Ice Cream Party
- Uncle Wiggily's Woodland Games
- Uncle Wiggily on the Flying Rug
- Uncle Wiggily at the Beach
- Uncle Wiggily and the Pirates
- Uncle Wiggily's Funny Auto
- Uncle Wiggily on Roller Skates
- Uncle Wiggily Goes Swimming

3K1415
Each..**35c**
Two for..**68c**

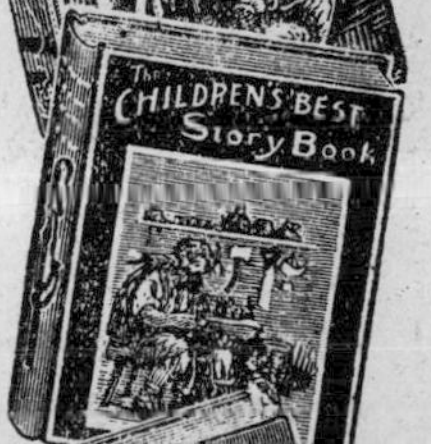
THE CHILDREN'S BEST STORY BOOK

The Children's Best Story Book

A collection of twenty-seven of the old favorite tales. Over 100 illustrations. Colored board cover. Cloth back. 384 pages. Printed from extra large type. Size, 7¾x9¾ inches. 1⅞ inches thick. Shpg. wt., 2½ pounds.

3K1510 **95c**

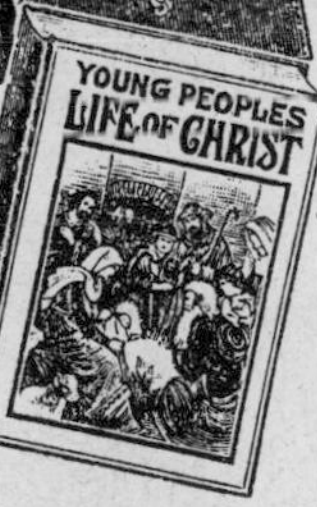
YOUNG PEOPLES LIFE OF CHRIST

Young People' Life of Christ

An exceptionally interesting and vivid account of the life of our Lord, from the manger to the cross. Every child should have the opportunity of reading this story. Illustrated. Cloth. 256 pages. Size, 7x9½ in. Shpg. wt., 1¾ lbs.

3K1779
89c

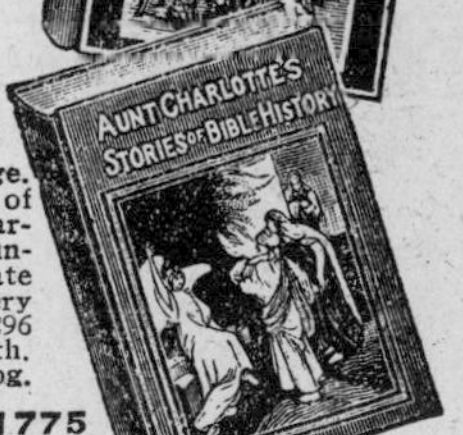
AUNT CHARLOTTE'S STORIES of BIBLE HISTORY

Aunt Charlotte's Stories of Bible History

By Charlotte M. Yonge. An interesting series of Bible stories, so arranged that every Sunday has its appropriate tale. A new story every Sunday for a year. 296 pages. Illustrated. Cloth. Size, 7x9¼ inches. Shpg. wt., 1½ pounds.

3K1775
89c

Books for Cut Out and Painting for Children 6 to 11 Years Old

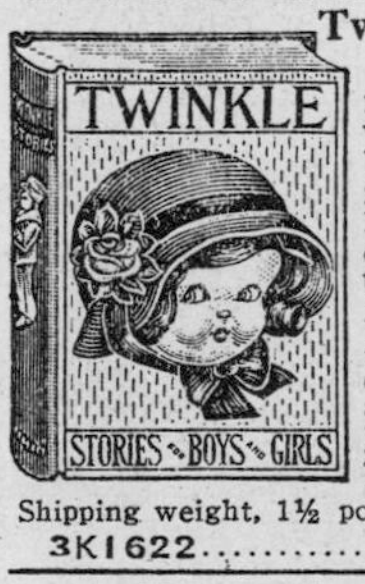
TWINKLE
STORIES FOR BOYS AND GIRLS

Twinkle

Contains simple little stories which can either be read by the youngster just learning to read, or can be read to them by their parents. The book is illustrated throughout with black and white illustrations. About 200 pages. Cloth. Size, 7½x10 in. Shipping weight, 1½ pounds.

3K1622....................**98c**

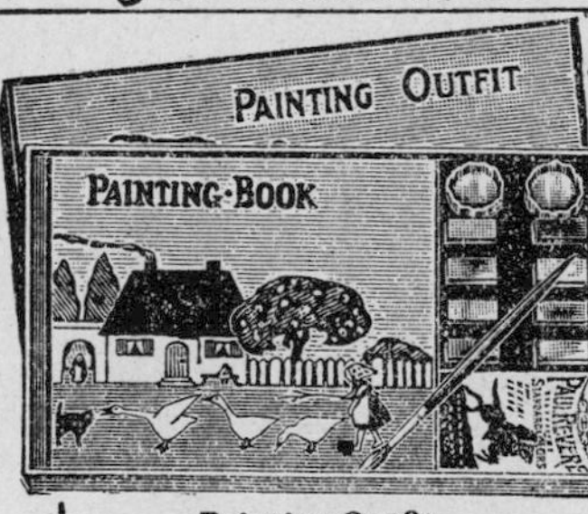
PAINTING OUTFIT
PAINTING-BOOK

Painting Outfit

This outfit contains one painting book of 60 pages, 25 of which are outline drawings to color and 4 are colored illustrations, and 31 are blank pages. Paint set of 8 colors, with two pans for water, and brush, also 1 box of 8 colored crayons. Size, 9x14½ inches. Shipping weight, 1½ pounds.

3K1765....................**79c**

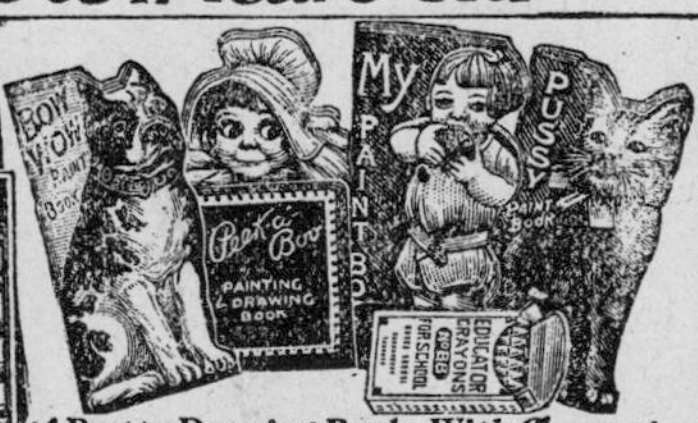
PAINTING DRAWING BOOK

4 Pretty Drawing Books With Crayon

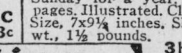

Brightly colored covers. Size, about 5½x10½ inches. 15 pages each. Box of colored wax crayons with each set. Shpg. wt., per set, ¾ lb.

3K1500—Set of 4 for......**39c**

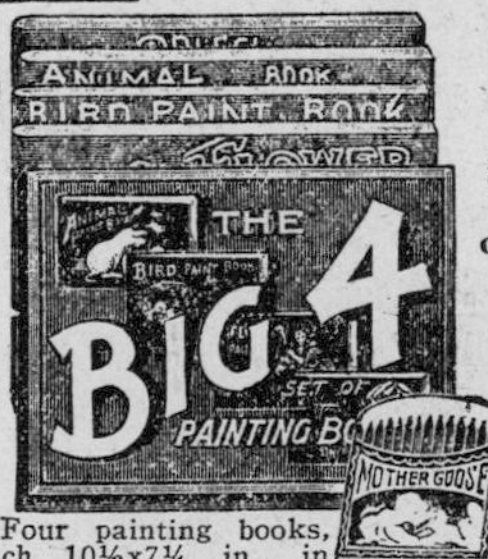
THE BIG 4
PAINTING BOOKS
MOTHER GOOSE

The Big Four Set of Painting Books With Box of Colored Crayons

Four painting books, each 10½x7¼ in., in carton. Covers in colors. Contains sketches ready to color; also pages in colors to show results that can be obtained. Shpg. wt., 1 lb.

3K1559—Per set of 4..........**23c**

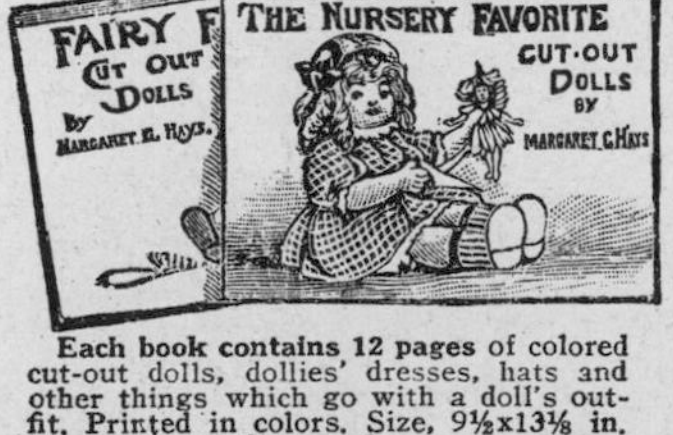
FAIRY CUT OUT DOLLS
BY MARGARET E. HAYS
THE NURSERY FAVORITE CUT-OUT DOLLS BY MARGARET G. HAYS

Favorite Cut-Out Dolls

Each book contains 12 pages of colored cut-out dolls, dollies' dresses, hats and other things which go with a doll's outfit. Printed in colors. Size, 9½x13⅜ in. Shipping wt., ⅜ pound.

3K1454—2 for..............**29c**

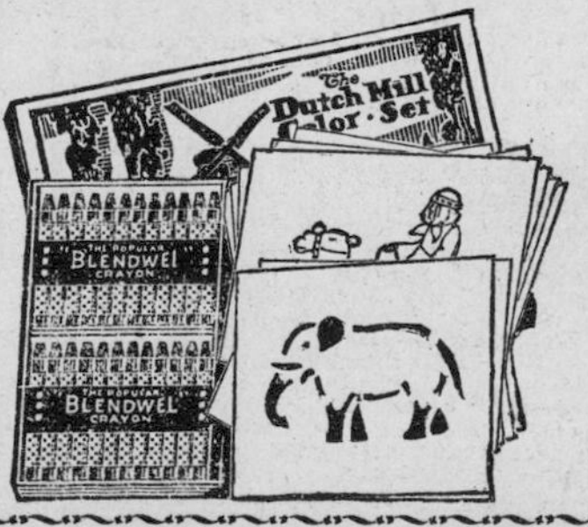
Dutch Mill Color Set
BLENDWEL CRAYON

Dutch Mill Color Set

Set contains 24 colored crayons, 8 outline drawings to color, 6 sheets of plain drawing paper and stencils. An outfit that will greatly please the child. Size, 7½x10½ in. Shipping wt., ⅜ lb.

3K1771..............**49c**

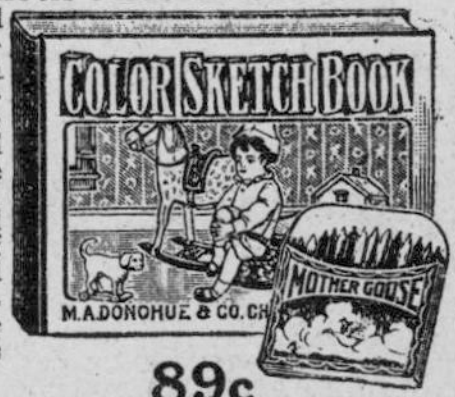
COLOR SKETCH BOOK
MOTHER GOOSE
M. A. DONOHUE & CO.

The Mammoth Color Sketch Book

Over a hundred pages. Many color pictures, each with an accompanying picture in black and white for the child to color. Colored board covers. Box of fourteen colored crayons. Size, 9x12 in. Shipping weight, 2½ pounds.

3K1553..............**89c**

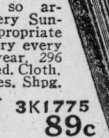

Charming Tales for the Little Ladies

The Bobbsey Twins

For Little Men and Women From 5 to 10 Years of Age
By Laura Lee Hope

Delightful stories for children. The Bobbsey Twins are very human and very mischievous little people, and their pranks are genuinely comical. Ideal for the smaller girls, for whom it is usually so hard to procure suitable reading. They charm the hearts of the little ones with stories of which they never tire. Bound in cloth. Size, 5¼x7⅞ inches. Average 220 pages. Shipping weight, each, 1 pound.

The Bobbsey Twins at Cherry Corners
The Bobbsey Twins Camping Out
The Bobbsey Twins in a Great City
The Bobbsey Twins on Blueberry Island
The Bobbsey Twins on the Deep Blue Sea
The Bobbsey Twins
The Bobbsey Twins in the Country
The Bobbsey Twins at School
The Bobbsey Twins at the Seashore
The Bobbsey Twins at Snow Lodge
The Bobbsey Twins and Baby May
The Bobbsey Twins Keeping House

The Bobbsey Twins on a Houseboat
The Bobbsey Twins at Meadow Brook
The Bobbsey Twins at Home
The Bobbsey Twins in Washington
The Bobbsey Twins in the Great West
The Bobbsey Twins at Cedar Camp
The Bobbsey Twins at the Country Fair

3K1717—Each..................48c
Any two for.......................93c

39c EACH

An Old Fashioned Girl

Little Men

Little Women

By Louisa M. Alcott

Bound in cloth. Size, 5¼x7¾ inches. Average 400 pages. Shpg. wt., each, 1 lb.
3K1686—Little Women........................$0.39
3K1620—An Old Fashioned Girl..............39
3K1656—Little Men..........................39
3K6231—Set of 3 books....................1.15

The Ruth Fielding Series

For Girls From 8 to 12 Years
By Alice B. Emerson

Delightful, interesting and exciting stories. Bound in cloth. Size, 5¼x7⅝ inches. Average 200 pages. Illustrated.

Ruth Fielding at Golden Pass
Ruth Fielding Treasure Hunting
Ruth Fielding of the Red Mill
Ruth Fielding at Briarwood Hall
Ruth Fielding at Snow Camp
Ruth Fielding at Lighthouse Point
Ruth Fielding at Silver Ranch
Ruth Fielding at Cliff Island
Ruth Fielding at Sunrise Farm
Ruth Fielding and the Gypsies
Ruth Fielding in Moving Pictures
Ruth Fielding Down in Dixie
Ruth Fielding at College
Ruth Fielding in the Saddle

Ruth Fielding in the Red Cross
Ruth Fielding at the War Front
Ruth Fielding Homeward Bound
Ruth Fielding Down East
Ruth Fielding in the Great Northwest
Ruth Fielding on the St. Lawrence
Ruth Fielding in the Far North

Ruth Fielding at Snow Camp
ALICE B. EMERSON

3K1698—Each....(Shipping wt., each, 1 lb.)....48c
Any two for.......................93c

Mrs. L. T. Meade Books

For Girls From 8 to 12 Years

These are excellent stories from the pen of this famous writer of girls' books who is as popular with the girls of today as she was with their mothers. Bound in cloth. Size, 5¼x7⅝ inches. Average 275 pages.

DADDY'S GIRL

Bad Little Hannah
Bunch of Cherries
Daddy's Girl
Deb and the Duchess
Frances Kane's Fortune
Girl in Ten Thousand

Girl of the True Blue
Good Luck
Heart of Gold
Little Mother to the Others
Modern Tomboy
Polly, a New Fashioned Girl
Sweet Girl Graduate
Wild Kitty
World of Girls

3K1722—Each..(Shpg. wt., ea., 1 lb.)48c
Any two for.......................93c

Heidi

By Johanna Spyri

An appealing tale of child life in the mountains of Switzerland. Cloth. 5x7½ in., 420 pages. Shpg. wt., 1 lb.

3K1690 48c

Hans Brinker,

or the Silver Skates. Mary Mapes Dodge. Size, 5x7½ in. Cloth. Shpg. wt., 1 lb.

3K1489 48c

The Marjorie Dean Series

By Pauline Lester Size, 5x7½ inches. Average 300 pages. Bound in cloth. Shpg. wt., 1¼ lbs.

Marjorie Dean, Post Graduate
Marjorie Dean, Marvelous Manager
Marjorie Dean at Hamilton Arms
Marjorie Dean's Romance
Marjorie Dean Macy
Marjorie Dean, College Freshman
Marjorie Dean, College Sophomore
Marjorie Dean, College Junior
Marjorie Dean, College Senior

3K1715—Any one of the above books.....48c
Set of four....................$1.89

The Mary Jane Series

By Clara Ingram Judson

For girls from 5 to 9. Average 200 pages. Bound in cloth. Illustrated. Shipping weight, each, 1 pound.

Mary Jane; Her Book
Mary Jane; Her Visit
Mary Jane's Kindergarten
Mary Jane Down South
Mary Jane's City Home
Mary Jane in New England
Mary Jane's Country Home
Mary Jane at School

3K1699—Each..................48c
Any two for.......................93c

See Box Paper on page 790.

Pinocchio

By C. Collodi. This story of the wooden man who came to life and had a series of marvelous experiences is a standard classic that every boy and girl should own. An illustrated edition. Bound in cloth. Size, 5¼x7½ inches. 264 pages. Shpg. wt., 1¼ lbs.

3K1491 48c

Five Little Peppers and How They Grew

By Margaret Sidney. The brightest of girls' stories. The tale of the life of the Pepper family, of Ben, Polly, Joel, Phronsie and David, is the kind that girls follow with delight. Illustrated. Bound in cloth. Size, 4¾x6½ inches. 427 pages. Shipping weight, 1 pound.

3K1712.......52c

The Barton Books

By May Hollis Barton

New style writer for girls whose style is somewhat of a mixture of Louise M. Alcott and Mrs. L. T. Meade, but thoroughly up to date in plot and action. Bound in cloth. Average 210 pages. Shipping weight, 1¼ pounds.

The Girl from the Country
Three Girl Chums at Laurel Hill
Bell Grayson's Ranching Days
Four Little Women of Roxby
Plain Jane and Pretty Betty

3K1619—Any one of the above books.....48c
Any two for.......................93c

The Honey Bunch Books

New, fascinating tales for little girls. Size, 5x7½ inches. Average 275 pages. Bound in cloth. Shipping weight, 1½ lbs.

Honey Bunch, Her First Trip on the Ocean
Honey Bunch, Just a Little Girl
Honey Bunch, Her First Visit to the City
Honey Bunch, Her First Days on the Farm
Honey Bunch, Her First Visit to the Seashore
Honey Bunch, Her First Little Garden
Honey Bunch, Her First Days in Camp
Honey Bunch, Her First Auto Tour

3K1702—Any one of the above books.....48c
Any two for.......................93c

Camp Fire Girls Series

A CAMPFIRE GIRL ON A HIKE

They bubble over with high spirits and good times. Bound in board covers, in imitation of cloth. Size, 5x7½ in. Shpg. wt., each, ¾ lb.

The Camp Fire Girls in the Allegheny Mountains
The Camp Fire Girls in the Country
The Camp Fire Girls' Trip Up the River
The Camp Fire Girls' Outing
The Camp Fire Girls on a Hike
The Camp Fire Girls at Twin Lakes

3K1762—Each..................14c
Three for 39c; six for.............75c

Elsie Dinsmore

By Martha Finley

(Author of the famous Elsie Books.) Elsie's difficulties, her trials and troubles and her courageous and triumphant conquering form a most alluring tale. All girls love this story. Bound in cloth. Size, 5¼x7½ inches. Average 300 pages. Shipping weight, 1 pound.

ELSIE DINSMORE
MARTHA FINLEY

3K1707..................48c
3K1711—Elsie's Holidays at Roseland..........48c
Both books for..............93c

The Children's Book Shelf

ROBIN HOOD

Here are sixteen books that every child should read. They have been carefully selected from the large number of children's books published with the view in mind of giving the child the best reading matter possible. Each volume contains from 262 to 320 pages. Lavishly illustrated and handsomely bound in cloth. Size, 6¼x8¾ inches. Beautifully colored illustration on front cover. Each book has an attractive paper jacket in colors. Shipping weight, each, 2 pounds.

Little Women
Tales From Shakespeare
Treasure Island
Robin Hood
Grimm's Fairy Tales
Pinocchio
Heidi
The Man Without a Country

Mother Goose Nursery Rhymes
The Wonder Book of Bible Stories
Favorite Fairy Tales
Alice in Wonderland
Arabian Nights
Hans Brinker
Robinson Crusoe
Kidnapped

3K1617—Any one of the above books........98c
Any two for.......................$1.93

Young People's Library

For Boys and Girls From 9 to 15 Years
Books All Children Love

Bound in tan cloth with allover design on both covers in two colors. Each book has colored end sheets and beautifully colored jacket. Printed on fine white paper from new plates. Size, 7¾x4¾ inches. Average 256 pages. Shipping weight, 1¼ pounds.

A Child's Garden of Verses. Stevenson
Alice in Wonderland. Carroll
Andersen's Fairy Tales. Andersen
Black Beauty. Sewel
Christmas Stories. Dickens
Children's Stories. R. Kipling
Helen's Babies. Habeston
Kidnapped. Stevenson
Lamplighter, The. Cummins
Last of the Mohicans. Cooper
Little Lame Prince, The. Mulock
Master of Ballantrae. Stevenson
Pathfinder, The. Cooper
Pilgrim's Progress. Bunyan
Pinocchio. Collodi
Robinson Crusoe. Defoe
Spy, The. Cooper
Swiss Family Robinson. Wyse
Tale of Two Cities. Dickens
Tales From Shakespeare. Chas. and Mary Lamb
Deerslayer, The. Cooper
Grimm's Fairy Tales. Grimm
Gulliver's Travels. Swift
Hans Brinker. Dodge
Heidi. Spyri
Tanglewood Tales. Hawthorne
Tom Brown's School Days. Hughes
Treasure Island. Stevenson
Uncle Tom's Cabin. Stowe
Wonder Book, The. Hawthorne

3K1768—Any one of the above books..................39c
Two for.......................75c

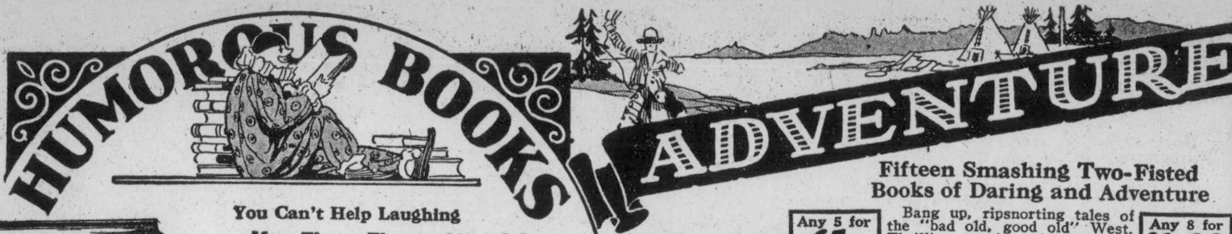

You Can't Help Laughing

More Than a Thousand New Jokes and Stories

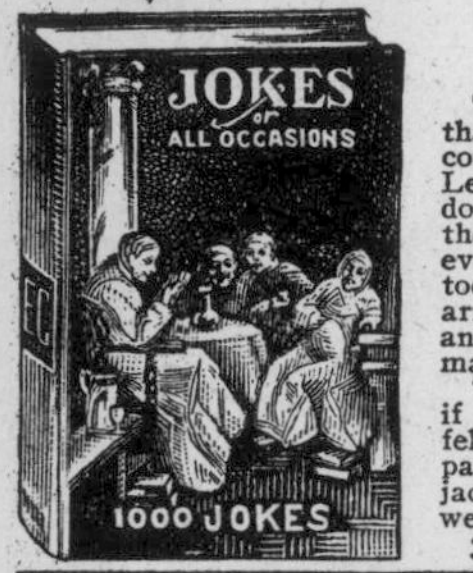

These are really funny jokes and stories, the kind that make you roar with glee. Not the old moss covered stuff from the time of Artemus Ward and Lew Dockstader, but fresh, bright and snappy anecdotes that have made a hit with all who have heard them. Read it to the family. It will provide many evenings of merry laughter and enjoyment. It's useful, too. All the jokes and stories are alphabetically arranged by subjects so that you can find a tale to fit any occasion. Read the ones about love, lunacy, lying, manners, marriage, etc.

This is a mighty nice old world in which to live if you can laugh now and then. This book fills a long felt want, for it is the very best of its kind. 368 pages, bound in cloth, with an attractive pictorial jacket in bright colors. Size, 5¼x7⅝ inches. Shipping weight, 1½ pounds.

3K3268........ **89c**

Fifteen Smashing Two-Fisted Books of Daring and Adventure

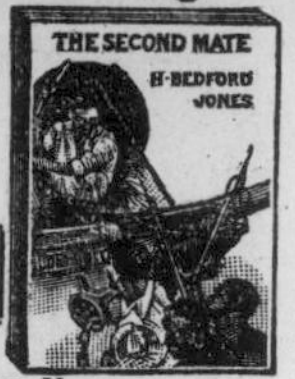

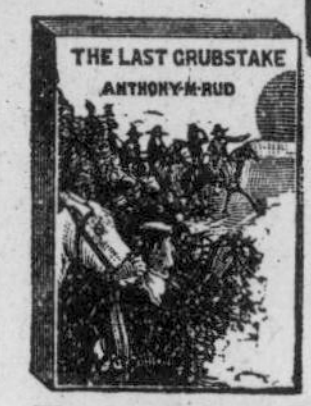

Any 5 for 65c **Any 8 for $1.00**

Bang up, ripsnorting tales of the "bad old, good old" West. Thrilling stories of adventure, by famous authors. Each book bound in heavy paper, with individual cover design in colors. Size, 5x7⅜ inches.

- **The Last Grubstake.** Anthony M. Rud.
- **The Second Mate.** H. Bedford-Jones.
- **The Seven Pearls of Shandi.** Magruder Maury.
- **Texas Men and Texas Cattle.** E. E. Harriman.
- **The Scourge of the Little "C."** J. E. Grinstead.
- **The Lone Hand Tracker.** Wm. W. Winter.
- **When Death Rode the Range.** Wm. W. Winter.
- **Raw Gold.** Clem Yore.
- **Don Quickshot Looking for Trouble.** Stephen Chalmers.
- **The Last Shot.** Wm. MacLeod Raine.
- **Straight Shooting.** W. C. Tuttle.
- **Sad Sontag Plays His Hunch.** W. C. Tuttle.
- **The Sentence of the Six Gun.** Anthony M. Rud.
- **The Outlaws of Flowerpot Canon.** Frank C. Robertson.
- **The Cleanup on Dead Man.** Frank C. Robertson.

3K1239—Any 5 for........ **65c**
Any 8 for........ **$1.00**
Shipping weight of five, 1¼ pounds.

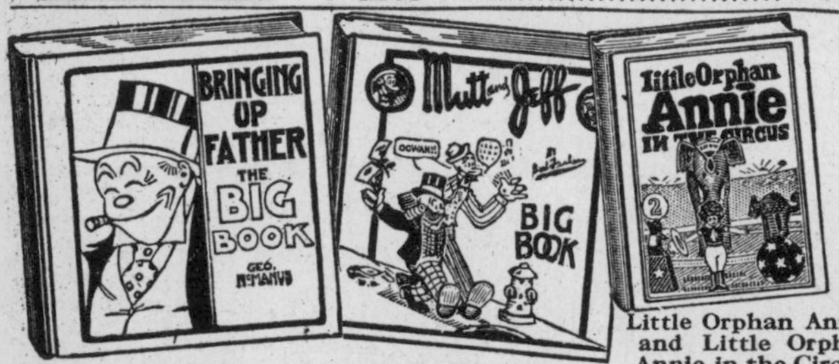

Christmas Cards Printed With Your Own Name. See Page 776.

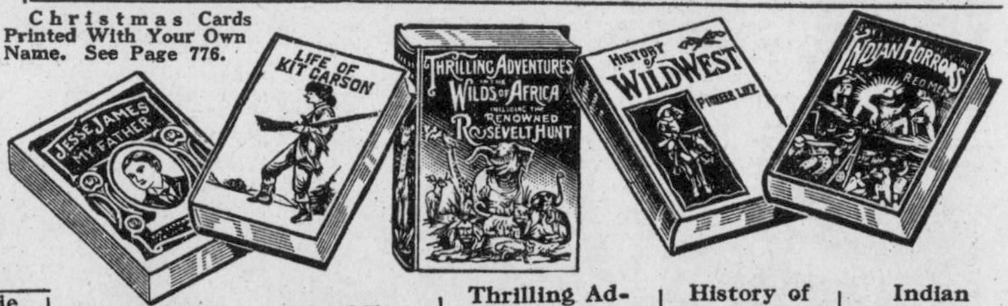

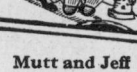

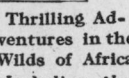

Father's Big Book

By Geo. McManus

Here is a big book containing a collection of cartoons featuring "Jiggs" and "Maggie" by the well known creator of Bringing Up Father. Bound in colored board covers. 144 pages. Size, 10x10 inches. Shpg. wt., 1¼ lbs.

3K3121....... **69c**

Mutt and Jeff Big Book

This new big book of Mutt and Jeff contains 144 pages of Bud Fisher's well known characters. Bound in colored board covers. Size, 10x10 inches. Shipping wt., 1¼ pounds.

3K3135... **69c**

Little Orphan Annie and Little Orphan Annie in the Circus

By Harold Gray

Follow Little Orphan Annie through her thrilling days with the circus. 86 pages of real entertainment. Bound in colored board covers. Size, 6¾x8½ in. Shpg. wt., 1 lb.

3K5998—Little Orphan Annie.... **49c**
3K5893
Little Orphan Annie in the Circus 49c
Both books for.... 95c

Jesse James, My Father

The first and only true story of Jesse James and his adventures. A very fascinating book, 189 pages. Colored paper cover. Size, 5x7½ in. Shpg. wt., ¾ lb.

3K1844 **21c**

Life of Kit Carson

By Edward S. Ellis

Adventure and excitement galore. 247 pages. Cloth. Size, 5¼x7½ in. Shipping weight, 1 pound.

3K1670 **48c**

Thrilling Adventures in the Wilds of Africa

Including the Renowned Roosevelt Hunt

558 pages. Over 200 illustrations. Cloth. Size, 6¾x9 inches. Shpg. wt., 3 pounds.

3K1802 **$1.69**

History of Our Wild West and Stories of Pioneer Life

354 pages. Illustrated. Cloth. Size, 6¼ x 8⅛ in. Shpg. wt., 1¾ pounds.

3K1815 **69c**

Indian Horrors

Fully illustrated. 600 pages. Cloth. Size, 5⅜x7⅝ inches. Shipping weight, 1¾ pounds.

3K1805 **97c**

Funny Cartoons

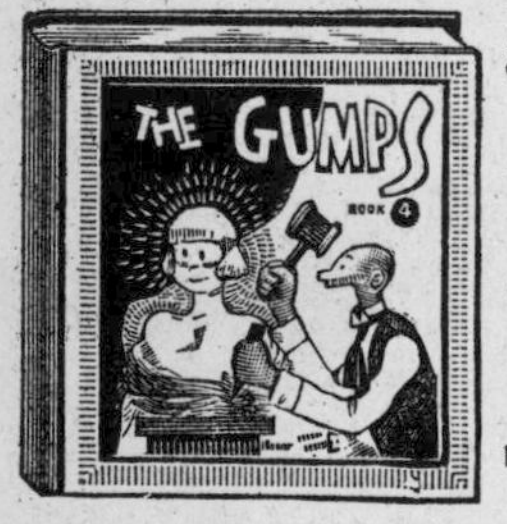

Each book contains 48 pages of cartoons. Size, 9⅞x9¹⁵⁄₁₆ inches. Colored board covers. Shipping weight, ¾ lb.

- 3K3138—Bringing Up Father, Book 7.
- 3K3139—Bringing Up Father, Book 8.
- 3K2510—Bringing Up Father, Book 11.
- 3K2367—Bringing Up Father, Book 12.
- 3K4000—The Gumps, Book 1.
- 3K2379—The Gumps, Book 2.
- 3K2474—The Gumps, Book 4.
- 3K1826—Mutt and Jeff, Book 10.
- 3K2508—Mutt and Jeff, Book 11.
- 3K2509—Mutt and Jeff, Book 12.
- 3K2472—Barney Google, Book 2.
- 3K2473—Barney Google, Book 3.
- 3K2500—Tillie the Toiler, Book 2.

Any one of the above books........ **20c**
Any three of the above books....$0.57
Any six of the above books...... 1.10

Pigs Is Pigs

By Ellis Parker Butler

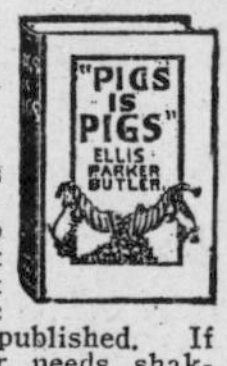

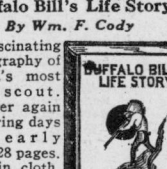

This is acknowledged to be the best short comic story published. If your liver needs shaking up, don't miss it. Bound in cloth. Size 4½x7 inches. About 50 pages. Shipping weight, 3 pounds.

3K3293..... **48c**

Buffalo Bill's Life Story

By Wm. F. Cody

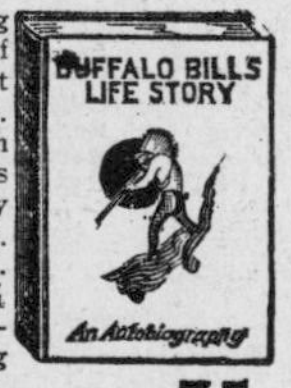

A fascinating autobiography of America's most famous scout. Live over again the stirring days of the early West. 328 pages. Bound in cloth. Size, 5½x7¾ inches. Illustrated. Shipping weight, 1¼ lbs.

3K1634.............. **75c**

See Page 776 for Gift Books.

History of the Great World War

A Comprehensive and Authentic History of the War by Land, Sea and Air.

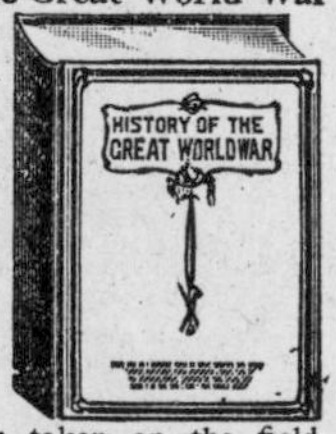

A book that covers the war period from its beginning. Fully illustrated with hundreds of half-tone pictures, many taken on the field of battle. Bound in cloth. 620 pages. 7x6 in. Shpg. wt., 3¼ lbs.

3K6160........ **$1.35**

Skeezix Story Books

By Mr. King

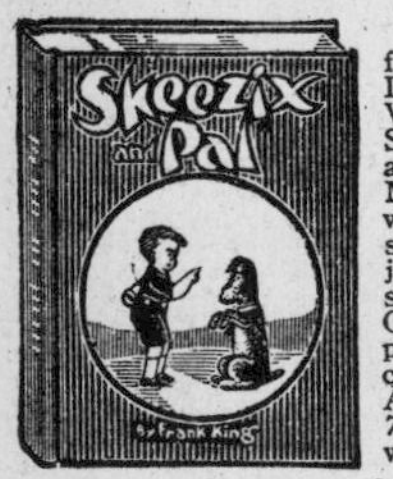

The originator of the famous Gasoline Alley. Delightful tales of Uncle Walt and the beloved Skeezix. Fun for kiddies and grownups as well. Made up in story form which are fun filled, whimsical and chock full of just the things youngsters like to read about. Colored pictures on every page. Bound in cloth with colored picture on cover. Average 105 pages. Size, 7¼x9½ inches. Shipping weight, each, 1 pound.

Skeezix and Uncle Walt
Skeezix and Pal
Skeezix at the Circus

3K6162—Each................ **85c**
Set of three.................. **$2.50**

Witty Stories and Toasts for All Occasions and How to Tell Them

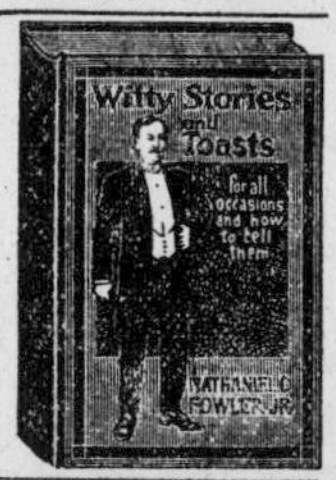

Bright, breezy and up to the minute matter for instantaneous use. Also contains several chapters of general suggestions for successful dinners. 216 pages. Bound in cloth. Size, 5⅝x7⅝ in.

3K4017
Shpg. wt., 1¼ lbs.. **79c**

Adventure and Frontier Series

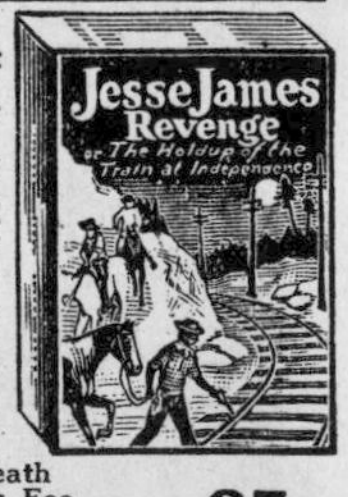

Paper bound. Average 200 pages. Size, 4⅞x7 inches.

- Border Outlaw
- Harry Tracy
- The James Boys
- Jesse James' Daring Raid
- Younger Brothers
- Dalton Brothers
- Rube Burrow, Outlaw King
- Tracy the Bandit
- Heroes of the Plains
- The James Boys of Old Missouri
- Jesse James' Surprise
- Jesse James' Daylight Foray
- Jesse James' Dash for Fortune
- Jesse James' Midnight Raid
- Jesse James' Great Haul
- Jesse James' Battle for Freedom
- Jesse James' Revenge
- Jesse James' Race for Life
- Jesse James' Midnight Attack
- Jesse James' Narrow Escape
- Jesse James' Ring of Death
- Jesse James' Mysterious Foe

3K1639—Shipping weight, of two, 1½ pounds. Any 2 for.... **27c**

Peck's Bad Boy Books

Give Them to the Boys

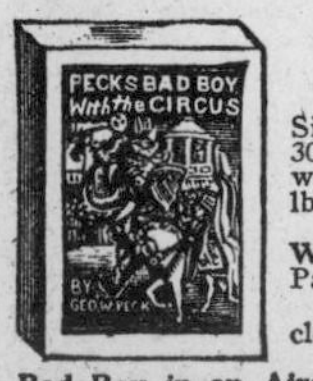

Colored paper or cloth covers. Size, 3⅛x7½ inches. Average 300 pages. Illustrated. Shipping weight, with paper covers, ¾ lb.; with cloth covers, 1 lb.

3K3112—Peck's Bad Boy With the Circus. Paper covers........ **28c**
3K3304—Same as above, cloth covers..................79c
3K3118—Peck's Bad Boy in an Airship. Paper covers..... **28c**
3K3305—Same as above, cloth covers..79c
3K3111—Peck's Bad Boy Abroad. Paper covers................ **28c**
3K3310—Same as above, cloth covers...79c
3K3113—Peck's Bad Boy With the Cowboys. Paper covers.............. **28c**
3K3311—Same as above, cloth covers...79c

The Nebbs Jr. and His Dog Spot, by Sol Hess

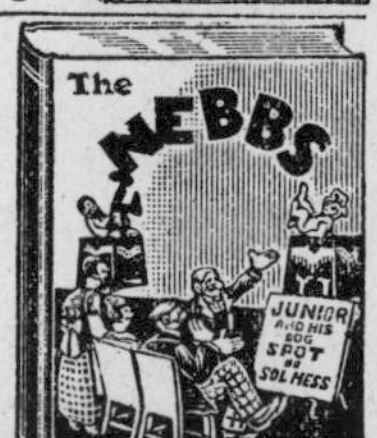

Every boy will want to read the interesting story written around this character. Cloth bound, 92 pages, size, 7¼x9½ inches. Shipping weight, 1 pound.

3K2289... **89c**

Celebrated Crimes and Their Solution

By George Barton

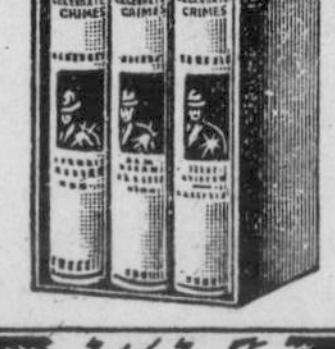

A 3-volume cloth bound set consisting of Famous Detective Mysteries, Great Cases of Famous Detectives and Adventures of the World's Greatest Detectives. Each book averages 250 pages. Size, 5½x7¾ in. Shpg. wt., 5 lbs.

3K1356
Per set........ **$2.29**

Frontier Series

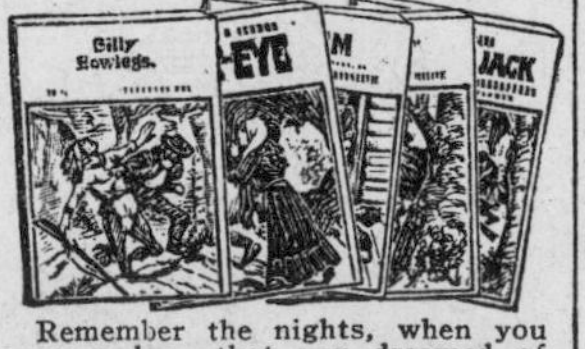

Remember the nights, when you were a boy, that you dreamed of the wild, terrible, fascinating western frontier?

The Frontier Series of good, clean, amazing adventure in the Old West will bring them back to you. A paper bound series which are of interest to the young folks. We are offering these in groups of five. Size of each book, 5¼x7 inches. Average, 100 pages. Shipping weight, of five books, ¾ lb.

3K1351—Series of 5 books.................. **29c**

Deadwood Dick Series

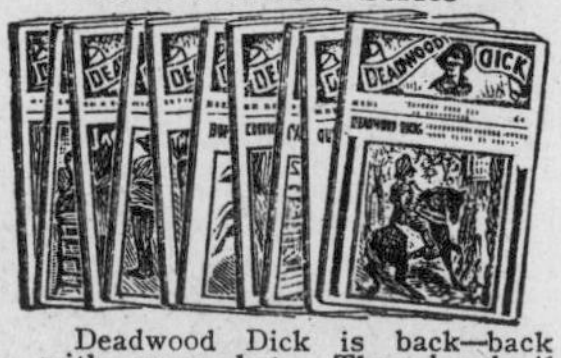

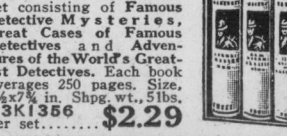

Deadwood Dick is back—back with guns hot. The daredevil Lancelot of Wild West days, plunging his way through breathtaking adventure.

Handsome tri-color covers. Through special arrangement with the publisher we are offering these books in groups of ten assorted titles. Each book contains an average of 32 pages; size, 5½x7⅞ inches. Shipping weight of ten books, ¾ pound.

3K1350—Series of 10 titles................ **39c**

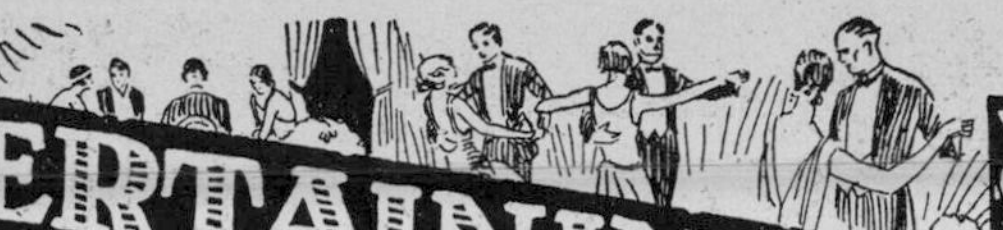

ENTERTAINING

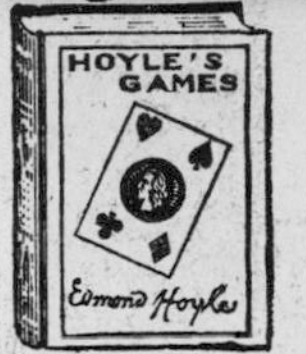

Hoyle's Games, Autograph Edition

The newest up to date edition revised by R. F. Foster, the leading authority on all indoor games, including the latest ideas in Auction Bridge and other card games; Backgammon, Chess and Checkers, Dice Games, Dominoes, with the official laws for all forms of Billiards and Bowling. Size, 5½x7 inches. 431 pages. Illustrated. Cloth bound. Shipping weight, 1½ pounds.
3K3904 .... 89c

Hoyle's Games, Paper Bound

311 pages. Size, 5x7⅜ inches. Shipping weight, 1 lb.
3K3923 .... 45c

Auction Bridge Complete

By Milton C. Works. Authoritative and up to date rules for both beginners and experts. Bound in cloth. 500 pages. Size, 5½x7⅝ in. Shpg. wt., 1 lb.
3K4298 .... $1.85

Learn Latest Dance Steps Easily

Dance Well and Be Popular—Learn All the Latest Steps

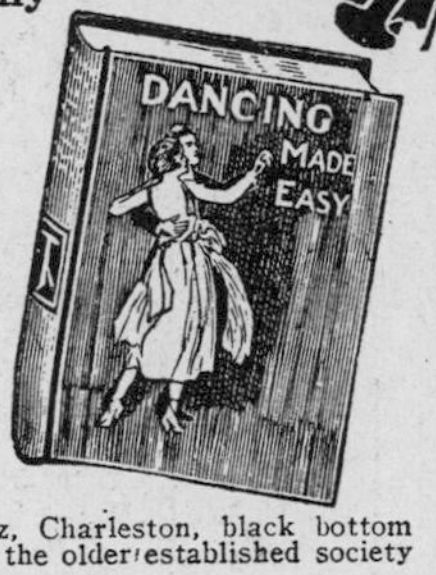

Get this marvelous, up to the minute book, "Dancing Made Easy." All the latest steps simply explained. You can learn them easily in one evening. This remarkable book sets forth new steps that are being danced, with illustrations and diagram charts. It will teach you the **latest variations** of jazz, the toddle, the camel walk, the canter, pivot, the one-step, the fox-trot, two-step, waltz, Charleston, black bottom and Valencia, as well as the older established society dances.

Remember, too, that every dance is carefully explained with pictorial diagrams that make the dances so easy to learn from this book. 277 pages. Cloth. Size, 5⅛x7½ in. Shpg. wt., 1 lb.
3K3997—Dancing Made Easy 89c

ETIQUETTE

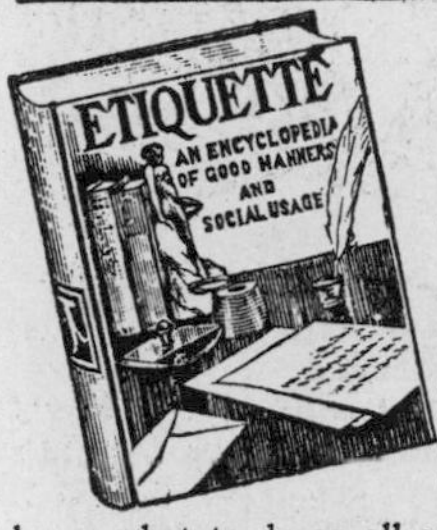

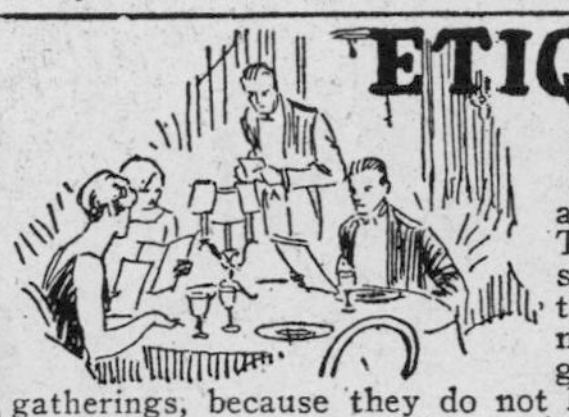

An Encyclopedia of Good Manners and Social Usage

There are some persons who are never at ease before people. They are awkward, self conscious, fearful all the time that they will do something that is not right. They are afraid to go to receptions, balls, informal gatherings, because they do not know how to act. They have a haunting fear of making social blunders. They don't know how to acknowledge formal invitations, they do not know the social customs that every man and woman should know.

With the aid of **"Etiquette"** you need never be at a loss to know what to do on all occasions. This book will give you the key to what is proper to do, to write, to wear, to say, no matter where you are or what situation may arise. 378 pages. Cloth. Size, 5⅛x7½ inches. Shipping weight, 1 pound.
3K3500 .... 89c

The books listed below will average from 200 to 300 pages. Size, 5½x7 inches. Bound in cloth. Shipping weight, 1¼ pounds.

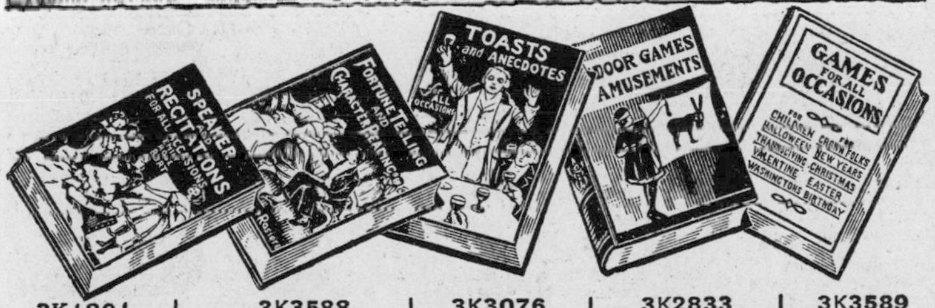

3K1891 Speaker and Recitations 69c	3K3588 Fortune Telling and Character Reading 89c	3K3076 Toasts and Anecdotes 69c	3K2833 Indoor Games and Amusements 98c	3K3589 Games for All Occasions 85c

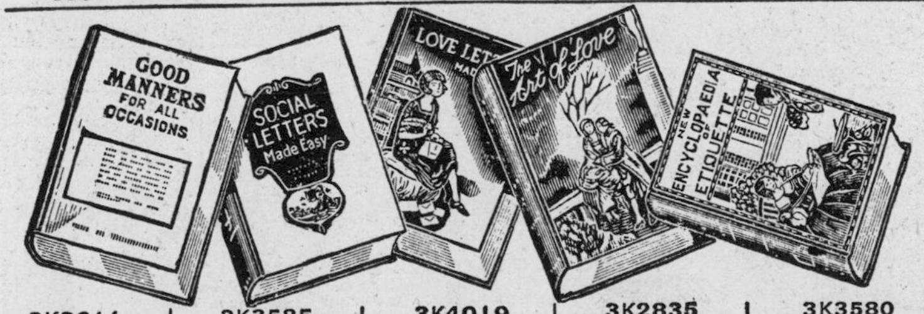

3K3611 Good Manners for All Occasions 89c	3K3585 Social Letters Made Easy 68c	3K4019 Love Letters Made Easy 69c	3K2835 The Art of Love 69c	3K3580 New Encyclopedia of Etiquette $1.65

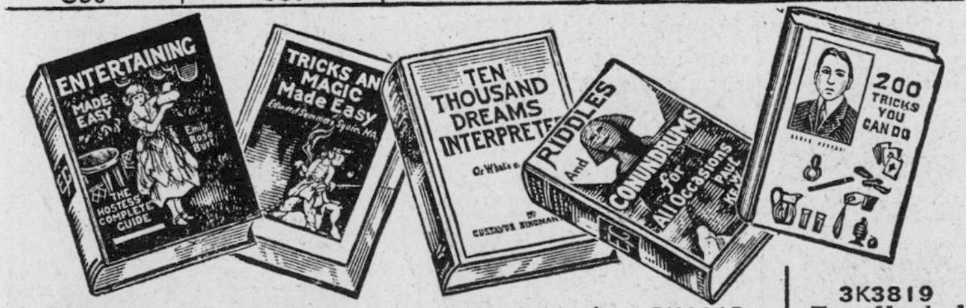

3K3900 Entertaining Made Easy 89c	3K3830 Tricks and Magic Made Easy 69c	3K4145 Ten Thousand Dreams Interpreted 98c	3K4012 Riddles and Conundrums 69c	3K3819 Two Hundred Tricks You Can Do. By Howard Thurston 89c

MEDICAL BOOKS

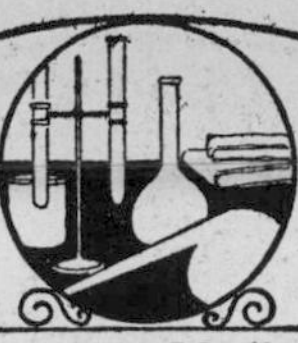

The World's Great Medical Adviser

By William A. Evans, M. D.

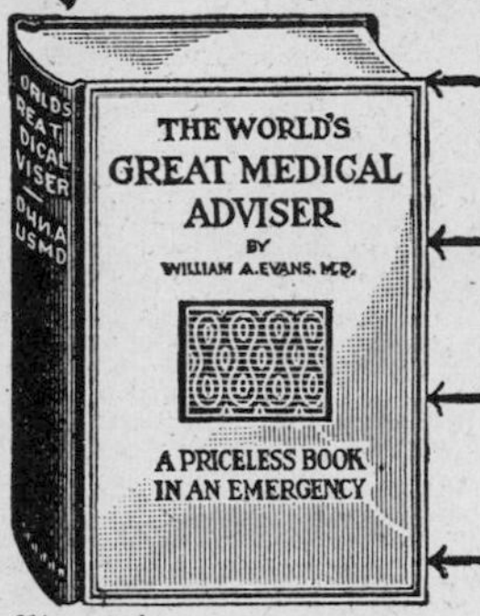

Bound in cloth.

Printed in large, easily read type.

1,040 pages.

400 practical and useful illustrations.

This great book may mean the difference between life and death.

In it nearly every known disease and ailment to which human beings are subject is frankly and ably discussed. Contains thousands of questions asked Dr. Evans by thousands of people seeking the road to health, together with the physician's answers. So varied are the topics covered that, without doubt, the very question that you want to ask yourself or some one in your family is here answered.

Bound in cloth. Size, 10x7 inches. 1,040 pages and over 400 illustrations. Shipping weight, 3½ pounds.
3K5946—Our special low price $1.75

Sex Hygiene Books

Facts for the Married

By Dr. William Lee Howard

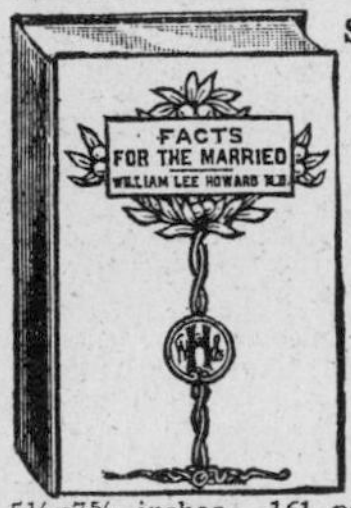

Ghastly tragic are the records of failure in marriage in this country. Scientists tell us the great cause is ignorance of sex. Now comes a book of sex constructively solving these fateful problems. Bound in cloth. Size, 5⅛x7⅝ inches. 161 pages.
3K3758—Shpg. wt., 1 lb. 89c

Sex Problems Solved for Every Married Couple

By Dr. William Lee Howard

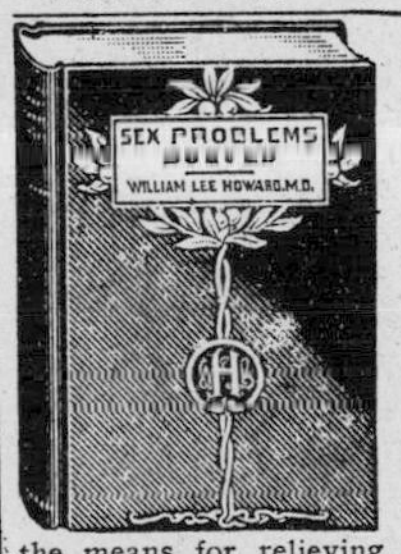

Every married couple should have this wonderful book if they want to get the very most out of life as it unfolds. Dr. Howard bares the causes for many forms of nervous and mental disorders and recommends the means for relieving them. Bound in cloth. Size, 5⅛x7⅝ inches. 204 pages. Shipping weight, 1 pound.
3K3756 .... 89c

Plain Facts on Sex Hygiene

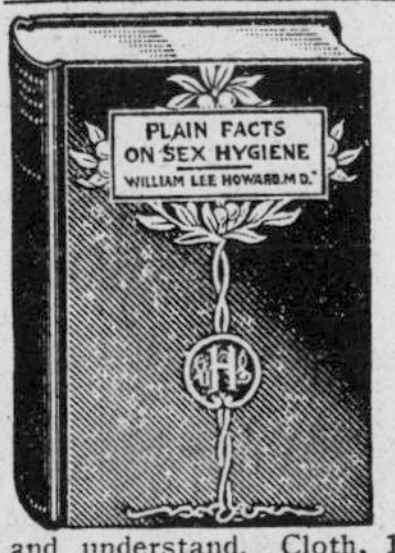

By Dr. William Lee Howard, WILL do much toward preventing childless marriages and subnormal children, Dr. Howard fixes your attention upon his revelations, uses plain words, shuns no details, evades no questions, but flattens out facts for all to read and understand. Cloth, 171 pages. Size, 5⅛x7⅞ in. Shpg. wt., 1 lb.
3K3754 .... 89c

A Complete and Authoritative Library on Sex Knowledge

The three books described above. Shipping weight, 3 pounds.
3K3765—Special reduced price for this 3-volume set $2.50

Getting Ready to Be a Mother

By Carolyn C. Van Blarcom, R. N.

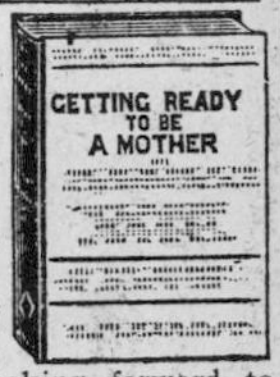

For the young woman who is looking forward to motherhood. If every expectant mother followed the simple, practical advice which this book offers, the rate of injury and death among our mothers and babies would be materially lessened.

Bound in cloth. Size, 5¼x7⅝ inches. 237 pages, 75 illustrations. Shipping wt., 1 lb.
3K3704 .... 98c

Husband and Wife

By Lyman B. Sperry, M. D.

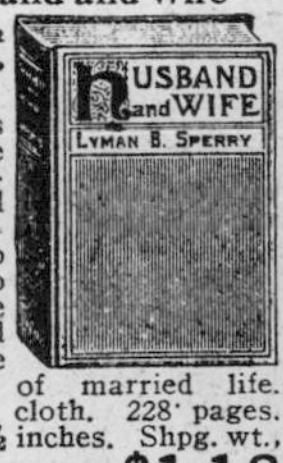

Gives valuable instructions and suggestions to those who have entered upon the relations of married life. Bound in cloth. 228 pages. Size, 5x7½ inches. Shpg. wt., 1¼ lbs.
3K3752 .... $1.18

The Care and Feeding of Children

New 13th Edition Revised and Enlarged. By L. Emmett Holt, M.D., LL.D. 215 pages. Cloth. Size, 4⅞x6¾ inches. Shipping weight, 1 pound.
3K3537 .... 87c

Feeding and Caring for the Baby

By M. C. Pease Jr., M. D., D. Sc.

A reliable guide for the mother from the birth of the baby and before, through the early years of childhood. Cloth. Size, 4¾x6⅝ in. 256 pages. Shpg. wt., ¾ lb.
3K3122 .... 43c

Standard Home Medical Guide

By Dr. A. F. Voak. Valuable information concerning the more common diseases and their treatment. 114 pages. Cloth. Size, 3⅞x7 inches. Shipping weight, 8 ounces.
3K6164 .... 39c

Household Library

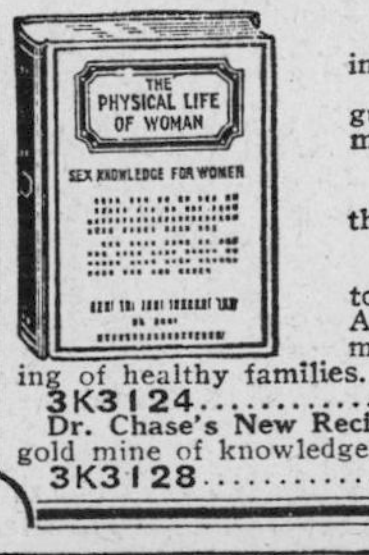

Bound in cloth. Average 300 pages. Size, 5⅛x7½ inches. Shipping weight, 1½ pounds.

Physical Life of Woman. Plain and practical language on the delicate physiology of women during maiden hood, matrimony and maternity.
3K3126 .... 98c

The Transmission of Life. A manual for men on the peculiar function of the male.
3K3125 .... 98c

The Family Physician, or every man his own doctor. Will help promote health and prolong life. Also an analysis of things relating to courtship, marriage, and the production, management and rearing of healthy families.
3K3124 .... 98c

Dr. Chase's New Recipe Book and Medical Adviser. A regular gold mine of knowledge.
3K3128 .... 98c

Webster's Revised Unabridged Dictionary

(Genuine G and C Merriam Edition)

Up to Date Department of All Modern Words

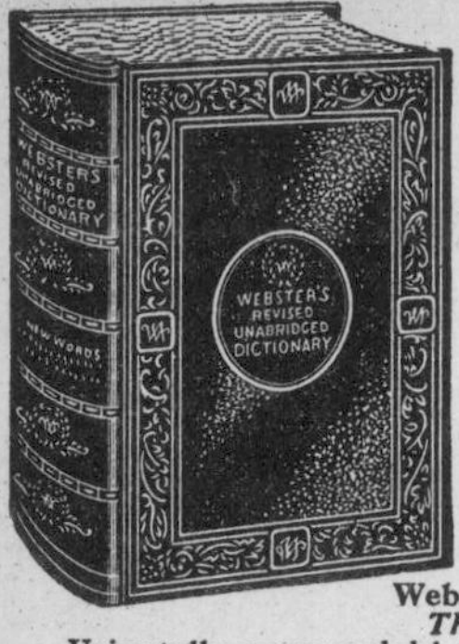

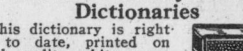

This great dictionary is without doubt the most comprehensive and complete ever compiled, containing positively every word in the English language, together with pages of derivities, classical and modern. This dictionary is accepted everywhere by colleges, schools and educational authorities as standard in all its phases.

2,120 pages. Printed on thin Bible paper and is only 2½ inches thick. Index cut in on edge, marbled edges and end sheets. Size, 11½x8¾x2½ inches.

Bound in wine color artificial leather, morocco grained, with handsomely embossed border. Title stamped in gold on side and back.

Shipping weight, either style, 7¾ pounds.

3K6809—Webster's Unabridged Dictionary. Bound in artificial leather, morocco grained........ **$7.35**

For the benefit of public libraries, schools and those people who expect to subject the dictionary to extra hard usage we also list the Unabridged bound in green, pebbled finish cloth.

3K6810—Webster's Unabridged Dictionary. Bound in cloth........ **$6.75**

Webster's New International Dictionary

The Merriam Webster Latest Edition

Universally recommended by statesmen, college presidents, educators and authors. Contains 400,000 vocabulary terms, 30,000 geographical subjects, 12,000 biographical entries. Thousands of other references, 6,000 illustrations, 2,700 pages, colored plates and engravings. Size, 9½x12½ inches. Shipping weight, 14 pounds.

3K6982—Bound in buff buckram. Marbled edges, indexed........ **$15.60**

3K6991—Bound in full tan sheep. Marbled edges, indexed........ **$19.60**

Winston Simplified Dictionary

Encyclopedia Edition

Edited by

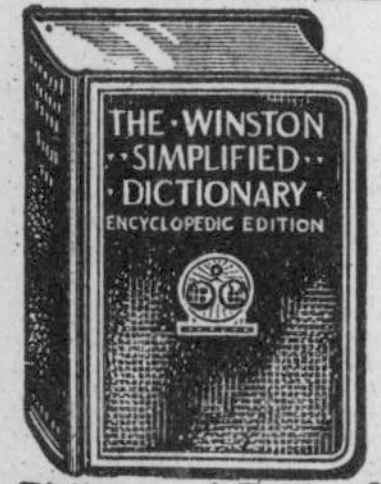

William Dodge Lewis, Pd.D., Litt.D., Henry Seidel Canby, Ph.D., and Thomas Kite Brown, Jr., Ph.D.

The objectives in this new work have been ease of reference, simplicity, completeness, and accuracy of definitions, and the highest scholarship. It also has the following features:

History of the Development of the English Language.
Dictionary of the English Language.
Dictionary of Signs and Symbols.
Dictionary of Foreign Words and Phrases.
Dictionary of Persons and Places.
Dictionary of Phrases.
Dictionary of Scottish Terms.
Dictionary of Christian Names of Men and Women.
Dictionary of Historical Events.
How to Write and Speak English.
Atlas and Gazetteer of the World.

1,500 pages, 3,000 illustrations, 8 color plates, 32 pages of maps in color. Bound in flexible art canvas. Title stamped in gold, indexed. Size, 6½x8½ inches. Shipping weight, 3½ pounds.

3K6217........ **$4.79**

Webster's Handy Service Dictionaries

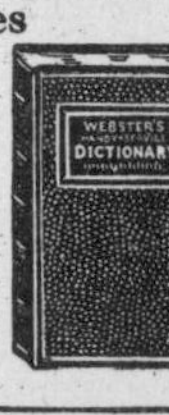

This dictionary is right up to date, printed on good quality white paper from **brand new plates.** Size, 4x5¾ inches. Over 246 pages. Shipping wt., 8 ounces.

3K6319—Bound in black cloth..... **23c**

3K6781—Bound in artificial leather..... **29c**

Name stamped in gold, 20c extra.

Cushing's Manual

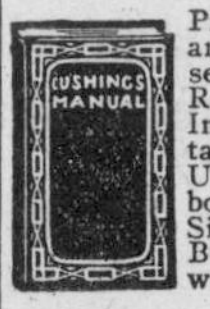

Manual of Parliamentary Practice. Rules of Proceeding and Debate in Deliberative Assemblies, by Luther S. Cushing. Revised to date by John James Ingalls. Also an appendix containing the Constitution of the United States. A copy of this book should be in every home. Size, 3½x5¾ inches. 244 pages. Bound in cloth. Shipping weight, 1 lb.

3K6218........ **49c**

Webster's New Popular Dictionary

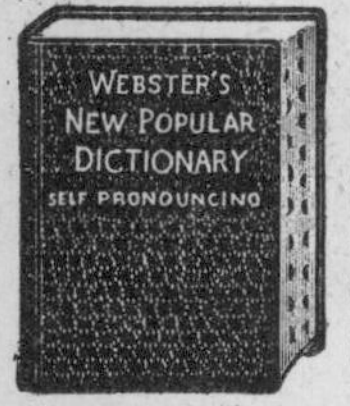

Self pronouncing, newly revised and corrected. In addition to all usual dictionary features, it contains many additional ones. 830 pages. Size, 5¼x7½ inches. Bound in cloth. Shipping weight, 1¾ pounds.

3K6811..... **89c**

3K6812—Same as above, but bound in good quality black artificial leather. Gold stamped. Red edges **$1.15**

3K6858—Same as 3K6812, but with patent index cut in on the edge........ **$1.39**

Name stamped in gold, 20 cents extra.

Foreign Language Dictionaries

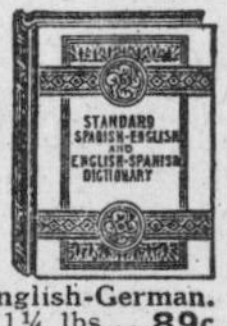

Six complete and accurate dictionaries which were compiled expressly to meet the requirements of increasing intercourse and trade. Full and complete vocabularies. Cloth.

3K6814—Spanish - English and English-Spanish. 218 pages. Size, 4⅝x6 inches. Shpg. wt., ¾ pound........ **89c**

3K6815—German-English and English-German. 700 pages. Size, 4¾x6 in. Shpg. wt., 1¼ lbs....**89c**

3K6816—French-English and English-French. 411 pages. Size, 5¼x7 in. Shpg. wt., 1¼ lbs....**89c**

3K6213—Italian-English and English-Italian Dictionary. Average, 400 pages. Size, 4¾x6⅝ inches. Shipping weight, 1 pound........**89c**

3K6214—Latin-English and English-Latin Dictionary. 225 pages. Size, 4¾x6⅝ inches. Shipping weight, 1 pound........**89c**

3K6215—Swedish-English and English-Swedish Dictionary. 225 pages. Size, 4¾x6⅝ inches. Shipping weight, 1 pound........**89c**

Special Offer to Nature Lovers

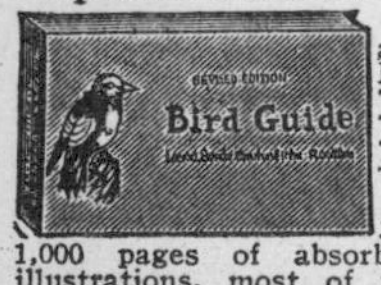

Four master keys to almost every secret Nature holds.
The Bird Guide
The Tree Guide
The Flower Guide
The Butterfly Guide

Each book is 5⅝x3⅝x½ inches. Nearly 1,000 pages of absorbing text, with 789 illustrations, most of them in full natural colors. Shipping weight, 2½ pounds.

3K5656—Four Volumes Pocket Nature Library in Tan Flexible Cloth Binding........ **$3.75**

3K5657—Same as above, but bound in Black Flexible Artificial Leather Binding. **$4.95**

The New Peerless Atlas of the World

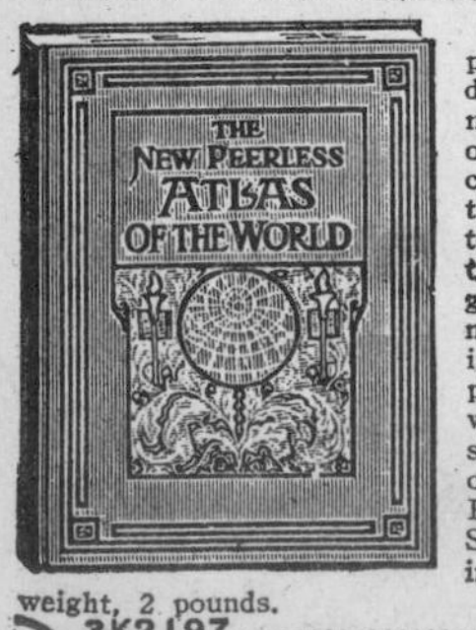

Ninety-six pages of up to date colored maps. 64 pages of index to cities and towns. Gazetteer—index of the world and general information. To keep in step with progress of the world you should have one of these books. Bound in cloth. Size, 9¾x12½ inches. Shipping weight, 2 pounds.

3K2197........ **$1.55**

Educational

Home and School Encyclopedia

The Source of Invaluable Information

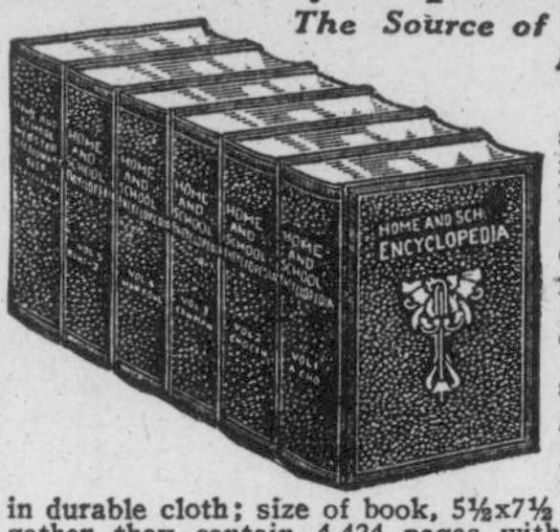

Complete in six volumes, including a large dictionary—covers all departments of human development and achievement since the dawn of civilization. The volumes are each artistically bound in durable cloth; size of book, 5½x7½ inches. Altogether they contain 4,424 pages with 50 full page maps, all absolutely up to date.

Home and School Webster's Dictionary

Self Pronouncing Type

It has 1,024 pages, 851 of which are devoted to the regular dictionary of words; the balance of the pages are devoted to special educational features and useful information. Shpg. wt., 9 lbs.

3K2148—Six-Volume Set........ **$5.95**

New All Steel Dictionary Holder

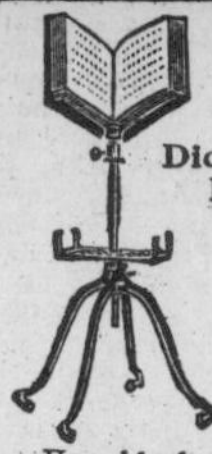

Has black japanned frame, oxidized finish center rod and polished quartered oak book leaves. Revolving book shelf and leaf supports are also japanned. Legs have metal casters, adjustable to any angle. Extended height, 39 inches. Shipping wt., 18 lbs.

3K4.. **$5.75**

3K10—New Unbreakable All Steel Dictionary Holder in japanned and oxidized finish. Shipping wt., 18 lbs....... **$7.25**

Biggest Value Ever Offered

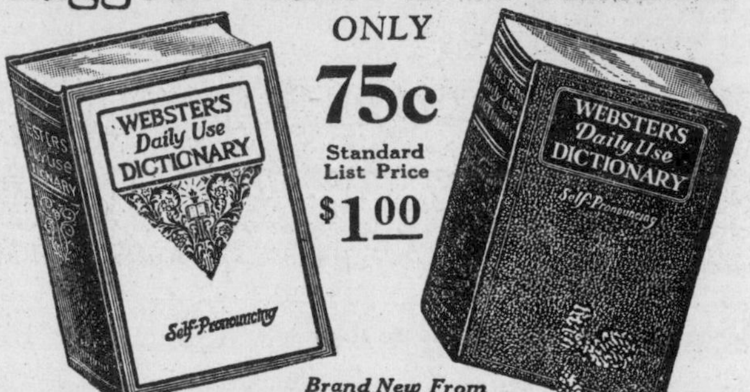

ONLY 75c

Standard List Price $1.00

Brand New From Cover to Cover

New Revised Edition of Webster's Daily Use Dictionary

The entire book has been reset and, although the last edition of this dictionary is less than three years old, it has been revised from cover to cover. This new book has 800 pages. In this new edition we have added to the text, the definitions of 2,185 additional words. The new appendix is changed from that of the usual "catch all" of information thrown together for advertising purposes, to an appendix of essentially literary character, which makes "The Daily Use Dictionary" of greater value to the student, reader and general user. This appendix contains the following:

List of Foreign Expressions.
Full Working List of Abbreviations.
A Good, Comprehensive Set of Rules of Punctuation with Examples.
Table of Weights and Measures.
Brief Business Laws, Etc.

Shipping Weight, 1½ pounds.

3K6808—Webster's Daily Use Dictionary (often sells elsewhere for $1.00). Bound in cloth........ **75c**

3K6859—Webster's Daily Use Dictionary. Same as above, bound in flexible artificial leather. (Others often ask $1.50). Our price......**$1.00**

Cook Books for Better Meals

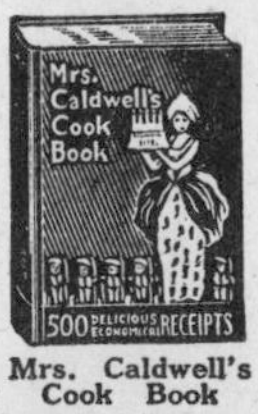

Mrs. Caldwell's Cook Book

Contains 500 practical, tested recipes, gathered from the best recipes used by the most skillful home cooks, will enable the average family to have the most delicious foods at an economical cost. Bound in white cloth, 128 pages, size 4¾x7¼ inches. Shipping wt., 1 lb.

3K3774 Each........ **43c**

Candies and Bonbons and How to Make Them. Illustrated with sixteen illustrations. Bound in cloth. Size, 5½x7¾ in. 256 pages. Shpg. wt., ¾ lb.

3K3821.. **$1.35**

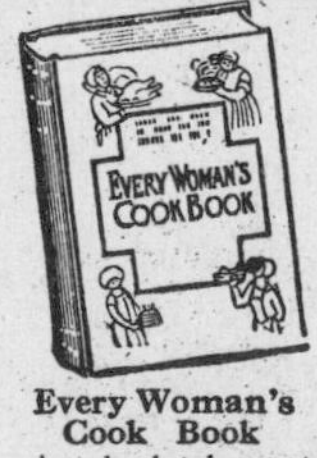

Every Woman's Cook Book

An absolutely up to date cook book of over 700 pages. Contains 3,000 new, thoroughly tested recipes. Housewives will appreciate the chapters on "Left Over Dishes" and "Facts Worth Knowing." Food values have received especial attention. Invalid cookery, hot and cold platter arrangements, southern and Jewish dishes are among the many new features included. Table decorations and menus for every occasion are offered. White oil cloth cover trimmed in blue. Size, 5⅜x8¼ inches. Shipping wt., 2 lbs.

3K3766 **$2.25**

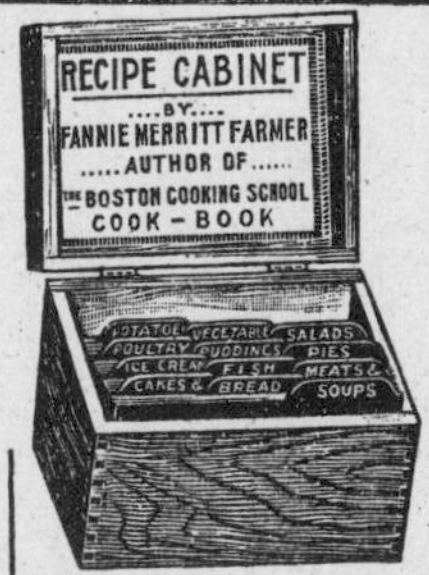

Fannie Merritt Farmer's Handy Recipe Cabinet

Author of Boston Cooking School Cook Book. A nicely finished oak cabinet, containing 200 recipes not contained in the Boston Cooking School Cook Book and a generous supply of blank cards for the busy housewife's own special recipes. Size of box, 4½x5½x4½ inches. Shipping weight, 2 pounds.

3K3525 **$1.85**

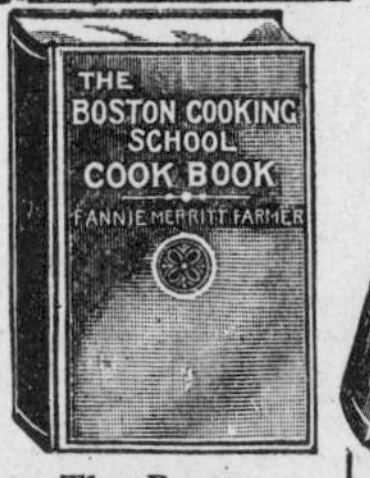

The Boston Cooking School Cook Book

By Fannie Merritt Farmer

New Revised Edition

Contains 2,677 recipes, ranging from the simple and economical to the elaborate and expensive, with 122 halftone illustrations, 806 pages. Cloth. Size, 5¼x7⅝ in. The best of all cook books. Shipping weight, 2 pounds.

3K3532
$2.25

White House Cook Book

New and Thoroughly Revised Edition

Every woman who owns a White House Cook Book swears by it. It is written by Hugo Ziemann, former steward of the White House, and Mrs. F. L. Gillette, revised by Mrs. Mary E. Dague.

Bound in white enamel cloth. Size, 7⅛x9¾ inches, 2 inches thick. Shipping weight, 3½ pounds.

3K3512..... **95c**

Mechanical

The Steel Square

Two Volumes, 633 Pages, 500 Illustrations

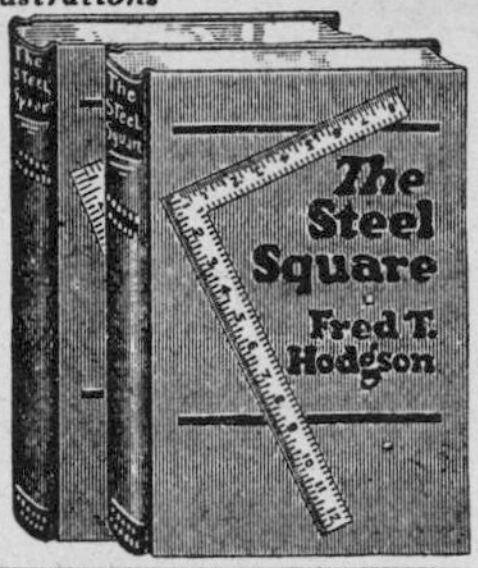

Including pitches and roof framing, the laying of rafters, hoppers, bevels, combination square, polygons and miters. Special chapters are devoted to stair building, finding length of jacks, securing bevels, practical calculations, showing how to measure solids, surfaces and distances, with miscellaneous rules and examples. Special chapters on wood finishing. A complete, thoroughly up to date encyclopedia on the practical uses of the steel square, showing how it can be used by the carpenter. Treats of all subjects to which the steel square can be applied. 500 practical and instructive illustrations are scattered throughout the book. The set (two volumes, each; size, 4½x7 inches) contains 633 pages. Bound in cloth. Shipping weight, 2 pounds.

3K9102—Per set (2 volumes) **$1.98**

Modern Carpentry

Two Volumes, 775 Pages, 600 Illustrations

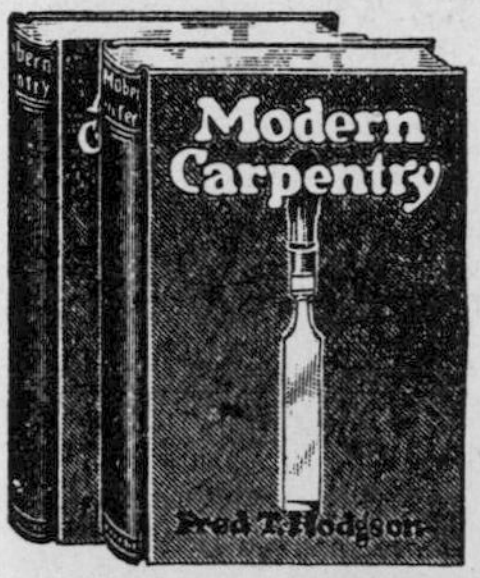

A practical, up to date treatise on carpentry and joinery, including layout of roofs, rafters, stairs, hoppers, bevels, mitering, coping, circle work, flooring, splayed work, hand railing, cornicing and dovetailing. A complete, up to date explanation of modern carpentry. An encyclopedia of the modern methods used in the erection of buildings from the laying of the foundation to the delivery of the building to the painter, with complete questions for review. We guarantee this work to contain unusually good, quick and practical methods for doing all kinds of joinery and carpentry work. Many special instructions are in this work, many of them covering an entire page. Every method of construction described is illustrated. The set (two volumes, size, 4½x7 inches); contains 775 pages. Bound in cloth. Shipping weight, 2 pounds.

3K9104—Per set (2 volumes). **$1.98**

Radio Books

Radio Cyclopedia

A Complete, Correct and Non-Technical Work. Easy to Read and Easy to Use

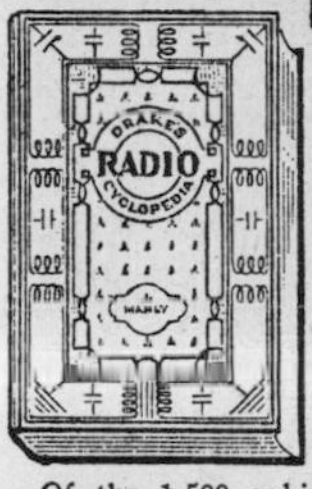

Comprising Over 1,500 Articles Arranged Alphabetically, and 1,000 Definitions, Terms, Abbreviations and Symbols.

Designed for Set Owners and Operators, Set Builders and Designers, Service and Repair Men, Salesmen and Dealers, Experimenters and Inventors, Students of Radio.

By Harold P. Manly

A complete and technical instruction book for every-one interested in radio. Covers every type of radio in every detail. Full instructions as to construction, operation and repair. Shows how and why every kind of radio operates. Invaluable to service and repair men.

Of the 1,500 subjects, 155 are especially for students of radio; 162 for experimenters and inventors; 75 for salesmen and dealers; 159 for service and repair men; 129 for builders and designers; 73 for owners and operators. Many of the subjects contain 18 pages. There are 1,003 definitions and references to words, terms, abbreviations and symbols; 125 tables, lists; graphic curves and simplified formulas of useful information. 870 pages; 6½x9 inches.

Illustrated with 950 illustrations and diagrams; all made especially for this book, and 125 tables, lists, graphic curves and simplified formulas of useful information. Shipping weight, 5 pounds.

3K4621 **$5.98**

Radio—Up to the Minute

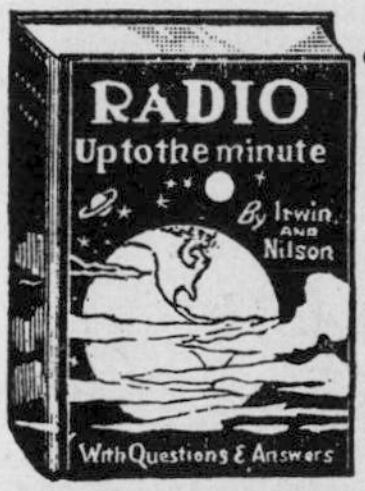

Revised Edition describes completely the new startling triumphs of radio research. Tells how to build all kinds of receiving sets. 402 pages and many illustrations. Bound in cloth. Size, 5x7½ inches. Shipping wt., 1¼ lbs.

3K4616 **89c**

Radio Experimenters' Library

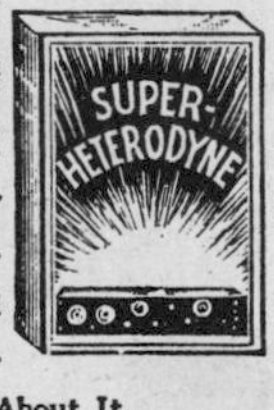

Here are some of the latest and most up to date books on radio, Paper covers. Average 45 pages. Size, about 5x7 in. Shpg. wt., each, 6 oz.

Radio Questions Answered.
Radio Frequency Amplification.
Reflex Radio Receivers.
How to make Practical Radio Receiving Sets.
How to Locate Troubles in Your Radio Set.
The Neutrodyne—All About It.
Tips for the Radio Amateur Constructor.
100 Radio Hook Ups.
How to Tune Your Radio Set.
The Super-Heterodyne.

3K4624—Any one of the above books **19c**
Any 2 of the above books **$0.37**
Entire set of 11 books **2.00**

Practical Heating Systems, Trouble Jobs and Ventilation

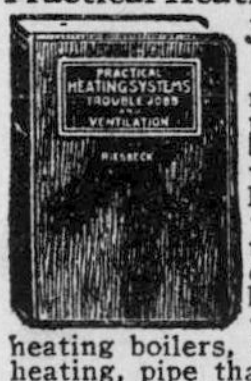

Covers the fundamental principles and practical installation of hot water, steam, vapor, vacuum and air line heating systems, and the principles of ventilation. With special chapters on radiation, boilers, oil burners, copper radiators, electric heating boilers, steam traps, greenhouse heating, pipe thawing by electricity.

Special emphasis is laid upon heating troubles and their remedies. Every sort of problem is discussed and solved; all in non-technical language.

The book contains 61 tables of useful information and 82 illustrations. By E. W. Riesbeck, M.E., Consulting Engineer.

Bound in limp leatherette. 277 pages. Size, 5x7½ inches. Shipping weight, 1½ pounds.

3K4314 **$3.98**

Basic Lettering

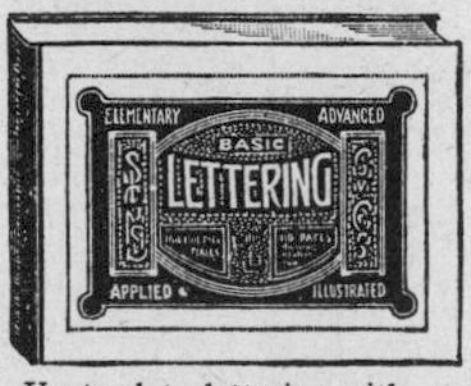

Up to date lettering with pen and brush for Show Card Work. Writing and Sign Painting. 164 pages of text, designs, monograms and layouts. Colors, their preparation and uses. Rope splicing illustrated. Cross indexed. Size, 9x12 inches. Cloth. Shipping wt., 3¼ lbs.

3K4619 **$2.89**

Earn Big Money as an Auto Mechanic!

2,000,000 Automobiles Sold Yearly

Big Demand—Bigger Pay for Automobile Mechanics

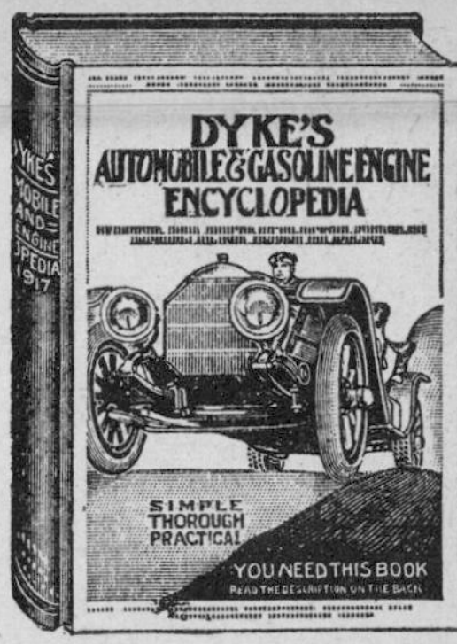

Dyke's Automobile and Gasoline Engine Encyclopedia gives you the chance to easily learn this fascinating and profitable trade. It will show you how to repair any automobile.

You Can Get This Book for Only $5.50

Dyke's Automobile Encyclopedia is a practical book. It teaches the fundamental principles of each and every part of an automobile in a simplified manner. Contains the latest information on Repairing, Electrical Systems, Ignition, Carburetion, Storage Batteries, Tire Repairing, etc., how to adjust engine bearings, valve clearance, valve timing, ignition timing, carburetors, rear axles, drive pinions, etc. Book is 7x10x2¼ inches, contains 1,249 pages, 4,200 illustrations, 87 instructions and 15,000 lines of index which makes it easy to locate any subject. Shipping weight, 5 pounds.

3K4868—Cloth Binding **$5.50**
3K4907—Flexible American Morocco Leather **$6.50**

Armature and Magnet Winding

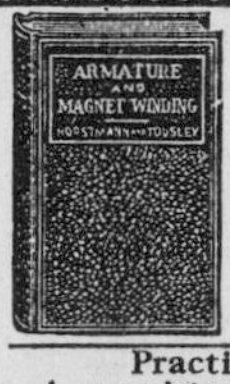

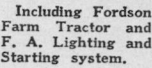

By Hortsmann and Tousley. Over 250 pages, 159 illustrations and 15 tables. Bound in cloth. Size, 4½x6¾ inches. Shipping weight, 1¼ pounds.

3K4310 **$1.18**

Practical Applied Electricity

A complete Standard Reference Work and Guide for the Practical Worker and Student in Electrical Engineering.

By D. P. Moreton, B.S., E.E., Armour Institute., 442 pages with 323 illustrations and diagrams. Cloth. Size, 4¾x7 inches. Shipping weight, 1½ pounds.

3K4308 **$1.65**

Electric Motors, Direct and Alternating, by Prof. D. P. Moreton. 250 pages, cloth binding. Size, 4¾x7 inches. Shpg. wt., 1¼ lbs.

3K4309 **$1.18**

Telephony, Including Automatic Switching, by A. B. Smith, E. E. 500 pages, 263 illustrations and wiring diagrams. Limp leatherette binding. Size, 4¾x7 inches. Shpg. wt., 1½ lbs.

3K5831 **$2.25**

Automobile Battery Care and Repair

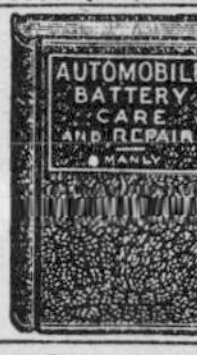

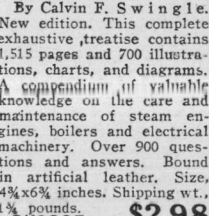

335 pages, 160 illustrations. Bound in artificial leather. Size 4⅝x6⅝ inches. Shipping weight, 1¼ lbs.

3K4629 **$1.60**

The Amateur Mechanic

By A. Frederick Collins. A very valuable handbook for anyone who wants to know how to use and repair mechanical devices. 205 pages. Illustrated. Cloth. Size, 5⅛x7⅞ inches. Shipping weight, 1¼ pounds.

3K4634 **98c**

Automobile Starting, Lighting and Ignition

826 pages, hundreds of illustrations and wiring diagrams. Artificial leather. Size, 4⅝x6⅝ inches. Shpg. wt., 1¼ lbs.

3K4631 **$2.55**

Sheet Metal Workers' Manual

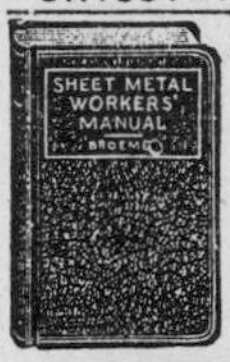

Contains 552 pages and 375 illustrations. It explains sheet metal work. Artificial leather. Size, 4½x6⅝ inches. Shipping weight, 1 lb.

3K4615 Only **$1.65**

The Model T Ford Car and Trouble Chart

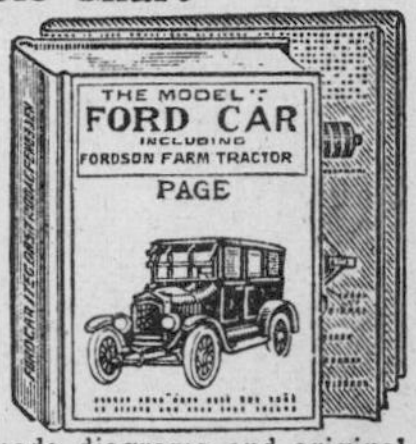

Including Fordson Farm Tractor and F. A. Lighting and Starting system.

Latest Edition

By Victor W. Page, M.E. New revised edition. Explains the operating principles of all parts of the Ford automobile. 495 pages, 188 specially made diagrams and original photographs of actual parts. Cloth. Size, 5⅛x7½ inches. Shipping weight, 1½ pounds.

Trouble Chart for Ford Cars

Tells how to find and remedy engine trouble on Ford cars. Size, 25x38 inches. Not illustrated.

3K4884—Book and Chart for **$1.35**

Swingle's Handbook for Steam Engineers and Electricians

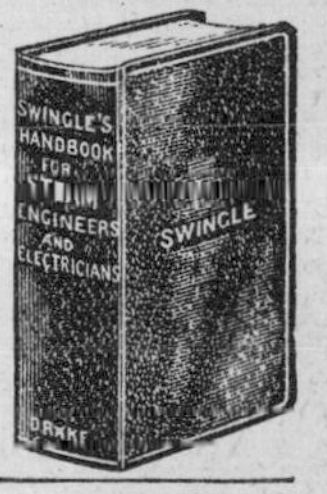

By Calvin F. Swingle. New edition. This complete exhaustive treatise contains 1,515 pages and 700 illustrations, charts, and diagrams. A compendium of valuable knowledge on the care and maintenance of steam engines, boilers and electrical machinery. Over 900 questions and answers. Bound in artificial leather. Size, 4¾x6⅝ inches. Shipping wt., 1¾ pounds.

3K9205 **$2.98**

Complete Examination Questions and Answers for Marine and Stationary Engineers

By Calvin F. Swingle. 400 pages. 212 illustrations. Bound in artificial leather. Size, 4½x6⅝ inches. Shpg. wt., 1½ lbs.

3K4698 **$1.58**

Steam Boilers. Their Construction, Care and Operation, With Questions and Answers, by C. F. Swingle, 305 pages, 170 illustrations. Size, 4¼x6⅝ inches. Shipping weight, 1¼ pounds.

3K5890 **$1.58**

Oxy-Acetylene Welding and Cutting, by H. P. Manly. 215 pages. Illustrated. Cloth binding. Size, 5x7 inches. Shipping weight, 1 pound.

3K4761 **$1.00**

Hand Books for Painters

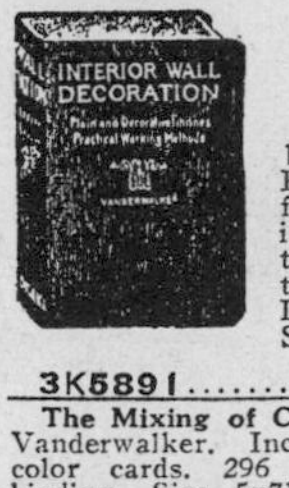

Interior Wall Decoration, by F. N. Vanderwalker. Practical working methods for plain and decorative finishes, new and standard treatments. 450 pages, illustrated. Size, 5x7½ inches. Limp leatherette binding. Shipping weight, 2 lbs.

3K5891 **$3.89**

The Mixing of Colors and Paints, by F. N. Vanderwalker. Includes color formulas and color cards. 296 pages. Illustrated. Cloth binding. Size, 5x7½ inches. Shipping weight, 1½ pounds.

3K6165 **$1.89**

Wood Finishing, Plain and Decorative, by F. N. Vanderwalker. Formulas and detailed instruction in method, tools and materials. 360 pages. Illustrated. Cloth binding. Size, 5x7½ inches. Shpg. wt., 1½ lbs.

3K5895 **$1.89**

House Painting Methods, by F. N. Vanderwalker. Includes both brush and spray painting. 386 pages. 140 illustrations and color chart. Cloth binding. Size, 5x7 inches. Shipping weight, 1½ pounds.

3K4315 **$1.89**

Modern Painters' Cyclopedia

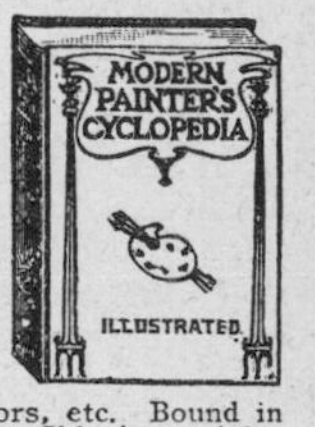

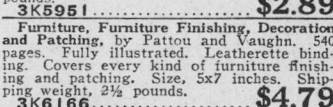

Contains 464 pages, 106 illustrations. Covers fully: Paints—their mixing and adulteration—color harmony, testing, estimating, kalsomining, gilding, varnishing, house painting, brushes, oil and dryers, water colors, etc. Bound in cloth. Size, 5⅝x7½ inches. Shipping weight, 1¾ pounds.

3K4302 **$1.65**

Studio Handbook, Letter and Design, by Samuel Welo. Hand lettered from cover to cover. A complete book for commercial artists. 233 pages. Limp leatherette binding. Size, 5x7 inches. Shipping weight, 1¼ pounds.

3K5951 **$2.89**

Furniture, Furniture Finishing, Decoration and Patching, by Pattou and Vaughn. 540 pages. Fully illustrated. Leatherette binding. Covers every kind of furniture finishing and patching. Size, 5x7 inches. Shipping weight, 2½ pounds.

3K6166 **$4.79**

The Greatest Bible Offer Ever Made

Beautiful Combination Bible, Durably and Handsomely Bound. Has Special Individual Features—1,800 Pages—Rich in Illustrations

Priced Very Low

You will have every reason to be proud of this beautiful book—both for its exceptionally fine appearance and for its unequaled merits as a Bible. You will find it more instructive, more conveniently arranged, more fascinating than any Bible you have ever had.

It Is Really Two Bibles in One

Both the King James version, unchanged, and the changed or revised version are shown on the same page. This feature alone will prove invaluable to the Bible teacher and student, since it shows at a glance what changes, additions and omissions were made by the revisers.

To further aid in its study and thorough understanding there are more than 60,000 center column marginal references and over 400 pages of helps to Bible students, including a complete concordance to the Holy Scriptures, together with a comprehensive dictionary of Scriptural proper names.

- 64 Full Page Illustrations. About 1,800 Pages.
- "Holy Bible" Embossed in Letters of Gold on Side and Back.
- Bound in Genuine Seal Grain Leather, Cloth Lined.
- Edges: Rich Gold Over Red—Dignified and Beautiful. White, Tough Paper.
- Full Divinity Circuit (Overlapping Covers).

Fully illustrated with a halftone frontispiece and sixty-four full page illustrations of important places and events of Bible times. Also, thirty-one full page plates of monuments, money, inscriptions, etc. Twelve full page colored maps.

Study the Features—They Are Important

1—Self pronouncing text, clear large type. 2—Rich in references, complete in every sense. 3—Both unchanged and revised version on same page, facilitating instant comparison. 4—Size, 6x8⅜ inches; 2¼ inches thick; compact, easily carried and easily read. 5—Student helps, 400 pages, aside from column references, contain essential information for intelligent Bible study. Our Special Teachers' Bible, leather binding, seal grained. Full divinity circuit (overlapping covers). Headband and marker. Round corners. Red under burnished gold edges. This style contains the full helps described above and, in addition, 5,000 Questions and Answers on the Old and New Testament, and Smith's Complete Illustrated Bible Dictionary.

	$4.75
3K8025—Shipping weight, 3½ pounds.	$4.75
3K8026—Same as 3K8025, but with index cut in on edge	$4.98
3K8030—Same as 3K8025, but with full leather lining to edge	5.35
3K8031—Same as 3K8030, but with index cut in on edge	5.58
3K8000—Bound in artificial leather	3.75
3K8005—Same as 3K8000, but with index cut in on edge	3.98

Our Special Teachers' Bible

Red Letter Edition. Bound in leather, seal grained. This superb edition is exactly the same as 3K8025, except that all the words spoken by Christ are printed in red. **$4.95**

3K8060—Shipping weight, 3½ pounds.	$4.95
3K8065—Same as 3K8060, but with full leather lining to edge	$5.45
3K8066—Same as 3K8065, but with index cut in on edge	5.68

TESTAMENTS

Vest Pocket Testaments

Nonpareil self pronouncing type. Gilt side title. Size, 2⅞x4⅜ inches. Shipping weight, any style, 6 oz.
3K8918—Leather, morocco grained, limp; gold edges. **79c**

3K8920—Leather, morocco grained. Divinity circuit (overlapping covers); red under gold edges.$1.13

3K8922—Leather, morocco grained, limp. Words of Christ printed in red, Round corners, gold edges $1.15

3K8924—Leather, morocco grained. Divinity circuit (overlapping covers). Words of Christ printed in red. Red under gold edges..........$1.35

3K8917—Same as 3K8918, but illustrated with pictures of the Holy Land printed on enameled paper and red under gold edges.........98c

Ruby Type Testaments

Artificial leather, square corners, red edges. Size, 2⅞x4 in. Shpg. wt., any style, 4 oz.
3K8902 ....**39c**

Self pronouncing type. Semi-flexible cloth. Size, 2⅞x4 in. Shipping weight, 5 oz.
3K8836 ....**29c**

Old Folks' Self Pronouncing Red Letter Testament With Psalms

3K8904 ....68c
Leather, morocco Grained, limp, gilt edges.

3K8906 ....$1.15
Leather, morocco Grained. Divinity circuit; round corners, gold edges. Self pronouncing type.

Large pica type. All words of Christ printed in red. Size, 5⅝x¾ inches. Grained cloth. Red edges. Shpg. wt., 1½ lbs.
3K8615 ....$1.35

New Testament

De Luxe Small Testaments. Size, 4¼x2¾ inches. Handy to carry and to use at church or in the home. Suitable as gifts for children to use in Sunday School and home. Shipping weight, each, 8 ounces.

3K8068—Bound in artificial leather, semi-flexible covers, red edges. Each 32c; 6 for.................$1.85
3K9099—Bound in genuine leather, pin seal grain, title stamped in genuine gold leaf. Full gold edges, and has silk ribbon marker. Each in box. Each, 55c; 6 for......$3.25

Selected Prayers for all Occasion
Compiled by A. L. Clinton, D. D.

A help for private devotion, giving suggestive prayers for family worship and public prayer. Bound in cloth. Size, 2⅞x5½ inches. 161 pages. Shipping wt., 3 oz.
3K8823...............**23c**

American Standard Revised Bible

Edited by the American Revision Committee. Large self pronouncing type; 32 full page illustrations. Contains selected Bible helps, including 4,000 questions and answers. Size, 4¾x7 inches. Moroccotal (artificial leather), divinity circuit, round corners, red under gold edges. Shipping weight, 2 pounds.
3K7998.....................**$2.45**

Children's Bibles

Charming Bible Stories for Children

It carries the child through the Bible in fifty-two interestingly told story lessons. Fifty full page designs. Bound in semi-limp artificial morocco leather. Stamped in gold leaf. Burnished red edges. 636 pages. 411 illustrations. Size, 6½x9⅛ in. Shpg. wt., 3¼ lbs.
3K1777......**$1.58**

Children's Illustrated Gift Bible
King James Version

Has 24 beautiful full page colored illustrations. On fine white paper. Also contains 67 pages of Practical Aids for Sunday School scholars prepared especially to assist young people in the study of the Bible, and 5 pages of colored maps. Bound in artificial leather, red under gold edges. Size, 3¾x5½ inches. Shpg. wt., 1 lb.
3K1948......................**$1.98**
3K2721—Same as 3K1948, but bound in genuine leather with red under gold edges.........$2.98

We will print any name in Gold Letters on the cover of any Leather Bound Bible for 20 cents extra. Print name carefully.

BIBLES for the Home

The Scofield
$2.58 Reference Bible
Authorized Edition

An invaluable help to Bible students. Best described by the phrase "Helps, at the place where needed." This new and improved edition contains many features which impart Bible study an increased interest. By the new system of connected topical references in the center of each page, all the greater themes of divine revelations are traced through the entire Bible. Helps and explanations have been furnished available for instant reference on the very page where help is needed. This is done by footnotes on every page where there is anything obscure or needing explanation and comment. Each of the sixty-six books of the Bible is divided with an introduction and an analysis and sub-heads which greatly facilitate the study and comprehension of the book. Entire Bible has been divided into paragraphs by italicized sub-heads, but still preserves the chapter and verse division. This Bible has been enthusiastically received by many famous preachers, evangelists and Bible students generally. Bound in cloth or genuine leather. Sizes, 5⅛x7⅛ inches. Shpg. wt., 2 lbs.
3K2703—Cloth binding...............................**$2.58**
3K2704—Genuine Leather Divinity Circuit...**$5.28**

The New Testament
An American Translation *By Edgar J. Goodspeed*

There have been many translations of the New Testament in English since 1525, but in the American translation, Edgar J. Goodspeed has sought to give American readers of the 20th Century the clearest conception possible of the meaning of these documents as the early Greeks wrote them. The early New Testaments were translated from not over 40 manuscripts of the 10th century, while this one is translated from over 4,000. Cloth. Size, 4¾x6½ inches. 481 pages. Shipping wt., ¾ lb. **$1.48**
3K8525

SPECIAL VALUE
The Holy Bible With Ideal Helps for Only 98c

King James Version. Black Print, Medium Large Type A home or Sunday School Bible. Has 8 full page black and white illustrations, and 16 pages of colored maps; also contains teachers' and readers' helps for the study of the Bible. Comprising Dictionary of Scripture Proper Names; Great Periods of Bible History; How to Believe; Measures, Weights and Money; Promises and Warnings of Our Lord; Calendar for Daily Reading of Scripture; Chapters for Special Occasions; Christian Worker and His Bible; Aids for Social and Private Prayer; History of the Bible; Parables and Miracles; Sunday School Teachers' Use of the Bible; Dictionary of Foreign Words, Etc. Size, each, 5x7¼ inches. Shipping weight, 2½ pounds.
3K7990—Black Cloth stiff covers, red edges, gilt stamped......**98c**
3K7991—Textile leather (artificial leather) divinity circuit (overlapping covers), red edges, round corners........$1.35
3K7992—Same as 3K7991, but bound in genuine leather......1.85
3K7993—Same as 3K7992, but with red under gold edges......2.25

Red Letter Reference Bible
King James Version

Printed in bold minion type, all the words and sayings of Christ distinguished from the context by being printed in red. Has 60,000 center marginal references. Old Testament passages generally regarded as prophetic of our Savior are indicated by a star. Contains 36 pages of Bible Readers' Aids and 16 pages of colored maps. Size, 6¾x4⅜ inches. Shipping weight, each, 2½ pounds.
3K2712—Bound in artificial leather, divinity circuit (overlapping covers), round corners, red edges...........**$1.85**
3K2713—Same as 3K2712, but with red under gold edges.............$2.50
3K2714—Same as 3K2713, but bound in Genuine Leather and contains 8 beautiful full page colored illustrations. Also has index cut in on edge....$3.85

India Paper Gift Bible
King James Version

With 32 Tissot illustrations, reproduced in the rich coloring of their priceless originals.

Nothing so clearly conveys the Bible stories as these wonderful pictures. Direct, simple and irresistible are these Tissot pictures to young and old. Descriptive verse under practically all pictures. Printed on Cambridge India paper in clear minion type. Has complete references and 12 full pages of colored maps. Size, 4¾x6⅞ inches. Only ¾ inch thick. Bound in leather, seal grained divinity circuit (overlapping covers), red under gold edges. Shipping weight, 1¼ pounds.
3K8576.................................**$4.98**

Sunday School Scholars' Bible
With Full Helps—An Ideal Hand Bible

Plain nonpareil type, easily read. Full divinity circuit (overlapping covers). King James version. Adapted to general reader as well as Sunday School scholar. Red under gold edges.

Headband and marker, 14 colored maps and 32 full page illustrations. Size, 5¾x7½ inches. 1,068 pages. Shipping wt., any style, 2¼ pounds.
3K8625
Artificial leather..........**$2.35**
3K8626—Same as 3K8625, but with index cut in on edge......$2.45
3K8630—Leather, morocco grained.........$2.95
3K8631—Same as 3K8630, but with index cut in on edge.........$3.15
3K8635—Leather, morocco grained, full leather lining......$3.28
3K8636—Same as 3K8635, but with index cut in on edge.........$3.48

Pocket Bibles
King James Version

Bound in artificial leather, in grained leather effect; divinity circuit (overlapping covers), red edges. Size, 4x5⅜ in. Shpg. wt., 1 lb. **75c**
3K2719
3K2720—Same as 3K2719, but with red under gold edges.............98c
3K2718—Same as 3K2719, but bound in genuine leather.......................$1.48

Student and Teacher

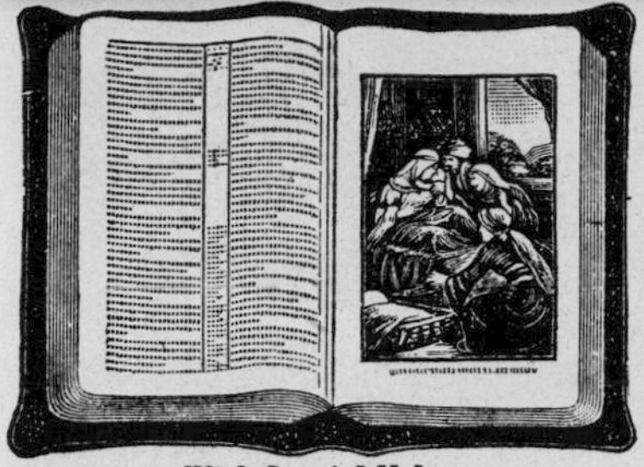

With Special Helps

> We will print any name in Gold Letters on the cover of any Leather Bound Bible for 20 cents extra. Print name carefully.

Big Value in a Large Print Bible

Self Pronouncing Teachers' Bible

Size, 5½x8 in. Contains over 1,300 pages, of which 1,272 are text. King James version, printed in large, clear, self-pronouncing type, with 60,000 center marginal references, and special features, such as:

- All passages in the Old Testament, prophetic of the coming of Christ, marked with a star.
- All difficult words in both Testaments made self pronouncing by diacritical marks.
- Synopsis of the Books of the Bible.
- Sunday School Teachers' Use of Bible.
- Authentic Bible Statistics and Information.
- Biblical Weights and Measures.
- Christian Worker and His Bible.
- How to Study the Bible.
- Hundreds of Helps and References.
- Family Register of Births, Marriages and Deaths.
- Proving the Old Testament. Half-tone Illustrations, etc.

3K2705—Bound in artificial leather. Divinity circuit (overlapping covers), round corners, red edges. Shipping weight, 2½ pounds **$2.10**
3K2706—Same as 3K2705, but Red Letter Edition **$2.29**

Colored Illustrated Edition

3K2707—Same as 3K2705, but with 8 beautiful, full page colored illustrations and bound in genuine leather **2.79**
3K2708—Same as 3K2707, but Red Letter Edition, all the words and sayings of Christ distinguished from the context by being printed in red **2.99**
3K2709—Same as 3K2707, but with red under gold edges and with index cut in on edge **3.80**

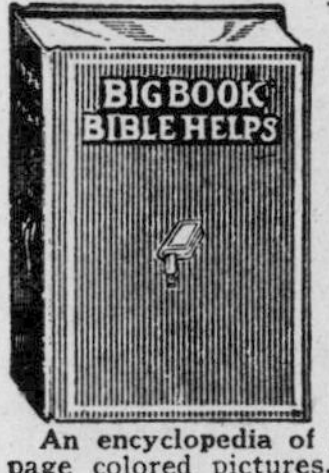

Big Book of Bible Helps

Contains: Standard helps to the study of the Bible; full concordance for reference; 5,000 questions and answers; illustrated dictionary of the Bible, including proper names with their pronunciations and meaning; aids for Sunday school scholars, also the museum of the Bible showing historical prints of manuscripts, inscriptions, etc. Fully illustrated. Bound in cloth. Size, 7x9¾ inches. 592 pages. Shipping weight, 3½ pounds.
3K7999 .... **$1.38**

Key to the Bible

New Edition, Printed on Thin Bible Paper

An encyclopedia of persons, places and things in the Bible. 16 full page colored pictures. Over 400 text illustrations. With this book, understanding and study of the Bible become very simple. 447 pages. Illustrated. Bound in flexible cloth. Size, 7½x9¾ inches. Shipping weight, 2½ pounds.
3K8220 .... **$1.35**

The Workers' and Home Illustrated Teachers' Bible

New Black Face Self Pronouncing Type
Forty-Nine Full Page Illustrations

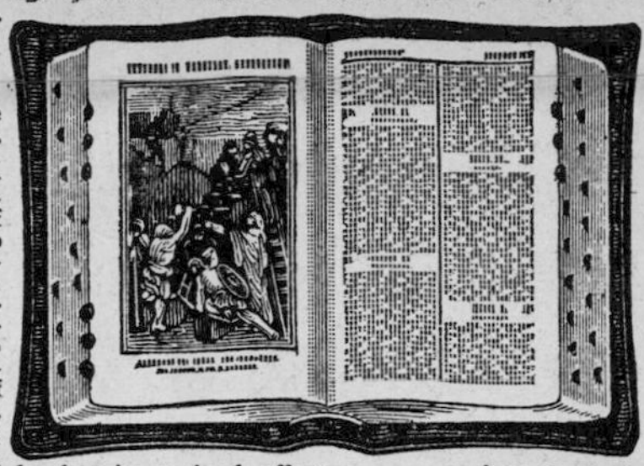

Large nonpareil black face self pronouncing type edition, suitable alike for old and young. Contains the King James version of the Old and New Testaments with nearly 200 pages of **valuable and complete helps** to the study of the Bible, including 4,500 questions and answers. **Sixteen full page colored illustrations,** with the verse underneath, and in addition thirty-two full page black and white illustrations. Has fourteen pages of colored maps; 1,022 pages. Size, 5¼x7¼ in. Shpg. wt., each, 2½ lbs.; six, 15 lbs.; twelve, 32 lbs.

3K8825—Bound in artificial leather in grained effect. Each, **$2.30; 6** for **$13.50; 12** for **$26.00**
3K8822—Same as 3K8825, but with index cut in on edge. Each, **$2.45; 6** for **$14.50; 12** for **$28.00**
3K8520—Same as 3K8825, but bound in leather, morocco grained, divinity circuit (overlapping covers), round corners, red under gold edges, headband and marker. Each, **$2.78; 6** for **$16.50; 12** for **$32.00**
3K8521—Same as 3K8520, but with index cut in on edge. Each, **$2.98; 6** for **$17.50; 12** for **$33.50**

When Our Eyes Begin to Fail

Old Folks' Bibles. Extra Large Type. Ideal for the Home

All the Good Features That Made the Family Bible So Popular

King James Version. Pica type Reference Bible with 60,000 references. Extra large type, perfectly readable for even very weak eyes.

Maps printed in colors. Size, 6½x9¼ in. Shipping wt., any style, 3½ lbs.

3K8585—Bound in cloth. Red edges **$2.75**
3K8586—Bound in artificial leather, limp covers. Red edges **$2.98**
3K8587—Limp leather, morocco grained. Red under gold edges **4.35**
3K8589—Leather, morocco grained. Full divinity circuit (overlapping covers), red under gold edges, headband and marker, grained lining **4.95**
3K8592—Same as 3K8589, but with full leather lining **5.55**

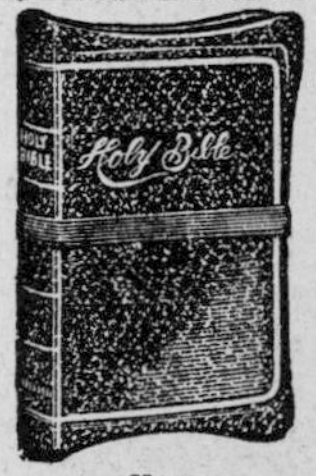

3K8589

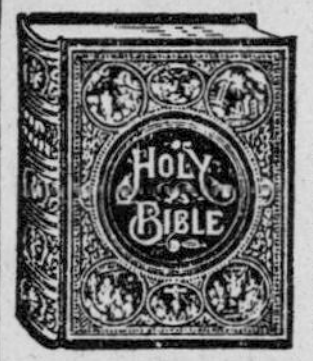

Red Letter Self Pronouncing Family Bible

(King James Version)

Artificial morocco grained leather, embossed on back and front, together with title in full gilt. Size, 12¼x10¼x2¼ in. Full gilt edges. 60,000 references. All words spoken by Christ printed in red. Complete helps, 105 beautiful pictures. Shpg. wt., 8 lbs.
3K8545 .... **$4.98**

Family Bible

King James version with thousands of marginal references, a full concordance, table of proper names, chronological index, marriage certificate and family record. The type is large and clear and makes reading easy. Has 16 full page illustrations, printed on a fair grade of paper. Bound in black cloth. Red edges. Size, 10x12x2 inches. Shipping weight, 6 pounds.
3K8533 .... **$2.59**

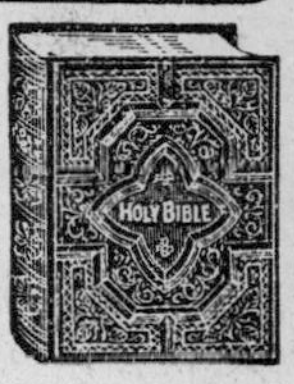

Catholic Religious Goods

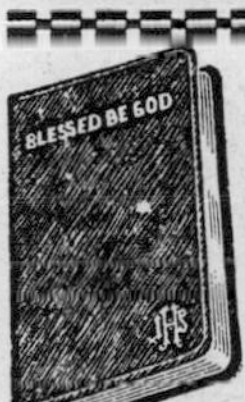

The New Prayer Book, "Blessed Be God"

By Rev. Chas. J. Callan, O. P. and Rev. John A. McHugh, O. P.

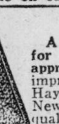

This new and complete prayer book will instruct and enlighten everyone who uses it. With it, it is easy to follow the inspiring ceremonies of the Church. With its aid one can perform his private devotions both intelligently and fruitfully. This is a most complete prayer book, containing besides the usual devotions found in prayer books many new Litanies and Novenas, including one to St. Therese; also mediations, devout reflections, and the Epistles and Gospels. Printed in type that makes it unusually easy to read for both old and young. Size, 4½x6½ inches. 780 pages, illustrated. Shipping weight, each, ¾ pound.

3K9086—Imitation leather, gold title on cover **$2.39**
3K9087—Genuine Morocco leather, I. H. S. in gold on cover **$3.29**
3K9088—Egyptian seal, leather lined, name in gold on cover **4.29**
3K9089—Black Morocco, gold cross and title on cover **4.89**
3K9090—Black Morocco, leather lined, gold title on cover **5.79**

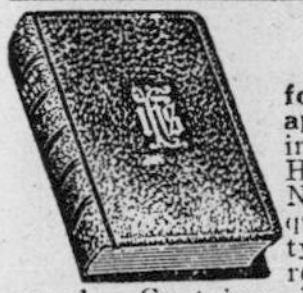

Key of Heaven

A select manual of prayers for daily use compiled from approved sources. Has the imprimatur of Patrick J. Hayes, D. D., Archbishop of New York. Printed on high quality thin paper from large type, which makes it easy to read, particularly for older people. Contains, in addition to the usual prayers, the Epistles and Gospels. Bound in imitation leather, red under gold edges. Contains 903 pages. Shpg. wt., ¾ lb.
3K9084 .... **$1.29**

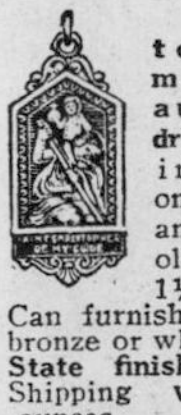

St. Christopher's medal for automobile drivers with inscription on back, "I am a Catholic." Size, 1½ x ⅝ in. Can furnish in either bronze or white metal. **State finish wanted.** Shipping weight, 3 ounces.
3K9085 ... **19c**

St. Therese

Home Blessing

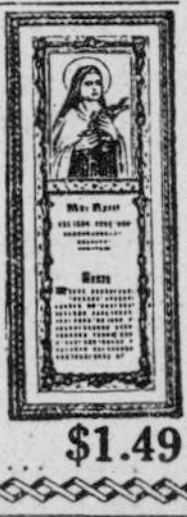

Illuminated picture prayer of the Little Flower of Jesus. Decorative border, beautiful gilt frame. Size, 7⅞ x 18½ inches. Shipping wt., 3 lbs.
3K9091 .... **$1.49**

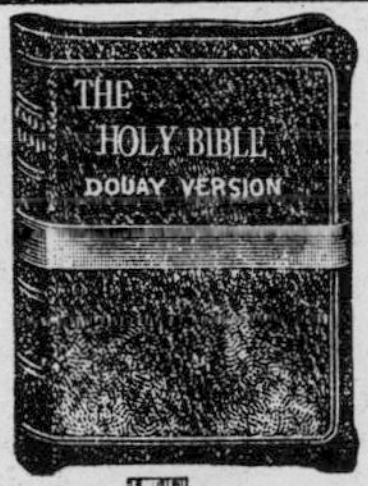

The Catholic Holy Bible

Douay Version. A Bible for Catholics, published with the imprimatur and approbation of His Eminence, the late John Cardinal Farley, Archbishop of New York. Many illustrations and 17 colored maps. Large clear type. Bound in leather, seal grain, gold edges, 1,400 pages. Size, 6x8¼ inches. Shpg. wt., 3 lbs.
3K8621 .... **$3.85**

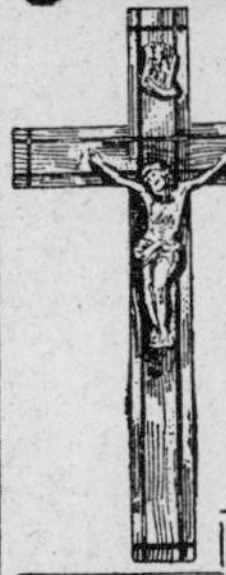

Fine Imported Rosewood Crucifixes

These crucifixes are made of the finest rosewood, inlaid with brass; corpus in bronze.

3K9081—8-in. Shpg. wt., 8 oz. **$1.29**
3K9082—12-in. Shipping weight, 1 lb. **$1.79**
3K9083—14-in. Shipping weight, 1¼ lbs. **$1.98**

Gift Outfits

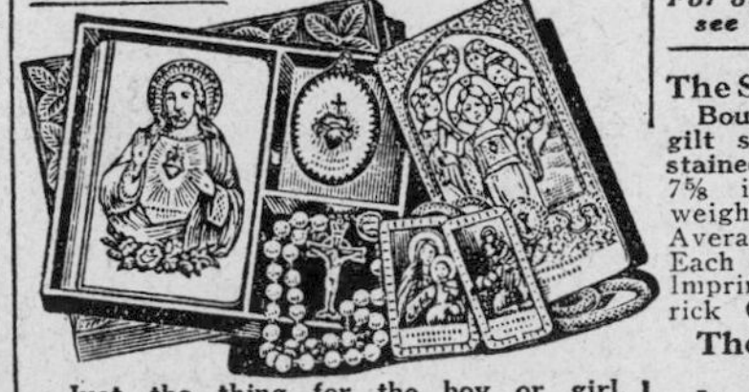

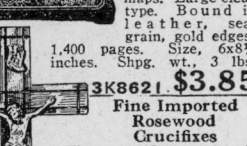

Just the thing for the boy or girl. The girls' set contains one white prayer book, also one white rosary, one pair of scapulars, one sacred heart badge and one colored holy picture. These articles come packed in a box, making a very appropriate gift. The boys' set is the same as above with the exception of the prayer book, which is of black leather. Shipping weight, 6 ounces.

3K9170—Girls' Outfit with White Prayer Book **$1.39**
3K9210—Boys' Outfit with Black Leather Prayer Book **1.39**

Statues

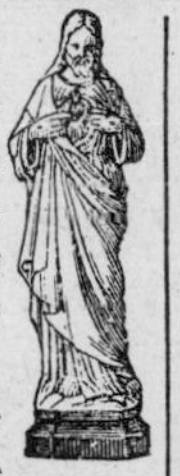

Imported High Grade Ivorene Statues. Made of composition plaster, finished in delicate cream.

Height, 12 inches. Shipping weight, 3½ lbs. Can furnish in any of the following subjects:

Sacred Heart of Jesus	Mother of Grace
Sacred Heart of Mary	Our Lady of Lourdes
St. Joseph	St. Anthony

Immaculate Conception
St. Therese, The Little Flower
St. Anne

3K9080—Any one of the above statues. **State choice.** Each **$2.29**

Same subjects as 3K9080, but 6in. high. State choice. Shpg. wt., 1½ lbs.
3K9079—Each **69c**

Luminous Crucifix

Shines in the Dark

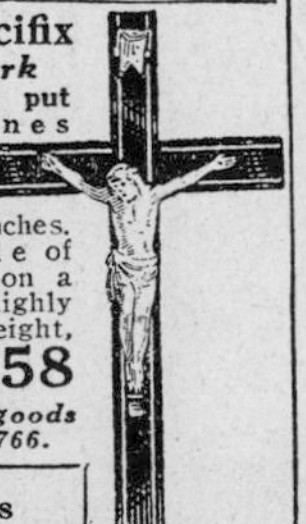

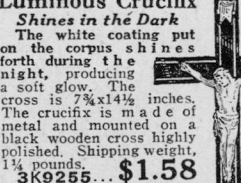

The white coating put on the corpus shines forth during the night, producing a soft glow. The cross is 7¾x14½ inches. The crucifix is made of metal and mounted on a black wooden cross highly polished. Shipping weight, 1¼ pounds.
3K9255 .... **$1.58**

For other religious goods see pages 750 and 766.

The Splendid Books

Bound in silk cloth, gilt stamping, yellow stained tops. Size 5¼x7⅝ inches. Shipping weight, 1½ pounds. Average 250 pages. Each book carries the Imprimatur of Patrick Cardinal Hayes.

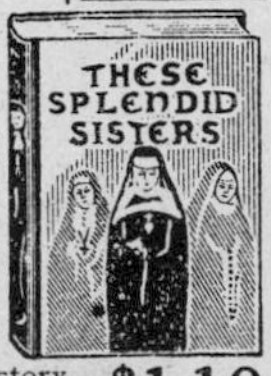

These Splendid Priests

In this book are found glowing accounts of those priests, who by their noble qualities of charity, dominate many a page of history.
3K2821—Each **$1.10**

These Splendid Sisters

Inspiring accounts of the unselfish devotion to humanity by Sisters of the Church. Women of indubitable courage and incomparable achievements.
3K2715—Each **$1.10**

Vest Pocket Prayer Books for Men

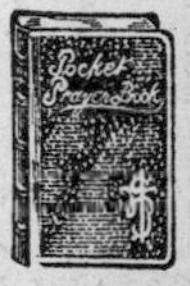

Vest Pocket Manual of Devotions, with Epistles and Gospels. Leather, seal grained, limp, red under gold edges. Shipping wt., 8 oz.
3K9076 .... **78c**
3K9097—Same as 3K9076, but bound in artificial leather, and without Epistles and Gospels **45c**

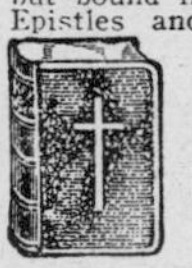

Large Type Key of Heaven. With Epistles and Gospels, and complete Manual of Prayer. Leather, seal grained, limp, red under gold edges. 537 pages. Size, 3x4⅝ inches; ⅝ inch thick. Shipping weight, 8 oz.
3K9071 .... **98c**

The Key of Heaven

With epistles and gospels. Over 600 pages. Size, 2½x3⅝ inches. Shipping weight, 8 oz.

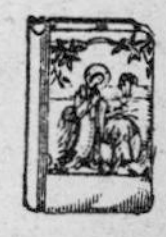

An Ideal First Communion Prayer Book

3K9098 — Celluloid cover with colored design. Crucifix with indulgenced prayer on inside front cover. Shpg. weight, 8 ounces **$1.35**

3K9073—A serviceable leather book strongly bound. Black seal grain. No crucifix in cover. Red under gold edges. Shpg. wt., 8 ounces **78c**

3K9078—Same as 3K9098, but bound in black padded leather, handsomely embossed. Especially suitable for boys, First communion **$1.18**

Children's Prayer Books

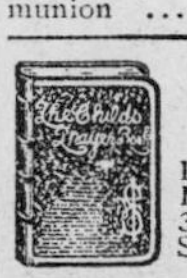

With 36 full page illustrations of the Holy Mass. Size, about 2½x3⅝ inches. 288 pages. Shipping wt., each, 6 oz.

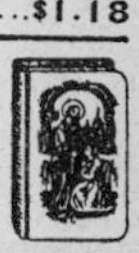

3K9052—Colored celluloid binding. With round corners. Beautiful colored picture on cover. (Assorted pictures.). Gold edges **78c**
3K9050—Embossed leather, limp. Round corners, gold design on side; red under gold edges **69c**
3K9095—Same as 3K9050, but bound in artificial leather **39c**

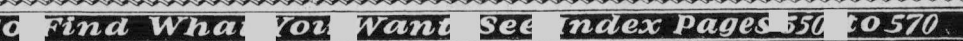

Remington Rebuilt Typewriter

CASH PRICE $40.00

Time Payment Price $45.00

EVERYONE can profitably use a good typewriter—it is a modern necessity in every business, institution and home. It is indispensable to students, writers, teachers, business men and professional men—every occupation imperatively feels its need. YOU NEED ONE.

You can have a famous machine—nationally known for its reliability, versatility, quickness and ease of operation—and

at a price less than one-half originally asked.

We offer you here the Genuine Remington Typewriter, complete in every feature, that has made it the foremost machine in the typewriter world. This machine is yours for the unbelievably low price of $40.00 cash—or $45.00 on our liberal deferred payment plan.

Years of Service Guaranteed

This splendid machine has been so thoroughly rebuilt, so completely reconstructed—every part showing the least sign of wear being replaced by parts absolutely new—that it is to all intents and purposes new. It looks exactly like new, it operates like new, and it will wear and give precisely the same service as a brand new machine. The only practical difference between it and a brand new typewriter is the price. The manufacturer has always asked around $102.50 for a new No. 10 Remington. The rebuilt machine we offer you here is alike in every respect, is equally good, is covered by the same broad guarantee, but costs you fifty-seven dollars and fifty cents less—a saving of more than half.

Our Stock Is Limited—Send Your Order Now

Our price is positively the lowest ever offered on any high grade standard make rebuilt typewriter. Supply is limited and we advise you to order early and avoid any possibility of disappointment. Make sure of this exceptional saving.

You can't make a mistake. The guarantee of the World's Largest Store—the surest and broadest guarantee in the world—is behind this great machine, and that means it has to satisfy you according to your own standards.

Look at the Features

Positively nothing is lacking. Every typewriter requirement is met with super efficiency. Shipping weight, 55 pounds.

3K6049— Elite Type   Cash price................$40.00
3K6048— Pica Type   Cash price................40.00

Be sure to state catalog number and style of type desired.
Terms, either style, $45.00. Send only $5.00 with order and $5.00 a month until Time Payment price has been paid. Use Time Payment Order Blank on page 1092.

Special Features of the Remington

1—**Light feathery touch.** Responds instantly, assures maximum speed with little effort.

2—**Key Board:** Standard, single shift, has 84 characters, scientifically positioned for greatest efficiency, so simple anyone can easily become familiar with them.

3—**Stencil Device:** Provides for speed and sharpness in cutting stencils without removing ribbon.

4—**Ribbon:** Two-color, self-reversing ribbon, automatically winds from one spool to the other.

5—**Marginal Stops:** In plain view. Line lock functions with absolute reliability. Release button located for easy, quick operation.

6—**Five self-starting marginal keys** for tabulating and instant selection of all indentations used in letter writing.

7—**Ultra Rapid Line Spacer:** Operates on ball bearings, no friction.

8—**Line Space Lever:** Same motion returning carriage to end of line turns roller and paper to next writing line.

9—**Oil Can:** Bottle of oil, type brush, cleaning brush and cover with each machine.

10—**Shift Lock:** Sturdily constructed, positive, holds carriage rigidly in place.

11—**Paper Roll:** Easily accommodates paper of any width up to width of carriage; accepts and releases sheet with amazing facility.

Typewriter Supplies

Stenographers' Note Books

Good quality note books. Shipping weight, for 12, 4 lbs.
3K12281—Plain ruling, pencil. 60 leaves. 12 for....45c
3K12282—Plain ruling, ink, 60 leaves, 12 for..85c
3K12596—Same as 3K12282 but has red center line. 60 leaves.
12 for....85c

Onion Skin Second Sheets

A high grade light weight white sheet, especially designed for making carbon copies. Shipping weight, 3 pounds.
3K9954—Size, 8½x11 inches. Package of 500 sheets....79c

Manila Second Sheets

A good grade of yellow Manila for carbon copies and scratch paper. Shipping weight, 3 pounds.
3K9957—Size, 8½x11 inches. Package of 500 sheets....45c

Very Fine Quality Carbon Paper

For typewriter work. Makes clear cut impressions. Will not blur or smear. State size wanted. Shipping weight, 25 sheets, 8 ounces; 100 sheets, 1½ pounds.
Black. Size, 8½x11 inches.
Black. Size, 8½x13 inches.
3K9975—Per roll of 25 sheets..25c
3K9976—Box of 100 sheets......85c

Metal Valuable Paper or Bond Box

A place to put valuable papers. Made of heavy gauge sheet metal, is lacquered in black with gilt marking, with lock and keys. Shipping weight, 2 pounds.
Size, 11½x5½x3 inches.
3K17505................98c

Typewriter Ribbons

A first class ribbon. Colors: Black, black and red, purple or blue. State color wanted.
3K9800—Harris, ½-inch. (Not in two colors.)
3K9801—Corona, ½-inch.
3K9802—Underwood, ½-inch.
3K9803—Oliver, 7⁄16-inch. (Not in two colors.)
3K9804—Oliver, 9⁄16-inch.
3K9805—Remington, ½-inch.
3K9806—L. C. Smith, ½-inch.
3K6857—Royal, ½-inch.
Each....(Shpg. wt., each, 4 oz.)....39c
Per dozen, any of the above ribbons. Shipping weight, 3½ pounds............$4.49

Heavy Duty Ribbon, 85c

We recommend this superfine ribbon for all general purposes where the typewriter is in continued daily use. Can furnish for same machines and in same colors as listed above. State machine and color. Shpg. wt., 4 oz.
3K9808................85c

Economy Typewriter Tablet

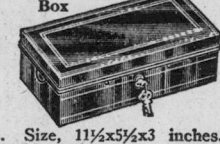

A very handy tablet for home or office. Contains 100 sheets good quality white bond paper. Size, 8⅜x11 inches. Shipping weight of three, 2 pounds.
3K12595
3 for................69c

Cico—New Liquid Paste

A pearly white liquid paste, always ready for use; requires no water, does not dry up. 5-oz. opal jar, equipped with air-tight cover and adjustable brush. A good economical paste. Shipping weight, 7 ounces.
3K3303................32c

For Photo Paste and Mucilage see page 801

Carter's Glue Pencil

For mending almost anything, wood, cloth, paper, china, and so on. Shipping weight, 4 ounces.
3K3302................19c

Riverside Typewriter Papers

"Typewriter Papers With a Reputation"

Excellent quality white bond paper for personal or business use. These papers are manufactured especially for typewriter use, but the smooth, hard surface is suitable for pen and ink writing.

"DORADO BOND"
A Very Good Quality of White Bond Paper
Light Weight
3K9700—Size, 8½x11 inches. 500 sheets................$0.85
3K9701—Size, 8½x13 inches. 500 sheets..$1.15
Shipping weight, per box, 4½ pounds.
3K9702—Size, 8½x11 inches. 500 sheets................$0.87
3K9703—Size, 8½x13 inches. 500 sheets..$1.18
Shipping weight, 6 pounds.
Heavy Weight
3K9704—Size, 8½x11 inches. 500 sheets................$1.08
3K9705—Size, 8½x13 inches. 500 sheets..$1.32
Shipping weight, 7 pounds.

"CHARA BOND"
A Fine Quality of White Woven Bond Paper
Light Weight
3K9963—Size, 8½x11 inches. 500 sheets................$1.65
3K9964—Size, 8½x13 inches. 500 sheets..$2.00
Shipping weight, 4½ pounds.
Medium Weight
3K9965—Size, 8½x11 inches. 500 sheets................$1.70
3K9966—Size, 8½x13 inches. 500 sheets..$2.10
Shipping weight, 6 pounds
Heavy Weight
3K9967—Size, 8½x11 inches. 500 sheets................$2.10
3K9968—Size, 8½x13 inches. 500 sheets. Shpg. wt., 7 lbs..$2.70

ENVELOPES
3K9980—To match "Dorado Bond" 3K9703. Box of 500 envelopes.
Shipping weight, 5 pounds....$1.40
3K9981—To match "Dorado Bond" 3K9705. Box of 500 envelopes.
Shipping weight, 6 pounds....$1.75
3K9982—To match "Chara Bond" 3K9966. Box of 500 envelopes.
Shipping weight, 5 pounds....$1.90
3K9983—To match "Chara Bond" 3K9968. Box of 500 envelopes.
Shipping weight, 6 pounds....$2.20

Typewriter cabinet containing 100 sheets of the well known Hammermill paper, size 7x10½ inches, and 72 envelopes to match, size 7½x4 inches. Put up in a cabinet which makes it very convenient and economical for desk or table. Can be refilled when empty. Shipping weight, 3 pounds.
3K24413—Typewriter Cabinet................$1.79

Send Sufficient Money for Postage on Parcel Post Shipments. Any Surplus Will Be Returned

Box Paper

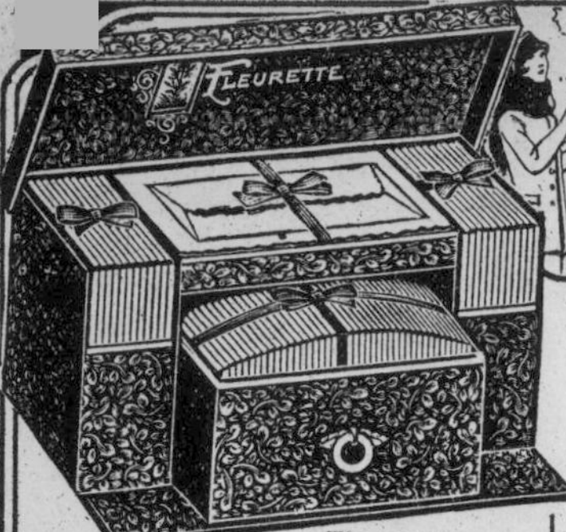

Fleurette

A handsome box covered with red paper with fancy design. 48 sheets unruled, white linen finish paper, gold deckled edge paper, 5¼x6½ inches, and 24 gold edged cards. 72 gold deckled edge envelopes. Box, 6x11x5½ inches. Shipping weight, 2½ lbs.

3K9262........................**$1.89**

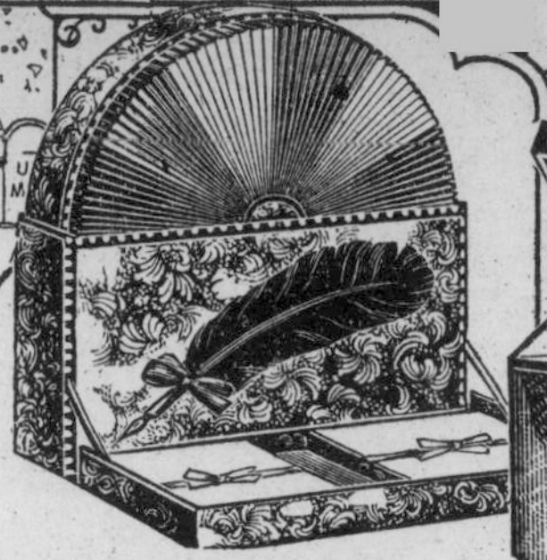

A Dandy Gift Box

Hinge top with semicircle swinging drawer. Swinging drawer contains 72 envelopes, 12 each of the following colors: Green, white, orchid, blue, sand and buff. Drop front contains 72 sheets unruled vellum finish paper, 5¼x6½ inches, 12 each of the colors above. Each box contains feather penholder with pen. Size of box, when closed, 7¼x13¼x4¼ inches. Shipping weight, 2 pounds.

3K9270...........**$1.98**

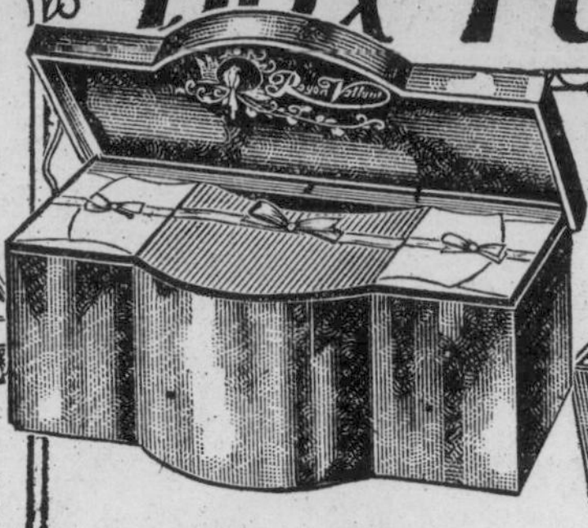

Rayon Vellum

Fancy gift box of stationery, containing 24 sheets each of white, blue and pink linen finish paper, size 5¼x6½ inches, with envelopes to match. Paper and envelopes ribbon tied. Size of box, 13½x6¼x5¼ inches. Shipping weight, 3 pounds.

3K9281....................**$1.59**

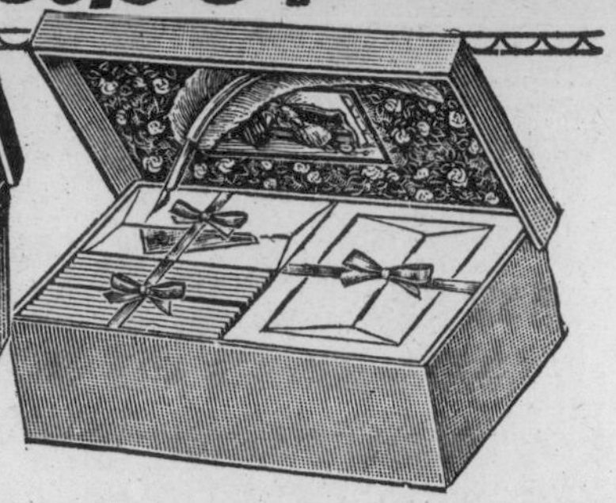

Hinged top cabinet with large 10-inch feather penholder with gold plated pen inside cover to match color of paper. Contains 24 sheets of fine quality unruled linen finish paper, 5⅛x6½ in.; 24 gilt edge correspondence cards; 48 envelopes to match. Ribbon tied. Can furnish in white, blue, buff or pink. **Specify color.** Size of box, 3½x7x11¼ in. Shpg. wt., 1½ lbs.

3K9280...................**98c**

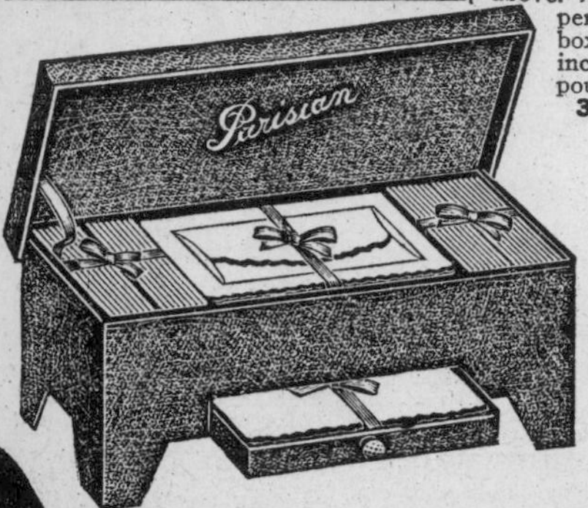

Parisian

Covered with "Old Blue" leather effect paper. 24 sheets fine quality white unruled, linen finish, gold deckled edge paper. Size, 5¼x6½ inches. Envelopes to match. 24 gold edge cards, 48 envelopes. Ribbon tied. Box, 6x12½x5¾ inches. Shipping weight, 3 pounds.

3K9263.....**$1.98**

Pine Lodge

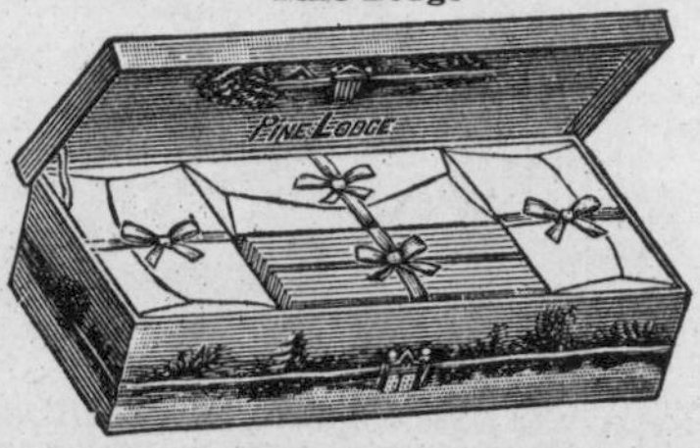

A real Christmas box. Winter scene on side and cover. Contains 24 sheets good quality unruled white linen finish paper, size 5⅛x6½ inches, 24 gilt edge correspondence cards and 48 envelopes. Tied with ribbon. Size, 5¾x13¾x3⅛ inches. Shipping weight, 1¾ pounds.

3K9282..........................**98c**

A Gift Box

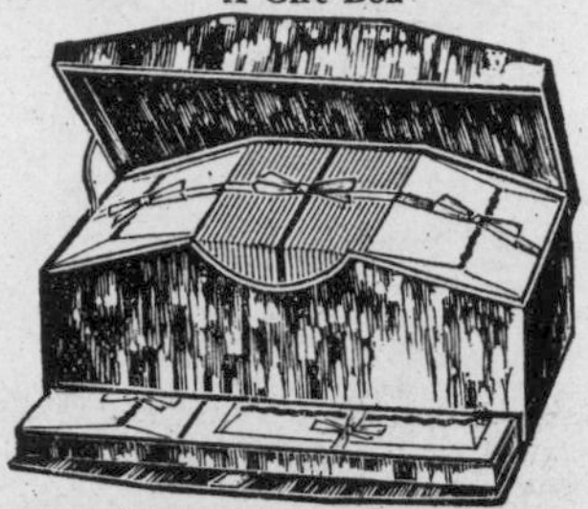

Contains 36 sheets of gold deckled edge vellum finish paper, size 5¼x6½ inches folded, and 12 gold edge correspondence cards, size, 3¼x5¼ inches. White only. Envelopes to match. Packed in gift box which has cover with gold and blue design paper. Shpg. wt., 2 lbs.

3K9261.......................**$1.69**

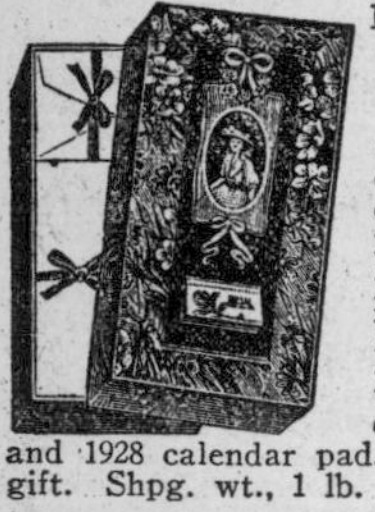

Floral Box With 1928 Calendar

Contains 24 sheets of good quality unruled cloth finish white paper, 5x6⅜ in. 24 envelopes to match. Size of box, 5¾x10¾ in. Floral covered top with inlay colored picture and 1928 calendar pad. Makes a nice gift. Shpg. wt., 1 lb.

3K18710......................**49c**

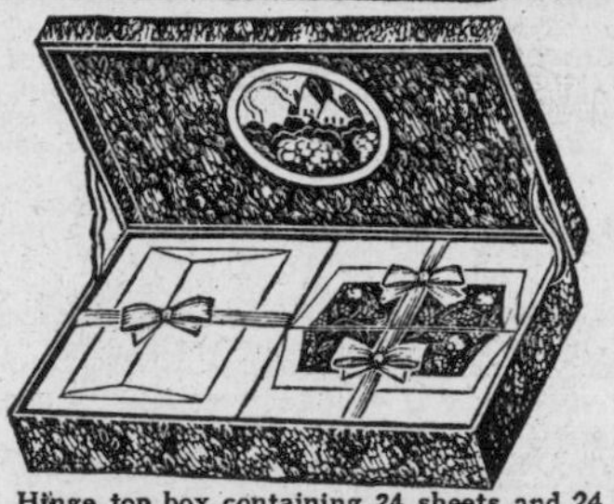

Hinge top box containing 24 sheets and 24 envelopes of high quality linen finish paper. Size of paper, 5x6½ in. Ribbon tied. Packed in box, 7x10¾ in. Can furnish in blue, white, or pink. **State color wanted.**

3K9268—Shpg. wt., 1 lb.........**55c**

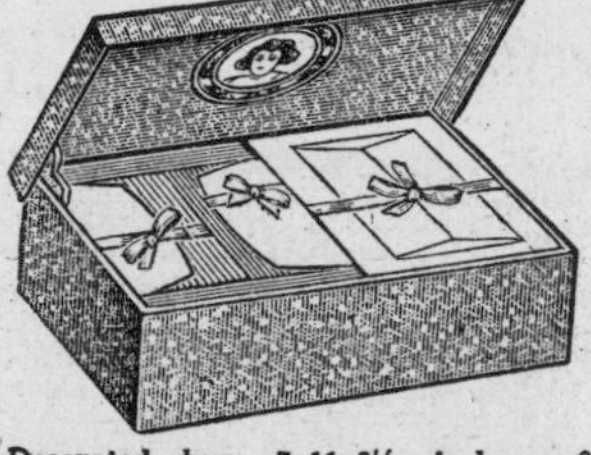

Decorated box, 7x11x3½ inches. 24 sheets good quality linen finish paper, 5⅛x6½ inches; 12 cards; 36 envelopes. Can furnish in blue, pink, buff or white tints. **Specify color.** Shipping weight, 2 pounds.

3K18699.......................**69c**

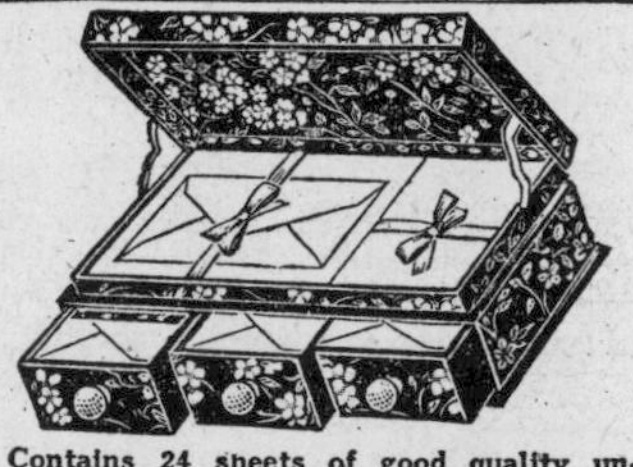

Contains 24 sheets of good quality unruled cloth finish paper, size 5⅛x6½ in.; 12 cards and 36 envelopes in either white, pink or blue tint. **Specify color wanted.** Box, 5¾x11x2⅞ in. Covered with fancy color design paper. Shpg. wt., 1½ lbs.

3K18708...........................**98c**

Lysette

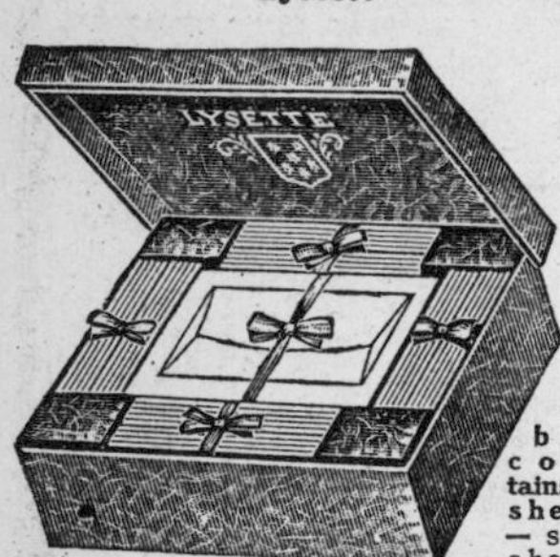

Gift box contains 24 sheets—six sheets each of white, blue, sand and buff color high quality paper, size 5x6½ inches. Six gilt edge correspondence cards of each color, and envelopes to match. Ribbon tied. Size of box, 10⅛x9x3½ in.

3K9265—Shpg. wt., 1½ lbs...**98c**

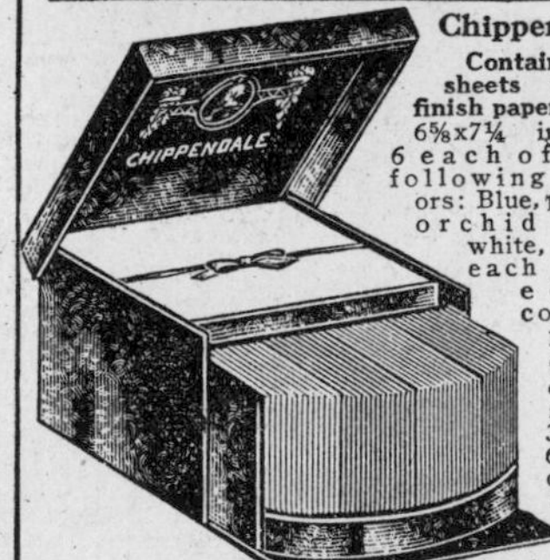

Chippendale

Contains 24 sheets ripple finish paper, size 6⅝x7¼ inches, 6 each of the following colors: Blue, peach, orchid and white, and 6 each gilt edge correspondence cards, size 3⅝ x 6⅝in., of the same colors with 6 envelopes of each color to match cards and paper. Size of box, 7x8¾x4⅝ inches. Shipping wt., 2½ pounds.

3K9275.........................**$1.15**

3-Drawer Bureau Stand Cabinet

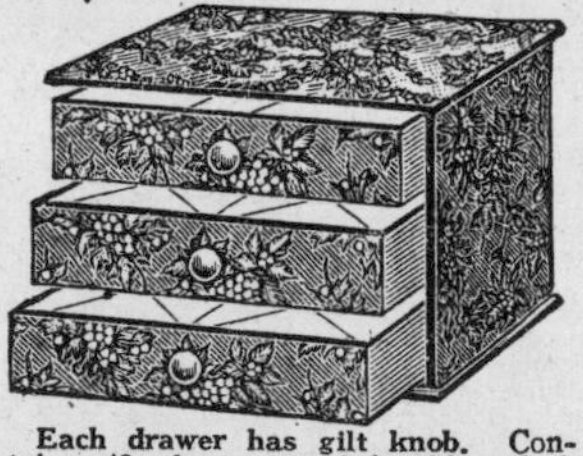

Each drawer has gilt knob. Contains 48 sheets unruled white cloth finish paper, size 4¾x6½ in., and 48 envelopes. Size of box, 7¼x5⅞x4⅝ inches. Shpg. wt., 1½ lbs.

3K9277..........................**73c**

Lockmoor

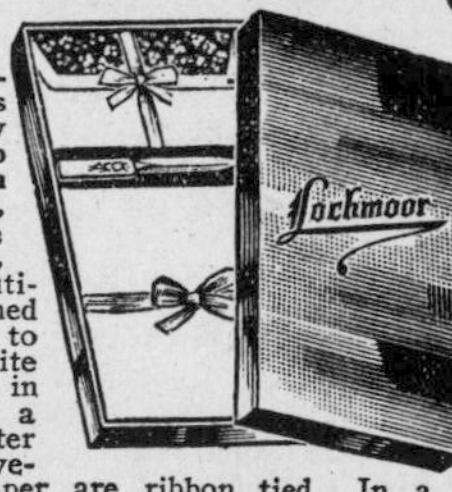

A gift package of 24 sheets of the new popular club size vellum finish paper, size 6¼x7½ inches, folded, with 24 beautiful tissue lined envelopes to match. White only. Packed in each box is a beautiful letter opener. Envelopes and paper are ribbon tied. In a white covered box, size, 7x12¾ inches. Shipping weight, 2 pounds.

3K9269............................**98c**

Fairland Linen Correspondence Cards

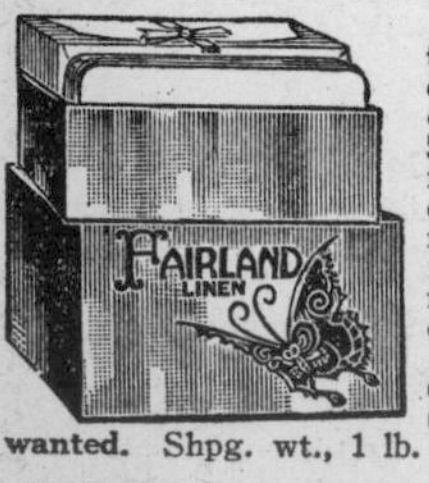

Box contains 24 folded gilt edge cards (size, 5⅛x3¼ inches folded), with envelopes to match. Can furnish in the following colors: White, peach, orchid or gray. **Specify color wanted.** Shpg. wt., 1 lb.

3K18701......................**59c**

A Big Value

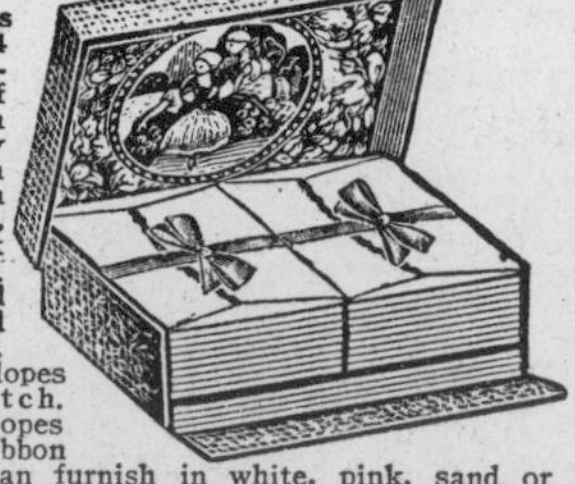

24 sheets and 24 envelopes of high quality smooth finish paper, size 5x6¾ in. Gold deckled edges. 24 envelopes to match. Envelopes are ribbon tied. Can furnish in white, pink, sand or gray. **State color wanted.**

3K9273—Shpg. wt., ¾ lb.......**49c**

Three-Drawer Holly Box

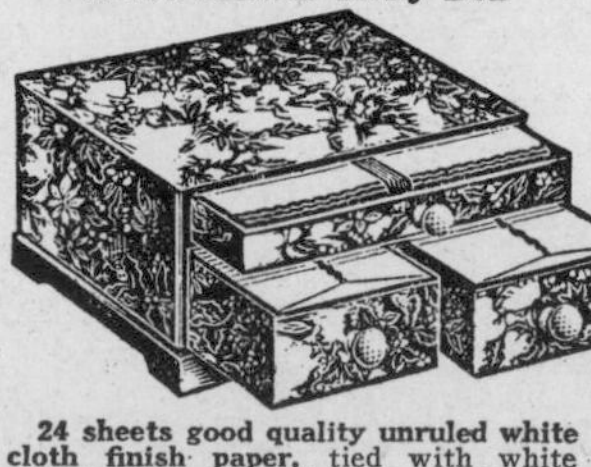

24 sheets good quality unruled white cloth finish paper, tied with white ribbon, size 5⅛x6¼ in., and 24 envelopes. Size of box, 5½x6½x3 in. Shipping wt., 1¼ lbs.

3K9278......................**75c**

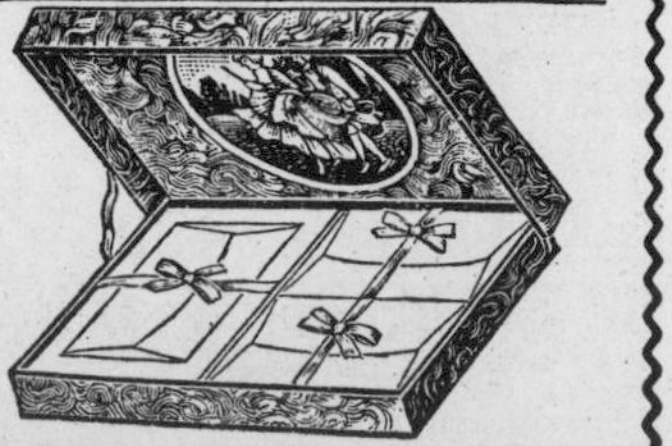

Contains 24 sheets of good quality unruled cloth finish paper, size 5x6½ inches, and 24 envelopes to match. Daintily tinted in blue, buff, heliotrope, pink or white. **State color.** Size of box, 7x11x1⅛ inches. Shipping weight, 2 pounds.

3K18723......................**43c**

A Lovely Gift

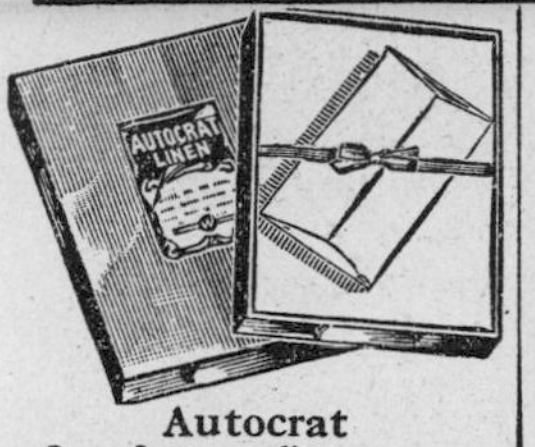

Autocrat

Our first quality paper, made from mixed rag stock. Size of sheets, 7x10½ in. Envelopes, 4x7½ in. 24 sheets and 24 envelopes to box. Can furnish in vellum or linen finish in either white, tan or gray tints. **Specify color wanted.** Shipping wt., 2 lbs.

3K18698—Linen finish 75c
3K18700—Vellum finish 75c

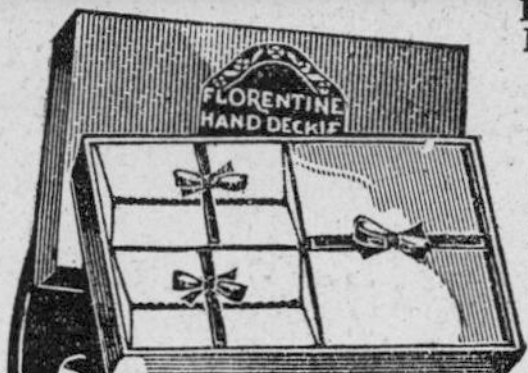

Florentine Hand Deckled Vellum Paper

24 sheets fine quality hand deckled edge vellum paper, 6½x5¼ in., with envelopes to match. Can furnish in white, gray, pink, peach or heliotrope. **State color.** Shipping weight, 1¼ pounds.

3K18713 — With silver deckled edge 47c
3K18714—With gold deckled edge 47c

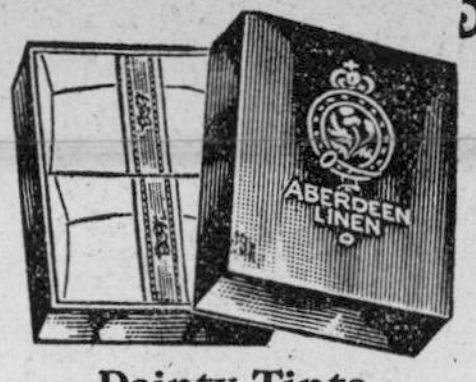

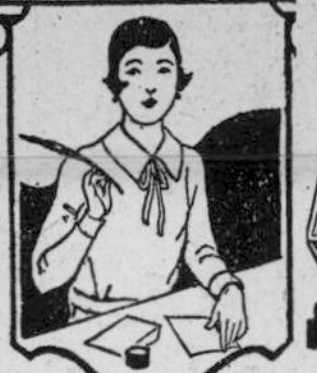

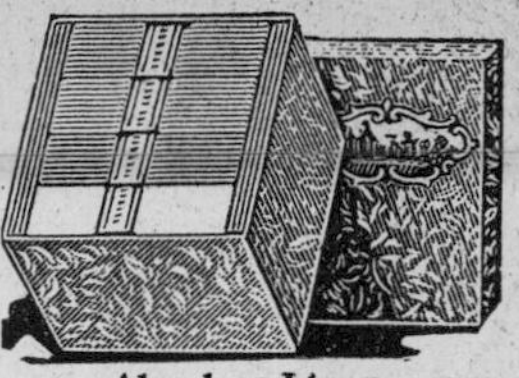

Dainty Tints

A box containing 24 sheets of good quality unruled paper, size 5⅛x6⅝ inches, with 24 envelopes to match. Can furnish in either of following finishes: Cloth or vellum. White pink, blue or gray. **Specify color wanted.** Shipping weight, 1 pound.

3K17952—Cloth finish...23c
3K17953—Vellum finish.23c

Aberdeen Linen

Twelve sheets each of white, blue, buff and pink good quality unruled cloth finish paper, with 48 envelopes to match. Size of paper, 5⅛x6⅝ inches. Shipping weight 1 lb.

3K18705 ....39c

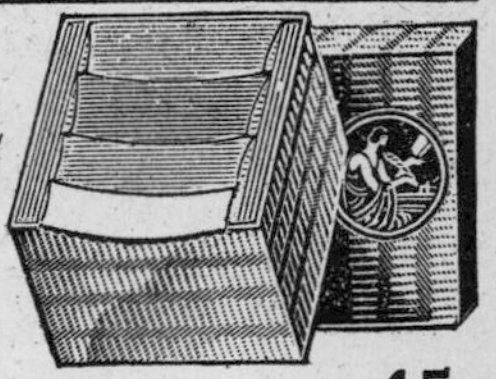

Twelve sheets each of white, blue, buff and pink high quality ripple finish paper, with gold deckled edge. Envelopes to match. Size of paper, 5¼ x 6½ inches. Shipping weight, 1¼ lbs.

3K18715 ....45c

Correspondence Cards

Box contains 24 cards size 4x5½ inches and 24 envelopes. We can furnish in either white, blue, pink or gray. **Specify color.** Linen finish. Shpg. wt., ¾ lb.

3K17956 ....23c
3K17957—Same as above, but with gold edges on cards.28c

Traymore

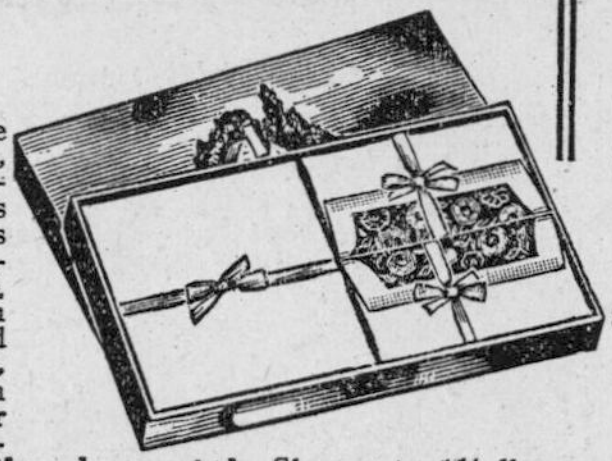

Beautiful fine quality, fancy finish, linen laid paper, unruled. 24 sheets size 6⅝x7½ inches folded and 24 envelopes size 3⅞x6¾ inches lined with handsomely colored tissue. Size of box, 8¼x13⅞ inches. Can furnish in either white, peach, lavender or green. **Specify color wanted.** Shpg. wt., 1½ lbs.

3K9254 ....89c

For Other Gift Suggestions See Page 776

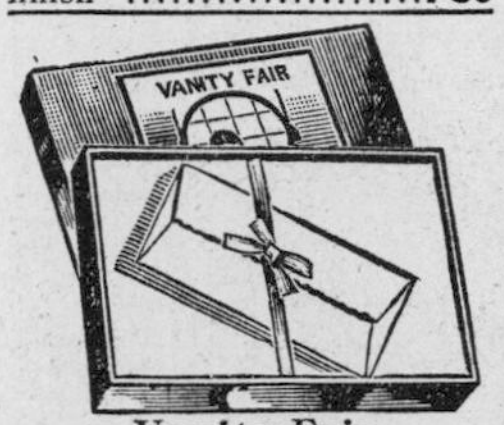

Vanity Fair

Our second quality paper. Size of sheet, 7⅛x10½ in. Envelopes 3⅞x7½ in. 24 sheets and 24 envelopes in box. Can furnish in vellum, cloth or ripple finish, in the following colors: White, gray or peach. **State color wanted.** Shpg. wt., 2 lbs.

3K17949—Vellum finish 45c
3K17950—Cloth finish.45c
3K17951 — Ripple finish 45c

Juvenile Stationery

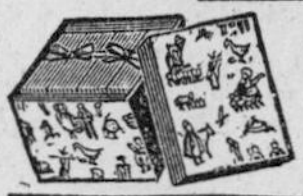

Package of juvenile stationery containing 48 sheets and 48 envelopes, 12 each of sand, blue, white and pink. All the kiddies enjoy this kind of stationery. Size of sheet, 3x4½ inches. Ribbon tied. Packed in box 4½x5 inches. Shpg. wt., ¾ lb.

3K18695 ....29c

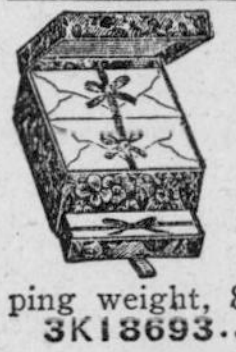

Floral Hinge Top Pull Drawer Box

24 sheets unruled white cloth finish paper, 3⅛ x 4½ in., and 24 envelopes, ribbon tied. Shipping weight, 8 ounces.

3K18693 ....35c

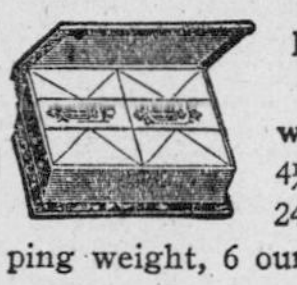

Book Shape Box

24 sheets of ruled white paper, 3¼x4½ inches, with 24 envelopes. Shipping weight, 6 ounces.

3K18691 ....23c

Envelopes—Plain or Printed

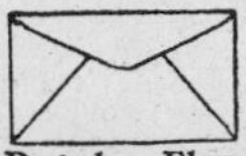

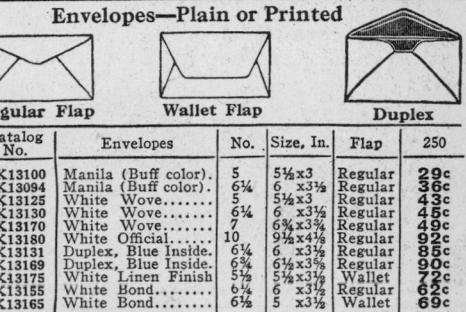

Regular Flap

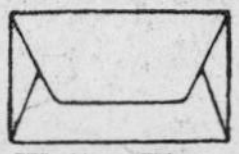

Wallet Flap

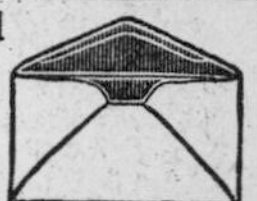

Duplex

Catalog No.	Envelopes	No.	Size, In.	Flap	250
3K13100	Manila (Buff color).	5	5½x3	Regular	29c
3K13094	Manila (Buff color).	6¼	6 x3½	Regular	36c
3K13125	White Wove.......	5	5½x3	Regular	43c
3K13130	White Wove.......	6¼	6 x3½	Regular	45c
3K13170	White Wove.......	7	6¾x3¾	Regular	49c
3K13180	White Official......	10	9½x4⅛	Regular	92c
3K13131	Duplex, Blue Inside.	6¼	6 x3½	Regular	85c
3K13169	Duplex, Blue Inside.	6¾	6½x3⅝	Regular	90c
3K13175	White Linen Finish	5½	5½x3⅓	Wallet	72c
3K13155	White Bond........	6¼	6 x3½	Regular	62c
3K13165	White Bond........	6½	5 x3½	Wallet	69c

Shipping weight, box of 250, 3 pounds.

WE WILL PRINT your name and address in neat type with dark blue ink in the upper left hand corner of any of the above envelopes, excepting numbers 3K13100 and 3K13094, at an additional charge of 85 cents for 250.

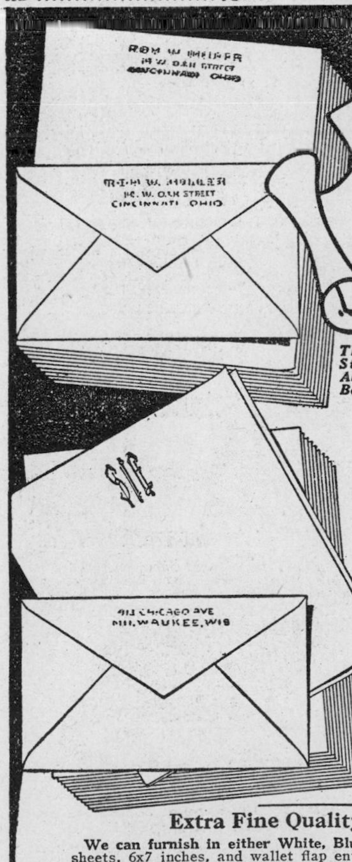

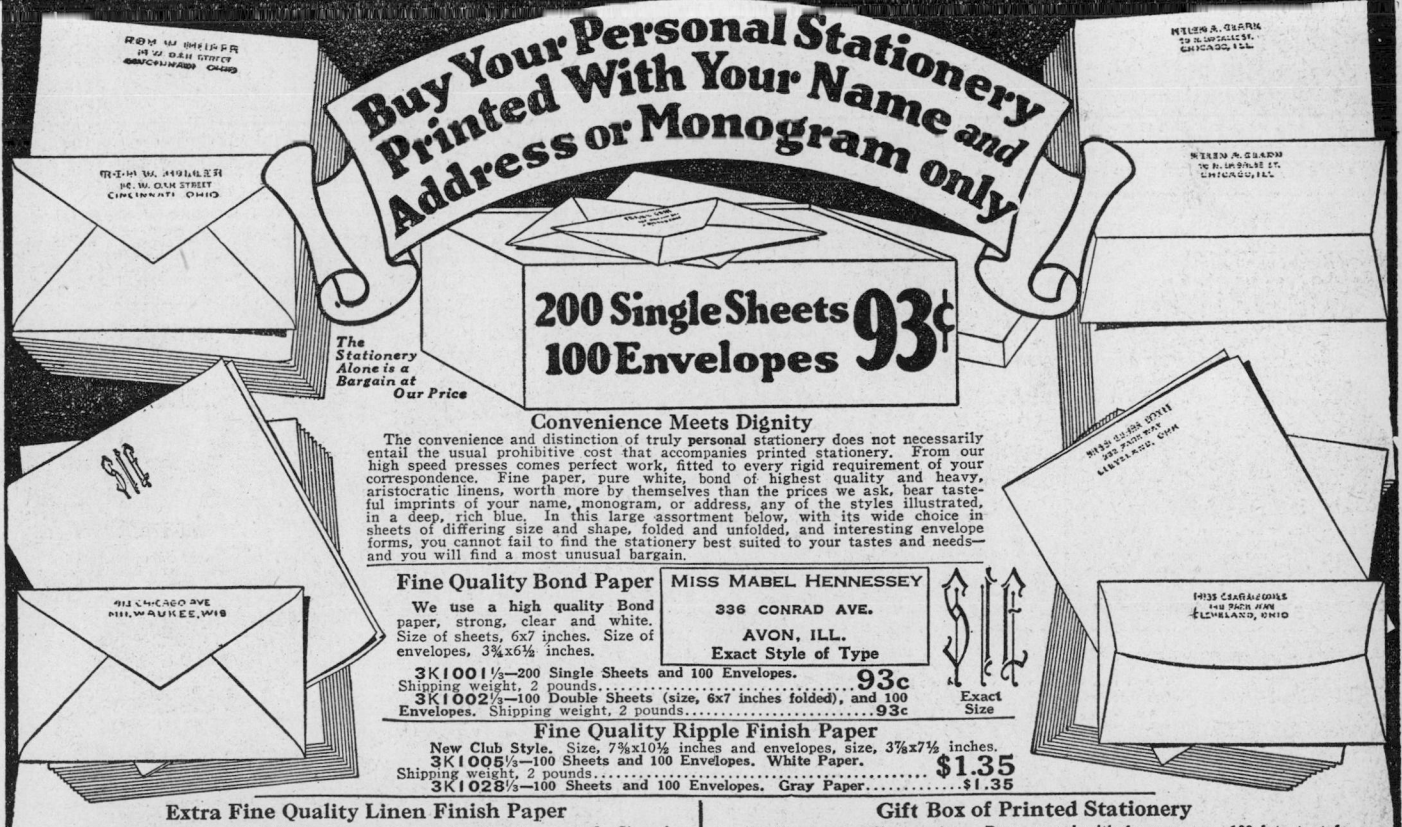

Buy Your Personal Stationery Printed With Your Name and Address or Monogram only

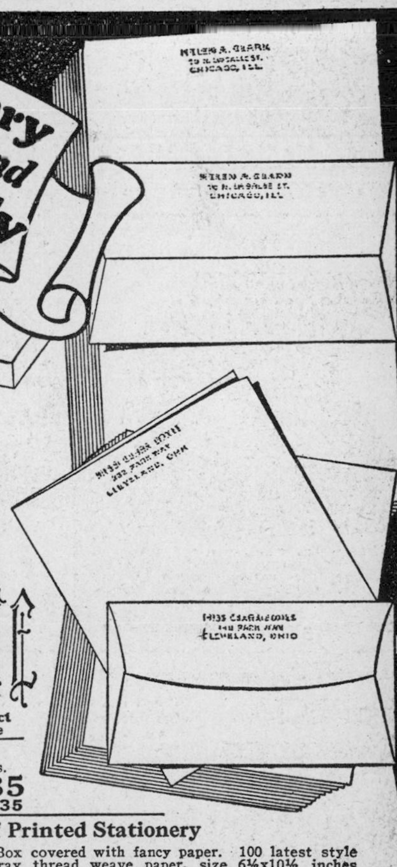

200 Single Sheets 100 Envelopes 93¢

The Stationery Alone is a Bargain at Our Price

Convenience Meets Dignity

The convenience and distinction of truly personal stationery does not necessarily entail the usual prohibitive cost that accompanies printed stationery. From our high speed presses comes perfect work, fitted to every rigid requirement of your correspondence. Fine paper, pure white, bond of highest quality and heavy, aristocratic linens, worth more by themselves than the prices we ask, bear tasteful imprints of your name, monogram, or address, any of the styles illustrated, in a deep, rich blue. In this large assortment below, with its wide choice in sheets of differing size and shape, folded and unfolded, and interesting envelope forms, you cannot fail to find the stationery best suited to your tastes and needs—and you will find a most unusual bargain.

Fine Quality Bond Paper

We use a high quality Bond paper, strong, clear and white. Size of sheets, 6x7 inches. Size of envelopes, 3⅝x6½ inches.

MISS MABEL HENNESSEY
336 CONRAD AVE.
AVON, ILL.
Exact Style of Type

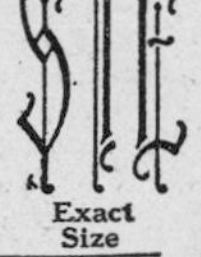

Exact Size

3K1001⅓—200 Single Sheets and 100 Envelopes. Shipping weight, 2 pounds 93c
3K1002⅓—100 Double Sheets (size, 6x7 inches folded), and 100 Envelopes. Shipping weight, 2 pounds 93c

Fine Quality Ripple Finish Paper

New Club Style. Size, 7⅜x10½ inches and envelopes, size, 3⅞x7½ inches.

3K1005⅓—100 Sheets and 100 Envelopes. White Paper. Shipping weight, 2 pounds $1.35
3K1028⅓—100 Sheets and 100 Envelopes. Gray Paper $1.35

Extra Fine Quality Linen Finish Paper

We can furnish in either White, Blue or Gray. **Specify color wanted.** Size of sheets, 6x7 inches, and wallet flap envelopes, size, 3⅝x6½ inches.

3K1003⅓—200 Single Sheets and 100 Envelopes. Linen Finish $1.25
3K1004⅓—100 Double Sheets (size, 6x7 inches folded), and 100 Envelopes. Linen Finish. Shipping weight, any of the above, 2 pounds $1.25
3K1029⅓—100 Correspondence Cards. Linen finish, white. Size, 3¼x5¼ inches. Envelopes to match. Shipping weight, 1¼ pounds $1.35

Gift Box of Printed Stationery

A gift anyone will appreciate. Box covered with fancy paper. 100 latest style flat sheets of extra fine quality gray thread weave paper, size 6½x10½ inches and 50 envelopes, 3⅞x6¾ inches. **Any name and address printed.**

3K1021⅓—Shipping weight, 2½ pounds $1.85
3K1022⅓—Same style as above but contains an extra fine quality of white vellum paper. Shipping weight, 2½ pounds $1.85

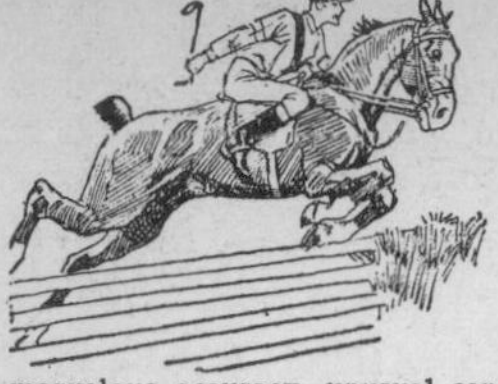

Truphoto Cameras

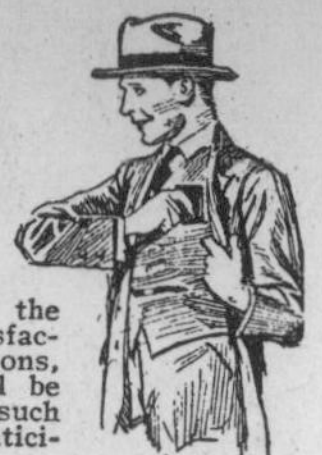

Combining Efficiency With Convenience

In answer to an insistent demand for a camera combining unsurpassed performance with extraordinary compactness, we confidently introduce our New Truphoto Cameras. In them, alone, will be found marvelous accuracy, unusual sensitiveness to detail, **together with utmost carrying convenience.**

Only that which contributes to better, clearer pictures is incorporated in Truphoto—all unnecessary, cumbersome parts are eliminated. Only features that **add to efficiency** are included in this NEW PRODUCT of an old, reliable concern.

We know that real photography pleasure awaits the buyer of the cameras offered on this page. Avail yourself of the genuine satisfaction that they place before you. Try them out under **any** conditions, on **any** subject. You will be pleased beyond words, and you will be amazed that we can offer you a camera of such exceptional merit at such a low price. **Production** answers that—tremendous production, anticipating tremendous demand!

Our popular little Kewpie Kamera, too, has received its share of Truphoto refinements. It is a bigger bargain than ever; possessing, as it now does, the remarkable features that are sure to make Truphoto Cameras the greatest camera values offered anywhere.

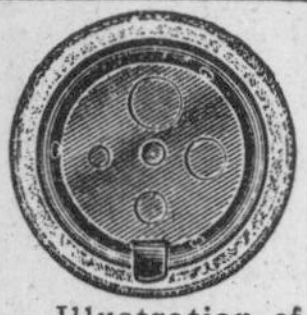

Illustration of the four diaphragm stops or openings on all Kewpies except the No. 2. These enable you to take pictures on dull days as well as bright.

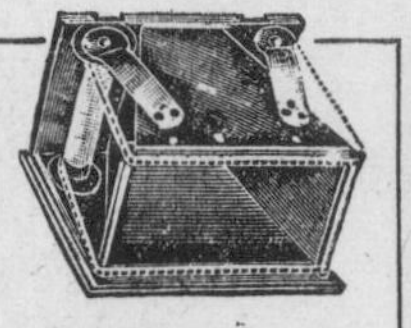

Illustration showing simple construction of the reloading device.

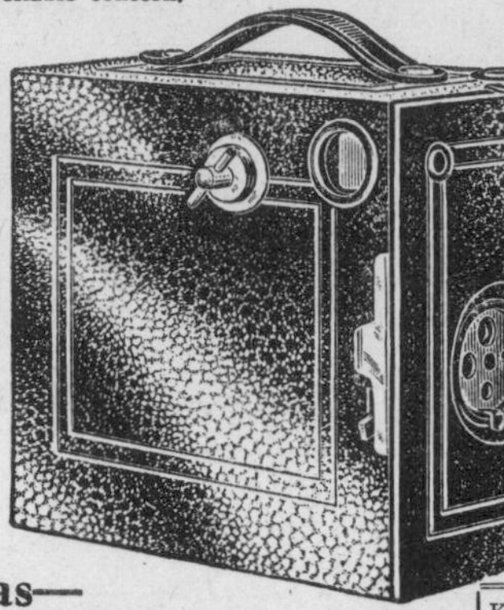

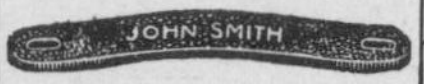
JOHN SMITH

Illustrates name on handle. Your name stamped in gold on handle of camera at no extra charge if you want it. Print name wanted carefully.

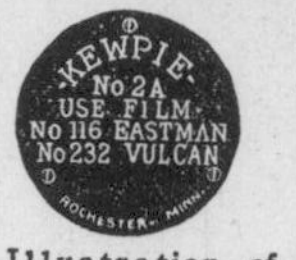
KEWPIE
No 2A
USE FILM
No 116 EASTMAN
No 232 VULCAN
ROCHESTER · MINN

Illustration of name plate placed on every one of our Truphoto Kewpie Kameras. When you see the name Truphoto on a camera, it is like having a guarantee for perfection.

COMPARE THESE LOW PRICES

LOWER PRICED THAN EVER

Better Than Ever

Cameras of quality, equal to the Truphoto, regularly sell elsewhere for at least one-third more.

Truphoto Kewpie Kameras—

"They Get the Picture"

When you have a Truphoto camera, you have the acme of perfection in camera construction and execution. You are positively assured of clear, sharp, true reproductions.

Made with a rigid light weight wood frame of ebony finish hardwood, covered with black artificial leather, seal grain. Looks well and wears well. Equipped with two finders, one for horizontal and one for vertical pictures. **Shutter has two speeds, instantaneous and time,** which enables you to take pictures under all conditions. **Has four stops or diaphragms** for controlling the light on extremely bright days. The lens is a single achromatic lens especially developed for this camera. The film holder device is of rigid construction, and yet so simple that a child can load it. Illustrated instruction book and Truphoto photographic exposure guide included with each Kewpie Kamera.

Kewpie Kamera	Catalog No.	Size of Picture, Inches	Size of Camera, Inches	Net	Shipping Weight	For Film See Bottom of This Page	
No. 2	3K41200	2¼x3¼	3¼x4⅛x5⅝	14 oz.	2 lbs.	3K42678 or 3K41032	$1.85
No. 2A	3K41220	2½x4¼	3½x5¼x5⅞	18 oz.	2¼ lbs.	3K42679 or 3K41033	2.65
No. 3	3K41240	3¼x4¼	4½x5¼x5⅞	22 oz.	2¾ lbs.	3K42682 or 3K41036	3.60
No. 3A	3K41260	3¼x5½ Post Card size	4¾x6½x6¾	31 oz.	3 lbs.	3K42685 or 3K41039	4.25

Truphoto Folding Cameras

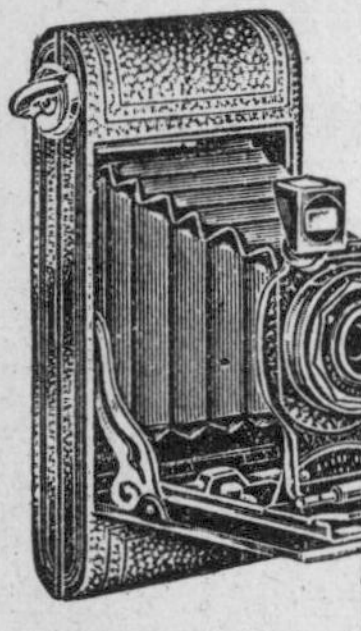

To those who want the best possible in a roll film hand camera, we recommend these models. Sturdy in construction, elegant in appearance with good quality shutters, single achromatic lenses, with the exception of the 3A, which has F:8 rapid rectilinear lens. Focusing is easily and satisfactorily taken care of by a new and positive focusing device. The single achromatic lens, F:16, with Wollensak shutter, will take either snap shots or time exposures. The thin model permits the camera to be carried easily in the coat pocket. The illustration shown above is of the No. 2 size, which takes a picture 2¼x3¼ inches. We can furnish this Truphoto Camera in three sizes:

3K47712—Truphoto Vest Pocket Camera. Takes pictures size 1⅝x2½ inches. Shpg. wt., 1 lb. **$4.39**

3K47713—Truphoto Camera No. 2. Takes pictures 2¼x3¼ inches. Shipping weight, 2 pounds **$5.98**

3K42826—Truphoto Camera No. 3A. Takes pictures 3¼x5½ inches. Shipping weight, 4¾ pounds............**$12.49**

Complete Camera Outfit

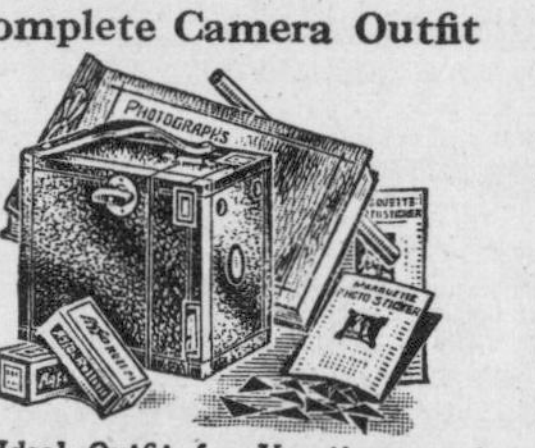
PHOTOGRAPHS

An Ideal Outfit for Vacations or to Take on That Auto Trip

Nothing more to buy. With this outfit you are ready to take pictures. And when the pictures are finished, you have in this outfit everything necessary to make a permanent record of your vacation, your children, your trip, etc. The biggest photographic value that has been offered in many a day.

Outfit contains a camera that takes pictures, size 2½x4¼ inches, a dandy album of seal grain imitation leather with 50 black leaves, 200 black mounting corners, a white pencil and 2 rolls of 6-exposure film.

3K45451—Shipping wt., 3 pounds.............**$2.25**

Citex Camera

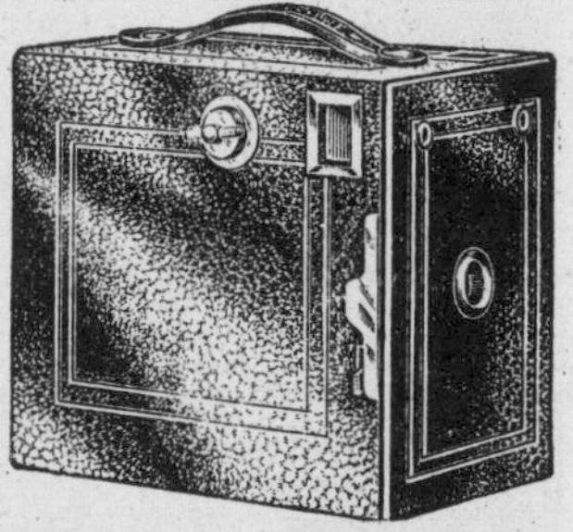

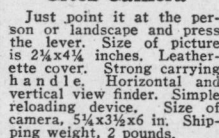

Just point it at the person or landscape and press the lever. Size of picture is 2¼x4¼ inches. Leatherette cover. Strong carrying handle. Horizontal and vertical view finder. Simple reloading device. Size of camera, 5¼x3½x6 in. Shipping weight, 2 pounds.

3K41550 Citex Camera.... **$1.39**

Same as above, except with one view finder. Takes pictures 2¼x3¼ in. Shipping weight, 1¾ pounds.

3K41551 Citex Camera.... **$1.25**

Our Baby Camera—*A Real Camera For Only 79c*

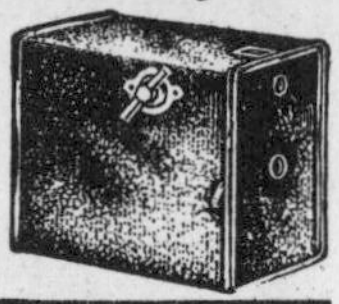

A good looking camera that takes real pictures, size 1⅝x2½ inches, from any regular vest pocket size film roll. It measures 2¼x3⅛ inches. Of durable steel construction, covered with attractive imitation leather. Has one view finder; single meniscus lens. Takes instantaneous pictures only. No adjustment necessary. Shipping weight, 1 pound.

3K47714 ....**79c**

Photographic Film

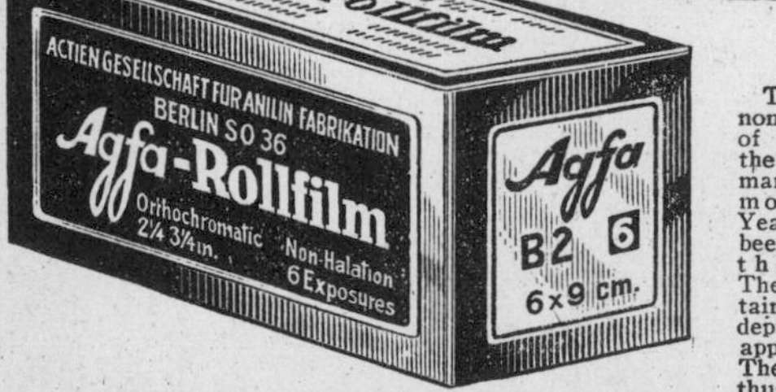
Agfa-Rollfilm
ACTIEN GESELLSCHAFT FUR ANILIN FABRIKATION
BERLIN SO 36
Agfa-Rollfilm
Orthochromatic
2¼ 3¼ in.
Non-Halation
6 Exposures
Agfa
B2
6
6x9 cm.

Agfa Rollfilms

Imported

These films are second to none in the excellent quality of their results. They are the finest products of Germany's greatest and foremost film manufacturers. Years of experimenting have been devoted to obtaining their absolute perfection. They produce negatives retaining all the color value, depths and subtle contrasts appearing in the subject. They will receive the enthusiastic endorsement of all photographers, including the most discriminating. They are exceptionally fast, enabling you to obtain correctly timed negatives, even under poor lighting conditions. Once you have used these films you will use no other. They are non-curling, very rapid, free from halation and orthochromatic. We particularly recommend them to you.

All films listed below may be used in Autographic Kodaks, but no record or title can be made on the film at the time of exposure, except with Autographic film. Shipping weights, 3 to 4 ounces.

For 1⅝x2½ Pictures
3K42676—Agfa. 8-Exp. Roll....**22c**

For 2¼x2¼ Pictures
3K42677—Agfa. 6-Exp. Roll....**18c**

For 2¼x3¼ Pictures
3K42678—Agfa. 6-Exp. Roll....**23c**

For 2½x4¼ Pictures
3K42679—Agfa. 6-Exp. Roll....**27c**

For 2⅞x4⅞ Pictures
3K42680—Agfa. 6-Exp. Roll....**41c**

For 3½x3½ Pictures
3K42681—Agfa. 6-Exp. Roll....**32c**

For 3¼x4¼ Pictures
3K42682—Agfa. 6-Exp. Roll....**41c**

For 3¼x4¼ Pictures and Stereos
3K42683—Agfa. 6-Exp. Roll....**38c**

For 3¼x5½ Pictures
3K42685—Agfa. 6-Exp. Roll....**50c**

For 4x5 Pictures and 3½x12 Panoramas
3K42686—Agfa. 6-Exp. Roll....**50c**

Eastman Film

The Film in the Yellow Box

It is non-curling, extremely rapid and free from halation. It is orthochromatic and will give good color values.

When ordering film, measure the length of the empty spool in your camera. Spool lengths are stated for each style. If you are not sure of the film number, tell us the name, model and size of your camera. We will send the **correct film.** Shipping weights, 3 to 4 ounces.

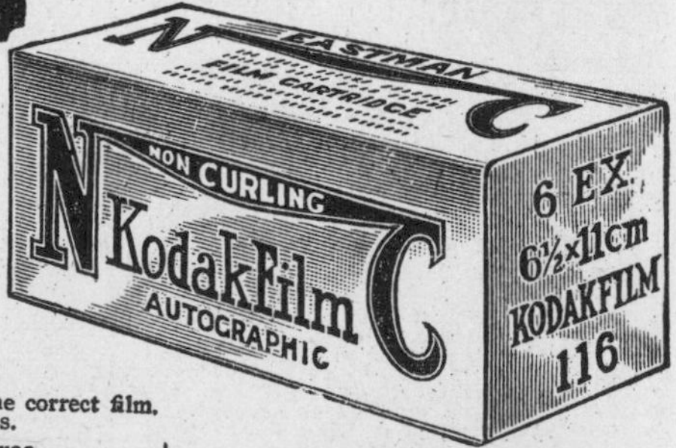
EASTMAN
FILM CARTRIDGE
N
NON CURLING
Kodak Film
AUTOGRAPHIC
C
6 EX.
6½x11cm
KODAK FILM
116

For 1⅝x2½ Pictures
3K41030—Eastman Autographic Film. 127. 8-Exp. Roll.......................**22c**

For 2¼x2¼ Pictures
3K41031—Eastman N. C. Film. 117. 6-Exp. Roll.......................**18c**

For 2¼x3¼ Pictures
3K41032—Eastman Autographic Film. 120. 6-Exp. Roll.......................**23c**

For 2½x4¼ Pictures
3K41033—Eastman Autographic Film. 116. 6-Exp. Roll.......................**27c**

For 2⅞x4⅞ Pictures
3K41037—Eastman N. C. Film. 130. 6-Exp. Roll.......................**41c**

For 3½x3½ Pictures
3K41034—Eastman N. C. Film. 101. 6-Exp. Roll.......................**32c**

For 3¼x4¼ Pictures
3K41036—Eastman N. C. Film. 124. 6-Exp. Roll.......................**41c**

For 3¼x4¼ Pictures and Stereos
3K41035—Eastman N. C. Film. 118. 6-Exp. Roll.......................**41c**

For 3¼x5½ Pictures and Stereos
3K41039—Eastman N. C. Film. 125. 6-Exp. Roll.......................**50c**

For 3¼x5½ Pictures
3K41038—Eastman N. C. Film. 122. 6-Exp. Roll.......................**50c**

For 4x5 Pictures and 3½x12 Panoramas
3K41040—Eastman Panorama N. C. Film. 103. 6-Exp. Roll...........**50c**

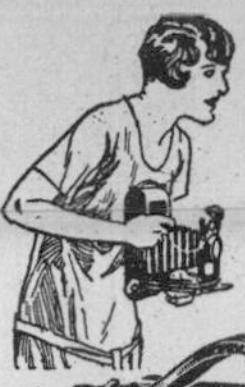

Kodaks and Eastman Cameras

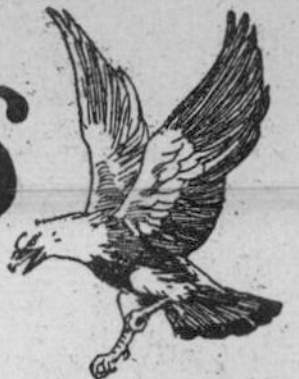

The enviable reputation of Eastman Cameras and Kodaks is world wide. Wherever you go, you find the name Eastman synonymous with high quality, beauty and efficiency. When you purchase an Eastman product you know that you are getting your money's worth—and when you purchase it from Sears, Roebuck and Co. you are doubly sure, because our liberal guarantee, behind everything we sell, makes your satisfaction positive. The Cameras and Kodaks shown on this page are true representatives of Eastman Kodak Company's sterling products.

Brownie Box Cameras

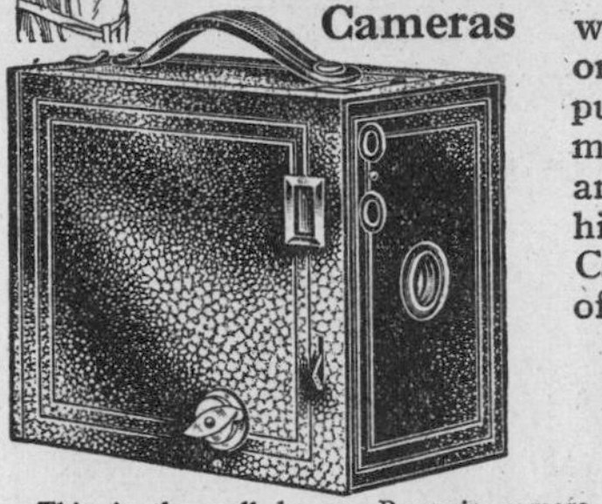

This is the well known Brownie camera which has satisfied tens of thousands of users. It is well constructed, and simple to operate. Has two shutter speeds—instantaneous and time, and has different diaphragm stops so that you can readily control light conditions. Shpg. wt., 2½ lbs.

3K41050—No. 2 Box Brownie. Takes picture size 2¼x3¼ inches.......................... **$2.29**

3K41052—No. 2A Box Brownie. Takes picture size 2½x4¼ inches.......................... **$3.19**

3K41053—No. 3 Box Brownie. Takes picture size 3¼x4¼ inches.......................... **$3.98**

3K41054—No. 2C Box Brownie. Takes picture size 2⅞x4⅞ inches.......................... **$4.49**

Vest Pocket Kodak

Picture size 1⅝x2½ inches

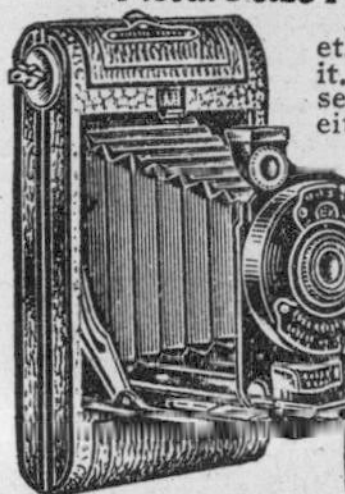

Small as a vest pocket. This camera will fit it. No focusing—just set the adjustment for either instantaneous or time, point the lens at the object to be photographed, and "click," the picture is yours. Like all other Kodaks, it is autographic, and the lens and shutters are carefully tested. Will hold an 8-exposure film. Equipped with Meniscus lens and rotary shutter, four diaphragm stops, two speeds, instantaneous and time. Brilliant reversible finder for vertical or horizontal pictures. Made of metal, covered with durable imitation leather. Trimmings finished in nickel and black enamel, one tripod socket. Shipping weight, 1 pound.

3K41011—Vest Pocket Kodak, Single Lens.......... **$ 4.45**

3K41012—Vest Pocket Kodak, Kodar Lens.......... **8.95**

3K41013—Vest Pocket Kodak, F.6.3................ **13.45**

Kodak Series III

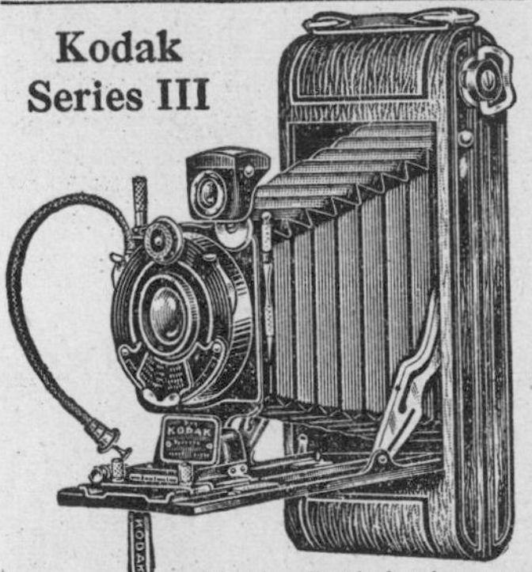

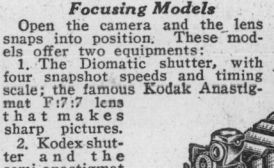

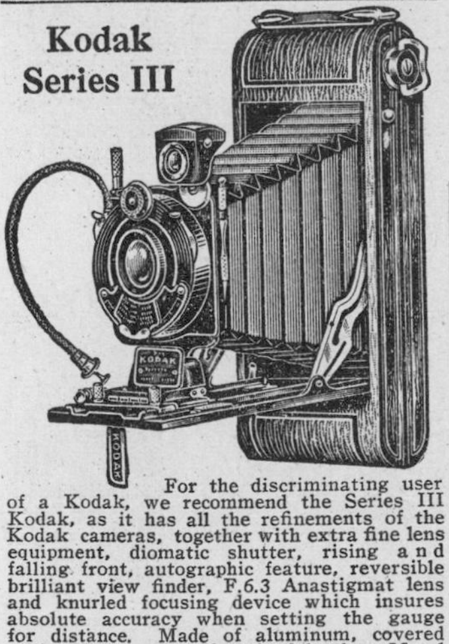

For the discriminating user of a Kodak, we recommend the Series III Kodak, as it has all the refinements of the Kodak cameras, together with extra fine lens equipment, diomatic shutter, rising and falling front, autographic feature, reversible brilliant view finder, F.6.3 Anastigmat lens and knurled focusing device which insures absolute accuracy when setting the gauge for distance. Made of aluminum, covered with a fine quality of grained leather. Metal parts highly nickeled. Has handle so that it can be easily carried. Furnished in four sizes. Shipping weight, 3 pounds.

3K41020—No. 1 Pocket Kodak. Takes picture size 2¼x3¼ inches, F.6.3........................ **$22.50**

3K41021—No. 1A Pocket Kodak. Takes picture size 2½x4¼ inches, F.6.3........................ **$25.50**

3K41022—No. 2C Pocket Kodak. Takes picture size 2⅞x4⅞ inches, F.6.3........................ **$28.00**

3K41023—No. 3 Pocket Kodak. Takes picture size 3¼x4¼ inches, F.6.3........................ **$26.50**

HAWKEYE CAMERAS

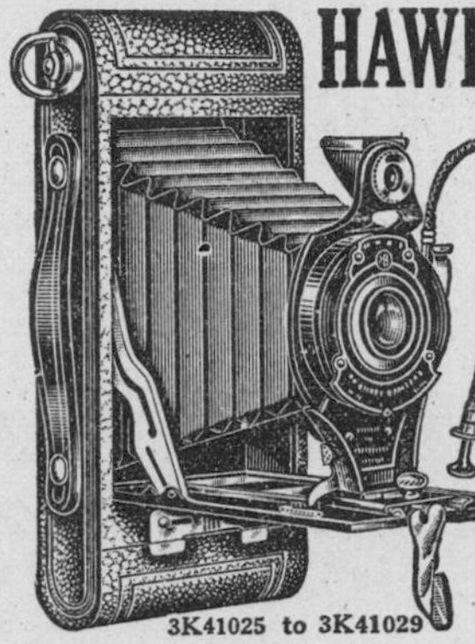

3K41025 to 3K41029

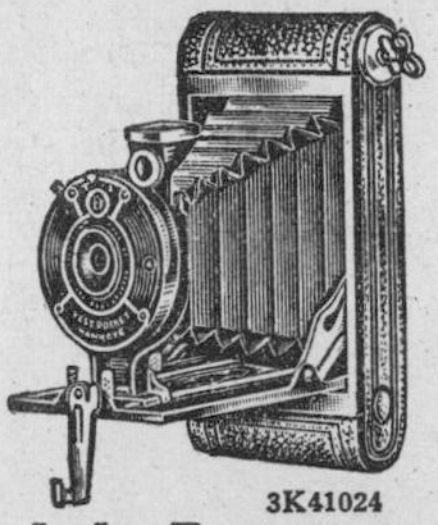

3K41024

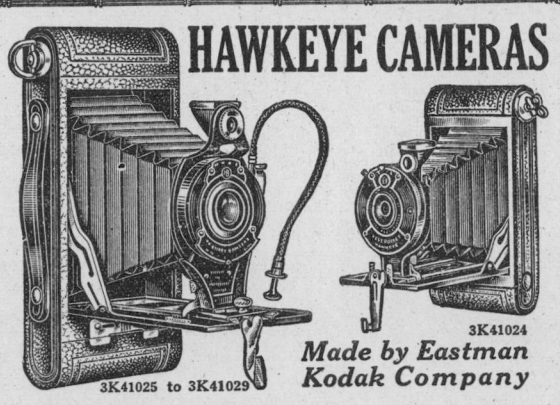

Made by Eastman Kodak Company

So exact in detail, so true in reproduction, it is readily understood why the Famous Hawkeye Camera has such a large following. With them even a beginner can be sure of obtaining excellent pictures, sure to please immeasurably with their marvelous fidelity to any subject chosen. True to the high standards of the Eastman Company's workmanship, these exceptional cameras are handy, compact and beautiful, as well as remarkably durable and efficient. Here is a camera you will be proud of, both for its appearance and the results it obtains for you.

All load with Kodak roll film, obtainable anywhere.

The reliable Kodex shutter appears on all sizes with two accurate snapshot speeds in addition to time and bulb settings. Exposures are made either with a lever or with the cable release supplied with each camera. The focus is adjustable. It is aided by an accurate scale and a handy focusing lock. The finder is reversible for horizontal or vertical views, and alternate sockets permit the use of a tripod in either position.

The cameras are covered with fine grain black imitation leather, handsomely embossed. Exposed metal parts are trimmed in durable black crystal lacquer, nickel and brass.

3K41024—Hawkeye Vest Pocket. Shpg. wt., 1 lb. Single Lens. Takes picture size 1⅝x2½ inches........ **$ 4.25**

3K41025—No. 2 Folding Hawkeye. Shpg. wt., 2 lbs. Single Lens. Takes picture size 2¼x3¼ inches.......... **6.45**

3K41026—No. 2 Folding Hawkeye. Shpg. wt., 2 lbs. Rapid Rectilinear Lens. Takes picture size 2¼x3¼ inches. **8.45**

3K41027—No. 2A Folding Hawkeye. Shpg. wt., 2½ lbs. Single lens. Takes picture size 2½x4¼ inches........... **7.65**

3K41028—No. 2A Folding Hawkeye. Shpg. wt., 2½ lbs. Rapid Rectilinear Lens. Takes picture size 2½x4¼ inches. **9.35**

3K41029—No. 3A Folding Hawkeye. Shpg. wt., 4¾ lbs. Rapid Rectilinear Lens. Takes picture size 3¼x5½ inches. **12.85**

CINE KODAKS

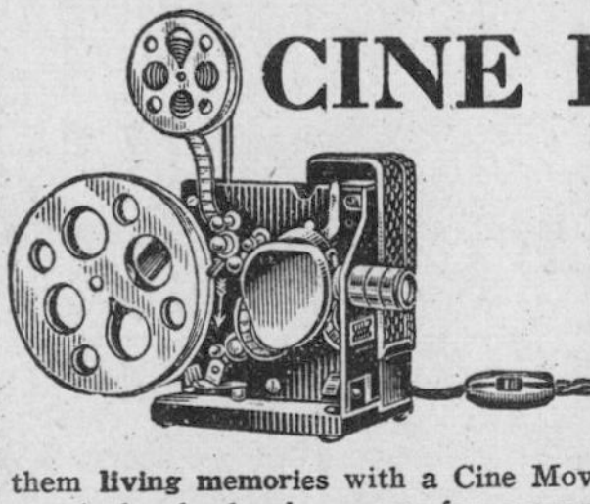

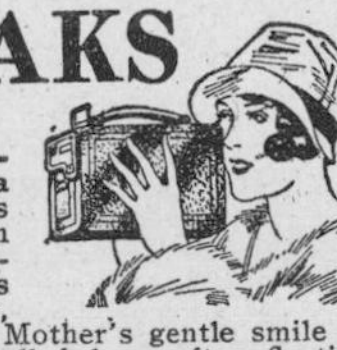

A Moving Picture Camera such as this makes life's high lights yours forever. Baby's cute gestures, always yours. Mother's gentle smile to be actually recalled long after fleeting years slip by. That boy of yours—exuberant, overflowing—perpetual motion. Preserve those priceless moments, make them **living memories** with a Cine Moving Picture Camera.

A handy hand camera for personal movies designed for simplicity and economy in operation. Has spring motor which eliminates hand cranking. Ready for instant use, as it requires no tripod.

3K43247—Cine Kodak, Model B, with Kokad Anastigmat Lens, F:3.5. Shpg. wt., 3½ lbs.......................... **$89.00**

3K43248—Kodascope, Model C Propector. Shipping weight, 6 pounds.. **54.00**

3K43251—Complete Outfit, Camera and projector.. **141.50**

3K41043—Cine Kodak, Model B, F:6.5. Shipping weight, 4 pounds.......................... **$69.00**

3K41046—Screen, 22x30 inches. Shipping weight, 2½ pounds.......................... **9.75**

3K41047—Screen, 30x30 inches. Shipping weight, 3½ pounds.......................... **13.50**

3K41048—Combination Case Holding Cine Kodak and two rolls of film. Shipping weight, 3 pounds...... **9.75**

3K43249—Cine Film, including processing, 50 feet. Shipping weight, 4 ounces.......................... **3.60**

3K43250—Cine Film, including processing, 100 feet. Shipping weight, 6 ounces.......................... **5.40**

Eastman Kodaks

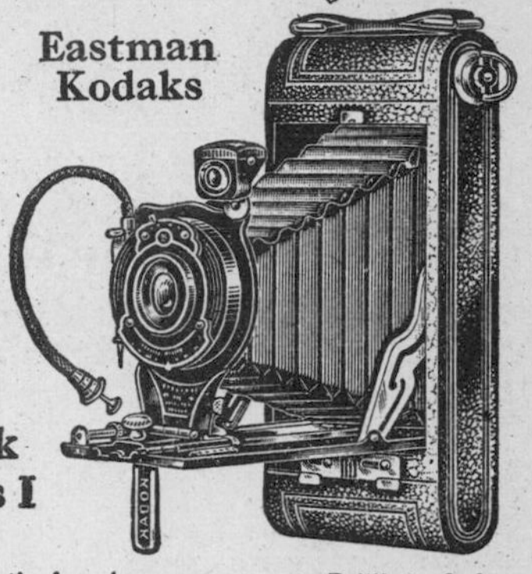

Kodak Series I

Automatic focusing arrangement. Brilliant finder, reversible for vertical or horizontal pictures. Two tripod sockets, body is made of aluminum, covered with fine leather, seal grained. Metal parts finished in nickel and black enamel. Rising, falling and sliding front. Black bellows. Has autographic feature which enables you to make a permanent record on each film. Shutters have the following speeds: Kodex shutter, time bulb, 1/25, 1/50 second; Ilex Universal shutter time bulb, 1, 1/2, 1/5, 1/10, 1/25, 1/100 second. Both are equipped with finger and cable release. Shipping weights: No. 1, 2 lbs.; No. 1A, 2½ lbs.; 3A, 4¾ lbs.

3K41000—No. 1, Series I, Single Lens. Takes picture size 2¼x3¼ in.. **$ 8.15**

3K41001—No. 1, Series I, Kodar Lens. Takes picture size 2¼x3¼ in.... **10.85**

3K41002—No. 1, Series I, F:7.7. Takes picture 2¼x3¼ inches......... **13.45**

3K41003—No. 1A, Series I, Single Lens. Takes picture size 2½x4¼ in.. **8.95**

3K41004—No. 1A, Series I, Kodar Lens. Takes picture size 2½x4¼ in... **11.65**

3K41005—No. 1A, Series I, F:7.7. Takes picture size 2½x4¼ inches..... **14.35**

3K41006—No. 3A, Series I, Kodar Lens. Takes picture size 3¼x5½ in... **16.15**

3K41009—No. 3A, Series I, F:7.7. Takes picture size 3¼x5½ inches..... **17.95**

Pocket Kodaks—Series II

Focusing Models

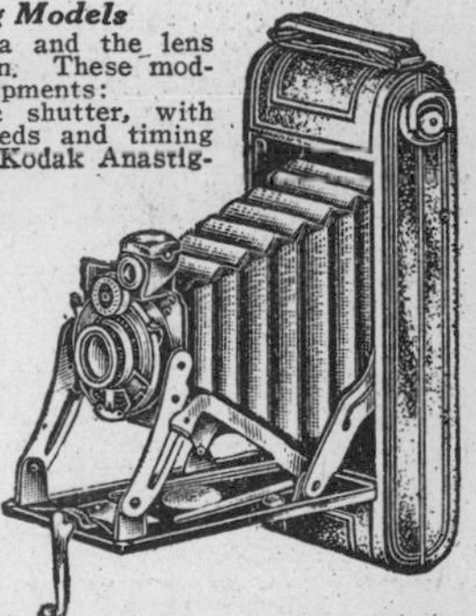

Open the camera and the lens snaps into position. These models offer two equipments:

1. The Diomatic shutter, with four snapshot speeds and timing scale; the famous Kodak Anastigmat F:7:7 lens that makes sharp pictures.

2. Kodex shutter and the semi-anastigmat lens, Kodar F:7.9—adequate equipment for average work.

Both models of the Pocket Kodaks, Series II, **are autographic; both** fit the pocket.

Capacity: No. 1, 6 exposures; No. 1A, 12 exposures. **Focus:** Fixed or adjustable. **Lenses:** Kodar F:7.9, or Kodak Anastigmat F:7.7. **Shutters:** Kodex, speeds 1/25, and 1/50 second; Diomatic, speeds 1/10, 1/25, 1/50 and 1/100 second; both with finger release, time and bulb actions. Brilliant finder, reversible for horizontal or vertical pictures. Two tripod sockets. **Body:** Aluminum. **Covering:** Leather; metal parts finished in nickel and black enamel. Black bellows. Autographic feature. Shpg. wt., 3 lbs.

3K41014—No. 1 Pocket Kodak, Series II, Single Lens. Takes picture size 2¼x3¼ inches.......................... **$11.25**

3K41015—No. 1 Pocket Kodak, Series II, Kodar Lens. Takes picture size 2¼x3¼ inches.......................... **$14.35**

3K41016—No. 1 Pocket Kodak, Series II, F:7.7. Takes picture size 2¼x3¼ inches.......................... **$18.95**

3K41017—No. 1A Pocket Kodak, Series II, Single Lens. Takes picture size 2½x4¼ inches.......................... **$12.55**

3K41018—No. 1A Pocket Kodak, Series II, Kodar Lens. Takes picture size 2½x4¼ inches.......................... **$16.15**

3K41019—No. 1A, Pocket Kodak, Series II, F:7.7. Takes picture size 2½x4¼ inches.......................... **$20.65**

Carrying Cases

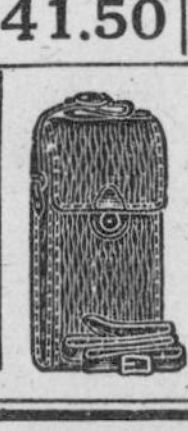

3K42818—Imitation Leather Carrying Case, with shoulder strap, for No. 2 Size Conley Cameras. Shpg. wt., ¾ lb...... **$1.80**

3K42822—Imitation Leather Carrying Case, with shoulder strap, for No. 2A Size Conley Cameras. Shpg. wt., 1¼ lbs.... **$1.98**

3K42825—Imitation Leather Carrying Case, with shoulder strap, for No. 3 Size Conley Cameras. Shpg. wt., 1½ lbs.... **$2.15**

3K42828—Imitation Leather Carrying Case with shoulder strap, for No. 3A Size Conley Cameras. Shpg. wt., 1¾ lbs.... **$2.25**

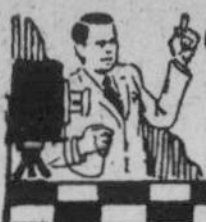

Photographers' Supplies ~

Darko Developing Papers

Red Label Papers and Post Cards
Contrast Emulsion for Soft Negatives

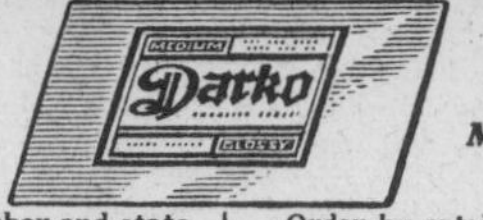

Order by catalog number and state size.

Papers
Glossy surface 3K42641
Velvet surface 3K42642

Post Cards
Glossy surface 3K42660
Velvet surface 3K42661
See price list below.

Green Label Papers and Post Cards
Medium Emulsion for Normal Negatives

Order by catalog number and state size.

Papers
Glossy surface 3K42646
Velvet surface 3K42647

Post Cards
Glossy surface 3K42663
Velvet surface 3K42664
See price list below.

Price List for Improved Darko Papers and Post Cards
Order by catalog number and state size

Size	Shpg. Wt.	Per Doz.	Shpg. Wt.	Per 2 Doz.	Shpg. Wt.	Per One-Half Gross	Shpg. Wt.	Per Gross
2¼x3¼	Not furnished		2 oz.	13c	These sizes not furnished in one-half gross packages. Less than one gross furnished only at 2-dozen rate.		8 oz.	$0.56
2½x4¼			2 oz.	17c			¾ lb.	.68
3¼x4¼			3 oz.	17c			¾ lb.	.90
2⅞x4⅞			3 oz.	17c			1 lb.	.90
4 x5			4 oz.	25c			1 lb.	1.15
3¼x5½			4 oz.	21c			1 lb.	1.07
4 x6	3 oz.	13c	These sizes not furnished in 2-dozen packages. Less than half gross furnished only at dozen rate.		¾ lb.	$0.68	1¼ lbs.	1.30
5 x7	6 oz.	21c			1 lb.	1.02	1¾ lbs.	1.95
6½x8½	7 oz.	34c			1½ lbs.	1.70	2¾ lbs.	3.20
8 x10	8 oz.	47c			1¾ lbs.	2.38	3¾ lbs.	4.50
Post Cards	4 oz	17c	5 oz.	29c	¾ lb.	.77	1¾ lbs.	1.44

Send Us Your Orders for Developing, Printing and Enlarging
We Save You Money
Postage Paid by Us on All Photo Finishing

Prices for developing roll films, any size roll, or number of exposures, per roll, 9c. This does not include any prints from the negative.

Prices for prints and post cards.

Size	Velvet Prints Unmounted, Each	Glossy Prints Unmounted Each
1⅝x2½	4c	5c
2¼x3¼	4c	5c
2½x4¼	5c	6c
3½x3½	5c	6c
3¼x4¼	5c	6c
2⅞x4⅞	6c	7c
4 x5	6c	7c
3¼x5½	6c	7c
Post Cds.	8c	9c

Prices for Enlargements

The average negative, provided it is reasonably sharp, gives fine results when enlarged about four times. For example, an 8x14-inch enlargement from a 2¼x3¼-inch negative.

Size of Enlargement	Black and White: Unmounted, Each	Black and White: Mounted, Each	Sepia: Unmounted, Each	Sepia: Mounted, Each	Hand Colored, Each
5x7 or smaller	$0.33	$0.42	$0.44	$0.52	$1.20
6½x8½	.47	.57	.59	.69	1.35
6x10	.56	.68	.65	.78	1.70
8x10	.58	.74	.70	.86	1.75
7x12	.64	.81	.76	.90	1.85
8x14	.69	.95	.86	1.10	1.95
10x12	.85	1.14	1.01	1.30	2.15
11x14	1.06	1.39	1.24	1.57	2.40
10x17	1.52	2.02	1.77	2.27	3.25
14x17	1.59	2.14	1.84	2.39	3.35
12x20	1.79	2.39	2.15	2.74	3.60
16x20	1.89	2.53	2.25	2.87	3.75

Send Money for Finishing in a Separate Envelope Marked Sears, Roebuck and Co., Chicago, Ill., Dept. 3. Ship Orders and Films Marked the Same Way.

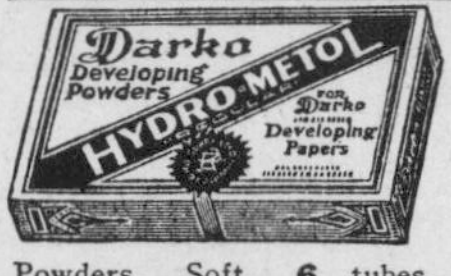

Developers for Paper

3K41936
Hydro - Metol Powders. Contrast.
6 tubes ...**23c**
3K41937
Hydro - Metol Powders. Soft. **6** tubes..............**23c**
3K41938—Amidol Powders. **6** tubes.**23c**
Shipping weight, 5 ounces.

Acid Hypo, 19c a pound

The usual selling price elsewhere of an acid hypo of this grade is from 25c to 35c per lb.
3K41985—Per pound.
(Shipping weight, 1½ lbs.)........... **19c**

Ronix Self Toning Daylight Printing Out Papers

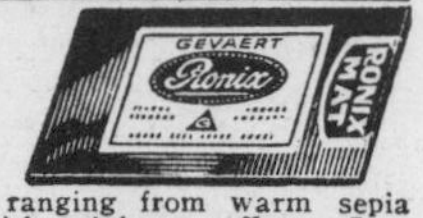

Imported from Belgium. Makes beautiful prints ranging from warm sepia to cold blues with minimum effort. Just print in daylight and fix in ordinary hypo. No other chemicals necessary. No darkroom, no fuss, no complicated processes. Shipping weight, 4 ounces.

	Size	Per Doz.
3K42841	2½x4¼	18c
3K42842	3¼x4¼	20c
3K42843	3¼x5½	25c
3K42844	4 x5	25c
3K42846	Post Cards	30c

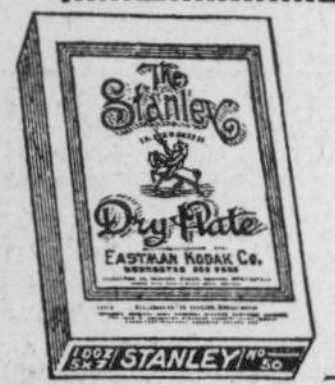

Stanley "Regular" Dry Plates
3K41778

Size	Weight, per Dozen	Shpg. Wt., per Dozen	Per Dozen
3½x3½	16 oz.	1½ lbs.	$0.44
3¼x4¼	17 oz.	1½ lbs.	.52
4 x5	1½ lbs.	2 lbs.	.72
3¼x5½	1⅜ lbs.	1¾ lbs.	.72
4¼x6½	2 lbs.	2¾ lbs.	1.04
5 x7	2⅝ lbs.	3½ lbs.	1.16
6½x8½	4 lbs.	5¾ lbs.	1.76
8 x10	5¾ lbs.	8 lbs.	2.56

Filmpacks

By the use of a film pack adapter you can instantly convert any plate camera, up to the 5x7 size, into a daylight loading film camera. Instead of two exposures with a plate holder, a film pack adapter occupying no more space gives you twelve exposures without reloading camera. Each pack contains twelve films.

Agfa Filmpacks are made in Germany and our tests show that they are by far the finest and fastest film packs on the market. In metal cans from which any single film can be removed without disturbing the remaining films. Speed 400 H and D.

Agfa Filmpacks also fit film pack cameras without an adapter.

*The 3x5¼ Filmpack fits all 3¼x5½ cameras except the Premo and Seneca models of 1913 and later. These cameras take the full 3¼x5½ size.

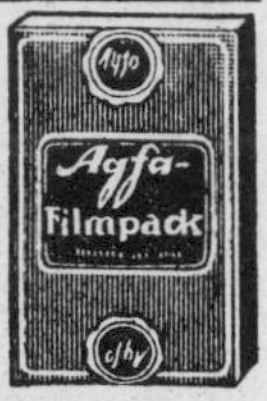

Catalog No.	Size	Shpg. Wt.	Each
3K42669	2¼x3¼	4 ounces	$0.47
3K42670	2½x4¼	5 ounces	.57
3K42671	3¼x4¼	6 ounces	.86
3K42672	4 x5	7 ounces	1.04
3K42673	*3 x5¼	7 ounces	.95
3K42674	*3¼x5½	7 ounces	1.04
3K42675	5 x7	¾ lb.	1.79

Photo Frames
Something New! Something Better!

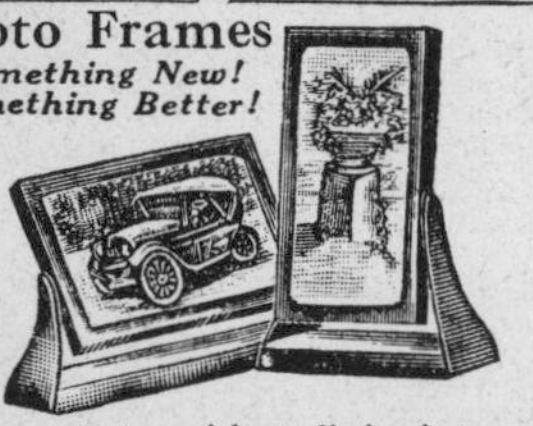

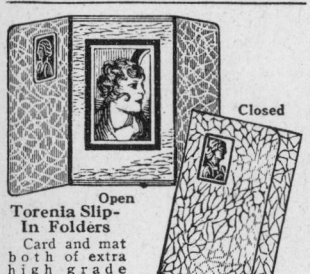

The neatest, quickest little frames for 2¼x4¼-inch (2A) pictures. The base snaps off the frame, the back can be removed, the picture inserted, and the back and base replaced in a few seconds, and your picture is permanently and handsomely framed. Made of all metal in **gold** or **black** color. **Be sure to specify color wanted.** Shipping weight, 6 ounces.
3K43098—Frame for Horizontal Pictures.............. **23c**
3K43097—Frame for Vertical Pictures **23c**

Our Best Trimming Boards

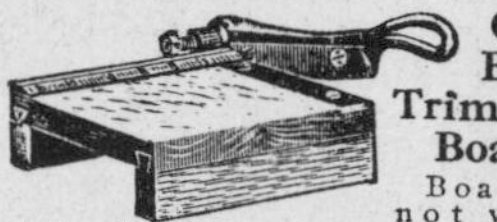

Board will not warp.
Spring joint keeps the two cutting edges always in contact. **3K41472**
Length of blade, 6½ in. Shipping weight, 3¼ lbs..... **$1.80**
Length of blade, 8½ inches. Shipping weight, 4½ pounds.............**$2.40**
Length of blade, 10½ inches. Shipping weight, 6 pounds.....................**$2.80**
Length of blade, 12½ inches. Shipping weight, 8¾ pounds.............**$3.50**

Glass Trays

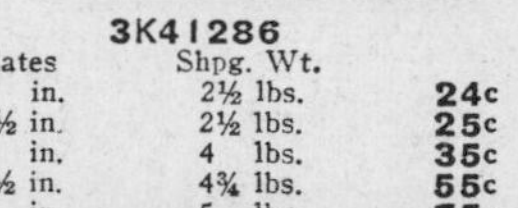

3K41286

For Plates	Shpg. Wt.	
4 x 5 in.	2½ lbs.	24c
3¼x 5½ in.	2½ lbs.	25c
5 x 7 in.	4 lbs.	35c
6½x 8½ in.	4¾ lbs.	55c
8 x10 in.	5 lbs.	75c

Waterproofed Apron

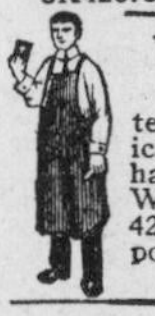

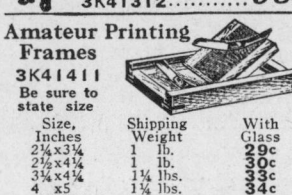

Made of rubber sheeting. Protects the clothing from chemical stains and dirt. Made for hard usage. An excellent value. Will give long service. Length, 42 inches. Shipping weight, 1 pound.
3K41312.......... **95c**

Measuring Glasses

Tumbler shape, for liquids; 2 and 4 ounces; graduated in ounces and drams; the 8-ounce in ounces and ½ and ¼ pints. Very low priced. **State size wanted.**

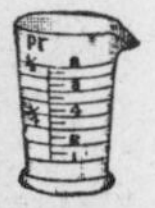

3K41241

Capacity	Shpg. Wt.	
2-oz.	1¼ lbs.	10c
4-oz.	2 lbs.	13c
8-oz.	2¾ lbs.	17c

Amateur Printing Frames

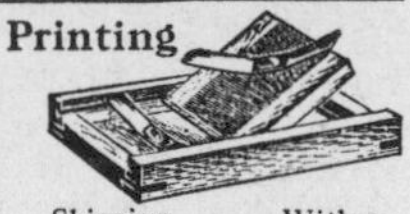

3K41411
Be sure to state size

Size, Inches	Shipping Weight	With Glass
2¼x3¼	1 lb.	29c
2½x4¼	1 lb.	30c
3¼x4¼	1¼ lbs.	33c
4 x5	1¼ lbs.	34c
3¼x5½	1¾ lbs.	36c
3⅝x6	2 lbs.	39c
5 x7	2 lbs.	42c

NOTE—For printing post cards from negatives 3¼x5½ or smaller, use a 3⅝x6 frame with glass.

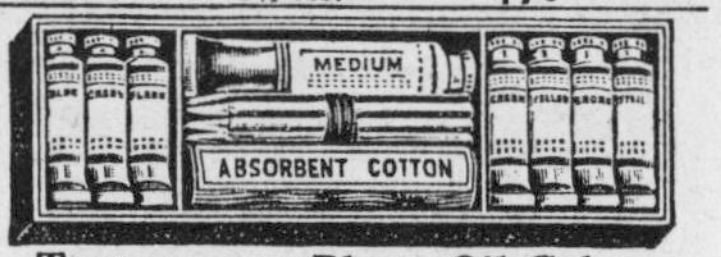

Transparent Photo Oil Colors

Exceptionally easy to use. No skill or artistic ability required to attain really beautiful results. This is the modern way of tinting photographs. Unsurpassed for brilliancy, quality and permanence. Set consists of 7 tubes of high grade transparent oil colors, 1 tube of medium, 6 stumps, and 1 roll of cotton. Size, 7½x2¼ in. Shipping weight, 1 lb.
3K48584.................... **$1.89**

Folders and Mounts

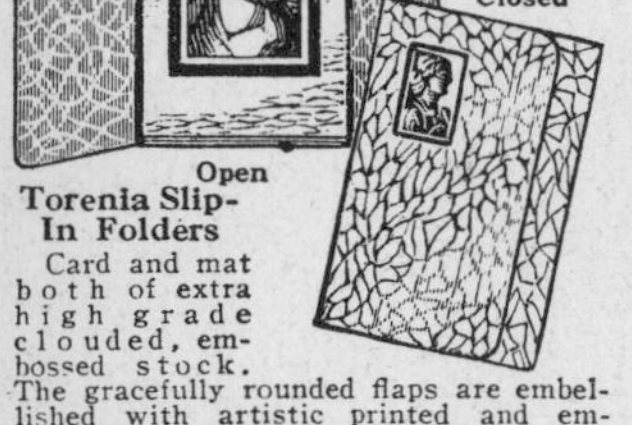

Closed

Open

Torenia Slip-In Folders

Card and mat both of extra high grade clouded, embossed stock.

The gracefully rounded flaps are embellished with artistic printed and embossed designs. Mat has either square or oval opening. Opening is ¼ to ½ inch smaller on each dimension than size print for which it is listed. Horizontal style has square opening only. Sold only in original sealed packages. **Brown only.**

Square Opening	Oval Opening	Size, Closed	For Photos	Per Doz.
3K43214	3K43217	4¼x6	3 x4	70c
3K43215	3K43218	5⅛x7⅛	3½x5	79c
3K43216	3K43219	5⅞x9¼	4 x6	98c

Shipping weight, 3x4, 1 lb.; 3½x5, 1¼ lbs.; 4x6, 1¾ pounds.

Horizontal Opening

3K43107	10 x8	7x5	$1.48
3K43108	11½x9¾	10x8	2.36

Shpg. wt., 7x5, 2¼ lbs.; 10x8, 3 lbs.

Coleus Slip-In Easel Mounts
Just the Thing for Amateur Photos!

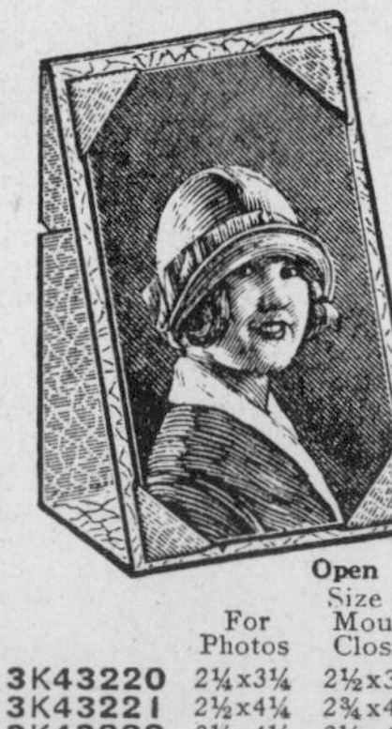

Open

A dainty easel folder mount. May be used either as easel or folder, as shown in illustrations. Picture is held by slipunder corners, no pasting required. Amounting for small pictures that for appearance and ease in using cannot be surpassed.

Made of fine grade stock in two colors, gray or brown. **State color.**

	For Photos	Size of Mount Closed	Shpg. Wt., per Doz.	Per ½ Gross	Per Doz.
3K43220	2¼x3¼	2½x3½	7 oz.	$1.98	36c
3K43221	2½x4¼	2¾x4½	¾ lb.	2.48	44c
3K43222	3¼x4¼	3½x4½	¾ lb.	2.69	48c
3K43223	3¼x5½	3½x5¾	1 lb.	2.98	52c

Magnolia Combination Folder and Easel

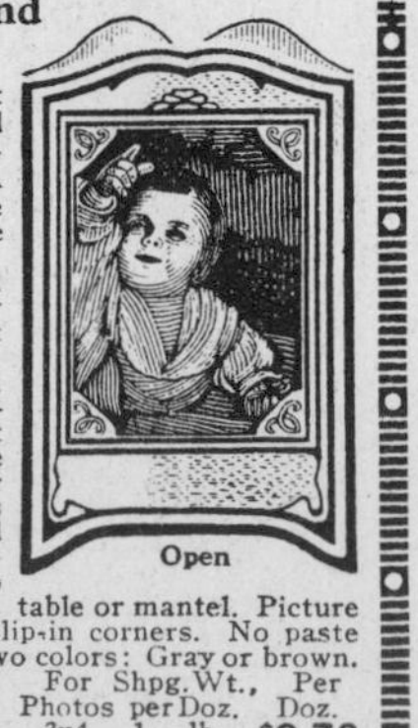

Open

Our best looking and most practical easel. A handsome two-tone easel folder. Will stand up strongly without warping. Professional photographers ask far more than our price. This mount will be an ornament to any dresser, table or mantel. Picture is held by slip-in corners. No paste required. Two colors: Gray or brown. **State color.**

	For Photos	Shpg. Wt. per Doz.	Per Doz.
3K43236	3x4	1 lb.	$0.79
3K43237	3x5	1 lb.	.98
3K43238	4x6	1½ lbs.	1.18

Iris Slip-In Post Card Folders

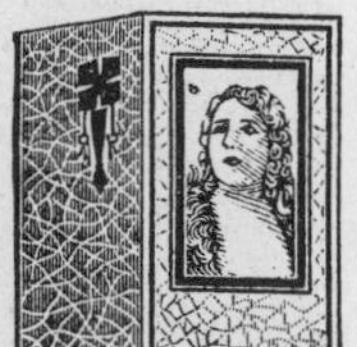

Open

A beautiful slip-in post card folder consisting of a single piece of heavy rough surfaced stock, folded to produce a cut-out mat. Cover is embellished with printed double line border and embossed, printed corner design. Double lines, one wide, one narrow, extend around the picture opening and a double line border is embossed around the outside edge of the mat. The panel shape of this mounting lends distinction to the post card. Shipping wt., per dozen, 1½ pounds.

Colors: Gray or brown. **State color wanted.**

3K43206—Size, closed, 4½x9 inches; opening, 2¾x5 inches; for photos, 3¼x5½ inches.
Per dozen.................. **59c**
Per ½ gross..................**$3.29**
Sold only in original sealed packages.

Lace Curtains at Low Prices

Filet Net Curtains

Unusually attractive pattern in good wearing Filet Net Curtains. At our low price this is excellent value. Size of each curtain about 35 inches wide by 2½ yards long. State catalog number of color wanted. Shipping weight, 1 lb.
24K4298—White
24K4299—Beige
Per pair......$1.98

Silk Fringe

Real value in serviceable quality Filet Net Single Curtain. Will look very neat at your windows. Trimmed with silk bullion fringe. Size, about 35 inches wide by 2½ yards long. State catalog number of color wanted.
24K4426—Ivory.
24K4427—Beige. Each. $1.19
Comes also in size, 44 inches wide by 2½ yards long.
24K4428—Ivory.
24K4429—Beige. Each. $1.39

Big Savings Assured

Curtains offered on this and the following pages are made for us by the leading curtain manufacturers. Our enormous output enables us to buy goods at low prices and offer them direct, to you at money saving prices. Whether you buy the lowest priced or most expensive, you will get real value for your money. Our guarantee of complete satisfaction or money back protects you fully.

ABOUT COLORS AND SIZES. The following are colors of lace curtains and curtain materials: Going from light to dark, ivory is the first shade darker than white. Cream is slightly darker than ivory. Drapery ecru comes next, a soft warm shade of light tan. Beige is a little darker in color than drapery ecru. Curtains may vary from 1 to 2 inches from sizes given; for due to the finishing process they either shrink or stretch slightly. In ordering curtains bear this in mind.

Filet Net Curtains

One of the most popular styles of Filet Net Curtains. Trimmed with silk bullion fringe. Size, about 35 inches wide by 2¼ yards long. State catalog number of color wanted. Shipping weight, ¾ pound.
24K4584—Ivory.
24K4585—Beige. Each.. 90c
Also comes in size 44 inches wide by 2¼ yards long.
24K4586—Ivory.
24K4587—Beige. Ea. $1.19

Silk Fringe

Neatly designed Filet Net Curtain with plain top. Good quality that will give excellent service. A real bargain at our price. Trimmed with silk bullion fringe. Size, about 39 inches wide by 2½ yards long. State catalog number of color wanted. Shpg. wt., 1 lb.
24K4454—Ivory.
24K4455—Beige.
Each......$1.98

Silk Fringe

Popular style of Filet Net Single Curtain. Scalloped at bottom and trimmed with silk bullion fringe. Size, about 35 inches wide by 2¼ yards long. State catalog number of color wanted. Shipping weight, 1 pound.
24K4414—Ivory.
24K4415—Beige. Each... 89c
Comes also in size 44 inches wide by 2¼ yards long.
24K4416—Ivory.
24K4417—Beige. Each $1.15

Filet Net Curtains that are excellent value. The design is especially pleasing and the substantial quality will give good service. Size of each curtain, about 25 inches wide by 2¼ yards long. State catalog number of color wanted. Shipping weight, ¾ pound.
24K4054—White.
24K4055—Beige. Per pr. $1.09

Low priced Filet Net Curtains at a big saving. Will look very attractive at your windows. Substantial quality. Size of each curtain, about 23 inches wide by 2¼ yards long. Loops not included. State catalog number of color wanted. Shipping weight, ¾ pound.
24K4092—White.
24K4093—Beige. Per pair.. 95c

Filet Net Panel

For those who want serviceable, good looking curtains at low prices, this is just the number to buy. Scalloped at bottom and trimmed with silk bullion fringe. Size, about 35 in. wide by 2¼ yards long. State catalog number of color wanted. Shipping weight, 1 pound.
24K4422—Ivory.
24K4423—Beige. Each.. 82c
Comes also in size 43 in. wide by 2¼ yards long.
24K4424—Ivory.
24K4425—Beige. Each. 98c

Sash Curtain

Durable quality Filet Net Sash Curtain made with loops at top ready to hang. Effectively designed and low priced. Size, about 34 inches wide by 29 inches long. Shipping weight, 5 ounces.
24K5091—White only.
Each.................. 35c

Durable quality Single Nottingham Curtain, woven in a design to give the effect of a pair of curtains, but really only one curtain. Size, about 48 inches wide by 2½ yards long. State catalog number of color wanted. Shipping weight, 1 pound.
24K4012—White.
24K4013—Beige. Each 90c

Practical Single Nottingham Lace Curtain, made to use one at a window. An especially pleasing design. Size, about 44 inches wide by 2½ yards long. State catalog number of color wanted. Shipping weight, ¾ pound.
24K4026—White.
24K4027—Beige. Each ... 75c

Lace Lambrequin

Attractive Lace Lambrequin. Made of a serviceable quality of shadow lace in an artistic design. Size, about 48 inches wide by 40 inches long. Shipping weight, 8 ounces.
24K5097—White only.
Each......................50c

You Can Make
Attractive Curtains
Very Easily

20c

18c

Ruffled Marquisette

Good grade Mercerized Curtain Marquisette with hemstitched taped edges. Comes in white, cream or beige. State color. Width, about 36 inches. Shipping weight, per yard, 5 oz.
24K6825—Per yd. **20c**

Fine Quality
Mercerized Hemstitched Curtain Voile with taped edges. Colors: White, cream or beige. State color. Width, 34 in. Shpg. wt., per yard, 4 oz.
24K6811—Per yard.. **20c**

Sunfast Jacquard Gauze
Lustrous quality Rayon Gauze. Made on a cotton warp. Very stylish and popular. Colors: Gold or natural tan. State color. Width, about 35 inches. Shipping weight, per yard, 3 ounces.
24K6330—Per yard.... **28c**

Plain Gauze
Same quality and width as 24K6330 but comes plain. Colors: Rose, blue, gold or natural tan. State color. Shipping wt., per yard, 3 ounces.
24K6331—Per yard.... **28c**

Splendid quality Ruffled Crossbar Curtain Marquisette. White only. Width, about 29 inches. Shipping weight, per yard, 4 oz.
24K6948 Per yard **18c**

Excellent value in checked Ruffled Scrim. White only. Width, about 30 in. Shpg. wt., per yard, 3 oz.
24K6933 Per yard **17c**

Woven Dot Ruffled Curtain Marquisette. Fine quality which will make up into dainty ruffled curtains.
24K6964—Comes in white with fast color dots of pink, blue or gold. State color. Width, about 27 inches. Shipping weight, per yard, 4 ounces. Per yard.................. **32c**
24K6963—Comes in white dots only. Width, about 34 inches. Per yard................. **29c**

FIGURED MARQUISETTE

25c

24K6868   24K6867

24K6869 Width, about 39 inches. Shpg. wt., per yard, 4 oz. Per yard..... **25c**
Comes in white only. Be sure to state catalog number of pattern wanted. Pleasing designs in serviceable quality Curtain Marquisette. Excellent value at our low price.

Ruffled Marquisette
Dainty figured Marquisette that is easily made up into pretty ruffled curtains. Hemstitched band and fast color ruffles of gold, pink or blue. State color. Width, about 34 inches. Shpg. wt., per yard, 4 oz.
24K6940 Per yard....... **35c**

Good quality Crossbar Curtain Marquisette. Comes in white, cream or beige. State color wanted. Width, about 35 inches. Shipping weight, per yard, 4 ounces.
24K6839 Per yard........... **10½c**
Very fine quality Crossbar Curtain Marquisette. White, cream or beige. State color. Width, about 36 inches. Shipping weight, per yard, 4 ounces.
24K6833 Per yard...... **18c**

Artificial Leather Gimp
Matches artificial leathers listed on this page; width, about ½ in. Shpg. wt., per roll, 1¼ lbs. Sold in rolls of 25 yds.
24K685—Per roll............ **30c**
For other Gimp see page 1003.

Colored Check Curtain Voile. Has fancy drawnwork stripes. Colors: Blue, pink or gold. State color. Width, about 35 in. Shpg. wt., yd., 4 oz.
24K6921 Per yard.. **21c**

Artificial Leathers

Artificial Upholstery Leather, used for all kinds of upholstering. Will give excellent service. Comes in black in plain leather finish or tan in Spanish finish. Be sure to state catalog number of color wanted. Width, about 50 inches. Shipping wt., per yard, 1½ pounds.
24K6393¼—Black, plain leather finish. Per yd.. **98c**
24K6381¼—Tan, Spanish finish. Per yard **$1.05**

Chase's Best Quality Extra Heavy Artificial Upholstery Leather that looks and feels like genuine leather. Will not peel or fade, and is unaffected by extreme temperature. Width, about 50 inches. Comes in tan, Spanish finish; also in black, plain leather finish. Be sure to state catalog number of color wanted. Shpg. wt., per yard, 2 lbs.
24K6383¼—Tan, Spanish finish. Per yd.. **$1.80**
24K6384¼—Black, plain leather finish. Per yard.. **$1.70**

Artificial Spanish Leather Oilcloth
This Spanish Leather Oilcloth has a finish and grain which closely resembles that of the real Spanish leather. Heavy drill back, which makes it very serviceable and practical. Suitable for use on desk tops, counters or baseboards; also can be used for furniture upholstering, automobiles and numerous other purposes. At our low price this is exceptional value. Be sure to state catalog number of color wanted. Width, about 50 in. Shpg. wt., per yd., 1½ lbs.
24K6377¼—Black. Per yard....**65c**
24K6378¼—Brown. Per yard.....**65c**
24K6379¼—Blue. Per yard.....**65c**

Metalene Nails
24K690—For upholstering purposes. Colors: Blue, black or tan. State color. Shipping wt., 4 ounces. Package of 100. **10c**

New Novelty Curtain Material usually known as "Ruflette." Made of crossbar scrim with colored openwork stripe and border finished with fancy scallop edge. Comes in white with pink, blue or gold borders. State color wanted. Width, about 30 inches. Shipping weight, per yard, 4 oz.
24K6828—Per yard........ **15c**

Printed Coin Spot Muslin
Durable quality with the popular coin spot. Colors: Blue, pink or gold dots. State color. Width, 34 inches. Shipping weight, per yard, 4 ounces.
24K6930—Per yard......... **14c**
Ruffled Coin Spot Muslin
Same quality and colors as above. Width, 30 inches.
24K6932—Per yard........ **19c**

MONKS CLOTH

Plain Rep Tapestry. Suitable for curtain drapes, furniture coverings, piano covers, table covers, etc. Colors: Myrtle green, mulberry, blue, natural tan or brown. Mention color. Width, about 49 inches. Shpg. wt., per yard, 1 lb.
24K6310—Per yard....... **65c**

TAPESTRIES

Splendid quality heavy mercerized Verdure Tapestry. Beautifully designed and woven with colorings that blend harmoniously. Very popular for upholstery purposes. One color combination of blue, mulberry, green and tan. Width, about 50 inches. Shipping weight, per yard, 1¾ pounds.
24K6336—Per yard...... **$2.85**

Heavy quality Verdure Tapestry that is priced remarkably low. Can be used for upholstering, also for portieres, table covers, etc. Comes in one color combination to harmonize with all furnishings: Black ground with blue, mulberry and tan. Width, about 50 inches. Shipping weight, per yard, 1¾ lbs.
24K6333—Per yard...... **$1.75**

Heavy quality Monk's Cloth made in the basket weave. Suitable for fancywork, drapes, hangings, etc. Comes in natural tan only. Width, about 50 in. Shpg. wt., per yard, 1¼ lbs.
24K6346—Per yard...... **65c**

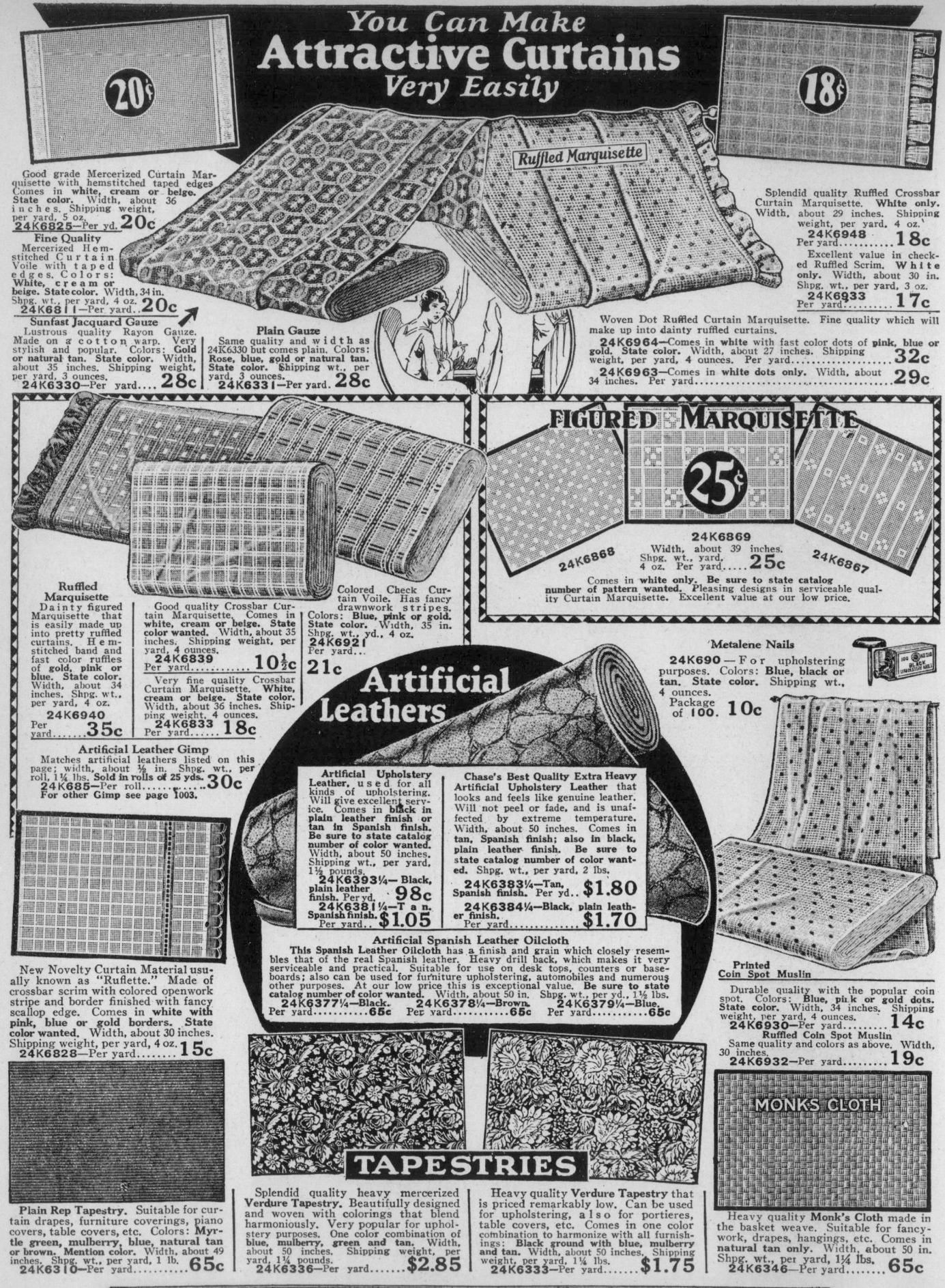

Send Sufficient Money for Postage on Parcel Post Shipments. Any Surplus Will Be Returned

813

Drapery Materials to Beautify the Home

For Information About the Names of Colors, See Page 549

Shantung

Fast Color Damask

Damask *Rayon*

24K6889

Rayon Taffeta
Made of Rayon on cotton warp. Priced very low for this fine quality. Dainty colors of blue, rose, gold or natural tan. State color. Width, about 35 inches. Shipping weight, per yard, 4 ounces.
24K6318—Per yd......45c

Drapery Taffeta
Fine quality highly lustrous Taffeta made of Rayon and cotton. Suitable for bedspreads, drapes, etc. Changeable colors of rose and gold, orchid and gold, blue and gold, or green and gold. State color. Width, about 45 inches. Shipping weight, per yard, 5 ounces.
24K6349—Per yard $1.10

Striped Drapery Damask
Made of Rayon and cotton. Perfectly blended fast color combinations in which following colors predominate: Black, blue, rose or green. State color. Width, 36 in. Shpg. wt., per yd., 8 oz.
24K6314 87c Yard

Crinkled Austrian Cloth
Made of Rayon and cotton. Suitable for drapes, bedspreads, etc. Rose, blue, gold or orchid (lavender). State color. Width, 40 in. Shipping weight, per yard, ¾ pound.
24K6324 Per yard.....59c

Fine quality Crinkled Cotton Material in striped design. Width, 40 inches.
24K6323—Comes in natural tan. Per yard...49c

Austrian Cloth

Fast Color Damask
The Rayon makes it so lustrous and the cotton warp makes it more serviceable. Colors: Blue, rose, mulberry or black predominating. State color. Width, 36 in. Shpg. wt., yd., 8 ounces.
24K6315 Per yard.....87c
24K6889—Cornice Description and Price.

Lustrous Rayon
Woven on cotton warp. A beautiful drapery material at a big saving in price. Colors: Gold, blue, mulberry or rose. State color. Width, about 36 in. Shpg. wt., per yard, 4 oz.
24K6302 Per yard 79c
Fringe. See Below for Price.

Good quality, highly mercerized Cotton Shantung. Colors: Natural tan, brown, rose or blue. State color. Width, about 35 inches. Shpg. wt., yard, 6 oz.
24K6361—Per yard.....37c

Sunfast Drapery Shantung of excellent quality, priced exceptionally low. A serviceable, practical drapery material; also suitable for blouses, dresses, etc. Colors: Natural tan, brown, rose or blue. State color. Width, 35 inches. Shipping weight, yard, 6 ounces.
24K6371—Per yard.....49c

Tussah Silk

Pongee

Velour

Tussah Silk
Drapery Tussah, made of Tussah Silk on a cotton warp. The woven design makes this a very effective drapery material. Colors: Blue, rose, gold or natural tan. State color. Width, about 36 inches. Shpg. wt., yd., 5 oz.
24K6338 Per yard. 45c

Sunfast Velour
Extra good quality Sunfast Cotton Velour Plush. Suitable for making portieres, drapes, hangings, table runners, upholstery, etc. Velour is especially desirable just at present for decorative purposes. Rich, high grade drapery material, priced very low for this wonderful quality. Comes in blue, mulberry, brown, rose or taupe gray. State color. Width, about 54 inches. Shipping weight, 1½ pounds.
24K6385—Per yard.....$1.98

Woven Figures
Mercerized Denim with woven figures. Can be used for covers, drapes, fancywork, etc. Comes in blue, mulberry, brown or green. State color wanted. Width, about 36 in. Shpg. wt., per yd., ¾ lb.
24K6298 Per yard.........32c

Pongee
Half Silk Tussah Pongee, the ever popular drapery material. Colors: Rose, blue, natural tan or mulberry. State color. Width, about 35 in. Shipping weight, per yard, 4 ounces.
24K6360—Per yard.........38c

Excellent quality Pongee, made of silk and cotton tussah, better quality than 24K6360 above. Comes in natural tan only. Width, about 35 inches. Shipping weight, per yard, 4 ounces.
24K6363—Per yard.........64c

Damask

Poplin

Fast Color Striped Damask
Exceptionally fine quality. Lustrous Rayon combined with highly mercerized cotton yarns are woven to give a delightful effect. Color combinations to harmonize with all decorative schemes: Blue and mulberry; black and gold; rose and taupe, or taupe and blue. State color. Width, 50 inches. Shipping weight, per yard, ¾ pound.
24K6353—Per yard. $1.95
24K6354—Fast color Damask. Same high quality as 24K6353 listed above, but comes in allover design. Colors: Black, blue, mulberry or taupe grounds. State color. Width, 50 in. Shpg. wt., per yard, ¾ lb. Per yard. **$1.95**

12 in.

Sold By the Scallop Only
Tapestry Valance
Beautiful fast color polychrome colorings on black ground will harmonize with any decorative scheme. Firmly woven of cotton yarns and decorated with lustrous Rayon. Trimmed with silk bullion fringe. Depth, 14 inches. Pattern repeats itself every 12 inches. Shpg. wt., 6 oz.
24K6307—Per scallop (12 in.)..57c

Cornice Fringe
An attractive new style to replace the wood cornices and shaped valances. Made of Rayon bullion fringe with fancy heading. Can be used over any kind of curtains or drapes. Will make your window treatment look ever so much more effective. Nine inches deep and comes in six beautiful polychrome color combinations in which the following colors predominate. Rose, blue, black, green, mulberry or taupe to harmonize with any color scheme. State color wanted. Made with a pocket attachment on back to slip over your curtain rod. Shpg. wt., per yd., 4 oz.
24K6889—Per yard...$1.19

Drapery Poplin
Splendid quality, highly mercerized. Will make up into very attractive drapes; also suitable for many other purposes. Colors: Blue, rose, brown, natural tan or green. State color. Width, about 36 inches. Shipping weight, per yard, 8 ounces.
24K6357—Yard.........52c
See 24K6884 to the right for Edge to match.

Room Arrangements
What Furnishings to Use
How to Select Colors
by an
Expert Interior Decorator
See Page 1017

Cotton Edging
Cotton Edging to match drapery materials. Colors: Copenhagen blue, dark blue, rose, brown, green, mulberry or natural linen. State color. Width, ⅝ inch. Shipping weight, per yard, 1 ounce.
24K6884—Per yard...4c
Cotton Edging similar to above, but 1 in. wide. Colors to match all cretonnes and drapery materials. State color. Shpg. wt., per yd., 1 oz.
24K6885—Per yard.....5c

Rayon Bullion Fringe
Fast Color Bullion Fringe. Furnished to match drapery materials and curtain nets. State color. Shpg. wt., per yard, 2 oz.
24K6887 Width, 2 in. Per yard......19c
24K6888 Width, 3 in. Per yard....25c

Rayon Edge
Sunfast Rayon and Cotton Edging to match our drapery materials. Width, ¾ inch. State color. Shpg. wt., per yard, 1 oz.
24K6886—Per yd......9c

Ball Fringe to match curtain scrim and cretonnes. State color. Will not match silks. Shipping weight, per yard, 1 ounce.
24K6880—Per yard....7c

Attractive Portieres
Priced Very Low

Velour Portieres

Beautiful, heavy quality, Double Faced Velour Portieres, a different color on each side. These high grade portieres are priced much lower than you would be able to purchase them elsewhere. Finished with French hem. Color combinations of **rose and blue; mulberrry and blue; gold and blue,** or **taupe and blue.** State color combination wanted.

24K3750—Size of each portiere, about 33 inches wide by 7½ feet long. Shipping weight, per pair, 6½ pounds.
Per pair.......................... **$15.50**

24K3753—Size of each portiere, about 47 inches wide by 7½ feet long. Shipping weight, per pair, 8 pounds.
Per pair.......................... **$20.50**

Grenadine Portieres

Striped Snowflake Grenadine Portieres of excellent quality. Make a suitable light weight hanging between doors or at your windows. Size of each portiere, about 36 inches wide by 2½ yards long. Colors: **Light tan ground with stripes of blue, rose, brown or green.** State color. Shpg. wt., 1¼ lbs.
24K3009—Per pair................................. **$2.25**

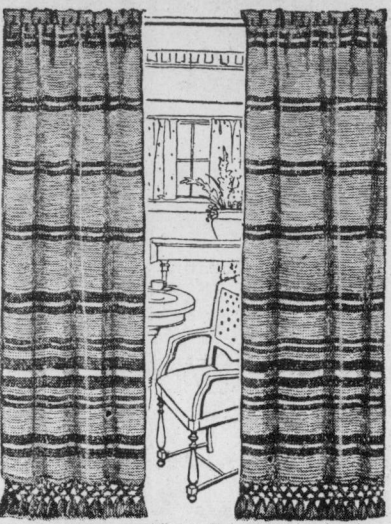

Grenadine Portieres

Light Weight Grenadine Portieres with Rayon stripes. Can be used between doors and also at your windows. Headed ready to hang. Size of each portiere, 36 inches wide by 2½ yards long. Colors: **Blue, rose, tan or green.** State color. Shipping weight, 1 lb.

24K3010—Per pair........ **$1.65**

$2⁴⁹

Fringed Tapestry Portieres

These are excellent value. The strong, heavy yarns are woven into a design that is very attractive. Colors: **Plain brown or plain mulberry;** also color combinations of **green and red; brown and green,** or **blue and gold.** State color. Size of each portiere, about 30 inches wide by 9 feet long, including fringe. Shipping weight, 3 lbs.

24K3011—Per pair.............. **$2.49**

For information about the names of colors see page 549

$5⁷⁵

Tapestry Portieres

Attractively designed. Carefully w o v e n a n d finished to give the best possible service. You will be well pleased when you see the beautiful quality of these portieres. Colors: **Mulberry, blue, brown or green.** State color wanted. Size of each portiere, about 50 inches wide by 9 feet long, including fringe. Shipping weight, 5 pounds.

24K3073—Per pair..................... **$5.75**

How to Choose Colors and Furnishings for Your Home Told by an Expert Interior Decorator. See Page 1017

$3⁴⁹

Tapestry Portieres

The dependable quality and the popular price make these Tapestry Portieres especially desirable. Richly designed and finished with knotted fringe. Plain colors of **brown or green;** also color combinations of **blue and gold; brown and green,** or **green and red.** State color. Size of each portiere, about 38 inches wide by 8½ feet long, including fringe. Shipping weight, 3 pounds.

24K3021—Per pair.......... **$3.49**

Brighten Up Your Home With These Couch Covers and Drapes

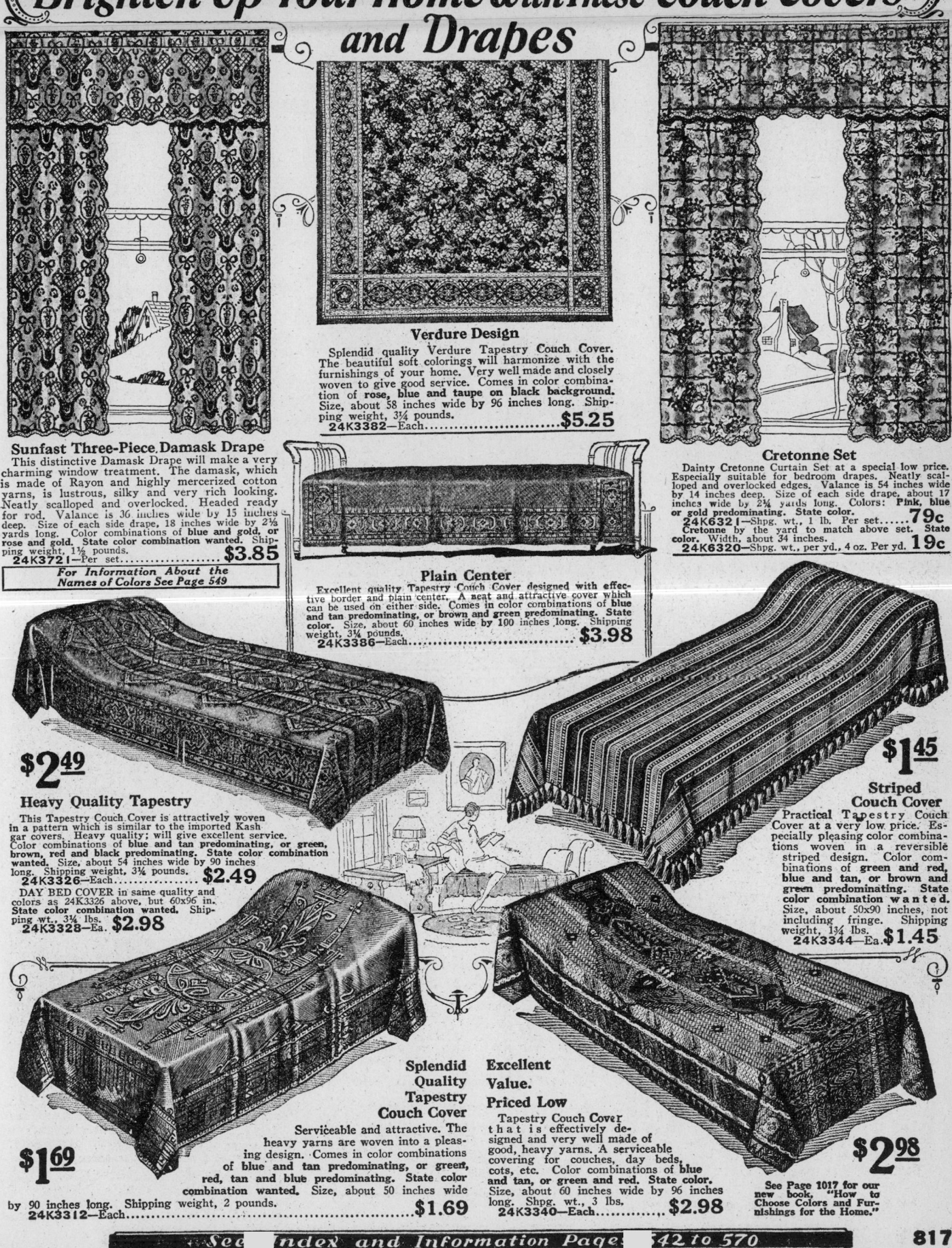

Verdure Design

Splendid quality Verdure Tapestry Couch Cover. The beautiful soft colorings will harmonize with the furnishings of your home. Very well made and closely woven to give good service. Comes in color combination of rose, blue and taupe on black background. Size, about 58 inches wide by 96 inches long. Shipping weight, 3¾ pounds.
24K3382—Each.......................$5.25

Sunfast Three-Piece Damask Drape

This distinctive Damask Drape will make a very charming window treatment. The damask, which is made of Rayon and highly mercerized cotton yarns, is lustrous, silky and very rich looking. Neatly scalloped and overlocked. Headed ready for rod. Valance is 36 inches wide by 15 inches deep. Size of each side drape, 18 inches wide by 2⅓ yards long. Color combinations of blue and gold, or rose and gold. State color combination wanted. Shipping weight, 1½ pounds.
24K3721—Per set.....................$3.85

For Information About the Names of Colors See Page 549

Cretonne Set

Dainty Cretonne Set at a special low price. Especially suitable for bedroom drapes. Neatly scalloped and overlocked edges. Valance is 54 inches wide by 14 inches deep. Size of each side drape, about 17 inches wide by 2¼ yards long. Colors: Pink, blue or gold predominating. State color.
24K6321—Shpg. wt., 1 lb. Per set......79c
Cretonne by the yard to match above set. State color. Width, about 34 inches.
24K6320—Shpg. wt., per yd., 4 oz. Per yd. 19c

Plain Center

Excellent quality Tapestry Couch Cover designed with effective border and plain center. A neat and attractive cover which can be used on either side. Comes in color combinations of blue and tan predominating, or brown and green predominating. State color. Size, about 60 inches wide by 100 inches long. Shipping weight, 3¼ pounds.
24K3386—Each.......................$3.98

$2.49 — Heavy Quality Tapestry

This Tapestry Couch Cover is attractively woven in a pattern which is similar to the imported Kashgar covers. Heavy quality; will give excellent service. Color combinations of blue and tan predominating, or green, brown, red and black predominating. State color combination wanted. Size, about 54 inches wide by 90 inches long. Shipping weight, 3¼ pounds.
24K3326—Each.......................$2.49
DAY BED COVER in same quality and colors as 24K3326 above, but 60x96 in. State color combination wanted. Shipping wt., 3¼ lbs.
24K3328—Ea. $2.98

$1.45 — Striped Couch Cover

Practical Tapestry Couch Cover at a very low price. Especially pleasing color combinations woven in a reversible striped design. Color combinations of green and red, blue and tan, or brown and green predominating. State color combination wanted. Size, about 50x90 inches, not including fringe. Shipping weight, 1¾ lbs.
24K3344—Ea. $1.45

$1.69 — Splendid Quality Tapestry Couch Cover

Serviceable and attractive. The heavy yarns are woven into a pleasing design. Comes in color combinations of blue and tan predominating, or green, red, tan and blue predominating. State color combination wanted. Size, about 50 inches wide by 90 inches long. Shipping weight, 2 pounds.
24K3312—Each.......................$1.69

$2.98 — Excellent Value. Priced Low.

Tapestry Couch Cover that is effectively designed and very well made of good, heavy yarns. A serviceable covering for couches, day beds, cots, etc. Color combinations of blue and tan, or green and red. State color. Size, about 60 inches wide by 96 inches long. Shpg. wt., 3 lbs.
24K3340—Each............,.$2.98

See Page 1017 for our new book, "How to Choose Colors and Furnishings for the Home."

Big Values ~ Unequaled Elsewhere

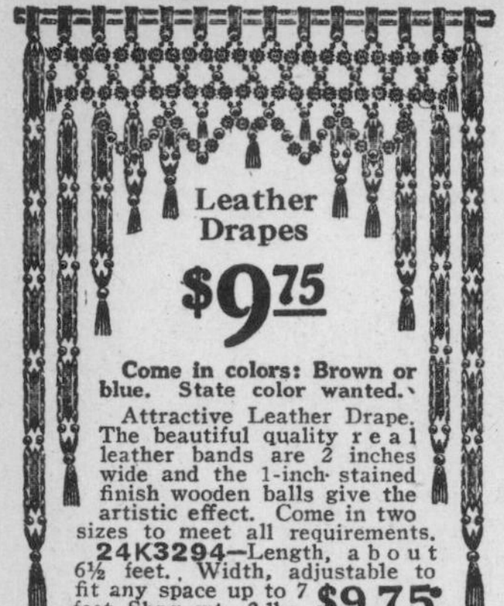

Leather Drapes

$9.75

Come in colors: Brown or blue. State color wanted.

Attractive Leather Drape. The beautiful quality real leather bands are 2 inches wide and the 1-inch stained finish wooden balls give the artistic effect. Come in two sizes to meet all requirements.

24K3294—Length, about 6½ feet. Width, adjustable to fit any space up to 7 feet. Shpg. wt., 3 lbs. **$9.75**

24K3293—Length, about 5 feet. Width, adjustable to fit any space up to 5 feet. Shipping weight, 2½ lbs. **$6.75**

Leather Valance. To match above drape. **State color.**

24K3284—Length, 42 inches. Width, adjustable to fit any space up to 7 feet. Shipping weight, 2¾ lbs. **$8.25**

24K3283—Length, 32 inches. Width, adjustable to fit any space up to 5 feet. Shipping weight, 1½ lbs. **$5.65**

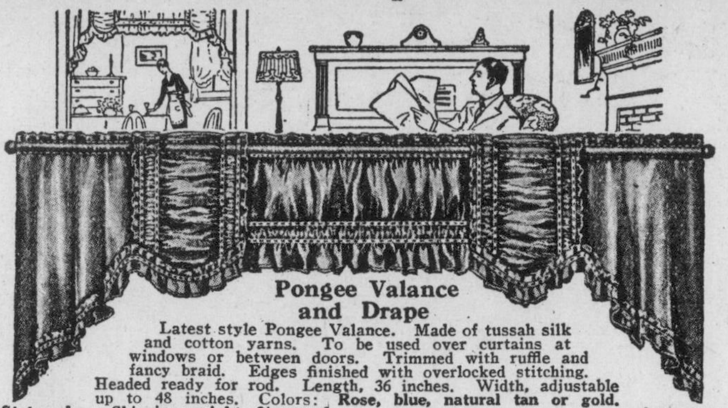

Pongee Valance and Drape

Latest style Pongee Valance. Made of tussah silk and cotton yarns. To be used over curtains at windows or between doors. Trimmed with ruffle and fancy braid. Edges finished with overlocked stitching. Headed ready for rod. Length, 36 inches. Width, adjustable up to 48 inches. Colors: **Rose, blue, natural tan or gold. State color.** Shipping weight, ¾ pound.

24K3732—Each **$2.98**

Three-Piece Pongee Drape. To match above valance. Set consists of valance, 17 inches long, width, adjustable up to 48 inches and side drapes each 16 inches wide by 2¼ yards long. Tiebacks included. **State color.** Shipping weight, 1¼ lbs.

24K3742—Per set **$4.75**

$1.98

24K3180—Three color combinations: **Blue and gold; brown and green, or green and red. State color combination wanted.** Length, 30 inches. Width, adjustable up to 5 feet. Shipping weight, 2 pounds.

Attractive Rope Valance which will give excellent service. Made with eight ¾-inch strands of chenille cord and eleven ⅝-inch strands of plain twisted cord.

$2.75

24K3190—Three color combinations: **Blue and gold; brown and green, or green and red. State color combination wanted.** Length, 32 inches. Width, adjustable up to 6 feet. Shipping weight, 2½ pounds.

Excellent quality Rope Valance Drapery. Will look very attractive as a drapery at your doors. Heavy strands are ¾-inch chenille cords and center strands are ⅝-inch plain cord. Tapestry bands are 3¾ in. wide.

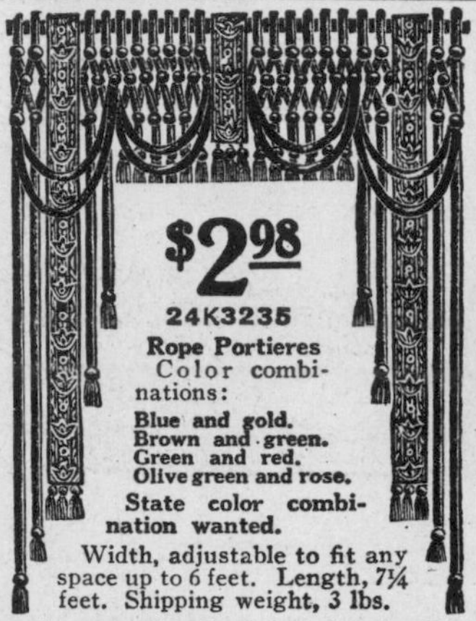

$2.98

24K3235

Rope Portieres

Color combinations:

Blue and gold.
Brown and green.
Green and red.
Olive green and rose.

State color combination wanted.

Width, adjustable to fit any space up to 6 feet. Length, 7¼ feet. Shipping weight, 3 lbs.

An exceptionally low price for this Rope Portiere. The 4-inch tapestry bands are combined with heavy ⅝-in. chenille cords. A serviceable and effective drapery.

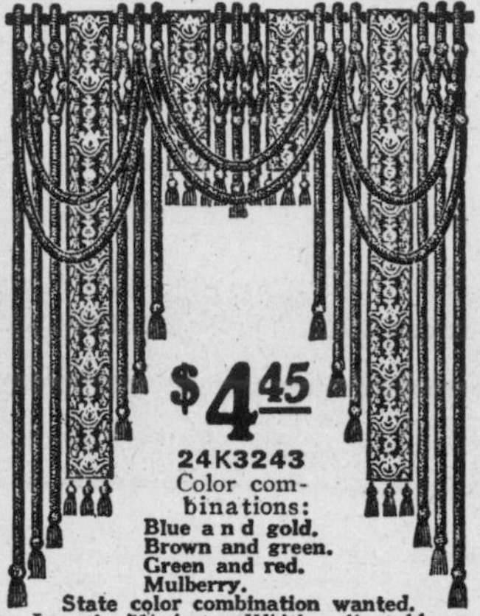

$4.45

24K3243

Color combinations:

Blue and gold.
Brown and green.
Green and red.
Mulberry.

State color combination wanted.

Length, 7¼ feet. Width, adjustable up to 7 feet. Shipping weight, 3¾ pounds.

Rope Portiere of splendid quality in a very effective overdrape design. The 4½-inch tapestry bands and the ⅞-inch chenille cords combine to make an attractive drapery for your doors.

Order Blanks Are in Back of This Catalog

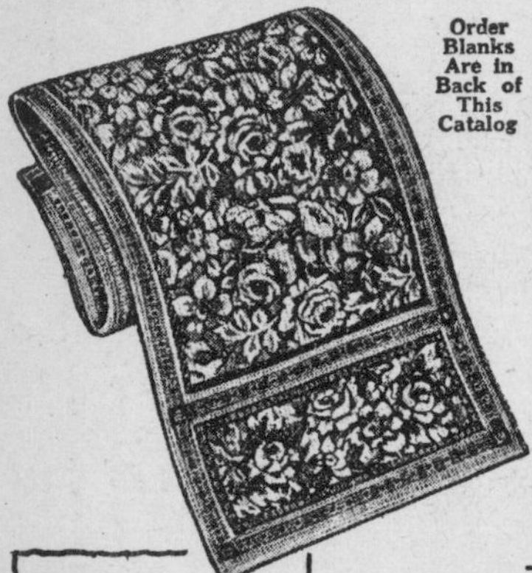

Imported Table Runner

A pretty table runner will add much to the decoration of your room. A wonderfully low price for this Washable Tapestry Table Runner. The attractive verdure design combines very effectively the following color combinations: **Rose or Blue predominating on green ground. State color wanted.** Size, about 16x50 in. Shpg. wt., ¾ lb.

24K3452
Each **98c**

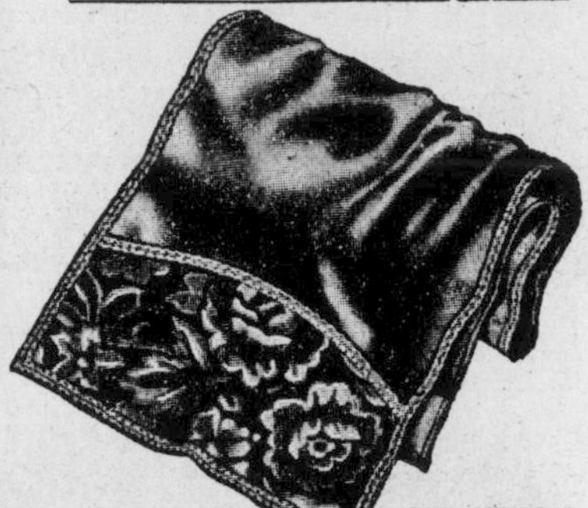

Velour and Tapestry Table Runner

An effective decoration. Made of beautiful quality velour with rich heavy tapestry at both ends. Trimmed all around with fancy braid. Colors: **Blue, brown, mulberry or taupe. State color.** Size, 16x54 in. Shipping weight, 1 pound.

24K3472
Each **$2.98**

Piano Scarf to match above. **State color.** Size, 16x72 inches.

24K3473
Each **$3.65**

Smaller Size

Same as above, but smaller size to be used for end tables, radio cabinets, stands, etc. Size, about 10x20 inches. Colors: **Blue, brown, mulberry or taupe. State color:** Shpg. wt., 8 oz.

24K3474
Each **$1.19**

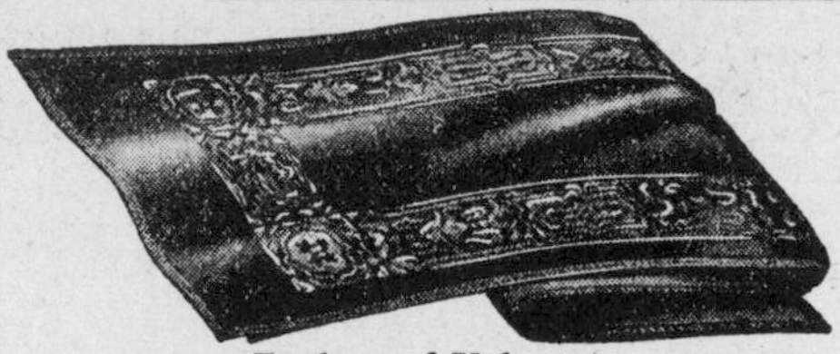

Embossed Velour

High Grade Table Runner made of beautiful quality velour with attractive embossed border. Neatly overlocked all around. Colors: **Blue, mulberry or taupe. State color.**

Cat. No.	Size	Shpg. Wt.	Each
24K3490	16x36 in.	1 lb.	$1.15
24K3491	16x50 in.	1 lb.	1.49
24K3492	16x72 in.	1¼ lbs.	1.98

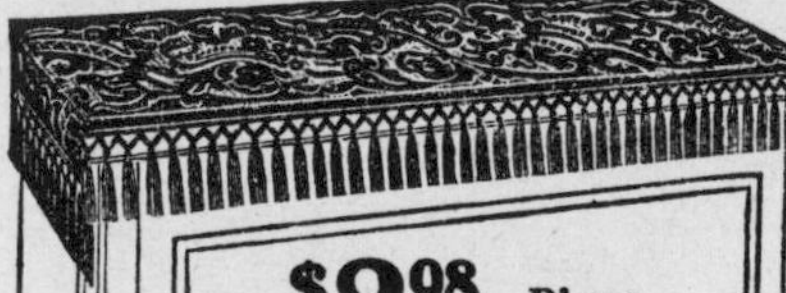

$2.98 **Piano Drape**

Brocaded Cotton Velour Piano Drape in a beautifully embossed design. Trimmed with 5-inch silk fringe. Colors: **Blue, rose, green or brown. State color wanted.** Size, about 24x90 inches, including fringe. Shipping weight, 1¼ pounds.

24K3475 .... **$2.98**

See Page 1017 for our new book, "How to Choose Colors and Furnishings for the Home.

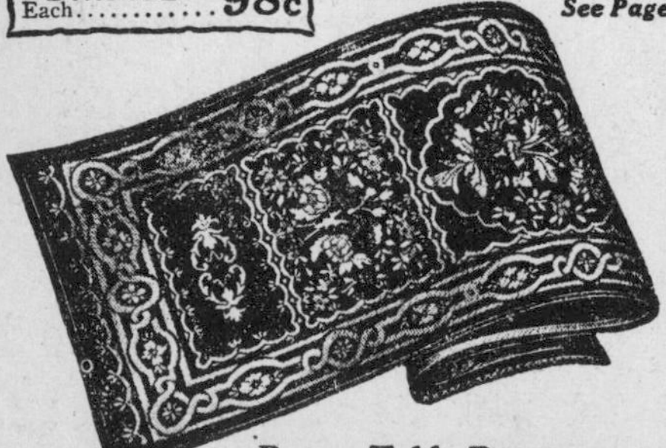

Rayon Table Runner

Lustrous, silky Table Runner that is rich looking and very decorative. Made of Rayon (artificial silk) and cotton and neatly overlocked all around. You can't appreciate the beauty and effectiveness of this latest style runner unless you see it yourself. Comes in one beautifully blended color combination of black, gold, rose and blue. Size, about 17x52 in. Shpg. wt., ¾ lb.

24K3455—Each **$1.89**

Radio Scarf

Same quality and color as above, but comes in a smaller size, suitable to be used on your radio cabinets, end tables, etc. Size, abt. 9x36 in. Shpg. wt., 6 oz.

24K3456—Each **98c**

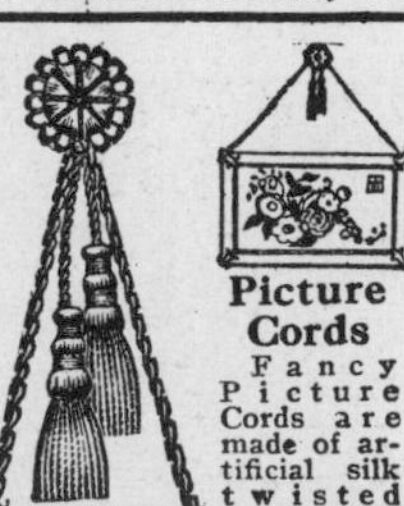

Picture Cords

Fancy Picture Cords are made of artificial silk twisted cords with picture wire foundation. Have two beautiful tassels of bullion fringe. Molding hook attached. They are high grade and add to the decoration of your rooms. Cords are 48 inches long. Color combinations: **Black and gold; blue and gold; sand and blue, or taupe and blue; also plain solid colors of French gray, old gold or mulberry. State color wanted.** Shipping weight, 4 ounces.

24K762—Each... **75c**

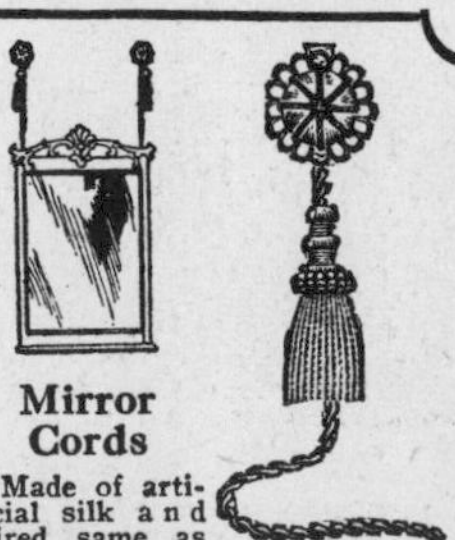

Mirror Cords

Made of artificial silk and wired same as picture cords. Come with fancy ornament and moulding hook attached. Have beautiful bullion fringe tassel. Length, 48 inches. Color combinations: **Black and gold; blue and gold; sand and blue, or taupe and blue; also plain solid colors of French gray, old gold or mulberry. State color wanted.** Shipping wt., 6 oz.

24K758—Pair.... **$1.10**

Mirrors Are on Page 908

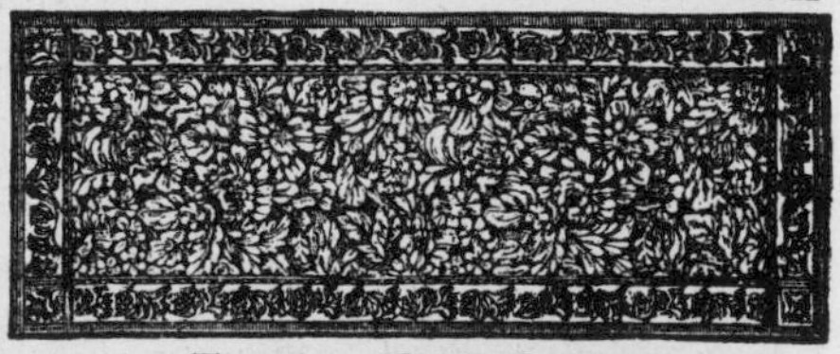

Tapestry Table Runner and Piano Scarf

Excellent quality. The rich verdure design is offset by a neat border. **Comes in one color combination only in which blue, tan, mulberry and black are blended effectively.** Shipping weight, 1 lb.

24K3466—Table Runner. Size about 19x50 inches **$1.50**

24K3467—Piano Scarf to match. Size, about 19x72 inches **2.25**

For Other Table Scarfs See Pages 244 and 245

We Make Our Own Window Shades

6 Easy Points of Information

Needed to Fill Your Order for Shades Correctly

1—**Catalog Number** of the quality and style you wish. If number has a fraction in it be sure to include it.

2—**Quantity.** State how many you need of each size.

3—**Widths.** Be sure to tell us whether the widths are cloth measure or tip to tip of roller. Read carefully instructions for measuring on page 821.

4—**Brackets.** For outside brackets give cloth measure. For inside brackets give tip to tip measure of roller, including the small metal tips which fit into the brackets. State whether you wish **outside** or **inside brackets.** Refer to Diagrams No. 1 and No. 2 on page 821. If shades are to hang on the face of window casings specify **outside brackets.** If shades are to be placed inside the casings specify **inside brackets.**

5—**Lengths.** Give lengths. Measure from top to bottom of windows and add 6 inches to allow easy raising and lowering.

6—**Color.** State color. Select from colors listed in the quality and style that you wish.

Water Color Opaque Shades

Machine Oil Opaque Shades

Plain and Fringed
Water Color Opaque Shades

Good quality, mounted on patent spring, nickel trimmed rollers. While excellent shades and very good quality for the money, we recommend our Oil Opaque Shades, listed at the right, for greater economy and service. Water Color Opaque Shades are furnished 36 inches wide, or less, and in the following colors: Sand, light brown, buff, white, slate, olive green or dark green. State color and size wanted and be sure to state whether measurements are for inside or outside brackets. Shipping weight, 1¾ pounds.

We can furnish Water Color Opaque Shades plain or trimmed with cotton bullion fringe as listed below.

Width of Cloth	Length	Plain Shades	Each	Fringed Shades	Each
36 inches	5 feet	24K1005¼	45c	24K1066¼	58c
36 inches	6 feet	24K1000¼	52c	24K1061¼	65c
36 inches	7 feet	24K1020¼	59c	24K1081¼	72c
36 inches	8 feet	24K1040¼	66c	24K1101¼	79c

Cut down less than 36 inches wide. Be sure to state width.

Width	Length	Plain Shades	Each	Fringed Shades	Each
Less than 36 inches	5 feet	24K1015½	48c	24K1076½	63c
Less than 36 inches	6 feet	24K1010½	55c	24K1091½	70c
Less than 36 inches	7 feet	24K1030½	62c	24K1091½	77c
Less than 36 inches	8 feet	24K1050½	69c	24K1111½	84c

The above shades are not made wider than 36 inches.

Plain and Fringed
Machine Oil Opaque Shades

Made from high quality machine made oil opaque cloth and mounted on substantial nickel trimmed rollers. Colors: Sand, light brown, buff, white, slate, olive green or dark green. State color and size wanted; also specify whether measurements are for inside or outside brackets. Shipping weight, 1¾ lbs.

We can furnish our Machine Oil Opaque Shades plain or trimmed with cotton bullion fringe as listed below.

Width of Cloth	Length	Plain Shades	Each	Fringed Shades	Each
36 inches	5 feet	24K1125¼	59c	24K1196¼	$0.75
36 inches	6 feet	24K1120¼	71c	24K1191¼	.85
36 inches	7 feet	24K1140¼	81c	24K1211¼	.95
38 inches	7 feet	24K1160¼	92c	24K1231¼	1.05
		24K1182¼	95c	24K1283¼	1.10

Cut down less than 36 inches wide. Be sure to state width.

Width	Length	Plain Shades	Each	Fringed Shades	Each
Less than 36 inches	5 feet	24K1135½	62c	24K1206½	$0.80
Less than 36 inches	6 feet	24K1130½	74c	24K1201½	.90
Less than 36 inches	7 feet	24K1150½	84c	24K1221½	1.00
Less than 36 inches	8 feet	24K1170½	95c	24K1241½	1.10

For shades over 38 inches wide see 24K1300½ and 24K1500½ on page 820 and add price of 24K1311½ or 24K1511½ extra for fringe.

Shade Pulls

Cotton Covered Ring Shade Pull with Cord to match our window shades. State color. Shpg. wt., 2 oz. 24K730 Each.....2c	High Grade Rayon Shade cord and Tassel. Tassel is 5 inches long. Dark green, olive green, buff, cream, white, sand or light brown. State color. 24K747 Each...................15c	Shipping weight, 2 ounces.	Solid Steel Ring Shade Pull. 1 inch in diameter. Bright polished finish. Same as furnished with our shades. Shpg. wt., per dozen, ¾ pound. 24K705 Doz......10c

Scalloped Machine Oil

Domestic Holland

Superior Quality Smooth Finish Shades
Mounted on Nickel Trimmed Rollers

These very popular shades resemble closely the well known high grade Holland shades. A special finishing process gives them a smooth texture and remarkable wear resisting qualities. Not to be confused with cheaper grades offered elsewhere. Exceptionally low prices. Colors: White, ecru or linen color. State color and size wanted and be sure to state whether measurements are for inside or outside brackets. Shipping weight, 1¾ lbs.

Catalog No.	Width of Cloth	Length	Each
24K1260¼	36 inches	5 feet	65c
24K1261¼	36 inches	6 feet	75c
24K1262¼	36 inches	7 feet	85c

Cut down less than 36 inches wide.

Catalog No.	Width	Length	Each
24K1263½	Less than 36 in.	5 ft.	69c
24K1264½	Less than 36 in.	6 ft.	79c
24K1265½	Less than 36 in.	7 ft.	89c

The above shades are not made wider than 36 inches.

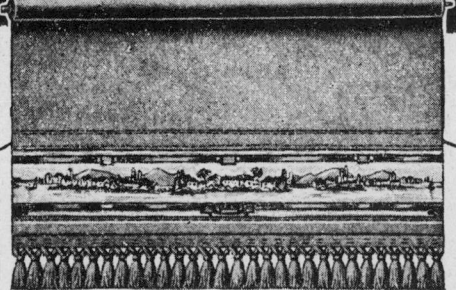

Venetian Design Art Panel Window Shades

Machine Oil Quality mounted on nickel trimmed rollers. These art panel window shades are wonderful values at our low prices. Very well made of extra fine quality machine oil opaque shade cloth. Art panel is 6 inches wide. Colors: Sand, buff, olive green, dark green or white. Shipping weight, 1¾ pounds.

24K1644¼—Trimmed with knotted cotton fringe. Size, 36 inches wide by 6 feet long. Each **$1.15**

24K1645¼—Same as above, but without fringe. Size, 36 inches wide by 6 feet long. Each **.98**

Scalloped and Trimmed
With Cotton Bullion Fringe

This popular style of shade will give a very pleasing appearance to your windows. They are made from an excellent quality of machine made oil opaque shade cloth and are mounted on nickel trimmed rollers. Come in dark green, olive green, buff, white, sand color or light brown. Be sure to state color wanted and whether measurements are for inside or outside brackets. Shipping weight, 1¾ pounds.

Catalog No.	Width of Cloth	Length	Each
24K1669¼	36 inches	5 feet	$0.80
24K1672¼	36 inches	6 feet	.90
24K1673¼	36 inches	7 feet	1.00

Cut down less than 36 inches wide. (State width.)

Catalog No.	Width	Length	Each
24K1670½	Less than 36 inches	5 feet	$0.90
24K1671½	Less than 36 inches	6 feet	1.00
24K1674½	Less than 36 inches	7 feet	1.10

For extra size Scalloped Shades, see price list of 24K1312½, Machine Oil Opaque Quality, listed on page 820.

Big Values in Floor Coverings

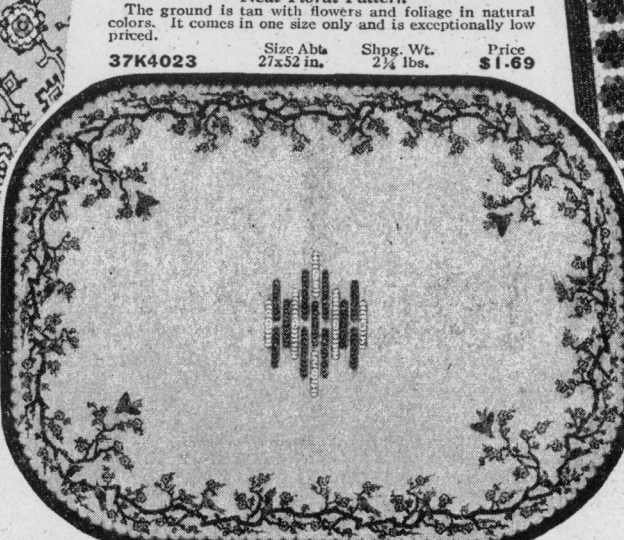

Tapestry Brussels Rug
Neat Floral Pattern
The ground is tan with flowers and foliage in natural colors. It comes in one size only and is exceptionally low priced.

	Size Abt.	Shpg. Wt.	Price
37K4023	27x52 in.	2¼ lbs.	$1.69

Bargain of Bargains
Seamless Tapestry Brussels Rug
If you are in need of a good grade large size Seamless Tapestry Brussels Rug, this is your opportunity to make a big saving. These rugs were purchased way below their usual price and we are offering them to you on the same low basis as they were purchased. We guarantee this is value that we will not again be able to repeat. Tan ground with old rose, blue and black figures with a neat border in contrasting colors.

	Size, Abt.	Shpg. Wt.	
37K5786	11¼x12 ft.	30 lbs.	$17.95

OVAL JAPANESE GRASS RUG
New Imported Grass Rug unusual in shape and design. Its beauty will renew the attractiveness of your sunparlor. Made of finest specially selected rice straw, with strong double cotton warp binder. Brown and blue design on natural tan ground. Blue border.

	Size, About	Shpg. Wt.	
37K2720	9 x12 ft.	20 lbs.	$5.65
37K2721	4½x 7½ ft.	7 lbs.	1.69
37K2722	6 x 9 ft.	10 lbs.	2.98
37K2726	30 x60 in.	3 lbs.	.98

Genuine Printed Linoleum Rug
The country's biggest value in a Genuine Printed Linoleum Rug. This guaranteed linoleum rug is a typical Sears value. It simply can't be equaled elsewhere. The pattern is essentially a kitchen design and one of the most effective ever produced. The dark figures in both the center and border are in a deep blue coloring; the lighter figures are in cream coloring outlined in black.

	Size, Abt.	Shpg.Wt.	
37K2590	9x12 ft.	56 lbs.	$8.75
37K2592	6x 9 ft.	29 lbs.	4.50
37K2595	9x10½ ft.	48 lbs.	7.95

Good Grade Seamless Japanese Grass Rug
Always popular. Make housework easy, especially during the summer months. Particularly appropriate for informal rooms, bedrooms, porches and summer cottages. Made of a good grade rice straw securely bound together with a good double warp cotton binder. Natural tan ground, figures in blue, green and brown and border to match.

	Size, Abt.	Shpg. Wt.	
37K2700	9x12 ft.	22 lbs.	$4.45
37K2703	5½x 9 ft.	10 lbs.	2.25
37K2705	8x10 ft.	19 lbs.	3.45
37K2707	3x 6 ft.	4 lbs.	.79

Genuine Fiber Rug
We are introducing an entirely new rug in this book which we know will interest you. It's an unusually durable floor covering flatly woven of specially treated fiber which gives it unusual resistance against the elements. The colors are fast—a damp mop cleans the rug and doesn't hurt it. Comes in two color combinations: Tan, brown and taupe, or blue, taupe and green. **State color combination.**

	Size, Abt.	Shpg. Wt.	
37K3350	9x12 ft.	22 lbs.	$9.98
37K3351	4x 7 ft.	7 lbs.	3.49
37K3352	6x 9 ft.	11 lbs.	6.25
37K3359	9x15 ft.	28 lbs.	13.95
37K1305	30x60 in.	3 lbs.	2.29

Biggest Bargain in Imported Grass Rug
Our highest grade seamless Imported Grass Rug. Durability, service and beauty are woven right into it; it is a suitable floor covering for any room. The rice straw is uniformly high grade, woven with a strong durable cotton warp. Jaspe taupe ground, figures in blue and brown, blue border.

	Size, Abt.	Shpg. Wt.	
37K2710	9x12 ft.	22 lbs.	$5.65
37K2711	4x 7 ft.	7 lbs.	1.59
37K2712	6x 9 ft.	12 lbs.	2.95

WOOL and FIBER RUGS

Jute Tapestry Brussels Rug at a Very Low Price
You will not find a better bargain in a printed Jute Tapestry Brussels Rug than this. A delightfully bright rug. Will add attractiveness to any interior. Tan and blue combination.

	Size, About	Shpg. Wt.	
37K1374	27x54 in.	2 lbs.	98c

A Typical Sears Value
Best Seamless Jute Tapestry Rug Made
Here is the best Jute Tapestry Rug in the country at a lower price than you can obtain this quality anywhere else. We know you are getting more than your money's worth when you buy this rug. You can match it up with any rug of its kind for quality and price in any store and we are confident that you will find it supreme. Taupe ground with figures in blue and brown.

37K3400—Size, about 9x12 ft. Shpg. wt., 19 pounds. **$11.50**

37K1384—Size, about 27x54 inches. Shpg. wt., 2 lbs.. **$1.05**

Another Big Value in a Floral Seamless Jute Tapestry Rug
Here is another wonderful buy in America's best Seamless Jute Tapestry Rug at a price usually paid for rugs of inferior foreign make. We know that there are no imported jute tapestry brussels rugs that can compare with what we offer you here. If you want a low priced rug you can't go wrong on this beautiful floral design. Ground color is dark tan with flowers and foliage in natural colors.

37K3410—Size, about 9x12 ft. Shpg. wt., 19 lbs. **$11.65**

37K1364—Size, about 27x54 in. Shpg. wt., 2 lbs. **$1.10**

Our Best Quality Wool and Fiber Rug
Whatever your color scheme, this fine quality Wool and Fiber Rug is sure to add charm to your room. You will marvel at the service this rug will give. Comes in three color combinations: Brown, blue and gray with border of contrasting color. **State color.**

	Size, About	Shpg. Wt.	
37K3480	9 x12 ft.	24 lbs.	$14.95
37K3481	4½x 7½ ft.	8 lbs.	7.69
37K3484	7½x 9 ft.	15 lbs.	11.98

Latest Design—Wool and Fiber
A Seamless Wool and Fiber Rug of guaranteed good quality at this price is a rare opportunity for saving. The taupe ground and blue and tan figures of this new pattern are woven of good grade wool and fiber yarns.

	Size, About	Shpg. Wt.	
37K3570	9 x12 ft.	20 lbs.	$11.50
37K3574	7½x 9 ft.	13 lbs.	8.95

Great Bargain! Wool and Fiber Rug
Where else could you buy a real serviceable rug in the 9x12-ft. size for $5.95? Comes in blue and tan or green and red. **State color combination in ordering.**

	Size, About	Shpg. Wt.	
37K3000	9 x12 ft.	13 lbs.	$5.95
37K3004	7½x 9 ft.	8 lbs.	3.98
37K3005	8¼x10½ ft.	12 lbs.	5.65
37K3007	12 x12 ft.	17 lbs.	9.75

High in Quality—Low in Price
An extra heavy Seamless Wool and Fiber Rug that will give a distinct note of beauty to your home. It is easy to clean, will lie flat and stand hard wear. Two-tone blue ground, figures in tan and blue.

	Size, About	Shpg. Wt.	
37K3590	9 x12 ft.	24 lbs.	$10.45
37K3592	6 x 9 ft.	12 lbs.	6.25
37K3595	8¼x10½ ft.	18 lbs.	9.95
37K3598	12 x15 ft.	24 lbs.	20.45

Wonderful Value—Wool and Fiber Rug
This beautiful Seamless Wool and Fiber Rug comes in the new two-tone tan combination. It is a serviceable floor covering at an unusually low price.

	Size, About	Shpg. Wt.	
37K3030	9 x12 ft.	16 lbs.	$7.45
37K3034	7½x 9 ft.	9 lbs.	4.95
37K3033	9 x 9 ft.	10 lbs.	6.25

We Guarantee Safe Delivery of All Our Shipments

Genuine Linoleum RUGS

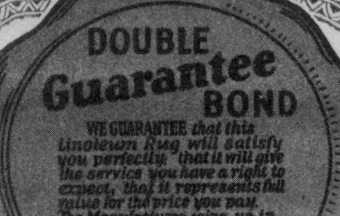

DOUBLE Guarantee BOND
WE GUARANTEE that this Linoleum Rug will satisfy you perfectly; that it will give the service you have a right to expect, that it represents full value for the price you pay. The Manufacturer joins us in this double Guarantee.
SEARS, ROEBUCK AND CO.

Genuine Jaspe Linoleum Rugs
Guaranteed the Best. Here we have for you an entirely new idea in decoration—a Jaspe Linoleum Rug with plain band borders and graceful floral pattern. The jaspe ground wears like inlaid linoleum. Comes in tan or taupe. **State color.**

	Size		Shpg. Wt.	
37K2820	9	x12 ft.	61 lbs.	$15.50
37K2822	7½x 9 ft.		37 lbs.	9.50
37K2825	9 x10½ ft.		56 lbs.	13.95
37K2826	12 x12 ft.		88 lbs.	19.75
37K2828	12 x15 ft.		98 lbs.	25.50

LOOK FOR OUR DOUBLE GUARANTEE BOND

When you buy Genuine Linoleum Rugs you are buying the greatest wear giving fabric ever made. There is no substitute! We guarantee these splendid linoleum rugs to outwear any other hard surface rugs made. Coined names—all names ending in "o-leum"—do not give you what linoleum, the one and only genuine, insures.

Listed on this page is an assortment of the finest linoleum rugs made—printed, inlaid and the latest style jaspe rugs with figured ornamentations. The last mentioned is entirely new and the World's Largest Store is the only mail order house in America to show it. All at Sears prices, which means big savings.

Artistic Linoleum Rug
The most beautiful and exquisitely decorated printed Linoleum Rug we've ever seen. Rose or taupe. Fully guaranteed, yet priced to fit a modest income. **State color.**

	Size		Shpg. Wt.	
37K2840	9 x12 ft.		56 lbs.	$13.50
37K2842	7½x 9 ft.		35 lbs.	8.75
37K2845	9 x10½ ft.		48 lbs.	11.85
37K2846	12 x12 ft.		77 lbs.	17.95
37K2848	12 x15 ft.		93 lbs.	21.95

Very Latest Design
We know this is a big bargain in a guaranteed printed Linoleum Rug. Bright and neat and easy to keep clean.

	Size		Shpg. Wt.	
37K2460	9 x12 ft.		56 lbs.	$12.75
37K2462	6 x 9 ft.		29 lbs.	6.50
37K2464	7½x 9 ft.		35 lbs.	8.25
37K2465	9 x10½ ft.		48 lbs.	11.50

Genuine Jaspe Linoleum Rugs
Guaranteed the best. Quality of material, artistry of workmanship and economy of purchase combine to make this Rug a floor covering that takes its place with the finest. The beautiful jaspe ground wears like inlaid linoleum, and has figured ornaments in new rich colors. Taupe or blue. **State color.**

	Size		Shpg. Wt.	
37K2810	9 x12 ft.		61 lbs.	$15.50
37K2812	6 x 9 ft.		32 lbs.	7.25
37K2814	7½x 9 ft.		37 lbs.	9.50
37K2815	9 x10½ ft.		56 lbs.	13.95

Chinese Design on Printed Linoleum
A most satisfactory Rug from the practical point of view. The jaspe ground and all over Chinese pattern does not show soil and cleans easily. Makes any room cozy. Tan or blue. **State color.**

	Size		Shpg. Wt.	
37K2860	9x12 ft.		56 lbs.	$11.50
37K2862	6x 9 ft.		29 lbs.	5.75
37K2865	9 10½ ft.		48 lbs.	10.25

← Genuine Linoleum Rug
Who else but the World's Largest Store can offer you a value like this in a genuine, heavy printed Linoleum Rug?

	Shpg. Size, Wt., Ft. Lbs.	
37K2550	9x12 56	$8.95
37K2554	7½x9 35	5.85
37K2556	12x12 103	13.50
37K2558	12x15 124	16.50

Genuine Inlaid Linoleum Rugs →
For beauty, service and quality genuine Inlaid Rugs have no equal. The designs and colorings go through to the burlap back, which assures years of hard service. We guarantee this rug to satisfy you in every respect.

	Shpg. Size, Wt., Ft. Lbs.	
37K2880	9x12 70	$19.85
37K2886	12x12 97	27.75

Special!

37K503
84¢
24x36 in.

The Country's leading value—Hit and Miss Rugs—woven of fine, clean rags

Rag Rug or Runner

37K677
$1.59
27x90 in.
37K519
39¢
18x36 in.

RAG RUGS

37K631
$1.19
24x36 in.
A
37K661
98¢
37K494
$2.59
27x54 in.
T
B
D
37K471
89¢
18x36 in.
37K601
$1.29
20x30 in.
C
E
F
R
G
37K643
$1.79
24x36 in.
S
37K663
$2.25
24x36 in.
I
P
Q
H
37K614
$1.39
25x50 in.
37K404
$1.29
25x50 in.
L
O
J
37K1804
$2.98
30x54 in.
37K671
$1.69
18x30 in.
N
M
K
37K194
$2.59
27x48 in.

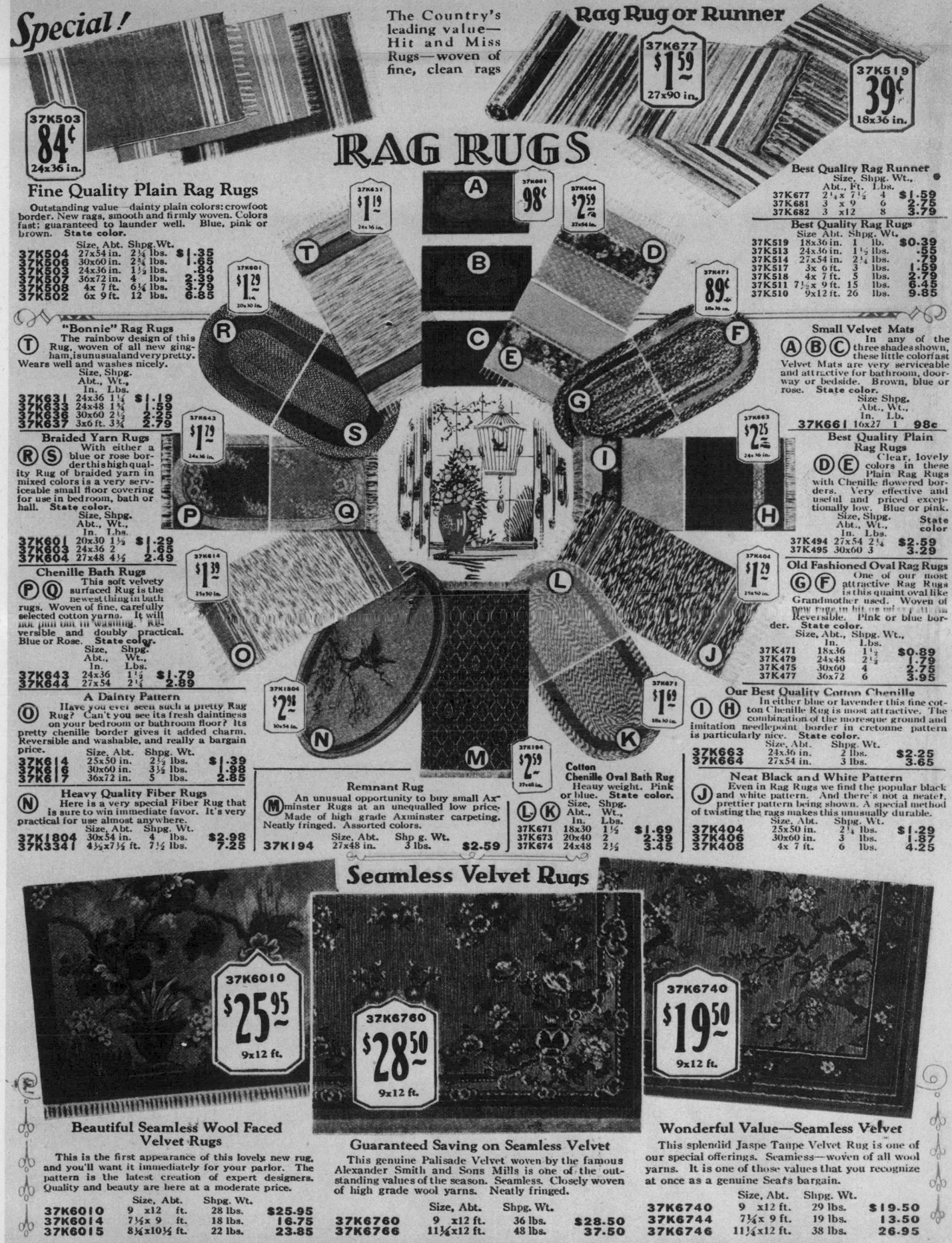

Fine Quality Plain Rag Rugs

Outstanding value—dainty plain colors: crowfoot border. New rags, smooth and firmly woven. Colors fast; guaranteed to launder well. Blue, pink or brown. **State color.**

	Size, Abt.	Shpg. Wt.	
37K504	27x54 in.	2¼ lbs.	$1.35
37K506	30x60 in.	2¾ lbs.	1.65
37K503	24x36 in.	1½ lbs.	.84
37K507	36x72 in.	4 lbs.	2.39
37K508	4x 7 ft.	6¼ lbs.	3.79
37K502	6x 9 ft.	12 lbs.	6.85

"Bonnie" Rag Rugs

(T) The rainbow design of this Rug, woven of all new gingham, is unusual and very pretty. Wears well and washes nicely.

	Size, Abt., In.	Shpg. Wt., Lbs.	
37K631	24x36	1¼	$1.19
37K633	24x48	1¾	1.59
37K636	30x60	2½	2.25
37K637	3x6 ft.	3¾	2.79

Braided Yarn Rugs

(R) (S) With either a blue or rose border this high quality Rug of braided yarn in mixed colors is a very serviceable small floor covering for use in bedroom, bath or hall. **State color.**

	Size, Abt., In.	Shpg. Wt., Lbs.	
37K601	20x30	1½	$1.29
37K603	24x36	2	1.65
37K604	27x48	4½	2.49

Chenille Bath Rugs

(P) (Q) This soft velvety surfaced Rug is the newest thing in bath rugs. Woven of fine, carefully selected cotton yarns. It will not pull out in washing. Reversible and doubly practical. Blue or Rose. **State color.**

	Size, Abt., In.	Shpg. Wt., Lbs.	
37K643	24x36	1½	$1.79
37K644	27x54	2¼	2.89

A Dainty Pattern

(O) Have you ever seen such a pretty Rag Rug? Can't you see its fresh daintiness on your bedroom or bathroom floor? Its pretty chenille border gives it added charm. Reversible and washable, and really a bargain price.

	Size, Abt.	Shpg. Wt.	
37K614	25x50 in.	2½ lbs.	$1.39
37K616	30x60 in.	3½ lbs.	1.98
37K617	36x72 in.	5 lbs.	2.85

Heavy Quality Fiber Rugs

(N) Here is a very special Fiber Rug that is sure to win immediate favor. It's very practical for use almost anywhere.

	Size, Abt.	Shpg. Wt.	
37K1804	30x54 in.	4 lbs.	$2.98
37K3341	4½x7½ ft.	7½ lbs.	7.25

Remnant Rug

(M) An unusual opportunity to buy small Axminster Rugs at an unequalled low price. Made of high grade Axminster carpeting. Neatly fringed. Assorted colors.

	Size, Abt.	Shpg. Wt.	
37K194	27x48 in.	3 lbs.	$2.59

Cotton Chenille Oval Bath Rug

(L) (K) Heavy weight. Pink or blue. **State color.**

	Size, Abt., In.	Shpg. Wt., Lbs.	
37K671	18x30	1½	$1.69
37K673	20x40	2	2.39
37K674	24x48	2½	3.45

Best Quality Rag Runner

	Size, Abt., Ft.	Shpg. Wt., Lbs.	
37K677	2¼x 7½	4	$1.59
37K681	3 x 9	6	2.75
37K682	3 x12	8	3.79

Best Quality Rag Rugs

	Size Abt.	Shpg. Wt.	
37K519	18x36 in.	1 lb.	$0.39
37K513	24x36 in.	1½ lbs.	.55
37K514	27x54 in.	2¼ lbs.	.79
37K517	3x 6 ft.	3 lbs.	1.59
37K518	4x 7 ft.	5 lbs.	2.79
37K511	7½x 9 ft.	15 lbs.	6.45
37K510	9x12 ft.	26 lbs.	9.85

Small Velvet Mats

(A) (B) (C) In any of the three shades shown, these little colorfast Velvet Mats are very serviceable and attractive for bathroom, doorway or bedside. Brown, blue or rose. **State color.**

	Size Abt., In.	Shpg. Wt., Lb.	
37K661	16x27	1	98c

Best Quality Plain Rag Rugs

(D) (E) Clear, lovely colors in these Plain Rag Rugs with Chenille flowered borders. Very effective and useful and priced exceptionally low. Blue or pink. State color

	Size, Abt., In.	Shpg. Wt., Lbs.	
37K494	27x54	2¼	$2.59
37K495	30x60	3	3.29

Old Fashioned Oval Rag Rugs

(G) (F) One of our most attractive Rag Rugs is this quaint oval like Grandmother used. Woven of new rags in hit or miss pattern. Reversible. Pink or blue border. **State color.**

	Size, Abt., In.	Shpg. Wt., Lbs.	
37K471	18x36	1½	$0.89
37K479	24x48	2½	1.79
37K475	30x60	4	2.75
37K477	36x72	6	3.95

Our Best Quality Cotton Chenille

(I) (H) In either blue or lavender this fine cotton Chenille Rug is most attractive. The combination of the moresque ground and imitation needlepoint border in cretonne pattern is particularly nice. **State color.**

	Size, Abt.	Shpg. Wt.	
37K663	24x36 in.	2 lbs.	$2.25
37K664	27x54 in.	3 lbs.	3.65

Neat Black and White Pattern

(J) Even in Rag Rugs we find the popular black and white pattern. And there's not a neater, prettier pattern being shown. A special method of twisting the rags makes this unusually durable.

	Size, Abt.	Shpg. Wt.	
37K404	25x50 in.	2¼ lbs.	$1.29
37K406	30x60 in.	3 lbs.	1.87
37K408	4x 7 ft.	6 lbs.	4.25

Seamless Velvet Rugs

37K6010
$25.95
9x12 ft.
37K6760
$28.50
9x12 ft.
37K6740
$19.50
9x12 ft.

Beautiful Seamless Wool Faced Velvet Rugs

This is the first appearance of this lovely new rug, and you'll want it immediately for your parlor. The pattern is the latest creation of expert designers. Quality and beauty are here at a moderate price.

	Size, Abt.	Shpg. Wt.	
37K6010	9 x12 ft.	28 lbs.	$25.95
37K6014	7½x 9 ft.	18 lbs.	16.75
37K6015	8¼x10½ ft.	22 lbs.	23.85

Guaranteed Saving on Seamless Velvet

This genuine Palisade Velvet woven by the famous Alexander Smith and Sons Mills is one of the outstanding values of the season. Seamless. Closely woven of high grade wool yarns. Neatly fringed.

	Size, Abt.	Shpg. Wt.	
37K6760	9 x12 ft.	36 lbs.	$28.50
37K6766	11¼x12 ft.	48 lbs.	37.50

Wonderful Value—Seamless Velvet

This splendid Jaspe Taupe Velvet Rug is one of our special offerings. Seamless—woven of all wool yarns. It is one of those values that you recognize at once as a genuine Sears bargain.

	Size, Abt.	Shpg. Wt.	
37K6740	9 x12 ft.	29 lbs.	$19.50
37K6744	7¼x 9 ft.	19 lbs.	13.50
37K6746	11¼x12 ft.	38 lbs.	26.95

SMALL RUGS

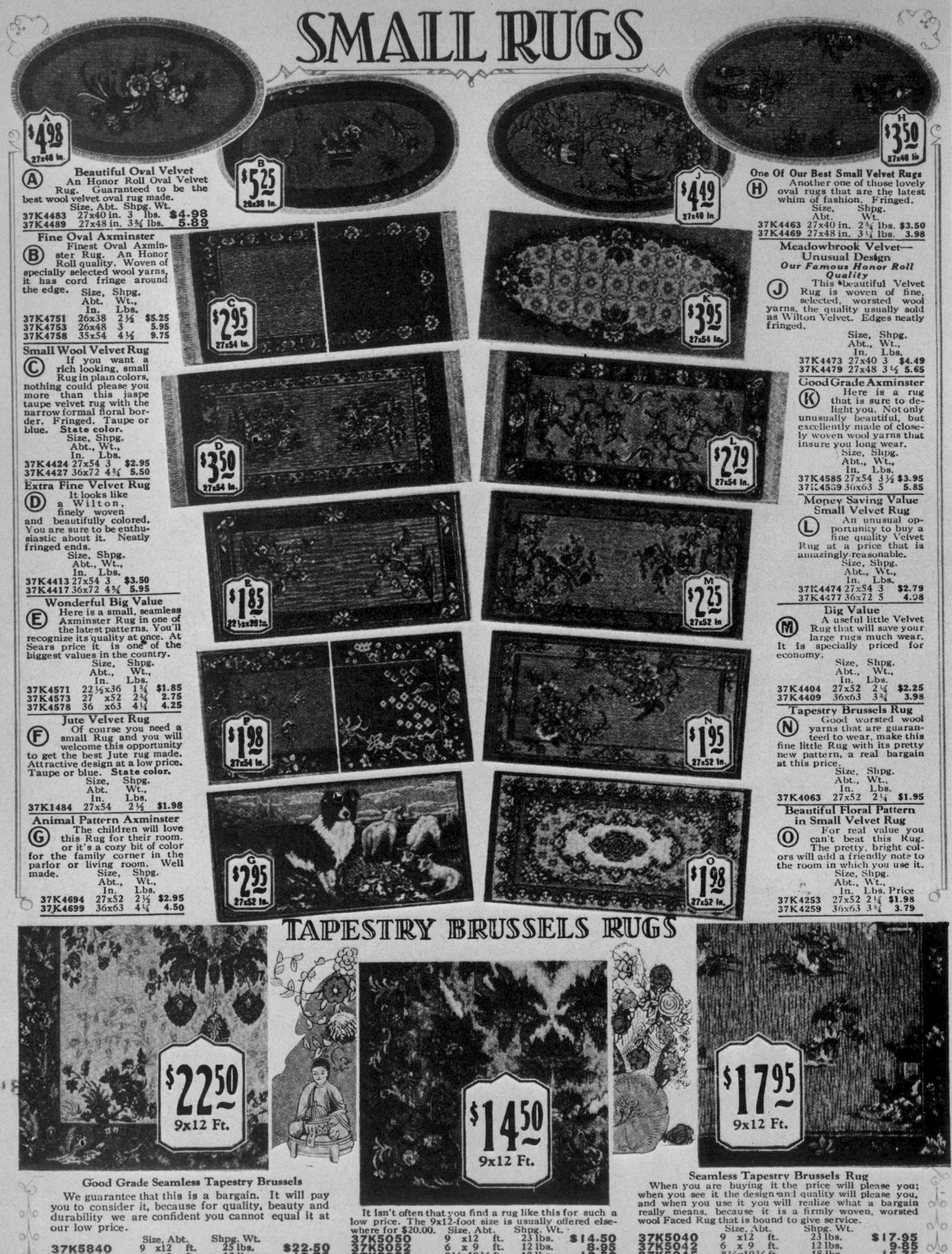

A
$4.98
27x40 In.

B
$5.25
26x38 In.

J
$4.49
27x40 In.

H
$3.50
27x40 In.

(A) Beautiful Oval Velvet
An Honor Roll Oval Velvet Rug. Guaranteed to be the best wool velvet oval rug made.

	Size, Abt.	Shpg. Wt.	
37K4483	27x40 in.	3 lbs.	$4.98
37K4489	27x48 in.	3¾ lbs.	5.89

(B) Fine Oval Axminster
Finest Oval Axminster Rug. An Honor Roll quality. Woven of specially selected wool yarns, it has cord fringe around the edge.

	Size, Abt. In.	Shpg. Wt., Lbs.	
37K4751	26x38	2½	$5.25
37K4753	26x48	3	5.95
37K4758	35x54	4½	9.75

(C) Small Wool Velvet Rug
If you want a rich looking, small Rug in plain colors, nothing could please you more than this jaspe taupe velvet rug with the narrow formal floral border. Fringed. Taupe or blue. **State color.**

	Size, Abt., In.	Shpg. Wt., Lbs.	
37K4424	27x54	3	$2.95
37K4427	36x72	4¾	5.50

(D) Extra Fine Velvet Rug
It looks like a Wilton, finely woven and beautifully colored. You are sure to be enthusiastic about it. Neatly fringed ends.

	Size, Abt., In.	Shpg. Wt., Lbs.	
37K4413	27x54	3	$3.50
37K4417	36x72	4¾	5.95

(E) Wonderful Big Value
Here is a small, seamless Axminster Rug in one of the latest patterns. You'll recognize its quality at once. At Sears price it is one of the biggest values in the country.

	Size, Abt., In.	Shpg. Wt., Lbs.	
37K4571	22½x36	1¾	$1.85
37K4573	27 x52	2¾	2.75
37K4578	36 x63	4¼	4.25

(F) Jute Velvet Rug
Of course you need a small Rug and you will welcome this opportunity to get the best Jute rug made. Attractive design at a low price. Taupe or blue. **State color.**

	Size, Abt. In.	Shpg. Wt., Lbs.	
37K1484	27x54	2½	$1.98

(G) Animal Pattern Axminster
The children will love this Rug for their room, or it's a cozy bit of color for the family corner in the parlor or living room. Well made.

	Size, Abt., In.	Shpg. Wt., Lbs.	
37K4694	27x52	2½	$2.95
37K4699	36x63	4¼	4.50

C
$2.95
27x54 In.

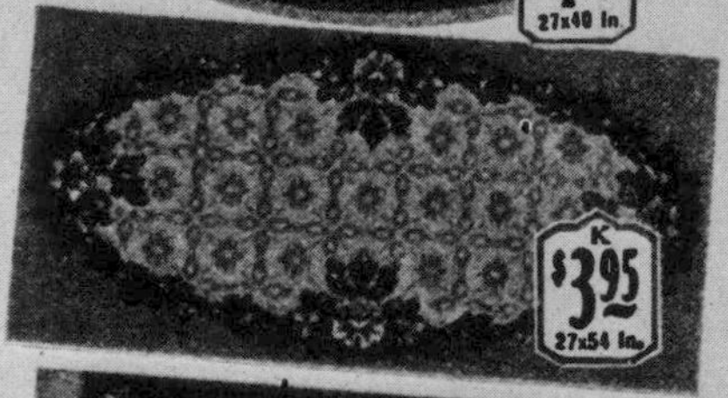

K
$3.95
27x54 In.

D
$3.50
27x54 In.

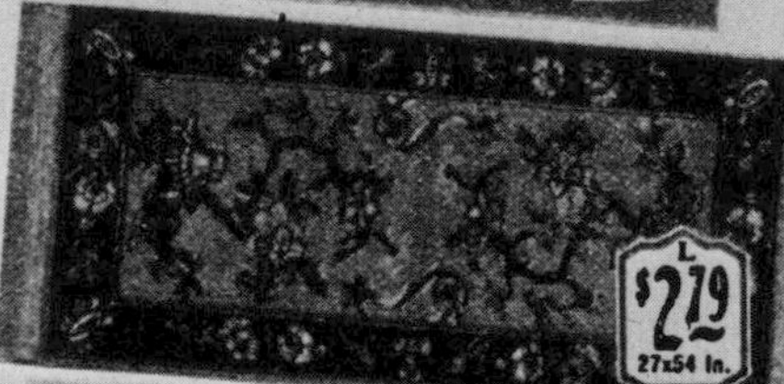

L
$2.79
27x54 In.

E
$1.85
22½x36 In.

M
$2.25
27x52 In.

F
$1.98
27x54 In.

N
$1.95
27x52 In.

G
$2.95
27x52 In.

O
$1.98
27x52 In.

(H) One Of Our Best Small Velvet Rugs
Another one of those lovely oval rugs that are the latest whim of fashion. Fringed.

	Size, Abt.	Shpg. Wt.	
37K4463	27x40 in.	2¾ lbs.	$3.50
37K4469	27x48 in.	3¼ lbs.	3.98

(J) Meadowbrook Velvet—Unusual Design
Our Famous Honor Roll Quality
This beautiful Velvet Rug is woven of fine, selected, worsted wool yarns, the quality usually sold as Wilton Velvet. Edges neatly fringed.

	Size, Abt., In.	Shpg. Wt., Lbs.	
37K4473	27x40	3	$4.49
37K4479	27x48	3½	5.65

(K) Good Grade Axminster
Here is a rug that is sure to delight you. Not only unusually beautiful, but excellently made of closely woven wool yarns that insure you long wear.

	Size, Abt., In.	Shpg. Wt., Lbs.	
37K4585	27x54	3½	$3.95
37K4539	36x63	5	5.85

(L) Money Saving Value Small Velvet Rug
An unusual opportunity to buy a fine quality Velvet Rug at a price that is amazingly reasonable.

	Size, Abt., In.	Shpg. Wt., Lbs.	
37K4474	27x54	3	$2.79
37K4477	36x72	5	4.98

(M) Big Value
A useful little Velvet Rug that will save your large rugs much wear. It is specially priced for economy.

	Size, Abt., In.	Shpg. Wt., Lbs.	
37K4404	27x52	2¼	$2.25
37K4409	36x63	3¾	3.98

(N) Tapestry Brussels Rug
Good worsted wool yarns that are guaranteed to wear, make this fine little Rug with its pretty new pattern, a real bargain at this price.

	Size, Abt., In.	Shpg. Wt., Lbs.	
37K4063	27x52	2¼	$1.95

(O) Beautiful Floral Pattern in Small Velvet Rug
For real value you can't beat this Rug. The pretty, bright colors will add a friendly note to the room in which you use it.

	Size, Abt., In.	Shpg. Wt., Lbs.	Price
37K4253	27x52	2¼	$1.98
37K4259	36x63	3¾	3.79

TAPESTRY BRUSSELS RUGS

$22.50
9x12 Ft.

$14.50
9x12 Ft.

$17.95
9x12 Ft.

Good Grade Seamless Tapestry Brussels
We guarantee that this is a bargain. It will pay you to consider it, because for quality, beauty and durability we are confident you cannot equal it at our low price.

	Size, Abt.	Shpg. Wt.	
37K5840	9 x12 ft.	25 lbs.	$22.50
37K5842	6 x 9 ft.	13 lbs.	12.75
37K5845	8¼x10½ ft.	20 lbs.	20.75

It isn't often that you find a rug like this for such a low price. The 9x12-foot size is usually offered elsewhere for $20.00.

	Size, Abt.	Shpg. Wt.	
37K5050	9 x12 ft.	23 lbs.	$14.50
37K5052	6 x 9 ft.	12 lbs.	8.95
37K5055	8¼x10½ ft.	18 lbs.	13.50
37K5056	11¼x12 ft.	30 lbs.	19.50

Seamless Tapestry Brussels Rug
When you are buying it the price will please you; when you see it the design and quality will please you, and when you use it you will realize what a bargain really means, because it is a firmly woven, worsted wool Faced Rug that is bound to give service.

	Size, Abt.	Shpg. Wt.	
37K5040	9 x12 ft.	23 lbs.	$17.95
37K5042	6 x 9 ft.	12 lbs.	9.85
37K5045	8¼x10½ ft.	18 lbs.	16.75
37K5046	11¼x12 ft.	30 lbs.	23.95

TAPESTRY BRUSSELS RUGS

Honor Roll $24.50
9x12-Ft.

$19.95 9x12-Ft.

$21.00 9x12-Ft.

$18.65 9x12-Ft.

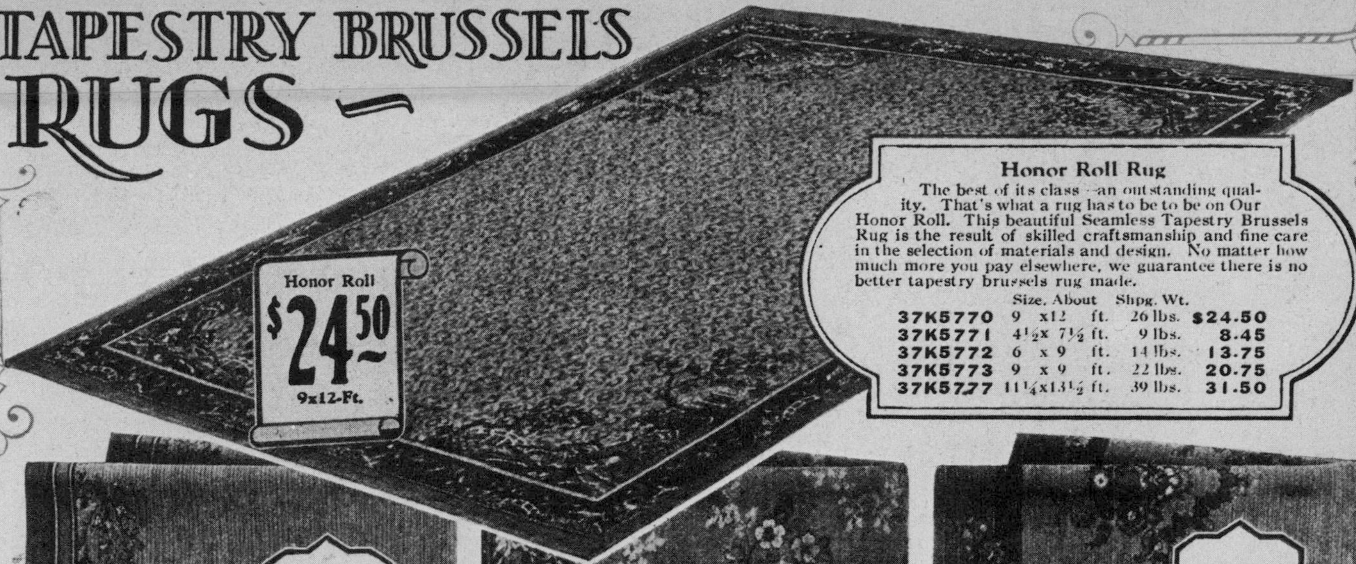

Honor Roll Rug

The best of its class—an outstanding quality. That's what a rug has to be to be on Our Honor Roll. This beautiful Seamless Tapestry Brussels Rug is the result of skilled craftsmanship and fine care in the selection of materials and design. No matter how much more you pay elsewhere, we guarantee there is no better tapestry brussels rug made.

	Size. About		Shpg. Wt.	
37K5770	9 x 12	ft.	26 lbs.	$24.50
37K5771	4½x 7½	ft.	9 lbs.	8.45
37K5772	6 x 9	ft.	14 lbs.	13.75
37K5773	9 x 9	ft.	22 lbs.	20.75
37K5777	11¼x13½	ft.	39 lbs.	31.50

Seamless Tapestry Brussels Rug

Modern in beauty of design and coloring, this Rug offers an old fashioned hundred cents to the dollar in value. Woven of worsted wool yarns. This quality usually sells for at least $24.00 in the 9x12-foot size.

	Size. About		Shpg. Wt.	
37K5850	9 x12	feet	29 lbs.	$19.95
37K5854	7½x9	feet	18 lbs.	14.95
37K5855	8¼x10½	feet	24 lbs.	18.75
37K5856	11¼x12	feet	36 lbs.	27.00
37K4003	27x52	inches	2¼ lbs.	2.15

Seamless Tapestry Brussels
A Guaranteed Value

Manufactured by a concern with many years' experience in weaving fine Tapestry Brussels Rugs, this rug is another new creation that will delight your eye with its beauty and your purse with its value.

	Size. About		Shpg. Wt.	
37K5880	9 x12	feet	25 lbs.	$21.00
37K5885	8¼x10½	feet	20 lbs.	19.75
37K5888	11¼x15	feet	40 lbs.	34.50

Something New in Seamless Tapestry Brussels

Color is the magic means of creating beauty in this Rug. The exquisite patterning is something entirely new in rug design, and it is woven of best quality worsted wool yarns that give excellent service.

	Size. About		Shpg. Wt.	
37K5080	9 x12	feet	29 lbs.	$18.65
37K5082	6 x 9	feet	15 lbs.	10.95
37K5085	8¼x10½	feet	24 lbs.	17.25
37K4043	27x52	in.	2¼ lbs.	2.00

$16.95 9x12-Ft.

$18.75 9x12-Ft.

$14.85 9x12-Ft.

Seamless Tapestry Brussels

One of the newest Wilton patterns worked out in good grade Seamless Tapestry Brussels in captivating colors. Here you can have the lovely Wilton effect at a low price; that's a value that will appeal to every thrifty woman.

	Size. About		Shpg. Wt.	
37K5740	9 x12	feet	21 lbs.	$16.95
37K5744	7½x9	feet	11 lbs.	12.50
37K5745	8¼x10½	feet	18 lbs.	15.75
37K5746	11¼x12	feet	26 lbs.	22.95

Popular Floral Design

The leader in Seamless Tapestry Brussels Floral Designs. One of the most popular patterns in our catalog. For service, workmanship and materials there is no better rug made for such low prices.

	Size. About		Shpg. Wt.	
37K5150	9 x12	feet	25 lbs.	$18.75
37K5152	6 x 9	feet	13 lbs.	11.25
37K5155	8¼x10½	feet	20 lbs.	17.50
37K5156	11¼x12	feet	33 lbs.	25.75
37K5158	11¼x15	feet	40 lbs.	31.50

Seamless Tapestry Brussels
Woven by the Mohawk Mills

Here is a fine rug whose lovely colorings and pattern will attract your attention. Quality—service—design—at prices that only Sears-Roebuck can make are guaranteed in this splendid Rug.

	Size. About		Shpg. Wt.	
37K5830	9 x12	feet	21 lbs.	$14.85
37K5834	7½x 9	feet	11 lbs.	11.50
37K5836	11¼x12	feet	26 lbs.	20.50

Your Orders Shipped Within 24 Hours!

High Grade Rugs

Descriptions and Prices on Opposite Page

Sears Greatest Rug Exhibit

A nation-wide showing of new patterns. Gorgeous, new Rugs of dependable quality that are incomparable bargains at Sears low prices. And there's the finest collection of them right here that ever has been offered. When you buy one of these rugs you have a guaranteed value that insures latest design, finest workmanship and lifelong service.

Honor Roll
37K6960
$45.50
9x12-Ft.

Honor Roll
37K9870
$57.50
9x12-Ft.

37K8930
$35.00
9x12-Ft.

37K8100
$42.95
9x12-Ft.

37K6910
$36.50
9x12-Ft.

37K6950
$39.50
9x12 Ft.

37K8900
$39.85
9x12 Ft.

37K8910
$41.00
9x12 Ft.

THE BEAUTY of a room depends on its rugs—they have to stand more wear than anything in your home and they are always on display. Therefore you should consider very carefully before buying. We have selected this fine group of rugs for you because we know they are the best value for your money both in quality and pattern. They are the greatest collection of medium priced rugs that it has ever been our privilege to offer you—greatest in the real sense of the word, since every one of them is a guaranteed bargain in beauty and service. We have investigated them, the materials and every detail of their manufacture, and that is why we are glad to place our guarantee on them, and offer you an assured saving.

Greatest test of all —Actual use! Sears rugs will give more than usual wear—extra quality is there and the prices are reasonable.

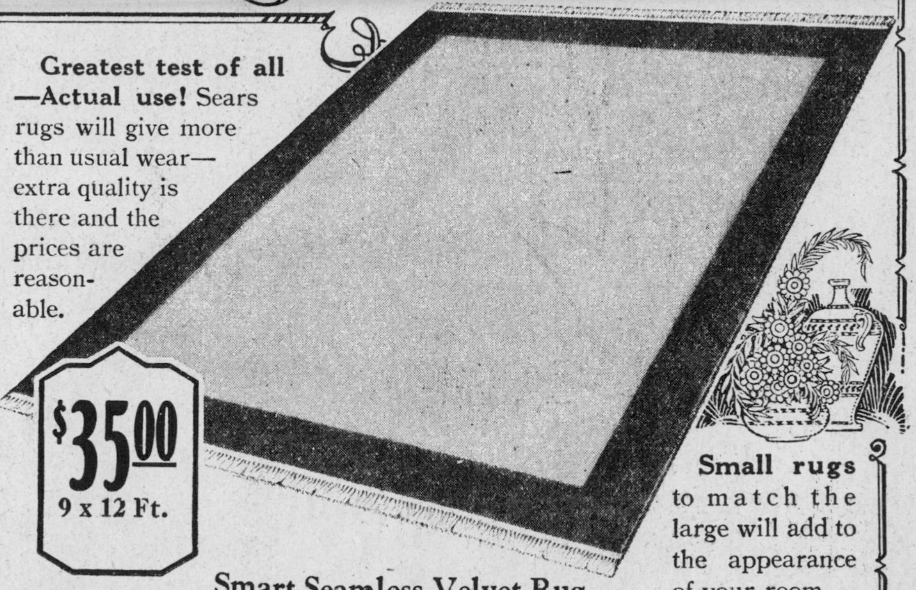

$35.00 9 x 12 Ft.

Small rugs to match the large will add to the appearance of your room.

Smart Seamless Velvet Rug
Newest Style in Plain Colors

A two-tone taupe Velvet Rug at prices far below those usually quoted on this quality. The trend of fashion has definitely swung to the use of plain hued floor covering and it is recognized as a mark of excellent taste in any room. Fringed, and closely woven, insuring long wear.

	Size, Abt.	Shipping Weight	
37K6500	9 x12 ft.	36 lbs.	$35.00
37K6502	6 x 9 ft.	18 lbs.	18.95
37K6505	8¼x10½ ft.	28 lbs.	32.50
37K6509	9 x15 ft.	43 lbs.	48.00
37K4423	27 x54 in.	3½ lbs.	3.65

Prices and Descriptions of Rugs Shown on Opposite Page

A The Best Quality Seamless Velvet Rug
A Genuine Wilton Design
One of Our Famous Honor Roll Rugs

This rug measures up to every standard set by Sears, Roebuck and Co. as worthy of being placed on our Honor Roll. We, of course, guarantee every rug on these pages, but any rug placed on our Honor Roll not only carries the usual guarantee, but is also guaranteed to be the best rug of its particular quality and type. This design is the very latest—a one-way pattern which does not repeat itself anywhere throughout the rug, woven very firmly and has an unusually close wool face. The ends are nicely finished with Linen fringe. Corners guaranteed not to curl.

	Size, Abt.	Shpg. Wt., Lbs.	
37K6960	9 x12 ft.	40	$45.50
37K6962	6 x 9 ft.	19	25.50
37K6964	7½x 9 ft.	24	31.95
37K6965	8¼x10½ ft.	29	41.95
37K4371	22½x36 in.	2¼	2.75
37K4374	27 x54 in.	4	4.75
37K4379	36 x63 in.	5½	7.25

B Highest Grade Wool Velvet Rug Made
A Big Value at Our Prices
Another One of Our Famous Honor Roll Rugs

This new Irvington Seamless Velvet Rug made by the Famous Alexander Smith Mills is another achievement in rug making. Here again we present to you something entirely new. It is our motto to lead and never follow. We want the customers of the World's Largest Store to have an opportunity to buy all the really good things that the market affords. This is an unusual rug; first, because of the fine workmanship; second, because the pattern is absolutely new; and third, because of the deep pile which gives it that luxurious effect. We know that it will cost you a great deal more to buy this fine rug elsewhere. This rug merits a place on our Honor Roll, because it is the best wool-faced velvet rug made in America. Fringed.

	Size, Abt.	Shpg. Wt., Lbs.	
37K9870	9 x12 ft.	56	$57.50
37K9875	8¼x10½ ft.	45	48.50
37K4943	27 x54 in.	5	6.50

C New Oriental Axminster
Of Very Good Quality
Another Alexander Smith Production

The World's Largest Store not only leads in big values, but also in style and pattern. This splendid Seamless Axminster Rug is a reproduction of a famous Chinese rug. Because this pattern was one of our biggest sellers this spring, we felt obligated to show it again in the fall season, as there are undoubtedly many of our customers who were not in a position to take advantage of this truly wonderful offer during the spring season. Its long wearing quality is one of its best points, for the quality is without an equal in rugs selling anywhere near this price. Where else could you buy this famous Carlton Axminster at anything like our prices? We are so certain of this value that we challenge all competition.

	Size, Abt.	Shpg. Wt., Lbs.	
37K8930	9 x12 ft.	34	$35.00
37K8932	6 x 9 ft.	19	19.50
37K8935	8¼x10½ ft.	29	31.75
37K4644	27 x54 in.	3¼	3.25

D Seamless High Grade Axminster Rug
A Size for Every Room

Here is another example of Sears leadership in the floor covering field. A new and modern thought in rug making. Something that is rich and handsome at a price that spells real economy. This is a distinctly European type of design and recommended particularly for homes with large families. It is both beautiful and serviceable because of its unusual color combination. Will not show the soil readily and will give years of hard and satisfactory wear.

	Size, Abt.	Shpg. Wt., Lbs.	
37K8100	9 x12 ft.	37	$42.95
37K8101	4½x 6½ ft.	12	12.25
37K8104	7½x 9 ft.	24	29.25
37K8103	9 x 9 ft.	29	38.75
37K8105	8¼x10½ ft.	32	39.00
37K8106	11¼x12 ft.	47	57.50
37K8108	11¼x15 ft.	60	69.85
37K4501	22½x36 in.	2¼	2.75
37K4505	27 x54 in.	3	4.00
37K4509	36 x63 in.	5	5.85

E Something New and Beautiful
Seamless Velvet Rug

Here is a rug of quality, workmanship and design at a price that only Sears can make. It would be equally appropriate for simple or elaborate interior, and its durability will delight you. The lovely pattern is of Chinese origin and typical of the high development of rug art in the Orient. Woven very firmly—has a well covered wool face. We recommend this rug as a splendid value. Fringed.

	Size, Abt.	Shpg. Wt., Lbs.	
37K6910	9 x12 ft.	36	$36.50
37K6912	6 x 9 ft.	18	19.50
37K6915	8¼x10½ ft.	28	32.95
37K4333	27 x54 in.	3½	3.75

F Gorgeous Seamless Velvet Rug
Often Sold as a Wilton Velvet

This rug is a bargain in every size and it comes in a size for every room. It can't fail to attract you at once. The artistic pattern and fresh, soft colors give it charm and individuality. And you can't excel the workmanship in this type of rug. It's made by experts who put the experience of years into every rug they make for you. A rug so durable and satisfactory would cost much more elsewhere. Neatly fringed, except 27x54-inch size.

	Size, Abt.	Shpg. Wt., Lbs.	
37K6950	9 x12 ft.	35	$39.50
37K6951	4½x 6½ ft.	10	12.95
37K6954	7½x 9 ft.	22	28.50
37K6953	9 x 9 ft.	33	35.50
37K6955	8¼x10½ ft.	28	37.00
37K6957	11¼x13½ ft.	49	56.95
37K4364	27 x54 in.	3	4.50

G New Seamless Axminster Rug
Woven by the Mohawk Mills

It's your living room that your guests really see and examine critically. And if you have this gorgeous new Axminster Rug on the floor they can't help admiring your taste and envying your good fortune. But what they'll never believe is that you could purchase it so reasonably. Look again at the new openwork design on the plain ground and the richness of the coloring, and you'll know it's a super-value because it's woven of the best yarns obtainable with a deep plush-like pile.

	Size, Abt.	Shpg. Wt., Lbs.	
37K8900	9 x12 ft.	35	$39.85
37K8901	4½x 6½ ft.	11	11.95
37K8902	6 x 9 ft.	19	22.00
37K8905	8¼x10½ ft.	29	36.50
37K4604	27 x54 in.	3	3.85
37K4609	36 x63 in.	5	5.65

H High Grade Seamless Axminster
A Big New Value

Here is a pattern that will lend dignity to a room without making it somber. The picture cannot do justice to the rich, handsome coloring any more than it can to the thick softness of the closely woven pile which is luxuriantly long. It is a rug of real distinction that marks your taste as faultless and, at the same time, it is a satisfaction to your pocketbook. The 11¼x12 foot size is seamed.

	Size, Abt.	Shpg. Wt. Lbs.	
37K8910	9 x12 ft.	37	$41.00
37K8914	7½x 9 ft.	25	27.95
37K8916	11¼x12 ft.	48	49.00
37K4614	27 x54 in.	3	4.00
37K4619	36 x63 in.	5	5.75

Seamless Velvet

37K6870
$32.50
9x12-Ft.

Beautiful Chinese Pattern Fine Grade Seamless Velvet Rug

This fine, soft, Jaspe velvet rug is luxuriantly beautiful and blends with any color combination. Woven of all wool yarns, it is guaranteed to prove serviceable. Fringed.

	Size, About	Shpg. Wt.	
37K6870	9 x12 ft.	36 lbs.	$32.50
37K6872	6 x 9 ft.	20 lbs.	18.35
37K6874	7½x 9 ft.	24 lbs.	23.55
37K6875	8¼x10½ ft.	30 lbs.	29.65
37K4243	27 x54 in.	3 lbs.	3.20

New Ideas in Floor Coverings

Beauty in Patterns

Quality in Values

Reasonable Prices

Built to Endure

See page 831 for other Velvet Rugs

37K6020
$24.75
9x12-Ft.

New Pattern in Seamless Velvet Rugs

A truly admirable rug. Beauty of coloring and dignity are blended with notable effect. If you want a medium priced seamless rug that is at the same time good looking and dependable this rug will appeal to you. It is usually offered by others as at least a $30.00 value in the 9x12-ft. size.

	Size, About	Shpg. Wt.	
37K6020	9 x12 ft.	28 lbs.	$24.75
37K6025	8¼x10½ ft.	22 lbs.	22.75
37K6026	11¼x12 ft.	35 lbs.	34.50

37K6860
$29.85
9x12-Ft.

Seamless Velvet Rugs

Good Quality and Low Price

One of the most popular patterns we ever had. Combines maximum service with minimum cost. One of our biggest values. Fringed. Recommended for hard service.

	Size, About	Shpg. Wt.	
37K6860	9 x12 ft.	36 lbs.	$29.85
37K6864	7½x 9 ft.	24 lbs.	22.50
37K6865	8¼x10½ ft.	30 lbs.	28.65
37K4224	27 x54 in.	3 lbs.	3.15
37K4227	36 x72 in.	5 lbs.	5.45

37K6000
$21.95
9x12-Ft.

Seamless Velvet Rug Mohawk Woven

If you appreciate a good looking seamless Velvet rug that is serviceable and at the same time medium priced, this rug will make a big appeal to you. It is sturdily woven with a wool face, and the ends are neatly fringed.

	Size, About	Shpg. Wt.	
37K6000	9 x12 ft.	27 lbs.	$21.95
37K6005	8¼x10½ ft.	22 lbs.	19.95

37K6900
$33.75
9x12-Ft.

Guaranteed Bargain—Seamless Velvet

Usually sells for $40.00 in the 9x12-ft. size. Fringed. Corners guaranteed not to curl. (Patented process.)

	Size, About	Shpg. Wt.	
37K6900	9 x12 ft.	32 lbs.	$33.75
37K6904	7½x 9 ft.	21 lbs.	23.75
37K6909	9 x15 ft.	39 lbs.	47.50
37K6906	11¼x12 ft.	40 lbs.	42.50
37K6908	12 x15 ft.	54 lbs.	61.50
37K4323	27 x54 in.	3 lbs.	3.35
37K4327	36 x72 in.	5 lbs.	5.75

37K6060
$20.50
9x12-Ft.

Fashionable Blue Chinese Seamless Velvet Rug

Woven in the lovely blue that is fashion's latest choice, this rich looking rug gives just the right warmth of color for the room you want to be the coziest. In the 9x12-ft. size it frequently sells up to $26.00 elsewhere.

	Size, About	Shpg. Wt.	
37K6060	9 x12 ft.	29 lbs.	$20.50
37K6064	7½x 9 ft.	19 lbs.	14.95
37K6065	8¼x10½ ft.	23 lbs.	18.75
37K4384	27 x52 in.	2¼ lbs.	1.95

37K6840
$23.50
9x12-Ft.

Fine Seamless Velvet Ru;

Rich, quiet colors. A flower design on the border gives it character without changing its lovely simplicity. An extra fine value, ordinarily offered in the 9x12-ft. size at from $6.00 to $8.00 more elsewhere. Real wearing service, and the jaspe ground does not readily show soil. Fringed. Corners guaranteed not to curl. (Patented process.)

	Size, About	Shpg. Wt.	
37K6840	9 x12 ft.	28 lbs.	$23.50
37K6842	6 x 9 ft.	15 lbs.	13.85
37K6845	8¼x10½ ft.	22 lbs.	21.65
37K6846	11¼x12 ft.	34 lbs.	30.75

and Axminster Rugs

Four Reasons Why
Our Floor Coverings Are Unexcelled!

1. Quality—Stands up.
2. Patterns—Best in America.
3. Service—Second to none.
4. Values—Outstanding.

37K8870
$37.95
9x12-Ft.

Fine Quality Seamless Axminster

On a soft rose taupe damask ground with a darker border are luxuriant figures in tropical design. The rich pleasing colors of this rug will give life and character to the dullest room. With a plush-like pile of all wool yarns, this rug is guaranteed to be one of the best buys in the country. Discriminating women will appreciate its value and its beauty.

	Size, About	Shpg. Wt.,	
37K8870	9 x12 ft.	34 lbs.	$37.95
37K8875	8¼x10½ ft.	28 lbs.	35.00
37K4584	27 x52 in.	3 lbs.	3.45

37K8130
$34.50
9x12-Ft.

37K8140
$29.85
9x12-Ft.

37K8850
$33.75
9x12-Ft.

Seamless Axminster Rug

This seamless rug with its beautiful soft pile will give splendid service. Latest design—which is particularly attractive.

		Size, About	Shpg. Wt.	
37K8130		9 x12 ft.	32 lbs.	$34.50
37K8134		7½x 9 ft.	21 lbs.	24.95
37K8135		8¼x10½ ft.	27 lbs.	31.50
37K8136	Seamed	11¼x12 ft.	41 lbs.	43.95

Wonderful Value—Seamless Axminster Rug

Good grade Seamless Axminster. Latest pattern. You could not duplicate these values at anything like our low prices. The 9x12 size usually sells for $39.50 elsewhere.

		Size, About	Shpg. Wt.	
37K8140		9 x12 ft.	32 lbs.	$29.85
37K8142		6 x 9 ft.	17 lbs.	17.65
37K8144		7½x 9 ft.	21 lbs.	21.95
37K8145		8¼x10½ ft.	27 lbs.	27.95
37K8146	Seamed	11¼x12 ft.	41 lbs.	39.50
37K4575		27 x52 in.	2¾ lbs.	2.70
37K4579		36 x63 in.	4¼ lbs.	4.45

Seamless Axminster Rug
Woven by the Mohawk Mills

This rug combines quality and design at low price. The pattern is fashionable and the quality the best that can be had, price considered. Sells up to $41.50 elsewhere in the 9x12 foot size.

	Size, About	Shpg. Wt.	
37K8850	9 x12 ft.	31 lbs.	$33.75
37K8852	6 x 9 ft.	17 lbs.	18.50
37K8855	8¼x10½ ft.	26 lbs.	30.95
37K4563	27 x52 in.	2½ lbs.	3.15

37K8020
$26.95
9x12-Ft.

37K8030
$26.95
9x12-Ft.

37K8860
$31.95
9x12-Ft.

The Famous Seamless Ardsley Axminster Rug

America's most popular Axminster at the lowest price ever offered anywhere. Just imagine Alexander Smith and Sons Carpet Co.'s seamless rug for $26.95. This is truly America's wonder bargain.

		Size, About	Shpg. Wt.	
37K8020		9 x12 ft.	31 lbs.	$26.95
37K8026	Seamed	11¼x12 ft.	40 lbs.	35.75

Another Famous Ardsley Axminster Bargain

Good grade Seamless Axminster Rug. The biggest value in the country at Sears low prices. Seamless; woven of good grade wool yarn. Taupe or blue. **State color wanted.**

	Size, About	Shpg. Wt.	
37K8030	9 x12 ft.	31 lbs.	$26.95
37K8032	6 x 9 ft.	16 lbs.	15.75
37K8035	8¼x10½ ft.	26 lbs.	24.50
37K4533	27 x52 in.	2¾ lbs.	2.65

A Wonderful Big Value

Here is a rug that fairly sparkles with quality, a good grade Seamless Axminster.

	Size, About	Shpg. Wt.	
37K8860	9 x12 ft.	32 lbs.	$31.95
37K8864	7½x 9 ft.	21 lbs.	23.50
37K8866	11¼x12 ft. (Seamed)	41 lbs.	42.50
37K4571	22½x36 in.	1¾ lbs.	1.85
37K4573	27 x52 in.	2¾ lbs.	2.75
37K4578	36 x63 in.	4¼ lbs	4.25

Your Orders Shipped Within 24 Hours!

Plain Carpets

Carpet and Border

$1.98 A Yd.

Reasonably Priced Plain Velvet Carpet
37K1621 —Width, about 27 inches.
Shipping weight per yard, 1¾ lbs. **$1.98**

$2.25 A Yd.

Good Quality
Plain Velvet Carpet
37K1613 —Width, about 27 inches.
Shipping weight, per yard, 1¾ lbs. **$2.25**

$4.75 A Yd.

Fine Worsted Wilton
37K1135 —Width, about 27 inches.
Shipping weight, per yard, 3½ lbs. **$4.75**

89c A Ft.   **$1.45 A Ft.**

BROADLOOM CARPETS

Claremont Quality
A good grade Velvet Broadloom Carpet. The color, a heather mixture, has a beautiful taupe effect that will not show soil. Send for sample. Shpg. Wt.,

	Width	Per Ft.
37K1177½	9 ft. 4 lbs.	$3.75
37K1178	27 in. 1½ lbs.	.89

Wide width of Broadloom carpet shipped only from CHICAGO, ILL.

Brewster Quality
One of the finest qualities in heavy Seamless Broadloom Velvet Carpets. Jade green or raisin taupe. State color. Send for sample. Shpg. W.,

	Width	Per Ft.
37K1179	9 ft. 5 lbs.	$6.35
37K1180	27 in. 1½ lbs.	1.45

Wide width shipped from CHICAGO, ILL.

$2.98 A Yd.

Good Quality Velvet Carpet and Border
37K1130 --Carpet.   37K1130 -Border.
Wth., 27 in. Shpg.wt.,   Width,22 ½ in. Shpg.
yd., 1¾ lbs. **$2.98**   wt., yd., 1 lb. **$2.98**

$2.45 A Yd.

Pretty Velvet Carpet
—Neat Design
37K1619 —Width, about 27 inches.
Shipping wt., per yard, 1½ lbs. **$2.45**

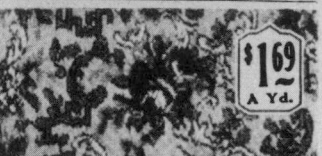

$1.69 A Yd.

Worsted Face Floral Tapestry
37K1517 —Width, about 27 inches.
Shipping wt., per yard, 1½ lbs. **$1.69**

Stair Carpets

Room Carpets

$1.59 A Yd.

Fine Velvet Stair Carpet
37K1692 —Width, about 27 in. Shipping weight, per yard, 1¾ lbs. **$1.59**

65c A Yd.

Jute Tapestry Brussels Stair Carpet
37K1514 —Width, about 27 in. Shipping weight, per yard, 1½ lbs. **65c**

$1.10 A Yd.

Jute Velvet Stair Carpet
37K1602 —Width, about 27 in. Shpg. wt., per yard, 1¾ lbs. **$1.10**

$1.98 A Yd.

Wool Velvet—Taupe or Blue Border
37K1650 —State color. Width, 27 inches. Shpg. wt., 1¾ lbs. **$1.98**

$1.85 A Yd.

Firmly Woven Velvet Stair Carpet
37K1604 - Width about 27 in. Shpg. wt., per yd., 1¾ lbs. **$1.85**

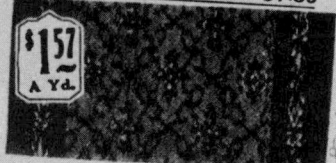

$1.57 A Yd.

37K1518—Tapestry brussels, Width, about 27 in. Shipping weight, per yard, 1¾ lbs. **$1.57**

$2.95 A Yd.

Long Wearing Velvet Carpeting
37K1616 —Width, about 27 in. Shpg. wt., per yd., 1½ lbs. **$2.95**

$2.59 A Yd.

Beautifully Designed Velvet Carpet
37K1609 Width, about 27 in. Shpg. wt., per yd., 1½ lbs. **$2.59**

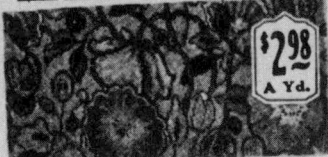

$2.98 A Yd.

Allover Floral Pattern Axminster
37K1226 —Width, about 27 in. Shpg. wt., per yd., 1¾ lbs. **$2.98**

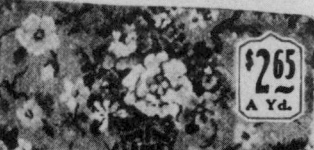

$2.65 A Yd.

Introducing a New Floral Velvet
37K1611 —Width, about 27 in. Shipping weight, per yard, 1½ lbs. **$2.65**

$2.39 A Yd.

Good Quality Axminster Carpet
37K1224 —Width, about 27 in. Shipping weight, per yard, 1½ lbs. **$2.39**

$2.85 A Yd.

Chinese Pattern Axminster Carpet
37K1225 Width, about 27 in. Shpg. wt., yd., 1¾ lbs. **$2.85**

Ingrain Carpets

36c A Yd.

Practical Granite Stair Carpet
37K1780 —Width, about 27 in. Shipping weight, per yard, 8 oz. **36c**

$1.10 A Yd.

Good Quality Ingrain Carpet
37K705 —Width, about 36 in. Shipping weight, per yard, 1¼ lbs. **$1.10**

47c A Yd.

Our Best Granite Carpet, Reversible
37K1789 —Width, about 27 in. Shipping weight, per yard, 1 lb. **47c**

$1.35 A Yd.

Finest Quality Ingrain Carpet
All Wool
Red or taupe ground. State color.
37K707 —Width, about 36 in. Shipping weight, per yard, 1¼ lbs. **$1.35**

95c A Yd.

Standard Quality Ingrain Carpet
37K703 —Width, about 36 in. Shipping wt., per yd., 1¼ lbs. **95c**

$1.20 A Yd.

Good Wearing Quality Ingrain
37K706 —Width, about 36 in. Shipping weight, per yard, 1¼ pounds **$1.20**

69c A Yd.

Our Best Grade Rag Carpet, Reversible
37K606 —Width, about 36 in. Shipping weight, per yard, 2½ lbs. **69c**

79c A Yd.

Ingrain Carpet
37K704 —Width, about 36 in. Shipping weight, per yard, 1½ lbs. **79c**

No Job is Too Big for Our ~~~
Up-to-date Carpet Work Room

We Guarantee Every Job

These two pictures show portions of our carpet workrooms which are fully equipped with the latest electric sewing machines that enable us to turn out work in the shortest possible time. Our cutters and hand sewers are of long experience in all kinds of carpet work, so that every job sent out by us is perfect according to specifications or we make it right. We are ready to serve you at any time; to give estimates on any job, to help you decide the **best and most economical way** of covering your floors, to send samples immediately upon request, and to give you the best quality work at the lowest prices. If you are considering any kind of new floor covering at all, carpets or rugs, let us at least make an estimate for you on carpeting. All you need to do is measure off your room, and let us know what carpeting from the catalog you would choose and we will send you as close an estimate as possible of what the cost would be to cover your floor with fashionable new carpeting.

One of Our Modern Sewing Machines

View of A Portion of Our Cutting Room

Beauty, wear and Sears, Roebuck and Co.'s low prices are the ideals of our floor covering department. Imagine how richly beautiful is the room laid with a single tone carpet or the cheerfulness of a well chosen figured design. What a full spacious effect it gives. What an air of comfort and good taste. The patterns selected on the opposite page are the finest carpet the American market has to offer at prices within the reach of the average home.

We are eager for you to know the quality of our carpets and to impress upon you the exceptional values we are offering. So we have arranged this season to send on request **free samples** of any carpetings you desire. A sample of any carpet or carpets illustrated in this book will be furnished upon request. Simply write to Jane Austin, Rug and Carpet Department, Sears, Roebuck and Co., Chicago, giving the catalog numbers of the carpets you prefer. If possible send an outline or diagram of the room to be carpeted and we will be glad to give you an accurate estimate of the cost of the carpet you have selected. Remember, we guarantee the quality of our carpets and we also guarantee a big saving as well.

In ordering carpets to cover the entire room, we strongly advise and recommend that you allow us to size your carpet. This makes the task of laying your carpet very much easier, as the process of sizing takes out all the fullness which would otherwise have to be taken out with a carpet stretcher at the time of laying. The nominal charge of 8c per yard for sizing is well spent, because it eliminates the greatest difficulty in laying your carpet.

Hall and Room Carpet

Cut to Measure

Beautiful floors at small cost—that is the service of carpet department. In making up carpets to cover your entire room, there is no need for the services of a high priced estimator. All that you need to do is to send us a diagram of the hall or room you wish to cover, giving us the dimensions and noting any fireplaces or irregularities. Our special service department will then (without charge) cut your carpet so that it will fit exactly. The only extra charge we will make is for sewing, 4c a yard for carpets, 10c a yard for special size rugs (made of carpet and border to match).

Chinese Matting
A Bargain in Imported Matting

Nothing quite takes the place of neat fresh matting for it is pretty, serviceable and easy to keep clean. This style features a blue and light green stripe on a natural tan ground. Reversible so that it has a double life. An exceptional value for the money. Shpg. wt., per yard, 1¾ lbs. Per roll, 70 lbs.

37K2802—36 in. wide.
Per yard $0.25
Per roll, 40 yards 9.50

Cotton Carpet Binding

Used principally for binding ends and edges of carpet. Width, about 1 inch. Comes in about 10¼-yd. rolls. Green, brown, taupe or red. **State color.** Shipping weight, 3 oz.

37K19
Per roll..........27c

Broadloom Carpet

Again we are proving our value and quality leadership in the entire floor covering field. Again we are demonstrating to our millions of customers that they can buy floor coverings from the World's Largest Store at prices which mean bigger savings than they can make anywhere else. Quality for quality and price for price we believe that you cannot duplicate our value at any other mail order or retail store in the world.

The vogue for plain color floor coverings has gained great popularity within the last year, because of its practicality, its effectiveness as a setting for any color scheme, and its economy. There is no finer seamless carpet at a price within the reach of the average home than our Brewster Broadloom carpet. We will serge the ends of your Broadloom carpets without charge or finish them with a neat cotton binding for $1.50 in the 9-foot size.

Carpet and Border

If standard size rugs are the wrong size or shape for your room, but still you don't want to cover the entire floor with carpeting, let us make you a rug in just the size and shape you want of 37K1130, on page 840. A rug made to order for your room can't fail to enhance its beauty and make you very happy. All you need to do (we'll be glad to send you a sample before you order) is to send us a diagram giving us the dimensions of the rug you wish made. No charge for cutting and only 10c a yard for sewing. We recommend sizing at 8c a yard to insure the rug lying flat.

Ingrain Carpet

Good quality, long wearing carpeting in allover designs that are ideal for real service at a very low price. You can cover your floor with a truly practical carpet at the lowest possible cost. Any one of the patterns shown on the opposite page makes a pretty floor covering, one that does not show soil and gives long wear.

Stair Pads

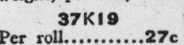

Well Padded With Soft Cotton.

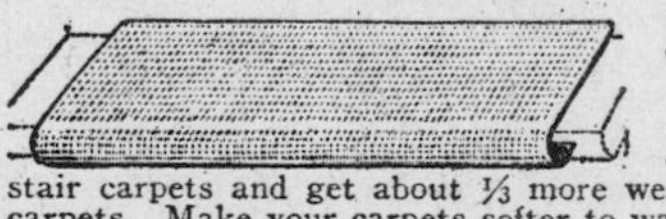

Put these stair pads underneath your stair carpets and get about ⅓ more wear out of your carpets. Make your carpets softer to walk on and give them a better appearance. One size only, about 22½ in. long and 8 in. wide. Weight, 7 ounces.

37K15—Each 12c

Stair Carpet

Treat your stairs with the same care and consideration that you do your room floors. Beautifully covered stairs lend an air of distinction to your home. We have in our carpet department a wide selection (as shown on page 840) of high quality stair carpets in fine patterns at our usual low prices. For a small cost you can have your stairway beautifully covered. Let us send you samples of the designs you like best so that you can see what really fine bargains they are.

We also have a complete stock of all the things you may need in laying the carpet. Either lining or stair pads will soften it considerably and add to its long life, while stair rods for fastening the carpet will insure its never coming loose.

Nuhair Rug and Carpet Cushion

Lay Your Rugs Over Nu-Hair Cushion

Adds materially to the life of your floor covering and gives that soft, luxurious effect. Nu-hair will last a lifetime and can be taken up, cleaned and relaid just like a rug. Mothproof, superior quality.

	Size, Feet	Shpg. Wt., Lbs.	
37K390	9 x12	24	$10.50
37K392	6 x 9	13	5.50
37K394	7½ x 9	15	6.85
37K395	8¼ x10½	20	8.75
37K396	11¼ x13	27	13.65
37K389	For 27-in. carpet	1¼	.59

Genuine Hair—Do not confuse with cheaper substitutes.

The Happiest Surprise of Her Life!

For the First Time in Years the World's Largest Store Is Offering This Marvelous Kitchen Cabinet
on Easy Payment Terms Every Woman Can Afford

No more do you have to wait until you have the full purchase price of this splendid kitchen cabinet before you can enjoy its use. Why not let it work for you in your home as you pay for it? A small down payment and equally small payments every month now put this cabinet within reach of every home. Days of kitchen drudgery can now be lightened. We feel sure you can't do better elsewhere, price for price and quality for quality. Why put off ordering? Eventually you'll have a kitchen cabinet; why not today?

Every feature is arranged to make kitchen work easier. Sanitary and moisture proof glass containers for coffee, tea, and spices. Bill hooks, cook book holder and metal coin tray on insides of doors; menu card, cooking time table, table of weights and measures, receipt file. Three removable and washable shelves in right hand upper compartment, useful for groceries, dishes, etc. One large removable shelf in the upper middle compartment for dishes and sundries. **And, in addition, the ten big special features described separately.**

1—Easy filling flour bin. Capacity, 50 pounds. Patent style lowering rods bring bin down to convenient level for filling. Has handy patent sifter.

2—Spacious, uncluttered work table with genuine "Crysteel" porcelain top, approved by Good Housekeeping institute and famous for durability, splendid appearance and easy to clean features. Closed working surface, 16x48 inches. Sliding extension porcelain table top, pulled forward, increases the working surface to 24x48 inches, giving additional working space of 384 square inches. Height of table top, 34 inches.

3—Removable bread board slides into receptacle under porcelain table top.

4—Sliding shelf in bottom of cupboard in base section and sliding pan tray.

5—Roll drop curtain. Opens without disturbing contents of cupboard.

6—Deep bread drawer, metal lined with ventilated sliding cover. Right hand top drawer partitioned for cutlery.

7—Strongly braced block for food chopper.

8—Swinging sugar jar equipped with patent catch.

9—Meal bin. Capacity, 20 pounds.

10—Easy to clean, no dirt gathering crevices and corners.

Thousands of women who today are using this model are highly pleased at the wonderful efficiency of this cabinet. Everything needed within arm's reach. At this amazingly low price you actually save about one-third compared to prices ordinarily asked elsewhere.

The construction of this cabinet is a positive insurance against warping or shrinkage from kitchen heat or moisture. The back and panels are of 3-ply wood. Mortised joints throughout. All nickeled hardware fittings. Mounted on casters. A slight push moves the cabinet easily, so that every particle of dust that has gathered underneath can easily be removed. Shipping weight, 315 pounds.

Terms: $5.00 with order and $5.00 a month until paid.

Measurements: 72 inches high, 48 inches wide and 27 inches deep. Shipped from our store for prompt delivery. Shipping weight, 315 pounds.

1K2191	Cash Prices	Easy Payment Prices
Golden oak, white enamel interior	$39.95	$43.95
White enamel throughout	44.35	48.75
Gray enamel throughout	44.45	48.85

When ordering on easy payments, use Time Payment Blanks on page 1092.

$5.00 DOWN

STOP! Thousands of tiresome steps every day are needless.

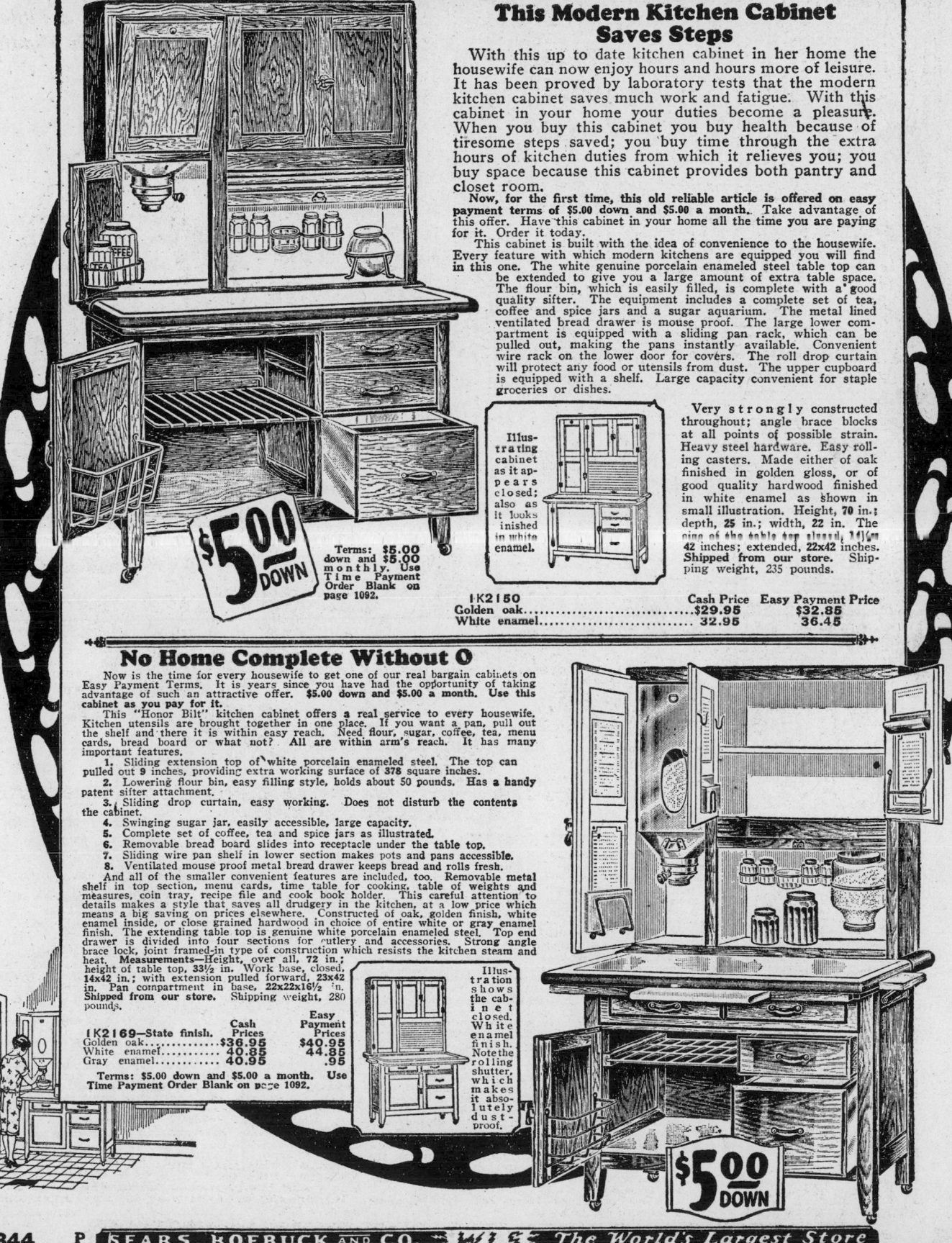

This Modern Kitchen Cabinet Saves Steps

With this up to date kitchen cabinet in her home the housewife can now enjoy hours and hours more of leisure. It has been proved by laboratory tests that the modern kitchen cabinet saves much work and fatigue. With this cabinet in your home your duties become a pleasure. When you buy this cabinet you buy health because of tiresome steps saved; you buy time through the extra hours of kitchen duties from which it relieves you; you buy space because this cabinet provides both pantry and closet room.

Now, for the first time, this old reliable article is offered on easy payment terms of $5.00 down and $5.00 a month. Take advantage of this offer. Have this cabinet in your home all the time you are paying for it. Order it today.

This cabinet is built with the idea of convenience to the housewife. Every feature with which modern kitchens are equipped you will find in this one. The white genuine porcelain enameled steel table top can be extended to give you a large amount of extra table space. The flour bin, which is easily filled, is complete with a good quality sifter. The equipment includes a complete set of tea, coffee and spice jars and a sugar aquarium. The metal lined ventilated bread drawer is mouse proof. The large lower compartment is equipped with a sliding pan rack, which can be pulled out, making the pans instantly available. Convenient wire rack on the lower door for covers. The roll drop curtain will protect any food or utensils from dust. The upper cupboard is equipped with a shelf. Large capacity convenient for staple groceries or dishes.

Illustrating cabinet as it appears closed; also as it looks finished in white enamel.

Very strongly constructed throughout; angle brace blocks at all points of possible strain. Heavy steel hardware. Easy rolling casters. Made either of oak finished in golden gloss, or of good quality hardwood finished in white enamel as shown in small illustration. Height, 70 in.; depth, 25 in.; width, 22 in. The size of the table top closed, 14½ x 42 inches; extended, 22x42 inches. Shipped from our store. Shipping weight, 235 pounds.

1K2150	Cash Price	Easy Payment Price
Golden oak	$29.95	$32.85
White enamel	32.95	36.45

Terms: $5.00 down and $5.00 monthly. Use Time Payment Order Blank on page 1092.

No Home Complete Without O

Now is the time for every housewife to get one of our real bargain cabinets on Easy Payment Terms. It is years since you have had the opportunity of taking advantage of such an attractive offer. $5.00 down and $5.00 a month. Use this cabinet as you pay for it.

This "Honor Bilt" kitchen cabinet offers a real service to every housewife. Kitchen utensils are brought together in one place. If you want a pan, pull out the shelf and there it is within easy reach. Need flour, sugar, coffee, tea, menu cards, bread board or what not? All are within arm's reach. It has many important features.

1. Sliding extension top of white porcelain enameled steel. The top can be pulled out 9 inches, providing extra working surface of 378 square inches.
2. Lowering flour bin, easy filling style, holds about 50 pounds. Has a handy patent sifter attachment.
3. Sliding drop curtain, easy working. Does not disturb the contents of the cabinet.
4. Swinging sugar jar, easily accessible, large capacity.
5. Complete set of coffee, tea and spice jars as illustrated.
6. Removable bread board slides into receptacle under the table top.
7. Sliding wire pan shelf in lower section makes pots and pans accessible.
8. Ventilated mouse proof metal bread drawer keeps bread and rolls fresh.

And all of the smaller convenient features are included, too. Removable metal shelf in top section, menu cards, time table for cooking, table of weights and measures, coin tray, recipe file and cook book holder. This careful attention to details makes a style that saves all drudgery in the kitchen, at a low price which means a big saving on prices elsewhere. Constructed of oak, golden finish, white enamel inside, or close grained hardwood in choice of entire white or gray enamel finish. The extending table top is genuine white porcelain enameled steel. Top end drawer is divided into four sections for cutlery and accessories. Strong angle brace lock, joint framed-in type of construction which resists the kitchen steam and heat. **Measurements**—Height, over all, 72 in.; height of table top, 33½ in. Work base, closed, 14x42 in.; with extension pulled forward, 23x42 in. Pan compartment in base, 22x22x16½ in. **Shipped from our store.** Shipping weight, 280 pounds.

1K2169—State finish.	Cash Prices	Easy Payment Prices
Golden oak	$36.95	$40.95
White enamel	40.85	44.85
Gray enamel	40.95	.95

Terms: $5.00 down and $5.00 a month. Use Time Payment Order Blank on page 1092.

Illustration shows the cabinet closed. White enamel finish. Note the rolling shutter, which makes it absolutely dust-proof.

$5.00 DOWN

Headquarters for Kitchen Furniture Because Our Prices Are Right

Kitchen Cupboard

A style of kitchen cupboard which offers an opportunity for thrifty buyers to save money. After seeing the price of this high quality cupboard you will agree that here is a big value. Made of hardwood. Finish—Golden gloss. Stands 71½ inches high and is 38½ inches wide and 16¾ inches deep, extreme outside measurements. Upper compartment has two inside shelves and the lower compartment has one. Drawers have knobs. Packed to secure lowest transportation rates. Easily put together. Shipped from factory in INDIANA. Shpg. wt., 140 lbs.
1K2218⅓........................ **$11.95**

See Order Blanks in Back of Catalog

Kitchen Cupboard

A big value in a kitchen cupboard that cannot be beat for convenience or low price. Made of hardwood. Finish—Golden gloss. 71½ inches high, 38½ inches wide and 16¾ inches deep, extreme outside measurements. Top section has glass panel doors and the inside is fitted with two shelves. Inside below is fitted with a shelf. Two roomy drawers. Wood knobs. Packed to secure lowest transportation rates. Easily put together. Shipped from factory in INDIANA. Shipping weight, 140 pounds.
1K2223⅓........................ **$12.75**

Buy at the World's Largest Store and SAVE

Table Values

Medicine Cabinets

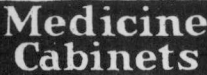

Wood cabinet. White enameled inside and outside. Has two shelves. Door equipped with catch. Plain plate mirror, 10 x14 in. Height, 16½ in.; width, 12½ in.; depth, 5¾ in. Shipping weight, 18 pounds. Can be shipped by parcel post.
1K4143.............. **$3.25**

Wood cabinet. You will be delighted with this big value in a useful and conveniently arranged medicine cabinet. An essential in every household. White enamel finish inside and out. Has two shelves and one drawer. Door is fitted with nickel lock catch. Plate glass mirror, 10x14 inches. Height, 21½ inches. Width, 13½ inches. Depth, 5¾ inches. Shipping weight, 22 pounds. Can be shipped by parcel post.
1K4144.............. **$5.25**

Made of sheet steel, outside and inside finished in white gloss enamel. Plain plate mirror in door. Two stationary steel shelves. Height, 19 inches; width, 13¼ inches. Mirror, 8x13 inches; depth, 4¾ inches. Shipping weight, 16 lbs. Can be shipped by parcel post.
1K4146.............. **$3.65**

Our largest and best cabinet finished in white gloss enamel. Has two steel shelves. Plain plate mirror. Height, 20 in. Width, 15 in. Depth, 6 in. Large mirror, 11x16 in. Shpg. wt., 26 lbs. Can be shipped by parcel post.
1K4151.............. **$5.65**

Especially attractive kitchen cabinet values are shown on pages 842, 843 and 844. You are sure of getting the lowest prices here.

White Porcelain Enameled Steel Top Table

Will give years of service. Hardwood frame, finished in white enamel. Sanitary and easy to keep clean. Securely jointed and screwed. Sliding casters. Large drawer with metal pull. Top 25x40 in. or 25x48 in. Height, 30 in. Packed to secure lowest transportation rates. Easily put together. Shipped from our store. Shipping weights, 40 and 45 pounds, respectively.
1K2407
25x40-inch top....... **$4.75**
1K2400—25x48-inch top. The same as 1K2407, except that it has two drawers......**$9.35**

$7 35
Golden Gloss

Drop Leaf Table

Made of hardwood. Choice of finished or unfinished tops. Completely finished in golden gloss, or with white top with apron and legs varnished or white enameled. Size of top, with leaves down, 40x22 inches; with leaves up, 44x40 inches; size of each leaf, 11x40 inches. Height, 30 inches. Legs, 1¾ inches square. Packed to secure lowest transportation rates. Easily put together. Shipped from our store.

1K2410—Completely finished in golden gloss. Shipping weight, 60 pounds.......... **$7.35**
1K2411—Apron and legs varnished; unfinished top. Shpg. wt., 45 lbs...**$5.95**
1K2412—Apron and legs white enameled; unfinished top. Shipping weight, 45 pounds **$6.75**

Good Quality Hardwood Kitchen Table

Every kitchen needs one of these tables and we know you cannot buy a better one elsewhere for the money. Made of hardwood, golden gloss finish except top, which is made of unfinished soft wood. Top, 24¾ x 41 inches. Strongly constructed with bolted leg fasteners. Packed to secure lowest transportation rates. Easily put together. Shipped from our store. Shpg. wt., 33 lbs.
1K2402..... **$2.95**

$2 95
Big Bargain

Drop Leaf Kitchen Table With End Drawer

$7 75
Unfinished Top
Golden Oak Trim

Every housewife will want one of these low priced drop leaf tables. Made of kiln dried hardwood. Size of top, with leaves down, 39¾x22 inches; with leaves up, 39¾x43¾ inches. A convenient feature is the end drawer, 10¾x13¾x2¾ inches. Height, 30 inches. Packed to secure lowest transportation rates. Easily put together. Shipped from our store. Shipping weight, 85 pounds.
1K2401—White unfinished top; golden oak trim and legs..... **$7.75**
White enameled throughout........**$9.75**

Other Splendid Offers

Kitchen Stool

Choice of Golden Oak or White Enamel

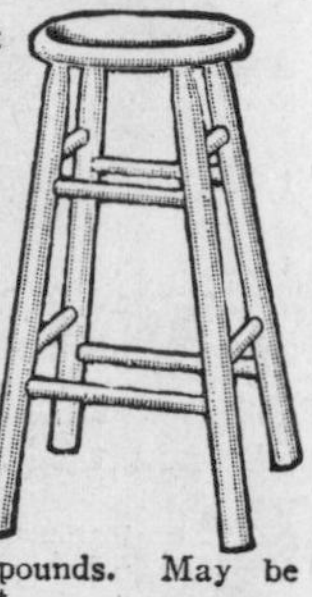

You should certainly have a kitchen stool. It is so much easier to do your work when seated. This stool is made of hardwood, finished in white enamel or golden gloss oak. It has a 13-in. seat and is 24 inches high. Legs strongly braced by **eight** deep doweled rungs. Shipping weight, 6 pounds. May be shipped by parcel post.
1K307—Oak.............. **$1.45**
White enamel.........**$1.55**

White Enameled Metal Stool

Height, 24 inches; 11-inch top. Steel throughout. Angle steel electrically welded construction. Legs supported by **eight** steel cross pieces. Absolutely rigid. Will last a lifetime. Weight, 10 pounds. Can be shipped by parcel post.
1K300
95c

Handy Indexed Cooking Recipe Outfit

Consists of cabinet, with 20 classified guides, indexed bread, cake, etc., and 100 ruled blank cards, 3x5 inches. Recipes not furnished. Capacity, 250 cards. Shipping weight, 1¾ pounds. Can be shipped by parcel post.
1K3901—Oak finish........ **49c**
1K3903—White enamel........ **79c**

Did you notice the kitchen lockers we are now offering on our kitchen furniture page 845?

Great Values
in Matched Dining Pieces

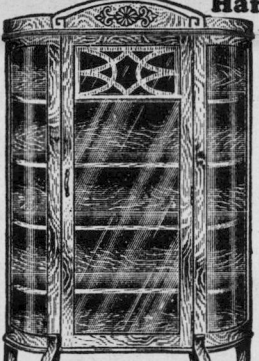

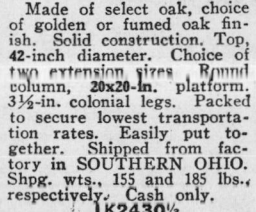

Dining and Kitchen

When you want dependable merchandise in a hurry, send your order to Sears, Roebuck and Co. **WE GUARANTEE SATISFACTION.**

Here Are Leader Values

Matched chair and arm chair at prices that will surprise you. These are splendid quality chairs, made of genuine quarter sawed oak in choice of golden or fumed finishes. Genuine box style slip seats, covered with genuine leather, brown Spanish grained. Size of seat, 16¾x16 in.; height of back, 20 in. Shipping weights, 13 and 15 pounds, respectively.

	Golden	Fumed
1K159—Chair	$3.45	$3.50
Arm Chair	6.45	6.50

Low in Price~ High in Value

A Wonder Value

Made of genuine quarter sawed oak, golden or fumed finish. Comfortable seat upholstered in genuine leather, brown Spanish grained. Box style slip seat, continuous steam bent back posts, all parts strongly doweled and glued. Size of seat, 16½x16½ in. Height of back, 21 in. Shipping wt. 13 pounds.

1K160—Golden oak.... $2.95
Fumed oak.... $3.00

Slip Seat Dining Chair

Solid oak, golden or fumed finish. Has a comfortable genuine leather slip seat, brown Spanish grained. Box style seat construction; steam bent continuous back posts. Size of seat, 17¾x14¼ in. Height of back from seat, 21 in. Entire height, 38½ in. Shpg. wt., each, 12 lbs.

1K197—Golden oak.... $2.65
Fumed oak........$2.70

Breakfast and

Wood Seat Dining Chair

A comfortable wood seat diner in design to match the one shown at the left. Just as strongly made and as neatly finished. Made of oak in choice of golden or fumed finishes. Saddle shaped wood seat. Size of seat, 18x15¼ in. Height of back, 21½ in. Shipping weight, 13 lbs.

1K147—Golden oak.....................$1.85
Fumed oak.....................1.90

White Enameled Kitchen or Breakfast Room Chair

Nothing adds more to the appearance of your kitchen than some of these good looking, washable, white enamel chairs. Four of these chairs, with one of the white porcelain enameled steel top kitchen tables described on page 846 makes an inexpensive breakfast set.

Attractive Colonial style, with the saddle shaped seat, the fancy back and the arrangement of the stretchers. Well built of hardwood, smoothly enamel coated. Size of seat, 16½x15½ in. Height of back from seat, 17¾ in. Entire height, 34¼ in. Shipping weight, each, 11 pounds.

1K14...... $2.85

Genuine Leather Seat Diner

Full box style slip seat, softly padded and upholstered in genuine leather, brown Spanish grained. Strongly made of oak, in choice of golden or fumed finishes. A neat design that will fit in well with other dining room furniture. Size of seat, 16½x15 in. Height of back, 22 in. Shpg. wt., 13 lbs.

1K191—Golden oak.......... $2.35
Fumed oak.............$2.40

Bentwood Chair

Comfortable, serviceable, sturdy. Will answer every home need. Also in demand for halls, cafeterias and any place a strong chair is needed. Back legs and back posts are one continuous tapered piece. Back legs steel braced to circular frame. All parts screwed. Seat, 16 in. diameter. Ht. of back, 18½ in. Made of solid oak, finished golden, or hardwood in mahogany or walnut finish. Shipping weight, 9 pounds.

1K50—Golden gloss....$3.55
Mahogany finish....$3.60
Walnut finish......3.65

These Pages Show Big Savings!

$1¹⁸

$1⁴⁵

$1¹⁸

A Kitchen Chair You'll Like

It's well made, neatly finished and a big value. Made of hardwood, in neat golden finish. Legs are double stretcher braced on three sides. Four-spindle back. Saddle shaped seat, 15½ in. square. Height of back, 21½ in. Packed to secure lowest transportation rates. Easily put together. Shpg. wt., 12 lbs.

1K3.............$1.18

This Chair Is Strong

Has continuous back posts, braced to the seat. Legs are double braced on three sides. Heavy seat. Triple slat back. Seat braced underneath to prevent cracking. Made of hardwood, in golden finish. Size of seat, 15½x16¼ in. Height of back, 18¾ in. Shipping weight, 12 pounds.

1K13..........$1.45

Unfinished Kitchen Chair

Well designed of unfinished hardwood. Has an unusually high, comfortable back and a saddle-shaped seat. Size of seat, 15½x 15⅝ in. Height of back from seat, 21½ in. Packed to secure lowest transportation rates. Easily put together. Shpg. wt., 9 lbs.

1K5.............$1.18

Chairs ~Priced Low~

On These Pages You Are Sure to Find the Chairs You Need at Prices You Can Afford to Pay

$3⁸⁵ Chair

Matched Chair and Arm Chair

Made of genuine quarter sawed oak, in choice of golden or fumed finishes. Seats are upholstered in genuine leather, brown Spanish grained. Full box slip seat style of construction. Strong, continuous back posts. Size of chair: Seat, 16½x16½ in.; height of back, 21 in. Shipping weights, 13 and 15 pounds, respectively.

	Golden	Fumed
1K187—Chair	$3.85	$3.90
Arm chair	6.85	6.90

$6⁸⁵ Arm Chair

Pad Seat Dining Chair

A husky, well made, neat appearing chair you will find an exceptional value at our price. Made of quarter sawed oak, golden or fumed finishes. The pad seat is genuine leather, brown Spanish grained. Size of seat, 17½x16½ in. Height of back, 20½ in. Shipping weight, 13 pounds.
1K161—Golden oak.... **$2.45**
Fumed oak.......$2.50

Our Best Quality Diner

Full box type removable slip seat, upholstered in heavy genuine leather, brown Spanish grained. Made of oak, in choice of golden or fumed finishes or of fine hardwood smoothly finished in walnut. Size of seat, 15x17 in. Height of back from seat, 22¼ in. Entire height, 39¼ in. Shipping wt., each, 15 lbs.
1K153—Golden oak.... **$3.65**
Fumed oak.......$3.70
Walnut finish...... 3.75

Headquarters for Better Dining Chairs

Kitchen Chairs

Unfinished Breakfast Room Chair

The beautiful cathedral style now so popular for breakfast set design. It has exceptionally fine lines; the legs and back slats neatly turned. Very strongly made of hardwood; stout construction seldom, if ever, found in a chair of this style at anywhere near our low price. Smoothly sanded; ready for your paint brush. Saddle seat, size, 16x15 in. Height of back from seat, 20 in. Entire height, 38 in. Packed to secure lowest transportation rates. Easily put together. Shipping weight, 10 pounds.
1K13............**$1.85**

Queen Anne Style Dining Chair

Sound construction, with full box type slip seat and continuous back posts. Upholstered in genuine leather, brown Spanish grained. Made of quarter sawed oak in golden or fumed finishes or hardwood in smooth walnut finish. Size of seat, 16x14 in. Height of back from seat, 21 in. Shipping weight, each, 12 pounds.
1K144—Golden oak.. **$2.85**
Fumed oak......$2.90
Walnut finish... 2.95

Solid Oak Chair

For a serviceable dining chair you need look no further. Neat in appearance and very strong. Continuous back posts; legs strongly braced. Made of oak, in choice of golden and fumed finishes. Saddle shaped seat, 17¾x14¼ in. Height of back, 36 in. Shipping weight, 13 pounds.
1K62—Golden oak...........**$1.95**
Fumed oak $2.00

Big Value Folding Chairs

$1⁴⁵

$1⁵⁹

$1⁵⁵

Low Back Style

Exceptionally well made with legs double braced all around. **Has bow back**—an added feature. Unfinished hardwood, smoothly sanded, ready for your paint brush. Saddle seat, 15½x15½ in. Height of back, 16 in. Packed to secure lowest transportation rates. Easily put together. Shipping weight, 12 lbs.
1K42.............**$1.45**

Popular Model

All hardwood, golden gloss finish. Saddle shaped seat. Very strongly constructed; back posts braced to seat, double stretchers between legs. Size of seat, 15½x 15¾ in. Height of back from seat, 21¾ in. Packed to secure lowest transportation rates. Easily put together. Shipping weight, 10 pounds.
1K8.............**$1.59**

Kitchen or Dining Chair

Made of hardwood, golden gloss finish. Saddle shaped seat. Very strongly made, with **eight stretchers** supporting the legs and angle braces connecting the seat and back. Size of seat, 15⅝x15½ in. Height of back from seat, 20¾ in. Packed to secure lowest transportation rates. Easily put together. Shipping wt., 10 lbs.
1K2.............**$1.55**

Made of smooth, non-splintering hardwood, natural light golden finish. All joints are deep doweled and nailed. All moving parts are riveted—no bolts to work loose or tear clothing. Seat has metal braces under the middle cross slats. Folds flat with one smooth, non-balking action. Can be stacked in space 1½x16x40 in. Size of seat, 13x13½ in. Height of back from seat, 17¼ in. Entire height, 32½ in. Shipping weight, each, 9 pounds.
1K1—Each..................**$1.08**
Per dozen $12.75
In lots of 100, shipped from factory near Chicago $105.00

Beautiful Breakfast Sets

Buy This Set on Time Payments of
$5.00 Down and $5.00 a Month

$5.00 Down

This breakfast set with the extension table makes a particular appeal as a dining set where space or funds prevent the purchase of regular dining room furniture. Closed, the table has the desired compactness; extended, it meets every requirement of the ordinary dining table, accommodating six people comfortably. This set is finished in choice of handsome frosted silver gray two-tone or frosted golden brown two-tone. The deep color of the two-tone effect on the table top and chairs is offset with line routing.

THE TABLE—Very strongly constructed; the top is screwed to the rim; the legs are bolted to the rim. Legs equipped with sliding casters. Extension supports are absolutely rigid. Size of the table, closed, 43x32 in.; extended, 60½x32 in. Complete with two leaves. Packed to secure lowest transportation rates. Easily put together. Shipping weight, 100 pounds.

THE CHAIRS—Strong, continuous bent back posts; stretcher braced legs. Seat, 16½x14 in. Height of back, 17¼ in. Shpg. wt., each, 15 lbs.

1K2530—Pieces may be purchased separately for cash.

	CASH PRICE		EASY PAYMENT PRICE	
	Frosted Silver Gray Oak Two-Tone	Frosted Golden Brown Two-Tone	Frosted Silver Gray Oak Two-Tone	Frosted Golden Brown Two-Tone
Chairs, each.........	$ 4.10	$ 4.15		
Table	13.25	13.30		
Complete set; table and four chairs....	28.65	28.90	$31.50	$31.85

Easy Payment Terms: Complete set, $5.00 down and $5.00 monthly. Use Time Payment Order Blank on Page 1092.

Beautiful Two-Tone Finishes

Table open illustrating leaves in use.

Use This Set as You Pay for It

A handsome set richly enameled in washable ivory, trimmed with dark blue. A beautiful design and finish sure to prove entirely satisfactory. Our price is exceptionally low considering the quality. This set is well made of fine hardwood and will give perfect service and satisfaction.

THE TABLE—The leaves are triple hinged; when up, they fit flush and tight with the top. Fancy corners, beveled edges, very strong box type construction. Legs are bolted to the top. Size of top, with leaves closed, 20¾x36 in.; with leaves extended, 42½x36 in. Packed to secure lowest transportation rates. Easily put together. Shipping weight, 60 pounds.

THE CHAIRS—Fancy cut-out design in back panel. Saddle shape seat. Legs are double stretcher braced. Size of seat, 16x15½ in. Height of the back, 17¾ in. Shipping weight, each, 11 pounds.

1K2510—Pieces may be purchased separately for cash.

	CASH PRICE	EASY PAYMENT PRICE
Chairs, each.................................	$ 2.95	....
Table	10.65	
Complete set, table and four chairs..................	20.95	$23.25

Easy Payment Terms: Complete set, $5.00 down and $5.00 monthly. Use Time Payment Order Blank on Page 1092.

$5.00 Down
and $5.00 a Month for Complete Set

Unfinished Breakfast Set Very Low Priced

You will not only experience the enjoyment of painting this breakfast set exactly the way you want to, but you will get the same quality. A set of this quality, decorated, would cost $25.00 or more elsewhere. Made of fine hardwood, smoothly finished and sanded, ready to enamel. The same fine construction has gone into this set as into the higher priced sets we sell. All joints are securely glued and braced.

THE TABLE—The legs are bolted to the table box. Leaves are triple hinged. Size of top, with leaves down, 21½x36 in.; with leaves up, 41½x36 in. Packed to secure lowest transportation rates. Shipping weight, 50 pounds.

THE CHAIRS—The bow backs are of square material, preferred by many to the round material backs. Seats are saddle shape, fancy turned stretchers between the legs. Size of seat, 15¾x14½ in. Height of the back, 18 in. Packed to secure lowest transportation rates. Easily put together. Shipping weight, each, 10 pounds.

1K2517—Pieces may be purchased separately.

Chairs, each... Cash only.............	$ 1.85
Table .... Cash only.............	4.95
Complete set, table and four chairs....................... Cash only.............	11.95

For Enamel to Finish This Set, See Page 1026

at Very Low Prices

$5.00 A Month

An Old Favorite Now Offered on Easy Payments

One of our best values in breakfast sets because of its extra compactness. An ideal set for the very small home that cannot accommodate the larger dining set. Will fit snugly into the modern breakfast nook. Extremely well made of fine hardwood, richly finished in washable ivory enamel, trimmed with blue, or washable gray enamel trimmed with blue. Pretty floral transfer patterns in bright colors on backs of chairs and on table legs.

THE TABLE—This popular drop leaf style is extra compact when folded. Size of top, with leaves down, only 8x36 in.; will open up to big size of 43x36 inches. Gate leg supports hold the leaves flush with the top. Leaves put together. Shipping weight, 75 pounds.

THE CHAIRS—Very strongly made with continuous bent back posts. Box style seat construction. Legs are stretcher braced. Size of seat, 15x15 in. Height of the back, 18 in. Chairs are shipped set up. Shipping weight, each, 10 pounds.

1K2538—Pieces may be purchased separately for cash.

	CASH PRICE		EASY PAYMENT PRICE	
	Ivory and Blue	Gray and Blue	Ivory and Blue	Gray and Blue
Chairs, each	$ 3.15	$ 3.20	....	....
Table	10.25	10.35	....	....
Complete set, table and chairs	22.45	22.55	$24.75	$24.85

Easy Payment Terms: Complete set, $5.00 down and $5.00 monthly. Use Time Payment Order Blank on Page 1092.

Smart New Breakfast Set

We are showing this beautiful set for the first time and are offering it on attractive **easy payment** prices. Don't put off ordering—you can have this set in your home all the time you are paying for it. Beautifully made of oak, finished in choice of frosted silver gray two-tone, blending to black at the edges, or frosted brown two-tone, blending to deeper color at the edges. The leaves and the back panels of the chairs have pretty colored transfer patterns.

THE TABLE—Extension slats hold the triple hinged leaves flush with the top. The top is screwed to the box; the legs are bolted to steel angle braced corners. Size of top, with leaves down, 23x36 in.; with leaves up, 41½x36 in. Packed to secure lowest transportation rates. Easily put together. Shipping weight, 65 pounds.

THE CHAIRS—Fancy four spindle backs; saddle shaped seats, double stretcher braced legs. Size of seat, 16½x16½ in. Height of back, 17 in. Packed to secure lowest transportation rates. Easily put together. Shipping weight, each, 12 pounds.

1K2545—Pieces may be purchased separately for cash.

	CASH PRICE		EASY PAYMENT PRICE	
	Frosted Silver Gray Two-Tone	Frosted Golden Brown Two-Tone	Frosted Silver Gray Two-Tone	Frosted Golden Brown Two-Tone
Chairs, each	$ 3.35	$ 3.40	....	....
Table	9.75	9.85	....	....
Complete set; table and four chairs	22.25	22.35	$24.45	$24.55

Easy Payment Terms: $5.00 down and $5.00 a month. Use Time Payment Order Blank on Page 1092.

The Very Newest in Breakfast Sets

The actual grain of burl walnut is exactly reproduced on this set. You have all the rare beauty of costly woods without paying high prices. The table top and the inset of the chair panels is of reproduction burl walnut. All other parts are finished in choice of Chinese red or sage green. The back rails and feet of the chairs and the edges and feet of the table are finished in black. All pieces are well built of hardwood.

THE TABLE—Well made and strongly braced. Size of the top open, 40x36 in. Size, with leaves down, 27½x36 in. Height, 30 in. Packed to secure lowest transportation charges. Easily put together. Shipping weight, 55 pounds.

THE CHAIRS—Fancy Windsor pattern with wide, shallow seats, 18x14½ in. Continuous back posts of square material; legs are braced with fancy stretchers. Height of back, 17½ in. Entire height, 35 in. Shipping weight, each, 10 pounds.

1K2531

	CASH PRICE		EASY PAYMENT PRICE	
	Chinese Red	Sage Green	Chinese Red	Sage Green
Chairs, each	$ 4.10	$ 4.15	....	....
Table	11.55	11.65	....	....
5-Piece Set	27.25	27.35	$29.85	$29.95

ONLY the complete set sold on Time Payments. Terms: $5.00 down and $5.00 a month. Use Time Payment Order Blank on page 1092.

Easy to Buy On Easy Payments

$5.00 **DOWN**

and easy monthly payments will buy any piece of this set as explained below

$44.75 Cash Price

Beautiful Walnut Buffet—The top and front are of **five-ply** sliced walnut veneers, finished in nut brown. Each door has an overlay of butt walnut; the top drawer has a most attractive overlay of genuine birdseye maple. The back rail and the base rail have overlays of satinwood. All other parts are of fine hardwood, finished to match the veneers. The back is veneered hardwood. Drawer bottoms are mahogany veneered. Lower drawer has a velvet lined silverware tray. Massive built-up posts, beautifully shaped and turned. **Newest style receding top, 66x22 in.**

$39.85 Cash Price

Fancy new style china cabinet with the canopy top. The front is of **five-ply** nut brown sliced walnut veneer overlaid with decorations of butt walnut. The center lower panel has a small overlay of birdseye maple. The beautifully cut wood grille has a small overlay decoration of satinwood. Sides are **three-ply** walnut veneer. All other parts are of hardwood finished to match. Apron and fancy carved stretcher have satinwood overlays. Beautifully turned and fluted front legs. Height, 66 inches; top, 41x19 inches.

For Table Pads, Protectors, See Page 224

$39.50 Cash Price

An attractive, sturdy dining table, in the latest fashion. The top is genuine nut brown **five-ply** sliced walnut veneer; the rest of the table is of hardwood, finished to match. The legs are massive, beautifully shaped and turned. Supporting them are gracefully cut stretchers, which add greatly to the strength of the table. This is an extra small size table, which closed measures only 54x45 in. Can be extended to 66 inches. Complete with leaves.

$20.85 Cash Price

Beautiful Server—Every dining room should have one. Very necessary and a part of every complete dining set. The top and front are of nut brown **five-ply** sliced walnut veneer; the ends are **three-ply**. Each door has an overlay of butt walnut; the small center panel has an overlay of genuine birdseye maple; back rail and base rail have overlays of fine satinwood. The back is veneered hardwood. All other parts are of solid hardwood, finished to match the veneers. Size of top, 41x19 in.

$5.95 Cash Price

Chair and Host Chair—Very strongly made of hardwood, finished to match veneered surfaces of the other pieces. The back panels are veneered with sliced walnut, decorated with birdseye maple and satinwood overlays. Front legs are beautifully turned and fluted. Seats are softly padded and upholstered in a harmonizing color Jacquard velour. A set of these chairs will add to the attractiveness of your dining room whether or not you buy them with the complete dining room set.

This set is the very newest thing. We wish especially to call your attention to the new style buffet and china cabinet. As well as being strictly up to the minute every piece is very strongly made and beautifully finished. Chair and host chair shipped from our store, other pieces from factory near CHICAGO or NORTH CAROLINA whichever is nearer you.

1K2390½	Shpg. Wt.	Cash Prices	Easy Payment Prices
Buffet	220 lbs.	$44.75	$49.45
Table	230 lbs.	39.50	43.45
China Cabinet	180 lbs.	39.85	43.85
Server	100 lbs.	20.85	22.95
Chair	25 lbs.	5.95	6.55
Host Chair	30 lbs.	9.25	10.15

Easy Payment Terms

	Down	Monthly
Any single piece	$ 5.00	$ 5.00
Any two pieces	8.00	8.00
Any three pieces	12.00	12.00
Any four pieces	16.00	16.00
Complete set	20.00	20.00

Set of chairs is considered as one piece, and is sold on Time Payments only when purchased with one or more larger pieces. A set consists of six chairs, or five chairs and host chair. Use Time Payment Order Blank on page 1092.

852 P SEARS, ROEBUCK AND CO. *The World's Largest Store*

These Perfectly Matched Pieces Sold Separately

or as a Complete Set

ORDER this set on our recommendation for its beauty, its durability and its low price. If it is not the greatest value in a dining set you ever saw, we will take it back without question and return your money in full, including all freight and drayage. The trial will not cost you one penny.

$39.50 Cash Price

$35.00 Cash Price

$9.95 Cash Price

$8.00 DOWN

and easy monthly payments will buy any piece in this set

$6.95 Cash Price

$46.85 Cash Price

$16.45 Cash Price

This Spanish Renaissance Dining Set

Now Offered on Easy Monthly Payments

The same style that has graced the halls of the Spanish Grandees of old Castile and Valencia. The rich carvings, the massiveness of design, the same solidity—all are faithfully reproduced in this handsome period style. And this distinctive set, ordinarily found only in the homes of the wealthy, can now be afforded by all. Let it add to the beauty of your home. Beautifully high lighted veneers of genuine walnut (5-ply tops and fronts, 3-ply ends). All other parts are hardwood, exposed parts finished to match. The turnings in the legs of all pieces are of a light contrasting golden hue; the interior of the scroll work, the deep flutings on the legs and the bronzed drawer pulls are touched with a deep blood red. All drawer bottoms are genuine 3-ply mahogany veneer. All drawers are dovetailed with dustproof partitions between. Triple drawer guides prevent balking. Glued blocks at all points of strain. Handsome bronzed drawer pulls. All pieces equipped with easy rolling casters or metal glides. Gracefully designed stretchers on all pieces.

BUFFET—Comes with or without mirror, as you prefer. (Illustrated both ways.) Top, 20x60 inches. Height, 41 inches. Center drawer is partitioned. Has plush lined sliding tray for silverware.

SERVER—Top, 38x19 inches. Height, 38 inches.

CHINA CABINET—Choice of paneled wood doors, decorated in color, or grilled glass doors. The china cabinet with wood doors shown in the panel is of a delightfully different design. The upper section is finished in a red blended lacquer in grained leather design. The top, back and interior are in plain red lacquer. The doors have large scroll plate hinges and knob plates. The cabinet with the grille covered glass doors is finished inside in natural stained finish. Height, 60 inches; top, 42x15½ inches.

TABLE—Top, 45x60 inches, in either 6 or 8-foot extension.

CHAIR—Seat, 18x15 inches. Height of back from seat, 22 inches. Upholstered in Jacquard velour, blue and taupe combination.

HOST CHAIR—Seat, 16x19 inches. Height of back from seat, 22 inches. Upholstered to match chair.

1K2351⅓—Chair and Host Chair shipped from our store. Other pieces from factory in INDIANA.

	Shpg. Wt.	Cash Prices	Easy Payment Prices
BUFFET—Without mirror	200 lbs.	$41.95	$46.25
With mirror	220 lbs.	46.85	51.65
SERVER	105 lbs.	16.45	18.25
CHINA CABINET—With wood doors	180 lbs.	42.75	47.25
CHINA CABINET—With glass doors	180 lbs.	39.50	43.50
TABLE—6-foot extension	210 lbs.	35.00	38.50
8-foot extension	225 lbs.	41.00	45.25
CHAIR	25 lbs.	6.95	7.65
HOST CHAIR	30 lbs.	9.95	10.95

Easy Payment Terms for Dining Furniture

	Down	Monthly
Any single piece	$ 8.00	$ 8.00
Any two pieces	12.00	12.00
Any three pieces	16.00	16.00
Any four pieces	20.00	20.00
Complete set	24.00	24.00

Server Sold Separately for Cash Only

Set of chairs is considered as one piece and is sold on Time Payments only when purchased with one or more larger pieces. Use Time Payment Order Blank on Page 1092.

Exceptional Values—Separately or in Combination

An exceptional opportunity to buy a beautiful bedroom set, or single pieces, on attractive Easy Payment Terms. Spread the purchase price over several months. Use and enjoy this set as you pay for it. Please note our Easy Payment Terms, below.

$6.00 DOWN
and $6.00 a Month Will Buy Any Piece in This Set

This handsome set is right up to the minute in style. Notice the new fashionable box end bed and the single mirror vanity dresser.

This dresser can be had in two mirror styles: The stationary fancy curved type, or the swinging mirror type with straight sides shown above in the small panel.

Genuine Mahogany and Butt Walnut

A combination of fine quality and workmanship—tops, fronts and sides of pieces are of genuine mahogany veneers; the top drawers and fancy overlays are of handsome butt walnut. All parts not veneered are of fine quality cabinet hardwood. All pieces are finished in a rich brown mahogany. The bottoms of all pieces are attractively offset with fancy scroll decorations. All drawers have genuine mahogany veneer drawer bottoms. The dresser, vanity dresser and chest of drawers have dustproof partitions under top and bottom drawers. All cabinet pieces are smoothly finished inside. Handles are heavy cast metal in the Early English finish. All pieces except the vanity bench are equipped with steel casters; the bench has metal glides.

THE BED—Handsome box end style. Wood side rails. Width, 54 in. Height, 51 in. Spring and bedding not included.

VANITY DRESSER—Featuring the new stationary single mirror style. Beautifully designed. Size of top, 48x 18 in. Genuine plate mirror, 36x26 in.

VANITY BENCH—Size of top, 27x 14 in. Correct height to match the vanity dresser.

CHEST OF DRAWERS—With or without mirror as you prefer. Mirror must be ordered separately. See price list. Size of top, 36x19 in. Genuine plate mirror in stationary standard, 18x14 in.

WARDROBE—One side is equipped with clothing trays; the other side as a wardrobe compartment. Size of top, 36x19 in. Height, 65 in.

DRESSERS—Two styles choice of stationary or swinging mirror. Size of top, 50x21 in. Size of stationary mirror, 38x30 in. Size of swinging mirror, 36x30 in.

All pieces shipped from factory in WISCONSIN except vanity bench which is shipped from our store. **Pieces may be purchased separately.**

1 K 4375⅓

	Shpg. Wt., Lbs.	Cash Price	Easy Payment Price
Bed	245	$33.75	$37.25
Vanity Dresser ..	195	49.50	54.50
Vanity Bench ...	20	7.95	8.75
Chest of Drawers	185	29.85	32.85
Mirror	20	6.45	7.15
Wardrobe ..	225	39.85	43.85
Dresser, Swinging Mirror ...	185	51.45	56.65
Dresser, Stationary Mirror ...	210	51.95	57.25

Easy Payment Terms

	Down	Monthly
Any single piece	$ 6.00	$ 6.00
Any two pieces	10.00	10.00
Any three pieces	14.00	14.00
Any four pieces	18.00	18.00
Complete set	22.00	22.00

The vanity bench and lowboy mirror are not considered as separate pieces and are sold on easy payments only when ordered with companion pieces. **Use Time Payment Order Blank on page 1092.**

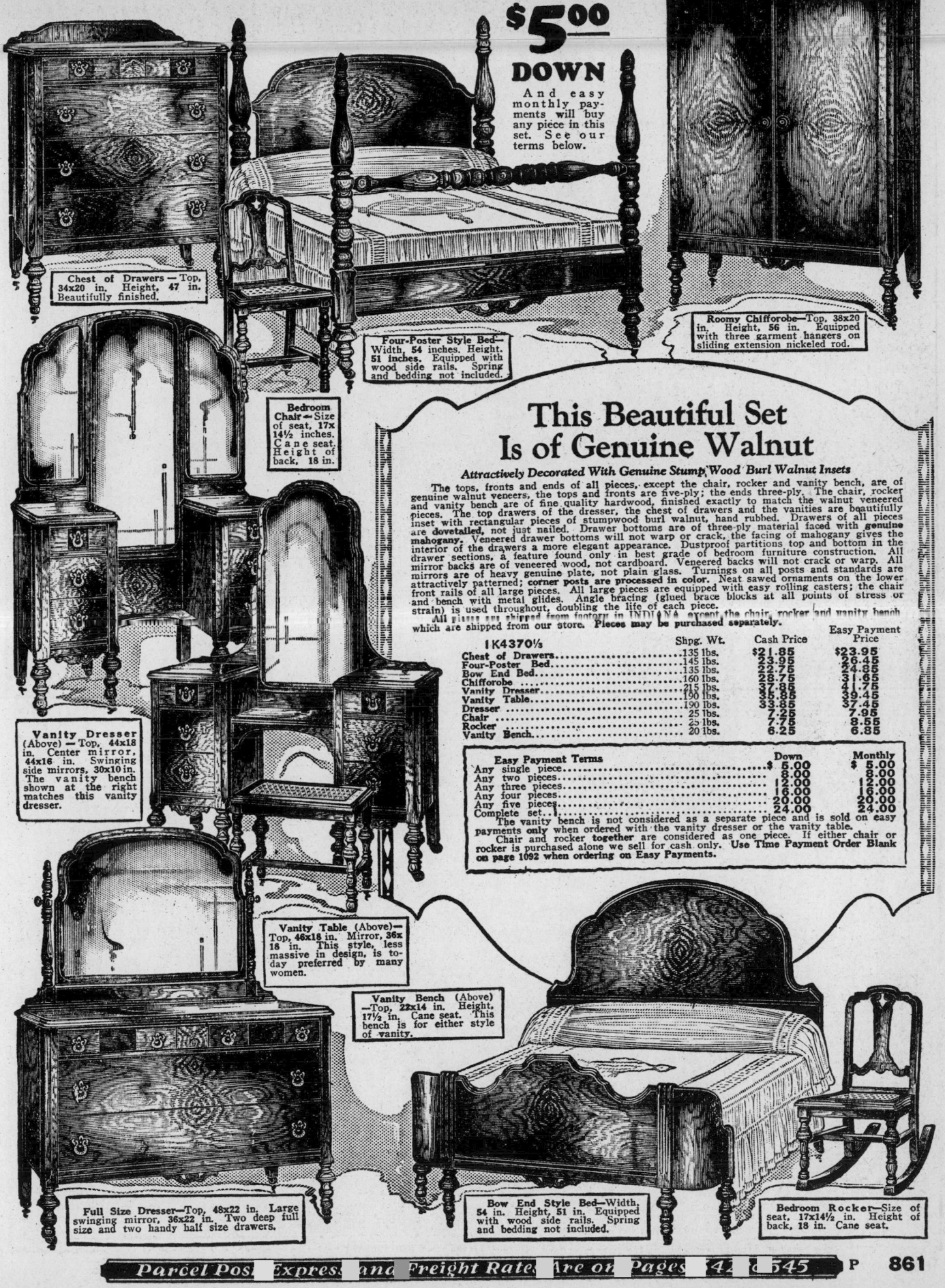

Beautiful Blended Walnut Bedroom Set

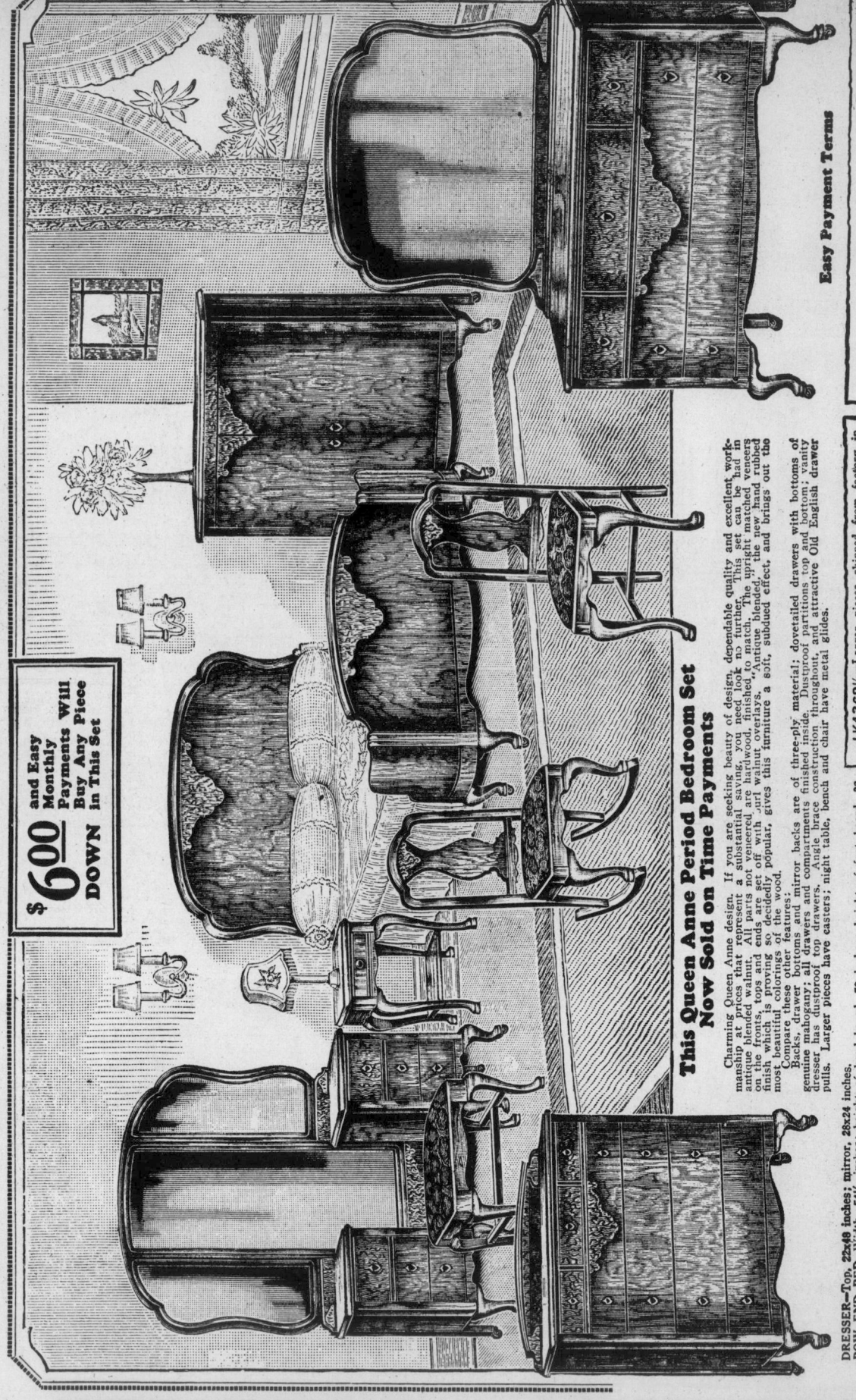

$6.00 and Easy Monthly Payments Will Buy Any Piece DOWN in This Set

This Queen Anne Period Bedroom Set Now Sold on Time Payments

Charming Queen Anne design. If you are seeking beauty of design, dependable quality and excellent workmanship at prices that represent a substantial saving, you need look no further. This set can be had in antique blended walnut. All parts not veneered are hardwood, finished to match. The upright matched veneers on the fronts, tops and ends are set off with burl walnut overlays. "Antique blended," the new hand rubbed finish which is proving so decidedly popular, gives this furniture a soft, subdued effect, and brings out the most beautiful colorings of the wood.

Compare these other features:

Backs, drawer bottoms and mirror backs are of three-ply material; dovetailed drawers with bottoms of genuine mahogany; all drawers and compartments finished inside. Dustproof partitions top and bottom; vanity dresser has dustproof top drawers. Single drawer construction throughout, and attractive Old English drawer pulls. Larger pieces have casters; night table, bench and chair have metal glides.

DRESSER—Top, 22x48 inches; mirror, 28x24 inches.
BOW END BED—Width, 54½ inches; height of head board, 50 inches; height of foot board, 33 inches. Springs and bedding not included. Wood side rails.
CHEST OF DRAWERS—Top, 20x42 inches; height, 52 inches.
VANITY DRESSER—Top, 19x48 inches; center mirror, 20x48 inches; wing mirrors, each, 10x31 in.
CHIFFOROBE—Top, 20x38 inches; height, 56 inches. Right side has garment space; left side has four trays.
NIGHT TABLE—Top, 14x17 inches; height, 28 inches.
BENCH—Top, 31½x21 inches; height, 18 inches. Upholstered in Jacquard velour.
CHAIR—Width of seat, 16 inches; height of back above seat, 20½ inches. Upholstered in Jacquard velour.
ROCKER—Width of seat, 16½ inches; depth of seat, 14 inches; height of back above seat, 20½ inches. Upholstered in Jacquard velour.

1K4362½—Larger pieces shipped from factory in INDIANA; chair, rocker and bench shipped from our store.

	Shpg. Wt., Lbs.	Cash Prices	Easy Payment Prices
Dresser	220	$42.75	$46.85
Bow End Bed	150	32.45	35.45
Chest of Drawers	210	34.85	38.45
Vanity Dresser	235	51.75	56.85
Chifforobe	200	33.75	36.85
Night Table	20	9.95	10.85
Bench	20	7.95	8.75
Chair	25	8.45	9.35
Rocker	25	8.95	9.85

Easy Payment Terms

	Down	Monthly
Any single piece	$ 6.00	$ 6.00
Any two pieces	10.00	10.00
Any three pieces	14.00	14.00
Any four pieces	18.00	18.00
Any five pieces	22.00	22.00
Complete set	26.00	26.00

Chair, rocker and night table are considered as one piece, and are sold only as a group on time payments. Vanity bench is considered as one piece with vanity dresser. Sold separately for cash only.
Use Time Payment Order Blank on page 1092.

Genuine Matched Walnut Set

$8.00 Down, $8.00 a Month

buys any two pieces

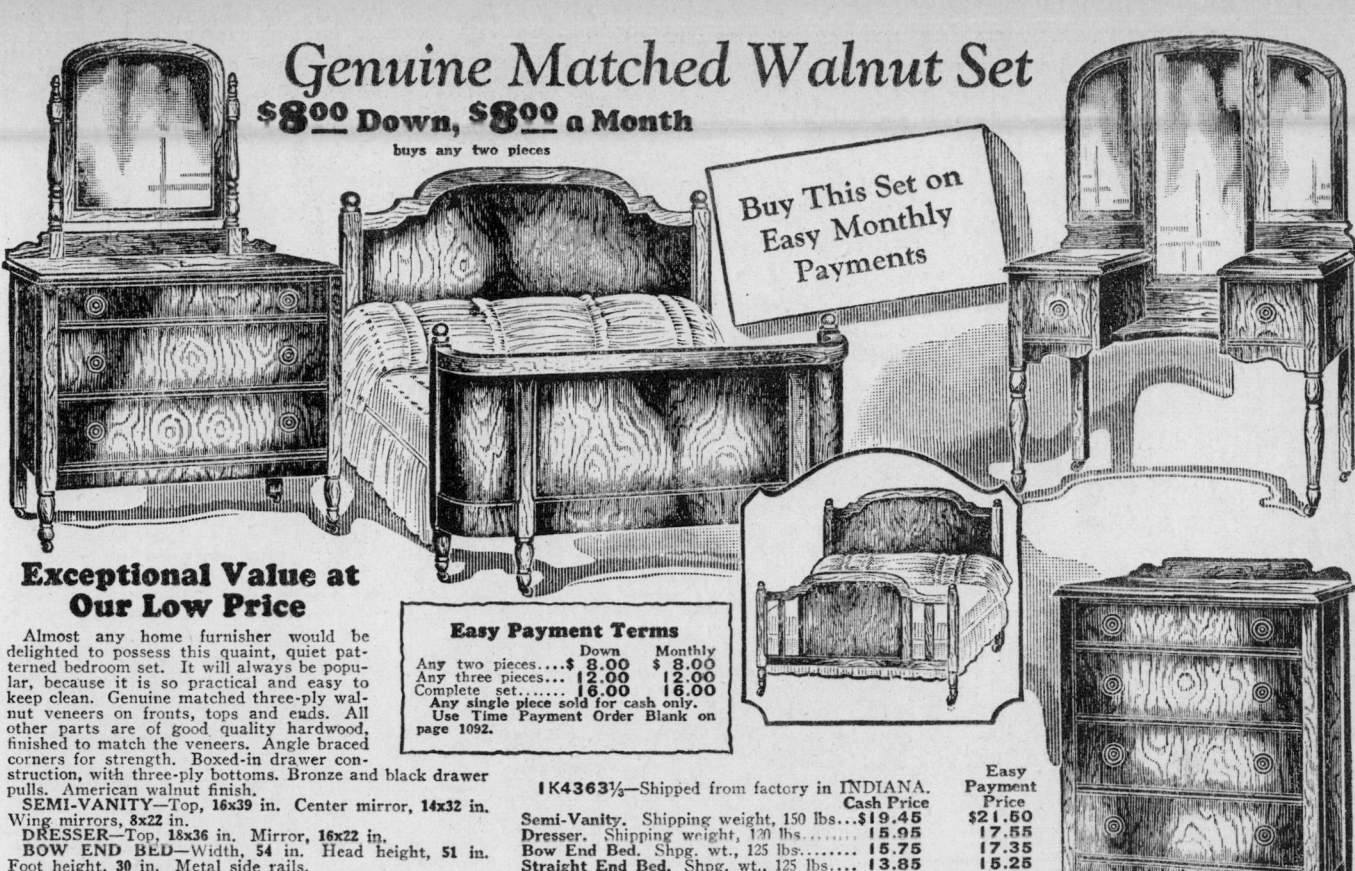

Buy This Set on Easy Monthly Payments

Exceptional Value at Our Low Price

Almost any home furnisher would be delighted to possess this quaint, quiet patterned bedroom set. It will always be popular, because it is so practical and easy to keep clean. Genuine matched three-ply walnut veneers on fronts, tops and ends. All other parts are of good quality hardwood, finished to match the veneers. Angle braced corners for strength. Boxed-in drawer construction, with three-ply bottoms. Bronze and black drawer pulls. American walnut finish.

SEMI-VANITY—Top, 16x39 in. Center mirror, 14x32 in. Wing mirrors, 8x22 in.

DRESSER—Top, 18x36 in. Mirror, 16x22 in.

BOW END BED—Width, 54 in. Head height, 51 in. Foot height, 30 in. Metal side rails.

STRAIGHT END BED—Width, 54 in. Head height, 51 in. Foot height, 33½ in. Metal side rails.

CHEST OF DRAWERS—Height, 47 in. Width, 30 in. Depth, 16 in.

Easy Payment Terms

	Down	Monthly
Any two pieces....	$ 8.00	$ 8.00
Any three pieces...	12.00	12.00
Complete set......	16.00	16.00

Any single piece sold for cash only. Use Time Payment Order Blank on page 1092.

1K4363⅓—Shipped from factory in INDIANA.

	Cash Price	Easy Payment Price
Semi-Vanity. Shipping weight, 150 lbs...	$19.45	$21.50
Dresser. Shipping weight, 120 lbs......	15.95	17.55
Bow End Bed. Shpg. wt., 125 lbs........	15.75	17.35
Straight End Bed. Shpg. wt., 125 lbs....	13.85	15.25
Chest of Drawers. Shpg. wt., 120 lbs....	12.65	13.95

Any of these pieces may be purchased separately for cash

Wardrobes and Chifforobes

Inexpensive Chifforobe

This handsome chifforobe can be had with or without mirror in the door. Three-ply golden oak, gloss finish, or three-ply hardwood, semi-gloss walnut finish. Choice of styles: With small mirror only, and solid front door, or with small mirror and full size mirror in door. Equipped with two garment hangers on pull-out slide. Glued block construction, insuring a very rigid case. Height, 66 inches; width, 40 inches; depth, 18 inches. Mirrors, 12x16 inches, and 14x40 inches. Shipped with legs detached. Shipping weight, 125 pounds. Shipped from factory in INDIANA.

	Golden Oak	Walnut Finish
1K4723⅓—Without mirror in door.....	$17.65	$17.75
1K4724⅓—With both mirrors..........	23.75	23.85

Cash Only

Chifforobe Bargains

Three-ply golden oak, gloss finish, or three-ply hardwood, semi-gloss walnut finish. Choice of styles: Without either mirror; with small door mirror only and solid front door, or with mirrors in **both doors.** Equipped with two garment hangers on pull-out slide. Height, 63 inches; width, 40 inches; depth, 18 inches. Plain plate mirrors, 9½x9½ inches and 14x40 inches. Shipping weight, 125 lbs. Shipped from factory in INDIANA.

1K4720⅓—Without mirror.
Golden oak.... **$15.75**
Walnut finish..... **$15.85**

1K4721⅓— Small mirror only.
Golden oak.... **$17.35**
Walnut finish..... **$17.45**

1K4722⅓—Both mirrors.
Golden oak............. **$23.85**
Walnut finish......... **$23.95**

Cash Only

Cash Only

Combination Secretary and Wardrobe

One side a full length closet equipped with garment hangers on a sliding rod; the other side a convenient arrangement of upper locker, desk space with drop leaf and three drawers below. Fine cabinet work throughout; made of oak, golden finish, or hardwood, walnut finish. Fitted with graceful Queen Anne style front legs. Height, 63 inches; width, 38 inches; depth, 17½ inches. Shipping weight, 125 pounds. Shipped from factory in INDIANA.

1K4719⅓ — Oak, golden finish.... **$18.65**
Hardwood, walnut finish......$18.75

Big Value Wardrobe or Front Hall Closet

Convenient arrangement of drawer and shelf space. At this low price there is a big saving for you in this good size wardrobe. A guaranteed value in a wonderfully convenient style. Golden finish, with select solid oak front. Inside has full width shelf near top with clothes hooks. Bottom equipped with two handy drawers. Height, 83 in.; width, 42 in.; depth, 19½ in. (Extreme outside measurements.) Packed to secure lowest transportation rates. Easily put together. Shipped from factory INDIANA. Shipping wt., 170 pounds.

1K4911⅓.... **$17.85**
Sold for Cash Only

This Wardrobe Provides Extra Closet Space

This handsome wardrobe will solve the problem. Equipped with sliding metal rods fitted to top, with wire coat hangers. Will prove entirely satisfactory. It has a very large capacity. Inside height, 51 in. Inside depth, 16 in. Made of oak, golden finish, or hardwood, walnut finish. Height, 63 in.; width, 38 in.; depth, 17½ in. Shpg. weight, 100 pounds. Shipped from factory in INDIANA.

1K4725⅓
Oak, golden finish.... **$14.65**
Hardwood, walnut finish..........$14.75

Cash Only

Save ONE-HALF on Wall Paper. See Pages 1018-1019

2865

Buy Now on Easy Payments

$8.00 DOWN and $8.00 a month will buy any two pieces of this set. See terms

$26.75 Cash Price

Spring and Bedding Not Included

$18.45 Cash Price

$21.85 Cash Price

$13.50 Cash Price

Genuine American Walnut Set

An unusual opportunity to secure this set on easy monthly payments. Use and enjoy it as you pay for it. Our prices for these bedroom pieces are low, much lower than others ask for the same or lower quality.

All pieces are blended walnut, with overlays of walnut veneer in scroll design. The dresser, vanity and chest of drawers have 5-ply blended walnut veneer tops; 3-ply fronts and ends. All drawers are dovetailed with side guides, guaranteeing smooth performance. All parts not veneered are of cabinet hardwood, finished in walnut to match the veneers. Angle braced construction throughout for greater strength. Equipped with bronze and black metal drawer pulls. Casters. Vanity and dresser have genuine plate mirrors.

The Dresser—Size of top, 40x22 inches. Height to dresser top, 35 inches. Entire height, 65 inches. Size of mirror, 26x24 inches. The Vanity—Size of top, 44x18 inches. Entire height, 66 inches. Center mirror, 36x16 inches; wing mirrors, 24x8 inches. Chest of Drawers—Size of top, 34x20 inches. Height, 47 inches. Bed—Full width, 54 inches. Height of head end, 50 inches; foot end, 30 inches. Reversible steel side rails.

1K4300⅓—All pieces shipped from factory in INDIANA. Pieces may be purchased separately.

	Shpg. Wt. Lbs.	Cash Price	Easy Payment Price
Dresser	140	$21.85	$24.00
Vanity	175	26.75	29.50
Chest of Drawers	130	13.50	14.85
Bed	130	18.45	20.35

Big Selection of Matched Bedroom Pieces~Lowest Prices

These Matched Pieces Are Practical and Inexpensive

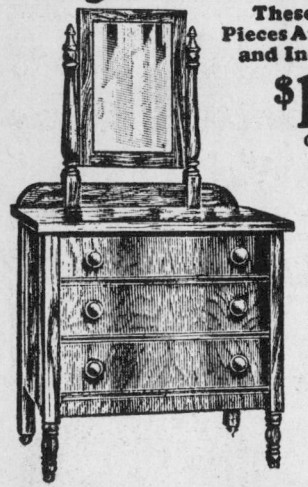

$10.85

Golden Gloss

Nothing stylish about them, but they are well made and neatly finished. Will give first class service and are very useful and practical. Made either of plain sawed oak in golden gloss finish, or good grade hardwood in dark walnut finish. Drawers are dovetailed and will stand the service required of them. They are equipped with drawer guides which guarantee smooth non-balking performance. Neat wood drawer knobs. Easy rolling casters.

THE DRESSER—Size of top, 36x18 in. Genuine plate mirror, 12x20 inches. Shipped from factory in NORTH CAROLINA. Shipping weight, 125 pounds.

THE CHEST OF DRAWERS—Size of top, 28x15½ inches, height, 41 inches. Shipped from factory in NORTH CAROLINA. Shipping weight, 110 pounds.

1K4401⅓—Dresser.
Golden Gloss Oak	Walnut Finish Hardwood
$10.85	$10.95

1K4700⅓ Chest of Drawers.
Golden Gloss Oak	Walnut Finish Hardwood
$9.65	$9.75

Matched Colonial Dresser and Chiffonier

$21.85

A new style in matched bedroom furniture design that you will like. The massive colonial style will add to the attractiveness of the bedroom. These pieces are made of solid oak, well finished in golden gloss. Drawers are deep and roomy. Easy sliding. Both pieces are strongly constructed. Both are equipped with genuine plate mirrors.

THE DRESSER—Size of top, 38x20 in. Size of mirror, 24x20 in. Shipped from factory in NORTH CAROLINA. Shipping wt., 135 lbs.

THE CHIFFONIER—Size of top, 30x20 in. Size of mirror, 18x12 in. Height, 48 in. Shipped from factory in NORTH CAROLINA. Shipping wt., 140 lbs.

1K4402⅓—Dresser ..$21.85
1K4701⅓—Chiffonier.18.95

Matched Dresser and Chest of Drawers

$11.75

Golden Gloss

Durable and sturdy pieces; roomy, attractive, low priced. One or both will prove a welcome addition to your other bedroom furniture. They provide an ample amount of extra drawer space, so much needed by most housewives. These pieces are made either of oak, golden gloss finish, or of good quality hardwood, rich walnut finish. Strongly constructed. Easy sliding drawers. Both pieces equipped with casters.

THE DRESSER—Size of top, 42x19 inches. Genuine plate swinging mirror, 24x20 in. Entire height, 65 in. Shipped from factory in INDIANA. Shipping weight, 135 pounds.

THE CHEST OF DRAWERS — Size of top, 34x19 in. Height, 51 in. Shipped from factory in INDIANA. Shipping wt., 130 lbs.

1K4414⅓—Dresser.
Golden Gloss Oak	Walnut Finish Hardwood
$19.85	$19.95

1K4713⅓ Chest of Drawers.
Golden Gloss Oak	Walnut Finish Hardwood
$11.75	$11.85

Here Are the Hidden Qualities that Make Real Value

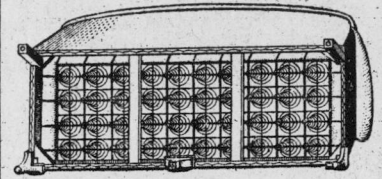

This illustrates the spring construction in the bottom of the Davenport. Note how the springs are locked together at the top.

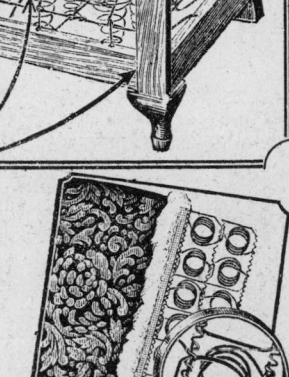

Loose cushions, spring filled
All - steel underckonstruction
Wide, heavy resilient springs
Hardwood frame, very strong

In upholstered living room furniture **the most important parts of the structure are those parts which cannot be seen.** You have a right to know what is under the cover, and because we know that the construction of our upholstered furniture is honest and without covered up faults, we take pride in illustrating and telling about these "hidden qualities."

The frame is of high grade hardwood; not only the exposed parts, but the parts which you don't see. No soft lumber is used. The frame is strongly cross braced and corner blocked and all joints are deep doweled and glued. The result is a dependable long lived structure.

Spring steel underconstruction, is absolutely trouble proof. Steel crossbars form a foundation to which the under construction springs are interlocked at their intersections. The springs hold firmly upright and cannot buckle or get out of alignment. The tops of the springs are flexibly interlocked with steel tie wires, giving a uniform surface and action.

Cushion springs are in most of our upholstered numbers, as illustrated at the right. Cushions are filled with the small, highly resilient coils, each interlocked to its neighbor, resulting in a fine uniformity of action. Since each spring is locked to its neighbor, buckling or disarrangement of alignment becomes impossible. The small illustration gives you an idea of just how many springs are used in one cushion alone.

Filling materials are of high grade sterilized two, germ cured moss and clean, white felted cotton. Heavy sheeting is used over the springs.

Davenport Mattresses
Sold for Cash Only
20-Pound Felted Cotton Mattress. Fitted with tapes for attaching to davenport spring. It has 2-in. box edges. Securely tufted. Good quality floral art ticking. Size, 48x72 in. Wt. 20 lbs. Shpg. wt., 22 lbs.
1K7213.. $4.45
25-Pound Felted Cotton Mattress. Securely tufted; has 2½-in. box edges with extra row side stitching. Serviceable grade of floral art ticking. Very attractive. Size, 48x72 in. Weighs full 25 pounds. Shpg. wt., 27 lbs.
1K7214.. $5.65
Our Finest Davenport Mattress. Full 35 pounds, fine quality all felted cotton. High quality ticking. Tufts are securely bound and evenly placed. Has 3½-in. roll edges. Size. 47x72 in. Weighs full 35 lbs. Shpg. wt., 37 lbs.
1K7223.. $6.95

Coverings are of long wearing fabrics of exquisite design and colorings that fashion and good taste approve. Every yard of fabric used is selected on two points, beauty and quality. The material is closely inspected for defects before it is applied.

The illustrations of construction were made from a davenport set we list in our catalog. It is representative of practically our complete listing of overstuffed furniture. We contract only with the largest manufacturers of overstuffed furniture and we refuse to cheapen our quality to make lower prices. You can be sure of excellent quality when you buy overstuffed furniture from the World's Largest Store.

Reversible Cushions
Can be had with any of our velour or mohair upholstered sets. We can furnish cushions upholstered on the reverse side in lustrous cotton damask at $1.35 per cushion extra; in harmonizing tapestry at $1.95 per cushion extra.

This illustrates the Spring construction of the cushion unit. Note how the springs are locked together so as to allow individual performance.

Attractive Easy Payment Terms Make This Parlor Set Easy to Own---Order Today

Easy Payment Terms

	Artificial Leather		Genuine Leather or Jacquard Velour	
	Down	Monthly	Down	Monthly
Chair or Rocker..	(Cash only)		$5.00	$5.00
Davenport ....$	8.00	$ 8.00	10.00	10.00
Any two pieces..	10.00	10.00	12.00	12.00
Complete set	12.00	12.00	14.00	14.00

Use Time Payment Order Blank on page 1092.

$12.00 Down
And $12.00 a Month Will Buy This Complete Set in Artificial Leather

A splendid, low priced set, well made and comfortable, that will meet with your entire approval. All pieces are neat in appearance, with the new style swell fronts, rapidly becoming popular. Pieces are spring filled and deeply padded. Upholstered in a selection of materials from which you are certain to pick that most suited to your home furnishing needs and your pocketbook.

This set is furnished in the following selection of upholsteries: Artificial leather, brown Spanish grained; genuine leather, brown Spanish grained, and good quality Jacquard velour in choice of blue, taupe or mulberry shades. **If ordering Jacquard velour be sure to state choice of color.** The frames of all pieces are of good quality kiln dried hardwood, the exposed parts in mahogany finish. All joints are deep doweled and glued. Frame is strongly braced. All pieces have spring filled backs and seats, covered with a soft padding of combination tow and cotton felt. Springs are firmly fastened into place and cannot work loose.

THE DAVENPORT—The seat has 24 springs; the back, 12 springs. Entire width, 72½ in. Size of seat, 60x22 in. Height of back, 21 in. Deep padded and very comfortable. Equipped with metal glides.

CHAIR AND ROCKER—Seat has 6 springs; back, 4 springs. Size of seat, 21½x19½ in. Height of back, 21 in. Chair is equipped with metal glides.

All pieces are packed to secure lowest transportation rates. Easily put together. Shipped from **our store** or from factory in **WESTERN NEW YORK.**

For Time Payment Order Blank, See Page 1092

1K1908½—If ordering velour upholstery, state color.	Shpg. Wt., Lbs.	Cash Prices			Easy Payment Prices		
		Artificial Leather	Genuine Leather	Jacquard Velour	Artificial Leather	Genuine Leather	Jacquard Velour
Davenport 140	140	$28.95	$43.95	$41.25	$31.75	$48.35	$45.35
Chair 65	65	14.35	23.25	21.15	15.65	25.55	23.25
Rocker 65	65	14.45	23.35	21.25	15.75	25.65	23.35

Attractive Parlor Sets

For the First Time We Offer This Attractive Set on Easy Payments

You will find this an exceptionally attractive set. All pieces are upholstered to order to insure new, fresh material. Please allow ten to fifteen days extra for upholstering. If you desire this set, or any piece of it, with reversible cushions, they can be ordered separately at a small additional charge. See page 867 for information about the extra cost.

Frames are birch, exposed parts mahogany finish. The spring construction and filling materials are as illustrated on page 867. This set is upholstered in choice of **Jacquard Velour or Mohair**. The velour set is furnished in the following color combinations: taupe with blue background, taupe with rose background or chestnut brown with mulberry background. The mohair set is furnished in choice of blue with rose background or taupe with rose background. The back of the backs of all pieces and the ends beneath the arms are upholstered in plain velour except the back of the bed davenport which is upholstered in black denim. Be sure to state color wanted.

BED DAVENPORT—Steel construction of seat contains 36 springs, the back has 18 springs. Each of the three loose seat cushions contains 42 fine wire springs. The bed opens out, as illustrated, giving a sleeping surface of 72x48 in. Equipped with a cable wire bed spring. Outside length, 91 in.; entire height, 33½ in.; height of back from seat, 15½ inches. Size of seat, 75x21 inches.

STATIONARY DAVENPORT—The seat has a steel construction of 30 springs; the back contains 18 springs; each of the three loose cushions contains 36 fine wire springs. Length, outside, 81 in.; entire height, 33 in.; height of back from seat, 15 in. Size of seat, 64x20½ in.

CHAIR AND ROCKER—The seat has a steel construction of 9 springs. The back has 6 springs. The loose cushions have 30 springs. Width, 34½ in.; entire height, 32 in.; height of back from seat, 14 in. Size of seat, 20½x19 in.

WING CHAIR—The seat has 9 springs, the back, 9 springs, the loose cushion, 30 springs. Width, 34½ in.; entire height, 36 in.; height of back from seat, 18 in. Size of seat, 20½x19 in.

All pieces shipped set up, except bed davenport, which is packed to secure lowest transportation rates. Easily put together.

Easy Payment Terms

Reversible cushions can be furnished at a small additional cost per cushion. Be sure to specify for what pieces the reversible cushions are wanted. See page 867.

Shipped from factory near CHICAGO or from factory in WESTERN NEW YORK, whichever is nearer you.

	Velour		Mohair	
	Down	Monthly	Down	Monthly
Any Chair or Rocker	$5.00	$5.00	$6.00	$6.00
Stationary Davenport only	7.00	7.00	9.00	9.00
Bed Davenport only	10.00	10.00	12.00	12.00
Complete Three-Piece Set with Stationary Davenport	15.00	15.00	20.00	20.00
Complete Three-Piece Set with Bed Davenport	20.00	20.00	25.00	25.00

When Ordering on Easy Payments Use Time Payment Order Blank on Page 1092.

1K1922⅓—Pieces may be purchased separately. Be sure to state kind of upholstery wanted.

		CASH PRICES		EASY PAYMENT PRICE	
	Shpg. Wt.	Jacquard Velour	Mohair	Jacquard Velour	Mohair
Chair	105 lbs.	$27.75	$39.50	$30.55	$43.45
Rocker	105 lbs.	27.85	39.60	30.65	43.55
Wing Chair	110 lbs.	30.65	42.85	33.75	47.15
Stationary Davenport	215 lbs.	49.00	69.00	53.90	75.90
Bed Davenport	330 lbs.	71.00	91.50	78.10	100.65

Buy This Popular Parlor Set Now on Easy Monthly Payments

Our Monthly Easy Payment Terms

	Down	Monthly
Chair only	$5.00	$5.00
Rocker only	5.00	5.00
Davenport only	8.00	8.00
Complete Set	15.00	15.00

When Ordering on Easy Payments Use Time Payment Order Blank on Page 1092.

We do not believe you can match this value anywhere else—comfort, style, construction and low price all considered. For the family of limited means, that wants a really splendid parlor set, we heartily recommend this one.

The frames of all pieces are of kiln dried hardwood, with the same careful attention to construction as in our highest priced sets. All exposed parts are finished in dull mahogany. Over the springs are soft fillings of wood wool and cotton, forming an even, comfortable surface. Deep, oil tempered coil springs in the seats and backs of the pieces are supported on heavy wood slats, insuring absolute rigidity at the base and making it impossible for the springs to buckle or get out of line. Offered in choice of four upholsteries: In artificial leather, brown Spanish grained; upholstered in genuine and artificial leather, brown Spanish grained (the back of the back and the outside of the arms of pieces being the artificial leather); embossed velour in blue, taupe or mulberry colors, or Jacquard velour in taupe with blue background, taupe with rose background or taupe with mulberry background colors. (Outside of arms and back are plain velour.)

If ordering either velour upholstery, be sure to state color wanted.

STATIONARY DAVENPORT—Length, outside, 80 inches. Entire height, 35 inches. Size of seat, 64x24 inches. Has 24 springs in seat, 18 springs in back. Equipped with metal glides.

CHAIR AND ROCKER—Entire height, 36½ inches. Height of back from seat, 22 inches. Seat sizes, 22x21 inches. Chair equipped with metal glides.

1K1943⅓—Shipped from factory in WESTERN NEW YORK or INDIANA. Pieces may be purchased separately. If ordering velour upholstery, be sure to state color.

Only $15.00 DOWN for Complete Set Upholstered in Velour

	Shipping Weight	CASH PRICES				EASY PAYMENT PRICES			
		Artificial Leather	Genuine Leather	Embossed Velour	Jacquard Velour	Artificial Leather	Genuine Leather	Embossed Velour	Jacquard Velour
Chair	70 lbs.	$17.65	$24.75	$21.75	$26.65	$19.45	$27.25	$23.95	$29.35
Rocker	70 lbs.	17.75	24.85	21.85	26.75	19.55	27.35	24.05	29.45
Davenport	195 lbs.	34.75	49.50	46.45	51.75	38.25	54.45	51.10	56.95

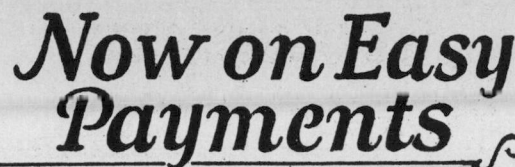

Now on Easy Payments

For Davenport Pad Mattresses to Fit, See Page 867.

This Magnificent Set Comes in Wide Selection

Choice of long bed style or shorter stationary style davenport; choice of two styles of chairs; choice of two grades of upholstery, each in several attractive shades. Buy to meet your needs, at a price you can afford.

Frames are of birch, exposed parts of select birch, finished brown mahogany. The spring construction and filling materials are exactly as illustrated on page 867.

This set is upholstered in choice of JACQUARD VELOUR or MOHAIR. The velour set is furnished in the following color combinations: taupe with blue background, taupe with rose background or chestnut brown with mulberry background. The mohair set is furnished in choice of blue with rose background or taupe with rose background. The back of the backs of all pieces and the ends beneath the arms are upholstered in plain velour except the back of the bed davenport which is upholstered in black denim. BE SURE TO STATE COLOR WANTED. Reversible cushions, upholstered in choice of damask or tapestry, can be had for a small additional cost. See page 867 for particulars.

BED DAVENPORT—Steel construction of seat contains 36 springs, the back has 18 springs. The back of the back is upholstered in denim. Each of the three loose cushions contains 42 fine wire springs, padded with high grade felted cotton. The bed opens out to long bed style, giving a generous sleeping surface of 44x72 in. Equipped with a highly flexible cable wire bed spring. Outside length, 89 in. Entire height, 32½ in. Height of back from seat, 14½ in. Size of seat, 75x22 in.

STATIONARY DAVENPORT—The seat has a steel construction of 30 springs; the back contains 18 springs. Each of the three loose cushions contains 36 fine wire springs. Length, outside, 80 in.; entire height, 33 in.; height of back from seat, 15 in. Size of seat, 64x21 in.

CHAIR AND ROCKER—The seat has a steel construction of 9 springs. The back has 6 springs. The loose cushion has 30 springs. Width, 34 in.; entire height, 33 in.; height of back from seat, 15 in. Size of seat, 20½x18 in.

WING CHAIR—The seat has 9 springs, the back 6 springs. Width, 34 in.; entire height, 37 in. Height of back from seat, 19 in. Size of seat, 20½x18 in.

1K1935⅓—Shipped from factory near CHICAGO or factory in WESTERN NEW YORK, whichever is nearer you. All pieces are set up, except bed davenport, which is packed to secure lowest transportation rates. Easily put together. Pieces may be purchased separately. Be sure to state color of upholstery wanted.

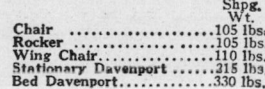

	Shpg. Wt.	CASH PRICES		EASY PAYMENT PRICES	
		Velour	Mohair	Velour	Mohair
Chair	105 lbs.	$31.75	$44.75	$34.95	$49.25
Rocker	105 lbs.	31.85	44.85	35.05	49.35
Wing Chair	110 lbs.	34.95	48.50	38.45	53.35
Stationary Davenport	215 lbs.	59.00	83.00	64.90	91.30
Bed Davenport	330 lbs.	79.00	105.00	86.90	115.50

All pieces are upholstered to order, insuring you clean, fresh merchandise. Allow 10 to 15 days for upholstering.

Only $15.00 DOWN
for Complete Set Upholstered in Velour

Only $21.00 DOWN
for Complete Set Upholstered in Mohair

Enjoy This Set as You Pay for It -- Use Our Easy Payment Offer

The home that appreciates good furniture will welcome this massive, deeply upholstered set. The rich pattern in soft color glows with warmth; the wide spread, welcoming arms invite rest. Offered in a splendid choice of colors, fabrics and pieces at prices easily afforded.

Upholstered in blue, taupe or mulberry velour; or mohair in choice of blue with rose background or taupe with rose background. Be sure to state color. The pattern of the rich velour, or mohair is a beautiful floral design. Tassels on the arms of all pieces enhance the beauty and add to the distinction of the set. Frames are of birch, finished in mahogany. Back of the backs and the outside of arms of pieces are upholstered in velour.

DAVENPORT—Height, 33 inches. Length, 82 inches. Height of back from seat, 18 inches. Seat, 22x63 inches. Has 24 double steel coil springs in seat, 27 coil springs in back; each of the three loose cushions contains 36 fine wire springs.

ROCKER AND CHAIR—Height, 33 inches. Height of back from seat, 18 inches. Seat, 20x22 inches. Nine double cone springs in seat, 9 double cone springs in back. Loose cushion seats, each containing 36 steel springs.

WING CHAIR—Height, 39 inches. Height of back from seat, 24 inches. Seat, 20x22 inches. Nine double cone springs in seat, 12 double cone springs in back. Loose cushion seat contains 36 steel springs.

For full details and illustrations showing construction of overstuffed sets, see page 867.

All our parlor sets are upholstered to order, insuring our customers clean, fresh merchandise. It requires ten to fifteen days to upholster the set of your choice.

Seat cushions can be furnished with reversible coverings for an extra charge. See page 867 for particulars.

Shipped from factory near CHICAGO or from factory in WESTERN NEW YORK. Pieces may be purchased separately. Be sure to state color of upholstery wanted.

1K1975⅓	Shipping Weight	Cash Prices		Easy Payment Prices	
		Velour	Mohair	Velour	Mohair
Chair	130 lbs.	$34.75	$ 57.75	$38.25	$ 63.55
Rocker	130 lbs.	34.85	57.85	38.35	63.65
Wing Chair	140 lbs.	37.50	61.65	41.25	67.85
Davenport	230 lbs.	63.75	109.50	70.15	120.45

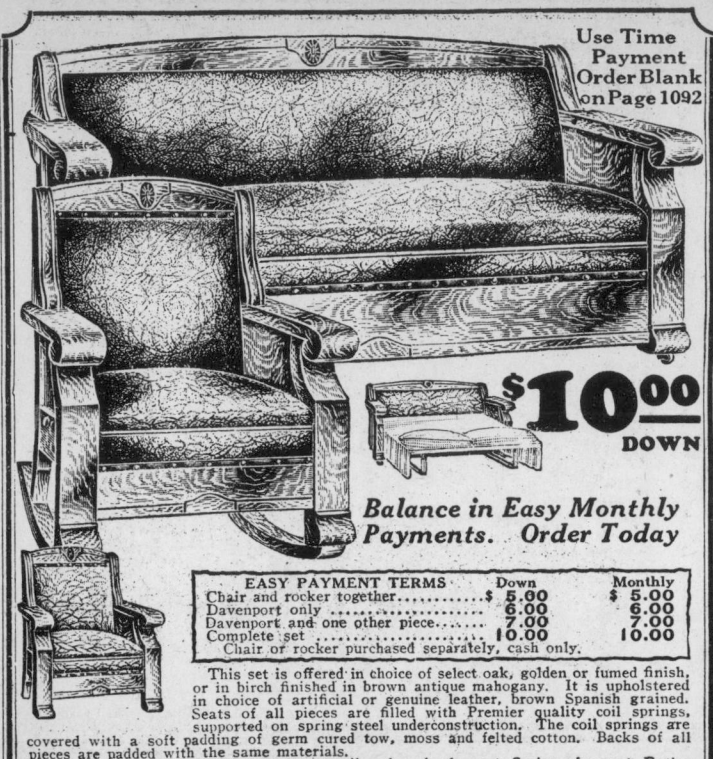

Low Priced and Comfortable

Big Value Parlor Set— Buy It On Easy Payments

$10.00 DOWN And $10.00 A Month Will Buy This Complete Set

All pieces softly padded with wood wool and cotton; all seats and backs are spring filled. Upholstered in artificial or genuine leather, brown Spanish grained. Frames of all pieces are of kiln dried hardwood, exposed parts finished in dull mahogany.

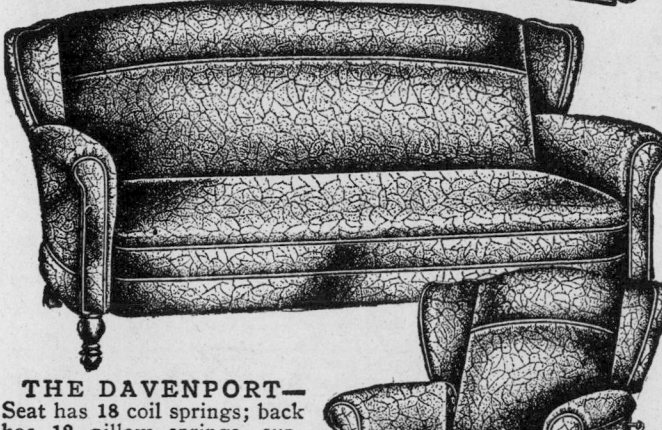

THE DAVENPORT—Seat has **18** coil springs; back has **12** pillow springs, supported on steel bands. Entire width, **63** in. Size of seat, **52x22** in. Height of back, **23½** in.

FOOT REST ROCKER—Back is adjustable; foot rest can be folded out of sight. Seat has 5 coil springs; the back has 4 pillow springs. Size of seat, 21x19 in. Height of back 26 in.

CHAIR The seat has 5 coil springs. The back has 14 pillow springs. Size of seat, 22x20 inches. Height of back, 22½ inches.

All pieces packed to secure lowest transportation rates. Easily put together. **Shipped from our store.**

IK1901	Shpg. Wt., Lbs.	Cash Prices Artificial Leather	Genuine Leather	Easy Payment Prices Artificial Leather	Genuine Leather
Davenport	145	$24.85	$38.95	$27.35	$42.85
Foot Rest Rocker	85	14.45	21.75	15.85	23.95
Chair	75	14.35	21.65	15.75	23.85

EASY PAYMENT TERMS

Chair or rocker purchased separately, cash only.

	Down	Monthly
Chair and rocker purchased together	$5.00	$5.00
Davenport only	5.00	5.00
Davenport and one other piece	8.00	8.00
Complete set	10.00	10.00

Use Time Payment Order Blank on Page 1092

Buy Now! Only **$5.00 DOWN** And $5.00 a Month

Birch frame veneered with oak, golden or fumed finished. Choice of upholsteries as listed below. The body contains 28 steel double cone shape springs; head 6 steel double cone shape springs. Length, 72 inches. Shipping weight, 95 pounds. Shipped from our store.

For Time Payment Order Blank See Page 1092.

IK1541	Cash Prices Golden	Fumed	Easy Payment Prices Golden	Fumed
Black artificial leather	$31.35	$31.45	$34.55	$34.65
Artificial leather, brown spanish grained	31.85	31.95	35.05	35.15
Black genuine leather	44.40	44.50	48.85	48.95
Genuine leather, brown Spanish grained	44.90	45.00	49.35	49.45

$5.00 DOWN And $5.00 A Month Buy on Easy Payments

Use Time Payment Order Blank on Page 1092

Birch frame, veneered with oak, in choice of golden or fumed finish. Choice of upholsteries as listed below. There are 28 steel coil cone shape springs in the body, and 6 in the head. Length, 78 inches; width, 27 inches. Shipping weight, 120 lbs. Shipped from our store.

IK1535	Cash Prices Golden	Fumed	Easy Payment Prices Golden	Fumed
Black artificial leather	$27.45	$27.55	$30.25	$30.35
Artificial leather, brown Spanish grained	27.95	28.05	30.75	30.85
Black Genuine leather	34.45	34.55	37.85	37.95
Genuine leather, brown Spanish grained	34.95	35.05	38.35	38.45

This Couch Low Priced and Comfortable. Sold for Cash Only

Well built and very durable. Frame made of hardwood, with a facing of figured quarter sawed oak veneer. Choice of golden or fumed finish. Upholstered in black artificial leather, or artificial leather, brown Spanish grained. Made with 18 steel coil springs in the body and 3 springs in the head, resting on slats securely anchored to the frame. Length, 73 inches. Width, 26 inches. Shipping weight, 80 pounds. Shipped from our store.

IK1512—Sold for Cash Only.	Golden Finish	Fumed Finish
Black artificial leather	$18.35	$18.45
Artificial leather, brown Spanish grained	18.85	18.95

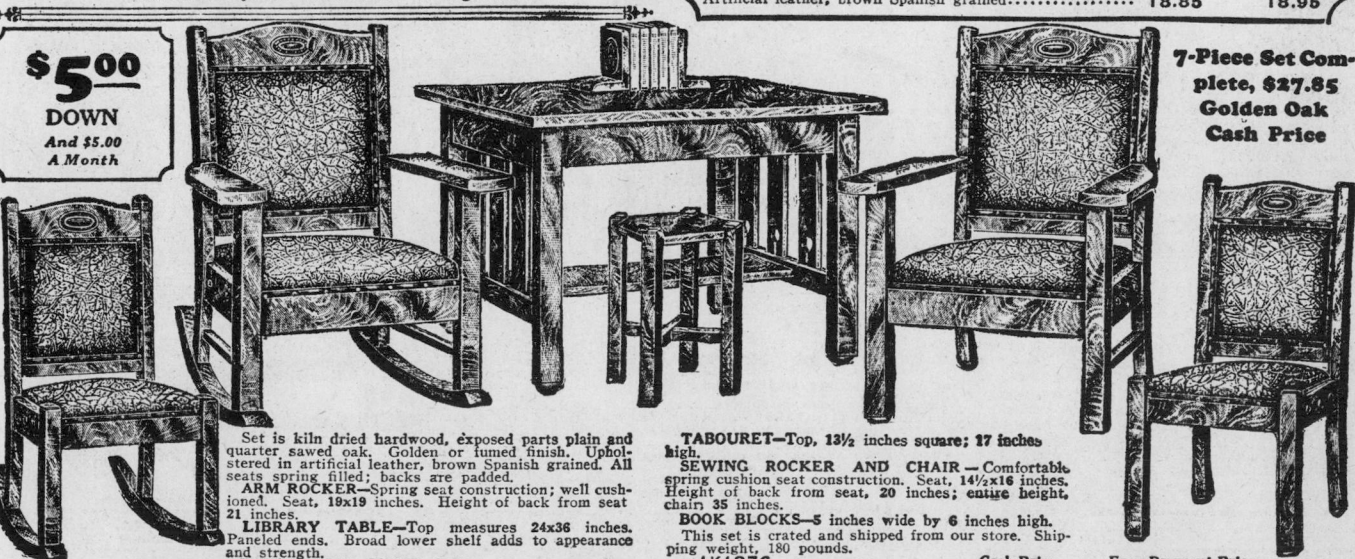

$5.00 DOWN And $5.00 A Month

7-Piece Set Complete, $27.85 Golden Oak Cash Price

Set is kiln dried hardwood, exposed parts plain and quarter sawed oak. Golden or fumed finish. Upholstered in artificial leather, brown Spanish grained. All seats spring filled; backs are padded.

ARM ROCKER—Spring seat construction; well cushioned. Seat, 19x19 inches. Height of back from seat 21 inches.

LIBRARY TABLE—Top measures 24x36 inches. Paneled ends. Broad lower shelf adds to appearance and strength.

LARGE ARM CHAIR—Spring seat construction. Noiseless, gliding casters. Seat measures 19x19 inches. Height of back from seat, 21 inches; entire height, 37 inches.

TABOURET—Top, 13½ inches square; 17 inches high.

SEWING ROCKER AND CHAIR—Comfortable, spring cushion seat construction. Seat, 14½x16 inches. Height of back from seat, 20 inches; entire height, chair 35 inches.

BOOK BLOCKS—5 inches wide by 6 inches high. This set is crated and shipped from our store. Shipping weight, 180 pounds.

IK1276	Cash Price	Easy Payment Price
Complete set, golden oak	$27.85	$30.75
Complete set, fumed oak	27.95	30.85

To Find What You Want See Index Pages 550 to 570

A Splendid Selection

Windsor Style Matched Chair and Rocker

Sold for Cash Only

Just different enough in design to add a distinctive note to the furnishings of your living room. You'll like the solid appearance of the wide spread legs supported by the double cross stretchers. The slanting back rail that helps to form the sides is exceptionally comfortable. The backs are just the right height for complete relaxation. The saddle shape seats are deep and comfortable. In these pieces, in typical colonial style, the seats are lower. Strongly, carefully constructed of hardwood, in choice of mahogany or walnut finishes. Size of seat, 19x17½ inches. Height of the back, 24 inches. Height of seat from floor, 17½ inches. Shipping weight, each piece, 25 lbs.

	Mahogany Finish	Walnut Finish
1K1461—Chair	$6.25	$6.35
1K1462—Rocker	6.35	6.45

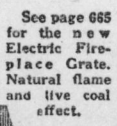

See page 665 for the new Electric Fireplace Grate. Natural flame and live coal effect.

Our Finest Rocker Built for Style and Comfort

Sag Seat Style

$13.45

The sag seat is supported on a criss-cross webbing base. Upholstered in an attractive pattern of velour in choice of blue or mulberry. The back of the back is plain velour. The frame is of fine hardwood finished in dark walnut. Very strongly constructed; the arms are connected to the front posts by steel braces. Size of seat, 22½x19½ inches. Height of back, 22½ inches. Shipping weight, 30 pounds. Be sure to state choice of upholstery color.

1K545—Cash only $13.45

Comfortably Designed —Beautifully Upholstered

Spring Cushion Seat

$8.95

Cash Only

Has a genuine auto type spring seat, upholstered in fine quality blue velour, and supported by 9 cushion springs. The frame is of fine kiln dried hardwood finished in dull walnut. The frame is exceptionally well made with steel corner angle braces supporting the underconstruction of the seat and the arms and front posts. High comfortable back. Size of seat, 19x17 inches. Height of back, 22 inches. Shipping weight, 24 pounds.

1K1469 ....$8.95

Auto Type Spring Filled Cushion

$9.35

Tapestry

Cash Only

Full box type of upholstered cushion with 9 springs in the seat. The center spring is extra deep, allowing extra "give" at the center of the cushion. Form fitting curved back. The runners are broad, long and smoothly turned, allowing smooth rocking action. The frame is made of quality hardwood, finished in walnut. The seat is upholstered in tapestry or choice of blue, taupe or mulberry velour. Size of seat, 19x18 inches. Height of back, 21½ inches. Shipping weight, 27 pounds.

1K581—Tapestry seat $9.35
Velour seat. State choice of color. 9.45

Genuine Leather Seat Rocker

Genuine Auto Type Spring Seat

$9.95

Cash Only

Every home has need of such a restful, decorative rocker. It is just one outstanding example of the savings you can make when you buy furniture here. Solidly constructed of kiln dried hardwood, satin finish in walnut. Two-tone back. The seat is supported by 9 springs and is upholstered in genuine leather, brown Spanish grained. Size of seat, 18¾x17 inches. Height of back, 22¼ inches. Shipping weight, 28 pounds.

1K1458 ....$9.95

Cash Only

Comfortable Deep Upholstered Wing Rocker

Neat in appearance and very comfortable. Deep padded wings and back; the seat is supported by 6 coil springs fastened to steel bands. The back is reinforced by steel bands. The frame is of kiln dried hardwood richly finished in mahogany. Upholstered all over in artificial leather, brown Spanish grained, or with the back, the seat and arms in genuine leather, brown Spanish grained, and the balance in artificial leather. Size of seat, 22x20 in. Height of back, 25 in. Shipping weight, 65 pounds. Packed to secure lowest transportation charges. Easily put together.

1K1471—Artificial leather $11.25
Genuine leather 17.35

Cash Only

Relax in This Rocker
Has an Extension Foot Rest and Reclining Back

The reclining back is adjustable to three positions; the foot rest, which folds out of sight when not in use, is extended to a comfortable "stretch out" length. The seat is supported by 4 deep spiral springs. The seat and back are softly padded. Mahogany finish hardwood frame. Upholstered in choice of imitation or genuine leather, brown Spanish grained, or blue or taupe velour. Seat, 19x18 in. Height of back, 23½ in. Shipping weight, 55 pounds. Packed to secure lowest transportation rates. Easily put together.

1K1429—Imitation leather $12.55
Genuine leather 17.85
Blue or taupe velour. State color 16.35

$5.00 DOWN $5.00 MONTH

This rocker suggests luxurious rest. So wide, deep and inviting, and so softly upholstered.

Spring Filled Seat and Back

The cushion seat has 9 springs; the back has 11 springs. All parts are softly padded. The frame is of kiln dried hardwood, finished in mahogany. Upholstered in genuine leather, brown Spanish grained, with the outside of the arms and back in artificial leather. Size of seat, 20x19 inches. Height of back, 25 inches. Shipping weight, 95 pounds. Shipped set up.

1K1479—Genuine brown Spanish leather. Cash price $30.85
Genuine brown Spanish leather. Easy payment price 33.95

Terms: $5.00 down and $5.00 a month. Use Time Payment Order Blank on page 1092.

of Comfortable Rockers

A Splendid Rocker
Found Nowhere Else

A Fine Value at

$9⁴⁵

Has an extremely comfortable spring seat. For the living room you couldn't make a happier selection than this rocker, which so emphatically suggests good taste, good material and good workmanship. The luxurious removable auto type seat is cushioned with 9 steel coil springs and is covered with long wearing velour furnished in choice of blue or mulberry. The hardwood frame is excellently finished in walnut. Height of back, 25 inches. Size of seat, 21x18½ inches. Shipping weight, 30 pounds.

1K500—Blue or mulberry velour. State choice.. $9.45

Matched Bedroom Pieces

Chair, Rocker and Vanity Chair

Every bedroom needs one or more of the styles offered here. The straight, high back chair can always do double duty as a dining room chair, while the rocker is very convenient for sewing. The Queen Anne period pattern harmonizes with other bedroom furnishings. Made of hardwood, walnut finish. Comes in choice of cane or wood seat styles. Height of backs: Chair, 19 in.; rocker, 19 in.; vanity chair, 13½ in. Size of seat, all pieces, 16¼x16½ in. Pieces may be purchased separately.

1K427	Shpg. Wt.	Wood Seat	Cane Seat
Chair	11 lbs.	$4.85	$5.25
Rocker	13 lbs.	5.35	5.75
Vanity chair	10 lbs.	4.95	5.35

Because we are the World's Largest Store we can name the World's Lowest Prices. When you buy from these pages you are sure of a saving.

You'll Like the Restful High Back of This Rocker

$12³⁵

Oak, Upholstered in Tapestry

The back is softly padded, offering a most attractive rocker for those who prefer the higher back. The box type spring cushion seat has a 9 coil spring unit, exceptionally resilient. Back of the back is also upholstered. Fancy braid trimming on the back and seat adds to the attractiveness of the rocker. Frame made of oak, golden finish, or hardwood, walnut finish. Choice of upholsteries: Genuine brown Spanish grain leather, tapestry in harmonizing colors, or Jacquard velour in choice of blue or mulberry. Size of seat, 20x16 in. Height of back from seat, 23 in. Entire height, 36 in. Shipping wt., 40 lbs.

1K580	Oak	Walnut
Genuine leather	$12.25	$12.35
Tapestry	12.35	12.45
Blue or mulberry velour. State choice	12.45	12.55

Rockers That Satisfy!

We feel sure you will be satisfied with any rocker or chair you may purchase from these pages. Quality and comfort, combined with low prices, is the foundation for our tremendous sales. Our rockers are shipped so carefully wrapped it is almost impossible for them to come to you scratched or marred. Most of them are shipped with the runners detached to lower transportation rates. Runners are easily put on.

Comfortable Wing Rocker

13³⁵

Artificial Leather

The seat is supported with 6 deep coil springs supported on steel bands. The back is filled with 6 pillow springs, very resilient and comfortable. The wings, arms, seat and back are all softly padded. Upholstered in choice of all artificial leather, brown Spanish grain, or genuine Spanish leather on the seat, arms and back, the balance of artificial leather. Size of seat, 26x19 in. Ht. of back, 24½ in. Shpg. wt. 75 lbs. Shipped set up.

1K472—All artificial leather......................... $13.35

Genuine and artificial leather combination $20.45

A Coxwell Chair Offers Supreme Comfort

A deep, low chair that invites complete relaxation. The widespread, welcoming arms, the tall back, the deep seat and the short legs, together form a combination of chair comfort impossible of production in any other style. The seat is filled with 9 highly resilient springs, the back with 4 pillow springs. Soft padded seat, back and arms. Figured blue or mulberry Jacquard velour upholstery, or tapestry. High quality hardwood frame, all exposed parts finished in mahogany. Seat, 24x24½ in. Entire height, 34 in. Shipping weight, 110 pounds.

1K1416
Jacquard velour, blue or mulberry. (State color) $25.45
Tapestry $23.45

Patterned After Original Old English Design

Buy one or both pieces. An unusual feature, common to this type of construction, are the arms which continue around as a part of the back. Note the fine construction, the shaped arms and seats, the extra long runners of the rocker attached to the posts in the original cleft style of old English craftsmanship. Hardwood, beautifully finished in antique mahogany or walnut. Size of seats, 20x17 inches. Shipping weight, each, 25 pounds.

	Mahogany Finish	Walnut Finish
1K598—Chair	$9.25	$9.35
1K599—Rocker	9.35	9.45

What Furnishings to Use
How to Select Colors
by an
Expert Interior Decorator
See Page 1017

$7⁵⁵

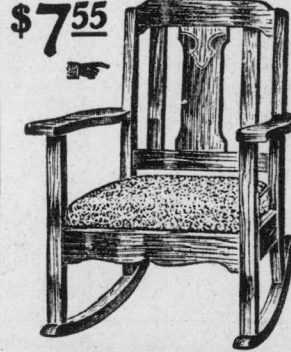

An Old Favorite

Auto type spring seat upholstered in genuine leather. Sturdy, comfortable, low priced and of a pleasing appearance. Kiln dried hardwood frame, finished in walnut. The auto type removable seat is supported with 9 coil springs. Upholstered in genuine leather, brown Spanish grained. The back panel is decorated in handsome two-tone effect. Size of seat, 19x17 in. Height of back, 25 in. Shpg. wt., 30 lbs.

1K561......... $7.55

Substantial Rockers

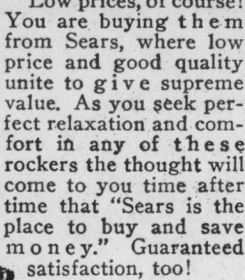

Low priced rockers selected for comfort and durability

Low prices, of course! You are buying them from Sears, where low price and good quality unite to give supreme value. As you seek perfect relaxation and comfort in any of these rockers the thought will come to you time after time that "Sears is the place to buy and save money." Guaranteed satisfaction, too!

Our Rockers are shipped carefully wrapped to insure safe delivery

Save Money On This Quality Rocker

A Big Value Rocker in Genuine Leather Upholstering

The same quality for which others usually ask $10.00, or more. A roomy sturdily built rocker worth investigating and worth owning. So solid it will stand every kind of hard usage; the genuine leather upholstered seat is thoroughly comfortable having nine springs. Made of a good quality hardwood in choice of golden or fumed finish. The seat is softly padded and upholstered in genuine leather, brown Spanish grained. Size of seat, 17x19 inches. Height of back from seat, 23½ inches. Shipping weight, set up, 35 lbs.

1 K563—Golden gloss finish....... **$7.25**
Fumed finish $7.35

Inexpensive Bedroom Rocker
$2.85

Golden Oak. Very well made and comfortable. A rocker that will give you perfect service and satisfaction. It has the correctly curved back and the saddle shape seat; it is low, as a bedroom rocker should be. Made of oak, in choice of golden or fumed finish. Seat, 15¾x16¾ in. Height of back from seat, 21 in. Packed to secure lowest transportation rates. Easily put together. Shipping weight, 12 pounds.

1 K405—Golden oak **$2.85**
Fumed oak $2.90

Bedroom or Sewing Rocker
$2.35

A very convenient style of bedroom or sewing rocker at an unusually low price. A popular and handy style, strongly built and very comfortable. Made of hardwood in imitation quarter sawed oak, high golden gloss finish. Saddle shape seat, 16x17 in. Height of back, 22½ inches. Packed to secure lowest transportation rates. Easily put together. Shipping wt., 14 lbs.

1 K453............... **$2.35**

Always Popular and a Big Bargain
$4.15
Golden Oak

Solid comfort! Real service! Two features you will expect in any rocker you buy, and this rocker has those two features **plus a bargain price.** Curved shape top panel. Comfortable rolling curved seat. Artistic design. Made of kiln dried durable oak in choice of golden gloss or fumed finish. Very strongly put together. It should give many years of satisfactory service. Seat measures 19x20 inches; height of back from seat, 24 inches. Packed to secure lowest transportation rates. Easily put together. Shpg. wt., 21 lbs.

1 K523—Golden oak **$4.15**
Fumed oak $4.20

This Rocker Built for Comfort
Padded Back Spring Filled Seat

The head rest is extra deeply padded, the back and seat are all comfortably padded, the seat is supported on 5 deep tempered coil springs fastened to steel bands. The frame is made of kiln dried hardwood, in choice of golden or fumed finish. Wide, comfortable arms.

Upholstered in artificial brown Spanish leather

Long runners. Size of seat, 19½x17 inches. Height of back, 24 inches. Packed to secure lowest transportation rates. Easily put together. Shpg. wt., 30 lbs.

1 K1233

Golden finish...................................... **$4.85**
Fumed finish....................................$4.90

Inexpensive Upholtered Rocker

An especially big value in an oak rocker with high back. Golden or fumed oak finish. One of the biggest bargains we have ever offered in this style. Genuine or artificial leather seat, brown Spanish grained. Seat, 18x19¾ inches. Height of back from seat, 25 inches. Entire height, 38½ in. Packed to secure lowest transportation rates. Easily put together. Shipping wt., 25 pounds.

Golden Oak
Artificial Leather

1 K567

	Golden Oak	Fumed Oak
Artificial leather, brown Spanish grained	$5.85	$5.95
Genuine leather, brown Spanish grained	6.85	6.95

All Oak Rocker—An Extra Value
$3.35
Golden Oak

The biggest value on the market in an all oak rocker! Search anywhere and you will soon be convinced that for a solid oak rocker in fumed or golden oak finish, his price breaks the record. Sturdy, well built, comfortable and a big bargain. Notice the size of this rocker as compared with others. Height of back, 23½ inches above seat. Size of seat, 20¾x18¼ inches. Packed to secure lowest transportation rates. Easily put together. Shipping weight, 21 pounds.

1 K522
Golden oak.................. **$3.35**
Fumed oak $3.40

Oak and Hardwood Rocker
Spring Filled Padded Leather Seat

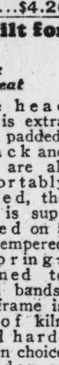

Appearance, comfort and low price are again paramount here. The frame is of thoroughly kiln dried hardwood, the exposed parts being of genuine oak. Comes in choice of golden or fumed finish. The seat is upholstered in artificial leather, brown Spanish grained. It is softly padded and is supported by 4 tempered coil springs which are fastened to steel bands. Size of seat, 17½x16 in. Height of back, 22 in. Packed to secure lowest transportation rates. Easily put together. Shipping weight, 25 pounds.

1 K568—Golden oak finish.................. **$3.75**
Fumed oak finish..................$3.80

"How to Choose Colors and Furnishings for Your Home." See page 1017 about this wonderful new book —at a bargain price.

Here's Comfortable All Hardwood Rocker
$5.45

Imitation quarter sawed oak finish. A pleasing design with graceful lines. A striking example of the unusually big values we offer in rockers. This substantial, well made rocker is priced very low. Made of hardwood, in imitation quarter sawed oak, high gloss finish. Height of back from seat, 24 inches. Curved back has broad top panel and shaped center panel. Saddle shape seat, 19x20½ inches. Packed to secure lowest transportation rates. Shipping weight, 23 pounds.

1 K520 .... **$5.45**

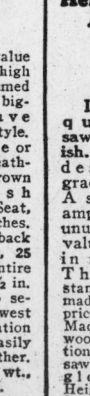

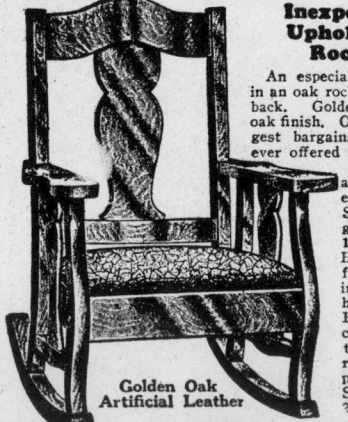

REED FURNITURE
at Lowest Prices!

Every day reed furniture becomes more popular for general home furnishing needs. Thousands of young married couples all over America are starting out with it—because it's bright and cheerful, it's comfortable, and it's inexpensive. Replace the old fashioned, out of date, comfortless furniture with new, practical pieces from these pages.

$13.95

Reed Bird Cage and Fernery

This combination piece offers brightness and cheer to the home, especially during the dark indoor days of winter. The bird cage is artistically woven of reed. It is completely equipped with a removable metal bottom, **two** porcelain seed cups and a swing. It is 10 in. in diameter, and 13 in. high. The fernery is equipped with a removable metal tray. Size, 28x11 in. Entire height, 61 in. Smoothly finished in rich brown enamel. Made of carefully woven reed in an artistic design over a sturdy hardwood frame. The legs and arch are strongly braced. Shipping weight, 60 lbs. Shipped from our store. Ferns are not included at the price we quote. Sold for cash only.

1K973—Brown enamel finish..........$13.95

Strong Square Style Fernery

Made of closely woven reed over a fancy turned hardwood frame which resembles reed wrapping. Pretty cross woven pattern between the center upright sections. Fancy woven braiding around the bottom of the basket. Convenient handles for lifting. Legs braced by cross stretcher pieces. Complete with a metal watering pan. Comes in choice of brown or ivory enamel finishes. Length, 27½ inches; width, 10½ inches; height, 31 inches. Shipping weight, 16 pounds. **Prices do not include ferns.**

1K971—Sold for cash only.
Brown enamel finish..............**$4.75**
Ivory enamel finish..............$4.95

DO YOU KNOW
How to Choose Furnishings and Colors for Your Home
See page 1017

Look at This Reed Rocker Value!

There's quality and comfort clear through in this splendid Rocker. Removable auto type spring filled seat cushion and padded back covered with attractively colored cretonne. Deep, wide back and flat arms. Seat contains 9 steel coil springs and measures 18x20 in. Attractive tightly woven reed pattern, over a steel braced hardwood frame. Choice of bright enamel finishes. Height of back from seat, 17 in.; total height, 29 in. Shipping weight, 24 lbs.

1K983—Sold for cash only.
Golden brown finish......................$8.35
Ivory enamel finish......................8.85
Frosted mahogany finish..................9.35

Now You Can Buy This Attractive Reed Set
On Easy Monthly Payments

No need to put off buying till you have the full cash price. Enjoy this set in your home while paying for it. Order today. Gracefully designed of reed, extremely comfortable, remarkably well built. And this set has the dash of color that makes a room warm and cheery. The back pads and the cushions are covered in a cheerful bright floral cretonne. **The cushions of all pieces are removable auto type, spring filled.** The weaving of the pieces is carefully and tightly done over metal braced hardwood frames. Into the fronts and backs of all pieces an attractive design has been woven, lending a touch of individuality. All pieces are enameled in rich golden brown.
CHAIR AND ROCKER—Seat measures, 19x19 inches. Height of back from seat, 22 inches. Removable cushion has 13 steel coil springs. Shipping weight, each, 28 pounds.
SETTEE—Seat measures, 60 x 20 inches. Height of back from seat, 22 inches. Cushions made in three sections; 15 coil springs in end sections, 16 coil springs in center. Shipping weight, 120 pounds.

1K999	Cash Price	Easy Payment Price
Chair	$14.85	$16.35
Rocker	14.95	16.45
Settee	35.45	38.95

Easy Payment Terms

Chair or rocker purchased separately, cash only.

	Down	Monthly
Settee only................	$5.00	$5.00
Chair and Rocker together	5.00	5.00
Settee and one other piece	8.00	8.00
Complete set..............	10.00	10.00

When Ordering on Easy Payments Use Time Payment Order Blank on Page 1092

Porch Furniture

Sun Parlor Swing

Smoothly sanded non-splintering oak, golden gloss finish. Seat 17 in. deep. Back, 20 in. high from seat. Complete with hooks, screws and chains, ready for hanging. Packed to secure lowest transportation rates. Easily put together.
1K1192—Sold for cash only.

Size	Shpg. Wt.	
4 ft.	35 lbs.	$4.95
4½ ft.	40 lbs.	5.65
5½ ft.	45 lbs.	6.45

Comfortable Cane Seat and Back

A neat appearing, comfortable rocker equally popular for indoor or outdoor use. The woven cane seat and high back are springy, comfortable and durable. Broad, flat arms. Strong, thoroughly seasoned maple frame, long runners. Legs are braced with double stretchers. Natural varnish finish. Size of seat, 22x17 in. Height of back, 30 in. Shpg. wt., 25 lbs.
1K179—Cash only...............$4.95

Popular Sun Porch Rocker

A neat appearing, comfortable rocker. The durable construction assures years and years of service. Made of maple, natural finish, with comfortable cane seat, and high slat back. Strong 2-in. posts. Legs are double stretcher braced. Long runners. Seat is 16x21 in. Height of back from seat, 30 in. Shipping weight, 20 pounds.
1K178—Cash only...............$4.45

Comfortable Armless Rocker

A small, inexpensive, comfortable rocker that will meet many needs in the home, for bedroom, sun porch or sewing room. Has a double cane herringbone woven seat, much stronger than ordinary basket woven seat. Runners are fitted into cleft feet. Natural varnish finish. Size of seat, 16½x14 in. Height of back, 19 in. Shpg. wt., 10 lbs.
1K1111
$1.45

Cash Only

Woven Seat Chair

Has a double cane herringbone woven seat. Taper legs; continuous back posts. Double stretcher bracing all around. Natural varnish finish. Size of seat, 16¼x12¾ in. Height of back, 15 in. Shipping wt., 9 lbs.
1K1112... $1.10

Cash only

Comfortable Arm Rocker

Strong, well made and comfortable. Has a double cane herringbone woven seat, a high back and flat, broad arms. Runners fit into cleft feet. Legs are double stretcher braced. Natural varnish finish. Size of seat, 19¼x15 in. Height of back, 21½ in. Shipping wt., 15 lbs.
1K1113
$2.65

Cash only

FIBRE-CRAFT *Furniture*

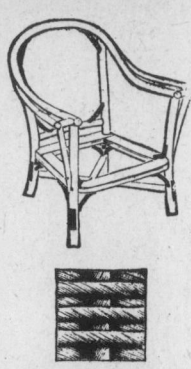

Sound construction in the frame insures exceptionally long life in all our Fibre-Craft Furniture. Frame is all hardwood, deep doweled and glued. Every joint is steel braced, insuring absolute rigidity. Made in the world's largest furniture weaving factories.

The illustrations of weaving show the actual size of the machine woven fiber weave, and the steel stakes about which the individual strands of hand woven fiber are twisted for lifelong strength. Is it any wonder our Fibre-Craft Furniture is so durable? Woven in the world's largest furniture weaving factory.

This Beautiful Set Now Sold on Easy Payments

The enamel finish of the bodies of the pieces is strikingly offset by the contrasting color designs and trimmings. The cretonne covered spring filled loose cushions are in a quiet pretty design. The chair, rocker and davenport are woven of fiber, in form fitting style, for comfort. Choice of two color combinations—brown trimmed with red or cream-ivory trimmed with blue.

DAVENPORT—Two loose cushions, each filled with 29 coil springs. Underconstruction, very strong. Length, 52½ in. Entire height, 31¾ in. Size of seat, 46x21 in. Back, 20 in. high.

CHAIR AND ROCKER—Seat cushions filled with 13 coil springs. Entire height, 31¾ in. Height of back, 19 in. Size of seat, 18 in.

FERNERY—Height, 28 in. Length, 28 in. Width, 11 in. Complete with galvanized watering pan. Ferns not included.

TABLE—Top, 24 in. diameter. Height, 28 in.

Easy Payment Terms

	Down	Monthly
Any three pieces	$ 8.00	$ 8.00
Any four pieces	8.00	8.00
Complete set	12.00	12.00

Fewer than three pieces, sold for cash only. When ordering on Easy Payments use Time Payment Order Blank on page 1092.

1K978

Pieces may be purchased separately for cash.	Shpg. Wt.	Cash Prices Brown and Red	Cash Prices Ivory and Blue	Easy Payment Prices Brown and Red	Easy Payment Prices Ivory and Blue
Davenport	87 lbs.	$21.85	$22.85	$24.25	$25.25
Chair	24 lbs.	10.45	10.85	11.55	11.95
Rocker	26 lbs.	10.55	10.95	11.65	12.05
Fernery	15 lbs.	6.25	6.75	6.95	7.45
Table	15 lbs.	6.85	7.25	7.55	7.95

Cash Only

Beautiful Matched Desk and Chair of Woven Fiber

Charmingly designed in a pretty pattern, and very handy for the smaller home which has no room for the larger secretary. Why not place this pretty set in your sun room or living room? It will add a note of brightness you are sure to like. Both pieces are of tightly woven fiber over strong hardwood frames. Finished in a quiet golden brown enamel. The desk has a 30x18 genuine quarter sawed oak veneer writing surface, gloss finish. Entire height, 36½ in. The size of the chair seat is 16x13½ in. Height of back, 17½ in. Pieces may be purchased separately.

1K956—Desk. Shipping weight, 51 pounds. **$11.95**

1K957—Chair. Shipping weight, 13 pounds. **$5.95**

Cash Only

New Beautiful Woven Fiber Set on Easy Payments

All pieces have cretonne covered cushion upholstered backs and loose auto type spring filled removable seat cushions. The pieces of this set are tightly hand woven of steel stake fiber described above. The seat cushions are built in the best fashion; the springs are fastened to steel strips, which are supported by hardwood frames. Finished in golden brown enamel.

DAVENPORT—Has two removable cushions, each with 12 coil springs. Length, 58 in. Entire height, 34 in. Height of back, 21 in. Size of seat, 48x20 in.

CHAIR AND ROCKER—Cushions have 9 coil springs. Entire height, 34 in. Height of back, 21 in. Size of seat, 19x18 in.

Easy Payment Terms

	Down	Monthly
Davenport and one other piece	$5.00	$5.00
Complete set	8.00	8.00

Any single piece, cash only. When ordering on Easy Payments use Time Payment Order Blank on page 1092.

1K900

Pieces may be purchased separately for cash only.	Shpg. Wt.	Cash Prices	Easy Payment Prices
Davenport	45 lbs.	$17.35	$19.25
Chair	24 lbs.	9.35	10.35
Rocker	26 lbs.	9.45	10.45

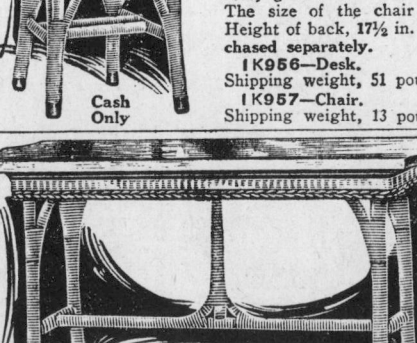

Cash Only

Fibre-Craft Davenport or Library Table

Just one more proof that Fibre-Craft is being used for the general home furnishing scheme. Legs very strongly braced by attractive stretchers and center pedestal which are tightly wrapped at the joints. Box style top orated in woven fiber and banded with braid. Graceful legs and stretchers are turned to resemble fiber. Top of quarter sawed oak, golden finish. Size, 48x18 in. Height, 30 in. Shipping weight, 75 pounds.

1K980—Finished in golden brown. **$12.95**

Is Bright and Cheerful

Square Fiber Fernery

This handy design will fit nicely in many places where the larger ferneries will not. Has a large fern capacity. 28 in. high, 11 in. square. Inside fitted with galvanized steel pan. Tightly woven fiber over a strong hardwood frame. Shipping weight, 9 pounds. Can be shipped by parcel post. Ferns not included.
1K911—Golden brown finish. **$2.45**

Cash only

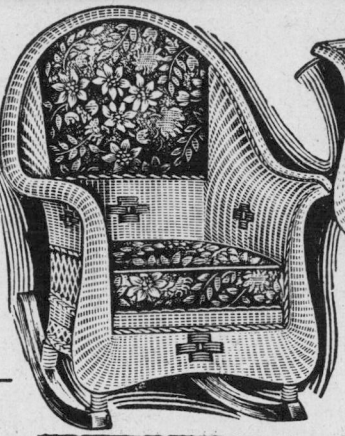

Easy to Buy on Easy Payments

Finished in attractive cafe au lait (coffee cream color). The attractive floral pattern cretonne upholstering helps to brighten up the room. Investigate this big value!

CHAIR AND ROCKER—Seats measure 19x19 in. Height of back from seat, 25 in. Removable upholstered cushions have 13 steel coil springs.

DAVENPORT—Seat, 60 in. wide and 21 in. deep. Height of back from seat, 24 in. Removable upholstered spring seat cushions. End cushions have 15 steel coil springs; center cushion, 10 steel coil springs.

1K944—Pieces may be purchased separately for cash.

	Shpg. Wt.	Cash Prices	Easy Payment Prices
Chair	30 lbs.	$18.45	$20.35
Rocker	30 lbs.	18.55	20.45
Davenport	120 lbs.	38.85	42.75

Easy Payment Terms on Above Set

Chair or rocker purchased separately, cash only.

	Down	Monthly
Davenport	$5.00	$5.00
Chair and rocker together	5.00	5.00
Davenport and one other piece	7.00	7.00
Complete set	9.00	9.00

When ordering on Easy Payments Use Time Payment Order Blank on page 1092.

Another Fernery Value

This beautiful and practical fiber fernery will fit harmoniously into your home. A choice between golden brown finish and artistic ivory enamel. We are quoting some remarkably low prices here on this substantial and attractive piece of furniture. Width, 11¼ in.; length, 27½ in.; height, 28 in. Has galvanized steel pan. Shipping weight, 13 pounds. Price does not include ferns.
1K938—Golden brown finish........**$3.65**
Ivory enamel finish........ **3.85**

Cash only

Useful Magazine Stand

Very convenient and attractive; you will find many uses for the pretty stand. Handy for books, magazines or a lamp. Large, roomy compartments. Quarter sawed oak veneer top and shelves. Tightly woven fiber over a hardwood frame. Trimmed with pretty braid. Top, 16 in. square; shelves, 12 in. square; entire height, 29½ in. Finished in golden brown. Shipping weight, 20 pounds.
1K920........**$7.25**

Cash only

Handy Small Table

For Sun porch, lawn or living room. There are many small odd corners in the home where this table could be fitted in. Convenient for a lamp or magazines. Beautifully woven, gracefully designed and strongly built. Artistically designed top, veneered in genuine quarter sawed oak. Top measures 34x18 inches. Height, 28 inches. Shipping weight, 30 lbs.
1K930—Finished in golden brown........ **$8.45**

Cash only

This Stunning Rocker

Will add a distinctive touch to any living room. It's a beautiful piece, fashionable and comfortable. Back fully upholstered and softly padded. Removable auto type, spring filled, loose seat cushion. Back and seat upholstered in bright cretonne. Choice of two attractive finishes — golden brown or frosted mahogany. Entire height, 36 inches. Height of back, 22½ inches. Size of seat, 19 x 19½ inches. Shipping weight, 32 pounds.
1K997
Golden brown finish........**$12.75**
Frosted mahogany finish **$12.95**

Cash only

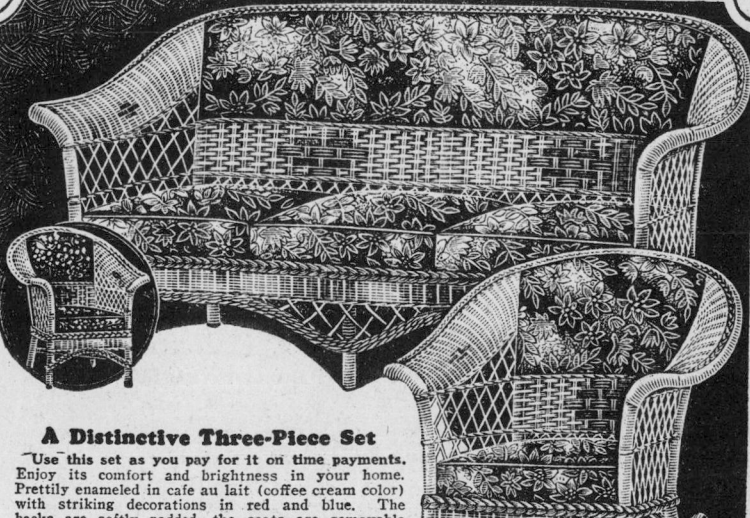

Fan Back Style

Very attractively designed. With a pretty running woven stripe. Wide sloping arms, comfortable back and seat. This style fits in exceptionally well as an odd piece in any room furnishing scheme. A new design in a type of construction usually priced much higher. Entire height, 37 inches. Height of back, 25½ inches. Size of seat, 19 inches wide. Shipping weight, 22 lbs.
1K975
Finished golden brown... **$8.25**

Cash only

A Distinctive Three-Piece Set

Use this set as you pay for it on time payments. Enjoy its comfort and brightness in your home. Prettily enameled in cafe au lait (coffee cream color) with striking decorations in red and blue. The backs are softly padded, the seats are removable auto type, coil spring filled. Upholstery is in a bright pattern cretonne.

THE DAVENPORT—Has three removable cushions, each with 9 coil springs. Entire height, 34 in. Entire length, 69 in. Height of back, 21 in. Size of seat, 58x21 in.

CHAIR AND ROCKER—Cushions have 9 coil springs. Width, 25 in. Entire height, 34 in. Height of backs, 21 in. Size of seats, 19x18 in.

1K901
Pieces may be purchased separately for cash.

	Shpg. Wt.	Cash Prices	Easy Payment Prices
Davenport	110 lbs.	$23.85	$26.25
Chair	28 lbs.	11.85	13.10
Rocker	30 lbs.	11.95	13.20

Easy Payment Terms

Chair or rocker purchased separately, cash only.

	Down	Monthly
Davenport	$5.00	$5.00
Chair and rocker together	5.00	5.00
Davenport and one other piece	7.00	7.00
Complete set	9.00	9.00

When ordering on Easy Payments Use Time Payment Order Blank on Page 1092.

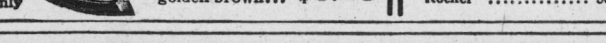

Still Lower Prices

Beauty and Comfort Combined in This All Ivory Enameled Crib

Attractiveness combined with comfort are the outstanding features of this crib. The price and quality, too, are remarkable. Dainty in appearance, yet substantially constructed to give lasting service. Made of thoroughly seasoned hardwood, finished in washable ivory enamel. Steel cane panels with polychrome ornaments on both ends that add to the attractive appearance. Equipped with strong, comfortable, sagless link steel fabric spring firmly fastened to steel frame with helical (coil) springs. Patent drop side; a slight pressure on the foot lever automatically drops the side; shock absorbers eliminate the noise. Side locks automatically when raised again. Mounted on easy rolling casters. Height, 41 inches; length, 54 inches; width, 30 inches; depth of sides, 24 inches. Packed to secure lowest transportation rates. Easily put together. Shpg. wt., 85 lbs.

1K5912..**$15.45**

For Comfortable Felted Cotton Pad Crib Mattress and Pillows to fit this crib, see bottom of page. Takes 30x54-inch mattress.

We are America's Headquarters for cribs and bassinets because we sell good quality at surprisingly low prices. Every crib and bassinet we sell will long outlast the infant years of the little fellow.

The Crib That Will Please You

Ivory enamel finish over kiln dried hardwood. Attractive steel cane panels with neat polychrome decoration on foot end panel and decorated top rail at head. Patent drop side; a slight pressure on the foot lever automatically drops the side; shock absorbers eliminate the noise. Side locks automatically when raised again. Equipped with strong, comfortable, sagless link fabric spring, firmly fastened to steel frame with helical (coil) springs. Length, 45 inches; width, 23 inches; height, 40 inches; depth of sides, 20 inches. The stamped steel swivel wheels with rubber tires allow this crib to be moved about with perfect ease. Packed to secure lowest transportation rates. Easily put together. Shipping weight, 40 pounds.

1K5913......................................**$12.45**

1K7265—Pad mattress to fit. Floral art ticking. Actual weight, 6 pounds. Shipping weight, 7 pounds. Can be mailed parcel post......................................**$2.25**

Very Attractive Crib

Those who are willing to spend a little more for the very best will be delighted with this artistically designed crib. Has attractive steel cane panels, the two end panels are decorated with pleasing polychrome ornaments. Exceptionally well constructed of selected hardwood and finished in glossy washable ivory enamel. Fitted with patent drop side; a slight pressure on the foot lever automatically drops the side; shock absorbers eliminate the noise. Side locks automatically when raised again. Strong, comfortable sagless link steel fabric spring, firmly fastened to steel frame with helical (coil) springs. Easy rolling casters. Length, 55 inches; width, 30 in.; height, 40 in.; depth of sides, 21¼ in. Packed to secure lowest transportation rates. Easily put together. Shipping weight, 70 lbs.

1K5911......................................**$11.95**

For comfortable Felted Cotton Pad Crib Mattress and Pillows to fit this crib, see bottom of page. Takes 30x54-inch size mattress.

Buy at This Low Price

A firmly made bassinet finished in washable ivory enamel over hardwood frame. Steel cane panels decorated with pretty juvenile pictures. Comfortable woven steel spring bottom. Length, 35 in.; width, 20 in.; height, 32 in.; depth of sides, 13 in. 6-in. stamped steel wheels with rubber tires. Easy rolling and noiseless. Packed to secure lowest transportation rates. Easily put together. This is a wonder value you are sure to appreciate. Shipping weight, 20 pounds.

1K5919.........**$5.45**

1K7251—Pad mattress to fit. Size, 18x34 in. Floral art ticking. Actual weight, 3 lbs. Shpg. wt., 5 lbs. Can be mailed parcel post.......................**$1.75**

Another Typical Sears Value

Wide steel panels with the beautiful polychrome decorations on the end panels and a distinctive touch to this well-proportioned crib. Made of seasoned hardwood finished in a rich washable ivory enamel. Strong, comfortable, woven wire spring. Has one-piece spot welded steel swivel wheels with rubber tires, easy rolling and noiseless. Length, 40 in.; width, 23 in.; height, 37 in.; depth of sides, 16 in. Packed to secure lowest transportation rates. Easily put together. Shpg. wt., 26 lbs.

1K5920......................................**$9.45**

1K7258—Pad mattress to fit. Fancy art ticking. Actual weight, 6 pounds. Shipping weight, 8 pounds. Can be mailed parcel post.................**$2.35**

CRIB MATTRESSES

Felted Crib Mattresses

All new cotton, covered with juvenile art ticking, three-inch box edges. Two smallest sizes can be shipped parcel post. For shipping weight add 1½ lbs. to actual weight stated.

1K7272

30x54 in.	Actual wt., 14 lbs.	.$3.95
30x60 in.	Actual wt., 16 lbs.	.4.75
30x64 in.	Actual wt., 17 lbs.	.5.10
36x60 in.	Actual wt., 19 lbs.	.5.60
40x60 in.	Actual wt., 21 lbs.	.6.35

Art Ticking Crib Mattress

(Not illustrated.) Good quality felted cotton filling, 3-in. box edges. Fancy art pattern ticking. Can ship small size by parcel post. For shipping weight, add 1½ pounds to actual weight.

1K7267

30x54-inch.	Actual wt., 12 lbs.	.$3.65
36x60-inch.	Actual wt., 16 lbs.	.4.45

A Crib for the Infant—A Bed for the Growing Child

Why buy both when this fine youths' bed meets both purposes? Large enough so that the average child of twelve can sleep in it comfortably. A low style for mothers' convenience; a drop side is not necessary. It is made of selected hardwood with washable ivory enamel finish. Steel cane panels with composition ornaments add to its attractiveness. Equipped with strong, comfortable, sagless link steel fabric spring firmly fastened to steel frame with helical (coil) springs. Equipped with easy rolling casters. The construction is the best throughout, strong and durable. The very best workmanship has been put in this crib, so that you will be fully satisfied when you buy this wonderful value. Length, 65 inches; width, 33 inches; height, 44½ inches. Packed to secure lowest transportation rates. Easily put together. We recommend this bed to those who want the best at lowest prices. Shpg. wt., 80 lbs.

1K5914.........**$12.85**

Comfortable Felted Cotton Pad Crib Mattress and Pillows to fit this bed shown at the right. Takes 30x64-inch mattress.

Soft Crib Pillows

Filled with fluffy half down turkey feather mixture. Good grade art ticking cover. Can be mailed parcel post.

1K7149—10x15-inch. Actual weight, 8 oz. Shpg. wt., ¾ lb. Each.....45c

1K7150—14x18-inch. Actual weight, 1¼ lbs. Shpg. wt., 2 lbs. Each.....65c

on Cribs and Bassinets

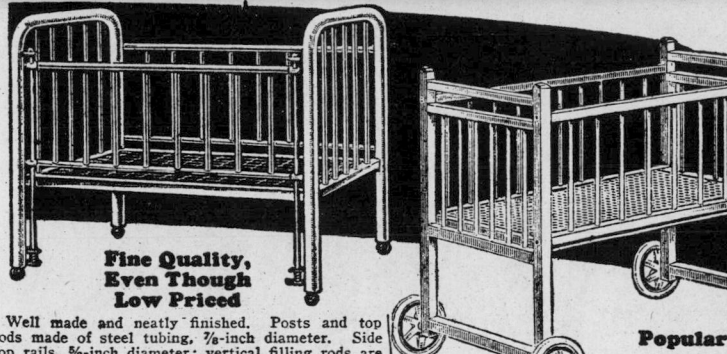

Fine Quality, Even Though Low Priced

Well made and neatly finished. Posts and top rods made of steel tubing, 7/8-inch diameter. Side top rails, 5/8-inch diameter; vertical filling rods are 1/4-inch diameter. One stationary and one sliding drop side, 14½ inches high. Height, 37½ inches. Equipped with strong, comfortable, sagless link steel fabric spring, firmly fastened to steel ends with helical (coil) springs. No projections on which baby may injure himself. At lower prices than are asked elsewhere. Shipping weights, 50 and 55 pounds, respectively.

	Brown Enamel	Ivory Enamel
1K5976		
Size, 30x54-inch	$6.75	$6.35
Size, 36x60-inch	7.15	6.75

1K7267—Felted Cotton Mattress to fit.
30x54-inch. Actual weight, 12 pounds.
  Shipping weight, 14 pounds.................$3.65
36x60-inch. Actual weight, 12 pounds.
  Shipping weight, 18 pounds........... 4.45

One of Our Most Popular Cribs at an Extra Low Price

Here is a good looking, well built crib that is an exceptional value. Made of kiln dried hardwood finished in washable ivory enamel. Has one sliding drop side, 21¼ in. high. Patent drop side; a slight pressure on the foot lever automatically releases the side. Shock absorbers eliminate the noise. Side locks automatically when raised again. Fitted with strong, comfortable, sagless link steel fabric spring, fastened to ends with helical (coil) springs. Height of ends, 40 inches; length, 54 inches; width, 30 inches. Packed to secure lowest transportation rates. Easily put together. Shipping weight, 60 pounds.

1K5935......................................$7.45
For Comfortable Felted Cotton Pad Crib Mattress and Pillows to fit this crib, see bottom of page. Takes 30x54-inch pad.

Popular Priced Bassinet

Mothers will appreciate this fine quality bassinet at a low price. It is easy to move about the home. Strongly made and neatly finished in washable ivory enamel over hardwood. Comfortable woven wire spring bottom. Equipped with 6-inch stamped steel, easy rolling, noiseless wheels with rubber tires. Length, 35 in.; height, 32 in.; width, 20 in.; depth of sides from spring, 12½ in. Packed to secure lowest transportation rates. Easily put together. Shpg. wt., 18 lbs.

1K5907—Bassinet.......$3.75
1K7251—Comfortable Cotton Pad Mattress, 18x34 in. Actual weight, 3 pounds. Shipping weight, 5 pounds.....................$1.75

Beautiful Wheeled Bassinet

Low priced serviceable, high grade bassinet that you are sure to appreciate. Sturdy hardwood construction, finished in rich washable ivory enamel. Perforated cane panels, with polychrome decorations. Equipped with comfortable wire spring, 6-inch rubber tire steel swivel wheels, noiseless and easy rolling. Height, 35 inches; length, 40 inches; width, 23 inches; depth of sides, 13 inches. This is truly a good buy; being America's headquarters for cribs and bassinets, we are able to give you the best quality at a minimum cost. Packed to secure lowest transportation rates. Easily put together. Shipping wt., 25 pounds.

1K5929—Crib. $8.45
1K7265—Soft Felted Cotton Pad Mattress covered with pretty floral art ticking to fit. Actual weight, 6 lbs. Shipping wt., 7 lbs. Can be shipped by parcel post.$2.25

Our Best All Steel Crib

Sensible half drop side crib, priced low. • Extra well finished.

Here is an exceptionally good buy that you will never regret. The wide perforated steel cane panels, ornamented with fancy medallion centers add a distinctive touch to this well proportioned, attractive crib. Has one stationary side and one patented half drop side. The lower section remains stationary, making the ends very rigid. A touch of the hand and the drop section swings out and down. It closes as easily. No noise, no rattle, no bothersome catches, no bolts to come loose and no projections on which baby may injure himself. Nicely finished in washable ivory or brown enamel, fitted with strong, comfortable, sagless link steel fabric spring, firmly fastened to steel frame with helical (coil) springs. Height, 46 inches; sides are 23½ inches high. Continuous corner posts are 1 1/16-inch. Packed to secure lowest transportation rates. Easily put together. Priced to make you a big saving. Shipping weights, 70 and 80 pounds, respectively.

	Brown Enamel	Ivory Enamel
1K5999		
Size, 30x54-inch	$12.85	$12.45
Size, 36x60-inch	13.35	12.95

For Comfortable Felted Cotton Pad Crib Mattress and Pillows to fit this crib, see bottom of page.

Big Crib Value for Thrifty Buyers

Value for your money is guaranteed when you buy this fine steel drop side crib; a most desirable style, priced low. Latest style steel cane panel ends with medallion centers. Has 7/8-inch continuous posts and top rails. Fillers are 5/16-inch tubing. Height of ends, 44½ inches; sides, 21½ inches. Equipped with strong, comfortable, sagless link steel fabric spring, firmly fastened to steel frame with helical (coil) springs. Packed to secure lowest transportation rates. Easily put together. Shipping weights, 65 and 75 pounds, respectively. State finish.

	Brown Enamel	Ivory Enamel	Vernis Martin
1K5995			
Size, 30x54-inch	$9.85	$9.45	$9.75
Size, 36x60-inch	10.35	9.95	10.25

Save on This Drop Side Steel Crib

A high grade crib at a price much lower than you would expect to pay for this quality. The construction is equal to that used on all our high quality steel beds. Has 7/8-in. continuous end posts; fillers are 5/16-in. tubing. Height of ends, 45 in.; depth of sides, 21½ in. One stationary and one sliding drop side. Choice of three finishes, as listed below. Equipped with strong, comfortable, sagless link steel fabric spring firmly fastened to steel frame with helical (coil) springs. Packed to secure lowest transportation rates. Easily put together. Shipping weights, 53 and 75 pounds, respectively.

	Brown Enamel	Ivory Enamel	Vernis Martin
1K5992			
Size, 30x54-in.	$8.25	$7.85	$8.10
Size, 36x60-in.	8.75	8.35	8.60

1K7267—Felted Cotton Crib Mattress to fit.
Size, 30x54-in. Actual weight, 12 pounds.....................$3.65
Size, 36x60-in. Actual weight, 16 pounds..................... 4.45

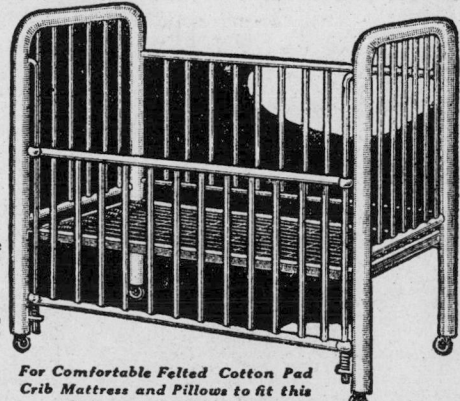

For Comfortable Felted Cotton Pad Crib Mattress and Pillows to fit this Crib, see left of page.

AND PILLOWS

Much lighter than cotton and more springy and buoyant. Deep tufted; 2½-in. box edge. Covered with a pretty juvenile art ticking. The two smaller sizes can be mailed parcel post.

1K7263
30x54-inch. Actual weight, 7 lbs. Shpg. wt., 8½ lbs...........$4.95
30x64-inch. Actual weight, 8 lbs. Shpg. wt., 9½ lbs........... 5.85
36x60-inch. Actual weight, 9 lbs. Shpg. wt., 11 lbs........... 6.35

This Mattress Is Filled With Genuine Japara Kapok

Filled with domestic all goose down. Imported linen striped ticking. Actual weight, 4 and 11 oz. Shipping wts., 5 oz. and ¾ lb. respectively.

Filled with one-half choice duck half down, one-fourth turkey down and one-fourth turkey half down. Best quality satin finish ticking. Actual wts., 11 and 19 oz. Shpg. wts., ¾ lb. and 1¼ lbs.

1K7159	1K7160	1K7153	1K7154
10x15-in....95c	14x18-in..$1.58	10x15-in....68c	14x18-in..$1.08

Save ONE-HALF on Wall Paper. See Pages 1018-1019

Outfit the Nursery From These Pages

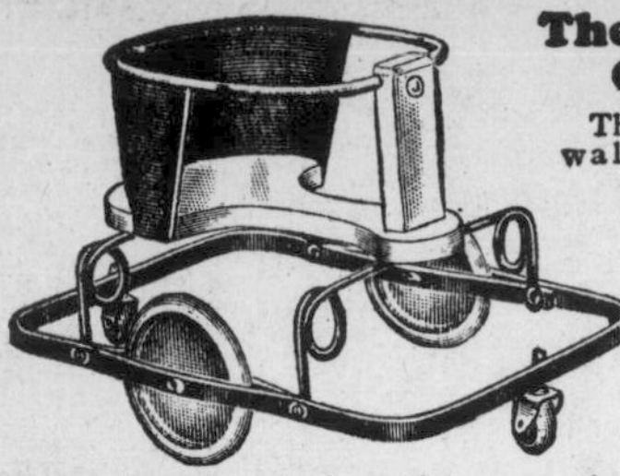

The New Jaunty Car Junior

The newest thing in baby walkers, scientifically designed to teach baby how to walk correctly. This Jaunty Car is made of spring steel and wood; rubber bumpers front and rear. Rubber tired 6-in. disc wheels and swivel casters front and rear. The casters are placed higher than the wheels so the car can be easily turned. All edges are beveled, no sharp corners. Beautifully finished in washable enamel colors. Complete with easily attached handle for pulling. Length, 22 inches; width, 15 inches; height of seat, 7½ inches. Shipping weight, 10 pounds.

1K251....................................$3.15

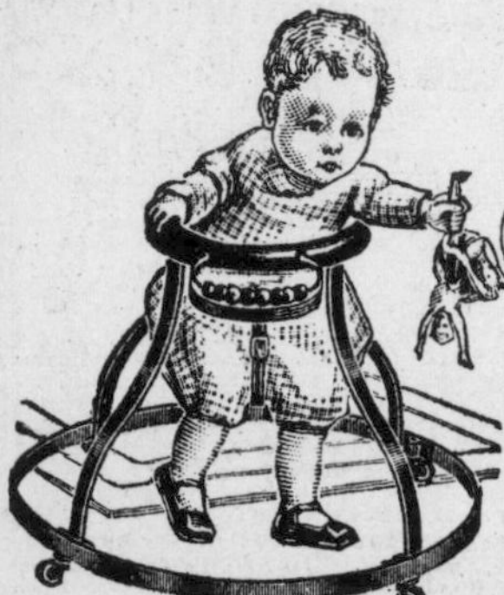

Baby Walker

Black enameled steel frame, smoothly rounded. Polished mahogany finish wood top. Seat suspended by three spiral springs and is adjustable to various heights. Ball bearing casters. Has tray decorated with colored beads for amusing baby. Height, 17 inches; base, 25 inches diameter. Can be sent parcel post. Shipping wt., 7 lbs.

1K240............ $2.15

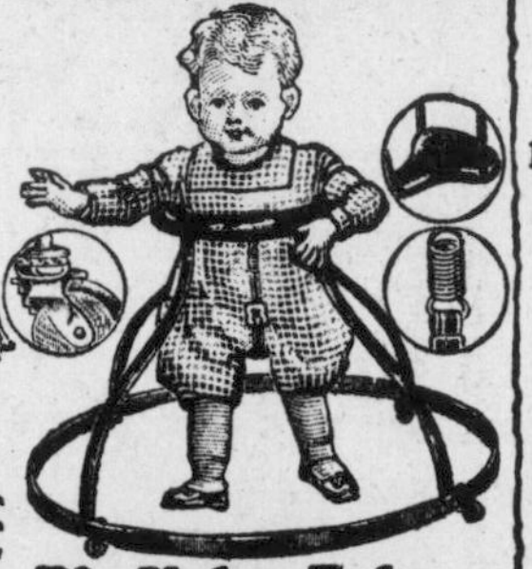

Big Value Baby Walker

It teaches baby how to walk and keeps him out of mischief. Black enameled steel frame, smoothly rounded. Polished mahogany finish wood top. Seat suspended by straps attached to three spiral springs, and is adjustable to various heights. Ball bearing casters. Height, 17 inches; base, 25 inches diameter. **Can be shipped parcel post.** Shipping weight, 7 pounds.

1K238............ $1.75

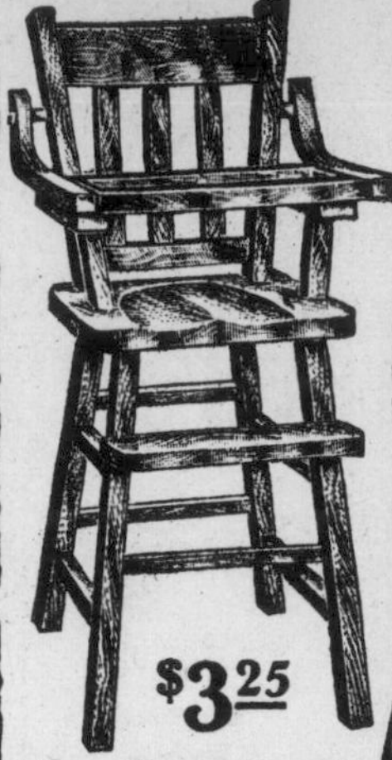

$3.25

Made Extra Strong

Sturdily constructed, solid high chair that will give excellent service. Large size tray that swings over back of chair. Comfortable shape seat and foot rest. Strongly braced legs. Made of hardwood, finished in golden gloss. Height, 41 inches. Height of seat, 22¾ inches. Shipped set up. A good quality high chair for less. Shipping weight, 13 lbs.

1K270....... $3.25

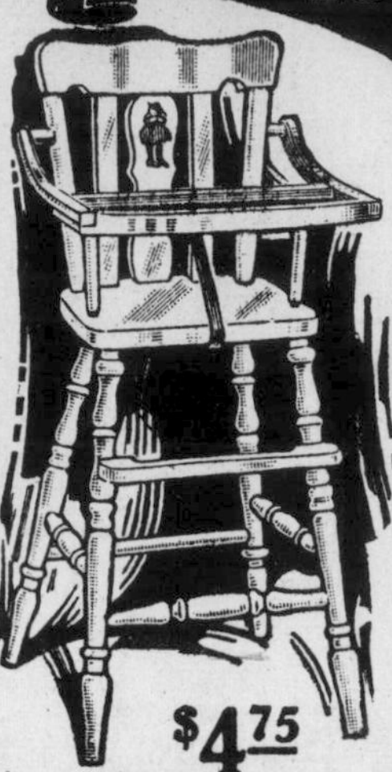

$4.75

A High Chair of Graceful Design

Now is your opportunity to secure an attractive high chair at a bargain price you cannot afford to overlook. Artistic transfer picture on back panel. Made of durable hardwood, finished in rich ivory enamel. Easy to keep clean. Blue enameled table swings back of chair. Equipped with safety strap to prevent baby from sliding out. Comfortable foot rest. Height, 38 in. Seat, 14½x13 in. Height of back from seat, 15¼ in. Shipped set up. Shipping wt., 12 lbs.

1K272... $4.75

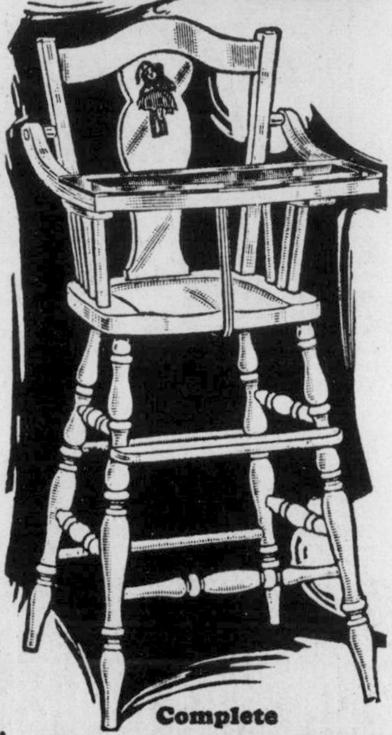

Complete With Aluminum Tray

Made of selected kiln dried hardwood finished in ivory enamel with an attractive transfer picture on the back panel. The handy removable, aluminum tray is easily cleaned. Table swings back of chair. Safety leather strap is fitted to prevent baby from sliding out. Height, over all, 39½ inches. Seat, 14¼x12½ inches. Height to seat, 23¼ inches. Shipped set up. Shipping weight, 16 pounds.

1K268................ $5.75

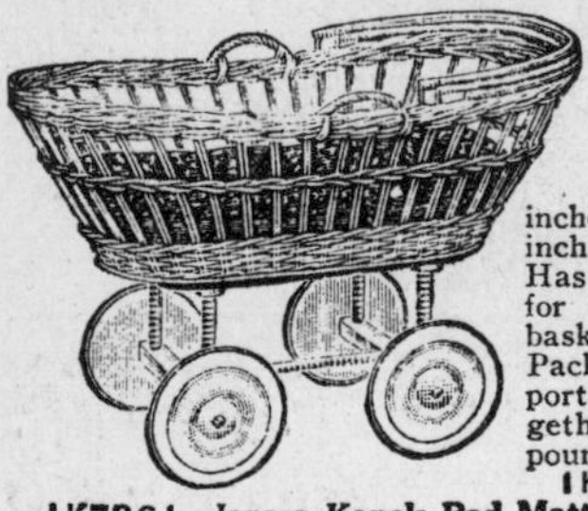

All Reed Bassinet

Cream Ivory Finish

Inside measurements, 13 x 27 inches; depth, 11 inches; height, 27¾ inches. 9½-inch rubber tired disc wheels. Has three adjustable reed bows for hood cover. Removable basket equipped with handles. Packed to secure lowest transportation rates. Easily put together. Shipping weight, 20 pounds.

1K5901............ $8.95

1K7261—Japara Kapok Pad Mattress to fit. Weight, 1½ lbs. Shipping weight, 2¼ pounds. Can be sent by parcel post............................ $1.65

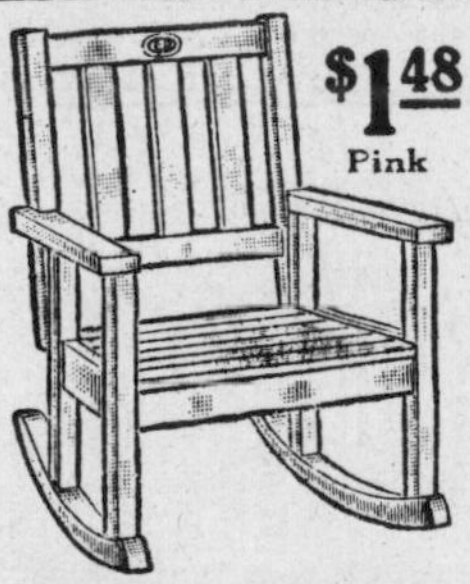

$1.48 Pink

Children's Brightly Enameled Rocker

Finished in choice of rich pink or blue washable enamel, with pretty transfer pattern of contrasting color on the top rail. Strongly made of hardwood; will stand children's rough treatment. Size of seat, 14x12 in. Height of back, 15 in. Packed to secure lowest transportation rates. Easily put together. Shipping weight, 9 pounds.

1K207
Pink enamel......... $1.48
Blue enamel............. $1.50

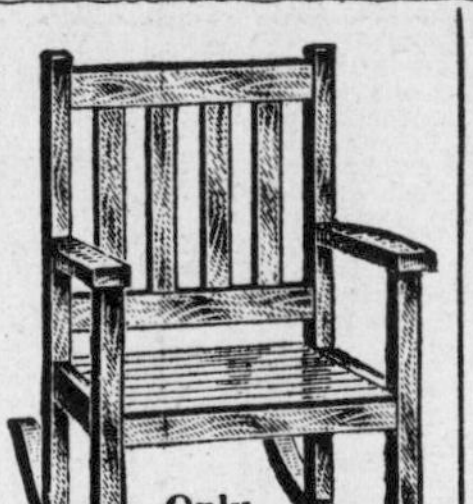

Only $1.05

Child's Rocker

It will stand hard usage, constructed of hardwood in dull golden shade. Measurements—Seat, 10½x13½ in. Height of back from seat, 13½ inches. Height, over all, 20 inches. Packed to secure lowest transportation rates. Easily put together. **Can be shipped by parcel post.** Shipping weight, 8 pounds.

1K231...... $1.05

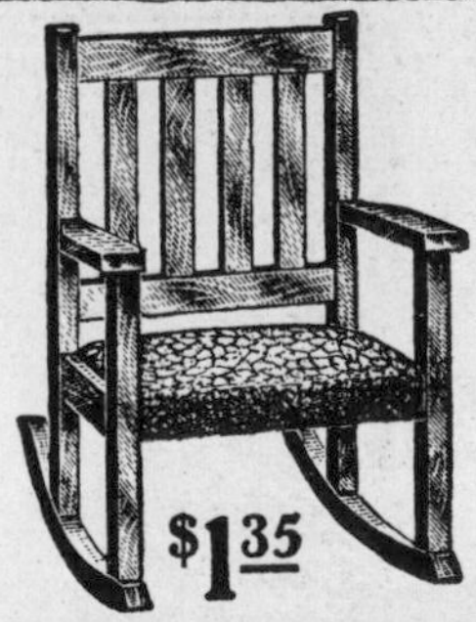

$1.35

Upholstered Seat Rocker

Made of oak, finished in dull golden shade. Pad seat upholstered in imitation brown Spanish leather. Seat size, 11¼x13½ inches. Height of back from seat, 13 inches. Packed to secure lowest transportation rates. Easily put together. **Can be shipped by parcel post.** Shipping weight, 9 pounds.

1K233........... $1.35

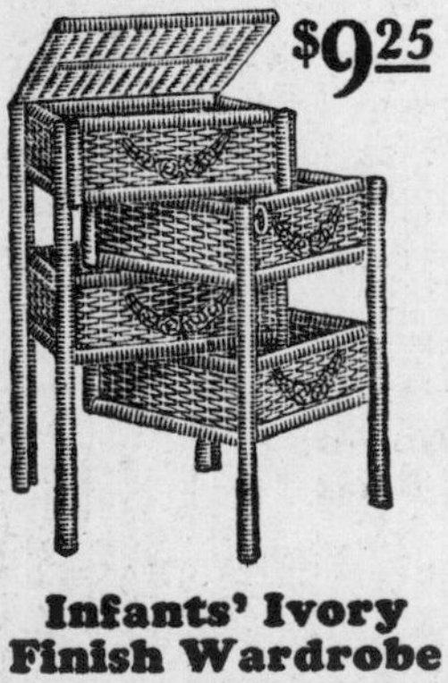

$9.25

Infants' Ivory Finish Wardrobe

A most attractive wardrobe which has ample storage space for baby's clothes. Folds into compact space. Can readily be moved about. Strongly made of half round reed and wood, all ivory enameled, with tinted ornaments. Top basket has cover. 18x18 inches square. Height, 33 inches. Shipping wt., 20 pounds.

1K223......... $9.25

Folding Play Yard Complete With Floor Cloth

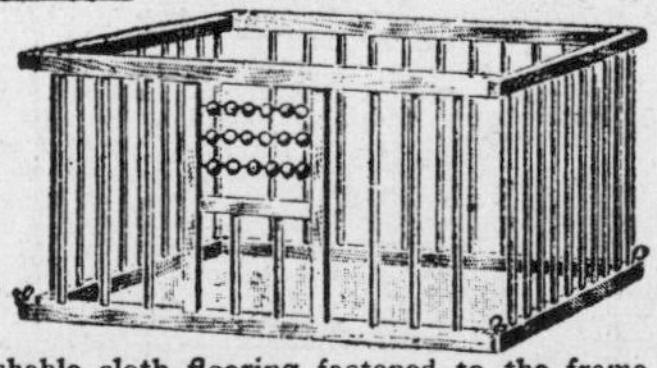

An ideal play yard made of hardwood finished in natural gloss; all parts smoothly beveled, sanded and shellacked, making it free from splinters. Riveted throughout, making it strong and rigid. Has washable cloth flooring fastened to the frame work with tapes. Has twenty-four varied colored wooden beads on three metal rods. 39¾ inches square; height, 24 inches. Packed to secure lowest transportation rates. Easily put together. Shipping weight, 17 pounds.

1K227...................... $3.65

Made same as described above, only smaller size and without beads. 38½ in. square. Height, 23½ inches. Packed to secure lowest transportation rates. Easily put together. Shpg. wt., 16 lbs.

1K219...................... $2.95

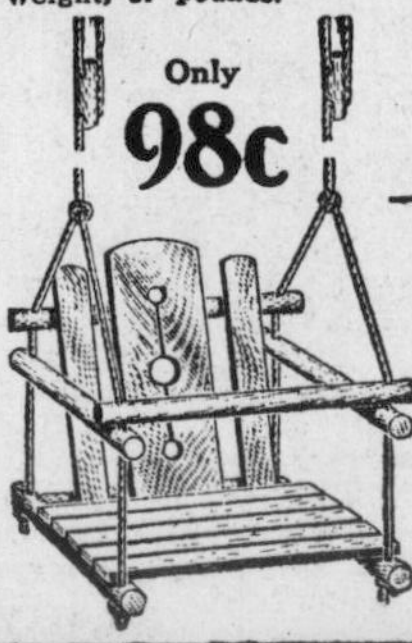

Only 98c

Baby Swing

Hang it anywhere; on the porch or in the house. Keep baby off the floor and keep him happy. Comfortable and strong. Natural finish hardwood frame suspended by strong cord with adjustable straps. Protection bar across the front. Seat, 9½x12¼ inches. Back, 12 inches. Complete, ready to hang. **Can be shipped by parcel post.** Shipping weight, 4 lbs.

1K244......................... 98c

Safety Gate

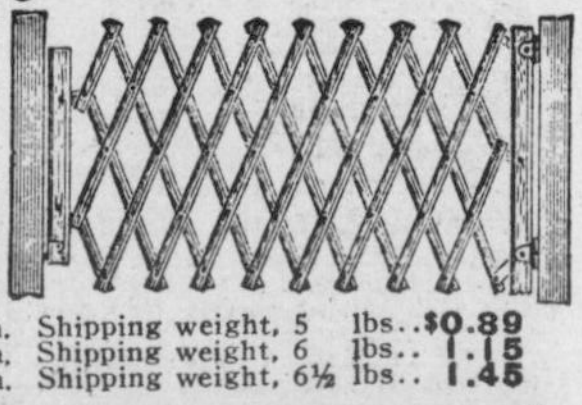

Hardwood, golden finish. All parts are riveted, smoothly sanded and free from splinters. Comes complete with hinges for hanging. Spring lock which baby cannot operate. Folds into compact size when not in use. Height, 33½ inches. Comes in three sizes extending from 7¼ inches to 4 feet; 9 inches to 5½ feet, or 10½ inches to 7½ feet. **Can be shipped by parcel post.**

1K220—Size, 4 -ft. extension. Shipping weight, 5 lbs.. $0.89
Size, 5½-ft. extension. Shipping weight, 6 lbs.. 1.15
Size, 7½-ft. extension. Shipping weight, 6½ lbs.. 1.45

Because Our Prices Are America's Lowest

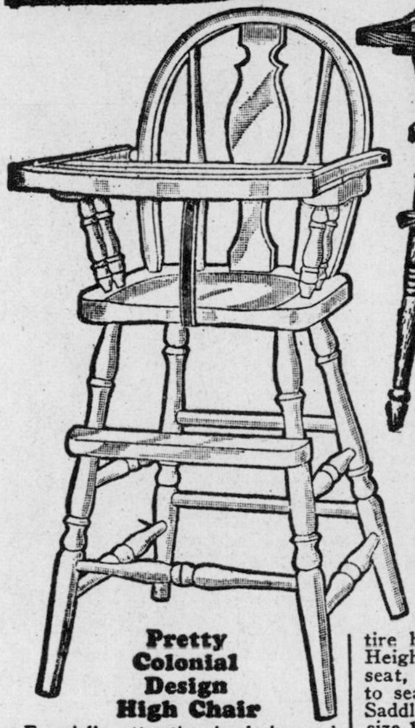

Fiber Style Rocker
High in Quality, Low in Price

Will stand all the rough treatment youngsters give their playthings, and will retain its neat appearance indefinitely. Made of tightly woven fiber finished in rich coffee cream color. Frame of exceptionally sturdy hardwood and braced with six steel braces. Legs wrapped with flat reed. Fancy woven fiber braided trimming on front of arms and the top of the back. One of the most popular features is the cretonne covered padded seat. Exceptionally long runners that make it almost impossible to tip backwards. Height of back from seat, 15 inches; seat, 12x12 inches. Entire height, 21¾ inches. Shipping weight, 10 pounds.
1K260.......... $4.45

$2.45

Inexpensive High Chair
Made of hardwood, golden gloss finish in a popular style. Large drop table swings back of chair. This chair is well braced and will give excellent service. Has saddle shape seat. Height, over all, 39 inches. Height to seat, 23½ inches; height of back from seat, 15 inches. Seat, 13¼x13½ inches. Packed to secure lowest transportation rates. Easily put together. Can be shipped by parcel post. Shipping weight, 12 pounds.
1K266............ $2.45

Children's Reed Rocker
Strong durable reed construction over hardwood frame; fancy braided reed on the front, the arms and across the back. Finished in cream ivory. Cretonne covered padded cushion. Height of back from seat, 15 in.; size of seat, 12x13 in. Entire height, 23 in. Shipping wt., 9 pounds.
1K256.. $4.15

Combination Bathtub and Dressing Table
Heavy pre-shrunken white duck top. Folds compactly. White enameled frame. Bathtub is a superior grade of pure white rubber, durable and will not leak. The apron contains pockets for toilet articles. Dressing table part, 26½x28 in. Tub, 22x24½ in. and 9 in. deep, 29¼ in. high. Can be shipped by parcel post. Shipping weight, 13 pounds.
1K282.................. $6.25

Low Priced— Big Value
For our low price you will find this a splendid value. Strongly constructed of all hardwood, finished in golden gloss. Entire height, 39½ in. Height of back from seat, 15½ in. Height to seat, 23¼ inches. Saddle shape seat, size, 13¼x13¼ inches. Large drop table swings back of chair. You make a big saving on this high chair. Packed to secure lowest transportation rates. Easily put together. May be shipped by parcel post. Shipping weight, 13 lbs.
1K271.. $2.95

Pretty Colonial Design High Chair
Especially attractive in design and finished in rich washable ivory enamel, trimmed in dark blue. The bow back is of square (not round) material. The legs are prettily turned; they are wide spread for safety. Large size tray swings back of seat. Equipped with safety strap to keep the child from sliding out of seat, or raising the tray. Shaped seat, 14x13 inches. Height of back, 17½ inches. Entire height, 42½ inches. Shipping weight, 15 pounds.
1K242.............. $5.25
See the Children's Rocker to match, 1K212, shown in center of page.

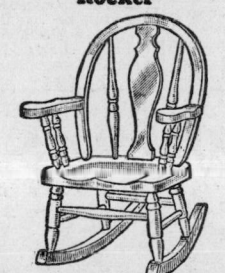

Children's Colonial Rocker
The pattern matches our high chair 1K242 shown in upper left of page. Strongly made of hardwood, finished in washable ivory enamel trimmed in dark blue. Shaped seat, 14x13 in. Height of back, 17½ in. Shipping weight, 10 pounds.
1K212............ $4.55

Infants' Dressing Table
Folds up into compact space, as shown in small illustration. The table top is an extra heavy grade of pre-shrunken white duck. The apron contains four pockets for toilet articles. The table top is easily removed for washing. The stand is smoothly white enameled hardwood. Top, 20¾x37 inches, 29½ inches high. Can be shipped by parcel post. Shipping weight, 9 pounds.
1K280 $4.25

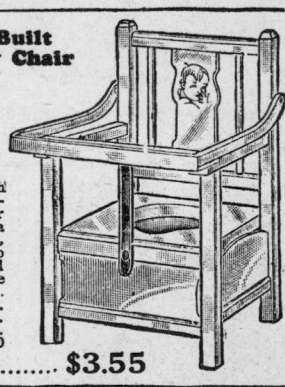

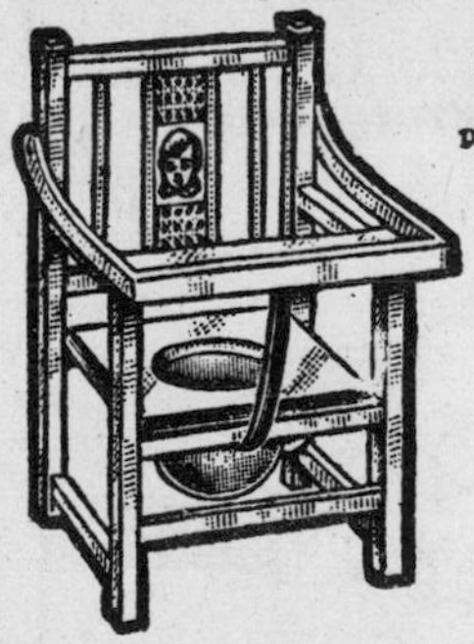

Big Value Nursery Chair
The perforated steel panel in back has a decorative transfer. Safety strap fitted to prevent baby from sliding out. Handy tray. Furnished either with or without removable chamber. Made of selected, kiln dried hardwood in ivory enamel finish. Size of seat, 11x11 in. Height, 21½ in. Shpg. wt., 8 lbs. Can be shipped by parcel post.
1K214
Without vessel.... $2.65
1K198
With vessel.. $3.15

Well Built Nursery Chair
Made of hardwood, finished in washable ivory enamel. The back panel is decorated with a cunning juvenile transfer pattern. Has a swinging tray, a safety strap and shaped seat. Complete with chamber. Height, 20½ in. Width, 14 in. Depth, 10 in. Shpg. wt., 10 pounds.
1K200............ $3.55

Children's Dining Chair
Strongly made; legs are stretcher braced. Oak seat, 16x16½ inches. Height of back from seat, 20 inches. Height of seat from floor, 21 inches. Choice of finishes. Shipped set up. Shipping wt., 15 lbs.
1K26
Golden gloss.... $2.15
Fumed oak $2-20

Kindergarten Chair
Has comfortable bow back and 13-in. seat. Height of back over seat, 14½ in.; total height, 28¼ in. Height of seat from floor, 14 in. Golden gloss finish hardwood. Very strongly made. Can be shipped by parcel post. Shipped set up. Shipping weight, 7 pounds.
1K205............ $1.35

Priced Low
Made of light, strong 3-ply hardwood. Finished in natural color varnish. Legs are strongly bolted to seat with smooth head bolts. Swing back tray and hinged seat cover. Height, 21 in. Seat, 11x12¼ in. Packed to secure lowest transportation rates. Easily put together. Shipping wt., 8 lbs. Can be shipped by parcel post.
1K226—Golden oak.. $1.95

Reed Nursery Chair
Substantially made hardwood frame and seat, covered with flat woven fiber reed below and with the back and sides of round woven fiber reed. Wooden tray with peg, which prevents baby from slipping out of seat. Height, 17 inches. Opening in seat. Can be shipped by parcel post. Shipping weight, 7 lbs.
1K208.............. $1.89

Nursery Chair
The tray swings to one side on a hinge and is fitted with patent spring lock that baby cannot open. Hardwood construction, natural color varnish finish. Seat, 10½x9¾ inches. Packed to secure lowest transportation rates. Easily put together. Shipping weight, 5 pounds.
1K204.............. $1.10

Toilet Seats
Fits over ordinary toilet seat with spring clamp. Made of hardwood, golden gloss finish. Width, inside, 9½ in. Opening in seat, 5½x7¼ in. Hinged guard tray with lock, 4½x10⅞ in. Height of back, 6¾ in. Can be shipped by parcel post. Shipping weight, 3 pounds.
1K210.................. $1.75

Spring Clamp Toilet Seat
Three-ply hardwood veneer, natural gloss finish. Fits over ordinary toilet seat, with spring clamp. Opening measures, 5¼x7¼ in. Size, over all, 11½x11¼ in. Can be shipped by parcel post. Shipping weight, 1 pound.
1K201.................. 65c

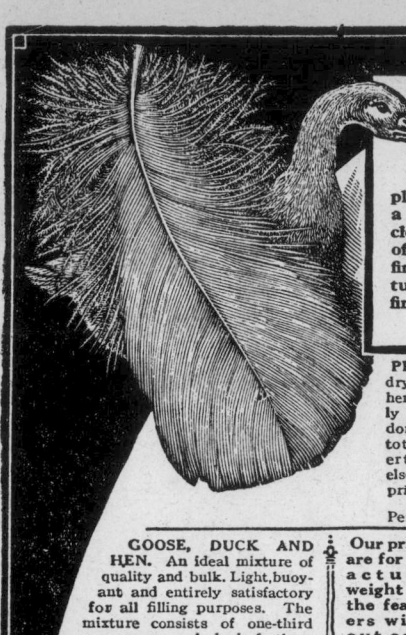

Guaranteed New Sanitary Feathers

We unqualifiedly guarantee all our feathers to be new; freshly plucked from live fowl. All feathers are sterilized and blown into a cooling process to dry and then ozonized to insure permanently clean, odorless and dustless feathers. We are the largest retailers of feathers and feather pillows in the world, and can give you the finest quality at prices which cannot be duplicated. The manufacturer joins us in our guarantee to you that these feathers are the finest, cleanest and best you can buy according to the grade wanted.

Be Sure to Read Page 892

For Ticking See Page 181

PRIME HEN. Prime, dry picked, western hen feathers, thoroughly renovated and deodorized. Far superior to the average hen feather that is usually offered elsewhere at the same price.
1K7103 Per pound..... 23c

ALL WHITE HEN. Beautiful, all white, processed hen feathers. The best hen feathers procurable, specially treated to make them full and fluffy. The finest hen feathers we have ever sold. Note our low price per pound.
1K7137 Per pound....... 48c

TURKEY AND HEN. A fine mixture, containing three-fourths selected, dry picked, turkey feathers of fine quality with one-fourth, light color, hen feathers. A grade we recommend highly as a filling mixture. As far as possible, the small and medium turkey feathers are selected.
1K7138 Per pound........ 39c

GOOSE, DUCK AND HEN. An ideal mixture of quality and bulk. Light, buoyant and entirely satisfactory for all filling purposes. The mixture consists of one-third gray goose and duck feathers and two-thirds prime hen feathers. The duck feathers are small and of silky texture. The hen feathers are white and colored in equal proportions.
1K7112—Per pound.... 65c

Our prices are for the actual weight of the feathers without containers. Put up in 1, 2, 3, 5 and 10-pound cloth sacks.

ALL WHITE GOOSE. A good grade of white China goose, ordinarily sold elsewhere as best quality goose. China goose feathers are big and springy, with a good proportion of down texture, but they are not as desirable as domestic white goose feathers. At the price this is a value without an equal.
1K7139 Per pound....... $1.39

GOOSE, DUCK AND HEN. The finest mixture of this kind we have ever handled. The finer quality feathers predominate in this filling—the mixture consisting of three-fourths gray goose and gray duck with one-fourth hen (just enough to give bulk and body). In this mixture you will find a soft, downy blend almost impossible to improve upon.
1K7115 Per pound..... 89c

All cushions, bulk feathers and pillows may be shipped parcel post. Add ½ pound for shipping weight.

OUR BEST ALL WHITE DOWN. After careful study of the requirements of our customers we have decided to list this one grade only because it has proved so satisfactory in past years. Our best grade down, white as snow. Consists of one-half extra choice domestic white goose down and one-half white selected hen down. It is the finest kind of mixture and we unreservedly recommend it.
1K7120 Per pound..... $1.59

GOOSE AND DUCK. For those of our customers who prefer a higher quality mixture we recommend this one. The mixture consists of one-half choice, downy, light goose and duck feathers and one-half choice gray duck feathers. Only light, downy domestic feathers are used and the equal mixture makes a good body, especially suitable for pillows or feather mattresses. Fewer pounds of this mixture give more bulk than other cheaper mixtures.
1K7100—Per pound.................................$1.09

FINEST DOMESTIC DOWNY WHITE GOOSE. We unreservedly guarantee that this is the finest feather filling we have ever handled. These domestic, downy white, goose feathers are hand picked and hand selected. Only those that are full size are used. Every feather is snow white. This domestic feather is larger, fluffier and has more down than the imported China goose feather many others sell for their best quality. More expensive, but well worth the price difference as fewer pounds go a longer way.
1K7121—Per pound.................................$1.98

Cushions
White Cambric Covers

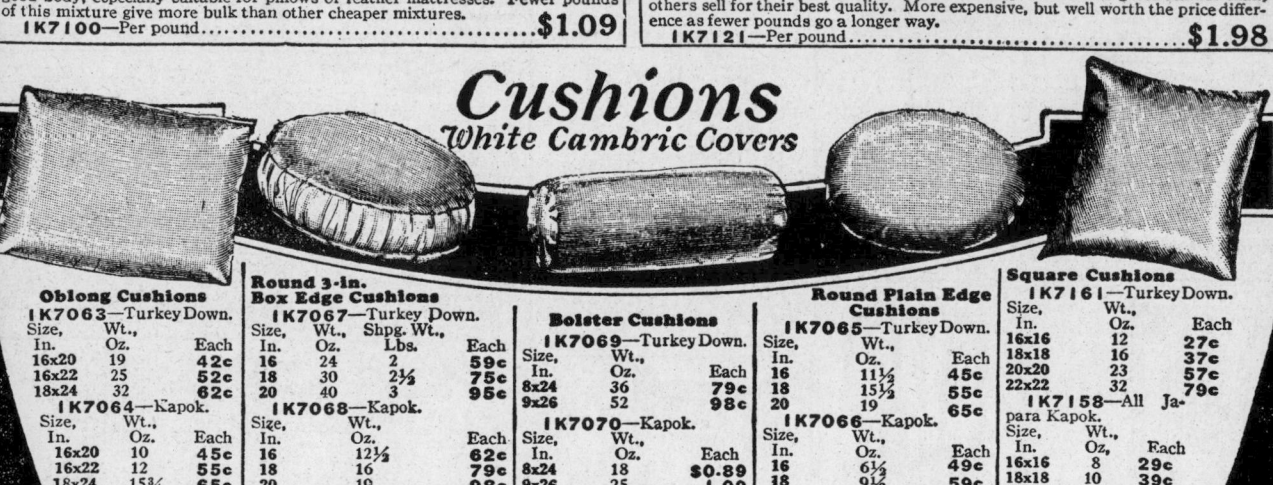

Oblong Cushions

1K7063—Turkey Down.

Size, In.	Wt., Oz.	Each
16x20	19	42c
16x22	25	52c
18x24	32	62c

1K7064—Kapok.

Size, In.	Wt., Oz.	Each
16x20	10	45c
16x22	12	55c
18x24	15¾	65c

Round 3-in. Box Edge Cushions

1K7067—Turkey Down.

Size, In.	Wt., Oz.	Shpg. Wt., Lbs.	Each
16	24	2	59c
18	30	2½	75c
20	40	3	95c

1K7068—Kapok.

Size, In.	Wt., Oz.	Each
16	12½	62c
18	16	79c
20	19	98c

Bolster Cushions

1K7069—Turkey Down.

Size, In.	Wt., Oz.	Each
8x24	36	79c
9x26	52	98c

1K7070—Kapok.

Size, In.	Wt., Oz.	Each
8x24	18	$0.89
9x26	25	1.09

Round Plain Edge Cushions

1K7065—Turkey Down.

Size, In.	Wt., Oz.	Each
16	11½	45c
18	15½	55c
20	19	65c

1K7066—Kapok.

Size, In.	Wt., Oz.	Each
16	6½	49c
18	9½	59c
20	13	69c

Square Cushions

1K7161—Turkey Down.

Size, In.	Wt., Oz.	Each
16x16	12	27c
18x18	16	37c
20x20	23	57c
22x22	32	79c

1K7158—All Japara Kapok.

Size, In.	Wt., Oz.	Each
16x16	8	29c
18x18	10	39c
20x20	14	59c
22x22	18	82c

These Cushions can all be mailed parcel post. For mailing weights of cushions, add 8 oz. to the weights given.

America's Headquarters for Feathers and Pillows!

Seat Cushions

Not tufted. Ready for you to cover and tuft with buttons or ribbons.

1K7079—Turkey Down.

Size, In.	Wt., Oz.	Each
16x19	20	48c
18x19	22	58c

1K7080—Kapok.

Size, In.	Wt., Oz.	Each
16x19	10	59c
18x19	12	79c

Half Moon Cushions

The half moon shape is very popular. It is offered only in 100 per cent Japara kapok.

1K7074—Kapok.

Size, In.	Wt., Oz.	Each
14x22	9	69c
16x24	12	89c

These Cushions are filled **only** with choice turkey down, (the small, soft, turkey feathers scientifically curled into a fluffy mass), or No. 1 grade prime 100% Japara kapok. They are covered with a good quality white cambric.

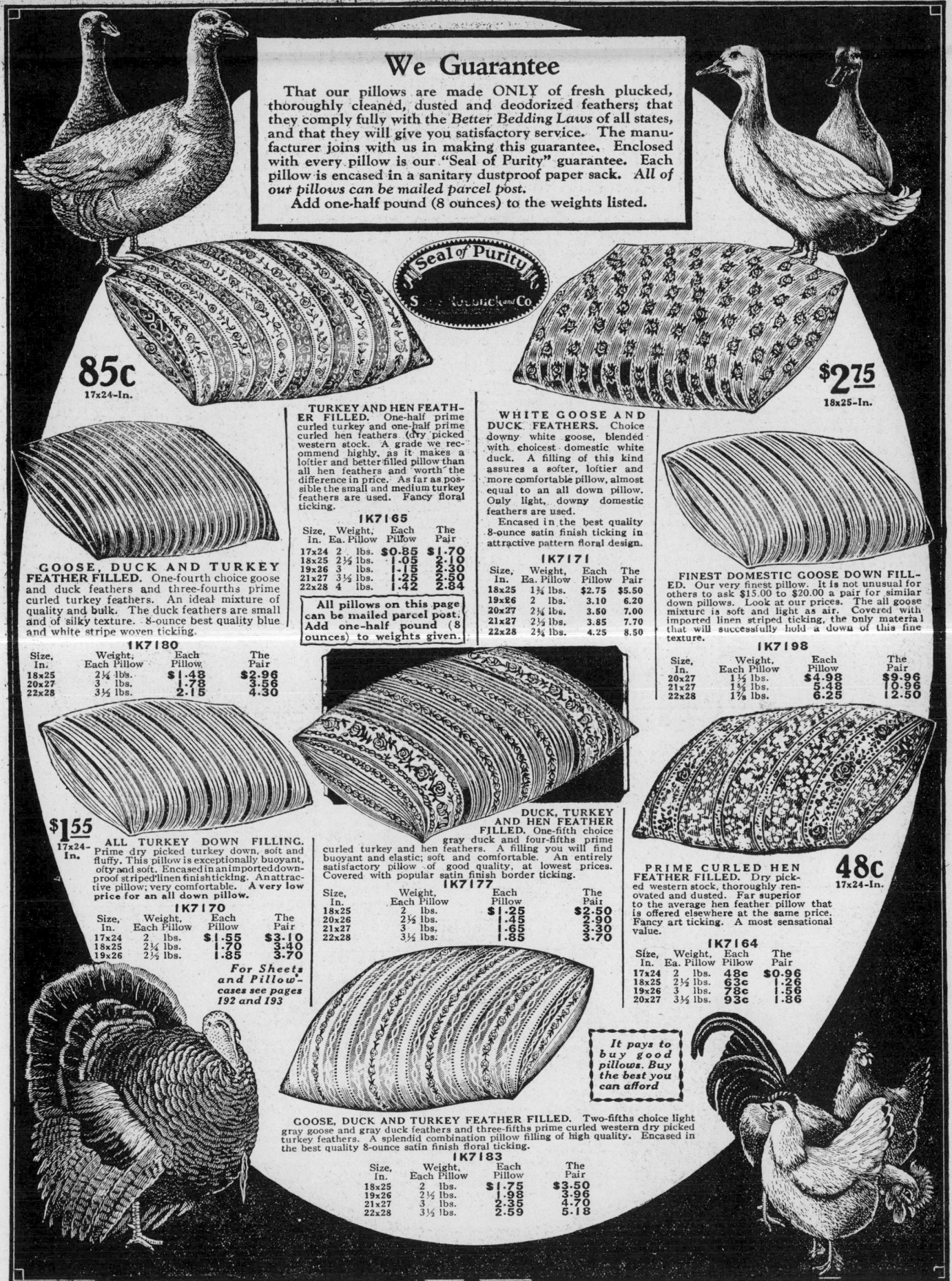

85c 17x24-In.

$2.75 18x25-In.

GOOSE, DUCK AND TURKEY FEATHER FILLED. One-fourth choice goose and duck feathers and three-fourths prime curled turkey feathers. An ideal mixture of quality and bulk. The duck feathers are small and of silky texture. 8-ounce best quality blue and white stripe woven ticking.

Size, In.	Weight, Each Pillow	Each Pillow	The Pair
18x25	2¼ lbs.	$1.48	$2.96
20x27	3 lbs.	1.78	3.56
22x28	3½ lbs.	2.15	4.30

1K7180

TURKEY AND HEN FEATHER FILLED. One-half prime curled turkey and one-half prime curled hen feathers (dry picked western stock). A grade we recommend highly, as it makes a loftier and better filled pillow than all hen feathers and worth the difference in price. As far as possible the small and medium turkey feathers are used. Fancy floral ticking.

1K7165

Size, In.	Weight, Ea. Pillow	Each Pillow	The Pair
17x24	2 lbs.	$0.85	$1.70
18x25	2½ lbs.	1.05	2.10
19x26	3 lbs.	1.15	2.30
21x27	3½ lbs.	1.25	2.50
22x28	4 lbs.	1.42	2.84

All pillows on this page can be mailed parcel post. Add one-half pound (8 ounces) to weights given.

WHITE GOOSE AND DUCK FEATHERS. Choice downy white goose, blended with choicest domestic white duck. A filling of this kind assures a softer, loftier and more comfortable pillow, almost equal to an all down pillow. Only light, downy domestic feathers are used. Encased in the best quality 8-ounce satin finish ticking in attractive pattern floral design.

1K7171

Size, In.	Weight, Ea. Pillow	Each Pillow	The Pair
18x25	1¾ lbs.	$2.75	$5.50
19x26	2 lbs.	3.10	6.20
20x27	2¼ lbs.	3.50	7.00
21x27	2½ lbs.	3.85	7.70
22x28	2¾ lbs.	4.25	8.50

FINEST DOMESTIC GOOSE DOWN FILLED. Our very finest pillow. It is not unusual for others to ask $15.00 to $20.00 a pair for similar down pillows. Look at our prices. The all goose mixture is soft and light as air. Covered with imported linen striped ticking, the only material that will successfully hold a down of this fine texture.

1K7198

Size, In.	Weight, Each Pillow	Each Pillow	The Pair
20x27	1½ lbs.	$4.98	$9.96
21x27	1⅝ lbs.	5.48	10.96
22x28	1⅞ lbs.	6.25	12.50

$1.55 17x24-In.

ALL TURKEY DOWN FILLING. Prime dry picked turkey down, soft and fluffy. This pillow is exceptionally buoyant, ofty and soft. Encased in an imported downproof striped linen finish ticking. An attractive pillow; very comfortable. A very low price for an all down pillow.

1K7170

Size, In.	Weight, Each Pillow	Each Pillow	The Pair
17x24	2 lbs.	$1.55	$3.10
18x25	2¼ lbs.	1.70	3.40
19x26	2½ lbs.	1.85	3.70

For Sheets and Pillowcases see pages 192 and 193

DUCK, TURKEY AND HEN FEATHER FILLED. One-fifth choice gray duck and four-fifths prime curled turkey and hen feathers. A filling you will find buoyant and elastic; soft and comfortable. An entirely satisfactory pillow of good quality, at lowest prices. Covered with popular satin finish border ticking.

1K7177

Size, In.	Weight, Each Pillow	Each Pillow	The Pair
18x25	2 lbs.	$1.25	$2.50
20x26	2½ lbs.	1.45	2.90
21x27	3 lbs.	1.65	3.30
22x28	3½ lbs.	1.85	3.70

PRIME CURLED HEN FEATHER FILLED. Dry picked western stock, thoroughly renovated and dusted. Far superior to the average hen feather pillow that is offered elsewhere at the same price. Fancy art ticking. A most sensational value.

48c 17x24-In.

1K7164

Size, In.	Weight, Ea. Pillow	Each Pillow	The Pair
17x24	2 lbs.	48c	$0.96
18x25	2½ lbs.	63c	1.26
19x26	3 lbs.	78c	1.56
20x27	3½ lbs.	93c	1.86

It pays to buy good pillows. Buy the best you can afford

GOOSE, DUCK AND TURKEY FEATHER FILLED. Two-fifths choice light gray goose and gray duck feathers and three-fifths prime curled western dry picked turkey feathers. A splendid combination pillow filling of high quality. Encased in the best quality 8-ounce satin finish floral ticking.

1K7183

Size, In.	Weight, Each Pillow	Each Pillow	The Pair
18x25	2 lbs.	$1.75	$3.50
19x26	2½ lbs.	1.98	3.96
21x27	3 lbs.	2.35	4.70
22x28	3½ lbs.	2.59	5.18

Seat Cushions

Cretonne Seat Cushion

Four-button tufted, very firm and soft. Dark ground colors with many bright colors in contrast. Will not soil readily. Weight, 1¼ and 2 pounds, respectively. Add ¼ pound for mailing weights. **Can be shipped parcel post.**
1K7041—19x16 inches.................... 65c
21x20 inches.............................. 98c

Every Home Needs Cretonne Cushions

Parrot Decorations
Black and gold color scheme with reproduction of a parrot surrounded by a bower of roses in twelve distinct colorings. Same pattern both sides. 16 inches square. Weight, 1¼ pounds. Shpg. wt., 1½ lbs.
1K7078—Can be shipped by parcel post.. 59c
Square Cushion. Assorted color combinations. 16 inches square. Not illustrated. Wt., 1¼ lbs. Shpg. wt., 1½ lbs.
1K7027—Can be shipped by parcel post.. 49c

Pretty Round Shape
Heavy cretonne material in bright colors, a gray background predominating. Can be had with or without 2-inch gold sateen ruffle. Size, 16 inches. Weight, 1¼ lbs. Shipping weight, 1½ pounds. **Can be shipped parcel post.**
1K7025—Without ruffle.................. 55c
With ruffle.......... 65c

Bar Harbor Cushions

Can be had in choice of bright cretonne on both sides; one side of green corduroy and reverse side in sateen, or in red Duco leather. Firmly filled with new cotton. 3-inch box edge. 8-button tufted. Actual weight, 4 pounds. Shipping weight, 4½ pounds.
1K7026—All cretonne.................. $1.25
Corduroy one side and sateen reverse side..$2.75
Red Duco leather all over...................... 2.35

All of these cushions, except those filled with Kapok and silk, are solidly filled with clean, new cotton that will not pack or mat, but will retain its fluffy fullness.

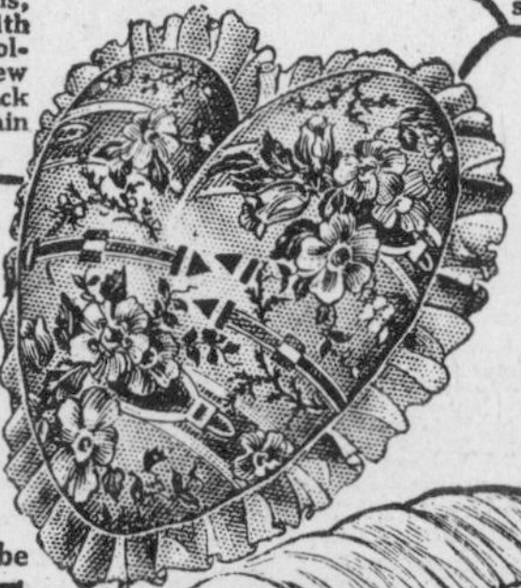

Pretty Heart Shape
A multicolor effect in cretonne, offset with a 2-inch sateen rose color ruffle. Size, 21x19 inches. Weight, 1¼ pounds. Shipping weight, 1½ pounds.
1K7000 — Can be shipped by parcel post... $1.05

Kapok and Silk Filled Bolster
Just the right size for the day bed or davenport. Bright cretonne, sunburst style pleated ends with button tuft. **Filled with kapok and silk.** Size, 8x24 in. Weight, 21 oz. Shipping weight, 1¾ pounds.
1K7056—Can be shipped by parcel post 98c

Corded Center
Dark background, colored in pink, orange and other contrasting colors. Corded center one side, other side plain. 2-inch sateen ruffle of blue. Weight, 1¼ pounds. Shipping weight, 1½ pounds.
1K7081—Can be shipped by parcel post.................. 75c

Beautiful Puffed Ends
Cretonne center with 5-inch sateen puffed ends, in rose color. Reverse side is all cretonne. Size, 24x16 in. Weight, 2 lbs. Shipping weight, 2¼ pounds.
1K7030—Can be shipped by parcel post...... 98c

A cushion here and there—on the window seat, the davenport or the chairs—will do much to make the home more cheerful and bright. And the investment is so small—why not buy several? You're sure to like the effect

Kapok and Silk
Bright overlay floral pattern in twelve colors. Pleats run to center in sunburst effect. 18-inch diameter, 4-inch boxed edge. Kapok and silk filled. Weight, 2 pounds. Shipping weight, 2¼ pounds.
1K7054—Can be sent by parcel post. $1.25

Serving Trays

Fancy Octagon Shape
Handsome nickeled non-rustable metal frame and one-piece rail. Beautiful imported glass panel, hand painted in bird and floral design in rich colors of lavender, yellows and greens, with genuine mother of pearl inlay. Size, 17¾x11¾ inches. Shipping weight, 8 pounds. **Can be shipped by parcel post.**
1K4186............................ $2.20

A Striking Subject

A fifteenth century ship offers a new and novel tray design. The imported glass panel is **hand painted** in exquisite combinations of purple, yellow, orange and blue with genuine mother of pearl inlay. Nickeled non-rustable metal frame; rubber feet. Size, 17¾x11¾ in. Shipping weight, 8 pounds. **Can be shipped parcel post.**
1K4185.................................. $1.89

A Tremendous Value
Here is a non-rustable nickel plated metal tray with glass panel. Parrot design in combination colorings of blue, black and gold. Size, 17¾x11¾ inches. **Can be shipped by parcel post.** Makes an ideal gift. Shipping weight, 8 pounds.
1K4170.................................... $1.19

For other serving trays see pages 614, 965 and 967

Framed Tapestries

Fireplace or Buffet Piece
Genuine imported Flemish tapestry exquisitely framed. Frame is colored in gold and mottled brown, touched with contrasting colors. Ornamental top and corners. **An assortment of subjects,** all reproductions of masterpieces; all from life. Sharp patterns; tightly framed; cardboard backs. Tapestry is 58x18 inches. Entire size, 61x28 inches. Shipping weight, 45 pounds.
1K4141 $7.65

Popular Picture Size
Beautifully framed in gilt and brown, touched with other colors. Genuine Flemish tapestries, in an **assortment of life subjects.** Tapestry size, 18 inches square. Entire size, 23x20½ inches. Shipping weight, 5 pounds.
1K4142.......................... $3.15

A Beautiful Medium Size
Genuine Flemish importation in an **assortment of appropriate life subjects** that will fit in nicely anywhere in the home. Beautifully framed in stippled gold, striped with dark blue. All are tightly framed, with cardboard backs. Tapestry size, 38x18 inches. Size, 42x25 in. Shipping weight, 30 pounds.
1K4165.................................... $5.98

Folding Beds and Cots-Mattresses to Fit

Every Home Needs a Folding Bed

A bed in which service and comfort are combined. Steel construction throughout. Neatly finished in a handsome dark gray enamel. Comfortable, sagless steel wire link fabric spring anchored to angle ends with helical (coil) springs. Spring is elevated 4 in. above side rails and 16½ in. from floor. The side rails are of angle steel. Height, head and foot ends, 30 in.; length, over all, 76¼ in. Folds into compact size. All parts strongly riveted, not bolted. Comes in two widths.

1K5891—30 inches wide. Shipping weight, 62 pounds........... $7.25
36 inches wide. Shipping weight, 64 pounds............. ..$7.75

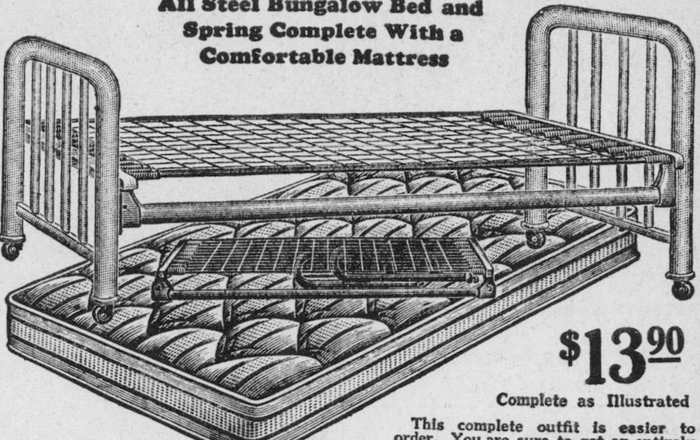

Big Values in a Well Made Folding Bed

Strongly built with graceful curved ends. Comfortable steel wire link fabric spring anchored to the ends with helical (coil) springs. 1⅝ in. steel bands at the sides of spring protect the fabric and keep it from sagging. The spring is elevated 4½ in. above side rails, giving greater comfort. Height of ends, 35 in. Continuous posts and top rails of steel tubing 1 1/16 in. thick. Straight vertical filling rods, 5/16 in. thick. Length, over all, 74½ in. Gray enamel finish. Very compact when folded.

1K5898—30 inches wide. Shipping wt., 62 lbs....... $8.75
36 inches wide. Shipping wt., 66 lbs....... ..$9.75

All Steel Bungalow Bed and Spring Complete With a Comfortable Mattress

$13.90

Complete as Illustrated

This complete outfit is easier to order. You are sure to get an entirely satisfactory combination.

The Bungalow Bed is complete with a comfortable link fabric spring, anchored to angle steel ends with helical (coil) springs. The spring fabric is elevated 3½ inches above the side rails and 16 inches above the floor. The continuous end posts are 1¼ inches thick. Height of both head and foot ends, 29 inches. Vertical filler posts are ½ inch thick. Bottom cross rods are ¾ inch thick. Comes in 30 and 36-inch widths. Complete with easy rolling casters. Finished in handsome brown enamel. Shipping weights, 60 and 65 pounds, respectively. Can be compactly folded when not in use.
Mattress to fit is a good quality box edge style, filled with all new, clean fluffy cotton. Covered with a good grade art ticking and deep tufted for firmness. Actual weights, 18 and 23 pounds. Shipping weights, 20 and 25 pounds.

1K5887—Bed and spring only. 30 inches wide...................... $ 9.25
36 inches wide...................... 9.75
1K7227—Mattress only. 30 inches wide...................... 4.75
36 inches wide...................... 5.45
1K5620—Combination offer. 30-inch bed, spring and mattress.............. 13.90
36-inch bed, spring and mattress.............. 15.10

BUILT for COMFORT

Handy Steel Folding Bed

As Comfortable as the Average Bed

A popular style that many of our customers use as an everyday bed. It is every bit as comfortable as the average bed and makes a neat, attractive appearance. If not in use all the time it can easily be folded and stored into a small space. Equipped with comfortable, steel fabric spring firmly anchored to angle steel ends with helical (coil) springs. Angle steel side rails make this bed very strong. Spring is elevated 4 in. above side rails and 16½ in. from floor, assuring greater comfort. 1⅝-in. steel bands at each side of spring protect the spring fabric. All parts riveted, not bolted. Height of head end, 36 in.; foot end, 30 in. Corner posts, 1 1/16 in. diameter. Length, over all, 75¾ in. Widths, 30 and 36 in. Inside length, 72¾ in. Dark gray enamel finish. Folds flat.

$7.45
30-Inch Size

1K5895—30 in. wide. Shipping weight, 64 pounds $7.45
36 in. wide. Shipping weight, 67 pounds.. ..$7.95

Pad Mattresses for Folding Beds and Cots

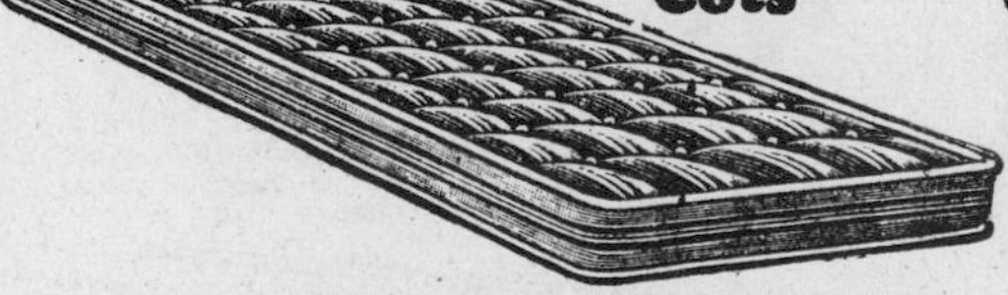

A Medium Priced Pad Mattress
Extremely Comfortable

Made of built-up layers of cotton felted stock, the same as our regular high grade cotton felted mattress. Our same Seal of Purity protects you. Tufts are evenly placed and strongly bound. Firmly woven twill ticking. Has 2-inch box edges.

1K7230
Size, 30x72 in. Actual wt., 14 lbs. Shipping wt., 16 lbs. (Can be shipped by parcel post)............... $4.28
Size, 36x72 in. Actual wt., 16 lbs. Shpg. wt., 18 lbs..... ...$4.78
Size, 42x72 in. Actual wt., 19 lbs. Shpg. wt., 21 lbs..... 5.28

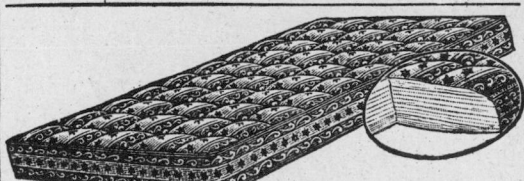

Felted Cotton Pad Mattress

This mattress is filled with guaranteed quality felted cotton (see small illustration in oval). Fleeced, worked and fitted into loose, fluffy layers and encased in the ticking. The construction is the same as our regular high grade cotton felted mattress. Full tufted with biscuit tufts. The same Seal of Purity protects you. 3-in. box edge. Fancy art pattern ticking.

1K7237
Size, 30x72 in. Actual wt., 18 lbs. Shipping wt., 20 pounds. (Can be shipped by parcel post)............ $4.75
Size, 36x72 in. Actual wt., 23 lbs. Shpg. wt., 25 lbs.......$5.45

Steel construction throughout. Continuous posts and top rail of 1 1/16-in. steel. Steel wire fabric spring fastened to angle ends and side rods with helical (coil) springs. Finished in dark gray enamel. Height of head and foot ends, 26½ in. Entire length, 76¾ in. Spring fabric is 16 in. from floor. Exceptionally strong and will give good service. Folds to 1½ in. thickness. Made in 30 and 36-in. widths. 73¾ in. long inside.

1K5889—30 in. wide. Shipping weight, 41 lbs.... $4.35
36 in. wide. Shpg. wt., 44 lbs. ..$4.85

Army Style Steel Cot

Only $4.35
30-Inch Size

Low Priced Wooden Cot

A handy cot for the unexpected visitor. Made of hardwood in neat varnish finish. Upright posts are firmly braced and all parts securely joined. Closely woven, comfortable fabric spring, 16½ in. from floor. Length, over all, 74½ in.; inside length, 71 in. Folds flat.

Folds Very Compactly

For Other Folding Cots, See Page 499

1K5854
30 in. wide. Shipping wt., 28 lbs..$2.95
36 in. wide. Shipping wt., 36 lbs $3.45

Buy Day Beds Now

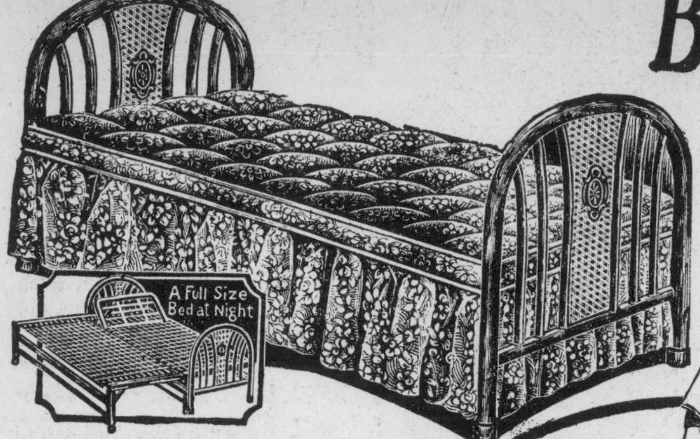
A Full Size Bed at Night

Beautiful Windsor Slide Out Style, Walnut Finish

$18.45 Cash Only

This handsome day bed is being offered at most attractive cash prices. Where else can you purchase a day bed of this up-to-date style and quality for less than $20.00 and complete with a 25-pound felted cotton mattress? Ready for use as a roomy bed in an instant. Slide out style—lower section slides out smoothly on easy rolling casters, forming a large size double bed. Strongly constructed with 4 beautifully curved filler rods ⅜ inch thick; bottom cross rods ⅝ inch thick, and an artistic steel cane panel decorated with a composition ornament. Equipped with a comfortable reclining head rest. Good quality link fabric wire spring anchored to the ends by helical (coil) springs. Continuous end posts, 1 1/16 inches thick. Ends, 32 inches high. Size, closed, 26x72¾ inches; as full size bed, 48x72¼ inches. Handsome walnut finish. 25-pound all felted cotton mattress, covered with floral design cretonne, included with day bed. Shipping weight, 100 pounds.

Sold for Cash Only.

1K5825—Day Bed and Mattress........ **$18.45**

1K7053—Japara Kapok filled Bolster to match. 8x24 in. Shpg. wt., 2lbs.... **$1.25**

Bright cretonne sofa cushions are shown on page 886.

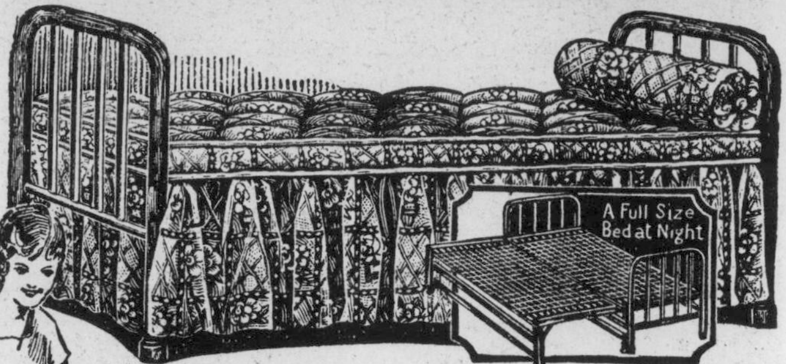
A Full Size Bed at Night

Cash Only

Slide Out Style Day Bed

Just as convenient—just as comfortable—at a big saving in price. Lower section slides forward smoothly on easy rolling casters, forming a large three-quarter size bed. Frame made of steel, ends finished in choice of mahogany or walnut. Has comfortable steel double wire fabric spring anchored to end angle irons with helical (coil) springs. Couch comes complete with felted cotton mattress, covered with high quality floral pattern cretonne. When closed for day use the bed measures 25x72¾ inches. When open as a bed, it is 46x72¾ inches. The ends are 29 inches high. Continuous corner posts, 1 1/16 inches thick. Filler posts are 5/16 in. thick. Bottom cross rods are ⅝ inch thick. Extreme outside length, 75 inches. Packed to secure lowest transportation rates. Easily put together. Shpg. wt., 98 lbs.

1K5817

Day bed, complete with cretonne covered mattress. Mahogany finish, **$14.85**

Walnut finish, **$14.95**

1K7057

Japara Kapok filled bolster to match. Size, 8x24 inches. Shipping weight, 2 pounds. **$1.25**

$5.00 Down *and $5.00 a Month*

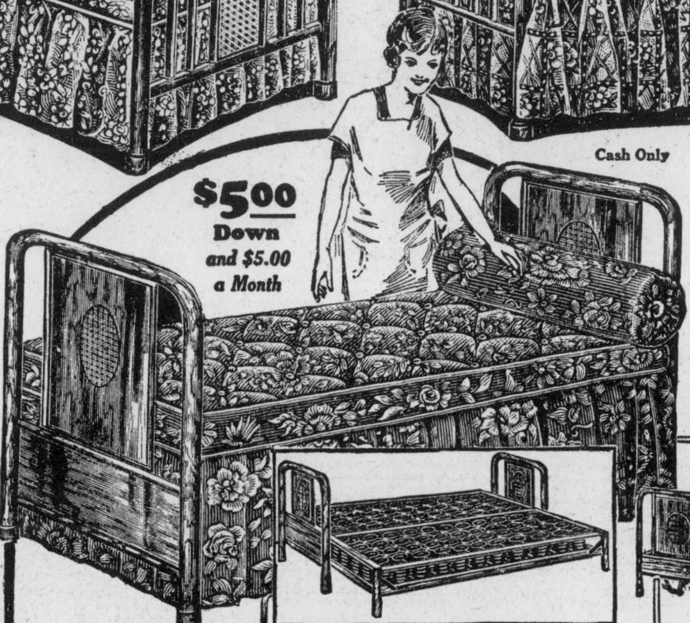

Our Easy Payment Terms Make This Automatic Style Day Bed Easy to Own

Only $5.00 down and $5.00 a month. Enjoy the use of this comfortable day bed in your home as you pay for it. **Has the same type of coil spring as the most comfortable beds.** The solid steel panel ends, carefully finished in hand grained walnut and offset by the ornamental perforated cane panel insets, make this day bed an unusually attractive style. Operates automatically by spring adjustment which eliminates the weight of lifting (a child can operate). Frame of angle steel, reinforced at all points of strain. All parts riveted—no bolts to work loose. Each section has 44 oil tempered coil springs, 6 inches deep. These coil springs are tied at the top with 60 interlocking helical (coil) springs which form an unbroken sleeping surface. Each section has a base structure of angle steel and is surrounded at the top with a 5/16-in. border wire. This border wire, in turn, is anchored by strong helical springs to the supporting frame work. Width, closed, 26 in.; open, 48½ in. Length inside, 76½ in. Height of ends, 32 in. Continuous end posts, 1 1/16 in. thick. Bottom cross rod, ¾ in. Complete with 28-lb. felted cotton mattress covered with floral pattern cretonne. Shipped with ends detached to save transportation charges. Easily put on. Shpg. wt., 157 lbs.

	Cash Prices	Easy Payment Prices
1K5845—Day Bed, complete with mattress.....	**$29.85**	**$32.85**
1K7055—Japara Kapok filled bolster to match. 8x24 in. Shipping weight, 2 lbs......	**$1.25**	**$1.40**

Bolster sold separately for cash only.

Easy Payment Terms: $5.00 down and $5.00 monthly. Use Time Payment Order Blank on page 1092.

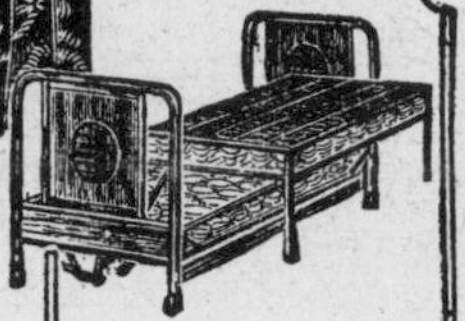

Illustrating the Automatic Style of Operation

Heavy springs eliminate the weight of lifting so that a child can operate. Simply lift the top section up and out. No rumpled rugs; no scratched floors with this style.

How to Choose Colors and Furnishings for Your Home. See page 1017 about this wonderful book at a bargain price. Be sure to order one.

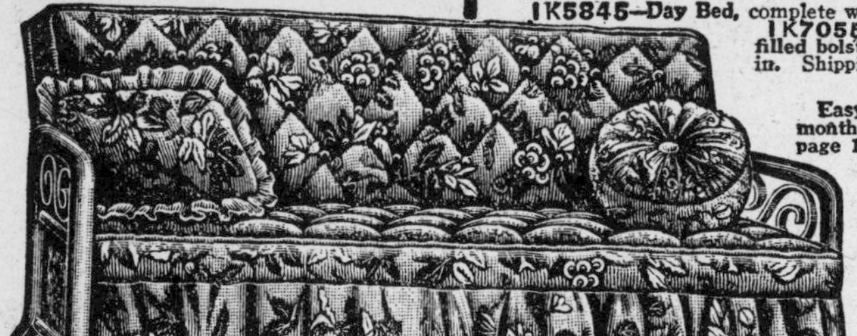

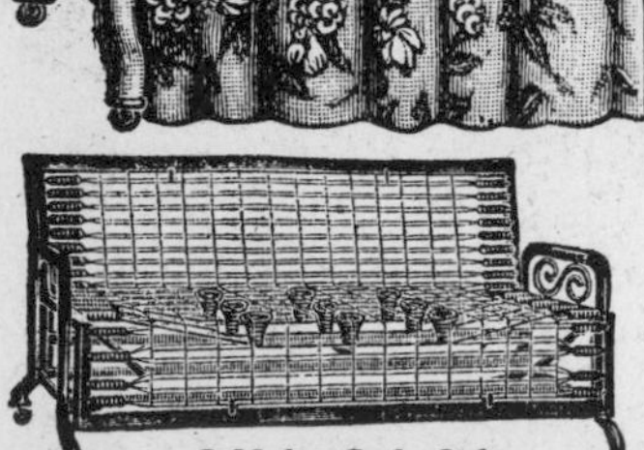

Sold for Cash Only

Combination Davenport or Bed

The back extension can be raised to form a back—or it can be dropped to seat level. The front drop side can be raised to seat level. Heavy 1⅛ inch tubular ends with a foot spread of 34 inches. The seat is supported by **nine 5-inch coil springs that double the comfort and life of the davenport.** Fabric is anchored to angle steel ends with helical (coil) springs. Size as a davenport, 23x72 inches; height of back from seat, 18 inches. Opened as a bed, 54x72 inches; width outside, 75 inches. Packed with legs detached to secure lowest transportation rates. Easily put on. Shipping weight, 72 pounds.

1K5819—Steel Davenport Bed only.............................. **$8.25**

1K7222—Felted cotton pad mattress, covered with olive green denim ticking. Square box edges; tufted top. Hood and tapes for fastening to davenport frame. Shipping weight, 23 pounds.............. **$4.95**

1K7220—Felted Cotton pad mattress, covered with cretonne ticking with flounce. Square box edges; tufted top. Hood and tapes for fastening to davenport frame. Shipping weight, 24 pounds.............. **$7.45**

Desirable Sanitary Couch

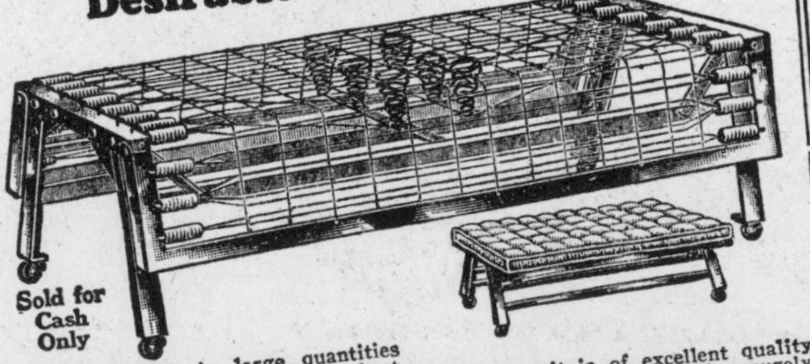

Sold for Cash Only

By purchasing in large quantities we are able to offer you the very best at an exceptionally low price. Although priced low, it is of excellent quality and will give satisfactory service. Frame strongly made of angle steel, securely riveted and braced. Finished in gray enamel. Comfortable link wire fabric with anti-rust coating, supported underneath with two rows of cone shape springs swung on heavy wire cables. The spring fabric is anchored to the angle ends by helical (coil) springs. Easy rolling casters. Size as a couch, 72½x23¼ in. Size as a bed, 44x72½ in. Height from floor, 18½ in. Packed to secure lowest transportation rates. Easily put together. Shpg. wt., 53 lbs.

1K5802—Sanitary Steel Couch, as illustrated........ **$3.95**

1K7211—Pad Mattress to fit. Felted cotton covered with olive green denim ticking. Tufted top and bottom and fitted with tapes for attaching to couch. Shipping weight, 16 pounds.............. **$4.18**

Biggest Values

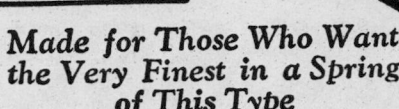

$15⁴⁵

One Hundred and Sixty-Five Triple Cone Coil Springs Make This the Most Comfortable Bed Spring We Have Ever Offered Our Customers

Made for Those Who Want the Very Finest in a Spring of This Type

A sensational value that can't be matched ANYWHERE. A bed spring of super-comfort at lower prices than usually asked for 99-coil or 140-coil styles.

This bed spring is made to our own specifications. Every comfort feature has been included; every device recommended by doctors who look on restful sleep as the cure for many ailments.

Proper rest is vital to our continued usefulness in the world and our present efficiency. With the right kind and amount of rest many of our present-day ills will vanish. The bed spring, the "resting foundation" for the sleeper, is the most important consideration. With a modern scientifically constructed spring that is free from squeaks and rattles and that, due to its coils, has full resilience without any possibility of sagging, is the kind of bed spring doctors recommend. It permits quiet unbroken sleep, and supports the body in its natural position.

A wonderful bed spring! The full 54-inch size has 165 triple cone coil springs, seven inches deep. These coil springs are securely fastened at the bottom to steel foundation cross braces. At their tops they are held in place by 280 interlocking helical (coil) springs which form a practically solid sleeping surface of springs. The triple cone coil springs are of lighter wire than the ordinary bed spring coils because there are so many more of them. Each coil has less weight to support; therefore it can be made lighter. And because each coil is of lighter wire it is just that much springier.

Every coil spring is tied at the center to the springs next to it, as is illustrated in the small panel on the opposite page. This eliminates the side sway or vibration so common to the ordinary spring. And as an added feature this spring is equipped with automatic operating side braces which not only check side sway but protect the edges and keep them from sagging when sitting on the side of the bed. This feature is illustrated in panel above at left.

The spring foundation is a frame of angle steel with thirteen individual cross braces. The corners are round, not square. Round corners not only eliminate sharp edges that tear bedding, but they prevent the sagging of mattress and bedding. The coil springs are enclosed at the top by an extra heavy 5/16-inch border wire to which the coil springs are securely clipped. Length, 73½ inches.

1K5797—Style to fit straight end beds with steel side rails. Comes in 54, 48, and 39-inch widths. Shipping weights, 85, 75 and 65 pounds, respectively. **$15.45** State width wanted.
Style to fit straight end beds with wood side rails. Width, 52 inches. Shipping weight, 85 pounds **$15.43**
1K5798—Style to fit bow end beds with steel side rails. Comes in **$15.85** 54-inch width only. Shipping weight, 85 pounds . . . .
Style to fit bow end beds with wood side rails. Width, 52-inch. Shipping weight, 85 pounds **$15.83**

How to Order a Bed Spring

State whether spring is wanted for wood or metal bed. Give the exact length and width of your bed.

If you want a spring for a metal bed, to obtain the width measure from one outside edge to the outside edge of the opposite rail. For the length, measure the length of the side rail.

If you want a spring for an ordinary wood bed, give the length of the cross slat for the width, and the length of the side rail for the length. If for wood bed fitted with square wood rails or with steel rails, where the spring rests on the rails instead of on slats, for the width give measurement from one outside edge to the outside edge of the opposite rail. For length, give length of side rail.

Another Astounding Bed Spring Value!

Buy and Compare

$9⁹⁵

Not a sale price on this fine spring—just the regular low price that only the World's Largest Store can name. A better quality than often sells at $12.00 or more.

Has the latest, newest features of bed spring construction. The full 54-inch size has 140 tempered coil cone shape deep springs securely fastened to individual steel bottom slats and locked at the top with interlocking helical (coil) springs, which forms an unbroken spring surface supremely comfortable. This spring has the improved round corner frame. The elimination of sharp corners means the end of torn bedding and sagging mattress. Heavy angle steel frame, gray enamel finish. Invest in sleeping comfort; you'll feel amply repaid in restful vigor the next day. A Wonderful Value! Length, 73 inches.

1K5794—Style to fit straight end beds with steel side rails. Comes in 54, 48 and 39-inch widths. Shipping weights, 70, 65 and 55 pounds, respectively. State width wanted **$9.95**
Style to fit straight end beds with wood side rails. 52-inch width only. Shipping weight, 70 pounds **9.93**
1K5795—Style to fit bow end beds with steel side rails. 54-inch width only. Shipping weight, 70 pounds **10.25**
Style to fit bow end beds with wood side rails. 52-inch width only. Shipping weight, 70 pounds **10.23**

Every spring shown on these two pages is a value worth consideration. Our policy of highest quality at lowest prices was never more apparent. It pays to buy bed springs at the World's Largest Store.

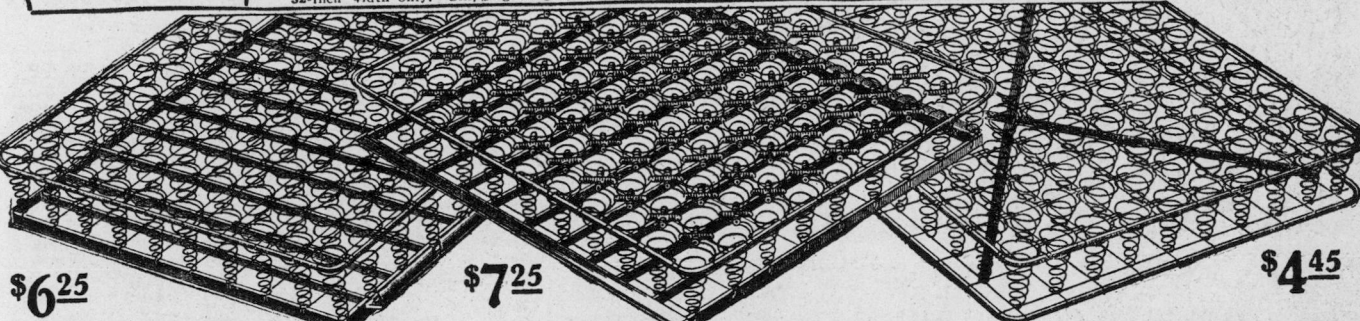

$6²⁵

Our Lowest Price for This Quality

This good quality bed spring, in the full 54-inch width, has 120 cone shape coil springs of medium weight wire fastened at the bottom to steel crossbars and locked together at the top by a patent interlocking top. A good, lively spring with years of service in it. Strongly riveted angle steel frame. Finished all over in gray enamel. No slats needed for metal beds. For use on wood beds three ordinary slats are necessary. When ordering state size and kind of bed for which the spring is ordered. Length, 74 in.

1K5765—Style to fit straight end beds with steel side rails. Comes in 54, 48, 42, and 39-inch widths. Shipping weights, 63, 56 and 46 pounds, respectively. **$6.25** State width.
Style to fit straight end beds with wood side rails. Comes in 52, 50 and 46-inch widths. Shipping weights, 63, 56 and 54 pounds, respectively. State width **$6.23**

$7²⁵

A Genuine 99-Coil Bed Spring With Full Helical (Coil) Spring Top

For less than you would pay elsewhere for a wire fabric spring nowhere near as comfortable or as durable. This bed spring has 99 deep, oil tempered cone shape coil springs securely locked to foundation cross braces at the bottom and to each other by crossed helical (coil) springs at the top, providing a sleeping surface both durable and very comfortable. At the price, an exceptional bargain! Heavy angle steel frame; heavy border wire at the top. Gray enamel finish. Length, 72½ in.

1K5776—Style for straight end beds with steel side rails. Size to fit 54-inch bed only. Shipping weight, 63 pounds **$7.25**
Style for straight end beds with wood side rails. 52-in. width only. Shpg. wt., 63 lbs **7.23**

$4⁴⁵

A Sensational Bed Spring Value!

This spring has ONE HUNDRED AND TWENTY cone shape coil springs six inches deep, of a heavier gauge wire than is ordinarily found in lower priced styles. The springs are fastened to a crosswire bottom with an added support of metal cross strips and are locked firmly together to the top with a patent interlocking wire construction. The border wires, top and bottom, are ¼-inch thick and seamless; the corners are rounded so as not to tear bedding. Length, 73 in. These springs cannot be used without bed slats. Bed slats not furnished.

1K5758—Made only to fit straight end beds with steel side rails. 54-inch width. **$4.45** Shipping weight, 37 pounds . . . .
1K5754—Similar spring but lighter weight to fit straight end beds with wood side rails. 52-inch width. Not illustrated. Shipping weight, 22 pounds . . . **$2.15**

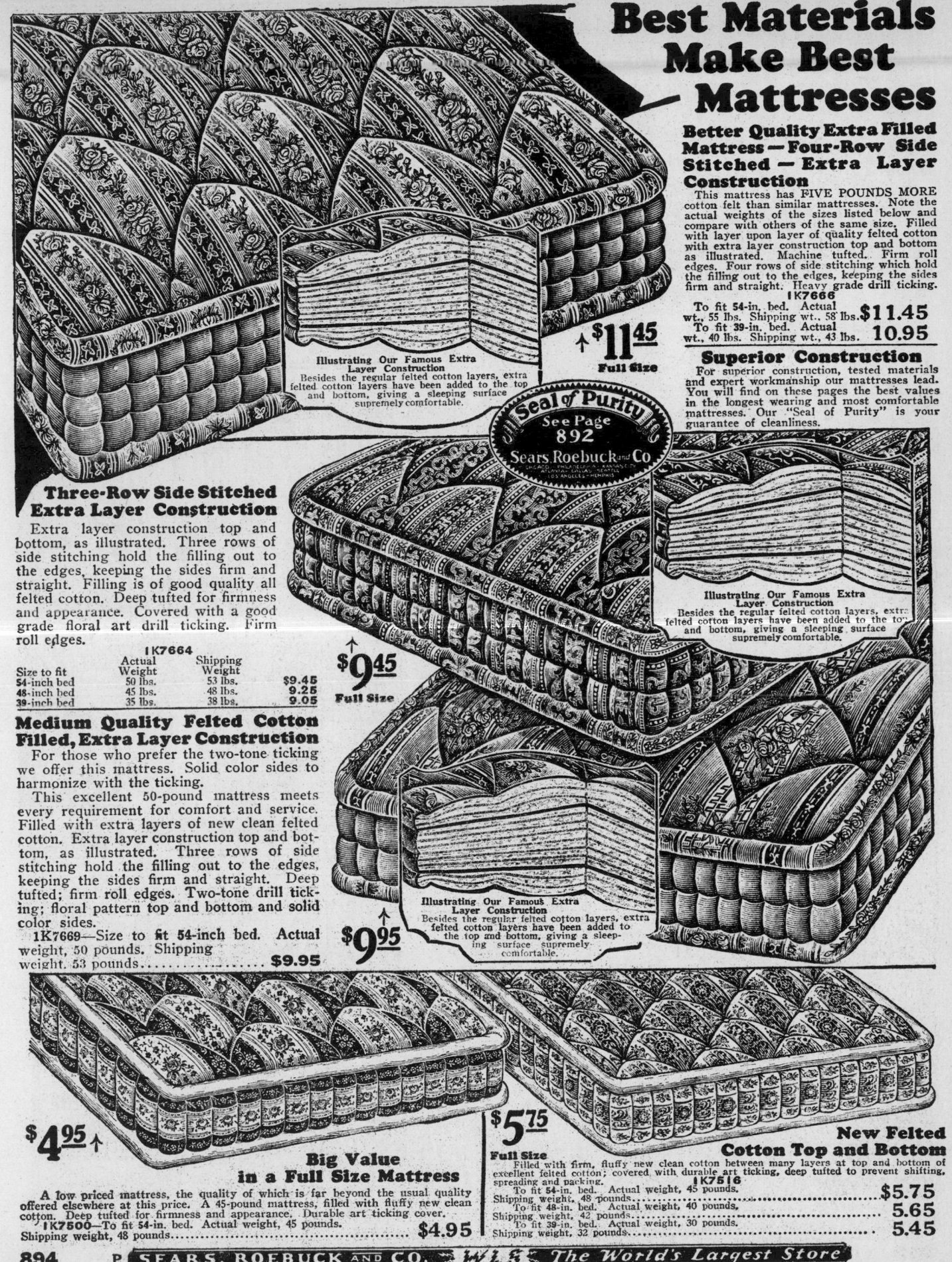

Best Materials Make Best Mattresses

Better Quality Extra Filled Mattress — Four-Row Side Stitched — Extra Layer Construction

This mattress has FIVE POUNDS MORE cotton felt than similar mattresses. Note the actual weights of the sizes listed below and compare with others of the same size. Filled with layer upon layer of quality felted cotton with extra layer construction top and bottom as illustrated. Machine tufted. Firm roll edges. Four rows of side stitching which hold the filling out to the edges, keeping the sides firm and straight. Heavy grade drill ticking.

1K7666

To fit 54-in. bed. Actual wt., 55 lbs. Shipping wt., 58 lbs. **$11.45**
To fit 39-in. bed. Actual wt., 40 lbs. Shipping wt., 43 lbs. **10.95**

↑$11.45 Full Size

Illustrating Our Famous Extra Layer Construction
Besides the regular felted cotton layers, extra felted cotton layers have been added to the top and bottom, giving a sleeping surface supremely comfortable.

Superior Construction

For superior construction, tested materials and expert workmanship our mattresses lead. You will find on these pages the best values in the longest wearing and most comfortable mattresses. Our "Seal of Purity" is your guarantee of cleanliness.

Seal of Purity See Page 892 Sears, Roebuck and Co. CHICAGO · PHILADELPHIA · KANSAS CITY · ATLANTA · DALLAS · SEATTLE · LOS ANGELES · MEMPHIS

Three-Row Side Stitched Extra Layer Construction

Extra layer construction top and bottom, as illustrated. Three rows of side stitching hold the filling out to the edges, keeping the sides firm and straight. Filling is of good quality all felted cotton. Deep tufted for firmness and appearance. Covered with a good grade floral art drill ticking. Firm roll edges.

Size to fit	1K7664 Actual Weight	Shipping Weight	
54-inch bed	50 lbs.	53 lbs.	$9.45
48-inch bed	45 lbs.	48 lbs.	9.25
39-inch bed	35 lbs.	38 lbs.	9.05

↑ $9.45 Full Size

Illustrating Our Famous Extra Layer Construction
Besides the regular felted cotton layers, extra felted cotton layers have been added to the top and bottom, giving a sleeping surface supremely comfortable.

Medium Quality Felted Cotton Filled, Extra Layer Construction

For those who prefer the two-tone ticking we offer this mattress. Solid color sides to harmonize with the ticking.

This excellent 50-pound mattress meets every requirement for comfort and service. Filled with extra layers of new clean felted cotton. Extra layer construction top and bottom, as illustrated. Three rows of side stitching hold the filling out to the edges, keeping the sides firm and straight. Deep tufted; firm roll edges. Two-tone drill ticking; floral pattern top and bottom and solid color sides.

1K7669—Size to fit 54-inch bed. Actual weight, 50 pounds. Shipping weight, 53 pounds.................**$9.95**

↑ $9.95

Illustrating Our Famous Extra Layer Construction
Besides the regular felted cotton layers, extra felted cotton layers have been added to the top and bottom, giving a sleeping surface supremely comfortable.

Big Value in a Full Size Mattress

$4.95 ↑

A low priced mattress, the quality of which is far beyond the usual quality offered elsewhere at this price. A 45-pound mattress, filled with fluffy new clean cotton. Deep tufted for firmness and appearance. Durable art ticking cover.

1K7500—To fit 54-in. bed. Actual weight, 45 pounds. Shipping weight, 48 pounds.................**$4.95**

New Felted Cotton Top and Bottom

$5.75 Full Size

Filled with firm, fluffy new clean cotton between many layers at top and bottom of excellent felted cotton; covered with durable art ticking, deep tufted to prevent shifting, spreading and packing.

1K7516
To fit 54-in. bed. Actual weight, 45 pounds. Shipping weight, 48 pounds.................**$5.75**
To fit 48-in. bed. Actual weight, 40 pounds. Shipping weight, 42 pounds.................**5.65**
To fit 39-in. bed. Actual weight, 30 pounds. Shipping weight, 32 pounds.................**5.45**

Finest Steel Beds

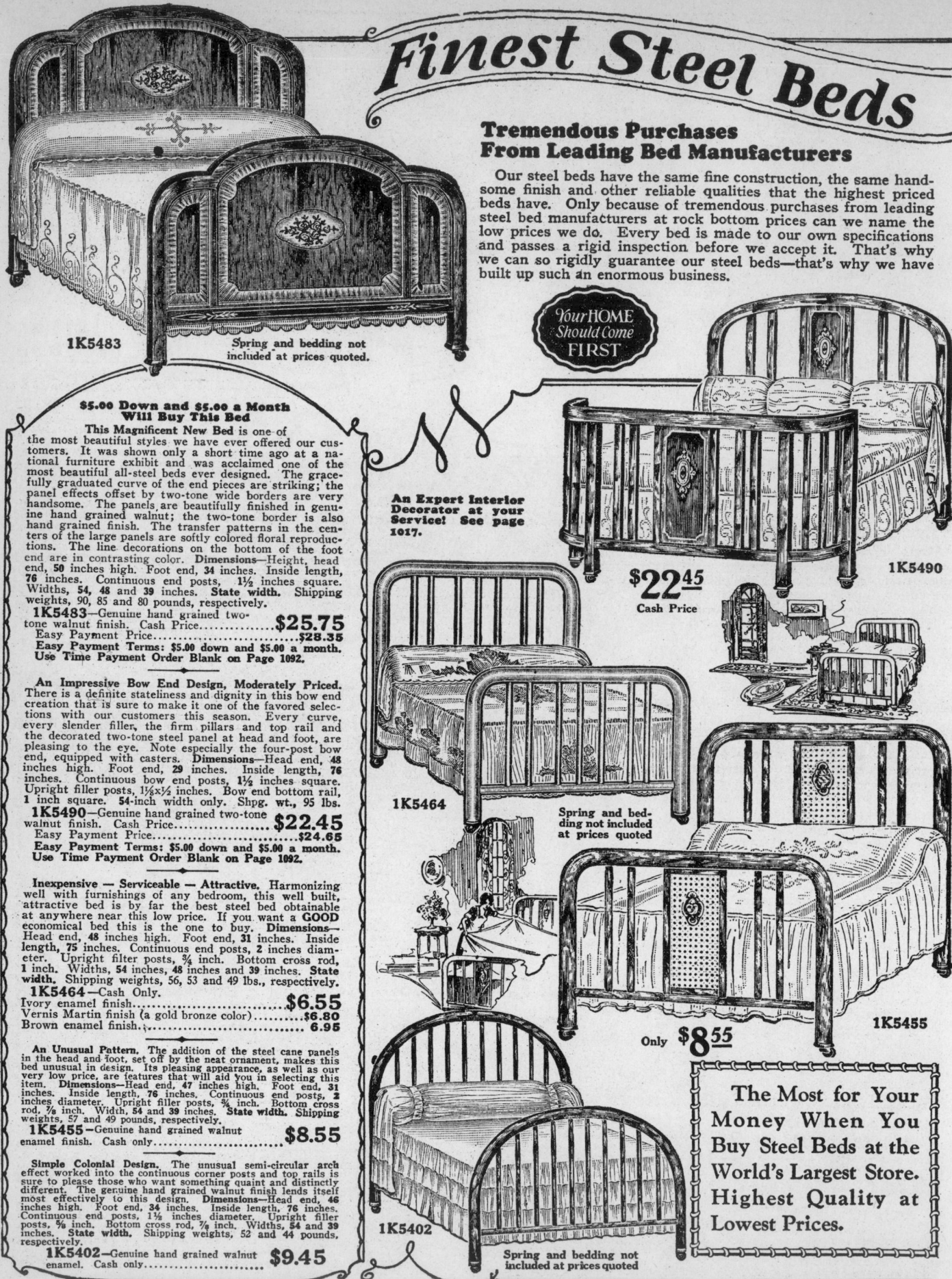

Tremendous Purchases From Leading Bed Manufacturers

Our steel beds have the same fine construction, the same handsome finish and other reliable qualities that the highest priced beds have. Only because of tremendous purchases from leading steel bed manufacturers at rock bottom prices can we name the low prices we do. Every bed is made to our own specifications and passes a rigid inspection before we accept it. That's why we can so rigidly guarantee our steel beds—that's why we have built up such an enormous business.

Your HOME Should Come FIRST

An Expert Interior Decorator at your Service! See page 1017.

1K5483
Spring and bedding not included at prices quoted.

$5.00 Down and $5.00 a Month Will Buy This Bed

This Magnificent New Bed is one of the most beautiful styles we have ever offered our customers. It was shown only a short time ago at a national furniture exhibit and was acclaimed one of the most beautiful all-steel beds ever designed. The gracefully graduated curve of the end pieces are striking; the panel effects offset by two-tone wide borders are very handsome. The panels are beautifully finished in genuine hand grained walnut; the two-tone border is also hand grained finish. The transfer patterns in the centers of the large panels are softly colored floral reproductions. The line decorations on the bottom of the foot end are in contrasting color. Dimensions—Height, head end, 50 inches high. Foot end, 34 inches. Inside length, 76 inches. Continuous end posts, 1½ inches square. Widths, 54, 48 and 39 inches. State width. Shipping weights, 90, 85 and 80 pounds, respectively.

1K5483—Genuine hand grained two-tone walnut finish. Cash Price.............**$25.75**
Easy Payment Price......................**$28.35**
Easy Payment Terms: $5.00 down and $5.00 a month. Use Time Payment Order Blank on Page 1092.

An Impressive Bow End Design, Moderately Priced. There is a definite stateliness and dignity in this bow end creation that is sure to make it one of the favored selections with our customers this season. Every curve, every slender filler, the firm pillars and top rail and the decorated two-tone steel panel at head and foot, are pleasing to the eye. Note especially the four-post bow end, equipped with casters. Dimensions—Head end, 48 inches high. Foot end, 29 inches. Inside length, 76 inches. Continuous bow end posts, 1½ inches square. Upright filler posts, 1½x½ inches. Bow end bottom rail, 1 inch square. 54-inch width only. Shpg. wt., 95 lbs.
1K5490—Genuine hand grained two-tone walnut finish. Cash Price....................**$22.45**
Easy Payment Price......................**$24.65**
Easy Payment Terms: $5.00 down and $5.00 a month. Use Time Payment Order Blank on Page 1092.

Inexpensive — Serviceable — Attractive. Harmonizing well with furnishings of any bedroom, this well built, attractive bed is by far the best steel bed obtainable at anywhere near this low price. If you want a **GOOD** economical bed this is the one to buy. Dimensions— Head end, 48 inches high. Foot end, 31 inches. Inside length, 75 inches. Continuous end posts, 2 inches diameter. Upright filter posts, ¾ inch. Bottom cross rod, 1 inch. Widths, 54 inches, 48 inches and 39 inches. **State width.** Shipping weights, 56, 53 and 49 lbs., respectively.
1K5464—Cash Only.
Ivory enamel finish............................**$6.55**
Vernis Martin finish (a gold bronze color)..........**$6.80**
Brown enamel finish................................ **6.95**

An Unusual Pattern. The addition of the steel cane panels in the head and foot, set off by the neat ornament, makes this bed unusual in design. Its pleasing appearance, as well as our very low price, are features that will aid you in selecting this item. Dimensions—Head end, 47 inches high. Foot end, 31 inches. Inside length, 76 inches. Continuous end posts, 2 inches diameter. Upright filler posts, ¾ inch. Bottom cross rod, ⅜ inch. Width, 54 and 39 inches. **State width.** Shipping weights, 57 and 49 pounds, respectively.
1K5455—Genuine hand grained walnut enamel finish. Cash only....................**$8.55**

Simple Colonial Design. The unusual semi-circular arch effect worked into the continuous corner posts and top rails is sure to please those who want something quaint and distinctly different. The genuine hand grained walnut finish lends itself most effectively to this design. Dimensions—Head end, 46 inches high. Foot end, 34 inches. Inside length, 76 inches. Continuous end posts, 1½ inches square. Upright filler posts, ⅝ inch. Bottom cross rod, ⅜ inch. Widths, 54 and 39 inches. **State width.** Shipping weights, 52 and 44 pounds, respectively.
1K5402—Genuine hand grained walnut enamel. Cash only.......................**$9.45**

$22⁴⁵ Cash Price

1K5490

1K5464

Spring and bedding not included at prices quoted

Only **$8⁵⁵**

1K5455

1K5402
Spring and bedding not included at prices quoted

The Most for Your Money When You Buy Steel Beds at the World's Largest Store. Highest Quality at Lowest Prices.

Carriages and Go-Carts at Lowest Prices

← **$11**⁴⁵   ► Brown Finish

$7⁹⁵

Handsome Fiber Stroller

Neat in appearance, very well made and most attractively priced. The hood, sides and dash are of closely woven fiber. The back, seat and hood are upholstered in a good grade material that looks like corduroy. Back and dash can be adjusted to reclining position. Body is 14 in. wide; seat, 13½x11 in. Length, 32 in. Continuous tubular steel pusher handles add to the strength of the carriage. Front wheels are 10 in. diameter. Rear wheels, 12 in.; ½-in. rubber tires. Strong foot brake. Shipping wt. 45 lbs.

1K7785—Brown body, gear and
upholstery. Cash only...................... **$11.45**
  Gray body, gear and
upholstery. Cash only...................... 11.55
  Cafe au lait body, gear and
upholstery. Cash only...................... 11.65

Comfortable Folding Go-Cart

Back and dash are adjustable so that the child can lie down. Folding adjustable hood. Spring shock absorbers under the seat. Sides, front and back are of fiber board. Steel frame, black enameled. Long flat steel pusher handle, with one-piece black enameled hand grips. Covering is a serviceable grade of black artificial leather. Go-cart folds into compact form; 10-in. wheels with ½-in. rubber tires. Size of body inside with back down, 31 in. long and 14 in. wide. Shpg. wt., 35 lbs.

1K7715—Cash only................. **$7.95**

$14³⁵ Brown Finish

This Beautiful Carriage Can Be Bought on Easy Payments of

$5.00 Down and $5.00 a Month

Our newest model, fashionably designed and handsomely finished. Has every feature of sound construction and comfort. The body and hood of tightly woven fiber over steel upright foundation wires. Body and hood are lined with a good quality genuine corduroy to match the finish. Bottom and back rest are softly padded. The body of this carriage is reversible. The body, which is held firmly in position by a spring adjustment, can be released by a slight foot pressure and swung around so that the baby faces the mother. Continuous tubular steel pusher handles form the foundation for the gear, making an exceptionally strong carriage. Easy riding floating type springs. Positive foot brake. 14-inch military wheels. Has a metal well under the flooring of the front part of the carriage, convenient for baby's wet clothing or extra bedding. Adjustable hood; glass windows, equipped with draft or storm curtain of same material as the carriage lining. Back rest is adjustable to sitting and reclining positions. Choice of gray or cafe au lait (coffee cream color) finish; body, upholstery and gear are all of one color. Length of bottom, 25 in.; width, 13 in. Length with back rest completely reclined, 33 in. Shpg. wt., 66 lbs.

1K7731	Gray	Cafe
Cash price	$22.65	$22.75
Easy payment price	24.85	24.95

Easy Payment Terms: $5.00 down and $5.00 a month. Time Payment Order Blank is on page 1092.

$20⁶⁵ Brown Finish

$5⁹⁵

Our Low Price Leader

A good carriage, exceptional at our price, neat appearing, well made and comfortable. The same type and quality that usually sells as high as $16.00 elsewhere. The body is made of strong woven fiber, richly enameled in choice of brown, gray or cafe au lait. The hood is adjustable. Equipped with a draft or storm curtain. Has a metal wall under the flooring of the front part of the carriage. Hood and body are lined with a durable material resembling corduroy; the draft curtain is of the same material. Back and bottom are softly padded. Back is adjustable to three positions. Strong tubular steel pusher handles; riveted steel gear. Large size 12-in. wheels with ½-in. rubber tires. Nickeled hub caps. Positive foot brake. Length inside at bottom, 20 in.; width, 12½ in. Length inside with the back extended, 32 in. Entire length, 42 in.; entire height, 33 in. Shipping wt., 70 lbs.

1K7875—Brown finish. Cash only. **$14.35**
  Gray finish.
Cash only........................... 14.45
  Cafe au lait (coffee cream color).
Cash only........................... 14.55

This Carriage Has a Reversible Body

The whole body can be swung around so that the baby will face the mother. The body is held firmly in position by a spring adjustment, but is released by a slight foot pressure. This carriage also has every other fine feature of construction and equipment. Fourteen-inch military wheels with ½-inch rubber tires. Metal well beneath the flooring. Draft or storm shield. Adjustable hood. Continuous hollow steel pushers which run the full length of the carriage, adding greatly to the strength of the gear. Genuine corduroy lining throughout. Storm shield of same material. Glass windows in hood. Choice of brown, gray or cafe au lait (coffee and cream) color finish; body, upholstery and gear are all of one color. Length of bottom, 20½ in.; width, 13 in. Length with the back completely reclined, 32½ in. Entire height, 41 in. Entire length, 41 in. Shipping weight, 70 pounds.

1K7877—Brown finish. Cash only **$20.65**
  Gray finish.
Cash only........................... 20.75
  Cafe au lait.
Cash only........................... 20.85

Two Attractive Values

Sold for Cash Only

Handsome Sulky

Attractive style, adjustable back and adjustable folding hood. Woven fiber sides give this sulky a most attractive appearance. Black enameled steel framework. Long curved handle. Black artificial leather hood and seat; 10-in. wheels, ½-in. rubber tires. Small steel rear wheels, 2½ in. high. Seat, 9½x12 in. Shipping weight, 22 pounds.

1K7754—Brown
finish.................. **$5.85**
  Cafe au lait (rich
coffee cream color).... 5.95

Big Value Folding Go-Cart

$5⁹⁵   The same style that often sells elsewhere for as high as $7.50 or more. Has all steel black enameled frame and a one-piece wood handle. Dash, seat, back, sides and hood are upholstered in good quality black leather cloth. Body, 14 in. wide; seat, 10 in.; dash up and back reclining, 31 in. long. Wheels, 10 in. with ⅜-in. rubber tires. Packed in carton. Shipping weight, 28 pounds.

1K7701—Cash only.............. **$5.95**

Library and Davenport Tables

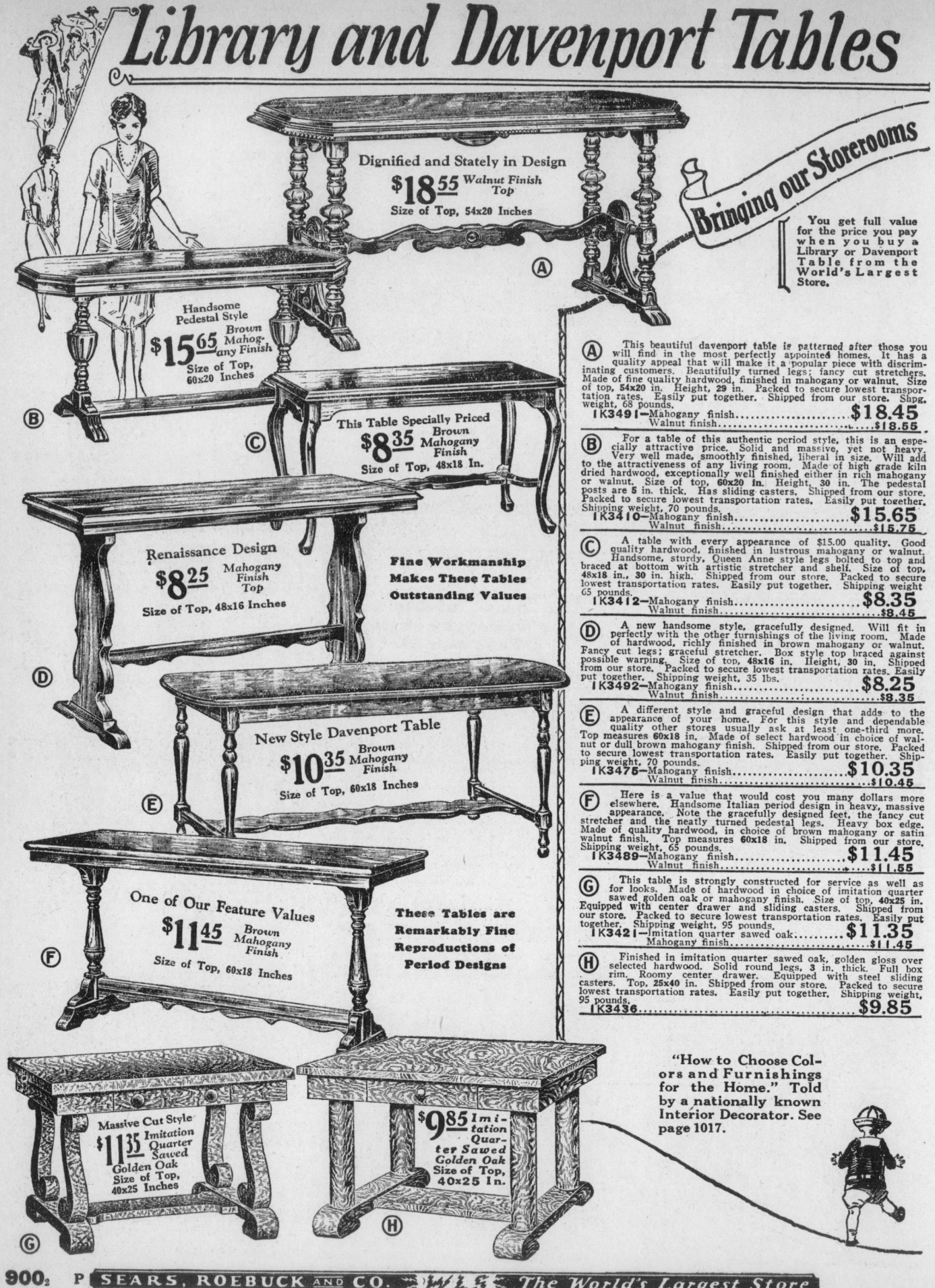

Dignified and Stately in Design
$18⁵⁵ *Walnut Finish Top*
Size of Top, 54x20 Inches
Ⓐ

Bringing our Storerooms

You get full value for the price you pay when you buy a Library or Davenport Table from the World's Largest Store.

Handsome Pedestal Style
$15⁶⁵ *Brown Mahogany Finish*
Size of Top, 60x20 Inches
Ⓑ

This Table Specially Priced
$8³⁵ *Brown Mahogany Finish*
Size of Top, 48x18 In.
Ⓒ

Renaissance Design
$8²⁵ *Mahogany Finish Top*
Size of Top, 48x16 Inches
Ⓓ

Fine Workmanship Makes These Tables Outstanding Values

New Style Davenport Table
$10³⁵ *Brown Mahogany Finish*
Size of Top, 60x18 Inches
Ⓔ

One of Our Feature Values
$11⁴⁵ *Brown Mahogany Finish*
Size of Top, 60x18 Inches
Ⓕ

These Tables are Remarkably Fine Reproductions of Period Designs

Massive Cut Style
$11³⁵ *Imitation Quarter Sawed Golden Oak*
Size of Top, 40x25 Inches
Ⓖ

$9⁸⁵ *Imitation Quarter Sawed Golden Oak*
Size of Top, 40x25 In.
Ⓗ

Ⓐ This beautiful davenport table is patterned after those you will find in the most perfectly appointed homes. It has a quality appeal that will make it a popular piece with discriminating customers. Beautifully turned legs; fancy cut stretchers. Made of fine quality hardwood, finished in mahogany or walnut. Size of top, 54x20 in. Height, 29 in. Packed to secure lowest transportation rates. Easily put together. Shipped from our store. Shpg. weight, 68 pounds.
1K3491—Mahogany finish......................$18.45
Walnut finish................................$18.55

Ⓑ For a table of this authentic period style, this is an especially attractive price. Solid and massive, yet not heavy. Very well made, smoothly finished, liberal in size. Will add to the attractiveness of any living room. Made of high grade kiln dried hardwood, exceptionally well finished either in rich mahogany or walnut. Size of top, 60x20 in. Height, 30 in. The pedestal posts are 5 in. thick. Has sliding casters. Shipped from our store. Packed to secure lowest transportation rates. Easily put together. Shipping weight, 70 pounds.
1K3410—Mahogany finish......................$15.65
Walnut finish................................$15.75

Ⓒ A table with every appearance of $15.00 quality. Good quality hardwood, finished in lustrous mahogany or walnut. Handsome, sturdy, Queen Anne style legs bolted to top and braced at bottom with artistic stretcher and shelf. Size of top, 48x18 in., 30 in. high. Shipped from our store. Packed to secure lowest transportation rates. Easily put together. Shipping weight 65 pounds.
1K3412—Mahogany finish......................$8.35
Walnut finish................................$8.45

Ⓓ A new handsome style, gracefully designed. Will fit in perfectly with the other furnishings of the living room. Made of hardwood, richly finished in brown mahogany or walnut. Fancy cut legs; graceful stretcher. Box style top braced against possible warping. Size of top, 48x16 in. Height, 30 in. Shipped from our store. Packed to secure lowest transportation rates. Easily put together. Shipping weight, 35 lbs.
1K3492—Mahogany finish......................$8.25
Walnut finish................................$8.35

Ⓔ A different style and graceful design that adds to the appearance of your home. For this style and dependable quality other stores usually ask at least one-third more. Top measures 60x18 in. Made of select hardwood in choice of walnut or dull brown mahogany finish. Shipped from our store. Packed to secure lowest transportation rates. Easily put together. Shipping weight, 70 pounds.
1K3475—Mahogany finish......................$10.35
Walnut finish................................$10.45

Ⓕ Here is a value that would cost you many dollars more elsewhere. Handsome Italian period design in heavy, massive appearance. Note the gracefully designed feet, the fancy cut stretcher and the neatly turned pedestal legs. Heavy box edge. Made of quality hardwood, in choice of brown mahogany or satin walnut finish. Top measures 60x18 in. Shipped from our store. Shipping weight, 65 pounds.
1K3489—Mahogany finish......................$11.45
Walnut finish................................$11.55

Ⓖ This table is strongly constructed for service as well as for looks. Made of hardwood in choice of imitation quarter sawed golden oak or mahogany finish. Size of top, 40x25 in. Equipped with center drawer and sliding casters. Shipped from our store. Packed to secure lowest transportation rates. Easily put together. Shipping weight, 95 pounds.
1K3421—Imitation quarter sawed oak..........$11.35
Mahogany finish.............................$11.45

Ⓗ Finished in imitation quarter sawed oak, golden gloss over selected hardwood. Solid round legs, 3 in. thick. Full box rim. Roomy center drawer. Equipped with steel sliding casters. Top, 25x40 in. Shipped from our store. Packed to secure lowest transportation rates. Easily put together. Shipping weight, 95 pounds.
1K3436......................................$9.85

"How to Choose Colors and Furnishings for the Home." Told by a nationally known Interior Decorator. See page 1017.

900₂ P SEARS, ROEBUCK AND CO. WLS The World's Largest Store

Sturdy, Graceful, Low Priced

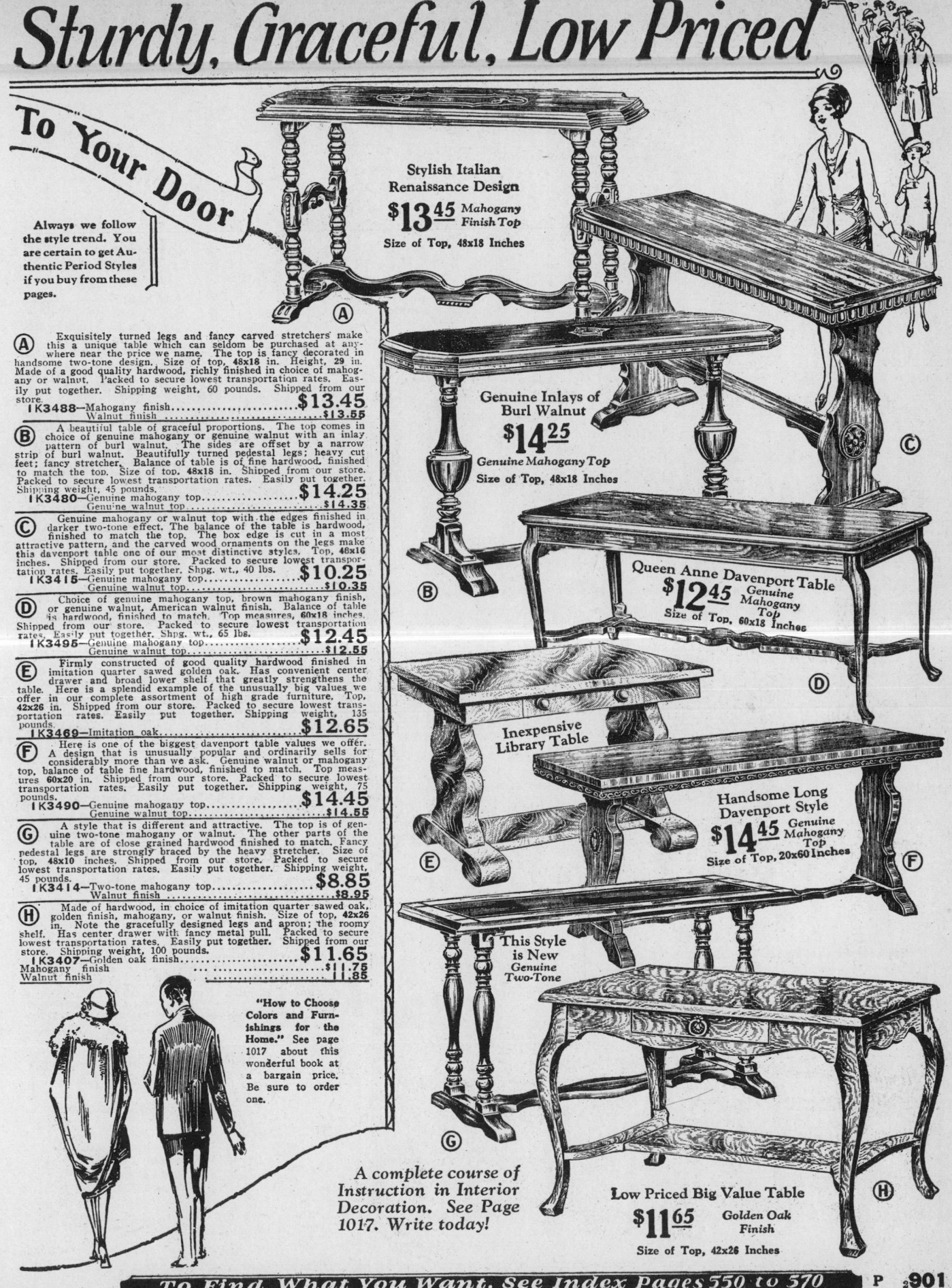

To Your Door

Always we follow the style trend. You are certain to get Authentic Period Styles if you buy from these pages.

Stylish Italian Renaissance Design
$13.45 Mahogany Finish Top
Size of Top, 48x18 Inches

Genuine Inlays of Burl Walnut
$14.25 Genuine Mahogany Top
Size of Top, 48x18 Inches

Queen Anne Davenport Table
$12.45 Genuine Mahogany Top
Size of Top, 60x18 Inches

Inexpensive Library Table

Handsome Long Davenport Style
$14.45 Genuine Mahogany Top
Size of Top, 20x60 Inches

This Style is New Genuine Two-Tone

Low Priced Big Value Table
$11.65 Golden Oak Finish
Size of Top, 42x26 Inches

(A) Exquisitely turned legs and fancy carved stretchers make this a unique table which can seldom be purchased at anywhere near the price we name. The top is fancy decorated in handsome two-tone design. Size of top, 48x18 in. Height, 29 in. Made of a good quality hardwood, richly finished in choice of mahogany or walnut. Packed to secure lowest transportation rates. Easily put together. Shipping weight, 60 pounds. Shipped from our store.
1K3488—Mahogany finish..................$13.45
Walnut finish..................$13.55

(B) A beautiful table of graceful proportions. The top comes in choice of genuine mahogany or genuine walnut with an inlay pattern of burl walnut. The sides are offset by a narrow strip of burl walnut. Beautifully turned pedestal legs; heavy cut feet; fancy stretcher. Balance of table is of fine hardwood, finished to match the top. Size of top, 48x18 in. Shipped from our store. Packed to secure lowest transportation rates. Easily put together. Shipping weight, 45 pounds.
1K3480—Genuine mahogany top...................$14.25
Genuine walnut top..................$14.35

(C) Genuine mahogany or walnut top with the edges finished in darker two-tone effect. The balance of the table is hardwood, finished to match the top. The box edge is cut in a most attractive pattern, and the carved wood ornaments on the legs make this davenport table one of our most distinctive styles. Top, 48x16 inches. Shipped from our store. Packed to secure lowest transportation rates. Easily put together. Shpg. wt. 40 lbs.
1K3415—Genuine mahogany top...................$10.25
Genuine walnut top..................$10.35

(D) Choice of genuine mahogany top, brown mahogany finish, or genuine walnut, American walnut finish. Balance of table is hardwood, finished to match. Top measures, 60x18 inches. Shipped from our store. Packed to secure lowest transportation rates. Easily put together. Shpg. wt. 65 lbs.
1K3495—Genuine mahogany top...................$12.45
Genuine walnut top..................$12.55

(E) Firmly constructed of good quality hardwood finished in imitation quarter sawed golden oak. Has convenient center drawer and broad lower shelf that greatly strengthens the table. Here is a splendid example of the unusually big values we offer in our complete assortment of high grade furniture. Top, 42x26 in. Shipped from our store. Packed to secure lowest transportation rates. Easily put together. Shipping weight, 135 pounds.
1K3469—Imitation oak...................$12.65

(F) Here is one of the biggest davenport table values we offer. A design that is unusually popular and ordinarily sells for considerably more than we ask. Genuine walnut or mahogany top, balance of table fine hardwood, finished to match. Top measures 60x20 in. Shipped from our store. Packed to secure lowest transportation rates. Easily put together. Shipping weight, 75 pounds.
1K3490—Genuine mahogany top...................$14.45
Genuine walnut top..................$14.55

(G) A style that is different and attractive. The top is of genuine two-tone mahogany or walnut. The other parts of the table are of close grained hardwood finished to match. Fancy pedestal legs are strongly braced by the heavy stretcher. Size of top, 48x10 inches. Shipped from our store. Packed to secure lowest transportation rates. Easily put together. Shipping weight, 45 pounds.
1K3414—Two-tone mahogany top...................$8.85
Walnut finish...................$8.95

(H) Made of hardwood, in choice of imitation quarter sawed oak, golden finish, mahogany, or walnut finish. Size of top, 42x26 in. Note the gracefully designed legs and apron; the roomy shelf. Has center drawer with fancy metal pull. Packed to secure lowest transportation rates. Easily put together. Shipped from our store. Shipping weight, 100 pounds.
1K3407—Golden oak finish...................$11.65
Mahogany finish..................$11.75
Walnut finish..................$11.85

"How to Choose Colors and Furnishings for the Home." See page 1017 about this wonderful book at a bargain price. Be sure to order one.

A complete course of Instruction in Interior Decoration. See Page 1017. Write today!

-Odd Pieces-Informal, Colorful and Warm-

Handsome Center Table

A most attractive center table that will find many uses in the home. Strongly, neatly made of hardwood, finished in choice of walnut or Chinese red or jade green lacquers. Size of the top, 28 in. diameter. Height, 30 in. Shipping weight, 20 pounds.

1K3615	
Walnut finish	$7.15
Red lacquer finish	7.25
Green lacquer finish	7.35

$4.75
Red Lacquer

End Table With Book Trough

Well made of hardwood in Chinese red or jade green lacquer. Top is decorated with colored floral pattern. Very strongly built. Top, 24x12 in.; height, 24 in. Shpg. wt. 20 lbs.

1K3666	
Red lacquer finish	$4.75
Green lacquer finish	$4.85

$17.55
Parchment Finish

This illustration shows parchment decorated finish.

Gateleg Drop Leaf Table

So very popular now in the up to date home. The advantages of the gateleg table have brought them into big demand. This is an especially desirable design, popularly priced. Made of kiln dried hardwood in mahogany, walnut or parchment color, the latter with beautiful decorative transfers as illustrated. Size, open, 32 x 40 inches; size, closed, 32 x 12 inches. Height, 30 inches. Shipping weight, 60 pounds. State finish.

1K3629

Mahogany finish	$14.85
Walnut finish	$14.95
Parchment color	17.55

$4.85
Red Lacquer

New Attractive Style End Table

Hardwood, choice of Chinese red or jade green lacquer finishes, offset by pretty transfer pattern in colors on the top. Gracefully turned legs and stretcher; wide spread feet. Top, 24x14 in.; height, 23 in. Shpg. wt. 20 lbs.

1K3667	$4.85
Red lacquer	$4.85
Green lacquer	$4.95

Two-Piece Lacquered Console Set

A lovely set for front hall or living room. Table and mirror frame of hardwood in choice of Chinese red or jade green lacquer; table has attractive contrasting floral transfer pattern. Genuine plate glass mirror. The frame is finished to match the table. Mirror size, 20x10 inches. Size of table top, 24x12 inches; height, 30 inches. Shipping weight, 25 pounds, complete.

1K3668	
Red lacquer	$8.35
Green lacquer	$8.45

Pieces are not sold separately

$8.35
2 Pc. Set
Red Finish

$2.55
Mahogany Finish

This Attractive Table Low Priced

Every home should have one or two of these handy and stylish end tables when they can be bought at such low prices. Mahogany or walnut finish over gumwood. Size of top, 12¾x24 inches. Height, 24½ inches. Can be shipped by parcel post. Packed to secure lowest transportation rates. Easily put together. Shipping wt., 12 lbs.

1K3637	
Mahogany finish	$2.55
Walnut finish	$2.65

$3.15
Red Lacquer

$3.25
Green Lacquer

Red or Green Lacquer Finishes

Beautifully finished hardwood end tables in choice of Chinese red or jade green lacquer finishes offset with transfer pattern in colors. Neatly turned, slender legs, strongly supported by fancy stretchers. Top, 24x12 in.; height, 24 in. Shipping wt., 15 lbs.

1K3669	
Red lacquer	$3.15
Green lacquer	$3.25

Single Drop Leaf Gateleg Table

A small size that will fill many needs in the home. When the drop leaf is lowered this table can be placed against the wall and used with a mirror as a console set. A low height, convenient for placing beside the arm of a chair or davenport. Made of hardwood, in choice of Chinese red or jade green lacquer finishes. The top is attractively decorated with a colored floral transfer pattern. The gateleg holds the drop leaf flush with the top when open. Size of the top when leaf is up, 24x24 inches; with the leaf down, 24x12 inches. Height, 24 inches. Shipping wt., 25 lbs.

1K3616	
Red lacquer	$7.25
Green lacquer	$7.35

Gateleg Table With Double Drop Leaf

Makes a beautiful library table, a small sized dining table or a splendid sewing or utility table. Another example of the latest styles and lowest prices that you will always find at Sears. This pretty and useful table, with its spacious 42x36-inch top, when open, will serve many needs. Closes to only 13½x36 in. Height, 29 inches. Made of hardwood. Shipping weight, 80 pounds.

1K3630	
Mahogany finish	$13.25
Walnut finish	$13.35

Handsome Tea Cart

Drop leaves, removable glass top serving tray, rubber tire swivel wheels. Made of hardwood in mahogany and walnut veneers or in Chinese red or jade green lacquers. Size of top with leaves down, 26x15½ in.; with leaves up, 36x26 in. Height, 31 in. Shipping wt., 40 lbs.

$12.65
Mahogany Veneer

1K3672	
Mahogany veneer	$12.65
Walnut veneer	$12.75
Red lacquer	13.65
Green lacquer	13.75

Four-Pocket Magazine Stand

Hardwood, gracefully designed in a most attractive new style pattern. Handsomely finished in Chinese red or jade green lacquer, with pretty floral transfer. A most attractive and useful piece of furniture; will hold all standard size magazines. Top, 12x10 inches; height, 19 inches. Shipping weight, 15 lbs.

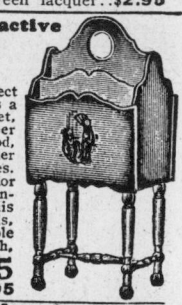

1K3673	
Red lacquer	$2.85
Green lacquer	$2.95

A New Attractive Style of Magazine Stand

You do not have to stoop over to select your favorite magazine. Note that this is a four-pocket size instead of the two-pocket which is so often sold at the same or higher prices. Well made of good quality hardwood, in choice of Chinese red or jade green lacquer finishes, shading to black at the edges. Beautifully decorated in a contrasting color oriental transfer pattern. The sides and center partition which form the pockets of this stand are fitted into grooves at the ends, making an extra strong and serviceable stand. Height, 27 in.; width, 12½ in., depth, 10½ in. Shipping wt., 8½ lbs.

1K3663	
Red lacquer	$4.85
Green lacquer	$4.95

The Latest in Magazine Baskets

All metal; gracefully designed; handsomely finished. Made of heavy gauge steel, all edges smoothly turned. Fancy twisted handle. Finished in two-tone lacquer, as listed below. Floral decorations in contrasting colors. Height, 13½ inches; width, 13 inches; depth, 8¼ inches. Shipping weight, 6½ lbs. Can go parcel post.

1K3671	
Red and black lacquer	$1.65
Green and black lacquer	$1.70
Bronze and black lacquer	1.75

Fernery

Simple, neat, construction, handsomely finished to match every taste. Well built, strongly braced. Complete with galvanized self watering pan. Size of top, 30x12 in.; height, 30 in. Shpg. wt., 40 lbs.

**Mahogany Finish
Walnut Finish
Red Lacquer
Green Lacquer**

1K3670	
Mahogany finish	$8.25
Walnut finish	$8.35
Red lacquer	$9.25
Green lacquer	$9.35

Matting Covered Utility Boxes

Save $2.00 to $3.00 over prices often asked elsewhere. These attractive bamboo trimmed utility boxes, lined with red fir and covered with high grade Japanese white matting, will be found practical, useful and economical for clothes and linens. They are equipped with strong hinges, lid stay and wood handles. Although strongly constructed these boxes are exceedingly light and easy to move about. Will not mar polished floors. At our especially low prices you will find these utility boxes unusually big values.

1K3774

Size.	Height.	Shpg. Wt.	
28 x15¼ in.	14 in.	17 lbs.	$4.85
36 x16½ in.	16 in.	26 lbs.	7.35
42½x17½ in.	16 in.	40 lbs.	8.85

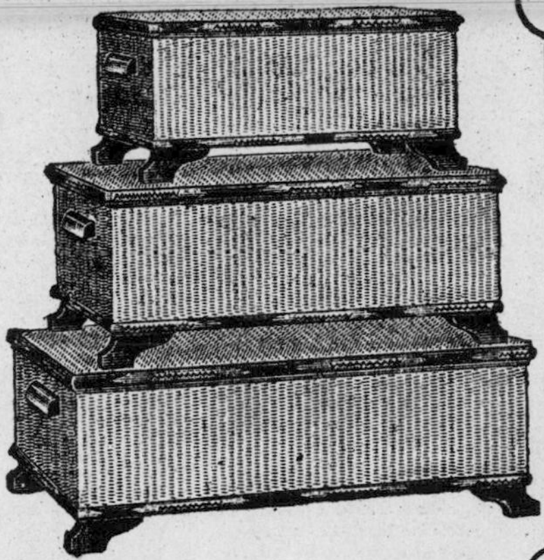

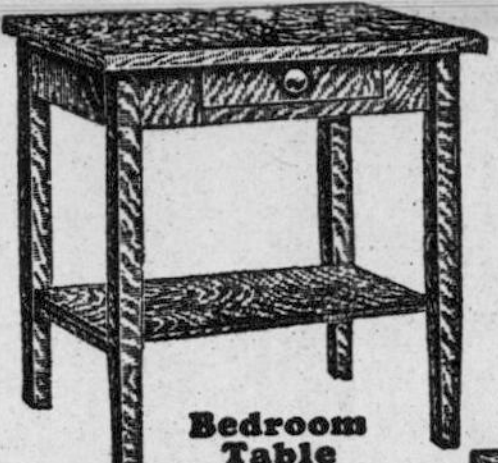

Bedroom Table

Made of hardwood, finished in choice of golden oak, walnut or white enamel. Full box rim, lower shelf strongly braced. Convenient small drawer. Top, 18x24 inches. Height, 28 inches. Shipping weight, 35 lbs.

1K3538
Golden oak.........$5.25
Walnut $5.35

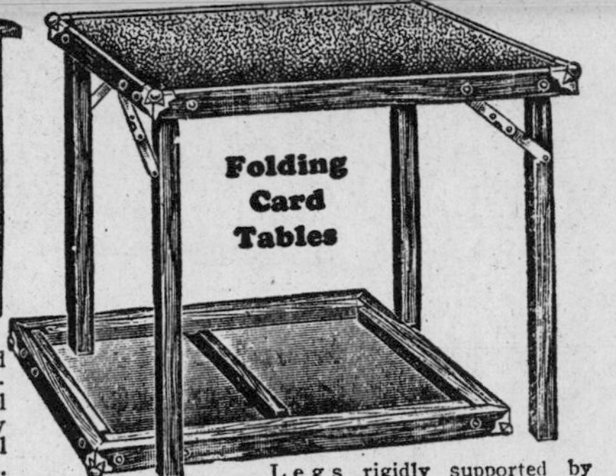

Folding Card Tables

Legs rigidly supported by positive locking steel braces. Neat fitting metal corners. Heavy hardwood frame, mahogany finish. Underside of top braced to prevent warping. Top covered with artificial leather. Top, 28¾ in. square. Height, 26 in. Shipping wt., 11 lbs.

1K3748—Artificial leather top...$2.10

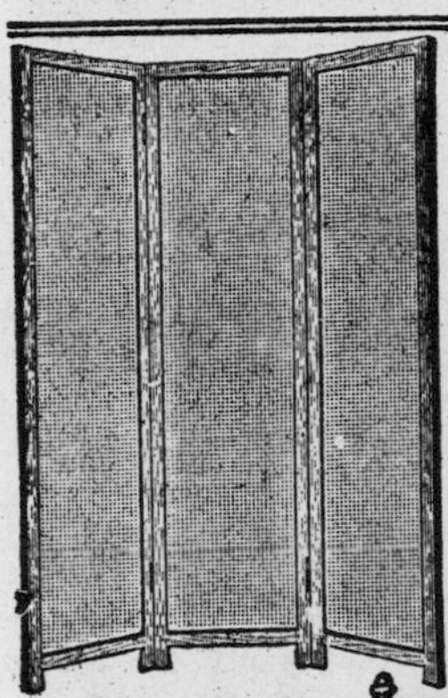

Fumed Oak 3-Wing Screen

Solid oak frame, substantially built, fumed finish. Strong, two-way hinges. Filling is dark green burlap, closely woven. Has three 17¾-inch wings. Height, 67 in. Total width, opened, 53¼ inches. Shipping weight, 24 pounds.

1K3717... $4.85

Martha Washington Sewing Cabinet

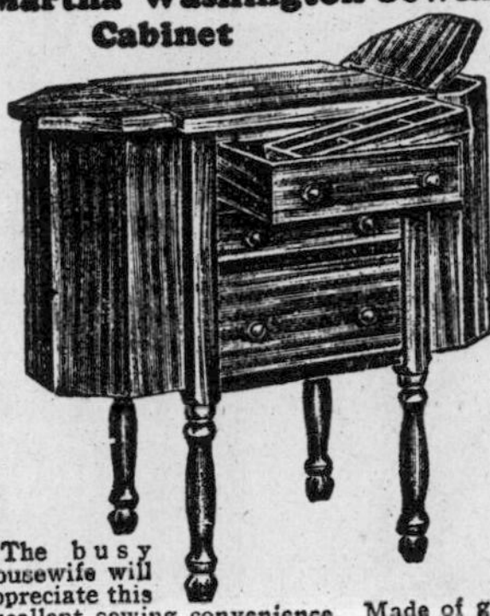

The busy housewife will appreciate this excellent sewing convenience. Made of gum-wood in brown mahogany or dull American walnut finishes. Top measures 23¾x12 in.; height, 29 in. Has deep 5-cornered side pockets, 9¾x5⅜x15 in., and three drawers with a divided compartment in the top one. Shipped with legs detached; made to screw in place. Shpg. wt., 40 lbs.

1K3614—Mahogany finish...$9.25
Walnut finish...............$9.35

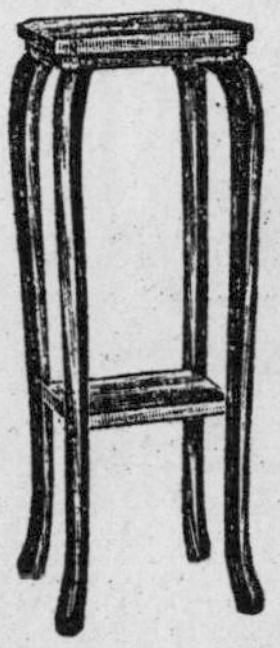

Queen Anne Stand

Made of hardwood, golden gloss finish or mahogany finish. Top, 12 x 12 in. Shelf, 10x10 in. Height, 34 in. Handy for a fern or lamp. Packed to secure lowest transportation rates. Easily put ogether. May be shipped by parcel post. Shipping wt., 25 pounds.

1K3782
Golden oak...... $4.10
Mahogany finish $4.15

Parlor Table

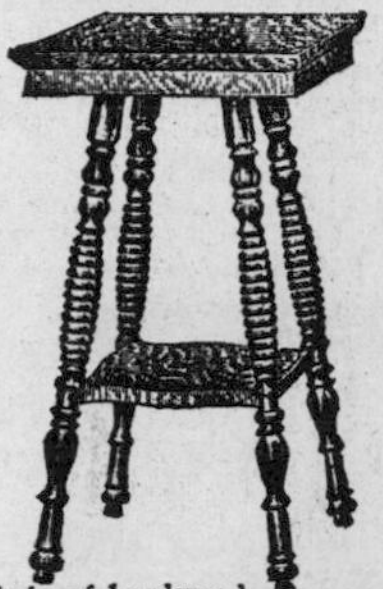

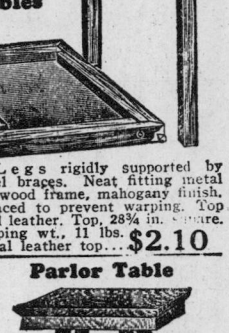

Made of hardwood in imitation quarter sawed oak, golden gloss finish. Size of top, 15x15 in. Height, 30 in. Packed to secure lowest transportation rates. Easily put together. May be shipped by parcel post. Shipping weight, 17 lbs.

[illegible].......$1.75

3 and 5-Wing Screens

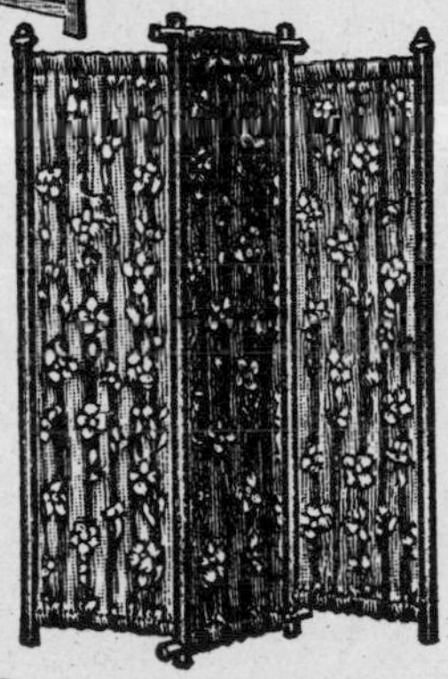

Hardwood frame, high golden gloss finish. Fitted with a superior quality floral pattern cretonne in assorted colors, shirred on rods at top and base. Two-way hinges. Height, 61 inches; width, open, three wings, 55½ inches; five wings; 91½ in. Shipping weights, 12 and 16 pounds, respectively.

1K3713
Three wings........$3.85
Five wings.....$6.25

Spread Leg Table

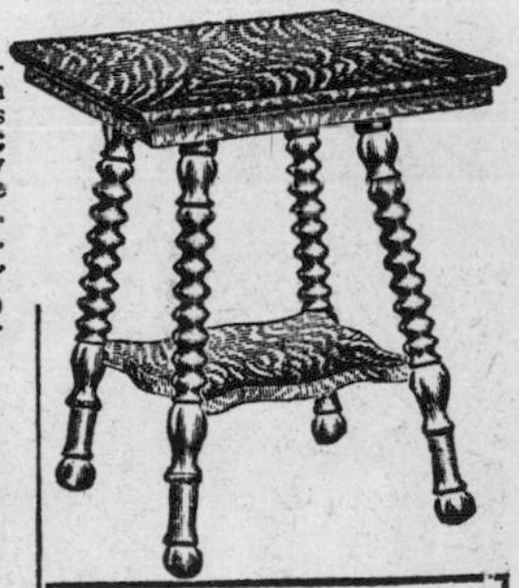

Made of hardwood in imitation quarter sawed oak, golden gloss finish. The spread legs make this a very solid table; one that will not tip. Handy shelf below. Packed to secure lowest transportation rates. Easily put together. Top, 24 in. square; height, 30 in. Shpg. wt., 32 pounds.

1K3523.........$2.75

Priscilla Sewing Cabinet

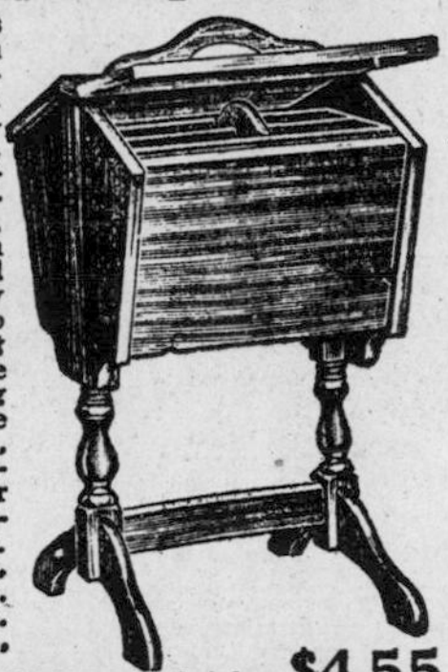

At prices every woman can well appreciate. A pretty, attractive cabinet, very convenient for sewing needs. Equipped with a partitioned sliding tray and a deep compartment below. Handle for moving about. Made of gumwood, brown mahogany or American walnut finish. Top measures, 12½x11½ in. Height, 24 in. Shipping wt., 18 pounds.

1K3609—Mahogany finish...$4.55
Walnut finish...............$4.65

Pedestal

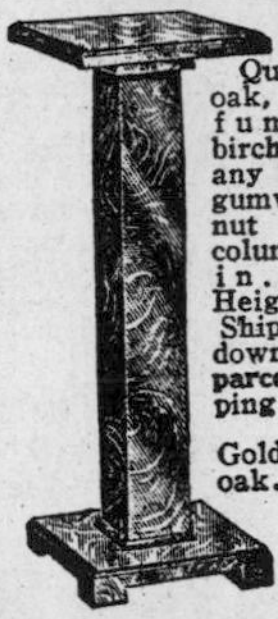

Quarter sawed oak, golden or fumed finish; birch in mahogany finish, or gumwood in walnut finish. 4-in. column. Top, 12 in. square. Height, 36½ in. Shipped knocked down. Can go parcel post. Shipping wt., 25 lbs.

1K3783
Golden oak... $3.90
Fumed oak. $4.00
Mahogany finish. $4.10
Walnut finish...........$4.20

An Expert Interior Decorator at You Service!
How to Choose Furnishings, Color Harmony, Room Decorations—See Page 1017.

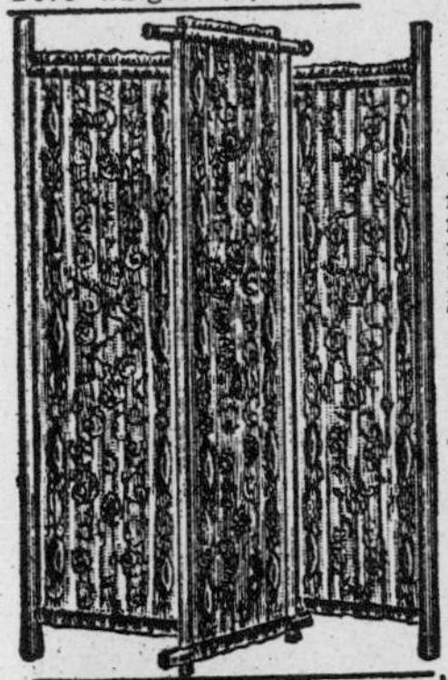

Three-Wing Golden Oak Screen

Frame made of hardwood, golden oak gloss finish. Has an attractive floral pattern cretonne filling in green with red flowers, shirred on wood rods at the top and base. Two-way hinges. Height, 61 in. Width, 49 in., open. Shipping weight, 12 pounds.

1K3704...$2.35

Folding Sewing Table

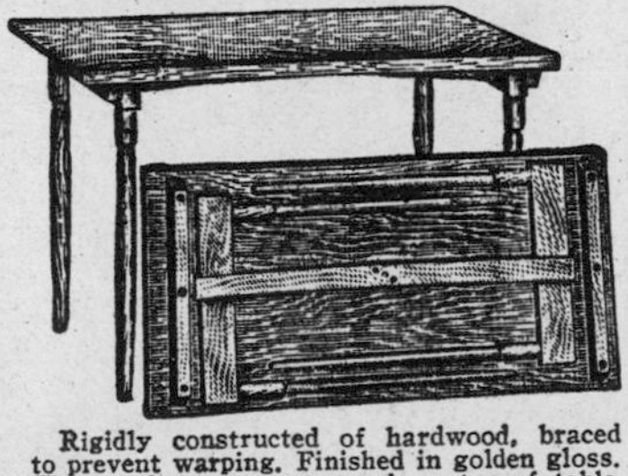

Rigidly constructed of hardwood, braced to prevent warping. Finished in golden gloss. Has yard measure stamped on top of table. Can be used as a card table. Size of top, 18x36 inches. Height, 25¾ inches. Shipping weight, 14 lbs. May be shipped by parcel post.

1K3738.....................$2.10

Commode

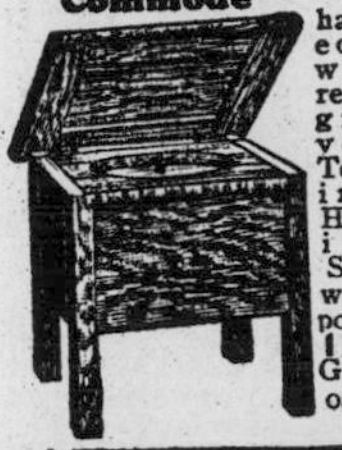

Made of hardwood, equipped with removable granite vessel. Top, 16x16 inches. Height, 17 inches. Shipping weight, 29 pounds.

1K4806
Golden oak finish. $7.25

Shoe Shining Box

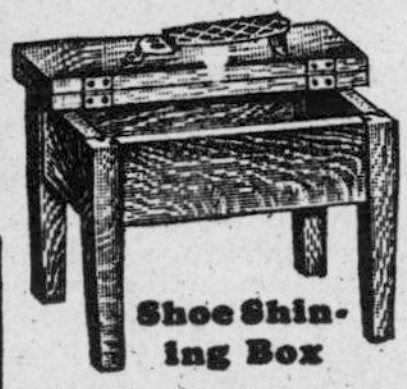

Made of oak, golden gloss finish. Length, 16¾ in.; width, 11 in.; height, 14 in. Large roomy compartment for holding brushes and polish. Equipped with shoe stand. Can be shipped by parcel post. Shpg. wt., 16 lbs.

1K4829... $1.95

Graceful Pedestal

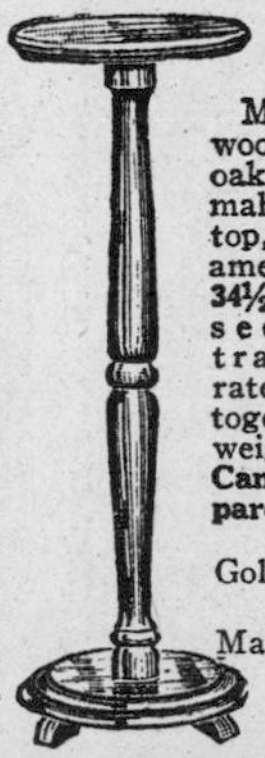

Made of hardwood, finished in oak, walnut or mahogany. Round top, 11 inches diameter; height, 34½ in. Packed to secure lowest transportation rates. Easily put together. Shipping weight, 10 pounds. Can be shipped by parcel post.

1K3780
Golden oak finish, $3.45
Mahogany finish, $3.55
Walnut finish, $3.65

Costumers

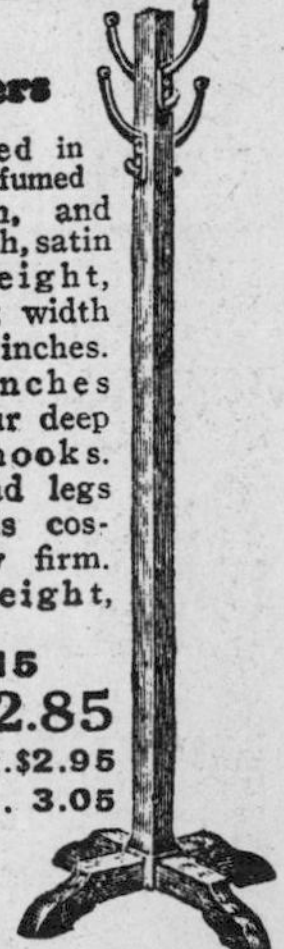

Furnished in golden or fumed oak finish, and walnut finish, satin rubbed. Height, 69½ inches; width of base, 20 inches. Staff, 1¾ inches square. Four deep double hooks. Wide spread legs make this costumer very firm. Shipping weight, 10 pounds.

1K1215
Golden oak.... $2.85
Fumed oak. $2.95
Walnut 3.05

HOME LOVERS WILL FIND
~Smoking Stands and Music Cabinets~

Handsome, Convenient Smoker

Everything a man desires in a smoking stand; a large top surface for trays, cigarette holders, etc. and below, side shelves and a large storage cabinet. The storage cabinet is copper lined, making it easier to keep moist and cool. Complete with three nickel plated ash trays, large tray, match box holder and crystal cigarette holder. Made of hardwood, finished in choice of walnut or red or green lacquer finishes. Overlay pattern on the door is of striking contrasting color. Fancy lock catch. Size of the top, 24x12 in. Height, 26 in. Shipping weight, 40 pounds.

1K3659—Walnut finish...... **$11.45**
Red lacquer finish.....$12.45
Green lacquer finish.....12.55

Copper Lined Humidor Style Smoking Stand

A new different style, sure to be liked. You'll notice the enclosed cabinet is below, the top affording an extra shelf. Equipped with nickel covered glass cigarette humidor, nickeled tray, match box stand and ash tray. The copper lined cabinet section is easy to keep moist and cool, making an ideal humidor. Fitted with nickel catch and hinges. Side handles make this an easy stand to move about. Hardwood, finished in choice of mahogany, walnut or red or green lacquers. Shipping weight, 40 pounds.

Height, 27¼ in. Width, 13¼ in. Depth, 11 in.
1K3675
Mahogany finish........................ **$10.45**
Walnut finish.....................$10.55
Red lacquer finish................11.55
Green lacquer finish..............11.65

Complete Smokers' Set

Equipped complete as shown, with two extra stands fitted with nickel plated crystal lined ash trays; individual nickel plated ash tray, match box holder, large tray and crystal cigarette holder. Deep lower shelf convenient for many smokers' articles; large top surface. The cabinet section is copper lined, making it easier to keep moist and cool. Made of hardwood, in choice of walnut or red or green lacquer finishes. The fancy overlay is in contrasting color. Size of top, 18x12 in. Height, 28 in. The stands are 20 in. high and have a 6½ in. base. Shpg. wt. 30 lbs.

1K3658—Walnut finish........... **$12.25**
Red lacquer finish............................$13.25
Green lacquer finish...........................13.35

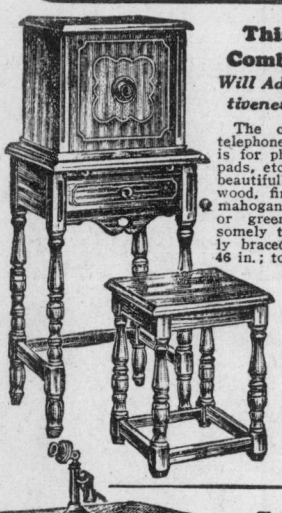

This Beautiful Combination Set
Will Add to the Attractiveness of Any Home

The cabinet is for the telephone; the drawer below is for phone books, scratch pads, etc. A graceful style, beautifully worked hardwood, finished in choice of mahogany, walnut or red or green lacquer. Handsomely turned legs, strongly braced. Cabinet, height, 46 in.; top, 15x12¾ in. Stool seat size, 12x12 in. Shipping wt., two-piece set, 45 lbs. Pieces are not sold separately.

1K3674
Mahogany finish. **$15.65**
Walnut finish. $15.75
Red Lacquer. $17.15
Green Lacquer. $17.25

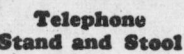

Telephone Stand and Stool

All oak, in choice of golden gloss or fumed finishes. The stand is 30 inches high, with 12x17-inch top. Stool seat is 12x12 inches. Very strongly made; neat in appearance. Shipping weight, 17 pounds. Pieces are not sold separately.

1K3546
Golden oak...... **$3.15**
Fumed oak..........$3.20

Telephone Set

Desk and bench, made of hardwood in choice of mahogany or walnut finishes. The desk has a large, handy 14x22-inch top and a shelf for the telephone book. Bench top is 10¾x16 inches. Height, 33½ inches. Shipping weight, 47 pounds. Pieces are not sold separately.

1K3549
Mahogany finish.......**$8.25**
Walnut finish..$8.35

Quality Smoking Stand

Made of hardwood in choice of walnut or mahogany finishes. Satin silver finish lock, brass hinges, glass ash tray and nickel finish match box holder. Top, 11¾x11¾ inches; height, 23 inches. Shipping weight, 19 pounds. Can be shipped by parcel post.

1K3654
Mahogany finish........... **$7.15**
Walnut finish......$7.25

Neat and Handy

A small, convenient size that will fit in anywhere. Has drawer for pipes and cigarettes, and a lower shelf for jar. Complete with nickeled metal ash tray and match holder. Height, 25 inches. Top, 9x9 inches. Made of hardwood, in choice of mahogany or walnut finishes. Shipping weight, 12 pounds.

1K3653
Mahogany finish......... **$3.75**
Walnut finish....$3.85

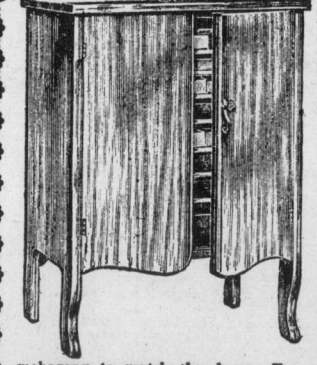

Smoking Stand With Handle

Made of hardwood, in choice of mahogany or walnut finishes. Complete with nickel plated red inset ash tray. Handy shelf for pipes and cigarettes. Height, 30 inches. Size of shelf, 8x8 inches. Packed to secure lowest transportation rates. Easily put together. Shipping wt., 10 lbs.

1K3656
Mahogany finish......... **$2.10**
Walnut finish....$2.15

A Popular Smoking Stand—Moderately Priced

Real smokers' furniture! Keep your pipes, cigars and cigarettes close by, yet out of sight in the compartment and your humidor on the lower shelf. Complete with nickel plated ash tray with red glass inset, cigar rests and match box holder. Made of hardwood in choice of mahogany or walnut finishes. Cabinet, 9x9 in.; 8¾ in. high. Total stand height, 27½ in. Shpg. wt., 15 lbs.

1K3650
Mahogany finish......... **$4.25**
Walnut finish....$4.35

For Records —For Sheet Music For Music Rolls

Genuine mahogany or walnut veneered doors. At our very low price this is truly a fine opportunity to buy the record or music cabinet you have wanted. Nine spacious compartments. Doors are genuine veneered walnut or mahogany. Remainder of cabinet of select kiln dried hardwood, finished in walnut or mahogany to match the doors. Top measures 31x16½ in.; height, 41 in. Shipping weight, 100 lbs.

1K3859
Mahogany veneered.......... **$21.75**
Walnut veneered.....$21.85

Convenient Smaller Size Music Cabinet

Choice of two finishes: The top and door are of walnut veneer with the balance in hardwood finished to match; or of quarter-sawed oak, golden finished with the balance in plain oak. A well made, nicely polished, inexpensive music cabinet. Height, 40 inches; width, 20 inches; depth, outside, 14 inches; inside, depth of shelves, 12 inches. Shipping weight, 60 pounds.

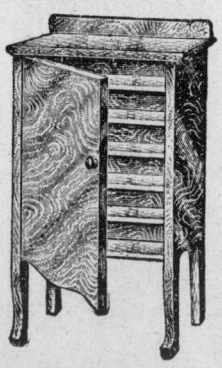

1K3857
Quarter sawed oak veneered...... **$13.85**
Walnut veneered........$13.95

REMARKABLE VALUES HERE
- Bookcases and Secretaries -

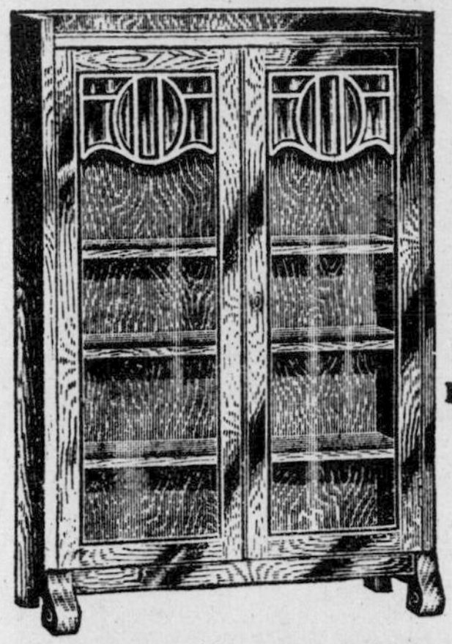

Sold On Easy Monthly Payments

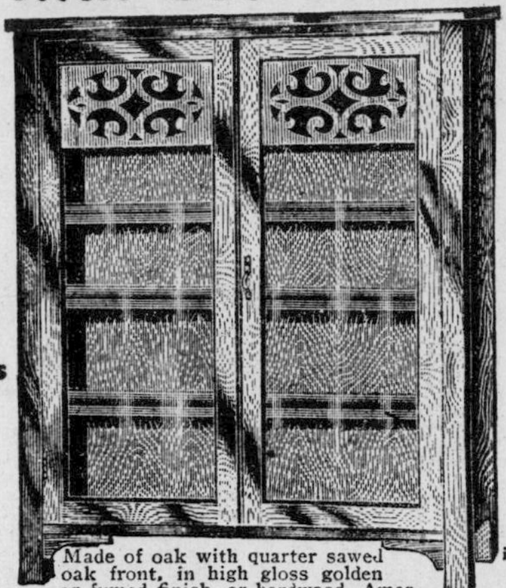

Shipped from Factory in ROCKFORD, ILL.

Made of oak, with quarter sawed oak front in golden gloss or fumed finish, or hardwood in mahogany or walnut finish. Glass paneled doors with fancy grilles. Four adjustable shelves. Will hold about 150 average size books. Height, 53½ in.; width, 32 in.; outside depth, 13 in.; inside depth, 10¼ in. Shpg. wt., 100 lbs. Shipped from factory in ROCKFORD, ILL. **Sold for cash only.**

1K3212½—Golden oak.........$17.45
Fumed oak.......... 17.55
Mahogany finish... 17.65
Walnut finish....... 17.75

Made of oak with quarter sawed oak front, in high gloss golden or fumed finish, or hardwood, American walnut finish. Has four adjustable sleeves; will hold about 190 average size books. Glass paneled doors decorated with fancy grills. Height, 54 in.; width, in.; outside depth, 12¼ in.; inside depth, 10½ in. Shipping weight, 130 pounds.

		Cash Price	Easy Payment Price
1K3213½—	Golden oak.......	$22.65	$24.95
	Fumed oak.......	22.75	25.05
	Walnut finish......	22.95	25.15

Terms: $5.00 down and $5.00 a month. Time Payment Order Blank on page 1092.

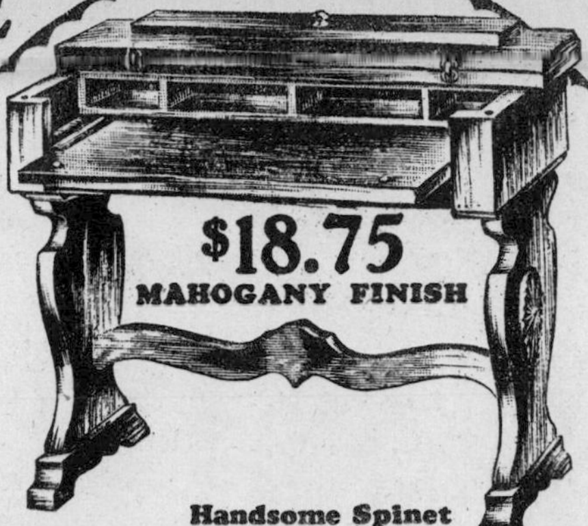

Handsome Spinet Desk

You will find this neat appearing desk a splendid value. It is fashioned in the true spinet design; very strongly made and excellently finished. The arrangement of the interior is ideal. The writing board can be pulled out 7 in., giving a solid writing surface, 27½x16 in. The writing board needs no support. Four wide pigeonholes provide ample space for stationery; two side trays are for pens and pencils. Writing board has brass fitted fingerholes. Hinged top is equipped with piano hinges, invisible from the outside. When closed, this desk can be used as a beautiful table, with a 20x34-in. top. Made of fine hardwood, in choice of mahogany or walnut finishes. Composition overlays on the legs. Height, 31 in. Shipping weight, 80 pounds. **Sold for cash only.**

1K3830—Mahogany finish..................$18.75
Walnut finish.................... 18.85

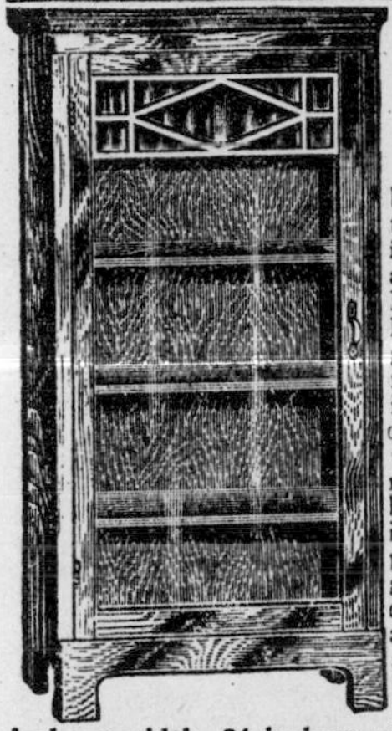

Student Size Bookcase

A narrow bookcase that will fit in almost anywhere. Made of oak, high gloss golden or fumed finish; or good quality hardwood in walnut or mahogany finish. Fancy pattern wood grille on the door. Holds about 75 average size books. Height, 53½ inches; width, 24 inches; outside depth, 12 inches; inside depts, 10¼ inches. Shipping weight, 85 pounds. Shipped from factory in ROCKFORD, ILL. **Sold for cash only.**

1K3211⅓—Golden oak $11.45
Fumed oak 11.55
Mahogany finish 11.65
Walnut finish 11.75

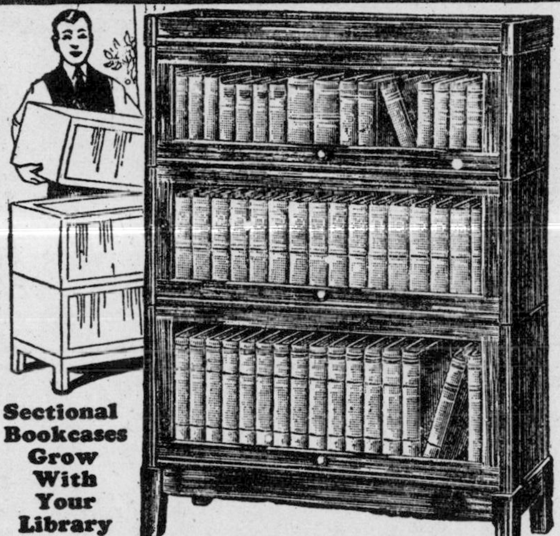

Sectional Bookcases Grow With Your Library

The sectional bookcase is made up of one No. 5 top section, one No. 7 base section and book sections in sizes as follows: No. 9, ht., inside, 9 in; No. 11, ht., inside, 11 in.; No. 13, ht., inside, 13 in. Width of sections, 34 in.; depth, 10½ in. **When ordering be sure to specify the book section numbers and quantities of each.** We recommend no more than four sections for one base and top. Comes in hardwood, brown mahogany or walnut finish, or quarter sawed oak in golden, fumed or office golden finishes. Shipped from factory in INDIANA. **Sold for cash only.**

1K3275⅓—Pieces may be purchased separately.

	Shpg. Wt.	Golden Oak	Fumed Oak	Office Golden	Mahogany Finish	Walnut Finish
No. 5 Top Section...	6 lbs.	$3.35	$3.40	$3.45	$3.50	$3.60
No. 7 Base Section...	6 lbs.	3.45	3.50	3.55	3.60	3.70
No. 9 Book Section...	22 lbs.	5.40	5.45	5.50	5.55	5.65
No. 11 Book Section...	25 lbs.	5.50	5.55	5.60	5.65	5.75
No. 13 Book Section...	28 lbs.	5.60	5.65	5.70	5.75	5.85

Business Men and Women Will Like This Desk

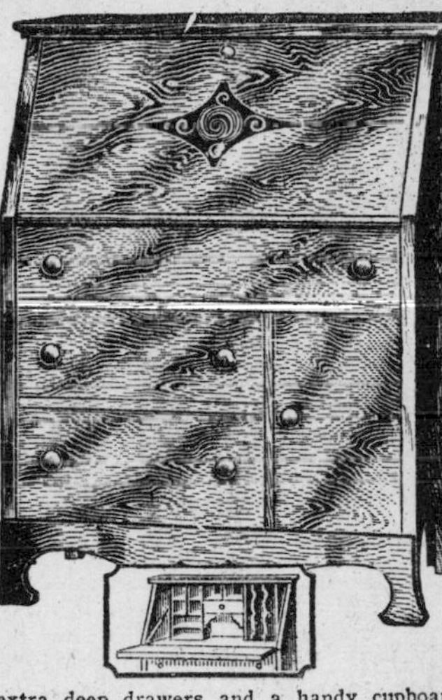

This style is equally adaptable for either social or business use. Designed for the home, but so completely equipped it can be used in the office. Made of oak in golden gloss or fumed finish, or hardwood, walnut finish. Below desk are three extra deep drawers and a handy cupboard with drawer and box letter file. The desk cover is decorated with an embossed engraving. Wood knobs. Ht., 46 in.; width, 31½ in.; depth, 15½ in. Shpg. wt., 115 lbs. Shipped from factory near CHICAGO.

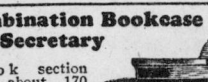

		Cash Price	Easy Payment Price
1K3300⅓—	Golden oak....	$22.65	$24.95
	Fumed oak....	22.75	25.05
	Walnut	22.85	25.15

Terms: $5.00 down and $5.00 a month. Use Time Payment Order Blank on page 1092.

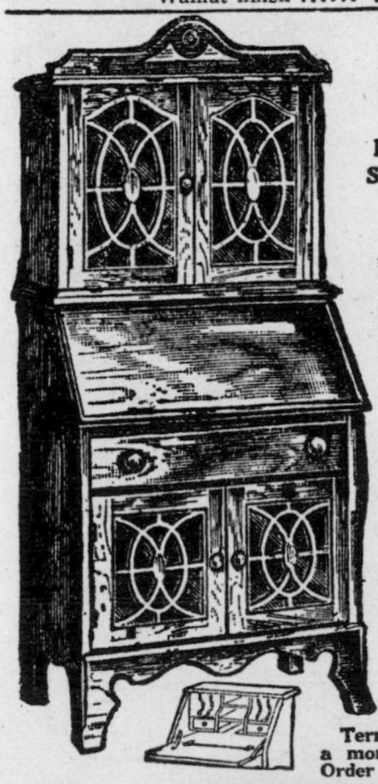

Every Home Needs a Secretary

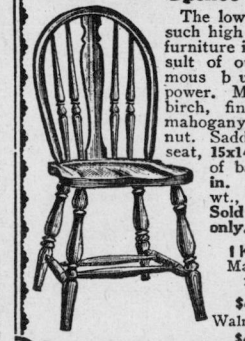

One of the handiest furniture pieces in the living room—a bookcase, a desk and a cupboard. The upper section is equipped with shelves. The glass doors are decorated with a fancy pattern wood grille. The desk section interior is as illustrated below. Strongly braced writing top. Lower cupboard has glass doors covered with fancy grilles. Made of hardwood, well finished in choice of mahogany or walnut. Height, 70 in.; width, 30 in.; depth, 15 in. Shpg. wt., 150 lbs. Shipped from factory in INDIANA.

1K3233⅓

	Cash Price	Easy Payment Price
Mahogany Finish	$29.65	$32.65
Walnut Finish	29.75	32.75

Terms: $5.00 down and $5.00 a month. Use Time Payment Order Blank on Page 1092.

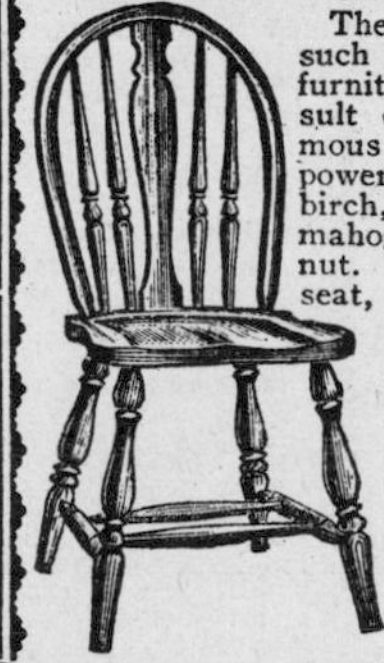

Spinet Chair

The low price of such high grade furniture is the result of our enormous buying power. Made of birch, finished in mahogany or walnut. Saddle shape seat, 15x14 in.; ht. of back, 18½ in. Shipping wt., 10 lbs. **Sold for cash only.**

1K3800
Mahogany finish
$4.65
Walnut finish
$4.75

Combination Bookcase and Secretary

Book section holds about 170 average size books. Four adjustable shelves. Desk section has pigeonhole case with imitation drawer. Above desk is cupboard with mirrored door covered with a fancy cut grille. Made of oak, golden gloss or fumed finish, or of hardwood, walnut or mahogany finish. Height, 62 in.; width, 36 in. Mirror, 9x15 in. Shipping weight, 140 pounds. Shipped from factory in ROCKFORD, ILL.

1K3120⅓

Cash Price
Golden oak......$22.65
Fumed oak........ 22.75
Mahogany finish. 22.85
Walnut finish.....22.95

Easy Payment Price
Golden oak......$24.95
Fumed oak........ 25.05
Mahogany finish. 25.15
Walnut finish.... 25.25

Terms: $5.00 down and $5.00 a month. Time Payment Order Blank Found on Page 1092.

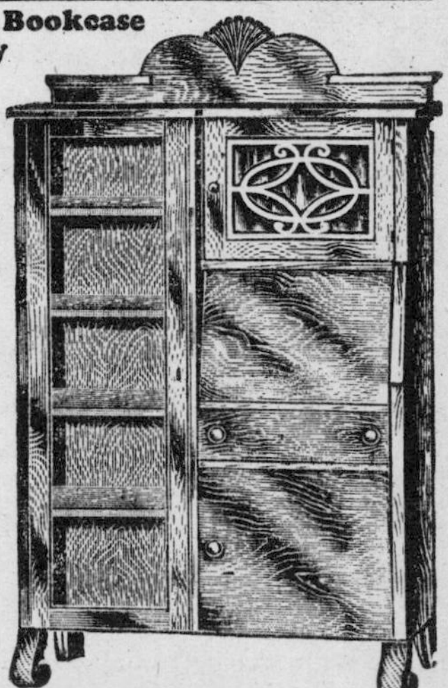

We Guarantee Safe Delivery of All Our Shipments

Solid Cedar and

Practical Protection

Clothing and fur insurance are what you buy when you invest in a cedar chest, a safe, mothproof storage space, beautiful as well as practical. The moths that you see flying around do no damage; it is the young moth worms, deposited as eggs in dark and concealed places that destroy clothing. The United States Government Department of Agriculture has definitely ascertained that cedar chests have a pronounced killing effect on moth worms. It is recommended that in using a cedar chest for the protection of clothing, fabrics and furs, special care should be taken to prevent undue escape of the aroma. The chests should remain tightly closed as much as possible. All the chests on these pages are made either entirely of cedar or cedar lining on the inside.

Popular Priced Chest of Beautiful Appearance—Big Value

Another pleasing chest in the ever popular Queen Anne design. Made of hardwood with handsome walnut finish. Attractive overlays on front add greatly to the beauty of this chest. Back and bottom cedar lined. Graceful polished legs with sliding casters. One lid stop. Cylinder lock with key. Triple hinges. Dust proof lid. The whole chest is finished in genuine Duco, giving it a hard and most durable surface. This is truly an artistic chest which may be had at the World's Largest Store at much below the usual prices asked elsewhere.

1 K3764—Walnut Finish

Size	Height	Shipping Weight	
45x18 inches	18 inches	90 pounds	$18.55

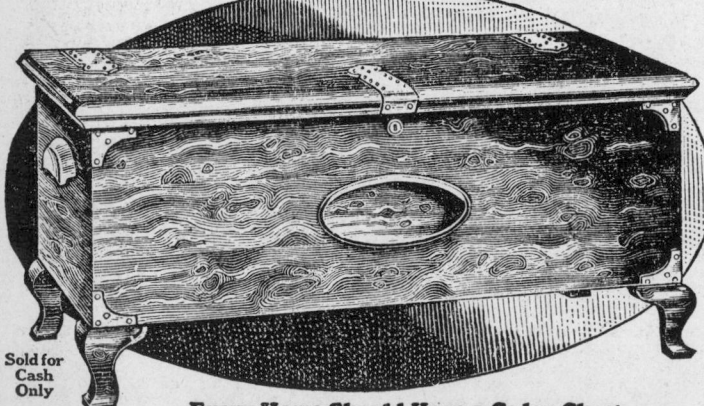

Every Home Should Have a Cedar Chest

Exceptional value in this Queen Anne style. Where can you get such an attractive solid Red Cedar Chest elsewhere at this remarkable price? A handsome chest in natural finish that will look well in any room. Genuine copper trimmings, studded with round copper head nails, add greatly to its beauty. Oval panel wood overlay. Wood handles. Inside dustproof lid construction; fitted with cylinder lock and key. Chest is finished in genuine Duco, giving it a hard and durable surface. Furnish your home now with one of these splendid chests. The price is low for the service it will give you. Choice of three sizes.

1 K3757—Solid Cedar

Size	Height	Shipping Weight	
42x19 inches	19 inches	85 pounds	$14.65
45x19 inches	19 inches	90 pounds	17.15
48x19 inches	19 inches	95 pounds	19.95

Beautiful Queen Anne Chest of Unusually Graceful Design

A much desired and popular departure from the massive style. Made of hardwood in a rich shade of walnut; back and bottom lined with red cedar. This chest will fit into almost any scheme of home decoration. Two-tone effect, the panel being darker in shade than the body of the chest. A hard and most durable surface of genuine Duco is the finishing touch of this chest. The clover and fleur de 'lis decorations are imitation ebony. Panel and designs are outlined in old gold color. Metal glides. Substantial lock. Double hinges, sliding lid stop. At the low prices we name this is a splendid value. Terms, $5.00 down and $5.00 a month.

1 K3798—Walnut Finish

Size	Height	Shipping Weight	Cash Price	Easy Payment Price
40x19 inches	21 inches	85 pounds	$22.75	$25.15
45x20 inches	22 inches	90 pounds	26.85	29.55

When Ordering on Easy Payments Use Time Payment Order Blank on Page 1092.

This Splendid Chest at Lower Prices Than Are Usually Asked Elsewhere

In quality, design and finish we know this value cannot be duplicated. The richness of the exquisite color pattern design, framed by a handsome diamond pattern wood molding adds a mark of refinement which is found only in expensive furniture. Made of hardwood; interior lined with genuine red cedar, insuring absolute protection. Reproduction butt walnut finish on lid. Sides beautifully finished in imitation walnut, having every appearance of the genuine wood. The whole chest is finished in genuine Duco. Braced corners, triple hinges, cylinder lock, double lid top, rolling casters. Lid fits closely with tapered tip, making it dustproof. An exceptional value at an unusually low price.

1 K3763—Full Cedar Lined

Size	Height	Shipping Weight	Cash Price	Easy Payment Price
45x21 inches	21 inches	100 pounds	$22.95	$25.25
48x21 inches	21 inches	105 pounds	24.95	27.45

Terms, $5.00 down and $5.00 a month.

Beautiful Simplicity in This Genuine Red Cedar Chest

The beautiful natural graining of red cedar is popular with many women who love its simplicity and color charm. Made of genuine red cedar. Constructed with interlocking corners and joints, and dustproof lid. Has substantial lock, hinges, lid stay and casters. Wood handles. Finished in genuine Duco. Largest size can be had with tray. An exceedingly good value at our low price.

1 K3756—Solid Cedar

Size	Height	Shipping Weight	
36x18 inches	18 inches	70 pounds	$ 8.25
42x19 inches	19 inches	85 pounds	12.45
45x19 inches	19 inches	90 pounds	14.95
48x19 inches	19 inches	95 pounds	17.95
54x21 inches	21 inches	110 pounds. Without tray	23.95
54x21 inches	21 inches	115 pounds. With tray	25.85

Sold for Cash Only

Cedar Lined Chests *Protect your Clothes!*

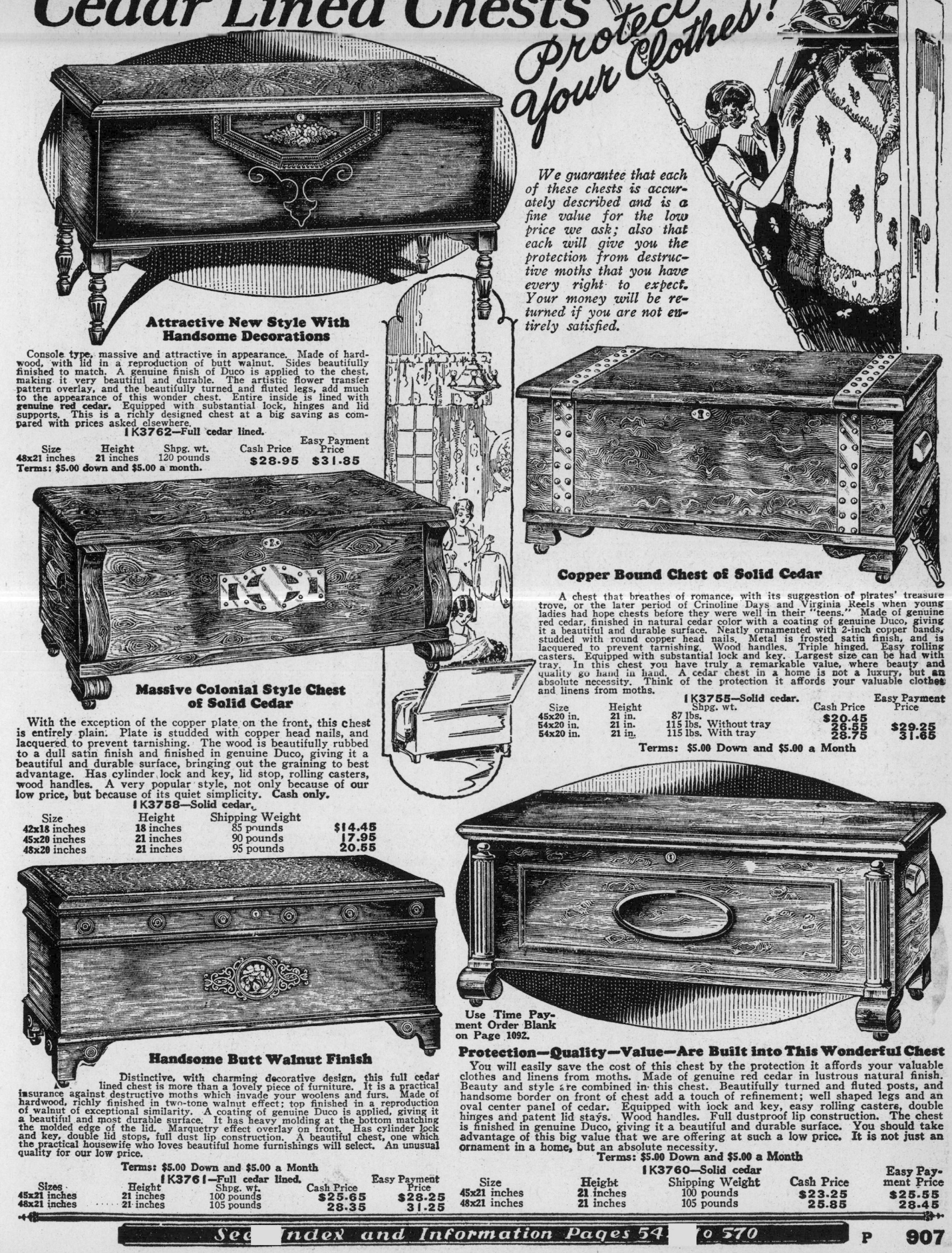

Attractive New Style With Handsome Decorations

Console type, massive and attractive in appearance. Made of hardwood, with lid in a reproduction of butt walnut. Sides beautifully finished to match. A genuine finish of Duco is applied to the chest, making it very beautiful and durable. The artistic flower transfer pattern overlay, and the beautifully turned and fluted legs, add much to the appearance of this wonder chest. Entire inside is lined with genuine red cedar. Equipped with substantial lock, hinges and lid supports. This is a richly designed chest at a big saving as compared with prices asked elsewhere.

1K3762—Full cedar lined.

Size	Height	Shpg. wt.	Cash Price	Easy Payment Price
48x21 inches	21 inches	120 pounds	$28.95	$31.85

Terms: $5.00 down and $5.00 a month.

Massive Colonial Style Chest of Solid Cedar

With the exception of the copper plate on the front, this chest is entirely plain. Plate is studded with copper head nails, and lacquered to prevent tarnishing. The wood is beautifully rubbed to a dull satin finish and finished in genuine Duco, giving it a beautiful and durable surface, bringing out the graining to best advantage. Has cylinder lock and key, lid stop, rolling casters, wood handles. A very popular style, not only because of our low price, but because of its quiet simplicity. **Cash only.**

1K3758—Solid cedar.

Size	Height	Shipping Weight	
42x18 inches	18 inches	85 pounds	$14.45
45x20 inches	21 inches	90 pounds	17.95
48x20 inches	21 inches	95 pounds	20.55

Copper Bound Chest of Solid Cedar

A chest that breathes of romance, with its suggestion of pirates' treasure trove, or the later period of Crinoline Days and Virginia Reels when young ladies had hope chests before they were well in their "teens." Made of genuine red cedar, finished in natural cedar color with a coating of genuine Duco, giving it a beautiful and durable surface. Neatly ornamented with 2-inch copper bands, studded with round copper head nails. Metal is frosted satin finish, and is lacquered to prevent tarnishing. Wood handles. Triple hinged. Easy rolling casters. Equipped with substantial lock and key. Largest size can be had with tray. In this chest you have truly a remarkable value, where beauty and quality go hand in hand. A cedar chest in a home is not a luxury, but an absolute necessity. Think of the protection it affords your valuable clothes and linens from moths.

1K3755—Solid cedar.

Size	Height	Shpg. wt.		Cash Price	Easy Payment Price
45x20 in.	21 in.	87 lbs.		$20.45	
54x20 in.	21 in.	115 lbs.	Without tray	26.55	$29.25
54x20 in.	21 in.	115 lbs.	With tray	28.75	31.65

Terms: $5.00 Down and $5.00 a Month

Handsome Butt Walnut Finish

Distinctive, with charming decorative design, this full cedar lined chest is more than a lovely piece of furniture. It is a practical insurance against destructive moths which invade your woolens and furs. Made of hardwood, richly finished in two-tone walnut effect; top finished in a reproduction of walnut of exceptional similarity. A coating of genuine Duco is applied, giving it a beautiful and most durable surface. It has heavy molding at the bottom matching the molded edge of the lid. Marquetry effect overlay on front. Has cylinder lock and key, double lid stops, full dust lip construction. A beautiful chest, one which the practical housewife who loves beautiful home furnishings will select. An unusual quality for our low price.

Terms: $5.00 Down and $5.00 a Month

1K3761—Full cedar lined.

Sizes	Height	Shpg. wt.	Cash Price	Easy Payment Price
45x21 inches	21 inches	100 pounds	$25.65	$28.25
48x21 inches	21 inches	105 pounds	28.35	31.25

Use Time Payment Order Blank on Page 1092.

Protection—Quality—Value—Are Built into This Wonderful Chest

You will easily save the cost of this chest by the protection it affords your valuable clothes and linens from moths. Made of genuine red cedar in lustrous natural finish. Beauty and style are combined in this chest. Beautifully turned and fluted posts, and handsome border on front of chest add a touch of refinement; well shaped legs and an oval center panel of cedar. Equipped with lock and key, easy rolling casters, double hinges and patent lid stays. Wood handles. Full dustproof lip construction. The chest is finished in genuine Duco, giving it a beautiful and durable surface. You should take advantage of this big value that we are offering at such a low price. It is not just an ornament in a home, but an absolute necessity.

Terms: $5.00 Down and $5.00 a Month

1K3760—Solid cedar

Size	Height	Shipping Weight	Cash Price	Easy Payment Price
45x21 inches	21 inches	100 pounds	$23.25	$25.55
48x21 inches	21 inches	105 pounds	25.85	28.45

Genuine Heavy Plate Mirrors

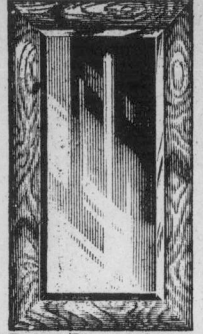

Bevel Plate Mirror

You will find many uses for this large size mirror in the home. Choice of imitation quarter sawed oak, mahogany or walnut finishes. Heavy bevel plate mirror. Frame, 23¼x45½ in. Width of frame, 2⅞ in. Mirror, 40x18 in. Shipping wt., 40 lbs.

1K4113
Oak finish........$9.65
Mahogany finish.. 9.75
Walnut finish... 9.85

Venetian Mirrors

Genuine plate glass, with etched design. Felted back. Furnished with loops ready for hanging. A real bargain. Shipping wts., 20 and 25 lbs.

1K4109
12x22 in...$3.65
14x26 in... 4.75

This Style Very Popular Now

A magnificent new style hall or parlor mirror, with a beautiful gold and brown carved frame decorated with soft contrasting colors. The side panel mirrors are hand etched in frosted effect. One of the greatest mirror values we have ever offered. Width, 34 in.; heigth, 20 in. Shipping weight, 45 pounds.
1K4160.................................$9.85

Big Mirror Value

Polychrome stippled frame with brown corners and top ornaments. Genuine heavy plain plate mirror, 10x20 in. Frame 12½x26 in. over all. Shipping weight, 22 lbs.

1K4116
$3.25

New Semi-Venetian Style

A handsome carved wood frame, finished in silver with high lights and shadings. The mirror is an extra heavy plate, ¼ in. thick, and is beautifully etched at the top and bottom. A large size. Height, 30 in.; width, 14½ in. Shipping wt., 35 lbs.

1K4162
$10.25

Gold bronze Cord and tassel, with fancy ornamental hooks. Length, 48 in. Shipping weight, 6 oz.
24K766
Per pair.... **89c**

New Fancy Center Panel Design

A frame of striking appearance in mottled old gold and brown, offset with a striping of black. Handsome scholl design at the top. Center panel decoration in frosted etching. Width, 50 in.; height, 21 in. Shipping weight, 45 pounds.
1K4166...........$11.45

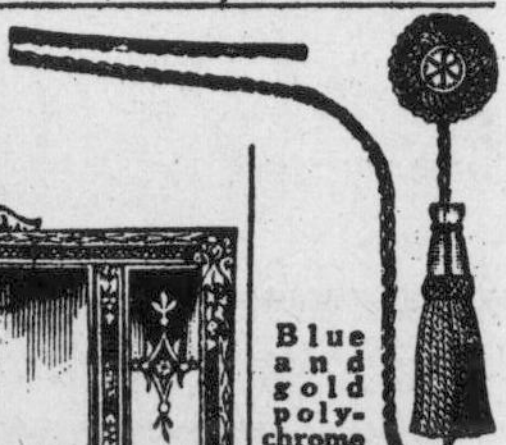

Blue and gold polychrome cord and tassel, with ornamental hook. Length, 48 in. Shipping weight, 6 oz.
24K765
Per pair $1.19

A Mirror of Quality

Handsome brown and gold frame, decorated in contrasting floral design. The side panels are hand etched in frosted effect. A beautiful design. Width, 46 in.; height, 16½ inches. Shipping weight, 30 pounds.
1K4164..................$5.95

Tapestry and Mirror

A combination mirror and tapestry. The top panel is decorated with an imported Flemish tapestry. Size of tapestry, 9½x9½ in. The lower panel is genuine plate mirror. Size of mirror panel, 17¼x9½ in. Makes a most attractive decoration in the home. Handsome gold and brown mottled frame in stippled effect, touched with soft contrasting colors. Height, 33 in.; width, 12 in. Shpg. wt., 25 lbs.
1K4169
$4.25

A Very Popular Style

Beautiful brown and gold frame, touched with bright contrasting colors. The small side panels are beautifully hand etched in frosted effect. Handsome carved decoration at the top. Width, 33 in.; height, 15 in. Shipping weight, 25 lbs.
1K4168..................$4.25

Combination Mirror and Coat Rack

An exceptionally convenient piece in homes that lack front hall closet space, or room for a costumer. Very heavily constructed to withstand the weight of outer wraps. Strong golden oak frame, set with oxidized finish. Genuine heavy plate mirror. Frame, 16x24 in. Width of molding, 2½ in. Mirror, 12x20 in. A very popular style of wall rack which at our low price is a splendid bargain. Shipping weight, 36 lbs.
1K4108..................$5.35

The fancy mirrors shown on this page are of a better and heavier quality than you ordinarily get at these prices. All of our etching is done from the back of the glass in frosted effect—the mirror surface is not cut, therefore, it will not catch dust

Plate Glass Mirrors

High gloss oak frame or hardwood white enameled. Carefully fitted corners. Six smallest sizes can be shipped by parcel post.

1K4102

Size, Mirror	Shpg. Wt.	Oak Frames Plain Edges	Oak Frames Bevel Edges	White Enamel Bevel Edges
7x 9 in.	5 lbs.	$0.65	......	......
8x10 in.	5½ lbs.	.85	......	......
9x12 in.	6 lbs.	.98	$1.35	......
10x14 in.	7½ lbs.	1.35	1.95	$2.10
12x20 in.	19 lbs.	2.45	3.25	3.75
14x24 in.	24 lbs.	3.45	......	......
16x28 in.	28 lbs.	5.75	......	......
18x40 in.	45 lbs.	8.95	......	......

High Grade Chairs for School and Office

$10⁷⁵
Golden Oak

$5⁶⁵
Golden Oak

$6⁷⁵
Golden Oak

Tablet Arm Chair Convenient for Home, Office or School Use

$4⁸⁵

Swivel Arm Chair

Revolving Office or Desk Chair. Matches Arm Chair 1K302, shown at the right. Made of quarter sawed oak, golden finish, or hardwood in choice of mahogany or walnut finishes. Saddle shape seat is 18x19½ in. Back is 19¼ in. high from seat. Shpg. wt., 47 lbs.
1K301—Golden oak..$10.75
Mahogany finish............10.85
Walnut finish............... 10.95

Office Chair

Very strongly constructed to stand the hard usage all office furniture gets. Deep doweled joints, strong bracing and gluing at all points of strain. Made of quarter sawed oak, golden finish or hardwood in choice of mahogany or walnut finishes. Saddle shape seat is 15½x17 in. Back, 18 in. high from seat. Shipping weight, 18 lbs.
1K303—Golden oak......$5.65
Mahogany finish $5.75
Walnut finish 5.85

Comfortable Arm Chair

Made of quarter sawed oak, golden finish, or hardwood in choice of mahogany or walnut finishes. Very comfortable and unusually low priced. Matches Revolving Chair 1K301, at extreme left of this page. Saddle shape seat is 17¾x20 in. Back is 19¼ in. high from seat. Shipping weight, 32 pounds.
1K302—Arm Chair,
Golden oak...............$6.75
Mahogany finish..............$6.85
Walnut finish 6.95

Very strongly made of select oak in choice of golden or fumed finishes. The wide tablet arm is of genuine quarter sawed oak, insuring a perfect writing surface. Fitted with rack below for books or packages. Comfortable saddle shaped seat. Form fitting curved back. Full box seat construction. All parts are deep doweled and glued. Size of the seat is scientifically determined to comfortably seat the average student. Height of the back, 19½ in. Size of the tablet arm, 23x11 in. Shipped from our store. Shipping weight, 23 pounds.
1K36—Singly. Each............$4.85
Lots of 100. Each............$4.45

MODERN OFFICE FURNITURE *at* SURPRISINGLY LOW PRICES!

When ordering on easy payments use time payment order blank on page 1092

Terms: $5.00 Down and $5.00 a Month

Terms: $5.00 down and $5.00 a month

A Real Economy Desk in Choice of Roll or Flat Top Style

Medium Size Desk for the Business Man

Choice of rolled top or flat top styles. A popular size in a big choice of finishes, and styles sure to appeal to the keen business man. We feel sure that quality for quality and price for price we are offering you more desk for your money. This desk is made of select oak, golden gloss finish, or of select close grained hardwood finished in handsome walnut or mahogany. Very strongly constructed; all legs are 2x2-in. posts; all joints are mortised and tenoned and carefully glued. The 5-ply veneered top is 13/16 in. thick. The 3-ply veneered panels in the back and ends are 3/16 in. thick. The back of the desk is finished. Equipped with a special deep drawer at the left for filing away long books or letter files. Has a sliding, finished writing board. Brass trimmings. Equipped with nickeled metal glides.

1K3991⅓—Rolled top style. Handy arrangement of pigeonholes with small drawers. Locks on rolled top and for small side drawer. Height, 42 in.; width, 48 in.; depth, 23 in. Shipped from factory in INDIANA. Shpg. wt., 190 lbs.

Sold for cash or on easy payment terms: $5.00 down; $5.00 a month.

1K3992⅓—Flat top style. Has lock on small top drawer. Height, 31 in.; width, 48 in.; depth, 23 in. Shipped from factory in INDIANA. Shpg. wt., 135 lbs.

Sold For Cash Only

top is 13/16 inch thick. The three-ply ends and back are 3/16 inch thick. The back of the desk is finished. Brass trimmings. Equipped with nickeled metal glides.

1K3993⅓—Roll top style. Has an easy rolling dustproof roll curtain. Upper section equipped with pigeonholes with a small drawer in the pigeonhole compartment. Height, 40 in.; width, 40 in.; depth, 23 in. Shipped from factory in INDIANA. Shipping weight, 135 pounds.

If you buy this desk you save valuable space in your office or home, not to speak of the many dollars you save when you buy the same desk at Sears. It has all the essentials. For the one who wishes to purchase a well constructed, efficient desk we can recommend this style highly. Made of oak, golden gloss finish, or close grained hardwood in choice of mahogany or walnut finishes. The legs are 2x2 in. square. The five-ply veneered panels are 3/16 inch thick. The back of the desk is finished.

1K3994⅓—Flat top style. Height, 29 in.; width, 40 in.; depth, 23 inches. Shipped from factory in INDIANA. Shipping weight, 95 pounds.

	Cash Prices	Easy Payment Prices
Golden oak	$32.65	$35.75
Mahogany finish	32.75	35.85
Walnut finish	32.85	35.95

	Cash Prices	Easy Payment Prices
Golden oak	$21.75	$23.75
Mahogany finish	21.85	23.85
Walnut finish	21.95	23.95

	Cash Prices	Easy Payment Prices
Golden oak	$20.75	$22.75
Mahogany finish	20.85	22.85
Walnut finish	20.95	22.95

	Cash Only
Golden oak	$13.35
Mahogany finish	16.45
Walnut finish	16.55

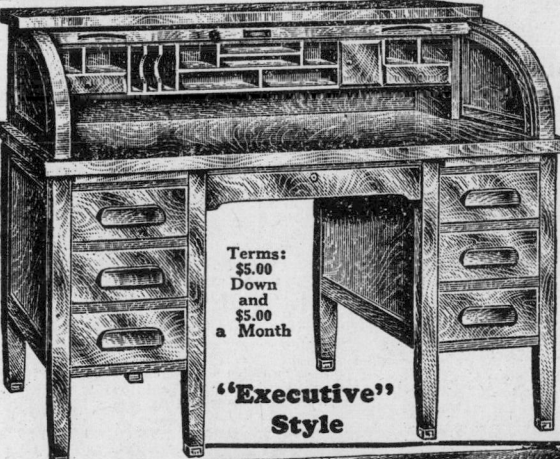

Terms: $5.00 Down and $5.00 a Month

"Executive" Style

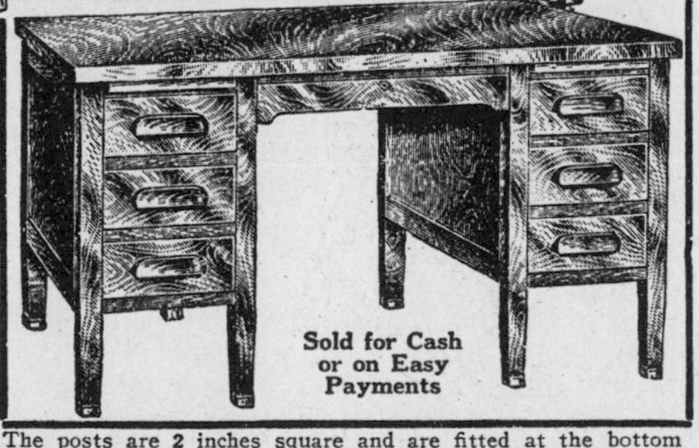

"Non-Skid" Chair Pad

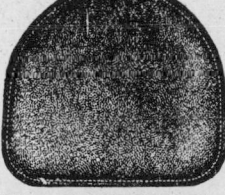

The top is of high quality, fine wool green felt. The bottom of a special non-skid art leather prevents this pad from skidding, eliminating the straps or tacks that are usually necessary to hold the seat pad in place. The filling is a pure padding felt that will wear and keep its shape for years. Shipping weights, 1 and 1½ lbs., respectively. Can be shipped parcel post.

1K312—15⅛ in. wide; 14½ in. long $1.35
1K313—18 in. wide; 16 in. long $1.75

Terms: $5.00 down; and $5.00 a month

This Roll Top Desk Especially Low Priced

You can't buy as big a bargain anywhere else in a roll top desk. A good solid oak construction, finished in dull golden office color. Roll top curtain, knee drawer and top side drawer equipped with separate locks. Plenty of space; many compartments. Legs are 1¾ in. square, tapered at the bottom. Scroll ends of solid oak, 1 in. thick. Panels of three-ply built up construction. Dovetailed drawer construction. Metal corner braces on each leg, the same as the highest priced desks have. Top size, 42x30 in. Height, 44 in. Has noiseless sliding casters. Shipping weight, 195 pounds. Shipped from factory in INDIANA.

1K3959⅓—Cash Price........$23.95   Easy Payment Price......$26.45

In choice of roll top or flat top styles. The handiest style of desk for the person who has more than an ordinary amount of business. Large amount of drawer space, with three pedestal drawers on the left hand side, a wide center drawer and two pedestal drawers on the right; the lower one double depth for filing purposes. Very strongly made of oak, office golden finish, with brass caps. Panels are three-ply ⅜ inch thick. Furnished in two sizes. Shipped from factory in INDIANA.

1K3957⅓—Roll top style. Has easy sliding roll curtain. Excellent arrangement of pigeonholes, with one private locker. Roll curtain controlls the locking device on the pedestal drawers. Center drawer has separate lock.

Sold for Cash or on Easy Payments

The posts are 2 inches square and are fitted at the bottom with brass caps. Panels are three-ply ⅜ inch thick. The five-ply veneered top is 13/16

	Cash Prices	Easy Payment Prices
Size, 30x52 in. Height, 44 in. Shipping wt., 240 lbs....$39.45		$43.45
Size, 30x60 in. Height, 44 in. Shipping wt., 250 lbs.... 41.45		45.55

1K3954⅓—Flat top style. Center drawer has lock.

	Cash Prices	Easy Payment Prices
Size, 30x52 in. Height, 30 in. Shipping wt., 170 lbs.... 26.45		28.85
Size, 30x60 in. Height, 30 in. Shipping wt., 180 lbs.... 28.95		31.75

Card Index File

Handy desk index consisting of A-Z index file and 100 ruled cards. Box, 5½x3¼ in. Cards are 3x5 in. Well made box smoothly finished in golden oak. Can be shipped parcel post. Shipping weight, 1¾ pounds.

1K3900—Cash only........55c

Hardwood Stools

Made of hardwood, light golden finish or white enameled finish. Seat, 13 in. in diameter. Cash only.

1K305
White enamel finish. One size only; 24 in. high. Shpg. wt., 6½ lbs. $1.79
Golden gloss finish.

Ht. In.	Wt. Lbs.	
18	6	$1.29
24	6½	1.45
30	7½	1.65
36	8½	1.85

18 and 24 in. sizes are shipped by parcel post.

ELECTRIC WASHER
New! Latest Approved AGITATOR

$5.00 DOWN

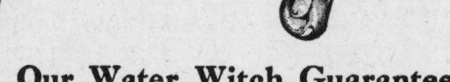

The latest addition to our large line of Washing Machines. The most modern, up to the minute washing principle applied with many refinements and exclusive features. Only in this new Water Witch can you get the ideal combination of the vibrator propeller action, the extra wide and convenient top opening, the self oiling bearings, the splashproof motor, the all metal wringer and the lifetime power unit. The Water Witch brings you all of these, at a price which is sensationally low when you compare it with other makes.

Here is an electric washer which we believe is destined to revolutionize the washing machine industry! A finer, more modern machine was never built. A more thorough washer has never been designed. Nor has the same huge value ever been offered in the history of electric washing machines. We know! From the first, we believed that electric washers could be made and sold, with a reasonable profit, at a great deal less money than the public was being asked to pay. We proved that years ago! We sold thousands and thousands of washers and our customers saved hundreds of thousands of dollars. Today, in the Water Witch we have incorporated all our many years experience in designing and manufacturing electric washers, we have concentrated all our huge buying power to give you the last big dollar of saving. We are proud of this new triumph of efficiency and we are backing it to the limit with our guarantee. You will be equally proud to have it in your home where it will solve, at once and forever, all your washing problems.

The propeller action has been definitely proven as the most desirable from every viewpoint. In the Water Witch we have developed a propeller of special design that surges through the water with a powerful wavelike motion, which cleans the clothes in far less time than was ever required before! The Water Witch washes a big batch of clothes with a speed almost magical!

Self Oiling Bearings

What could be simpler than to pour hot water into the big roomy tub, add soap or washing powder, put in the clothes, put on the lid and press a button? No need to first look around, a searchlight in one hand, an oil can in the other, and go on a still hunt for oil holes. Not in the Water Witch! If this washer were like the ordinary kind you'd be continually fussing and bothering with oil and grease, worrying about the places you've overlooked. And well you might worry! For washers of that type don't last long. The bearings you miss and those which don't get sufficient lubrication wear away in a hurry. Many manufacturers don't use self oiling bearings because they cost more money, but if you're a careful buyer, you'll have no other kind. When you buy a Water Witch your investment is safe!

New Perfection, New Beauty

The big, copper tub of the Water Witch is positively leakproof. The specially designed propeller has watertight connections. The heavy vertical supports hold the washer rigid and add to its stanch, sturdy reliability. The power unit which oscillates the propeller back and forth is exactly the same as we use in our other washers, the duplicate in every proven detail of construction. The splashproof motor and the all metal wringer, too, are the same high quality equipment that has demonstrated its serviceability through the years. The Water Witch, while built for service, is also attractively and pleasingly finished. Because it is practically noiseless and vibrationless, you can use it in the kitchen where the clean, bright appearance will not be out of place.

The easy payment plan on which the Water Witch may be purchased permits you to have the comfort and convenience of this remarkable home servant for only $5.00 down. Then when the machine arrives, you can try it for four weeks, putting it to every test on every kind of washing task you may have. At the end of the trial, after you have compared, examined and tested every feature to your complete satisfaction, you start paying for it in small monthly amounts. In this way there is no difficulty in buying an electric washer and your payments are less than you are now paying for laundry charges or a laundress.

For Laundry Tubs See Page 1010

Our Water Witch Guarantee

We guarantee this electric washing machine will satisfy you in every way. We guarantee that it will wash your clothes quickly and clean, to your entire satisfaction. We guarantee the Water Witch to be made of first quality materials and will replace without cost to you any part which should prove to be defective in material or workmanship. The entire resources of Sears, Roebuck and Co. are back of your purchase when you buy this washer, together with our nation wide reputation for fair and square dealing.

Extra Wide Tub

Measure the top opening of the Water Witch and you'll find it is 24 inches across. This is an important feature, because it means that to get the desired tub capacity we don't have to build the washer so high you are inconvenienced when you reach into the tub for the clothes. Again, you have plenty of elbow room, with no cramping to get at the clothes. The tub holds a big batch of clothes. Measuring the capacity in sheets, the tub will hold seven large, full size sheets at one time.

$92.00 Cash

SPLASHPROOF Motor

The very best obtainable splashproof motor is used on our washers. Manufactured especially for washing machine use by one of the oldest and largest manufacturers of fractional horse-power motors in America. An exceptionally high grade motor that is not subject to damage or injury when water is carelessly splashed or spilled on it. The thorough waterproof construction protects at all times the parts that are liable to damage or injury from water. Designed with sufficient capacity to drive both the washer and wringer at the same time, without danger of overloading the motor. Absolutely trouble-proof, full capacity 1/4 horse-power motor.

Catalog No.	Water Witch Electric Washer	Cash Price	Easy Payment Price	Payment With Order	Monthly Payment
26K570	With Motor for Alternating Current; 105 to 115 volts, 60 cycles.	$92.00	$101.50	$5.00	$7.00

Shipped from our store. Shipping weight, 285 pounds.

Special Voltage Motors

If the electric current supplied to you is different from the standard 105 to 115 volts, 60 cycles, alternating current, we charge $4.00 more for the washing machine because the motor manufacturers make an extra charge for these special voltage motors. When writing your order, be sure to mention whether you use direct or alternating current, and the voltage and cycles. This information will be found on your electric meter.

When Ordering on Easy Payment Plan Use Order Blank on Page 1092

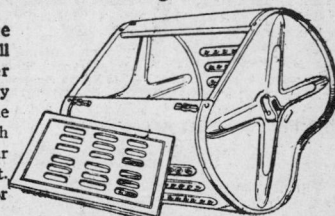

Introducing a *New Simplified* ELECTRIC IRONER

$5.00 Down $7.50 A Month

Superior Features of the Liberty

Wide Wooden Padded Roll. The roll on the Liberty is 26 inches wide, which means that the machine is of sufficient size to iron single folded the largest pieces you may have, such as bedspreads, sheets, large tablecloths and the like. It is made of selected seasoned poplar, which we have found is the most satisfactory construction for the purpose. The roll is covered with padding and white muslin, which can be conveniently removed for airing and fluffing and then reapplied. There is an even, positive pressure the full length of the roll against the shoe, assuring uniform beauty of the finished work. You have instant and absolute control of the rotation of the roll at all times by means of the control board or the table. Roll cannot start until you tilt this table up. To stop, merely press it down.

Safe, Simple Control—There are no confusing levers or bars to reach for and it is impossible to make a mistake. This control has been approved by the leading authorities of the country. The diameter of the roll and its number of revolutions per minute were determined to insure maximum ironing efficiency.

Gas or Electrically Heated!

$88.25 Cash With Gas Heater

$91.25 Cash Electrically Heated

We can furnish the Liberty with either GAS or ELECTRIC heating element. With the former, it is only necessary to attach the rubber hose connection to your gas jet. A standard 8-foot length of hose is furnished with each gas heated ironer. With the electric heating element all you do is plug in on your electric house circuit and turn the switch on the ironer. Either element will give you years of service. If your electric current is other than the standard 60-cycle A. C. current, order ironer with gas heater. Be sure to specify type of current you use.

Electric Motor—Standard, powerful motor which we know will give you the service you expect. When ordering Electric Ironer be sure to mention whether you use direct or alternating current, and the voltage and cycles. This information will be found on your electric meter.

A real, automatic, simplified, improved HOME IRONER. The biggest advance in design and efficiency yet made in this greatest labor saver of the home. Ironing is now reduced to its simplest form—ALL of the hard, back breaking drudgery of ironing by hand is removed. You actually rest while doing something which formerly was the hardest kind of work; manual labor which no woman ever should be asked to do. Everything is automatic with the new Liberty Ironer—there are no gears or levers to operate with hands, feet or knees—yet the control of starting or stopping is instantaneous.

With the Liberty you can iron those pieces which were formerly impossible to iron satisfactorily on an ironing machine. You will see from the illustration at the extreme left how simple it is to iron even the most complicated apparel on the Liberty. No matter how intricate the ruffle or flounce, the Liberty will iron it just right. All those pieces which you probably thought HAD to be ironed by hand are ironed on the Liberty quickly, easily, beautifully.

30 Days' Free Trial
Guaranteed to Satisfy—a Whole Year to Pay

Order the Liberty Electric Ironer today. See how easy it is to operate. How easily, quickly and well it can iron your clothes. Try it in YOUR home, on your ironing for four weeks. Compare the Liberty, if you wish, with other ironers, no matter how much higher priced. Then, after the trial, if you are not convinced that the Liberty can save you all the hard work of ironing day, giving you many, many more hours of leisure, or if you do not think the Liberty is the biggest value obtainable, send it back. We will then return every cent you have paid, plus transportation charges, and the trial will not have cost you one cent.

You need not pay cash when you buy the Liberty. Our Easy Payment Plan enables you to purchase on terms which bring the ownership of this greatest labor saving appliance within the reach of everyone.

We guarantee to satisfy you and save you money. The Liberty is a quality product, built to endure through the years. It will serve you until there can be no question but that it has returned your investment over and over again.

Shipped from our store. Shipping weight, 225 pounds.
26K800—Liberty Ironer With Gas Heater. Cash...**$88.25**
Time Payment Price.................................**$98.25**
TERMS: $5.00 down and $7.50 a month.
26K801—Liberty Ironer With Electric Heater for standard 105 to 115 volts, 60-cycle A. C. current. Cash...**$91.25**
Time Payment Price.................................**$99.75**
TERMS: $5.00 down and $7.50 a month.
When ordering on easy payments use Time Payment Order Blank on Page 1092.

Low in Price—Big in Value

The Homan Washer is the acme of simplicity. It is operated by the old reliable lever movement. Operation consists simply of side to side movement of the lever which rotates the dolly. This simple and durable construction insures long life. Nothing to get out of order.

Just think, only $8.95 for this high grade Homan Washer. Only the World's Largest Store could sell a washing machine of this quality at such a low price. At this price no home need be without a washing machine. We have sold thousands of these machines and their popularity is well deserved.

The tub is corrugated on the inside and smoothly finished to prevent tearing of clothes. Diameter of tub is 22½ inches; depth, 11¼ inches, inside measurements. It is nicely finished in natural wood color. Sturdily constructed throughout. Our low price offers a big saving over similar washers of this type, sold elsewhere. Get rid of the washboard! Enjoy life! Prompt shipment of the Homan from our store. Shipping weight, 58 pounds.
26K525—Homan Washing Machine.............**$8.95**

Easy to Buy—
Easy to Operate

The Quick and Easy Washer is all that its name implies. It does your washing quickly, easily and well. It is exceptionally well made of high quality materials. Simple as the Quick and Easy Washer is, you will find it a great improvement over the washboard. Health is wealth—protect yours. Use a washing machine. **Shipped from our store.** The Quick and Easy Washer is made in two sizes. Both machines are 25 inches high. Sold for cash only.

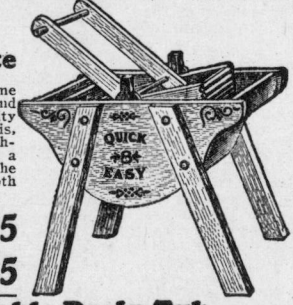

26K530—Size, 19x28½x14 inches inside measure. Shipping weight, 45 pounds............................ **$4.95**
26K535—Size, 22x28½x14 inches inside measure. Shipping weight, 50 pounds............................ **6.45**

Portable Drain Tub

This Portable Drain Tub will save you many needless steps on washday. It is built high enough to save stooping. The Portable Drain Tub is mounted on easy rolling casters. It saves the lifting or carrying of water or clothes. It is equipped with a large drain faucet with standard hose connection.

The Portable Drain Tub used in connection with stationary tubs increases the efficiency of the stationary tubs 50 per cent. This fact is attested to by housewives who have used both the Portable Drain Tubs and stationary tubs.

Order one of these Portable Drain Tubs for your next washday. You will marvel at the work it will save you. At our low price no home need be without this great washday convenience. You deserve one! **Shipped from our store. Sold for cash only.**
26K4002—Portable Drain Tub. Finished in battleship gray. Steel construction throughout. Height, 33½ inches; width, 16¾ inches; length, 21¾ inches. Capacity, 19 gallons. Shipping weight, 40 pounds......... **$4.85**

The Best Hand Power Washer Made!

$15.95

No need to dread the work of washday. This High Speed Wizard uses the simplest principles to make your washing easy. The slight touch of your hand on the handle transfers enormous forces of leverage to smooth running gears, rotating the dolly at high speed with hardly any effort on your part. Your washing is done, and done well, in a mere fraction of time usually necessary. There's nothing complicated, nothing to get out of order. No other hand operated machine can offer so much of efficiency and ease. Every latest device that adds to your convenience is incorporated in the High Speed Wizard. A special frame for attaching a hand wringer is placed at one side of the tub in a position that reduces the work of wringing to a minimum. The lid fastens with a strong hasp and is quickly lifted and out of the way when wringing.

In every way the High Speed Wizard is the superior hand operated washer. Send in your order and take advantage of this new, low price.

Built for Long Service

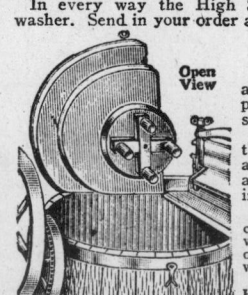

Open View

The construction and material of this washer are far superior to the ordinary machine of this price. Heavier parts and wood from specially selected stock give lasting satisfaction.

Every detail is made well. The gearing is the result of years of experimenting. A special arrangement of the handle socket permits operation from a standing or sitting position, making it easy to operate.

Inside of the full size, six-sheet capacity tub, is corrugated, which means cleaner clothes and quicker washing. Metal drain cock is conveniently located on side of tub. Shipped from our store. Shipping weight, 115 pounds. Sold for cash only.
26K514—High Speed Wizard Washer............. **$15.95**

To Find What You Want, See Index Pages 550 to 570   P 913

Exquisite American Dinnerware of Semi-Porcelain

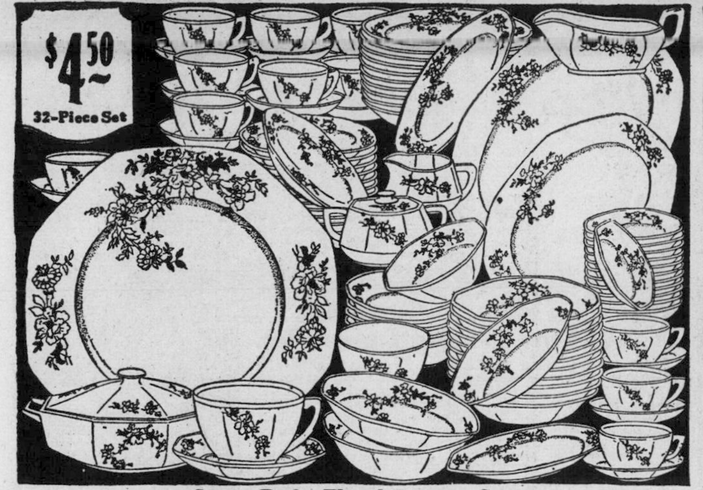

$4.50
32-Piece Set

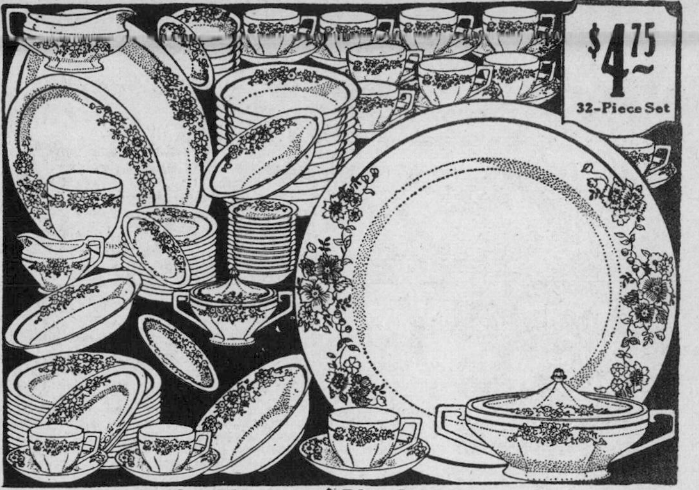

$4.75
32-Piece Set

Ivory Body Floral Dinner Set

Floral decorated dinnerware at exceptionally low prices. Decorated with a conventional floral design of yellow flowers with burnt orange colored centers, slate colored stems and small leaves which adds contrast to the beautiful color of the flowers. Made of the new ivory semi-porcelain in an octagon shape.

35K338—Ivory Body Floral Dinnerware. Complete sets and open stock. For list of pieces in the complete sets see page 914.

32-Piece Dinner Set. Wt., 26 lbs.	$ 4.50
66-Piece Dinner Set. Wt., 51 lbs.	12.65
53-Piece Dinner Set. Wt., 42 lbs.	$10.50
90-Piece Dinner Set. Wt., 75 lbs.	15.85

	Size, Abt.	Set of Six
Tea Cups and Saucers	......	$1.48
Coffee Cups and Saucers	......	1.71
Bread and Butter Plates	6 in.	.68
Pie Plates	7 in.	.75
Tea or Breakfast Plates	8 in.	.93
Dinner Plates	9 in.	1.18
Dinner Plates, extra large	9¾ in.	1.40
Soup Plates (coupe shape)	8 in.	1.15
Sauce Dishes	5 in.	.50
Oatmeal Dishes	6 in.	1.03
Oyster Bowls	......	1.30

	Size Abt.	Each
Covered Vegetable Dish	......	$1.35
Gravy or Sauce Boat	......	.49
Platter, small	11¼ in.	.35
Platter, medium	13½ in.	.58
Platter, large	15¼ in.	.92
Cream Pitcher	......	.37
Pitcher	3¼ pts.	.63
Bowl	1 pt.	.27
Covered Sugar Bowl	......	.68
Pickle Dish	......	.37
Covered Butter Dish	......	1.02
Oval Open Vegetable Dish	9 in.	.40
Round Deep Salad Bowl	9¼ in.	.59

Garden Flower and Blue Line Dinner Set

A popular style of dinnerware decoiated with sprays of blue, pink and yellow garden flowers and buds with green leaves connected with a blue line forming a border. Made of American pure white semi-porcelain in a plain edge shape.

35K340—Garden Flower and Blue Line Dinnerware. Complete sets and open stock. For list of pieces in the complete sets see page 914.

32-Piece Dinner Set. Wt., 26 lbs.	$ 4.75
66-Piece Dinner Set. Wt., 51 lbs.	12.98
53-Piece Dinner Set. Wt., 42 lbs.	$10.65
90-Piece Dinner Set. Wt., 75 lbs.	16.35

	Size Abt.	Set of Six
Tea Cups and Saucers	......	$1.55
Coffee Cups and Saucers	......	1.83
Bread and Butter Plates	6 in.	.73
Pie Plates	7 in.	.80
Tea or Breakfast Plates	8 in.	.98
Dinner Plates	9 in.	1.23
Dinner Plates, extra large	9¼ in.	1.48
Soup Plates (coupe shape)	8 in.	1.20
Sauce Dishes	5 in.	.53
Oatmeal Dishes	6 in.	1.08
Oyster Bowls	......	1.38

	Size Abt.	Each
Covered Vegetable Dish	......	$1.25
Gravy or Sauce Boat	......	.52
Platter, small	11¼ in.	.38
Platter, medium	13½ in.	.59
Platter, large	15¼ in.	.95
Cream Pitcher	......	.39
Pitcher	3¼ pts.	.67
Bowl	1 pt.	.27
Covered Sugar Bowl	......	.72
Pickle Dish	......	.22
Covered Butter Dish	......	1.09
Oval Open Veg. Dish	9 in.	.42
Round Deep Salad Bowl	9¼ in.	.61

Gold Band Patterns Always Attractive

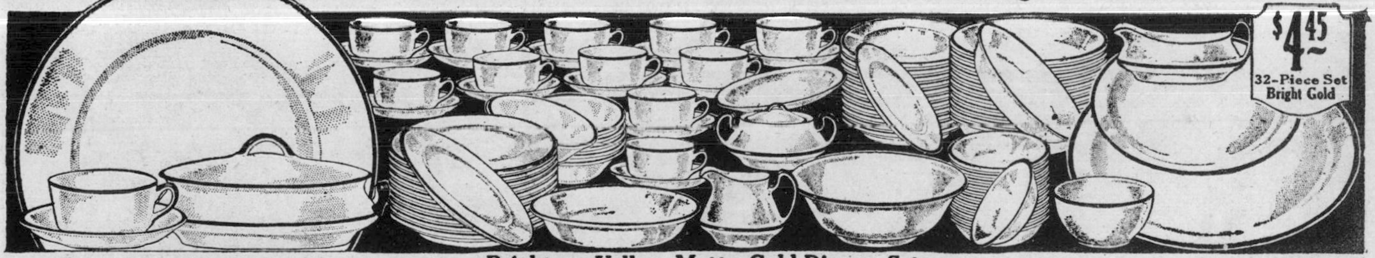

$4.45
32-Piece Set
Bright Gold

Bright or Yellow Matte Gold Dinner Sets

Choice of either bright gold or 18-karat yellow matte gold dinnerware. No. 35K246 Dinnerware is a bright gold band with bright gold traced handles. No. 35K234 Dinnerware is an 18-karat yellow matte gold band, handles heavily covered with gold.

The matte gold is the satin finished gold used on the highest priced sets. The ware of both sets is of first quality American pure white semi-porcelain in a plain edge shape. Complete sets and open stock. For list of pieces in the complete sets see page 914.

	35K246		35K234	
32-Piece Dinner Set. Wt., 26 lbs.	Bright Gold	$ 4.45	Matte Gold	$ 7.75
53-Piece Dinner Set. Wt., 42 lbs.	Bright Gold	10.35	Matte Gold	17.75
66-Piece Dinner Set. Wt., 51 lbs.	Bright Gold	$12.50	Matte Gold	$21.75
90-Piece Dinner Set. Wt., 75 lbs.	Bright Gold	15.75	Matte Gold	25.75

	Size, Abt.	35K246 Bright Gold Set of Six	35K234 Matte Gold Set of Six
Tea Cups and Saucers	......	$1.53	$2.63
Coffee Cups and Saucers	......	1.78	3.08
Bread and Butter Plates	6 in.	.70	1.14
Pie Plates	7 in.	.78	1.38
Tea or Breakfast Plates	8 in.	.95	1.63
Dinner Plates	9 in.	1.19	1.88
Dinner Plates, extra large	10 in.	1.45	2.25
Soup Plates (coupe shape)	8 in.	1.20	1.88

	Size, Abt.	35K246 Bright Gold	35K234 Matte Gold
Sauce Dishes, Set of 6	5 in.	$0.49	$0.98
Oatmeal Dishes. Set of 6	6 in.	1.08	1.75
Oyster Bowls, Set of 6	......	1.35	2.13
Covered Vegetable Dish, Each	......	1.25	2.40
Gravy (Sauce) Boat, Each	......	.48	.95
Platter, small, Each	11¼ in.	.32	.49
Platter, medium, Each	13½ in.	.55	.89
Platter, large, Each	15¼ in.	.86	1.54

	Size, Abt.	35K246 Bright Gold Each	35K234 Matte Gold Each
Cream Pitcher	......	$0.37	$0.60
Pitcher	3¼ pts.	.60	1.25
Bowl	1 pt.	.25	.40
Covered Sugar Bowl	......	.72	1.37
Pickle Dish	......	.20	.37
Covered Butter Dish	......	1.06	1.85
Oval Open Veg. Dish	9 in.	.38	.60
Round Deep Salad Bowl	9¼ in.	.56	.90

The Beautiful Colonial Shape Gold Band Set

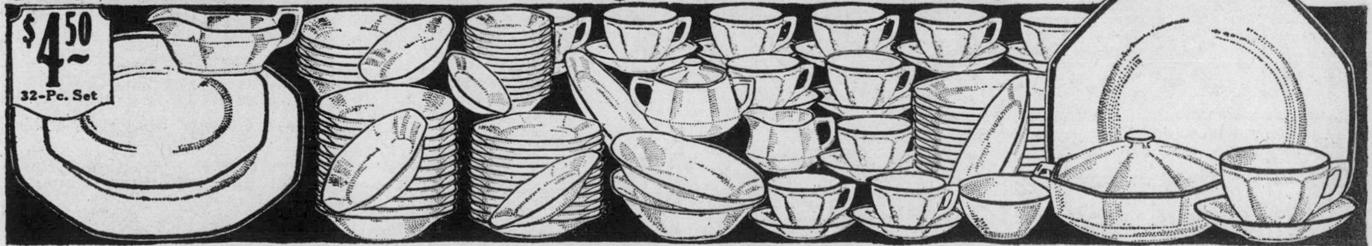

$4.50
32-Pc. Set

Ivory Body Gold Band Dinner Set

Remindful of rare ivory, grown mellow with the touch of years is this beautiful Gold Band Dinner Set. The bright gold band on the cream colored ivory semi-porcelain body blends most harmoniously, giving the appearance of a rich matte gold. Handles of each piece are traced in gold. The dinnerware is made in the popular octagon shape.

35K242—Ivory Body, Gold Band Dinnerware. Complete sets and open stock. For list of pieces in the complete sets see page 914.

32-Piece Dinner Set. Wt., 26 lbs.	$ 4.50
53-Piece Dinner Set. Wt., 42 lbs.	10.75
66-Piece Dinner Set. Wt., 51 lbs.	$12.75
90-Piece Dinner Set. Wt., 75 lbs.	16.25

	Size, Abt.	Set of Six
Tea Cups and Saucers	......	$1.49
Coffee Cups and Saucers	......	1.73
Bread and Butter Plates	6 in.	.69
Pie Plates	7 in.	.77
Tea or Breakfast Plates	8 in.	.93
Dinner Plates	9 in.	1.20
Dinner Plates (extra large)	10 in.	$1.43
Soup Plates (coupe shape)	8 in.	1.18
Sauce Dishes	5 in.	.50
Oatmeal Dishes	6 in.	1.05
Oyster Bowls	......	1.33
Covered Vegetable Dish.	Each	1.39

	Size Abt.	Each
Gravy, or Sauce Boat	......	$0.50
Platter, small	11¼ in.	.36
Platter, medium	13½ in.	.58
Platter, large	15¼ in.	.92
Cream Pitcher	......	.38
Pitcher	3¼ pts.	.65
Bowl	1 pt.	$0.27
Covered Sugar Bowl	......	.70
Pickle Dish	......	.38
Covered Butter Dish	......	1.05
Oval Open Veg. Dish	9 in.	.45
Round Deep Salad Bowl	9¼ in.	.60

Your Orders Shipped Within 24 Hours!

Imported English Semi-Porcelain Dinnerware

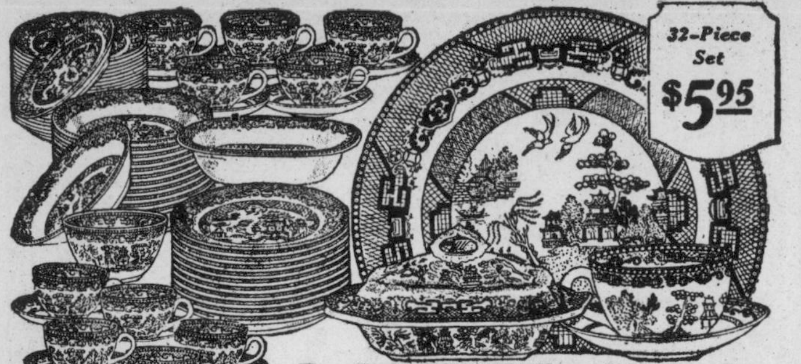

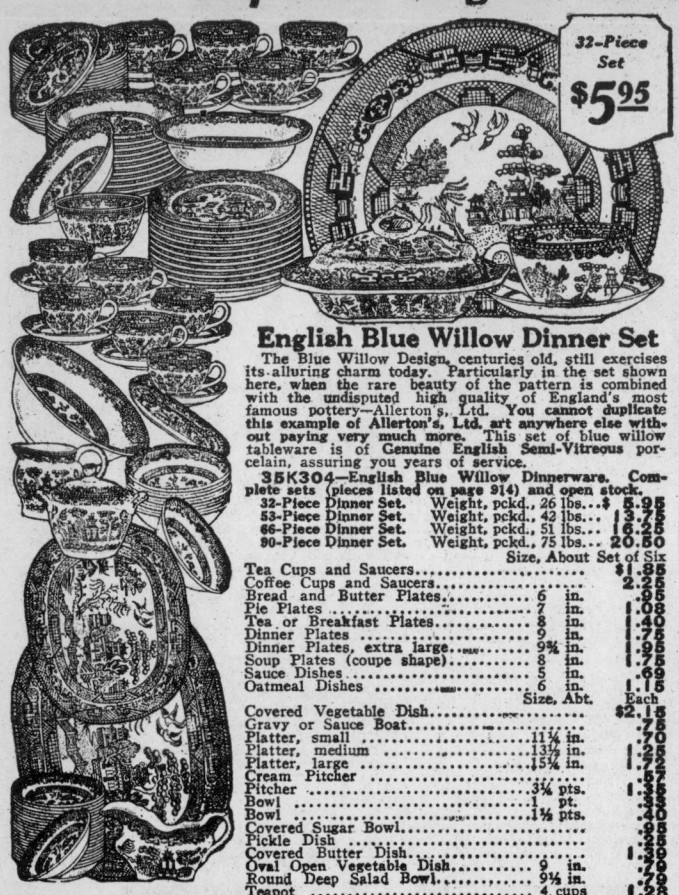

32-Piece Set
$5.95

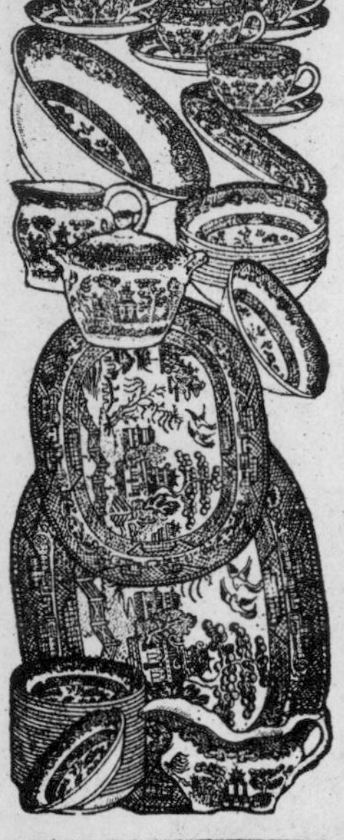

English Blue Willow Dinner Set

The Blue Willow Design, centuries old, still exercises its alluring charm today. Particularly in the set shown here, when the rare beauty of the pattern is combined with the undisputed high quality of England's most famous pottery—Allerton's, Ltd. **You cannot duplicate this example of Allerton's, Ltd. art anywhere else without paying very much more.** This set of blue willow tableware is of **Genuine English Semi-Vitreous** porcelain, assuring you years of service.

35K304—English Blue Willow Dinnerware. Complete sets (pieces listed on page 914) and open stock.

32-Piece Dinner Set.	Weight, pckd., 26 lbs...	$ 5.95
53-Piece Dinner Set.	Weight, pckd., 42 lbs...	13.75
66-Piece Dinner Set.	Weight, pckd., 51 lbs...	16.25
90-Piece Dinner Set.	Weight, pckd., 75 lbs...	20.50

	Size, About	Set of Six
Tea Cups and Saucers		$1.85
Coffee Cups and Saucers		2.25
Bread and Butter Plates	6 in.	.95
Pie Plates	7 in.	1.08
Tea or Breakfast Plates	8 in.	1.40
Dinner Plates	9 in.	1.75
Dinner Plates, extra large	9¾ in.	1.95
Soup Plates (coupe shape)	8 in.	1.75
Sauce Dishes	5 in.	.69
Oatmeal Dishes	6 in.	1.15

	Size, Abt.	Each
Covered Vegetable Dish		$2.15
Gravy or Sauce Boat		.75
Platter, small	11¼ in.	.70
Platter, medium	13½ in.	1.25
Platter, large	15¼ in.	1.72
Cream Pitcher		.57
Pitcher	3¼ pts.	1.35
Bowl	1 pt.	.33
Bowl	1½ pts.	.40
Covered Sugar Bowl		.95
Pickle Dish		.25
Covered Butter Dish		1.39
Oval Open Vegetable Dish	9 in.	.79
Round Deep Salad Bowl	9½ in.	.79
Teapot	4 cups	1.28

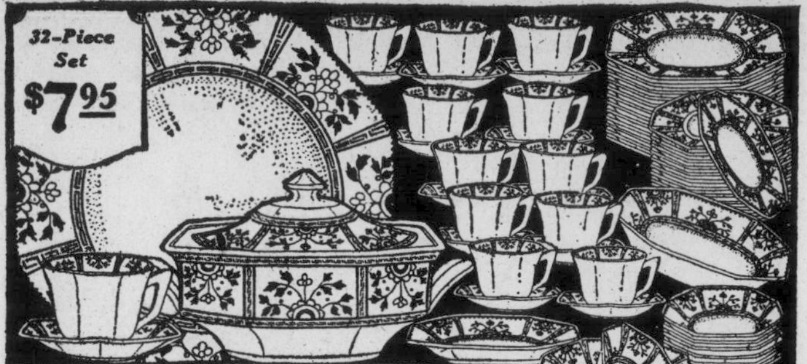

32-Piece Set
$7.95

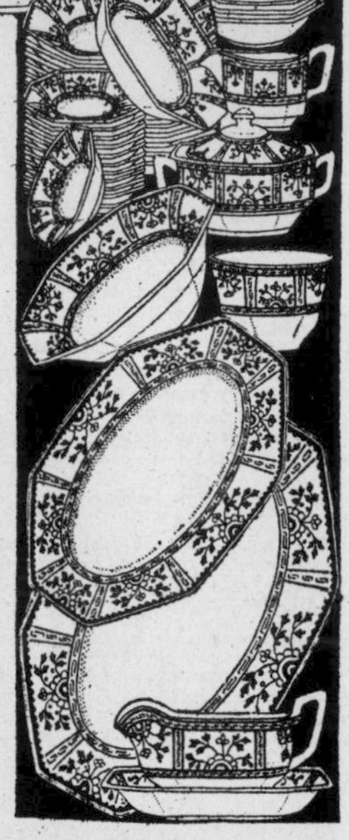

English Blue Paneled Dinner Set

True to England's tradition of "correctness," this Blue Paneled Dinner Set possesses the dainty delicacy required by unerring good taste. The royal blue floral design, contrasting with the subdued ivory tint of the ware, will never lose its strong appeal. This dinner set is a product of John Maddock and Sons, Ltd., England, and because it is of genuine English Semi-Vitreous Porcelain, it will serve you for years. Handles and knobs are traced with blue. Shape is the new Pagoda.

35K331—English Blue Paneled Dinnerware. Complete sets (pieces listed on page 914) and open stock.

32-Piece Dinner Set.	Weight, pckd., 26 lbs...	$ 7.95
53-Piece Dinner Set.	Weight, pckd., 42 lbs...	17.85
66-Piece Dinner Set.	Weight, pckd., 51 lbs...	21.00
90-Piece Dinner Set.	Weight, pckd., 75 lbs...	25.75

	Size, Abt.	Set of Six
Tea Cups and Saucers		$2.48
Coffee Cups and Saucers		2.93
Bread and Butter Plates	5¾ in.	1.23
Pie Plates	6¾ in.	1.40
Tea or Breakfast Plates	7½ in.	1.88
Dinner Plates	8½ in.	2.33
Dinner Plates, extra large	9½ in.	2.83
Soup Plates (coupe shape)	8 in.	2.33
Sauce Dishes	5 in.	.93
Oatmeal Dishes	6 in.	1.55

	Size, Abt.	Each
Covered Vegetable Dish		$2.80
Gravy or Sauce Boat		1.10
Platter, small	10⅛ in.	.69
Platter, medium	12 in.	1.00
Platter, large	14¼ in.	1.65
Cream Pitcher		.75
Pitcher	2¼ pts.	1.20
Bowl	1 pt.	.45
Bowl	1½ pts.	.55
Covered Sugar Bowl		1.25
Pickle Dish		.35
Covered Butter Dish		1.87
Oval Open Vegetable Dish	9 in.	.68
Round Deep Salad Bowl	9¼ in.	1.02

English Floral Spray Dinner Set

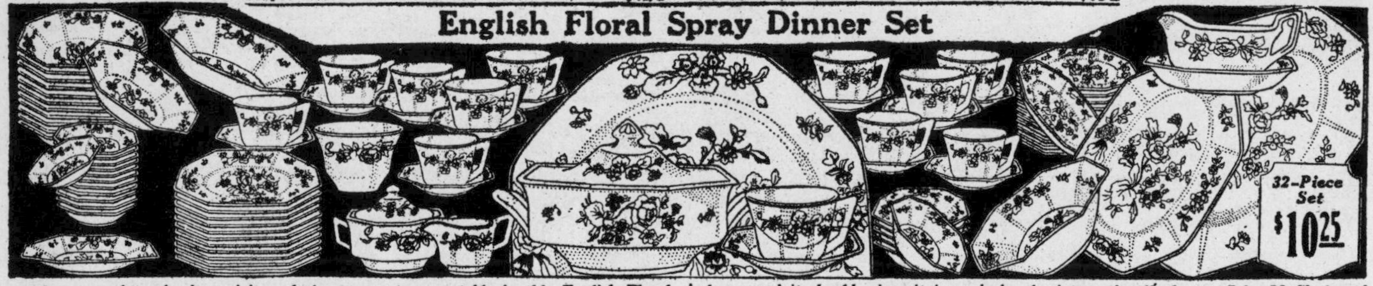

32-Piece Set
$10.25

An unusual touch of exquisite coloring comes to your table in this English Floral Spray Dinner Set. The old fashioned garden flowers in natural colors are treated so masterfully that they actually appear to be hand painted. The edges of each piece are traced in bright green, as are the handles and knobs. This set will win your lasting favor, and it should, since it is made by the internationally known John Maddock and Sons, Ltd., England. The ware is genuine ivory body English semi-vitreous porcelain in the new Pagoda shape.

35K236—English Floral Spray Dinnerware. Complete sets and open stock. For list of pieces in the complete sets see page 914.
32-Piece Dinner Set. Wt., 26 lbs..$10.25—**53-Piece Dinner Set.** Wt., 42 lbs..$23.50—**66-Piece Dinner Set.** Wt., 51 lbs..$28.75—**90-Piece Dinner Set.** Wt., 75 lbs..$35.75

	Size, Abt.	Per Set of Six
Tea Cups and Saucers		$3.49
Coffee Cups and Saucers		4.13
Bread and Butter Plates	5¾ in.	1.70
Pie Plates	6¾ in.	1.98
Tea or Breakfast Plates	7½ in.	2.63
Dinner Plates	8½ in.	3.27
Dinner Plates, extra large	9½ in.	3.93

	Size, Abt.	
Soup Plates. (Coupe Shape) Set of 6	8 in.	$3.25
Sauce Dishes. Set of six	5 in.	1.33
Oatmeal Dishes. Set of six	6 in.	2.18
Covered Vegetable Dish. Each		3.95
Gravy or Sauce Boat. Each		1.50

	Size, Abt.	Each
Platter, small	10⅛ in.	$0.98
Platter, Medium	12 in.	1.39
Platter, large	14¼ in.	2.27
Cream Pitcher		1.05
Pitcher	2¼ pts.	1.68
Bowl	1 pt.	.65

	Size, Abt.	Each
Bowl	1½ pts.	$0.78
Covered Sugar Bowl		1.75
Pickle Dish		.49
Covered Butter Dish		2.65
Oval Open Veg. Dish	9 in.	1.05
Round Deep Salad Bowl	9¼ in.	1.29

English Fruit Pattern Dinnerware

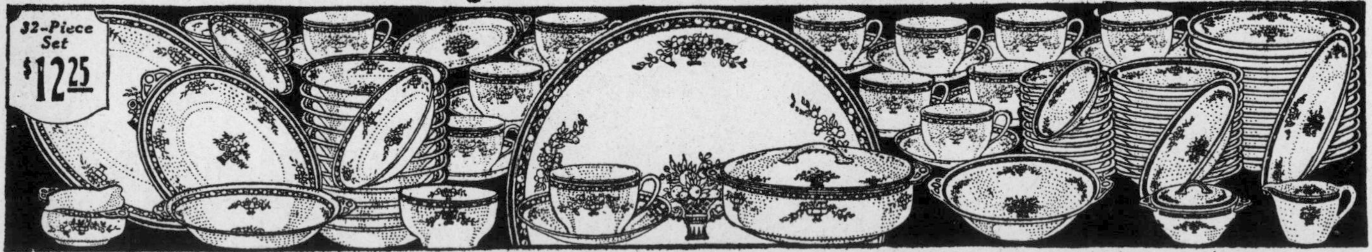

32-Piece Set
$12.25

The clear brilliancy of color—orange, yellow and blue in the small fruit peeping from green leaves on the border—lends individual smartness to each piece, while the borders, black background between dark yellow bands, give just enough contrast for utmost effectiveness. In the center of the pieces are blue and black compotes filled with colored fruits and blossoms. Gold is traced on border and handles of each piece. The ware is ivory body English semi-vitreous porcelain in a plain edge shape, a product of Johnson Bros.

35K241—Fruit Pattern Dinnerware. Complete sets and open stock. For list of pieces in the complete sets see page 914.
32-Piece Dinner Set. Wt., 26 lbs...$12.25—**53-Piece Dinner Set.** Wt., 42 lbs...$29.50—**66-Piece Dinner Set.** Wt., 51 lbs..$36.75—**90-Piece Dinner Set.** Wt., 75 lbs..$45.00

	Size, Abt.	Set of Six
Tea Cups and Saucers		$3.73
Coffee Cups and Saucers		4.40
Bread and Butter Plates	6 in.	1.88
Pie Plates	7 in.	2.13
Tea or Breakfast Plates	8 in.	2.80
Dinner Plates	9 in.	3.48

	Size, Abt.	Set of Six
Dinner Plates, extra large	9¾ in.	$4.23
Soup Plates (coupe shape)	8 in.	3.48
Sauce Dishes	5 in.	1.43
Oatmeal Dishes	6 in.	2.35
Round Covered Vegetable Dish. each		4.75
Gravy or Sauce Boat. Each		1.60

	Size, Abt.	Each
Platter, small	11¼ in.	$1.05
Platter, medium	13½ in.	1.45
Platter, large	15¼ in.	2.45
Cream Pitcher		1.10
Pitcher	3¼ pts.	1.80
Bowl	1 pt.	.69

	Size, Abt.	Each
Bowl	1½ pts.	$0.85
Covered Sugar Bowl		1.90
Pickle Dish		1.00
Covered Butter Dish		2.88
Ovel Open Veg. Dish	9 in.	1.05
Round Deep Salad Bowl	9¼ in.	1.48

Imported German and French China Dinnerware

$12.75 32-Piece Set

$11.25 32-Piece Set

The loveliness only associated with costly Old World china is instantly evident in these two exquisite dinner sets, products of a famous old German pottery. The chaste simplicity of the Gold Line and Gold Band Dinner Set and the brilliancy of the softly colored design in the Pink Rose Border Set exert an appeal that becomes ever stronger —for here are works of real art.

This Gold Band and Gold Line China Dinner Set is ever popular and always in good taste. It consists of a wide band and hairline of bright gold around the outside edge of each piece and a gold hairline around the shoulder of each piece. The handles are also traced with gold. The shape is plain, as illustrated above.

35K351—Gold Band China Dinner Set. Complete sets and open stock. For list of pieces in the complete sets see page 914.

Most pleasing and effective is this Pink Rose Border China Dinner Set. It consists of a border pattern in panel design with dainty pink roses on a delicate blue background, with a tan and green conventional design between each panel. The edge of each piece has a gold line, and the handles are traced with gold. The shape is plain, as illustrated above.

35K352—Pink Rose Border China Dinner Set. Complete sets and open stock. For list of pieces in the complete sets see page 914.

| 32-Pc. Dinner Set. Wt., pkd., 26 lbs. | $12.75 | 66-Pc. Dinner Set. Wt., pkd., 51 lbs. | $34.45 |
| 53-Pc. Dinner Set. Wt., pkd., 42 lbs. | 28.15 | 90-Pc. Dinner Set. Wt., pkd., 75 lbs. | 42.50 |

	Per Set Size, Abt. of Six		Size, Abt. Each
Tea Cups and Saucers	$3.08	Gravy or Sauce Boat	$1.98
Coffee Cups and Saucers	3.72	Platter, small........13 in.	1.60
Bread and Butter Plates...6 in.	1.60	Platter, medium.......4½ in.	2.40
Pie Plates........7¾ in.	2.28	Platter, large.......16½ in.	3.48
Tea or Breakfast Plates..8½ in.	2.65	Cream Pitcher	.59
Dinner Plates........9½ in.	3.72	Bowl...........1 pt.	.86
Soup Plates (coupe shape).8 in.	2.82	Covered Sugar Bowl	1.05
Sauce Dishes........5 in.	.80	Pickle Dish	.18
Oatmeal Dishes........6 in.	2.12	Covered Butter Dish	.80
Oval Covered Vegetable Dish. Each	3.48	Oval Open Vegetable Dish..9½ in.	1.02
Round Covered Vegetable Dish. Each	3.48	Round Deep Salad Bowl..9¾ in.	1.18

| 32-Pc. Dinner Set. Wt., pkd., 26 lbs. | $11.25 | 66-Pc. Dinner Set. Wt., pkd., 51 lbs. | $30.50 |
| 53-Pc. Dinner Set. Wt., pkd., 42 lbs. | 24.85 | 90-Pc. Dinner Set. Wt., pkd., 75 lbs. | 37.65 |

	Per Set Size, Abt. of Six		Size, Abt. Each
Tea Cups and Saucers	$2.65	Gravy or Sauce Boat	$1.88
Coffee Cups and saucers	3.35	Platter, small........13 in.	1.39
Bread and Butter Plates...6 in.	1.42	Platter, medium......14½ in.	2.08
Pie Plates........7¾ in.	2.00	Platter, large.......16½ in.	3.08
Tea or Breakfast Plates..8½ in.	2.35	Cream Pitcher	.53
Dinner Plates........9½ in.	3.25	Bowl...........1 pt.	.80
Soup Plates (coupe shape).8 in.	2.55	Covered Sugar Bowl	.96
Sauce Dishes........5 in.	1.35	Pickle Dish	.70
Oatmeal Dishes........6 in.	1.89	Covered Butter Dish	.08
Oval Covered Vegetable Dish. Each	3.05	Oval Open Vegetable Dish..9½ in.	.92
Round Covered Vegetable Dish. Each	3.05	Round Deep Salad Bowl..9¾ in.	1.10

Genuine Haviland at a NEW LOW PRICE

$25.75 32-Pc. Set

Haviland Pink Rose and Conventional Border Dinner Set. Beauty of design—unquestioned leadership in high quality accounts for the world wide popularity of Haviland China—and the set shown here is particularly worthy of the name. Small pink and yellow roses with green leaves inside a conventional border of ochre and soft blue form the

35K357—Pink Rose and Conventional Border Dinnerware. Complete Sets and Open Stock. For list of pieces in the complete sets see page 914.

pleasing decoration theme. Supplementing the border proper is another smaller one, consisting of narrow egg and dart with a matte gold band. Each flat piece has a small rose design in its center. All handles are covered with gold. Produced by Haviland and Co., Limoges, France.

| 32-Piece Dinner Set. Wt., 26 lbs. | $25.75 | 53-Piece Dinner Set. Wt., 42 lbs. | $59.75 | 66-Piece Dinner Set. Wt., 51 lbs. | $72.50 | 90-Piece Dinner Set. Wt., 75 lbs. | $88.75 |

	Per Set Size, Abt. of Six		Per Set Size, Abt. of Six		Size, Abt. Each		Size, Abt. Each
Tea Cups and Saucers	$7.25	Dinner Plates, extra large..10¼ in.	$6.98	Gravy or Sauce Boat, Fast Stand	$6.95	Bowl.........1 pt.	$1.65
Coffee Cups and Saucers	8.75	Soup Plates (coupe shape)..8 in.	4.75	Platter, small........11½ in.	2.40	Covered Sugar Bowl	3.25
Bread and Butter Plates..6¼ in.	4.23	Sauce Dishes........5 in.	3.38	Platter, medium......13¾ in.	3.85	Pickle Dish	1.55
Pie Plates........7½ in.	4.25	Oatmeal Dishes........6 in.	4.63	Platter, large........16 in.	5.40	Covered Butter Dish	4.65
Tea or Breakfast Plates..8½ in.	5.38	Round Covered Vegetable Dish. Each	7.65	Cream Pitcher	2.25	Oval Open Vegetable Dish.10 in.	3.00
Dinner Plates........9% in.	5.83			Pitcher.........3 pts.	4.50	Round Deep Salad Bowl..8½ in.	3.00

Haviland Dinner Ware ~ The Desire of Every Woman

$13.95 32-Pc. Set

Genuine Haviland China Dinner Set. Another example of the striking originality and superb skill of Haviland artists. In this china dinner set, large and small spraying of beautiful flowers are perfectly blended with green and tan-yellow leaves. A tan line

35K354—Haviland China Dinner Set. Complete Sets and Open Stock. For list of pieces in the complete sets see page 914.

around the edges, and handles decorated with a wide band of 18-karat matte gold, complete the decoration. Here, you will find, too, the incomparable hardness of body, depth and quality of glaze, brilliancy of finish present in all Haviland, Limoges, France, products.

| 32-Piece Dinner Set. Wt., 26 lbs. | $13.95 | 53-Piece Dinner Set. Wt., 42 lbs. | $33.50 | 66-Piece Dinner Set. Wt., 51 lbs. | $42.95 | 90-Piece Dinner Set. Wt., 75 lbs. | $50.75 |

	Per Set Size, Abt. of Six		Per Set Size, Abt. of Six		Size, Abt. Each		Size, Abt. Each
Tea Cups and Saucers	$4.08	Dinner Plates, extra large..10¼ in.	$3.68	Gravy or Sauce Boat, Fast Stand	$3.65	Bowl.........1 pt.	$1.15
Coffee Cups and Saucers	5.33	Soup Plates (coupe shape)..8 in.	3.75	Platter, small........11½ in.	1.50	Covered Sugar Bowl	1.95
Bread and Butter Plates..6¼ in.	2.43	Sauce Dishes........5 in.	1.98	Platter, medium......13¾ in.	2.60	Pickle Dish	1.10
Pie Plates........7¾ in.	2.75	Oatmeal Dishes........6 in.	2.58	Platter, large........16 in.	3.95	Covered Butter Dish	3.10
Tea or Breakfast Plates..8½ in.	2.88	Oval Covered Vegetable Dish. Each	4.60	Cream Pitcher	1.25	Oval Open Vegetable Dish.10 in.	2.20
Dinner Plates........9% in.	3.05	Round Covered Vegetable Dish. Each	4.60	Pitcher.........3 pts.	2.50	Round Deep Salad Bowl..8½ in.	1.85

Parcel Post, Express and Freight Rates Are on Pages 542 to 545

Fine Quality Cut and Etched Crystal Clear Glass Tableware

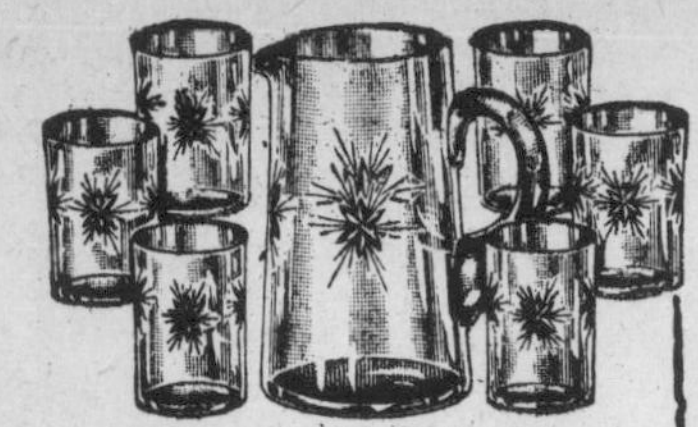

7-Piece Star Cut Water Set
Two-quart 8½-inch tankard shape pitcher and six ½-pint tumblers. Thin blown crystal glass, highly polished. Cut with three six-pointed sunburst stars with rays. Weight, packed, 8 pounds.
35K1405—Per set... **$1.80**

Star Cut Stemware

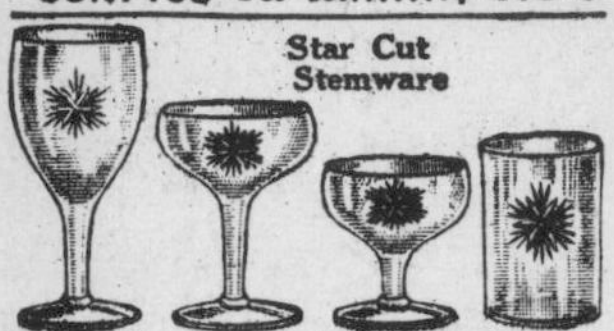

Thin blown crystal glass, highly polished, with one-piece drawn stems. Each piece is cut with three 6-point polished stars with cut silver gray rays. Popular Fifth Avenue shape.
35K1400—Water Goblet. Height, 6¼ in. Weight, packed, 4½ lbs. Per set of six... **$1.83**
35K1401—Tall Footed Sherbet. Height, 4½ in. Weight, packed, 4¼ pounds. Per set of six... **$1.80**
35K1402—Low Footed Sherbet. Height, 3⅜ in. Weight, packed, 4 lbs. Per set of six... **$1.73**
35K1403—Standard Table Tumbler. Height, 4⅛ in. Weight, packed, 3¾ lbs. Per set of six... **89c**
35K1404—Tall Lemonade or Ice Tea Tumbler. Height, 5⅝ in. Weight, packed, 4½ lbs. Per set of six... **$1.15**

Poinsettia Cut Stemware

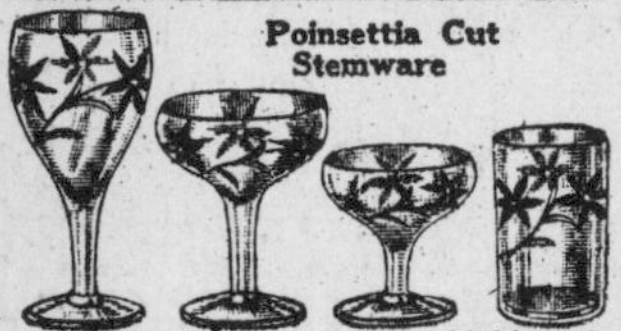

Thin blown crystal glass, highly polished, with one-piece drawn stems. Each piece is cut with three large silver gray poinsettias with silver gray leaves and stems. The popular Fifth Avenue shape.
35K1410—Water Goblet. Height, 6⅞ in. Weight, packed, 4¾ lbs. Per set of six... **$1.80**
35K1411—Tall Footed Sherbet. Height, 4⅞ in. Weight, packed, 4½ pounds. Per set of six... **$1.76**
35K1412—Low Footed Sherbet. Height, 3⅜ inches. Weight, packed, 4 pounds. Per set of six... **$1.72**
35K1413—Standard Table Tumbler. Height, 3¾ in. Weight, packed, 4 lbs. Per set of six... **85c**
35K1414—Tall Lemonade or Iced Tea Tumbler. Height, 5½ in. Weight, packed, 4¼ lbs. Per set of six... **$1.25**

Daisy Cut Stemware

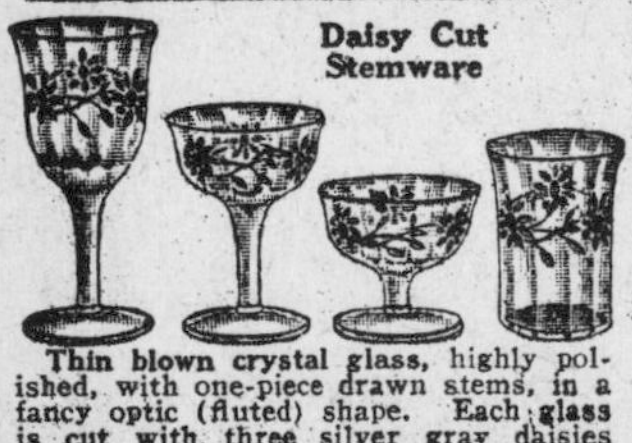

Thin blown crystal glass, highly polished, with one-piece drawn stems, in a fancy optic (fluted) shape. Each glass is cut with three silver gray daisies **with** bright polished centers and silver **gray** leaves and stems on a new and **graceful** shape.
35K1420—Water Goblet. Height, 6½ in. Wt., packed, 5 lbs. Per set of six... **$2.20**
35K1421—Tall Footed Sherbet. Height, 4⅛ in. Wt., packed, 4½ lbs. Per set of six... **$2.18**
35K1422—Low Footed Sherbet. Height, 3 in. Weight, packed, 4 lbs. Per set of six... **$2.15**
35K1423—Standard Table Tumbler. Height, 3¾ in. Weight, packed, 4½ lbs. Per set of six... **$1.15**
35K1424—Tall Lemonade or Iced Tea Tumbler. Height, 5½ in. Weight, packed, 4¾ lbs. Per set of six... **$1.63**

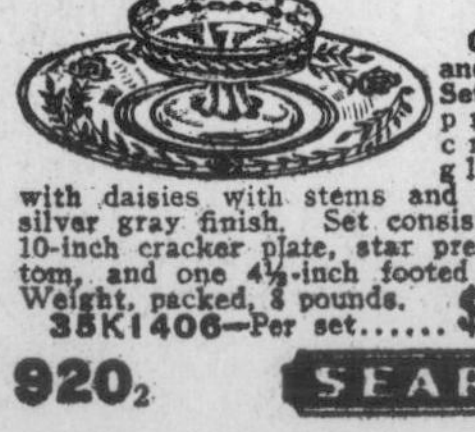

Cheese and Cracker Set. Thin pressed crystal glass cut with daisies with stems and leaves in silver gray finish. Set consists of one 10-inch cracker plate, star pressed bottom, and one 4½-inch footed compote. Weight, packed, 3 pounds.
35K1406—Per set... **$1.35**

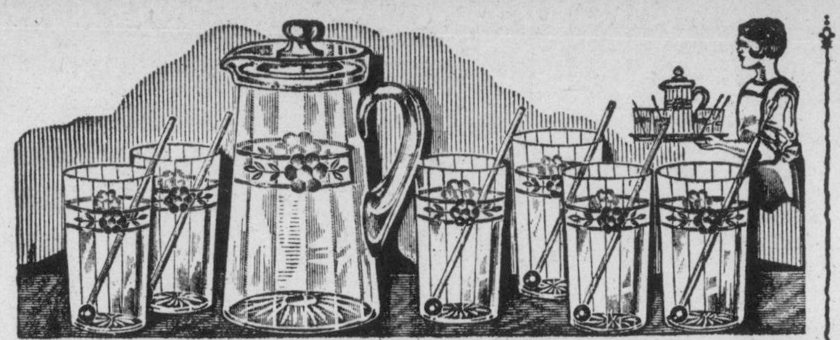

14-Piece Iced Tea or Lemonade Set. One 10-inch optic covered pitcher, six tall iced tea or lemonade glasses and six sippers with red bulbs representing cherries. Cut glass conventional floral border and bands in silver gray finish. Wt., pckd., 14 lbs.
35K1407... **$2.50**

GENUINE HEAVY CUT GLASS

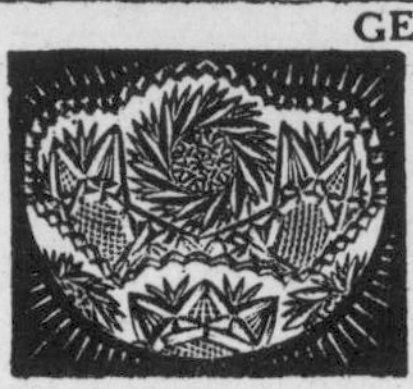

8-In. Buzz Star Salad Bowl
Cut around the side with three large buzz stars and deep cut and polished miter lines forming hob stars with hob nail center. Bottom cut with large hob star with deep cut and polished lines. Notched cut edge. Weight, pkd., 6 pounds.
35K1408... $2.98

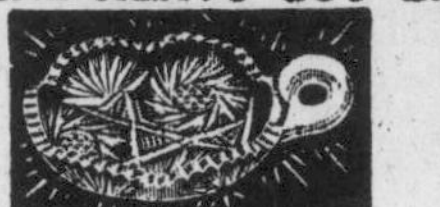

Handled Nappies
Cut with three whirling stars and three fan cuttings with heavy mitered lines, all highly polished notched cut edge.
35K1415—5-inch. Weight, packed, 3 pounds... **$1.75**
35K1416—6-inch. Weight, packed, 3½ pounds... **$2.10**

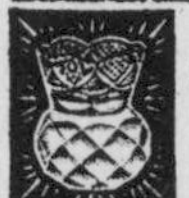

Toothpick Holder
Clear crystal glass highly polished. Diamond cut bottom. Fancy pressed top, notched edge. Weight, packed, 1 pound.
35K1417... 65c

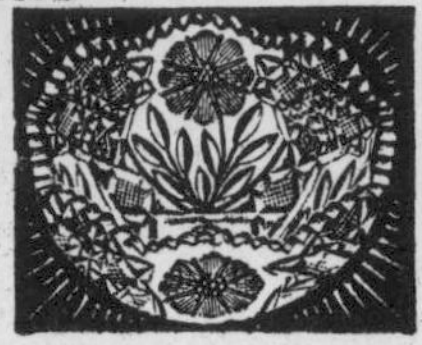

8-Inch Daisy Salad Bowl
Cut around the side and bottom with five large silver gray daisies with polished centers and deep cut and polished leaves and stems. Between the daisies is a diamond and hob star cutting. Notched cut edge. Weight, packed, 6 pounds.
35K1409... $4.25

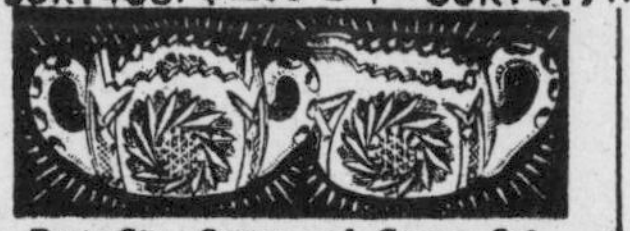

Buzz Star Sugar and Cream Set
Cut on each side with a large buzz star with silver gray rays and polished diamond and miter cut lines. The bottom is cut with large hob star and polished miter lines. Notched cut edge and handles. Height, 3 in. Wt., pkd., 4 lbs.
35K1418—Per set... **$3.98**

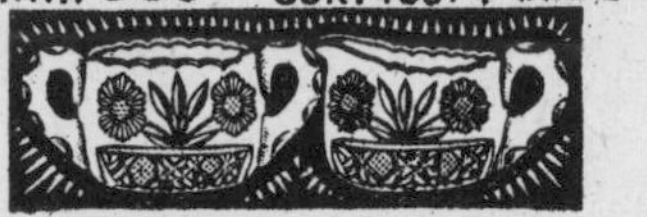

Floral Sugar and Cream Set
Cut with two large silver gray daisies with bright polished leaves and stems. Diamond design and miter cut border around the bottom. Cut star bottom and notched cut edge and handles. Height, 3 inches. Weight, packed, 5 pounds.
35K1419—Per set... **$4.75**

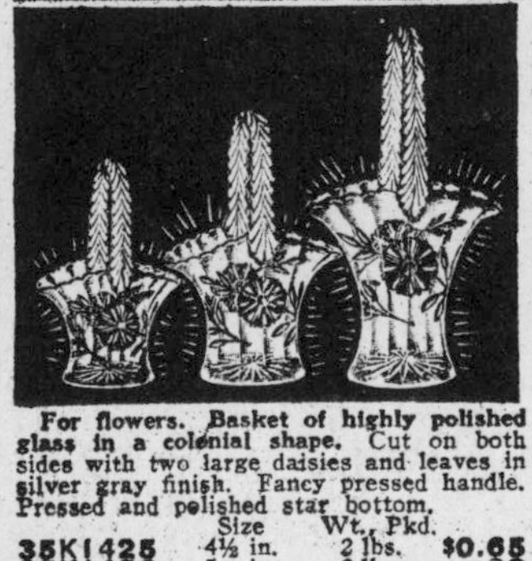

For flowers. Basket of highly polished glass in a colonial shape. Cut on both sides with two large daisies and leaves in silver gray finish. Fancy pressed handle. Pressed and polished star bottom.

	Size	Wt., Pkd.	
35K1425	4½ in.	2 lbs.	$0.65
35K1426	5 in.	3 lbs.	[illegible]
35K1427	6 in.	4 lbs.	1.[illegible]

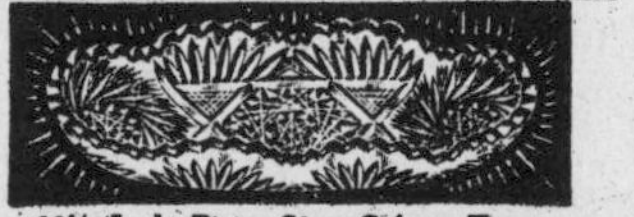

10½-Inch Buzz Star Celery Tray
Cut on each end with a large buzz star with deep cut and polished miter lines, large hob star with deep cut and polished lines in center. Notched cut edges. Weight, packed, 5 pounds.
35K1428... $2.35

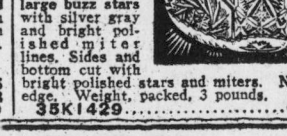

8-Inch Bon-bon Dish
Cut with two large buzz stars with silver gray and bright polished miter lines. Sides and bottom cut with bright polished stars and miters. Notched cut edge. Weight, packed, 3 pounds.
35K1429... $1.98

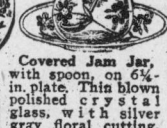

Footed Whipped Cream Set. 5-inch footed bowl, one 6½-inch plate and a spoon. Made of thin pressed glass cut with sprays of roses in silver gray finish. Wt., packed, 4 pounds.
35K1435
$1.25

Daisy Cut Salad or Desert Plates. Thin pressed crystal glass. Each piece has three sprays consisting of daisies with stems and leaves in silver gray finish. Pressed star bottom. Set consists of six 8-inch plates. Weight, packed, 6 pounds.
35K1436—Per set of six... **$3.35**

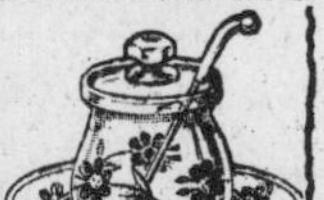

Covered Jam Jar, with spoon, on 6¼-in. plate. Thin blown polished crystal glass, with silver gray floral cutting. Wt., pkd., 4 lbs.
35K1437. Per set... **75c**

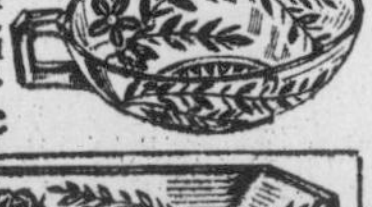

6-Inch Handled Nappy. Cut with a rose and leaf design in silver gray finish on both sides. Pressed star bottom. Weight, packed, 2 lbs.
35K1438... 75c

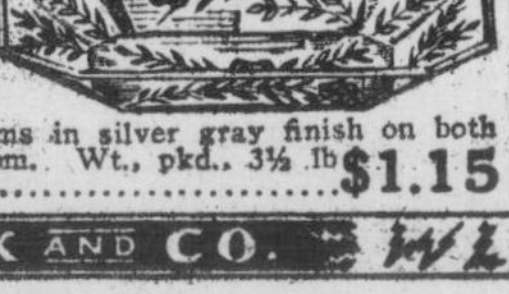

10½-Inch Octagon Shape Celery Tray. With three sprays of rambler rose design with leaves and stems in silver gray finish on both sides and bottom. Wt., pkd., 3½ lb.
35K1439... $1.15

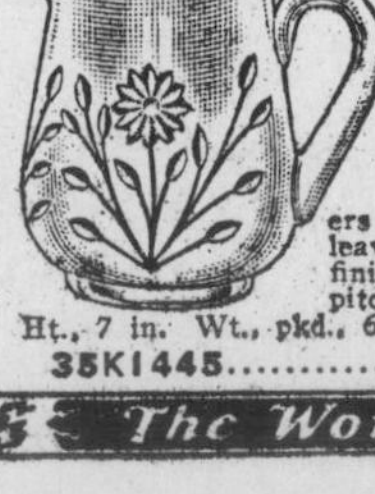

Cut Glass Water Pitcher
Thin blown crystal glass, cut with three sprays of flowers with stems and leaves in silver gray finish. Capacity of pitcher, ½ gallon. Ht., 7 in. Wt., pkd., 6 lbs.
35K1445... 98c

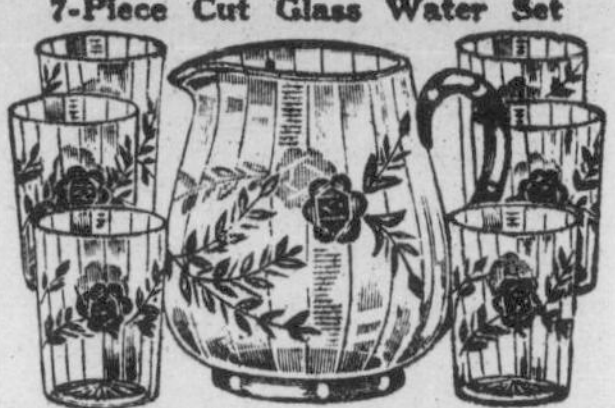

7-Piece Cut Glass Water Set
Two-quart 7½-inch fancy shape pitcher and six ½-pint tumblers. Each piece is cut with a spray of conventional flowers with stems and leaves in silver gray finish. Wt., packed, 8 lbs.
35K1446... $1.98

Conventional Floral Cut Stemware

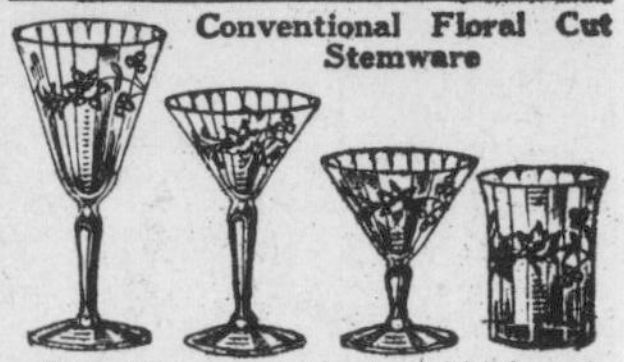

Thin blown crystal glass highly polished with one-piece drawn stem in fancy optic (fluted) cone shape. Each glass is cut with three flowers and buds and stems in silver gray finish.
35K1430—Water Goblets. Height, 7 inches. Weight, packed, 4½ lbs. Per set of six... **$2.38**
35K1431—Tall Footed Sherbets. Height, 4½ inches. Weight, packed, 4½ lbs. Per set of six... **$2.35**
35K1432—Low Footed Sherbets. Height, 3½ inches. Weight, packed, 4 lbs. Per set of six... **$2.33**
35K1433—Standard Table Tumblers. Height, 4 inches. Weight, packed, 4 lbs. Per set of six... **$1.48**
25K1434—Tall Lemonade or Iced Tea Tumblers. Height, 5⅝ in. Weight, packed, 4¼ lbs. Per set of six... **$1.65**

Plate Etched Stemware

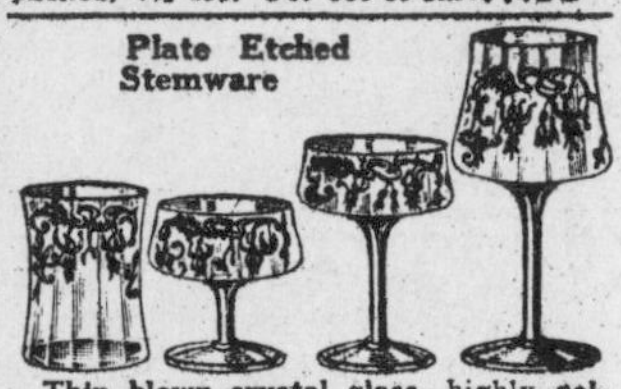

Thin blown crystal glass, highly polished, in a new aristocratic optic (fluted) shape. Solid one-piece drawn stems. Beautifully decorated with a genuine plate etched border in fuchsia design. A very high grade line. Rich and handsome glassware.
35K1440—Water Goblet. Height, 7 inches. Weight, packed, 5½ lbs. Per set of six... **$4.20**
35K1441—Tall Footed Sherbet. Height, 4½ inches. Weight, packed, 4¾ lbs. Per set of six... **$4.18**
35K1442—Low Footed Sherbet. Height, 3½ inches. Weight, packed, 4¼ lbs. Per set of six... **$4.08**
35K1443—Standard Table Tumbler. Height, 3¾ inches. Weight, packed, 4½ lbs. Per set of six... **$2.58**
35K1444—Tall Lemonade or Iced Tea Tumbler. Height, 5½ in. Weight, packed, 5 lbs. Per set of six... **$3.00**

Floral Cluster Cut Stemware

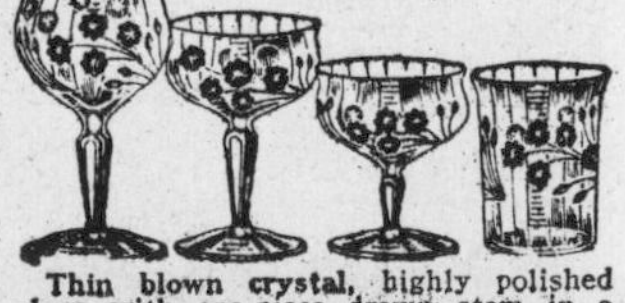

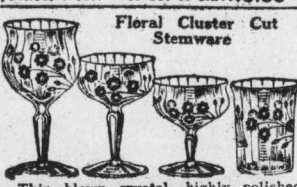

Thin blown crystal, highly polished glass with one-piece drawn stem in a fancy optic (fluted) shape. Each piece is cut with three sprays of flowers, leaves and stems in silver gray finish. The leaves are cut and polished.
35K1450—Water Goblets. Height, 6½ inches. Weight, packed, 5 lbs. Per set of six... **$3.13**
35K1451—Tall Footed Sherbets. Height, 5¼ inches. Weight, packed, 4½ lbs. Per set of six... **$3.10**
35K1452—Low Footed Sherbets. Height, 3½ inches. Weight, packed, 4 lbs. Per set of six... **$3.08**
35K1453—Standard Table Tumblers. Height, 4⅛ inches. Weight, packed, 4½ lbs. Per set of six... **$2.13**
35K1454—Tall Lemonade or Iced Tea Tumblers. Height, 5⅝ in. Weight, packed, 4¾ lbs. Per set of six... **$2.38**

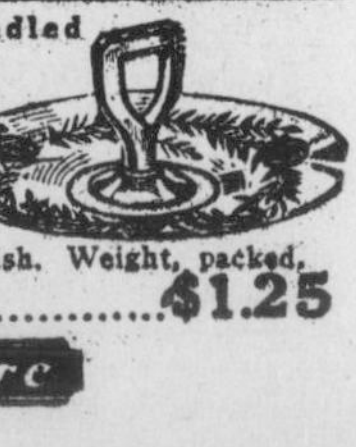

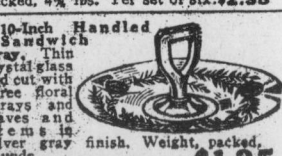

10-Inch Handled Sandwich Tray. Thin crystal glass and cut with three floral sprays and leaves and stems in silver gray finish. Weight, packed, 3 pounds.
35K1447... $1.25

Choice Pieces for Your Table

Your Choice 98¢

Seven-Piece Cut Glass Water Set, 98c
The biggest and best value ever offered in a cut glass water set. Often sold elsewhere for as high as $1.50. Thin crystal glass and cut with a beautiful conventional design in silver gray finish. One 2-quart 8-inch tankard pitcher and six tumblers to match. Weight, packed, 9 pounds.
35K1600—Per set.........98c

11-Inch Sandwich Tray. Thin rose color glass in satin finish with two cut-out handles.
35K1601 ....98c

Fancy Elephant Ornament. Imported china decorated in natural color with an iridescent glaze. Height, 4½ inches. Weight, packed, 1¼ lbs.
35K1602 ....98c

Individual Salt Dips. Pressed clear crystal glass, cut with polished star and fern leaf between silver gray vertical lines. Notched cut edge. Weight, packed, 2 pounds.
35K1603—Set of 6........98c

8½-Inch Pie Plate. Mounted in a pierced solid brass nickel plated frame with metal handles and feet. The dish is of clear glass of heat resisting quality in optic fluted shape. The corrugated glass bottom permits the heat to circulate and bake an even crust top and bottom. Weight, packed, 4 pounds.
35K1604 ....98c

3½-Inch Candlesticks. Pea green colored glass in satin finish, in the new opera squat shape, five inches across bottom of base. Weight, packed, 4 pounds.
35K1605—Per pair.98c

Tall 16½-Inch Flower Vase, in a trumpet shape made of tangerine iridescent glass. Weight, packed, 5½ pounds.
35K1606 ....98c

8-Inch Sweet Pea Vase. Rolled edge and optic fluted design in burnt orange color. Decorated around the top edge with a black border with imitation enameled flowers and yellow lines. Wt., packed, 4 lbs.
35K1607
98c

Glass Candy Jar. Pressed blue iridescent color glass in colonial design. Height, 9 inches. Capacity, ½ pound. Wt., 4 lbs.
35K1608 98c

Artificial Fruit Assortment. Very ornamental when used in fruit bowls for table decorations. One each, apple, orange, tangerine, peach, pear, plum, banana and a bunch of grapes. Weight, packed, 1 pound.
35K1611—Per box.........98c

Floral Sugar and Cream Set. Pressed rose colored crystal glass. Each piece is cut on both sides with floral sprays and leaves in silver gray finish. Height 3 in. Weight, packed, 4 pounds.
35K1612 Per set 98c

4-Inch Jardiniere with Roses. Rose color pottery, glazed inside and out. Fitted with five artificial roses, ferns and moss. Can also be used as a bulb bowl. Wt., pkd., 2 lbs.
35K1613 ....98c

Colonial Footed Sherbet

For ice cream or sundaes. Pressed crystal glass, highly polished, in colonial shape. Heavy pressed crystal bottom. Height, 3 inches. Weight, per dozen, 8 pounds.
35K1614—Per dozen.................98c

5-Piece Smoker Set. Blue colored iridescent pressed glass. One 5-inch ash tray with cigarette snuffer, match box holder and four individual ash trays. Weight, packed, 4 pounds.
35K1615 ....98c

18-Piece Tumbler Assortment

Clear thin pressed crackle glass design. Six 5-ounce grape juice glasses, six 9-ounce table tumblers and six 12-ounce iced tea or lemonade tumblers. Weight, packed, 14 pounds.
35K1617—Tumbler Assortment 98c

Tall Footed Sherbets. Pressed glass in crackle effect. Star pressed bottom. Wt., packed, 9 lbs.
35K1616 98c Set of 10...

Sherbet Set
Clear pressed glass in crackle glass design. Six cone shape sherbets and six 6¼-inch plates. Weight, packed, 10 pounds.
35K1619 Per set.........98c

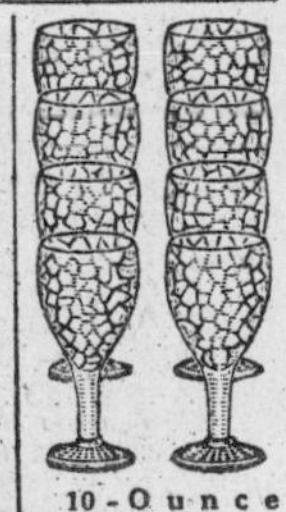

10-Ounce Pressed Glass Tall Footed Goblets. Thin pressed glass in crackle design. Star pressed bottom. Weight, packed, 9 lbs.
35K1618 Set of 8 goblets.98c

8½-Inch Footed Colored Glass Fruit or Flower Bowl. Burnt orange colored glass decorated around the edge with an enameled floral decoration on a black border between two gold lines. Height of bowl, 5 inches. Weight, packed, 6 pounds.
35K1610 ....98c

7-Piece Celery Set. Clear pressed glass in colonial shape. One 10¼-inch celery tray with pressed design in bottom and six footed and handled individual salt dips. Weight, pkd., 5 lbs.
35K1620.................98c

10-Inch Handled Sandwich or Lunch Tray. Thin pea green colored glass in satin finish in a colonial shape. Weight, pkd., 7 lbs.
35K1621.................98c

Hand Painted Bon Bon

6-Inch Heart Shape Handled Bon Bon Dish. Pea green satin finish colored glass and decorated with three hand painted rose and floral decoration. Weight, packed, 2 pounds.
35K1622 ....98c

Salt and Pepper Shakers. Cut and pressed design. Fitted with glass tops. Height, 3 inches. Weight, packed, 1½ pounds.
35K1623...98c

Whipped Cream or Mayonnaise Set. One 6-inch dish and glass spoon made of pressed tangerine colored glass in crackle effect. Weight, packed, 5 pounds.
35K1624 ....98c

Bed Room Water Bottle and Tumbler. Thin blown burnt orange colored glass, decorated with a cockatoo and black lines. The tumbler acts as a cover when not in use. Weight, packed, 4 pounds. 
35K1625 Per set.........98c

9-Inch Bud Vases. Glass, in two-tone color, amethyst top and green foot. Cut with a floral spray with leaves in silver gray finish. Weight, packed, 3 pounds.
35K1626 Per set of two vases.....98c

98¢ Special Bargains in Plain White Tableware 98¢

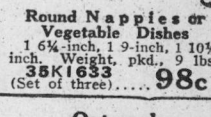

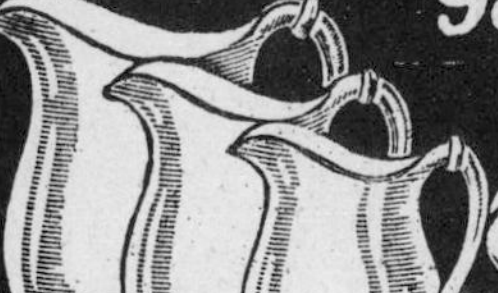

Milk or Cream Pitcher Set. Capacity 1-pint, 3-pint and 4-pint. Weight, packed, 10 pounds.
35K1627—(Set of three) 98c

Plates. 7½-inch Pie Plates. Weight, packed, 5 pounds.
35K1628—1 doz. 98c
Plates. 9¼-inch Dinner Plates. Weight, packed, 11 pounds.
35K1629 (Set of eight) 98c

Ovide Tea Cups and Saucers. Size, ½-pint. Weight, packed, 6 pounds.
35K1630 (Set of six) 98c

Oyster or Soup Bowls. Capacity, 1½ pints. Weight, pkd., 6 pounds.
35K1631 (Set of six)....98c

9½-Inch Rim Shape Soup Plates. Weight, packed, 9 pounds.
35K1632 (Set of six) 98c

Round Nappies or Vegetable Dishes. 1 6¼-inch, 1 9-inch, 1 10¼ inch. Weight, pkd., 9 lbs.
35K1633 (Set of three).....98c

Mush and Milk Bowls. Size, ¾-pint. Weight, packed, 7 pounds.
35K1634 (Set of six) 98c

FOR EVERYDAY USE
Pure white semi-porcelain in plain edge shape. For a larger assortment of plain white tableware see page 914.

Oatmeal Dishes. Size, 5½ inches. Wt., packed, 4 pounds.
35K1635 (Set of twelve)..98c

Useful Gifts at Unusual Prices

White Marble Figures

11-Inch Golden Iridescent Glass Footed Fruit Bowl. Deer, holly leaves and berries in raised relief. Height, 3½ in. Wt., packed, 4 lbs.
35K2100... **65c**

For Other Vases See Pages 765 and 766

Composition marble, representing a boy and girl reading from books. Height, 10 inches. Wt., packed, 8 pounds.
35K2110 Per pair..... **$1.75**

Composition marble, representing two girls reading from a book. Height, 11 inches. Weight, pkd., 7 lbs.
35K2111 **$1.50**

White Figure. Of composition marble, representing child and dog at play with ball. Size, 7x 11½ in. Weight, packed, 10 pounds.
35K2112.... **$1.48**

White Fern or Flower Urn. Composition marble. 12-inch bowl with four removable doves. Set on 7-inch pedestal. Filled with green air fern and artificial red roses. Weight, pkd., 11 pounds.
35K2113 Complete... **$2.95**

Composition marble, representing a boy and girl carrying fruit. Height, 9½ inches. Weight, packed, 7 pounds.
35K2114 Per pair **$1.45**

11-Inch Cut Glass Cake Plate and Pearl Handled Cake Server. Cut with four large silver gray daisies. The plated cake server has a mother of pearl handle. Wt., packed, 6 pounds.
35K2130 Per set **$2.75**

10-Inch Chromo Glass Flower Vase. Decorated with birds and flowers in many colors. Wt., pkd., 4¼ lbs.
35K2131 **55c**

10½-Inch Cut Glass Bud Vase. Thin blown crystal glass with gray floral cutting. Fitted with artificial color rosebuds. Weight, packed, 2 lbs.
35K2101 **95c**

Three-Piece Console Set 
Golden Iridescent Glass in Colonial Shape. One 12-inch fruit or flower bowl and two 11-inch flower vases to match. Weight, packed, 12 pounds.
35K2102—Set... **$1.65**

Hand Painted Glassware

Hand Painted Vanity Box. Clear glass. Has powder, rouge and lip stick compartments. Decorated with red roses and green leaves and gold band. Length, 6½ inches. Weight, packed, 4 pounds.
35K2115... **$2.35**

Hand Painted Powder and Puff Box. Thin satin finish glass with blue, pink and golden colors. Puff in each box. Diameter, 4 in. Wt., pkd., 1 lb.
35K2116 **$1.75**

Hand Painted Powder Box. Rose pink satin finish glass with pink roses and blue flowers. Puff in each box. Height, 6 in. Wt., pkd., 3 lbs.
35K2117 **$2.75**

3-Piece Smoker Set. Green satin finish glass with hand painted yellow daisies and black leaves. One 6¼-inch tray, match holder, cigarette holder and ash tray with snuffers. Wt., pkd., 4 lbs.
35K2118... **$1.85**

Hand Painted Powder and Puff Box With Puff. Thin glass, satin finish. Pink flower and green leaves. Diam. box. 4 in. Wt., pkd., 1 lb.
35K2119 **$1.00**

Hand Painted Glass Powder Box. Hand painted floral design. Height and width, 3 inches. Wt. pkd., 3 lb.
35K2120 **50c**

Glass Aquariums
Mounted in a metal frame with four feet and decorated in olive green. The sides are clear glass.
35K2132—2-Gallon Capacity. Size 11x8x7 inches. Weight, packed, 9½ lbs. **$2.98**
35K2133—3-Gallon Capacity. Size, 12x8x8 inches. Weight, packed, 10½ pounds. **$3.65**
35K2134—4-Gallon Capacity. Size, 13x9x9 inches. Weight, packed, 12 pounds. **$4.25**

Salt and Pepper Shakers. White china covered with yellow matte gold. Height, 3¾ inches. Wt., pkd., 2 lbs.
35K2103 Per set **$2.25**

Salt and Pepper Shakers. White china covered with yellow matte gold. Height, 3½ inches. Wt., packed, 2 lbs.
35K2104 Per set **$2.75**

Salt and Pepper Shakers. White china. Tops are covered with yellow matte gold. Height, 3¼ in. Wt., pkd., 2 lbs.
35K2105 Per pair **$1.00**

Polychrome Book Ends. Of conventional design. The finish is antique verdigris bronze. Weight, pkd., 4 pounds.
35K2106...... **$1.25**

Hand Painted Candlesticks. Green satin finish glass decorated with black leaves. Height, 2¼ inches. Weight, packed, 2 pounds.
35K2121 Per pair **$1.35**

Satin finish glass. Decorated with a pink rose and green leaves. Powder box with puff and two perfume bottles.
35K2122... **$2.50**

3-Piece Rose Pink Vanity Set Wt. pkd., 10 lbs.

Rolled Edge Baby Plate and Handled Mug. Of cream color pottery and decorated with small "bunnies." The rolled edge prevents food from sliding off the plate. Wt., packed, 5 lbs.
35K2135 **$1.00**

Children's Cup and Saucer and Plate Set. One 7½-inch plate and a small cup and saucer. Of white semi-porcelain. Decorated with children in colors at play. Wt., pkd., 4 lbs.
35K2136 **58c**

Children's Cereal Set. One 6½-inch cereal bowl and handled mug, of white semi-porcelain. Decorated with children in colors at play. Weight, packed, 3 pounds.
35K2137......... **65c**

For other gift suggestions see page 924

Individual Salt Shaker Set. Six individual shakers with glass top. Hand painted rose with green leaves. Wt., pkd., 3 lbs.
35K2123......... **$3.50**

Salt and Pepper Shakers. Glass in a white satin finish and decorated with hand painted pink roses and green leaves. Glass tops. Ht., 3 in. Wt., pkd., 2 lbs.
35K2124—Pr.. **$1.25**

Glass Sherbet Set. Iridescent glass with rainbow luster finish in optic (fluted) effect. Six 4-inch sherbets and six 6-in. plates. Weight, packed, 8 pounds.
35K2138 Per set... **$1.25**

Grape Juice Set. Heavy pressed crystal glass, floral decoration. 10-inch glass tray, grape juice bottle and stopper and six footed grape juice glasses. Wt., pkd., 10¾ lbs.
35K2107—Per set....... **$1.35**

7-Piece Salad or Berry Set. Of American pure white semi-porcelain. Tan lattice border with panels of pink roses and a gold band. 8¾-inch bowl and six 5-inch berry dishes. Weight, packed, 10 lbs.
35K2125.................. **$1.38**

7-Piece Cold Meat Set. Of English ivory body semi-porcelain in an octagon shape and decorated in blue paneled design. 12-inch meat platter and six 8-inch plates. Weight, packed, 8 pounds.
35K2126.................. **$2.95**

3-Piece Console Set. Made of glass decorated in solid burnt orange color with black lines.

Three-Piece Table or Console Set. 10-inch compote and two 8-inch candlesticks, red candles. Jade green glass with black base. Weight, packed, 9 pounds.
35K2108 Three-piece set... **$1.45**
35K2109—Banquet Candles. Box of 12. Weight, packed, 2¼ pounds.... **35c**

8-Inch Cut Glass Candlesticks. Of clear pressed glass, in a Colonial style. Weight, packed, 5¼ pounds.
35K2127—Set.. **$1.65**

5-Piece Console Set. Burnt orange color glass. 8-inch flower bowl with glass removable flower holder. Removable black base and four 3½-in. candlesticks. Weight, packed, 12 pounds.
35K2128......... **$1.50**

5-Inch Colonial Candlesticks. Of crystal glass, cut with silver gray flowers, leaves and stems. Weight, packed, 3 pounds.
35K2129 **75c**

One 6-inch flower bowl with black base and two 7½-inch candlesticks with pair red candles. Weight, packed, 4 lbs.
35K2139.... **$1.25**

Gifts for All Occasions

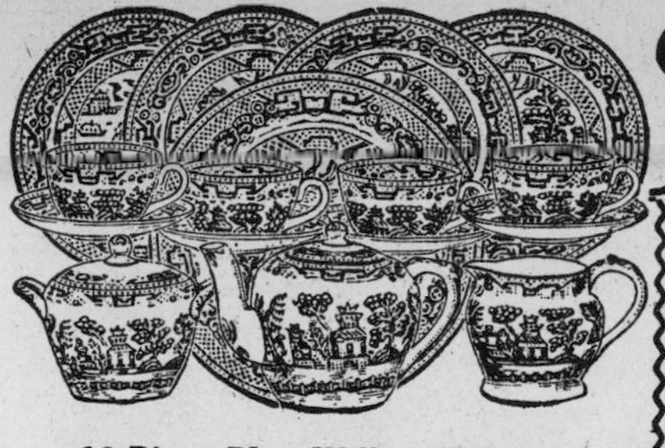

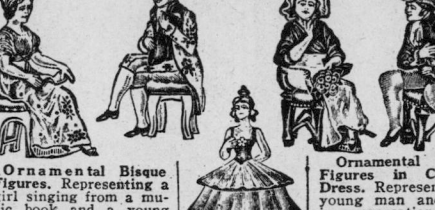

18-Piece Blue Willow Tea Set

Four tea cups and saucers, four 8-inch breakfast plates, one 9¾-inch cake plate, one teapot (2-pieces) 4-cup capacity, one covered sugar bowl (2-pieces) and one cream pitcher. Imported English semi-porcelain. The decoration is the old and popular design and very appropriate for a tea set. Weight, packed, 15 pounds.

35K2500—Per set **$5.12**

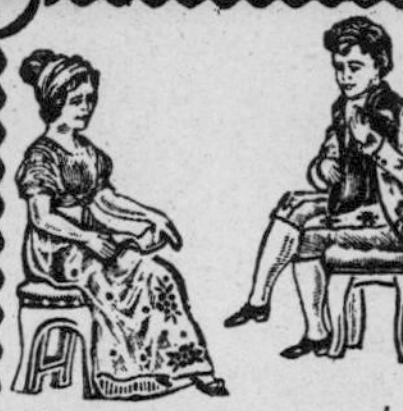

Ornamental Bisque Figures. Representing a girl singing from a music book and a young man playing a string instrument. Imported china. Decorated in blue and pink colors. Height, 7½ in. Wt., pkd., 5 lbs.

35K2504 Per pair.... **$3.35**

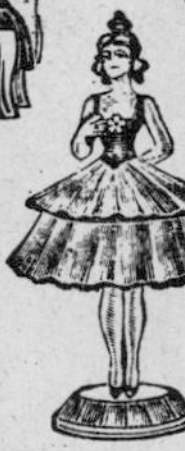

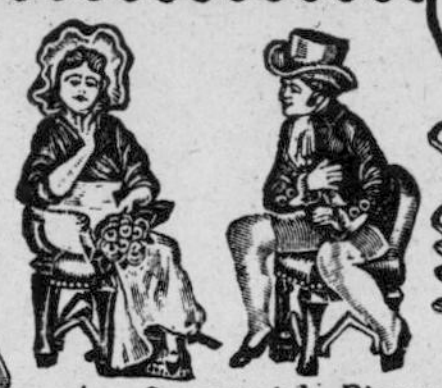

Ornamental Bisque Figures in Colonial Dress. Representing a young man and lady in conversation. Imported china and decorated in red, blue and tan colors. Height, 7¼ inches. Weight, packed, 5 pounds.

35K2506 Per pair.... **$3.85**

Ornamental Bisque Figured Puff Box. Representing a young lady in a party dress of light green, standing on a pedestal of luster green and black. The top ruffle of the dress is the cover of the powder box. Imported china. Height, 8 in. Weight, packed, 2½ pounds.

35K2505—Each **$1.98**

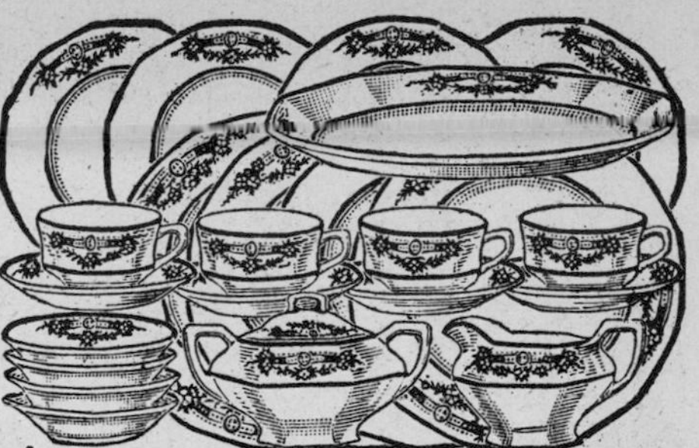

24-Piece Apple Blossom and Gold Dinner Set

Decoration of delicate tan color scrolls with a small pink rose on a blue background, in the center. Garlands of pink apple blossoms with green foliage suspend from each end of the scrolls. Each piece is trimmed with bright gold. Made of American semi-porcelain in a colonial shape. Set consists of:

4 Tea Cups
4 Tea Saucers
4 Pie Plates
4 Dinner Plates
4 Sauce Dishes
1 Sugar Bowl (2-pcs.)
1 1-Pt. Cream Pitcher
1 11½-Inch Platter

Weight, packed, 17 pounds.

35K2519—Per set **$4.60**

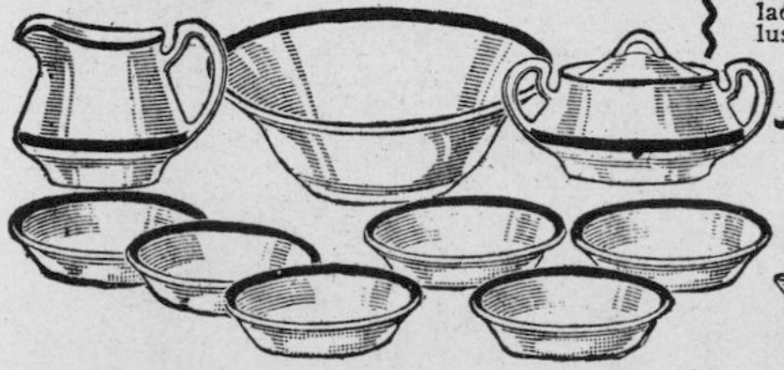

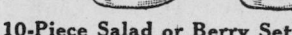

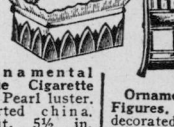

10-Piece Salad or Berry Set

8½-inch salad or berry bowl, six 5-inch sauce dishes, covered sugar bowl (2-pieces) and 1-pint cream pitcher. American semi-porcelain. Decorated with a band of bright gold. Weight, packed, 8 pounds.

35K2501 .... **$1.95**

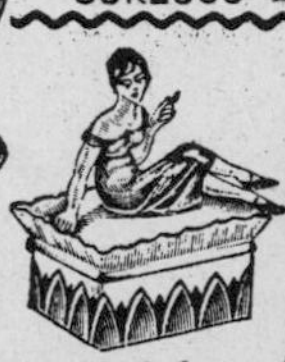

Ornamental Bisque Cigarette Box. Pearl luster. Imported china. Height, 5½ in. Weight, packed, 2½ pounds.

35K2507 Each.... **$1.75**

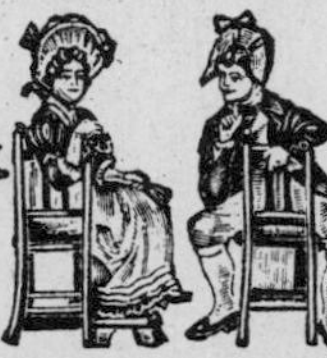

Ornamental Bisque Figures. Imported china decorated in red, blue and pink. Height, 6 in. Wt., packed, 4½ lbs.

35K2508 Per pair.... **$2.25**

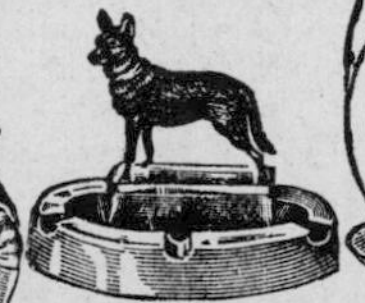

Ornamental Bisque Cigar and Ash Tray. Imported china, with metal police dog in bronze color. Height, 5¼ in. Width of tray, 6½ in. Weight, packed, 3 pounds.

35K2509 Each.... **$2.75**

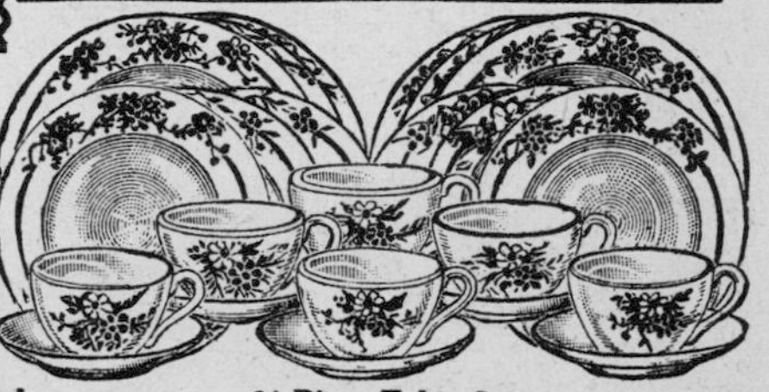

24-Piece Table Set

Decorated with sprays of small blue, pink and yellow garden flowers and buds with green and black leaves. The decorations are connected with blue lines forming a border. The ware is of first quality American semi-porcelain. Weight, packed, 14 pounds.

6 Tea Cups
6 Tea Saucers
6 Bread and Butter Plates
6 Tea or Salad Plates

35K2520—Set.................... **$3.20**

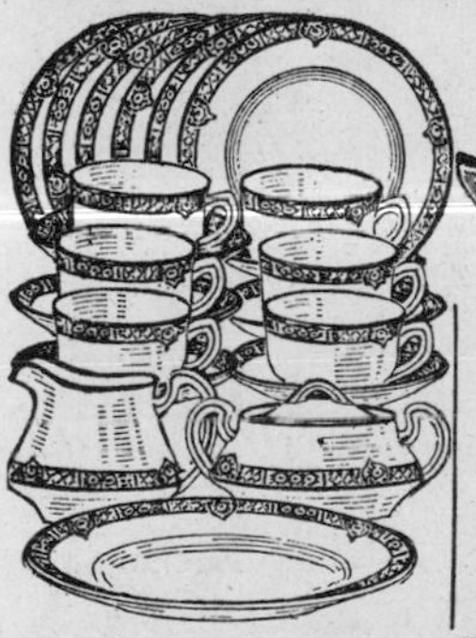

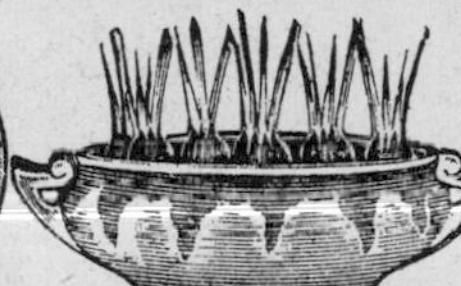

7½-Inch Bulb Bowl. Earthenware with fancy handles. Decorated in a pale blue matte glaze with darker blue border. Height of bowl, 3½ in. Wt., pkd., 4 lbs.

35K2510 Each.... **$1.98**

Bulbs not included in price.

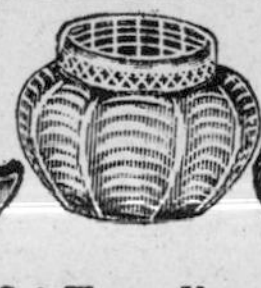

Cut Flower Vase. Imported heavy glass in a pearl luster with a removable plated metal frame which holds the cut flowers upright. Height, 4½ inches; width, 6½ inches. Wt., packed, 5 lbs.

35K2511 Each.... **$2.25**

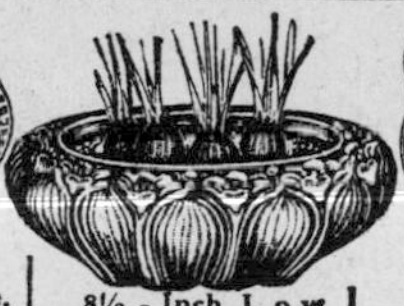

8½-Inch Low Footed Bulb Bowl. Earthenware in brown and blue colors in embossed flower and leaf design. Opening is 6¼ in. Height, 3 in. Wt., packed, 4½ lbs.

35K2512 Each.... **$1.19**

Bulbs not included in price.

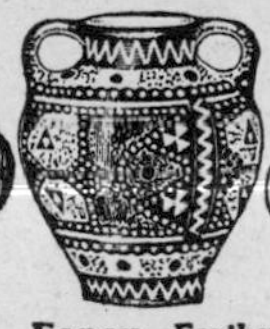

Fancy Earthenware Flower Vase. Of imported earthenware and decorated with a mottled blue and tan decoration. Height, 7 inches. Weight, packed, 6½ pounds.

35K2513 Each.... **$1.75**

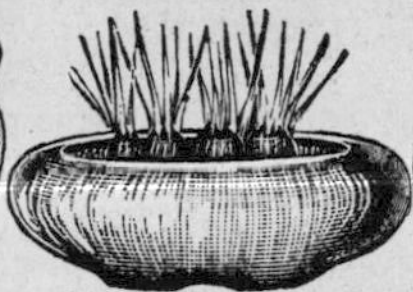

9-Inch Low Footed Bowl. Earthenware in a mixed gray and green color. The opening is 6¾ in. Height, 3 inches. Weight, packed, 4½ pounds.

35K2514 Each.... **$1.50**

Bulbs not included in price.

22-Piece Lunch Set

Six tea cups and saucers, six 8-inch tea plates, covered sugar bowl (2 pieces), 1-pint cream pitcher and 11½-inch platter. American semi-porcelain. Decorated with a black and tan lattice border with panels of pink roses. Bright gold line around edge of each piece. Wt., packed, 16 lbs.

35K2502 Per set **$5.85**

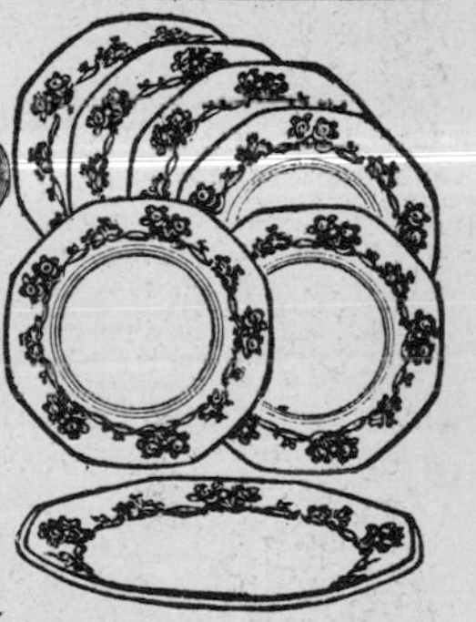

7-Piece Cake Set

9½-inch cake plate and six 7-inch serving plates. Of American semi-porcelain. Decorated with a border of sprays of large red conventional flowers with black leaves. The back of the leaves are yellow and part of them are turned over to show a yellow color. Each cluster of flowers is connected with slate color stems. Weight, packed, 9 lbs.

35K2521 Per set......... **$1.50**

Our Famous 48-Piece White Set

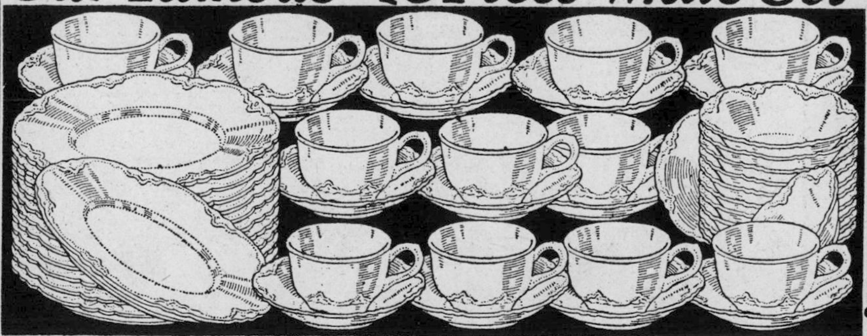

Look—Less Than 9c Apiece

Will give maximum service since it is made of pure, non-pourous semi-porcelain, noted for strength and durability. Attractively embossed around edges, and you can easily match additional pieces at a very small cost from our Snowflake White Dinnerware, described on page 914, to complete this set.

You will never tire of this practical and artistic pure white dinnerware. A most remarkable value, since it comprises 48 of those pieces most frequently used. 12 dinner plates, 12 sauce dishes, 12 tea cups, 12 tea saucers. 48 pieces in all for only $3.95.

35K2515—48-Piece Assortment of White Semi-Porcelain Dinnerware. Weight, packed for shipment, 35 pounds.............................. **$3.95**

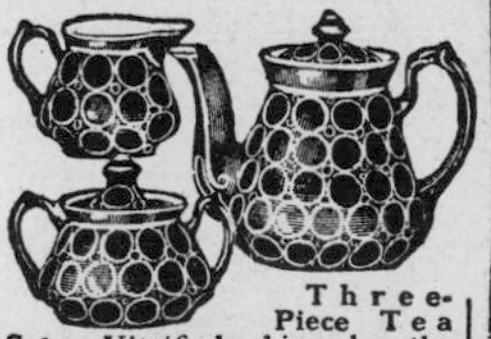

Three-Piece Tea Set. Vitrified china by the Hall China Company. Set consists of one 5-cup teapot, sugar bowl and cream pitcher. Decorated all over in cobalt blue with circles of bright gold. Gold traced handles. Weight, packed, 9 lbs.

35K2503—Per set **$3.75**
35K2525—Teapot only. Wt., packed, 5 lbs.... **$1.98**
35K2527—Sugar and Cream Set only. Weight, packed, 4 pounds...... **$1.80**

Imported English Jet Teapot

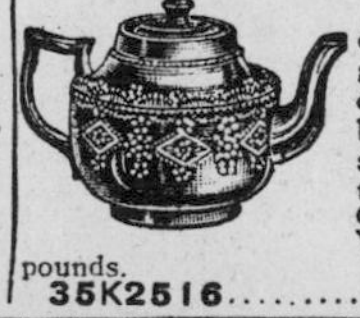

Earthenware, decorated with a green design with colored enamel beading. Handle, spout and cover traced with gold. Capacity, 6 cups. Weight, packed, 5 pounds.

35K2516 .... **$1.25**

English Style Tea Pot

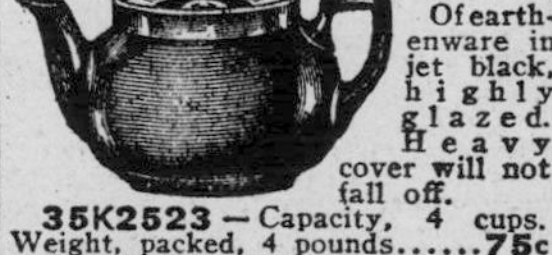

Of earthenware in jet black, highly glazed. Heavy cover will not fall off.

35K2523—Capacity, 4 cups. Weight, packed, 4 pounds...... **75c**
35K2524—Capacity, 6 cups. Weight, packed, 5 pounds...... **85c**

Imported English Jet Teapot

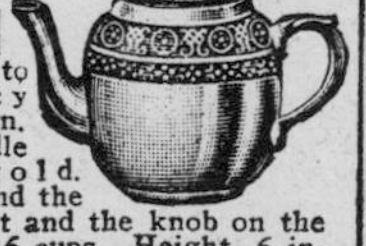

Decorated with colored enamel beads to form a fancy border design. Spout and handle traced with gold. Gold line around the body of the pot and the knob on the lid. Capacity, 6 cups. Height, 6 in. Weight, packed, 4 pounds.

35K2518 .... **98c**

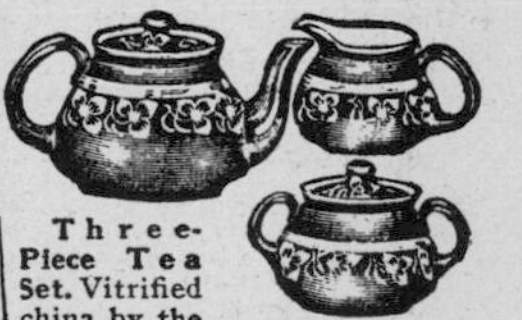

Three-Piece Tea Set. Vitrified china by the Hall China Company. Set consists of 4-cup teapot, sugar bowl and cream pitcher. Decorated all over in a red brown color with gold bands and clover leaves. Gold trimmed edges and handles. Weight, packed, 9 pounds.

35K2522 Per set **$3.25**
35K2526—Teapot only. (Wt., pkd., 5 lbs.).. **$1.80**
35K2528—Sugar and Cream Set only. Weight, packed, 4 pounds.... **$1.48**

Imported German Fancy China

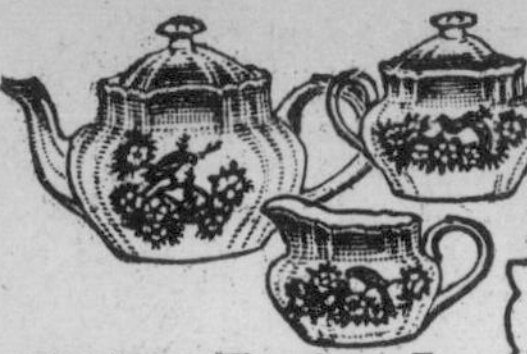

Three-Piece Tea Sets. Teapot, sugar bowl and cream pitcher of translucent china and decorated with assorted birds and flowers. Light gray luster around top edges. Weight, pkd., 6 pounds.
35K3600—Per set **$1.48**

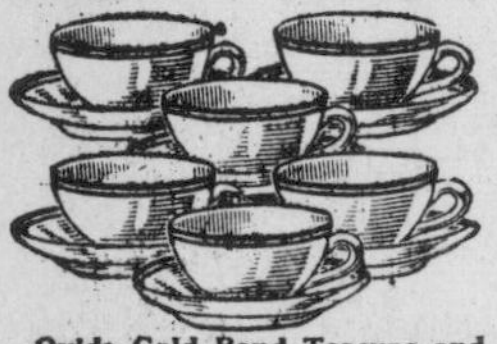

Ovide Gold Band Teacups and Saucers decorated with a wide band and a hairline of bright gold. Capacity, ⅓ pint. Weight, packed, 6 pounds.
35K3601—Set of 6 cups and saucers. **$1.72**

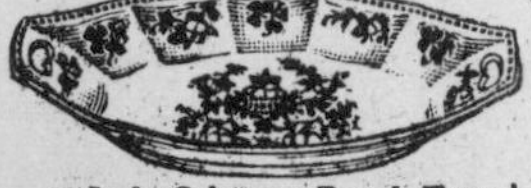

13-Inch Cake or Bread Tray with open handles decorated with a conventional floral design of many colors. Alternating in the panels are gold and floral sprays. Weight, packed, 5 pounds.
35K3602 ...... **$1.25**

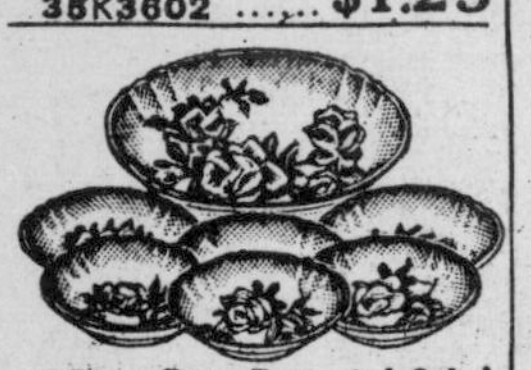

7-Piece Rose Decorated Salad or Berry Set. 9-inch bowl and six 5½-inch sauce dishes decorated with large red and pink roses and green leaves. Weight, packed, 8 pounds.
35K3603—Set... **$1.50**
35K3604—Salad Bowl only. (Weight, packed, 3½ pounds) **65c**

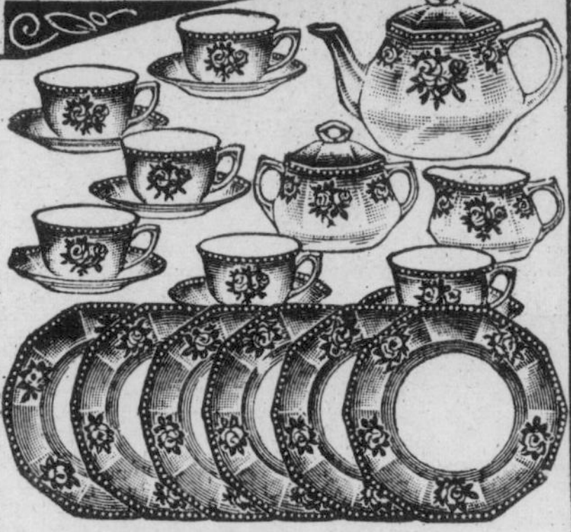

23-Piece China Tea Set

Imported china in a plain edge shape. Decoration of yellow and burnt orange between black hairlines and floral spray of conventional flowers. Teapot, covered sugar bowl, cream pitcher, six tea cups and saucers and six tea plates. Weight, packed, 18 lbs.
35K3608—Per set........ **$6.75**

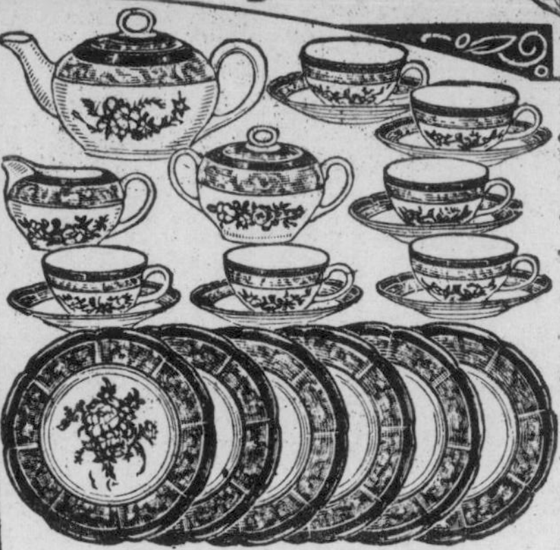

23-Piece China Tea Set

Imported china in a fancy shape. Decoration of conventional flower designs of red, yellow, lavender and green on a burnt orange luster. Teapot, covered sugar bowl, cream pitcher, six tea cups and saucers and six tea plates. Weight, packed, 18 lbs.
35K3609 .... **$3.98**

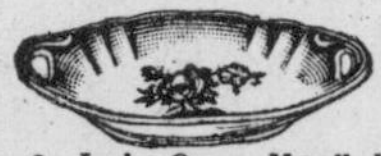

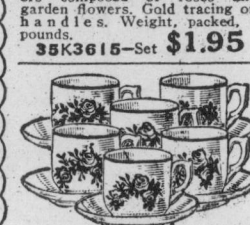

9-Inch Open Handled Spoon Tray or Olive Dish. Decorated with a tan luster and center with sprays of garden flowers. Wt., pkd., 2 lbs.
35K3605 .... **55c**

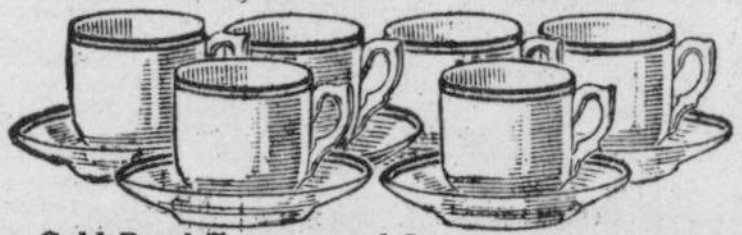

Gold Band Teacups and Saucers decorated with a wide band and a hairline of gold. Capacity, ⅓ pint. Weight, packed, 6 pounds.
35K3610—Set of 6 cups and saucers........................ **$1.59**

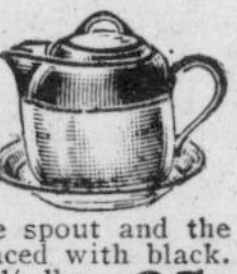

Syrup Pitcher and Plate. Decorated in pale blue luster with a burnt orange border, a black line around the spout and the handles are traced with black. Wt., packed, 2½ lbs.
35K3612 .... **85c**

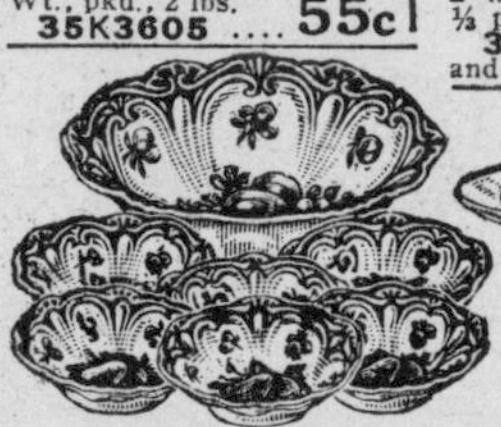

7-Piece Fancy Shape Salad or Berry Set. Large 10½-inch bowl and six 5½-inch sauce dishes, fancy decorations. Wt., packed, 8 lbs.
35K3606—Per set... **$1.98**
35K3607—Salad Bowl only. Wt., packed., 4 lbs.... **93c**

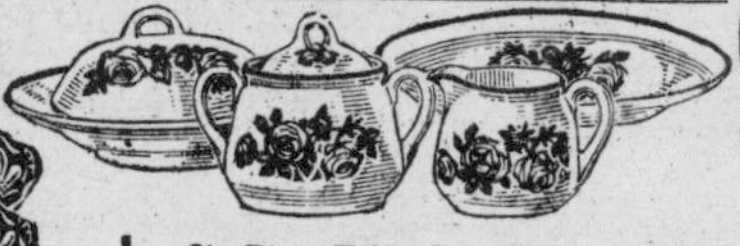

Six-Piece Table Set. Imported white china decorated with red and pink roses and rosebuds with green leaves and bright gold lines, handles traced with gold. Covered butter dish, covered sugar bowl, cream pitcher and a spoon tray. Wt., pkd., 8 lbs.
35K3611.................. **$1.25**

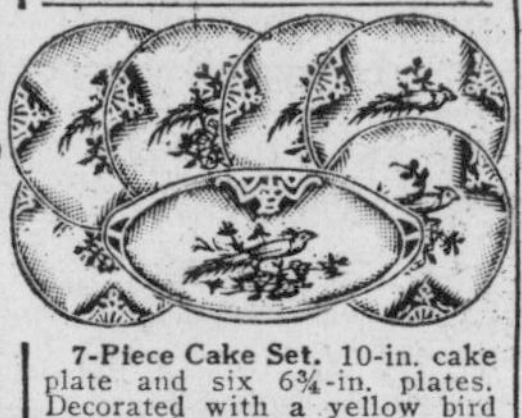

7-Piece Cake Set. 10-in. cake plate and six 6¾-in. plates. Decorated with a yellow bird and flowers on a background of green and tan luster. Wt., packed, 6 lbs.
35K3613—Set **$2.25**
35K3614—Cake Plate only. (Weight, packed, 2 pounds)............ **82c**

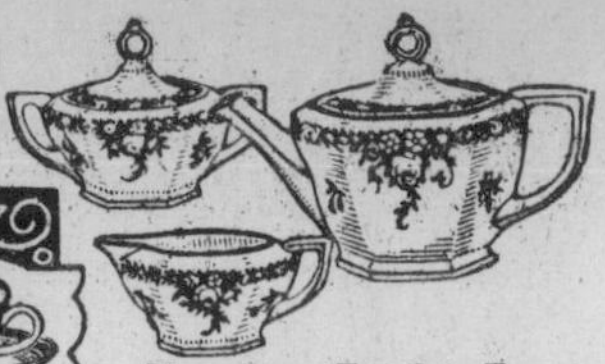

Three-Piece Tea Set. Teapot, covered sugar bowl and cream pitcher. Translucent white china decorated with sprays and borders composed of roses and garden flowers. Gold tracing on handles. Weight, packed, 6 pounds.
35K3615—Set **$1.95**

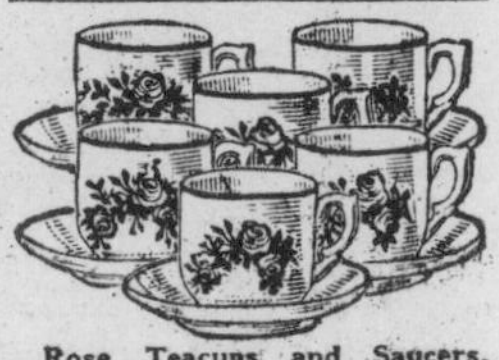

Rose Teacups and Saucers. Decorated with pink roses and blue forget-me-nots. Gold traced handles. Capacity, ⅝-pint. Wt., packed, 6 pounds.
35K3616—Set, 6 cups and saucers. **$1.85**

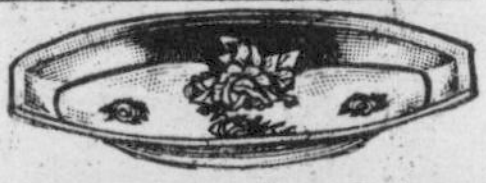

12-Inch Celery Tray. Decorated with a spray of yellow tea roses over a light blue border. Weight, packed, 3 lbs.
35K3617 .... **67c**

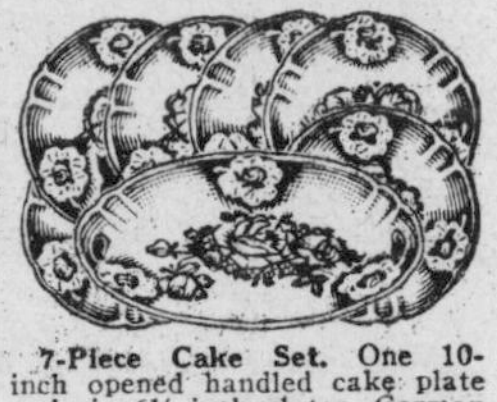

7-Piece Cake Set. One 10-inch opened handled cake plate and six 6½-inch plates. German china decorated with red and pink roses on a tan and green background. Weight, packed, 6 pounds.
35K3618—Set **$2.00**
35K3619—Cake Plate only. (Weight, packed, 2 pounds) **70c**

Imported Japanese China

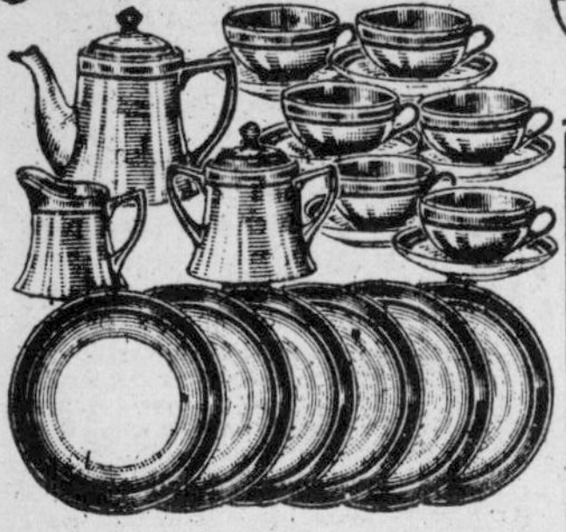

23-Piece China Tea Set

Imported china in a plain edge shape with tankard shape teapot, sugar bowl and cream pitcher. Decorated with a tan luster with blue luster band and black lines. Teapot, covered sugar bowl, cream pitcher, six tea cups and saucers and six tea plates. Weight, packed, 18 pounds.
35K4600 .... **$4.95**

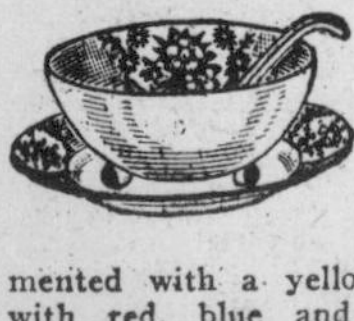

Mayonnaise Dish and Plate With Ladle. Tan luster border between a bright gold and a black hairline. Ornamented with a yellow basket design with red, blue and yellow flowers. Weight, packed, 3 pounds.
35K4601..................... **$1.75**

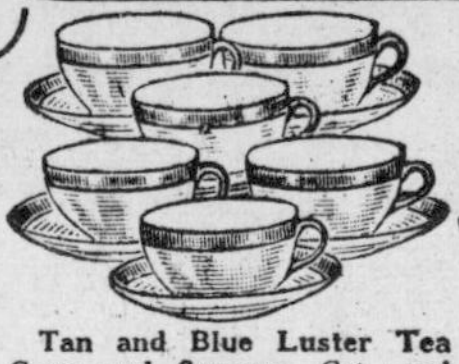

Tan and Blue Luster Tea Cups and Saucers. Cup and saucer have a blue luster band and a black hairline. Capacity, ½ pint. Wt., pkd., 6 lbs.
35K4602—Set, 6 cups and saucers............ **$1.88**

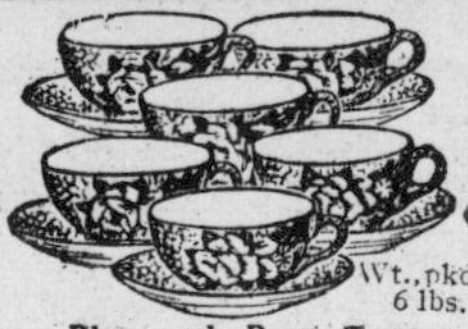

Wt., pkd., 6 lbs.

Blue and Rose Teacups and Saucers. Decorated all over with a mottled light blue color and one yellow rose. Black line aroung edge. Capacity, ½ pint.
35K4603—Set of 6 cups and saucers **$1.75**

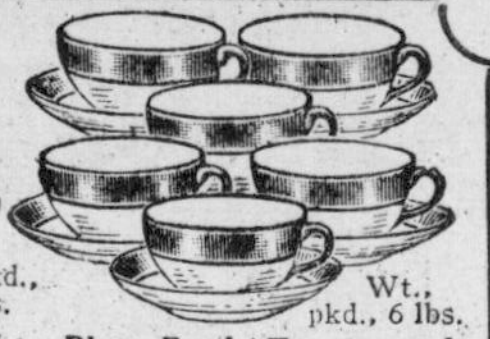

Wt., pkd., 6 lbs.

Blue Band Teacup and Saucer Set. Decorated with a wide blue luster band and black line. Capacity, ½-pint.
35K4604—Set of 6 cups and saucers... **$1.48**

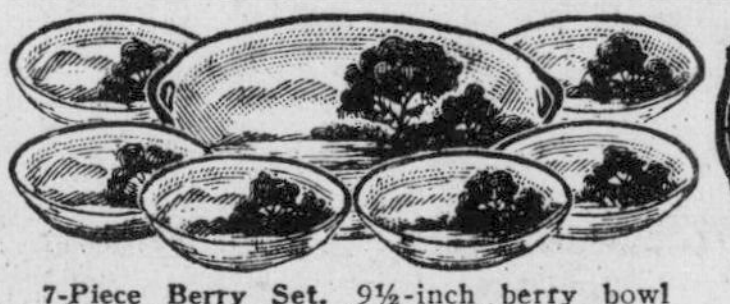

7-Piece Berry Set. 9½-inch berry bowl and six 5-inch sauce dishes. Hand painted scenic design in many colors. Gold decorated handles. Weight, pkd., 8 lbs.
35K4605—Set **$3.48**
35K4606—Salad Bowl only. (Weight, packed, 3 lbs.)........ **1.69**

7-Piece Cake Set

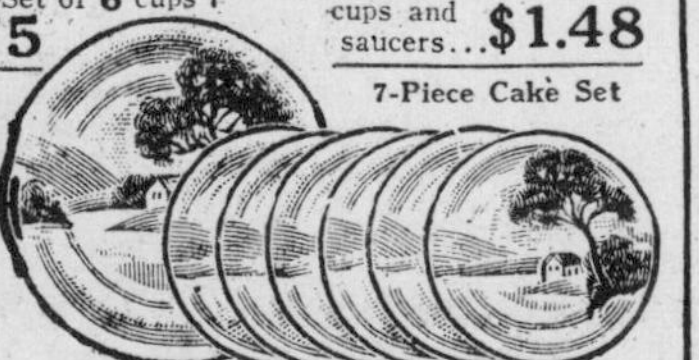

9½-inch cake plate with gold decorated handles and six 6¼-inch plates. Hand painted scenic design in many colors. Wt. packed, 7 lbs.
35K4607—Set.................. **$3.45**
35K4608—Cake Plate only. (Weight, packed, 2 lbs.).............. **1.65**

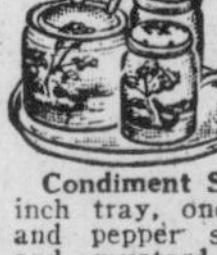

Wt. pkd., 2½ lbs.

Condiment Set. 5-inch tray, one salt and pepper shaker and mustard with spoon. Scenic design.
35K4609 **$1.00**

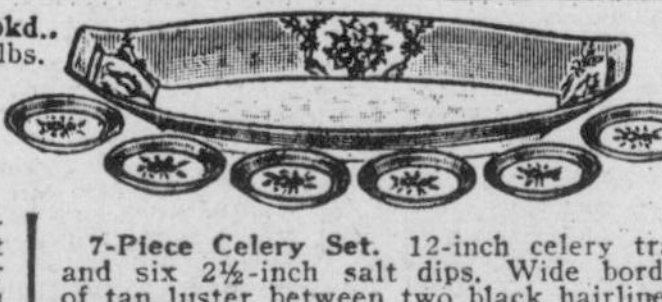

7-Piece Celery Set. 12-inch celery tray and six 2½-inch salt dips. Wide border of tan luster between two black hairlines. Ornamented with red, blue and yellow flowers. Weight, pkd., 4 lbs.
35K4610 .... **$2.75**

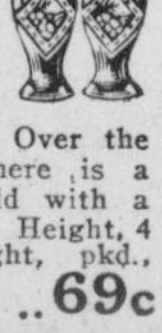

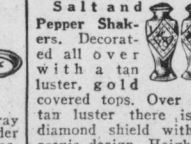

Salt and Pepper Shakers. Decorated all over with a tan luster, gold covered tops. Over the tan luster there is a diamond shield with a scenic design. Height, 4 inches. Weight, pkd., 1½ lbs.
35K4611 .. **69c**

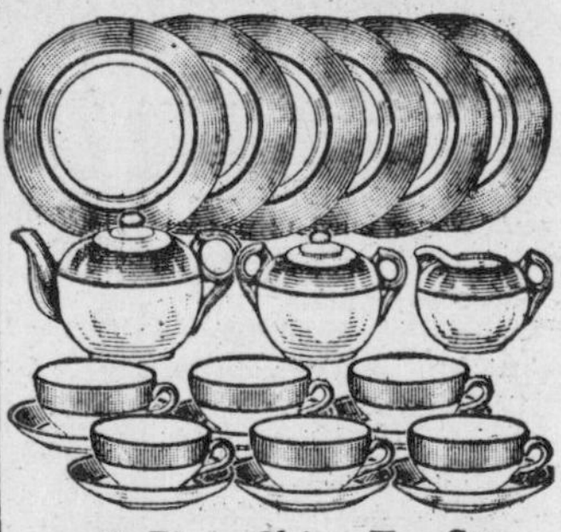

23-Piece China Tea Set

Imported china in a plain edge shape. The decoration consists of a blue luster band with a black line. One teapot, covered sugar bowl, cream pitcher, six tea cups and saucers and six tea plates. Weight, packed, 18 pounds.
35K4612 .... **$4.25**

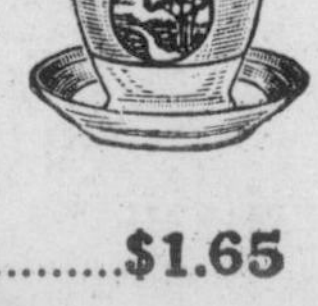

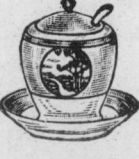

Jam Jar With Plate and Ladle. Decorated with a tan luster with green luster bands between black lines and a scenic medallion in hand painted design. Height, on plate, 5½ in. Weight, packed, 3½ lbs.
35K4613............... **$1.65**

Colored Glassware Is Correct

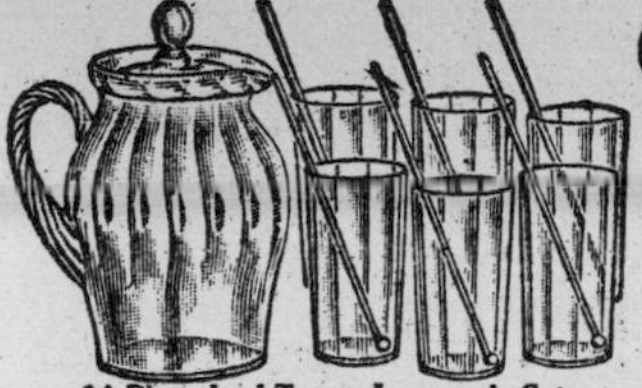

14-Piece Iced Tea or Lemonade Set
Rose pink or green colored thin glass; 4-pint pitcher and cover, six 12-ounce iced tea or lemonade tumblers, six glass spoon sippers. Weight, packed, 16 pounds.
35K5000—Rose Pink Set.....**$2.75**
35K5001—Emerald Green Set. **2.75**

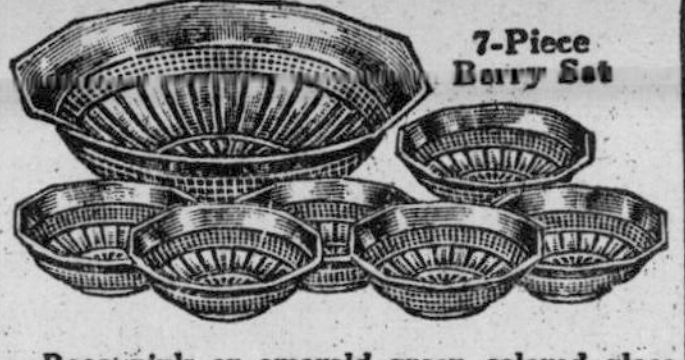

7-Piece Berry Set
Rose pink or emerald green colored glass with pressed paneled and border design. One 9½-inch berry bowl and six 4¾-inch sauce dishes to match. Weight, packed, 10 lbs.
35K5028—Rose Pink. Per set..**$1.89**
35K5029—Emerald Green. Set.. **1.89**

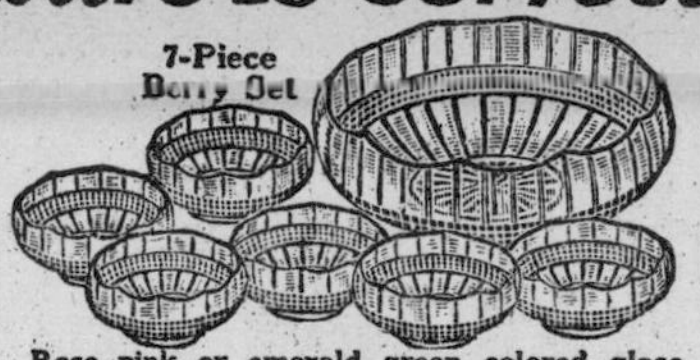

7-Piece Berry Set
Rose pink or emerald green colored glass. Decorated with cut lines forming panels, and a pressed design forming a border. Pressed star in bottom. One 8½-inch berry or salad bowl and six 4-inch sauce dishes to match. Weight, packed, 10 pounds.
35K5031—Rose Pink Set.........**$2.75**
35K5032—Emerald Green Set...... **2.75**

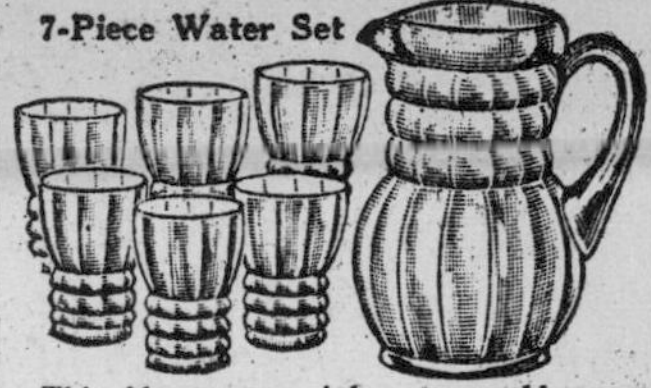

7-Piece Water Set
Thin blown rose pink or emerald green colored glass in a fancy shape optic (fluted) design. Set consists of one 4-pint fancy shape pitcher, 9 inches high, and six ½-pint tumblers to match. Weight, packed, 10 pounds.
35K5080—Rose Pink.......**$2.25**
35K5081—Emerald Green... **2.25**

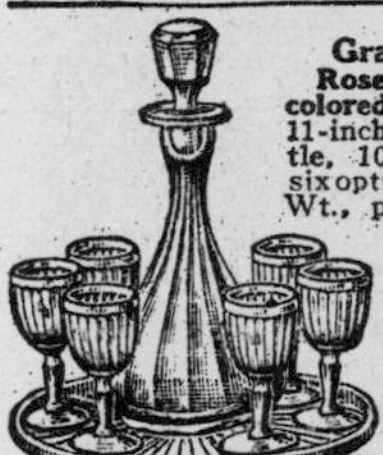

8-Piece Grape Juice Set
Rose pink or green colored pressed glass; 11-inch grape juice bottle, 10½-inch tray and six optic (fluted) glasses. Wt., packed, 10 lbs.
35K5003 Rose Pink Set **$2.40**
35K5004 Emerald Green Set **$2.40**

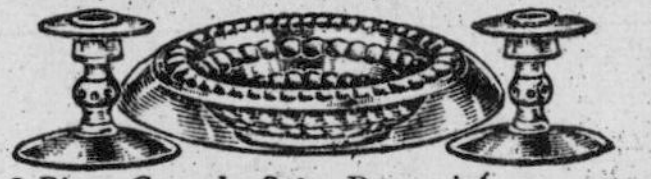

3-Piece Console Set. Rose pink or emerald green colored glass. One 11-inch rolled edge bowl with pressed design, that reflects the light, and two 4-inch candlesticks with wide bases. Wt., packed, 7 pounds.
35K5034—Rose Pink. Per Set..**$2.25**
35K5035—Emerald Green. Set.. **2.25**

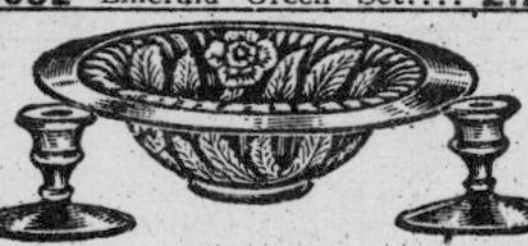

3-Piece Console Set. Rose pink or emerald green colored glass. One large 12½-in. bowl with rock crystal design in silver gray finish and two 3½-in. candlesticks with wide bases. Weight, packed, 9 pounds.
35K5041—Rose Pink..............**$2.75**
35K5042—Emerald Green.......... **2.75**

35K5037—10-inch pink or blue candles for above. Set of **2.** **State color.** Weight, packed, 1 pound..**25c**

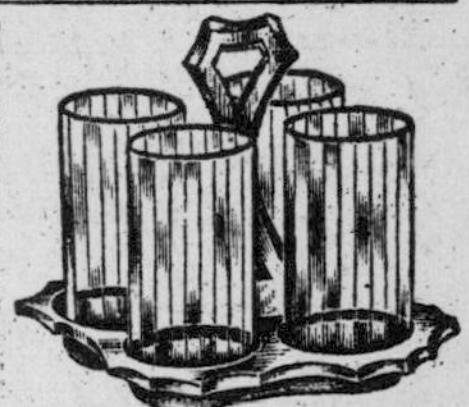

5-Piece Bridge Sets. Crystal glass in rose pink or emerald green color. Four-compartment handled tray and four 10-ounce optic (fluted) tumblers. Wt., packed, 8 lbs.
35K5083—Pink Rose Set....**$1.98**
35K5084—Emerald Green Set **1.98**

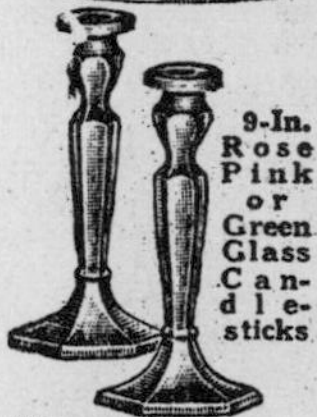

9-In. Rose Pink or Green Glass Candlesticks
Wt., pkd., 6 lbs.
35K5006—Rose Pink. Pair...**$1.50**
35K5007—Jade Green. Pair.**$1.50**

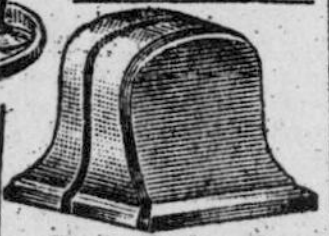

Book Ends. Rose pink or emerald green colored glass in satin finish. Size of base, 2½x7 in., and heavy enough to hold a number of books without falling over. Weight, packed, 9 lbs.
35K5022 Rose Pink. Per pair **$2.98**
35K5023 Emerald Green. Per pair **$2.98**

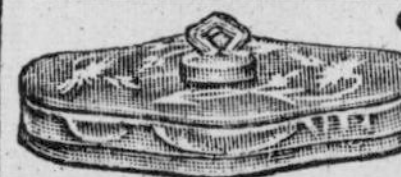

Covered Vanity Set or Compact. Clear rose pink or green colored glass and cut on top with a floral design. Compartment for puff, rouge, and lipstick. Weight, packed, 5 pounds.
35K5098—Rose Colored Set.....**$1.48**
35K5099—Emerald Green Colored Set **$1.48**

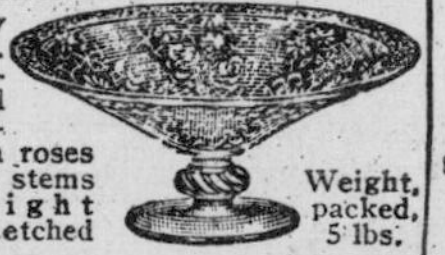

10½-Inch Low Footed Compote. Rose pink or emerald green colored thin glass, and decorated all over with roses and daisies with stems and leaves in a light pressed design, in etched effect. Weight, packed, 5 lbs.
35K5046—Rose Pink **$1.89**
35K5047—Emerald Green **1.89**

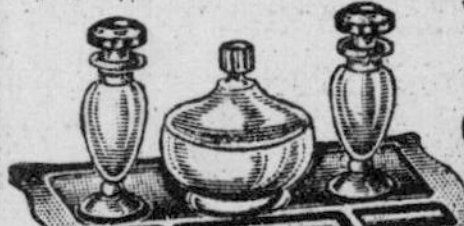

4-Piece Vanity Set. Rose pink or green colored glass in satin finish. One 11-inch compartment tray, one 4-in. powder box and two 5-in. perfume bottles with ground stopper droppers. Wt., packed, 10 lbs.
35K5086—Satin Finish Rose Pink Set.**$2.50**
35K5087—Satin Finish Green Set....**$2.50**

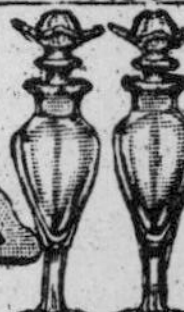

Perfume Bottles With Droppers. Rose pink or emerald green colored glass with a brilliant luster. The top of the dropper forms a rosebud. Ht., 7 in. Wt., per pair, packed, 2 lbs.
35K5089 Rose Pink. Per pair ..**$1.45**
[illegible] Emerald green. Per pr.**$1.45**

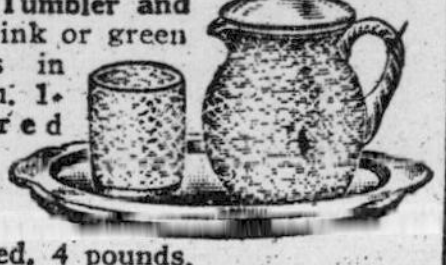

Bedroom Set. Water Pitcher with Tumbler and Tray. Rose pink or green colored glass in crackled design. 1-pint covered pitcher, ½-pint tumbler and 11-inch [illegible] Weight, packed, 4 pounds.
35K5009—Rose Pink. Per set.**$2.10**
35K5010—Emerald Green. Set. **2.10**

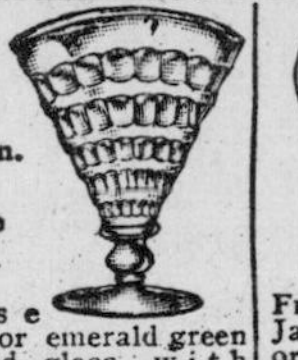

7½-In. Fan Shape Vase. Rose pink or emerald green colored glass, with bright pressed panels which reflect the light and adds brilliancy to the vase. Width at top, 6 in. Weight, packed, 3 pounds.
35K5051 Rose Pink.......**89c**
35K5052 Emerald Green...**89c**

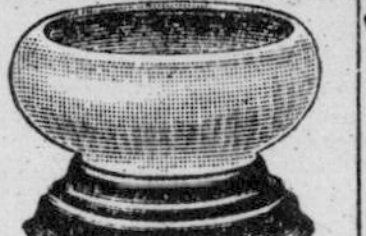

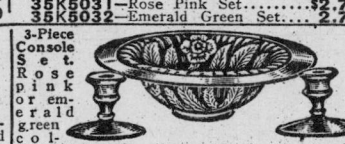

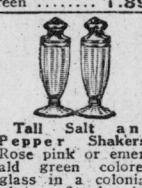

7-Inch Colored Glass Fruit or Flower Bowls. Jade green, pink luster or blue colored glass, and mounted on an ebony glass detachable base. Height, 5¼ in. Wt., packed, 6 lbs.
35K5054 — Jade Green Bowl.....**$1.25**
35K5055 — Pink Luster Bowl.....**$1.25**
35K5056 — Blue Color Bowl......**$1.25**

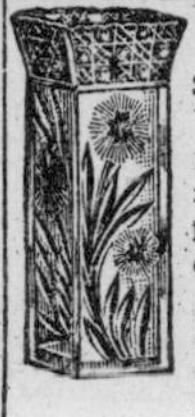

10-In. Square Vase, pressed rose pink colored glass. Sides cut with flowers in silver gray finish. Pressed and cut border design around top. Weight, packed, 7 lbs.
35K5057 $1.48

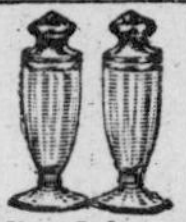

Tall Salt and Pepper Shakers. Rose pink or emerald green colored glass in a colonial shape, fitted with heavy silver plated tops. Height, 4¼ inches. Wt., packed, 2 pounds.
35K5095—Rose Pink. Per pair.. ....**$1.25**
35K5096 Emerald Green. Per pair **$1.25**

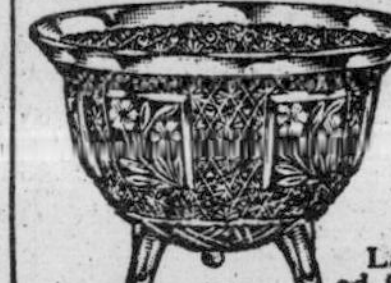

Large 10-Inch Footed Orange or Fruit Bowl, Rose pink colored glass in a brilliant pressed glass design. Around the bowl there are six panels, each showing two cut flowers in silver gray finish. Height, 6¾ in. Weight, packed, 10 lbs.
35K5105 ....**$1.75**

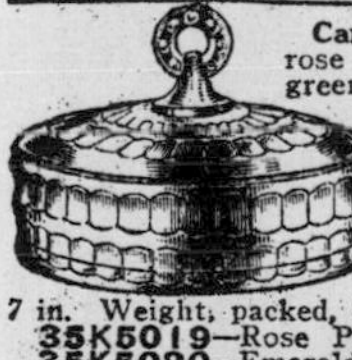

Candy Box. Pressed rose pink or emerald green colored glass, with two pressed borders and pressed design in bottom. Three compartments. Fitted with a handled cover. Ht., 5 in.; diameter, 7 in. Weight, packed, 6 pounds.
35K5019—Rose Pink **$1.25**
35K5020—Emerald Green.... **1.25**

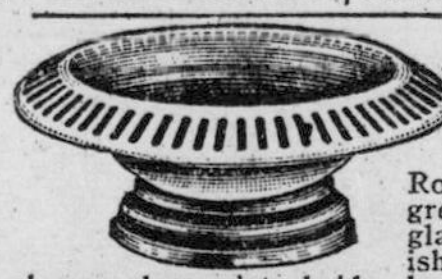

10-Inch Fruit or Flower Bowl. With removable flower holder. Rose pink or jade green colored glass in satin finish mounted on ebony glass detachable base. Perforated around the edge of bowl border. Height, 4 inches. Weight, packed, 8 pounds.
35K5011—Rose Pink Flower Bowl.**$2.30**
35K5012—Emerald Green Flower Bowl **2.30**

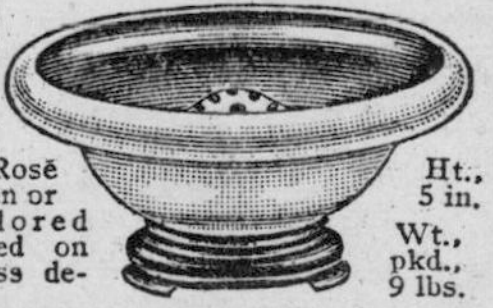

10½ - Inch Colored Glass Fruit or Flower Bowls, with removable flower holders. Rose pink, jade green or tangerine colored glass, mounted on an ebony glass detachable base. Ht., 5 in. Wt., pkd., 9 lbs.
35K5092—Rose Pink Fruit Bowl .**$1.65**
35K5093—Jade Green Fruit Bowl. **1.65**
35K5094—Tangerine Fruit Bowl.. **1.65**

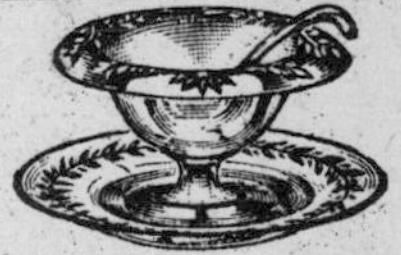

Mayonnaise Dish and Plate With Spoon. Thin pressed glass with rose pink or green color. Rolled edge dish cut with floral spray. Plate has border of cut leaves and stems. One 6½-in. dish, 8-in. plate and ladle. Weight, packed, 4 pounds.
35K5064—Rose Pink.......**$1.45**
35K5065—Emerald Green... **1.45**

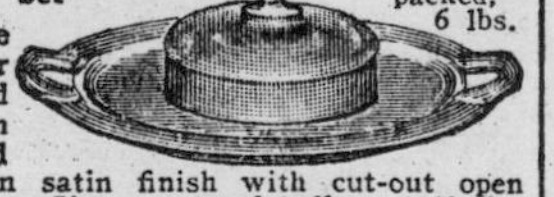

Cheese and Cracker Set Rose pink or emerald green colored glass in satin finish with cut-out open handles. Size across handles, 11½ in. Weight, packed, 6 lbs.
35K5106—Rose Pink.........**$1.75**
35K5107—Emerald Green..... **1.75**

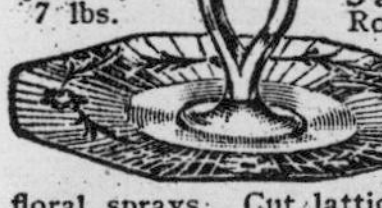

10 - Inch Handled Sandwich Tray. Rose pink or green colored thin glass, octagon shape, cut with floral sprays. Cut lattice background. Weight, packed, 7 lbs.
35K5016—Rose Pink.........**$1.35**
35K5017—Emerald Green..... **1.35**

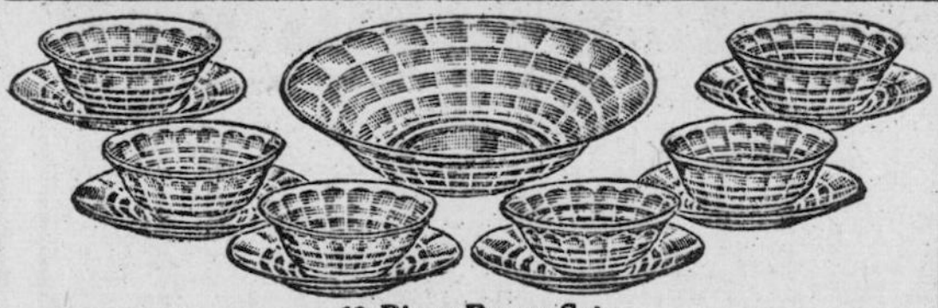

13-Piece Berry Set
Rose pink or emerald green colored glass in an optic (fluted) colonial shape. One 9½-inch berry bowl, six 4½-inch sauce dishes and six 6¾-inch saucers for the sauce dishes. Weight, packed, 12 pounds.
35K5069—Rose Pink. Per set..............................**$2.75**
35K5070—Emerald Green. Per set.......................... **2.75**

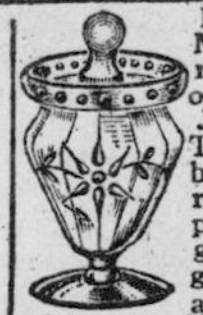

Footed Marmalade or Jam Jars. Thin blown rose pink or green glass and cut with a poinsettia flower in a silver gray finish. Ht., 5½ in. Wt., pkd., 3 pounds.
35K5013—Rose Pink Jar.....**78c**
35K5014 Emerald Green Jar **78c**

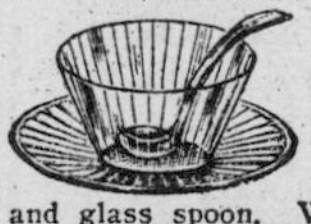

Whipped Cream or Mayonnaise Set. Thin blown rose pink or emerald green colored glass in optic (fluted) design. One 4½-inch dish, 6¼ - inch plate and glass spoon. Wt., packed, 4 lbs.
35K5102—Rose Pink Set......**88c**
35K5103—Emerald Green Set..**88c**

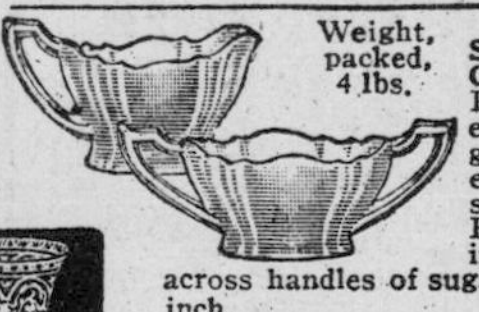

Colonial Sugar and Cream Set. Rose pink or emerald green colored glass in satin finish. Height, 2½ in.; width across handles of sugar bowl, 7¼ inch. Weight, packed, 4 lbs.
35K5067—Rose Pink. Per set **98c**
35K5068 — Emerald Green. Per set **98c**

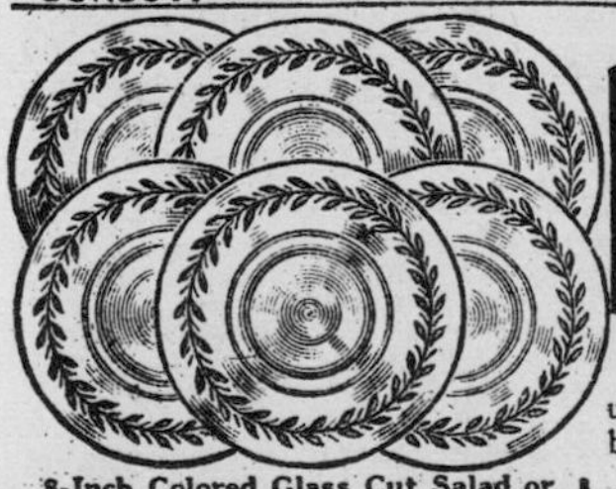

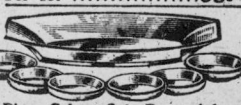

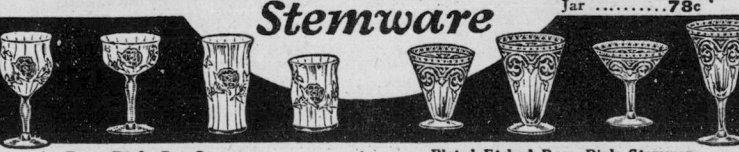

8-Inch Colored Glass Cut Salad or Dessert Plates. Thin pressed glass, either rose pink or emerald green color. Cut with a border of leaves and stems in silver gray finish. Weight, packed, 6 pounds.
35K5025—Rose Pink Salad Plates. Set of 6...........**$2.35**
35K5026—Emerald Green Salad Plates. Set of 6...........**$2.35**

Stemware

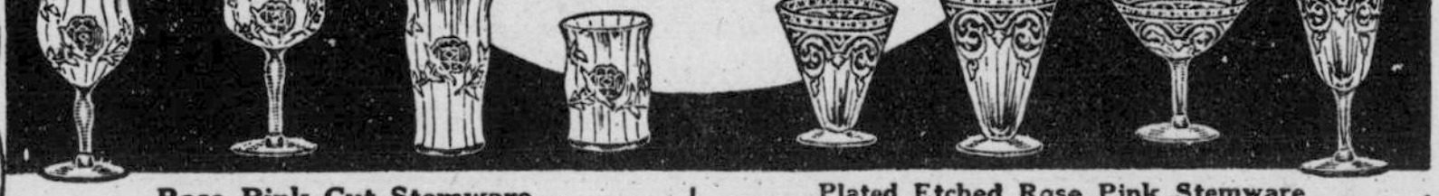

Rose Pink Cut Stemware
Thin blown rose pink colored glass in a popular optic (fluted) shape and cut with a rambler rose design.
35K5072—**Water Goblets.** Height, 6½ inches. Weight, packed, 6 pounds. Per set of six..**$3.00**
35K5073—**Tall Footed Sherbets.** Height, 5½ in. Wt., packed, 5 lbs. Per set of six...**$2.95**
35K5074—**Standard Table Tumblers.** Height, 4 in. Wt., packed, 4 lbs. Per set of six..**$2.50**
35K5075—**Lemonade or Iced Tea Tumblers.** Height, 5⅝ inches. Weight, packed 5 pounds. Per set of six.........................**$2.60**

Plated Etched Rose Pink Stemware
Thin blown rose pink colored glass, highly polished in an exceptionally delicate optic (fluted) shape. The goblets and tall sherbets have one-piece drawn stems. The table and iced tea tumblers are the new cone shape. The decoration is of fine plate etching, as the illustration shows.
35K5076—**Water Goblets.** Height, 7 in. Wt., packed, 6 lbs. Per set of six..................**$3.85**
35K5077—**Tall Footed Sherbets.** Ht., 4½ in. Wt., packed, 5 lbs. Per set of six...............**$3.80**
35K5078—**Table Tumblers.** Height, 4½ in. Wt., packed, 4 lbs. Per set of six...................**$3.75**
35K5079—**Lemonade or Iced Tea Tumblers.** Height, 5½ inches. Wt., packed, 5 lbs. Per set of six..............................**$3.90**

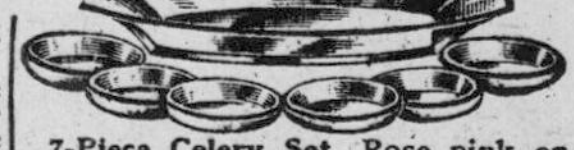

7-Piece Celery Set. Rose pink or emerald green colored celery set. One 11¼-inch oblong tray and six 2½-inch oval individual salt dips. Weight, packed, 3½ pounds.
35K5108 Rose Pink. Per set........**$1.32**
35K5109 Emerald Green. Per set.... **1.32**

Tulip Water Jug Earthenware, highly glazed inside and out. Decorated with two tulips in colors. Capacity, 5 pints. Weight, packed, 6 pounds.

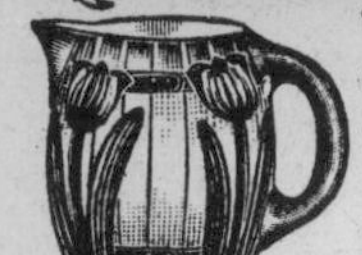

35K6100 **98c**

Wood Covered Salt Box. Earthenware and decorated with scenes in delft blue and wide blue bands at top and bottom. Weight, packed, 5 pounds.

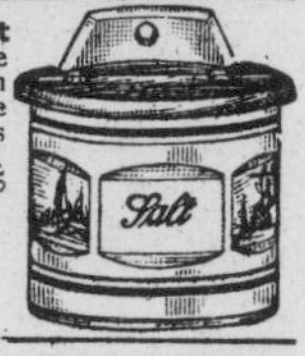

35K6101 **85c**

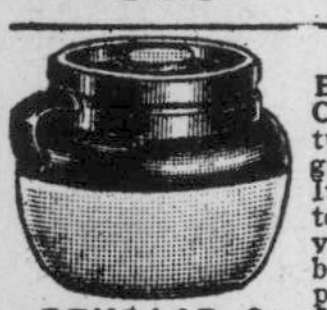

Half-Gallon Baked Bean Pot With Cover. Stoneware in two colors, natural gray and dark brown. It is not necessary to dwell on the advantage of baking beans in this style pot. Wt., pkd., 8 lbs.

35K6145—One-Half Gallon Bean Pot **45c**

Refrigerator Set

Clear pressed glass, consisting of three 5¾-inch jars, 2½ inches high. One jar acts as a cover for the one below, the top jar having a handled cover. Saves space in the refrigerator or ice box. You can see the contents at a glance. Weight, packed, 9 lbs.

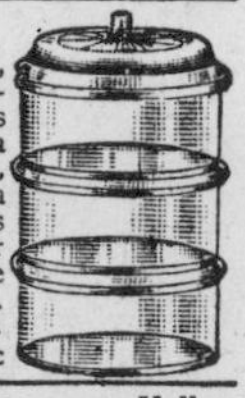

35K6102 .....55c

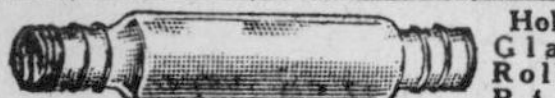

Hollow Glass Rolling Pin. Pressed glass, with a cork-lined metal cap. The rolling pin may be filled with cold water. This is to keep the pie crust cold and also prevents the dough from adhering to the roller. Weight, packed, 3½ pounds.

35K6103.................. **43c**

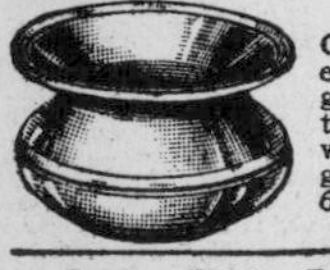

Gold Decorated Cuspidor. Brown earthenware, highly glazed. Center and top edges have a wide band of bright gold. Wt., packed, 6 lbs.

35K6104 **55c**

Sanitary Chicken Feeder or Fountain

Gray color stoneware, glazed inside and out. Much better than metal. Each fountain contains two pieces, the container and tray. Capacity, ½ gallon. Weight, packed, 10 lbs.

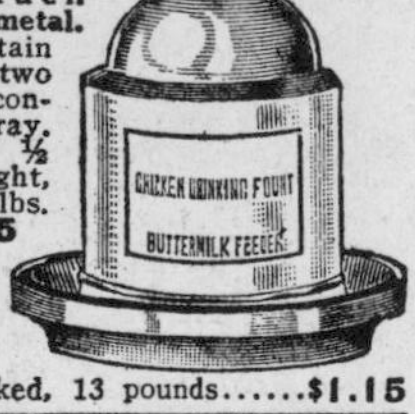

35K6105 **85c**

35K6146 Capacity, 1 gallon. Weight, packed, 13 pounds......$1.15

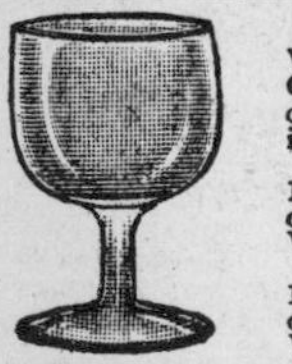

Hoffman House Water or Iced Tea Goblets. Extra heavy, clear glass, are carried in two sizes only.

35K6106 12-ounce. Per half dozen ....90c Wt., packed, 10 lbs.

35K6107 17-ounce. Per half dozen ....$1.08 Wt., packed, 12 lbs.

Colonial Footed Sherbet

For ice cream or sundaes. Pressed crystal glass. Height, 3 in. Wt. pkd., per half dozen, 6 pounds.

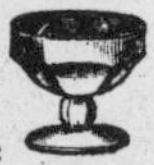

35K6108—Half doz..49c

Clear, thin blown optic tumblers. Cut with a grape design. Capacity, ½ pint. Wt., packed, per half dozen, 3 lbs.

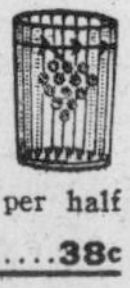

35K6111—Half doz..41c

Same tumbler as above, without grape design. Capacity, ½ pint. Weight, packed, per half dozen, 3 pounds.

35K6110—Half dozen..........38c

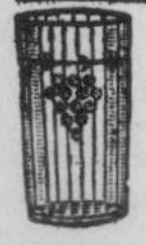

Grape design thin clear glass iced tea tumblers. Capacity, 12 oz. Weight, packed, per half dozen, 4 pounds.

35K6112—Half doz..54c

Fifteen-Piece Imported Cereal or Spice Set

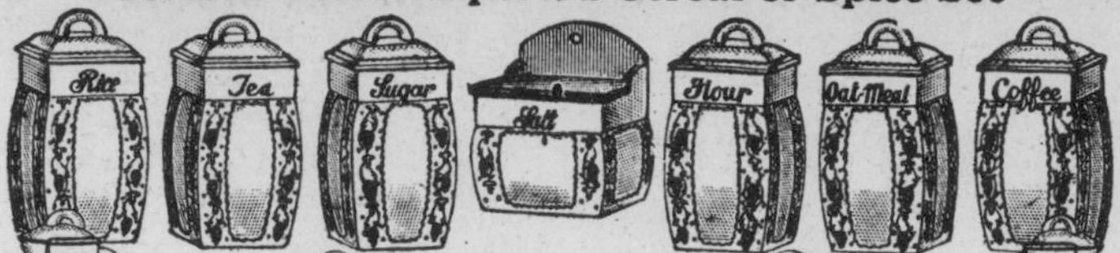

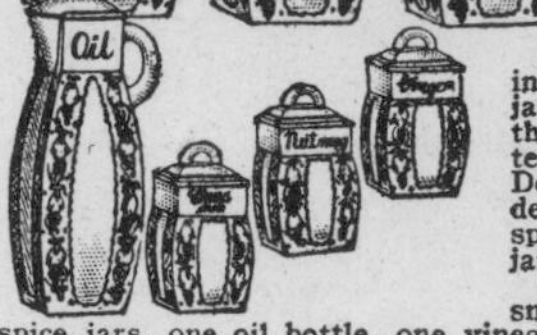

Imported earthenware in a Colonial shape. The jars are economical in that they keep the contents fresh and clean. Decorated with a grape design in blue. Name of spice or cereal on each jar in black.

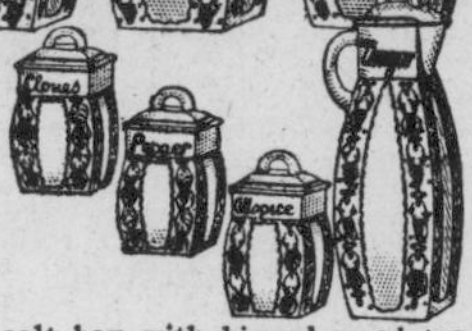

Six large and six small covered cereal or spice jars, one oil bottle, one vinegar bottle and one large salt box with hinged wood top.

35K6114—Fifteen-Piece Cereal or Spice Set. Without rack. Weight, packed, 25 pounds..........$4.90

35K6115—Rack only, made of metal in white enamel finish, to hold above set. Weight, packed, 10 pounds..........$2.75

35K6113—Fifteen-Piece Cereal or Spice Set. Complete with rack. Weight, packed, 35 pounds. Per set.......... **$7.50**

Latest Improved Butter Churn

Manufactured in America

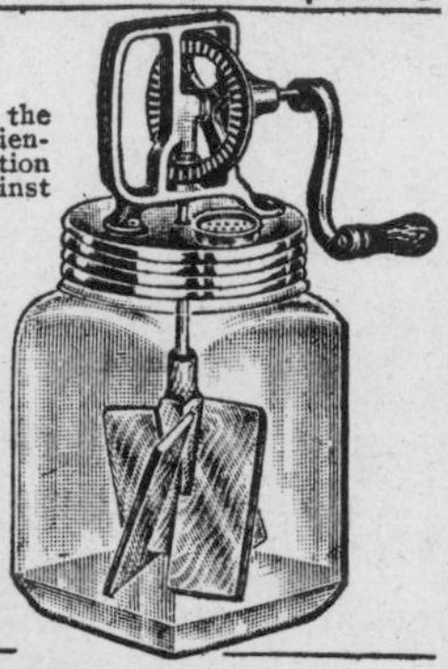

Makes butter out of cream in 8 to 10 minutes. This is the style churn used by the Agricultural Colleges for their scientific experiments in butter making. The peculiar construction of the dasher, giving a rotary motion to the cream against the square sides of the churn, is what makes this the best churn ever made. A child can operate it. Easy running, strongly made, easily cleaned. A perforated draining cap in lid permits the buttermilk to be poured out and cold water poured in to wash the butter without removing the top. Extra heavy flint glass jars with rounded corners. The 4-blade dasher is made of hard maple. Castings and gears accurately fitted and light running. Used also for beating eggs, mixing cake batter and salad dressings. Will churn one-half the capacity of churn. Can merge fresh milk with butter. 1 pound butter and 1 pint milk churned for a few minutes make about 2 pounds of milk-charged butter.

35K6116—Capacity, 4 quarts. Weight, packed, 9 pounds..........$1.95

35K6117—Capacity, 6 quarts. Weight, packed, 10 pounds..........$2.45

35K6118—Capacity, 8 quarts. Weight, packed, 12 pounds..........$3.15

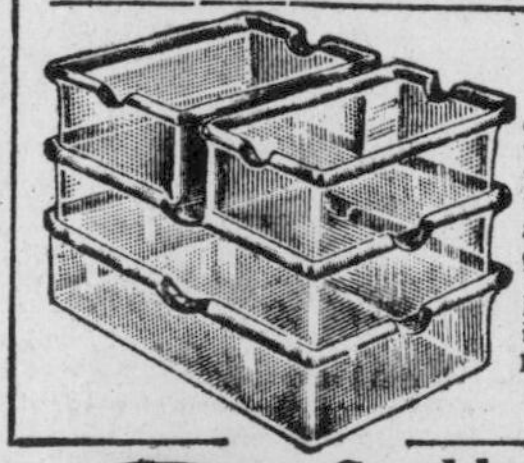

Space Saver Ice Box Dish

The four dishes do not take up any more space than does one dish of the same size of any other kind. They are just the thing for the left overs. Being made of glass, they are transparent and you can see at a glance what each one contains. They are square shape, fit one on top of the other, and have an opening on each end to permit circulation of cold air. They keep the food fresh and free from mold. Your ice box will not be too small if you use Space Saver Ice Box Dishes. Set consists of two small dishes, 3½x4 inches, and two large dishes, 4½x7½ inches. Weight, packed, 8½ pounds.

35K6119—Per set.......... **94c**

Crackle and Needle Etched Glass Goblets—Sherbets—Tumblers

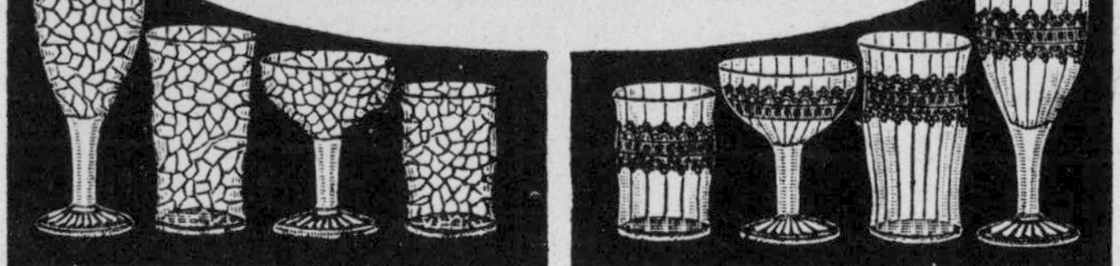

Thin pressed clear glass in crackle glass design in a popular shape. Good, everyday, useful glassware.

35K6120—Water Goblets. Height, 7 inches. Weight, packed, per half dozen, 4 pounds. Per half dozen..........86c

35K6121—Tall Footed Sherbets. Height, 4⅝ inches. Weight, packed, per half dozen, 3½ lbs. Per half dozen..69c

35K6122—Table Tumblers. Height, 4 inches. Weight, packed, per half dozen, 2½ pounds. Per half dozen..........29c

35K6123—Tall Lemonade or Iced Tea Tumblers. Height, 5¼ inches. Weight, packed, per half dozen, 3½ pounds. Per half dozen..........73c

Thin pressed clear glass in the old standard needle etched pattern which has always been popular. Good, everyday, useful glassware.

35K6124—Water Goblets. Height, 7 inches. Weight, packed, per half dozen, 4 pounds. Per half dozen.......$1.00

35K6125—Tall Footed Sherbets. Height, 4⅝ inches. Weight, packed, per half dozen, 3½ lbs. Per half dozen..85c

35K6126—Table Tumblers. Height, 4 inches. Weight, packed, per half dozen, 2½ pounds. Per half dozen..........48c

35K6127—Tall Lemonade or Iced Tea Tumblers. Height, 5¼ inches. Weight, packed, per half dozen, 3½ lbs. Per half dozen..........83c

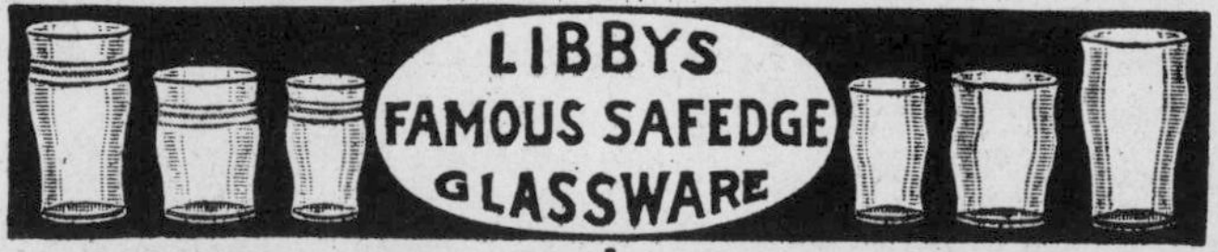

Libby-Safedge Nonik Tumblers. Clear glass decorated with a wide engraved band and two hair lines. The tumblers are reinforced around the edge which prevents them from chipping. Thin but strong and durable.

35K6128—Engraved Band 5-Ounce Grape Juice Tumblers. Weight, packed, 3 pounds. Per half dozen tumblers..60c

35K6129—Engraved Band 10-Ounce Table Tumblers. Weight, packed, 4 pounds. Per half dozen tumblers...63c

35K6130—Engraved Band 12-Ounce Iced Tea Tumblers. Weight, packed, 5 pounds. Per half dozen tumblers....82c

Libby-Safedge Nonik Tumblers. Same as tumblers at the left, but having no decorated band. Reinforced around the edge which prevents them from chipping.

35K6131—Plain 5-Ounce Grape Juice Tumblers. Weight, packed, 3 lbs. Per half dozen tumblers..........54c

35K6132—Plain 10-Ounce Table Tumblers. Weight, packed, 4 pounds. Per half dozen tumblers..........58c

35K6133—Plain 12-Ounce Iced Tea Tumblers. Weight, packed, 5 pounds. Per half dozen tumblers..........75c

Five-Piece Blue Band White Mixing Bowl Set. White earthenware, highly glazed. Decorated with blue bands. Set contains the following bowls:

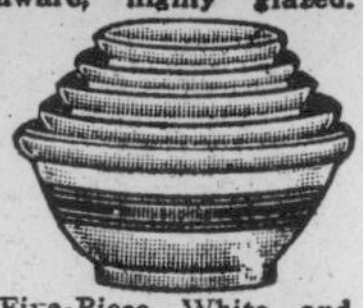

Size Inches	Capacity Pints
5	1
6	1½
7	2
8	2½
9	4

35K6134—Five-Piece White and Blue Mixing Bowl Set. Weight, packed, 13 pounds. Per set..........$1.50

Three-Piece Blue Band White Mixing Bowl Set White earthenware, highly glazed. Decorated with blue bands. Set contains the following bowls:

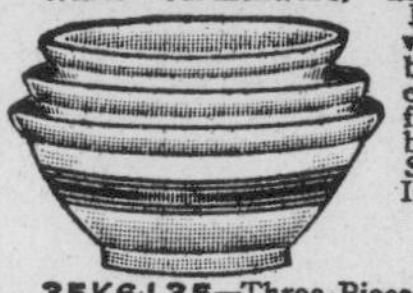

Size Inches.	Capacity Pints
10	5
11	7½
12	9¼

35K6135—Three-Piece White and Blue Mixing Bowl Set. Weight, packed, 20 pounds. Per set..........$2.57

Five-Piece Yellow Mixing Bowl Set

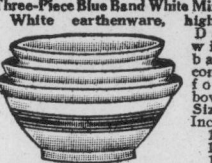

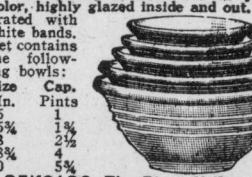

Good quality earthenware in yellow color, highly glazed inside and out. Decorated with white bands. Set contains the following bowls:

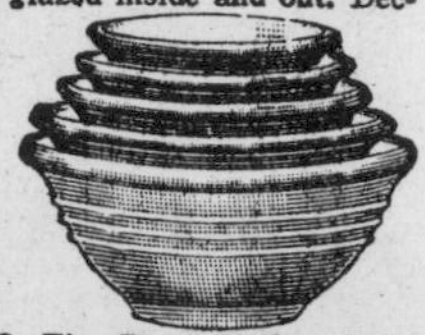

Size In.	Cap. Pints
6	1
6¾	1¾
8	2½
8¾	4
10	5¾

35K6136—Five-Piece Yellow Mixing Bowl Set. Weight, packed, 12 lbs. Per set..........$1.28

Five-Piece Sanitary Glass Mixing Bowl Sets

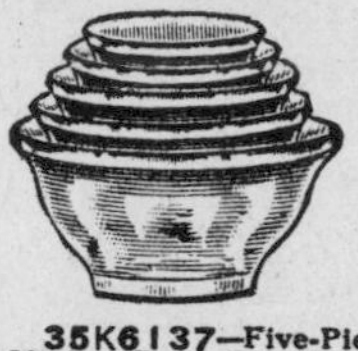

Heavy, clear glass, sanitary and easy to clean. Set contains the following bowls:

Size In.	Capacity Pints
5	¾
6	1⅛
7	2
8	3
9	4

35K6137—Five-Piece Sanitary Glass Mixing Bowl Set. Weight, packed, 10 pounds. Per set..........67c

English Earthenware Bowls

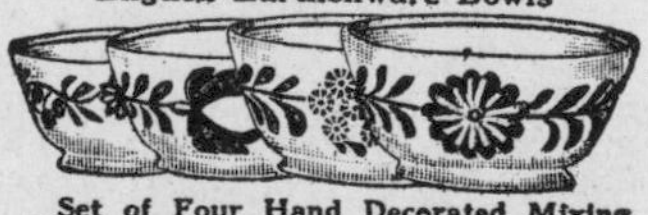

Set of Four Hand Decorated Mixing Bowls. English earthenware, highly glazed. Size of bowl, 5½, 6, 6½ and 7½ in. Wt., pkd., per set, 7 lbs.

35K6138—Per set.... **$1.08**

Seven-Piece Kitchen Set

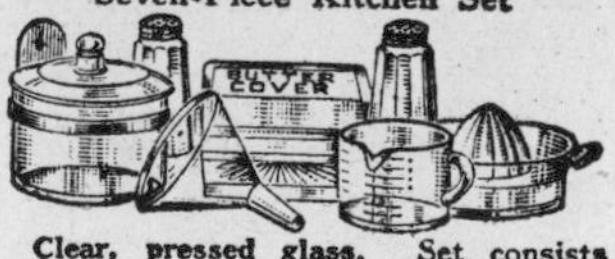

Clear, pressed glass. Set consists of one covered salt box with metal frame, one covered 1-pound butter jar with pressed design in bottom, one graduated ½-pint measuring glass, one orange reamer, one 4½-inch glass funnel and one salt and one pepper shaker with embossed aluminum tops. Weight, packed, 9 pounds.

35K6139—Per set.... **$1.15**

Plain Footed Sherbet

Pressed crystal glass, highly polished. For sundaes, ice cream and sherbets. Height, 3 inches. Weight, per half dozen, 4 pounds.

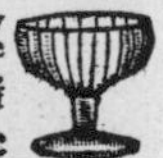

35K6140—Half doz. **50c**

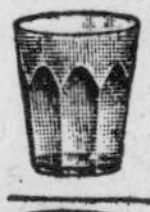

Colonial Pressed Glass Common Tumbler. Medium weight glass. Can also be used as a jelly tumbler. Capacity, ½ pint. Weight, packed, per half dozen, 5 pounds.

35K6141—Per half dozen **20c**

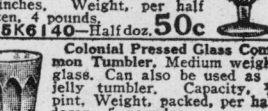

Nine-Ounce Fancy Barrel Shape Hotel Tumbler. Pressed crystal glass. Full finish. Non-nesting, with fluted heavy bottom. Weight, packed, per half dozen, 5 pounds.

35K6143—Per half dozen **39c**

35K6142—Straight shape hotel tumbler. Per half dozen.. **38c**

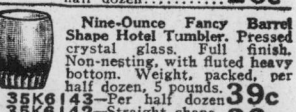

Colonial Iced Tea Tumblers

Light weight pressed glass in narrow fluted design. Capacity, ¾ pint. Weight, per half dozen, packed, 7 pounds.

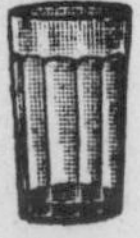

35K6144 Per half dozen..... **44c**

13-Piece Border Pattern Water Set

Pressed polished glass in a colonial shape with a diamond design border and a pressed star bottom. One 2-pint water pitcher and twelve ½-pint tumblers to match. Weight, packed, 16 pounds.
35K6800 .... **$1.89**

7-Piece Iridescent Glass Water Set

Gold color iridescent pressed glass. Decorated with fruits and butterflies in raised relief. One 2½-pint pitcher and six tumblers to match. Weight, packed, 12 pounds.
35K6801
Per set **$1.58**

7-Piece Optic Water Set

Thin pressed crystal glass, highly polished in optic (fluted) design. One 3-pint pitcher and six bell shaped tumblers, with pressed star bottom. Strong handle. Weight, packed, 8 pounds.
35K6802—Per set **98c**

7-Piece Glass Water Set

Wt., pkd., 8 lbs.

Crackle Glass Design. Medium weight pressed glass. Three-pint tankard shape pitcher and six ½-pint tumblers.
35K6803—Per set **85c**
35K6831—8-Piece Iced Tea or Lemonade Set. Same as above, with fancy covered pitcher. Weight, pkd., 10 lbs **$1.40**

8-Piece Punch Bowl Set

Heavy clear pressed glass. Imitation cut. For grape juice, punch, orangeade, etc. Deep bowl, 12½ inches wide, with foot, and six cups. Weight, packed, 20 lbs.
35K6804—Per set ... **$1.58**

6-Piece Colonial Table Set

Covered butter dish (2 pieces), covered sugar bowl (2 pieces), one spoonholder and one cream pitcher. Pressed glass. Weight, packed, 12 pounds.
35K6805—Per set **75c**

6-Piece Pressed Floral Design Table Set

Covered butter dish (two pieces), covered sugar bowl (two pieces), cream pitcher and spoonholder. Polished crystal glass. Weight, packed, 13 pounds.
35K6806—Per set **92c**

Refrigerator Water Bottle

Clear pressed glass in a square shape. Grape design cut on sides. Fitted with a patented watertight metal cover, easy to remove; allows bottle to be laid on side. Capacity, 1 qt. Wt., pkd., 3 pounds.
35K6807
49c

Round Glass Covered Cracker or Cookie Jar

Clear glass with handled cover. Keeps cookies or crackers fresh. Can be used as a sugar or flour jar. Capacity, 1 gallon. Weight, packed, 8 pounds.
35K6808
88c

Daisy Cut Sugar and Cream Set

Colonial Shape Footed Sugar and Cream Set. Polished crystal glass in panel effect, cut with flowers and leaves in silver gray finish. Height, 3½ in. Wt., packed, 4 lbs.
35K6809—Per set **65c**

Colonial Shape Ice Water Pitcher.

Heavy glass. Turned over edges prevent the ice and liquid from spilling over the sides when poured. Capacity, 3 pints. Height, 7 in. Shipping wt., 7 lbs.
35K6810
55c

6-Piece Gold Iridescent Table Set

Pressed glass. Decorated with fruits and butterflies, covered butter dish (two pieces), covered sugar bowl (two pieces), spoonholder and cream pitcher. Weight, packed, 10 pounds.
35K6811—Per set **$1.75**

Covered Water or Iced Tea Pitcher.

Pressed glass in optic (fluted) design. Star pressed bottom. Capacity, 3 pints; height, 10 inches. Shpg. wt., 7 lbs.
35K6812 ..... **75c**

11½-Inch Handled Sandwich Tray.

Polished crystal glass. Pressed floral design on a beaded background, has silvery effect. Weight, packed, 4 pounds.
35K6813 .... **62c**

Round Glass Fish Bowls or Aquariums

Clear glass, in following sizes:
35K6814—Capacity, 1 gallon. Weight, packed, 6½ pounds **72c**
35K6815—Capacity, 2 gallons. Weight, packed, 9½ pounds **$1.15**

Candy Jar

Clear glass. Pressed triangle design. Capacity, 1 pound. Height, 10½ in. Weight, packed, 5 pounds.
35K6824
69c

Footed Cake Salver

Pressed crystal glass, with Colonial shape stem. Pressed star bottom. Size, 9 inches. Ht., 4½ inches. Weight, packed, 5½ lbs.
35K6818 ... **55c**

11-Inch Cake Salver.

Green or amber pressed glass with flowers and leaves in rock crystal effect. Weight, packed, 5 lbs.
35K6819—Green Color Salver **$1.10**
35K6820—Amber Color Salver **$1.10**

20-Piece Green Colored Glassware Set

Clear transparent green colored fire polished press glass in colonial and diamond design. The set consists of pieces that are useful every day in the year.

1 Seven-Piece Water Set	1 Seven-Pc. Berry Set
1 Covered Butter Dish, (2 pieces)	1 Covered Sugar Bowl (2 pieces)
1 Cream Pitcher	1 Spoon Holder

Weight, packed, 25 pounds.
35K6817—Per set **$2.50**

7-Piece Footed Iridescent Berry Set

Gold color iridescent pressed glass. Decorated with fruits and butterflies in raised relief. The set consists of one 8-inch footed berry bowl and six 4¾-inch sauce dishes.
35K6821—Weight, packed, 10 pounds **$1.75**

13-Piece Colonial Berry Set

Eight-inch berry bowl and twelve 4¼-inch sauce dishes to match. Made of pressed glass in colonial pattern. Pressed star in the bottom of each piece. Weight, packed, 10 pounds.
35K6822 .... **78c**

16-Piece Border Pattern Berry Set

Pressed polished glass in a colonial shape with a diamond design border and a pressed star bottom. One deep berry bowl, twelve sauce dishes, one covered sugar bowl and one cream pitcher. Wt., packed, 16 lbs.
35K6823—Per set **$1.75**

5-Piece Table Set

Clear glass salt and pepper shakers with nickel plated tops, vinegar bottle, syrup pitcher and 6½-inch tray, cut with a grape design in silver gray finish. Wt. pkd., 5½ lbs. **$1.18**
35K6825
35K6827—1-Quart Fruit Jars. (Wt., packed, 25 pounds.) Per dozen ... **$1.12**
8K405—Mason Jar Caps. Weight, packed, 1¾ pounds. Per dozen **27c**

Sanitary Mason Fruit Jars

Clear glass. Strong shoulder. Fitted with a non-corroding opal glass lined metal top and red rubber fruit jar ring. The screw top jar is much safer than the wire clamped jars.
35K6826—1-Pint Fruit Jars. (Weight, packed, 15 lbs.) Per dozen **98c**

Footed Square Shape Honey or Jelly Dish

Pressed glass, in floral design. Size, 5½ inches square. Height to top of handled cover, 5½ in. Weight, packed, 4 pounds.
35K6829
39c

16-Piece Berry Set

Clear pressed glass, pressed diamond design. Eight-inch berry or salad bowl, twelve 4½-inch sauce dishes, one covered and handled sugar bowl and creamer to match. Pressed star bottoms. Weight, packed, 15 pounds.
35K6830—Per set **$1.35**

Table, Baking and Cooking Glassware

High Grade Nickel Plated Tableware

With first quality glass inserts. Made of heavy gauge brass heavily nickel plated. The embossing stands out in relief and the deep etched effect looks like engraving.

Handled Relish Dish. Nickel plated frame. Around the outside of the frame there is an embossed border. Fitted with a 4-inch green glass relish dish. Wt., packed, 4½ lbs.
35K7800
89c

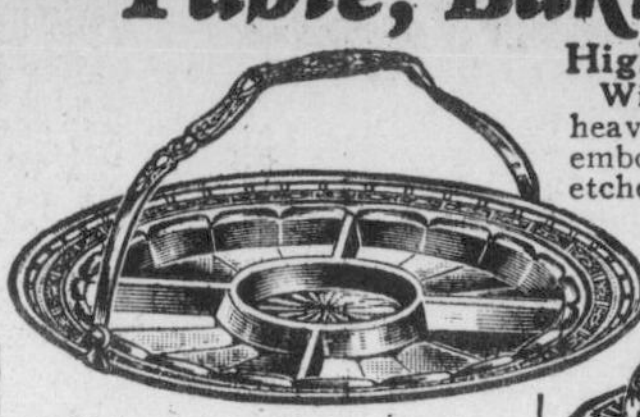

12¾-Inch Handled Five-Compartment Relish Dish. Nickel plated frame. Glass dish insert is of green color fluted glass with a pressed star in center. Pierced and embossed border. The fancy handle has an etched design and is also pierced. Wt., packed, 6 pounds.
35K7801.........**$2.98**

10-Inch Handled Cheese and Cracker Tray. Nickel plated with covered glass cheese dish. Embossed and pierced border. The handle is also decorated with a design and pierced. Wt., packed, 3 pounds.
35K7802.........**$1.65**

13-Inch Bread Tray. Nickel plated. Rolled edge with a fancy embossing around the side and ends and a floral effect design covering the bottom of the tray. Wt., packed, 2 lbs.
35K7803.............**85c**

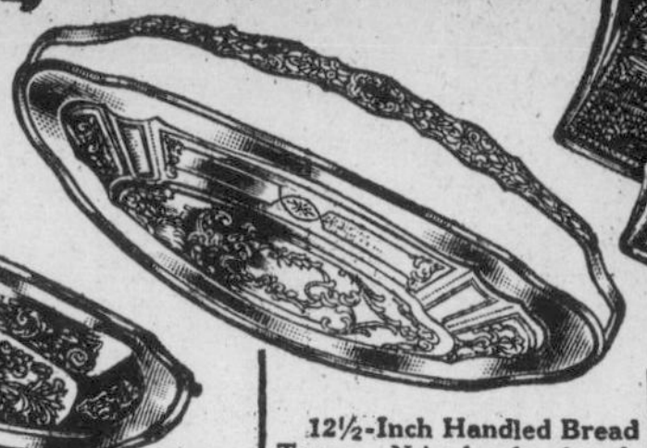

12½-Inch Handled Bread Tray. Nickel plated. Rolled edge with a fancy panel design around the sides and etched effect in bottom. The fancy handle is covered with a pressed design. Weight, packed, 2 pounds.
35K7804.**$1.25**

Crumb Tray Set. Nickel plated. Consisting of a tray and scraper with open handle decorated in chased effect with a Japanese garden scene in an embossed frame. Wt., packed, 1½ lbs.
35K7805
Per set.....**$1.25**

Serving Trays. Nickel plated. Rolled edge with Holland scenes in the center, in chased effect. In addition to the scenes, the large tray has scroll design in each corner of the center.
35K7806—Size, 9x14 in. Wt. pkd., 2 lbs. **$1.35**
35K7807 — Size, 11½x16½ in. Weight, packed, 3 pounds... **$2.50**

Mounted Glass Baking Dishes

Mounted in solid brass nickel plated frames with metal handles and feet

These dishes are made of clear glass of high heat resisting quality in what is known as the optic shape, which combines great strength with low expansion under heat. The corrugated bottom permits the heat to circulate and bake an even crust top and bottom. Clean and economical in service. In baking, oven heat is transmitted to the food uniformly on all sides.

12 and 13-Inch Round Serving Trays. Nickel plated with rolled edge. Plain without embossing but highly polished. The old standard shape. You should have one of each size.
35K7808—12-inch Tray. Wt., pkd., 2 lbs. **$1.29**
35K7809—13-inch Tray. Wt., pkd., 2½ lbs. **$1.50**

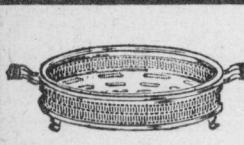

Glass Pie Plate, in nickel plated frame. 9½ in. Height of plate, 1¾ inches.
35K7810—Shpg. weight, 4 lbs....... **$1.65**

8-Inch Round Glass Casserole in nickel plated frame. Capacity, 3 pts. Shipping wt., 5½ lbs.
35K7811.............. **$2.75**
9-Inch Round Glass Casserole in nickel plated frame. Capacity, 3½ pints. Shpg. wt., 8 lbs.
35K7812.............. **$3.35**

10½-In. Muffin Pan. In nickel plated frame. Eight compartment glass dish is made of cooking glass. Size of dish, 10½x6¾ inches. The frame also fits our 35K7817 Baked Apple Dish shown below in our cooking glassware line.
35K7813—Muffin Pan. Weight, packed, 8 pounds. **$2.95**

8-Inch Oval Casserole in nickel plated frame. Capacity, 2 pints. Shipping wt., 5½ lbs. **$2.50**
9-Inch Oval Casserole in nickel plated frame. Capacity, 3½ pints. Shipping wt., 7 lbs. **$3.45**
35K7815.............

10-Inch Oval Steak Casserole in nickel plated frame. 7¾ in. wide. Capacity, 2½ pints. Weight, packed, 9 lbs. **$2.95**
35K7816.............

Cooking and Baking Glassware

These dishes are made of clear glass of high heat resisting quality in what is known as the optic shape, which combines great strength with low expansion under heat. The corrugated bottom permits the heat to circulate and bake an even crust top and bottom. Clean and economical in service. For other Glass or Baking Dishes see page 763.

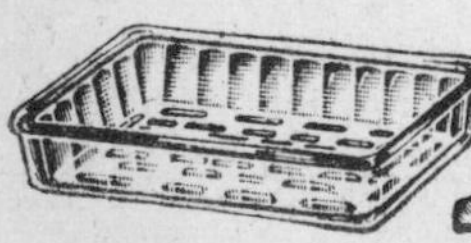

35K7817—6 x 10 x 2-Inch Brown Betty or Baked Apple Dish. Weight, packed, 5¼ pounds.............**80c**

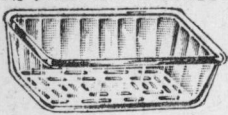

35K7818—Bread Pan or Pound Cake Dish. 5 x 9 x 3 inches. Weight, packed, 4½ pounds..............**62c**

35K7827—Eight-Compartment Muffin Dish. Size, 10½ x 6¾ in. Wt., pkd., 3 lbs.**$1.25**

35K7819 — 7-Inch Pudding Dish. Weight, packed, 3 lbs.....**69c** 
35K7830—Custard Cups. 4 oz. Weight, pkd., 3½ lbs. Set of 6 ....**83c**
35K7831—Custard Cups. Capacity, 6 oz. Wt., half dozen, 4 lbs. Set of 6 ....**$1.15**

35K7828 — Round Pie Plate. 8½-inch. Weight, packed, 4 pounds........**60c**

35K7820 — Oval Casserole With Cover. 5¾ x 8 inches. Capacity, 2 pints. Wt., packed, 7 lbs.....**$1.25**
35K7821 — Oval Casserole With Cover. 9½ x 7 inches. Capacity, 3½ pints. Wt., packed, 6¾ lbs. **$1.55**

35K7822—Round Casserole With Cover. 8¼ in. Capacity, 3 pints. Weight, packed, 6¾ lbs.....**$1.35**
35K7823—Round Casserole With Cover. 9 in. Capacity, 3½ pints. Weight, packed, 7 pounds...**$1.58**

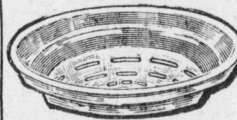

"Save-All" Pie Plate. The edge keeps juice in pie and prevents mussy oven or gummed pan. Size, 8½ inches. Wt., packed, 4¾ lbs.
35K7829
75c

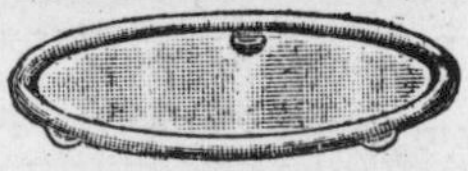

35K7825 — Hot Dish with three ball feet. Size, 8¼ inches. Very useful for teapots or unmounted dishes containing hot food. Weight, packed, 1 pound......**58c**

35K7824—Oval Steak Casserole With Cover. Size, 10x7¾ inches. Capacity, 2½ pints. Weight, packed, 7 lbs...**$1.45**

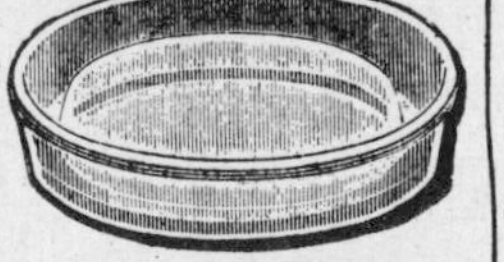

Mary Ann Cake Pan. Makes a wonderful cake which can be filled with fruit, custards or meringue. Wt., packed, 5¼ lbs.
35K7832—Size, 8½ inches. **$1.15**

35K7826—Angel Food Tube Cake Pan. Size, 3½x8 inches. Weight, packed, 6¾ pounds.......**$1.58**

35K7833—9-Inch Cake Plate. Weight, packed, 4¼ pounds **60c**

Tea or Serving Trays

Large Oval Shape Tea or Serving Tray.
14-Inch Oval Shape Tea or Serving Tray.

Mahogany Finish Serving Tray. Made of wood with strong handles. The glass covered bottom represents mahogany wood with inlaid border and center design. Size of tray, 17½x11½ in. Weight, packed, 8 lbs.
35K7834............. **95c**

Frame is hard composition and finished in the new Japanese red. Glass covered bottom is also finished in Japanese red with embossed design in the center. Strong wood and fiber handles. Weight, packed, 5¾ pounds.
35K7835....... **$1.25**

Mahogany Finish Serving Tray. A reproduction of an oil painting of flowers and a vase in natural colors. The frame is made of wood in two tones of coloring. Strong metal bound handles. Size, 17½x11½ in. Weight, packed, 4 lbs.
35K7836............ **$1.65**

For other Serving Trays see pages 614, 965 and 967

A hard composition in a maroon color finish with wood handles. Glass covered bottom in maroon finish, shading to Japanese red with two hand painted gilt designs in the center. Size tray, 19x13 inches. Wt., pkd., 8 lbs.
35K7837.......... **$2.15**

Mahogany Finish Serving Tray. A reproduction of an oil painting and garden flowers in natural colors. The frame is made of wood in two tones of coloring. Size, 17½x11½ inches. Weight, packed, 4 pounds.
35K7838........... **$1.45**

Brighten Your Home

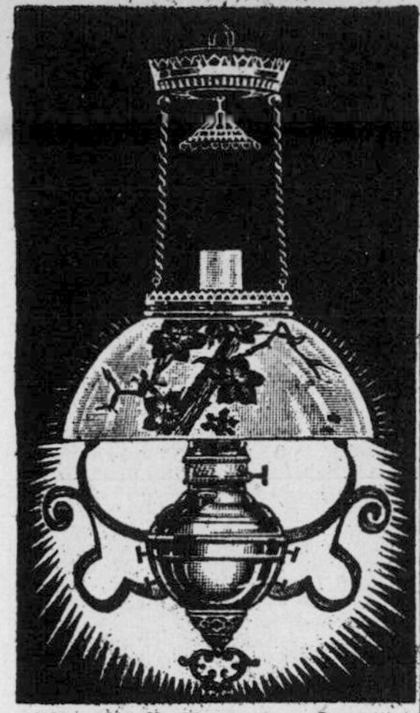

"Sunglow" Extension Lamp

Fitted with brass extension frame, brass oil fount holder with bottom pull ornament, embossed brass crown, smoke bell and ceiling plate. The removable brass oil pot is fitted with No. 2 center draft burner, No. 2 Rochester chimney and wick. The 14-inch opal glass dome shade is decorated with flowers. Automatic extension lowers lamp from 33 to 65 inches. Weight, packed, 40 pounds.
35K8100.......**$10.98**

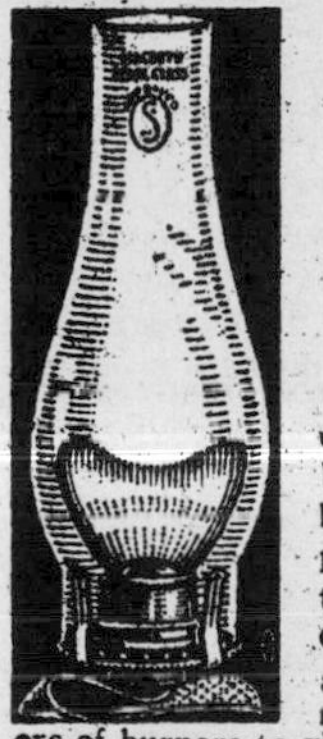

No Smoke No Flicker More Light Steady Flame

Improved Burner and Chimney

This is the improved chimney and burner which has been perfected by the Standard Oil Company and the manufacturers of burners to give the users of oil lamps the maximum amount of light. The old style chimney and burner will not permit this.

You cannot use satisfactorily the new burner and the old crimp top chimney, neither can you use an old burner with an approved chimney. To obtain this bigger and better light, **it is necessary to use both the improved No. 2 Brass Burner and the approved Straight Top Chimney.**

35K8101—No. 2 Brass Burner, Wick and Lead Glass Chimney. Weight, packed, 2½ pounds **38c**

35K8102—Chimneys only. Weight, 2½ pounds. Per ½ dozen **$1.30**

35K8103—Burner only. Weight, ¾ pound. Each....**12c**

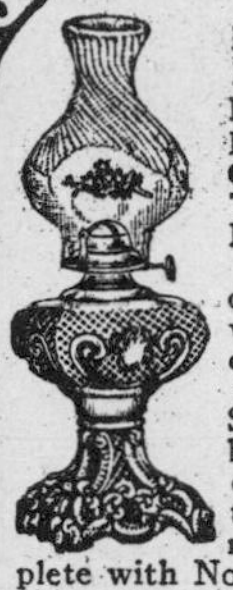

Richly Embossed Large Ruby and Gold Color Table Lamp. Chimney decorated with ruby color flowers. Solid gilded base with embossing tinted ruby, complete with No. 3 burner, chimney and wick. Oil cap., 2½ pts. Clinch collar. Height, 19 in. Wt., packed, 9 lbs.
35K8107 **$1.19**

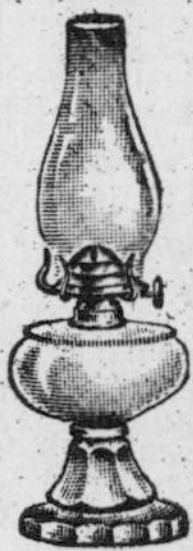

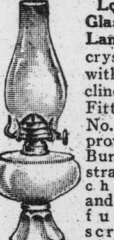

Low Footed Glass Table Lamp. Clear crystal glass with brass clinch collar. Fitted with No. 2 Improved Brass Burner and straight top chimney and wick, fully described on this page. Ht. 17½ in. Capacity 1½ pints. Wt., packed, 6½ lbs.
35K8108.....**80c**

Famous Angle Wall Lamp Single Burner

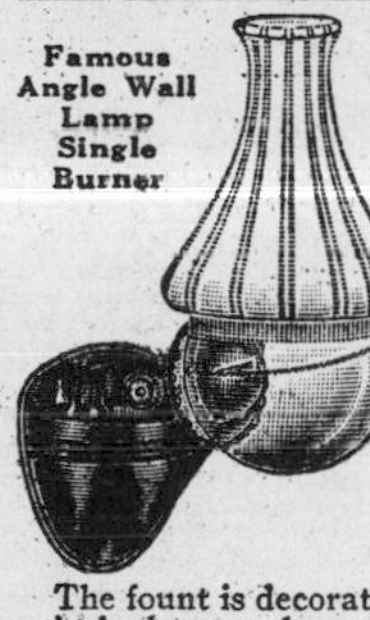

The fount is decorated with bronze lacquer. Capacity of oil fount, 20 oz. Weight, packed, 10 pounds.
35K8109. **$4.45**

Top and Bottom Globes

35K8110—Plain White Opal Glass Top (chimney). Weight, packed, 5 pounds. Each **95c**

35K8111—Clear Crystal Glass Bottom Globe. Weight, packed, 3½ pounds. Each **75c**

35K8112—Flat Wicks. Weight, packed, per six, 8 ounces..........**25c**

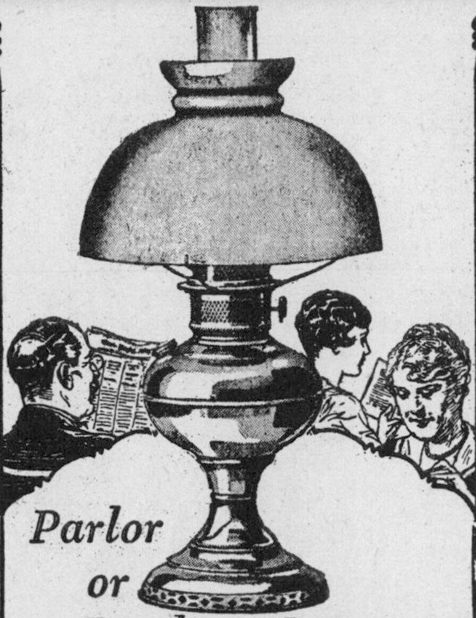

Parlor or Reading Lamp

Simple—Economical—Smokeless—Odorless—Standard Rochester

The Old Reliable "Rochester" Lamp at an Exceptionally Low Price

This lamp has been the standard reading and sewing lamp for forty years or more and is probably the best known lamp ever produced. Its main features are **simplicity, durability and fine strong light.**

Simplicity. The lamp is so constructed that there are no complicated parts to get out of order. To operate it after it is lit, all the user has to do is to turn the wick.

Durability. It is scientifically made of heavy gauge brass, nickel plated, and with proper care will last a lifetime.

Light. The lamp is fitted with a No. 2 center draft burner, No. 2 Rochester chimney and wick, which produces a clear, strong and steady tulip shape white flame, equal in brilliancy to more than forty candle power.

The lamp is an ideal one for reading or sewing; it is efficient and economical to maintain. The oil capacity is 1 quart. Height, 21 in.

The price we ask—$3.45—for the lamp complete, including chimney, wick, 10-inch tripod and 10-inch opal glass dome shade, is very low. It is probably about one-half the present price elsewhere. Weight, packed, 10 pounds.

35K8113—"Rochester" Reading Lamp...............................**$3.45**

35K8114—"Rochester" Reading Lamp With Green Shade. Weight, packed, 10 lbs...............................**$4.25**

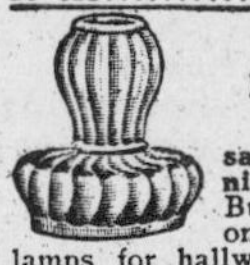

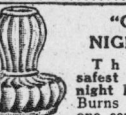

"GLOW" NIGHT LAMP

The thriftiest, safest and handiest night lamp made. Burns 100 hours for one cent. Just the lamps for hallways, stairs, bathrooms, bedrooms or sick chamber. It is simple and practical. All glass, both fount and globe, with a one-piece glass burner which does not burn oil directly but generates a vapor that feeds the flame; comes in two styles—table and bracket.

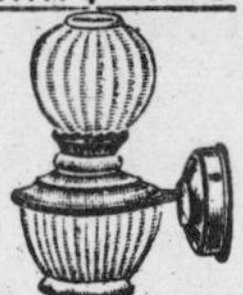

35K8115—"Glow" Night Table Lamp. Weight, packed, 3 lbs...............**48c**

35K8116—"Glow" Night Bracket Lamp, complete with brushed brass bracket for hanging. Weight, packed 3 lbs...............**95c**

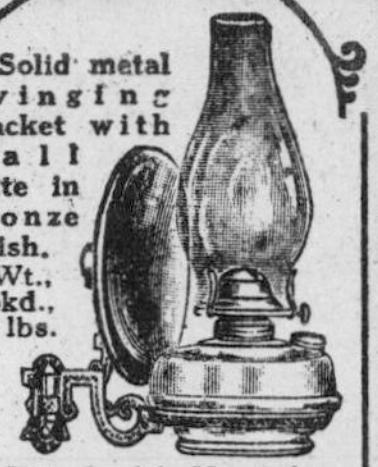

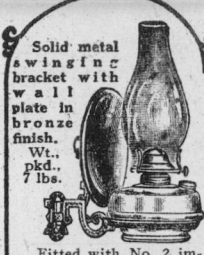

Solid metal swinging bracket with wall plate in bronze finish. Wt., pkd., 7 lbs.

Fitted with No. 2 improved brass burner and straight top chimney. Wick and removable crystal glass fount. Back of the lamp, attached to the bracket frame, is a 7-inch mirrored glass reflector.
35K8117
$1.25

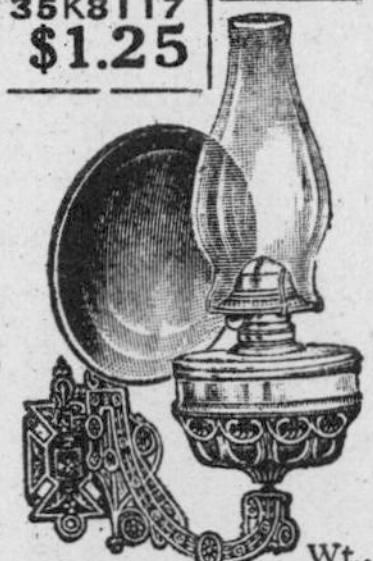

Wt., pkd., 9 lbs.

Fancy ornamental heavy solid metal swinging bracket with wall plate and fount holder in bronze gilt finish. Fitted with No. 2 improved brass burner and straight top chimney, wick and removable crystal glass fount. Adjustable 8-inch mirrored glass reflector back of lamp. Capacity, 1½ pints.
35K8118
$1.45

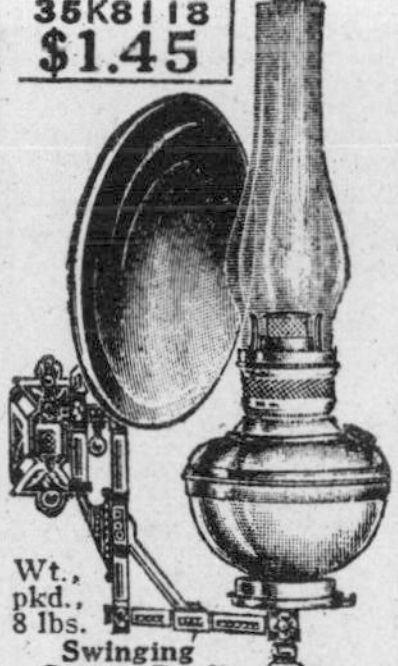

Wt., pkd., 8 lbs.

Swinging Center Draft Brass Bracket Lamp

Ornamental solid metal swinging bracket with wall plate in gilt finish. Fitted with polished brass removable oil fount and No. 2 center draft burner, chimney and wick. Adjustable 10-inch mirrored glass reflector. Capacity, 2½ pints.
35K8119..**$3.95**

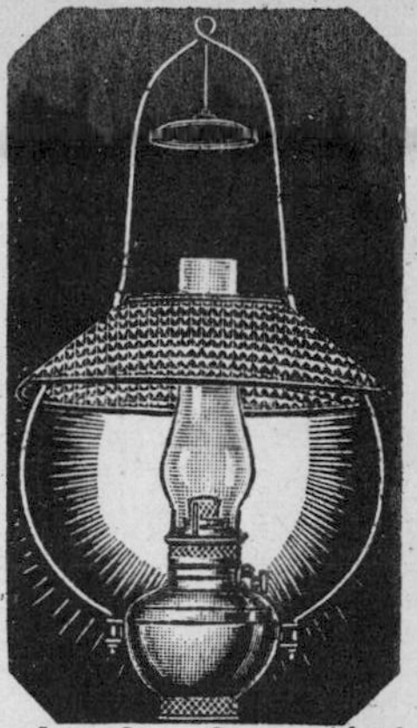

Juno Store Lamp without extension. Steel, brass plated frame, removable brass fount fitted with No. 2 center draft burner, 15-inch tin shade (outside enameled green, inside nickel plated finish), metal smoke bell, No. 2 Rochester chimney and wick. Wt., packed, 20 lbs.
35K8120....**$4.25**

Extension

For hanging lamps; to raise and lower for lighting, cleaning, filling, etc. Permits 3-ft. extension. Brass finish. Wt., packed, 5 lbs.
35K8134....**$2.75**

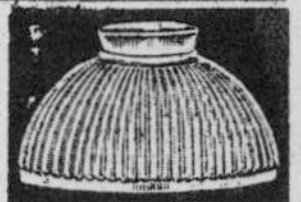

10-inch Fluted White Opal Glass Shade. Wt. packed 6½ lbs. Each.
35K8121 **75c**

35K8122—10-in. Fluted Green Glass Shade. White lined. Wt., pkd., 6½ lbs. Each.....**$1.65**

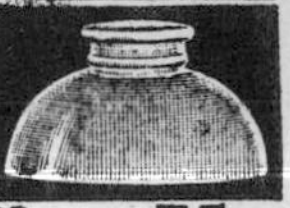

10-in. Plain White Opal Glass Shade. Each.
35K8123 **75c**

35K8124—10-inch Plain Green Opal Glass Shade. White lined. Each..........**$1.65**
Weight, packed, 6 pounds.

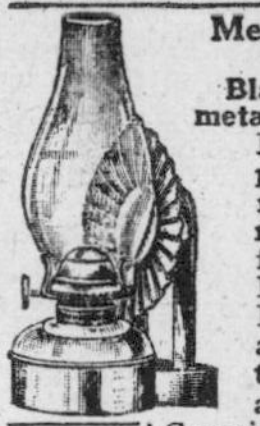

Metal Bracket Lamp

Black enameled metal frame. Fitted with polished tin reflector, removable glass fount, No. 2 Improved Brass Burner and straight top chimney and wick. Capacity, 1 pint. Height, 12½ in. Wt., pkd., 5¼ lbs.
35K8125 ...**78c**

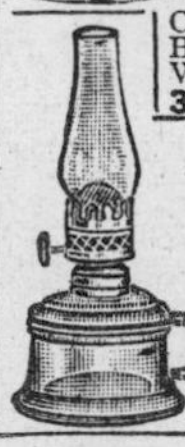

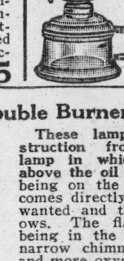

Handled Night Lamp. Green color glass fount fitted with brass burner and a wick ¼ inch wide, clear glass Chimney. Ht., 7 in. Wt., pkd., 2½ lbs.
35K8126
39c

Ever-Brite Gasoline Table Lamp

Lights With a Match—Clean—Safe—Economical

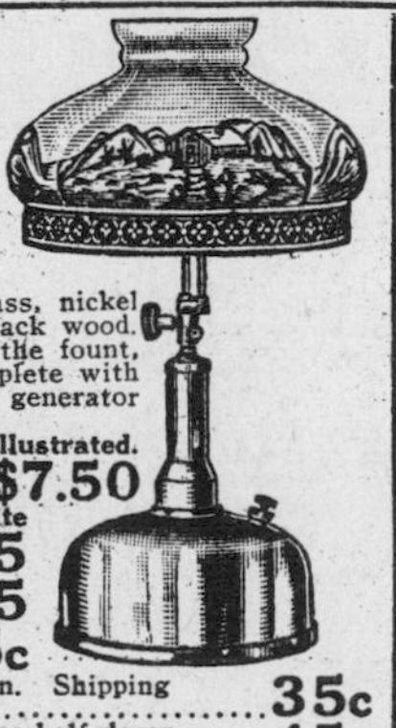

Produces a light of unusually high candle power. **Its consumption of fuel is very small.** It is fitted with two mantles, and casts no shadows.

It lights almost instantly with an ordinary parlor match. Anyone can operate it. No complicated parts to get out of order. Requires filling only once a week.

Absolutely safe. The fuel has only one outlet—a tiny hole in the generator. It has no wick to trim, no chimney to clean or break. It cannot leak or become oily.

"Ever-Brite" Lamp base and burner are made of heavy brass, nickel plated. The standard is made of brass covered with heavy black wood. Height, 20 in., and the diameter of the base, which contains the fount, is 8 inches. Capacity of fount, 3 pints. It is furnished complete with two extra mantles, air pump, wrench, cleaning pick, extra generator and extra tip.

35K8127—Improved "Ever-Brite" Lamp with shade illustrated. Weight, packed, 12 pounds. Complete...............................**$7.50**

35K8128—Improved "Ever-Brite" Lamp with fancy white shade. Weight, packed, 10 pounds. Complete...............................**$6.75**

35K8129—10-Inch Fancy Decorated Shade. Weight, packed, 7 pounds. Each...................**1.45**

35K8133—10-Inch White Fancy Shade. Weight, packed, 7 pounds. Each...................**95c**

35K8130—"Ever-Brite" Gasoline Mantles. Per half dozen. Shipping weight, 4 ounces...............................**35c**

35K8131—Regular Size Mantles for gasoline systems. Per half dozen. Shipping weight, 4 ounces...............................**45c**

35K8132—Generator for "Ever-Brite" Gasoline Lamp. Shipping weight, 3 ounces. Each...............................**28c**

The Famous Double Burner Angle Lamp

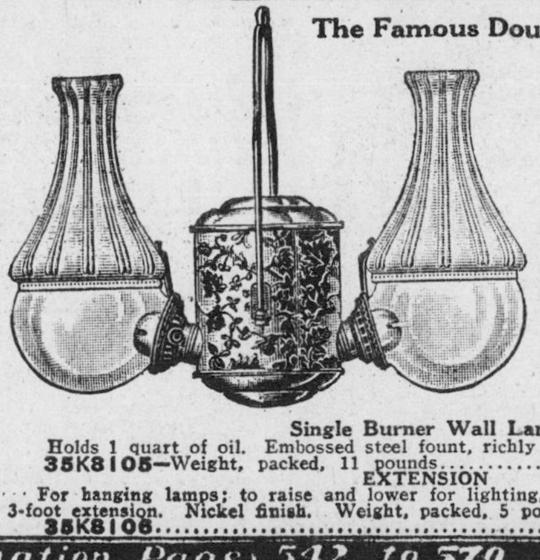

These lamps differ in construction from the ordinary lamp in which the burner is above the oil tank. The burner being on the side all the light comes directly down where it is wanted and there are no shadows. The flame of the lamp being in the bowl instead of a narrow chimney burns less oil and more oxygen. The bowl being below, the flame cannot smoke the chimney and cut off the light. The lamp is easy to fill, light and keep clean.

DOUBLE BURNER LAMP

Holds 3 quarts of oil. Embossed steel fount, richly nickel plated. Weight, packed, 18 lbs.
35K8104....**$9.25**

Single Burner Wall Lamp

Holds 1 quart of oil. Embossed steel fount, richly nickel plated.
35K8105—Weight, packed, 11 pounds...............................**$5.75**

EXTENSION

For hanging lamps; to raise and lower for lighting, cleaning, filling, etc. Permits 3-foot extension. Nickel finish. Weight, packed, 5 pounds.
35K8106...............................**$3.25**

See Index and Information Pages 542 to 570

THE DAUNTLESS *Will Always Rank as* AMERICA'S GREATEST WARM AIR CIRCULATOR

20,000 Enthusiastic Users the First Year

WHEN Winter Comes—That's the time our customers will rise up and thank us for supplying them with the Dauntless Warm Air Circulator. Let it rain—let it snow—let it hail—let it freeze and you will always find the Dauntless on the job ready to keep your rooms properly heated with a small amount of fuel.

From Coast to Coast, from border to gulf, in cities, towns and hamlets, thousands of users claim the Dauntless Warm Air Furnace the most efficient and most wonderful heating device they have ever seen or used.

Built for lifetime service. Takes the place of two or three ordinary stoves.

Our Dauntless Warm Air Circulator operates on the warm air furnace principle and supplies a volume of warm, healthful heat into every nook and corner of the rooms, making it possible to keep an **entire home of five or six rooms, upstairs and downstairs,** comfortably warm in zero weather. Beyond question of doubt, this method of warm air circulation is the most healthful, sanitary and modern way of home heating known.

Principle of Operation

The Dauntless Warm Air Circulator is equipped with an extra heavy steel plate combustion chamber incased in an outer porcelain enameled casing with scientifically constructed air space between. The cold air, drawn from the floor, flows up from the bottom of the Circulator through the special designed chamber. As it comes in contact with the heating element, the cold air is instantly heated and distributed through the top from room to room, circulating healthful, sanitary heat throughout the house. **The action of the flow of air is the same as in warm air furnaces.**

The Humidifier or Water Pan furnishes the required amount of humidity, creating a most comfortable feeling of warmth with a minimum amount of fuel. **It is** located in a readily accessible place and can be filled when necessary with a dipper, pitcher or other container. If necessary, it can be removed and filled and then replaced without effort.

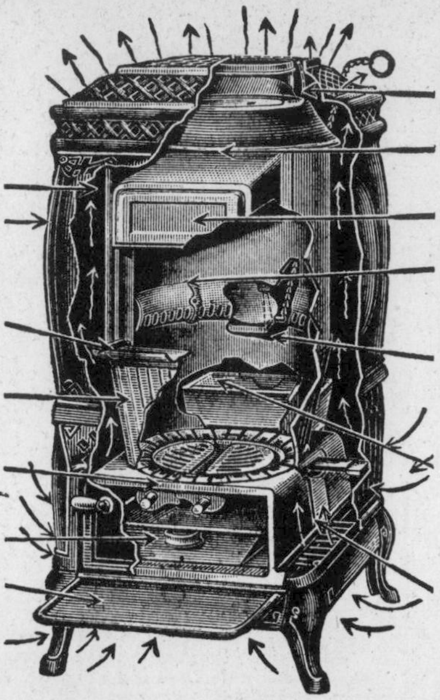

Extra wide space between fire chamber and outer casing, permitting a large volume of warm air to pass through and circulate to all corners of the house.
Heavy cast iron outer casing.
Coal chute for feeding coal. Not needed on stove fitted with magazine for burning hard coal and is not furnished.
Heavy ribbed cast iron fire pot.
Two-bar duplex grate for burning any kind of coal, lignite, coke or wood.
Large and roomy ashpan equipped with heavy handle.
Ash tray to prevent ashes from falling on floor while being removed.
Reversible flue collar with sliding check damper. Pipe can be run straight in or up as desired.
Heavy gauge steel combustion chamber.
Smoke screen to prevent smoke coming into room during refueling.
Hot blast ring permits air to mix with smoke and gases, getting every bit of heat from fuel. Not needed on stove with magazine for burning hard coal and is not furnished.
Hot blast damper. Operated by chain pull from top of stove.
Large capacity water pan. Easily refilled or removed for cleaning.
Large one-piece ashpit. Absolutely airtight.

See Large Illustration on Opposite Page

Educative View Showing Details of Construction

The extraordinary durable iron used as the base for the rich grained Porcelain Enamel finish, is not the ordinary commercial kind, but is produced by blending of several different kinds of iron selected for their special qualities, and a proved formula that produce a metal so durable that we can **unconditionally guarantee the Dauntless** to withstand the hardest kind of usage for practically a lifetime.

Closely fitted doors, special designed **smoke outlet** and perfect **dampers** give positive control of the fire. Tests made have shown a saving of one-third to one-half of the fuel required to heat the same amount of space as an ordinary stove.

Large feed door accommodates large chunks of coal or wood. **Smoke Screen** is provided inside of feed door and keeps the smoke out of the room when the feed door is open.

The inner body is rugged in construction and dome shape in design. Heavy steel plate dome or combustion chamber is securely bolted to outside of fire pot, preventing bolts from coming in contact with flame and burning off. All joints are hand ground and securely fitted together with best quality cement, giving an absolutely airtight construction. Damper construction permits regulating the heater to produce almost any degree of heat.

Holds fire for almost forty-eight hours without attention. The firepot is made extra heavy, similar to those found in hot air furnaces. **The hot blast** feature consumes the gas arising from the fuel and causes the heat to be thrown against the body instead of into the center of the heater. Combustion takes place in a complete circle against the firepot, the entire radiating surface is uniformly heated, producing almost complete radiation. **The hot blast feature and coal chute are not needed on stoves fitted with magazine for burning hard coal and are not furnished.**

Measurements of the Dauntless: Height from floor, 51 inches. Diameter of fire box, 16½ inches. Feed door, 10½x14 inches. Floor space, 25x25 in. Takes 7-inch stovepipe. Shpg. wt., 468 lbs.

Order now. Don't wait.

The Logical Successor to the Old Fashioned Heating Stove

The Dauntless Warm Air Circulator requires less attention than any other heating **appliance.** Most users find a scuttle of coal twice a day is practically all the fueling it requires, **and** will hold fire for almost forty-eight hours without attention.

Unconditionally Guaranteed. Special 30-Day Trial Offer

Every stove we sell is covered by our binding guarantee and we are pleased to ship you a Dauntless Warm Air Circulator with the understanding and agreement that it must reach your station in perfect order. You can give it 30 days' trial, during which time you can put it to every possible test, and if you do not find it better, stronger, handsomer, better made and better finished and more economical in the consumption of fuel than any similar heating device you could buy at home or elsewhere at almost double our price, you can return it to us at our expense and we will immediately return your money.

Lasts a Lifetime—You do not purchase a furnace or heating appliance for five or even ten years and for that reason the questions of Durability, Economy of Fuel and Efficiency are most important.

There is but one way the purchaser can intelligently determine the size and kind of heating device to buy, and that is by thoroughly investigating the construction of the many appliances on the market and determining from that investigation whether it will heat the home perfectly in all kinds of weather and give years and years of satisfactory service.

The Dauntless is made in our own foundry by men with more than forty years of stove making experience. The materials used are absolutely the best obtainable, regardless of price.

No other dealer or manufacturer dare make this offer, for we are the only ones, that we know of, that use Solid Cast Iron for the outer casing. Steel, the material generally used, will not stand up as cast iron does.

22K1678—Dauntless Warm Air Circulator, for soft coal, lignite or wood. Cash price **$79.85**
Easy Time Payment price **$89.50**

22K1680—Dauntless, fitted with magazine for burning hard coal or coke. Cash price **$83.85**
Time Payment price **$93.50**

If you prefer to buy on time, only a few cents each day will bring you the joy, comfort and happiness of our Dauntless Warm Air Circulator. Special Low Terms of $5.00 with order and $5.00 a month until full time payment price has been paid. When ordering on Easy Payments, use Time Payment Order Blank on page 1092.

The Freight Charges on the Dauntless are small when you consider the big saving you make in price. This is another outstanding example of Sears leadership in producing the finest stoves at the lowest prices.

Floor Tray, a Valuable Accessory for the Dauntless. Be sure to order one.

Protect your floor covering with the beautiful mahogany finish floor tray as illustrated on opposite page. Made of heavy gauge steel finished in rich brown grained mahogany enamel to match the Dauntless. The smooth, glass-like finish is easy to clean, simply wipe with a cloth. Can also be furnished in plain black as shown below at left. A thing of beauty and joy forever. Measures 29½x29½ inches. Shipping weight, 18 pounds.

22K1973—Enameled Floor Tray **$4.50**
22K1977—Plain Black Floor Tray **$2.25**

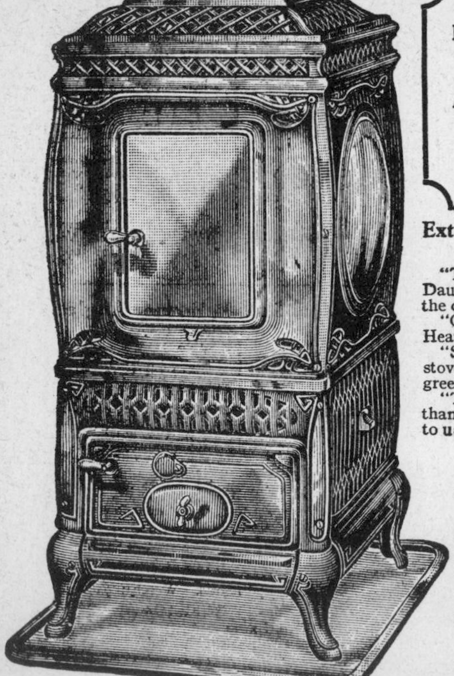

Dauntless Warm Air Circulator

Enormous Stocks
Low Freight Charges
Prompt Shipments

From one of the following cities, whichever is nearest you:

Philadelphia, Pa. **Springfield, Mass.**
Harrisburg, Pa. **Newark, Ohio**

Extracts from a few of the many thousands of letters received from satisfied users.

"Two stoves failed to keep two rooms comfortable. The Dauntless does the work and keeps the whole house warm even in the coldest weather."

"One big stove heated half of my rooms; I find the Dauntless Heater warms my whole house and uses less fuel."

"Since I started using the Dauntless I have thrown out two stoves and am now keeping five large rooms at from 70 to 72 degrees and have made a big saving in my fuel bills."

"The Dauntless Circulating Heater heats our five rooms better than they were heated when we had two stoves and does not begin to use as much fuel."

(Names and Addresses on Request)

Plain Black Finish Dauntless

Shipped from factory in Newark, Ohio.

Made exactly like our enameled Dauntless. Finished in plain black. Can be blackened just like any other plain stove. Just the type for stores, offices, warehouses, etc. The measurements and the terms are just the same, and it is also backed by the same unconditional guarantee as our enameled Dauntless. Tray not included. See 22K1977, above at right. Shipping wt., 468 lbs.

22K1683—Plain Black Dauntless for soft coal, lignite or wood.
Cash price **$63.50**
Time payment price **$70.50**

22K1684—Plain Dauntless, with magazine for burning hard coal or coke.
Cash price **$67.50**
Time payment price **$74.50**

Colonial Fire Set

See Illustration on Opposite Page

For the small sum of $8.50 we will send you this beautiful wrought iron Colonial Design Fire Set, consisting of strong well made shovel with wide blade, brush with extra long bristles, tongs with wide opening to handle big chunks of coal and poker of proper length and shape to stir the burning coals and remove clinkers. The complete outfit is made of solid brass finished to harmonize with the stove. Do not confuse this beautiful fire set with the ordinary set sold by most dealers, as it is made extra heavy and will stand years of the hardest kind of usage. In durability, beauty and finish it is the equal of sets selling at double our price. Shpg. wt., 33 lbs.

22K1984—Colonial Fire Set **$8.50**

An Indispensable Accessory

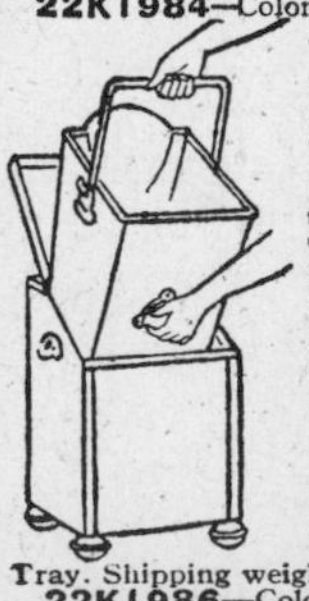

This Colonial Porcelain Mahogany Coal Chest makes your heating outfit complete for parlor, dining room, library or living room and we are not making a strong statement when we say that it is beyond question of doubt the most beautiful and most serviceable outfit of its kind on the market. The inside container is made of extra heavy gauge steel and is guaranteed to withstand the hardest kind of usage. Do not confuse this Colonial Coal Chest with the ordinary kind. It is made in our own factory, the design and construction harmonizes with furnishings in any room and corresponds in color and finish with the Dauntless and Floor Tray. Shipping weight 41 pounds.

22K1986—Colonial Coal Chest **$9.00**

Be sure to order the Coal Chest, Fire Set and Enameled Floor Tray with your Dauntless. If Dauntless is wanted with magazine for burning hard coal only add $4.00 to prices below.

22K1698—Dauntless, including Coal Chest, Fire Set and Floor Tray. Shpg. wt., 571 lbs.
Cash price **$101.85**
Time Payment price **$111.50**

Terms: $5.00 with order, $5.00 a month. If ordering on Easy Terms use Time Payment Order Blank on page 1092.

Single pieces can be had at catalog price. We recommend present owners of the Dauntless order these beautiful accessories.

DAUNTLESS

Warm Air Circulator
Looks like a Phonograph!
Heats like a Furnace!

Heats the Whole House in the Coldest Weather. Harmonizes With Any Furnishings

Heats Upstairs and Down

Suitable for Schools, Churches, Stores and Public Halls

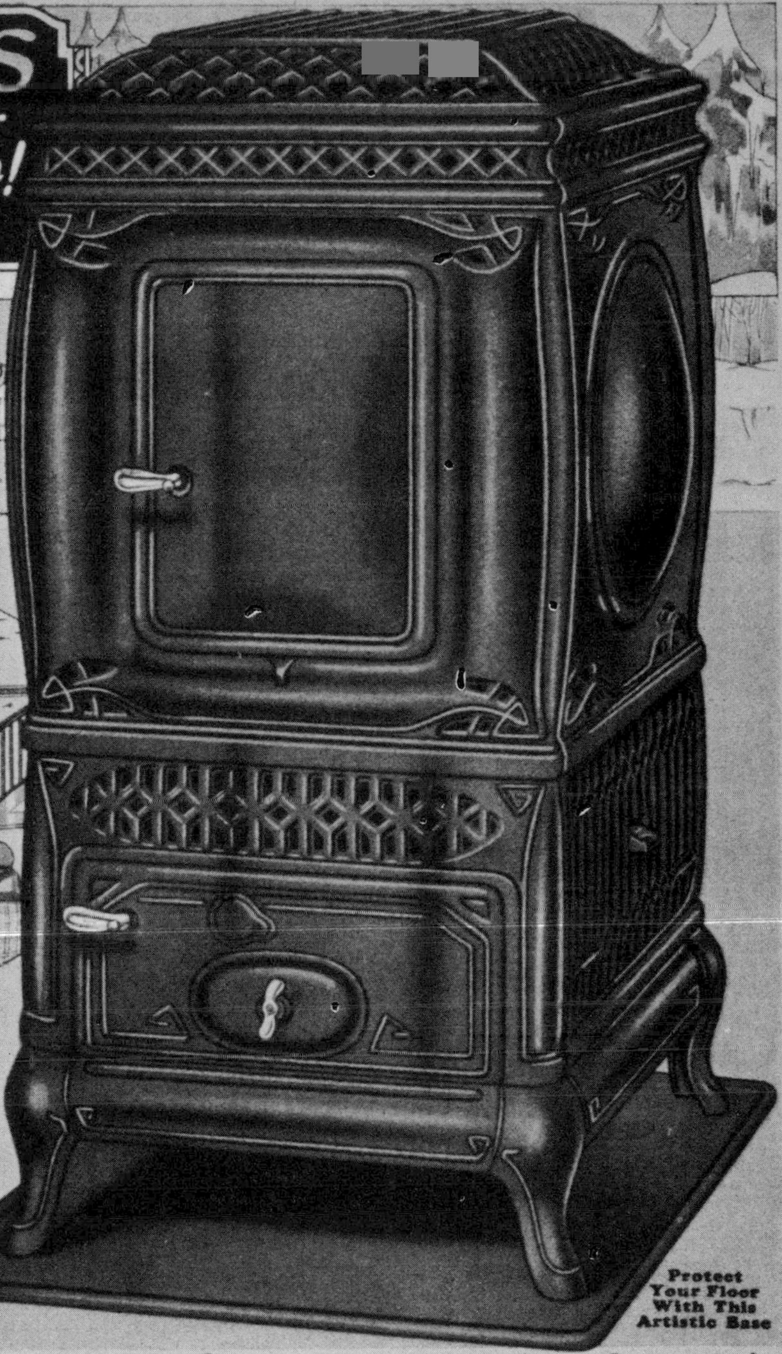

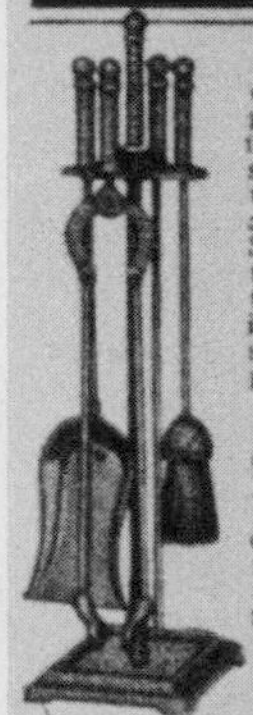

An accessory indispensable for complete enjoyment of the Dauntless. Consists of shovel, tongs, brush, poker and stand, made of Solid Brass, finished to harmonize with the Dauntless. Easily cleaned. Described on opposite page.

This Handsome, Convenient and Practical Coal Chest is described on the opposite page. Order it and these other accessories for the stove you intend to buy or for the one you now own. Our prices are lowest.

CASH PRICE,
$79.85

Huge Stocks Prompt Shipment

Protect Your Floor With This Artistic Base

~$5.00 Down ~$5.00 a Month

A few of the many reasons why our Dauntless is the Nation's Greatest Warm Air Circulator

Made in our own factory and sold direct to our customers at less than wholesale prices.

Endorsed by thousands as the logical successor to the old fashioned heating stove.

Cast iron, extra heavy and strong, built throughout for lifetime service. Takes the place of two or three ordinary heating stoves.

Heats five to seven rooms in the coldest weather with a small amount of fuel.

Every particle of fuel is turned into healthful heat. Burns hard coal (anthracite), coke, soft coal, lignite, wood, or any kind of fuel that any heating stove will burn.

A miser for saving fuel. Holds fire 36 to 48 hours without attention.

The heating element has a capacity like furnaces used for heating the average size home.

The same design grate as used with high price furnaces. Airtight doors and damper keep fire under constant control.

Genuine porcelain enameled grained mahogany finish. Beautiful enough for the finest home. Stain proof, easy to keep clean.

A most dependable warm air circulator, that circulates fresh, healthful, sanitary heat to every corner of the rooms.

See opposite page for details of construction

Made in OUR OWN FOUNDRY

$34.75 CASH
And Up

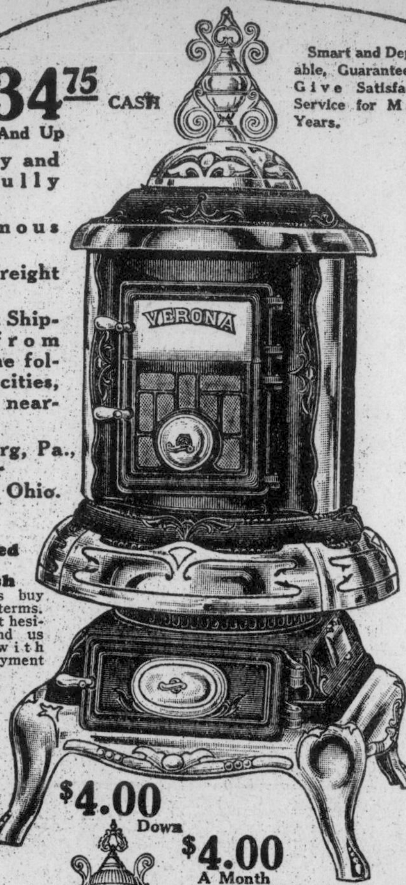

Smart and Dependable, Guaranteed to Give Satisfactory Service for Many Years.

Securely and Carefully Crated.

Enormous Stocks.

Low Freight Charges.

Prompt Shipments from one of the following cities, the one nearer you: Harrisburg, Pa., or Newark, Ohio.

You Need Not Pay Cash
Thousands buy on easy terms. You need not hesitate to send us your order with the first payment of $4.00.

$4.00 Down
$4.00 A Month

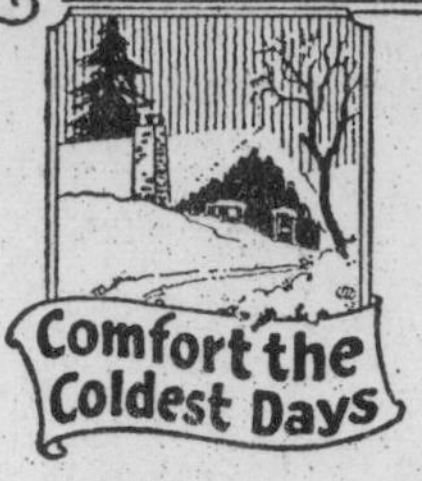

This Big Double Downstairs and Upstairs Heater Defies the Coldest Winter Days

Heats a Big House, Downstairs and Upstairs Without Forcing. Burns Hard (Anthracite) Coal, Soft Coal, Lignite, or Wood.

Best principles of heating require a constant and steady circulation of warm air to every part of the room from floor to ceiling.

This stove has two steel bodies with an air space or flue between which draws air from near the floor, and as the air passes upward between the bodies it becomes highly heated and passes out very hot from the hot air collar, furnishing a steady circulation of heated air.

Heats a big house, downstairs and upstairs. Heats an upstairs room or two without extra fuel cost by connecting a stovepipe from the hot air collar to a register in floor above. Register for this purpose is listed on page 976.

Strongly Made—Bright, Smooth Nickel Plated Trimmings

Whole stove strongly made of cast iron with steel drums around the fire chamber. Made to stand hard firing and last for years. The base made positively airtight and gastight by our famous Wehrle machine fitting system, makes this double heater the most wonderful fire keeper and fuel saver ever made.

Fire pot and easy working roller bearing grates are extra strong to stand hard firing and intense heat. The kind used on high priced base burners. Two feed doors make a big opening for putting in large chunks of wood. Mica windows to radiate firelight around room. Bright and snappy nickel plated base and legs, foot rails and trimmings. A very beautiful stove, good enough for the nicest homes.

The freight charges amount to next to nothing compared to the big saving in price. This big double heater can be depended upon to give long, economical service as well as low first price.

All sizes take 6-inch pipe. **Terms: $4.00 cash and $4.00 a month until paid. If ordering on easy payments, use Time Payment Blank on page 1092.**

Self feeding magazine for burning hard coal can be furnished for only $3.25 extra.

Made in Two Sizes, Order by Number	Diameter Fire Pot, Inches	Cash Price	Time Payment Price	Height, Floor to Urn Base, Inches	Floor Space, Inches	Shipping Weight, Pounds
22K1558	15¾	$34.75	$39.75	48	26x26	284
22K1559	17½	39.50	44.50	52	28x28	345

$6.75
AND UP

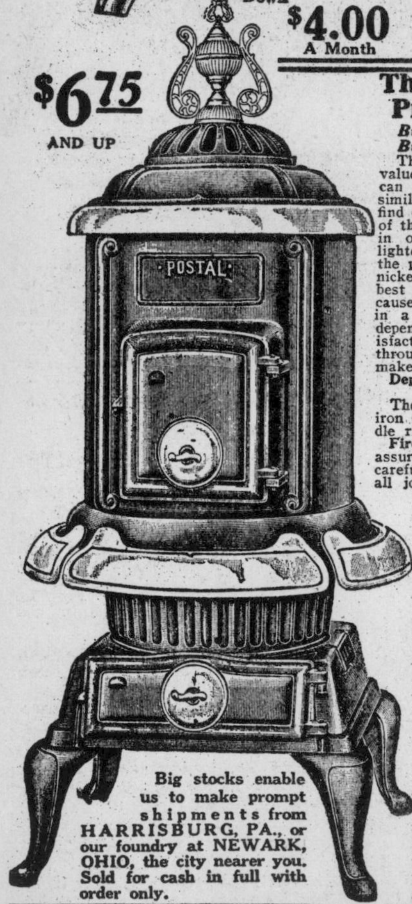

The Leader of All Low Priced Oak Heaters

Burns Anything That Can Be Burned in Any Heating Stove

This heater offers you the best value that a small amount of money can buy. Match it with others of similar size and weight and you will find our prices very attractive. Made of the same quality materials we use in our more expensive stoves, but lighter in weight. We have kept down the price by using just a few simple nickel plated trimmings. One of the best values we offer this season, because it gives you everything needed in a heating stove—pleasing style, dependable construction, assured satisfaction in heating and keeping fire through the night—at prices that make it a dominant value.

Dependable Construction—Efficient Heating Service

The whole stove is made of cast iron except the upper drum and middle ring, which are steel.

Fire pot is made of tested cast iron, assuring long service. Steel body is carefully fitted and securely bolted at all joints. Fire easily controlled by screw draft in ash door and check draft in feed door. Draw center grate furnished to burn hard and soft coal, coke, wood and corn cobs. Ashpan is furnished. Removable lid opening in top to feed hard coal when magazine is used. Be sure to buy a size large enough to heat your rooms without firing hard in cold weather. **Self feeding magazine can be furnished only for the three larger sizes.** If self feeding magazine is wanted, add $2.75 to price. We do not furnish magazine for 22K1592 or 22K1591. At our low prices you can afford to buy one of the larger sizes.

Heating capacities. Be sure to order a stove large enough. Stove 22K1591 will heat only a small bedroom. Stove 22K1592 will heat a medium size room. Stove 22K1593 will heat a large room. Stoves 22K1594 and 22K1595 will heat several rooms, **and are our most popular and desirable sizes.**

Freight charges amount to little compared to the saving you make in buying this heater from us.

Big stocks enable us to make prompt shipments from HARRISBURG, PA., or our foundry at NEWARK, OHIO, the city nearer you. Sold for cash in full with order only.

Made in Five Sizes. Order by Number	Diameter, Fire Pot Inches	For Coal and Wood, Without Magazine	Height, Floor to Urn Base, Inches	Size of Feed Door Opening, Inches	Floor Space, Inches	Size Pipe, Inches	Shpg. Wt., Lbs.
22K1591	9¼	$ 6.75	37¼	5½x7½	14x14	5	70
22K1592	11¼	8.85	39½	6½x7¾	16x16	5	90
22K1593	13¼	10.90	42	7½x8	18x18	6	113
22K1594	15	12.90	44½	8 x9	21x21	6	151
22K1595	17	16.75	47½	8¾x9½	23x23	7	189

Popular Priced Soft Coal Hot Blast Heater

Guaranteed to Please in Looks, Price and Service

Burns Soft Coal, Siftings, Slack, Lignite, Coke, Hard Coal or Cobs. Made airtight so fire is under positive control at all times. Holds fire all night. NOT A WOOD BURNER

$22.75

Has the "Right of Way" Over All Low Priced Hot Blast Heaters

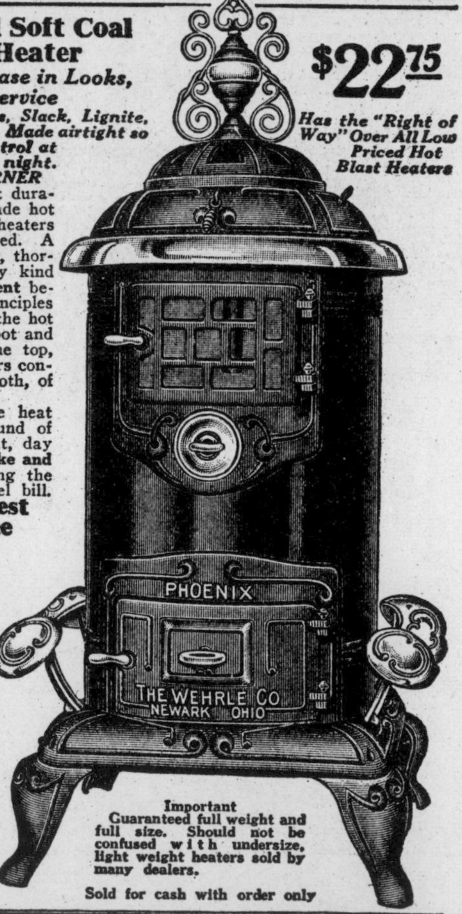

Combines the best, most durable features that have made hot blasts such popular heaters wherever soft coal is burned. A quick and powerful heater, thoroughly dependable in any kind of weather. **Doubly efficient** because it combines both principles of hot blast construction, the hot blast ring above the fire pot and hot blast tube from the top, while most hot blast heaters contain either one, but not both, of these features.

This stove gets all the heat possible out of every pound of fuel and gives steady heat, day and night. **Consumes smoke and gases,** greatly increasing the heat and reducing the fuel bill.

Features of Interest and Convenience

Fire pot is of extra heavy cast iron, large and deep. Heavy cast iron lining above fire pot adds protection to body. Latest type draw center grate, made extra heavy for years of service.

Attractive in appearance, with bright, snappy nickel plated trimmings and foot rails, and mica door that radiates the firelight out into the room. Good materials and excellent workmanship make this a first class stove. Ashpan and ash chutes are furnished (many makes do not have these, so that removal of ashes is a dusty, mussy job). Shaker door in ash door.

Big stocks and prompt shipment from our foundry at NEWARK, OHIO. Freight charges amount to little no matter where you live.

Important
Guaranteed full weight and full size. Should not be confused with undersize, light weight heaters sold by many dealers.

Sold for cash with order only

Made in Three Sizes. Order by Number	Diameter of Fire Pot, Inches	Each	Height of Urn Base, Inches	Floor Space, Inches	Size of Mica Door Opening, Inches	Size Pipe, Inches	Shpg. Wt., Lbs.
22K1602	13½	$22.75	45	23 x23	9 x6½	6	172
22K1603	15¼	24.85	46¼	25¼x25¼	10½x6¾	6	214
22K1604	17½	26.90	48	26½x26½	10½x6¾	7	251

Money Saved Is Money Earned

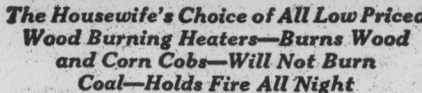

$13.95

An Unusually Low Price

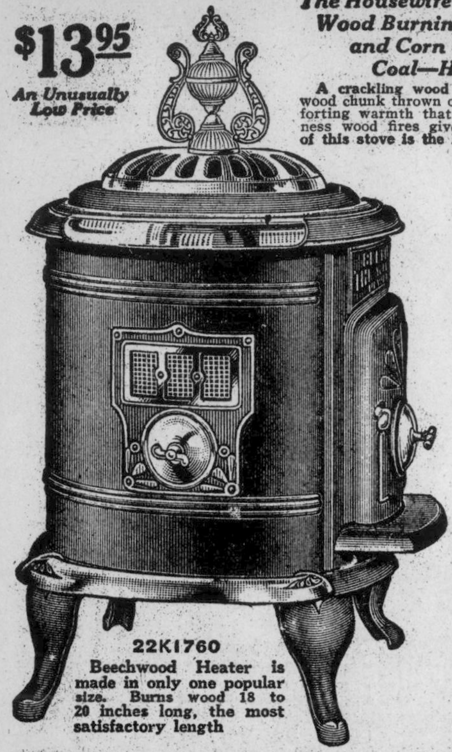

22K1760

Beechwood Heater is made in only one popular size. Burns wood 18 to 20 inches long, the most satisfactory length

The Housewife's Choice of All Low Priced Wood Burning Heaters—Burns Wood and Corn Cobs—Will Not Burn Coal—Holds Fire All Night

A crackling wood fire started in a hurry, a big dry wood chunk thrown on a few minutes later means a comforting warmth that has no substitute for the friendliness wood fires give in the winter. **The chief feature of this stove is the large front feed door, big enough to** take in good size chunks and blocks of wood. There is also a removable lid under the swing top so that fuel can be fed through this opening when desired. This is one of our best sellers and we recommend it as your selection.

Body is made of heavy gauge uniform blue steel bolted and cemented airtight to the cast iron top, bottom and front. Measures inside, 21 x 14½ inches. Floor space, 27x19 inches. **Total height of stove to urn base, 32 inches.**

Main bottom is heavy cast iron, corrugated for burning wood.

Cheerful mica fire door shows the comforting fire.

Front feed door is large enough to take big chunks and blocks of wood. Measures 12x8 inches.

Removable lid under swing top is very convenient for feeding the wood through the opening when so desired and is a good feature for boiling water. **The following parts are nickel plated:** Swing top, front top band, draft doors, mica frame and foot rail. Takes 6-inch stovepipe.

Shipped from PHILADELPHIA, PA., SPRINGFIELD, MASS., or NEWARK, OHIO.

This new model is sure to find thousands of satisfied users and friends. Shipping weight, 108 pounds.

22K1760 Beechwood Heater... **$13.95**

E-Z-est-WAY

New and Improved Giant Kerosene (Oil) Heater

A Style of Finish to Suit Your Purpose

Burns common kerosene oil, obtainable almost anywhere. Does the work of two or three ordinary oil heaters. **Big capacity tank—holds five full quarts.** For homes, offices, warehouses, shipping rooms, shops, garages and other places where additional heat is required. **A big help to your heating problems,** during the bitter cold of winter, and when your stove or furnace will not supply sufficient heat, **our Giant Oil Heater finds a real welcome.** During the damp, chilly days of early spring, when stove or furnace heat is not required, the Giant Oil Heater affords the safest, sanest and most economical comfort.

Odorless, Smokeless, Reliable, Clean and Sanitary. Easily carried into any part of the building where additional heat is required. Flame in plain sight and flame control conveniently located.

Never Fail Lock—All E-Z-est Way Giant Oil Heaters are equipped with a New and Improved Latch that never fails to lock the drum securely into place.

Radiating Fire Bowl completely surrounds the flame and distributes the heat uniformly throughout the room. A big improvement in oil heater construction.

Heavy Metal Oil Tank—The tank is made of extra heavy metal and, in addition, a rust preventative is applied to the inner surface, an additional guard against rusting.

Extra Large Wicks—The Wicks are extra large and heavy and can easily be renewed. They come ready trimmed, securely fastened to a metal carrier which engages with the cogs on the spindle. The construction is such that inserting or replacing the wick is very simple.

Patented Air Distributor—The Air Distributor or Flame Spreader is the heart of the oil heater. It rests upon the wick and regulates the amount of air fed into the flame. The air distributor used in our Giant Oil Heater is said to deliver a larger, steadier and more perfectly balanced supply of oxygen to the flame than any other type of oil heater. This construction means perfect combustion and greater heating efficiency.

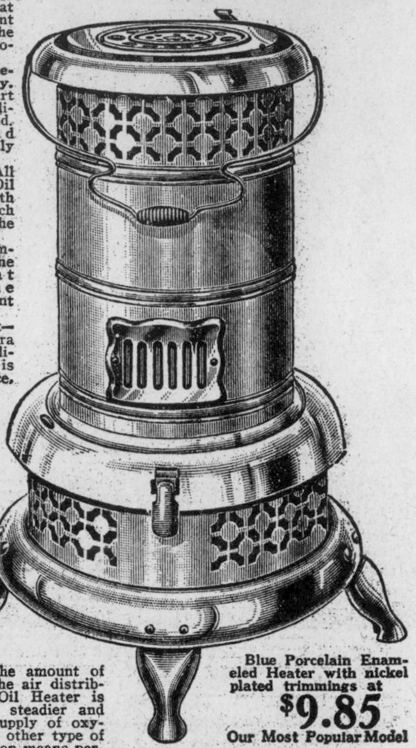

Blue Porcelain Enameled Heater with nickel plated trimmings at **$9.85**

Our Most Popular Model

Base and Legs made of heavy steel. Always stands strong and firm.

Adjustable Ventilating Damper, in top of heater, permits control of heat. **Guaranteed** just the same as all stoves we sell, to give absolute satisfaction or your money back.

All three models are 26 inches high. Shipping weight 20 pounds. Shipped from our PHILADELPHIA store. Sold for cash with order.

Blue Porcelain Enameled Heater With Nickel Plated Trimmings

Upper and lower drums are finished in robin's egg blue porcelain enamel. Rustproof. Top, middle ring, base and legs are nickel plated. An especially handsome heater.

22K2857........ **$9.85**

Plain Heater With Nickel Plated Trimmings

Upper and lower drums are made of plain steel. Top, middle ring, base and legs are nickel plated.

22K2856 **$8.85**

Plain Heater With Black Enameled Trimmings

Upper and lower drums are made of plain steel. Top, middle ring, base and legs are black enamel finish.

22K2855 **$7.85**

Order Extra Wicks for Future Use

Giant Heater Wicks furnished complete with holder, ready for use. Made extra large and heavy for E-Z-est-Way Oil Heater only and will not fit any other stoves.

22K2849—Each... **60c**

Stovepipe and Elbows

We do not sell made up (put together) stovepipe. Our pipe, 24 in. long, has seam formed and edges turned over, ready to put together. Simply joint the edges and tighten the seam with a hammer. Not the light gauge pipe sold by some for higher prices. Shipped from PHILADELPHIA, PA., or NEWARK, OHIO.

Order by Number	Pipe, Size, In.	Smooth Black Steel Each	Polished Blue Steel Each	Shpg. Wt., Lbs., Each
22K5907	5	20c	30c	1¾
22K5908	6	22c	35c	2¼
22K5909	7	25c	40c	2¾
22K5916	7x6	26c	42c	2½

Order by Number	Size	Smooth Black Steel, Each	Polished Blue Steel, Each	Shpg. Wt., Lbs.
22K5919	5-inch Elbow	15c	28c	1¼
22K5920	6-inch Elbow	18c	36c	1½
22K5921	7-inch Elbow	22c	44c	1¾

Stove Mica (or Isinglass)

Can be cut easily with a pair of shears. Mailing weight, 2 ounces per dozen pieces.

Order by No.	Size, In.	6 Pcs.	12 Pcs.
22K4937	2 x3	....	$0.25
22K4938	2½x2½	....	.35
22K4939	2½x4	....	.55
22K4940	3 x4	....	.75
22K4941	3 x5	50c	.95
22K4942	3½x4½	55c	1.05
22K4943	3½x5	60c	1.15
22K4944	4 x5	65c	1.25

Stove Putty or Cement

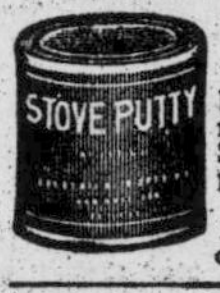

Used for closing joints between castings to make them airtight. Shipping weight, 1¼ pounds.

22K2936 1-pound can............ **16c**

Iron Repair Cement

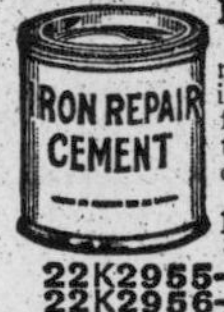

Quick hardening; for repairing leaks or breaks in castings, water fronts, for pipe and screw thread joints and seams or boilers and tanks. Shipping weights: 1-lb. package, 1¼ lbs.; ½-lb. package, ¾ lb.

22K2955—1-lb. package 35c

22K2956—½-lb. package 18c

Famous S-R Stove Polish

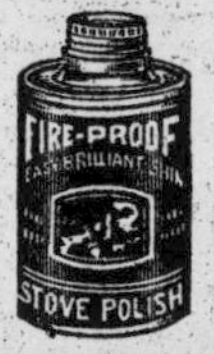

Buy three **full half-pint** cans of this famous fireproof, non-freezing polish. Apply **whether stove is warm or cold;** polishes quickly to a brilliant black luster without dust or odor. Adheres to iron—not to the hands. Shpg. wt., 3½ lbs.

22K2959 3 cans............**37c**

Serviceable and Quick Heating Hot Blast Airtight Wood Burners

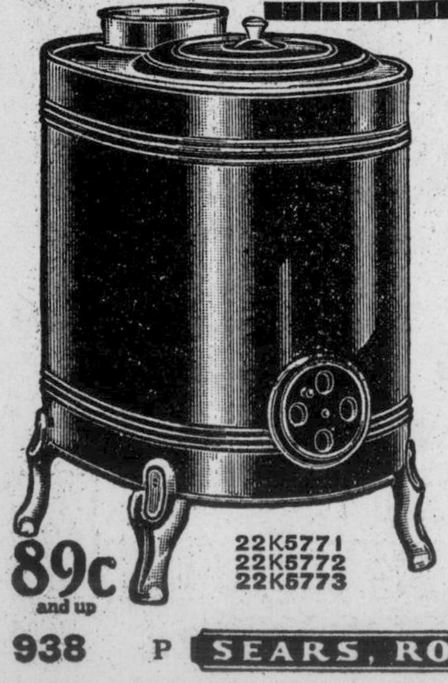

89c and up

22K5771
22K5772
22K5773

Steel body stove of the better kind, with hot blast, by which all air entering stove through upper draft is heated before reaching fire, making it burn steadily and give the greatest amount of heat from fuel. This valuable feature is usually found only in stoves of this type selling at much higher prices. Makes control of fire easy. Draft register and ash cover can be closed airtight so that the fire will burn for several hours without attention.

The stove is made with inner steel lining 12 inches high. Can be furnished in smooth steel or polished steel; the polished steel requires no blackening. All sizes take 6-inch stovepipe. Height, floor to urn top, 32¾ to 37 inches.

Order by Number	Size of Body, Inches	Smooth Steel: With Foot Rails	Smooth Steel: Without Foot Rails	Polished Steel: With Foot Rails	Polished Steel: Without Foot Rails	Shpg. Wt., Lbs.
22K5774	20 x16½	$4.15	$2.85	$4.90	$3.60	35
22K5775	23¼x16¾	4.65	3.35	5.50	4.20	40
22K5776	29¼x16¾	5.25	3.95	6.25	4.95	49

Small Steel Airtight Wood Burner

Satisfactory for small rooms. We recommend our larger and better airtight heaters shown at the right. Smallest size takes 5-inch pipe; others 6-inch pipe.

Made in Three-Sizes. Order by Number	Circumference of Body, Inches	Each	Height, Top, Inches	Shpg. Wt., Lbs.
22K5771	50¾	$0.89	27	24
22K5772	56½	1.35	32½	30
22K5773	60½	1.95	37	35

Prompt shipment from PHILADELPHIA, PA., or NEWARK, OHIO.

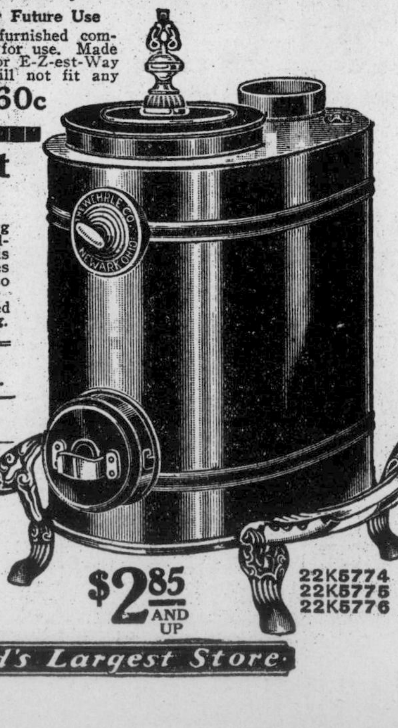

$2.85 AND UP

22K5774
22K5775
22K5776

LOW PRICES *Save You Almost Half*

No Smoke! Heat! *When You Want It Where You Want It* No Odor!

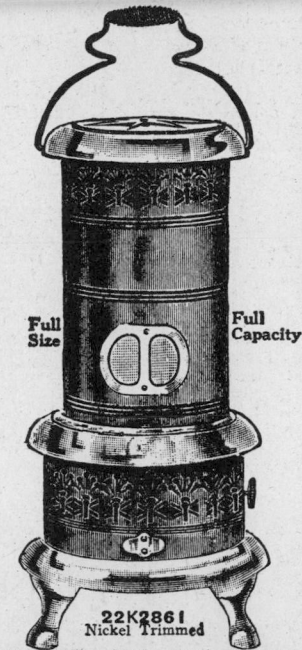

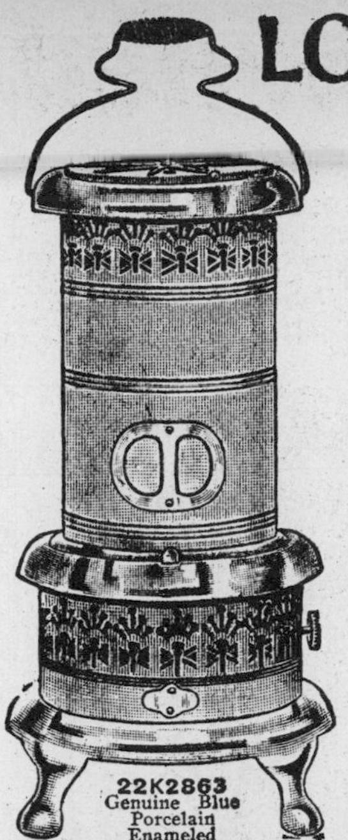

The convenience of these fine oil heaters during the seasons of sudden temperature changes makes them worth much more than their purchase price. In warmth and fuel economy they assure satisfaction in the days "before it's time to light the fire," or in places where heat cannot be had by other methods. E-Z-est-Way Oil Heaters are in every way the best made, in their respective classes. Full size and full capacity. Do not confuse with the light weight, short capacity heaters sold by many dealers.

Our construction makes them sturdy and substantial. We call particular attention to the one-piece base and legs, the legs being formed as part of the base. This base is much stronger than the ordinary base with bolted legs, for it prevents the leg from becoming twisted or getting out of alignment. The heater will always stand solid and steady.

Our patented wick stop prevents turning flame too high. A marvel in simplicity and easy lighting. Nothing about our Oil Heaters to get out of order. Guaranteed smokeless and odorless.

22K2863
Genuine Blue Porcelain Enameled

Blue Porcelain Enameled Heater With Nickel Plated Trimmings
Upper and lower drums are finished in robin's egg blue porcelain enamel. Rustproof. Top, middle ring and one-piece base and legs are nickel plated. An especially handsome heater. Shipping weight, 17 pounds.
22K2863 ....$6.75

Full Size **Full Capacity**

22K2861
Nickel Trimmed

A style of finish to suit your purpose; otherwise the three heaters are identically made. Will heat a medium size room very comfortably. Height to main top, 24¼ inches. Full size tank, when full, will run heater about 8½ hours. Takes 8-inch round wick. All three styles are shipped from our PHILADELPHIA store. Sold for cash with order.

Plain Heater With Nickel Plated Trimmings
Upper and lower drums are made of plain steel. Top, middle ring and one-piece base and legs are nickel plated. Shipping wt., 17 lbs.
22K2861.....$5.25

Plain Heater With Black Enameled Trimmings
Upper and lower drums are made of plain steel. Top, middle ring and one-piece base and legs are black enamel finish.
22K2859—Shipping weight, 17 pounds........$3.95

22K2859
Plain Black

Order Extra Wicks for Future Use
Furnished complete with holder, ready for use. Made for E-Z-est-Way Oil Heater only and will not fit any other stoves.
22K2865—Each......................35c

Beautiful Period Model Radiant Gas Heaters

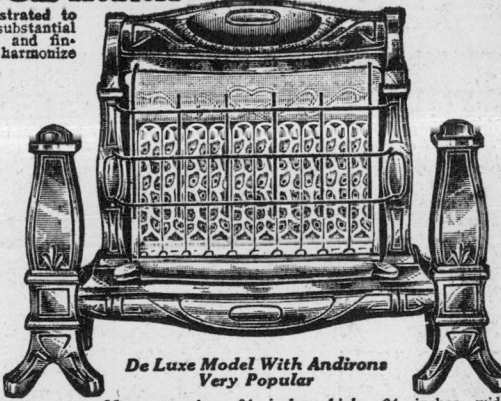

A Combination of Beauty, Efficiency and Economy. The new and very attractive model illustrated to the left is beautifully and tastefully finished in genuine mahogany porcelain enamel, a joy for any home. Designed to fit in with almost any interior decorating scheme. The ten fireclay heat distributing radiants are so constructed that the entire surface is brilliantly and evenly heated, the upper portion glowing as brightly as the lower. Clean and odorless, consuming all the gas

Genuine Mahogany Porcelain Enamel Finish

fumes, leaving the air in room clean and refreshing.
The burner is scientifically constructed to produce perfect combustion. The air and gas is mixed at one point, allowing an even flow of gas to each opening. Burns natural or manufactured gas. Will not burn gasoline or acetylene gas. Flame can be easily regulated to any degree of heat desired.
Shipped from PHILADELPHIA, PA., or NEWARK, OHIO.
Measurements: 20 inches high, 25 inches wide, 6 inches deep; 3-inch pipe collar. Shipping weight, 90 pounds.
Heaters of This Type Often Sell Elsewhere up to $25.00.
22K1804—Solid Cast Iron Heater with 10 Fireclay Mantles $12.85

The De Luxe model illustrated to the right is equipped with substantial Andirons. Colonial design and finished in statuary bronze to harmonize with the furnishings in almost any home.
The soft, golden radiance diffused by this heater lend an indescribable charm to its surroundings. The elements are provided with a large number of radiating points that insure the entire surface becoming brilliantly and evenly heated, the upper portion glowing as brightly as the bottom. Clean and odorless, consuming all the gas fumes, leaving the air in room clean and refreshing.
The burner is scientifically constructed to produce perfect combustion. The air and gas is mixed at one point, allowing an even flow of gas to each opening. Flame can be easily regulated to any degree of heat desired.

De Luxe Model With Andirons Very Popular

Measurements: 24 inches high, 24 inches wide, 10 inches deep; 3-inch pipe collar. Shipping wt., 90 lbs.
Heaters of This Type Often Sell Elsewhere up to $30.00.
Burns natural or manufactured gas. Will not burn gasoline or acetylene gas.
Prompt shipment from PHILADELPHIA, PA., or NEWARK, OHIO.
22K1803—Solid Cast Iron Heater with 10 Fireclay Mantles $19.85

Flexible Steel Gas Tubing
Has rubber ends. Shipping wt., 2 oz. per foot.
22K2928—4-foot length	35c
22K2928—6-foot length	50c
22K2928—8-foot length	75c
22K2928—10-foot length	90c

Quick, Clean, Healthful Heat

Our Low Prices Mean a Big Saving

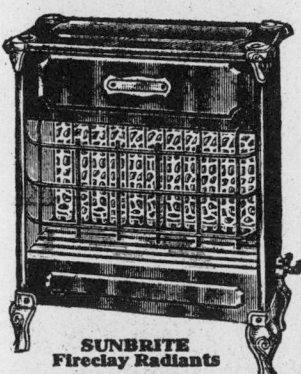

The Acknowledged Leaders Among the Better Gas Heaters
Equipped With Latest and Improved Type Bunsen Burners
The most popular and widely known gas heaters made. Bunsen Tube Burners have separate mixers and orifice openings for each tube, a construction that insures the greatest efficiency and satisfactory operation with a minimum of gas consumption. They give your rooms the temperature you want quickly after they have been lighted. With the especially designed reflector and back construction, they continue to throw off heat a long time after the gas has been turned off.
Made in two styles and a popular assortment of sizes. One style is furnished with clay radiants which turn to a glowing red quickly after being lighted. These clay radiants immediately radiate clean, healthful heat straight out into the room on every side. The other style is furnished with an asbestos back radiation element that serves a purpose similar to the clay radiants described above. The asbestos glows like smouldering moss while the heater is lit. The selection of either type is a matter of personal choice; we recommend either. Only be sure you have selected a heater large enough to suit your needs. Shipped from PHILADELPHIA, PA., or NEWARK, OHIO, whichever is nearer you.
Heater bodies are heavy gauge blue steel polished, with rolled top and panel front, nickel plated legs, valve and corner ornaments. Corrugated copper deflector and adjustable valve. Wire dress guard. Valve has pipe or tubing connection. Equipped with 3-inch flue vent.

SUNBRITE Fireclay Radiants

These Heaters Are Not Mailable
Both the Sunbrite Radiant and Judge Bunsen Gas Heaters burn either natural or manufactured gas and extract every particle of heat from it. Will not burn gasoline or acetylene gas. Our low price brings their comfort and convenience within the reach of all.

JUDGE Asbestos Back

	Order by Number	No. of Jets	Each	Size of Body, Inches	Total Height, Inches	Shpg. Wt., Lbs.		Order by Number	No. of Jets	Each	Size of Body, In.	Total Height, In.	Shpg. Wt., Lbs.
SUN-BRITE Fireclay Radiants	22K5841	7	$6.50	12¾x7½	22¼	14	JUDGE Asbestos Back	22K5838	7	$4.50	12¾x7½	22¼	14
	22K5842	10	7.50	17¼x7½	22¼	16		22K5839	9	5.00	15¾x7½	22¼	16
	22K5843	13	8.50	22 x7½	22¼	18		22K5840	11	6.00	18¾x7½	22¼	18

To Find What You Want, See Index Pages 550 to 570

P 939

"FIDELITY" ELECTRIC RANGE

Cooking Satisfaction Heretofore Unheard Of

So sure are we of the quality and efficiency of our Fidelity Electric Ranges that we will send the model shown in large illustration to you upon receipt of $79.50 cash price, or $5.00 as an initial payment, if you prefer our time payment plan, with the distinct understanding that you may use it in your home 30 days, judging for yourself on its quality and efficiency. If at any time during the 30 days you become dissatisfied and feel that you could secure any other Electric Range that would suit you better and find you have not saved a large amount of money, write us and we will give you instructions how to return the range and cheerfully return all the money you have paid, including all freight charges.

Tested by National Board of Fire Underwriters

The Underwriter Laboratory is a chartered corporation authorized to establish and maintain laboratories for the examination and testing of appliances, and to bring to the user the best obtainable opinion on the merits of appliances and devices in respect to life and fire hazards and accident prevention.

1,000 Watts burning for one hour equals 1 Kilowatt Hour, the unit under which you buy current. Average current consumption per month for a family of four to six is only 100 to 175 kilowatt hours (KWH). Electric Ranges require a special power line, giving you the advantage of lowest current rates. Inquire of your local electrician as to cost, which varies according to local conditions.

Only $5.00 A Month

Buys This Magnificent Genuine Porcelain Enameled Electric Range

Know Real Cooking Comfort

Unless you have tasted foods baked or cooked the electric way you cannot appreciate the flavory, tempting, delicious difference over cooking by any other method. Less water is required, no chance for boiling over, and full flavor and juices are retained without the usual shrinkage. There are no fuel gases to be absorbed by the foods and no uncertain temperatures to contend with. Have you noticed that toast made the electric way is far superior to any other? The difference is more pronounced where savory meat juices or airy pastries are freed from fuel odors and gases by electric cooking.

Special Details of Construction

Fidelity Enameled Ranges are built unusually stanch and rigid for years of hard and satisfactory service. Sold under our absolute guarantee of satisfaction or your money back.

Cooking Top. Made of heavy cast iron, finished in lustrous baked-on black enamel and equipped with three 8-inch removable radiant type, surface heating, 1,500-watt heat units, affording maximum utensil capacity.

The Coils are arranged spirally in deeply grooved vitreous clay product, unaffected by water, juices or acids, and cannot be harmed by boiling over of fluids. Terminal connections are made extra heavy; maximum capacities, 1,500 watts each. Each heating unit is connected with a three-heat switch reading HIGH, MEDIUM and LOW.

Utility Plug for attaching vacuum cleaner, electric iron or toaster.

Baking Oven is made of heavy gauge refined iron, has double walls, heavily insulated with thick mineral wool on top, bottom, back and side, making it absolutely a perfect heat retainer. Will hold baking temperature for a long period after current is turned off.

Back Wall is constructed with a vent near the top so the odor from cooking passes to the flue, making the oven absolutely sanitary. Equipped with two removable heating units of the radiant type, one located at the top and the other at the bottom of oven. Each of these units is connected with a three-heat switch, reading HIGH, MEDIUM and LOW. The upper unit can be used for broiling steaks and other meats.

Oven Door is made of cast iron, beautifully finished in French gray porcelain enamel, with white porcelain enamel panel, heavily insulated and made to fit absolutely airtight. It is balanced by use of a spring, and, when open, forms a convenient shelf.

Switch Panel is made of heavy cast iron, finished in French gray porcelain enamel, furnished with a switch for each heating unit with indicators designating HIGH, MEDIUM, LOW or OFF.

Entire Range finished in white porcelain enamel with gray enameled trimmings. Ranges furnished for 110-220-volt three-wire, or 110-volt two-wire systems, for A. C. or D. C., single phase. Be sure to state the type of wiring and current you intend using.

Measurements: Oven, 16x16x12 inches; cooking top, 21x21 inches; height to cooking top, 29¾ inches; floor space, 22x44 inches. Shipping weight, 225 pounds.

Shipped direct from our factory in NEWARK, OHIO.

Furnished with oven on right hand side only.

22K1711—Electric Range. Cash price...... **$79.50**
Time payment price.................... **$88.50**
Terms: $5.00 down, $5.00 a month. Use Time Payment Order Blank on Page 1092.

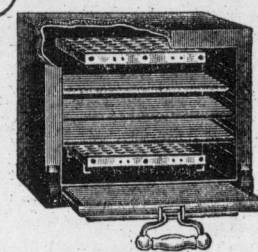

Perfect Baking Oven and Broiler Combined

Measures 16x16x12 inches. Has removable upper and lower interchangeable 3-heat square heating elements of same capacities as those on cooking top. Upper unit highly effective for broiling. Entire oven of heavy metal construction, airtight, with interior walls and door of special non-rusting alloy, and heavily heat insulated with 2 inches of rock wool. Heat retained long after current is turned off. Marvelous results which electricity only can give.

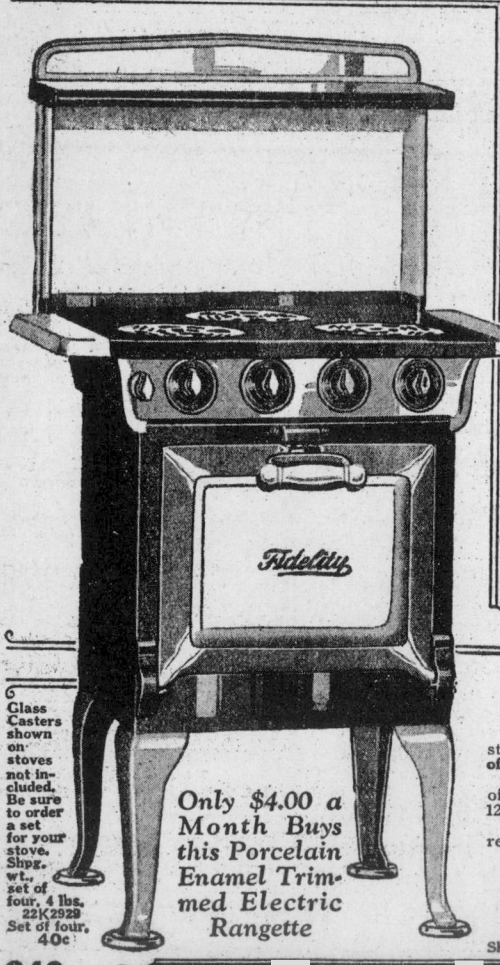

Glass Casters shown on stoves not included. Be sure to order a set for your stove. Shpg. wt., set of four, 4 lbs. 22K2929 Set of four, 40c

Only $4.00 a Month Buys this Porcelain Enamel Trimmed Electric Rangette

Fidelity Electric Rangette
Built for Speed and Comfort—Priced Within the Reach of All
Tested by National Board of Fire Underwriters

This very popular Fidelity Electric Rangette embodies the best features and improvements of today's styles. Wired for 110 to 220 volts. Uses either direct or alternating current. Be sure to state the type of wiring and current you intend using.

Baking Oven is heavily insulated, a perfect heat retainer. Powerful 1,500 watt heating unit in center of oven bottom, provided with positive three-heat switch. Measures 16 inches wide, 12 inches deep, 12 inches high.

Cooking Top is made of heavy cast iron, finished in baked-on black enamel. Equipped with three 8-inch removable radiant type, surface heating, 1,500-watt heat units. Measures 18x23 inches.

Each Burner is equipped with a positive three-heat switch, registering HIGH, MEDIUM and LOW. Burners are of the latest and most improved design. Capacity, 1,500-watts each.

22K1712—Electric Range, as illustrated. Shipping wt., 155 lbs. Cash price............ **$48.50**
Mantel Shelf, genuine white porcelain enameled.
22K1712—Time payment price.........................**$53.50**
Terms: $4.00 with order and $4.00 a month until paid. Use Time Payment Order Blank on page 1092.
Shipped direct from our factory in NEWARK, OHIO.

Our *Elite* Porcelain Enameled GAS RANGE and KITCHEN HEATER Combined

A beautiful white enameled pearl gray trimmed four-burner gas range with a fine, dependable oven and broiler! A practical and thoroughly efficient kitchen heater and rubbish burner of equal beauty! Combined into one solid utility unit to meet the needs and desires of thousands of housewives. The heater uses a minimum of fuel and disposes of waste and rubbish that would be a nuisance to destroy otherwise. Does wonders in the way of cooking and heating and will keep the kitchen warm and comfortable in zero weather. Burns Hard or Soft Coal, Coke or Wood.

Notice the roomy gray enameled UTILITY DRAWER of a thousand and one uses. You will greatly appreciate the convenience of this handy compartment for keeping the knives, forks, and other cooking equipment close to the stove, where they belong. This stove has the same easy sliding grates, the same rounded, smooth flowing surfaces as described on page 942 under our ELITE Gas Range.

The gas section has four heat diffusing burners, including three full size burners and one large giant burner, an oven that bakes as beautifully as it looks and has all the features of the up to date stove. If you have been considering either a kitchen heater or a new beautiful gas range, why not get both in one? At our price the cost is very low and the satisfaction great. The space under the cooking burners is white porcelain enameled, easy to keep clean and convenient for storing cooking utensils.

Measurements: Baking oven, 16x17⅝x13 inches; broiling oven, 16x17⅝x8 inches; cooking top, 32x19½ inches, including shelf. Height to cooking top, 33¼ inches. Length, over all, 52 inches. Floor space, 20x52 inches. Take 6-inch pipe. Heater has special drop coal feed door; top, 14½x19½ inches. Two 8-inch lids. Length for wood, 15½ inches. Shipping wt., 370 lbs.

Terms: $5.00 with order and $5.00 a month until full price has been paid. The easy and pleasant way to pay for kitchen comfort. Use Time Payment Order Blank on page 1092. Shipped promptly from our factory in NEWARK, OHIO.

22K99—Water coil to fit fire box to heat boiler. Shipping weight, 20 pounds. **$5.25**
Made only with oven on right.

22K1316—Combination heater and gas range. **$77.85**
Cash price............................
Time payment price............................**$86.85**

New and Improved Oven Heat Regulator insures 100% correct cooking by scientific time and temperature control. Be sure to order your range with oven heat regulator as shown on illustration and described on page 943.
Price only............................**$8.00**

Freight charges for shipping this beautiful combination are even lower than you might expect and are actually a trifle when you consider the great saving you make in buying direct from us.

Made in Our Own Foundry

Sanitary Clear Glass Stove Casters, not included in price. Protect floor, rugs or linoleum from being marred. Easy to clean. Order a set for your stove. Shipping weight, per set of four, 4 lbs.
22K2929 Set of 4 Casters, 40c

You need not pay cash in full

$5.00 DOWN
$5.00 A MONTH

A—White porcelain enameled splasher cleans like a china dish.
B—Extra wide cooking top. Slide-easy top grates for gas section, two lids in coal section for cooking. Cook and heat with the same stove and fuel.
C—Large ashpan easily removed without fuss or mess.
D—Roomy utility drawer for storing cooking accessories.
E—Roomy shelf on top with back rail, making it safe and convenient to hold dishes and utensils.
F—Never fail, heat retaining oven constructed to insure the heat reaching all parts of the oven. Even heat for baking or roasting assured.
G—Note white enameled broiling pan.
H—Strong and sturdy legs. Easy to clean under the stove.

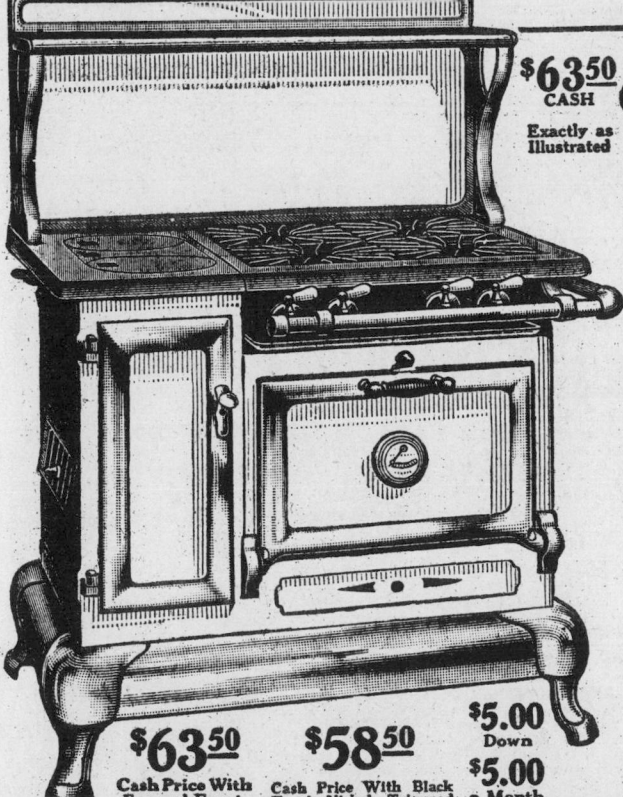

$63.50 CASH

Exactly as Illustrated

Combination GAS RANGE and KITCHEN HEATER With White Porcelain Enameled Front

And White Porcelain Enameled Mantle Shelf

This range is a combination of a kitchen heater and a gas range built into a single body. Very compact, takes up only a small amount of space.

Gas baking oven operates entirely independent from the coal section of the range. Guaranteed to do very fine work, both baking and roasting. It is not a combination oven and cannot be heated by the coal fire. The coal and wood fire cooks and heats, but does not bake. Uses gas only for baking.

You can cook with two fuels at the same time, using all six lids at a time when desired. Has two coal and wood lids and four gas cooking burners, including three full size and one Giant burner.

The coal and wood compartment may be used as an incinerator as well. Burn all your refuse, garbage and waste without odor; an easy, profitable way to dispose of such refuse.

Fire box burns hard or soft coal, coke, short wood, corn cobs, rubbish and kitchen waste. Cooks quickly and will furnish plenty of heat to warm your kitchen in the coldest weather.

The stove body is made of heavy gauge steel. Oven, 18x19 inches. Top, 34½x21½ inches. Fire box length for wood, 16 inches. Takes 6-inch stovepipe. Shpg. wt., 360 lbs.

Be sure to state whether you burn manufactured or natural gas. Range will not burn acetylene or gasoline gas. We will ship range for manufactured gas unless otherwise specified.

Range With White Enameled Front and Mantle Shelf.
22K1310—Range, as illustrated. Cash price............................**$63.50**
22K1310—Range, as illustrated. Time payment price............................**$69.50**
Range, Plain Black, Nickel Trimmed, and Mantle Shelf.
22K1311—Range. Cash price............................**58.50**
22K1311—Range. Time payment price............................**64.50**
22K1900—Automatic Lighter for top burners............................**1.25**

When you consider the great saving our factory prices give you, it is easy to figure the difference between our low prices and those asked by others.
Shipped promptly from our factory in NEWARK, OHIO.

You need not Pay Cash in full. Terms: $5.00 with order, $5.00 a month until time payment price is paid. Use Time Payment Order Blank on page 1092.
22K97—Water front to fit in fire box to heat hot water boiler. **$4.75**
Shipping weight, 20 pounds.

Sanitary Clear Glass Stove Casters. Protect floor, rugs or linoleum from being marred. Easy to clean. Be sure to order a set for your stove. Shipping weight, per set of four, 4 lbs.
22K2929—Set of 4 Casters............................40c

$63.50
Cash Price With Enamel Front

$58.50
Cash Price With Black Front Nickel Trimmed

$5.00 Down
$5.00 a Month

NEW PEERLESS
COMBINATION
Coal and Gas Range
Pearl Gray Enameled

The Very Acme of Perfection
Two Perfect and Complete
Ranges Combined in One
Brightly Polished Cooking Top
Requires No Blacking

Distinctive in Appearance and Superior to Similar Ranges Selling for From $15.00 to $20.00 More Than Our Price

Made especially to meet the demand for a highly satisfactory combination gas and coal range. A gas range and a coal range built into a single body to economize in space and cost. You get all the conveniences of both.

Think of Its Double Convenience and Splendid Features

Comfort, winter and summer. In winter, with a coal fire to warm the kitchen, the coal heated oven is always ready. If more cooking is needed, the gas oven may be used, and on special baking days both ovens are available. In summer the gas oven is most convenient.

The Pearl Gray Porcelain Enamel Finish requires very little care to keep it clean and spotless. The enamel is fused into the iron castings, and with the same amount of care given any porcelain dish, will last as long as the range. The right end of the range is plain black.

To keep the enamel clean and brilliant, simply use hot water and soap. Apply with a soft cloth when the range is cold.

A Few of the Many Desirable Peerless Features

Improved, fuel saving, quick baking gas oven. Measures 13½ inches deep, 18 inches wide. Oven rack easily adjusted to desired height. Convenient thermometer in door to guide one in good baking.

Splasher back of genuine white porcelain enamel. Sanitary. Easily cleaned with a damp cloth.

Gas section cooking top has four powerful heat diffusing burners, including one giant burner. Room enough for all kinds and sizes of utensils. Top measures 24½x20 inches.

Gas valves of approved type; absolutely reliable, easy to adjust, and positively, non-leakable.

Porcelain enamel drip pan easily removed for cleaning.

Touch-a-button automatic lighter instantly lights any or all burners in the cooking top without the use of matches.

Sturdy gray porcelain enameled base and legs, built for strength and durability, in keeping with the pleasing design and massiveness of the whole range. Back base strip is black.

Perfected, easily controlled coal or wood baking oven; measures 18 inches deep, 18 inches wide. Surrounded by full size flues.

Fuel saving fire box with extra heavy cast iron linings and duplex grate for burning fuels of all kinds—hard coal, soft coal, coke, wood or corn cobs.

Coal feed door, large and ample for easy feeding of coal or coke into fire. Conveniently located at left end of stove.

Heat retaining warming oven, very convenient to keep cooked foods warm until ready to serve.

Brightly polished. Coal or wood cooking section measures 24½x21½ inches, every square inch usable. Four full size accurately fitted griddle lids, including one three-ring sectional lid and one anti-scorch lid for cooking cereals, etc.

Two separate ovens and big double cooking top with which you can prepare a great big dinner for extra company as easily as you prepare an ordinary meal on an ordinary cook stove. Each oven is designed for its particular fuel and will do the most satisfactory work. No parts to change or move. The gas oven is located in the right hand side of the high closet, a very convenient height to reach easily. A complete gas oven in itself. Length for wood, 18 inches. Stove body made of extra heavy cast iron, strong and durable. Built for lifetime service.

22K98—Water front, for heating Range Boiler. (Shipping weight, 25 pounds) **$4.75**

$5.00 DOWN $5.00 MONTH

You Need Not Pay Cash. Thousands Buy on Our Easy Terms.

Priced Very Low
$94.50 CASH

Made in Our Own Foundry

Glass casters shown on stove not included. Order 22K2929. Shpg. wt. 4 lbs. Set of four casters. 40c

When ordered for burning hard (anthracite) coal, the fire box is equipped with our new and improved dockash grate and firebrick linings. Be sure to state whether you burn hard or soft coal.

Measurements: Coal oven, 18 inches deep by 18 inches wide by 10 inches high. Gas oven, 13½ inches deep by 18 inches wide, 9½ inches high. Cooking top, 24½x40½ inches. Height, 33 inches. Takes 7-inch stovepipe. Shipping weight, 583 pounds.

Be sure to state whether you burn manufactured or natural gas. Range will not burn acetylene or gasoline gas. We will ship range for manufactured gas unless otherwise specified.

22K1312—New and Improved Peerless Combination Coal and Gas Range. **$94.50**
Cash price
Time payment price **$104.50**
Terms: $5.00 with order, $5.00 a month until time payment price is paid. Use Time Payment Order Blank on page 1092.

We make shipment from PHILADELPHIA, PA., HARRISBURG, PA., SPRINGFIELD, MASS., or NEWARK, OHIO.

The freight charges on the New Peerless are unusually low, especially when you consider the saving you make by buying directly from us. Nowhere else can you duplicate this fine range at so low a price.

KITCHEN HEATER and RUBBISH BURNER

White Enamel Front or Plain Black
Burns Any Kind of Coal or Wood

Thoroughly efficient and made throughout of heavy cast iron. One of the most satisfactory stoves ever designed for this purpose. Small and compact, it takes up just a little room, but it will do wonders in the way of heating and cooking, using a minimum amount of fuel and disposing of waste and rubbish that would be a nuisance to throw away or destroy otherwise. Will keep kitchen warm and comfortable in zero weather. Every inch of the stove radiates heat. Will heat a great big room on a small amount of fuel. The fire box is made just like our big coal ranges and burns any kind of coal, coke, wood, corn cobs and rubbish. Has special drop door for feeding coal. Conveniently located on front of stove.

Gas lighter for fire box can be connected with gas stove or direct to gas supply pipe. Furnished for $1.75 added to prices given below.

Water front to fit in fire box to heat 40-gallon water boiler can be furnished if wanted. Add $4.50 to prices given below.

Shipped from HARRISBURG, PA., or NEWARK, OHIO. Sold only for cash in full with order.

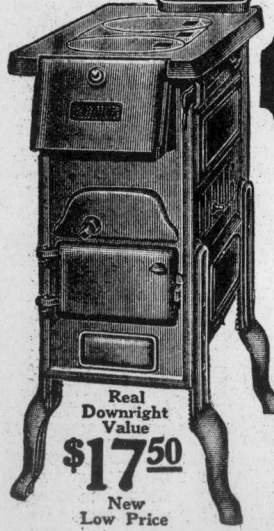

Real Downright Value
$17.50
New Low Price

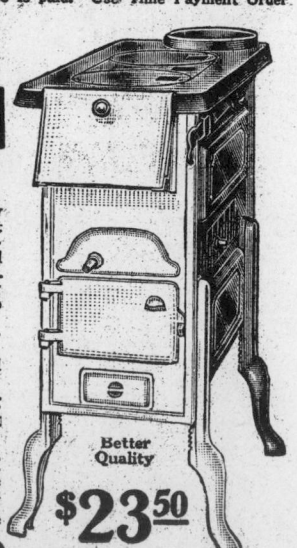

Better Quality
$23.50

Both Models Are Equipped With Legs Adjustable to Any Height Desired
22K6280—Plain Black. Length for wood, 14 inches. Stove is made of cast iron, much stronger and more lasting than similar stoves made with steel body. Adjustable legs permit setting stove at any height wanted, or to line up with top of gas stove. Top, 12x24 inches. Two No. 8 lids. Takes 6-inch stovepipe. Shipping weight, 199 pounds.
Stove only **$17.50**

Both Models Are Made Entirely of Cast Iron. Hold Fire All Night
22K6281—White Porcelain Enameled Front. Genuine full white porcelain enameled front. Especially suited to stand alongside of your white enameled range. Made of heavy cast iron. Length for wood, 14 inches. Top, 12x24 inches. Two No. 8 lids. Has adjustable legs to accommodate the height of any gas stove. Takes 6-inch stovepipe. Shipping weight, 199 pounds.
Stove only **$23.50**

COLUMBIA Porcelain Enameled Cast Iron Range

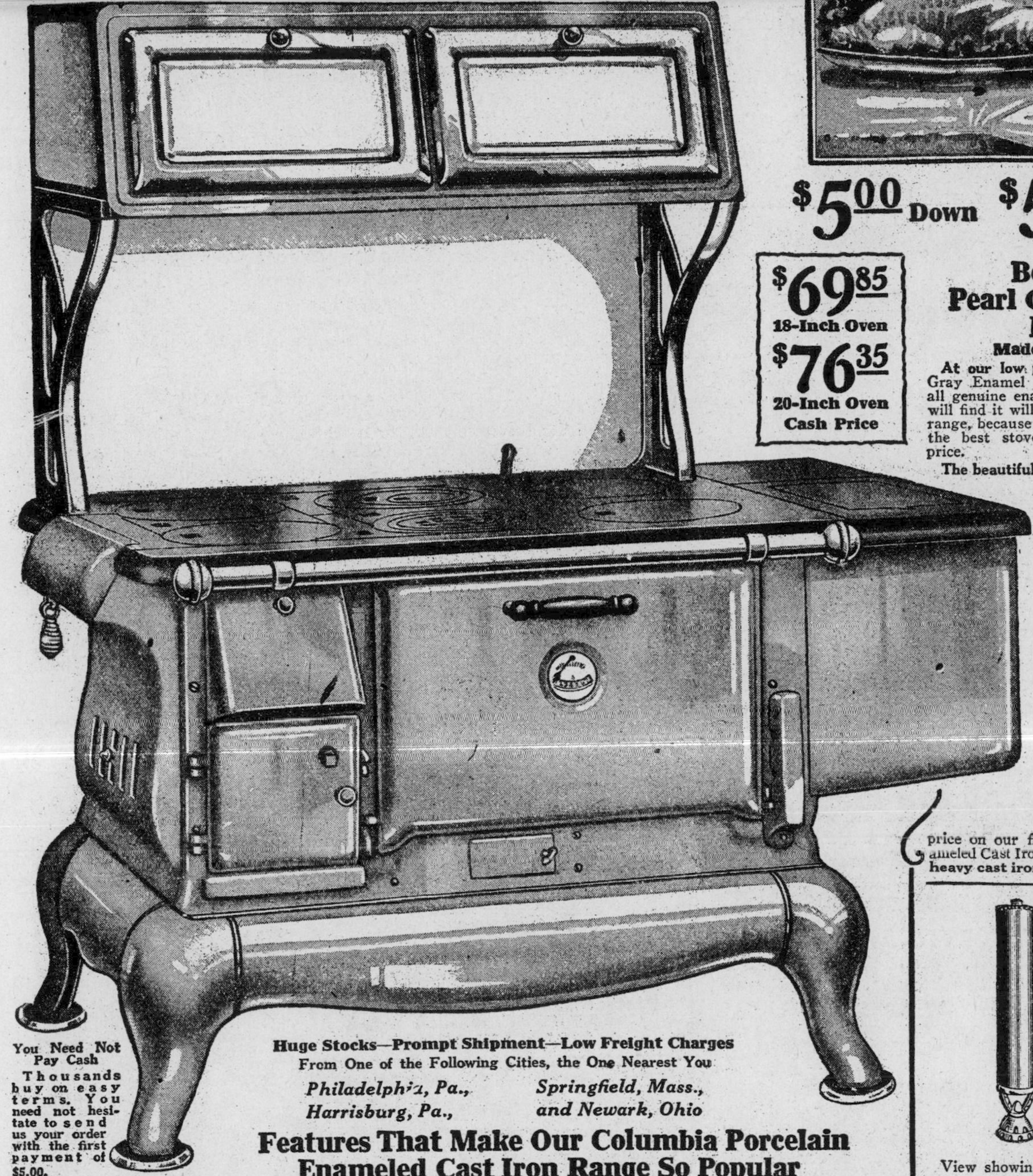

$5.00 Down $5.00 A Month

$69.85 18-Inch Oven
$76.35 20-Inch Oven Cash Price

Beautiful Pearl Gray Enamel Finish
Made In Two Sizes

At our low price this beautiful Pearl Gray Enamel Range is the greatest of all genuine enameled stove values. You will find it will pay you to invest in this range, because it is true economy to buy the best stove, especially at our low price.

The beautiful, soft pearl gray porcelain enamel finish is sure to please you, not only because of its attractive appearance, but because it is so easily cleaned. The whole range has a massive dignity and, with its many special conveniences, and lasting built-in quality, is sure to be the pride of the kitchen.

You might easily pay $30.00 to $50.00 more elsewhere for a range of this quality and finish.

The easiest range to keep spotlessly clean that has ever been built. Grease, soot and dirt can be wiped off quickly with a damp cloth, as if it were a china dish.

Unusually liberal terms and fair, low price on our finest Gray Porcelain Enameled Cast Iron Range. A range made of heavy cast iron, built to last a lifetime.

You Need Not Pay Cash

Thousands buy on easy terms. You need not hesitate to send us your order with the first payment of $5.00.

Huge Stocks—Prompt Shipment—Low Freight Charges
From One of the Following Cities, the One Nearest You

Philadelphia, Pa., *Springfield, Mass.,*
Harrisburg, Pa., *and Newark, Ohio*

Features That Make Our Columbia Porcelain Enameled Cast Iron Range So Popular

Body, made of solid cast iron, built to last a lifetime. Every part carefully tested; every joint ground and fitted perfectly.

Cooking top, ground and polished to a mirror finish. Always looks neat and sanitary. No polishing required, simply wipe with a cloth. Six 8-inch lids, including one three-ring sectional lid to fit different size cooking utensils, and one anti-scorch lid, which prevents burning of cereals during long cooking. Highly nickel plated towel bar. Height to cooking top, 31 inches.

Large Uniform Baking Oven, made in two sizes and is guaranteed to do the very best baking or roasting. Construction is such that you get the full measure of heat directly into the oven. Oven door is strongly built, extra thick and ground to a perfect fit. When opened forms a convenient shelf. Reliable thermometer tells the heat of oven at all times. A convenient feature.

Fire Box, is worthy of special consideration; designed for the most satisfactory work with the least amount of fuel. Extra heavy cast iron three-section linings and two-bar easy working duplex grate that burns any kind of coal, wood, coke or corn cobs. Fire box length for wood, 17½ and 19½ in., according to size.

Large Flues, scientifically constructed for all fuels. This is an important feature and every stove user should be sure that this detail has been perfected in the range you buy. Takes 7-inch stovepipe.

Large Ash Pan, so located that the ashes fall directly into the pan and not around it.

Convenient Drafts, of generous capacity, conveniently located for quick and easy adjustment.

Reservoir, made of extra heavy pure copper. Will not rust. Holds 8 full gallons. Heats by contact and keeps water boiling hot at all times. Easily removed for cleaning.

Warming Closet, big capacity and very convenient for keeping foods warm until ready to serve.

Sturdy base and legs, built for strength and durability. Back base strip and legs are plain black, rest of base and legs finished in genuine pearl gray enamel.

Our tremendous stocks enable us to make prompt shipment from a city near you.

Freight charges on this heavy, well made cast iron range amount to nothing compared to the big saving you make in price. It more than pays you to consider Sears as your stove headquarters. Terms: $5.00 with order and $5.00 a month. Use Time Payment Order Blank on Page 1099.

Made in Two Sizes as Listed Below.

View showing range with water front connected to range boiler for heating water. Water front may be used only where there is a constant pressure through the pipes. You do not require a reservoir with a water front, although water fronts can be fitted to either type. Range boiler is not furnished at this price. For range boilers see page 1009. Shipping weight, 25 pounds.

22K98—Large capacity water front.................. **$4.75**

Anti-Scorch Lid very convenient for cooking cereals, etc., and keep them from burning.

Three-Ring Sectional Lid. Sections can be removed to fit different size utensils.

Range With Reservoir			Range Without Reservoir			Measurements of the Two Sizes					
Catalog No.	Cash Price	Time Payment Price	Catalog No.	Cash Price	Time Payment Price	Size Lids. In.	Size Oven. In.	Size Cooking Top, In.	Height to Cooking Top, In.	Shpg. Wt. With Reservoir	Shpg. Wt. Without Reservoir
22K1132	$69.85	$77.85	22K1143	$65.85	$73.85	8	18x17	42½x24½	31	405	370
22K1187	76.35	84.35	22K1188	72.35	80.35	8	20x20	42½x26	31	450	415

Sanitary Clear Glass Stove Casters. Not included in price of above range. Protect floor, rugs or linoleum from being marred. Easy to clean. Be sure to order a set for your stove. Shipping weight, set of four, 4 pounds.

22K2929—Set of four Glass Casters.................................. **40c**

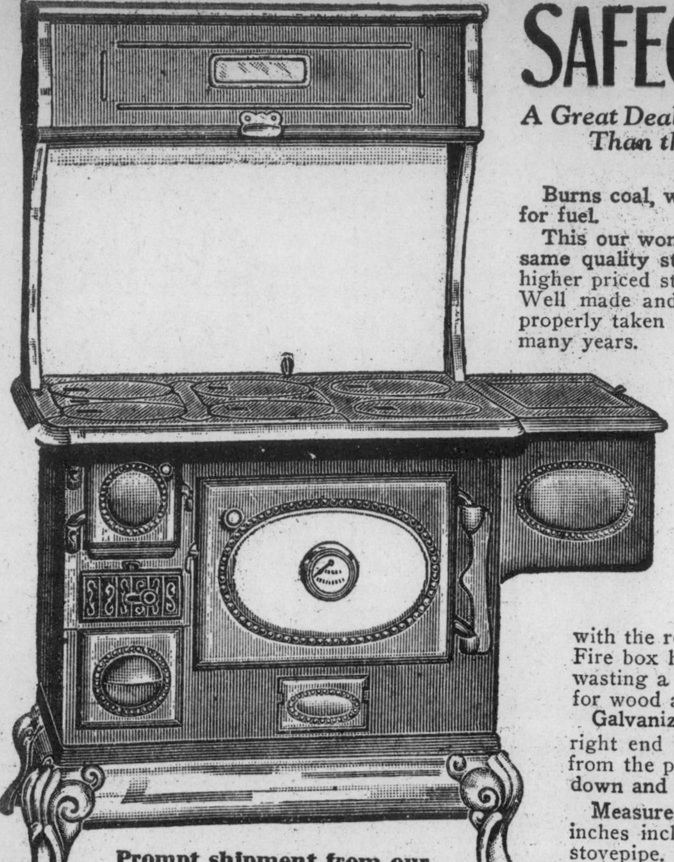

Prompt shipment from our foundry at Newark, Ohio

Only $4.00 Down.
Only $4.00 a Month

SAFEGUARD *Your* DOLLARS

A Great Deal More Quality in This Steel Range Than the Low Price Indicates. Will Last a Long Time

Burns coal, wood, corn cobs, chips or anything used for fuel.

This our wonder six-hole steel range is made of the same quality steel plate as is used in our larger and higher priced steel ranges, only it is not quite so thick. Well made and will stand up under hard usage. If properly taken care of, this range will last for a good many years.

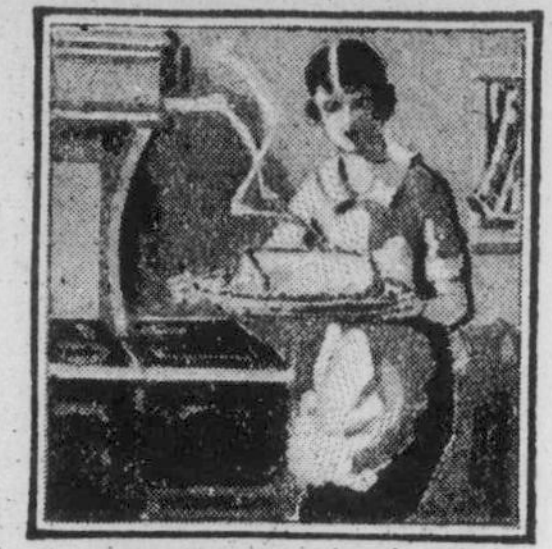

Sanitary White Porcelain Enameled Splasher and Oven Door Panel

White porcelain enameled trimmings are in demand today and we call your attention to these particular features in this dandy range. Easily cleaned with a damp cloth and will always look neat and sanitary.

Oven a Quick and Sure Baker

Good size oven that will heat quickly and give satisfactory baking results all the time. Equipped with an oven thermometer that is a big aid in good baking. You will be more than pleased with the results you will obtain from this stove the first day that you use it. Fire box has cast iron linings and is large enough to do good work without wasting a lot of fuel. Furnished with flat dumping and shaking grates, one for wood and one for coal.

Galvanized iron reservoir with a capacity of 21 quarts is attached to the right end of the range. If range is wanted without reservoir, deduct $1.75 from the price. We cannot furnish a waterfront for this stove. **Terms: $4.00 down and $4.00 a month.** Use Time Payment Order Blank on page 1092.

Measurements: Oven, 16x18 inches. Six No. 8 lids. Cooking top, 38¾x20¼ inches including reservoir. Height to cooking top, 32 inches. Takes 6-inch stovepipe. Shipping weight, 246 pounds. **Prompt shipment from our foundry at NEWARK, OHIO. Safe delivery guaranteed.**

22K1249—Range for Coal and Wood, with Reservoir and Warming Closet.

Low cash price.. **$29.85**

Liberal time payment price.. **33.50**

The Leader of All Low Priced Steel Coal and Wood Cook Stoves

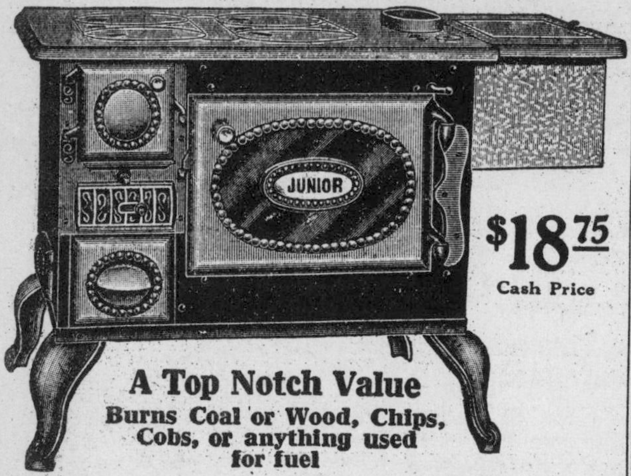

$18.75
Cash Price

A Top Notch Value

Burns Coal or Wood, Chips, Cobs, or anything used for fuel

Body is made of good quality rust-resisting steel. Oven is a sure and satisfactory baker and roaster. Reservoir made of heavy galvanized iron and can be detached and used on top of the stove or hooked to either end of the stove. Reservoir is packed inside the oven for shipment, and holds 5 full gallons. If stove is wanted without reservoir deduct $1.00 from price below. Has four 8-inch lids and takes 6-inch pipe. Fire box has cast iron linings and flat shaking and dumping grate. Fire box length for wood, 17¾ inches. **Shipped from Newark, Ohio. Sold only for cash with order.**

With Reservoir		Oven, Inches	Cooking Top, Inches	Height to Cooking Top, Inches	Shpg. Wt., Pounds
22K1299	**$18.75**	16x18	29¼x20¼	26½	180

The Leader of All Low Priced Cast Iron Coal and Wood Cook Stoves

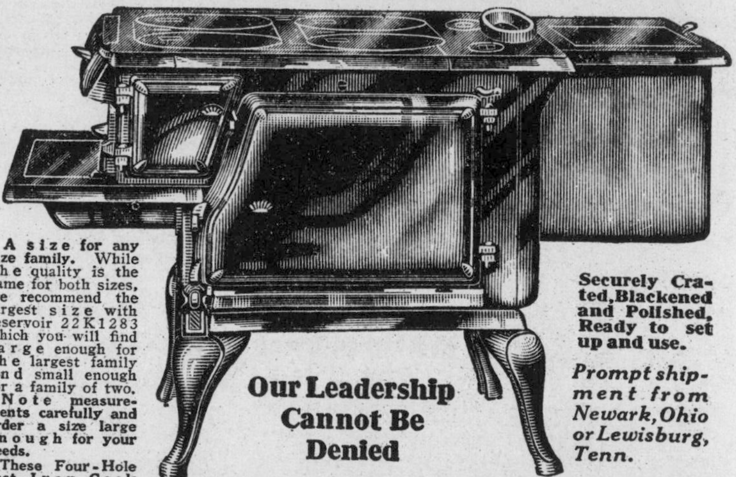

Securely Crated, Blackened and Polished, Ready to set up and use.

Prompt shipment from Newark, Ohio or Lewisburg, Tenn.

Our Leadership Cannot Be Denied

A size for any size family. While the quality is the same for both sizes, we recommend the largest size with reservoir 22K1283 which you will find large enough for the largest family and small enough for a family of two.

Note measurements carefully and order a size large enough for your needs.

These Four-Hole Cast Iron Cook Stoves with or without reservoir are offered to those who desire to make only a small investment and, at the same time, obtain a perfect working, splendid looking Cook Stove, at an enormous saving of money.

While inexpensive, the stove is entirely practical, economical in operation, substantial and neat appearing. Sold under our absolute **guarantee of satisfaction or your money back.** Our prices are made possible by factory facilities, which make it plainer than ever what splendid values we are now offering. Send your order today—don't wait.

Made of cast iron, every piece and part the right weight and thickness to give good wear. The baking and roasting oven does splendid work, quickly and without waste of fuel. Has two oven doors, a feature seldom found on stoves of this type. The lids and cooking top are made the proper thickness and will give years of satisfactory service. Reservoir is made of heavy galvanized iron, and heats by contact. Reservoir for 22K1275 holds **15 quarts,** for 22K1283 holds **32 quarts.**

Fire box has cast iron grates and cast iron fireback. Coal feed door furnished on stove when ordered for burning coal and wood. On wood burning model the coal feed door is not needed, therefore they are not furnished. Takes 6-inch pipe. **Sold for cash only.**

Order by Number	Style	Size of Lids, In.	Oven, Measures, Inches	Stove for Coal and Wood	Stove for Wood Only	Cooking Top, In. Without Reservoir	Fire Box Length for Wood,	Shpg. Wt., Lbs.
22K1274	Without reservoir	8	17x14¾x10½	$19.85	$19.75	26½x21¾	18½ in.	190
22K1275	With reservoir...	8	17x14¾x10½	21.85	21.75	26½x21¾	18½ in.	200
22K1282	Without reservoir	8	20x15 x11	22.50	22.40	28 x23	18½ in.	245
22K1283	With reservoir...	8	20x15 x11	24.50	24.40	28 x23	18½ in.	270

LOWEST PRICED and BETTER QUALITY LAUNDRY STOVES

$3.00

Stovepipe Baking Oven

We especially recommend that in ordering a laundry stove or a small heating stove you order a Stovepipe Baking Oven. Not recommended for use with Water Heaters 22K1480 and 22K1499 listed on page 953.

Oven measures 9 inches wide by 17¾ inches long inside; holds two 8-in. pie plates or an 8x17-inch baking and roasting pan. Pipe collar on top and bottom to fit 6-inch stovepipe. Shipping weight, 21 pounds. Sold only for cash with order. Shipped from PHILADELPHIA, PA., or NEWARK, OHIO.

22K5500—Stovepipe Baking Oven.... **$3.00**
22K5894—Special joint of pipe for drum oven.22c

Heats 8 Sadirons

$6.75

Burns Coal, Corn Cobs or Wood

No other Laundry Stove of this type compares with it in weight, size or measurements

Utility Four-Lid Laundry Stove and Sadiron Heater

Quality, workmanship and capacity same as our Moose at right. Convenient to heat sadirons while cooking or heating a wash boiler. Sadiron not included in price. Large fire pot is strongly made to stand intense heat and hard firing. Grate is shaking and dumping style.

Fire pot diameter at top, 12 inches. Cooking surface, 20¾x21½ inches. Height, floor to top, 23½ inches. Takes 6-inch stovepipe. Shipping weight, 112 pounds.

22K5490—UTILITY Stove......... **$6.75**
Shipped from PHILADELPHIA, PA., NEWARK, OHIO, or LEWISBURG, TENN. Sold only for cash with order.

$5.75

Quality and Satisfaction Sell This Stove Our Own Foundry Saves You Money

Our Wonder Laundry Stove
The "Moose"

This Four-Hole Coal Burning Laundry Stove is the very best coal laundry stove manufactured in any stove foundry in the world. It far outclasses any other laundry stove on the market in every respect, regardless of name, make or price. There is no laundry stove that compares with it either in quality of materials, size, attractiveness of design, special grate features, etc. And as a big, well made, perfect laundry stove we guarantee it to give absolute satisfaction. At our low price it is really a most wonderful value.

It has a very large top, carrying four covers, each fitting in a No. 8 cooking hole. Top measurement, over all, is 20¾x21½ inches, big enough to accommodate a big wash boiler and cooking utensils at the same time. It will also take the new style steel or galvanized iron tubs now in common use. Its arrangement of fire pot and construction of main top is such that the heat is evenly distributed, and it is a quick heater, economical in the use of fuel and a splendid up to date laundry stove, with all the good features of every laundry stove on the market and the defects of none. Burns coal, corn cobs, coke and short wood. Fire pot diameter at top, 12 inches. Cooking top measures 20¾x21½ inches. Four No. 8 lids. Height, from floor to top, 22¼ inches. Takes 6-inch stovepipe.

Shipped from PHILADELPHIA, PA., NEWARK, OHIO, or LEWISBURG, TENN., whichever is nearest you. Sold for cash with order only. Shipping weight, 116 pounds.
22K5494—MOOSE Stove..**$5.75**

$4.60
Shipped From LEWISBURG, TENN.

4-Hole Laundry Stove

Priced Amazingly Low!

We do not offer this Laundry Stove as the equal of our Moose Four-Hole Laundry Stove illustrated at left, but we do guarantee it to be just as good as similar stoves selling at much higher prices by other dealers. Therefore, and wholly in your own interest, we ask you to read the description of our Moose, as we feel that for the slight difference in price you can well afford to send us your order for the better and higher grade stove.

Made of cast iron. Top measures 19½x19½ inches. Height, 23 inches. Fire pot diameter at top, 12 inches. Four 7-inch lids. Takes 6-inch pipe. Shipping weight, 90 pounds.

22K1479—Four-Hole Laundry Stove......................**$4.60**

Two-Hole Stove
Top measures: 19½x13 inches. Has two 7-inch lids. Height, 23 inches. Diameter of fire pot, 12 inches. Shipping weight, 80 pounds.
22K1474..................**$4.20**

One of our best values. Made exactly like our 22K5494 at left, and of the same quality of materials. If you do not need a four-lid stove you will make no mistake in ordering this stove. Has front feed door for feeding fuel without lifting utensils or lid. Flat shaking and dumping grate. All parts are good weight and the stove is well made. Burns coal, coke, corn cobs and short wood. Height, 22 inches. Diameter of fire pot, at top, 12 inches. Two No. 8 lids. Top measures 19x11 inches. Takes 6-inch stovepipe. Shipping weight, 85 pounds.

22K1498—PET Stove....... **$5.25**
Shipped from stock in PHILADELPHIA, PA., NEWARK, OHIO, or LEWISBURG, TENN. Sold only for cash with order.

$7.25 2-Hole Size

$8.75 4-Hole Size

Securely crated, blackened and polished. Ready to set up and use. Prompt shipment from PHILADELPHIA, PA., NEWARK, OHIO, or LEWISBURG, TENN., whichever is nearest you.

The Greatest Combination Laundry, Cooking and Heating Stove Value We Have Ever Offered

Burns Coal, Coke, Wood, Chips, Blocks or Corn Cobs. Made With Either Four or Two Cooking Holes

Marvel Combination Coal and Wood Laundry Stove, with the improved Oblong Fire Pot and Long, Flat Double Trunnion Dump Grate, burns coal, coke, wood, chips or corn cobs.

We recommend the 4-hole size for use with the largest size wash boiler. (See illustration at right.) A convenient drop end feed door makes fueling easy. This feature makes it easy to add fuel without removing wash boiler or cooking utensils from the top. Both sizes have 7-inch lids.

You will find its features the biggest improvements known in Laundry Stoves. Big, roomy oblong fire pot, and trunnion dump grate for burning long sticks of wood, coal, chips or any kind of fuel. Fire pot measures 9½x18 inches.

We recommend that when you order this stove you include one of our stovepipe ovens and get the fullest benefits from your fuel on wash day, or whenever the stove is in use.

Drum Oven measures 9 inches wide and 17¾ inches long inside; will hold two 8-inch pie plates, or an 8x17-inch baking or roasting pan. Top and bottom pipe collar takes 6-inch stovepipe. See top of page for further information about oven.

Order the complete baking outfit as listed below for a real economy combination outfit.

Large size with 4 cooking holes—our most popular seller

Order by Number	No. Lids	Stove Only	Stove with Drum Oven	Size Top, In.	In. Ht.	Shpg. Wt. Lbs.
22K1489	2	$7.25	$10.25	13x19½	21½	100
22K1478	4	8.75	11.75	18x18	21½	110

Illustration showing big capacity of the 4-hole size, 22K1478. Articles shown are not included in price.

The GREATEST OIL STOVE Success
America Has Ever Known!

$38.50
CASH PRICE

$4.00 DOWN

$4.00 A MONTH

You Need Not Pay Cash

Thousands buy on easy terms. You need not hesitate to send us your order with the first payment of $4.00.

Famous Cook Uses and Recommends the E-Z-estWay

Spacious shelf space for keeping cooked food and dishes warm.

Genuine Porcelain enameled splasher and oven side, acid proof and stainless. Cleans like a china dish.

Big capacity top with three additional cooking holes heated by one burner. Parts easily removed for cleaning.

Genuine Porcelain enameled valve handles for simple and easy adjustment of flame to any desired heat.

Perfect bake easy oven, like on high priced gas ranges. Bakes and roasts to perfection. Enameled oven door with thermometer. Easy to keep clean.

Shipped direct from our Philadelphia Store

The Only Range Made With Five Three-in-One HIGH SPEED Heat Diffusing Wickless Giant Burners

Built Like a Gas Range.   Reliable as a Compass

Makes Its Own Gas From Common Kerosene [Coal Oil]

EXCLUSIVE PATENTED FEATURES

View showing section of heavy heat resisting steel anchor plate cooking top removed for cleaning, an exclusive Sears feature you will not find on any other stove. Simply lift off the stove and set in dishpan and wash just as you do the dishes. Made of heavy heat resisting steel plate, guaranteed never to warp or buckle.

View of New and Improved Three-In-One High Speed Heat Diffusing Giant Burner, only one of the many E-Z-est-Way Wickless Oil Range Features. Burns common kerosene (coal oil). Odorless and smokeless. Easy to keep in good condition. Easily controlled and easily regulated from an intense frying heat to a low simmering flame. The ideal burner for grilling minute steaks, preparing roasts or baking and preserving of any kind. All done in proper time.

Fast or slow, an intense searing flame or mild simmering heat, depending upon the operation. No other oil burner made has such a wide range of flame adjustment and control.

Educative view showing the scientific flue construction of cooking top, on Our Big Wickless Oil Range, by which the surplus heat from each burner is diverted to the rear warming holes and enables you to prepare a large meal in less time and with less fuel than any other oil stove made. In addition, the arrangement supplies sufficient heat to the shelf for keeping food and dishes warm.

An oil stove should not be bought with the thought of using it one, two or even five years, and for that reason the initial cost, question of durability, efficiency of burners, baking qualities of oven, economy of fuel and cost of repairs are the all important factors to consider. No more can be had out of any stove than has been built into it, and for that reason the splendid quality built into the E-Z-est-Way Oil Range **will pay you the biggest dividend** with years and years of satisfactory service.

Tens of thousands of women in city, suburban and farm homes are enthusiastic users of Our Wickless Range. The powerful "burn like gas" burners are the reason for their success, making them an ideal stove for year around use. Their speed, intensity and wide range of good, clean wholesome cooking heat are unsurpassed by that of any other oil stove.

You can use the range the year around and every day, for cooking, frying, laundry work, preserving—every use to which a cook stove is put—and we guarantee it to meet every kitchen requirement.

Every range is tested in the factory before you receive it and is absolutely guaranteed to give satisfaction or we will return your money.

The glistening snow white, acid proof, stainless porcelain enamel is easily kept spick and span, and cleans like a china dish. The attractive two-tone battleship gray and lustrous baked-on black enamel harmonizes with the best kitchen surroundings.

The five powerful three-in-one high speed heat diffusing giant burners provide speed and comfort in cooking, without smoke, odor or soot.

The cooking top is extra wide to accommodate large size cooking utensils and made in three anchor plate sections, easily removed for cleaning. The material is heavy, heat resisting steel plate, guaranteed to remain level and never warp or buckle. Every inch of space can be utilized for cooking or for keeping food warm. The slide easy cast iron grates permit cooking utensils to be moved from place to place with no danger of spilling their contents. Other splendid features are the rear holes for extra cooking and the sectional cast iron grid to accommodate different size cooking utensils.

The big capacity top provides ample space for a wash boiler and large cooking utensils, all to be used at one and the same time. The end shelf is a convenient extension to the top and serves as a guard for the glass oil container.

Measurements: Oven, 19 inches deep, 14 inches wide, 12 inches high. Cooking top, 36x20 inches, including end shelf. Height to cooking top, 32 inches. Total length of range, 56 inches. Shipping weight, 208 pounds. Prompt shipment from our PHILADELPHIA Store.

22K1409—Range with built-on oven

Low Cash Price...**$38.50**

Special Time Payment Price...42.50

TERMS: $4.00 with order and $4.00 each month until balance is paid. **Use Time Payment Order** Blank on page 1092.

E-Z-est-Way Wickless Oil Range uses asbestos lighting rings instead of wicks. Order an extra supply and have them when needed.

22K2401—Dozen...**$1.10**

Sanitary Clear Glass Stove Casters. Not included in price. Protects floor, rugs or linoleum from being marred. Easy to clean. Be sure to order a set for your stove. Shpg. wt., per set of four, 4 lbs.

22K2929—Set of 4...**40c**

We Guarantee to Satisfy You and Save You Money

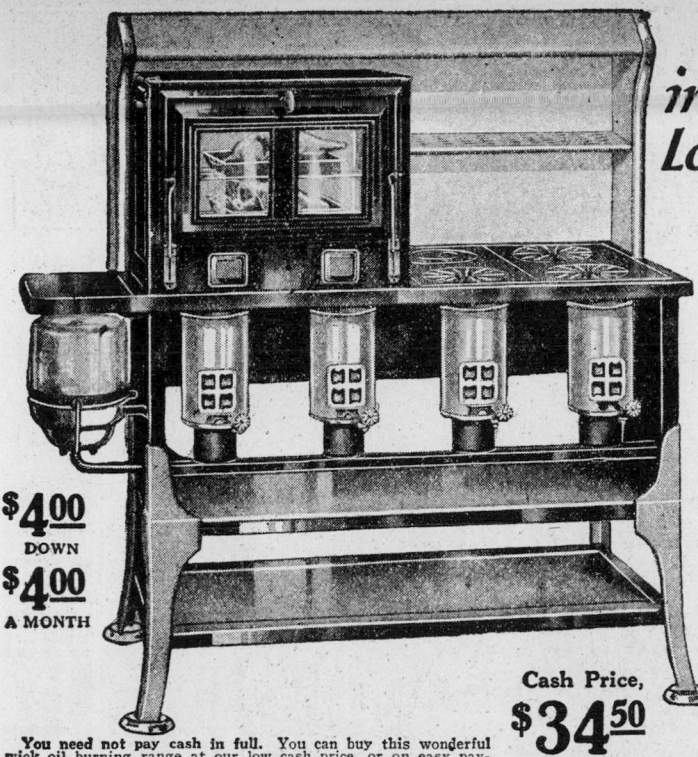

The Last Word
in WICK OIL STOVES With
Long Blue Enameled Chimneys

E-Z-est-Way Wick Oil Range With Direct Action Triplex Heat Diffusing Giant Burners

The wonderful three-in-one, direct action, triple heat generating burners light like a lamp and produce a clean, steady, brisk, brilliant, snappy blue flame and concentrate the heat directly on the cooking utensils like the modern gas and electric burners. Will do the work in less time, with less kerosene, and at a lower cost than any other wick burning oil stove on the market, regardless of name or make. One burner does the work of three.

The perfect flame control prevents turning the flame too high and eliminates the continuous fussing over wick adjustments. The wick cannot creep while the stove is in use. The new straightline body design is very attractive, and the pleasing two-tone color scheme harmonizes with the best of kitchen surroundings.

The body is made of extra heavy stamped steel, very sturdy, and the entire range, is unexcelled for workmanship, quality, convenience of operation and general cooking and baking satisfaction.

Big capacity, heat retaining daylight baking oven. Has patented tongue and groove construction on door to insure a heat-tight fit. Notice the big capacity; also the Ventilators under door to give the best results with baking or roasting.

Solid brass burner securely locked to feed pipe and heavy band iron brace—no chance for becoming out of alignment. Used on E-Z-est-Way Stoves only.

The heat retaining warming cabinet is very convenient to keep cooked food warm until ready to serve, and provides a place to keep dishes warm. Shelf for that purpose drops down when oven is removed.

The cooking top is extra wide, made in three anchor plate sections, and easily removed for cleaning. The material is heavy heat resisting steel plate, guaranteed to remain level and never warp or buckle. Every inch of space can be utilized for cooking or for keeping food warm. The slide easy cast iron grates permit cooking utensils to be moved from place to place with no danger of spilling their contents. Other splendid features are the rear holes for extra cooking and keeps the whole meal warm for late arrivals. Has sectional cast iron grid to accommodate different size cooking utensils.

The big and roomy top provides ample space for a wash boiler, oven and large cooking utensils, all to be used at one and the same time. The end shelf is a convenient extension to the top and serves as a guard for the glass oil container.

Cooking Top measures 51x20 inches with End Shelf, on eight-hole size.
Cooking Top measures 42x20 inches with End Shelf, on six-hole size.

Order extra wicks with your stove.

22K2463—Twelve wicks $3.00
Six wicks 1.50
Three wicks .... .75

$4.00 DOWN
$4.00 A MONTH

Cash Price, $34.50

8-Hole Model With Canopy Shelf and Baking Oven

You need not pay cash in full. You can buy this wonderful wick oil burning range at our low cash price, or on easy payments. Terms: $4.00 with order and $4.00 a month until paid in full. Use Time Payment Order Blank on page 1092.

Shipped from our PHILADELPHIA store.
The four-burner model has eight cooking holes.
The three-burner model has six cooking holes.
Shipping weight of eight-hole stove, 155 pounds; of six-hole stove, 135 pounds.

Range with eight cooking holes.
22K1445—Cash price $34.50
Time payment price 38.50

Range with six cooking holes.
22K1446—Cash price $30.25
Time payment price 34.25

Stove Casters as illustrated on stove not included.
22K2929—Set of 4. Shipping weight, 4 pounds .... .40

Positively the Best and Strongest All Purpose Heavy Duty Wickless Oil Stove Made

Equipped With Giant Super-Heat Diffusing Burners

Priced especially low and built to serve nearly every purpose, is this fine, substantial wickless low type Oil Stove. The frame is made of heavy gauge angle iron, securely welded together, and will easily support a weight of five hundred pounds. It is furnished with heavy square grates and has a large top surface. You will find this model especially suitable for the farm and laundry, for use in restaurants, and places where a stove is put to extra hard usage. It is equipped with the same powerful giant super-heat diffusing burners illustrated and described on page 955. The chimneys are finished in blue porcelain enamel.

Wickless stoves use asbestos rings instead of wicks. Order an extra dozen; have them when needed.
22K2401—Per dozen $1.10

Sold for Cash Only
Shipped from our Philadelphia store

Catalog No.	No. of Burners		Top Measures, Inches	Height	Shipping Weight
22K1453	2	$ 9.25	12x24	18	35 lbs.
22K1450	3	12.25	12x29¾	21	52 lbs.

E-Z-est-Way Wickless Stove With Giant Heat Diffusing Burner

Ideal for camps, outings, dairies, picnics, parties, yachts and general utility.

The construction is very sturdy; instead of legs it stands solidly on a strong circular base. A steel shield forms the body and protects the flame against wind and drafts. An ideal model for picnic parties, camping trips, outings and other purposes when only a small fire is needed. Equipped with the same quick acting giant heat diffusing burner used on our large and higher priced stoves and should not be compared with the undersized burner sold by many dealers.

Oven with glass door, 22K5473, shown on page 957, will be found very convenient for baking, roasting and toasting. We positively guarantee perfect operation and satisfaction or your money back. Measurements of stove: Height, 10¾ in.; diameter, 9½ in. Shipped from our PHILADELPHIA store. Sold for cash only.
22K1427—Stove, as illustrated. Shipping weight, 14 lbs.... $3.25

The Only Low Priced Wickless Cooking Outfit Made With Giant Heat Diffusing Burners and Extra Wide and Extra Long Cooking Top

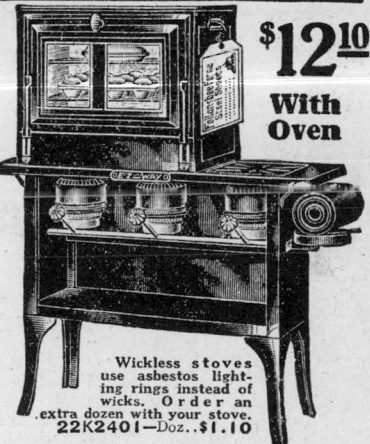

$12.10 With Oven

Cook and bake with this E-Z-est-Way Wickless Oil Stove in your own home for thirty days and you will readily see why it is one of our most popular cooking outfits. A first class stove in every detail. Has the same giant super-heat diffusing burners as used on our larger and higher priced oil stoves; made of the same high quality materials and finished in baked-on black enamel. Guaranteed to give satisfaction.

There's a world of comfort in using an E-Z-est-Way Wickless Oil Stove. Order one of these stoves and see the difference. Oven is a sure and satisfactory baker.

This is our 22K5464 oven shown on page 957. Top measures 37x14 inches. Height, 30½ inches. Shipping weight of stove, with oven, 68 pounds; without oven, 43 pounds.

Shipped from PHILADELPHIA, PA. Sold only for cash in full with order.
22K5415—Stove with oven. $12.10
22K5415—Stove without oven 8.85

Wickless stoves use asbestos lighting rings instead of wicks. Order an extra dozen with your stove.
22K2401—Doz..$1.10

E-Z-est WAY OVENS

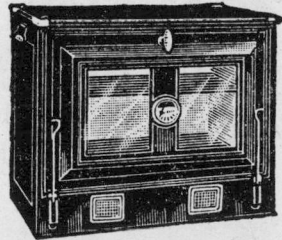

Our Best Oven With Heat Indicator

Made of genuine Follansbee forged blue polished steel. Every part made to fit perfectly. Daylight two-panel glass door with oven heat indicator. Lined with bright corrugated tin, insulated with heavy asbestos on sides, top and back. Two oven racks furnished. Measurements, inside: 18 inches wide, 12 inches high, 11½ inches deep. Shpg. wt.. 28 lbs. Not mailable. Sold for cash only.
22K6466 .... $4.60

Very Popular Model

Large clear two-panel glass door. Asbestos lined. Ventilators below door for supplying fresh air to oven, insuring perfect baking. Inside measurements: 18 inches wide, 11½ inches deep, 12 inches high. Shipping weight, 27 pounds. Not mailable. Sold for cash only.
22K5468 .... $3.75

The HERCULES Furnace

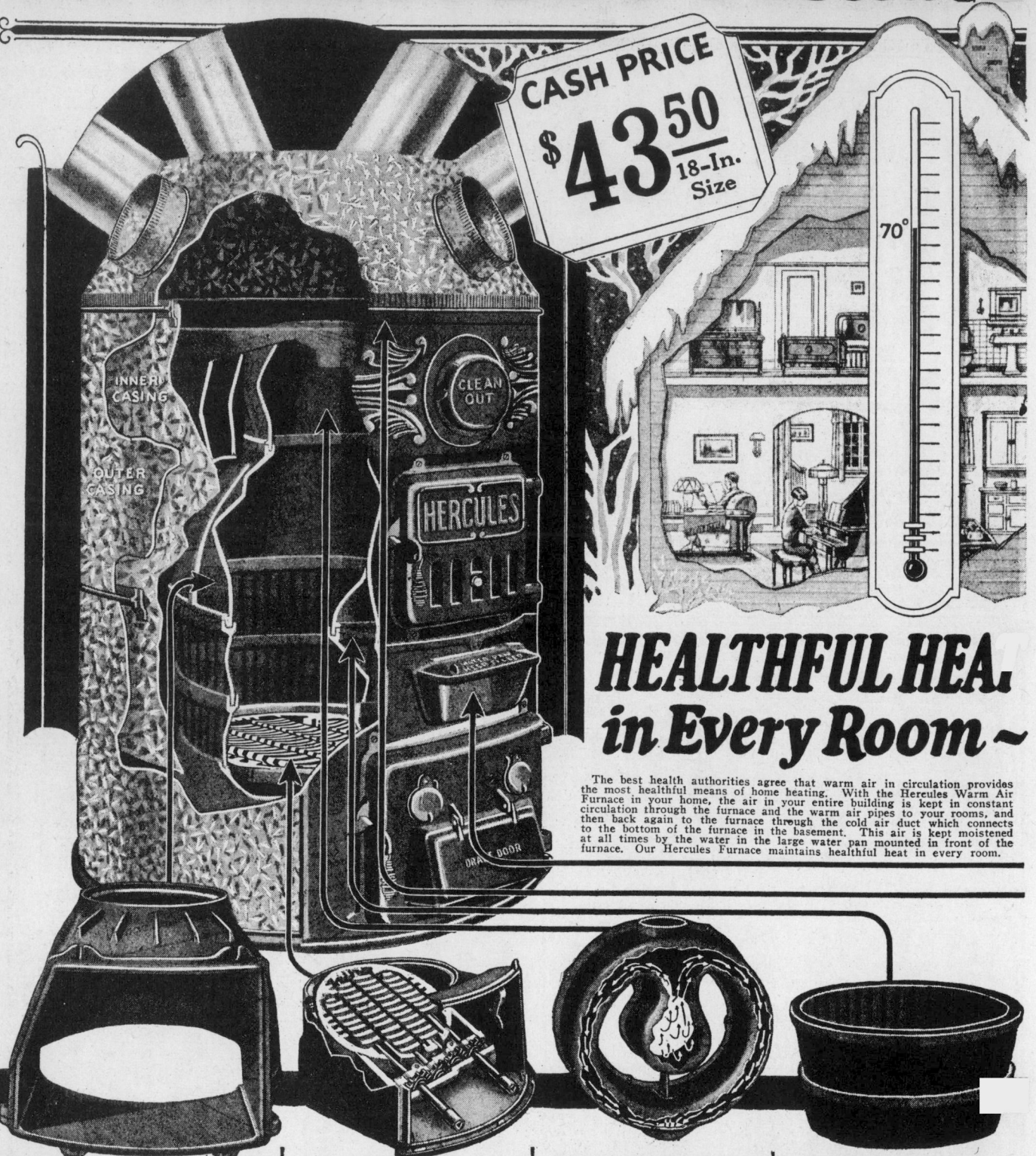

CASH PRICE
$43.50
18-In. Size

70°

HEALTHFUL HEAT in Every Room ~

The best health authorities agree that warm air in circulation provides the most healthful means of home heating. With the Hercules Warm Air Furnace in your home, the air in your entire building is kept in constant circulation through the furnace and the warm air pipes to your rooms, and then back again to the furnace through the cold air duct which connects to the bottom of the furnace in the basement. This air is kept moistened at all times by the water in the large water pan mounted in front of the furnace. Our Hercules Furnace maintains healthful heat in every room.

INNER CASING

OUTER CASING

CLEAN OUT

HERCULES

DRAFT DOOR

Above illustration shows the construction of the high ribbed cast iron fire dome of this furnace. The unusually h i g h combustion chamber provides ample space for the proper combustion of the fuel so that you get the most efficient heating results. Notice the large size feed throat on this fire door section, which provides a feed door opening large enough to admit large chunks of wood or coal. The raised ribs around this fire dome add to the heating surface and strengthen the casting.

The entire grate section of our Hercules Warm Air Pipe Furnace is made up in one assembly, resting on a hinge support at the back of the ashpit and supported by two cast iron hooks in front. By pulling these hooks forward at the front, the entire assembly can be lowered on the rear hinge so that grate bars can be removed and replaced with little effort. You just insert the grate bar and then lift up the grate frame, the hooks automatically fall into place and the furnace is ready for use. Grates are triangular revolving type, clinkers are easily ground up and discharged into the ashpit.

The above illustration shows the construction of the large circular cast iron radiator on this furnace. The entire top and sides are made in one casting and the bottom plate of the radiator is another. This bottom plate is very firmly cemented and bolted to the bottom of the radiator with a deep tongue and groove joint. This radiator is of unusually large proportions and is unusually high providing the necessary heating surface for greatest heating efficiency. The smoke collar is connected at the back of the radiator and there is a cleanout opening in the front, through which it can be thoroughly cleaned.

The fire pot is made in two sections, which fit together with deep tongue and groove joints. These castings are made from high grade iron for greatest durability, and are heavily corrugated to provide an extra large amount of heating surface. The two-piece construction of this fire pot provides ample leeway for expansion and contraction and reduces to a minimum the possibility of castings cracking. These castings are made from accurate patterns so that perfect fit is assured.

M[illegible]us a Big S[illegible]ving of Fuel

Solid Comfort All Winter Long With Our Hercules Warm Air Pipe Furnace

EASY PAYMENTS
$10.00 DOWN
$10.00 A MONTH

Your furnace outfit is, without any question, the most important piece of equipment in your entire building. Fuel economy is a most important factor. Remember, your furnace will be in operation for many years. Each year it will be either burning fuel economically or wasting it.

The furnace you select should be designed for greatest heating efficiency. It should have ample heating surface in proportion to grate area and it should have ample air chamber capacity and ample fire travel to obtain the full benefit of all available heat units in the fuel.

A High Grade Furnace Built for Service

Our Hercules Warm Air Pipe Furnace has all of these features worked out to a high degree of perfection. It is a strictly high quality furnace designed for greatest efficiency and durability. It is a furnace that will continue to give you satisfactory service for very many years with a minimum amount of attention and minimum expense for fuel.

When you can buy a furnace which is always the best in these three features at the price quoted on our Hercules you have secured the greatest of heating values. Constant use by thousands of our customers has proved the Hercules the best value in furnaces. It has stood the test in all types of homes, in every kind of weather and has always lived up to expectations.

Yearly improvements have made our Hercules the nearest thing to perfection. Our ability to buy material in great quantities and the rapid sale of our furnaces have enabled us to quote such a low price. Only the World's Largest Store can do this.

Every Hercules Heating System Guaranteed

Our guarantee protects you in your purchase of this heating plant. We are willing to guarantee you satisfaction or return your money—that certainly is proof that we have faith in the Hercules, that we are sure it will live up to all of our claims. Years of experience in the furnace business has taught us and thousands of satisfied customers to expect the utmost in heating perfection from our Hercules Warm Air Pipe Furnace—that is what we are offering you, heating perfection at a price usually paid for a far inferior product.

Prices and Dimensions Hercules Warm Air Furnace

Shipped From Factory in OHIO

Catalog No.	Diam. Fire Pot, In.	Size, Smoke Collar, In.	Size, Feed Door, Inches	Ht., With Casing, In.	Diam. Casing, In.	Shpg. Wt., Lbs.	Cash	Easy Payments
42K3983⅓	18	7	8¾x11½	56½	36	720	$ 43.50	$ 48.00
42K3984⅓	20	8	10½x12½	60½	38	820	51.75	57.00
42K3985⅓	22	8	11 x13	63½	43	915	64.00	70.50
42K3986⅓	24	8	11 x13	65½	45	1,080	75.00	82.50
42K3987⅓	26	9	11 x13	68	50	1,350	87.00	96.00
42K3988⅓	28	9	10½x12½	72½	54⅜	1,525	109.50	120.50
42K3989⅓	30	10	10½x12½	73¾	58	1,650	133.35	147.00

Terms: $10.00 Down and $10.00 per Month.

Above prices include furnace complete with galvanized top and casing, but warm air pipe, registers, smoke pipe, smoke damper, etc., are not included. Smoke pipe, smoke damper, hot water coil and wood burning grate listed at right.

If wanted with gas burner in addition to coal grate write for prices.

If ordering on easy payments please fill out special easy payment order blank on page 1092. To take advantage of our easy payment offer it is necessary that you hold title to the building in which the furnace is to be installed. No interest or other expense to be added to monthly payment prices.

Let Us Send You an Estimate on a Modern Warm Air Heating System for Your Home

Our experience in the development, perfection and distribution of our Hercules Warm Air Heating Systems extends over a period of over twenty-five years.

We have proved to many thousands of our customers that our Hercules Warm Air Furnaces are easy to install. That they fulfill every claim we make for them. That the broad guarantee under which they are sold and our liberal merchandising policy are a reliable assurance of satisfaction.

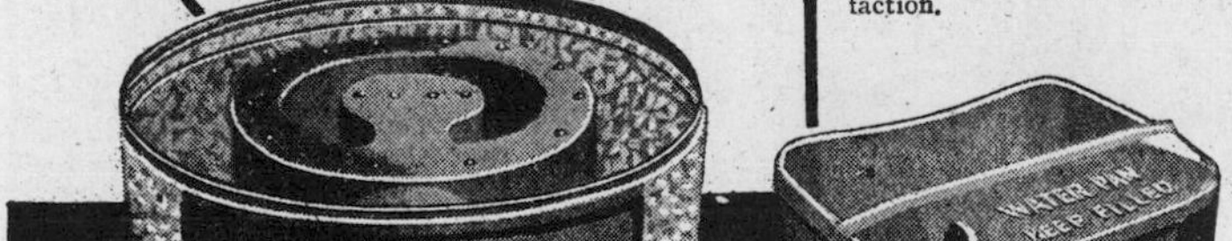

WATER PAN KEEP FILLED

The above illustration shows in detail the air space casing insulation of our Hercules Pipe Furnace. The outer casing is made of strong gauge galvanized sheet metal in two sections, an upper section and a lower section. Inside of this outer casing and spaced one inch apart from around the entire furnace, there is suspended an inner casing also made of galvanized iron, which extends down to a level with the top of the ashpit, providing a one inch insulating space around the entire heating body of the furnace. Effectively preventing the loss of heat through the furnace casing, this one-inch insulating air space is a big coal saving feature on this furnace for the reason that it prevents heat loss in the basement.

Above illustration shows the large capacity cast iron water pan supplied with this furnace. This water pan is mounted in the front casting just beneath the fire door and directly opposite the fire pot castings where the fire is hottest, thus insuring sufficiently rapid evaporation to provide the proper degree of moisture to the air as it circulates through the furnace and up to your rooms.

The water pan is, of course, open inside the furnace air heating chamber. The part of the pan which projects out through the front of the furnace, however, is provided with a hinged cast iron cover. When filling, this cover is simply raised and pushed aside and the water poured right in, making a very convenient arrangement.

Our Heating Offer Can't Be Beat

Only the finest quality material is used on Hercules Heating Systems. We design your system for you. You get free engineering service. You get specially prepared plans. You get a complete instruction book covering every phase and every detail of the installation. You have an opportunity to save from $100.00 to $200.00 on the installation cost alone by looking after the work yourself. You get a strictly modern heating system unexcelled by any in the country for fine quality material and heating efficiency. In short, you get service and quality, and you get it at a price that spells dollars in your pocket. That's what you get when you order a Hercules Heating System, and that's why we say our proposition cannot be beat. **Write for our special Plumbing and Heating Catalog 548K. Get our estimate and judge for yourself.**

Peerless Flue Cleaner

$1.45

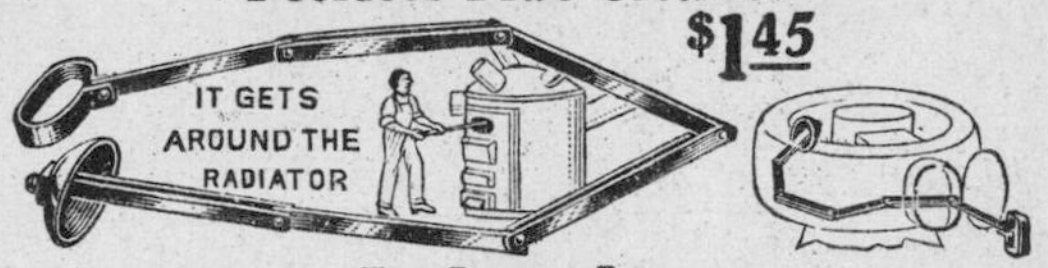

IT GETS AROUND THE RADIATOR

The Greatest Ever

Here is the most practical and efficient furnace flue cleaner on the market. It is flexible in one direction only. It is absolutely rigid in the other, so that it is always under complete control of the person using it. All of the soot in any furnace radiator can be easily removed in a few minutes. We know of no other flue cleaner on the market that can possibly compare with this in actual results. It will pay for itself in one month in fuel saved. You will make a big saving in your coal bills by keeping your furnace radiator clean.

42K165¼—Shipping weight, 4½ pounds.............. **$1.45**

Hercules Automatic Water Pan Filler Saves Time and Labor

$4.95 Complete

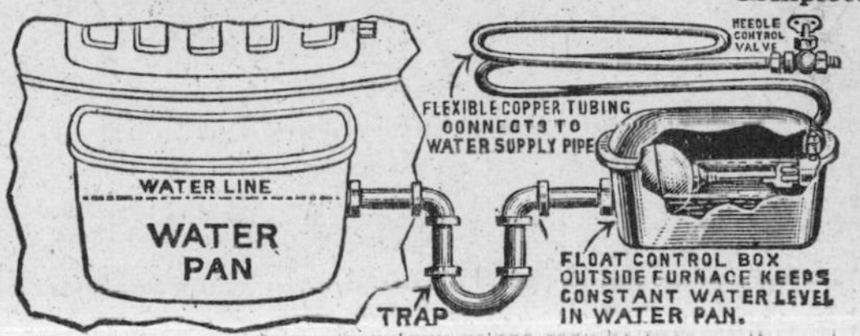

NEEDLE CONTROL VALVE
FLEXIBLE COPPER TUBING CONNECTS TO WATER SUPPLY PIPE
WATER LINE
WATER PAN
TRAP
FLOAT CONTROL BOX OUTSIDE FURNACE KEEPS CONSTANT WATER LEVEL IN WATER PAN.

This device completely relieves you of the task of keeping the water pan on your furnace filled. It is easily attached to any furnace by simply tapping into the water pan and making the connection. The flexible copper water supply tube is then connected at some convenient point on your water supply pipe. Once installed, it requires no more attention, operates constantly throughout the entire heating season and it will last for many years without attention.

You are always assured of correct humidity as the water pan can never run dry. Equipment includes bronze float valve with Monel metal needle point, 3-inch copper float, brass float chamber, five feet ¼-inch flexible copper tubing, needle control valve, and trap.

42K121—Shipping weight, 5 pounds.................. **$4.95**

Hot Water Coil

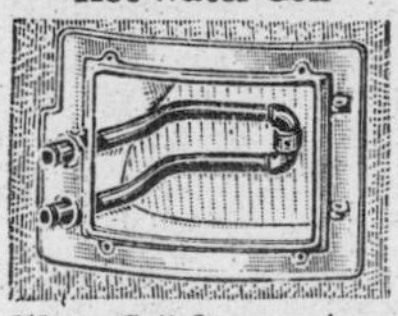

Hot Water Coil fits any pipe or pipeless furnace we sell. **Be sure to state fire pot diameter of furnace.** Shipping weight, 10 pounds.

42K1675¼........... **$1.85**

Wood Burning Grate

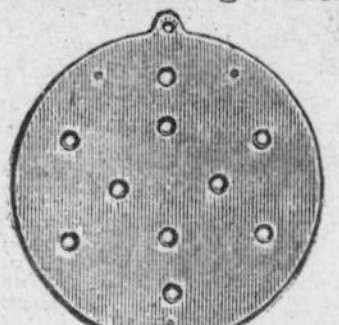

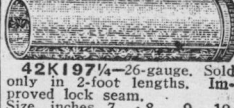

Cast iron, sets on top of regular furnace grate. **Be sure to state fire pot diameter of furnace.** Shipping weight, 12 pounds. **Shipped from factory in OHIO.**

42K1674⅓... **$2.25**

Asbestos Paper

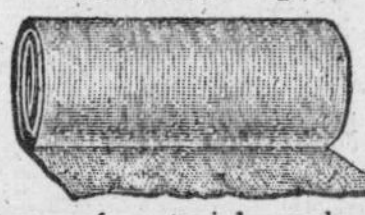

A fireproof material, made of natural mineral asbestos fibers reduced to a pulp and spread out into a sheet of uniform thickness. It is usually applied with starch paste, or the special Asbestos Paste listed below.

In addition to covering furnace pipes, asbestos paper is used for covering walls, partitions and ceilings exposed to heat, and as a lining for floors and ceilings. It comes in rolls 36 inches wide. Shipped from our store. Prices subject to market changes.

42K193¼—10-yard roll. Shipping weight, 11 pounds.............. **$1.00**

42K194¼—50-yard roll. Shipping weight, 52 pounds.............. **$3.95**

Cold Water Paste

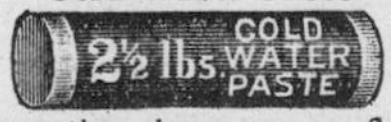

2½ lbs. COLD WATER PASTE

For pasting down canvas flaps on Air Cell pipe covering. Used also for pasting asbestos paper to tin furnace pipes on warm air heating systems. Simply mix with cold water and use. Comes in 2½-pound package.

42K195—Per package **35c**

Galvanized Smoke Pipe

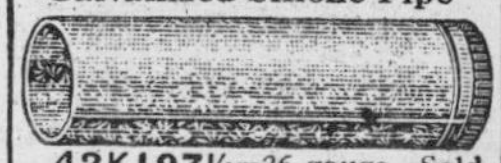

42K197¼—26-gauge. Sold only in 2-foot lengths. Improved lock seam.

Size, inches	7	8	9	10
Shpg. wt., lbs., per length	3½	4	4½	5
Per length	44c	47c	50c	54c

Galvanized Adjustable Smoke Pipe Elbows

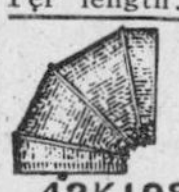

42K198¼—26-gauge. Adjustable to any angle.

Size, inches	7	8	9	10
Shpg. wt., lbs.	2	2¼	2½	3
Each	38c	42c	48c	60c

Smoke Pipe Dampers

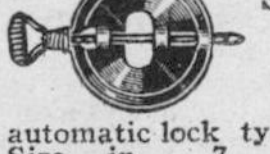

42K199 Cast iron automatic lock type.

Size, in.	7	8	9	10
Shpg. wt., lbs.	½	¾	1	1¼
Each	22c	30c	45c	60c

HERCULES Heating Systems

We Sell Coal Direct From Mines to You. See Page 647.

You Can Make a BIG SAVING *On Your* Heating System

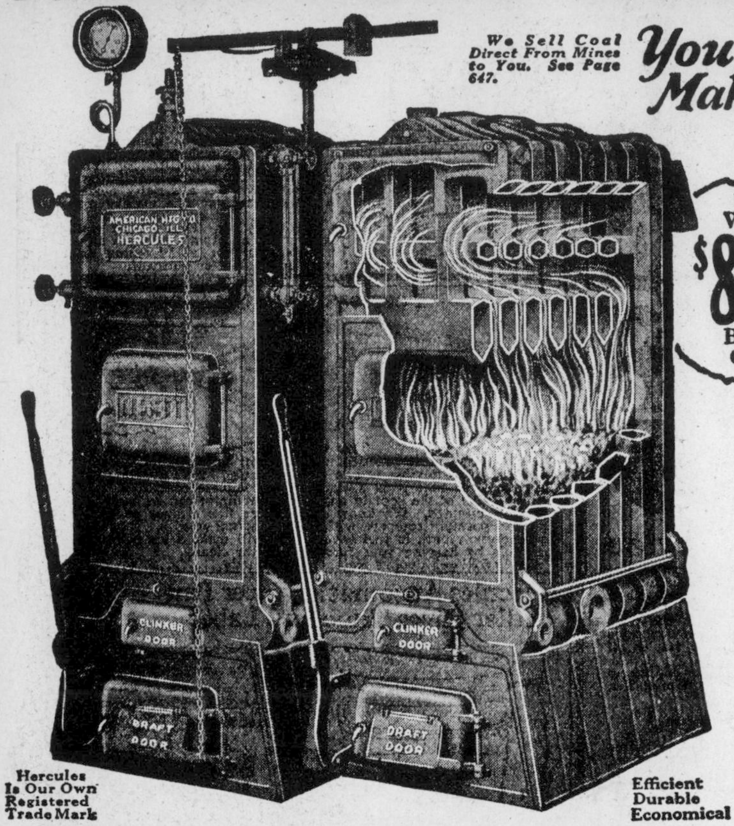

Hercules Is Our Own Registered Trade Mark

Efficient Durable Economical

Hot Water $81.75 and up Boiler Only

Why Be Without This Great Home Comfort?

If you haven't a Hercules Heating System in your home you are missing one of the greatest of all modern comforts. Just think of what it means to have your entire house heated to a comfortable and even temperature throughout the coldest winter weather; only one fire to attend to, no smoke, dust or gas in your living rooms, no carrying of coal and ashes over your rugs and carpets. On the coldest winter morning you can get up in a nice warm bedroom. You can use a modern oil or gas stove for cooking in the kitchen if you want to and still be warm and comfortable. This great comfort and convenience is easily within your means.

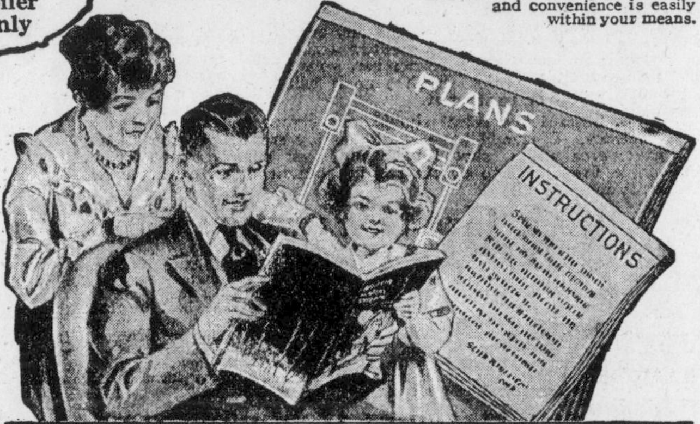

Boiler Ratings

All our Hercules Boilers both Square and Round are rated according to the regular standard as adopted by boiler manufacturers throughout the country. In these ratings no allowance has been made for heat losses from exposed mains and branch pipes, fittings, etc. In selecting a boiler add 100 per cent to the amount of radiation you have to supply and select a boiler rated accordingly; for instance, if you have 400 square feet of radiation to heat, you should have a boiler rated 800 square feet at least. We strongly advocate ample boiler capacity on any heating system. It is always far better to have a boiler a little over size than too small.

HERCULES Square Boiler

Illustrations on this and the opposite page show our Hercules Round and Square Boilers for steam or hot water heating. From a standpoint of heating efficiency a choice between these boilers would be hard to make. That is largely a matter of opinion. Some people prefer a round boiler, others prefer the square. Nevertheless, whichever boiler you select, we believe we are offering you the best. The fundamental principle of these boilers is right. Notice the large amount of heating surface directly over the fire. The boiler is the heart of your heating system. For many years it will be burning coal economically or wasting it. A heating system for your home is an investment that you will make probably once in a lifetime. An inefficient boiler on your heating system is a poor investment at any price. With a Hercules Boiler in your home you will get the utmost heat out of the fuel you burn.

Our Hercules Square Boilers shown in the above illustration are made of cast iron, the boiler being assembled in vertical sections as shown. The vertical sections are interconnected with tapered push nipples and the sections are held together with draw rods at three points.

These boilers burn hard coal, soft coal, wood or coke and embody the very latest improvements in home heating boiler design. The V shape construction of the individual sections, directly over the fire and in the firepot itself, presents the greatest amount of heating surface where the heat is most effective.

The prices as given below on the steam boilers include steam trimmings complete. Prices on hot water boilers are for boilers only without fittings. Boilers are all 58 inches high over all and take 9-inch smoke pipe. Firing tools include the hoe, poker, rake and flue brush with handle furnished with each boiler. Shipped from factory in WESTERN NEW YORK. Prices subject to market changes.

No.	Rating, Hot Water	Rating, Steam	Size of Fire Pot, Inches	Flow and Return Tappings	Shpg. Wt., Hot Water	Shpg. Wt., Steam	42K3973⅓ Hot Water: Cash Price	42K3973⅓ Hot Water: Price on Easy Payments	42K3972⅓ Steam: Cash Price	42K3972⅓ Steam: Price on Easy Payments
517	1,000	600	17x16½	2-2½ in.	900	940	$ 81.75	$ 90.00	$96.75	$106.50
617	1,250	750	17x20½	2-2½ in.	1,050	1,090	94.85	104.50	109.85	121.00
717	1,500	900	17x25	3-2½ in.	1,190	1,230	107.95	119.00	122.95	135.00
817	1,750	1,050	17x29	3-2½ in.	1,350	1,400	122.35	134.50	137.35	151.50

When writing for our estimate be sure to state whether Round or Square Boiler is preferred. Where no preference is stated square boiler will be figured on estimates. If you wish to purchase boiler on easy payments write for special terms.

Cast Iron Radiators for Steam or Hot Water Systems

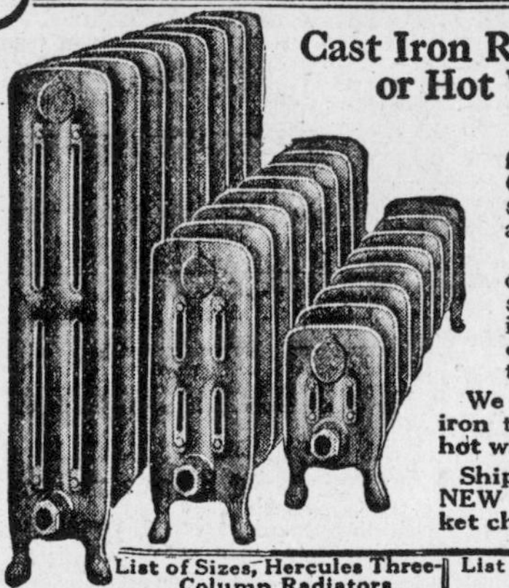

Good quality cast iron carefully machined and tested. Graceful, plain design. The smooth surfaces do not collect dust and dirt, and appeal to the housekeeper.

Only three and five-column radiators are listed below. For other styles send for our Special Plumbing and Heating Catalog. When ordering state number of sections and height wanted.

We can also furnish new style cast iron tubular radiators for steam or hot water. Prices given on request.

Shipped from factory in WESTERN NEW YORK. Prices subject to market changes.

List of Sizes, Hercules Three-Column Radiators

	38 In. High	26 In. High	22 In. High
42K3998⅓ Steam. Per sq. ft.....	30c	39½c	44c
42K3999⅓ Hot Water. Per sq. ft.....	30c	39½c	44c

List of Sizes, Hercules Five-Column Radiators

	22 In. High	18 In. High	14 In. High
42K4002 Steam. Per sq. ft.....	47c	53c	57c
42K4003 Hot Water. Per sq. ft.....	47c	53c	57c

Radiator Air Moisteners

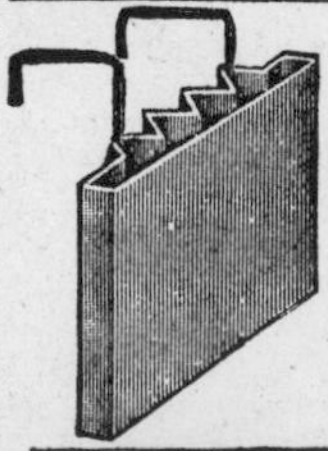

The best health authorities agree that proper moistening of the air in your home during the winter time is necessary to health and comfort.

Our Hercules Air Moistener keeps air moistened by evaporation of water. Filled with water and hung back of radiator, out of the way and out of sight. Galvanized sheet metal. Shipping weight, 4 pounds.

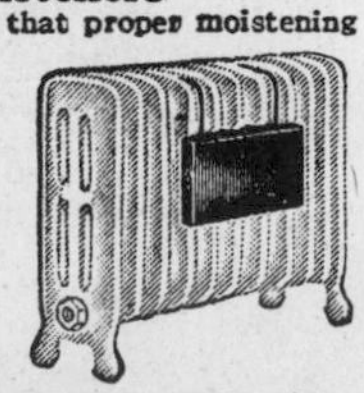

42K157—With gold bronze finish......... **50c**

Asbestos Cement

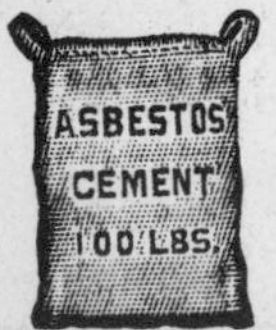

For covering heating or power boilers, galvanized range boilers, smoke pipes and elbows and tees on heating systems, etc. Prevents loss of heat. Pays for itself in one or two seasons. Composed of asbestos fiber and a cement compound. Mixed and applied like ordinary plaster to a thickness of about 1½ in. Comes in 100-lb. bags. One bag covers about 11 square feet to a thickness of about 1½ in.

42K196⅓—Per bag....... **$1.65**

Shipped from factory in NORTHWESTERN INDIANA or PHILADELPHIA, PA., whichever is nearer to you.

Air Cell Asbestos Pipe Covering

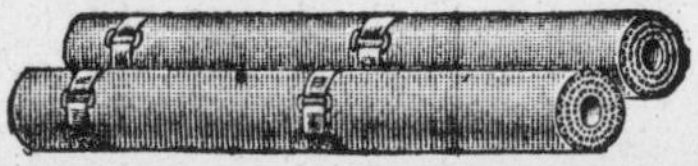

For covering pipes on heating systems; also cold water pipes to prevent freezing. Easily applied after pipes are in place. Sold only in 3-foot lengths, 1 inch thick. **Shipped from factory in NORTHWESTERN INDIANA or PHILADELPHIA, PA., whichever is nearer to you.**

42K4046⅓

For Pipe Size, In.	Shpg. Wt., Lbs.	Per 3-Ft. Lgth.	For Pipe Size, In.	Shpg. Wt., Lbs.	Per 3-Ft. Lgth.
½	1¾	24c	2	3½	40c
¾	2	27c	2½	4	45c
1	2¼	30c	3	4½	50c
1¼	2¾	33c	3½	5	56c
1½	3	37c	4	5½	67c

Steel Wire Flue Brush

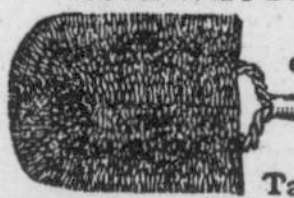

A very effective cleaner for cast iron heating boilers, round or square.

Size, 1¾x4½x5½ in. Tapped for ¾-inch pipe connection. Shipping weight, 1 lb.

42K168.................. **70c**

Siphon Air Valve

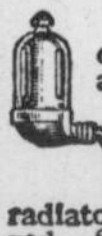

Here is a valve that you can depend upon to open and close at the proper time and keep the radiators on your steam heating plant operating at all times to their highest efficiency. No more air trapped radiators. Cannot become water logged. Saves fuel.

42K119—Shpg. wt., 4 oz. **65c**

for G[illegible]test Wint[illegible]r Comfort

Round or Square Boilers

Cash or Easy Payment Terms

Our Hercules Heating Systems are sold for cash or on easy payment terms. You need not wait until you have accumulated sufficient funds to pay cash in full. You can install your heating system right now. A moderate payment down is all that is necessary to bring you one of our complete Hercules Heating Systems and you can enjoy this great comfort and convenience in your home while paying for it in small monthly payments easily within your means.

Every Hercules Heating System Guaranteed

We have the facilities and the organization which assure you of satisfactory service. Our responsibility removes the risk. You can place your order with us feeling confident that you will obtain a heating system that will prove satisfactory in every respect. Our Hercules Heating Systems are sold under the same broad and binding guarantee as every other item of merchandise in our catalog. That is, if for any reason whatever you are not satisfied with your purchase, you may return the material to us at our expense and we will return your money, including all transportation charges you have paid.

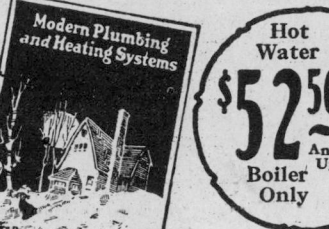

Write for Our **Special Heating and Plumbing Catalog 548 K**

Sent Postpaid on Request

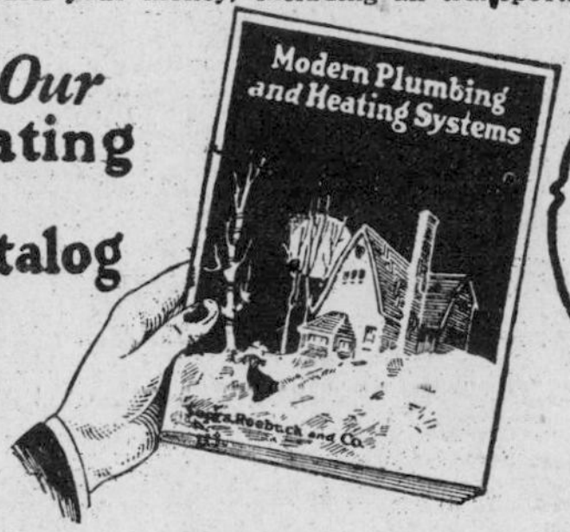

Hot Water **$52.50** And Up Boiler Only

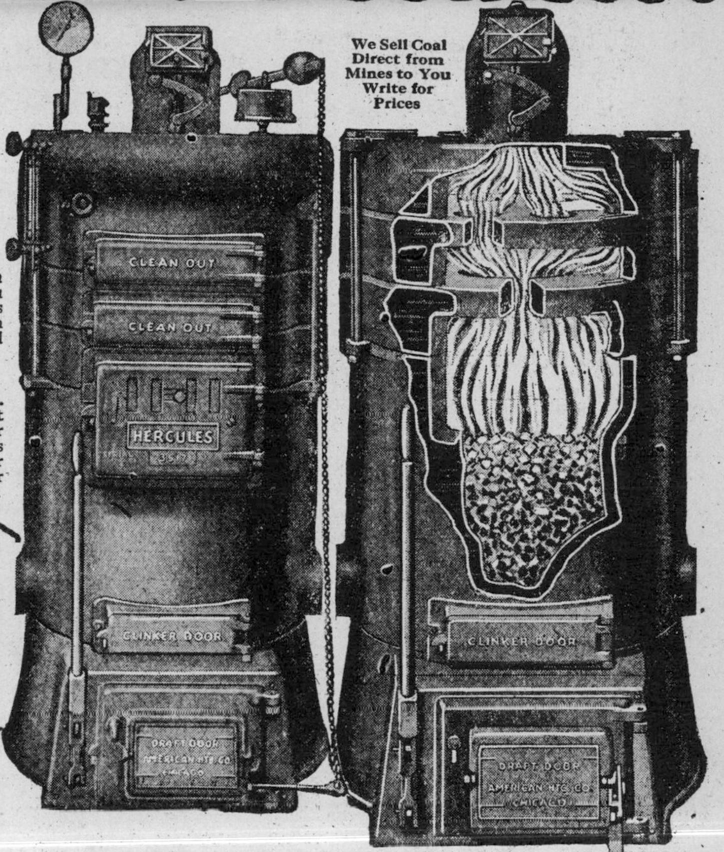

Complete Estimates Cheerfully Furnished

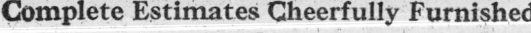

We will gladly send you an estimate on a complete steam or hot water heating system without obligating you in the least. Write immediately for one of our Special Plumbing and Heating Catalogs. Fill out the special information blank that you will find enclosed with this book, giving us the necessary information in regard to your building, and our complete estimate will be promptly sent to you. We will estimate on either a round or a square boiler, whichever type you prefer. Our engineers will estimate the exact size radiators and boiler, piping, etc., required for your building and you will be surprised at the big saving you can make. Any handy man can install any of our heating systems by following the simple plans and instructions which we furnish. All main pipes are cut to fit. All you have to do is to screw them together as indicated on the plans. **When writing for our estimate please state if round or square boiler is wanted. Where no preference is stated square boiler will be figured on estimates.**

HERCULES Round Boiler

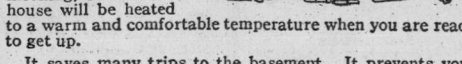

Scientifically designed for greatest heating efficiency, our Hercules Cast Iron Round Boilers are unexcelled for economical home heating. These Hercules Boilers are equal to the best on the market in workmanship, finish and material. They are built to a very high quality standard, the grates, door, castings and other parts being of heavy construction so that the boiler, with ordinary care, will last a lifetime. All doors are ground to a very accurate fit, reducing air leakage to a minimum. Ample cleanout openings have been provided, making the boiler easily accessible for cleaning at all points. There is a liberal size feed door and a very deep fire pot, which makes this one of the most economical home heating boilers on the market. The grate bars are of the rocking type. The entire grate can be easily shaken by moving the long lever handle at the front of the boiler backward and forward. Each boiler has tappings to receive a coil for heating water for domestic purposes.

The illustrations above show boilers having three sections above the fire pot. These boilers are also furnished with only two sections above the fire pot and with three sections above the fire pot, depending, of course, upon the heating capacity required.

We offer you these boilers with the assurance that they represent the maximum in fuel economy and home comfort.

When writing for our estimate be sure to state whether round or square boiler is preferred. Where no preference is stated square boiler will be figured on estimates.

Both Cash and Easy Payment Prices are given below. Write for special terms if you wish to purchase on easy payments.

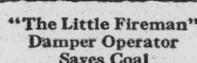

Please Read Information on Opposite Page Regarding Boiler Ratings

Prices and Dimensions—Hercules Round Boilers

The prices, as given below on the steam boilers, include steam trimmings complete. Prices on hot water boilers are for boilers only without fittings. Firing tools include the hoe, poker, rake and flue brush with handle furnished with each boiler. Shipped from warehouse in WESTERN NEW YORK.

42K3978⅓—Hot Water Boiler. State size wanted.

Size of Grate	Sections Above Fire Pot	Size Tappings, Feed and Return	Size of Smoke Collar	Rated Capacity, Sq. Ft.	Height to Feed Outlet, Inches	Shpg. Wt., Lbs.	Cash Price	Easy Payment Price
17-Inch Diameter	2	2½ in.	7 in.	550	42½ in.	625	$ 52.50	$ 58.00
	3	2½ in.	7 in.	650	47½ in.	730	67.50	74.50
20-Inch Diameter	2	2½ in.	8 in.	800	45 in.	745	70.50	77.50
	3	2½ in.	8 in.	900	50 in.	850	82.50	91.00
23-Inch Diameter	2	3 in.	8 in.	1100	45 in.	910	97.50	107.50
26-Inch Diameter	2	3 in.	10 in.	1450	45 in.	1090	112.50	124.00
	3	3 in.	10 in.	1550	50 in.	1230	135.00	148.50
29-Inch Diameter	2	4 in.	10 in.	1900	46 in.	1300	142.50	157.00
	3	4 in.	10 in.	2050	51 in.	1490	165.00	181.50

42K3979⅓—Steam Boiler. State size wanted.

Size of Grate	Sections Above Fire Pot	Size Tappings, Feed and Return	Size of Smoke Collar	Rated Capacity, Sq. Ft.	Height to Feed Outlet, Inches	Shpg. Wt., Lbs.	Cash Price	Easy Payment Price
17-Inch Diameter	2	2½ in.	7 in.	350	46½ in.	725	$ 60.00	$ 66.00
	3	2½ in.	7 in.	400	51½ in.	830	75.00	82.50
20-Inch Diameter	2	2½ in.	8 in.	500	51½ in.	850	82.50	91.00
	3	2½ in.	8 in.	550	56½ in.	950	94.50	104.00
23-Inch Diameter	2	3 in.	8 in.	675	51½ in.	1050	115.50	127.00
26-Inch Diameter	2	3 in.	10 in.	900	51½ in.	1210	139.50	153.50
	3	3 in.	10 in.	1000	56½ in.	1350	162.00	178.50
29-Inch Diameter	2	4 in.	10 in.	1150	52½ in.	1500	177.00	195.00
	3	4 in.	10 in.	1225	57½ in.	1680	199.50	219.50

The Hercules Thermostat Heat Regulator Saves Coal

$29.95 Complete

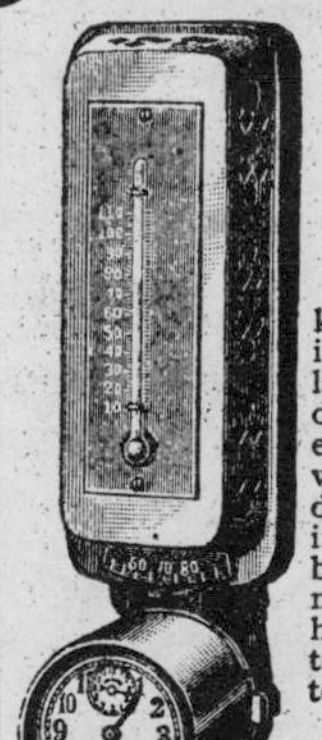

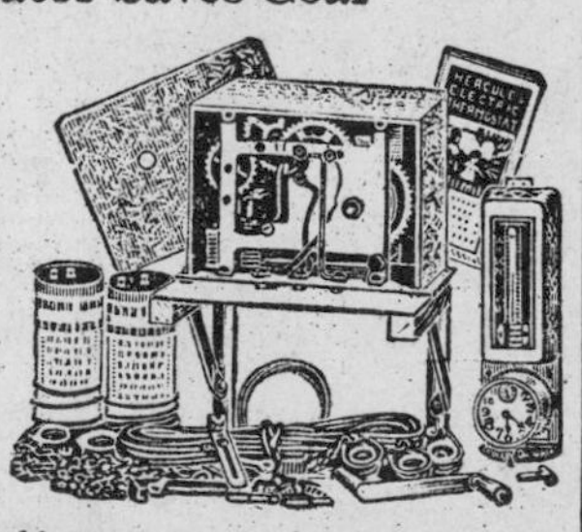

This device will keep the temperature in your rooms regulated to an exact degree throughout the entire winter, and it will open up the dampers on your heating system one hour before you arise in the morning, so that the house will be heated to a warm and comfortable temperature when you are ready to get up.

It saves many trips to the basement. It prevents your rooms from cooling off, as it opens the dampers automatically as soon as the temperature drops below 70 degrees, or whatever you have set it for, and it prevents overheating your rooms, because it closes the dampers as soon as the temperature goes above that degree.

It saves coal. **Complete instructions for installing furnished with each outfit.**

42K1174¼ — Outfit, complete, ready to install. Shipping weight, 30 pounds....... **$29.95**

"The Little Fireman" Damper Operator Saves Coal

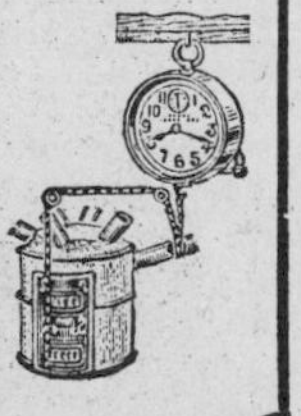

Opens the dampers on your heating system an hour before you get up in the morning, so that when you rise, every room in your house will be warm and cozy. Outfit includes clock, pulleys and 18 feet of chain ready to install with full instructions. Shipping wt., 6 lbs.
42K1172... **$3.95**

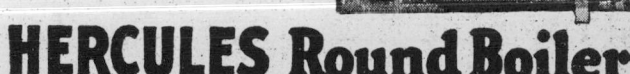

"Hi-Grade" Aluminum Ware at America's Lowest Prices

"Hi-Grade" ware is pure aluminum, hard and durable. It is several gauges heavier than many competitive makes, and will give excellent service.

Because of our immense purchases of this ware, we are able to offer it at less than usual dealers' costs. Compare and note the big savings you can make here. Every piece is GUARANTEED EXTRA VALUE.

For extra heavy aluminum ware that will last a lifetime, we recommend the "Best Made" shown on the opposite page.

65c 4-Qt. Kettle Bargains of a Lifetime

Our Prices Save You Money!

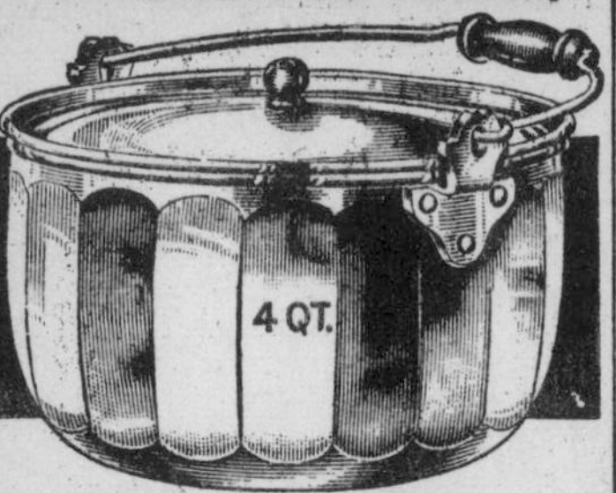

Paneled Convex Kettles

"Hi-Grade," paneled, heavy pure aluminum kettles, with cover, wood grip, long wearing, serviceable. Unusual values.

	Cap.	Shpg. Wt.	
99K922	4 qts.	1 pound	$0.65
99K952	6 qts.	2 pounds	.79
99K953	8 qts.	2 pounds	.99
99K954	10 qts.	3 pounds	1.25

Preserving Kettles

45c 4-Qt. "Hi-Grade" pure aluminum, paneled, nicely finished, remarkable saving in price, among our very best sellers.

99K928—Cap., 4 qts. Weight, ¾ lb....45c
99K955—Cap., 6 qts. Weight, 2 lbs...69c
99K956—Cap., 8 qts. Weight, 3 lbs...85c
99K957—Cap., 10 qts. Weight, 3 lbs...95c

Large Preserving Kettles With Covers

$1.60 12-Qt. "Hi-Grade" pure aluminum, smooth finish, plain sides. Ideal for preserving, stewing and soup making. Shipping weight, 4 pounds.

	Capacity	
99K997	12 quarts	$1.60
99K998	14 quarts	2.25
99K999	16 quarts	2.60

Improved Double Boiler

$1.40 "Hi-Grade" pure aluminum, can be used as a pudding pan, casserole, open saucepan, convex saucepan or double boiler. Cap., upper, 2 qts.; lower, 3 qts. Interchangeable cover. Shipping wt., 3 lbs.
99K2408...$1.40

Double Boilers

79c "Hi-Grade" pure aluminum, just the thing for cereals, 1½-Qt. milk, puddings, custards, etc., paneled sides.
9K929—Capacity of inset, 1½ quarts. Weight, 1½ lbs...........79c
99K964—Capacity of inset, 2 quarts. Shpg. wt., 2 lbs.........$1.10
99K965—Capacity of inset, 3 quarts. Shipping weight, 2½ pounds.........$1.50

Wash Basins

39c 11½-In. "Hi-Grade" pure aluminum, smooth finish.
9K900—Diameter, 11½ in. Weight, ¾ lb..39c
9K901—Diameter, 13¼ in. Weight, 1 lb..49c

DISH PAN BARGAINS

Serviceable Pans at Saving Prices — 85c 10-Qt. Round

"Hi-Grade" pure aluminum, surprise you at the amount of wear and tear they stand, maximum service at minimum cost, there is no better "buy" in the country.

Handles securely riveted, sturdy, one-piece body, highly polished.

		Capacity	Shpg. Wt.	
99K978	Round	10 qts.	2½ lbs.	$0.85
99K980	Round	14 qts.	3 lbs.	1.00
99K981	Round	17 qts.	3½ lbs.	1.45
99K982	Oval	10 qts.	2½ lbs.	.95
99K983	Oval	12 qts.	3 lbs.	1.25

PERCOLATORS for Thrifty Housewives

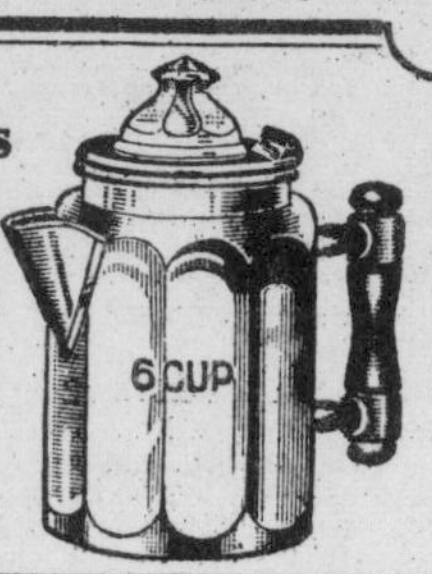

65c 6-Cup. "Hi-Grade" pure aluminum, paneled, surprising quality at these prices. They are not "cheap," but real worth while values. Sturdy, rigid construction, handsomely polished surface, glass top, ebonized handle. Easy to keep clean; make excellent coffee. Superb percolators at unusually low prices. Weight, 2 pounds.

	Capacity	
9K902	3 pints or 6 cups	$0.65
9K903	4 pints or 9 cups	.79
9K904	6 pints or 12 cups	1.00

9K2806—Extra glass tops. Weight, 1¼ pounds. 6 for...........15c

For Electric Percolators, see page 663.

Coffeepots

75c 9-Cup. "Hi-Grade" pure aluminum, paneled sides, ebonized handle. Wt., 2 lbs.
9K908—Capacity, 4 pints or 9 cups.........75c
9K909—Capacity, 6 pints or 12 cups.......$1.25

Teapots

89c 6-Cup. "Hi-Grade" pure aluminum, paneled sides, welded spout, ebonized handle. Weight, 2 lbs.
9K926 Cap., 3 pts. or 6 cups...89c
9K927 Cap., 4 pts. or 9 cups...98c

Convex Saucepans *With Cover*

48c 3-Qt. "Hi-Grade" pure aluminum, straight style, paneled sides. Highly polished.

	Capacity	Weight	
9K923	3 qts.	1 lb.	48c
9K924	4 qts.	1 lb	65c
9K925	6 qts.	1¼ lbs.	85c

Colanders

49c 9¼-In. "Hi-Grade" pure aluminum. Shipping weight, 2 pounds.
99K988—Diameter, 9¼ in. Capacity, 3 quarts...........49c
99K989—Diameter, 11¼ in. Capacity, 5 quarts...........69c

Double Lipped Saucepans

19c 1-Qt. "Hi-Grade" pure aluminum, seamless, easy to clean, two lips make pouring easy.

	Capacity	Weight	
9K946	1 qt.	5 oz.	19c
9K947	2 qts.	8 oz.	29c
9K948	3 qts.	¾ lb.	44c
9K949	4 qts.	1 lb.	55c

Set of 4 Pot Covers in Wire Rack

68c "Hi-Grade" pure aluminum. One-piece covers, securely fastened ring handles. Sizes, 8, 8½, 9½ and 10½ in. Weight, ¾ pound.
9K945—Set of 4, with rack..68c

Water or Milk Pails

79c 8-Qt. "Hi-Grade" pure aluminum, smooth polished finish. Shipping weight, 3 lbs.
99K991 Cap., 8 qts. 79c
99K992 Cap., 10 qts. $1.00
99K993 Cap., 12 qts. $1.20

Combination Funnel

22c "Hi-Grade" pure aluminum. Fruit funnel, dipper, strainer funnel, and jar filler all in one. Various screens make possible fine or coarse straining. Top diam., 5¼ in. Weight, 8 ounces.
9K913—Each...........22c

Water or Milk Pitchers

65c 2½ Qt. "Hi-Grade" pure aluminum, paneled sides, seamless. Weight, 2 lbs.
9K933—Cap., 2½ qts....65c
9K934—Cap., 4 qts.....79c

Milk Pails

45c 1-Qt. "Hi-Grade" pure aluminum, highly polished.
9K930—Cap., 1 qt. Wt., 6 oz..45c
9K931—Cap., 2 qts. Wt., 8 oz. 65c
9K932—Cap., 4 qts. Wt., 1 lb. 95c

Muffin Pans

63c 9-Cup. "Hi-Grade" pure aluminum, smooth finish.

	Capacity	Weight	
9K916	6 cups	6 ounces	42c
9K917	9 cups	8 ounces	63c

Aluminum Cleaners and Polishers

Beaver 19c Removes stains, grease and dirt. Large size, 12 pads and 2 cakes of cleaner. Weight, 7 ounces.
9K2849—Per package...19c

S.O.S. *The Magic Cleaner of Pots and Pans*

Large Pkg. 21c It's easy to keep your aluminum spick and span with S.O.S. 6 cakes in package. Weight, 3 oz.
9K2853—Per package...21c

Colonial Style Teakettles

89c 5-Qt. In spite of the amazingly low prices on these "Hi-Grade" pure aluminum teakettles, they are not to be confused with cheap, inferior quality goods! If you want inexpensive, good quality, serviceable teakettles—here they are! Beautifully and sturdily designed.

Colonial style, seamless. Easily cleaned and sanitary; brightly polished surface. Ebonized cover knob and handle. Flat bottom. Shipping weight, 3 pounds.

	Capacity	
99K974	5 quarts	$0.89
99K976	6½ quarts	1.25

Round Roaster

"Hi-Grade" pure aluminum. 85c Size, 7x10½ inches over all. Practical and convenient small roaster. Shipping wt., 2 lbs.
99K986...........85c

Oval Roasters

98c 15x8¾x6¾

"Hi-Grade" pure aluminum, equipped with tight fitting cover. Self basting. Remarkable value.

	Size, Over All	Shpg. Wt.	
99K994	15 x 8¾x6¾	1¾ lbs.	$0.98
99K995	17¼x10 x7½	2½ lbs.	1.35
99K996	19 x11¾x7¾	3 lbs.	1.85

Cake Pan

"Hi-Grade" pure aluminum, diameter, 9½ inches. Weight, 2 oz. 15c
9K912...........15c

Pie Plates

"Hi-Grade" pure aluminum, smooth finish. Weight, 2 ounces. 10c 9-In.

	Diameter	
9K910	9 inches	10c
9K911	10 inches	15c

Mixing Bowls

"Hi-Grade" pure aluminum, highly polished. 39c 3-Qt.

	Capacity	Diameter	Weight	
9K905	3 qts.	9¾ in.	8 oz.	39c
9K906	4 qts.	10½ in.	¾ lb.	48c
9K907	5 qts.	11½ in.	1 lb.	55c

Pudding Pans

"Hi-Grade" pure aluminum, durable and bright finish. 15c 1-Qt.

	Capacity	Weight	
9K918	1 quart	3 ounces	15c
9K919	2 quarts	4 ounces	25c
9K920	3 quarts	5 ounces	35c
9K921	4 quarts	7 ounces	45c

Bread and Cake Pan

"Hi-Grade" pure aluminum, highly polished. Size, 9⅝x5⅝x2¾ inches. Weight, 4 oz. 35c
9K914.........35c

Set of 3 Saucepans

"Hi-Grade" pure aluminum, three handy sizes for everyday use (1½, 2 and 3 qts.), double lipped to permit pouring from either side. Seamless and strongly made. Weight, 3 pounds. 85c
9K942—Per set..85c

High Quality Ironware at Substantial Savings

Ground Smooth—Highly Polished

SELF-BASTING COVER

Skillets $1.48 No. 8

Snug fitting, self basting cover retains heat at steady, even temperature. Cooks food in most appetizing and delicious manner.

Skillet and Cover Complete

No.	Diam., Top	Shpg. Wt.	
99K2797	8	10½ in.	7½ lbs.	$1.48
99K2798	9	11¼ in.	7¾ lbs.	1.75
99K2799	10	11¾ in.	8¼ lbs.	2.30

Skillet Only

9K2725	8	10½ in.	4 lbs.	.72
9K2726	9	11¼ in.	4½ lbs.	.92
9K2727	10	11¾ in.	5 lbs.	1.30

Waffle Irons $1.35 Low Style

BALL JOINT — RING GROOVED BASE CATCH'S GREASE

Famous Puritan ball joint type, making possible turning of waffle by only slightly raising the handles—no weight or strain, and can be done in an instant. Fine quality, heavy, smoothly finished castings. Will hold heat well. Ring grooved base catches all the grease. 7¾ inches diameter.

99K2708—Low style. Shipping weight, 11 pounds. ... $1.35

99K2707—High style. Especially suitable for gas stoves. Shpg. wt., 14 lbs. ... 1.78

Dutch Ovens

With Self Basting Cover and Tinned Grate $2.35 4-Qt.

Finest Quality. Full Polished.

	Cap	Shpg. Wt.	
99K2713	4 qts.	11 lbs.	$2.35
99K2714	6 qts.	13 lbs.	2.85
99K2715	8 qts.	17 lbs.	3.35

Regular Good Quality

99K2710	4 qts.	12 lbs.	$1.98
99K2711	6 qts.	16 lbs.	2.45
99K2712	8 qts.	18 lbs.	2.85

Stove Kettles $2.15 7-Qt.

Finest quality, cast iron, heavy, ground smooth inside, flat bottom.

99K2716—Capacity, 7 qts. Shipping weight, 8 lbs. ... $2.15

99K2717—Capacity, 9 qts. Shipping weight, 9 lbs. ... $2.65

Long Griddles $1.38 22x9⅛ inches

High quality, smooth finish and polished, long enough to cover two burners or stove holes. Handles are reinforced.

9K2737 — Size, 22x9⅛ inches. Weight, 8 pounds. ... $1.38

9K2738 — Size, 24x10¾ inches. Weight, 12 pounds. ... $1.78

Handled Griddle 88c

Finest quality, cast iron. Smooth ground top, raised edge.

9K2731 — Diameter, 10¼ inches. Weight, 4¼ lbs. 88c

REGULAR GOOD QUALITY IRONWARE

Skillets 55c No. 8

Regular good grade iron skillets without covers.

	No.	Diam., In.	Wt., Lbs.	
9K2734	8	10½	4	55c
9K2735	9	11½	5½	75c
9K2736	10	11¾	6¼	89c

Smooth Finish Large Kettles

Regular good quality iron, used as sugar, wash or butcher's kettle. Flange around rim. Not mailable.

	Cap. Gal.	Shp. Wt. Lbs.	
99K2725	13	42	$4.25
99K2726	19	60	6.80
99K2727	27	83	7.85

For Larger Kettles See Page 1066

Ham or Wash Boilers $2.45 7-Gal.

Good quality, smooth cast iron, flat bottom.

99K2720 Size, 22x12½x8¾ inches; capacity, 7 gal.; shipping weight, 24 lbs. ... $2.45

99K2721 Size, 24x13½x9¾ inches; capacity, 9 gal.; shipping weight, 28 lbs. ... $2.85

SUPER VALUES IN HEAVY STEEL WARE

Ovenette Kooker Saves Fuel! 98c

For Roasting, Baking, Etc., on Top of Gas, Gasoline or Oil Stove

Cooks without heating the kitchen. Bakes potatoes, apples, bread, biscuits, pies, etc.; also for roasting, broiling, frying and toasting, heating flatirons, etc. Diameter of plate, 10¼ inches; seamless tinned steel cover, 5 inches high. Shpg. wt., 3 lbs.

99K2700—Complete with plate rack and cover. ... 98c

Covered Roasting Pans 49c 10x15x7 In.

VENT

Splendid, practical pans at surprisingly low prices. Guaranteed to give satisfactory service. Vent in top. Good quality smooth steel. With drip rack to prevent burning and sticking. Self basting cover.

	Size, In.	Wt., Lbs.	
9K2765	10x15x7	3½ lbs.	49c
9K2766	11x17x8	4 lbs.	58c
9K2767	13x18x8	5 lbs.	75c

Open Roasting or Baking Pans 9c And Up

Good quality, smooth finish, heavy sheet steel, seamless.

	Size, In.	Wt., Lbs.	
9K2741	7x10	¾	9c
9K2743	10x14	1¼	15c
9K2745	14x17	1¾	34c

Skillets 24c 10¼-In. Cool Handle

Smooth steel, seamless, good quality, 10¼-in. top diam. Wt. 1½ lbs.

9K2759 ... 24c

Heavy seamless steel, ground and polished inside; 10½-in. top diam. Wt., 2 lbs.

9K2760 ... 29c

Nickel Plated Copper Teakettles

Try to Match These Values!

$1.25 3½-Qt.

NICKEL PLATED COPPER

Supreme quality, strong shouldered, sturdy, unusually durable teakettles with beautifully finished nickel plate over copper. Deep set covers that will not come off while pouring. Highly polished surface will not tarnish. Tinned inside. Black enameled wood handles and knobs. Flat bottom. It is values such as these that give us the leadership in selling high quality goods at greatly reduced prices.

	Capacity, Qts.	Shpg. Wt. Lbs.	
99K2336	3½	2¾	$1.25
99K2338	6	3	1.50
99K2339	7½	4	1.70

Nickel Plated Copper Coffee Pots $1.30 4½-Pt.

Unusually sturdy construction, solid copper, tinned inside and polished nickel on the outside. Hinged cover and tip on spout to keep coffee from cooling. Wood handle and knob. Flat bottom. Weight, 2 lbs.

	Cap., Pts.	
9K2330	4½	$1.30
9K2331	5	1.60

Nickel Plated Copper Percolators $1.89 6-Cup

Sturdily constructed, solid copper, heavily nickel plated. Highly polished. Aluminum inset, glass top, wood handle.

	Cap. Cups	Wt. Lbs.	
9K2332	6	2¼	$1.89
9K2333	9	2½	2.10

For Electric Percolators See Page 663

CAST ALUMINUM WARE

$3.95 6-Qt. Teakettle

6QT. CAST ALUMINUM

Strongly made but light in weight. Durable single piece construction, with no joints or seams. Smoothly cast. Highly polished. Sliding cover and flat bottom. May be filled through large spout. Holds heat and is a great fuel saver. Shipping weight, 5 pounds.

99K2372 ... $3.95

Skillets $1.88 10½-In.

Highly polished. Easy to clean and to keep clean. Cast in one piece. Hard, smooth finish. Heats rapidly. Will last a lifetime. Cool handle securely fastened with eyelet for hanging. You save materially when you invest your money in this value. Wt., 1¾ lbs.

	Diameter	
9K2279	10½ in.	$1.88
9K2280	11¼ in.	2.18

SOLID COPPER WARE

6-Gallon Kettle $2.85

SOLID COPPER CAPACITY 6 GALLONS

6-gal. cap. solid copper. Ideal for preserving fruits, canning vegetables and boiling ham. Tight fitting cover, convenient handles, seams well soldered. Diam., 11 in. Shpg. wt., 7 lbs.

99K2048 ... $2.85

Large Open Kettles $9.95 12-Gal.

SOLID COPPER

Strong and substantial, will not discolor foods. Extra heavy iron bails, ears and rims. State size. Not mailable.

	Cap. Gal.	Shpg. Wt.	
99K2730	12	44 lbs.	$9.95
99K2731	16	54 lbs.	1.85
99K2732	20	70 lbs.	4.75
99K2733	25	74 lbs.	6.85
99K2734	36	102 lbs.	9.90

Serviceable Kitchen Utensils

Dish Dryer 98c

DISH DRYER

Extra heavy, retinned. Size of tray, 12x17x4 in. Length, over all, 20¾ inches. Shpg. wt., 4 lbs.

99K2178 ... 98c

Round Dish Drainer Set 95c

Includes round dish drainer, soap saver, dish mop and vegetable brush. Drainer is heavy tinned wire with basket in center. Shpg. wt., 2¼ lbs.

9K2558—Complete set. ... 95c

Corn Poppers

Steel, for use on any stove, no shaking required, just turn the crank. 6 in. diameter, 8½ in. high over all. Shpg. wt., 3 lbs.

9K2750 ... 95c

Pops and butters corn, separates popped from unpopped kernels. Pan, 7x9x3½ in. Length, over all, 25 in.

99K2704—Regular quality. Shpg. wt., 2 pounds. ... 35c

99K2705—Extra quality. Shipping weight, 3 pounds. ... 49c

Japanned Tea Tray

Excellent serving trays. Decoration around edge; black japan finish.

	Lgth.	Weight	
9K2598	14 in.	8 oz.	15c
9K2599	16 in.	1 lb.	22c
9K2600	20 in.	1½ lbs.	35c

For Other Serving Trays See Pages 614 and 928

Puritan Bread Mixer and Kneader $2.45 12-Qt. Size

Wonderful time and labor saver. Takes only five minutes instead of half an hour as when done by the old method. Clean and sanitary. Sturdily constructed of heavy polished tin with steel kneading arm and table clamp. Will last a lifetime. Complete instructions and recipes are furnished with each mixer.

	Qts.	Loaves	Wt., Lbs.	
99K2180	12	2 to 6	5	$2.45
99K2181	20	4 to 10	13	3.45

High Grade Flour Sifter 34c

Well made, of heavy highly polished tin. Improved style. Ebony finish handle. Weight, 1 pound.

9K2590 ... 34c

Tin Cake Pans

Absolutely sanitary, heavy rounded corners. Wired rim.

9K2580—Small loaf. Dimensions, 8¾x4¾x2¾ in. Wt., 8 oz. Each ... 7c

9K2581—Medium loaf. Dim., 9½x 5½x2½x3 in. Wt., ¾ lb. Each ... 9c

9K2584—Loaf cake. Dimensions, 9¾x4¾x3 in. Wt., ¾ lb. Each ... 11c

Tin Muffin Pans 9K2585 State size.

8 cups. Wt., 8 oz. Each ... 15c

12 cups. Wt., 12 oz. Each ... 22c

Polished Maple Rolling Pin 20c

Excellent quality. Revolving handles. Length, over all, 17¾ in. Wt., 1½ lbs.

9K2604 ... 20c

Household Strainer Set 58c

Reinforced tinned steel, heavy rim. Wire and wood handles. Includes extension, bowl and teastrainers.

9K2550—Wt., 1 lb. Set ... 58c

Animal Tin Cake Cutters 48c

9K2563—Wt., ¾ lb. Dz., asstd. 48c

Handy Pot Cover Outfit 30c

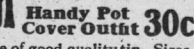

Made of good quality tin. Sizes, 9, 9½, 10, 10½, 11 and 11½ inches. Wire rack for hanging included. Wt., per set, 2 lbs.

9K2594—Set of 6 ... 30c

Oblong Tin Dinner Pail 50c

Well made; reinforced sides. Handle securely riveted. Two compartments. Size, 9x6 inches; 6½ inches high. Weight, 1½ pounds.

9K2577 ... 50c

Never Burn Hot Plate

Our Price, 69c

Nationally Advertised to Sell for $1.00

An entirely new invention, scientifically constructed. Use on any stove. Prevents scorched food or ruined cooking utensils. Any kind of food such as cereals, rice, milk or preserves, etc., can be cooked without danger of burning. Saves its cost in fuel many times a year. Cast metal, aluminum finish. Diameter, 7¾ inches. Shipping weight, 3 pounds.

9K2720 ... 69c

Buy Here for Less Money

$1.40
No. 10

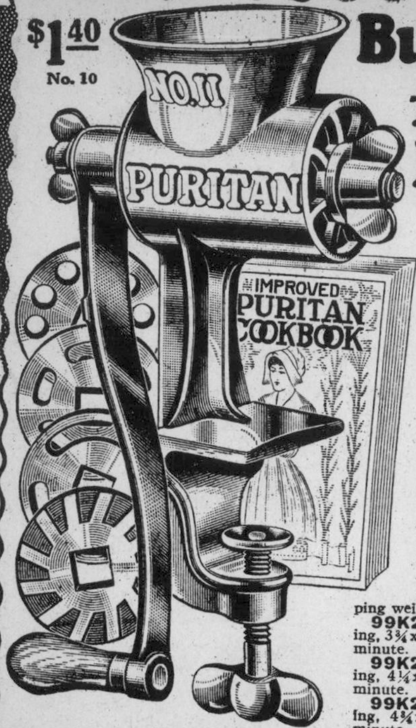

"Puritan" Food and Meat Choppers

Do not mash or tear foods. Will cut meats, vegetables, fruits, nuts, bread, crackers, etc. Cutters provided with each machine for chopping fine, medium or coarse. Extra large choppers.

Heavy one-piece barrels, straight ribbed inside. Heavily tinned to prevent rusting. Three self-sharpening knives and one pulverizer made from special steel and ground true. Easily cleaned. Extra long handle. Size No. 11 is for average size family. Improved Puritan cook book included with each chopper.

99K2820—No. 10. Top opening, 3⅛x2⅛ in. 2 pounds per minute. Shipping weight, 4 pounds....$1.40
99K2821—No. 11. Top opening, 3¾x2⅞ inches. 2½ pounds per minute. Shpg. wt., 5 lbs....$1.75
99K2822—No. 12. Top opening, 4¼x3⅛ inches. 3 pounds per minute. Shpg. wt., 6 lbs....$2.10
99K2823—No. 13. Top opening, 4¾x4 inches. 4 pounds per minute. Shpg. wt., 8 lbs...$2.65

SAVE on Genuine Enterprise Choppers

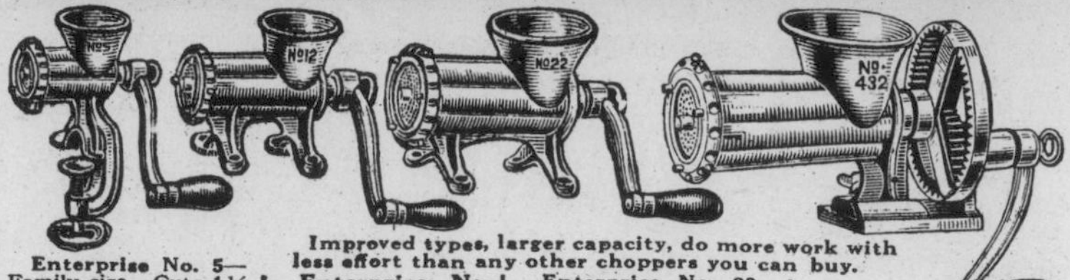

Improved types, larger capacity, do more work with less effort than any other choppers you can buy.

Enterprise No. 5—Family size. Cuts 1½ lbs. a minute. Shpg. wt., 6 lbs.
99K2826...$2.90
Enterprise No. 10—Large family size. Cuts 3 lbs. a minute. Shpg. wt., 14 lbs.
99K2827...$4.90

Enterprise No. 12—Large family size. Cuts 3 lbs. a minute. Shpg. wt., 12 lbs.
99K2828
$4.67

Enterprise No. 22—Butcher shop and farmers' size. Chops 4 lbs. a minute. Shpg. wt., 19 lbs.
99K2829...$8.00
Enterprise No. 32—Extra size, chops 5 lbs. a minute. Shpg. wt., 25 lbs.
99K2830...$9.79

Enterprise No. 432—Extra size with gear drive. Chops 5 lbs. a minute. Shpg. wt., 46 lbs.
99K2832. $15.10

Power Pulleys $1.80

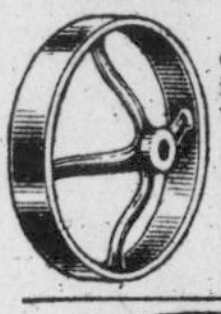

For Enterprise Choppers. 12x2-inch face. Shpg. wt., 8 lbs.
99K2835—Fits No. 12..$1.80
99K2836—Fits No. 22..$1.80
99K2837—Fits No. 32..$1.80

Extra Parts for Enterprise Choppers

Be sure to state number of choppers for which parts are wanted

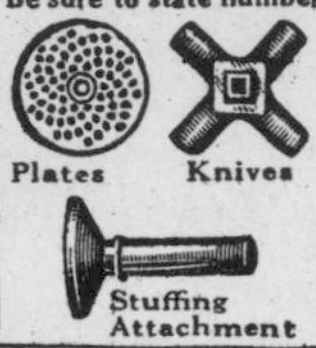

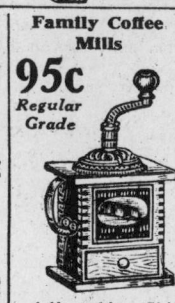

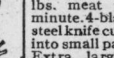

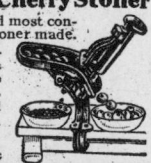

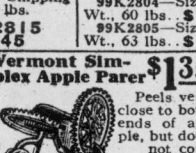

For Chopper	Knives 9K2667	Plates 9K2659 3/16-In. Holes	Plates 9K2662 3/8-In. Holes	Stuffing Attachment 9K2645 ¾-In. Tube
Wt.	2 Oz.	8 Oz.	8 Oz.	2 Oz.
No. 5	40c	$0.55	$0.60	$0.89
No. 10	45c	1.00	1.10	.95
No. 12	45c	1.00	1.10	.95
No. 22	60c	1.50	1.65	1.10
No. 32	90c	2.25	2.50	1.48
No. 432	90c	2.25	2.50	1.48

Fruit Juice and Jelly Press

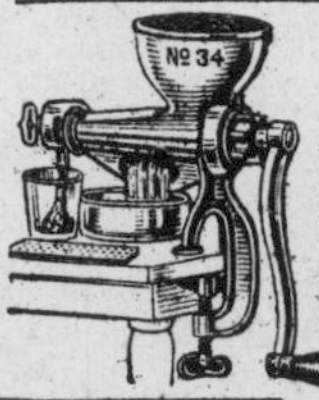

For making jellies, fruit butter, etc. Spiral core extracts juice and discharges pulp and seed. Juice passes through strainer before it leaves press. Heavily tinned, easily opened, long crank. 1-qt. capacity. Shipping wt., 22 lbs.
99K2815
$6.45

Genuine Enterprise Lard and Fruit Presses

$10.24
4-Qt.

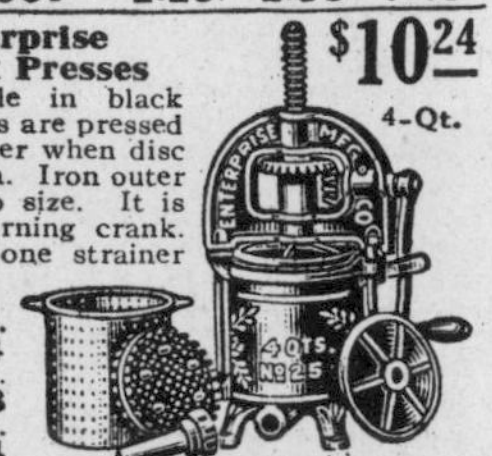

Strong and durable in black japanned finish. Juices are pressed from contents in hopper when disc at top is screwed down. Iron outer cylinder bored true to size. It is easily operated by turning crank. One solid plate and one strainer plate with each size.

99K2803—Size, 4 qts. Wt., 45 lbs..$10.24
99K2804—Size, 6 qts. Wt., 60 lbs..$11.13
99K2805—Size, 8 qts. Wt., 63 lbs..$12.24

Retinned Food Chopper 98c

Usually Sells for $1.50 Elsewhere

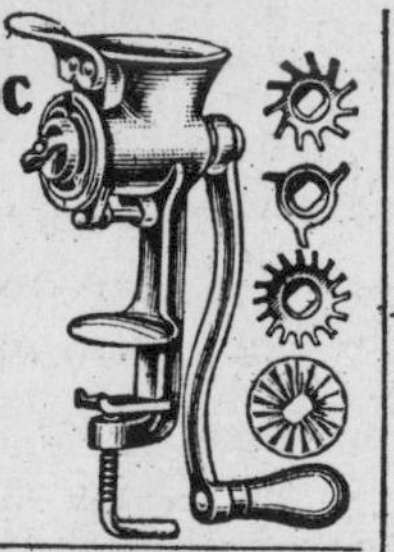

Four self-sharpening knives: Fine, medium, coarse and pulverizer. Opens for washing. Top, 3⅝-2¾ in. 2 coats block tin, will not rust. Shpg. wt., 4 lbs.
99K2818
Each........98c

Butchers' Style Meat and Food Chopper

For Household Use

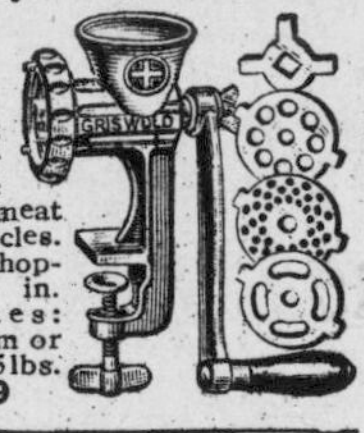

Cuts about 3 lbs. meat per minute. 4-blade steel knife cuts meat into small particles. Extra large hopper, 3¾x2⅞ in. 3 steel plates: Coarse, medium or fine. Shpg. wt., 5 lbs.
99K2819
$1.95

Rotary Knife Peach and Apple Parer

$1.75

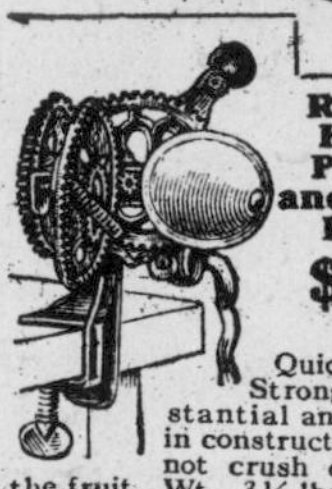

Quick acting. Strong, substantial and simple in construction. Does not crush or waste the fruit. Wt., 3½ lbs.
9K2787.......$1.75

Vermont Simplex Apple Parer $1.35

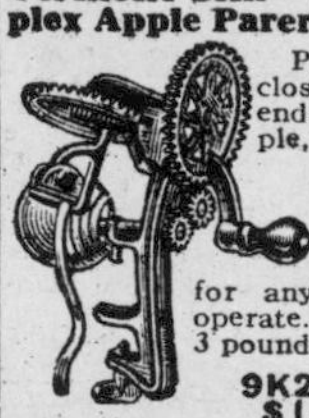

Peels very close to both ends of apple, but does not core or slice. Very simple and easy for anybody to operate. Weight, 3 pounds.
9K2790
$1.35

Vermont Apple Parer 95c

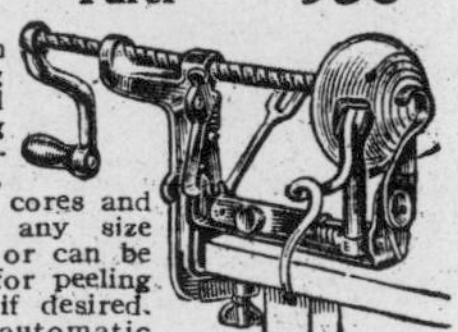

With slicing and coring attachment. Peels, cores and slices any size apple or can be used for peeling only, if desired. Has automatic push off. Weight, 2 pounds.
9K2793.................95c

"See Thru" Coffee Mill

$1.24

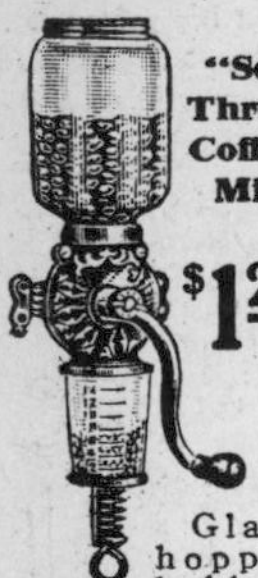

Glass hopper holds 1 pound coffee; airtight screw cover. Perfect adjustment for coarse or fine grinding. Graduated measuring cup. Screws furnished for attaching. Shipping wt., 7 lbs.
99K2445—With tumbler.....$1.24

Family Coffee Mills

95c
Regular Grade

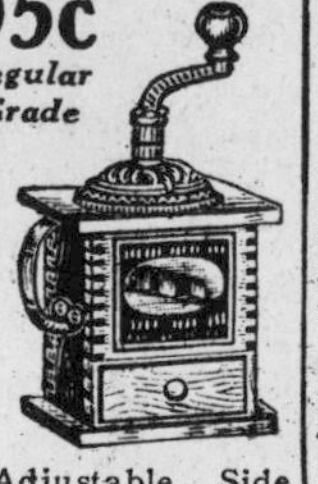

Adjustable. Side handle for holding. Holds 1 lb. Size, 7x7x7 inches. Wt., 5 lbs.
9K2825—Regular construction. Flat top. 95c
9K2826—Extra quality, as illustrated. $1.25

Sausage Stuffers

$1.65
Family Size

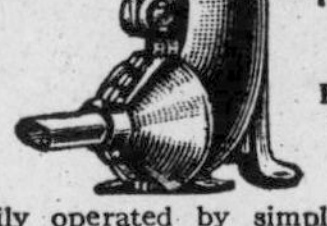

Easily operated by simply filling hopper with sausage meat and pressing lever. It is a time and money saver and is absolutely sanitary in construction. Strong black japanned iron with tin spout.
99K2808—Family size. Shipping weight, 10 pounds.....$1.65
99K2809—Butchers' size. Shipping weight, 14 pounds.....$2.25

Our Home Cherry Stoner

The fastest and most convenient cherry stoner made.

Pits two cherries with each thrust of the plunger. Simple, easy to use and easy to clean. Weight, 2¼ lbs.
9K2797 .90c

Lard and Jelly Presses

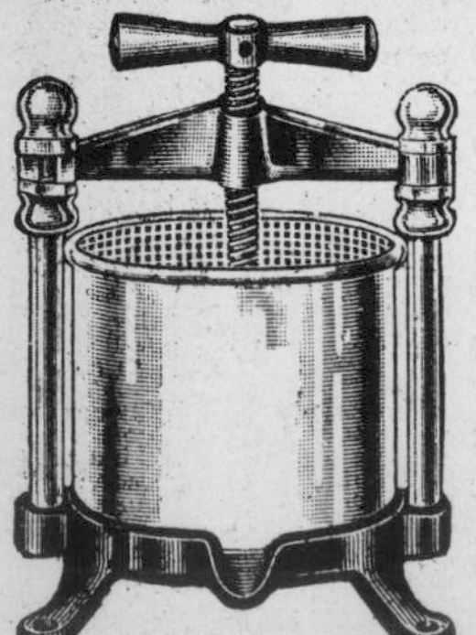

$2.80
2-Qt. Size

Buy From Sears and Save About One-Third Over Prices Elsewhere

Strong—Sturdy—Dependable Construction

Well made, durable household presses, with heavy tin cylinders and deep, well cut threads on steel screws that will not slip and that give tremendous pressure in extracting all the juices from either meats or fruits. Disc top screws down tightly. All three sizes at low prices. All sizes furnished with screws for attaching.

99K2811—2-quart size. Shipping weight, 12 pounds..........$2.80
99K2812—4-quart size. Shipping weight, 28 pounds..........$4.25
99K2813—10-quart size. Shipping weight, 41 pounds..........$5.95

Bottling Goods

Crown Cap Glass Bottles

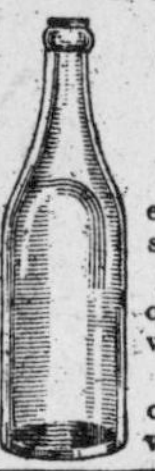

$1.90
2 Doz.

Capacity, each, 24 ounces. For beverages, catsup, etc. Good quality, well shaped.
99K2575—Carton of 2 dozen. Shipping weight, 40 lbs..$1.90
99K2576—Crate of 6 dozen. Shipping weight, 120 lbs.$5.25

Bottle Capper

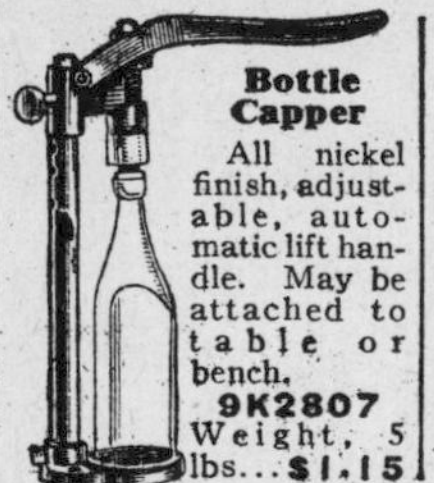

All nickel finish, adjustable, automatic lift handle. May be attached to table or bench.
9K2807 Weight, 5 lbs...$1.15

Bottle Capper Improved

All Steel

98c

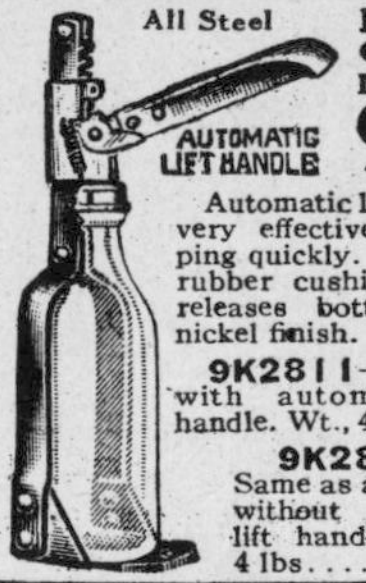

Automatic lift handle, very effective in capping quickly. Head has rubber cushion which releases bottle. All nickel finish.
9K2811—Capper with automatic lift handle. Wt., 4 lbs. 98c
9K2809
Same as above, but without automatic lift handle. Wt., 4 lbs........78c

Crown Bottle Caps

Standard Size for Crown Cap Bottles

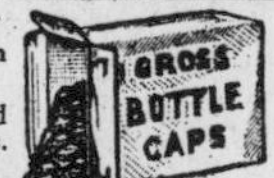

Fully lacquered, cork lined tight fitting metal caps. Weight, 1 gross, 1¼ lbs.
9K2801—1 gross...22c
9K2800—10 gross...........$2.15

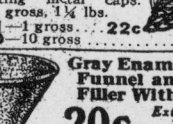

Siphon Bottle Filler

75c

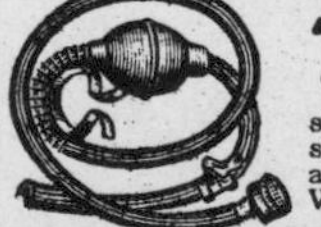

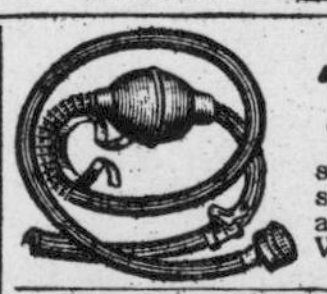

Made of heavy red rubber hose, 5 feet long. Fitted with bulb starter, nickel plated brass shut-off, spring hose holder and aluminum filter end. Weight, ¾ pound.
9K2816.............75c

Gray Enameled Steel Funnel and Bottle Filler With Handle

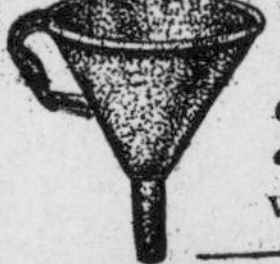

20c

Extra Quality Two-Coat Enamel

Diameter, 4½ inches. Weight, 8 ounces.
9K2030..........20c

Hardwood Spigot

19c

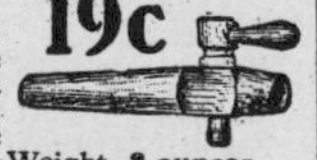

Smooth finish, hardwood spigot with cork lined valve seat. Long spout makes it handy for filling bottles. Length, 8 inches, and fits hole ⅞ to 1¼ inches in diameter. Weight, 8 ounces.
9K2805.........................19c

Grape and Fruit Crusher

For Making Grape Juice

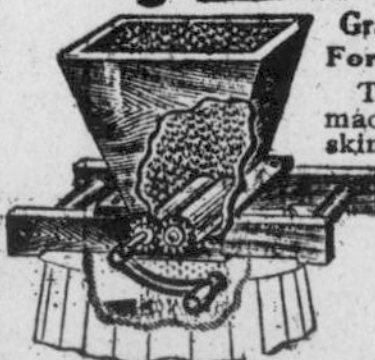

The best grape juice is made from the whole fruit, skin, pulp and seeds. This crusher is designed for just that purpose. Its two adjustable corrugated hardwood rolls crush the whole fruit, releasing all the juice. Sets on any standard pail. Made of hardwood. Size of hopper, 8¼x9x7 in. deep, outside. Ht., over all, 8¼ in. Shpg. wt., 7 lbs.
99K2660—Each...............$3.45

Plain and Charred White Oak Kegs

Extra quality. Non-porous staves, kiln dried. Riveted steel hoops. Bung included.

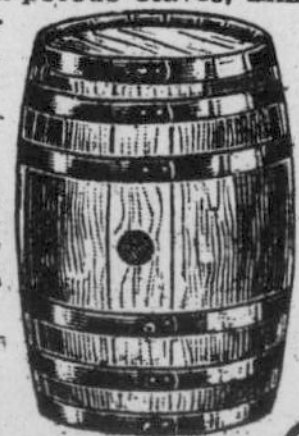

Plain	Cap., Gal.	Shpg. Wt.	
99K2536	5	12 lbs.	$1.75
99K2537	10	19 lbs.	2.50
99K2538	15	26 lbs.	2.95
99K2539	30	30 lbs.	3.95

Charred. Kiln dried, selected quality.

Charred	Cap., Gal.	Shpg. Wt.	
99K2546	5	12 lbs.	$2.15
99K2547	10	19 lbs.	2.90
99K2548	15	26 lbs.	3.35
99K2549	30	30 lbs.	4.35

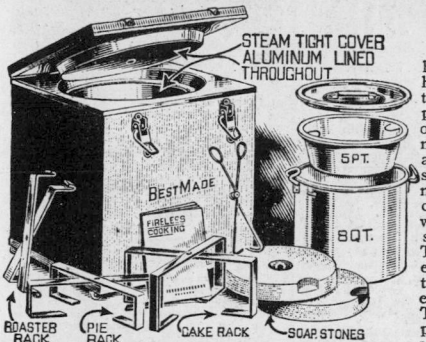
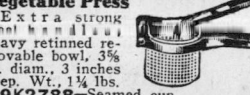

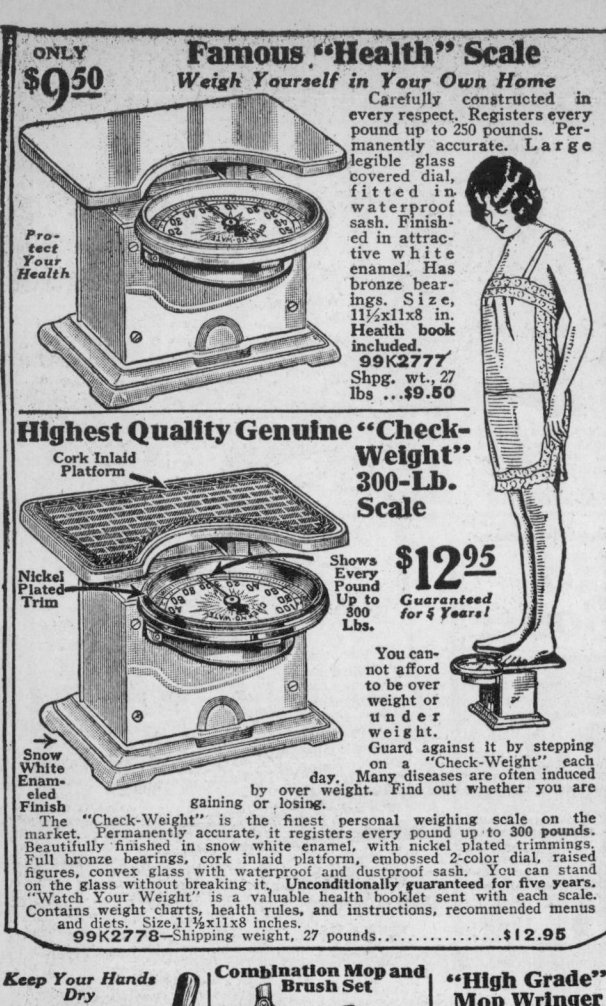

Famous "Health" Scale

ONLY **$9.50**

Weigh Yourself in Your Own Home

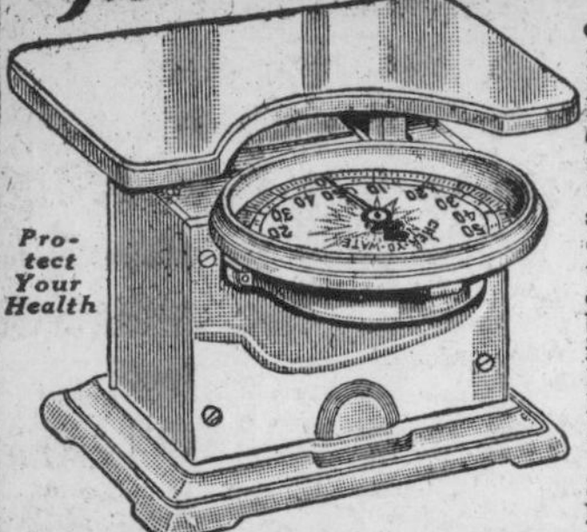

Protect Your Health

Carefully constructed in every respect. Registers every pound up to 250 pounds. Permanently accurate. Large legible glass covered dial, fitted in waterproof sash. Finished in attractive white enamel. Has bronze bearings. Size, 11½x11x8 in. Health book included.

99K2777 Shpg. wt., 27 lbs ...$9.50

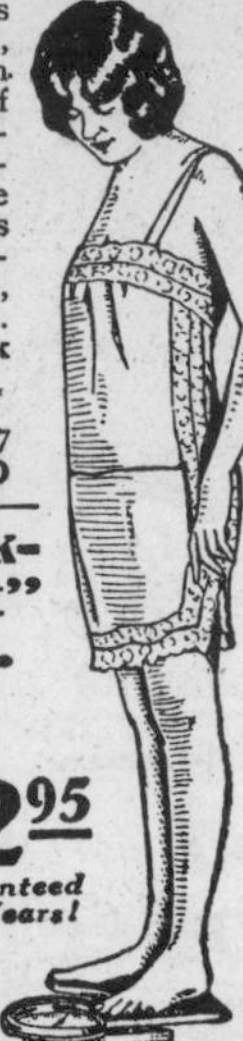

Highest Quality Genuine "Check-Weight" 300-Lb. Scale

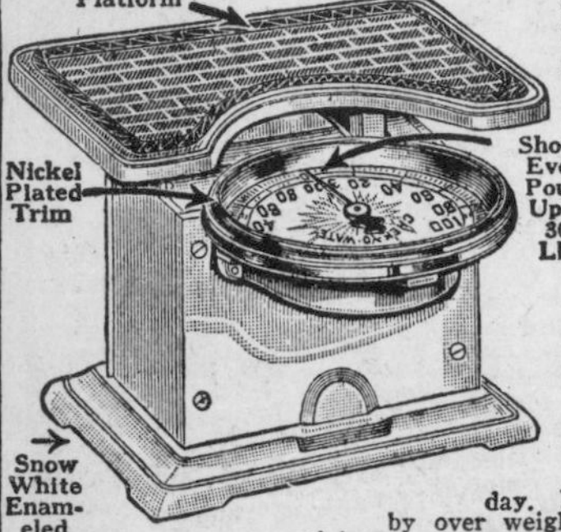

Cork Inlaid Platform
Nickel Plated Trim
Shows Every Pound Up to 300 Lbs.
Snow White Enameled Finish

$12.95 *Guaranteed for 5 Years!*

You cannot afford to be over weight or under weight. Guard against it by stepping on a "Check-Weight" each day. Many diseases are often induced by over weight. Find out whether you are gaining or losing.

The "Check-Weight" is the finest personal weighing scale on the market. Permanently accurate, it registers every pound up to 300 pounds. Beautifully finished in snow white enamel, with nickel plated trimmings. Full bronze bearings, cork inlaid platform, embossed 2-color dial, raised figures, convex glass with waterproof and dustproof sash. You can stand on the glass without breaking it. **Unconditionally guaranteed for five years.** "Watch Your Weight" is a valuable health booklet sent with each scale. Contains weight charts, health rules, and instructions, recommended menus and diets. Size, 11½x11x8 inches.

99K2778—Shipping weight, 27 pounds................$12.95

Scales At Big Savings

Family Spring Scale

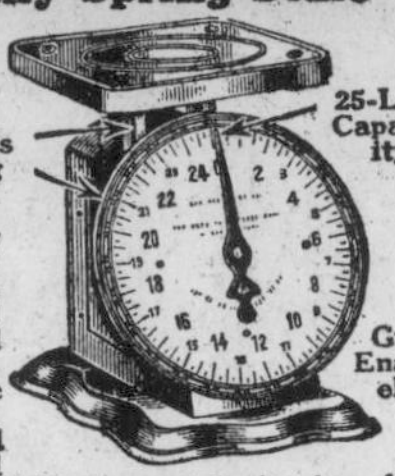

Double Standards Slanting Dial
25-Lb. Capacity
Gray Enameled

Gray enameled steel body and platform. Double standards. Tempered steel spring. White enameled slanting dial with plain figures. Thumbscrew for balancing. Height, 8½ in. Capacity, 25 lbs. by oz. Not legal for use in trade in some states. Shipping wt., 5 pounds.

99K2781 ....$1.10

Extra Grade Family Spring Scale

25 Lbs. by Oz.

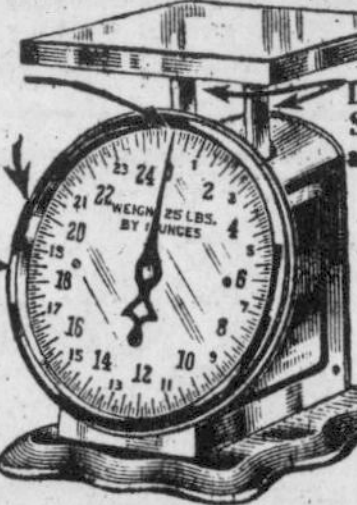

Slanting Dial Easy to Read
Glass Front
Double Standards

$1.95

Sheet steel, light blue enamel. White enameled dial, black figures. Diam., 6½ in. Removable white tile platform. Height, 8½ in. Not legal for use in trade in some states. Shipping weight, 6 pounds.

99K2784 ....$1.95

60-Lb. Household or Family Scale

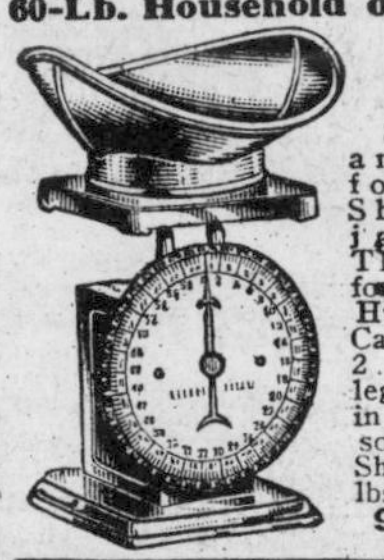

Double Standards

Satisfactory and accurate for home. Sheet steel, japaned. Thumbscrew for balancing. Ht., 10¾ in. Cap., 60 lbs. by 2 oz. Not legal for use in trade in some states. Shpg. wt., 10 lbs.

99K2785 $2.95

Watch Your Baby's Health!

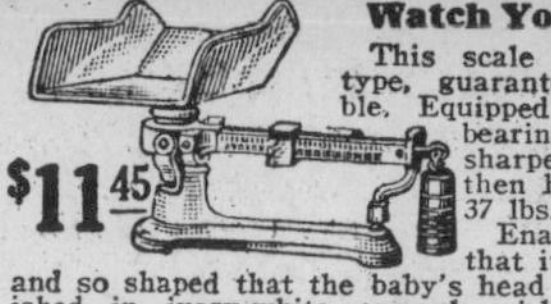

$11.45

This scale is of the brass beam type, guaranteed accurate and durable. Equipped with finest tool steel bearings and pivots, which are sharpened to knife edge and then hardened. Weighs up to 37 lbs. by ¼ oz. Enameled tray attached so that it cannot tip off the scale and so shaped that the baby's head rests comfortably. Finished in ivory-white enamel, nickel plated brass beam. Weight and age table from birth to school age included.

99K2779—Shipping weight, 25 pounds.......$11.45

For Other Nursery Supplies See Pages 588, 589, 639, 880 to 883.

"High Grade" Beam Counter Scales

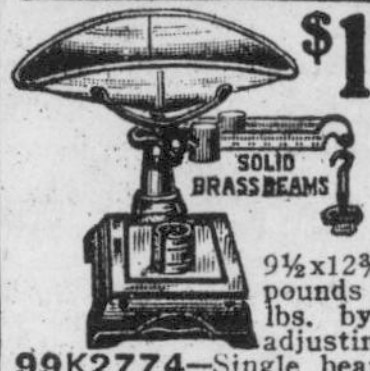

SOLID BRASS BEAMS

$12.40

Single Beam

These scales are legal in all states for use in trade and are an excellent scale for general use. Finished in red. Platform measures 9½x12¾ inches. Capacity of scoop, 30 pounds by ½ oz. Capacity of platform, 240 lbs. by ¼ lbs. Poises are equipped with adjusting screws.

99K2774—Single beam. Shpg. wt., 53 lbs....$12.40
99K2775—Double beam. Shpg. wt., 56 lbs... 14.90

Scale Beams With Two Poises

Not Legal for Use in Trade

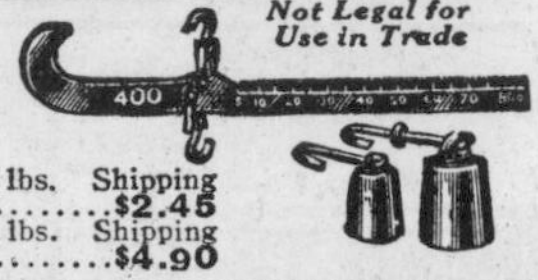

Heavy strong beam for rough weighing. Black enameled finish.

99K2791—Cap., 200 lbs. Shipping weight, 8 pounds $2.45
99K2793—Cap., 400 lbs. Shipping weight, 19 pounds.............$4.90

"High Grade" Mop Outfit

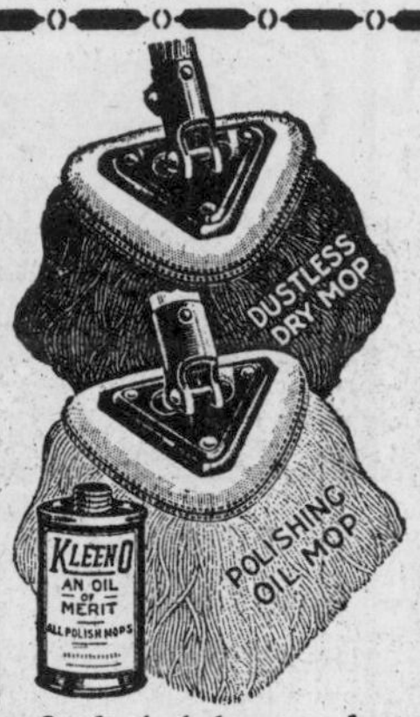

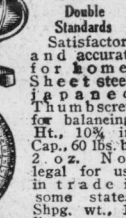

DUSTLESS DRY MOP
POLISHING OIL MOP
KLEENO AN OIL OF MERIT

95c Complete

Ideal for Polishing —No Stooping—Saves Your Knees

Absolutely no better value in mops anywhere for downright economy and usefulness than this "Best Made" outfit. Meets with instant approval. Makes housework lighter and easier and saves your strength and disposition.

Outfit includes two long wearing mops, triangularly shaped, to get into corners; one light and fluffy to pick up dust and lint, the other large and of fine texture to spread oil evenly on the floor; a 16-ounce can (one pint) of best grade oil for re-oiling mop, and two 48-inch handles. Handles are adjustable, so that any place can be reached in cleaning. Easily washed when soiled. Steel frame around mop is cushioned to protect woodwork and furniture.

99K2155—Shipping weight, 4 pounds. Complete.............................. 95c

Extra Grade, Highest Quality Sets. Similar to above, except oversized, finest quality mop heads and varnished handles.

99K2153—Shipping weight, 5 pounds. Complete..................................$1.35

Keep Your Hands Dry

Use a "Sanitary Self Wringing Mop" 75c

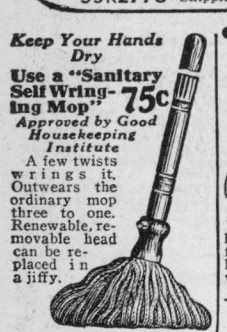

Approved by Good Housekeeping Institute

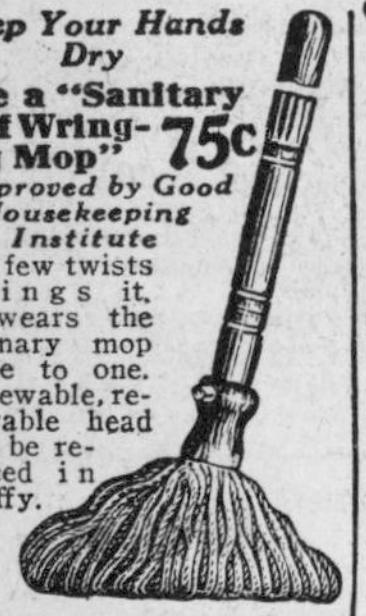

A few twists wrings it. Outwears the ordinary mop three to one. Renewable, removable head can be replaced in a jiffy.

Shipping weight, 2 lbs.

99K2163 ....75c

Extra high grade, with button device and non-rusting revolving twin sleeve to aid in wringing. 48-in handle. Shipping weight, 2 pounds.

99K2166 ....$1.35

Extra mop head for 99K2166. Weight, ¾ lb.

9K2870 ....70c

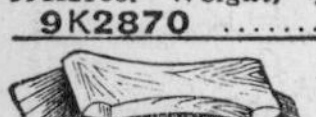

Combination Mop and Brush Set

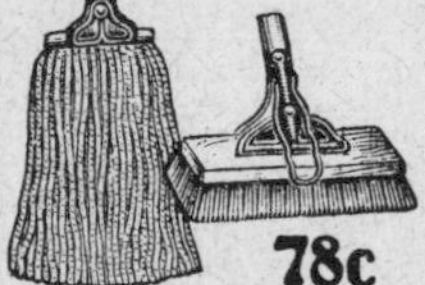

78c

Holds either mop or brush. Set includes one high grade cotton mop, one fiber brush and one 48-inch handle or holder. Shipping weight, 2 pounds.

99K2165 ....78c

Mop Head

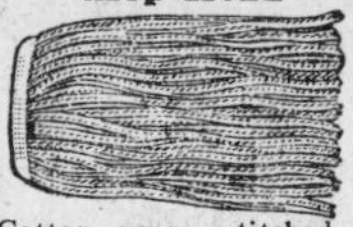

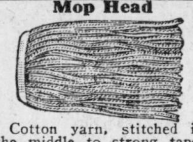

Cotton yarn, stitched in the middle to strong tape. Fastens to any ordinary mop handle. Wt., 1 lb.

9K2862—Without handle 25c

"High Grade" Mop Wringer Bucket

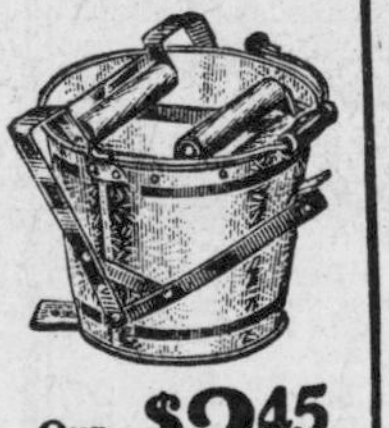

Our Price, **$2.45**

Has hardwood rolls attached to extra heavy galvanized pail with metal frame. Strong and durable, will outlast two or three ordinary wood wringer buckets. Shipping wt., 13 pounds.

99K2098...$2.45

"Best Made" Reversible Extra Size Dust Mop

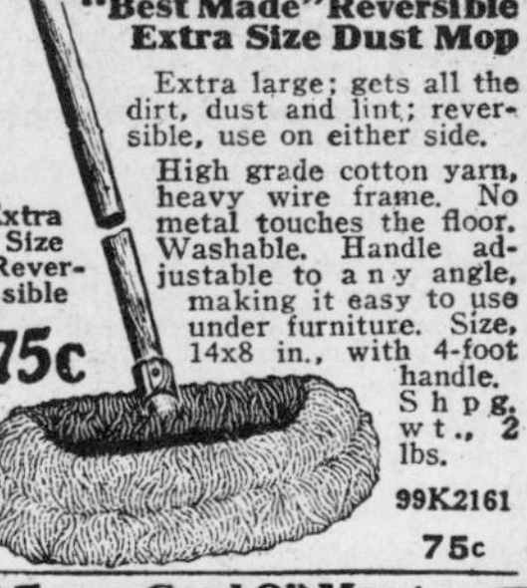

Extra Size Reversible **75c**

Extra large; gets all the dirt, dust and lint; reversible, use on either side.

High grade cotton yarn, heavy wire frame. No metal touches the floor. Washable. Handle adjustable to any angle, making it easy to use under furniture. Size, 14x8 in., with 4-foot handle. Shpg. wt., 2 lbs.

99K2161 75c

Fiber Scrub Brush

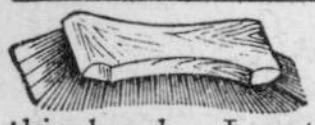

15c

Necessary in every household. You'll be surprised at the long wear you get out of this brush. Length, 8½ inches. Palmyra fiber. Weight, ¾ pound.

9K2868 ....15c

Good Oil Mop

45c

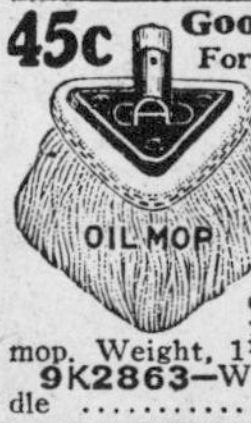

For Use on All Hardwood Floors

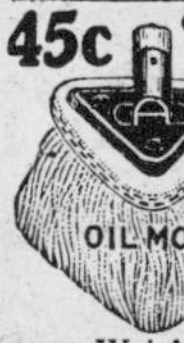

OIL MOP

Good quality cotton. Washable. Use an old mop handle with this mop. Weight, 1½ pounds.

9K2863—Without handle 45c

Dustless Dry Mop

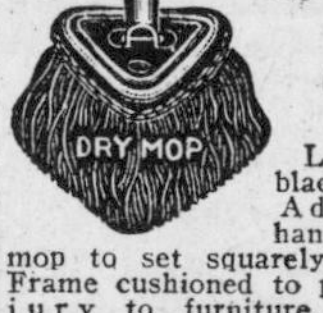

DRY MOP

49c

Long fiber black yarn. Adjustable handle permits mop to set squarely on floor. Frame cushioned to prevent injury to furniture. Shipping weight, 2 pounds.

99K2151 With 48-inch handle.......49c

Extra Large Oil Polish Mop

72c

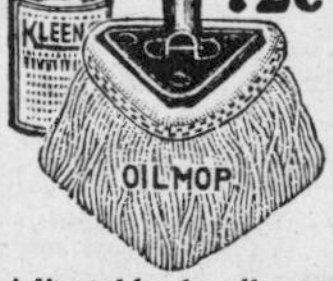

OIL MOP
KLEEN

An extra large, long cotton fiber oil mop. Heavily cushioned to prevent scratching furniture. Adjustable handle permits mop to set squarely on floor. With 48-inch handle and ½-pint mop oil for renewing mop. Shpg. wt., 3 lbs.

99K2152 ....72c

Floor Brush With Handle

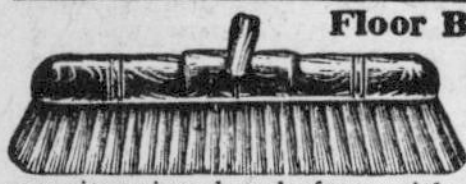

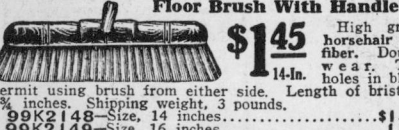

$1.45 14-In.

High grade horsehair and fiber. Double wear. Two holes in block permit using brush from either side. Length of bristles, 2¾ inches. Shipping weight, 3 pounds.

99K2148—Size, 14 inches..................$1.45
99K2149—Size, 16 inches..................1.75

Fiber House Brooms

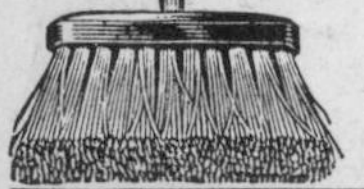

Three rows India fiber. Width of head, 10 in. Length of fiber, 5 in. Complete with 48-in. handle. Shipping weight, 2 pounds.

99K2144—1 broom......47c
99K2145—2 brooms.....92c

Dust Pans

15c

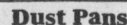

Heavy gauge steel, not easily dented or bent. Black japanned. Wt., 1¼ lbs.

9K2879—Regular quality. Ea..15c
9K2880—Extra heavy Quaker pattern. Finest quality. Each.........35c

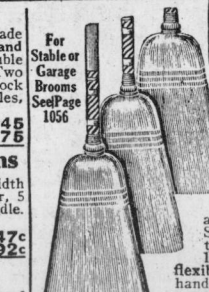

For Stable or Garage Brooms See Page 1056

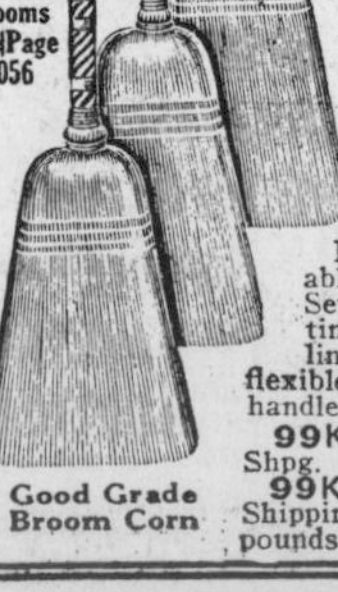

Good Grade Broom Corn

Remarkable Broom Value

39c EACH

Three Brooms for the Usual Price of Two

Made of good durable broom corn. Sewed across four times with strong linen twine. Long flexible sweep. Smooth handles.

99K2122—1 broom. Shpg. wt., 1¾ lbs. 39c
99K2121—3 brooms. Shipping weight, 5½ pounds $1.15

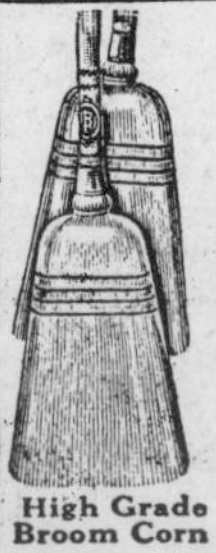

High Grade Broom Corn

High Grade House Brooms

55c EACH

Made by experienced workmen of high grade broom corn. Carefully stitched four times and securely fastened to polished maple handle. Long sweep.

99K2124
1 broom. Shpg. wt., 1¾ lbs.........$0.55
99K2123
2 brooms. Shpg. wt., 3½ lbs.. 1.00

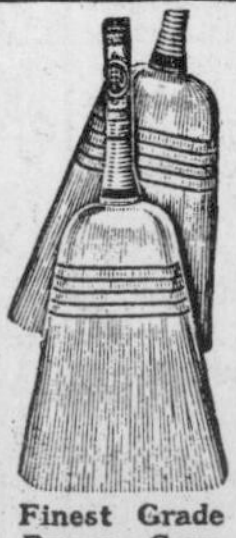

Finest Grade Broom Corn Obtainable

Extra High Grade Fancy Carpet Brooms

79c EACH

A real broom, made by expert workmen, of the very best materials obtainable. Every broom is carefully inspected before leaving the factory. Extra strong. Five linen stitchings. Long pliable sweep. Smooth enameled hard maple handle.

99K2126—1 broom. Shpg. wt., 2¼ lbs..79c
99K2125—2 brooms. Shipping weight, 4½ pounds $1.50

EQUIP YOUR DAIRY AT BIG SAVINGS

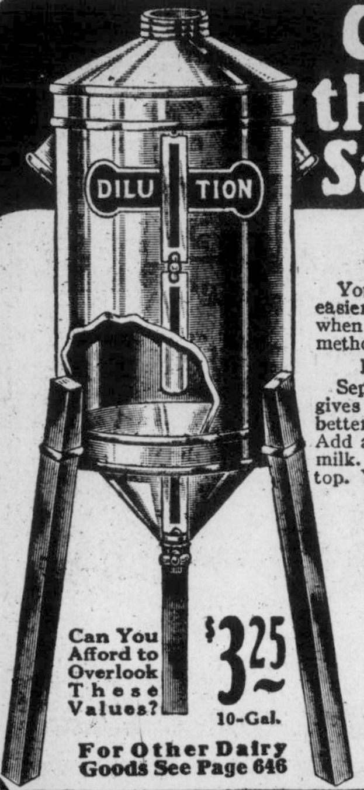

Compare this Money Saving Price

Dilution Cream Separator

You get more cream, get it quicker, easier and more conveniently than when you resort to the old skimming methods.

Does the Work Quickly

Separates in three to four hours, and gives a sweet diluted milk that is much better for stock feeding than sour milk. Add an equal quantity of water to the milk. Cream separates and rises to top. You can watch separation through glass gauges in side of tank. Milk is drawn off through deep cone bottom faucet without disturbing cream.

Made of heavy tin plate. Seamed and well soldered throughout. Beautifully blue enameled outside. Prices include tank, tin tubes, strainer faucet and hardwood legs.

Can You Afford to Overlook These Values?

$3.25 10-Gal.

	Cap.	Shpg. Wt.	
99K2550	10 gal.	14 lbs.	$3.25
99K2551	*14 gal.	16 lbs.	4.15
99K2552	*18 gal.	20 lbs.	5.15
99K2553	*24 gal.	22 lbs.	6.30
99K2554	*32 gal.	31 lbs.	6.90

*Not mailable.

For Other Dairy Goods See Page 646

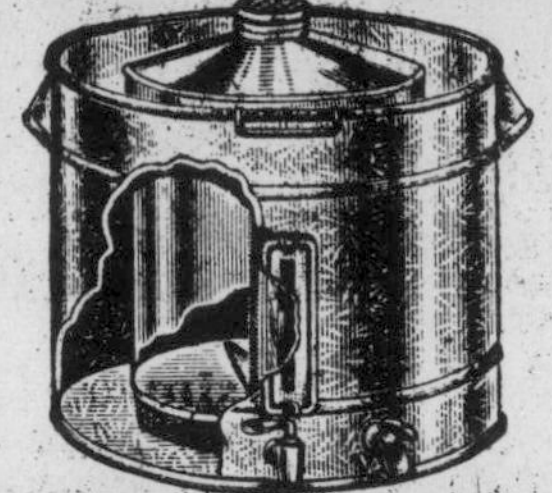

Double Can Cream Separators

$5.50 4-Gal.

Keeps cream cold and separates cream from milk in four to six hours in warm or cold weather. Removable inner can makes cleaning easy. Glass gauges show depth of cream. Water does not mix with milk or cream. Has separate faucets for drawing off milk and water. Inner can heavy tin plate. Outer can galvanized iron.

	Capacity of Inner Can	Shipping Weight	
99K2562	4 gal.	14 lbs.	$5.50
99K2563	* 6 gal.	17 lbs.	6.20
99K2564	* 8 gal.	20 lbs.	6.70
99K2565	*10 gal.	21 lbs.	7.25
99K2566	*12 gal.	23 lbs.	7.80

*Not mailable.

Our Improved Milk Coolers and Aerators

$6.40 Size No. 2

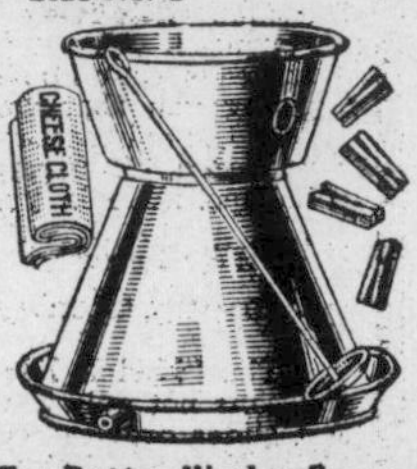

Milk Keeps Better if Cooled as Soon as Milked!

Pour milk or cream in at top through strainer and it comes out cool, sweet and clean. Cools milk quickly; aerates it, removing animal odors. Simple in construction. Easy to clean. Heavy tin plate with galvanized steel bottom. Use ice or cold running water. With double cheesecloth strainer, spring holding pins and directions. **Not mailable.**

99K2532—Size No. 2. Receiver holds 18 quarts. For 5 to 25 cows. Shipping weight, 25 pounds............$6.40
99K2533—Size No. 3. Receiver holds 34 quarts. For 25 to 50 cows. Shipping weight, 33 pounds............$7.80
99K2534—Size No. 4. Receiver holds 52 quarts. For 50 to 100 cows. Shipping weight, 40 pounds............$9.30

For Butter Worker See Page 926

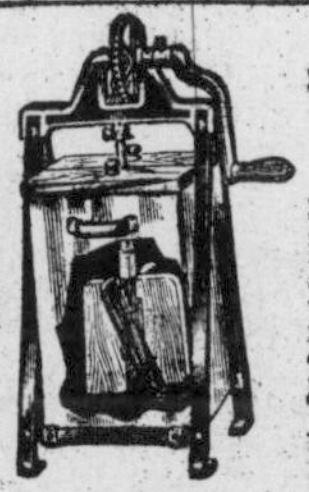

Elgin Metal Churn

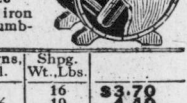

$2.65 2-Gal.

Gets all the butter from the cream in from 8 to 10 minutes. A well constructed churn with can of heavy steel, triple tinned and rust-proof. Cover is of natural finish, selected hardwood. Frame is of steel. Castings have aluminum finish. Legs and standards strongly riveted steel. The gears, wheels and top castings are accurately fitted and run smoothly. Has removable dasher, making it easy to clean. Our prices are the lowest.

	Cap.	Shpg. Wt	
99K2596	2 gal.	9 lbs.	$2.65
99K2597	3 gal.	13 lbs.	3.45
99K2598	4 gal.	14 lbs.	3.95
99K2599	6 gal.	18 lbs.	4.70

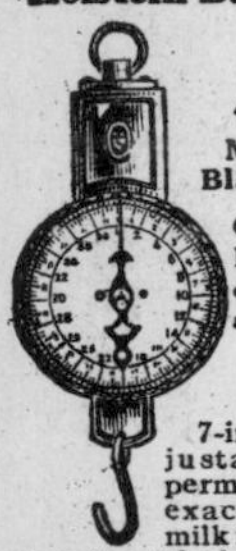

Holstein Dairy Scales

$3.50 40-Lb. Size

Milk Record Blank Included

Comply With Department of Weights and Measures Requirements

7-inch dial. Adjustable pointer permits obtaining exact weight of milk in pail. Directions furnished. Wt., 4 lbs.

9K2898—Cap., 40 lbs. by tenths of a lb....$3.50
9K2899—Cap., 60 lbs. by tenths of a lb....$4.50
9K2897—Milk Record Blanks. Seven-day sheet for keeping daily record of milk output for each cow. Wt., 1 lb. Per 100 sheets......48c

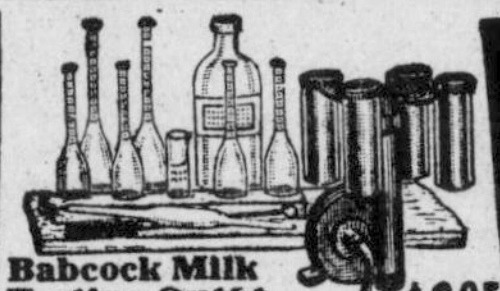

Babcock Milk Testing Outfit

$6.85

Dairy authorities recommend the Babcock Test. Prices include test bottles, brush, acid measure, pipette and directions for making tests. Acid not included. Shpg. wt., 19 lbs.

99K2573—Four-bottle size....................$6.85

Extra Glassware for Babcock Testers

9K2882—50 per cent cream bottles Wt., 2 oz..........30c
9K2884—10 per cent milk bottles. Wt., 2 oz..........28c
9K2886—50/100 of 1 per cent skim milk bottles. Wt. 2 oz..75c
9K2888—17.6-18-C. C. combination milk and cream pipettes. Weight, 3 ounces..........24c
9K2890—17.5-C. C. acid measures. Weight, 1 oz....15c

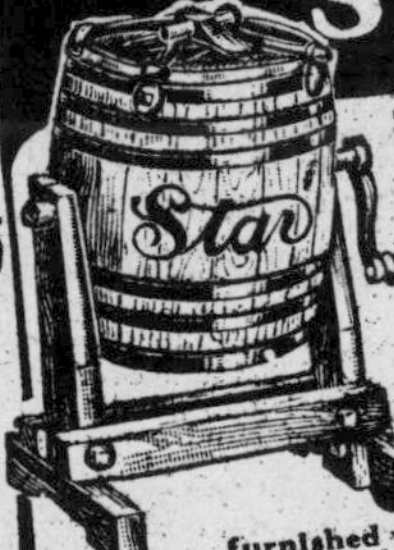

"STAR" BARREL CHURNS

$5.40 6-Gal.

Barrel of oak. Varnished. Not mailable.

99K2592—Holds 6 gallons. Churns up to 3 gallons. Shipping weight, 30 pounds..........$5.40
99K2593—Holds 10 gallons. Churns up to 5 gallons. Shipping weight, 36 lbs. $6.15
99K2594—Holds 15 gallons. Churns up to 7 gallons. Shipping weight, 41 lbs. $7.00
99K2595—Holds 20 gallons. Churns up to 10 gallons. Shipping weight, 51 lbs. $7.90

Power churns below are furnished with 12-inch tight and loose pulleys, which take a 2-inch belt. Shipped direct from factory in NORTHERN ILLINOIS.

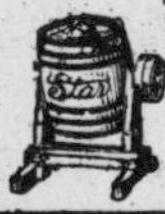

Not Mailable	Holds, Gal.	Churns, Gal.	Wt., Lbs.	
99K8348⅓	15	7	60	$10.40
99K8349⅓	20	10	70	11.75
99K8350⅓	25	12	90	13.65
99K8351⅓	35	16	100	16.50

Cedar Cylinder Churns

$3.70 3-Gal. Size

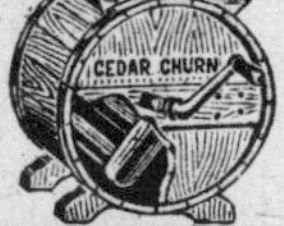

Has 4-paddle dasher, making butter quickly. Made of clear straight grained cedar. Hoops are galvanized iron. Crank is heavily tinned cast iron and is locked to churn with thumbscrews and clamp.

	No.	Holds, Gal.	Churns, Gal.	Shpg. Wt., Lbs.	
99K2613	1	3	2	16	$3.70
99K2614	2	4	2½	19	4.40
99K2615*	3	7	4	24	5.15
99K2616*	4	10	6	27	6.40

*Not mailable.

OUR PRICES ON CATTLE ACCESSORIES SAVE YOU MONEY

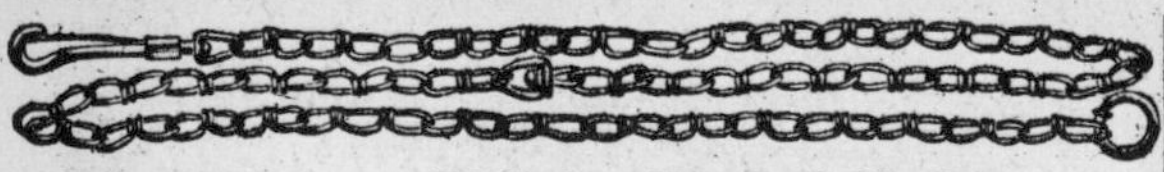

Picket or Tie Out Chains

42c And Up

Heavy gauge steel chain with swivel snap on one end and 1¾-inch ring on other. Swivel in center to avoid tangling.

9K6035—Size 0 or about ⅛ in. diam., 20 feet long. Wt., 4 lbs..42c
9K6037—Size 2-0 or about 9/64 in. diam., 30 feet long. Wt., 6 lbs..65c
9K6038—Size 3-0 or about 5/32 in. diam., 30 feet long. Wt., 7 lbs..89c

For Cattle Halters and Ropes see page 1053.

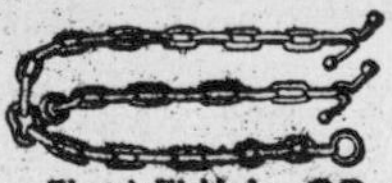

Electric Welded Straight Link Cow Ties

23c

Links are extra strong. Size 2-0. About ⅛ inch in diameter, 4½ ft. long. Weight, 2 pounds.

	Each	Doz.
9K6034	23c	$2.65

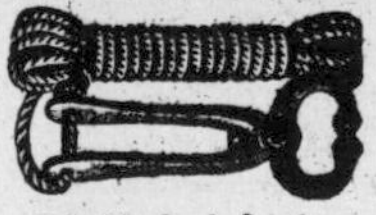

Sensible Cattle Leaders

Malleable iron. Length, 8½ inches.

9K6086—With 10 ft. ⅝-in. rope..........35c
9K6087—Leader only..............25c

Self Piercing Bull Ring

25c

Copper. Better than old style rings. ¼x2¾-inch. Weight, 4 ounces.

9K6076.....25c

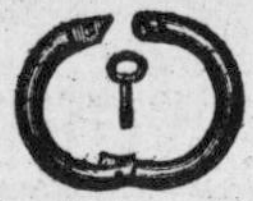

Prize Bull Ring

45c

Large size, self piercing. extra heavy solid copper, beautifully finished. Size, ⅜x3 in. Weight, 6 ounces.

9K6075......45c

Buy An ANTI-KICKING COW CHAIN HERE FOR LESS MONEY

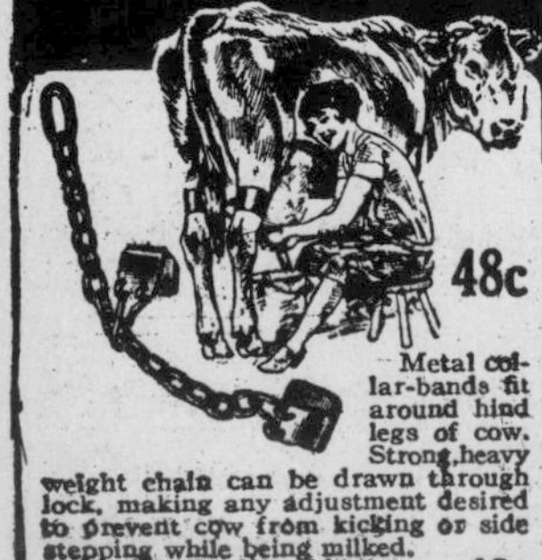

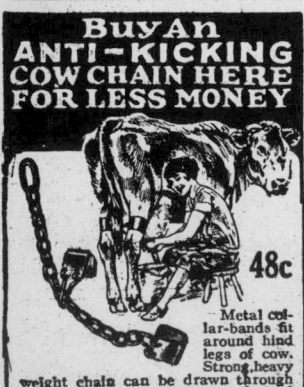

48c

Metal collar-bands fit around hind legs of cow. Strong, heavy weight chain can be drawn through lock, making any adjustment desired to prevent cow from kicking or side stepping while being milked.

9K6043—Wt., 1½ lbs.....48c

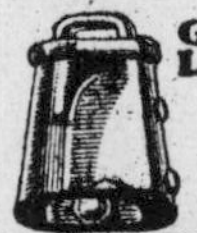

Genuine Kentucky Loud Speaker Cow Bells

25c And Up

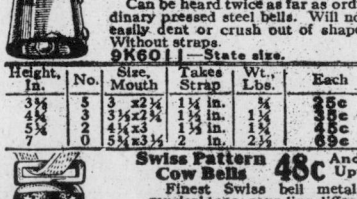

Can be heard twice as far as ordinary pressed steel bells. Will not easily dent or crush out of shape. Without straps.

9K6011—State size.

Height, In.	No.	Size, Mouth	Takes Strap	Wt., Lbs.	Each
3⅝	5	3 x2¼	1¼ in.	⅝	25c
4¾	3	3½x2¾	1½ in.	1¼	35c
5¼	2	4¼x3	1½ in.	1¾	45c
7	0	5¾x3½	2 in.	2½	69c

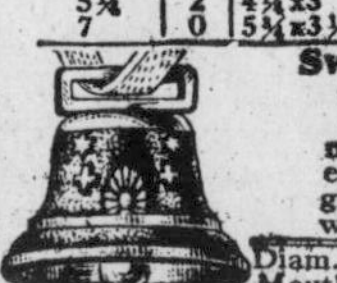

Swiss Pattern Cow Bells

48c And Up

Finest Swiss bell metal, musical tone, sounding different than ordinary bells. Will give years of service. Comes without straps.

		Diam. Mouth	Takes Strap	Weight, Lbs.	
9K601	3	3⅛ in.	1¼ in.	¾	$0.48
9K601	4	3⅝ in.	1½ in.	1	.72
9K601	5	5 in.	2¼ in.	2	1.24

Leather Cow Bell Straps, 40 Inches Long

Width, inches......	1¼	1½	2	2¼
Weight..............	7 oz.	8 oz.	¾ lb.	¾ lb.
10K2601........	39c	45c	54c	65c

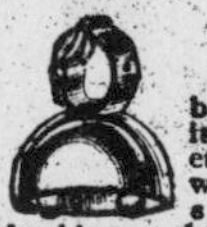

Turkey Bell

15c

Solid brass, polished. Diameter, 1⅜ in., with leather strap and buckle as shown. Wt., each, 3 oz.

	Each	Doz.
9K6002	15c	$1.75

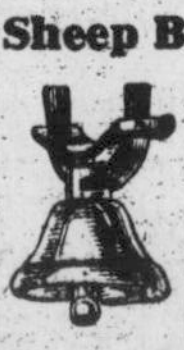

Sheep Bell With Strap

30c

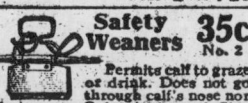

Diameter, 2⅞ inches, with strap as shown. Wt., each, 5 oz.

	Each	Doz.
9K6004	30c	$2.90

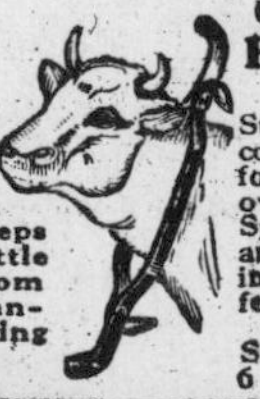

Cow Poke

2 for 72c

Keeps Cattle From Wandering

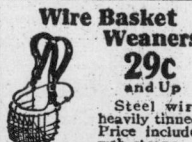

Will not chafe. Strong, light and comfortable; long forks. Length, over all, 36 in. Spur points stop animal from forcing way through fence.

99K6274
Shipping weight, 6 lbs. 2 for 72c

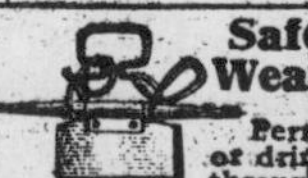

Safety Weaners

35c No. 2

Permits calf to graze or drink. Does not go through calf's nose nor make it sore. Galvanized metal. Side projection prevents calf sucking sidewise. Parcel post weight, 1 pound.

9K6094—State size.

Size	For	Wt.	
2	Large Calves	4 oz.	35c
3	Yearlings	6 oz.	40c
4	2-Yr. Olds and Cows	8 oz.	45c

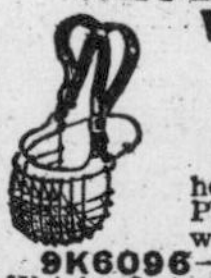

Wire Basket Weaners

29c and Up

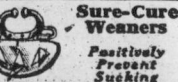

Steel wire, heavily tinned. Price includes web straps.

9K6096—Calves. Weight, 8 ounces..29c
9K6097—Yearlings. Weight, 1 pound...32c
9K6098—Cows. Weight, 1 pound...40c

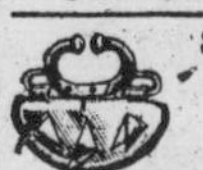

Sure-Cure Weaners

Positively Prevent Sucking

Adjustable nose ring fitted with smooth ball tips. Easily applied. Made of malleable iron and steel heavily tinned.

9K6092—Calves. Weight, 4 ounces..40c
9K6093—Cows. Weight, 8 ounces..50c

QUALITY DAIRY NEEDS AT LOWER PRICES

Clear Glass Milk Bottles

HALF PINTS	PINTS	QUARTS
$1.00 Per Two Doz.	$1.33 Per Two Doz.	$1.70 Per Two Doz.

Best quality clear flint glass, not easily broken. Uniform size, properly annealed. Smoothly finished inside and out. Will stand a great deal of rough handling. Take standard caps shown on this page. Accurate, comply with all legal requirements.

HALF PINTS
99K2570—Per crate of 2 doz. Shpg. wt., 20 lbs. **$1.00**
99K2580—Per crate of 6 doz. Shpg. wt., crate, 55 lbs. Not mailable.......**$2.68**

PINTS
99K2571—Per crate of 2 doz. Shpg. wt., 30 lbs. **$1.33**
99K2581—Per crate of 6 doz. Shpg. wt., crate, 85 lbs. Not mailable.......**$3.48**

QUARTS
99K2572—Per crate of 2 doz. Shpg. wt., 48 lbs...**$1.70**
99K2582—Per crate of 6 doz. Shpg. wt., crate, 135 lbs. Not mailable. **$4.70**

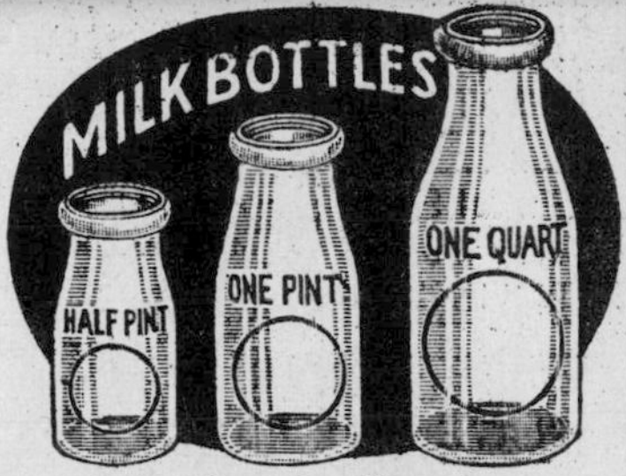

MILK BOTTLES
HALF PINT
ONE PINT
ONE QUART

Best Quality—
None Better Made

STRONG STURDY and RIGID!

Milwaukee Pattern Riveted Milk Cans

$2.65 5-Gallon

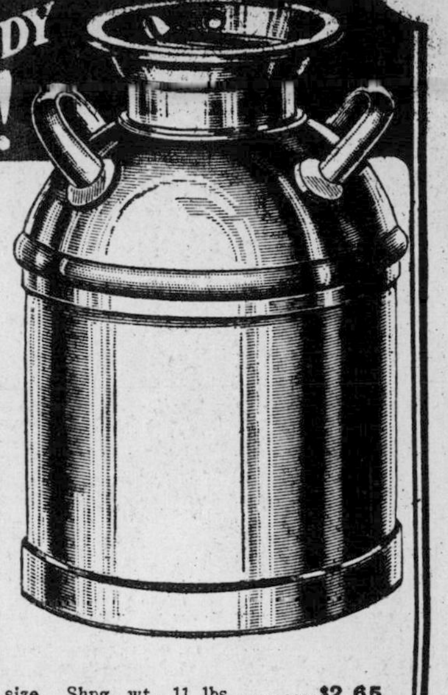

Well made of smooth sheet steel, double seamed and riveted throughout. Neck and bowl drawn in one piece. Reinforced breast is joined to body in such a manner as to form a very strong and rigid joint. Heavy steel bottom is riveted to body and reinforced with outside bottom hoop. Round handles are welded on. Seamless 6-inch plug type cover. Cans are carefully tinned and retinned, and inside seams are well loaded with solder. Full, rounded breast and bottom, easy to clean.

99K2500—5-gallon size. Shpg. wt., 11 lbs..........**$2.65**
99K2501—8-gallon size. Shpg. wt., 16 lbs..........**3.15**
99K2502—10-gallon size. Shpg. wt., 18 lbs..........**3.35**

For Dairy Thermometers see page 772

Bristle Milk Bottle Brush **13c**

Bristles, securely fastened. Stiff tampico tufts. Length, 16 inches. Weight, 2 ounces.
9K2876 ....**13c**

Printed Milk Bottle Caps

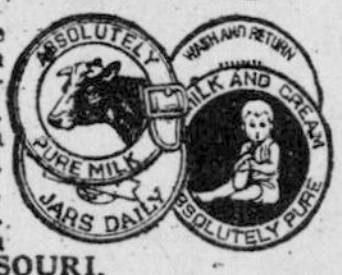

ABSOLUTELY PURE MILK
JARS DAILY
MILK AND CREAM
ABSOLUTELY PURE

Send sample of lettering. Can be printed either red or blue. 50,000 packed in barrel. Shpg. weight, 135 lbs. State color. Shipped from factory in MISSOURI.
99K8000⅓ **$13.75**

We can furnish stock designs similar to those shown without extra cost. Write for circular.

Extra Heavy Tinned Dairy Pails

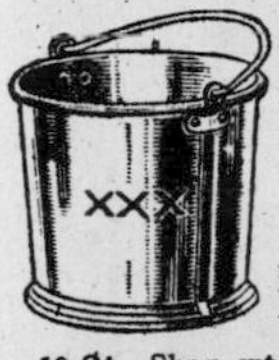

50c 10-Qt.

Heavy wired top rim and bail. Extra strong heavy tinned ears.

10-Qt. Shpg. wt., each, 3¼ lbs.
99K2907—Each **$0.50**
99K2910—3 for..........**1.40**
12-Quart. Shpg. wt., each, 3½ lbs.
99K2908—Each **$0.60**
99K2911—3 for..........**1.70**
14-Quart. Shpg. wt., each, 3¾ lbs.
99K2909—Each **$0.65**
99K2912—3 for..........**1.85**

Heavy Tin Milk Pail

39c

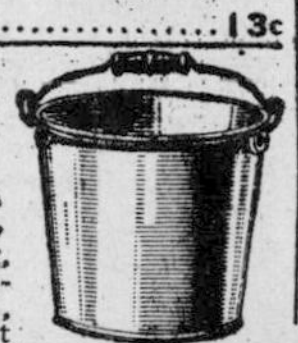

Strong, serviceable, bright heavy tin plate. Inside seams soldered. Heavy wire bail, wood grip. Cap., 12 qts. Shpg. wt., 1¾ lbs.
99K2902 Each **39c**
99K2904 2 for......**69c**

Waterproof Caps for Milk Bottles

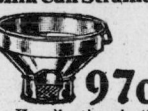

65c 2,000 Plain Caps

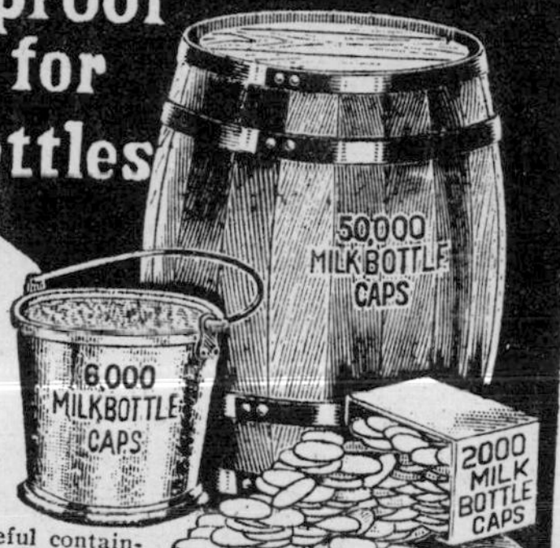

50,000 MILK BOTTLE CAPS
6,000 MILKBOTTLE CAPS
2000 MILK BOTTLE CAPS

Save money on first quality milk bottle caps. Absolutely waterproof, paraffined on both sides. Will fit standard size milk bottles. Packed in handy useful containers which are always in demand about the farm or dairy. Thrifty dairymen all over the country regularly buy from Sears because they know they get extra grade goods; that they get them quicker and for less money than elsewhere.

9K2893—In packages containing 2,000 plain caps. Weight, 5 pounds..**65c**
99K2587—In 20-quart extra heavy and extra large galvanized pail, containing about 6,000 plain caps. Shipping wt., 17 pounds..**$2.25**
99K2585—In barrels containing about 50,000 plain caps. Shipping weight, 133 pounds. Not mailable..........**$12.75**

New Jersey Pattern R. R. Milk Cans

We Recommend These Cans for Shipping Purposes

$2.85 5-Gal.

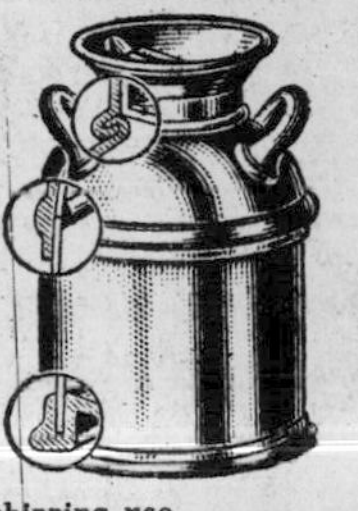

Great savings in this wonderfully well made heavy steel plate milk can. Seamed, riveted and heavily tinned with solder floated into the seams, inside and out. Is absolutely sanitary and easy to clean, as there are no crevices in which the germs or dirt can collect. Reinforced body and bottom are rolled together to form durable, rigid joints. Breast and bottom are full rounded with lock joint, making them especially rigid. Smooth inside finish. **Built for hard usage.** Seamless 6-inch plug type cover. **The ideal cans for shipping use.**

99K2506—5-gal. size. Shpg. wt., 12 lbs.**$2.85**
99K2507—8-gal. size. Shpg. wt., 20 lbs. **3.75**
99K2508—10-gal. size. Shpg. wt., 23 lbs. **3.95**

Sanitary Strainer Pails

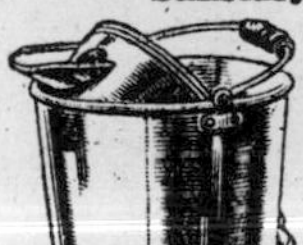

92c 12-Qt.

Soldered seams, sanitary finish, fine mesh copper strainer. Heavy bail with handle at bottom helps in tipping. Flat bottom.
9K2900—State size.

Cap., Qts.	Wt., Lbs.	Each
12	3¼	92c
14	3½	98c

Milk Can Strainer

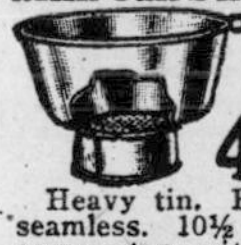

48c

Heavy tin. Bowl is seamless. 10½ inches across top with 4½-inch brass strainer cloth. Well made and unusually low priced. Buy at Sears and save. Wt., 1 lb.
9K2896......**48c**

Extra Quality Milk Can Strainer

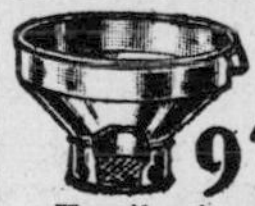

97c

Heavily tinned. 4½-inch brass strainer, removable hoop for attaching cheesecloth. Diameter, 11 inches. Weight, 3 lbs.
9K2895 ....**97c**

Lock Cover Cream Setting Cans

$1.35 For 3 14-Qt.

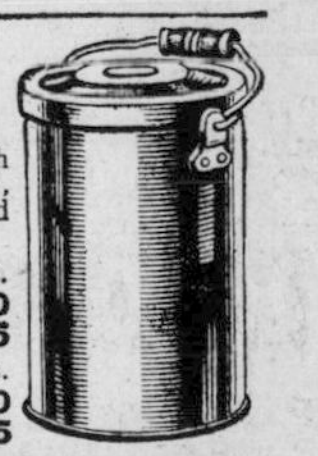

Patent cover. Well riveted ears with wood grip wire bail. With raised bottom, carefully soldered. Special prices quoted below on three cans. Not mailable.

14-Quart Size. Shpg. wt., each, 12 lbs.
99K2529—Each **$0.50**
99K2527—3 for..............**1.35**
20-Quart Size. Shpg. wt., each, 14 lbs.
99K2530—Each **$0.60**
99K2528—3 for..............**1.65**

POWERFUL QUICK CUTTING DEHORNERS and HOG ACCESSORIES

Aluminum Ear Buttons

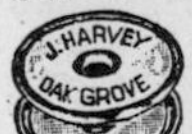

J. HARVEY
OAK GROVE

Made to order, with name and address (not over 15 letters) on one side and name of farm or ranch and any number or series of numbers up to 999 on reverse side. **Shipped from factory in NORTHERN ILLINOIS.**
99K8329⅓—State name and number.

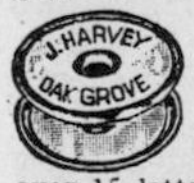

Lots of	Shpg. Weight	Each
25	3 oz.	$ 1.20
50	5 oz.	1.80
100	¾ lb.	3.10
500	3 lbs.	15.00
999	6 lbs.	24.50

Combination Punch and Pliers

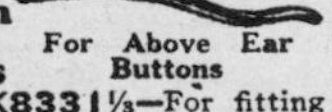

For Above Ear Buttons

99K8331⅓—For fitting buttons shown above to ears. Shpg. wt., ¾ lb.**$1.20**

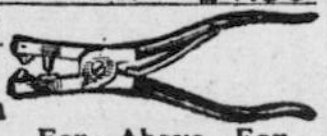

Copper Plated Rings

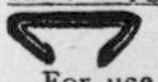

For use only with 9K6065 Hog Ringer shown to right.
9K6066—Hog Size.
9K6067—Shoat Size.
9K6068—Pig Size.
Box of 100 any size. Wt., 7 ounces......................**8c**
Doz. boxes, wt., 6 lbs..**95c**

Metal Ear Labels

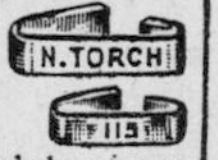

N. TORCH
115

Not more than 11 large letters can be put on sheep sizes; 15 on cattle or extra cattle sizes; 22 on cattle and extra cattle sizes, in smaller type. We do not furnish less than 25 labels of one name. **State name and numbers. Shipped from factory in NORTHEASTERN ILL.**

99K8319⅓—Sheep and Hog size.

Lots of	Shpg. Wt.	Name and No.	Name Only	No. Only
25	3 oz.	$0.75	$0.58	$0.55
50	6 oz.	1.25	.98	.95
100	¾ lb.	1.80	1.58	1.50
99K8321⅓—Cattle Size.				
25	8 oz.	$0.95	$0.85	$0.80
50	¾ lb.	1.50	1.15	1.10
100	1½ lbs.	1.95	1.75	1.70
99K8323⅓—Extra Cattle Size.				
25	¾ lb.	$1.00	$0.95	$0.90
50	1¼ lbs.	1.60	1.45	1.40
100	2½ lbs.	2.25	2.25	2.10

Oval Hole Ear Punches

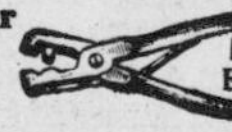

For Above Ear Labels

Punches hole and closes label.
99K8325⅓
Regular Cattle, Sheep and Hog Size. Shipping weight, ¾ pound......**$1.35**
99K8327⅓—Extra Cattle Size. Shipping weight, ¾ pound......**$2.10**

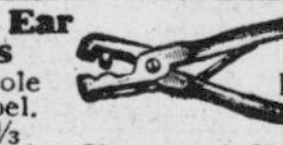

Hog Ringer

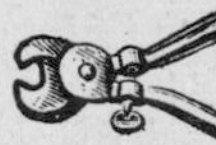

Fitted with thumbscrew. Wt., ¾ lb.
9K6065....**13c**

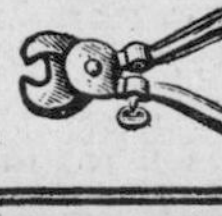

"Can't Root" Combined Hog Tamer and Ear Marker

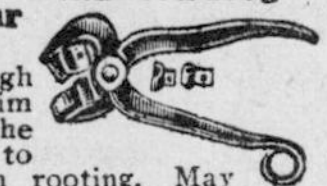

Cuts cleanly through the muscles in the rim of hog's nose, the only perfect way to prevent a hog from rooting. May also be used for hog or cattle ear notchers. Two different size steel cutters included. Length, 10 inches.
9K6044—Wt., 1¼ lbs..........**$1.20**

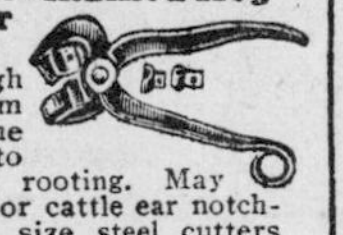

Stock Marking Punch With Steel Cutting Dies

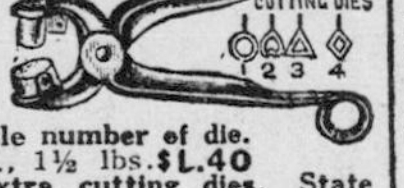

CUTTING DIES
1 2 3 4

Interchangeable tempered dies. Lgth., 11 in. One die included with each punch. **State style number of die.**
9K6050—Wt., 1½ lbs.**$1.40**
9K6051—Extra cutting dies. State style number of dies. Wt., 1 oz. Each.**34c**

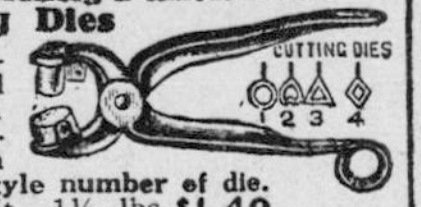

Tattoo Stock Marker With Interchangeable ½-Inch Letters and Figures

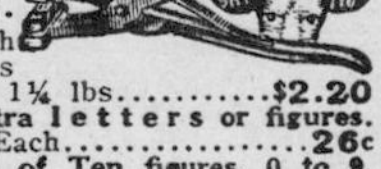

Full directions. State letters or figures wanted.
9K6045—With any three letters or figures. Wt., 1¼ lbs..........**$2.20**
9K6046—Extra letters or figures. Weight, 1 oz. Each..........**26c**
9K6047—Set of Ten figures, 0 to 9. Weight, ¾ pound. Per set..........**$2.55**
9K6048—Tattoo Oil, Black. Marks 500 ears. Weight, 4 oz. Per bottle..**45c**

Genuine Leavitt Guaranteed Dehorner Knives Cut on Four Sides

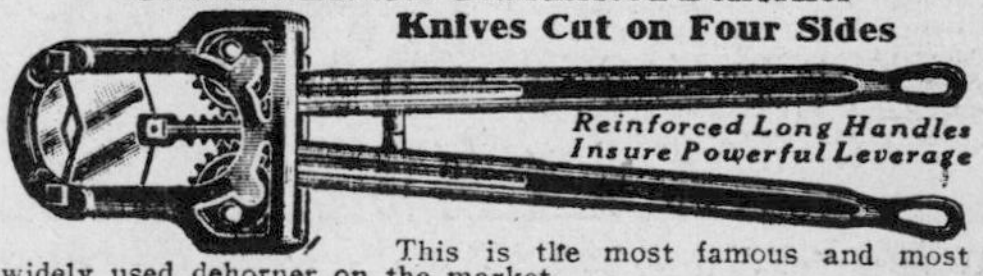

Reinforced Long Handles Insure Powerful Leverage

This is the most famous and most widely used dehorner on the market.
99K5908—No. 2. Medium size. Opening, 3x3 in. Length over all, 37½ in. Knives included. Shpg. wt., 14 lbs...**$2.85**
9K5942—Extra sliding knife. Weight, ¾ pound.....**45c**
9K5941—Extra stationary knife. Weight, 8 ounces...**40c**
99K5909—No. 3. Large size. Opening, 4x4 in. This dehorner will do the work of the No. 2 or smaller dehorner. Length over all, 37½ in. Knives included. Shpg. wt., 15 lbs...**$3.60**
9K5944—Extra sliding knife. Weight, 1 pound......**50c**
9K5943—Extra stationary knife. Weight, ¾ pound..**45c**

Highest Grade Genuine Keystone Dehorner

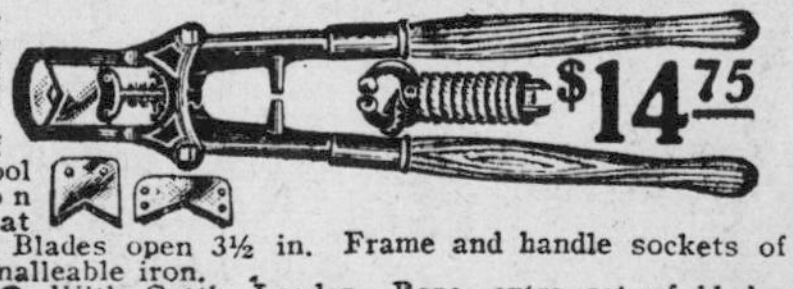

$14.75

Greater cutting power at beginning of stroke. Knives of tempered tool steel, cut on four sides at same time. Blades open 3½ in. Frame and handle sockets of high grade malleable iron.
99K5900—With Cattle Leader. Rope, extra set of blades and screws. Lgth., 47½ in. Shpg. wt., 20 lbs.......**$14.75**

Dehorning Saw

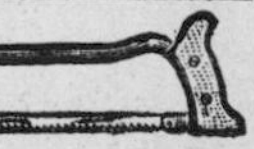

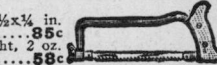

Malleable iron frame; blade, 9½x¼ in.
9K6090—Wt., 1¼ lbs..........**85c**
9K6091—Extra blades. Weight, 2 oz. 4 for..........**58c**

See Index and Information Pages 542 to 570

Attractive Prices on Lock Sets

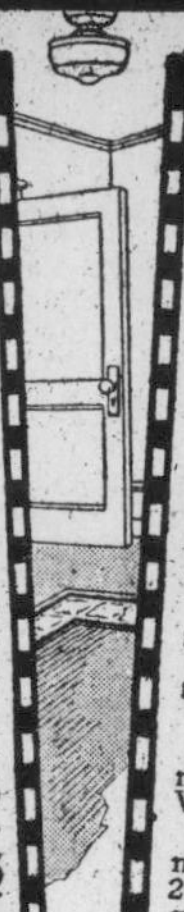

Chicago Design

Steel Lock Sets for Inside Doors

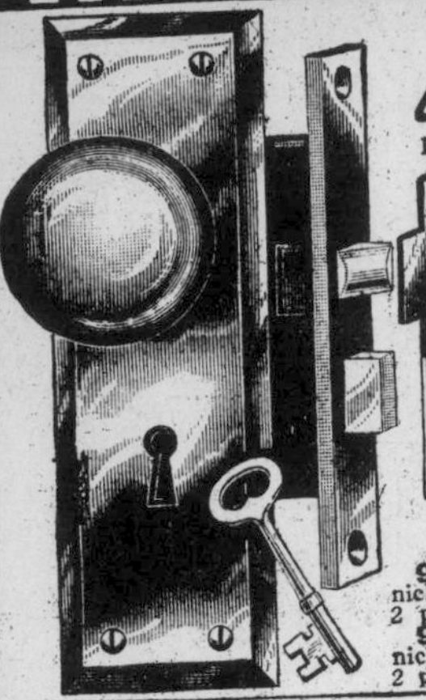

49c Per Set

Reversible mortise lock, 3¾x3¼ inches. 2¼-inch knobs. Heavy beveled edge escutcheons, 7x2¼ inches. Nickel plated key. Weight, 2 pounds.

9K4619—Lemon brass finish on steel. Per set.....49c
9K4679—Old copper finish on steel. Per set.....49c

Genuine Solid Bronze Sets

"The Enduring Metal"

Easy spring mortise lock, 3¾x3¼ inches, with cast bronze face bolts and strike. Genuine bronze, 2¼-inch knobs. Beveled bronze escutcheons, 7x2¼ inches. Nickel plated key. Weight, 2 pounds.

9K4620—Lemon brass finish on genuine bronze. Per set.......$1.49
9K4680—Old copper finish on genuine bronze. Per set.......$1.49

Genuine Bronze Bathroom Sets

9K4419—Lemon brass finish on outside, nickel plated inside, with thumb turn. Weight, 2 pounds. Per set.......$1.90
9K4421—Old copper finish on outside, nickel plated inside, with thumb turn. Weight, 2 pounds. Per set.......$1.90

Stratford Design

Steel Lock Sets for Inside Doors

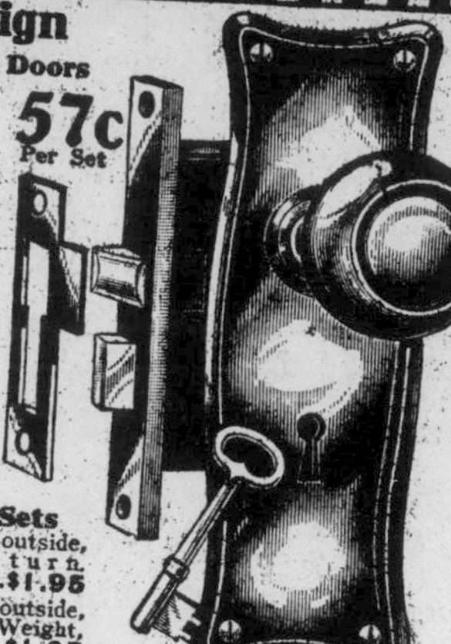

57c Per Set

Reversible mortise lock; size, 3¾x3¼ inches. Knob, 2¼ inches. Escutcheons, 7⅝x2⅝ inches. Nickel plated key. Weight, 2¼ pounds.

9K4570—Lemon brass finish on steel. Per set.....57c
9K4728—Old copper finish on steel. Per set.....57c

Genuine Solid Bronze Sets

"The Lifetime Hardware"

Easy spring mortise lock, 3¾x3¼ in., with cast bronze face, bolt and strike. Genuine bronze, 2¼-inch knobs. Bronze escutcheons; size, 7⅝x2⅝ inches. Nickel plated key. Weight, 2¼ pounds.

9K4571—Lemon brass finish on genuine bronze. Per set.....$1.65
9K4729—Old copper finish on genuine bronze. Per set.....$1.65

Genuine Bronze Bathroom Sets

9K4420—Lemon brass finish on outside, nickel plated inside, with thumb turn. Weight, 2¼ pounds. Per set.......$1.95
9K4422—Old copper finish on outside, nickel plated inside, with thumb turn. Weight, 2¼ pounds. Per set.......$1.95

Cylinder Front Door Lock Sets

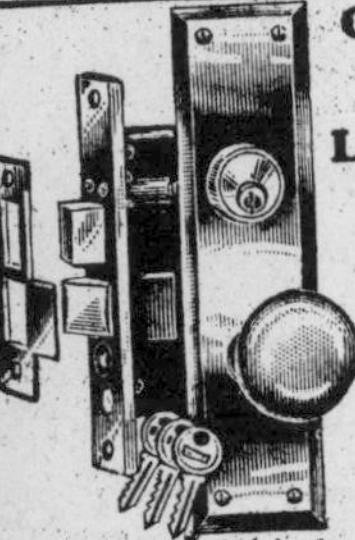

$7.00 Per Set

Reversible mortise lock, 5⅝x3¾ inches. Genuine bronze front, bolts and strike. Genuine bronze 2¼-inch knobs, and escutcheons; outside, 10½x2¼ inches; inside, 7x2¼ inches. One key operates both bolts from outside. Thumb turn on inside. Complete with screws and three keys. Weight, 5¼ pounds.

9K4624—Genuine bronze, lemon finish. Per set.......$7.00
9K4676—Genuine bronze, old copper finish. Set.......$7.00

Three-Tumbler Front Door Lock Sets

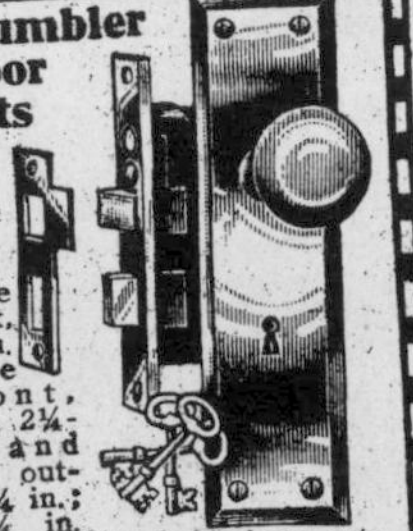

$3.20 Per Set

Reversible mortise lock, 5⅛ x 3½ in. Genuine bronze front, bolts, strike, 2¼-in. knobs and escutcheons; outside, 10½x2¼ in.; inside, 7x2¼ in. One key operates both bolts from outside. Thumb turn on inside. Complete with screws and three keys. Wt., 4 lbs.

9K4626—Genuine bronze lemon finish. Per set.......$3.20
9K4674—Genuine bronze old copper finish. Per set.......$3.20

One-Tumbler Lock. Has electro plated steel front, escutcheons and knobs.

9K4627—Lemon brass finish. Set.......$1.75
9K4675—Old copper finish. Per set.......$1.75

Three-Tumbler Front Door Lock Sets

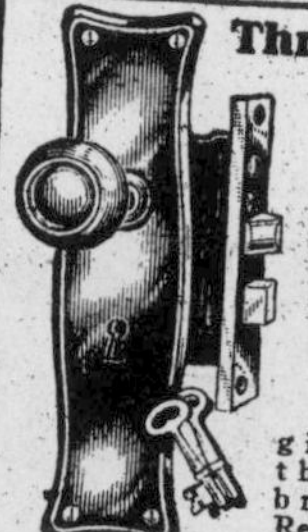

$3.20 Per Set

The massive construction gives strength to the durable heavy bronze material. Reversible mortise lock, 5x3½ inches. Genuine bronze front, bolts, strike, 2¼-inch knobs and escutcheons; outside, 12x3 inches; inside, 7⅝x2⅝ in. One key operates both bolts from outside. Thumb turn on inside. Complete with screws and three keys. Wt., 4 lbs.

9K4576—Genuine bronze lemon finish. Per set.......$3.20
9K4724—Genuine bronze old copper finish. Per set.......$3.20

Cylinder Front Door Lock Sets

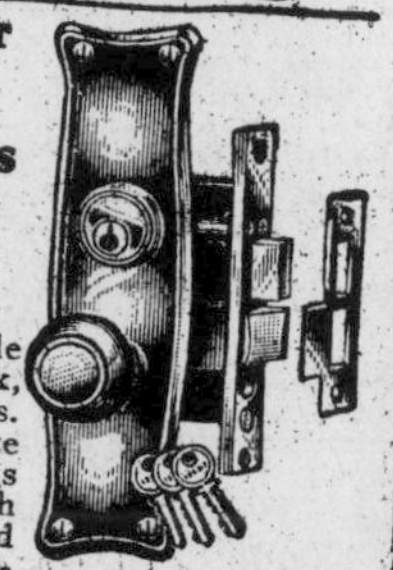

$7.00 Per Set

Reversible mortise lock, 5⅝x3¾ inches. Genuine bronze front, bolts strike, 2¼-inch knobs and and escutcheons; outside, 12x3 in.; inside, 7⅝x2⅝ in. One key operates both bolts from outside. Thumb turn on inside. Complete with screws and three keys. Weight, 5 pounds.

9K4574—Genuine bronze, lemon finish. Per set.......$7.00
9K4726—Genuine bronze, old copper finish. Per set.......$7.00

Door Checks

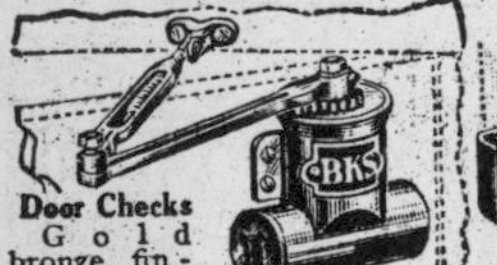

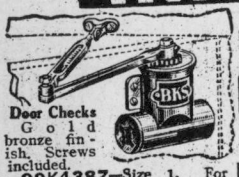

Gold bronze finish. Screws included.

99K4387—Size 1. For light inside doors. Shpg wt., 7 pounds.......$3.20
99K4388—Size 2. For medium inside doors. Shpg. wt., 11 pounds.......$3.70
99K4389—Size 3. For medium inside and light outside doors. Shipping weight, 12 pounds.......$4.20
99K4390—Size 4. For heavy doors up to 3x7 ft. by 2 in. Shpg. wt., 15 lbs.$5.65

Floor Spring Hinges

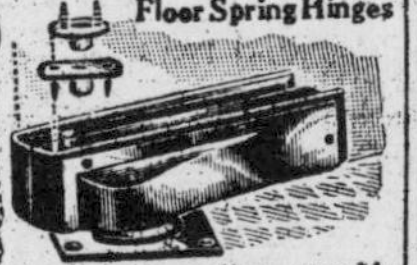

Extra quality, trouble free set. Heavy and strong enough to stand hardest service. This quality often sells elsewhere at $1.50. For doors 1⅜ to 1¾ in. thick. Weight, 4 lbs.

9K4657—Lemon brass. Per set.....98c
9K4844—Old copper finish. Per set.....98c

Glass Push Plates

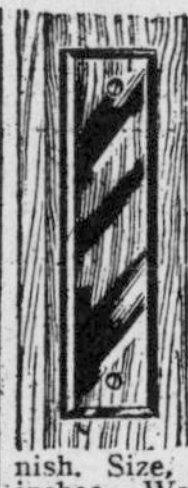

65c Pair

Beveled Edge Plate Glass

Easily cleaned. Nothing to discolor or tarnish. Size, about 3x12 inches. Weight, per pair, 2 pounds.

9K4719 Pair.......65c

Door Holders

Rubber tipped. Holds door in any position. Wt., ¾ lb.

9K4498 Lemon brass finish. 85c
9K4794 Old copper polished finish...85c

Rubber Tipped Metal Base Knobs

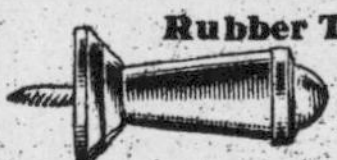

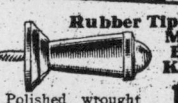

12c

Polished wrought steel, electro plated. Length, 2⅜ in. Weight, 3 oz.

9K4456—Lemon brass finish.......12c
9K4828—Old copper polished finish.......12c

Rubber Tipped Birch Base Knobs

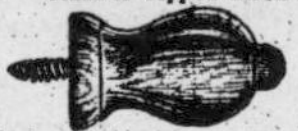

28c Doz.

Strong screw, good quality tip. Weight, per dozen, 1½ lbs.

9K4087—Per dozen.....28c

$2.25 French Window and Screen Door Lock

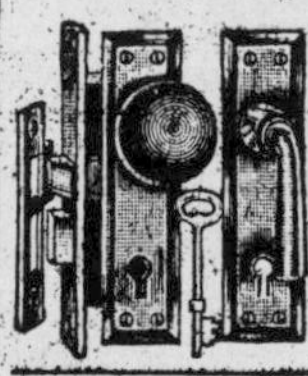

Genuine Bronze Flat Front Mortise Locks

For Flat Front French Windows and Doors.

Escutcheons are 4⅝x1⅛ inches. Lock, 3⅝x1½ inches. Knob, 1⅞ inches. Weight, 1¼ pounds.

9K4527—Genuine bronze, lemon finish.......$2.25
9K4755—Genuine bronze, old copper finish.......$2.25

Mortise Door Bolts

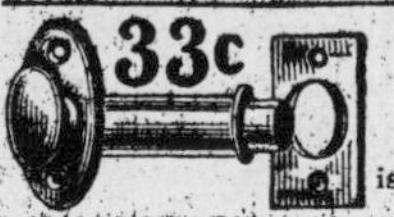

33c

Solid Bronze Knob and Escutcheon

Weight, 4 ounces.

9K4496—Lemon brass finished knob and escutcheon. Each.......33c
9K4800—Old copper finished knob and escutcheon. Each.......33c

Window Hardware

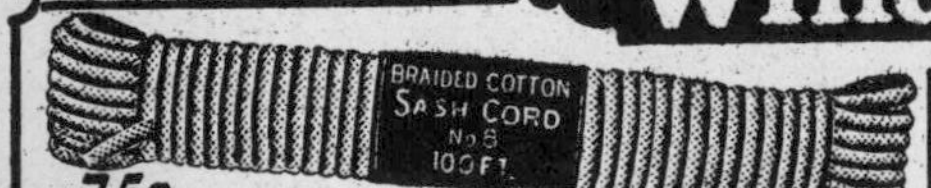

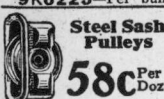

75c Per 100 Feet

No. 8 Braided Sash Cord

A very superior quality. Made from selected long staple cotton. Size, ¼ inch. Put up in bundles of 100 feet. Also makes a very high quality clothes line.

9K6225—Per bundle.......(Wt., 2¼ lbs.).......75c

Steel Sash Pulleys

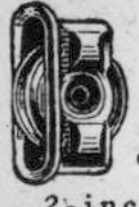

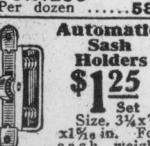

58c Per Doz.

2-inch wheel. Weight, per dozen, 1½ pounds.

9K4256 Per dozen.......58c

All Steel Spring Sash Balances

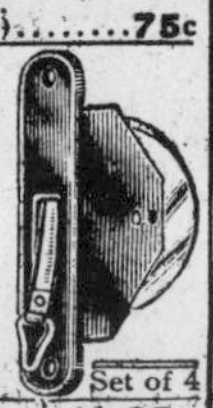

Rustless Metal Tape

9K4258

State size wanted

Size No.	Wt., Lbs.	Balances Sash	Set of 4
1	3	6 to 7 lbs.	$1.88
2	3½	8 to 9 lbs.	2.00
3	3⅝	10 to 11 lbs.	2.20
4	3¾	12 to 13 lbs.	2.40
5	4	14 to 15 lbs.	2.55
6	4½	16 to 17 lbs.	2.70

Automatic Sash Holders

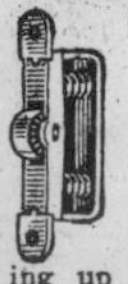

$1.25 Set

Size, 3¼x⅞x1⁵⁄₁₆ in. For sash weighing up to 30 pounds each. Weight, 1¾ lbs.

9K4262 Set of 4.....$1.25

Stop Bead Screws and Washers

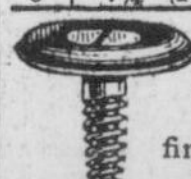

Weight, per doz., 2 oz.

9K4512—Lemon finish. Dozen.......10c
9K4780—Old copper finish. Dozen.......10c

Crescent Sash Fasteners

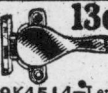

9K4518—Lemon brass finish.......7c
9K4772—Old copper finish.......7c
9K4410—Nickel plated finish.....8c
9K4566—Sanded old brass finish.8c

Side Sash Fasteners

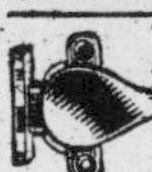

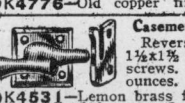

13c

Cam action, holds sash firmly and prevents rattling. Cast iron. Packed with screws. Wt., 2 oz.

9K4514—Lemon brass finish...13c
9K4776—Old copper finish.......13c

Casement Fasteners

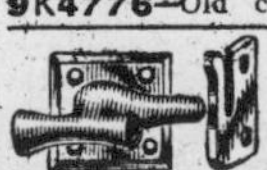

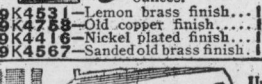

Reversible. Size, 1½x1⅝ in. With screws. Weight, 4 ounces.

9K4531—Lemon brass finish...14c
9K4768—Old copper finish.......14c
9K4416—Nickel plated finish...18c
9K4567—Sanded old brass finish.18c

Universal Casement Adjuster

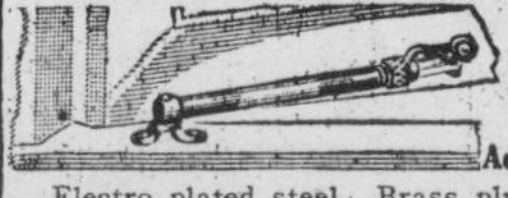

Electro plated steel. Brass plunger. Locks. Lgth., 12 in. Wt., ¾ lb.

9K4533—Lemon brass finish.$1.05
9K4751—Old copper finish.......1.05

Sash Lifts

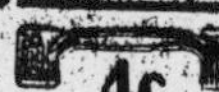

4c Each

Plated cast iron. Size, 3½ inches. Weight, 2 ounces.

9K4530—Lemon brass finish.4c
9K4760—Old copper finish.......4c
9K4565—Sanded old brass finish.......5c

Hook Sash Lifts

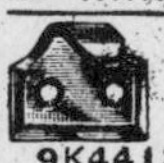

6 For 13c

Bevel edges. Size, 1½ inches. Wt. of six, 6 oz.

9K4413—Nickel plated finish. Each.......10c

Electro Plated Steel

9K4522—Lemon brass finish. Six for.......13c
9K4768—Old copper polished finish. Six for.......13c

Genuine Brass

9K4524—Lemon brass finish. Six for.......42c
9K4770—Polished old copper finish. Six for.......42c

Galvanized Non-Rust Cellar Window Set

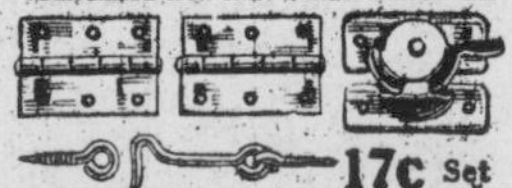

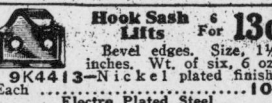

17c Set

Pair of 2½-inch steel butts, one steel sash fastener and one 2½-inch hook and eye. Complete with screws.

9K4382—Set..(Wt., 7 oz.)..17c

Barrel Bolts

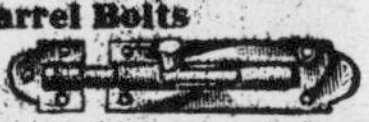

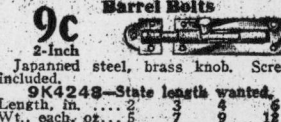

9c 2-Inch

Japanned steel, brass knob. Screws included.

9K4248—State length wanted.

Length, in.	2	3	4	6
Wt., each, oz.	5	7	9	12
Each	9c	11c	13c	17c

For Lumber, Millwork, Roofing and Complete Homes See Pages 1077 to 1091.

Coat and Hat Hooks

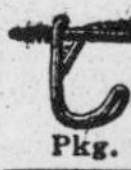

30c Pkg. 3 Doz.

Copper plated steel wire, threaded point. Length, 3 inches. Wt., 2 lbs.

9K4197—Pkg. of 3 doz.....30c

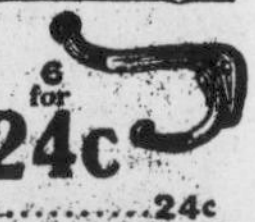

6 for 24c

Electro plated. With screws. Lgth., 3 in. Wt., ¾ lb.

9K4458—Lemon brass finish. 6 for.......24c
9K4824—Old copper finish. 6 for.......24c

Coat Hangers Tinned Steel Wire

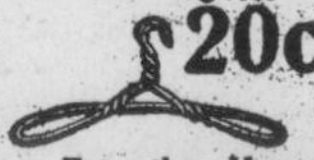

6 for 20c

9K2808 Wt., per set, 1¼ lbs. Set of 6...20c

For other Hangers see page 254

Highest Quality Lock Sets

Colonial Glass Knob Lock Set

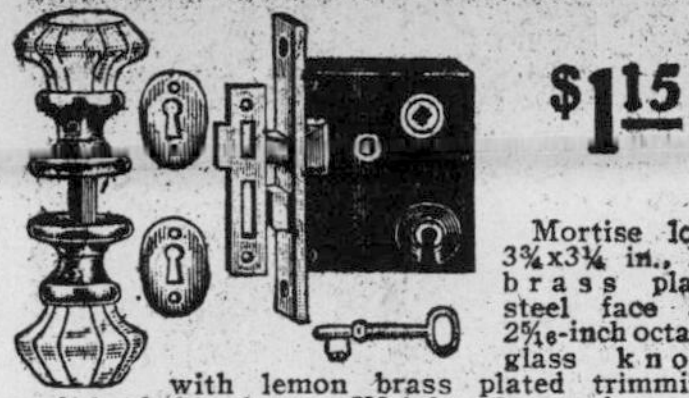

$1.15

Mortise lock, 3¾x3¾ in., has brass plated steel face and 2⅛-inch octagon glass knobs with lemon brass plated trimmings and keyhole plates. Weight, 2 pounds.
9K4645 ....$1.15

Extra Quality, same as above, but solid brass trim and keyhole plates. Mortise lock has heavy cast brass front. Glass knobs. Weight, 2½ pounds.
9K4649 ....$1.65

Glass Knobs only, lemon brass trimmings.
9K4060—Wt., per pr., 1 lb. Per pair..95c
Mortise Lock only, steel face. Wt., 1¼ lbs.
9K4644—Each 43c

Cylinder Rim Night Latch With 3 Keys

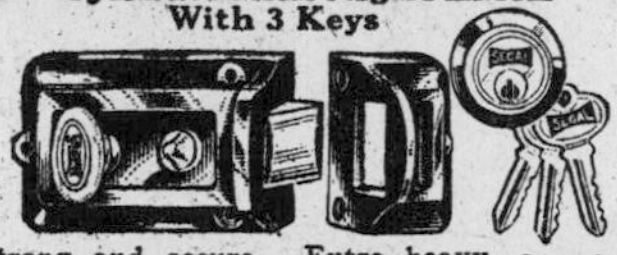

Strong and secure. Extra heavy japanned iron case. Cast brass turn, bolt and cylinder. Night latch has extra long throw with dead bolt locking device. For doors ⅞ to 2⅜ in. thick. Size of case, 3⅝x2⅝ in. Wt., 2 lbs.

$1.38

9K4021 ....$1.38

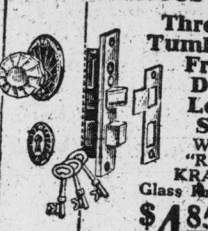

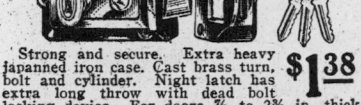

Tubular Rim Night Latch

With 2 Keys **58c**

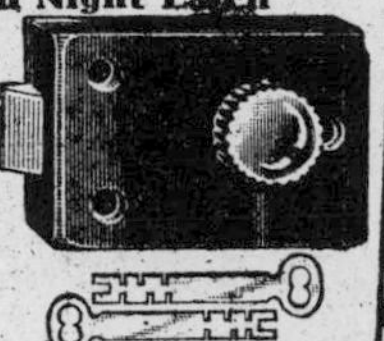

Japanned case. 3x2 inches. For doors up to 1¾ inches thick. Brass escutcheon, plated bolt and knob. Two keys. Weight, 1 pound.

9K4019 ....58c

Rim Lock Set

Reversible

38c Size, 4¼x3¼ in., with stop, iron bolts, tinned key, jet black knobs and keyhole plate.

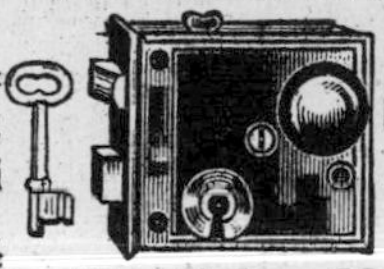

9K4045 — Set. Weight, 2 lbs...38c
9K4044—Lock only. Wt., 1¼ lbs....28c
9K4061—Knobs only. Weight, 1 pound. Per pair..............................15c

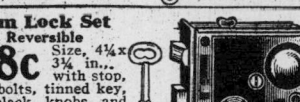

Rim Latch Set

Reversible

50c Size, 4x2¾ inch. Iron bolts, japanned case, jet black knobs.

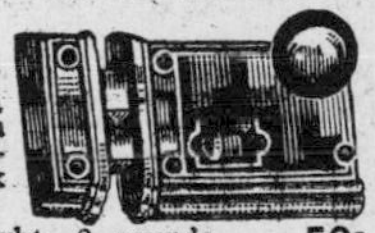

9K4027—Set. Weight, 2 pounds......50c
9K4026—Latch only. Weight, 1 lb......34c

Sets That Add $500.00 to the Sales of Your Home

"NARCISSUS" Three-Tumbler Front Door Lock Set

With "RICH KRAFT" Glass Knobs

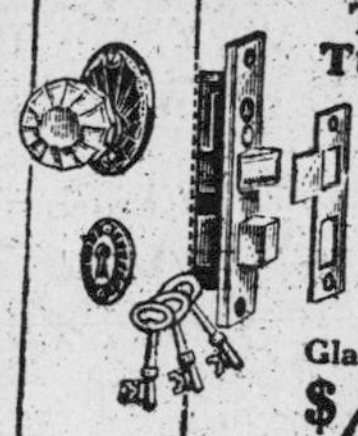

$4.85 Per Set

Strong lock for front door. Size, 5x3½ in. Heavy solid brass front bolts and strike. "RICH KRAFT" glass knobs on inside with solid cast bronze knob and trimmings on outside. Bronze key escutcheon. Sanded old brass finish. Wt., 4 lbs.
9K4552—Complete set with 3 keys $4.85

"NARCISSUS" Cylinder Front Door Lock Set

With "RICH KRAFT" Glass Knobs

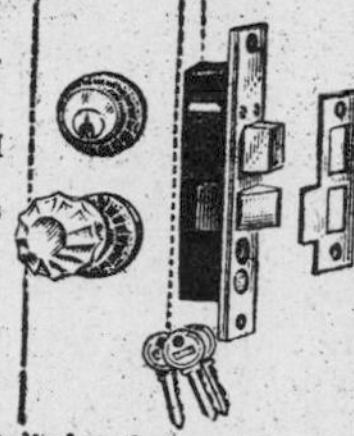

$9.25 Per Set

Thief-proof cylinder lock. Newest type. Size, 5½x3¼ in. Heavy solid brass front bolts and strike. Both bolts operated by one key. Handsome "RICH KRAFT" glass knobs on inside with solid cast bronze knob and trimmings on outside. Bronze key escutcheon. Sanded old brass finish. Wt., 5¼ lbs.
9K4550—Complete set with 3 keys $9.25

"NARCISSUS" French Window Lock Set

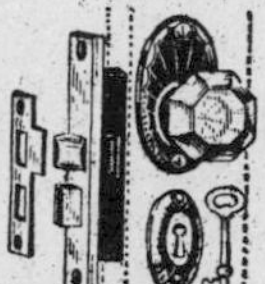

$3.50 Per Set

The "Narcissus" lock set on your French windows adds to their effectiveness and charm and increases the value of your home. Glass knob on outside with bronze key escutcheon. Genuine bronze lever handle and key plate on inside. Lock, 3⅝x1½ inches. Sanded old brass finish. Wt., 1¼ lbs.
9K4556 ....$3.50

"NARCISSUS" Cylinder Lock Set

For Entrance Doors

Ideal for bungalows. Strong cylinder lock, 5x3⅝ in., operated by thumb piece and "RICH KRAFT" glass knob from inside, key and solid bronze handle and thumb lever from outside. Heavy cast bronze trim. Sanded old brass finish. Wt., 7¼ lbs.

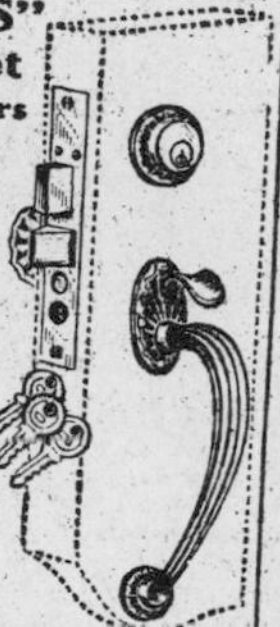

9K4551.$9.75

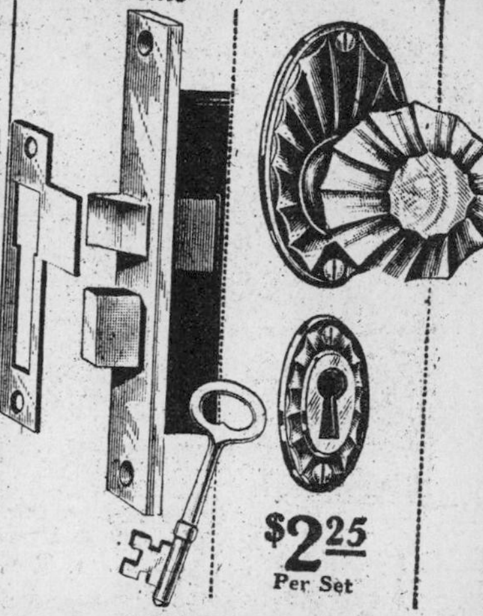

$2.25 Per Set

"NARCISSUS" Lock Sets for Inside Doors

With "RICH KRAFT" Glass Knobs

Extra quality values in artistic door sets. Easy spring lock. Size, 3⅜x3¾ in. Heavy cast brass face, bolts and strike. Knob trimmings and key plates are solid bronze. Sanded old brass finish. Weight, 2 pounds.
9K4553—Complete set for inside door.$2.25

Closet Door Set

Same as above but with bronze turn on inside of door in place of glass knob. Sanded old brass finish. Wt., 2 lbs.
9K4554.....$1.65

Bathroom Door Set

Similar to inside door set with nickel finish and thumbpiece on inside in place of key. Weight, 2 lbs.
9K4555...$2.65

Trunk Locks

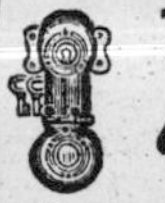

45c

Sturdy, attractive locks with two keys. Size, 6¼x1¾ inches. Weight, ⅝ pound.
9K4336—Brass plated steel...45c
9K4337—Solid brass $1.35

Foot Scraper 45c

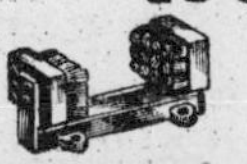

Brushes on each end of metal scraper, japanned finish. Complete with screws.
9K4186 — Weight, 2¼ pounds..............45c

DOOR BUTTS

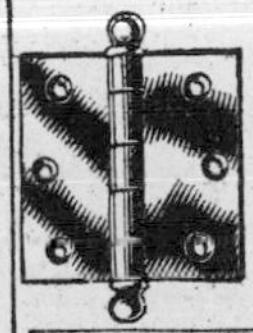

Non-Rising Loose Pin Plated

State size.
9K4568—Sanded Old Brass Finish.
9K4832 — Old Copper Finish.
9K4651—Lemon Finish

Size	Weight	9K4568 Per Pair	9K4832 9K4651 Per Pair
2½x2½ in.	8 oz.	17c	16c
3 x3 in.	1 lb.	18c	17c
3½x3½ in.	1¼ lbs.	19c	18c
4 x4 in.	2 lbs.	29c	28c
4½x4½ in.	2½ lbs.	50c	48c

9K4424—Nickel plated. Size, 3½x3½ in., for bathroom doors. Weight, 1¼ lbs. Pair 30c

Half Mortise

Size given is length of joint. State size.
9K4838—Old copper.
9K4654—Lemon brass.

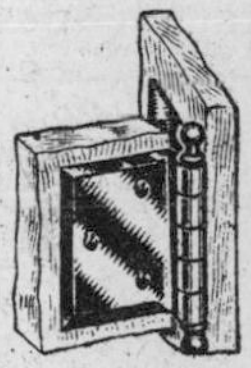

Size	Weight	Per Pair
1½ in.	4 oz.	18c
2 in.	4 oz.	23c
2½ in.	1 lb.	25c
3 in.	1 lb.	27c
3½ in.	1½ lbs.	28c
4 in.	2 lbs.	38c

9K4428—Nickel plated steel.

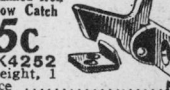

Size	Weight	Per Pair
2 in.	4 oz.	35c
3½ in.	1½ lbs.	45c

PADLOCKS for Every Purpose

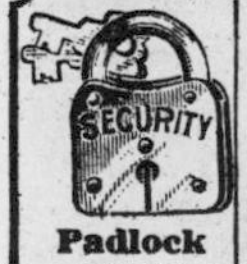

Padlock

All steel, brass plated. Two keys. Size, 2x2⅞ in. Wt., 4 oz.
9K4358 15c

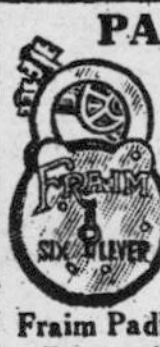

Fraim Padlock

Brass plated steel. Six lever. 2x3 in. Two keys. Wt., 5 oz.
9K4352 28c

Heavy cast brass case, nickel steel spring shackle. Two keys. Size, 2x2⅞ in. Wt., 7 oz.
9K4353 54c

Cylinder Padlock

Case hardened, file and saw proof, steel shackle. Two keys. Heavy cast bronze case. Size, 2 in. Wt., 1 lb.
9K4363.$1.65

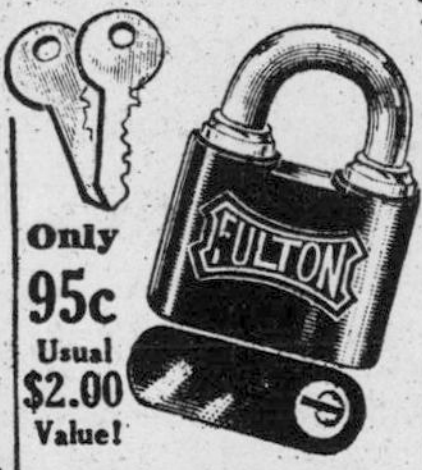

Only 95c Usual $2.00 Value!

Pin tumbler cylinder. Means safety for barn, garage or spare tire. No duplicate keys. Rust-proof malleable iron case. Genuine phosphor bronze spring shackle. With two keys. Width, 2 inches. Wt., 1 lb.
9K4355 ......95c

Corbin's Best $2.25

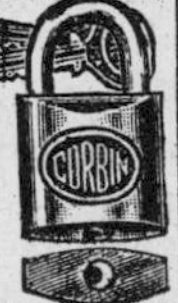

Most secure padlock made. Solid brass bored out. Two keys. Size, 1¾ in. wide, 2¾ inches long. Weight, 1 pound.
9K4366 ......$2.25

Combination Padlock

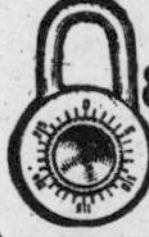

85c No keys needed. Size, 1¾ in. Wt., 6 oz.
9K4368—Steel case and shackle, brass knob 85c
9K4369—Brass case, steel shackle......$1.10

DRAWER LOCKS AND PULLS

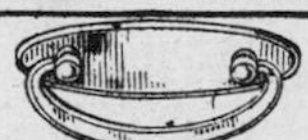

35c Brass Drop Handles

Plate, 3½ inches long. Weight, 2 ounces.
9K4812—Old copper. Each 35c
9K4482 — Lemon brass. Each 35c
9K4404 — Nickel plated. Each 40c

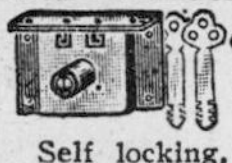

Chest Lock

Self locking, brass. For wood, 1 inch thick. Width, 3½ in. Wt., 2 oz.
9K4324 With screws. $1.40

Steel Drawer Lock

For wood, ⅞ inch thick, 1¾ in. wide. Brass cylinder. Wt., 2 oz.
9K4326 With screws....42c

Drawer Handles

Brass plate and brass plated steel handle. Bolts, 3 in. center to center.
9K4472
Wt., 6 oz. 6 for.40c

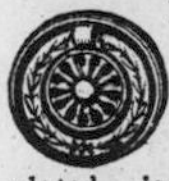

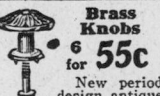

Ring Drawer Pulls 68c

Antique brass finish. Brass plated ring 1⅝ inch in diameter. Weight of six, 6 ounces.
9K4471–6 for..68c

Brass Box Corners

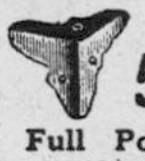

4 for 53c

Full Polished
9K4342
Size, 1¾x1¾ in. Wt., 4 oz. Pkg. of 4...53c

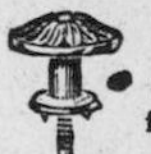

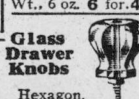

Brass Knobs

6 for 55c

New period design antique brass knob. Size, 1¼ in. Wt. of six, 5 oz.
9K4467
6 for 55c

Glass Drawer Knobs

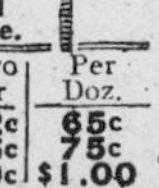

Hexagon.
9K4461
State size.

Size, In.	Wt., Oz.	Two for	Per Doz.
⅞	1	12c	65c
1⅛	2	15c	75c
1⅜	2	20c	$1.00

Cupboard Hardware

Fast Joint Narrow Steel Butts

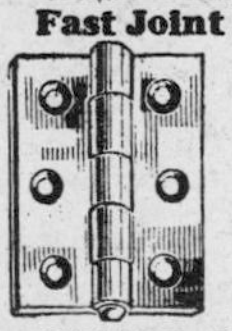

3 Pairs 1-INCH 10c

9K4388—Plain finish. With screws.

L'gth	Wt., 3 Prs.	3 Prs.
1 in.	2 oz.	10c
1½ in.	4 oz.	13c
2 in.	7 oz.	18c
2½ in.	¾ lb.	23c

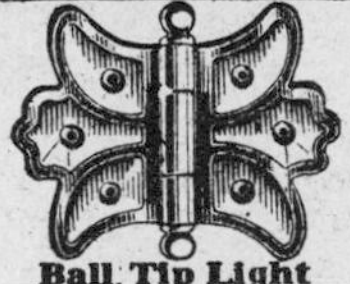

Ball Tip Light Cupboard Butts

For cupboards and china cabinets. Width, open, 2⅝ in. Weight, pair, 2 ounces.
9K4842—Old copper finish. Per pair..$0.12
Per doz. pairs. 1.28
9K4656—Lemon brass finish. Pair.$0.12
Per doz. pairs. 1.28

Drawer Pulls

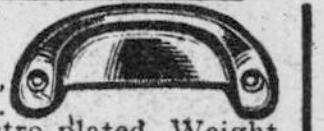

Length, 3½ in. Steel, electro plated. Weight of six, 6 ounces.
9K4816—Old copper polished finish. 6 for...19c
9K4480—Lemon brass finish. 6 for............19c

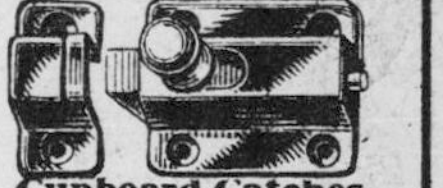

Cupboard Catches

Steel electro plated. Wt., 2 oz.
9K4792—Old copper polished finish 9c
9K4500—Lemon brass finish 9c

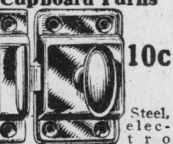

Light Cupboard Butts With Loose Pins

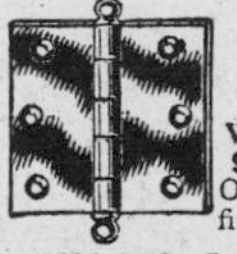

Wt., 5 oz.
9K4836
Old copper finish.
9K4653—Lemon brass.
Size, 2x2 in. Per pr..16c
Size, 2½x2 in. Per pr..18c
Size, 2½x2½ in. Pair..20c
9K4426—Nickel plated finish. Size, 2½x2 in., for medicine cases. Per pr..25c
9K4569—Sanded old brass finish. Size, 2½x2 inches. Per pair.........20c

Cupboard Turns

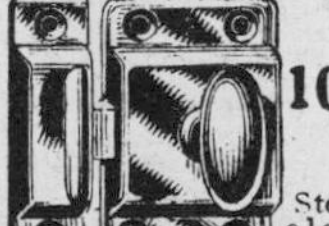

10c

Steel, electro plated. Size, 1¾x1⅞ in. Weight, each, 2 ounces.
9K4790—Old copper polished. 10c
9K4502—Lemon brass 10c
9K4408—Nickel plated 15c

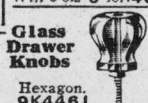

Japanned Iron Elbow Catch

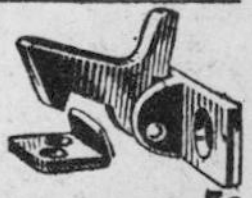

5c
9K4252
Weight, 1 ounce 5c

Cast Japanned Door Buttons

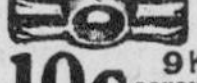

10c 9K4205 — With screws. State size.
Length, 1½ in.
Per Doz. Wt., 6 oz. Doz. 10c
Length, 2 in. Wt., ¾ lb.
Per dozen.........................12c

To Find What You Want, See Index Pages 550 to 570

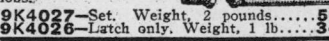

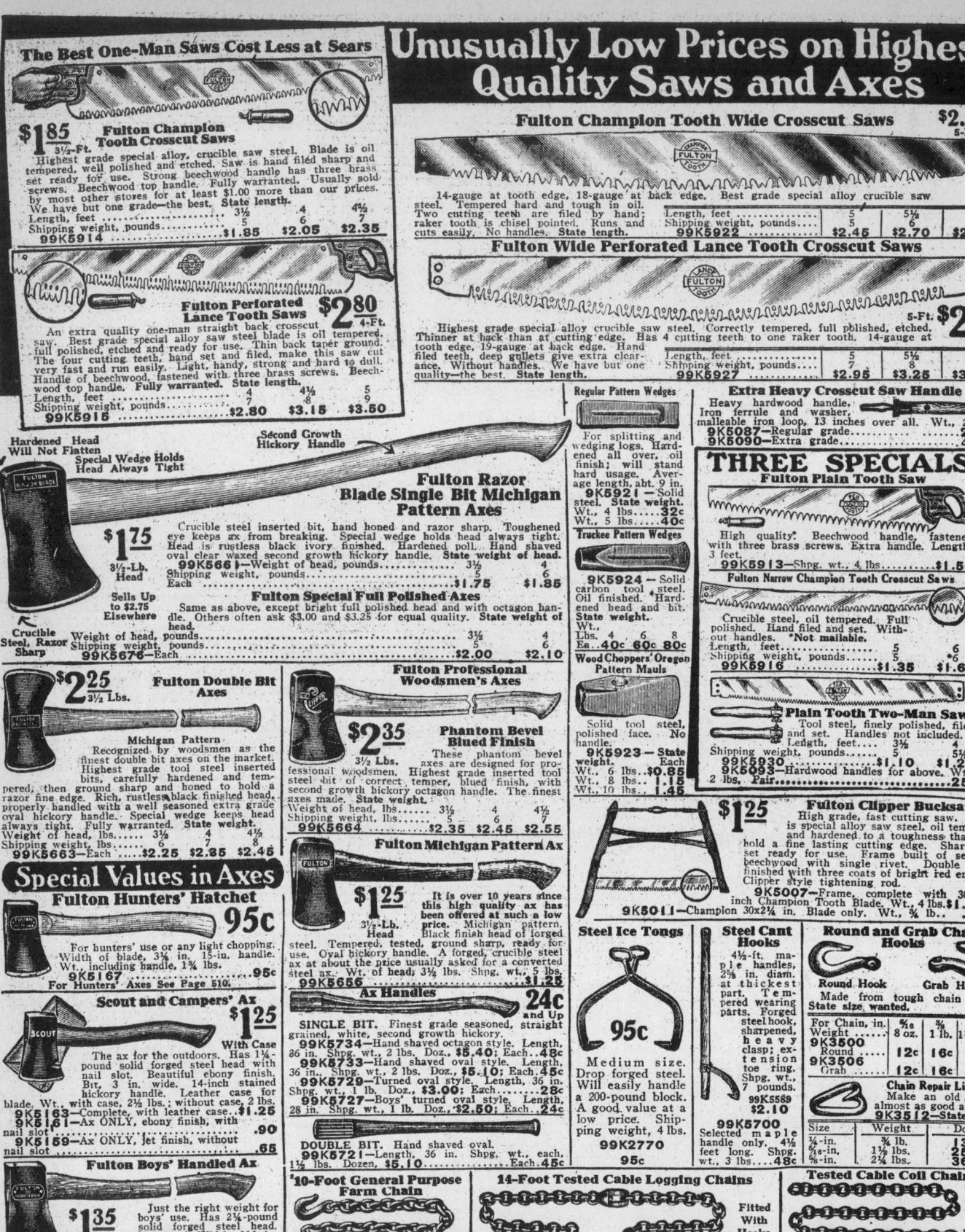

Famous Fulton Quality Circular Saws

Fulton Cut Off Saws · **Fulton Rip Saws** · **Fulton Cordwood Saws**

High grade crucible saw steel, accurately gauged and tempered. Carefully hammered, blocked, filed and set. Best results obtained when run at rated speed. We will supply saws with special size holes at no extra charge. Not mailable.

Dia., In.	G'ge	Arbor Hole, In.	Rev. per Minute	Wt., Lbs.	9K5000 Cut-off Saw Teeth	9K5000 Cut-off Saw Each	9K5001 Rip Saw Teeth	9K5001 Rip Saw Each
6	18	¾	4,800	1	100	$1.25	36	$1.25
8	18	⅞	4,500	1	100	1.75	36	1.75
10	16	1	4,000	1½	90	2.10	36	2.10
12	15	1	3,300	3	90	2.60	36	2.60
14	15	1⅛	2,800	4	90	3.20	36	3.20

Larger Sizes. ★Not Mailable

Dia., In.	G'ge	Arbor Hole, In.	Rev. per Minute	Shpg. Wt., Lbs.	99K5955 Cut-Off Saw Teeth	99K5955 Cut-Off Saw Each	99K5953 Rip Saw Teeth	99K5953 Rip Saw Each
16	14	1⅛	2,500	6	90	$3.95	36	$3.95
18	13	1¼	2,250	8	80	4.75	36	4.75
20	13	1⅝	1,950	12	80	5.50	36	5.50
24	11	1⅜	1,600	18	72	6.50	36	6.50
★26	11	1⅜	1,500	21	72	7.60	36	7.60
★28	10	1⅜	1,400	26	72	8.90	36	8.90
★30	10	1⅜ or 1½	1,300	29	72	9.85	36	9.85
★32	10	1⅝	1,120	38	72	10.75	36	10.75
★36	9	1⅝	1,000	50	80	13.90	36	13.90

Fulton Steel Band Saw Blades

Special saw steel. Filed and set. NOT BRAZED. We braze any length wanted at 35c per saw.

99K8130½—State width and length

Size, Band Saw	¼ in.	⅜ in.	½ in.	⅝ in.	¾ in.	1 in.
Shpg. Wt. per ft.	1 oz.	2 oz.	2 oz.	2 oz.	2 oz.	3 oz.
Per foot	7c	8c	9c	10c	11c	12c

Shipped from factory at CINCINNATI, OHIO.

9K5990—Silver Solder for Brazing Band Saw Blades. Per oz. $1.20

Saw Sets

9K5102—Size 3. For Lance tooth and single tooth long saws and small circular saws, from 20 to 14 gauge. Has sliding gauge thumbscrew adjustment. Length, 9½ in. Wt., 2 lbs. 95c

9K5103 — Size 4. For Champion wide tooth and crosscut saws from 20 to 14 gauge. Sliding gauge thumbscrew adjustment. Length, 9½ in. Weight, 2 pounds. 98c

9K5108—Size 5. For large circular saws, from 6 to 14 gauge. Screw adjustment. Length, 15 in. Weight, 3 pounds $2.10

$18.75 Foot Power

Manual Trainer Band Saw

Angle steel frame; 18x20-in. steel table top, 30 in. from floor. Ht., over all, 45 in., 11-in. swing. Three ¼-in. band saws furnished. Shipped from factory at CINCINNATI, OHIO.

99K8643⅓ — Foot power, as illustrated. Shpg. wt., 130 lbs. $18.75

99K8644⅓ — With 5½x2-in. pulley for power. Shpg. wt., 120 lbs. $16.75

Extra Blades for Above. Size ¼ x 66 in.:

99K8647⅓ — Pkg. of 3 blades, Shpg. wt., 1 lb. $1.35

Fulton Circular Cordwood Saw

$2.25 20-Inch

For Use on Saw Mandrels, Cordwood and Pole Sawing Machines

As the best cordwood saw that money can buy, we offer our Fulton at a real economy price. Material and workmanship of the finest. Meets every requirement of the professional wood cutter and stands up under every demand.

Finer Cordwood Saws Are Not Made

Guaranteed in Every Respect

Made of special analysis guaranteed first quality saw steel, hand smithed, blocked, filed and set. Of uniform gauge, or thickness, properly ground, tempered and well balanced; holds edge for a long time. Our special tooth, with deep round gullet, gives plenty of sawdust clearance.

99K5957—Furnished with standard 1⅜-inch diameter arbor hole. **We supply any size hole without extra charge. For crosscut sawing only.**

Diam. In.	20	24	★26	★28	★30	★32	★36
Gauge	13	11	11	10	10	9	9
Teeth in Saw	60	60	64	64	72	72	80
Shpg. wt., lbs.	11	17	19	24	29	35	42
1⅜-in. hole	$2.25	$3.25	$3.95	$4.45	$4.95	$5.90	$7.90

★Not mailable.

Circular Saw Mandrels

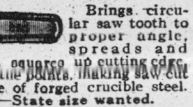

Pulley on End

State Size

Pulley in Center

Carefully machined. Fully warranted. Babbitted bearings. Arbors have left hand threads. Bolts for attaching. ★ Not mailable.

Size No.	Pulley, Diam. Face, In.	Shaft, In.	For Saws, Diam., In.	Size, Saw Hole, In.	Shpg. Wt., Lbs.	99K5574 Pulley on End	99K5573 Pulley in Center
0	2 x3	16½x ⅞	6	¾	18	$2.55	$2.58
1	2½x3½	16½x1 1/16	10	1	26	2.75	2.78
2	3 x4	19 x1 3/16	14	1⅛	31	3.70	3.75
3	3½x4½	21½x1 5/16	18	1¼	41	4.70	4.75
6	5 x6	28 x1 7/16	24	1⅜	55	7.20	7.25
7	5½x6½	30½x1 7/16	26	1⅝	61	8.40	8.45
★8	6 x7½	32½x1 9/16	30	1½	95	9.30	9.35

Saw Swages or Upsets

Brings circular saw tooth to proper angle, spreads and shapes point, squares up cutting edge, gives body to the points, making saw cut easily. Made of forged crucible steel.

9K5113—State size wanted.

Size	For Saws	Weight	
No. 1	5 to 10-gauge	1¼ lbs.	$4.40
No. 2	9 to 12-gauge	8 oz.	3.65
No. 3	12 to 14-gauge	4 oz.	2.90

For Tilting Table Saws

Steel plate holding boxes firmly for mounting on frame.

[illegible] Right hand saw mandrel with connecting box for mounting on frame with 60-lb. flywheel, Shpg. wt., 140 lbs. $11.20

99K8166⅓— Right hand saw mandrel with connection box for mounting on frame with 95-lb. flywheel. Shipping wt., 175 lbs. $13.15

Mandrel Sets

Have babbitted bearing boxes. 60 or 95-lb. flywheel, 5-in. pul[illegible] 48 in. long. **Left hand mandrels at same prices. Shipped from SO. WISC. or CENTRAL PA., whichever is nearer.**

For Flat Table Saws

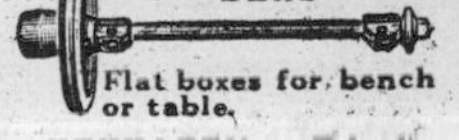

Flat boxes for bench or table.

99K8163⅓ — Right hand saw mandrel for flat table, with 60-lb. flywheel. Shpg. wt., 125 lbs. $9.75

99K8164⅓ — Right hand saw mandrel for flat table, with 95-lb. flywheel. Shpg. wt., 160 lbs. $11.75

Sawing Attachment for the Fordson Tractor

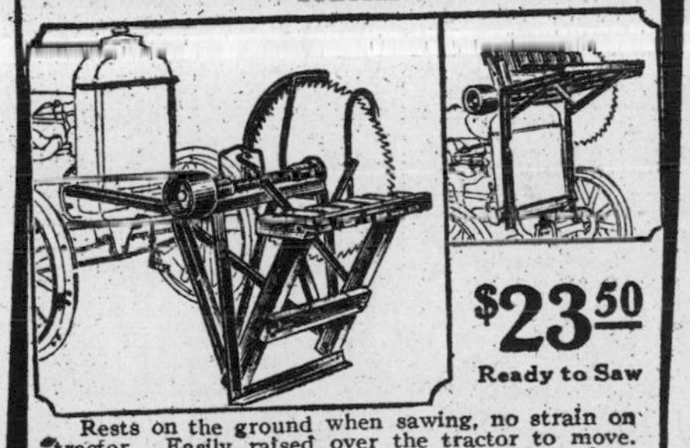

$23.50 Ready to Saw

Rests on the ground when sawing, no strain on tractor. Easily raised over the tractor to move. **Easily attached and ready for work in less than 5 minutes.** Mandrel—cold rolled shaft, 38 in. long, 1½-in. diam. Bearings babbitted and grooved for proper lubrication. Pulley, 10-in. diam., 6-in. face. **Shipped from factory in SOUTHERN WISCONSIN.**

99K8162⅓—Shpg. wt., 136 lbs. $23.50

$18.75 Without Saw

99K 8155⅓

60-Pound Balance Wheel

Tilting Table Saw Frame for Cordwood and Pole Sawing

Strong, sturdy and will give you long service. For cordwood saws with 1⅜-inch hole. Mandrels, cold rolled steel, 1½-in. diam., 48 in. long. Fitted with safety saw guards. Will take saws from 20 to 30 inches in diameter. Pulley, 5-in. diameter, 6-inch face. Shpg. wt., 275 lbs. **Shipped from factory in SOUTHERN WISCONSIN.**

99K8155⅓—Without saw $18.75

99K8161⅓—Same as 99K8155⅓, except with pole extension as shown in smaller cut. Without saw. Shipping wt., 295 lbs. $20.75

Pole Saw Frame

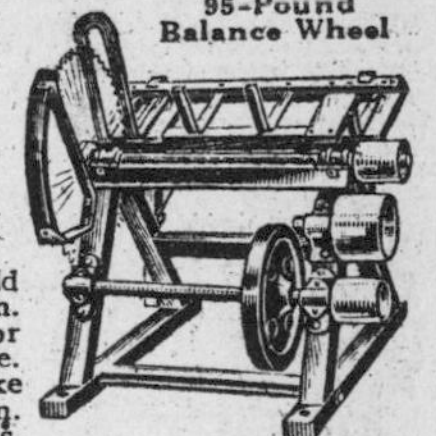

95-Pound Balance Wheel

Balance wheel on separate shaft out of the way; long poles or heavy cordwood, sawed easily. Upper and lower pulleys, 5-in. diam., with 6-in. face. Center pulley, 8-in. diam. with 6-in. face. Mandrels, cold rolled steel, 1½-in. diam., 48 in. long, for saws with 1⅜-in. hole. Safety saw guards. Take saws 20 to 30 in. diam. Shipping wt., 365 lbs. **Shipped from factory in SOUTHERN WISC.**

99K8150⅓—Without saw $27.50

Big Savings on Woodworking Machinery

DIAMOND 16-Inch Band Saw Machine

For Our Full Line of Woodworking Machinery Write for Our Catalog No. 528K

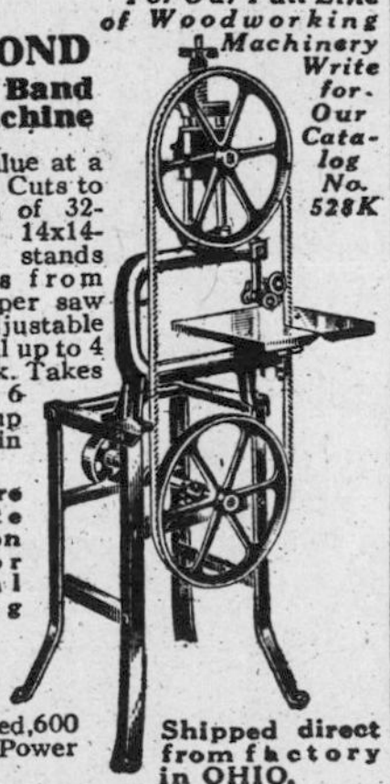

A big value at a low price. Cuts to the center of 32-inch circle. 14x14-inch table stands 40 inches from floor. Upper saw guide is adjustable for material up to 4 inches thick. Takes saws 10 ft. 6 in. long up to ½ inch in width.

For more complete description send for Special Catalog 528K.

Shpg. wt., 200 lbs. 5x2-inch pulley Speed, 600 R. P. M. Power ½ H.-P.

Shipped direct from factory in OHIO.

99K8222⅓ — Complete with one ⅛-inch band saw $42.50

Simplex Lathe Set
Consists of Metal Parts Only

Will swing material up to 11 in. in diam. Bed can be made as long as desired.

Spindle—1 in. in diam., threaded for face plate, taper socket for spur center. Nut and collar at both ends for circular saw or emery wheel up to 10 in. in diam., by 1 in. thick with ⅞-in. hole. Size of pulley, 3-in. diam., by 2-in. face. Ball bearing. Shipping wt., 60 lbs. **Shipped direct from factory in OHIO.**

99K8625⅓—Complete with spur center, 4¾-in. face plate and two chisel rests $13.50

Turning Chisels With Handle

99K8632⅓—Turning Chisels.

Size	Shpg. Wt.	
¼ in.	6 oz.	$0.80
½ in.	8 oz.	.85
¾ in.	¾ lb.	.90
1 in.	1 lb.	1.15
1½ in.	1¼ lbs.	1.35

Turning Gouges With Handle

99K8633⅓—Turning Gouges.

Size	Shpg. Wt.	
¼ in.	6 oz.	$0.90
½ in.	8 oz.	1.00
¾ in.	¾ lb.	1.15
1 in.	1 lb.	1.35
1½ in.	1 lb.	1.60

Shipped direct from factory in OHIO.

Gem Mortising and Tenoning Machine

Makes mortises up to 10 in. wide by 1 in. thick. Makes tenons up to 5 in. wide from one edge or 10 in. wide by reversing work and cutting from both edges and from ¼ to ⅝ in. thick with 1-in. shoulder on each side. Height, 6 ft. 3 in. Guide bed stands 32 in. from floor and tilts to angle up to 45 degrees. Floor space required, 2 ft. 4 in. x 2 ft. 6 in. Shpg. wt., 150 lbs.

Shipped direct from factory in OHIO.

99K8635⅓ With tenon tool and one ⅜-in. mortise chisel. $25.50

For Foot Power

Planing Mill Special

For Our Full Line of Woodworking Machinery Write for our Catalog No. 528K.

$495.00 Eight Machines in One

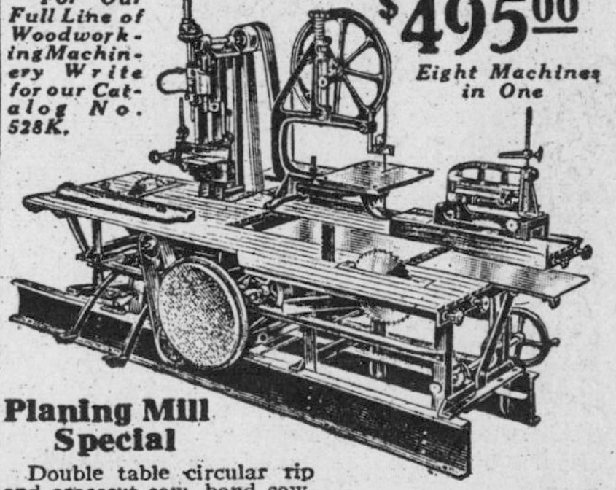

Double table circular rip and crosscut saw, band saw, swing cut-off saw, 12-inch jointer, tenoner, upright hollow chisel mortiser and borer, reversible spindle shaper and sanding machine. Shipping weight, 1,900 pounds. Floor space, 4 ft. 10 in. x 9 ft. 6 in. Tight and loose drive pulley, 10x4 in. face. Speed, 550 R.P.M. Power, 5 to 7½ H.-P. **Shipped direct from factory in OHIO.**

99K8685⅓—With one 12-inch cut-off saw, one 12-inch rip saw, one 10-inch crosscut saw, one ⅜-inch band saw and five belts $495.00

Order Blanks Are in Back of This Catalog

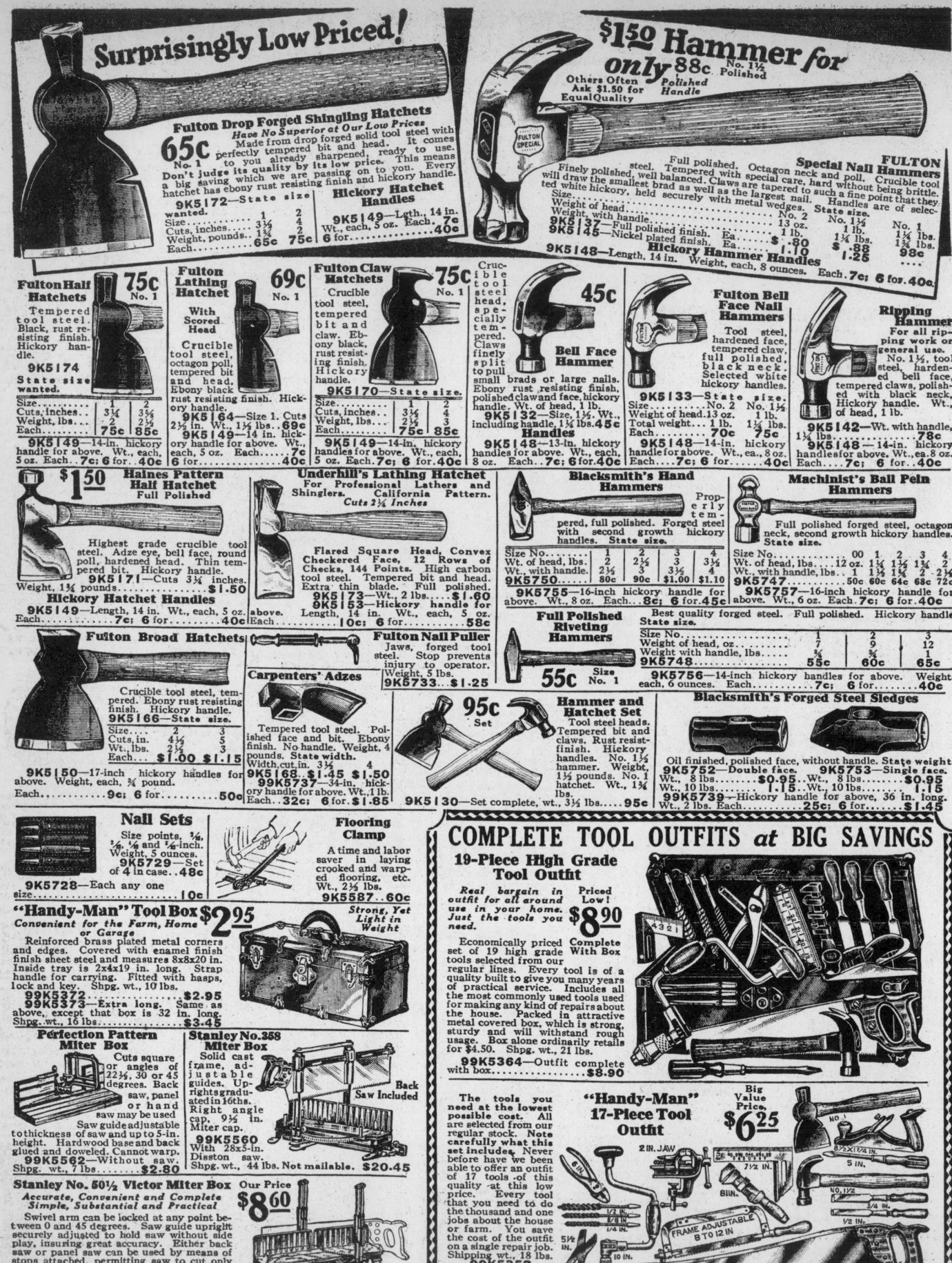

Absolutely Accurate LEVELS and RULES

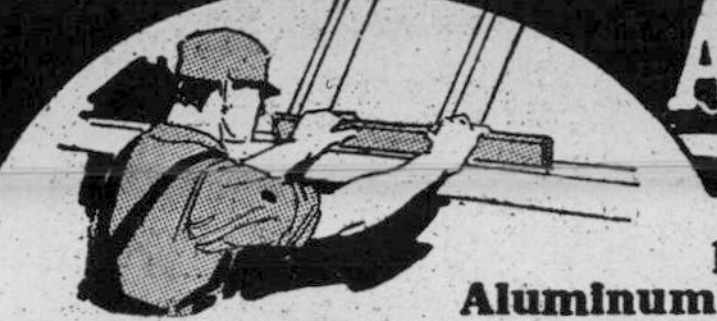

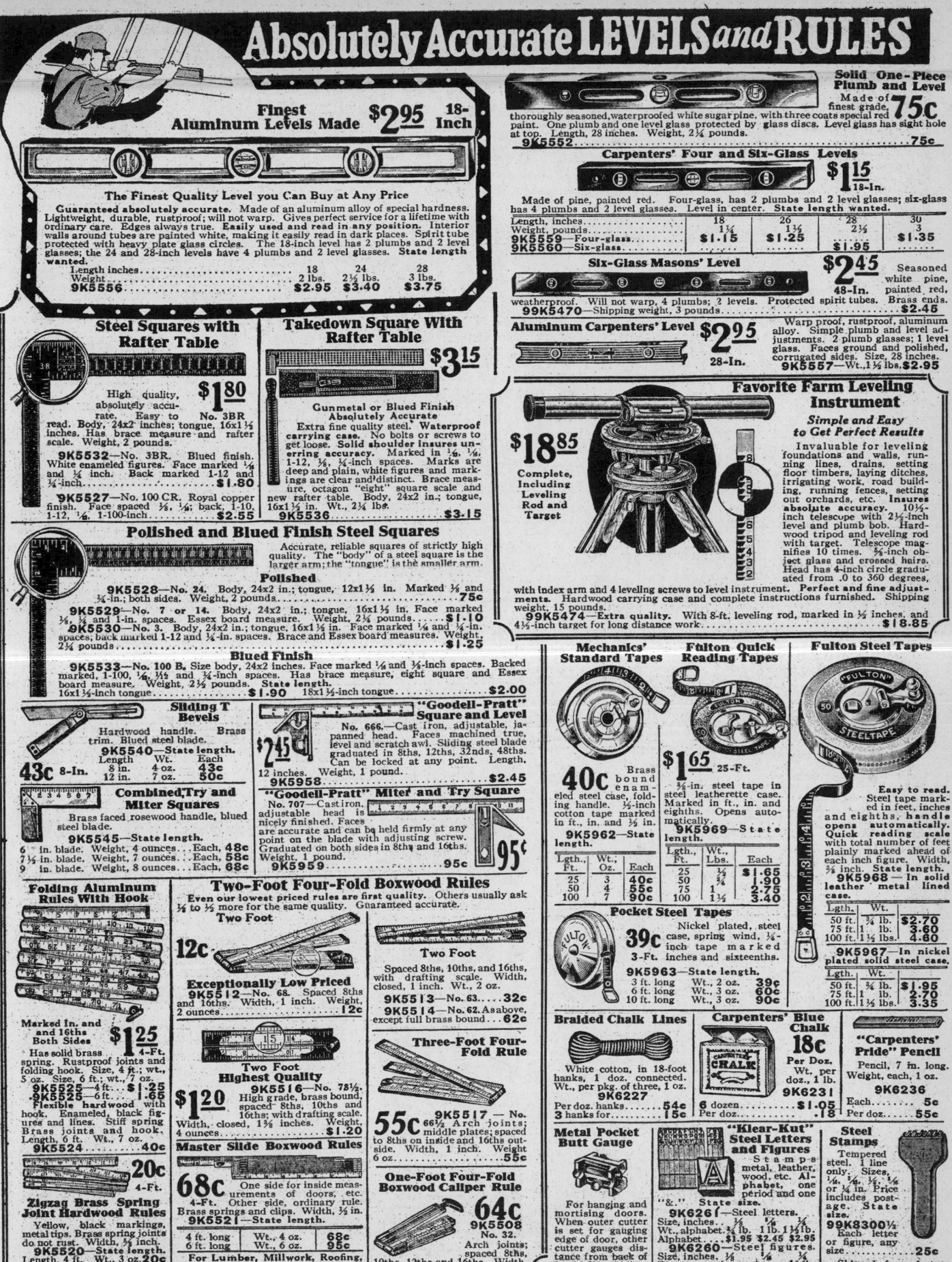

Finest Aluminum Levels Made $2.95 18-Inch

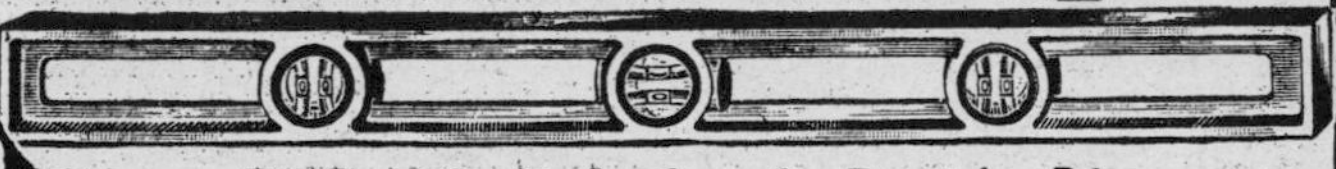

The Finest Quality Level you Can Buy at Any Price

Guaranteed absolutely accurate. Made of an aluminum alloy of special hardness. Lightweight, durable, rustproof; will not warp. Gives perfect service for a lifetime with ordinary care. Edges always true. **Easily used and read in any position.** Interior walls around tubes are painted white, making it easily read in dark places. Spirit tube protected with heavy plate glass circles. The 18-inch level has 2 plumbs and 2 level glasses; the 24 and 28-inch levels have 4 plumbs and 2 level glasses. **State length wanted.**

Length inches	18	24	28
Weight	2 lbs.	2½ lbs.	3 lbs.
9K5556	$2.95	$3.40	$3.75

Solid One-Piece Plumb and Level

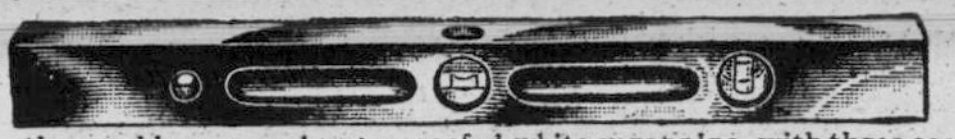

Made of finest grade, thoroughly seasoned, waterproofed white sugar pine, with three coats special red paint. One plumb and one level glass protected by glass discs. Level glass has sight hole at top. Length, 28 inches. Weight, 2¼ pounds. **75c**

9K5552 .... 75c

Carpenters' Four and Six-Glass Levels

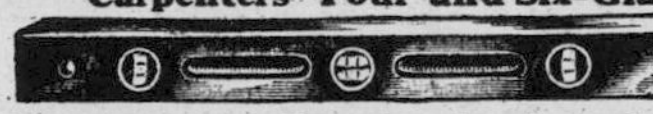

$1.15 18-In.

Made of pine, painted red. Four-glass, has 2 plumbs and 2 level glasses; six-glass has 4 plumbs and 2 level glasses. Level in center. **State length wanted.**

Length, inches	18	26	28	30
Weight, pounds	1¼	1⅓	2½	3
9K5559—Four-glass	$1.15	$1.25	....	$1.35
9K5560—Six-glass	....	....	$1.95	....

Six-Glass Masons' Level

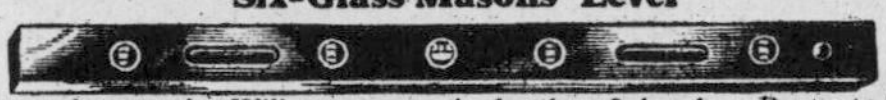

$2.45 48-In.

Seasoned white pine, painted red, weatherproof. Will not warp, 4 plumbs; 2 levels. Protected spirit tubes. Brass ends.

99K5470—Shipping weight, 3 pounds $2.45

Aluminum Carpenters' Level

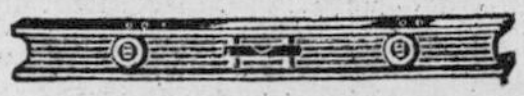

$2.95 28-In.

Warp proof, rustproof, aluminum alloy. Simple plumb and level adjustments. 2 plumb glasses; 1 level glass. Faces ground and polished, corrugated sides. Size, 28 inches.

9K5557—Wt., 1½ lbs. $2.95

Steel Squares with Rafter Table

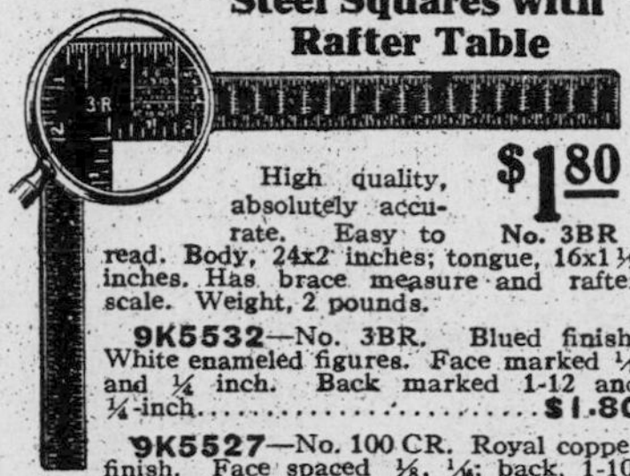

$1.80 No. 3BR

High quality, absolutely accurate. Easy to read. Body, 24x2 inches; tongue, 16x1½ inches. Has brace measure and rafter scale. Weight, 2 pounds.

9K5532—No. 3BR. Blued finish. White enameled figures. Face marked 1/16 and ¼ inch. Back marked 1-12 and ¼-inch $1.80

9K5527—No. 100 CR. Royal copper finish. Face spaced ⅛, 1/16; back, 1-10, 1-12, 1/16, 1-100-inch $2.55

Takedown Square With Rafter Table

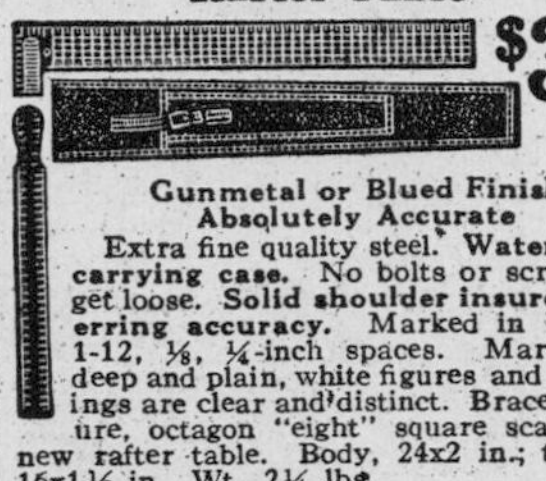

$3.15

Gunmetal or Blued Finish Absolutely Accurate

Extra fine quality steel. **Waterproof carrying case.** No bolts or screws to get loose. **Solid shoulder insures unerring accuracy.** Marked in 1/16, 1/16, 1-12, ⅛, ¼-inch spaces. Marks are deep and plain, white figures and markings are clear and distinct. Brace measure, octagon "eight" square scale and new rafter table. Body, 24x2 in.; tongue, 16x1½ in. Wt., 2¼ lbs.

9K5536 .... $3.15

Favorite Farm Leveling Instrument

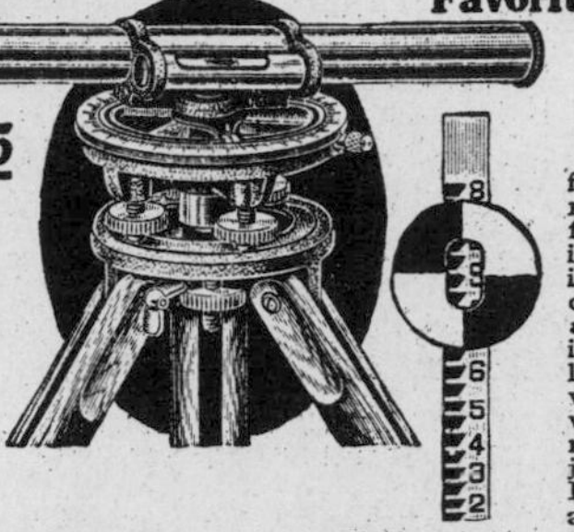

$18.85 Complete, Including Leveling Rod and Target

Simple and Easy to Get Perfect Results

Invaluable for leveling foundations and walls, running lines, drains, setting floor timbers, laying ditches, irrigating work, road building, running fences, setting out orchards, etc. **Insures absolute accuracy.** 10½-inch telescope with 2½-inch level and plumb bob. Hardwood tripod and leveling rod with target. Telescope magnifies 10 times. ⅝-inch object glass and crossed hairs. Head has 4-inch circle graduated from .0 to 360 degrees, with index arm and 4 leveling screws to level instrument. **Perfect and fine adjustments.** Hardwood carrying case and complete instructions furnished. Shipping weight, 15 pounds.

99K5474—**Extra quality.** With 8-ft. leveling rod, marked in ½ inches, and 4½-inch target for long distance work $18.85

Polished and Blued Finish Steel Squares

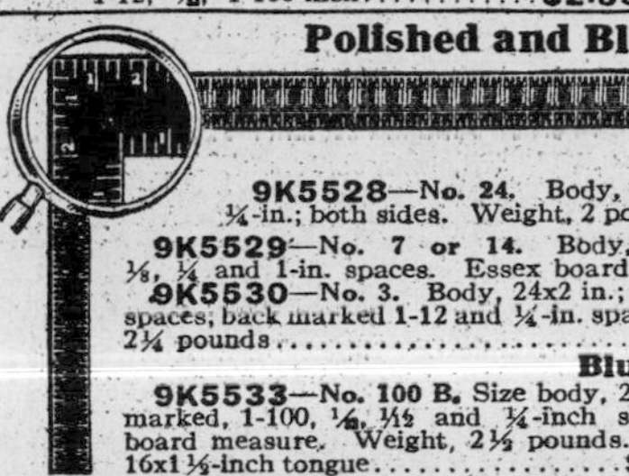

Accurate, reliable squares of strictly high quality. The "body" of a steel square is the larger arm; the "tongue" is the smaller arm.

Polished

9K5528—No. 24. Body, 24x2 in.; tongue, 12x1½ in. Marked ⅛ and ¼-in.; both sides. Weight, 2 pounds 75c

9K5529—No. 7 or 14. Body, 24x2 in.; tongue, 16x1½ in. Face marked ⅛, ¼ and 1-in. spaces. Essex board measure. Weight, 2¼ pounds $1.10

9K5530—No. 3. Body, 24x2 in.; tongue, 16x1½ in. Face marked 1/16 and ¼-in. spaces; back marked 1-12 and ¼-in. spaces. Brace and Essex board measures. Weight, 2¼ pounds $1.25

Blued Finish

9K5533—No. 100 B. Size body, 24x2 inches. Face marked 1/16 and ⅛-inch spaces. Backed marked, 1-100, 1/16, 1/12 and ¼-inch spaces. Has brace measure, eight square and Essex board measure. Weight, 2½ pounds. **State length.**
16x1½-inch tongue .... $1.90 18x1½-inch tongue $2.00

Sliding T Bevels

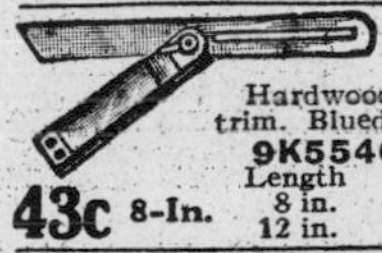

Hardwood handle. Brass trim. Blued steel blade.

9K5540—State length.

43c 8-In.

Length	Wt.	Each
8 in.	4 oz.	43c
12 in.	7 oz.	50c

"Goodell-Pratt" Square and Level

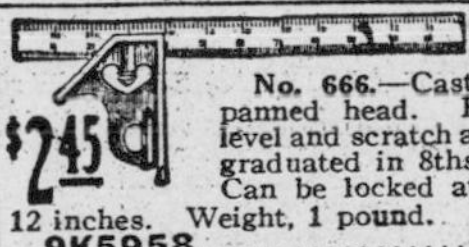

$2.45

No. 666.—Cast iron, adjustable, japanned head. Faces machined true, level and scratch awl. Sliding steel blade graduated in 8ths, 12ths, 32nds, 48ths. Can be locked at any point. Length, 12 inches. Weight, 1 pound.

9K5958 .... $2.45

Combined Try and Miter Squares

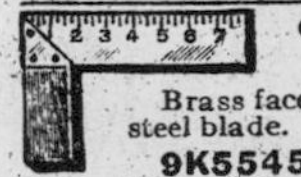

Brass faced rosewood handle, blued steel blade.

9K5545—State length.

6 in. blade. Weight, 4 ounces... Each, 48c
7½ in. blade. Weight, 7 ounces... Each, 58c
9 in. blade. Weight, 8 ounces... Each, 68c

"Goodell-Pratt" Miter and Try Square

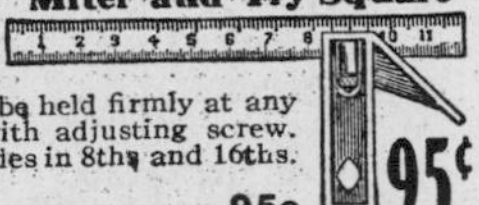

No. 707—Cast iron, adjustable head is nicely finished. Faces are accurate and can be held firmly at any point on the blade with adjusting screw. Graduated on both sides in 8ths and 16ths. Weight, 1 pound.

9K5959 .... 95c

95¢

Folding Aluminum Rules With Hook

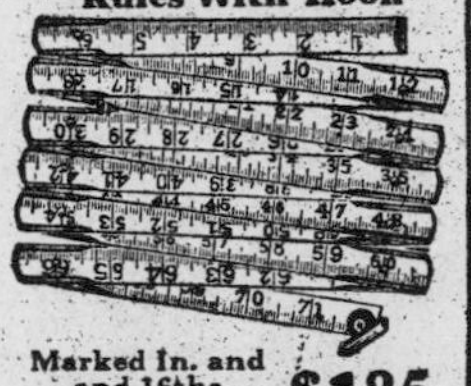

Marked In. and and 16ths Both Sides

$1.25 4-Ft.

Has solid brass spring. Rustproof joints and folding hook. Size, 4 ft.; wt., 5 oz. Size, 6 ft.; wt., 7 oz.

9K5525—4 ft. ... $1.25
9K5525—6 ft. ... 1.65

Flexible hardwood with hook. Enameled, black figures and lines. Stiff spring Brass joints and hook. Length, 6 ft. Wt., 7 oz.

9K5524 .... 40c

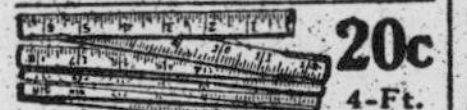

20c 4-Ft.

Zigzag Brass Spring Joint Hardwood Rules

Yellow, black markings, metal tips. Brass spring joints do not rust. Width, ⅝ inch.

9K5520—State length.
Length, 4 ft. Wt., 3 oz. 20c
Length, 6 ft. Wt., 4 oz. 30c
Length, 8 ft. Wt. 5 oz. 40c

Two-Foot Four-Fold Boxwood Rules

Even our lowest priced rules are first quality. Others usually ask ⅛ to ½ more for the same quality. Guaranteed accurate.

Two Foot

12c

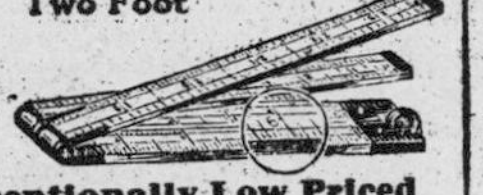

Exceptionally Low Priced

9K5512—No. 68. Spaced 8ths and 16ths. Width, 1 inch. Weight, 2 ounces 12c

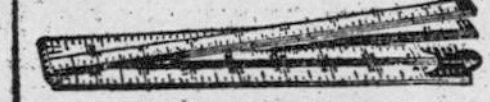

Two Foot

Spaced 8ths, 10ths, and 16ths, with drafting scale. Width, closed, 1 inch. Wt., 2 oz.

9K5513—No. 63 ..... 32c

9K5514—No. 62. As above, except full brass bound ... 62c

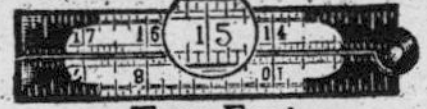

Two Foot Highest Quality

$1.20

9K5516—No. 78½. High grade, brass bound, spaced 8ths, 10ths and 16ths; with drafting scale. Width, closed, 1⅜ inches. Weight, 4 ounces $1.20

Three-Foot Four-Fold Rule

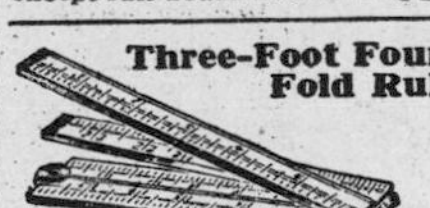

55c

9K5517 — No. 66½ Arch joints; middle plates; spaced to 8ths on inside and 16ths outside. Width, 1 inch. Weight 6 oz 55c

Master Slide Boxwood Rules

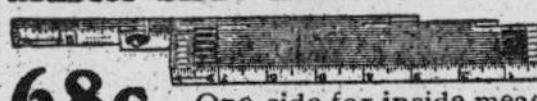

68c 4-Ft.

One side for inside measurements of doors, etc. Other side, ordinary rule. Brass springs and clips. Width, ½ in.

9K5521—State length.

4 ft. long	Wt., 4 oz.	68c
6 ft. long	Wt., 6 oz.	95c

For Lumber, Millwork, Roofing, and Complete Homes, See Pages 1077 to 1091.

One-Foot Four-Fold Boxwood Caliper Rule

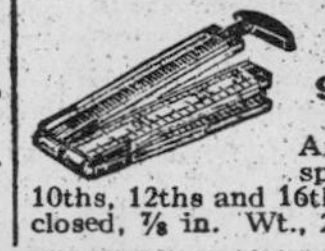

64c

9K5508 No. 32.

Arch joints; spaced 8ths, 10ths, 12ths and 16ths. Width, closed, ⅞ in. Wt., 2 oz. . 64c

Mechanics' Standard Tapes

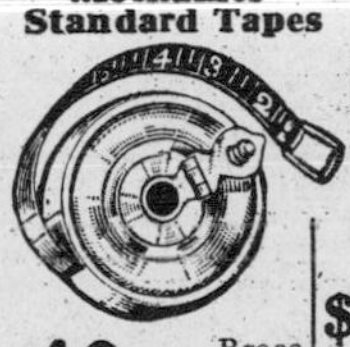

40c

Brass bound enameled steel case, folding handle. ½-inch cotton tape marked in ft., in. and ½ in.

9K5962—State length.

Lgth., Ft.	Wt., Oz.	Each
25	3	40c
50	4	55c
100	7	90c

Fulton Quick Reading Tapes

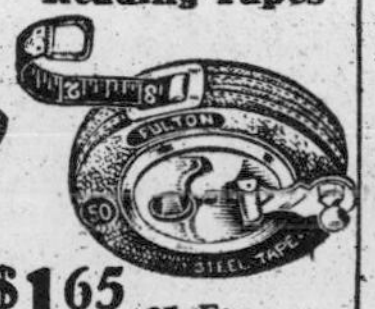

$1.65 25-Ft.

⅜-in. steel tape in steel leatherette case. Marked in ft., in. and eighths. Opens automatically.

9K5969—State length.

Lgth., Ft.	Wt., Lbs.	Each
25	½	$1.65
50	¾	1.90
75	1	2.75
100	1½	3.40

Fulton Steel Tapes

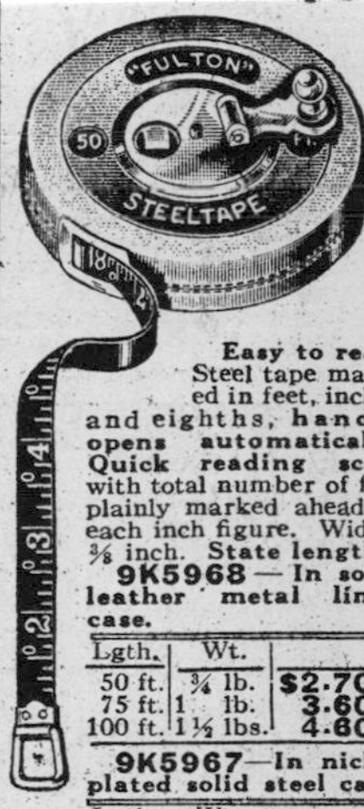

Easy to read. Steel tape marked in feet, inches and eighths, handle opens automatically. Quick reading scale with total number of feet plainly marked ahead of each inch figure. Width, ⅜ inch. State length.

9K5968 — In solid leather metal lined case.

Lgth.	Wt.	
50 ft.	¾ lb.	$2.70
75 ft.	1 lb.	3.60
100 ft.	1½ lbs.	4.60

9K5967—In nickel plated solid steel case.

Lgth.	Wt.	
50 ft.	¾ lb.	$1.95
75 ft.	1 lb.	2.70
100 ft.	1½ lbs.	3.35

Pocket Steel Tapes

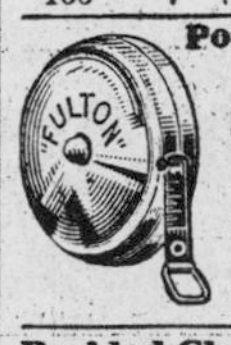

39c 3-Ft.

Nickel plated, steel case, spring wind, ¼-inch tape marked inches and sixteenths.

9K5963—State length.

3 ft. long	Wt., 2 oz.	39c
6 ft. long	Wt., 3 oz.	60c
10 ft. long	Wt., 3 oz.	90c

Braided Chalk Lines

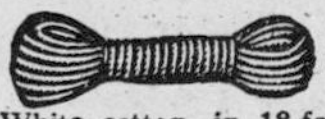

White cotton, in 18-foot hanks, 1 doz. connected. Wt., per pkg. of three, 1 oz.

9K6227
Per doz. hanks 54c
3 hanks for 15c

Carpenters' Blue Chalk

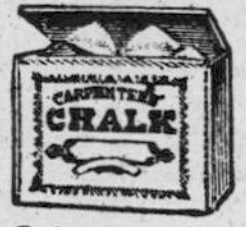

18c Per Doz.

Wt. per doz., 1 lb.

9K6231
6 dozen $1.05
Per doz. .... .18

"Carpenters' Pride" Pencil

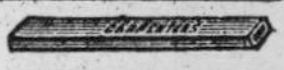

Pencil, 7 in. long. Weight, each, 1 oz.

9K6236
Each 5c
Per doz. 55c

Metal Pocket Butt Gauge

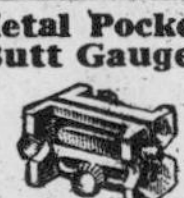

For hanging and mortising doors. When outer cutter is set for gauging edge of door, other cutter gauges distance from back of jamb. Wt., ¾ lb.

9K5504 $1.20

"Klear-Kut" Steel Letters and Figures

Stamps metal, leather, wood, etc. Alphabet, one period and one "&." State size.

9K6261—Steel letters.

Size, inches	⅛	3/16	¼
Wt., alphabet	¾ lb.	1 lb.	1½ lb.
Alphabet	$1.95	$2.45	$2.95

9K6260—Steel figures.

Size, inches	⅛	3/16	¼
Wt., per set	4 oz.	6 oz.	¾ lb.
Set of 9	65c	80c	95c

Steel Stamps

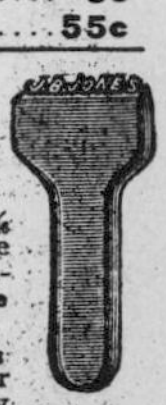

Tempered steel. 1 line only. Sizes, 1/16, 3/32, ⅛, 3/16 or ¼ in. Price includes postage. State size.

99K8300⅓
Each letter or figure, any size 25c

Shipped from factory in IOWA.

Genuine "FULTON" Highest Quality SCREW PLATES

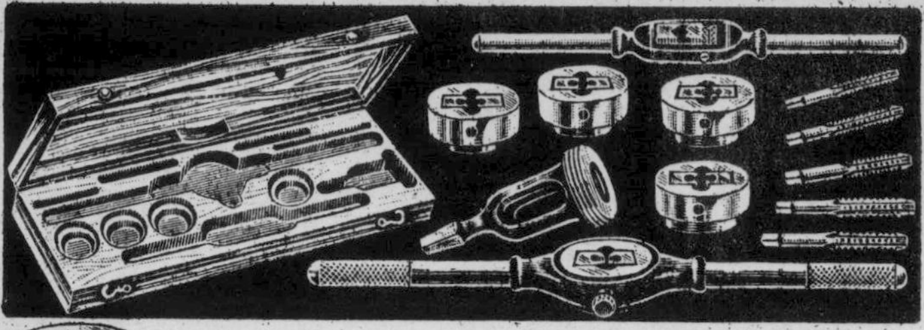

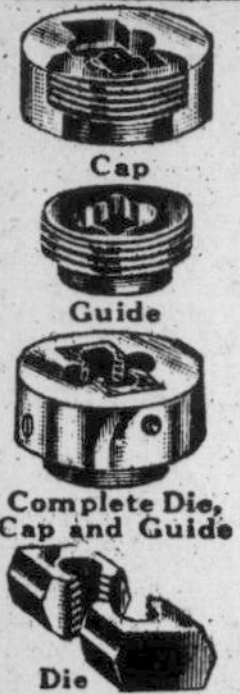

Cap

Guide

Complete Die, Cap and Guide

Die

Highest quality at lowest prices. Priced one-third or better under usual dealers' prices. Reversible type dies give the use of another set of cutting edges when one becomes worn. Bit brace attachment included for work in close quarters. Dies are tool steel in one piece. Adjustable for tight or loose fits on rods, bolts, etc. Mottled finish, polished knurled handles. Packed in varnished hardwood case.

$9.50 And Up

Sets with U. S. Standard Threads Cut 5 Sizes

99K5125—No. 1. One stock, length, 16 inches. One adjustable tap wrench, 11 inches long. Cuts sizes ¼^{20}, 5/16^{18}, ⅜^{16}, 7/16^{14} and ½^{13}. Complete with 5 taps and 5 dies. Dies and collets are 2 inches in diameter. Shipping weight, 11 pounds. Per set........ **$9.50**

Cut 7 Sizes

99K5126—No. 5. One stock, length, 23 inches; tap wrench, 15½ inches long. Cuts sizes ¼^{20}, 5/16^{18}, ⅜^{16}, 7/16^{14}, ½^{13}, ⅝^{11} and ¾^{10}. Complete with 7 taps and 7 dies. Dies and collets are 2¾ inches in diameter. Shipping weight, 20 pounds. Per set........ **$13.90**

Cut 9 Sizes

99K5127—No. 7. One stock, length, 26 inches. Adjusted tap wrench, 21 inches long. Cuts sizes ¼^{20}, 5/16^{18}, ⅜^{16}, 7/16^{14}, ½^{13}, ⅝^{11}, ¾^{10}, ⅞^{9} and 1^{8}. Complete with 9 taps and 9 dies. Dies and collets are 2¾ inches in diameter. Shipping weight, 27 pounds. Per set........ **$23.40**

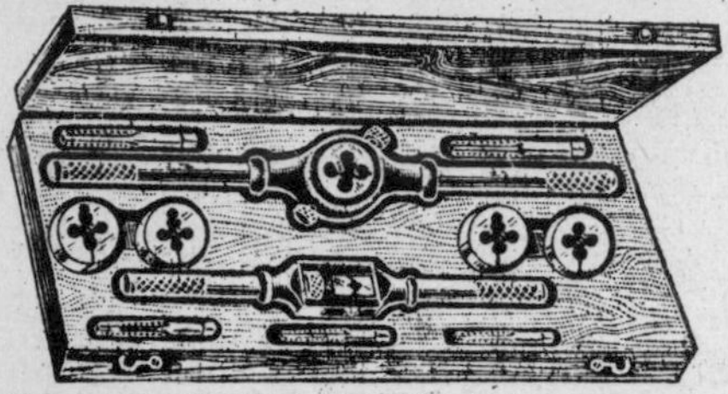

Fulton Screw Plates

Packed in varnished hardwood case

99K5116—No. 1. Cuts 5 sizes U. S. Standard Threads as follows: ¼^{20}, 5/16^{18}, ⅜^{16}, 7/16^{14} and ½^{13}. One 16-in. stock. Adjustable 11-in tap wrench. Shpg. wt., 8 lbs... **$7.25**

99K5117—No. 31. Cuts 5 sizes S. A. E. Threads as follows: ¼^{28}, 5/16^{24}, ⅜^{24}, 7/16^{20} and ½^{20}. All other parts similar to set above. Shipping weight, 8 pounds........ **$7.30**

99K5118—No. 5. Cuts 7 sizes U. S. Standard Threads as follows: ¼^{20}, 5/16^{18}, ⅜^{16}, 7/16^{14}, ½^{13}, ⅝^{11} and ¾^{10}. One 23½-in. stock. Adjustable 15-in. tap wrench. Shipping weight, 15 pounds........ **$10.75**

99K5119—No. 35. Cuts 7 sizes S. A. E. Threads as follows: ¼^{28}, 5/16^{24}, ⅜^{24}, 7/16^{20}, ½^{20}, ⅝^{18} and ¾^{16}. All other parts similar to set above. Shipping weight, 15 pounds........ **$10.80**

99K5120—No. 7. Cuts 9 sizes U. S. Standard Threads as follows: ¼^{20}, 5/16^{18}, ⅜^{16}, 7/16^{14}, ½^{13}, ⅝^{11}, ¾^{10}, ⅞^{9} and 1^{8}. One 26-in. stock. 11 and 19-in. tap wrenches. Shpg. wt., 27 lbs.. **$16.95**

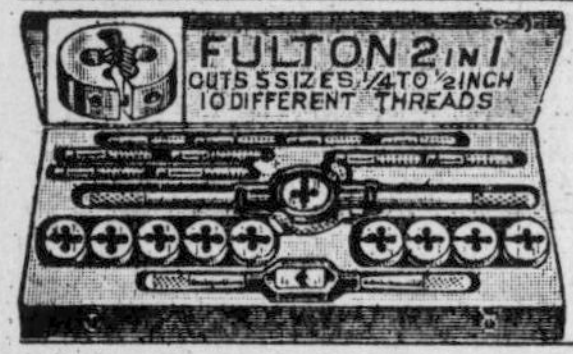

FULTON 2 in 1 Combination Screw Plate

Both U. S. Standard and S. A. E. Threads

99K5122—Cuts 5 sizes, 10 different threads. U. S. Standard. Size, in., ¼^{20}, 5/16^{18}, ⅜^{16}, 7/16^{14} and ½^{13}. S. A. E. Thread. Size, in., ¼^{28}, 5/16^{24}, ⅜^{24}, 7/16^{20}, ½^{20}. With 10 taps and 10 dies. Dies, 1½ in. in diam. Adjustable 11-in. tap wrench. Adjustable 16-in. guide stock. In varnished hardwood case. Shipping weight, 8 pounds........ **$11.95**

Greenfield Button Die Screw Plates

$4.95

U. S. Standard Threads. Tap wrench, round, adjustable dies, 13/16-inch in diameter. Stock, 6¼ inches long. Weight, per set, 2 pounds.

9K5658—No. DD6. Fractional sizes. Cuts 6 sizes as follows: 7/64^{48}, ⅛^{40}, 5/32^{36}, 3/16^{24}, 7/32^{24} and ¼^{20}.
Per set........ **$4.95**

9K5659—No. D10. Machine screw sizes. Cuts 10 sizes as follows: 2^{56}, 3^{48}, 4^{36}, 5^{30}, 6^{32}, 8^{32}, 10^{24}, 10^{32}, 12^{24} and 14^{20}
Per set........ **$7.95**

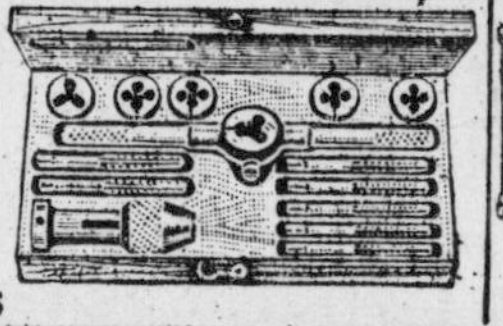

Blacksmiths' Stocks and Dies

Genuine Butterfield Blacksmiths' Stocks and Dies

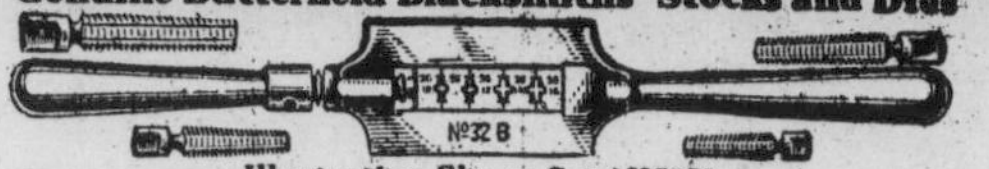

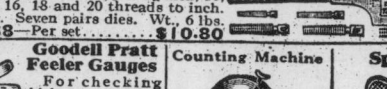

Illustration Shows Set 9K5673

Stock and die sets of high quality that offer the thrifty a wonderful opportunity to save. Taps and dies are made of hardened tempered steel. Perfect fit and adjustment. All parts guaranteed against defective material or workmanship.

U. S. Standard — Factory No. 41L. 3 taps, 3 dies. Cuts ⅜^{16}, 5/16^{18}, ¼^{20} threads to inch. Weight, 2½ pounds. **9K5669** Per set........ **$4.50**

V-Thread — Factory No. 32B. 4 taps, 4 dies. Cuts ¾ to ¼ inch. 10, 12, 14 and 16 threads to inch. Weight, 6 pounds. **9K5673** Per set........ **$5.80**

U. S. Standard — Factory No. 32E. 4 taps, 4 dies. Cuts ⅜^{16}, ½^{13}, ⅝^{11}, ¾^{10} threads to inch. Weight, 6 pounds **9K5676** Per set........ **$6.65**

Butterfield's Blacksmiths' Separate Plate, Stock and Dies V-Thread—Taps and Dies

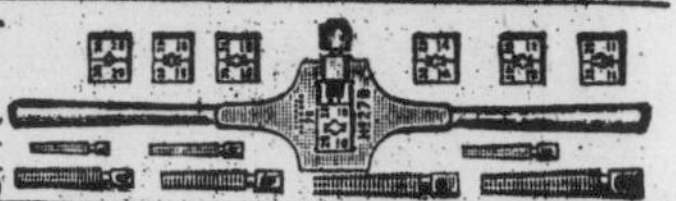

Factory No. 27D, cuts ¾ to 5/16 inch, 10, 11, 12, 14, 16, 18 and 20 threads to inch. Seven taps. Seven pairs dies. Wt., 6 lbs.
9K5668—Per set........ **$10.80**

Goodell Pratt Feeler Gauges

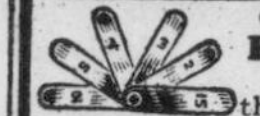

For checking thickness, gauging exhaust and valve openings. Marked by thousandths.

9K5985—State No. of leaves wanted.

Six leaves, .002, .003, .004, .005, .010 and .015. Length, 2¼ inches. Shpg. wt., 1 oz.... **44c**

Twenty-four leaves, .002 to .025 inch. Length, 2¾ inches. Shipping weight, 2 oz.... **$1.90**

Counting Machine

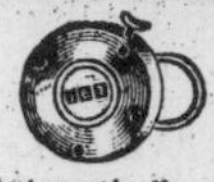

Automatically registers from 1 to 999. Can be set to zero at will. Nickel plated. Weight, 4 ounces.
9K5989 **$3.80**

Speed Indicator

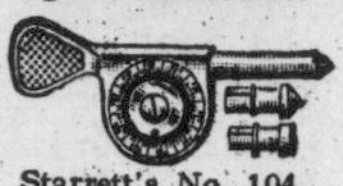

Starrett's No. 104. Metal handle. Graduations show every revolution. Wt., 4 oz.
9K5984—With two rubber tips........ **95c**

Starrett's No. 9 Combination Set

$4.95

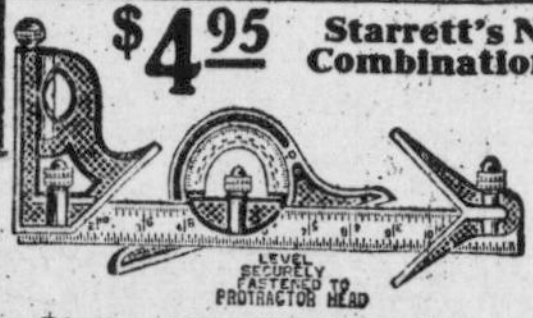

Blade graduated in 8ths, 16ths, 32nds and 64ths. Miter head, bevel protractor head, level attachment and center head. Wt., 2 lbs.
9K5961........ **$4.95**

Blacksmiths' Taper Taps

9K5679—Highly tempered steel. Easy cutting. Right hand. State size and number of threads.

Size, in.	¼	5/16	⅜	7/16	½	⅝
Threads to inch	20	18	16	14-16	12-14	12
Wt., oz.	1	1	1	2	2	2
Each	32c	35c	40c	43c	50c	64c

Kurled Center Punch

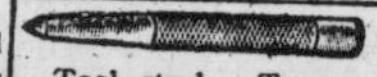

Tool steel. Tempered at both ends. Diameter, ⅜ inch. Weight, 2 ounces.
9K5734........ **10c**

CALIPERS and DIVIDERS

Starrett's Yankee Calipers

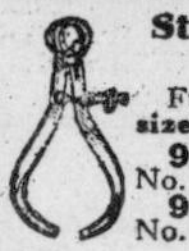

Full polished. State size.

9K5974—Outside. No. 79.

9K5975—Inside. No. 73 Spring Nut.

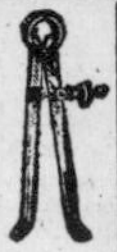

Size, Inches	4	6	8
Weight, ounces	3	5	6
Each	80c	90c	$1.05

Starrett's Perfect Firm Joint Screw Adjusting Calipers

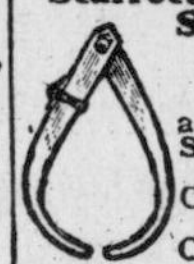

Full Polished

High grade steel. Quick, accurate adjustment. State size.

9K5976—Outside Calipers. No. 34.

9K5977—Inside Calipers. No. 35.

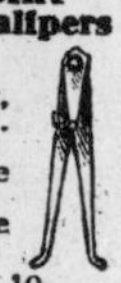

Size, inches	6	8	10
Weight	4 oz.	6 oz.	¾ lb.
Each	90c	$1.12	$1.35

Forged Steel Wing Calipers

Polished high quality tool steel.
9K5496—State size.

Size	Weight	Each
6 in.	4 oz.	48c
8 in.	6 oz.	65c
10 in.	8 oz.	85c

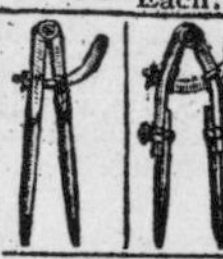

Extension Dividers

9K5498—State size. Polished.

Size, In.	Scribes Circle	Wt., Lb.	Each
6	17 in.	½	$1.00
8	22 in.	¾	1.20
10	24 in.	1	1.30

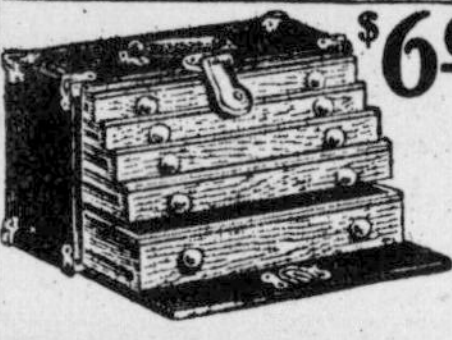

$6.65

Machinists' and Pattern Makers' Metal Covered Tool Case

5 Standard Size Drawers

A convenient chest for carrying tools from job to job. Covered with baked enameled steel, olive color. Light in weight, yet strong enough to stand the knocks and bumps of everyday use. Lid slides back out of the way and when closed swings up in front of drawers, locking all of them. Has five drawers of standard size, sturdy construction and bottoms are lined with green cloth. Size Size, 12x7¾x20 inches. Shpg. wt., 16 lbs.
99K5374........ **$6.65**

GUARANTEED FILES AT LOWEST PRICES

Fulton Handy File Set

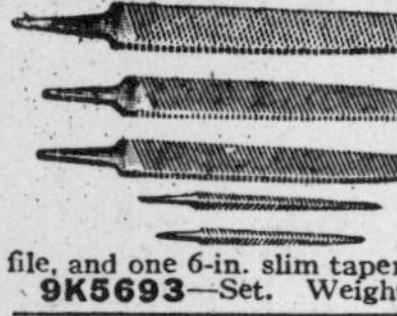

5 High Quality Files

Useful around the home, shop or farm. Well tempered, fast free cutting files. One each 8-in., 10-in. and 12-in. mill files; one 5-in. slim taper saw file, and one 6-in. slim taper saw file.
9K5693—Set. Weight, 1¾ pounds........ **65c**

Slim Taper Files

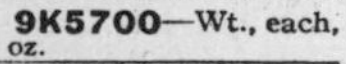

9K5700—Wt., each, 1 oz.

Size	Each	Six for
4 in.	8c	45c
5 in.	9c	50c
6 in.	12c	68c

Extra Slim Taper Files

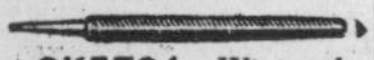

9K5701—Wt., each, 1 oz.

Size	Each	Six for
4 in.	8c	46c
6 in.	10c	56c

Weeds Special Slim Hand Saw Files

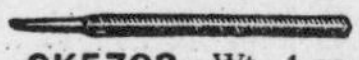

9K5702—Wt., 1 oz.

Size	Each	Six for
5 in.	15c	$0.85
6 in.	20c	1.14

Fulton Round Bastard Files

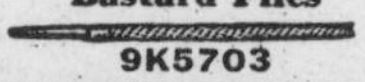

9K5703

Size	Wt.	Each	Six
4 in.	1 oz.	8c	$0.45
6 in.	2 oz.	12c	.68
8 in.	4 oz.	15c	.85
10 in.	4 oz.	18c	1.00
12 in.	8 oz.	22c	1.25

Fulton Guaranteed Mill Files

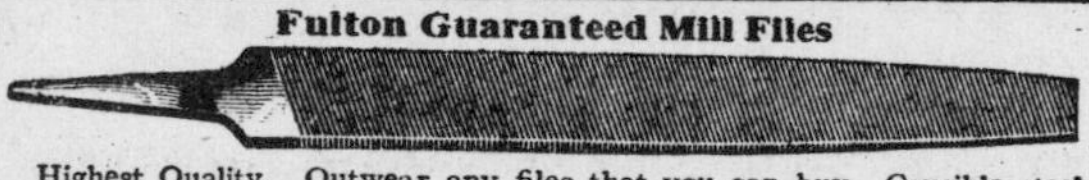

Highest Quality. Outwear any files that you can buy. Crucible steel, hardened and tempered. State length.

Size, inches	6	8	10	12	14	16
Weight	2 oz.	5 oz.	9 oz.	¾ lb.	1¼ lbs.	1¾ lbs.
9K5704—Each	9c	13c	18c	24c	33c	45c
Six for	50c	72c	$1.00	$1.35	$1.88	$2.57
9K5705—1 Round Edge. Each	14c	20c	26c	......	......	
Six for	78c	$1.14	$1.46	......	......	

Fulton Half Round Bastard Files

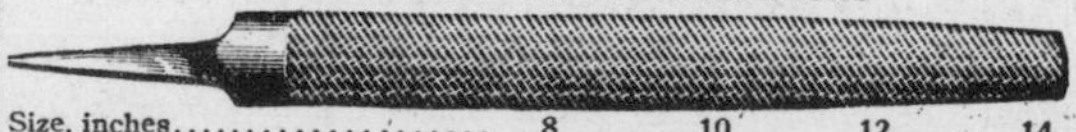

Size, inches	8	10	12	14
Weight	4 oz.	8 oz.	¾ lb.	1½ lbs.
9K5708—State size. Each	20c	26c	38c	48c
Six for	$1.18	$1.49	$2.18	$2.75

Fulton Flat Bastard Files—Coarse Cut

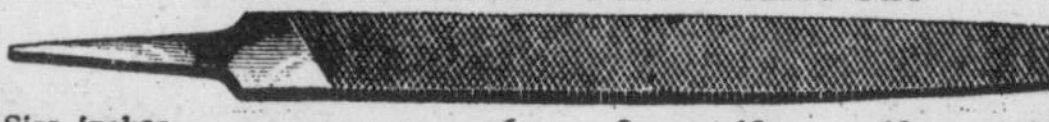

Size, inches	6	8	10	12	14
Weight	2 oz.	6 oz.	¾ lb.	1 lb.	1½ lbs.
9K5707—State size. Each	12c	17c	22c	30c	40c
Six for	68c	97c	$1.25	$1.70	$2.25

Fulton Half Round Wood Rasp

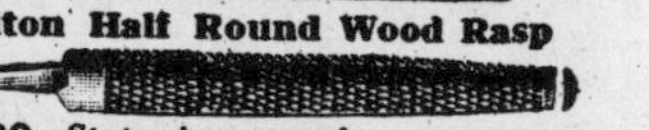

9K5709—State size wanted.

Size	Weight	Each	Six for
10 in.	8 oz.	44c	$2.50
12 in.	1 lb.	58c	3.35
14 in.	1¼ lbs.	78c	4.45

Fulton E-Z-Cut Horse Rasp

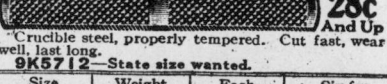

28c And Up

Crucible steel, properly tempered. Cut fast, wear well, last long.
9K5712—State size wanted.

Size	Weight	Each	Six for
12 in.	1½ lbs.	28c	$1.60
14 in.	2 lbs.	36c	2.05
16 in.	3 lbs.	48c	2.74
18 in.	3½ lbs.	65c	3.72

Magneto File

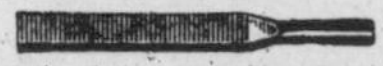

For filing magneto points. Width, ¼ in.; lgth., 5½ in. Wt., each, 1 oz. **9K5706**
Each........ **10c**
Six for........ **50c**

File Handle 9c

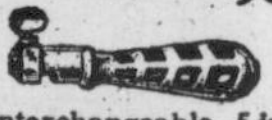

Interchangeable, 5 in. long. Wt., 4 oz.
9K5696.... **9c**

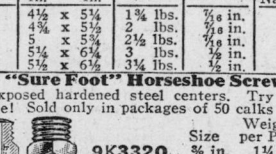

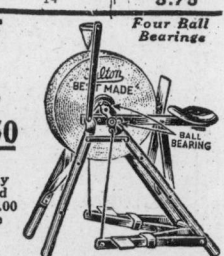

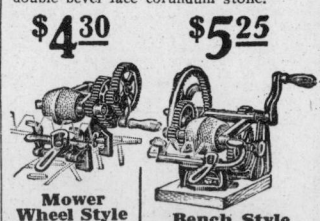

Mail Boxes Made According to U.S. Gov't Regulations

PRICED LOW

89c

Galvanized sheet steel box for ordinary mail only. High quality, extra strong, most popular style made. Buy a box that will last for years. It's long enough to take newspapers and periodicals. **Has coin holder. Turned edges; riveted joints.** Nail holes already punched for quickly mounting box on board or post. **If requested we stencil your name on both sides and send you cardboard stencil free.** This stencil can be used in marking bags, boxes, implements, etc., with your name. Inside measurements, 18½ inches long, 6¼ inches wide, 7½ inches high. Shipping weight, 9 pounds.

99K2845.................................... **89c**

Rural Delivery Box No. 2

$2.80

Extra Large Size for Parcel Post Mail. Made According to U. S. Government Regulations.

When requested we stencil customer's name on both sides of box and send cardboard stencil without extra charge. Large size, for parcel post packages as well as ordinary mail. Measures 23½ inches long, 11 inches wide and 14 inches high, inside measurements. Has signal flag, letter drop in door, door catch and coin holder. Shipping weight, 22 pounds.

99K2846 ....$2.80

De Luxe House Mail Boxes 68c

Practical and good looking. Furnished with lock and two keys. Glass panel and name holder. Spring clip at bottom to hold papers. Screws for attaching are included.

9K2920—Heavy steel, black finish. Size, 12x5⅝x2¼ in. Wt., 1½ lbs. **68c**

9K2918—Extra quality, galvanized iron, aluminum finished. Size, 11x6x2½ inches. Weight, 2 pounds.... **88c**

50c R. F. D. Mail Box Lock With Chain

Cast brass case with steel shackle, self locking. Made especially for R. F. D. boxes. Price includes two regular keys. Wt., 5 oz.

9K4347......... **50c**

Shovels and Spades

95c Spading Forks — **Square Point Spade**

Steel D Handles — *Invincible Steel D Handle*

11½-inch tempered tines, diamond shape back, 34-in. selected handle, strapped ferrule.

99K6862—Regular grade. Light steel D head. Shipping weight, 3½ pounds........ **95c**

99K6861—Extra quality. Polished, heavy steel D head. Shipping weight, 4 lbs... **$1.45**

95c *Square Point Spade—Full Polished*

Plain back, steel blade. Size, 7x12 in. Selected, 27-inch handle. Shpg. wt., 5 lbs.

99K6654 .... **95c**

Square Point Shovel — **Steel Furnace Scoop**

79c *Invincible Steel D Handle*

Plain back, steel blade. Size, 9½x11½ inches. Selected 26-inch hardwood handle. Shipping weight, 5 pounds.

99K6660........... **79c**

Hardwood D Handle **59c**

Hollow back. Fits any furnace door. Selected 28-in. handle. Blade, 13¾ in. long; 9¾-in. mouth. Shpg. wt., 5 lbs.

99K6695........... **59c**

Invincible Round Point Shovels

Long Handle — Steel D Handle

79c Extra grade, plain back, steel blade. Size, 11¾ inches. Selected 51-inch handle. Shipping weight, 5 pounds.

99K6670—Black blade.......... **79c**

99K6671—Full polished blade. **95c**

79c Plain black, steel blade. Size, 9x12½ in. Selected, 26-in. hardwood handle. Shipping weight, 5 lbs.

99K6668—Black.... **79c**

Invincible Steel D Handle Spades

Post Hole — Drain Spade

Full polished steel blade. Straight grain 27-in. hardwood handle. Size, 6x18 in. Shipping weight, 6 lbs.

99K6699 .... **$1.25**

Has plain back and 26-in. hardwood handle. Full polished concave steel blade tapers from 6 inches at step to 4¾ inches near point. Length, 18 inches. Shpg. wt., 5 lbs.

99K6700 .... **$1.25**

Steel Grain Scoop — **Steel General Purpose Shovel**

Hollow back. Extra wide mouth. Full polished. High quality tempered steel blade. Steel D head. Hardwood handle.

99K6685—No. 8. Handle, 27½ in. long. Blade, 13½ in. wide, 16½ in. long. Shpg. wt., 5¾ lbs............ **$1.25**

99K6686—No. 10. Handle, 26 in. long. Blade, 14 in. wide, 17½ in. long. Shipping weight, 6 pounds........... **$1.35**

45c Good quality 44-in. handle which avoids stooping. Broad blade, 11¾x14 in., hollow back.

99K6694.. **45c**

Hay and Manure Forks

95c 99K6815 Hay Fork. Three 12-inch spring steel tines and 4½-foot handle. Shpg. wt., 3 lbs....... **95c**

99K6817—D Handle Manure Fork. Four 12-in. spring steel tines and malleable D handle. Shipping weight, 4 pounds...... **98c**

97c 99K6816 Manure Fork. Four 12-inch spring steel tines and 4½-ft. handle. Shpg. wt., 4 lbs....... **97c**

Scoop Fork — **Coke Fork** Extra Size

$2.35 Flat tipped, oval steel tines, 30-inch selected D handle. Ten tines, 15½ in. long, 14 in. wide. **Not mailable.** Shipping wt., 8 lbs.

99K6853............... **$2.35**

Forged steel; square tines; strapped ferrule and 30-inch selected D handle. 12 tines, 17 inches long, 18 inches wide. **Not mailable.** Shipping weight, 8 pounds.

99K6856........... **$2.65**

Hay and Manure Fork Handles

4½ feet long, selected, well seasoned northern ash, bent. Shipping weight, 2 pound

Regular grade. Bored and chucked without strap or ferrule.

99K5701—For Hay Fork.............. **25c**

99K5703—For Manure Fork.......... **25c**

Extra quality. Strapped and capped.

99K5702—For Hay Fork.............. **45c**

99K5704—For Manure Fork.......... **45c**

D Handle Head

Malleable iron, hardwood grip. Wt., 8 oz.

9K6112 **12c**

Pick and Mattock Handles

Selected quality. Lgth., 36 in.

99K5715—Shpg. wt., 2 lbs. **45c**

Regular grade. Lgth. 36 in.

99K5716—Shpg. wt., 2 lbs. **28c**

26-In. Shovel D Handle

99K5711—Hardwood. Shpg. wt., ea., 2 lbs..... **48c**

Long Cutter Mattock

Forged steel. 16 in. long.

9K5929—Wt., 6 lbs **89c**

Long Shovel Handle

Hardwood, 4½ feet long. Shipping weight, 2 pounds.

99K5713 .... **33c**

Galvanized Measure

50c

Capacity, ½ bushel. Shipping weight, 3 lbs.

99K2170 **50c**

Galvanized Feed Baskets

69c One-Bushel

99K2173 Capacity, 1 bu. Shpg. wt., 5 lbs. **Not mailable.** **69c**

99K2174 Capacity, 1½ bu. Shpg. wt., 6 lbs. **Not mailable.** **$1.00**

Adjustable Husking Hooks

Double strapped leather wrist band, curved palm plate. Right hand ONLY.

9K6136 Single steel hook. Wt., 2 oz. Each....... **15c**

9K6138 Double malleable hooks. Wt., 4 oz. Each.. **39c**

Husking Pin 10c

Steel pin mounted on good quality leather with laced thong adjustment. Weight, 1 oz.

9K6132. **10c**

Box Truck $3.95

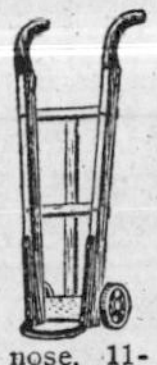

Hardwood with 3 ft. 10 in. bent handles. 17 in. between handles and 12 in. across nose. 11-in. straps, ¾-in. square axle and 6-in. wheels. Shpg. wt., 21 lbs.

99K6740—Not mailable..... **$3.95**

Wire Chain Seed Corn Hangers

$1.60 Doz.

Holds 20 ears. Made of galvanized wire. Length, 18 inches; 2¾-in. prongs. Weight, per dozen, 7 lbs.

9K6131 Per dozen.. **$1.60**

Fulton Defiance Lawn Mowers

Ball Bearing—Smooth Running

All Our Mowers Cut Full Swaths—14-In., 16-In. and 18-In.

$7.95 14-Inch

Strong, sturdy and substantial, yet easy to run and designed for a wide range of work. Built to give you maximum service at a big saving. Finished in gold and silver with black and red trimmings.

Highest quality steel ball bearings make the Fulton Defiance the lightest, smoothest, easiest running mower you can buy at anywhere near our price. All bearings are perfectly ground and are dustproof throughout. **Fulton Defiance Mowers** are unusually good and constructed on the very finest mechanical principles. Revolving cutters that cannot be thrown out of alignment and do not leave the grass ragged as in the types which have lighter cutters.

Self-Sharpening—9-In.x1¼-in. Oversize Wheels—Four Spiral Blades

Fulton Defiance Mowers never need filing or sharpening: the revolving blades sharpen themselves as you cut the grass. Handsome, splendidly made machines; all materials used in construction are first quality, all parts are carefully machined and hand fitted. Every Fulton Defiance Mower has oversize wheels and four spiral cutting knives.

	Cuts	Shpg. Wt.	Each
99K6506	14 in.	45 lbs.	$7.95
99K6507	16 in.	50 lbs.	8.70
99K6508	18 in.	55 lbs.	9.45

Grass Catchers

Extra heavy canvas. Galvanized bottom. Shpg. wt., 5 lbs.

99K6555—For 12 to 16-inch mowers.............. **95c**

99K6556—For 18 to 20-inch mowers.............. **$1.00**

Steel Garden Rake 88c 12 Teeth

5½-ft. hardwood handle. Shpg.wt.,3 lbs.

99K6872 12 teeth.. **88c**

99K6873—14 teeth......... **98c**

Super Spray Nozzle

Forged from solid bar of brass, extra large waterway. Fits all ¾-inch couplings. Shipping weight, 8 ounces.

9K7092 .... **45c**

Garden Hoe 85c

Not riveted. Polished blade. Solid socket and shank. Width of blade, 6 inches. Length of hardwood handle, 4½ feet. Shipping wt., 2 lbs.

99K6840 .... **85c**

Lawn Sprinkler

Arm Spread 12 Inches **$1.15**

Solid polished brass arms and head, 10¼ in. high. Wt., 4 lbs.

9K7088..... **$1.15**

9c Per Ft. Black

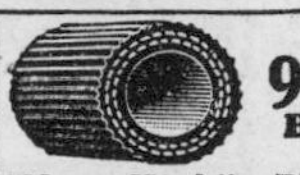

Heavy Corrugated Rubber Garden Hose

Heavy double braided jackets, non-kinkable, ¾-in. couplings. Order any length from 10 to 500 feet.

"Not-a-Kink"—Black

99K7250—Size, inside, ½ in. Shpg. wt., per. ft., 5 oz. Per ft.. **9c**

99K7249—Size, inside, ⅝ in. Shpg. wt., per ft., 6 oz. Per ft..... **10c**

99K7255—Size, inside, ¾ in. Shpg. wt., per ft., 7 oz. Per ft..... **11c**

"Best Made"—Red

99K7251—Size, inside, ⅝ in. Wt., per ft., 6 oz. Per ft.... **12c**

99K7253—Size, inside, ¾ in. Wt., per ft., 8 oz. Per ft.... **15c**

Spraying Hose, Page 1015

Large Size Molded Water Hose

1-Inch Inside Diameter

20c Per Foot

Heavy double braided. For contractors, greenhouses, parks, garages, etc. Suitable for any water pressure. Any length desired. Price does not include couplings. Shipping weight, per foot, 8 ounces.

99K7244—Per foot..... **20c**

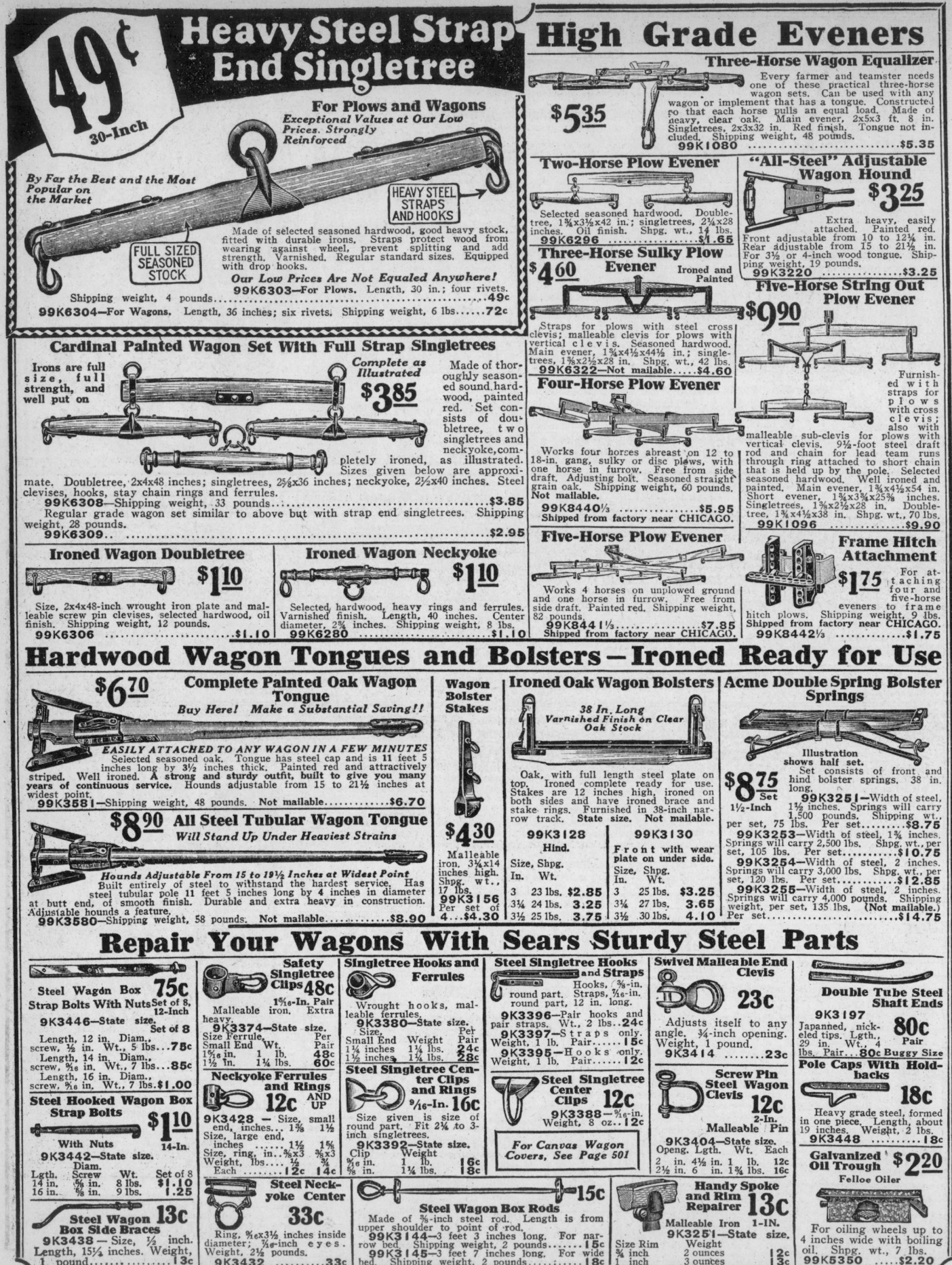

49¢ 30-Inch

Heavy Steel Strap End Singletree

For Plows and Wagons

Exceptional Values at Our Low Prices. Strongly Reinforced

By Far the Best and the Most Popular on the Market

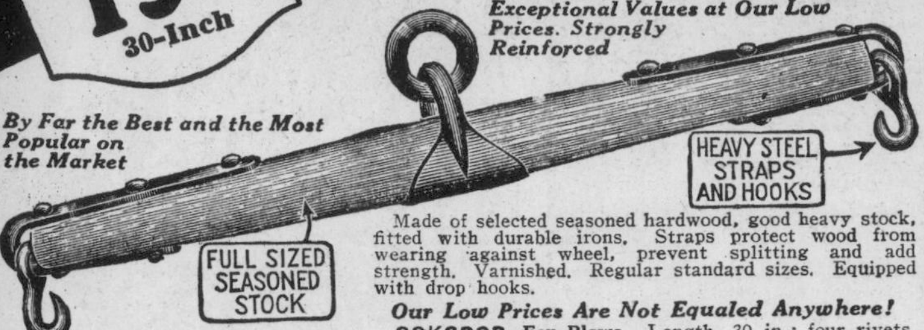

Made of selected seasoned hardwood, good heavy stock, fitted with durable irons. Straps protect wood from wearing against wheel, prevent splitting and add strength. Varnished. Regular standard sizes. Equipped with drop hooks.

Our Low Prices Are Not Equaled Anywhere!

99K6303—For Plows. Length, 30 in.; four rivets. Shipping weight, 4 pounds 49c

99K6304—For Wagons. Length, 36 inches; six rivets. Shipping weight, 6 lbs...... 72c

High Grade Eveners

Three-Horse Wagon Equalizer

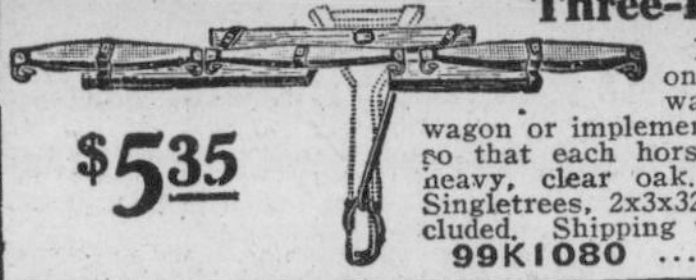

$5.35

Every farmer and teamster needs one of these practical three-horse wagon sets. Can be used with any wagon or implement that has a tongue. Constructed so that each horse pulls an equal load. Made of heavy, clear oak. Main evener, 2x5x3 ft. 8 in. Singletrees, 2x3x32 in. Red finish. Tongue not included. Shipping weight, 48 pounds.

99K1080 .... $5.35

Two-Horse Plow Evener

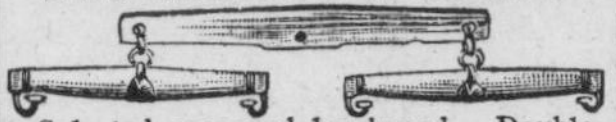

Selected seasoned hardwood. Doubletree, 1¾x3½x42 in.; singletrees, 2¼x28 inches. Oil finish. Shpg. wt., 14 lbs.

99K6296 .... $1.65

"All-Steel" Adjustable Wagon Hound

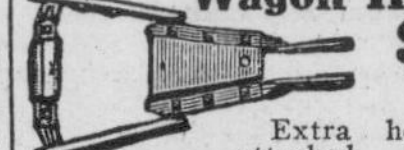

$3.25

Extra heavy, easily attached. Painted red. Front adjustable from 10 to 12¾ in. Rear adjustable from 15 to 21½ in. For 3½ or 4-inch wood tongue. Shipping weight, 19 pounds.

99K3220 .... $3.25

Three-Horse Sulky Plow Evener

$4.60 Ironed and Painted

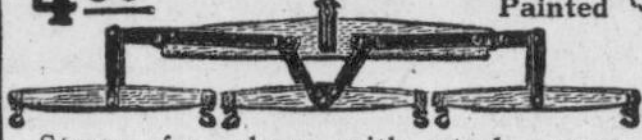

Straps for plows with steel cross clevis; malleable clevis for plows with vertical clevis. Seasoned hardwood. Main evener, 1¾x4½x44½ in.; singletrees, 1⅜x2½x28 in. Shpg. wt., 42 lbs.

99K6322—Not mailable..... $4.60

Five-Horse String Out Plow Evener

$9.90

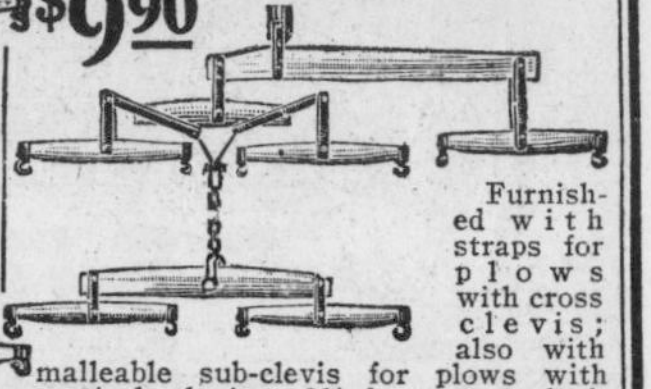

Furnished with straps for plows with cross clevis; also with malleable sub-clevis for plows with vertical clevis. 9½-foot steel draft rod and chain for lead team runs through ring attached to short chain that is held up by the pole. Selected seasoned hardwood. Well ironed and painted. Main evener, 1¾x4½x54 in. Short evener, 1¾x3¾x25⅜ inches. Singletrees, 1⅜x2½x28 in. Doubletree, 1¾x4½x38 in. Shpg. wt., 70 lbs.

99K1096 .... $9.90

Cardinal Painted Wagon Set With Full Strap Singletrees

Irons are full size, full strength, and well put on

Complete as Illustrated $3.85

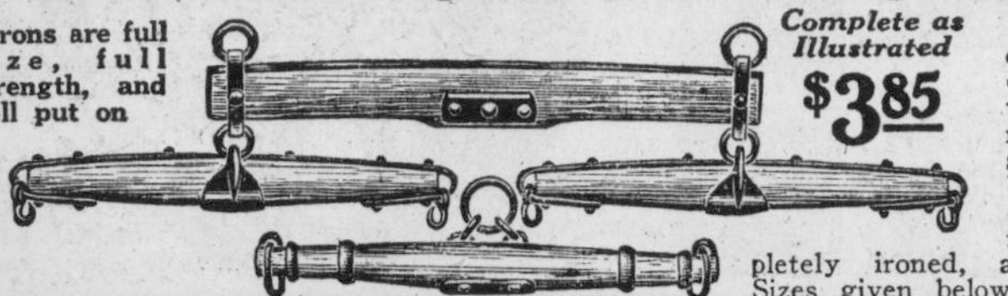

Made of thoroughly seasoned sound hardwood, painted red. Set consists of doubletree, two singletrees and neckyoke, completely ironed, as illustrated. Sizes given below are approximate. Doubletree, 2x4x48 inches; singletrees, 2⅝x36 inches; neckyoke, 2½x40 inches. Steel clevises, hooks, stay chain rings and ferrules.

99K6308—Shipping weight, 33 pounds $3.85

Regular grade wagon set similar to above but with strap end singletrees. Shipping weight, 28 pounds.

99K6309 .... $2.95

Four-Horse Plow Evener

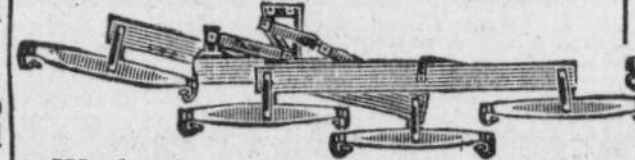

Works four horses abreast on 12 to 18-in. gang, sulky or disc plows, with one horse in furrow. Free from side draft. Adjusting bolt. Seasoned straight grain oak. Shipping weight, 60 pounds. Not mailable.

99K8440⅓ $5.95

Shipped from factory near CHICAGO.

Ironed Wagon Doubletree

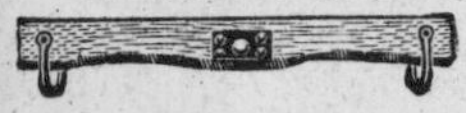

$1.10

Size, 2x4x48-inch wrought iron plate and malleable screw pin clevises, selected hardwood, oil finish. Shipping weight, 12 pounds.

99K6306 .... $1.10

Ironed Wagon Neckyoke

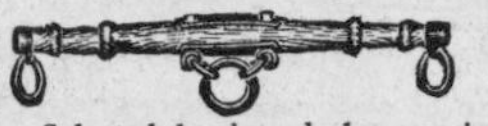

$1.10

Selected hardwood, heavy rings and ferrules. Varnished finish. Length, 40 inches. Center diameter, 2⅝ inches. Shipping weight, 8 lbs.

99K6280 .... $1.10

Five-Horse Plow Evener

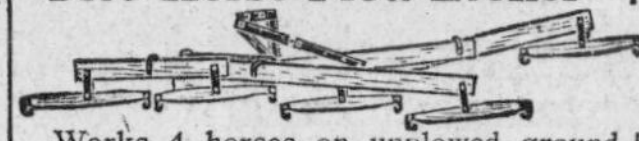

Works 4 horses on unplowed ground and one horse in furrow. Free from side draft. Painted red. Shipping weight, 82 pounds.

99K8441⅓ $7.85

Shipped from factory near CHICAGO.

Frame Hitch Attachment

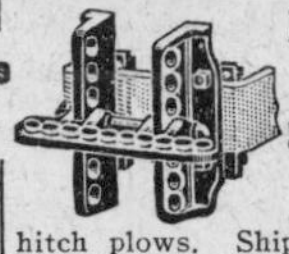

$1.75

For attaching four and five-horse eveners to frame hitch plows. Shipping weight, 9 lbs. **Shipped from factory near CHICAGO.**

99K8442⅓ $1.75

Hardwood Wagon Tongues and Bolsters—Ironed Ready for Use

Complete Painted Oak Wagon Tongue

$6.70

Buy Here! Make a Substantial Saving!!

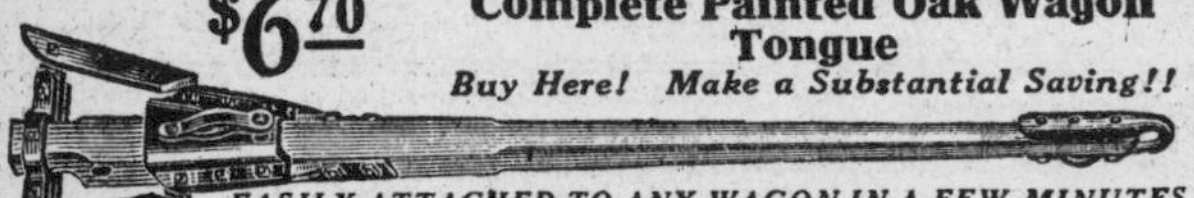

EASILY ATTACHED TO ANY WAGON IN A FEW MINUTES

Selected seasoned oak. Tongue has steel cap and is 11 feet 5 inches long by 3½ inches thick. Painted red and attractively striped. Well ironed. **A strong and sturdy outfit, built to give you many years of continuous service.** Hounds adjustable from 15 to 21½ inches at widest point.

99K3581—Shipping weight, 48 pounds. Not mailable $6.70

$8.90 All Steel Tubular Wagon Tongue

Will Stand Up Under Heaviest Strains

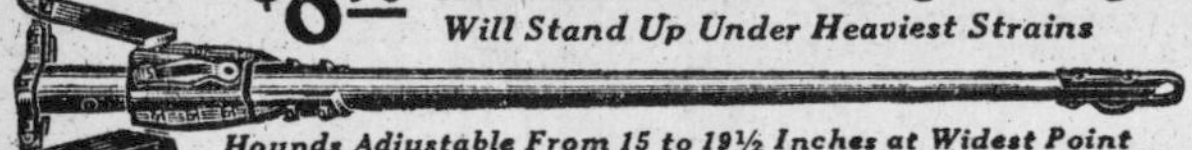

Hounds Adjustable From 15 to 19½ Inches at Widest Point

Built entirely of steel to withstand the hardest service. Has steel tubular pole 11 feet 5 inches long by 4 inches in diameter at butt end, of smooth finish. Durable and extra heavy in construction. Adjustable hounds a feature.

99K3580—Shipping weight, 58 pounds. Not mailable $8.90

Wagon Bolster Stakes

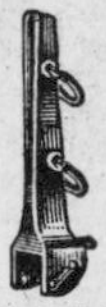

$4.30

Malleable iron, 3¼x14 inches high. Shpg. wt., 17 lbs.

99K3156 Per set of 4...$4.30

Ironed Oak Wagon Bolsters

38 In. Long Varnished Finish on Clear Oak Stock

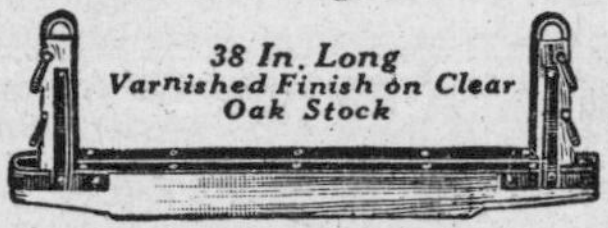

Oak, with full length steel plate on top. Ironed complete ready for use. Stakes are 12 inches high, ironed on both sides and have ironed brace and stake rings. Furnished in 38-inch narrow track. **State size. Not mailable.**

99K3128 Hind.

Size, In.	Shpg. Wt.	
3	23 lbs.	$2.85
3¼	24 lbs.	3.25
3½	25 lbs.	3.75

99K3130 Front with wear plate on under side.

Size, In.	Shpg. Wt.	
3	25 lbs.	$3.25
3¼	27 lbs.	3.65
3½	30 lbs.	4.10

Acme Double Spring Bolster Springs

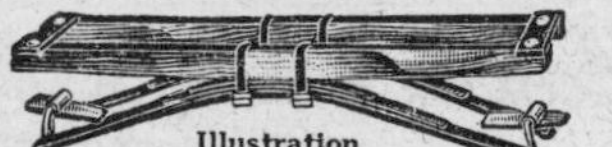

Illustration shows half set.

$8.75 Set 1½-Inch

Set consists of front and hind bolster springs. 38 in. long.

99K3251—Width of steel, 1½ inches. Springs will carry 1,500 pounds. Shipping wt., per set, 75 lbs. Per set $8.75

99K3253—Width of steel, 1¾ inches. Springs will carry 2,500 lbs. Shpg. wt., per set, 105 lbs. Per set $10.75

99K3254—Width of steel, 2 inches. Springs will carry 3,000 lbs. Shpg. wt., per set, 120 lbs. Per set $12.85

99K3255—Width of steel, 2 inches. Springs will carry 4,000 pounds. Shipping weight, per set, 135 lbs. **(Not mailable.)** Per set $14.75

Repair Your Wagons With Sears Sturdy Steel Parts

Steel Wagon Box Strap Bolts With Nuts

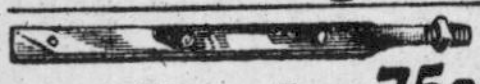

75c Set of 8, 12-Inch

9K3446—State size. Set of 8

Length, 12 in. Diam., screw, ½ in. Wt., 5 lbs... **75c**

Length, 14 in. Diam., screw, 9/16 in. Wt., 7 lbs... **85c**

Length, 16 in. Diam., screw, 9/16 in. Wt., 7 lbs. **$1.00**

Steel Hooked Wagon Box Strap Bolts

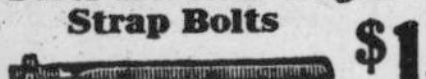

With Nuts $1.10 14-In.

9K3442—State size.

Lgth.	Diam. Screw	Wt.	Set of 8
14 in.	⅝ in.	8 lbs.	$1.10
16 in.	⅝ in.	9 lbs.	1.25

Steel Wagon Box Side Braces

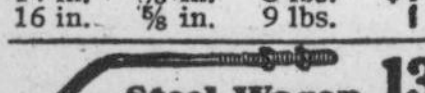

13c

9K3438—Size, ½ inch. Length, 15¼ inches. Weight, 1 pound 13c

Safety Singletree Clips

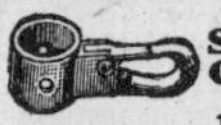

48c 1 5/16-In. Pair

Malleable iron. Extra heavy.

9K3374—State size.

Size Ferrule, Small End	Wt.	Per Pair
1 5/16 in.	1 lb.	48c
1½ in.	1¼ lbs.	60c

Neckyoke Ferrules and Rings

12c AND UP

9K3428 — Size, small end, inches... 1⅜ 1½

Size, large end, inches 1½ 1⅝

Size, ring, in.. ⅜x3 ⅜x3

Weight, lbs.... ½ ¾

Each **12c** **14c**

Steel Neckyoke Center

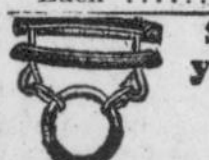

33c

Ring, 9/16x3½ inches inside diameter; 7/16-inch eyes. Weight, 2½ pounds.

9K3432 .... 33c

Singletree Hooks and Ferrules

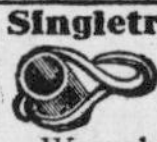

Wrought hooks, malleable ferrules.

9K3380—State size.

Size, Small End	Weight	Per Pair
1¼ inches	1¼ lbs.	24c
1½ inches	1¼ lbs.	28c

Steel Singletree Center Clips and Rings

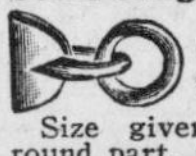

9/16-In. 16c

Size given is size of round part. Fit 2¼ to 3-inch singletrees.

9K3392—State size.

Clip	Weight	
9/16 in.	1 lb.	16c
⅝ in.	1¼ lbs.	18c

Steel Wagon Box Rods

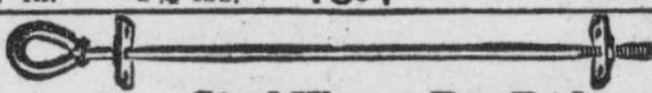

15c

Made of ⅜-inch steel rod. Length is from upper shoulder to point of rod.

99K3144—3 feet 3 inches long. For narrow bed. Shipping weight, 2 pounds....... 15c

99K3145—3 feet 7 inches long. For wide bed. Shipping weight, 2 pounds........ 18c

Steel Singletree Hooks and Straps

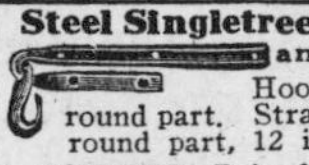

Hooks, ⅜-in. round part. Straps, 7/16-in. round part, 12 in. long.

9K3396—Pair hooks and pair straps. Wt., 2 lbs.. **24c**

9K3397—Straps only. Weight, 1 lb. Pair...... **15c**

9K3395—Hooks only. Weight, 1 lb. Pair...... **12c**

Steel Singletree Center Clips

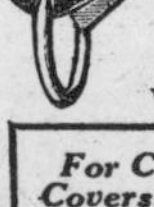

12c

9K3388—9/16-in. Weight, 8 oz.. **12c**

For Canvas Wagon Covers, See Page 501

Swivel Malleable End Clevis

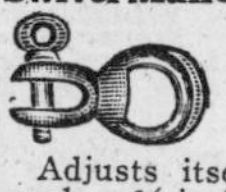

23c

Adjusts itself to any angle. ¾-inch opening. Weight, 1 pound.

9K3414 .... 23c

Screw Pin Steel Wagon Clevis

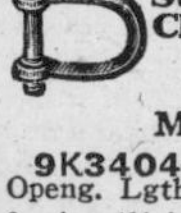

12c 2-In. Malleable Pin

9K3404—State size.

Openg.	Lgth.	Wt.	Each
2 in.	4½ in.	1 lb.	12c
2½ in.	6 in.	1¾ lbs.	16c

Handy Spoke and Rim Repairer

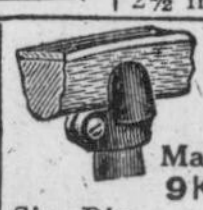

13c Malleable Iron 1-IN.

9K3251—State size.

Size Rim	Weight	
¾ inch	2 ounces	12c
1 inch	3 ounces	13c

Double Tube Steel Shaft Ends

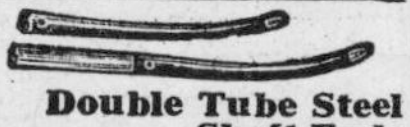

9K3197

Japanned, nickeled tips. Lgth., 29 in. Wt., 4 lbs. Pair... **80c** 80c Pair Buggy Size

Pole Caps With Holdbacks

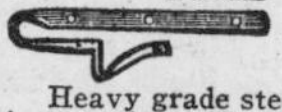

18c

Heavy grade steel, formed in one piece. Length, about 19 inches. Weight, 2 lbs.

9K3448 .... 18c

Galvanized Oil Trough $2.20

Felloe Oiler

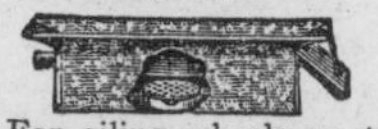

For oiling wheels up to 4 inches wide with boiling oil. Shpg. wt., 7 lbs.

99K5350 ..... $2.20

Extra Heavy White Cotton Duck or Canvas

65c #6-In.

No. 8, first quality. Used for covering grain and hay stacks, farm machinery, etc., for making wagon top covers, cushions, awnings and luggage covers, etc., for covering new cement work, etc. Hard twist and close weave, sheds water as no other canvas will. Suitable for sail making.

NOTE—This is a high quality extra heavy duck. Actual weight, 17 ounces per square yard.

Close Weave Hard Twist

Width, inches	36	54	72
Shipping weight, yard, ounces	18	27	36
99K7580—Per yard	65c	95c	$1.25

Black Oiled Cotton Duck *For Wagon Covers*

Regular $1.25 A YD.

Absolutely waterproof. Heavily coated on one side with thick black oil which when dried becomes very tough and smooth. Flexible; oil will not crack or peel off. Use to cover wagons, hay stacks, construction work, farm machinery, etc. Width, 50 in. Shpg. wt., per yd., 2 lbs.

99K7586—Regular grade, No. 12. Per yard $1.25
99K7585—Extra grade, No. 10. Per yard 1.35

Spanish Grain Artificial Leather

$1.65 A YD.

Heavy sateen back. Will not crack or peel. For auto tops, cushions, etc. Write for free samples. Shipping weight, per yard, 1 pound.

99K7502—Tan. Per yard $1.65
9K3196—Gimp to match. Roll, 25 yards. Tan. Wt., 5 oz. Per roll 30c
9K3188—Buttons. Tan. Weight, 4 oz. Package of 100 ....23c
9K3194—Nails. Tan. Weight, 4 oz. Package of 100 .....14c

Extra Heavy Bronco Artificial Leather

$2.35 A YARD

Positively will not crack or peel. Easily applied. 50 inches wide. Shipping weight, per yard, 2 pounds.

99K7506—Black, leather grain. Per yard $2.25
99K7507—Tan, beautiful Spanish grain. Per yard 2.35

Morocco Grain Artificial Leather

Regular 95c A YD.

Made of heavy tough cloth, colored back, flexible, weatherproof, will not peel, blister, fade or crack. For auto or buggy cushions, for reupholstering chairs, book covers, etc. Looks and feels like genuine leather, is pliable and sanitary. Write for free samples. Regular grade. Shipping weight, per yard, 1 lb.

99K7516—Black. Per yard 95c
Extra quality. Shipping weight, per yard, 1 pound.
99K7511—Black. Per yard $1.35
99K7513—Tan. Per yard 1.00
99K7515—Special for upholstering. Black, dull finish 1.35

Genuine Chase "Drednaut" Auto Fabric

$1.65 Per Yard

DOUBLE TEXTURE 64 INCHES WIDE

"Dreadnaut" Rubberized Top Recovering Material

Standard Equipment on Best Closed Cars

Double texture, leakproof, waterproof and sunproof. Will not crack, peel, blister or fade. Heavy white twill back, Victoria long grain black rubber outside coating. Recover your closed car! No sewing necessary, simply remove drip molding and old cover and apply new. 64 inches wide, suitable for all cars. Be sure to include needed amount for trimming.
99K7571—Shipping weight, per yard, 3 pounds. Per yard $1.65

Genuine Chase "Drednaut" Motor Topping

$1.35 Per Yard

Ideal top, curtain or cushion material for auto and buggy coverings. Double texture fabric, handsomely grained black rubber outside coating, drab color back. Water and sunproof. Standard equipment on America's highest grade vehicles and automobiles. 54 inches wide. Shipping weight, per yard, 2 pounds.
99K7570—Per yard $1.35

DOUBLE TEXTURE 54 INCHES WIDE

Genuine Chase Rubber Drill

85c A YARD

Water shedding, rubber fabric especially adapted to recovering Ford tops. Same quality as material furnished with Ford cars. Made of best quality rubber cemented to hard twisted, close woven American drill; strong but pliable. Width, 54 inches. Black back. Shipping weight, per yard, 2¼ pounds.
99K7565—34-ounce. Black back. Per yard 85c
99K7540—20-ounce. White back. Per yard, 70c
99K7542—24-ounce. White back. Per yard, 80c
99K7550—22-ounce. Dark back. Per yard, 80c

RUBBER FOR FORD CARS

Metaline Nails

Used to fasten gimp on edge of seats, tables, etc. Package of 100. Colors: Black or tan. State color. Weight, 4 ounces.
9K3193—Per package ...9c

Trimmers' Gimp

Used to cover seams and edges. In rolls of 25 yards. Colors: Black or tan. State color. Width, ½ in. Weight, per roll, 6 ounces.
9K3195—Per roll ...28c

Wood Rims for Buggies, Wagons and Trucks

Not Mailable

Slightly oversize in length, to allow for cutting and fitting
Selected, seasoned, XXX extra grade hickory, for buggies and wagons. Full set of eight pieces, enough for two front and two hind wheels. State height wanted.

	Tread, In.	Depth, In.	Heights in Stock, Inches	Shpg. Wt. per Set Lbs.	¼ of Set	Per Set
99K8445⅓	⅞	1	36, 38, 40, 42, 44, 46	19 lbs.	$0.70	$2.50
99K8446⅓	1	1⅛	36, 38, 40, 42, 44, 46, 48	23 lbs.	.85	2.95
99K8447⅓	1¼	1¼	36, 38, 40, 42, 44, 46, 48	30 lbs.	.95	3.35
99K8448⅓	1¼	1⅜	36, 38, 40, 42, 44, 46, 48	34 lbs.	1.15	3.98
99K8449⅓	1⅜	1½	36, 38, 40, 42, 46, 48	39 lbs.	1.30	4.70
99K8450⅓	1½	1⅝	36, 38, 46, 48	47 lbs.	1.60	5.70

SELECTED SEASONED OAK for wagons and trucks. Full set of eight pieces, enough for two front and two hind wheels. State height wanted.

	Tread, In.	Depth, In.	Height in Stock, Inches	Shpg. Lbs. Wt.	¼ of Set	Per Set
99K8455⅓	1½	2	36, 40, 42, 46, 48, 52, 54	52	$1.25	$4.55
99K8456⅓	1¾	2	36, 40, 42, 48, 50, 52, 54	60	1.40	5.10
99K8457⅓	1¾	2¼	40, 42, 48, 50, 52, 54	75	1.59	5.95
99K8458⅓	2	2¼	42, 44, 52, 54	82	1.75	6.50
99K8459⅓	2½	2	36, 40, 42, 48, 50, 52, 54	89	1.90	6.95
99K8460⅓	4	2	36, 38, 40, 42, 48, 50, 52, 54	120	2.15	8.00
99K8461⅓	4	2	36, 38, 40, 42, 48, 50, 52, 54	150	2.90	11.00

Finished Tongue Hounds

85c

Made of seasoned selected stock. Size, 2x3½x30 inches. Shipping wt., 6 lbs.
99K8517⅓ Per pair 85c

Wagon Hounds

$1.45

Finished Hind Hounds. Selected stock; rounded and planed smooth. Size, 2x3½x47 inches. Shipping wt., 12 lbs.
99K8518⅓ Per pair ...$1.45

Bent Oak Wagon Hounds

$2.10 Narrow Track

Seasoned selected grain timber, steam bent.
99K8535⅓—For narrow track. Size, 2x3 inches. Shipping weight, 18 pounds $2.10
99K8536⅓—For wide track. Size, 2x3 inches. Shipping weight, 18 pounds $2.20

Wagon Sand Boards

Seasoned selected stock. Narrow. Length, 3 feet 9 inches.

	Size, In.	Shpg. Wt., Lbs.	
99K8515⅓	3x3	9	$0.95
99K8516⅓	3x3½	12	1.10

High Grade Surrey or Buggy Poles

Not Mailable

Straight grain hickory. Ironed complete. Size, 2x2½ inches. Shipping weight, 40 pounds.
99K8560⅓—Unpainted $8.90
99K8561⅓—Red finish 9.90
99K8562⅓—Black finish 9.95

Buggy and Wagon Poles

Selected hickory. Finished, double bent. Not mailable.

	Size, In.	Shpg. Wt.	Per Set
99K8546⅓	1¾x2¼	13 lbs.	$4.50
99K8547⅓	2 x2½	15 lbs.	4.80
99K8548⅓	2 x3	18 lbs.	5.90

Braced Heel Buggy Shafts

Bradley Eye

Seasoned hickory, leather loops. 21 in. imitation patent leather ends. Size, 1⅜x2 in. Shpg. wt., 21 lbs.

Kind of Eye	Plain	Bradley
99K8555⅓—Unpainted	$4.70	$4.90
99K8556⅓—Red finish	5.80	6.00
99K8557⅓—Black finish	5.90	6.10

Buggy and Wagon Shafts

Seasoned hickory. Not mailable.

	Size, In.	Shpg. Wt.	Per Set
99K8485⅓	1⅜x1⅞	13 lbs.	$3.20
99K8486⅓	1½x2	15 lbs.	3.40
99K8487⅓	1½x2¼	19 lbs.	3.60

Plain Oak Wagon Spokes

Front spokes measure 22 inches long. Hind spokes measure 26 inches long. Set consists of 24 front and 28 hind spokes. Be sure to state size; also, if ordering less than full set, state whether spokes are wanted for front or hind wheels.

99K8475⅓—XX Grade.

Size, inches	1¾	1⅞	2	2¼	2⅜	2½
Shpg. wt., per full set	52 lbs.	58 lbs.	64 lbs.	70 lbs.	76 lbs.	89 lbs.
Per ¼ set, 14 spokes	$1.05	$1.30	$1.40	$1.50	$1.60	$1.90
Per full set	3.65	4.60	4.95	5.40	5.70	6.90

99K8476⅓—XXX Extra Grade.

Per ¼ set, 14 spokes	$1.60	$1.90	$2.10	$2.25	$2.45	$2.85
Per full set	5.55	6.90	7.60	7.95	8.70	10.25

Extra Grade Oak Wagon Tongues

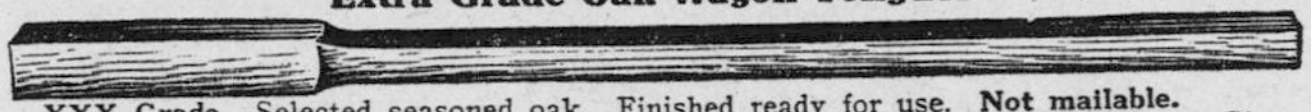

Seasoned oak. Finished ready for use. Not mailable.
XXX Grade. Selected seasoned oak.
99K8540⅓ — Size, 3 in. Shpg. wt., 31 lbs. $2.40
99K8541⅓ — Size, 3½ in. Shpg. wt., 40 lbs. $2.45
99K8542⅓ — Size, 4 in. Shpg. wt., 60 lbs. $2.95

Wagon Bolsters

Seasoned stock, rounded and finished, 48 inches long.

Front	Size, In.	Wt., Lbs.	
99K8508⅓	3 x4	14	$1.00
99K8509⅓	3¼x4¼	17	1.20
99K8510⅓	3½x4¼	21	1.40
Hind			
99K8505⅓	3 x4	15	1.10
99K8506⅓	3¼x4½	18	1.25
99K8507⅓	3 x6	21	1.50

Wagon and Plow Oval Singletrees

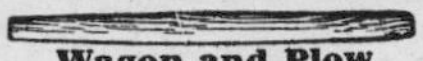

Wagon. Length, 36 in.

	Size, In.	Shpg. Wt., Lbs.	
99K8531⅓	2¼	3	30c
99K8532⅓	2¾	3	35c
99K8533⅓	3	4	39c
99K8534⅓	3	4	

Plow. Size, 2¼x30 inches. Shpg. wt., 2 lbs. ...16c

Finished Wagon Axles

Seasoned straight grain stock. Narrow. Length, 5 feet 1 inch.

	Size, In.	Shpg. Wt., Lbs.	
99K8496⅓	2¾	16	$1.55
99K8497⅓	3	19	1.65
99K8498⅓	3¼	22	1.95
99K8499⅓	3½	24	2.55

Turned Neckyokes

48c 38-Inch   **65c 42-Inch**

Selected seasoned stock.

	Size	Shpg. Wt.	
99K8520⅓	2½x38 in.	5 lbs.	48c
99K8521⅓	2⅝x40 in.	6 lbs.	55c
99K8522⅓	2¾x42 in.	6 lbs.	65c

Wagon Eveners

69c 2 x 4 In.   **98c 2½x4½ In.**

Selected seasoned stock. 48 in. long.

	Size, In.	Shpg. Wt., Lbs.	
99K8525⅓	2 x4	10	69c
99K8526⅓	2 x4½	12	79c
99K8527⅓	2½x4½	13	98c

All Wagon Wood Stock Listed on This Page Shipped From Factory in OHIO.

Modern Bathroom Outfits

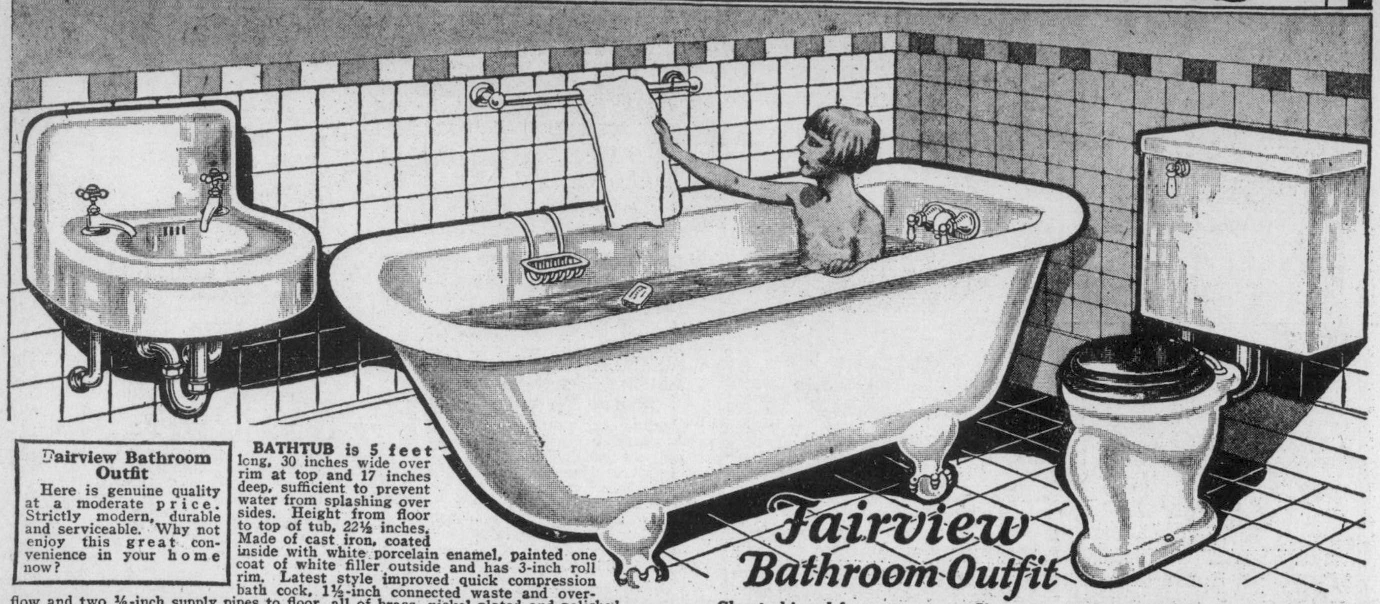

Fairview Bathroom Outfit

Here is genuine quality at a moderate price. Strictly modern, durable and serviceable. Why not enjoy this great convenience in your home now?

BATHTUB is 5 feet long, 30 inches wide over rim at top and 17 inches deep, sufficient to prevent water from splashing over sides. Height from floor to top of tub, 22½ inches. Made of cast iron, coated inside with white porcelain enamel, painted one coat of white filler outside and has 3-inch roll rim. Latest style improved quick compression bath cock, 1½-inch connected waste and overflow and two ½-inch supply pipes to floor, all of brass, nickel plated and polished.

LAVATORY is 18 inches from front to back, 21 inches wide and has 8-inch high back and roll or turnover rim 4 inches deep. Bowl, 10½x14½ inches. Soap cup cast in top directly above overflow. 1¼-inch trap with outlet, two compression faucets with china tops, one marked "hot," the other "cold," and two ⅜-inch supply pipes. All trimmings of the latest design, made of brass, nicely nickel plated.

CLOSET—The closet combination is the special feature of this bathroom outfit. Has siphon washdown bowl of vitreous earthenware, highly polished mahogany finish seat with nickel plated brass hinges and large capacity white china tank with china handle flush lever and nickel plated supply pipe to floor. This vitreous china tank is artistically designed. It is a beautiful sanitary closet outfit that is easily kept clean and white and will add greatly to the appearance of your bathroom.

Closet shipped from our store. Shpg. wt., 130 lbs. **Bathtub and lavatory from HARRISBURG, PA., or SPRINGFIELD, MASS.** Shipping weight, 410 lbs.

42K3664¼—Fairview Bathroom Outfit (bathtub, lavatory and closet), with lavatory supply and waste pipes to wall, as illustrated..... **$64.75**

42K3665¼—Fairview Bathroom Outfit (bathtub, lavatory and closet), with lavatory supply and waste pipes to floor.......... **65.20**

If wanted with supply and waste pipes threaded for iron pipe, add $1.50 extra.

Prices for above outfits do not include Towel Bar or Soap Dish. For Bathroom Trimmings see page 1010.

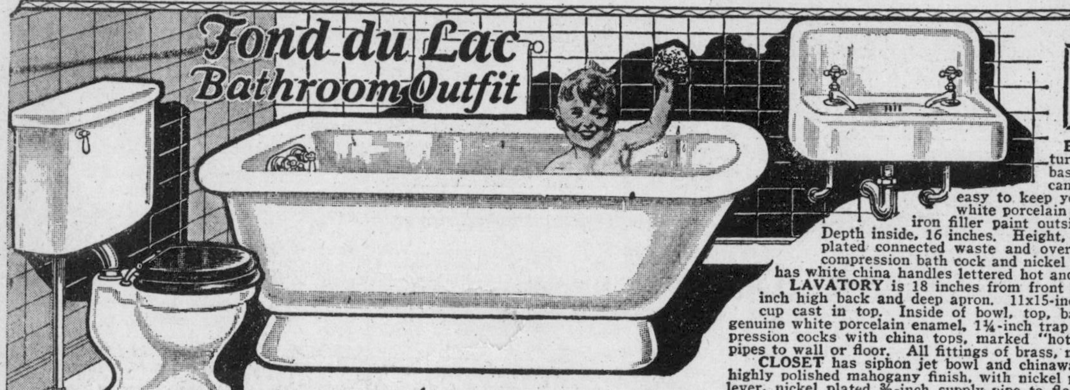

Fond du Lac Bathroom Outfit

White vitreous china closet tank. Siphon jet closet bowl and large square lavatory are special features of this outfit.

BATHTUB is a beautiful sanitary fixture mounted on a dustproof cast iron base. Dust or other foreign substances cannot collect beneath this tub. Makes it easy to keep your bathroom clean. Tub is cast iron, white porcelain enameled inside, painted one coat white iron filler paint outside. Length, 5 feet. Width, 30 inches. Depth inside, 16 inches. Height, 22 inches. Fitted complete with nickel plated connected waste and overflow, latest design nickel plated rapid compression bath cock and nickel plated supply pipes to floor. Bath cock has white china handles lettered hot and cold.

LAVATORY is 18 inches from front to back, 24 inches wide and has a 10-inch high back and deep apron. 11x15-inch bowl. Made of cast iron with soap cup cast in top. Inside of bowl, top, back and outside of apron glazed with genuine white porcelain enamel, 1¼-inch trap with outlet to wall or floor, two compression cocks with china tops, marked "hot" and "cold," and two ⅜-inch supply pipes to wall or floor. All fittings of brass, nicely nickel plated.

CLOSET has siphon jet bowl and chinaware tank. Seat of seasoned birchwood, highly polished mahogany finish, with nickel plated brass hinges. China handle flush lever, nickel plated ⅜-inch supply pipe to floor.

Closet shipped from our store. Shpg. wt., 150 lbs. **Bathtub and lavatory shipped from HARRISBURG, PA., or SPRINGFIELD, MASS.** Shipping weight, 555 pounds.

42K3658¼—Fond du Lac Bathroom Outfit (bathtub, lavatory and closet), with supply and waste pipes of lavatory to wall, as illustrated.................... **$82.95**

If wanted with waste and supply pipes threaded for connecting to iron pipe, allow $1.50 extra.

Prices do not include Towel Bar. For Bathroom Trimmings see page 1010.

42K3659¼—Fond du Lac Bathroom Outfit (bathtub, lavatory and closet), with supply and waste pipes of lavatory to the floor.................... **$83.35**

Ambassador Bathroom Outfit

Here is an outfit at a moderate price that would be appropriate for the finest mansion. What a pride it will be for you to have this beautiful outfit installed in your home.

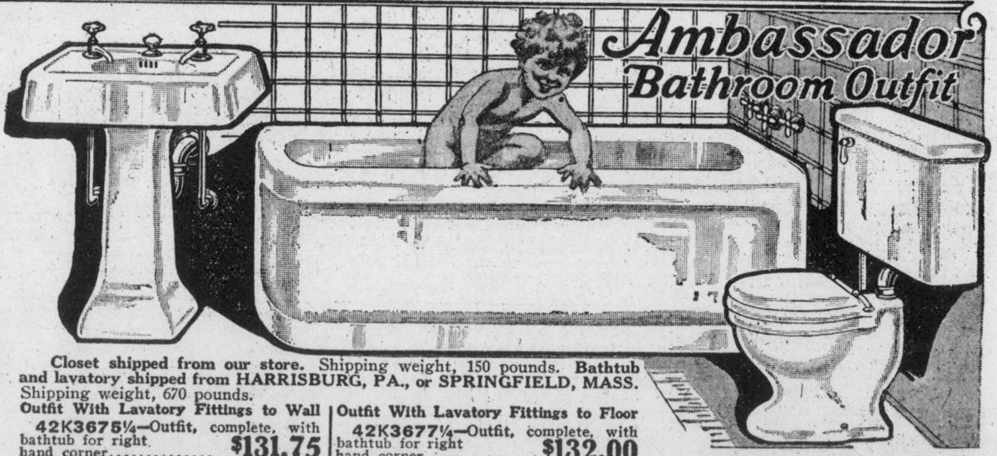

BATHTUB is 5 feet long, 30 inches wide over all at top and 17 inches deep inside. This beautiful corner bathtub is cast in one solid piece; genuine white porcelain enamel all over. It is designed to be built in solid in the corner of the room, as shown. Illustration shows tub in right hand corner. Can also be furnished for left hand corner if desired. Waste and supply fittings are of solid brass, concealed in the wall so that only the controlling knobs and china handles protrude.

LAVATORY is of the square pattern, with top measuring 20 inches from front to back and 24 inches wide. Square pedestal. Inside, top and apron of lavatory and pedestal are coated with white porcelain enamel. 1¼-inch trap with outlet to floor or wall. Has latest improved pop-up waste; two latest style compression cocks with china handles, marked "hot" and "cold" and two ⅜-inch supply pipes. All trimmings solid brass nickel plated.

CLOSET has siphon jet bowl of vitreous earthenware and chinaware tank. Seat is of solid birchwood with hand rubbed ivory-white finish, fitted with nickel plated brass hinges. China handle flush lever, nickel plated; ⅜-inch supply pipe from tank to floor.

Closet shipped from our store. Shipping weight, 150 pounds. **Bathtub and lavatory shipped from HARRISBURG, PA., or SPRINGFIELD, MASS.** Shipping weight, 670 pounds.

Outfit With Lavatory Fittings to Wall

42K3675¼—Outfit, complete, with bathtub for right hand corner.............. **$131.75**

42K3674¼—Outfit, complete, with bathtub for left hand corner.............. **$131.75**

Outfit With Lavatory Fittings to Floor

42K3677¼—Outfit, complete, with bathtub for right hand corner.............. **$132.00**

42K3676¼—Outfit, complete, with bathtub for left hand corner.............. **$132.00**

If wanted with waste and supply pipes threaded for iron pipe, allow $1.50 extra.

Unexcelled Quality - Big Savings!

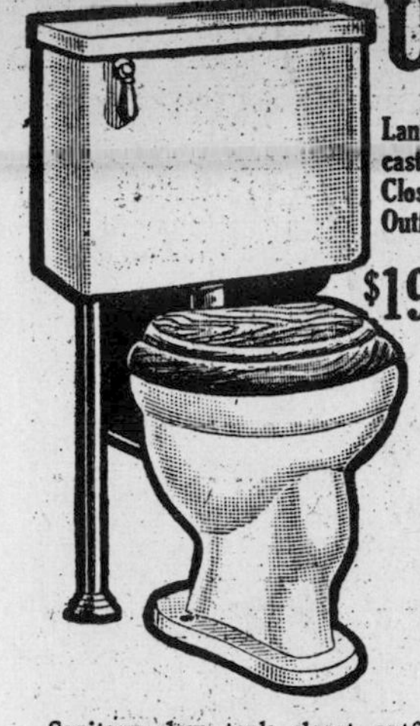

Lancaster Closet Outfit

$19.45

Sanitary, low tank closet outfit with all white composition tank made of a special composition material, the base of which is asbestos. It is impervious to moisture and very durable. It will not deteriorate, break or crack, and is far superior to the old style wooden tanks. The tank has Douglas ball type flushing valve with overflow and refill tube, white china lever pull and nickel plated brass supply pipe to floor. Seat is of birch, mahogany finish, with brass bar hinge. Siphon washdown, vitreous earthenware bowl. Shpg. wt., 95 lbs.

42K2021¼ $19.45

Edgewood Closet Outfit

This outfit is the same as our Lancaster Closet Outfit described above, except that bowl is siphon jet pattern the same as furnished with our Oakdale Closet Outfit illustrated at center of page. The siphon jet style bowl is almost noiseless in its flushing action. Shipping weight, 105 pounds.

42K2023¼ $24.85

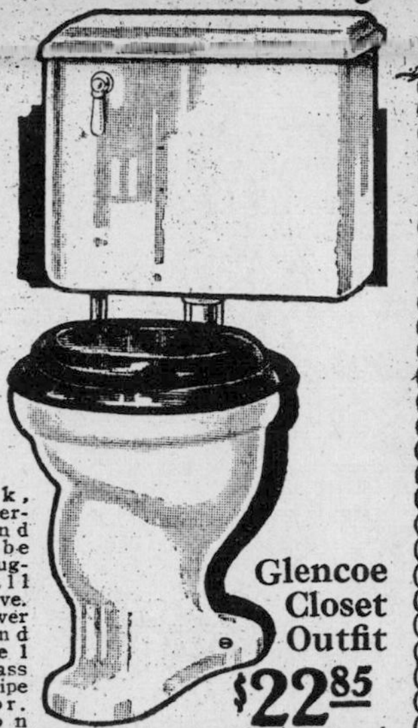

Has sanitary cast iron genuine white porcelain enameled tank equipped with latest improved brass flushing mechanism. Copper ball float, compound lever ball cock, brass overflow and refill tube and Douglas ball flush valve. China lever pull and nickel plated brass supply pipe to floor. Siphon washdown vitreous earthenware bowl. Seat and cover of birch, with mahogany finish and nickel plated brass bar hinge.

Glencoe Closet Outfit

$22.85

42K2002¼—Shpg. wt., 130 lbs.. $22.85

42K2010¼—Outfit same as above, except with genuine celluloid covered white seat. Shpg. wt., 130 lbs...... **$24.95**

42K1880¼—Tank only, for siphon washdown bowl. Shpg. wt., 83 lbs... 13.50

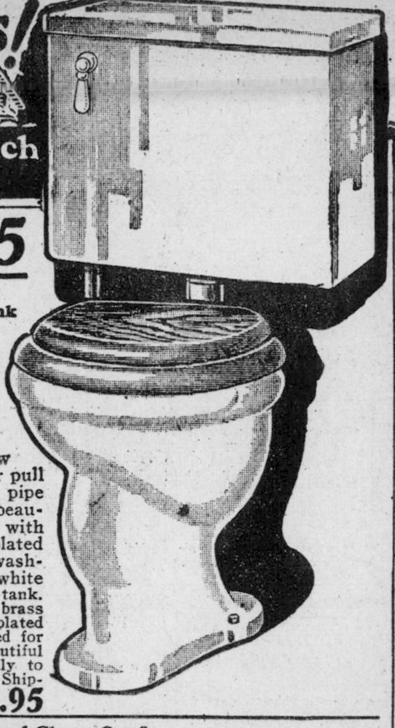

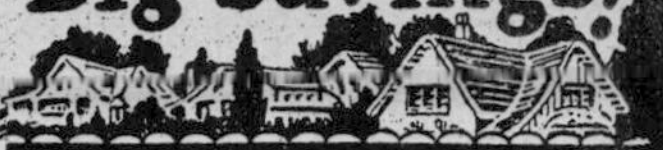

Nowhere Else Such a Value as This

Fairfield Closet Outfit $20.95

Has Beautiful White Vitreous Tank

A strictly modern low tank closet outfit. Tank is made of white vitreous earthenware with latest improved brass flushing mechanism, copper ball float and compound lever ball cock. Has Douglas ball type flushing valve with overflow and refill tube, white china lever pull and nickel plated brass supply pipe to floor. Seat is of solid birch, beautifully finished in mahogany, with solid brass bar hinge, nickel plated and polished. Bowl is siphon washdown pattern made of sanitary white vitreous earthenware to match tank. Tank connects to bowl with solid brass nickel plated elbow. Nickel plated brass screws and washers furnished for attaching bowl to floor. This beautiful sanitary outfit will add wonderfully to the appearance of your bathroom. Shipping weight, 130 pounds.

42K2000¼ $20.95

Ridgeland Closet Outfit

This outfit is same as our Fairfield Closet Outfit described above, except that it has a beautiful snow white seat to match tank and bowl. Seat is coated by a special process with genuine white celluloid and has hand rubbed finish.

42K2008¼—Shipping weight, 130 pounds.............. $22.90

Another Real Value

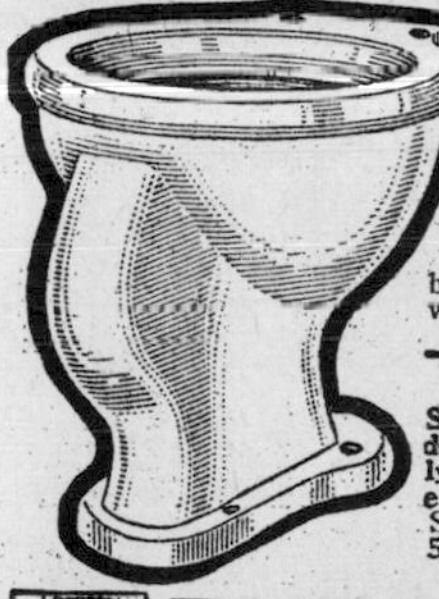

42K1888¼—Composition White Tank only, to fit washdown bowl. Shpg. wt., 40 lbs. **$9.95**

42K1889¼ Composition Tank only, to fit siphon jet bowl. Shipping weight, 40 lbs. **$10.00**

42K1894¼ Siphon Washdown Bowl only. Vitreous earthenware. Shipping weight, 50 pounds. **$6.95**

Oakdale Closet Outfit

Same as our Fairfield Closet Outfit at right, except bowl is siphon jet pattern instead of siphon washdown. Almost noiseless in its flushing action. Siphon jet bowl, in addition to the regular siphon flushing action, has small jet which projects a solid stream of water at high velocity through the trap of bowl in same directions as flow of water so that flushing action is greatly enhanced. Shipping weight, 50 lbs.

42K2001¼—Outfit complete, as illustrated.............. $26.75

Avondale Closet Outfit With Genuine White Celluloid Coated Seat

Same as Oakdale Closet Outfit described above, illustrated at right, except it is equipped with finest quality genuine white celluloid coated seat, hand rubbed finish. Shipping weight, 150 pounds.

42K2009¼ $28.85

42K1877¼—China Tank only, to fit siphon jet bowl. Shpg. wt., 65 lbs.......... **$12.35**

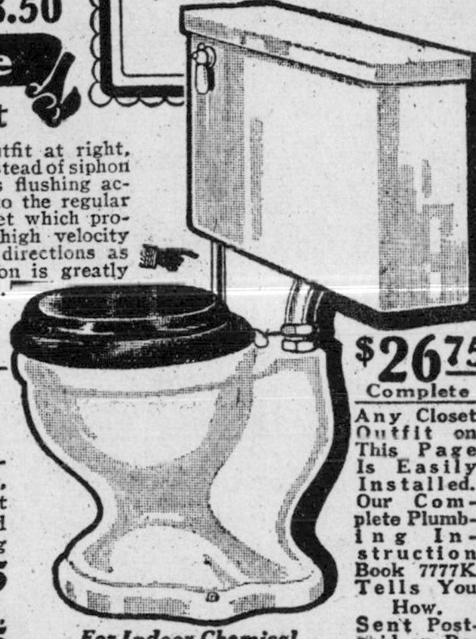

$26.75 Complete

Any Closet Outfit on This Page Is Easily Installed. Our Complete Plumbing Instruction Book 7777K Tells You How. Sent Postpaid on Request.

For Indoor Chemical Closets See Page 644

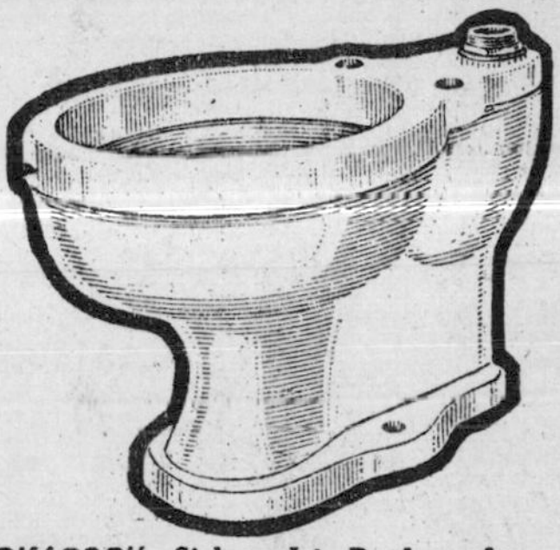

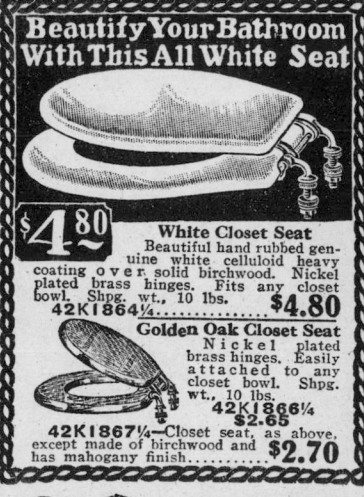

42K1898¼—Siphon Jet Bowl only. Vitreous earthenware. Shipping weight, 60 pounds.............. **$12.25**

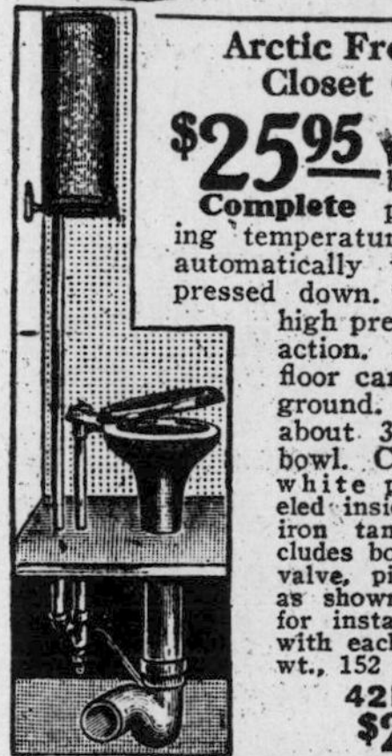

Arctic Frostproof Closet Outfit

$25.95 Complete

For unheated rooms or outbuildings exposed to freezing temperatures. Operates automatically when seat is pressed down. Has strong, high pressure flushing action. Parts below floor can be buried in ground. Trap comes about 3 feet below bowl. Cast iron bowl, white porcelain enameled inside. Galvanized iron tank. Outfit includes bowl, seat, tank, valve, piping and trap, as shown. Instructions for installing furnished with each outfit. Shpg. wt., 152 lbs.

42K1860¼ $25.95

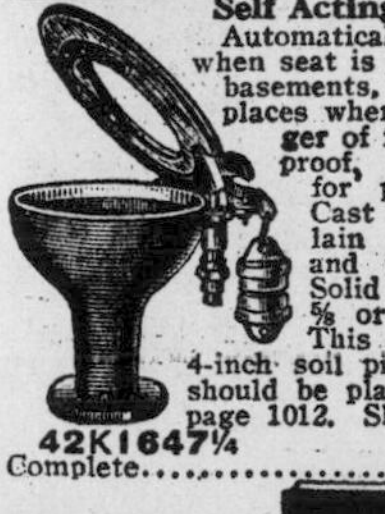

Self Acting Hopper Closet

Automatically flushes bowl when seat is pressed down. For basements, factories and places where there is no danger of freezing. Not frostproof. Especially suited for public places, etc. Cast iron bowl, porcelain enameled inside and painted outside. Solid oak seat. For ½, ⅝ or ¾-inch lead pipe. This bowl has no trap. 4-inch soil pipe trap 42K1540¼ should be placed under it. See page 1012. Shpg. wt., 45 lbs.

42K1647¼ Complete.......... $8.75

Hercules Septic Tank for Sewage Disposal

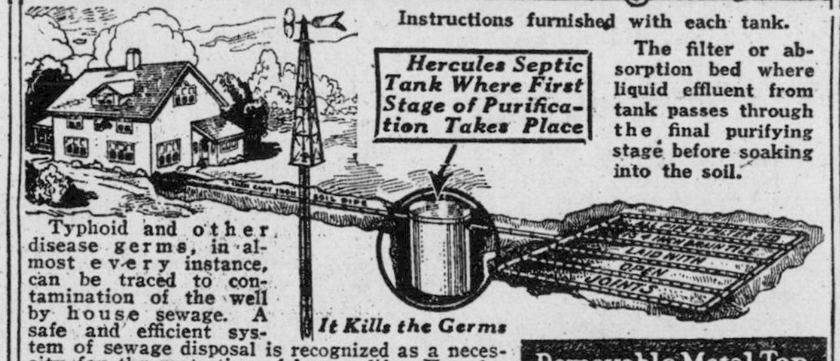

Hercules Septic Tank Where First Stage of Purification Takes Place
It Kills the Germs

Instructions furnished with each tank.

The filter or absorption bed where liquid effluent from tank passes through the final purifying stage before soaking into the soil.

Typhoid and other disease germs, in almost every instance, can be traced to contamination of the well by house sewage. A safe and efficient system of sewage disposal is recognized as a necessity for the protection of human life. Hercules Septic Tank is adapted for sewage disposal from any building where running water is available. The natural process of bacterial action provides a safe, effectual and inexpensive means of sewage disposal, as well as an effective protection for your water supply. Hercules tanks are built from high quality Copper Bearing Steel Plate, unexcelled for rust resistance. In addition to this, they are coated with a special rust resisting preservative, making them very durable.

Catalog No.	Diameter, Inches	Height, Inches	Total Cap., Gals.	Shipping Weight	Capacity Home Use, Number Persons	
42K3562⅓	30½	48	153	165	4	$20.65
42K3563⅓	36	48	212	205	6	22.40
42K3564⅓	45	48	331	300	8	28.00

Above prices do not include drain tile.

Shipped from factory in WESTERN NEW YORK or NORTHERN ILLINOIS whichever is nearer you.

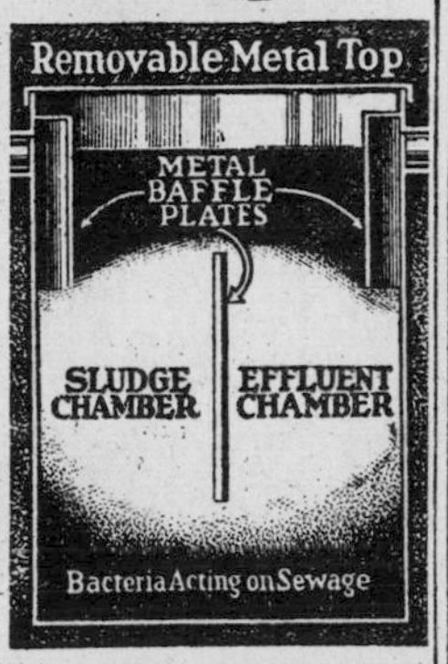

Removable Metal Top
METAL BAFFLE PLATES
SLUDGE CHAMBER
EFFLUENT CHAMBER
Bacteria Acting on Sewage

Beautify Your Bathroom With This All White Seat

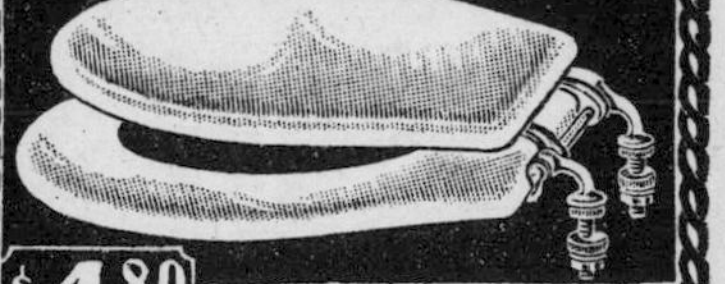

$4.80

White Closet Seat

Beautiful hand rubbed genuine white celluloid heavy coating over solid birchwood. Nickel plated brass hinges. Fits any closet bowl. Shpg. wt., 10 lbs.

42K1864¼ $4.80

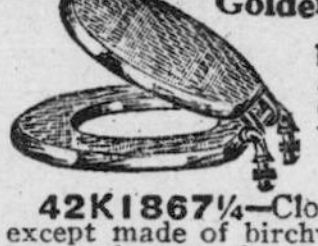

Golden Oak Closet Seat

Nickel plated brass hinges. Easily attached to any closet bowl. Shpg. wt., 10 lbs.

42K1866¼ $2.65

42K1867¼—Closet seat, as above, except made of birchwood and has mahogany finish.......... **$2.70**

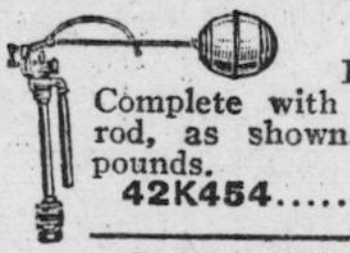

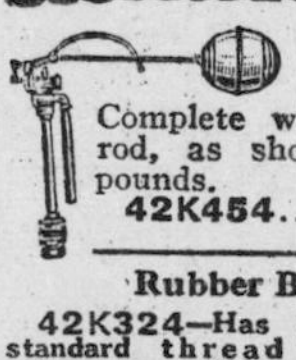

Brass Ball Cock

For low closet tank. Complete with copper ball float and rod, as shown. Shipping weight, 3 pounds.

42K454 .... $1.30

Rubber Ball Valve

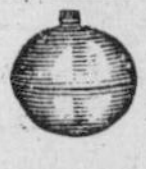

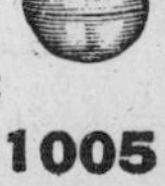

42K324—Has brass insert with standard thread for attaching to valve stem. Shpg. wt., 6 oz.

2-inch. **22c** 2½-inch. **25c** 2¾-inch. **29c**

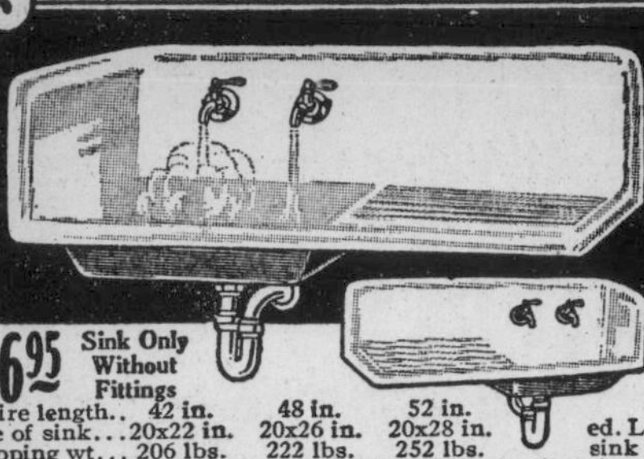

Magnolia Corner Sink

Cast iron white porcelain enameled. Fittings include ½-inch flanged faucets with white china indexed handles latest improved boltless strainer and 1½-inch trap to floor or wall. All fittings solid brass, nickel plated. Large illustration shows sink with left hand end piece and right hand drain board. Small illustration shows sink with right hand end piece and left hand drain board. Be very careful to order correct sink.

$26.95 Sink Only Without Fittings

Entire length..	42 in.	48 in.	52 in.
Size of sink...	20x22 in.	20x26 in.	20x28 in.
Shipping wt...	206 lbs.	222 lbs.	252 lbs.

Shipped from HARRISBURG, PA., or SPRINGFIELD, MASS.

Length of Sink	With Left Hand End Piece and Right Hand Drain Board Like Large Illustration			With Right Hand End Piece and Left Hand Drain Board Like Small Illustration		
	42K3804⅓ Sink Complete With Fittings to Wall	42K3809⅓ Sink Complete With Fittings to Floor	42K3811⅓ Sink only, Without Strainer, Trap or Faucets	42K3803⅓ Sink Complete With Fittings to Wall	42K3805⅓ Sink Complete With Fittings to Floor	42K3810⅓ Sink Only, Without Strainer, Trap or Faucets
42	$31.35	$31.95	$26.95	$31.35	$31.95	$26.95
48	34.00	34.65	29.60	34.00	34.65	29.60
52	35.90	36.50	31.50	35.90	36.50	31.50

NOTE—At an extra charge of $3.50 over price of sink complete we can furnish our new style swing spout faucet with white glass soap dish.

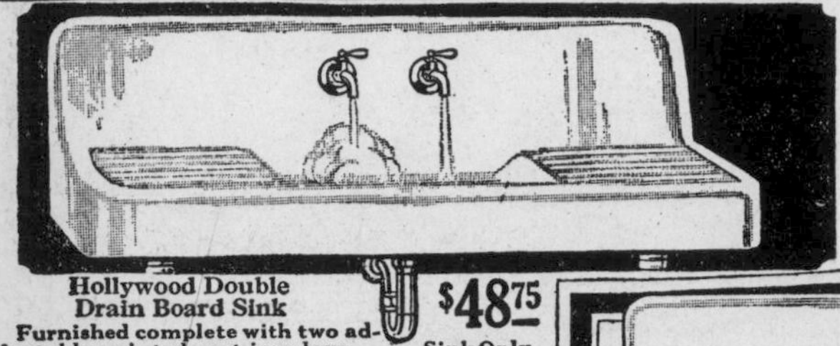

Hollywood Double Drain Board Sink

$48.75 Sink Only Without Fittings

Furnished complete with two adjustable painted cast iron legs and concealed wall hangers. Fittings include ½-inch flanged faucets, with white china indexed handles, latest improved boltless strainer and trap to wall or floor, all solid brass, nickel plated. Cast iron, white porcelain enameled, double drain board sink with apron. Furnished in two sizes, 62 inches long and 74 inches long.

Length over all, 62 in.	Length over all, 74 in.
Size of sink, 20x26 in.	Size of sink, 22x26 in.
Drain boards, 20x18 in.	Drain boards, 22x24 in.
Shipping weight, 300 lbs.	Shipping wt., 333 lbs.

Be sure to state size wanted	Size, 62 Inches	Size, 74 Inches
42K3830⅓–Sink complete with faucets and trap to wall..........	$52.20	$80.25
42K3831⅓–Sink complete with faucets and trap to floor..........	52.75	80.75
42K3832⅓–Sink with legs—no fittings........	48.75	76.85

For iron pipe threads add 75c to price of sink with fittings. For porcelain enameled legs instead of painted, add $3.50. Shipped from HARRISBURG, PA., or SPRINGFIELD, MASS.

NOTE—At an extra charge of $3.50 over price of sink complete we can furnish our new style swing spout faucet with white glass soap dish.

Just Think of the Saving You Make

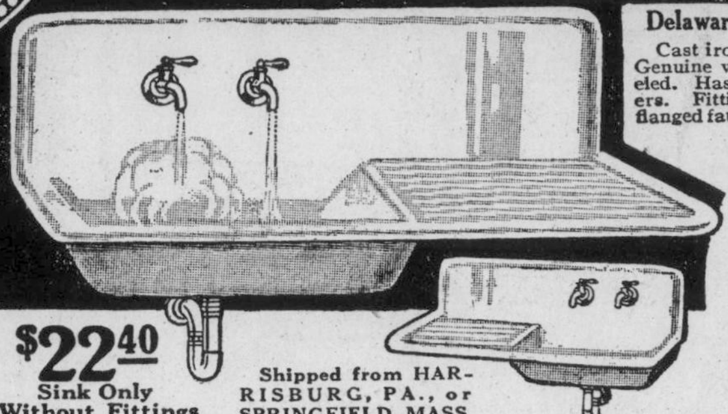

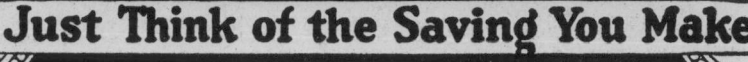

Delaware Roll Rim Sink

Cast iron, in one solid piece. Genuine white porcelain enameled. Has concealed wall hangers. Fittings include ½-inch flanged faucets, with white china indexed handles, latest improved boltless strainer and 1½-inch trap to floor or wall. All fittings solid brass, nickel plated.

NOTE—At an extra charge of $3.50 over price of sink complete we can furnish our new style swing spout faucet with white glass soap dish.

$22.40 Sink Only Without Fittings

Shipped from HARRISBURG, PA., or SPRINGFIELD, MASS.

For iron pipe connections add 75c to price of sink with fittings.

Entire length.....	42 in.	48 in.	52 in.
Size of sink......	20x24 in.	20x26 in.	20x28 in.
Drain board......	20x18 in.	20x22 in.	20x24 in.
Shipping weight...	186 lbs.	215 lbs.	215 lbs.

Large illustration shows sink with right hand drain board. Small illustration shows sink with left hand drain board. Be very careful to order correct sink.

Lgth. of Sink	With Right Hand Drain Board Like Large Illustration			With Left Hand Drain Board Like Small Illustration		
	42K3859⅓ Sink Complete With Fittings to Wall	42K3862⅓ Sink Complete With Fittings to Floor	42K3864⅓ Sink Only Without Strainer, Trap or Faucets	42K3860⅓ Sink Complete With Fittings to Wall	42K3861⅓ Sink Complete With Fittings to Floor	42K3863⅓ Sink Only, Without Strainer, Trap or Faucets
42	$26.75	$27.35	$22.40	$26.75	$27.35	$22.40
48	29.75	30.35	25.25	29.75	30.35	25.25
52	31.25	31.85	26.75	31.25	31.85	26.75

Big Value

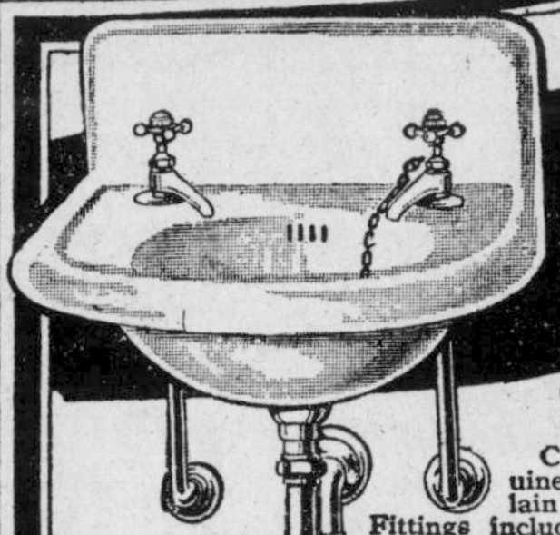

Champlain Lavatory

Cast iron genuine white porcelain enameled. Fittings include compression basin cocks with white china index buttons lettered hot and cold, trap and supply pipes to floor or wall. All fittings solid brass, nickel plated.
Shipped from HARRISBURG, PA., or SPRINGFIELD, MASS.

Size of slab, 17x19 inches. 10x14-inch bowl. Back, 6 inches high. Shpg. wt., 56 lbs.

42K3720⅓—With fittings to wall as shown.......................... $11.35
42K3721⅓—With fittings to floor. 11.65
42K3722⅓—Without fittings..... 5.75

Size of slab, 18x21 inches. Bowl, 10½x14½ inches. Back, 8 inches high. Shpg. wt., 82 lbs.

42K3775⅓—With fittings to wall.. $12.95
42K3776⅓—With fittings to floor. 13.35
42K3777⅓—Without fittings..... 7.85

For iron pipe threads add 75 cents to price of lavatory with fittings.

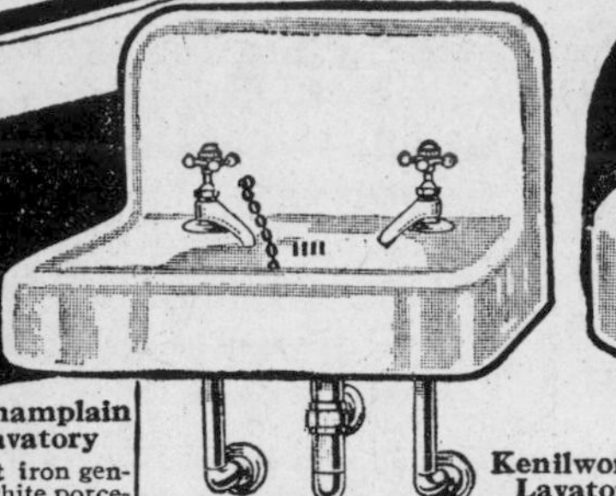

Kenilworth Lavatory

Cast iron, genuine white porcelain enameled. Fittings include compression basin cocks with china index buttons lettered hot and cold, trap and supply pipes to floor or wall. All fittings are solid brass, nickel plated. Shipped from HARRISBURG, PA., or SPRINGFIELD, MASS. Shpg. wt., 93 lbs.

Size of slab, 17½x21 inches. Bowl, 10x14 inches. Back, 8 inches high.

42K3750⅓—With fittings to wall as shown........................ $13.95
42K3751⅓—With fittings to floor........................ 14.25
42K3752⅓ — Without fittings........................ 8.95

Size of slab, 18x24 in. Bowl, 11x15 in. Back, 10 in. high. Shpg. wt., 105 lbs.

42K3732⅓—With fittings to wall as shown........................ $16.65
42K3733⅓—With fittings to floor........................ 16.95
42K3734⅓ — Without fittings........................ 11.25

For iron pipe threads add 75 cents to price of lavatory with fittings.

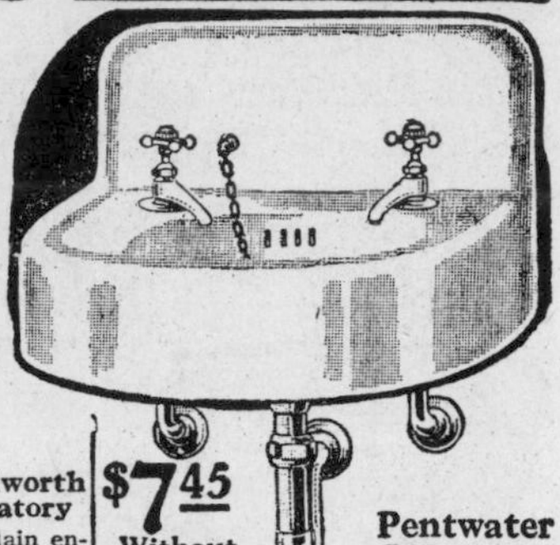

Pentwater Lavatory

$7.45 Without Fittings

Cast iron. Genuine white porcelain enameled. Has deep apron. Fittings include compression basin cocks lettered hot and cold, trap and supply pipes to floor or wall. All fittings brass, nickel plated. Shipped from HARRISBURG, PA., or SPRINGFIELD, MASS. Shpg. wt., 68 lbs.

Size of slab, 17x19 inches. Bowl, 10½x13½ in. Back, 6 in. high.

42K3741⅓ — With fittings to wall as shown........... $12.65
42K3742⅓—With fittings to floor.......... 12.95
42K3743⅓—Without fittings.............. 7.45

Size of slab, 18x21 inches. Bowl, 10½x14½ inches. Back, 8 inches high. Shipping weight, 82 pounds.

42K3744⅓ — With fittings to wall as shown........... $13.50
42K3745⅓—With fittings to floor.......... 13.90
42K3746⅓ — Without fittings.............. 8.45

For iron pipe threads add 75 cents to price of lavatory with fittings.

Splendid Roll Rim Sink

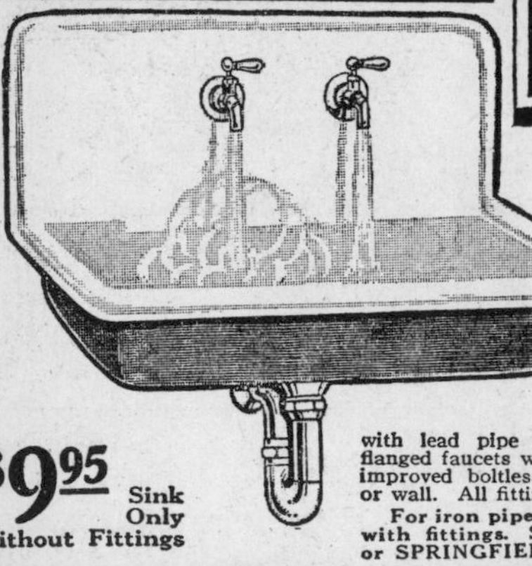

Milburn Roll Rim Sink

Any roll rim cast iron sink on this page can be furnished with painted cast iron legs at $1.25 extra for each leg or with porcelain enameled legs at $3.00 extra for each leg.

Cast iron one-piece white porcelain enameled. Furnished complete with concealed wall hangers. Prices are for sinks with lead pipe connection. Fittings include ½-inch flanged faucets with white china indexed handles, latest improved boltless strainer and 1½-inch trap to floor or wall. All fittings solid brass, nickel plated.

For iron pipe connection add 75c to price of sink with fittings. Shipped from HARRISBURG, PA., or SPRINGFIELD, MASS.

$9.95 Sink Only Without Fittings

Size of Sink	42K3800⅓ Sink Complete With Faucets and Trap to Wall as Shown		42K3801⅓ Sink Complete With Fittings, Faucets and Trap to Floor		42K3802⅓ Sink Only Without Strainer, Trap or Faucets	
	Shpg. Wt., Lbs.		Shpg. Wt., Lbs.		Shpg. Wt., Lbs.	
18x24	96	$14.25	100	$14.75	88	$ 9.95
20x24	104	15.50	108	16.00	103	10.95
18x30	125	15.65	129	16.25	110	11.45
20x30	130	17.45	134	17.95	118	13.15
20x36	145	19.25	149	19.75	140	14.95
22x42	200	23.50	204	24.25	182	19.00

NOTE—At an extra charge of $3.50 over price of sink complete we can furnish our new style swing spout faucet with white glass soap dish.

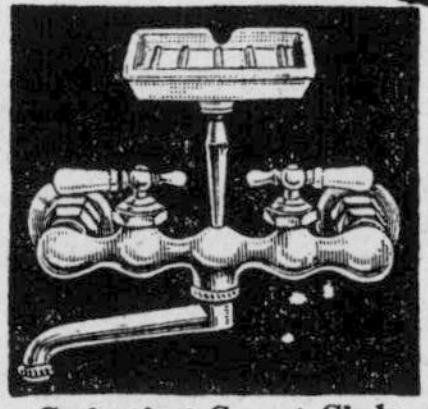

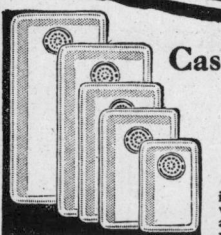

Swinging Spout Sink Faucet

$5.50

New style combination sink faucet with swinging spout. Brass, nickel plated. Spout has removable brass strainer. Fits ½-inch pipe. Has white china handles marked hot and cold and white opal glass soap dish. Modern, beautiful and attractive. Shpg. wt., 6 lbs.

42K387........$5.50

Same as above, except without soap dish. Shipping weight, 3½ pounds.

42K383........$4.35

For other Sink Faucets see page 1012.

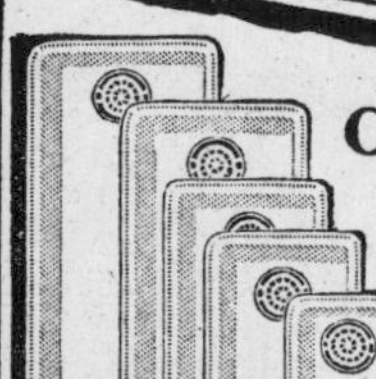

Cast Iron Flat Rim Kitchen Sinks

$2.65 and Up

Practical, serviceable, moderate in cost. Furnished with genuine white porcelain enamel finish inside and painted finish outside; also with painted finish inside and outside. Threaded for 1¼ or 1½-inch iron waste pipe, 25c extra.

42K1640¼—Painted inside and out.

Size, over all..........................	16x24	18x30
Shipping weight, pounds..................	46	62
Each....................................	$2.65	$3.45

42K1642¼—Porcelain enameled inside, painted outside.

Size, Over All	Shpg. Wt., Lbs.		Size, Over All	Shpg. Wt., Lbs.	
16x24	46	$4.90	20x36	75	$ 7.45
18x30	60	4.95	20x40	80	10.15
20x30	63	5.95			

For Sink Faucets see page 1012.

on These Sanitary, Easy to Clean Sinks!

Hiawatha Apron Sink

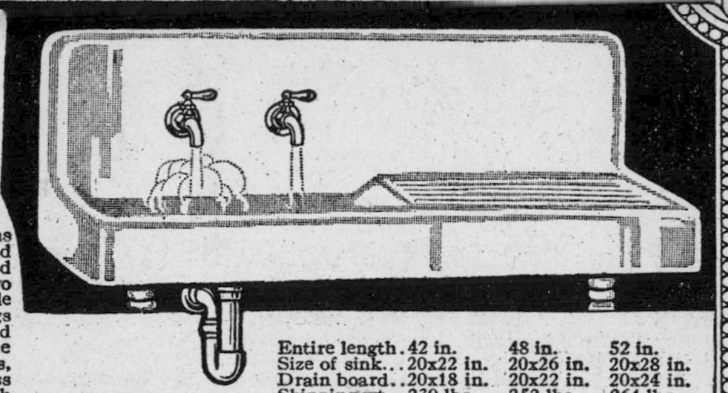

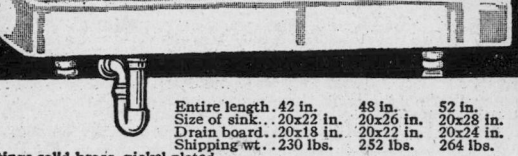

Here is one of the most elegant sinks you could possibly select. Cast iron in one piece, genuine white porcelain enameled.

Has deep apron as shown. Furnished complete with concealed wall hangers and two cast iron adjustable painted legs. Fittings include ½-inch flanged faucets, with white china indexed handles, latest improved boltless strainer and 1½-inch trap to floor or wall. All fittings solid brass, nickel plated.

Illustration shows sink with right hand drain board. Also furnished with left hand drain board. Be very careful to order correct sink. For iron pipe threads add 75c to price of sink with fittings. Shipped from HARRISBURG, PA., or SPRINGFIELD, MASS.

Entire length.	42 in.	48 in.	52 in.
Size of sink...	20x22 in.	20x26 in.	20x28 in.
Drain board.	20x18 in.	20x22 in.	20x24 in.
Shipping wt.	230 lbs.	252 lbs.	264 lbs.

	With Right Hand Drain Board			With Left Hand Drain Board		
Length of Sink	42K3888½ Sink Complete With Fittings to Wall	42K3890½ Sink Complete With Fittings to Floor	42K3892½ Sink Only, Without Strainer, Trap or Faucets	42K3889½ Sink Complete With Fittings to Wall	42K3891½ Sink Complete With Fittings to Floor	42K3893½ Sink Only, Without Strainer, Trap or Faucets
42	$33.50	$34.25	$29.25	$33.50	$34.25	$29.25
48	40.75	41.25	36.45	40.75	41.25	36.45
52	43.75	44.20	39.25	43.75	44.20	39.25

NOTE—At an extra charge of $3.50 over price of sink complete we can furnish our new style swing spout faucet with white glass soap dish.

Claremont Corner Sink

Cast iron genuine white porcelain enameled. Furnished complete with concealed wall hangers and two cast iron painted adjustable legs. Fittings include ½-inch flanged faucets, with white china indexed handles, latest improved boltless strainer and 1½-inch trap to floor or wall. All fittings solid brass, nickel plated. Be very careful to order correct sink. For iron pipe threads add 75c to price of sink with fittings. If white porcelain enameled legs are wanted instead of painted, add $3.50.

Shipped from HARRISBURG, PA., or SPRINGFIELD, MASS.

Large illustration shows sink with right hand end piece and left hand drain board. Small illustration shows sink with left hand end piece and right hand drain board.

Entire length.	42 in.	48 in.	52 in.
Size of sink...	20x22 in.	20x26 in.	20x28 in.
Shipping weight.	254 lbs.	276 lbs.	290 lbs.

	With Right Hand End Piece and Left Hand Drain Board			With Left Hand End Piece and Right Hand Drain Board		
Length of Sink	42K3794½ Sink Complete With Fittings to Wall	42K3796½ Sink Complete With Fittings to Floor	42K3798½ Sink Only, Without Fittings	42K3795½ Sink Complete With Fittings to Wall	42K3797½ Sink Complete With Fittings to Floor	42K3799½ Sink Only, Without Fittings
42	$36.50	$37.10	$33.00	$36.50	$37.10	$33.00
48	44.30	44.90	40.00	44.30	44.90	40.00
52	47.95	48.65	43.75	47.95	48.65	43.75

NOTE—At an extra charge of $3.50 over price of sink complete we can furnish our new style swing spout faucet with white glass soap dish.

Lavatories

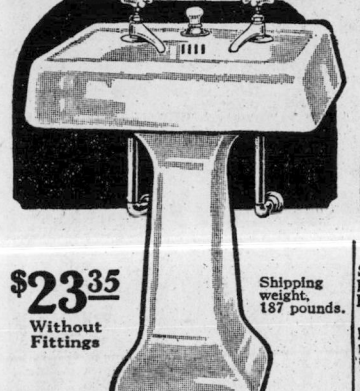

$23 35 Without Fittings

Shipping weight, 187 pounds.

Montrose Pedestal Lavatory

Size, 20x24 inches. 11x15-inch bowl. Beautiful, sanitary cast iron, genuine white porcelain enameled from floor up. Large roomy slab gives ample room for shaving mug, toilet articles, etc. Fittings include compression faucets with white china handles, trap and supply pipes to floor or wall and improved pop-up waste. All fittings are solid brass, nickel plated. Shipped from HARRISBURG, PA., or SPRINGFIELD, MASS.

42K3756½—Complete with fittings with pipes to wall, as shown.......$30.35
42K3757½—Complete with fittings, with pipes to floor........$30.65
For iron pipe threads add 75 cents to price of lavatory with fittings.
42K3758½—Lavatory only..$23.35

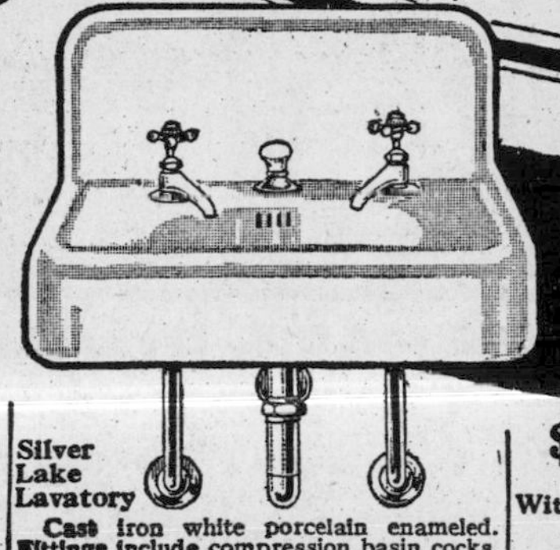

Silver Lake Lavatory

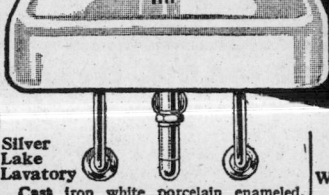

Cast iron white porcelain enameled. Fittings include compression basin cocks, pop-up waste with china handle, trap and supply pipes to floor or wall, all of solid brass, nickel plated. Shipped from HARRISBURG, PA., or SPRINGFIELD, MASS. Shpg. wt. 97 lbs. Size of slab, 17½x21 in. Bowl, 10x14 in. Back, 8 in. high.

42K3753½ With Fittings to Wall as Shown	42K3754½ With Fittings to Floor	42K3755½ Without Fittings
$16.65	$16.95	$9.75

Size of slab, 18x24 in. Bowl, 11x15 in. Back, 10 in. high. Shipping wt., 102 lbs.

42K3738½ With Fittings to Wall as Shown	42K3739½ With Fittings to Floor	42K3740½ Without Fittings
$22.00	$22.50	$13.25

For iron pipe threads add 75 cents to price of lavatory with fittings.

Pocahontas Lavatory

$7 95 Without Fittings

Length on side, 18¾ inches. Bowl, 10x14 inches. Back, 6 inches high. Cast iron, genuine white porcelain enameled. Fittings include compression basin cocks, lettered hot and cold, trap and supply pipes to wall or floor. All fittings solid brass, nickel plated. Shipped from HARRISBURG, PA., or SPRINGFIELD, MASS. Shipping weight, 60 pounds.

42K3772½—Lavatory complete with fittings, with pipes to wall, as shown.................$13.10
42K3773½—Complete with fittings, with pipes to floor.....$13.60
For iron pipe threads add 75 cents to price of lavatory with fittings.
42K3774½ Lavatory only...............$7.95

$35 25 Sink Only Without Fittings

Elmwood Double Drain Board Roll Rim Sink

Same as our Hollywood sink described on opposite page, except that it has roll rim instead of deep apron. Furnished complete with painted legs. For porcelain enameled legs, add $3.50. Length, over all, 62 inches. Size sink, 20x26 inches. Drain boards, 20x18 inches. Shipping weight, 312 pounds.

42K3812½—Complete with faucets and trap to wall.........$39.85
42K3813½—Complete with faucets and trap to floor.........$40.50
42K3814½—Sink only with legs, no fittings............$35.25
For iron pipe threads, add 75c to price of sink with fittings.

NOTE—At an extra charge of $3.50 over price of sink complete we can furnish our new style swing spout faucet with white glass soap dish.

Shipped from HARRISBURG, PA., or SPRINGFIELD, MASS.

Kitchen Sink and Pump Outfit

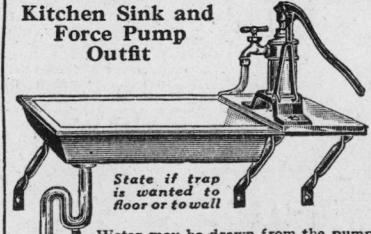

Includes cast iron flat rim sink, porcelain enameled inside, 3-inch pitcher spout pump with iron cylinder, 1½-inch cast iron sink trap to floor or wall fitted for iron pipe connections, pump bracket, two sink brackets. Pump threaded for 1¼-inch iron suction pipe. Waste pipe or suction pipe not included.

42K2029¼—Outfit complete as described.

Size of sink, in.	18x30	20x30	20x36	20x40
Shpg. wt., lbs.	95	97	110	115
With trap to wall...	$8.55	$9.60	$11.10	$13.80
With trap to floor...	9.85	10.90	12.40	15.10

If pump with brass lined cylinder is wanted instead of iron, add 90c to prices.

State if trap is wanted to floor or to wall

Brass Sink Strainer

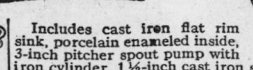

Strainer, new style with tailpiece. Fits cast iron roll rim and apron sinks shown on this and the opposite page. Shipping weight, ¾ pound.
42K386.................. 55c

Cast Iron Sink Backs

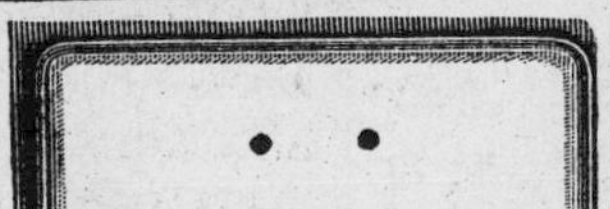

42K1643¼—Porcelain enameled, for flat rim sinks. 12 inches high and 2¼ inches thick.

Length, in..	24	30	36	40
Shpg. wt., lbs......	35	38	51	53
Each......	$3.90	$3.95	$5.95	$6.40

Drain Boards

$5 55 Up

Reversible cast iron enameled drain board. With iron bracket. State size.
42K1645¼

Size, 18x20 in.	Shpg. wt., 46 lbs.	$5.55
Size, 18x24 in.	Shpg. wt., 56 lbs.	5.60
Size, 20x24 in.	Shpg. wt., 62 lbs.	5.95

Roll Rim Steel Sink

Heavily galvanized inside and out. Brackets are listed below.

Size, over all, inches...	16x24	18x30
Shipping weight, pounds...	20	28
42K1636½—Galvanized......	$3.00	$4.15

For iron pipe connection, add 25c.

Flat Rim Steel Sinks

If wanted for 1½-inch iron pipe connection, add 25c

Size, over all, inches....	16x24	18x30
Shipping weight, pounds...	10	14½
42K1630¼—Painted......	$2.35	$2.85
42K1632¼—Galvanized...	2.55	3.30

Steel Sink Brackets

Used with flat rim cast iron and flat and roll rim steel sinks. Very neat in appearance. Shpg. wt., pair, 3 lbs.
42K350—No. 1 Plain, for 16 or 18-inch sinks.
Per pair.....................35c
42K351—No. 2 Plain, for 20-inch sinks and larger.
Per pair.....................40c

Kitchen Sink and Force Pump Outfit

Includes cast iron flat rim sink, porcelain enameled inside, 3-inch brass body cistern force pump with cock spout threaded for hose connection, three sink brackets, oak pump board, 1½-inch cast iron trap, fitted for iron pipe connection. No pipe included.

State if trap is wanted to floor or to wall

Water may be drawn from the pump spout, forced into an attic tank or used for sprinkling, etc. Pump has 1¼-inch suction and 1-inch discharge for iron pipe connection.

42K2031¼

Size of sink, in....	18x30	20x30	20x36	20x40
Shpg. wt., lbs.....	92	97	101	111
With trap to floor.	$13.00	$14.15	$15.65	$18.30
With trap to wall..	11.70	12.85	14.35	17.00

Parcel Post, Express and Freight Rates Are on Pages 542 to 545

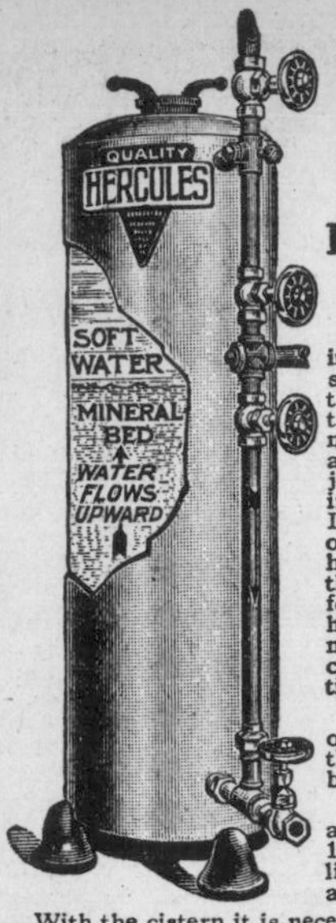
QUALITY
HERCULES
SOFT WATER
MINERAL BED
WATER FLOWS UPWARD

$89.75 Necessities for the Home The Best at Lowest Prices

20,000-Grain Capacity

Hercules Water Softener

Better Than a Cistern

The Hercules Water Softener is installed in the basement, and the hard water piped so as to pass through it. As the water passes through the mineral bed in the softener, all the hardness is caught and held. The mineral absorbs the hardness like a sponge absorbs water. No chemicals are added—just the hardness is removed. The mineral in time takes up all the hardness it can hold. It is then necessary to put about 10 pounds of salt in the softener, which releases the hardness and is flushed to the sewer with the salt. Salt must be added every two to four weeks, depending on the amount of hardness in the water. The mineral does not lose its efficiency; it is permanent, because it is insoluble in water and will continue to soften water for years.

A cistern is a catch-all place for the dirt of the roof and gutters; each rain washes the accumulation of bugs, chimney soot and bird wastage into the family wash water.

A Hercules Water Softener costs less than a cistern and gives an unlimited supply of 100 per cent soft, pure, untainted and delightfully clear water, good for drinking, and a pleasure in doing all household tasks.

With the cistern it is necessary to have a separate pump and storage tank. The Hercules Water Softener eliminates this. It is easily connected to your plumbing system in a few hours' time. Any handy man can install it by following out simple instructions. It is shipped complete, ready to use, there is nothing to be added after you get it.

SPECIFICATIONS

Size of tank, 14 inches in diameter; height of shell, 48 inches, guaranteed to stand 125 pounds pressure. Built of heavy, rust resisting steel and coated inside and out with a specially prepared material which absolutely prevents rusting. The fittings are ¾-inch in size. The valves are the best obtainable. A 3-inch brass plug with rubber seated gasket on head of tank; 2-cubic feet of high capacity, white synthetic mineral. THE HERCULES WATER SOFTENER CARRIES OUR MONEY BACK GUARANTEE.

42K2520½—Shipping weight, 330 pounds.. ....**$89.75**

Shipped from factory warehouses at WESTERN KANSAS, SOUTHERN MINNESOTA or CENTRAL OHIO.

42K1465¼—Hercules Water Softener Salt. Prepared especially for water softener use. Comes in 100-pound bags. Per bag.......... **$1.75**

Stoneware Laundry Tubs

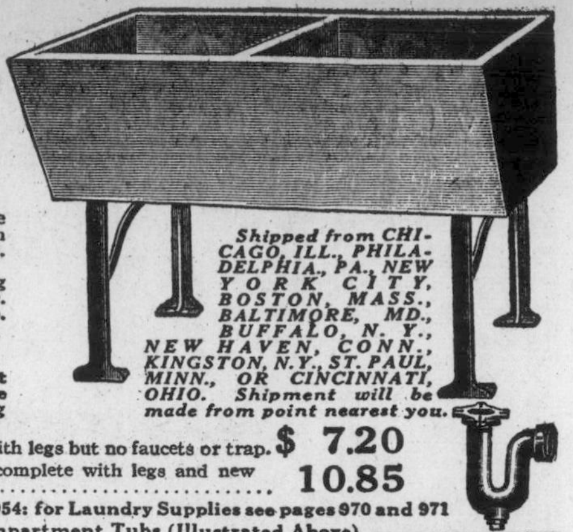
Shipped from CHICAGO, ILL., PHILADELPHIA, PA., NEW YORK CITY, BOSTON, MASS., BALTIMORE, MD., BUFFALO, N. Y., NEW HAVEN, CONN., KINGSTON, N.Y., ST. PAUL, MINN., OR CINCINNATI, OHIO. Shipment will be made from point nearest you.

Molded in one solid piece from special granitine composition material. No seams to leak or catch grease or dirt. Tubs have metal rims and guards. Ornamental cast iron legs.

Small illustrations show trap and new style swinging spout faucet furnished when tub is ordered complete. One and two-part tubs require one faucet and one trap. Three-part tubs require one faucet and two traps.

One-Compartment Laundry Tubs (Not illustrated.)

Same as 42K3897½ illustrated at right except with only one compartment. Made in one size only, 24x24 inches. Tub is 14 inches deep. Shipping weight, 235 pounds.

42K3868½—One-Compartment Laundry Tub with legs but no faucets or trap. **$7.20**

42K3869½—One-Compartment Laundry Tub complete with legs and new style swinging arm faucet and trap.......... **10.85**

For Laundry Stoves see page 954: for Laundry Supplies see pages 970 and 971

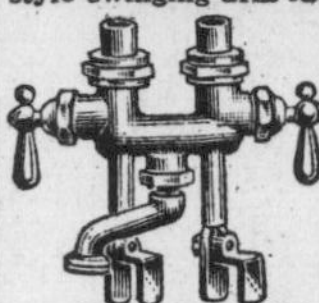

Two-Compartment Tubs (Illustrated Above)

Length over all, inches..........	48	54	60
Size, each tub, over all, inches..........	24x24x15½	24x27x15½	24x30x15½
Shipping weight, pounds..........	380	450	500
42K3897½—Tubs with legs but no faucet or trap..........	$9.75	$10.95	$12.45
42K3781½—Tubs complete with legs, new style swinging spout faucet and trap..........	13.25	14.25	15.75

Three-Compartment Laundry Tubs Without Back (Not Illustrated)

Same as 42K3897½ illustrated above, except with three compartments. Made in one size only, 72 inches long. Each tub measures 24x24x15½ inches over all. Shipping weight, 550 pounds.

42K3879½—Three-Compartment Laundry Tub with legs but no faucet or trap.......... **$15.35**

42K3784½—Three Compartment Laundry Tub complete with legs and new style swinging spout faucet with extension for three tubs and two traps.......... **19.95**

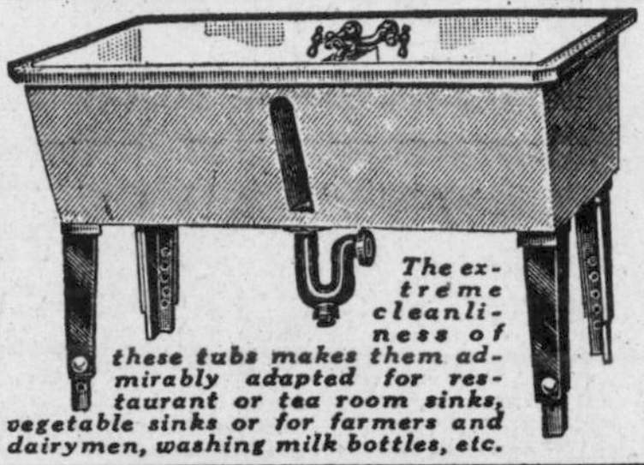

The extreme cleanliness of these tubs makes them admirably adapted for restaurant or tea room sinks, vegetable sinks or for farmers and dairymen, washing milk bottles, etc.

Porcelain Enameled Steel Laundry Tubs

These tubs are made of 14-gauge steel, heavily coated with genuine porcelain enamel, both inside and out. The inside of both tubs is coated with white porcelain enamel, and the outside is coated with agate gray porcelain enamel. The legs are coated with black porcelain enamel, and are adjustable to any desired height. The faucet being placed down below the top of the tubs permits you to put on a wooden cover or table top so that the tubs may be used as a work table in your kitchen when not used for washing. Each tub furnished complete with combination brass faucet and cast iron trap as shown. Shipping weight, 106 pounds.

42K3914½—Size, 24x48 inches over all. Height is adjustable within wide range.......... **$27.95**

Shipped from factory in WESTERN PENNSYLVANIA or EASTERN OHIO.

For Washing Machines, see page 910 to 913.
For Coal Burning Water Heaters, see page 953.

SNOW WHITE FIXTURES FOR THE BATHROOM BEAUTIFUL

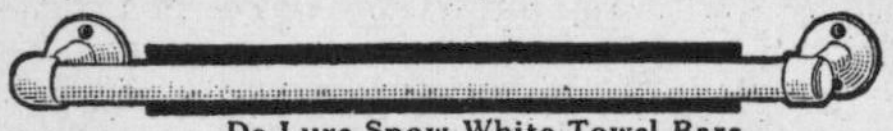

De Luxe Snow White Towel Bars

42K290—¾ in. diameter.	Shpg. Wt.		42K289—1¼ in. diameter.	Shpg. Wt.	
15 in.	2½ lbs.	$0.78	18 in.	2¾ lbs.	$0.85
18 in.	2¾ lbs.	.80	24 in.	4 lbs.	1.05
24 in.	3½ lbs.	.95	30 in.	4¼ lbs.	1.25

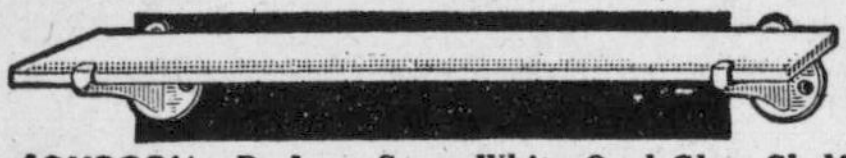

42K288¼—De Luxe Snow White Opal Glass Shelf. Has cast iron, hard porcelain enameled brackets. Opal glass shelf with rounded and ground edges and corners.
5x18 inches. Shpg. wt., 6¾ pounds.. $1.65
5x24 inches. Shpg. wt., 8 pounds.. 1.80

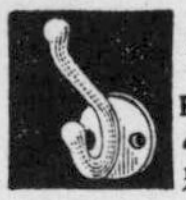

De Luxe Snow White Double Bathrobe Hook. Shipping weight, each, 4 ounces.
42K291—Each.......... 16c
½ dozen.......... 90c

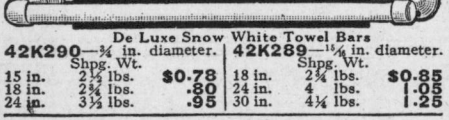

You will surely appreciate the massive beauty and remarkable durability of these high grade fixtures. Do not confuse them with soft finish or painted fixtures. The coating on these fixtures is genuine hard white porcelain enamel, smooth and hard as glass, just like your bathtub. Easy to clean and keep clean. The designs are the very latest and are strikingly artistic. They will last a lifetime. Special white enameled capped screws included with each fixture.

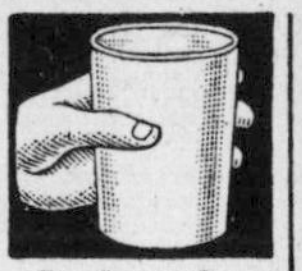

De Luxe Snow White Glass Tumbler. Fits any holder on this page. Shipping wt., ¾ lb.... 42K231.. **18c**

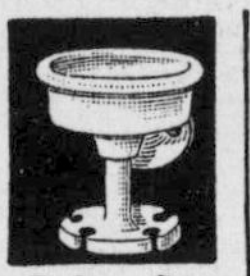

De Luxe Snow White Tooth Brush and Tumbler Holder. Shpg. wt., 1¾ lbs. 42K286.. **64c**

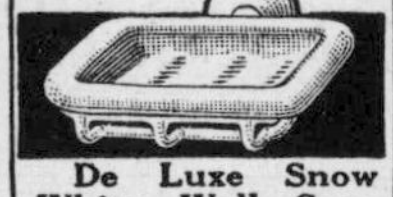

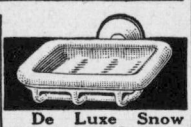

De Luxe Snow White Wall Soap Dish with removable Opal Glass Tray. Size, 4⅜x5½ inches. Shipping weight, 1½ pounds. 42K284.. **85c**

Bevel Plate Mirror

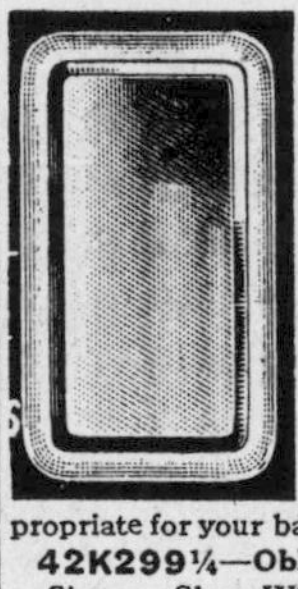

Made of high quality polished and beveled plate glass. Frames are of wood and are beautifully finished in snow white enamel. These mirrors are especially appropriate for your bathroom.

42K299¼—Oblong Style.

Size	Shpg. Wt.	
12x16 in.	16 lbs.	$3.60
12x20 in.	23 lbs.	4.85
14x24 in.	28 lbs.	5.95

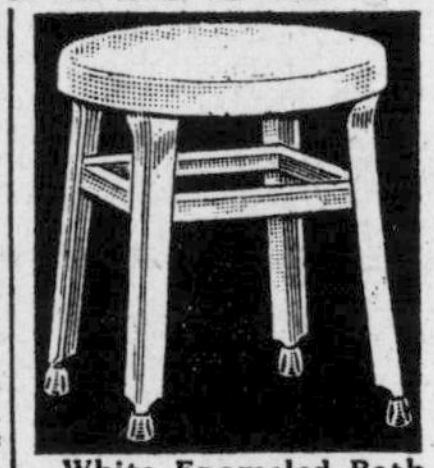

White Enameled Bath Stool. Strong and well made of steel. Has beautiful white finish. Used in or out of tub. Rubber tipped legs. Practical; sanitary and attractive, 15 in. high. Diameter, top 12 in. Should be in every bathroom. Shipping weight, 6 pounds. 42K297¼ **$1.45**

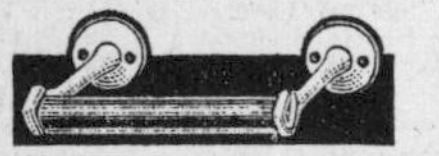

De Luxe Snow White Toilet Paper Holder. Has black wood roller. Shipping weight, 1 pound.
42K282.......... **30c**

High Grade Bath Spray

60c

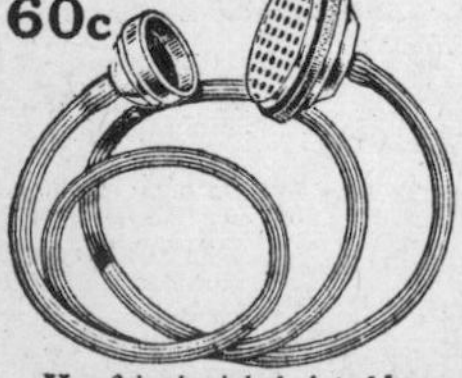

Has 3-inch nickel plated brass spr ayhead with rubber ring protector easily attached to bathtub faucet. Five feet ⅜-in. red rubber tubing. Shipping weight, 1 pound.
42K261.......... **60c**
Same as above except has 4-in. spray head and corrugated hose.
42K260—Shipping weight, 1¼ pounds.......... **98c**

NICKEL PLATED FIXTURES MADE OF BRASS

High quality. Made of brass, except where otherwise stated. Nickel plated screws furnished with each fixture.

Nickel Plated Brass Towel Bars

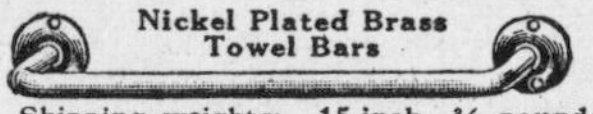

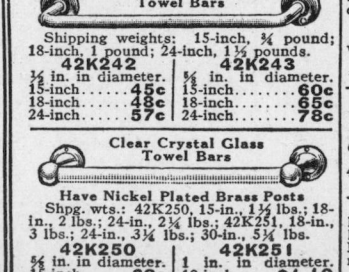

Shipping weights: 15-inch, ¾ pound; 18-inch, 1 pound; 24-inch, 1½ pounds.

42K242 ⅜ in. in diameter.		42K243 ⅝ in. in diameter.	
15-inch......	45c	15-inch......	60c
18-inch......	48c	18-inch......	65c
24-inch......	57c	24-inch......	78c

Clear Crystal Glass Towel Bars

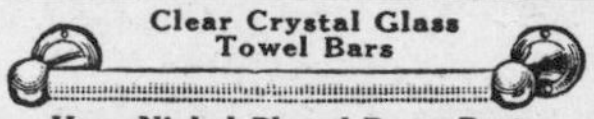

Have Nickel Plated Brass Posts

Shpg. wts.: 42K250, 15-in., 1½ lbs.; 18-in., 2 lbs.; 24-in., 2¼ lbs.; 42K251, 18-in., 3 lbs.; 24-in., 3¼ lbs.; 30-in., 5¼ lbs.

42K250 ⅝ in. in diameter.		42K251 1 in. in diameter.	
15-inch......	68c	18-inch......	$1.10
18-inch......	75c	24-inch......	1.20
24-inch......	80c	30-inch......	1.35

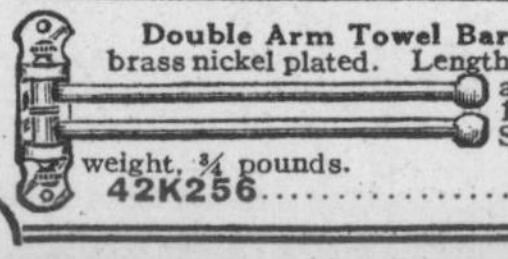

Double Arm Towel Bar. Solid brass nickel plated. Length over all about 12 in. Shipping weight, ¾ pounds. 42K256.......... **85c**

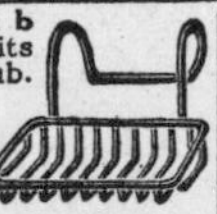

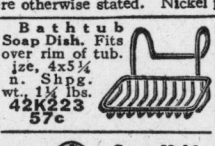

Bathtub Soap Dish. Fits over rim of tub. Size, 4x5¼ in. Shpg. wt., 1¼ lbs. 42K223 **57c**

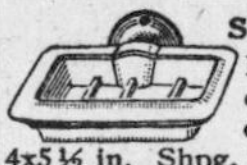

Soap Holder Removable opal glass dish. Size, 4x5½ in. Shpg. wt., 1½ lbs. 42K213.......... **65c**

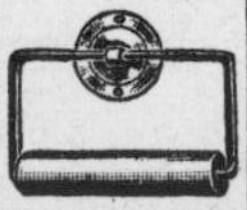

Toilet Paper Holder. Black wood roller. Shpg. Wt., 4 oz. 42K276 **24c**

Soap Dish Held between faucets with springs. Size, 4¾x6 inches. 42K219—Shipping weight, 8 ounces. **72c**

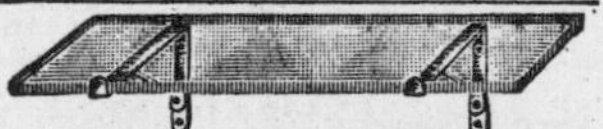

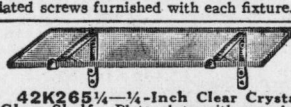

42K265¼—¼-Inch Clear Crystal Glass Shelf. Plate glass with rounded and ground outside edges and corners. Nickel plated brass brackets.
5x18 inches. Shipping wt., 5 lbs. $1.05
5x24 inches. Shipping wt., 6 lbs.. 1.15

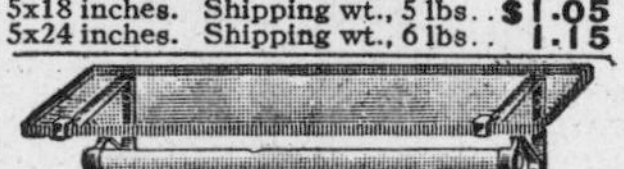

42K266¼—Crystal Glass Shelf and Towel Bar. Same as above, except has glass towel bar under shelf.
5x18 inches. Shipping wt., 6½ lbs. $2.25
5x24 inches. Shipping wt., 6½ lbs. 2.50

White Bathtub Seat

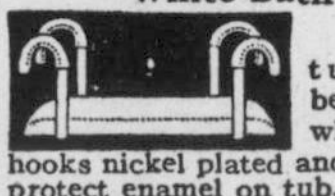

Hooks over rim of tub. Hardwood beautifully finished in white enamel. Steel hooks nickel plated and rubber covered to protect enamel on tub. Shipping weight, 4¾ pounds. 42K263.......... **98c**

Siphon Bath Spray Brush

$2.85

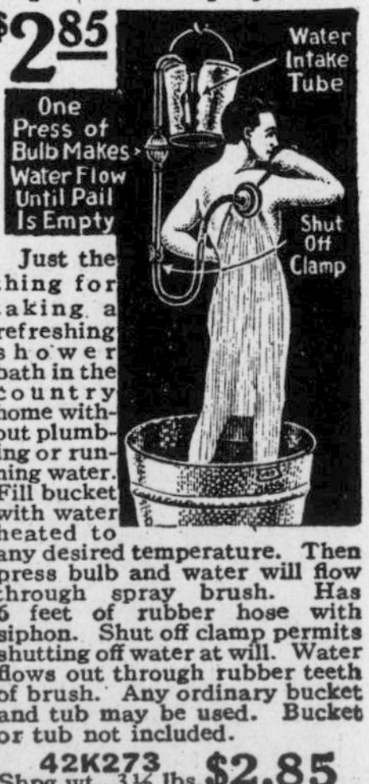
Water Intake Tube
One Press of Bulb Makes Water Flow Until Pail Is Empty
Shut Off Clamp

Just the thing for taking a refreshing shower bath in the country home without plumbing or running water. Fill bucket with water heated to any desired temperature. Then press bulb and water will flow through spray brush. Has 6 feet of rubber hose with siphon. Shut off clamp permits shutting off water at will. Water flows out through rubber teeth of brush. Any ordinary bucket and tub may be used. Bucket or tub not included.
42K273 Shpg.wt., 3½ lbs. **$2.85**

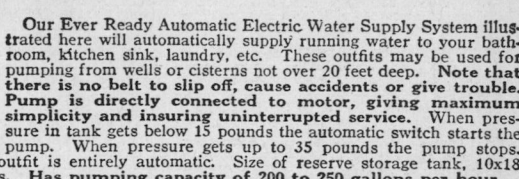

"Ever Ready" Electric Water Supply System

It Has No Belt to Slip Off or Give Trouble ☛

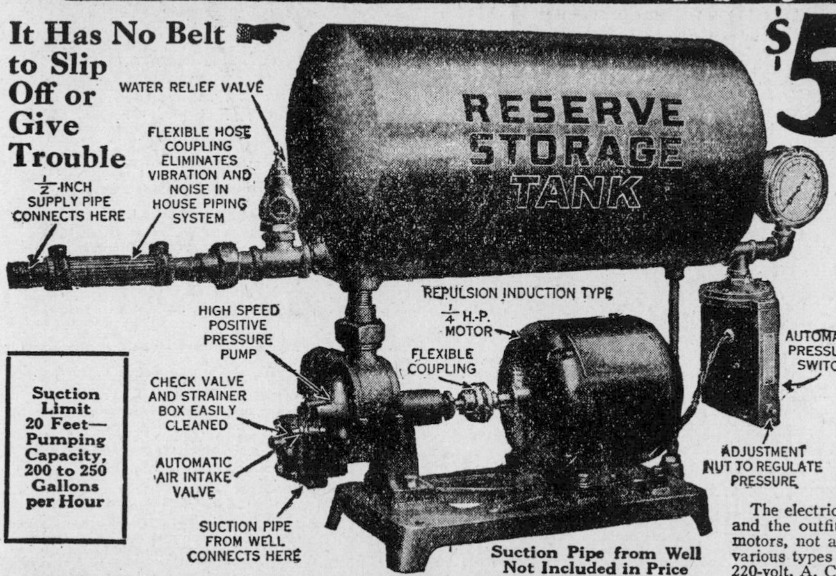

WATER RELIEF VALVE
FLEXIBLE HOSE COUPLING ELIMINATES VIBRATION AND NOISE IN HOUSE PIPING SYSTEM
½-INCH SUPPLY PIPE CONNECTS HERE
RESERVE STORAGE TANK
REPULSION INDUCTION TYPE ¼ H.-P. MOTOR
HIGH SPEED POSITIVE PRESSURE PUMP
FLEXIBLE COUPLING
CHECK VALVE AND STRAINER BOX EASILY CLEANED
AUTOMATIC AIR INTAKE VALVE
SUCTION PIPE FROM WELL CONNECTS HERE
AUTOMATIC PRESSURE SWITCH
ADJUSTMENT NUT TO REGULATE PRESSURE

Suction Limit 20 Feet—Pumping Capacity, 200 to 250 Gallons per Hour

Suction Pipe from Well Not Included in Price

$59.70 CASH

Ready to Install~

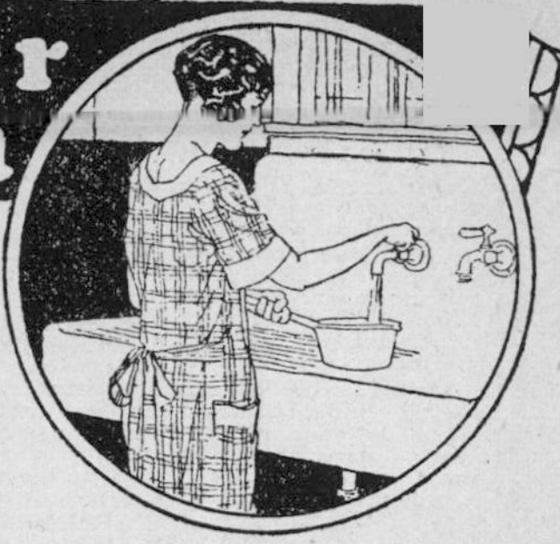

Our Ever Ready Automatic Electric Water Supply System illustrated here will automatically supply running water to your bathroom, kitchen sink, laundry, etc. These outfits may be used for pumping from wells or cisterns not over 20 feet deep. **Note that there is no belt to slip off, cause accidents or give trouble. Pump is directly connected to motor, giving maximum simplicity and insuring uninterrupted service.** When pressure in tank gets below 15 pounds the automatic switch starts the pump. When pressure gets up to 35 pounds the pump stops. The outfit is entirely automatic. Size of reserve storage tank, 10x18 inches. **Has pumping capacity of 200 to 250 gallons per hour.**

A Strictly High Grade Outfit

This is a strictly high grade outfit, built for long service. Equipment includes a ½-inch water relief valve, set at 60 pounds to prevent excessive pressure in tank.

The electric motor is a strictly high grade ¼ H.-P. repulsion induction type motor and the outfit should not be confused with cheaper outfits which have split phase motors, not at all satisfactory for this kind of service. Motor can be furnished for various types of electric current, as follows: 105-volt, 110-volt, 115-volt, 120-volt and 220-volt, A. C., single phase, 60-cycle; 110-volt and 220-volt, D. C.; also at additional cost as quoted at left we can furnish motor for 32-volt, D. C., same as furnished by ordinary farm electric lighting plants. **When ordering be sure to state which is wanted.**

You can get this information from the people who supply you with electric current. Special quotations for outfits with motors for current other than above given on request.

Pump is tapped for ¾-inch Suction Pipe, Discharge Connection from Tank is for ½-inch Iron Pipe. Outfit includes Pump, Motor, Base, Tank, Automatic Switch, Pressure Gauge, Flexible Hose Coupling and Combination Check Valve and Strainer Box as shown.

We can furnish pneumatic water supply systems for deep wells, gasoline engine or windmill driven; also hand power outfits for deep wells. Prices quoted on request.

PRICES—Outfits With Water Relief Valve, Foot Valve and Strainer, for Connection to Dug or Drilled Wells, Lakes, Streams, Springs, etc.

	Kind of Current	Cash Price	Easy Payment Price	Payment Down	Payment, per Month
42K3636¼	105 to 220-volt 60-cycle A. C..	$59.95	$66.00	$10.00	$6.00
42K3637¼	110-volt D. C.	59.95	66.00	10.00	6.00
42K3642¼	220-volt D. C.	59.95	66.00	10.00	6.00
42K3638¼	Farm Lighting Plant, 32-volt	61.95	68.50	10.00	7.50

PRICES—Outfits Same as Above Without Foot Valve for Connection to Drive Well Pipe.

	Kind of Current	Cash Price	Easy Payment Price	Payment Down	Payment, per Month
42K3639¼	105 to 220-volt 60-cycle A. C..	$59.70	$65.50	$10.00	$6.00
42K3640¼	110-volt D. C.	59.70	65.50	10.00	6.00
42K3643¼	220-volt D. C.	59.70	65.50	10.00	6.00
42K3641¼	Farm Lighting Plant, 32-volt.	61.70	68.00	10.00	7.50

Economical to Operate—Easy to Install

Figuring cost of current at 10 cents per kilowatt hour, it will cost you only 14 cents to pump 1,000 gallons of water. Maximum working pressure, 35 lbs. Outfit may be placed any distance within about 100 feet from the well or cistern, but pump should not be more than 20 feet above lowest water level. Any handy man can easily install this outfit by following the simple instructions which we furnish.

Shipping weight, complete outfit, 83 pounds.

If ordering on monthly payment plan, use time payment order blank on page 1092.

$62.50 Cash Price Deep Well Electric Water Supply System

for Pumping Head Only

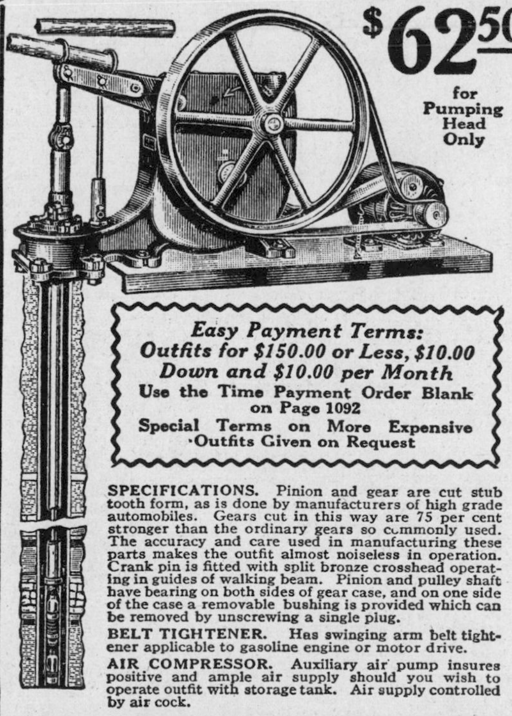

Oil cased, deep well pump for wells up to 200 feet in depth. Pumping capacity, 120 gallons per hour. Sufficient for all home requirements or light farm pumping where water is over twenty feet below surface and our shallow well outfit quoted above cannot be used. Has 6-inch stroke.

SPLASH OILED. The main driving mechanism is incased in an oiltight, dustproof housing which is partly filled with oil. The lower part of the gear and walking beam are immersed in this oil bath at all times, and as the gears revolve the oil is carried upwards and distributed over all moving parts within the housing, giving every moving part and bearing an oil bath at each revolution, insuring positive lubrication.

NOISELESS. The simplicity of design followed in this pump reduces the moving parts to a minimum. There are only three moving parts in the complete transmission, the pinion and gear with crank pin fitted with split bronze crosshead which operates in a slotted lever of bell crank type. All gears being machine cut and are gauged and finished to an accurate fit, insuring a smooth and quiet running outfit free from vibration.

ECONOMICAL. In this outfit friction is reduced to the minimum, and the design is such as to give the most efficient transmission of power from motor to pump plunger. The high efficiency of this outfit makes it very economical of current, and makes it especially desirable for use with private home electric lighting plants as well as where the current is brought from a local company.

ENGINE OR MOTOR DRIVE. Pumping head may be operated by electric motor or gasoline engine. Special estimates given on complete outfits with gasoline engine drive for any depth of well. Drive pulley is 16 inches in diameter and has 2¾-inch face.

42K3625¼—Working Head only, including flat face pulley without steel base, belt tightener or electric motor, for gasoline engine or electric motor drive. Shipping weight, 158 pounds.
Cash Price.......... **$62.50**
Easy Payment Price.......... **69.00**

Note: Outfits below include working head and motor assembled on steel base, pump rod and galvanized drop pipe, plunger and brass cylinder, size 1¾x24 inches; driving belt and automatic belt tightener, complete as shown, for depths of well specified. **All outfits have discharge outlet threaded for 1-inch iron pipe.** 2-inch drop pipe and 1⅛-inch wood pump rod.

42K3626¼—Complete Pumping Outfit, as described and illustrated, with ¼ horse-power electric motor for 21-foot well. Shpg. wt., 275 lbs.
Cash Price.......... **$109.10**
Easy Payment Price.......... **120.10**

For each additional foot of well depth up to 35 feet, add 37 cents to cash price, 41 cents to easy payment price and 2¼ pounds to shipping weight. For wells over 35 feet deep use outfit 42K3627¼. ☛

42K3627¼—Complete Pumping Outfit, same as 42K3626¼, except with ⅓ horse-power motor for wells 36 feet deep. Shpg. wt., 280 lbs.
Cash Price.......... **$132.60**
Easy Payment Price.......... **146.20**

For each additional foot of well depth up to 95 feet, add 37 cents to cash price, 41 cents to easy payment price and 4¼ lbs. to shipping weight. For wells over 95 feet deep use outfit 42K3628¼. ☛

42K3628¼—Complete Outfit, same as 42K3626¼, except with ½ horse-power motor for wells 96 feet deep. By adding extra pipe and pump rod as quoted below, this outfit can be used for wells up to 200 feet deep. Shipping weight, 295 pounds.
Cash Price.......... **$154.80**
Easy Payment Price.......... **170.85**

For each additional foot of well depth up to 200 feet, add 37 cents to cash price, 41 cents to easy payment price and 4¼ lbs. to shipping weight.

If Ordering on Easy Terms, Use Time Payment Order Blank on Page 1092

Below we quote the price for automatic switch and galvanized storage tanks, which should be added in case you wish to make the outfit automatic; also anti-freezing set length attachment which you can attach to take off water pipe connection under ground, making the outfit anti-freezing.

42K3629¼—Electric Automatic Switch. Shipping weight, 5 pounds.......... **$6.90**

Galvanized Storage Tank	Size Tank	Capacity, Gallons	Shpg. Wt., Lbs.	Tank Only
42K3652¼	18 in. x 4 ft.	53	105	$16.25
42K3653¼	20 in. x 5 ft.	82	150	19.00

42K147 — Pressure Gauge for Water Supply Systems. Indicates up to 100 lbs. pressure. Shpg.wt., 2 lbs. **$1.30**
For prices on pipe, pipe fittings and glass water gauges, see page 1013.

42K3631¼—Anti-Freezing Set Length Attachment. Includes all machined rods and parts necessary to extend pipe head and stuffing box underground so that pipe connection can be taken off below frost line, making outfit anti-freezing. Shipping weight, 55 pounds.......... **$11.30**

Easy Payment Terms:
Outfits for $150.00 or Less, $10.00 Down and $10.00 per Month
Use the Time Payment Order Blank on Page 1092
Special Terms on More Expensive Outfits Given on Request

SPECIFICATIONS. Pinion and gear are cut stub tooth form, as is done by manufacturers of high grade automobiles. Gears cut in this way are 75 per cent stronger than the ordinary gears so commonly used. The accuracy and care used in manufacturing these parts makes the outfit almost noiseless in operation. Crank pin is fitted with split bronze crosshead operating in guides of walking beam. Pinion and pulley shaft have bearing on both sides of gear case, and on one side of the case a removable bushing is provided which can be removed by unscrewing a single plug.

BELT TIGHTENER. Has swinging arm belt tightener applicable to gasoline engine or motor drive.

AIR COMPRESSOR. Auxiliary air pump insures positive and ample air supply should you wish to operate outfit with storage tank. Air supply controlled by air cock.

OTHER FEATURES. Equipped with handle for emergency hand operation. Pump rod and plunger easily removed for repairs without removing pump head or drop pipe. Outfit can be made anti-freezing at slight extra cost. Unquestionably, this is one of the most satisfactory deep well pumping outfits on the market.

MOTOR. Repulsion induction type for single phase, 60-cycle, 110 or 220-volt, 60-cycle A. C. current. Also, furnished for 32-volt, 110-volt or 220-volt D. C. current. **In ordering complete outfits, state kind of current you have.**

EVER READY Hand Power Water Supply System

Cash or Easy Payments **$44.85**

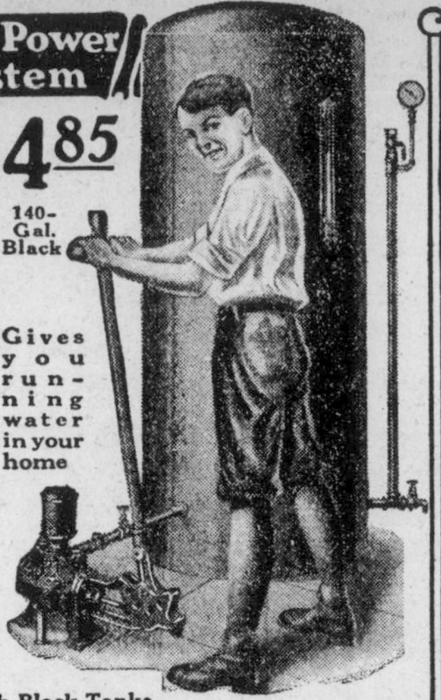

140-Gal. Black

Gives you running water in your home

Our Ever Ready Hand Power Water Supply System has easy working geared head drive, hand force pump with brass cased piston rod, brass air attachment. Pumps air and water at the same time. Has 3-inch brass lined cylinder and large air chamber, well made and carefully machined.

Fifteen minutes' pumping each day supplies sufficient water for the ordinary household. Complete outfit includes tank, pump and all necessary valves, gauges and connections, etc., as shown. Suction pipe to well or cistern or water supply pipe to plumbing fixtures not included. Order 1¼-inch galvanized pipe to connect pump with well, and ¾-inch galvanized pipe to make connection between tank and plumbing fixtures. Tanks on all outfits quoted below are **shipped from factory in NORTHERN ILLINOIS or warehouse near PHILADELPHIA.** Pump with fittings **shipped from our store.** Any of the outfits listed below can easily be converted into a power outfit for gasoline engine drive by attaching our 23K312 Pump Jack, page 1044.

If ordering on easy payments use time payment order blank on page 1092.

Outfits With Black Tanks

	Diam. In.	Lgth. Feet	Cap. Gal.	Shpg. Wt., Lbs.	Cash Price	Price on Easy Payments	Payment Down	Payment per Month
42K3612¼	24	6	140	320	$44.85	$49.50	$10.00	$5.00
42K3614¼	30	6	220	510	59.75	66.00	10.00	6.00
42K3616¼	36	6	315	600	67.25	74.00	10.00	7.00
Outfits With Galvanized Tanks								
42K3613¼	24	6	140	330	$51.85	$57.00	$10.00	$ 7.50
42K3615¼	30	6	220	515	76.75	84.50	10.00	9.50
42K3617¼	36	6	315	610	88.25	97.00	10.00	12.00

Extra Heavy Hand Force Pump

$8.20 2½x10-In.

Takes 1¼-Inch Well Pipe

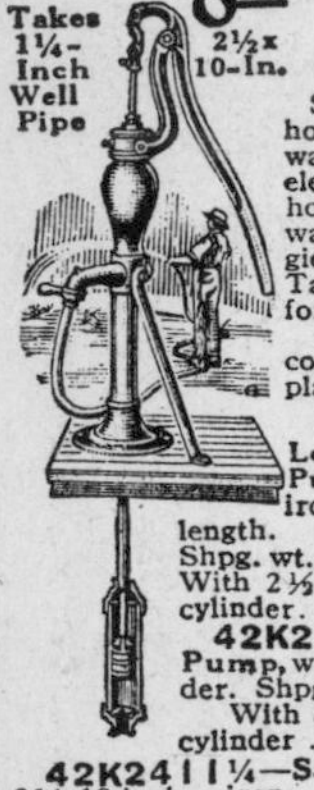

Spout has shutoff and hose clevis, so that water can be forced to elevated tank or through hose for sprinkling, washing windows, buggies, automobiles, etc. Tapped in back of spout for 1-inch pipe.

Bottom of cylinder comes 4 feet below pump platform. 6-inch stroke.

42K2409¼—Set Length Hand Force Pump with 2½x10-in. iron cylinder, 4-ft. set length. Shpg. wt., 76 lbs.. **$8.20**

With 2½x10-inch brass lined cylinder............**$9.90**

42K2410¼ — Same Pump, with 3x10-inch iron cylinder. Shpg. wt., 85 lbs. **$8.25**

With 3x10-inch brass lined cylinder............**$9.95**

42K2411¼—Same Pump, with 3½x10-inch iron cylinder. Shipping weight, 90 pounds............**$8.95**

With 3½x10-inch brass lined cylinder............**$10.75**

42K2413¼—Pump Standard only. Six-inch stroke. Tapped for 1¼-inch pipe. Shpg. wt., 45 lbs......**$6.35**

Prices given below are for pumps complete with iron cylinder, black pipe and pump rod all cut and fitted ready to install in depths of well specified. For shipping weights allow for weight of pump as given above and add 2½ pounds for foot.

Depth of Well	42K2409¼ With 2½x10 In. Iron Cylinder. For Brass Lined Cylinder Add $1.70	42K2410¼ With 3x10-Inch Iron Cylinder. For Brass Lined Cylinder Add $1.80	42K2411¼ With 3½x10-In. Iron Cylinder. For Brass Lined Cylinder Add $1.80
10 ft.	$ 8.85	$ 8.90	$ 9.60
15 ft.	9.40	9.45	10.15
20 ft.	9.95	10.00	10.75
25 ft.	10.50	10.55	11.25
30 ft.	13.15	13.20	13.90
35 ft.	14.10	14.15	14.85
40 ft.	15.05	15.10	15.80
45 ft.	16.00	16.05	16.75
50 ft.	16.95	17.00	17.70
55 ft.	17.90	17.95	18.65
60 ft.	18.85	18.90	19.60
65 ft.	19.80	19.85	19.55
70 ft.	20.75	20.80	21.50
75 ft.	21.70	21.75	22.45

If galvanized pipe is wanted on above outfits instead of black, add 3 cents per foot. Outfits quoted above for wells over 25 feet deep have cylinder at bottom of pipe. Outfits for wells 25 feet deep and under have cylinder 4 feet below pump platform.

Spiral Earth Augers

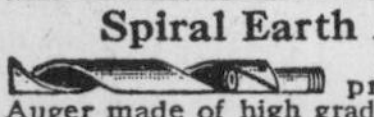

For boring wells, prospecting, etc., Auger made of high grade steel with pipe shank. Shank is threaded for standard 1-inch pipe. Auger works inside of 2-in. pipe casing, and as hole increases in depth, casing is driven down following auger. Extra lengths of pipe are added to casing as hole gets deeper, and extra lengths of 1-in. pipe added to shank so that auger may be turned. Length of auger, 26 in.; outside diam., 1⅞ in. Shpg. wt., 7 lbs.

42K1140¼............**$6.30**

Extra Heavy Windmill Set Length Force Pump

$9.55 2½x 10-In.

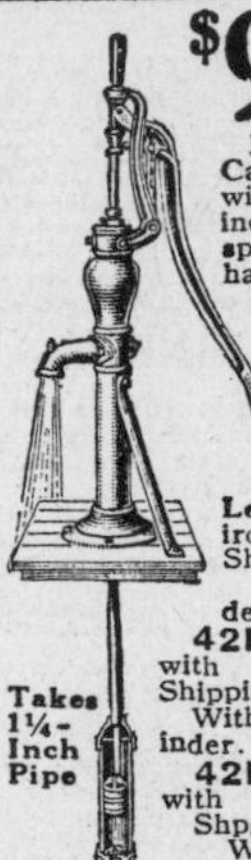

Takes 1¼-Inch Pipe

For wells up to 150 ft. deep. Can be operated by hand, windmill or pump jack. Six-inch stroke. Tapped back of spout for 1¼-inch pipe. Spout has shut off and hose clevis, so that water can be forced to elevated tank or through hose for sprinkling, washing windows, buggies, automobiles, etc. Bottom of cylinder, 4 feet below pump. Stroke, 6 inch.

42K2392¼—4 Ft. Set Length Pump with 2½x10-in. iron cylinder. Shpg. wt., 100 lbs. **$9.55**

With brass lined cylinder............**$11.25**

42K2393¼—Same Pump with 3x10-inch iron cylinder. Shipping weight, 105 lbs. **$9.60**

With 3x10-inch brass lined cylinder............**$11.30**

42K2394¼—Same Pump with 3½x10-inch iron cylinder. Shpg. wt., 110 lbs. **$10.30**

With 3½x10-inch brass lined cylinder............**$12.10**

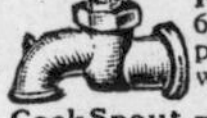

Cock Spout, $1.65 Extra

42K2396¼—Windmill Force Pump Standard only. 6-in. stroke. Tapped for 2-inch pipe or smaller. Shipping weight, 65 pounds............**$7.25**

42K2397¼—Windmill Force Pump Standard only. 10-in. stroke. Tapped for 2-in. pipe or smaller. Shipping weight, 70 pounds.......**$7.95**

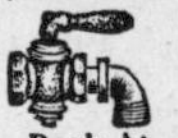

Back Attachment, $1.50 Extra

Prices below are for pumps complete with iron cylinder, black pipe and pump rod all cut and fitted ready to install in depths specified. For shpg. wt. allow for wt. of pump as given above and add 2½ lbs. per foot.

Depth of Well	42K2392¼ With 2½x10-In. Iron Cylinder. For Brass Lined Cylinder Add $1.70	42K2393¼ With 3x10-In. Iron Cylinder. For Brass Lined Cylinder Add $1.80	42K2394¼ With 3½x10-In. Iron Cylinder. For Brass Lined Cylinder Add $1.80
10 ft.	$10.20	$10.25	$10.95
15 ft.	10.75	10.80	11.50
20 ft.	11.30	11.35	12.05
25 ft.	11.85	11.90	12.60
30 ft.	14.50	14.55	15.25
35 ft.	15.45	15.50	16.20
40 ft.	16.40	16.45	17.15
45 ft.	17.35	17.40	18.10
50 ft.	18.30	18.35	19.05
55 ft.	19.25	19.30	20.00
60 ft.	20.20	20.25	20.95

If galvanized pipe is wanted on above outfits instead of black, add 3 cents per foot.

Outfits quoted above for wells over 25 feet deep have cylinder at bottom of pipe. Outfits for wells 25 feet deep and under have cylinder 4 feet below pump platform.

WaterConductors

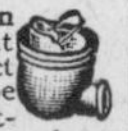

Hang on pump spout and connect with iron pipe for conducting water to tank or trough. **State size.** Shpg. wt., 5¼ lbs.

42K856

1¼-inch pipe... **42c**

1½-inch pipe... **45c**

Galvanized Foot Valves

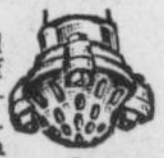

Screwed on end of pump suction pipe. Acts as a check valve. Galvanized. Pipe size, 1¼ in. Shipping weight, 3¼ pounds.

42K858 **75c**

Striking Values

Set Length Lift Pump

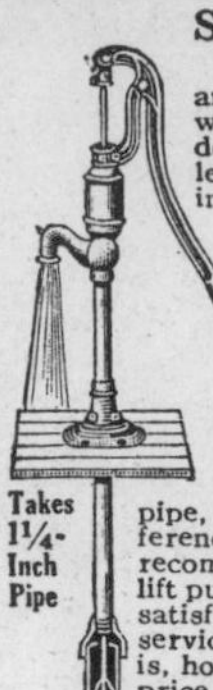

Takes 1¼-Inch Pipe

Medium weight; anti-freezing; for wells up to 30 feet deep. Four-foot set length pump. Six-inch stroke. Takes 1¼-inch pipe. Cylinder comes four feet below pump platform.

$4.20 4-Ft. Set Length

While we guarantee this pump to be equal to some competitive pumps offered at higher prices than we ask here, and while we guarantee this pump to be suitable for wells up to 30 feet deep by adding extra pipe, still, considering the small difference in price, we would strongly recommend our extra heavy weight lift pump quoted below as being a more satisfactory pump for general farm service. This medium weight pump is, however, a remarkable value at the price we offer it.

42K2349¼—With 3x10-in. iron cylinder. Four-foot set length. Shpg. wt., 50 lbs. **$4.20**

Heavy Weight Lift Pump

$5.85 4-Ft. Set Length

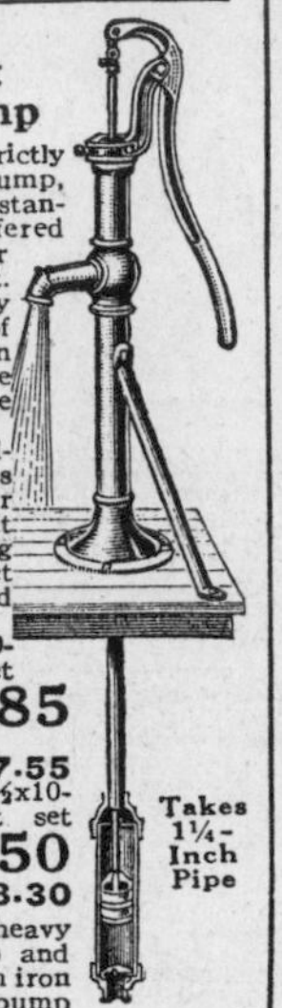

Takes 1¼-Inch Pipe

Here is a strictly high grade pump, strong and substantially built, offered at a price usually asked for pumps of much lighter weight. Do not confuse this heavy weight pump with pumps of lighter construction offered on the market at about the price we ask for this high grade article.

Made up complete with cylinder, pipe and pump rod, as shown. Cylinder comes four feet below pump platform. It is sufficiently heavy and strong for use in wells up to 60 feet deep by adding extra pipe and pump rod.

42K2351¼—With 3x10-inch iron cylinder. 4-foot set length as shown. Shpg. wt., 60 lbs..... **$5.85**

With brass lined cylinder............**$7.55**

42K2352¼—With 3½x10-inch iron cylinder, 4-foot set length. Shipping wt., 65 pounds............**$6.50**

With brass lined cylinder. **$8.30**

Prices below are for heavy weight pumps all made up and ready to install complete with iron cylinder black pipe and pump rod for depths of well specified. For shipping weights, allow for weight of pump as given above and add 2½ pounds per foot for extension.

Depth of Well	42K2351¼ With 3x10-In. Iron Cylinder. For Brass Lined Cylinder Add $1.80	42K2352¼ With 3½x10-In. Iron Cylinder. For Brass Lined Cylinder Add $1.80
10 feet	$ 6.50	$ 7.15
15 feet	7.05	7.70
20 feet	7.60	8.25
25 feet	8.15	8.80
30 feet	10.80	11.45
35 feet	11.75	12.40
40 feet	12.70	13.35
45 feet	13.65	14.30
50 feet	14.60	15.25

42K2355¼—Pump Standard only, without cylinder pipe or pump rod. Shipping weight, 40 pounds...... **$3.15**

If galvanized pipe is wanted on above outfits instead of black, add 3c per foot.

How to Order Your Pump Outfit

If the distance from pump platform to the lowest water level is less than 25 feet, you can use one of our 4-foot set length pumps, quoted on this page, and order sufficient extra pipe o reach about 3 feet below water.

If the distance to the lowest water level is over 25 feet, cylinder must be placed below water. Lift pumps draw water to the pump spout only. If you want to force the water to an elevated tank or a pressure tank, order a force pump.

We charge 2 cents per foot in addition to cost of pump rod and pipe for cutting and fitting pump outfits to specifications

We have listed a number of pumps on this page, completely made up, with pipe, pump rod and cylinder cut and fitted for depths of well specified. Prices given on these outfits include all cos for cutting and fitting. Measure distance from pump platform to water level in well during dry season, and order outfit 5 feet longer than this so cylinder will come below water line Outfits for wells 25 feet deep and under have cylinder placed 4 feet below pump. For deeper wells cylinder is placed at bottom of extension pipe and pump rod is extended down.

Galvanized Round Steel Pump Rod

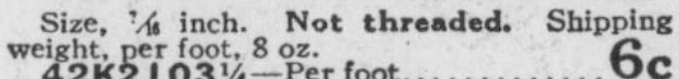

Size, ⅜ inch. **Not threaded.** Shipping weight, per foot, 8 oz.

42K2103¼—Per foot............**6c**

Threads, extra, per cut............5c

Galvanized Pump Rod Couplings

To fit above pump rod.

42K822—Shipping weight, 4 oz..... **7c**

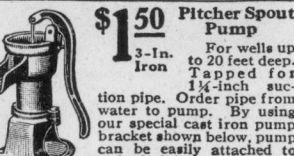

Cistern Force Pump

$4.65 3-In. Plain Spout

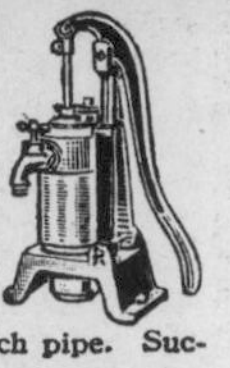

For wells or cisterns 20 feet deep or less. Has solid brass cylinder, valve seat and stuffing nut. Gooseneck spout fitted with hose coupling or faucet spout, as illustrated. Tapped for 1¼-inch suction. Top outlet is tapped for 1-inch pipe. Suction pipe not included.

42K2377¼—With plain spout and 3-inch cylinder. Shipping weight, 26 pounds............**$4.65**

42K2379¼—With faucet spout and 3-inch cylinder. Shpg. wt., 24 lbs. **$5.25**

Pitcher Spout Pump

$1.50 3-In. Iron

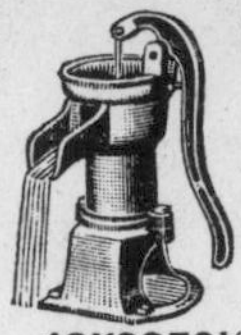

For wells up to 20 feet deep. Tapped for 1¼-inch suction pipe. Order pipe from water to pump. By using our special cast iron pump bracket shown below, pump can be easily attached to end of sink.

42K2370¼—3-inch iron cylinder. Shipping wt., 22 lbs. **$1.50**

42K2371¼—3-inch brass lined cylinder. Shipping weight, 23 pounds. **$2.40**

42K2372¼—3½-inch iron cylinder. Shipping weight, 23 pounds...... **$1.84**

42K2373¼—3½-inch brass lined cylinder. Shipping weight, 24 pounds. **$2.75**

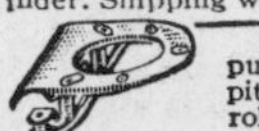

42K390—Cast iron pump bracket. For attaching pitcher spout pumps to flat or roll rim sinks. Shipping weight, 5 pounds.. **$1.10**

Rotary Barrel Pump

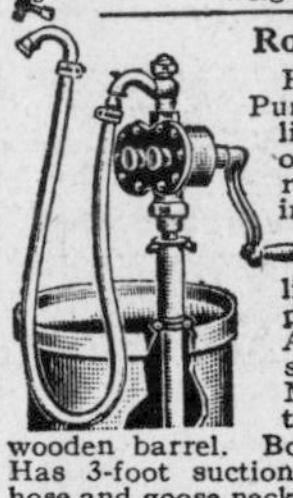

Hand Rotary Barrel Pump. For pumping gasoline, motor oil, syrup or other liquids out of barrels. Much used for filling gasoline tanks on traction engines, automobiles, etc. Forces liquids 15 to 20 feet above pump. Works same as Acme Rotary Pump shown on opposite page. Made of iron. Furnished to fit steel barrel or wooden barrel. Both types quoted below. Has 3-foot suction pipe, 5-foot discharge hose and goose neck. Pumps 13 gallons per minute. Shipping weight, 65 lbs.

42K2259¼—With attachment for steel barrel as shown............**$12.75**

42K2260¼—With attachment for wooden barrel............**$12.65**

For Barrel Pumps Also, See Page 456

Double Acting Pump

A very efficient hand force pump for use where suction lift does not exceed 20 feet. All brass valves and geared head drive. Pumps liquid only, no air. Much used for pumping water to elevated tanks, cleaning, filling and testing boilers and tanks, for fire protection and as a deck pump. Has 1¼-inch suction and 1-inch discharge. Shipping weight, 65 lbs.

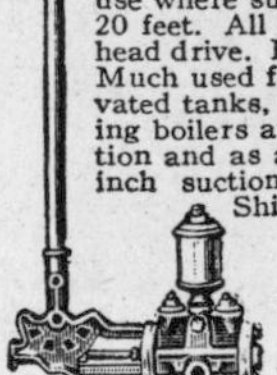

42K2187¼ With 3-inch brass lined cylinder. **$11.95**

Air and Water Force Pump

Same as 42K2187¼, except that it has brass air pump attachment for use with pneumatic water systems. 1¼-inch suction and 1-inch discharge. 4-inch stroke, 3-inch brass lined cylinder. Suction limit, 20 feet. Shipping weight, 76 pounds.

42K2188¼—Pump, as described............**$12.95**

Large Capacity Tank Pump

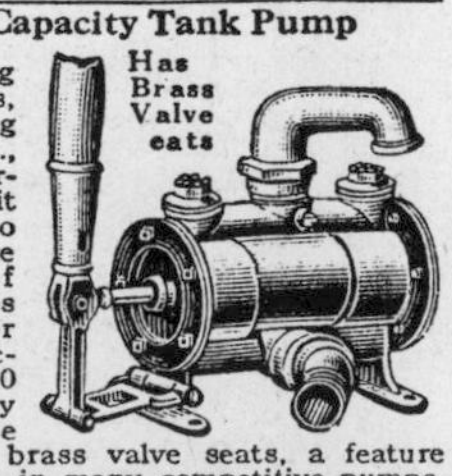

Has Brass Valve eats

For filling thresher tanks, for emptying cesspools, etc., or for any purpose where it is desired to pump a large volume of water. Pumps 50 gallons per minute. Suction limit, 20 feet. A strictly high grade pump. Has brass valve seats, a feature not contained in many competitive pumps. Cylinder, 5 inches in discharge, 5-inch stroke; suction and discharge, 2 in. Has extra connection for discharge to connect 1-inch hose for sprinkling, etc. Shipping weight, 78 pounds.

42K2266¼—Pump as described............**$9.85**

42K828—5-Inch Crimped Plunger Leathers. Shpg. wt., 8 oz. Set of two. **65c**

Galvanized Malleable Strainers

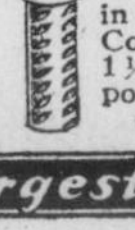

Placed at end of pump suction pipe in well to keep out foreign matter. Covered with brass wire cloth. Size, 1¼-inch. Shipping weight, 1¾ pounds.

42K826............**46c**

Sprayers-Pumps

$6.65 Barrel Spray Pump

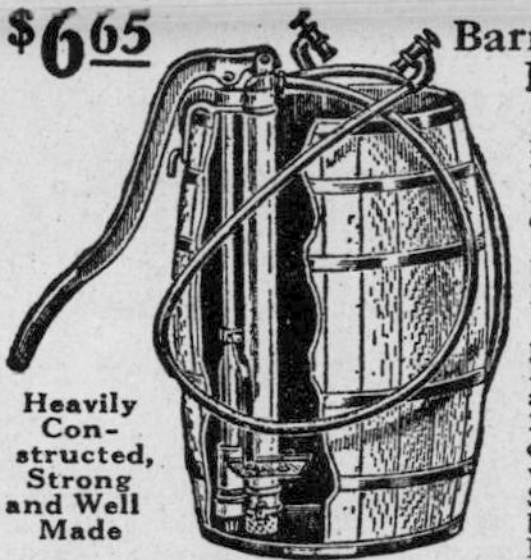

Heavily Constructed, Strong and Well Made

For spraying or whitewashing. Nothing to catch on low hanging branches. Develops 125 lbs. pressure. Height, over all, 37 inches. 2-inch brass cylinder and valve seats. Solid bronze ball valves. Not affected by strong solutions. Has brass connection for ½-inch hose coupling and brass strainer in base. Two paddle dash agitator. Easily attached to any barrel. Prices do not include hose, shutoffs, nozzles or barrel. Large boiler tube air chamber, 1¾x35 inches high. Shpg. wt., 40 lbs.

42K939¼—Perfection Barrel Sprayer With Dash Agitator. Fitted for one lead of ½-inch hose. No hose included.... **$6.65**

42K941¼—Perfection Barrel Sprayer. Fitted for two leads of ½-inch hose. No hose included.................... **$7.55**

Hose Extensions for Barrel Sprayers

½-Inch Five-Ply Spray Hose Complete with Misty Nozzle and Shut Off Cock.

	Length	Shpg. Wt.	
42K1012¼	5 ft.	3 lbs.	$1.75
42K1014¼	10 ft.	6 lbs.	2.40
42K1016¼	25 ft.	13 lbs.	4.35

High Grade Spray Hose

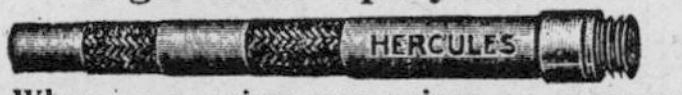

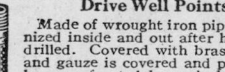

When comparing our prices on sprayer hose remember we furnish two couplings with each length of hose.

Half-inch hose furnished with standard ½ or ¾-inch hose connections, ⅜-inch hose furnished with standard ¼-inch connections. Be sure to order correct size hose to fit your sprayer.

42K961¼—Perfection 5-Ply Sheeting Smooth Spray Hose for 100 pounds pressure. Comes only in lengths specified below. **Furnished complete with coupling connections.** Shipping weight, per foot, 4½ ounces.

Lgth., ft.	5	10	15	25	50
⅜-inch...	60c	$1.00	$1.45	$2.30	$4.35
½-inch...	70c	1.15	1.60	2.50	4.75

42K950¼—Perfection Double Braid Smooth Spray Hose for 150 pounds pressure. Comes only in lengths specified below. **Furnished complete with coupling connections.** Shipping weight, per foot, 5 ounces.

Lgth., ft.	5	10	15	25	50
⅜-inch...	78c	$1.35	$1.90	$3.00	$5.90
½-inch...	84c	1.44	2.10	3.25	6.25

42K952¼—Hercules ½-Inch Double Braid Corrugated Spray Hose for 225 pounds working pressure, special seamless braided, high quality. Comes only in lengths specified below. **Furnished complete with coupling connections.** Shipping weight, per foot, 5 ounces.

Lgth., 10 feet.. $1.85 | Lgth., 25 feet.. $4.25
Lgth., 15 feet.. 2.65 | Lgth., 50 feet.. 8.25

For Garden Hose See Page 999.

Barrel and Bucket Spray Pump

Only $3.95

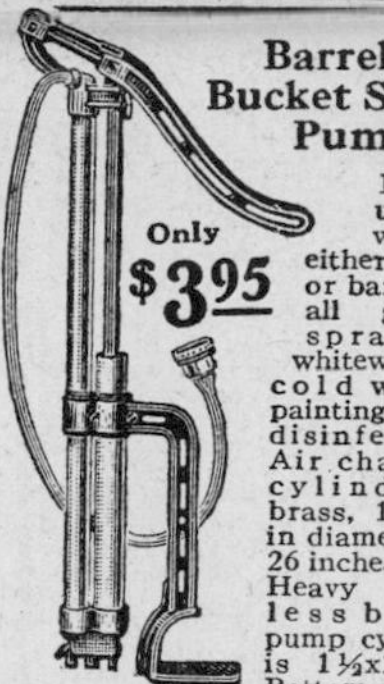

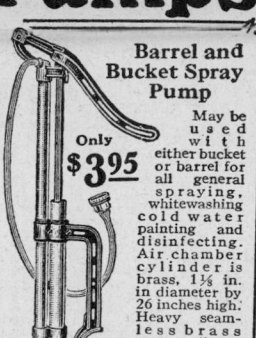

May be used with either bucket or barrel for all general spraying, whitewashing cold water painting and disinfecting. Air chamber cylinder is brass, 1⅛ in. in diameter by 26 inches high. Heavy seamless brass pump cylinder is 1½x12 in. Bottom casting and valves are brass. Produces large, powerful continuous spray with slow pumping. Has 3 feet of ⅜-inch hose and combination nozzle for fine spray or solid stream. Air jet agitator. Height over all, 31 inches. **Mailable.**

42K905¼
Shpg. wt., 11 lbs.... **$3.95**

$10.75 Complete — A Big Labor and Time Saver

Monarch Wheelbarrow Sprayer

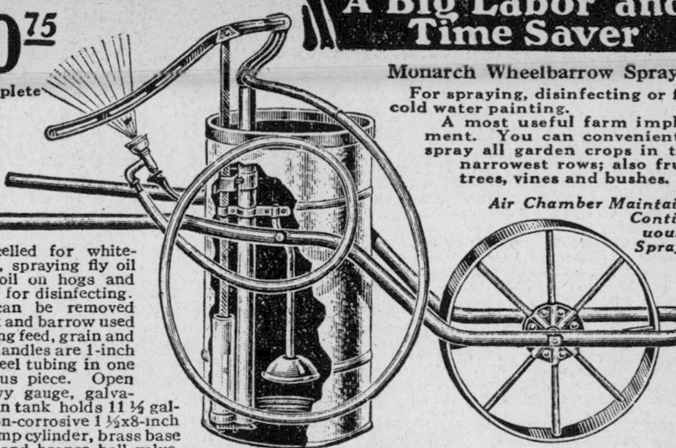

For spraying, disinfecting or for cold water painting.

A most useful farm implement. You can conveniently spray all garden crops in the narrowest rows; also fruit trees, vines and bushes.

Air Chamber Maintains Continuous Spray

Unexcelled for whitewashing, spraying fly oil or lice oil on hogs and cattle or for disinfecting. Pump can be removed and tank and barrow used for carting feed, grain and slops. Handles are 1-inch heavy steel tubing in one continuous piece. Open top, heavy gauge, galvanized iron tank holds 11½ gallons. Non-corrosive 1½x8-inch brass pump cylinder, brass base castings and bronze ball valve. Produces a pressure of 150 pounds. Has 4¼-inch vacuum cup agitator, 8 feet of ⅜-inch hose, automatic shut off cock and nozzle.

42K949¼—Shipping weight, 50 pounds.................. **$10.75**

42K922¼—**Hercules Wheelbarrow Sprayer** same as above, except that the pump is of much heavier construction; and has 12½ feet of spray hose with 4-foot extension rod and automatic cock. Has 20 inch wheel with 2-inch tire. Has larger air chamber and double paddle agitators on each side of pump. A high grade quality sprayer equal to the best on the market. For high quality and durability, this sprayer is unexcelled. Shipping weight, 56 pounds.................. **$14.95**

Double Acting Tubular Sprayer

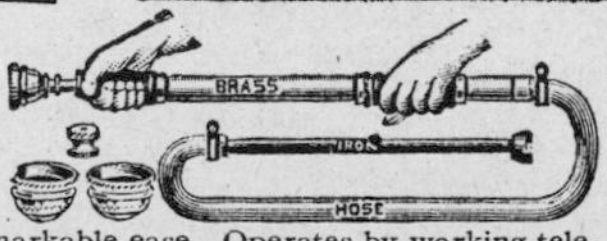

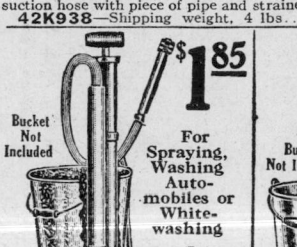

For spraying, whitewashing and applying disinfectants. Gives powerful continuous spray. Develops 200 pounds pressure with remarkable ease. Operates by working telescoping tubes forward and backward. Has nozzles for coarse spray, fine spray and solid stream. Made of brass. Has wood handle and ½-inch suction hose with piece of pipe and strainer on end.

42K938—Shipping weight, 4 lbs.................. **$3.35**

$1.85 For Spraying, Washing Automobiles or Whitewashing

Bucket Not Included

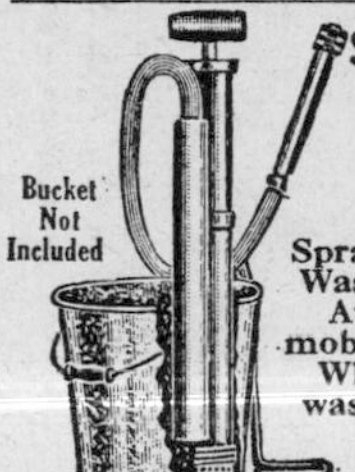

Galvanized iron. Has large ball valves with rubber seats and brass strainer in brass cage with brass screw cap easily removed for cleaning. Large air chamber maintains continuous spray. Includes 3 feet of ¼-in. hose, 1 foot brass extension pipe and nozzle for both a coarse and fine spray. Shipping weight, 4¼ pounds.

42K919¼...... **$1.85**

Big Value $2.40 Bucket Sprayer and Whitewasher

Bucket Not Included

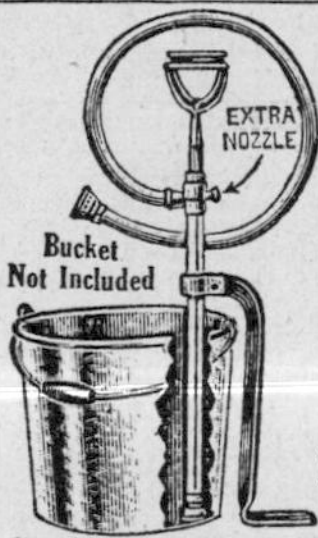

Double acting. Gives steady spray. Made of brass and has iron handle and foot rest. Has 3 feet of ⅜-inch hose and two nozzles, one for spraying, the other a straight stream nozzle for sprinkling. May be used for spraying or whitewashing. Shipping weight, 6 pounds.

42K947¼—Bucket Whitewash Sprayer.. **$2.40**

Hercules Compressed Air Sprayer

For Spraying or Whitewashing

No Better Spray Pump Than This Made or Sold by Anyone. Cam Lock Type

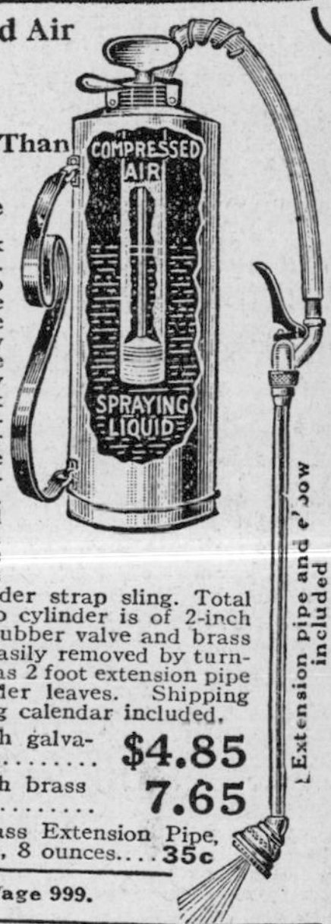

Has latest improved quick acting lever cam pump lock. Gives continuous spray. Do not confuse this high grade article with cheap competitive sprayers made to sell at a low price. Furnished complete with 2 feet of ½-inch heavy spray hose with non-kink guard, and automatic adjustable cock equipped with lever shutoff and strainer. Three gallons of liquid can be sprayed with three charges of air. Heavy gauge galvanized steel tank with interlocked and riveted seam. Tank is 7 inches in diameter and 19 inches high. Easily carried by shoulder strap sling. Total capacity, 3¼ gallons. Pump cylinder is of 2-inch seamless brass tubing with rubber valve and brass valve spring. Entire pump easily removed by turning quick acting cam lock. Has 2 foot extension pipe and elbow for spraying under leaves. Shipping weight, 10 pounds. Spraying calendar included.

42K951¼—Sprayer with galvanized tank and extension pipe........ **$4.85**

42K953¼—Sprayer with brass tank and brass pipe................ **7.65**

42K944¼—Straight Brass Extension Pipe, 2 feet long. Shipping weight, 8 ounces... **35c**

For Pruning Shears See Page 999.

Acme Rotary Power Force Pump $12.95

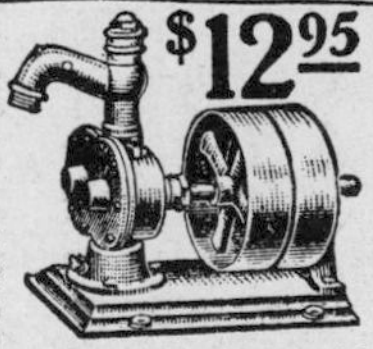

Will force water a horizontal distance of 200 feet and throw a solid stream 20 feet. An excellent pump for raising a large amount of water with minimum amount of power where lift is not over 15 feet and elevated tank into which water is forced not over 50 feet above pump. Reliable protection in case of fire. Driving shaft made long enough to allow use of balance wheel with handle so pump may be worked by hand when desired. Spout threaded for iron pipe at end and also at top where it connects to pump. Can be run at 300 revolutions per minute without injury, although 200 is recommended. High speed permits belting direct to engine. If wanted with balance wheel and handle for hand power, allow $5.50 extra. Prices quoted do not include pipe or belt. If you wish to pump gasoline or benzine, or other such light bodied liquids, be sure to order the special gasoline pump quoted below. **Order by catalog number, and specify capacity of pump desired.**

Gallons per Min.	H-P.	Pipe Size, In.		Pulley, In.	Shpg. Wt.	42K2268¼ For Water and Heavier Liquids.	42K2269¼ Special for Gasoline, Each
		Inlet	Outlet				
13	1	1¼	1	10x3	80 lbs.	$12.95	$15.20
17	1	1½	1¼	10x3	98 lbs.	16.40	18.65
36	3	2	2	12x3½	175 lbs.	36.25	38.50

Hercules Centrifugal Pumps

Shipped from factory in NORTHERN INDIANA.

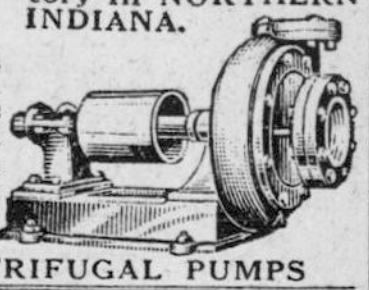

Simplest and most practical pump on the market for irrigation or wherever a large volume of water is to be handled against a total head not exceeding 65 feet. Must be placed not more than 20 feet above water. Scientifically designed for greatest efficiency. It is a strictly high grade pump in every way. Two smallest sizes have bronze bearings. All other sizes have ring oiled pedestal bearings. Extra long stuffing box reduces wear. Built for high speed which permits belting direct to line shaft, engine or tractor. **Complete instructions for installing and operating furnished with each pump.**

PRICES AND DIMENSIONS OF HERCULES CENTRIFUGAL PUMPS

Catalog No.	Size No.	Cap. per Min., in Gal.	Diam. Suction in In.	Diam. Discharge In.	Shpg. Wt., Lbs.	Pulley, Diam. Face, In.	Each
42K2329⅓	¾	15	1	¾	25	3x2	$12.50
42K2330⅓	1	25	1¼	1	45	4x3	15.00
42K2332⅓	1½	70	2	1½	65	4x4	25.95
42K2333⅓	2	120	2½	2	85	4x4	33.95
42K2334⅓	2½	185	3	2½	160	6x6	49.50
42K2335⅓	3	285	4	3	205	7x6	58.65
42K2337⅓	4	470	5	4	356	8x8	74.95

Pump Cylinders

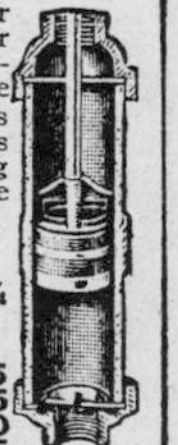

10-in. cylinders have 6-in. stroke and 16-in. a 10-in. stroke. Cylinders 3½ in. in diameter, fitted for 1½-in. pipe; 4 in. in diameter for 2-in. pipe; all others fitted for 1¼-in. pipe. 10-in. cylinders have one leather on plunger. 16-in. cylinders have two. Brass lined cylinders have seamless brass tubular lining and have brass cage and brass valve in plunger.

Iron Cylinders

Dim., In.	Wt., Lbs.	42K1105¼ 10 In. Long	Wt., Lbs.	42K1107¼ 16 In. Long
2½	11	$1.45	16	$2.35
3	12	1.70	18	2.65
3½	15	2.50	24	3.80
4	21	3.00	30	4.95

Brass Lined Cylinders

Weights same as Iron Cylinders.

Diam.	42K1126¼ 10 In. Long	42K1128¼ 16 In. Long
2½ in.	$3.15	$4.15
3 in.	3.50	4.50
3½ in.	4.15	5.45
4 in.	5.15	7.25

New Process Pump Leathers

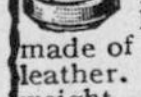

42K828 Plunger leathers made of good quality leather. Shipping weight, 8 ounces. **State size wanted.**

42K830 Check valve leathers, made of very tough, good quality leather. Shipping weight, 4 ounces. **State size wanted.**

Inside Diam. of Barrel of Cylinder Which Leather Will Fit	Each	Actual Outside Diameter of Leather	Each
2	7c	2½	4c
2¼	8c	2¾	5c
2½	10c	3	6c
2¾	11c	3¼	7c
3	12c	3½	8c
3¼	14c	3¾	10c
3½	16c	4	11c
3¾	20c	4¼	13c
4	22c	4½	14c

Little Giant Pipe Holder

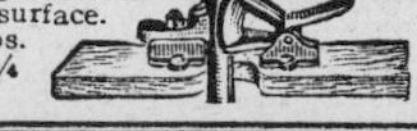

Harder the pull, tighter the grip. For 1, 1¼, 1½ and 2-inch pipe. Dog has corrugated chilled surface. Shpg. wt., 35 lbs.

42K1134¼
$2.85

Well Boring Outfit

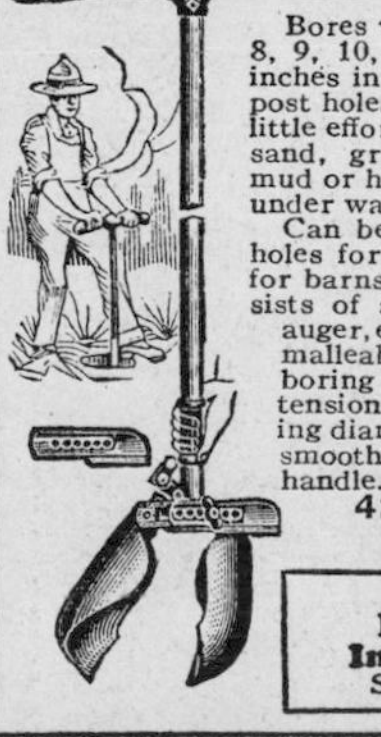

Bores wells 25 feet deep, 8, 9, 10, 11, 12, 13 or 14 inches in diameter, or digs post holes quickly and with little effort. Bores through sand, gravel, sticky clay, mud or hard pan. Will dig under water.

Can be used for digging holes for foundation piling for barns, etc. Outfit consists of a new type earth auger, extension rods with malleable couplings for boring down 25 feet, extension blade for increasing diameter of hole and a smooth finish hardwood handle. Shpg. wt., 50 lbs.

42K1861¼
$6.95

For Other **Posthole Implements** See Page 999

Drive Well Points

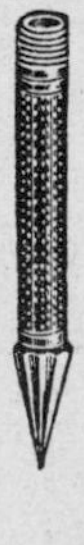

Made of wrought iron pipe, galvanized inside and out after holes are drilled. Covered with brass gauze, and gauze is covered and protected by a perforated brass jacket. No. 60 gauze is used for coarse and No. 100 gauze for fine sand.

42K1136¼—60-Gauze.
42K1138¼—100-Gauze.

Diameter, In.	Lgth., In.	Shpg. Wt., Lbs.	60-Gauze	100-Gauze
1¼	24	5	$1.35	$3.05
1¼	30	6¼	1.70	3.80
1¼	36	7½	2.10	4.55
1¼	42	8¾	2.45	5.35
1½	36	9	2.70	5.40
2	36	14	3.90	7.20
2	48	16	4.98	9.45

Malleable Iron Driving Caps

42K834—Screwed on top of pipe to protect threads when driving it down.

Size, inches....	1¼	1½	2
Shpg. wt., lbs...	1½	2	2¾
Each..........	30c	36c	66c

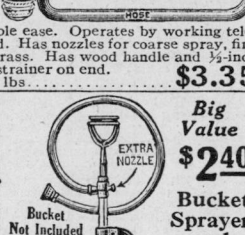

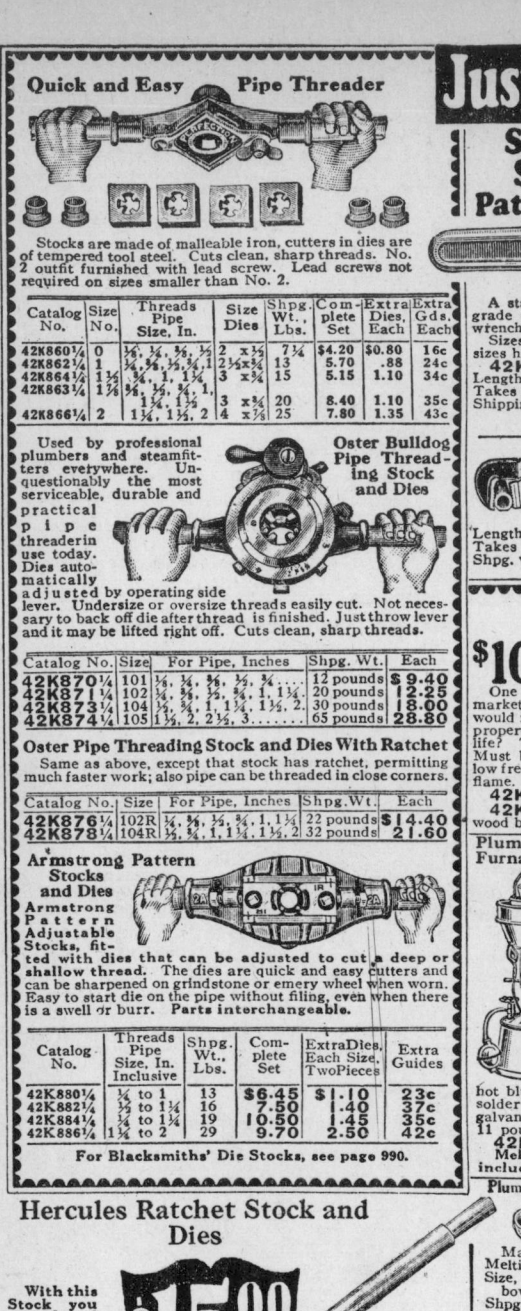
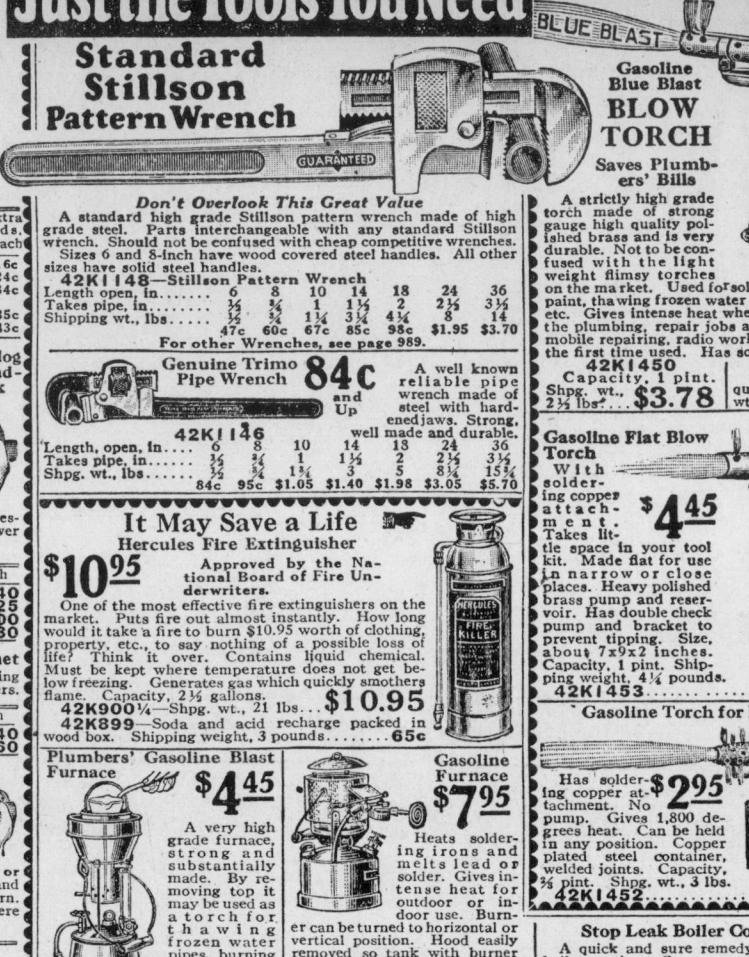

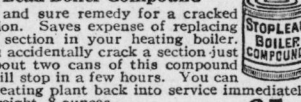

BE YOUR OWN INTERIOR DECORATOR

NEW, Enlarged, Revised Edition of the popular Book "HOW TO CHOOSE COLORS AND FURNISHINGS FOR YOUR HOME" by Hazel H. Adler.

Last year we sold thousands of copies of this inspiring book and had to reprint several editions to fill the demand. We received hundreds of letters of appreciation from women who read the book and profited by its valuable advice and suggestions.

This practical book was prepared especially for our customers by Hazel H. Adler, America's foremost Interior Decorator and an international color authority. It contains many elaborate color illustrations, color charts, plans, sketches and budgets. It will tell you all the things you have always wanted to know about furnishing a tasteful and artistic home which all your friends will admire, and within your price limit.

The book explains in a clear, interesting manner:

1. How to plan color schemes, select paint or wall paper; decide on floor coverings and furniture;

2. How to choose and make curtains and draperies and add those little touches which give charm and distinction to a home;

3. How to arrange furniture in a sociable and hospitable manner.

Full decorating plans are provided for every room in the house. Suggestions for this purpose are beautifully illustrated in colors and a patented Interior Decoration Color Harmony Chart assures a wide selection of varied and interesting color combinations.

Include this book in your next order. **Be sure to order it under the following catalog number:**

3K4117—"Colors and Furnishings." Sent anywhere in the United States, postpaid........................**29c**

NOTE: If you are anxious to get this book immediately and are not sending in an order for other merchandise, you can use the coupon below.

INTERIOR DECORATION IN TWELVE EASY LESSONS

$4.95

A complete course of instruction in interior decoration written and supervised by Hazel H. Adler, a nationally known authority on that fascinating subject. After completing this study in 12 simple, easy lessons you will be thoroughly competent to plan and carry out to successful completion any decoration project for your home. You will know how to make your home interesting, distinctive, beautiful. You will be accomplished in every phase of room arrangement, you will know how to make curtains, draperies, lamp shades, how to treat walls and woodwork. Moreover, you can undertake Interior Decoration as a means of making extra money in your spare time.

For only $4.95 this course teaches you the following:

1—How to Plan Decorations of New Rooms and Old.
2—Color Harmony.
3—Walls and Woodwork.
4—Floors and Floor Covering.
5—Furniture.
6—Curtains and Drapery.
7—Decorative Accessories.
8—Living Rooms.
9—Bedrooms.
10—Dining, Breakfast and Sun Rooms.
11—Kitchen and Bathrooms.
12—How to Apply your Knowledge of Interior Decoration.

The course includes a Color Harmony Chart, usually retailing at $2.00, printed and illustrated pamphlets, problem sheets, scrapbook, loose leaf binder, pocket file, cutouts; also a special feature and sealed answers with each lesson. After you have completed the course you are entitled to consult Mrs. Adler on any problems which have come up in connection with the course or on your own Interior Decoration work.

3K2290—Interior Decorating Course. Shipping weight, 4 pounds...........................**$4.95**

Fill Out and Mail the Coupon TODAY!

29¢

WALL PAPER Store

for This Big FREE Wall Paper Book

More on Your Paper!

Send for This Big Wall Paper Book Today It's FREE!

We make our wall paper, owning and operating one of the largest, best equipped mills in the country. We make and sell millions of rolls of wall paper every month, being the world's largest wall paper dealers. We sell direct to you, saving you all the usual middlemen's profits. We furnish our wall paper ready trimmed, making it easy to hang. We offer you exclusive patterns, showing the latest ideas of the foremost designers. We give all our patterns a ground coat before the color design is applied, insuring lasting color and long life. This feature, usually found only in high priced papers, keeps the paper fresh appearing, makes it more durable and easy to clean.

Prove to your own satisfaction the big savings we make you and the attractive variety of designs we offer you. Fill out the coupon on the post card above and mail it for a FREE copy of our latest big Wall Paper Sample Book. Ask for it TODAY! You can't afford to overlook the amazingly large savings our low prices make you on every pattern shown.

YOU CAN select from a wide range of attractive designs. We sell wall paper for as little as 3c a single roll—enough paper for a whole room for only 65c! Elsewhere you would often be asked 75c a roll or more for some of the artistic creations we sell at 30c a roll. You owe it to yourself to get a FREE copy of this splendid catalog. Fill out the coupon on the post card and mail it TODAY for YOUR copy.

WALL PAPER SAMPLES

Sears, Roebuck and Co.
The World's Largest Store

A Weather-Tight Roof
Makes a Snug Home

Asbestos Fiber Liquid Roof Coating

Made of Genuine Long Fiber Asbestos and Guaranteed Gilsonite Asphaltum

Use this splendid roof coating to make your roof long lasting and leak proof. It will penetrate every crack, joint, nail hole or rust spot in any flat or steep roof, whether composition, felt, p a p e r, gravel or metal. Comes in thick liquid form, readily spread over the old roof. (Use our Special Roof Brush 30K3170, shown below.) It will not run or sag in hot weather nor crack in cold weather. This roof coating has no superior for dampproofing exterior foundations and underground s t e e l or wood tanks. One gallon will cover about 65 square feet, applied about one-sixteenth of an inch thick. Any color of this roof coating will give the same high grade service, although the color of the red or green coating requires making it on a different formula.

38c a Gallon in 50-Gal. Barrels (Black)

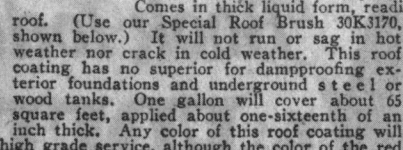

	Shpg. Wt., Lbs.	30K3479 Black	Shpg. Wt., Lbs.	30K3480 Red	30K3481 Dark Green
1 gallon	13	72c	14	$1.60	$1.73
5 gallons. Per gallon	45	57c	60	1.50	1.63
★30-gallon half barrel. Per gallon	265	40c	350	1.15	1.24
★50-gallon barrel. Per gallon	425	38c	565	1.09	1.20

★Shipped from factory in NEW JERSEY.

Asbestos Fiber Roof Cement

There is nothing better for patching chimney flashings, holes, gaps or repairing around gutters and skylights. Apply it one-eight to one-fourth inch thick, depending on the size and the kind of repair. As easy to use as putty. Can be used with excellent results as a covering for the entire roof; ten pounds will cover about 25 square feet of smooth surface. Most conveniently applied over large surfaces with a trowel—see opposite page.

$1.80 Black, 25 Pounds

	30K3477 Black	30K3478 Red	30K3483 Dark Green	Shpg. Wt., Lbs.
5-pound can	$ 0.48	$ 0.87	$ 0.98	10
10-pound can	.87	1.45	1.75	15
25-pound pail	1.80	3.60	4.25	29
50-pound pail	3.15	6.50	7.25	55
★300-pound half barrel	2.60	29.20	33.20	340
★550-pound barrel	8.40	48.25	55.00	620

★Shipped from factory in NEW JERSEY.

Rufix
A Splendid Roof Paint

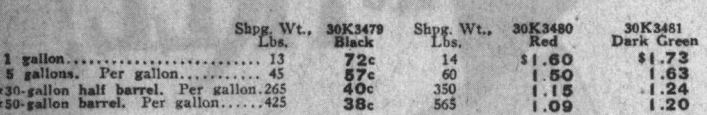

Black and Maroon
Sold Under Our Own Trade Mark, Registered in the U. S. Patent Office

70c a Gallon in 50-Gal. Barrels (Black)

A coat of Rufix NOW will protect your roof from leaking and keep its appearance attractive for years to come. You can STOP LEAKS, too, that may have already developed in your roof. Before applying Rufix all nail holes and bad leaks should be filled with our Asbestos Fiber Roof Cement 30K3477, shown at the left. Rufix forms a tough, elastic, weatherproof coating, being a combination of weather resisting gums and oils. It is NOT made of cheap coal tar products usually offered at about our Rufix prices. It will not soften even during extremely hot weather. You can readily apply Rufix yourself. To secure best results, use the special Roof Paint Brush shown at left below, Rufix being somewhat thick to use with an ordinary paint brush. We guarantee Rufix to give service equal to that of the highest priced roof paints on the market or we will replace it free of charge. One gallon will cover approximately 250 square feet, one coat, on smooth surfaces.

	Shpg. Wt. Lbs.	30K1910 Black Per Gal.	Shpg. Wt., Lbs.	30K1920 Maroon Per Gal
1-gallon can	12	98c	14	$1.27
5-gallon can	43	92c	63	1.22
★25-gallon half barrel	275	78c	375	.98
★50-gallon barrel	500	70c	720	.93

★Shipped from factory in NORTHEASTERN ILLINOIS.

Roof Paint Brush

The brush we recommend for all heavy tar p a i n t s, roof coatings and heavy painting material. Bound with wire and carefully cemented into a hardwood head, 3¼-inch bristles. Long lasting, will not check or crack.

75c THREE KNOTS

30K3170

Two Knots. Shpg. wt., 1 lb....................55c
Three Knots. Shpg. wt., 1¼ lbs............75c
Four Knots. Shpg. wt., 1¾ lbs............90c

Creosote Wood Preserver
75¢ One Gal.

Lengthens the Life of Wood Surfaces

You can make wood fence posts, sills, joists, etc., last much longer by treating them with this splendid Wood Preserver. Use it for treating soft woods, too. Made of pure creosote oil, recommended by the United States Government as the best possible wood preservative. It is also a splendid stain and preservative for shingled roofs. We are offering it at the lowest price at which pure creosote oil wood preserver is ever sold. Do not confuse it with adulterated creosote oils sometimes offered at prices lower than these. One gallon of this preservative will cover 80 square feet with two coats, or will treat about twenty ordinary fence posts to the height of 2½ feet.

30K1947—Creosote Wood Preserver.
1-gal. can ......(Shpg. wt., 14 lbs.)..............75c
5-gal. can .....(Shpg. wt., 59 lbs.) Gal...72c
★25-gal. half bbl...(Shpg. wt., 245 lbs.) Gal...66c
★50-gal. barrel ...(Shpg. wt., 510 lbs.) Gal...63c
★Shipped from factory in NORTHEASTERN ILLINOIS.

Seroco Shingle Stain

85c 1 Gal.

You can weatherproof your roofs, shingled walls and rough wood sidings at small expense and make them attractive appearing. This splendid stain contains a high proportion of Creosote Oil, making it an excellent preservative. One gallon covers about 80 square feet of shingles, two coats, or 125 to 150 square feet of fir siding and similar soft woods, two coats. 1,000 4x16-inch shingles can be dipped two-thirds of their length with 2½ or 3 gallons of this stain; apply two coats to obtain a lasting color. See directions for measuring your roof on page 1021. NOTE—Only the Bungalow Brown color can be used on hardwood. For actual color of Seroco Shingle Stain see page 1023.

Stain for New, Clean Shingles

30K1181—Moss Green.	30K1186—Bungalow Brown.	30K1185—Red.	
1-gallon can	(Shipping weight, 14 pounds)		85c
5-gallon can	(Shipping weight, 55 pounds)		Per gallon 83c
★25-gallon half barrel	(Shipping weight, 250 pounds)		Per gallon 73c
★50-gallon barrel	(Shipping weight, 500 pounds)		Per gallon 68c

★Shipped from factory in NORTHEASTERN ILLINOIS.

Special Stain for Old Weathered Shingles

Your old shingles will look like new when covered with this splendid double strength stain. It covers and protects the surface thoroughly. Our prices on this stain make it an unusually big value.

30K1191—Moss Green.	30K1195—Red.	30K1196—Bungalow Brown.	
Order the above numbers to obtain the special stain made with double strength color for old and weathered shingles.

1-gallon can	(Shipping weight, 14 pounds)		$1.21
5-gallon can	(Shipping weight, 59 pounds)		Per gallon 1.16
★25-gallon half barrel	(Shipping weight, 250 pounds)		Per gallon 1.00
★50-gallon barrel	(Shipping weight, 500 pounds)		Per gallon .95

★Shipped from factory in NORTHEASTERN ILLINOIS.

Liquid Coal Tar

Protect water tanks, metal fence posts, and other metal surfaces against rust with this excellent preparation; widely used by professional roofers for recoating gravel roofs; sometimes used for pruning and tree wound dressing. May be applied cold, but gives best results when heated to a boiling temperature.

63c 1 Gal.

30K3468			
1-gallon can	(Shipping weight, 14 pounds)		63c
5-gallon can	(Shipping weight, 55 pounds)		Per gallon 55c
★25-gallon half barrel	(Shipping weight, 250 pounds)		Per gallon 29c
★50-gallon barrel	(Shipping weight, 425 pounds)		Per gallon 23c

★Shipped from factory in SOUTHEASTERN PENNSYLVANIA.

Seroco BARN PAINT

A Better Paint for Barns

Don't put "any old paint" on your barns and outbuildings because it is cheap. Good paint PAYS! You KNOW it is good economy to keep frame buildings well painted. It preserves the life of the wood, protects the surfaces from weather and decay and gives the buildings thus painted an attractive appearance and greater value.

$1.30 per Gal. in 5-Gal. Cans
Except French Gray

Seroco Barn Paint is a high grade paint that spreads easily, evenly and smoothly and wears for years. BEST OF ALL, it costs you no more than inferior barn paints that do not give you the excellent appearance and wearing qualities of Seroco Barn Paint. We make it in our big modern paint factory and make it like a high grade house paint, grinding every particle of oxide with the oil. The result is a smooth, even paint with unusually good covering capacity and uniform color. Contrast this modern Pebble Mill Grinding Process with the usual barn paint formula—simply **pigment mixed in oil.** We make millions of gallons of paint a year, manufacturing it under modern scientific methods, economically and uniformly, using the best proven ingredients for the purpose.

We sell this splendid paint direct from the factory to the user, at remarkably low prices that give you the benefit of our skilled methods, big output and one moderate profit. Every brushful of Seroco Barn Paint saves you money, both during the painting and through the after years. It will cover better, spread more widely, last longer and look better longer than any other barn paint you may have used. Try it under our amazingly liberal PAINT GUARANTEE (see page 1022). For best results we recommend using 30K3087 Brush, 4½-inch size, or 30K3101 Brush, 6-inch size (see pages 1028 and 1029).

Seroco Barn Paint PAYS both when you paint and while it wears. **Our low prices mean money saved**—our high quality means satisfaction.

30K830—Yellow. 30K850—Maroon. 30K800—Red.

5-gallon can. Shipping weight, 67 pounds. Per gallon	$1.30
3-gallon can. Shipping weight, 40 pounds. Per gallon	1.33
1-gallon can. Shipping weight, 16 pounds.	1.35

NOTE—We do not furnish Barn Paint in containers larger than 5 gallons, as it is impractical to stir paint successfully in larger size containers.

Special French Gray Barn Paint

A special Gray Barn Paint of unusual quality. Superior to the ordinary barn paints and to many of the house paints frequently offered at much higher prices.

30K820

5-gallon can. Shpg. wt., 80 lbs. Per gallon	$1.81
3-gallon can. Shpg. wt., 49 lbs. Per gallon	1.86
1-gallon can. Shipping weight, 19 pounds	1.90

Our iron paint paddle for mixing paints is included with all 3 and 5-gallon cans. For Color Samples See Page 1023.

See page 1022 for Linseed Oil and Paint Thinner (Substitute for turpentine.)

HOW TO MEASURE YOUR BUILDING FOR PAINTING

To Find How Many Gallons Are Needed

Measure the length, width and height of the building. Add together the total length in feet of the two sides and two ends of the building. Multiply this by the height of the building at the eaves with two feet added for cornice. This gives you number of square feet of surface to be painted.

For example, suppose your building measures 26 feet wide, 33 feet long and 22 feet high, you would figure it as shown at right.

No. 1—For poor surfaces where no paint has been applied for 12 to 18 years, and the wood is bare and porous, for three coats divide the number of square feet by 100. Three coats are necessary for a surface of this kind. If only two coats are applied, chalking and spotting are sure to follow.

No. 2—For fair surfaces where paint film is worn thin and chalking rapidly. For two coats divide the number of square feet by 180, for three coats divide by 125.

No. 3—For new wood three coats are always necessary. Divide the number of square feet by 165.

No. 4—For good surfaces where paint film is unbroken and is chalking only slightly. For two coats divide the number of square feet by 250, for one coat divide by 500.

In figuring the amount of trimming required the rule of 1 gallon trimming to 5 gallons of body is usually followed.

Remember This:

The square feet of covering capacity of any paint varies with the kind of surface over which it is applied. A badly weathered and very porous surface will require twice as much paint as another surface which is in good condition. So in judging your surface we give you the table at left to guide you in estimating the number of gallons you will need.

Do not be deceived by different claims made for the spreading capacities of various paints, for common sense will tell you that the larger the surface over which you spread a gallon of paint the thinner the film will be, and the thinner the film the more easily will it be destroyed by the weather. Seroco Paint will go just as far as any other paint with the right thickness of film. We give you the covering capacities which will insure you a paint film with maximum protection and endurance.

Front	26 feet
One side	33 feet
Rear	26 feet
Other side	33 feet
Total	118 feet

Multiply this by height with two feet added for cornice | 24 feet

Total | 2,832 sq. ft.

Barn Painting

If you have taken the height of your barn to the eaves and it has a high gable, you will have to allow paint for this space. Multiply width of barn by the height of gable above the corner post. Divide the number of square feet by the covering capacity, and this gives you the amount of paint needed for both gables. The amount of trimming required for a barn is about 1 gallon of trimming to 10 gallons of body.

In figuring roof paint or stain, multiply the length of the house by the width, then add one-third that amount and the total will be approximate area of roof. Now divide by covering capacity per gallon of paint or stain you wish to use. The result will be the number of gallons required.

Wagon Paint

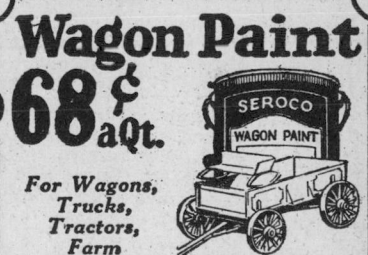

68¢ a Qt.

For Wagons, Trucks, Tractors, Farm Implements and Milk Cans

This high grade paint applied to your farm vehicles and implements will prevent them from being ruined by rust. Its use may save you many dollars in repairs. One gallon is often enough to refinish every implement on the farm. Use it on milk cans to prevent rust and to identify your own cans.

30K1854—Red.
30K1855—Blue.
30K1856—Green.
30K1857—Yellow.
30K1858—Vermilion.
30K1859—Black.

1-quart can. Shipping weight, 4 pounds	$0.68
½-gallon can. Shipping weight, 9 pounds	1.31
1-gallon can. Shipping weight, 14 pounds	2.47

Asphalt Roof Paint

Second only to our Rufix Paint (see opposite page), for felt or composition roofs, warehouses, iron roofs, trestles, sheds, etc. Better than coal tar type roof paints; often sold elsewhere for $1.00 or more a gallon. One gallon will cover about 200 square feet of smooth surface or 150 square feet of rough surface, one coat.

30K1941—Asphalt Roof Paint. Black only.

1-gallon can. (Shipping weight, 12 pounds)	74c
5-gallon can. (Shipping weight, 45 pounds). Per gallon	71c
★25-gallon half barrel. (Shipping weight, 215 pounds). Per gallon	60c
★50-gallon barrel. (Shipping weight, 425 pounds). Per gallon	53c

★Shipped from factory in NORTHEASTERN ILLINOIS.

6-Inch Trowel

45c

Made of steel ground smooth and well shaped. Especially recommended for applying Asbestos Fiber Roof Cement. Weight, 3 ounces.

9K5886 .... **45c**

It's Easy to Order From the World's Largest Store. See Page 546

1021

Seroco HOUSE PAINT

Only $2.20 Per Gallon

IN 5 GALLON CANS

A Better Paint for Less Money!

WE sell high grade House Paint under the strongest paint guarantee in the world! That proves OUR confidence in its quality. ONE trial of this splendid paint will establish YOUR confidence in its excellence.

Seroco House Paint offers you ALL the features you expect from the highest priced brands of paint offered elsewhere and our prices often save you from one-third to one-half over the prices many dealers ask! You will get exceptional wearing qualities, smooth glossy surfaces, fresh easy flowing paint, when you buy Seroco House Paint under our amazingly liberal guarantee, shown at the left.

Paint is an investment, not an expense. It prevents decay, protects the wood surfaces, makes the home more attractive and adds to its value. It is false economy to permit a building to become shabby, dilapidated or weather beaten. Good paint, properly applied, will restore it to its original well kept appearance and "keep it young." Get the fullest economy paint can offer you by using Seroco House Paint. You will never regret it!

We offer you thirty-five attractive shades of Seroco House Paint on the opposite page, in actual colors. Note carefully the big saving our prices make you, and remember that the highest prices asked elsewhere cannot possibly represent any higher quality paint than we offer you, direct from our modern paint factory.

All we ask is—simply apply Seroco Paint according to the plain directions we furnish. We know that the results will more than please you.

5-gallon can. Shipping weight, 80 pounds. Per gallon	$2.20
3-gallon can. Shipping weight, 50 pounds. Per gallon	2.23
1-gallon can. Shipping weight, 19 pounds	2.29
½-gallon can. Shipping weight, 10 pounds	1.20
1-quart can. Shipping weight, 6 pounds	.65

Our iron paint paddle for stirring paints is included with all 3 and 5-gallon cans.

NOTE—We do not furnish Seroco House Paint in containers larger than 5 gallons, as it is impractical to stir paint successfully in larger size containers.

35 Colors of Seroco House Paint

30K209—Beaver Brown.	30K253—Golden Green.	30K204—Pea Green.
30K239—Black.	30K221—Leather Brown.	30K208—Pearl Gray.
30K218—Buff.	30K207—Dark Stone Gray.	30K217—Pure Blue.
30K206—Canary.	30K223—Light Blue.	30K263—Russet Brown.
30K230—Chocolate Brown.	30K259—Light Steel Gray.	30K258—Seal Brown.
30K246—Colonial Yellow.	30K235—Light Stone Gray.	30K233—Slate.
30K254—Cream.	30K224—Maroon.	30K203—Straw Yellow.
30K237—Dark Steel Gray.	30K244—Pale Green.	30K219—Terra Cotta.
30K202—Dove.	30K232—Myrtle Green.	30K256—Ivory-White.
30K236—Emerald Green.	30K213—Nile Green.	30K226—Willow Green.
30K216—Fawn.	30K229—Oxide Red.	30K257—White (Inside).
30K201—French Gray.		30K243—White (Outside).

Colors Are Shown on Opposite Page

We Guarantee

to furnish new paint free of charge, ship it to you at our expense and PAY FOR PUTTING IT ON YOUR BUILDING, if Seroco Paint does not give you the service you have a right to expect when carefully applied according to our directions—two coats to painted surfaces in fairly good condition, three coats to new surfaces and old painted and unpainted surfaces in bad condition—with raw linseed oil and turpentine added as per instructions on the containers, depending on the condition of the surface.

Or, if after applying a portion of any Seroco Paint you are not satisfied in every way, you may send back the remainder, and we will return the price you paid for the entire quantity, including all shipping charges.

We guarantee Seroco Paint to represent good honest value; that it will make a nice appearing job; will fully protect the surface on which it is applied; is easy to apply and will give you the service you have a right to expect of any paint, regardless of price.

Sears, Roebuck and Co.
The World's Largest Store

SEROCO THE LONGLIFE HOUSE-PAINT
READY MIXED — FORMULA — GUARANTEED
SEARS ROEBUCK AND CO.

Only $2.20 Per Gal. In 5-Gal. Cans

See pages 1028 and 1029 for a full line of brushes; order them with your paint.

You May Need Some Linseed Oil

On painted surfaces in fairly good condition apply two coats of Seroco Ready Mixed House Paint with the first coat thinned with ½ pint of turpentine to each gallon of paint. On surfaces that have never been painted and on old porous surfaces badly in need of paint, three coats should be applied, the first coat thinned in proportion of about two quarts of pure raw linseed oil to each gallon of Ready Mixed Paint. On new surfaces of pitchy lumber, that have never been painted, you will need about one quart of turpentine and one quart of linseed oil per gallon for the first coat.

Seroco Substitute for Turpentine
Paint Thinner

An economical thinner to be used in place of turpentine in paints on old surfaces and for cleaning brushes. Guaranteed satisfactory. Write for prices on Pure Turpentine.

30K3462

1-quart can (Shipping weight, 3 pounds)		20c
½-gallon can (Shipping weight, 6 pounds)		35c
1-gallon can (Shipping weight, 10 pounds)		48c
5-gallon can (Shipping weight, 37 pounds)	Per Gallon	43c

Pure Linseed Oil

The price of Linseed Oil is changing constantly. Send us a post card, and immediately upon receipt of it we will send you our regular quotation card, quoting the lowest prevailing prices, which we will guarantee for a stated period.

Seroco Brush Lacquer

Every Brushful a Stroke of Beauty

The popular new finish—so easy to apply and so quick to dry! The convenience and beauty of paint, the durable luster of varnish and the hard-wearing gloss of enamel, combined into a quick drying finish of rare beauty—this is **Brush Lacquer.** With it, a few quick strokes transforms as with a brush of magic. A kitchen table or chair lacquered in the afternoon can be safely used for the evening meal. A floor or flight of stairs refinished after supper can be used freely before bedtime. Redecorated playthings can be freely handled an hour after being refinished.

Brush Lacquer adds new charm to furniture or any interior woodwork. Use it either on new unfinished wood surfaces, **(if not stained)** or over painted, varnished or enameled surfaces, carefully following the directions furnished. It is adapted for practically any home furnishings or fittings, except those with metal surfaces.

Brush Lacquer is similar in type to the widely used Automobile Lacquer, but is applied with a brush instead of being sprayed on. It should be applied in generous quantities with quick brush strokes over a small area. **It is NOT an automobile finish.**

Allow an hour between coats for thorough drying and to prevent a damp undercoat from "loosening" or "rolling up." Put on the necessary number of coats required to secure the best results. The covering capacity is about 250 square feet per gallon, two coats. A pint and a half will refinish a large breakfast set.

For Colors See Opposite Page

95¢ Per Pint

Use our Brush Lacquer Thinner if the Lacquer tends to thicken. Use the Thinner, too, to clean the brush. **Turpentine, naphtha, alcohol, benzine, etc., cannot be used to thin Brush Lacquer.** We recommend brushes 30K3025 or 30K3033, page 1029, for use with this Lacquer.

Choose Seroco Brush Lacquer From These Colors

30K2075—Light Ivory.	30K2080—Turkey.	30K2085—Marine.
30K2076—Wheat.	30K2081—Chocolate.	30K2086—Apple Green.
30K2077—Fawn.	30K2082—Cloud Gray.	30K2087—Black.
30K2078—Lemon.	30K2083—Deep Buff.	30K2088—White.
30K2079—Tangerine.	30K2084—Turquoise.	30K2089—Clear.
½-pint can......**55c** (Shipping weight, 1¾ lbs.)	1-pint can.......**95c** (Shipping weight, 2½ lbs.)	1-quart can.. **$1.70** (Shipping weight, 4 lbs.)

30K2090—Brush Lacquer Thinner

½-pint can. Shipping weight, 1¾ pounds.......... **40c**
1-pint can. Shipping weight, 2½ pounds.......... **55c**
1-quart can. Shipping weight, 4 pounds.......... **95c**

Gold Bronze and Aluminum Radiator Enamels

The Finishes of Countless Uses

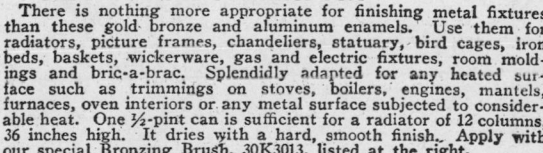

There is nothing more appropriate for finishing metal fixtures than these gold bronze and aluminum enamels. Use them for radiators, picture frames, chandeliers, statuary, bird cages, iron beds, baskets, wickerware, gas and electric fixtures, room moldings and bric-a-brac. Splendidly adapted for any heated surface such as trimmings on stoves, boilers, engines, mantels, furnaces, oven interiors or any metal surface subjected to considerable heat. One ½-pint can is sufficient for a radiator of 12 columns, 36 inches high. It dries with a hard, smooth finish. Apply with our special Bronzing Brush, 30K3013, listed at the right.

30K2123—Gold Bronze Enamel.		30K2122—Aluminum Enamel.	
⅛-pint can (Shpg. wt., 1 lb.)	$0.22	⅛-pint can (Shpg. wt., 1 lb.)	$0.20
¼-pint can (Shpg. wt., 1¼ lbs.)	.32	¼-pint can (Shpg. wt., 1¼ lbs.)	.25
½-pint can (Shpg. wt., 1¾ lbs.)	.45	½-pint can (Shpg. wt., 1¾ lbs.)	.34
1-pint can (Shpg. wt., 2½ lbs.	.60	1-pint can (Shpg. wt., 2½ lbs.)	.50
1-quart can (Shpg. wt., 4½ lbs.)	1.15	1-quart can (Shpg. wt., 4 lbs.)	.94

Vernis Martin (Gold Bronze) Finish Outfit

Widely used for giving new beauty to iron beds, etc. The outfit comprises 4-ounce can of Mixing Liquid, 1¾-ounce can of Bronzing Powder, 4-ounce can of Lacquer and brush. Easily applied, very satisfactory and big value at our price. Shipping weight, 2 pounds.

30K2128.......... **62c**

Painters' Time Saver

For quickly and neatly painting, enameling or varnishing window sash, door casings, baseboards, moldings, etc. Saves soiling walls, floors or windows. Handy when washing woodwork, too. Shpg. wt., 8 oz.

30K2980.......... **12c**

Radiator Bronzing Brush

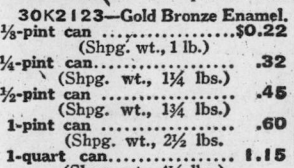

Width, 1½ inches; length, 9½ inches. Shpg. wt., 2 oz.

30K3013.......... **30c**

Bronzing Brush

Soft hair brushes for applying gold and silver paints, bronzing, etc. Shipping weight, each, 1 ounce.

30K3011

Size, inch	⅜	½	¾	1
Each	9c	12c	14c	18c

Gold Bronze Powder

Comes in bright gold, rich brass or Roman gold color. (Not illustrated.) **State color wanted.** Mix with Bronzing Liquid 30K2167 (at right), using 7 ounces of Bronze Powder to each pint of Bronzing Liquid.

30K2190

4-ounce can. (Shpg. wt., 6 oz.)... **34c**
8-ounce can. (Shipping weight, 1 pound).... **62c**

Aluminum or Silver Color Powder

Mix with Bronzing Liquid 30K2167 (at right), using 3 ounces of powder to each pint of Liquid. (Not illustrated.)

30K2194

4-ounce can. (Shipping weight, 6 ounces)...... **34c**
8-ounce can. (Shipping wt., 1 lb.).. **60c**

Bronzing Liquid

For mixing with gold, aluminum or other bronze powders. (Not illustrated.) More desirable than banana liquid, being equally efficient, less expensive and having no offensive odor.

30K2167

1-pint can. (Shipping weight, 1¾ pounds)... **36c**
1-quart can. (Shpg. wt., 3½ lbs)...... **58c**

Steel Wool and Shavings

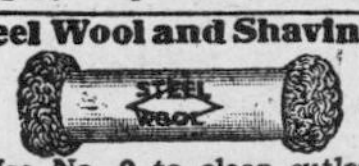

Use No. 0 to clean cutlery, aluminum ware, etc.; **No. 1** for floors, woodwork, linoleum, etc.; **No. 3** for stoves, ranges, etc. **Steel Shavings** used for removing rust from iron preparatory to painting. **State size number.**

9K6265—Steel Wool.

No.	Grade	Equal to	Per 1-Lb. Pkg.
0	Very Fine	No. 00 Sandpaper	45c
1	Fine	Nos. 0 and ½ Sandpaper	40c
3	Medium	No. 1½ Sandpaper	30c

9K6264—Steel Shavings. (For rougher work.) 1-pound package...... **30c**

For all grades of sand paper see page 987.

Do You Know?

How to paint your home;
What colors to use;
How to refinish old woodwork and floors;
How to lacquer furniture.

See page 1017

DECALCOMANIA TRANSFERS

Up to Date, Stylish Decoration for Furniture

The latest design furniture pieces are usually sold decorated with Decalcomania Transfers. Bring your own furniture pieces or sets up to date by putting on these transfers yourself. Apply them with Le Page's Liquid Glue, 30K3218. (Shipping weight, 1 pound. Price per ¼-pint can, 25c.) Washing or varnishing the furniture will not affect their lasting color or finish if you coat them with our Decalcomania Varnish 30K2725. (Shipping weight, 1 pound. Price, per ¼-pint can, 21c.) Complete directions furnished for applying transfers.

30K16—1 sheet composed of 15 transfers, light pink and yellow rose designs, 4 baskets, drops, corners and other pieces to complete a bedroom set. Shipping weight, 8 ounces.......... **$1.00**

30K18—Pink rose and tiny blue forget-me-not design, 1½x15 inches. Each.......... **10c**

30K20—Pink rose and tiny blue and white flower design, 1¼x12 inches. Each.......... **10c**

30K22—Blue thistle and pink rose design, 1½x9 inches. Each.......... **10c**

30K24—Nasturtium design. Natural coloring, 1½x12 inches. Each.......... **10c**

30K26—Pink rose design, 1½x15 inches. Each.......... **10c**

30K28—Nursery Holland Characters (choice of Boy, Girl, Mother, Father), 4 inches high. Each.......... **10c**
Shipping weight, each, 2 ounces.

30K14—One sheet composed of eleven transfers, yellow and rose floral decorations with green shaded sprays. Four flower receptacles and seven smaller floral pieces, enough to decorate the average set of furniture. Shipping weight, 8 ounces.......... **$1.00**

30K12—One sheet of fourteen transfer pieces, apple blossom pattern. Two large sprays, twelve smaller ones. Pink and green blended shades. Shipping wt., 8 ounces.......... **$1.00**

30K23—Complete set of nineteen appropriate transfers for children's room or nursery furniture or painted nursery walls. Shpg. wt., 8 oz.. **$1.00**

30K25—Set of ten figures selected from 30K23 Set. Shpg. wt., 5 oz.... **.50**

30K27—Set of four figures from 30K23 Set. Shpg. wt., 3 oz....... **.30**

30K29—Set of five figures from 30K23 Set. Shpg. wt., 4 oz....... **.40**

We will send our illustrated Decalcomania Transfer circular DT30PK on request.

Use Good Brushes

Popular Paint Brush

$1.50 4-Inch

This is our most popular brush and **a big value.** We recommend it very highly for the man who has occasional painting jobs around the home. It is of a quality to insure dependable service. Medium long black Chinese bristles, **secured in vulcanized rubber.** Heavy tin ferrule, nailed and soldered; hardwood handle.

30K3087—Shipping weight, ¾ pound.

Width	Length	
3 Inches	3⅝ Inches	$0.83
3½ Inches	3⅝ Inches	1.17
4 Inches	3¾ Inches	1.50
4½ Inches	4 Inches	2.25

$1.43 4-Inch

RUBBERSET TRADE MARK

Big Value Paint Brush

A low priced genuine Rubberset Brush, an exceptional value at these prices. A favorite among home owners who want a good grade inexpensive brush. Has white Russian bristles, brass bound. A handy brush for any painting job.

30K3081—Shpg. wt., ¾ lb.

W'th, In.	L'gth, In.	
3	3⅛	$0.92
3½	3¼	1.07
4	3⅝	1.43

$3.20 4-Inch

High Grade Extra Long Bristle Paint Brush

Favorite Among Professional Painters

Another high grade brush, widely used by professional painters. Has extra long selected black Chinese bristles **secured in vulcanized rubber.** The average home owner prefers a brush with shorter bristles.

30K3082—Shpg. wt., ¾ lb.

W'th, In.	L'gth, In.	
3	3⅞	$1.75
3½	4⅛	2.35
4	4½	3.20

66c 4-Inch

Challenge Paint Brush—A Big Value

Our lowest priced brush and a big value. Suitable for ordinary use. Has bristles **secured in vulcanized rubber,** tin ferrule. Our higher priced brushes, of course, are even bigger values and will give even more satisfactory results.

30K3084

W'th, In.	L'gth, In.	Shpg. Wt.	
2½	2⅛	8 oz.	35c
3	2⅓	¾ lb.	45c
3½	2⅝	¾ lb.	54c
4	2⅝	¾ lb.	66c
4½	2¾	¾ lb.	80c

$3.55 4-Inch

RUBBERSET TRADE MARK

Our Very Best Paint Brush

This brush is a favorite among professional painters who want the very best; worth one-third to one-half more. Long, heavy, selected black Chinese bristles. It will give you amazingly long, dependable service.

30K3083—Shipping weight, ¾ pound.

Width, In.	Length, In.	
3	4⅞	$2.60
3½	4¾	2.95
4	4¾	3.55
4½	4¾	3.78

$2.15 4-Inch

Our Medium Priced Favorite

Our most popular medium priced brush. Very satisfactory for both the professional painter and the home owner. Has long, black Chinese bristles, **secured in vulcanized rubber;** hardwood handle. A remarkably big value.

30K3080

Shipping weight, ¾ lb.

Width, In.	Length, In.	
3	3½	$1.15
3½	3½	1.45
4	4	2.15

Two Handy Brushes

75c 4-Inch

Big Value Paint Brush

A splendid brush at a ridiculously low price. Selected Chinese bristles in a big variety of lengths.

30K3093

W'h, In.	Lgt., In.	Shpg. Wt.	
2½	2⅜	8 oz.	40c
3	2⅝	¾ lb.	50c
3½	2¾	¾ lb.	59c
4	3	¾ lb.	75c
4½	3¼	¾ lb.	95c

85c 3-Inch

Varnish Brush

A very popular, satisfactory, yet inexpensive brush for home varnishing. Extra thick black selected soft Chinese bristles, **set in vulcanized rubber.** Double nickel plated ferrule, well nailed.

30K3037

W'h. In.	Lgt., In.	Shpg. Wt.	
1	2	4 oz.	26c
1½	2⅜	6 oz.	38c
2	2¼	7 oz.	50c
2½	2¾	8 oz.	72c
3	2⅞	¾ lb.	85c

Brush Outfit

Handy, Inexpensive, Complete Painting Outfit for the Home Owner

This outfit includes the following: 2 Chinese Bristle Chiseled Sash Brushes, 1 each ½ and 1 inch wide; 2 Chinese Black Bristle Flat Paint Brushes, 1 each 3½ and 4 inches wide; Chinese Bristle Varnish Brush, 2½ inches wide; Curved Back Steel Wire Brush; Painters' Duster; Putty Knife; Paint Paddle; 2 Paint Pot Hooks; Painters' Time Saver; Scraping Knife. Shipping weight, 6 lbs.

30K2953—Complete outfit........ **$5.35**

Painters' Dusters

Not for Paint

Mixed gray horsehair. A very good duster for removing dust and dirt from surfaces before painting, etc. Diameter, 2½ inches; length, 3½ in. Shpg. wt., ¾ lb.

30K3128........ **70c**

A fine duster. Extra quality black and gray bristles **secured in vulcanized rubber.** Diameter, 2⅜ in.; length, 4 in. Shpg. wt., ¾ lb.

30K3127...... **$1.50**

Roof Seam Brush

Especially made for applying liquid roof cement and coal tar on seams in roofing material. Selected Tampico bristles, 3¼ in. long. Diameter, 1⅝ in.; over all length, 10½ inches. Shipping weight, ¾ pound.

30K3172........ **48c**

RUBBERSET TRADE MARK

Plasterers' or Cement Workers' Brush

All gray stiff Russian bristles set in hard rubber and solidly bound with leather. The center row of bristles set in metal, securely attached to the block. Width, 8 in. Length of bristles, 4 inches. Shipping weight, 2½ pounds.

30K3125........ **$5.28**

Kalsomine Brushes

Popular Low Priced Brush

$2.45 7¾-Inch

Our lowest priced and most popular kalsomine brush. Especially adapted for the home owners' use, well made and a remarkably big value. Others regularly ask one-half more for a brush of this quality. All black, pure Chinese bristles **secured in vulcanized rubber.** Shipping weight, all sizes, 1½ pounds.

30K3100

Width, In.	Length, In.	
5¾	3¼	$1.56
6¾	3¾	1.88
7¾	3¾	2.45

RUBBERSET TRADE MARK

Two Splendid Brushes

A high grade Rubberset Kalsomine Brush which, properly cared for, will give the home owner many years' satisfactory service. Extra long all black bristles. Especially recommended for the man who kalsomines frequently.

30K3106

Width, In.	L'gth, In.	Shpg. Wt., Lbs.	
5¾	4⅛	2	$2.79
6¾	4½	2¼	3.62
7¾	4¾	2½	4.77

Our finest Rubberset Kalsomine Brush; made with the highest quality mixed Russian bristles of a length to handle easily. Worth easily one-half more.

30K3108

W'h, In.	L'h, In.	Shpg. Wt., Lbs.	
5¾	4¼	2	$3.11
6¾	4½	2¼	4.16
7¾	4¾	2½	5.75

Glass Cutters and Scrapers

Graduated scale on bar. Cuts circles from 3 to 22 inches in diameter. Cutter can be taken off and used for straight cutting. Shpg. wt., ¾ lb.

30K2877 **38c**

30K2873—Extra wheels. Shipping weight, 2 ounces........ 3 for **9c**

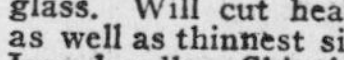

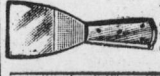

Extra quality cutting wheel for cutting plate, art and rough glass. Will cut heaviest plate as well as thinnest single glass. Iron handle. Shipping weight, 3 ounces.

30K2875........ **9c**

Six cutting wheels in a turret head. Each wheel will cut 500 feet. Shipping weight, 3 ounces.

30K2876........ **20c**

It pays to buy your paints and painting supplies from the World's Largest Store!

Wall Scraping Knife. Stiff blade, 3-inch square point, made of high grade steel. Blade runs through handle. Shipping weight, 6 ounces.

30K2925........ **40c**

Professional Painters' High Grade Wall Scraping Knife. Stiff blade, square point, made of high grade steel. Steel bolster. Blade runs through bakelite handle.

30K2924—3-inch blade. Shipping weight, 5 ounces........ **60c**

4-inch blade. Shipping weight, ¾ pound........ **70c**

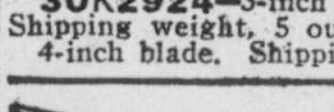

Wall Scraping Knife. Stiff blade. 3⅝-inch square point. Hardwood handle. Shipping weight, 8 ounces.

30K2926........ **12c**

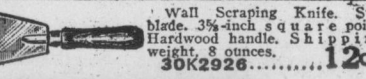

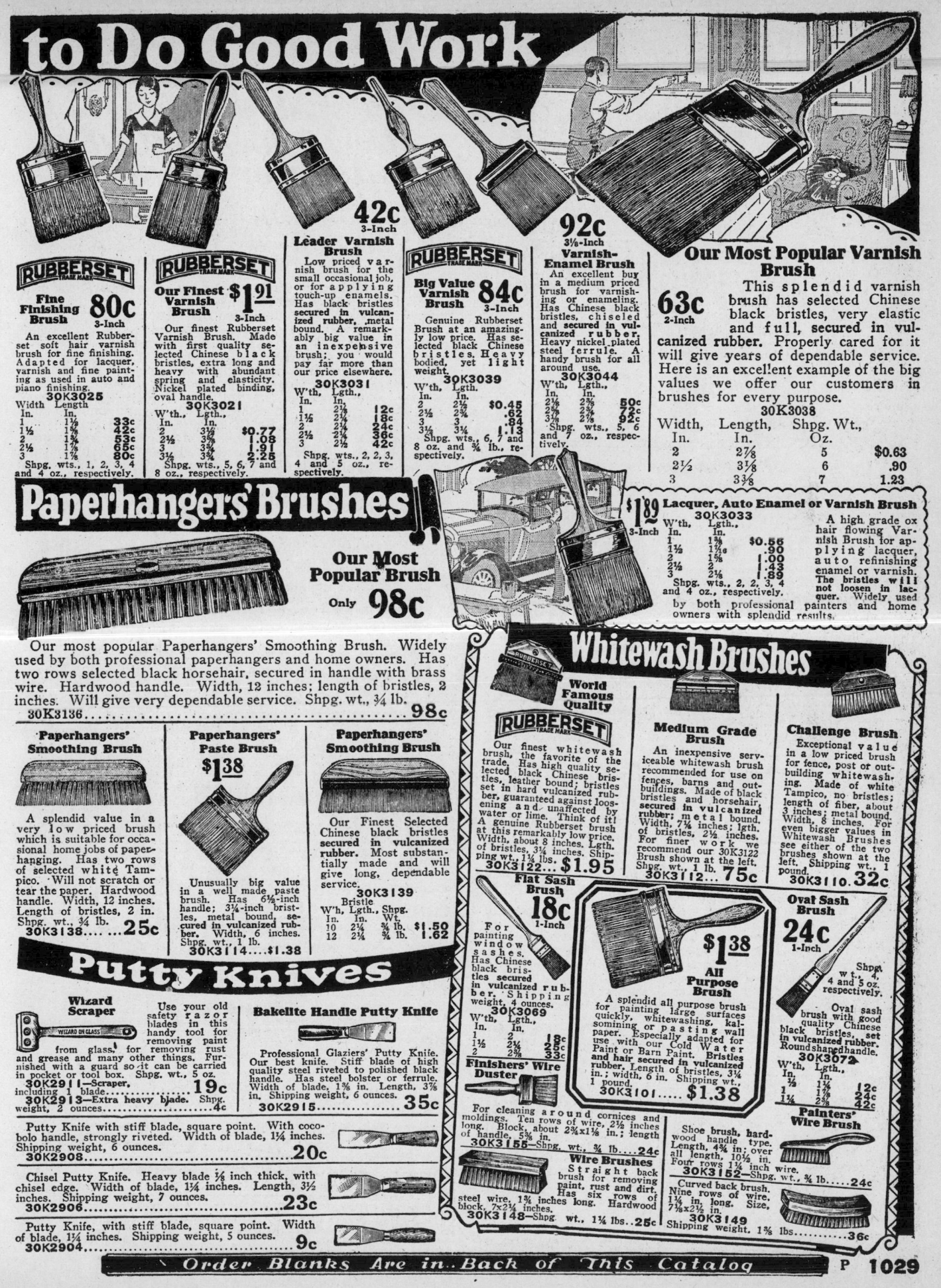

CHINESE GLOSS LACQUER

New Colors for Old Furniture or Woodwork

$2.30 Per Gal.

Think of it! You can refinish all your old furniture pieces to match, quickly, easily, satisfactorily and at small expense. All your dining room pieces in one harmonious color combination—your bedroom pieces likewise. You can also refinish the woodwork to match the room furniture. You can have the pleasing effect of new perfectly matched furniture sets at only a small fraction of the cost of new furniture! Don't regret the mismatched dining table, buffet or chairs, the bed, dresser or chifforobe of unmatched finishes. Refinish them in any of the popular wood finishes you prefer, we list them all. Best of all, it is so easy to make the change, you can do the work yourself without difficulty, and see the quickly transformed pieces and woodwork glow with a new harmonious beauty.

Chinese Gloss Lacquer is a high grade color varnish. We sell it at amazingly low prices, made possible by making it in our big modern varnish factory and selling it direct to you with no dealer's profits added to our price. One gallon will cover at least 600 square feet, one coat. We recommend applying it with Brush 30K3038, see page 1029. If you wish to refinish dark finish pieces with a lighter color, it is absolutely necessary to apply one or more coats of our 30K2697 Undercoat, listed at the left, before applying the lacquer. Best results can be obtained by using this undercoat even when applying dark colors of this finish.

See Actual Colors on Page 1024

30K2689—Brown Mahogany.   30K2692—Red Mahogany.
30K2690—Light Oak.   30K2693—Cherry.
30K2691—Dark Oak.   30K2694—Walnut.

1-pint can...........(Shipping weight, 3 pounds).........$0.40
1-quart can..........(Shipping weight, 4 pounds).......... .65
1-gallon can........(Shipping weight, 12 pounds).......... 2.30

How to Choose Colors and Furnishings for the Home. See Page 1017 About This Wonderful Book at a Bargain Price. Be Sure to Order One.

Undercoat for Chinese Gloss Lacquer

This undercoat or ground color is absolutely necessary when changing the color of your furniture, floor or woodwork from a dark to a lighter color. You will get the very best results by using it even with the dark finish lacquers. This opaque yellow paint completely covers the original finish and forms an excellent foundation for new finishes. Is also well adapted as a base for graining colors. One gallon will cover about 600 square feet, one coat.

30K2697

1-pint can.   Shipping weight, 3 pounds..........35c
1-quart can.   Shipping weight, 5 pounds........$0.63
1-gallon can.   Shipping weight, 18 pounds........ 2.18

63c 1 QT.

Sero-Var *The Universal Varnish*

Sero-Var Is Our Own Trade Mark, Registered in U. S. Pat. Off.

Made in Our Own Splendidly Equipped Up to Date Factory and Guaranteed to Be the Equal of Any of the Nationally Advertised "_____ Spar" Varnishes Often Sold at $5.00 to $7.00 Per Gallon Elsewhere.

Wherever you think of varnish, for either inside or outside use, think of Sero-Var. It will give your dining room, kitchen or nursery furniture a desirable glossy finish, making old furniture look like new. It will give amazingly long wear when used on porches, doors, boats, etc. It has no superior as a floor varnish except our splendid Seroco Floor Varnish shown on the opposite page. Sero-Var is easily applied, dries hard over night, holds its color and is absolutely unaffected by hot or cold water. It is clear and transparent, and will not change the color of the wood. It differs from the widely advertised "spar" varnishes in only one respect—lower price. You get exactly the same high quality materials, lasting service and finish, but you save one-half or more on the price. We sell it direct to you from our factory, with no middlemen's profits included in our price. Apply with a good flat varnish brush (see page 1029).

One gallon of Sero-Var will cover about 500 square feet, one coat.

30K2727

1-pint can..........(Shpg. wt., 2½ lbs.)......$0.50
1-quart can.........(Shpg. wt., 3½ lbs.)...... .78
½-gallon can.......(Shpg. wt., 6½ lbs.)...... 1.45
1-gallon can........(Shpg. wt., 12 lbs.)...... 2.55
5-gallon can, per gal.(Shpg. wt., 50 lbs.)...... 2.30

Interior Varnish

75c 1 QT.

A splendid varnish for use on all inside woodwork or over graining. It dries in about twenty-four hours, produces a fine gloss and is a most durable finish. One gallon will cover about 500 square feet, one coat.

30K2718
Pint $0.48
Quart .... .75
½ Gallon.. 1.30
1 Gallon.. 2.35

Seat Varnish

Especially adapted for chairs; invaluable, too, for church and school seats. Dries hard and durable, will not soften up under body heat. Dries free from dust in a few hours, hardens in forty-eight hours. One quart will refinish six dining room chairs and the dining table one coat.

30K2721
1 Pint....$0.48
1 Quart... .85
½ Gallon.. 1.55

Hard Oil Finish Varnish

Extra Light

65c 1 QT.

An unusually light hard oil finish varnish for finishing woodwork. It preserves the natural grain and color of the wood, works freely and dries in about twenty-four hours with a high gloss. One gallon will cover about 500 square feet, one coat.

30K2710
Quart $0.65
½ Gallon.. 1.10
1 Gallon.. 1.95

FOR SHIPPING WEIGHTS OF VARNISHES SEE 30K2727 AT LEFT

Transparent Tile Varnish

For varnished tile paper, white or ivory enameled surfaces or light color painted walls. Do not use on natural wood finish surfaces. Transparent and will not discolor the surfaces for whose use it is recommended. Has a good body and dries well. One gallon will cover about 500 square feet, one coat.

30K2725
1 Pint....$0.45
1 Quart... .75
½ Gallon.. 1.35
1 Gallon.. 2.43

Seroco Dye Stains

49c 1 QT.

An excellent penetrating wood stain, imparting a rich, natural color to new woodwork, floors or furniture. You can obtain a splendid finish by applying a coat of white or orange shellac over the newly stained wood; then a coat of varnish or wax. Apply it only on new wood surfaces that have not been treated with any other finish. **It must not be used on painted, varnished or enameled surfaces.** On open grained hardwood, best results are obtained by first filling the wood with Seroco Paste Wood Filler (see page 1027). Put Seroco Dye Stains on with a varnish brush. One gallon will cover about 400 square feet, one coat.

1-pint can. Shpg. wt., 2 lbs.....30c
1-quart can. Shpg. wt., 3 lbs.....49c
1-gallon can. Shpg. wt., 11 lbs.$1.63

30K2643—Light Golden Oak.   30K2648—Mahogany.
30K2647—Medium Golden Oak.   30K2649—Walnut.
30K2645—Dark Golden Oak.   30K2644—Weathered or Mission
30K2646—Fumed or Brown Oak.   Oak.

Paint and Varnish Remover

One of the best paint and varnish removers on the market. Guaranteed to remove paint, varnish or oil from wood or iron without damage to the wood veneer, glue or filler. Free from caustics, carbolic acid, lye or any other injurious ingredient. Saves the tedious, unsatisfactory scraping of the old finish by hand. Directions on can.

30K2770
Pint. Shipping weight, 2½ lbs.....34c
Quart. Shipping weight, 4 lbs.....56c
Gallon. Shpg. wt., 11 lbs...$1.85

PAINT YOUR OWN CAR!

Auto Top Dressing

You can greatly improve the appearance of the car and increase its weather resisting qualities by refinishing leather and imitation leather tops with this dressing. Dries over night; the finish will not crack or peel. One quart will cover the top of an average touring car, two coats. Apply with a good varnish brush (see 30K3031, page 1029).

30K3428—Gloss Jet Black.
1-pint can ......(Shipping weight, 2 pounds)............42c
1-quart can ......(Shipping weight, 3 pounds)............78c

Quick Drying Auto Seat Dressing

Gives leather and imitation automobile seats a greatly improved appearance. Dries in one hour without danger of injuring the most delicate fabric. Be sure to apply in a warm, dry temperature and have the leather surface perfectly clean and dry. Will not peel off and dust will not stick to the refinished surface. Apply with a varnish brush (see page 1029).

30K3423—Gloss Jet Black.
1-pint can ......(Shipping weight, 2 pounds)............ 48c

Aut-O-Sek for Waterproofing Auto Tops

You can waterproof old leather, imitation leather, mohair, pantasote or canvas auto tops with this excellent dressing. Apply it with a sponge, rag or brush for a lasting finish. Unaffected by folding, bending or creasing the top. Dries in 12 to 24 hours; it is NOT a varnish "top dressing." The black finish produces a rich black luster, not a shiny finish. Use the khaki color to renew a faded khaki top.

30K3425—Black.   30K3426—Khaki.
1-quart can.........(Shipping weight, 3 pounds)........ $1.10

Special Painting Outfit For Fords

For Complete Description and Larger Illustration See Page 457.

Furnished in Black Only.

We furnish enough material to finish the body and fenders of a Ford car, two coats; the top, seats and engine, one coat.

30K1699 — Complete outfit as illustrated. (Shipping wt., 14 lbs.)

$2.85

Complete Refinishing Outfits for All Cars

For Complete Description and Larger Illustration See Page 457.

Colors:
30K1773—Black.   30K1789—Brewster Green.
30K1775—Russet Tan.   30K1785—Vermilion.
30K1777—Sea Blue.   30K1787—Dark Wine.
30K1791—Dark Blue.   30K1793—Auto Gray.
Shipping weight, outfit, 17 pounds.
Complete outfit. State color.............. **$4.45**

COLORS in OIL

For coloring or tinting when mixing paint. These colors are ground in pure linseed oil and are strong and permanent. Some of the harder pigments are ground several times, greatly increasing the tinting power. Put up in 1-pound cans. Shipping weight, 1¼ pounds.

	Per Lb.		Per Lb.
30K2230—Lampblack	28c	30K2248—Blind or Chrome	
30K2231—Coach Black	25c	Green	25c
30K2232—Ivory Black	25c	30K2253—English Venetian Red.	18c
30K2233—Drop Black	22c	30K2254—Indian Red	21c
30K2235—American (Prussian)		30K2255—Tuscan Red	39c
Blue	46c	30K2256—Unfading Red	31c
30K2236—Ultramarine Blue	39c	30K2259—Scarlet Vermilion	30c
30K2237—Cobalt Blue	45c	30K2262—Chrome Yellow, Light.	28c
30K2240—Raw Umber	21c	30K2263—Chrome Yellow,	
30K2241—Burnt Umber	21c	Medium	28c
30K2242—Raw Sienna	22c	30K2264—Chrome Yellow,	
30K2243—Burnt Sienna	22c	Orange	28c
		30K2265—French Yellow, Ochre.	18c

Black Touch-Up Varnish

An excellent varnish for touching up scratches or marks on the car. Produces a tough, durable finish. Dries dust free in two hours; hardens in six hours. Apply with a varnish brush (see 30K3025, page 1029).

30K1850
1-pint can ......(Shipping weight, 2 pounds)............45c
1-quart can ......(Shipping weight, 3¼ pounds)............80c

AUTOMOBILE ENAMEL

You can bring back a large measure of the original attractive appearance of your car at a trifling expense with a few hours' pleasant work. No matter how dilapidated it now appears, regardless of how flat and dull the finish, Seroco Auto Enamel will give it a lasting luster and bright appearance beyond belief.

This splendid enamel is a special paint for automobiles. It flows freely, spreads evenly and stays on. It will not chip, crack or peel. It dries with a smooth, mirror-like gloss, with pure, non-fading colors. You can buy automobile enamel elsewhere at twice our price or more, but you cannot buy another enamel that will give you more lasting satisfaction.

About three quarts are sufficient to refinish the body and gear of the average car, two coats. Remove any gloss from the old finish by rubbing it down with steel wool or sandpaper. Complete directions furnished for applying Seroco Auto Enamel. Use a good varnish brush (see 30K3038 and 30K3033, page 1029).

For color samples see page 1024.

30K1706—Russet Tan.	30K1735—Brewster Green.	30K1705—Vermilion.
30K1760—Auto Gray.	30K1755—Dark Blue.	30K1715—Dark Wine.
	30K1740—Black.	30K1707—Sea Blue.
	30K1725—Cream.	

1-pint can............(Shipping weight, 2 pounds)...................$0.43
1-quart can ....(Shipping weight, 3½ pounds)................. .75
½-gallon can ....(Shipping weight, 8 pounds)................. 1.44
1-gallon can ....(Shipping weight, 13 pounds)................. 2.75

Lamp and Fender Lacquer

Refinish the fenders and lamps on your car with this high grade, durable, weather resisting lacquer. Their improved appearance will repay you many fold. One coat will usually remove all the signs of the hard usage fenders regularly receive. Apply with a good Varnish Brush, 30K3033 (see page 1029.)

30K2185—Black. High gloss.
½-pint can ......(Shipping weight, 1¼ pounds)............30c
1-pint can ......(Shipping weight, 2 pounds)............45c
1-quart can ......(Shipping weight, 3¼ pounds)............80c

Auto Refinishing Varnish

This excellent varnish will revive the original gloss finish if the car paint is in good condition. It is very pale, transparent and durable and will not darken any light shade of body paint. Dries in about 16 hours—hardens in three days. We recommend 30K3033 Varnish Brush, page 1029.

30K2740
1-pint can ......(Shipping weight, 2¼ pounds)............52c
1-quart can ......(Shipping weight, 3½ pounds)............$0.84
½-gallon can ......(Shipping weight, 6 pounds)............ 1.50

Engine and Radiator Enamel

Keep your engine and radiator clean and free from rust with this splendid heat resisting enamel. It will not readily blister, peel or rub off; its glossy surface is easy to keep free from grease and dirt. Here is a value you should not overlook. Apply with a good varnish brush (see 30K3031 page 1029.)

30K3416—Black.   30K3417—Gray.
½-pint can ......(Shipping weight, 1¼ pounds)............29c
1-pint can ......(Shipping weight, 2¼ pounds)............48c

Powdered Pumice Stone

(Not Illustrated)

Especially adapted for rubbing furniture, woodwork, etc., either before or after varnishing. A high grade powdered domestic product. Shipping weight, 1½ pounds.
30K2673—1 pound............9c

Graining Rollers

You can grain your wainscoting, floors, woodwork or furniture successfully with this set, imitating any growth of wood. No experience is required. Complete directions for using. Set of 3 rubber rollers. Length, 4¾ in. Shpg. wt., ¾ lb.
30K2964............93c

Graining Tools

Use this set of two rollers, length 5 in., and one steel comb, for imitating heart of oak grain. Shipping weight, 8 oz.
30K2967......83c

Undercoat or Ground Color

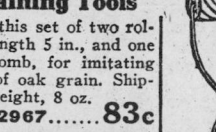

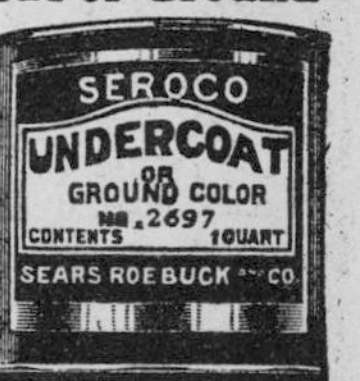

Use this opaque yellow paint as a ground coat when graining your floors or woodwork a lighter shade. It covers the original finish and permits successful graining in a lighter color when dry. One quart will cover about 150 square feet, one coat.

30K2697
1-pint can. Shpg. wt. 3 lbs............35c
1-quart can. Shpg. wt. 5 lbs............$0.63
1-gallon can. Shpg. wt. 18 lbs............2.18

Interior Decoration

By a Famous Authority

Hazel H. Adler

How to refinish old woodwork. How to refinish old floors. How to lacquer furniture.

See Page 1017

Ready Mixed Graining Colors in Oil

53c 1 Quart

Furnished ready for use, being mixed with liquid in the proper proportion. Apply like paint or varnish with a similar brush and grain at once with graining tool. If you wish to grain your floors or woodwork a lighter shade apply 30K2697 Undercoat (at extreme right) as a base for the graining color.

30K2274—Light Golden Oak.
30K2275—Dark Golden Oak.
30K2276—Medium Golden Oak.
1-pint can ......(Shipping weight, 2¼ pounds)............32c
1-quart can ......(Shipping weight, 3½ pounds)............$0.53
1-gallon can ......(Shipping weight, 13 pounds)............2.05

A small, handy tool for ordinary graining work. Width, 3 in. Shipping wt., 7 oz.
30K2965
32c

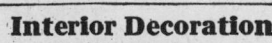

Your Orders Shipped Within 24 Hours!

P 1035

Reach the Goal of Greater Profits

DON'T Lose the Hidden Dollars
No Middleman's Profit Here

$5.00
Brings Any Dairy Size Separator

We make it easy for you to become the owner of an Economy Cream Separator. If you prefer to buy any of the dairy sizes on monthly payment terms just fill out the Time Payment Order Blank on page 1092 and send it to us together with a deposit of $5.00 (or $10.00 if you order an Electric Drive Separator). Once a month, starting after thirty days' trial, send us a payment of the amount stated under the price of the size selected and in a few months the separator is paid for and is your property. Should you prefer to send cash with the order, as most of our customers do, you can make a saving by taking advantage of our somewhat lower cash prices.

Take Thirty Days' Farm Trial

There are hundreds of thousands of Economy Kings in daily use throughout the United States and a little inquiry will no doubt show that many of your own neighbors are using them. We will be glad to have you guide yourself by their opinion but it is not necessary to take anyone else's word, as we send every Economy King out on thirty days' trial.

You may test the Economy King alongside any other cream separator regardless of price; compare them in ease of running, closeness of skimming, and in any way you see fit. If this thirty-day test does not prove the Economy King to be not only the lowest in price, but the best at any price, you can send it back to us and we will return your money, including any freight charges you have paid. The test costs you not a penny if you do not keep the machine.

A farm trial will prove that the Economy King saves both money and time.

Our Guarantee

When we ship you a cream separator no salesman goes along to call your attention only to its good features. You buy the separator on trial and it must sell itself to you on its own merit, after you have tested it carefully and given it a most searching examination. This makes it necessary for us to build and test our separators with greatest care. Each one is run and tested by a skilled expert, and when he puts his O. K. on the machine you may be sure that it is perfect in every way. To still futher protect you, you will receive a written guarantee which protects you against defects in workmanship and material during all the years you use the separator.

Order an Economy King on thirty days' trial, test it alongside of any other separator made and decide for yourself which is best.

For Cream Separator Oil, See Page 456

WHY NOT FARM FOR CREAM?

Your main crop may be corn, wheat or hay, or perhaps it is hogs, beef cattle or other stock, but no matter what it is, it will pay you well to keep cows and farm for cream, even if only as a side line.

Field crops are subject to weather conditions. A hail storm, flood or an early frost may in a few hours wipe out the result of a season's toil and planning. If crops are good they are usually harvested and turned into cash but once a year, and bring no further income until the next year. Live stock is subject to wide fluctuations in market price and often, after all the time and care needed to bring it to marketable condition, sells for no more than the cost of raising.

The cream crop, on the other hand, can be harvested twice every day in the year and turned into cash as fast as sent to the market. Prices are not only published daily but broadcasted by radio also, so that you are sure of getting the full value. Cream brings its highest price in the winter when you have little else to sell and, because of its high value in proportion to weight, you can ship it hundreds of miles if desirable, to take advantage of a better market condition.

Selling only the cream, the dairyman has an ample supply of fresh, sweet skim milk, one of the best foods in the world for raising young stock and chickens economically. The grain fed to dairy cattle enriches the soil in the form of manure so that better and larger crops are produced from year to year. Dairying brings prosperity to the farm and the farmer. Tenants become owners and those already owning their land obtain more of the comforts and pleasures in life through the regular cash income from the sale of cream and butter.

Use an Economy King to Get the Best Results

Cream is so valuable you cannot afford to waste even a spoonful a day. An Economy King Cream Separator will skim the cream to the last drop, from warm or cold milk. It skims milk from cows on dry feed, cows far advanced in lactation and from breeds whose milk is hardest to skim, giving you a smooth, clean, aerated cream, free from froth and in elegant condition after cooling to ship long distances or to ripen for home butter making. It will skim a thin cream for ice cream makers or for retail sale, an extra heavy cream for shipping economically, or any grade in between, all instantly regulated by the user.

Housewives Are Delighted With the Economy King

The easy cleaning features of the Economy King make a big hit with the housewife. The bowl is easy to take apart and the skimming discs are rinsed in a jiffy on the handy disc washer we supply with it. The bowl shell, supply tank and covers are smoothly retinned with rounding corners and without dirt collecting crevices, so the whole washing operation takes but a few minutes. The frame of the machine is smooth and rounding and the base is open, making it easy to sweep or mop under and with no place for dampness or mold to collect. A drip shelf prevents oil stains on the floor. Economy Separators turn very easily and all but the larger sizes are well adapted for operation by women or even well grown children.

Quick Delivery Direct From Our Factory

To insure quick delivery and make the freight charges you pay a very small amount, we ship Economy Separators direct from the factory at Buffalo, N. Y. Mail your order to Sears, Roebuck and Co., Philadelphia, and we will ship promptly from our factory stock.

GOOD POINTS EVERYWHERE

Bearings Flooded With Oil

The rim of the bronze worm wheel runs in a basin of oil, throwing off a fine mist or spray. This oil is collected in pockets and fed into the bearings through passages so that they run in a constant bath of fresh oil. A glass oiling indicator shows you that the oiling system is working properly.

No-Splash Supply Tank

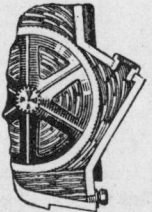

Made with full curving sides and convex bottom so that milk will not splash over no matter how hastily it is poured into tank. Broad top rim is easily grasped for lifting. Feet are provided to protect faucet if set on a flat surface.

Easy to Replace Bearing

Lower bowl spindle bearing is removed from the outside. Putting in a new one, if ever necessary, is the work of but a few minutes. In many separators this bearing is removable only after taking out both worm wheel and pinion, which is much more difficult.

Oil Circulating System

Bearings are of extra length and provided with an oil circulating system so that oil reaching the end of the shaft does not leak out but is collected and drained back into the oil basin. The circulating bath of fresh oil in which they run makes them nearly frictionless.

With Our Famous Economy King

MADE AND SOLD ONLY
by Sears, Roebuck and Co.

in Your Cream Pail!!!
Thirty Days' Trial-Only $5.00 Down

COMPARE PRICES BEFORE BUYING

We build our Economy King Cream Separators in our own big factory at Buffalo, N. Y., and we sell to you at real factory prices. In buying from us you save the profits and expenses of agents, retailers and jobbers and keep this money right at home, in your own pocketbook. Nothing is added to a cream separator after it leaves the factory except those extra profits between maker and user and, while they do not add a cent to the value of any separator, they do add a lot to the price you pay when you buy in the ordinary way.

You must sell your farm products at producers' prices so why not buy at producers' prices also? You cannot afford to market your crops at one profit and pay three or four profits on the articles you must buy. Just match the factory prices on our Special Economy Kings listed below with agents' and dealers' prices for machines of equal capacity and quality and you will quickly see the saving you make in buying from us at these real factory prices.

400-Pound Capacity Separator for $38.25

This special Economy King has all our latest improvements, including sanitary loose disc bowl that skims warm or cold, new or old milk to perfection. Perfect oil splash lubricating system with patented oiling indicator; seamless, no-splash supply tank; handy disc washer; simple crank speed timer and every convenience. Very easy to run, to clean and to care for. Well adapted for use by women and girls who cannot easily handle a heavier separator.

It has all the big features of our standard Economy King line and although somewhat lighter in construction, is heavy enough to give many years of splendid service with ordinary care. **Shipped from Buffalo, N. Y.**

23K5824—Special Economy King Cream Separator No. 24. Skims 400 pounds or 190 quarts an hour. Adapted for a dairy of from two to six or seven cows. Shipping weight, 155 pounds. Cash price..........................**$38.25**

Time payment price, **$5.00** with order and balance in monthly payments of **$4.00** each, starting after 30 days..................................... **43.20**

Fast Skimming, 600-Pound Size for $50.75

This fast skimming Special Economy King handles 600 pounds or about 290 quarts an hour. It skims a milk pail full every two minutes, saving time and labor every day you use it. Handles a big milk flow when necessary and enables you to increase your herd and hence your profits, without buying a larger separator later on.

It has all the latest Economy King improvements and conveniences, but is somewhat lighter in construction than our regular Standard Economy King Cream Separator, which we always recommend for those who want the best. These special separators, however, are better than those commonly sold and will give you years of satisfactory service with ordinary care.

They skim warm or cold milk to a trace and give you a smooth, even cream of any wished for thickness. Sent on 30 days' trial and guaranteed to please. **Shipped from Buffalo, N. Y.**

23K5826—Special Economy King Cream Separator No. 26. Skims 600 pounds or about 290 quarts an hour. For dairies of from three to twelve or fifteen cows. Shipping weight, 190 pounds. Cash price......................**$50.75**

Time payment price, **$5.00** with order, balance in monthly payments of **$5.50** each..................................... **56.75**

When Ordering on Easy Payments Use Time Payment Order Blank on Page 1092

Cash or Time Payments

400-Lb. $38.25 Cash Price

MANY EXCLUSIVE FEATURES

Flexible Spindle Bearing

This bearing is of an expensive anti-friction alloy designed to prevent wear on the bowl spindle. In operation a stream of fresh oil is fed between the bearing surfaces constantly and reduces friction to almost nothing. A multiplex spring with flexible spring steel tongues cushions and centers the bowl.

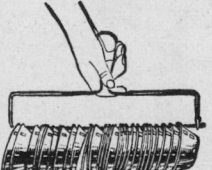

Cleaning the Skimming Discs

Discs for cleaning are transferred to the disc washer with almost the ease and speed of a single piece. This permits you to clean each separately or rinse all at once, after which they can be spread out on the washer and hung up to dry and air.

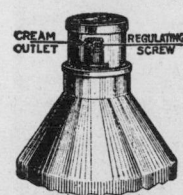

Light or Heavy Cream

CREAM OUTLET   REGULATING SCREW

Our cream screw is quickly regulated to give you any cream from the thinnest to the heaviest. It is extra large and substantial and much more durable than the small light cream screws necessary to save space in some separators, and which, if lost or mutilated, prevent the use of the separator until replaced.

Bowl Lifts Off Spindle

Bowl lifts off driving spindle for emptying and washing. This makes it lighter and easier to handle and avoids damaging spindle or driving worm which remain in the machine. An improved bowl seating key enables you to seat the bowl on the spindle instantly.

Join the Big Army of Prosperous Economy King Users. Order on Trial Today

Our SANITARY Skimming Bowl

Easy to Clean and Handle

Takes the Cream to the Last Drop

Here are the parts of our sanitary, loose disc bowl. They are all heavily double tinned, giving a smooth, bright, rust resisting finish. Very easy to take apart, wash and assemble.

Our bowls purify and cleanse the milk, removing any dirt, hair or insects that may have fallen into it, so that both cream and skim milk leave the separator in better condition than the original whole milk. In the operation of separating the butter fat globules are unbroken and the cream, after cooling, is in elegant condition for shipping or to ripen for home butter making.

For Cream Separator Oil, See Page 456

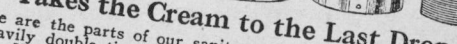

See Index and Information Pages 542 to 570

P 1037

Greater Dairy *Profits* Assured

250-lb. Size $40⁸⁰ Cash Price

Our Standard Economy King

For Those Who Want the Best

For Cream Separator Oil See Page 456

See page 1039 for description of Electric Drive Separators.

$5.⁰⁰ Brings Any Hand Driven Separator

$10.00 Brings Any Electric Drive Separator on 30 Days' Trial.

No matter what cream separator you favor or have used in the past, we believe that we can prove to you by an actual farm test that in our Standard Economy King Separators, as listed on this and the following page, we give you more exclusive improvements and convenient features than can be obtained in any other separator, regardless of price.

These Standard Economy Kings are built heavier and more substantial and have wider gears and bigger shafting than even the most expensive separators of equal capacity sold by agents and dealers. They have valuable patented conveniences not to be had in other machines, including our accurate crank speed timer, oiling indicator, wide range cream regulation, instant bowl seating device and other original improvements.

Standard Economy King No. 12
Skimming Capacity, 250 Pounds (About 120 Quarts) an Hour

This is the smallest of our regular dairy machines with stand and will give good satisfaction where the herd is small, two to four cows, and you do not intend to increase it. This size is easy to run, handle and to keep clean. It skims any quantity of milk from 1 gallon up and has all our latest features, including crank speed timer and detachable spindle loose disc skimming bowl.

23K1252—Economy King Cream Separator No. 12, with stand. Skimming capacity, 250 pounds of milk an hour. Shipping weight, 165 pounds. **Shipped from BUFFALO, N. Y.**
Cash price..........................**$40.80**
Time payment price, **$5.00** with order and balance in monthly payments of **$4.00** each, starting after 30 days......................**45.20**
23K11252—Standard Economy King No. 12, with electric drive, for 110-volt alternating or 32-volt direct current. **In ordering specify kind of electric current used.** Skimming capacity, 250 pounds an hour. Shipping weight, 225 pounds. **Shipped from BUFFALO, N. Y. Cash price**..................**$70.75**
Time payment price, **$10.00** with order and balance in monthly payments of **$7.00** each......................**78.15**

Standard Economy King No. 14
Skimming Capacity, 375 Pounds (About 180 Quarts) an Hour

A very good size for any herd of from two to five or six cows. For more than five cows we always recommend the No. 16 machine, listed on opposite page as it does any skimming in two-thirds the time or less, saving a world of time and labor in the course of a year. This size, however, will give splendid satisfaction with a small herd. It is a substantial, well built machine adapted for hard everyday dairy use and a splendid skimmer, taking practically every drop of cream from the milk in any condition in which milk can be skimmed.

23K1254—Economy King Cream Separator No. 14, with stand. Skimming capacity, 375 pounds of milk an hour. Shipping weight, 175 pounds. **Shipped from BUFFALO, N. Y.** Cash price......................**$51.15**
Time payment price, **$5.00** with order and balance in monthly payments of **$5.50** each, starting after 30 days......................**57.00**
23K11254—Standard Economy King No. 14, with electric drive, for 110-volt alternating or 32-volt direct current. **In ordering specify kind of electric current used.** Skimming capacity, 375 pounds an hour. Shipping weight, 235 pounds. **Shipped from BUFFALO, N. Y.** Cash price......................**$81.50**
Time payment price, **$10.00** with order and balance in monthly payments of **$8.50** each......................**89.00**
When Ordering on Easy Payments, Use Time Payment Order Blank on Page 1092

The Best Size to Order

There are many good reasons for selecting a cream separator of ample capacity, as any experienced cream separator user will tell you. The larger sizes skim the milk much more quickly, saving time and labor every day in the year. They are cleaned about as quickly as the smaller sizes and are practically as easy to run and care for. They easily handle the big milk flow you will have at certain times of the year and save much valuable time in the planting and harvest seasons when every moment counts.

Another advantage of these larger sizes is that they will last longer than the smaller machines. A cream separator, like any other machine, only wears as it is used, and as the larger sizes do any skimming in about one-half the time of the smaller sizes, they are used only about half as long each day and naturally will run about twice as many days before wearing out or needing repairs, so that although the price is a little higher in the first place, in the long run they cost you less per year than the smaller sizes.

Shipped Complete With Everything Needed

Each Economy King Cream Separator is packed complete with all the needed tools and supplies for setting up, cleaning and operating. We include cleaning brushes, a supply of separator oil, wrench, cream screw and bowl seating keys, bowl vise, rubber bowl rings, screws for fastening to floor and everything necessary.

We also send directions for setting up and operating the machine, giving you full and complete instructions on every point, telling you all you need to know about the separator in a plain simple way that you will find easy to understand and follow, even though you know nothing about a cream separator and have never seen one in operation.

Table Sizes for Home Use

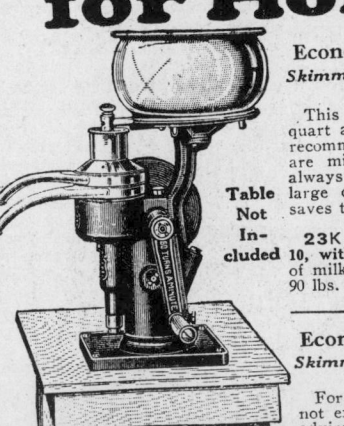

Economy King Cream Separator No. 10
Skimming Capacity, 135 Lbs. (About 65 Qts.) an Hour

This size skims at the rate of a trifle over a quart a minute. Because of its small capacity, we recommend its use where only one or two cows are milked and the quantity to be skimmed is always small. In most cases it is better to buy the large capacity table machine, listed below, as it saves time with every skimming.

Table Not Included 23K1250—Economy King Cream Separator No. 10, without stand. Skimming capacity, 135 pounds of milk an hour. Shipping weight, 90 lbs. **Sold for cash only**............**$29.50**

Economy King Cream Separator No. 11
Skimming Capacity, 200 Lbs. (About 95 Qts.) an Hour

For dairies of one to three cows, which you do not expect to enlarge later on, this is the size we advise buying. Before ordering, however, be sure to figure on future additions to your herd, which may make your purchase of a larger size advisable.

23K1251—Economy King Cream Separator No. 11, without stand. Skimming capacity, 200 pounds of milk an hour. Shipping weight, 95 lbs. **Sold for cash only**............**$33.35**
Shipped from BUFFALO, N. Y.

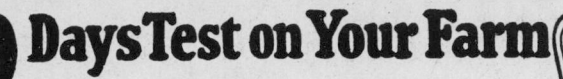

The Separators We Recommend

30 Days Test on Your Farm

The Standard Economy King

alongside of any separator made, regardless of price, will prove to you that money cannot buy a better separator than our Standard Economy King listed below. This test costs you nothing if you do not keep the separator and we let you be the sole judge.

Standard Economy King No. 16

Skimming Capacity, 600 Pounds (About 290 Quarts) of Milk an Hour

This is the best size for dairies of from three to twelve or fifteen cows, and is the size selected by most of our customers. It skims at the rate of a milk pail full every two minutes and does a big skimming in short order.

If you have a small or medium size herd, this is the Economy King we recommend. It saves time and labor daily, and because of its big capacity handles the big spring milk flow easily. Should you enlarge your herd in coming seasons, as you will be more than likely to do, it will take care of the extra milk up to a herd of eighteen or twenty cows, if necessary, and save you the expense of buying a separator of larger capacity.

It is a wonderfully close skimmer and takes the cream to a trace from warm or cold milk, gives you a cream of any wished for density, from the thinnest to the heaviest, and cleanses and aerates both the cream and skim milk.

This No. 16 Economy King has all our latest improvements and conveniences. We fully guarantee it and allow you full thirty days for trial, giving you plenty of time to prove its worth in your own dairy.

23K1256—Economy King Cream Separator No. 16, with stand. Skimming capacity, 600 lbs. of milk an hour. Shpg. wt., 225 lbs. Shipped from BUFFALO, N. Y.
Cash price.. **$60.95**
Time payment price, $5.00 with order and balance in monthly payments of $6.50 each, starting after 30 days.............. **68.40**

23K11256—Standard Economy King No. 16, with electric drive, for 110-volt alternating or 32-volt direct current. In ordering specify kind of electric current used. Skimming capacity, 600 pounds an hour. Shipping weight, 285 lbs. Shipped from BUFFALO, N. Y.
Cash price.. **$91.00**
Time payment price, $10.00 with order and balance in monthly payments of $10.00 each................................ **98.65**

Standard Economy King No. 18

Skimming Capacity, 800 Pounds (About 390 Quarts) of Milk an Hour

We advise buying this size for herds of ten or twelve to fifty cows or more. It readily takes care of an extra large milk flow when the cows are fresh or on spring pasture, because of its big capacity. It runs so easily that you can handle a large quantity of milk without the use of power, if desired.

It skims at the rate of six and one-half quarts a minute, or a pailful in about one and one-half minutes. City milk dealers and ice cream makers who must separate large quantities of milk without loss of time will find this size just what they need.

It is well adapted for use with power because of its heavy frame and base and substantial construction throughout.

We guarantee this Economy King to please you in every way. Send us your trial order today.

23K1258—Economy King Cream Separator No. 18 with stand. Skimming capacity, 800 pounds of milk an hour. Shipping weight, 235 pounds. Shipped from BUFFALO, N. Y.
Cash price.. **$71.85**
Time payment price, $5.00 with order and balance in monthly payments of $7.50 each, starting after 30 days.......... **78.85**

23K11258—Standard Economy King No. 18, with electric drive, for 110-volt alternating or 32-volt direct current. In ordering specify kind of electric current used. Skimming capacity, 800 pounds an hour. Shipping weight, 295 lbs. Shipped from BUFFALO, N. Y.
Cash price.. **$101.50**
Time payment price, $10.00 with order and balance in monthly payments of $11.00 each................................ **109.00**

SEE BELOW FOR DESCRIPTION OF ELECTRIC DRIVE SEPARATORS

Electric Power Is the Best

If you have a home electric lighting plant or can buy electric current, we always recommend the purchase of our Electric Drive Economy Kings, listed above and also on opposite page.

Our electrically operated separators are provided with special heavy duty motors, mounted on a bracket below the drip shelf, and drive through a pulley on the pinion shaft. They do not interfere with hand operation and if the power is off, separating can be done by turning the hand crank.

In ordering, give voltage and say whether you have direct or alternating current. If alternating current, find out from your electric company the number of cycles or frequencies. The 32-volt motor equipment includes knife switch, fuse plugs and 40 feet of insulated wire. (Extra wire, if wanted, 3 cents per foot.) Alternating current motor equipment includes 10 feet of cord with attachment plug for lamp socket. If your electric current is different from those listed, write for special prices. We can also supply electric equipment for the dairy size Economy King you are now using. If interested, write us.

$5.00 Down
Easy Monthly Payments

When Ordering on Easy Payments Use Time Payment Order Blank on Page 1092

Easy to Buy Easy to Use

Saves Its Cost the First Season

Other farm machines are used for a few days to a few weeks during their season and then put aside until the following season, but an Economy King Cream Separator saves time and makes money for its user the year around.

Twice every day it skims the cream from the milk to the last drop. It gives you the cream smooth, purified, aerated and in the best condition after cooling to bring the highest market price. The warm, sweet, skim milk with a little corn or oil meal added is a wonderful food for young stock and makes them grow like magic.

An Economy King will save its cost the first season, with a small herd, in the extra cream it gives you over old methods, and it continues to make and save for all the years you use it. Three cows and an Economy King will pay you better than four cows without one and you save the care and feed of the extra cow.

It reduces the dairy work from hours to minutes daily and takes away the hard, disagreeable part of it. It insures a cash income every week in the year, turns waste into profit and brings prosperity to its owner. Order an Economy King on thirty days' trial and find out by an actual farm test the money making and time saving advantages of dairying in the Economy way.

Frank Frosts Milkers Have Valuable Exclusive Features

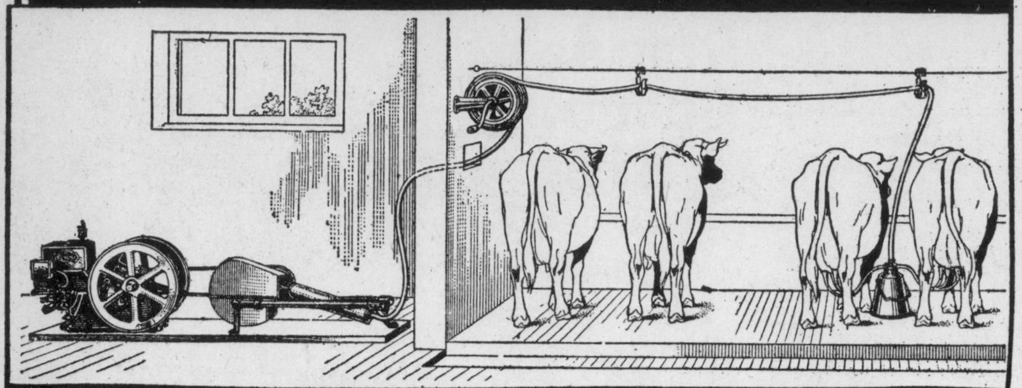

Are You Still Milking by Hand in the Old Fashioned Way?

Turn a Hard Job Into an Easy One

FRANK FROST'S MILKERS make time wasting, finger cramping, hand milking unnecessary. They replace man power with motor or engine power, make milking easy and pleasant instead of a hard, monotonous grind, and save time in handling the dairy herd. The larger the herd, the greater the saving of time and labor, but even with a milking herd of nine or ten cows it will pay you to use the Frost Milker.

Frost's Milkers are wonderfully simple and can be set up ready for use in an hour or two and taken down just as quickly. In moving from one barn to another or changing the arrangement of the cows in a barn, there is nothing to throw away and nothing new for you to buy. There are no iron pipe lines to fit and install, no vacuum tank or heavy complicated air pump, no pump rods working back and forth in barn, no delicate or unreliable pulsator and no gauges to watch.

Frank Frost has shown that all this machinery and fitting is unnecessary, yet his milker will do all that the most costly pipe line milkers will do, and do it just as quickly and just as well. Others have always found it necessary to run two or three tubes from the milk chamber to the teat cup cluster in order to get a massaging action on the cow's teats while milking, but Frost gets the same massaging action with a single tube.

Frank Frost has spent most of his life in making things easier for dairymen, and his improved milking machines have years of experience and testing behind them. Frost has put the advantages of the milking machine within the reach of tenants or renters who are likely to move and those who plan to build new barns or change the old ones, as his milkers can be moved and installed with little time and at practically no cost.

Frost's Improved Model Milking Machine is adapted for use with any form of power. The engine drive style can be operated with any two or four-cycle gasoline engine of 1 horse-power and upward, or we supply our regular 1¾ Horse-Power Economy Gasoline Engine to run it, if preferred. If engine operated, the engine and pump can be located in another room or outside shed, which is always best. The electric drive outfit can be operated by home electric lighting plant or purchased electric current.

It milks two cows at the same time or one cow, if desired, and will milk from 12 to 20 cows an hour, depending on how much milk they give and also how much you strip.

It will milk one or two rows of cows up to about 50 feet long. Consists of a vacuum pump, a flexible rubber suction or air hose, mounted on a revolving reel and supporting wire with roller hose hangers. Includes a 6-gallon milk pail with positive automatic milk valve and regulated suction releasing means in the cover, and two sets of teat cups with the necessary rubber hose connections; also belting for engine or motor.

In operation, the milking is usually started with the two cows at the end of the row, nearest the hose reel and, as each pair of cows is milked, the air hose is pulled along on the roller bearing supporting hooks attached to the wire above the cows. After the milking is finished, a few turns of the handle winds the air hose back on the reel. A second row of cows can now be milked in the same way.

Two sets of Frost Teat Cups are included which, in milking, gently massage the teats from the top downward, just as is done in hand milking or the same as the action of the calf's mouth in feeding, keeping the teats in a healthy, normal condition. Does not require a cord or surcingle to hold teat cups on the cow. Sights are provided in the pail cover, so that the flow of milk from each cow can be seen at all times. Pump should run at 40 pulsations a minute.

23K12—Frost's Engine Drive Milker, complete with belt but without engine. Shipping weight, 135 pounds........ **$98.00**

23K14—Frost's Engine Drive Milker, complete with 1¾ Horse-Power Economy Gasoline Engine and belt. Shipping weight, 415 pounds.......... **$145.00**

23K16—Frost's Electric Drive Milker with ⅓ Horse-Power Motor, mounted on pump frame. Shipping weight, 165 pounds.................... **$123.00**

In ordering electric drive milker specify voltage and current used and, if alternating current, give number of cycles also.

Milker shipped from NORTHEASTERN ILLINOIS. Engine shipped from HARRISBURG, PA.

Send for Frost Milker Direction Sheet

We do not print a direction book for the Frost Milker because it is so simple that the 30 to 50-page direction book usually sent out with other milkers is unnecessary. We, however, issue a 4-page leaflet of instructions for users of Frost Milkers. This leaflet tells how to install the milker; just how to handle it in milking the cows, how to keep it clean and whatever it is necessary to know. It will give you a better idea of the operation of the Frost Milker than any advertisement and we will gladly send it free and postpaid, on request. Just write us asking for a copy of Instruction Circular 2793PK covering Frost Milker.

For Cream Separator Oil See Page 456

Rubber Bowl Rings

Important Notice—Rubber bowl rings will only fit the size and style of separator they are intended for. Be careful in ordering to insure getting the correct rings for your separator.

Rubber Bowl Rings to Fit Economy King Separators. (Will Not Fit Improved Economy or Economy Chief.)

Catalog No.	Size No.	Per Pkg. of 6 Rings	Shipping Weight, Ounces
23K820	10 or 11	36c	3
23K822	2 or 4, 12 or 14, 24 or 40	39c	3
23K826	6-16 or 26	42c	4
23K828	8 or 18	47c	4

Rubber Bowl Rings to Fit Any Size Improved Economy or Economy Chief Cream Separators. (Will Not Fit the Economy King.)

Catalog No.	Size No.	Per Pkg. of 6 Rings	Shipping Weight, Ounces
23K667	Any Size	37c	3

We sell Rubber Bowl Rings only in packages of six rings and we do not break packages. Directions for care of rings are printed on every package.

Our Flexible Power Drive

$12.50 And Up

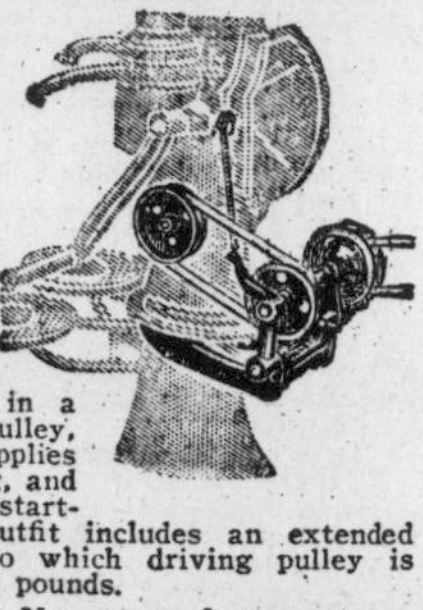

For running Economy King Cream Separators with a gasoline engine, either by direct belt connection or countershaft. A flexible steel spring shaft absorbs all the shock and jar of the engine explosions and applies the power to the separator in a smooth, even flow. A pulley, mounted on a rocker arm, applies the power gradually in starting, and tight and loose pulleys permit starting and stopping engine. Outfit includes an extended pinion shaft for separator, to which driving pulley is attached. Shipping weight, 40 pounds.

23K782—Flexible drive for Nos. 12, 14 and 26 Economy King.............. **$12.50**

23K786—Flexible Drive for Nos. 16 and 18 Economy King.............. **12.80**

Shipped from BUFFALO, N. Y.

Pulleys for Power

$3.90 And Up

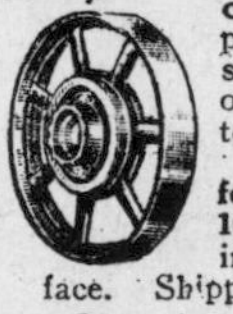

Applied to separator by removing crank and replacing it with the pulley. To be used with a countershaft and cannot be belted to a gasoline engine direct, as engine runs too fast.

23K1135—Friction Clutch Pulley for Economy King Separators Nos. 10, 11, 12, 14, 24 or 26. Size, 14 inches in diameter, 1½-inch face. Shipping weight, 17 lbs.... **$3.90**

Give size of separator used when ordering.

23K1130—Friction Clutch Pulley for Economy King Separators Nos. 16 or 18. Size, 14 inches in diameter, 2-inch face. Shipping weight, 20 pounds.............. **$4.25**

Give size of separator used when ordering.

Shipped from BUFFALO, N. Y.

Repairs

Repairs cost nothing if they come under the terms of our guarantee. If, however, it is necessary to replace a part giving out through natural wear, or a part broken through accident, we supply the needed piece promptly and at a very low price.

We carry a complete stock of repairs for Economy Separators at Philadelphia, and, of course, another stock at the factory. In addition, we have complete repair shops at Buffalo, N. Y., where we are equipped to do bowl repairing and rebalancing and Economy Separator repairing of all kinds skillfully and at reasonable prices.

In the instruction booklet we supply with each separator you will find a repair list showing a picture of each part, together with a price list which makes it very easy to order just the part needed.

Frost's Teat Cups

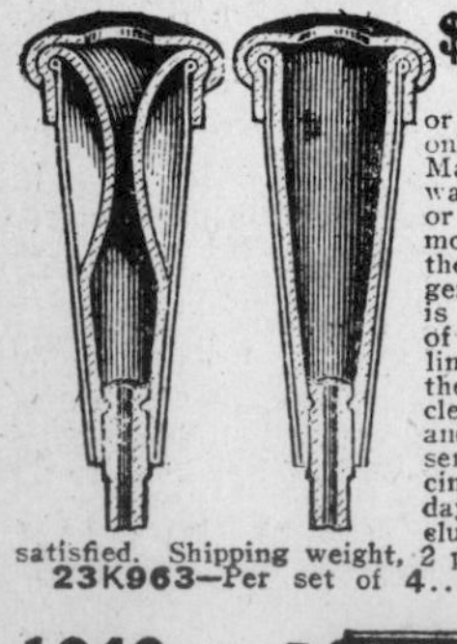

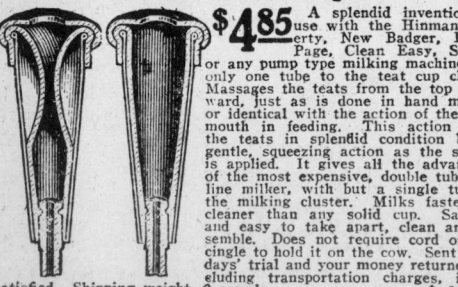

$4.85 A splendid invention for use with the Hinman, Liberty, New Badger, Burton Page, Clean Easy, Success or any pump type milking machine with only one tube to the teat cup cluster. Massages the teats from the top downward, just as is done in hand milking or identical with the action of the calf's mouth in feeding. This action keeps the teats in splendid condition by its gentle, squeezing action as the suction is applied. It gives all the advantages of the most expensive, double tube pipe line milker, with but a single tube to the milking cluster. Milks faster and cleaner than any solid cup. Sanitary and easy to take apart, clean and assemble. Does not require cord or surcingle to hold it on the cow. Sent on 30 days' trial and your money returned, including transportation charges, if not satisfied. Shipping weight, 2 pounds.

23K963—Per set of 4.............................. **$4.85**

Cleaning Brushes

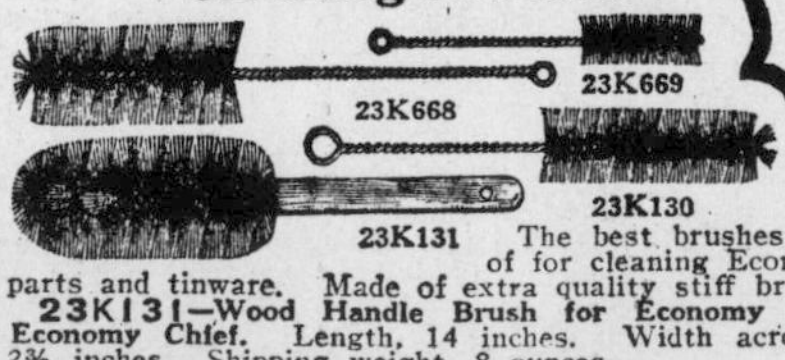

The best brushes we know of for cleaning Economy bowl parts and tinware. Made of extra quality stiff brush stock.

23K131—Wood Handle Brush for Economy King and Economy Chief. Length, 14 inches. Width across brush, 2⅜ inches. Shipping weight, 8 ounces.................. **22c**

23K668—Wire Handle Brush for Economy Chief. Length, 13½ inches. Width across brush, 2 in. Shpg. wt., 7 oz.. **15c**

23K130—Wire Handle Brush for Economy King. Length, 12 inches. Width across brush, 1½ in. Shpg. wt., 6 oz.. **15c**

23K132—Wire Handle Tube Brush for Economy King. Same style as 23K130. Length, 12 inches. Width across brush, ⅞ inch. Shipping weight, 4 ounces.............. **10c**

23K669—Small Wire Handle Brush for Economy Chief. Length, 8½ inches. Width across brush, ⅝ inch. Shipping weight, 2 ounces.............................. **5c**

Milking Machine Tubing

High grade red rubber Milking Machine Tubing, especially compounded to resist the oil of the butter fat in the milk. Will stand up perfectly under Board of Health requirements, which include sterilization of the tubing after use in water heated to 170 degrees and allowed to cool. Sizes to fit all milking machines. **State length and size wanted.**

	Inside Diameter	Thickness of Wall	Per Foot
23K862	7/32 inch	5/32 inch	18c
23K864	5/16 inch	11/64 inch	25c
23K866	⅜ inch	11/64 inch	29c
23K868	7/16 inch	7/32 inch	33c

Shipping weight, per foot, 4 ounces

Hand Engine Trucks

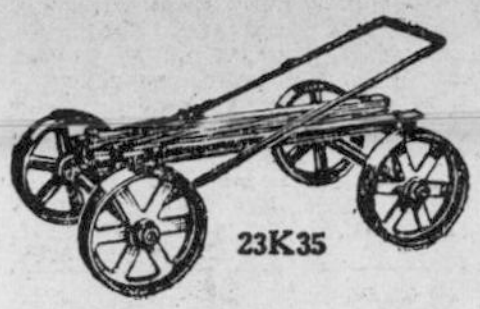
23K35

If you have several jobs for an engine to do you should have a hand truck to move the engine from one place to another. The 23K35 trucks as illustrated are all steel, painted red and have holes drilled and bolts furnished ready to fasten engine to truck. Can be used for any engine up to 6 horse-power by boring new holes to fit.

The 23K01 Truck (not illustrated) has front and rear bolsters to bolt to engine base. An adjustable tie rod connects them. Frame not included as engine base acts as frame. Bolsters 18 inches wide, wheels 9x2 inches.

The 23K35 Truck has an angle steel frame, 36 inches long; 1⅜-inch solid steel axle, 30 inches wide; steel wheels, 14 inches in diameter with 2½-inch tires; for use with our 3½ and 6 horse-power engines.

23K01—Engine Truck without frame for engines weighing up to 500 lbs. Shipping weight, 55 pounds........**$3.75**

Shipped from BELLEVILLE, PA.

23K35—All Steel Hand Truck for any 2½ to 6 horse-power engines. Shipping weight, 118 pounds......**$13.90**

Shipped from HARRISBURG, PENNSYLVANIA.

Real Time and Money Saver
Sears ECONOMY Log Sawing Outfit

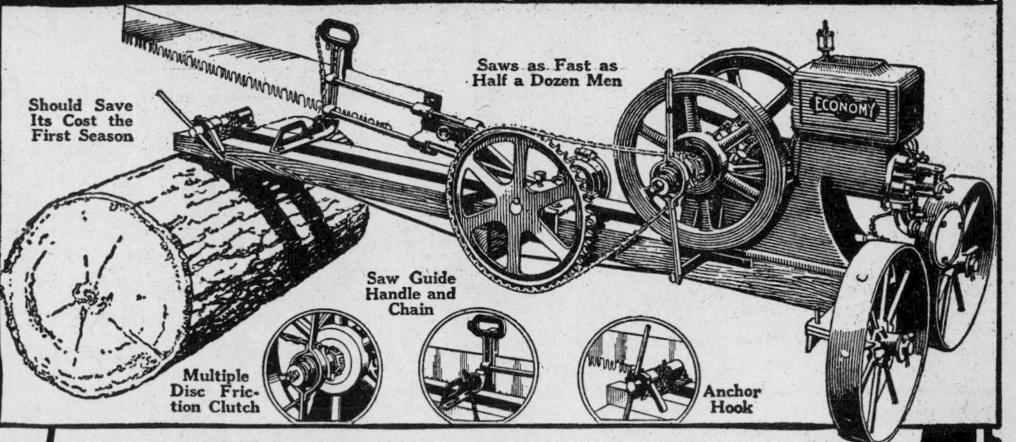
Should Save Its Cost the First Season
Saws as Fast as Half a Dozen Men
ECONOMY
Saw Guide Handle and Chain
Multiple Disc Friction Clutch
Anchor Hook

The Economy Drag Saw Outfit is complete with a 1¾ horse-power engine mounted on a 9-foot hardwood frame, with a 5-foot saw blade and multiple disc lever clutch. The multiple disc lever clutch enables the operator to start the engine without starting the saw or to stop the saw without stopping the engine and prevents damage to saw blade in case it binds in the cut. The two all steel wheels, 18 inches in diameter, with 3-inch tires, are mounted on swivel axles that can be easily changed, so the outfit may be drawn from one place to another or moved from cut to cut along the log. Saw blade is 5 feet long, made of high grade saw steel and is filed and set, ready for use. Length of stroke, 20 inches; saw operates at 170 strokes per minute.

Engine will operate saw successfully on any log from 8 inches up to 3 feet in diameter in either hard or soft wood. Exhaustive tests show that one man can cut through a 2-foot log in two minutes, while it requires two men ten minutes to cut the same log with hand crosscut saw. Outfit will pay for itself in a very short time, as it will saw as much wood in one week as three men would handle in four weeks with hand crosscut saw. Saw is held by guide, which holds the saw rigid while outfit is being moved. A truss rod extends full length of the frame, strengthening the outfit and preventing vibration.

The anchor hook holds outfit to the log, is easily handled and prevents slipping. Standard No. 51 binder or shredder chain is used for driving saw, as chain drive is very flexible and easy to handle.

Engine can be removed from the saw frame and used for pumping water or any other work. Pulley furnished at extra price, so that engine can be used for other work when not sawing wood. Weight, complete, 490 pounds; crated for shipment, 525 pounds. Full instructions accompany the outfit, telling how to set it up, how to start and run the engine. If ordered without engine, clutch cannot be supplied, as clutch is part of flywheel of engine. Should not be used with engines weighing over 300 pounds. **Shipped complete from factory at EVANSVILLE, INDIANA.**

23K2232—**Economy Portable Drag Saw Outfit,** including engine and 5-foot saw. Shipping weight, 525 pounds........**$89.50**

23K2233—**Drag Saw Outfit** only with Saw but without engine or friction clutch. Shipping weight, 250 pounds. **Be sure to give horse-power of engine and size of engine shaft; also size of key way in shaft.** (Engine shaft must not be more than 1½ inches in diameter.)........................**$35.00**

23K229—**5-Foot Extra Saw Blade** for Economy Drag Saw only. Weight, 15 pounds........**$4.50**

23K404—**4x4-Inch Pulley** to run other machines, extra. Weight, 10 pounds................**$1.25**

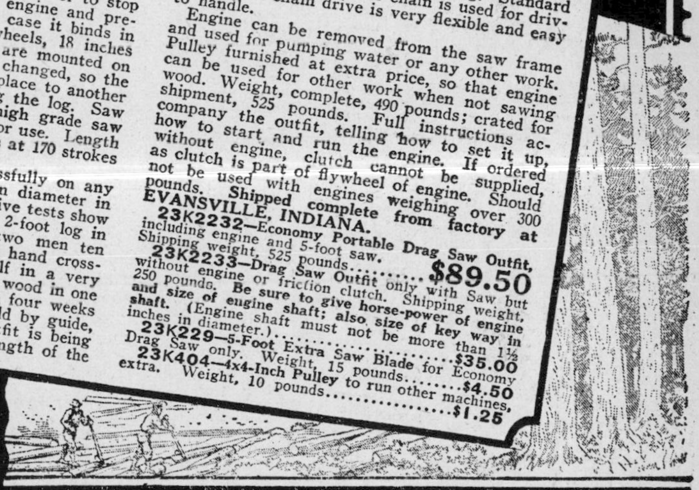

Speed Governing Line Shaft

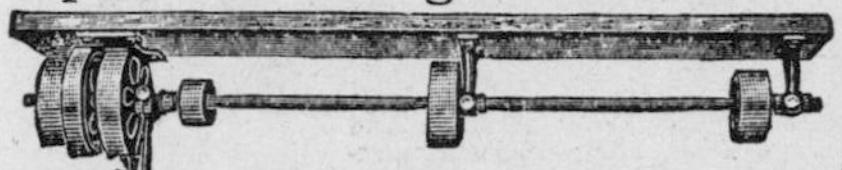

Complete with speed governor and clutch control. Can be used with any engine up to 3½ horse-power, to run the cream separator, churn, washing machine, pump jack or any small machine, as the speed governor takes care of variations in speed of engine and size of engine pulley. It can be set permanently for any desired speed, or can be increased or decreased as desired. Full instructions with each outfit. **Shipped from factory in NORTHERN IOWA.**

23K321—**8-Foot Shaft, Speed Governor, one 4-inch, one 6-inch, two 8-inch Pulleys and two Hangers, mounted on 8-foot wood base.** Weight, 115 pounds..........**$20.85**

23K322—**12-Foot Shaft, Speed Governor, one 4-inch, two 6-inch, three 8-inch Pulleys and three Hangers, mounted on 12-foot wood base.** Weight, 150 pounds..............................**$25.90**

Portable Engines and Pole Saw Rigs

$197.00

6 Horse-Power

All Steel Truck and Saw Frame.

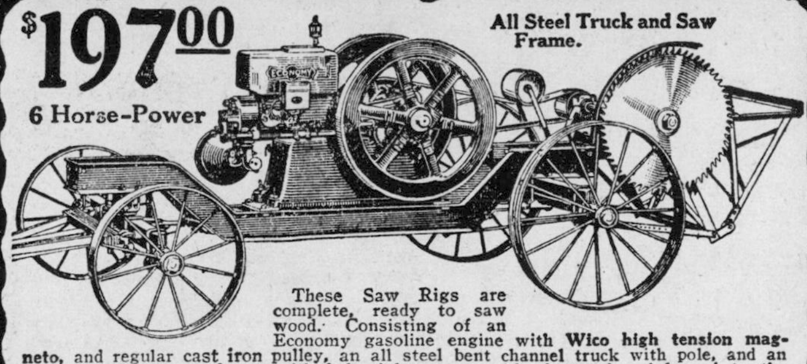
ECONOMY

These Saw Rigs are complete, ready to saw wood. Consisting of an Economy gasoline engine with **Wico high tension magneto,** and regular cast iron pulley, an all steel bent channel truck with pole, and an all steel tilting saw frame with belt tightener securely fastened and braced to the back of the truck, saw blade and belt. Saw frame is easily removed when it is desired to use the engine for other work.

The truck is of special construction, with bent channel steel frame. Axles are all solid steel, 1⅝ inches in diameter, reinforced with 3-inch I beam. Wheels are all steel, 24 inches front, 32 inches rear with 4x⅜-inch grooved tire. On the 6 and 8 horse-power truck we furnish a 5-inch steel channel frame 8½ feet long, on the larger sizes a 6-inch steel channel frame 9 feet long.

Sawing Outfit Complete

23K4573—**Portable Sawing Outfit with 6 Horse-Power Engine, 10x6-Inch Pulley,** Saw Table, 26-Inch Saw and Belt. Shipping weight, 1,703 pounds..............**$197.00**

10x8-Inch Friction Clutch Pulley in place of regular, add..........**10.70**

23K4773—**Portable Sawing Outfit with 8 Horse-Power Engine, 16x6-Inch Pulley,** Saw Table, 30-Inch Saw and Belt. Shipping weight 2,043 pounds..........**$228.00**

16x8-Inch Friction Clutch Pulley in place of regular, add..........**18.45**

Engine and Truck Only

23K457—**6 Horse-Power Engine and Truck.** Shipping weight, 1,447 pounds..............**$167.75**

23K477—8 Horse-Power Engine and Truck. Shipping wt., 1,787 lbs.....**$199.00**

23K4978—10 Horse-Power Engine and Truck. Shipping wt., 2,633 lbs.....**269.00**

23K41278—14 Horse-Power Engine and Truck. Shpg. wt., 3,248 lbs.....**348.00**

The 6 horse-power engine is shipped from HARRISBURG, PA., warehouse. Larger engines are shipped from EVANSVILLE, IND. Trucks and saw frame shipped from NORTHERN ILLINOIS factory.

Economy Auto-Powered Sawing Machine

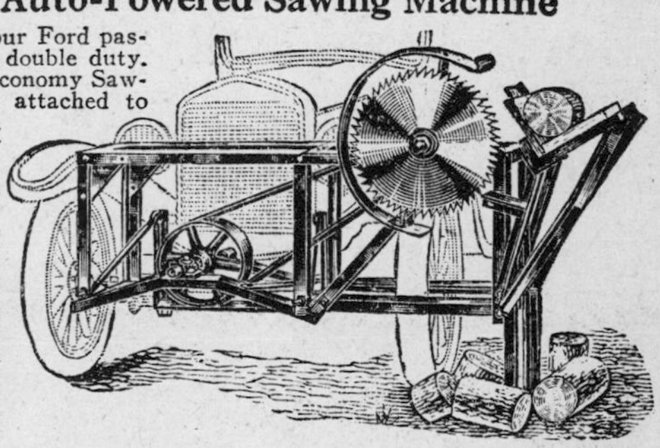

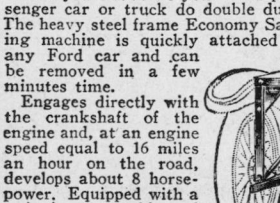

Now you can make your Ford passenger car or truck do double duty. The heavy steel frame Economy Sawing machine is quickly attached to any Ford car and can be removed in a few minutes time.

Engages directly with the crankshaft of the engine and, at an engine speed equal to 16 miles an hour on the road, develops about 8 horse-power. Equipped with a swinging saw table and a 24-inch crosscut saw that easily handles poles, limbs, posts, ties or slabs up to 10 inches, greatest diameter.

Runs at moderate speed, no weight on the crankshaft, no strain on the car, no loss of power. Engine can be cranked with hand crank if necessary, either with or without the saw frame attached. Fan belt pulley is removed and replaced with another pulley of same size containing the attaching coupling. This requires less than an hour the first time, after which saw frame can be removed or replaced in a few minutes.

Car travels over any ordinary surface with saw frame attached so you can saw where most convenient. In operation, the folding steel supports, resting on the ground, take nearly all weight off car. Braces attached to frame prevent any weight or strain on crankshaft.

This is the handiest sawing machine ever built and will do the work of half a dozen men, sawing by hand. Can be attached to Ford passenger cars or trucks of all models, or to Chevrolet passenger cars and one-half ton or one-ton trucks of 1925 model or later. **When ordering, the year and model of your car should be given.** Not adapted for other makes or models of cars.

Complete with 24-inch saw and necessary attachments. Shipping weight, 200 pounds. **Shipped from factory in SOUTHEASTERN MICHIGAN.**

23K555..**$74.00**

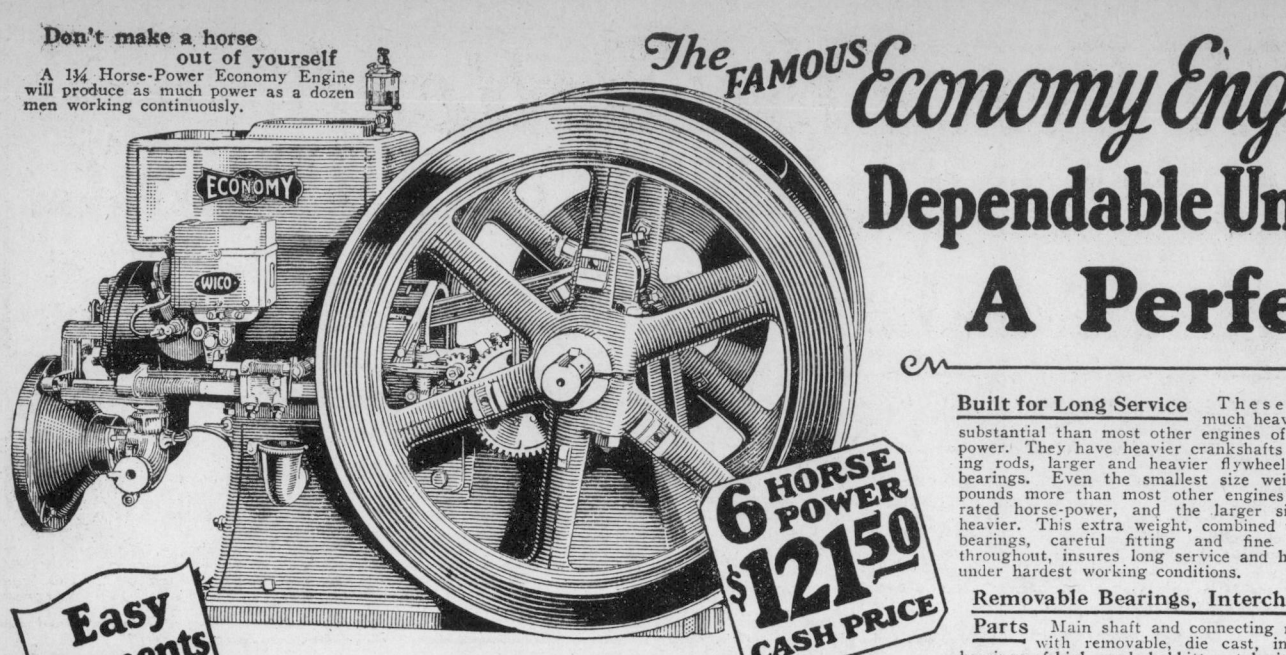
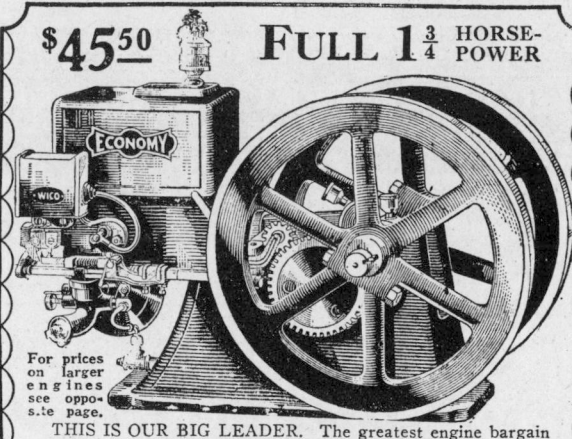

Will Serve You Better!

All Conditions-Economical to Operate Engine *for the* Farm-Fully Guaranteed

Starts Easily
More Power
Less Fuel
All Sizes

MONTHLY PAYMENT TERMS make it easy for you to become the owner of a powerful, reliable Economy Engine even though you do not have the ready cash on hand. See price list below for easy terms and surprisingly low prices.

PROMPT DELIVERY FROM A NEARBY WAREHOUSE

For the convenience of our customers and to make the freight charges a small item, we carry Economy Engines in the 1¾, 2¼, 3½ and 6 horse-power sizes in warehouse at Harrisburg, Pa. **Send your order to Sears, Roebuck and Co., Philadelphia, Pa., and we will ship promptly from our HARRISBURG, Pa., warehouse stock so that the engine will usually be in your hands in just a few days' time—you pay only the freight from our Harrisburg warehouse, and it is a small sum in nearly every case.**

The 8, 10 and 14 horse-power engines are not carried in stock in our Harrisburg warehouse, but are shipped from the factory in EVANSVILLE, IND.

ECONOMY GASOLINE ENGINE

With WICO High Tension Magneto

In the larger sizes (see preceding page for the 1¾ Horse Power Economy)

23K9225—2¼ Horse-Power Economy Gasoline Engine with 5x4-inch pulley. Shipping weight, 300 pounds. **Shipped from Harrisburg, Pa.**
Cash price **$64.50**
Time payment price, **$7.00** with order and balance in monthly payments of **$9.00** each........ **74.00**

23K9035—3½ Horse-Power Economy Gasoline Engine with 8x4-inch pulley. Shipping weight, 520 pounds. **Shipped from Harrisburg, Pa.**
Cash price **$84.75**
Time payment price, **$10.00** with order and balance in monthly payments of **$12.00** each........ **97.50**

23K9060—6 Horse-Power Economy Gasoline Engine with 10x6-inch pulley. Shipping weight, 860 pounds. **Shipped from Harrisburg, Pa.**
Cash price **$121.50**
Time payment price, **$14.00** with order and balance in monthly payments of **$17.00** each........ **139.50**
For 10x8-inch Friction Clutch Pulley in place of regular solid pulley, add $10.70.

23K9080—8 Horse-Power Economy Gasoline Engine with 16x6-inch pulley. Shipping weight, 1,200 pounds. **Shipped from Evansville, Ind.**
Cash price **$157.00**
Time payment price, **$20.00** with order and balance in monthly payments of **$25.00** each........ **180.00**
For 16x8-inch Friction Clutch Pulley in place of regular solid pulley, add $18.45.

23K9100—10 Horse-Power Economy Gasoline Engine with 16x8-inch Friction Clutch pulley. Shipping weight, 1,985 pounds. **Shipped from Evansville, Ind.**
Cash price **$209.00**
Time payment price, **$30.00** with order and balance in monthly payments of **$33.00** each........ **240.00**

23K9140—14 Horse-Power Economy Gasoline Engine with 20x8-inch friction clutch pulley. Shipping weight, 2,600 pounds. **Shipped from Evansville, Ind.**
Cash price **$295.00**
Time payment price, **$40.00** with order and balance in monthly payments of **$45.00** each........ **336.00**

When Ordering on Time Payments Use the Easy Payment Order Blank on Page 1092

ECONOMY ENGINE SPECIFICATIONS SHOW HIGH QUALITY

Guaranteed Horse-Power	Cylinder Bore, Inches	Stroke of Piston, Inches	Engine Speed R. P. M.	FLYWHEELS Diameter, Inches	FLYWHEELS Weight, Pounds	Crankshaft Diameter, Inches	Actual Engine Wt., Lbs.
1¾	3¼	5	600	18	43	1¼	246
2¼	3⅝	5	600	19¾	52	1⅜	295
3½	4¼	6	550	22	88	1⅝	483
6	5	7½	500	28	168	2	777
8	5¾	9	400	34	242	2¼	1,107
10	6½	11	360	38	386	2½	1,823
14	7½	12	350	44	530	2¾	2,433

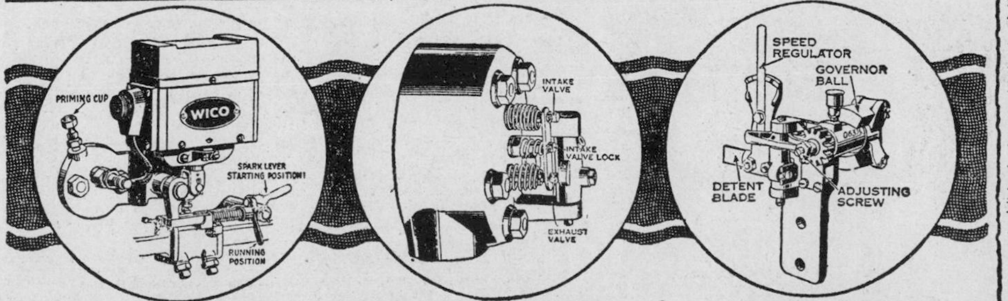

WICO SURE FIRE MAGNETO

Water, oil and dustproof with only one moving part. Gives a big, flamy spark no matter how slow you turn the engine over.

BIG FUEL SAVING FEATURE

Improved valve lock on cylinder head holds intake tightly closed when exhaust valve is open. Prevents blow-back through mixer and saves gas.

SPEED EASY TO REGULATE

You can change speeds while engine is running by shifting regulator. Gives a reduction up to about 125 revolutions per minute from high speed.

Clutch Pulleys

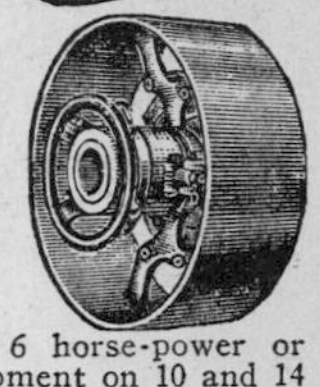

Bolts to the spokes of the flywheel and enables the operator to start the engine without starting the machine or having to disconnect the belt. You can also stop the machine without stopping the engine.

Recommended on all engines of 6 horse-power or larger. Furnished as standard equipment on 10 and 14 Horse-Power Economy Gasoline Engines. **Shipped from EVANSVILLE, IND.** For price in place of regular pulley, see engine prices at the left.

	Diameter, In.	Face, In.	Shpg. Wt., Lbs.	Each
23K510	10	8	83	**$13.90**
23K512	12	6	83	**17.80**
23K516	16	8	100	**21.50**
23K520	20	8	210	**28.50**
23K524	24	8	225	**29.00**
23K530	30	8	235	**31.00**

Clutch Pulleys for Small Engines

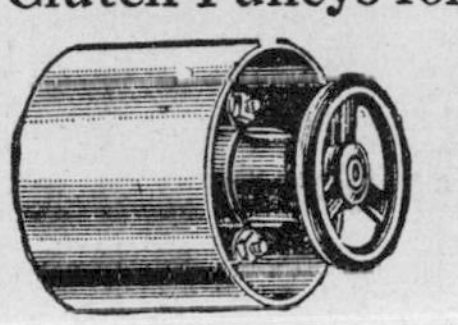

Adapted to attach to crankshaft of 1¼, 2¼ or 3½ Horse-Power Economy Engines, replacing regular solid pulley. Can also be used on other engines with crankshafts of 1¼ to 1⅝ in. in diameter. These handy pulleys disconnect power from machinery at any time. Make cranking the engine easy, start the load without jerk or jar, and make it possible to stop machinery without stopping engine. Also do away with the need of tight and loose pulleys.

If used on an Economy Engine, give horse-power when ordering. On other engines, give diameter of crankshaft extension. **Shipped from HARRISBURG, PA.**

	Diam.	Face	Weight	Each
23K507	5 in.	4 in.	14 lbs.	**$ 7.20**
23K508	6 in.	5 in.	16 lbs.	**8.70**
23K509	8 in.	5 in.	21 lbs.	**10.25**

Direct Connected Gear Driven Pumping Outfits

$65.75

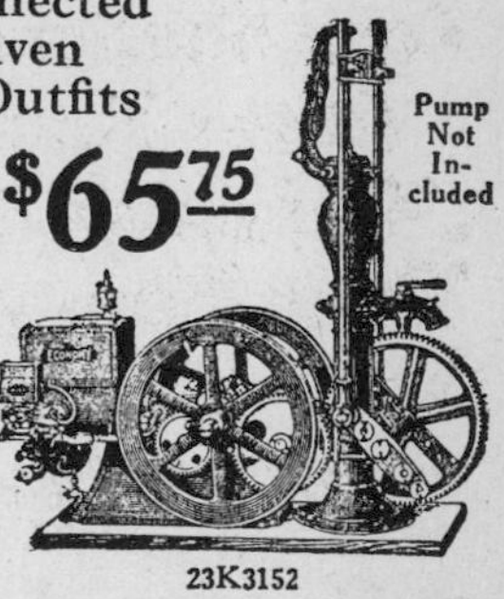

Pump Not Included

23K3152

These outfits consist of a 1¾ Horse-Power Economy Gasoline Engine with **Wico Magneto,** 4x4-inch Pulley and Pump Jack, fastened by four cap screws to the base of the engine so that the jack with babbitt bearings is driven by machine cut gears instead of a belt, with four strokes, 5, 6, 8 and 10 inches, running pump about 40 strokes per minute.

The vertical jack, shown above, is built to clamp around the body of any ordinary hand or windmill force pump, and is furnished with long iron pipe pitman rods and crosshead. Will handle up to 300-foot well. Width over all, 22 inches; length, 45 inches.

The horizontal jack shown below has a stand that holds the outer end of the jack and short rods with a clamp to fasten to the handle of any force pump. Width over all, 22 inches; length, 59 inches.

Engine can be detached from the jack and used for other work. Shipping weight, 390 pounds.

23K3152—1¾ Horse-Power Direct Connected Vertical Pumping Outfit with 4x4-inch Pulley........ **$65.75**

23K3153—1¾ Horse-Power Direct Connected Horizontal Pumping Outfit with 4x4-inch Pulley........ **$65.75**

Shipped complete from EVANSVILLE, IND., only.

23K3153

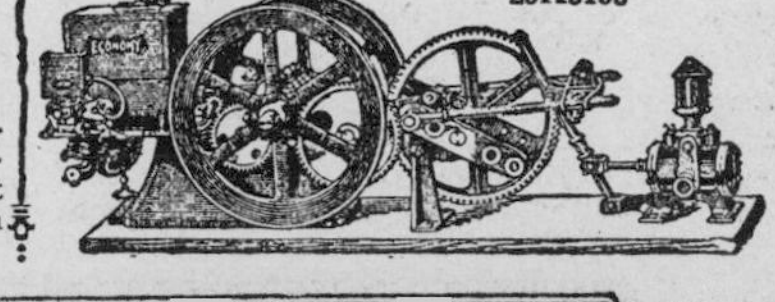

Pump Not Included

Pump Jacks Stylish Buggies and Carts

Double Gear Pump Jack

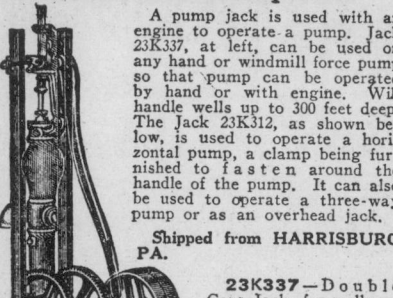

A pump jack is used with an engine to operate a pump. Jack 23K337, at left, can be used on any hand or windmill force pump so that pump can be operated by hand or with engine. Will handle wells up to 300 feet deep. The Jack 23K312, as shown below, is used to operate a horizontal pump, a clamp being furnished to fasten around the handle of the pump. It can also be used to operate a three-way pump or as an overhead jack.

Shipped from HARRISBURG, PA.

23K337—Double Gear Jack, for wells up to 300 feet deep. Shipping weight, 90 pounds....**$6.95**

23K312—Double Gear Horizontal Jack, with hand clamp and stand support. Shipping weight, 95 pounds....**$7.95**

23K370—11 feet of 2-inch Rubber Belt with fastener to use with pump jack. Wt., 2 lbs. **$1.50**
Both jacks are back geared four to one, with three strokes, 4½, 7 and 9½ inches, equipped with 13-inch tight and loose pulleys, 2¼-inch face. Should run about 150 revolutions per minute, operating the pump about 35 strokes a minute.

Pump Not Included

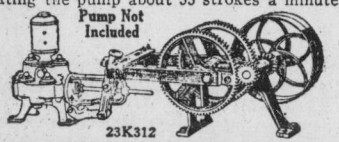

23K312

Self-Oiling Worm Drive Jack With Enclosed Gears

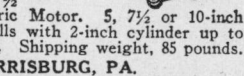

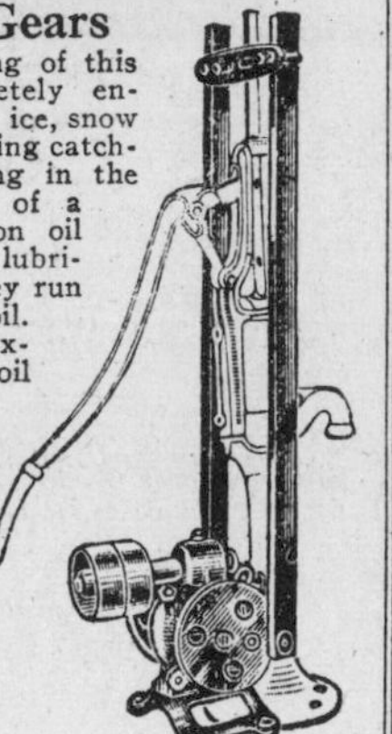

The worm drive gearing of this efficient jack is completely enclosed, protecting it from ice, snow and dust and also preventing catching of fingers or clothing in the gears. Three-quarters of a pint of good transmission oil poured into the gear case lubricates all gears so that they run in a constant bath of oil. No attention required except to change the oil every six months.

Jack is back geared 16 to 1 with 4-inch tight and loose pulleys for engine drive, or a 10-inch single pulley for electric motor drive. Pulleys have 2¼-in. face. We recommend using our 1¾ Horse-Power Economy or similar small engine, or ½ Horse-Power Electric Motor. 5, 7½ or 10-inch stroke. Pumps wells with 2-inch cylinder up to 200 to 250 feet deep. Shipping weight, 85 pounds.

Shipped from HARRISBURG, PA.

23K334—Worm Drive Jack with 4-inch tight and loose pulleys for gasoline engine drive...........**$8.60**
23K335—Worm Drive Jack with one 10-inch pulley for electric motor drive.... **8.65**

Double Back Geared Jack $8.50

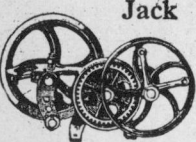

For use with engine on very deep wells, where slow speed is required or electric motor. Will handle a 2-inch cylinder or less on wells up to 350 feet deep, back geared, sixteen to one, with three strokes, 5, 7½ and 10 inches. 13-inch Center Drive Pulley with clutch for starting and stopping. Pulley should run about 560 R. P. M. with electric motor to run pump 35 strokes per minute. With engine for deep wells pulley should run about 480 R.P.M., running pump 30 strokes per minute. Will fit any pump standard up to 4 inches in diameter. Gears completely covered with steel gear guard. **Shipped from HARRISBURG, PA.**

23K339—Double Back Geared Center Drive Clutch Jack, with Steel Gear Guard. Weight, 100 pounds................**$8.50**
23K371—Clamp for attaching jack to handle when used with horizontal pump. Wt., 1 lb..65c

Our American Beauty

Our up to date American Beauty is strongly made from high quality materials and will give splendid service. Has up to date automobile style seat, 32½ inches across top of cushion. Upholstered in high grade artificial leather, tufted spring cushion and back. Three-bow top, auto skeleton style, black auto rubber with tan inside. Side curtains and storm apron. **Body**—Piano style, 23 inches wide, 56 inches long. **Wheels**—Sarven's patent style, 39 inches front and 43 inches rear. ⅞-inch screwed rims with ⁵⁄₁₆-inch oval edge steel tires. Curved, patent leather dash with hand holes and line rail, rubber mat. Body painted plain black; gear, Brewster green, neatly striped. **Track**—4 feet 8 inches narrow or 5 feet 2 inches wide. Weight, 400 pounds. **Shipped from HUNTINGBURG, IND.**

23K3508—American Beauty Buggy with triple braced, selected hickory shafts and steel tires. State width of track. Shipping weight, 500 pounds....................**$88.50**
   23K900—Pole in place of shafts, add.....**$3.65**
   23K901—Pole and shafts, add.............. 8.90
   23K902—For ⅞-inch high grade rubber tires, add 9.70

Our Farm Service Buggy

A big, roomy rig for stout people or those who are in the habit of carrying cream cans, egg baskets or other parcels to market, bringing home groceries, etc. Has piano style body, 26 inches wide, 56 inches long, up to date auto style seat, 34½ inches across top of cushion; wheels have 1-inch steel tires. In all other respects has the same specifications and finished in the same high grade manner as our American Beauty Buggy listed above. Track, 4 feet 8 inches narrow or 5 feet 2 inches wide. Weight, 420 pounds.
23K3507—Farm Service Buggy with triple braced shafts and steel tires. State width of track. **Shipped from HUNTINGBURG, IND.** Shipping weight, 525 pounds....**$85.00**

Our Standard Top Buggy

A strong, comfortable, light running buggy, built for long use. Seat has solid panel back with arm rails, 30½ inches across. Upholstered in black imitation leather with tufted back and spring cushion. Three-bow skeleton auto style, auto rubber top with waterproof side curtains. **Wheels**—39 inches front, 43 inches rear, with screwed rims and ⁵⁄₁₆-inch steel tires. **Body**—Piano style, 23x56 inches. **Body**—Plain black; gear, Brewster green, neatly striped. Patent leather padded dash; rubber mat; storm apron. **Track**—4 feet 8 inches narrow, or 5 feet 2 inches wide. Weight, 400 pounds. Shipping weight, 500 pounds.
23K3501—Standard Top Buggy with triple braced shafts and steel tires (not illustrated). State width of track...................**$83.00**
Shipped from HUNTINGBURG, IND.
Price of extra pole and rubber tires same as for American Beauty Buggy above.

$8850

Skeleton Road Cart $23.85

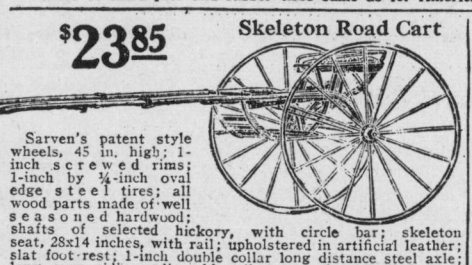

Sarven's patent style wheels, 45 in. high; 1-inch screwed rims; 1-inch by ¼-inch oval edge steel tires; all wood parts made of well seasoned hardwood; shafts of selected hickory, with circle bar; skeleton seat, 28x14 inches, with rail; upholstered in artificial leather; slat foot-rest; 1-inch double collar long distance steel axle; long easy riding adjustable oil tempered spring. Painted carmine red with black striping. **TRACK**—4 feet 8 inches, narrow, or 5 feet 2 inches wide. Net weight, 145 pounds. **Shipped from HUNTINGBURG, IND.**
23K34—Skeleton Road Cart. State width of track. Shipping weight, 265 pounds.........**$23.85**

Phaeton Body Road Cart

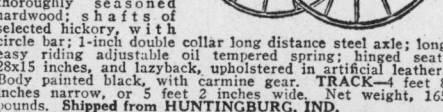

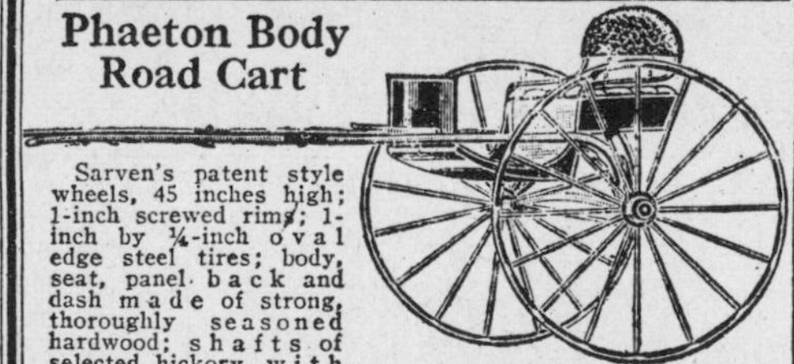

Sarven's patent style wheels, 45 inches high; 1-inch screwed rims; 1-inch by ¼-inch oval edge steel tires; body, seat, panel back and dash made of strong, thoroughly seasoned hardwood; shafts of selected hickory, with circle bar; 1-inch double collar long distance steel axle; long easy riding adjustable oil tempered spring; hinged seat, 28x15 inches, and lazyback, upholstered in artificial leather. Body painted black, with carmine gear. **TRACK**—4 feet 8 inches narrow, or 5 feet 2 inches wide. Net weight, 165 pounds. **Shipped from HUNTINGBURG, IND.**
23K135—Phaeton Road Cart. State width of track. Shipping weight, 285 lbs......**$29.90**

PONY CART

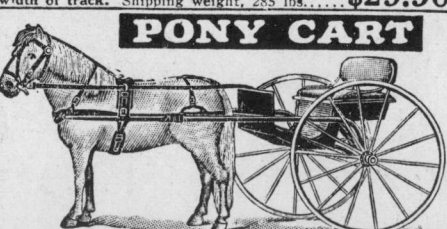

Regular cart body. Seat, 28 inches wide, upholstered with artificial leather, will hold two people comfortably. Painting—Body, black; gear and shafts, red. **Track**—3 feet 9 inches. Shipping weight, 155 pounds.

	Ht. of Pony	Shafts	Wheels	
23K2020	33 to 42 in.	56 in.	30 in.	$30.75
23K2021	42 to 50 in.	60 in.	34 in.	31.75
23K2022	Over 50 in.	66 in.	38 in.	32.75

Shipped from CINCINNATI, OHIO.

American Beauty Runabout $59.90

The body and running gear of this runabout are exactly the same as our American Beauty Buggy described on this page. The seat is bent panel, 31 inches across top of cushion, upholstered in black artificial leather with tufted back and spring cushion. **Painting**—Body and seat, plain black; gear, Brewster green. **Track**—4 feet 8 inches narrow, or 5 feet 2 inches wide. Weight, 335 pounds.

23K3515—American Beauty Runabout with triple braced shafts and steel tires. State width of track. **Shipped from HUNTINGBURG, IND.** Shipping weight, 450 pounds...............**$59.90**

Our Utility Market Wagon $76.75

Shipped from HUNTINGBURG, IND.

Has panel seat with lazyback, 34 inches across. Upholstered in black artificial leather. **Body**—76 inches long by 32 inches wide; hardwood frame and panels, ironed and braced; drop endgate. **Wheels**—39 inches front, 43 inches rear, 1-inch screwed rims, ⁵⁄₁₆-inch oval edge steel tires. Body painted dark green, striped with black molding; gear, green striped. **Track**—4 feet 8 inches narrow, 5 feet 2 inches wide. Weight, 415 pounds.

23K502—Market Wagon with triple braced shafts and steel tires, one seat. State width of track. Shipping weight, 650 pounds........**$76.75**
   23K904—Extra seat in back, add.........**$12.75**
   23K900—Pole in place of shafts, add...... 3.65
   23K901—Pole and shafts, add.......... 8.90
   23K903—1-inch high grade rubber tires in place of steel, add.......................... 10.65
   23K905—Panel back seat with top in place of regular seat, add...................... 19.75
   23K906—Hand brake, add.............. 6.95

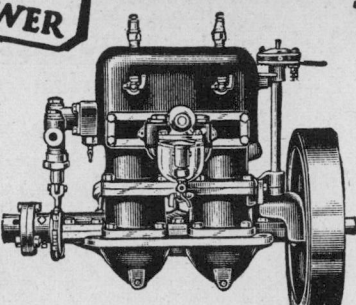

CUSTOM QUALITY

Improved breast strap snaps with loop for pole strap. Does away with collar strap.

$5.00 Down—$5.00 a Month

General Farm or Wagon Harness

This Harness is sold on easy monthly payments; thirty days' trial; priced unusually low; a harness made according to Sears, Roebuck and Co.'s high standard of quality. It's the lowest price at which a harness of this quality has been offered for years. We made our terms very easy, too—only $5.00 a month—so that everyone can take advantage of this opportunity.

Compare—and Satisfy Yourself

When you get this harness, examine it carefully. Compare it with other makes selling at from $10.00 to $15.00 more than our price. Compare the leather, the hardware, the workmanship. Compare, also, the size and thickness of our straps with others. Only because we buy so many are we able to offer you this low price.

Try this harness on your own team. Use it for thirty days. Then if you do not find it exactly as represented and satisfactory in every way, box it up and send it back to us at our expense. We will then return every cent you have paid, including transportation charges.

$53.25
Cash Price

Here Are the Strong Points
Below Are the Specifications. Note the Size of the Straps and You Will Realize What a Good Substantial Harness Is Here Offered

BRIDLES—⅝-inch short cheeks with nosebands; Concord blinds; combination front and winker brace, ring crowns, round reins, complete with two check-up straps.
LINES—Strong and well made, 1⅛ inches wide, 20 feet long.
TRACES—6 feet long, 1¾ inches wide, very carefully fitted and stitched with three rows of stitching, fancy scalloped safe; extra heavy bellyband billet; 6-link swivel heel chain.
HAMES—Steel, bolt, brass ball top, four well made hame straps, two spread straps with rings, folded bellybands.
BREECHING—Wide heavy folded body with 1¼-inch layer, 1¼-inch side straps, three-ring style, adjustable hip straps, 1¼ inches wide, with trace carrier; 1¼-inch backstraps to hames, equipped with metal wear loops.

PADS—Extra wide leather body, swell shape and leather lined with 1½-inch market straps and metal bridges.
MARTINGALES—1½ inches wide.
BREAST STRAPS—1½ inches wide, with snaps and improved rollers. These straps are cut from heavy stock, and with the new style of combination breast strap and martingale snap it does away with the collar straps and makes a more substantial job.
TRIMMINGS—Black japanned, with brass balls on the hames.
10K650¼—Double Harness, without collars. Shipping weight, 95 pounds. Time payment price.................................... **$58.50**
Terms: $5.00 with your order and $5.00 a month until easy payment price has been paid. Use Time Payment Order Blank on page 1092.
10K651¼—Same Harness, cash in full with order................. **53.25**

"New England" Farm Harness

$59.95

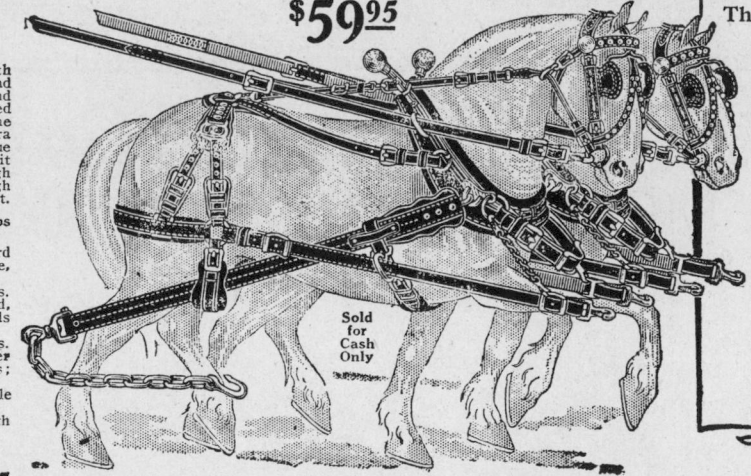

Sold for Cash Only

Just compare our price on this harness with that usually asked by others, and you will find that we make you a saving of $10.00 to $25.00 and even more per set. Remember, nothing is added to the cost of our harness after it leaves the factory, except our own small profit. Extra profits do not add one cent to the actual value of any harness. When we ship you a harness it must appeal to you by its own merit, its high quality, after you have given it a most thorough examination and put it to every reasonable test.

Flesh Side of Straps Is Not Blacked—All Straps Have Creased Edges
BRIDLES—⅝-inch box loop cheeks; Concord (sensible) blinds, spotted front and face piece, round reins; two check-up straps.
HAMES—Steel clip and staple with brass balls.
TRACES—1¾-inch double and three-row stitched, 6 feet long, clipped to hames, folded bellybands with 1½-inch buckles.
LINES—1 inch wide, 20 feet long, stitched laps.
BREECHING—Folded body, 1½-inch layer stitched full length; flange breeching layer loops; 1-inch hip straps and double backstraps.
SIDEBACKERS OR JOCKEY STRAPS—Single strap, 1½ inches wide.
BREAST STRAPS—Heavy single strap with leather loops, 1¾ inches wide, snaps and slides.
TRIMMINGS—Black japanned, brass spots.
Weight, packed for shipment, 95 pounds.
10K691¼—Double harness without collars. Cash only................$59.95

This Explains Why We Sell Harness So Cheap

In buying our harness you pay only one profit above manufacturing cost. Our Harness is designed and constructed by skilled mechanics and of selected materials. Finished sets are examined by experts of long experience, so that we can AND DO guarantee that any harness you buy from us will stand up to its work and satisfy you every way.

Every farmer should give Sears harness a trial on his own farm and in his own way. We will gladly send a set for a full month's trial without risk to you. If you find the harness to be all we claim for it on quality and value, you will want to keep it, but if you are not perfectly satisfied, just send it back, and we will promptly return all the money you have paid on it and the shipping charges also. By becoming the only sales medium between the factory and you, we save you the selling expense of jobbers, dealers and agents, and you keep this saving right in your own pocket.

"Aroostook" Custom Built Harness
Harness That Will Stand the Test

$82.50

Sold for Cash Only

You'll like the leather in this harness—thick, heavy straps, heavy three-ply traces, built to stand the hardest pulls. The leather was tanned right from selected No. 1 northern steer hides by the good old fashioned bark process. This takes longer time and costs more, but it puts longer life and greater strength into the leather. Here is workmanship, too, of the same expert character that has established such a wonderful reputation for our harness wherever it has been used. You look for long wear, even with the hardest use, in a Sears, Roebuck and Co. harness. This harness will satisfy you. This we guarantee.

This type of harness is popular in the Eastern States, especially in the great potato growing districts. Farmers use it for field or wagon work. Its quality is of the kind that gives years of satisfactory service.
BRIDLES—⅝-inch box loop cheeks, sensible blinds, spotted fronts, fancy face pieces; short flat reins.
LINES—Extra good quality and well made; 1 inch wide; 18 feet long; buckle and billet ends with snaps to bit.
HAMES—No. 10 Concord bolt; wood, brass long spot; 4 heavy hame straps; ⅝-inch spread straps.
TRACES—2¼ inches wide, double and stitched; 4 feet 8 inches long with hook ends, (no chains).
PADS—Harness leather scalloped body, with layer, full brass spotted; 1¾-inch billets; 1½-inch folded bellybands with layer.
BREAST STRAPS—1¾ inches wide with leather loops; snaps and slides.
SIDEBACKERS—1¾-inch single strap body with snaps to neckyokes; 1-inch carrying straps.
BREECHING—Single strap body, with layer at each end; 3-ring stay lead-up; fancy tapered hip strap; spotted back straps to hames; padded rump safes; 1¾-inch lazy straps.
TRIMMINGS—Brass buckles and spots. Weight, boxed for shipment, 100 lbs.
10K685¼—Double harness, without collars. Cash only........................ **$82.50**

PRICES LOW!

$5.00 Down—$5.00 a Month

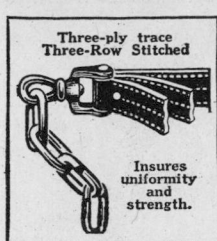

Three-ply trace Three-Row Stitched.
Insures uniformity and strength.

"Farm King" Metal-to-Metal Harness

Why is "Metal-to-Metal" Construction the Best?

Look at your old harness. It wears out first where there is the greatest friction of metal against leather. Friction is the greatest destroyer of harness. This new improved harness has the latest and best special "metal-to-metal" features. Where there is likely to be see-saw wear or friction, metal wears against metal; the leather is protected. None but the choicest No. 1 heavy northern steer hides are used. Tanned by the old fashioned bark process; a long process and the most costly, but the best one. This leather will stand the hardest test.

Special Easy Terms Offer

Don't wait until your old harness breaks and stops your work. All you need right now is $5.00, then pay the balance in small monthly payments of $5.00 each. Take advantage of this Special Easy Terms offer. Send your order, with only $5.00, now, and have a sturdy, dependable harness on hand when you need it.

$63.25 Cash Price

Read in Detail What a Splendid Harness This Is

BRIDLES—1-inch, double cheeks, with heavy 1¼-inch crown straps, in the popular ring crown style.
LINES—Selected with extra care. Made from heavy stock, 1⅛ inches wide and 20 feet long. A 1⅛-inch line in this grade of stock is as good as the majority of 1¼-inch lines.
TRACES—Heavy three-ply leather, 1¾ inches wide, three-row stitch, with extra heavy 1½-inch bellyband billets. Bellybands made with layer for extra strength. Six-link swivel heel chains sewed in.
BREECHING—Very heavy, folded body, 2½ inches wide with 1¼-inch layer. The fold is filled with harness leather, making it extra strong. The back straps are selected heavy leather, 1⅛ inches wide, protected at all points of wear by special "metal-to-metal" fittings. Side straps are very heavy, 1¼ inches wide, and are also protected by "metal-to-metal" fittings.

SIDEBACKERS—Very heavy leather, 1¾-inch body, 1⅛-inch carrying straps, combination snap and loop to neckyoke, "metal-to-metal" fittings.
BACK PADS—5 inches wide, swell shape, harness leather top, leather lined bottom with heavy 1½-inch layer, extra heavy 1½-inch market straps, all protected by "metal-to-metal" fittings.
HAMES—Steel Concord bolt, brass ball top; one of the strongest hames made. Trims up the harness and shows off your team to the best advantage.

10K605¼—Double harness, without collars. Shipping weight, 95 pounds. Time payment price............................ **$69.50**
Terms: $5.00 down and $5.00 a month until full easy payment price has been paid. Use Time Payment Order Blank on page 1092.
10K606¼—Price of harness, cash in full with order................ **63.25**

Reliable Quality at Low Cost

That's what you expect when you buy harness and saddlery from Sears, Roebuck and Co., and that's just what you'll get if you make up your order from this catalog.

Quality that is reliable results from the manner in which the leather is tanned that goes into the manufacture of our harness, strap work and saddles, the old time bark tannage, proved the best by countless numbers of our customers, over the 35-year period during which we have been selling harness.

Low cost is made certain by large quantity production, modern methods of manufacture, purchase of supplies for cash and economical distribution.

Thus when you order from this catalog you know in advance that quality and price are both right, and this is further assured to you through our nationally known guarantee.

$61.25

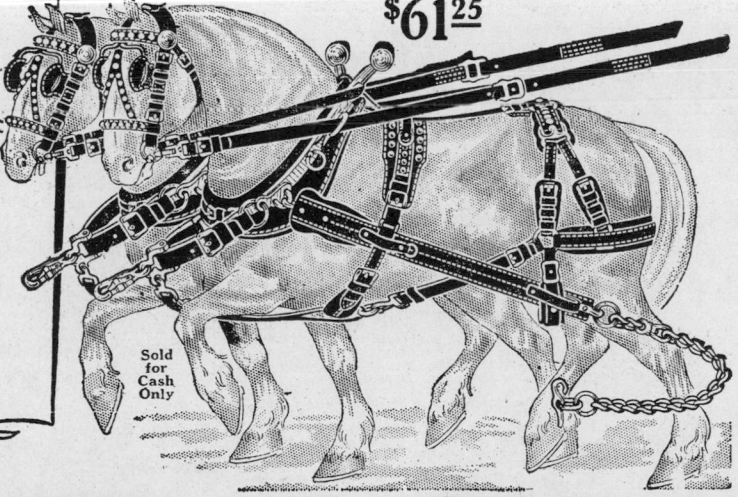

Sold for Cash Only

"East Lynn" Heavy Wagon Harness

BRIDLES—⅞-inch long cheeks; Concord blinds; combination nose band and face pieces, spotted front; flat reins. **LINES**—Our best and heaviest 1½ or 1¼ inches wide, 20 feet long. **TRACES**—4½ feet long and 2¼ inches wide; three-row stitching; short scalloped safe; 1½-inch bellyband billet; 42-inch chain. **HAMES**—Steel, clip, dandy brass ball top, four hame straps, two spread straps with rings; 1½-inch folded bellybands. **BREECHING**—Folded body, 2½ inches wide with 1¼-inch layer; 1 or 1¼-inch side straps; three-ring style double hip straps, 1 or 1¼ inches wide, with hip strap trace carrier; 1½-inch back straps to hames; padded rump safe. **PADS**—4 inches wide, tapering to 3 inches; 1½-inch layer and billet. **MARTINGALES**—1¾ inches wide. **BREAST STRAPS**—1¾ inches wide with roller snaps. **TRIMMINGS**—Black japanned; brass spots.
Weight of harness, packed for shipment, 90 lbs.
10K863¼—Double harness, with 1⅛-inch lines, and breeching with 1-inch hip and side straps, without collars..... **$61.25**
10K864¼—Double harness, with 1¼-inch lines, and breeching with 1¼-inch hip and side straps, without collars..... **$63.50**
If either of the above harness is wanted with sidebackers in place of breast straps, martingales and side straps, add.........**$3.75**
You may buy the breeching of this harness separately. Order:
10K2483—Complete breeching, with 1-inch hip and side straps and body for two horses. Shipping weight, 17 pounds. Per set..........**$14.95**
10K2484—Complete breeching with 1¼-inch hip and side straps and body for two horses. Shipping weight, 18 pounds. Per set..........**$15.95**

$65.50

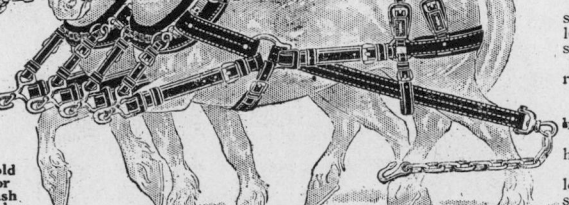

Sold for Cash Only

"White Mountain" Boston Truck Harness

To Possess Good Work Harness Is Highly Profitably

Don't overlook quality—that which gives good harness its value. The real test of harness is in the length of service and quality of service it gives. This can be decided only by actual use. We give you the privilege of using the harness for a reasonable time and agree to replace free of charge any part of it that wears out because of poor quality of material or workmanship. Thus customers have the opportunity to judge the quality of our harness by the actual service it gives.

We suggest your careful consideration of the harness shown here. It represents a popular style used extensively throughout the New England States, and is a decided bargain. The leather is of selected quality with flesh finish back and narrow creased edges. Harness is splendidly made.
BRIDLES—¾-inch cheeks with box loops, Concord (sensible) blinds; face pieces and flat reins.
LINES—1-inch wide, 16 feet long; heavy leather, sewed laps; buckle, billet and snap ends.
HAMES—Concord bolt, wood, with steel back, long spot, Dandy brass ball tops. Heavy hame straps and spread straps.
TRACES—Double and 3-row stitched, 2 inches wide at front end, 1¾-inch rear with dee, hook and 24-inch chain; folded bellybands with return billets.
BREECHING—Wide folded body with 1½-inch layer; heavy lead-ups with safes and box loops; 1½-inch side straps extending to dee in trace; 1-inch double backstraps and double hip straps; padded rump safe.
JOCKEY STRAPS—1½-inch wide, single strap with hook and ring; 1-inch carrying straps.
TRIMMINGS—Black japanned, brass spots.
10K857¼—Double harness, without collars. Shipping weight, 95 pounds..... **$65.50**

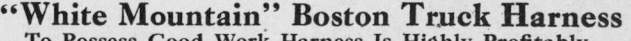

We Guarantee to Satisfy You and Save You Money

P 1047

Harness of Quality for Light or Heavy Work

"Benton" Single Buggy Harness

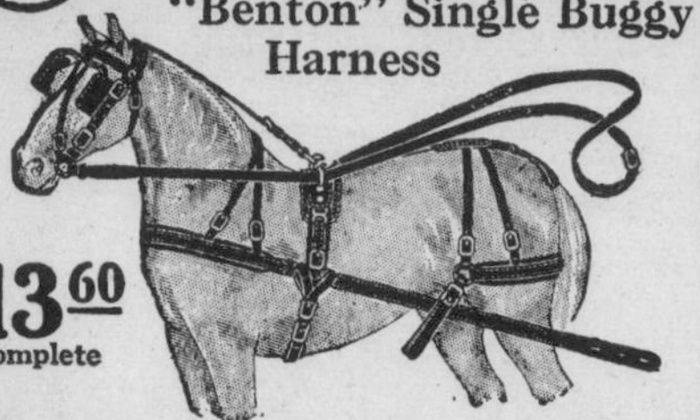

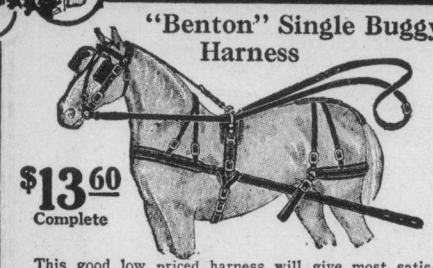

$13.60 Complete

This good low priced harness will give most satisfactory service. Has ¾-inch bridle, 1-inch lines, 1¼-inch traces, folded breeching and heavy gig saddle. Other parts made in proportion. Japan trimmed. You may buy parts of this harness, if wanted. Order:

10K23B—Bridle. Shpg. wt., 3 lbs. **$2.35**
10K23L—Lines. Shpg. wt., 2½ lbs. **2.20**
10K23BC—Breast Collar and Traces. Shipping weight, 5 pounds **$3.55**
10K23SS—Strap Saddle, Shaft Tugs and Bellyband. Shipping weight, 6 pounds **$3.00**
10K23PS—Padded Saddle, Shaft Tugs and Bellyband. Shipping weight, 6 pounds **$5.00**
10K23BG—Breeching. Shipping wt., 5 lbs. **2.50**
10K23¼—Complete harness, with strap saddle. Shipping weight, 16 pounds..... **$13.60**

"Zeno" Express Harness

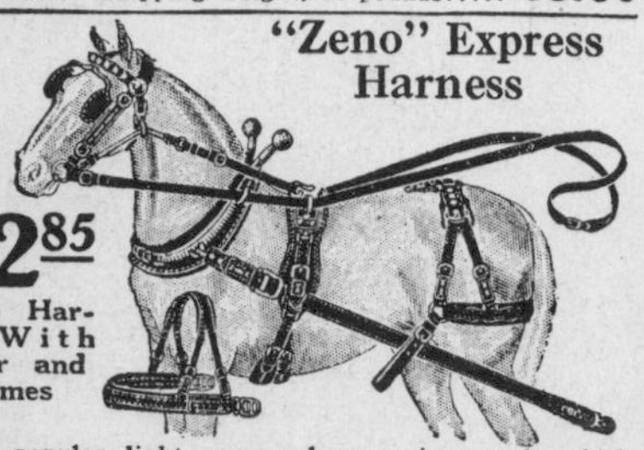

$32.85 Single Harness With Collar and Hames

This popular light express harness is a style which we have sold for many years. Many use it as a buggy or spring wagon harness, work for which it is entirely suitable. The leather used in its construction is of quality that wears splendidly, and we are careful to see that all parts are extra strong.

10K147B—BRIDLE—¾-inch box loop cheeks. Shipping weight, 5 pounds **$3.95**
10K147C—COLLAR—Leather, light express weight. Sizes, 17 to 22 inches. **State size.** Shipping weight, 9 pounds **$3.25**
10K147L—LINES—1 inch wide, 13½ feet long. Shipping weight, 4 pounds **$2.75**
10K147HT—HAMES—Ball top; hame tugs with box loops, two hame straps. Shpg. wt., 10 lbs. .. **$4.15**
10K147T—TRACES—1½-inch, double and stitched, 6 feet long. Shipping weight, 5 pounds **$3.85**
10K147S—SADDLE—4½-inch leather skirts, cloth lined pad. Shipping weight, 7 pounds **$6.65**
10K147SB—DEE SHAFT TUGS AND BELLYBANDS—Shipping weight, 3 pounds **$3.00**
10K147BG—BREECHING—Folded leather body with layer, ⅞-inch hip straps; 1⅛-inch side straps; 1⅛-inch turnback. Shipping weight, 8 pounds **$5.40**
TRIMMINGS—Black Japan.
10K147¼—Single harness, with collar and hames. Collar size, 17 to 22 inches. **State size.** Shipping weight, 46 pounds **$32.85**
10K148¼—Single harness, with breast collar. Shipping weight, 40 pounds **$29.20**
10K148BC—Breast Collar only. Shipping weight, 5 pounds **$3.75**

"Pellico" Chain Harness

$36.50 Without Collars

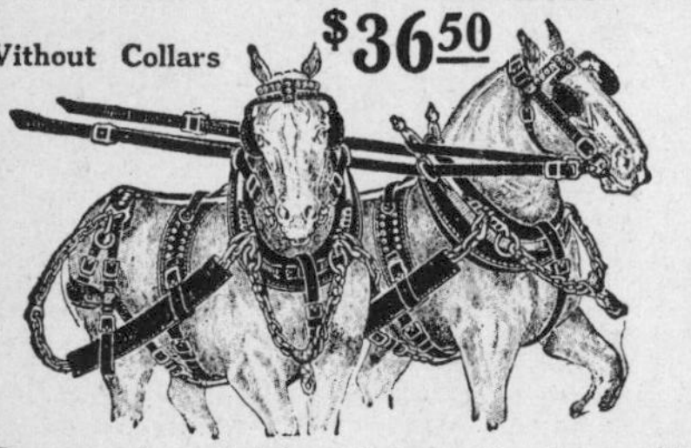

Farmers of good judgment invariably choose this when looking for a serviceable harness at medium price. In this harness we combine real service value with low cost very satisfactorily, resulting in a strong and practical set for general farming purposes.

BRIDLES—1¼-inch double and stitched cheeks; Concord or pigeon wing blinds. **State choice. LINES**—1⅛ inches wide, 18 feet long. **HAMES**—Adjustable draft, ball tops; hame straps; spread straps; Trilby breast chains; 1½-inch pole straps. **TRACES**—Heavy links; No. 1 wire; 7 feet long. **CHAIN PIPING**—Leather, 36 or 42 inches long; flat bellybands. **PADS**—Wide leather body, felt lined. **BREECHING**—Heavy folded body with layer, 1¼-inch hip straps, back straps and side straps, or furnished without breeching, but with single hip straps.

10K430¼—Double Harness, without breeching or pole straps, with hip straps and 36-inch chain piping, without collars. Shipping weight, 75 pounds **$27.95**
10K431¼—Double Harness, with breeching, pole straps and 42-inch chain piping, without collars. Shipping weight, 85 pounds **$36.50**

"Midget" Shetland Pony Harness

For Ponies Weighing 200 to 400 Pounds

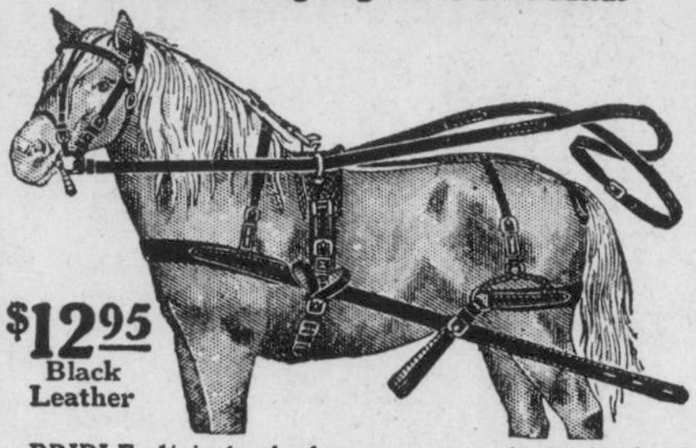

$12.95 Black Leather

BRIDLE—½-inch cheeks, open; overcheck; headstall adjustable from 26 to 32 inches. **LINES**—9 feet 10 inches long; ¾-inch fronts; ⅞-inch hand parts. **BREAST COLLAR**—1⅜-inch single strap; 1-inch single strap traces; full length of breast collar and traces, 10 feet 8 inches. **GIG SADDLE**—2¼-inch flexible tree; single strap skirts. **BREECHING**—1¼-inch single strap; ½-inch hip straps; ¾-inch side straps; ⅝-inch turnback, with crupper. **TRIMMINGS**—Nickel plated. **GIRTH MEASUREMENTS**—Adjustable from 47 to 54 inches. Weight of harness packed for shipment, 10 pounds.

10K184¼—Single harness, black leather... **$12.95**
10K185¼—Single harness, russet leather..... **$13.75**

The "Improved Buster" Indian or Mustang Pony Harness With Breast Collar

For Ponies Weighing 500 to 800 Pounds. Shipping weight, 13 pounds.

10K188¼ Black leather.. **$17.50**
10K189¼ Russet leather. **$18.95**

"Drayman" Heavy Express Harness

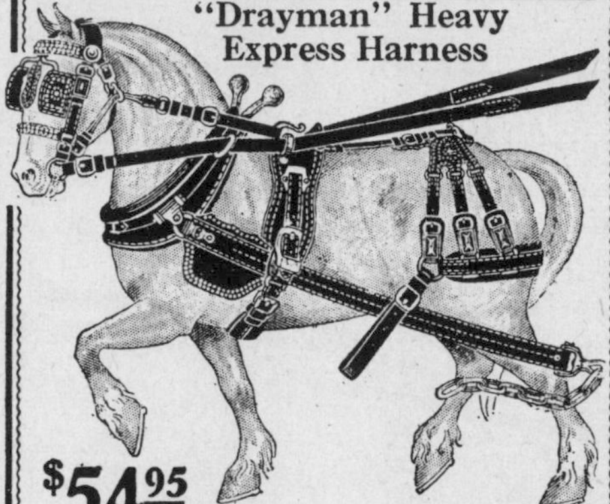

$54.95 Complete

Dealers in fuel, ice, milk, building material, etc., will find this harness just suited to their work. All straps are cut extra heavy to insure reliability for such service. It is an attractive set that will show your horse to its best advantage and prove a paying advertisement for your business. For general express work it is a leader in every respect.

BRIDLE—⅞-inch short cheeks, wide crown; double and stitched front, round winker brace; spotted blinds. **LINES**—1-inch front, 1⅛-inch hand parts. **HAMES**—Heavy wood, painted red, brass long spot, 1-inch hame straps. **TRACES**—2-inch double and stitched, clip to hames; leather part, 6 feet long, large fenders. **SADDLE**—6-inch heavy leather skirts; wool kersey lined pad, well stuffed; running bearers, 1½-inch shaft tugs; folded bellybands. **BREECHING**—Folded body with 1½-inch layer box loop lead ups; 1¼-inch back straps; 1½-inch side straps; padded rump safe. Weight, boxed for shipment, 60 pounds. For collar to use with this harness see Collar page 1049.

10K165¼—Single harness, brass trimmed, without collar **$54.95**

Goat or Dog Harness

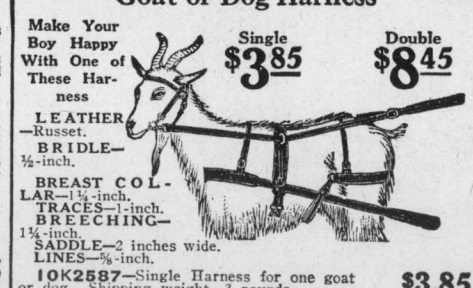

Make Your Boy Happy With One of These Harness

Single **$3.85** Double **$8.45**

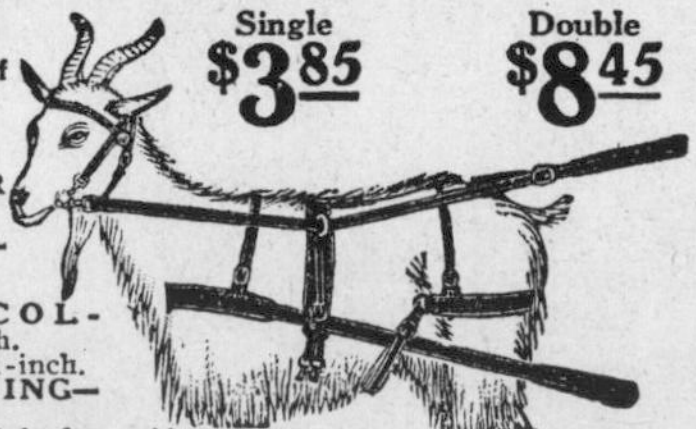

LEATHER—Russet. **BRIDLE**—½-inch. **BREAST COLLAR**—1¼-inch. **TRACES**—1-inch. **BREECHING**—1¼-inch. **SADDLE**—2 inches wide. **LINES**—⅝-inch.

10K2587—Single Harness for one goat or dog. Shipping weight, 3 pounds **$3.85**
10K2588—Double Harness for two goats or two dogs. Shipping weight, 5 pounds **8.45**

"Winford" Single Buggy Harness

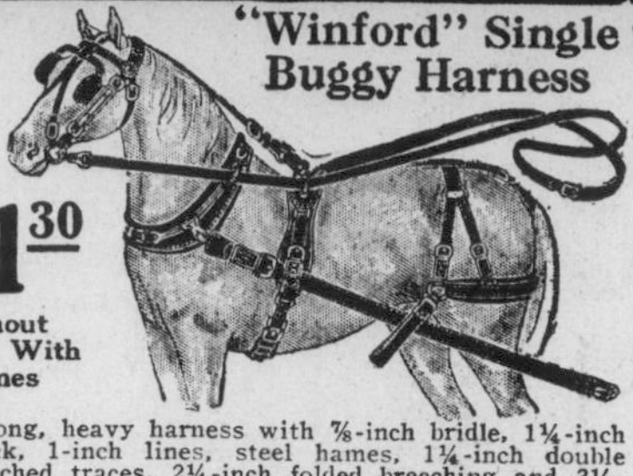

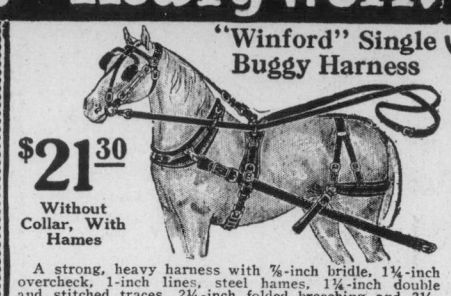

$21.30 Without Collar, With Hames

A strong, heavy harness with ⅞-inch bridle, 1¼-inch overcheck, 1-inch lines, steel hames, 1¼-inch double and stitched traces, 2¼-inch folded breeching and 3½-inch saddle. Japan trimmed. Kip leather collar in sizes 17 to 22 inches.

Prices of complete set with padded saddle

10K16¼—Single harness with collar and hames. Shipping weight, 30 lbs. **State size of collar.. $24.15**
10K18¼—Single harness without collar, with hames. Shipping weight, 25 lbs. **State size of hames.. $21.30**

You may buy parts of this harness, if wanted. Order:

10K13B—Bridle. Shipping wt., 3 lbs.... **$3.45**
10K16L—Lines. Shipping wt., 2½ lbs.. **$2.25**
10K16C—Collar. Shipping weight, 5 lbs. **State size** **$2.85**
10K16H—Hames, hame straps and hame tugs. Shipping weight, 7 pounds **$2.00**
10K16T—Traces. Shipping wt., 6 lbs... **$3.35**
10K16SS—Strap saddle with shaft tugs and bellyband. Shipping wt., 5 pounds **$4.75**
10K16PS—Padded saddle with shaft tugs and bellyband. Shipping wt., 5 pounds **$6.25**
10K16BG—Breeching. Shpg wt., 5 lbs... **$4.00**

"Utility" Single Farm Harness

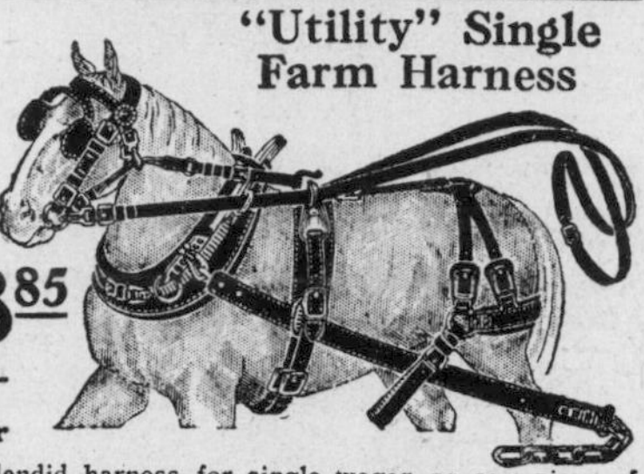

$18.85 Without Collar

A splendid harness for single wagon or any piece of farm machinery that can be pulled by one horse. The leather is tanned firm and strong, all parts carefully cut, fitted and finished. **Sold complete for one horse or by the part, as wanted.**

10K2065—BRIDLE—⅞-inch cheeks, round side reins. Shpg. wt., 5 lbs. **$3.50**
10K259L—LINES—1 inch wide, 13 feet long. Shipping weight, 4 pounds **$2.60**
10K259HH—HAMES, HAME STRAPS AND TRACES—Wood hames, high or low top **(state choice)**, adjustable draft; ⅞-inch hame straps. Traces, 1½ inches wide, 6 feet long, double and stitched. Shipping weight, 15 pounds **$5.95**
10K2581—PAD AND BREECHING—3¾-inch harness leather pad, stuffed bottom; iron tree, strap skirts, 1-inch shaft tugs, double bellyband. Breeching, folded body with layer, 1-inch backstrap, ⅞-inch hip straps. Shipping weight, 12 pounds **$6.95**
10K260C—COLLAR—Split rim and shoulder, chrome face, 16½-inch draft. Sizes, 17 to 22 inches. **State size.** Shipping weight, 10 pounds **$2.40**
10K259¼—Single harness without collar. Shipping wt., 40 lbs. **$18.85**
10K260¼—Single harness with collar. **State size of collar.** Shipping weight, 45 pounds **$21.25**

"Reliance" Chain Farm Harness

It Can't Be Beat at the Price

$20.95 Without Collars

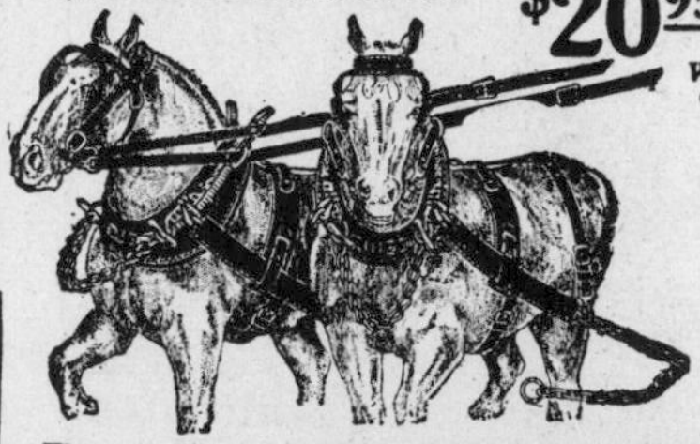

There is always much rough work to be done around a farm that requires the use of a strong harness, but often the question of cost is to be considered. In such cases the purchase of a good chain harness similar to this is advised. This "rough and ready" work harness is suitable for either horses or mules, and will be found both practical and very economical.

BRIDLES—⅞-inch cheeks. **LINES**—⅞ inch wide, 15 feet long, riveted. **HAMES**—Adjustable draft; hame straps; spread straps; 26-inch breast chains. **TRACES**—Straight link chains, No. 2 wire, 7 feet long; 24-inch leather piping, 1¼-inch bellybands. **BACKBANDS**—4 inches wide, harness leather. **HIP AND BACK STRAPS**—⅞-inch hip and back straps, riveted laps; buckle cruppers. Weight, packed for shipment, 55 pounds.

10K422¼—Harness for two horses, without collars **$20.95**
10K2505—Hip Breeching, with 1½-inch body; ⅞-inch side straps, with snaps. Shipping weight, 3½ pounds. Per set **$3.25**

A Sears Collar Assures Good Fit and Big Saving

The "Jackson" Horse Collar

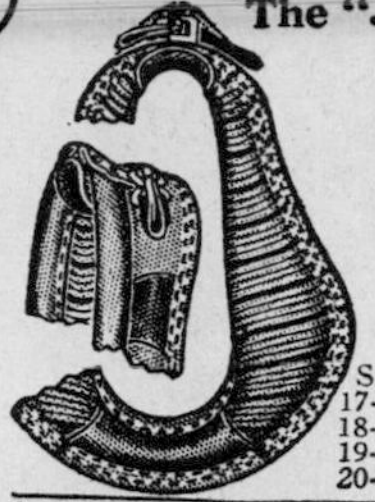

Canvas collar with heavy web rim. Half Sweeney pattern, for horses with thick necks and big shoulders; wide leather top pad, buckle top; split wear leathers at hame terrets and draft, around entire bottom of collar; cloth face, 18-inch draft. Well stuffed and splendidly made throughout. Shipping weight, 9 lbs.

10K3404¼

Size	Each	Size	Each
17-in.	$2.59	21-in.	$2.67
18-in.	2.61	22-in.	2.69
19-in.	2.63	23-in.	2.73
20-in.	2.65	24-in.	2.79

The "Lankford" Horse Collar

$1.27 AND UP

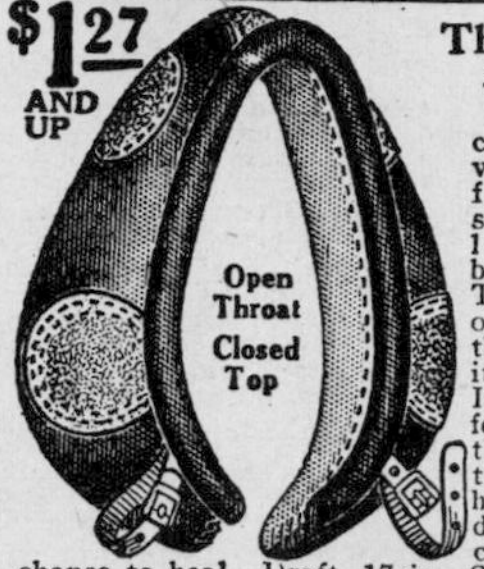

Open Throat
Closed Top

An easy wearing plow collar with brown canvas rim shoulder; duck face, cotton fiber stuffed; hame wear leathers, straps to buckle around hames. There are three grades of collars of this style that are of lower quality than those we offer. In this grade we are offering our customers the greatest value for their money. If your horse has sore shoulders, the use of this collar will give them a chance to heal. Draft, 17 in. Shpg. wt., each, 9½ lbs.

10K3469¼

Size	Each	Size	Each
17-inch	$1.27	22-inch	$1.39
18-inch	1.30	23-inch	1.42
19-inch	1.33	24-inch	1.45
20-inch	1.35	25-inch	1.48
21-inch	1.37		

"Lankford Gall Chaser." A humane plow collar similar to the above, but all white and lighter in weight. Stuffed with medicated cotton and straw. Sizes, 17 to 25 in. **State size.** Shpg. wt., 5 lbs.
10K3468¼—Each $1.15

The "Lewis" Collar

$2.25 AND UP

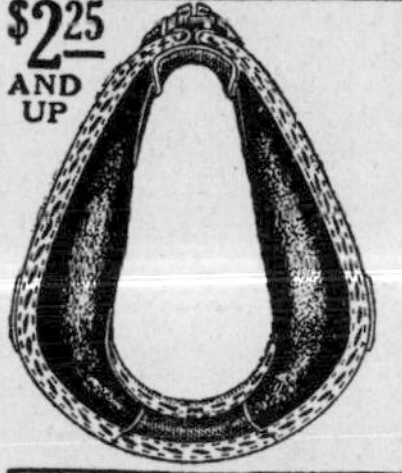

Brown split leather rim and shoulder; chrome face; thong stitched; leather top pad; buckle top; 16½-inch draft. Weight, about 7½ pounds. Shpg. wt., 9 lbs.

10K3420¼

Size	Each
17-inch	$2.25
18-inch	2.27
19-inch	2.30
20-inch	2.32
21-inch	2.35
22-inch	2.38
23-inch	2.65
24-inch	2.95

The "Stanley" Collar

$4.85 AND UP

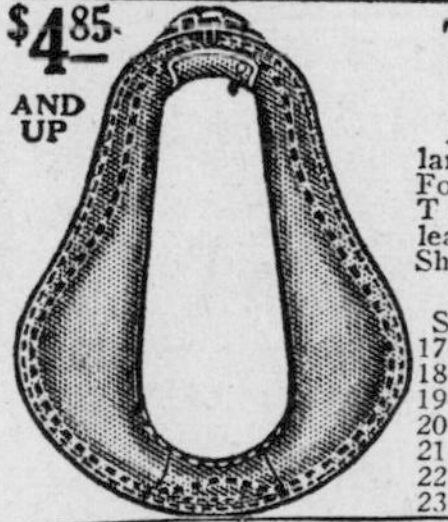

A strong, well made collar, half Sweeney pattern. For horses with thick necks. Thong sewed; buckle top, leather pad. Draft, 17 in. Shipping weight, 7¾ pounds.

10K3427¼

Size	Each
17-inch	$4.85
18-inch	4.90
19-inch	4.95
20-inch	5.10
21-inch	5.20
22-inch	5.30
23-inch	5.40

"Triplex" Felted Sweat Pad

49c AND UP

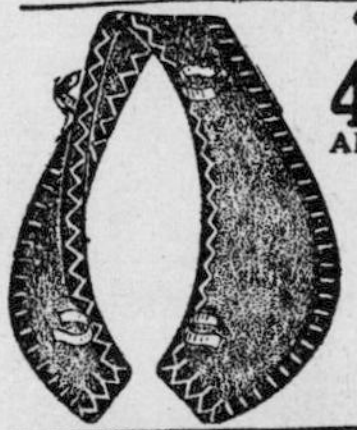

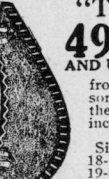

Picked and felted pad. Prevents collar from chafing the horse. Absorbs the moisture and keeps the shoulder cool. Draft, 10 inches. Shpg. wt., 1½ lbs.

10K3677

Size	Each	Size	Each
18-inch	49c	22-inch	53c
19-inch	50c	23-inch	54c
20-inch	51c	24-inch	55c
21-inch	52c	25-inch	56c

The Genuine "Dura" Sweat Pad

43c AND UP

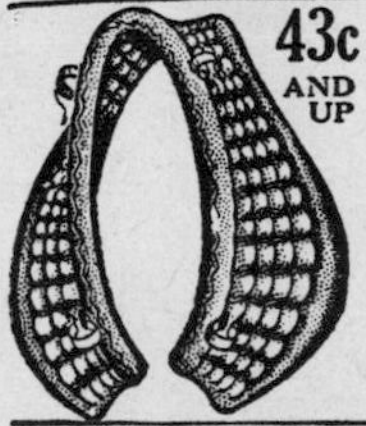

Made of gold color drilling, with red felt edge, quilted and stuffed. About 12-inch draft. Shipping weight, 3¾ pounds.

10K3693

Size	Each	Size	Each
18-inch	43c	22-inch	51c
19-inch	45c	23-inch	53c
20-inch	47c	24-inch	55c
21-inch	49c	25-inch	57c

"Irving" Curled Hair Sweat Pads

Very comfortable, springy and cool. Draft, 12 in. Shipping weight, 3¼ pounds.

10K3694

Size	Each	Size	Each	Size	Each
18-inch	$1.35	21-inch	$1.49	24-inch	$1.64
19-inch	1.39	22-inch	1.54	25-inch	1.69
20-inch	1.44	23-inch	1.59		

"Fitzall" Adjustable Horse Collar

THE CHAMPION OF ALL

A Good Thing Is Often Imitated but Seldom Equaled

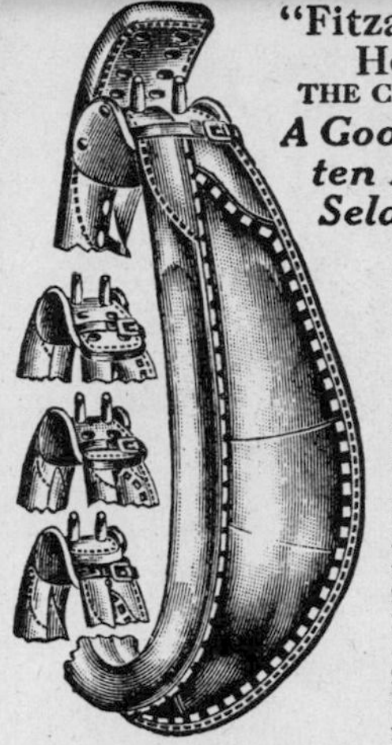

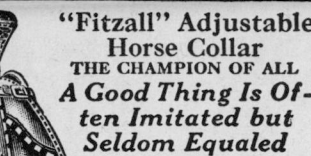

"Fitzall" collars are good collars and they are made to meet the changing conditions of horses' shoulders caused by alternate seasons of light and heavy work. With a "Fitzall" collar these changes can be met and the shoulders properly fitted at all times. We have sold thousands of these collars and have abundant faith in them, due to the many letters of praise received from our customers; so we do not hesitate to recommend them as the ideal horse collars to use. It is not only humane but good business to provide the best possible collar for your horse which serves you so well.

These collars are made of heavy, firm collar leather, thong stitched; the top of the collar is not stuffed, but stiffened by several layers of leather stitched together; the large draft is well stuffed and shaped to fit the hollow of the neck snugly and comfortably. The top of the collar is unstuffed and flexible and has four pairs of adjusting holes on each side. You **adjust the steel pegs in the holes on both sides,** thereby lengthening or shortening the collar without changing the width at the top. This adjusting is easily and quickly done, and affords a practical method of changing the size of a collar so that it will always fit properly. Each collar can be adjusted to four different sizes. The smooth leather pad at the top fits the top of the neck, reduces friction and prevents binding. The "Fitzall" Horse Collars are made in three grades. Comparison of prices will show that the cost of these collars is very little higher than ordinary one-size collars of equal quality.

Order your "Fitzall" today, remember the guarantee of the World's Largest Store assures you absolute satisfaction so that you run no risk in making your purchase.

10K3431¼—Made with split leather shoulder and rim; russet face, well stuffed; 17-inch draft. Shipping weight, 9 pounds.

Size Adjustable From	Each	Size Adjustable From	Each
17 to 20 inches	$5.45	20 to 23 inches	$5.85
18 to 21 inches	5.55	21 to 24 inches	6.00
19 to 22 inches	5.70	22 to 25 inches	6.15

10K3432¼—Made with black collar leather shoulder, kip rim; russet face; draft, 17 in. Shpg. wt., 9½ lbs.

Size Adjustable From	Each	Size Adjustable From	Each
17 to 20 inches	$5.95	20 to 23 inches	$6.35
18 to 21 inches	6.15	21 to 24 inches	6.40
19 to 22 inches	6.25	22 to 25 inches	6.55

10K3433¼—Made of all russet collar leather; draft, 17 inches. Shipping weight, 10 pounds.

Size Adjustable From	Each	Size Adjustable From	Each
17 to 20 inches	$6.50	20 to 23 inches	$6.80
18 to 21 inches	6.55	21 to 24 inches	6.95
19 to 22 inches	6.70	22 to 25 inches	7.15

Extra leather top pads for "Fitzall" Collars. Shipping weight, ¾ pound.
10K3601—Each $1.00

How to Measure

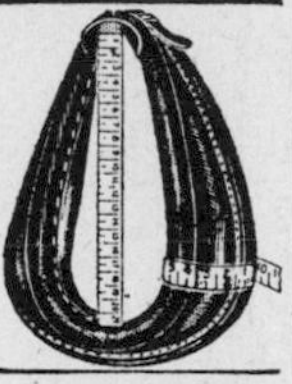

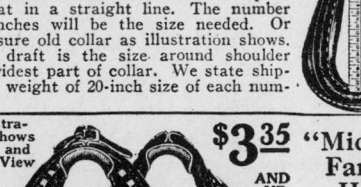

Measure horse's neck from top to throat in a straight line. The number of inches will be the size needed. Or measure old collar as illustration shows. The draft is the size around shoulder at widest part of collar. We state shipping weight of 20-inch size of each number.

"Mid-West Farms" Horse Collar

$3.35 AND UP

Illustration Shows Face and Back View

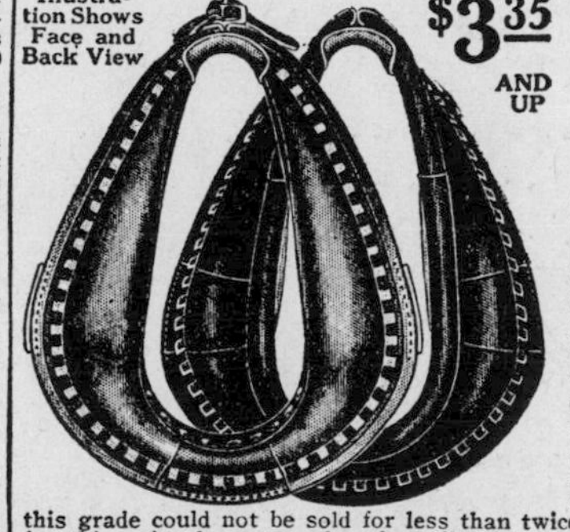

Examination of the material and workmanship of this collar will surely please and satisfy the most critical that it is one of the best low priced leather collars you can buy. Split leather is used at the rim and shoulder, enabling us to make so low a price. A grain leather collar of this grade could not be sold for less than twice the price we ask for this. At the outer edge the collar is ribbon thong stitched; the middle seam is also thong sewed and the throat built up full and stuffed; open top fitted with a heavy sole leather top pad; the draft is 16½ in. Weight, about 7½ lbs. Shpg. wt., 9 lbs.

10K3428¼

Size	Each	Size	Each
17-inch	$3.35	21-inch	$3.55
18-inch	3.40	22-inch	3.60
19-inch	3.45	23-inch	3.75
20-inch	3.50	24-inch	4.15

The "Gladstone" Collar

$4.15 AND UP

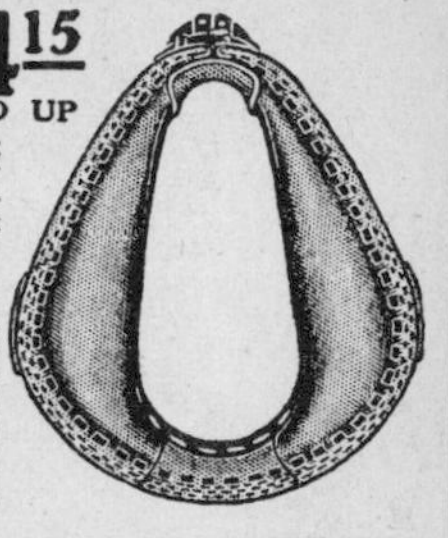

Black collar leather shoulder and rim with well stuffed russet face; thong stitched. middle seam and outer edge; pieced shoulder; leather top pad; buckle top; 16½-inch draft. Weight, about 8 lbs. Shpg. wt., 9½ lbs.

10K3425¼

Size	Each
17-inch	$4.15
18-inch	4.20
19-inch	4.30
20-inch	4.40
21-inch	4.50
22-inch	4.60
23-inch	4.75
24-inch	4.95

Drayman's Special Horse Collars

$7.25 AND UP

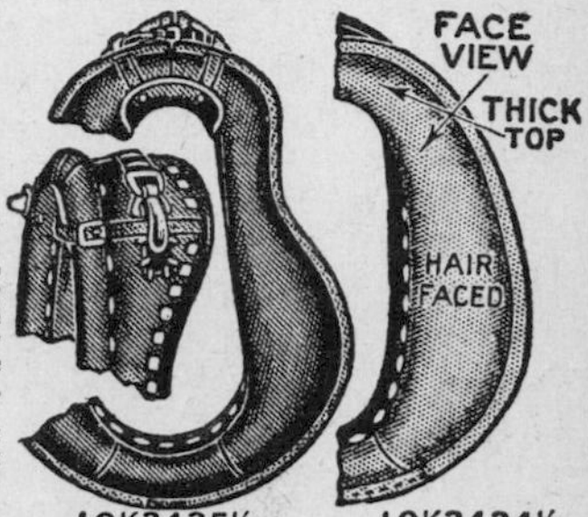

FACE VIEW
THICK TOP
HAIR FACED

All black kip leather, Concord style, with heavy rim and shoulder; Irish top finish; thong middle seam; hair face; large top cap, strapped on; single patent fastener at top; draft, about 18½ in. Shipping wt., 13 lbs.

10K3435¼ Half Sweeney — **10K3434¼** Straight Pattern

Size	Each	Size	Each
18-inch	$7.25	22-inch	$7.75
19-inch	7.35	23-inch	7.85
20-inch	7.50	24-inch	7.95
21-inch	7.65		

The "Weston" Horse Collar

$1.95 AND UP

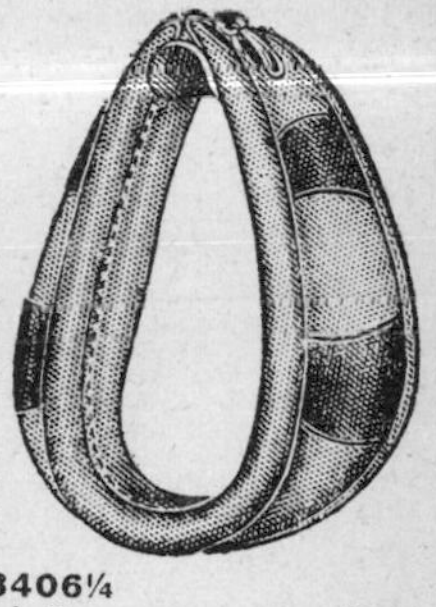

Heavy canvas collar with web rim; split wear leathers at draft and hame terrets; well stuffed shoulder and face; leather top, cap; patent fastener at top, riveted on; draft, about 17½ inches. Shipping weight, 7½ pounds.

10K3406¼

Size	Each	Size	Each
17-inch	$1.95	21-inch	$2.05
18-inch	1.97	22-inch	2.10
19-inch	1.99	23-inch	2.15
20-inch	2.00	24-inch	2.20

"Watson" Team Collar

$5.95 AND UP

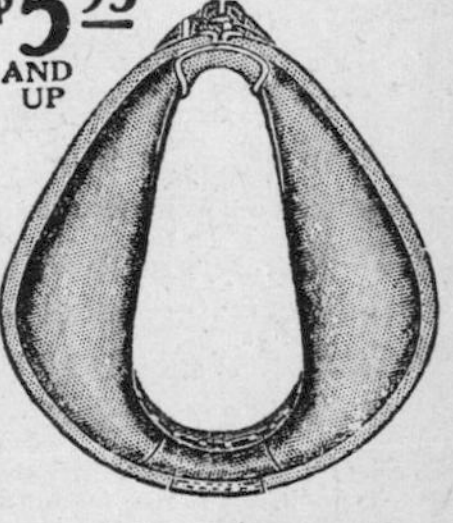

Heavy russet grain leather team collar; full rim and shoulder; ribbon thong stitched; heavy sole leather top pad; buckle top; 18-in. draft; smooth, well stuffed face. An extra good collar priced extra low. Shipping weight, 13 lbs.

10K3440¼

Size	Each
18-inch	$5.95
19-inch	6.00
20-inch	6.05
21-inch	6.10
22-inch	6.15

Genuine Irish Case Collar

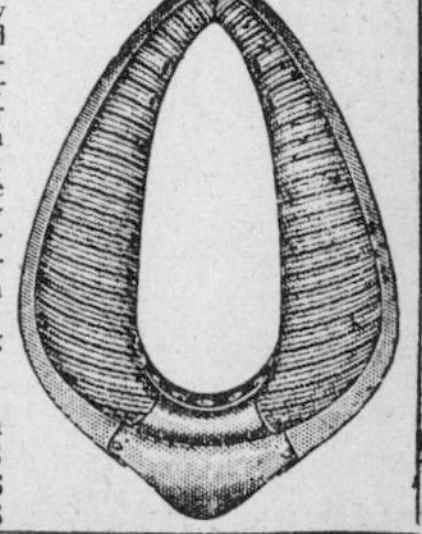

Special heavy draft dray collar with full rim and shoulder of selected kip collar leather; wide flange or fender and large leather apron; thong stitched; open top with single fastener. Heavy hair stuffed face covered with XX quality blue and white tick securely sewed onto a special liner and tufted at top; 19-inch draft.

10K3455¼ — Shipping weight, 13 pounds.

Size, In.	Each	Size, In.	Each
18	$7.95	22	$8.35
19	8.05	23	8.65
20	8.15	24	8.95
21	8.25		

Dependable Saddles ~ Prices Low ~

Only the World's Largest Store Can Make Such Low Prices

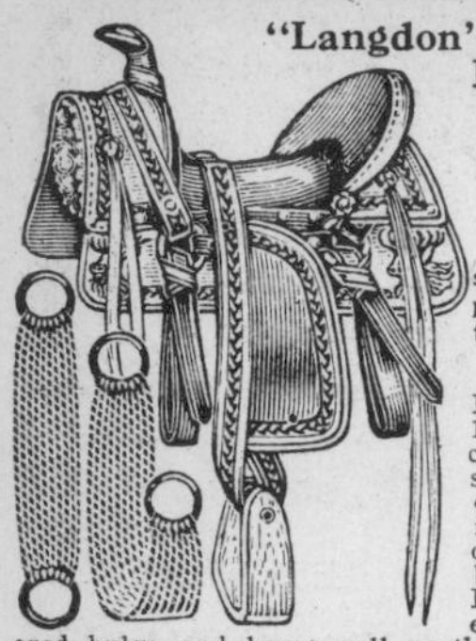

"Langdon" Low Priced Farm Saddle

$15.75

Wise economy should induce the purchase of one of these saddles.

LEATHER—Russet. **TREE**—13½ in. Canvas covered Steel fork sheepskin wool covered bars, making the saddle easy on the horse's back. **SEAT**—Half leather covered bulge and horn; leather covered; roll cantle. **SKIRTS**—20¼ inches long. **RIGGING**—Double cinch rigged, with 1-inch tie straps, to tie; 4-inch cinches. **STIRRUP STRAPS**—1¾ inches wide, full length to buckle; fenders, 6 inches wide, 13 inches long, attached; 3-inch Texas bolt stirrups. Weight of saddle, about 14 pounds.

Packed for shipment, 20 pounds.

10K1310¼..........................**$15.75**

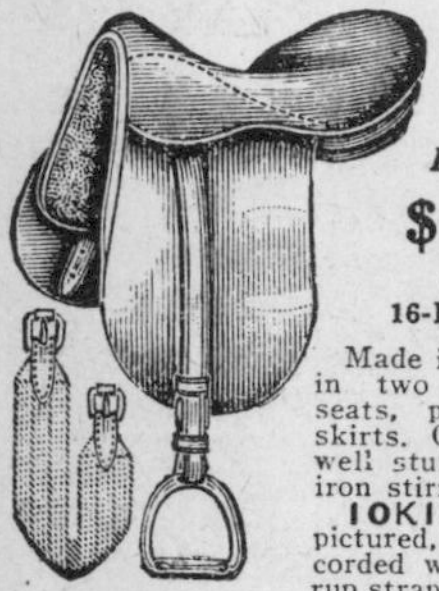

"National Park" English Style Saddles

For Men and Women.

$11.85

16-Inch Tree

Made in russet leather only, in two sizes. Kip leather seats, pigskin impression skirts. Cotton serge covered, well stuffed pad; web girths, iron stirrups.

10K1208¼—Saddle, as pictured, with 16-inch tree, corded web girth, 1-inch stirrup straps. Shipping weight, 15 pounds..**$11.85**

10K1209¼—Smaller saddle, with 15-inch tree, plain web girth, ⅞-inch stirrup straps. Shipping weight, 10 pounds.....**$8.75**

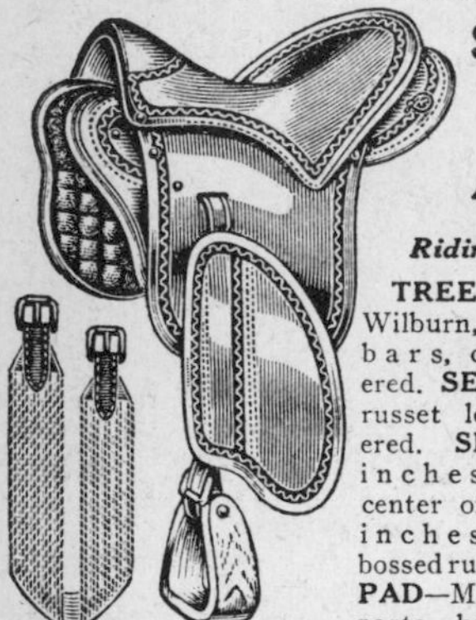

"Buna Vista" Saddle

$17.25

These Saddles Are Famous for Their Riding Comfort

TREE — 16½-inch Wilburn, extended bars, canvas covered. **SEAT**—Large, russet leather covered. **SKIRTS** — 17 inches long from center of seat, 11½ inches wide, embossed russet leather. **PAD**—Made in two parts, hair stuffed, serge covered, full stitched. **STIRRUP STRAPS**—1 inch wide with heavy piped fenders, 9½x14 inches. 4-inch wood stirrups and cord girth. Weight, about 16 pounds. Shipping weight, 22 pounds.

10K1227¼..........................**$17.25**

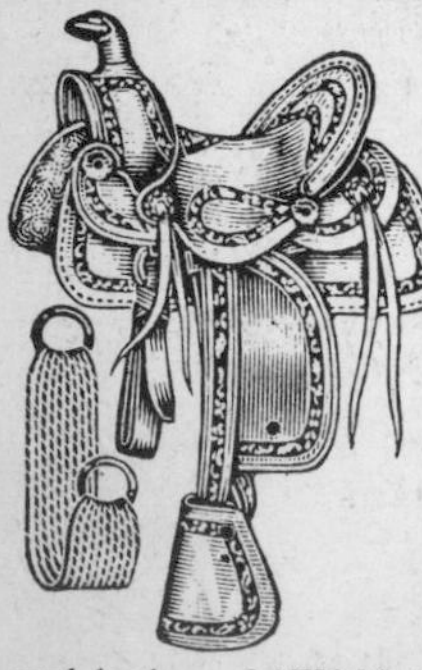

A Reliable Pony Stock Saddle

A saddle that everyred blooded boy or girl would like to own.

$16.65

TREE — 12-inch, Omaha, canvas covered, with steel fork. **SEAT**—Full; leather jockeys, horn and fork full leather covered. **CANTLE**—Bound, front lined and stitched. **HORN** — Covered and stitched, with cap. **SKIRTS**—Round corners and felt lined, good leather. **LATIGOS**—1¼-in. Single leather. **CINCH**—4-inch, hard hair. **STIRRUP STRAPS**—1¼-inch, to buckle. **STIRRUPS**—2½-inch hooded. Weight, packed for shipment, 16 lbs.

10K1219¼..........................**$16.65**

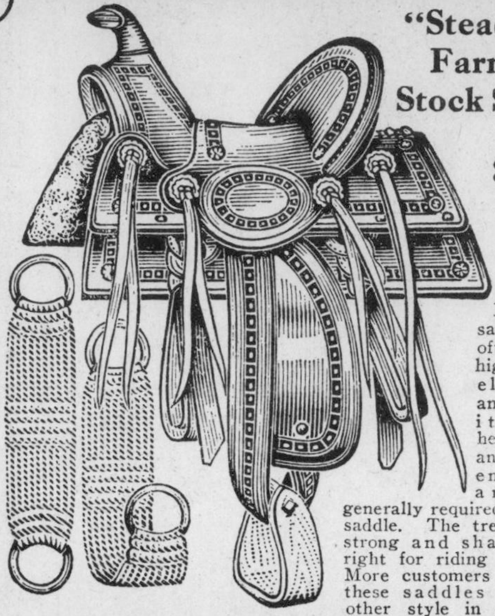

"Steadfast" Farm or Stock Saddle

$17.25

Here is a saddle that often sells as high as $25.00 elsewhere, and it's worth it, being heavy enough and strong enough for any work generally required of a farm saddle. The tree is extra strong and shaped just right for riding comfort. More customers are using these saddles than any other style in our entire line.

LEATHER—Fine russet, fancy stamped border. **TREE**—13½ inches, leather covered horn, steel fork. **SEAT**—Full; seat, jockey and cantle in one piece; leather bound cantle. **SKIRTS**—Wool lined, 20 inches long. **CINCHES**—4-inch cotton, 1-inch tie straps. **STIRRUP STRAPS**—1½ inches wide to buckle, with fenders, (7x13 inches) attached. Weight, about 18 pounds. Shipping weight, 24 pounds.

10K1485¼—Each..........................**$17.25**

"Fletcher" Stock Saddle

$35.95 **15-Inch Double Cinch**

LEATHER—Extra fine quality, bark tanned, russet saddle skirting, fancy stamped. **TREE**—15 or 16-inch, hide covered 14-inch bulge, steel fork and horn, leather covered. **SKIRTS**—13x26 inches, felt lined. **STIRRUP STRAPS**—3 inches wide, ox bow stirrups, fenders; 8x15 inches. **CINCHES**—15-strand, mixed wool and hair, double or single. **LATIGO STRAPS**—1½ inches wide on the near side and 1¾ inches on the off side. Weight, about 28 pounds. Shipping weight, 36 pounds.

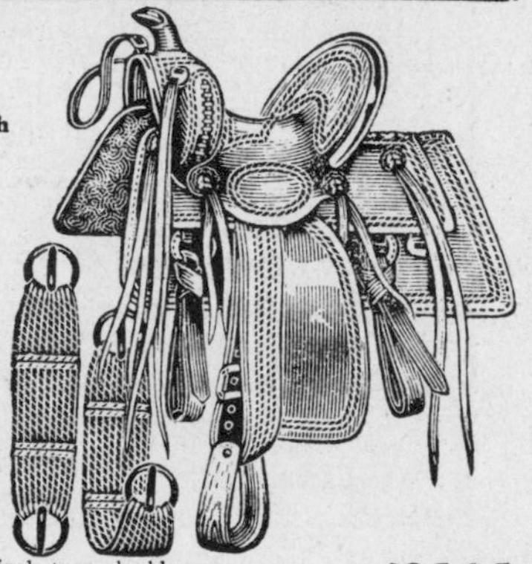

10K1465¼—With 15-inch tree, double cinch..........................**$35.95**
10K1466¼—With 16-inch tree, double cinch..........................**$36.00**
10K1467¼—With 15-inch tree, single cinch..........................**35.85**
10K1468¼—With 16-inch tree, single cinch..........................**35.75**

The "Westridge" Stock Saddle

$37.95 **Double Cinch**

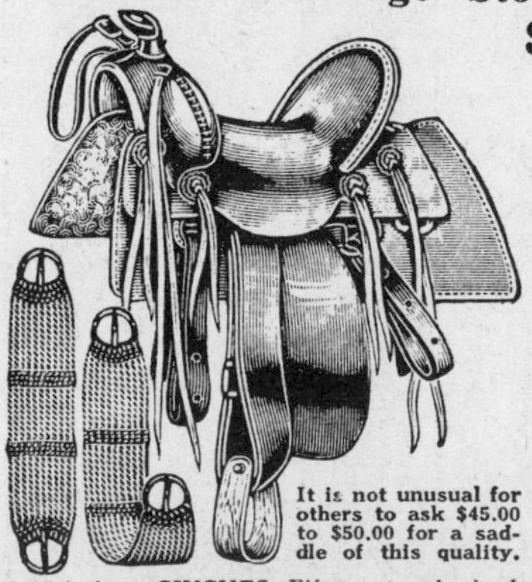

Double Cinch Rigged

Those who prefer a plain, unstamped saddle will be very highly pleased with the quality and construction of this one. Indeed, it is one of the best saddles for general riding purposes that we have ever offered at so low a price, and we recommend its purchase very highly.

LEATHER—Extra fine quality bark tanned, russet saddle skirting, plain, no stamping. **TREE**—15-inch hide covered, 14-inch bulge, steel fork and horn. **SKIRTS**—13 inches wide, 26 inches long, wool lined, round corners. **STIRRUP STRAPS**—3 inches wide, ox bow stirrups; fenders, 8x15 inches. **CINCHES**—Fifteen-strand mixed wool and hair, with buckle tongue. **LATIGO STRAPS**—1½ inches wide on near side, 1¾ inches on off side. Weight, 28 pounds; shipping weight, 36 pounds.

It is not unusual for others to ask $45.00 to $50.00 for a saddle of this quality.

10K1463¼—Double Cinch Rigged..........................**$37.95**
10K1464¼—Single Cinch Rigged, round skirts..........................**$37.75**

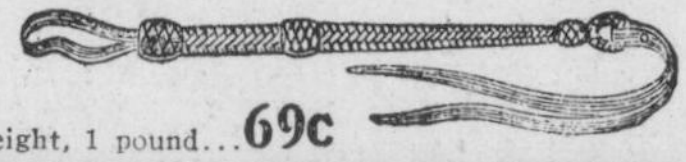

Mexican Quirt. Eight-plait, braided russet leather body, Iron spike. Full length, about 34 inches.

10K6270—Shipping weight, 1 pound...**69c**

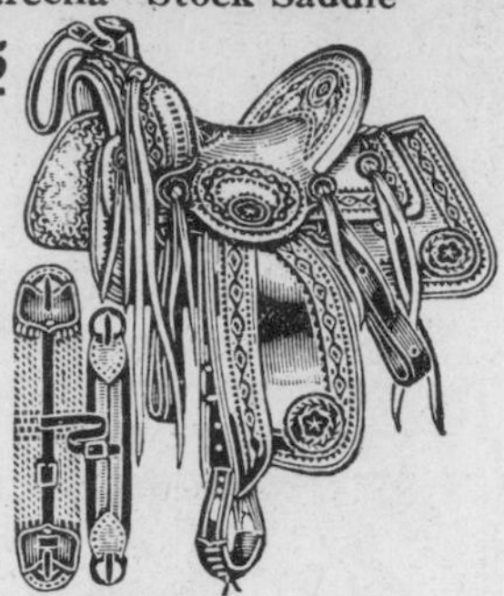

"Marcella" Stock Saddle

$49.95

15-Inch Tree

TREE—15 or 16-inch, hide covered steel fork, leather covered horn; 16-inch bulge. **SEAT**—Full; leather covered, with seat, jockey and cantle in one piece; bound cantle. **SKIRTS**—14x28 inches, wool lined; or short, round skirts. **RIGGING**—Double cinch rigged, with 6-inch cord front cinch and 4-inch web rear cinch. **STIRRUP STRAPS**—3 inches wide buckled, with fenders 9 inches wide and 16½ inches long; ox bow stirrups, brass bound. **LATIGO STRAPS**—1½ inches wide on near side, 1¾ inches wide on off side.

10K1374¼—With 15-in. tree. Weight, about 34 pounds. Shipping weight, 42 pounds..........................**$49.95**

10K1377¼—With 16-in. tree. Weight, about 36 pounds. Shipping weight, 44 pounds..........................**$49.98**

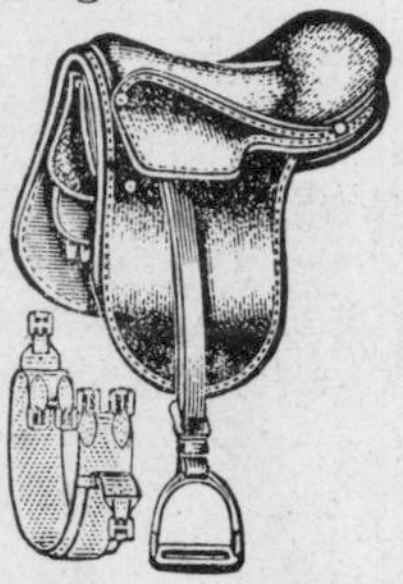

English Riding Saddle

The style preferred by riding schools and clubs, for the use of men or women. Extensively used on the bridle paths of town and city. **TREE**—18-inch, with soft leather covered pad. Genuine pigskin seat; with pigskin impression jockey. **SKIRTS**—11x20 inches, hogskin impression. **CINCHES**—Double, Fitzwilliam style, white cotton serge; inside, 5 inches wide; outside, 3 inches wide. **STIRRUP STRAP**—1⅛ inches wide, with nickel plated iron stirrups. Weight of saddle, about 13½ lbs. Shipping weight, 19½ lbs.

10K1210¼
$35.95

10K1211¼—Saddle, similar to 10K1210¼ but imported from England. Shipping weight, 21 pounds ...**$49.75**

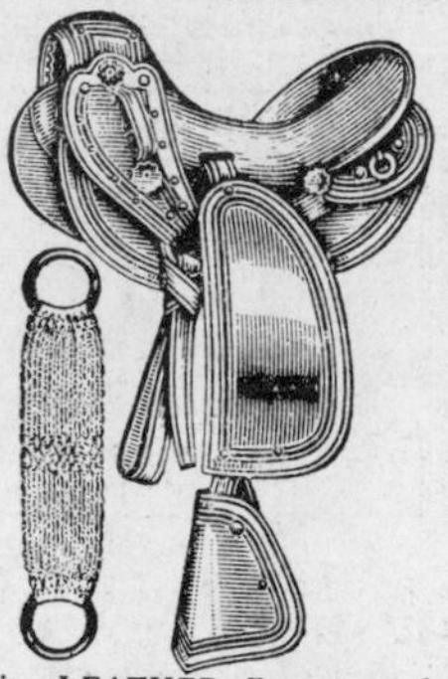

"Roslyn" Single Rigged Saddle

$11.50

TREE—13-inch, canvas covered, muley style. **SEAT**—Full leather covered. **STIRRUP STRAPS** — 1⅛ inches wide, to buckle, with fenders, 7x14 inches. **STIRRUPS**—3 inch, wood, leather hooded. **CINCH** — 4 inches wide, with rings. **LATIGO STRAPS**—1⅛ inches wide to tie. **LEATHER**—Russet, good quality embossed border. Flat handhold on near side. Weight, about 11 pounds; packed for shipment, 17 pounds.

10K1285¼..........................**$11.50**

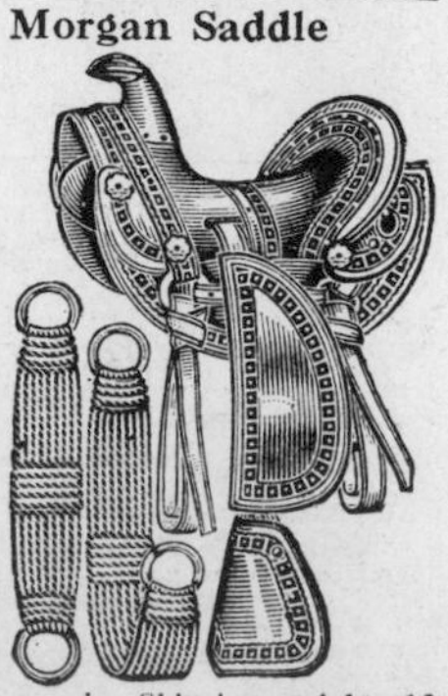

"Oliver" Morgan Saddle

Russet Leather For Boys and Girls

$11.45

Single Cinch

TREE—12-inch canvas covered, Morgan style, leather covered round horn. **SEAT** — Half leather covered, round skirts. **STIRRUP STRAPS**—1 inch wide, full length, to buckle; fenders, 6x13 inches, attached; 3-inch wood stirrups, leather hooded. **RIGGING** — Double or single cinch rigged; corded cinches, with rings; 1-inch tie straps. Weight, about 10½ pounds. Shipping weight, 16 pounds.

10K1215¼—With single cinch..**$11.45**
10K1217¼—With double cinch....**$12.45**

Riding Equipment That Satisfies

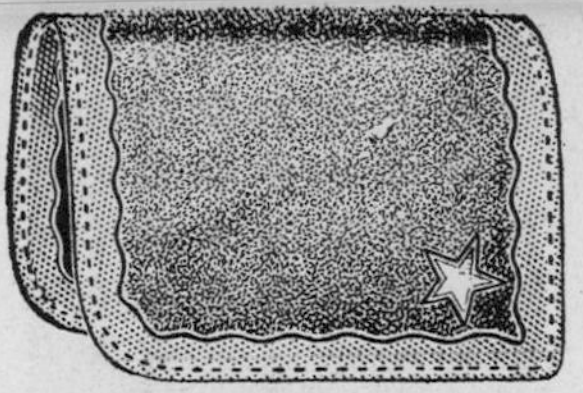

Gray Felt Saddle Blanket

$1.10

Scalloped border, edges trimmed with assorted color braid. Size, 24 inches long, 16 inches wide from center. Shpg. wt., 1 lb.
10K5810—Each **$1.10**
10K5811—Pony size, 24 inches long, 10 inches wide from center. Each .... **.89**

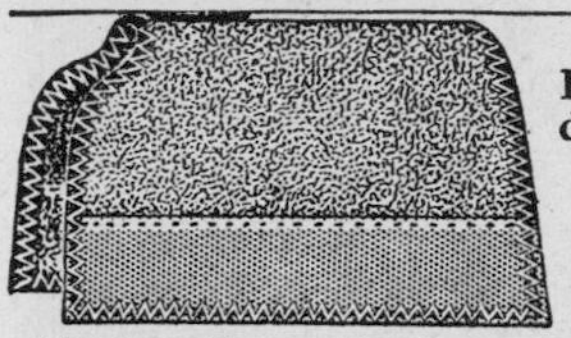

"Triplex" Fabric Saddle Blanket

$1.95

Shaped Saddle Blanket

"Triplex" fabric saddle blankets consist of wool, hair and cotton, picked and felted, and makes a serviceable, well-wearing pad. Keeps the back cool.
10K5841—Plain Cut Saddle Blanket. Size 26x35 inches. Shpg. wt., 1 pound. Each **$1.55**
10K5842—Shaped Saddle Blanket. Size 32x36 inches. Shipping weight, 1½ pounds. Each **$1.95**

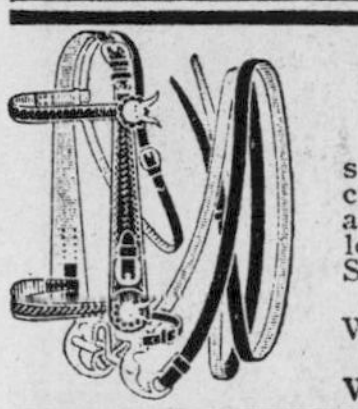

Great Western Cowboy Bridle

Russet leather, pointed and stamped cheeks, adjustable crown, nickel plated buckles and ornaments. Reins, 6 feet long, ⅞ inch wide; noseband. Shipping weight, 3½ pounds.
10K1781 Without bit **$4.25**
10K1782 With bit **4.75**

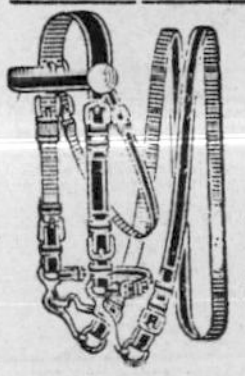

English Style Riding Bridle

Russet leather, creased edges, wide crown, ⅞-inch cheeks with small leather loops, ⅝-inch throatlatch, ½-inch curb strap, port bit, 6-foot rein, center laced; nickel plated trimmed. Shipping weight, 3 lbs.
10K1744 .... **$2.65**

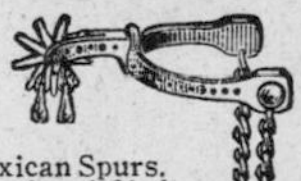

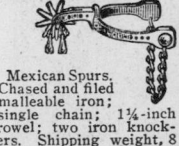

Mexican Spurs. Chased and filed malleable iron; single chain; 1¼-inch rowel; two iron knockers. Shipping weight, 8 ounces.
10K8022 Per pair **89c**

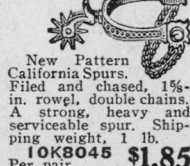

New Pattern California Spurs. Filed and chased, 1⅝-in. rowel, double chains. A strong, heavy and serviceable spur. Shipping weight, 1 lb.
10K8045 Per pair **$1.85**

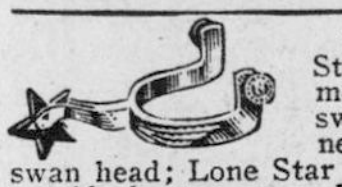

Medium Weight Hand Forged Steel Spurs. ⅝-inch band ornamented with sterling silver swan's wing; 2¼-inch swan neck shank with gold plated swan head; Lone Star ornamented rowel, 1⅜ inches; outside button on each spur has silver plated ornament. Shipping weight, 1 pound.
10K8053—Per pair **$3.75**

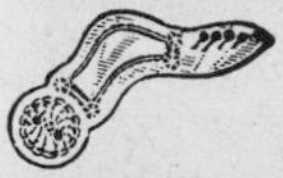

"Irwin" Russet Leather Shaped Spur Straps. Cut to fit over the instep. Can be used on any button spur. Shipping weight, 6 ounces.
10K8017 Per pair **36c**

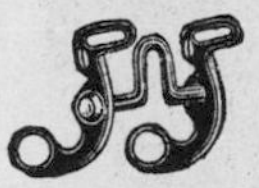

Fine Blued Mexican Curb Bit. Short port on mouth bar without roller. Shpg. wt., 1 lb.
10K8140 .... **45c**
Same as 10K8140, but with roller in mouth bar. Shipping weight, 1 pound.
10K8141 .... **50c**

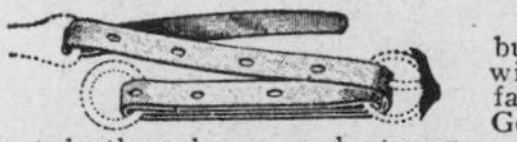

Latigo straps for buckle cinch ring with lace strings to fasten, for near side. Good quality russet leather, heavy and strong.
10K3036—Latigoes about 5½ feet long.
Width 1½ in. Shpg. wt., ¾ lb. Each **75c**
Width 2 in. Shpg. wt., 1 lb. Each **98c**
Latigo straps for tie cinch ring, with lace strings to fasten. Made of russet skirting leather or pliable latigo leather.
10K3043—Skirting leather latigo, 1¼ in. wide, 5 ft. long. Shpg. wt., ¾ lb. Each **57c**
10K3047—Pliable latigo leather, 1½ in. wide, abt. 5½ ft. long. Shpg. wt., ¾ lb. Ea. **55c**

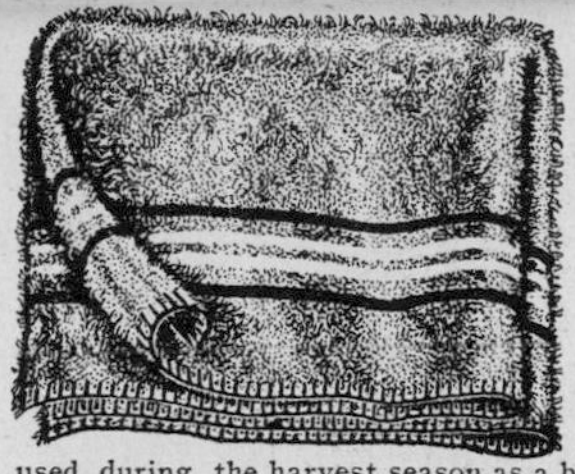

Northwest Combination Folded Saddle Blanket

$1.85

Made with the popular gray body and an attractive contrasting border. A saddle blanket of fine quality, well made and of good appearance which can also be used during the harvest season as a bunk blanket or camping blanket.
10K5820—Size, 60x80 inches. Weight, about 3 pounds. Shipping weight, 4 pounds. Each **$1.85**

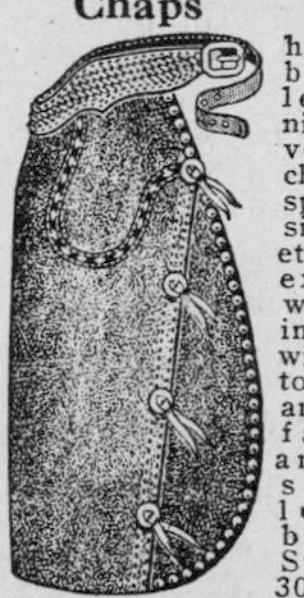

"Cheyenne" Riding Chaps

Made of heavy brown leather, nickel silver conchas and spots, inside pockets, wide extended wings, 25-inch thigh, wide bottoms, snap and ring fastener and heavy stamped leather belt. Sizes, 28, 30, 32 and 34 inches leg measurement at inseam. **State size.** Shipping weight, 9 pounds.
10K3074 Per pair **$19.95**

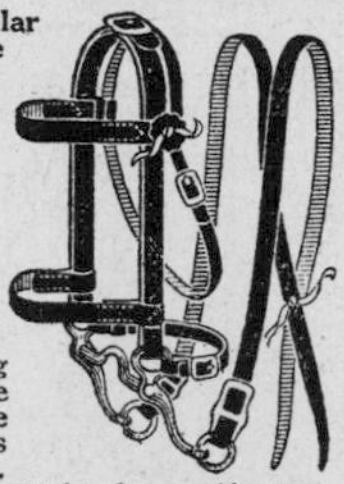

Russet Leather Bridle

Our Most Popular Riding Bridle

The splendid quality of this bridle will show after long service. This is your assurance of a genuine bargain.

Light weight but strong western style bridle for the use of farmers and other riders. Well tanned russet leather, uniformly cut, carefully finished. Adjusts to fit large or small horses; ¾-inch double headstall to buckle on top; noseband; ¾-inch reins, 6 feet long, to loop in bit; port bit and curb strap. Shpg. wt., 3 lbs.
10K1754 .... **$1.89**

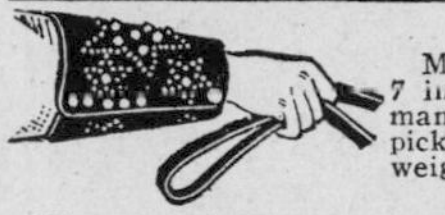

Riding Cuffs

Made of good leather, 7 inches long. Used by many farmers when picking corn. Shipping weight, 1 pound.

Five-star design; four small stars, one large; snap fastening.
10K3180—Black. Per pair **$2.48**
10K3191—Russet. Per pair **2.48**

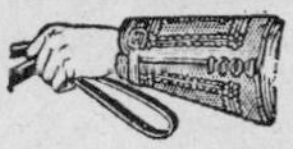

Leather, creased. Rawhide laced top. Buckle and billet at wrist.
10K3174—Russet. Per pair **$1.49**
10K3179—Black. Per pair **1.49**

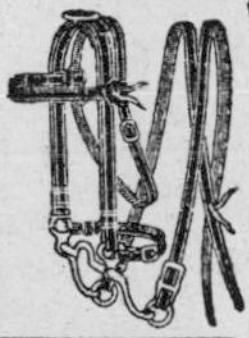

Shetland Pony Bridles

Pony bridle, as pictured. Russet leather only. ⅝-inch cheeks, double headstall. 4½-foot reins; port bit. Shpg. wt., 2½ lbs.
10K1814 .... **$1.65**
Russet or black leather pony bridles, ⅝-inch bridle with reins 4 feet long, nickel plated buckles, snaffle bit. **Not illustrated.** Shpg. wt., 2½ lbs.
10K1812—Russet. Each **$1.65**
10K1813—Black. Each **1.65**

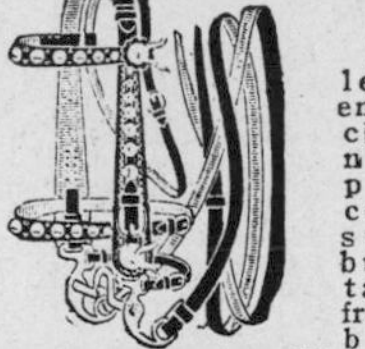

"Sioux" Cowboy Riding Bridles

Russet leather, embossed cheeks, nickel plated conchas, swedge buckles, tapered front, sunburst spots; 1-in. reins, 6½ feet long. Shipping weight, 4 lbs.
10K1779 Without bit **$5.15**
10K1780 With bit **5.60**

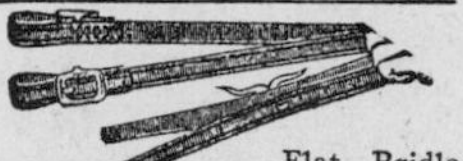

Flat Bridle Reins with buckle and billet ends, ⅞-inch medium weight russet leather, 7 feet long. Shipping weight, 1 pound.
10K1712—Pair **$1.05**

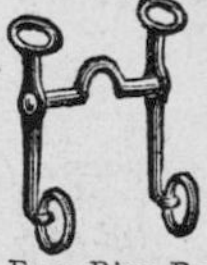

Port Bit. Malleable iron. Straight posts, low port. One of the most popular riding bridle bits made. Shipping weight, ¾ pound.
10K8272 .... **28c**
Nickel Plated Four-Ring Port Bit. For double rein riding bridles. Shipping weight, 1 pound.
10K8184 .... **$1.25**

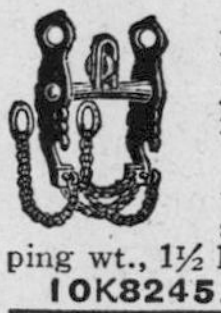

California Heavy Cowboy Bit. Patent port, complete with rein chains and roller. A very heavy and strong bit. Shipping wt., 1½ lbs.
10K8245 .... **$1.25**

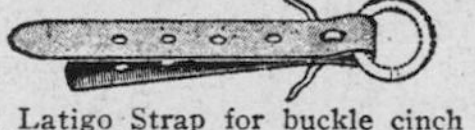

Latigo Strap for buckle cinch ring, with lace strings to fasten. Russet leather. For off side. Two in. wide, 36 in. long doubled (18 in. long). Shipping weight, ¾ pound.
10K3045—Each **75c**

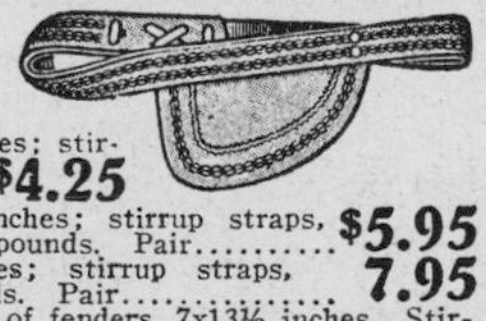

Fenders and Stirrup Leathers. Russet leather, embossed border; stirrup straps, 5 feet 6 inches long; lace strings. The grade used on our heavy stock saddles.
10K3048—Fenders, 7x13½ inches; stirrup straps, 2 inches. Shipping weight, 3½ pounds. Pair **$4.25**
10K3049—Fenders, 7½x14½ inches; stirrup straps, 2½ inches. Shipping weight, 4¼ pounds. Pair **$5.95**
10K3051—Fenders, 9x16 inches; stirrup straps, 3 inches. Shipping weight, 6 pounds. Pair **7.95**
Fenders and Stirrup Straps. Size of fenders, 7x13½ inches. Stirrup straps, 1½ inches wide, 5 feet 4 inches long, to buckle. Russet leather. Embossed border. Shipping weight, 2¼ pounds.
10K3037—Per pair **$3.25**

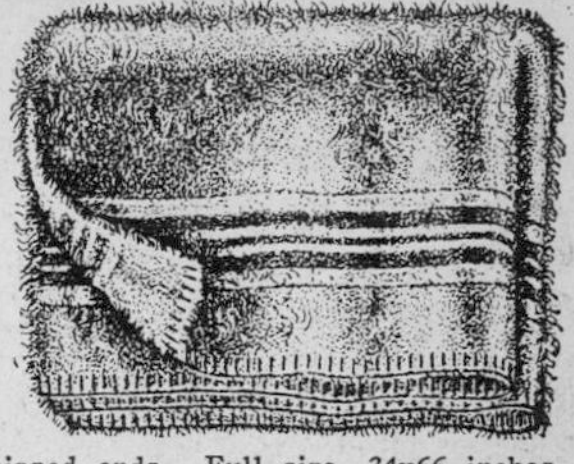

Folded Saddle Blanket

$1.65

Manufactured from a mixture of wool, hair and cotton; soft and absorbent. Gray body with striped headings. Whipped ends. Full size, 34x66 inches. When folded for use under saddle it measures 34x33 inches. Weight, about 2½ pounds. Shipping weight, 3 pounds.
10K5818—Each **$1.65**

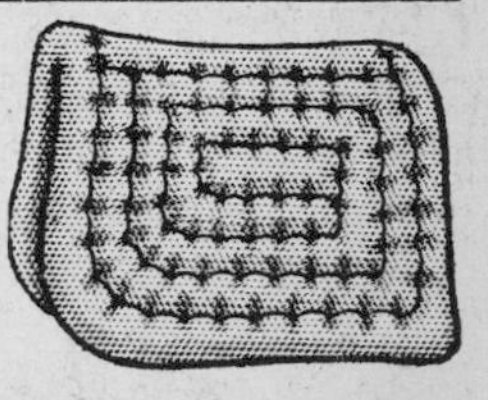

Quilted Saddle Blanket

80c

Drill covered, composite stuffing. Will protect the back and keep horse comfortable. Size, 24x30 inches made up. Shipping weight, 4¾ pounds.
10K5850—Each **80c**

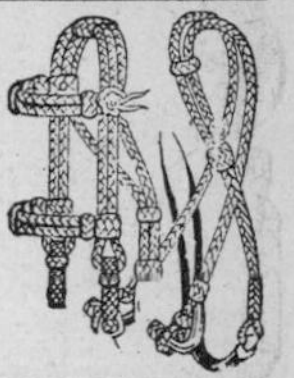

Braided Leather Bridle

Fancy leather braided Western Riding Bridle of brown and white leather. Made with double headstall, front and noseband, overhead throatlatch and 7-foot reins with romal quirt ends; without bit. Trimmed with braided knots and leather fringe. Shipping weight, 4¼ pounds.
10K1743—Each ... **$4.25**

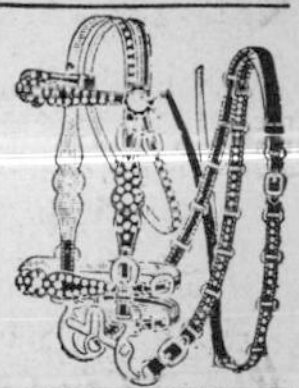

"Rocky Mountain" Riding Bridle

Russet leather. Spotted cheeks, noseband and front. Nickel plated buckles; ring, link reins, quirt ends. Bit furnished. Shipping weight, 4 pounds.
10K1778 Complete bridle **$7.85**
10K1777—Reins only. Shipping weight, 1½ pounds **$2.95**

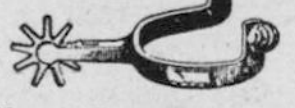

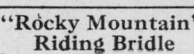

Hand Forged Steel Spurs; ½-in. band, sterling silver mounted; silver mounted buttons; 2-inch shank; 1½-inch rowel, silver mounted pin. Shipping weight, 1 pound.
10K8051 Per pair **$2.95**

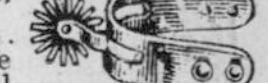

"Eureka" Spurs. Wide steel heel band, nickel plated 1⅝-inch rowel. Shipping weight, ¾ lb.
10K8009 Per pair **98c**
Spur Straps. To be used with 10K8009 Spurs. Shipping weight, 7 oz.
10K8011 Per pair **40c**

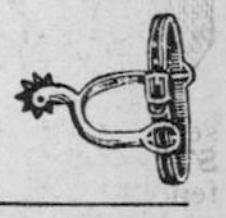

English Style Spurs

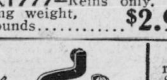

Malleable iron; XC white metal plated, with spur straps. A neat, light spur for dress wear. Shipping weight, ¾ pound.
10K8025—Per pair **$0.59**
Polished brass with steel rowel.
10K8026—Per pair **1.15**

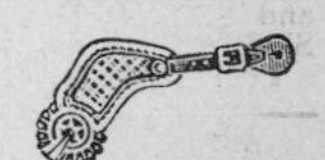

"Jasper" Russet Leather Fancy Stamped Spur Straps. Adjustable buckle and billet. For use on any button spurs. Shpg. wt., ¾ lb.
10K8029—Per pair **85c**

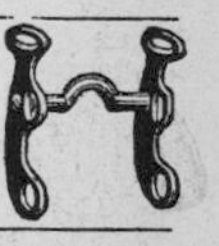

Fine Wrought Iron Mouthpiece Port Bit. Japanned finish, strong and heavy bit for hard mouthed horses or mules. Shipping weight, 1 pound.
10K8187 .... **43c**

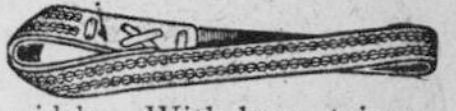

California Style Stirrup Straps, 5 feet 6 inches long and in three different widths. With lace strings. Extra heavy russet leather. For high class stock saddles.

10K3046

Size, In.	Shpg. Wt.	Per Pair
2	2¼ lbs.	$2.85
2½	3 lbs.	3.62
3	3¾ lbs.	4.75

Russet Leather Stirrup Straps for light weight saddles, 4 feet 8 inches long, with buckle. Good leather and well made. Shipping wt., 1¼ lbs.
10K3039—Per pair, 1-inch **$1.17**
Per pair, 1¼-inch **$1.47**

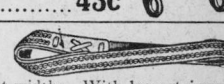

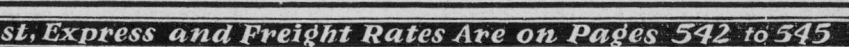

Parcel Post, Express and Freight Rates Are on Pages 542 to 545

We Serve 1,500,000 Harness Customers Annually

Manila Rope Lariats

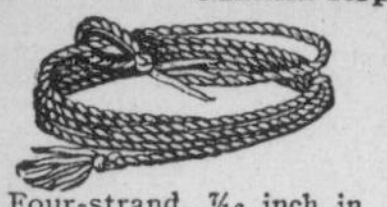

Four-strand, 7/16 inch in diameter, braided tassel, brass honda, braided loop at back end to fasten to horn of saddle.

10K3127
Length, 30 ft. Shpg. wt., 2½ lbs. Each.......... $1.55
Length, 35 ft. Shpg. wt., 3 lbs. Each.......... $1.70
Length, 40 ft. Shpg. wt., 3½ lbs. Each.......... $1.85

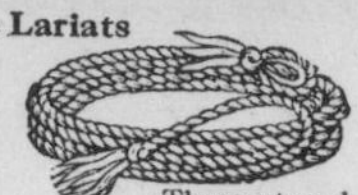

Three-strand Long Silk Fiber Manila Rope Lariat. Extra quality. 7/16 inch. Solid brass honda slips freely, braided loop at back end.

10K3128
Length, 30 ft. Shpg. wt., 2¾ lbs. Each...... $2.25
Length, 35 ft. Shpg. wt., 3¼ lbs. Each...... $2.45
Length, 40 ft. Shpg. wt., 3½ lbs. Each...... $2.75

For Lariat Rope by the foot see page 1000

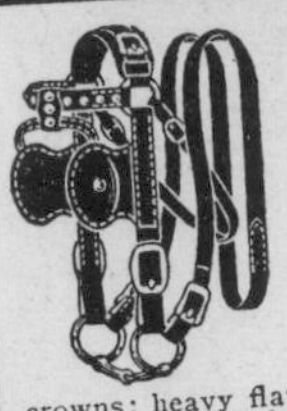

$2.99 With Sensible Blinds

Our Two Most Popular Team Bridles

Many thousands of these bridles have been sold and they always give satisfaction. We make sure that the leather going into them is good, thereby assuring reliable wearing quality. The bridles have heavy 1¼-inch stitched cheeks; folded ring crowns; heavy flat reins to throw over hames; extra strong, improved winker brace connected to front. Shipping weight, 5 pounds.

10K2071—With pigeon wing blinds. Each.......... $2.98
10K2072—With sensible (cupped) blinds. Each.......... $2.99

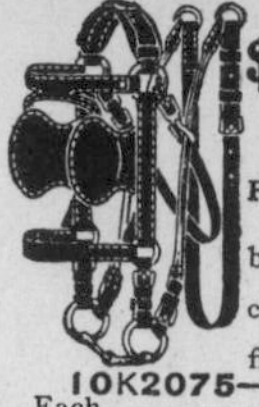

$3.75 7/8-Inch Cheeks Flat Rein

Ring Crown Bridles

Extra heavy, improved folded ring crown, very strong, and adjustable for large or small horses; double billets; short cheeks; sensible, cupped blinds; combination front and winker brace. Shipping weight, each, 6¼ pounds.

10K2060—With 7/8-in. cheeks., short flat rein. Each.......... $3.75
10K2061—With 1-inch cheeks, short flat rein. Each.......... $3.85
10K2075—With 7/8-inch cheeks, long round front rein. Each.......... $4.25
10K2076—With 1-inch cheeks, long round front rein. Each.......... $4.35

Double Cinch

For heavy stock saddles. Consists of eighteen strands hard hair in each cinch, with two bars of soft hair holding them together; leather chafes and connecting straps. Shipping weight, 4 pounds.

10K3230
Per pair.......... $3.65

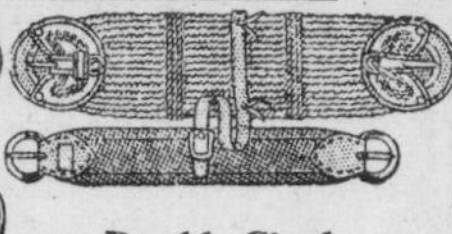

Double Cinch

For heavy stock saddles; 6-inch cotton cord front cinch with two bars connecting the strands; heavy leather shields under buckles. Rear cinch of strong belting web, 4 in. wide. Shipping wt., 4 lbs.

10K3232
Per pair.......... $2.85

For lightweight stock or farm saddles. Each cinch is made of strongly woven belting web, 3½ inches wide, leather chafes under rings; connecting straps. Shipping weight, 3 pounds.

10K3234—Double Cinch. Per pair (not illustrated).......... $1.35

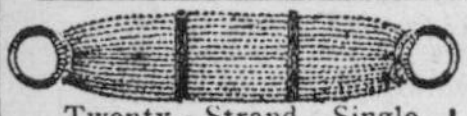

Twenty-Strand Single Cinch, made of hemp, cotton, wool and hair. Cinch is regular length and can be used on any saddle that is fitted with latigo straps to tie. Shipping wt., 1¾ lbs.

10K3240
Each, 75c

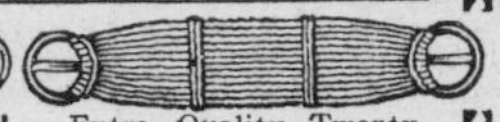

Extra Quality Twenty-Strand Four-Cord Hair Single Cinch with buckle tongues. Two bars hold strands together. Shpg. wt., 1¾ lbs.

10K3245
Each, $1.25

Texas Style Cotton Girth

Twenty-Strand Soft Texas Cotton Girth. No 1 grade with buckle tongues. Shipping weight, 1¼ pounds.

10K3239
Each (not illustrated) 50c

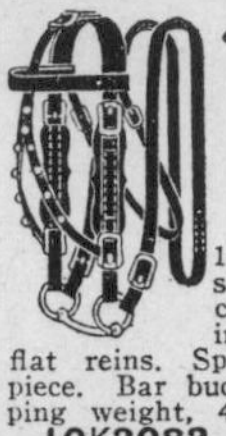

"Alonzo" Team Bridle

$1.98

Open, 1¼-inch sewed cheeks, 1-inch short flat reins. Spotted facepiece. Bar buckles. Shipping weight, 4¼ pounds.

10K2082
Each.......... $1.98

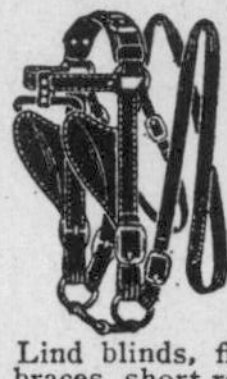

"Topsy" Team Bridle

$1.98

7/8-inch cheeks, folded ring crown. Jenny Lind blinds, flat winker braces, short reins. Furnished with bit. Shpg. wt., 4½ lbs.

10K2070
Each.......... $1.98

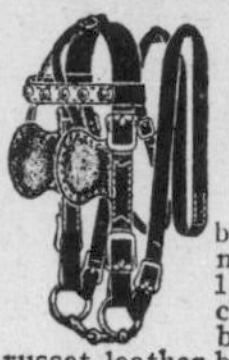

Special Team Bridle

$1.75

Low priced bridles, made with 1¾-inch cheeks, bar buckles, russet leather blinds, brass spotted russet brow band, short reins. Shpg. wt., 4½ lbs.

10K2014—Each $1.75
10K2019—Same as above, but all black and without spotting on brow band. Each.......$1.59

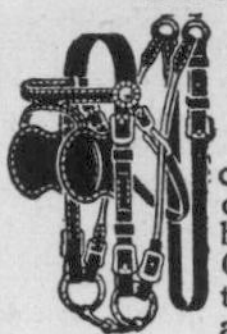

"Antony" Team Bridle

$3.50

7/8-in. long cheeks, cupped blinds. Combination front and winker braces, long round reins. Shipping weight, 5¼ lbs.

10K2065
Each.......... $3.50

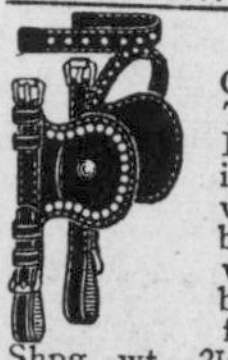

Bridle Outfit for Team Bridle, 7/8-in. cheeks with sensible blinds; winker brace and front. Shpg. wt., 2¼ lbs.

10K2046—With japanned buckles. Pair, for one bridle.......$2.15

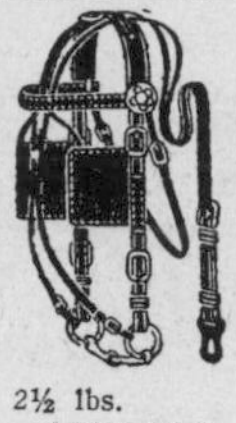

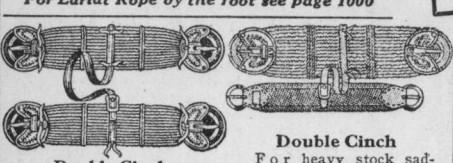

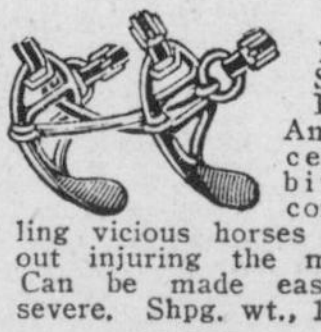

Buggy Bridle

$1.97

Buggy bridle with 5/8-inch flat cheeks and winker brace. Shpg. wt., 2½ lbs.

10K1860
Overcheck Bridle. $1.97
10K1861—Side Check Bridle.......... $1.99

Fine 5/8-inch open bridle, noseband overcheck. Shipping wt., 2 lbs.

10K1863.... $2.15

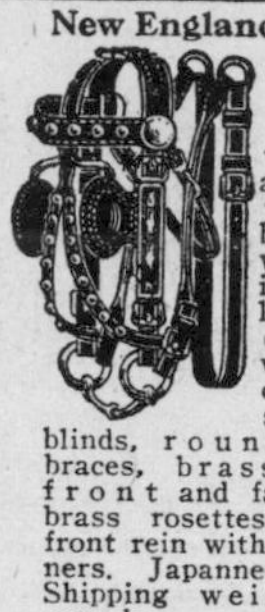

"New England" Style Team Bridle

Strong, well made and attractive bridle with 3/4-inch box loop, long cheeks, wide crown, sensible blinds, round winker braces, brass spotted front and face piece, brass rosettes, round front rein with gag runners. Japanned buckles. Shipping weight, 5½ pounds.

10K2038.. $4.45

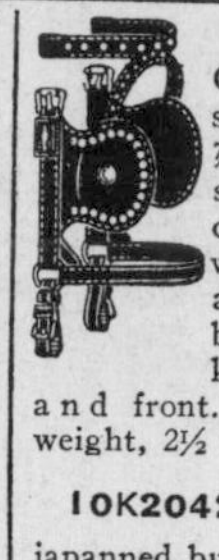

Bridle Outfit, consisting of 7/8-inch short cheeks with blinds and noseband, winker brace and front. Shipping weight, 2½ pounds.

10K2042—With japanned buckles.

Pair for one bridle.... $2.45

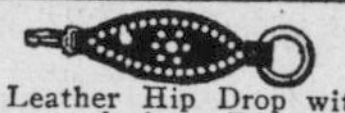

Leather Hip Drop with snap and ring. For tying up the hitching strap. Makes fine spreader. Shipping weight, 6 ounces.

10K2021—With nickel plated spots.......... 82c
10K2022—With brass spots.......... 82c

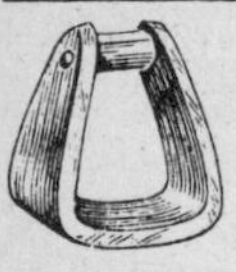

Heavy Wood Stirrup, 4 in. wide. Bolt through the bar and stirrup, making it very strong. Suitable for heavy saddles, with stirrup straps up to 3 inches wide. Shpg. wt., 2 lbs.

10K3093
Pair.......... 30c

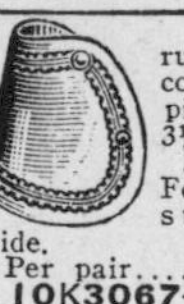

Wood Stirrups. Leather covered. Shipping wt., pair, 3½ lbs.

10K3066—For stirrup straps, 2 in. wide. Per pair.......... $1.50
10K3067—For stirrup straps 3 in. wide. Per pair.......... $1.75
10K3095—For stirrup straps 1 to 1½ in. wide. Shpg. wt., 2 lbs. Per pair.......... $1.30

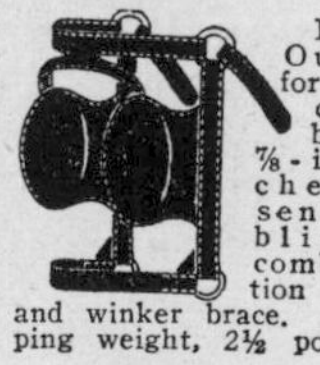

Bridle Outfit for ring crown bridle, 7/8-inch cheeks, sensible blinds, combination front and winker brace. Shipping weight, 2½ pounds.

10K2040
Per pair for one bridle.......... $1.95

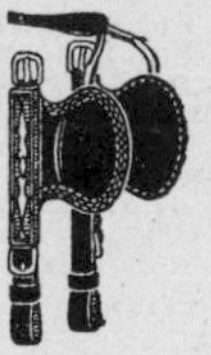

Bridle Outfit for express bridle, 3/4-inch box loop cheeks. Shipping wt., 2 lbs.

10K2045
Imitation rubber trimmed. Per pair, for one bridle.......... $1.75

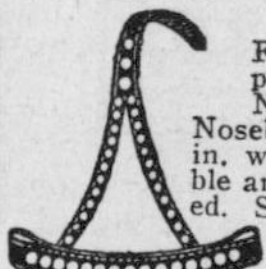

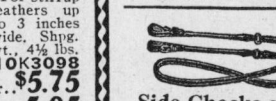

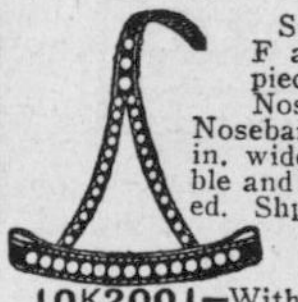

Spotted Face-piece and Noseband. Noseband is 1 in. wide, double and stitched. Shpg. wt., 7 oz.

10K2001—With brass spots. Each. 65c
10K2002—With nickel plated spots. Each.......... 65c

Facepiece Without Noseband; ¾ inch at the top with 5/8-inch billets. Shipping wt., 5 oz.

10K2005—With brass spots. Each. 27c
10K2006—With nickel plated spots. Each.......... 27c

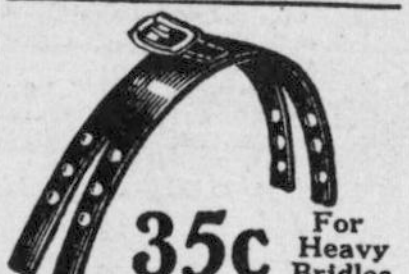

35c For Heavy Bridles

Heavy Leather Bridle Crownpieces for repairing bridles. 24 in. long.

10K2430—For heavy bridles. 1¾ inches wide, 7/8-inch billets. Shipping weight, 7 ounces. Each.......... 35c
10K2431—For buggy bridles, 1⅛ inches wide, 5/8-inch billets. Shipping weight, 6 oz. Each.......... 42c

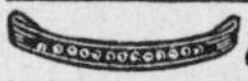

45c Bridle fronts for team or express bridles; double and stitched; 1 inch wide, 17 inches long; spotted. Shipping weight, each, 5 oz.

10K2442 — With nickel plated spots. Each.......... 45c
10K2443 — With brass spots. Each.......... 45c

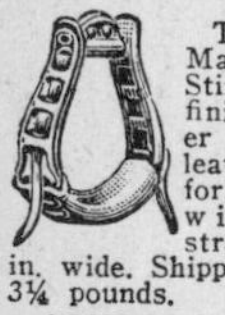

Texas Style Malleable Iron Stirrups. XC finish. Leather lined and leather bottom for saddles with stirrup straps up to 3 in. wide. Shipping weight, 3¼ pounds.

10K3094
Per pair.......... $2.40

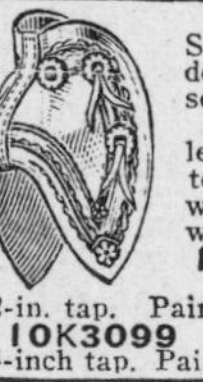

Colorado Style Tapideros. Russet leather. For stirrup leathers up to 3 inches wide. Shpg. wt., 4½ lbs.

10K3098
12-in. tap. Pair.. $5.75
10K3099
14-inch tap. Pair. 5.95

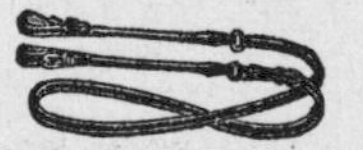

Side Checks and Rounds for Team Bridles

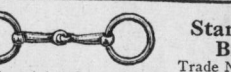

Heavy Harness Side Check, ¾-inch billets and center check, long rounds. Shipping weight, 1¼ lbs.

10K2063
Each.......... $1.50
10K2062 — Rounds only. Shpg. wt., ¾ lb. Each.......... 45c

Solid Head Bit. No. 1 wire. Trade No. 90. 3-inch loose rings, 5-in. stiff mouthpiece. Gives splendid service. Shpg. wt., 1¼ lbs.

10K8215—Ea. 35c

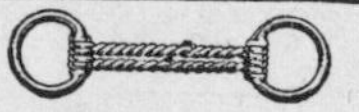

Double Jointed. Shpg. wt., 8 oz.

10K8205—Ea.. 24c

Single Jointed. Shpg. wt., 6 oz.

10K8206.......... 19c

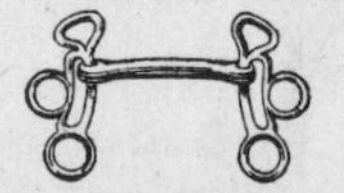

Buckeye Safety Bit

For use on work bridles or for breaking young horses. Has sure controlling power. Loose bar. Shipping weight, 1¼ lbs.

10K8101
Jointed mouthpiece. 50c
10K8102
Stiff mouthpiece... 50c

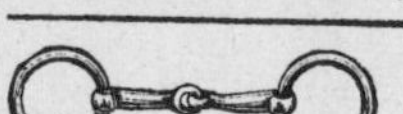

Standard Team Bridle Bits

Trade No. 47, 2¾-inch ring, stiff or jointed mouthpiece. Shpg. wt., ¾ lb.

10K8221—Jointed.
10K8222—Stiff. Each.......... $0.13
Per dozen.......... $1.45

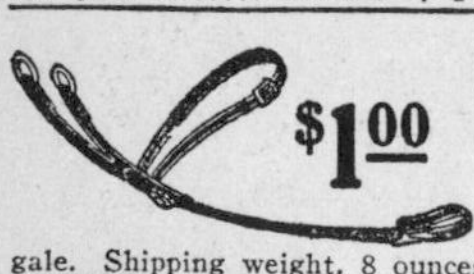

$1.00

Riding Martingale. Heavy russet leather, with flat neck strap. XC buckles. Shipping wt., ¾ lb.

10K2517
Each.......... $1.00

Extra fine russet leather riding martingale. Shipping weight, 8 ounces.

10K2518—Each.......... $1.50

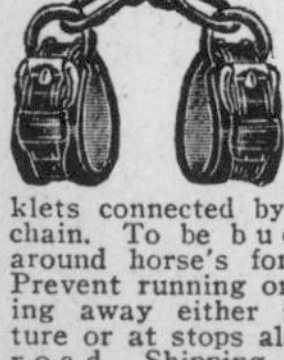

Horse Hobbles. Consist of two leather anklets connected by swivel chain. To be buckled around horse's fore legs. Prevent running or straying away either in pasture or at stops along the road. Shipping weight, 1½ pounds.

10K3100...... 83c

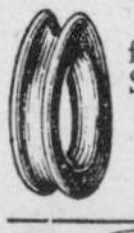

Brass Honda for lariat, 7/16 in. Shpg. wt., 3 oz.

10K3119
Each, 12c

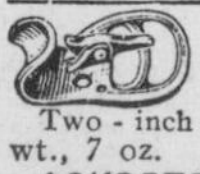

Cinch Buckle

Two-inch loops. Shpg. wt., 7 oz.

10K3278
Each.......... 39c

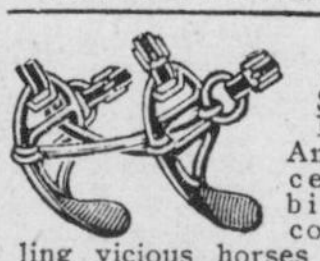

Jay-Eye-See Bit. An excellent bit for controlling vicious horses without injuring the mouth. Can be made easy or severe. Shpg. wt., 1 lb.

10K8285
XC white metal plated.......... 35c

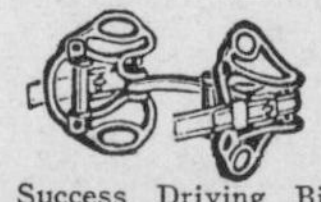

Success Driving Bit. Has a steel bar. Good controlling power without injuring mouth. Shipping wt., 1¾ lbs.

10K8291—XC white metal plated.......... 89c

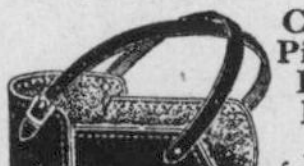

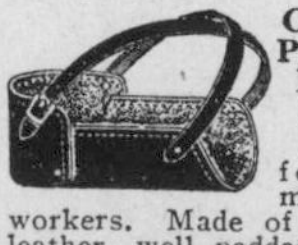

Cotton Pickers Knee Pads

Also for cement workers. Made of heavy leather, well padded with heavy felt. Size, 7x7 in.; ½-in. adjusting straps. Shpg. wt., each, 2 lbs.

10K5300—Ea.... 38c
2 for.......... 75c

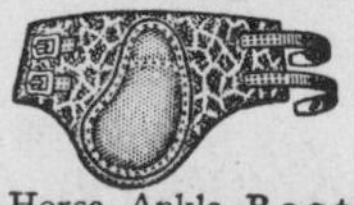

Horse Ankle Boot. Heavy cupped body, well padded and lined. Sold in pairs only. Shipping weight, 1 pound.

10K5636
Per pair.......... $1.39

Check Up Your Needs-Put Your Harness in A-1 Shape

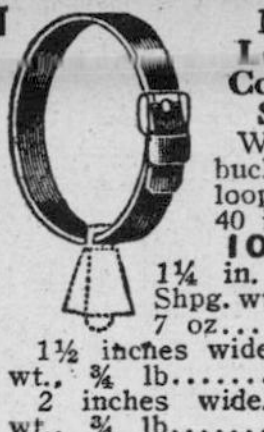

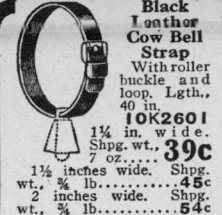

Black Leather Cow Bell Strap

With roller buckle and loop. Lgth., 40 in.

10K2601 1¼ in. wide. Shpg. wt., 7 oz..... **39c**

1½ inches wide. Shpg. wt., ¾ lb.........**45c**

2 inches wide. Shpg. wt., ¾ lb.........**54c**

2¼ inches wide. Shpg. wt., 1 lb.........**65c**

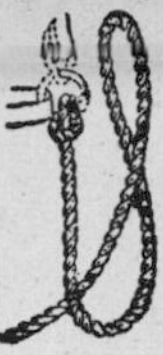

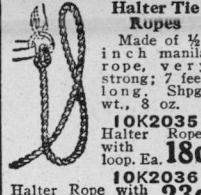

Halter Tie Ropes

Made of ½-inch manila rope, very strong; 7 feet long. Shpg. wt., 8 oz.

10K2035 Halter Rope, with loop. Ea. **18c**

10K2036 Halter Rope with snap. Each....... **23c**

For Cattle Leaders and Chain Ties see page 974.

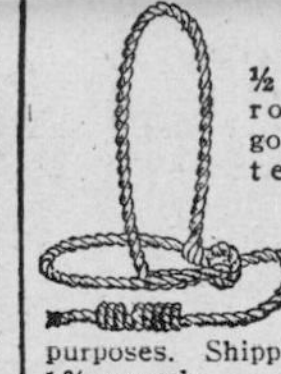

Strong Rope Halter

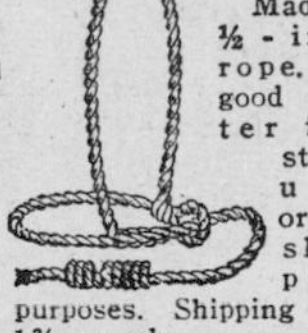

Made of ½-inch rope. A good halter for stable use or for shipping purposes. Shipping wt., 1¾ pounds.

10K2041.... **26c**

Rope Ties for Horses and Cattle

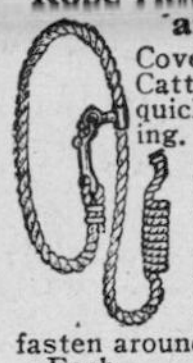

Covert's Horse and Cattle Ties. For quick, safe hitching. Made of ½-inch rope; long lead. Shpg. wt., 1¾ lbs.

10K2037 For horses or cattle. With one snap to fasten around neck. Each........... **36c**

10K2039—For horses. With extra snap to snap in bit. Each... **50c**

Avoid Breaks When Time Means Money to You-*Buy Now!*

$3.98 And Up

"Hagerman" Double Lines

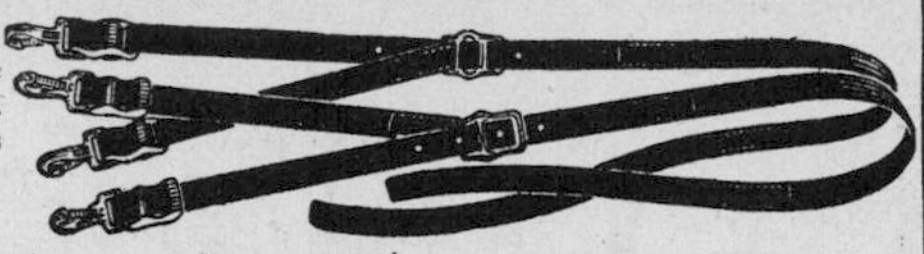

Made of black harness leather, the kind used in medium priced team harness. Special buckles and snaps at the bits. Buckle in the center.

10K2155—1 inch wide.

15 ft. long. Shpg. wt., 5 lbs..**$3.98**
18 ft. long. Shpg. wt., 5½ lbs.. **4.55**
20 ft. long. Shpg. wt., 6 lbs.. **4.85**
22 ft. long. Shpg. wt., 6½ lbs.. **5.10**

10K2170—1⅛ inches wide.
18 feet long. Shipping weight, 7 pounds **$5.15**
20 feet long. Shipping weight, 7½ pounds **$5.45**
22 feet long. Shipping weight, 8 pounds **$5.95**

10K2171—1¼ inches wide.
18 feet long. Shipping weight, 7½ pounds **$5.75**
20 feet long. Shipping weight, 8 pounds **$5.95**

$5.65 And Up

"Jackson" Farm Harness Lines

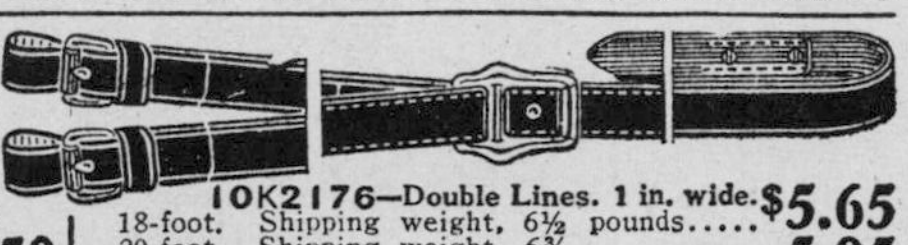

Extra good quality stock, double and stitched at the center; stitched and riveted laps; heavy japanned roller buckles at bits, special center buckle.

10K2174—Double Lines. 1⅛ in. wide.
18-foot. Shipping weight, 7 pounds...... **$6.25**
20-foot. Shipping weight, 7¾ pounds........................ **$6.50**

10K2176—Double Lines. 1 in. wide.
18-foot. Shipping weight, 6½ pounds..... **$5.65**
20-foot. Shipping weight, 6¾ pounds.......................... **5.95**

Standard Team Lines for Double Harness

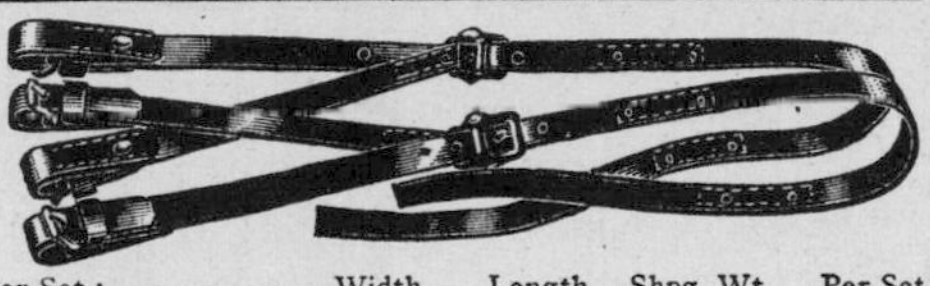

Firm uniform leather tanned just right to insure strength and long service; stitched and riveted laps; buckles and billets at bits; Moline center buckles.

	Width	Length	Shpg. Wt.	Per Set
10K2165	1 inch	18 feet	5½ lbs.	$5.65
10K2166	1 inch	20 feet	6 lbs.	5.85
10K2167	1⅛ inch	18 feet	6 lbs.	$5.95
10K2168	1⅛ inch	20 feet	6½ lbs.	6.35

$4.60 And Up

"Drexel" Team Lines

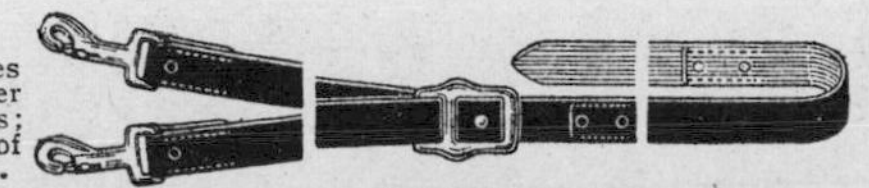

Good quality, heavy weight, double lines with stitched and riveted laps, Moline center buckles that will not catch in your fly nets; heavy bolt snaps sewed and riveted on. Made of firm uniform stock. **These lines are excellent values.**

10K2175—1-Inch Lines.
18 feet long. Shipping weight, 6½ pounds **$4.60**
20 feet long. Shipping weight, 7 pounds **$4.95**

10K2178—1⅛-Inch Lines.
18 feet long. Shipping weight, 7½ pounds **$5.25**
20 feet long. Shipping weight, 8 pounds **$5.65**

10K2179—1¼-Inch Lines.
18 feet long. Shipping weight, 8½ pounds **$5.95**
20 feet long. Shipping weight, 9 pounds **$6.15**

Team Housings of Double and Stitched Harness Leather

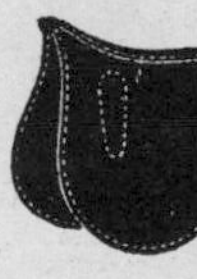

12¾ x 16 in. from center; unspotted. Shpg. wt., 4½ lbs.

10K2363 Each............. **$3.95**

Same as above, only larger, 14½x18 inches from center. Shipping weight, 7½ pounds.

10K2364 Each.............. **$5.25**

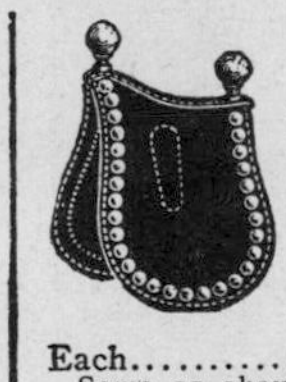

Size, 13 x 16 in. to center. Brass balls and spots. Shpg. wt., 5 lbs.

10K2367 Each............ **$5.60**

Same as above, but 14½x 18 inches. Shipping weight, 8 pounds.

10K2368 Each............. **$6.65**

Single Driving Lines. 12½ Feet Long

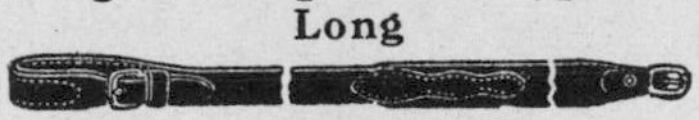

With ⅞-in. fronts, 1-in. hand parts. Shpg. wt., 2½ lbs.
10K2150 Per pair.... **$2.75**

With 1-inch fronts, 1⅛-inch hand parts. Shpg. wt., 2½ lbs.
10K2152 Per pair.... **$3.10**

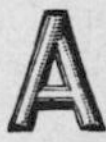

Brass letters, 1½ inches high. **State letters wanted.** We cannot put more than ten letters on each side of housing. Shpg. wt., 2 oz.

10K2374—Each letter........... **12c**

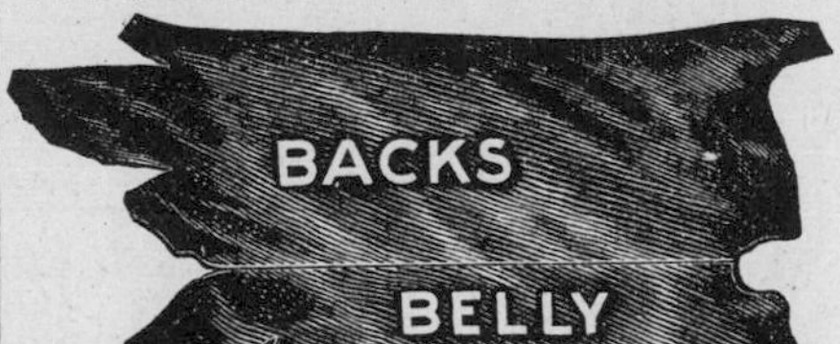

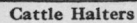

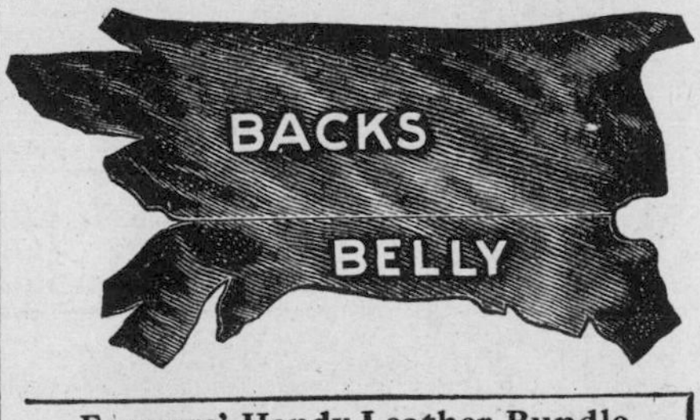

Bark Tanned Black Harness Leather

Our leather is noted for its strength of fiber and unexcelled wearing qualities. It is the same high grade that we use in our sets of harness and miscellaneous strap work; is tanned by the old bark process, in use for over fifty years, and never fails to give satisfaction. We will send you as near the weight you order as we can and charge for the quantity we send, but we do not cut the sides, backs or pieces into straps.

10K7763¼—Full Sides, weighing from 16 to 19 pounds each. Pound.........................**52c**

10K7764¼—Full Sides, weighing from 20 to 24 pounds each. Pound.........................**53c**

10K7767¼—Backs only, weighing from 13 to 16 pounds. Pound.........................**60c**

10K7768¼—Backs only, heavy trace leather, weighing from 17 to 19 pounds. Per pound....**62c**

Leather Bellies. Used for repairing or making light strap work. Pieces weigh from 4 to 8 pounds each.

10K7771—Per pound.................. **29c**

For Harness Oil see page 456

Farmers' Handy Leather Bundle

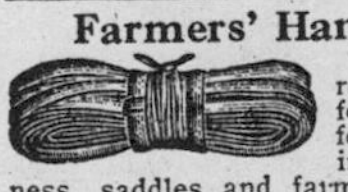

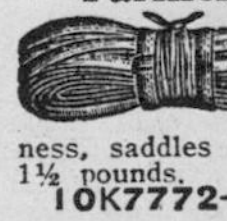

Contains 1 pound of assorted rawhide leather strips, in different lengths and widths. Used for many purposes, such as making quick repairs about harness, saddles and farm machinery. Shipping weight, 1½ pounds.

10K7772—Per bundle......................... **32c**

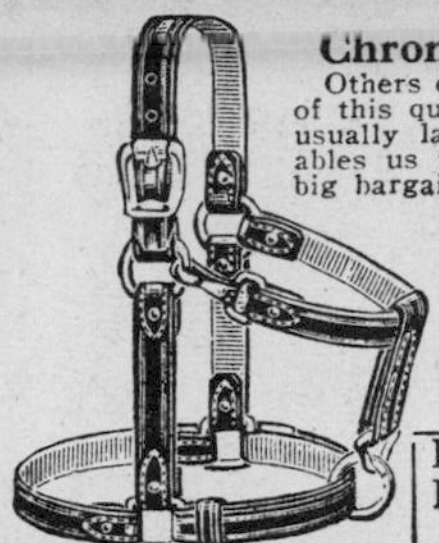

Chrome Leather Halter

Others often ask $2.00 for a halter of this quality. Purchase of an unusually large quantity for cash enables us to offer them as an extra big bargain. Made 1¼ inches wide, 5-ring style, with sewed and riveted laps. Standard size, suitable for the average horse. A strong, well made halter that will give splendid service. Shipping weight, 3¼ pounds.

10K1966 Each............. **$1.15**

Black Leather Five-Ring Halter

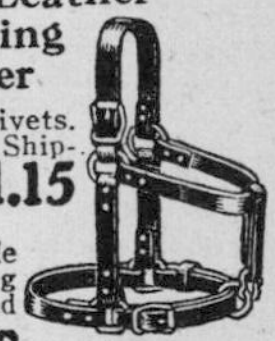

Laps riveted with double headed rivets. These are halters of splendid value. Shipping weight, 3 pounds.

10K1984—1¼-inch halter..... **$1.15**

Black Leather Colt Halter

1-inch straps, five-ring style. Made on the same style and just as strong as our horse halters. Laps riveted with double headed rivets.

10K1988—Shpg. wt., 1¾ lbs. **89c**

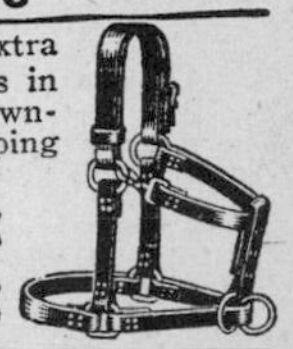

Heavy Black Leather Halter. Extra strong, four double headed rivets in each lap, six rings, double crownpiece, snap throatlatch. Shipping weight, 3½ pounds.

10K1998 1¼-inch halter........... **$1.75**

10K1999 1½-inch halter........... **1.95**

Cattle Halters

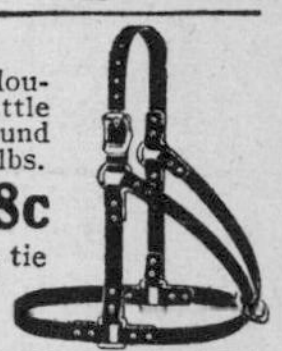

Good quality. Laps riveted with double headed rivets. Adjustable for cattle of various sizes. Will not chafe around the horns. 1 in. wide. Shpg. wt., 2½ lbs.

10K2000 Leather Cow Halter............... **78c**

Heavy woven web halters with rope tie snapped on. Shpg. wt., 2 lbs.

10K1978—Cow Halter... **64c**

10K1979—Calf halter......**55c**

Assorted Color Web Halters

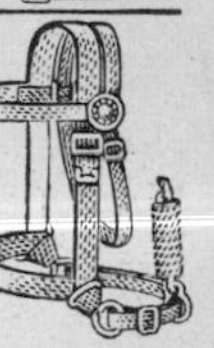

Heavy 13-cord web, adjustable chin strap, rope tie. Long throatlatch. Shipping weight, 2¼ pounds.

10K1974.................... **55c**

Web Halter. 1½ inch headstall. No brow band. Shpg. wt., 2 lbs.

10K1970.................... **39c**

Woven Web Colt or Pony Halter

With rope tie. A low priced halter that will be found very useful. Shipping weight, 2 pounds.

10K1981.................... **50c**

Halters, 1¼ Inches Wide, 5-Ring Style, Riveted

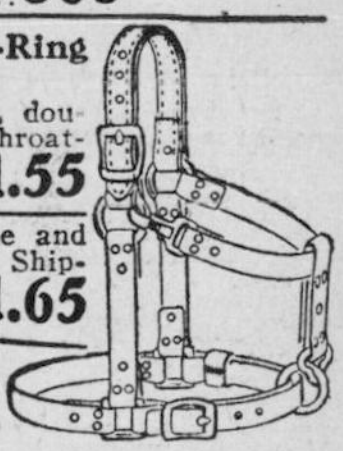

Indian Surface Tanned Halter, double and stitched crown, snap throatlatch. Shipping wt., 3¼ lbs.

10K1967—Each......... **$1.55**

Chrome Tanned Halter, double and stitched crown, snap throatlatch. Shipping weight, 2¾ pounds.

10K1968—Each......... **$1.65**

Rawhide Halter, double and stitched crown, snap throatlatch. Shpg. wt., 3¼ lbs.

10K1969—Each.... **$1.85**

Horse Roaching Shears

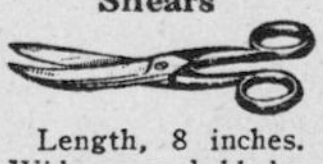

Length, 8 inches. Wide curved blades of well tempered steel. For clipping the mane, tail and fetlocks. Shipping weight, 1 pound.

10K4815 Each....... **$1.25**

Stockmen's Show Halters

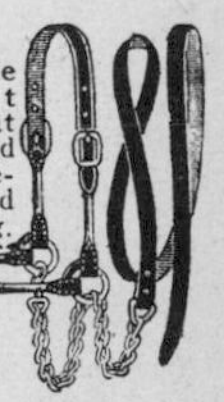

Standard Cattle Halter. Russet leather. With flat crown, round cheeks and noseband; 1⅛-inch lead rein, 5 feet long. Brass buckles and rings; 18-inch chains. Shpg. wt., 2 lbs.

10K1989 **$2.85**

Hercules Bull Tie

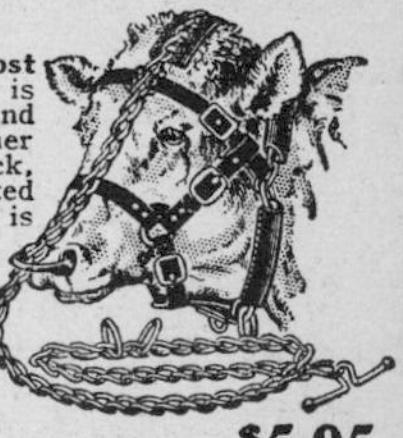

Designed to hold the most vicious bulls. This Bull Halter is constructed of stout chain and bark tanned leather. The leather encased chain encircles the neck, locked underneath by a patented clasp. To this chain another is attached which passes over the poll, down the forehead and through the nose ring by which the bull is tied. A quick jerk will spend its effects, not on the ring, but over the poll to the neck chain.

10K1993—Shipping weight, 8 pounds... **$5.95**

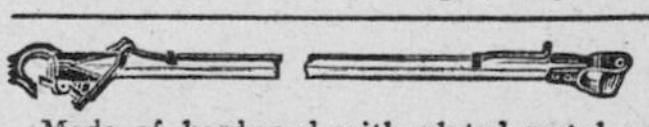

Hercules Bull Staff

Made of hardwood with plated metal parts of malleable iron; snaps into ring in bull's nose; snap is operated from metal rod ending at thumbscrew which when turned down, holds lock securely. Simple, easy working and safe, with great controlling power.

10K4200—Shipping weight, 5½ lbs...... **$4.75**

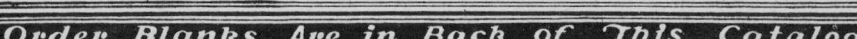

Here's Warmth and Comfort for Your Horses

"Renown" Horse Blanket

$2.25 And Up

For blankets of exceptional value we highly recommend these. So popular was this number last year in the small size that we are now having it made in two larger sizes so that more of our customers may get the benefit of a truly amazing bargain. Long wearing quality and unusual strength are its features. Soft, fluffy and warm. The body of the blanket is of two shades of brown with a heading border of gray and red, which make an attractive combination. We are sure that every customer purchasing these blankets will be delighted with their quality and coloring.

10K9900¼—Size, 72x74 inches. Shipping weight, 4½ lbs. Each...$2.25
10K9901¼—Size, 76x80 inches. Shipping weight, 6 lbs. Each... 2.75
10K9902¼—Size, 80x84 inches. Shipping weight, 7 lbs. Each... 3.25

$4.65

"Reliance" Horse Blanket

Buy and examine these blankets; note especially their firm texture and splendid finish. Put one on your horse; you will be very pleased with its appearance and pronounce it the most remarkable blanket value you ever received. Not only is it a desirable horse blanket, but it may be used very satisfactorily as a camping blanket, or for general outdoor use. Quality considered our price is very low. The body of the blanket is reddish brown with contrasting head stripes of beautiful colors.

10K9924¼—Size, 84x90 inches. Weight, about 8 pounds. Shipping weight, 9½ pounds. Each.................$4.65

$4.95

"Wonderland" Fancy Plaid

A blanket made as this one is, always satisfies; about two-thirds wool, just right for both strength and warmth and the pretty plaid pattern of dark blue, brown and gold is one we know you will like. You'll like, also, the soft, fluffy, wool-like finish of this blanket and the splendid service it will give you. Plaid blankets are always popular, and usually high priced, but not here. Investigate and you'll find that we save you from $2.00 to $3.00 compared with the price asked by others for similar quality. Made by L. C. Chase.

10K9935¼—Size, 80x84 inches. Shipping weight, 7 pounds. Each.................$4.95
10K9936¼—Size, 84x90 inches. Shpg. wt., 8 lbs. Each.....$5.50

$1.65 And Up

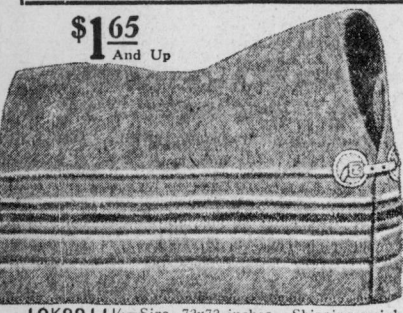

Favorite Low Priced Horse Blankets

Strongly woven cotton blankets which give surprisingly good service. They represent value that is hard to beat and will be found satisfactory for occasional use or where climate is not too severe. It pays to keep horses covered even in moderately cold weather and, when blankets can be bought as cheaply as these, there is no real economy in being without them. The body color is gray with striped heading.

10K9911¼—Size, 72x72 inches. Shipping weight, 5 lbs. Each.....$1.65
10K9912¼—Size, 76x80 inches. Shipping weight, 6 lbs. Each..... 2.25
10K9913¼—Size, 80x84 inches. Shipping weight, 6½ lbs. Each..... 2.55

$2.85

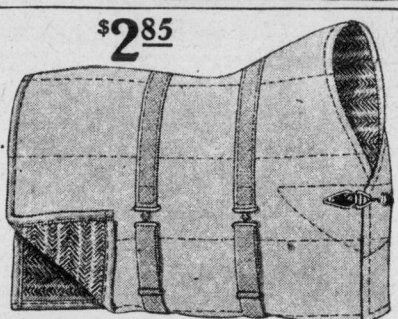

"Sovereign" Horse Blanket

A Great Big Bargain. We honestly believe these blankets to be worth $4.00 to $4.50 to any horse owner. Buy it, examine it, use it and you will think so too. Made from heavy brown duck, lined with a warm blanket lining and reinforced. Wide surcingles. Suitable for horses of average size. Can be used as an outside blanket as well as a stable blanket and, at this low price, you can afford to buy for the future as well as for your present needs.

10K9730¼—76-in. blanket. Shpg. wt., 7 lbs. Each........$2.85
10K9731¼—80-in. blanket. Shpg. wt., 9 lbs. Each.........$3.15

Leather or Woven Web Carrying Straps

With metal handle. Suitable for carrying school books, messenger bags, auto robes, etc. Straps are 48 inches long. Blanket not included. Shpg. wt., 1 lb.
10K9300—With two web straps, ⅞-inch...................35c
10K9301—With two leather straps, ¾-inch.................75c

The "Milton" Stable Blankets

These blankets are made of strong, heavy burlap, fabric lined, well stitched all around; buckle and billet front fastener, neck correctly shaped; full quilted body fitted with two wide surcingles. For good, well made blankets order these.

10K9724¼—76-inch blanket. Weight, about 7¼ lbs. Shpg. wt., 8½ lbs. Each...$2.75
10K9725¼—80-in. blanket. Wt., about 8 lbs. Shpg. wt., 9½ lbs. Each...$2.95

Unlined Stable Sheets

Made of mangled burlap in three sizes. Two surcingles, with stay extending to first surcingle; hemmed neck and front. The right kind to keep your horse clean in the stable. Shpg. wt., each, 3 lbs.

10K9702—72-inch blanket. Weight, about 2¼ pounds...$1.55
10K9703—76-inch blanket. Weight, about 2½ pounds...$1.65
10K9704—80-inch blanket. Weight, about 2½ pounds... 1.75

Quality Brushes and Curry Combs

"Sherman" Horse Brush

Fine quality genuine bristles. A high class brush at a low price. Flexible leather block well stitched. Seventeen rows of stiff black bristles, brass wire drawn. Oval shape, flat face; leather strap. Will adjust to the horse's body with pressure of hand. Size, 9x4½ inches.
10K5121—Shpg. wt., 1 lb.........$1.25

Steel Curry Comb

Solid back, eight bars, wrought shank through the handle, strong brace. Shipping weight, 2 pounds.
10K4922 Plain Steel...18c

"Dandy" Curry Comb

Five bars, closed back double wire shank running through handle and riveted; lacquered finish. Shipping wt., each, ¾ lb.; per dozen, 6 lbs.
10K4925 Each...10c
Per dozen.....$1.00

Humane Corrugated Steel Curry Comb

Loosens the dirt without irritating flesh. Has no sharp teeth, therefore no place for hair to clog. Slight tap rids it of dirt. Shpg. wt., ¾ lb.
10K4929 Each.....15c

Perfection Steel Curry Comb

Made with mane comb. Back grasp, six-bar lacquered steel. Wire shank through handle and riveted. Shpg. wt., 1 lb.
10K4930...20c

Stable or Garage Broom

Contains broom corn and enough split reeds to make it strong and elastic. Wire binding and extra rows of stitching stiffen broom. Shipping wt., 3¾ lbs.
10K5163¼...$1.10

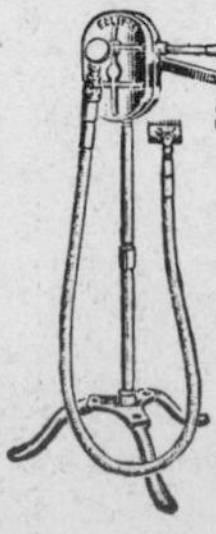

Improved "Scratcher" Horse Brush.

Combines curry comb and brush. Gets hard dirt out of fetlocks easily. Wood back, 8½x4 in. Leather strap.
10K5001 Shpg. wt., 1 lb.
23c

Rice Root Horse Brush.

Tufts firmly stapled in block. Size, 10x2¾ in. Polished top. Leather thumb and finger guards.
10K5091 Shpg. wt., 1 lb.
59c

"Gilbert" Horse Brush.

Fifteen rows gray tampico, wire drawn, oval face, leather strap; 9 in. long, 4¾ in. wide.
10K5095 Shpg. wt., 1¼ lbs.
90c

Stable or Garage Broom

14-inch wood block; four rows bass, about 48 tufts, wire stapled. Shipping weight, 2¾ lbs.
10K5167—Without handle...75c
10K5170—Handle. Shipping weight, 2 pounds.......12c

For Other Brooms See Page 972

"Eclipse" Clean Cutting Horse, Cattle and Sheep Clipping Machines
Makes Clipping an Easy Task

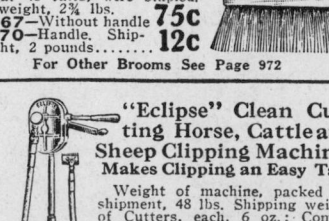

Weight of machine, packed for shipment, 48 lbs. Shipping weight of Cutters, each, 6 oz.; Combs, each, 6 oz.

10K4680¼—Horse and Cattle Clipping Machine, complete.........$11.75
10K4682—Extra Cutter..$1.20
10K4684—Extra Comb... 1.65
10K4880¼—Sheep Shearing Machine, complete........$19.50
10K4883—Extra Cutter..25c
10K4884—Extra Comb...85c

From FACTORY TO YOU!
Big SAVINGS Guaranteed

OUR SHOE FACTORY IN THE EAST — OUR PLUMBING GOODS FACTORY — OUR CREAM SEPARATOR FACTORY — OUR PAINT FACTORY — OUR FULTON TENT FACTORY — OUR BRADLEY IMPLEMENT FACTORY — ANOTHER OF OUR SHOE FACTORIES — OUR MILLWORK FACTORY IN OHIO — OUR STOVE FOUNDRY — OUR WIRE FENCING FACTORY — OUR OIL STOVE FOUNDRY — OUR WALL PAPER MILL — OUR MILLWORK FACTORY IN NEW JERSEY — OUR LUMBER PLANT IN ILLINOIS

We Manufacture Much of Our Merchandise in Our Own Factories

Naturally, because we supply eleven million families with a large share of their needs, the volume enables us to run our business more economically and buy and sell for less than any other source of supply you could possibly have. One of the ways in which we make you a large saving is by doing our own manufacturing.

Some of the more important goods we thus produce are:

Shoes — Building Material — Paint
Stoves — Wall Paper — Cream Separators
Plumbing Goods — Tents — Wire Fencing
Farm Implements

An idea of the quantities we manufacture may be gathered from the fact that every year our Wall Paper Mill makes upwards of twenty million 8-yard rolls of wall paper and our Paint Factory upwards of one million gallons of paint, while our Millwork Factories produce many millions of dollars' worth of building material.

Not only do we cut our costs and handling expenses by this plan, but we are able to insure a higher and more uniform standard of quality.

When you buy merchandise of this class from our catalog, it is equal to buying direct from the factory. You pay only one profit from the time the raw material is received at the factory until the finished merchandise arrives at your home.

In addition to the money saving we make you through our own manufacturing, we make you a large saving on other merchandise by contracting for the entire output or a large share of the output of other large factories, both in the United States and foreign countries. These factories naturally trim their profits to the minimum and enable us to secure high standard merchandise at the lowest prices for which it can be bought.

Whether we do our own manufacturing or buy from other factories we cut out every possible penny of unnecessary profit and expense and give you the full benefit in rock bottom prices.

You can easily see how the World's Largest Store can guarantee to satisfy you and save you money.

Sears, Roebuck and Co.
The World's Largest Store

37,500 OF OUR MODERN HOMES have been built in the U. S. A. This is an illustration of one of them. The millwork and lumber for all these were produced in our own factories. Be sure to see our building material pages in this catalog.

HOUSE PAINT — WALLPAPER — LUMBER

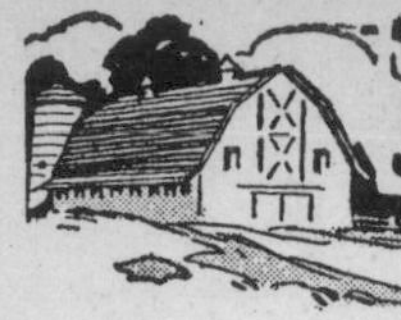

David Bradley Implements

Unexcelled Repair Service
Complete repair stocks of Bradley parts carried at our Philadelphia store insure prompt service to any Bradley user.

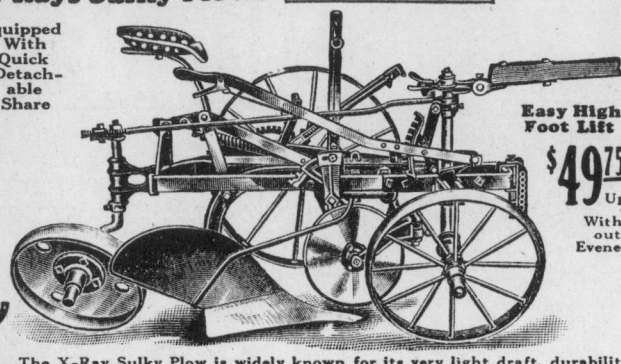

David Bradley X-Rays Sulky Plows

Equipped With Quick Detachable Share

Easy High Foot Lift

$49.75 Up Without Eveners

The X-Ray Sulky Plow is widely known for its very light draft, durability, perfect scouring and easy handling. A boy can handle it with ease. Perfectly balanced high lift. This plow has been a leader in its field for many years. Bottoms are the famous **garden city clipper** shape built of soft center steel, famous for perfect work. **Quick detachable shares** of hard tempered soft center steel, can be removed in a few moments.

Prices are for plows complete with pole, neckyoke, rolling coulter, weed hook and wrench. Evener not included in the price of plow, as many already have a good evener on hand, making it unnecessary to buy another. If needed, see list of eveners below for either 3 or 4 horses. Will furnish a jointer instead of a coulter if so desired. Can furnish combination coulter and jointer instead at $1.50 extra.

Catalog No.	Size, In.	Style of Garden City Clipper Bottom	Wt., Lbs.	Shipped From BRADLEY, ILL. Plow, Each	Extra Shares, Each: Soft Center Steel, Quick Detachable	Extra Shares, Each: Solid Steel Quick Detachable
32K240	12	Stubble..........	472	$49.75	$3.15	$2.35
32K241	12	General Purpose..	474	50.25	3.15	2.35
32K242	14	Stubble..........	477	50.50	3.60	2.65
32K243	14	General Purpose..	479	51.00	3.60	2.65
32K244	16	Stubble..........	482	51.25	4.10	2.95
32K245	16	General Purpose..	487	51.75	4.10	2.95

Eveners for Sulky Plows

Catalog No.	Description	Weight, Lbs.: Wood	Weight, Lbs.: Steel	Shipped From BRADLEY, ILL.: Wood	Shipped From BRADLEY, ILL.: Steel
32K255	3-Horse Abreast.........	38	45	$3.75	$5.25
32K250	4-Horse Abreast.........	56	·85	6.70	9.55

David Bradley Garden City Clipper Walking Plows

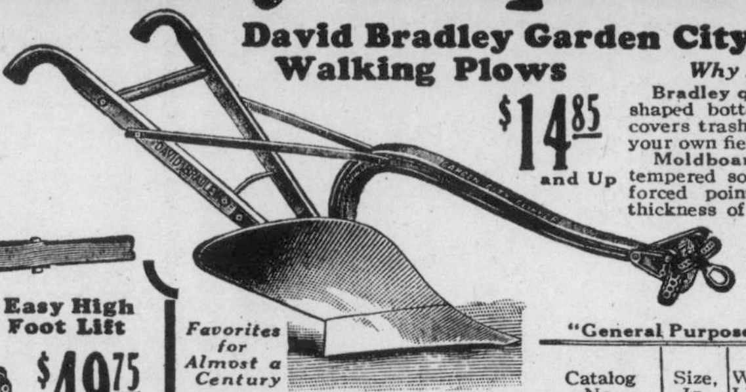

Favorites for Almost a Century

$14.85 and Up

Why Pay More for Any Plow?

Bradley quality is unsurpassed. Correctly shaped bottom turns the soil clear over and covers trash with the least draft. Try one in your own field. Satisfaction guaranteed.

Moldboard, share and landside of hard tempered soft center steel. **Shares** have reinforced points. **Moldboards** have an extra thickness of hard steel welded on front where wear is greatest. Entire bottom carefully ground and polished. Guaranteed to scour. Steel beam highly arched to clear trash. **Shipped from our Philadelphia store.**

"General Purpose" or "Stubble and Sod" Shape

Catalog No.	Size, In.	Wt., Lbs.	Plow	Extra Shares, Each: Soft Center Steel	Extra Shares, Each: Solid Steel
72K105¼	12	113	$14.85	$3.15	$2.35
72K106¼	14	122	16.90	3.60	2.57
72K107¼	16	128	18.95	4.10	2.95
"Stubble" or "Old Ground" Shape					
72K102¼	14	120	$16.85	$3.60	$2.57

David Bradley Royal Blue Plow

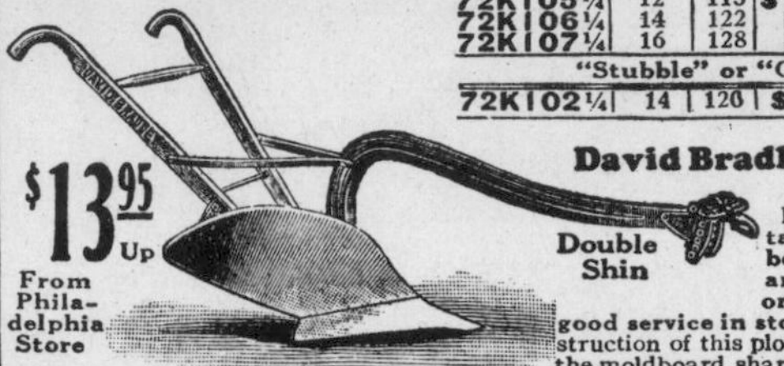

$13.95 Up From Philadelphia Store

Double Shin

Does fine work in stubble or tame sod and, as the moldboard, landside and share are solid steel, with mild or natural temper, it gives good service in stony land. The bottom construction of this plow is one of its special features, the moldboard, share and landside being securely bolted to a steel frog, and outer landside secured to a cast inner landside which has an adjustable slip heel. **Bottoms** are perfectly ground and highly polished. **Moldboards** are double shinned on top, insuring great wearing qualities. **Beam** is heavy double beaded steel, highly arched so as not to foul in trashy land. **Handles** are of first quality oak, well braced to beam and adjustable. **Shipped from our store.**

Catalog No.	Size, Inches	Weight, Pounds	Plow	Extra Share
72K125¼	10	95	$13.95	$1.77
72K126¼	12	100	15.90	2.08
72K127¼	14	110	17.50	2.50

Attachments for Plows

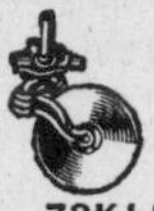

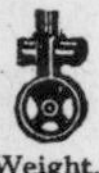

For either steel or wood beam plows. If ordered without plow, state whether for wood or steel beam, right or left hand and kind of plow. Shipped from our store.

72K115¼—13-Inch Bradley Caster Rolling Coulter for walking plows. Large chilled bearings, convenient to oil. Weight, 26 pounds.................................... **$3.35**

72K113¼—15-Inch Bradley Caster Rolling Coulter for riding plows. Weight, 22 pounds.................................... **$4.00**

72K114¼—Knife Coulter for walking plows. Weight, 9 pounds.......... **1.55**

72K116¼—Quincy Reversible Coulter for walking plows. Weight, 9 lbs. **1.45**

72K117¼—Fin Cutter. For David Bradley Stubble General Purpose and Royal Blue Walking Plows. When not ordered with plow be sure to state number appearing on bottom of your old share. Can furnish in blank to fit any walking plow. Weight, 4 pounds.................................... **$0.95**

72K118¼—Steel Moldboard Jointer for walking plows. Weight, 15 lbs.. **2.40**

72K119¼—Gauge Wheel for steel beam walking plow. Weight, 11 pounds **1.05**

72K123¼—Gauge Wheel for wood beam walking plow. Weight, 11 pounds. **1.06**

David Bradley Cast Plow

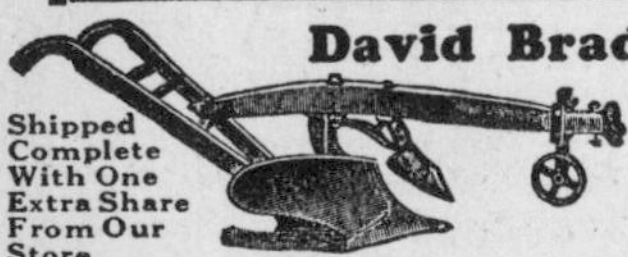

Shipped Complete With One Extra Share From Our Store

For Use in Sandy, Gravelly or Gritty Soils Only

Noted for their perfect shape, scouring qualities and light draft. The share and shin (sometimes called cutter shares) are in one piece, so in renewing one you renew the other. Materials used in the bottoms are a special mixture of metals of extreme hardness, yet possessed of strength and toughness. **Beam** is first quality oak, bolted to slotted braces on the handles, making it adjustable for more or less land. **Handles** are thoroughly seasoned oak, braced by heavy rounds and a steel stay rod. A jointer should be used with the two larger sizes when plowing trashy ground. The bottom of share measures about 2 inches less than the full cut of plow. Jointer and gauge wheel must be purchased extra at prices shown below. **Shipped from our Philadelphia store.**

Catalog No.	Size	Wt., Lbs.	Plow	Extra Share
72K170¼	DA2- 6 in.	50	$ 7.25	$0.60
72K175¼	D20-10 in.	108	13.65	.97
72K176¼	D40-11½ in.	135	15.95	1.22

72K178¼—Jointer. Weight, 12 pounds. Extra.................................... **$1.90**

72K179¼—Gauge Wheel. Weight, 11 pounds. Extra.................................... **.99**

Riding Attachment for Walking Plows

Dust-proof Hubs

$15.90

Price Does Not Include Plow

Time and Labor Saver

Easily attached to any wood or steel beam plow. No extra burden for your team. Can be set for any depth furrow. Being tongueless, the attachment cannot be backed up by the team; neither does it carry the plow high from the ground. Made of iron and steel. Regular type of riding plow wheels with wide oval tires. Not intended for use on smaller than 10-inch plows nor rod breakers. **Shipped from our Philadelphia store.**

72K192¼—For right hand plows. Weight, 147 pounds.................................... **$15.90**

72K193¼—For left hand plows. Weight, 147 pounds.................................... **15.95**

One-Horse or Pony Plows

$4.58 7-In. *Wood Beam*

Steel or Wood Beams

For use wherever a light one or two-horse plow is required. Mol[illegible]board, shares and landsides hardened steel. Adjustable slip heel. Price includes one extra share. **Shipped from our store.**

Catalog No.	Size		Wt., Lbs.	Each
Steel Beam Plows				
72K4190¼	Pony,	7-inch	60	$5.90
72K4191¼	A. O.,	8-inch	65	6.60
72K4192¼	B. O.,	9-inch	70	7.35
72K4193¼	C. O.,	10-inch	85	8.95
Wood Beam Plows				
72K4195¼	Pony,	7-inch	42	4.58
72K4196¼	A. O.,	8-inch	45	5.25
Extra Shares for Above				
72K4180¼	Pony,	7-inch	2½	55c
72K4181¼	A. O.,	8-inch	3	65c
72K4182¼	B. O.,	9-inch	3½	75c
72K4183¼	C. O.,	10-inch	5	85c

David Bradley Hillside Plows

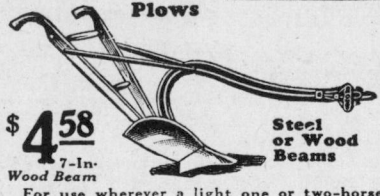

$10.75 and Up

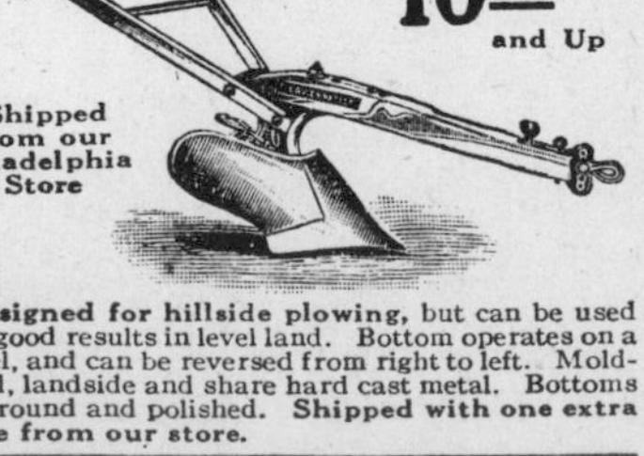

Shipped from our Philadelphia Store

Designed for hillside plowing, but can be used with good results in level land. Bottom operates on a swivel, and can be reversed from right to left. Moldboard, landside and share hard cast metal. Bottoms are ground and polished. **Shipped with one extra share from our store.**

Catalog No.	Size, In.	Wt., Lbs.	Plow	Extra Share
72K181¼	8	80	$10.75	$1.05
72K182¼	10	115	13.95	1.35
72K183¼	12	145	17.25	1.95

Coulter Harrow and Pulverizer

$11.75 Up

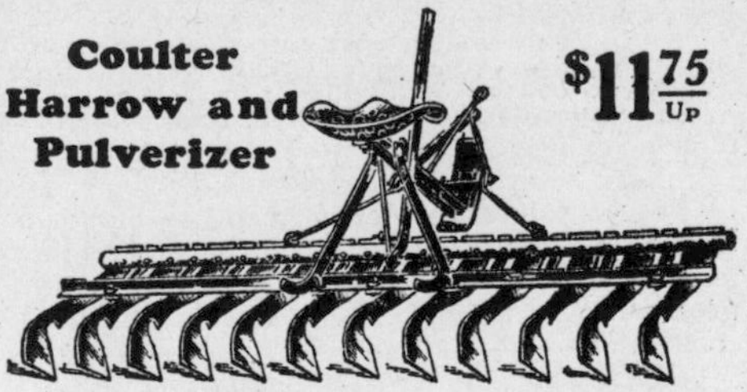

This very popular harrow and pulverizer will work successfully in any kind of soil, and on flat, rolling or hilly ground. Almost every farm has need for one. Truck gardeners and cotton growers find them indispensable. The long curving coulters or knives are very effective for producing perfect seed beds. The blades completely pulverize, level the surface and form a mulch at one operation, without packing the soil. Angle of penetration of the blades may be adjusted by lever within easy reach of operator. The action of the blades is like that of a knife. They cut down through the furrows, thoroughly cutting up the sod, stubble or cover crop that has been plowed down, so it rots quickly and adds humus to the soil. In connection with the short floats between each pair of coulters the front ends of the coulters crush the clods and lumps, compacting the whole plowed depth, leaving it in perfect condition for seeding. Construction extra strong, being made entirely of steel. Nothing to wear out but the coulters or blades and they will last for many years. Suitable hitch is provided for clevis at the front end of drawbar. Furnished in three sizes. **Shipped from factory in NEW YORK.**

32K392—One-Section One-Horse Walking Harrow. Equipped with 6 coulters and 5 floats and handles. Cuts 3 feet wide. Wt., 60 lbs. **$11.75**

32K393—One-Section One-Horse Riding or Walking Harrow. Equipped with 8 coulters and 7 floats, handles and seat. Cuts 4 feet 4 inches wide. Weight, 100 pounds......... **$18.50**

32K394—One-Section Two-Horse Riding Harrow. Equipped with 12 coulters and 10 floats and seat. Cuts 6 feet 6 inches wide. Weight, 115 pounds.................... **$19.95**

32K395—Extra Coulters or Blades. Weight, 3 pounds.................................... **72c**

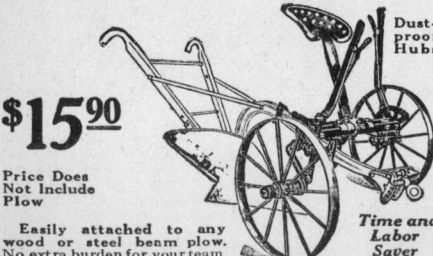

Standard *for* Almost a Century

David Bradley Tractor Disc Harrows

A One-Man Outfit

For Use With Fordson and Other Tractors

Better till-age in half the time. In no other tractor disc harrow will you find better quality, more simplicity in operating or greater efficiency. Inner ends of front gang roll against each other, equalizing thrust; no strain on bearings. A flexible swiveling chain connection between rear gangs equalizes end pull, while cross arm trailer connection enables the disc to turn very short and prevents buckling up in center; this also forces gangs to cut a uniform depth. Oil soaked hard maple liners, with hard oil cups at all bearings. Forward frame and stub pole made of heavy angle steel in one solid unit. Disc blades highest quality steel, fully tempered and highly polished. Throwoff levers free scrapers from the discs when not needed. Ropes to scraper levers not furnished.

TANDEM DISC HARROWS COMPLETE AS ILLUSTRATED

Catalog No.	No. of Disc	Width of Cut	Weight, Lbs. Without Scrapers	Weight, Lbs. With Scrapers	From Bradley, Ill. Without Scrapers	From Bradley, Ill. With Scrapers
32K299	24	6 feet	633	725	$65.50	$71.50
32K300	28	7 feet	690	792	71.75	78.25
32K301	32	8 feet	780	890	78.75	85.75
32K303	40	10 feet	970	1110	89.85	98.75

Single Tractor Disc Harrows. Consisting of Everything Shown Above, Excepting the Rear Gangs and Connections. Shipped from BRADLEY, ILL.

Catalog No.	No. of Disc	Width Cut	Without Scrapers Wt., Lbs.	Without Scrapers Price	With Scrapers Wt., Lbs.	With Scrapers Price
32K310	12	6 ft.	337	$34.00	377	$37.00
32K311	14	7 ft.	380	37.30	429	40.55
32K312	16	8 ft.	424	41.00	476	44.50
32K313	20	10 ft.	527	46.70	589	51.15

Rear Gangs or Trailer Complete With Connections for Attaching to Forward Gangs of Either Our Horse Drawn or Tractor Harrows. Shipped from BRADLEY, ILL.

Catalog No.	No. of Disc	Width Cut	Without Scrapers Wt., Lbs.	Without Scrapers Price	With Scrapers Wt., Lbs.	With Scrapers Price
32K314	12	6 ft.	298	$31.50	388	$34.50
32K315	14	7 ft.	348	34.45	397	37.70
32K316	16	8 ft.	394	37.75	446	41.25
32K317	20	10 ft.	479	43.15	541	47.60

Steel Frame Spring Tooth Harrows

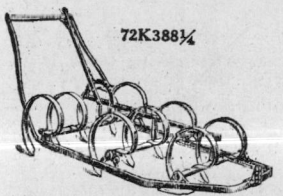

72K388¼

72K389¼

Favorites in truck gardens, orchards, timber countries and stony or stumpy ground. Thoroughly pulverizes the soil and digs up weeds, vines and grasses. Of latest design with inner bar of one section cut off at forward hinge and bridged over the top to rear hinge, thus preventing clogging between the bars. Heavy angle steel frames. Teeth of standard design. Each section cuts 3 feet. Single section harrow shows steel handles, furnished at extra price. **The three and four-section harrows are especially designed for use with tractors.** Sections are hinged at center. For 50 cents per section extra we will furnish harrow with special pointed teeth for cultivating alfalfa. **Shipped from our Philadelphia store.**

Catalog No.	No. Teeth	No. Sections	Wt., Lbs.	Each
72K388¼	9	1	135	$12.40
72K389¼	17	2	270	22.80
72K398¼	26	3	400	35.70
72K400¼	35	4	500	47.75

72K390¼—Extra Spring Teeth. Weight, 5 pounds. Each............54c
72K391¼—Extra Alfalfa Teeth. Weight, 5 pounds. Each............67c
72K399¼—Steel Handles for 9-Tooth Harrow. Weight, 15 pounds...........................**$1.35**

David Bradley Triple Lever Disc Harrows

$39.45 And Up

4, 5 and 6-ft. Disc Harrow shipped from Philadelphia store. Other sizes from factory at Bradley, Ill.

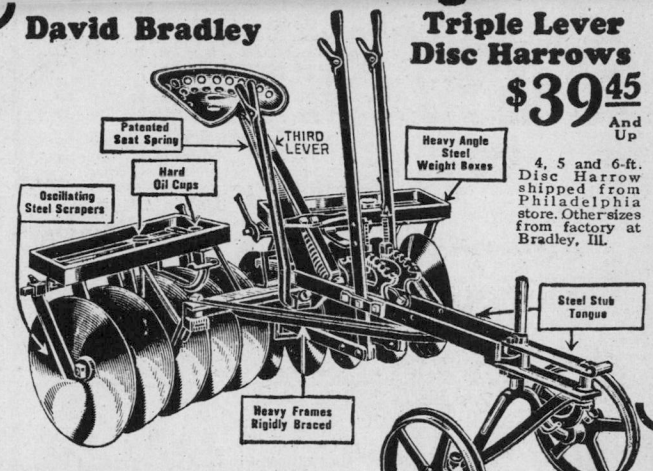

Buy a Bradley and enjoy real Disc Harrow satisfaction. You can pay more, but you can buy no better disc harrows than the David Bradley. It embodies many features of real merit not found in any other disc harrow.

Made in our own big Bradley Implement Factory and sold direct to you, eliminating the profits of all middlemen, which explains why we can sell these high class Bradley tools at such low prices. Buy one. Test it in your own field. If you are not convinced that the Bradley is superior to any Harrow you have ever used, and the biggest value you have ever seen, send it back and your money will be returned including transportation charges.

An all steel harrow of true bumper type. Gangs roll together without buckling or riding each other. Even penetration of ground its entire width.

Flexible gangs operated by independent levers.

Bumper washers on inner ends of gangs.

Oil soaked maple linings in all bearing boxes. Hard oil cups.

Oscillating spring steel scrapers are operated by foot levers and disengaged by hand throw-off levers.

Patented seat spring insures easier riding and greater safety.

Third lever enables the operator instantly to adjust the disc more closely to the ground, securing even penetration the full length of both gangs. Prevents buckling up in the center.

All the way through, construction is of the best. Built for long, satisfactory service.

David Bradley Disc Harrows are shipped complete with eveners, scrapers, weight boxes, third lever and tongue truck at the following prices:

Catalog No.	No. of Discs	Width of Cut	Size Hitch	16-Inch Discs Wt. Lbs.	16-Inch Discs Shipped From Our Store	16-Inch Discs Shipped From Bradley, Ill.	18-Inch Discs Wt. Lbs.	18-Inch Discs Shipped From Our Store	18-Inch Discs Shipped From Bradley, Ill.
72K330¼	8	4 ft.	2-Horse	400	$39.45		415	$41.65	
72K331¼	10	5 ft.	2-Horse	430	42.60		450	45.35	
72K332¼	12	6 ft.	3-Horse	490	46.75		525	50.00	
32K333	14	7 ft.	4-Horse	535	$46.95		575	$50.45	
32K334	16	8 ft.	4-Horse	590		51.75	635		55.75
32K322	18	9 ft.	4-Horse	650		56.50	700		61.00
32K319	20	10 ft.	4-Horse	722		61.25	700		66.25

Reversible Disc Harrow and Cultivator

A harrow and cultivator combined that has always been a great favorite for berry cultivation, rowed crops, tobacco fields trenching and filling. Easily adjusted to throw dirt to or from the row. Can be set together for harrowing or separated to straddle the row. Distance between gangs adjustable from 6 to 18 inches. Highly polished steel 16-inch disc blades. Bearing lubricated by hard grease cups. When discs are set close together the 6-disc harrow cuts about 3 feet wide, the 8-disc about 4 feet wide. Shipped complete with neckyoke, pole and two-horse hitch, from our Philadelphia store.

Catalog No.	No. of Discs	Weight Pounds	Shipped From Our Store Less Scrapers	Shipped From Our Store With Scrapers
72K345¼	6	217	$23.15	$24.65
72K346¼	8	238	25.55	27.65

David Bradley Shaker Potato Digger

Equal of Any Walking Shaker Digger Made

$15.50 Without Truck

The rolling weed fender parts the weeds and vines, leaving way clear for blade. Flat blade of polished steel is 17 inches wide and 15 inches long. Strong shaker rods, 20 inches. Heavy steel bars, high arched, will not clog. Truck straddles row and holds digger to even depth. Shipped from our Philadelphia store.

Catalog No.	Description	Wt., Lbs.	Each
72K437¼	Potato Digger without Truck	125	$15.50
72K438¼	Potato Digger with Truck	160	18.95

David Bradley Steel Beam Potato Hillers and Diggers

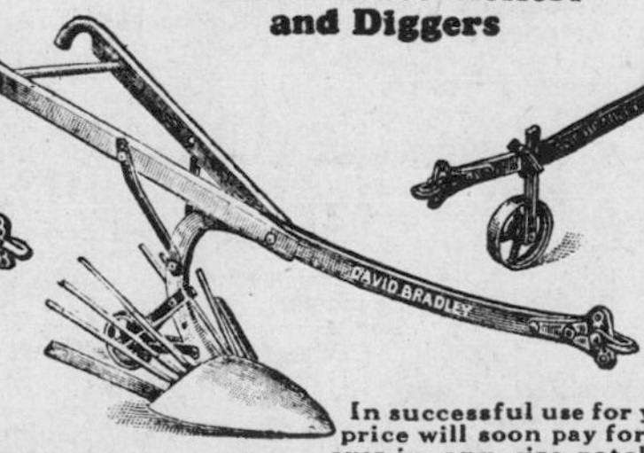

In successful use for years and at our low price will soon pay for itself several times over in any size patch. Forged steel beam digger. Adjustable rear gauge wheel regulates depth of digger. Polished steel digger blade throws potatoes out of ground without cutting them. Hiller blade has hinged wings adjustable for width. Gauge wheel shown on hiller is extra at price shown below. Either hiller or digger blade can be easily and quickly attached to the same beam. Handles rigidly braced are adjustable for height. Buy the combined hiller and digger and you have a combination potato cultivator and digger.

highly arched to clear trash.

Catalog No.	Description	Wt., Lbs.	From Philadelphia store
72K432¼	Potato Digger only	100	$ 9.50
72K433¼	Potato Hiller only	73	9.80
72K434¼	Combined Potato Hiller and Digger	118	13.70
72K435¼	Front Gauge Wheel, extra	11	.98

David Bradley Steel Guarded End Lever Harrow

Guarded frame prevents catching on trees, stumps, stones or other obstructions. The U shape steel tooth bars are fastened to the heavy I beam frame at each end. A very rigid construction. Triangular 7-inch swedged teeth are headed; can't drop out. Single section harrows shipped with draw irons; other sizes with drawbar and irons. Shipped from our Philadelphia store.

Catalog No.	No. Teeth	No. Sections	Width, Cut, Ft.	Wt., Lbs.	Each
72K362¼	25	1	4	90	$ 7.25
72K363¼	30	1	4¾	97	7.95
72K364¼	50	2	8	185	15.60
72K365¼	60	2	9½	210	17.00
72K366¼	75	3	12	275	23.40
72K367¼	90	3	14¼	310	26.40

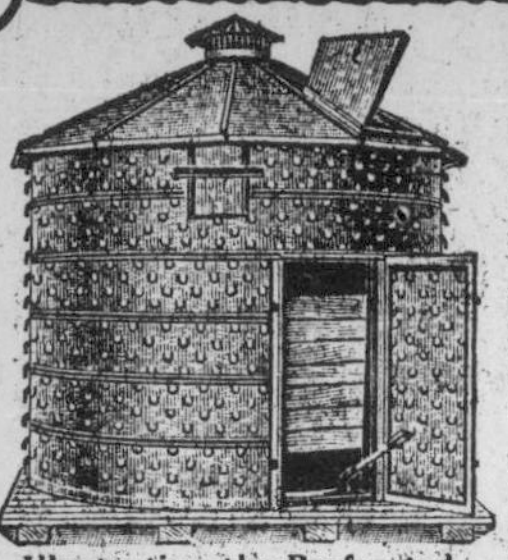

Illustrating the Perforated Corn Cribs

Galvanized Steel Corn Cribs and Grain Bins

Corn or grain stored in these steel bins is kept in perfect condition. Rainproof, ratproof and fireproof; lightning will not harm them. Made from 22-gauge galvanized steel for the body and 26-gauge for the roof. The sheets extend horizontally around body, forming a corrugated overlapping joint. Steel circles extend around top and bottom of body inside and the sheets are bolted to these circles. Easily set up.

Door frames strongly formed, and doors equipped with strong hinges and double steel hasps which can be fastened with padlock. Sectional roof joined by standing seams, fastened with bolted clamps and bolted to body.

Hinged door in roof has hasp for locking. Perforated ventilating pipe extends from floor to top ventilator. The body perforations are eliptical, slightly larger at top than at bottom. The tongues of metal are punched out far enough to provide full ventilation, yet the projecting tongues prevent rain beating in.

Bottoms of corn cribs are extra. Bolts and anchors are furnished for setting on concrete or wooden floor. **Shipped from factory in CENTRAL OHIO.**

Grain Bin

Prices of Perforated Corn Cribs

Catalog No.	Diameter	Height	Capacity, Ear Corn, Bushels	Wt., Lbs.	Each Crib	Wt. of Bottoms, Lbs.	Each Bottom
32K1487	7 ft. 11½ in.	7 ft. 8 in.	180	760	$ 72.85	90	$ 9.00
32K1488	7 ft. 11½ in.	10 ft. 2 in.	230	860	89.50	90	9.00
32K1480	10 ft. 4 in.	7 ft. 8 in.	305	1,000	93.75	115	14.50
32K1481	10 ft. 4 in.	10 ft. 2 in.	400	1,150	109.85	115	14.50
32K1482	12 ft. 9 in.	7 ft. 8 in.	475	1,180	113.75	180	18.00
32K1483	12 ft. 9 in.	10 ft. 2 in.	615	1,350	130.00	180	18.00

Prices of Grain Bins (Bodies Not Perforated)

Catalog No.	Diameter	Height	Capacity, Winchester Bushels	Wt., Lbs.	Each Bin	Wt. of Bottoms, Lbs.	Each Bottom
32K1494	7 ft. 11½ in.	7 ft. 8 in.	320	750	$ 77.25	90	$ 9.00
32K1495	7 ft. 11½ in.	10 ft. 2 in.	420	850	89.50	90	9.00
32K1490	10 ft. 4 in.	7 ft. 8 in.	516	1,000	92.50	115	14.50
32K1491	10 ft. 4 in.	10 ft. 2 in.	685	1,150	108.65	115	14.50
32K1492	12 ft. 9 in.	7 ft. 8 in.	785	1,180	112.50	180	18.00
32K1493	12 ft. 9 in.	10 ft. 2 in.	1,040	1,350	128.75	180	18.00

Make Your Cribs and Bins Ratproof. See Page 1075

Portable Wood and Wire Corn Crib $4.65 UP

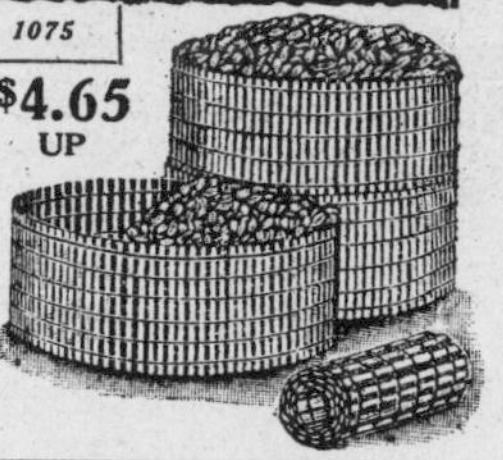

Made of heavy fence lath, 4 feet long, securely woven together with five pairs of No. 12 galvanized wires, by automatic machinery. Single section crib consists of one single section, 4 feet high. Double section crib consists of two sections, making crib 8 feet high. All single section and 400 and 600-bushel double section cribs are shipped in one bundle. Other sizes in two bundles. Capacity figured at 2 cubic feet to bushel. **Shipped from factory near CHICAGO.**

Single Section Cribs

Catalog No.	Cap., Bu.	Diam. Feet	Lineal Feet	Wt., Lbs.	Each
32K1484	400	16	48	175	$4.65
32K1485	500	18	55	200	5.45
32K1486	600	21	67	225	6.15

Double Section Cribs

Catalog No.	Cap., Bu.	Diam. Feet	Lineal Feet	Wt., Lbs.	Each
32K1473	800	15½	99	325	$ 9.45
32K1474	400	12	74	280	6.95
32K1475	600	14	88	340	8.50
32K1476	1,000	18	115	385	10.95
32K1477	1,200	20	124	485	12.35
32K1478	1,500	22	138	540	13.85

When not used as a crib, they make a good garden fence.

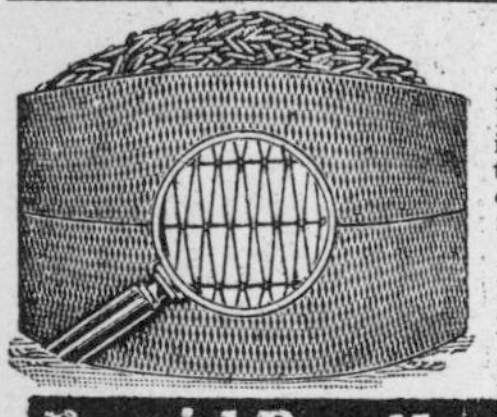

Portable Woven Wire Corn Crib

Top and bottom wires, No. 12½ gauge; intermediate horizontal wires, No. 14 and transverse wires, No. 14½ gauge galvanized wires forming meshes 2 inches wide. Ends of crib fasten together. (Illustration shows double section crib.) When not used as a crib, makes good garden fence. **Shipped from factory near CHICAGO.**

32K1460—Single Section. 400-bushel capacity, 15 ft. 6 in. in diam. Height, 4 ft. 1 in. Wt., 49 lbs. . **$3.50**

32K1461—Double Section. 400-bushel capacity, 11 ft. 8 in. in diam. Height, 8 ft. 2 in. Wt., 73 lbs. . **$5.15**

32K1462—Double Section. 800-bushel capacity, 15 ft. 6 in. in diam. Height, 8 ft. 2 in. Wt., 100 lbs. **$6.90**

David Bradley Two-Hole Corn Sheller

Requires only one horse-power engine or motor

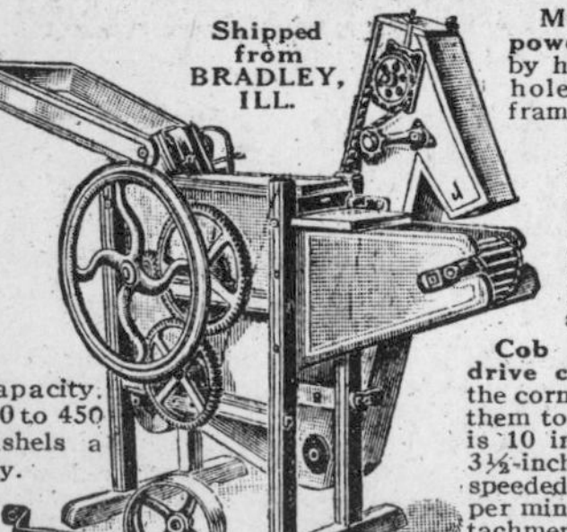

Shipped from BRADLEY, ILL.

Capacity. 350 to 450 bushels a day.

Made of extra heavy parts throughout for power use, yet so well balanced that it runs as easily by hand as the lighter two-hole machines. Hardwood frame is strongly bolted and braced. Balance wheel is extra heavy. Rag irons and springs are adjustable and can be set so machine will shell clean either small or large ears of corn. Delivers corn free from dirt and chaff.

Cob carrier has heavy drive chain, which separates the corn from cobs and delivers them to rear of sheller. Pulley is 10 inches in diameter with 3½-inch face and should be speeded about 350 revolutions per minute for best results. Attachments illustrated with sheller are extra. Price of sheller includes crank, pulley, fan and feed table.

	Description	Weight, Pounds	Each
32K1408	Two-Hole Sheller..........	290	$31.90
32K1409	6-Foot Cob Stacker..........	35	9.10
32K1410	5-Foot Sacking Elevator......	65	14.35
32K1411	8-Foot Wagon Elevator.....	90	20.05

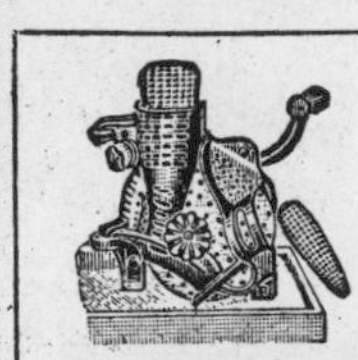

Adjustable Corn Sheller

Complete with cob guide; also has butting and tipping attachment. For removing imperfect grains at ends, when shelling seed corn. Adjustable spring tension **—takes all size ears.** Clamps to any box. **Shipped from our store.** Wt., 22 lbs.

72K1413¼ Complete.... **$1.90**

Always the Best

Knife on Flywheel Type Feed Cutters

For Stock and Poultry

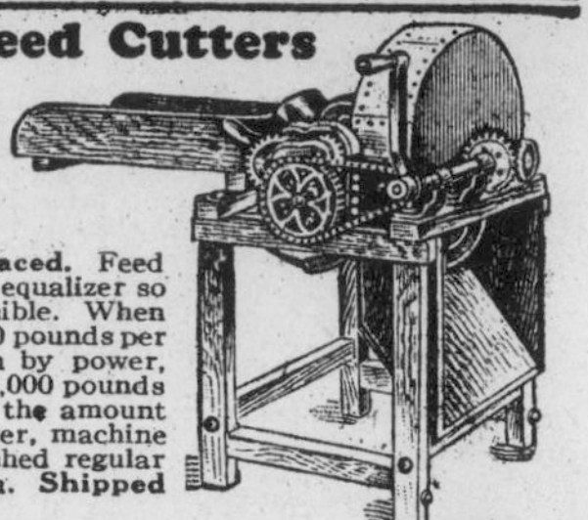

The knife on flywheel type is very efficient and preferred by many. This construction permits unusually easy operation with large capacity which has made this type very popular. Convenient cone gear provides quick change of length of cut adjustable to ⅛ inch, ⅜ inch or ¹¹⁄₁₆ inch.

Frame extra strong, made of hardwood, well braced. Feed table is broad and deep. Feed rolls are governed by an equalizer so both ends are raised equally—no binding in boxes possible. When run by hand, capacity dry fodder, No. 6 cutter, 400 to 600 pounds per hour; No. 9, 600 to 800 pounds per hour. When run by power, capacity No. 6 cutter, 600 to 800 pounds; No. 9, 800 to 1,000 pounds per hour. Capacity for green fodder is about double the amount given for dry fodder. When operating cutters by power, machine should run 200 to 400 revolutions per minute. Furnished regular with crank for hand operation. Pulley for power is extra. **Shipped from factory near CHICAGO.**

32K1522—No. 6 Cutter, equipped with two 9-inch knives. Weight, 220 pounds.......... **$31.95**

32K1523—No. 9 Cutter, equipped with two 10-inch knives. Weight, 240 pounds.......... **34.80**

32K1524—10x4-Inch Pulley. Weight, 13 pounds.......... **2.50**

Hand Feed Cutters for Stock and Poultry

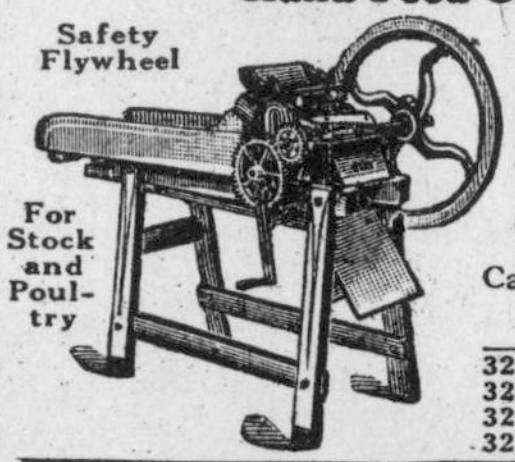

Safety Flywheel

For Stock and Poultry

Durable and efficient cutters at very low prices. Removing one knife doubles length of cut. Instantaneous lever control. Two tempered steel knives make a downward shearing cut against a hardened cutting bar. Capacities per hour given based on hand operation. Running by power more than doubles capacity. Pulley for power extra. **No. 7 Cutter recommended for cutting feed for poultry.** Capacity of green fodder is double the amount shown below for dry fodder.

Catalog No.	Size No.	Size Knife	Cap., Lbs., Dry Fodder	Length of Cut, In.	Wt., Lbs.	From Factory Near Chicago
32K1519	7	8½ in.	150 to 200	⅛, ⁵⁄₁₆, ½	150	$18.95
32K1515	8	8½ in.	200 to 300	½, ⅝, 1	175	21.75
32K1516	10	10 in.	300 to 450	½, ⅝, 1	290	31.50
32K1517	10x3-in. Pulley. State size cutter.				10	1.12

Power Feed Cutters

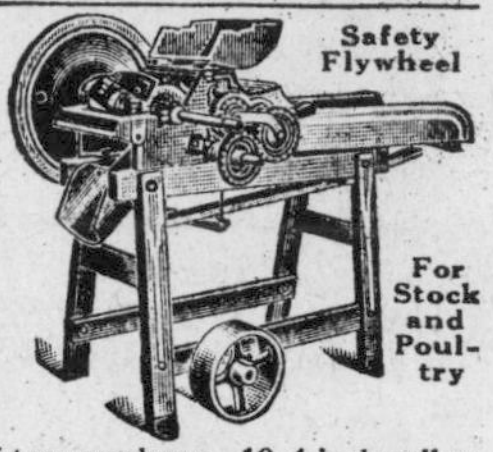

Safety Flywheel

For Stock and Poultry

Large capacity. Requires 1 to 2 horse-power engine. Heavy hardwood frame strongly braced. Feed rolls driven by expansion gearing. Pressure controlled by an equalizer and spring board. Friction balance wheel, safety stop lever and sliding cone gear for changing length of cut. Capacity of green feed is double the amount given below for dry fodder. By removing two opposite knives on No. 11 Cutter, length of cut is doubled. **No. 10½ Cutter is especially designed for cutting feed for poultry.**

32K1520—No. 10½ Cutter has three 10½-inch steel knives. Length of cut, ⅜, ¼ and ⅜ inch. Capacity, dry fodder, 800 to 1,200 pounds per hour. 10x4-inch pulley. Speed, 300 to 400 revolutions per minute. Weight, 300 lbs. **Shipped from factory near CHICAGO.. $35.25**

32K1530—No. 11 Cutter has four 11-inch steel knives. Length of cut, ¼, ⅝ and 1 inch. Capacity, dry fodder, 1 to 1½ tons per hour. 10x4-inch pulley. Speed, 400 to 500 revolutions per minute. Weight, 380 pounds. **Shipped from OHIO factory..........$41.75**

32K1531—Crank for hand use. Weight, 8 pounds.......... **1.25**

No. 5 Hand Feed Cutter

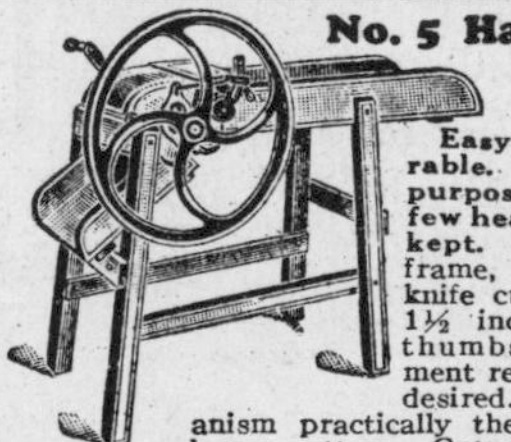

Easy running, durable. Answers every purpose where but a few head of cattle are kept. Heavy cast end frame, 11-inch cutting knife cuts from ⅓ to 1½ inches long. A thumbscrew adjustment regulates size cut desired. Feeding mechanism practically the same as our larger cutters. Capacity, 150 to 200 pounds dry fodder and 300 to 400 pounds green fodder per hour. Weight, 150 pounds. **Shipped from our store.**

72K1505¼.......... **$17.75**

Bradley Lever Feed Cutter

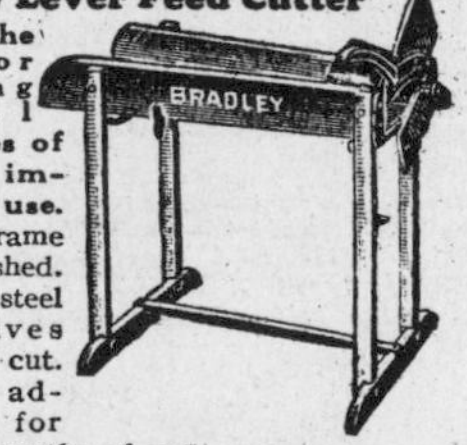

Just the size for cutting small quantities of feed for immediate use. Heavy frame well finished. Curved steel knife gives shearing cut. Positive adjustment for different lengths of cut. **Shipped from our store.**

72K1500¼—Weight, 65 pounds.......... **$6.65**

Root Cutters

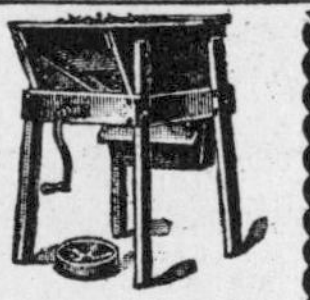

Cuts roots and vegetables into long half round pieces for feeding cattle, hogs and sheep. Knives easily replaced or sharpened. **Shipped from factory in NORTHERN OHIO.**

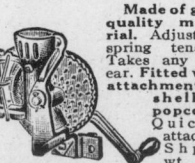

32K1395—With crank for hand power. Capacity, 30 to 50 bushels per hour. Weight, 100 pounds.. **$13.35**

32K1396—With crank and pulley. Capacity, by power, 60 to 80 bushels per hour. Weight, 110 pounds.......... **$14.95**

Hustler Corn Sheller

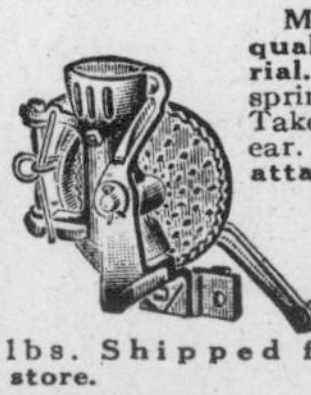

Made of good quality material. Adjustable spring tension. Takes any size ear. **Fitted with attachment for shelling popcorn.** Quickly attached. Shpg. wt., 16 lbs. **Shipped from our store.**

72K1414¼.......... **$1.35**

All Steel One-Hole Corn Sheller

Better Work and Greater Capacity

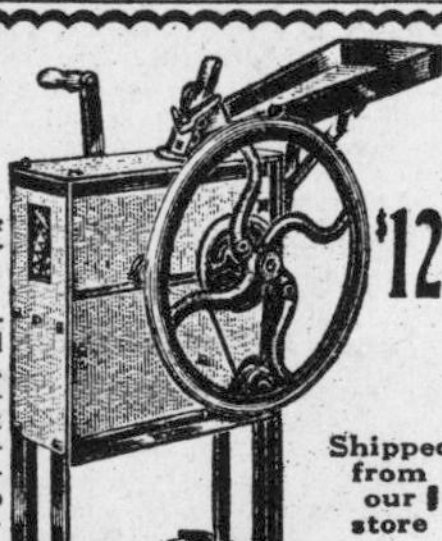

$12.95

Shipped from our store

For poultrymen and small farms. A marked improvement over the ordinary wood construction, no warping or decay. Permanent alignment of all working parts and a clean job of shelling insured. Sheller is of the rapid feed type. A new style of construction of the feed spout permits ears to pass through to the shelling discs without being hindered by any obstruction or opening in the wall of the throat. No wedging. Heavy angle iron frame strongly braced. Sides of heavy galvanized sheet steel. Shaft is cold rolled steel; all bearings accurately fitted, permitting easy operation. Adjustable to take large or small ears. Heavy balance wheel. Fan has strong blast and delivers corn free from chaff and dirt. Capacity, 10 to 20 bushels per hour depending on speed and condition of the corn. **Shipped from our store.**

72K1406¼—One-Hole Sheller, complete with steel feed table and fan. Weight, 175 pounds.......... **$12.95**

72K1403¼—8-Inch Pulley for power. Weight, 6 pounds.......... **90c**

at Lowest Prices

Hand Grist Mills
$2.65
Size 1½

Every country home needs a grist mill. Grind corn, small grain, roots, bark, dry bone and shells, rock salt, coffee, etc. Adjustable to grind coarse, medium or fine. Made of iron throughout, except shaft, which is steel. Long wearing steel alloy burrs. Large heavy balance wheel makes mill easy running. Shipped from our store.

72K6133¼—Size No. 1½. Grinds about 2 pounds corn in 5 minutes. Shipping weight, 25 pounds........ **$2.65**

72K6134¼—Size No. 2. Grinds about 4 pounds corn in 5 minutes. Shipping weight, 42 pounds........ **4.60**

72K6135¼—Size No. 3. Grinds about 6 pounds corn in 5 minutes. Shipping weight, 74 pounds........ **7.65**

Extra Burrs

72K6140¼—For No. 1½ size grist mill. Weight, 1¼ pounds. Per pair........ **60c**

72K6141¼—For No. 2 size grist mill. Weight, 2¾ pounds. Per pair........ **95c**

72K6142¼—For No. 3 size grist mill. Weight, 6½ pounds. Per pair........ **$1.25**

Tools for Farm and Garden

One-Horse Steel Cultivator
With Lever Expander
$8.85

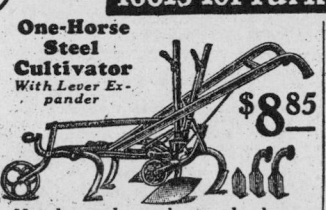

Has horse hoes, lever wheel, rear wheel depth regulator and outside handle braces. Solid and rigid in construction. Lever wheel and rear wheel depth regulator control depth of cultivation, enabling cultivator to run steadily. Lever expander widens or narrows width of cultivator to suit widths of rows. Shipping weight, 85 pounds. Shipped from our store.

72K6231¼—Complete.... **$8.85**

Steel Cultivator
With Lever Expander
$5.25
Without Wheel

Adjustable from 10 to 26 in. wide from center to center of teeth, outside handle braces. Has five 2½-in. teeth. Shpg. wt., 50 pounds.

Shipped from our store.

72K6306¼—Without Front Wheel........ **$5.25**

72K6227¼—With Front Wheel........ **$5.95**

72K6174—2½-Inch Cultivator Teeth. Weight, ¾ pound. Each........ **15c**

72K6176—10-Inch Cultivator Sweeps. Wt., 1½ lbs. Each........ **30c**

14-Tooth Steel Harrow
$5.55
Without Front Wheel

Equipped with lever expander with which you can adjust harrow from 11 to 33 inches in width; also has outside handle braces and front wheel. Diamond shape teeth, ⅝x⅝ inch. Weight, 52 pounds. Shipped from our store.

72K6307¼—Without Front Wheel........ **$5.55**

72K6235¼—With Front Wheel. Weight, 64 pounds........ **$6.25**

72K6172—Extra Teeth. Weight, 1 pound. Each........ **15c**

Steel Beam Double Shovel Plow
$3.90

Extra heavy beams, 1¾x¾ in. Steel blades, 6x11 inches. Handles have bolt as well as wood brace. Plow has adjustable clevises. Shipped from our store. Shipping weight, 32 pounds.

72K6204¼........ **$3.90**

Push Bar Garden Cultivator
$3.87

Can be used as plow, cultivator or weeder. The plow can be shifted from side to side independently of the course of the wheel. 18-inch wheel. Furnished with five cultivator teeth, plow, weeder attachment and wrench. Shipped from our store. Shipping weight, 25 pounds.

72K6211¼—Complete.... **$3.87**

Balance Frame Garden Cultivator
$2.98

With complete set of attachments. Constructed with center of weight directly over wheel axle, making it self-balancing. Slotted foot permits changing draft on attachments to suit light or heavy soils. 24-inch wheel and ¼x1-inch steel frame. Shipping weight, 22 pounds. Shipped from our store.

72K6240¼........ **$2.98**

High Wheel Garden Plow and Cultivator

Can be used as a garden plow, cultivator or hoe. Moldboard sweep, reversible shovel and wrench furnished with each implement. Shipping weight, 20 lbs. Shipped from our store.

72K6209¼—Complete...... **$2.65**

Five-Tooth Cultivator Hoe Attachment

Tempered Steel With Forged Points

Can be used with 72K6209¼ and 72K6240¼ or any Cultivator having slotted foot. Middle prong removable. Shipping wt., 2½ lbs. Shipped from our store.

72K6241¼........ **65c**

Triple-Geared Hand Seeder

Gauge regulates seed. Duck bag. Shipped from our store. Shipping weight, 5¼ lbs.

$1.75

Steel Singletrees

Shipped from our store.
Solid Center

Catalog No.	Size In.	Wt., Lbs.	Each
72K2396¼	26	4½	48c
72K2398¼	36	4½	80c

Swivel Center

Catalog No.	Size In.	Wt., Lbs.	Each
72K2397¼	26	4½	53c
72K2399¼	36	4½	85c

David Bradley Cob Crusher Feed Grinder
$25.95
Shipped From Our Store

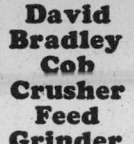

Grinds corn on the cob (without the shuck), shelled corn, oats or other small grain to most any degree of fineness from cracked feed to table meal. Cob breakers on the shaft and the worm feed constitute a force feed, giving grinder large capacity and making it an excellent mill for grinding small grain and shelled corn, as well as ear corn.

Extra heavy frame, cast in one piece, has hinged bottom with wood break pins.

Cold rolled steel shaft, 1⅛ inches in diameter, with ball bearing end thrust. Large bearings lined with engine babbitt and fitted with hard oil cups.

Large capacity sheet steel hopper. Ear corn will not bridge or choke.

Angle steel legs strongly braced.

Pulley is 12 inches in diameter with 6-inch face and should run from 300 to 500 revolutions per minute to give best results. Requires 4 to 6 horse-power engine. Can also furnish either 8x6, 10x6 or 14x6-inch pulley instead, without extra charge. State size of your engine pulley and its speed and we will equip the grinder with the proper size pulley. Capacity depends on power, speed and kind of grain. Grinds 10 to 25 bushels of dry ear corn, or 10 to 40 bushels of shelled corn, wheat, oats or barley per hour.

Large Grinding Capacity With Small Power

Instantaneous Hand Lever Adjustment

The 8-inch burrs are self aligning, self adjusting and extra heavy. A convenient lever regulates fineness of grinding and can be thrown off instantly, separating the burrs. Shipped complete with one set of coarse burrs for crushing or cracking ear and shelled corn for rough feed and one set of medium burrs for finer grinding of shelled corn and small grain. Special oats burrs, which are also suitable for grinding table meal, are extra at prices given below. Shipped from our store.

Grinder With Sacking Elevator

Catalog No.	Description	Wt. Lbs.	
72K1690¼	Cob Crusher Feed Grinder.	280	$25.95
72K1694¼	5-Foot Sacking Elevator	70	13.25
72K1697¼	Pair of Regular Burrs (state coarse or medium)	7	
72K1700¼	Pair of Special Oats Burrs.	7	.30
72K1701¼	Pair of Slice Cut Burrs.	7	.33

David Bradley Small Grain Grinder
$14.25

Feed Grinder, Family Mill and Flour Mill Combined

Requires Only 1 H.-P. Motor or Engine. Thousands in use. Grinds cornmeal and graham flour for table use, as well as coarse feed for cattle. Heavy cast iron frame strongly bolted. A slide in steel hopper regulates flow of grain. Pulley is 4x4 inches and should run from 700 to 750 revolutions per minute to give best results. Self aligning burrs, 5¼ inches, mounted in a dust tight case. Handwheel adjustment for fineness of grinding. One set coarse burrs for grinding shelled corn, oats and other small grains for feed, and one set fine burrs for grinding meal and flour for table use furnished with each mill. Capacity, 5 to 15 bushels per hour, depending on fineness of grinding, condition of grain and power used.

Prices Include Bolting Attachment

Catalog No.	Description	Wt., Lbs.	Shipped From Our Store
72K1660¼	Without Legs or Flywheel.......	72	$10.35
72K1661¼	With Legs and No Flywheel.......	83	11.95
72K1662¼	With Flywheel and No Legs.......	90	12.65
72K1663¼	With Flywheel and Legs.........	103	14.25
72K1664¼	Extra Burrs (State coarse or fine)	4	.87

Crystalline Metal Bells

School and Church Bells
$10.65 and Up

Cast from a special mixture of metal of high quality. We guarantee superior tone, volume and quality over composition bells of any other make. Thirty-eight inch and larger bells mounted on roller bearings enable one person to easily ring our largest bells. Bells 24 inches and larger fitted with improved spring clapper, insuring full stroke without possibility of a second stroke. Shipped complete with frame, wheels and wood sills, from factory in OHIO.

Farm Bells
$3.95 and Up

Every farm should have a good bell. The metal in these bells is the same as in our school and church bells. Large size recommended for use on the average farm. Shipped from factory in OHIO.

School and Factory Bells

Catalog No.	Dia. In.	Wt., Lbs.	Each
32K2800	20	165	$10.65
32K2801	22	205	13.50
32K2802	24	250	17.00
32K2803	26	350	26.15
32K2804	28	450	33.50
32K2805	30	555	43.75

Church Bells, With Tolling Hammers

Catalog No.	Dia. In.	Wt., Lbs.	Each
32K2822	24	260	$19.50
32K2823	26	365	29.55
32K2824	28	465	36.95
32K2825	30	570	46.70
32K2826	32	640	52.50
32K2827	34	765	63.15
32K2828	36	950	76.40
32K2829	38	1,010	87.25
32K2830	40	1,300	105.50
32K2834	48	2,280	180.00

Farm Bells

Catalog No.	Diam. In.	Wt., Lbs.	Each
32K2835	16	58	$3.95
32K2836	18	73	5.65
32K2837	19½	112	7.50

High Grade Farm Wagons *and* Trucks

Champion Two-Horse Standard Farm Wagons

$87.50 Up

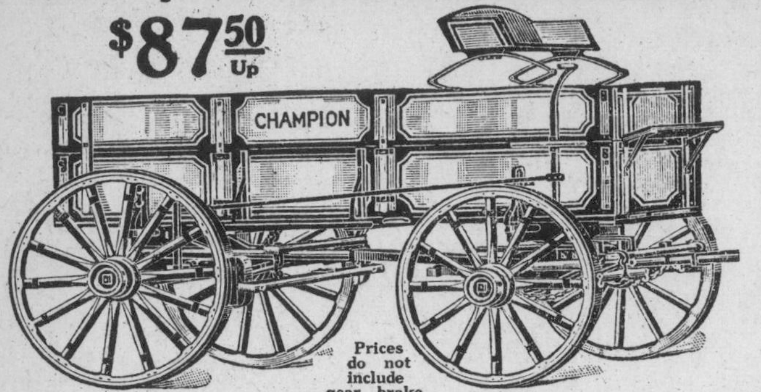

Prices do not include gear brake.

Champion in quality and workmanship. Guaranteed to give the utmost of service. Our low prices give you a substantial saving. Note carefully the features of superior construction.

GEAR—All gear woods including reaches, bolsters and hounds are seasoned selected oak. Heavy steel bolster, sand and bolster plates.

AXLES of best grade hickory. Dust-proof skeins have extra large bells and are set in red lead. Level bearing-weight distributed entire length of skein.

BOX flooring is of selected yellow pine, grooved and matched; sides of seasoned wood guaranteed not to warp or split. Top sides securely held with cleats; double bottom over bolsters and box fasteners on each side. Boxes are 10½ feet long, equipped with comstock type endgate.

WOOD WHEELS of highest quality material. Oak spokes, rims and hubs. Hubs bored true to rims. Steel tires securely bolted to rim.

TRACK—Narrow track wagons measure 4 feet 6 inches wide from center to center of tires at bottom of wheels. Wide track wagons measure 5 feet wide from center to center of tires at bottom of wheels. Be sure to specify width desired.

Read Before Ordering

Champion Wagons are shipped regular with 40-inch front and 44-inch rear wheels, and with drop tongue and neck yoke. We can furnish instead wagons with 36-inch front wheels, 40-inch rear wheels or 42-inch front and 48-inch rear wheels without extra charge. **Be sure to state when special height wheels are desired. Will furnish stiff detachable tongue with tongue chains instead of drop tongue and neck yoke when desired. Do not fail to specify width track wanted.**

Wagons shipped complete with seat, grain cleats, spreader chains, side box fasteners, drop tongue, doubletrees and neck yoke from factory near LOUISVILLE, KY.

Catalog No.	Size of Skein	Size of Tires	Depth of Box	Estimated Capacity, Pounds	Weight, Gear and Box, Lbs.	Price, Gear Only	Wagon Complete
32K1060⅓	2½x8	1½x½	20 inches	2,500	900	$64.75	$ 87.50
32K1032	3x9	2 x½	24 inches	3,000	1,000	71.50	96.95
32K1033	3x9	2½x½	24 inches	3,000	1,100	75.00	100.80
32K1034	3¼x10	2½x½	26 inches	4,000	1,200	76.25	101.50
32K1035	3¼x10	3 x½	26 inches	4,000	1,275	78.00	104.00

If higher box is wanted than listed add 80c per inch. Weights of wagon gear only are about 300 to 350 pounds less than above weights.

Extra Attachments

32K1079—Gear Brake, complete. Weight, 70 pounds.......... **$6.50**

32K1080—Lock Chains. Wt., 15 pounds.................. **$1.50**

32K1802—Set Doubletrees and Neck yoke. Weight, 34 lbs.......... **$4.10**

32K1081—10-Inch Tip Top box. Weight, 80 pounds.......... **$7.65**

32K1082—12-Inch Tip Top box. Weight, 90 pounds.......... **$8.85**

Handy Platform Cart

Useful for handling milk cans, barrels, sprayers, etc. Steel frame strongly bolted and braced. Woodplatform, 32x28 inches, set close to ground. Detachable chain across front of cart to hold load on platform. Wheels, 36 inches in diameter; 2-inch wide tires. Removable side and end boards, forming a box 11¾ inches deep furnished at extra price. **Shipped from our store.**

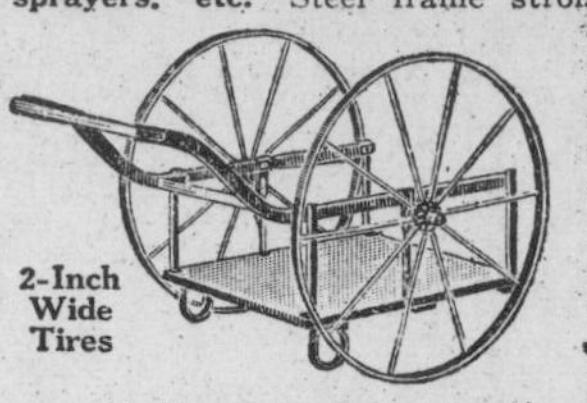

2-Inch Wide Tires

72K2236¼—Weight, 100 lbs... **$8.45**

72K2237¼—Removable Box. Weight, 27 pounds.......................... **$2.20**

Hand Cart

For Farm or City Delivery Use

Wheels run smoothly on sidewalks and pavement as well as soft ground. Has large, deep selected wood box. 1-inch steel axle. Wheels, 36 inches high with 2-inch wide tires. Box, 36 inches long, 21 inches wide, 9 inches deep inside. Ends and sides can be removed, leaving bottom flat. Top extension box shown in illustration extra at price shown below. **Shipped from our store.**

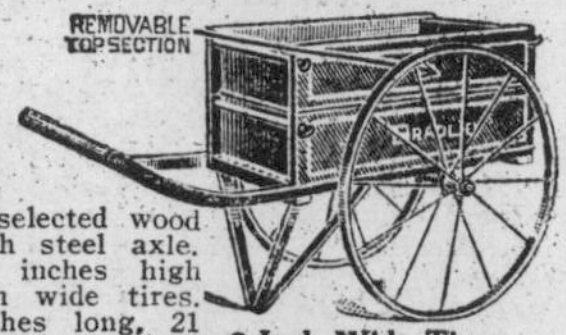

2-Inch Wide Tires

72K2227¼—Hand Cart. Weight, 100 pounds.................. **$9.75**

72K2228¼—Top Extension Box. Weight, 15 pounds.......................... **$1.50**

One-Horse Farm Wagons

$59.75

WAGON COMPLETE

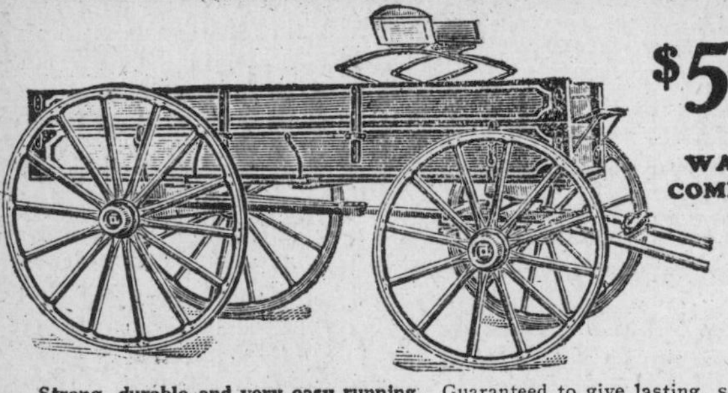

Strong, durable and very easy running. Guaranteed to give lasting, satisfactory service.

Axles and spokes of seasoned hickory. Hubs, rims, bolsters and gear woods made of seasoned oak. Rims securely riveted at spokes. Gear and box substantially ironed and nicely painted. Height of wheels, front, 40 inches; rear, 44 inches. Length of box, standard size, 8 feet 6 inches. Extra heavy size, 9 feet 10 inches.

Track. Narrow, 4 feet 8 inches. **Wide,** 5 feet between wheel centers.

Bolsters for narrow track measure 38 inches between stakes; for wide track, 42 inches. **Specify width wanted. Prices given below include shafts. Shipped from factory near LOUISVILLE, KY.**

One-Horse Wagon, Wood Axle, Cast Skeins and Wood Hub Wheels

	Size, Skein	Size, Tires	Depth, Box	Capacity	Weight, Gear Only	Weight, Wagon, Complete
Standard size..	2¼x7 in.	1¼x⅜ in.	14 in.	1,500 lbs.	450 lbs.	550 lbs.
Extra heavy size	2½x8 in.	1⅜x⁷⁄₁₆ in.	18 in.	2,000 lbs.	660 lbs.	700 lbs.

32K1010—Standard size Gear only, with shafts.......................**$42.50**

32K1011—Standard size Wagon, complete with box and seat....... **59.75**

32K1012—Extra heavy Gear only, with shafts...................... **47.65**

32K1013—Extra heavy Wagon, complete with box and seat......... **66.50**

32K1014—Extra for Gear Brake.................................. **6.75**

32K1015—Extra for Box Brake.................................... **6.55**

32K1016—Extra for Pole in place of shafts....................... **2.45**

Standard One-Horse Wagon With Sarven Patent Wheels

Similar to our 32K1010 and 32K1011, with the exception that it has solid steel axles instead of wood and Sarven patent wheels instead of wood hub wheels.

32K1019—Gear only. Capacity, 1,700 pounds.......................**$42.65**

32K1020—Wagon complete with box and seat. Capacity, 1,700 lbs... **59.95**

If complete wagon is wanted without spring seat deduct $4.65 from prices shown.

One-Horse Handy Dump Cart

Can Be Used in Places Inaccessible to a Wagon

$27.75

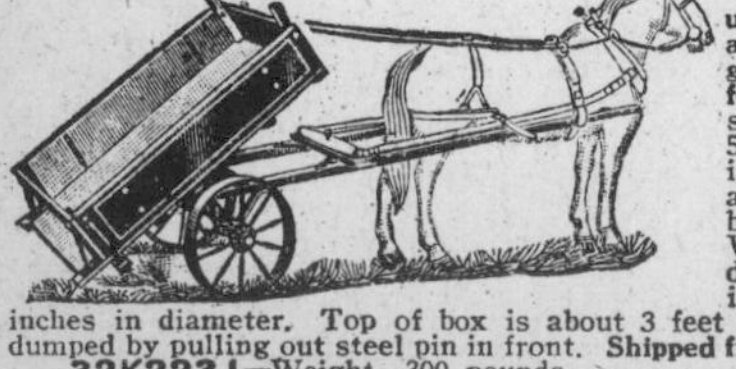

A light one-horse cart, suitable for use in fence building, gathering fruit and truck crops, hauling manure for gardens, light loads of dirt, stone, fodder, etc. Strongly built of good sound lumber, well painted. Box is 5 feet long, 3 feet 4 inches wide, 11½ inches deep, inside measurements, and made of ⅞-inch material, well braced. Bottom is strongly framed. Wheels are heavy steel, 24 inches in diameter, 3-inch tires, and the tread is 48 inches. Solid steel axle, 1⅜ inches in diameter. Top of box is about 3 feet high from the ground. Box can be dumped by pulling out steel pin in front. **Shipped from BRADLEY, ILL.**

32K2231—Weight, 300 pounds.......... **$27.75**

Steel Frame Barrel and Spray Cart

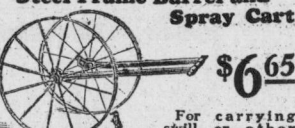

$6.65

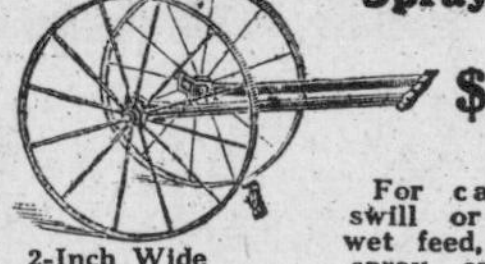

2-Inch Wide Tires

For carrying swill or other wet feed, orchard spray cart, etc. Steel wheels are 36 inches high with 2-inch tires. Frame bolted to axle castings, made to fit the sides of a barrel to which they are bolted. Price includes bolts, one bracket or rest for bottom of barrel. **Shipped from our store.**

72K2225¼—Weight, 66 pounds.......... **$6.65**

Milk Can Barrow

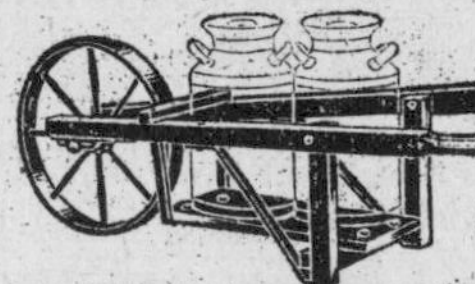

$4.85

A strongly built barrow with low platform that will save the high lifts. The handiest barrow for handling milk or cream cans, grain, potatoes, feed for stock, etc. Heavy hardwood frame strongly braced. Platform, 24 inches long and 10 inches wide. Heavy 20-inch steel wheel with 2-inch tires. Price does not include cans. **Shipped from factory in OHIO.**

32K2226⅓—Wt., 50 lbs... **$4.85**

Four and Six-Knee Bench Sleds

$27.75 Four-Knee Sled

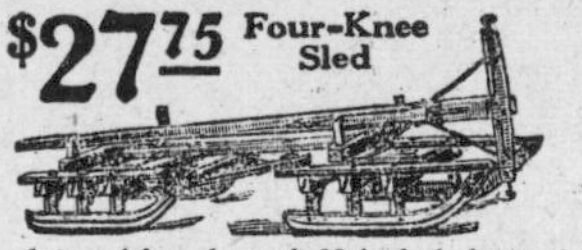

These are well constructed bobsleds and are the most popular sizes and styles of this type of sled we have ever sold. Made of thoroughly seasoned hard sled stock. **RUNNERS**—2x3-inch stock, 4 feet 8 inches long. **KNEES**—2½x3 inches. **SHOES**—3 feet 3 inches long; very heavy; cast in one piece. **BEAMS**—2½x3 inches. **RAVES**—1¼x5 inches. **PAINTING**—Bright red. **TRACK**—37 inches. Complete with pole and 38-inch bolsters. **Shipped from factory in OHIO.**

32K4904—Four-Knee Bench Sled. Weight, 350 pounds.......... **$27.75**

32K4905—Six-Knee Bench Sled (as illustrated above). Weight, 370 pounds.......... **30.00**

Can furnish 42-inch bolsters instead of 38-inch, extra.......... **$1.50**

Extra for shafts, in place of pole.......... **5.50**

Wood Knee Cutter Gear

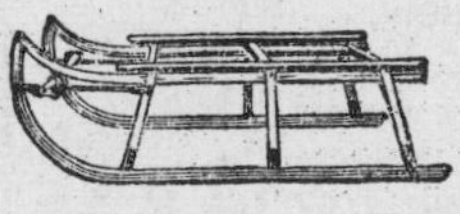

Easily fastens to your buggy body. Strongly made from seasoned hardwood sled stock, well braced. Has drawbar and shaft, shackles for standard width of shaft or pole. Hitch can be made to center or side. Wood runners, raves and knees, 1x⅝-inch stock. Runners have steel shoes. Gear is 17 inches high and about 5 feet long; 37-inch track. **Shipped from OHIO factory.**

32K4919 Weight, 50 lbs... **$7.95**

Light Spring Wagon Bobsled

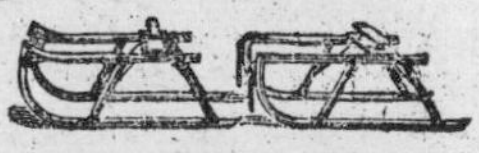

Height, 18 inches from the ground. The runners are 3 feet 1 inch long. Front runners furnished with common drawbar and shaft shackle so common width of shaft or pole can be attached either front or side. Runners painted dark red and fitted with hardened steel shoes. **BEAMS**—1¾x6 inches; wood runners, raves and knees of seasoned sled stock. **TRACK**—37 inches. **Shipped from factory in OHIO.**

32K4910—Weight, 100 pounds.... **$10.50**

Bobsled Runners

$3.25

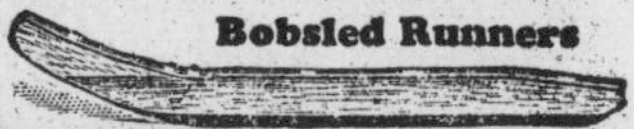

For repairing any make sled. Selected hardwood, painted. Channel iron reinforced nose. Heavy cast shoe attached with smooth head tire bolts. Our 1⅞-inch runners are commonly known to the trade as 2-inch. **Shipped from our store.**

Catalog No.	Actual Measure	Weight, Each	Each
72K4915¼	1⅞x5 in. x 4 ft. 7 in...	30 lbs.	$3.25
72K4916¼	1⅞x6 in. x 5 ft. 9 in...	42 lbs.	3.80
72K4917¼	1⅞x6 in. x 6 ft. 7½ in...	52 lbs.	4.15
72K4918¼	2½x6 in. x 6 ft. 7½ in...	75 lbs.	5.95

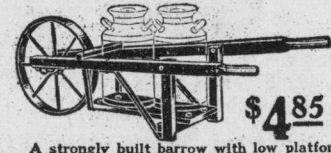

Built to Stand Hardest Wear

Steel and Wood Wheel Farm Trucks

Ringed Bolster Stakes

Grooved Steel Tires

Trussed Axles

$39⁷⁵ and Up

Metal Wheel

To stand the gaff of rough usage the year around, a farm truck must be built of the best material. The trucks we offer are built according to standards adopted by leading farm wagon manufacturers and guaranteed to give the limit of service. Every point of strain securely trussed and braced. All parts perfectly fitted. Made of first quality seasoned lumber, high grade iron and steel by expert wagon manufacturers, and have every feature found in the very best trucks. Easy running and built low for easy loading. Order this truck and compare it with the best and highest priced trucks. If it is not the biggest bargain you have ever seen return it to us.

Standard Oak Drop Tongue furnished regular with trucks. Can furnish stiff tongue instead for $2.00 extra.

AXLES—Heavy select quality hickory with strong steel truss rods underneath, giving additional strength.
SKEINS—Standard cast iron, 3¼x10 inches. Set in red lead and forged on axles by hydraulic pressure.
REACH—Selected oak, 10 feet long.
BOLSTERS—Narrow, measure 38 inches between stakes. **Wide**, 42 inches between bolster stakes. **State width desired.**
TRACK—Narrow, 4 feet 8 inches between wheel centers. **Wide**, 5 feet between wheel centers.
WHEELS—Metal Wheels, full forged, have 4x⅜-inch grooved steel tires; steel spokes are forged into hubs. Guaranteed never to come loose. Front wheels, 28 inches high; rear wheels, 32 inches high. **Wood Wheels**—Built of carefully selected hardwood. Steel tires, 3x⅜-inch, securely set to oak rims. Front wood wheels are 36 inches high; rear wood wheels, 40 inches high.
PAINTING—Gearing on both wood and steel wheel trucks nicely painted dark orange color. Metal wheels painted black; wood wheels, dark orange color.

Can furnish these trucks with Round Steel Angle Hounds for drop tongue in place of Square Wood Hounds at same prices. If wanted be sure to specify when ordering.

Wood Wheel Truck $52⁸⁰

Catalog No.	Description	Wt., Lbs.	Ship'd from Fact. Nr. Louisville, Ky.
32K1800A	Wood Wheel Farm Truck, Wide Track..	660	$52.95
32K1800B	Wood Wheel Farm Truck, Narrow Track	650	52.80
32K1801A	Steel Wheel Farm Truck, Wide Track..	550	39.90
32K1801B	Steel Wheel Farm Truck, Narrow Track	540	39.75
32K1802	Set doubletrees and neckyoke............	34	4.10
32K1803	Brakes with box attachment............	75	7.75
32K1804	Brakes without box attachment........	65	5.75

Steel Wheel Farm Truck

$34⁹⁵

Standard quality truck somewhat lighter than the one shown as the truss rods are omitted and it has a plain front gear and crossbar tongue. Capacity, 4,000 pounds. Handy truck for about the farm and for general hauling. Built low for easy loading. This truck will give years of satisfactory service. Hickory axles. All other wood parts seasoned oak. Skeins, standard cast iron, 3¼x10 inches. **Bolsters, narrow,** measure 38 inches between stakes; **wide** —42 inches between stakes. **Track, narrow,** 4 feet 8 inches between wheel centers; **wide**—5 feet between wheel centers. **Metal wheels,** good quality, have 4x⅜ inch grooved steel tires; size, front, 28 inches high; rear, 32 inches high. **Painting**—gearing dark orange color, wheels black. **Shipped from factory near LOUISVILLE, KY.**

32K1830—Narrow Track. Weight, 510 pounds...............$34.95
32K1831—Wide Track. Weight, 515 pounds.................. 35.50

Grain Tight Wagon Box $23⁵⁰

26x38-Inch

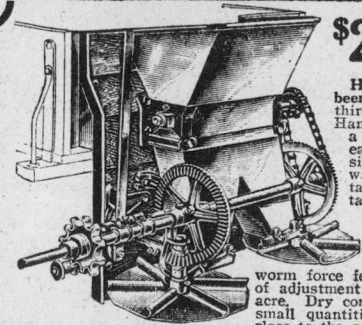

Complete with Comstock hinged endgate, grain cleats, spreader chain and side box fasteners.

A **first class, substantial box** of standard construction at a price that saves you money. Such quality, construction, equipment and general finish are found only in the best grade wagon boxes.

The floor is made of selected seasoned material, tongued, grooved and strongly braced. Selected wood sides, will not warp and are free from knots. All outside cleats hardwood, securely riveted and nailed at both ends. Cast iron wearing plates, reinforced bolsters. Double edge irons on top of sides and ends. All joints between top boards and box completely covered by strong cleats, making the box grain tight. 10½ feet long, 26 or 28 inches deep.

Catalog No.	Description	Depth, Inches	Width, Inches	Weight, Pounds	Shipped From Factory Near Louisville, Ky.
32K1805	Wagon Box........	26	38	350	$23.50
32K1809	Wagon Box........	26	42	355	24.00
32K1810	Wagon Box........	28	38	360	24.25
32K1811	Wagon Box........	28	42	365	24.75
32K1806	Tip Top Box......	10	..	75	6.75
32K1812	Tip Top Box......	12	..	80	7.25
32K1807	Spring Seat.......	..	..	35	5.45

Force Feed Lime and Fertilizer Sowers

$44⁸⁵

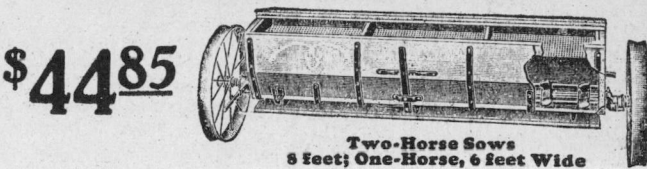

Two-Horse Sows 8 feet; One-Horse, 6 feet Wide

Handles all kinds of commercial fertilizers, ashes, lime, marl and pulverized limestone. Hand lever regulates sowing of any desired quantity. The agitator and force feed consist of heavy cast paddles mounted on the 1¼ inch square steel shaft axles and driven from both wheels. Drive shaft has a center bearing and each wheel drives half the shaft independently of the other half. A clutch in each wheel enables operator to throw out one or both drives. The feed wheels are spread 6 inches apart the entire length of hopper, one directly over each discharge opening in hopper bottom. Two steel rods extending full length pass through each feed wheel and, in addition to strengthening the feed, they serve as agitators. This arrangement gives a steady uniform feed of any weight material.

Hopper holds 10 bushels, is strongly built of good lumber, well braced, with hinged lid and heavy sheet iron bottom and ends. A removable galvanized screen keeps out obstructions which would not pass through discharge openings. Extra large grease cups on bearings provide thorough lubrication. Steel wheels, 30 inches in diameter; 4-inch wide concave tires. Price includes pole, but no neckyoke or eveners. **Shipped from factory near CHICAGO.**
32K1133—Two-Horse Spreader. Width of sowing, 8 feet.
Weight, 456 pounds...................................$44.85

One-Horse Lime and Fertilizer Sowers

Similar in construction to above. Sows lime and fertilizer same as 2-Horse Spreader and in addition has special feature for top dressing for growing plants, all but four openings can be closed, allowing a top dressing on two rows 3 feet apart. Openings for each row are about 6 inches apart, so dressing will fall on either side of plant in the row. Can Furnish plate for drilling 3½ feet apart instead of 3 feet if so stated on your order. Steel wheels 36 inches high with 3-inch tires. Price includes shafts but no evener. **Shipped from factory near PHILADELPHIA.**
32K1154—One-Horse Spreader. Width of sowing, 6 feet.
Weight, 355 pounds...................................$41.75

Endgate Lime and Fertilizer Spreader

$29⁹⁵ **The Use of Lime and Fertilizer Means a Bigger Yield and Increased Profits**

Here is an Endgate Spreader you have been waiting for. Our price saves you one-third or more over ordinary retail prices. Handles all kinds of commercial fertilizer and pulverized lime in the quickest, easiest and cheapest way. Material is simply shoveled into the hopper from wagon box. No clogging or caking. Attaches to the rear end of any wagon box, taking the place of endgate. Installed or removed in a few minutes' time. No holes to bore. A sturdy, light draft, high quality spreader. No complicated parts. Guaranteed to stand up under the most severe usage. Has positive worm force feed. Regulator slides permit big range of adjustment for spreading the desired amount per acre. Dry commercial fertilizer can be applied in as small quantities as 150 pounds to the acre. Sows close to the ground. All bearings are on outside, dust and dirt free, easily oiled. Protector board or shield extending below the revolving discs prevent interference with even sowing by wind, cornstalks or other obstructions in the field. Double revolving discs with fins driven by balanced gears insure an even, uniform spread up to approximately 20 feet in width depending on weight and condition of material. The long control lever permits operator to quickly and conveniently throw in or out of gear. Price includes large sprocket wheel with clips for attaching to wagon wheel, also chain for driving. **Shipped from factory near FORT WAYNE, INDIANA.**
32K1153—Weight, 200 pounds.....................$29.95

Let Sears Save You Money

FARMERS' FRIEND

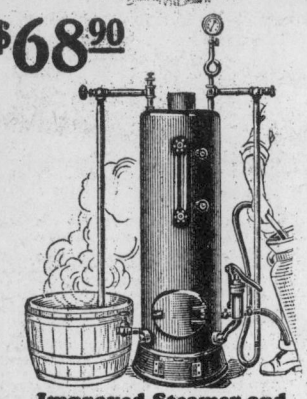

$68.90

Improved Steamer and Feed Cooker

Used for a variety of purposes on the farm, dairies, etc., wherever steam is required for cooking feed, scalding hogs, washing or renovating purposes.

Will burn coal, wood, cobs, etc. Are very quick steamers and will furnish a continuous supply of steam under pressure as long as fuel and water are supplied. Can be used anywhere. Shell is made of genuine boiler plate steel ¼-inch thick, with heads of ⅛-inch fire box steel. No small flues to clog or burn out. Water completely surrounds fire box. Heads are securely welded to shell. Cast iron base and dump grate.

Equipped with pop safety valve set at 15 pounds, steam gauge, water gauge, two sets of half-inch steam pipes with shut-off valves, two try cocks, hand pump and hand pump hose. Diameter of boiler, 17 inches.

Catalog No.	Boiler Cap.	Ht. In.	Wt. Lbs.	From Southern Michigan Factory
32K1888	30 gal.	56	430	$68.90
32K1889	40 gal.	68	485	77.00

Sanitary Watering Fountain

For hogs, sheep and other small stock. Automatic feed. Galvanized steel with top and bottom double seamed. Top is pressed into funnel shape and has brass filling plug. Mounted on heavy angle steel sled. Fountain with heater has base enclosed; furnished with a three-burner kerosene heater. Shipped from factory in EASTERN OHIO.

Catalog No.	Cap. Gal.	Wt. Lbs.	Without Heater	With Heater
32K1860	65	105	$9.85	$17.65
32K1861	85	105	10.95	18.75
32K1862	100	110	12.00	

Dewey Automatic Stock Waterer

Easily attached to open tank or barrel. Regulated by brass float. Cast iron trough, 11½x6x4½ inches high outside. Furnished complete with gaskets, strainer, wood block and directions for attaching.

72K990¼—Weight, 14 lbs...... **$1.90**

Automatic Regulator Valve and Float

$2.50

A universal valve that will work either under gravity or pressure feed. Easily installed in any trough or tank, and will maintain a constant supply of fresh water. Valves are brass, of heavy pattern.

The small valve is for hog troughs, the large valve where a large amount of water is needed, as in large troughs or cattle tanks. Either valve can be connected to any size pipe by using ordinary pipe reducers.

Shipped from our store, complete with copper float, locknuts and pipe nipple.

72K1978—½-inch valve. **$2.50**
Weight, 3 pounds..........
72K1979—¾-inch valve. Weight, 5 pounds. **$3.50**

CALDRON COOKER AND FURNACE

$7.60 and Up

Give your hogs cooked feed and get greater profits. Cooker can also be used for rendering lard, boiling sap, making soap, etc. Has no bottom. Sets on the ground. For indoor use, set cooker on brick or concrete base. Jacket is made of heavy, rolled steel plate supported at bottom by heavy iron bands.

When ordering jacket only, be sure to tell us the exact circumference of your kettle underneath the flange. Kettles are fine grained iron with black lead finish inside, giving a smooth surface. Rim rests on top of jacket, and is easily removed. Coal grates, cover and pipes are extra at prices given below. Shipped from factory in CENTRAL OHIO.

FULL CAPACITY GUARANTEED

Cap. Gal.	Cir. In.	Cookers, Complete			Steel Jackets Only			Kettles Only		
		Catalog No.	Wt. Lbs.	Each	Catalog No.	Wt. Lbs.	Each	Catalog No.	Wt. Lbs.	Each
16	70¼	32K1920	97	$7.60	32K1944	43	$3.95	32K1950	54	$3.65
23	79¼	32K1921	120	9.50	32K1945	46	4.55	32K1951	74	4.95
31	87¾	32K1922	150	12.40	32K1946	63	5.60	32K1952	87	6.80
48	101½	32K1923	201	14.75	32K1947	80	6.20	32K1953	121	8.55
64	109¾	32K1924	267	19.60	32K1948	86	7.15	32K1954	188	12.45
78	116¾	32K1925	305	21.85	32K1949	91	7.85	32K1955	204	14.00

32K1937—Coal Grate for 16 and 23-Gallon Cookers. Weight, 41 lbs. **$3.70**
32K1938—Coal Grate for 31, 48, 64 and 78-Gallon Cookers. Weight, 63 pounds. **$5.80**
32K1940—Wood Hinged Cover for 16, 23 and 31-Gallon Cookers. Weight, 10 pounds. **95c**
32K1941—Wood Hinged Cover for 48, 64 and 78-Gallon Cookers. Weight, 16 pounds. **$1.30**
32K1942—Elbow, one joint of pipe and damper for use with 16 and 23-Gallon Cookers. Weight, 5 pounds. **75c**
32K1943—Elbow, one joint of pipe and damper for use with 31, 48, 64 and 78-Gallon Cookers. Weight, 6 pounds. **80c**

For Other Copper and Iron Kettles See Page 967

Kenwood Agricultural Boilers

$19.25 16-Gal.

Popular With Both Farmers and Butchers.

A strictly high grade boiler, and our own exclusive design. Can be used for any purpose where a fine smooth kettle is required, such as rendering lard, cooking feed for stock or boiling sap. Caldrons are of fine grade smooth iron, with black lead finish inside. Furnaces are all cast iron. Price is for furnace and caldron complete as shown, but without pipe. Furnaces for coal burning use iron grate and heavy firebrick lining which can be taken out and replaced through the door. Shipped from factory in CENTRAL OHIO.

FULL CAPACITY GUARANTEED

Wood Burning Boilers					Coal Burning Boilers				
Catalog No.	Size Gal.	Size Pipe	Wt. Lbs.	Each	Catalog No.	Size Gal.	Size Pipe	Wt. Lbs.	Each
32K2000	16	5 in.	233	$19.25	32K2006	16	5 in.	262	$20.90
32K2001	23	6 in.	276	21.95	32K2007	23	6 in.	311	23.55
32K2002	31	6 in.	341	25.25	32K2008	31	6 in.	389	27.85
32K2003	48	7 in.	406	29.85	32K2009	48	7 in.	459	32.45
32K1904	60	7 in.	629	39.80	32K1911	60	7 in.	654	42.50
32K1905	75	8 in.	707	43.70	32K1912	75	8 in.	754	45.85

Feed Cooker and Water Heater

A strongly made cooker, built to give long service. Burns coal, wood or cobs. Body is made of heavy No. 16 gauge blue steel, all joints and seams securely welded. Boiler is made of No. 20 gauge galvanized steel. Fire door is large enough to put in large chunks of wood. Grate is large; either wood or coal can be burned. Body sets on strong steel legs so furnace can be used in a building. Complete with grate, one joint 6-inch pipe and elbow. Shipped from factory in CENTRAL OHIO.

Catalog No.	Capacity, Gal.	Width, In.	Length, In.	Wt., Lbs.	Price
32K1966	40	22	30	210	$14.75
32K1967	60	22	36	225	17.80
32K1968	90	22	54	260	21.50
32K1969	120	22	70	300	24.50

Handy Feed Cookers

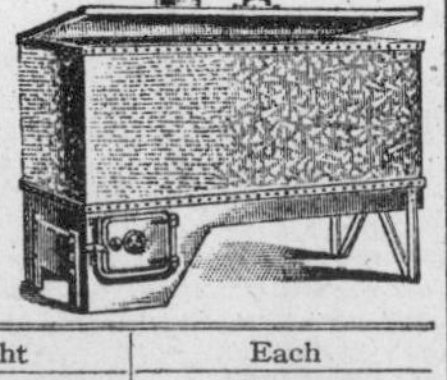

A large capacity cooker for cooking feed, boiling water, etc. Heavy galvanized sheet steel boiler strongly bound at top and bottom, and has a close fitting hinged cover. Fire box is No. 16 gauge blue annealed steel. Fire flue is 4 inches deep and extends entire length of boiler. Heavy cast iron grate will burn coal, wood or cobs.

Price Includes One Joint of 6-Inch Pipe.
Shipped from NORTHEASTERN INDIANA.

Catalog No.	Capacity	Weight	Each
32K1970	60 gallons	180 pounds	$14.95
32K1971	90 gallons	190 pounds	16.50
32K1972	115 gallons	206 pounds	18.45
32K1973	160 gallons	245 pounds	22.25

Automatic Hog Feeder

Your hogs will gain weight faster if they have free access to feed at all times than if they are fed at intervals. And they will actually eat less. Thousands of hog raisers have installed these automatic feeders. The two sides prevent crowding, save labor and keep food clean. Feeder strongly made of high grade clear lumber, guaranteed to give complete satisfaction. Built in sections to be bolted together. Packed to secure lowest transportation rates. Easily put together. Shipped from factory near CHICAGO.

32K1876—3-ft. 8-in. size, capacity 12 bushels, one compartment, with removable board. Wt., 160 lbs. **$7.75**

32K1875—6-foot size, capacity 25 bushels, 3 compartments, with removable board above trough for feeding ear corn. Weight, 300 pounds. **$10.85**

Rotary Hog Oiler

Every hog raiser needs a good hog oiler. Over 30,000 in use. No valves or springs. When hog rubs, wheels rotate, picking up oil from basin, surplus oil returning to basin. No waste. Made of heavy cast iron. Animal cannot tip it over. Entire oiler is 13½ inches high and 13½ inches wide. Shipped from our store.

72K1768¼—Weight, 87 lbs...... **$9.10**

Hog Oil, Medicated

For killing and preventing lice. Used both as a spray and for all hog oilers.

30K3329—Hog Oil.	Shpg. Wt.	Per Gal.
5-gallon can	40 lbs.	40c
10-gallon can	80 lbs.	35c
*30-gal. steel bbl., with faucet.	250 lbs.	35c
*50-gal. steel bbl., with faucet.	430 lbs.	33c

*Shipped from factory in NORTHEASTERN ILLINOIS.

Combination Hog Scalder and Watering Tank

$10.25 and Up

Can also be used for other purposes. Made of No. 20 gauge galvanized steel. Chains are extra at prices shown below. Shipped from factory in EASTERN INDIANA.

Catalog No.	Width In.	Depth In.	Length Ft.	Wt. Lbs.	Each
32K1865	28	18	5	90	$10.25
32K1866	30	20	6	115	11.00
32K1867	30	24	6	125	11.75

32K1880—Two heavy chains, 7 feet long with hooks. Weight, 14 pounds.......... **$1.45**

Portable Hog House

$23.00

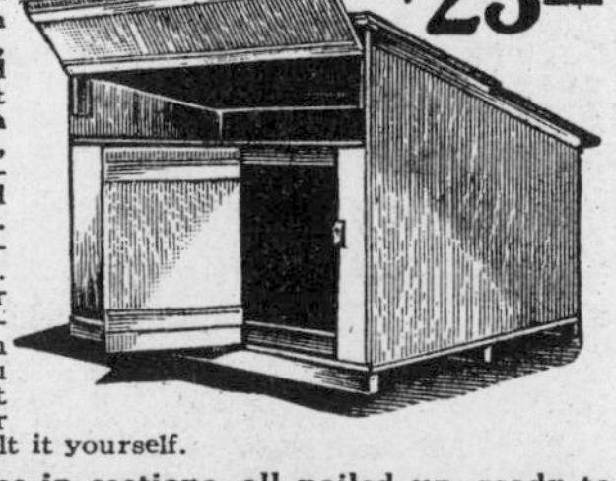

Made from 1-inch pine, dressed about ⅞-inch thick, tongued and grooved. Weathertight. Cheaper and better than if you bought lumber and built it yourself.

Comes in sections, all nailed up, ready to bolt together. Can be taken down and moved or stored. Warm, dry, easily cleaned. Ventilation by long door at top across front, or roof section can be raised. Service door, 24x36 inches. Roof supported by three 2x4 timbers. Drop door at top is 15 inches high, 6 feet 4 inches long, with strap hinges.

Floor supported by three 2x4 timbers and sets at slight angle for drainage.

Dimensions of house, 5 feet wide, 6 feet 6 inches long. Height, front. 61 inches; back, 41 inches. Shipped unpainted from NORTHERN INDIANA.
32K1877—Wt., 480 pounds.. **$23.00**

1066₃ P SEARS, ROEBUCK AND CO. *The World's Largest Store*

on Efficient Equipment

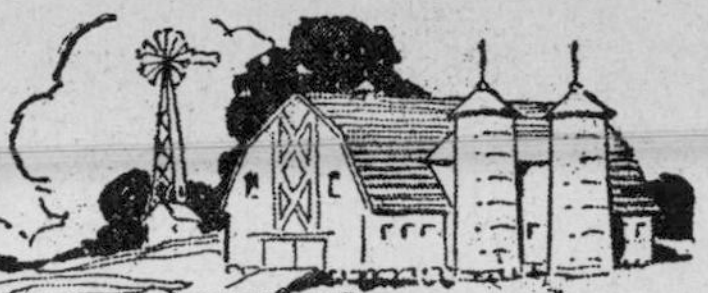

Heavy Galvanized Hog Troughs

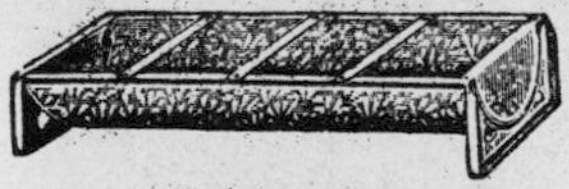

$1.35 And Up

One-piece rounded bottom, easily kept clean. Crossbars, 1 foot apart. No sharp edges to injure stock. Troughs are 12 inches wide, 5 inches deep. **Shipped from our store.**

Catalog No.	Length, Feet	Weight, Lbs.	Each
72K4457¼	4	12½	$1.35
72K4458¼	6	18	1.95
72K4459¼	8	24	2.55

Round Storage Tanks

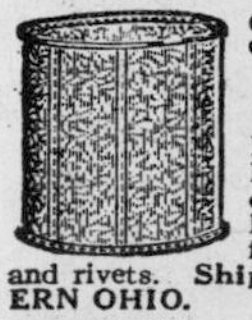

$28.55 And Up

Made from No. 20-gauge galvanized steel, but, can be made from No. 18-gauge at prices 30 per cent higher. Shipped set up unless otherwise ordered. They do not have lock seams, but are punched for rivets. Prices include solder and rivets. **Shipped from factory in NORTHERN OHIO.**

Catalog No.	Diam. Ft.	Ht., Ft.	Cap., Gal.	Wt., Lbs.	Each
32K4388	6	6	1,200	265	$28.55
32K4389	6	8	1,600	330	36.25
32K4392	8	5	1,800	330	39.25
32K4393	8	6	2,133	375	44.50

Wagon Tanks

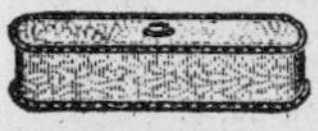

Sides flanged over and riveted to top and bottom between two flat steel bands. Carefully soldered. Watertight top and seams. Splash board or bulkhead. Round 14-in. manhole with cover, 1-inch pipe connection in end. All sizes, 2 feet high. **Shipped set up from factory in NORTHERN OHIO.**

Catalog No.	Lgth., Ft.	Wth., Ft.	Cap., Gal.	Wt., Lbs.	Each
32K4439	4	2	110	85	$ 9.75
32K4440	6	2	144	120	12.85
32K4441	8	2	197	155	15.90
32K4442	8	2½	245	170	18.35
32K4443	8	3	295	190	19.95
32K4444	10	3	378	235	23.25

Wood Stock and Storage Tanks

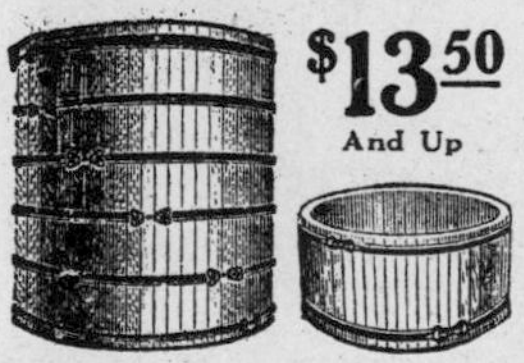

$13.50 And Up

Furnished with flat bands and adjustable draw lugs. Round hoops at same price if so ordered. Shipped flat, unpainted. Weights are for 1½-inch cypress. Add 15 per cent for weights of 2-inch cypress. Complete instructions furnished for setting up tanks. **Shipped from factory in Baltimore, Md.**

Catalog No.	Ht., Ft.	Diam., Feet	Capacity, Gallons	Wt. of 1½ In. Lbs.	Cypress 1½-Inch	Cypress 2-Inch
32K4460	2	4	176	180	$ 13.50	$ 16.25
32K4461	4	4	284	260	23.65	28.50
32K4462	2	5	200	210	13.75	20.60
32K4463	5	5	600	500	32.75	42.00
32K4464	2	6	315	265	21.00	25.75
32K4466	2	7	441	340	28.00	32.00
32K4468	2	8	567	390	32.00	38.45
32K4470	2	10	872	595	39.50	54.00
32K4472	6	6	1,100	655	49.85	60.50
32K4473	8	6	1,445	860	70.00	79.00
32K4474	6	8	1,966	970	69.00	83.50
32K4475	8	8	2,645	1,200	90.00	106.00
32K4476	10	10	5,300	1,700	133.25	192.00

Submersible Tank Heater

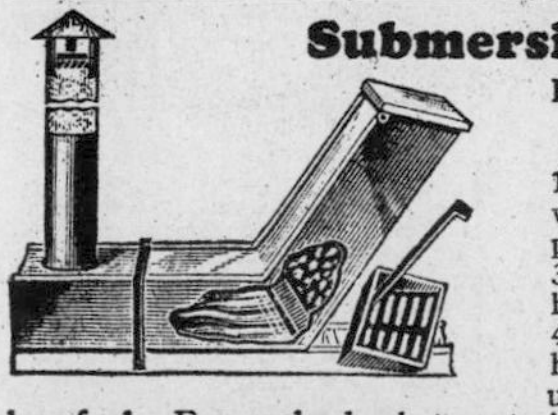

For Heating Outdoor Stock Watering Tanks—Burns Any Kind of Fuel

The submersible heater is made of 14-gauge boiler plate with all seams welded, doing away with rivets, bolts or packing. Heat chest and fire box are each 30 inches long, 12 inches wide and 8 inches high, joined together at an angle of about 45 degrees. The heating chamber lying horizontal on the bottom of the tank and all under water saves more heat and requires less fuel. For coal a basket grate is provided, but for wood or other fuels no grate is needed, and it burns wood 30 inches long. It sets flat on the tank bottom, with weights placed on its top, or strapped to a platform, as shown in the illustration. The strap is furnished, but the platform is not. **Shipped from factory in WESTERN OHIO.**

32K4493—Submersible Tank Heater, without grate. Wt., 75 lbs... **$7.75**
32K4494—Submersible Tank Heater, with coal grate. Wt., 85 lbs. **9.25**

PEERLESS Windmills

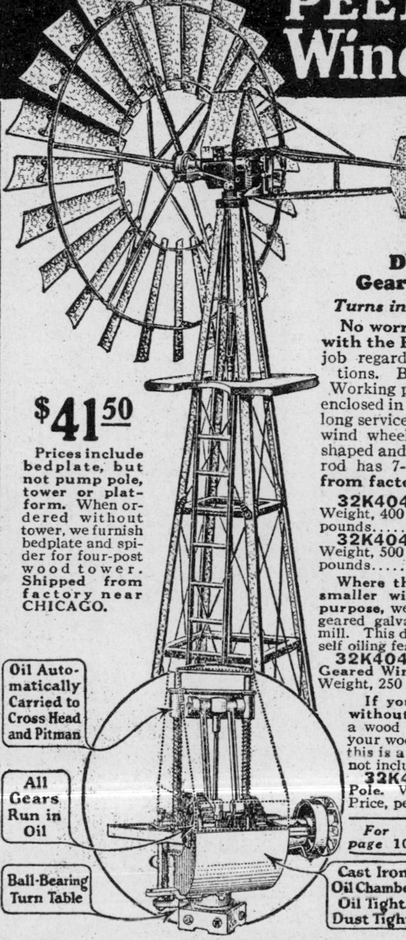

PEERLESS
DOUBLE GEARED
SELF OILING
Oil Automatically Carried to Cross Head and Pitman
All Gears Run in Oil
Ball-Bearing Turn Table
Cast Iron Oil Chamber Oil Tight Dust Tight

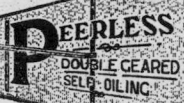

$41.50

Prices include bedplate, but not pump pole, tower or platform. When ordered without tower, we furnish bedplate and spider for four-post wood tower. **Shipped from factory near CHICAGO.**

Double Back Geared, Self Oiling

Turns in the Slightest Breeze

No worry about water supply with the Peerless. Always on the job regardless of weather conditions. Ball bearing turntable. Working parts run in oil and are enclosed in dusttight case. Built for long service. Heavy galvanized steel wind wheel and rudder, correctly shaped and strongly braced. Pump rod has 7-inch stroke. **Shipped from factory near CHICAGO.**

32K4041—8-Foot Windmill. Weight, 400 pounds......... **$41.50**
32K4042—10-Foot Windmill. Weight, 500 pounds......... **$54.00**

Where the work is light and a smaller windmill will serve the purpose, we can supply 6-foot single geared galvanized steel wheel windmill. This does not have the enclosed self oiling feature.

32K4040—6-Foot Single Geared Windmill. Weight, 250 lbs......... **$25.50**

If you order your windmill without steel tower, or to go on a wood tower, be sure to order your wood pump pole extra, as this is a part of the tower, and is not included with the windmill.

32K4043—Wood Pump Pole. Weight, per foot, 1 pound. Price, per foot......... **5c**

For Windmill Pumps see page 1014.

Galvanized Steel Towers

Strongly constructed and well braced. Price includes anchor posts.

Catalog No.	Ht., Feet	Wt., Lbs.	Each	Catalog No.	Ht., Feet	Wt., Lbs.	Each
Tower for 6 and 8-Ft. Windmills				Tower for 10-Foot Windmills			
32K4156	20	350	$27.95	32K4160	20	390	$31.75
32K4157	30	535	41.35	32K4161	30	560	44.00
32K4158	40	700	56.75	32K4162	40	745	58.65
32K4159	50	940	74.50	32K4163	50	1,000	78.75

Lock Seam Galvanized Hog Troughs

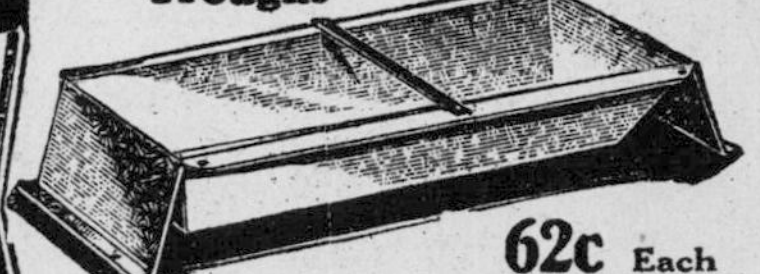

62c Each in Lots of 6

Shipped Set-Up and Nested at a Saving of One-Half in Freight Charges

Leakproof, rustproof and freezeproof. The only trough made which can be shipped completely set up and yet nested in a compact bundle, thus saving you one-half in freight charges. A bundle of six can also be sent by parcel post.

Made of galvanized sheet steel, is liquid tight, formed from one piece with footpiece locked seamed. Sanitary. No deep crevices to gather food—no sharp corners or exposed edges. Easily fastened to plank singly or in rows. Crossbars are spaced 12 inches apart. Troughs are 13 inches across the top, 5 inches high. **Shipped from our store.**

Catalog No.	Size, Feet	Wt., Each, Lbs.	Single	Lots of Six, Ea.
72K4400¼	2	5½	64c	62c

General Utility and Pig Feeding Pans

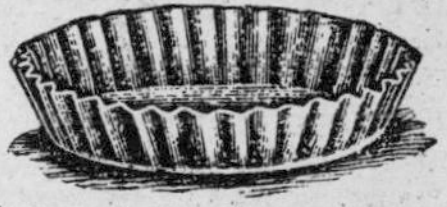

Handy for feeding small stock and for many farm purposes; also in households, shops, garages, etc. **Strong and rigid.** Cannot be damaged by freezing. Pressed from one piece of 22-gauge galvanized steel without seam or solder. Diameter, top, 17 inches; bottom, 14 inches. Depth, 3½ inches. **Shipped from our store, nested,** insuring safe delivery and saving in shipping costs. Weight, 3¼ pounds.

72K3256¼—Single......... **47c**
72K3257¼—Lots of 6. Weight, 21 lbs. Each......... **45c**

Cast Iron Hog Troughs

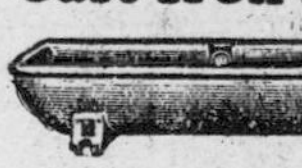

Width, 12 in. **Shipped from factory in CENTRAL PENNSYLVANIA.**

Catalog No.	Length	Cross-bars	Wt., Lbs.	Each
32K4495	2 ft.	....	25	$1.55
32K4496	3 ft.	1	35	2.35
32K4497	4 ft.	2	55	3.50
32K4499	6 ft.	3	78	4.45

All tanks on this page made of 20-gauge galvanized steel, unless otherwise stated. Will make of 18-gauge steel at prices 30 per cent higher, or No. 16-gauge at prices 60 per cent higher. Measurements given in all cases are outside over all.

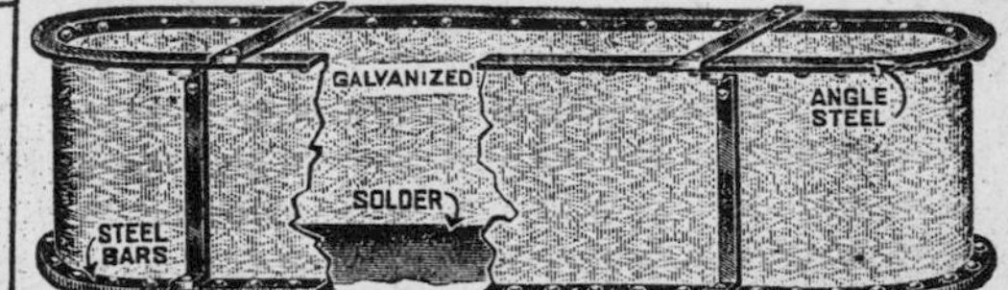

GALVANIZED
ANGLE STEEL
SOLDER
STEEL BARS

Galvanized Steel Stock Tanks

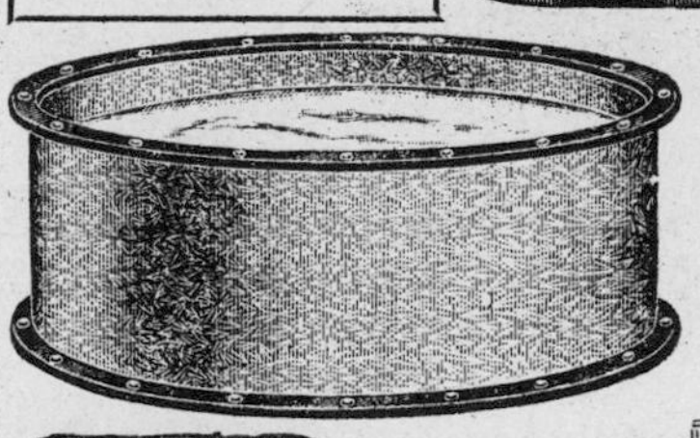

We offer you only the best in quality and workmanship at prices that give you a worth while saving. Bottoms of all plain tanks over 1 foot high are secured between two pieces of flat steel or bound with angle steel, depending on size and shape of tank. Firmly braced sides. Corrugated tanks have seams packed with elastic packing, then riveted, and they do not have the side braces.

Shipped from NORTHERN OHIO factory.

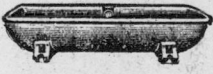

Round Tanks

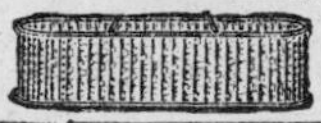

Catalog No.	Diam. Ft.	Ht. Ft.	Cap. Gal.	Wt., Lbs.	Plain Tank	Corrugated Tank
32K4310	4	2	166	80	$ 7.50	$ 6.90
32K4311	4	2½	215	90	8.55	....
32K4312	4	3	254	100	10.40	....
32K4313	4	4	338	125	12.70	....
32K4314	5	2	262	110	10.35	9.50
32K4316	5	3	411	135	12.60	....
32K4317	5	4	548	160	16.25	....
32K4318	5	5	675	185	19.50	....
32K4320	6	2	384	140	12.75	12.20
32K4322	6	3	583	170	16.50	....
32K4323	6	4	768	200	20.70	....
32K4324	6	5	966	235	25.00	....

Round End Tanks

Catalog No.	Lgth Ft.	Wth Ft.	Ht. Ft.	Cap., Gal.	Wt., Lbs.	Plain Tank	Corrugated Tank
32K4330	4	2	1	45	45	$ 4.75	....
32K4331	6	2	1	70	65	6.40	....
32K4332	8	2	1	100	85	7.95	....
32K4334	4	2	2	91	61	5.50	$ 4.95
32K4336	6	2	2	144	90	7.80	7.25
32K4337	8	2	2	197	120	9.75	9.15
32K4339	8	2½	2	245	135	11.45	10.35
32K4340	8	2½	2½	310	145	12.75	....
32K4341	8	3	2	295	140	12.95	11.50
32K4342	8	3	2½	375	155	14.25	....
32K4343	8	4	2	386	150	14.65	13.45
32K4347	10	3	2	384	170	14.95	13.75
32K4350	10	4	2	496	195	17.40	15.75
32K4351	10	4	2½	625	220	19.95	....
32K4354	10	6	2	813	230	22.75	....
32K4356	16	4	2	826	300	27.85	25.35
32K4357	16	5	2	1,072	335	33.25	31.25

Peerless Dairy Barn Equipment

Peerless Cow Stanchions

Install Peerless Stanchions in your barns. Their adjustable width holds the animal securely and yet allows for comfort and freedom of movement. You cannot find better quality than in the Peerless. We offer several designs at special low prices that will yield you substantial savings.

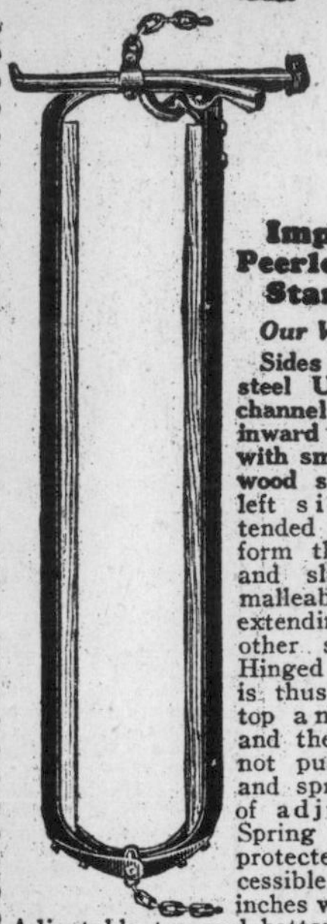

Improved Peerless Steel Stanchion
Our Very Best

Sides are heavy steel U-bars, the channel turned inward and lined with smooth hardwood strips. The left side is extended around to form the top bar and slides in a malleable iron loop extending from the other side bar. Hinged side bar is thus supported top and bottom, and the cow cannot push against and spring it out of adjustment. Spring latch is protected, yet accessible. Opens 24 inches wide at top. Adjustable top and bottom for neck space. Height inside, 48 inches; chains, 6 inches long. Finished in black japan. **Shipped from our PHILADELPHIA store.**
72K2209¼
Weight, 25 pounds........**$3.10**

Oval Steel Stanchions

Furnished with or without wood lining. Side bars are heavy U-bar steel. Lined stanchions have smooth rounded hardwood strips. The channel of the steel U-bars, being turned inward, the wood linings are firmly supported by the steel. Unlined stanchions have flat side of the steel U-bars turned inward, allowing smooth, flat surface against the animal's neck. Hinge, latch and top are malleable castings. Adjustable top and bottom for neck space; 48 inches inside. Chains, 6 inches long. Durably finished in black japan. **Shipped from our PHILADELPHIA store.**
72K2214¼—Steel Stanchion with wood lining. Wt., 21 lbs...**$2.65**
72K2213¼—Steel Stanchion without wood lining. Weight, 17 pounds............**$2.30**
72K2273—6-Inch Hook Bolt for attaching stanchion to wood frames. Wt., 1 lb....**10c**
72K2220—Bottom Anchor, for fastening stanchion to concrete curb. (For any chain hanging stanchion). Weight, 1½ lbs....**28c**
72K2221—Malleable Clamp with bolts for hanging stanchion to pipe frame (1⅝-inch outside diameter.) Weight, 8 ounces........**28c**

Steel Stall Partitions for Wood Frames

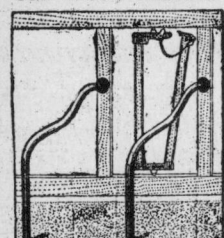

Same as used with our complete steel stalls. If you prefer wood frames you can buy the steel partitions separately. Prices do not include stanchion or framework and are for one partition only. Shipped from our PHILADELPHIA store.
72K2270¼—Partition with flange and screws for attaching to frame. Weight, 15 pounds........**$1.95**
72K2272—Flange for wood floor. Weight, 3 pounds..**45c**

Wood Bar Stanchions $2.45
Used for Many Years and Still in Great Demand

Side bars are clear white hardwood, rounded, smoothed and oiled. Tops and bottoms heavy malleable. Adjustable for neck space.

Stanchions, 49 inches high inside. Chains, 6 inches long. Shipped from our PHILADELPHIA store.

72K2216¼—Wood Stanchion, Chain Hanger.
Weight, 17 lbs.........**$2.45**

Send for This Free Catalog 476K

Every dairyman should have this book. It shows larger illustrations, other style stalls and litter carriers, mangers, pens, and a complete line of Peerless Dairy Barn Equipment.

Peerless Steel Stalls

Substantial, simple and practical and contain all features necessary for cleanliness and convenience. Built of heavy, 1⅝-inch outside diameter, brazed steel tubing. All parts securely bolted together, with heavy malleable iron fittings. Upright posts stand 5 feet 5 inches high above floor with 5 inches additional imbedded in concrete. The triple bend partitions extend back 42 inches from uprights and 42 inches high from floor, and have flange riveted to bottom to secure them in concrete. Stalls are finished in blue gray enamel paint.
Model A Stall (at right below), the strongest and most popular type ever made, can be furnished 3 feet 6 inches to 4 feet wide. Price includes top rail, two uprights, one bent partition, necessary clamps and bolts, and one stanchion with anchor.
Model C Stalls (below), suited for small cows, or where a low cost stall is wanted, made any width from 3 to 4 feet. State width. Price includes top rail, one side upright and partition, stanchion with anchor and necessary clamps and bolts.

READ BEFORE ORDERING

When ordering stalls give us this information:
Into how many rows will stalls be divided? The desired width of stalls.
Will rows join building wall at one end or both ends?
Also furnish a pencil drawing showing number of stalls in each row, the location, size and kind of any posts that may be in the way of the rows, and the distance between centers of posts. An extra charge is made for special fittings needed where stalls must be connected to posts.

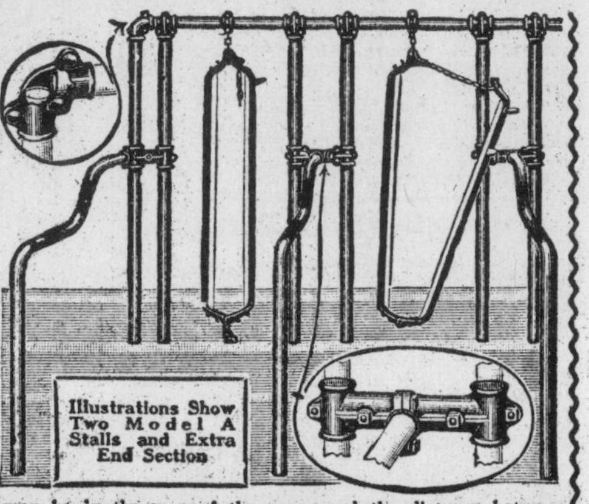

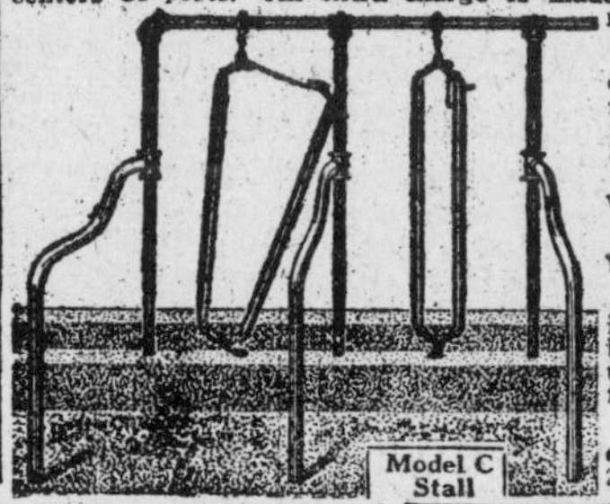

Illustrations Show Two Model A Stalls and Extra End Section

The stanchion regularly furnished in either stall is our 72K2214¼. We will furnish stalls with our 72K2209¼, if desired, at an extra price of 30 cents per stall. Shipped from factory near CHICAGO.
32K2263—Model A Stall. Weight, 75 pounds............**$8.15**
32K2267—Model C Stall. Weight, 56 pounds............**6.35**
Where both ends of a row of stalls are independent and do not join the wall of building, one extra section composed of an upright and bent partition is required for finishing the end of row.
32K2268—Extra End Section for either model. Shipping weight, 25 pounds...............**$2.85**

Model C Stall

Detachable Water Bowls

Automatic in action. Require no attention except occasional cleaning. Attach to either steel or wood posts. A storage tank (elevated a few feet) provides all the pressure necessary, or can be connected to city water. Water can be piped from either above or below. When piped from below two ordinary elbows and a short nipple are required. These are not included in the price of the bowl nor are the pieces of pipe and coupling shown above bowl in illustration.
Quickly detached for cleaning by removing one bolt, which locks the bowl securely in place. Bowl is cast iron, 10 inches in diameter and 4¼ inches deep with rolled edges. Shipped complete with clamps from our PHILADELPHIA store. Wt., 12 lbs.
72K2240¼—Bowl for Steel Stalls.....**$2.50**
72K2241¼—Bowl for Wood Stalls.................**2.50**

Litter Carriers, Track and Attachments

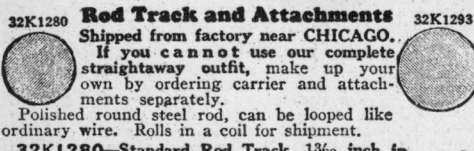

I-Beam Track

Rod Track and Attachments
32K1280 ... **32K1293**

Shipped from factory near CHICAGO. If you cannot use our complete straightaway outfit, make up your own by ordering carrier and attachments separately.
Polished round steel track can be looped like ordinary wire. Rolls in a coil for shipment.
32K1280—Standard Rod Track, 13/32 inch in diameter. Weight, per foot, ⅓ pound. Per foot........**4c**
32K1293—Heavy Rod Track, 15/32 inch in diameter. Weight, per foot, ½ pound. Per foot.....**5½c**

Tension Bolt

One required at each end of rod track. Welded eye. Size, ⅞x30 inches, with nut and washer. Wt., 7 lbs.
32K1282....**95c**

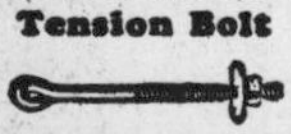

End Loop Clamps
One required at each end of rod track. They hook into tension bolt for stretching the track.
32K1281—Weight, 2 pounds...........**28c**

Anchor Loop
(Not Illustrated)
Necessary where rod track attaches to post. Includes 20 feet heavy rod, two loop clamps, turnbuckle and ¾ inch by 6 feet anchor rod. Weight, 20 pounds.
32K1284.....**$2.95**

Curve or Switch
(Not Illustrated)
For turning a square corner with rod track. Made of angle steel with malleable points. Wt., 25 lbs.
32K1285.......**$3.75**

Carrier With Automatic Lift
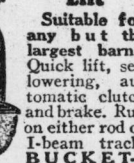

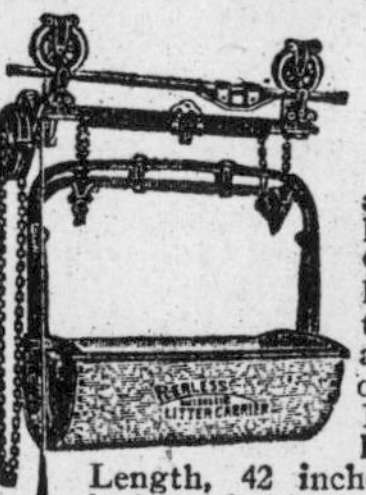

Suitable for any but the largest barns. Quick lift, self lowering, automatic clutch and brake. Run on either rod or I-beam track.
BUCKET—Length, 42 inches; width, 24 inches; depth, 16 inches. Body is one-piece 18-gauge galvanized steel; ends 16-gauge, reinforced all around with steel angle. Heavy 2-inch steel channel bail, adjustable for height. TRACK WHEELS—Malleable, with steel roller bearings. Shipped from factory near CHICAGO. Weight, 215 lbs.
32K1246............**$35.50**

Complete Litter Carrier Outfit
This style for use in barns with low ceilings or doorways. Bucket, 42 inches long, 24 inches wide, 16 inches deep. Galvanized steel, hardwood ends. Complete with 100 feet Standard rod track, anchor loop, clamps, turnbuckle and anchor rod. For additional track see prices at left, or if the heavy rod track is wanted, allow 1½ cents per foot extra.
Shipped from factory near CHICAGO.
32K1275—Outfit complete. Weight, 200 lbs...**$27.50**
32K1278—Carrier only. Weight, 135 pounds.............**$18.75**

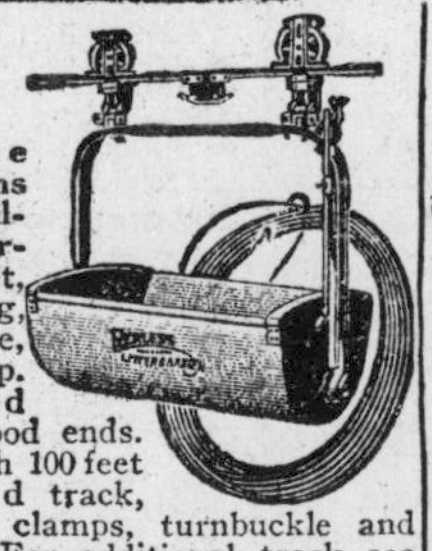

Made of 2-inch round edge, high carbon steel. Can be bent cold to form curves or turns. Supported by malleable hangers which can be screwed to ceiling or joist, but usually joist brackets are used, being more convenient. Splice connections with bolts, as shown in illustration, furnished for coupling track joints. Order one hanger and bracket for each 4 feet of track. All tracks and attachments shipped from factory near CHICAGO.
32K1214—Rail Track. Weight, per foot, 1½ pounds. Per foot....**11c**
32K1216—Malleable Hanger, 9 inches long. Weight, 1¾ pounds.........**25c**
32K1217—Joist Bracket for track running across joist. Weight, 1 pound.
Bracket only **7c**
32K1218—Joist Bracket for track running parallel with joist. Weight, 1 pound.
Bracket only **7c**

11c Per Ft.

How to Order a Litter Carrier
For each line of rod track, order two Tension Bolts (32K1282) and two End Loop Clamps (32K1281). If track extends to a post, order Anchor Loop (32K1284). If rod track turns a square corner, two independent lines of rod track are necessary, each with tension bolts and end loop clamps; also a Curve or Switch (32K1285).

Low Prices on Cider Mills *and* Fruit Presses

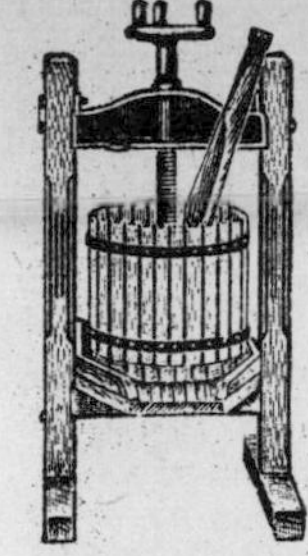

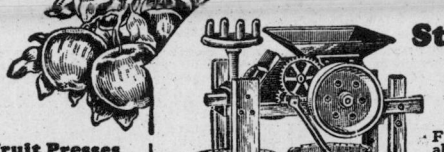

Fruit Presses

These are high class and must not be confused with lighter grade presses. Withstand great pressure and get all the juice from the fruit. Hardwood frame firmly bolted together. Heavy iron crosshead has accurately threaded screw arbor. Smooth hardwood tubs strongly bound by wrought iron hoops. Easy to clean. Tub sizes given below are outside measurements. **Shipped from factory in EASTERN PENNSYLVANIA.**

Catalog No.	Ht., In.	Size Tub, In.	Wt., Lbs.	Each
32K2380	40	10x10	75	$ 6.98
32K2381	44	12x12	105	9.25
32K2382	51	16x14	180	14.95

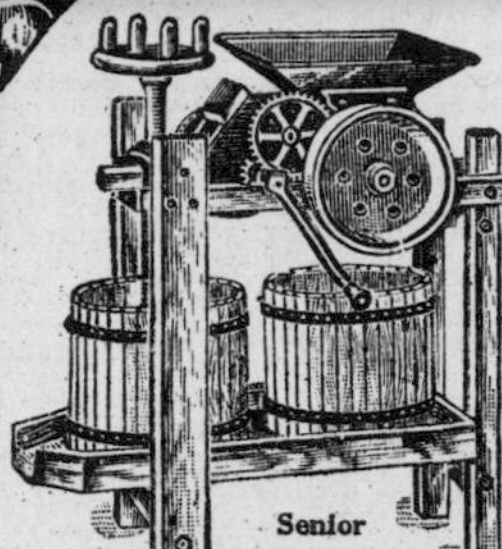

Senior

Standard Cider Mills

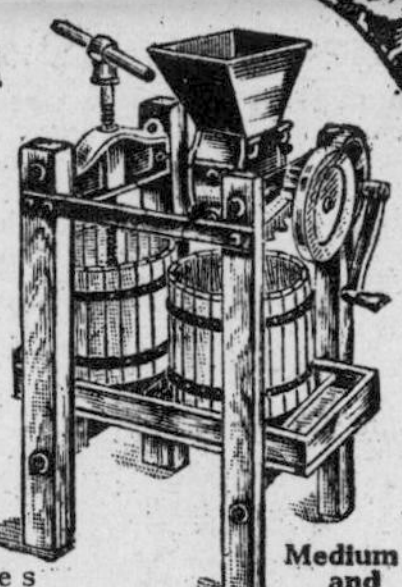

Medium and Junior

Positive Force Feed. Grinds all size apples without clogging. Strictly high grade in every particular and guaranteed to give perfect satisfaction. Grinds grapes as well as apples. Heavy hardwood frames strongly bolted together. Large capacity hopper. A steel spider shape agitator automatically forces the apples against the steel grinding cylinder, grinding them to a pulp. Heavy cast screw arbor with steel press screw accurately threaded. The medium and senior size have heavy balance wheel 13½x3⅛, with wide face, and can be driven by belt from engine. The junior and medium mills are of same general construction, differing only in size, and are operated by a crank. The senior mill is much larger and has a larger capacity. Tubs are of selected hardwood with heavy iron hoops. **Shipped from PENNSYLVANIA factory.**

Catalog No.	Size	Capacity, Cider, per Day	Size Tubs, Inches	Wt., Lbs.	Each
32K2387	Junior	2 to 4 barrels	10x12	165	$19.65
32K2388	Medium	3 to 6 barrels	12x14	256	24.25
32K2389	Senior	6 to 12 barrels	14x17	337	33.70

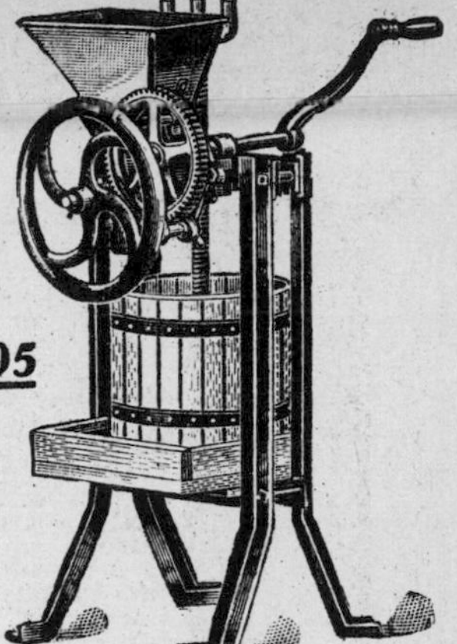

$15.95

Shipped From Our Philadelphia Store

Steel Frame Family Cider Mill and Press

Agitator Hopper Will Not Clog Force Feed

The heavy steel frame and legs and heavy steel crosshead make this an extra strong and rigid outfit which will outlast any wood frame press. Mill is geared, has a large agitator hopper with extra wide adjustable throat and will grind larger apples than any other type of single tub mill. Oscillating hopper sides automatically force fruit against the cast iron grinding cylinder until it is reduced to a pulp. Grinding part can be detached, making a press only. Heavy steel press screw accurately threaded and fitted. Hardwood slatted tub, 10x10½ inches, reinforced by heavy wrought iron hoops securely riveted. Capacity, 1 to 2 barrels per day. **Shipped from our store.**

72K2386¼—Weight, 140 lbs......**$15.95**

Household Fruit Press

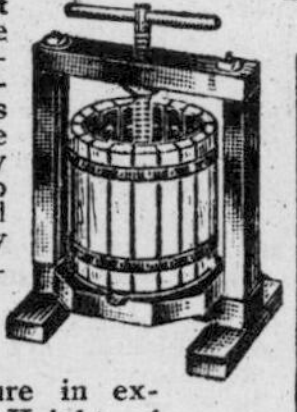

A well made, durable fruit press just the right size for home use. Frame made entirely of hardwood, securely held together by two long bolts running through entire side frame making a very rigid construction. No wobble. Smooth hardwood tubs, reinforced with heavy iron hoops securely riveted to slats. Steel press screw, ¾x15 in. long accurately threaded, gives tremendous pressure in extracting all the juices. Height of frame, 18 in.; width, 14⅛ in. Size tub, 9x 9¼ in. Holds about 8 qts. **Packed in carton for parcel post shipment. Shipped from our store.**

72K2383¼—Weight, 23 lbs....**$2.95**

Grape and Berry Crusher

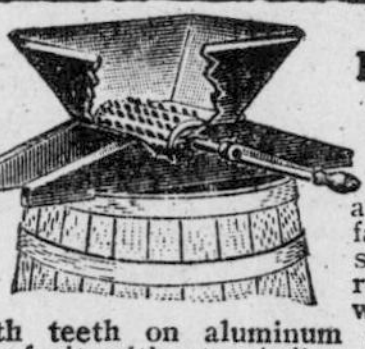

Grinding parts of aluminum, will not rust, easy to keep clean. The 4½x9 aluminum roll firmly fastened to a ⅝-inch steel shaft, has 12 rows of strong teeth which mesh closely with teeth on aluminum side plate. Mashes the fruit without grinding seeds, reducing all to a pulp from which juice can easily be extracted by a press. Large capacity hopper. All wood parts are selected wood, nicely finished. Cannot be used for apples, pears or other hard fruit. **Shipped from our store.**

72K2384¼—Weight, 22 lbs........**$5.98**

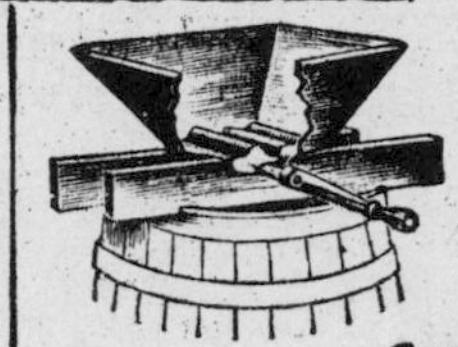

Grape and Berry Crusher

A strongly built and efficient crusher. Has two cast rollers, Italian type, 5 inches long, working in steel bearing plates which insure easy running. Mashes the grapes and berries, reducing all to a pulp from which juice can easily be extracted by a press. Will not crack the seeds. Wood hopper, 15¼x 8⅛ inches; holds ½ bushel. Side rails, 24 inches long. **Shipped from our store.**

72K2377¼—Weight, 21 pounds....................**$4.10**

Bee Keepers' Supplies

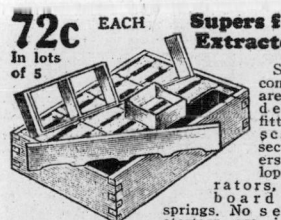

Supers for Comb or Extracted Honey

72c EACH In lots of 5

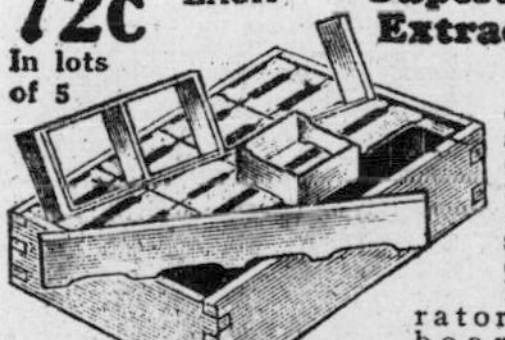

75c EACH In Lots of 5

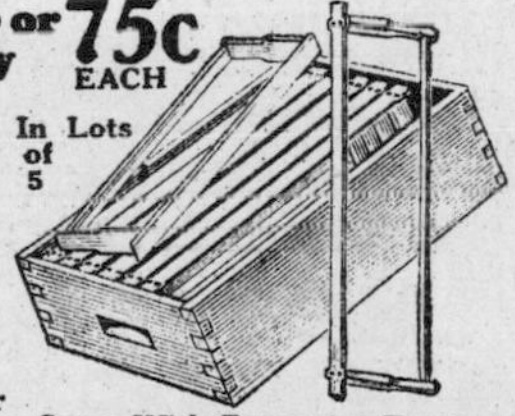

Super With Extracting Frames.

Supers for comb honey are 4¾ in. deep and fitted with scalloped section holders, scalloped separators, follower board and flat springs. No sections or starters are included, except that sections are included with the single supers. Scalloped sections, 4¼x4¼x 1⅞ inches, can only be used with this furniture.

Supers for Comb Honey. The sections or honey boxes shown in illustration must be ordered separately.

72K3504¼—Crate of five 8-Frame Supers for Comb Honey. Without sections. Weight, 36 pounds..................**$3.60**

72K3509¼—Crate of five 10-Frame Supers for Comb Honey. Without sections. Weight, 39 pounds..................**$3.95**

72K3490¼—Single 8-Frame Super for Comb Honey. Includes 24 4¼x 4¼x1⅞ sections. Weight, 8 pounds..................**$1.25**

72K3491¼—Single 10-Frame Super for Comb Honey. Includes twenty-eight 4¼x4¼x1⅞ sections. Weight, 10 pounds..........**$1.35**

Supers for extracted honey are 5⅝ in. deep and are complete with 5⅜-inch shallow frames. No wax foundation is included.

72K3512¼—Crate of five 8-Frame Supers for Extracted Honey. With frame. Wt., 36 lbs........**$3.75**

72K3516¼—Crate of five 10-Frame Supers for Extracted Honey. With frames. Wt., 39 lbs.....**$4.25**

72K3492¼—Single 8-Frame Super for Extracted Honey. With frames. Weight, 7 pounds........**90c**

72K3493¼—Single 10-Frame Super for Extracted Honey. With frames. Weight, 9 pounds.......**$1.10**

One-Story Dovetailed Bee Hives

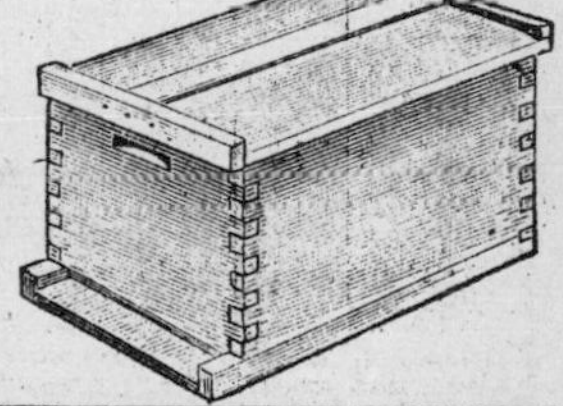

Standard hives—universally used by bee keepers. Fitted with Hoffman frames, which are pierced for wiring, excelsior cover and reversible bottom. Made of clear white pine. No knots, splits or sap. Every piece fitting each other with perfect accuracy. No foundation, starters or division board furnished. The metal roofed double cover, furnished at an additional price, has telescoping sides, which fit down over the hive, and an inner wood cover which can be used as an escape board. Shipped in flat, to be put together by purchaser. Necessary nails and instructions included.

Supers or upper stories are not included. To make 1½-story hives, order also the styles of super desired. **Shipped from our store.**

Catalog No.	Description	Weight, Pounds	Wood Cover	Metal Cover
72K3501¼	Crate of five 8-Frame, 1-Story Hives..........	113	$10.25	$12.50
72K3508¼	Crate of five 10-Frame, 1-Story Hives..........	123	11.25	14.10
72K3498¼	Single 1-Story 8-Frame Hive..........	25	2.45	....
72K3499¼	Single 1-Story 10-Frame Hive..........	26	2.65	....

Hoffman Self Spacing Frames

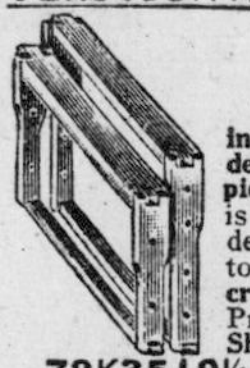

The deep frame is 17⅝ inches long by 9⅛ inches deep, with 18¾-inch top piece. The shallow frame is 17⅝ inches long, 5⅜ in deep and has 18½-inch top piece. **Sold only in full crates.** Shipped in flat. Price includes nails. **Shipped from our store.**

72K3519¼—Crate of 50 Shallow Frames. Wt., 14 lbs..**$2.05**

72K3520¼—Crate of 100 Shallow Frames. Wt., 28 lbs..**3.75**

72K3518¼—Crate of 50 Deep Hoffman Frames. Wt., 24 lbs..**2.90**

72K3521¼—Crate of 100 Deep Hoffman Frames. Wt., 45 lbs..**5.60**

Honey Storage Tanks

$9.75 UP

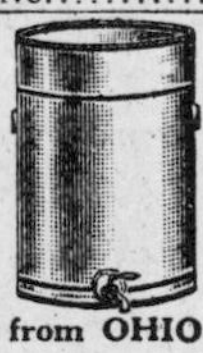

Strongly made of **galvanized steel, painted outside.** Steel band around top, and heavy wire welded into bottom edge make them rigid. Have tinned handles and full flow honey gate. **Shipped from OHIO factory.**

	Gal.	Ht. In.	Dia. In.	Wt. Lbs.	
32K3400	40	21	29½	50	$ 9.75
32K3401	60	24	31½	65	12.40
32K3402	100	31	35½	85	15.75

Wax Comb Foundation

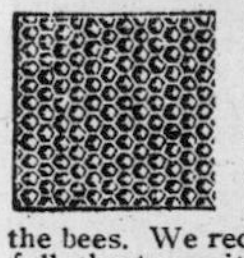

We offer only the best, sweet, clean, genuine Weed process foundation, made from pure domestic beeswax. Tough, clear and easily worked by the bees. We recommend the use of full sheets as it eliminates an excess of drone comb and over production of drones. This permits bees using all their energy in producing honey. Order now at these low prices and add to your honey profits. Medium Brood Foundation Sheets are about 7⅝x16¾ inches and run 7 sheets to the pound. Thin super foundation sheets are 3⅞x15½ inches and run about 28 sheets to the pound. Shipping weight, 1-pound boxes, 2 pounds; 5-pound boxes, 6½ lbs. **Shipped from our store.**

72K3528—Medium Brood, 5 pounds, **$3.60**; per pound..................**75c**

72K3529—Thin Super, 5 pounds, **$4.10**; per pound..................**85c**

Section Honey Boxes

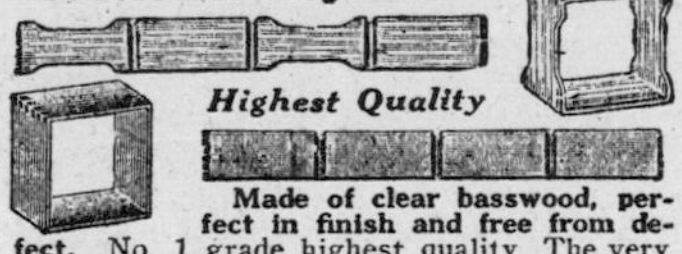

Highest Quality

Made of clear basswood, perfect in finish and free from defect. No. 1 grade highest quality. The very close sorting leaves sections a little darker in color, which we offer as No. 2 grade. Sold only in full packages as listed below. **Shipped from our store.**

Scalloped Sections

72K3524¼

No. 1 grade. Size, 4¼x4¼x1⅞ inches.

Per package of 100. Wt., 6½ lbs. **$1.10**

Per package of 250. Weight, 19 pounds **$2.75**

Per crate of 500. Wt., 35 lbs..**$5.20**

72K3530¼

No. 2 grade. Size, 4¼x4¼x1⅞ inches.

Per crate of 500. Weight, 35 pounds ...**$4.75**

Plain Sections

72K3526¼

No. 1 grade. Size, 4¼x4¼x1⅞ inches.

Per package of 250. Wt., 17 pounds **$2.25**

Per crate of 500. Wt., 30 lbs..**$4.75**

72K3522¼

No. 1 grade. Size, 4x5x1⅜ inches.

Per package of 250. Wt., 16 lbs. ...**$2.50**

Per crate of 500. Wt., 31 lbs...**$4.75**

Bee Smokers

Every Bee Keeper Needs a Good Smoker

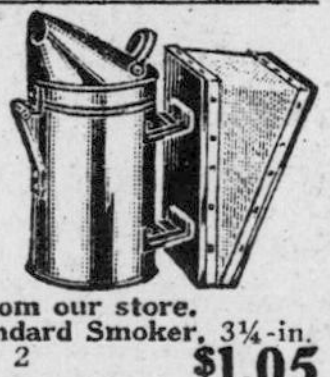

Have flexible hinge which permits close, tight fit of nozzle over fire chamber. Made of heavy tin. Guaranteed perfect. **Shipped from our store.**

72K3471—Standard Smoker, 3¼-in. diameter. Weight, 2 pounds..................**$1.05**

72K3472—Jumbo Smoker, 4-inch diameter. Wt., 2 lbs. **1.20**

Canvas Bee Gloves

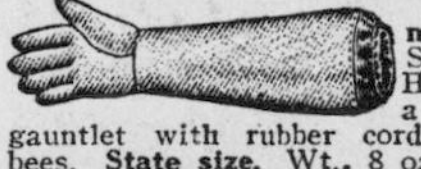

Large or medium sizes. Stingproof. Have fingers and long gauntlet with rubber cord to exclude bees. **State size.** Wt., 8 oz.

72K3546—Per pair..........**75c**

Honey Extractors

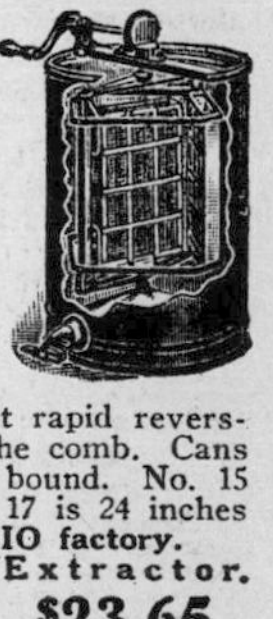

Standard in every respect. Have slip gear which throws crank and pinion out of gear at maximum speed, allowing reel to continue in motion with crank hanging loose. Have ball bearings top and bottom. Frames of comb baskets are heavily galvanized. The wire cloth against which the combs rest can be easily removed for cleaning. Improved pocket hinges permit rapid reversing to extract both sides of the comb. Cans are galvanized steel, strongly bound. No. 15 is 21 inches in diameter. No. 17 is 24 inches in diameter. **Shipped from OHIO factory.**

32K3475—No. 15 2-Frame Extractor. Comb pockets, 9⅝x16 inches. Weight, 95 pounds..................**$23.65**

32K3476—No. 17 2-Frame Extractor. Pockets, 12x16 inches. Weight, 120 pounds..................**$28.95**

See Index and Information Pages 542 to 570

Super-Hatcher HOT WATER Incubators

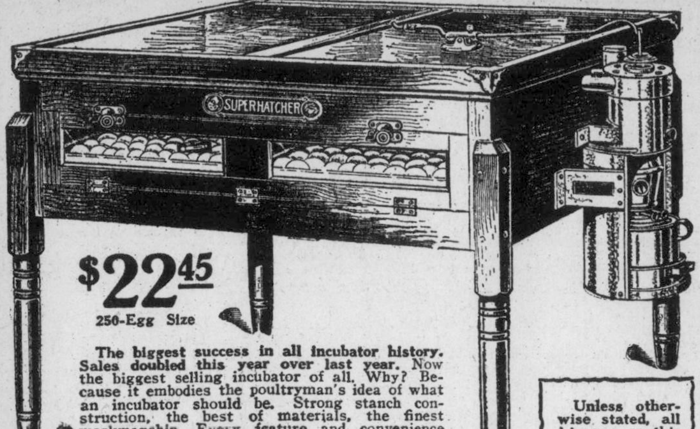

$22.45
250-Egg Size

The biggest success in all incubator history. Sales doubled this year over last year. Now the biggest selling incubator of all. Why? Because it embodies the poultryman's idea of what an incubator should be. Strong stanch construction, the best of materials, the finest workmanship. Every feature and convenience we know of to make hatches better, and to save time, labor, eggs and fuel.

Buy your Super-Hatcher early and get the early chicks which are the most profitable.

Unless otherwise stated, all items on this page shipped from our PHILADELPHIA store.

Note some of the super features of Super-Hatcher construction. Thick, double wall California redwood case, well insulated. Three-ply laminated top—will never check, warp or split. Copper hot-water heating tank of generous proportions. Heavy non-leakable lamp, 2-quart capacity, with highest grade burner provides abundant heat. Automatic, reliable regulator maintains uniform temperature. Strong egg trays, equipped with patented egg turning device. Ample nursery space underneath egg tray.

Every Super-Hatcher bears the label of the Underwriters' Laboratories, showing that the National Board of Fire Underwriters has inspected, tested and approved the Super-Hatcher construction, and this label certifies to its safety and fireproof qualities. With this label you are always entitled to the lowest insurance rates.

Each incubator complete with thermometer, egg tester and instructions for operating.

Catalog No.	Capacity, Eggs	Egg Trays	Size, Each Tray, In.	Size, Over All, Inches Length	Width	Height	Wt., Lbs.	Each
72K3084¼	155	1	24¼x22¾	38	27	32½	95	$17.45
72K3085¼	250	2	17½x27¼	48	32	32½	125	22.45
72K3086¼	400	3	17½x27¼	67	31½	32½	180	32.50
72K3087¼	600	4	24¼x22¾	63	49	32½	225	48.50

Double Deck Super-Hatcher Incubators

The 400-egg and the 600-egg size incubators can be used in pairs, double decked, thus giving increased capacity without additional floor space. When so used, extra heavy and shorter legs are furnished. Total height, 48 inches.

72K3088¼—800-egg capacity (two No. 72K3086¼ double decked). Weight, 380 pounds.......... **$65.00**

72K3089¼—1,200-egg capacity (two No. 72K3087¼ double decked). Weight, 470 pounds.......... **97.00**

Buy at Sears and

Little Brown Hen Incubator

The Time Tried Original of Its Type

Over 300,000 Satisfied Users

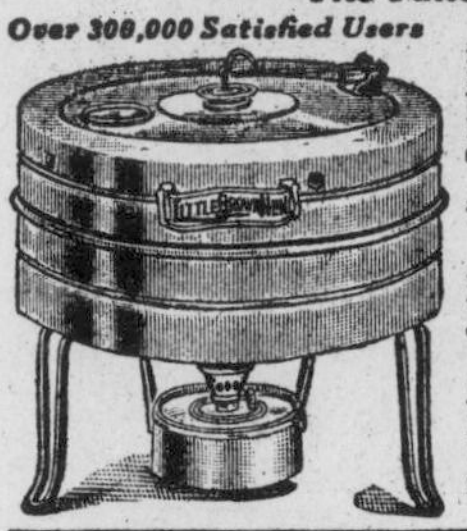

The acknowledged leader in its field. More of them in use than any other incubator of similar capacity. Simple, convenient and easy to care for; it has become famous for the healthy, vigorous chicks it hatches. Used by large and small poultry raisers everywhere.

Diameter, 18 inches; height, 15 inches. Holds fifty average size hens' eggs. Regulator is of brass wafer type, sensitive and reliable. Furnished complete with lamp, thermometer, moisture pan and instructions for operating. Strongly made of metal with felt lined nest. Nicely finished in brown enamel.

Give the Little Brown Hen a fair trial and if it does not satisfy you send it back and we will return your money with transportation charges. Can be shipped by parcel post, freight or express. When ordered by parcel post be sure to send amount of postage extra.

72K3011¼—Weight, 14 pounds.. **$4.95**

Sectional Metal Trap Nests

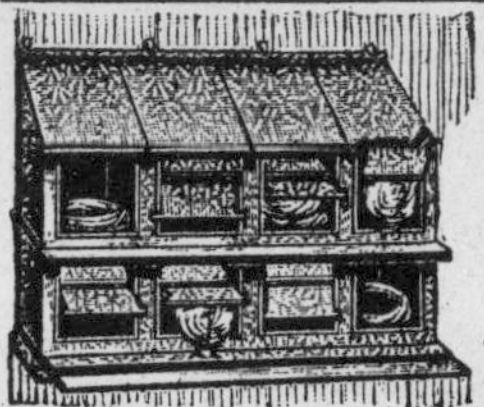

$3.40 UP

Avoid feeding poor laying hens during winter months. Trap nests cull out the poor layers; aid in breeding only heavy egg producers. Sanitary, easily cleaned, no place for mites and lice to hide. Sloping top prevents roosting on top. All sizes, 48 inches long, 13 inches deep. Ample ventilation provided for hen in each nest. **Not mailable.**

Catalog No.	No. of Nests	Height Front	Back	Wt., Lbs.	
72K3252¼	4	14	19	28	$3.40
72K3253¼	8	28	33	45	6.50

Trap Nest Fronts

Galvanized trap nest fronts, same as used in trap nests shown above. You make the nest box yourself from boards. Size, front, 15 inches high, 12 inches wide; opening, 9x11 inches. Sold only in sets of 6 fronts.

72K3254¼—6 Trap Nest Fronts. Weight, 11 pounds.... **$2.00**

Sanitary Wire Hens' Nest

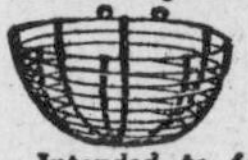

Keeps down Vermin

Intended to fasten to wall by hooks or screws. Should be lined with straw and supported at bottom. Heavy steel wire, copper plated, reinforced. Diameter, 14 inches. Shpg. wt., per dozen, 7 lbs.

72K3190¼
Per dozen........ **$1.95**

Galvanized Steel Hens' Nests

$3.10

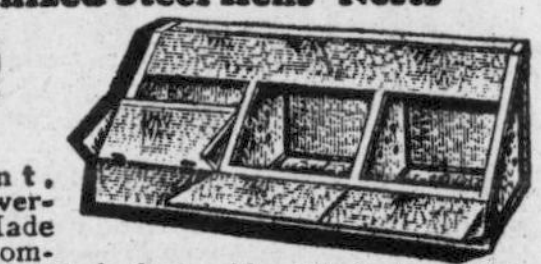

Convenient, sanitary and vermin proof. Made in three compartments, each 11 inches wide, 13 inches deep, 12¾ inches high. Set on a shelf or hang against wall. Doors form a perch for hens to fly on when entering nest. Weight, 30 pounds.

72K3249¼.......... **$3.10**

Dry Mash Hopper Feeders

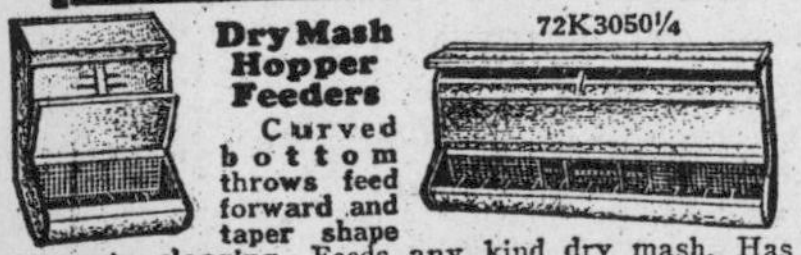

Curved bottom throws feed forward and taper shape **prevents clogging.** Feeds any kind dry mash. Has partitions and swinging front, hinged lid over hopper and trough keeps out rats and vermin. The 36-inch size has five soldered partitions. The 36-inch size is not mailable.

Catalog No.	Width	Weight	Each
72K3113¼	12 in.	6 lbs.	$1.35
72K3114¼	24 in.	11 lbs.	1.85
72K3050¼	36 in.	20 lbs.	3.65

Big Capacity Dry Mash Hopper

Capacity, 100 Lbs.

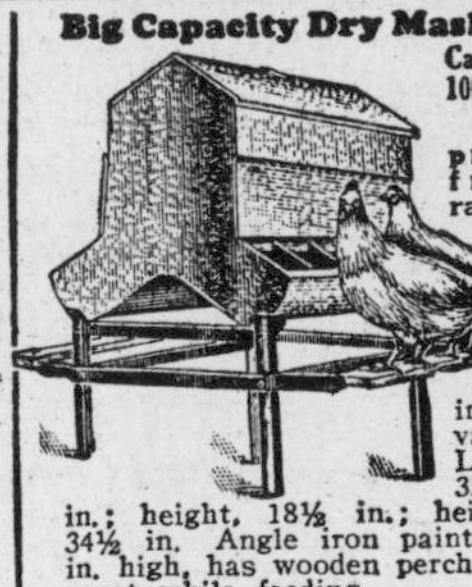

Hinged cover protects food from weather, rats and mice. Cuts down waste. Saves valuable floor scratching space. Galvanized steel. Length, hopper, 35 in.; width, 21 in.; height, 18½ in.; height, over all, 34½ in. Angle iron painted stand, 15½ in. high, has wooden perch for poultry to roost while feeding.

72K3117¼—Wt., 50 lbs. **$8.75**

Poultry Grit and Shell Boxes

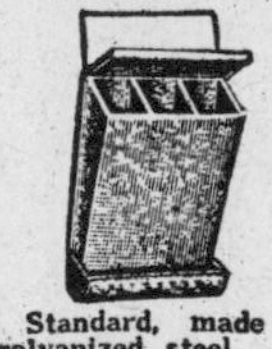

Standard, made of galvanized steel.

72K3161—Three-compartment size. Weight, 3 pounds....... **65c**

72K3162—Four-compartment size. Weight, 3½ pounds.. **85c**

Improved Metal Egg Carriers

$1.25 and up

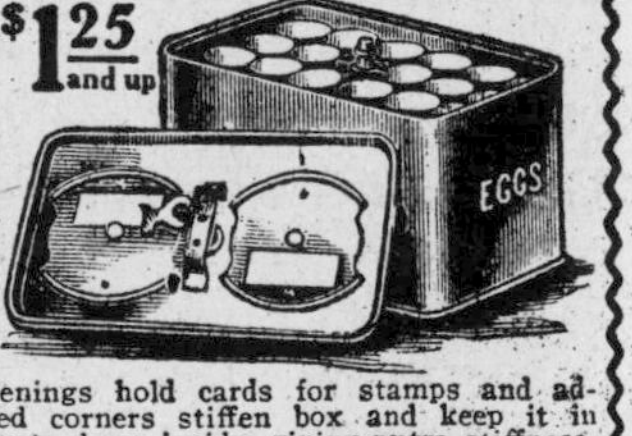

For parcel post delivery. Light, safe, durable. Can also be used as combination egg, butter or poultry package. Baked-on aluminized finish, will not rub off. Fillers, heavy cardboard. Two revolving discs with openings hold cards for stamps and address. Rounded corners stiffen box and keep it in shape. Cover sets down inside, giving extra stiffness. Cover fastens to the center spindle by the friction clamp. No hinges to get twisted out of place.

Catalog No.	Size	Weight	Each
72K3124¼	2 dozen	3 lbs.	$1.25
72K3125¼	4 dozen	5 lbs.	1.70
72K3126¼	6 dozen	6 lbs.	2.15

Big Capacity Round Hopper Feeder

Holds 100 Pounds Feed

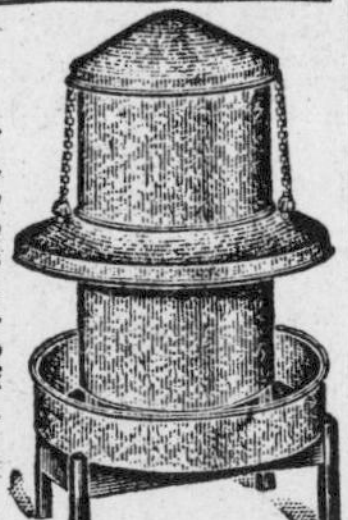

Ideal hopper for feeding dry mash for large flocks of fowls. Round shape enables fowls to eat all around in a circle. No crowding. Feed pan, 22 inches in diameter, 3½ inches deep. Cover can be closed over openings on feed trough to keep out mice and rats. Made of heavy galvanized steel.

72K3118¼
Weight, 65 lbs... **$5.75**

2-In-1 Poultry and Chick Feeder

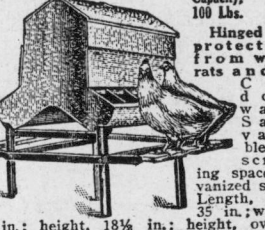

A Popular Choice and a Big Value

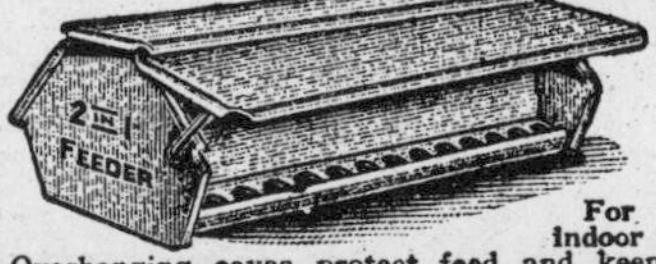

For chicks or fowls, indoor and outdoor use.

Overhanging eaves protect feed and keep hens out when used for chicks. Raise cover and set feeder higher as birds grow larger. Extra feed guards furnished for baby chicks. Sliding cover, 30 inches long, 21 inches wide; holds about 1 bushel. Feeds from both sides. Will feed 300 chicks. Galvanized steel.

72K3116¼—Weight, 18 pounds.......... **$3.50**

Egg Cartons

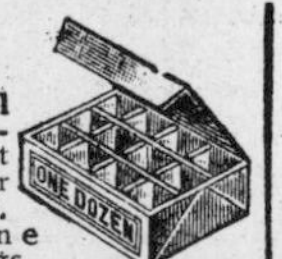

For local delivery only. Not suitable for parcel post. Holds one dozen eggs. Made of stiff cardboard.

72K3250¼—Bundle of 100. Weight, 13 lbs.. **85c**

72K3251¼—Bundle of 250. Weight, 34 pounds...... **$2.00**

Egg Case Cartons

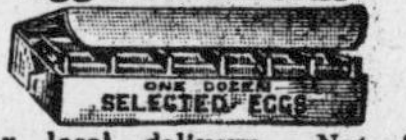

For local delivery. Not for parcel post. Fit standard Egg Cases. Protect and display eggs attractively. Each holds one dozen eggs.

72K3178¼
Bundle of 100. Wt., 16 pounds.......... **$1.30**

72K3186¼
Bundle of 250. Wt., 39 pounds.......... **3.10**

Wet Mash Feeder

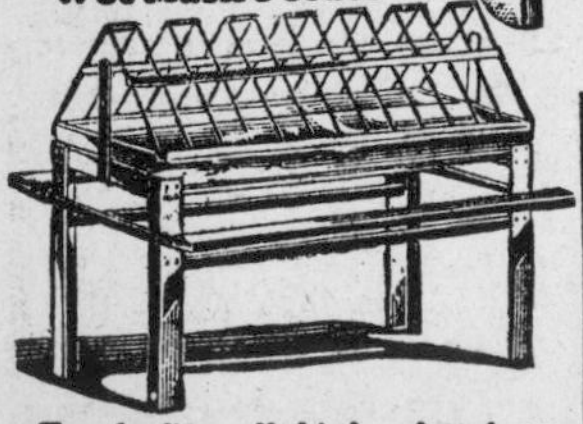

For feeding all kinds of wet or dry feeds, green feed, cut roots or buttermilk. Trough is double, feeding from both sides, with inverted V bottom. Made of heavy charcoal tin, 3¾ inches deep, 30 inches long, 18 inches wide. Grate keeps feed clean and prevents waste. Grate is galvanized rod, removable for filling or cleaning. Metal stand well braced, has folding perches. Weight, 30 pounds.

72K3120¼.......... **$5.98**

Poultry Shipping Coop

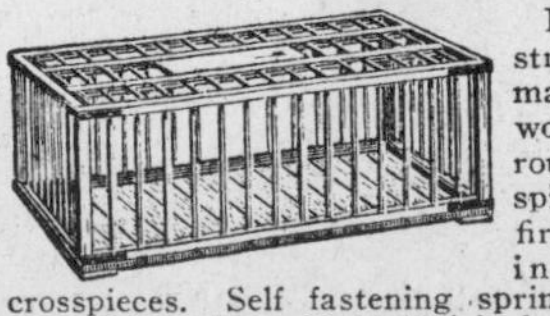

Light and strong. Well made of hard wood. The round wood spindles are firmly set into strong crosspieces. Self fastening spring door in top. Dimensions, 36x24x12½ inches. Shipped flat to save freight charges. Easily put together. Shipped from our store or factories in Northeastern Pennsylvania and Northern Virginia. We advise the purchase of these in lots of six to deliver them at lowest cost or freight charges. **Not mailable.**

72K3342¼—Weight, 16 lbs.
Price, each.......... **$1.35**

Running Board Coops

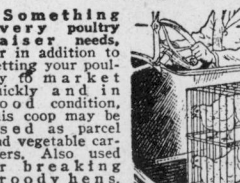

Something every poultry raiser needs, for in addition to getting your poultry to market quickly and in good condition, this coop may be used as parcel and vegetable carriers. Also used for breaking broody hens. Made of very heavy galvanized wires welded at intersections. Two strong wood decks. Height, 24 inches; width, 12 inches; length, 40 inches. Collapsible and shipped folded flat, insuring delivery to you in perfect condition. Easily put together. **Not mailable.** Weight, 20 pounds.

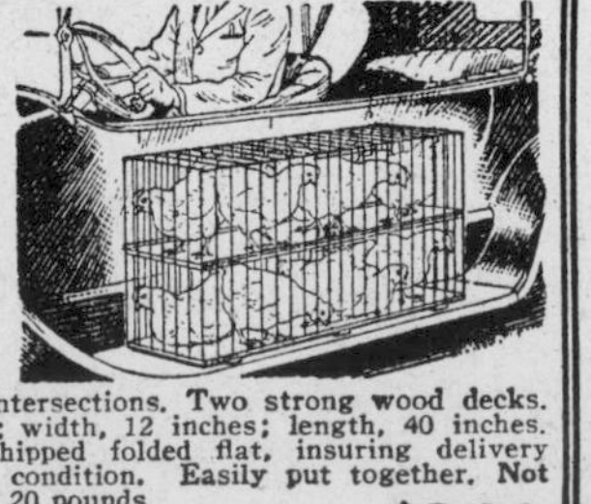

72K3341¼.......... **$2.90**

Folding Egg Carriers

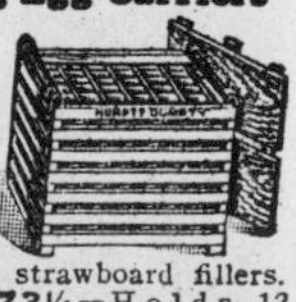

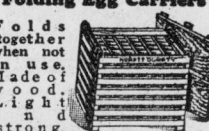

Folds together when not in use. Made of wood. Light and strong. Collapsible strawboard fillers.

72K3173¼—Holds 12 dozen, single compartment. Shipping weight, 6½ pounds.......... **48c**

72K3103¼—Holds 6 dozen, single compartment. Shipping weight, 4 pounds.......... **43c**

72K3165¼—Extra Fillers for 36 doz. eggs. (Three complete replacements). Weight, 2 pounds... **35c**

Increase Your Profits

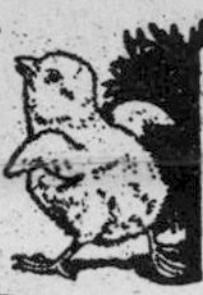

Big Gray Hen Incubator

100-Egg Capacity

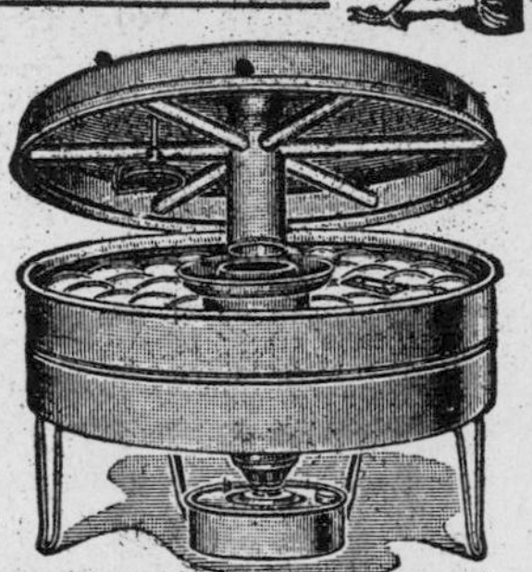

Made on same principles that have made the Little Brown Hen so successful. If you want an incubator larger than the Little Brown Hen and less expensive than our larger Super-Hatcher Incubators, the Big Gray Hen will suit you. While low in price, it is a high quality machine and easily maintains even hatching temperature under the most difficult conditions. All metal, strong and durable. It has double insulated walls. Regulator is the brass wafer type, sensitive and reliable. Nest lined with felt. Glass window in top permits easy reading of thermometer. Finished in gray enamel. **Shipped complete with thermometer, moisture pan and directions for operating.** Weight, 40 pounds.

72K3016¼ **$8.95**

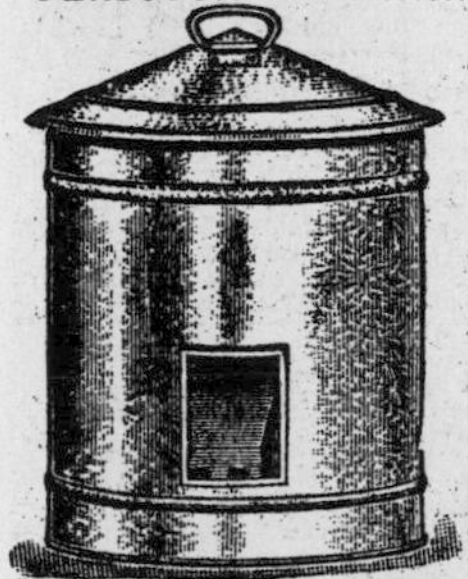

The All-Year Poultry Waterer

$1.90 UP

Keeps water warm in winter and cool in summer. Non-freezing. No lamp required. Supply your poultry with fresh, clean water at the proper temperature and increase egg production. Keeps water at practically the same temperature for 12 hours or longer. Substantially built of heavy galvanized steel with double walls, heavily insulated. Cone shape prevents fowls from roosting on tops. Has handle for carrying.

72K3134¼—2-gallon size. Weight, 22 pounds **$1.90**
72K3135¼—3-gallon size. Weight, 25 pounds **2.10**
72K3136¼—5-gallon size. Weight, 26 pounds **2.45**

Top Fill Non-Freeze Poultry Fountain

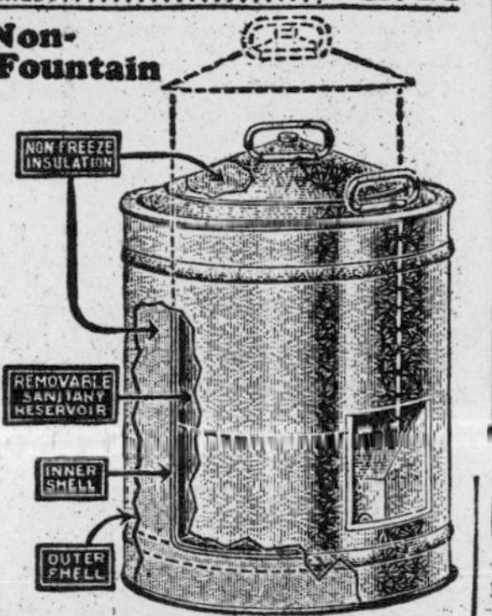

Here is what progressive poultry raisers have long been waiting for—a non-freezing fountain with packed double wall, strictly sanitary, easily cleaned, scalded and filled—at a popular price. Heretofore such a fountain has been obtainable only at a very high price. This fountain is high quality in every respect, and costs but a little more than the ordinary type insulated fountain now in general use. It is made in two sections of galvanized steel, with double walls, heavily packed to keep water cool in summer and from freezing in winter. Cone shaped top heavily insulated. Simply lift out inner tank and fill from top. Our biggest value in a poultry fountain. Made in 5-gallon size only.

72K3144¼—Weight, 30 pounds **$3.55**

Large Capacity Fountain and Heater

12-Gallon Capacity

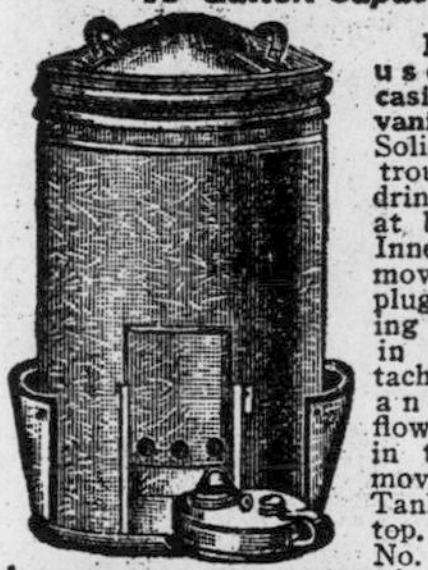

For all year use. Outside casing of galvanized steel. Solid cast iron trough forms drinking cups at both ends. Inner tank removable, and has plug for cleaning out. Valve in bottom attaches to float and regulates flow of water in trough. Removable cover. Tank fills from top. Lamp with No. 2 Zenith burner prevents water from freezing.

72K3129¼—Weight, 50 pounds **$8.45**

Automatic Poultry Waterer

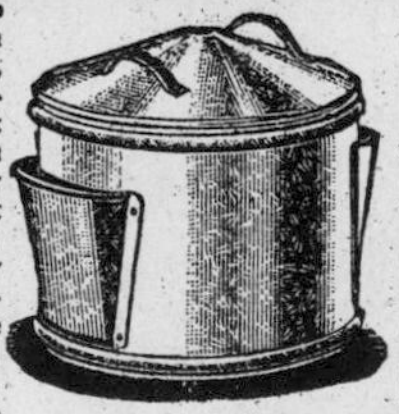

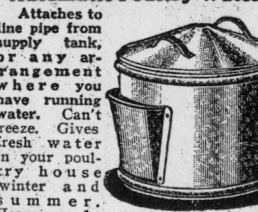

Attaches to line pipe from supply tank, or any arrangement where you have running water. Can't freeze. Gives fresh water in your poultry house winter and summer. Heavy galvanized box 17 inches in diameter, 13 inches deep. Cast iron trough on both sides; brass float valve. Works under any pressure up to 80 pounds. Kerosene lamp sets under trough, prevents freezing.

72K4450¼—Weight, 30 pounds **$8.25**

End Fill Poultry Fountain

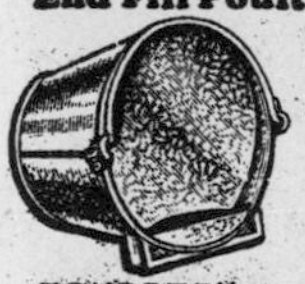

Our biggest bargain in a big capacity fountain. Strongly made from galvanized steel with bail for carrying. Stand on end to fill. Holds 12 quarts.

72K3275¼ Weight, 3 pounds **88c**

Combination Poultry Fountain and Heater

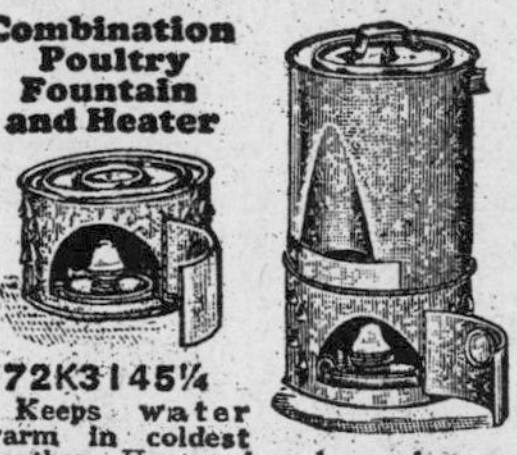

72K3145¼

Keeps water warm in coldest weather. Heater has brass burner. Oil reservoir holds kerosene to burn about one week. Simple and safe. Heater can also be used for brooding small chicks, sprouting oats, etc. Fountain can be used separately if desired. Galvanized steel.

72K3143¼—Complete 5-gallon capacity. Weight, 10 pounds **$2.95**
72K3138¼—Complete, 10-gallon capacity. Weight, 15 pounds **$3.85**
72K3145¼—Heater only. Wt., 4½ pounds **$1.60**

Top Fill Poultry Fountain

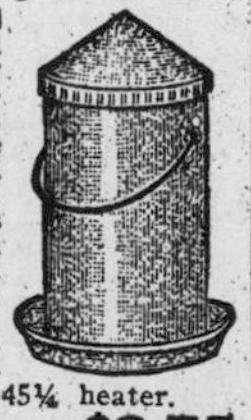

Easy to fill and clean. The top and the water container are separate telescoping cylinders making a double wall fountain. Pan is 13 inches in diameter. Chickens drink all around. A strongly made, high quality fountain. Holds 5 gallons. Makes a good winter fountain in combination with 72K3145¼ heater.

72K3330¼ Weight, 12 pounds...... **$2.75**

Improved Radio Blue Flame Oil Brooder

$9.95 AND UP

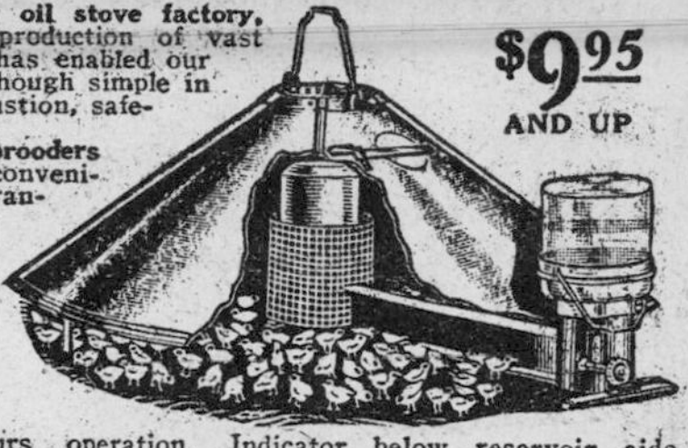

Developed and made in our own big oil stove factory, where our experience gained in the production of vast numbers of the finest oil stoves made has enabled our engineers to produce a brooder, which, though simple in principle, gives perfect, economical combustion, safety and dependability.

You can entrust your chicks to these brooders with perfect confidence and enjoy the convenience, cleanliness and labor saving advantages of kerosene oil fuel.

The wickless burner gives plenty of heat without smoke, fumes or odor. The combustion tube burns all the oil with a hot blue flame and can be closely regulated and needs readjustment only occasionally. The flame is regulated by a hand wheel which raises and lowers the reservoir. Glass oil reservoir holds one gallon, enough for 20 to 24 hours operation. Indicator below reservoir aids easy adjustment. Oil pipe is seamless copper tubing and has no packed or screwed joints, thus eliminating all danger of leaks. Canopy is designed to deflect and spread heat, and has adjustable damper at top, providing ventilation and circulation of fresh air. Burner is blue enameled outside. Brooder is finished in black japan; canopy is galvanized.

Catalog No.	Capacity, Chicks	Size, Canopy	Wt., Lbs.	Each
72K3040¼	500	42 in.	55	$ 9.95
72K3041¼	1,000	52 in.	60	10.95

72K3078 — Package 12 extra lighting rings, for Radio Brooder. Wt., 12 oz. **$1.10**

Imperial Stove Brooders

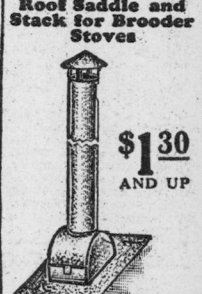

Shipped from our store.

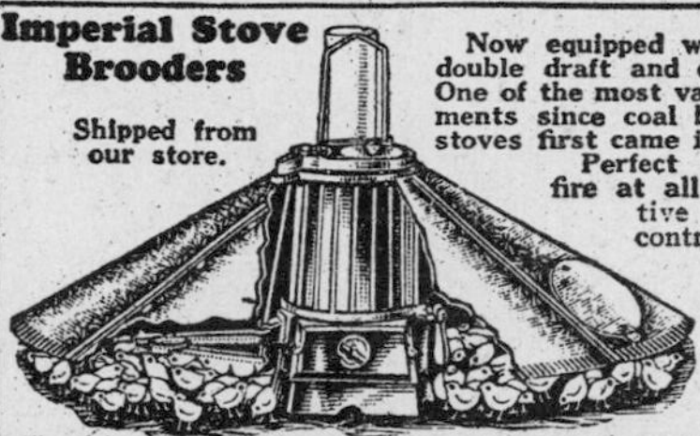

Now equipped with our new double draft and damper control. One of the most valuable improvements since coal burning brooder stoves first came into use.

Perfect control of the fire at all times. Sensitive heat regulator controlling the draft is automatic and positive in maintaining an even temperature. Your chicks are safe with this reliable brooder. Stoves are strongly built of cast iron, with rocking grates, canopies are galvanized steel. Stoves burn either hard or soft coal and come in three sizes:

No. 1—18 inches high and 11 inches in diameter; 9-inch grate, 4-inch pipe collar, 42-inch canopy for 500 chicks.
No. 2—22 inches high and 12 inches in diameter; 10¼-inch grate, 4-inch pipe collar, 52-inch canopy for 1,000 chicks.
No. 3—24 inches high and 13 inches in diameter; 11½-inch grate, 5-inch pipe collar, 60-inch canopy for 1,200 chicks.

72K2995¼—No. 1 Stove Brooders. Wt., 80 lbs.... **$11.25**
72K2996¼—No. 2 Stove Brooders. Wt., 105 lbs... **14.50**
72K2997¼—No. 3 Stove Brooders. Wt., 130 lbs... **17.85**

Pipe, Elbows and Dampers for Above Stoves

Size	72K3002¼ Black Pipe 2-Foot Lengths		72K3006¼ Black Steel Elbows		72K3007 Pipe Damper	
	Weight	Each	Weight	Each	Weight	Each
4-inch	3 lbs.	18c	1 lb.	[illegible]	[illegible]	[illegible]
5-inch	3 lbs.	20c	1 lb.	15c	4 oz.	17c

Roof Saddle and Stack for Brooder Stoves

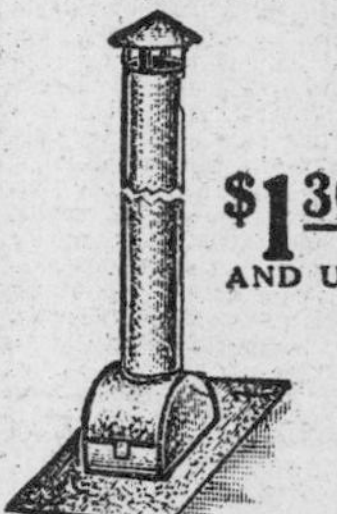

$1.30 AND UP

Adjustable for roof pitch. Keeps out rain and prevents down draft. Stack is so supported it will stand without wiring. Made of galvanized steel. Price includes saddle, 2-foot stack and rain cap. Wt., each, 8 lbs.

72K3005¼
For 4-in. pipe. $1.30
For 5-in. pipe. 1.50

Aluminum Poultry Leg Bands

Pliable aluminum. Fit any size fowl. Weight, per 100, 3 ounces. Numbered as follows:

72K3205—50 bands, 1 to 50 .... **25c**
72K3206—100 bands, 1 to 100 .... **40c**
72K3204—200 bands, 1 to 200 .... **80c**

Poultry Punch

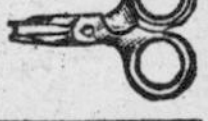

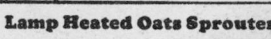

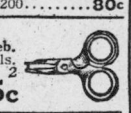

Will not pinch or tear the web. Used for either chicks or fowls. Nickel plated finish. Weight, 2 ounces.

72K3195 .... **35c**

Celluloid Leg Bands

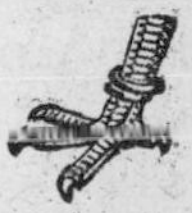

Packages of 100. All one color. Colors: Red, blue, yellow, green or black. **State color.**

72K3317—¼ inch. Baby chick size. Pkg., wt., 4 oz.. **30c**
72K3318—5/16 inch. For small breeds. Package, wt., 4 oz. **40c**
72K3319—11/16 inch. For American breeds. Package, wt., 4 oz.... **45c**
72K3320—¾ inch. For Asiatic breeds. Package, wt., 4 oz. **50c**

Square Pan Oats Sprouter

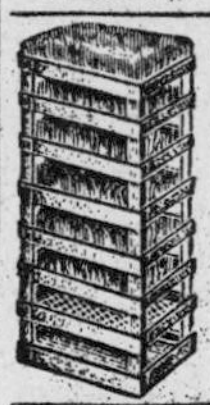

Feed green sprouted grain and increase egg production. No lamp or fuel required. Consists of series of perforated galvanized pans and one bottom drip pan.

Pans of the first size, 11x15 inches; large size, 11x32 inches. Each pan firmly supported by galvanized steel legs. Can be shipped by parcel post. **Shipped from our store.**

Catalog No.	No. Pans	Capacity Size Flock	Wt., Lbs.	Each
72K7067¼	8	Medium	14	$2.98
72K7068¼	8	Large	25	5.60

Lamp Heated Oats Sprouter

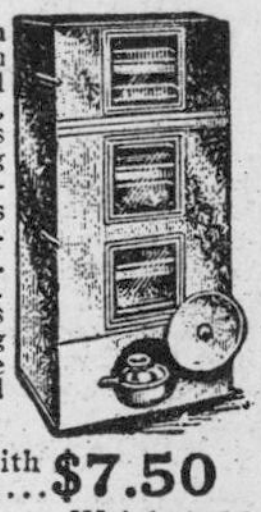

Made of galvanized steel in two sections. Base section with lamp only is for small flocks. It is 35 inches high, 23 inches wide, 18 inches deep. Holds four sprouting trays 17x21 inches and moisture pan. For larger flocks purchase the extra top section. Large glass doors. Perforated top is removable. Upper section, 13 inches high, has two sprouting trays. Shipped flat, to save you freight charges. **Shipped from ILLINOIS factory.**

32K7600—(Base section with lamp.) Weight, 45 pounds.......... **$7.50**
32K7601—Extra top section. Weight, 16 pounds **$4.35**

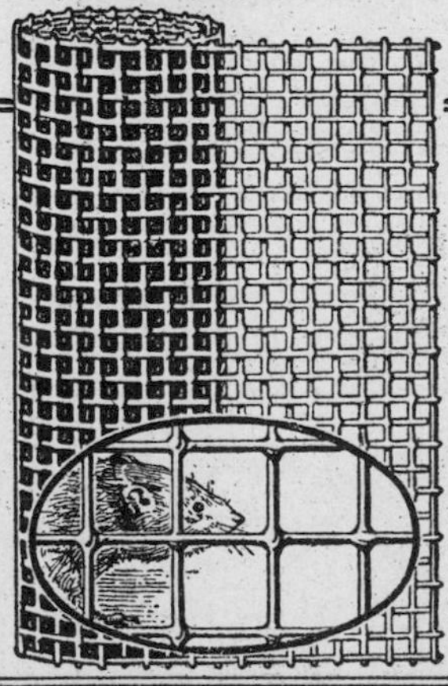

Galvanized Square Mesh Hardware Cloth

Make your poultry houses, grain bins and corn cribs rat and mouse proof. **The small cost will more than be offset by the saving in grain and poultry;** also extensively used for window guards, cages, screening equipment, fruit evaporators, repairing incubator egg trays, etc. Uniform mesh of heavy wire heavily galvanized after weaving. **Be sure to state height and number of mesh to the inch wanted.**

72K5423¼—Shipped from our store.

No. Mesh to In.	Gauge	Width, In.	Sq. Ft. in 100-Foot Roll	Wt., per 100-Foot Roll	Per 50-Foot Roll	Per 100-Foot Roll
2	19	24	200	57 lbs.	$4.05	$ 7.85
2	19	30	250	70 lbs.	5.10	9.80
2	19	36	300	85 lbs.	6.10	11.75
3	21	24	200	58 lbs.	4.40	8.55
3	21	30	250	73 lbs.	5.50	10.65
3	21	36	300	90 lbs.	6.60	12.80
4	23	24	200	52 lbs.	4.75	9.25
4	23	30	250	65 lbs.	5.95	11.50
4	23	36	300	84 lbs.	7.15	13.85

Road Scrapers

The Highest Grade Scrapers Made

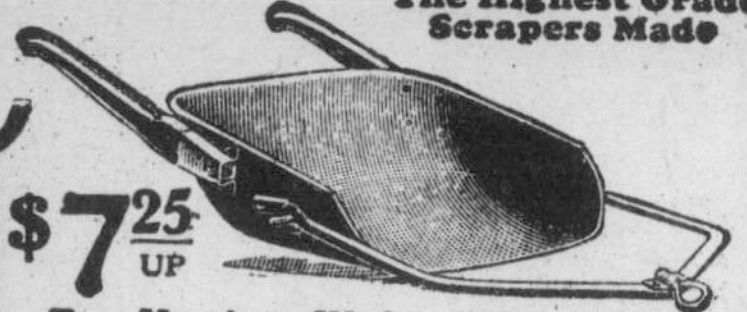

$7$25 UP

For Heaviest Work of Farmers, Contractors, Railroads and Townships.

Heavy gauge steel. Bowls are pressed from a single sheet of special high carbon scraper steel. Full thickness of steel at the point of greatest wear. Scrapers fill and clean easily. Bail and swivel are heavy forged steel.

Hardwood handles. Double runner scrapers have two runners of hardened steel riveted to bottom; double bottom scrapers, an extra bottom plate of hardened steel, riveted to bottom. **Shipped from warehouse at HARRISBURG, PA.**

Size	Width, Inches	Dpth., In.	Cap. Cub. Ft.	Gauge Steel	Weight, Pounds
No. 3	27	10	3½	10	80 to 85
No. 2	30	10½	5	10	90 to 95
No. 1	32	11	7	10	100 to 105

Cat. No.	Style Bottom	No. 3	No. 2	No. 1
32K2503	Double Runner.	$7.60	$7.75	$8.10
32K2506	Double Bottom.	8.95	9.20	9.55

For small contractors and farmers whose work is not very heavy or for occasional jobs, our 32K2507 will serve every purpose. It is well made of good materials and will be found durable and satisfactory for any but the heaviest class of work. Weight, 75 pounds. **Shipped from warehouse at HARRISBURG, PA.**
32K2507—No. 2 Double Runner Scraper............... **$7.25**

Cast Iron Boat Head

Make your own stone boat. Use any straight plank. Will outwear several sets of plank. Head, heavy and strong, 29 inches wide. Will last a lifetime. Shipped from factory in CENTRAL PENNSYLVANIA.
32K2550—Weight, 70 pounds.... **$3.85**

Portable Platform Scales

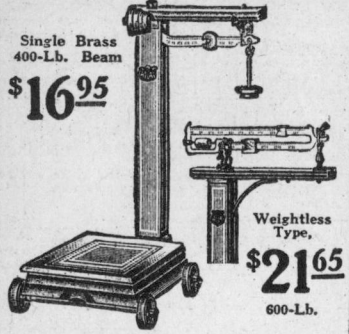

Single Brass 400-Lb. Beam

$16$95

Weightless Type,

$21$65

600-Lb.

Portable Platform Scales

Sealed to U. S. Standard. Guaranteed accurate, close weighing and durable. They can be used in buying and selling anywhere. Single beam scales have hardwood pillar, solid brass beam, and are graduated to ½-pound and sliding poise. Frame and levers strong and heavy. Nicely painted and varnished. Except for the beam, the weightless type scales are the same as our single beam scales. The upper bar is graduated by ½-pound marks to 100 pounds. The lower bar has large poise which engages notches, weighing by 100 pounds to full capacity of scales. Shipped from factory in CENTRAL NEW YORK.

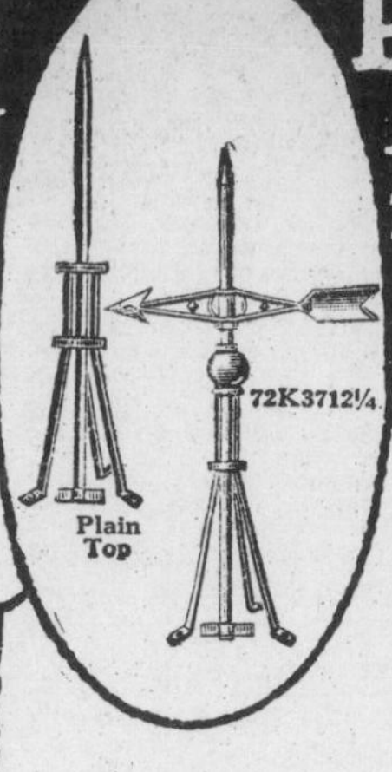

Single Beam Scales

Catalog No.	Cap., Lbs.	Platform, In.	Shpg. Wt., Lbs.	Each
32K1791	400	15½x24	145	$16.95
32K1792	600	16 x24	150	17.35
32K1793	800	17 x25	160	19.65
32K1794	1,000	18 x25	165	22.40
32K1799	1,200	18 x26	175	25.00

Weightless Type Scales

Catalog No.	Cap., Lbs.	Platform, In.	Shpg. Wt., Lbs.	Each
32K1795	600	16x24	160	$21.65
32K1796	800	17x25	170	23.50
32K1797	1,000	18x25	180	26.25
32K1798	1,200	18x26	190	28.75

32K1774—50-Pound Sealed Test Weight. Guaranteed accurate. Used for testing any scale. Shipped from factory in CENTRAL NEW YORK......... **$3.75**

Power Take-Off and Clutch Pulley for Fordson Tractor

$29$85

With this attachment you can put your Fordson to the fullest use. Permanently attached to your tractor, it is always ready for work and in a few minutes you can have your Fordson grinding, cutting wood, pumping or doing any work where belt power is necessary. Bolts on in place of the foot rest. Automatically locked, it can only be thrown into motion by the operator. Belt can be put on or removed without stopping engine, without danger to operator or of breaking or throwing belt. Engine can be cranked without removing belt.

This attachment will soon pay for itself as it saves time, and enables one to get the fullest use from his Fordson for all belt power purposes. Will last for years as it is substantially built of best materials, and is a mechanical job of the highest quality.

Patented clutch throws in or out of gear easily and without clashing. Is easy to install, simply bolting on in place of foot rest. Automatically lubricated and is dirt and dust proof. Oil seal prevents throwing oil. Heavy one-piece housing. Working parts made of alloy steel, hardened and carefully fitted. Runs on high quality ball bearing. Fiber pulley, 9½ inches in diameter with 6½-inch face included. Guaranteed to give you satisfaction and good service or your money refunded. Shipped from our store.
72K2230¼—Weight, 60 pounds.................**$29.85**

Atlas Improved Wagon and Stock Scales

Good marketing requires accurate weighing. Our Atlas Scales are sealed to U. S. Standard; guaranteed accurate. Full capacity, compound beams, no loose weights. Directions included for building and setting up. Shipped from factory near KANSAS CITY, MO.

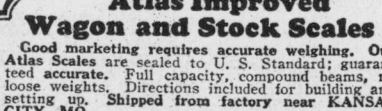

Shallow Pit Scales

Recommended for permanent setting, all around heavy duty, and longest service.

These are known as five-lever scales, the most modern type of heavy scale construction.

Two main levers, one at each end, extend across the platform and rest on heavy bearing chairs. Another lever extends from each main lever and carries the weight to the fifth lever, which transmits it to the weigh beam.

The great advantage of this type scale is that the entire lever system always remains stationary, whereas in scales of the hanging lever type the levers swing with the platform, causing extra wear on knife edges and bearings.

Pit Wagon Scales

Catalog No.	Capacity	Size, Platform	Wt., Lbs.	Each
32K1786	4 tons	14x8 ft.	670	$ 60.00
32K1787	5 tons	14x8 ft.	680	63.50
32K1788	6 tons	14x8 ft.	720	69.75
32K1789	10 tons	22x8 ft.	1,400	124.00

Pit Motor Truck Scales

Catalog No.	Capacity	Size, Platform	Wt., Lbs.	Each
32K1790	10 tons	16x8 ft.	1,420	$150.00
32K1841	15 tons	18x9 ft.	1,800	245.00

Pitless Wagon and Stock Scales

Require no pit, but set right on top of the ground. Easily set up, and can be moved from one location to another with little trouble.

They come with full steel frame, and steel platform joists, ready to put together—all complete except platform.

We recommend pit scales for all public weighing.

Pitless Scales are designed particularly for farm use and are recommended for their convenience. No pit, no wall, wood frame timbers or platform joists are needed. Simply bolt steel together, hang in scale irons, lay on platform plank—and your scale is set. The lever construction is on the same principle as our Shallow Pit Scales.

Shipped from factory near KANSAS CITY, MO.

Catalog No.	Capacity	Size Platform	Weight, Pounds	Each
32K1781	4 tons	14x8 ft.	1,375	$101.00
32K1782	5 tons	14x8 ft.	1,400	104.50
32K1783	6 tons	14x8 ft.	1,420	107.00

High Grade Friction Hoist

$33$75

Useful to the farmer in hoisting hay, raising barns, dragging logs, moving buildings; in fact, any drag or hoisting jobs. To contractors, for excavating with scraper or drag line, hoisting materials on jobs, or in lumber yards.

A strongly constructed, well made hoist at a very low price.

Length over all, 54 inches; drum, 22 inches long, 4 inches diameter. Brake drum, 12 inches, wood lined. Drum shaft, 2 inches in diameter. Capacity, 400 feet ¾-inch rope; speed lift, 35 feet per minute. Geared 4 to 1 and requires 2½ to 4 horse-power engine. Drive pulley, 4 inches in diameter, 6-inch face. Friction drum is operated by shifting clutch. For lowering loads, a foot brake is rigged to operate against the flange of drum. Shipped from OHIO factory.
32K2610—Friction Hoist. Weight, 365 pounds............**$33.75**

Low Prices on Wall Board

WOOD FIBER WALL BOARD, as its name implies, is made of wood fiber. This material, under another name, sells at a much higher price, and is in great demand for new buildings and the remodeling of old ones. It is clean, dry, sanitary and durable. Can be painted or tinted any color desired and is especially treated for waterproof quality. Any handy person can apply it with satisfactory results. Can be sawed and solidly nailed without danger of splitting. Rooms are ready for occupancy as soon as applied.

Suitable for schools, lodge halls, office buildings, garages and stores where quick work, decorative possibilities and warmth are desired. We suggest using the wood panel strips over the joints. Standard size, ⅝x1¾ inches.

Wall board comes in sheets 32 or 48 inches wide, ⅜6 inch thick, and in various lengths from 6 to 12 feet. Carefully bundled for shipment.

Shipped from factory in WESTERN NEW YORK, SOUTHERN ILLINOIS, or KANSAS CITY, MO., only. When ordering be sure to give size of sheets wanted.

48K3196—Plain Light Cream Finish. Both Sides Alike.

This illustration shows the exact thickness of our Wall Board.

W'th, In.	Lgth, Feet	No. of Square Feet to the Sheet	Shpg. Wt., per Sheet, Pounds	Per Sheet	W'th, In.	Lgth, Feet	No. of Square Feet to the Sheet	Shpg. Wt., per Sheet, Pounds	Per Sheet
32	6	16	9	$0.48	48	6	24	14	$0.72
32	7	18⅔	11	.56	48	7	28	16	.84
32	8	21⅓	12	.64	48	8	32	18	.96
32	9	24	14	.72	48	9	36	20	1.08
32	10	26⅔	15	.80	48	10	40	22	1.20
32	12	32	18	.96	48	12	48	27	1.44

Wood Panel Strips

For Use With Wood Fiber Wall Board
Wood Panel Strips Shipped From CINCINNATI, OHIO, SOUTHERN ILLINOIS, KANSAS CITY, MO., or NEWARK, N. J.

48K7922—Yellow Pine. Per 100 feet. Shipping weight, 12 pounds......................$1.30

It's Easy to Order From the World's Largest Store
See Order Blanks in Back of Catalog

Goodwall SHEET PLASTER

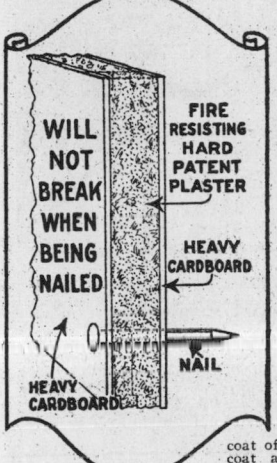

WILL NOT BREAK WHEN BEING NAILED

FIRE RESISTING HARD PATENT PLASTER

HEAVY CARDBOARD

NAIL

HEAVY CARDBOARD

Goodwall Sheet Plaster is a fire resisting gypsum rock composition plaster of even thickness between two sheets of heavy cardboard. These cardboards are so saturated with the fire resisting gypsum composition that they make Goodwall Sheet Plaster far more fire resisting than regular lath and plaster.

Illustration at right shows Goodwall Sheet Plaster applied to studding. It can be plastered with specially prepared Hard Plaster Finish, which will give results equal to lath and plaster job. It can also be wallpapered without the use of Hard Plaster.

For best results we recommend a ⅜-inch coat of Hard Plaster for first coat and ⅛-inch Top Coat Finish for second coat.

Here are its Many Advantages

It enables you to do a better job for less money and can be applied by yourself.

It is equal in service and strength to a lath and plaster wall.

It does away with lath stains and hair cracks.

It deadens sound as effectively as lath and plaster.

It is vermin proof and can be painted, papered or kalsomined.

It can be covered with a plaster coat of any thickness, but ⅜ of an inch hard plaster for first coat and ⅛ of an inch top coat finish for second coat will be sufficient to make a smooth and seamless wall.

It is dry. No need to wait for weeks to drive the dampness out.

It is clean. No muss and dirt when you apply it.

It is strong. Send for a sample and try to break it with your hands.

It cuts out cost of lath; none needed with Goodwall Sheet Plaster.

It will not break when being nailed.

It can be cut with a saw, or broken with a clean edge by scoring the cardboard on both sides with a knife, breaking where scored.

EASILY APPLIED

Quick Delivery at Low Freight Charges From Many Shipping Points: Grand Rapids, Mich., Oakfield, N. Y., Fort Dodge, Iowa, Gypsum, Ohio, Sweetwater, Texas, or Plasterco, Va.

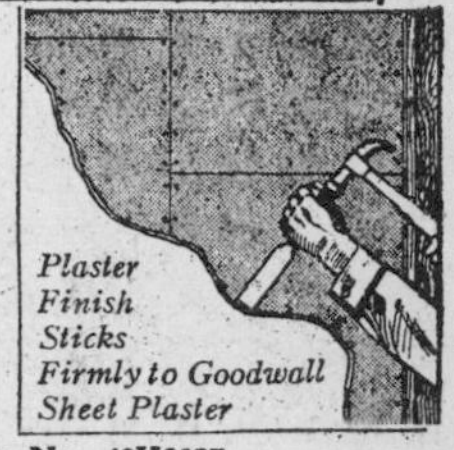

Plaster Finish Sticks Firmly to Goodwall Sheet Plaster

Order by Catalog No. 48K3027

At the left is illustrated a piece of Goodwall Sheet Plaster in actual thickness of the ⅜-inch sheets. The large sheets can be used same as any wall board without the use of plaster finish and in that case we recommend that you use our Joint finisher listed below to fill up the joints between the sheets.

Size, In.	Thickness, In.	Sq. Ft. per Sheet	Shpg. Wt., Crated, per Sheet	Per Sheet
32x 48	⅜	10⅔	20 lbs.	$0.26
48x 72	⅜	24	52 lbs.	.91
48x 84	⅜	28	60 lbs.	1.04
48x 96	⅜	32	68 lbs.	1.21
48x108	⅜	36	77 lbs.	1.37
48x120	⅜	40	86 lbs.	1.52

48K2995—Joint Finisher. Per 5-pound package..80c
Five pounds will fill the joints on 500 square feet of sheet plaster. Shipped with sheet plaster.

SPECIALLY PREPARED HARD PLASTER
(For First Coat)

Shipped in Good Strong Bags With Sheet Plaster
Quantity required to cover 100 square feet, ⅜-inch coat, 150 pounds.
Shipped from GRAND RAPIDS, MICH., OAKFIELD, N. Y., FORT DODGE, IOWA, GYPSUM, OHIO, PLASTERCO, VA., or SWEETWATER, TEXAS.

48K2999—Per 100-pound bag..................65c

SPECIALLY PREPARED TOP COAT PLASTER

For second coat. Shipped in good strong bags with Sheet Plaster from all points, except Sweetwater, Texas. If you want a real white finish, order our white top coat, listed below.
Quantity required to cover 100 square feet, ⅛-inch coat, 50 pounds. Shipped from Grand Rapids, Mich., Oakfield, N. Y., Fort Dodge, Iowa, Plasterco, Va., Gypsum, Ohio.

48K2997—White Top Coat. Per 100-pound bag.............$1.45

Nails—One pound will be required for 12 sheets of Goodwall Sheet Plaster, 32x48 inches. Ordinary 3-penny nails can be used, placed not more than 4 inches apart.

BUILDING PAPERS *and* FELTS

Blue Plaster Cardboard

Less than one-half of a cent a square foot for our Fulton Brand Blue Plaster Cardboard. Used in camps, cottages, etc., as a low priced material for ceiling and above wainscoting. Also used in buildings where a low cost interior finish is desired. Good for lining garages. Keeps out wind and cold.

It is a heavy paper, about the thickness of ordinary cardboard with smooth surface. Made only in "A" grade from carefully selected stock. Strong and durable. Comes in a pleasing shade of blue. Easily put on with ordinary large headed tacks or 6-ounce billposter's tacks. For sheathing purposes it would be hard to obtain a warmer, stronger or tougher material. Rolls are 36 inches wide. It can be included in your order for wall paper or other merchandise.

48K3012—Blue Plaster Cardboard. 250 square feet per roll. Weight, per roll, 30 lbs. 78c

48K3013—Blue Plaster Cardboard. 500 square feet per roll. Weight, per roll, 60 lbs.....$1.50

Tarred Felt

Tarred felt is one of the best kinds of building paper for lining floors and for use between sheathing and siding. Can be used under stucco and brick veneers. It is also used for gravel roofs. Made of carefully selected felt, thoroughly saturated with redistilled American coal tar.

48K3050—Tarred Felt. 250 square feet per roll. Weight, per roll, 60 pounds............$2.00
We recommend this for all first class jobs, because it is the thickest. Used extensively for roofing temporary buildings. It makes an excellent insulating felt and should be used under all floors.

48K3054—Tarred Felt. 400 square feet per roll. Weight, per roll, 60 pounds............$2.00
Tarred Felt, medium thickness. This thickness of tarred felt is used for gravel roofing where several layers are specified. It is not as thick as 48K3050 but is very satisfactory where a medium grade of work is required.

48K3055—Tarred Felt. 500 square feet per roll. Weight, per roll, 60 pounds..............$2.00

Deadening Felt

Homan Brand Deadening Felt is used to deaden the sound between floors and in walls. It serves as a layer under floor linoleums, oilcloths or rugs. Formerly only the more expensive buildings were equipped with it. Now it is unusual when deadening felt is not used. Our low price is all the more reason for its usefulness for building purposes. It is made of a good grade of felt, soft and pliable, and will add much to the warmth and value of your building. We recommend the heavier felt, 48K3006. It makes the floors more soundproof and warmer. Homan Brand Deadening Felt should be under every floor. All rolls are 36 inches wide and contain about 450 square feet of Deadening Felt.

48K3004—Deadening Felt. Shipping weight, per roll, 50 pounds. Per roll......$2.20

48K3006—Deadening Felt. Shipping weight, per roll, 75 pounds. Per roll.........$3.50

Red Rosin Paper

Red Rosin Sized Building Paper should be used under siding and between floors of all residences. It makes the dwelling warmer, drier and more healthful. The valuation on any home is increased when it is insulated to make it warm in winter and cool in summer. The cost is so small when compared to the gain that it is now used more than ever. It is rosin sized. We recommend our Leader Brand, weighing 40 pounds per roll, as it is thick, tough, durable and of sufficient weight to give the most satisfaction. Our competition Brand is a fair grade and weighs 20 pounds to the roll. However, no matter which brand you choose, you can rest assured of obtaining a splendid value for the money.

48K3000—Leader Brand. 36 inches wide. Weight, 40 pounds. Per roll...............98c

48K3007—Competition Brand. 36 inches wide. Weight, 20 pounds. Per roll..............49c

All Building Papers and Felts Shipped From Chicago or Philadelphia

It's Easy to Order From the World's Largest Store. See Page 546

Guaranteed
Highest Grade

APPROVED BY NATIONAL BOARD OF FIRE UNDERWRITERS

TWO-INCH WATER-TIGHT LAP JOINT

Oriental
Slate Surfaced Roofing
Approved by the National Board of Fire Underwriters

Guaranteed 17 Years

Oriental Slate Surfaced Asphalt Roofing has a beautiful red or green slate color, that will not fade, and is an excellent value.

Thousands of customers heartily recommend our Oriental Slate Surfaced Asphalt Roofing for its wonderful wearing quality, fine appearance, and the saving made on the cost. **Roofing not as good as this sells throughout the country for $3.00 to $3.50 per roll.**

The outstanding features that make this roofing so satisfactory are: Fabricated of high quality waterproof and fire resisting materials, **heavy roofing felt, imported asphalt and genuine crushed,** natural color, green or red slate. Either color is permanent. Never needs paint.

It is extra heavy and durable. Snowproof and sunproof. Rain only washes it clean. Good in every climate. Better than wood shingles. Can be laid over old shingles, saving the expense and dirt in tearing them off. Suitable for buildings with a roof having a pitch of 1½ inches or more to each running foot.

Oriental Roofing protects your house from fire, whereas sparks from a chimney may destroy wood shingles.

Weight: Average weight, per roll, 90 pounds, including nails and cement. Contains 108 square feet and will cover 100 square feet, all in one piece.

CAUTION! Buy Only Roofing With 2-Inch Watertight Lap Joint. If slate or pebbles lie between the two layers of roofing, the joints will loosen up and leak.

Oriental Slate Surfaced Roofing, complete with 1-inch large headed galvanized roofing nails and cement for laps. 48K2163—Red. 48K2162—Green. **Guaranteed 17 Years**	**Per Roll** $2.20	Complete with 1¾-inch large headed galvanized roofing nails to lay over old shingles and cement for laps. 48K1479—Red. 48K1476—Green. **Guaranteed 17 Years**	**Per Roll** $2.30

Quick Service—Low Freight Rates

We are close neighbors, regardless of where you live. Our roofing warehouses are located in all sections of the country. Each warehouse is the shipping point for the territory nearest to it with lowest freight rates for roofing materials.

Below we list locations and shipping points of our largest roofing factories and warehouses. See how close we are to your home! You save on price of the good roofing, and you also save money on the short haul freight charges.

Shipped from CHICAGO, ILL., PHILADELPHIA, PA., KANSAS CITY, MO., ATLANTA, GA., NEWARK, N. J., YORK, PA., WESTERN NEW YORK, EASTERN MASSACHUSETTS, SOUTHERN OHIO, SOUTHERN ILLINOIS, NORTHERN ILLINOIS, OR ST. PAUL, MINN.

$2.20 Per Roll

Our Liberal Guarantee for Roofing

is the outgrowth of over 25 years' experience in the manufacture and sale of ready roofing by the World's Largest Store. It is with the knowledge of high and long lasting quality that we can guarantee our roofing for a longer period, because our roofing lasts longer than we claim.

Sears, Roebuck and Co. were first to guarantee ready roofing for a term of years. Our first guarantee was for 12 years. The weight of our Oriental Roofing when first guaranteed was only 80 pounds per roll. Yet, customers have written that this roofing lasts much longer.

We have gradually improved the quality and increased the weight of our roofing until now the average weight per roll is 90 pounds, and with each change in quality, we extended the number of years in our guarantee, until now Oriental and Fire-Chief Roofings, the best prepared roofings made, are guaranteed for 17 years! Right now, there are more than one million roofs covered with Sears, Roebuck and Co.'s roofing.

SAMPLES We guarantee that you will be satisfied with our roofing, but if you prefer to see samples before sending us your order, ask for Free Roofing Samples 8573K.

Steel Roofing and Siding

2½ and 1¼-Inch Corrugated Steel

2½-INCH AND 1¼-INCH CORRUGATED SHEETS are furnished in sheets which actually measure 26 inches wide. Both have a covering width of only 24 inches on account of the side lap. When ordering, allow from 4 to 6 inches for end laps, depending upon the pitch of roof. For siding, a 2-inch end lap is sufficient. When ordering allow 5 sheets to cover 100 square feet of surface; this does not include the end laps.

Two-V and Three-V Crimp Steel

Two-V and Three-V Crimp Steel Roofing have a covering width of 24 inches after lapping one crimp over the other. Requires no soldering, folding or hammering of seams or joints; anyone who has ordinary mechanical ability can put it on.

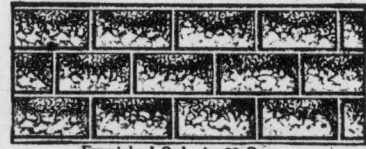

Prices of 2½-Inch Corrugated Steel

Catalog No.	Per 5-Ft. Sheet	Per 6-Ft. Sheet	Per 7-Ft. Sheet	Per 8-Ft. Sheet	Per 9-Ft. Sheet	Per 10-Ft. Sheet	Per 12-Ft. Sheet	Wt., per 100 Sq. Feet
48K3105—28-Gauge Painted Red.	31c	38c	44c	50c	56c	$0.62	$0.79	68 lbs.
48K3106—28-Gauge Galvanized.	50c	60c	70c	80c	90c	1.00	1.24	84 lbs.
48K3123—26-Gauge Galvanized.	55c	66c	77c	88c	99c	1.10	1.36	98 lbs.

Prices of 1¼-Inch Corrugated Steel

Catalog No.	Per 5-Ft. Sheet	Per 6-Ft. Sheet	Per 7-Ft. Sheet	Per 8-Ft. Sheet	Per 9-Ft. Sheet	Per 10-Ft. Sheet	Per 12-Ft. Sheet	Wt., per 100 Sq. Feet
48K3107—28-Gauge Painted Red.	32c	39c	46c	52c	$0.58	$0.64	$0.81	68 lbs.
48K3108—28-Gauge Galvanized.	51c	62c	72c	82c	.92	1.02	1.28	84 lbs.
48K3125—26-Gauge Galvanized.	56c	68c	79c	90c	1.01	1.12	1.40	98 lbs.

Prices of Two-V Crimp Steel

Catalog No.	Per 5-Ft. Sheet	Per 6-Ft. Sheet	Per 7-Ft. Sheet	Per 8-Ft. Sheet	Per 9-Ft. Sheet	Per 10-Ft. Sheet	Per 12-Ft. Sheet	Wt., per 100 Sq. Feet
48K3077—28-Gauge Painted Red.	29c	35c	41c	47c	53c	$0.58	$0.73	69 lbs.
48K3078—28-Gauge Galvanized.	47c	57c	67c	76c	85c	.94	1.08	85 lbs.
48K3080—26-Gauge Galvanized.	51c	62c	72c	82c	92c	1.02	1.28	98 lbs.

Prices of Three-V Crimp Steel

Catalog No.	Per 5-Ft. Sheet	Per 6-Ft. Sheet	Per 7-Ft. Sheet	Per 8-Ft. Sheet	Per 9-Ft. Sheet	Per 10-Ft. Sheet	Per 12-Ft. Sheet	Wt., per 100 Sq. Feet
48K3086—28-Gauge Galvanized.	48c	58c	68c	78c	87c	$0.96	$1.20	86 lbs.
48K3083—26-Gauge Galvanized.	53c	64c	75c	86c	96c	1.06	1.32	100 lbs.

Pressed Brick Face Steel Siding

Size of single brick, 2¾x8½ inches. In sheets, 60x28 inches. Pressed Brick Steel Siding after painting resembles pressed brick. Sold only in full sheets, painted red, or galvanized, as quoted below.

Painted, 64 pounds per 100 square feet; galvanized, 78 pounds per 100 square feet. Furnished only in 28-gauge.

Catalog No.	Pressed Brick Face Steel Siding	Per Sheet, 60x28 Inches
48K3116	Painted Red	36c
48K3117	Galvanized	56c

Rock Face Steel Siding

Size of single stone, 7x12 inches. In sheets, 60x28 inches.

An elegant facing for stone fronts. Easily applied. Weight, painted, 64 pounds; galvanized, 78 pounds per square of 100 square feet.

Furnished Only in 28-Gauge.

Catalog No.	Rock Face Steel Siding	Per Sheet, 60x28 Inches
48K3142	Painted Red	38c
48K3143	Galvanized	57c

Galvanized and Black Sheet Steel

48K3225—Galvanized Flat Sheet Steel, standard grade. Size of sheet, 28x96 inches. State gauge wanted.

No. of gauge	28	26	24
No. of sheets per bundle	10	8	7
Wt., per bundle, lbs.	146	135	151
Per sheet	$0.80	$0.87	$1.04
Per bundle	7.55	6.90	7.25

48K3222—Black Sheet Steel.

No. of gauge	28	26	24
No. of sheets per bundle	10	8	7
Wt., per bundle, lbs.	117	112	131
Per sheet	$0.46	$0.53	$0.68
Per bundle	4.55	4.20	4.75

Beaded Steel for Ceilings or Sidings

Made from U. S. Standard 28-gauge steel, painted on both sides with iron oxide paint, ground in linseed oil. Sheets cover 24 inches from center of outside beads and can be furnished in 5, 6, 8 and 10-foot lengths. The beads are small corrugations, ⅝ inch wide by ⅜ inch deep and 3 inches from center to center.

Always allow for end lap.

48K3115—Beaded Steel Siding or Ceiling. Weight, painted, 70 pounds per square of 100 square feet.

Length, feet	5	6	8	10
Per sheet	32c	38c	51c	64c

All Articles Listed Above Shipped From CENTRAL OHIO or NORTHERN KENTUCKY

Galvanized Steel Valley

Made of a good grade of galvanized steel in a continuous strip, locked joints. Full lengths are 25 feet and 50 feet. Width, 14 inches.

48K3197—Galvanized Steel Valley in rolls, 28-gauge.
25-foot roll. Weight, 20 lbs.............$1.75
50-foot roll. Weight, 40 lbs............. 3.50

Shipped from CHICAGO or PHILADELPHIA store.

Galvanized Steel Ventilators

Extra heavy, 22, 24 and 26-gauge galvanized steel is used in the manufacture of our Majestic Ventilators, according to size.

Majestic Ventilators are equipped with four stay rods which hold them securely in place on the roof. A wire screen is provided to keep birds out.

Your choice of gold bronzed horse or cow weather vane.

Prices of Majestic Ventilators for large buildings:

Catalog No.	Size Flue	Size Base	Height	Wt., Lbs.	No. Cattle	
48K657	18 in.	26 in.	7 ft. 6 in.	115	4	$22.00
48K652	20 in.	29 in.	8 ft. 8 in.	155	6	25.60
48K653	24 in.	36 in.	9 ft. 5 in.	182	8	29.20
48K654	28 in.	40 in.	10 ft. 4 in.	235	12	34.95
48K655	30 in.	44 in.	10 ft. 9 in.	252	14	37.35
48K656	36 in.	55 in.	11 ft. 3 in.	396	20	45.60

Prince Galvanized Steel Ventilators

Suitable for small buildings such as small barns, hog houses and poultry houses.

Prices of Prince Ventilators for small buildings:

Catalog No.	Size of Flue, In.	Size of Base, In.	Height	Wt., Lbs.	
48K650	16	22	3 ft. 5 in.	55	$9.90
48K651	22	24	3 ft. 6 in.	58	12.10

All Ventilators Shipped From CENTRAL OHIO

High Grade Metal Ceilings

$6.98 Per 100 Square Feet

LINCOLN DESIGN

Deeply embossed, intended for residences, churches, lodge halls or public buildings. The cornice drops 9 inches on the side wall. Send us a rough drawing of your ceiling, giving measures of ceiling and of all offsets in wall, and our ceiling experts will quote you the price on your requirement. Shipping weight, 60 pounds to the square.

48K11694—Lincoln Design. Per 100 sq. ft., including nails... $6.98
Shipped from steel mills in CENTRAL OHIO.

$3.60 Per 100 Square Feet

Suitable for Large or Small Rooms

This neat and tastefully designed steel ceiling is used very extensively for stores and moderate priced buildings. It is of a neat, small pattern which will be appropriate for any size room.

48K3114½—Steel Siding or Ceiling Covering. Sold at this price only in sheets of 24x96 inches, which includes allowances made for side and end laps as beaded on the sheets. Weight, per square, 56 pounds. Painted in a light drab color on both sides.
Per sheet, 58c; per 100 square feet.......... $3.60
48K3118—Egg and Dart Design Border. Width, 3 inches. Per 4-foot length....... 15c
Shipped from CENTRAL OHIO or NORTHERN KENTUCKY.

The two illustrations of metal ceilings shown are our two most popular designs. However, our Building Material Catalog shows other attractive designs. If you want more designs to select from write for our Building Material, Millwork and Roofing Catalog 547K. Sent postpaid on request.

No Soldering—The Joints Slip Together and Stay

Corrugated Conductor

Makes a stiff, strong pipe, and is easily put together. Furnished only in 10-foot lengths. They are made to fit the following eaves troughs:

| Size of eaves troughs, inches | 3½ | 4 | 5 | 6 |
| Size of conductor, inches | 2 | 2 | 3 | 4 |

48K1278—Full Weight, U. S. Standard 28-Gauge.

Size, inches	2	★3	4
Weight, per length, lbs.	4½	6½	9
Per 10-foot length	43c	54c	68c

48K3303—Extra Heavy Weight, U. S. Standard 26-Gauge Galvanized Steel.

Size, inches	2	3	4
Weight, per length, lbs.	6	7½	10
Per 10-foot length	53c	65c	85c

Patent Slip Joint Eaves Troughs

Furnished with the **slip joint** connection that will fit at either end of each piece no matter which way the water runs. No bother about right hand or left hand eaves trough. Just order the number of pieces you need and put them on.

FULL WEIGHT, U. S. STANDARD 28-GAUGE GALVANIZED
48K1279

Width, across top or size, inches	3½	4	★5	6
Weight, per length, pounds	4½	5	6½	8
Per 10-foot length	38c	44c	55c	68c

EXTRA HEAVY WEIGHT, U. S. STANDARD 26-GAUGE GALVANIZED STEEL
48K3304

Width across top or size, inches	3½	4	5	6
Weight, per length, pounds	5½	6	7½	9
Per 10-foot length	43c	55c	65c	78c

ORDER BY SIZE AND NUMBER.

Extra Heavy Gauge Eaves Trough Corners or Miters

Inside Corner Miter 48K3309   Outside Corner Miter 48K3310

Furnished only in extra heavy 26-gauge galvanized steel, because more strength is required at corners of eaves trough, where ice and snow are likely to collect. Therefore, we furnish only extra heavy 26-gauge corners to use with the 28 or 26-gauge eaves trough.

Complete with **slip joint** connections that fit at either end of the corner so that it can be connected with either right or left hand eaves trough. Be sure to state whether you want outside or inside corners.

48K3309—Inside Corner.
48K3310—Outside Corner.

Width across top or size, inches	3½	4	★5	6
Weight, each, ounces	11	13	17	19
Each	25c	28c	30c	38c

Outlet

Illustration represents outlet in position, can be connected anywhere to suit down spout. No soldering needed.

48K3308—Extra Heavy 26-Gauge Galvanized Steel Outlets.

Size, inches	3½	4	★5	6
Fitted for conductor, size, in.	2	2	3	4
Weight, each, ounces	7	8	11	12
Each	15c	20c	23c	24c

End Cap Slip Joint

For either eaves troughs or our adjustable outlet.

48K3307—Extra Heavy 26-Gauge Galvanized Steel.

Size, inches	3½	4	★5	6
Weight, ounces	2	2	3	3
Each	9c	9c	12c	14c

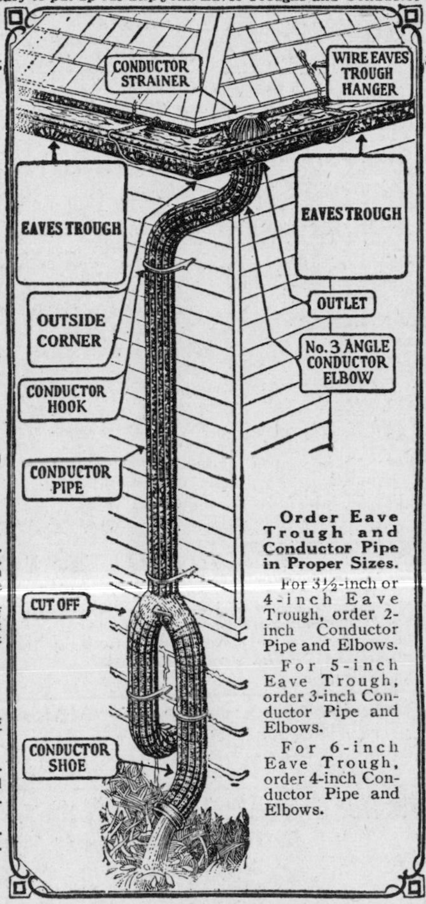

Galvanized Steel, Rust Resisting

WE FURNISH TWO THICKNESSES: Heavy (United States Standard 28-gauge) and extra heavy (United States Standard 26-gauge) which is 20 per cent thicker and heavier than the standard 28-gauge. We recommend the extra heavy grade or 26-gauge in preference to the 28-gauge weight, as it costs but little more, costs no more to hang and gives at least double the wear. All articles on this page are shipped from CHICAGO or PHILADELPHIA and all items marked (★) are also shipped from NEWARK, N. J.

OUR SLIP JOINT REQUIRES NO SOLDER. No experience necessary to put up our Slip Joint Eaves Troughs and Conductor Pipes.

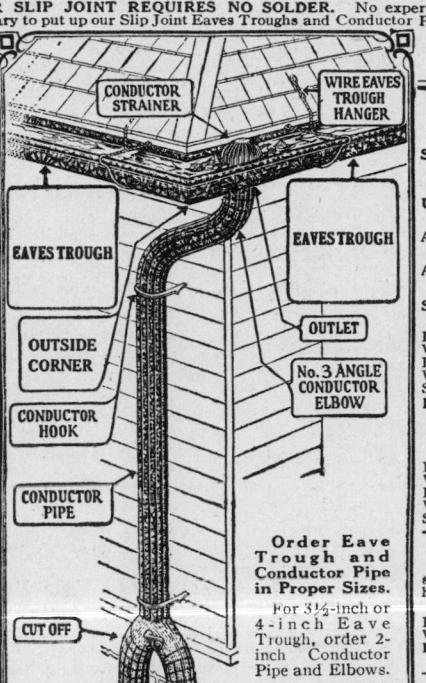

CONDUCTOR STRAINER · WIRE EAVES TROUGH HANGER · EAVES TROUGH · EAVES TROUGH · OUTSIDE CORNER · OUTLET · CONDUCTOR HOOK · No. 3 ANGLE CONDUCTOR ELBOW · CONDUCTOR PIPE · CUT OFF · CONDUCTOR SHOE

Order Eave Trough and Conductor Pipe in Proper Sizes.

For 3½-inch or 4-inch Eave Trough, order 2-inch Conductor Pipe and Elbows.

For 5-inch Eave Trough, order 3-inch Conductor Pipe and Elbows.

For 6-inch Eave Trough, order 4-inch Conductor Pipe and Elbows.

Wire Eaves Trough Hangers

48K3170—Every 4 feet of trough requires one hanger.

Size, in.	3½	4	★5	6
Wt., per doz., lbs.	1	1¼	1¾	1¾
Per doz.	22c	26c	29c	34c

Hooks for Conductors

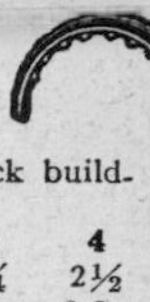

48K3188—Tinned Conductor Hooks for conductor pipe.
Can be used on frame or brick buildings.

Size, inches	2	★3	4
Weight, per dozen, lbs.	1¼	1¾	2½
Per dozen	50c	63c	90c

Ridge Roll Finial

Galvanized Steel Finial to be used with our Ridge Roll 48K3337 and 48K3152. This finial is to be used at the ends of the ridge.

48K3168★—Standard Gauge Galvanized Finial.
Weight, each, 1 pound. Each....40c

Galvanized Steel Elbows and Shoes

Specify Angle and Number in Catalog

FULL WEIGHT U. S. Standard 28-Gauge
48K3182—Elbow, Angle No. 2.
48K3183—Elbow, Angle No. 3.
48K3184—Conductor Shoe.

No. 2 Angle No. 3 Angle Shoe

Diameter or size, inches	2	★3	4
Weight, each, ounces	6	7	11
Elbow	14c	17c	26c
Weight, each, ounces	6	8	12
Shoe	20c	24c	35c

EXTRA HEAVY WEIGHT, U. S. STANDARD 26-GAUGE GALVANIZED STEEL
48K3312—Elbow. Angle No. 2.
48K3313—Elbow. Angle No. 3.
48K3314—Conductor Shoe.

Diameter or size, inches	2	★3	4
Weight, each, ounces	10	14	15
Elbow	21c	23c	38c
Weight, each, ounces	7	12	20
Shoe	33c	40c	55c

Rain Water Cut-Offs

For Corrugated Conductor. Fits corresponding size of conductor pipe. A turn of the handle diverts water to cistern or overflow pipe.

48K3306

| Diameter of spout, inches | 2 | ★3 | 4 |
| Weight, each, ounces | 8 | 12 | 21 |

Extra Heavy U. S. Standard 26-Gauge. Each....57c 59c 83c

V-Angle Ridge Cap

Used on steel, slate or shingle roofs. Comes in 10-foot lengths. 8-inch girth, in our full weight 28-gauge or extra heavy weight 26-gauge.

Standard 28-Gauge
48K3167★—Per length, galvanized. Weight, per length, 5 pounds....45c

Extra Heavy 26-Gauge
48K3341—Per length, galvanized. Weight, per length, 7 pounds....55c

Round Roll Ridge Cap

Diameter of roll, 2 in.; width of apron, 2½ in.; girth, 10 inches. Made only in 10-foot lengths.

Full Weight 28-Gauge
48K3152★—Per length, galvanized. Weight, per length, 5½ pounds....48c

Extra Heavy 26-Gauge
48K3337—Per length, galvanized. Weight, per length, 8 pounds....65c

Conductor Funnel

For running two conductors into one. Size indicates size of lower spout.

48K3305—No. 26-Gauge Galvanized Steel.

Size, in.	2	★3	4
Wt., ea., oz.	9	12	17
Each	26c	33c	43c

Conductor Strainers

48K3194—Galvanized Wire Conductor Strainers, placed in the outlet of eaves trough, prevents leaves, etc., stopping up the conductor. The size given designates the size outlet strainer will fit.

Size, inches	2	★3	4
Weight, each, oz.	1	2	3
Each	8c	9c	13c

Sheet Zinc

Suitable for covering table tops, stove boards, heat shields, etc. No. 9—Size of sheet, 36 by 84 inches. Weight, per sheet, 14 lbs.

48K4601—Per sheet....$1.95

Tin Shingles

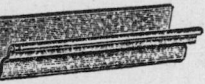

Made of a good grade of roofing tin. Useful for repairing old roofs and making a tight joint around chimney, etc. Painted on both sides.

48K3199—Size, 5x7 inches. Each....2c
Per 100. (Shipping weight, 15 pounds)....$1.30

O. G. Box Style Eaves Trough and Fittings
LAP JOINT FOR SOLDERING

Eaves Trough

Made of heavy 26-gauge galvanized steel, plain joints for soldering. Size across at top, 5 inches. Weight, per 10-foot length, 10 lbs.

48K3401★—10-foot length....95c
Conductor pipe No. 48K3303, size 3 in., is suitable to use with this eaves trough.

Outside Corner Miters

Size, 5 in. Weight, each, 1 pound.
48K3405★ Each....83c

Inside Corner Miters

Size, 5 inches. Weight, each, 1 pound.
48K3406★ Each....83c

End Caps

End Cap for left hand end of O. G. Eaves Trough. Size, 5 inches. Weight, each, 2 ounces.
48K3404★ Left Hand. Each....15c

End Cap for right hand end of O. G. Eaves Trough. Size, 5 in. Weight, each, 2 oz.
48K3403★ Right Hand. Each....15c

Hangers

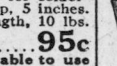

Hangers for O. G. Eaves Trough. Length, 13 in. Weight, each, 3 ounces.
48K3821★ Each....6c

Outlet Tube

Size, 3 inches. Wt., each, 3 ounces.
48K3402★ Each....10c

Fire-Place Furnishings

QUALITY FULLY GUARANTEED

Fireplace furnishings are shipped from PHILADELPHIA store, or from factory in OHIO, whichever is nearer you, unless otherwise stated.

Andirons $4.50

Colonial Design
Cast Iron Andirons. Ball top ebony (black) finish. Height, 18 inches. Ball, 3 inches in diameter. Matches Fire Set 63K4160. Weight, boxed, 40 lbs.
63K3901........ $4.50

Gas Logs

Made of clay. Decorated and colored to represent real oak logs. Each log consists of three-stick formation as illustrated. Packed complete with stand and air mixer.
63K4183 — Length, 16 inches. Weight, 50 pounds. $6.50
63K4184 — Length, 18 inches. Weight, 60 lbs...$7.15
63K4185 — Length, 20 inches. Weight, 90 lbs...$8.35
63K4186 — Length, 22 inches. Weight, 105 lbs..$8.75
63K4187 — Length, 24 inches. Weight, 125 lbs,..$9.60

Cast Iron Automatic Ash Dump

Mailable. Size, 6x8 inches. Weight, 3 pounds.
63K4176...........45c

Four-Piece Fire Set
Round Head Handle Wrought Iron Fire Set. Complete with stand, shovel, tongs and poker. Suitable for colonial or mission fireplace. Burnt brass or black finish handles. Total height, 25 inches. Matches Andirons 63K3901, 63K4802 and 63K4805. Shipping weight, 15 pounds. Mailable.
63K4160—Black finish. $3.30
63K4161—Black with burnt brass finish handles............ $3.60

Folding Spark Screens

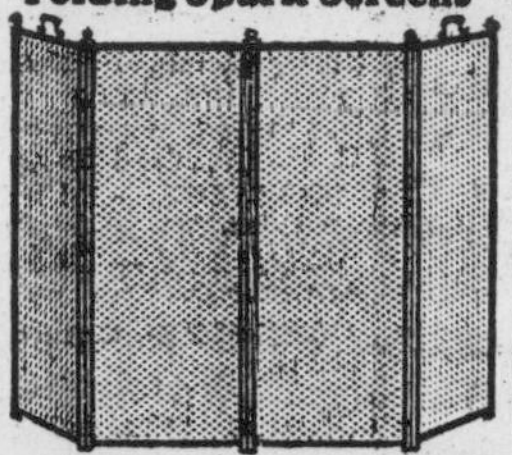

These screens are very attractive in addition to the protection they afford. Made up of four folds. Each fold 12 in. wide, 30 in. high. Mailable. Wt., packed, 15 lbs. Shipped from our PHILADELPHIA store.
63K4211—Heavy Black Spiral Weave Fabric, with round black frame trimmed with brass handles, hinge caps and knobs.. $4.95
63K4214—Heavy Black Fabric with hammered brass finish frame.. $7.75

Andirons $2.85 AND UP

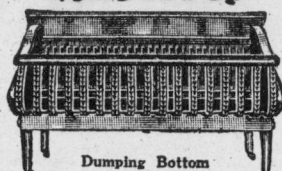

Hand Wrought Iron Art Nouveau Design Andirons. Burnt brass or black finish. Total height, 13½ inches; depth from front to back, 20 inches. Shipping weight, 25 pounds. Mailable.
63K4802—Black finish. Per pair.......... $2.85
63K4805—Burnt brass finish. Per pair....... 3.75

Portable Grates $5.15 and Up

Dumping Bottom

For use in open fireplace, will burn wood or coal. Made of cast iron. Ebony (black) finish. Depth, front to back, 13 inches.

	Total Length, Inches	Wt. Lbs.	
63K4070	19	40	$5.15
63K4071	20¾	45	5.35
63K4072	23¾	50	5.50
63K4073	25¼	55	5.75
63K4074	28	60	6.50
63K4075	31	70	7.25

Five-Piece Fire Set
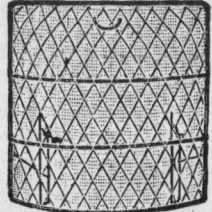
Square Head Wrought Iron Fire Set, ebony (black) finish, complete with stand, shovel, brush, tongs and poker. Matches Andirons 63K4126. Height, 29 inches. Shipping weight, 25 pounds. Mailable.
63K4170
Per set, $5.45

Wire Spark Guards

Heavy crimped copper plated 1¼-inch wire mesh, lined with fine wire cloth. Weight, packed, 15 pounds. Shipped from our PHILADELPHIA store.
63K4215—Size 24x30 inches..... $2.20
63K4216 Size, 30x30 inches...$2.60
63K4217 Size, 36x30 inches... 2.95
63K4218 Size, 36x36 inches... 3.65

Andirons $3.85

Square Top, Ebony (black) Finish Cast Iron Andirons. Height, 18 inches. Posts, 3 inches. Head, 5 inches. Matches Fire Set 63K4170. Wt., boxed, 40 lbs.
63K4126...... $3.85

Mantel Grates

Our Best Coal Grate. All cast iron, oxidized copper plated finish. Needs no firebrick setting. Has double drafts and dampers. Shipped from foundry in OHIO. Wt., crated, 210 lbs.
63K4020—Fireplace Grate, 24½ in. wide, 30¼ in. high. Fire basket 20 in. wide, 12 in. deep. $24.50
63K4021—Fireplace Grate, 30½ in. wide, 30¼ in. high. Fire basket, 24 in. wide, 12 in. deep.. $27.00

Cast Iron Throat Damper

Size Over All	Wt.	
34x13 in.	50 lbs.	$5.10
40x13 in,	56 lbs.	5.95
63K4175

Concrete Mixer and Block Machine

ONLY $25.95

63K5998

The Triumph Concrete Mixer

Especially built for farm needs. The Triumph Mixer is an ideal mixer for the countless small jobs that can be easily done during spare hours.
Here are some of the uses it can be put to: Building—Concrete Foundations; Floors; Feed and Water Troughs; Sidewalks; Culverts; Fence Posts; Roadways; Fruit and Vegetable Cellars; Porches; Porch Steps, etc.
This Triumph Concrete Mixer will pay for itself on any one job. It thoroughly MIXES CONCRETE, MORTAR OR PLASTER wet or dry. A GOOD FEED MIXER.
Design—Tilting drum permits loading on one side and discharging on the other. Material—Made of the best grade of gray iron castings, heavy sheet and heavy angle plates, well braced. Capacity—1½ to 2 cubic feet per batch (a wheelbarrow load). Power—Equipped with 12-inch pulley, 3-inch face; can be operated with 1 horsepower engine; also handle furnished for hand power. Frame—Made of 1½x1½-inch angle steel. General Dimensions—Length, 3 feet; width, 2 feet 10 inches; height, 4 feet 6 inches; shoveling height, 35 inches. Drum—Heavy 16-gauge sheet steel, with cast iron bottom, 22 inches deep, 18 inches in diameter at top, 23 inches in diameter at bottom, inside measurements. Shipping weight, 250 pounds.
63K5998—Triumph Concrete Mixer on Stand............. $25.95
Shipped from factory in OHIO.

You Save Money Here
Do Your Own Concrete Work

Concrete will not rust or rot. It needs no paint to preserve it or keep it looking good. Neither fire nor storm destroys it. When you build with concrete you build to stay. It practically eliminates repairs, replacement and upkeep expenses. You can build with concrete many of the needed improvements about your farm for less money than in any other way.

Write for Your Copy of Our Concrete Machinery Catalog 532PK

If the concrete machine or mixer illustrated and priced here does not suit your requirements, then write for our Catalog of Concrete Machinery 532PK. It shows a large variety of molds for concrete products, including block machines, urn, chimney column, pier, baluster, brick and silo molds, automatic block tampers, pallets, sill and cap machines, and 5 and 10-foot concrete mixers. It is yours for the asking; sent postpaid.

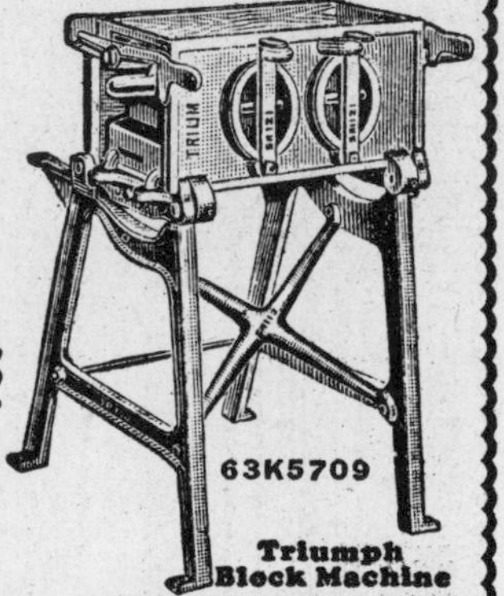

ONLY $25.65

63K5709

Triumph Block Machine

A good block making outfit at a moderate price for anyone wishing to make concrete blocks for his own use. No experience needed. Makes blocks face down, using a wood pallet. Makes 8x8x16-inch blocks with rock face and double air space. Flask is locked with simple latches attached to endgate. Two men can make from 100 to 125 blocks per day. Mounted on substantial iron stand as shown. Each outfit contains: One Rock Face Plate for whole blocks; one Rock Face Plate for half and quarter blocks; two Rock Endgates; two Core Endgates; two Dividing Plates; one Gable Block Dividing Plate for making gable blocks; two Joint Block Attachments; Plugs for making solid blocks; one striker; one Double End Tamper; one Sample Wood Pallet. Additional parts and attachments can be furnished extra.
63K5709 — Triumph Block Machine for 8x8x16-inch blocks, on iron stand, as illustrated. Shpg. wt., 165 lbs. $25.65
Shipped from factory in OHIO.
For Cement Workers' Tools see Page 999

Going to Build?

Buy Your Material at Factory Prices

For Builders' Hardware and Tools, See Pages 978, 979 and 984 to 991

Send for This Free Book

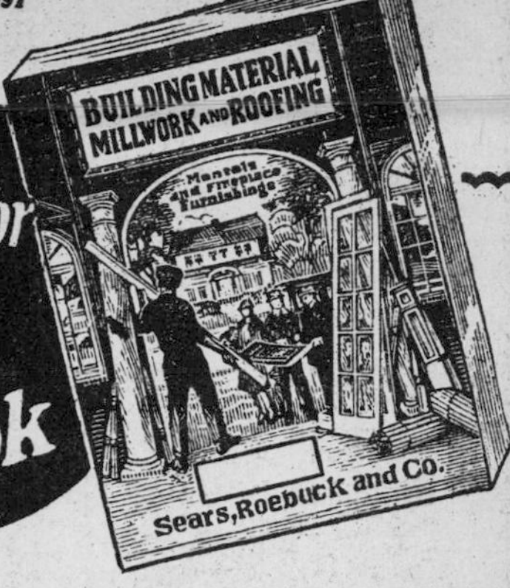

Our Building Material Catalog Illustrates and Describes Everything in Building Material at Strictly Factory Prices—Shows Latest Designs in

Doors, Windows, Moldings, Columns, Porches, Stairs, Cabinets, Buffets, Mantels, Window Frames, Door Frames, Interior Trim, Front Entrances, Breakfast Alcoves, Medicine Cases, Kitchen Cabinets, Roofing, Sash, Pergolas, Newels, Colonnades, Built-In Ironing Boards, Fireplace Furnishings, Builders' Hardware, Etc., Lumber, Lath, Shingles, Siding, Studding, Flooring, Metal Ceilings and Side Walls

Ask for Catalog P547K. THIS CATALOG CONTAINS 3,500 BUILDING BARGAINS!

If you are building on a large or small scale, and require building material and millwork not listed on this or the following two pages, then send for this catalog. A post card stating "Send me your Building Material Catalog, P547K" will bring it to you by return mail.

Glazed Storm Sash and Storm Doors

Two-Light Storm Sash

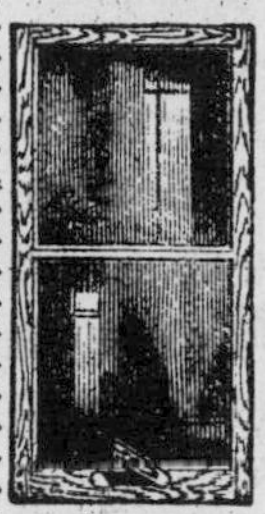

1⅛ inches thick. Carried in stock in the following sizes. Prices do not include ventilators. Ventilators, 15 cents each, extra.

For Check Rail Windows, See Page 1086

Shipped from our own factory in NEWARK, N. J.

Sizes Not Priced Are Not Carried in Stock at Factory

Size of Glass In.	Outside Measurement of Sash: Width Ft.	Width In.	Height Ft.	Height In.	63K7292 Glazed Single Strength Glass	Wt., Lbs.	63K7293 Glazed Double Strength Glass	Wt., Lbs.
12x20	1	4½	3	11⅝	$1.24	23	....	....
12x24	1	4½	4	7⅝	1.39	26	....	....
12x26	1	4½	4	11⅝	1.45	27	....	....
12x28	1	4½	5	3⅝	1.51	29	....	....
14x20	1	6½	3	11⅝	1.32	23	....	....
14x24	1	6½	4	7⅝	1.48	27	....	....
14x28	1	6½	5	3⅝	1.73	30	....	....
16x20	1	8½	3	11⅝	1.42	25	$1.65	27
16x24	1	8½	4	7⅝	1.56	29	....	....
16x26	1	8½	4	11⅝	1.76	30	....	....
16x28	1	8½	5	3⅝	1.84	32	....	....
16x30	1	8½	5	7⅝	1.92	34	....	....
18x20	1	10½	3	11⅝	1.51	27	1.76	29
18x22	1	10½	4	3⅝	1.70	29	1.98	31
18x24	1	10½	4	7⅝	1.76	31	....	....
18x26	1	10½	4	11⅝	1.86	32	2.19	34
18x28	1	10½	5	3⅝	1.94	34	2.30	36
18x30	1	10½	5	7⅝	2.08	36	....	....
18x32	1	10½	5	11⅝	....	....	2.58	39
20x20	2	0½	3	11⅝	1.58	29	1.82	31
20x22	2	0½	4	3⅝	1.76	31	2.05	33
20x24	2	0½	4	7⅝	1.78	33	2.10	35
20x26	2	0½	4	11⅝	1.86	33	2.19	35
20x28	2	0½	5	3⅝	1.94	34	2.30	36
20x30	2	0½	5	7⅝	2.13	35	....	....
20x32	2	0½	5	11⅝	2.36	37	....	....
22x20	2	2½	3	11⅝	1.72	31	2.03	33
22x22	2	2½	4	3⅝	1.89	33	2.22	35
22x24	2	2½	4	7⅝	1.91	35	2.24	37
22x26	2	2½	4	11⅝	1.98	35	2.35	37
22x28	2	2½	5	3⅝	2.11	36	2.51	38
22x30	2	2½	5	7⅝	2.27	37	2.72	39
22x32	2	2½	5	11⅝	2.50	39	....	....
24x20	2	4½	3	11⅝	1.72	33	2.03	35
24x22	2	4½	4	3⅝	1.89	35	....	....
24x24	2	4½	4	7⅝	1.95	36	2.34	38
24x26	2	4½	4	11⅝	1.98	37	2.35	39
24x28	2	4½	5	3⅝	2.11	38	2.51	39
24x30	2	4½	5	7⅝	2.27	39	2.72	41
24x32	2	4½	5	11⅝	2.60	40	3.10	42
24x36	2	4½	6	7⅝	2.96	45	....	....
26x24	2	6½	4	7⅝	2.02	38	2.40	40
26x26	2	6½	4	11⅝	2.11	39	2.51	41
26x28	2	6½	5	3⅝	2.32	40	2.75	42
26x30	2	6½	5	7⅝	2.50	41	2.99	43
26x32	2	6½	5	11⅝	2.76	43	3.28	45
28x24	2	8½	4	7⅝	2.17	40	2.59	42
28x26	2	8½	4	11⅝	2.32	41	2.75	43
28x28	2	8½	5	3⅝	2.44	42	2.91	45
28x30	2	8½	5	7⅝	2.50	43	2.98	45
28x32	2	8½	5	11⅝	3.02	45	3.62	47
30x24	2	10½	4	7⅝	2.27	39	2.72	41
30x26	2	10½	4	11⅝	2.50	41	2.99	43
30x28	2	10½	5	3⅝	2.54	43	3.02	45
30x30	2	10½	5	7⅝	2.85	45	3.42	47
32x30	3	0½	5	7⅝	....	....	3.73	49
32x32	3	0½	5	11⅝	....	....	4.10	51
36x26	3	4½	4	11⅝	....	....	3.73	49
36x28	3	4½	5	3⅝	....	....	4.00	51
40x28	3	8½	5	3⅝	....	....	4.66	57

For Double Hung Check Rail Windows See Page 1086

Glazed storm sash. Made of clear soft pine in a most substantial manner. High grade window glass is carefully secured with good putty and points; furnished "in the white." Not varnished or painted.

Size of our sash is sufficient to allow for trimming. In some cases a little trimming would avoid the necessity of ordering special sizes. In ordering give number in catalog of the storm sash wanted and the exact size of opening and we will send you sash which may be trimmed to fit.

Shipped from our own factory in NEWARK, N. J.

When Ordering Give Width First

Four-Light Storm Sash

1⅛ inches thick. Carried in stock in sizes shown below. Prices do not include ventilators. Ventilators, 15c each, extra.

For Check Rail Windows, See Page 1086

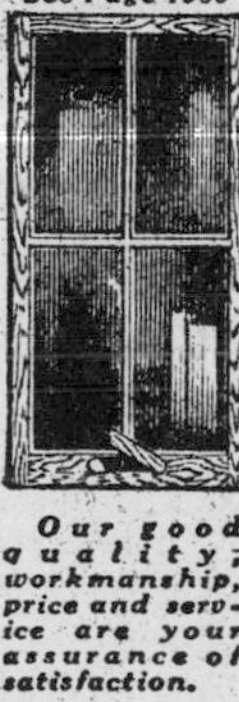

Our good quality; workmanship, price and service are your assurance of satisfaction.

Size of Glass	Outside Measurement of Sash: Width Ft.	Width In.	Height Ft.	Height In.	63K7295 Single Strength Glass	Wt., Lbs.
10x20	2	1	3	11⅝	$1.73	36
10x22	2	1	4	3⅝	1.75	38
10x24	2	1	4	7⅝	1.83	40
10x26	2	1	4	11⅝	2.03	41
10x28	2	1	5	3⅝	2.07	42
10x32	2	1	5	11⅝	2.29	45
12x20	2	5	3	11⅝	1.72	38
12x22	2	5	4	3⅝	1.94	40
12x24	2	5	4	7⅝	1.98	42
12x26	2	5	4	11⅝	2.06	43
12x28	2	5	5	3⅝	2.14	44
12x30	2	5	5	7⅝	2.54	45
12x32	2	5	5	11⅝	2.80	47
14x20	2	9	3	11⅝	2.05	40
14x22	2	9	4	3⅝	2.22	42
14x24	2	9	4	7⅝	2.24	44
14x26	2	9	4	11⅝	2.32	45
14x28	2	9	5	3⅝	2.58	46
14x30	2	9	5	7⅝	2.79	47
14x32	2	9	5	11⅝	2.96	49
15x24	2	11	4	7⅝	2.43	44
15x26	2	11	4	11⅝	2.79	46
15x28	2	11	5	3⅝	2.91	47
15x30	2	11	5	7⅝	3.04	48
15x32	2	11	5	11⅝	3.24	50

Eight-Light Storm Sash

1⅛ inches thick. Carried in stock in the following sizes. Prices do not include ventilators. Ventilators, 15 cents each, extra.

For Check Rail Windows, See Page 1086

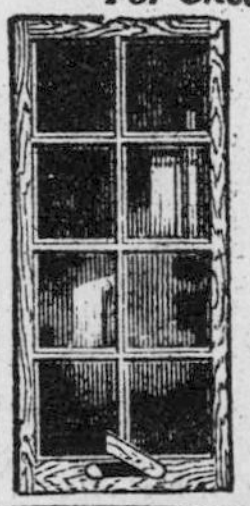

Size of Glass	Outside Measurement of Sash: Width Ft.	Width In.	Height Ft.	Height In.	63K7300 Single Strength Glass	Wt., Lbs.
9x12	1	11	4	7⅝	$1.72	33
9x14	1	11	5	3⅝	1.86	35
10x12	2	1	4	7⅝	1.72	37
10x14	2	1	5	3⅝	1.95	39
10x16	2	1	5	11⅝	2.28	41
12x14	2	5	5	3⅝	2.16	42
12x16	2	5	5	11⅝	2.50	43
12x18	2	5	6	7⅝	2.72	45
14x16	2	9	5	11⅝	2.74	46
14x18	2	9	6	7⅝	2.93	49
14x20	2	9	7	3⅝	3.21	51

Twelve-Light Storm Sash

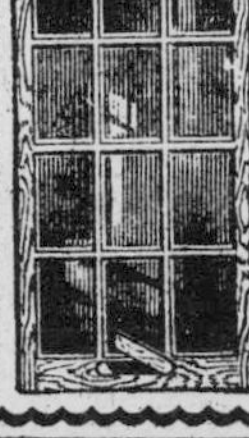

1⅛ inches thick. Carried in stock in the following sizes. Ventilators, 15 cents each, extra.

For Check Rail Windows, See Page 1086

Size of Glass	Outside Measurement of Sash: Width Ft.	Width In.	Height Ft.	Height In.	63K7305 Single Strength Glass	Wt., Lbs.
8x10	2	4¾	3	11	$1.78	44
8x12	2	4¾	4	7	1.98	46
9x12	2	7¾	4	7	2.11	48
9x14	2	7¾	5	3	2.38	50
10x12	2	10¾	4	7	2.19	50
10x14	2	10¾	5	3	2.43	52
10x16	2	10¾	5	11	2.80	54

High Grade Storm Doors

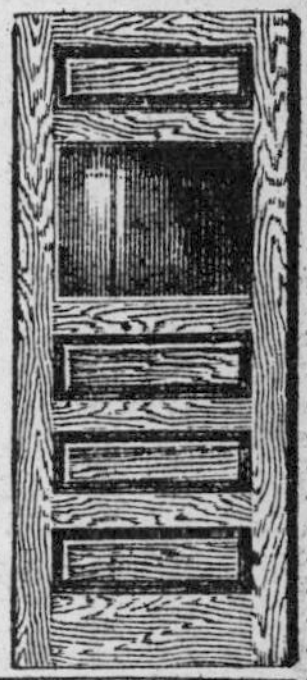

Carefully made of clear soft wood. Perfect coping and sanding. Shipped in the white, suitable either for paint or natural finish. Glazed with high grade double strength glass.

Painted Doors

Made from the same grade of lumber usually used in painted doors. While not made of clear lumber, doors are strong and durable, and very carefully painted. Glazed with double strength glass.

Shipped from our own factory in NEWARK, N. J.

Size of Door. 1⅛ Inches Thick: Width Ft.	Width In.	Height Ft.	Height In.	63K6808 No. 1 Quality, Glazed Double Strength Glass	63K6800 Painted Doors, Glazed Double Strength Glass	Shipping Wt., Lbs.
2	6¼	6	7	$5.00	$4.15	58
2	8¼	6	9	5.30	4.40	63
2	10¼	6	11	5.80	4.95	68
3	0¼	7	1	5.95	5.10	73

Double Duty Combination Storm and Screen Doors

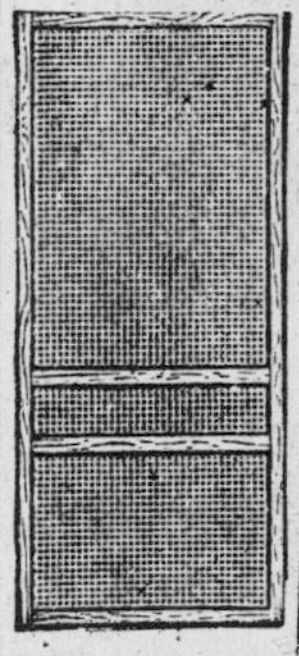

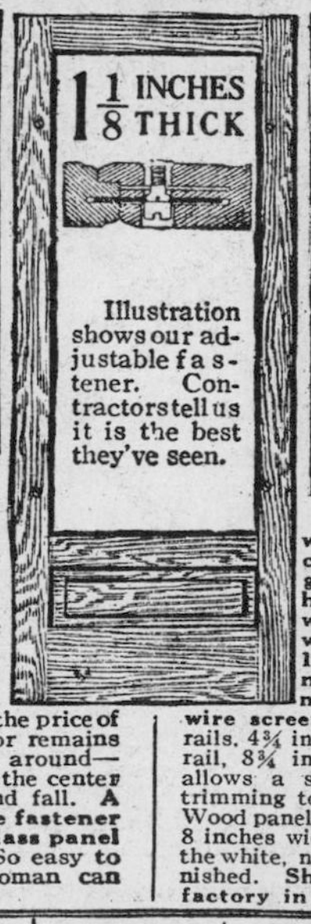

Illustration shows our adjustable fastener. Contractors tell us it is the best they've seen.

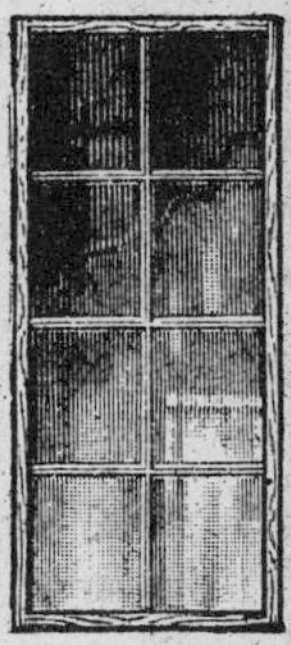

Here's the highest class combination screen and storm door made. A high grade screen door in summer — a substantial storm door in winter—at the price of one door. The door remains on hinges all year around—you simply change the center panel in spring and fall. **A strong, adjustable fastener holds screen or glass panel firmly in place.** So easy to operate that a woman can make the change.

Made of clear white pine, with clear window glass securely held in place with wood stops and with high grade 14-mesh galvanized or 16-mesh bronze wire screen. Side and top rails, 4¾ inches wide; bottom rail, 8¾ inches wide. This allows a small margin for trimming to insure snug fit. Wood panel at bottom of door, 8 inches wide. Furnished in the white, not painted or varnished. Shipped from our factory in NEWARK, N. J.

Size, 1⅛ Inches Thick: Width Ft.	Width In.	Height Ft.	Height In.	63K2410 14-Mesh Galv. Wire Screen Panel	63K2412 16-Mesh Bronze Wire Screen Panel	Shpg. Wt., Lbs.
2	8¼	6	9	$7.30	$8.05	50
2	8¼	7	1	7.55	8.30	65
2	10¼	6	11	7.90	8.65	68
2	10¼	7	1	8.05	8.80	75
3	0¼	7	1	8.20	8.95	78

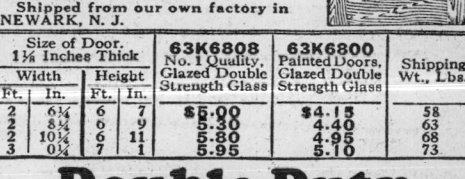

Windows, Frames and Cabinets

FOR STORM WINDOWS AND DOORS SEE PAGE 1085

Check-Rail Windows and Frames

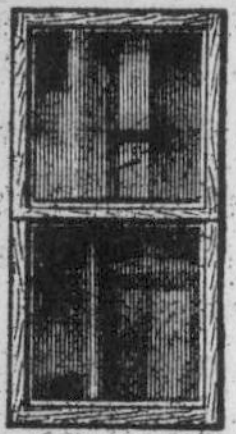

63K7186
63K7187

Two-Light Check-Rail Windows

1⅜ in. thick. Price includes top and bottom sash, glazed with clear glass and best putty.

Frames Including Pulleys

Jambs, 5¼ inches, includes blind stop. Outside casing made of cypress, 1⅛x4¼ in. Plain drip cap. Leakproof sill, 1¾x7½ in. Shpg. wt., 30 lbs.

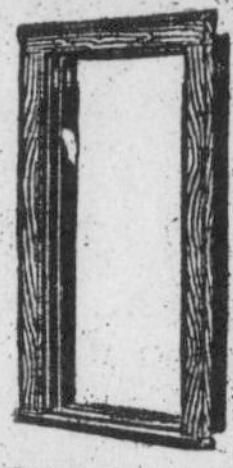

63K9944

SIZE of GLASS Inches	Outside Measurement of Entire Window: Width Ft.	Width In.	Height Ft.	Height In.	Weight of Two-Light Windows: S. S. Glass Lbs.	D. S. Glass Lbs.	WINDOW: Glazed Single Strength Glass 63K7186	Glazed Double Strength Glass 63K7187	FRAME 63K9944
12x20	1	4⅛	3	10	12	......	$1.20	......	$2.30
12x24	1	4⅛	4	6	12	......	1.34	......	2.59
12x28	1	4⅛	5	2	14	......	1.46	......	2.89
14x20	1	6⅛	3	10	12	......	1.28	......	2.37
14x24	1	6⅛	4	6	13	......	1.43	......	2.64
16x20	1	8⅛	3	10	14	15	1.37	$1.60	2.42
18x20	1	10⅛	3	10	14	15	1.46	1.71	2.49
18x24	1	10⅛	4	6	16	18	1.70	1.98	2.73
20x20	2	0⅛	3	10	15	16	1.52	1.77	2.50
20x24	2	0⅛	4	6	17	19	1.70	1.98	2.95
20x26	2	0⅛	4	10	19	21	1.79	2.12	2.99
20x28	2	0⅛	5	2	20	22	1.87	2.23	3.13
22x20	2	2⅛	3	10	16	17	1.66	1.97	2.88
22x24	2	2⅛	4	6	18	20	1.82	2.17	3.00
22x28	2	2⅛	5	2	20	22	2.04	2.43	3.19
24x20	2	4⅛	3	10	17	19	1.66	1.97	2.65
24x24	2	4⅛	4	6	19	21	1.88	2.26	3.05
24x26	2	4⅛	4	10	21	23	1.92	2.28	3.10
24x28	2	4⅛	5	2	22	25	2.04	2.43	3.24
24x30	2	4⅛	5	6	23	26	2.19	2.64	3.34
26x24	2	6⅛	4	6	21	22	1.95	2.33	3.11
26x26	2	6⅛	4	10	22	24	2.04	2.43	3.20
26x28	2	6⅛	5	2	23	26	2.23	2.67	3.30
28x24	2	8⅛	4	6	22	24	2.10	2.51	3.16
28x26	2	8⅛	4	10	24	26	2.23	2.67	3.27
28x28	2	8⅛	5	2	25	28	2.36	2.82	3.35
28x30	2	8⅛	5	6	26	29	2.42	2.88	3.44
30x24	2	10⅛	4	6	24	27	2.19	2.64	3.22
30x26	2	10⅛	4	10	25	28	2.42	2.90	3.30
30x28	2	10⅛	5	2	27	30	2.45	2.93	3.41
30x30	2	10⅛	5	6	30	33	2.75	3.32	3.50

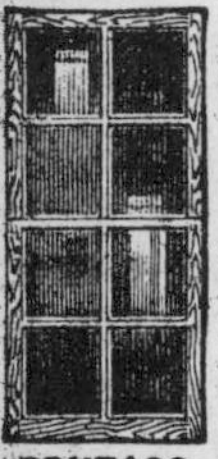

63K7192

Eight-Light Check-Rail Windows

1⅜ in. thick. Price includes top and bottom sash, glazed with clear glass and best putty.

Frames Including Pulleys

Jambs, 5¼ inches, includes blind stop. Outside casing made of cypress, 1⅛x4¼ in. Plain drip cap. Leakproof sill, 1¾x7½ in. Shpg. wt., 30 lbs.

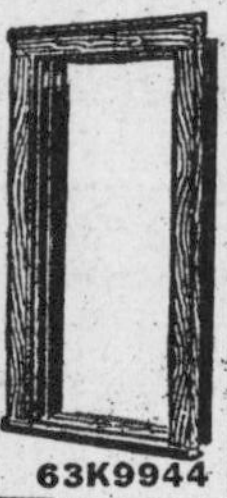

63K9944

SIZE OF GLASS Inches	Outside Measurement of Entire Window: Width Ft.	Width In.	Height Ft.	Height In.	Weight of Eight-Light Windows, Pounds	WINDOW Glazed Single Strength Glass 63K7192	FRAME 63K9944
9x12	1	11	4	6	17	$1.66	$2.85
10x12	2	1	4	6	18	1.68	3.04
12x14	2	5	5	2	23	2.08	3.31
12x16	2	5	5	10	24	2.42	3.48

Built-In Ironing Board Outfit

A Combination of Useful Features

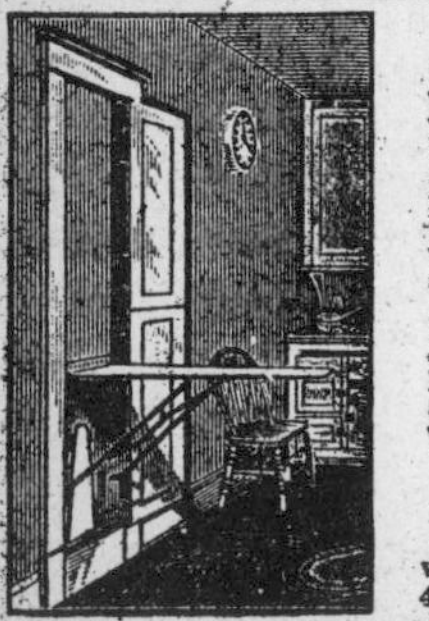

A complete full size Ironing Board, including sleeve board, always ready for use, yet never in the way. A labor saving feature. Usually installed with electric light socket in the compartment, so electric iron is always convenient. ALL SET UP READY TO INSTALL. Only work necessary on job is to fit door and outside trim. Includes cabinet backed with bead ceiling, door, round edge casing trim, all hardware except door hinges and latch. Door hinges and latch should be ordered separately to match the other hardware in your house.

Description

Made of clear Fir. Opening in wall, 14 inches wide, 80 inches high, 4½ inches deep. Will fit between studding placed 16 inches on center. Ironing board is 11½ inches wide by 49 inches long, 32 inches from floor. Sleeve board, 5 inches wide, 23 inches long. 3⅝-inch casing with two base blocks furnished for trimming.

63K376—Complete Built-In Ironing Board Outfit, clear Fir, as described. Shipping weight, 80 lbs. **$11.30**

Shipped From Our Own Factory in NEWARK, N. J.

Description

GLAZED WINDOWS AND SASH—Made of CLEAR SOFT WHITE PINE, seasoned and kiln dried, carefully machined and sandpapered. Glazed with good quality clear glass held in place with zinc diamond points and good putty.

WINDOW FRAMES—We use a very high grade of lumber in our frames. The workmanship is perfect. OUTSIDE CASINGS ARE 1⅛ INCHES THICK, **made of Clear Cypress, a wood best suited to withstand the elements and which takes paint readily.** The pulley stiles, parting stops and blind stops are made of clear fir. Equipped with steel pulleys fastened into place. Frames are rabbeted or grooved and finished ready to nail together, without sawing. Stud opening should be 6 inches wider and 5 inches higher than opening size of window. Frames are packed to secure lowest transportation rates. Easily put together.

Easy to Order Windows and Frames

from the tables. The column of sizes under the heading of "Size of Glass" shows the size of glass in inches in each sash of the window, and all the prices on the same line in the other columns refer to windows or frames to fit this particular size. For example: Take a two-light window, glass size 24x28 inches; the size of the opening in the frame for this same window is 2 feet 4⅛ inches by 5 feet 2 inches. The price of a window this size glazed single strength is $2.04. Price of a pulley frame for this size window is $3.24. Weight of window is 22 pounds.

All items of Millwork including doors, windows, frames, moldings, porch work, storm windows, storm doors, etc. (pages 1085, 1086 and 1087) are **shipped direct to you from our own factory** in NEWARK, N. J.

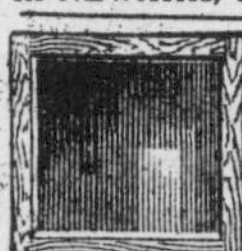

One-Light Glazed Attic Sash

1⅜ INCHES THICK
With 3-Inch Bottom Rail

SIZE OF GLASS, Inches	Outside Measurement of Sash: Width Ft.	Width In.	Height Ft.	Height In.	Wt., Lbs.	Glazed Single Strength Glass 63K7211
16 x 20	1	8	2	1	10	$0.70
20 x 20	2	0	2	1	14	.79
20 x 24	2	0	2	5	17	.87
24 x 20	2	4	2	1	17	.87
24 x 24	2	4	2	5	20	.97
24 x 30	2	4	2	11	26	1.17

Four-Light Glazed Barn Sash

1⅛ INCHES THICK
With 3-Inch Bottom Rail

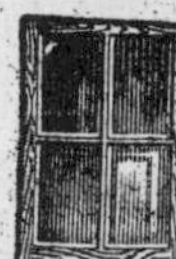

SIZE OF GLASS, Inches	Outside Measurement of Sash: Width Ft.	Width In.	Height Ft.	Height In.	Wt., Lbs.	Glazed Single Strength Glass 63K7261
8 x 10	1	8	2	1	12	65c
9 x 12	1	10	2	5	14	68c
9 x 14	1	10	2	9	16	82c
10 x 12	2	0	2	5	16	78c

Sash Weights

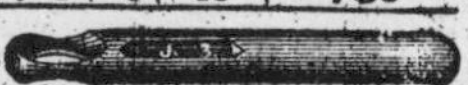

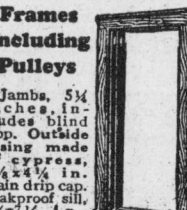

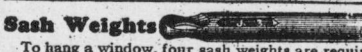

To hang a window, four sash weights are required, each weighing one-fourth the weight of entire window. Our weights are standard diameter and length, according to weight. **We ship sash weights from factory in PENNSYLVANIA.** Sizes, from 3 to 8½ pounds by half pounds, and from 9 to 26 pounds by pounds. **State weight.**

63K7200—Per pound **2½c**

Built-In Medicine Case

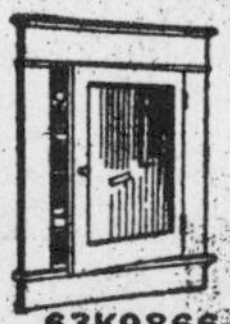

Made of clear Fir. Plain plate mirror, 14 inches wide by 18 inches high. Three adjustable wood shelves. Furnished with trim as illustrated, except hardware. Recess opening in wall, 1 foot 8 inches wide by 2 feet 4½ inches high. Depth over all, 4 inches. Size of door, 1 foot 6 inches wide by 1 foot 11 inches high. Glazed with plain plate mirror. Shipping weight, 30 pounds.

63K9866—Clear Fir.
Each **$7.30**

Floor Tile

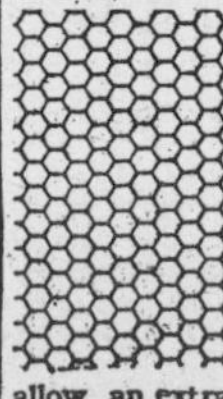

Tile for use in bathrooms, kitchens and vestibules makes an excellent floor. It is very easy to keep clean. Tile floors never wear out. They require no expense and upkeep. They are vermin proof and sanitary in every way.

Our floor tile is made in 1-inch hexagons and ¾-inch squares. It is furnished pasted on sheets of paper about 1 foot wide by 2 feet long.

Note: When ordering, always allow an extra foot or two for fitting. Shipping weight, per square foot, 3½ pounds.

63K1000—Plain White Hexagon Floor Tile, per square foot **30c**

63K1001—Plain White Square Floor T[ile], per square foot **30c**

Shipped from factory in OHIO.

Write for TILE LIST P622K for our complete showing. Sent free and postpaid on request.

Check-Rail Windows and Frames

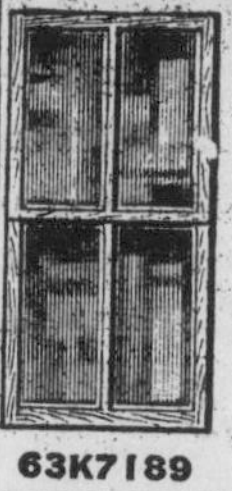

63K7189

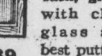

Four-Light Check-Rail Windows

1⅜ inches thick. Price includes top and bottom sash, glazed with clear glass and best putty.

Frames Including Pulleys

Jambs, 5¼ inches, includes blind stop. Outside casing made of cypress, 1⅛x4¼ in. Plain drip cap. Leakproof sill, 1¾x7½ in. Shipping wt., 30 lbs.

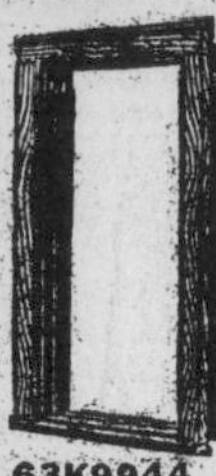

63K9944

SIZE OF GLASS Inches	Outside Measurement of Entire Window: Width Ft.	Width In.	Height Ft.	Height In.	Weight of Four-Light Windows, Pounds	WINDOW Glazed Single Strength Glass 63K7189	FRAME 63K9944
10x20	2	1	3	10	19	$1.67	$2.60
10x24	2	1	4	6	21	1.76	3.00
10x28	2	1	5	2	22	1.96	3.19
12x20	2	5	3	10	19	1.66	2.70
12x24	2	5	4	6	21	1.87	2.96
12x26	2	5	4	10	21	1.99	3.20
12x28	2	5	5	2	22	2.07	3.32
14x20	2	9	3	10	22	1.98	3.05
14x24	2	9	4	6	23	2.16	3.29
14x26	2	9	4	10	23	2.23	3.37
14x28	2	9	5	2	24	2.49	3.48
14x30	2	9	5	6	26	2.69	3.56

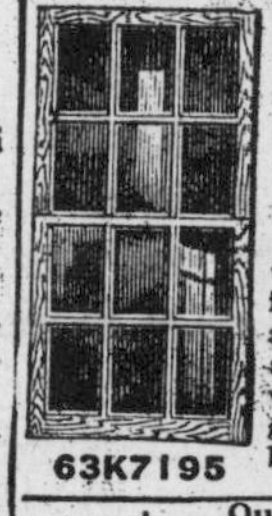

63K7195

Twelve-Light Check-Rail Windows

1⅜ inches thick. Price includes top and bottom sash, glazed with clear glass and best putty.

Frames Including Pulleys

Jambs, 5¼ inches, includes blind stop. Outside casing made of cypress, 1⅛x4¼ in. Plain drip cap. Leakproof sill, 1¾x7½ in. Shipping wt., 30 lbs.

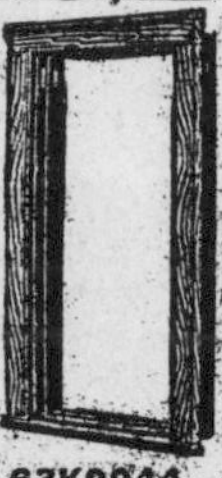

63K9944

SIZE OF GLASS, Inches	Outside Measurement of Entire Window: Width Ft.	Width In.	Height Ft.	Height In.	Weight of Twelve-Light Windows, Pounds	WINDOW Glazed Single Strength Glass 63K7195	FRAME 63K9944
8x10	2	4½	3	10	19	$1.72	$2.65
8x12	2	4½	4	6	20	1.92	3.05
9x12	2	7½	4	6	22	2.04	3.16
10x12	2	10½	4	6	23	2.11	3.22

Three-Light Glazed Cellar Sash

1⅜ INCHES THICK
With 3-Inch Bottom Rails
With Frames to Match
For Stone, Concrete or Brick Wall

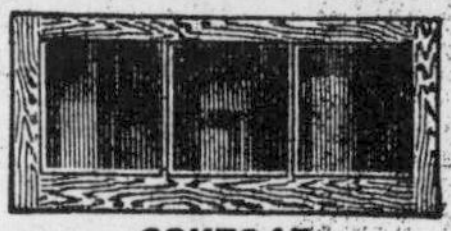

63K7245

SIZE OF GLASS, Inches	Outside Measurement of Sash: Width Ft.	Width In.	Height Ft.	Height In.	Wt., Lbs.	Glazed Sash 63K7245	FRAME 63K7898
8x10	2	4	1	3	12	62c	$1.48
9x12	2	7	1	5	16	71c	1.52
10x12	2	10	1	5	18	78c	1.56
10x16	2	10	1	9	22	87c	1.60

Colonial Breakfast Alcove

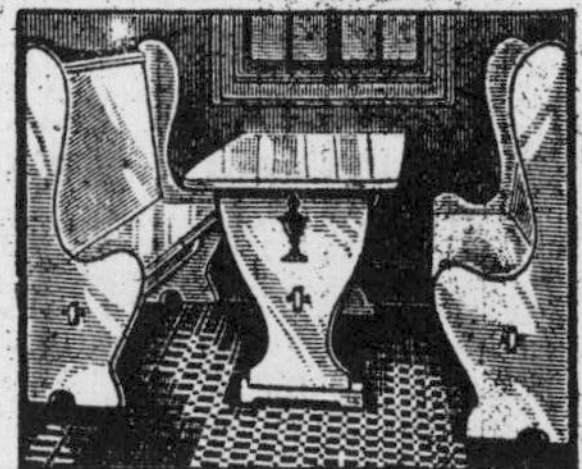

A new and very desirable design. One of the new features is a drawer right under the table top. Made of Clear Fir and sandpapered ready for finish. **ALL SET UP READY TO INSTALL.** Seating capacity of four, requiring floor space 6 feet wide by 4 feet deep. Equally desirable when set up in a corner, or against a wall in your kitchen. Shipped in the white without paint or varnish. Wrapped in tough paper and crated.

Description

TABLE: Width, 2 feet 6 inches; length, 3 feet 8 inches; height from floor to top, 2 feet 6 inches. Has drawer 14 inches wide by 14 inches long by 4 inches deep, under table top. EACH BENCH: Width on seat, 1 foot 1⅛ inches; length, 3 feet 8 inches, height, over all, 4 feet. Shipping weight, 225 pounds.

63K9870—Colonial Breakfast Alcove, clear Fir, as described above **$26.00**

Highest Quality Millwork　　　　　**Best Values and Service**

We carry in stock 150 kinds and sizes of exterior doors and over 140 kinds and sizes of inside panel doors, all of which are illustrated and described in our Building Material Catalog, 547K (illustrated on page 1085). We show on this page such articles as doors, moldings, frames, porch material, etc., that are in the greatest demand. Make your selection from these pages, as every article represents our very best values in Building Material, Millwork and Roofing. All items of Millwork including doors, windows, frames, moldings, porch work, storm windows,

storm doors, etc. (pages 1085, 1086 and 1087) are shipped direct to you from our own factory in NEWARK, N. J.

All our millwork is shipped bright and clean, and, as a rule, of better quality than can be purchased locally.

If you intend to build on a larger scale, and require a vast assortment of designs to select from, write for our special Building Material Catalog 547K (illustrated and described on page 1085). If time does not permit your waiting for the catalog, make your selection from these pages.

Clear Fir Front Doors

Made of Clear Fir pine, 1⅜ inches thick. Will not warp, shrink or check. Carefully sanded. Can be stained and varnished or painted. Glazed with selected glass by competent workmen. Shipped in the white without paint or varnish.

SIZES 1⅜ Inches Thick				Glass Size in Inches	Wt. Lbs.	63K9860 Glazed Clear Double Strength Glass (as illustrat'd)	63K9850 Glazed With Leaded Crystal Glass
Width		Height					
Ft.	In.	Ft.	In.				
2	6	6	6	21⅝x24	70	$4.85	$7.25
2	8	6	8	23⅝x26	75	5.20	7.95
2	10	6	10	25⅝x28	85	5.75	8.80
3	0	7	0	27⅝x30	90	6.25	9.30

63K9860

Back Band Molding

Prices quoted include only the back band. Casing must be ordered separately.

Back Band can be used with Round Edge Casing to make a neat and tasty design of door and window trim. Size, 1¼x1¼ inches. Weight, per 100 feet, 20 pounds.

63K9934—Clear Fir. Per 100 lineal feet.......$2.23
63K7553—Clear Red Oak. Per 100 lineal feet.....4.95

Round Edge Casing

Size, ¾x3⅝ inches. Weight, per 100 feet, 65 pounds.
63K9932—Clear Fir. Per 100 lineal feet.....$3.67
63K7597—Clear Oak. Per 100 lineal feet.....8.82

Quarter Round Moulding

Used for base shoe or to cover joints in corners. Size, ¾x¾ inch. Weight, per 100 ft., 15 lbs.
63K9928
Clear Fir. Per 100 lineal feet.....78c
63K7788
Clear Oak. Per 100 lineal feet.....$2.10

Cove Moulding

Used the same as quarter round and is used under stair treads, steps, stools etc. Size, ⅝x⅞ inch. Price, per 100 feet. Weight, 15 lbs.
63K9929 — Clear Fir.....78c
63K7819 Clear Oak.....$2.10

Baseboard

Size, ¾x7¼ inches. Weight, per 100 feet, 130 lbs. Per 100 Lineal Ft.
63K9936—Clear Fir.....$ 7.34
63K7540—Clear Oak.....16.80
Base Shoe or Carpet Strip
Size, ½x¾ inch. Weight, per 100 feet, 15 pounds. Per 100 Lineal Ft.
63K9935—Clear Fir.....78c
63K7532—Clear Oak.....$2.10

Picture Moulding

Size, ¾x1¾ inches. Weight, per 100 ft., 35 lbs. Per 100 Lineal Ft.
63K9933—Clear Fir.....$1.56
63K7800—Clear Oak..4.20

Round Edge Door and Window Stops

Weight, per 100 feet, 15 lbs.

Size, Inches	63K9863 Clear Fir Per 100 Lineal Feet	63K17778 Clear Oak Per 100 Lineal Feet
⅜x1⅛	78c	$2.10
⅜x1⅝	86c	2.31

Door Frames

All our frames are made of carefully selected, kiln dried lumber. The outside casings are made of Clear Cypress, which is finished to 1⅜ inch thick. The door jambs are Clear Fir. Our frames are conceded by experienced builders to be the best on the market.

All frames are packed to secure lowest transportation rates. Easily put together.

Sizes of Materials
Drip Cap.................1¼x1⅝ inches
Head Casing..............1⅜x4¼ inches
Outside Casing...........1⅜x4¼ inches
Jambs...................1⅜x5¼ inches
Sill....................1¾ inches thick
Weight, 60 pounds
High Quality Drip Cap Frame
63K9949—With Softwood Sill. Any size up to 3 ft. x 7 ft.....$3.95
63K9950—With Oak Sill. Any size up to 3 ft. x 7 ft.....4.70

Inside Door Jambs

Finest grade, sanded as smooth as glass. Made of clear Fir or Oak. The side jambs are perfectly dadoed. The head jamb fits into this dado tightly.

IMPORTANT — The jamb is ¾x5¼ inches. If wanted wider than 5¼ inches add for each additional inch or fraction thereof, 40 cents for Fir and 70 cents for Oak.

Weight, 18 pounds.

SIZE				63K9943 Clear Fir	63K7952 Clear Oak
Width		H'g't			
Ft.	In.	Ft.	In.		
2	8	6	8	$0.95	2.40
3	0	7	0	1.10	2.55

FINEST GRADE, 95c AND UP

Front Doors

CLEAR FIR 1⅜ Inches Thick

Made of Clear Fir. Can be exposed to the weather. Will not warp or shrink when finished. Takes stain and varnish and is an ideal wood for white paint or enamel. Perfect workmanship guaranteed. Carefully sanded. Glazed with best quality double strength glass.

OAK VENEER

1¾ Inches Thick Made of the choicest oak veneers, which are selected for grain and color. The cores are built up of California Pine, lock jointed and glued under enormous pressure. Superior to a solid door and more beautiful in appearance. Glazed with highest grade beveled plate glass.

63K60

SIZES				Glass Size in Inches	Clear Fir 1⅜ Inches Thick		Oak Veneered, 1¾ Inches Thick	
Width		Height			Wt. Lbs.	63K391 Glazed Double Strength Glass	Wt. Lbs.	63K60 Glazed Bevel Plate Glass
Ft.	In.	Ft.	In.					
2	8	6	8	20x56	80	$7.30	120	$23.40
3	0	7	0	24x60	95	8.60	140	28.60

High Grade Inside Doors

Clear Fir Stiles and Rails With Figured Panels
63K192
Five-cross panel doors made of clear kiln dried Fir Lumber. Panels are 3-ply flat laminated, beautiful in figured grain and color.

Oak Veneered
63K6250
Oak veneered five-panel doors made of choicest Oak veneers selected for grain and color, which are glued onto a White Pine core under enormous pressure, and guaranteed not to warp, twist or crack.

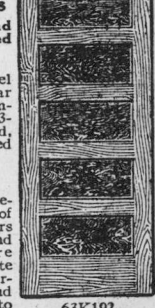

63K192 or 63K6250

SIZES 1⅜ in. thick				Clear Fir		Veneered Oak	
Width		H'g't		Wt. Lbs.	63K192	Wt. Lbs.	63K6250
Ft.	In.	Ft.	In.				
2	4	6	8	50	$3.10	73	$7.95
2	6	6	8	53	3.15	75	8.25
2	8	6	8	54	3.23	78	8.25
2	8	6	8	58	3.38	84	8.60
2	6	7	0	57	3.48		
2	8	7	0	61	3.63	88	9.30

Door and Window Trim
IN SETS READY TO NAIL IN PLACE

These door and window sets are made in Clear Fir and Clear Oak. All parts of each trim set are carefully sandpapered and carefully wrapped, one set in a carton (see illustration above), free from dirt and ready to nail into place. All moldings are cut to exact size. The head trim, consisting of three moldings nailed together, for over doors and windows, has a cap with molded edge and returned at the ends. All moldings in these sets are full standard size. See illustrations.

TO ORDER, give size of the door or window you want to trim, and mention the width first.

1¼x2 inches
¾x4⅝ inches
7⅞x1 inch.
CAP
HEAD CASING
FILLET
CASING ¾x4¼ in.
4⅝x10x1⅝ inches
63K9904
63K7591

1¼x2 inches
¾x4⅝ inches
⅞x1 inch
CAP
HEAD CASING
FILLET
CASING ¾x4¼ in.
STOOL
1⅛x3⅜ in.
APRON ¾x3⅝ in.

PRICE OF TRIM FOR DOORS
Price Quoted covers any size door up to 3 feet wide by 7 feet high. Outside doors require one side of trim and inside doors two sides. Weight, 25 pounds.
63K9904—Clear Fir Inside Door Trim. Per set.....$1.85
63K7591—Clear Oak Inside Door Trim. Per set.....$3.25

PRICE OF TRIM FOR WINDOWS
Prices quoted cover any sizes of windows up to and including opening size 2 feet 10⅜ inches wide by 5 feet 6 inches high. Weight, 35 lbs.
63K9903
63K7578
63K9903—Clear Fir Inside Window Trim. Per set.....$1.95
63K7578—Clear Oak Inside Window Trim. Per set.....$3.30

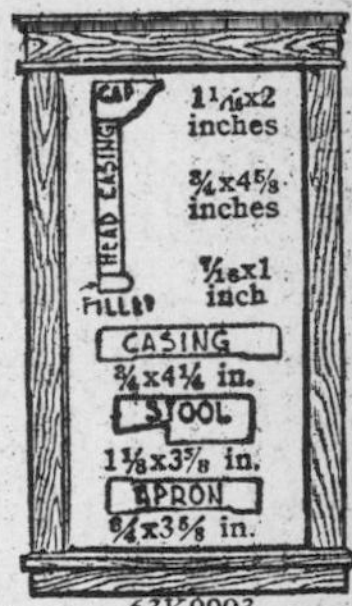

Colonial Columns

Lock Joint Built-Up Columns of Clear Fir Lumber. Most generally used for all types of porches. Should be painted as soon as received. Carefully crated, guaranteed to reach you in good condition. For splitting columns, add 20 cents extra.

Diameter of Shaft at Base	Ht., Over All	Wt., Lbs.	63K8070 Includes Plain Cap and Base, Each
6 in.	6 ft.	27	$2.59
6 in.	8 ft.	33	2.95
6 in.	9 ft.	36	3.15
8 in.	6 ft.	40	3.25
8 in.	8 ft.	46	3.65
8 in.	9 ft.	50	4.20
8 in.	10 ft.	53	4.75
10 in.	6 ft.	53	4.80
10 in.	8 ft.	62	4.95
10 in.	9 ft.	66	5.25

63K8070

Porch Rail

Made of clear fir. Size, 1¾x3⅝ in. Weight, per foot, 1 pound.

63K8191
TOP PORCH RAIL
63K8191—Per lineal foot. 6½c
BOTTOM PORCH RAIL
63K8193—Per lineal foot. 6½c

Round Porch Newel

Colonial design, made of clear fir, with turned cap and square base.
63K8150
Diameter of shaft at base, 7 inches. Length, 4 feet. Weight, 23 pounds.
Each.........$2.90

63K8150

Square Balluster Stock

Made of clear fir. Size, 1¾x1¾ inches. 32 inches long. Weight, each, 1 pound.

63K8110—Each....9½c

Square and Turned Porch Newels

Made of clear fir, the best known wood for porch material. Carefully turned and smoothed.

Shaft, In.	Lgth., Ft.	Wt., Lbs.	63K8182 Each
4x4	4	11	$0.66
5x5	4	15	1.05
6x6	4	24	1.49

63K8182 can be used with 63K8175 columns. 
63K8182

Solid Turned Columns

Made of clear fir. Ends bored to prevent checking. For splitting, add 10 cents extra.

Size, In.	Lgth., Ft.	Wt., Lbs.	63K8175 Each
4x4	8	20	$1.23
5x5	8	27	1.94
5x5	9	37	2.21
6x6	8	48	2.84

ESTIMATES
cheerfully given. Send us your list if you cannot find your requirements here.

63K8175

All Items On This Page Are Shipped From Our Own Factory in NEWARK, N. J.

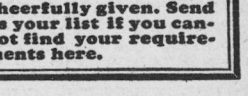

LUMBER
LATH AND SHINGLES AT WHOLESALE PRICES
We Make FREE Estimates

Here are items of lumber generally required. For complete assortment, write for Lumber List 8852K or send list of material you require for total price delivered to your station, freight prepaid.

All lumber shown on this page will be shipped from our new 40-acre lumber plant in New Jersey. The assortments carried have been carefully selected to give the best service and value. Our Fir and Pacific Coast Hemlock come from the virgin forests of Washington and Oregon, and are far superior to Tamarack, Norway Pine and Northern Hemlock.

There is no better wood known than Cypress for outside purposes, due to its wonderful weather and time resisting qualities. Note the fine selection of Cypress shown on this page.

See Pages 1090 and 1091 About Complete Houses

See Page 1089 About Complete Barns

ACTUAL THICKNESS OF ¾ INCH FLOORING

ACTUAL THICKNESS OF 13/16-INCH FLOORING

Hardwood Flooring

Clear Grade Oak or Maple Flooring, our highest grade. All flooring furnished in standard lengths only.

How to Lay Hardwood Flooring

Lay dampproof paper or tarred felt between hardwood flooring and subfloors. See page 1077. Nail ¾-inch flooring every 8 inches with fourpenny casing nails; 13/16-inch, every 10 inches with eightpenny flooring nails, 1½-inch face flooring counted 2 inches wide; 2-inch face is counted 2½ inches wide; 2¼-inch face is counted 3 inches wide. Order one-third extra to allow for tongue and groove.

Weight, per 100 Square Feet, 100 Lbs.

Catalog No.	Grade	Kind	Size, Inches	Per 100 Sq. Ft.
56K28	Clear	Maple	⅜x1½ or 2	$8.25
56K29	Select	Maple	⅜x1½ or 2	6.50
56K21	Clear	Plain Oak	⅜x1½ or 2	8.00
56K22	Select	Plain Oak	⅜x1½ or 2	6.50
56K25	Clear	Quar. Sawed Oak	⅜x1½ or 2	10.95
56K26	Select	Quar. Sawed Oak	⅜x1½ or 2	8.00

Weight, per 100 Square Feet, 200 Lbs.

Catalog No.	Grade	Kind	Size, Inches	Per 100 Sq. Ft.
56K30	Clear	Maple	13/16x2¼	$10.80
56K31	Select	Maple	13/16x2¼	9.20
56K23	Clear	Plain Oak	13/16x2¼	10.90
56K24	Select	Plain Oak	13/16x2¼	9.50
56K27	Clear	Quarter Sawed Oak	13/16x2¼	12.50

Finishing Lumber

Planed four sides. Clear Grade is the highest grade. Select is the second grade, suitable for outside finish. We recommend Cypress for outside use.

Size, In.	56K134 Fir, Clear, per 100 Lin. Ft.	56K135 Fir, Select, per 100 Lin. Ft.	56K136 Cypress, Clear, per 100 Lin. Ft.	56K137 Cypress, Select, per 100 Lin. Ft.	Wt., Lbs. per 100 Lin. Ft.
1x3	$1.90	$1.60	$3.05	$2.45	65
1x4	2.50	2.10	4.05	3.20	85
1x5	3.55	3.05	5.05	4.05	100
1x6	3.75	3.15	6.05	4.85	125
1x8	5.05	4.20	8.00	6.45	165
1x10	7.20	6.15	10.50	8.50	210
1x12	8.60	7.35	13.15	10.70	250

Shingle Bargains
Large Bundles

Extra Clear Red Cedar Shingles measure 2 inches thick at butts to five shingles. Extra *A* Shingles measure 2 inches thick at butts to six shingles. Perfection Shingles measure 2¼ inches thick at the butts to five shingles. Four bundles when laid 5 inches to the weather will cover 125 square feet.

Length, Inches	56K146 Grade	Per Bundle	Wt., per Bundle, Lbs.
16	Extra *A* Red Cedar	$1.03	35
16	Extra Clear Red Cedar	1.24	40
18	Perfection Red Cedar	1.85	55

Bevel Siding

Clapboards or Weather Boards

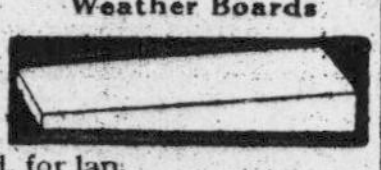

Clear, our highest grade. Select, our second grade. Finished to ½x5½ inches. When ordering, add one-third for 4-inch, one-fourth for 6-inch, to total number of square feet to be covered, for lap.

56K114—Weight, per 100 Square Feet, 80 Pounds.

Grade and Kind of Wood	½x4 per 100 Sq. Ft.	½x6 per 100 Sq. Ft.	⅝x8 per 100 Sq. Ft.	⅝x10 per 100 Sq. Ft.
Clear Cypress	$5.20	$5.20	$8.00	$8.00
Select Cypress	4.85	4.85		
Red Cedar			6.50	7.00
Clear Fir	4.10	4.10		

Partition and Ceiling

Clear, our highest grade. No. 1, our next grade. Order one-fourth extra to allow for tongue and groove.

Fir or Pacific Coast Hemlock	Size, Inches	56K115 Clear Grade, per 100 Sq. Ft.	56K116 No. 1 Grade, per 100 Sq. Ft.	Weight, per 100 Sq. Ft. Pounds
Ceiling	⅜x4	$5.10	$4.60	140
Partition	¾x4	5.80	5.10	180

Garages—Write for Catalog 446K

Studding, Joists and Rafters

56K101 — Fir or Pacific Coast Hemlock Planed to Standard Size

Size, In.	Lgth., Feet	No. 1 Grade, Each Piece	Wt., Lbs. Each Piece	Size, In.	Lgth., Feet	No. 1 Grade, Each Piece	Wt., Lbs. Each Piece
2x4	8	20c	13	2x8	14	$0.77	47
2x4	9	24c	15	2x8	16	.87	53
2x4	10	27c	17	2x8	18	1.06	60
2x4	12	33c	20	2x8	20	1.18	67
2x4	14	38c	23				
2x4	16	44c	27	2x10	8	.50	35
2x4	18	53c	30	2x10	10	.70	45
2x4	20	59c	33	2x10	12	.84	52
				2x10	14	.98	61
2x6	8	27c	20	2x10	16	1.12	69
2x6	10	38c	25	2x10	18	1.36	78
2x6	12	45c	30	2x10	20	1.50	87
2x6	14	53c	35				
2x6	16	61c	40	2x12	8	.65	42
2x6	18	71c	45	2x12	10	.88	52
2x6	20	80c	50	2x12	12	1.06	62
				2x12	14	1.23	72
2x8	8	39c	27	2x12	16	1.40	83
2x8	10	55c	33	2x12	18	1.70	94
2x8	12	66c	40	2x12	20	1.89	104

Dressed and Matched
Fir or Pacific Coast Hemlock

No. 1 Grade we recommend for barn boards and hay mow floors. No. 2 Grade we recommend for sheathing, subflooring and roof boards.

Weight, per 100 square feet, 210 pounds. Order one-fifth extra for tongue and groove.

Size, Inches	56K109 No. 1 Grade, per 100 Sq. Ft.	56K110 No. 2 Grade, per 100 Sq. Ft.	Size, After Planing
1x6	$5.25	$3.60	5¼-inch face
1x8	5.25	3.85	7¼-inch face
1x10	5.25	3.85	9¼-inch face

Fir or Pacific Coast Hemlock Shiplap

Weight, per 100 square feet, 210 pounds. Order one-fifth extra to allow for lap.

Size, Inches	56K106 No. 1 Grade, per 100 Sq. Ft.	56K107 No. 2 Grade, per 100 Sq. Ft.	Size, After Planing
1x8	$5.25	$3.85	7⅛-inch face
1x10	5.25	3.85	9⅛-inch face

Boards Planed on Both Sides
Weight, per 100 Square Feet, 250 Lbs.

Size, Inches	56K140 No. 1 Grade Cypress, per 100 Sq. Ft.	56K103 No. 1 Grade Fir or Pacific Coast Hemlock, per 100 Sq. Ft.	56K104 No. 2 Grade Fir or Pacific Coast Hemlock, per 100 Sq. Ft.
1x4	$6.10	$5.05	$3.20
1x6	6.10	5.25	3.60
1x8	6.10	5.25	3.65
1x10	6.10	5.25	3.85
1x12	7.30	6.30	4.05

Pacific Coast Hemlock and Fir Flooring

Clear is the highest grade. No. 1 Grade, our next grade below clear, No. 2, our lowest grade, can be used with economy for inexpensive work by cutting out some defects. Allow one-fourth extra for tongue and groove.

56K118 — Weight, per 100 Square Feet, 200 Pounds.

Trade Size	Grade	Kind of Wood	Actual Finished Size	Per 100 Square Feet
1x4	Clear	Flat Grain	3¼-inch face	$5.80
1x4	No. 1	Flat Grain	3¼-inch face	5.10
1x4	No. 2	Flat Grain	3¼-inch face	4.20
1x3	Clear	Flat Grain	2⅜-inch face	6.00
1x3	No. 1	Flat Grain	2⅜-inch face	5.30
1x3	No. 2	Flat Grain	2⅜-inch face	4.40
1x4	Clear	Edge Grain	3¼-inch face	6.90
1x4	No. 1	Edge Grain	3¼-inch face	5.80
1x3	Clear	Edge Grain	2⅜-inch face	7.40
1¼x4	Clear	Edge Grain	3¼-inch face	9.50

Fir and Pacific Coast Hemlock Lath

56K143 Figure 1,550 lath to 100 square yds. Nail ⅜ inch apart.

Kind of Wood	Lgth. Feet	Grade	Price, per 1000 Pieces	Weight Pounds
Fir or Pacific Coast Hemlock	4	No. 1	$7.35	500
Fir or Pacific Coast Hemlock	4	No. 2	6.15	500
Cypress	4	No. 1	11.10	500
Cypress	4	No. 2	9.10	500
Spruce	4	No. 1	10.00	500
Spruce	4	No. 2	7.30	500

Drop Siding

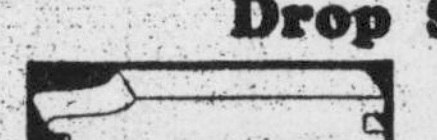

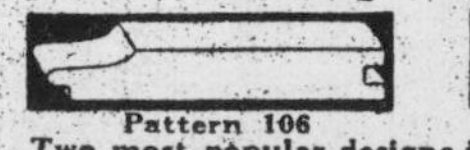

Pattern 106   Pattern 117

Two most popular designs illustrated. Other designs can be furnished at 30c per 100 feet extra. Weight, per 100 square feet, 180 pounds. Allow one-fifth for lap or tongue and groove. State pattern wanted.

56K112

Size, Inches	Kind of Wood	Grade	Per 100 Square Feet
1x6	Fir	Clear	$6.40
1x6	Fir	No. 1	5.65
1x6	Fir	No. 2	4.10
1x6	Cypress	Select	9.25
1x6	Cypress	No. 1	6.10

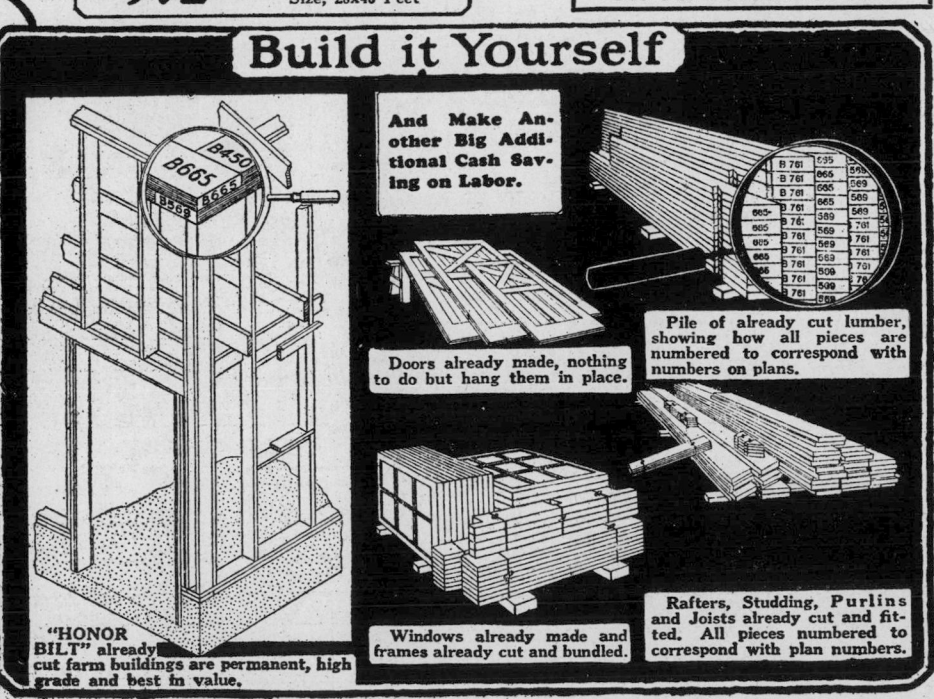

Save $500

"Honor Bilt"

YOU are sure of real satisfaction when you buy your home from Sears, Roebuck and Co. You profit by our enormous buying ability and extraordinary factory facilities. You gain by our successful system of "HONOR BILT" Modern Homes.

When you buy your home from us you will save about one-half the cost of labor; save all architects' fees; save because there are no extras; no waste of surplus materials; save by avoiding poor workmanship and faulty construction. In short, "HONOR BILT" modern home advantages are multiplied over and over. They are modern, high grade, permanent homes designed by leading architects. "HONOR BILT" modern homes have been successfully built by more than 37,500 families; 25,400 were built by the owners themselves.

Easy Payments

Our book, "HONOR BILT" Modern Homes, 598PK, explains our successful system of home ownership on the cash or easy payment plan. Write for your free copy of this interesting book.

One Order Brings It All!

No need to shop about in a dozen places. When you purchase a home from us you dispose of the entire transaction in a few minutes. On acceptance of your order we ship at factory prices all the material to build your house complete. See partial list on opposite page.

Our Guarantee Is Backed by More Than $100,000,000.00

We guarantee every "HONOR BILT" Modern Home to be exactly as represented and to give perfect satisfaction. We guarantee to furnish sufficient material to complete the house you select according to our plans and specifications. We guarantee safe delivery. We guarantee satisfaction or will return your money promptly, including freight charges. This guarantee is backed by our entire organization with a capital of over $100,000,000.00.

From Our Own Mills Direct to You

Letters from "HONOR BILT" Home customers tell of saving from $500.00 to $2,000.00. Such big savings are effected because we operate our own large mills and lumber yards on modern principles, and sell direct to you.

Saved $1,000.00

Sears, Roebuck and Co.

I want you to know how pleased I am with my Modern Home, purchased from you. The Ready-Cut material fit perfectly and I never worked with or saw better material. Many people remarked about the fine quality of material. I figure I saved $1,000.00 to $1,200.00 building the "Honor Bilt" way.

HERMAN THOMPSON.

Address Furnished on Request.

Left—The Martha Washington, 7 Rooms and Bath, under construction.

Build Your Home the Skyscraper Way

Skyscraper construction saves time and money. Why? Because all materials come ready cut from the mills. This modern and approved principle of economy and better construction is used when you build the "Honor Bilt" way. Our "Honor Bilt" Modern Homes are high grade, permanent, warm and convenient. They are recognized as the best made frame houses on the market.

The Crescent. FIVE ROOMS AND BATH

$2,436 MONTHLY PAYMENTS **$40**

Two Extra Rooms in Attic, $347 extra

The Gladstone

SIX ROOMS and BATH

$2,025

MONTHLY PAYMENTS **$35**

Saved $2,000

Sears, Roebuck and Co.

I am very well pleased with my "Honor Bilt" Home. Your material is of the very best and the Ready-Cut method is sure a great way of building. I saved about $2,000.00 and have a much better home than if I would have built the other way. I thank you for your excellent service.

WERNER P. BURKE.

Address Furnished on Request

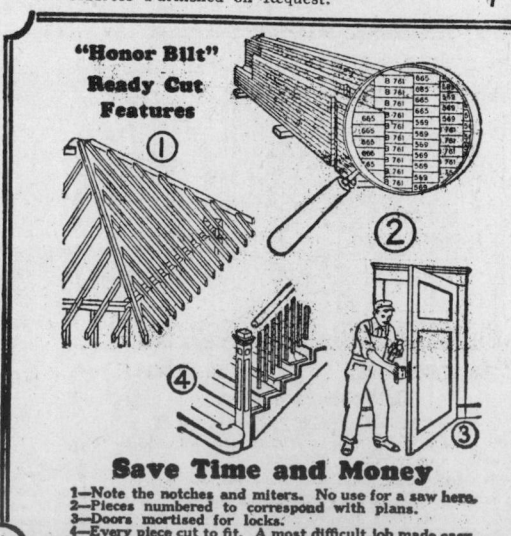

"Honor Bilt" Ready Cut Features

Save Time and Money

1—Note the notches and miters. No use for a saw here.
2—Pieces numbered to correspond with plans.
3—Doors mortised for locks.
4—Every piece cut to fit. A most difficult job made easy.

to $2,000 on a Complete Home
EASY PAYMENTS - FACTORY TO YOU

Modern Homes

"HONOR BILT" means a more Substantial Home—a Warm and Comfortable Home—Superior Home for you—and at a big saving in money and time!

They are permanent, high grade homes. "HONOR BILT" Homes are furnished ready cut and fitted. They have double floors, double walls and 2x4-inch studding.

Highest Quality Material

The lumber furnished for "Honor Bilt" homes is bright and new, fine, dry No. 1 framing, clear Cypress for outside finish, and clear siding. Expert mechanics, modern machinery and good materials insure perfectly made millwork. Oak, Birch, Fir or Yellow Pine (as specified) for interior finish—the kind of material that will prove to be a little better than generally used in home construction. Every detail is a quality product.

Easy Payments

If you own a good, well located building lot and have some cash, you can buy an "HONOR BILT" Modern Home, including the Heating, Plumbing and Lighting Fixtures; arrange Easy Monthly Payment Terms, and (in some instances) we will advance part of the cash for labor and such materials as we do not furnish—brick, cement, etc. The monthly payments shown do not include our low interest.

Many of our customers build their own "Honor Bilt" homes, doing part or all of the work themselves, in which case they do not need to put in much cash, as we consider the value of their work the same as cash.

Prices for "HONOR BILT" Modern Homes shown on these pages include the following items:

Lumber	Molding	Hardware
Lath	Flooring	Nails
Millwork, such as:	Medicine Case	Eaves Trough
Doors	Porch Material	Down Spout
Windows	Building Paper	Paint and Varnish

Shingles or Roofing as specified.
We guarantee enough material to finish the house complete, except cement, brick and plaster.

Save From $500.00 to $2,000.00

You need our Book of "HONOR BILT" Modern Homes. It will save you $500.00 to $2,000.00, depending upon the size house you build. It illustrates 100 designs of homes for city, suburb and farm. Each home is priced, completely illustrated and described. Floor plans are shown for every design. Just a few of the "Honor Bilt" Modern Homes are shown here.

Proofs of Satisfied Customers

We have thousands of letters from customers who have not only saved from $500.00 to $2,000.00, but who happily tell us that ours are the best homes in their locality.

Saved $1,500.00

Sears, Roebuck and Co.

I wish to take this opportunity to express my appreciation of the courtesy and fair treatment you have accorded me. As near as I can estimate I saved about $1,500.00 through building one of your "Honor Bilt" Homes and, as I know very little about carpenter work, I think that a very remarkable saving.

LESLIE F. DRESSLER.

Address Furnished on Request.

The Puritan. SEVEN ROOMS AND BATH
$2,504   MONTHLY PAYMENTS $40

The Conway. FIVE ROOMS AND BATH
$1,614   MONTHLY PAYMENTS $30

Standard Built Homes From $520 to $1,041
Choice of 4, 5 or 6 Rooms With Bath

The Grant. SIX ROOMS AND BATH
$1,041   MONTHLY PAYMENTS $25

"Honor Bilt" Modern Home Conveniences

Above—"HONOR BILT" Kitchen De Luxe White Tile Sink and Drain Board. White Enamel Cupboards.

We feature in addition: A breakfast alcove, wardrobe, clothes closets, folding built-in ironing boards, coal chutes, wall safes, broom closets, etc.

This Free Book of 100 Homes!

Our "Book of Modern Homes, 598K," contains over 100 designs from $520.00 to $4,652.00. Choose from One and Two-story Houses, Bungalows, Income Bungalows, Two-Flat Buildings, Colonials, English, Mission and American types.

It explains our free Architectural Service. Easy Payment Plan, and our successful "Honor Bilt" System.

A magnificent book! Many pages of beautiful color illustrations of exteriors, rotogravure illustrations of furnished interiors and floor plans.

Included are: Sectional Summer Cottages, designed for woods or seashore, from $298.00 up; also 31 wood and steel garages for $86.50 and up.

Ask for "Book of Modern Homes, 598K."

Free Home Exhibits in These Cities

Chicago, Ill., Store, Arthington St. and Central Park Ave. Downtown Exhibit, 30 N. Dearborn St.

Cincinnati, Ohio, 131 W. 4th St.

Cleveland, Ohio, 1013-1017 Euclid Ave., Wurlitzer Bldg.

Columbus, Ohio, 78 S. Third St.

Dayton, Ohio, 49 East 2d St., Columbia Bldg.

Detroit, Mich., 704 Penobscot Bldg., 143-147 Fort St. W.

New York, N. Y., 115 Fifth Ave.

Philadelphia, Pa., Store, 4640 Roosevelt Blvd. Downtown Exhibit, 312 S. Broad St.

Pittsburgh, Pa., 3016-3018 Jenkins Arcade.

Washington, D. C., 704 Tenth St., N. W.

Get this FREE Book of HOMES

Honor Bilt MODERN HOMES Sears, Roebuck and Co

Ask for 598K

It's Easy to Measure for Clothing

Our clothing is carefully made according to correct size standards. You do not need to order larger sizes than we specify. Our descriptions tell you the size range and you can order with the assurance that, if your size is listed, we guarantee the garment will fit you. Our sizes are obtained by securing the average of thousands of men, women and children in each size, and we believe are the most accurate standards in the country.

We Guarantee to Fit and Please You

Men's, Young Men's and Youths' Clothing

Figure 1

How to Take the Measurements

Stand in your natural way, breathe regularly and do not expand chest; also take everything bulky out of your pockets.

Chest. Take measurement over vest. Measure all around body at chest, close up under arms, snug but not tight. Tape measure should be over shoulder blades at the back. See line marked A on Figure 1.

Waist. If you wear a belt, take it off and take your measure over trousers all around body at waist. Your waistline is just above hip bones. Feel sides for location of hip bones. See line marked B on Figure 2.

Inseam. This is to show length of trousers leg. Stand straight and draw trousers well up in crotch. Measure from close up in crotch to bottom of trousers, at length desired. See line marked C on Figure 2. For cuff bottom trousers measure 1 inch shorter than for regular trousers.

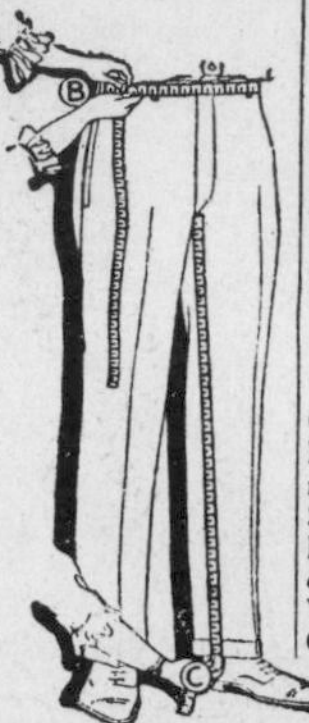

Figure 2

What Measurements to Give in Your Order

Suits. Give chest and waist measures and length of inseam; also height, weight and age.

Coats of All Kinds, Jackets, Raincoats and Overcoats. State chest measure taken over vest; also height, weight and age.

Vests. Give chest and waist sizes; also height, weight and age.

Pants (Both Dress and Work Pants) and Overalls. Give waist size and length of inseam; also height, weight and age.

WOMEN'S, MISSES' and JUNIORS'

Coats, Dresses, Knickers, Blouses, Raincoats, etc.

HOW TO TAKE MEASUREMENTS:

Always Pull Tape Close but Not Tight.

Do Not Allow. We Will Make All Necessary Allowances.

Give Each Measurement as Stated in Description of Garment You Are Ordering.

Actual Bust Measurement
For any garment, be sure to measure over very largest part of bust with dress or blouse on. Tapeline in back must run on shoulder blades and not below them.

Actual Waist Measurement
This measurement is very important when ordering knickers and skirts. Please do not allow *extra*. Give actual tape measurement, over dress or blouse.

Actual Lower-Hip Measurement
This means very *largest* part of figure below waist. Do not "allow." We will make all necessary allowances. Measure over dress or skirt.

Length Garment Desired
For dresses, coats or raincoats, measure down back from neckline to hem, as shown in small diagram, N to L.
For skirts measure down front from waist, as shown (W to S).

Height
Knowing your height, we can use the very best judgment in sending you the proper dress, coat, suit or knicker. Give weight, also, if you desire best possible fit

Tell Us This—Do you like to wear your garments loose-fitting or close-fitting? See space for answer on order blank.

Use Clothing Order Blank on Other Side of This Sheet

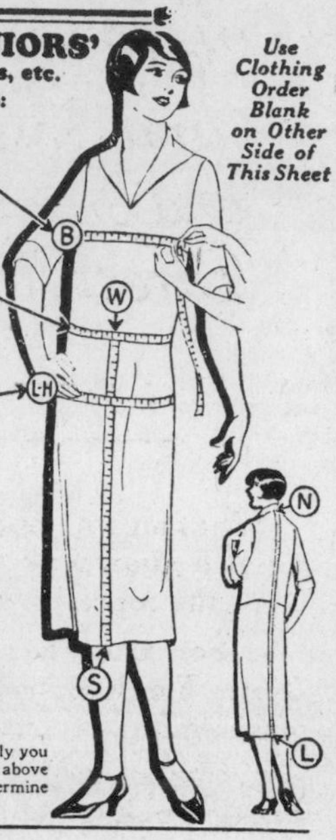

You Will Be Delighted! To learn how easily and quickly you can be correctly fitted when above information is given to us. Our years of experience enables us to determine from these measurements exactly what size garment will fit you.

Boys' and Girls' Clothing

GIVE AGE SIZE. To find AGE SIZE, take the boy's or girl's chest measure, then consult boys' or girls' scale of sizes below.

Before ordering a boy's or girl's garment it is necessary to know the chest measure in order to know the proper AGE SIZE to order, as boys of the same age will vary very greatly in size, and the same with girls. For example, a boy only 10 years of age may be as large as the average boy of 12, or, on the other hand, he may be as small as the average boy of 9 years. Girls of the same age also vary in size. The size scales herewith show the average chest measure of boys and girls of each age. These have been compiled from the measurements of many thousands of boys and girls of each age.

HOW TO MEASURE. **For a boy:** If a long pants suit is wanted see instructions along with Figure 7. If a knee pants suit is wanted see "D" on Figure 5. Measure all around body at chest over his shirt or blouse. **For a girl**, see "L" on Figure 6. Measure all around body at chest over her dress or blouse. In either case, see that the tape measure is well up under arms and that it is over shoulder blades at the back. After you have the measurement, see boys' or girls' scale to find what age size to order.

To Measure for Boys' Long Trousers and Long Trouser Suits

Figure 7.

For suits, measure boy's chest, waist and inseam, as shown in this long trouser picture. For trousers, measure waist and inseam only. Our boys' long trousers and long trousers suits are sold according to age size and measurement. The table below shows you the measurements of the different age sizes. For example: If your boy's chest measure is 27 inches, waist measure 25½ inches and inseam 23 inches, order size 10. If you find that your boy's measurements do not agree with age sizes given in the table, send us the boy's chest, waist and inseam measurements and state his height and weight and we will send a garment that will fit him.

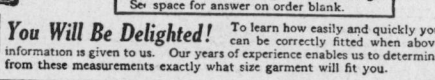

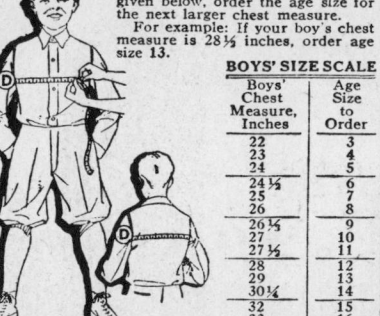

Age Size to Order	5	6	7	8	9	10
Chest Measure, Inches	24	24½	25	26	26½	27
Waist Measure, Inches	23½	24	24	24½	25	25½
Inseam Measure, Inches	18	19	20	21	22	23
Age Size to Order	11	12	13	14	15	16
Chest Measure, Inches	27½	28	29	30¼	32	33
Waist Measure, Inches	26	27	27½	28	29	30
Inseam Measure, Inches	24	25	26	27	28	29

Boys' or Little Fellows'

Knee Pants, Suits, Overcoats, Raincoats, Mackinaw Coats, Blouses and Underwear

How to Use Size Scale

For example: If your boy's chest measure is 24 inches, order age size 5, or if your boy's chest measure is 30¼ inches, order age size 14.

In case your boy's chest measure is between two of the measurements given below, order the age size for the next larger chest measure.

For example: If your boy's chest measure is 28½ inches, order age size 13.

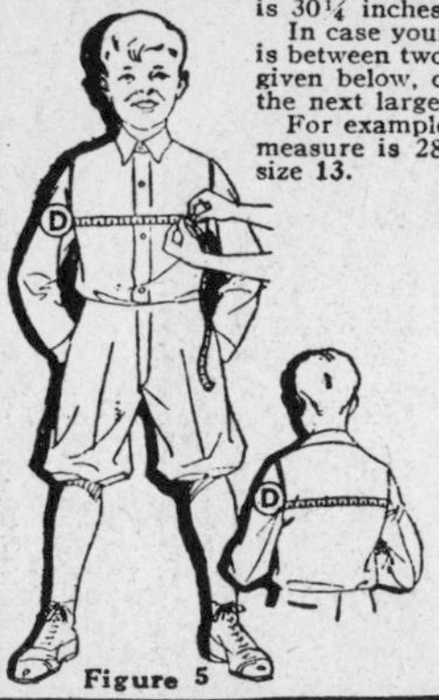

Figure 5

BOYS' SIZE SCALE

Boys' Chest Measure, Inches	Age Size to Order
22	3
23	4
24	5
24½	6
25	7
26	8
26½	9
27	10
27½	11
28	12
29	13
30¼	14
32	15
33	16
34	17

Girls' or Children's

Dresses, Blouses, Middies, Raincoats and Underwear

How to Use Size Scale

For example: If your girl's chest measure is 22 inches, order age size 3, or if your girl's chest measure is 31 inches, order age size 12.

In case your girl's chest measure is between two of the measurements given below, order the age size for the next larger chest measure.

For example: If your girl's chest measure is 26½ inches, order age size 8.

GIRLS' SIZE SCALE

Girls' Chest Measure Inches	Age Size to Order	Lgth. of Dress In.
21	2	20
22	3	22
23	4	23
24	5	24
25	6	26
26	7	27
27	8	28
29	10	32
31	12	36
33	14	40

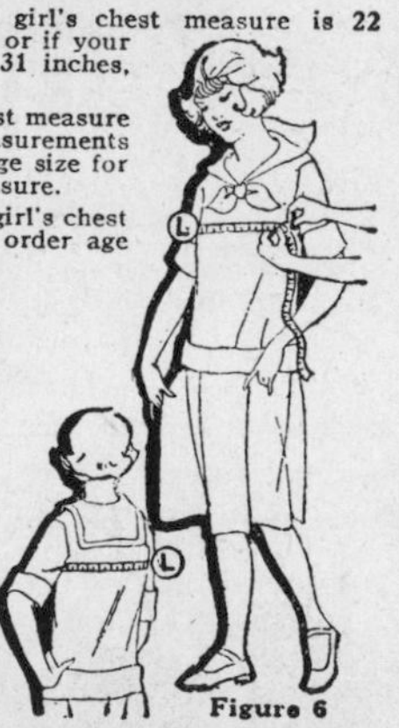

Figure 6

Parcel Post Rates—It's Easy to Figure Them—Allow Enough. We'll Return Any Balance

1. Ask your postmaster in what zone you live, measuring from the city where our nearest store is located; or, if you have one of our big General Catalogs, the map on the parcel post rate page will help you find the zone.

2. Add up the weights of the articles you are ordering and find the total weight of your shipment; weights are given in descriptions.

3. Then look at the table at the right for the rates to your zone. The upper row of rates shows the postage on the first pound of your order according to your zone, and the rate in the lower row shows the postage to be added for each additional pound according to your zone.

For example: If the total weight of the goods you order is over 11 pounds but not over 12 pounds and you live in the 3d zone from the city where our store is located, you will see by referring to the rates in the upper row that the rate of the first pound for the 3d zone is 8 cents and by referring to the lower row of rates you will see that each additional pound for the 3d zone costs 2 cents more. There being 11 additional pounds, this would make 22 cents, which, added to the 8 cents for the first pound makes 30 cents, which will be the total required for your shipment.

4. Packages weighing up to 8 ounces may be mailed for 1½ cents for each 2 ounces; books consisting of 24 or more pages up to and including 8 ounces, at the rate of 1 cent for 2 ounces. Everything over that weight takes pound rate.

Always send enough money extra to pay postage on parcel post shipments. We'll return any balance due you.

FOR FREIGHT AND EXPRESS RATES SEE PAGE 544 IN THIS CATALOG OR ASK YOUR STATION AGENT

Local Zone If you live in a city where one of our stores is located and order goods by mail from that store, the rate for the first pound is 7 cents and you add 1 cent for each additional 2 pounds, or a fraction thereof. For example: If you order goods weighing over 14 pounds but not over 15 pounds, the parcel post charge is 7 cents for the first pound and 1 cent more for each additional 2 pounds. There being 14 additional pounds this would be 7 cents, making a total of 14 cents.

LOCAL ZONE See explanation above.	ZONE 1 Not over 50 miles from Our Store	ZONE 2 Not over 150 miles from Our Store	ZONE 3 151 to 300 miles from Our Store	ZONE 4 301 to 600 miles from Our Store	ZONE 5 601 to 1,000 miles from Our Store	ZONE 6 1,000 to 1,400 miles from Our Store
For weights over 8 ounces up to 1 pound the postage is	7c	7c	8c	9c	10c	11c
For each additional pound or fraction of a pound, add	1c	1c	2c	4c	6c	8c

LIMIT IN WEIGHT. Packages up to 70 pounds are carried in zones 1, 2 and 3; in all other zones 50 lbs. is the limit in weight.

LIMIT IN SIZE. Packages up to 7 feet in length and girth combined will be carried by Parcel Post. Nothing larger. Heavier and larger articles may be shipped economically by express or freight.

A Fashion Review of Unusual Interest

On the Pages to Follow You'll Find the Latest and Smartest Spring and Summer Apparel Direct From New York

What an assurance of authentic designing—what a guarantee of quality and what a saving that represents to you.

For truly these models are direct from New York—in styling—in selection—in making.

Furthermore, there is no premium for New York style or tailoring when you buy from us, but merely one small profit added to the maker's cost.

Thus, our low prices permit you to purchase more apparel and more stylish apparel for your money than you can buy elsewhere.

31H6000
All Silk
Crepe Satin
or All Silk
Flat Crepe
$14⁷⁵

A Stunning New York Style Frock

This lovely frock is offered in your choice of lustrous *All Silk Crepe Satin* or in lovely *All Silk Flat Crepe;* both enhanced with contrasting color self material used for a chic pleated jabot frill and attractive cuffs. The skirt has a double tier of pleated flouncing at front, trimmed on top with clusters of contrasting chain stitching; matching the adornment on the cuffs. A bow finish on one side of the bodice, novelty buttons on the jabot and a girdle with a handsome buckle adornment, all unite in making this frock exceedingly smart and appealing.

Women's and Misses' Sizes—34, 36, 38, 40, 42 and 44 inches bust measure. Length from back of neck to hem 44 inches only, with deep basted hem (about 5 inches) so dress can easily be made longer or shorter. **State size.** Shipping wt., 1½ lbs.

Crepe Satin		Flat Crepe	
31H6000—Navy.	$14⁷⁵	31H6002—Claret Red.	$14⁷⁵
31H6001—Black.		31H6003—Queen Blue.	
		31H6004—Black.	

See Index and Information Pages 459 to 485

Charming New Frocks for the Summer Season

31H6050
All Wool Light Weight Summer Flannel
$9.98

31H6045
Rayon Plaid Gingham
$3.98

31H6055
Printed Washable "Gloria" Voile
$3.89

The Latest Tailored Mode

More pleasing than ever are the tailored frocks this season, having assumed a more feminine and graceful silhouette, such as you see in the smart model, shown above. This frock is fashioned of *All Wool Flannel*, and has a prettily trimmed bodice, and a swagger, pleated skirt. Contrasting two-tone *Flannel* was used for the collar, vestee and attractive undersleeves. Has chic trimming of novelty metal ball buttons and a buckle adjusted leather belt.
Women's and Misses' Sizes—34, 36, 38 and 40 inches bust measure. Length from back of neck to hem, 42 inches only, with deep 5-inch hem, making length easy to alter. State size. Shpg. wt., 1½ lbs. **$9.98**
31H6050—Light Green.

Descriptions of Dresses Shown on Opposite Page

Tailored—Yet Dressy in Effect

A new and individual treatment of tucking and pleating is featured in the design of this handsome frock. Although the style is of tailored inspiration, the model is quite dressy and lovely, due to its fabric of richly lustrous *All Silk Flat Crepe* and trimming of contrasting color ribbon. The belt is adorned with a novelty clasp buckle.
Women's and Misses' Sizes—34, 36, 38, 40, 42 and 44 inches bust measure. Length from back of neck to hem, 44 inches only, with deep 5-inch hem, making length easy to alter. State size. Shipping weight, 1½ pounds.
31H6060—Cedarwood.
31H6061—Queen Blue.
31H6062—Black. **$8.98**

Fashioned of an Attractive Fabric

Such charm and smartness are seldom found in a frock so moderately priced and for this reason we especially recommend this attractive model for your selection. Gracefully fashioned of pleasing quality *Printed All Silk Crepe de Chine* it features front pleats on the skirt and a chic, double tiered button enhanced jabot frill on the bodice. Has trimming of solid color silk *Crepe* and the belt shows an ornamental buckle.
Women's and Misses' Sizes—34, 36, 38 and 40 inches bust measure. Length from back of neck to hem, 43 inches only, with deep 5-inch hem, making length easy to alter. State size. Shipping weight, 1½ lbs. **$9.98**
31H6065—Rose Fancy.

One of New York's Very Latest

This beautiful frock is artfully fashioned of extra good quality *All Silk Flat Crepe*. It has an attractive bodice with diamond shaped tucking, front and back; a cascade drape frill at one side and an ornamental flower at the shoulder. Box pleating on the skirt achieves a silhouette of graceful animation, and a final smart note is lent by a gypsy sash enhanced with a jeweled pin.
Women's and Misses' Sizes—34, 36, 38 and 40 inches bust measure. Length from back of neck to hem, 43 inches only, with deep 5-inch hem, making length easy to alter. State size. Shipping weight, 1½ pounds.
31H6070—Queen Blue.
31H6071—Rose Beige (Pinkish Tan). **$16.95**

New and Decidedly Smart

Richly lustrous *All Silk Crepe Satin* in chic combination with contrasting color *All Silk Flat Crepe* fashions this stunning frock. Graceful overdrape panels and a wide girdle are new and interesting features in its design. Effectively trimmed with beautiful embroidered braid bandings, novelty metal buttons and a handsome ornamental buckle.
Women's and Misses' Sizes—36, 38, 40, 42 and 44 inches bust measure. Length from back of neck to hem, 42 and 44 inches only, with deep 5-inch hem, making length easy to alter. State size and length. Shipping weight, 1½ pounds.
31H6075—Rose Beige (Pinkish Tan). **$16.98**

Practical for Many Occasions

For general everyday service, when you need a good looking, neatly styled frock, you will be pleased to have this practical, inexpensive model. The material is attractive *Silk Warp Crepe Adora*, adapted on becoming lines and enhanced with solid color silk warp crepe. Smartness is lent to the bodice by a jaunty tie, and to the skirt by shirring in the center and graceful pleats on either side. Composition buttons and a novelty buckle are pleasing finishing details.
Women's and Misses' Sizes—36, 38, 40, 42 and 44 inches bust measure. Length from back of neck to hem, 44 inches only, with deep 5-inch hem, making length easy to alter. State size. Shipping weight, 1½ pounds.
31H6080—Tan Fancy. **$5.98**

Trimmed With Dainty Net Frilling

This charming frock portrays the popular mode of the day, having a softly bloused bodice with puffed, long sleeves; a skirt showing graceful pleats at front and a sash tie belt at the waistline. It is smartly adapted in a pleasing quality *All Silk Flat Crepe*, and has adornment of self covered buttons on the skirt, while the bodice is enhanced with ecru *Venise* pattern lace and fluted, dainty net frilling piped with the silk.
Women's and Misses' Sizes—34, 36, 38 and 40 inches bust measure. Length from back of neck to hem, 42 inches only, with deep 5-inch hem, making length easy to alter. State size. Shipping weight, 1½ pounds.
31H6085—American Beauty.
31H6086—Queen Blue. **$9.98**

Plaid Fabrics Are Popular

Smart, practical and very inexpensive, is this frock of woven *Plaid Rayon* (artificial silk) *Gingham;* a washable fabric of attractive appearance.
Fashioned on becoming lines, the frock boasts a clever new treatment in the styling of the collar; made with long strap ends, that have piped and button trimmed openings at the waistline, serving as slits for the wide girdle, which fastens with a metal buckle. The skirt has box pleating on either side, and a trim finishing note is lent by a silk ribbon bow at the neck.
Women's and Misses' Sizes—36, 38, 40, 42 and 44 inches bust measure. Length from back of neck to hem, 44 inches only, with deep 5-inch hem, making length easy to alter. State size. Shipping weight, 1½ pounds.
31H6045—Blue Plaid. **$3.98**

Surprisingly Low in Price

That one can't judge the merits of a frock by its price is well proved by this attractive model, which boasts a smart style, neat workmanship, a fabric of pleasing quality, yet for all that, costs only $3.89.
Made of washable "Gloria" Cotton Voile, of a charming new pattern; the frock is gracefully fashioned with scalloped border tunic panels and is effectively trimmed with pin tucked solid color *Voile* and piping. It has a grosgrain ribbon tie with pretty bead drops, and shows further adornment of novelty glass buttons and a metal edged composition clasp buckle.
Women's and Misses' Sizes—36, 38, 40, 42 and 44 inches bust measure. Length from back of neck to hem, 44 and 46 inches, with deep 5-inch hem, making length easy to alter. State size and length. Shipping weight, 1½ pounds.
31H6055—Tan and Copenhagen Blue Fancy.
31H6056—Tan and Navy Blue Fancy. **$3.89**

31H6065
Printed
All Silk
Crepe
de Chine
$9⁹⁸

31H6075
Good Quality
All Silk
Crepe Satin
$16⁹⁸

31H6070
Good
Quality
All Silk
Flat Crepe
$16⁹⁵

31H6060
All Silk
Flat Crepe
$8⁹⁸

31H6080
Silk Warp
Crepe Adora
$5⁹⁸

31H6085
All Silk
Flat Crepe
$9⁹⁸

For Descriptions of These
Dresses See Opposite Page

Order Blanks Are in Back of This Catalog

New Fabrics – Chic Designs Selected in New York for the Well Dressed Miss

Dresses on this and the opposite page, except 31H6300, come with deep 5-inch basted hem, making length easy to alter.

All Silk Washable Broadcloth, so practical and smart for summer frocks, fashions this good looking two-piece effect model. The bodice has a ribbon tie and adornment of attractive embroidery, while the skirt shows pleating at front. Frock comes with a buckle trimmed sash tie belt.
Misses' and Small Women's Sizes—16 to 22 years. Bust measure, 34 to 40 inches. Length, from back of neck to hem, 43 inches only, with deep 5-inch basted hem, making length easy to alter. **State age size and bust measure.** See size scale. Shipping weight, 1½ pounds.
31H6310—Powder Blue.
31H6311—Salmon. **$7.39**

This inexpensive washable frock is fashioned of linen finished *Printed Kotolin*, which is both good looking and serviceable. The style is appealingly youthful, showing *Rayon* (artificial silk) braid edged, pointed folds at front and rows of shirring below the waistline. Has trimming of solid color mercerized cotton *Pongee* and a fancy ribbon tie.
Misses' and Small Women's Sizes—14 to 22 years. Bust measure, 32 to 40 inches. Length, from back of neck to hem, 44 inches only, with deep 5-inch hem, making length easy to alter. **State age size and bust measure.** See size scale. Shpg. wt., 1½ lbs.
31H6315—Blue Fancy.
31H6316—Tan Fancy. **$2.98**

31H6310
All Silk Washable Broadcloth
$7.39

31H6315
Guaranteed Washable Fast Color Kotolin
$2.98

Fashioned of sheer dainty *All Silk Georgette Crepe*. Made with a basque bodice and a scalloped edge full cut skirt, it shows lavish adornment of pearl and silver bead embroidery in combination with studded brilliants, and has a fancy *Georgette* and feather rosette on the shoulder. Comes with an extra pair of detachable sleeves and a slip of *All Silk Crepe de Chine*.
Misses' and Small Women's Sizes—14 to 22 years. Bust measure, 32 to 40. Lengths, from back of neck to hem, 41 and 43 inches. **State age size, bust measure and length.** See size scale. Shipping weight, 1½ pounds.
31H6300—Coral Blush.
31H6301—Light Green. **$16.95**

This frock is made of lustrous *All Silk Crepe Satin* in a style that is smart and youthful. It portrays popular fashion themes, in the form of double tiered, scalloped edged flounces on the skirt, and a graceful streamer sash tie on the bodice. Contrasting color silk *Georgette* was used as trimming. Has all around fancy metal buckled belt.
Misses' and Small Women's Sizes—16 to 22 years. Bust measure, 34 to 40. Length, from back of neck to hem, 42 inches. Has deep 5-inch basted hem, making length easy to alter. See size scale. Shpg. wt., 1½ lbs.
31H6305—Claret Red.
31H6306—Black. **$12.75**

31H6300
All Silk Georgette Crepe Party Dress
$16.95

31H6305
All Silk Crepe Satin
$12.75

Fancy check silk warp *Crepe Adora* is offered here. Contrasting solid color silk warp *Crepe* was used for the front tying sash belt and as a loose fold on the gracefully pleated skirt. Handsomely trimmed with fancy embroidered net collar and cuffs.
Misses' and Small Women's Sizes—14 to 22 years. Bust measure, 32 to 40. Length, from back of neck to hem, 43 inches, with deep 5-inch basted hem. **State age size and bust measure.** See size scale. Shipping weight, 1½ pounds.
31H6320—Red Fancy.
31H6321—Green Fancy. **$5.95**

This one has been fashioned of lustrous *All Silk Flat Crepe* and attractively trimmed with banding of multicolored *Rayon* (artificial silk) embroidered net. The skirt shows box pleating on either side, and the frock is further enhanced with a silk flower at one shoulder.
Misses' and Small Women's Sizes—14 to 22 years. Bust measure, 32 to 40. Length, from back of neck to hem, 43 inches, with deep 5-inch basted hem. **State age size and bust measure.** See size scale. Shipping weight, 1½ pounds.
31H6325—French Blue.
31H6326—Rosewood.
31H6327—Navy. **$8.98**

We offer this lovely frock of sheer dainty *All Silk Georgette Crepe* at a great saving. It has an attractive yoke and cuffs of lustrous crepe satin cut in uneven points and outlined with fancy *Rayon* (artificial silk) stitching. The skirt has rows of shirring and a chic note is lent by a wide girdle with flower ornament. *Tub Silk Slip* included.
Misses' and Small Women's Sizes—14 to 22 years. Bust measure, 32 to 40 inches. Length, from back of neck to hem, 43 inches, with deep 5-inch basted hem. **State age size and bust measure.** See size scale. Shipping weight, 1½ pounds.
31H6330—Nile Green.
31H6331—Rosewood. **$15.98**

It is fashioned of good quality *All Silk Flat Crepe* with a double inverted kick pleat on sides and a sash tie belt at the waistline. Trimming is provided by contrasting silk *Crepe* and multicolored embroidered bands on the collar and cuffs, and smartly placed pin tucking.
Misses' and Small Women's Sizes—16 to 22 years. Bust measure, 34 to 40 inches. Lengths, from back of neck to hem, 42 and 44 inches, with deep 5-inch basted hem. **State age size, bust measure and length.** See size scale. Shipping weight, 1½ lbs.
31H6335—Oak Buff.
31H6336—Rosewood.
31H6337—Black. **$13.95**

Adapted in good looking *Rayon* (artificial silk) *Warp Crepe*, it has a V shaped neck bodice with pin tucking at either side. The frock shows chic trimming of three-tone silk and velvet ribbon and has a pretty flower ornament.
Misses' and Small Women's Sizes—14 to 22 years. Bust measure, 32 to 40 inches. Length, from back of neck to hem, 43 inches, with deep 5-inch basted hem. **State age size and bust measure.** See size scale. Shipping weight, 1½ pounds.
31H6340—Leaf Green.
31H6341—Tan. **$6.48**

It is fashioned in youthful two-piece effect of *All Silk Flat Crepe*; a combination that makes this frock smart and desirable. The bodice shows adornment and *Rayon* (artificial silk) embroidery. Box pleating on the skirt. Collar and cuffs are finished with two-tone silk piping.
Misses' and Small Women's Sizes—16 to 22 years. Bust measure, 34 to 40 inches. Length, from back of neck to hem, 43 inches, with deep 5-inch basted hem. **State age size and bust measure.** See size scale. Shipping weight, 1½ pounds.
31H6345—Briar Rose.
31H6346—Queen Blue. **$9.98**

This good looking frock is designed in the popular two-piece effect of lustrous, washable woven check *Rayon* (artificial silk) *Crepe* with smart trimming of contrasting silk *Crepe de Chine*.
Misses' and Small Women's Sizes—14 to 22 years. Bust measure, 32 to 40 inches. Length, from back of neck to hem, 43 inches only, with 5-inch hem, making length easy to alter. **State age size and bust measure.** See size scale. Shpg. wt., 1½ lbs.
31H6350—Medium Blue Check.
31H6351—Red Check. **$4.98**

All Silk Printed Crepe de Chine is the fabric that fashions this graceful frock. The model is also made youthful and charming by having a lovely ecru lace vestee outlined with net frilling and a "Pierrot" double ruffle collar of matching net.
Misses' and Small Women's Sizes—14 to 20 years. Bust measure, 32 to 38 inches. Lengths, from back of neck to hem, 43 inches, with deep 5-inch basted hem. **State age, size and bust measure.** See size scale. Shpg. wt., 1½ lbs.
31H6355—Tan Fancy. **$8.95**

Misses' Sizes 14-16-18-20-22 Years
Bust Measures 32-34-36-38-40 Inches

Smartly Styled Spring and
Summer Frocks for Misses

31H6320
Silk Warp
Crepe
Adora
$5.95

31H6325
All Silk
Flat
Crepe
$8.98

31H6330
All Silk
Georgette
Crepe
$15.98

31H6335
Good Quality
All Silk
Flat Crepe
$13.25

31H6340
Rayon Warp
Crepe
$6.48

31H6345
All Silk
Flat Crepe
$9.98

31H6350
Woven
Rayon
Crepe
$4.98

31H6355
Novelty Printed
All Silk
Crepe de Chine
$8.25

These Frocks Are Fully Described
on Opposite Page

Order Blanks Are in Back of This Catalog

Low Priced — Well Made Sports Wear

27H8015
Fancy Knitted Sport Blouse
$1.98

27H8005
Khaki Jean Sport Shirt
$1.39
Women's and Misses' Sizes

27H8270
All Wool Knitted Worsted Two-Piece "TOM-BOY" Sport Suit
$5.98

27H8020
Mercerized English Broadcloth Blouse
98c

How to Order

In ordering any of the Sport Apparel shown on pages 60, 61, 62, 63 and 64, be sure to give your exact waist measure, drawing tape firmly around waist above hips. Do not "allow" as these garments are cut over full standard patterns and are not skimped in any way.

In ordering Waists or Middies, give exact bust measure.

Women's and Misses' Sizes

27H8215
All Wool Fancy Tweed Knickers
$2.98

27H8200
Khaki Cloth or Cotton Tweed Knickers
98c

27H8250 $2.98
Corduroy Knickers

Sturdy and Durable

These good looking knickers are fashioned of strong, sturdy quality *Velour Corduroy*. They have buttoned knee cuffs and an adjustable belt.
Women's and Misses' Regular Sizes—24 to 34 inches waist measure. **State exact waist measure.** Shipping weight, 2 pounds.
27H8250 $2.98
Tobacco Brown.

Women's and Misses' Sizes

Misses Sizes

Misses Sizes

27H8220
Imported Linen Sport Outfit
$4.98
Knickers Alone $2.98

Ages 7 to 14 Years

27H8205
Khaki Jean "TOM-BOY" Suit
$1.98

Shirt Alone 98c
Skirt Alone $1.00

Correct Sport Garments

Mannish tailored sport shirt of sturdy *Khaki Jean Cloth*. Tie included.
Women's and Misses' Sizes—34 to 44 inches bust measure. **State size.** Shipping weight, ¾ pound.
27H8005—Khaki Tan. $1.39
Smartly styled, comfortable knickers, in your choice of strongly woven *Khaki Cloth* or cotton *Tweed*. Made with adjustable belt and buttoned knee cuffs.
Women's and Misses' Regular Sizes—24 to 34 inches waist measure. **State exact waist measure.** Shipping weight, 2 pounds.
27H8200—Tan Khaki. 98c
27H8201—Gray Tweed.

Smart for Outdoors

Attractive knitted blouse (one-third wool, balance cotton) with fancy pattern of lustrous *Rayon* (artificial silk).
Women's and Misses' Sizes—34 to 44 inches bust measure. **State size.** Shipping weight, ¾ pound.
27H8015—Buff, Tan and Blue Combination. $1.98
Correctly styled knickers of sturdy quality *All Wool Fancy Tweed*. With fitted knee cuffs and an adjustable belt.
Women's and Misses' Regular Sizes—24 to 34 inches waist measure. **State exact waist measure.** Shipping weight, 2 lbs.
27H8215—Tan.
27H8216—Gray. $2.98

"Tom Boy" Knitted Suit

A swagger "Tom Boy" sport suit of fine quality knitted *All Worsted* yarn. Made in clever two-piece style, it consists of a slip-on blouse with a smart woven stripe pattern, while the skirt is of harmonizing solid color. Has attractive adjustable belt, with leather ends and a buckle.
Misses' Sizes—34, 36, 38 and 40 inches bust measure. **State size.** Shipping weight, 2 pounds.
27H8270—Robinhood Green.
27H8271—Tan. $5.98

Fashion's Very Latest

Two-piece sport outfit of woven check, *Imported White Linen*. Consists of sleeveless jacket and well tailored knickers.
Misses' Sizes—34, 36, 38 and 40 inches bust measure. Knickers, 24 to 34 inches waist measure. **State bust and exact waist measure.** Shipping weight of outfit, 3 lbs.; knickers, 1½ lbs.
27H8220—Two-Piece Outfit. White with black check. $4.98
27H8221—Knickers Alone. White with black check. 2.98
Tailored blouse of *English Broadcloth* shown with above outfit.
Sizes—34 to 44 inches bust measure. **State size.** Shipping weight, 10 ounces.
27H8020—White. 98c

Girls' Practical Outfit

This two-piece "Tom Boy" outfit of sturdy quality, *Tan Khaki Jean Cloth*, consists of a separate sport shirt, and "Tom Boy" style skirt which has fancy belt finished with leather ends and a buckle.
Ages—7, 8, 10, 12 and 14 years. **State age and exact waist measure.** Shpg. wt., 1½ lbs.
27H8205—Khaki Tan Two-Piece Outfit. $1.98
27H8010 98c   **27H8210** 1.00
Shirt Alone...   Skirt Alone.

Practical and Inexpensive

An ideal play costume for young girls. Consists of a separate blouse and knickers fashioned of durable *Hill's Tan Khaki Jean Cloth*. The blouse has embroidered ornament; knickers have separate belt and buttoned knee cuffs.
Ages—7, 8, 10, 12 and 14 years. **State age and waist measure.** Shpg. wt., 2 lbs.
31H6650—Two-Piece Outfit. $1.98
31H6651—Knickers Alone. 1.00

Ages 7 to 14 Years

31H6650
Hill's Khaki Jean Play Suit
$1.98
Knickers Alone $1.00

CHARMING STYLE and Priced so Low!

I know you will all be delighted with this 1927 spring and summer line I have selected for you. These new hats are beautiful, the smartest assortment I have ever assembled. And the prices! You will hardly believe your eyes! You, no doubt, have impressions of values in millinery, but when you see the stunning latest style hats we are offering you this season you will be really amazed. Only Sears, Roebuck and Co., could give such high quality materials and full selections of fashionable colors in the many head sizes at the low prices you will find quoted in these 17 pages. From the vast offerings of the world's greatest makers, I selected models for all types, from the very little girls to women of mature years, so every one of you will be immensely pleased, I am sure.

Pauline

America's Best Known Milliner

— and only $3.48 !

Makes a charming picture, does it not? And we guarantee that the quality, workmanship and materials throughout will satisfy the most discriminating.

We invite comparisons with hats selling elsewhere at prices far, far above our price. The graceful wide brim shape (14¾ inches across) is of fine quality imported **piping straw braid.** This braid makes that very rich looking glossy hat. Trimmed handsomely with wide, high grade cire satin ribbon, expertly draped. Stunning, huge, flat rose of novelty pattern made of sheer organdy and shaded Rayon plush. Trim is finished by a clever double strand silverlike cord across the front. Fitted with attractive silk lining. Especially designed for the stylish young woman and miss. **In two head sizes.**

Colors: **Black with shaded tiger lily (new salmon shade) flower or black with shaded rose-pink color flower.** Measure and state color. Shipping weight, 2½ pounds.

78H9002—This fits 21¾ to 22 inches head size. **$3.48**
78H9003—This fits 22¾ to 23 inches head size. 3.48

It Is Easy to Measure Your Headsize—See Page 72

78H8005
$2.98
This fits from 21¾ to 21¾ inches head size.

Colors: **French beige (sand), Copenhagen blue, gooseberry (light) green or black.** Measure and state color. Shipping wt., 1¾ lbs.

Draped toque crown is a popular style this season. Very smart and unusually becoming to small features. Made of fine quality **Rayon faille.** Several rows of rich looking ribbon, having metallic border, give a striking two-tone effect. Ribbon also binds brim and sets off odd, self wing design at side. Brilliant, brooch style trimming pin. Silk lined.

Rayon Is the Trade Name for Artificial Silk

78H9007—Medium size. Fits 21½ to 22 inches head size. **$2.98**
Colors: **Orchid (lavender), cameo pink (light), Copenhagen blue or wild honey (light brown).** Measure and state color. Shipping weight, 1¾ pounds.
Daintiest of this summer's styles are made of transparent braid. This lovely new shape is of very fine genuine **Swiss hair braid.** Stylish, close fitting brim, with close roll at back, has facing of good quality silk crepe de chine. Fine, novelty flower appliques form an attractive trimming across front. Note clever dent across crown, 'tis very smart indeed.

78H8009—Small size. Fits from 21 to 21¾ inches head size. **$1.98**
Colors: **Gooseberry (light) green, French beige (sand), briar rose (new rose color), bright red or black.** Measure and state color. Shipping weight, 1¾ pounds.
One of our smartest tailored models and a feature value. Chic New Yorkers are wearing this new tam style, which adapts itself handsomely in this fine soft quality **Jap Swiss hemp straw braid.** Good looking trimming of grosgrain ribbon, set off with odd little straw ornaments. Neat, tailored binding along brim edge. Silk lined.

We Guarantee to Satisfy You and Save You Money

Bridal Wreath

Ornamental Shrubs, Hedges, Evergreens, Vines

Rose of Sharon

The Finishing Touches of Flower and Foliage

Beautiful shrubs are a most important ornament and, properly diversified in shape and variation of bloom, will add marked beauty to any home. They are invaluable for flowering effects, for attractiveness of foliage, to mellow sharp angles or lines, to relieve the harshness where house and lawn meet, as screens against objectionable views, etc. We offer only first quality shrubs. Planting suggestions and pruning instructions sent with each shipment. **Shipping weights, each, 2 pounds; 3 plants, 4 pounds.**

Varieties

Althea (Rose of Sharon). This shrub makes a compact upright growth of from 8 to 12 feet. Abundance of white, pink or red flowers, according to variety, from July to September. Extra heavy, 2 to 3 years old.
71H1520⅓—Each....**45c** 3 for....**$1.25**

Barberry (Japanese). One of the best shrubs for all purposes. Will grow in almost any soil, in sun or shade. Dense grower, 3 to 5 feet high. The leaves are small, turning scarlet in fall. Twigs are thorny and covered with scarlet berries in fall and winter. Very good for planting next to foundation of house. Heavy, 18 to 24-inch plants.
71H1500⅓—Each..........**45c** 3 for..........................**$1.25**

Bridal Wreath (Spirea Van Houttei). One of the prettiest and most popular shrubs. Very attractive with its mass of white flowers in April. The profusion of bloom weighs the branches down and covers the bush with a canopy of white. Never fails to attract attention. Grows 6 to 8 feet tall.
71H1527⅓—Each..........**45c** 3 for..........................**$1.25**

Butterfly Bush. Very attractive. Grows 3 to 6 feet tall and is valued for its very conspicuous dark blue "Lilac" flowers borne in late July and August. Will make a quick bushy growth in spring. Heavy, 18 to 24-inch plant.
71H1501⅓—Each..........**45c** 3 for..........................**$1.25**

Deutzia (Pride of Rochester). Upright fast grower, 6 to 8 feet. Flowers in large panicles or clusters in late May. White tinged with pink. Heavy, 18 to 24-inch plants. Very hardy.
71H1522⅓—Each..........**48c** 3 for..........................**$1.29**

Golden Bell (Forsythia Intermedia). Hardy, fast growing shrubs with good foliage which follows the showy yellow bell shaped flowers. This variety is the tallest grower of any Golden Bell. 18 to 24-inch plants. Grows 6 to 8 feet.
71H1523⅓—Each..........**45c** 3 for..........................**$1.25**

Honeysuckle (Fragrantissama). The bush honeysuckle is a hardy, fast growing shrub with very deep green glossy foliage. Grows 6 to 8 feet broad and spreading. Very fragrant. White flowers followed by attractive red berries that hang on into the winter. Heavy No. 1 plants, 2 to 3 feet.
71H1507⅓—Each..........**45c** 3 for..........................**$1.25**

Hydrangea A. G. (Hills of Snow). The Hydrangeas are valuable for show flowers in mid and late summer and are used separately or in groups. Hills of Snow have huge dense balls of small white flowers in June and July. Grow 4 to 6 feet tall and should be pruned severely in late winter or early spring to produce large flowers. Heavy plants, 18 to 24 inches high.
71H1516⅓—Each....**48c** 3 for...**$1.29**

Japan Quince. Used as specimens and for hedges. Grows 4 to 6 feet. Attractive scarlet crimson flowers in April and glossy green foliage which hangs on till late in the fall. Heavy, 18 to 24-inch plants.
71H1525⅓—Each..........**59c** 3 for..........................**$1.55**

Hydrangea P. G. Very handsome shrub. Larger than the Hydrangea A. G. Large clusters of very showy white flowers, turning pink and bronze later in season. Begins to bloom early in August and continues for several weeks. Grows 6 to 8 feet tall but new growth should be cut back about one half each fall for large flowers next season. Stands drought well. 18 to 24-inch plants.
71H1506⅓—Each..........**48c** 3 for..........................**$1.29**

Lilac (Purple). The well known common variety with its purple fragrant flowers. 2 to 3-foot plants.
71H1508⅓—Each..........**59c** 3 for..........................**$1.55**

Snowball. Used mostly as a screen or hedge. Noted for its clusters of handsome globular pure white flowers in May. No. 1 heavy plants, 18 to 24 inches high.
71H1526⅓—Each..........**59c** 3 for..........................**$1.55**

Spirea (Anthony Waterer). Compact low growing shrub, 2 to 3 feet, with dense deep green foliage. Bright pink flowers in full flat clusters. If the flowers are cut away when they fade the shrub will sometimes bloom again. 12 to 18-inch plants.
71H1528⅓—Each..........**48c** 3 for..........................**$1.29**

Syringa (Mock Orange). These old fashioned shrubs are justly popular for attractive foliage and flowers. They are strong growers in sun or partial shade. 18 to 24-inch plants.
71H1519⅓—Each..........**45c** 3 for..........................**$1.25**

Weigelia (Pink). Abundant, showy flowers that vary from deep rose pink blooms in May and June. Grows 6 to 8 feet. Very effective in group plantings. 18 to 24-inch plants.
71H1529⅓—Each..........**45c** 3 for..........................**$1.25**

Shipped from Nurseries in NEW JERSEY

No orders accepted for less than $1.00 worth of nursery stock

Grass Seed

There are two types of grass seed mixtures. One is a quality mixture made up of only the better grasses which are generally slow in starting growth, but which make a beautiful, permanent lawn. The other is a cheap mixture of quick growing low priced grasses like timothy, which make a lawn quickly, but one which is good for only one season. In the past, we have offered only a fine quality mixture which cannot profitably be sold for less than our price. Now we are offering along with this quality seed, a mixture containing timothy on which we are able to make a very attractive price.

De Luxe Quality Lawn Seed The One We Recommend

Expert blend of the very finest recleaned imported and domestic varieties of true turf grasses. Makes a solid, velvety green lawn that will withstand trampling, maintain its fine texture and color through periods of drought and heat, and last indefinitely with a little care. Contains no timothy. Usually retails for 60c a pound elsewhere.

71H3000—1-pound package....**$0.39**
71H3001—3-pound package.... **1.10**
71H3002—5-pound package.... **1.79**

Special Green Cover Mixture To Meet Price Competition

Where quick but not lasting results are wanted use our Green Cover Mixture. This is a blend of the more common grasses, such as timothy that are noted for their quick growth. Will not make nearly as fine and permanent a lawn as our De Luxe Quality mixture. Where a quick turf is wanted use this mixture. Usually retails from 35c to 40c a pound elsewhere.

71H3003—1-pound package....**$0.27**
71H3004—3-pound package.... **.75**
71H3005—5-pound package.... **1.19**

White Clover

We offer only a choice grade of clean white clover. **Although it is not a grass, many** people like to have it to dress up their lawns. One-pound packages only.
71H3006—1-pound package white clover..............................**59c**
Shipping weights: 1-pound carton, 1½ pounds; 3-pound bag, 3½ pounds; 5-pound bag, 6 pounds.

Shipped from stock

Plant More Ornamental Hedges

Cheaper and more attractive than wooden or iron fences. Sizes, 12 to 18 inches have 3 canes, and 18 to 24 inches, three or more canes. Planting and pruning instructions with each shipment.

California Privet: The popular hedge plant, with glossy thick, deep green leaves. Most generally planted ornamental hedge. Grows very rapidly and should be planted whenever quick hedge is wanted without expense or trouble. Easily trimmed. Holds foliage very late. All good, strong, quick growing plants. Plant 6 to 10 inches apart. Will not stand severe freezing. Plant Amoor River in cold sections.

Amoor River Privet: North. Has boxlike leaves and forms a dense and handsome hedge. Very hardy. Grows 8 to 12 feet. Has numerous white flowers during June and late autumn. Vines covered with pretty steel blue berries. A strong healthy hedge for Central and Northern States. Plant 6 to 10 inches apart.

Spirea V. H. (Bridal Wreath): Not only noted for its beauty as shrub, but also makes beautiful hedge. Plant 18 to 24 inches apart. Grows 6 to 8 feet high.

Japanese Barberry: Grows 3 to 4 feet. The best small hedge. Also used for edging walks, drives and for garden borders. Have small red berries in fall and winter.

Catalog No.	Variety	Size	12	25	50
71H1555⅓	Calif. Privet	12 to 18 in.	$0.59	$0.98	$1.69
71H1556⅓	Calif. Privet	18 to 24 in.	.79	1.48	2.25
71H1557⅓	Amoor Privet	12 to 18 in.	1.59	2.79	3.98
71H1558⅓	Amoor Privet	18 to 24 in.	1.79	2.98	4.98
71H1560⅓	Spirea V. H.	12 to 18 in.	1.79	3.39	5.98
71H1561⅓	Spirea V. H.	18 to 24 in.	2.39	3.98	6.98
71H1559⅓	Japanese Bar.	12 to 18 in.	1.89	3.59	6.48

Shipping weights, 12 to 18 inches: 12 plants, 4 lbs.; 25 plants, 8 lbs.; 50 plants, 20 lbs.; 18 to 24 inches: 12 plants, 5 lbs.; 25 plants, 10 lbs.; 50 plants, 25 lbs.

Shipped from Nurseries in NEW JERSEY

Shade Trees

Ornamental trees bring natural beauty where ever used for shelter or cooling shade, screening objectionable views, beautifying your home grounds, and for backgrounds they are indispensable. Plant the hardwood types for permanency. Although they grow slower, when you think of their longevity, beauty of form and foliage, they are the best. Planting instructions accompany each shipment.

Varieties

Ash (White) (American): A stately quick growing tree with broad spreading limbs. Good for shade or street planting; grows over 60 feet.

Maple (Silver or Soft): A fast growing good foliage and very popular tree, producing quick shade. Leaves are bright green above and silvery beneath. Turn beautiful yellow in fall. Over 60 feet.

Elm (American): Nothing compares with the American Elm for restful beauty and a permanent tree for shade. It is majestic and graceful with wide spreading head borne on straight shapely trunk.

Poplar (Lombardy): A tall upright narrow width tree that is well known to most everyone. Easy to transplant and a rapid grower. Valuable as screens or backgrounds in mixed plantings. or to offset straight lines. Does not shed its leaves early.

State Variety Wanted.

Cat. No.	Size	Each	For 3
71H1420⅓	6 to 8 feet	$0.98	$2.25

On account of size these trees cannot be shipped except by express. Shipped from nurseries in NEW JERSEY.
Shipping weights: 6 to 8-foot trees, packed, 5 pounds each.

Climbing Vines

Hardy Vines and Creepers

Nothing contributes more to the charm of the home surroundings than a good show of hardy climbing vines covering the walls, or adorning the summer houses and the verandas.
Full planting and pruning instructions sent with each shipment.

Boston Ivy: This beautiful self clinging vine is noted for its ability to cover walls of stone or brick. Dense bright green attractive foliage turning crimson in fall. Hardy.
71H1240⅓—Each.................**39c**

Clematis Paniculata (Japanese): Bright foliage with countless small star shape white sweet scented flowers, which are beautiful both in foliage and blossom; bloom late. Support on trellis. Grows 10 to 15 feet.
71H1244⅓—Each.................**39c**

Clematis Jackmanni: Large, rich, velvety violet-plum flowers in solid masses. The most popular variety.
71H1246⅓—Each.................**79c**

Honeysuckle (Hall's): The popular evergreen honeysuckle, so extensively used for screen, fragrance and beauty. Shiny green foliage. Pure white trumpet shape flowers. Sweetly perfumed. Blooms continuously. Easily grown. Hardy. Endures heavy soil. Heavy 2 to 3-year old plants.
71H1241⅓—Each.................**39c**

Trumpet Vine: A strong, healthy woody vine, twining tightly with numerous tendrils among its stems. Largely used and very desirable for covering arbors, summer cottages, rustic bridges, etc. Orange scarlet flowers in midsummer. Bright green foliage.
71H1249⅓—Each.................**39c**

Wisteria (Japanese): We offer only root cuttings which are sure to bloom. A heavy climbing vine. Beautiful foliage, long clusters of pea shape purple flowers. Grows very tall.
71H1243⅓—Each.................**39c**

Shpg. wt., each, 1 lb. Shipped from nurseries in NEW JERSEY.

See Index and Information Pages 459 to 485

New Improved Models

Besides being the most attractive couches ours are most comfortable.

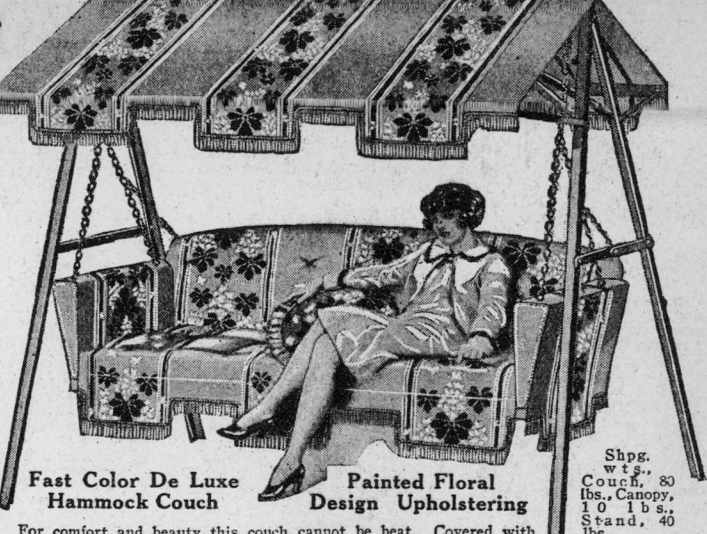

"LUXURY" UPHOLSTERED SPRING BACK HAMMOCK COUCH
comfortable. All angle steel frame. Canvas covering is made of good quality heavy duck, blue and gray with white stripes. Fast color. A very striking pattern. Length of couch is 72 inches; seat is 24 inches wide and back is 18 inches high. Equipped with sufficient chains to hang from stand only. Magazine pocket.

6H5900¼—Hammock Couch only.....(Shipping weight, 70 pounds). **$14.95**
6H5901¼—Canopy to match couch......(Shipping weight, 10 pounds)....**$5.89**
6H5918¼—Folding Iron Stand........(Shipping weight, 40 pounds).......3.95

One of the latest styles. A hammock couch with both seat and back made of wire link fabric springs with helical (coil) spring extensions. Padded seat and back with wood wool filling, making couch invitingly comfortable.

Fast Color De Luxe Hammock Couch   **Painted Floral Design Upholstering**

For comfort and beauty this couch cannot be beat. Covered with 8-ounce painted duck, green with orange and dark green floral design; a very pretty pattern. Cotton filled padded back and mattress, deep valance, scalloped and fringed. Frame is of angle iron construction with wire fabric springs in both back and seat. Couch is 72 inches long and 24 inches wide. Equipped with sufficient chains to hang from stand only.

Shpg. wts., Couch, 80 lbs., Canopy, 10 lbs., Stand, 40 lbs.

6H5925¼—Couch only................................**$24.95**
6H5937¼—Canopy to match above couch, made of same material.............**$8.45**
6H5918¼—Folding Iron Stand only........................3.95

Oval Pillow
Made of same material to match the above couch hammock. Ruffled edge, filled with new, clean and lofty Kapok. Size, 24x16 inches. Shipping weight, 2 pounds.
6H5923¼ **$1.98**

Priced Very Low!

"LEADER" HAMMOCK
Only **$3⁶⁹**

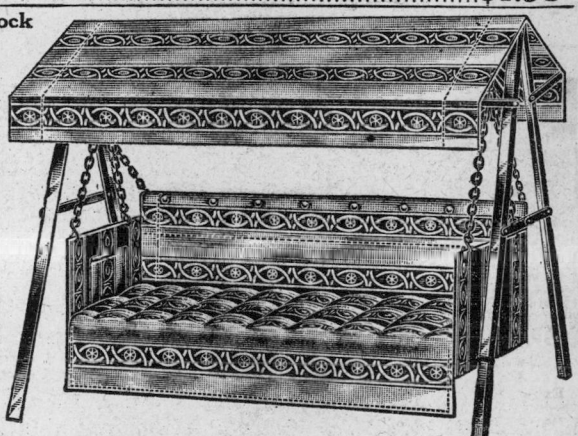

Made from a good weight, plain weave fabric in a popular Tartan plaid effect, pleasing colors. Full fringed curtain, large, upholstered throwback pillow, good weight rope, varnished wood foot spreader, concealed head spreader. Size of bed part, about 74x34 inches. Shpg. wt., 6½ lbs. **$3.69**
6H5104¼

JACQUARD WEAVE HAMMOCK
Well woven of strong warp yarn. Harmonious colors are rich brown with green. Conventional floral effect, leaf design and Jacquard weave. Fitted with upholstered throwback pillow ornamented with tassels and straight spreader at head. Suspension cords at foot divided with turned wood spreader.

Size of bed part, 72 in. long and 32 in. wide. Shpg. wt., 5 lbs.
6H5102 **$2⁹⁸**

"Comfort" Hammock Couch
Good quality heavy drill green with white fancy stripes, fast color. Steel frame, fitted with wire link fabric springs, helical (coil) springs at both ends. Full tufted covered wood wool mattress. Removable padded back rail. Ends of couch are constructed so they will not pull away from canvas. Equipped with sufficient chains to hang from stand only. Length, 72 inches; width, 24 inches.

6H5905¼—Hammock Couch only. Shipping wt., 55 lbs. **$9.98**
6H5906¼—Canopy to match. Shipping wt., 10 lbs. **$4.45**
6H5918¼—Folding Angle Iron Stand only. Shipping wt., 40 lbs........**$3.95**

Built to Stand Wear!

$11⁴⁵ Complete

Shipped direct from factory in WISCONSIN or PENNSYLVANIA.

Folding Wood Lawn Settee
Heavy hardwood frame with ⅝-inch slats, painted in green and well varnished in natural finish. Length, 42 inches. Shipping weight, 17 lbs.
6H5495¼....... **$1.79**

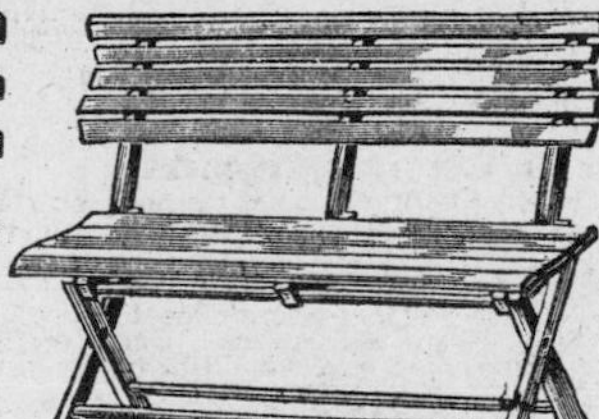

Folding Lawn Settee
Wood curved seat; designed to make you comfortable. Made of heavy selected hardwood, frame and back slats painted green and the seat slats are varnished natural color. Center support for both the seat and back slats; length, 44 inches. Shipping weight, 20 pounds. **$2.79**
6H5491¼...................

Steel Lawn Swing
A Lawn Swing made of steel at a popular price. Ideal for lawns, parks and playgrounds and will last many years. Noiseless and safe. Framework made of steel and painted green. Seats, platform and arm rests made of hardwood, natural finish. Height is 7 feet. Floor space required, 5x8 feet. Seats are 30 inches wide; back, 29 inches high. Easily erected. Instructions for erecting furnished with swing. Shipped from factory in PENNSYLVANIA.

6H5904⅓—Without canopy. Shpg. wt., 150 lbs.. **$15.98**
6H5908⅓—With canopy. Shipping weight, 170 pounds............**$17.98**

Hardwood Lawn Swing
This swing is made of selected hardwood. All connections and braces are fastened with bolts and nuts. Fitted with adjustable seats. This is an extra large, roomy, comfortable swing with plenty of space between the seats. It will comfortably seat four adults or six children. The slats in the seats, back and foot rest are strong and securely fastened. The derrick or upright frame is about 8 feet high and occupies a space about 5x8 feet. The seats are 34 inches wide. Frame is painted bright red, while the hangers, seats and foot rests are thoroughly varnished in a natural wood finish.

6H5902⅓—Lawn Swing without canopy. Shipping wt., 110 lbs.**$7.98**
6H5903⅓—Lawn Swing with canopy. Shipping wt., 125 lbs...**$11.45**

Steel Slat Settees
Ideal for outdoor use. Full size, well built. Strongly braced, nicely finished in green paint. Built of ⅞x⁵⁄₁₆-inch steel. Braces, 1x¼-inch flat steel. Packed to secure lowest transportation rates. Easily put together. From factory in OHIO VALLEY.
6H5488½—4 feet long. Shipping weight, 70 pounds.......... **$5.98**
6H5489½—5 feet long. Shipping weight, 80 pounds.......... 7.98

Children's Swing. Same style as above, but smaller in size. Stands 5 feet high and occupies a space 40 by 60 inches. Seats measure 10 inches deep and have 18-inch backs. Frame painted green, hangers and seats are varnished natural finish. Ideal for the little tots, ages 3 to 10 years.
6H5950⅓—Shipping weight, 35 pounds................... **$4.98**

PRIZE WINNERS ~ Popular Styles From Famous Beaches

For Men and Boys

$2.98

Boys' and Men's Athletic Two-Piece Bathing Suits

Very latest style. When ordering complete suit, give catalog number, size and color of shirt and size and kind of trunks wanted. Shpg. wt., each garment, ¾ lb.

Heavy Weight All Wool Worsted Supporter Shirt
6H2144—Men's Solid White Shirt. Sizes, 34 to 42 in. chest measure. **$1.98**
6H2143—Boys' Solid White Shirt. Sizes, 28, 30 and 32 in. chest measure. **$1.79**
6H2141—Navy and White Striped Shirt. Sizes, 34 to 42 in. chest measure. **$2.12**
6H2142—Navy Blue and Orange Striped Shirt. Sizes, 34 to 42 in. chest measure. **$2.12**

Navy Blue Knitted All Wool Worsted Trunks
Fly front, with white web belt. State size.
6H2145—Men's, 32 to 44 inches waist. **$1.98**
6H2146—Boys' sizes, 26, 28 and 30 inches waist. **$1.79**

Navy Blue All Wool Flannel Trunks. Fly front, fast color, white web belt. 30 to 44 in. waist.
6H2147. **$1.98**

Juvenile One-Piece All Worsted

Upper part either white or jockey red, lower part navy blue. Sizes, 22 to 28 in. chest. State size. Shipping weight, 1 pound.
6H2122—White and Navy Blue. **$1.29**
6H2119—Jockey Red and Navy Blue. **$1.29**

Juvenile All Wool Worsted
Fine quality yarns. Plain colors. Sizes, 22 to 28 in. chest. State size.
6H2124 Jockey Red. **$1.15**
6H2118 Peacock Blue. **$1.15**
Cotton Bathing Suit, same style and size as above. Jockey red. State size.
6H2159. **39c**

Flapper Style All Wool Worsted Bathing Suits

Medium weight, popular style, trunks sewed to skirt. Sizes, 34 to 46 in. bust. State size.
6H2149—Peacock blue with black and white stripes. **$2.98**
6H2154—Jockey red with black and white skirt stripes. **$2.98**
6H2150—Navy blue with white skirt stripes. **$2.98**
6H2155—Kelly green with orange and white skirt stripes. **$2.98**

Women's Heavy Ribbed All Wool Worsted Bathing Suits
Solid colors. California style. Sizes, 34 to 42 inches bust measure. State size. Shipping weight, 2 lbs.
6H2152—Jockey red color. **$3.79**
6H2153—Peacock blue. **$3.79**
6H2156—Black. **3.79**

Extra Large Size Women's All Wool Worsted
Medium weight. Trunk sewed to skirt, round neck, winged sleeve. Sizes, 46 to 54 in. bust measure. State size.
6H2163—Navy blue with white trimming. **$3.98**

Women's Cotton Bathing Suit
Medium weight, navy blue with trimmings of contrasting colors. Sizes, 36 to 46 inches bust measure. State size.
6H2160. **89c**

Shipping weight, 1¾ lbs.

Be Sure to State Size Wanted

Men's Medium Weight All Wool Worsted Bathing Suit
Navy blue with white skirt stripes. Sizes, 36 to 46 in. chest measure.
6H2140. **$2.89**

Men's Heavy Elastic Ribbed All Wool Worsted Suit
Navy blue with white and orange skirt stripes. Sizes, 34 to 46 in. chest.
6H2148. **$3.98**

Men's Cotton Suit
Medium weight. Style as above. Navy blue with trimming of contrasting color. Sizes, 36 to 46 in. chest.
6H2139. **79c**

Misses' All Wool Worsted Bathing Suit
Medium weight. California style. Very attractive. Sizes, 28 to 34 in. bust measure. Shpg. wt., 1¾ lbs.
6H2193—Peacock blue with black and white skirt stripes. **$2.48**
6H2192—Jockey red with black and white skirt stripes. **$2.48**
6H2191—Kelly green with black and white skirt stripes. **$2.48**

Misses' Cotton Bathing Suit
Navy blue with trimming of contrasting colors. Sizes, 28 to 34 inches bust. State size. Shpg. wt., 1¾ lbs.
6H2187. **69c**

Boys' All Wool Worsted Bathing Suit
Medium weight. California style. Sizes, 28 to 34 in. chest measure. Shipping weight, 1 pound.
6H2123—Maroon with orange and royal blue chest stripes. **$2.39**
6H2120—Navy blue with white and old gold chest stripes. **$2.39**

Boys' Cotton Bathing Suit
Navy blue with trimming of contrasting colors. Sizes, 28 to 34 in. chest. Shipping weight, 1 pound.
6H2131. **68c**

Boys' All Wool Worsted Bathing Suit
Can also be worn by girls. California style suit. White or Jockey red upper and Navy blue web belt. Sizes, 28 to 34 in. chest measure. State size. Shipping weight, 1 pound.
6H2130—White and navy blue. **$2.59**
6H2138—Jockey red and navy blue. **$2.59**

Boys' Cotton Bathing Suit
Same style and sizes as above (no belt). White upper and Navy blue bottom. State size.
6H2158. **68c**

Women's Novelty Bathing Suit
Highest quality heavy all wool worsted yarn. California style suit with all-over novelty pattern. Sizes, 34 to 42 in. bust measure. State size. Shpg. wt., 2 lbs.
6H2171—Jockey red and white color combination. **$4.40**
6H2170—Peacock blue and gray color combination. **$4.40**

Men's Medium Weight All Wool Worsted Bathing Suit
Dark brown color with orange and royal blue chest stripes. A very attractive color combination. Sizes, 36 to 46 inches chest measure. State size. Shpg. wt., 1¾ lbs.
6H2125 **$2.98**

Submarine Bathing Cap
Regular $1.50 Retail Value
For men and women. Shipping wt., 6 oz.
6H2135—Red. **98c**
6H2136—Blue. **98c**
6H2137—Green. **98c**

Fancy Brocaded Diver
Regular 50c retail value. New and beautiful appearance. For men and women. Shipping weight, 3 oz.
6H2100—Blue. **39c**
6H2103—Red. **39c**

Plain Rubber Diver
With slight white trim at edge.
6H2101—Blue. **18c**
6H2104—Red. **18c**

Aviators' Style Beautiful Moire Design
Regular 75c Retail Value. Heavy rubber. For men and women. Shpg. wt., 4 oz.
6H2112—Navy blue. **59c**
6H2113—Red. **59c**
6H2114—Green. **59c**
6H2106—White. **59c**

Aviators' Style Plain Cap
6H2109—Natural color. Pure para rubber. **47c**

Children's Butterfly Design Rubber Diving Cap
Shpg. wt., 3 oz.
6H2116
Red and white trimmed. **21c**
6H2115—Blue and white trimmed. **21c**

Women's Big Bow Brocaded Diving Cap
Regular 75c Retail Value
Shpg. wt., 3 oz.
6H2132 Blue with blue bow. **49c**
6H2133—Red with red bow. **49c**
6H2134—Green with green bow. **49c**

Bathers' White Web Belt
Nickel plated; non-tarnishable buckle. Adds style to suits. Sizes 26 to 44 in. waist measure. State size. Shipping weight, 5 oz.
6H2195. **15c**

Women's Rubber Bathing Slippers
Made entirely of rubber. Sizes, 3, 4, 5, 6 and 7. No half sizes. State size. Shpg.wt.,1 lb.
6H2189 Red. **79c**
6H2186—Green. **79c**
6H2185—Blue. **79c**
Children's Rubber Bathing Slippers, same as above, in color red only. Sizes, 11, 12, 13, 1 and 2. State size.
6H2190. **69c**

Aviators' Style Bathing Cap and Slipper Set
An opportunity to get a bathing cap to match slippers. Sizes of slippers, 3, 4, 5, 6 and 7. No half sizes. State size. Shipping weight, 1 pound.
6H2183 Red. **$1.29**
6H2184 Blue. **$1.29**

When inflated will properly support for swimming an adult of 200 pounds. Shipping wt., 4 oz.
6H2121 Per pair. **35c**

In Less Than a Day Your Order's on Its Way

P